Profiles of Indiana

2019

Fifth Edition

Profiles of Indiana

A UNIVERSAL REFERENCE BOOK

Grey House Publishing

PRESIDENT: Richard Gottlieb
PUBLISHER: Leslie Mackenzie
EDITORIAL DIRECTOR: Laura Mars
SENIOR EDITOR: David Garoogian
PRODUCTION MANAGER: Kristen Hayes
MARKETING DIRECTOR: Jessica Moody

Grey House Publishing, Inc.
4919 Route 22
Amenia, NY 12501
518.789.8700 • FAX 845.373.6390
www.greyhouse.com • books@greyhouse.com

First edition published 2007
Printed in Canada

Publisher's Cataloging-In-Publication Data
(Prepared by The Donohue Group, Inc.)

Names: Grey House Publishing, Inc., publisher.
Title: Profiles of Indiana.
Description: Millerton, N.Y. : Grey House Publishing, 2007- | Place of publication varies. | "A Universal Reference Book." | "History, statistics, demographics for 714 populated places in Indiana including comparative statistics & rankings."
Identifiers: ISSN 1939-6007
Subjects: LCSH: Cities and towns--Indiana--Statistics--Periodicals. | Cities and towns--Indiana--History--Periodicals.
Classification: LCC HA361 .P76 | DDC 317.72--dc23
ISBN: 978-1-64265-327-4

Table of Contents

Introduction . . . vii

Researchers' Guide to Data . . . ix

Facts & Photos
Introduction and Table of Contents . . . 1
State Emblems, Key Facts, and Locator Map . . . 2
Photo Gallery . . . 4
History of Indiana . . . 10
Timeline of Indiana History . . . 13

Government
Introduction and Table of Contents . . . 17
A Guide to Indiana State Government . . . 19
Congressional Districts . . . 22

Demographic Maps
Introduction and Table of Contents . . . 23
Population . . . 25
Percent White . . . 26
Percent Black . . . 27
Percent Asian . . . 28
Percent Hispanic . . . 29
Median Age . . . 30
Median Household Income . . . 31
Median Home Value . . . 32
High School Graduates . . . 33
College Graduates . . . 34
Voted for Donald Trump in 2016 . . . 35

Geography
Introduction and Table of Contents . . . 37
Land and Natural Resources . . . 39
Geographical Characteristics of the 50 Most Populated Places in Indiana . . . 40
Populated Places, Transportation and Physical Features . . . 41
Federal Lands and Indian Reservations . . . 42
Satellite View . . . 43

Energy
Introduction and Table of Contents . . . 45
Quick Facts . . . 47
Overview . . . 47
Coal . . . 47
Electricity . . . 47
Renewable Energy . . . 48
Petroleum . . . 49
Natural Gas . . . 49

Climate
Introduction and Table of Contents . . . 53
User Guide . . . 55
Indiana Physical Features and Climate Narrative . . . 59
State Relief Map . . . 60
Weather Stations Map . . . 61
Weather Stations by County . . . 62

Weather Stations by City . . . 63
Weather Stations by Elevation . . . 64
National Weather Service Stations . . . 65
Cooperative Weather Stations . . . 69
Weather Station Rankings . . . 79

Comparative Statistics
Introduction and Table of Contents . . . 91
Comparative Statistics of 100 Largest Communities . . . 92

Community Rankings
Introduction and Table of Contents . . . 121
Rankings of Top/Bottom 150 Communities with Population of 2,500 or More . . . 123

Education
Introduction and Table of Contents . . . 249
User Guide . . . 251
Public School Educational Profile . . . 257
School District Rankings . . . 258
National Assessment of Educational Progress (NAEP) . . . 274
State Report Card . . . 282

Ancestry, Ethnicity and Race
Introduction and Table of Contents . . . 285
User Guide . . . 287
State Profile . . . 295
County Profiles . . . 296
Place Profiles . . . 388
Ancestry Group Rankings . . . 403
Hispanic Origin Rankings . . . 423
Racial Group Rankings . . . 428

Profiles: Combined Statistical Data of Counties and Places
Introduction and Table of Contents . . . 445
User Guide . . . 447
Core Based Statistical Areas (CBSAs) and Counties . . . 460
County and Place Profiles . . . 461

Index
County and Place Name . . . 717

Introduction

Welcome to the 5th edition of *Profiles of Indiana* from Grey House Publishing. The state profile series—now 15 books strong—was developed in 2006, derived from the award-winning 4-volume *Profiles of America*, which compiles data on more than 43,000 places in the United States.

This new edition of *Profiles of Indiana* includes all the valuable, in-depth and up-to-date information that these works are known for, but now, this rich content has been reorganized and rearranged, and is fully illustrated with images to support the text and statistics. It is easier to use and more accessible for a variety of users—from high school students to relocation professionals.

Starting with this edition, all the state profiles will benefit from a new design, more data, more photos, and a new, thoughtful arrangement that makes the content more accessible and easy-to-use. There are more helpful features, like thumb tabs to help keep you oriented in each chapter—now 11—and chapter leader pages that include a specific Introduction, Table of Contents and, in many cases, a unique User Guide, paving the way for the researcher to take full advantage of every last piece of data presented. *Profiles of Indiana* includes hundreds of statistical data points, tables and charts that provide solid, fact-based research, and dozens of maps and photos.

Here is an overview of the new chapter arrangement:

About Indiana: Facts & Photos
This 4-color chapter provides a real sense of the state from a variety of historical and physical vantage points. It includes Indiana history and geography, plus a photo gallery that includes not only sights unique to the state, but also its state flag, seal, motto, bird, flower, and more. This chapter also includes a timeline of political and newsworthy events from Indiana's founding to the present day.

Government: A State Guide
This is an important and detailed look at the history and structure of Indiana's government, including discussion of the state's legislative, judicial and executive branches and various types of local government. The chapter ends with a map of Indiana's 9 US Congressional Districts.

Demographic Maps
These 11 colorful, full-page maps help to anchor the researcher to the state's diverse population, illustrating population, race and ethnic makeup (white, black, Asian, Hispanic), age, home values, household income, high school graduates, college graduates, and presidential election results.

Geography
This chapter explores Indiana's physical features, natural resources, federal land, and Indian reservations, including a satellite view of the state. In addition to providing a visual sense of the state, this data contributes to a better understanding of settlement patterns, economic development, and state resources that are vital for the state's continued growth.

Energy
This is a detailed look at Indiana's energy needs, uses and available resources—including petroleum, natural gas, coal, electricity and renewable energy. The energy sector is a significant economic driver for the state, and plays a big part in the overall lifestyle of its residents.

Climate
This chapter starts with a summary of Indiana's climate, which is followed by three colorful climate maps and profiles of both National and Cooperative Weather Stations. In addition, there are Weather Station Rankings with hundreds of interesting details, such the highest annual snowfall—reported at 67.3 inches at South Bend Michiana Regional.

Comparative Statistics for Indiana's 100 Largest Communities
This chapter makes it easy to compare statistics for Indiana's 100 largest communities by dozens of data points, including density of people per square mile, land area, population size, ethnic percentages, household size, education level and much more. This is a treasure trove of data for grant writers, government researchers and demographers.

Top and Bottom Rankings of Indiana Places over 2,500
This chapter includes rankings for dozens of categories, for both the top 150 and bottom 150 communities with population over 2,500. Explore everything from places at highest elevation (Union City at 1,122 feet above sea level) to lowest elevation (Evansville at 387 feet above sea level). Other topics ranked include employment, household income, population size and many more.

Education
This chapter begins with an Educational State Profile that summarizes number of schools, students, diplomas granted and educational dollars spent. Also included are School District Rankings for 16 topics from Teacher/Student Ratios to High School Drop-Out Rates. Following these rankings are statewide assessment results from the *Indiana Statewide Testing for Educational Progress-Plus (ISTEP+).*

Ancestry, Ethnicity and Race

This chapter gives details about the ancestral, Hispanic and racial makeup of Indiana's 200+ ethnic categories. Profiles are included for the state, its 92 counties, and its places with 50,000 or more residents. In the ranking section, data is displayed three ways: 1) by number, based on all places regardless of population; 2) by percent, based on all places regardless of population; 3) by percent, based on places with populations of 50,000 or more. You will discover, for example, that Crown Point has the greatest number of Macedonians in the state (901), and that 84.6% of the population of Raglesville are of French ancestry.

Profiles

This chapter is arranged alphabetically by county, then by place—for a total of 784 places and 92 counties. These detailed place profiles compile dozens of data points based on the U.S. Census Bureau's American Community Survey and other current government sources such as the Federal Bureau of Investigation, the U.S. Department of Education, and the U.S. Environmental Protection Agency. New categories to this edition include data on selected monthly owner costs with and without a mortgage, the number of dentists per capita, and annual median and maximum Air Quality Index values. These unique place profiles pull together statistical and descriptive information on every Census-recognized place in Indiana plus 105 unincorporated communities.

Profiles of Indiana ends with an **Index of County and Place Names**. This index makes it easy to find the specific profile for a specific county or place.

Researchers' Guide to Data

The following text is designed to support the user in getting the most out of the immense amount of data presented in this newly designed *Profiles of Indiana*. The Introduction that precedes this Researchers' Guide summarizes the 11 chapter topics and arrangement, giving an overview of the content contained within. The individual chapters include their own Introduction, Table of Contents and, in many cases, User Guide with specific guidelines about the data.

What follows here is more specific information on the places in Indiana that are covered and how they are designated. In addition, this Researchers' Guide outlines various uses for the data, from student research papers to government grants to relocation proposals.

Places Covered in *Profiles of Indiana*

All 92 counties.

567 incorporated municipalities. Includes 119 cities, 447 towns, and one consolidated city-county.

112 Census Designated Places (CDP). The U.S. Bureau of the Census defines a CDP as "a statistical entity, defined for each decennial census according to Census Bureau guidelines, comprising a densely settled concentration of population that is not within an incorporated place, but is locally identified by a name. CDPs are delineated cooperatively by state and local officials and the Census Bureau, following Census Bureau guidelines."

105 unincorporated communities. The communities included have statistics for their ZIP Code Tabulation Area (ZCTA) available from the Census Bureau. They are referred to as "postal areas." A ZCTA is a statistical entity developed by the Census Bureau to approximate the delivery area for a US Postal Service 5-digit or 3-digit ZIP Code in the US and Puerto Rico. A ZCTA is an aggregation of census blocks that have the same predominant ZIP Code associated with the mailing addresses in the Census Bureau's Master Address File. Thus, the Postal Service's delivery areas have been adjusted to encompass whole census blocks so that the Census Bureau can tabulate census data for the ZCTAs. ZCTAs do not include all ZIP Codes used for mail delivery and therefore do not precisely depict the area within which mail deliveries associated with that ZIP Code occur. Additionally, some areas that are known by a unique name, although they are part of a larger incorporated place, are also included as "postal areas."

Important Notes

- Since the last decennial census, the U.S. Census replaced the long-form sample with the American Community Survey (ACS), which uses a series of monthly samples to produce annually updated estimates for the same areas. ACS estimates are based on data from a sample of housing units and people in the population, not the full population. ACS sampling error (uncertainty of data) is greater for those areas with smaller populations.
- *Profiles of Indiana* uses the term "community" to refer to all places except counties. The term "county" is used to refer to counties and county-equivalents. All places are defined as of the 2010 Census.
- If a community spans multiple counties, the community will be shown in the county that contains its largest population.
- In each community profile, only school districts that have schools that are physically located within the community are shown. In addition, statistics for each school district cover the entire district, regardless of the physical location of the schools within the district.
- Special care should be taken when interpreting certain statistics for communities containing large colleges or universities. College students were counted as residents of the area in which they were living while attending college (as they have been since the 1950 census). One effect this may have is skewing the figures for population, income, housing, and educational attainment.
- Some information (e.g. income) is available for both counties and individual communities. Other information is available for just counties (e.g. election results), or just individual communities (e.g. crime rates). Please refer to the User Guide in the Profiles chapter for a complete listing.

Research Support

Profiles of Indiana is designed to provide just the right data and insight into the make-up of the state of Indiana. It offers the detail and demographic information that researchers and grant writers need, as well as curriculum support for high school and college students doing state research, comparing the state with other states, and investigating civic topics. This data provides the critical information that translates into successful outcomes related to community or government grants and funding, or research on political science, sociology, history, civics, current events and more.

Users will find that by working their way through the 11 chapters and using the Comparative Section and the Ranking Section in conjunction with specific information in the Profile Section, they can develop strong, statistical-based insights into every populated place in Indiana.

Funding & Grants

This research is crucial for accurate journalism, and offers the necessary knowledge in relation to government initiatives and public works projects. Not only does this extensive data pinpoint specific information necessary to succeed on a wide range of government and non-profit grant applications, but it is the kind of data than helps make sense of trends and needs throughout Indiana.

Curriculum-Based Projects

Just as important to successful funding and grant applications is how *Profiles of Indiana* supports a wide range of curriculum at the high school and college level. Using this work develops an understanding of how to compare and rank statistical information, tasks that strengthen the important critical and analytical thinking skills necessary for students at all levels.

In addition to the wide reaching benefits, *Profiles of Indiana* also shows how to translate the story of statistics into awareness about where we live, how we live there, and how we are affected by current trends in education, crime, health, health insurance and income.

Environmental studies students will benefit from the statistics on land area, water area, transportation, elevation and typography, natural resources and, of course, climate. Access to this data in one place, thoughtfully arranged, with ranking statistics, not only help develop an environmental profile that is unique, but is a game changer for a variety of environmental initiatives. Plus, working with these statistical tables and charts and comparative data and rankings offer great benefit to students working on mathematics and statistical course assignments.

Economic and Business Benefit

The demographics and statistics in *Profiles of Indiana* can help Chambers of Commerce, business councils and others develop supportive materials on the uniqueness of their area for strong job development, relocation, investment, and tourism. *Profiles of Indiana* provides the hard data that businesses turn to when making those critical decisions—data that is thorough, accurate, thoughtfully presented and necessary for important projection and marketing materials.

In summary, *Profiles of Indiana* and its immense amount of thoughtfully arranged content is a valuable resource for a wide variety of uses, from student research papers to corporate relocation professionals.

Facts & Photos

This four-color chapter includes a little bit of everything "Indiana"—state emblems, general map, photos, state history and a timeline. It provides an excellent grounding before digging into the statistics, charts, and rankings that follow.

State Emblems 2

Key Facts 3

Locator Map 3

Photo Gallery 4

History of Indiana 10

Timeline of Indiana History 13

The Hoosier State

The Crossroads of America

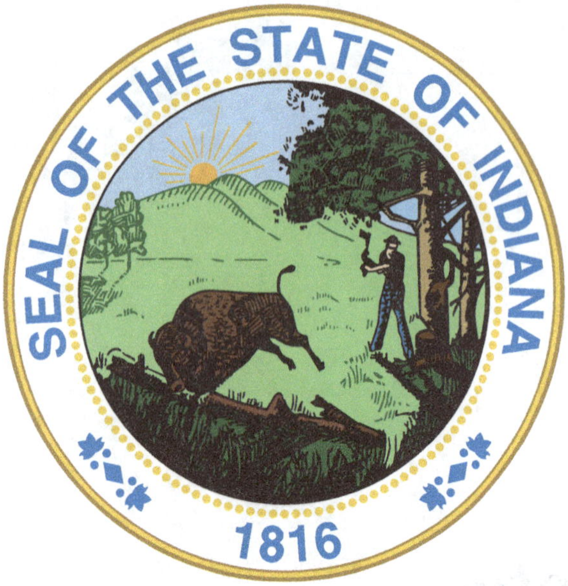

State seal

State flag

State motto, "The Crossroads of America"

State bird, Northern Cardinal (Cardinalis cardinalis)

State flower, Peony (Paeonia)

State insect, Say's Firefly (Pyractomena angulata)

Governor	**Eric Joseph Holcomb (R)**
Lieutenant Governor	**Suzanne Crouch (R)**
State Capital	Indianapolis
Date of Statehood	December 11, 1816 (19th state)
Before Statehood	Indiana Territory
Largest City	Indianapolis
Demonym	Hoosier (official)
Highest Point	Hoosier Hill (1,257 feet)
Lowest Point	Confluence of Ohio River and Wabash River (320 feet)
Time Zone	Eastern (80 counties); Central (12 counties)
State Emblems	
State Bird	Cardinal (*Richmondena cardinalis cardinalis*)
State Flower	Peony (*Paeonia*)
State Insect	Say's Firefly (*Pyractomena angulata*)
State Motto	"The Crossroads of America"
State Nickname	"The Hoosier State"
State Pie	Sugar Cream Pie
State Poem	"Indiana" by Arthur Franklin Mapes
State Rifle	Grouseland Rifle
State River	Wabash River
State Soil	Miami soil (brown silt loam)
State Song	"On the Banks of the Wabash, Far Away" by Paul Dresser
State Stone	Salem Limestone
State Tree	Tulip Tree (*Liriodendron tulipifera*)

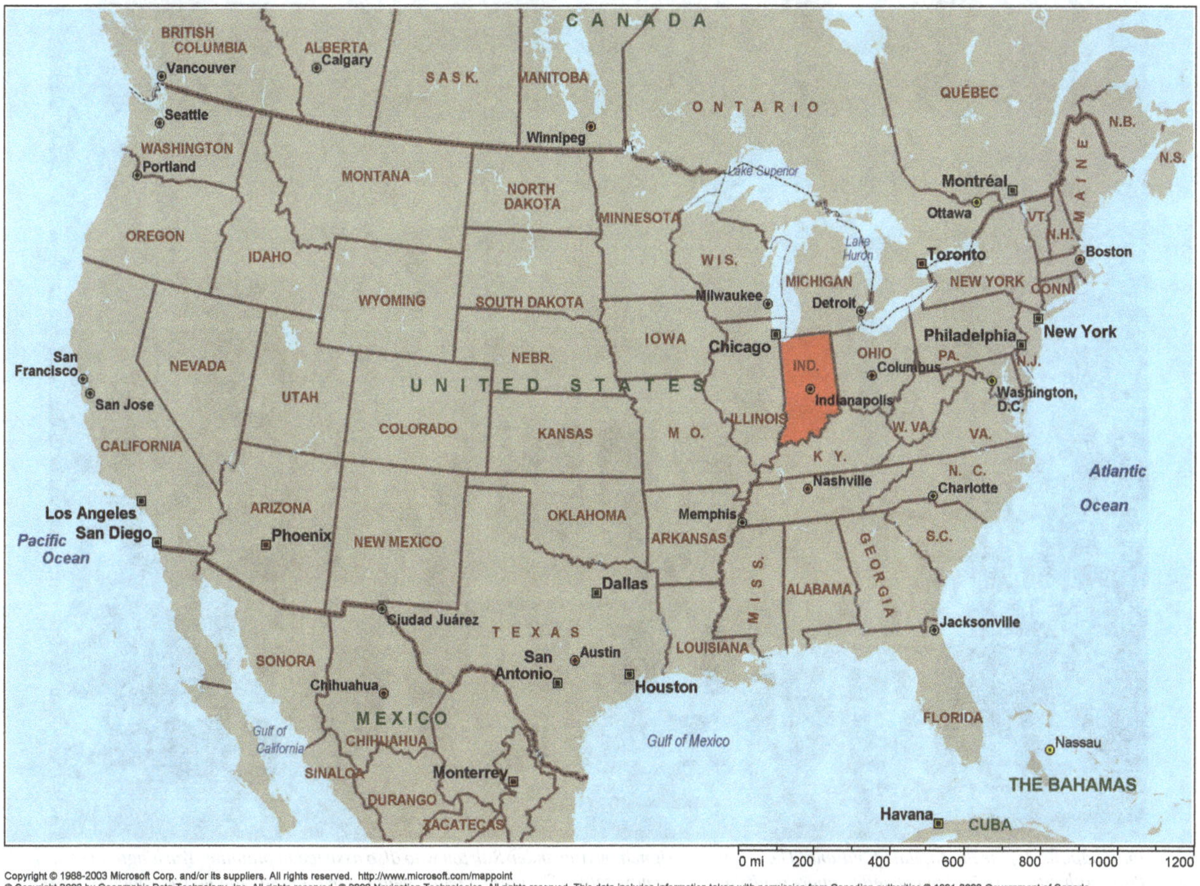

Indianapolis, top, is the capital of Indiana. The city was designed by Alexander Ralston who also assisted in planning Washington D.C.; thus, both cities are laid out on mile-square grids and easily navigable. The bottom photo details the Indiana Statehouse, which is also shown in the foreground of the top photo. It was designed by Edwin May and Adolf Scherer, and built in 1878-1879. In 1975, it was added to the National Register of Historic Places.

Indiana's history with auto racing is steeped in the Indianapolis 500, top. The race happens every Memorial Day weekend, and attracts over 250,000 spectators, making it the largest, single day sporting event in the world. The bottom photo is of Lake Michigan, viewed from Indiana Dunes State Park, whose 250-foot high dunes are the result of glacial sand being forced from the lake by high winds and waves—a natural process that happens nowhere else on earth.

The William Henry Harrison Mansion and Museum in Vincennes, Indiana, top, was built in 1804 for Harrison during his term as governor. It was nicknamed Grouseland, *for the many grouse—large, peasant-like birds—in the area. The bottom photo shows the domed atrium of the West Baden Springs Hotel, built in 1902, and the largest free-spanning dome in the United States until 1955. Both the resort, known for its mineral baths, and* Grouseland, *are national Historic Landmarks.*

Charles C. Deam Wilderness area, top, was designated a wilderness in 1982 and encompasses nearly 13,000 acres of the Hoosier National Forest. With 37.3 miles of trails for hiking, backpacking and horseback riding, it is located in the Indiana Uplands in the northern section of the state. Clifty Creek Power Plant, bottom, is a coal-fired electric plant in Madison. Plants like these provide about 85 percent of Indiana's energy supply.

The University of Notre Dame, whose main building is pictured in the top photo, is ranked among the top 20 universities in the United States. It contains an endowment of nearly $12 billion, the largest in the state. Notre Dame Stadium, bottom, is home to the school's Fighting Irish football team. It was built in 1930, with capacity of 60,000. Today the stadium holds 77,622 and, in 2014, the playing surface was changed from natural grass to FieldTurf.

This Basilica of the Sacred Heart is part of the University of Nortre Dame, a Catholic research university just north of the city of South Bend. Founded in 1842 as an all-male institution, it began enrolling women in 1972. It is considered one of the "Big Three" universities in American Roman Catholic higher education and its athletic teams are members of the NCAA Division I, and known as the Fighting Irish.

History of Indiana

Aboriginal Inhabitants

The first inhabitants in what is now Indiana were the Paleo-Indians, who arrived about 8000 BC after the melting of the glaciers at the end of the Ice Age. Divided into small groups, the Paleo-Indians were nomads who hunted large game such as mastodons. They created stone tools made out of chert by chipping, knapping and flaking. The Archaic period, which began between 5000 and 4000 BC, covered the next phase of indigenous culture. The people developed new tools as well as techniques to cook food, an important step in civilization. Such new tools included different types of spear points and knives, with various forms of notches. They made ground-stone tools such as stone axes, woodworking tools and grinding stones. During the latter part of the period, they built earthwork mounds and middens, which showed that settlements were becoming more permanent. The Archaic period ended at about 1500 BC, although some Archaic people lived until 700 BC. Afterward, the Woodland period took place in Indiana, where various new cultural attributes appeared. During this period, the people created ceramics and pottery, and extended their cultivation of plants. An early Woodland period group named the Adena people had elegant burial rituals, featuring log tombs beneath earth mounds. In the middle portion of the Woodland period, the Hopewell people began developing long-range trade of goods. Nearing the end of the stage, the people developed highly productive cultivation and adaptation of agriculture, growing such crops as corn and squash. The Woodland period ended around 1000 AD. The Mississippian culture emerged, lasting from 1000 until the 15th century, shortly before the arrival of Europeans. During this stage, the people created large urban settlements designed according to their cosmology, with large mounds and plazas defining ceremonial and public spaces. The concentrated settlements depended on the agricultural surpluses. One such complex was the Angel Mounds. They had large public areas such as plazas and platform mounds, where leaders lived or conducted rituals. Mississippian civilization collapsed in Indiana during the mid-15th century for reasons that remain unclear. The historic Native American tribes in the area at the time of European encounter spoke different languages of the Algonquian family. They included the Shawnee, Miami, and Illini. Later they were joined by refugee tribes from eastern regions including the Delaware who settled in the White and Whitewater River Valleys.

European Exploration and Sovereignty

In 1679 the French explorer René-Robert Cavelier, Sieur de La Salle was the first European to cross into Indiana after reaching present-day South Bend at the Saint Joseph River. He returned the following year to learn about the region. French-Canadian fur traders soon arrived, bringing blankets, jewelry, tools, whiskey and weapons to trade for skins with the Native Americans. By 1702, Sieur Juchereau established the first trading post near Vincennes. In 1715, Sieur de Vincennes built Fort Miami at Kekionga, now Fort Wayne. In 1717, another Canadian, Picote de Beletre, built Fort Ouiatenon on the Wabash River, to try to control Native American trade routes from Lake Erie to the Mississippi River. In 1732, Sieur de Vincennes built a second fur trading post at Vincennes. French Canadian settlers, who had left the earlier post because of hostilities, returned in larger numbers. In a period of a few years, British colonists arrived from the East and contended against the Canadians for control of the lucrative fur trade. Fighting between the French and British colonists occurred throughout the 1750s as a result.

The Native American tribes of Indiana sided with the French Canadians during the French and Indian War (also known as the Seven Years' War). With British victory in 1763, the French were forced to cede all their lands in North America east of the Mississippi River and north and west of the colonies to the British crown.

The tribes in Indiana did not give up; they destroyed Fort Ouiatenon and Fort Miami during Pontiac's Rebellion. The British royal proclamation of 1763 designated the land west of the Appalachians for Indian use, and excluded British colonists from the area, which the Crown called Indian Territory. In 1775, the American Revolutionary War began as the colonists sought for more self-government and independence from the British. The majority of the fighting took place near the East Coast, but the Patriot military officer George Rogers Clark called for an army to help fight the British in the west. Clark's army won significant battles and took over Vincennes and Fort Sackville on February 25, 1779. During the war, Clark managed to cut off British troops who were attacking the eastern colonists from the west. His success is often credited for changing the course of the American Revolutionary War. At the end of the war, through the Treaty of Paris, the British crown ceded their claims to the land south of the Great Lakes to the newly formed United States, including American Indian lands.

The Frontier

In 1787 the US defined present-day Indiana as part of its Northwest Territory. In 1800, Congress separated Ohio from the Northwest Territory, designating the rest of the land as the Indiana Territory. President Thomas Jefferson chose William Henry Harrison as the governor of the territory and Vincennes was established as the capital. After Michigan Territory was separated and the Illinois Territory was formed, Indiana was reduced to its current size and geography.

Starting with the Battle of Fallen Timbers in 1794 and Treaty of Greenville, 1795, Indian titles to Indiana lands were extinguished by usurpation, purchase, or war and treaty. About half the state was acquired in the St. Mary's Purchase from the Miami in 1818. Purchases weren't complete until the Treaty of Mississinwas in 1826 acquired the last of the reserved Indian lands in the northeast.

A portrait of the Indiana frontier about 1810: The frontier was defined by the treaty of Fort Wayne in 1809, adding much of southwestern lands around Vincinnes and southeastern lands adjacent to Cincinnati, to areas along the Ohio River as part of U.S. territory. Settlements were military outposts, Fort Ouiatenon in the northwest and Fort Miami (later Fort Wayne) in the northeast, Fort Knox and Vincinnes settlement on the lower Wabash, Clarksville (across from Louisville), Vevay, and Corydon along the Ohio River, the Quaker Colony in Richmond on the eastern border, and Conner's Post (later Connersville) on the east central frontier. Indianapolis wouldn't be a populated place for 15 more years, and central and northern Indiana Territory remained savage wilderness. Indian presence was waning, but still a threat to settlement. Only two counties, Clark and Dearborn in the extreme southeast, had been organized. Land titles issued out of Cincinnati were sparse. Migration was chiefly by flatboat on the Ohio River westerly, and wagon trails up the Wabash/White River Valleys (west) and Whitewater River Valleys (east).

In 1810, the Shawnee chief Tecumseh and his brother Tenskwatawa encouraged other tribes in the territory to resist European settlement. Tensions rose and the US authorized Harrison to launch a preemptive expedition against Tecumseh's Confederacy; the US gained victory at the Battle of Tippecanoe on November 7, 1811. Tecumseh was killed in 1813 during the Battle of Thames. After his death, armed resistance to United States control ended in the region. Most Native American tribes in the state were later removed to west of the Mississippi River in the 1820s and 1830s after US negotiations and purchase of their lands.

Statehood and Settlement

In order to decrease the threat of Indian raids following the Battle of Tippecanoe, Corydon, a town in the far southern part of Indiana, was named the second capital of the Indiana Territory in May 1813. Two years later, a petition for statehood was approved by the territorial general assembly and sent to Congress. An Enabling Act was passed to provide an election of delegates to write a constitution for Indiana. On June 10, 1816, delegates assembled at Corydon to write the constitution, which was completed in 19 days. President James Madison approved Indiana's admission into the union as the nineteenth state on December 11, 1816. In 1825, the state capital was moved from Corydon to Indianapolis.

Many European immigrants went west to settle in Indiana in the early 19th century. The largest immigrant group to settle in Indiana were Germans, as well as numerous immigrants from Ireland and England. Americans who were primarily ethnically English migrated from the Northern Tier of New York and New England, as well as the mid-Atlantic state of Pennsylvania. The arrival of steamboats on the Ohio River in 1811, and the National Road at Richmond in 1829 greatly facilitated settlement of northern and western Indiana.

Following statehood, the new government worked to transform Indiana from a frontier into a developed, well-populated, and thriving state, beginning significant demographic and economic changes. The state's founders initiated a program, Indiana Mammoth Internal Improvement Act, that led to the construction of roads, canals, railroads and state-funded public schools. The plans bankrupted the state and were a financial disaster, but increased land and produce value more than fourfold. In response to the crisis and in order to avert another, in 1851, a second constitution was adopted. Among its provisions were a prohibition on public debt and extension of suffrage to African-Americans.

Civil War

During the American Civil War, Indiana became politically influential and played an important role in the affairs of the nation. As the first western state to mobilize for the United States in the war, Indiana had soldiers participating in all of the major engagements. The state provided 126 infantry regiments, 26 batteries of artillery and 13 regiments of cavalry to the cause of the Union. In 1861, Indiana was assigned a quota of 7,500 men to join the Union Army. So many volunteered in the first call that thousands had to be turned away. Before the war ended, Indiana contributed 208,367 men to fight and serve in the war. Casualties were over 35% among these men: 24,416 lost their lives in the conflict and over 50,000 more were wounded. The only Civil War battle fought in Indiana was the Battle of Corydon, which occurred during Morgan's Raid. The battle left 15 dead, 40 wounded, and 355 captured.

Indiana remained a largely agricultural state; post-war industries included food processing, such as milling grain, distilling it into alcohol, and meatpacking; building of wagons, buggies, farm machinery, and hardware.

Early 20th century

With the onset of the industrial revolution, Indiana industry began to grow at an accelerated rate across the northern part of the state. With industrialization, workers developed labor unions and suffrage movements arose in relation to the progress of women. The Indiana Gas Boom led to rapid industrialization during the late 19th century by providing cheap fuel to the region. In the early 20th century, Indiana developed into a strong manufacturing state with ties to the new auto industry. Haynes-Apperson, the nation's first commercially successful auto company, operated in Kokomo until 1925. The construction of the Indianapolis Motor Speedway and the start of auto-related industries were also related to the auto industry boom.

During the 1930s, Indiana, like the rest of the nation, was affected by the Great Depression. The economic downturn had a wide-ranging negative impact on Indiana, such as the decline of urbanization. The Dust Bowl further to the west resulted in many migrants fleeing into the more industrialized Midwest. Governor Paul V. McNutt's administration struggled to build a state-funded welfare system to help the overwhelmed private charities. During his administration, spending and taxes were both cut drastically in response to the Depression, and the state government was completely reorganized. McNutt ended Prohibition in the state and enacted the state's first income tax. On several occasions, he declared martial law to put an end to worker strikes. World War II helped lift the economy in Indiana, as the war required steel, food and other goods that were produced in the state. Roughly 10 percent of Indiana's population joined the armed forces, while hundreds of industries earned war production contracts and began making war material. Indiana manufactured 4.5 percent of total United States military armaments produced during World War II, ranking eighth among the 48 states. The expansion of industry to meet war demands helped end the Great Depression.

Modern Era

With the conclusion of World War II, Indiana rebounded to levels of production prior to the Great Depression. Industry became the primary employer, a trend that continued into the 1960s. Urbanization during the 1950s and 1960s led to substantial growth in the state's cities. The auto, steel and pharmaceutical industries topped Indiana's major businesses. Indiana's population continued to grow during the years after the war, exceeding five million by the 1970 census. In the 1960s, the administration of Matthew E. Welsh adopted its first sales tax of two percent. Indiana schools were desegregated in 1949. In 1950, the Census Bureau reported Indiana's population as 95.5% white and 4.4% black. Governor Welsh also worked with the General Assembly to pass the Indiana Civil Rights Bill, granting equal protection to minorities in seeking employment.

Beginning in 1970, a series of amendments to the state constitution were proposed. With adoption, the Indiana Court of Appeals was created and the procedure of appointing justices on the courts was adjusted.

The 1973 oil crisis created a recession that hurt the automotive industry in Indiana. Companies such as Delco Electronics and Delphi began a long series of downsizing that contributed to high unemployment rates in manufacturing in Anderson, Muncie, and Kokomo. The restructuring and deindustrialization trend continued until the 1980s, when the national and state economy began to diversify and recover.
Source: Wikipedia

Timeline of Indiana History

1614-1615
Samuel de Champlain, New France governor, explored Maumee River region

1671
Simon de Saint-Lusson claimed most of the area for France

1679
Rene-Robert Cavelier de La Salle, Louis de Baude de Frontenac, planned for control of Maumee-Wabash trade route; plans included relocation of Miami Indians to headwaters of Maumee River

1728-1732
Vincennes established on Wabash River by France, first European settlement in area

1747
British convinced Huron Indian Chief, King Nicolas, to attack French-owned Fort Miami

1752-1753
Smallpox epidemic devastated local Indian population

1754-1763
France and Indian War

1763
England gained control of Vincennes and Indiana area; Proclamation of 1763 forbade settlement west of Appalachian Mountains; British sent Indian war parties to attack settlers who disobeyed proclamation

1772
General Gage ordered France to leave settlements in Wabash Valley, demanded land deeds

1774
British Parliament passed Quebec Act, French settlements, including Indiana, were included in province of Quebec

1775-1783
Revolutionary War

1777
British encouraged Indians to attack settlers George Rogers Clark

1778
Colonel George Rogers Clark's expedition captured Fort Sackville at Vincennes; Indiana became part of Virginia; British Governor Henry Hamilton overtook Fort Sackville

1779
British at Fort Sackville surrendered to Colonel George Rogers Clark, his expedition and Francis Vigo

1783
Treaty of Paris gave modern-day Indiana lands to United States

1787
Continental Congress created Northwest Territory; territory to be governed by a governor, three judges; laws prohibited slavery, encouraged public education, guaranteed religious freedom and civil rights

1794
Anthony Wayne overwhelmed Shawnee Indians, led by Tecumseh, in battle near rapids of Maumee River; Anthony Wayne established fort, named Fort Wayne

1800
Indiana Territory established from Northwest Territory; William Henry Harrison first Governor; Vincennes named capital

1803
Indians signed treaties ceding land in Indiana

1805
Michigan Territory separated from Indiana Territory

1809
Illinois Territory separated from Indiana Territory

1811
Chief Tecumseh and Indians defeated in Battle of Tippecanoe

1812-1814
War of 1812

1813
Chief Tecumseh killed at Battle of the Thames; Indiana Territory capital moved to Corydon

1814
Treaty of Ghent ended War of 1812

1816
Indiana became 19th U. S. state; Jonathan Jennings first Governor; Abraham Lincoln and family moved to Indiana

1818
Indians gave up claims to portion of central Indiana, "New Purchase"

1825
State capital moved to Indianapolis

1835
Wabash and Erie Canal opened from Fort Wayne to Huntington

1842
University of Notre Dame founded

1851
State Consitution adopted, included measure protecting property rights of married women

1861-1865
Civil War

1889
Standard Oil Co. built refinery in Whiting

1897
Tribal status of Miami Indians terminated

1906
U. S. Steel Company built plant, founded Gary

1908
Serial killer, Belle Gunness, died in fire at her farm in LaPorte

1911
First Indy 500 auto race occurred

1915
Workmen's Compensation Act enacted

1925
Tri-State tornado struck Indiana, Illinois, Missouri; many dead

1930
Mob broke into Marion jail, beat two young black men to death, hung them from tree

1937
Ohio River flooded causing severe damage in southern Indiana

1956
Northern Indiana Toll Road completed

1963
Studebaker Automobile Corporation ceased auto production at South Bend plant

1974
Series of 148 tornadoes struck the Midwest and Southern states (including Indiana); many killed with severe property damage

1980
Indianapolis businessman, Herbert Baumeister, killed 16 men, most gay

1984
NFL Baltimore Colts moved to Indianapolis

1985
AIDS patient, Ryan White, barred from attending public school

1987
Air Force jet crashed into Ramada Inn near Indianapolis Airport, ten killed

1988
Indianian J. Danforth Quayle, elected U. S. Vice President

1998
Explosion at Southern Energy Co. in Hammond killed 16

1999
Lilly Endowment Inc. presented $50 million grant to Hispanic Scholarship Fund

2001
Cicero's town president, nine others, charged with stealing $10 million in taxpayer monies; Oklahoma City bomber, Timothy McVeigh, executed at Federal Penitentiary in Terre Haute

2003
Governor Frank O'Bannon suffered massive stroke, died

2004
Indianapolis Colts' Peyton Manning broke Dan Marino's pass record

2005
Measles outbreak among school children; tornado struck Evansville, 22 killed, 200 injured

2007
Indianapolis Colts won Super Bowl XLI

2010
Eight teenagers shot at skating rink during concert in Gary

2011
Five people killed, more than 40 injured in stage collapse at Indiana State Fair

2012
Series of powerful storms and tornadoes left 13 dead, destroyed town of Marysville

Indiana Governor Mitch Daniels signed legislation making Indiana the 23rd right-to-work state

New York Giants quarterback Eli Manning led his team to a 21-17 victory over the New England Patriots in Super Bowl XLVI at Lucas Oil Stadium in Indianapolis.

BP agreed to spend over $400 million to settle legal complaints about chronic pollution problems at its refinery in northwest Indiana.

Mike Pence, a Republican congressman, was elected state governor.

2013
Floodwaters swelled the Mississippi River and other Midwestern rivers following days of torrential rains. Two flood related deaths were in Indiana.

2014
U.S. health officials reported the first time that Middle East respiratory syndrome (MERS) spread from one person to another in the U.S. when an Indiana man (the first US case of MERS) spread the virus to an Illinois man.

The U.S. Supreme court denied review of cases that limited marriage to opposite sex couples, in effect, granting equal marriage rights to gays and lesbians in Indiana and four other states.

2015
Theodore Hesburgh (b.1917), former president of Notre Dame University (1952-1987), died. He was awarded the Presidential

Medal of Freedom in 1964 and the Congressional Gold Medal in 2000.

Indiana governor Mike Pence signed into law a religious objections bill that opponents worry could allow discrimination against gays and lesbians.

2016
Indiana Gov. Mike Pence signed a bill that broadly limited women's access to abortions, prohibiting abortions on the grounds of Down's syndrome or any other disability. The American Civil Liberties Union and Planned Parenthood of Indiana and Kentucky sued Indiana over the law.

GOP front runner Donald Trump named Indiana Gov. Mike Pence as his running mate.

2017
Former Indiana governor and congressman Mike Pence becomes vice president.

Republican Eric Holcomb became Indiana's 51st governor and quickly reversed several of Pence's policies, declaring an emergency in East Chicago over lead contamination, pardoning wrongly convicted Keith Cooper and canceling a plan to lease the state's cell phone towers.

Takuma Sato became the first Japanese driver to win the Indianapolis 500.

A federal judge blocked Indiana from enforcing a law banning abortions due to fetal genetic abnormalities and requiring that aborted fetuses be buried or cremated.

2018
State lawmakers passed a bill legalizing the sale of alcohol on Sundays.

CBD oil becomes legal in Indiana.

South Bend Democratic Mayor Pete Buttigieg married his same-sex partner at the Cathedral of Saint James Episcopal Church in South Bend.

2019
South Bend Mayor Pete Buttigieg becomes a candidate for President in 2020.
Source: www.worldatlas.com; www.timelinesdb.com

Government

This chapter summarizes how the government of Indiana works, including details of the state's legislative, judicial and executive branches, descriptions of different types of local government—county, town, city, township—and a Congressional District map.

Overview 19
Legislature 19
Judiciary 19
Executive 19
Checks and Balances 19
How a Bill Becomes a Law—Constitutional Requirements 19
County Government 20
Town Government 20
City Government 20
Township Government 21
Congressional District Map 22

The Hoosier State

The Crossroads of America

A Guide to Indiana State Government

Overview

The government of Indiana is established and regulated by the Constitution of Indiana. The state-level government consists of three branches, the judicial branch, the legislative branch, and the executive branch. The three branches balance share power and jointly govern the state of Indiana. County and local governments are also constitutional bodies with limited authority to levy taxes, pass legislation, and create and maintain local public infrastructure.

The government of Indiana was first formed in December 1816 and replaced the government of the Indiana Territory. The early government came under criticism beginning as early as the 1820s for having many public offices filled by appointment and lack of delegation of authority to lower officials, requiring state level legislation for things like divorce approval. In 1851 a new constitution was adopted by the state remedying many of these problems and opening more offices to public election. Significant government reforms were enacted again in 1971 when the state courts were reorganized and new powers were granted to the governor which had historically been a weak institution.

Elections to fill positions in Indiana's government are held biennally on Election Day, with special elections being occasionally held to fill unexpected vacancies. State representatives serve two-year terms, while all other elected state, county, and municipal officials serve four-year terms. Most of the positions in the government bureaucracy are filled through the state merit system or the state patronage system.

The government provides a wide range of services including law enforcement, infrastructure construction and maintenance, licensing and registration of numerous things, tax collection, fire protection, business and utility regulation, utility services, and park and conversation maintenance efforts.

The government of Indiana sits in the state capital of Indianapolis. Each of the three branches operates out of the Indiana Statehouse. The state maintains several office buildings that hold many of its bureaus and departments. Most of the state's bureaus are located in the Indiana Government Center North, a high-rise tower in downtown Indianapolis.

Legislature

The Indiana General Assembly is the legislative branch of the state of Indiana. It is a bicameral legislature that consists of a lower house, the Indiana House of Representatives, and an upper house, the Indiana Senate. The General Assembly meets annually at the Indiana State House in Indianapolis.

Members of the General Assembly are elected from districts that are realigned every ten years. Representatives serve two-year terms; senators serve four-year terms. Both houses must pass a bill before it can be submitted to the governor and enacted into law.

Judiciary

The Supreme Court of Indiana is the highest judicial body in Indiana. The court oversees the lower courts and commissions that jointly make up the judicial branch. The other courts include the Indiana Tax Court, the Indiana Court of Appeals, and circuit, superior, and city or town courts. The courts are assisted by several commissions that are also part of the judicial branch, including the Judicial Nominating Commission.

Executive

The Governor of Indiana is the chief executive officer of the government of Indiana. Elected to a four-year term, the Governor is responsible for overseeing the day-to-day management of the functions of the state government. The governor is assisted by other officials elected to the executive branch including the Lieutenant Governor and the Attorney General.

Checks and Balances

The Constitution of Indiana has several checks and balances built into its clauses to prevent any one branch of the government from becoming dominant. The governor has the power to veto any bill passed by the General Assembly. The General Assembly has the power to override a veto with a simple majority. The courts have the authority to declare laws unconstitutional and revoke them, while the General Assembly has the power to initiate an amendment to the constitution to override the decision of the courts. The courts judges are appointed by a commission made of representatives of the governor and the courts, and their jurisdictions can be regulated by the General Assembly.

How a Bill Becomes a Law—Constitutional Requirements

INTRODUCTION

"The style of every law shall be: 'Be it enacted by the General Assembly of the State of Indiana'; and no law shall be enacted, except by bill. Bills may originate in either House, but may be amended or rejected in the other; except that bills for raising revenue shall originate in the House of Representatives" Art. 4. Sec. 1; Art. 4, Sec. 17

CONSIDERATION

"Every bill shall be read, by title, on three several days, in each House; unless, in case of emergency, two-thirds of the House where such bill may be pending shall, by a vote of yeas and nays, deem it expedient to dispense with this rule; but the reading of a bill, by title, on its final passage, shall, in no case, be dispensed with; and the vote on the passage of every bill or joint resolution shall be taken by yeas and nays" Art. 4. Sec. 18

PASSAGE

"A majority of all the members elected to each House, shall be necessary to pass every bill or joint resolution; and all bills and joint resolutions so passed, shall be signed by the Presiding Officers of the respective Houses" Art. 4, Sec. 25

PRESENTMENT

"Every bill which shall have passed the General Assembly shall be presented to the Governor" Art. 5, Sec. 14

FILING

"Every bill presented to the Governor which is signed by him or on which he fails to act within said seven days after presentment shall be filed with the Secretary of State within ten days of presentmentàIn the event a bill is passed over the Governor's veto, such bill shall be filed with the Secretary of State without further presentment to the Governor" Art. 5, Sec. 17

CIRCULATION

"No act shall take effect, until the same shall have been published and circulated in the several counties of the State, by authority, except in case of emergency, which emergency shall be declared in the preamble, or in the body, of the law" Art. 5, Sec. 17

County Government

County governments are made up of two bodies:

County Council—A county council of seven to fifteen members controls all spending and revenue of the county government. Four of the representatives are elected from county districts; the other three representatives are elected at large. The council members serve four year terms. They are responsible for setting salaries, the annual budget, and special spending. The council also has limited authority to impose local taxes, usually in the form of an income tax that is subject to state level approval, excise taxes, or service taxes, like those on dining or lodging.

Commissioners—The executive body consists of three to five commissioners. The commissioners are elected county wide, usually in staggered terms, and serve four-year terms. One of the commissioners, typically the most senior, serves as president. They are charged with executing the acts legislated by the council and managing the day-to-day functions of the county government.

Counties also have employee boards to oversee different aspects of the county. These boards are usually filled by direct election from the public, appointment by the commission, or a combination of both methods. Boards typically oversee management of water facilities, public roads, and new projects, among others tasks. Each school district has a board that is elected by public election. County school boards are responsible for funding and management of the public school system within their district. The majority of school funding comes from property taxes imposed by the board on the district. The tax rate is subject to state level approval and is capped, by law, at 1% of property value.

Court: Each county forms a Judicial Circuit of the state, and has a Circuit Court. Some counties also have Superior Courts. These are the courts of general jurisdiction. Marion County also has dedicated small claims courts.

County Officials: The county has several other elected offices, including sheriff, coroner, auditor, treasurer, recorder, surveyor, and circuit court clerk. Each of these elected officers serves a term of four years and oversees a different part of the county government. Members elected to county government positions are required to declare party affiliations and to be residents of the county.

Town Government

Many small communities in Indiana are incorporated as towns. A town has a council-manager form of government, with a three- or five-member Town Council serving as primarily the legislature function of government. For practical reasons, the Town Council may share in some of the executive functions. However, under statute, the role of the executive officer belongs to the President of the Town Council. The President of the Town Council is an elected member of the town selected by his fellow town councilmen to lead the council. The council may appoint a non-partisan town manager to oversee the day-to-day operations of the municipal government. The council is responsible for setting the town's budget and tax rates, and appointing all town employees.

Unlike some states, Indiana council members must declare a political party affiliation, if any, when they file to run for office. Upon election in November, they are sworn in before January 1 of the following year and serve a four-year term. There are no state term limits affecting how many times a candidate may run for reelection to office.

A town also elects a clerk/treasurer, who manages the town's finances. As an elected official, the clerk/treasurer is solely executive in function and operates independently of the town council, but operates within the council-approved budget.

City Government

Most larger communities are incorporated as cities. A city can be either a third-class city or a second-class city (the first-class designation is reserved for Indianapolis). An Indiana city has a mayor-council form of government, but a third-class city may appoint a city manager. The mayor, elected to a four-year term, serves as the executive. Most mayors in Indiana are elected in partisan elections. The legislative branch consists of a five-, seven-, or nine-member City Council. Council members serve four-year terms, and may be elected by geographic districts or at-large. Most cities in Indiana use districts.

Township Government

A township trustee administers the civil government of the township. The trustee is elected by the residents of the township to a term of four years. The trustee is responsible for providing fire protection and ambulance service to unincorporated areas, providing relief for those living in poverty and burial of the indigent, maintaining cemeteries and burial grounds, resolving fencing disputes between neighbors, investigating claims of livestock killed by dogs, controlling weeds, managing the township budget and financial records, and preparing an annual financial report. The trustee also acts as the property tax assessor. Other public matters in which a trustee may sometimes be involved include zoning, parks, libraries, schools, shelters and community centers.

The trustee is assisted by a three-member Township Board whose members are elected to four-year terms. Duties of the board include adopting the annual budget, serving as a board of finance and approving township contracts. In January of each year, the trustee presents to the board an annual report showing the receipts, expenditures, investments and debts of the township. The approved report is then published in local papers for public inspection.
Source: State of Indiana, http://www.in.gov; Wikipedia, http://en.wikipedia.org/wiki/Government_of_Indiana

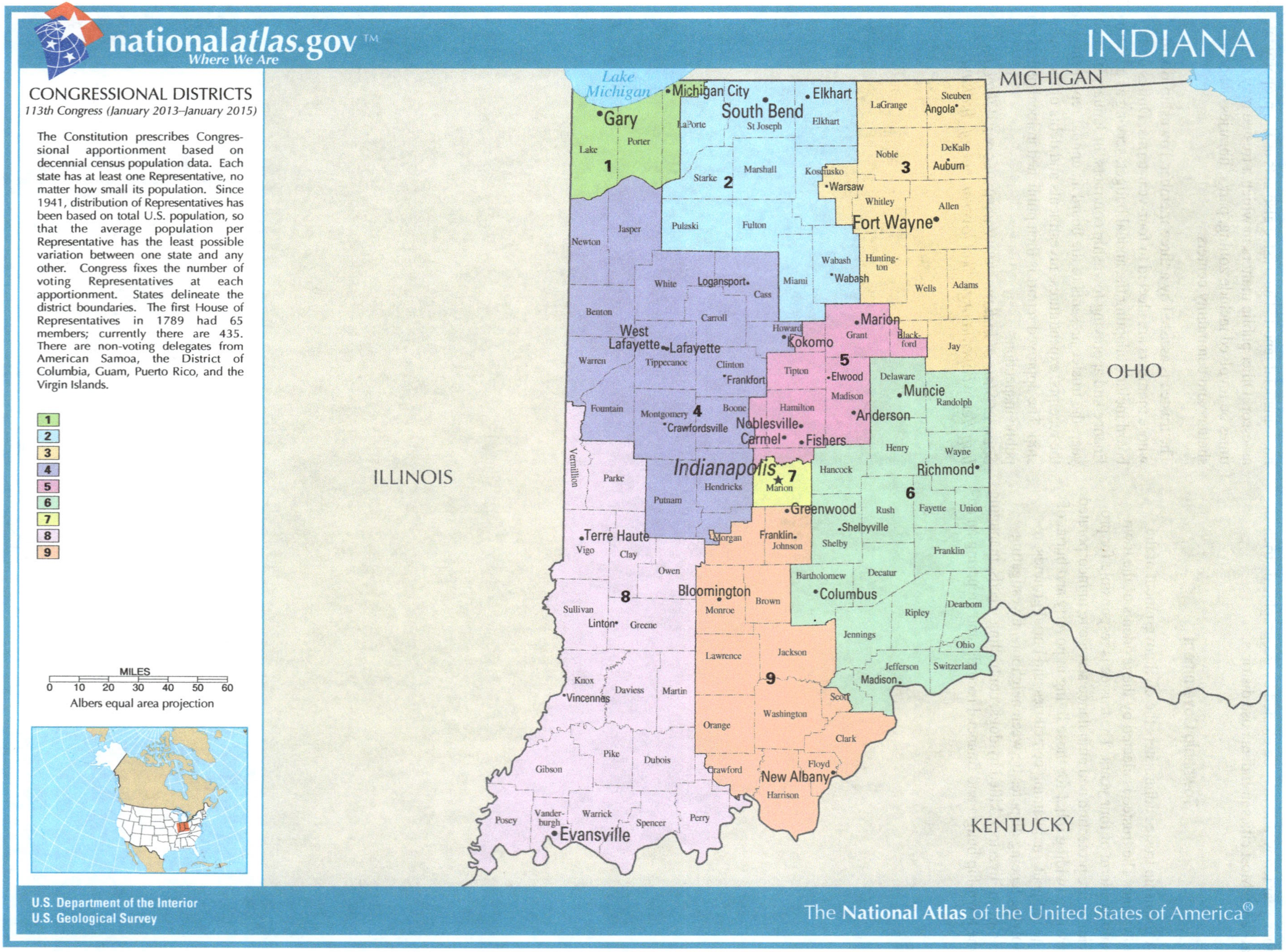
nationalatlas.gov™
Where We Are
INDIANA
CONGRESSIONAL DISTRICTS
113th Congress (January 2013–January 2015)
The Constitution prescribes Congressional apportionment based on decennial census population data. Each state has at least one Representative, no matter how small its population. Since 1941, distribution of Representatives has been based on total U.S. population, so that the average population per Representative has the least possible variation between one state and any other. Congress fixes the number of voting Representatives at each apportionment. States delineate the district boundaries. The first House of Representatives in 1789 had 65 members; currently there are 435. There are non-voting delegates from American Samoa, the District of Columbia, Guam, Puerto Rico, and the Virgin Islands.
1
2
3
4
5
6
7
8
9
MILES
0 10 20 30 40 50 60
Albers equal area projection
Lake Michigan
MICHIGAN
OHIO
ILLINOIS
KENTUCKY
Gary
Michigan City
South Bend
Elkhart
Fort Wayne
Angola
Auburn
Warsaw
Wabash
Logansport
Kokomo
Marion
West Lafayette
Lafayette
Frankfort
Elwood
Muncie
Anderson
Noblesville
Carmel
Fishers
Crawfordsville
Indianapolis
Richmond
Greenwood
Shelbyville
Franklin
Terre Haute
Bloomington
Columbus
Linton
Vincennes
Madison
New Albany
Evansville
Lake
Porter
LaPorte
St Joseph
Elkhart
LaGrange
Steuben
Noble
DeKalb
Kosciusko
Whitley
Allen
Starke
Marshall
Pulaski
Fulton
Newton
Jasper
White
Cass
Miami
Wabash
Huntington
Wells
Adams
Benton
Carroll
Howard
Grant
Blackford
Jay
Warren
Tippecanoe
Clinton
Tipton
Madison
Delaware
Randolph
Fountain
Montgomery
Boone
Hamilton
Henry
Wayne
Vermillion
Parke
Putnam
Hendricks
Marion
Hancock
Rush
Fayette
Union
Vigo
Clay
Morgan
Johnson
Shelby
Franklin
Owen
Monroe
Brown
Bartholomew
Decatur
Dearborn
Sullivan
Greene
Ripley
Jennings
Ohio
Lawrence
Jackson
Jefferson
Switzerland
Knox
Daviess
Martin
Scott
Washington
Orange
Clark
Gibson
Pike
Dubois
Crawford
Floyd
Harrison
Posey
Vanderburgh
Warrick
Spencer
Perry
U.S. Department of the Interior
U.S. Geological Survey
The National Atlas of the United States of America®

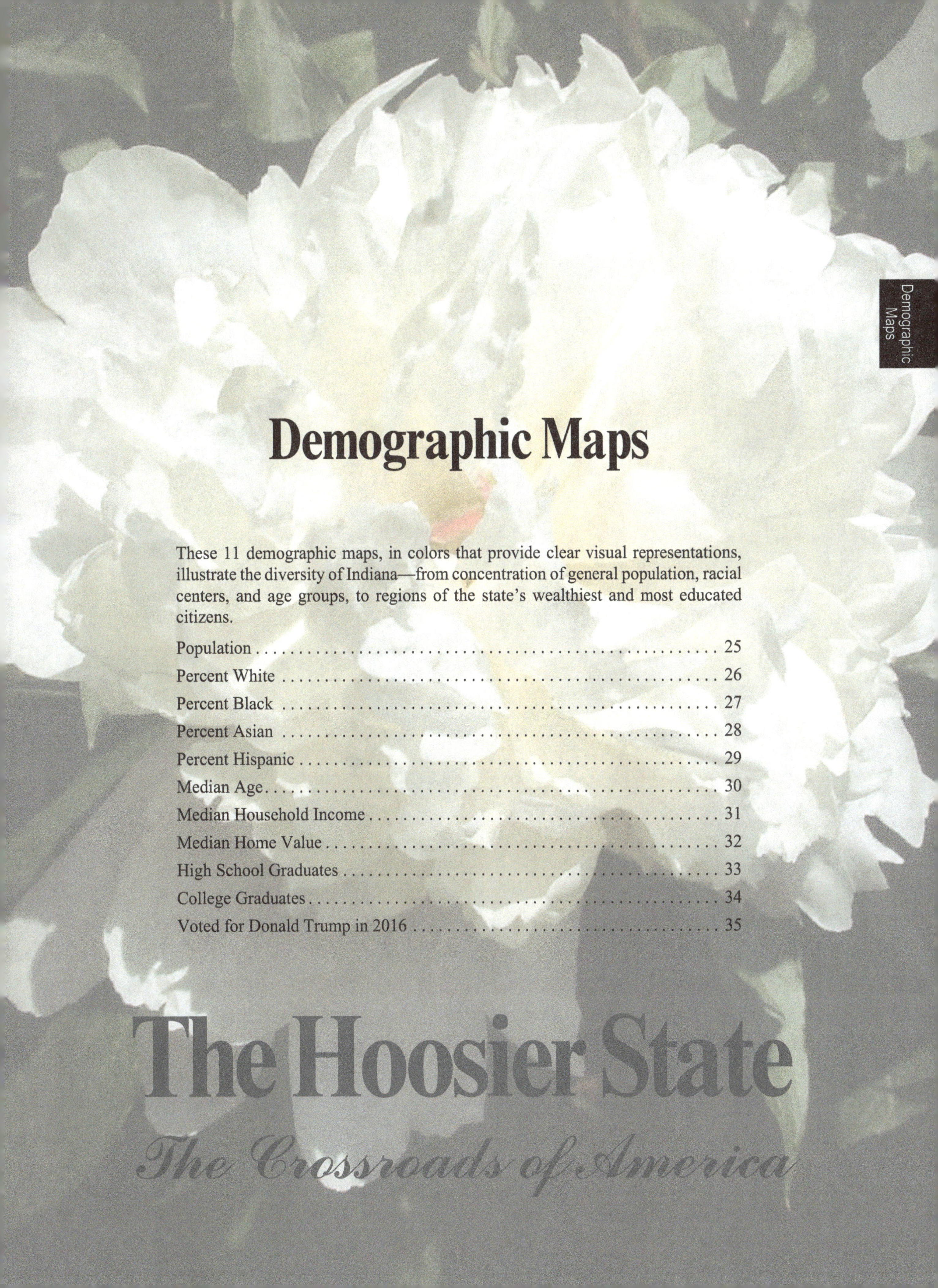

Demographic Maps

These 11 demographic maps, in colors that provide clear visual representations, illustrate the diversity of Indiana—from concentration of general population, racial centers, and age groups, to regions of the state's wealthiest and most educated citizens.

Population 25
Percent White 26
Percent Black 27
Percent Asian 28
Percent Hispanic 29
Median Age 30
Median Household Income 31
Median Home Value 32
High School Graduates 33
College Graduates 34
Voted for Donald Trump in 2016 35

Population

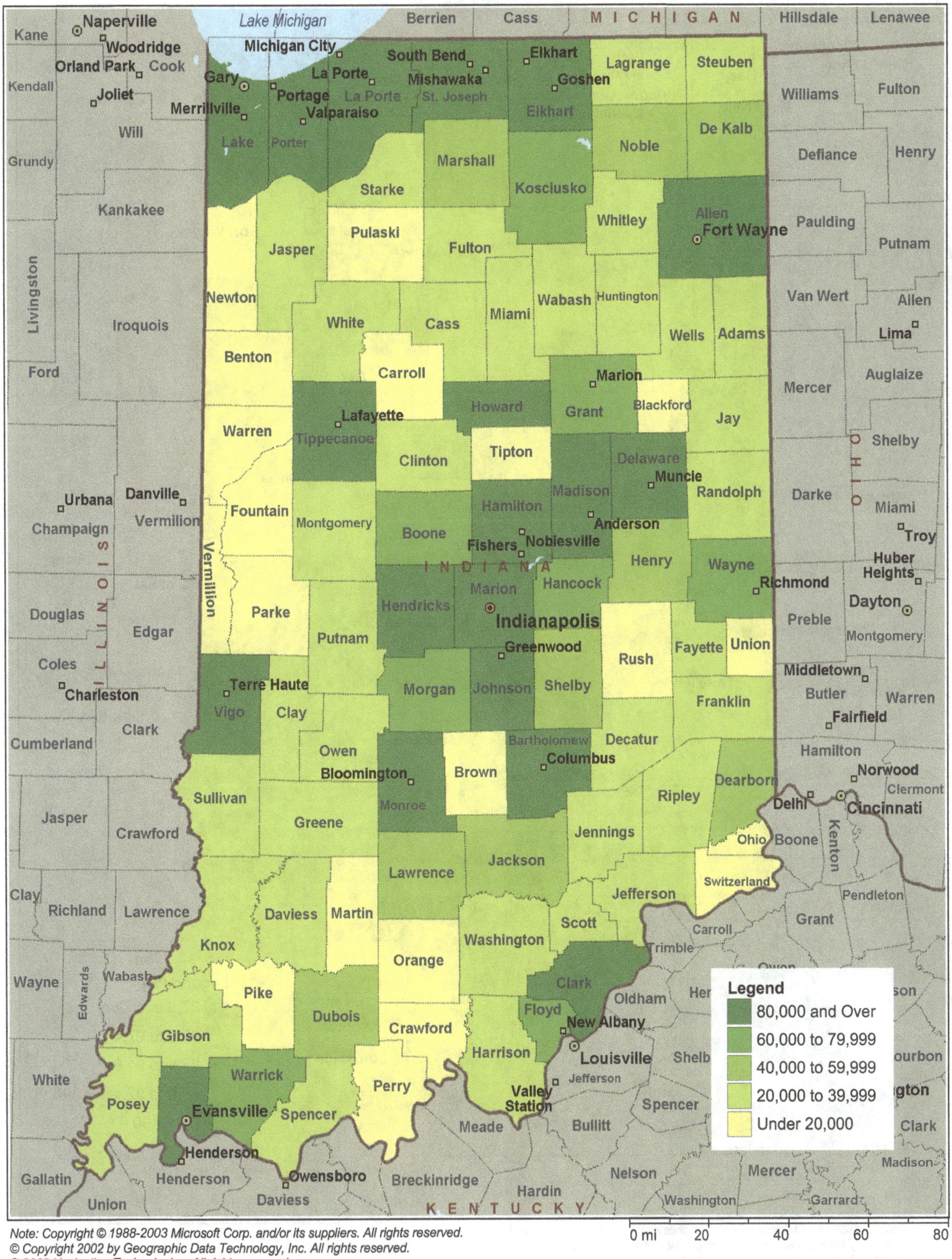
Lake Michigan
MICHIGAN
INDIANA
ILLINOIS
OHIO
KENTUCKY
Michigan City
South Bend
Elkhart
Goshen
Mishawaka
La Porte
Gary
Portage
Merrillville
Valparaiso
Lake
Porter
St. Joseph
Lagrange
Steuben
Noble
De Kalb
Marshall
Kosciusko
Starke
Pulaski
Jasper
Fulton
Whitley
Allen
Fort Wayne
Newton
White
Cass
Miami
Wabash
Huntington
Wells
Adams
Benton
Carroll
Marion
Grant
Blackford
Jay
Howard
Lafayette
Tippecanoe
Warren
Clinton
Tipton
Delaware
Muncie
Randolph
Madison
Hamilton
Fountain
Montgomery
Boone
Anderson
Fishers
Noblesville
Henry
Wayne
Richmond
Vermillion
Hendricks
Hancock
Parke
Indianapolis
Putnam
Rush
Fayette
Union
Greenwood
Vigo
Terre Haute
Clay
Morgan
Johnson
Shelby
Franklin
Owen
Bloomington
Monroe
Brown
Bartholomew
Columbus
Decatur
Dearborn
Ripley
Sullivan
Greene
Jennings
Ohio
Switzerland
Lawrence
Jackson
Jefferson
Knox
Daviess
Martin
Scott
Washington
Orange
Clark
Pike
Dubois
Floyd
New Albany
Louisville
Crawford
Harrison
Gibson
Warrick
Posey
Evansville
Spencer
Perry
Henderson
Owensboro
Cincinnati
Dayton
Lima
Legend
80,000 and Over
60,000 to 79,999
40,000 to 59,999
20,000 to 39,999
Under 20,000
0 mi 20 40 60 80

Percent White

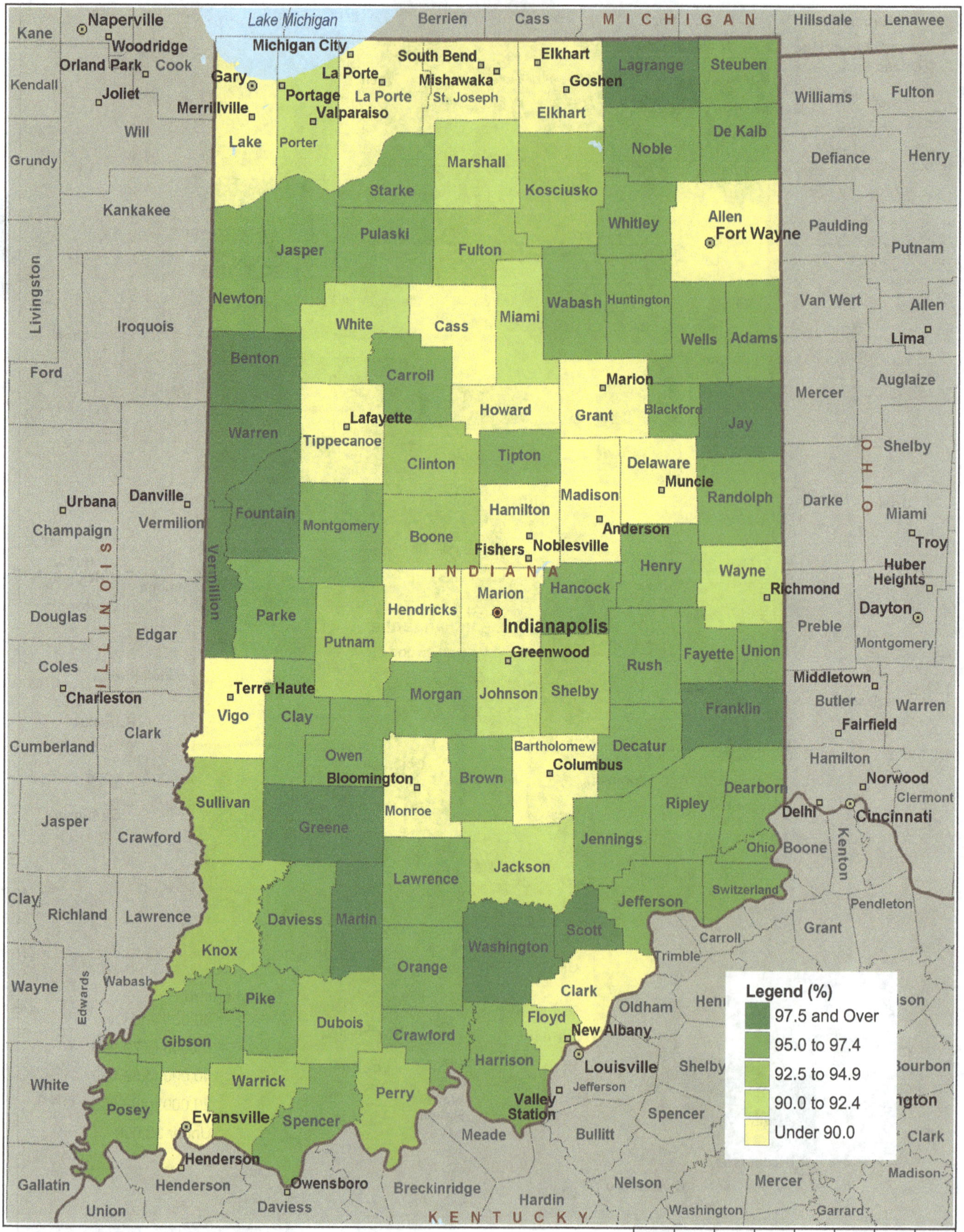

0 mi 20 40 60 80

Percent Black

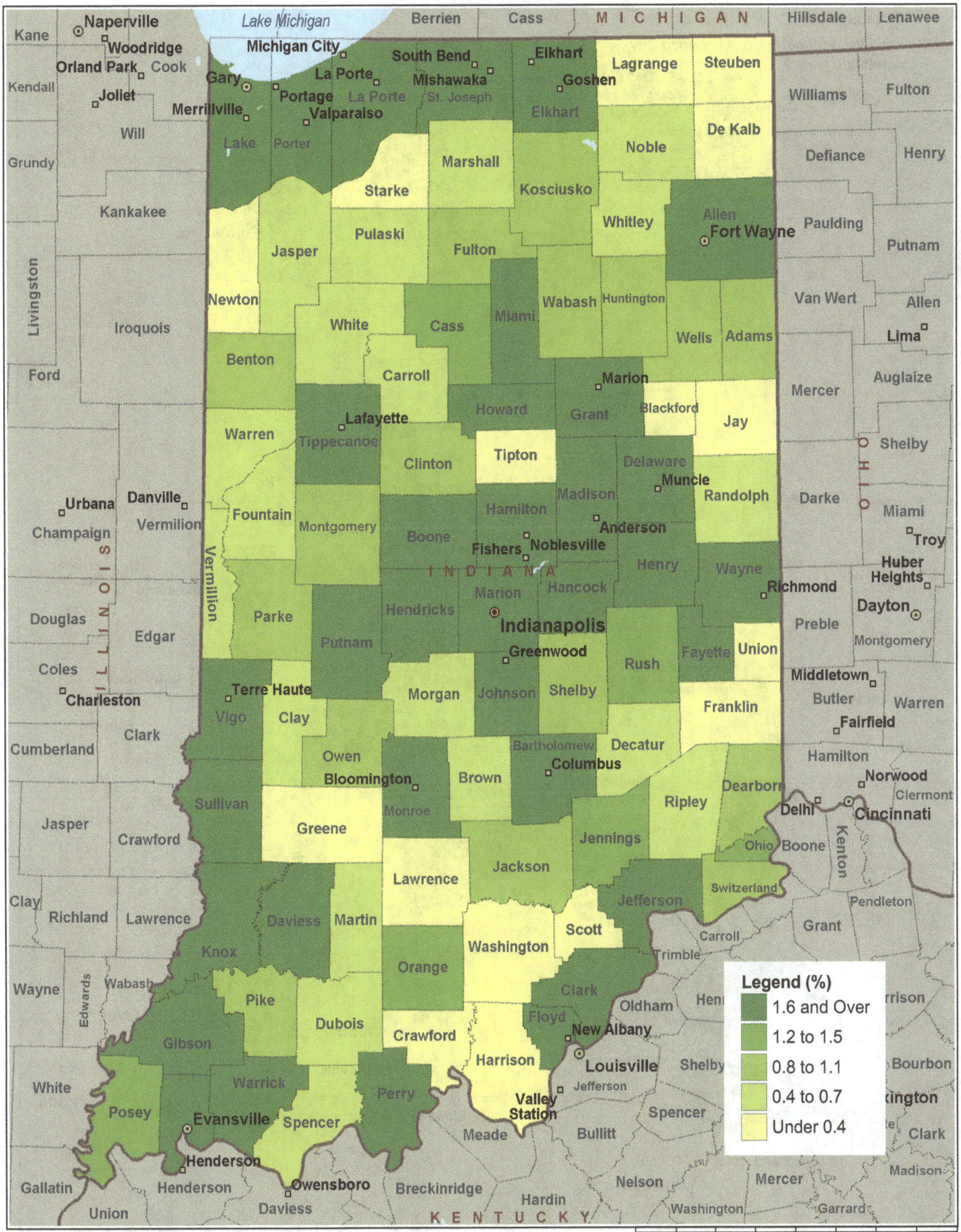

0 mi 20 40 60 80

Percent Asian

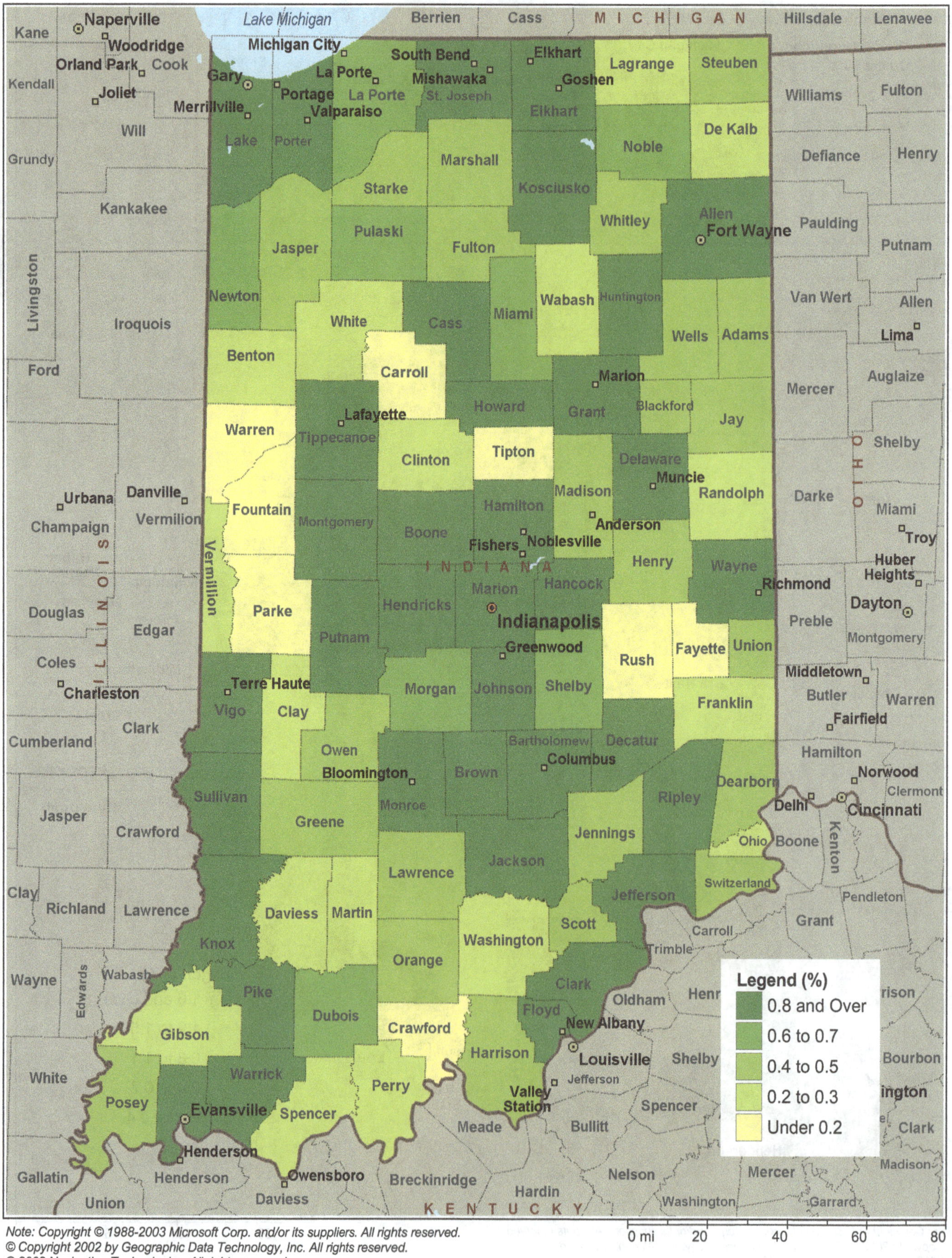

Percent Hispanic

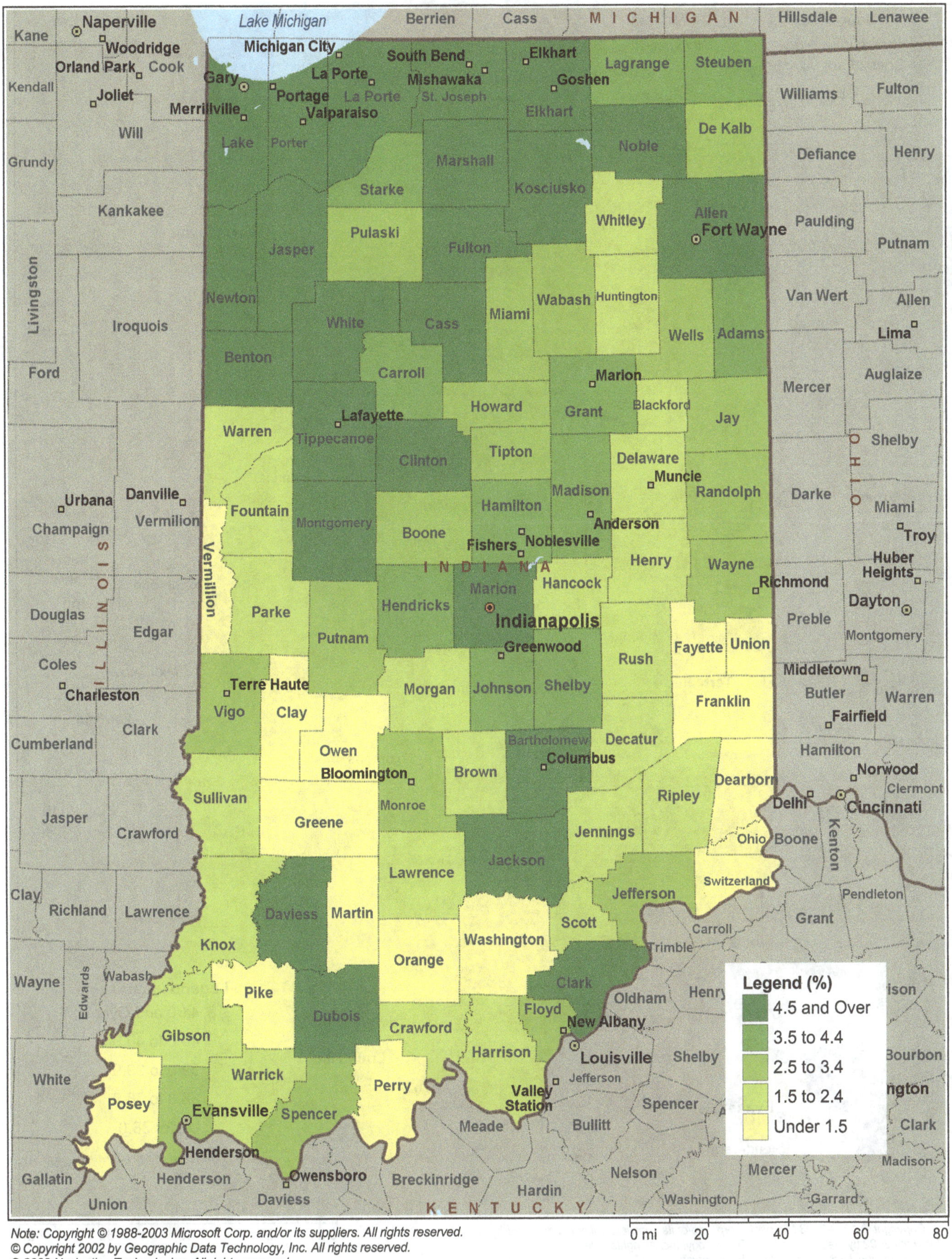

Median Age

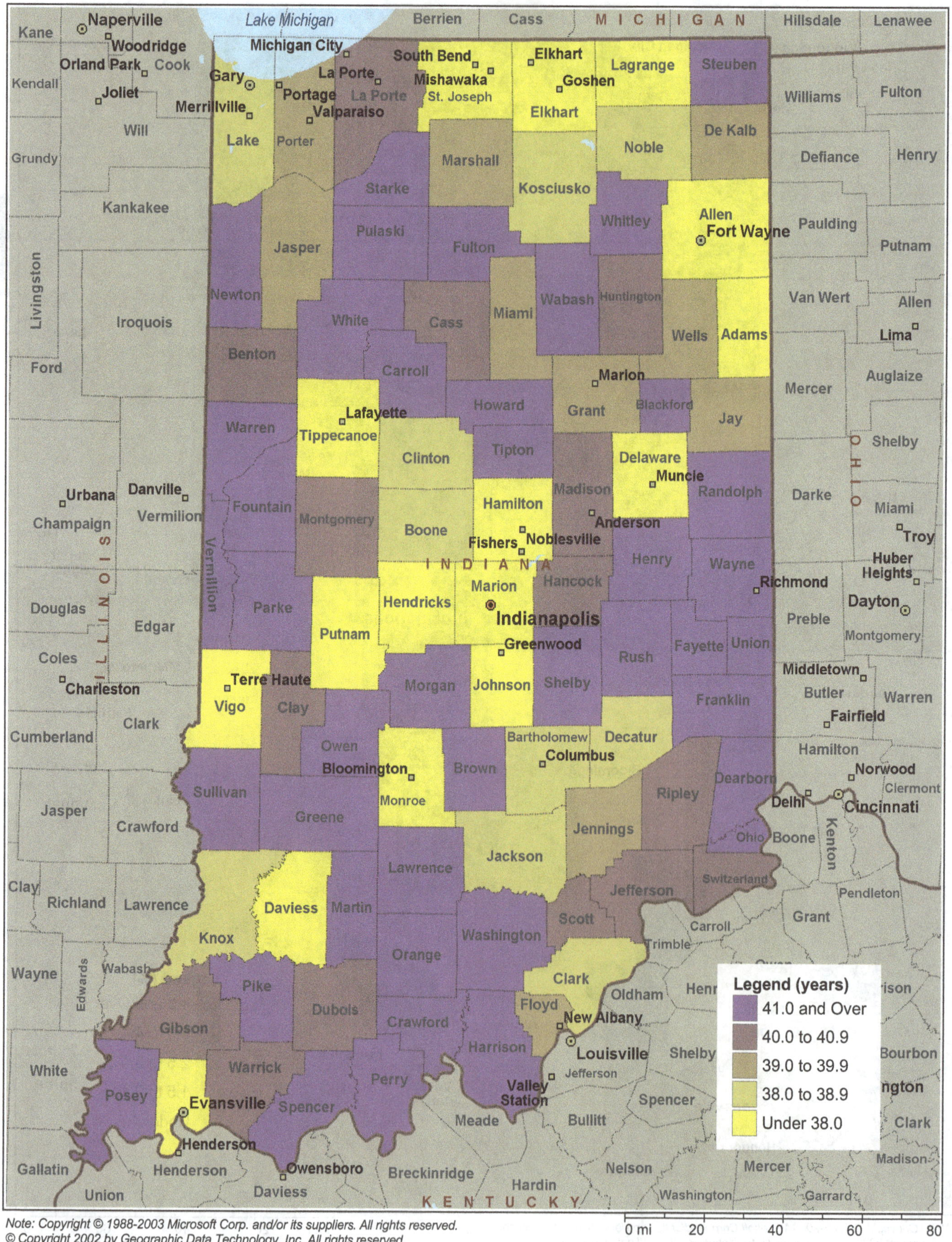

Lake Michigan
M I C H I G A N
I N D I A N A
I L L I N O I S
O H I O
K E N T U C K Y
Legend (years)
41.0 and Over
40.0 to 40.9
39.0 to 39.9
38.0 to 38.9
Under 38.0
0 mi
20
40
60
80
Naperville
Kane
Woodridge
Orland Park
Cook
Kendall
Joliet
Will
Grundy
Kankakee
Livingston
Iroquois
Ford
Urbana
Champaign
Danville
Vermilion
Douglas
Edgar
Coles
Charleston
Clark
Cumberland
Jasper
Crawford
Clay
Richland
Lawrence
Wayne
Edwards
Wabash
White
Gallatin
Union
Berrien
Cass
Hillsdale
Lenawee
Williams
Fulton
Defiance
Henry
Paulding
Putnam
Van Wert
Allen
Lima
Mercer
Auglaize
Shelby
Darke
Miami
Troy
Huber Heights
Dayton
Preble
Montgomery
Middletown
Butler
Warren
Fairfield
Hamilton
Norwood
Clermont
Delhi
Cincinnati
Boone
Kenton
Pendleton
Grant
Carroll
Trimble
Oldham
Henr
Shelby
Louisville
Jefferson
Spencer
Bullitt
Nelson
Mercer
Washington
Garrard
Madison
Clark
Bourbon
ngton
rison
Meade
Hardin
Breckinridge
Henderson
Daviess
Owensboro
Henderson
Michigan City
Gary
La Porte
South Bend
Mishawaka
Portage
Valparaiso
Merrillville
Lake
Porter
La Porte
St. Joseph
Elkhart
Goshen
Elkhart
Lagrange
Steuben
Noble
De Kalb
Marshall
Starke
Kosciusko
Whitley
Allen
Fort Wayne
Jasper
Pulaski
Fulton
Newton
White
Cass
Miami
Wabash
Huntington
Wells
Adams
Benton
Carroll
Marion
Grant
Blackford
Jay
Howard
Warren
Lafayette
Tippecanoe
Clinton
Tipton
Delaware
Muncie
Randolph
Fountain
Montgomery
Boone
Hamilton
Madison
Anderson
Fishers
Noblesville
Vermillion
Henry
Wayne
Richmond
Hancock
Parke
Putnam
Hendricks
Marion
Indianapolis
Greenwood
Rush
Fayette
Union
Terre Haute
Vigo
Clay
Morgan
Johnson
Shelby
Franklin
Owen
Bartholomew
Columbus
Decatur
Bloomington
Brown
Sullivan
Greene
Monroe
Ripley
Dearborn
Jennings
Ohio
Jackson
Lawrence
Switzerland
Jefferson
Daviess
Martin
Knox
Scott
Washington
Orange
Clark
Pike
Dubois
Floyd
New Albany
Crawford
Gibson
Harrison
Warrick
Perry
Valley Station
Posey
Evansville
Spencer

Median Household Income

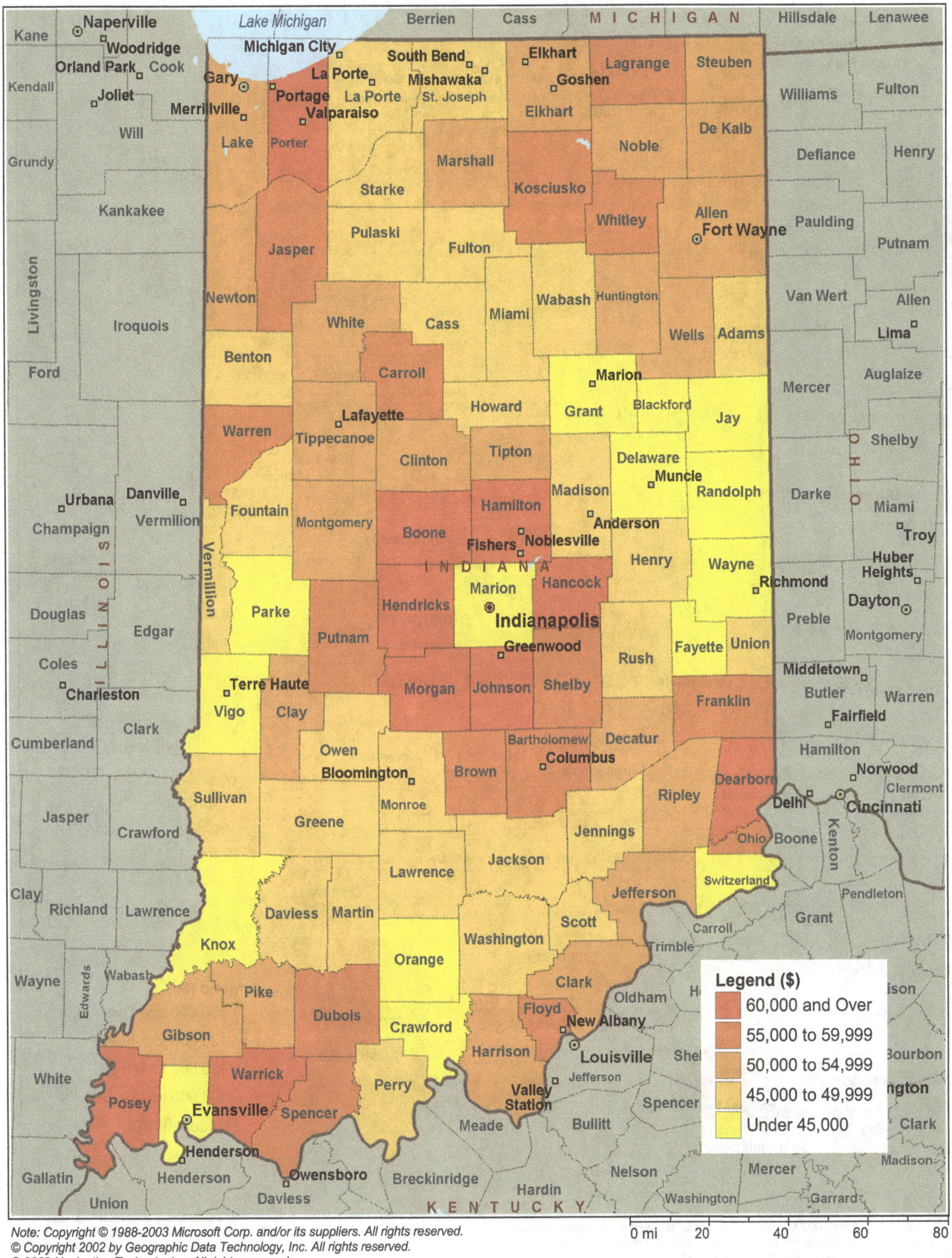

Median Home Value

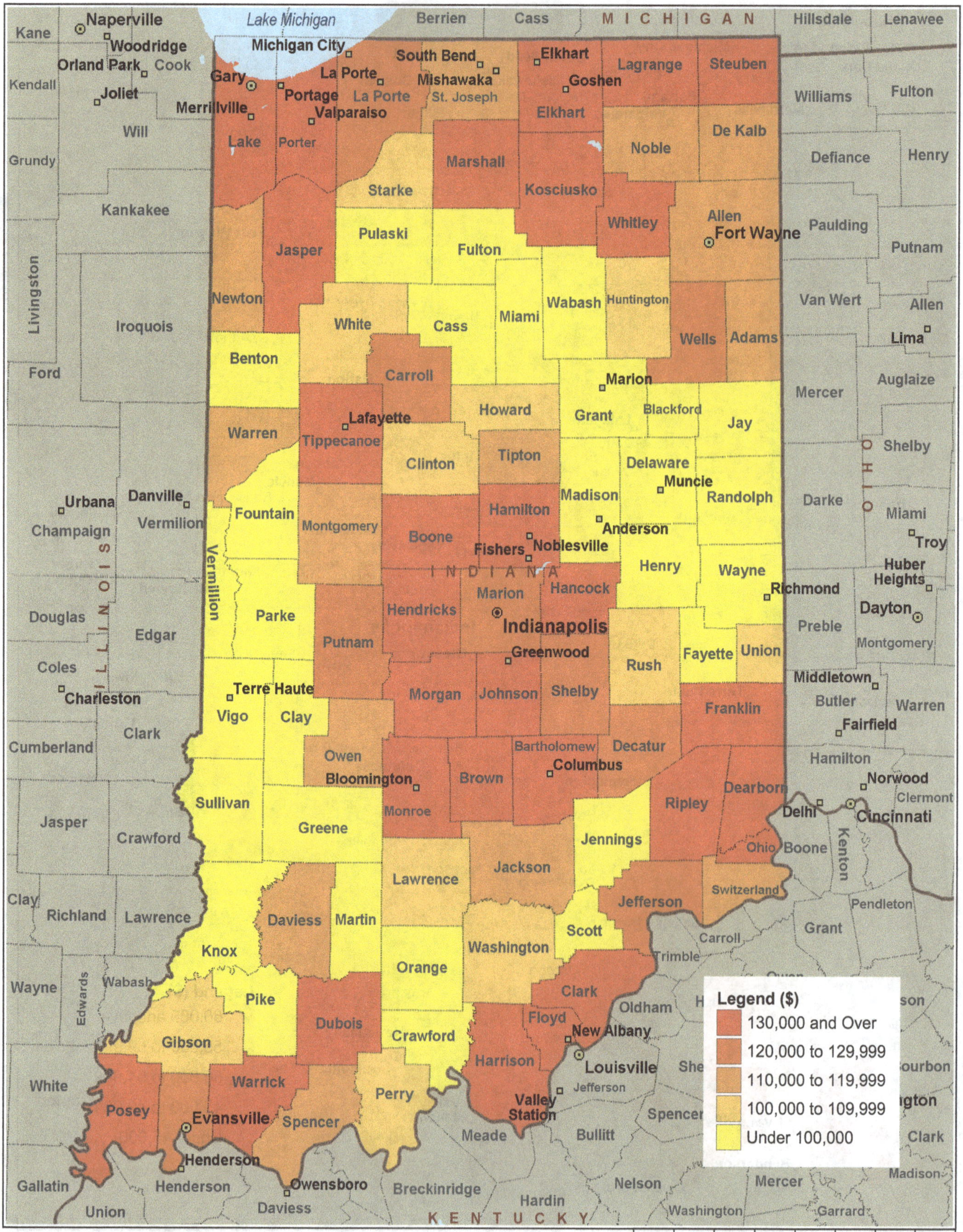

0 mi 20 40 60 80

High School Graduates*

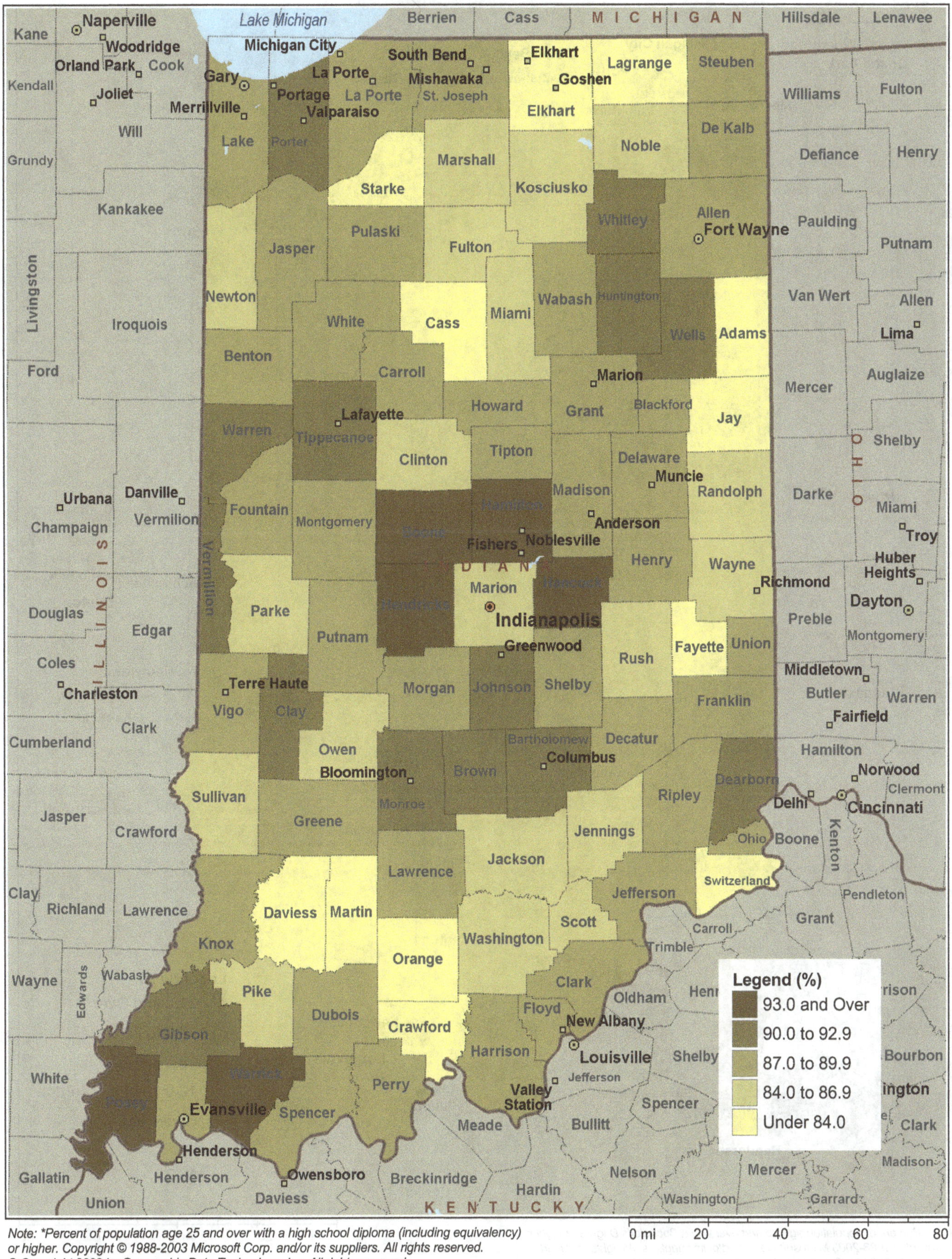

Note: *Percent of population age 25 and over with a high school diploma (including equivalency) or higher.

College Graduates*

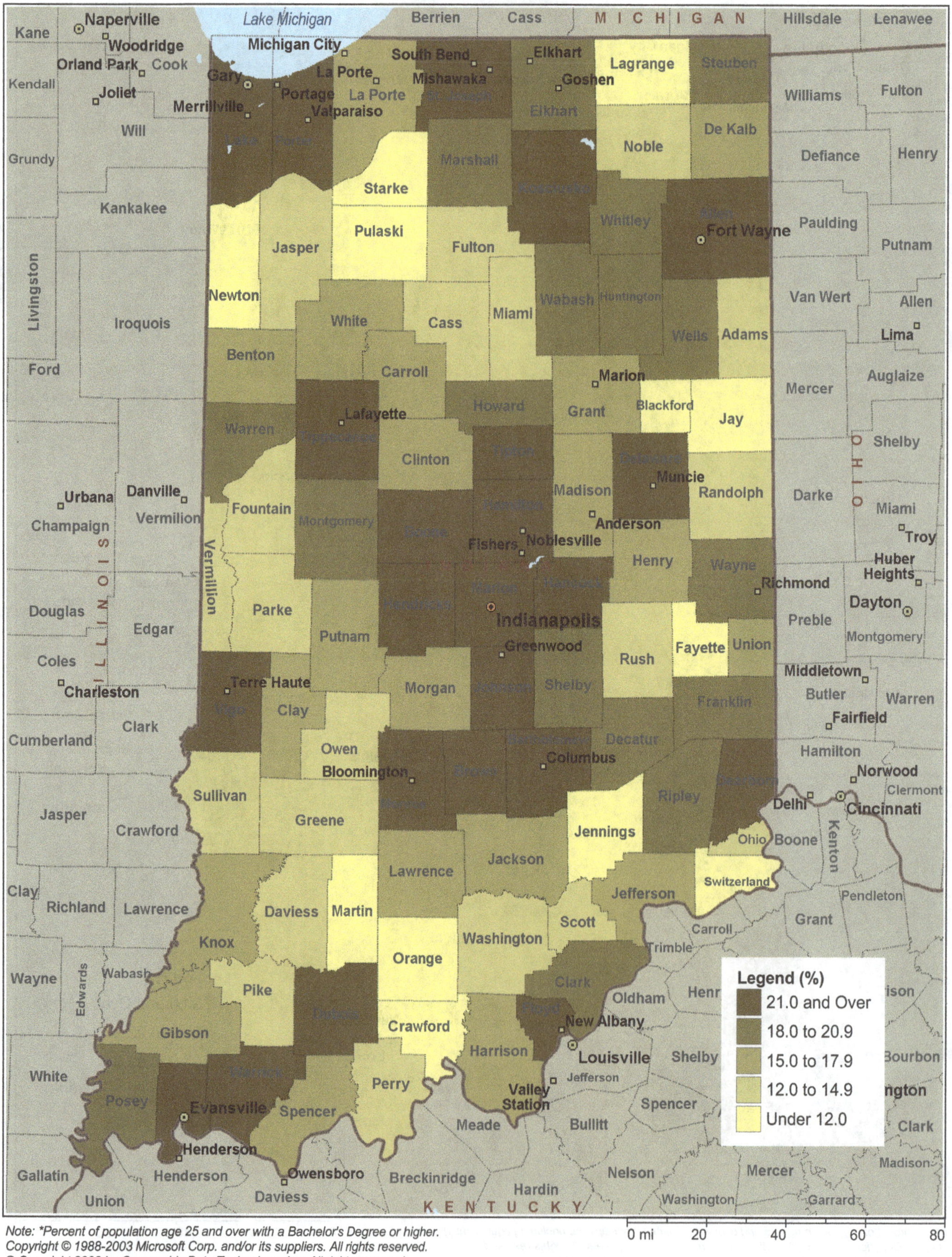

*Note: *Percent of population age 25 and over with a Bachelor's Degree or higher.*

Voted for Donald Trump in 2016

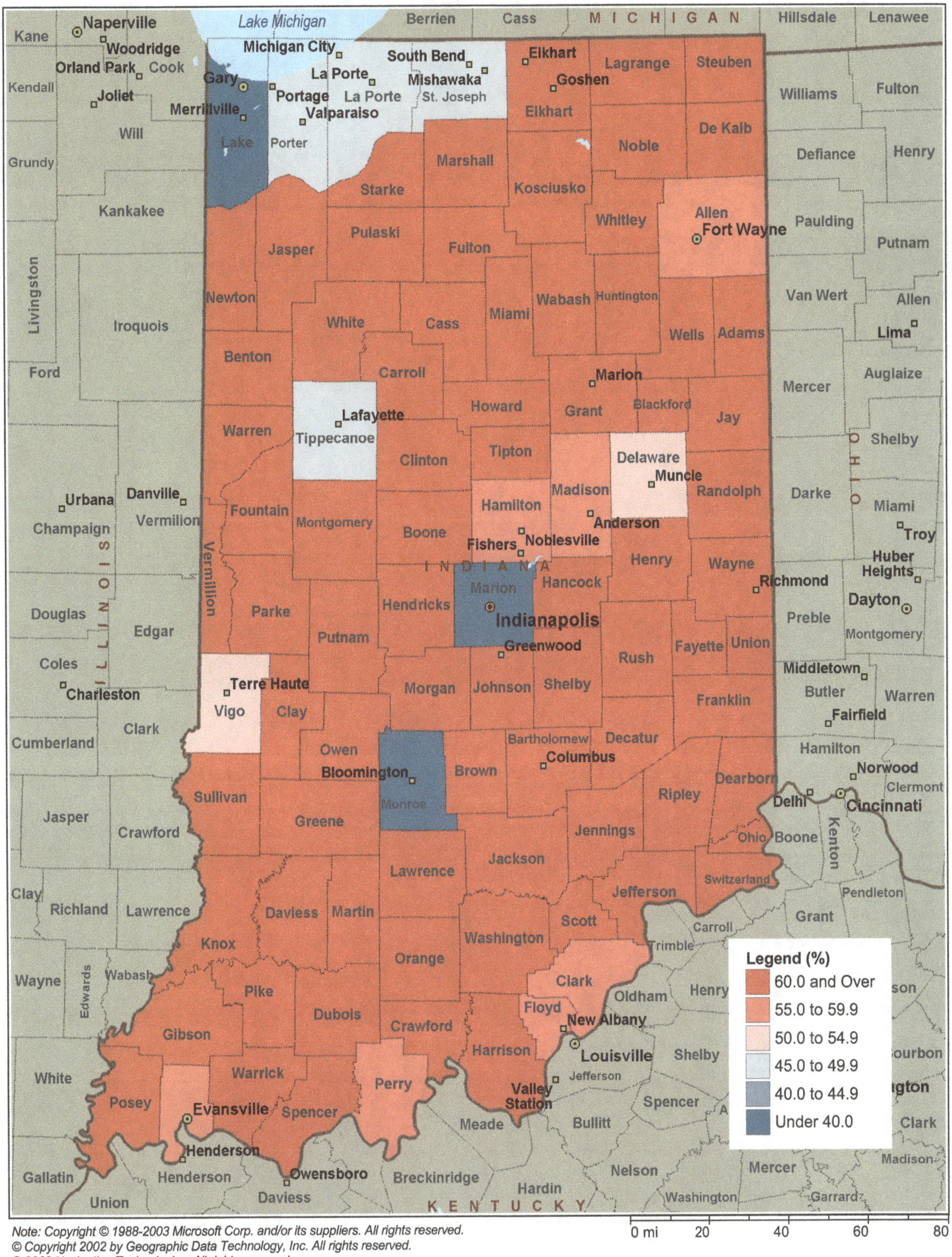

Demographic Maps

Geography

This chapter identifies Federal lands, Native American Reservations, physical characteristics, and an account of Indiana's land and natural resources, and ends with a satellite view of the state.

Land and Natural Resources 39

Geographical Characteristics of the 50 Most Populated Places in Indiana 40

Populated Places, Transportation and Physical Features 41

Federal Lands and Indian Reservations 42

Satellite View 43

The Hoosier State

The Crossroads of America

Geography

[illegible]

Land and Natural Resources

Topic	Value	Time Period
Total Surface Area (acres)	23,158,400	2015
Land	22,772,400	2015
Federal Land	479,300	2015
Non-Federal Land	22,293,100	2015
Developed	2,541,100	2015
Rural	19,752,000	2015
Cropland	13,325,000	2015
CRP Land	93,600	2015
Pastureland	1,756,700	2015
Rangeland	0	2015
Forest Land	3,913,300	2015
Other Rural Land	663,400	2015
Water	386,000	2015
World Heritage Sites	0	September 30, 2018
National Heritage Areas	0	September 30, 2018
National Natural Landmarks	30	September 30, 2018
National Historic Landmarks	42	September 30, 2018
National Register of Historic Place Listings	1,921	September 30, 2018
National Parks	3	September 30, 2018
Wild and Scenic Rivers Managed by the NPS	0	September 30, 2018
National Trails Managed by the NPS	1	September 30, 2018
Archeological Sites in National Parks	230	September 30, 2018
Visitors to National Parks	2,027,770	September 30, 2018
Economic Benefit from National Park Tourism (dollars)	115,400,000	September 30, 2018
Land and Water Conservation Fund Grants (dollars)	89,639,503	Since 1965
Historic Preservation Grants (dollars)	28,391,821	Since 1969
Community Conservation and Recreation Projects	48	Since 1987
Federal Acres Transferred for Local Parks and Recreation	16,019	Since 1948
Crude Oil Production (thousand barrels per year)	1,779	2017
Crude Oil Reserves, Proved (million barrels)	5	December 31, 2017
Natural Gas Marketed Production (million cubic feet per year)	5,914	2017
Natural Gas Proved Reserves, Dry (billion cubic feet)	Not Available	December 31, 2017
Coal Production (thousand short tons per year)	31,472	2017
Coal Reserves, Recoverable (million short tons)	456	2017

Sources: *U.S. Department of the Interior, National Park Service, State Profiles; United States Department of Agriculture, Natural Resources Conservation Service, 2015 National Resources Inventory; Department of Energy, Energy Information Administration, Coal, Natural Gas, Petroleum and Other Liquids Production and Reserves*

Geographical Characteristics of the 50 Most Populated Places in Indiana

Place	Land Area (square miles)	Water Area (square miles)	Elevation (feet)	Latitude (degrees)	Longitude (degrees)
Anderson city *Madison Co.*	41.371189	0.108860	879	40.08976560	-85.68944850
Bloomington city *Monroe Co.*	23.158400	0.198624	771	39.16370030	-86.52426420
Brownsburg town *Hendricks Co.*	11.075891	0.076134	883	39.83959290	-86.39279690
Carmel city *Hamilton Co.*	47.463255	1.084934	853	39.96547940	-86.14836880
Clarksville town *Clark Co.*	9.973374	0.203056	456	38.32208180	-85.76757640
Columbus city *Bartholomew Co.*	27.497203	0.386019	627	39.20968400	-85.91780160
Crown Point city *Lake Co.*	17.712548	0.015148	732	41.41710230	-87.34742320
East Chicago city *Lake Co.*	14.087685	2.064571	591	41.65045880	-87.45112310
Elkhart city *Elkhart Co.*	23.452990	0.966700	751	41.69116660	-85.96513200
Evansville city *Vanderburgh Co.*	44.153398	0.472082	387	37.98773390	-87.53470300
Fishers city *Hamilton Co.*	33.585447	2.248735	817	39.95988870	-85.97029180
Fort Wayne city *Allen Co.*	110.618437	0.213678	810	41.08817290	-85.14388000
Franklin city *Johnson Co.*	13.006337	0.000000	725	39.49348590	-86.05407520
Gary city *Lake Co.*	49.865047	7.310393	600	41.59588270	-87.34485350
Goshen city *Elkhart Co.*	16.229340	0.355243	801	41.57492130	-85.83079260
Granger cdp *Saint Joseph Co.*	25.566932	0.001439	801	41.73603380	-86.13582990
Greenfield city *Hancock Co.*	12.550920	0.112348	883	39.79328270	-85.77254840
Greenwood city *Johnson Co.*	21.230337	0.000727	804	39.60953080	-86.10723990
Hammond city *Lake Co.*	22.775573	2.105784	600	41.62166280	-87.49459060
Highland town *Lake Co.*	6.935746	0.022619	623	41.54649060	-87.45721270
Hobart city *Lake Co.*	26.331259	0.375365	623	41.51353000	-87.27639950
Indianapolis city *Marion Co.*	361.433182	6.591785	718	39.77666440	-86.14593550
Jeffersonville city *Clark Co.*	34.064321	0.293625	446	38.33340220	-85.69721070
Kokomo city *Howard Co.*	18.497005	0.058645	810	40.47531690	-86.13276320
La Porte city *LaPorte Co.*	11.660397	0.710303	814	41.60789610	-86.71360560
Lafayette city *Tippecanoe Co.*	27.742275	0.000000	702	40.39942500	-86.86169940
Lawrence city *Marion Co.*	20.131522	0.109716	873	39.86595650	-85.98964620
Logansport city *Cass Co.*	8.747675	0.222377	640	40.75018240	-86.35618220
Marion city *Grant Co.*	15.710841	0.083735	814	40.54958160	-85.65922490
Merrillville town *Lake Co.*	33.215668	0.035112	656	41.47268720	-87.31807040
Michigan City city *LaPorte Co.*	19.587608	3.265320	627	41.71251180	-86.87614390
Mishawaka city *Saint Joseph Co.*	16.997103	0.347792	722	41.67173330	-86.16629560
Muncie city *Delaware Co.*	27.196445	0.192048	951	40.19897810	-85.39334590
Munster town *Lake Co.*	7.570203	0.081086	610	41.54751020	-87.50326850
New Albany city *Floyd Co.*	14.938541	0.170544	449	38.30745630	-85.82705270
New Castle city *Henry Co.*	7.294752	0.021151	1,063	39.91983540	-85.37006400
Noblesville city *Hamilton Co.*	31.374480	1.415179	764	40.03697920	-86.00719190
Plainfield town *Hendricks Co.*	22.273822	0.108504	732	39.70146850	-86.37293620
Portage city *Porter Co.*	25.628113	1.983519	636	41.59161380	-87.17893750
Richmond city *Wayne Co.*	23.914754	0.157105	981	39.83207920	-84.88969890
Schererville town *Lake Co.*	14.712073	0.053047	669	41.48516810	-87.44338370
Seymour city *Jackson Co.*	11.422108	0.004672	600	38.94481850	-85.89239310
Shelbyville city *Shelby Co.*	11.563837	0.284932	764	39.53381920	-85.77369660
South Bend city *Saint Joseph Co.*	41.457771	0.417313	692	41.67684970	-86.26904300
Terre Haute city *Vigo Co.*	34.536271	0.732308	502	39.46554190	-87.37592440
Valparaiso city *Porter Co.*	15.530254	0.048243	794	41.47982350	-87.05226440
Vincennes city *Knox Co.*	7.411728	0.068011	420	38.67610090	-87.51111880
West Lafayette city *Tippecanoe Co.*	7.615278	0.009926	610	40.45524470	-86.91182540
Westfield city *Hamilton Co.*	26.838109	0.240548	886	40.02848050	-86.15662080
Zionsville town *Boone Co.*	10.256802	0.038018	843	39.95922800	-86.27114950

SOURCE: U.S. Census Bureau, Census 2010

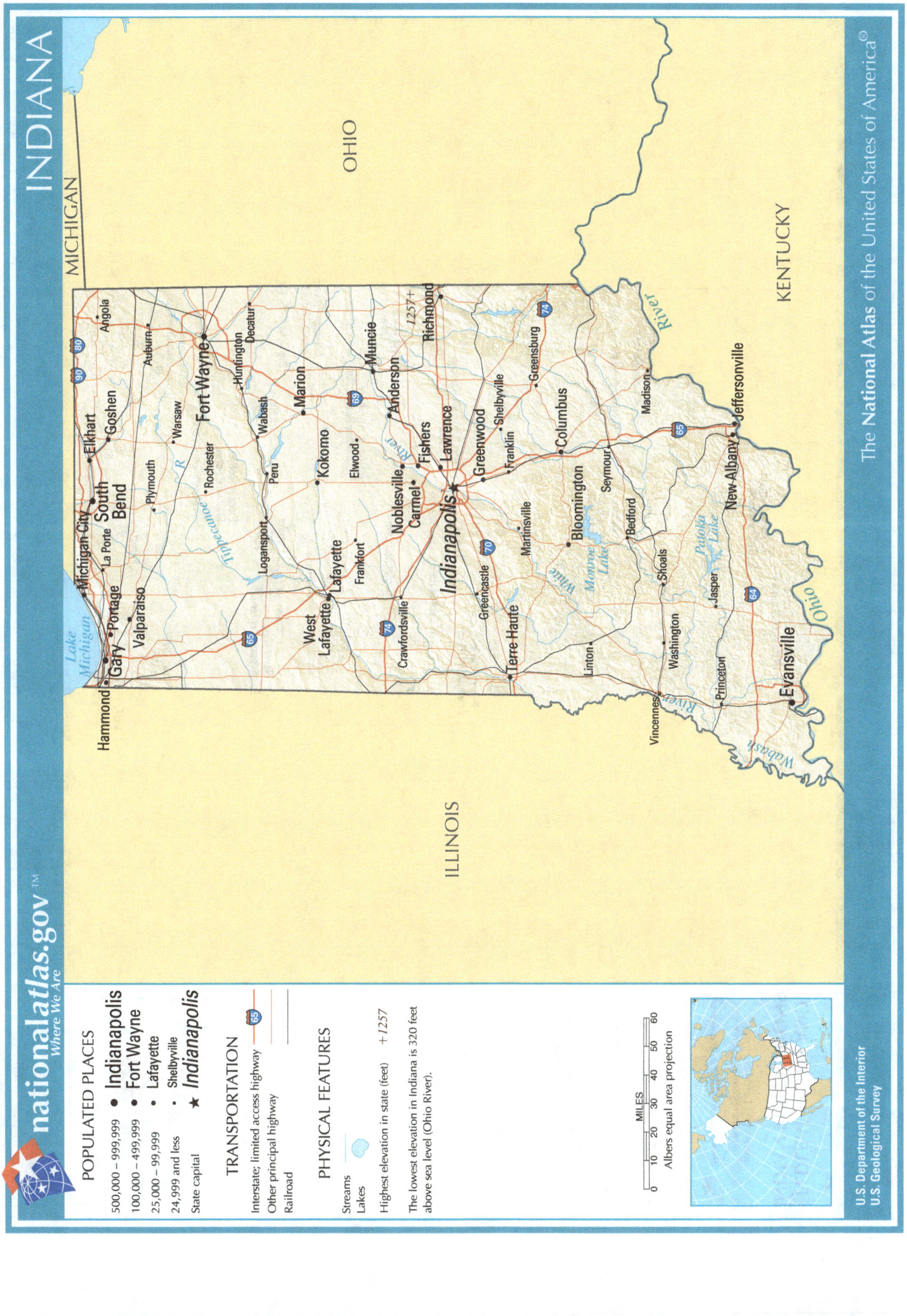
INDIANA
nationalatlas.gov™
Where We Are
POPULATED PLACES
500,000 – 999,999 • Indianapolis
100,000 – 499,999 • Fort Wayne
25,000 – 99,999 • Lafayette
24,999 and less • Shelbyville
State capital ★ Indianapolis
TRANSPORTATION
Interstate; limited access highway
Other principal highway
Railroad
PHYSICAL FEATURES
Streams
Lakes
Highest elevation in state (feet) +1257
The lowest elevation in Indiana is 320 feet above sea level (Ohio River).
MILES
0 10 20 30 40 50 60
Albers equal area projection
U.S. Department of the Interior
U.S. Geological Survey
The National Atlas of the United States of America®
MICHIGAN
OHIO
KENTUCKY
ILLINOIS
Lake Michigan
Hammond
Gary
Portage
Valparaiso
Michigan City
La Porte
South Bend
Elkhart
Goshen
Angola
Auburn
Plymouth
Warsaw
Fort Wayne
Huntington
Decatur
Rochester
Wabash
Peru
Marion
Logansport
Kokomo
Elwood
Muncie
Anderson
Richmond
1257+
West Lafayette
Lafayette
Frankfort
Noblesville
Carmel
Fishers
Lawrence
Indianapolis
Greenwood
Shelbyville
Franklin
Greensburg
Crawfordsville
Greencastle
Martinsville
Columbus
Bloomington
Seymour
Madison
Terre Haute
Linton
Bedford
Shoals
Washington
Jasper
Vincennes
Princeton
Evansville
New Albany
Jeffersonville
Tippecanoe
White
Monroe Lake
Patoka Lake
Wabash
Ohio
River
90
80
65
69
70
74
64

INDIANA
nationalatlas.gov™
Where We Are
FEDERAL LANDS AND INDIAN RESERVATIONS
Department of Defense (includes Army Corps of Engineers lakes)
Fish and Wildlife Service / Wilderness
Forest Service / Wilderness
National Park Service / Wilderness
Some small sites are not shown, especially in urban areas.
MILES
0 10 20 30 40 50 60
Albers equal area projection
Abbreviations
NWR National Wildlife Refuge
MICHIGAN
OHIO
ILLINOIS
KENTUCKY
Gary
Indiana Dunes National Lakeshore
Michigan City
La Porte Outdoor Training Facility
South Bend
Elkhart
Angola
Auburn
Warsaw
Fort Wayne
Huntington Lake
Salamonie Lake
Mississinewa Lake
Wabash
Marion
Grissom Air Force Base (Closed)
Logansport
Kokomo
Elwood
Muncie
Anderson
Richmond
West Lafayette
Lafayette
Frankfort
Noblesville
Carmel
Fishers
Fort Benjamin Harrison (Closed)
Indianapolis
Cecil M Harden Lake
Crawfordsville
Newport Army Ammunition Plant
Greenwood
Shelbyville
Franklin
Brookville Lake
Camp Atterbury Military Reservation
Columbus
Cagles Mill Lake
Terre Haute
Bloomington
Monroe Lake
Hoosier National Forest
Linton
Crane Naval Weapons Support Center
Jefferson Proving Ground (Closed)
Big Oaks NWR
Muscatatuck NWR
Madison
Pioneer Mothers Memorial Forest
Paoli Experimental Forest
Indiana Arsenal Army Ammuniton Plant (Closed)
New Albany
Patoka Lake
Vincennes
Patoka River NWR
Evansville
White
Wabash
River
Ohio
The National Atlas of the United States of America®
U.S. Department of the Interior
U.S. Geological Survey

nationalatlas.gov™
Where We Are

INDIANA

SATELLITE VIEW

In 1972, Landsat began transmitting views of our planet back to Earth. The first Landsat and its five successors (two of them are in operation now) have delivered millions of images from a satellite orbiting 438 miles above the Earth. Landsat's orbit enables a new image to be recorded every sixteen days of any area on the Earth's surface. The satellite view on this map was created from a mosaic of many Landsat images joined together. Colors were selected to better show variations in the landscape. Relief shading was added to enhance the terrain and make the landforms of each state more apparent.

MILES
0 10 20 30 40 50 60
Albers equal area projection

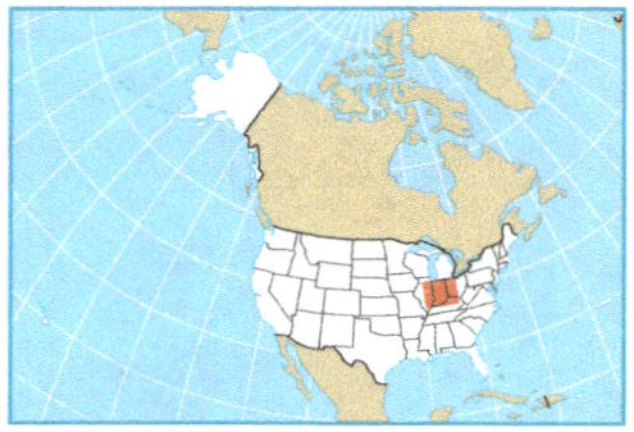

U.S. Department of the Interior
U.S. Geological Survey

The **National Atlas** of the United States of America®

Geography

Energy

This chapter offers a state summary of this crucial industry, from a general overview to details about the major energy sources.

Quick Facts 47
Overview 47
Coal 47
Electricity 47
Renewable Energy 48
Petroleum 49
Natural Gas 49

The Hoosier State

The Crossroads of America

Indiana Energy Profile

Quick Facts

- Indiana is the fifth-largest producer of ethanol in the nation and makes about 1.2 billion gallons per year, almost 8% of the nation's total.
- In 2017, Indiana ranked eighth among the states in coal production and second in coal consumption, after Texas. In 2018, coal fueled 69% of Indiana's net electricity generation and provided coke to the state's steel industry.
- The industrial sector, which includes chemicals, steel, and agriculture, is the largest end-use energy consuming sector in Indiana and accounts for almost half the energy used in the state.
- The Whiting refinery, which can process about 413,500 barrels of crude oil per calendar day, is the largest inland oil refinery in the nation. Only six Gulf Coast refineries can process more crude.
- Wind power provided about 5% of Indiana's electricity generation in 2018, while solar, biomass, and hydropower combined accounted for slightly more than 1% of generation.

Overview

Indiana, located in the nation's Interior Plains just west of the Appalachian Mountains, extends from Lake Michigan south to the Ohio River.[1,2] Sediments deposited over millions of years,[3] when the state was covered by inland seas and later by lush swamps,[4,5] became the geologic layers that contain Indiana's fossil fuel resources, predominantly coal but also crude oil and some natural gas.[6,7,8] The flat plains and slightly rolling terrain in the northern two-thirds of the state are the result of the 2,000-foot-thick glacier that covered much of the state during the Ice Ages. The retreat of the glacier more than 10,000 years ago left behind the excellent topsoil that supports Indiana's agriculture.[9] Ample summer rainfall and rich prairie soils allow Indiana farmers to produce abundant corn and soybean crops that make the state a major producer of ethanol and biodiesel.[10,11,12,13,14] Indiana's open farmland also has substantial wind energy resources, and most of the state's wind farms are in the central and western part of the state.[15,16]

Although Indiana is one of the smallest states in land area west of the Appalachian Mountains, it has a varied climate because of its length from north to south. In the north, Indiana experiences lake-effect snows and winds off Lake Michigan. In the south, the hilly terrain creates localized weather variations. The climate statewide is influenced by the interplay of polar air moving south from Canada and warm, moist air moving north from the Gulf of Mexico. Indiana's winters can be bitterly cold, spring weather often includes tornadoes, and summer days may have oppressive humidity and heat.[17] In part because of those weather extremes, Indiana ranks among the top 10 states in total and residential energy use per capita.[18,19] The industrial sector is the state's largest end-use energy consuming sector, using almost half of the energy consumed in the state.[20] Indiana's industrial activities include the energy-intensive chemical, petroleum, and steelmaking industries.[21,22] Overall, more than three times as much energy is consumed in the state as is produced there.[23]

Coal

Indiana has about 1.5% of U.S. economically recoverable coal reserves[24] and is the nation's eighth-largest coal producer. The state accounts for nearly 3% of U.S. coal production. Bituminous coal is produced from almost 20 surface and underground mines located in southwestern Indiana within the Indiana portion of the coal-rich Illinois Basin.[25,26,27] About one-fourth of the approximately 30 million tons of coal produced annually in Indiana is shipped to a dozen other states by rail, barge, and truck.[28,29] A small amount of Indiana coal is exported to other countries.[30]

Even though Indiana is one of the top coal producers in the nation, state production does not meet state demand.[31,32] In 2017, Indiana's total coal consumption ranked second after Texas.[33] Additional coal arrives by rail and barge from mines primarily in West Virginia, Illinois, Kentucky, and Wyoming.[34] The amount of coal Indiana consumes for electricity generation ranks third in the nation, after Texas and Missouri. The state is also third, after Pennsylvania and North Dakota, in the amount of coal used by the industrial sector.[35,36] Because Indiana is a leader in steel manufacturing, nearly one-tenth of the coal used in the state is delivered to coking plants that supply the state's steel industry.[37,38,39,40] However, the industrial sector's coal consumption has declined every year, except for one, since 2005.[41] A very small amount of coal is used in the commercial sector and no appreciable coal is used in the residential sector, where 0.1% of households heat with coal.[42,43]

Electricity

Indiana is among the top five states in the share of its electricity that is generated from coal. Although coal-fired electricity generation has declined by 30% in the past decade, about 70% of the state's electricity was still generated from coal in 2018.[44,45] Eight of Indiana's 10 largest power plants are coal-fired,[46] but more than 3,300 megawatts of coal-fired capacity have retired since 2010.[47] The share of the state's net generation from natural gas has increased more than fourfold during the same period, reaching more than one-fifth of state generation in 2018.[48,49] Almost nine-tenths of the nearly 1,600 megawatts of new generating capacity that was brought online in Indiana during 2018 was powered by natural gas, while the rest of the new generation was powered by renewable energy sources.[50] Wind provided 5% of Indiana's electricity generation in 2018, and other renewable resources—biomass, solar, and hydroelectric power—together accounted for slightly more than 1% of the state's utility-scale net generation. Nearly all of Indiana's solar generation comes from larger, utility-scale facilities. The rest of the state's net electricity generation comes from other gases, other energy sources, and petroleum liquids.[51]

As coal-fired generation has decreased, Indiana's total generation has decreased. Indiana consumers use more electricity than in-state generators can supply. To meet power demand in 2017, one-tenth of Indiana's electricity supply came from other states.[52] Out-of-state power supplies are delivered by the two interstate power grids serving Indiana: the PJM Interconnect in the northeast corner of the state and the Midcontinent Independent System Operator in the west and south.[53] Indiana is among the top six states in electricity retail sales to the industrial sector.[54] Total electricity consumption from all sectors in Indiana is in the top one-fourth of the states.[55] Three in 10 Indiana households rely on electricity as their primary energy source for home heating.[56]

Renewable Energy

Indiana is among the nation's top producers of liquid biofuels. The state's abundant corn and soybean crops provide the feedstock for biofuel production.[57] Indiana's 14 fuel ethanol plants use corn as their feedstock, and the biodiesel plants use soy oil and other feedstocks.[58,59,60] Indiana is the fifth-largest producer of ethanol in the nation and makes about 1.2 billion gallons per year, almost 8% of the nation's total.[61] The state also has the sixth-largest production capacity for biodiesel at more than 100 million gallons per year.[62]

Renewable energy supplied more than 6% of Indiana's net electricity generation in 2018. Wind is the state's primary renewable resource used for electric power generation, and 5% of Indiana's net electricity generation came from wind turbines in 2018.[63] Indiana's first utility-scale wind project, the 103.5-megawatt Benton County Wind Farm, came online in 2008.[64] Currently, wind turbines stretch across central Indiana, and the state has more than 2,300 megawatts of wind capacity, up from 2,100 megawatts in 2017.[65]

Additional small amounts of electricity are generated from solar, biomass, and hydroelectric facilities.[66] Extreme southwestern Indiana has the state's best solar resources, but solar facilities are found statewide.[67,68] The state's biomass resources include crop and forest residues, animal waste, and solid biomass resources.[69] Most of Indiana's biomass power plants are landfill gas facilities located in the northern half of the state.[70] There are also three small wood pellet plants in Indiana that convert wood waste into pellets used for heating and electricity generation. They have a combined manufacturing capacity of about 47,000 tons of pellets per year.[71] The state's only large hydroelectric power plant is on the Ohio River at Indiana's southeastern boundary.[72,73]

Although Indiana's geothermal energy resources are modest,[74] the state has one large geothermal installation, located at Ball State University in Muncie. That system was designed to replace aging coal-fired boilers and provide heating and cooling to 47 university buildings.[75]

In 2011, Indiana's legislature created a voluntary clean energy portfolio standard; however, as of 2018, no Indiana utility had chosen to participate.[76] If an electric utility elected to participate, they had to agree to acquire an average of 4% of the electricity they sold to customers from clean energy sources between 2013 and 2018. In 2019 the target increased to 7%, and in 2025 the target will rise to 10%.[77] Among the eligible sources are wind, solar, coalbed methane, clean coal technology, nuclear energy, combined heat and power systems, and natural gas plants built after July 1, 2011 that displace electricity generation from coal.[78]

Indiana utilities are required to offer net metering for customer-sited renewable generating facilities with less than 1 megawatt of capacity. Customers are compensated for any electricity they generate that is in excess of what they use. At the end of 2017, 49 megawatts of customer-sited capacity were connected under the net metering program. In 2017, the legislature increased the limit on a utility's net metered connections from 1% to 1.5% of the utility's peak summer load. The law reserves 40% of the 1.5% of capacity for residential customers and 15% of the 1.5% for organic biomass. There are no restrictions on the remainder. In 2017, the Indiana legislature also reduced the rate customers receive from utilities for their distributed (small-scale, customer-sited) generation. Compensation was switched from a system based on a higher retail rate for electricity to one linked to the lower wholesale power rate.[79]

Petroleum

Indiana's proved crude oil reserves are small and have declined from about 40 million barrels in 1979 to 5 million in 2017.[80,81] The Trenton Field, discovered in east-central Indiana in 1876, was the nation's first oil field to produce more than 100 million barrels of crude oil. The field ceased production in the early 20th century, and the center of the state's crude oil production moved to the Illinois Basin in southwestern Indiana, where output peaked in 1956.[82] Although advanced drilling technology had increased Indiana's crude oil production in recent years,[83] the state's production dropped to its lowest level in more than 35 years in 2018.[84,85] Indiana crude oil production now accounts for less than 0.1% of the nation's total oil production.[86]

The Whiting refinery, located in northwest Indiana, is one of the state's two petroleum refineries and is one of the oldest U.S. refineries, having opened in 1889. Whiting is the largest inland crude oil refinery in the nation; only six Gulf Coast refineries have higher capacities.[87] The Whiting refinery can process about 413,500 barrels of crude oil per calendar day and produces large quantities of motor gasoline, diesel fuel, and jet fuel as well as about 5% of the nation's asphalt.[88,89] A second, small refinery is located in Mount Vernon at the southern tip of Indiana. That refinery processes Illinois Basin crude oil from southern Indiana, southern Illinois, and western Kentucky. Its refined products—motor gasoline, diesel fuel, and lubricants—are delivered to customers in Indiana, Illinois, Michigan, Ohio, and Kentucky.[90] A plastics-to-fuel plant that will be able to process 100,000 tons of non-recycled plastic waste into 18 million gallons of ultra-low sulfur diesel fuel is in development in Indiana.[91]

Nearly half of the Indiana's petroleum consumption is in the form of motor gasoline, and three-tenths is distillate fuel oil, including diesel fuel.[92] Although conventional motor gasoline can be used in most of Indiana, reformulated motor gasoline blended with ethanol is required in the state's northwest corner near Chicago. In addition, motor gasoline formulated to reduce emissions that contribute to ground-level ozone is required during the summer months in southeast Indiana near Louisville, Kentucky.[93,94] Most of the petroleum not used by the transportation sector is used by industry. The rest is used in the commercial and residential sectors, which consume almost equal amounts.[95] Distillate fuel (heating oil) sales to the residential sector have declined over the past three decades.[96] Currently, nearly 1% of Indiana households use fuel oil or kerosene for home heating, and 7% use hydrocarbon gas liquids, mostly propane.[97] A small amount (less than 0.2%) of Indiana's electricity is petroleum-fired.[98]

Natural Gas

Indiana has minor natural gas reserves, and, in 2017, the state's annual natural gas production was only 0.02% of the U.S. total.[99,100] There was a brief spike in production in 2011 when the number of wells completed using hydraulic fracturing, which improved initial production, increased.[101,102] Most of the state's natural gas fields are in the east central part of the state where natural gas was first discovered in the mid-1870s.[103] The availability of advanced drilling technologies has created renewed interest in a shallow natural gas play in the Albany Shale in southwestern Indiana, which, along with potential coalbed methane resources, could add new natural gas reserves.[104]

Indiana is crossed by nine interstate natural gas pipelines. Those pipelines bring natural gas produced in Appalachia, the Gulf Coast, and western Canada into the state.[105] Natural gas enters Indiana primarily from Illinois and Ohio, and about one-fourth of that natural gas is used in Indiana. Most of the rest is sent on to Michigan and Ohio.[106] Some of the natural gas that enters Indiana is put in storage. The state has 21 natural gas storage fields with a combined total capacity of 113 billion cubic feet.[107,108]

Indiana's natural gas consumption is much greater than state production.[109,110] The industrial sector is the largest natural gas consumer in Indiana and accounts for more than half of the natural gas used in the state.[111] The state's electric power sector has experienced an almost five-fold increase in the use of natural gas for electricity generation in the past decade.[112] Since 2016, the electric power sector's natural gas consumption has exceeded the residential sector's use. The residential sector uses one-sixth of the natural gas consumed in Indiana. Three-fifths of the state's households use natural gas for home heating.[113,114]

Endnotes

[1] U.S. Geological Survey, Geology and National Parks, Geologic Provinces of the United States: Interior Plain Province, updated April 21, 2017.
[2] World Atlas, Indiana Geography, accessed April 18, 2019.
[3] U.S. Geological Survey, Geology and National Parks, Geologic Provinces of the United States: Interior Plain Province, updated April 21, 2017.

[4] Gray, Henry H., Nautiloids: Shelled Marauders of Indiana's Ordovician Seas, Indiana Geological and Water Survey, accessed April 18, 2019.
[5] Indiana Department of Natural Resources, Division of Reclamation, Facts about Coal in Indiana, accessed April 18, 2019.
[6] U.S. Energy Information Administration (EIA), Annual Coal Report 2017 (November 2018), Table 15, Recoverable Coal Reserves at Producing Mines, Estimated Recoverable Reserves, and Demonstrated Reserve Base by Mining Method, 2017.
[7] U.S. EIA, Crude Oil Proved Reserves, Reserves Changes, and Production, Proved Reserves as of December 31, 2017.
[8] U.S. EIA, U.S. Crude Oil and Natural Gas Proved Reserves, Year-end 2017, Table 16, Coalbed methane proved reserves, reserves changes, and production, 2017.
[9] City-Data, Indiana-Topography, accessed April 18, 2019.
[10] Indiana State Climate Office, About Indiana Climate, updated December 2002.
[11] U.S. Department of Agriculture, 2018 State Agriculture Overview, Indiana, accessed April 18, 2019.
[12] "U.S. Ethanol Plants, RINs, Operational," Ethanol Producer Magazine, updated September 6, 2018.
[13] U.S. EIA, U.S. Fuel Ethanol Plant Production Capacity, Detailed nameplate capacity of fuel ethanol plants by Petroleum Administration for Defense District (PADD District), Nameplate Capacities of Fuel Ethanol Plants, January 2018 (Excel File).
[14] U.S. EIA, Monthly Biodiesel Production Report, U.S. biodiesel production capacity, 2018.
[15] U.S. Department of Energy, Office of Energy Efficiency and Renewable Energy, WINDExchange, Wind Energy in Indiana, accessed April 18, 2019.
[16] U.S. EIA, Indiana Profile Overview, Wind Power Plant Map Layer, accessed April 18, 2019.
[17] Indiana State Climate Office, About Indiana Climate, updated December 2002.
[18] U.S. EIA, State Energy Data System, 1960-2016 estimates, Key Statistics and Indicators, Total energy consumption per capita by end-use sector and Total energy consumption per capita in the residential sector, 1960-2016.
[19] U.S. EIA, State Energy Data System, Table C13, Energy Consumption Estimates per Capita by End-Use Sector, Ranked by State, 2016.
[20] U.S. EIA, State Energy Data System, Table C1, Energy Consumption Overview: Estimates by Energy Source and End-Use Sector, 2016.
[21] U.S. Bureau of Economic Analysis, Interactive Data, Regional Data, GDP & Personal Income, Annual Gross Domestic Product (GDP) by State, GDP in Current Dollars, Classification NAICS, Indiana, All statistics in the table, 2016, 2017.
[22] Pete, Joseph, "Indiana Remains National Champion of Steel Production," nwitimes.com (March 12, 2016).
[23] U.S. EIA, State Energy Data System, Table P3, Total Primary Energy Production and Total Energy Consumption Estimates in Trillion Btu, 2016.
[24] U.S. EIA, Annual Coal Report 2017 (November 2018), Table 15, Recoverable Coal Reserves at Producing Mines, Estimated Recoverable Reserves, and Demonstrated Reserve Base by Mining Method, 2017.
[25] U.S. EIA, Annual Coal Report 2017 (November 2018), Table 6, Coal Production and Number of Mines by State and Coal Rank, 2017.
[26] Indiana Department of Natural Resources, Active Mining Permits Map, accessed April 18, 2019.
[27] U.S. EIA, Energy Explained, Coal Explained, Where Our Coal Comes From, accessed April 19, 2019.
[28] U.S. EIA, Annual Coal Report 2017 (November 2018), Table 1, Coal Production and Number of Mines by State and Mine Type, 2017 and 2016.
[29] U.S. EIA, Annual Coal Distribution Report 2017 (November 2018), Domestic distribution of coal by origin State, Indiana, Table OS-7, Domestic Coal Distribution, by Origin State, 2017.
[30] U.S. EIA, Annual Coal Distribution Report 2017 (November 2018), U.S. Domestic and Foreign Coal Distribution by State of Origin, Domestic and Foreign Distribution of U.S. Coal by State of Origin, 2017.
[31] U.S. EIA, Annual Coal Report 2017 (November 2018), Table 6, Coal Production and Number of Mines by State and Coal Rank, 2017.
[32] U.S. EIA, Annual Coal Report 2017 (November 2018), Table 26, U.S. Coal Consumption by End Use Sector, Census Division, and State, 2017 and 2016.
[33] U.S. EIA, State Energy Data System, Table F23, Coal Consumption Estimates and Imports and Exports of Coal Coke, 2017.
[34] U.S. EIA, Annual Coal Distribution Report 2017 (November 2018), Domestic distribution of coal by destination State, Indiana, Table DS-13, Domestic Coal Distribution, by Destination State, 2017.
[35] U.S. EIA, Annual Coal Report 2017 (November 2018), Table 26, U.S. Coal Consumption by End Use Sector, Census Division, and State, 2017 and 2016.
[36] U.S. EIA, State Energy Data System, Table F23, Coal Consumption Estimates and Imports and Exports of Coal Coke, 2017.
[37] Pete, Joseph, "Indiana Remains National Champion of Steel Production," nwitimes.com (March 12, 2016).
[38] U.S. EIA, Annual Coal Distribution Report 2017 (November 2018), Domestic distribution of coal by destination State, Indiana, Table DS-13, Domestic Coal Distribution, by Destination State, 2017.
[39] "The Roles of Coal and Coke in Steelmaking," Heyl & Patter Blog (July 16, 2014).
[40] SteelWorks, Where Steel is Made, Steel Plants of North America (June 2013).
[41] U.S. EIA, State Energy Consumption Estimates, 1960 Through 2016, DOE/EIA-0214(2016) (June 2018), Indiana Table CT6, p. 179.
[42] U.S. EIA, State Energy Data System, Table F23 Coal Consumption Estimates and Imports and Exports of Coal Coke, 2017.
[43] U.S. Census Bureau, American FactFinder, Indiana, Table B25040, House Heating Fuel, 2017 American Community Survey 1-Year Estimates.
[44] U.S. EIA, Electric Power Monthly (February 2019), Tables 1.3.B, 1.4.B.
[45] U.S. EIA, Indiana Electricity Profile 2017, Table 5, Electric power industry generation by primary energy source, 1990 through 2017.
[46] U.S. EIA, State Electricity Profiles, Indiana Electricity Profile 2017, Tables 2A, Ten Largest Plants by Capacity, 2017, and 2B, Ten Largest Plants by Generation, 2017 .
[47] U.S. EIA, Electricity, Form EIA-860 detailed data with previous form data (EIA-860A/860B), 2017 Form EIA-860 Data, Schedule 3, 'Generator Data' (Retired & Canceled Units Only).
[48] U.S. EIA, Electric Power Monthly (February 2019), Tables 1.3.B, 1.7.B.
[49] U.S. EIA, Indiana Electricity Profile 2017, Table 5, Electric power industry generation by primary energy source, 1990 through 2017.
[50] U.S. EIA, Electric Power Monthly (February 2019), Table 6.3.
[51] U.S. EIA, Electric Power Monthly (February 2019), Tables 1.3.B, 1.5.B, 1.8.B, 1.10.B, 1.11.B, 1.13.B, 1.14.B, 1.15.B, 1.17.B.
[52] U.S. EIA, Indiana Electricity Profile 2017, Table 10, Supply and disposition of electricity, 1990 through 2017.
[53] U.S. Federal Energy Regulatory Commission, Regional Transmission Organizations (RT)/Independent System Operators (ISO), updated October 18, 2018.
[54] U.S. EIA, Electric Power Monthly (February 2019), Table 5.4.B.
[55] U.S. EIA, State Energy Data System, Table F20, Electricity Consumption Estimates, 2017.
[56] U.S. Census Bureau, American FactFinder, Indiana, Table B25040, House Heating Fuel, 2017 American Community Survey 1-Year Estimates.
[57] NETSTATE, Indiana Economy, accessed April 22, 2019.
[58] U.S. EIA, U.S. Fuel Ethanol Plant Production Capacity, Detailed nameplate capacity of fuel ethanol plants by Petroleum Administration for Defense District (PADD District), Nameplate Capacities of Fuel Ethanol Plants, January 2018 (Excel File).
[59] "U.S. Ethanol Plants, RINs, Operational," Ethanol Producer Magazine, updated September 6, 2018.
[60] "U.S. Biodiesel Plants, operational," Biodiesel Magazine, updated December 13, 2017.
[61] U.S. EIA, State Energy Data System, Table P1, Primary Energy Production Estimates in Physical Units, 2016.
[62] U.S. EIA, Monthly Biodiesel Production Report (March 2019), Table 4, Biodiesel producers and production capacity by state, January 2019.
[63] U.S. EIA, Electric Power Monthly (February 2019), Tables 1.3.B, 1.10.B, 1.11.B, 1.14.B.
[64] Benton County, Indiana, Wind Farms, Benton County Wind Farm, accessed April 24, 2019.
[65] U.S. EIA, Electric Power Monthly (March 2019), Table 6.2.B.
[66] U.S. EIA, Electric Power Monthly (February 2019), Tables 1.3.B, 1.10.B, 1.15.B, 1.17.B.
[67] National Renewable Energy Laboratory, Geospatial Data Science, Solar Maps, U.S. State Solar Resource Maps, Direct Normal Solar Resource of Indiana (April 4, 2017).
[68] U.S. EIA, Indiana Profile Overview, Solar Power Plant Map Layer, accessed April 24, 2019.
[69] Human, Dan, "Biomass could power 1/3 of Hoosier homes, report says," Indianapolis Business Journal (November 16, 2013).
[70] U.S. EIA, Indiana Profile Overview, Biomass Power Plant Map Layer, accessed April 24, 2019.
[71] "U.S. Pellet Plants," Biomass Magazine, updated September 21, 2018.
[72] U.S. EIA, Indiana Profile Overview, Hydroelectric Power Plant Map Layer, accessed April 24, 2019.
[73] U.S. EIA, Electricity, Form EIA-860 detailed data with previous form data (EIA-860A/860B), 2017 Form EIA-860 Data, Schedule 3, 'Generator Data' (Operating Units Only).
[74] National Renewable Energy Laboratory, Geospatial Data Science, Geothermal Maps, Resource Potential, accessed April 25, 2019.
[75] Ball State University, Geothermal Energy System, accessed April 25, 2019.
[76] Indiana Utility Regulatory Commission, 2018 Annual Report, p. 36.
[77] Indiana Office of Energy Development, Indiana Choice Program, accessed April 25, 2019.
[78] Indiana Office of Energy Development, CHOICE Program FAQ, accessed April 25, 2019.
[79] Indiana Utility Regulatory Commission, 2018 Annual Report, p. 33-35.
[80] U.S. EIA, Crude Oil Proved Reserves, Reserves Changes, and Production, Annual, Proved Reserves as of December 31, 2017.
[81] U.S. EIA, Indiana Crude Oil Proved Reserves, Annual, 1977-2017.
[82] Indiana Geological Survey, Oil and Gas, A Brief Overview of the History of the Petroleum Industry In Indiana, Trenton Field, accessed April 22, 2019.
[83] McDivitt, Herschel, Hydraulic Fracturing 101, Indiana Division of Oil and Gas, slide 35, Indiana Hydraulic Fracturing Trends, updated October 15, 2014.
[84] U.S. EIA, Indiana Field Production of Crude Oil, Annual, 1981-2017.
[85] U.S. EIA, Indiana Field Production of Crude Oil, Monthly, January 1981-January 2019.
[86] U.S. EIA, U.S. Field Production of Crude Oil, Monthly, January 1920-January 2019.
[87] U.S. EIA, Oil: Crude and Petroleum Products Explained, Refining Crude Oil, Top 10 U.S. refineries operable capacity, as of January 1, 2018.
[88] U.S. EIA, Refinery Capacity Report (June 2018), Table 3, Capacity of Operable Petroleum Refineries by State as of January 1, 2018.
[89] BP, United States, Whiting Refinery, accessed April 22, 2019.
[90] CountryMark, About Us, Refinery, accessed April 22, 2019.
[91] Zimmerman, Cindy, "Plastics-to-Fuel Plant Planned for Indiana," Energy.AGwired (November 14, 2018).

[92] U.S. EIA, State Energy Data System, Table C3, Primary Energy Consumption Estimates, 2016.
[93] American Fuel & Petrochemical Manufacturers, State Motor Fuels Specifications, Indiana, updated September 2017.
[94] American Petroleum Institute, U.S. Gasoline Requirements, Map, updated January 2018.
[95] U.S. EIA, State Energy Data System, Table F15, Total Petroleum Consumption Estimates, 2017.
[96] U.S. EIA, Indiana Total Distillate Sales/Deliveries to Residential Consumers, 1984-2017.
[97] U.S. Census Bureau, American FactFinder, Indiana, Table B25040, House Heating Fuel, 2017 American Community Survey 1-Year Estimates.
[98] U.S. EIA, Electric Power Monthly (February 2019), Tables 1.3.B, 1.5.B.
[99] U.S. EIA, Natural Gas Reserves Summary as of December 31, Wet NG, Annual, 2012-17.
[100] U.S. EIA, Natural Gas Gross Withdrawals and Production, Gross Withdrawals, Annual, 2013-18.
[101] Indiana Department of Natural Resources, Oil and Gas Division, Annual Well Completions and Hydraulic Fracturing Data, 2005 to 2012.
[102] U.S. EIA, Indiana Natural Gas Gross Withdrawals, 1967-2017.
[103] Rupp, John A., Oil and Gas, A Brief Overview of the History of the Petroleum Industry in Indiana, Indiana Geological Survey, accessed April 26, 2019.
[104] Indiana Geological Survey, Oil and Gas, Indiana Petroleum History, A Brief Overview of the History of the Petroleum Industry in Indiana, Current Activity and Future Prospects, accessed April 26, 2019.
[105] U.S. EIA, Indiana Profile Overview, Natural Gas Inter/Intrastate Pipeline Map Layer, accessed April 26, 2019.
[106] U.S. EIA, International and Interstate Movements of Natural Gas by State, Indiana, Annual, 2012-17.
[107] U.S. EIA, Underground Natural Gas Storage Capacity, Total Number of Existing Fields, Annual, 2012-17.
[108] U.S. EIA, Underground Natural Gas Storage Capacity, Total Storage Capacity, Annual, 2012-17.
[109] U.S. EIA, Natural Gas Consumption by End Use, Total Consumption, Annual, 2013-18.
[110] U.S. EIA, Indiana Natural Gas Gross Withdrawals, 1967-2017.
[111] U.S. EIA, Natural Gas Consumption by End Use, Indiana, Annual, 2013-18.
[112] U.S. EIA, Indiana Natural Gas Deliveries to Electric Power Consumers, 1997-2018.
[113] U.S. EIA, Natural Gas Consumption by End Use, Indiana, Annual, 2013-18.
[114] U.S. Census Bureau, American FactFinder, Indiana, Table B25040, House Heating Fuel, 2017 American Community Survey 1-Year Estimates.

Source: U.S. Energy Information Administration, State Profile and Energy Estimates, May 16, 2019

Climate

Starting with a user guide to interpret the climate data, this chapter discusses Indiana's physical features, including relief and weather station maps, and goes on to include all the state's weather stations, listed in a number of ways, plus rankings.

User Guide. 55

Indiana Physical Features and Climate Narrative 59

State Relief Map 60

Weather Stations Map 61

Weather Stations by County 62

Weather Stations by City. 63

Weather Stations by Elevation 64

National Weather Service Stations 65

Cooperative Weather Stations 69

Weather Station Rankings 79

The Hoosier State

The Crossroads of America

User Guide

SOURCES OF THE DATA

The National Climactic Data Center (NCDC) has two main classes or types of weather stations; first-order stations which are staffed by professional meteorologists and cooperative stations which are staffed by volunteers. All National Weather Service (NWS) stations included in this book are first-order stations.

The data in the climate section is compiled from several sources. The majority comes from the original NCDC computer tapes (DSI-3220 Summary of Month Cooperative). This data was used to create the entire table for each cooperative station and part of each National Weather Service station. The remainder of the data for each NWS station comes from the International Station Meteorological Climate Summary, Version 4.0, September 1996, which is also available from the NCDC.

WEATHER STATION TABLES

The weather station tables are grouped by type (National Weather Service and Cooperative) and then arranged alphabetically. The station name is almost always a place name, and is shown here just as it appears in NCDC data. The station name is followed by the county in which the station is located (or by county equivalent name), the elevation of the station (at the time beginning of the thirty year period) and the latitude and longitude.

The National Weather Service Station tables contain 32 data elements which were compiled from two different sources, the International Station Meteorological Climate Summary (ISMCS) and NCDC DSI-3220 data tapes. The following 13 elements are from the ISMCS: maximum precipitation, minimum precipitation, maximum snowfall, maximum 24-hour snowfall, thunderstorm days, foggy days, predominant sky cover, relative humidity (morning and afternoon), dewpoint, wind speed and direction, and maximum wind gust. The remaining 19 elements come from the DSI-3220 data tapes. The period of record (POR) for data from the DSI-3220 data tapes is 1980-2009. The POR for ISMCS data varies from station to station and appears in a note below each station.

The Cooperative Station tables contain 19 data elements which were all compiled from the DSI-3220 data tapes with a POR of 1980-2009.

WEATHER ELEMENTS (NWS AND COOPERATIVE STATIONS)

The following elements were compiled by the editor from the NCDC DSI-3220 data tapes using a period of record of 1980-2009.

The average temperatures (maximum, minimum, and mean) are the average (see Methodology below) of those temperatures for all available values for a given month. For example, for a given station the average maximum temperature for July is the arithmetic average of all available maximum July temperatures for that station. (Maximum means the highest recorded temperature, minimum means the lowest recorded temperature, and mean means an arithmetic average temperature.)

The extreme maximum temperature is the highest temperature recorded in each month over the period 1980-2009. The extreme minimum temperature is the lowest temperature recorded in each month over the same time period. The extreme maximum daily precipitation is the largest amount of precipitation recorded over a 24-hour period in each month from 1980-2009. The maximum snow depth is the maximum snow depth recorded in each month over the period 1980-2009.

The days for maximum temperature and minimum temperature are the average number of days those criteria were met for all available instances. The symbol ≥ means greater than or equal to, the symbol ≤ means less than or equal to. For example, for a given station, the number of days the maximum temperature was greater than or equal to 90°F in July, is just an arithmetic average of the number of days in all the available Julys for that station.

Heating and cooling degree days are based on the median temperature for a given day and its variance from 65°F. For example, for a given station if the day's high temperature was 50°F and the day's low temperature was 30°F, the median (midpoint) temperature was 40°F. 40°F is 25 degrees below 65°F, hence on this day there would be 25 heating degree days. This also applies for cooling degree days. For example, for a given station if the day's high temperature was 80°F and the day's low temperature was 70°F, the median (midpoint) temperature was 75°F. 75°F is 10 degrees above 65°F, hence on this day there would be 10 cooling degree days. All heating and/or cooling degree days in a month are summed for the month giving respective totals for each element for that month. These sums for a given month for a given station over the past thirty years are again summed and then arithmetically averaged. It should be noted that the heating and cooling degree days do not cancel each other out. It is possible to have both for a given station in the same month.

Precipitation data is computed the same as heating and cooling degree days. Mean precipitation and mean snowfall are arithmetic averages of cumulative totals for the month. All available values for the thirty year period for a given month for a given station are summed and then divided by the number of values. The same is true for days of greater than or equal to 0.1", 0.5",and 1.0" of precipitation, and days of greater than or equal to 1.0" of snow depth on the ground. The word trace appears for precipitation and snowfall amounts that are too small to measure.

Finally, remember that all values presented in the tables and the rankings are averages, maximums, or minimums of available data (see Methodology below) for that specific data element for the last thirty years (1980-2009).

WEATHER ELEMENTS (NWS STATIONS ONLY)

The following elements were taken directly from the International Station Meteorological Climate Summary. The periods of records vary per station and are noted at the bottom of each table.

Maximum precipitation, minimum precipitation, maximum snowfall, maximum snow depth, maximum 24-hour snowfall, thunderstorm days, foggy days, relative humidity (morning and afternoon), dewpoint, prevailing wind speed and direction, and maximum wind gust are all self-explanatory.

The word trace appears for precipitation and snowfall amounts that are too small to measure.

Predominant sky cover contains four possible entries: CLR (clear); SCT (scattered); BRK (broken); and OVR (overcast).

INCLUSION CRITERIA—HOW STATIONS WERE SELECTED

The basic criteria is that a station must have data for temperature, precipitation, heating and cooling degree days of sufficient quantity in order to create a meaningful average. More specifically, the definition of sufficiency here has two parts. First, there must be 22 values for a given data element, and second, ten of the nineteen elements included in the table must pass this sufficiency test. For example, in regard to mean maximum temperature (the first element on every data table), a given station needs to have a value for every month of at least 22 of the last thirty years in order to meet the criteria, and, in addition, every station included must have at least ten of the nineteen elements with at least this minimal level of completeness in order to fulfill the criteria. We then removed stations that were geographically close together, giving preference to stations with better data quality.

METHODOLOGY

The following discussion applies only to data compiled from the NCDC DSI-3220 data tapes and excludes weather elements that are extreme maximums or minimums.

The data is based on an arithmetic average of all available data for a specific data element at a given station. For example, the average maximum daily high temperature during July for any given station was abstracted from NCDC source tapes for the thirty Julys, starting in July, 1980 and ending in July, 2009. These thirty figures were then summed and divided by thirty to produce an arithmetic average. As might be expected, there were not thirty values for every data element on every table. For a variety of reasons, NCDC data is sometimes incomplete. Thus the following standards were established.

For those data elements where there were 26-30 values, the data was taken to be essentially complete and an average was computed. For data elements where there were 22-25 values, the data was taken as being partly complete but still valid enough to use to compute an average. Such averages are shown in ***bold italic*** type to indicate that there was less than 26 values. For the few data elements where there were not even 22 values, no average was computed and 'na' appears in the space. If any of the twelve months for a given data element reported a value of 'na', no annual average was computed and the annual average was reported as 'na' as well.

Thus the basic computational methodology used is designed to provide an arithmetic average. Because of this, such a pure arithmetic average is somewhat different from the special type of average (called a "normal") which NCDC procedures produces and appears in federal publications.

Perhaps the best outline of the contrasting normalization methodology is found in the following paragraph (which appears as part of an NCDC technical document titled, CLIM81 1961-1990 NORMALS TD-9641 prepared by Lewis France of NCDC in May, 1992):

> Normals have been defined as the arithmetic mean of a climatological element computed over a long time period. International agreements eventually led to the decision that the appropriate time period would be three consecutive decades (Guttman, 1989). The data record should be consistent (have no changes in location, instruments, observation practices, etc.; these are identified here as "exposure changes") and have no missing values so a normal will reflect the actual average climatic conditions. If any significant exposure changes have occurred, the data record is said to be "inhomogeneous," and the normal may not reflect a true climatic average. Such data need to be adjusted to remove the nonclimatic inhomogeneities. The resulting (adjusted) record is then said to be "homogeneous." If no exposure changes have occurred at a station, the normal is calculated simply by averaging the appropriate 30 values from the 1961-1990 record.

In the main, there are two "inhomogeneities" that NCDC is correcting for with normalization: adjusting for variances in time of day of observation (at the so-called First Order stations data is based on midnight to midnight observation times and this practice is not necessarily followed at cooperative stations which are staffed by volunteers), and second, estimating data that is either missing or incongruent.

The editors had some concerns regarding the comparative results of the two methodologies. Would our methodology produce strikingly different results than NCDC's? To allay concerns, results of the two processes were compared for the time period normalized results are available (1971-2000). In short, what was found was that the answer to this question is no. Never the less, users should be aware that because of both the time period covered (1980-2009) and the methodology used, data is not compatible with data from other sources.

POTENTIAL CAUTIONS

First, as with any statistical reference work of this type, users need to be aware of the source of the data. The information here comes from NOAA, and it is the most comprehensive and reliable core data available. Although it is the best, it is not perfect. Most weather stations are staffed by volunteers, times of observation sometimes vary, stations occasionally are moved (especially over a thirty year period), equipment is changed or upgraded, and all of these factors affect the uniformity of the data. The editors do not attempt to correct for these factors, and this data is not intended for either climatologists or atmospheric scientists. Users with concerns about data collection and reporting protocols are both referred to NCDC technical documentation.

Second, users need to be aware of the methodology here which is described above. Although this methodology has produced fully satisfactory results, it is not directly compatible with other methodologies, hence variances in the results published here and those which appear in other publications will doubtlessly arise.

Third, is the trap of that informal logical fallacy known as "hasty generalization," and its corollaries. This may involve presuming the future will be like the past (specifically, next year will be an average year), or it may involve misunderstanding the limitations of an arithmetic average, but more interestingly, it may involve those mistakes made most innocently by generalizing informally on too broad a basis. As weather is highly localized, the data should be taken in that context. A weather station collects data about climatic conditions at that spot, and that spot may or may not be an effective paradigm for an entire town or area.

Indiana Physical Features and Climate Narrative

PHYSICAL FEATURES AND GENERAL CLIMATE. Indiana has an invigorating climate of warm summers and cool winters, because of its location in the middle latitudes in the interior of a large continent. Imposed on the well-known daily and seasonal changes of temperature are changes occurring every few days as surges of polar air move southeastward or air of tropical origin moves northeastward. These outbreaks are more frequent and pronounced in the winter than in the summer. A winter may be unusually cold or a summer cool if the influence of polar air is rather continuous. Likewise, a summer may be unusually warm or a winter mild if air of tropical origin predominates. The action between these two air masses with a contrast in temperature and density fosters the development of low pressure centers which in moving generally eastward frequently pass through or near Indiana, resulting in normally abundant rain. The cyclones are least active and frequently pass north of Indiana in midsummer. Thunderstorms, often local in areal coverage, are important at such times when evaporation and loss of moisture from the soil and vegetation exceeds rainfall. Major climatological variations within the State are caused by differences of latitude, elevation, terrain, soil, and lakes.

The effect of the Great Lakes and more specifically, Lake Michigan, on the climate of northern Indiana is most pronounced just inland from the Lake Michigan shore and diminishes to insignificance in central Indiana. The result of cold air passing over the warmer lake water of Lake Michigan induces precipitation in the lee of Lake Michigan in fall and winter. Average daily minimum temperatures in the fall are higher and daily maximum temperatures in the spring are lower in northwestern Indiana than farther south. Winter precipitation, especially snowfall, is several times greater in the counties of Lake, Porter, and LaPorte as the result of this phenomena. Lake related snowfall and cloudiness often extends to central Indiana in the winter. Very local severe snowstorms have occurred just inland from Lake Michigan.

Another important variable in the composition of Indiana weather is the topography of the State. Elevations range from a little more than 300 feet at the mouth of the Wabash in the southwest corner of the State, to a little over 1,200 feet in the east-central portion (Randolph County) and northeastern section (Steuben County). Differences of terrain affect the climate considerably. South-central Indiana is unglaciated and has the most rugged relief. The Kankakee Valley in the northwest has but little slope to the west and drains what was formerly marshlands. Many small lakes abound in northeastern Indiana among numerous glacial moraines and hills. Most of the north, central, and southwest is rolling country.

TEMPERATURE. Variations of temperature and precipitation occur in short distances where terrain is hilly. On calm, clear nights the valley bottoms have lower temperatures than the slopes and tops of the surrounding hills. Mean maximum as well as mean minimum temperatures decrease from south to north with latitude and decrease from west to east with elevation. Near Lake Michigan temperatures average higher than expected for the latitude in the fall and winter, and lower than expected for the latitude in the spring and summer.

The average date of the last freezing temperature in the spring ranges from the first week of April in the Ohio River Valley of the southwest to the second week of May in the extreme northeast. The usual trend of a later date toward the north is reversed in extreme northwestern Indiana, where the average date is about April 30 near Lake Michigan. In the fall the average date of the first temperature of 32°F. or colder is from October 7 in the extreme northeast to October 26 along the Ohio River in the southwest.

Spring freezes are later in valleys and hollows and fall freezes are earlier. Longer freeze-free periods occur on ridges and hills. Southern Indiana has much of this type of terrain. The gradual slope upward from southwestern Indiana to northeastern Indiana results in lower minimum temperatures and shorter growing seasons in the east compared to the west at the same latitude. In the Kankakee Valley, peat or muck lands experience late spring and early fall frosts because of the radiative characteristic of the soil.

PRECIPITATION. Average annual rainfall ranges from 36 inches in northern Indiana to 43 inches in southern Indiana. July rainfall averages about the same in all areas. The greater precipitation in the south compared with the north comes in the winter months. Southern Indiana has the greatest rainfall in March and the least in October. The wettest month in northern and central Indiana is June and the driest is February. A drought occasionally occurs in the summer when evaporation is highest and dependence on rainfall is greatest.

Most of the state is drained by the Wabash River system. Other river basins are the Maumee in the extreme northeast, the St. Joseph (Lake Michigan) and Kankakee (Illinois River) in the north-central and northwest, and some Ohio River drainage in the extreme south and southeast. Floods occur in some part of the State nearly every year and have occurred in every month of the year. The season of greatest flood frequency is during the winter and spring months. The primary cause of floods is prolonged periods of heavy rains, although occasionally the rains falling on a snow cover and the formation of ice jams are an added factor. The most common type of flood-producing storm in the area is that having a quasi-stationary front oriented from west-southwest to east-northeast with a series of waves or perturbations moving to the east along the front.

Average annual snowfall increases from about 10 inches in southern Indiana to 40 inches in the northern portion of the State and higher in the three county areas along Lake Michigan. From year to year snowfall varies greatly, depending both on temperatures and the frequency of winter storms. At a given latitude in central and southern Indiana snowfall is greatest toward the east because of higher elevation.

OTHER CLIMATIC ELEMENTS. Cloudiness is least in the fall and greatest in the winter. The north is cloudier than the south, particularly in the winter when the Great Lakes have the greatest effect upon the weather.

Average relative humidity differs very little at night over Indiana. During the day relative humidity is usually lower in the south than in the north. This is true for all seasons. However, the simultaneous occurrence of high temperatures and high relative humidity is most frequent in the south.

Prevailing winds are from the southwest quadrant throughout most of the year. Winds from the northern quadrant occur in the winter and persist for a longer time in the north. Along the shore of Lake Michigan the sea-breeze effect is observed in the summer when winds in central United States are light or calm. Vertical currents from the heating of land during the day cause wind near the ground to flow from over water to land reducing the maximum temperature of the day. At night the breezes are in the opposite direction or from the land to water because of land cooling. These breezes are important in limiting extremely high temperatures of a summer day and account for rapid changes in short distances within a mile or so of the lake shore. Winds meet less friction passing over water so off-lake winds have a considerably higher speed than those off or over land.

Severe storms are most frequent in the spring. About one-half of the tornadoes occur between 2 p.m. and 6 p.m. and nearly three-fourths between 10 a.m. and 10 p.m. Hail falls occasionally in very local areas.

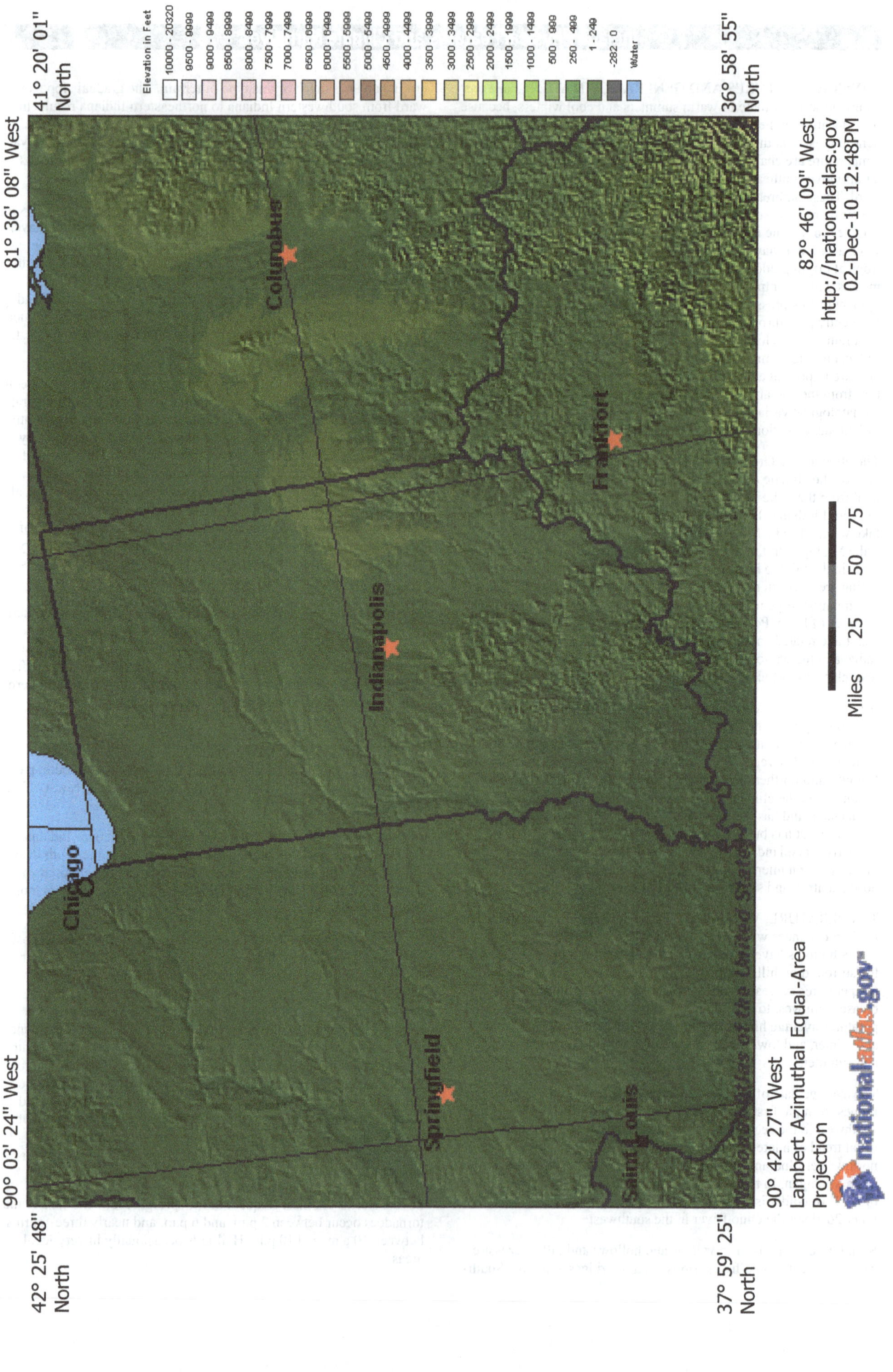
41° 20' 01" North
81° 36' 08" West
42° 25' 48" North
90° 03' 24" West
37° 59' 25" North
90° 42' 27" West
36° 58' 55" North
82° 46' 09" West
Elevation in Feet
10000 - 20320
9500 - 9999
9000 - 9499
8500 - 8999
8000 - 8499
7500 - 7999
7000 - 7499
6500 - 6999
6000 - 6499
5500 - 5999
5000 - 5499
4500 - 4999
4000 - 4499
3500 - 3999
3000 - 3499
2500 - 2999
2000 - 2499
1500 - 1999
1000 - 1499
500 - 999
250 - 499
1 - 249
-282 0
Water
Columbus
Frankfort
Indianapolis
Chicago
Springfield
Saint Louis
National Atlas of the United States
Miles 25 50 75
Lambert Azimuthal Equal-Area Projection
http://nationalatlas.gov
02-Dec-10 12:48PM
nationalatlas.gov

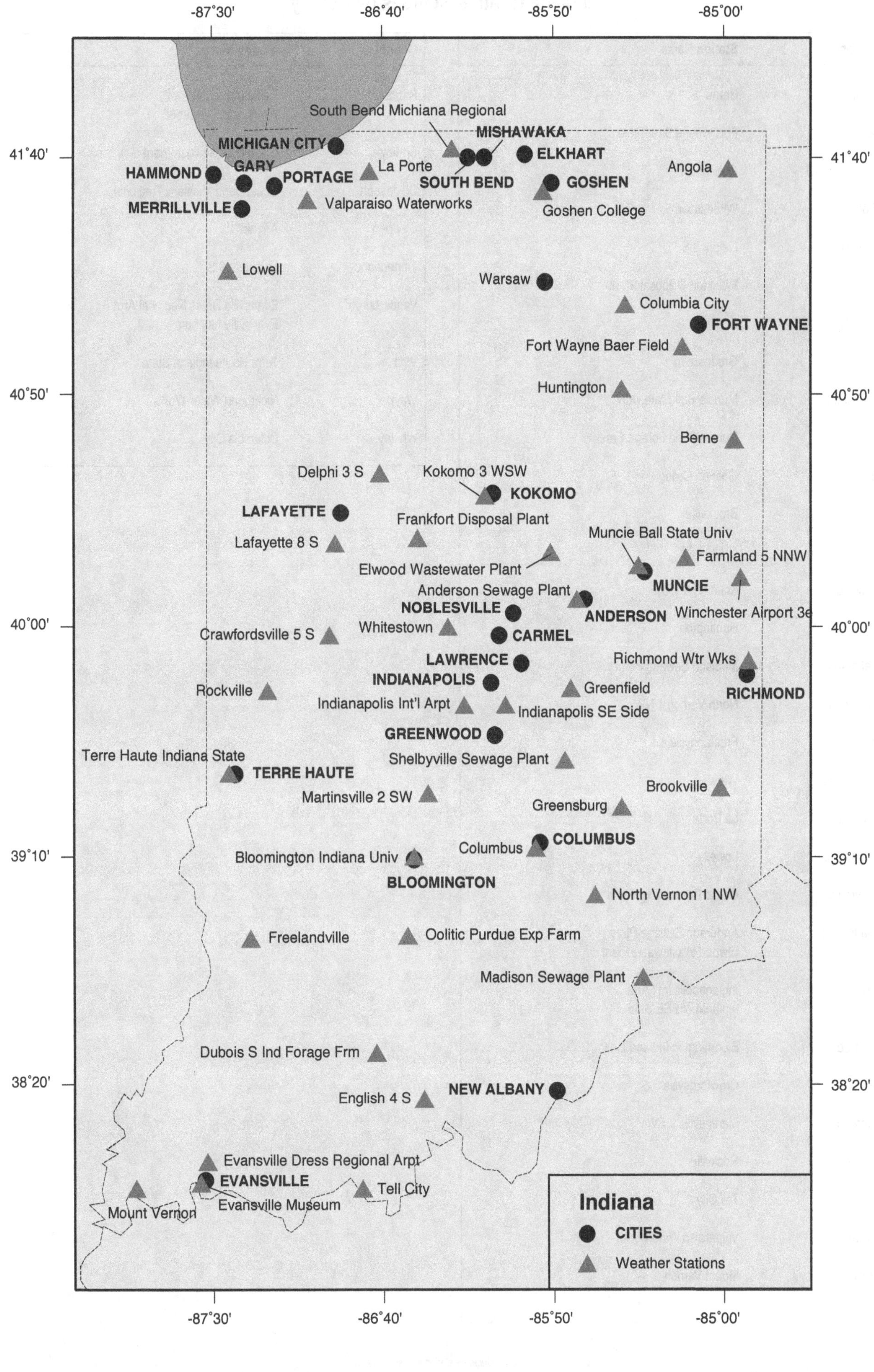
-87°30'
-86°40'
-85°50'
-85°00'
41°40'
40°50'
40°00'
39°10'
38°20'
South Bend Michiana Regional
MICHIGAN CITY
MISHAWAKA
ELKHART
HAMMOND
GARY
PORTAGE
La Porte
SOUTH BEND
GOSHEN
Angola
MERRILLVILLE
Valparaiso Waterworks
Goshen College
Lowell
Warsaw
Columbia City
FORT WAYNE
Fort Wayne Baer Field
Huntington
Berne
Delphi 3 S
Kokomo 3 WSW
KOKOMO
LAFAYETTE
Frankfort Disposal Plant
Lafayette 8 S
Muncie Ball State Univ
Farmland 5 NNW
Elwood Wastewater Plant
Anderson Sewage Plant
MUNCIE
NOBLESVILLE
ANDERSON
Winchester Airport 3e
Crawfordsville 5 S
Whitestown
CARMEL
LAWRENCE
Richmond Wtr Wks
INDIANAPOLIS
RICHMOND
Rockville
Greenfield
Indianapolis Int'l Arpt
Indianapolis SE Side
GREENWOOD
Terre Haute Indiana State
Shelbyville Sewage Plant
TERRE HAUTE
Brookville
Martinsville 2 SW
Greensburg
COLUMBUS
Columbus
Bloomington Indiana Univ
BLOOMINGTON
North Vernon 1 NW
Freelandville
Oolitic Purdue Exp Farm
Madison Sewage Plant
Dubois S Ind Forage Frm
English 4 S
NEW ALBANY
Evansville Dress Regional Arpt
EVANSVILLE
Tell City
Evansville Museum
Mount Vernon
Indiana
CITIES
Weather Stations

Indiana Weather Stations by County

County	Station Name
Adams	Berne
Allen	Fort Wayne Baer Field
Bartholomew	Columbus
Boone	Whitestown
Carroll	Delphi 3 S
Clinton	Frankfort Disposal Plant
Crawford	English 4 S
Decatur	Greensburg
Delaware	Muncie Ball State Univ
Dubois	Dubois S Ind Forage Frm
Elkhart	Goshen College
Franklin	Brookville
Hancock	Greenfield
Howard	Kokomo 3 WSW
Huntington	Huntington
Jefferson	Madison Sewage Plant
Jennings	North Vernon 1 NW
Knox	Freelandville
Kosciusko	Warsaw
La Porte	La Porte
Lake	Lowell
Lawrence	Oolitic Purdue Exp Farm
Madison	Anderson Sewage Plant Elwood Wastewater Plant
Marion	Indianapolis Int'l Arpt Indianapolis SE Side
Monroe	Bloomington Indiana Univ
Montgomery	Crawfordsville 5 S
Morgan	Martinsville 2 SW
Parke	Rockville
Perry	Tell City
Porter	Valparaiso Waterworks
Posey	Mount Vernon

County	Station Name
Randolph	Farmland 5 NNW Winchester Airport 3E
Shelby	Shelbyville Sewage Plant
St. Joseph	South Bend Michiana Regional
Steuben	Angola
Tippecanoe	Lafayette 8 S
Vanderburgh	Evansville Dress Regional Arpt Evansville Museum
Vigo	Terre Haute Indiana State
Wayne	Richmond Water Works
Whitley	Columbia City

See User Guide for station inclusion criteria.

Indiana Weather Stations by City

City	Station Name	Miles
Anderson	Anderson Sewage Plant	1.9
	Elwood Wastewater Plant	14.6
	Greenfield	22.1
	Muncie Ball State Univ	16.2
Bloomington	Bloomington Indiana Univ	0.5
	Martinsville 2 SW	16.9
	Oolitic Purdue Exp Farm	19.3
Carmel	Anderson Sewage Plant	22.3
	Elwood Wastewater Plant	24.4
	Greenfield	22.9
	Indianapolis Int'l Arpt	19.6
	Indianapolis SE Side	17.8
	Whitestown	13.1
Columbus	Columbus	1.5
	Greensburg	23.4
	North Vernon 1 NW	19.3
	Shelbyville Sewage Plant	21.6
Elkhart	Goshen College	10.2
	South Bend Michiana Regional	18.9
	Three Rivers, MI	24.3
Evansville	Evansville Museum	1.5
	Evansville Dress Regional Arpt	5.1
	Mount Vernon	18.7
	Henderson 7 SSW, KY	16.4
Fishers	Anderson Sewage Plant	18.3
	Elwood Wastewater Plant	22.9
	Greenfield	18.3
	Indianapolis Int'l Arpt	21.5
	Indianapolis SE Side	17.0
	Whitestown	18.2
Fort Wayne	Columbia City	19.5
	Fort Wayne Baer Field	7.1
Gary	Park Forest, IL	18.5
	Lowell	21.9
	Valparaiso Waterworks	16.5
Goshen	Goshen College	3.2
	Warsaw	24.2
Greenwood	Greenfield	22.8
	Indianapolis Int'l Arpt	10.6
	Indianapolis SE Side	7.6
	Martinsville 2 SW	23.1
	Shelbyville Sewage Plant	19.1
Hammond	Chicago Midway Arpt, IL	17.4
	Park Forest, IL	12.3
	Lowell	23.8
	Valparaiso Waterworks	24.5
Indianapolis	Greenfield	20.9
	Indianapolis Int'l Arpt	8.5
	Indianapolis SE Side	6.8
	Whitestown	17.9
Kokomo	Elwood Wastewater Plant	20.9
Kokomo *(cont.)*	Frankfort Disposal Plant	22.2
	Kokomo 3 WSW	1.9
Lafayette	Delphi 3 S	14.0
	Frankfort Disposal Plant	20.6
	Lafayette 8 S	7.6
Lawrence	Anderson Sewage Plant	21.8
	Greenfield	14.1
	Indianapolis Int'l Arpt	17.8
	Indianapolis SE Side	11.0
	Whitestown	21.1
Merrillville	Park Forest, IL	17.2
	Lowell	16.0
	Valparaiso Waterworks	16.5
Michigan City	La Porte	10.0
	Valparaiso Waterworks	15.1
Mishawaka	Goshen College	16.9
	South Bend Michiana Regional	8.7
Muncie	Anderson Sewage Plant	18.3
	Elwood Wastewater Plant	24.6
	Farmland 5 NNW	13.4
	Muncie Ball State Univ	1.9
New Albany	Louisville Standiford Field, KY	9.7
Noblesville	Anderson Sewage Plant	16.7
	Elwood Wastewater Plant	17.6
	Greenfield	23.5
	Indianapolis SE Side	23.1
	Whitestown	17.5
Portage	La Porte	23.6
	Lowell	24.2
	Valparaiso Waterworks	8.8
Richmond	Richmond Water Works	3.8
	Winchester Airport 3E	24.5
South Bend	Goshen College	20.8
	South Bend Michiana Regional	4.6
Terre Haute	Rockville	22.3
	Terre Haute Indiana State	1.4

Note: Miles is the distance between the geographic center of the city and the weather station.

Indiana Weather Stations by Elevation

Feet	Station Name
1,109	Winchester Airport 3E
1,015	Richmond Water Works
1,009	Angola
964	Farmland 5 NNW
939	Muncie Ball State Univ
935	Greensburg
935	Whitestown
875	Goshen College
865	Greenfield
859	Berne
850	Columbia City
845	Anderson Sewage Plant
845	Indianapolis SE Side
839	Elwood Wastewater Plant
834	Frankfort Disposal Plant
830	Bloomington Indiana Univ
819	Kokomo 3 WSW
810	La Porte
810	Warsaw
799	Valparaiso Waterworks
792	Indianapolis Int'l Arpt
791	Fort Wayne Baer Field
772	South Bend Michiana Regional
762	Crawfordsville 5 S
750	Shelbyville Sewage Plant
745	North Vernon 1 NW
732	Lafayette 8 S
725	Huntington
689	Dubois S Ind Forage Frm
689	Rockville
670	Delphi 3 S
665	Lowell
649	Oolitic Purdue Exp Farm
629	Brookville
621	Columbus
609	Martinsville 2 SW
549	Freelandville
509	English 4 S
506	Terre Haute Indiana State
459	Madison Sewage Plant
419	Mount Vernon
399	Tell City
380	Evansville Dress Regional Arpt
379	Evansville Museum

See User Guide for station inclusion criteria.

Evansville Regional Airport

Evansville, Indiana, is located on the Ohio River. The country around Evansville ranges from level to areas of rolling terrain near the river. Dress Regional Airport, where weather observations are taken, is located in a shallow valley with low hills to the east and west which parallel the valley, but slope down to the south. There are hills five miles to the north which are about 100 feet higher than the field. The open end of the valley slopes down and south toward the city of Evansville and the Ohio River.

Prevailing wind direction is from the south-southwest. The strongest winds occur during a deep winter storm passage through the Lower Ohio Valley. Strong and cold north to northwest winds occur from late autumn to early spring, most often, in January and February, as large domes of arctic high pressure moves into the midwest.

Geographically, Evansville lies in the path of moisture-bearing low pressure formations that move from the western Gulf region, northeastward over the Mississippi and Ohio Valleys to the Great Lakes and northern Atlantic Coast. Much of the precipitation results from these storm systems, especially in the cooler part of the year.

Both temperature and precipitation are closely related to the movement of the polar front and the storms which move along the front. This is especially true in the winter and spring months. In summer and early autumn changes are less severe and periods of polar air invasions are less prolonged. There is considerable variation in seasonal and monthly temperature and precipitation from year to year as these factors depend greatly on the frequency of storm and frontal passages.

Convective thunderstorms, developing in the maritime tropical air from the Gulf of Mexico and squall line activity, combine to supply the summer rainfall. The greatest precipitation intensities for short periods of time come in the months of greatest thunderstorm frequency. The greatest intensities for 24 hours or more are confined to the winter months.

Severe storms are rather infrequent but thunderstorms cause some wind damage each year. Hail often occurs with the stronger thunderstorms. Evansville is in tornado alley with the most frequent occurrence in early spring and late fall.

Snowfall varies greatly from season to season, as do rainfall and temperature. Snowfalls of two or more inches are very infrequent, and these amounts are usually melted within a day or two.

The growing season averages 199 days, but has been as long as 250 days and as short as 169 days.

Evansville Regional Airport *Vanderburgh County* Elevation: 380 ft. Latitude: 38° 03' N Longitude: 87° 32' W

	JAN	FEB	MAR	APR	MAY	JUN	JUL	AUG	SEP	OCT	NOV	DEC	YEAR
Mean Maximum Temp. (°F)	41.1	45.8	56.3	67.3	76.7	85.3	88.5	87.8	81.2	69.5	56.3	44.3	66.7
Mean Temp. (°F)	33.0	36.7	46.1	56.1	65.9	74.8	78.3	77.0	69.4	57.8	46.7	36.1	56.5
Mean Minimum Temp. (°F)	24.9	27.7	35.7	44.9	55.0	64.3	68.1	66.0	57.5	46.0	36.9	27.9	46.2
Extreme Maximum Temp. (°F)	71	77	84	91	94	101	102	104	100	93	82	77	104
Extreme Minimum Temp. (°F)	-18	-8	3	23	34	42	51	43	34	23	11	-15	-18
Days Maximum Temp. ≥ 90°F	0	0	0	0	1	9	14	12	5	0	0	0	41
Days Maximum Temp. ≤ 32°F	7	4	1	0	0	0	0	0	0	0	0	5	17
Days Minimum Temp. ≤ 32°F	24	19	13	3	0	0	0	0	0	2	11	21	93
Days Minimum Temp. ≤ 0°F	1	0	0	0	0	0	0	0	0	0	0	1	2
Heating Degree Days (base 65°F)	984	793	585	285	78	5	0	1	41	249	545	889	4,455
Cooling Degree Days (base 65°F)	0	0	4	26	113	307	420	378	179	32	1	0	1,460
Mean Precipitation (in.)	3.07	3.16	4.25	4.35	5.39	3.90	3.95	3.02	3.12	3.28	4.12	3.73	45.34
Maximum Precipitation (in.)*	13.5	7.3	12.8	10.3	13.5	6.9	9.7	8.4	7.0	7.9	8.5	8.2	63.1
Minimum Precipitation (in.)*	0.5	0.6	1.3	1.1	0.9	0.6	0.2	0.2	0.5	trace	0.9	0.6	27.9
Extreme Maximum Daily Precip. (in.)	3.72	3.38	6.40	6.04	4.92	3.67	2.95	3.03	2.83	2.45	3.48	2.30	6.40
Days With ≥ 0.1" Precipitation	6	5	7	7	8	6	6	5	5	6	6	7	74
Days With ≥ 0.5" Precipitation	2	2	3	3	4	3	3	2	2	2	3	3	32
Days With ≥ 1.0" Precipitation	1	1	1	1	1	1	1	1	1	1	1	1	12
Mean Snowfall (in.)	3.4	3.8	***1.3***	***0.2***	***trace***	***trace***	***0.0***	***0.0***	***trace***	***0.2***	***0.1***	2.4	***11.4***
Maximum Snowfall (in.)*	21	18	20	9	0	0	0	0	0	5	7	10	36
Maximum 24-hr. Snowfall (in.)*	8	11	8	9	0	0	0	0	0	4	7	7	11
Maximum Snow Depth (in.)	8	12	10	3	trace	trace	0	0	trace	2	***1***	7	***12***
Days With ≥ 1.0" Snow Depth	4	4	1	0	0	0	0	0	0	0	***0***	3	***12***
Thunderstorm Days*	1	1	4	5	6	7	7	5	3	2	2	1	44
Foggy Days*	12	12	12	9	11	11	13	16	15	12	11	13	147
Predominant Sky Cover*	OVR	OVR	OVR	OVR	OVR	OVR	SCT	CLR	CLR	CLR	OVR	OVR	OVR
Mean Relative Humidity 7am (%)*	80	80	78	73	75	75	78	82	83	83	80	81	79
Mean Relative Humidity 4pm (%)*	66	61	56	50	52	52	54	54	52	50	59	67	56
Mean Dewpoint (°F)*	24	27	35	44	54	63	67	66	58	46	36	28	46
Prevailing Wind Direction*	NW	NW	NW	SSW	S	SW	SW	SW	S	NW	S	NW	NW
Prevailing Wind Speed (mph)*	12	12	12	13	9	9	8	8	8	7	10	10	10
Maximum Wind Gust (mph)*	55	53	52	63	71	76	56	46	59	52	70	56	76

Note: (*) Period of record is 1948-1995

Fort Wayne Baer Field

Fort Wayne is located at the junction of the St. Marys, St. Joseph, and Maumee Rivers in northeastern Indiana. The surrounding area is generally level south and east of the city. Southwest and west, the terrain is somewhat rolling, while to the northwest and a few miles north from the city, it becomes quite hilly. The highest point in the general area is about 40 miles due north of Fort Wayne, near Angola, Indiana. At this point, the elevation rises to 1,060 feet above sea level.

The climate is representative of northeastern Indiana and is influenced to some extent by the Great Lakes. It does not differ greatly from the climates of other mid-western cities of the same general latitude. Temperature differences between daily highs and lows are invigorating and average about 20 degrees. The average occurrence of the last freeze in the spring is late April, and the first freeze in the fall is mid-October, making the average freeze-free period 173 days. The length of the growing season is favorable for the maturing of all crops and vegetables normally grown in the midwest.

Annual precipitation is well distributed, with somewhat larger monthly amounts falling in late spring and early summer. Damaging hailstorms occur at an average of about twice a year. One of the most notable storms caused severe damage to property, many thousands of trees, and power and telephone lines in the area. Severe flooding has also occurred in the area. Snow usually covers the ground for about 30 days during the winter months, but heavy snowstorms are not frequent.

Except for the considerable cloudiness that occurs during the winter months, Fort Wayne enjoys a good midwestern average sunshine. Heavy fog occurrence is infrequent.

Fort Wayne Baer Field *Allen County* Elevation: 791 ft. Latitude: 41° 00' N Longitude: 85° 12' W

	JAN	FEB	MAR	APR	MAY	JUN	JUL	AUG	SEP	OCT	NOV	DEC	YEAR
Mean Maximum Temp. (°F)	32.4	36.1	47.6	60.7	71.6	80.8	84.3	82.1	75.9	63.1	49.6	36.4	60.0
Mean Temp. (°F)	25.2	28.4	38.3	49.9	60.6	70.1	73.7	71.7	64.5	52.7	41.5	29.6	50.5
Mean Minimum Temp. (°F)	17.9	20.6	28.9	39.1	49.5	59.4	63.1	61.2	53.1	42.2	33.4	22.8	40.9
Extreme Maximum Temp. (°F)	66	73	82	88	94	106	102	99	97	89	77	71	106
Extreme Minimum Temp. (°F)	-22	-18	-7	7	27	38	45	40	29	19	10	-18	-22
Days Maximum Temp. ≥ 90°F	0	0	0	0	1	4	6	3	1	0	0	0	15
Days Maximum Temp. ≤ 32°F	15	11	3	0	0	0	0	0	0	0	1	11	41
Days Minimum Temp. ≤ 32°F	28	24	20	7	0	0	0	0	0	4	15	26	124
Days Minimum Temp. ≤ 0°F	4	2	0	0	0	0	0	0	0	0	0	2	8
Heating Degree Days (base 65°F)	1,229	1,029	823	455	183	27	2	9	94	387	697	1,091	6,026
Cooling Degree Days (base 65°F)	0	0	1	9	52	188	279	223	86	10	0	0	848
Mean Precipitation (in.)	2.26	2.08	2.76	3.50	4.13	4.15	4.28	3.68	2.83	2.88	2.98	2.82	38.35
Maximum Precipitation (in.)*	9.7	6.8	5.3	7.1	8.8	8.3	11.0	7.7	6.8	9.3	8.0	7.6	54.6
Minimum Precipitation (in.)*	0.4	0.3	0.7	1.3	1.0	0.8	0.4	0.4	0.3	0.1	0.6	0.4	24.4
Extreme Maximum Daily Precip. (in.)	1.79	3.03	1.96	2.57	4.35	4.40	2.83	3.40	2.13	2.69	2.44	1.79	4.40
Days With ≥ 0.1" Precipitation	5	5	6	8	8	7	7	6	5	6	7	7	77
Days With ≥ 0.5" Precipitation	1	1	2	2	3	3	3	3	2	2	2	2	26
Days With ≥ 1.0" Precipitation	0	0	0	1	1	1	1	1	1	1	1	0	8
Mean Snowfall (in.)	10.2	7.8	4.1	1.1	trace	trace	trace	trace	trace	0.4	2.0	8.2	33.8
Maximum Snowfall (in.)*	30	17	20	12	trace	0	0	0	0	8	14	20	62
Maximum 24-hr. Snowfall (in.)*	11	8	13	6	trace	0	0	0	0	6	6	11	13
Maximum Snow Depth (in.)	12	20	9	6	trace	trace	trace	trace	trace	3	4	9	20
Days With ≥ 1.0" Snow Depth	15	12	4	0	0	0	0	0	0	0	1	9	41
Thunderstorm Days*	< 1	1	2	4	5	7	7	6	4	2	1	< 1	39
Foggy Days*	14	13	13	11	12	10	14	17	14	14	13	15	160
Predominant Sky Cover*	OVR	OVR	OVR	OVR	OVR	OVR	SCT	SCT	OVR	OVR	OVR	OVR	OVR
Mean Relative Humidity 7am (%)*	81	81	80	78	77	78	82	86	87	85	83	83	82
Mean Relative Humidity 4pm (%)*	72	67	62	54	52	52	53	55	53	54	67	74	60
Mean Dewpoint (°F)*	18	20	28	38	48	57	62	61	54	43	33	23	41
Prevailing Wind Direction*	W	W	W	SW	SW	SW	SW	SW	SW	SW	SW	W	SW
Prevailing Wind Speed (mph)*	14	14	14	14	12	12	9	9	10	12	13	13	12
Maximum Wind Gust (mph)*	69	54	59	61	59	64	67	59	53	63	58	58	69

Note: (*) Period of record is 1948-1995

Indianapolis Int'l Airport

Indianapolis is located in the central part of the state and is situated on level or slightly rolling terrain. The greater part of the city lies east of the White River which flows in a general north to south direction.

The National Weather Service Forecast Office is located approximately seven miles southwest of the central part of the city at the Indianapolis International Airport. From a field elevation of 797 feet above sea level at the Indianapolis International Airport the terrain slopes gradually downward to a little below 645 feet at the White River, then upward to just over 910 feet in the northwest corner and eastern sections of the county. The street elevation at the former city office located in the Old Federal Building is 718 feet.

Indianapolis has a temperate climate, with very warm summers and without a dry season. Very cold temperatures may be produced by the invasion of continental polar air in the winter from northern latitudes. The polar air can be quite frigid with very low humidity. The arrival of maritime tropical air from the Gulf in the summer brings warm temperatures and moderate humidity. One of the longest and most severe heat waves brought temperatures of 100 degrees or more for nine consecutive days.

Precipitation is distributed fairly evenly throughout the year, and therefore there is no pronounced wet or dry season. Rainfall in the spring and summer is produced mostly by showers and thunderstorms. A rainfall of about two and a half inches in a 24-hour period can be expected about once a year. Snowfalls of three inches or more occur on an average of two or three times in the winter.

Local levees and/or channel improvements now protect some formerly flood-prone areas.

Based on the 1951-1980 period, the average first occurrence of 32 degrees Fahrenheit in the fall is October 20 and the average last occurrence in the spring is April 22.

Indianapolis Int'l Airport *Marion County* Elevation: 792 ft. Latitude: 39° 43' N Longitude: 86° 16' W

	JAN	FEB	MAR	APR	MAY	JUN	JUL	AUG	SEP	OCT	NOV	DEC	YEAR
Mean Maximum Temp. (°F)	36.0	40.5	51.5	63.3	73.1	82.0	85.3	84.1	77.8	65.3	52.3	39.4	62.5
Mean Temp. (°F)	28.3	32.2	42.0	52.9	62.8	72.0	75.5	74.2	67.0	55.0	43.7	32.0	53.1
Mean Minimum Temp. (°F)	20.5	23.8	32.4	42.4	52.5	61.9	65.8	64.3	56.2	44.5	35.0	24.6	43.7
Extreme Maximum Temp. (°F)	68	76	85	86	93	102	103	102	96	91	79	74	103
Extreme Minimum Temp. (°F)	-27	-21	-7	18	29	37	48	42	32	20	10	-23	-27
Days Maximum Temp. ≥ 90°F	0	0	0	0	0	3	7	6	2	0	0	0	18
Days Maximum Temp. ≤ 32°F	12	7	2	0	0	0	0	0	0	0	1	8	30
Days Minimum Temp. ≤ 32°F	26	22	16	4	0	0	0	0	0	3	13	23	107
Days Minimum Temp. ≤ 0°F	2	1	0	0	0	0	0	0	0	0	0	1	4
Heating Degree Days (base 65°F)	1,131	922	709	371	132	15	1	3	66	323	634	1,015	5,322
Cooling Degree Days (base 65°F)	0	0	2	15	72	231	334	296	133	18	0	0	1,101
Mean Precipitation (in.)	2.67	2.35	3.60	3.77	4.98	4.06	4.55	3.39	3.21	3.14	3.60	3.13	42.45
Maximum Precipitation (in.)*	12.7	5.3	10.7	8.1	9.3	7.4	11.8	8.3	8.1	7.8	8.5	7.7	55.8
Minimum Precipitation (in.)*	0.4	0.4	0.9	1.0	1.1	0.4	1.2	0.7	0.2	0.2	0.8	0.4	27.9
Extreme Maximum Daily Precip. (in.)	2.70	2.03	2.54	2.34	3.80	3.09	5.09	3.81	7.20	2.74	4.15	1.74	7.20
Days With ≥ 0.1" Precipitation	6	5	7	8	9	7	7	6	5	5	6	7	78
Days With ≥ 0.5" Precipitation	2	1	2	3	4	3	3	2	2	2	2	2	28
Days With ≥ 1.0" Precipitation	0	0	1	1	1	1	1	1	1	1	1	1	10
Mean Snowfall (in.)	8.5	6.4	2.7	0.3	trace	trace	0.0	trace	trace	0.4	0.8	6.4	25.5
Maximum Snowfall (in.)*	31	18	11	4	trace	0	0	0	0	9	8	28	45
Maximum 24-hr. Snowfall (in.)*	10	8	6	3	trace	0	0	0	0	8	8	10	10
Maximum Snow Depth (in.)	11	13	8	1	trace	trace	0	trace	trace	2	4	9	13
Days With ≥ 1.0" Snow Depth	10	8	2	0	0	0	0	0	0	0	0	6	26
Thunderstorm Days*	1	1	3	5	6	7	8	6	3	2	1	< 1	43
Foggy Days*	15	13	13	11	13	12	16	18	15	13	14	15	168
Predominant Sky Cover*	OVR	OVR	OVR	OVR	OVR	OVR	SCT	SCT	CLR	OVR	OVR	OVR	OVR
Mean Relative Humidity 7am (%)*	81	81	79	77	80	80	84	88	87	85	83	83	82
Mean Relative Humidity 4pm (%)*	69	64	59	54	53	53	56	56	53	53	63	70	59
Mean Dewpoint (°F)*	20	23	31	40	51	60	65	64	56	44	34	25	43
Prevailing Wind Direction*	WSW	WNW	WNW	SW	SW	SW	SW	SW	SW	SW	SW	SW	SW
Prevailing Wind Speed (mph)*	12	13	14	13	10	9	8	8	9	10	12	12	10
Maximum Wind Gust (mph)*	60	62	75	75	69	70	81	70	74	64	79	64	81

Note: (*) Period of record is 1948-1995

Climate

South Bend Michiana Regional

South Bend is located on the Saint Joseph River in the northern portion of Saint Joseph County, situated on mostly level to gently rolling terrain and some former marshland. Drainage for the area is through the Saint Joseph River and Kankakee River.

South Bend is under the climatic influence of Lake Michigan with its nearest shore 20 miles to the northwest. The lake has a moderating effect on the temperature. Temperatures of 100 degrees or higher are rare and cold waves are less severe than at many locations at the same latitude. This results in favorable conditions for orchard and vegetable growth.

Based on the 1951-1980 period, the average first occurrence of 32 degrees Fahrenheit in the fall is October 18 and the average last occurrence in the spring is May 1.

Precipitation is fairly evenly distributed throughout the year with the greatest amounts during the growing season. The predominant snow season is from November through March, although there are also generally lighter amounts in October and April.

Winter is marked by considerable cloudiness and rather high humidity along with frequent periods of snow. Heavy snowfalls, resulting from a cold northwest wind passing over Lake Michigan are not uncommon.

South Bend Michiana Regional *St. Joseph County* Elevation: 772 ft. Latitude: 41° 42' N Longitude: 86° 20' W

	JAN	FEB	MAR	APR	MAY	JUN	JUL	AUG	SEP	OCT	NOV	DEC	YEAR
Mean Maximum Temp. (°F)	31.9	35.6	46.7	59.6	70.5	79.8	83.3	81.2	74.5	61.8	48.5	35.8	59.1
Mean Temp. (°F)	25.0	28.1	37.7	49.2	59.6	69.3	73.3	71.6	64.2	52.3	41.0	29.3	50.1
Mean Minimum Temp. (°F)	18.0	20.6	28.6	38.8	48.7	58.8	63.3	61.9	53.9	42.8	33.5	22.7	41.0
Extreme Maximum Temp. (°F)	65	74	85	89	91	104	102	103	95	88	76	70	104
Extreme Minimum Temp. (°F)	-21	-13	-3	13	26	36	42	42	32	20	7	-15	-21
Days Maximum Temp. ≥ 90°F	0	0	0	0	1	4	6	3	1	0	0	0	15
Days Maximum Temp. ≤ 32°F	16	12	4	0	0	0	0	0	0	0	2	11	45
Days Minimum Temp. ≤ 32°F	28	24	21	8	0	0	0	0	0	3	15	26	125
Days Minimum Temp. ≤ 0°F	3	2	0	0	0	0	0	0	0	0	0	2	7
Heating Degree Days (base 65°F)	1,234	1,035	841	477	211	39	4	11	105	396	712	1,100	6,165
Cooling Degree Days (base 65°F)	0	0	1	10	51	175	270	223	89	10	0	0	829
Mean Precipitation (in.)	2.29	1.95	2.47	3.26	3.68	3.80	3.96	3.99	3.65	3.37	3.23	2.68	38.33
Maximum Precipitation (in.)*	5.3	4.5	8.0	6.0	6.9	10.9	7.5	8.3	9.0	9.8	6.7	5.5	55.6
Minimum Precipitation (in.)*	0.7	0.5	0.5	0.5	0.8	0.5	1.2	0.3	trace	0.4	1.4	0.7	25.1
Extreme Maximum Daily Precip. (in.)	1.80	1.70	1.41	2.48	2.79	3.51	3.64	3.96	6.58	3.47	3.92	2.45	6.58
Days With ≥ 0.1" Precipitation	6	5	6	7	7	7	7	7	6	7	7	7	79
Days With ≥ 0.5" Precipitation	1	1	1	2	3	2	3	3	2	2	2	1	23
Days With ≥ 1.0" Precipitation	0	0	0	1	1	1	1	1	1	1	1	0	8
Mean Snowfall (in.)	20.3	15.1	7.4	1.5	trace	trace	trace	trace	trace	0.5	5.0	17.5	67.3
Maximum Snowfall (in.)*	86	35	34	14	1	0	0	0	0	9	30	42	142
Maximum 24-hr. Snowfall (in.)*	16	12	9	8	1	0	0	0	0	7	15	11	16
Maximum Snow Depth (in.)	18	23	9	6	trace	trace	trace	trace	trace	6	8	14	23
Days With ≥ 1.0" Snow Depth	20	15	5	1	0	0	0	0	0	0	2	12	55
Thunderstorm Days*	< 1	< 1	2	4	5	8	7	6	4	2	1	< 1	39
Foggy Days*	15	14	15	13	13	12	14	18	16	16	15	17	178
Predominant Sky Cover*	OVR	OVR	OVR	OVR	OVR	OVR	OVR	OVR	OVR	OVR	OVR	OVR	OVR
Mean Relative Humidity 7am (%)*	82	82	80	77	76	78	82	86	86	84	83	83	82
Mean Relative Humidity 4pm (%)*	73	69	62	55	53	52	55	57	55	57	68	75	61
Mean Dewpoint (°F)*	18	20	28	37	47	57	62	62	54	43	33	23	41
Prevailing Wind Direction*	SW	SW	SW	NNW	SSW	SSW	SW	SW	SSW	SSW	SW	SW	SW
Prevailing Wind Speed (mph)*	13	13	13	13	12	10	9	9	10	12	12	13	12
Maximum Wind Gust (mph)*	67	58	55	66	86	71	66	59	63	59	74	69	86

Note: (*) Period of record is 1948-1995

The period of record for National Weather Service station data is 1980 – 2009 except where noted. See User Guide for detailed explanation of data.

Anderson Sewage Plant *Madison County* Elevation: 845 ft. Latitude: 40° 06' N Longitude: 85° 43' W

	JAN	FEB	MAR	APR	MAY	JUN	JUL	AUG	SEP	OCT	NOV	DEC	YEAR
Mean Maximum Temp. (°F)	34.4	39.0	49.2	61.6	71.9	80.7	83.8	82.3	76.2	63.9	50.8	37.9	61.0
Mean Temp. (°F)	27.1	31.2	40.3	51.4	61.7	70.7	74.0	72.5	65.4	53.8	42.8	31.0	51.8
Mean Minimum Temp. (°F)	19.8	23.3	31.4	41.2	51.3	60.6	64.2	62.6	54.7	43.6	34.8	24.0	42.6
Extreme Maximum Temp. (°F)	65	73	81	87	93	101	103	101	95	90	80	75	103
Extreme Minimum Temp. (°F)	-24	-12	-7	17	31	37	45	40	31	20	10	-22	-24
Days Maximum Temp. ≥ 90°F	0	0	0	0	0	4	6	4	1	0	0	0	15
Days Maximum Temp. ≤ 32°F	13	9	3	0	0	0	0	0	0	0	1	10	36
Days Minimum Temp. ≤ 32°F	27	22	18	5	0	0	0	0	0	4	14	24	114
Days Minimum Temp. ≤ 0°F	3	1	0	0	0	0	0	0	0	0	0	1	5
Heating Degree Days (base 65°F)	1,167	952	761	412	164	23	3	7	85	357	659	1,048	5,638
Cooling Degree Days (base 65°F)	0	0	2	12	67	200	289	246	105	17	1	0	939
Mean Precipitation (in.)	2.39	2.28	3.26	3.83	4.39	4.21	4.40	3.49	2.99	3.10	3.66	3.09	41.09
Extreme Maximum Daily Precip. (in.)	3.00	2.37	3.30	2.00	2.69	3.51	3.06	2.70	4.21	1.91	3.42	2.00	4.21
Days With ≥ 0.1" Precipitation	5	5	7	9	8	7	7	6	5	6	6	7	78
Days With ≥ 0.5" Precipitation	2	1	3	3	3	3	4	2	2	2	3	2	30
Days With ≥ 1.0" Precipitation	0	0	1	1	1	1	1	1	1	1	1	1	10
Mean Snowfall (in.)	7.2	4.2	1.6	0.2	0.0	0.0	0.0	0.0	0.0	0.1	0.5	4.1	17.9
Maximum Snow Depth (in.)	***18***	***12***	8	1	0	0	0	0	0	trace	3	***16***	***18***
Days With ≥ 1.0" Snow Depth	***7***	4	2	0	0	0	0	0	0	0	0	4	***17***

Angola *Steuben County* Elevation: 1,009 ft. Latitude: 41° 38' N Longitude: 84° 59' W

	JAN	FEB	MAR	APR	MAY	JUN	JUL	AUG	SEP	OCT	NOV	DEC	YEAR
Mean Maximum Temp. (°F)	30.3	33.9	44.3	57.7	68.8	78.2	81.8	80.1	73.3	60.4	47.4	34.4	57.5
Mean Temp. (°F)	22.5	25.1	34.4	46.7	57.8	67.5	71.3	69.4	61.8	49.6	38.8	27.3	47.7
Mean Minimum Temp. (°F)	14.7	16.3	24.5	35.7	46.7	56.6	60.7	58.6	50.2	38.7	30.1	20.1	37.7
Extreme Maximum Temp. (°F)	63	71	78	85	90	101	98	97	93	86	75	69	101
Extreme Minimum Temp. (°F)	-27	-14	-10	4	22	32	41	37	27	16	9	-19	-27
Days Maximum Temp. ≥ 90°F	0	0	0	0	0	2	3	2	0	0	0	0	7
Days Maximum Temp. ≤ 32°F	18	13	5	0	0	0	0	0	0	0	3	13	52
Days Minimum Temp. ≤ 32°F	29	27	25	12	1	0	0	0	0	9	19	28	150
Days Minimum Temp. ≤ 0°F	5	4	0	0	0	0	0	0	0	0	0	2	11
Heating Degree Days (base 65°F)	1,310	1,122	943	546	250	53	11	23	144	476	781	1,163	6,822
Cooling Degree Days (base 65°F)	0	0	1	6	33	134	212	166	54	4	0	0	610
Mean Precipitation (in.)	2.27	2.10	2.69	3.40	4.25	3.81	4.12	4.18	3.30	3.01	3.07	2.81	39.01
Extreme Maximum Daily Precip. (in.)	1.67	1.75	2.11	2.52	4.10	3.55	3.55	3.78	2.41	3.19	2.35	2.36	4.10
Days With ≥ 0.1" Precipitation	6	5	6	7	8	7	7	7	6	6	7	7	79
Days With ≥ 0.5" Precipitation	1	1	2	2	3	3	3	3	2	2	2	2	26
Days With ≥ 1.0" Precipitation	0	0	0	1	1	1	1	1	1	1	0	0	7
Mean Snowfall (in.)	10.6	8.4	4.8	1.0	trace	0.0	0.0	0.0	0.0	0.3	2.1	9.2	36.4
Maximum Snow Depth (in.)	23	22	13	6	trace	0	0	0	0	3	5	20	23
Days With ≥ 1.0" Snow Depth	18	15	6	1	0	0	0	0	0	0	2	11	53

Berne *Adams County* Elevation: 859 ft. Latitude: 40° 40' N Longitude: 84° 57' W

	JAN	FEB	MAR	APR	MAY	JUN	JUL	AUG	SEP	OCT	NOV	DEC	YEAR
Mean Maximum Temp. (°F)	33.7	37.5	48.4	61.1	71.8	81.0	84.6	82.8	76.6	63.7	50.3	37.2	60.7
Mean Temp. (°F)	26.6	29.5	39.0	50.7	61.3	70.9	74.6	72.8	65.7	53.7	42.3	30.4	51.5
Mean Minimum Temp. (°F)	19.4	21.5	29.5	40.2	50.7	60.7	64.6	62.6	54.9	43.7	34.1	23.5	42.1
Extreme Maximum Temp. (°F)	65	74	82	88	94	104	101	99	96	89	77	72	104
Extreme Minimum Temp. (°F)	-24	-13	-4	10	29	39	47	42	31	20	11	-19	-24
Days Maximum Temp. ≥ 90°F	0	0	0	0	0	4	7	4	1	0	0	0	16
Days Maximum Temp. ≤ 32°F	14	10	3	0	0	0	0	0	0	0	1	10	38
Days Minimum Temp. ≤ 32°F	27	23	20	6	0	0	0	0	0	3	14	25	118
Days Minimum Temp. ≤ 0°F	3	2	0	0	0	0	0	0	0	0	0	1	6
Heating Degree Days (base 65°F)	1,185	998	803	435	171	24	2	6	81	361	677	1,067	5,810
Cooling Degree Days (base 65°F)	0	0	2	11	62	207	306	253	109	16	0	0	966
Mean Precipitation (in.)	2.38	2.33	2.75	3.80	3.89	4.31	4.44	3.61	2.78	2.90	3.08	2.79	39.06
Extreme Maximum Daily Precip. (in.)	1.94	1.69	1.95	2.11	2.42	4.20	3.46	3.62	2.45	2.21	2.07	2.02	4.20
Days With ≥ 0.1" Precipitation	6	5	6	8	8	8	7	6	5	6	7	6	78
Days With ≥ 0.5" Precipitation	1	2	2	2	3	3	3	2	2	2	2	2	26
Days With ≥ 1.0" Precipitation	0	0	0	1	1	1	1	1	1	1	1	0	8
Mean Snowfall (in.)	8.2	7.3	4.1	0.8	0.0	0.0	0.0	0.0	0.0	0.3	1.6	5.9	28.2
Maximum Snow Depth (in.)	24	25	11	5	0	0	0	0	0	1	3	9	25
Days With ≥ 1.0" Snow Depth	13	10	4	0	0	0	0	0	0	0	1	8	36

Bloomington Indiana Univ *Monroe County* Elevation: 830 ft. Latitude: 39° 10' N Longitude: 86° 31' W

	JAN	FEB	MAR	APR	MAY	JUN	JUL	AUG	SEP	OCT	NOV	DEC	YEAR
Mean Maximum Temp. (°F)	37.4	42.2	52.2	63.9	73.6	81.8	85.4	84.9	78.2	66.0	53.9	40.8	63.4
Mean Temp. (°F)	29.4	33.0	42.1	53.3	63.2	71.9	75.7	74.6	67.2	55.3	44.9	32.9	53.6
Mean Minimum Temp. (°F)	21.2	23.9	31.9	42.6	52.8	62.0	65.8	64.2	56.1	44.5	35.9	25.0	43.8
Extreme Maximum Temp. (°F)	69	76	83	87	93	101	104	100	98	90	79	74	104
Extreme Minimum Temp. (°F)	-21	-13	-2	18	31	38	48	44	33	23	13	-20	-21
Days Maximum Temp. ≥ 90°F	0	0	0	0	0	3	7	7	2	0	0	0	19
Days Maximum Temp. ≤ 32°F	11	6	2	0	0	0	0	0	0	0	1	8	28
Days Minimum Temp. ≤ 32°F	27	22	17	5	0	0	0	0	0	2	13	23	109
Days Minimum Temp. ≤ 0°F	2	1	0	0	0	0	0	0	0	0	0	1	4
Heating Degree Days (base 65°F)	1,098	896	706	365	126	16	1	3	62	316	596	988	5,173
Cooling Degree Days (base 65°F)	0	0	3	20	78	232	338	307	134	21	1	0	1,134
Mean Precipitation (in.)	3.11	2.72	3.60	4.49	5.80	4.73	4.60	3.62	3.75	3.70	3.81	3.55	47.48
Extreme Maximum Daily Precip. (in.)	2.44	2.14	2.91	3.65	3.50	2.67	3.12	3.75	4.00	4.15	2.98	2.50	4.15
Days With ≥ 0.1" Precipitation	6	6	7	8	9	7	7	5	5	6	6	7	79
Days With ≥ 0.5" Precipitation	2	2	2	3	4	3	3	2	3	3	3	2	32
Days With ≥ 1.0" Precipitation	1	1	1	1	2	1	1	1	1	1	1	1	13
Mean Snowfall (in.)	***5.2***	2.7	0.9	trace	0.0	0.0	0.0	0.0	0.0	0.2	0.0	3.9	***12.9***
Maximum Snow Depth (in.)	***13***	***9***	***14***	1	0	0	0	0	0	2	trace	***15***	***15***
Days With ≥ 1.0" Snow Depth	***6***	4	1	0	0	0	0	0	0	0	0	4	***15***

The period of record for all cooperative weather station data is 1980 – 2009. See User Guide for detailed explanation of data.

Climate

Brookville *Franklin County* Elevation: 629 ft. Latitude: 39° 25' N Longitude: 85° 01' W

	JAN	FEB	MAR	APR	MAY	JUN	JUL	AUG	SEP	OCT	NOV	DEC	YEAR
Mean Maximum Temp. (°F)	37.9	42.0	52.6	65.0	74.7	83.3	86.8	86.0	79.6	66.9	54.7	41.3	64.2
Mean Temp. (°F)	28.9	31.8	41.0	52.3	62.1	71.0	74.8	73.8	66.2	53.9	43.8	32.5	52.7
Mean Minimum Temp. (°F)	19.8	21.5	29.3	39.5	49.6	58.6	62.8	61.5	52.8	40.8	32.9	23.7	41.1
Extreme Maximum Temp. (°F)	67	76	84	89	94	102	102	103	99	92	82	76	103
Extreme Minimum Temp. (°F)	-31	-15	-9	16	29	38	45	41	30	17	9	-20	-31
Days Maximum Temp. ≥ 90°F	0	0	0	0	0	6	10	9	3	0	0	0	28
Days Maximum Temp. ≤ 32°F	10	6	1	0	0	0	0	0	0	0	1	7	25
Days Minimum Temp. ≤ 32°F	27	24	20	7	1	0	0	0	0	7	16	24	126
Days Minimum Temp. ≤ 0°F	3	2	0	0	0	0	0	0	0	0	0	1	6
Heating Degree Days (base 65°F)	1,113	931	739	387	146	20	1	5	75	354	629	1,000	5,400
Cooling Degree Days (base 65°F)	0	0	2	12	65	206	312	284	120	18	1	0	1,020
Mean Precipitation (in.)	3.04	2.61	3.64	4.14	5.09	3.72	4.37	3.44	2.62	3.24	3.55	3.40	42.86
Extreme Maximum Daily Precip. (in.)	2.85	2.02	3.18	3.35	4.03	2.35	3.88	3.20	2.94	3.80	2.23	2.57	4.03
Days With ≥ 0.1" Precipitation	6	5	7	9	9	7	7	5	5	6	7	7	80
Days With ≥ 0.5" Precipitation	2	2	2	3	3	3	3	2	2	2	3	2	29
Days With ≥ 1.0" Precipitation	1	0	1	1	1	1	1	1	1	1	1	1	11
Mean Snowfall (in.)	4.2	4.0	1.5	0.1	trace	0.0	0.0	0.0	0.0	0.1	0.6	3.7	14.2
Maximum Snow Depth (in.)	10	9	7	1	trace	0	0	0	0	na	6	na	na
Days With ≥ 1.0" Snow Depth	7	7	1	0	0	0	0	0	0	0	0	4	19

Columbia City *Whitley County* Elevation: 850 ft. Latitude: 41° 09' N Longitude: 85° 29' W

	JAN	FEB	MAR	APR	MAY	JUN	JUL	AUG	SEP	OCT	NOV	DEC	YEAR
Mean Maximum Temp. (°F)	31.6	35.4	46.4	59.1	70.3	79.5	82.7	81.1	75.0	61.9	49.1	36.2	59.0
Mean Temp. (°F)	24.0	26.8	36.6	48.3	59.2	68.6	72.0	70.3	63.3	50.9	40.3	28.8	49.1
Mean Minimum Temp. (°F)	16.1	18.1	26.9	37.4	48.0	57.7	61.2	59.5	51.6	39.9	31.4	21.3	39.1
Extreme Maximum Temp. (°F)	66	72	80	88	92	103	101	98	95	89	77	70	103
Extreme Minimum Temp. (°F)	-24	-16	-6	7	24	36	44	36	27	17	8	-22	-24
Days Maximum Temp. ≥ 90°F	0	0	0	0	0	3	4	2	1	0	0	0	10
Days Maximum Temp. ≤ 32°F	16	11	4	0	0	0	0	0	0	0	2	11	44
Days Minimum Temp. ≤ 32°F	28	24	23	9	1	0	0	0	0	7	17	26	135
Days Minimum Temp. ≤ 0°F	4	3	0	0	0	0	0	0	0	0	0	2	9
Heating Degree Days (base 65°F)	1,264	1,073	873	503	214	41	7	17	117	437	733	1,117	6,396
Cooling Degree Days (base 65°F)	0	0	1	7	40	157	230	190	74	8	0	0	707
Mean Precipitation (in.)	2.34	1.85	2.79	3.52	4.13	4.41	4.03	3.91	3.33	3.05	3.26	2.85	39.47
Extreme Maximum Daily Precip. (in.)	2.58	1.39	2.14	2.54	2.52	4.48	3.09	4.30	3.20	2.39	3.57	1.70	4.48
Days With ≥ 0.1" Precipitation	6	5	6	7	8	7	7	6	6	6	7	7	78
Days With ≥ 0.5" Precipitation	1	1	2	2	3	3	3	3	2	2	2	2	26
Days With ≥ 1.0" Precipitation	0	0	1	1	1	1	1	1	1	1	1	0	9
Mean Snowfall (in.)	8.8	6.7	3.5	0.7	0.0	0.0	0.0	0.0	0.0	0.2	1.2	6.4	27.5
Maximum Snow Depth (in.)	11	16	7	6	0	0	0	0	0	1	4	11	16
Days With ≥ 1.0" Snow Depth	15	10	4	0	0	0	0	0	0	0	1	8	38

Columbus *Bartholomew County* Elevation: 621 ft. Latitude: 39° 12' N Longitude: 85° 55' W

	JAN	FEB	MAR	APR	MAY	JUN	JUL	AUG	SEP	OCT	NOV	DEC	YEAR
Mean Maximum Temp. (°F)	37.6	42.0	52.2	64.1	73.6	82.2	85.4	84.7	78.4	66.5	54.0	41.0	63.5
Mean Temp. (°F)	29.3	32.8	41.8	53.0	63.1	72.0	75.5	74.1	66.8	54.7	44.2	33.0	53.4
Mean Minimum Temp. (°F)	21.0	23.4	31.3	41.9	52.5	61.8	65.5	63.5	55.0	42.9	34.4	24.8	43.2
Extreme Maximum Temp. (°F)	68	76	83	86	91	100	103	103	97	91	80	73	103
Extreme Minimum Temp. (°F)	-26	-14	-6	18	31	41	51	43	34	21	11	-20	-26
Days Maximum Temp. ≥ 90°F	0	0	0	0	0	4	7	7	2	0	0	0	20
Days Maximum Temp. ≤ 32°F	10	6	1	0	0	0	0	0	0	0	1	7	25
Days Minimum Temp. ≤ 32°F	26	23	18	4	0	0	0	0	0	4	14	23	112
Days Minimum Temp. ≤ 0°F	2	1	0	0	0	0	0	0	0	0	0	1	4
Heating Degree Days (base 65°F)	1,099	905	715	367	125	15	1	3	64	329	616	987	5,226
Cooling Degree Days (base 65°F)	0	0	2	15	72	232	332	292	124	18	0	0	1,087
Mean Precipitation (in.)	2.85	2.63	3.71	4.54	5.25	3.87	4.10	3.67	3.05	3.24	3.66	3.45	44.02
Extreme Maximum Daily Precip. (in.)	2.76	2.17	2.67	3.99	3.01	2.72	6.37	4.11	2.72	3.20	2.30	2.25	6.37
Days With ≥ 0.1" Precipitation	5	5	7	8	9	7	6	6	5	5	6	7	76
Days With ≥ 0.5" Precipitation	2	2	3	3	4	3	3	3	2	2	3	3	33
Days With ≥ 1.0" Precipitation	1	0	1	1	1	1	1	1	1	1	1	1	11
Mean Snowfall (in.)	5.1	3.5	2.1	0.1	trace	0.0	0.0	0.0	0.0	0.1	0.1	3.4	14.4
Maximum Snow Depth (in.)	16	9	10	1	trace	0	0	0	0	1	1	19	19
Days With ≥ 1.0" Snow Depth	6	4	1	0	0	0	0	0	0	0	0	4	15

Crawfordsville 5 S *Montgomery County* Elevation: 762 ft. Latitude: 39° 58' N Longitude: 86° 56' W

	JAN	FEB	MAR	APR	MAY	JUN	JUL	AUG	SEP	OCT	NOV	DEC	YEAR
Mean Maximum Temp. (°F)	34.7	39.0	49.9	62.0	72.0	81.6	84.4	83.2	77.7	65.4	51.2	37.9	61.6
Mean Temp. (°F)	25.8	29.3	38.8	50.1	60.1	70.0	72.8	70.9	64.0	52.6	41.3	29.0	50.4
Mean Minimum Temp. (°F)	16.9	19.5	27.7	38.2	48.1	58.3	61.2	58.7	50.3	39.7	31.4	20.1	39.2
Extreme Maximum Temp. (°F)	65	74	83	87	93	102	99	101	96	89	80	74	102
Extreme Minimum Temp. (°F)	-31	-24	-12	3	28	32	41	36	23	18	3	-24	-31
Days Maximum Temp. ≥ 90°F	0	0	0	0	0	4	6	4	2	0	0	0	16
Days Maximum Temp. ≤ 32°F	13	9	3	0	0	0	0	0	0	0	1	10	36
Days Minimum Temp. ≤ 32°F	27	25	22	9	1	0	0	0	1	8	17	26	136
Days Minimum Temp. ≤ 0°F	4	3	0	0	0	0	0	0	0	0	0	3	10
Heating Degree Days (base 65°F)	1,207	1,002	806	449	193	31	7	15	109	390	702	1,110	6,021
Cooling Degree Days (base 65°F)	0	0	1	11	46	187	255	207	85	13	0	0	805
Mean Precipitation (in.)	2.48	2.46	2.94	4.01	4.66	4.53	4.44	3.70	3.20	3.33	4.16	3.10	43.01
Extreme Maximum Daily Precip. (in.)	2.70	2.98	2.10	2.75	3.50	3.28	2.71	4.35	2.25	3.76	2.65	3.20	4.35
Days With ≥ 0.1" Precipitation	5	5	6	8	9	8	7	5	5	6	7	7	78
Days With ≥ 0.5" Precipitation	2	2	2	3	3	3	3	3	2	2	3	2	30
Days With ≥ 1.0" Precipitation	0	1	0	1	1	1	1	1	1	1	1	0	9
Mean Snowfall (in.)	na	5.4	2.7	0.2	trace	0.0	0.0	0.0	0.0	trace	0.6	4.7	na
Maximum Snow Depth (in.)	na	na	na	3	trace	0	0	0	0	1	5	na	na
Days With ≥ 1.0" Snow Depth	na	na	1	0	0	0	0	0	0	0	0	4	na

The period of record for all cooperative weather station data is 1980 – 2009. See User Guide for detailed explanation of data.

Delphi 3 S *Carroll County* Elevation: 670 ft. Latitude: 40° 33' N Longitude: 86° 41' W

	JAN	FEB	MAR	APR	MAY	JUN	JUL	AUG	SEP	OCT	NOV	DEC	YEAR
Mean Maximum Temp. (°F)	34.6	39.0	50.7	64.0	74.2	82.8	85.4	83.8	78.3	65.5	52.1	38.3	62.4
Mean Temp. (°F)	26.9	30.5	40.9	52.3	62.5	71.4	74.3	72.6	65.9	54.1	43.4	31.0	52.1
Mean Minimum Temp. (°F)	19.3	22.1	30.9	40.5	50.7	59.9	63.2	61.5	53.5	42.7	34.6	23.6	41.9
Extreme Maximum Temp. (°F)	67	73	84	89	96	105	103	100	96	89	78	71	105
Extreme Minimum Temp. (°F)	-24	-16	0	10	30	36	44	38	27	18	9	-21	-24
Days Maximum Temp. ≥ 90°F	0	0	0	0	1	5	7	5	2	0	0	0	20
Days Maximum Temp. ≤ 32°F	13	8	2	0	0	0	0	0	0	0	1	8	32
Days Minimum Temp. ≤ 32°F	27	23	18	7	0	0	0	0	0	5	13	24	117
Days Minimum Temp. ≤ 0°F	3	2	0	0	0	0	0	0	0	0	0	2	7
Heating Degree Days (base 65°F)	1,174	968	744	389	142	19	2	7	75	347	643	1,048	5,558
Cooling Degree Days (base 65°F)	0	0	2	15	71	216	298	250	109	17	1	0	979
Mean Precipitation (in.)	2.15	2.05	2.76	3.49	4.37	4.00	4.57	3.68	2.74	2.98	3.12	2.61	38.52
Extreme Maximum Daily Precip. (in.)	2.07	2.42	2.03	2.59	3.00	3.00	3.55	2.64	4.78	2.78	2.50	2.44	4.78
Days With ≥ 0.1" Precipitation	5	4	6	7	8	6	7	6	5	6	6	6	72
Days With ≥ 0.5" Precipitation	1	1	2	3	3	3	3	3	2	2	2	2	27
Days With ≥ 1.0" Precipitation	1	0	1	1	1	1	1	1	1	1	1	0	10
Mean Snowfall (in.)	5.6	4.8	2.4	0.5	trace	0.0	0.0	0.0	0.0	0.2	0.5	4.6	18.6
Maximum Snow Depth (in.)	18	17	10	4	trace	0	0	0	0	4	2	9	18
Days With ≥ 1.0" Snow Depth	10	8	2	0	0	0	0	0	0	0	0	6	26

Dubois S Ind Forage Frm *Dubois County* Elevation: 689 ft. Latitude: 38° 27' N Longitude: 86° 42' W

	JAN	FEB	MAR	APR	MAY	JUN	JUL	AUG	SEP	OCT	NOV	DEC	YEAR
Mean Maximum Temp. (°F)	39.6	44.4	54.4	65.4	74.6	82.8	86.4	86.3	79.4	67.8	55.8	43.4	65.0
Mean Temp. (°F)	30.7	34.4	43.6	54.5	63.7	72.2	76.0	75.1	67.7	56.1	45.7	34.3	54.5
Mean Minimum Temp. (°F)	21.7	24.3	32.8	43.5	52.8	61.6	65.5	63.8	55.9	44.4	35.6	25.3	43.9
Extreme Maximum Temp. (°F)	70	76	83	88	92	101	102	102	99	92	81	75	102
Extreme Minimum Temp. (°F)	-25	-12	0	17	29	40	46	42	33	18	10	-20	-25
Days Maximum Temp. ≥ 90°F	0	0	0	0	0	5	9	10	3	0	0	0	27
Days Maximum Temp. ≤ 32°F	8	5	1	0	0	0	0	0	0	0	0	6	20
Days Minimum Temp. ≤ 32°F	26	22	16	4	0	0	0	0	0	4	13	23	108
Days Minimum Temp. ≤ 0°F	2	1	0	0	0	0	0	0	0	0	0	1	4
Heating Degree Days (base 65°F)	1,058	859	659	334	120	15	1	2	60	296	574	944	4,922
Cooling Degree Days (base 65°F)	0	0	4	24	87	238	348	322	147	28	2	0	1,200
Mean Precipitation (in.)	3.27	2.97	4.20	4.63	5.80	4.32	4.31	3.21	3.91	3.73	4.03	3.68	48.06
Extreme Maximum Daily Precip. (in.)	4.20	2.39	4.82	5.66	3.90	5.38	3.45	2.76	3.00	4.12	4.25	3.18	5.66
Days With ≥ 0.1" Precipitation	5	5	7	8	9	7	7	6	5	6	7	6	78
Days With ≥ 0.5" Precipitation	2	2	3	3	4	3	3	2	3	3	3	3	34
Days With ≥ 1.0" Precipitation	1	1	1	1	2	1	1	1	1	1	1	1	13
Mean Snowfall (in.)	2.4	2.7	1.5	trace	0.0	0.0	0.0	0.0	0.0	0.2	trace	2.3	9.1
Maximum Snow Depth (in.)	8	10	14	trace	0	0	0	0	0	0	1	18	18
Days With ≥ 1.0" Snow Depth	4	3	1	0	0	0	0	0	0	0	0	3	11

Elwood Wastewater Plant *Madison County* Elevation: 839 ft. Latitude: 40° 16' N Longitude: 85° 51' W

	JAN	FEB	MAR	APR	MAY	JUN	JUL	AUG	SEP	OCT	NOV	DEC	YEAR
Mean Maximum Temp. (°F)	33.5	38.1	48.8	61.6	72.3	81.3	84.7	83.3	77.5	64.5	51.2	37.6	61.2
Mean Temp. (°F)	25.2	29.1	38.5	50.0	60.9	70.1	73.5	71.7	64.9	52.4	41.7	29.4	50.6
Mean Minimum Temp. (°F)	16.8	20.0	28.2	38.2	49.4	58.8	62.4	60.1	52.2	40.3	32.2	21.3	40.0
Extreme Maximum Temp. (°F)	65	74	81	87	93	102	101	99	96	92	79	72	102
Extreme Minimum Temp. (°F)	-24	-23	-8	12	28	38	44	38	29	18	5	-20	-24
Days Maximum Temp. ≥ 90°F	0	0	0	0	0	4	6	5	2	0	0	0	17
Days Maximum Temp. ≤ 32°F	14	9	3	0	0	0	0	0	0	0	1	9	36
Days Minimum Temp. ≤ 32°F	28	24	21	8	0	0	0	0	0	7	17	26	131
Days Minimum Temp. ≤ 0°F	4	2	0	0	0	0	0	0	0	0	0	2	8
Heating Degree Days (base 65°F)	1,229	1,010	816	454	177	30	3	12	94	394	692	1,095	6,006
Cooling Degree Days (base 65°F)	0	0	1	9	57	189	275	227	96	11	0	0	865
Mean Precipitation (in.)	2.55	2.04	2.87	3.69	4.28	4.36	4.34	3.77	3.35	2.79	3.56	3.02	40.62
Extreme Maximum Daily Precip. (in.)	2.90	1.30	1.95	2.60	2.80	4.65	4.25	3.97	5.01	2.15	3.50	2.50	5.01
Days With ≥ 0.1" Precipitation	5	4	7	8	8	7	7	6	5	5	7	7	76
Days With ≥ 0.5" Precipitation	1	2	2	3	3	3	3	2	2	2	2	2	27
Days With ≥ 1.0" Precipitation	0	0	1	1	1	1	1	1	1	0	1	1	9
Mean Snowfall (in.)	na	na	0.8	trace	0.0	0.0	0.0	0.0	0.0	trace	0.1	2.8	na
Maximum Snow Depth (in.)	na	na	10	4	0	0	0	0	0	trace	trace	na	na
Days With ≥ 1.0" Snow Depth	na	na	1	0	0	0	0	0	0	0	0	2	na

English 4 S *Crawford County* Elevation: 509 ft. Latitude: 38° 17' N Longitude: 86° 28' W

	JAN	FEB	MAR	APR	MAY	JUN	JUL	AUG	SEP	OCT	NOV	DEC	YEAR
Mean Maximum Temp. (°F)	41.9	48.2	57.6	68.3	76.9	84.4	88.0	87.1	80.8	69.8	57.5	45.1	67.1
Mean Temp. (°F)	32.1	36.9	44.9	54.7	63.5	71.6	75.8	74.2	66.8	55.5	45.9	35.2	54.7
Mean Minimum Temp. (°F)	22.3	25.5	32.1	40.9	50.1	58.8	63.5	61.3	52.7	41.1	34.3	25.2	42.3
Extreme Maximum Temp. (°F)	72	76	85	91	93	102	104	102	98	88	84	76	104
Extreme Minimum Temp. (°F)	-30	-15	-2	15	26	36	41	35	28	14	4	-21	-30
Days Maximum Temp. ≥ 90°F	0	0	0	0	0	6	13	11	3	0	0	0	33
Days Maximum Temp. ≤ 32°F	6	3	0	0	0	0	0	0	0	0	0	5	14
Days Minimum Temp. ≤ 32°F	25	21	17	7	1	0	0	0	0	7	14	22	114
Days Minimum Temp. ≤ 0°F	2	1	0	0	0	0	0	0	0	0	0	1	4
Heating Degree Days (base 65°F)	1,012	789	620	322	113	14	1	3	68	306	566	919	4,733
Cooling Degree Days (base 65°F)	0	0	3	18	73	219	341	295	127	17	1	1	1,095
Mean Precipitation (in.)	3.53	3.54	4.45	4.45	5.66	4.45	4.00	3.31	3.64	3.47	4.24	3.91	48.65
Extreme Maximum Daily Precip. (in.)	5.50	4.30	3.01	3.82	4.06	3.29	3.65	2.95	3.55	2.50	2.93	2.65	5.50
Days With ≥ 0.1" Precipitation	6	7	8	8	9	7	6	5	5	6	7	7	81
Days With ≥ 0.5" Precipitation	2	2	3	3	4	3	3	2	2	2	3	3	32
Days With ≥ 1.0" Precipitation	1	1	1	1	2	1	1	1	1	1	1	1	13
Mean Snowfall (in.)	1.0	na	0.1	trace	0.0	0.0	0.0	0.0	0.0	trace	trace	2.0	na
Maximum Snow Depth (in.)	10	15	14	trace	0	0	0	0	0	1	trace	22	22
Days With ≥ 1.0" Snow Depth	5	3	1	0	0	0	0	0	0	0	0	3	12

The period of record for all cooperative weather station data is 1980 – 2009. See User Guide for detailed explanation of data.

Climate

Evansville Museum *Vanderburgh County* Elevation: 379 ft. Latitude: 37° 58' N Longitude: 87° 34' W

	JAN	FEB	MAR	APR	MAY	JUN	JUL	AUG	SEP	OCT	NOV	DEC	YEAR
Mean Maximum Temp. (°F)	42.9	47.8	59.1	70.2	78.7	87.4	90.0	90.0	83.3	71.6	58.9	46.1	68.8
Mean Temp. (°F)	35.2	38.7	48.5	59.1	68.0	76.7	80.0	79.6	72.2	60.6	49.7	38.2	58.9
Mean Minimum Temp. (°F)	27.2	29.5	38.2	47.9	57.2	66.1	70.0	69.1	61.1	49.4	40.6	30.2	48.9
Extreme Maximum Temp. (°F)	71	78	86	91	95	101	102	102	100	95	85	78	102
Extreme Minimum Temp. (°F)	-17	-8	5	24	36	45	47	46	37	22	13	-15	-17
Days Maximum Temp. ≥ 90°F	0	0	0	0	2	12	17	17	7	1	0	0	56
Days Maximum Temp. ≤ 32°F	5	3	0	0	0	0	0	0	0	0	0	3	11
Days Minimum Temp. ≤ 32°F	21	16	10	1	0	0	0	0	0	1	7	16	72
Days Minimum Temp. ≤ 0°F	1	0	0	0	0	0	0	0	0	0	0	0	1
Heating Degree Days (base 65°F)	917	738	509	216	52	2	0	0	26	186	455	824	3,925
Cooling Degree Days (base 65°F)	0	0	6	44	152	361	473	459	245	56	4	0	1,800
Mean Precipitation (in.)	2.97	3.35	4.48	4.34	4.96	3.55	4.25	3.31	3.57	3.55	4.17	3.79	46.29
Extreme Maximum Daily Precip. (in.)	2.81	2.83	3.84	5.47	2.97	3.77	5.74	4.00	5.34	2.57	4.10	3.15	5.74
Days With ≥ 0.1" Precipitation	5	6	7	7	8	6	6	5	5	6	6	6	73
Days With ≥ 0.5" Precipitation	2	2	3	3	3	2	3	2	2	2	3	2	29
Days With ≥ 1.0" Precipitation	0	1	1	1	1	1	1	1	1	1	1	1	11
Mean Snowfall (in.)	3.1	2.9	1.5	0.1	trace	0.0	0.0	0.0	0.0	trace	0.1	3.3	11.0
Maximum Snow Depth (in.)	6	9	6	trace	trace	0	0	0	0	trace	trace	22	22
Days With ≥ 1.0" Snow Depth	3	4	1	0	0	0	0	0	0	0	0	3	11

Farmland 5 NNW *Randolph County* Elevation: 964 ft. Latitude: 40° 15' N Longitude: 85° 09' W

	JAN	FEB	MAR	APR	MAY	JUN	JUL	AUG	SEP	OCT	NOV	DEC	YEAR
Mean Maximum Temp. (°F)	33.9	37.6	48.1	61.0	71.6	80.7	84.0	82.6	76.9	64.4	51.1	37.9	60.8
Mean Temp. (°F)	25.6	28.5	37.9	49.7	60.5	69.9	73.1	71.2	64.2	52.4	41.6	29.8	50.4
Mean Minimum Temp. (°F)	17.3	19.3	27.5	38.5	49.4	58.9	62.1	59.7	51.5	40.4	32.1	21.7	39.9
Extreme Maximum Temp. (°F)	66	74	81	85	94	102	100	98	95	90	79	72	102
Extreme Minimum Temp. (°F)	-25	-21	-16	10	28	37	40	38	27	17	5	-21	-25
Days Maximum Temp. ≥ 90°F	0	0	0	0	0	4	6	5	2	0	0	0	17
Days Maximum Temp. ≤ 32°F	14	10	4	0	0	0	0	0	0	0	1	10	39
Days Minimum Temp. ≤ 32°F	28	25	22	8	1	0	0	0	0	7	17	26	134
Days Minimum Temp. ≤ 0°F	4	2	0	0	0	0	0	0	0	0	0	2	8
Heating Degree Days (base 65°F)	1,214	1,026	836	460	187	33	5	15	106	397	695	1,084	6,058
Cooling Degree Days (base 65°F)	0	0	1	9	54	185	263	214	90	13	0	0	829
Mean Precipitation (in.)	2.11	1.94	2.83	3.65	4.28	4.23	4.77	3.60	2.98	2.95	3.26	2.61	39.21
Extreme Maximum Daily Precip. (in.)	3.31	2.09	2.24	2.36	2.51	3.73	4.40	3.02	3.18	2.73	3.01	2.40	4.40
Days With ≥ 0.1" Precipitation	5	5	7	8	8	7	7	5	5	6	6	6	75
Days With ≥ 0.5" Precipitation	1	1	2	2	3	3	3	3	2	2	2	2	26
Days With ≥ 1.0" Precipitation	0	0	0	1	1	1	1	1	1	1	1	0	8
Mean Snowfall (in.)	7.0	5.9	3.0	0.4	trace	0.0	0.0	0.0	0.0	0.3	1.0	4.8	22.4
Maximum Snow Depth (in.)	16	16	11	5	trace	0	0	0	0	3	4	7	16
Days With ≥ 1.0" Snow Depth	12	10	4	0	0	0	0	0	0	0	1	7	34

Frankfort Disposal Plant *Clinton County* Elevation: 834 ft. Latitude: 40° 19' N Longitude: 86° 30' W

	JAN	FEB	MAR	APR	MAY	JUN	JUL	AUG	SEP	OCT	NOV	DEC	YEAR
Mean Maximum Temp. (°F)	33.9	37.9	49.0	61.8	72.1	81.0	83.9	82.3	76.7	64.0	50.5	37.3	60.9
Mean Temp. (°F)	26.5	29.8	39.6	51.0	61.3	70.5	73.6	72.0	65.2	53.5	42.2	30.1	51.3
Mean Minimum Temp. (°F)	19.0	21.6	30.2	40.2	50.5	59.8	63.4	61.5	53.6	42.9	33.8	22.8	41.6
Extreme Maximum Temp. (°F)	66	73	83	87	92	101	105	98	95	90	77	72	105
Extreme Minimum Temp. (°F)	-25	-14	-13	16	30	36	44	38	28	20	9	-26	-26
Days Maximum Temp. ≥ 90°F	0	0	0	0	0	4	6	4	1	0	0	0	15
Days Maximum Temp. ≤ 32°F	14	9	3	0	0	0	0	0	0	0	1	10	37
Days Minimum Temp. ≤ 32°F	27	24	19	6	0	0	0	0	0	4	14	25	119
Days Minimum Temp. ≤ 0°F	3	2	0	0	0	0	0	0	0	0	0	2	7
Heating Degree Days (base 65°F)	1,188	989	782	422	167	24	3	9	87	364	678	1,076	5,789
Cooling Degree Days (base 65°F)	0	0	1	11	59	195	277	232	99	14	0	0	888
Mean Precipitation (in.)	2.29	2.21	3.01	3.66	4.25	4.42	4.34	3.91	2.96	3.08	3.53	2.94	40.60
Extreme Maximum Daily Precip. (in.)	1.90	3.12	2.80	2.74	3.47	4.30	3.38	4.25	3.50	3.30	3.15	2.27	4.30
Days With ≥ 0.1" Precipitation	5	5	7	8	9	7	7	6	5	6	7	7	79
Days With ≥ 0.5" Precipitation	1	1	2	2	3	3	3	3	2	2	2	2	26
Days With ≥ 1.0" Precipitation	0	0	1	1	1	1	1	1	1	1	1	0	9
Mean Snowfall (in.)	7.5	6.1	2.7	0.4	trace	0.0	0.0	0.0	0.0	0.4	0.5	5.0	22.6
Maximum Snow Depth (in.)	13	18	14	7	trace	0	0	0	0	7	3	7	18
Days With ≥ 1.0" Snow Depth	10	8	3	0	0	0	0	0	0	0	0	7	28

Freelandville *Knox County* Elevation: 549 ft. Latitude: 38° 52' N Longitude: 87° 19' W

	JAN	FEB	MAR	APR	MAY	JUN	JUL	AUG	SEP	OCT	NOV	DEC	YEAR
Mean Maximum Temp. (°F)	37.1	41.8	52.5	64.3	73.8	82.7	85.7	84.9	78.5	66.4	53.5	40.1	63.5
Mean Temp. (°F)	29.7	33.4	42.7	53.8	63.7	72.9	76.0	74.6	67.4	55.7	44.6	32.5	53.9
Mean Minimum Temp. (°F)	22.2	24.9	32.9	43.3	53.6	63.1	66.3	64.3	56.2	45.0	35.6	24.9	44.3
Extreme Maximum Temp. (°F)	69	75	82	86	92	101	101	99	97	90	80	72	101
Extreme Minimum Temp. (°F)	-21	-11	7	21	33	41	50	45	35	25	10	-23	-23
Days Maximum Temp. ≥ 90°F	0	0	0	0	0	4	7	6	2	0	0	0	19
Days Maximum Temp. ≤ 32°F	11	6	2	0	0	0	0	0	0	0	1	8	28
Days Minimum Temp. ≤ 32°F	25	22	16	4	0	0	0	0	0	2	12	23	104
Days Minimum Temp. ≤ 0°F	2	1	0	0	0	0	0	0	0	0	0	1	4
Heating Degree Days (base 65°F)	1,089	887	686	347	113	12	1	3	61	305	607	1,000	5,111
Cooling Degree Days (base 65°F)	0	0	3	19	81	257	349	309	139	24	1	0	1,182
Mean Precipitation (in.)	2.77	2.73	3.73	4.16	5.66	3.80	4.77	3.22	3.49	3.93	4.14	3.32	45.72
Extreme Maximum Daily Precip. (in.)	2.57	2.04	2.69	3.14	3.30	3.36	3.37	3.01	3.81	3.52	2.80	2.19	3.81
Days With ≥ 0.1" Precipitation	6	5	7	8	8	7	7	5	5	6	7	7	78
Days With ≥ 0.5" Precipitation	2	2	2	3	4	3	3	2	2	3	3	3	32
Days With ≥ 1.0" Precipitation	1	1	1	1	2	1	1	1	1	1	1	1	13
Mean Snowfall (in.)	4.5	3.5	1.5	trace	0.0	0.0	0.0	0.0	0.0	0.1	0.2	4.1	13.9
Maximum Snow Depth (in.)	11	7	8	trace	0	0	0	0	0	2	1	12	12
Days With ≥ 1.0" Snow Depth	5	3	1	0	0	0	0	0	0	0	0	4	13

The period of record for all cooperative weather station data is 1980 – 2009. See User Guide for detailed explanation of data.

Goshen College *Elkhart County* Elevation: 875 ft. Latitude: 41° 33' N Longitude: 85° 53' W

	JAN	FEB	MAR	APR	MAY	JUN	JUL	AUG	SEP	OCT	NOV	DEC	YEAR
Mean Maximum Temp. (°F)	32.2	36.0	47.5	60.6	71.6	80.5	83.6	81.6	75.2	62.5	49.2	35.9	59.7
Mean Temp. (°F)	25.2	28.3	38.2	49.9	60.4	69.8	73.3	71.4	64.4	52.6	41.5	29.5	50.4
Mean Minimum Temp. (°F)	18.2	20.5	28.9	39.1	49.2	58.9	62.8	61.3	53.6	42.7	33.7	23.0	41.0
Extreme Maximum Temp. (°F)	63	73	81	93	92	102	100	99	95	88	76	69	102
Extreme Minimum Temp. (°F)	-24	-14	-3	1	28	37	41	37	29	18	11	-18	-24
Days Maximum Temp. ≥ 90°F	0	0	0	0	0	4	5	3	1	0	0	0	13
Days Maximum Temp. ≤ 32°F	16	11	3	0	0	0	0	0	0	0	1	11	42
Days Minimum Temp. ≤ 32°F	28	24	20	7	0	0	0	0	0	4	14	26	123
Days Minimum Temp. ≤ 0°F	3	2	0	0	0	0	0	0	0	0	0	2	7
Heating Degree Days (base 65°F)	1,228	1,031	825	455	187	30	4	11	98	386	700	1,094	6,049
Cooling Degree Days (base 65°F)	0	0	1	8	52	179	266	217	86	9	0	0	818
Mean Precipitation (in.)	2.17	2.08	2.54	3.47	3.85	3.96	4.28	4.24	3.52	3.23	3.02	2.67	39.03
Extreme Maximum Daily Precip. (in.)	3.02	2.19	2.31	3.18	2.93	3.36	6.65	3.79	3.31	3.05	2.18	2.58	6.65
Days With ≥ 0.1" Precipitation	5	6	7	7	7	7	6	6	6	6	7	7	77
Days With ≥ 0.5" Precipitation	1	1	1	2	3	3	3	3	2	2	2	1	24
Days With ≥ 1.0" Precipitation	0	0	0	1	1	1	1	1	1	1	1	0	8
Mean Snowfall (in.)	10.9	9.0	5.0	1.3	trace	0.0	0.0	0.0	0.0	0.4	3.1	10.6	40.3
Maximum Snow Depth (in.)	17	14	8	4	trace	0	0	0	0	5	4	17	17
Days With ≥ 1.0" Snow Depth	16	12	4	0	0	0	0	0	0	0	1	10	43

Greenfield *Hancock County* Elevation: 865 ft. Latitude: 39° 47' N Longitude: 85° 45' W

	JAN	FEB	MAR	APR	MAY	JUN	JUL	AUG	SEP	OCT	NOV	DEC	YEAR
Mean Maximum Temp. (°F)	34.8	38.9	49.6	62.1	72.2	81.5	84.7	83.6	77.6	65.0	51.5	38.4	61.6
Mean Temp. (°F)	26.8	30.1	39.8	51.6	62.0	71.2	74.6	73.3	66.3	54.0	42.6	30.6	51.9
Mean Minimum Temp. (°F)	18.8	21.3	30.1	41.1	51.7	60.9	64.5	62.9	54.9	42.9	33.6	22.8	42.1
Extreme Maximum Temp. (°F)	65	73	84	87	93	103	102	101	95	90	79	72	103
Extreme Minimum Temp. (°F)	-29	-19	-6	16	30	39	48	41	31	20	10	-19	-29
Days Maximum Temp. ≥ 90°F	0	0	0	0	0	4	6	5	2	0	0	0	17
Days Maximum Temp. ≤ 32°F	13	8	3	0	0	0	0	0	0	0	1	9	34
Days Minimum Temp. ≤ 32°F	27	24	19	6	0	0	0	0	0	4	15	24	119
Days Minimum Temp. ≤ 0°F	3	2	0	0	0	0	0	0	0	0	0	2	7
Heating Degree Days (base 65°F)	1,178	979	774	408	156	23	2	6	74	352	666	1,060	5,678
Cooling Degree Days (base 65°F)	0	0	1	13	69	216	307	270	118	17	0	0	1,011
Mean Precipitation (in.)	2.69	2.36	3.56	4.32	5.48	4.59	5.11	3.86	3.47	3.42	3.82	3.22	45.90
Extreme Maximum Daily Precip. (in.)	2.43	1.67	2.41	3.80	3.41	3.85	4.37	4.71	3.13	4.10	3.00	3.41	4.71
Days With ≥ 0.1" Precipitation	6	5	7	8	9	8	7	6	6	6	7	7	82
Days With ≥ 0.5" Precipitation	2	2	2	3	4	3	4	3	2	2	3	2	32
Days With ≥ 1.0" Precipitation	1	0	1	1	2	1	2	1	1	1	1	0	12
Mean Snowfall (in.)	5.8	3.5	1.7	0.1	0.0	0.0	0.0	0.0	0.0	0.1	0.6	3.9	15.7
Maximum Snow Depth (in.)	15	12	8	3	0	0	0	0	0	3	5	10	15
Days With ≥ 1.0" Snow Depth	10	7	2	0	0	0	0	0	0	0	1	6	26

Greensburg *Decatur County* Elevation: 935 ft. Latitude: 39° 21' N Longitude: 85° 30' W

	JAN	FEB	MAR	APR	MAY	JUN	JUL	AUG	SEP	OCT	NOV	DEC	YEAR
Mean Maximum Temp. (°F)	35.8	40.5	50.6	62.8	72.8	81.6	84.8	83.8	77.4	65.2	52.4	39.7	62.3
Mean Temp. (°F)	28.4	32.0	41.3	52.8	63.0	71.8	75.2	73.9	66.9	54.8	43.8	32.3	53.0
Mean Minimum Temp. (°F)	20.9	23.5	32.0	42.9	53.2	62.0	65.6	63.8	56.2	44.4	35.1	24.8	43.7
Extreme Maximum Temp. (°F)	66	74	82	88	93	101	101	101	96	91	79	73	101
Extreme Minimum Temp. (°F)	-24	-14	-12	19	30	39	46	42	32	17	12	-21	-24
Days Maximum Temp. ≥ 90°F	0	0	0	0	0	4	6	6	1	0	0	0	17
Days Maximum Temp. ≤ 32°F	12	8	2	0	0	0	0	0	0	0	1	8	31
Days Minimum Temp. ≤ 32°F	26	22	17	4	0	0	0	0	0	4	13	24	110
Days Minimum Temp. ≤ 0°F	2	1	0	0	0	0	0	0	0	0	0	1	4
Heating Degree Days (base 65°F)	1,127	925	728	376	133	18	1	5	70	329	631	1,009	5,352
Cooling Degree Days (base 65°F)	0	0	3	18	79	230	324	285	132	21	1	0	1,093
Mean Precipitation (in.)	2.92	2.45	3.69	4.42	5.52	4.45	4.01	3.93	3.08	3.24	3.65	3.38	44.74
Extreme Maximum Daily Precip. (in.)	3.09	2.02	2.48	4.00	2.78	5.00	2.76	4.21	3.54	3.60	2.15	2.25	5.00
Days With ≥ 0.1" Precipitation	6	6	7	9	9	7	7	6	5	6	7	7	82
Days With ≥ 0.5" Precipitation	2	2	3	3	4	3	3	2	2	2	3	2	31
Days With ≥ 1.0" Precipitation	1	0	1	1	1	1	1	1	1	1	1	1	11
Mean Snowfall (in.)	5.5	3.8	2.2	0.3	trace	0.0	0.0	0.0	0.0	0.2	0.2	4.2	16.4
Maximum Snow Depth (in.)	16	8	10	3	0	0	0	0	0	1	1	21	21
Days With ≥ 1.0" Snow Depth	7	5	1	0	0	0	0	0	0	0	0	4	17

Huntington *Huntington County* Elevation: 725 ft. Latitude: 40° 51' N Longitude: 85° 30' W

	JAN	FEB	MAR	APR	MAY	JUN	JUL	AUG	SEP	OCT	NOV	DEC	YEAR
Mean Maximum Temp. (°F)	33.1	37.0	47.6	61.2	72.4	81.7	85.3	83.7	76.9	63.7	50.5	37.1	60.9
Mean Temp. (°F)	25.3	28.0	37.5	49.7	60.4	70.0	73.8	72.2	64.4	52.1	41.4	29.5	50.4
Mean Minimum Temp. (°F)	17.3	18.8	27.5	38.2	48.5	58.3	62.3	60.6	51.8	40.4	32.2	21.8	39.8
Extreme Maximum Temp. (°F)	66	75	82	89	94	105	105	103	96	92	79	71	105
Extreme Minimum Temp. (°F)	-28	-16	-11	6	26	37	43	38	28	16	9	-24	-28
Days Maximum Temp. ≥ 90°F	0	0	0	0	1	5	8	5	2	0	0	0	21
Days Maximum Temp. ≤ 32°F	15	9	3	0	0	0	0	0	0	0	1	10	38
Days Minimum Temp. ≤ 32°F	28	25	22	9	1	0	0	0	0	7	16	26	134
Days Minimum Temp. ≤ 0°F	4	2	0	0	0	0	0	0	0	0	0	2	8
Heating Degree Days (base 65°F)	1,226	1,040	846	462	188	32	3	10	101	404	703	1,094	6,109
Cooling Degree Days (base 65°F)	0	0	1	10	54	191	284	239	90	11	0	0	880
Mean Precipitation (in.)	2.25	2.00	2.62	3.50	4.33	4.17	4.05	3.74	2.99	3.07	3.02	2.69	38.43
Extreme Maximum Daily Precip. (in.)	1.65	2.41	1.94	2.33	2.80	3.08	5.53	4.15	2.80	3.36	3.07	2.21	5.53
Days With ≥ 0.1" Precipitation	6	5	6	8	8	7	6	6	6	6	6	7	77
Days With ≥ 0.5" Precipitation	1	1	2	2	3	3	3	2	2	2	2	2	25
Days With ≥ 1.0" Precipitation	0	0	0	1	1	1	1	1	1	1	1	0	8
Mean Snowfall (in.)	9.7	7.1	3.2	0.8	0.0	0.0	0.0	0.0	0.0	0.2	1.0	7.3	29.3
Maximum Snow Depth (in.)	***10***	15	***10***	9	0	0	0	0	0	3	4	***8***	***15***
Days With ≥ 1.0" Snow Depth	***7***	6	2	0	0	0	0	0	0	0	0	6	***21***

The period of record for all cooperative weather station data is 1980 – 2009. See User Guide for detailed explanation of data.

Indianapolis SE Side *Marion County* Elevation: 845 ft. Latitude: 39° 43' N Longitude: 86° 04' W

	JAN	FEB	MAR	APR	MAY	JUN	JUL	AUG	SEP	OCT	NOV	DEC	YEAR
Mean Maximum Temp. (°F)	35.0	39.2	49.6	61.9	72.2	81.2	84.3	83.3	77.1	64.7	51.6	38.6	61.6
Mean Temp. (°F)	27.2	30.6	40.0	51.6	61.9	71.2	74.5	73.1	66.0	54.1	42.8	30.9	52.0
Mean Minimum Temp. (°F)	19.4	21.9	30.3	41.4	51.6	61.2	64.7	63.0	54.9	43.4	33.8	23.1	42.4
Extreme Maximum Temp. (°F)	65	74	83	87	92	104	103	100	94	89	82	73	104
Extreme Minimum Temp. (°F)	-22	-12	2	18	29	35	44	45	30	20	8	-20	-22
Days Maximum Temp. ≥ 90°F	0	0	0	0	0	3	6	5	1	0	0	0	15
Days Maximum Temp. ≤ 32°F	13	8	3	0	0	0	0	0	0	0	1	9	34
Days Minimum Temp. ≤ 32°F	27	24	19	5	0	0	0	0	0	4	15	25	119
Days Minimum Temp. ≤ 0°F	3	1	0	0	0	0	0	0	0	0	0	2	6
Heating Degree Days (base 65°F)	1,166	966	772	407	154	22	3	6	78	347	661	1,050	5,632
Cooling Degree Days (base 65°F)	0	0	2	13	66	216	304	265	115	17	0	0	998
Mean Precipitation (in.)	2.33	2.09	3.25	4.10	4.99	4.33	4.71	3.38	2.95	3.24	3.63	3.11	42.11
Extreme Maximum Daily Precip. (in.)	1.94	1.96	2.25	2.80	2.55	3.57	4.16	3.90	4.03	3.04	3.11	2.73	4.16
Days With ≥ 0.1" Precipitation	5	5	7	8	8	7	7	5	5	5	6	7	75
Days With ≥ 0.5" Precipitation	2	1	2	3	4	3	3	2	2	2	3	2	29
Days With ≥ 1.0" Precipitation	1	0	1	1	1	1	1	1	1	1	1	1	11
Mean Snowfall (in.)	***5.0***	3.6	1.0	0.1	trace	0.0	0.0	0.0	0.0	0.2	0.2	3.3	***13.4***
Maximum Snow Depth (in.)	13	12	9	1	0	0	0	0	0	trace	3	15	15
Days With ≥ 1.0" Snow Depth	8	6	2	0	0	0	0	0	0	0	0	5	21

Kokomo 3 WSW *Howard County* Elevation: 819 ft. Latitude: 40° 28' N Longitude: 86° 10' W

	JAN	FEB	MAR	APR	MAY	JUN	JUL	AUG	SEP	OCT	NOV	DEC	YEAR
Mean Maximum Temp. (°F)	32.2	36.3	47.6	61.0	71.4	80.6	83.8	82.3	76.5	63.8	50.2	36.1	60.2
Mean Temp. (°F)	24.3	27.6	37.6	49.6	60.1	69.7	73.0	71.3	64.2	52.2	41.1	28.6	49.9
Mean Minimum Temp. (°F)	16.4	18.8	27.5	38.2	48.8	58.7	62.1	60.2	51.9	40.6	31.8	21.0	39.7
Extreme Maximum Temp. (°F)	65	74	82	88	92	104	102	100	95	91	81	71	104
Extreme Minimum Temp. (°F)	-26	-20	-10	8	28	34	43	37	27	17	3	-24	-26
Days Maximum Temp. ≥ 90°F	0	0	0	0	0	4	6	4	2	0	0	0	16
Days Maximum Temp. ≤ 32°F	16	11	4	0	0	0	0	0	0	0	2	11	44
Days Minimum Temp. ≤ 32°F	28	25	22	9	0	0	0	0	0	7	17	27	135
Days Minimum Temp. ≤ 0°F	5	3	0	0	0	0	0	0	0	0	0	2	10
Heating Degree Days (base 65°F)	1,256	1,051	845	466	194	35	6	14	106	402	712	1,123	6,210
Cooling Degree Days (base 65°F)	0	0	1	11	50	182	260	215	90	13	0	0	822
Mean Precipitation (in.)	2.61	2.48	2.99	3.87	4.47	4.41	4.78	3.98	3.51	3.27	3.56	3.19	43.12
Extreme Maximum Daily Precip. (in.)	1.94	2.66	2.40	2.40	3.54	4.90	8.82	3.56	6.37	3.54	2.83	3.00	8.82
Days With ≥ 0.1" Precipitation	6	6	7	8	9	8	7	6	6	6	7	8	84
Days With ≥ 0.5" Precipitation	1	1	2	3	3	3	3	3	2	2	3	2	28
Days With ≥ 1.0" Precipitation	1	0	0	1	1	1	1	1	1	1	1	1	10
Mean Snowfall (in.)	11.1	10.4	5.2	1.1	trace	0.0	0.0	0.0	0.0	0.4	1.3	8.8	38.3
Maximum Snow Depth (in.)	17	24	14	8	trace	0	0	0	0	7	3	9	24
Days With ≥ 1.0" Snow Depth	14	11	4	0	0	0	0	0	0	0	1	9	39

La Porte *La Porte County* Elevation: 810 ft. Latitude: 41° 37' N Longitude: 86° 44' W

	JAN	FEB	MAR	APR	MAY	JUN	JUL	AUG	SEP	OCT	NOV	DEC	YEAR
Mean Maximum Temp. (°F)	31.3	35.0	45.6	58.4	69.8	78.9	82.3	80.4	74.1	61.7	48.1	35.4	58.4
Mean Temp. (°F)	24.6	28.0	37.3	49.1	59.9	69.5	73.4	71.8	64.7	52.8	41.0	29.1	50.1
Mean Minimum Temp. (°F)	17.8	20.9	29.0	39.8	50.0	60.0	64.4	63.2	55.3	43.8	33.9	22.7	41.7
Extreme Maximum Temp. (°F)	64	71	82	90	91	101	101	100	95	89	75	72	101
Extreme Minimum Temp. (°F)	-23	-16	-6	16	30	38	47	44	35	24	10	-18	-23
Days Maximum Temp. ≥ 90°F	0	0	0	0	0	3	4	3	1	0	0	0	11
Days Maximum Temp. ≤ 32°F	17	12	4	0	0	0	0	0	0	0	2	11	46
Days Minimum Temp. ≤ 32°F	28	24	21	6	0	0	0	0	0	2	14	25	120
Days Minimum Temp. ≤ 0°F	3	2	0	0	0	0	0	0	0	0	0	2	7
Heating Degree Days (base 65°F)	1,247	1,040	852	480	204	37	3	9	94	383	713	1,106	6,168
Cooling Degree Days (base 65°F)	0	0	1	9	52	178	269	228	92	10	0	0	839
Mean Precipitation (in.)	2.63	2.28	2.94	3.55	3.82	4.21	4.26	4.40	3.68	3.75	3.86	3.18	42.56
Extreme Maximum Daily Precip. (in.)	2.34	1.70	1.77	2.56	3.23	3.62	4.59	3.49	6.73	2.81	5.00	2.13	6.73
Days With ≥ 0.1" Precipitation	8	6	7	8	8	7	7	7	6	7	8	8	87
Days With ≥ 0.5" Precipitation	1	1	2	3	3	3	3	3	2	2	2	2	27
Days With ≥ 1.0" Precipitation	0	0	1	1	1	1	1	1	1	1	1	1	10
Mean Snowfall (in.)	20.6	13.9	7.2	1.4	trace	0.0	0.0	0.0	0.0	0.4	3.8	14.9	62.2
Maximum Snow Depth (in.)	18	24	11	6	trace	0	0	0	0	1	10	14	24
Days With ≥ 1.0" Snow Depth	20	14	5	1	0	0	0	0	0	0	2	11	53

Lafayette 8 S *Tippecanoe County* Elevation: 732 ft. Latitude: 40° 18' N Longitude: 86° 54' W

	JAN	FEB	MAR	APR	MAY	JUN	JUL	AUG	SEP	OCT	NOV	DEC	YEAR
Mean Maximum Temp. (°F)	33.4	37.7	48.9	61.5	72.5	81.6	84.3	82.9	77.6	64.8	51.2	37.2	61.1
Mean Temp. (°F)	25.4	28.8	39.2	50.9	61.7	70.9	73.9	72.2	65.6	53.6	42.2	29.4	51.1
Mean Minimum Temp. (°F)	17.3	19.9	29.4	40.1	50.9	60.2	63.5	61.6	53.6	42.4	33.2	21.5	41.1
Extreme Maximum Temp. (°F)	65	74	82	89	93	104	102	98	96	91	80	71	104
Extreme Minimum Temp. (°F)	-25	-19	-8	4	29	36	44	37	26	19	7	-25	-25
Days Maximum Temp. ≥ 90°F	0	0	0	0	1	5	6	4	2	0	0	0	18
Days Maximum Temp. ≤ 32°F	14	10	3	0	0	0	0	0	0	0	1	10	38
Days Minimum Temp. ≤ 32°F	27	25	20	7	0	0	0	0	0	5	15	26	125
Days Minimum Temp. ≤ 0°F	4	3	0	0	0	0	0	0	0	0	0	2	9
Heating Degree Days (base 65°F)	1,221	1,017	796	431	165	27	3	10	87	363	676	1,098	5,894
Cooling Degree Days (base 65°F)	0	0	2	14	70	210	287	241	111	17	0	0	952
Mean Precipitation (in.)	2.07	1.96	2.73	3.37	4.60	4.44	4.08	3.76	2.79	2.81	3.24	2.59	38.44
Extreme Maximum Daily Precip. (in.)	2.30	2.26	3.30	3.44	4.14	4.51	2.50	3.66	3.72	2.19	2.35	2.02	4.51
Days With ≥ 0.1" Precipitation	5	4	6	7	8	7	7	6	5	5	6	6	72
Days With ≥ 0.5" Precipitation	1	1	2	2	3	3	3	2	2	2	2	2	25
Days With ≥ 1.0" Precipitation	0	0	0	0	1	1	1	1	1	1	1	0	7
Mean Snowfall (in.)	6.9	5.3	2.4	0.6	trace	0.0	0.0	0.0	0.0	0.5	0.5	5.1	21.3
Maximum Snow Depth (in.)	18	19	10	5	trace	0	0	0	0	5	4	9	19
Days With ≥ 1.0" Snow Depth	11	9	3	0	0	0	0	0	0	0	0	8	31

The period of record for all cooperative weather station data is 1980 – 2009. See User Guide for detailed explanation of data.

Lowell *Lake County* Elevation: 665 ft. Latitude: 41° 16' N Longitude: 87° 25' W

	JAN	FEB	MAR	APR	MAY	JUN	JUL	AUG	SEP	OCT	NOV	DEC	YEAR
Mean Maximum Temp. (°F)	31.5	35.9	47.5	60.6	71.8	81.0	84.0	82.1	76.5	63.6	49.4	35.4	59.9
Mean Temp. (°F)	23.3	27.0	37.5	49.3	60.0	69.6	73.1	71.2	64.2	52.0	40.4	27.2	49.6
Mean Minimum Temp. (°F)	15.0	18.1	27.6	37.9	48.2	58.2	62.1	60.2	51.9	40.3	31.3	19.3	39.2
Extreme Maximum Temp. (°F)	66	73	84	91	93	104	101	104	98	91	76	69	104
Extreme Minimum Temp. (°F)	-25	-21	-9	7	27	36	42	38	28	18	6	-20	-25
Days Maximum Temp. ≥ 90°F	0	0	0	0	1	5	7	3	2	0	0	0	18
Days Maximum Temp. ≤ 32°F	16	11	3	0	0	0	0	0	0	0	1	11	42
Days Minimum Temp. ≤ 32°F	29	25	23	9	1	0	0	0	0	6	17	27	137
Days Minimum Temp. ≤ 0°F	5	3	0	0	0	0	0	0	0	0	0	3	11
Heating Degree Days (base 65°F)	1,286	1,068	845	474	200	37	5	13	105	408	733	1,165	6,339
Cooling Degree Days (base 65°F)	0	0	1	9	52	182	261	211	88	11	0	0	815
Mean Precipitation (in.)	1.91	1.68	2.65	3.73	4.33	4.53	3.85	4.15	3.23	3.45	3.42	2.52	39.45
Extreme Maximum Daily Precip. (in.)	2.81	1.89	2.19	3.88	2.91	3.85	3.64	3.53	3.20	2.92	5.14	2.96	5.14
Days With ≥ 0.1" Precipitation	5	4	6	7	8	7	7	6	5	6	7	6	74
Days With ≥ 0.5" Precipitation	1	1	2	2	3	2	3	3	2	2	2	1	24
Days With ≥ 1.0" Precipitation	0	0	0	1	1	1	1	1	1	1	1	1	9
Mean Snowfall (in.)	9.4	9.1	3.6	0.3	trace	0.0	0.0	0.0	0.0	0.2	0.8	7.4	30.8
Maximum Snow Depth (in.)	na	na	***9***	***1***	***trace***	***0***	***0***	***0***	***0***	***1***	***4***	na	na
Days With ≥ 1.0" Snow Depth	na	***7***	***2***	0	0	0	0	0	0	0	0	***8***	na

Madison Sewage Plant *Jefferson County* Elevation: 459 ft. Latitude: 38° 44' N Longitude: 85° 24' W

	JAN	FEB	MAR	APR	MAY	JUN	JUL	AUG	SEP	OCT	NOV	DEC	YEAR
Mean Maximum Temp. (°F)	41.0	45.3	55.3	66.5	75.0	83.1	86.7	86.0	79.5	68.2	56.1	44.1	65.6
Mean Temp. (°F)	32.8	35.8	44.8	55.0	64.1	72.5	76.6	75.6	68.6	57.2	46.4	35.9	55.4
Mean Minimum Temp. (°F)	24.5	26.3	34.0	43.5	53.1	61.8	66.4	65.2	57.7	46.0	36.6	27.5	45.2
Extreme Maximum Temp. (°F)	68	76	84	91	93	103	103	104	99	93	84	77	104
Extreme Minimum Temp. (°F)	-17	-8	-2	19	31	40	51	43	33	23	11	-18	-18
Days Maximum Temp. ≥ 90°F	0	0	0	0	0	4	10	9	3	0	0	0	26
Days Maximum Temp. ≤ 32°F	6	4	0	0	0	0	0	0	0	0	0	5	15
Days Minimum Temp. ≤ 32°F	24	20	14	3	0	0	0	0	0	1	11	21	94
Days Minimum Temp. ≤ 0°F	1	0	0	0	0	0	0	0	0	0	0	1	2
Heating Degree Days (base 65°F)	991	820	623	305	105	11	0	1	44	260	553	897	4,610
Cooling Degree Days (base 65°F)	0	0	2	15	82	242	365	338	160	25	1	0	1,230
Mean Precipitation (in.)	3.40	2.96	4.19	4.33	5.32	4.21	4.55	4.11	3.23	3.79	3.69	3.76	47.54
Extreme Maximum Daily Precip. (in.)	4.00	2.60	3.10	2.20	2.80	2.90	3.65	4.97	5.16	5.00	2.80	2.60	5.16
Days With ≥ 0.1" Precipitation	6	6	8	9	9	8	7	6	5	6	7	7	84
Days With ≥ 0.5" Precipitation	2	2	3	3	4	3	3	3	2	3	3	2	33
Days With ≥ 1.0" Precipitation	1	1	1	1	2	1	2	1	1	1	1	1	14
Mean Snowfall (in.)	4.3	3.9	1.3	0.1	trace	0.0	0.0	0.0	0.0	0.1	trace	3.4	13.1
Maximum Snow Depth (in.)	***10***	16	8	1	trace	0	0	0	0	4	trace	***15***	***16***
Days With ≥ 1.0" Snow Depth	***4***	4	1	0	0	0	0	0	0	0	0	2	***11***

Martinsville 2 SW *Morgan County* Elevation: 609 ft. Latitude: 39° 24' N Longitude: 86° 27' W

	JAN	FEB	MAR	APR	MAY	JUN	JUL	AUG	SEP	OCT	NOV	DEC	YEAR
Mean Maximum Temp. (°F)	36.6	41.1	51.5	63.2	72.7	81.1	84.7	84.1	78.0	65.5	53.1	40.3	62.7
Mean Temp. (°F)	27.9	31.4	40.6	51.5	61.3	70.2	73.9	72.5	65.1	52.9	42.8	31.7	51.8
Mean Minimum Temp. (°F)	19.1	21.5	29.6	39.7	49.7	59.2	63.0	60.9	52.2	40.3	32.5	23.0	40.9
Extreme Maximum Temp. (°F)	67	75	83	88	92	101	101	100	95	89	81	75	101
Extreme Minimum Temp. (°F)	-35	-20	-15	12	29	35	45	38	28	19	9	-22	-35
Days Maximum Temp. ≥ 90°F	0	0	0	0	0	2	6	6	2	0	0	0	16
Days Maximum Temp. ≤ 32°F	11	7	2	0	0	0	0	0	0	0	1	8	29
Days Minimum Temp. ≤ 32°F	27	24	20	7	1	0	0	0	0	7	16	25	127
Days Minimum Temp. ≤ 0°F	3	2	0	0	0	0	0	0	0	0	0	2	7
Heating Degree Days (base 65°F)	1,145	945	753	411	162	25	3	8	90	380	659	1,027	5,608
Cooling Degree Days (base 65°F)	0	0	1	12	53	187	285	248	101	12	0	0	899
Mean Precipitation (in.)	2.65	2.42	3.42	4.41	5.29	4.57	4.31	3.83	3.50	3.42	3.64	3.23	44.69
Extreme Maximum Daily Precip. (in.)	2.16	2.34	2.20	3.50	2.83	8.02	3.85	5.82	4.12	4.76	3.40	2.92	8.02
Days With ≥ 0.1" Precipitation	5	5	7	8	9	7	7	5	5	5	6	7	76
Days With ≥ 0.5" Precipitation	2	2	2	3	4	3	3	3	2	2	3	2	31
Days With ≥ 1.0" Precipitation	1	0	1	1	1	1	1	1	1	1	1	1	11
Mean Snowfall (in.)	5.6	4.2	2.0	0.1	0.0	0.0	0.0	0.0	0.0	0.2	0.3	3.6	16.0
Maximum Snow Depth (in.)	***16***	***9***	***10***	1	0	0	0	0	0	0	***4***	***13***	***16***
Days With ≥ 1.0" Snow Depth	***5***	***3***	1	0	0	0	0	0	0	0	0	3	***12***

Mount Vernon *Posey County* Elevation: 419 ft. Latitude: 37° 57' N Longitude: 87° 53' W

	JAN	FEB	MAR	APR	MAY	JUN	JUL	AUG	SEP	OCT	NOV	DEC	YEAR
Mean Maximum Temp. (°F)	40.7	45.2	55.1	66.2	76.0	84.7	88.0	87.4	81.2	69.2	56.7	44.3	66.2
Mean Temp. (°F)	32.5	36.2	45.3	55.8	65.9	74.8	78.2	77.0	69.8	58.0	47.3	36.3	56.4
Mean Minimum Temp. (°F)	24.3	27.2	35.3	45.3	55.7	64.9	68.3	66.4	58.4	46.7	37.9	28.2	46.6
Extreme Maximum Temp. (°F)	71	76	83	90	93	101	102	104	99	90	82	77	104
Extreme Minimum Temp. (°F)	-16	-7	7	25	36	44	51	45	32	22	12	-16	-16
Days Maximum Temp. ≥ 90°F	0	0	0	0	1	8	13	12	4	0	0	0	38
Days Maximum Temp. ≤ 32°F	7	5	1	0	0	0	0	0	0	0	0	5	18
Days Minimum Temp. ≤ 32°F	24	19	12	2	0	0	0	0	0	1	10	20	88
Days Minimum Temp. ≤ 0°F	1	1	0	0	0	0	0	0	0	0	0	1	3
Heating Degree Days (base 65°F)	1,000	807	608	295	79	6	0	1	39	246	525	884	4,490
Cooling Degree Days (base 65°F)	0	0	3	26	113	307	416	379	191	34	2	0	1,471
Mean Precipitation (in.)	3.48	3.07	4.26	4.39	5.66	3.94	3.83	2.92	3.02	3.42	4.01	3.92	45.92
Extreme Maximum Daily Precip. (in.)	4.69	2.52	6.29	7.40	3.42	3.73	3.40	3.28	3.57	4.06	3.20	3.70	7.40
Days With ≥ 0.1" Precipitation	5	5	7	7	8	7	6	5	5	5	6	7	73
Days With ≥ 0.5" Precipitation	2	2	3	3	4	3	3	2	2	2	3	3	32
Days With ≥ 1.0" Precipitation	1	1	1	1	2	1	1	1	1	1	1	1	13
Mean Snowfall (in.)	2.3	3.2	1.3	0.1	0.0	0.0	0.0	0.0	0.0	0.1	0.0	1.8	8.8
Maximum Snow Depth (in.)	6	9	8	3	0	0	0	0	0	3	1	6	9
Days With ≥ 1.0" Snow Depth	4	3	1	0	0	0	0	0	0	0	0	2	10

The period of record for all cooperative weather station data is 1980 – 2009. See User Guide for detailed explanation of data.

Climate

Muncie Ball State Univ *Delaware County* Elevation: 939 ft. Latitude: 40° 13' N Longitude: 85° 25' W

	JAN	FEB	MAR	APR	MAY	JUN	JUL	AUG	SEP	OCT	NOV	DEC	YEAR
Mean Maximum Temp. (°F)	33.4	38.2	47.9	60.7	71.8	81.0	84.8	82.8	76.5	64.2	50.6	37.9	60.8
Mean Temp. (°F)	25.4	29.5	38.2	50.0	61.4	70.5	74.2	72.1	64.6	52.9	41.6	30.1	50.9
Mean Minimum Temp. (°F)	17.3	20.8	28.6	39.2	51.0	60.1	63.5	61.3	52.7	41.5	32.5	22.1	40.9
Extreme Maximum Temp. (°F)	64	74	80	86	90	102	100	99	96	88	79	71	102
Extreme Minimum Temp. (°F)	-29	-13	-8	10	25	36	40	39	27	18	9	-21	-29
Days Maximum Temp. ≥ 90°F	0	0	0	0	0	4	7	4	2	0	0	0	17
Days Maximum Temp. ≤ 32°F	14	9	4	0	0	0	0	0	0	0	2	9	38
Days Minimum Temp. ≤ 32°F	28	24	21	8	0	0	0	0	0	5	17	26	129
Days Minimum Temp. ≤ 0°F	4	2	0	0	0	0	0	0	0	0	0	2	8
Heating Degree Days (base 65°F)	1,222	997	824	454	170	29	3	9	103	382	696	1,076	5,965
Cooling Degree Days (base 65°F)	0	0	1	10	65	202	294	236	99	14	0	0	921
Mean Precipitation (in.)	1.88	2.12	2.91	3.45	4.56	4.51	4.59	3.14	3.25	2.70	3.52	2.86	39.49
Extreme Maximum Daily Precip. (in.)	1.38	2.05	1.83	na	2.52	4.74	3.10	2.92	4.14	2.13	2.69	3.09	na
Days With ≥ 0.1" Precipitation	5	5	7	7	8	7	7	5	5	5	7	7	75
Days With ≥ 0.5" Precipitation	1	1	2	2	3	3	3	2	2	2	3	2	26
Days With ≥ 1.0" Precipitation	0	0	0	1	1	1	1	1	1	1	1	0	8
Mean Snowfall (in.)	7.4	6.0	2.7	0.5	trace	0.0	0.0	0.0	0.0	0.3	1.0	6.1	24.0
Maximum Snow Depth (in.)	10	16	9	6	trace	0	0	0	0	3	4	10	16
Days With ≥ 1.0" Snow Depth	10	8	3	0	0	0	0	0	0	0	1	7	29

North Vernon 1 NW *Jennings County* Elevation: 745 ft. Latitude: 39° 02' N Longitude: 85° 38' W

	JAN	FEB	MAR	APR	MAY	JUN	JUL	AUG	SEP	OCT	NOV	DEC	YEAR
Mean Maximum Temp. (°F)	40.3	45.2	55.2	67.1	75.0	83.4	86.3	85.2	79.2	67.8	55.4	43.2	65.3
Mean Temp. (°F)	32.0	35.5	44.6	55.2	63.7	72.2	75.6	74.3	67.7	56.3	45.9	34.7	54.8
Mean Minimum Temp. (°F)	23.6	26.0	33.9	43.3	52.2	61.0	64.8	63.3	56.0	44.7	36.3	26.4	44.3
Extreme Maximum Temp. (°F)	67	75	85	87	90	101	102	103	96	91	80	74	103
Extreme Minimum Temp. (°F)	-22	-12	-6	19	30	39	47	40	33	23	8	-22	-22
Days Maximum Temp. ≥ 90°F	0	0	0	0	0	4	8	6	2	0	0	0	20
Days Maximum Temp. ≤ 32°F	7	5	1	0	0	0	0	0	0	0	0	5	18
Days Minimum Temp. ≤ 32°F	23	19	15	4	0	0	0	0	0	4	12	21	98
Days Minimum Temp. ≤ 0°F	1	1	0	0	0	0	0	0	0	0	0	1	3
Heating Degree Days (base 65°F)	1,015	826	630	311	113	11	0	3	55	288	569	932	4,753
Cooling Degree Days (base 65°F)	0	0	5	24	79	235	335	299	139	25	1	0	1,142
Mean Precipitation (in.)	2.40	2.63	3.70	4.49	5.03	3.96	4.44	4.60	3.20	3.69	3.88	3.59	45.61
Extreme Maximum Daily Precip. (in.)	2.09	2.10	3.92	4.00	2.90	3.63	3.47	4.55	3.51	4.02	2.27	2.14	4.55
Days With ≥ 0.1" Precipitation	5	5	6	8	8	6	6	5	4	5	6	7	71
Days With ≥ 0.5" Precipitation	2	2	3	3	3	2	3	3	2	2	3	2	30
Days With ≥ 1.0" Precipitation	1	0	1	1	1	1	1	1	1	1	1	1	11
Mean Snowfall (in.)	2.7	3.1	1.5	trace	trace	0.0	0.0	0.0	0.0	0.0	0.0	3.5	10.8
Maximum Snow Depth (in.)	11	7	12	trace	trace	0	0	0	0	0	1	na	na
Days With ≥ 1.0" Snow Depth	4	4	1	0	0	0	0	0	0	0	0	2	11

Oolitic Purdue Exp Farm *Lawrence County* Elevation: 649 ft. Latitude: 38° 53' N Longitude: 86° 33' W

	JAN	FEB	MAR	APR	MAY	JUN	JUL	AUG	SEP	OCT	NOV	DEC	YEAR
Mean Maximum Temp. (°F)	38.2	43.3	53.0	64.3	73.6	82.0	85.5	84.9	78.8	66.6	54.5	41.7	63.9
Mean Temp. (°F)	29.2	33.0	41.7	52.5	62.1	71.0	74.7	73.5	66.2	54.0	43.9	32.6	52.9
Mean Minimum Temp. (°F)	20.0	22.7	30.3	40.6	50.6	59.9	63.9	62.1	53.6	41.5	33.2	23.5	41.8
Extreme Maximum Temp. (°F)	68	75	82	88	91	102	102	102	99	91	81	75	102
Extreme Minimum Temp. (°F)	-29	-16	-4	15	29	38	47	41	31	16	8	-23	-29
Days Maximum Temp. ≥ 90°F	0	0	0	0	0	3	7	7	2	0	0	0	19
Days Maximum Temp. ≤ 32°F	10	6	1	0	0	0	0	0	0	0	1	7	25
Days Minimum Temp. ≤ 32°F	27	23	19	6	0	0	0	0	0	6	16	24	121
Days Minimum Temp. ≤ 0°F	3	1	0	0	0	0	0	0	0	0	0	2	6
Heating Degree Days (base 65°F)	1,103	898	718	383	144	18	1	4	75	347	628	996	5,315
Cooling Degree Days (base 65°F)	0	0	2	14	62	205	309	275	118	15	0	0	1,000
Mean Precipitation (in.)	2.92	2.74	3.83	4.43	5.76	4.07	4.53	3.65	3.17	3.70	3.70	3.51	46.01
Extreme Maximum Daily Precip. (in.)	3.06	2.67	2.90	4.80	3.18	4.05	3.78	4.61	2.57	3.80	2.83	2.48	4.80
Days With ≥ 0.1" Precipitation	6	5	7	9	8	7	7	6	5	6	7	6	79
Days With ≥ 0.5" Precipitation	2	2	3	3	4	3	3	2	2	3	2	3	32
Days With ≥ 1.0" Precipitation	1	0	1	1	2	1	1	1	1	1	1	1	12
Mean Snowfall (in.)	4.6	4.1	2.0	0.1	trace	0.0	0.0	0.0	0.0	0.1	0.1	3.9	14.9
Maximum Snow Depth (in.)	12	8	10	1	trace	0	0	0	0	1	1	16	16
Days With ≥ 1.0" Snow Depth	7	6	2	0	0	0	0	0	0	0	0	4	19

Richmond Water Works *Wayne County* Elevation: 1,015 ft. Latitude: 39° 53' N Longitude: 84° 53' W

	JAN	FEB	MAR	APR	MAY	JUN	JUL	AUG	SEP	OCT	NOV	DEC	YEAR
Mean Maximum Temp. (°F)	35.6	39.8	50.4	62.7	72.6	81.3	84.5	83.2	76.9	64.5	51.7	39.0	61.8
Mean Temp. (°F)	27.4	30.9	40.2	51.3	61.4	70.1	73.6	72.2	65.0	53.2	42.5	31.2	51.6
Mean Minimum Temp. (°F)	19.2	22.0	30.0	39.9	50.0	58.9	62.6	61.2	53.2	41.9	33.3	23.3	41.3
Extreme Maximum Temp. (°F)	66	74	82	94	92	99	100	100	96	90	78	72	100
Extreme Minimum Temp. (°F)	-27	-20	-9	14	29	37	43	41	32	18	10	-22	-27
Days Maximum Temp. ≥ 90°F	0	0	0	0	0	4	6	5	1	0	0	0	16
Days Maximum Temp. ≤ 32°F	12	8	2	0	0	0	0	0	0	0	1	9	32
Days Minimum Temp. ≤ 32°F	27	23	19	6	0	0	0	0	0	5	15	25	120
Days Minimum Temp. ≤ 0°F	3	2	0	0	0	0	0	0	0	0	0	1	6
Heating Degree Days (base 65°F)	1,159	958	763	412	163	25	2	7	88	372	667	1,041	5,657
Cooling Degree Days (base 65°F)	0	0	1	9	57	185	276	238	96	14	0	0	876
Mean Precipitation (in.)	2.73	2.25	3.19	3.84	4.72	4.30	4.02	3.49	2.75	3.15	3.36	2.90	40.70
Extreme Maximum Daily Precip. (in.)	3.19	1.80	2.12	2.79	2.41	3.12	3.38	2.86	2.41	4.53	2.41	2.27	4.53
Days With ≥ 0.1" Precipitation	6	5	7	8	9	8	6	5	5	6	6	6	77
Days With ≥ 0.5" Precipitation	2	1	2	2	3	3	3	2	2	2	2	2	26
Days With ≥ 1.0" Precipitation	1	0	1	1	1	1	1	1	1	1	1	1	11
Mean Snowfall (in.)	5.9	3.6	1.6	0.2	trace	0.0	0.0	0.0	0.0	0.2	0.4	3.8	15.7
Maximum Snow Depth (in.)	21	13	5	2	trace	0	0	0	0	2	5	20	21
Days With ≥ 1.0" Snow Depth	8	6	1	0	0	0	0	0	0	0	0	5	20

The period of record for all cooperative weather station data is 1980 – 2009. See User Guide for detailed explanation of data.

Rockville *Parke County* Elevation: 689 ft. Latitude: 39° 46' N Longitude: 87° 14' W

	JAN	FEB	MAR	APR	MAY	JUN	JUL	AUG	SEP	OCT	NOV	DEC	YEAR
Mean Maximum Temp. (°F)	36.9	42.0	53.5	66.0	75.7	84.1	86.9	85.5	79.2	67.2	53.6	40.1	64.2
Mean Temp. (°F)	28.8	32.9	43.2	54.4	63.9	72.7	76.0	74.5	67.3	55.8	44.6	32.4	53.9
Mean Minimum Temp. (°F)	20.5	23.8	32.8	42.7	52.1	61.2	64.9	63.5	55.4	44.4	35.5	24.6	43.5
Extreme Maximum Temp. (°F)	66	74	84	89	93	103	104	102	96	90	79	74	104
Extreme Minimum Temp. (°F)	-25	-18	-4	17	27	37	43	41	31	19	8	-21	-25
Days Maximum Temp. ≥ 90°F	0	0	0	0	1	7	10	7	2	0	0	0	27
Days Maximum Temp. ≤ 32°F	11	6	1	0	0	0	0	0	0	0	1	7	26
Days Minimum Temp. ≤ 32°F	26	22	16	5	0	0	0	0	0	4	13	23	109
Days Minimum Temp. ≤ 0°F	3	2	0	0	0	0	0	0	0	0	0	1	6
Heating Degree Days (base 65°F)	1,117	900	673	334	112	12	1	2	59	300	607	1,005	5,122
Cooling Degree Days (base 65°F)	0	0	3	22	86	250	347	304	135	23	1	0	1,171
Mean Precipitation (in.)	2.83	2.51	3.44	4.14	5.39	4.55	5.13	4.01	3.31	3.80	4.21	3.56	46.88
Extreme Maximum Daily Precip. (in.)	2.60	3.18	3.10	2.20	8.05	5.00	3.45	4.73	5.46	3.00	4.15	3.03	8.05
Days With ≥ 0.1" Precipitation	6	5	7	9	9	8	7	6	5	6	7	7	82
Days With ≥ 0.5" Precipitation	2	2	3	3	4	3	3	3	3	3	3	3	35
Days With ≥ 1.0" Precipitation	1	1	1	1	2	1	2	1	1	1	1	1	14
Mean Snowfall (in.)	5.1	2.9	1.6	0.0	trace	0.0	0.0	0.0	0.0	trace	0.1	3.9	13.6
Maximum Snow Depth (in.)	15	18	12	1	trace	0	0	0	0	1	4	12	18
Days With ≥ 1.0" Snow Depth	9	6	1	0	0	0	0	0	0	0	0	6	22

Shelbyville Sewage Plant *Shelby County* Elevation: 750 ft. Latitude: 39° 31' N Longitude: 85° 47' W

	JAN	FEB	MAR	APR	MAY	JUN	JUL	AUG	SEP	OCT	NOV	DEC	YEAR
Mean Maximum Temp. (°F)	36.2	40.4	51.3	63.2	73.1	82.3	85.3	83.7	78.3	66.0	***52.8***	39.4	***62.7***
Mean Temp. (°F)	28.0	31.2	41.0	52.4	62.6	71.9	74.9	72.9	66.4	54.3	***43.5***	31.4	***52.5***
Mean Minimum Temp. (°F)	19.7	22.0	30.7	41.6	52.1	61.4	64.4	62.0	54.4	42.6	***34.2***	23.5	***42.4***
Extreme Maximum Temp. (°F)	66	74	81	85	91	102	102	100	98	90	***80***	75	***102***
Extreme Minimum Temp. (°F)	-25	-16	0	17	31	41	48	46	32	20	***12***	-22	***-25***
Days Maximum Temp. ≥ 90°F	0	0	0	0	0	4	7	4	2	0	***0***	0	***17***
Days Maximum Temp. ≤ 32°F	11	7	2	0	0	0	0	0	0	0	***1***	8	***29***
Days Minimum Temp. ≤ 32°F	27	24	19	5	0	0	0	0	0	5	***14***	25	***119***
Days Minimum Temp. ≤ 0°F	3	2	0	0	0	0	0	0	0	0	***0***	1	***6***
Heating Degree Days (base 65°F)	1,141	950	737	386	137	16	1	6	71	343	***638***	1,036	***5,462***
Cooling Degree Days (base 65°F)	0	0	2	14	70	229	314	258	119	17	***0***	0	***1,023***
Mean Precipitation (in.)	2.80	2.35	3.28	4.20	4.99	4.11	4.00	3.27	2.99	2.93	3.23	3.00	41.15
Extreme Maximum Daily Precip. (in.)	2.58	2.03	1.84	3.62	3.49	***3.54***	3.35	3.96	3.15	4.43	***2.70***	2.50	***4.43***
Days With ≥ 0.1" Precipitation	6	5	7	8	8	7	7	6	5	5	***6***	6	***76***
Days With ≥ 0.5" Precipitation	2	2	3	3	4	3	3	2	2	2	***2***	2	***30***
Days With ≥ 1.0" Precipitation	1	0	1	1	1	1	1	1	1	1	1	1	11
Mean Snowfall (in.)	***2.4***	***1.7***	***0.8***	trace	0.0	0.0	0.0	0.0	0.0	trace	***trace***	***0.8***	***5.7***
Maximum Snow Depth (in.)	***8***	***11***	***7***	trace	0	***0***	0	***0***	0	***1***	***trace***	na	na
Days With ≥ 1.0" Snow Depth	***2***	***2***	1	0	0	0	0	0	0	0	***0***	***1***	***6***

Tell City *Perry County* Elevation: 399 ft. Latitude: 37° 57' N Longitude: 86° 46' W

	JAN	FEB	MAR	APR	MAY	JUN	JUL	AUG	SEP	OCT	NOV	DEC	YEAR
Mean Maximum Temp. (°F)	41.9	46.0	56.0	67.1	76.1	84.1	87.5	87.2	80.8	69.5	57.3	45.1	66.5
Mean Temp. (°F)	34.1	37.2	45.9	56.2	65.5	74.1	77.9	76.9	69.8	58.4	48.0	37.3	56.8
Mean Minimum Temp. (°F)	26.3	28.4	35.7	45.2	54.8	64.0	68.3	66.7	58.6	47.2	38.7	29.3	46.9
Extreme Maximum Temp. (°F)	71	74	84	89	91	99	103	100	100	92	83	77	103
Extreme Minimum Temp. (°F)	-17	-5	-1	22	34	43	52	46	36	22	14	-14	-17
Days Maximum Temp. ≥ 90°F	0	0	0	0	0	6	12	11	4	0	0	0	33
Days Maximum Temp. ≤ 32°F	6	4	1	0	0	0	0	0	0	0	0	4	15
Days Minimum Temp. ≤ 32°F	22	19	12	3	0	0	0	0	0	1	8	18	83
Days Minimum Temp. ≤ 0°F	1	0	0	0	0	0	0	0	0	0	0	0	1
Heating Degree Days (base 65°F)	950	779	591	286	85	7	0	1	39	235	505	854	4,332
Cooling Degree Days (base 65°F)	0	0	4	27	107	286	407	378	188	37	3	0	1,437
Mean Precipitation (in.)	3.31	3.18	4.25	4.25	5.78	4.38	4.47	3.35	3.59	3.40	3.78	4.10	47.84
Extreme Maximum Daily Precip. (in.)	3.51	3.09	4.75	3.34	3.93	4.37	3.20	3.27	4.43	2.72	3.10	2.25	4.75
Days With ≥ 0.1" Precipitation	6	6	7	7	9	7	7	5	5	5	6	7	77
Days With ≥ 0.5" Precipitation	2	2	2	3	4	3	3	2	2	2	3	3	32
Days With ≥ 1.0" Precipitation	1	1	1	1	2	1	1	1	1	1	1	1	13
Mean Snowfall (in.)	1.8	2.2	0.4	trace	0.0	0.0	0.0	0.0	0.0	0.0	0.1	0.8	5.3
Maximum Snow Depth (in.)	7	10	5	1	0	0	0	0	0	0	trace	21	21
Days With ≥ 1.0" Snow Depth	2	2	0	0	0	0	0	0	0	0	0	0	4

Terre Haute Indiana State *Vigo County* Elevation: 506 ft. Latitude: 39° 28' N Longitude: 87° 25' W

	JAN	FEB	MAR	APR	MAY	JUN	JUL	AUG	SEP	OCT	NOV	DEC	YEAR
Mean Maximum Temp. (°F)	***37.7***	42.1	53.3	65.3	75.8	84.4	***88.0***	***86.5***	***80.7***	***68.3***	***54.4***	***41.1***	***64.8***
Mean Temp. (°F)	***28.4***	32.2	42.6	54.0	64.0	73.0	***76.8***	***74.8***	***67.8***	***55.4***	***43.9***	***31.9***	***53.7***
Mean Minimum Temp. (°F)	***19.2***	22.2	32.3	42.6	52.2	61.4	***65.5***	***63.0***	***54.9***	***42.6***	***33.3***	***22.6***	***42.6***
Extreme Maximum Temp. (°F)	69	***76***	***84***	***89***	***99***	***102***	***102***	***102***	***100***	***91***	***82***	***74***	***102***
Extreme Minimum Temp. (°F)	-18	***-20***	***1***	***17***	***29***	***36***	***41***	***42***	***27***	***19***	***5***	***-22***	***-22***
Days Maximum Temp. ≥ 90°F	0	0	0	0	1	8	12	***10***	***4***	***0***	0	0	***35***
Days Maximum Temp. ≤ 32°F	10	6	1	0	0	0	0	***0***	***0***	***0***	1	6	***24***
Days Minimum Temp. ≤ 32°F	26	23	17	5	0	0	0	***0***	***0***	***5***	15	24	***115***
Days Minimum Temp. ≤ 0°F	***2***	2	0	0	0	0	0	***0***	***0***	***0***	0	1	***5***
Heating Degree Days (base 65°F)	***1,125***	922	688	346	113	13	***1***	***3***	***60***	***312***	***626***	***1,017***	***5,226***
Cooling Degree Days (base 65°F)	***0***	0	2	23	90	259	***372***	***314***	***149***	***23***	***0***	***0***	***1,232***
Mean Precipitation (in.)	***2.56***	2.53	3.49	4.49	5.04	4.50	4.42	3.36	***3.51***	***3.65***	3.57	3.12	***44.24***
Extreme Maximum Daily Precip. (in.)	***2.50***	***2.81***	***2.72***	***2.87***	***3.00***	***4.59***	na	***2.70***	***5.30***	na	***2.00***	***2.31***	na
Days With ≥ 0.1" Precipitation	5	5	6	8	8	6	7	5	***5***	***5***	6	5	***71***
Days With ≥ 0.5" Precipitation	2	2	2	3	3	3	3	2	***2***	***2***	2	2	***28***
Days With ≥ 1.0" Precipitation	1	1	1	1	1	1	1	1	***1***	***1***	1	1	***12***
Mean Snowfall (in.)	***3.9***	***3.3***	***1.0***	***0.0***	0.0	0.0	0.0	0.0	***0.0***	***0.0***	***0.3***	2.9	***11.4***
Maximum Snow Depth (in.)	***12***	na	***6***	***1***	***0***	***0***	***0***	***0***	***0***	***0***	***2***	na	na
Days With ≥ 1.0" Snow Depth	***6***	na	***1***	0	0	0	0	0	***0***	***0***	***0***	***4***	na

The period of record for all cooperative weather station data is 1980 – 2009. See User Guide for detailed explanation of data.

Climate

Valparaiso Waterworks *Porter County* Elevation: 799 ft. Latitude: 41° 31' N Longitude: 87° 02' W

	JAN	FEB	MAR	APR	MAY	JUN	JUL	AUG	SEP	OCT	NOV	DEC	YEAR
Mean Maximum Temp. (°F)	31.6	36.9	47.3	60.2	71.2	79.6	83.1	81.0	74.6	63.1	48.9	35.9	59.5
Mean Temp. (°F)	24.4	29.0	38.1	49.6	60.1	68.9	73.2	71.2	64.3	53.0	41.3	29.3	50.2
Mean Minimum Temp. (°F)	17.1	21.1	28.9	39.0	48.9	58.1	63.2	61.5	53.9	42.9	33.5	22.6	40.9
Extreme Maximum Temp. (°F)	63	71	83	88	90	100	99	99	93	85	74	68	100
Extreme Minimum Temp. (°F)	-25	-18	-5	14	30	35	44	39	32	20	8	-20	-25
Days Maximum Temp. ≥ 90°F	0	0	0	0	0	3	4	3	1	0	0	0	11
Days Maximum Temp. ≤ 32°F	17	10	3	0	0	0	0	0	0	0	1	11	42
Days Minimum Temp. ≤ 32°F	28	23	21	7	0	0	0	0	0	4	15	26	124
Days Minimum Temp. ≤ 0°F	4	2	0	0	0	0	0	0	0	0	0	2	8
Heating Degree Days (base 65°F)	1,253	1,011	828	465	197	40	4	12	104	374	706	1,100	6,094
Cooling Degree Days (base 65°F)	0	0	1	10	52	164	264	210	90	10	0	0	801
Mean Precipitation (in.)	2.16	1.91	2.56	3.54	4.13	4.51	4.24	3.91	3.29	3.22	3.81	2.64	39.92
Extreme Maximum Daily Precip. (in.)	1.76	1.59	1.99	2.07	2.20	5.28	7.34	4.42	2.52	2.64	4.05	2.33	7.34
Days With ≥ 0.1" Precipitation	5	5	6	7	8	7	7	6	7	6	7	6	77
Days With ≥ 0.5" Precipitation	1	1	2	2	3	3	3	2	2	2	2	2	25
Days With ≥ 1.0" Precipitation	0	0	0	1	1	1	1	1	1	1	1	1	9
Mean Snowfall (in.)	12.6	8.1	6.0	1.1	trace	0.0	0.0	0.0	0.0	0.2	2.2	9.5	39.7
Maximum Snow Depth (in.)	20	24	16	6	trace	0	0	0	0	3	6	22	24
Days With ≥ 1.0" Snow Depth	20	12	5	0	0	0	0	0	0	0	2	10	49

Warsaw *Kosciusko County* Elevation: 810 ft. Latitude: 41° 14' N Longitude: 85° 52' W

	JAN	FEB	MAR	APR	MAY	JUN	JUL	AUG	SEP	OCT	NOV	DEC	YEAR
Mean Maximum Temp. (°F)	32.3	36.1	47.1	59.7	70.8	79.9	82.9	81.2	74.7	62.3	49.3	36.1	59.4
Mean Temp. (°F)	24.9	28.1	37.9	49.5	59.9	69.3	72.8	71.3	64.0	52.2	41.1	29.3	50.0
Mean Minimum Temp. (°F)	17.5	20.1	28.7	39.2	49.0	58.8	62.7	61.3	53.3	42.1	32.7	22.0	40.6
Extreme Maximum Temp. (°F)	63	73	82	87	91	102	102	98	95	90	76	69	102
Extreme Minimum Temp. (°F)	-25	-13	-9	8	28	37	43	37	29	20	9	-20	-25
Days Maximum Temp. ≥ 90°F	0	0	0	0	0	3	4	2	1	0	0	0	10
Days Maximum Temp. ≤ 32°F	16	11	3	0	0	0	0	0	0	0	1	11	42
Days Minimum Temp. ≤ 32°F	28	24	21	7	0	0	0	0	0	5	16	26	127
Days Minimum Temp. ≤ 0°F	3	2	0	0	0	0	0	0	0	0	0	2	7
Heating Degree Days (base 65°F)	1,236	1,036	834	469	200	32	5	10	107	399	712	1,102	6,142
Cooling Degree Days (base 65°F)	0	0	1	9	49	168	252	213	83	9	0	0	784
Mean Precipitation (in.)	2.10	1.69	2.17	3.58	4.23	4.31	4.05	4.38	3.11	3.29	2.88	2.59	38.38
Extreme Maximum Daily Precip. (in.)	2.20	1.53	1.87	3.42	2.93	4.87	4.32	4.33	2.43	3.69	2.50	3.90	4.87
Days With ≥ 0.1" Precipitation	5	5	5	8	8	7	7	7	6	6	6	6	76
Days With ≥ 0.5" Precipitation	1	1	1	2	3	3	3	3	2	2	2	2	25
Days With ≥ 1.0" Precipitation	0	0	0	1	1	1	1	1	1	1	1	0	8
Mean Snowfall (in.)	na	na	1.7	0.3	0.0	0.0	0.0	0.0	0.0	trace	0.3	4.3	na
Maximum Snow Depth (in.)	na	na	6	4	0	0	0	0	0	trace	2	na	na
Days With ≥ 1.0" Snow Depth	na	na	1	0	0	0	0	0	0	0	0	6	na

Whitestown *Boone County* Elevation: 935 ft. Latitude: 40° 00' N Longitude: 86° 21' W

	JAN	FEB	MAR	APR	MAY	JUN	JUL	AUG	SEP	OCT	NOV	DEC	YEAR
Mean Maximum Temp. (°F)	35.1	40.2	51.4	64.4	74.3	83.0	85.7	84.3	78.5	66.0	52.1	38.6	62.8
Mean Temp. (°F)	27.1	31.2	41.1	52.8	62.8	71.6	74.6	73.0	66.2	54.7	43.2	31.1	52.4
Mean Minimum Temp. (°F)	19.0	22.2	30.8	41.2	51.2	60.2	63.5	61.6	53.9	43.3	34.3	23.5	42.0
Extreme Maximum Temp. (°F)	65	74	82	88	94	104	103	100	96	88	78	73	104
Extreme Minimum Temp. (°F)	-27	-20	-10	15	30	35	43	37	28	20	6	-22	-27
Days Maximum Temp. ≥ 90°F	0	0	0	0	1	5	8	6	2	0	0	0	22
Days Maximum Temp. ≤ 32°F	13	8	2	0	0	0	0	0	0	0	1	9	33
Days Minimum Temp. ≤ 32°F	27	23	18	6	0	0	0	0	0	5	14	24	117
Days Minimum Temp. ≤ 0°F	3	2	0	0	0	0	0	0	0	0	0	2	7
Heating Degree Days (base 65°F)	1,169	949	736	376	138	18	2	7	75	331	648	1,045	5,494
Cooling Degree Days (base 65°F)	0	0	2	17	75	223	307	261	118	19	0	0	1,022
Mean Precipitation (in.)	2.69	2.55	3.40	3.91	4.84	4.06	4.31	3.33	3.39	3.06	3.68	3.29	42.51
Extreme Maximum Daily Precip. (in.)	2.22	3.12	2.66	1.80	2.65	2.95	3.43	3.89	5.46	2.36	3.73	2.45	5.46
Days With ≥ 0.1" Precipitation	6	5	7	9	9	7	7	5	5	6	7	7	80
Days With ≥ 0.5" Precipitation	2	2	2	3	3	3	3	2	3	2	2	2	29
Days With ≥ 1.0" Precipitation	0	0	1	1	1	1	1	1	1	1	1	1	10
Mean Snowfall (in.)	8.0	6.4	2.4	0.3	0.0	0.0	0.0	0.0	0.0	0.3	0.7	5.8	23.9
Maximum Snow Depth (in.)	14	22	11	2	0	0	0	0	0	5	2	9	22
Days With ≥ 1.0" Snow Depth	11	8	2	0	0	0	0	0	0	0	0	7	28

Winchester Airport 3E *Randolph County* Elevation: 1,109 ft. Latitude: 40° 11' N Longitude: 84° 55' W

	JAN	FEB	MAR	APR	MAY	JUN	JUL	AUG	SEP	OCT	NOV	DEC	YEAR
Mean Maximum Temp. (°F)	33.0	36.9	47.4	60.4	70.8	79.7	82.9	81.5	75.7	63.1	49.9	37.0	59.9
Mean Temp. (°F)	25.4	28.5	38.2	50.3	60.9	69.9	73.0	71.3	64.8	53.0	41.5	29.7	50.5
Mean Minimum Temp. (°F)	17.8	20.1	28.9	40.1	50.9	60.1	63.1	61.1	53.9	42.7	33.0	22.3	41.2
Extreme Maximum Temp. (°F)	64	73	80	85	89	101	100	97	93	89	77	71	101
Extreme Minimum Temp. (°F)	-26	-15	-11	12	29	40	46	39	29	19	9	-22	-26
Days Maximum Temp. ≥ 90°F	0	0	0	0	0	2	4	2	1	0	0	0	9
Days Maximum Temp. ≤ 32°F	15	10	4	0	0	0	0	0	0	0	2	11	42
Days Minimum Temp. ≤ 32°F	28	25	21	6	0	0	0	0	0	4	16	26	126
Days Minimum Temp. ≤ 0°F	4	2	0	0	0	0	0	0	0	0	0	2	8
Heating Degree Days (base 65°F)	1,220	1,025	826	445	179	31	4	12	95	381	698	1,087	6,003
Cooling Degree Days (base 65°F)	0	0	1	11	58	185	260	216	96	15	0	0	842
Mean Precipitation (in.)	2.07	1.73	2.74	3.71	4.36	4.45	4.36	3.47	2.92	3.04	3.27	2.78	38.90
Extreme Maximum Daily Precip. (in.)	2.64	1.80	2.46	2.58	2.47	6.45	2.90	3.53	3.00	2.68	3.52	2.52	6.45
Days With ≥ 0.1" Precipitation	5	4	6	8	8	7	7	6	5	5	7	6	74
Days With ≥ 0.5" Precipitation	1	1	2	2	3	3	3	2	2	2	2	2	25
Days With ≥ 1.0" Precipitation	1	0	0	1	1	1	1	1	1	1	1	0	9
Mean Snowfall (in.)	5.9	5.4	2.5	0.3	0.0	0.0	0.0	0.0	0.0	0.1	0.5	3.8	18.5
Maximum Snow Depth (in.)	21	19	11	5	0	0	0	0	0	2	2	14	21
Days With ≥ 1.0" Snow Depth	11	10	3	0	0	0	0	0	0	0	1	6	31

The period of record for all cooperative weather station data is 1980 – 2009. See User Guide for detailed explanation of data.

Indiana Weather Station Rankings

Annual Extreme Maximum Temperature

Highest			Lowest		
Rank	Station Name	°F	Rank	Station Name	°F
1	Fort Wayne Baer Field	106	1	Richmond Water Works	100
2	Delphi 3 S	105	1	Valparaiso Waterworks	***100***
2	Frankfort Disposal Plant	105	3	Angola	101
2	Huntington	105	3	Freelandville	101
5	Berne	104	3	Greensburg	101
5	Bloomington Indiana Univ	104	3	La Porte	101
5	English 4 S	***104***	3	Martinsville 2 SW	101
5	Evansville Dress Regional Arpt	104	3	Winchester Airport 3E	101
5	Indianapolis SE Side	104	9	Crawfordsville 5 S	102
5	Kokomo 3 WSW	104	9	Dubois S Ind Forage Frm	102
5	Lafayette 8 S	104	9	Elwood Wastewater Plant	102
5	Lowell	104	9	Evansville Museum	***102***
5	Madison Sewage Plant	104	9	Farmland 5 NNW	102
5	Mount Vernon	104	9	Goshen College	102
5	Rockville	104	9	Muncie Ball State Univ	***102***
5	South Bend Michiana Regional	104	9	Oolitic Purdue Exp Farm	102
5	Whitestown	104	9	Shelbyville Sewage Plant	***102***
18	Anderson Sewage Plant	103	9	Terre Haute Indiana State	***102***
18	Brookville	103	9	Warsaw	102
18	Columbia City	103	20	Anderson Sewage Plant	103
18	Columbus	103	20	Brookville	103
18	Greenfield	103	20	Columbia City	103
18	Indianapolis Int'l Arpt	103	20	Columbus	103
18	North Vernon 1 NW	103	20	Greenfield	103
18	Tell City	103	20	Indianapolis Int'l Arpt	103

Annual Mean Maximum Temperature

Highest			Lowest		
Rank	Station Name	°F	Rank	Station Name	°F
1	Evansville Museum	***68.8***	1	Angola	57.5
2	English 4 S	***67.1***	2	La Porte	58.4
3	Evansville Dress Regional Arpt	66.7	3	Columbia City	59.0
4	Tell City	66.5	4	South Bend Michiana Regional	59.1
5	Mount Vernon	66.2	5	Warsaw	***59.4***
6	Madison Sewage Plant	65.6	6	Valparaiso Waterworks	***59.5***
7	North Vernon 1 NW	***65.3***	7	Goshen College	59.7
8	Dubois S Ind Forage Frm	65.0	8	Lowell	59.9
9	Terre Haute Indiana State	***64.8***	8	Winchester Airport 3E	59.9
10	Brookville	64.2	10	Fort Wayne Baer Field	60.0
10	Rockville	64.2	11	Kokomo 3 WSW	60.2
12	Oolitic Purdue Exp Farm	63.9	12	Berne	60.7
13	Columbus	63.5	13	Farmland 5 NNW	60.8
13	Freelandville	63.5	13	Muncie Ball State Univ	***60.8***
15	Bloomington Indiana Univ	63.4	15	Frankfort Disposal Plant	60.9
16	Whitestown	62.8	15	Huntington	60.9
17	Martinsville 2 SW	62.7	17	Anderson Sewage Plant	61.0
17	Shelbyville Sewage Plant	***62.7***	18	Lafayette 8 S	61.1
19	Indianapolis Int'l Arpt	62.6	19	Elwood Wastewater Plant	61.2
20	Delphi 3 S	62.4	20	Crawfordsville 5 S	***61.6***
21	Greensburg	62.3	20	Indianapolis SE Side	61.6
22	Richmond Water Works	61.8	22	Greenfield	61.7
23	Greenfield	61.7	23	Richmond Water Works	61.8
24	Crawfordsville 5 S	***61.6***	24	Greensburg	62.3
24	Indianapolis SE Side	61.6	25	Delphi 3 S	62.4

Rankings include 25 highest/lowest stations. If state has less than 25 stations, all stations are included. The period of record is 1980–2009. See User Guide for detailed explanation of data.

Annual Mean Temperature

Highest			Lowest		
Rank	Station Name	°F	Rank	Station Name	°F
1	Evansville Museum	***58.9***	1	Angola	47.7
2	Tell City	56.8	2	Columbia City	49.1
3	Evansville Dress Regional Arpt	56.5	3	Lowell	49.6
4	Mount Vernon	56.4	4	Kokomo 3 WSW	49.9
5	Madison Sewage Plant	55.4	5	Warsaw	***50.0***
6	English 4 S	***54.8***	6	La Porte	50.1
6	North Vernon 1 NW	***54.8***	6	South Bend Michiana Regional	50.1
8	Dubois S Ind Forage Frm	54.5	8	Valparaiso Waterworks	***50.2***
9	Freelandville	53.9	9	Crawfordsville 5 S	***50.4***
9	Rockville	53.9	9	Farmland 5 NNW	50.4
11	Terre Haute Indiana State	***53.7***	9	Goshen College	50.4
12	Bloomington Indiana Univ	53.6	9	Huntington	50.4
13	Columbus	53.4	13	Fort Wayne Baer Field	50.5
14	Indianapolis Int'l Arpt	53.1	13	Winchester Airport 3E	50.5
15	Greensburg	53.0	15	Elwood Wastewater Plant	50.6
16	Oolitic Purdue Exp Farm	52.9	16	Muncie Ball State Univ	***50.9***
17	Brookville	52.7	17	Lafayette 8 S	51.2
18	Shelbyville Sewage Plant	***52.5***	18	Frankfort Disposal Plant	51.3
18	Whitestown	52.5	19	Berne	51.5
20	Delphi 3 S	52.2	20	Richmond Water Works	51.6
21	Indianapolis SE Side	52.0	21	Anderson Sewage Plant	51.8
22	Greenfield	51.9	21	Martinsville 2 SW	51.8
23	Anderson Sewage Plant	51.8	23	Greenfield	51.9
23	Martinsville 2 SW	51.8	24	Indianapolis SE Side	52.0
25	Richmond Water Works	51.6	25	Delphi 3 S	52.2

Annual Mean Minimum Temperature

Highest			Lowest		
Rank	Station Name	°F	Rank	Station Name	°F
1	Evansville Museum	***48.9***	1	Angola	37.8
2	Tell City	46.9	2	Columbia City	39.1
3	Mount Vernon	46.6	3	Crawfordsville 5 S	***39.2***
4	Evansville Dress Regional Arpt	46.2	3	Lowell	39.2
5	Madison Sewage Plant	45.2	5	Kokomo 3 WSW	39.7
6	Freelandville	44.4	6	Huntington	39.8
7	North Vernon 1 NW	***44.3***	7	Farmland 5 NNW	39.9
8	Dubois S Ind Forage Frm	43.9	8	Elwood Wastewater Plant	40.0
9	Bloomington Indiana Univ	43.8	9	Warsaw	40.6
10	Greensburg	43.7	10	Fort Wayne Baer Field	40.9
10	Indianapolis Int'l Arpt	43.7	10	Martinsville 2 SW	40.9
12	Rockville	43.5	10	Muncie Ball State Univ	***40.9***
13	Columbus	43.2	10	Valparaiso Waterworks	***40.9***
14	Anderson Sewage Plant	42.6	14	Goshen College	41.0
14	Terre Haute Indiana State	***42.6***	14	South Bend Michiana Regional	41.0
16	Indianapolis SE Side	42.4	16	Brookville	41.1
16	Shelbyville Sewage Plant	***42.4***	16	Lafayette 8 S	41.1
18	English 4 S	***42.3***	18	Winchester Airport 3E	41.2
19	Berne	42.1	19	Richmond Water Works	41.3
19	Greenfield	42.1	20	Frankfort Disposal Plant	41.6
19	Whitestown	42.1	21	La Porte	41.7
22	Delphi 3 S	41.9	22	Oolitic Purdue Exp Farm	41.8
23	Oolitic Purdue Exp Farm	41.8	23	Delphi 3 S	41.9
24	La Porte	41.7	24	Berne	42.1
25	Frankfort Disposal Plant	41.6	24	Greenfield	42.1

Rankings include 25 highest/lowest stations. If state has less than 25 stations, all stations are included. The period of record is 1980–2009. See User Guide for detailed explanation of data.

Annual Extreme Minimum Temperature

Highest			Lowest		
Rank	Station Name	°F	Rank	Station Name	°F
1	Mount Vernon	-16	1	Martinsville 2 SW	-35
2	Evansville Museum	***-17***	2	Brookville	-31
2	Tell City	-17	2	Crawfordsville 5 S	-31
4	Evansville Dress Regional Arpt	-18	4	English 4 S	***-30***
4	Madison Sewage Plant	-18	5	Greenfield	-29
6	Bloomington Indiana Univ	-21	5	Muncie Ball State Univ	***-29***
6	South Bend Michiana Regional	-21	5	Oolitic Purdue Exp Farm	-29
8	Fort Wayne Baer Field	-22	8	Huntington	-28
8	Indianapolis SE Side	-22	9	Angola	-27
8	North Vernon 1 NW	-22	9	Indianapolis Int'l Arpt	-27
8	Terre Haute Indiana State	***-22***	9	Richmond Water Works	-27
12	Freelandville	-23	9	Whitestown	-27
12	La Porte	-23	13	Columbus	-26
14	Anderson Sewage Plant	-24	13	Frankfort Disposal Plant	-26
14	Berne	-24	13	Kokomo 3 WSW	-26
14	Columbia City	-24	13	Winchester Airport 3E	-26
14	Delphi 3 S	-24	17	Dubois S Ind Forage Frm	-25
14	Elwood Wastewater Plant	-24	17	Farmland 5 NNW	-25
14	Goshen College	-24	17	Lafayette 8 S	-25
14	Greensburg	-24	17	Lowell	-25
21	Dubois S Ind Forage Frm	-25	17	Rockville	-25
21	Farmland 5 NNW	-25	17	Shelbyville Sewage Plant	***-25***
21	Lafayette 8 S	-25	17	Valparaiso Waterworks	***-25***
21	Lowell	-25	17	Warsaw	-25
21	Rockville	-25	25	Anderson Sewage Plant	-24

July Mean Maximum Temperature

Highest			Lowest		
Rank	Station Name	°F	Rank	Station Name	°F
1	Evansville Museum	***90.0***	1	Angola	81.8
2	Evansville Dress Regional Arpt	88.5	2	La Porte	82.3
3	English 4 S	88.0	3	Columbia City	82.7
3	Mount Vernon	88.0	4	Warsaw	82.9
3	Terre Haute Indiana State	***88.0***	4	Winchester Airport 3E	82.9
6	Tell City	87.5	6	Valparaiso Waterworks	***83.1***
7	Rockville	86.9	7	South Bend Michiana Regional	83.3
8	Brookville	86.8	8	Goshen College	83.6
9	Madison Sewage Plant	86.7	9	Anderson Sewage Plant	83.8
10	Dubois S Ind Forage Frm	86.4	9	Kokomo 3 WSW	83.8
11	North Vernon 1 NW	***86.3***	11	Frankfort Disposal Plant	83.9
12	Freelandville	85.7	12	Farmland 5 NNW	84.0
12	Whitestown	85.7	12	Lowell	84.0
14	Oolitic Purdue Exp Farm	85.5	14	Fort Wayne Baer Field	84.3
15	Bloomington Indiana Univ	85.4	14	Indianapolis SE Side	84.3
15	Columbus	85.4	14	Lafayette 8 S	84.3
15	Delphi 3 S	85.4	17	Crawfordsville 5 S	84.4
18	Huntington	85.3	18	Richmond Water Works	84.5
18	Indianapolis Int'l Arpt	85.3	19	Berne	84.6
18	Shelbyville Sewage Plant	85.3	20	Elwood Wastewater Plant	84.7
21	Greensburg	84.8	20	Greenfield	84.7
21	Muncie Ball State Univ	***84.8***	20	Martinsville 2 SW	84.7
23	Elwood Wastewater Plant	84.7	23	Greensburg	84.8
23	Greenfield	84.7	23	Muncie Ball State Univ	***84.8***
23	Martinsville 2 SW	84.7	25	Huntington	85.3

Rankings include 25 highest/lowest stations. If state has less than 25 stations, all stations are included. The period of record is 1980–2009. See User Guide for detailed explanation of data.

January Mean Minimum Temperature

Highest			Lowest		
Rank	Station Name	°F	Rank	Station Name	°F
1	Evansville Museum	***27.2***	1	Angola	14.7
2	Tell City	26.3	2	Lowell	15.0
3	Evansville Dress Regional Arpt	24.9	3	Columbia City	16.1
4	Madison Sewage Plant	24.5	4	Kokomo 3 WSW	16.4
5	Mount Vernon	24.4	5	Elwood Wastewater Plant	16.8
6	North Vernon 1 NW	***23.6***	6	Crawfordsville 5 S	***16.9***
7	English 4 S	22.3	7	Valparaiso Waterworks	17.1
8	Freelandville	22.2	8	Farmland 5 NNW	17.3
9	Dubois S Ind Forage Frm	21.7	8	Huntington	17.3
10	Bloomington Indiana Univ	21.2	8	Lafayette 8 S	17.3
11	Columbus	21.0	8	Muncie Ball State Univ	***17.3***
12	Greensburg	20.9	12	Warsaw	17.5
13	Indianapolis Int'l Arpt	20.5	13	La Porte	17.8
13	Rockville	20.5	13	Winchester Airport 3E	17.8
15	Oolitic Purdue Exp Farm	20.1	15	Fort Wayne Baer Field	17.9
16	Anderson Sewage Plant	19.8	16	South Bend Michiana Regional	18.0
16	Brookville	19.8	17	Goshen College	18.2
18	Shelbyville Sewage Plant	19.7	18	Greenfield	18.8
19	Berne	19.4	19	Frankfort Disposal Plant	19.0
19	Indianapolis SE Side	19.4	19	Whitestown	19.0
21	Delphi 3 S	19.3	21	Martinsville 2 SW	19.1
22	Richmond Water Works	19.2	22	Richmond Water Works	19.2
22	Terre Haute Indiana State	***19.2***	22	Terre Haute Indiana State	***19.2***
24	Martinsville 2 SW	19.1	24	Delphi 3 S	19.3
25	Frankfort Disposal Plant	19.0	25	Berne	19.4

Number of Days Annually Maximum Temperature ≥ 90°F

Highest			Lowest		
Rank	Station Name	Days	Rank	Station Name	Days
1	Evansville Museum	***56***	1	Angola	7
2	Evansville Dress Regional Arpt	41	2	Winchester Airport 3E	9
3	Mount Vernon	38	3	Columbia City	10
4	Terre Haute Indiana State	***35***	3	Warsaw	10
5	English 4 S	***33***	5	La Porte	11
5	Tell City	33	5	Valparaiso Waterworks	***11***
7	Brookville	28	7	Goshen College	13
8	Dubois S Ind Forage Frm	27	8	Anderson Sewage Plant	15
8	Rockville	27	8	Frankfort Disposal Plant	15
10	Madison Sewage Plant	26	8	Fort Wayne Baer Field	15
11	Whitestown	22	8	Indianapolis SE Side	15
12	Huntington	21	8	South Bend Michiana Regional	15
13	Columbus	20	13	Berne	16
13	Delphi 3 S	20	13	Crawfordsville 5 S	16
13	North Vernon 1 NW	20	13	Kokomo 3 WSW	16
16	Bloomington Indiana Univ	19	13	Martinsville 2 SW	16
16	Freelandville	19	13	Richmond Water Works	16
16	Oolitic Purdue Exp Farm	19	18	Elwood Wastewater Plant	17
19	Indianapolis Int'l Arpt	18	18	Farmland 5 NNW	17
19	Lafayette 8 S	18	18	Greenfield	17
19	Lowell	18	18	Greensburg	17
22	Elwood Wastewater Plant	17	18	Muncie Ball State Univ	***17***
22	Farmland 5 NNW	17	18	Shelbyville Sewage Plant	***17***
22	Greenfield	17	24	Indianapolis Int'l Arpt	18
22	Greensburg	17	24	Lafayette 8 S	18

Rankings include 25 highest/lowest stations. If state has less than 25 stations, all stations are included. The period of record is 1980–2009. See User Guide for detailed explanation of data.

Number of Days Annually Maximum Temperature ≤ 32°F

Highest			Lowest		
Rank	Station Name	Days	Rank	Station Name	Days
1	Angola	52	1	Evansville Museum	***11***
2	La Porte	46	2	English 4 S	***14***
3	South Bend Michiana Regional	45	3	Madison Sewage Plant	15
4	Columbia City	44	3	Tell City	15
4	Kokomo 3 WSW	44	5	Evansville Dress Regional Arpt	17
6	Goshen College	42	6	Mount Vernon	18
6	Lowell	42	6	North Vernon 1 NW	18
6	Valparaiso Waterworks	***42***	8	Dubois S Ind Forage Frm	20
6	Warsaw	42	9	Terre Haute Indiana State	***24***
6	Winchester Airport 3E	42	10	Brookville	25
11	Fort Wayne Baer Field	41	10	Columbus	25
12	Farmland 5 NNW	39	10	Oolitic Purdue Exp Farm	25
13	Berne	38	13	Rockville	26
13	Huntington	38	14	Bloomington Indiana Univ	28
13	Lafayette 8 S	38	14	Freelandville	28
13	Muncie Ball State Univ	***38***	16	Martinsville 2 SW	29
17	Frankfort Disposal Plant	37	16	Shelbyville Sewage Plant	***29***
18	Anderson Sewage Plant	36	18	Indianapolis Int'l Arpt	30
18	Crawfordsville 5 S	36	19	Greensburg	31
18	Elwood Wastewater Plant	36	20	Delphi 3 S	32
21	Greenfield	34	20	Richmond Water Works	32
21	Indianapolis SE Side	34	22	Whitestown	33
23	Whitestown	33	23	Greenfield	34
24	Delphi 3 S	32	23	Indianapolis SE Side	34
24	Richmond Water Works	32	25	Anderson Sewage Plant	36

Number of Days Annually Minimum Temperature ≤ 32°F

Highest			Lowest		
Rank	Station Name	Days	Rank	Station Name	Days
1	Angola	150	1	Evansville Museum	***72***
2	Lowell	137	2	Tell City	83
3	Crawfordsville 5 S	136	3	Mount Vernon	88
4	Columbia City	135	4	Evansville Dress Regional Arpt	93
4	Kokomo 3 WSW	135	5	Madison Sewage Plant	94
6	Farmland 5 NNW	134	6	North Vernon 1 NW	98
6	Huntington	134	7	Freelandville	104
8	Elwood Wastewater Plant	131	8	Indianapolis Int'l Arpt	107
9	Muncie Ball State Univ	***129***	9	Dubois S Ind Forage Frm	108
10	Martinsville 2 SW	127	10	Bloomington Indiana Univ	109
10	Warsaw	127	10	Rockville	109
12	Brookville	126	12	Greensburg	110
12	Winchester Airport 3E	126	13	Columbus	112
14	Lafayette 8 S	125	14	Anderson Sewage Plant	114
14	South Bend Michiana Regional	125	14	English 4 S	***114***
16	Fort Wayne Baer Field	124	16	Terre Haute Indiana State	***115***
16	Valparaiso Waterworks	***124***	17	Delphi 3 S	117
18	Goshen College	123	17	Whitestown	117
19	Oolitic Purdue Exp Farm	121	19	Berne	118
20	La Porte	120	20	Frankfort Disposal Plant	119
20	Richmond Water Works	120	20	Greenfield	119
22	Frankfort Disposal Plant	119	20	Indianapolis SE Side	119
22	Greenfield	119	20	Shelbyville Sewage Plant	***119***
22	Indianapolis SE Side	119	24	La Porte	120
22	Shelbyville Sewage Plant	***119***	24	Richmond Water Works	120

Rankings include 25 highest/lowest stations. If state has less than 25 stations, all stations are included. The period of record is 1980–2009. See User Guide for detailed explanation of data.

Number of Days Annually Minimum Temperature ≤ 0°F

Highest			Lowest		
Rank	Station Name	Days	Rank	Station Name	Days
1	Angola	11	1	Evansville Museum	***1***
1	Lowell	11	1	Tell City	1
3	Crawfordsville 5 S	10	3	Evansville Dress Regional Arpt	2
3	Kokomo 3 WSW	10	3	Madison Sewage Plant	2
5	Columbia City	9	5	Mount Vernon	3
5	Lafayette 8 S	9	5	North Vernon 1 NW	3
7	Elwood Wastewater Plant	8	7	Bloomington Indiana Univ	4
7	Farmland 5 NNW	8	7	Columbus	4
7	Fort Wayne Baer Field	8	7	Dubois S Ind Forage Frm	4
7	Huntington	8	7	English 4 S	***4***
7	Muncie Ball State Univ	***8***	7	Freelandville	4
7	Valparaiso Waterworks	***8***	7	Greensburg	4
7	Winchester Airport 3E	8	7	Indianapolis Int'l Arpt	4
14	Delphi 3 S	7	14	Anderson Sewage Plant	5
14	Frankfort Disposal Plant	7	14	Terre Haute Indiana State	***5***
14	Goshen College	7	16	Berne	6
14	Greenfield	7	16	Brookville	6
14	La Porte	7	16	Indianapolis SE Side	6
14	Martinsville 2 SW	7	16	Oolitic Purdue Exp Farm	6
14	South Bend Michiana Regional	7	16	Richmond Water Works	6
14	Warsaw	7	16	Rockville	6
14	Whitestown	7	16	Shelbyville Sewage Plant	***6***
23	Berne	6	23	Delphi 3 S	7
23	Brookville	6	23	Frankfort Disposal Plant	7
23	Indianapolis SE Side	6	23	Goshen College	7

Number of Annual Heating Degree Days

Highest			Lowest		
Rank	Station Name	Num.	Rank	Station Name	Num.
1	Angola	6,822	1	Evansville Museum	***3,925***
2	Columbia City	6,396	2	Tell City	4,332
3	Lowell	6,339	3	Evansville Dress Regional Arpt	4,455
4	Kokomo 3 WSW	6,210	4	Mount Vernon	4,490
5	La Porte	6,168	5	Madison Sewage Plant	4,610
6	South Bend Michiana Regional	6,165	6	English 4 S	***4,733***
7	Warsaw	***6,142***	7	North Vernon 1 NW	***4,753***
8	Huntington	6,109	8	Dubois S Ind Forage Frm	4,922
9	Valparaiso Waterworks	***6,094***	9	Freelandville	5,111
10	Farmland 5 NNW	6,058	10	Rockville	5,122
11	Goshen College	6,049	11	Bloomington Indiana Univ	5,173
12	Fort Wayne Baer Field	6,026	12	Columbus	5,226
13	Crawfordsville 5 S	***6,021***	12	Terre Haute Indiana State	***5,226***
14	Elwood Wastewater Plant	6,006	14	Oolitic Purdue Exp Farm	5,315
15	Winchester Airport 3E	6,003	15	Indianapolis Int'l Arpt	5,322
16	Muncie Ball State Univ	***5,965***	16	Greensburg	5,352
17	Lafayette 8 S	5,894	17	Brookville	5,400
18	Berne	5,810	18	Shelbyville Sewage Plant	***5,462***
19	Frankfort Disposal Plant	5,789	19	Whitestown	5,494
20	Greenfield	5,678	20	Delphi 3 S	5,558
21	Richmond Water Works	5,657	21	Martinsville 2 SW	5,608
22	Anderson Sewage Plant	5,638	22	Indianapolis SE Side	5,632
23	Indianapolis SE Side	5,632	23	Anderson Sewage Plant	5,638
24	Martinsville 2 SW	5,608	24	Richmond Water Works	5,657
25	Delphi 3 S	5,558	25	Greenfield	5,678

Rankings include 25 highest/lowest stations. If state has less than 25 stations, all stations are included. The period of record is 1980–2009. See User Guide for detailed explanation of data.

Number of Annual Cooling Degree Days

Highest Rank	Highest Station Name	Num.	Lowest Rank	Lowest Station Name	Num.
1	Evansville Museum	***1,800***	1	Angola	610
2	Mount Vernon	1,471	2	Columbia City	707
3	Evansville Dress Regional Arpt	1,460	3	Warsaw	***784***
4	Tell City	1,437	4	Valparaiso Waterworks	***801***
5	Terre Haute Indiana State	***1,232***	5	Crawfordsville 5 S	***805***
6	Madison Sewage Plant	1,230	6	Lowell	815
7	Dubois S Ind Forage Frm	1,200	7	Goshen College	818
8	Freelandville	1,182	8	Kokomo 3 WSW	822
9	Rockville	1,171	9	Farmland 5 NNW	829
10	North Vernon 1 NW	***1,142***	9	South Bend Michiana Regional	829
11	Bloomington Indiana Univ	1,134	11	La Porte	839
12	Indianapolis Int'l Arpt	1,101	12	Winchester Airport 3E	842
13	English 4 S	***1,095***	13	Fort Wayne Baer Field	848
14	Greensburg	1,093	14	Elwood Wastewater Plant	865
15	Columbus	1,087	15	Richmond Water Works	876
16	Shelbyville Sewage Plant	***1,023***	16	Huntington	880
17	Whitestown	1,022	17	Frankfort Disposal Plant	888
18	Brookville	1,020	18	Martinsville 2 SW	899
19	Greenfield	1,011	19	Muncie Ball State Univ	***921***
20	Oolitic Purdue Exp Farm	1,000	20	Anderson Sewage Plant	939
21	Indianapolis SE Side	998	21	Lafayette 8 S	952
22	Delphi 3 S	979	22	Berne	966
23	Berne	966	23	Delphi 3 S	979
24	Lafayette 8 S	952	24	Indianapolis SE Side	998
25	Anderson Sewage Plant	939	25	Oolitic Purdue Exp Farm	1,000

Annual Precipitation

Highest Rank	Highest Station Name	Inches	Lowest Rank	Lowest Station Name	Inches
1	English 4 S	***48.65***	1	South Bend Michiana Regional	38.33
2	Dubois S Ind Forage Frm	48.06	2	Fort Wayne Baer Field	38.35
3	Tell City	47.84	3	Warsaw	38.38
4	Madison Sewage Plant	47.54	4	Huntington	38.43
5	Bloomington Indiana Univ	47.48	5	Lafayette 8 S	38.44
6	Rockville	46.88	6	Delphi 3 S	38.52
7	Evansville Museum	***46.29***	7	Winchester Airport 3E	38.90
8	Oolitic Purdue Exp Farm	46.01	8	Angola	39.01
9	Mount Vernon	45.92	9	Goshen College	39.03
10	Greenfield	45.90	10	Berne	39.06
11	Freelandville	45.72	11	Farmland 5 NNW	39.21
12	North Vernon 1 NW	45.61	12	Lowell	39.45
13	Evansville Dress Regional Arpt	45.34	13	Columbia City	39.47
14	Greensburg	44.74	14	Muncie Ball State Univ	***39.49***
15	Martinsville 2 SW	44.69	15	Valparaiso Waterworks	***39.92***
16	Terre Haute Indiana State	***44.24***	16	Frankfort Disposal Plant	40.60
17	Columbus	44.02	17	Elwood Wastewater Plant	40.62
18	Kokomo 3 WSW	43.12	18	Richmond Water Works	40.70
19	Crawfordsville 5 S	***43.01***	19	Anderson Sewage Plant	41.09
20	Brookville	42.86	20	Shelbyville Sewage Plant	41.15
21	La Porte	42.56	21	Indianapolis SE Side	42.11
22	Whitestown	42.51	22	Indianapolis Int'l Arpt	42.45
23	Indianapolis Int'l Arpt	42.45	23	Whitestown	42.51
24	Indianapolis SE Side	42.11	24	La Porte	42.56
25	Shelbyville Sewage Plant	41.15	25	Brookville	42.86

Rankings include 25 highest/lowest stations. If state has less than 25 stations, all stations are included. The period of record is 1980–2009. See User Guide for detailed explanation of data.

Annual Extreme Maximum Daily Precipitation

Highest

Rank	Station Name	Inches
1	Kokomo 3 WSW	8.82
2	Rockville	8.05
3	Martinsville 2 SW	8.02
4	Mount Vernon	7.40
5	Valparaiso Waterworks	***7.34***
6	Indianapolis Int'l Arpt	7.20
7	La Porte	6.73
8	Goshen College	6.65
9	South Bend Michiana Regional	6.58
10	Winchester Airport 3E	***6.45***
11	Evansville Dress Regional Arpt	6.40
12	Columbus	6.37
13	Evansville Museum	***5.74***
14	Dubois S Ind Forage Frm	5.66
15	Huntington	5.53
16	English 4 S	***5.50***
17	Whitestown	5.46
18	Madison Sewage Plant	5.16
19	Lowell	5.14
20	Elwood Wastewater Plant	5.01
21	Greensburg	5.00
22	Warsaw	4.87
23	Oolitic Purdue Exp Farm	4.80
24	Delphi 3 S	4.78
25	Tell City	4.75

Lowest

Rank	Station Name	Inches
1	Freelandville	3.81
2	Brookville	4.03
3	Angola	4.10
4	Bloomington Indiana Univ	4.15
5	Indianapolis SE Side	4.16
6	Berne	4.20
7	Anderson Sewage Plant	4.21
8	Frankfort Disposal Plant	4.30
9	Crawfordsville 5 S	***4.35***
10	Farmland 5 NNW	4.40
10	Fort Wayne Baer Field	4.40
12	Shelbyville Sewage Plant	***4.43***
13	Columbia City	4.48
14	Lafayette 8 S	4.51
15	Richmond Water Works	4.53
16	North Vernon 1 NW	***4.55***
17	Greenfield	4.71
18	Tell City	4.75
19	Delphi 3 S	4.78
20	Oolitic Purdue Exp Farm	4.80
21	Warsaw	4.87
22	Greensburg	5.00
23	Elwood Wastewater Plant	5.01
24	Lowell	5.14
25	Madison Sewage Plant	5.16

Number of Days Annually With ≥ 0.1 Inches of Precipitation

Highest

Rank	Station Name	Days
1	La Porte	87
2	Kokomo 3 WSW	84
2	Madison Sewage Plant	84
4	Greenfield	82
4	Greensburg	82
4	Rockville	82
7	English 4 S	***81***
8	Brookville	80
8	Whitestown	80
10	Angola	79
10	Bloomington Indiana Univ	79
10	Frankfort Disposal Plant	79
10	Oolitic Purdue Exp Farm	79
10	South Bend Michiana Regional	79
15	Anderson Sewage Plant	78
15	Berne	78
15	Columbia City	78
15	Crawfordsville 5 S	***78***
15	Dubois S Ind Forage Frm	78
15	Freelandville	78
15	Indianapolis Int'l Arpt	78
22	Fort Wayne Baer Field	77
22	Goshen College	77
22	Huntington	77
22	Richmond Water Works	77

Lowest

Rank	Station Name	Days
1	North Vernon 1 NW	71
1	Terre Haute Indiana State	***71***
3	Delphi 3 S	72
3	Lafayette 8 S	72
5	Evansville Museum	***73***
5	Mount Vernon	73
7	Evansville Dress Regional Arpt	74
7	Lowell	74
7	Winchester Airport 3E	74
10	Farmland 5 NNW	75
10	Indianapolis SE Side	75
10	Muncie Ball State Univ	***75***
13	Columbus	76
13	Elwood Wastewater Plant	76
13	Martinsville 2 SW	76
13	Shelbyville Sewage Plant	***76***
13	Warsaw	76
18	Fort Wayne Baer Field	77
18	Goshen College	77
18	Huntington	77
18	Richmond Water Works	77
18	Tell City	77
18	Valparaiso Waterworks	***77***
24	Anderson Sewage Plant	78
24	Berne	78

Rankings include 25 highest/lowest stations. If state has less than 25 stations, all stations are included. The period of record is 1980–2009. See User Guide for detailed explanation of data.

Number of Days Annually With ≥ 0.5 Inches of Precipitation

Rank	Station Name (Highest)	Days	Rank	Station Name (Lowest)	Days
1	Rockville	35	1	South Bend Michiana Regional	23
2	Dubois S Ind Forage Frm	34	2	Goshen College	24
3	Columbus	33	2	Lowell	24
3	Madison Sewage Plant	33	4	Huntington	25
5	Bloomington Indiana Univ	32	4	Lafayette 8 S	25
5	English 4 S	***32***	4	Valparaiso Waterworks	***25***
5	Evansville Dress Regional Arpt	32	4	Warsaw	25
5	Freelandville	32	4	Winchester Airport 3E	25
5	Greenfield	32	9	Angola	26
5	Mount Vernon	32	9	Berne	26
5	Oolitic Purdue Exp Farm	32	9	Columbia City	26
5	Tell City	32	9	Farmland 5 NNW	26
13	Greensburg	31	9	Frankfort Disposal Plant	26
13	Martinsville 2 SW	31	9	Fort Wayne Baer Field	26
15	Anderson Sewage Plant	30	9	Muncie Ball State Univ	***26***
15	Crawfordsville 5 S	***30***	9	Richmond Water Works	26
15	North Vernon 1 NW	30	17	Delphi 3 S	27
15	Shelbyville Sewage Plant	***30***	17	Elwood Wastewater Plant	27
19	Brookville	29	17	La Porte	27
19	Evansville Museum	***29***	20	Indianapolis Int'l Arpt	28
19	Indianapolis SE Side	29	20	Kokomo 3 WSW	28
19	Whitestown	29	20	Terre Haute Indiana State	***28***
23	Indianapolis Int'l Arpt	28	23	Brookville	29
23	Kokomo 3 WSW	28	23	Evansville Museum	***29***
23	Terre Haute Indiana State	***28***	23	Indianapolis SE Side	29

Number of Days Annually With ≥ 1.0 Inches of Precipitation

Rank	Station Name (Highest)	Days	Rank	Station Name (Lowest)	Days
1	Madison Sewage Plant	14	1	Angola	7
1	Rockville	14	1	Lafayette 8 S	7
3	Bloomington Indiana Univ	13	3	Berne	8
3	Dubois S Ind Forage Frm	13	3	Farmland 5 NNW	8
3	English 4 S	***13***	3	Fort Wayne Baer Field	8
3	Freelandville	13	3	Goshen College	8
3	Mount Vernon	13	3	Huntington	8
3	Tell City	13	3	Muncie Ball State Univ	***8***
9	Evansville Dress Regional Arpt	12	3	South Bend Michiana Regional	8
9	Greenfield	12	3	Warsaw	8
9	Oolitic Purdue Exp Farm	12	11	Columbia City	9
9	Terre Haute Indiana State	***12***	11	Crawfordsville 5 S	***9***
13	Brookville	11	11	Elwood Wastewater Plant	9
13	Columbus	11	11	Frankfort Disposal Plant	9
13	Evansville Museum	***11***	11	Lowell	9
13	Greensburg	11	11	Valparaiso Waterworks	***9***
13	Indianapolis SE Side	11	11	Winchester Airport 3E	9
13	Martinsville 2 SW	11	18	Anderson Sewage Plant	10
13	North Vernon 1 NW	11	18	Delphi 3 S	10
13	Richmond Water Works	11	18	Indianapolis Int'l Arpt	10
13	Shelbyville Sewage Plant	11	18	Kokomo 3 WSW	10
22	Anderson Sewage Plant	10	18	La Porte	10
22	Delphi 3 S	10	18	Whitestown	10
22	Indianapolis Int'l Arpt	10	24	Brookville	11
22	Kokomo 3 WSW	10	24	Columbus	11

Rankings include 25 highest/lowest stations. If state has less than 25 stations, all stations are included. The period of record is 1980–2009. See User Guide for detailed explanation of data.

Annual Snowfall

Highest			Lowest		
Rank	**Station Name**	**Inches**	**Rank**	**Station Name**	**Inches**
1	South Bend Michiana Regional	67.3	1	Tell City	5.3
2	La Porte	62.2	2	Shelbyville Sewage Plant	***5.7***
3	Goshen College	40.3	3	Mount Vernon	8.8
4	Valparaiso Waterworks	***39.7***	4	Dubois S Ind Forage Frm	***9.1***
5	Kokomo 3 WSW	38.3	5	North Vernon 1 NW	***10.8***
6	Angola	36.4	6	Evansville Museum	***11.0***
7	Fort Wayne Baer Field	33.8	7	Evansville Dress Regional Arpt	***11.4***
8	Lowell	30.8	7	Terre Haute Indiana State	***11.4***
9	Huntington	29.3	9	Bloomington Indiana Univ	***12.9***
10	Berne	28.2	10	Madison Sewage Plant	13.1
11	Columbia City	27.5	11	Indianapolis SE Side	***13.4***
12	Indianapolis Int'l Arpt	25.5	12	Rockville	13.6
13	Muncie Ball State Univ	***24.0***	13	Freelandville	13.9
14	Whitestown	23.9	14	Brookville	***14.2***
15	Frankfort Disposal Plant	22.6	15	Columbus	14.4
16	Farmland 5 NNW	22.4	16	Oolitic Purdue Exp Farm	14.9
17	Lafayette 8 S	21.3	17	Greenfield	15.7
18	Delphi 3 S	18.6	17	Richmond Water Works	15.7
19	Winchester Airport 3E	18.5	19	Martinsville 2 SW	16.0
20	Anderson Sewage Plant	17.9	20	Greensburg	16.4
21	Greensburg	16.4	21	Anderson Sewage Plant	17.9
22	Martinsville 2 SW	16.0	22	Winchester Airport 3E	18.5
23	Greenfield	15.7	23	Delphi 3 S	18.6
23	Richmond Water Works	15.7	24	Lafayette 8 S	21.3
25	Oolitic Purdue Exp Farm	14.9	25	Farmland 5 NNW	22.4

Annual Maximum Snow Depth

Highest			Lowest		
Rank	**Station Name**	**Inches**	**Rank**	**Station Name**	**Inches**
1	Berne	25	1	Mount Vernon	9
2	Kokomo 3 WSW	24	2	Evansville Dress Regional Arpt	***12***
2	La Porte	24	2	Freelandville	***12***
2	Valparaiso Waterworks	***24***	4	Indianapolis Int'l Arpt	13
5	Angola	23	5	Bloomington Indiana Univ	***15***
5	South Bend Michiana Regional	23	5	Greenfield	15
7	English 4 S	***22***	5	Huntington	***15***
7	Evansville Museum	***22***	5	Indianapolis SE Side	15
7	Whitestown	22	9	Columbia City	16
10	Greensburg	21	9	Farmland 5 NNW	16
10	Richmond Water Works	21	9	Madison Sewage Plant	***16***
10	Tell City	21	9	Martinsville 2 SW	***16***
10	Winchester Airport 3E	21	9	Muncie Ball State Univ	***16***
14	Fort Wayne Baer Field	20	9	Oolitic Purdue Exp Farm	16
15	Columbus	***19***	15	Goshen College	17
15	Lafayette 8 S	19	16	Anderson Sewage Plant	***18***
17	Anderson Sewage Plant	***18***	16	Delphi 3 S	18
17	Delphi 3 S	18	16	Dubois S Ind Forage Frm	***18***
17	Dubois S Ind Forage Frm	***18***	16	Frankfort Disposal Plant	18
17	Frankfort Disposal Plant	18	16	Rockville	18
17	Rockville	18	21	Columbus	***19***
22	Goshen College	17	21	Lafayette 8 S	19
23	Columbia City	16	23	Fort Wayne Baer Field	20
23	Farmland 5 NNW	16	24	Greensburg	21
23	Madison Sewage Plant	***16***	24	Richmond Water Works	21

Rankings include 25 highest/lowest stations. If state has less than 25 stations, all stations are included. The period of record is 1980–2009. See User Guide for detailed explanation of data.

Number of Days Annually With ≥ 1.0 Inch Snow Depth

Highest			Lowest		
Rank	**Station Name**	**Days**	**Rank**	**Station Name**	**Days**
1	South Bend Michiana Regional	55	1	Tell City	4
2	Angola	53	2	Shelbyville Sewage Plant	***6***
2	La Porte	53	3	Mount Vernon	10
4	Valparaiso Waterworks	***49***	4	Dubois S Ind Forage Frm	***11***
5	Goshen College	43	4	Evansville Museum	***11***
6	Fort Wayne Baer Field	41	4	Madison Sewage Plant	***11***
7	Kokomo 3 WSW	39	4	North Vernon 1 NW	***11***
8	Columbia City	38	8	English 4 S	***12***
9	Berne	36	8	Evansville Dress Regional Arpt	***12***
10	Farmland 5 NNW	34	8	Martinsville 2 SW	***12***
11	Lafayette 8 S	31	11	Freelandville	***13***
11	Winchester Airport 3E	31	12	Bloomington Indiana Univ	***15***
13	Muncie Ball State Univ	***29***	12	Columbus	***15***
14	Frankfort Disposal Plant	28	14	Anderson Sewage Plant	***17***
14	Whitestown	28	14	Greensburg	17
16	Delphi 3 S	26	16	Brookville	***19***
16	Greenfield	26	16	Oolitic Purdue Exp Farm	19
16	Indianapolis Int'l Arpt	26	18	Richmond Water Works	20
19	Rockville	22	19	Huntington	***21***
20	Huntington	***21***	19	Indianapolis SE Side	21
20	Indianapolis SE Side	21	21	Rockville	22
22	Richmond Water Works	20	22	Delphi 3 S	26
23	Brookville	***19***	22	Greenfield	26
23	Oolitic Purdue Exp Farm	19	22	Indianapolis Int'l Arpt	26
25	Anderson Sewage Plant	***17***	25	Frankfort Disposal Plant	28

Climate

Rankings include 25 highest/lowest stations. If state has less than 25 stations, all stations are included. The period of record is 1980–2009. See User Guide for detailed explanation of data.

Comparative Statistics

This chapter compares the 100 most populated cities in Indiana by 68 data points, such as language, ancestry, employment, education, and crime.

Population 92

Physical Characteristics. 94

Race/Hispanic Origin 96

Average Household Size, Age, and Male/Female Ratio 98

Foreign Born, Language Spoken, Disabled Persons, and Veterans . . 100

Five Largest Ancestry Groups. 102

Marriage Status 104

Employment by Occupation. 106

Educational Attainment 108

Health Insurance. 110

Income and Poverty 112

Housing 114

Commute to Work 116

Crime 118

The Hoosier State

The Crossroads of America

Population

Place	2000 Census	2010 Census	Current Estimate[1]	Population Growth Since 2000 (%)
Anderson city *Madison Co.*	59,734	56,129	54,986	-7.9
Angola city *Steuben Co.*	7,344	8,612	8,636	17.5
Auburn city *DeKalb Co.*	12,074	12,731	13,004	7.7
Avon town *Hendricks Co.*	6,248	12,446	16,479	163.7
Bargersville town *Johnson Co.*	2,120	4,013	6,919	226.3
Bedford city *Lawrence Co.*	13,768	13,413	13,292	-3.4
Beech Grove city *Marion Co.*	14,880	14,192	14,943	0.4
Bloomington city *Monroe Co.*	69,291	80,405	83,636	20.7
Bluffton city *Wells Co.*	9,536	9,897	9,823	3.0
Brazil city *Clay Co.*	8,188	7,912	8,384	2.3
Brownsburg town *Hendricks Co.*	14,520	21,285	24,625	69.5
Carmel city *Hamilton Co.*	37,733	79,191	88,595	134.7
Cedar Lake town *Lake Co.*	9,279	11,560	12,024	29.5
Charlestown city *Clark Co.*	5,993	7,585	8,079	34.8
Chesterton town *Porter Co.*	10,488	13,068	14,052	33.9
Clarksville town *Clark Co.*	21,400	21,724	21,228	-0.8
Columbia City city *Whitley Co.*	7,077	8,750	9,057	27.9
Columbus city *Bartholomew Co.*	39,059	44,061	46,926	20.1
Connersville city *Fayette Co.*	15,411	13,481	13,022	-15.5
Crawfordsville city *Montgomery Co.*	15,243	15,915	16,075	5.4
Crown Point city *Lake Co.*	19,806	27,317	28,952	46.1
Danville town *Hendricks Co.*	6,418	9,001	9,598	49.5
Decatur city *Adams Co.*	9,528	9,405	9,502	-0.2
Dyer town *Lake Co.*	13,895	16,390	16,077	15.7
East Chicago city *Lake Co.*	32,414	29,698	28,728	-11.3
Elkhart city *Elkhart Co.*	51,874	50,949	52,662	1.5
Elwood city *Madison Co.*	9,737	8,614	8,458	-13.1
Evansville city *Vanderburgh Co.*	121,582	117,429	119,806	-1.4
Fishers city *Hamilton Co.*	37,835	76,794	87,557	131.4
Fort Wayne city *Allen Co.*	205,727	253,691	262,450	27.5
Frankfort city *Clinton Co.*	16,662	16,422	16,226	-2.6
Franklin city *Johnson Co.*	19,463	23,712	24,489	25.8
Garrett city *DeKalb Co.*	5,803	6,286	6,762	16.5
Gary city *Lake Co.*	102,746	80,294	77,416	-24.6
Goshen city *Elkhart Co.*	29,383	31,719	33,583	14.2
Granger CDP *Saint Joseph Co.*	28,284	30,465	30,717	8.6
Greencastle city *Putnam Co.*	9,880	10,326	10,426	5.5
Greenfield city *Hancock Co.*	14,600	20,602	21,565	47.7
Greensburg city *Decatur Co.*	10,260	11,492	12,056	17.5
Greenwood city *Johnson Co.*	36,037	49,791	55,459	53.8
Griffith town *Lake Co.*	17,334	16,893	16,468	-5.0
Hammond city *Lake Co.*	83,048	80,830	77,827	-6.2
Highland town *Lake Co.*	23,546	23,727	22,938	-2.5
Hobart city *Lake Co.*	25,363	29,059	28,573	12.6
Huntertown town *Allen Co.*	1,771	4,810	6,857	287.1
Huntington city *Huntington Co.*	17,450	17,391	17,214	-1.3
Indianapolis city *Marion Co.*	781,870	820,445	853,431	9.1
Jasper city *Dubois Co.*	12,100	15,038	15,716	29.8
Jeffersonville city *Clark Co.*	27,362	44,953	46,840	71.1
Kendallville city *Noble Co.*	9,616	9,862	9,592	-0.2

Place	2000 Census	2010 Census	Current Estimate[1]	Population Growth Since 2000 (%)
Kokomo city *Howard Co.*	46,113	45,468	57,941	25.6
La Porte city *LaPorte Co.*	21,621	22,053	21,825	0.9
Lafayette city *Tippecanoe Co.*	56,397	67,140	72,174	27.9
Lake Station city *Lake Co.*	13,948	12,572	12,157	-12.8
Lakes of the Four Seasons CDP *Lake Co.*	7,291	7,033	7,061	-3.1
Lawrence city *Marion Co.*	38,915	46,001	48,081	23.5
Lebanon city *Boone Co.*	14,222	15,792	15,710	10.4
Logansport city *Cass Co.*	19,684	18,396	18,169	-7.7
Lowell town *Lake Co.*	7,505	9,276	9,502	26.6
Madison city *Jefferson Co.*	12,004	11,967	11,920	-0.7
Marion city *Grant Co.*	31,320	29,948	28,490	-9.0
Martinsville city *Morgan Co.*	11,698	11,828	11,647	-0.4
Merrillville town *Lake Co.*	30,560	35,246	35,183	15.1
Michigan City city *LaPorte Co.*	32,900	31,479	31,352	-4.7
Mishawaka city *Saint Joseph Co.*	46,557	48,252	48,582	4.3
Mooresville town *Morgan Co.*	9,273	9,326	9,571	3.2
Muncie city *Delaware Co.*	67,430	70,085	69,237	2.6
Munster town *Lake Co.*	21,511	23,603	23,005	6.9
Nappanee city *Elkhart Co.*	6,710	6,648	6,927	3.2
New Albany city *Floyd Co.*	37,603	36,372	36,548	-2.8
New Castle city *Henry Co.*	17,780	18,114	17,476	-1.7
New Haven city *Allen Co.*	12,406	14,794	15,895	28.1
Noblesville city *Hamilton Co.*	28,590	51,969	59,807	109.1
North Vernon city *Jennings Co.*	6,515	6,728	6,695	2.7
Notre Dame CDP *Saint Joseph Co.*	n/a	5,973	6,720	n/a
Peru city *Miami Co.*	12,994	11,417	11,510	-11.4
Plainfield town *Hendricks Co.*	18,396	27,631	31,012	68.5
Plymouth city *Marshall Co.*	9,840	10,033	10,011	1.7
Portage city *Porter Co.*	33,496	36,828	36,849	10.0
Princeton city *Gibson Co.*	8,175	8,644	8,573	4.8
Richmond city *Wayne Co.*	39,124	36,812	35,819	-8.4
Saint John town *Lake Co.*	8,382	14,850	16,391	95.5
Schererville town *Lake Co.*	24,851	29,243	28,778	15.8
Scottsburg city *Scott Co.*	6,040	6,747	6,687	10.7
Sellersburg town *Clark Co.*	6,071	6,128	8,806	45.0
Seymour city *Jackson Co.*	18,101	17,503	19,225	6.2
Shelbyville city *Shelby Co.*	17,951	19,191	19,034	6.0
South Bend city *Saint Joseph Co.*	107,789	101,168	101,928	-5.4
Speedway town *Marion Co.*	12,881	11,812	12,229	-5.0
Tell City city *Perry Co.*	7,845	7,272	7,295	-7.0
Terre Haute city *Vigo Co.*	59,614	60,785	60,691	1.8
Valparaiso city *Porter Co.*	27,428	31,730	32,501	18.5
Vincennes city *Knox Co.*	18,701	18,423	17,944	-4.0
Wabash city *Wabash Co.*	11,743	10,666	10,272	-12.5
Warsaw city *Kosciusko Co.*	12,415	13,559	14,797	19.1
Washington city *Daviess Co.*	11,380	11,509	11,999	5.4
West Lafayette city *Tippecanoe Co.*	28,778	29,596	45,110	56.7
Westfield city *Hamilton Co.*	9,293	30,068	35,956	286.9
Yorktown town *Delaware Co.*	4,785	9,405	11,200	134.0
Zionsville town *Boone Co.*	8,775	14,160	25,810	194.1

NOTE: (1) Current population is based on the American Community Survey's 2013-2017 Five-Year Estimate.
SOURCE: U.S. Census Bureau, Census 2010, Census 2000; U.S. Census Bureau, American Community Survey, 2013-2017 Five-Year Estimates

Physical Characteristics

Place	Density (persons per square mile)	Land Area (square miles)	Water Area (square miles)	Elevation (feet)
Anderson city *Madison Co.*	1,329.1	41.37	0.11	879
Angola city *Steuben Co.*	1,361.4	6.34	0.05	1,063
Auburn city *DeKalb Co.*	1,830.4	7.10	0.00	866
Avon town *Hendricks Co.*	1,157.2	14.24	0.10	833
Bargersville town *Johnson Co.*	1,404.6	4.93	0.00	820
Bedford city *Lawrence Co.*	1,093.0	12.16	0.00	686
Beech Grove city *Marion Co.*	3,400.3	4.39	0.00	804
Bloomington city *Monroe Co.*	3,611.5	23.16	0.20	771
Bluffton city *Wells Co.*	1,193.3	8.23	0.13	827
Brazil city *Clay Co.*	2,769.7	3.03	0.03	653
Brownsburg town *Hendricks Co.*	2,223.3	11.08	0.08	883
Carmel city *Hamilton Co.*	1,866.6	47.46	1.08	853
Cedar Lake town *Lake Co.*	1,463.0	8.22	1.39	709
Charlestown city *Clark Co.*	705.8	11.45	0.04	591
Chesterton town *Porter Co.*	1,505.7	9.33	0.11	640
Clarksville town *Clark Co.*	2,128.5	9.97	0.20	456
Columbia City city *Whitley Co.*	1,622.6	5.58	0.02	860
Columbus city *Bartholomew Co.*	1,706.6	27.50	0.39	627
Connersville city *Fayette Co.*	1,681.4	7.74	0.02	823
Crawfordsville city *Montgomery Co.*	1,757.5	9.15	0.00	794
Crown Point city *Lake Co.*	1,634.5	17.71	0.02	732
Danville town *Hendricks Co.*	1,385.0	6.93	0.05	955
Decatur city *Adams Co.*	1,644.7	5.78	0.01	801
Dyer town *Lake Co.*	2,633.9	6.10	0.00	640
East Chicago city *Lake Co.*	2,039.2	14.09	2.06	591
Elkhart city *Elkhart Co.*	2,245.4	23.45	0.97	751
Elwood city *Madison Co.*	2,241.2	3.77	0.00	863
Evansville city *Vanderburgh Co.*	2,713.4	44.15	0.47	387
Fishers city *Hamilton Co.*	2,607.0	33.59	2.25	817
Fort Wayne city *Allen Co.*	2,372.6	110.62	0.21	810
Frankfort city *Clinton Co.*	2,570.9	6.31	0.00	850
Franklin city *Johnson Co.*	1,882.9	13.01	0.00	725
Garrett city *DeKalb Co.*	1,756.1	3.85	0.00	883
Gary city *Lake Co.*	1,552.5	49.87	7.31	600
Goshen city *Elkhart Co.*	2,069.3	16.23	0.36	801
Granger CDP *Saint Joseph Co.*	1,201.4	25.57	0.00	801
Greencastle city *Putnam Co.*	1,988.9	5.24	0.05	843
Greenfield city *Hancock Co.*	1,718.2	12.55	0.11	883
Greensburg city *Decatur Co.*	1,300.6	9.27	0.05	958
Greenwood city *Johnson Co.*	2,612.3	21.23	0.00	804
Griffith town *Lake Co.*	2,129.6	7.73	0.00	630
Hammond city *Lake Co.*	3,417.1	22.78	2.11	600
Highland town *Lake Co.*	3,307.2	6.94	0.02	623
Hobart city *Lake Co.*	1,085.1	26.33	0.38	623
Huntertown town *Allen Co.*	1,803.4	3.80	0.01	833
Huntington city *Huntington Co.*	1,977.0	8.71	0.13	748
Indianapolis city *Marion Co.*	2,361.2	361.43	6.59	718
Jasper city *Dubois Co.*	1,199.3	13.10	0.09	466
Jeffersonville city *Clark Co.*	1,375.0	34.06	0.29	446
Kendallville city *Noble Co.*	1,586.8	6.04	0.22	988

Place	Density (persons per square mile)	Land Area (square miles)	Water Area (square miles)	Elevation (feet)
Kokomo city *Howard Co.*	3,132.5	18.50	0.06	810
La Porte city *LaPorte Co.*	1,871.7	11.66	0.71	814
Lafayette city *Tippecanoe Co.*	2,601.6	27.74	0.00	702
Lake Station city *Lake Co.*	1,465.4	8.30	0.13	620
Lakes of the Four Seasons CDP *Lake Co.*	2,634.0	2.68	0.42	764
Lawrence city *Marion Co.*	2,388.3	20.13	0.11	873
Lebanon city *Boone Co.*	1,010.0	15.55	0.02	942
Logansport city *Cass Co.*	2,077.0	8.75	0.22	640
Lowell town *Lake Co.*	1,834.4	5.18	0.09	669
Madison city *Jefferson Co.*	1,390.1	8.57	0.27	489
Marion city *Grant Co.*	1,813.4	15.71	0.08	814
Martinsville city *Morgan Co.*	2,594.2	4.49	0.02	604
Merrillville town *Lake Co.*	1,059.2	33.22	0.04	656
Michigan City city *LaPorte Co.*	1,600.6	19.59	3.27	627
Mishawaka city *Saint Joseph Co.*	2,858.3	17.00	0.35	722
Mooresville town *Morgan Co.*	1,522.8	6.28	0.06	718
Muncie city *Delaware Co.*	2,545.8	27.20	0.19	951
Munster town *Lake Co.*	3,038.9	7.57	0.08	610
Nappanee city *Elkhart Co.*	1,669.7	4.15	0.00	876
New Albany city *Floyd Co.*	2,446.6	14.94	0.17	449
New Castle city *Henry Co.*	2,395.7	7.29	0.02	1,063
New Haven city *Allen Co.*	1,610.9	9.87	0.01	758
Noblesville city *Hamilton Co.*	1,906.2	31.37	1.42	764
North Vernon city *Jennings Co.*	1,011.5	6.62	0.01	718
Notre Dame CDP *Saint Joseph Co.*	5,562.7	1.21	0.07	n/a
Peru city *Miami Co.*	2,254.7	5.10	0.07	653
Plainfield town *Hendricks Co.*	1,392.3	22.27	0.11	732
Plymouth city *Marshall Co.*	1,328.8	7.53	0.04	797
Portage city *Porter Co.*	1,437.8	25.63	1.98	636
Princeton city *Gibson Co.*	1,690.9	5.07	0.01	499
Richmond city *Wayne Co.*	1,497.8	23.91	0.16	981
Saint John town *Lake Co.*	1,439.4	11.39	0.09	725
Schererville town *Lake Co.*	1,956.1	14.71	0.05	669
Scottsburg city *Scott Co.*	1,323.4	5.05	0.02	564
Sellersburg town *Clark Co.*	2,233.5	3.94	0.03	486
Seymour city *Jackson Co.*	1,683.1	11.42	0.00	600
Shelbyville city *Shelby Co.*	1,646.0	11.56	0.28	764
South Bend city *Saint Joseph Co.*	2,458.6	41.46	0.42	692
Speedway town *Marion Co.*	2,570.1	4.76	0.01	748
Tell City city *Perry Co.*	1,609.0	4.53	0.11	420
Terre Haute city *Vigo Co.*	1,757.3	34.54	0.73	502
Valparaiso city *Porter Co.*	2,092.8	15.53	0.05	794
Vincennes city *Knox Co.*	2,421.0	7.41	0.07	420
Wabash city *Wabash Co.*	1,156.0	8.89	0.24	712
Warsaw city *Kosciusko Co.*	1,278.2	11.58	1.34	827
Washington city *Daviess Co.*	2,536.5	4.73	0.04	502
West Lafayette city *Tippecanoe Co.*	5,923.6	7.62	0.01	610
Westfield city *Hamilton Co.*	1,339.7	26.84	0.24	886
Yorktown town *Delaware Co.*	1,275.8	8.78	0.08	915
Zionsville town *Boone Co.*	2,516.4	10.26	0.04	843

SOURCE: U.S. Census Bureau, Census 2010; U.S. Census Bureau, American Community Survey, 2013-2017 Five-Year Estimates

Race/Hispanic Origin

Place	White[1] (%)	Black[1] (%)	Asian[1] (%)	AIAN[1,2] (%)	NHOPI[1,3] (%)	Two or More Races (%)	Hispanic[4] (%)
Anderson city *Madison Co.*	79.0	13.8	0.9	0.3	0.0	4.1	5.3
Angola city *Steuben Co.*	95.6	0.7	0.4	0.0	0.1	2.7	4.8
Auburn city *DeKalb Co.*	99.0	0.3	0.2	0.0	0.0	0.5	1.9
Avon town *Hendricks Co.*	84.0	7.4	3.0	0.4	0.0	4.6	8.6
Bargersville town *Johnson Co.*	98.3	1.1	0.2	0.0	0.0	0.4	0.0
Bedford city *Lawrence Co.*	95.3	0.6	0.5	0.5	0.2	1.9	2.1
Beech Grove city *Marion Co.*	89.8	6.9	0.5	0.0	0.0	1.8	3.9
Bloomington city *Monroe Co.*	81.7	4.3	9.6	0.3	0.0	3.5	4.2
Bluffton city *Wells Co.*	96.4	1.1	0.5	0.0	0.0	1.1	3.5
Brazil city *Clay Co.*	95.4	0.8	0.0	0.1	0.0	3.1	1.3
Brownsburg town *Hendricks Co.*	91.5	3.6	2.6	0.3	0.0	0.8	3.1
Carmel city *Hamilton Co.*	84.0	2.5	10.3	0.3	0.0	2.2	3.2
Cedar Lake town *Lake Co.*	94.0	0.6	0.3	0.1	0.0	2.9	5.5
Charlestown city *Clark Co.*	90.6	1.9	0.5	0.0	0.0	3.7	7.6
Chesterton town *Porter Co.*	94.3	1.1	2.0	0.2	0.0	2.1	7.4
Clarksville town *Clark Co.*	89.6	4.1	1.6	0.2	0.0	3.6	7.9
Columbia City city *Whitley Co.*	94.0	0.8	0.6	0.1	0.0	3.9	3.9
Columbus city *Bartholomew Co.*	81.4	2.5	10.4	0.2	0.1	2.1	5.7
Connersville city *Fayette Co.*	94.8	3.8	0.2	0.0	0.0	0.3	1.5
Crawfordsville city *Montgomery Co.*	93.0	1.7	0.9	0.4	0.0	3.5	8.5
Crown Point city *Lake Co.*	86.8	5.7	2.4	0.0	0.0	2.4	8.6
Danville town *Hendricks Co.*	95.7	2.0	1.8	0.0	0.0	0.5	1.1
Decatur city *Adams Co.*	94.3	2.2	0.4	0.2	0.0	0.5	7.6
Dyer town *Lake Co.*	83.9	4.6	3.1	0.7	0.0	1.3	10.1
East Chicago city *Lake Co.*	24.5	36.4	0.2	0.4	0.0	2.7	57.0
Elkhart city *Elkhart Co.*	74.5	14.9	1.7	0.2	0.1	3.4	23.0
Elwood city *Madison Co.*	98.2	0.3	0.2	0.1	0.0	0.9	3.5
Evansville city *Vanderburgh Co.*	81.7	12.6	0.7	0.3	0.2	3.3	3.0
Fishers city *Hamilton Co.*	84.0	5.6	6.8	0.0	0.0	2.8	3.8
Fort Wayne city *Allen Co.*	74.2	15.0	4.3	0.2	0.1	4.2	8.7
Frankfort city *Clinton Co.*	91.9	1.7	0.2	0.3	0.1	1.0	27.8
Franklin city *Johnson Co.*	95.7	1.5	0.7	0.0	0.0	0.6	2.7
Garrett city *DeKalb Co.*	97.8	0.3	0.1	0.0	0.0	1.5	2.2
Gary city *Lake Co.*	14.0	81.0	0.4	0.2	0.2	2.1	5.8
Goshen city *Elkhart Co.*	88.7	2.8	1.3	0.1	0.0	3.5	30.0
Granger CDP *Saint Joseph Co.*	87.2	3.6	6.7	0.2	0.2	1.9	2.6
Greencastle city *Putnam Co.*	92.8	2.1	2.6	0.0	0.1	1.9	3.7
Greenfield city *Hancock Co.*	97.0	0.9	1.3	0.0	0.1	0.6	2.0
Greensburg city *Decatur Co.*	94.6	1.1	2.8	0.0	0.0	0.7	2.0
Greenwood city *Johnson Co.*	86.2	4.4	5.7	0.4	0.0	1.1	6.1
Griffith town *Lake Co.*	73.5	15.8	1.7	0.0	0.0	2.3	15.9
Hammond city *Lake Co.*	51.5	21.4	1.3	0.3	0.0	3.9	36.6
Highland town *Lake Co.*	83.9	4.4	1.9	0.4	0.0	3.5	15.5
Hobart city *Lake Co.*	84.8	7.7	0.9	0.7	0.0	2.3	11.8
Huntertown town *Allen Co.*	88.5	3.5	2.7	0.2	0.0	5.1	3.7
Huntington city *Huntington Co.*	95.0	1.5	1.6	0.2	0.0	1.0	3.2
Indianapolis city *Marion Co.*	61.8	28.1	3.0	0.3	0.0	3.0	10.1
Jasper city *Dubois Co.*	94.6	0.9	0.8	0.0	0.0	0.3	8.1
Jeffersonville city *Clark Co.*	80.4	13.7	0.9	0.1	0.0	4.6	5.2
Kendallville city *Noble Co.*	95.8	1.0	1.2	0.1	0.0	1.8	4.0

Place	White[1] (%)	Black[1] (%)	Asian[1] (%)	AIAN[1,2] (%)	NHOPI[1,3] (%)	Two or More Races (%)	Hispanic[4] (%)
Kokomo city *Howard Co.*	84.3	10.0	1.6	0.4	0.1	2.6	3.8
La Porte city *LaPorte Co.*	88.4	2.8	0.3	0.3	0.1	2.4	12.3
Lafayette city *Tippecanoe Co.*	85.0	8.5	1.6	0.2	0.0	2.3	12.2
Lake Station city *Lake Co.*	81.1	3.2	0.8	1.0	0.0	5.3	33.0
Lakes of the Four Seasons CDP *Lake Co.*	94.2	1.3	0.4	0.0	0.0	1.8	10.8
Lawrence city *Marion Co.*	64.4	27.8	1.5	0.1	0.0	3.9	12.2
Lebanon city *Boone Co.*	95.7	1.2	0.0	0.0	0.0	2.9	4.0
Logansport city *Cass Co.*	71.0	2.2	2.2	0.3	0.2	4.0	27.0
Lowell town *Lake Co.*	95.0	0.2	0.1	0.2	0.2	0.6	6.9
Madison city *Jefferson Co.*	92.3	3.0	1.9	0.4	0.0	1.4	6.0
Marion city *Grant Co.*	77.6	15.9	1.4	0.1	0.0	4.0	5.7
Martinsville city *Morgan Co.*	95.3	1.6	0.2	0.2	0.0	2.0	1.4
Merrillville town *Lake Co.*	41.2	46.1	1.3	0.3	0.0	4.5	14.6
Michigan City city *LaPorte Co.*	63.2	28.7	0.9	0.2	0.0	5.5	6.1
Mishawaka city *Saint Joseph Co.*	84.9	7.2	1.9	0.8	0.1	3.9	6.3
Mooresville town *Morgan Co.*	99.5	0.0	0.0	0.0	0.0	0.5	2.0
Muncie city *Delaware Co.*	83.0	11.6	1.6	0.1	0.1	2.9	3.1
Munster town *Lake Co.*	84.2	3.0	4.8	0.2	0.1	1.4	14.5
Nappanee city *Elkhart Co.*	95.1	2.5	1.0	0.0	0.2	1.2	7.3
New Albany city *Floyd Co.*	85.4	9.2	0.7	0.4	0.0	2.8	4.4
New Castle city *Henry Co.*	95.7	1.5	0.7	0.1	0.0	1.6	1.5
New Haven city *Allen Co.*	95.1	2.6	0.3	0.1	0.0	1.3	5.7
Noblesville city *Hamilton Co.*	89.7	4.0	2.5	0.1	0.0	2.8	4.5
North Vernon city *Jennings Co.*	97.0	1.5	0.1	0.7	0.0	0.7	1.8
Notre Dame CDP *Saint Joseph Co.*	82.6	3.0	9.6	0.1	0.0	4.3	7.4
Peru city *Miami Co.*	88.1	7.4	0.7	1.5	0.0	1.7	4.7
Plainfield town *Hendricks Co.*	84.1	9.0	3.8	0.1	0.0	1.3	4.7
Plymouth city *Marshall Co.*	82.9	0.6	0.7	0.6	0.0	2.6	25.5
Portage city *Porter Co.*	83.7	9.6	1.9	0.2	0.1	2.3	19.3
Princeton city *Gibson Co.*	88.5	6.2	0.3	0.0	0.0	3.1	3.0
Richmond city *Wayne Co.*	84.6	8.3	1.6	0.2	0.0	3.5	4.5
Saint John town *Lake Co.*	94.2	0.6	0.7	0.1	0.0	2.9	9.1
Schererville town *Lake Co.*	82.6	5.1	3.3	0.4	0.0	3.5	11.8
Scottsburg city *Scott Co.*	97.4	0.9	0.3	0.2	0.0	1.0	2.9
Sellersburg town *Clark Co.*	93.2	1.1	0.2	0.0	0.0	3.2	4.0
Seymour city *Jackson Co.*	85.0	1.9	3.3	0.2	0.0	1.6	11.9
Shelbyville city *Shelby Co.*	89.7	2.1	1.3	0.3	0.0	1.4	8.4
South Bend city *Saint Joseph Co.*	63.1	26.4	1.4	0.5	0.1	4.2	14.4
Speedway town *Marion Co.*	64.4	21.4	4.1	0.1	0.2	4.9	9.2
Tell City city *Perry Co.*	95.1	1.2	0.2	0.6	0.0	2.7	1.7
Terre Haute city *Vigo Co.*	83.0	9.5	1.5	0.3	0.0	4.7	3.0
Valparaiso city *Porter Co.*	92.0	3.1	2.5	0.2	0.2	1.5	6.7
Vincennes city *Knox Co.*	91.0	5.9	0.9	0.1	0.1	1.4	2.4
Wabash city *Wabash Co.*	95.6	0.4	0.4	0.4	0.0	2.0	2.2
Warsaw city *Kosciusko Co.*	87.4	2.3	3.3	0.2	0.0	3.5	10.3
Washington city *Daviess Co.*	88.8	4.6	0.2	0.1	0.1	1.6	12.5
West Lafayette city *Tippecanoe Co.*	69.2	3.2	23.8	0.3	0.1	2.9	4.2
Westfield city *Hamilton Co.*	89.9	3.9	3.1	0.0	0.0	1.4	4.7
Yorktown town *Delaware Co.*	94.6	2.8	0.0	0.0	0.0	1.9	0.0
Zionsville town *Boone Co.*	91.5	1.6	5.0	0.1	0.0	1.5	2.5

NOTE: (1) Exclude multiple race combinations; (2) American Indian/Alaska Native; (3) Native Hawaiian/Other Pacific Islander; (4) May be of any race
SOURCE: U.S. Census Bureau, American Community Survey, 2013-2017 Five-Year Estimates

Average Household Size, Age, and Male/Female Ratio

Place	Average Household Size (persons)	Median Age (years)	Age Under 18 (%)	Age 65 and Over (%)	Males per 100 Females
Anderson city *Madison Co.*	2.25	37.4	22.2	17.0	93.0
Angola city *Steuben Co.*	2.33	29.8	20.8	16.5	108.3
Auburn city *DeKalb Co.*	2.31	39.8	23.2	17.7	100.3
Avon town *Hendricks Co.*	2.91	35.3	27.6	10.9	94.8
Bargersville town *Johnson Co.*	2.83	33.5	30.2	11.4	105.6
Bedford city *Lawrence Co.*	2.27	41.8	21.1	19.8	87.7
Beech Grove city *Marion Co.*	2.52	36.5	26.6	16.1	81.7
Bloomington city *Monroe Co.*	2.26	23.8	11.4	8.7	99.1
Bluffton city *Wells Co.*	2.28	38.6	25.2	18.5	93.5
Brazil city *Clay Co.*	2.35	35.1	26.5	14.3	95.8
Brownsburg town *Hendricks Co.*	2.69	37.3	24.3	13.3	97.0
Carmel city *Hamilton Co.*	2.66	39.5	26.8	12.9	93.8
Cedar Lake town *Lake Co.*	2.85	34.5	27.1	10.0	106.1
Charlestown city *Clark Co.*	2.71	36.1	26.4	10.0	84.7
Chesterton town *Porter Co.*	2.56	39.8	23.5	15.1	97.3
Clarksville town *Clark Co.*	2.38	41.5	19.0	18.2	90.1
Columbia City city *Whitley Co.*	2.21	37.8	21.1	16.8	84.2
Columbus city *Bartholomew Co.*	2.44	36.2	24.3	15.0	96.9
Connersville city *Fayette Co.*	2.33	41.7	21.4	20.2	91.2
Crawfordsville city *Montgomery Co.*	2.30	37.0	22.4	17.2	106.8
Crown Point city *Lake Co.*	2.47	41.5	21.9	19.0	93.0
Danville town *Hendricks Co.*	2.66	37.8	26.8	15.5	98.8
Decatur city *Adams Co.*	2.26	38.7	24.3	15.5	97.4
Dyer town *Lake Co.*	2.61	45.5	18.8	19.5	99.8
East Chicago city *Lake Co.*	2.79	31.7	30.1	12.3	86.3
Elkhart city *Elkhart Co.*	2.61	33.4	27.5	12.4	91.7
Elwood city *Madison Co.*	2.40	38.9	21.7	16.1	94.4
Evansville city *Vanderburgh Co.*	2.24	37.2	21.5	15.5	91.2
Fishers city *Hamilton Co.*	2.78	35.2	30.9	8.0	95.1
Fort Wayne city *Allen Co.*	2.46	34.9	25.7	13.4	93.5
Frankfort city *Clinton Co.*	2.68	34.0	28.6	14.8	94.4
Franklin city *Johnson Co.*	2.53	38.0	23.5	16.3	94.7
Garrett city *DeKalb Co.*	2.56	36.2	26.5	13.3	89.1
Gary city *Lake Co.*	2.43	38.6	25.4	17.2	84.3
Goshen city *Elkhart Co.*	2.59	35.6	26.2	17.2	97.6
Granger CDP *Saint Joseph Co.*	2.94	42.0	27.9	14.5	95.0
Greencastle city *Putnam Co.*	2.25	26.3	18.0	15.4	81.2
Greenfield city *Hancock Co.*	2.35	39.2	23.1	18.2	86.0
Greensburg city *Decatur Co.*	2.36	37.0	25.2	15.5	94.1
Greenwood city *Johnson Co.*	2.57	35.5	25.4	13.8	93.8
Griffith town *Lake Co.*	2.50	36.7	21.7	13.5	99.5
Hammond city *Lake Co.*	2.70	33.9	25.8	11.0	96.4
Highland town *Lake Co.*	2.40	42.5	20.8	18.7	93.1
Hobart city *Lake Co.*	2.53	39.1	23.1	16.7	88.4
Huntertown town *Allen Co.*	2.84	35.3	30.2	12.3	99.5
Huntington city *Huntington Co.*	2.39	35.7	22.4	14.4	88.8
Indianapolis city *Marion Co.*	2.51	34.1	24.7	11.5	93.3
Jasper city *Dubois Co.*	2.37	40.0	23.4	17.2	96.4
Jeffersonville city *Clark Co.*	2.54	38.2	22.9	14.5	90.8
Kendallville city *Noble Co.*	2.27	38.1	24.9	16.4	90.1

Place	Average Household Size (persons)	Median Age (years)	Age Under 18 (%)	Age 65 and Over (%)	Males per 100 Females
Kokomo city *Howard Co.*	2.25	39.9	22.5	18.0	92.5
La Porte city *LaPorte Co.*	2.31	36.5	25.2	17.7	93.5
Lafayette city *Tippecanoe Co.*	2.27	32.4	22.3	12.7	95.6
Lake Station city *Lake Co.*	2.97	35.4	28.1	13.0	106.2
Lakes of the Four Seasons CDP *Lake Co.*	2.76	44.0	20.4	14.8	91.5
Lawrence city *Marion Co.*	2.59	35.0	26.5	11.5	90.3
Lebanon city *Boone Co.*	2.18	40.5	21.1	15.9	98.0
Logansport city *Cass Co.*	2.55	35.4	26.0	14.3	94.1
Lowell town *Lake Co.*	2.79	37.3	26.4	15.2	98.5
Madison city *Jefferson Co.*	2.08	42.6	17.7	19.1	71.8
Marion city *Grant Co.*	2.26	35.1	20.1	16.7	82.3
Martinsville city *Morgan Co.*	2.50	39.9	21.3	16.0	92.2
Merrillville town *Lake Co.*	2.49	38.2	24.0	14.7	88.1
Michigan City city *LaPorte Co.*	2.22	37.1	22.2	14.0	102.8
Mishawaka city *Saint Joseph Co.*	2.31	35.4	22.7	15.4	91.5
Mooresville town *Morgan Co.*	2.45	43.9	20.5	18.6	81.9
Muncie city *Delaware Co.*	2.25	28.8	16.8	13.9	90.8
Munster town *Lake Co.*	2.59	45.2	20.8	19.4	99.5
Nappanee city *Elkhart Co.*	2.62	32.1	29.4	11.9	91.3
New Albany city *Floyd Co.*	2.33	38.2	20.7	15.3	91.2
New Castle city *Henry Co.*	2.38	40.8	22.6	18.0	93.2
New Haven city *Allen Co.*	2.60	35.1	26.3	14.8	94.0
Noblesville city *Hamilton Co.*	2.67	33.5	28.3	10.8	93.3
North Vernon city *Jennings Co.*	2.41	37.3	22.9	16.8	94.7
Notre Dame CDP *Saint Joseph Co.*	2.29	20.6	0.3	1.0	119.5
Peru city *Miami Co.*	2.42	38.0	24.4	15.4	93.7
Plainfield town *Hendricks Co.*	2.51	37.7	24.2	13.1	101.9
Plymouth city *Marshall Co.*	2.53	33.9	27.5	14.5	92.6
Portage city *Porter Co.*	2.55	39.1	22.1	14.4	89.5
Princeton city *Gibson Co.*	2.38	36.3	25.3	16.8	100.8
Richmond city *Wayne Co.*	2.33	39.3	21.2	18.4	90.5
Saint John town *Lake Co.*	2.88	43.6	26.0	14.7	94.3
Schererville town *Lake Co.*	2.46	43.2	20.1	17.9	100.0
Scottsburg city *Scott Co.*	2.48	37.2	20.3	15.9	91.3
Sellersburg town *Clark Co.*	2.76	36.1	27.5	12.5	114.2
Seymour city *Jackson Co.*	2.48	36.8	26.0	14.5	101.8
Shelbyville city *Shelby Co.*	2.40	36.7	24.6	14.2	90.8
South Bend city *Saint Joseph Co.*	2.54	33.4	26.8	12.6	93.4
Speedway town *Marion Co.*	2.36	33.5	23.6	15.3	85.6
Tell City city *Perry Co.*	2.29	40.1	23.4	19.4	103.1
Terre Haute city *Vigo Co.*	2.30	32.6	19.4	14.0	106.4
Valparaiso city *Porter Co.*	2.31	34.2	21.2	16.0	93.3
Vincennes city *Knox Co.*	2.21	34.0	19.1	15.3	102.2
Wabash city *Wabash Co.*	2.18	41.1	20.2	19.3	89.4
Warsaw city *Kosciusko Co.*	2.46	31.8	25.6	13.5	96.5
Washington city *Daviess Co.*	2.49	37.0	26.0	17.2	105.4
West Lafayette city *Tippecanoe Co.*	2.34	21.7	10.4	6.8	115.5
Westfield city *Hamilton Co.*	2.86	34.5	31.0	8.4	94.1
Yorktown town *Delaware Co.*	2.54	40.2	24.8	16.8	96.6
Zionsville town *Boone Co.*	2.79	38.1	29.9	10.0	97.1

SOURCE: U.S. Census Bureau, American Community Survey, 2013-2017 Five-Year Estimates

Foreign Born, Language Spoken, Disabled Persons, and Veterans

Place	Foreign Born (%)	Speak English Only at Home (%)	With a Disability (%)	Veterans (%)
Anderson city *Madison Co.*	3.00	94.6	21.2	9.2
Angola city *Steuben Co.*	2.90	94.9	17.8	6.5
Auburn city *DeKalb Co.*	1.20	97.5	16.1	8.6
Avon town *Hendricks Co.*	9.20	89.3	8.7	8.0
Bargersville town *Johnson Co.*	2.60	94.8	8.5	8.4
Bedford city *Lawrence Co.*	1.70	98.2	19.2	9.9
Beech Grove city *Marion Co.*	1.90	96.8	16.2	9.3
Bloomington city *Monroe Co.*	12.10	84.9	9.8	3.3
Bluffton city *Wells Co.*	0.70	97.1	14.9	8.2
Brazil city *Clay Co.*	0.20	98.5	23.0	9.6
Brownsburg town *Hendricks Co.*	5.00	93.8	12.5	9.4
Carmel city *Hamilton Co.*	11.60	87.0	6.1	5.4
Cedar Lake town *Lake Co.*	2.60	94.7	10.5	8.7
Charlestown city *Clark Co.*	4.50	94.2	17.3	7.1
Chesterton town *Porter Co.*	4.00	94.0	8.8	8.4
Clarksville town *Clark Co.*	5.90	92.6	17.9	10.7
Columbia City city *Whitley Co.*	1.00	98.3	20.1	6.9
Columbus city *Bartholomew Co.*	13.40	85.4	11.7	6.1
Connersville city *Fayette Co.*	0.60	99.1	20.6	9.6
Crawfordsville city *Montgomery Co.*	4.80	91.9	16.6	7.0
Crown Point city *Lake Co.*	7.90	87.8	11.2	8.6
Danville town *Hendricks Co.*	2.20	95.8	13.7	7.6
Decatur city *Adams Co.*	0.70	94.9	18.4	7.3
Dyer town *Lake Co.*	6.90	86.9	9.8	8.0
East Chicago city *Lake Co.*	15.70	55.1	18.5	4.6
Elkhart city *Elkhart Co.*	12.20	79.4	16.7	5.7
Elwood city *Madison Co.*	0.90	98.2	19.1	7.3
Evansville city *Vanderburgh Co.*	2.70	96.2	17.9	8.4
Fishers city *Hamilton Co.*	8.90	90.0	6.1	5.4
Fort Wayne city *Allen Co.*	7.80	88.0	13.3	7.3
Frankfort city *Clinton Co.*	13.50	73.2	14.1	6.5
Franklin city *Johnson Co.*	2.00	96.2	12.2	9.9
Garrett city *DeKalb Co.*	0.80	97.8	16.9	7.5
Gary city *Lake Co.*	2.00	95.3	18.3	8.6
Goshen city *Elkhart Co.*	15.00	71.9	13.7	6.2
Granger CDP *Saint Joseph Co.*	7.90	91.0	8.0	6.8
Greencastle city *Putnam Co.*	3.20	95.6	17.7	6.8
Greenfield city *Hancock Co.*	2.00	96.6	18.7	10.2
Greensburg city *Decatur Co.*	2.40	95.0	14.0	5.5
Greenwood city *Johnson Co.*	7.80	88.6	11.5	8.9
Griffith town *Lake Co.*	4.40	90.8	13.2	7.7
Hammond city *Lake Co.*	11.30	74.2	15.5	6.7
Highland town *Lake Co.*	5.90	88.5	13.3	8.6
Hobart city *Lake Co.*	2.80	93.5	13.2	10.3
Huntertown town *Allen Co.*	3.20	95.4	9.6	10.6
Huntington city *Huntington Co.*	2.40	95.5	16.5	7.4
Indianapolis city *Marion Co.*	9.30	86.7	13.7	7.0
Jasper city *Dubois Co.*	5.80	92.3	11.9	9.3
Jeffersonville city *Clark Co.*	3.30	94.9	15.4	9.0
Kendallville city *Noble Co.*	3.00	94.5	19.4	6.4

Place	Foreign Born (%)	Speak English Only at Home (%)	With a Disability (%)	Veterans (%)
Kokomo city *Howard Co.*	2.50	96.1	18.8	10.1
La Porte city *LaPorte Co.*	5.80	88.5	15.0	8.9
Lafayette city *Tippecanoe Co.*	7.10	88.1	15.2	7.6
Lake Station city *Lake Co.*	5.90	78.6	15.3	8.5
Lakes of the Four Seasons CDP *Lake Co.*	7.50	88.3	9.6	5.2
Lawrence city *Marion Co.*	8.00	86.5	13.5	9.3
Lebanon city *Boone Co.*	1.30	97.2	15.3	8.8
Logansport city *Cass Co.*	16.40	73.2	15.2	6.9
Lowell town *Lake Co.*	1.30	95.0	11.6	9.1
Madison city *Jefferson Co.*	1.80	97.1	18.0	9.6
Marion city *Grant Co.*	2.20	95.7	22.0	7.4
Martinsville city *Morgan Co.*	1.40	98.1	22.3	10.7
Merrillville town *Lake Co.*	4.90	90.2	13.3	8.6
Michigan City city *LaPorte Co.*	3.50	94.6	14.7	7.9
Mishawaka city *Saint Joseph Co.*	5.40	93.8	15.0	8.2
Mooresville town *Morgan Co.*	0.20	99.3	17.8	10.9
Muncie city *Delaware Co.*	2.70	95.6	17.1	6.1
Munster town *Lake Co.*	10.70	80.5	11.6	6.4
Nappanee city *Elkhart Co.*	2.60	94.3	12.8	6.1
New Albany city *Floyd Co.*	1.90	96.6	16.4	8.5
New Castle city *Henry Co.*	0.80	98.1	22.3	8.2
New Haven city *Allen Co.*	1.20	97.4	14.0	9.0
Noblesville city *Hamilton Co.*	3.90	94.1	9.5	7.2
North Vernon city *Jennings Co.*	0.70	98.7	19.7	6.7
Notre Dame CDP *Saint Joseph Co.*	10.00	84.9	5.9	1.0
Peru city *Miami Co.*	1.10	97.8	17.6	10.5
Plainfield town *Hendricks Co.*	6.70	89.7	13.2	8.4
Plymouth city *Marshall Co.*	9.30	79.2	16.1	8.5
Portage city *Porter Co.*	5.30	89.2	13.1	7.2
Princeton city *Gibson Co.*	3.80	94.4	16.4	8.9
Richmond city *Wayne Co.*	3.30	94.7	21.8	10.2
Saint John town *Lake Co.*	4.40	93.1	9.1	8.2
Schererville town *Lake Co.*	10.70	83.3	10.3	7.2
Scottsburg city *Scott Co.*	0.30	95.3	19.2	8.4
Sellersburg town *Clark Co.*	1.60	96.5	8.0	8.0
Seymour city *Jackson Co.*	8.80	87.6	15.5	7.8
Shelbyville city *Shelby Co.*	4.70	92.0	16.3	8.3
South Bend city *Saint Joseph Co.*	8.50	85.1	15.4	6.2
Speedway town *Marion Co.*	16.30	80.5	14.3	6.5
Tell City city *Perry Co.*	0.70	99.6	17.1	9.6
Terre Haute city *Vigo Co.*	3.10	94.9	20.4	7.5
Valparaiso city *Porter Co.*	5.20	92.8	10.9	6.1
Vincennes city *Knox Co.*	1.60	97.5	20.3	8.2
Wabash city *Wabash Co.*	1.00	96.2	14.5	9.1
Warsaw city *Kosciusko Co.*	7.50	87.6	14.3	6.8
Washington city *Daviess Co.*	5.30	87.0	19.4	9.9
West Lafayette city *Tippecanoe Co.*	24.50	71.3	6.2	2.0
Westfield city *Hamilton Co.*	5.70	91.6	8.6	5.6
Yorktown town *Delaware Co.*	0.60	99.0	11.8	8.9
Zionsville town *Boone Co.*	5.60	93.5	5.8	5.0

SOURCE: U.S. Census Bureau, American Community Survey, 2013-2017 Five-Year Estimates

Five Largest Ancestry Groups

Place	Group 1	Group 2	Group 3	Group 4	Group 5
Anderson city *Madison Co.*	German (17.8%)	Irish (11.0%)	American (9.2%)	English (6.5%)	Italian (2.6%)
Angola city *Steuben Co.*	German (30.9%)	Irish (12.2%)	English (10.6%)	American (7.9%)	European (7.2%)
Auburn city *DeKalb Co.*	German (38.0%)	English (14.0%)	Irish (12.5%)	American (12.5%)	European (4.2%)
Avon town *Hendricks Co.*	German (25.0%)	Irish (13.0%)	English (9.6%)	American (7.0%)	French (3.1%)
Bargersville town *Johnson Co.*	German (21.6%)	American (15.0%)	English (12.9%)	Irish (9.9%)	Polish (4.8%)
Bedford city *Lawrence Co.*	German (17.7%)	Irish (13.0%)	American (11.5%)	English (9.1%)	Italian (3.5%)
Beech Grove city *Marion Co.*	German (22.7%)	Irish (15.2%)	American (7.4%)	English (6.8%)	Italian (3.4%)
Bloomington city *Monroe Co.*	German (19.9%)	Irish (10.9%)	English (10.8%)	Italian (4.0%)	American (3.8%)
Bluffton city *Wells Co.*	German (29.2%)	American (12.5%)	English (7.8%)	Irish (7.4%)	Swiss (5.3%)
Brazil city *Clay Co.*	German (25.3%)	Irish (10.4%)	American (9.3%)	English (7.8%)	Dutch (3.4%)
Brownsburg town *Hendricks Co.*	German (21.5%)	American (15.9%)	Irish (11.3%)	English (9.7%)	French (3.2%)
Carmel city *Hamilton Co.*	German (24.8%)	Irish (14.5%)	English (12.3%)	American (9.6%)	Italian (4.0%)
Cedar Lake town *Lake Co.*	German (29.0%)	Irish (21.2%)	Polish (16.5%)	Italian (9.0%)	English (8.3%)
Charlestown city *Clark Co.*	German (19.4%)	American (14.5%)	Irish (11.8%)	English (8.1%)	French (7.3%)
Chesterton town *Porter Co.*	German (28.5%)	Irish (15.6%)	Polish (11.0%)	English (7.9%)	Italian (7.7%)
Clarksville town *Clark Co.*	German (19.0%)	Irish (12.2%)	English (8.6%)	American (8.4%)	French (3.8%)
Columbia City city *Whitley Co.*	German (25.6%)	American (9.8%)	English (9.2%)	Irish (7.3%)	French (2.8%)
Columbus city *Bartholomew Co.*	German (20.1%)	American (14.2%)	Irish (9.6%)	English (9.2%)	French (2.0%)
Connersville city *Fayette Co.*	German (18.4%)	American (14.9%)	Irish (11.3%)	English (5.8%)	French (2.4%)
Crawfordsville city *Montgomery Co.*	German (20.2%)	Irish (14.2%)	American (10.2%)	English (9.1%)	Polish (3.0%)
Crown Point city *Lake Co.*	German (22.3%)	Irish (13.8%)	Polish (11.8%)	Italian (8.4%)	English (6.2%)
Danville town *Hendricks Co.*	German (22.1%)	American (11.3%)	Irish (11.2%)	English (7.0%)	Scottish (4.1%)
Decatur city *Adams Co.*	German (30.6%)	American (12.4%)	English (9.5%)	Irish (7.5%)	Swiss (2.8%)
Dyer town *Lake Co.*	German (21.6%)	Polish (20.2%)	Irish (16.2%)	Italian (10.2%)	Dutch (6.3%)
East Chicago city *Lake Co.*	Polish (2.4%)	German (1.4%)	American (0.8%)	Irish (0.7%)	French (0.4%)
Elkhart city *Elkhart Co.*	German (16.4%)	Irish (8.1%)	American (6.7%)	English (4.8%)	European (2.9%)
Elwood city *Madison Co.*	German (21.4%)	American (15.6%)	Irish (12.5%)	English (5.2%)	European (2.6%)
Evansville city *Vanderburgh Co.*	German (25.7%)	Irish (11.6%)	English (11.3%)	American (7.1%)	French (1.7%)
Fishers city *Hamilton Co.*	German (27.0%)	Irish (12.0%)	English (10.0%)	American (9.9%)	Polish (5.2%)
Fort Wayne city *Allen Co.*	German (26.1%)	Irish (9.5%)	English (6.5%)	American (6.4%)	French (3.2%)
Frankfort city *Clinton Co.*	German (14.2%)	Irish (11.0%)	American (7.1%)	English (6.7%)	Scotch-Irish (1.8%)
Franklin city *Johnson Co.*	German (21.5%)	Irish (11.6%)	American (10.2%)	English (7.8%)	Italian (3.5%)
Garrett city *DeKalb Co.*	German (27.0%)	Irish (11.4%)	American (6.9%)	English (6.1%)	European (6.0%)
Gary city *Lake Co.*	German (2.6%)	Irish (2.1%)	American (2.0%)	English (1.0%)	Polish (0.9%)
Goshen city *Elkhart Co.*	German (22.7%)	American (8.9%)	Irish (7.2%)	English (4.7%)	Swiss (4.4%)
Granger CDP *Saint Joseph Co.*	German (24.6%)	Irish (13.0%)	Polish (11.4%)	English (9.6%)	American (7.0%)
Greencastle city *Putnam Co.*	German (17.6%)	Irish (9.6%)	English (8.6%)	American (8.1%)	European (3.7%)
Greenfield city *Hancock Co.*	German (22.6%)	American (15.8%)	Irish (12.2%)	English (10.0%)	Scottish (2.6%)
Greensburg city *Decatur Co.*	German (36.7%)	American (17.7%)	Irish (14.1%)	English (6.8%)	Italian (4.2%)
Greenwood city *Johnson Co.*	German (22.9%)	Irish (11.0%)	English (10.7%)	American (8.6%)	Scottish (2.3%)
Griffith town *Lake Co.*	German (21.8%)	Irish (13.0%)	Polish (11.4%)	English (5.5%)	Dutch (5.0%)
Hammond city *Lake Co.*	German (10.2%)	Irish (8.6%)	Polish (7.6%)	English (3.3%)	Italian (3.1%)
Highland town *Lake Co.*	German (21.7%)	Polish (18.0%)	Irish (13.8%)	English (6.7%)	Dutch (5.4%)
Hobart city *Lake Co.*	German (22.3%)	Irish (20.3%)	Polish (9.3%)	English (9.0%)	Italian (5.0%)
Huntertown town *Allen Co.*	German (28.0%)	American (16.5%)	Irish (10.2%)	English (8.9%)	French (5.1%)
Huntington city *Huntington Co.*	German (32.5%)	Irish (13.0%)	American (10.9%)	English (7.9%)	Italian (2.1%)
Indianapolis city *Marion Co.*	German (15.4%)	Irish (9.4%)	American (6.3%)	English (6.2%)	African (2.5%)
Jasper city *Dubois Co.*	German (42.8%)	Irish (11.6%)	American (8.4%)	English (7.8%)	Dutch (1.9%)
Jeffersonville city *Clark Co.*	German (20.2%)	Irish (13.9%)	English (8.7%)	American (7.2%)	Italian (3.1%)
Kendallville city *Noble Co.*	German (20.2%)	American (11.4%)	European (10.4%)	Irish (10.1%)	English (8.8%)

Place	Group 1	Group 2	Group 3	Group 4	Group 5
Kokomo city *Howard Co.*	German (19.1%)	American (11.3%)	Irish (10.8%)	English (8.4%)	Italian (2.3%)
La Porte city *LaPorte Co.*	German (29.4%)	Irish (14.7%)	Polish (11.5%)	English (7.1%)	American (5.6%)
Lafayette city *Tippecanoe Co.*	German (25.4%)	Irish (13.6%)	English (8.4%)	American (6.1%)	Dutch (2.6%)
Lake Station city *Lake Co.*	Irish (14.9%)	German (11.1%)	Polish (10.1%)	Italian (7.9%)	American (5.4%)
Lakes of the Four Seasons CDP *Lake Co.*	German (29.8%)	Irish (19.7%)	Polish (13.4%)	Croatian (6.3%)	English (5.3%)
Lawrence city *Marion Co.*	German (14.7%)	Irish (8.1%)	American (7.6%)	English (6.4%)	Italian (2.5%)
Lebanon city *Boone Co.*	German (19.6%)	American (15.1%)	Irish (10.8%)	English (9.6%)	Scottish (3.6%)
Logansport city *Cass Co.*	German (19.2%)	American (9.7%)	Irish (7.4%)	English (5.4%)	Italian (3.5%)
Lowell town *Lake Co.*	German (34.9%)	Irish (21.5%)	Polish (14.1%)	English (9.4%)	American (7.0%)
Madison city *Jefferson Co.*	German (22.1%)	Irish (12.8%)	English (12.5%)	American (6.5%)	Italian (2.6%)
Marion city *Grant Co.*	German (20.4%)	Irish (9.9%)	American (9.1%)	English (6.6%)	Italian (2.0%)
Martinsville city *Morgan Co.*	German (20.6%)	English (12.7%)	American (11.1%)	Irish (11.0%)	French (3.8%)
Merrillville town *Lake Co.*	German (11.1%)	Irish (8.6%)	Polish (4.9%)	Italian (2.5%)	English (2.5%)
Michigan City city *LaPorte Co.*	German (20.0%)	Irish (12.1%)	Polish (9.9%)	English (4.1%)	American (4.0%)
Mishawaka city *Saint Joseph Co.*	German (21.9%)	Irish (12.3%)	American (10.1%)	Polish (9.0%)	English (6.3%)
Mooresville town *Morgan Co.*	German (19.7%)	American (16.7%)	Irish (13.5%)	English (12.0%)	European (3.1%)
Muncie city *Delaware Co.*	German (17.8%)	Irish (12.5%)	American (9.8%)	English (7.2%)	Italian (2.3%)
Munster town *Lake Co.*	German (17.3%)	Irish (15.5%)	Polish (14.8%)	Italian (9.8%)	English (7.0%)
Nappanee city *Elkhart Co.*	German (28.8%)	Irish (10.6%)	English (6.2%)	Italian (6.2%)	American (6.0%)
New Albany city *Floyd Co.*	German (23.3%)	Irish (13.8%)	English (9.0%)	American (8.3%)	French (3.0%)
New Castle city *Henry Co.*	American (14.8%)	German (14.8%)	English (11.6%)	Irish (10.3%)	Dutch (1.8%)
New Haven city *Allen Co.*	German (33.2%)	American (11.7%)	Irish (11.2%)	English (6.8%)	French (3.8%)
Noblesville city *Hamilton Co.*	German (25.7%)	Irish (12.4%)	American (12.0%)	English (10.0%)	Italian (4.5%)
North Vernon city *Jennings Co.*	German (14.5%)	American (14.3%)	Irish (6.5%)	English (6.0%)	Dutch (3.4%)
Notre Dame CDP *Saint Joseph Co.*	Irish (25.5%)	German (20.0%)	Italian (12.2%)	Polish (6.3%)	English (5.0%)
Peru city *Miami Co.*	German (17.0%)	American (15.3%)	Irish (10.0%)	English (6.4%)	Dutch (2.9%)
Plainfield town *Hendricks Co.*	German (18.1%)	Irish (12.4%)	American (11.7%)	English (8.3%)	Italian (4.3%)
Plymouth city *Marshall Co.*	German (20.2%)	Irish (8.7%)	American (7.3%)	English (6.1%)	Polish (4.1%)
Portage city *Porter Co.*	German (18.0%)	Irish (13.1%)	Polish (10.5%)	English (5.9%)	Italian (4.0%)
Princeton city *Gibson Co.*	German (20.6%)	American (11.0%)	Irish (10.0%)	English (9.3%)	Polish (3.0%)
Richmond city *Wayne Co.*	German (18.3%)	Irish (13.4%)	English (9.0%)	American (8.5%)	Italian (2.3%)
Saint John town *Lake Co.*	German (22.6%)	Polish (18.8%)	Irish (16.4%)	Italian (11.3%)	English (7.5%)
Schererville town *Lake Co.*	German (22.1%)	Irish (17.1%)	Polish (16.9%)	Italian (7.2%)	English (4.7%)
Scottsburg city *Scott Co.*	German (15.8%)	English (15.7%)	Irish (11.8%)	American (10.3%)	Scottish (2.7%)
Sellersburg town *Clark Co.*	German (29.7%)	Irish (18.7%)	English (10.3%)	American (7.4%)	Scottish (1.7%)
Seymour city *Jackson Co.*	German (21.5%)	American (18.9%)	Irish (8.2%)	English (8.2%)	Scottish (2.1%)
Shelbyville city *Shelby Co.*	German (24.4%)	American (17.4%)	Irish (11.0%)	English (6.9%)	European (1.6%)
South Bend city *Saint Joseph Co.*	German (15.9%)	Irish (9.3%)	Polish (8.0%)	English (4.9%)	American (4.5%)
Speedway town *Marion Co.*	German (19.2%)	English (9.6%)	Irish (8.4%)	American (6.6%)	African (3.5%)
Tell City city *Perry Co.*	German (29.2%)	American (12.1%)	Irish (11.7%)	French (8.3%)	English (7.8%)
Terre Haute city *Vigo Co.*	German (18.6%)	American (11.6%)	Irish (10.1%)	English (8.0%)	French (2.6%)
Valparaiso city *Porter Co.*	German (28.0%)	Irish (19.3%)	Polish (10.2%)	English (9.6%)	Italian (6.3%)
Vincennes city *Knox Co.*	German (21.5%)	Irish (12.7%)	American (8.0%)	English (6.0%)	French (4.0%)
Wabash city *Wabash Co.*	German (26.8%)	Irish (13.8%)	American (13.7%)	English (7.1%)	Dutch (1.8%)
Warsaw city *Kosciusko Co.*	German (23.4%)	Irish (12.1%)	English (9.6%)	American (8.7%)	Italian (3.2%)
Washington city *Daviess Co.*	German (22.4%)	American (11.7%)	Irish (11.0%)	English (8.7%)	French (2.5%)
West Lafayette city *Tippecanoe Co.*	German (24.2%)	Irish (11.1%)	English (7.4%)	Polish (5.5%)	Italian (4.8%)
Westfield city *Hamilton Co.*	German (24.3%)	Irish (15.2%)	American (13.4%)	English (9.3%)	Italian (4.2%)
Yorktown town *Delaware Co.*	German (23.1%)	Irish (14.7%)	American (12.2%)	English (11.8%)	Scottish (2.9%)
Zionsville town *Boone Co.*	German (26.8%)	English (13.4%)	Irish (10.8%)	American (9.6%)	Italian (5.1%)

NOTE: "French" excludes Basque; Please refer to the User Guide for more information.
SOURCE: U.S. Census Bureau, American Community Survey, 2013-2017 Five-Year Estimates

Marriage Status

Place	Never Married (%)	Now Married[1] (%)	Separated (%)	Widowed (%)	Divorced (%)
Anderson city *Madison Co.*	32.8	40.8	2.3	7.3	19.1
Angola city *Steuben Co.*	38.3	40.2	2.5	7.5	14.0
Auburn city *DeKalb Co.*	30.2	45.9	0.7	9.7	14.1
Avon town *Hendricks Co.*	25.2	56.7	1.2	4.6	13.4
Bargersville town *Johnson Co.*	19.9	66.8	1.1	3.9	9.4
Bedford city *Lawrence Co.*	22.8	47.5	0.8	9.8	19.9
Beech Grove city *Marion Co.*	35.1	40.5	1.7	7.4	17.0
Bloomington city *Monroe Co.*	63.6	25.0	0.8	3.0	8.4
Bluffton city *Wells Co.*	26.9	51.7	1.6	8.2	13.2
Brazil city *Clay Co.*	28.4	47.7	1.8	6.5	17.4
Brownsburg town *Hendricks Co.*	23.2	60.3	2.7	5.9	10.6
Carmel city *Hamilton Co.*	23.9	64.4	0.5	3.8	7.9
Cedar Lake town *Lake Co.*	32.5	52.0	0.5	3.6	12.0
Charlestown city *Clark Co.*	28.6	46.8	2.1	8.0	16.5
Chesterton town *Porter Co.*	27.4	54.4	1.6	6.3	11.9
Clarksville town *Clark Co.*	28.0	44.3	2.5	11.0	16.7
Columbia City city *Whitley Co.*	30.5	47.0	0.9	6.4	16.1
Columbus city *Bartholomew Co.*	28.0	52.5	1.7	6.1	13.4
Connersville city *Fayette Co.*	26.2	44.1	1.4	9.5	20.2
Crawfordsville city *Montgomery Co.*	30.8	45.7	2.4	6.4	17.1
Crown Point city *Lake Co.*	26.8	54.1	0.5	8.4	10.7
Danville town *Hendricks Co.*	24.9	54.0	1.7	7.0	14.2
Decatur city *Adams Co.*	26.9	45.2	1.0	9.5	18.4
Dyer town *Lake Co.*	25.3	58.3	1.0	7.9	8.5
East Chicago city *Lake Co.*	46.7	36.3	2.3	6.6	10.5
Elkhart city *Elkhart Co.*	36.4	40.3	2.7	7.0	16.3
Elwood city *Madison Co.*	27.7	47.6	1.9	8.6	16.1
Evansville city *Vanderburgh Co.*	34.3	41.0	1.6	7.0	17.7
Fishers city *Hamilton Co.*	24.0	63.4	1.1	3.0	9.7
Fort Wayne city *Allen Co.*	34.8	46.2	1.4	5.9	13.2
Frankfort city *Clinton Co.*	28.0	49.3	3.1	8.6	14.1
Franklin city *Johnson Co.*	25.4	51.7	0.8	8.1	14.8
Garrett city *DeKalb Co.*	31.1	45.4	0.9	6.1	17.4
Gary city *Lake Co.*	45.1	31.4	2.7	9.1	14.3
Goshen city *Elkhart Co.*	32.2	49.2	1.8	6.5	12.1
Granger CDP *Saint Joseph Co.*	21.8	68.5	0.7	4.2	5.5
Greencastle city *Putnam Co.*	46.1	31.4	0.4	8.1	14.4
Greenfield city *Hancock Co.*	24.0	52.3	2.0	8.2	15.5
Greensburg city *Decatur Co.*	28.2	48.0	1.2	7.4	16.4
Greenwood city *Johnson Co.*	29.8	51.1	1.0	5.9	13.2
Griffith town *Lake Co.*	37.3	44.0	0.4	6.2	12.6
Hammond city *Lake Co.*	40.9	41.1	2.5	6.1	11.9
Highland town *Lake Co.*	28.6	50.6	1.2	7.6	13.2
Hobart city *Lake Co.*	28.1	53.0	1.7	6.9	12.0
Huntertown town *Allen Co.*	24.1	59.7	0.5	3.1	13.1
Huntington city *Huntington Co.*	33.7	46.1	1.1	7.3	12.9
Indianapolis city *Marion Co.*	41.4	40.3	2.0	5.2	13.1
Jasper city *Dubois Co.*	27.1	53.3	0.8	6.7	12.9
Jeffersonville city *Clark Co.*	31.2	47.7	1.9	6.0	15.1
Kendallville city *Noble Co.*	26.6	46.1	2.8	8.0	19.3

Place	Never Married (%)	Now Married[1] (%)	Separated (%)	Widowed (%)	Divorced (%)
Kokomo city *Howard Co.*	26.8	48.2	1.9	7.6	17.5
La Porte city *LaPorte Co.*	31.0	43.2	1.3	8.1	17.8
Lafayette city *Tippecanoe Co.*	37.0	42.4	1.6	5.1	15.5
Lake Station city *Lake Co.*	33.5	48.5	3.2	5.8	12.2
Lakes of the Four Seasons CDP *Lake Co.*	21.6	63.6	0.2	5.5	9.3
Lawrence city *Marion Co.*	34.8	48.6	1.6	5.5	11.2
Lebanon city *Boone Co.*	26.9	47.9	1.2	8.4	16.8
Logansport city *Cass Co.*	33.3	44.6	1.7	7.2	14.9
Lowell town *Lake Co.*	30.9	52.8	1.6	6.7	9.5
Madison city *Jefferson Co.*	29.6	42.0	1.7	8.5	19.9
Marion city *Grant Co.*	39.2	35.8	1.5	8.3	16.7
Martinsville city *Morgan Co.*	28.0	43.4	3.7	8.1	20.5
Merrillville town *Lake Co.*	35.3	44.6	2.0	6.7	13.3
Michigan City city *LaPorte Co.*	39.4	36.9	1.7	6.2	17.4
Mishawaka city *Saint Joseph Co.*	35.8	40.2	1.2	7.7	16.4
Mooresville town *Morgan Co.*	26.1	49.3	1.1	9.8	14.9
Muncie city *Delaware Co.*	48.4	32.5	1.3	6.2	12.9
Munster town *Lake Co.*	28.8	53.7	1.0	8.5	9.1
Nappanee city *Elkhart Co.*	23.3	59.1	5.0	4.2	13.3
New Albany city *Floyd Co.*	34.0	41.6	2.4	7.7	16.7
New Castle city *Henry Co.*	28.6	41.4	1.7	9.0	21.0
New Haven city *Allen Co.*	27.2	51.2	1.1	7.1	14.5
Noblesville city *Hamilton Co.*	25.9	57.9	1.3	4.5	11.6
North Vernon city *Jennings Co.*	29.5	42.6	2.6	8.9	19.1
Notre Dame CDP *Saint Joseph Co.*	97.7	0.7	0.0	0.3	1.4
Peru city *Miami Co.*	31.1	45.7	2.0	6.9	16.3
Plainfield town *Hendricks Co.*	29.9	49.1	1.3	5.7	15.3
Plymouth city *Marshall Co.*	33.5	44.8	1.4	6.6	15.0
Portage city *Porter Co.*	33.1	46.7	1.9	7.0	13.2
Princeton city *Gibson Co.*	30.6	43.4	1.9	7.0	19.0
Richmond city *Wayne Co.*	32.3	41.6	1.4	8.7	17.4
Saint John town *Lake Co.*	22.8	65.2	0.1	4.8	7.2
Schererville town *Lake Co.*	29.1	54.5	0.8	6.5	9.8
Scottsburg city *Scott Co.*	29.2	52.2	2.0	6.0	12.6
Sellersburg town *Clark Co.*	24.8	52.4	4.3	7.6	15.2
Seymour city *Jackson Co.*	22.5	53.6	2.0	8.3	15.6
Shelbyville city *Shelby Co.*	28.8	46.1	2.2	8.9	16.1
South Bend city *Saint Joseph Co.*	41.5	38.9	2.4	6.5	13.1
Speedway town *Marion Co.*	38.1	40.4	0.9	6.8	14.8
Tell City city *Perry Co.*	21.9	52.9	2.2	9.1	16.1
Terre Haute city *Vigo Co.*	43.0	35.9	1.6	6.2	14.9
Valparaiso city *Porter Co.*	37.4	43.8	1.4	6.4	12.5
Vincennes city *Knox Co.*	33.2	42.2	1.2	8.0	16.6
Wabash city *Wabash Co.*	26.4	49.3	1.3	7.2	17.1
Warsaw city *Kosciusko Co.*	30.8	47.8	1.4	5.8	15.7
Washington city *Daviess Co.*	30.0	46.2	1.4	9.2	14.5
West Lafayette city *Tippecanoe Co.*	72.1	22.2	0.3	2.7	2.9
Westfield city *Hamilton Co.*	24.8	63.0	0.7	3.4	8.8
Yorktown town *Delaware Co.*	21.5	58.9	1.1	6.2	13.4
Zionsville town *Boone Co.*	21.3	68.2	0.3	3.7	6.9

NOTE: (1) Includes separated.
SOURCE: U.S. Census Bureau, American Community Survey, 2013-2017 Five-Year Estimates

Comparative Statistics

Employment by Occupation

Place	MBF[1] (%)	CES[2] (%)	ELCAM[3] (%)	HPT[4] (%)	S[5] (%)	SO[6] (%)	NRCM[7] (%)	PTMM[8] (%)
Anderson city *Madison Co.*	8.0	2.6	8.7	5.6	25.0	23.9	8.1	18.0
Angola city *Steuben Co.*	7.4	6.5	12.9	3.4	16.5	23.3	5.7	24.2
Auburn city *DeKalb Co.*	12.0	3.1	9.6	5.0	15.3	20.3	4.4	30.4
Avon town *Hendricks Co.*	19.2	8.2	8.9	9.2	14.4	24.6	6.3	9.3
Bargersville town *Johnson Co.*	23.9	8.1	5.8	8.7	10.7	19.5	7.9	15.4
Bedford city *Lawrence Co.*	8.1	3.5	6.8	8.1	20.6	22.6	10.9	19.4
Beech Grove city *Marion Co.*	9.5	3.2	7.2	5.3	18.1	31.2	7.1	18.4
Bloomington city *Monroe Co.*	12.8	6.1	22.4	4.4	23.0	20.0	3.6	7.8
Bluffton city *Wells Co.*	10.2	2.6	5.1	7.1	19.9	22.4	6.5	26.2
Brazil city *Clay Co.*	8.9	0.9	11.3	3.6	23.1	19.9	7.7	24.7
Brownsburg town *Hendricks Co.*	16.4	4.1	9.2	8.8	17.8	26.4	6.0	11.3
Carmel city *Hamilton Co.*	26.3	11.0	15.6	9.5	8.6	21.9	2.7	4.5
Cedar Lake town *Lake Co.*	15.2	4.4	7.8	3.8	19.2	21.1	16.5	12.1
Charlestown city *Clark Co.*	12.7	3.5	5.3	9.9	16.1	21.5	8.1	22.9
Chesterton town *Porter Co.*	16.4	3.7	12.7	6.4	16.4	20.5	11.7	12.3
Clarksville town *Clark Co.*	12.2	3.4	4.9	6.0	21.5	26.7	7.6	17.7
Columbia City city *Whitley Co.*	14.5	1.7	7.2	7.4	17.1	22.7	6.2	23.1
Columbus city *Bartholomew Co.*	17.8	16.8	8.1	5.3	13.7	17.7	4.6	16.0
Connersville city *Fayette Co.*	6.3	3.1	5.9	7.7	20.7	23.6	6.4	26.3
Crawfordsville city *Montgomery Co.*	9.0	2.0	11.9	3.2	17.6	22.0	9.6	24.8
Crown Point city *Lake Co.*	15.7	4.1	10.6	9.3	15.7	21.8	9.0	13.9
Danville town *Hendricks Co.*	14.0	3.8	10.2	8.7	17.0	28.9	5.9	11.5
Decatur city *Adams Co.*	7.2	2.1	7.1	5.1	17.9	22.7	7.3	30.7
Dyer town *Lake Co.*	15.0	3.6	11.0	8.3	12.7	22.6	10.2	16.6
East Chicago city *Lake Co.*	7.6	0.9	7.0	3.5	27.9	19.6	8.3	25.1
Elkhart city *Elkhart Co.*	6.7	2.5	6.4	2.9	16.5	18.8	6.5	39.7
Elwood city *Madison Co.*	5.6	1.5	3.3	8.0	25.8	19.2	6.9	29.5
Evansville city *Vanderburgh Co.*	10.7	3.8	9.1	4.9	19.9	24.4	7.5	19.8
Fishers city *Hamilton Co.*	26.0	10.5	13.6	8.7	9.4	25.2	3.0	3.4
Fort Wayne city *Allen Co.*	12.0	4.6	10.4	5.6	17.6	24.7	7.0	18.2
Frankfort city *Clinton Co.*	5.6	1.7	6.7	3.6	16.1	17.4	9.9	39.0
Franklin city *Johnson Co.*	12.7	2.9	10.6	6.3	19.9	21.3	9.2	17.1
Garrett city *DeKalb Co.*	11.1	3.1	7.8	1.8	13.6	20.0	10.7	31.9
Gary city *Lake Co.*	7.6	1.4	9.0	4.6	29.9	23.1	5.9	18.6
Goshen city *Elkhart Co.*	7.7	3.8	9.9	4.0	15.0	21.1	8.6	29.9
Granger CDP *Saint Joseph Co.*	20.3	6.4	14.9	10.6	9.8	24.1	4.7	9.2
Greencastle city *Putnam Co.*	6.8	2.6	15.4	3.4	20.1	21.5	4.6	25.6
Greenfield city *Hancock Co.*	11.9	4.6	8.0	8.0	14.6	26.6	10.5	15.7
Greensburg city *Decatur Co.*	12.1	5.6	6.9	3.3	14.4	16.5	4.7	36.5
Greenwood city *Johnson Co.*	15.7	7.1	7.6	6.8	16.3	26.5	7.8	12.2
Griffith town *Lake Co.*	10.8	3.1	5.5	5.0	18.4	27.2	9.7	20.2
Hammond city *Lake Co.*	8.7	2.3	7.8	3.6	21.2	23.6	10.2	22.7
Highland town *Lake Co.*	14.9	3.7	8.3	5.4	17.2	24.8	9.4	16.2
Hobart city *Lake Co.*	12.0	3.3	10.2	6.2	19.0	22.6	9.1	17.5
Huntertown town *Allen Co.*	14.9	3.9	10.6	9.5	14.5	25.7	7.2	13.6
Huntington city *Huntington Co.*	6.6	1.3	9.3	4.1	18.8	22.5	8.7	28.9
Indianapolis city *Marion Co.*	14.0	4.7	9.8	6.3	17.8	25.0	7.3	15.1
Jasper city *Dubois Co.*	13.3	6.6	8.9	4.4	15.8	24.1	6.4	20.4
Jeffersonville city *Clark Co.*	14.1	3.8	8.0	5.4	17.6	25.9	5.6	19.7
Kendallville city *Noble Co.*	12.1	2.6	5.9	5.6	14.4	12.5	5.4	41.4

Place	MBF[1] (%)	CES[2] (%)	ELCAM[3] (%)	HPT[4] (%)	S[5] (%)	SO[6] (%)	NRCM[7] (%)	PTMM[8] (%)
Kokomo city *Howard Co.*	7.1	4.2	7.7	6.0	21.1	20.5	7.8	25.5
La Porte city *LaPorte Co.*	6.1	2.7	6.4	4.8	22.0	24.9	8.6	24.6
Lafayette city *Tippecanoe Co.*	10.6	5.7	8.8	5.9	19.1	21.9	7.1	20.9
Lake Station city *Lake Co.*	3.9	1.3	3.5	6.0	25.4	22.3	13.2	24.3
Lakes of the Four Seasons CDP *Lake Co.*	13.8	4.9	8.8	8.0	12.0	27.8	8.4	16.2
Lawrence city *Marion Co.*	15.7	6.0	10.1	5.7	16.3	24.7	11.0	10.6
Lebanon city *Boone Co.*	14.1	4.2	7.5	5.5	15.7	26.4	9.5	17.2
Logansport city *Cass Co.*	6.5	0.7	5.4	5.7	16.9	17.2	11.1	36.5
Lowell town *Lake Co.*	13.3	1.8	14.3	4.6	13.1	21.9	10.9	20.0
Madison city *Jefferson Co.*	11.1	3.4	10.3	5.8	19.1	16.0	6.5	27.8
Marion city *Grant Co.*	7.5	1.3	10.1	5.4	28.6	22.5	5.6	19.1
Martinsville city *Morgan Co.*	8.5	1.8	5.6	2.9	20.6	24.7	14.2	21.6
Merrillville town *Lake Co.*	10.9	2.8	9.1	6.8	17.4	24.7	9.4	18.9
Michigan City city *LaPorte Co.*	10.2	1.6	8.0	3.9	23.6	22.8	8.7	21.1
Mishawaka city *Saint Joseph Co.*	10.1	3.3	9.8	5.8	19.0	25.9	7.0	19.0
Mooresville town *Morgan Co.*	8.7	1.6	8.3	2.5	17.2	27.7	12.0	22.0
Muncie city *Delaware Co.*	10.1	2.7	12.6	4.8	26.0	24.8	6.5	12.6
Munster town *Lake Co.*	22.4	5.0	10.7	10.4	12.1	24.6	5.8	9.0
Nappanee city *Elkhart Co.*	9.9	2.7	9.7	2.2	12.7	28.7	3.5	30.6
New Albany city *Floyd Co.*	10.7	4.0	8.8	6.9	17.3	26.0	8.5	17.8
New Castle city *Henry Co.*	8.1	2.3	10.4	5.3	19.2	22.2	7.1	25.4
New Haven city *Allen Co.*	10.1	4.0	6.5	6.6	19.0	24.0	7.6	22.3
Noblesville city *Hamilton Co.*	19.8	6.5	10.3	6.7	14.4	29.0	5.8	7.6
North Vernon city *Jennings Co.*	9.8	2.8	5.7	2.9	17.1	18.7	9.0	34.0
Notre Dame CDP *Saint Joseph Co.*	5.3	6.6	32.4	0.4	20.1	30.2	2.0	3.0
Peru city *Miami Co.*	5.0	2.5	7.2	3.9	22.5	19.9	9.9	29.0
Plainfield town *Hendricks Co.*	15.0	6.6	11.6	6.5	15.0	25.4	7.0	12.9
Plymouth city *Marshall Co.*	7.7	0.8	9.4	3.6	16.1	20.6	4.8	36.9
Portage city *Porter Co.*	9.6	3.5	6.9	5.0	22.0	22.9	9.4	20.7
Princeton city *Gibson Co.*	9.4	4.3	3.9	5.6	18.1	17.7	11.6	29.4
Richmond city *Wayne Co.*	9.3	2.5	9.7	6.8	22.2	21.7	5.8	21.9
Saint John town *Lake Co.*	20.3	6.0	9.7	10.6	11.0	23.5	9.1	9.8
Schererville town *Lake Co.*	16.0	4.0	10.5	7.6	14.2	24.0	10.3	13.4
Scottsburg city *Scott Co.*	10.5	2.8	9.9	4.2	13.8	22.6	10.2	26.2
Sellersburg town *Clark Co.*	15.5	5.1	9.2	5.3	14.0	28.6	7.8	14.5
Seymour city *Jackson Co.*	10.4	5.3	8.0	4.5	17.0	20.9	6.8	27.2
Shelbyville city *Shelby Co.*	9.8	2.5	5.2	5.4	17.2	22.3	10.5	27.1
South Bend city *Saint Joseph Co.*	9.7	3.9	11.9	5.1	21.8	22.8	5.3	19.4
Speedway town *Marion Co.*	12.2	5.8	8.9	6.0	18.4	23.8	7.4	17.5
Tell City city *Perry Co.*	8.3	3.2	5.6	2.2	21.3	22.2	7.2	30.0
Terre Haute city *Vigo Co.*	8.9	4.1	13.0	5.3	23.2	23.0	6.3	16.2
Valparaiso city *Porter Co.*	14.7	5.3	16.0	6.5	15.5	25.9	5.7	10.4
Vincennes city *Knox Co.*	9.8	1.3	7.1	5.7	25.6	18.1	5.1	27.3
Wabash city *Wabash Co.*	11.0	0.9	8.7	5.7	22.3	21.4	6.4	23.7
Warsaw city *Kosciusko Co.*	12.0	7.7	9.2	5.4	10.0	21.5	6.6	27.7
Washington city *Daviess Co.*	9.0	1.4	8.0	5.1	18.9	19.3	11.3	27.0
West Lafayette city *Tippecanoe Co.*	8.8	12.7	29.4	3.2	19.6	18.5	3.5	4.3
Westfield city *Hamilton Co.*	22.7	9.4	12.2	7.8	10.7	25.0	5.0	7.2
Yorktown town *Delaware Co.*	13.3	7.7	9.5	12.7	16.5	24.7	5.8	9.8
Zionsville town *Boone Co.*	27.7	10.8	14.4	9.4	9.1	19.1	3.3	6.2

NOTES: (1) Management, business, and financial occupations; (2) Computer, engineering, and science occupations; (3) Education, legal, community service, arts, and media occupations; (4) Healthcare practitioners and technical occupations; (5) Service occupations; (6) Sales and office occupations; (7) Natural resources, construction, and maintenance occupations; (8) Production, transportation, and material moving occupations

SOURCE: U.S. Census Bureau, American Community Survey, 2013-2017 Five-Year Estimates

Comparative Statistics

Educational Attainment

Place	Percent of Population 25 Years and Over with:		
	High School Diploma or Higher[1]	Bachelor's Degree or Higher	Graduate/Professional Degree
Anderson city *Madison Co.*	84.8	14.5	4.8
Angola city *Steuben Co.*	87.2	23.1	10.3
Auburn city *DeKalb Co.*	91.2	23.4	6.8
Avon town *Hendricks Co.*	92.5	38.7	14.0
Bargersville town *Johnson Co.*	89.2	35.0	12.4
Bedford city *Lawrence Co.*	87.5	14.8	5.7
Beech Grove city *Marion Co.*	86.8	15.1	4.8
Bloomington city *Monroe Co.*	92.6	56.8	30.6
Bluffton city *Wells Co.*	90.8	16.6	6.3
Brazil city *Clay Co.*	86.7	14.8	3.9
Brownsburg town *Hendricks Co.*	92.7	35.6	11.5
Carmel city *Hamilton Co.*	97.9	71.0	29.0
Cedar Lake town *Lake Co.*	90.3	20.6	6.3
Charlestown city *Clark Co.*	81.9	13.7	4.1
Chesterton town *Porter Co.*	93.2	31.0	12.5
Clarksville town *Clark Co.*	86.2	17.9	4.5
Columbia City city *Whitley Co.*	87.5	23.4	7.8
Columbus city *Bartholomew Co.*	91.5	39.9	17.1
Connersville city *Fayette Co.*	78.2	9.5	2.4
Crawfordsville city *Montgomery Co.*	85.9	19.2	6.0
Crown Point city *Lake Co.*	91.9	33.3	10.0
Danville town *Hendricks Co.*	93.6	29.5	9.1
Decatur city *Adams Co.*	87.0	11.2	3.0
Dyer town *Lake Co.*	94.3	30.4	10.4
East Chicago city *Lake Co.*	72.1	8.6	2.9
Elkhart city *Elkhart Co.*	76.1	13.1	4.3
Elwood city *Madison Co.*	82.7	10.8	2.8
Evansville city *Vanderburgh Co.*	86.9	20.7	7.0
Fishers city *Hamilton Co.*	97.5	65.1	23.4
Fort Wayne city *Allen Co.*	88.6	26.8	9.2
Frankfort city *Clinton Co.*	79.3	11.3	3.9
Franklin city *Johnson Co.*	88.6	24.1	8.7
Garrett city *DeKalb Co.*	86.9	11.1	3.4
Gary city *Lake Co.*	84.9	12.8	4.8
Goshen city *Elkhart Co.*	76.9	21.9	10.0
Granger CDP *Saint Joseph Co.*	96.6	52.7	23.0
Greencastle city *Putnam Co.*	88.0	17.8	8.6
Greenfield city *Hancock Co.*	91.1	21.8	6.9
Greensburg city *Decatur Co.*	90.0	20.3	6.8
Greenwood city *Johnson Co.*	91.1	29.4	8.1
Griffith town *Lake Co.*	93.0	18.8	4.2
Hammond city *Lake Co.*	80.3	14.0	3.7
Highland town *Lake Co.*	93.1	26.7	8.0
Hobart city *Lake Co.*	89.9	21.5	6.6
Huntertown town *Allen Co.*	96.3	28.9	12.2
Huntington city *Huntington Co.*	86.5	15.5	6.9
Indianapolis city *Marion Co.*	85.5	29.7	10.5
Jasper city *Dubois Co.*	88.4	24.9	6.6
Jeffersonville city *Clark Co.*	90.7	21.1	6.9
Kendallville city *Noble Co.*	84.3	12.9	4.4

Place	Percent of Population 25 Years and Over with: High School Diploma or Higher[1]	Bachelor's Degree or Higher	Graduate/Professional Degree
Kokomo city *Howard Co.*	86.9	17.3	6.2
La Porte city *LaPorte Co.*	84.9	16.1	5.3
Lafayette city *Tippecanoe Co.*	87.6	24.5	8.4
Lake Station city *Lake Co.*	78.8	6.0	2.1
Lakes of the Four Seasons CDP *Lake Co.*	94.8	27.7	7.1
Lawrence city *Marion Co.*	86.0	32.8	10.6
Lebanon city *Boone Co.*	87.1	25.8	8.0
Logansport city *Cass Co.*	74.2	10.9	3.3
Lowell town *Lake Co.*	91.1	20.4	7.9
Madison city *Jefferson Co.*	89.4	18.8	7.9
Marion city *Grant Co.*	82.9	14.2	6.2
Martinsville city *Morgan Co.*	82.3	11.2	3.4
Merrillville town *Lake Co.*	92.0	23.4	8.4
Michigan City city *LaPorte Co.*	85.6	16.6	5.8
Mishawaka city *Saint Joseph Co.*	88.0	24.3	8.4
Mooresville town *Morgan Co.*	86.1	11.4	3.1
Muncie city *Delaware Co.*	86.7	23.6	10.5
Munster town *Lake Co.*	94.7	42.7	14.9
Nappanee city *Elkhart Co.*	86.9	17.2	6.6
New Albany city *Floyd Co.*	84.6	20.6	7.5
New Castle city *Henry Co.*	86.8	14.7	4.3
New Haven city *Allen Co.*	88.7	16.1	4.1
Noblesville city *Hamilton Co.*	94.6	45.8	13.3
North Vernon city *Jennings Co.*	81.6	12.6	4.7
Notre Dame CDP *Saint Joseph Co.*	96.1	76.5	37.1
Peru city *Miami Co.*	83.2	10.8	3.3
Plainfield town *Hendricks Co.*	92.8	30.3	11.3
Plymouth city *Marshall Co.*	80.6	17.4	7.0
Portage city *Porter Co.*	88.3	15.7	5.6
Princeton city *Gibson Co.*	87.9	10.4	3.4
Richmond city *Wayne Co.*	82.6	18.1	8.1
Saint John town *Lake Co.*	96.1	38.9	13.6
Schererville town *Lake Co.*	93.6	31.7	12.6
Scottsburg city *Scott Co.*	88.1	15.1	3.6
Sellersburg town *Clark Co.*	88.8	23.1	7.7
Seymour city *Jackson Co.*	84.7	19.2	6.2
Shelbyville city *Shelby Co.*	83.9	17.0	6.3
South Bend city *Saint Joseph Co.*	83.4	24.3	9.8
Speedway town *Marion Co.*	87.1	30.0	11.3
Tell City city *Perry Co.*	88.7	15.5	9.0
Terre Haute city *Vigo Co.*	85.0	22.1	9.0
Valparaiso city *Porter Co.*	94.7	39.5	14.4
Vincennes city *Knox Co.*	83.7	15.1	6.4
Wabash city *Wabash Co.*	86.5	12.3	4.2
Warsaw city *Kosciusko Co.*	84.9	28.4	10.1
Washington city *Daviess Co.*	79.6	15.4	4.8
West Lafayette city *Tippecanoe Co.*	94.7	71.9	45.6
Westfield city *Hamilton Co.*	96.2	56.5	17.4
Yorktown town *Delaware Co.*	95.3	28.0	10.5
Zionsville town *Boone Co.*	97.8	70.4	33.2

NOTE: (1) Includes General Equivalency Diploma (GED)
SOURCE: U.S. Census Bureau, American Community Survey, 2013-2017 Five-Year Estimates

Health Insurance

Place	Percent of Total Population with: Any Insurance	Private Insurance	Public Insurance	No Insurance	Percent of Population[1] Under Age 18 without Health Insurance
Anderson city *Madison Co.*	86.8	54.1	47.5	13.2	6.1
Angola city *Steuben Co.*	87.3	64.1	34.8	12.7	12.2
Auburn city *DeKalb Co.*	93.1	74.5	32.5	6.9	10.3
Avon town *Hendricks Co.*	93.0	84.5	18.2	7.0	1.8
Bargersville town *Johnson Co.*	97.9	89.8	19.8	2.1	0.6
Bedford city *Lawrence Co.*	89.8	63.4	41.6	10.2	6.2
Beech Grove city *Marion Co.*	89.7	56.4	45.8	10.3	3.7
Bloomington city *Monroe Co.*	90.8	77.3	20.1	9.2	5.8
Bluffton city *Wells Co.*	90.4	63.2	42.3	9.6	10.1
Brazil city *Clay Co.*	91.2	62.6	41.3	8.8	2.7
Brownsburg town *Hendricks Co.*	91.0	81.7	21.8	9.0	8.4
Carmel city *Hamilton Co.*	96.5	89.5	15.8	3.5	2.0
Cedar Lake town *Lake Co.*	91.7	78.5	22.5	8.3	6.4
Charlestown city *Clark Co.*	89.9	64.5	36.3	10.1	4.5
Chesterton town *Porter Co.*	95.4	84.5	23.0	4.6	1.8
Clarksville town *Clark Co.*	87.2	63.8	36.8	12.8	9.3
Columbia City city *Whitley Co.*	91.4	69.8	37.1	8.6	5.2
Columbus city *Bartholomew Co.*	90.1	75.3	27.7	9.9	9.7
Connersville city *Fayette Co.*	84.3	53.1	44.3	15.7	6.2
Crawfordsville city *Montgomery Co.*	85.3	63.3	34.1	14.7	8.6
Crown Point city *Lake Co.*	95.5	81.4	29.5	4.5	3.4
Danville town *Hendricks Co.*	91.5	76.0	25.3	8.5	5.2
Decatur city *Adams Co.*	95.4	72.0	36.3	4.6	6.4
Dyer town *Lake Co.*	96.3	84.4	26.3	3.7	0.9
East Chicago city *Lake Co.*	82.9	43.8	49.6	17.1	7.5
Elkhart city *Elkhart Co.*	82.4	49.5	41.9	17.6	7.9
Elwood city *Madison Co.*	86.6	58.3	41.4	13.4	4.1
Evansville city *Vanderburgh Co.*	88.3	61.1	39.9	11.7	4.9
Fishers city *Hamilton Co.*	95.9	90.5	11.5	4.1	4.2
Fort Wayne city *Allen Co.*	88.3	63.5	34.7	11.7	7.0
Frankfort city *Clinton Co.*	86.9	60.4	37.7	13.1	4.1
Franklin city *Johnson Co.*	90.9	76.7	27.2	9.1	7.4
Garrett city *DeKalb Co.*	88.3	67.0	34.9	11.7	6.4
Gary city *Lake Co.*	87.0	44.1	55.6	13.0	3.4
Goshen city *Elkhart Co.*	82.6	59.4	35.8	17.4	10.0
Granger CDP *Saint Joseph Co.*	95.8	87.0	19.5	4.2	3.8
Greencastle city *Putnam Co.*	91.9	72.1	33.9	8.1	3.4
Greenfield city *Hancock Co.*	92.1	72.0	34.7	7.9	6.6
Greensburg city *Decatur Co.*	91.2	72.2	30.4	8.8	6.2
Greenwood city *Johnson Co.*	90.0	71.3	30.6	10.0	6.4
Griffith town *Lake Co.*	92.1	70.3	32.7	7.9	3.9
Hammond city *Lake Co.*	84.9	57.2	37.6	15.1	6.5
Highland town *Lake Co.*	93.4	78.9	29.6	6.6	4.8
Hobart city *Lake Co.*	93.1	76.9	31.2	6.9	3.7
Huntertown town *Allen Co.*	95.8	82.8	23.7	4.2	2.3
Huntington city *Huntington Co.*	89.2	66.7	33.4	10.8	7.6
Indianapolis city *Marion Co.*	87.4	60.5	35.9	12.6	6.1
Jasper city *Dubois Co.*	92.7	80.5	24.0	7.3	5.0
Jeffersonville city *Clark Co.*	90.8	72.6	31.6	9.2	6.8
Kendallville city *Noble Co.*	86.9	64.7	36.1	13.1	7.0

Place	Percent of Total Population with: Any Insurance	Private Insurance	Public Insurance	No Insurance	Percent of Population[1] Under Age 18 without Health Insurance
Kokomo city *Howard Co.*	89.2	64.9	41.5	10.8	5.7
La Porte city *LaPorte Co.*	85.7	59.3	40.6	14.3	8.0
Lafayette city *Tippecanoe Co.*	86.7	62.9	33.8	13.3	5.5
Lake Station city *Lake Co.*	84.9	56.1	40.0	15.1	7.2
Lakes of the Four Seasons CDP *Lake Co.*	94.3	80.5	26.1	5.7	3.1
Lawrence city *Marion Co.*	86.3	63.5	31.8	13.7	6.3
Lebanon city *Boone Co.*	89.8	72.1	33.1	10.2	9.9
Logansport city *Cass Co.*	83.2	59.5	34.6	16.8	10.2
Lowell town *Lake Co.*	91.2	77.6	24.9	8.8	7.2
Madison city *Jefferson Co.*	91.7	68.5	41.6	8.3	0.6
Marion city *Grant Co.*	87.1	53.6	48.8	12.9	5.0
Martinsville city *Morgan Co.*	87.4	55.2	43.8	12.6	8.0
Merrillville town *Lake Co.*	90.4	71.6	30.2	9.6	6.6
Michigan City city *LaPorte Co.*	87.9	54.2	44.4	12.1	5.1
Mishawaka city *Saint Joseph Co.*	86.7	64.5	33.6	13.3	6.9
Mooresville town *Morgan Co.*	92.4	68.7	37.4	7.6	5.3
Muncie city *Delaware Co.*	88.9	65.3	34.8	11.1	5.4
Munster town *Lake Co.*	95.1	85.1	23.1	4.9	0.8
Nappanee city *Elkhart Co.*	86.0	74.0	23.0	14.0	9.4
New Albany city *Floyd Co.*	91.3	67.6	36.8	8.7	3.7
New Castle city *Henry Co.*	88.3	58.4	47.1	11.7	7.0
New Haven city *Allen Co.*	90.6	68.3	34.5	9.4	5.6
Noblesville city *Hamilton Co.*	92.6	82.4	19.5	7.4	4.5
North Vernon city *Jennings Co.*	87.8	58.6	39.2	12.2	10.2
Notre Dame CDP *Saint Joseph Co.*	97.5	95.4	4.3	2.5	0.7
Peru city *Miami Co.*	88.8	57.0	46.4	11.2	2.9
Plainfield town *Hendricks Co.*	93.1	75.1	30.2	6.9	5.7
Plymouth city *Marshall Co.*	85.4	53.1	43.2	14.6	12.3
Portage city *Porter Co.*	89.6	70.4	32.6	10.4	3.3
Princeton city *Gibson Co.*	91.4	67.8	36.8	8.6	6.5
Richmond city *Wayne Co.*	85.9	54.5	45.4	14.1	9.7
Saint John town *Lake Co.*	96.5	89.7	18.8	3.5	2.2
Schererville town *Lake Co.*	91.4	79.7	25.2	8.6	8.7
Scottsburg city *Scott Co.*	92.0	68.5	38.1	8.0	0.7
Sellersburg town *Clark Co.*	89.0	74.8	24.3	11.0	11.2
Seymour city *Jackson Co.*	89.1	67.1	31.9	10.9	6.1
Shelbyville city *Shelby Co.*	88.0	66.9	32.6	12.0	10.4
South Bend city *Saint Joseph Co.*	86.2	56.0	39.5	13.8	5.6
Speedway town *Marion Co.*	89.1	63.7	35.6	10.9	3.5
Tell City city *Perry Co.*	89.5	65.4	39.5	10.5	4.9
Terre Haute city *Vigo Co.*	88.4	61.0	39.7	11.6	5.7
Valparaiso city *Porter Co.*	91.1	75.2	26.8	8.9	3.0
Vincennes city *Knox Co.*	89.4	62.7	40.7	10.6	3.5
Wabash city *Wabash Co.*	89.6	66.1	37.8	10.4	4.0
Warsaw city *Kosciusko Co.*	88.0	72.5	25.4	12.0	13.2
Washington city *Daviess Co.*	88.0	56.6	44.0	12.0	7.1
West Lafayette city *Tippecanoe Co.*	94.5	89.6	11.2	5.5	5.1
Westfield city *Hamilton Co.*	93.3	86.3	15.0	6.7	3.3
Yorktown town *Delaware Co.*	95.2	81.8	29.8	4.8	1.1
Zionsville town *Boone Co.*	96.8	92.1	12.6	3.2	2.0

NOTE: (1) Civilian noninstitutionalized population.
SOURCE: U.S. Census Bureau, American Community Survey, 2013-2017 Five-Year Estimates

Comparative Statistics

Income and Poverty

Place	Average Household Income ($)	Median Household Income ($)	Per Capita Income ($)	Households w/$100,000+ Income (%)	Poverty Rate (%)
Anderson city *Madison Co.*	45,965	34,693	20,207	8.3	25.8
Angola city *Steuben Co.*	54,217	41,568	20,515	11.5	16.9
Auburn city *DeKalb Co.*	68,262	47,129	29,911	16.4	11.7
Avon town *Hendricks Co.*	98,463	85,433	34,913	42.8	5.4
Bargersville town *Johnson Co.*	110,158	81,673	39,347	38.6	6.4
Bedford city *Lawrence Co.*	53,289	40,076	23,627	10.5	17.9
Beech Grove city *Marion Co.*	49,446	37,819	20,388	11.0	21.1
Bloomington city *Monroe Co.*	55,113	33,172	21,972	15.5	37.5
Bluffton city *Wells Co.*	52,946	40,194	23,041	11.6	17.6
Brazil city *Clay Co.*	45,852	35,042	18,875	9.1	23.7
Brownsburg town *Hendricks Co.*	86,960	68,986	32,690	31.0	3.4
Carmel city *Hamilton Co.*	147,771	109,201	55,796	54.7	3.7
Cedar Lake town *Lake Co.*	85,043	70,702	30,271	25.9	9.9
Charlestown city *Clark Co.*	55,890	42,450	21,808	14.6	14.6
Chesterton town *Porter Co.*	92,194	66,861	36,568	32.5	8.1
Clarksville town *Clark Co.*	55,058	42,872	25,019	12.2	11.5
Columbia City city *Whitley Co.*	56,062	46,611	25,154	11.5	14.7
Columbus city *Bartholomew Co.*	76,343	57,535	31,895	24.7	12.2
Connersville city *Fayette Co.*	46,951	33,902	20,321	8.5	24.2
Crawfordsville city *Montgomery Co.*	50,570	40,899	21,057	10.3	15.5
Crown Point city *Lake Co.*	84,875	69,471	33,636	30.3	7.8
Danville town *Hendricks Co.*	76,663	64,074	29,591	28.2	7.2
Decatur city *Adams Co.*	49,965	41,004	22,146	8.4	20.2
Dyer town *Lake Co.*	104,417	79,167	40,173	37.3	3.6
East Chicago city *Lake Co.*	40,367	30,205	15,159	6.3	34.6
Elkhart city *Elkhart Co.*	47,042	37,121	18,426	8.2	24.8
Elwood city *Madison Co.*	50,921	36,342	21,425	9.7	22.5
Evansville city *Vanderburgh Co.*	50,350	36,956	22,375	9.9	23.3
Fishers city *Hamilton Co.*	128,847	101,469	46,619	50.9	3.3
Fort Wayne city *Allen Co.*	60,942	45,853	25,066	14.6	17.8
Frankfort city *Clinton Co.*	53,443	41,982	20,057	11.2	16.3
Franklin city *Johnson Co.*	67,641	56,367	26,647	22.5	10.4
Garrett city *DeKalb Co.*	48,393	42,277	19,143	3.1	20.1
Gary city *Lake Co.*	40,917	29,293	17,392	6.8	35.8
Goshen city *Elkhart Co.*	55,375	46,055	21,450	13.0	17.3
Granger CDP *Saint Joseph Co.*	131,022	100,182	45,182	50.1	4.1
Greencastle city *Putnam Co.*	58,373	46,029	19,689	9.7	13.8
Greenfield city *Hancock Co.*	60,664	52,130	26,025	16.3	12.9
Greensburg city *Decatur Co.*	59,478	50,781	24,929	13.1	12.5
Greenwood city *Johnson Co.*	70,416	55,274	28,078	20.4	12.2
Griffith town *Lake Co.*	67,290	57,452	27,430	21.7	8.9
Hammond city *Lake Co.*	53,796	44,427	20,337	11.4	22.2
Highland town *Lake Co.*	73,803	62,345	31,371	24.8	7.7
Hobart city *Lake Co.*	68,836	58,366	27,550	20.7	11.1
Huntertown town *Allen Co.*	91,876	74,575	32,241	31.5	5.4
Huntington city *Huntington Co.*	51,370	42,302	20,322	10.5	16.9
Indianapolis city *Marion Co.*	63,698	44,709	26,232	16.8	20.1
Jasper city *Dubois Co.*	77,946	55,878	31,993	20.2	11.0
Jeffersonville city *Clark Co.*	65,161	52,861	26,840	15.8	10.2
Kendallville city *Noble Co.*	47,133	37,232	20,960	8.1	19.0

Place	Average Household Income ($)	Median Household Income ($)	Per Capita Income ($)	Households w/$100,000+ Income (%)	Poverty Rate (%)
Kokomo city *Howard Co.*	55,147	41,366	24,463	12.8	20.4
La Porte city *LaPorte Co.*	47,451	36,734	19,980	7.5	22.4
Lafayette city *Tippecanoe Co.*	54,473	43,894	24,117	11.5	18.9
Lake Station city *Lake Co.*	50,090	41,930	17,217	8.7	25.4
Lakes of the Four Seasons CDP *Lake Co.*	91,926	89,906	33,764	40.2	5.4
Lawrence city *Marion Co.*	66,291	50,107	26,397	21.0	15.8
Lebanon city *Boone Co.*	65,359	47,234	29,462	16.4	9.3
Logansport city *Cass Co.*	46,665	35,603	18,442	8.6	18.3
Lowell town *Lake Co.*	70,662	62,574	25,645	22.0	9.1
Madison city *Jefferson Co.*	56,574	46,444	24,128	16.4	19.2
Marion city *Grant Co.*	43,029	32,879	17,631	6.5	26.4
Martinsville city *Morgan Co.*	51,695	42,092	20,753	11.3	21.6
Merrillville town *Lake Co.*	65,178	56,330	26,749	18.6	10.9
Michigan City city *LaPorte Co.*	50,213	38,631	20,279	9.5	25.5
Mishawaka city *Saint Joseph Co.*	50,312	39,821	22,124	9.8	18.8
Mooresville town *Morgan Co.*	58,076	52,513	24,105	14.1	14.1
Muncie city *Delaware Co.*	44,711	32,372	18,891	9.4	29.9
Munster town *Lake Co.*	100,558	78,251	39,915	38.2	4.8
Nappanee city *Elkhart Co.*	59,141	46,146	22,815	15.3	10.1
New Albany city *Floyd Co.*	56,147	43,914	25,266	13.3	18.3
New Castle city *Henry Co.*	46,700	36,655	20,110	6.9	23.3
New Haven city *Allen Co.*	54,413	47,649	21,278	10.7	12.3
Noblesville city *Hamilton Co.*	93,070	74,681	34,910	33.0	6.5
North Vernon city *Jennings Co.*	57,103	42,200	23,558	13.8	19.8
Notre Dame CDP *Saint Joseph Co.*	18,193	15,625	5,995	0.0	80.2
Peru city *Miami Co.*	46,776	34,991	19,905	7.1	22.7
Plainfield town *Hendricks Co.*	73,581	62,121	28,383	25.0	8.6
Plymouth city *Marshall Co.*	45,069	35,713	17,709	7.2	23.9
Portage city *Porter Co.*	62,924	54,566	25,498	19.2	17.2
Princeton city *Gibson Co.*	56,665	41,340	22,685	8.2	15.0
Richmond city *Wayne Co.*	50,371	33,381	20,907	11.1	23.4
Saint John town *Lake Co.*	121,622	103,701	42,503	53.4	3.2
Schererville town *Lake Co.*	89,007	68,166	36,641	32.5	4.5
Scottsburg city *Scott Co.*	57,702	46,090	23,077	20.8	15.4
Sellersburg town *Clark Co.*	75,526	61,617	28,471	21.5	8.5
Seymour city *Jackson Co.*	53,725	43,664	21,942	13.0	19.7
Shelbyville city *Shelby Co.*	59,757	48,071	24,675	15.3	16.2
South Bend city *Saint Joseph Co.*	52,434	37,441	21,100	10.9	25.4
Speedway town *Marion Co.*	51,534	40,109	22,873	11.3	21.0
Tell City city *Perry Co.*	52,072	42,145	22,152	11.5	20.0
Terre Haute city *Vigo Co.*	46,931	34,746	19,263	9.0	26.0
Valparaiso city *Porter Co.*	71,440	52,507	29,067	21.1	13.6
Vincennes city *Knox Co.*	46,187	36,724	19,529	7.4	22.9
Wabash city *Wabash Co.*	55,348	44,094	24,876	9.2	17.4
Warsaw city *Kosciusko Co.*	68,466	50,046	27,137	17.4	13.2
Washington city *Daviess Co.*	50,604	36,411	20,300	13.0	18.4
West Lafayette city *Tippecanoe Co.*	59,259	31,230	19,421	18.8	41.1
Westfield city *Hamilton Co.*	108,176	89,144	37,855	44.4	6.7
Yorktown town *Delaware Co.*	80,524	62,372	31,646	25.4	8.2
Zionsville town *Boone Co.*	169,680	127,152	60,565	60.6	2.6

SOURCE: U.S. Census Bureau, American Community Survey, 2013-2017 Five-Year Estimates

Housing

Place	Homeownership Rate (%)	Median Home Value ($)	Median Year Structure Built	Homeowner Vacancy Rate (%)	Median Gross Rent ($/month)	Rental Vacancy Rate (%)
Anderson city *Madison Co.*	56.0	70,500	1960	3.9	724	8.2
Angola city *Steuben Co.*	48.3	120,500	1981	6.1	725	1.5
Auburn city *DeKalb Co.*	69.5	106,400	1977	3.6	684	5.0
Avon town *Hendricks Co.*	80.9	185,200	2000	0.9	1,055	4.7
Bargersville town *Johnson Co.*	74.1	180,700	2003	0.0	955	4.4
Bedford city *Lawrence Co.*	64.9	87,600	1959	4.1	656	11.7
Beech Grove city *Marion Co.*	53.5	96,200	1961	2.0	753	1.8
Bloomington city *Monroe Co.*	34.5	176,300	1982	0.9	863	5.3
Bluffton city *Wells Co.*	66.2	94,900	1968	1.1	560	10.5
Brazil city *Clay Co.*	59.1	72,200	1953	4.3	616	0.0
Brownsburg town *Hendricks Co.*	75.0	163,600	1997	0.6	1,032	4.1
Carmel city *Hamilton Co.*	77.6	320,400	1994	2.4	1,150	8.4
Cedar Lake town *Lake Co.*	80.1	170,100	1975	3.6	861	11.6
Charlestown city *Clark Co.*	59.3	109,300	1962	3.9	764	4.3
Chesterton town *Porter Co.*	68.1	176,300	1980	0.0	885	1.0
Clarksville town *Clark Co.*	60.5	112,900	1970	3.9	767	10.3
Columbia City city *Whitley Co.*	64.2	106,200	1979	0.6	590	2.6
Columbus city *Bartholomew Co.*	63.6	148,500	1979	0.8	864	8.6
Connersville city *Fayette Co.*	57.7	68,500	1956	7.5	662	12.6
Crawfordsville city *Montgomery Co.*	55.8	91,700	1960	2.1	637	8.7
Crown Point city *Lake Co.*	79.0	178,400	1983	1.3	989	3.8
Danville town *Hendricks Co.*	67.8	152,800	1992	0.7	834	4.0
Decatur city *Adams Co.*	64.4	94,000	1959	0.0	565	6.9
Dyer town *Lake Co.*	91.0	199,400	1986	1.1	999	0.0
East Chicago city *Lake Co.*	43.8	73,300	1942	2.1	673	9.0
Elkhart city *Elkhart Co.*	46.8	87,700	1964	3.1	722	7.6
Elwood city *Madison Co.*	62.5	66,600	1942	3.9	683	5.9
Evansville city *Vanderburgh Co.*	54.5	89,700	1958	2.2	738	6.6
Fishers city *Hamilton Co.*	80.8	240,100	1999	0.4	1,175	10.8
Fort Wayne city *Allen Co.*	62.0	106,500	1970	1.8	708	7.6
Frankfort city *Clinton Co.*	62.5	79,000	1954	0.5	678	9.0
Franklin city *Johnson Co.*	63.1	119,200	1991	3.4	798	5.6
Garrett city *DeKalb Co.*	65.5	86,400	1957	0.0	686	6.2
Gary city *Lake Co.*	52.0	66,300	1955	3.2	751	8.4
Goshen city *Elkhart Co.*	55.5	111,000	1979	1.8	745	5.5
Granger CDP *Saint Joseph Co.*	95.5	203,500	1987	0.3	1,472	14.7
Greencastle city *Putnam Co.*	51.4	103,900	1963	2.1	689	5.5
Greenfield city *Hancock Co.*	58.2	132,000	1988	2.5	854	2.4
Greensburg city *Decatur Co.*	57.7	110,300	1972	0.0	758	6.8
Greenwood city *Johnson Co.*	57.6	143,100	1991	1.1	903	6.5
Griffith town *Lake Co.*	65.8	135,600	1967	0.2	857	6.2
Hammond city *Lake Co.*	59.7	87,600	1951	2.0	852	5.5
Highland town *Lake Co.*	78.4	155,400	1966	1.6	1,017	1.1
Hobart city *Lake Co.*	75.1	134,300	1966	1.0	873	5.2
Huntertown town *Allen Co.*	92.1	154,500	2004	1.7	968	0.0
Huntington city *Huntington Co.*	64.8	78,400	1941	1.9	678	4.9
Indianapolis city *Marion Co.*	53.4	123,500	1971	2.1	840	8.4
Jasper city *Dubois Co.*	72.5	151,000	1979	4.2	563	3.4
Jeffersonville city *Clark Co.*	70.2	128,300	1978	2.4	792	11.6
Kendallville city *Noble Co.*	57.1	92,900	1969	1.9	651	6.8

Place	Homeownership Rate (%)	Median Home Value ($)	Median Year Structure Built	Homeowner Vacancy Rate (%)	Median Gross Rent ($/month)	Rental Vacancy Rate (%)
Kokomo city *Howard Co.*	60.7	85,200	1965	3.2	672	7.1
La Porte city *LaPorte Co.*	57.2	93,400	1955	2.3	672	5.0
Lafayette city *Tippecanoe Co.*	46.6	105,300	1971	1.9	789	5.2
Lake Station city *Lake Co.*	69.2	78,700	1958	6.1	907	0.0
Lakes of the Four Seasons CDP *Lake Co.*	93.9	184,500	1978	0.0	1,193	0.0
Lawrence city *Marion Co.*	65.4	133,600	1991	3.4	823	6.9
Lebanon city *Boone Co.*	61.8	113,800	1978	1.4	758	9.3
Logansport city *Cass Co.*	59.8	65,400	Before 1940	1.4	631	4.7
Lowell town *Lake Co.*	81.0	152,200	1978	0.0	986	0.0
Madison city *Jefferson Co.*	58.4	125,000	1964	10.0	715	6.7
Marion city *Grant Co.*	55.9	65,400	1958	4.7	650	8.0
Martinsville city *Morgan Co.*	52.9	96,300	1958	0.0	689	9.9
Merrillville town *Lake Co.*	65.1	128,600	1974	1.0	1,026	7.7
Michigan City city *LaPorte Co.*	54.0	89,000	1961	2.1	741	5.6
Mishawaka city *Saint Joseph Co.*	50.2	93,300	1974	1.7	730	14.8
Mooresville town *Morgan Co.*	66.9	123,700	1977	0.0	770	5.4
Muncie city *Delaware Co.*	51.4	70,500	1960	3.6	714	8.5
Munster town *Lake Co.*	86.0	217,700	1971	1.6	1,072	0.0
Nappanee city *Elkhart Co.*	62.2	121,300	1974	1.8	668	8.6
New Albany city *Floyd Co.*	55.4	111,300	1962	2.4	753	10.0
New Castle city *Henry Co.*	58.2	71,700	1957	5.3	662	19.2
New Haven city *Allen Co.*	71.6	97,300	1973	0.5	750	4.7
Noblesville city *Hamilton Co.*	69.9	183,700	2000	1.4	993	3.3
North Vernon city *Jennings Co.*	51.9	86,100	1972	1.9	656	7.0
Notre Dame CDP *Saint Joseph Co.*	0.0	n/a	1993	0.0	646	3.2
Peru city *Miami Co.*	61.1	60,400	Before 1940	2.2	633	2.2
Plainfield town *Hendricks Co.*	68.6	155,100	1994	0.9	990	7.6
Plymouth city *Marshall Co.*	56.0	89,200	1969	4.9	670	7.7
Portage city *Porter Co.*	68.5	141,000	1978	1.6	884	4.8
Princeton city *Gibson Co.*	58.0	81,000	1959	3.9	644	5.7
Richmond city *Wayne Co.*	56.8	85,300	1956	3.1	653	18.0
Saint John town *Lake Co.*	98.3	274,300	1998	0.1	842	0.0
Schererville town *Lake Co.*	77.9	206,300	1987	1.3	940	4.6
Scottsburg city *Scott Co.*	59.9	97,200	1971	4.0	754	8.5
Sellersburg town *Clark Co.*	73.3	144,900	1977	0.0	936	4.9
Seymour city *Jackson Co.*	62.8	108,400	1973	3.0	746	4.9
Shelbyville city *Shelby Co.*	59.3	96,300	1967	1.2	757	11.3
South Bend city *Saint Joseph Co.*	57.2	81,100	1955	2.9	741	13.2
Speedway town *Marion Co.*	45.7	117,000	1962	4.0	741	6.5
Tell City city *Perry Co.*	69.5	91,000	1961	1.4	611	2.3
Terre Haute city *Vigo Co.*	51.7	76,600	1953	3.8	694	8.1
Valparaiso city *Porter Co.*	56.1	175,000	1976	1.9	897	6.4
Vincennes city *Knox Co.*	49.8	73,700	1957	1.9	673	9.6
Wabash city *Wabash Co.*	66.2	77,300	1949	4.3	640	5.8
Warsaw city *Kosciusko Co.*	56.2	124,300	1976	0.7	803	4.6
Washington city *Daviess Co.*	62.8	82,200	1957	1.7	622	12.6
West Lafayette city *Tippecanoe Co.*	34.4	192,600	1981	0.5	860	5.2
Westfield city *Hamilton Co.*	81.4	232,300	2002	0.3	1,162	5.6
Yorktown town *Delaware Co.*	81.3	133,900	1971	0.9	697	0.0
Zionsville town *Boone Co.*	80.7	360,100	1999	0.0	1,249	9.8

SOURCE: U.S. Census Bureau, American Community Survey, 2013-2017 Five-Year Estimates

Commute to Work

Place	Automobile (%)	Public Transportation (%)	Walk (%)	Work from Home (%)	Mean Travel Time to Work (minutes)
Anderson city *Madison Co.*	90.5	0.3	3.8	3.1	23.7
Angola city *Steuben Co.*	86.5	0.4	6.2	4.9	14.5
Auburn city *DeKalb Co.*	95.2	0.0	0.3	2.9	17.7
Avon town *Hendricks Co.*	92.4	0.0	0.6	6.1	29.5
Bargersville town *Johnson Co.*	94.0	0.4	1.1	4.5	27.6
Bedford city *Lawrence Co.*	94.4	0.0	2.4	2.5	18.9
Beech Grove city *Marion Co.*	93.3	1.7	2.2	2.0	22.7
Bloomington city *Monroe Co.*	72.0	6.7	12.8	4.1	16.1
Bluffton city *Wells Co.*	93.6	0.0	2.0	2.9	18.9
Brazil city *Clay Co.*	96.1	0.0	2.8	0.6	22.2
Brownsburg town *Hendricks Co.*	94.5	0.0	0.4	3.6	28.1
Carmel city *Hamilton Co.*	89.6	0.2	1.1	8.3	24.2
Cedar Lake town *Lake Co.*	93.0	1.2	1.1	3.8	34.7
Charlestown city *Clark Co.*	98.2	0.0	0.5	1.3	25.0
Chesterton town *Porter Co.*	90.2	2.3	1.4	5.7	26.3
Clarksville town *Clark Co.*	94.5	1.0	0.8	3.0	21.0
Columbia City city *Whitley Co.*	95.7	0.5	1.1	1.6	20.1
Columbus city *Bartholomew Co.*	93.9	0.9	1.3	2.6	17.3
Connersville city *Fayette Co.*	93.1	0.8	1.8	2.3	23.7
Crawfordsville city *Montgomery Co.*	91.0	0.0	6.2	1.5	16.8
Crown Point city *Lake Co.*	92.0	1.4	1.5	3.1	28.0
Danville town *Hendricks Co.*	92.0	0.0	2.3	5.1	25.0
Decatur city *Adams Co.*	95.8	0.0	1.9	1.4	20.2
Dyer town *Lake Co.*	92.0	3.0	1.1	2.8	29.9
East Chicago city *Lake Co.*	90.4	3.4	2.8	0.4	23.7
Elkhart city *Elkhart Co.*	91.7	1.4	2.7	2.0	19.2
Elwood city *Madison Co.*	92.4	0.0	1.7	2.6	23.3
Evansville city *Vanderburgh Co.*	91.9	2.4	2.5	1.7	18.7
Fishers city *Hamilton Co.*	90.2	0.3	0.4	8.6	27.5
Fort Wayne city *Allen Co.*	93.0	1.1	1.2	3.7	20.9
Frankfort city *Clinton Co.*	94.8	0.0	0.5	1.5	20.1
Franklin city *Johnson Co.*	95.2	0.4	1.7	1.8	23.1
Garrett city *DeKalb Co.*	95.8	0.0	1.0	2.4	23.0
Gary city *Lake Co.*	88.1	6.0	2.0	1.8	27.0
Goshen city *Elkhart Co.*	91.6	0.6	3.2	2.4	17.3
Granger CDP *Saint Joseph Co.*	93.1	0.2	0.4	6.0	23.3
Greencastle city *Putnam Co.*	70.8	0.0	24.4	3.0	15.6
Greenfield city *Hancock Co.*	97.5	0.0	0.9	1.4	22.1
Greensburg city *Decatur Co.*	94.3	0.4	2.5	2.3	17.4
Greenwood city *Johnson Co.*	93.9	0.4	1.2	3.8	25.3
Griffith town *Lake Co.*	91.8	2.9	0.4	2.6	25.7
Hammond city *Lake Co.*	92.7	3.0	2.4	1.2	26.7
Highland town *Lake Co.*	92.3	3.0	0.8	3.1	26.9
Hobart city *Lake Co.*	93.4	0.9	0.3	4.1	26.8
Huntertown town *Allen Co.*	97.3	0.0	0.0	2.6	25.7
Huntington city *Huntington Co.*	91.0	0.0	6.1	2.5	17.4
Indianapolis city *Marion Co.*	91.5	2.0	1.8	3.2	23.1
Jasper city *Dubois Co.*	93.3	0.1	2.0	4.1	16.7
Jeffersonville city *Clark Co.*	93.0	1.6	1.1	3.1	21.7
Kendallville city *Noble Co.*	96.0	0.0	2.2	0.9	20.5

Place	Automobile (%)	Public Transportation (%)	Walk (%)	Work from Home (%)	Mean Travel Time to Work (minutes)
Kokomo city *Howard Co.*	93.6	0.5	1.1	3.2	18.7
La Porte city *LaPorte Co.*	91.0	0.2	3.4	3.2	19.3
Lafayette city *Tippecanoe Co.*	89.4	3.6	2.3	2.4	16.7
Lake Station city *Lake Co.*	97.5	0.3	0.7	0.8	26.5
Lakes of the Four Seasons CDP *Lake Co.*	93.2	0.0	0.4	4.6	35.4
Lawrence city *Marion Co.*	93.1	0.4	1.1	4.6	27.4
Lebanon city *Boone Co.*	94.9	0.0	0.3	2.4	21.9
Logansport city *Cass Co.*	94.4	1.0	2.1	0.6	18.4
Lowell town *Lake Co.*	98.3	0.0	0.3	0.7	36.7
Madison city *Jefferson Co.*	91.4	0.1	3.2	3.0	18.0
Marion city *Grant Co.*	83.2	0.5	8.9	6.1	15.6
Martinsville city *Morgan Co.*	90.6	0.0	3.7	5.1	25.7
Merrillville town *Lake Co.*	93.1	1.8	0.5	2.4	27.3
Michigan City city *LaPorte Co.*	91.6	2.0	3.1	2.4	19.6
Mishawaka city *Saint Joseph Co.*	93.6	1.8	2.2	2.0	20.8
Mooresville town *Morgan Co.*	93.7	0.0	2.1	2.3	21.5
Muncie city *Delaware Co.*	83.5	3.2	7.5	3.3	18.9
Munster town *Lake Co.*	85.6	6.7	0.5	5.2	29.2
Nappanee city *Elkhart Co.*	94.2	0.0	2.2	1.3	21.7
New Albany city *Floyd Co.*	93.5	1.6	2.0	2.4	20.2
New Castle city *Henry Co.*	94.8	0.3	1.7	2.1	23.9
New Haven city *Allen Co.*	95.5	0.1	0.9	2.4	19.9
Noblesville city *Hamilton Co.*	91.0	0.0	1.1	7.6	26.1
North Vernon city *Jennings Co.*	95.8	0.0	2.7	0.9	23.3
Notre Dame CDP *Saint Joseph Co.*	10.4	0.2	70.5	12.3	10.6
Peru city *Miami Co.*	93.0	0.2	2.7	1.0	19.3
Plainfield town *Hendricks Co.*	91.9	0.0	1.2	5.2	21.7
Plymouth city *Marshall Co.*	94.2	0.2	3.2	1.2	18.4
Portage city *Porter Co.*	92.9	1.0	1.6	3.0	26.6
Princeton city *Gibson Co.*	90.9	0.4	6.6	0.6	18.2
Richmond city *Wayne Co.*	88.2	0.6	5.0	2.5	15.1
Saint John town *Lake Co.*	90.6	3.3	0.2	4.6	36.3
Schererville town *Lake Co.*	92.3	2.5	0.2	3.4	30.2
Scottsburg city *Scott Co.*	94.6	0.0	1.2	1.9	25.3
Sellersburg town *Clark Co.*	95.6	0.0	0.2	3.0	21.7
Seymour city *Jackson Co.*	93.5	0.2	1.4	1.4	17.8
Shelbyville city *Shelby Co.*	95.9	0.1	1.6	1.1	19.9
South Bend city *Saint Joseph Co.*	89.4	2.8	3.1	2.9	19.9
Speedway town *Marion Co.*	92.4	3.1	0.9	2.4	21.2
Tell City city *Perry Co.*	96.8	0.0	1.6	1.4	17.7
Terre Haute city *Vigo Co.*	87.6	1.6	5.4	3.9	17.8
Valparaiso city *Porter Co.*	86.2	1.3	5.5	4.8	22.0
Vincennes city *Knox Co.*	91.7	0.4	4.2	0.9	14.5
Wabash city *Wabash Co.*	94.0	0.6	2.9	2.0	16.7
Warsaw city *Kosciusko Co.*	93.0	0.0	1.9	2.9	13.5
Washington city *Daviess Co.*	92.4	0.3	4.2	1.3	19.8
West Lafayette city *Tippecanoe Co.*	57.7	6.1	26.6	4.8	15.6
Westfield city *Hamilton Co.*	91.7	0.0	0.7	6.6	23.8
Yorktown town *Delaware Co.*	97.7	0.0	0.2	0.8	20.6
Zionsville town *Boone Co.*	89.5	0.1	1.1	8.0	25.9

SOURCE: U.S. Census Bureau, American Community Survey, 2013-2017 Five-Year Estimates

Crime

Place	Violent Crime Rate (crimes per 10,000 population)	Property Crime Rate (crimes per 10,000 population)
Anderson city *Madison Co.*	47.3	440.0
Angola city *Steuben Co.*	n/a	n/a
Auburn city *DeKalb Co.*	n/a	n/a
Avon town *Hendricks Co.*	n/a	n/a
Bargersville town *Johnson Co.*	12.1	169.3
Bedford city *Lawrence Co.*	8.3	252.8
Beech Grove city *Marion Co.*	n/a	227.9
Bloomington city *Monroe Co.*	52.0	303.6
Bluffton city *Wells Co.*	7.0	n/a
Brazil city *Clay Co.*	n/a	n/a
Brownsburg town *Hendricks Co.*	n/a	114.5
Carmel city *Hamilton Co.*	1.8	74.7
Cedar Lake town *Lake Co.*	n/a	161.2
Charlestown city *Clark Co.*	n/a	155.2
Chesterton town *Porter Co.*	5.9	86.7
Clarksville town *Clark Co.*	49.7	546.3
Columbia City city *Whitley Co.*	n/a	n/a
Columbus city *Bartholomew Co.*	n/a	402.4
Connersville city *Fayette Co.*	n/a	n/a
Crawfordsville city *Montgomery Co.*	47.5	256.7
Crown Point city *Lake Co.*	3.4	113.3
Danville town *Hendricks Co.*	n/a	117.6
Decatur city *Adams Co.*	10.5	143.6
Dyer town *Lake Co.*	2.5	85.1
East Chicago city *Lake Co.*	66.6	345.6
Elkhart city *Elkhart Co.*	n/a	351.0
Elwood city *Madison Co.*	14.3	263.5
Evansville city *Vanderburgh Co.*	69.1	500.9
Fishers city *Hamilton Co.*	4.7	92.6
Fort Wayne city *Allen Co.*	35.8	318.0
Frankfort city *Clinton Co.*	9.5	315.6
Franklin city *Johnson Co.*	50.7	339.6
Garrett city *DeKalb Co.*	n/a	n/a
Gary city *Lake Co.*	62.1	340.5
Goshen city *Elkhart Co.*	n/a	336.8
Granger CDP *Saint Joseph Co.*	n/a	n/a
Greencastle city *Putnam Co.*	n/a	n/a
Greenfield city *Hancock Co.*	43.0	188.8
Greensburg city *Decatur Co.*	n/a	n/a
Greenwood city *Johnson Co.*	51.8	323.9
Griffith town *Lake Co.*	15.5	219.8
Hammond city *Lake Co.*	63.5	391.4
Highland town *Lake Co.*	15.9	325.6
Hobart city *Lake Co.*	33.1	416.5
Huntertown town *Allen Co.*	n/a	n/a
Huntington city *Huntington Co.*	n/a	n/a
Indianapolis city *Marion Co.*	133.4	441.2
Jasper city *Dubois Co.*	22.5	102.7
Jeffersonville city *Clark Co.*	14.1	302.4
Kendallville city *Noble Co.*	n/a	227.9

Place	Violent Crime Rate (crimes per 10,000 population)	Property Crime Rate (crimes per 10,000 population)
Kokomo city *Howard Co.*	72.2	289.0
La Porte city *LaPorte Co.*	47.5	254.6
Lafayette city *Tippecanoe Co.*	50.4	364.9
Lake Station city *Lake Co.*	12.7	280.1
Lakes of the Four Seasons CDP *Lake Co.*	n/a	n/a
Lawrence city *Marion Co.*	n/a	n/a
Lebanon city *Boone Co.*	n/a	n/a
Logansport city *Cass Co.*	13.6	372.9
Lowell town *Lake Co.*	2.1	6.3
Madison city *Jefferson Co.*	n/a	n/a
Marion city *Grant Co.*	34.2	372.4
Martinsville city *Morgan Co.*	n/a	n/a
Merrillville town *Lake Co.*	n/a	367.4
Michigan City city *LaPorte Co.*	n/a	n/a
Mishawaka city *Saint Joseph Co.*	21.5	n/a
Mooresville town *Morgan Co.*	7.2	288.4
Muncie city *Delaware Co.*	35.7	362.0
Munster town *Lake Co.*	10.1	201.8
Nappanee city *Elkhart Co.*	n/a	151.5
New Albany city *Floyd Co.*	n/a	n/a
New Castle city *Henry Co.*	n/a	n/a
New Haven city *Allen Co.*	24.5	216.4
Noblesville city *Hamilton Co.*	n/a	131.7
North Vernon city *Jennings Co.*	26.3	258.9
Notre Dame CDP *Saint Joseph Co.*	n/a	n/a
Peru city *Miami Co.*	n/a	396.0
Plainfield town *Hendricks Co.*	26.5	266.9
Plymouth city *Marshall Co.*	6.0	273.8
Portage city *Porter Co.*	n/a	n/a
Princeton city *Gibson Co.*	n/a	n/a
Richmond city *Wayne Co.*	n/a	n/a
Saint John town *Lake Co.*	1.2	83.5
Schererville town *Lake Co.*	n/a	n/a
Scottsburg city *Scott Co.*	n/a	460.3
Sellersburg town *Clark Co.*	7.9	97.3
Seymour city *Jackson Co.*	33.7	373.4
Shelbyville city *Shelby Co.*	n/a	279.8
South Bend city *Saint Joseph Co.*	104.5	500.7
Speedway town *Marion Co.*	31.3	410.7
Tell City city *Perry Co.*	6.8	179.0
Terre Haute city *Vigo Co.*	n/a	n/a
Valparaiso city *Porter Co.*	14.4	151.2
Vincennes city *Knox Co.*	13.4	572.6
Wabash city *Wabash Co.*	n/a	n/a
Warsaw city *Kosciusko Co.*	n/a	412.8
Washington city *Daviess Co.*	n/a	n/a
West Lafayette city *Tippecanoe Co.*	10.5	100.1
Westfield city *Hamilton Co.*	5.7	101.4
Yorktown town *Delaware Co.*	n/a	n/a
Zionsville town *Boone Co.*	n/a	n/a

NOTE: n/a not available.
SOURCE: Federal Bureau of Investigation, Uniform Crime Reports, 2017

Community Rankings

This chapter ranks incorporated places and CDPs (Census Designated Places) with populations of 2,500 or more. Most topics have two tables, one in descending order, and one in ascending order. Ten topics only include tables in descending order—Water Area, Ancestry (five tables), Black/ African American Population, Asian Population, American Indian/Alaska Native Population, Native Hawaiian/Other Pacific Islander, Homeowner Vacancy Rate, Rental Vacancy Rate, Population Under 18 Years Old with No Health Insurance, and Commute to Work: Public Transportation. This is because there are more than 150 communities that place at the bottom of these topics with zero numbers.

Land Area 123
Water Area 125
Elevation 126
Population 128
Population Growth Since 2000 130
Population Density 132
White Population 134
Black/African American Population 136
Asian Population 138
American Indian/Alaska Native Population 140
Native Hawaiian/Other Pacific Islander Population 141
Two or More Races 142
Hispanic Population 144
Average Household Size 146
Median Age 148
Population Under Age 18 150
Population Age 65 and Over 152
Males per 100 Females 154
Marriage Status: Never Married 156

The Hoosier State

The Crossroads of America

Marriage Status: Now Married . . . 158
Marriage Status: Separated . . . 160
Marriage Status: Widowed . . . 162
Marriage Status: Divorced . . . 164
Foreign Born . . . 166
Speak English-only at Home . . . 168
Individuals with a Disability . . . 170
Veterans . . . 172
Ancestry: German . . . 174
Ancestry: English . . . 175
Ancestry: American . . . 176
Ancestry: Irish . . . 177
Ancestry: Italian . . . 178
Employment: Management, Business, and Financial Occupations . . . 179
Employment: Computer, Engineering, and Science Occupations . . . 181
Employment: Education, Legal, Community Service, Arts, and Media Occupations . . . 183
Employment: Healthcare Practitioners . . . 185
Employment: Service Occupations . . . 187
Employment: Sales and Office Occupations . . . 189
Employment: Natural Resources, Construction, and Maintenance Occupations . . . 191
Employment: Production, Transportation, and Material Moving Occupations . . . 193
Per Capita Income . . . 195
Median Household Income . . . 197
Average Household Income . . . 199
Households with Income of $100,000 or More . . . 201
Poverty Rate . . . 203
Educational Attainment: High School Diploma or Higher . . . 205
Educational Attainment: Bachelor's Degree or Higher . . . 207
Educational Attainment: Graduate/Professional Degree or Higher . . . 209
Homeownership Rate . . . 211
Median Home Value . . . 213
Median Year Structure Built . . . 215
Homeowner Vacancy Rate . . . 217
Median Selected Monthly Owner Costs: With Mortgage . . . 218
Median Selected Monthly Owner Costs: Without Mortgage . . . 220
Median Gross Rent . . . 222
Rental Vacancy Rate . . . 224
Population with Health Insurance . . . 225
Population with Private Health Insurance . . . 227
Population with Public Health Insurance . . . 229
Population with No Health Insurance . . . 231
Population Under 18 Years Old with No Health Insurance . . . 233
Commute to Work: Car . . . 235
Commute to Work: Public Transportation . . . 237
Commute to Work: Walk . . . 238
Commute to Work: Work from Home . . . 240
Mean Travel Time to Work . . . 242
Violent Crime Rate per 10,000 Population . . . 244
Property Crime Rate per 10,000 Population . . . 246

Land Area

Top 150 Places Ranked in *Descending* Order

State Rank	Sq. Miles	Place
1	361.433	**Indianapolis** (city) Marion County
2	110.618	**Fort Wayne** (city) Allen County
3	49.865	**Gary** (city) Lake County
4	47.463	**Carmel** (city) Hamilton County
5	44.153	**Evansville** (city) Vanderburgh County
6	41.458	**South Bend** (city) Saint Joseph County
7	41.371	**Anderson** (city) Madison County
8	34.536	**Terre Haute** (city) Vigo County
9	34.064	**Jeffersonville** (city) Clark County
10	33.585	**Fishers** (city) Hamilton County
11	33.216	**Merrillville** (town) Lake County
12	31.374	**Noblesville** (city) Hamilton County
13	27.742	**Lafayette** (city) Tippecanoe County
14	27.497	**Columbus** (city) Bartholomew County
15	27.196	**Muncie** (city) Delaware County
16	26.838	**Westfield** (city) Hamilton County
17	26.331	**Hobart** (city) Lake County
18	25.628	**Portage** (city) Porter County
19	25.567	**Granger** (CDP) Saint Joseph County
20	23.915	**Richmond** (city) Wayne County
21	23.453	**Elkhart** (city) Elkhart County
22	23.158	**Bloomington** (city) Monroe County
23	22.776	**Hammond** (city) Lake County
24	22.274	**Plainfield** (town) Hendricks County
25	21.230	**Greenwood** (city) Johnson County
26	20.132	**Lawrence** (city) Marion County
27	19.588	**Michigan City** (city) LaPorte County
28	18.497	**Kokomo** (city) Howard County
29	17.713	**Crown Point** (city) Lake County
30	16.997	**Mishawaka** (city) Saint Joseph County
31	16.229	**Goshen** (city) Elkhart County
32	15.711	**Marion** (city) Grant County
33	15.555	**Lebanon** (city) Boone County
34	15.530	**Valparaiso** (city) Porter County
35	14.939	**New Albany** (city) Floyd County
36	14.712	**Schererville** (town) Lake County
37	14.241	**Avon** (town) Hendricks County
38	14.088	**East Chicago** (city) Lake County
39	13.105	**Jasper** (city) Dubois County
40	13.006	**Franklin** (city) Johnson County
41	12.551	**Greenfield** (city) Hancock County
42	12.548	**Bright** (CDP) Dearborn County
43	12.161	**Bedford** (city) Lawrence County
44	11.975	**Winfield** (town) Lake County
45	11.660	**La Porte** (city) LaPorte County
46	11.576	**Warsaw** (city) Kosciusko County
47	11.564	**Shelbyville** (city) Shelby County
48	11.446	**Charlestown** (city) Clark County
49	11.422	**Seymour** (city) Jackson County
50	11.387	**Saint John** (town) Lake County
51	11.166	**Pendleton** (town) Madison County
52	11.076	**Brownsburg** (town) Hendricks County
53	10.720	**Smithville-Sanders** (CDP) Monroe County
54	10.458	**Whitestown** (town) Boone County
55	10.257	**Zionsville** (town) Boone County
56	9.973	**Clarksville** (town) Clark County
57	9.867	**New Haven** (city) Allen County
58	9.332	**Chesterton** (town) Porter County
59	9.270	**Greensburg** (city) Decatur County
60	9.146	**Crawfordsville** (city) Montgomery County
61	8.886	**Wabash** (city) Wabash County
62	8.779	**Yorktown** (town) Delaware County
63	8.748	**Logansport** (city) Cass County
64	8.707	**Huntington** (city) Huntington County
65	8.575	**Madison** (city) Jefferson County
66	8.296	**Lake Station** (city) Lake County
67	8.232	**Bluffton** (city) Wells County
68	8.219	**Cedar Lake** (town) Lake County
69	8.070	**Roselawn** (CDP) Newton County
70	7.745	**Connersville** (city) Fayette County
71	7.733	**Griffith** (town) Lake County
72	7.615	**West Lafayette** (city) Tippecanoe County
73	7.570	**Munster** (town) Lake County
74	7.534	**Plymouth** (city) Marshall County
75	7.412	**Vincennes** (city) Knox County
76	7.295	**New Castle** (city) Henry County
77	7.104	**Auburn** (city) DeKalb County
78	6.936	**Highland** (town) Lake County
79	6.930	**Danville** (town) Hendricks County
80	6.619	**North Vernon** (city) Jennings County
81	6.443	**Santa Claus** (town) Spencer County
82	6.344	**Angola** (city) Steuben County
83	6.311	**Frankfort** (city) Clinton County
84	6.285	**Mooresville** (town) Morgan County
85	6.200	**Porter** (town) Porter County
86	6.104	**Dyer** (town) Lake County
87	6.087	**Batesville** (city) Ripley County
88	6.045	**Kendallville** (city) Noble County
89	5.777	**Decatur** (city) Adams County
90	5.712	**Greendale** (city) Dearborn County
91	5.582	**Columbia City** (city) Whitley County
92	5.242	**Greencastle** (city) Putnam County
93	5.180	**Lowell** (town) Lake County
94	5.105	**Peru** (city) Miami County
95	5.070	**Princeton** (city) Gibson County
96	5.061	**Huntingburg** (city) Dubois County
97	5.053	**Scottsburg** (city) Scott County
98	4.941	**Lawrenceburg** (city) Dearborn County
99	4.926	**Bargersville** (town) Johnson County
100	4.900	**Dunlap** (CDP) Elkhart County
101	4.758	**Speedway** (town) Marion County
102	4.731	**Washington** (city) Daviess County
103	4.701	**McCordsville** (town) Hancock County
104	4.691	**Rochester** (city) Fulton County
105	4.651	**Portland** (city) Jay County
106	4.556	**Gas City** (city) Grant County
107	4.534	**Tell City** (city) Perry County
108	4.490	**Martinsville** (city) Morgan County
109	4.395	**Beech Grove** (city) Marion County
110	4.240	**Ellettsville** (town) Monroe County
111	4.149	**Nappanee** (city) Elkhart County
112	4.138	**Hidden Valley** (CDP) Dearborn County
113	4.000	**Salem** (city) Washington County
114	3.943	**Sellersburg** (town) Clark County
115	3.920	**Knox** (city) Starke County
116	3.875	**Hartford City** (city) Blackford County
117	3.851	**Garrett** (city) DeKalb County
118	3.802	**Huntertown** (town) Allen County
119	3.800	**Rensselaer** (city) Jasper County
120	3.774	**Elwood** (city) Madison County
121	3.755	**Middlebury** (town) Elkhart County
122	3.743	**Paoli** (town) Orange County
123	3.713	**Leo-Cedarville** (town) Allen County
124	3.609	**De Motte** (town) Jasper County
125	3.568	**North Terre Haute** (CDP) Vigo County
126	3.564	**Simonton Lake** (CDP) Elkhart County
127	3.534	**North Manchester** (town) Wabash County
128	3.470	**Monticello** (city) White County
129	3.328	**Winchester** (city) Randolph County
130	3.276	**Mitchell** (city) Lawrence County
131	3.219	**Whiteland** (town) Johnson County
132	3.138	**Upland** (town) Grant County
133	3.109	**Edinburgh** (town) Johnson County
134	3.091	**Rushville** (city) Rush County
135	3.088	**Westville** (town) LaPorte County
136	3.027	**Brazil** (city) Clay County
137	3.022	**Linton** (city) Greene County
138	3.012	**Heritage Lake** (CDP) Putnam County
139	3.001	**Boonville** (city) Warrick County
140	2.976	**Fortville** (town) Hancock County
141	2.951	**Pittsboro** (town) Hendricks County
142	2.808	**Mount Vernon** (city) Posey County
143	2.763	**Winona Lake** (town) Kosciusko County
144	2.761	**Aurora** (city) Dearborn County
145	2.726	**Delphi** (city) Carroll County
146	2.715	**Bremen** (town) Marshall County
147	2.681	**Lakes of the Four Seasons** (CDP) Lake County
148	2.627	**Alexandria** (city) Madison County
149	2.577	**Austin** (city) Scott County
150	2.562	**Country Squire Lakes** (CDP) Jennings County

Note: *This section ranks incorporated places and CDPs (Census Designated Places) with populations of 2,500 or more. Unincorporated postal areas were not considered. Please refer to the User Guide for additional information.*

Land Area

Top 150 Places Ranked in *Ascending* Order

State Rank	Sq. Miles	Place
1	0.370	**Salt Creek Commons** (CDP) Porter County
2	1.097	**Fort Branch** (town) Gibson County
3	1.208	**Notre Dame** (CDP) Saint Joseph County
4	1.243	**South Haven** (CDP) Porter County
5	1.346	**Bicknell** (city) Knox County
6	1.357	**Osceola** (town) Saint Joseph County
7	1.361	**Melody Hill** (CDP) Vanderburgh County
8	1.361	**Winamac** (town) Pulaski County
9	1.366	**Greentown** (town) Howard County
10	1.406	**Newburgh** (town) Warrick County
11	1.429	**Ossian** (town) Wells County
12	1.461	**New Whiteland** (town) Johnson County
13	1.492	**Rockville** (town) Parke County
14	1.498	**Brookville** (town) Franklin County
15	1.567	**Loogootee** (city) Martin County
16	1.583	**Fairmount** (town) Grant County
17	1.588	**Brownstown** (town) Jackson County
18	1.600	**Attica** (city) Fountain County
19	1.649	**Corydon** (town) Harrison County
20	1.704	**Lagrange** (town) LaGrange County
21	1.708	**Cicero** (town) Hamilton County
22	1.787	**Syracuse** (town) Kosciusko County
23	1.798	**Whiting** (city) Lake County
24	1.876	**Sullivan** (city) Sullivan County
25	1.899	**Shorewood Forest** (CDP) Porter County
26	1.976	**Hebron** (town) Porter County
27	2.033	**Chandler** (town) Warrick County
28	2.049	**Georgetown** (town) Floyd County
29	2.058	**Cumberland** (town) Marion County
30	2.078	**Berne** (city) Adams County
31	2.093	**Butler** (city) DeKalb County
32	2.137	**Sheridan** (town) Hamilton County
33	2.200	**Union City** (city) Randolph County
34	2.238	**Clinton** (city) Vermillion County
35	2.267	**Highland** (CDP) Vanderburgh County
36	2.308	**Hanover** (town) Jefferson County
37	2.310	**Ligonier** (city) Noble County
38	2.404	**Centerville** (town) Wayne County
39	2.504	**Tipton** (city) Tipton County
40	2.562	**Country Squire Lakes** (CDP) Jennings County
41	2.577	**Austin** (city) Scott County
42	2.627	**Alexandria** (city) Madison County
43	2.681	**Lakes of the Four Seasons** (CDP) Lake County
44	2.715	**Bremen** (town) Marshall County
45	2.726	**Delphi** (city) Carroll County
46	2.761	**Aurora** (city) Dearborn County
47	2.763	**Winona Lake** (town) Kosciusko County
48	2.808	**Mount Vernon** (city) Posey County
49	2.951	**Pittsboro** (town) Hendricks County
50	2.976	**Fortville** (town) Hancock County
51	3.001	**Boonville** (city) Warrick County
52	3.012	**Heritage Lake** (CDP) Putnam County
53	3.022	**Linton** (city) Greene County
54	3.027	**Brazil** (city) Clay County
55	3.088	**Westville** (town) LaPorte County
56	3.091	**Rushville** (city) Rush County
57	3.109	**Edinburgh** (town) Johnson County
58	3.138	**Upland** (town) Grant County
59	3.219	**Whiteland** (town) Johnson County
60	3.276	**Mitchell** (city) Lawrence County
61	3.328	**Winchester** (city) Randolph County
62	3.470	**Monticello** (city) White County
63	3.534	**North Manchester** (town) Wabash County
64	3.564	**Simonton Lake** (CDP) Elkhart County
65	3.568	**North Terre Haute** (CDP) Vigo County
66	3.609	**De Motte** (town) Jasper County
67	3.713	**Leo-Cedarville** (town) Allen County
68	3.743	**Paoli** (town) Orange County
69	3.755	**Middlebury** (town) Elkhart County
70	3.774	**Elwood** (city) Madison County
71	3.800	**Rensselaer** (city) Jasper County
72	3.802	**Huntertown** (town) Allen County
73	3.851	**Garrett** (city) DeKalb County
74	3.875	**Hartford City** (city) Blackford County
75	3.920	**Knox** (city) Starke County
76	3.943	**Sellersburg** (town) Clark County
77	4.000	**Salem** (city) Washington County
78	4.138	**Hidden Valley** (CDP) Dearborn County
79	4.149	**Nappanee** (city) Elkhart County
80	4.240	**Ellettsville** (town) Monroe County
81	4.395	**Beech Grove** (city) Marion County
82	4.490	**Martinsville** (city) Morgan County
83	4.534	**Tell City** (city) Perry County
84	4.556	**Gas City** (city) Grant County
85	4.651	**Portland** (city) Jay County
86	4.691	**Rochester** (city) Fulton County
87	4.701	**McCordsville** (town) Hancock County
88	4.731	**Washington** (city) Daviess County
89	4.758	**Speedway** (town) Marion County
90	4.900	**Dunlap** (CDP) Elkhart County
91	4.926	**Bargersville** (town) Johnson County
92	4.941	**Lawrenceburg** (city) Dearborn County
93	5.053	**Scottsburg** (city) Scott County
94	5.061	**Huntingburg** (city) Dubois County
95	5.070	**Princeton** (city) Gibson County
96	5.105	**Peru** (city) Miami County
97	5.180	**Lowell** (town) Lake County
98	5.242	**Greencastle** (city) Putnam County
99	5.582	**Columbia City** (city) Whitley County
100	5.712	**Greendale** (city) Dearborn County
101	5.777	**Decatur** (city) Adams County
102	6.045	**Kendallville** (city) Noble County
103	6.087	**Batesville** (city) Ripley County
104	6.104	**Dyer** (town) Lake County
105	6.200	**Porter** (town) Porter County
106	6.285	**Mooresville** (town) Morgan County
107	6.311	**Frankfort** (city) Clinton County
108	6.344	**Angola** (city) Steuben County
109	6.443	**Santa Claus** (town) Spencer County
110	6.619	**North Vernon** (city) Jennings County
111	6.930	**Danville** (town) Hendricks County
112	6.936	**Highland** (town) Lake County
113	7.104	**Auburn** (city) DeKalb County
114	7.295	**New Castle** (city) Henry County
115	7.412	**Vincennes** (city) Knox County
116	7.534	**Plymouth** (city) Marshall County
117	7.570	**Munster** (town) Lake County
118	7.615	**West Lafayette** (city) Tippecanoe County
119	7.733	**Griffith** (town) Lake County
120	7.745	**Connersville** (city) Fayette County
121	8.070	**Roselawn** (CDP) Newton County
122	8.219	**Cedar Lake** (town) Lake County
123	8.232	**Bluffton** (city) Wells County
124	8.296	**Lake Station** (city) Lake County
125	8.575	**Madison** (city) Jefferson County
126	8.707	**Huntington** (city) Huntington County
127	8.748	**Logansport** (city) Cass County
128	8.779	**Yorktown** (town) Delaware County
129	8.886	**Wabash** (city) Wabash County
130	9.146	**Crawfordsville** (city) Montgomery County
131	9.270	**Greensburg** (city) Decatur County
132	9.332	**Chesterton** (town) Porter County
133	9.867	**New Haven** (city) Allen County
134	9.973	**Clarksville** (town) Clark County
135	10.257	**Zionsville** (town) Boone County
136	10.458	**Whitestown** (town) Boone County
137	10.720	**Smithville-Sanders** (CDP) Monroe County
138	11.076	**Brownsburg** (town) Hendricks County
139	11.166	**Pendleton** (town) Madison County
140	11.387	**Saint John** (town) Lake County
141	11.422	**Seymour** (city) Jackson County
142	11.446	**Charlestown** (city) Clark County
143	11.564	**Shelbyville** (city) Shelby County
144	11.576	**Warsaw** (city) Kosciusko County
145	11.660	**La Porte** (city) LaPorte County
146	11.975	**Winfield** (town) Lake County
147	12.161	**Bedford** (city) Lawrence County
148	12.548	**Bright** (CDP) Dearborn County
149	12.551	**Greenfield** (city) Hancock County
150	13.006	**Franklin** (city) Johnson County

Note: *This section ranks incorporated places and CDPs (Census Designated Places) with populations of 2,500 or more. Unincorporated postal areas were not considered. Please refer to the User Guide for additional information.*

Water Area

Top 150 Places Ranked in *Descending* Order

State Rank	Sq. Miles	Place
1	7.310	**Gary** (city) Lake County
2	6.592	**Indianapolis** (city) Marion County
3	3.265	**Michigan City** (city) LaPorte County
4	2.249	**Fishers** (city) Hamilton County
5	2.106	**Hammond** (city) Lake County
6	2.065	**East Chicago** (city) Lake County
7	1.984	**Portage** (city) Porter County
8	1.429	**Whiting** (city) Lake County
9	1.415	**Noblesville** (city) Hamilton County
10	1.387	**Cedar Lake** (town) Lake County
11	1.338	**Warsaw** (city) Kosciusko County
12	1.111	**Rochester** (city) Fulton County
13	1.085	**Carmel** (city) Hamilton County
14	0.967	**Elkhart** (city) Elkhart County
15	0.732	**Terre Haute** (city) Vigo County
16	0.710	**La Porte** (city) LaPorte County
17	0.490	**Winona Lake** (town) Kosciusko County
18	0.472	**Evansville** (city) Vanderburgh County
19	0.471	**Simonton Lake** (CDP) Elkhart County
20	0.469	**Heritage Lake** (CDP) Putnam County
21	0.421	**Santa Claus** (town) Spencer County
22	0.417	**South Bend** (city) Saint Joseph County
23	0.416	**Lakes of the Four Seasons** (CDP) Lake County
24	0.412	**Cicero** (town) Hamilton County
25	0.386	**Columbus** (city) Bartholomew County
26	0.375	**Hobart** (city) Lake County
27	0.366	**Syracuse** (town) Kosciusko County
28	0.355	**Goshen** (city) Elkhart County
29	0.348	**Mishawaka** (city) Saint Joseph County
30	0.338	**Shorewood Forest** (CDP) Porter County
31	0.327	**Aurora** (city) Dearborn County
32	0.294	**Jeffersonville** (city) Clark County
33	0.285	**Shelbyville** (city) Shelby County
34	0.284	**Porter** (town) Porter County
35	0.272	**Madison** (city) Jefferson County
36	0.270	**Lawrenceburg** (city) Dearborn County
37	0.270	**Hidden Valley** (CDP) Dearborn County
38	0.241	**Westfield** (city) Hamilton County
39	0.238	**Wabash** (city) Wabash County
40	0.224	**Kendallville** (city) Noble County
41	0.222	**Logansport** (city) Cass County
42	0.216	**Monticello** (city) White County
43	0.214	**Fort Wayne** (city) Allen County
44	0.213	**Huntingburg** (city) Dubois County
45	0.203	**Clarksville** (town) Clark County
46	0.199	**Bloomington** (city) Monroe County
47	0.192	**Muncie** (city) Delaware County
48	0.171	**New Albany** (city) Floyd County
49	0.157	**Richmond** (city) Wayne County
50	0.139	**Country Squire Lakes** (CDP) Jennings County
51	0.136	**Leo-Cedarville** (town) Allen County
52	0.134	**Huntington** (city) Huntington County
53	0.131	**Lake Station** (city) Lake County
54	0.129	**Bluffton** (city) Wells County
55	0.113	**Chesterton** (town) Porter County
56	0.112	**Greenfield** (city) Hancock County
57	0.110	**Lawrence** (city) Marion County
58	0.109	**Anderson** (city) Madison County
59	0.109	**Plainfield** (town) Hendricks County
60	0.105	**Tell City** (city) Perry County
61	0.102	**Avon** (town) Hendricks County
62	0.091	**Jasper** (city) Dubois County
63	0.091	**Saint John** (town) Lake County
64	0.086	**Lowell** (town) Lake County
65	0.084	**Marion** (city) Grant County
66	0.083	**Yorktown** (town) Delaware County
67	0.081	**Munster** (town) Lake County
68	0.079	**North Manchester** (town) Wabash County
69	0.076	**Brownsburg** (town) Hendricks County
70	0.075	**Greendale** (city) Dearborn County
71	0.073	**Peru** (city) Miami County
72	0.068	**Vincennes** (city) Knox County
73	0.067	**Pendleton** (town) Madison County
74	0.066	**Winfield** (town) Lake County
75	0.066	**Notre Dame** (CDP) Saint Joseph County
76	0.066	**Batesville** (city) Ripley County
77	0.060	**Rensselaer** (city) Jasper County
78	0.059	**Kokomo** (city) Howard County
79	0.057	**Mooresville** (town) Morgan County
80	0.053	**Schererville** (town) Lake County
81	0.051	**Greencastle** (city) Putnam County
82	0.050	**Mount Vernon** (city) Posey County
83	0.048	**Valparaiso** (city) Porter County
84	0.047	**Angola** (city) Steuben County
85	0.046	**Danville** (town) Hendricks County
86	0.045	**Greensburg** (city) Decatur County
87	0.043	**Brookville** (town) Franklin County
88	0.040	**Plymouth** (city) Marshall County
89	0.039	**Charlestown** (city) Clark County
90	0.038	**Zionsville** (town) Boone County
91	0.037	**Washington** (city) Daviess County
92	0.035	**Merrillville** (town) Lake County
93	0.030	**Sellersburg** (town) Clark County
94	0.028	**Brazil** (city) Clay County
95	0.023	**Highland** (town) Lake County
96	0.022	**Middlebury** (town) Elkhart County
97	0.021	**Columbia City** (city) Whitley County
98	0.021	**New Castle** (city) Henry County
99	0.021	**Hartford City** (city) Blackford County
100	0.019	**Scottsburg** (city) Scott County
101	0.019	**Clinton** (city) Vermillion County
102	0.018	**Martinsville** (city) Morgan County
103	0.018	**Bright** (CDP) Dearborn County
104	0.018	**Georgetown** (town) Floyd County
105	0.018	**Salem** (city) Washington County
106	0.016	**Melody Hill** (CDP) Vanderburgh County
107	0.016	**Lebanon** (city) Boone County
108	0.015	**Crown Point** (city) Lake County
109	0.015	**Connersville** (city) Fayette County
110	0.014	**Paoli** (town) Orange County
111	0.013	**Boonville** (city) Warrick County
112	0.013	**Winchester** (city) Randolph County
113	0.013	**Highland** (CDP) Vanderburgh County
114	0.012	**Roselawn** (CDP) Newton County
115	0.012	**Upland** (town) Grant County
116	0.011	**Fort Branch** (town) Gibson County
117	0.010	**Huntertown** (town) Allen County
118	0.010	**North Vernon** (city) Jennings County
119	0.010	**West Lafayette** (city) Tippecanoe County
120	0.010	**Dunlap** (CDP) Elkhart County
121	0.010	**Cumberland** (town) Marion County
122	0.009	**Union City** (city) Randolph County
123	0.009	**McCordsville** (town) Hancock County
124	0.008	**Ossian** (town) Wells County
125	0.008	**Speedway** (town) Marion County
126	0.007	**Fortville** (town) Hancock County
127	0.007	**Osceola** (town) Saint Joseph County
128	0.006	**Decatur** (city) Adams County
129	0.006	**Brownstown** (town) Jackson County
130	0.005	**Mitchell** (city) Lawrence County
131	0.005	**Princeton** (city) Gibson County
132	0.005	**New Haven** (city) Allen County
133	0.005	**Seymour** (city) Jackson County
134	0.004	**Bremen** (town) Marshall County
135	0.004	**Hanover** (town) Jefferson County
136	0.004	**Sheridan** (town) Hamilton County
137	0.004	**Loogootee** (city) Martin County
138	0.003	**Portland** (city) Jay County
139	0.003	**De Motte** (town) Jasper County
140	0.001	**Granger** (CDP) Saint Joseph County
141	0.001	**Newburgh** (town) Warrick County
142	0.001	**Greenwood** (city) Johnson County
143	0.001	**Centerville** (town) Wayne County
144	0.000	**Berne** (city) Adams County
145	0.000	**Ligonier** (city) Noble County
146	0.000	**Alexandria** (city) Madison County
146	0.000	**Attica** (city) Fountain County
146	0.000	**Auburn** (city) DeKalb County
146	0.000	**Austin** (city) Scott County
146	0.000	**Bargersville** (town) Johnson County

Note: *This section ranks incorporated places and CDPs (Census Designated Places) with populations of 2,500 or more. Unincorporated postal areas were not considered. Please refer to the User Guide for additional information.*

Elevation

Top 150 Places Ranked in *Descending* Order

State Rank	Feet	Place
1	1,122	**Union City** (city) Randolph County
2	1,093	**Winchester** (city) Randolph County
3	1,063	**Angola** (city) Steuben County
3	1,063	**New Castle** (city) Henry County
5	1,014	**Centerville** (town) Wayne County
6	988	**Kendallville** (city) Noble County
7	981	**Richmond** (city) Wayne County
8	971	**Batesville** (city) Ripley County
9	958	**Greensburg** (city) Decatur County
9	958	**Rushville** (city) Rush County
11	955	**Danville** (town) Hendricks County
12	951	**Muncie** (city) Delaware County
13	948	**Sheridan** (town) Hamilton County
14	942	**Lebanon** (city) Boone County
14	942	**Pittsboro** (town) Hendricks County
16	938	**Whitestown** (town) Boone County
17	935	**Upland** (town) Grant County
18	932	**Lagrange** (town) LaGrange County
19	922	**Bright** (CDP) Dearborn County
20	919	**Hartford City** (city) Blackford County
21	915	**Yorktown** (town) Delaware County
22	906	**Portland** (city) Jay County
23	886	**Westfield** (city) Hamilton County
24	883	**Brownsburg** (town) Hendricks County
24	883	**Garrett** (city) DeKalb County
24	883	**Greenfield** (city) Hancock County
27	879	**Anderson** (city) Madison County
27	879	**Syracuse** (town) Kosciusko County
29	876	**Ligonier** (city) Noble County
29	876	**Nappanee** (city) Elkhart County
31	873	**Fairmount** (town) Grant County
31	873	**Lawrence** (city) Marion County
33	869	**Alexandria** (city) Madison County
33	869	**Tipton** (city) Tipton County
35	866	**Auburn** (city) DeKalb County
35	866	**Butler** (city) DeKalb County
37	863	**Elwood** (city) Madison County
38	860	**Columbia City** (city) Whitley County
38	860	**Heritage Lake** (CDP) Putnam County
40	856	**Fortville** (town) Hancock County
40	856	**Gas City** (city) Grant County
42	853	**Bremen** (town) Marshall County
42	853	**Carmel** (city) Hamilton County
42	853	**Cumberland** (town) Marion County
45	850	**Frankfort** (city) Clinton County
45	850	**McCordsville** (town) Hancock County
47	846	**Berne** (city) Adams County
47	846	**Pendleton** (town) Madison County
49	843	**Greencastle** (city) Putnam County
49	843	**Zionsville** (town) Boone County
51	840	**Ossian** (town) Wells County
52	837	**Greentown** (town) Howard County
52	837	**Middlebury** (town) Elkhart County
54	833	**Avon** (town) Hendricks County
54	833	**Cicero** (town) Hamilton County
54	833	**Huntertown** (town) Allen County
57	827	**Bluffton** (city) Wells County
57	827	**Warsaw** (city) Kosciusko County
59	823	**Connersville** (city) Fayette County
60	820	**Bargersville** (town) Johnson County
61	817	**Fishers** (city) Hamilton County
61	817	**Winona Lake** (town) Kosciusko County
63	814	**La Porte** (city) LaPorte County
63	814	**Marion** (city) Grant County
65	810	**Fort Wayne** (city) Allen County
65	810	**Kokomo** (city) Howard County
67	807	**New Whiteland** (town) Johnson County
68	804	**Beech Grove** (city) Marion County
68	804	**Greenwood** (city) Johnson County
70	801	**Decatur** (city) Adams County
70	801	**Goshen** (city) Elkhart County
70	801	**Granger** (CDP) Saint Joseph County
73	797	**Leo-Cedarville** (town) Allen County
73	797	**Plymouth** (city) Marshall County
75	794	**Crawfordsville** (city) Montgomery County
75	794	**Valparaiso** (city) Porter County
75	794	**Westville** (town) LaPorte County
75	794	**Whiteland** (town) Johnson County
79	784	**Hanover** (town) Jefferson County
79	784	**Simonton Lake** (CDP) Elkhart County
81	781	**Rochester** (city) Fulton County
82	778	**Dunlap** (CDP) Elkhart County
83	774	**North Manchester** (town) Wabash County
84	771	**Bloomington** (city) Monroe County
85	764	**Lakes of the Four Seasons** (CDP) Lake County
85	764	**Noblesville** (city) Hamilton County
85	764	**Shelbyville** (city) Shelby County
88	758	**New Haven** (city) Allen County
89	751	**Elkhart** (city) Elkhart County
89	751	**Salem** (city) Washington County
91	748	**Huntington** (city) Huntington County
91	748	**Speedway** (town) Marion County
93	738	**Osceola** (town) Saint Joseph County
94	732	**Crown Point** (city) Lake County
94	732	**Plainfield** (town) Hendricks County
96	725	**Franklin** (city) Johnson County
96	725	**Saint John** (town) Lake County
98	722	**Georgetown** (town) Floyd County
98	722	**Mishawaka** (city) Saint Joseph County
98	722	**Shorewood Forest** (CDP) Porter County
101	718	**Indianapolis** (city) Marion County
101	718	**Mooresville** (town) Morgan County
101	718	**North Vernon** (city) Jennings County
104	712	**Knox** (city) Starke County
104	712	**Rockville** (town) Parke County
104	712	**Wabash** (city) Wabash County
107	709	**Cedar Lake** (town) Lake County
107	709	**Hebron** (town) Porter County
107	709	**Winfield** (town) Lake County
110	705	**Winamac** (town) Pulaski County
111	702	**Country Squire Lakes** (CDP) Jennings County
111	702	**Lafayette** (city) Tippecanoe County
113	696	**Ellettsville** (town) Monroe County
114	692	**South Bend** (city) Saint Joseph County
115	686	**Bedford** (city) Lawrence County
116	682	**Mitchell** (city) Lawrence County
116	682	**Roselawn** (CDP) Newton County
118	676	**Monticello** (city) White County
119	673	**Edinburgh** (town) Johnson County
120	669	**De Motte** (town) Jasper County
120	669	**Lowell** (town) Lake County
120	669	**Schererville** (town) Lake County
123	666	**Brookville** (town) Franklin County
124	663	**Rensselaer** (city) Jasper County
125	656	**Merrillville** (town) Lake County
126	653	**Brazil** (city) Clay County
126	653	**Peru** (city) Miami County
126	653	**South Haven** (CDP) Porter County
129	640	**Chesterton** (town) Porter County
129	640	**Dyer** (town) Lake County
129	640	**Logansport** (city) Cass County
129	640	**Porter** (town) Porter County
133	636	**Portage** (city) Porter County
134	630	**Griffith** (town) Lake County
135	627	**Columbus** (city) Bartholomew County
135	627	**Michigan City** (city) LaPorte County
137	623	**Brownstown** (town) Jackson County
137	623	**Highland** (town) Lake County
137	623	**Hobart** (city) Lake County
137	623	**Paoli** (town) Orange County
141	620	**Lake Station** (city) Lake County
142	610	**Munster** (town) Lake County
142	610	**West Lafayette** (city) Tippecanoe County
144	604	**Martinsville** (city) Morgan County
145	600	**Gary** (city) Lake County
145	600	**Hammond** (city) Lake County
145	600	**Seymour** (city) Jackson County
148	591	**Charlestown** (city) Clark County
148	591	**East Chicago** (city) Lake County
150	587	**Corydon** (town) Harrison County

Note: *This section ranks incorporated places and CDPs (Census Designated Places) with populations of 2,500 or more. Unincorporated postal areas were not considered. Please refer to the User Guide for additional information.*

Elevation

Top 150 Places Ranked in *Ascending* Order

State Rank	Feet	Place
1	387	**Evansville** (city) Vanderburgh County
2	394	**Newburgh** (town) Warrick County
3	400	**Mount Vernon** (city) Posey County
4	413	**Chandler** (town) Warrick County
5	420	**Tell City** (city) Perry County
5	420	**Vincennes** (city) Knox County
7	423	**Boonville** (city) Warrick County
8	427	**Melody Hill** (CDP) Vanderburgh County
9	446	**Jeffersonville** (city) Clark County
10	449	**Fort Branch** (town) Gibson County
10	449	**New Albany** (city) Floyd County
12	456	**Clarksville** (town) Clark County
13	466	**Jasper** (city) Dubois County
14	472	**Santa Claus** (town) Spencer County
15	479	**Lawrenceburg** (city) Dearborn County
16	482	**Highland** (CDP) Vanderburgh County
17	486	**Aurora** (city) Dearborn County
17	486	**Sellersburg** (town) Clark County
19	489	**Huntingburg** (city) Dubois County
19	489	**Madison** (city) Jefferson County
21	495	**North Terre Haute** (CDP) Vigo County
22	499	**Clinton** (city) Vermillion County
22	499	**Princeton** (city) Gibson County
24	502	**Terre Haute** (city) Vigo County
24	502	**Washington** (city) Daviess County
26	515	**Bicknell** (city) Knox County
27	528	**Greendale** (city) Dearborn County
27	528	**Sullivan** (city) Sullivan County
29	531	**Linton** (city) Greene County
30	538	**Loogootee** (city) Martin County
31	541	**Attica** (city) Fountain County
32	548	**Hidden Valley** (CDP) Dearborn County
33	558	**Austin** (city) Scott County
34	564	**Scottsburg** (city) Scott County
35	568	**Delphi** (city) Carroll County
36	587	**Corydon** (town) Harrison County
36	587	**Whiting** (city) Lake County
38	591	**Charlestown** (city) Clark County
38	591	**East Chicago** (city) Lake County
40	600	**Gary** (city) Lake County
40	600	**Hammond** (city) Lake County
40	600	**Seymour** (city) Jackson County
43	604	**Martinsville** (city) Morgan County
44	610	**Munster** (town) Lake County
44	610	**West Lafayette** (city) Tippecanoe County
46	620	**Lake Station** (city) Lake County
47	623	**Brownstown** (town) Jackson County
47	623	**Highland** (town) Lake County
47	623	**Hobart** (city) Lake County
47	623	**Paoli** (town) Orange County
51	627	**Columbus** (city) Bartholomew County
51	627	**Michigan City** (city) LaPorte County
53	630	**Griffith** (town) Lake County
54	636	**Portage** (city) Porter County
55	640	**Chesterton** (town) Porter County
55	640	**Dyer** (town) Lake County
55	640	**Logansport** (city) Cass County
55	640	**Porter** (town) Porter County
59	653	**Brazil** (city) Clay County
59	653	**Peru** (city) Miami County
59	653	**South Haven** (CDP) Porter County
62	656	**Merrillville** (town) Lake County
63	663	**Rensselaer** (city) Jasper County
64	666	**Brookville** (town) Franklin County
65	669	**De Motte** (town) Jasper County
65	669	**Lowell** (town) Lake County
65	669	**Schererville** (town) Lake County
68	673	**Edinburgh** (town) Johnson County
69	676	**Monticello** (city) White County
70	682	**Mitchell** (city) Lawrence County
70	682	**Roselawn** (CDP) Newton County
72	686	**Bedford** (city) Lawrence County
73	692	**South Bend** (city) Saint Joseph County
74	696	**Ellettsville** (town) Monroe County
75	702	**Country Squire Lakes** (CDP) Jennings County
75	702	**Lafayette** (city) Tippecanoe County
77	705	**Winamac** (town) Pulaski County
78	709	**Cedar Lake** (town) Lake County
78	709	**Hebron** (town) Porter County
78	709	**Winfield** (town) Lake County
81	712	**Knox** (city) Starke County
81	712	**Rockville** (town) Parke County
81	712	**Wabash** (city) Wabash County
84	718	**Indianapolis** (city) Marion County
84	718	**Mooresville** (town) Morgan County
84	718	**North Vernon** (city) Jennings County
87	722	**Georgetown** (town) Floyd County
87	722	**Mishawaka** (city) Saint Joseph County
87	722	**Shorewood Forest** (CDP) Porter County
90	725	**Franklin** (city) Johnson County
90	725	**Saint John** (town) Lake County
92	732	**Crown Point** (city) Lake County
92	732	**Plainfield** (town) Hendricks County
94	738	**Osceola** (town) Saint Joseph County
95	748	**Huntington** (city) Huntington County
95	748	**Speedway** (town) Marion County
97	751	**Elkhart** (city) Elkhart County
97	751	**Salem** (city) Washington County
99	758	**New Haven** (city) Allen County
100	764	**Lakes of the Four Seasons** (CDP) Lake County
100	764	**Noblesville** (city) Hamilton County
100	764	**Shelbyville** (city) Shelby County
103	771	**Bloomington** (city) Monroe County
104	774	**North Manchester** (town) Wabash County
105	778	**Dunlap** (CDP) Elkhart County
106	781	**Rochester** (city) Fulton County
107	784	**Hanover** (town) Jefferson County
107	784	**Simonton Lake** (CDP) Elkhart County
109	794	**Crawfordsville** (city) Montgomery County
109	794	**Valparaiso** (city) Porter County
109	794	**Westville** (town) LaPorte County
109	794	**Whiteland** (town) Johnson County
113	797	**Leo-Cedarville** (town) Allen County
113	797	**Plymouth** (city) Marshall County
115	801	**Decatur** (city) Adams County
115	801	**Goshen** (city) Elkhart County
115	801	**Granger** (CDP) Saint Joseph County
118	804	**Beech Grove** (city) Marion County
118	804	**Greenwood** (city) Johnson County
120	807	**New Whiteland** (town) Johnson County
121	810	**Fort Wayne** (city) Allen County
121	810	**Kokomo** (city) Howard County
123	814	**La Porte** (city) LaPorte County
123	814	**Marion** (city) Grant County
125	817	**Fishers** (city) Hamilton County
125	817	**Winona Lake** (town) Kosciusko County
127	820	**Bargersville** (town) Johnson County
128	823	**Connersville** (city) Fayette County
129	827	**Bluffton** (city) Wells County
129	827	**Warsaw** (city) Kosciusko County
131	833	**Avon** (town) Hendricks County
131	833	**Cicero** (town) Hamilton County
131	833	**Huntertown** (town) Allen County
134	837	**Greentown** (town) Howard County
134	837	**Middlebury** (town) Elkhart County
136	840	**Ossian** (town) Wells County
137	843	**Greencastle** (city) Putnam County
137	843	**Zionsville** (town) Boone County
139	846	**Berne** (city) Adams County
139	846	**Pendleton** (town) Madison County
141	850	**Frankfort** (city) Clinton County
141	850	**McCordsville** (town) Hancock County
143	853	**Bremen** (town) Marshall County
143	853	**Carmel** (city) Hamilton County
143	853	**Cumberland** (town) Marion County
146	856	**Fortville** (town) Hancock County
146	856	**Gas City** (city) Grant County
148	860	**Columbia City** (city) Whitley County
148	860	**Heritage Lake** (CDP) Putnam County
150	863	**Elwood** (city) Madison County

Note: *This section ranks incorporated places and CDPs (Census Designated Places) with populations of 2,500 or more. Unincorporated postal areas were not considered. Please refer to the User Guide for additional information.*

Population

Top 150 Places Ranked in *Descending* Order

State Rank	Number	Place
1	853,431	**Indianapolis** (city) Marion County
2	262,450	**Fort Wayne** (city) Allen County
3	119,806	**Evansville** (city) Vanderburgh County
4	101,928	**South Bend** (city) Saint Joseph County
5	88,595	**Carmel** (city) Hamilton County
6	87,557	**Fishers** (city) Hamilton County
7	83,636	**Bloomington** (city) Monroe County
8	77,827	**Hammond** (city) Lake County
9	77,416	**Gary** (city) Lake County
10	72,174	**Lafayette** (city) Tippecanoe County
11	69,237	**Muncie** (city) Delaware County
12	60,691	**Terre Haute** (city) Vigo County
13	59,807	**Noblesville** (city) Hamilton County
14	57,941	**Kokomo** (city) Howard County
15	55,459	**Greenwood** (city) Johnson County
16	54,986	**Anderson** (city) Madison County
17	52,662	**Elkhart** (city) Elkhart County
18	48,582	**Mishawaka** (city) Saint Joseph County
19	48,081	**Lawrence** (city) Marion County
20	46,926	**Columbus** (city) Bartholomew County
21	46,840	**Jeffersonville** (city) Clark County
22	45,110	**West Lafayette** (city) Tippecanoe County
23	36,849	**Portage** (city) Porter County
24	36,548	**New Albany** (city) Floyd County
25	35,956	**Westfield** (city) Hamilton County
26	35,819	**Richmond** (city) Wayne County
27	35,183	**Merrillville** (town) Lake County
28	33,583	**Goshen** (city) Elkhart County
29	32,501	**Valparaiso** (city) Porter County
30	31,352	**Michigan City** (city) LaPorte County
31	31,012	**Plainfield** (town) Hendricks County
32	30,717	**Granger** (CDP) Saint Joseph County
33	28,952	**Crown Point** (city) Lake County
34	28,778	**Schererville** (town) Lake County
35	28,728	**East Chicago** (city) Lake County
36	28,573	**Hobart** (city) Lake County
37	28,490	**Marion** (city) Grant County
38	25,810	**Zionsville** (town) Boone County
39	24,625	**Brownsburg** (town) Hendricks County
40	24,489	**Franklin** (city) Johnson County
41	23,005	**Munster** (town) Lake County
42	22,938	**Highland** (town) Lake County
43	21,825	**La Porte** (city) LaPorte County
44	21,565	**Greenfield** (city) Hancock County
45	21,228	**Clarksville** (town) Clark County
46	19,225	**Seymour** (city) Jackson County
47	19,034	**Shelbyville** (city) Shelby County
48	18,169	**Logansport** (city) Cass County
49	17,944	**Vincennes** (city) Knox County
50	17,476	**New Castle** (city) Henry County
51	17,214	**Huntington** (city) Huntington County
52	16,479	**Avon** (town) Hendricks County
53	16,468	**Griffith** (town) Lake County
54	16,391	**Saint John** (town) Lake County
55	16,226	**Frankfort** (city) Clinton County
56	16,077	**Dyer** (town) Lake County
57	16,075	**Crawfordsville** (city) Montgomery County
58	15,895	**New Haven** (city) Allen County
59	15,716	**Jasper** (city) Dubois County
60	15,710	**Lebanon** (city) Boone County
61	14,943	**Beech Grove** (city) Marion County
62	14,797	**Warsaw** (city) Kosciusko County
63	14,052	**Chesterton** (town) Porter County
64	13,292	**Bedford** (city) Lawrence County
65	13,022	**Connersville** (city) Fayette County
66	13,004	**Auburn** (city) DeKalb County
67	12,229	**Speedway** (town) Marion County
68	12,157	**Lake Station** (city) Lake County
69	12,056	**Greensburg** (city) Decatur County
70	12,024	**Cedar Lake** (town) Lake County
71	11,999	**Washington** (city) Daviess County
72	11,920	**Madison** (city) Jefferson County
73	11,647	**Martinsville** (city) Morgan County
74	11,510	**Peru** (city) Miami County
75	11,200	**Yorktown** (town) Delaware County
76	10,426	**Greencastle** (city) Putnam County
77	10,272	**Wabash** (city) Wabash County
78	10,011	**Plymouth** (city) Marshall County
79	9,823	**Bluffton** (city) Wells County
80	9,598	**Danville** (town) Hendricks County
81	9,592	**Kendallville** (city) Noble County
82	9,571	**Mooresville** (town) Morgan County
83	9,502	**Decatur** (city) Adams County
83	9,502	**Lowell** (town) Lake County
85	9,057	**Columbia City** (city) Whitley County
86	8,806	**Sellersburg** (town) Clark County
87	8,636	**Angola** (city) Steuben County
88	8,573	**Princeton** (city) Gibson County
89	8,458	**Elwood** (city) Madison County
90	8,384	**Brazil** (city) Clay County
91	8,079	**Charlestown** (city) Clark County
92	7,295	**Tell City** (city) Perry County
93	7,061	**Lakes of the Four Seasons** (CDP) Lake County
94	6,927	**Nappanee** (city) Elkhart County
95	6,919	**Bargersville** (town) Johnson County
96	6,857	**Huntertown** (town) Allen County
97	6,762	**Garrett** (city) DeKalb County
98	6,720	**Notre Dame** (CDP) Saint Joseph County
99	6,695	**North Vernon** (city) Jennings County
100	6,687	**Scottsburg** (city) Scott County
101	6,659	**Westville** (town) LaPorte County
102	6,633	**Huntingburg** (city) Dubois County
103	6,548	**Mount Vernon** (city) Posey County
104	6,542	**Ellettsville** (town) Monroe County
105	6,487	**Whitestown** (town) Boone County
106	6,389	**Batesville** (city) Ripley County
107	6,379	**Boonville** (city) Warrick County
108	6,191	**Salem** (city) Washington County
109	6,160	**Rushville** (city) Rush County
110	6,152	**North Manchester** (town) Wabash County
111	6,116	**McCordsville** (town) Hancock County
112	6,110	**Dunlap** (CDP) Elkhart County
113	6,068	**Portland** (city) Jay County
114	6,059	**Rochester** (city) Fulton County
115	6,002	**Hartford City** (city) Blackford County
116	5,920	**Gas City** (city) Grant County
117	5,881	**New Whiteland** (town) Johnson County
118	5,631	**Rensselaer** (city) Jasper County
119	5,566	**Cumberland** (town) Marion County
120	5,395	**Winfield** (town) Lake County
121	5,344	**Hidden Valley** (CDP) Dearborn County
122	5,326	**Bright** (CDP) Dearborn County
123	5,298	**Monticello** (city) White County
124	5,288	**Linton** (city) Greene County
125	5,151	**Tipton** (city) Tipton County
126	5,140	**Winona Lake** (town) Kosciusko County
127	5,064	**South Haven** (CDP) Porter County
128	5,061	**Winchester** (city) Randolph County
129	5,045	**Alexandria** (city) Madison County
130	4,981	**Lawrenceburg** (city) Dearborn County
131	4,880	**Cicero** (town) Hamilton County
132	4,858	**Whiting** (city) Lake County
133	4,855	**Porter** (town) Porter County
134	4,845	**Ligonier** (city) Noble County
135	4,796	**Edinburgh** (town) Johnson County
136	4,752	**Clinton** (city) Vermillion County
137	4,615	**Simonton Lake** (CDP) Elkhart County
138	4,594	**Roselawn** (CDP) Newton County
139	4,570	**Whiteland** (town) Johnson County
140	4,548	**Bremen** (town) Marshall County
141	4,539	**Highland** (CDP) Vanderburgh County
142	4,537	**Greendale** (city) Dearborn County
143	4,323	**Fortville** (town) Hancock County
144	4,280	**Mitchell** (city) Lawrence County
145	4,269	**Pendleton** (town) Madison County
146	4,231	**North Terre Haute** (CDP) Vigo County
147	4,122	**Sullivan** (city) Sullivan County
148	4,002	**Berne** (city) Adams County
149	3,992	**De Motte** (town) Jasper County
150	3,968	**Hebron** (town) Porter County

Note: *This section ranks incorporated places and CDPs (Census Designated Places) with populations of 2,500 or more. Unincorporated postal areas were not considered. Please refer to the User Guide for additional information.*

Population

Top 150 Places Ranked in *Ascending* Order

State Rank	Number	Place
1	2,512	**Shorewood Forest** (CDP) Porter County
2	2,515	**Salt Creek Commons** (CDP) Porter County
3	2,543	**Brookville** (town) Franklin County
4	2,562	**Rockville** (town) Parke County
5	2,579	**Centerville** (town) Wayne County
6	2,626	**Greentown** (town) Howard County
7	2,709	**Winamac** (town) Pulaski County
8	2,712	**Loogootee** (city) Martin County
8	2,712	**Osceola** (town) Saint Joseph County
10	2,738	**Santa Claus** (town) Spencer County
11	2,763	**Butler** (city) DeKalb County
12	2,802	**Lagrange** (town) LaGrange County
13	2,828	**Sheridan** (town) Hamilton County
14	2,873	**Syracuse** (town) Kosciusko County
15	2,952	**Brownstown** (town) Jackson County
16	2,957	**Fort Branch** (town) Gibson County
17	2,964	**Bicknell** (city) Knox County
18	2,976	**Fairmount** (town) Grant County
19	3,000	**Heritage Lake** (CDP) Putnam County
20	3,057	**Delphi** (city) Carroll County
21	3,116	**Corydon** (town) Harrison County
22	3,187	**Georgetown** (town) Floyd County
23	3,224	**Pittsboro** (town) Hendricks County
24	3,235	**Country Squire Lakes** (CDP) Jennings County
25	3,246	**Attica** (city) Fountain County
26	3,280	**Newburgh** (town) Warrick County
27	3,362	**Smithville-Sanders** (CDP) Monroe County
28	3,450	**Chandler** (town) Warrick County
29	3,483	**Hanover** (town) Jefferson County
30	3,505	**Union City** (city) Randolph County
31	3,520	**Knox** (city) Starke County
32	3,535	**Middlebury** (town) Elkhart County
33	3,625	**Melody Hill** (CDP) Vanderburgh County
34	3,642	**Upland** (town) Grant County
35	3,665	**Paoli** (town) Orange County
36	3,735	**Leo-Cedarville** (town) Allen County
37	3,770	**Aurora** (city) Dearborn County
38	3,899	**Ossian** (town) Wells County
39	3,960	**Austin** (city) Scott County
40	3,968	**Hebron** (town) Porter County
41	3,992	**De Motte** (town) Jasper County
42	4,002	**Berne** (city) Adams County
43	4,122	**Sullivan** (city) Sullivan County
44	4,231	**North Terre Haute** (CDP) Vigo County
45	4,269	**Pendleton** (town) Madison County
46	4,280	**Mitchell** (city) Lawrence County
47	4,323	**Fortville** (town) Hancock County
48	4,537	**Greendale** (city) Dearborn County
49	4,539	**Highland** (CDP) Vanderburgh County
50	4,548	**Bremen** (town) Marshall County
51	4,570	**Whiteland** (town) Johnson County
52	4,594	**Roselawn** (CDP) Newton County
53	4,615	**Simonton Lake** (CDP) Elkhart County
54	4,752	**Clinton** (city) Vermillion County
55	4,796	**Edinburgh** (town) Johnson County
56	4,845	**Ligonier** (city) Noble County
57	4,855	**Porter** (town) Porter County
58	4,858	**Whiting** (city) Lake County
59	4,880	**Cicero** (town) Hamilton County
60	4,981	**Lawrenceburg** (city) Dearborn County
61	5,045	**Alexandria** (city) Madison County
62	5,061	**Winchester** (city) Randolph County
63	5,064	**South Haven** (CDP) Porter County
64	5,140	**Winona Lake** (town) Kosciusko County
65	5,151	**Tipton** (city) Tipton County
66	5,288	**Linton** (city) Greene County
67	5,298	**Monticello** (city) White County
68	5,326	**Bright** (CDP) Dearborn County
69	5,344	**Hidden Valley** (CDP) Dearborn County
70	5,395	**Winfield** (town) Lake County
71	5,566	**Cumberland** (town) Marion County
72	5,631	**Rensselaer** (city) Jasper County
73	5,881	**New Whiteland** (town) Johnson County
74	5,920	**Gas City** (city) Grant County
75	6,002	**Hartford City** (city) Blackford County
76	6,059	**Rochester** (city) Fulton County
77	6,068	**Portland** (city) Jay County
78	6,110	**Dunlap** (CDP) Elkhart County
79	6,116	**McCordsville** (town) Hancock County
80	6,152	**North Manchester** (town) Wabash County
81	6,160	**Rushville** (city) Rush County
82	6,191	**Salem** (city) Washington County
83	6,379	**Boonville** (city) Warrick County
84	6,389	**Batesville** (city) Ripley County
85	6,487	**Whitestown** (town) Boone County
86	6,542	**Ellettsville** (town) Monroe County
87	6,548	**Mount Vernon** (city) Posey County
88	6,633	**Huntingburg** (city) Dubois County
89	6,659	**Westville** (town) LaPorte County
90	6,687	**Scottsburg** (city) Scott County
91	6,695	**North Vernon** (city) Jennings County
92	6,720	**Notre Dame** (CDP) Saint Joseph County
93	6,762	**Garrett** (city) DeKalb County
94	6,857	**Huntertown** (town) Allen County
95	6,919	**Bargersville** (town) Johnson County
96	6,927	**Nappanee** (city) Elkhart County
97	7,061	**Lakes of the Four Seasons** (CDP) Lake County
98	7,295	**Tell City** (city) Perry County
99	8,079	**Charlestown** (city) Clark County
100	8,384	**Brazil** (city) Clay County
101	8,458	**Elwood** (city) Madison County
102	8,573	**Princeton** (city) Gibson County
103	8,636	**Angola** (city) Steuben County
104	8,806	**Sellersburg** (town) Clark County
105	9,057	**Columbia City** (city) Whitley County
106	9,502	**Decatur** (city) Adams County
106	9,502	**Lowell** (town) Lake County
108	9,571	**Mooresville** (town) Morgan County
109	9,592	**Kendallville** (city) Noble County
110	9,598	**Danville** (town) Hendricks County
111	9,823	**Bluffton** (city) Wells County
112	10,011	**Plymouth** (city) Marshall County
113	10,272	**Wabash** (city) Wabash County
114	10,426	**Greencastle** (city) Putnam County
115	11,200	**Yorktown** (town) Delaware County
116	11,510	**Peru** (city) Miami County
117	11,647	**Martinsville** (city) Morgan County
118	11,920	**Madison** (city) Jefferson County
119	11,999	**Washington** (city) Daviess County
120	12,024	**Cedar Lake** (town) Lake County
121	12,056	**Greensburg** (city) Decatur County
122	12,157	**Lake Station** (city) Lake County
123	12,229	**Speedway** (town) Marion County
124	13,004	**Auburn** (city) DeKalb County
125	13,022	**Connersville** (city) Fayette County
126	13,292	**Bedford** (city) Lawrence County
127	14,052	**Chesterton** (town) Porter County
128	14,797	**Warsaw** (city) Kosciusko County
129	14,943	**Beech Grove** (city) Marion County
130	15,710	**Lebanon** (city) Boone County
131	15,716	**Jasper** (city) Dubois County
132	15,895	**New Haven** (city) Allen County
133	16,075	**Crawfordsville** (city) Montgomery County
134	16,077	**Dyer** (town) Lake County
135	16,226	**Frankfort** (city) Clinton County
136	16,391	**Saint John** (town) Lake County
137	16,468	**Griffith** (town) Lake County
138	16,479	**Avon** (town) Hendricks County
139	17,214	**Huntington** (city) Huntington County
140	17,476	**New Castle** (city) Henry County
141	17,944	**Vincennes** (city) Knox County
142	18,169	**Logansport** (city) Cass County
143	19,034	**Shelbyville** (city) Shelby County
144	19,225	**Seymour** (city) Jackson County
145	21,228	**Clarksville** (town) Clark County
146	21,565	**Greenfield** (city) Hancock County
147	21,825	**La Porte** (city) LaPorte County
148	22,938	**Highland** (town) Lake County
149	23,005	**Munster** (town) Lake County
150	24,489	**Franklin** (city) Johnson County

***Note:** This section ranks incorporated places and CDPs (Census Designated Places) with populations of 2,500 or more. Unincorporated postal areas were not considered. Please refer to the User Guide for additional information.*

Population Growth Since 2000

Top 150 Places Ranked in *Descending* Order

State Rank	Percent	Place
1	1,277.3	**Whitestown** (town) Boone County
2	439.3	**McCordsville** (town) Hancock County
3	287.2	**Huntertown** (town) Allen County
4	286.9	**Westfield** (city) Hamilton County
5	226.4	**Bargersville** (town) Johnson County
6	214.7	**Westville** (town) LaPorte County
7	194.1	**Zionsville** (town) Boone County
8	163.7	**Avon** (town) Hendricks County
9	134.8	**Carmel** (city) Hamilton County
9	134.8	**Winfield** (town) Lake County
11	134.1	**Yorktown** (town) Delaware County
12	131.4	**Fishers** (city) Hamilton County
13	109.2	**Noblesville** (city) Hamilton County
14	103.0	**Pittsboro** (town) Hendricks County
15	95.5	**Saint John** (town) Lake County
16	71.2	**Jeffersonville** (city) Clark County
17	69.6	**Brownsburg** (town) Hendricks County
18	68.6	**Plainfield** (town) Hendricks County
19	56.8	**West Lafayette** (city) Tippecanoe County
20	53.9	**Greenwood** (city) Johnson County
21	49.5	**Danville** (town) Hendricks County
22	47.7	**Greenfield** (city) Hancock County
23	46.2	**Crown Point** (city) Lake County
24	45.9	**Osceola** (town) Saint Joseph County
25	45.1	**Sellersburg** (town) Clark County
26	43.1	**Georgetown** (town) Floyd County
27	34.8	**Charlestown** (city) Clark County
28	34.3	**Leo-Cedarville** (town) Allen County
29	34.1	**Santa Claus** (town) Spencer County
30	34.0	**Chesterton** (town) Porter County
31	32.5	**Ossian** (town) Wells County
32	29.9	**Jasper** (city) Dubois County
33	29.6	**Cedar Lake** (town) Lake County
34	28.9	**Winona Lake** (town) Kosciusko County
35	28.8	**Ellettsville** (town) Monroe County
36	28.4	**New Whiteland** (town) Johnson County
37	28.1	**New Haven** (city) Allen County
38	28.0	**Columbia City** (city) Whitley County
38	28.0	**Lafayette** (city) Tippecanoe County
40	27.6	**Fort Wayne** (city) Allen County
41	27.5	**Fort Branch** (town) Gibson County
42	26.6	**Lowell** (town) Lake County
43	25.8	**Franklin** (city) Johnson County
44	25.7	**Kokomo** (city) Howard County
45	25.5	**Fortville** (town) Hancock County
46	23.6	**Lawrence** (city) Marion County
47	23.4	**De Motte** (town) Jasper County
48	22.9	**Hanover** (town) Jefferson County
49	21.0	**Hidden Valley** (CDP) Dearborn County
50	20.7	**Bloomington** (city) Monroe County
51	20.1	**Columbus** (city) Bartholomew County
52	19.6	**Middlebury** (town) Elkhart County
53	19.2	**Warsaw** (city) Kosciusko County
54	18.5	**Huntingburg** (city) Dubois County
54	18.5	**Valparaiso** (city) Porter County
56	18.2	**Melody Hill** (CDP) Vanderburgh County
57	17.6	**Angola** (city) Steuben County
58	17.5	**Greensburg** (city) Decatur County
59	16.8	**Roselawn** (CDP) Newton County
60	16.5	**Garrett** (city) DeKalb County
61	15.8	**Schererville** (town) Lake County
62	15.7	**Dyer** (town) Lake County
63	15.5	**Whiteland** (town) Johnson County
64	15.1	**Merrillville** (town) Lake County
65	14.8	**Corydon** (town) Harrison County
66	14.3	**Goshen** (city) Elkhart County
67	13.9	**Simonton Lake** (CDP) Elkhart County
68	13.4	**Cicero** (town) Hamilton County
69	12.7	**Hobart** (city) Lake County
70	12.2	**Sheridan** (town) Hamilton County
71	12.0	**Winamac** (town) Pulaski County
72	11.5	**Chandler** (town) Warrick County
73	11.2	**Ligonier** (city) Noble County
74	10.7	**Scottsburg** (city) Scott County
75	10.5	**Highland** (CDP) Vanderburgh County
75	10.5	**Lebanon** (city) Boone County
77	10.3	**Hebron** (town) Porter County
78	10.2	**Pendleton** (town) Madison County
79	10.0	**Portage** (city) Porter County
80	9.2	**Indianapolis** (city) Marion County
81	8.6	**Granger** (CDP) Saint Joseph County
82	7.7	**Auburn** (city) DeKalb County
83	6.9	**Munster** (town) Lake County
84	6.5	**Edinburgh** (town) Johnson County
85	6.4	**Rensselaer** (city) Jasper County
86	6.3	**Centerville** (town) Wayne County
86	6.3	**Lawrenceburg** (city) Dearborn County
88	6.2	**Newburgh** (town) Warrick County
88	6.2	**Seymour** (city) Jackson County
90	6.0	**Shelbyville** (city) Shelby County
91	5.9	**Batesville** (city) Ripley County
92	5.6	**Greendale** (city) Dearborn County
93	5.5	**Crawfordsville** (city) Montgomery County
93	5.5	**Greencastle** (city) Putnam County
95	5.4	**Washington** (city) Daviess County
96	4.9	**Princeton** (city) Gibson County
97	4.3	**Mishawaka** (city) Saint Joseph County
98	3.8	**Dunlap** (CDP) Elkhart County
99	3.2	**Mooresville** (town) Morgan County
99	3.2	**Nappanee** (city) Elkhart County
101	3.1	**Greentown** (town) Howard County
102	3.0	**Bluffton** (city) Wells County
103	2.8	**North Vernon** (city) Jennings County
103	2.8	**Rushville** (city) Rush County
105	2.7	**Muncie** (city) Delaware County
106	2.4	**Brazil** (city) Clay County
107	1.8	**Terre Haute** (city) Vigo County
108	1.7	**Plymouth** (city) Marshall County
109	1.5	**Elkhart** (city) Elkhart County
110	1.4	**Bremen** (town) Marshall County
110	1.4	**Butler** (city) DeKalb County
110	1.4	**Delphi** (city) Carroll County
113	1.2	**Cumberland** (town) Marion County
114	0.9	**La Porte** (city) LaPorte County
115	0.5	**Winchester** (city) Randolph County
116	0.4	**Beech Grove** (city) Marion County
117	0.3	**Salem** (city) Washington County
118	-0.2	**Kendallville** (city) Noble County
119	-0.3	**Decatur** (city) Adams County
119	-0.3	**Gas City** (city) Grant County
121	-0.4	**Martinsville** (city) Morgan County
122	-0.5	**Fairmount** (town) Grant County
123	-0.7	**Madison** (city) Jefferson County
124	-0.8	**Clarksville** (town) Clark County
125	-0.9	**Brownstown** (town) Jackson County
126	-1.0	**Country Squire Lakes** (CDP) Jennings County
126	-1.0	**Heritage Lake** (CDP) Putnam County
126	-1.0	**Notre Dame** (CDP) Saint Joseph County
126	-1.0	**Salt Creek Commons** (CDP) Porter County
126	-1.0	**Shorewood Forest** (CDP) Porter County
126	-1.0	**Smithville-Sanders** (CDP) Monroe County
132	-1.1	**Loogootee** (city) Martin County
133	-1.4	**Huntington** (city) Huntington County
134	-1.5	**Bright** (CDP) Dearborn County
134	-1.5	**Evansville** (city) Vanderburgh County
136	-1.7	**New Castle** (city) Henry County
136	-1.7	**North Manchester** (town) Wabash County
138	-1.9	**Tipton** (city) Tipton County
139	-2.4	**Porter** (town) Porter County
140	-2.6	**Frankfort** (city) Clinton County
140	-2.6	**Highland** (town) Lake County
142	-2.8	**New Albany** (city) Floyd County
143	-3.2	**Lakes of the Four Seasons** (CDP) Lake County
143	-3.2	**Union City** (city) Randolph County
145	-3.5	**Bedford** (city) Lawrence County
146	-3.6	**Berne** (city) Adams County
147	-4.0	**Lagrange** (town) LaGrange County
147	-4.0	**Vincennes** (city) Knox County
149	-4.1	**Brookville** (town) Franklin County
150	-4.2	**Upland** (town) Grant County

***Note:** This section ranks incorporated places and CDPs (Census Designated Places) with populations of 2,500 or more. Unincorporated postal areas were not considered. Please refer to the User Guide for additional information.*

Population Growth Since 2000

Top 150 Places Ranked in *Ascending* Order

State Rank	Percent	Place
1	-24.7	**Gary** (city) Lake County
2	-19.4	**Alexandria** (city) Madison County
3	-16.2	**Austin** (city) Scott County
4	-15.5	**Connersville** (city) Fayette County
5	-13.4	**Hartford City** (city) Blackford County
6	-13.1	**Elwood** (city) Madison County
7	-12.8	**Lake Station** (city) Lake County
8	-12.5	**Wabash** (city) Wabash County
9	-12.4	**Mount Vernon** (city) Posey County
10	-12.3	**Bicknell** (city) Knox County
11	-11.4	**East Chicago** (city) Lake County
11	-11.4	**Peru** (city) Miami County
13	-10.7	**Sullivan** (city) Sullivan County
14	-9.9	**South Haven** (CDP) Porter County
15	-9.0	**Marion** (city) Grant County
16	-8.4	**Linton** (city) Greene County
16	-8.4	**Richmond** (city) Wayne County
18	-8.1	**North Terre Haute** (CDP) Vigo County
19	-7.9	**Anderson** (city) Madison County
20	-7.7	**Logansport** (city) Cass County
21	-7.4	**Monticello** (city) White County
22	-7.3	**Clinton** (city) Vermillion County
22	-7.3	**Rockville** (town) Parke County
24	-7.0	**Attica** (city) Fountain County
24	-7.0	**Tell City** (city) Perry County
26	-6.7	**Boonville** (city) Warrick County
27	-6.3	**Hammond** (city) Lake County
27	-6.3	**Mitchell** (city) Lawrence County
29	-5.7	**Portland** (city) Jay County
30	-5.5	**Rochester** (city) Fulton County
31	-5.4	**Knox** (city) Starke County
31	-5.4	**South Bend** (city) Saint Joseph County
31	-5.4	**Syracuse** (town) Kosciusko County
31	-5.4	**Whiting** (city) Lake County
35	-5.1	**Speedway** (town) Marion County
36	-5.0	**Griffith** (town) Lake County
37	-4.9	**Aurora** (city) Dearborn County
38	-4.7	**Michigan City** (city) LaPorte County
38	-4.7	**Paoli** (town) Orange County
40	-4.2	**Upland** (town) Grant County
41	-4.1	**Brookville** (town) Franklin County
42	-4.0	**Lagrange** (town) LaGrange County
42	-4.0	**Vincennes** (city) Knox County
44	-3.6	**Berne** (city) Adams County
45	-3.5	**Bedford** (city) Lawrence County
46	-3.2	**Lakes of the Four Seasons** (CDP) Lake County
46	-3.2	**Union City** (city) Randolph County
48	-2.8	**New Albany** (city) Floyd County
49	-2.6	**Frankfort** (city) Clinton County
49	-2.6	**Highland** (town) Lake County
51	-2.4	**Porter** (town) Porter County
52	-1.9	**Tipton** (city) Tipton County
53	-1.7	**New Castle** (city) Henry County
53	-1.7	**North Manchester** (town) Wabash County
55	-1.5	**Bright** (CDP) Dearborn County
55	-1.5	**Evansville** (city) Vanderburgh County
57	-1.4	**Huntington** (city) Huntington County
58	-1.1	**Loogootee** (city) Martin County
59	-0.9	**Brownstown** (town) Jackson County
60	-0.8	**Clarksville** (town) Clark County
61	-0.7	**Madison** (city) Jefferson County
62	-0.5	**Fairmount** (town) Grant County
63	-0.4	**Martinsville** (city) Morgan County
64	-0.3	**Decatur** (city) Adams County
64	-0.3	**Gas City** (city) Grant County
66	-0.2	**Kendallville** (city) Noble County
67	0.3	**Salem** (city) Washington County
68	0.4	**Beech Grove** (city) Marion County
69	0.5	**Winchester** (city) Randolph County
70	0.9	**La Porte** (city) LaPorte County
71	1.2	**Cumberland** (town) Marion County
72	1.4	**Bremen** (town) Marshall County
72	1.4	**Butler** (city) DeKalb County
72	1.4	**Delphi** (city) Carroll County
75	1.5	**Elkhart** (city) Elkhart County
76	1.7	**Plymouth** (city) Marshall County
77	1.8	**Terre Haute** (city) Vigo County
78	2.4	**Brazil** (city) Clay County
79	2.7	**Muncie** (city) Delaware County
80	2.8	**North Vernon** (city) Jennings County
80	2.8	**Rushville** (city) Rush County
82	3.0	**Bluffton** (city) Wells County
83	3.1	**Greentown** (town) Howard County
84	3.2	**Mooresville** (town) Morgan County
84	3.2	**Nappanee** (city) Elkhart County
86	3.8	**Dunlap** (CDP) Elkhart County
87	4.3	**Mishawaka** (city) Saint Joseph County
88	4.9	**Princeton** (city) Gibson County
89	5.4	**Washington** (city) Daviess County
90	5.5	**Crawfordsville** (city) Montgomery County
90	5.5	**Greencastle** (city) Putnam County
92	5.6	**Greendale** (city) Dearborn County
93	5.9	**Batesville** (city) Ripley County
94	6.0	**Shelbyville** (city) Shelby County
95	6.2	**Newburgh** (town) Warrick County
95	6.2	**Seymour** (city) Jackson County
97	6.3	**Centerville** (town) Wayne County
97	6.3	**Lawrenceburg** (city) Dearborn County
99	6.4	**Rensselaer** (city) Jasper County
100	6.5	**Edinburgh** (town) Johnson County
101	6.9	**Munster** (town) Lake County
102	7.7	**Auburn** (city) DeKalb County
103	8.6	**Granger** (CDP) Saint Joseph County
104	9.2	**Indianapolis** (city) Marion County
105	10.0	**Portage** (city) Porter County
106	10.2	**Pendleton** (town) Madison County
107	10.3	**Hebron** (town) Porter County
108	10.5	**Highland** (CDP) Vanderburgh County
108	10.5	**Lebanon** (city) Boone County
110	10.7	**Scottsburg** (city) Scott County
111	11.2	**Ligonier** (city) Noble County
112	11.5	**Chandler** (town) Warrick County
113	12.0	**Winamac** (town) Pulaski County
114	12.2	**Sheridan** (town) Hamilton County
115	12.7	**Hobart** (city) Lake County
116	13.4	**Cicero** (town) Hamilton County
117	13.9	**Simonton Lake** (CDP) Elkhart County
118	14.3	**Goshen** (city) Elkhart County
119	14.8	**Corydon** (town) Harrison County
120	15.1	**Merrillville** (town) Lake County
121	15.5	**Whiteland** (town) Johnson County
122	15.7	**Dyer** (town) Lake County
123	15.8	**Schererville** (town) Lake County
124	16.5	**Garrett** (city) DeKalb County
125	16.8	**Roselawn** (CDP) Newton County
126	17.5	**Greensburg** (city) Decatur County
127	17.6	**Angola** (city) Steuben County
128	18.2	**Melody Hill** (CDP) Vanderburgh County
129	18.5	**Huntingburg** (city) Dubois County
129	18.5	**Valparaiso** (city) Porter County
131	19.2	**Warsaw** (city) Kosciusko County
132	19.6	**Middlebury** (town) Elkhart County
133	20.1	**Columbus** (city) Bartholomew County
134	20.7	**Bloomington** (city) Monroe County
135	21.0	**Hidden Valley** (CDP) Dearborn County
136	22.9	**Hanover** (town) Jefferson County
137	23.4	**De Motte** (town) Jasper County
138	23.6	**Lawrence** (city) Marion County
139	25.5	**Fortville** (town) Hancock County
140	25.7	**Kokomo** (city) Howard County
141	25.8	**Franklin** (city) Johnson County
142	26.6	**Lowell** (town) Lake County
143	27.5	**Fort Branch** (town) Gibson County
144	27.6	**Fort Wayne** (city) Allen County
145	28.0	**Columbia City** (city) Whitley County
145	28.0	**Lafayette** (city) Tippecanoe County
147	28.1	**New Haven** (city) Allen County
148	28.4	**New Whiteland** (town) Johnson County
149	28.8	**Ellettsville** (town) Monroe County
150	28.9	**Winona Lake** (town) Kosciusko County

Note: *This section ranks incorporated places and CDPs (Census Designated Places) with populations of 2,500 or more. Unincorporated postal areas were not considered. Please refer to the User Guide for additional information.*

Population Density

Top 150 Places Ranked in *Descending* Order

State Rank	Pop./ Sq. Mi.	Place
1	6,790.3	**Salt Creek Commons** (CDP) Porter County
2	5,923.6	**West Lafayette** (city) Tippecanoe County
3	5,562.7	**Notre Dame** (CDP) Saint Joseph County
4	4,074.8	**South Haven** (CDP) Porter County
5	4,024.3	**New Whiteland** (town) Johnson County
6	3,611.5	**Bloomington** (city) Monroe County
7	3,417.1	**Hammond** (city) Lake County
8	3,400.3	**Beech Grove** (city) Marion County
9	3,307.2	**Highland** (town) Lake County
10	3,132.5	**Kokomo** (city) Howard County
11	3,038.9	**Munster** (town) Lake County
12	2,858.3	**Mishawaka** (city) Saint Joseph County
13	2,857.1	**Cicero** (town) Hamilton County
14	2,769.7	**Brazil** (city) Clay County
15	2,728.7	**Ossian** (town) Wells County
16	2,713.4	**Evansville** (city) Vanderburgh County
17	2,704.2	**Cumberland** (town) Marion County
18	2,702.5	**Whiting** (city) Lake County
19	2,695.5	**Fort Branch** (town) Gibson County
20	2,664.1	**Melody Hill** (CDP) Vanderburgh County
21	2,634.0	**Lakes of the Four Seasons** (CDP) Lake County
22	2,633.9	**Dyer** (town) Lake County
23	2,612.3	**Greenwood** (city) Johnson County
24	2,607.0	**Fishers** (city) Hamilton County
25	2,601.6	**Lafayette** (city) Tippecanoe County
26	2,594.2	**Martinsville** (city) Morgan County
27	2,570.9	**Frankfort** (city) Clinton County
28	2,570.1	**Speedway** (town) Marion County
29	2,545.8	**Muncie** (city) Delaware County
30	2,536.5	**Washington** (city) Daviess County
31	2,516.4	**Zionsville** (town) Boone County
32	2,458.6	**South Bend** (city) Saint Joseph County
33	2,446.6	**New Albany** (city) Floyd County
34	2,421.0	**Vincennes** (city) Knox County
35	2,395.7	**New Castle** (city) Henry County
36	2,388.3	**Lawrence** (city) Marion County
37	2,372.6	**Fort Wayne** (city) Allen County
38	2,361.2	**Indianapolis** (city) Marion County
39	2,332.5	**Newburgh** (town) Warrick County
40	2,332.2	**Mount Vernon** (city) Posey County
41	2,254.7	**Peru** (city) Miami County
42	2,245.4	**Elkhart** (city) Elkhart County
43	2,241.2	**Elwood** (city) Madison County
44	2,233.5	**Sellersburg** (town) Clark County
45	2,223.3	**Brownsburg** (town) Hendricks County
46	2,201.8	**Bicknell** (city) Knox County
47	2,197.5	**Sullivan** (city) Sullivan County
48	2,156.5	**Westville** (town) LaPorte County
49	2,129.6	**Griffith** (town) Lake County
50	2,128.5	**Clarksville** (town) Clark County
51	2,125.5	**Boonville** (city) Warrick County
52	2,123.4	**Clinton** (city) Vermillion County
53	2,097.8	**Ligonier** (city) Noble County
54	2,092.8	**Valparaiso** (city) Porter County
55	2,077.0	**Logansport** (city) Cass County
56	2,069.3	**Goshen** (city) Elkhart County
57	2,057.3	**Tipton** (city) Tipton County
58	2,039.2	**East Chicago** (city) Lake County
59	2,029.0	**Attica** (city) Fountain County
60	2,008.3	**Hebron** (town) Porter County
61	2,002.0	**Highland** (CDP) Vanderburgh County
62	1,999.0	**Osceola** (town) Saint Joseph County
63	1,993.0	**Rushville** (city) Rush County
64	1,989.9	**Winamac** (town) Pulaski County
65	1,988.9	**Greencastle** (city) Putnam County
66	1,977.0	**Huntington** (city) Huntington County
67	1,956.1	**Schererville** (town) Lake County
68	1,926.2	**Berne** (city) Adams County
69	1,922.9	**Greentown** (town) Howard County
70	1,920.2	**Alexandria** (city) Madison County
71	1,906.2	**Noblesville** (city) Hamilton County
72	1,889.2	**Corydon** (town) Harrison County
73	1,882.9	**Franklin** (city) Johnson County
74	1,880.3	**Fairmount** (town) Grant County
75	1,871.7	**La Porte** (city) LaPorte County
76	1,866.6	**Carmel** (city) Hamilton County
77	1,860.4	**Winona Lake** (town) Kosciusko County
78	1,858.9	**Brownstown** (town) Jackson County
79	1,834.4	**Lowell** (town) Lake County
80	1,830.4	**Auburn** (city) DeKalb County
81	1,813.4	**Marion** (city) Grant County
82	1,803.4	**Huntertown** (town) Allen County
83	1,757.5	**Crawfordsville** (city) Montgomery County
84	1,757.3	**Terre Haute** (city) Vigo County
85	1,756.1	**Garrett** (city) DeKalb County
86	1,750.1	**Linton** (city) Greene County
87	1,740.6	**North Manchester** (town) Wabash County
88	1,730.6	**Loogootee** (city) Martin County
89	1,718.2	**Greenfield** (city) Hancock County
90	1,716.6	**Rockville** (town) Parke County
91	1,706.6	**Columbus** (city) Bartholomew County
92	1,697.1	**Brookville** (town) Franklin County
93	1,696.8	**Chandler** (town) Warrick County
94	1,690.9	**Princeton** (city) Gibson County
95	1,683.1	**Seymour** (city) Jackson County
96	1,681.4	**Connersville** (city) Fayette County
97	1,674.9	**Bremen** (town) Marshall County
98	1,669.7	**Nappanee** (city) Elkhart County
99	1,646.0	**Shelbyville** (city) Shelby County
100	1,644.7	**Decatur** (city) Adams County
101	1,644.6	**Lagrange** (town) LaGrange County
102	1,634.5	**Crown Point** (city) Lake County
103	1,622.6	**Columbia City** (city) Whitley County
104	1,610.9	**New Haven** (city) Allen County
105	1,609.0	**Tell City** (city) Perry County
106	1,607.7	**Syracuse** (town) Kosciusko County
107	1,600.6	**Michigan City** (city) LaPorte County
108	1,593.0	**Union City** (city) Randolph County
109	1,586.8	**Kendallville** (city) Noble County
110	1,555.3	**Georgetown** (town) Floyd County
111	1,552.5	**Gary** (city) Lake County
112	1,548.8	**Hartford City** (city) Blackford County
113	1,547.8	**Salem** (city) Washington County
114	1,543.0	**Ellettsville** (town) Monroe County
115	1,542.4	**Edinburgh** (town) Johnson County
116	1,536.7	**Austin** (city) Scott County
117	1,527.0	**Monticello** (city) White County
118	1,522.8	**Mooresville** (town) Morgan County
119	1,520.6	**Winchester** (city) Randolph County
120	1,509.2	**Hanover** (town) Jefferson County
121	1,505.7	**Chesterton** (town) Porter County
122	1,497.8	**Richmond** (city) Wayne County
123	1,481.8	**Rensselaer** (city) Jasper County
124	1,465.4	**Lake Station** (city) Lake County
125	1,463.0	**Cedar Lake** (town) Lake County
126	1,452.4	**Fortville** (town) Hancock County
127	1,439.4	**Saint John** (town) Lake County
128	1,437.8	**Portage** (city) Porter County
129	1,419.5	**Whiteland** (town) Johnson County
130	1,404.6	**Bargersville** (town) Johnson County
131	1,392.3	**Plainfield** (town) Hendricks County
132	1,390.1	**Madison** (city) Jefferson County
133	1,385.0	**Danville** (town) Hendricks County
134	1,375.0	**Jeffersonville** (city) Clark County
135	1,365.7	**Aurora** (city) Dearborn County
136	1,361.4	**Angola** (city) Steuben County
137	1,339.7	**Westfield** (city) Hamilton County
138	1,329.1	**Anderson** (city) Madison County
139	1,328.8	**Plymouth** (city) Marshall County
140	1,323.4	**Scottsburg** (city) Scott County
141	1,323.3	**Sheridan** (town) Hamilton County
142	1,323.1	**Shorewood Forest** (CDP) Porter County
143	1,320.0	**Butler** (city) DeKalb County
144	1,310.5	**Huntingburg** (city) Dubois County
145	1,306.5	**Mitchell** (city) Lawrence County
146	1,304.6	**Portland** (city) Jay County
147	1,301.0	**McCordsville** (town) Hancock County
148	1,300.6	**Greensburg** (city) Decatur County
149	1,299.3	**Gas City** (city) Grant County
150	1,295.0	**Simonton Lake** (CDP) Elkhart County

***Note:** This section ranks incorporated places and CDPs (Census Designated Places) with populations of 2,500 or more. Unincorporated postal areas were not considered. Please refer to the User Guide for additional information.*

Population Density

Top 150 Places Ranked in *Ascending* Order

State Rank	Pop./ Sq. Mi.	Place
1	313.6	**Smithville-Sanders** (CDP) Monroe County
2	382.3	**Pendleton** (town) Madison County
3	424.4	**Bright** (CDP) Dearborn County
4	425.0	**Santa Claus** (town) Spencer County
5	450.5	**Winfield** (town) Lake County
6	569.3	**Roselawn** (CDP) Newton County
7	620.3	**Whitestown** (town) Boone County
8	705.8	**Charlestown** (city) Clark County
9	783.1	**Porter** (town) Porter County
10	794.2	**Greendale** (city) Dearborn County
11	897.9	**Knox** (city) Starke County
12	941.3	**Middlebury** (town) Elkhart County
13	979.1	**Paoli** (town) Orange County
14	995.9	**Heritage Lake** (CDP) Putnam County
15	1,005.8	**Leo-Cedarville** (town) Allen County
16	1,008.1	**Lawrenceburg** (city) Dearborn County
17	1,010.0	**Lebanon** (city) Boone County
18	1,011.5	**North Vernon** (city) Jennings County
19	1,049.5	**Batesville** (city) Ripley County
20	1,059.2	**Merrillville** (town) Lake County
21	1,072.7	**Centerville** (town) Wayne County
22	1,085.1	**Hobart** (city) Lake County
23	1,092.5	**Pittsboro** (town) Hendricks County
24	1,093.0	**Bedford** (city) Lawrence County
25	1,106.2	**De Motte** (town) Jasper County
26	1,121.5	**Delphi** (city) Carroll County
27	1,156.0	**Wabash** (city) Wabash County
28	1,157.2	**Avon** (town) Hendricks County
29	1,160.6	**Upland** (town) Grant County
30	1,185.9	**North Terre Haute** (CDP) Vigo County
31	1,193.3	**Bluffton** (city) Wells County
32	1,199.3	**Jasper** (city) Dubois County
33	1,201.4	**Granger** (CDP) Saint Joseph County
34	1,246.8	**Dunlap** (CDP) Elkhart County
35	1,262.6	**Country Squire Lakes** (CDP) Jennings County
36	1,275.8	**Yorktown** (town) Delaware County
37	1,278.2	**Warsaw** (city) Kosciusko County
38	1,291.4	**Hidden Valley** (CDP) Dearborn County
39	1,291.7	**Rochester** (city) Fulton County
40	1,295.0	**Simonton Lake** (CDP) Elkhart County
41	1,299.3	**Gas City** (city) Grant County
42	1,300.6	**Greensburg** (city) Decatur County
43	1,301.0	**McCordsville** (town) Hancock County
44	1,304.6	**Portland** (city) Jay County
45	1,306.5	**Mitchell** (city) Lawrence County
46	1,310.5	**Huntingburg** (city) Dubois County
47	1,320.0	**Butler** (city) DeKalb County
48	1,323.1	**Shorewood Forest** (CDP) Porter County
49	1,323.3	**Sheridan** (town) Hamilton County
50	1,323.4	**Scottsburg** (city) Scott County
51	1,328.8	**Plymouth** (city) Marshall County
52	1,329.1	**Anderson** (city) Madison County
53	1,339.7	**Westfield** (city) Hamilton County
54	1,361.4	**Angola** (city) Steuben County
55	1,365.7	**Aurora** (city) Dearborn County
56	1,375.0	**Jeffersonville** (city) Clark County
57	1,385.0	**Danville** (town) Hendricks County
58	1,390.1	**Madison** (city) Jefferson County
59	1,392.3	**Plainfield** (town) Hendricks County
60	1,404.6	**Bargersville** (town) Johnson County
61	1,419.5	**Whiteland** (town) Johnson County
62	1,437.8	**Portage** (city) Porter County
63	1,439.4	**Saint John** (town) Lake County
64	1,452.4	**Fortville** (town) Hancock County
65	1,463.0	**Cedar Lake** (town) Lake County
66	1,465.4	**Lake Station** (city) Lake County
67	1,481.8	**Rensselaer** (city) Jasper County
68	1,497.8	**Richmond** (city) Wayne County
69	1,505.7	**Chesterton** (town) Porter County
70	1,509.2	**Hanover** (town) Jefferson County
71	1,520.6	**Winchester** (city) Randolph County
72	1,522.8	**Mooresville** (town) Morgan County
73	1,527.0	**Monticello** (city) White County
74	1,536.7	**Austin** (city) Scott County
75	1,542.4	**Edinburgh** (town) Johnson County
76	1,543.0	**Ellettsville** (town) Monroe County
77	1,547.8	**Salem** (city) Washington County
78	1,548.8	**Hartford City** (city) Blackford County
79	1,552.5	**Gary** (city) Lake County
80	1,555.3	**Georgetown** (town) Floyd County
81	1,586.8	**Kendallville** (city) Noble County
82	1,593.0	**Union City** (city) Randolph County
83	1,600.6	**Michigan City** (city) LaPorte County
84	1,607.7	**Syracuse** (town) Kosciusko County
85	1,609.0	**Tell City** (city) Perry County
86	1,610.9	**New Haven** (city) Allen County
87	1,622.6	**Columbia City** (city) Whitley County
88	1,634.5	**Crown Point** (city) Lake County
89	1,644.6	**Lagrange** (town) LaGrange County
90	1,644.7	**Decatur** (city) Adams County
91	1,646.0	**Shelbyville** (city) Shelby County
92	1,669.7	**Nappanee** (city) Elkhart County
93	1,674.9	**Bremen** (town) Marshall County
94	1,681.4	**Connersville** (city) Fayette County
95	1,683.1	**Seymour** (city) Jackson County
96	1,690.9	**Princeton** (city) Gibson County
97	1,696.8	**Chandler** (town) Warrick County
98	1,697.1	**Brookville** (town) Franklin County
99	1,706.6	**Columbus** (city) Bartholomew County
100	1,716.6	**Rockville** (town) Parke County
101	1,718.2	**Greenfield** (city) Hancock County
102	1,730.6	**Loogootee** (city) Martin County
103	1,740.6	**North Manchester** (town) Wabash County
104	1,750.1	**Linton** (city) Greene County
105	1,756.1	**Garrett** (city) DeKalb County
106	1,757.3	**Terre Haute** (city) Vigo County
107	1,757.5	**Crawfordsville** (city) Montgomery County
108	1,803.4	**Huntertown** (town) Allen County
109	1,813.4	**Marion** (city) Grant County
110	1,830.4	**Auburn** (city) DeKalb County
111	1,834.4	**Lowell** (town) Lake County
112	1,858.9	**Brownstown** (town) Jackson County
113	1,860.4	**Winona Lake** (town) Kosciusko County
114	1,866.6	**Carmel** (city) Hamilton County
115	1,871.7	**La Porte** (city) LaPorte County
116	1,880.3	**Fairmount** (town) Grant County
117	1,882.9	**Franklin** (city) Johnson County
118	1,889.2	**Corydon** (town) Harrison County
119	1,906.2	**Noblesville** (city) Hamilton County
120	1,920.2	**Alexandria** (city) Madison County
121	1,922.9	**Greentown** (town) Howard County
122	1,926.2	**Berne** (city) Adams County
123	1,956.1	**Schererville** (town) Lake County
124	1,977.0	**Huntington** (city) Huntington County
125	1,988.9	**Greencastle** (city) Putnam County
126	1,989.9	**Winamac** (town) Pulaski County
127	1,993.0	**Rushville** (city) Rush County
128	1,999.0	**Osceola** (town) Saint Joseph County
129	2,002.0	**Highland** (CDP) Vanderburgh County
130	2,008.3	**Hebron** (town) Porter County
131	2,029.0	**Attica** (city) Fountain County
132	2,039.2	**East Chicago** (city) Lake County
133	2,057.3	**Tipton** (city) Tipton County
134	2,069.3	**Goshen** (city) Elkhart County
135	2,077.0	**Logansport** (city) Cass County
136	2,092.8	**Valparaiso** (city) Porter County
137	2,097.8	**Ligonier** (city) Noble County
138	2,123.4	**Clinton** (city) Vermillion County
139	2,125.5	**Boonville** (city) Warrick County
140	2,128.5	**Clarksville** (town) Clark County
141	2,129.6	**Griffith** (town) Lake County
142	2,156.5	**Westville** (town) LaPorte County
143	2,197.5	**Sullivan** (city) Sullivan County
144	2,201.8	**Bicknell** (city) Knox County
145	2,223.3	**Brownsburg** (town) Hendricks County
146	2,233.5	**Sellersburg** (town) Clark County
147	2,241.2	**Elwood** (city) Madison County
148	2,245.4	**Elkhart** (city) Elkhart County
149	2,254.7	**Peru** (city) Miami County
150	2,332.2	**Mount Vernon** (city) Posey County

Note: *This section ranks incorporated places and CDPs (Census Designated Places) with populations of 2,500 or more. Unincorporated postal areas were not considered. Please refer to the User Guide for additional information.*

White Population

Top 150 Places Ranked in *Descending* Order

State Rank	Percent	Place
1	100.0	**Brookville** (town) Franklin County
2	99.7	**Cicero** (town) Hamilton County
3	99.5	**Mooresville** (town) Morgan County
3	99.5	**Whiteland** (town) Johnson County
5	99.3	**Heritage Lake** (CDP) Putnam County
6	99.1	**Alexandria** (city) Madison County
6	99.1	**Highland** (CDP) Vanderburgh County
8	99.0	**Auburn** (city) DeKalb County
9	98.9	**Brownstown** (town) Jackson County
10	98.7	**Chandler** (town) Warrick County
10	98.7	**Knox** (city) Starke County
12	98.6	**Corydon** (town) Harrison County
13	98.5	**Clinton** (city) Vermillion County
13	98.5	**Sheridan** (town) Hamilton County
15	98.3	**Bargersville** (town) Johnson County
15	98.3	**Fairmount** (town) Grant County
15	98.3	**Greentown** (town) Howard County
15	98.3	**Loogootee** (city) Martin County
15	98.3	**Salem** (city) Washington County
20	98.2	**Elwood** (city) Madison County
21	98.0	**Austin** (city) Scott County
21	98.0	**Linton** (city) Greene County
23	97.9	**Winona Lake** (town) Kosciusko County
24	97.8	**Garrett** (city) DeKalb County
25	97.7	**Attica** (city) Fountain County
25	97.7	**Bright** (CDP) Dearborn County
27	97.5	**Rochester** (city) Fulton County
27	97.5	**Santa Claus** (town) Spencer County
29	97.4	**Rockville** (town) Parke County
29	97.4	**Scottsburg** (city) Scott County
31	97.3	**Hidden Valley** (CDP) Dearborn County
32	97.2	**Aurora** (city) Dearborn County
33	97.1	**Paoli** (town) Orange County
34	97.0	**Greenfield** (city) Hancock County
34	97.0	**Hartford City** (city) Blackford County
34	97.0	**North Vernon** (city) Jennings County
37	96.9	**Pendleton** (town) Madison County
38	96.7	**Sullivan** (city) Sullivan County
39	96.4	**Bluffton** (city) Wells County
39	96.4	**Greendale** (city) Dearborn County
39	96.4	**Lawrenceburg** (city) Dearborn County
42	96.3	**Porter** (town) Porter County
43	96.2	**Ossian** (town) Wells County
44	96.1	**Bicknell** (city) Knox County
44	96.1	**Boonville** (city) Warrick County
44	96.1	**Ligonier** (city) Noble County
47	96.0	**North Terre Haute** (CDP) Vigo County
47	96.0	**Roselawn** (CDP) Newton County
49	95.8	**Kendallville** (city) Noble County
49	95.8	**Lagrange** (town) LaGrange County
51	95.7	**Butler** (city) DeKalb County
51	95.7	**Danville** (town) Hendricks County
51	95.7	**Franklin** (city) Johnson County
51	95.7	**Lebanon** (city) Boone County
51	95.7	**New Castle** (city) Henry County
51	95.7	**Smithville-Sanders** (CDP) Monroe County
57	95.6	**Angola** (city) Steuben County
57	95.6	**Wabash** (city) Wabash County
59	95.5	**Batesville** (city) Ripley County
59	95.5	**Union City** (city) Randolph County
61	95.4	**Brazil** (city) Clay County
61	95.4	**Portland** (city) Jay County
63	95.3	**Bedford** (city) Lawrence County
63	95.3	**Martinsville** (city) Morgan County
65	95.1	**Country Squire Lakes** (CDP) Jennings County
65	95.1	**De Motte** (town) Jasper County
65	95.1	**Nappanee** (city) Elkhart County
65	95.1	**New Haven** (city) Allen County
65	95.1	**Tell City** (city) Perry County
70	95.0	**Huntington** (city) Huntington County
70	95.0	**Lowell** (town) Lake County
72	94.9	**Berne** (city) Adams County
72	94.9	**Georgetown** (town) Floyd County
74	94.8	**Connersville** (city) Fayette County
74	94.8	**Melody Hill** (CDP) Vanderburgh County
74	94.8	**Syracuse** (town) Kosciusko County
74	94.8	**Tipton** (city) Tipton County
78	94.6	**Greensburg** (city) Decatur County
78	94.6	**Jasper** (city) Dubois County
78	94.6	**Leo-Cedarville** (town) Allen County
78	94.6	**Yorktown** (town) Delaware County
82	94.3	**Chesterton** (town) Porter County
82	94.3	**Decatur** (city) Adams County
82	94.3	**Winchester** (city) Randolph County
85	94.2	**Centerville** (town) Wayne County
85	94.2	**Lakes of the Four Seasons** (CDP) Lake County
85	94.2	**Saint John** (town) Lake County
88	94.0	**Cedar Lake** (town) Lake County
88	94.0	**Columbia City** (city) Whitley County
90	93.9	**Pittsboro** (town) Hendricks County
90	93.9	**Rushville** (city) Rush County
92	93.8	**Rensselaer** (city) Jasper County
92	93.8	**Salt Creek Commons** (CDP) Porter County
94	93.7	**Ellettsville** (town) Monroe County
94	93.7	**Mitchell** (city) Lawrence County
94	93.7	**Upland** (town) Grant County
97	93.5	**Hanover** (town) Jefferson County
98	93.4	**South Haven** (CDP) Porter County
99	93.2	**Sellersburg** (town) Clark County
100	93.1	**Fort Branch** (town) Gibson County
101	93.0	**Crawfordsville** (city) Montgomery County
101	93.0	**North Manchester** (town) Wabash County
103	92.8	**Greencastle** (city) Putnam County
104	92.6	**Mount Vernon** (city) Posey County
105	92.4	**Hebron** (town) Porter County
106	92.3	**Fortville** (town) Hancock County
106	92.3	**Madison** (city) Jefferson County
108	92.0	**Valparaiso** (city) Porter County
109	91.9	**Frankfort** (city) Clinton County
110	91.5	**Bremen** (town) Marshall County
110	91.5	**Brownsburg** (town) Hendricks County
110	91.5	**Zionsville** (town) Boone County
113	91.2	**Shorewood Forest** (CDP) Porter County
114	91.1	**Gas City** (city) Grant County
114	91.1	**Winamac** (town) Pulaski County
116	91.0	**New Whiteland** (town) Johnson County
116	91.0	**Osceola** (town) Saint Joseph County
116	91.0	**Vincennes** (city) Knox County
119	90.9	**Middlebury** (town) Elkhart County
120	90.6	**Charlestown** (city) Clark County
121	90.1	**Delphi** (city) Carroll County
122	89.9	**Westfield** (city) Hamilton County
123	89.8	**Beech Grove** (city) Marion County
123	89.8	**Newburgh** (town) Warrick County
125	89.7	**Dunlap** (CDP) Elkhart County
125	89.7	**Noblesville** (city) Hamilton County
125	89.7	**Shelbyville** (city) Shelby County
128	89.6	**Clarksville** (town) Clark County
129	88.8	**Washington** (city) Daviess County
130	88.7	**Goshen** (city) Elkhart County
131	88.5	**Huntertown** (town) Allen County
131	88.5	**Princeton** (city) Gibson County
133	88.4	**La Porte** (city) LaPorte County
134	88.1	**Peru** (city) Miami County
135	87.9	**McCordsville** (town) Hancock County
136	87.4	**Edinburgh** (town) Johnson County
136	87.4	**Warsaw** (city) Kosciusko County
138	87.2	**Granger** (CDP) Saint Joseph County
139	86.8	**Crown Point** (city) Lake County
140	86.5	**Simonton Lake** (CDP) Elkhart County
141	86.4	**Whitestown** (town) Boone County
142	86.2	**Greenwood** (city) Johnson County
143	85.4	**New Albany** (city) Floyd County
144	85.0	**Lafayette** (city) Tippecanoe County
144	85.0	**Seymour** (city) Jackson County
146	84.9	**Mishawaka** (city) Saint Joseph County
147	84.8	**Hobart** (city) Lake County
148	84.6	**Richmond** (city) Wayne County
149	84.3	**Kokomo** (city) Howard County
150	84.2	**Munster** (town) Lake County

Note: *This section ranks incorporated places and CDPs (Census Designated Places) with populations of 2,500 or more. Unincorporated postal areas were not considered. Please refer to the User Guide for additional information.*

White Population

Top 150 Places Ranked in *Ascending* Order

State Rank	Percent	Place
1	14.0	**Gary** (city) Lake County
2	24.5	**East Chicago** (city) Lake County
3	41.2	**Merrillville** (town) Lake County
4	51.5	**Hammond** (city) Lake County
5	61.8	**Indianapolis** (city) Marion County
6	63.1	**South Bend** (city) Saint Joseph County
7	63.2	**Michigan City** (city) LaPorte County
8	64.4	**Lawrence** (city) Marion County
8	64.4	**Speedway** (town) Marion County
10	69.2	**West Lafayette** (city) Tippecanoe County
11	71.0	**Logansport** (city) Cass County
12	72.2	**Westville** (town) LaPorte County
13	73.4	**Whiting** (city) Lake County
14	73.5	**Griffith** (town) Lake County
15	74.2	**Fort Wayne** (city) Allen County
16	74.5	**Elkhart** (city) Elkhart County
17	77.6	**Marion** (city) Grant County
18	79.0	**Anderson** (city) Madison County
19	79.5	**Huntingburg** (city) Dubois County
20	80.4	**Jeffersonville** (city) Clark County
21	80.7	**Winfield** (town) Lake County
22	81.1	**Lake Station** (city) Lake County
23	81.4	**Columbus** (city) Bartholomew County
24	81.7	**Bloomington** (city) Monroe County
24	81.7	**Evansville** (city) Vanderburgh County
26	82.6	**Cumberland** (town) Marion County
26	82.6	**Notre Dame** (CDP) Saint Joseph County
26	82.6	**Schererville** (town) Lake County
29	82.9	**Plymouth** (city) Marshall County
30	83.0	**Muncie** (city) Delaware County
30	83.0	**Terre Haute** (city) Vigo County
32	83.7	**Monticello** (city) White County
32	83.7	**Portage** (city) Porter County
34	83.9	**Dyer** (town) Lake County
34	83.9	**Highland** (town) Lake County
36	84.0	**Avon** (town) Hendricks County
36	84.0	**Carmel** (city) Hamilton County
36	84.0	**Fishers** (city) Hamilton County
39	84.1	**Plainfield** (town) Hendricks County
40	84.2	**Munster** (town) Lake County
41	84.3	**Kokomo** (city) Howard County
42	84.6	**Richmond** (city) Wayne County
43	84.8	**Hobart** (city) Lake County
44	84.9	**Mishawaka** (city) Saint Joseph County
45	85.0	**Lafayette** (city) Tippecanoe County
45	85.0	**Seymour** (city) Jackson County
47	85.4	**New Albany** (city) Floyd County
48	86.2	**Greenwood** (city) Johnson County
49	86.4	**Whitestown** (town) Boone County
50	86.5	**Simonton Lake** (CDP) Elkhart County
51	86.8	**Crown Point** (city) Lake County
52	87.2	**Granger** (CDP) Saint Joseph County
53	87.4	**Edinburgh** (town) Johnson County
53	87.4	**Warsaw** (city) Kosciusko County
55	87.9	**McCordsville** (town) Hancock County
56	88.1	**Peru** (city) Miami County
57	88.4	**La Porte** (city) LaPorte County
58	88.5	**Huntertown** (town) Allen County
58	88.5	**Princeton** (city) Gibson County
60	88.7	**Goshen** (city) Elkhart County
61	88.8	**Washington** (city) Daviess County
62	89.6	**Clarksville** (town) Clark County
63	89.7	**Dunlap** (CDP) Elkhart County
63	89.7	**Noblesville** (city) Hamilton County
63	89.7	**Shelbyville** (city) Shelby County
66	89.8	**Beech Grove** (city) Marion County
66	89.8	**Newburgh** (town) Warrick County
68	89.9	**Westfield** (city) Hamilton County
69	90.1	**Delphi** (city) Carroll County
70	90.6	**Charlestown** (city) Clark County
71	90.9	**Middlebury** (town) Elkhart County
72	91.0	**New Whiteland** (town) Johnson County
72	91.0	**Osceola** (town) Saint Joseph County
72	91.0	**Vincennes** (city) Knox County
75	91.1	**Gas City** (city) Grant County
75	91.1	**Winamac** (town) Pulaski County
77	91.2	**Shorewood Forest** (CDP) Porter County
78	91.5	**Bremen** (town) Marshall County
78	91.5	**Brownsburg** (town) Hendricks County
78	91.5	**Zionsville** (town) Boone County
81	91.9	**Frankfort** (city) Clinton County
82	92.0	**Valparaiso** (city) Porter County
83	92.3	**Fortville** (town) Hancock County
83	92.3	**Madison** (city) Jefferson County
85	92.4	**Hebron** (town) Porter County
86	92.6	**Mount Vernon** (city) Posey County
87	92.8	**Greencastle** (city) Putnam County
88	93.0	**Crawfordsville** (city) Montgomery County
88	93.0	**North Manchester** (town) Wabash County
90	93.1	**Fort Branch** (town) Gibson County
91	93.2	**Sellersburg** (town) Clark County
92	93.4	**South Haven** (CDP) Porter County
93	93.5	**Hanover** (town) Jefferson County
94	93.7	**Ellettsville** (town) Monroe County
94	93.7	**Mitchell** (city) Lawrence County
94	93.7	**Upland** (town) Grant County
97	93.8	**Rensselaer** (city) Jasper County
97	93.8	**Salt Creek Commons** (CDP) Porter County
99	93.9	**Pittsboro** (town) Hendricks County
99	93.9	**Rushville** (city) Rush County
101	94.0	**Cedar Lake** (town) Lake County
101	94.0	**Columbia City** (city) Whitley County
103	94.2	**Centerville** (town) Wayne County
103	94.2	**Lakes of the Four Seasons** (CDP) Lake County
103	94.2	**Saint John** (town) Lake County
106	94.3	**Chesterton** (town) Porter County
106	94.3	**Decatur** (city) Adams County
106	94.3	**Winchester** (city) Randolph County
109	94.6	**Greensburg** (city) Decatur County
109	94.6	**Jasper** (city) Dubois County
109	94.6	**Leo-Cedarville** (town) Allen County
109	94.6	**Yorktown** (town) Delaware County
113	94.8	**Connersville** (city) Fayette County
113	94.8	**Melody Hill** (CDP) Vanderburgh County
113	94.8	**Syracuse** (town) Kosciusko County
113	94.8	**Tipton** (city) Tipton County
117	94.9	**Berne** (city) Adams County
117	94.9	**Georgetown** (town) Floyd County
119	95.0	**Huntington** (city) Huntington County
119	95.0	**Lowell** (town) Lake County
121	95.1	**Country Squire Lakes** (CDP) Jennings County
121	95.1	**De Motte** (town) Jasper County
121	95.1	**Nappanee** (city) Elkhart County
121	95.1	**New Haven** (city) Allen County
121	95.1	**Tell City** (city) Perry County
126	95.3	**Bedford** (city) Lawrence County
126	95.3	**Martinsville** (city) Morgan County
128	95.4	**Brazil** (city) Clay County
128	95.4	**Portland** (city) Jay County
130	95.5	**Batesville** (city) Ripley County
130	95.5	**Union City** (city) Randolph County
132	95.6	**Angola** (city) Steuben County
132	95.6	**Wabash** (city) Wabash County
134	95.7	**Butler** (city) DeKalb County
134	95.7	**Danville** (town) Hendricks County
134	95.7	**Franklin** (city) Johnson County
134	95.7	**Lebanon** (city) Boone County
134	95.7	**New Castle** (city) Henry County
134	95.7	**Smithville-Sanders** (CDP) Monroe County
140	95.8	**Kendallville** (city) Noble County
140	95.8	**Lagrange** (town) LaGrange County
142	96.0	**North Terre Haute** (CDP) Vigo County
142	96.0	**Roselawn** (CDP) Newton County
144	96.1	**Bicknell** (city) Knox County
144	96.1	**Boonville** (city) Warrick County
144	96.1	**Ligonier** (city) Noble County
147	96.2	**Ossian** (town) Wells County
148	96.3	**Porter** (town) Porter County
149	96.4	**Bluffton** (city) Wells County
149	96.4	**Greendale** (city) Dearborn County

Note: *This section ranks incorporated places and CDPs (Census Designated Places) with populations of 2,500 or more. Unincorporated postal areas were not considered. Please refer to the User Guide for additional information.*

Black/African American Population

Top 150 Places Ranked in *Descending* Order

State Rank	Percent	Place
1	81.0	**Gary** (city) Lake County
2	46.1	**Merrillville** (town) Lake County
3	36.4	**East Chicago** (city) Lake County
4	28.7	**Michigan City** (city) LaPorte County
5	28.1	**Indianapolis** (city) Marion County
6	27.8	**Lawrence** (city) Marion County
7	26.4	**South Bend** (city) Saint Joseph County
8	24.2	**Westville** (town) LaPorte County
9	21.4	**Hammond** (city) Lake County
9	21.4	**Speedway** (town) Marion County
11	15.9	**Marion** (city) Grant County
12	15.8	**Griffith** (town) Lake County
13	15.0	**Fort Wayne** (city) Allen County
14	14.9	**Elkhart** (city) Elkhart County
15	13.8	**Anderson** (city) Madison County
16	13.7	**Jeffersonville** (city) Clark County
17	12.6	**Evansville** (city) Vanderburgh County
18	12.2	**Cumberland** (town) Marion County
19	11.6	**Muncie** (city) Delaware County
20	10.0	**Kokomo** (city) Howard County
21	9.6	**Portage** (city) Porter County
22	9.5	**Terre Haute** (city) Vigo County
23	9.2	**New Albany** (city) Floyd County
24	9.1	**Simonton Lake** (CDP) Elkhart County
25	9.0	**Plainfield** (town) Hendricks County
26	8.5	**Lafayette** (city) Tippecanoe County
27	8.3	**Richmond** (city) Wayne County
28	7.7	**Hobart** (city) Lake County
29	7.6	**Hebron** (town) Porter County
30	7.4	**Avon** (town) Hendricks County
30	7.4	**Peru** (city) Miami County
32	7.2	**Mishawaka** (city) Saint Joseph County
33	6.9	**Beech Grove** (city) Marion County
34	6.4	**Whitestown** (town) Boone County
35	6.2	**Princeton** (city) Gibson County
36	6.1	**Dunlap** (CDP) Elkhart County
36	6.1	**Winfield** (town) Lake County
38	5.9	**Vincennes** (city) Knox County
39	5.7	**Crown Point** (city) Lake County
40	5.6	**Fishers** (city) Hamilton County
41	5.3	**Hanover** (town) Jefferson County
42	5.1	**Schererville** (town) Lake County
43	5.0	**Melody Hill** (CDP) Vanderburgh County
44	4.7	**McCordsville** (town) Hancock County
45	4.6	**Dyer** (town) Lake County
45	4.6	**Washington** (city) Daviess County
47	4.4	**Greenwood** (city) Johnson County
47	4.4	**Highland** (town) Lake County
49	4.3	**Bloomington** (city) Monroe County
49	4.3	**South Haven** (CDP) Porter County
51	4.1	**Clarksville** (town) Clark County
51	4.1	**Mount Vernon** (city) Posey County
53	4.0	**Noblesville** (city) Hamilton County
54	3.9	**Newburgh** (town) Warrick County
54	3.9	**Rushville** (city) Rush County
54	3.9	**Westfield** (city) Hamilton County
57	3.8	**Connersville** (city) Fayette County
58	3.6	**Brownsburg** (town) Hendricks County
58	3.6	**Granger** (CDP) Saint Joseph County
60	3.5	**Huntertown** (town) Allen County
61	3.4	**Edinburgh** (town) Johnson County
61	3.4	**Shorewood Forest** (CDP) Porter County
63	3.3	**Pittsboro** (town) Hendricks County
63	3.3	**Whiting** (city) Lake County
65	3.2	**Lake Station** (city) Lake County
65	3.2	**West Lafayette** (city) Tippecanoe County
67	3.1	**Valparaiso** (city) Porter County
68	3.0	**Madison** (city) Jefferson County
68	3.0	**Munster** (town) Lake County
68	3.0	**Notre Dame** (CDP) Saint Joseph County
71	2.9	**Lawrenceburg** (city) Dearborn County
72	2.8	**Berne** (city) Adams County
72	2.8	**Goshen** (city) Elkhart County
72	2.8	**La Porte** (city) LaPorte County
72	2.8	**Yorktown** (town) Delaware County
76	2.7	**Rensselaer** (city) Jasper County
77	2.6	**New Haven** (city) Allen County
78	2.5	**Carmel** (city) Hamilton County
78	2.5	**Centerville** (town) Wayne County
78	2.5	**Columbus** (city) Bartholomew County
78	2.5	**Nappanee** (city) Elkhart County
82	2.3	**Warsaw** (city) Kosciusko County
83	2.2	**Decatur** (city) Adams County
83	2.2	**Fortville** (town) Hancock County
83	2.2	**Logansport** (city) Cass County
86	2.1	**Country Squire Lakes** (CDP) Jennings County
86	2.1	**Greencastle** (city) Putnam County
86	2.1	**Shelbyville** (city) Shelby County
89	2.0	**Danville** (town) Hendricks County
89	2.0	**Greendale** (city) Dearborn County
91	1.9	**Charlestown** (city) Clark County
91	1.9	**Seymour** (city) Jackson County
93	1.8	**New Whiteland** (town) Johnson County
94	1.7	**Crawfordsville** (city) Montgomery County
94	1.7	**Frankfort** (city) Clinton County
96	1.6	**Martinsville** (city) Morgan County
96	1.6	**Zionsville** (town) Boone County
98	1.5	**Franklin** (city) Johnson County
98	1.5	**Gas City** (city) Grant County
98	1.5	**Huntingburg** (city) Dubois County
98	1.5	**Huntington** (city) Huntington County
98	1.5	**New Castle** (city) Henry County
98	1.5	**North Vernon** (city) Jennings County
104	1.4	**Middlebury** (town) Elkhart County
104	1.4	**North Manchester** (town) Wabash County
106	1.3	**Lakes of the Four Seasons** (CDP) Lake County
106	1.3	**North Terre Haute** (CDP) Vigo County
108	1.2	**Delphi** (city) Carroll County
108	1.2	**Ellettsville** (town) Monroe County
108	1.2	**Lebanon** (city) Boone County
108	1.2	**Tell City** (city) Perry County
112	1.1	**Bargersville** (town) Johnson County
112	1.1	**Bluffton** (city) Wells County
112	1.1	**Chesterton** (town) Porter County
112	1.1	**Greensburg** (city) Decatur County
112	1.1	**Sellersburg** (town) Clark County
117	1.0	**Bicknell** (city) Knox County
117	1.0	**Kendallville** (city) Noble County
117	1.0	**Pendleton** (town) Madison County
117	1.0	**Upland** (town) Grant County
121	0.9	**Clinton** (city) Vermillion County
121	0.9	**Greenfield** (city) Hancock County
121	0.9	**Jasper** (city) Dubois County
121	0.9	**Scottsburg** (city) Scott County
125	0.8	**Brazil** (city) Clay County
125	0.8	**Columbia City** (city) Whitley County
125	0.8	**Portland** (city) Jay County
125	0.8	**Winamac** (town) Pulaski County
129	0.7	**Angola** (city) Steuben County
129	0.7	**Batesville** (city) Ripley County
129	0.7	**Linton** (city) Greene County
132	0.6	**Bedford** (city) Lawrence County
132	0.6	**Cedar Lake** (town) Lake County
132	0.6	**Plymouth** (city) Marshall County
132	0.6	**Saint John** (town) Lake County
136	0.5	**Attica** (city) Fountain County
136	0.5	**Boonville** (city) Warrick County
136	0.5	**Paoli** (town) Orange County
136	0.5	**Salt Creek Commons** (CDP) Porter County
136	0.5	**Winona Lake** (town) Kosciusko County
141	0.4	**Highland** (CDP) Vanderburgh County
141	0.4	**Loogootee** (city) Martin County
141	0.4	**Rochester** (city) Fulton County
141	0.4	**Salem** (city) Washington County
141	0.4	**Tipton** (city) Tipton County
141	0.4	**Wabash** (city) Wabash County
147	0.3	**Auburn** (city) DeKalb County
147	0.3	**Bremen** (town) Marshall County
147	0.3	**Butler** (city) DeKalb County
147	0.3	**Elwood** (city) Madison County

Note: *This section ranks incorporated places and CDPs (Census Designated Places) with populations of 2,500 or more. Unincorporated postal areas were not considered. Please refer to the User Guide for additional information.*

Black/African American Population

Top 150 Places Ranked in *Ascending* Order

State Rank	Percent	Place
1	0.0	**Alexandria** (city) Madison County
1	0.0	**Aurora** (city) Dearborn County
1	0.0	**Austin** (city) Scott County
1	0.0	**Bright** (CDP) Dearborn County
1	0.0	**Brookville** (town) Franklin County
1	0.0	**Cicero** (town) Hamilton County
1	0.0	**De Motte** (town) Jasper County
1	0.0	**Fairmount** (town) Grant County
1	0.0	**Hartford City** (city) Blackford County
1	0.0	**Heritage Lake** (CDP) Putnam County
1	0.0	**Hidden Valley** (CDP) Dearborn County
1	0.0	**Lagrange** (town) LaGrange County
1	0.0	**Leo-Cedarville** (town) Allen County
1	0.0	**Mooresville** (town) Morgan County
1	0.0	**Ossian** (town) Wells County
1	0.0	**Porter** (town) Porter County
1	0.0	**Rockville** (town) Parke County
1	0.0	**Roselawn** (CDP) Newton County
1	0.0	**Smithville-Sanders** (CDP) Monroe County
1	0.0	**Sullivan** (city) Sullivan County
1	0.0	**Union City** (city) Randolph County
1	0.0	**Whiteland** (town) Johnson County
23	0.1	**Chandler** (town) Warrick County
23	0.1	**Corydon** (town) Harrison County
23	0.1	**Knox** (city) Starke County
23	0.1	**Sheridan** (town) Hamilton County
27	0.2	**Brownstown** (town) Jackson County
27	0.2	**Georgetown** (town) Floyd County
27	0.2	**Greentown** (town) Howard County
27	0.2	**Ligonier** (city) Noble County
27	0.2	**Lowell** (town) Lake County
27	0.2	**Mitchell** (city) Lawrence County
27	0.2	**Monticello** (city) White County
27	0.2	**Santa Claus** (town) Spencer County
27	0.2	**Syracuse** (town) Kosciusko County
27	0.2	**Winchester** (city) Randolph County
37	0.3	**Auburn** (city) DeKalb County
37	0.3	**Bremen** (town) Marshall County
37	0.3	**Butler** (city) DeKalb County
37	0.3	**Elwood** (city) Madison County
37	0.3	**Fort Branch** (town) Gibson County
37	0.3	**Garrett** (city) DeKalb County
37	0.3	**Osceola** (town) Saint Joseph County
44	0.4	**Highland** (CDP) Vanderburgh County
44	0.4	**Loogootee** (city) Martin County
44	0.4	**Rochester** (city) Fulton County
44	0.4	**Salem** (city) Washington County
44	0.4	**Tipton** (city) Tipton County
44	0.4	**Wabash** (city) Wabash County
50	0.5	**Attica** (city) Fountain County
50	0.5	**Boonville** (city) Warrick County
50	0.5	**Paoli** (town) Orange County
50	0.5	**Salt Creek Commons** (CDP) Porter County
50	0.5	**Winona Lake** (town) Kosciusko County
55	0.6	**Bedford** (city) Lawrence County
55	0.6	**Cedar Lake** (town) Lake County
55	0.6	**Plymouth** (city) Marshall County
55	0.6	**Saint John** (town) Lake County
59	0.7	**Angola** (city) Steuben County
59	0.7	**Batesville** (city) Ripley County
59	0.7	**Linton** (city) Greene County
62	0.8	**Brazil** (city) Clay County
62	0.8	**Columbia City** (city) Whitley County
62	0.8	**Portland** (city) Jay County
62	0.8	**Winamac** (town) Pulaski County
66	0.9	**Clinton** (city) Vermillion County
66	0.9	**Greenfield** (city) Hancock County
66	0.9	**Jasper** (city) Dubois County
66	0.9	**Scottsburg** (city) Scott County
70	1.0	**Bicknell** (city) Knox County
70	1.0	**Kendallville** (city) Noble County
70	1.0	**Pendleton** (town) Madison County
70	1.0	**Upland** (town) Grant County
74	1.1	**Bargersville** (town) Johnson County
74	1.1	**Bluffton** (city) Wells County
74	1.1	**Chesterton** (town) Porter County
74	1.1	**Greensburg** (city) Decatur County
74	1.1	**Sellersburg** (town) Clark County
79	1.2	**Delphi** (city) Carroll County
79	1.2	**Ellettsville** (town) Monroe County
79	1.2	**Lebanon** (city) Boone County
79	1.2	**Tell City** (city) Perry County
83	1.3	**Lakes of the Four Seasons** (CDP) Lake County
83	1.3	**North Terre Haute** (CDP) Vigo County
85	1.4	**Middlebury** (town) Elkhart County
85	1.4	**North Manchester** (town) Wabash County
87	1.5	**Franklin** (city) Johnson County
87	1.5	**Gas City** (city) Grant County
87	1.5	**Huntingburg** (city) Dubois County
87	1.5	**Huntington** (city) Huntington County
87	1.5	**New Castle** (city) Henry County
87	1.5	**North Vernon** (city) Jennings County
93	1.6	**Martinsville** (city) Morgan County
93	1.6	**Zionsville** (town) Boone County
95	1.7	**Crawfordsville** (city) Montgomery County
95	1.7	**Frankfort** (city) Clinton County
97	1.8	**New Whiteland** (town) Johnson County
98	1.9	**Charlestown** (city) Clark County
98	1.9	**Seymour** (city) Jackson County
100	2.0	**Danville** (town) Hendricks County
100	2.0	**Greendale** (city) Dearborn County
102	2.1	**Country Squire Lakes** (CDP) Jennings County
102	2.1	**Greencastle** (city) Putnam County
102	2.1	**Shelbyville** (city) Shelby County
105	2.2	**Decatur** (city) Adams County
105	2.2	**Fortville** (town) Hancock County
105	2.2	**Logansport** (city) Cass County
108	2.3	**Warsaw** (city) Kosciusko County
109	2.5	**Carmel** (city) Hamilton County
109	2.5	**Centerville** (town) Wayne County
109	2.5	**Columbus** (city) Bartholomew County
109	2.5	**Nappanee** (city) Elkhart County
113	2.6	**New Haven** (city) Allen County
114	2.7	**Rensselaer** (city) Jasper County
115	2.8	**Berne** (city) Adams County
115	2.8	**Goshen** (city) Elkhart County
115	2.8	**La Porte** (city) LaPorte County
115	2.8	**Yorktown** (town) Delaware County
119	2.9	**Lawrenceburg** (city) Dearborn County
120	3.0	**Madison** (city) Jefferson County
120	3.0	**Munster** (town) Lake County
120	3.0	**Notre Dame** (CDP) Saint Joseph County
123	3.1	**Valparaiso** (city) Porter County
124	3.2	**Lake Station** (city) Lake County
124	3.2	**West Lafayette** (city) Tippecanoe County
126	3.3	**Pittsboro** (town) Hendricks County
126	3.3	**Whiting** (city) Lake County
128	3.4	**Edinburgh** (town) Johnson County
128	3.4	**Shorewood Forest** (CDP) Porter County
130	3.5	**Huntertown** (town) Allen County
131	3.6	**Brownsburg** (town) Hendricks County
131	3.6	**Granger** (CDP) Saint Joseph County
133	3.8	**Connersville** (city) Fayette County
134	3.9	**Newburgh** (town) Warrick County
134	3.9	**Rushville** (city) Rush County
134	3.9	**Westfield** (city) Hamilton County
137	4.0	**Noblesville** (city) Hamilton County
138	4.1	**Clarksville** (town) Clark County
138	4.1	**Mount Vernon** (city) Posey County
140	4.3	**Bloomington** (city) Monroe County
140	4.3	**South Haven** (CDP) Porter County
142	4.4	**Greenwood** (city) Johnson County
142	4.4	**Highland** (town) Lake County
144	4.6	**Dyer** (town) Lake County
144	4.6	**Washington** (city) Daviess County
146	4.7	**McCordsville** (town) Hancock County
147	5.0	**Melody Hill** (CDP) Vanderburgh County
148	5.1	**Schererville** (town) Lake County
149	5.3	**Hanover** (town) Jefferson County
150	5.6	**Fishers** (city) Hamilton County

Note: *This section ranks incorporated places and CDPs (Census Designated Places) with populations of 2,500 or more. Unincorporated postal areas were not considered. Please refer to the User Guide for additional information.*

Asian Population

Top 150 Places Ranked in *Descending* Order

State Rank	Percent	Place
1	23.8	**West Lafayette** (city) Tippecanoe County
2	10.4	**Columbus** (city) Bartholomew County
3	10.3	**Carmel** (city) Hamilton County
4	9.6	**Bloomington** (city) Monroe County
4	9.6	**Notre Dame** (CDP) Saint Joseph County
6	6.8	**Fishers** (city) Hamilton County
7	6.7	**Granger** (CDP) Saint Joseph County
8	6.3	**Newburgh** (town) Warrick County
9	5.7	**Greenwood** (city) Johnson County
10	5.6	**Osceola** (town) Saint Joseph County
11	5.0	**Whitestown** (town) Boone County
11	5.0	**Zionsville** (town) Boone County
13	4.8	**Munster** (town) Lake County
14	4.3	**Fort Wayne** (city) Allen County
15	4.1	**Shorewood Forest** (CDP) Porter County
15	4.1	**Speedway** (town) Marion County
17	3.8	**Plainfield** (town) Hendricks County
18	3.3	**Batesville** (city) Ripley County
18	3.3	**Schererville** (town) Lake County
18	3.3	**Seymour** (city) Jackson County
18	3.3	**Warsaw** (city) Kosciusko County
22	3.1	**Dyer** (town) Lake County
22	3.1	**Westfield** (city) Hamilton County
24	3.0	**Avon** (town) Hendricks County
24	3.0	**Indianapolis** (city) Marion County
24	3.0	**Winfield** (town) Lake County
27	2.8	**Aurora** (city) Dearborn County
27	2.8	**Greensburg** (city) Decatur County
29	2.7	**Huntertown** (town) Allen County
30	2.6	**Brownsburg** (town) Hendricks County
30	2.6	**Greencastle** (city) Putnam County
30	2.6	**Smithville-Sanders** (CDP) Monroe County
33	2.5	**Noblesville** (city) Hamilton County
33	2.5	**Simonton Lake** (CDP) Elkhart County
33	2.5	**Valparaiso** (city) Porter County
36	2.4	**Crown Point** (city) Lake County
37	2.2	**Logansport** (city) Cass County
38	2.1	**Sullivan** (city) Sullivan County
38	2.1	**Upland** (town) Grant County
40	2.0	**Chesterton** (town) Porter County
40	2.0	**Paoli** (town) Orange County
42	1.9	**Highland** (town) Lake County
42	1.9	**Madison** (city) Jefferson County
42	1.9	**Mishawaka** (city) Saint Joseph County
42	1.9	**Portage** (city) Porter County
46	1.8	**Danville** (town) Hendricks County
46	1.8	**Winamac** (town) Pulaski County
48	1.7	**Elkhart** (city) Elkhart County
48	1.7	**Griffith** (town) Lake County
48	1.7	**Huntingburg** (city) Dubois County
48	1.7	**Porter** (town) Porter County
52	1.6	**Clarksville** (town) Clark County
52	1.6	**Huntington** (city) Huntington County
52	1.6	**Kokomo** (city) Howard County
52	1.6	**Lafayette** (city) Tippecanoe County
52	1.6	**Muncie** (city) Delaware County
52	1.6	**Richmond** (city) Wayne County
58	1.5	**Lawrence** (city) Marion County
58	1.5	**Salt Creek Commons** (CDP) Porter County
58	1.5	**Terre Haute** (city) Vigo County
61	1.4	**Fairmount** (town) Grant County
61	1.4	**Marion** (city) Grant County
61	1.4	**South Bend** (city) Saint Joseph County
64	1.3	**Berne** (city) Adams County
64	1.3	**Goshen** (city) Elkhart County
64	1.3	**Greenfield** (city) Hancock County
64	1.3	**Hammond** (city) Lake County
64	1.3	**Merrillville** (town) Lake County
64	1.3	**Shelbyville** (city) Shelby County
70	1.2	**Kendallville** (city) Noble County
71	1.0	**Georgetown** (town) Floyd County
71	1.0	**Mitchell** (city) Lawrence County
71	1.0	**Nappanee** (city) Elkhart County
74	0.9	**Anderson** (city) Madison County
74	0.9	**Crawfordsville** (city) Montgomery County
74	0.9	**Hobart** (city) Lake County
74	0.9	**Jeffersonville** (city) Clark County
74	0.9	**Michigan City** (city) LaPorte County
74	0.9	**New Whiteland** (town) Johnson County
74	0.9	**Vincennes** (city) Knox County
81	0.8	**Jasper** (city) Dubois County
81	0.8	**Lake Station** (city) Lake County
81	0.8	**Ossian** (town) Wells County
81	0.8	**Rensselaer** (city) Jasper County
85	0.7	**De Motte** (town) Jasper County
85	0.7	**Dunlap** (CDP) Elkhart County
85	0.7	**Evansville** (city) Vanderburgh County
85	0.7	**Fort Branch** (town) Gibson County
85	0.7	**Franklin** (city) Johnson County
85	0.7	**New Albany** (city) Floyd County
85	0.7	**New Castle** (city) Henry County
85	0.7	**Peru** (city) Miami County
85	0.7	**Plymouth** (city) Marshall County
85	0.7	**Saint John** (town) Lake County
95	0.6	**Columbia City** (city) Whitley County
95	0.6	**Winchester** (city) Randolph County
97	0.5	**Bedford** (city) Lawrence County
97	0.5	**Beech Grove** (city) Marion County
97	0.5	**Bluffton** (city) Wells County
97	0.5	**Charlestown** (city) Clark County
97	0.5	**Country Squire Lakes** (CDP) Jennings County
97	0.5	**Gas City** (city) Grant County
97	0.5	**Highland** (CDP) Vanderburgh County
97	0.5	**Mount Vernon** (city) Posey County
97	0.5	**Whiteland** (town) Johnson County
106	0.4	**Angola** (city) Steuben County
106	0.4	**Decatur** (city) Adams County
106	0.4	**Gary** (city) Lake County
106	0.4	**Hartford City** (city) Blackford County
106	0.4	**Lakes of the Four Seasons** (CDP) Lake County
106	0.4	**Wabash** (city) Wabash County
112	0.3	**Attica** (city) Fountain County
112	0.3	**Cedar Lake** (town) Lake County
112	0.3	**Cicero** (town) Hamilton County
112	0.3	**Greentown** (town) Howard County
112	0.3	**La Porte** (city) LaPorte County
112	0.3	**Lagrange** (town) LaGrange County
112	0.3	**New Haven** (city) Allen County
112	0.3	**Princeton** (city) Gibson County
112	0.3	**Rochester** (city) Fulton County
112	0.3	**Scottsburg** (city) Scott County
112	0.3	**Syracuse** (town) Kosciusko County
112	0.3	**Westville** (town) LaPorte County
112	0.3	**Winona Lake** (town) Kosciusko County
125	0.2	**Auburn** (city) DeKalb County
125	0.2	**Bargersville** (town) Johnson County
125	0.2	**Connersville** (city) Fayette County
125	0.2	**Cumberland** (town) Marion County
125	0.2	**East Chicago** (city) Lake County
125	0.2	**Elwood** (city) Madison County
125	0.2	**Frankfort** (city) Clinton County
125	0.2	**Martinsville** (city) Morgan County
125	0.2	**Portland** (city) Jay County
125	0.2	**Sellersburg** (town) Clark County
125	0.2	**Sheridan** (town) Hamilton County
125	0.2	**Tell City** (city) Perry County
125	0.2	**Washington** (city) Daviess County
138	0.1	**Garrett** (city) DeKalb County
138	0.1	**Hanover** (town) Jefferson County
138	0.1	**Lowell** (town) Lake County
138	0.1	**North Vernon** (city) Jennings County
138	0.1	**South Haven** (CDP) Porter County
143	0.0	**Alexandria** (city) Madison County
143	0.0	**Austin** (city) Scott County
143	0.0	**Bicknell** (city) Knox County
143	0.0	**Boonville** (city) Warrick County
143	0.0	**Brazil** (city) Clay County
143	0.0	**Bremen** (town) Marshall County
143	0.0	**Bright** (CDP) Dearborn County
143	0.0	**Brookville** (town) Franklin County

Note: This section ranks incorporated places and CDPs (Census Designated Places) with populations of 2,500 or more. Unincorporated postal areas were not considered. Please refer to the User Guide for additional information.

Asian Population

Top 150 Places Ranked in *Ascending* Order

State Rank	Percent	Place
1	0.0	**Alexandria** (city) Madison County
1	0.0	**Austin** (city) Scott County
1	0.0	**Bicknell** (city) Knox County
1	0.0	**Boonville** (city) Warrick County
1	0.0	**Brazil** (city) Clay County
1	0.0	**Bremen** (town) Marshall County
1	0.0	**Bright** (CDP) Dearborn County
1	0.0	**Brookville** (town) Franklin County
1	0.0	**Brownstown** (town) Jackson County
1	0.0	**Butler** (city) DeKalb County
1	0.0	**Centerville** (town) Wayne County
1	0.0	**Chandler** (town) Warrick County
1	0.0	**Clinton** (city) Vermillion County
1	0.0	**Corydon** (town) Harrison County
1	0.0	**Delphi** (city) Carroll County
1	0.0	**Edinburgh** (town) Johnson County
1	0.0	**Ellettsville** (town) Monroe County
1	0.0	**Fortville** (town) Hancock County
1	0.0	**Greendale** (city) Dearborn County
1	0.0	**Hebron** (town) Porter County
1	0.0	**Heritage Lake** (CDP) Putnam County
1	0.0	**Hidden Valley** (CDP) Dearborn County
1	0.0	**Knox** (city) Starke County
1	0.0	**Lawrenceburg** (city) Dearborn County
1	0.0	**Lebanon** (city) Boone County
1	0.0	**Leo-Cedarville** (town) Allen County
1	0.0	**Ligonier** (city) Noble County
1	0.0	**Linton** (city) Greene County
1	0.0	**Loogootee** (city) Martin County
1	0.0	**McCordsville** (town) Hancock County
1	0.0	**Melody Hill** (CDP) Vanderburgh County
1	0.0	**Middlebury** (town) Elkhart County
1	0.0	**Monticello** (city) White County
1	0.0	**Mooresville** (town) Morgan County
1	0.0	**North Manchester** (town) Wabash County
1	0.0	**North Terre Haute** (CDP) Vigo County
1	0.0	**Pendleton** (town) Madison County
1	0.0	**Pittsboro** (town) Hendricks County
1	0.0	**Rockville** (town) Parke County
1	0.0	**Roselawn** (CDP) Newton County
1	0.0	**Rushville** (city) Rush County
1	0.0	**Salem** (city) Washington County
1	0.0	**Santa Claus** (town) Spencer County
1	0.0	**Tipton** (city) Tipton County
1	0.0	**Union City** (city) Randolph County
1	0.0	**Whiting** (city) Lake County
1	0.0	**Yorktown** (town) Delaware County
48	0.1	**Garrett** (city) DeKalb County
48	0.1	**Hanover** (town) Jefferson County
48	0.1	**Lowell** (town) Lake County
48	0.1	**North Vernon** (city) Jennings County
48	0.1	**South Haven** (CDP) Porter County
53	0.2	**Auburn** (city) DeKalb County
53	0.2	**Bargersville** (town) Johnson County
53	0.2	**Connersville** (city) Fayette County
53	0.2	**Cumberland** (town) Marion County
53	0.2	**East Chicago** (city) Lake County
53	0.2	**Elwood** (city) Madison County
53	0.2	**Frankfort** (city) Clinton County
53	0.2	**Martinsville** (city) Morgan County
53	0.2	**Portland** (city) Jay County
53	0.2	**Sellersburg** (town) Clark County
53	0.2	**Sheridan** (town) Hamilton County
53	0.2	**Tell City** (city) Perry County
53	0.2	**Washington** (city) Daviess County
66	0.3	**Attica** (city) Fountain County
66	0.3	**Cedar Lake** (town) Lake County
66	0.3	**Cicero** (town) Hamilton County
66	0.3	**Greentown** (town) Howard County
66	0.3	**La Porte** (city) LaPorte County
66	0.3	**Lagrange** (town) LaGrange County
66	0.3	**New Haven** (city) Allen County
66	0.3	**Princeton** (city) Gibson County
66	0.3	**Rochester** (city) Fulton County
66	0.3	**Scottsburg** (city) Scott County
66	0.3	**Syracuse** (town) Kosciusko County
66	0.3	**Westville** (town) LaPorte County
66	0.3	**Winona Lake** (town) Kosciusko County
79	0.4	**Angola** (city) Steuben County
79	0.4	**Decatur** (city) Adams County
79	0.4	**Gary** (city) Lake County
79	0.4	**Hartford City** (city) Blackford County
79	0.4	**Lakes of the Four Seasons** (CDP) Lake County
79	0.4	**Wabash** (city) Wabash County
85	0.5	**Bedford** (city) Lawrence County
85	0.5	**Beech Grove** (city) Marion County
85	0.5	**Bluffton** (city) Wells County
85	0.5	**Charlestown** (city) Clark County
85	0.5	**Country Squire Lakes** (CDP) Jennings County
85	0.5	**Gas City** (city) Grant County
85	0.5	**Highland** (CDP) Vanderburgh County
85	0.5	**Mount Vernon** (city) Posey County
85	0.5	**Whiteland** (town) Johnson County
94	0.6	**Columbia City** (city) Whitley County
94	0.6	**Winchester** (city) Randolph County
96	0.7	**De Motte** (town) Jasper County
96	0.7	**Dunlap** (CDP) Elkhart County
96	0.7	**Evansville** (city) Vanderburgh County
96	0.7	**Fort Branch** (town) Gibson County
96	0.7	**Franklin** (city) Johnson County
96	0.7	**New Albany** (city) Floyd County
96	0.7	**New Castle** (city) Henry County
96	0.7	**Peru** (city) Miami County
96	0.7	**Plymouth** (city) Marshall County
96	0.7	**Saint John** (town) Lake County
106	0.8	**Jasper** (city) Dubois County
106	0.8	**Lake Station** (city) Lake County
106	0.8	**Ossian** (town) Wells County
106	0.8	**Rensselaer** (city) Jasper County
110	0.9	**Anderson** (city) Madison County
110	0.9	**Crawfordsville** (city) Montgomery County
110	0.9	**Hobart** (city) Lake County
110	0.9	**Jeffersonville** (city) Clark County
110	0.9	**Michigan City** (city) LaPorte County
110	0.9	**New Whiteland** (town) Johnson County
110	0.9	**Vincennes** (city) Knox County
117	1.0	**Georgetown** (town) Floyd County
117	1.0	**Mitchell** (city) Lawrence County
117	1.0	**Nappanee** (city) Elkhart County
120	1.2	**Kendallville** (city) Noble County
121	1.3	**Berne** (city) Adams County
121	1.3	**Goshen** (city) Elkhart County
121	1.3	**Greenfield** (city) Hancock County
121	1.3	**Hammond** (city) Lake County
121	1.3	**Merrillville** (town) Lake County
121	1.3	**Shelbyville** (city) Shelby County
127	1.4	**Fairmount** (town) Grant County
127	1.4	**Marion** (city) Grant County
127	1.4	**South Bend** (city) Saint Joseph County
130	1.5	**Lawrence** (city) Marion County
130	1.5	**Salt Creek Commons** (CDP) Porter County
130	1.5	**Terre Haute** (city) Vigo County
133	1.6	**Clarksville** (town) Clark County
133	1.6	**Huntington** (city) Huntington County
133	1.6	**Kokomo** (city) Howard County
133	1.6	**Lafayette** (city) Tippecanoe County
133	1.6	**Muncie** (city) Delaware County
133	1.6	**Richmond** (city) Wayne County
139	1.7	**Elkhart** (city) Elkhart County
139	1.7	**Griffith** (town) Lake County
139	1.7	**Huntingburg** (city) Dubois County
139	1.7	**Porter** (town) Porter County
143	1.8	**Danville** (town) Hendricks County
143	1.8	**Winamac** (town) Pulaski County
145	1.9	**Highland** (town) Lake County
145	1.9	**Madison** (city) Jefferson County
145	1.9	**Mishawaka** (city) Saint Joseph County
145	1.9	**Portage** (city) Porter County
149	2.0	**Chesterton** (town) Porter County
149	2.0	**Paoli** (town) Orange County

Note: *This section ranks incorporated places and CDPs (Census Designated Places) with populations of 2,500 or more. Unincorporated postal areas were not considered. Please refer to the User Guide for additional information.*

American Indian/Alaska Native Population

Top 150 Places Ranked in *Descending* Order

State Rank	Percent	Place
1	1.5	**Peru** (city) Miami County
2	1.2	**Rochester** (city) Fulton County
3	1.1	**Loogootee** (city) Martin County
4	1.0	**Huntingburg** (city) Dubois County
4	1.0	**Lake Station** (city) Lake County
4	1.0	**Whitestown** (town) Boone County
7	0.9	**Austin** (city) Scott County
7	0.9	**Delphi** (city) Carroll County
7	0.9	**Hidden Valley** (CDP) Dearborn County
10	0.8	**Mishawaka** (city) Saint Joseph County
10	0.8	**Upland** (town) Grant County
12	0.7	**Dyer** (town) Lake County
12	0.7	**Heritage Lake** (CDP) Putnam County
12	0.7	**Hobart** (city) Lake County
12	0.7	**North Vernon** (city) Jennings County
16	0.6	**North Terre Haute** (CDP) Vigo County
16	0.6	**Plymouth** (city) Marshall County
16	0.6	**Shorewood Forest** (CDP) Porter County
16	0.6	**Tell City** (city) Perry County
20	0.5	**Bedford** (city) Lawrence County
20	0.5	**Dunlap** (CDP) Elkhart County
20	0.5	**South Bend** (city) Saint Joseph County
23	0.4	**Attica** (city) Fountain County
23	0.4	**Avon** (town) Hendricks County
23	0.4	**Crawfordsville** (city) Montgomery County
23	0.4	**East Chicago** (city) Lake County
23	0.4	**Greenwood** (city) Johnson County
23	0.4	**Highland** (town) Lake County
23	0.4	**Kokomo** (city) Howard County
23	0.4	**Madison** (city) Jefferson County
23	0.4	**New Albany** (city) Floyd County
23	0.4	**Schererville** (town) Lake County
23	0.4	**Smithville-Sanders** (CDP) Monroe County
23	0.4	**Sullivan** (city) Sullivan County
23	0.4	**Wabash** (city) Wabash County
36	0.3	**Anderson** (city) Madison County
36	0.3	**Bloomington** (city) Monroe County
36	0.3	**Boonville** (city) Warrick County
36	0.3	**Brownsburg** (town) Hendricks County
36	0.3	**Carmel** (city) Hamilton County
36	0.3	**Chandler** (town) Warrick County
36	0.3	**Evansville** (city) Vanderburgh County
36	0.3	**Frankfort** (city) Clinton County
36	0.3	**Hammond** (city) Lake County
36	0.3	**Indianapolis** (city) Marion County
36	0.3	**La Porte** (city) LaPorte County
36	0.3	**Logansport** (city) Cass County
36	0.3	**Merrillville** (town) Lake County
36	0.3	**Portland** (city) Jay County
36	0.3	**Santa Claus** (town) Spencer County
36	0.3	**Shelbyville** (city) Shelby County
36	0.3	**Syracuse** (town) Kosciusko County
36	0.3	**Terre Haute** (city) Vigo County
36	0.3	**West Lafayette** (city) Tippecanoe County
55	0.2	**Chesterton** (town) Porter County
55	0.2	**Clarksville** (town) Clark County
55	0.2	**Columbus** (city) Bartholomew County
55	0.2	**Decatur** (city) Adams County
55	0.2	**Edinburgh** (town) Johnson County
55	0.2	**Elkhart** (city) Elkhart County
55	0.2	**Fort Branch** (town) Gibson County
55	0.2	**Fort Wayne** (city) Allen County
55	0.2	**Gary** (city) Lake County
55	0.2	**Granger** (CDP) Saint Joseph County
55	0.2	**Hartford City** (city) Blackford County
55	0.2	**Huntertown** (town) Allen County
55	0.2	**Huntington** (city) Huntington County
55	0.2	**Lafayette** (city) Tippecanoe County
55	0.2	**Lowell** (town) Lake County
55	0.2	**Martinsville** (city) Morgan County
55	0.2	**Michigan City** (city) LaPorte County
55	0.2	**Munster** (town) Lake County
55	0.2	**Portage** (city) Porter County
55	0.2	**Porter** (town) Porter County
55	0.2	**Richmond** (city) Wayne County
55	0.2	**Scottsburg** (city) Scott County
55	0.2	**Seymour** (city) Jackson County
55	0.2	**Valparaiso** (city) Porter County
55	0.2	**Warsaw** (city) Kosciusko County
55	0.2	**Westville** (town) LaPorte County
81	0.1	**Brazil** (city) Clay County
81	0.1	**Cedar Lake** (town) Lake County
81	0.1	**Columbia City** (city) Whitley County
81	0.1	**Elwood** (city) Madison County
81	0.1	**Goshen** (city) Elkhart County
81	0.1	**Hanover** (town) Jefferson County
81	0.1	**Jeffersonville** (city) Clark County
81	0.1	**Kendallville** (city) Noble County
81	0.1	**Lawrence** (city) Marion County
81	0.1	**Marion** (city) Grant County
81	0.1	**Muncie** (city) Delaware County
81	0.1	**New Castle** (city) Henry County
81	0.1	**New Haven** (city) Allen County
81	0.1	**Noblesville** (city) Hamilton County
81	0.1	**Notre Dame** (CDP) Saint Joseph County
81	0.1	**Osceola** (town) Saint Joseph County
81	0.1	**Plainfield** (town) Hendricks County
81	0.1	**Saint John** (town) Lake County
81	0.1	**Speedway** (town) Marion County
81	0.1	**Vincennes** (city) Knox County
81	0.1	**Washington** (city) Daviess County
81	0.1	**Winona Lake** (town) Kosciusko County
81	0.1	**Zionsville** (town) Boone County
104	0.0	**Alexandria** (city) Madison County
104	0.0	**Angola** (city) Steuben County
104	0.0	**Auburn** (city) DeKalb County
104	0.0	**Aurora** (city) Dearborn County
104	0.0	**Bargersville** (town) Johnson County
104	0.0	**Batesville** (city) Ripley County
104	0.0	**Beech Grove** (city) Marion County
104	0.0	**Berne** (city) Adams County
104	0.0	**Bicknell** (city) Knox County
104	0.0	**Bluffton** (city) Wells County
104	0.0	**Bremen** (town) Marshall County
104	0.0	**Bright** (CDP) Dearborn County
104	0.0	**Brookville** (town) Franklin County
104	0.0	**Brownstown** (town) Jackson County
104	0.0	**Butler** (city) DeKalb County
104	0.0	**Centerville** (town) Wayne County
104	0.0	**Charlestown** (city) Clark County
104	0.0	**Cicero** (town) Hamilton County
104	0.0	**Clinton** (city) Vermillion County
104	0.0	**Connersville** (city) Fayette County
104	0.0	**Corydon** (town) Harrison County
104	0.0	**Country Squire Lakes** (CDP) Jennings County
104	0.0	**Crown Point** (city) Lake County
104	0.0	**Cumberland** (town) Marion County
104	0.0	**Danville** (town) Hendricks County
104	0.0	**De Motte** (town) Jasper County
104	0.0	**Ellettsville** (town) Monroe County
104	0.0	**Fairmount** (town) Grant County
104	0.0	**Fishers** (city) Hamilton County
104	0.0	**Fortville** (town) Hancock County
104	0.0	**Franklin** (city) Johnson County
104	0.0	**Garrett** (city) DeKalb County
104	0.0	**Gas City** (city) Grant County
104	0.0	**Georgetown** (town) Floyd County
104	0.0	**Greencastle** (city) Putnam County
104	0.0	**Greendale** (city) Dearborn County
104	0.0	**Greenfield** (city) Hancock County
104	0.0	**Greensburg** (city) Decatur County
104	0.0	**Greentown** (town) Howard County
104	0.0	**Griffith** (town) Lake County
104	0.0	**Hebron** (town) Porter County
104	0.0	**Highland** (CDP) Vanderburgh County
104	0.0	**Jasper** (city) Dubois County
104	0.0	**Knox** (city) Starke County
104	0.0	**Lagrange** (town) LaGrange County
104	0.0	**Lakes of the Four Seasons** (CDP) Lake County
104	0.0	**Lawrenceburg** (city) Dearborn County

Note: *This section ranks incorporated places and CDPs (Census Designated Places) with populations of 2,500 or more. Unincorporated postal areas were not considered. Please refer to the User Guide for additional information.*

Native Hawaiian/Other Pacific Islander Population

Top 150 Places Ranked in *Descending* Order

State Rank	Percent	Place
1	1.1	**Tipton** (city) Tipton County
2	0.3	**Linton** (city) Greene County
3	0.2	**Bedford** (city) Lawrence County
3	0.2	**Evansville** (city) Vanderburgh County
3	0.2	**Gary** (city) Lake County
3	0.2	**Granger** (CDP) Saint Joseph County
3	0.2	**Logansport** (city) Cass County
3	0.2	**Lowell** (town) Lake County
3	0.2	**Nappanee** (city) Elkhart County
3	0.2	**Speedway** (town) Marion County
3	0.2	**Valparaiso** (city) Porter County
3	0.2	**Whiting** (city) Lake County
13	0.1	**Angola** (city) Steuben County
13	0.1	**Columbus** (city) Bartholomew County
13	0.1	**Elkhart** (city) Elkhart County
13	0.1	**Fort Wayne** (city) Allen County
13	0.1	**Frankfort** (city) Clinton County
13	0.1	**Greencastle** (city) Putnam County
13	0.1	**Greenfield** (city) Hancock County
13	0.1	**Kokomo** (city) Howard County
13	0.1	**La Porte** (city) LaPorte County
13	0.1	**Mishawaka** (city) Saint Joseph County
13	0.1	**Muncie** (city) Delaware County
13	0.1	**Munster** (town) Lake County
13	0.1	**Portage** (city) Porter County
13	0.1	**South Bend** (city) Saint Joseph County
13	0.1	**Vincennes** (city) Knox County
13	0.1	**Washington** (city) Daviess County
13	0.1	**West Lafayette** (city) Tippecanoe County
13	0.1	**Westville** (town) LaPorte County
31	0.0	**Alexandria** (city) Madison County
31	0.0	**Anderson** (city) Madison County
31	0.0	**Attica** (city) Fountain County
31	0.0	**Auburn** (city) DeKalb County
31	0.0	**Aurora** (city) Dearborn County
31	0.0	**Austin** (city) Scott County
31	0.0	**Avon** (town) Hendricks County
31	0.0	**Bargersville** (town) Johnson County
31	0.0	**Batesville** (city) Ripley County
31	0.0	**Beech Grove** (city) Marion County
31	0.0	**Berne** (city) Adams County
31	0.0	**Bicknell** (city) Knox County
31	0.0	**Bloomington** (city) Monroe County
31	0.0	**Bluffton** (city) Wells County
31	0.0	**Boonville** (city) Warrick County
31	0.0	**Brazil** (city) Clay County
31	0.0	**Bremen** (town) Marshall County
31	0.0	**Bright** (CDP) Dearborn County
31	0.0	**Brookville** (town) Franklin County
31	0.0	**Brownsburg** (town) Hendricks County
31	0.0	**Brownstown** (town) Jackson County
31	0.0	**Butler** (city) DeKalb County
31	0.0	**Carmel** (city) Hamilton County
31	0.0	**Cedar Lake** (town) Lake County
31	0.0	**Centerville** (town) Wayne County
31	0.0	**Chandler** (town) Warrick County
31	0.0	**Charlestown** (city) Clark County
31	0.0	**Chesterton** (town) Porter County
31	0.0	**Cicero** (town) Hamilton County
31	0.0	**Clarksville** (town) Clark County
31	0.0	**Clinton** (city) Vermillion County
31	0.0	**Columbia City** (city) Whitley County
31	0.0	**Connersville** (city) Fayette County
31	0.0	**Corydon** (town) Harrison County
31	0.0	**Country Squire Lakes** (CDP) Jennings County
31	0.0	**Crawfordsville** (city) Montgomery County
31	0.0	**Crown Point** (city) Lake County
31	0.0	**Cumberland** (town) Marion County
31	0.0	**Danville** (town) Hendricks County
31	0.0	**De Motte** (town) Jasper County
31	0.0	**Decatur** (city) Adams County
31	0.0	**Delphi** (city) Carroll County
31	0.0	**Dunlap** (CDP) Elkhart County
31	0.0	**Dyer** (town) Lake County
31	0.0	**East Chicago** (city) Lake County
31	0.0	**Edinburgh** (town) Johnson County
31	0.0	**Ellettsville** (town) Monroe County
31	0.0	**Elwood** (city) Madison County
31	0.0	**Fairmount** (town) Grant County
31	0.0	**Fishers** (city) Hamilton County
31	0.0	**Fort Branch** (town) Gibson County
31	0.0	**Fortville** (town) Hancock County
31	0.0	**Franklin** (city) Johnson County
31	0.0	**Garrett** (city) DeKalb County
31	0.0	**Gas City** (city) Grant County
31	0.0	**Georgetown** (town) Floyd County
31	0.0	**Goshen** (city) Elkhart County
31	0.0	**Greendale** (city) Dearborn County
31	0.0	**Greensburg** (city) Decatur County
31	0.0	**Greentown** (town) Howard County
31	0.0	**Greenwood** (city) Johnson County
31	0.0	**Griffith** (town) Lake County
31	0.0	**Hammond** (city) Lake County
31	0.0	**Hanover** (town) Jefferson County
31	0.0	**Hartford City** (city) Blackford County
31	0.0	**Hebron** (town) Porter County
31	0.0	**Heritage Lake** (CDP) Putnam County
31	0.0	**Hidden Valley** (CDP) Dearborn County
31	0.0	**Highland** (CDP) Vanderburgh County
31	0.0	**Highland** (town) Lake County
31	0.0	**Hobart** (city) Lake County
31	0.0	**Huntertown** (town) Allen County
31	0.0	**Huntingburg** (city) Dubois County
31	0.0	**Huntington** (city) Huntington County
31	0.0	**Indianapolis** (city) Marion County
31	0.0	**Jasper** (city) Dubois County
31	0.0	**Jeffersonville** (city) Clark County
31	0.0	**Kendallville** (city) Noble County
31	0.0	**Knox** (city) Starke County
31	0.0	**Lafayette** (city) Tippecanoe County
31	0.0	**Lagrange** (town) LaGrange County
31	0.0	**Lake Station** (city) Lake County
31	0.0	**Lakes of the Four Seasons** (CDP) Lake County
31	0.0	**Lawrence** (city) Marion County
31	0.0	**Lawrenceburg** (city) Dearborn County
31	0.0	**Lebanon** (city) Boone County
31	0.0	**Leo-Cedarville** (town) Allen County
31	0.0	**Ligonier** (city) Noble County
31	0.0	**Loogootee** (city) Martin County
31	0.0	**Madison** (city) Jefferson County
31	0.0	**Marion** (city) Grant County
31	0.0	**Martinsville** (city) Morgan County
31	0.0	**McCordsville** (town) Hancock County
31	0.0	**Melody Hill** (CDP) Vanderburgh County
31	0.0	**Merrillville** (town) Lake County
31	0.0	**Michigan City** (city) LaPorte County
31	0.0	**Middlebury** (town) Elkhart County
31	0.0	**Mitchell** (city) Lawrence County
31	0.0	**Monticello** (city) White County
31	0.0	**Mooresville** (town) Morgan County
31	0.0	**Mount Vernon** (city) Posey County
31	0.0	**New Albany** (city) Floyd County
31	0.0	**New Castle** (city) Henry County
31	0.0	**New Haven** (city) Allen County
31	0.0	**New Whiteland** (town) Johnson County
31	0.0	**Newburgh** (town) Warrick County
31	0.0	**Noblesville** (city) Hamilton County
31	0.0	**North Manchester** (town) Wabash County
31	0.0	**North Terre Haute** (CDP) Vigo County
31	0.0	**North Vernon** (city) Jennings County
31	0.0	**Notre Dame** (CDP) Saint Joseph County
31	0.0	**Osceola** (town) Saint Joseph County
31	0.0	**Ossian** (town) Wells County
31	0.0	**Paoli** (town) Orange County
31	0.0	**Pendleton** (town) Madison County
31	0.0	**Peru** (city) Miami County
31	0.0	**Pittsboro** (town) Hendricks County
31	0.0	**Plainfield** (town) Hendricks County
31	0.0	**Plymouth** (city) Marshall County
31	0.0	**Porter** (town) Porter County

Note: *This section ranks incorporated places and CDPs (Census Designated Places) with populations of 2,500 or more. Unincorporated postal areas were not considered. Please refer to the User Guide for additional information.*

Two or More Races

Top 150 Places Ranked in *Descending* Order

State Rank	Percent	Place
1	7.4	**McCordsville** (town) Hancock County
2	6.9	**Middlebury** (town) Elkhart County
3	5.6	**Fortville** (town) Hancock County
4	5.5	**Fort Branch** (town) Gibson County
4	5.5	**Gas City** (city) Grant County
4	5.5	**Michigan City** (city) LaPorte County
7	5.3	**Lake Station** (city) Lake County
8	5.1	**Huntertown** (town) Allen County
9	4.9	**Speedway** (town) Marion County
10	4.7	**Terre Haute** (city) Vigo County
11	4.6	**Avon** (town) Hendricks County
11	4.6	**Jeffersonville** (city) Clark County
11	4.6	**New Whiteland** (town) Johnson County
14	4.5	**Merrillville** (town) Lake County
15	4.3	**Notre Dame** (CDP) Saint Joseph County
16	4.2	**Fort Wayne** (city) Allen County
16	4.2	**South Bend** (city) Saint Joseph County
18	4.1	**Anderson** (city) Madison County
19	4.0	**Logansport** (city) Cass County
19	4.0	**Marion** (city) Grant County
21	3.9	**Columbia City** (city) Whitley County
21	3.9	**Hammond** (city) Lake County
21	3.9	**Lagrange** (town) LaGrange County
21	3.9	**Lawrence** (city) Marion County
21	3.9	**Mishawaka** (city) Saint Joseph County
26	3.7	**Charlestown** (city) Clark County
26	3.7	**Winamac** (town) Pulaski County
28	3.6	**Bremen** (town) Marshall County
28	3.6	**Clarksville** (town) Clark County
30	3.5	**Bloomington** (city) Monroe County
30	3.5	**Crawfordsville** (city) Montgomery County
30	3.5	**Ellettsville** (town) Monroe County
30	3.5	**Goshen** (city) Elkhart County
30	3.5	**Highland** (town) Lake County
30	3.5	**Monticello** (city) White County
30	3.5	**Richmond** (city) Wayne County
30	3.5	**Schererville** (town) Lake County
30	3.5	**Warsaw** (city) Kosciusko County
39	3.4	**Cumberland** (town) Marion County
39	3.4	**Elkhart** (city) Elkhart County
39	3.4	**Ligonier** (city) Noble County
39	3.4	**Salt Creek Commons** (CDP) Porter County
43	3.3	**Centerville** (town) Wayne County
43	3.3	**Evansville** (city) Vanderburgh County
45	3.2	**Sellersburg** (town) Clark County
46	3.1	**Boonville** (city) Warrick County
46	3.1	**Brazil** (city) Clay County
46	3.1	**Princeton** (city) Gibson County
49	3.0	**Indianapolis** (city) Marion County
50	2.9	**Cedar Lake** (town) Lake County
50	2.9	**Huntingburg** (city) Dubois County
50	2.9	**Lebanon** (city) Boone County
50	2.9	**Muncie** (city) Delaware County
50	2.9	**Saint John** (town) Lake County
50	2.9	**Syracuse** (town) Kosciusko County
50	2.9	**West Lafayette** (city) Tippecanoe County
57	2.8	**Fishers** (city) Hamilton County
57	2.8	**Mount Vernon** (city) Posey County
57	2.8	**New Albany** (city) Floyd County
57	2.8	**Noblesville** (city) Hamilton County
57	2.8	**North Manchester** (town) Wabash County
57	2.8	**Tipton** (city) Tipton County
63	2.7	**Angola** (city) Steuben County
63	2.7	**East Chicago** (city) Lake County
63	2.7	**Osceola** (town) Saint Joseph County
63	2.7	**Tell City** (city) Perry County
67	2.6	**Dunlap** (CDP) Elkhart County
67	2.6	**Kokomo** (city) Howard County
67	2.6	**Plymouth** (city) Marshall County
67	2.6	**Rockville** (town) Parke County
71	2.5	**Butler** (city) DeKalb County
71	2.5	**Westville** (town) LaPorte County
71	2.5	**Whiting** (city) Lake County
74	2.4	**Crown Point** (city) Lake County
74	2.4	**Hartford City** (city) Blackford County
74	2.4	**La Porte** (city) LaPorte County
77	2.3	**Griffith** (town) Lake County
77	2.3	**Hobart** (city) Lake County
77	2.3	**Lafayette** (city) Tippecanoe County
77	2.3	**Mitchell** (city) Lawrence County
77	2.3	**Pittsboro** (town) Hendricks County
77	2.3	**Portage** (city) Porter County
77	2.3	**Winchester** (city) Randolph County
84	2.2	**Carmel** (city) Hamilton County
84	2.2	**Pendleton** (town) Madison County
84	2.2	**Winfield** (town) Lake County
87	2.1	**Chesterton** (town) Porter County
87	2.1	**Columbus** (city) Bartholomew County
87	2.1	**Gary** (city) Lake County
90	2.0	**Bicknell** (city) Knox County
90	2.0	**Edinburgh** (town) Johnson County
90	2.0	**Martinsville** (city) Morgan County
90	2.0	**North Terre Haute** (CDP) Vigo County
90	2.0	**Union City** (city) Randolph County
90	2.0	**Wabash** (city) Wabash County
96	1.9	**Bedford** (city) Lawrence County
96	1.9	**Georgetown** (town) Floyd County
96	1.9	**Granger** (CDP) Saint Joseph County
96	1.9	**Greencastle** (city) Putnam County
96	1.9	**Portland** (city) Jay County
96	1.9	**Upland** (town) Grant County
96	1.9	**Yorktown** (town) Delaware County
103	1.8	**Beech Grove** (city) Marion County
103	1.8	**Kendallville** (city) Noble County
103	1.8	**Lakes of the Four Seasons** (CDP) Lake County
103	1.8	**Simonton Lake** (CDP) Elkhart County
103	1.8	**South Haven** (CDP) Porter County
108	1.7	**Bright** (CDP) Dearborn County
108	1.7	**Peru** (city) Miami County
110	1.6	**New Castle** (city) Henry County
110	1.6	**Seymour** (city) Jackson County
110	1.6	**Washington** (city) Daviess County
113	1.5	**Garrett** (city) DeKalb County
113	1.5	**Valparaiso** (city) Porter County
113	1.5	**Zionsville** (town) Boone County
116	1.4	**Madison** (city) Jefferson County
116	1.4	**Munster** (town) Lake County
116	1.4	**Shelbyville** (city) Shelby County
116	1.4	**Vincennes** (city) Knox County
116	1.4	**Westfield** (city) Hamilton County
121	1.3	**Corydon** (town) Harrison County
121	1.3	**Dyer** (town) Lake County
121	1.3	**New Haven** (city) Allen County
121	1.3	**Plainfield** (town) Hendricks County
121	1.3	**Salem** (city) Washington County
126	1.2	**Greentown** (town) Howard County
126	1.2	**Leo-Cedarville** (town) Allen County
126	1.2	**Nappanee** (city) Elkhart County
129	1.1	**Bluffton** (city) Wells County
129	1.1	**Greenwood** (city) Johnson County
129	1.1	**Hidden Valley** (CDP) Dearborn County
129	1.1	**Linton** (city) Greene County
133	1.0	**De Motte** (town) Jasper County
133	1.0	**Frankfort** (city) Clinton County
133	1.0	**Huntington** (city) Huntington County
133	1.0	**Rensselaer** (city) Jasper County
133	1.0	**Santa Claus** (town) Spencer County
133	1.0	**Scottsburg** (city) Scott County
133	1.0	**Sheridan** (town) Hamilton County
133	1.0	**Smithville-Sanders** (CDP) Monroe County
141	0.9	**Brownstown** (town) Jackson County
141	0.9	**Chandler** (town) Warrick County
141	0.9	**Delphi** (city) Carroll County
141	0.9	**Elwood** (city) Madison County
141	0.9	**Porter** (town) Porter County
141	0.9	**Rushville** (city) Rush County
141	0.9	**Whitestown** (town) Boone County
141	0.9	**Winona Lake** (town) Kosciusko County
149	0.8	**Austin** (city) Scott County
149	0.8	**Brownsburg** (town) Hendricks County

Note: *This section ranks incorporated places and CDPs (Census Designated Places) with populations of 2,500 or more. Unincorporated postal areas were not considered. Please refer to the User Guide for additional information.*

Two or More Races

Top 150 Places Ranked in *Ascending* Order

State Rank	Percent	Place
1	0.0	**Aurora** (city) Dearborn County
1	0.0	**Berne** (city) Adams County
1	0.0	**Brookville** (town) Franklin County
1	0.0	**Cicero** (town) Hamilton County
1	0.0	**Clinton** (city) Vermillion County
1	0.0	**Country Squire Lakes** (CDP) Jennings County
1	0.0	**Greendale** (city) Dearborn County
1	0.0	**Hebron** (town) Porter County
1	0.0	**Heritage Lake** (CDP) Putnam County
1	0.0	**Highland** (CDP) Vanderburgh County
1	0.0	**Loogootee** (city) Martin County
1	0.0	**Melody Hill** (CDP) Vanderburgh County
1	0.0	**Newburgh** (town) Warrick County
1	0.0	**Whiteland** (town) Johnson County
15	0.1	**Knox** (city) Starke County
16	0.2	**Lawrenceburg** (city) Dearborn County
16	0.2	**Shorewood Forest** (CDP) Porter County
18	0.3	**Connersville** (city) Fayette County
18	0.3	**Fairmount** (town) Grant County
18	0.3	**Jasper** (city) Dubois County
21	0.4	**Bargersville** (town) Johnson County
21	0.4	**Ossian** (town) Wells County
23	0.5	**Auburn** (city) DeKalb County
23	0.5	**Batesville** (city) Ripley County
23	0.5	**Danville** (town) Hendricks County
23	0.5	**Decatur** (city) Adams County
23	0.5	**Mooresville** (town) Morgan County
23	0.5	**Paoli** (town) Orange County
23	0.5	**Rochester** (city) Fulton County
30	0.6	**Attica** (city) Fountain County
30	0.6	**Franklin** (city) Johnson County
30	0.6	**Greenfield** (city) Hancock County
30	0.6	**Lowell** (town) Lake County
34	0.7	**Alexandria** (city) Madison County
34	0.7	**Greensburg** (city) Decatur County
34	0.7	**North Vernon** (city) Jennings County
34	0.7	**Roselawn** (CDP) Newton County
38	0.8	**Austin** (city) Scott County
38	0.8	**Brownsburg** (town) Hendricks County
38	0.8	**Hanover** (town) Jefferson County
38	0.8	**Sullivan** (city) Sullivan County
42	0.9	**Brownstown** (town) Jackson County
42	0.9	**Chandler** (town) Warrick County
42	0.9	**Delphi** (city) Carroll County
42	0.9	**Elwood** (city) Madison County
42	0.9	**Porter** (town) Porter County
42	0.9	**Rushville** (city) Rush County
42	0.9	**Whitestown** (town) Boone County
42	0.9	**Winona Lake** (town) Kosciusko County
50	1.0	**De Motte** (town) Jasper County
50	1.0	**Frankfort** (city) Clinton County
50	1.0	**Huntington** (city) Huntington County
50	1.0	**Rensselaer** (city) Jasper County
50	1.0	**Santa Claus** (town) Spencer County
50	1.0	**Scottsburg** (city) Scott County
50	1.0	**Sheridan** (town) Hamilton County
50	1.0	**Smithville-Sanders** (CDP) Monroe County
58	1.1	**Bluffton** (city) Wells County
58	1.1	**Greenwood** (city) Johnson County
58	1.1	**Hidden Valley** (CDP) Dearborn County
58	1.1	**Linton** (city) Greene County
62	1.2	**Greentown** (town) Howard County
62	1.2	**Leo-Cedarville** (town) Allen County
62	1.2	**Nappanee** (city) Elkhart County
65	1.3	**Corydon** (town) Harrison County
65	1.3	**Dyer** (town) Lake County
65	1.3	**New Haven** (city) Allen County
65	1.3	**Plainfield** (town) Hendricks County
65	1.3	**Salem** (city) Washington County
70	1.4	**Madison** (city) Jefferson County
70	1.4	**Munster** (town) Lake County
70	1.4	**Shelbyville** (city) Shelby County
70	1.4	**Vincennes** (city) Knox County
70	1.4	**Westfield** (city) Hamilton County
75	1.5	**Garrett** (city) DeKalb County
75	1.5	**Valparaiso** (city) Porter County
75	1.5	**Zionsville** (town) Boone County
78	1.6	**New Castle** (city) Henry County
78	1.6	**Seymour** (city) Jackson County
78	1.6	**Washington** (city) Daviess County
81	1.7	**Bright** (CDP) Dearborn County
81	1.7	**Peru** (city) Miami County
83	1.8	**Beech Grove** (city) Marion County
83	1.8	**Kendallville** (city) Noble County
83	1.8	**Lakes of the Four Seasons** (CDP) Lake County
83	1.8	**Simonton Lake** (CDP) Elkhart County
83	1.8	**South Haven** (CDP) Porter County
88	1.9	**Bedford** (city) Lawrence County
88	1.9	**Georgetown** (town) Floyd County
88	1.9	**Granger** (CDP) Saint Joseph County
88	1.9	**Greencastle** (city) Putnam County
88	1.9	**Portland** (city) Jay County
88	1.9	**Upland** (town) Grant County
88	1.9	**Yorktown** (town) Delaware County
95	2.0	**Bicknell** (city) Knox County
95	2.0	**Edinburgh** (town) Johnson County
95	2.0	**Martinsville** (city) Morgan County
95	2.0	**North Terre Haute** (CDP) Vigo County
95	2.0	**Union City** (city) Randolph County
95	2.0	**Wabash** (city) Wabash County
101	2.1	**Chesterton** (town) Porter County
101	2.1	**Columbus** (city) Bartholomew County
101	2.1	**Gary** (city) Lake County
104	2.2	**Carmel** (city) Hamilton County
104	2.2	**Pendleton** (town) Madison County
104	2.2	**Winfield** (town) Lake County
107	2.3	**Griffith** (town) Lake County
107	2.3	**Hobart** (city) Lake County
107	2.3	**Lafayette** (city) Tippecanoe County
107	2.3	**Mitchell** (city) Lawrence County
107	2.3	**Pittsboro** (town) Hendricks County
107	2.3	**Portage** (city) Porter County
107	2.3	**Winchester** (city) Randolph County
114	2.4	**Crown Point** (city) Lake County
114	2.4	**Hartford City** (city) Blackford County
114	2.4	**La Porte** (city) LaPorte County
117	2.5	**Butler** (city) DeKalb County
117	2.5	**Westville** (town) LaPorte County
117	2.5	**Whiting** (city) Lake County
120	2.6	**Dunlap** (CDP) Elkhart County
120	2.6	**Kokomo** (city) Howard County
120	2.6	**Plymouth** (city) Marshall County
120	2.6	**Rockville** (town) Parke County
124	2.7	**Angola** (city) Steuben County
124	2.7	**East Chicago** (city) Lake County
124	2.7	**Osceola** (town) Saint Joseph County
124	2.7	**Tell City** (city) Perry County
128	2.8	**Fishers** (city) Hamilton County
128	2.8	**Mount Vernon** (city) Posey County
128	2.8	**New Albany** (city) Floyd County
128	2.8	**Noblesville** (city) Hamilton County
128	2.8	**North Manchester** (town) Wabash County
128	2.8	**Tipton** (city) Tipton County
134	2.9	**Cedar Lake** (town) Lake County
134	2.9	**Huntingburg** (city) Dubois County
134	2.9	**Lebanon** (city) Boone County
134	2.9	**Muncie** (city) Delaware County
134	2.9	**Saint John** (town) Lake County
134	2.9	**Syracuse** (town) Kosciusko County
134	2.9	**West Lafayette** (city) Tippecanoe County
141	3.0	**Indianapolis** (city) Marion County
142	3.1	**Boonville** (city) Warrick County
142	3.1	**Brazil** (city) Clay County
142	3.1	**Princeton** (city) Gibson County
145	3.2	**Sellersburg** (town) Clark County
146	3.3	**Centerville** (town) Wayne County
146	3.3	**Evansville** (city) Vanderburgh County
148	3.4	**Cumberland** (town) Marion County
148	3.4	**Elkhart** (city) Elkhart County
148	3.4	**Ligonier** (city) Noble County

Note: *This section ranks incorporated places and CDPs (Census Designated Places) with populations of 2,500 or more. Unincorporated postal areas were not considered. Please refer to the User Guide for additional information.*

Hispanic Population

Top 150 Places Ranked in *Descending* Order

State Rank	Percent	Place
1	59.9	**Ligonier** (city) Noble County
2	57.0	**East Chicago** (city) Lake County
3	36.7	**Whiting** (city) Lake County
4	36.6	**Hammond** (city) Lake County
5	33.0	**Lake Station** (city) Lake County
6	30.0	**Goshen** (city) Elkhart County
7	27.8	**Frankfort** (city) Clinton County
8	27.0	**Logansport** (city) Cass County
9	25.5	**Plymouth** (city) Marshall County
10	24.1	**Huntingburg** (city) Dubois County
11	23.0	**Elkhart** (city) Elkhart County
12	19.3	**Portage** (city) Porter County
13	18.8	**Delphi** (city) Carroll County
14	18.4	**Winfield** (town) Lake County
15	17.7	**Union City** (city) Randolph County
16	16.6	**Lagrange** (town) LaGrange County
17	16.4	**Bremen** (town) Marshall County
18	15.9	**Griffith** (town) Lake County
19	15.5	**Highland** (town) Lake County
20	15.1	**Monticello** (city) White County
21	14.6	**Merrillville** (town) Lake County
22	14.5	**Munster** (town) Lake County
23	14.4	**South Bend** (city) Saint Joseph County
24	12.5	**Washington** (city) Daviess County
25	12.3	**La Porte** (city) LaPorte County
26	12.2	**Lafayette** (city) Tippecanoe County
26	12.2	**Lawrence** (city) Marion County
26	12.2	**Porter** (town) Porter County
29	11.9	**Seymour** (city) Jackson County
30	11.8	**Hobart** (city) Lake County
30	11.8	**Middlebury** (town) Elkhart County
30	11.8	**Schererville** (town) Lake County
33	11.4	**Winona Lake** (town) Kosciusko County
34	11.3	**South Haven** (CDP) Porter County
35	10.8	**Lakes of the Four Seasons** (CDP) Lake County
35	10.8	**Syracuse** (town) Kosciusko County
37	10.3	**Warsaw** (city) Kosciusko County
38	10.1	**Dyer** (town) Lake County
38	10.1	**Indianapolis** (city) Marion County
40	9.8	**Edinburgh** (town) Johnson County
41	9.2	**Hebron** (town) Porter County
41	9.2	**Speedway** (town) Marion County
43	9.1	**Saint John** (town) Lake County
44	8.7	**Fort Wayne** (city) Allen County
45	8.6	**Avon** (town) Hendricks County
45	8.6	**Crown Point** (city) Lake County
47	8.5	**Crawfordsville** (city) Montgomery County
48	8.4	**Portland** (city) Jay County
48	8.4	**Shelbyville** (city) Shelby County
50	8.1	**Jasper** (city) Dubois County
50	8.1	**Roselawn** (CDP) Newton County
52	7.9	**Clarksville** (town) Clark County
52	7.9	**Dunlap** (CDP) Elkhart County
54	7.6	**Charlestown** (city) Clark County
54	7.6	**Decatur** (city) Adams County
56	7.4	**Chesterton** (town) Porter County
56	7.4	**Notre Dame** (CDP) Saint Joseph County
58	7.3	**Nappanee** (city) Elkhart County
59	7.1	**North Manchester** (town) Wabash County
60	6.9	**Lowell** (town) Lake County
61	6.8	**Country Squire Lakes** (CDP) Jennings County
61	6.8	**McCordsville** (town) Hancock County
61	6.8	**Westville** (town) LaPorte County
64	6.7	**Valparaiso** (city) Porter County
65	6.6	**Salt Creek Commons** (CDP) Porter County
66	6.3	**Mishawaka** (city) Saint Joseph County
67	6.1	**De Motte** (town) Jasper County
67	6.1	**Greenwood** (city) Johnson County
67	6.1	**Michigan City** (city) LaPorte County
70	6.0	**Madison** (city) Jefferson County
71	5.9	**Gas City** (city) Grant County
72	5.8	**Gary** (city) Lake County
73	5.7	**Columbus** (city) Bartholomew County
73	5.7	**Marion** (city) Grant County
73	5.7	**New Haven** (city) Allen County
73	5.7	**Rensselaer** (city) Jasper County
77	5.5	**Cedar Lake** (town) Lake County
77	5.5	**Leo-Cedarville** (town) Allen County
79	5.3	**Anderson** (city) Madison County
79	5.3	**Knox** (city) Starke County
79	5.3	**Mitchell** (city) Lawrence County
82	5.2	**Jeffersonville** (city) Clark County
83	5.0	**Cicero** (town) Hamilton County
84	4.9	**Osceola** (town) Saint Joseph County
85	4.8	**Angola** (city) Steuben County
86	4.7	**Fairmount** (town) Grant County
86	4.7	**Peru** (city) Miami County
86	4.7	**Plainfield** (town) Hendricks County
86	4.7	**Westfield** (city) Hamilton County
86	4.7	**Winamac** (town) Pulaski County
91	4.5	**Noblesville** (city) Hamilton County
91	4.5	**Richmond** (city) Wayne County
93	4.4	**Boonville** (city) Warrick County
93	4.4	**New Albany** (city) Floyd County
95	4.2	**Bloomington** (city) Monroe County
95	4.2	**Brookville** (town) Franklin County
95	4.2	**Pittsboro** (town) Hendricks County
95	4.2	**Simonton Lake** (CDP) Elkhart County
95	4.2	**West Lafayette** (city) Tippecanoe County
100	4.1	**Alexandria** (city) Madison County
100	4.1	**Hidden Valley** (CDP) Dearborn County
100	4.1	**Whitestown** (town) Boone County
103	4.0	**Kendallville** (city) Noble County
103	4.0	**Lebanon** (city) Boone County
103	4.0	**Sellersburg** (town) Clark County
106	3.9	**Beech Grove** (city) Marion County
106	3.9	**Columbia City** (city) Whitley County
108	3.8	**Attica** (city) Fountain County
108	3.8	**Fishers** (city) Hamilton County
108	3.8	**Kokomo** (city) Howard County
111	3.7	**Greencastle** (city) Putnam County
111	3.7	**Huntertown** (town) Allen County
113	3.6	**Austin** (city) Scott County
114	3.5	**Bluffton** (city) Wells County
114	3.5	**Elwood** (city) Madison County
116	3.3	**Ellettsville** (town) Monroe County
116	3.3	**Ossian** (town) Wells County
118	3.2	**Carmel** (city) Hamilton County
118	3.2	**Huntington** (city) Huntington County
120	3.1	**Brownsburg** (town) Hendricks County
120	3.1	**Muncie** (city) Delaware County
122	3.0	**Evansville** (city) Vanderburgh County
122	3.0	**New Whiteland** (town) Johnson County
122	3.0	**Princeton** (city) Gibson County
122	3.0	**Terre Haute** (city) Vigo County
126	2.9	**Cumberland** (town) Marion County
126	2.9	**Scottsburg** (city) Scott County
128	2.8	**Butler** (city) DeKalb County
128	2.8	**Georgetown** (town) Floyd County
128	2.8	**Rochester** (city) Fulton County
128	2.8	**Tipton** (city) Tipton County
132	2.7	**Clinton** (city) Vermillion County
132	2.7	**Franklin** (city) Johnson County
134	2.6	**Granger** (CDP) Saint Joseph County
135	2.5	**Hartford City** (city) Blackford County
135	2.5	**Zionsville** (town) Boone County
137	2.4	**Vincennes** (city) Knox County
138	2.3	**Rushville** (city) Rush County
139	2.2	**Garrett** (city) DeKalb County
139	2.2	**Wabash** (city) Wabash County
141	2.1	**Bedford** (city) Lawrence County
141	2.1	**Santa Claus** (town) Spencer County
143	2.0	**Greendale** (city) Dearborn County
143	2.0	**Greenfield** (city) Hancock County
143	2.0	**Greensburg** (city) Decatur County
143	2.0	**Mooresville** (town) Morgan County
147	1.9	**Auburn** (city) DeKalb County
148	1.8	**North Vernon** (city) Jennings County
148	1.8	**Sheridan** (town) Hamilton County
150	1.7	**Berne** (city) Adams County

Note: *This section ranks incorporated places and CDPs (Census Designated Places) with populations of 2,500 or more. Unincorporated postal areas were not considered. Please refer to the User Guide for additional information.*

Hispanic Population

Top 150 Places Ranked in *Ascending* Order

State Rank	Percent	Place
1	0.0	**Aurora** (city) Dearborn County
1	0.0	**Bargersville** (town) Johnson County
1	0.0	**Corydon** (town) Harrison County
1	0.0	**Fortville** (town) Hancock County
1	0.0	**Highland** (CDP) Vanderburgh County
1	0.0	**Whiteland** (town) Johnson County
1	0.0	**Yorktown** (town) Delaware County
8	0.1	**Paoli** (town) Orange County
9	0.3	**Chandler** (town) Warrick County
9	0.3	**Newburgh** (town) Warrick County
11	0.4	**Centerville** (town) Wayne County
11	0.4	**Loogootee** (city) Martin County
11	0.4	**North Terre Haute** (CDP) Vigo County
11	0.4	**Smithville-Sanders** (CDP) Monroe County
15	0.5	**Fort Branch** (town) Gibson County
16	0.6	**Lawrenceburg** (city) Dearborn County
16	0.6	**Salem** (city) Washington County
18	0.7	**Rockville** (town) Parke County
18	0.7	**Sullivan** (city) Sullivan County
20	0.8	**Batesville** (city) Ripley County
21	0.9	**Brownstown** (town) Jackson County
21	0.9	**Pendleton** (town) Madison County
21	0.9	**Upland** (town) Grant County
24	1.0	**Bright** (CDP) Dearborn County
24	1.0	**Linton** (city) Greene County
24	1.0	**Melody Hill** (CDP) Vanderburgh County
27	1.1	**Danville** (town) Hendricks County
27	1.1	**Mount Vernon** (city) Posey County
29	1.2	**Heritage Lake** (CDP) Putnam County
30	1.3	**Brazil** (city) Clay County
30	1.3	**Shorewood Forest** (CDP) Porter County
30	1.3	**Winchester** (city) Randolph County
33	1.4	**Martinsville** (city) Morgan County
34	1.5	**Bicknell** (city) Knox County
34	1.5	**Connersville** (city) Fayette County
34	1.5	**New Castle** (city) Henry County
37	1.6	**Hanover** (town) Jefferson County
38	1.7	**Berne** (city) Adams County
38	1.7	**Greentown** (town) Howard County
38	1.7	**Tell City** (city) Perry County
41	1.8	**North Vernon** (city) Jennings County
41	1.8	**Sheridan** (town) Hamilton County
43	1.9	**Auburn** (city) DeKalb County
44	2.0	**Greendale** (city) Dearborn County
44	2.0	**Greenfield** (city) Hancock County
44	2.0	**Greensburg** (city) Decatur County
44	2.0	**Mooresville** (town) Morgan County
48	2.1	**Bedford** (city) Lawrence County
48	2.1	**Santa Claus** (town) Spencer County
50	2.2	**Garrett** (city) DeKalb County
50	2.2	**Wabash** (city) Wabash County
52	2.3	**Rushville** (city) Rush County
53	2.4	**Vincennes** (city) Knox County
54	2.5	**Hartford City** (city) Blackford County
54	2.5	**Zionsville** (town) Boone County
56	2.6	**Granger** (CDP) Saint Joseph County
57	2.7	**Clinton** (city) Vermillion County
57	2.7	**Franklin** (city) Johnson County
59	2.8	**Butler** (city) DeKalb County
59	2.8	**Georgetown** (town) Floyd County
59	2.8	**Rochester** (city) Fulton County
59	2.8	**Tipton** (city) Tipton County
63	2.9	**Cumberland** (town) Marion County
63	2.9	**Scottsburg** (city) Scott County
65	3.0	**Evansville** (city) Vanderburgh County
65	3.0	**New Whiteland** (town) Johnson County
65	3.0	**Princeton** (city) Gibson County
65	3.0	**Terre Haute** (city) Vigo County
69	3.1	**Brownsburg** (town) Hendricks County
69	3.1	**Muncie** (city) Delaware County
71	3.2	**Carmel** (city) Hamilton County
71	3.2	**Huntington** (city) Huntington County
73	3.3	**Ellettsville** (town) Monroe County
73	3.3	**Ossian** (town) Wells County
75	3.5	**Bluffton** (city) Wells County
75	3.5	**Elwood** (city) Madison County
77	3.6	**Austin** (city) Scott County
78	3.7	**Greencastle** (city) Putnam County
78	3.7	**Huntertown** (town) Allen County
80	3.8	**Attica** (city) Fountain County
80	3.8	**Fishers** (city) Hamilton County
80	3.8	**Kokomo** (city) Howard County
83	3.9	**Beech Grove** (city) Marion County
83	3.9	**Columbia City** (city) Whitley County
85	4.0	**Kendallville** (city) Noble County
85	4.0	**Lebanon** (city) Boone County
85	4.0	**Sellersburg** (town) Clark County
88	4.1	**Alexandria** (city) Madison County
88	4.1	**Hidden Valley** (CDP) Dearborn County
88	4.1	**Whitestown** (town) Boone County
91	4.2	**Bloomington** (city) Monroe County
91	4.2	**Brookville** (town) Franklin County
91	4.2	**Pittsboro** (town) Hendricks County
91	4.2	**Simonton Lake** (CDP) Elkhart County
91	4.2	**West Lafayette** (city) Tippecanoe County
96	4.4	**Boonville** (city) Warrick County
96	4.4	**New Albany** (city) Floyd County
98	4.5	**Noblesville** (city) Hamilton County
98	4.5	**Richmond** (city) Wayne County
100	4.7	**Fairmount** (town) Grant County
100	4.7	**Peru** (city) Miami County
100	4.7	**Plainfield** (town) Hendricks County
100	4.7	**Westfield** (city) Hamilton County
100	4.7	**Winamac** (town) Pulaski County
105	4.8	**Angola** (city) Steuben County
106	4.9	**Osceola** (town) Saint Joseph County
107	5.0	**Cicero** (town) Hamilton County
108	5.2	**Jeffersonville** (city) Clark County
109	5.3	**Anderson** (city) Madison County
109	5.3	**Knox** (city) Starke County
109	5.3	**Mitchell** (city) Lawrence County
112	5.5	**Cedar Lake** (town) Lake County
112	5.5	**Leo-Cedarville** (town) Allen County
114	5.7	**Columbus** (city) Bartholomew County
114	5.7	**Marion** (city) Grant County
114	5.7	**New Haven** (city) Allen County
114	5.7	**Rensselaer** (city) Jasper County
118	5.8	**Gary** (city) Lake County
119	5.9	**Gas City** (city) Grant County
120	6.0	**Madison** (city) Jefferson County
121	6.1	**De Motte** (town) Jasper County
121	6.1	**Greenwood** (city) Johnson County
121	6.1	**Michigan City** (city) LaPorte County
124	6.3	**Mishawaka** (city) Saint Joseph County
125	6.6	**Salt Creek Commons** (CDP) Porter County
126	6.7	**Valparaiso** (city) Porter County
127	6.8	**Country Squire Lakes** (CDP) Jennings County
127	6.8	**McCordsville** (town) Hancock County
127	6.8	**Westville** (town) LaPorte County
130	6.9	**Lowell** (town) Lake County
131	7.1	**North Manchester** (town) Wabash County
132	7.3	**Nappanee** (city) Elkhart County
133	7.4	**Chesterton** (town) Porter County
133	7.4	**Notre Dame** (CDP) Saint Joseph County
135	7.6	**Charlestown** (city) Clark County
135	7.6	**Decatur** (city) Adams County
137	7.9	**Clarksville** (town) Clark County
137	7.9	**Dunlap** (CDP) Elkhart County
139	8.1	**Jasper** (city) Dubois County
139	8.1	**Roselawn** (CDP) Newton County
141	8.4	**Portland** (city) Jay County
141	8.4	**Shelbyville** (city) Shelby County
143	8.5	**Crawfordsville** (city) Montgomery County
144	8.6	**Avon** (town) Hendricks County
144	8.6	**Crown Point** (city) Lake County
146	8.7	**Fort Wayne** (city) Allen County
147	9.1	**Saint John** (town) Lake County
148	9.2	**Hebron** (town) Porter County
148	9.2	**Speedway** (town) Marion County
150	9.8	**Edinburgh** (town) Johnson County

Note: *This section ranks incorporated places and CDPs (Census Designated Places) with populations of 2,500 or more. Unincorporated postal areas were not considered. Please refer to the User Guide for additional information.*

Average Household Size

Top 150 Places Ranked in *Descending* Order

State Rank	Persons	Place
1	3.38	**Salt Creek Commons** (CDP) Porter County
2	3.16	**Middlebury** (town) Elkhart County
3	3.13	**Porter** (town) Porter County
4	3.10	**Georgetown** (town) Floyd County
4	3.10	**Winfield** (town) Lake County
6	3.07	**Hidden Valley** (CDP) Dearborn County
7	3.04	**Leo-Cedarville** (town) Allen County
8	3.01	**Dunlap** (CDP) Elkhart County
9	2.98	**Roselawn** (CDP) Newton County
10	2.97	**Lake Station** (city) Lake County
11	2.95	**Pittsboro** (town) Hendricks County
12	2.94	**Granger** (CDP) Saint Joseph County
13	2.92	**McCordsville** (town) Hancock County
13	2.92	**Osceola** (town) Saint Joseph County
15	2.91	**Avon** (town) Hendricks County
15	2.91	**Ligonier** (city) Noble County
17	2.89	**Whiteland** (town) Johnson County
18	2.88	**Saint John** (town) Lake County
19	2.86	**Westfield** (city) Hamilton County
20	2.85	**Butler** (city) DeKalb County
20	2.85	**Cedar Lake** (town) Lake County
20	2.85	**Whiting** (city) Lake County
23	2.84	**Huntertown** (town) Allen County
24	2.83	**Bargersville** (town) Johnson County
25	2.81	**Whitestown** (town) Boone County
26	2.79	**East Chicago** (city) Lake County
26	2.79	**Highland** (CDP) Vanderburgh County
26	2.79	**Lowell** (town) Lake County
26	2.79	**Zionsville** (town) Boone County
30	2.78	**Country Squire Lakes** (CDP) Jennings County
30	2.78	**Fishers** (city) Hamilton County
32	2.77	**Hebron** (town) Porter County
33	2.76	**Lakes of the Four Seasons** (CDP) Lake County
33	2.76	**Sellersburg** (town) Clark County
35	2.74	**Santa Claus** (town) Spencer County
36	2.73	**Huntingburg** (city) Dubois County
37	2.72	**New Whiteland** (town) Johnson County
38	2.71	**Charlestown** (city) Clark County
39	2.70	**Hammond** (city) Lake County
40	2.69	**Brownsburg** (town) Hendricks County
40	2.69	**Chandler** (town) Warrick County
40	2.69	**Cumberland** (town) Marion County
43	2.68	**Frankfort** (city) Clinton County
44	2.67	**Bright** (CDP) Dearborn County
44	2.67	**Noblesville** (city) Hamilton County
44	2.67	**Ossian** (town) Wells County
47	2.66	**Carmel** (city) Hamilton County
47	2.66	**Danville** (town) Hendricks County
47	2.66	**Fairmount** (town) Grant County
50	2.65	**Melody Hill** (CDP) Vanderburgh County
51	2.63	**Shorewood Forest** (CDP) Porter County
51	2.63	**South Haven** (CDP) Porter County
53	2.62	**Nappanee** (city) Elkhart County
53	2.62	**North Terre Haute** (CDP) Vigo County
55	2.61	**Dyer** (town) Lake County
55	2.61	**Elkhart** (city) Elkhart County
57	2.60	**Austin** (city) Scott County
57	2.60	**Brownstown** (town) Jackson County
57	2.60	**New Haven** (city) Allen County
60	2.59	**Fort Branch** (town) Gibson County
60	2.59	**Goshen** (city) Elkhart County
60	2.59	**Lawrence** (city) Marion County
60	2.59	**Munster** (town) Lake County
60	2.59	**Simonton Lake** (CDP) Elkhart County
65	2.57	**Greenwood** (city) Johnson County
66	2.56	**Chesterton** (town) Porter County
66	2.56	**Edinburgh** (town) Johnson County
66	2.56	**Garrett** (city) DeKalb County
66	2.56	**Heritage Lake** (CDP) Putnam County
66	2.56	**Upland** (town) Grant County
71	2.55	**Logansport** (city) Cass County
71	2.55	**Portage** (city) Porter County
73	2.54	**Alexandria** (city) Madison County
73	2.54	**Aurora** (city) Dearborn County
73	2.54	**Jeffersonville** (city) Clark County
73	2.54	**South Bend** (city) Saint Joseph County
73	2.54	**Yorktown** (town) Delaware County
78	2.53	**Franklin** (city) Johnson County
78	2.53	**Hobart** (city) Lake County
78	2.53	**Plymouth** (city) Marshall County
81	2.52	**Beech Grove** (city) Marion County
81	2.52	**Bicknell** (city) Knox County
81	2.52	**Knox** (city) Starke County
84	2.51	**Delphi** (city) Carroll County
84	2.51	**Indianapolis** (city) Marion County
84	2.51	**Plainfield** (town) Hendricks County
87	2.50	**Griffith** (town) Lake County
87	2.50	**Martinsville** (city) Morgan County
89	2.49	**Fortville** (town) Hancock County
89	2.49	**Hanover** (town) Jefferson County
89	2.49	**Merrillville** (town) Lake County
89	2.49	**Washington** (city) Daviess County
93	2.48	**Bremen** (town) Marshall County
93	2.48	**Centerville** (town) Wayne County
93	2.48	**Scottsburg** (city) Scott County
93	2.48	**Seymour** (city) Jackson County
97	2.47	**Cicero** (town) Hamilton County
97	2.47	**Crown Point** (city) Lake County
99	2.46	**Fort Wayne** (city) Allen County
99	2.46	**Schererville** (town) Lake County
99	2.46	**Warsaw** (city) Kosciusko County
102	2.45	**Mooresville** (town) Morgan County
103	2.44	**Columbus** (city) Bartholomew County
103	2.44	**Winona Lake** (town) Kosciusko County
105	2.43	**Gary** (city) Lake County
105	2.43	**Sheridan** (town) Hamilton County
107	2.42	**De Motte** (town) Jasper County
107	2.42	**Peru** (city) Miami County
109	2.41	**Lagrange** (town) LaGrange County
109	2.41	**North Vernon** (city) Jennings County
111	2.40	**Elwood** (city) Madison County
111	2.40	**Highland** (town) Lake County
111	2.40	**Shelbyville** (city) Shelby County
114	2.39	**Huntington** (city) Huntington County
115	2.38	**Boonville** (city) Warrick County
115	2.38	**Clarksville** (town) Clark County
115	2.38	**New Castle** (city) Henry County
115	2.38	**Paoli** (town) Orange County
115	2.38	**Princeton** (city) Gibson County
115	2.38	**Rensselaer** (city) Jasper County
121	2.37	**Gas City** (city) Grant County
121	2.37	**Greentown** (town) Howard County
121	2.37	**Jasper** (city) Dubois County
121	2.37	**Newburgh** (town) Warrick County
121	2.37	**Union City** (city) Randolph County
126	2.36	**Batesville** (city) Ripley County
126	2.36	**Greensburg** (city) Decatur County
126	2.36	**Speedway** (town) Marion County
129	2.35	**Brazil** (city) Clay County
129	2.35	**Greenfield** (city) Hancock County
129	2.35	**Monticello** (city) White County
129	2.35	**Mount Vernon** (city) Posey County
129	2.35	**Pendleton** (town) Madison County
129	2.35	**Syracuse** (town) Kosciusko County
129	2.35	**Westville** (town) LaPorte County
129	2.35	**Winamac** (town) Pulaski County
137	2.34	**Hartford City** (city) Blackford County
137	2.34	**West Lafayette** (city) Tippecanoe County
139	2.33	**Angola** (city) Steuben County
139	2.33	**Connersville** (city) Fayette County
139	2.33	**Ellettsville** (town) Monroe County
139	2.33	**Greendale** (city) Dearborn County
139	2.33	**Linton** (city) Greene County
139	2.33	**New Albany** (city) Floyd County
139	2.33	**Richmond** (city) Wayne County
146	2.32	**Tipton** (city) Tipton County
147	2.31	**Auburn** (city) DeKalb County
147	2.31	**La Porte** (city) LaPorte County
147	2.31	**Mishawaka** (city) Saint Joseph County
147	2.31	**Mitchell** (city) Lawrence County

Note: *This section ranks incorporated places and CDPs (Census Designated Places) with populations of 2,500 or more. Unincorporated postal areas were not considered. Please refer to the User Guide for additional information.*

Average Household Size

Top 150 Places Ranked in *Ascending* Order

State Rank	Persons	Place
1	2.08	**Madison** (city) Jefferson County
2	2.11	**Corydon** (town) Harrison County
2	2.11	**Sullivan** (city) Sullivan County
4	2.14	**Lawrenceburg** (city) Dearborn County
5	2.16	**Loogootee** (city) Martin County
6	2.18	**Lebanon** (city) Boone County
6	2.18	**Wabash** (city) Wabash County
8	2.19	**Clinton** (city) Vermillion County
8	2.19	**Salem** (city) Washington County
10	2.21	**Columbia City** (city) Whitley County
10	2.21	**Vincennes** (city) Knox County
12	2.22	**Attica** (city) Fountain County
12	2.22	**Brookville** (town) Franklin County
12	2.22	**Michigan City** (city) LaPorte County
15	2.23	**North Manchester** (town) Wabash County
15	2.23	**Rochester** (city) Fulton County
17	2.24	**Evansville** (city) Vanderburgh County
17	2.24	**Rockville** (town) Parke County
19	2.25	**Anderson** (city) Madison County
19	2.25	**Greencastle** (city) Putnam County
19	2.25	**Kokomo** (city) Howard County
19	2.25	**Muncie** (city) Delaware County
19	2.25	**Portland** (city) Jay County
24	2.26	**Bloomington** (city) Monroe County
24	2.26	**Decatur** (city) Adams County
24	2.26	**Marion** (city) Grant County
27	2.27	**Bedford** (city) Lawrence County
27	2.27	**Kendallville** (city) Noble County
27	2.27	**Lafayette** (city) Tippecanoe County
30	2.28	**Bluffton** (city) Wells County
31	2.29	**Notre Dame** (CDP) Saint Joseph County
31	2.29	**Tell City** (city) Perry County
33	2.30	**Berne** (city) Adams County
33	2.30	**Crawfordsville** (city) Montgomery County
33	2.30	**Rushville** (city) Rush County
33	2.30	**Smithville-Sanders** (CDP) Monroe County
33	2.30	**Terre Haute** (city) Vigo County
33	2.30	**Winchester** (city) Randolph County
39	2.31	**Auburn** (city) DeKalb County
39	2.31	**La Porte** (city) LaPorte County
39	2.31	**Mishawaka** (city) Saint Joseph County
39	2.31	**Mitchell** (city) Lawrence County
39	2.31	**Valparaiso** (city) Porter County
44	2.32	**Tipton** (city) Tipton County
45	2.33	**Angola** (city) Steuben County
45	2.33	**Connersville** (city) Fayette County
45	2.33	**Ellettsville** (town) Monroe County
45	2.33	**Greendale** (city) Dearborn County
45	2.33	**Linton** (city) Greene County
45	2.33	**New Albany** (city) Floyd County
45	2.33	**Richmond** (city) Wayne County
52	2.34	**Hartford City** (city) Blackford County
52	2.34	**West Lafayette** (city) Tippecanoe County
54	2.35	**Brazil** (city) Clay County
54	2.35	**Greenfield** (city) Hancock County
54	2.35	**Monticello** (city) White County
54	2.35	**Mount Vernon** (city) Posey County
54	2.35	**Pendleton** (town) Madison County
54	2.35	**Syracuse** (town) Kosciusko County
54	2.35	**Westville** (town) LaPorte County
54	2.35	**Winamac** (town) Pulaski County
62	2.36	**Batesville** (city) Ripley County
62	2.36	**Greensburg** (city) Decatur County
62	2.36	**Speedway** (town) Marion County
65	2.37	**Gas City** (city) Grant County
65	2.37	**Greentown** (town) Howard County
65	2.37	**Jasper** (city) Dubois County
65	2.37	**Newburgh** (town) Warrick County
65	2.37	**Union City** (city) Randolph County
70	2.38	**Boonville** (city) Warrick County
70	2.38	**Clarksville** (town) Clark County
70	2.38	**New Castle** (city) Henry County
70	2.38	**Paoli** (town) Orange County
70	2.38	**Princeton** (city) Gibson County
70	2.38	**Rensselaer** (city) Jasper County
76	2.39	**Huntington** (city) Huntington County
77	2.40	**Elwood** (city) Madison County
77	2.40	**Highland** (town) Lake County
77	2.40	**Shelbyville** (city) Shelby County
80	2.41	**Lagrange** (town) LaGrange County
80	2.41	**North Vernon** (city) Jennings County
82	2.42	**De Motte** (town) Jasper County
82	2.42	**Peru** (city) Miami County
84	2.43	**Gary** (city) Lake County
84	2.43	**Sheridan** (town) Hamilton County
86	2.44	**Columbus** (city) Bartholomew County
86	2.44	**Winona Lake** (town) Kosciusko County
88	2.45	**Mooresville** (town) Morgan County
89	2.46	**Fort Wayne** (city) Allen County
89	2.46	**Schererville** (town) Lake County
89	2.46	**Warsaw** (city) Kosciusko County
92	2.47	**Cicero** (town) Hamilton County
92	2.47	**Crown Point** (city) Lake County
94	2.48	**Bremen** (town) Marshall County
94	2.48	**Centerville** (town) Wayne County
94	2.48	**Scottsburg** (city) Scott County
94	2.48	**Seymour** (city) Jackson County
98	2.49	**Fortville** (town) Hancock County
98	2.49	**Hanover** (town) Jefferson County
98	2.49	**Merrillville** (town) Lake County
98	2.49	**Washington** (city) Daviess County
102	2.50	**Griffith** (town) Lake County
102	2.50	**Martinsville** (city) Morgan County
104	2.51	**Delphi** (city) Carroll County
104	2.51	**Indianapolis** (city) Marion County
104	2.51	**Plainfield** (town) Hendricks County
107	2.52	**Beech Grove** (city) Marion County
107	2.52	**Bicknell** (city) Knox County
107	2.52	**Knox** (city) Starke County
110	2.53	**Franklin** (city) Johnson County
110	2.53	**Hobart** (city) Lake County
110	2.53	**Plymouth** (city) Marshall County
113	2.54	**Alexandria** (city) Madison County
113	2.54	**Aurora** (city) Dearborn County
113	2.54	**Jeffersonville** (city) Clark County
113	2.54	**South Bend** (city) Saint Joseph County
113	2.54	**Yorktown** (town) Delaware County
118	2.55	**Logansport** (city) Cass County
118	2.55	**Portage** (city) Porter County
120	2.56	**Chesterton** (town) Porter County
120	2.56	**Edinburgh** (town) Johnson County
120	2.56	**Garrett** (city) DeKalb County
120	2.56	**Heritage Lake** (CDP) Putnam County
120	2.56	**Upland** (town) Grant County
125	2.57	**Greenwood** (city) Johnson County
126	2.59	**Fort Branch** (town) Gibson County
126	2.59	**Goshen** (city) Elkhart County
126	2.59	**Lawrence** (city) Marion County
126	2.59	**Munster** (town) Lake County
126	2.59	**Simonton Lake** (CDP) Elkhart County
131	2.60	**Austin** (city) Scott County
131	2.60	**Brownstown** (town) Jackson County
131	2.60	**New Haven** (city) Allen County
134	2.61	**Dyer** (town) Lake County
134	2.61	**Elkhart** (city) Elkhart County
136	2.62	**Nappanee** (city) Elkhart County
136	2.62	**North Terre Haute** (CDP) Vigo County
138	2.63	**Shorewood Forest** (CDP) Porter County
138	2.63	**South Haven** (CDP) Porter County
140	2.65	**Melody Hill** (CDP) Vanderburgh County
141	2.66	**Carmel** (city) Hamilton County
141	2.66	**Danville** (town) Hendricks County
141	2.66	**Fairmount** (town) Grant County
144	2.67	**Bright** (CDP) Dearborn County
144	2.67	**Noblesville** (city) Hamilton County
144	2.67	**Ossian** (town) Wells County
147	2.68	**Frankfort** (city) Clinton County
148	2.69	**Brownsburg** (town) Hendricks County
148	2.69	**Chandler** (town) Warrick County
148	2.69	**Cumberland** (town) Marion County

Note: *This section ranks incorporated places and CDPs (Census Designated Places) with populations of 2,500 or more. Unincorporated postal areas were not considered. Please refer to the User Guide for additional information.*

Median Age

Top 150 Places Ranked in *Descending* Order

State Rank	Years	Place
1	50.1	**Shorewood Forest** (CDP) Porter County
2	47.6	**Smithville-Sanders** (CDP) Monroe County
3	47.1	**Corydon** (town) Harrison County
4	45.5	**Dyer** (town) Lake County
5	45.2	**Munster** (town) Lake County
6	45.1	**Newburgh** (town) Warrick County
6	45.1	**Sullivan** (city) Sullivan County
8	44.0	**Lakes of the Four Seasons** (CDP) Lake County
8	44.0	**Rochester** (city) Fulton County
10	43.9	**Berne** (city) Adams County
10	43.9	**Mooresville** (town) Morgan County
12	43.8	**Hidden Valley** (CDP) Dearborn County
13	43.7	**Mitchell** (city) Lawrence County
14	43.6	**Highland** (CDP) Vanderburgh County
14	43.6	**Saint John** (town) Lake County
16	43.4	**Lawrenceburg** (city) Dearborn County
17	43.2	**Bright** (CDP) Dearborn County
17	43.2	**Schererville** (town) Lake County
19	43.1	**Heritage Lake** (CDP) Putnam County
20	42.6	**Linton** (city) Greene County
20	42.6	**Madison** (city) Jefferson County
22	42.5	**Highland** (town) Lake County
23	42.4	**Clinton** (city) Vermillion County
24	42.2	**Cicero** (town) Hamilton County
24	42.2	**Mount Vernon** (city) Posey County
26	42.0	**Batesville** (city) Ripley County
26	42.0	**Granger** (CDP) Saint Joseph County
28	41.9	**Fort Branch** (town) Gibson County
29	41.8	**Bedford** (city) Lawrence County
29	41.8	**Simonton Lake** (CDP) Elkhart County
31	41.7	**Connersville** (city) Fayette County
32	41.5	**Clarksville** (town) Clark County
32	41.5	**Crown Point** (city) Lake County
32	41.5	**Rushville** (city) Rush County
35	41.4	**Santa Claus** (town) Spencer County
36	41.2	**Melody Hill** (CDP) Vanderburgh County
37	41.1	**Rensselaer** (city) Jasper County
37	41.1	**Wabash** (city) Wabash County
39	40.8	**Brookville** (town) Franklin County
39	40.8	**Gas City** (city) Grant County
39	40.8	**New Castle** (city) Henry County
42	40.6	**Rockville** (town) Parke County
43	40.5	**Attica** (city) Fountain County
43	40.5	**Lebanon** (city) Boone County
45	40.3	**Boonville** (city) Warrick County
45	40.3	**Hartford City** (city) Blackford County
47	40.2	**Paoli** (town) Orange County
47	40.2	**Yorktown** (town) Delaware County
49	40.1	**Knox** (city) Starke County
49	40.1	**Tell City** (city) Perry County
51	40.0	**Jasper** (city) Dubois County
52	39.9	**Kokomo** (city) Howard County
52	39.9	**Martinsville** (city) Morgan County
54	39.8	**Auburn** (city) DeKalb County
54	39.8	**Chesterton** (town) Porter County
56	39.7	**Austin** (city) Scott County
56	39.7	**Greendale** (city) Dearborn County
56	39.7	**Salem** (city) Washington County
59	39.6	**Greentown** (town) Howard County
60	39.5	**Carmel** (city) Hamilton County
61	39.4	**Delphi** (city) Carroll County
61	39.4	**Loogootee** (city) Martin County
63	39.3	**Richmond** (city) Wayne County
64	39.2	**Greenfield** (city) Hancock County
65	39.1	**Hobart** (city) Lake County
65	39.1	**Portage** (city) Porter County
67	39.0	**Ellettsville** (town) Monroe County
68	38.9	**Elwood** (city) Madison County
68	38.9	**Pendleton** (town) Madison County
68	38.9	**Winamac** (town) Pulaski County
71	38.8	**Centerville** (town) Wayne County
71	38.8	**Fortville** (town) Hancock County
71	38.8	**Tipton** (city) Tipton County
74	38.7	**Decatur** (city) Adams County
75	38.6	**Bluffton** (city) Wells County
75	38.6	**Gary** (city) Lake County
77	38.5	**De Motte** (town) Jasper County
78	38.3	**Osceola** (town) Saint Joseph County
79	38.2	**Edinburgh** (town) Johnson County
79	38.2	**Jeffersonville** (city) Clark County
79	38.2	**Merrillville** (town) Lake County
79	38.2	**New Albany** (city) Floyd County
83	38.1	**Kendallville** (city) Noble County
83	38.1	**Monticello** (city) White County
83	38.1	**Winchester** (city) Randolph County
83	38.1	**Zionsville** (town) Boone County
87	38.0	**Franklin** (city) Johnson County
87	38.0	**Peru** (city) Miami County
89	37.9	**Fairmount** (town) Grant County
89	37.9	**South Haven** (CDP) Porter County
91	37.8	**Columbia City** (city) Whitley County
91	37.8	**Danville** (town) Hendricks County
93	37.7	**Plainfield** (town) Hendricks County
94	37.4	**Anderson** (city) Madison County
95	37.3	**Brownsburg** (town) Hendricks County
95	37.3	**Lowell** (town) Lake County
95	37.3	**North Vernon** (city) Jennings County
95	37.3	**Winfield** (town) Lake County
99	37.2	**Dunlap** (CDP) Elkhart County
99	37.2	**Evansville** (city) Vanderburgh County
99	37.2	**Roselawn** (CDP) Newton County
99	37.2	**Scottsburg** (city) Scott County
103	37.1	**Leo-Cedarville** (town) Allen County
103	37.1	**Michigan City** (city) LaPorte County
105	37.0	**Crawfordsville** (city) Montgomery County
105	37.0	**Greensburg** (city) Decatur County
105	37.0	**North Terre Haute** (CDP) Vigo County
105	37.0	**Union City** (city) Randolph County
105	37.0	**Washington** (city) Daviess County
110	36.8	**Seymour** (city) Jackson County
110	36.8	**Syracuse** (town) Kosciusko County
112	36.7	**Griffith** (town) Lake County
112	36.7	**Shelbyville** (city) Shelby County
114	36.5	**Beech Grove** (city) Marion County
114	36.5	**La Porte** (city) LaPorte County
116	36.3	**Princeton** (city) Gibson County
117	36.2	**Brownstown** (town) Jackson County
117	36.2	**Columbus** (city) Bartholomew County
117	36.2	**Garrett** (city) DeKalb County
120	36.1	**Bicknell** (city) Knox County
120	36.1	**Charlestown** (city) Clark County
120	36.1	**Sellersburg** (town) Clark County
123	36.0	**Aurora** (city) Dearborn County
124	35.9	**Lagrange** (town) LaGrange County
125	35.7	**Huntington** (city) Huntington County
126	35.6	**Goshen** (city) Elkhart County
127	35.5	**Cumberland** (town) Marion County
127	35.5	**Greenwood** (city) Johnson County
127	35.5	**Portland** (city) Jay County
130	35.4	**Lake Station** (city) Lake County
130	35.4	**Logansport** (city) Cass County
130	35.4	**Mishawaka** (city) Saint Joseph County
133	35.3	**Avon** (town) Hendricks County
133	35.3	**Huntertown** (town) Allen County
135	35.2	**Fishers** (city) Hamilton County
136	35.1	**Brazil** (city) Clay County
136	35.1	**Marion** (city) Grant County
136	35.1	**New Haven** (city) Allen County
136	35.1	**Westville** (town) LaPorte County
140	35.0	**Lawrence** (city) Marion County
141	34.9	**Fort Wayne** (city) Allen County
141	34.9	**Sheridan** (town) Hamilton County
143	34.6	**North Manchester** (town) Wabash County
143	34.6	**Whiteland** (town) Johnson County
145	34.5	**Cedar Lake** (town) Lake County
145	34.5	**Country Squire Lakes** (CDP) Jennings County
145	34.5	**Ossian** (town) Wells County
145	34.5	**Westfield** (city) Hamilton County
149	34.4	**Middlebury** (town) Elkhart County
149	34.4	**Whiting** (city) Lake County

Note: *This section ranks incorporated places and CDPs (Census Designated Places) with populations of 2,500 or more. Unincorporated postal areas were not considered. Please refer to the User Guide for additional information.*

Median Age

Top 150 Places Ranked in *Ascending* Order

State Rank	Years	Place
1	20.6	**Notre Dame** (CDP) Saint Joseph County
2	21.7	**West Lafayette** (city) Tippecanoe County
3	22.2	**Upland** (town) Grant County
4	23.8	**Bloomington** (city) Monroe County
5	24.8	**Hanover** (town) Jefferson County
6	26.3	**Greencastle** (city) Putnam County
7	28.8	**Muncie** (city) Delaware County
8	29.8	**Angola** (city) Steuben County
8	29.8	**Whitestown** (town) Boone County
10	30.1	**Winona Lake** (town) Kosciusko County
11	31.4	**Ligonier** (city) Noble County
12	31.7	**East Chicago** (city) Lake County
13	31.8	**Warsaw** (city) Kosciusko County
14	31.9	**McCordsville** (town) Hancock County
15	32.1	**Nappanee** (city) Elkhart County
16	32.4	**Lafayette** (city) Tippecanoe County
16	32.4	**Salt Creek Commons** (CDP) Porter County
18	32.6	**Huntingburg** (city) Dubois County
18	32.6	**Terre Haute** (city) Vigo County
20	32.7	**Hebron** (town) Porter County
21	32.8	**Porter** (town) Porter County
22	32.9	**Butler** (city) DeKalb County
23	33.4	**Chandler** (town) Warrick County
23	33.4	**Elkhart** (city) Elkhart County
23	33.4	**South Bend** (city) Saint Joseph County
26	33.5	**Bargersville** (town) Johnson County
26	33.5	**Georgetown** (town) Floyd County
26	33.5	**Noblesville** (city) Hamilton County
26	33.5	**Speedway** (town) Marion County
30	33.6	**Alexandria** (city) Madison County
30	33.6	**New Whiteland** (town) Johnson County
32	33.9	**Hammond** (city) Lake County
32	33.9	**Plymouth** (city) Marshall County
34	34.0	**Frankfort** (city) Clinton County
34	34.0	**Vincennes** (city) Knox County
36	34.1	**Indianapolis** (city) Marion County
36	34.1	**Pittsboro** (town) Hendricks County
38	34.2	**Bremen** (town) Marshall County
38	34.2	**Valparaiso** (city) Porter County
40	34.4	**Middlebury** (town) Elkhart County
40	34.4	**Whiting** (city) Lake County
42	34.5	**Cedar Lake** (town) Lake County
42	34.5	**Country Squire Lakes** (CDP) Jennings County
42	34.5	**Ossian** (town) Wells County
42	34.5	**Westfield** (city) Hamilton County
46	34.6	**North Manchester** (town) Wabash County
46	34.6	**Whiteland** (town) Johnson County
48	34.9	**Fort Wayne** (city) Allen County
48	34.9	**Sheridan** (town) Hamilton County
50	35.0	**Lawrence** (city) Marion County
51	35.1	**Brazil** (city) Clay County
51	35.1	**Marion** (city) Grant County
51	35.1	**New Haven** (city) Allen County
51	35.1	**Westville** (town) LaPorte County
55	35.2	**Fishers** (city) Hamilton County
56	35.3	**Avon** (town) Hendricks County
56	35.3	**Huntertown** (town) Allen County
58	35.4	**Lake Station** (city) Lake County
58	35.4	**Logansport** (city) Cass County
58	35.4	**Mishawaka** (city) Saint Joseph County
61	35.5	**Cumberland** (town) Marion County
61	35.5	**Greenwood** (city) Johnson County
61	35.5	**Portland** (city) Jay County
64	35.6	**Goshen** (city) Elkhart County
65	35.7	**Huntington** (city) Huntington County
66	35.9	**Lagrange** (town) LaGrange County
67	36.0	**Aurora** (city) Dearborn County
68	36.1	**Bicknell** (city) Knox County
68	36.1	**Charlestown** (city) Clark County
68	36.1	**Sellersburg** (town) Clark County
71	36.2	**Brownstown** (town) Jackson County
71	36.2	**Columbus** (city) Bartholomew County
71	36.2	**Garrett** (city) DeKalb County
74	36.3	**Princeton** (city) Gibson County
75	36.5	**Beech Grove** (city) Marion County
75	36.5	**La Porte** (city) LaPorte County
77	36.7	**Griffith** (town) Lake County
77	36.7	**Shelbyville** (city) Shelby County
79	36.8	**Seymour** (city) Jackson County
79	36.8	**Syracuse** (town) Kosciusko County
81	37.0	**Crawfordsville** (city) Montgomery County
81	37.0	**Greensburg** (city) Decatur County
81	37.0	**North Terre Haute** (CDP) Vigo County
81	37.0	**Union City** (city) Randolph County
81	37.0	**Washington** (city) Daviess County
86	37.1	**Leo-Cedarville** (town) Allen County
86	37.1	**Michigan City** (city) LaPorte County
88	37.2	**Dunlap** (CDP) Elkhart County
88	37.2	**Evansville** (city) Vanderburgh County
88	37.2	**Roselawn** (CDP) Newton County
88	37.2	**Scottsburg** (city) Scott County
92	37.3	**Brownsburg** (town) Hendricks County
92	37.3	**Lowell** (town) Lake County
92	37.3	**North Vernon** (city) Jennings County
92	37.3	**Winfield** (town) Lake County
96	37.4	**Anderson** (city) Madison County
97	37.7	**Plainfield** (town) Hendricks County
98	37.8	**Columbia City** (city) Whitley County
98	37.8	**Danville** (town) Hendricks County
100	37.9	**Fairmount** (town) Grant County
100	37.9	**South Haven** (CDP) Porter County
102	38.0	**Franklin** (city) Johnson County
102	38.0	**Peru** (city) Miami County
104	38.1	**Kendallville** (city) Noble County
104	38.1	**Monticello** (city) White County
104	38.1	**Winchester** (city) Randolph County
104	38.1	**Zionsville** (town) Boone County
108	38.2	**Edinburgh** (town) Johnson County
108	38.2	**Jeffersonville** (city) Clark County
108	38.2	**Merrillville** (town) Lake County
108	38.2	**New Albany** (city) Floyd County
112	38.3	**Osceola** (town) Saint Joseph County
113	38.5	**De Motte** (town) Jasper County
114	38.6	**Bluffton** (city) Wells County
114	38.6	**Gary** (city) Lake County
116	38.7	**Decatur** (city) Adams County
117	38.8	**Centerville** (town) Wayne County
117	38.8	**Fortville** (town) Hancock County
117	38.8	**Tipton** (city) Tipton County
120	38.9	**Elwood** (city) Madison County
120	38.9	**Pendleton** (town) Madison County
120	38.9	**Winamac** (town) Pulaski County
123	39.0	**Ellettsville** (town) Monroe County
124	39.1	**Hobart** (city) Lake County
124	39.1	**Portage** (city) Porter County
126	39.2	**Greenfield** (city) Hancock County
127	39.3	**Richmond** (city) Wayne County
128	39.4	**Delphi** (city) Carroll County
128	39.4	**Loogootee** (city) Martin County
130	39.5	**Carmel** (city) Hamilton County
131	39.6	**Greentown** (town) Howard County
132	39.7	**Austin** (city) Scott County
132	39.7	**Greendale** (city) Dearborn County
132	39.7	**Salem** (city) Washington County
135	39.8	**Auburn** (city) DeKalb County
135	39.8	**Chesterton** (town) Porter County
137	39.9	**Kokomo** (city) Howard County
137	39.9	**Martinsville** (city) Morgan County
139	40.0	**Jasper** (city) Dubois County
140	40.1	**Knox** (city) Starke County
140	40.1	**Tell City** (city) Perry County
142	40.2	**Paoli** (town) Orange County
142	40.2	**Yorktown** (town) Delaware County
144	40.3	**Boonville** (city) Warrick County
144	40.3	**Hartford City** (city) Blackford County
146	40.5	**Attica** (city) Fountain County
146	40.5	**Lebanon** (city) Boone County
148	40.6	**Rockville** (town) Parke County
149	40.8	**Brookville** (town) Franklin County
149	40.8	**Gas City** (city) Grant County

Note: *This section ranks incorporated places and CDPs (Census Designated Places) with populations of 2,500 or more. Unincorporated postal areas were not considered. Please refer to the User Guide for additional information.*

Population Under Age 18

Top 150 Places Ranked in *Descending* Order

State Rank	Percent	Place
1	35.1	**Whitestown** (town) Boone County
2	34.0	**Georgetown** (town) Floyd County
3	33.7	**Salt Creek Commons** (CDP) Porter County
4	32.4	**Hebron** (town) Porter County
5	31.8	**Huntingburg** (city) Dubois County
6	31.5	**Leo-Cedarville** (town) Allen County
6	31.5	**Union City** (city) Randolph County
8	31.4	**Ligonier** (city) Noble County
9	31.0	**Westfield** (city) Hamilton County
10	30.9	**Fishers** (city) Hamilton County
10	30.9	**Pittsboro** (town) Hendricks County
12	30.2	**Bargersville** (town) Johnson County
12	30.2	**Huntertown** (town) Allen County
14	30.1	**Chandler** (town) Warrick County
14	30.1	**East Chicago** (city) Lake County
14	30.1	**Middlebury** (town) Elkhart County
17	29.9	**Zionsville** (town) Boone County
18	29.4	**Cumberland** (town) Marion County
18	29.4	**Nappanee** (city) Elkhart County
20	29.1	**Sheridan** (town) Hamilton County
21	28.6	**Frankfort** (city) Clinton County
22	28.3	**New Whiteland** (town) Johnson County
22	28.3	**Noblesville** (city) Hamilton County
24	28.2	**Bremen** (town) Marshall County
25	28.1	**Hidden Valley** (CDP) Dearborn County
25	28.1	**Lake Station** (city) Lake County
25	28.1	**Winfield** (town) Lake County
28	27.9	**Granger** (CDP) Saint Joseph County
29	27.8	**McCordsville** (town) Hancock County
30	27.6	**Avon** (town) Hendricks County
30	27.6	**Ossian** (town) Wells County
32	27.5	**Elkhart** (city) Elkhart County
32	27.5	**Plymouth** (city) Marshall County
32	27.5	**Sellersburg** (town) Clark County
35	27.2	**Fairmount** (town) Grant County
35	27.2	**Porter** (town) Porter County
37	27.1	**Cedar Lake** (town) Lake County
37	27.1	**Dunlap** (CDP) Elkhart County
37	27.1	**Osceola** (town) Saint Joseph County
40	27.0	**Brownstown** (town) Jackson County
41	26.9	**Tipton** (city) Tipton County
42	26.8	**Carmel** (city) Hamilton County
42	26.8	**Danville** (town) Hendricks County
42	26.8	**Roselawn** (CDP) Newton County
42	26.8	**South Bend** (city) Saint Joseph County
46	26.6	**Beech Grove** (city) Marion County
47	26.5	**Brazil** (city) Clay County
47	26.5	**Garrett** (city) DeKalb County
47	26.5	**Lawrence** (city) Marion County
50	26.4	**Charlestown** (city) Clark County
50	26.4	**Lowell** (town) Lake County
52	26.3	**New Haven** (city) Allen County
52	26.3	**Syracuse** (town) Kosciusko County
54	26.2	**Centerville** (town) Wayne County
54	26.2	**Goshen** (city) Elkhart County
56	26.1	**Greentown** (town) Howard County
57	26.0	**Logansport** (city) Cass County
57	26.0	**Saint John** (town) Lake County
57	26.0	**Seymour** (city) Jackson County
57	26.0	**Washington** (city) Daviess County
61	25.9	**Bicknell** (city) Knox County
61	25.9	**De Motte** (town) Jasper County
63	25.8	**Hammond** (city) Lake County
64	25.7	**Fort Wayne** (city) Allen County
64	25.7	**Whiting** (city) Lake County
66	25.6	**Warsaw** (city) Kosciusko County
67	25.4	**Country Squire Lakes** (CDP) Jennings County
67	25.4	**Gary** (city) Lake County
67	25.4	**Greenwood** (city) Johnson County
67	25.4	**Santa Claus** (town) Spencer County
71	25.3	**Aurora** (city) Dearborn County
71	25.3	**Princeton** (city) Gibson County
73	25.2	**Austin** (city) Scott County
73	25.2	**Bluffton** (city) Wells County
73	25.2	**Boonville** (city) Warrick County
73	25.2	**Greensburg** (city) Decatur County
73	25.2	**La Porte** (city) LaPorte County
73	25.2	**Melody Hill** (CDP) Vanderburgh County
73	25.2	**Monticello** (city) White County
80	25.0	**Portland** (city) Jay County
81	24.9	**Gas City** (city) Grant County
81	24.9	**Kendallville** (city) Noble County
83	24.8	**Lagrange** (town) LaGrange County
83	24.8	**Yorktown** (town) Delaware County
85	24.7	**Indianapolis** (city) Marion County
85	24.7	**Loogootee** (city) Martin County
85	24.7	**Simonton Lake** (CDP) Elkhart County
88	24.6	**Shelbyville** (city) Shelby County
88	24.6	**Winamac** (town) Pulaski County
90	24.4	**Peru** (city) Miami County
91	24.3	**Brownsburg** (town) Hendricks County
91	24.3	**Columbus** (city) Bartholomew County
91	24.3	**Decatur** (city) Adams County
94	24.2	**Alexandria** (city) Madison County
94	24.2	**Plainfield** (town) Hendricks County
94	24.2	**Winchester** (city) Randolph County
97	24.0	**Butler** (city) DeKalb County
97	24.0	**Merrillville** (town) Lake County
99	23.9	**Ellettsville** (town) Monroe County
99	23.9	**Rensselaer** (city) Jasper County
101	23.8	**Hartford City** (city) Blackford County
102	23.7	**Highland** (CDP) Vanderburgh County
103	23.6	**Speedway** (town) Marion County
104	23.5	**Chesterton** (town) Porter County
104	23.5	**Franklin** (city) Johnson County
106	23.4	**Batesville** (city) Ripley County
106	23.4	**Jasper** (city) Dubois County
106	23.4	**North Terre Haute** (CDP) Vigo County
106	23.4	**Tell City** (city) Perry County
110	23.2	**Auburn** (city) DeKalb County
110	23.2	**Pendleton** (town) Madison County
112	23.1	**Delphi** (city) Carroll County
112	23.1	**Greenfield** (city) Hancock County
112	23.1	**Hobart** (city) Lake County
115	22.9	**Jeffersonville** (city) Clark County
115	22.9	**North Vernon** (city) Jennings County
117	22.7	**Bright** (CDP) Dearborn County
117	22.7	**Clinton** (city) Vermillion County
117	22.7	**Mishawaka** (city) Saint Joseph County
117	22.7	**South Haven** (CDP) Porter County
121	22.6	**Edinburgh** (town) Johnson County
121	22.6	**New Castle** (city) Henry County
123	22.5	**Kokomo** (city) Howard County
124	22.4	**Crawfordsville** (city) Montgomery County
124	22.4	**Huntington** (city) Huntington County
124	22.4	**Shorewood Forest** (CDP) Porter County
127	22.3	**Lafayette** (city) Tippecanoe County
128	22.2	**Anderson** (city) Madison County
128	22.2	**Michigan City** (city) LaPorte County
130	22.1	**Brookville** (town) Franklin County
130	22.1	**Portage** (city) Porter County
130	22.1	**Whiteland** (town) Johnson County
133	21.9	**Crown Point** (city) Lake County
133	21.9	**Fort Branch** (town) Gibson County
135	21.8	**Fortville** (town) Hancock County
135	21.8	**Rushville** (city) Rush County
137	21.7	**Elwood** (city) Madison County
137	21.7	**Griffith** (town) Lake County
137	21.7	**Linton** (city) Greene County
140	21.5	**Evansville** (city) Vanderburgh County
141	21.4	**Connersville** (city) Fayette County
142	21.3	**Martinsville** (city) Morgan County
142	21.3	**Salem** (city) Washington County
144	21.2	**North Manchester** (town) Wabash County
144	21.2	**Richmond** (city) Wayne County
144	21.2	**Valparaiso** (city) Porter County
147	21.1	**Bedford** (city) Lawrence County
147	21.1	**Columbia City** (city) Whitley County
147	21.1	**Lawrenceburg** (city) Dearborn County
147	21.1	**Lebanon** (city) Boone County

Note: *This section ranks incorporated places and CDPs (Census Designated Places) with populations of 2,500 or more. Unincorporated postal areas were not considered. Please refer to the User Guide for additional information.*

Population Under Age 18

Top 150 Places Ranked in *Ascending* Order

State Rank	Percent	Place
1	0.3	**Notre Dame** (CDP) Saint Joseph County
2	8.0	**Westville** (town) LaPorte County
3	10.4	**West Lafayette** (city) Tippecanoe County
4	11.4	**Bloomington** (city) Monroe County
5	14.1	**Upland** (town) Grant County
6	15.6	**Sullivan** (city) Sullivan County
7	16.5	**Corydon** (town) Harrison County
8	16.8	**Muncie** (city) Delaware County
9	17.5	**Smithville-Sanders** (CDP) Monroe County
10	17.7	**Madison** (city) Jefferson County
11	18.0	**Greencastle** (city) Putnam County
11	18.0	**Hanover** (town) Jefferson County
13	18.2	**Knox** (city) Starke County
14	18.3	**Winona Lake** (town) Kosciusko County
15	18.5	**Heritage Lake** (CDP) Putnam County
16	18.8	**Dyer** (town) Lake County
17	19.0	**Clarksville** (town) Clark County
18	19.1	**Vincennes** (city) Knox County
19	19.4	**Terre Haute** (city) Vigo County
20	19.6	**Mount Vernon** (city) Posey County
21	19.7	**Newburgh** (town) Warrick County
22	20.1	**Marion** (city) Grant County
22	20.1	**Paoli** (town) Orange County
22	20.1	**Schererville** (town) Lake County
25	20.2	**Wabash** (city) Wabash County
26	20.3	**Berne** (city) Adams County
26	20.3	**Rockville** (town) Parke County
26	20.3	**Scottsburg** (city) Scott County
29	20.4	**Attica** (city) Fountain County
29	20.4	**Lakes of the Four Seasons** (CDP) Lake County
31	20.5	**Mooresville** (town) Morgan County
32	20.6	**Rochester** (city) Fulton County
33	20.7	**Cicero** (town) Hamilton County
33	20.7	**New Albany** (city) Floyd County
35	20.8	**Angola** (city) Steuben County
35	20.8	**Highland** (town) Lake County
35	20.8	**Mitchell** (city) Lawrence County
35	20.8	**Munster** (town) Lake County
39	20.9	**Greendale** (city) Dearborn County
40	21.1	**Bedford** (city) Lawrence County
40	21.1	**Columbia City** (city) Whitley County
40	21.1	**Lawrenceburg** (city) Dearborn County
40	21.1	**Lebanon** (city) Boone County
44	21.2	**North Manchester** (town) Wabash County
44	21.2	**Richmond** (city) Wayne County
44	21.2	**Valparaiso** (city) Porter County
47	21.3	**Martinsville** (city) Morgan County
47	21.3	**Salem** (city) Washington County
49	21.4	**Connersville** (city) Fayette County
50	21.5	**Evansville** (city) Vanderburgh County
51	21.7	**Elwood** (city) Madison County
51	21.7	**Griffith** (town) Lake County
51	21.7	**Linton** (city) Greene County
54	21.8	**Fortville** (town) Hancock County
54	21.8	**Rushville** (city) Rush County
56	21.9	**Crown Point** (city) Lake County
56	21.9	**Fort Branch** (town) Gibson County
58	22.1	**Brookville** (town) Franklin County
58	22.1	**Portage** (city) Porter County
58	22.1	**Whiteland** (town) Johnson County
61	22.2	**Anderson** (city) Madison County
61	22.2	**Michigan City** (city) LaPorte County
63	22.3	**Lafayette** (city) Tippecanoe County
64	22.4	**Crawfordsville** (city) Montgomery County
64	22.4	**Huntington** (city) Huntington County
64	22.4	**Shorewood Forest** (CDP) Porter County
67	22.5	**Kokomo** (city) Howard County
68	22.6	**Edinburgh** (town) Johnson County
68	22.6	**New Castle** (city) Henry County
70	22.7	**Bright** (CDP) Dearborn County
70	22.7	**Clinton** (city) Vermillion County
70	22.7	**Mishawaka** (city) Saint Joseph County
70	22.7	**South Haven** (CDP) Porter County
74	22.9	**Jeffersonville** (city) Clark County
74	22.9	**North Vernon** (city) Jennings County
76	23.1	**Delphi** (city) Carroll County
76	23.1	**Greenfield** (city) Hancock County
76	23.1	**Hobart** (city) Lake County
79	23.2	**Auburn** (city) DeKalb County
79	23.2	**Pendleton** (town) Madison County
81	23.4	**Batesville** (city) Ripley County
81	23.4	**Jasper** (city) Dubois County
81	23.4	**North Terre Haute** (CDP) Vigo County
81	23.4	**Tell City** (city) Perry County
85	23.5	**Chesterton** (town) Porter County
85	23.5	**Franklin** (city) Johnson County
87	23.6	**Speedway** (town) Marion County
88	23.7	**Highland** (CDP) Vanderburgh County
89	23.8	**Hartford City** (city) Blackford County
90	23.9	**Ellettsville** (town) Monroe County
90	23.9	**Rensselaer** (city) Jasper County
92	24.0	**Butler** (city) DeKalb County
92	24.0	**Merrillville** (town) Lake County
94	24.2	**Alexandria** (city) Madison County
94	24.2	**Plainfield** (town) Hendricks County
94	24.2	**Winchester** (city) Randolph County
97	24.3	**Brownsburg** (town) Hendricks County
97	24.3	**Columbus** (city) Bartholomew County
97	24.3	**Decatur** (city) Adams County
100	24.4	**Peru** (city) Miami County
101	24.6	**Shelbyville** (city) Shelby County
101	24.6	**Winamac** (town) Pulaski County
103	24.7	**Indianapolis** (city) Marion County
103	24.7	**Loogootee** (city) Martin County
103	24.7	**Simonton Lake** (CDP) Elkhart County
106	24.8	**Lagrange** (town) LaGrange County
106	24.8	**Yorktown** (town) Delaware County
108	24.9	**Gas City** (city) Grant County
108	24.9	**Kendallville** (city) Noble County
110	25.0	**Portland** (city) Jay County
111	25.2	**Austin** (city) Scott County
111	25.2	**Bluffton** (city) Wells County
111	25.2	**Boonville** (city) Warrick County
111	25.2	**Greensburg** (city) Decatur County
111	25.2	**La Porte** (city) LaPorte County
111	25.2	**Melody Hill** (CDP) Vanderburgh County
111	25.2	**Monticello** (city) White County
118	25.3	**Aurora** (city) Dearborn County
118	25.3	**Princeton** (city) Gibson County
120	25.4	**Country Squire Lakes** (CDP) Jennings County
120	25.4	**Gary** (city) Lake County
120	25.4	**Greenwood** (city) Johnson County
120	25.4	**Santa Claus** (town) Spencer County
124	25.6	**Warsaw** (city) Kosciusko County
125	25.7	**Fort Wayne** (city) Allen County
125	25.7	**Whiting** (city) Lake County
127	25.8	**Hammond** (city) Lake County
128	25.9	**Bicknell** (city) Knox County
128	25.9	**De Motte** (town) Jasper County
130	26.0	**Logansport** (city) Cass County
130	26.0	**Saint John** (town) Lake County
130	26.0	**Seymour** (city) Jackson County
130	26.0	**Washington** (city) Daviess County
134	26.1	**Greentown** (town) Howard County
135	26.2	**Centerville** (town) Wayne County
135	26.2	**Goshen** (city) Elkhart County
137	26.3	**New Haven** (city) Allen County
137	26.3	**Syracuse** (town) Kosciusko County
139	26.4	**Charlestown** (city) Clark County
139	26.4	**Lowell** (town) Lake County
141	26.5	**Brazil** (city) Clay County
141	26.5	**Garrett** (city) DeKalb County
141	26.5	**Lawrence** (city) Marion County
144	26.6	**Beech Grove** (city) Marion County
145	26.8	**Carmel** (city) Hamilton County
145	26.8	**Danville** (town) Hendricks County
145	26.8	**Roselawn** (CDP) Newton County
145	26.8	**South Bend** (city) Saint Joseph County
149	26.9	**Tipton** (city) Tipton County
150	27.0	**Brownstown** (town) Jackson County

Note: *This section ranks incorporated places and CDPs (Census Designated Places) with populations of 2,500 or more. Unincorporated postal areas were not considered. Please refer to the User Guide for additional information.*

Population Age 65 and Over

Top 150 Places Ranked in *Descending* Order

State Rank	Percent	Place
1	24.6	**Berne** (city) Adams County
2	24.0	**Shorewood Forest** (CDP) Porter County
3	21.4	**Rochester** (city) Fulton County
4	20.8	**Delphi** (city) Carroll County
5	20.6	**North Manchester** (town) Wabash County
6	20.5	**Batesville** (city) Ripley County
6	20.5	**De Motte** (town) Jasper County
6	20.5	**Rushville** (city) Rush County
9	20.4	**Boonville** (city) Warrick County
10	20.3	**Brookville** (town) Franklin County
10	20.3	**Linton** (city) Greene County
12	20.2	**Connersville** (city) Fayette County
13	20.1	**Mitchell** (city) Lawrence County
13	20.1	**Salem** (city) Washington County
15	19.8	**Bedford** (city) Lawrence County
16	19.5	**Dyer** (town) Lake County
17	19.4	**Monticello** (city) White County
17	19.4	**Munster** (town) Lake County
17	19.4	**Sullivan** (city) Sullivan County
17	19.4	**Tell City** (city) Perry County
21	19.3	**Wabash** (city) Wabash County
22	19.2	**Corydon** (town) Harrison County
22	19.2	**Greentown** (town) Howard County
24	19.1	**Alexandria** (city) Madison County
24	19.1	**Madison** (city) Jefferson County
26	19.0	**Crown Point** (city) Lake County
27	18.9	**Rockville** (town) Parke County
28	18.8	**Clinton** (city) Vermillion County
29	18.7	**Highland** (town) Lake County
30	18.6	**Mooresville** (town) Morgan County
31	18.5	**Bluffton** (city) Wells County
32	18.4	**Richmond** (city) Wayne County
33	18.3	**Winchester** (city) Randolph County
34	18.2	**Clarksville** (town) Clark County
34	18.2	**Greenfield** (city) Hancock County
36	18.0	**Kokomo** (city) Howard County
36	18.0	**New Castle** (city) Henry County
36	18.0	**Newburgh** (town) Warrick County
36	18.0	**Paoli** (town) Orange County
40	17.9	**Schererville** (town) Lake County
41	17.8	**Greendale** (city) Dearborn County
41	17.8	**Mount Vernon** (city) Posey County
41	17.8	**Portland** (city) Jay County
44	17.7	**Auburn** (city) DeKalb County
44	17.7	**La Porte** (city) LaPorte County
46	17.6	**Ellettsville** (town) Monroe County
46	17.6	**Fort Branch** (town) Gibson County
46	17.6	**Simonton Lake** (CDP) Elkhart County
49	17.5	**Attica** (city) Fountain County
49	17.5	**Gas City** (city) Grant County
49	17.5	**Tipton** (city) Tipton County
52	17.4	**Centerville** (town) Wayne County
52	17.4	**Hidden Valley** (CDP) Dearborn County
52	17.4	**Smithville-Sanders** (CDP) Monroe County
55	17.3	**Hartford City** (city) Blackford County
56	17.2	**Crawfordsville** (city) Montgomery County
56	17.2	**Gary** (city) Lake County
56	17.2	**Goshen** (city) Elkhart County
56	17.2	**Jasper** (city) Dubois County
56	17.2	**Washington** (city) Daviess County
56	17.2	**Winamac** (town) Pulaski County
62	17.0	**Anderson** (city) Madison County
62	17.0	**Lagrange** (town) LaGrange County
64	16.8	**Columbia City** (city) Whitley County
64	16.8	**North Vernon** (city) Jennings County
64	16.8	**Pendleton** (town) Madison County
64	16.8	**Princeton** (city) Gibson County
64	16.8	**Yorktown** (town) Delaware County
69	16.7	**Hobart** (city) Lake County
69	16.7	**Marion** (city) Grant County
71	16.6	**North Terre Haute** (CDP) Vigo County
72	16.5	**Angola** (city) Steuben County
73	16.4	**Kendallville** (city) Noble County
74	16.3	**Franklin** (city) Johnson County
75	16.2	**Osceola** (town) Saint Joseph County
76	16.1	**Beech Grove** (city) Marion County
76	16.1	**Elwood** (city) Madison County
78	16.0	**Martinsville** (city) Morgan County
78	16.0	**Melody Hill** (CDP) Vanderburgh County
78	16.0	**Rensselaer** (city) Jasper County
78	16.0	**Syracuse** (town) Kosciusko County
78	16.0	**Valparaiso** (city) Porter County
83	15.9	**Lawrenceburg** (city) Dearborn County
83	15.9	**Lebanon** (city) Boone County
83	15.9	**Santa Claus** (town) Spencer County
83	15.9	**Scottsburg** (city) Scott County
87	15.7	**Austin** (city) Scott County
87	15.7	**Brownstown** (town) Jackson County
87	15.7	**Loogootee** (city) Martin County
87	15.7	**Sheridan** (town) Hamilton County
87	15.7	**Union City** (city) Randolph County
92	15.6	**Fairmount** (town) Grant County
93	15.5	**Danville** (town) Hendricks County
93	15.5	**Decatur** (city) Adams County
93	15.5	**Evansville** (city) Vanderburgh County
93	15.5	**Greensburg** (city) Decatur County
93	15.5	**Knox** (city) Starke County
98	15.4	**Greencastle** (city) Putnam County
98	15.4	**Heritage Lake** (CDP) Putnam County
98	15.4	**Mishawaka** (city) Saint Joseph County
98	15.4	**Peru** (city) Miami County
102	15.3	**Cicero** (town) Hamilton County
102	15.3	**New Albany** (city) Floyd County
102	15.3	**Speedway** (town) Marion County
102	15.3	**Vincennes** (city) Knox County
102	15.3	**Winfield** (town) Lake County
107	15.2	**Lowell** (town) Lake County
108	15.1	**Bright** (CDP) Dearborn County
108	15.1	**Chesterton** (town) Porter County
110	15.0	**Columbus** (city) Bartholomew County
111	14.9	**Ossian** (town) Wells County
112	14.8	**Bicknell** (city) Knox County
112	14.8	**Frankfort** (city) Clinton County
112	14.8	**Lakes of the Four Seasons** (CDP) Lake County
112	14.8	**New Haven** (city) Allen County
116	14.7	**Merrillville** (town) Lake County
116	14.7	**Saint John** (town) Lake County
118	14.6	**Highland** (CDP) Vanderburgh County
119	14.5	**Granger** (CDP) Saint Joseph County
119	14.5	**Jeffersonville** (city) Clark County
119	14.5	**Plymouth** (city) Marshall County
119	14.5	**Seymour** (city) Jackson County
123	14.4	**Huntington** (city) Huntington County
123	14.4	**Middlebury** (town) Elkhart County
123	14.4	**Portage** (city) Porter County
126	14.3	**Brazil** (city) Clay County
126	14.3	**Logansport** (city) Cass County
128	14.2	**Cumberland** (town) Marion County
128	14.2	**Huntingburg** (city) Dubois County
128	14.2	**Shelbyville** (city) Shelby County
131	14.1	**Edinburgh** (town) Johnson County
132	14.0	**Michigan City** (city) LaPorte County
132	14.0	**Terre Haute** (city) Vigo County
134	13.9	**Aurora** (city) Dearborn County
134	13.9	**Muncie** (city) Delaware County
136	13.8	**Bremen** (town) Marshall County
136	13.8	**Greenwood** (city) Johnson County
138	13.5	**Griffith** (town) Lake County
138	13.5	**Warsaw** (city) Kosciusko County
140	13.4	**Fort Wayne** (city) Allen County
141	13.3	**Brownsburg** (town) Hendricks County
141	13.3	**Garrett** (city) DeKalb County
141	13.3	**Hanover** (town) Jefferson County
144	13.1	**Plainfield** (town) Hendricks County
145	13.0	**Lake Station** (city) Lake County
146	12.9	**Carmel** (city) Hamilton County
146	12.9	**Fortville** (town) Hancock County
148	12.7	**Lafayette** (city) Tippecanoe County
149	12.6	**South Bend** (city) Saint Joseph County
150	12.5	**Roselawn** (CDP) Newton County

Note: *This section ranks incorporated places and CDPs (Census Designated Places) with populations of 2,500 or more. Unincorporated postal areas were not considered. Please refer to the User Guide for additional information.*

Population Age 65 and Over

Top 150 Places Ranked in *Ascending* Order

State Rank	Percent	Place
1	1.0	**Notre Dame** (CDP) Saint Joseph County
2	4.2	**Westville** (town) LaPorte County
3	4.6	**McCordsville** (town) Hancock County
4	5.2	**Salt Creek Commons** (CDP) Porter County
5	5.3	**Whitestown** (town) Boone County
6	6.8	**West Lafayette** (city) Tippecanoe County
6	6.8	**Whiteland** (town) Johnson County
8	8.0	**Fishers** (city) Hamilton County
8	8.0	**Porter** (town) Porter County
10	8.4	**Westfield** (city) Hamilton County
11	8.7	**Bloomington** (city) Monroe County
12	9.0	**Ligonier** (city) Noble County
13	9.3	**Georgetown** (town) Floyd County
13	9.3	**Whiting** (city) Lake County
15	10.0	**Cedar Lake** (town) Lake County
15	10.0	**Charlestown** (city) Clark County
15	10.0	**Zionsville** (town) Boone County
18	10.2	**Country Squire Lakes** (CDP) Jennings County
18	10.2	**Hebron** (town) Porter County
20	10.3	**Upland** (town) Grant County
21	10.4	**Chandler** (town) Warrick County
22	10.6	**Leo-Cedarville** (town) Allen County
23	10.8	**Noblesville** (city) Hamilton County
24	10.9	**Avon** (town) Hendricks County
25	11.0	**Hammond** (city) Lake County
26	11.4	**Bargersville** (town) Johnson County
27	11.5	**Indianapolis** (city) Marion County
27	11.5	**Lawrence** (city) Marion County
29	11.6	**Butler** (city) DeKalb County
29	11.6	**Winona Lake** (town) Kosciusko County
31	11.8	**Pittsboro** (town) Hendricks County
32	11.9	**Nappanee** (city) Elkhart County
33	12.2	**Dunlap** (CDP) Elkhart County
34	12.3	**East Chicago** (city) Lake County
34	12.3	**Huntertown** (town) Allen County
34	12.3	**New Whiteland** (town) Johnson County
34	12.3	**South Haven** (CDP) Porter County
38	12.4	**Elkhart** (city) Elkhart County
39	12.5	**Roselawn** (CDP) Newton County
39	12.5	**Sellersburg** (town) Clark County
41	12.6	**South Bend** (city) Saint Joseph County
42	12.7	**Lafayette** (city) Tippecanoe County
43	12.9	**Carmel** (city) Hamilton County
43	12.9	**Fortville** (town) Hancock County
45	13.0	**Lake Station** (city) Lake County
46	13.1	**Plainfield** (town) Hendricks County
47	13.3	**Brownsburg** (town) Hendricks County
47	13.3	**Garrett** (city) DeKalb County
47	13.3	**Hanover** (town) Jefferson County
50	13.4	**Fort Wayne** (city) Allen County
51	13.5	**Griffith** (town) Lake County
51	13.5	**Warsaw** (city) Kosciusko County
53	13.8	**Bremen** (town) Marshall County
53	13.8	**Greenwood** (city) Johnson County
55	13.9	**Aurora** (city) Dearborn County
55	13.9	**Muncie** (city) Delaware County
57	14.0	**Michigan City** (city) LaPorte County
57	14.0	**Terre Haute** (city) Vigo County
59	14.1	**Edinburgh** (town) Johnson County
60	14.2	**Cumberland** (town) Marion County
60	14.2	**Huntingburg** (city) Dubois County
60	14.2	**Shelbyville** (city) Shelby County
63	14.3	**Brazil** (city) Clay County
63	14.3	**Logansport** (city) Cass County
65	14.4	**Huntington** (city) Huntington County
65	14.4	**Middlebury** (town) Elkhart County
65	14.4	**Portage** (city) Porter County
68	14.5	**Granger** (CDP) Saint Joseph County
68	14.5	**Jeffersonville** (city) Clark County
68	14.5	**Plymouth** (city) Marshall County
68	14.5	**Seymour** (city) Jackson County
72	14.6	**Highland** (CDP) Vanderburgh County
73	14.7	**Merrillville** (town) Lake County
73	14.7	**Saint John** (town) Lake County
75	14.8	**Bicknell** (city) Knox County
75	14.8	**Frankfort** (city) Clinton County
75	14.8	**Lakes of the Four Seasons** (CDP) Lake County
75	14.8	**New Haven** (city) Allen County
79	14.9	**Ossian** (town) Wells County
80	15.0	**Columbus** (city) Bartholomew County
81	15.1	**Bright** (CDP) Dearborn County
81	15.1	**Chesterton** (town) Porter County
83	15.2	**Lowell** (town) Lake County
84	15.3	**Cicero** (town) Hamilton County
84	15.3	**New Albany** (city) Floyd County
84	15.3	**Speedway** (town) Marion County
84	15.3	**Vincennes** (city) Knox County
84	15.3	**Winfield** (town) Lake County
89	15.4	**Greencastle** (city) Putnam County
89	15.4	**Heritage Lake** (CDP) Putnam County
89	15.4	**Mishawaka** (city) Saint Joseph County
89	15.4	**Peru** (city) Miami County
93	15.5	**Danville** (town) Hendricks County
93	15.5	**Decatur** (city) Adams County
93	15.5	**Evansville** (city) Vanderburgh County
93	15.5	**Greensburg** (city) Decatur County
93	15.5	**Knox** (city) Starke County
98	15.6	**Fairmount** (town) Grant County
99	15.7	**Austin** (city) Scott County
99	15.7	**Brownstown** (town) Jackson County
99	15.7	**Loogootee** (city) Martin County
99	15.7	**Sheridan** (town) Hamilton County
99	15.7	**Union City** (city) Randolph County
104	15.9	**Lawrenceburg** (city) Dearborn County
104	15.9	**Lebanon** (city) Boone County
104	15.9	**Santa Claus** (town) Spencer County
104	15.9	**Scottsburg** (city) Scott County
108	16.0	**Martinsville** (city) Morgan County
108	16.0	**Melody Hill** (CDP) Vanderburgh County
108	16.0	**Rensselaer** (city) Jasper County
108	16.0	**Syracuse** (town) Kosciusko County
108	16.0	**Valparaiso** (city) Porter County
113	16.1	**Beech Grove** (city) Marion County
113	16.1	**Elwood** (city) Madison County
115	16.2	**Osceola** (town) Saint Joseph County
116	16.3	**Franklin** (city) Johnson County
117	16.4	**Kendallville** (city) Noble County
118	16.5	**Angola** (city) Steuben County
119	16.6	**North Terre Haute** (CDP) Vigo County
120	16.7	**Hobart** (city) Lake County
120	16.7	**Marion** (city) Grant County
122	16.8	**Columbia City** (city) Whitley County
122	16.8	**North Vernon** (city) Jennings County
122	16.8	**Pendleton** (town) Madison County
122	16.8	**Princeton** (city) Gibson County
122	16.8	**Yorktown** (town) Delaware County
127	17.0	**Anderson** (city) Madison County
127	17.0	**Lagrange** (town) LaGrange County
129	17.2	**Crawfordsville** (city) Montgomery County
129	17.2	**Gary** (city) Lake County
129	17.2	**Goshen** (city) Elkhart County
129	17.2	**Jasper** (city) Dubois County
129	17.2	**Washington** (city) Daviess County
129	17.2	**Winamac** (town) Pulaski County
135	17.3	**Hartford City** (city) Blackford County
136	17.4	**Centerville** (town) Wayne County
136	17.4	**Hidden Valley** (CDP) Dearborn County
136	17.4	**Smithville-Sanders** (CDP) Monroe County
139	17.5	**Attica** (city) Fountain County
139	17.5	**Gas City** (city) Grant County
139	17.5	**Tipton** (city) Tipton County
142	17.6	**Ellettsville** (town) Monroe County
142	17.6	**Fort Branch** (town) Gibson County
142	17.6	**Simonton Lake** (CDP) Elkhart County
145	17.7	**Auburn** (city) DeKalb County
145	17.7	**La Porte** (city) LaPorte County
147	17.8	**Greendale** (city) Dearborn County
147	17.8	**Mount Vernon** (city) Posey County
147	17.8	**Portland** (city) Jay County
150	17.9	**Schererville** (town) Lake County

Note: *This section ranks incorporated places and CDPs (Census Designated Places) with populations of 2,500 or more. Unincorporated postal areas were not considered. Please refer to the User Guide for additional information.*

Males per 100 Females

Top 150 Places Ranked in *Descending* Order

State Rank	Ratio	Place
1	333.2	**Westville** (town) LaPorte County
2	118.3	**West Lafayette** (city) Tippecanoe County
3	111.7	**Plainfield** (town) Hendricks County
4	111.5	**Notre Dame** (CDP) Saint Joseph County
5	106.8	**Terre Haute** (city) Vigo County
6	105.8	**Michigan City** (city) LaPorte County
7	104.8	**Bargersville** (town) Johnson County
8	102.9	**Roselawn** (CDP) Newton County
9	102.8	**Cedar Lake** (town) Lake County
10	102.7	**Heritage Lake** (CDP) Putnam County
11	102.4	**Angola** (city) Steuben County
11	102.4	**Osceola** (town) Saint Joseph County
13	102.3	**Country Squire Lakes** (CDP) Jennings County
14	101.9	**Whitestown** (town) Boone County
15	101.6	**Smithville-Sanders** (CDP) Monroe County
16	101.4	**Hidden Valley** (CDP) Dearborn County
16	101.4	**Syracuse** (town) Kosciusko County
18	101.1	**Bloomington** (city) Monroe County
18	101.1	**Vincennes** (city) Knox County
20	101.0	**Salt Creek Commons** (CDP) Porter County
21	100.4	**Crawfordsville** (city) Montgomery County
22	100.2	**Sheridan** (town) Hamilton County
23	100.0	**Crown Point** (city) Lake County
24	99.9	**Lake Station** (city) Lake County
25	99.6	**Edinburgh** (town) Johnson County
25	99.6	**Saint John** (town) Lake County
27	99.4	**Butler** (city) DeKalb County
27	99.4	**Fort Branch** (town) Gibson County
27	99.4	**Leo-Cedarville** (town) Allen County
30	99.1	**Ligonier** (city) Noble County
31	98.3	**Bright** (CDP) Dearborn County
32	98.2	**Granger** (CDP) Saint Joseph County
33	98.1	**Porter** (town) Porter County
34	97.4	**Aurora** (city) Dearborn County
35	97.2	**Logansport** (city) Cass County
36	97.1	**Dunlap** (CDP) Elkhart County
36	97.1	**Frankfort** (city) Clinton County
38	97.0	**Cicero** (town) Hamilton County
39	96.9	**Lowell** (town) Lake County
39	96.9	**North Terre Haute** (CDP) Vigo County
41	96.7	**Huntertown** (town) Allen County
41	96.7	**Jasper** (city) Dubois County
41	96.7	**Simonton Lake** (CDP) Elkhart County
44	96.6	**Whiting** (city) Lake County
45	96.4	**Warsaw** (city) Kosciusko County
45	96.4	**Whiteland** (town) Johnson County
47	96.3	**Lawrenceburg** (city) Dearborn County
47	96.3	**South Haven** (CDP) Porter County
49	96.2	**Hammond** (city) Lake County
50	96.0	**Lakes of the Four Seasons** (CDP) Lake County
51	95.9	**Highland** (CDP) Vanderburgh County
52	95.8	**Melody Hill** (CDP) Vanderburgh County
53	95.7	**Attica** (city) Fountain County
53	95.7	**Westfield** (city) Hamilton County
55	95.5	**Goshen** (city) Elkhart County
55	95.5	**Nappanee** (city) Elkhart County
57	95.4	**Jeffersonville** (city) Clark County
58	95.3	**Winamac** (town) Pulaski County
59	95.2	**Chandler** (town) Warrick County
59	95.2	**Shelbyville** (city) Shelby County
61	95.1	**Carmel** (city) Hamilton County
61	95.1	**Seymour** (city) Jackson County
63	95.0	**Winfield** (town) Lake County
64	94.9	**Bicknell** (city) Knox County
64	94.9	**Elwood** (city) Madison County
64	94.9	**Lafayette** (city) Tippecanoe County
64	94.9	**Zionsville** (town) Boone County
68	94.8	**Chesterton** (town) Porter County
69	94.7	**Austin** (city) Scott County
69	94.7	**Shorewood Forest** (CDP) Porter County
69	94.7	**Union City** (city) Randolph County
69	94.7	**Valparaiso** (city) Porter County
73	94.6	**Middlebury** (town) Elkhart County
73	94.6	**New Whiteland** (town) Johnson County
75	94.5	**Fishers** (city) Hamilton County
75	94.5	**Fortville** (town) Hancock County
77	94.4	**Martinsville** (city) Morgan County
77	94.4	**Sellersburg** (town) Clark County
79	94.3	**Fairmount** (town) Grant County
80	94.2	**Hobart** (city) Lake County
80	94.2	**Schererville** (town) Lake County
82	94.1	**Danville** (town) Hendricks County
83	93.9	**Columbus** (city) Bartholomew County
83	93.9	**Greenwood** (city) Johnson County
83	93.9	**Pittsboro** (town) Hendricks County
83	93.9	**South Bend** (city) Saint Joseph County
87	93.8	**Decatur** (city) Adams County
87	93.8	**Dyer** (town) Lake County
87	93.8	**Fort Wayne** (city) Allen County
87	93.8	**McCordsville** (town) Hancock County
87	93.8	**Noblesville** (city) Hamilton County
92	93.7	**Portage** (city) Porter County
93	93.6	**Speedway** (town) Marion County
94	93.5	**Hebron** (town) Porter County
94	93.5	**Indianapolis** (city) Marion County
96	93.4	**Avon** (town) Hendricks County
96	93.4	**Georgetown** (town) Floyd County
98	93.3	**Paoli** (town) Orange County
99	93.2	**La Porte** (city) LaPorte County
100	93.1	**Brownstown** (town) Jackson County
101	93.0	**Elkhart** (city) Elkhart County
101	93.0	**Gas City** (city) Grant County
101	93.0	**Kendallville** (city) Noble County
104	92.9	**Newburgh** (town) Warrick County
104	92.9	**Washington** (city) Daviess County
106	92.8	**Auburn** (city) DeKalb County
107	92.7	**Evansville** (city) Vanderburgh County
107	92.7	**Greenfield** (city) Hancock County
107	92.7	**New Haven** (city) Allen County
110	92.6	**Cumberland** (town) Marion County
111	92.5	**Munster** (town) Lake County
112	92.4	**Clarksville** (town) Clark County
113	92.3	**Bluffton** (city) Wells County
113	92.3	**Brazil** (city) Clay County
113	92.3	**Highland** (town) Lake County
116	92.2	**Brownsburg** (town) Hendricks County
116	92.2	**Lebanon** (city) Boone County
116	92.2	**Rensselaer** (city) Jasper County
119	92.1	**Garrett** (city) DeKalb County
120	91.9	**Anderson** (city) Madison County
120	91.9	**Greensburg** (city) Decatur County
120	91.9	**Plymouth** (city) Marshall County
120	91.9	**Rochester** (city) Fulton County
120	91.9	**Santa Claus** (town) Spencer County
125	91.8	**Delphi** (city) Carroll County
125	91.8	**Richmond** (city) Wayne County
127	91.7	**North Vernon** (city) Jennings County
128	91.6	**Alexandria** (city) Madison County
128	91.6	**Greendale** (city) Dearborn County
130	91.5	**Bremen** (town) Marshall County
131	91.4	**Mount Vernon** (city) Posey County
132	91.3	**Batesville** (city) Ripley County
132	91.3	**Franklin** (city) Johnson County
132	91.3	**Huntington** (city) Huntington County
132	91.3	**Loogootee** (city) Martin County
136	91.2	**Huntingburg** (city) Dubois County
136	91.2	**Upland** (town) Grant County
138	91.1	**Linton** (city) Greene County
138	91.1	**Princeton** (city) Gibson County
140	91.0	**Connersville** (city) Fayette County
140	91.0	**Winchester** (city) Randolph County
142	90.9	**Griffith** (town) Lake County
143	90.8	**Columbia City** (city) Whitley County
144	90.7	**Hanover** (town) Jefferson County
144	90.7	**Hartford City** (city) Blackford County
144	90.7	**Ossian** (town) Wells County
147	90.6	**Clinton** (city) Vermillion County
147	90.6	**Muncie** (city) Delaware County
149	90.5	**Charlestown** (city) Clark County
149	90.5	**Lawrence** (city) Marion County

Note: *This section ranks incorporated places and CDPs (Census Designated Places) with populations of 2,500 or more. Unincorporated postal areas were not considered. Please refer to the User Guide for additional information.*

Males per 100 Females

Top 150 Places Ranked in *Ascending* Order

State Rank	Ratio	Place
1	81.2	**Madison** (city) Jefferson County
2	84.0	**Corydon** (town) Harrison County
3	84.6	**North Manchester** (town) Wabash County
4	85.1	**Gary** (city) Lake County
5	85.2	**Greentown** (town) Howard County
6	85.6	**Berne** (city) Adams County
7	86.2	**Knox** (city) Starke County
8	86.3	**Boonville** (city) Warrick County
8	86.3	**Sullivan** (city) Sullivan County
10	86.8	**Beech Grove** (city) Marion County
11	86.9	**Mitchell** (city) Lawrence County
11	86.9	**Salem** (city) Washington County
13	87.1	**De Motte** (town) Jasper County
14	87.3	**Winona Lake** (town) Kosciusko County
15	87.5	**Ellettsville** (town) Monroe County
15	87.5	**Greencastle** (city) Putnam County
17	87.6	**New Castle** (city) Henry County
18	87.8	**Brookville** (town) Franklin County
18	87.8	**Lagrange** (town) LaGrange County
18	87.8	**Portland** (city) Jay County
18	87.8	**Rockville** (town) Parke County
22	88.0	**Kokomo** (city) Howard County
23	88.1	**East Chicago** (city) Lake County
24	88.4	**Tipton** (city) Tipton County
25	88.6	**Merrillville** (town) Lake County
26	88.8	**Marion** (city) Grant County
27	88.9	**Mishawaka** (city) Saint Joseph County
28	89.1	**Mooresville** (town) Morgan County
29	89.2	**Wabash** (city) Wabash County
30	89.7	**Pendleton** (town) Madison County
31	89.8	**Bedford** (city) Lawrence County
32	89.9	**Monticello** (city) White County
33	90.3	**Tell City** (city) Perry County
34	90.4	**Centerville** (town) Wayne County
34	90.4	**Peru** (city) Miami County
34	90.4	**Scottsburg** (city) Scott County
37	90.5	**Charlestown** (city) Clark County
37	90.5	**Lawrence** (city) Marion County
37	90.5	**New Albany** (city) Floyd County
37	90.5	**Rushville** (city) Rush County
37	90.5	**Yorktown** (town) Delaware County
42	90.6	**Clinton** (city) Vermillion County
42	90.6	**Muncie** (city) Delaware County
44	90.7	**Hanover** (town) Jefferson County
44	90.7	**Hartford City** (city) Blackford County
44	90.7	**Ossian** (town) Wells County
47	90.8	**Columbia City** (city) Whitley County
48	90.9	**Griffith** (town) Lake County
49	91.0	**Connersville** (city) Fayette County
49	91.0	**Winchester** (city) Randolph County
51	91.1	**Linton** (city) Greene County
51	91.1	**Princeton** (city) Gibson County
53	91.2	**Huntingburg** (city) Dubois County
53	91.2	**Upland** (town) Grant County
55	91.3	**Batesville** (city) Ripley County
55	91.3	**Franklin** (city) Johnson County
55	91.3	**Huntington** (city) Huntington County
55	91.3	**Loogootee** (city) Martin County
59	91.4	**Mount Vernon** (city) Posey County
60	91.5	**Bremen** (town) Marshall County
61	91.6	**Alexandria** (city) Madison County
61	91.6	**Greendale** (city) Dearborn County
63	91.7	**North Vernon** (city) Jennings County
64	91.8	**Delphi** (city) Carroll County
64	91.8	**Richmond** (city) Wayne County
66	91.9	**Anderson** (city) Madison County
66	91.9	**Greensburg** (city) Decatur County
66	91.9	**Plymouth** (city) Marshall County
66	91.9	**Rochester** (city) Fulton County
66	91.9	**Santa Claus** (town) Spencer County
71	92.1	**Garrett** (city) DeKalb County
72	92.2	**Brownsburg** (town) Hendricks County
72	92.2	**Lebanon** (city) Boone County
72	92.2	**Rensselaer** (city) Jasper County
75	92.3	**Bluffton** (city) Wells County
75	92.3	**Brazil** (city) Clay County
75	92.3	**Highland** (town) Lake County
78	92.4	**Clarksville** (town) Clark County
79	92.5	**Munster** (town) Lake County
80	92.6	**Cumberland** (town) Marion County
81	92.7	**Evansville** (city) Vanderburgh County
81	92.7	**Greenfield** (city) Hancock County
81	92.7	**New Haven** (city) Allen County
84	92.8	**Auburn** (city) DeKalb County
85	92.9	**Newburgh** (town) Warrick County
85	92.9	**Washington** (city) Daviess County
87	93.0	**Elkhart** (city) Elkhart County
87	93.0	**Gas City** (city) Grant County
87	93.0	**Kendallville** (city) Noble County
90	93.1	**Brownstown** (town) Jackson County
91	93.2	**La Porte** (city) LaPorte County
92	93.3	**Paoli** (town) Orange County
93	93.4	**Avon** (town) Hendricks County
93	93.4	**Georgetown** (town) Floyd County
95	93.5	**Hebron** (town) Porter County
95	93.5	**Indianapolis** (city) Marion County
97	93.6	**Speedway** (town) Marion County
98	93.7	**Portage** (city) Porter County
99	93.8	**Decatur** (city) Adams County
99	93.8	**Dyer** (town) Lake County
99	93.8	**Fort Wayne** (city) Allen County
99	93.8	**McCordsville** (town) Hancock County
99	93.8	**Noblesville** (city) Hamilton County
104	93.9	**Columbus** (city) Bartholomew County
104	93.9	**Greenwood** (city) Johnson County
104	93.9	**Pittsboro** (town) Hendricks County
104	93.9	**South Bend** (city) Saint Joseph County
108	94.1	**Danville** (town) Hendricks County
109	94.2	**Hobart** (city) Lake County
109	94.2	**Schererville** (town) Lake County
111	94.3	**Fairmount** (town) Grant County
112	94.4	**Martinsville** (city) Morgan County
112	94.4	**Sellersburg** (town) Clark County
114	94.5	**Fishers** (city) Hamilton County
114	94.5	**Fortville** (town) Hancock County
116	94.6	**Middlebury** (town) Elkhart County
116	94.6	**New Whiteland** (town) Johnson County
118	94.7	**Austin** (city) Scott County
118	94.7	**Shorewood Forest** (CDP) Porter County
118	94.7	**Union City** (city) Randolph County
118	94.7	**Valparaiso** (city) Porter County
122	94.8	**Chesterton** (town) Porter County
123	94.9	**Bicknell** (city) Knox County
123	94.9	**Elwood** (city) Madison County
123	94.9	**Lafayette** (city) Tippecanoe County
123	94.9	**Zionsville** (town) Boone County
127	95.0	**Winfield** (town) Lake County
128	95.1	**Carmel** (city) Hamilton County
128	95.1	**Seymour** (city) Jackson County
130	95.2	**Chandler** (town) Warrick County
130	95.2	**Shelbyville** (city) Shelby County
132	95.3	**Winamac** (town) Pulaski County
133	95.4	**Jeffersonville** (city) Clark County
134	95.5	**Goshen** (city) Elkhart County
134	95.5	**Nappanee** (city) Elkhart County
136	95.7	**Attica** (city) Fountain County
136	95.7	**Westfield** (city) Hamilton County
138	95.8	**Melody Hill** (CDP) Vanderburgh County
139	95.9	**Highland** (CDP) Vanderburgh County
140	96.0	**Lakes of the Four Seasons** (CDP) Lake County
141	96.2	**Hammond** (city) Lake County
142	96.3	**Lawrenceburg** (city) Dearborn County
142	96.3	**South Haven** (CDP) Porter County
144	96.4	**Warsaw** (city) Kosciusko County
144	96.4	**Whiteland** (town) Johnson County
146	96.6	**Whiting** (city) Lake County
147	96.7	**Huntertown** (town) Allen County
147	96.7	**Jasper** (city) Dubois County
147	96.7	**Simonton Lake** (CDP) Elkhart County
150	96.9	**Lowell** (town) Lake County

Note: *This section ranks incorporated places and CDPs (Census Designated Places) with populations of 2,500 or more. Unincorporated postal areas were not considered. Please refer to the User Guide for additional information.*

Rankings

Marriage Status: Never Married

Top 150 Places Ranked in *Descending* Order

State Rank	Percent	Place
1	97.7	**Notre Dame** (CDP) Saint Joseph County
2	72.1	**West Lafayette** (city) Tippecanoe County
3	63.6	**Bloomington** (city) Monroe County
4	57.4	**Upland** (town) Grant County
5	51.1	**Westville** (town) LaPorte County
6	48.4	**Muncie** (city) Delaware County
7	48.1	**Hanover** (town) Jefferson County
8	46.7	**East Chicago** (city) Lake County
9	46.1	**Greencastle** (city) Putnam County
10	45.1	**Gary** (city) Lake County
11	43.0	**Terre Haute** (city) Vigo County
12	41.6	**Whiting** (city) Lake County
13	41.5	**South Bend** (city) Saint Joseph County
14	41.4	**Indianapolis** (city) Marion County
15	40.9	**Hammond** (city) Lake County
16	39.4	**Michigan City** (city) LaPorte County
17	39.2	**Marion** (city) Grant County
18	38.7	**North Manchester** (town) Wabash County
19	38.3	**Angola** (city) Steuben County
20	38.1	**Speedway** (town) Marion County
21	37.4	**Valparaiso** (city) Porter County
22	37.3	**Griffith** (town) Lake County
23	37.0	**Lafayette** (city) Tippecanoe County
24	36.4	**Elkhart** (city) Elkhart County
25	36.1	**Cumberland** (town) Marion County
26	35.8	**Butler** (city) DeKalb County
26	35.8	**Knox** (city) Starke County
26	35.8	**Mishawaka** (city) Saint Joseph County
29	35.6	**Winona Lake** (town) Kosciusko County
30	35.3	**Merrillville** (town) Lake County
31	35.1	**Beech Grove** (city) Marion County
32	34.8	**Fort Wayne** (city) Allen County
32	34.8	**Lawrence** (city) Marion County
34	34.6	**Union City** (city) Randolph County
35	34.3	**Evansville** (city) Vanderburgh County
36	34.0	**New Albany** (city) Floyd County
37	33.7	**Huntington** (city) Huntington County
38	33.5	**Lake Station** (city) Lake County
38	33.5	**Plymouth** (city) Marshall County
40	33.3	**Logansport** (city) Cass County
41	33.2	**Lawrenceburg** (city) Dearborn County
41	33.2	**Vincennes** (city) Knox County
43	33.1	**Portage** (city) Porter County
44	32.8	**Anderson** (city) Madison County
45	32.5	**Cedar Lake** (town) Lake County
45	32.5	**De Motte** (town) Jasper County
47	32.3	**Richmond** (city) Wayne County
48	32.2	**Bremen** (town) Marshall County
48	32.2	**Goshen** (city) Elkhart County
50	32.0	**Edinburgh** (town) Johnson County
50	32.0	**Porter** (town) Porter County
52	31.9	**Ligonier** (city) Noble County
53	31.2	**Hebron** (town) Porter County
53	31.2	**Jeffersonville** (city) Clark County
55	31.1	**Garrett** (city) DeKalb County
55	31.1	**Peru** (city) Miami County
57	31.0	**La Porte** (city) LaPorte County
57	31.0	**Portland** (city) Jay County
59	30.9	**Lowell** (town) Lake County
59	30.9	**Salt Creek Commons** (CDP) Porter County
61	30.8	**Crawfordsville** (city) Montgomery County
61	30.8	**Warsaw** (city) Kosciusko County
63	30.7	**Bright** (CDP) Dearborn County
64	30.6	**Princeton** (city) Gibson County
65	30.5	**Columbia City** (city) Whitley County
66	30.2	**Auburn** (city) DeKalb County
67	30.0	**Washington** (city) Daviess County
68	29.9	**Plainfield** (town) Hendricks County
68	29.9	**Syracuse** (town) Kosciusko County
70	29.8	**Greenwood** (city) Johnson County
70	29.8	**Leo-Cedarville** (town) Allen County
72	29.6	**Madison** (city) Jefferson County
73	29.5	**North Vernon** (city) Jennings County
74	29.2	**Scottsburg** (city) Scott County
74	29.2	**Whiteland** (town) Johnson County
76	29.1	**Mount Vernon** (city) Posey County
76	29.1	**Schererville** (town) Lake County
78	28.8	**Chandler** (town) Warrick County
78	28.8	**Munster** (town) Lake County
78	28.8	**Shelbyville** (city) Shelby County
78	28.8	**Winamac** (town) Pulaski County
82	28.7	**Country Squire Lakes** (CDP) Jennings County
83	28.6	**Charlestown** (city) Clark County
83	28.6	**Highland** (town) Lake County
83	28.6	**New Castle** (city) Henry County
86	28.5	**Heritage Lake** (CDP) Putnam County
87	28.4	**Brazil** (city) Clay County
88	28.2	**Greensburg** (city) Decatur County
89	28.1	**Hobart** (city) Lake County
89	28.1	**New Whiteland** (town) Johnson County
89	28.1	**North Terre Haute** (CDP) Vigo County
92	28.0	**Clarksville** (town) Clark County
92	28.0	**Columbus** (city) Bartholomew County
92	28.0	**Frankfort** (city) Clinton County
92	28.0	**Martinsville** (city) Morgan County
96	27.7	**Clinton** (city) Vermillion County
96	27.7	**Elwood** (city) Madison County
96	27.7	**Fairmount** (town) Grant County
96	27.7	**Sheridan** (town) Hamilton County
100	27.6	**Bicknell** (city) Knox County
101	27.5	**Aurora** (city) Dearborn County
101	27.5	**Brownstown** (town) Jackson County
101	27.5	**Huntingburg** (city) Dubois County
104	27.4	**Chesterton** (town) Porter County
104	27.4	**Delphi** (city) Carroll County
106	27.2	**New Haven** (city) Allen County
107	27.1	**Jasper** (city) Dubois County
107	27.1	**McCordsville** (town) Hancock County
107	27.1	**Rensselaer** (city) Jasper County
110	27.0	**Dunlap** (CDP) Elkhart County
111	26.9	**Bluffton** (city) Wells County
111	26.9	**Decatur** (city) Adams County
111	26.9	**Lebanon** (city) Boone County
114	26.8	**Attica** (city) Fountain County
114	26.8	**Crown Point** (city) Lake County
114	26.8	**Kokomo** (city) Howard County
114	26.8	**South Haven** (CDP) Porter County
118	26.6	**Kendallville** (city) Noble County
119	26.4	**Fort Branch** (town) Gibson County
119	26.4	**Wabash** (city) Wabash County
121	26.2	**Connersville** (city) Fayette County
121	26.2	**Greendale** (city) Dearborn County
123	26.1	**Loogootee** (city) Martin County
123	26.1	**Mooresville** (town) Morgan County
123	26.1	**Paoli** (town) Orange County
126	26.0	**Alexandria** (city) Madison County
126	26.0	**Austin** (city) Scott County
128	25.9	**Lagrange** (town) LaGrange County
128	25.9	**Noblesville** (city) Hamilton County
130	25.7	**Berne** (city) Adams County
130	25.7	**Simonton Lake** (CDP) Elkhart County
132	25.6	**Winfield** (town) Lake County
133	25.4	**Franklin** (city) Johnson County
134	25.3	**Dyer** (town) Lake County
134	25.3	**Monticello** (city) White County
136	25.2	**Avon** (town) Hendricks County
136	25.2	**Osceola** (town) Saint Joseph County
136	25.2	**Winchester** (city) Randolph County
139	25.1	**Gas City** (city) Grant County
140	25.0	**Brookville** (town) Franklin County
140	25.0	**Tipton** (city) Tipton County
142	24.9	**Danville** (town) Hendricks County
143	24.8	**Rochester** (city) Fulton County
143	24.8	**Sellersburg** (town) Clark County
143	24.8	**Westfield** (city) Hamilton County
146	24.7	**Hartford City** (city) Blackford County
147	24.4	**Ellettsville** (town) Monroe County
147	24.4	**Smithville-Sanders** (CDP) Monroe County
149	24.2	**Newburgh** (town) Warrick County
150	24.1	**Huntertown** (town) Allen County

***Note:** This section ranks incorporated places and CDPs (Census Designated Places) with populations of 2,500 or more. Unincorporated postal areas were not considered. Please refer to the User Guide for additional information.*

Marriage Status: Never Married

Top 150 Places Ranked in *Ascending* Order

State Rank	Percent	Place
1	18.0	**Mitchell** (city) Lawrence County
2	18.3	**Middlebury** (town) Elkhart County
3	18.6	**Melody Hill** (CDP) Vanderburgh County
4	19.2	**Santa Claus** (town) Spencer County
5	19.4	**Pittsboro** (town) Hendricks County
6	19.7	**Boonville** (city) Warrick County
6	19.7	**Highland** (CDP) Vanderburgh County
8	19.9	**Bargersville** (town) Johnson County
8	19.9	**Shorewood Forest** (CDP) Porter County
10	20.6	**Batesville** (city) Ripley County
11	20.8	**Whitestown** (town) Boone County
12	20.9	**Ossian** (town) Wells County
13	21.2	**Pendleton** (town) Madison County
14	21.3	**Zionsville** (town) Boone County
15	21.4	**Roselawn** (CDP) Newton County
16	21.5	**Yorktown** (town) Delaware County
17	21.6	**Lakes of the Four Seasons** (CDP) Lake County
18	21.8	**Granger** (CDP) Saint Joseph County
19	21.9	**Tell City** (city) Perry County
20	22.0	**Centerville** (town) Wayne County
20	22.0	**Cicero** (town) Hamilton County
22	22.2	**Georgetown** (town) Floyd County
23	22.4	**Greentown** (town) Howard County
23	22.4	**Rushville** (city) Rush County
25	22.5	**Seymour** (city) Jackson County
26	22.6	**Linton** (city) Greene County
27	22.8	**Bedford** (city) Lawrence County
27	22.8	**Fortville** (town) Hancock County
27	22.8	**Saint John** (town) Lake County
30	23.1	**Hidden Valley** (CDP) Dearborn County
31	23.2	**Brownsburg** (town) Hendricks County
32	23.3	**Nappanee** (city) Elkhart County
33	23.5	**Rockville** (town) Parke County
34	23.6	**Salem** (city) Washington County
35	23.8	**Sullivan** (city) Sullivan County
36	23.9	**Carmel** (city) Hamilton County
36	23.9	**Corydon** (town) Harrison County
38	24.0	**Fishers** (city) Hamilton County
38	24.0	**Greenfield** (city) Hancock County
40	24.1	**Huntertown** (town) Allen County
41	24.2	**Newburgh** (town) Warrick County
42	24.4	**Ellettsville** (town) Monroe County
42	24.4	**Smithville-Sanders** (CDP) Monroe County
44	24.7	**Hartford City** (city) Blackford County
45	24.8	**Rochester** (city) Fulton County
45	24.8	**Sellersburg** (town) Clark County
45	24.8	**Westfield** (city) Hamilton County
48	24.9	**Danville** (town) Hendricks County
49	25.0	**Brookville** (town) Franklin County
49	25.0	**Tipton** (city) Tipton County
51	25.1	**Gas City** (city) Grant County
52	25.2	**Avon** (town) Hendricks County
52	25.2	**Osceola** (town) Saint Joseph County
52	25.2	**Winchester** (city) Randolph County
55	25.3	**Dyer** (town) Lake County
55	25.3	**Monticello** (city) White County
57	25.4	**Franklin** (city) Johnson County
58	25.6	**Winfield** (town) Lake County
59	25.7	**Berne** (city) Adams County
59	25.7	**Simonton Lake** (CDP) Elkhart County
61	25.9	**Lagrange** (town) LaGrange County
61	25.9	**Noblesville** (city) Hamilton County
63	26.0	**Alexandria** (city) Madison County
63	26.0	**Austin** (city) Scott County
65	26.1	**Loogootee** (city) Martin County
65	26.1	**Mooresville** (town) Morgan County
65	26.1	**Paoli** (town) Orange County
68	26.2	**Connersville** (city) Fayette County
68	26.2	**Greendale** (city) Dearborn County
70	26.4	**Fort Branch** (town) Gibson County
70	26.4	**Wabash** (city) Wabash County
72	26.6	**Kendallville** (city) Noble County
73	26.8	**Attica** (city) Fountain County
73	26.8	**Crown Point** (city) Lake County
73	26.8	**Kokomo** (city) Howard County
73	26.8	**South Haven** (CDP) Porter County
77	26.9	**Bluffton** (city) Wells County
77	26.9	**Decatur** (city) Adams County
77	26.9	**Lebanon** (city) Boone County
80	27.0	**Dunlap** (CDP) Elkhart County
81	27.1	**Jasper** (city) Dubois County
81	27.1	**McCordsville** (town) Hancock County
81	27.1	**Rensselaer** (city) Jasper County
84	27.2	**New Haven** (city) Allen County
85	27.4	**Chesterton** (town) Porter County
85	27.4	**Delphi** (city) Carroll County
87	27.5	**Aurora** (city) Dearborn County
87	27.5	**Brownstown** (town) Jackson County
87	27.5	**Huntingburg** (city) Dubois County
90	27.6	**Bicknell** (city) Knox County
91	27.7	**Clinton** (city) Vermillion County
91	27.7	**Elwood** (city) Madison County
91	27.7	**Fairmount** (town) Grant County
91	27.7	**Sheridan** (town) Hamilton County
95	28.0	**Clarksville** (town) Clark County
95	28.0	**Columbus** (city) Bartholomew County
95	28.0	**Frankfort** (city) Clinton County
95	28.0	**Martinsville** (city) Morgan County
99	28.1	**Hobart** (city) Lake County
99	28.1	**New Whiteland** (town) Johnson County
99	28.1	**North Terre Haute** (CDP) Vigo County
102	28.2	**Greensburg** (city) Decatur County
103	28.4	**Brazil** (city) Clay County
104	28.5	**Heritage Lake** (CDP) Putnam County
105	28.6	**Charlestown** (city) Clark County
105	28.6	**Highland** (town) Lake County
105	28.6	**New Castle** (city) Henry County
108	28.7	**Country Squire Lakes** (CDP) Jennings County
109	28.8	**Chandler** (town) Warrick County
109	28.8	**Munster** (town) Lake County
109	28.8	**Shelbyville** (city) Shelby County
109	28.8	**Winamac** (town) Pulaski County
113	29.1	**Mount Vernon** (city) Posey County
113	29.1	**Schererville** (town) Lake County
115	29.2	**Scottsburg** (city) Scott County
115	29.2	**Whiteland** (town) Johnson County
117	29.5	**North Vernon** (city) Jennings County
118	29.6	**Madison** (city) Jefferson County
119	29.8	**Greenwood** (city) Johnson County
119	29.8	**Leo-Cedarville** (town) Allen County
121	29.9	**Plainfield** (town) Hendricks County
121	29.9	**Syracuse** (town) Kosciusko County
123	30.0	**Washington** (city) Daviess County
124	30.2	**Auburn** (city) DeKalb County
125	30.5	**Columbia City** (city) Whitley County
126	30.6	**Princeton** (city) Gibson County
127	30.7	**Bright** (CDP) Dearborn County
128	30.8	**Crawfordsville** (city) Montgomery County
128	30.8	**Warsaw** (city) Kosciusko County
130	30.9	**Lowell** (town) Lake County
130	30.9	**Salt Creek Commons** (CDP) Porter County
132	31.0	**La Porte** (city) LaPorte County
132	31.0	**Portland** (city) Jay County
134	31.1	**Garrett** (city) DeKalb County
134	31.1	**Peru** (city) Miami County
136	31.2	**Hebron** (town) Porter County
136	31.2	**Jeffersonville** (city) Clark County
138	31.9	**Ligonier** (city) Noble County
139	32.0	**Edinburgh** (town) Johnson County
139	32.0	**Porter** (town) Porter County
141	32.2	**Bremen** (town) Marshall County
141	32.2	**Goshen** (city) Elkhart County
143	32.3	**Richmond** (city) Wayne County
144	32.5	**Cedar Lake** (town) Lake County
144	32.5	**De Motte** (town) Jasper County
146	32.8	**Anderson** (city) Madison County
147	33.1	**Portage** (city) Porter County
148	33.2	**Lawrenceburg** (city) Dearborn County
148	33.2	**Vincennes** (city) Knox County
150	33.3	**Logansport** (city) Cass County

Note: *This section ranks incorporated places and CDPs (Census Designated Places) with populations of 2,500 or more. Unincorporated postal areas were not considered. Please refer to the User Guide for additional information.*

Marriage Status: Now Married

Top 150 Places Ranked in *Descending* Order

State Rank	Percent	Place
1	71.0	**Middlebury** (town) Elkhart County
2	68.5	**Granger** (CDP) Saint Joseph County
3	68.2	**Santa Claus** (town) Spencer County
3	68.2	**Zionsville** (town) Boone County
5	67.1	**Hidden Valley** (CDP) Dearborn County
5	67.1	**Highland** (CDP) Vanderburgh County
7	66.8	**Bargersville** (town) Johnson County
8	66.3	**Pittsboro** (town) Hendricks County
9	66.1	**Shorewood Forest** (CDP) Porter County
10	65.2	**Roselawn** (CDP) Newton County
10	65.2	**Saint John** (town) Lake County
12	65.1	**Whitestown** (town) Boone County
13	64.6	**Melody Hill** (CDP) Vanderburgh County
14	64.4	**Carmel** (city) Hamilton County
15	63.6	**Lakes of the Four Seasons** (CDP) Lake County
16	63.4	**Fishers** (city) Hamilton County
17	63.0	**Westfield** (city) Hamilton County
18	62.9	**McCordsville** (town) Hancock County
19	62.7	**Georgetown** (town) Floyd County
20	61.0	**Batesville** (city) Ripley County
21	60.9	**Heritage Lake** (CDP) Putnam County
22	60.3	**Brownsburg** (town) Hendricks County
23	60.2	**Dunlap** (CDP) Elkhart County
23	60.2	**Winfield** (town) Lake County
25	59.9	**Osceola** (town) Saint Joseph County
26	59.8	**Ossian** (town) Wells County
27	59.7	**Huntertown** (town) Allen County
28	59.6	**Cicero** (town) Hamilton County
29	59.5	**Leo-Cedarville** (town) Allen County
30	59.1	**Nappanee** (city) Elkhart County
31	58.9	**Yorktown** (town) Delaware County
32	58.7	**Newburgh** (town) Warrick County
33	58.3	**Dyer** (town) Lake County
34	57.9	**Noblesville** (city) Hamilton County
35	57.7	**Smithville-Sanders** (CDP) Monroe County
36	57.5	**Porter** (town) Porter County
37	56.7	**Avon** (town) Hendricks County
38	56.5	**Pendleton** (town) Madison County
39	56.3	**Salt Creek Commons** (CDP) Porter County
40	56.0	**South Haven** (CDP) Porter County
41	55.7	**Berne** (city) Adams County
42	55.3	**Chandler** (town) Warrick County
43	54.9	**Fortville** (town) Hancock County
44	54.8	**Hartford City** (city) Blackford County
45	54.6	**Fort Branch** (town) Gibson County
46	54.5	**Schererville** (town) Lake County
47	54.4	**Boonville** (city) Warrick County
47	54.4	**Chesterton** (town) Porter County
49	54.1	**Crown Point** (city) Lake County
50	54.0	**Austin** (city) Scott County
50	54.0	**Danville** (town) Hendricks County
52	53.8	**Greentown** (town) Howard County
52	53.8	**Rensselaer** (city) Jasper County
54	53.7	**Munster** (town) Lake County
55	53.6	**Seymour** (city) Jackson County
56	53.3	**Jasper** (city) Dubois County
57	53.2	**Greendale** (city) Dearborn County
58	53.0	**Hobart** (city) Lake County
58	53.0	**Tipton** (city) Tipton County
60	52.9	**Tell City** (city) Perry County
60	52.9	**Winchester** (city) Randolph County
62	52.8	**Lowell** (town) Lake County
63	52.6	**Bright** (CDP) Dearborn County
64	52.5	**Columbus** (city) Bartholomew County
65	52.4	**Sellersburg** (town) Clark County
65	52.4	**Whiteland** (town) Johnson County
67	52.3	**Greenfield** (city) Hancock County
68	52.2	**Scottsburg** (city) Scott County
69	52.1	**Hebron** (town) Porter County
70	52.0	**Cedar Lake** (town) Lake County
70	52.0	**Fairmount** (town) Grant County
72	51.7	**Bluffton** (city) Wells County
72	51.7	**Franklin** (city) Johnson County
74	51.3	**Simonton Lake** (CDP) Elkhart County
75	51.2	**Huntingburg** (city) Dubois County
75	51.2	**New Haven** (city) Allen County
77	51.1	**Bremen** (town) Marshall County
77	51.1	**Greenwood** (city) Johnson County
79	50.8	**Aurora** (city) Dearborn County
80	50.6	**Highland** (town) Lake County
81	50.5	**Alexandria** (city) Madison County
81	50.5	**Rockville** (town) Parke County
83	50.4	**Mitchell** (city) Lawrence County
83	50.4	**Rushville** (city) Rush County
85	50.3	**Linton** (city) Greene County
86	50.2	**Ligonier** (city) Noble County
87	49.7	**Mount Vernon** (city) Posey County
88	49.4	**Winona Lake** (town) Kosciusko County
89	49.3	**Frankfort** (city) Clinton County
89	49.3	**Mooresville** (town) Morgan County
89	49.3	**Wabash** (city) Wabash County
92	49.2	**Goshen** (city) Elkhart County
93	49.1	**Brookville** (town) Franklin County
93	49.1	**Plainfield** (town) Hendricks County
95	49.0	**Bicknell** (city) Knox County
96	48.8	**Sheridan** (town) Hamilton County
97	48.6	**Lawrence** (city) Marion County
98	48.5	**Lake Station** (city) Lake County
99	48.2	**Cumberland** (town) Marion County
99	48.2	**Kokomo** (city) Howard County
101	48.0	**Greensburg** (city) Decatur County
102	47.9	**Lebanon** (city) Boone County
103	47.8	**Warsaw** (city) Kosciusko County
104	47.7	**Brazil** (city) Clay County
104	47.7	**Gas City** (city) Grant County
104	47.7	**Jeffersonville** (city) Clark County
107	47.6	**Elwood** (city) Madison County
108	47.5	**Bedford** (city) Lawrence County
108	47.5	**Centerville** (town) Wayne County
110	47.3	**Ellettsville** (town) Monroe County
111	47.1	**New Whiteland** (town) Johnson County
112	47.0	**Columbia City** (city) Whitley County
113	46.8	**Attica** (city) Fountain County
113	46.8	**Charlestown** (city) Clark County
113	46.8	**North Terre Haute** (CDP) Vigo County
116	46.7	**Portage** (city) Porter County
117	46.4	**Edinburgh** (town) Johnson County
118	46.3	**Winamac** (town) Pulaski County
119	46.2	**Fort Wayne** (city) Allen County
119	46.2	**Washington** (city) Daviess County
121	46.1	**Huntington** (city) Huntington County
121	46.1	**Kendallville** (city) Noble County
121	46.1	**Shelbyville** (city) Shelby County
124	45.9	**Auburn** (city) DeKalb County
125	45.7	**Crawfordsville** (city) Montgomery County
125	45.7	**Peru** (city) Miami County
127	45.4	**Brownstown** (town) Jackson County
127	45.4	**Garrett** (city) DeKalb County
129	45.2	**Corydon** (town) Harrison County
129	45.2	**Decatur** (city) Adams County
131	45.1	**Country Squire Lakes** (CDP) Jennings County
131	45.1	**De Motte** (town) Jasper County
131	45.1	**Lagrange** (town) LaGrange County
134	44.9	**Salem** (city) Washington County
135	44.8	**Plymouth** (city) Marshall County
136	44.6	**Delphi** (city) Carroll County
136	44.6	**Logansport** (city) Cass County
136	44.6	**Merrillville** (town) Lake County
139	44.3	**Clarksville** (town) Clark County
139	44.3	**Monticello** (city) White County
141	44.1	**Connersville** (city) Fayette County
142	44.0	**Griffith** (town) Lake County
143	43.8	**Valparaiso** (city) Porter County
144	43.4	**Martinsville** (city) Morgan County
144	43.4	**Princeton** (city) Gibson County
146	43.3	**Sullivan** (city) Sullivan County
147	43.2	**La Porte** (city) LaPorte County
148	42.6	**North Vernon** (city) Jennings County
148	42.6	**Portland** (city) Jay County
150	42.5	**Rochester** (city) Fulton County

Note: *This section ranks incorporated places and CDPs (Census Designated Places) with populations of 2,500 or more. Unincorporated postal areas were not considered. Please refer to the User Guide for additional information.*

Marriage Status: Now Married

Top 150 Places Ranked in *Ascending* Order

State Rank	Percent	Place
1	0.7	**Notre Dame** (CDP) Saint Joseph County
2	22.2	**West Lafayette** (city) Tippecanoe County
3	24.1	**Westville** (town) LaPorte County
4	25.0	**Bloomington** (city) Monroe County
5	31.4	**Gary** (city) Lake County
5	31.4	**Greencastle** (city) Putnam County
7	32.3	**Hanover** (town) Jefferson County
7	32.3	**Union City** (city) Randolph County
9	32.5	**Muncie** (city) Delaware County
10	32.9	**Upland** (town) Grant County
11	33.9	**Knox** (city) Starke County
12	34.4	**Lawrenceburg** (city) Dearborn County
13	35.8	**Marion** (city) Grant County
14	35.9	**Terre Haute** (city) Vigo County
15	36.3	**Clinton** (city) Vermillion County
15	36.3	**East Chicago** (city) Lake County
17	36.9	**Michigan City** (city) LaPorte County
18	37.9	**Butler** (city) DeKalb County
19	38.9	**South Bend** (city) Saint Joseph County
20	40.2	**Angola** (city) Steuben County
20	40.2	**Mishawaka** (city) Saint Joseph County
22	40.3	**Elkhart** (city) Elkhart County
22	40.3	**Indianapolis** (city) Marion County
24	40.4	**Speedway** (town) Marion County
25	40.5	**Beech Grove** (city) Marion County
25	40.5	**Loogootee** (city) Martin County
27	40.8	**Anderson** (city) Madison County
28	41.0	**Evansville** (city) Vanderburgh County
29	41.1	**Hammond** (city) Lake County
30	41.4	**New Castle** (city) Henry County
31	41.6	**New Albany** (city) Floyd County
31	41.6	**Paoli** (town) Orange County
31	41.6	**Richmond** (city) Wayne County
34	41.8	**North Manchester** (town) Wabash County
34	41.8	**Whiting** (city) Lake County
36	42.0	**Madison** (city) Jefferson County
37	42.2	**Vincennes** (city) Knox County
38	42.4	**Lafayette** (city) Tippecanoe County
38	42.4	**Syracuse** (town) Kosciusko County
40	42.5	**Rochester** (city) Fulton County
41	42.6	**North Vernon** (city) Jennings County
41	42.6	**Portland** (city) Jay County
43	43.2	**La Porte** (city) LaPorte County
44	43.3	**Sullivan** (city) Sullivan County
45	43.4	**Martinsville** (city) Morgan County
45	43.4	**Princeton** (city) Gibson County
47	43.8	**Valparaiso** (city) Porter County
48	44.0	**Griffith** (town) Lake County
49	44.1	**Connersville** (city) Fayette County
50	44.3	**Clarksville** (town) Clark County
50	44.3	**Monticello** (city) White County
52	44.6	**Delphi** (city) Carroll County
52	44.6	**Logansport** (city) Cass County
52	44.6	**Merrillville** (town) Lake County
55	44.8	**Plymouth** (city) Marshall County
56	44.9	**Salem** (city) Washington County
57	45.1	**Country Squire Lakes** (CDP) Jennings County
57	45.1	**De Motte** (town) Jasper County
57	45.1	**Lagrange** (town) LaGrange County
60	45.2	**Corydon** (town) Harrison County
60	45.2	**Decatur** (city) Adams County
62	45.4	**Brownstown** (town) Jackson County
62	45.4	**Garrett** (city) DeKalb County
64	45.7	**Crawfordsville** (city) Montgomery County
64	45.7	**Peru** (city) Miami County
66	45.9	**Auburn** (city) DeKalb County
67	46.1	**Huntington** (city) Huntington County
67	46.1	**Kendallville** (city) Noble County
67	46.1	**Shelbyville** (city) Shelby County
70	46.2	**Fort Wayne** (city) Allen County
70	46.2	**Washington** (city) Daviess County
72	46.3	**Winamac** (town) Pulaski County
73	46.4	**Edinburgh** (town) Johnson County
74	46.7	**Portage** (city) Porter County
75	46.8	**Attica** (city) Fountain County
75	46.8	**Charlestown** (city) Clark County
75	46.8	**North Terre Haute** (CDP) Vigo County
78	47.0	**Columbia City** (city) Whitley County
79	47.1	**New Whiteland** (town) Johnson County
80	47.3	**Ellettsville** (town) Monroe County
81	47.5	**Bedford** (city) Lawrence County
81	47.5	**Centerville** (town) Wayne County
83	47.6	**Elwood** (city) Madison County
84	47.7	**Brazil** (city) Clay County
84	47.7	**Gas City** (city) Grant County
84	47.7	**Jeffersonville** (city) Clark County
87	47.8	**Warsaw** (city) Kosciusko County
88	47.9	**Lebanon** (city) Boone County
89	48.0	**Greensburg** (city) Decatur County
90	48.2	**Cumberland** (town) Marion County
90	48.2	**Kokomo** (city) Howard County
92	48.5	**Lake Station** (city) Lake County
93	48.6	**Lawrence** (city) Marion County
94	48.8	**Sheridan** (town) Hamilton County
95	49.0	**Bicknell** (city) Knox County
96	49.1	**Brookville** (town) Franklin County
96	49.1	**Plainfield** (town) Hendricks County
98	49.2	**Goshen** (city) Elkhart County
99	49.3	**Frankfort** (city) Clinton County
99	49.3	**Mooresville** (town) Morgan County
99	49.3	**Wabash** (city) Wabash County
102	49.4	**Winona Lake** (town) Kosciusko County
103	49.7	**Mount Vernon** (city) Posey County
104	50.2	**Ligonier** (city) Noble County
105	50.3	**Linton** (city) Greene County
106	50.4	**Mitchell** (city) Lawrence County
106	50.4	**Rushville** (city) Rush County
108	50.5	**Alexandria** (city) Madison County
108	50.5	**Rockville** (town) Parke County
110	50.6	**Highland** (town) Lake County
111	50.8	**Aurora** (city) Dearborn County
112	51.1	**Bremen** (town) Marshall County
112	51.1	**Greenwood** (city) Johnson County
114	51.2	**Huntingburg** (city) Dubois County
114	51.2	**New Haven** (city) Allen County
116	51.3	**Simonton Lake** (CDP) Elkhart County
117	51.7	**Bluffton** (city) Wells County
117	51.7	**Franklin** (city) Johnson County
119	52.0	**Cedar Lake** (town) Lake County
119	52.0	**Fairmount** (town) Grant County
121	52.1	**Hebron** (town) Porter County
122	52.2	**Scottsburg** (city) Scott County
123	52.3	**Greenfield** (city) Hancock County
124	52.4	**Sellersburg** (town) Clark County
124	52.4	**Whiteland** (town) Johnson County
126	52.5	**Columbus** (city) Bartholomew County
127	52.6	**Bright** (CDP) Dearborn County
128	52.8	**Lowell** (town) Lake County
129	52.9	**Tell City** (city) Perry County
129	52.9	**Winchester** (city) Randolph County
131	53.0	**Hobart** (city) Lake County
131	53.0	**Tipton** (city) Tipton County
133	53.2	**Greendale** (city) Dearborn County
134	53.3	**Jasper** (city) Dubois County
135	53.6	**Seymour** (city) Jackson County
136	53.7	**Munster** (town) Lake County
137	53.8	**Greentown** (town) Howard County
137	53.8	**Rensselaer** (city) Jasper County
139	54.0	**Austin** (city) Scott County
139	54.0	**Danville** (town) Hendricks County
141	54.1	**Crown Point** (city) Lake County
142	54.4	**Boonville** (city) Warrick County
142	54.4	**Chesterton** (town) Porter County
144	54.5	**Schererville** (town) Lake County
145	54.6	**Fort Branch** (town) Gibson County
146	54.8	**Hartford City** (city) Blackford County
147	54.9	**Fortville** (town) Hancock County
148	55.3	**Chandler** (town) Warrick County
149	55.7	**Berne** (city) Adams County
150	56.0	**South Haven** (CDP) Porter County

Note: *This section ranks incorporated places and CDPs (Census Designated Places) with populations of 2,500 or more. Unincorporated postal areas were not considered. Please refer to the User Guide for additional information.*

Marriage Status: Separated

Top 150 Places Ranked in *Descending* Order

State Rank	Percent	Place
1	5.0	**Nappanee** (city) Elkhart County
2	4.3	**Sellersburg** (town) Clark County
3	3.9	**Whiting** (city) Lake County
4	3.7	**Martinsville** (city) Morgan County
5	3.3	**Ligonier** (city) Noble County
5	3.3	**North Manchester** (town) Wabash County
7	3.2	**Lake Station** (city) Lake County
8	3.1	**Frankfort** (city) Clinton County
9	2.9	**Attica** (city) Fountain County
9	2.9	**Dunlap** (CDP) Elkhart County
9	2.9	**Portland** (city) Jay County
12	2.8	**Kendallville** (city) Noble County
13	2.7	**Brownsburg** (town) Hendricks County
13	2.7	**Centerville** (town) Wayne County
13	2.7	**Elkhart** (city) Elkhart County
13	2.7	**Gary** (city) Lake County
17	2.6	**North Vernon** (city) Jennings County
17	2.6	**Westville** (town) LaPorte County
17	2.6	**Winona Lake** (town) Kosciusko County
20	2.5	**Angola** (city) Steuben County
20	2.5	**Bicknell** (city) Knox County
20	2.5	**Bremen** (town) Marshall County
20	2.5	**Clarksville** (town) Clark County
20	2.5	**Ellettsville** (town) Monroe County
20	2.5	**Fairmount** (town) Grant County
20	2.5	**Fortville** (town) Hancock County
20	2.5	**Hammond** (city) Lake County
20	2.5	**Mitchell** (city) Lawrence County
20	2.5	**Sheridan** (town) Hamilton County
30	2.4	**Batesville** (city) Ripley County
30	2.4	**Cicero** (town) Hamilton County
30	2.4	**Crawfordsville** (city) Montgomery County
30	2.4	**Greendale** (city) Dearborn County
30	2.4	**New Albany** (city) Floyd County
30	2.4	**South Bend** (city) Saint Joseph County
36	2.3	**Anderson** (city) Madison County
36	2.3	**Country Squire Lakes** (CDP) Jennings County
36	2.3	**East Chicago** (city) Lake County
36	2.3	**Lagrange** (town) LaGrange County
40	2.2	**Boonville** (city) Warrick County
40	2.2	**Shelbyville** (city) Shelby County
40	2.2	**Tell City** (city) Perry County
43	2.1	**Charlestown** (city) Clark County
44	2.0	**De Motte** (town) Jasper County
44	2.0	**Greenfield** (city) Hancock County
44	2.0	**Hartford City** (city) Blackford County
44	2.0	**Indianapolis** (city) Marion County
44	2.0	**Lawrenceburg** (city) Dearborn County
44	2.0	**Merrillville** (town) Lake County
44	2.0	**Peru** (city) Miami County
44	2.0	**Scottsburg** (city) Scott County
44	2.0	**Seymour** (city) Jackson County
44	2.0	**Winchester** (city) Randolph County
54	1.9	**Cumberland** (town) Marion County
54	1.9	**Elwood** (city) Madison County
54	1.9	**Jeffersonville** (city) Clark County
54	1.9	**Knox** (city) Starke County
54	1.9	**Kokomo** (city) Howard County
54	1.9	**Portage** (city) Porter County
54	1.9	**Princeton** (city) Gibson County
61	1.8	**Brazil** (city) Clay County
61	1.8	**Goshen** (city) Elkhart County
61	1.8	**Greentown** (town) Howard County
61	1.8	**New Whiteland** (town) Johnson County
65	1.7	**Beech Grove** (city) Marion County
65	1.7	**Columbus** (city) Bartholomew County
65	1.7	**Danville** (town) Hendricks County
65	1.7	**Hobart** (city) Lake County
65	1.7	**Logansport** (city) Cass County
65	1.7	**Madison** (city) Jefferson County
65	1.7	**Michigan City** (city) LaPorte County
65	1.7	**New Castle** (city) Henry County
73	1.6	**Aurora** (city) Dearborn County
73	1.6	**Bluffton** (city) Wells County
73	1.6	**Chesterton** (town) Porter County
73	1.6	**Delphi** (city) Carroll County
73	1.6	**Evansville** (city) Vanderburgh County
73	1.6	**Lafayette** (city) Tippecanoe County
73	1.6	**Lawrence** (city) Marion County
73	1.6	**Lowell** (town) Lake County
73	1.6	**Paoli** (town) Orange County
73	1.6	**Rushville** (city) Rush County
73	1.6	**South Haven** (CDP) Porter County
73	1.6	**Terre Haute** (city) Vigo County
85	1.5	**Alexandria** (city) Madison County
85	1.5	**Corydon** (town) Harrison County
85	1.5	**Marion** (city) Grant County
88	1.4	**Connersville** (city) Fayette County
88	1.4	**Fort Wayne** (city) Allen County
88	1.4	**Loogootee** (city) Martin County
88	1.4	**Plymouth** (city) Marshall County
88	1.4	**Richmond** (city) Wayne County
88	1.4	**Salem** (city) Washington County
88	1.4	**Valparaiso** (city) Porter County
88	1.4	**Warsaw** (city) Kosciusko County
88	1.4	**Washington** (city) Daviess County
88	1.4	**Whitestown** (town) Boone County
98	1.3	**Chandler** (town) Warrick County
98	1.3	**Georgetown** (town) Floyd County
98	1.3	**Hebron** (town) Porter County
98	1.3	**La Porte** (city) LaPorte County
98	1.3	**Muncie** (city) Delaware County
98	1.3	**Noblesville** (city) Hamilton County
98	1.3	**Plainfield** (town) Hendricks County
98	1.3	**Rensselaer** (city) Jasper County
98	1.3	**Roselawn** (CDP) Newton County
98	1.3	**Wabash** (city) Wabash County
108	1.2	**Austin** (city) Scott County
108	1.2	**Avon** (town) Hendricks County
108	1.2	**Berne** (city) Adams County
108	1.2	**Greensburg** (city) Decatur County
108	1.2	**Highland** (town) Lake County
108	1.2	**Lebanon** (city) Boone County
108	1.2	**Mishawaka** (city) Saint Joseph County
108	1.2	**Union City** (city) Randolph County
108	1.2	**Vincennes** (city) Knox County
117	1.1	**Bargersville** (town) Johnson County
117	1.1	**Butler** (city) DeKalb County
117	1.1	**Fishers** (city) Hamilton County
117	1.1	**Huntingburg** (city) Dubois County
117	1.1	**Huntington** (city) Huntington County
117	1.1	**Linton** (city) Greene County
117	1.1	**Mooresville** (town) Morgan County
117	1.1	**New Haven** (city) Allen County
117	1.1	**Yorktown** (town) Delaware County
126	1.0	**Decatur** (city) Adams County
126	1.0	**Dyer** (town) Lake County
126	1.0	**Greenwood** (city) Johnson County
126	1.0	**Hanover** (town) Jefferson County
126	1.0	**Munster** (town) Lake County
126	1.0	**Winamac** (town) Pulaski County
132	0.9	**Columbia City** (city) Whitley County
132	0.9	**Garrett** (city) DeKalb County
132	0.9	**Gas City** (city) Grant County
132	0.9	**Monticello** (city) White County
132	0.9	**Newburgh** (town) Warrick County
132	0.9	**Speedway** (town) Marion County
138	0.8	**Bedford** (city) Lawrence County
138	0.8	**Bloomington** (city) Monroe County
138	0.8	**Franklin** (city) Johnson County
138	0.8	**Jasper** (city) Dubois County
138	0.8	**Melody Hill** (CDP) Vanderburgh County
138	0.8	**Pendleton** (town) Madison County
138	0.8	**Pittsboro** (town) Hendricks County
138	0.8	**Schererville** (town) Lake County
138	0.8	**Tipton** (city) Tipton County
147	0.7	**Auburn** (city) DeKalb County
147	0.7	**Edinburgh** (town) Johnson County
147	0.7	**Granger** (CDP) Saint Joseph County
147	0.7	**Hidden Valley** (CDP) Dearborn County

Note: *This section ranks incorporated places and CDPs (Census Designated Places) with populations of 2,500 or more. Unincorporated postal areas were not considered. Please refer to the User Guide for additional information.*

Marriage Status: Separated

Top 150 Places Ranked in *Ascending* Order

State Rank	Percent	Place
1	0.0	**Highland** (CDP) Vanderburgh County
1	0.0	**Leo-Cedarville** (town) Allen County
1	0.0	**McCordsville** (town) Hancock County
1	0.0	**Middlebury** (town) Elkhart County
1	0.0	**Notre Dame** (CDP) Saint Joseph County
1	0.0	**Porter** (town) Porter County
1	0.0	**Rockville** (town) Parke County
8	0.1	**Osceola** (town) Saint Joseph County
8	0.1	**Saint John** (town) Lake County
10	0.2	**Brookville** (town) Franklin County
10	0.2	**Lakes of the Four Seasons** (CDP) Lake County
10	0.2	**North Terre Haute** (CDP) Vigo County
10	0.2	**Simonton Lake** (CDP) Elkhart County
10	0.2	**Upland** (town) Grant County
15	0.3	**Bright** (CDP) Dearborn County
15	0.3	**Shorewood Forest** (CDP) Porter County
15	0.3	**West Lafayette** (city) Tippecanoe County
15	0.3	**Zionsville** (town) Boone County
19	0.4	**Fort Branch** (town) Gibson County
19	0.4	**Greencastle** (city) Putnam County
19	0.4	**Griffith** (town) Lake County
19	0.4	**Ossian** (town) Wells County
19	0.4	**Rochester** (city) Fulton County
19	0.4	**Syracuse** (town) Kosciusko County
25	0.5	**Brownstown** (town) Jackson County
25	0.5	**Carmel** (city) Hamilton County
25	0.5	**Cedar Lake** (town) Lake County
25	0.5	**Clinton** (city) Vermillion County
25	0.5	**Crown Point** (city) Lake County
25	0.5	**Heritage Lake** (CDP) Putnam County
25	0.5	**Huntertown** (town) Allen County
25	0.5	**Salt Creek Commons** (CDP) Porter County
25	0.5	**Smithville-Sanders** (CDP) Monroe County
25	0.5	**Sullivan** (city) Sullivan County
35	0.6	**Santa Claus** (town) Spencer County
35	0.6	**Winfield** (town) Lake County
37	0.7	**Auburn** (city) DeKalb County
37	0.7	**Edinburgh** (town) Johnson County
37	0.7	**Granger** (CDP) Saint Joseph County
37	0.7	**Hidden Valley** (CDP) Dearborn County
37	0.7	**Mount Vernon** (city) Posey County
37	0.7	**Westfield** (city) Hamilton County
37	0.7	**Whiteland** (town) Johnson County
44	0.8	**Bedford** (city) Lawrence County
44	0.8	**Bloomington** (city) Monroe County
44	0.8	**Franklin** (city) Johnson County
44	0.8	**Jasper** (city) Dubois County
44	0.8	**Melody Hill** (CDP) Vanderburgh County
44	0.8	**Pendleton** (town) Madison County
44	0.8	**Pittsboro** (town) Hendricks County
44	0.8	**Schererville** (town) Lake County
44	0.8	**Tipton** (city) Tipton County
53	0.9	**Columbia City** (city) Whitley County
53	0.9	**Garrett** (city) DeKalb County
53	0.9	**Gas City** (city) Grant County
53	0.9	**Monticello** (city) White County
53	0.9	**Newburgh** (town) Warrick County
53	0.9	**Speedway** (town) Marion County
59	1.0	**Decatur** (city) Adams County
59	1.0	**Dyer** (town) Lake County
59	1.0	**Greenwood** (city) Johnson County
59	1.0	**Hanover** (town) Jefferson County
59	1.0	**Munster** (town) Lake County
59	1.0	**Winamac** (town) Pulaski County
65	1.1	**Bargersville** (town) Johnson County
65	1.1	**Butler** (city) DeKalb County
65	1.1	**Fishers** (city) Hamilton County
65	1.1	**Huntingburg** (city) Dubois County
65	1.1	**Huntington** (city) Huntington County
65	1.1	**Linton** (city) Greene County
65	1.1	**Mooresville** (town) Morgan County
65	1.1	**New Haven** (city) Allen County
65	1.1	**Yorktown** (town) Delaware County
74	1.2	**Austin** (city) Scott County
74	1.2	**Avon** (town) Hendricks County
74	1.2	**Berne** (city) Adams County
74	1.2	**Greensburg** (city) Decatur County
74	1.2	**Highland** (town) Lake County
74	1.2	**Lebanon** (city) Boone County
74	1.2	**Mishawaka** (city) Saint Joseph County
74	1.2	**Union City** (city) Randolph County
74	1.2	**Vincennes** (city) Knox County
83	1.3	**Chandler** (town) Warrick County
83	1.3	**Georgetown** (town) Floyd County
83	1.3	**Hebron** (town) Porter County
83	1.3	**La Porte** (city) LaPorte County
83	1.3	**Muncie** (city) Delaware County
83	1.3	**Noblesville** (city) Hamilton County
83	1.3	**Plainfield** (town) Hendricks County
83	1.3	**Rensselaer** (city) Jasper County
83	1.3	**Roselawn** (CDP) Newton County
83	1.3	**Wabash** (city) Wabash County
93	1.4	**Connersville** (city) Fayette County
93	1.4	**Fort Wayne** (city) Allen County
93	1.4	**Loogootee** (city) Martin County
93	1.4	**Plymouth** (city) Marshall County
93	1.4	**Richmond** (city) Wayne County
93	1.4	**Salem** (city) Washington County
93	1.4	**Valparaiso** (city) Porter County
93	1.4	**Warsaw** (city) Kosciusko County
93	1.4	**Washington** (city) Daviess County
93	1.4	**Whitestown** (town) Boone County
103	1.5	**Alexandria** (city) Madison County
103	1.5	**Corydon** (town) Harrison County
103	1.5	**Marion** (city) Grant County
106	1.6	**Aurora** (city) Dearborn County
106	1.6	**Bluffton** (city) Wells County
106	1.6	**Chesterton** (town) Porter County
106	1.6	**Delphi** (city) Carroll County
106	1.6	**Evansville** (city) Vanderburgh County
106	1.6	**Lafayette** (city) Tippecanoe County
106	1.6	**Lawrence** (city) Marion County
106	1.6	**Lowell** (town) Lake County
106	1.6	**Paoli** (town) Orange County
106	1.6	**Rushville** (city) Rush County
106	1.6	**South Haven** (CDP) Porter County
106	1.6	**Terre Haute** (city) Vigo County
118	1.7	**Beech Grove** (city) Marion County
118	1.7	**Columbus** (city) Bartholomew County
118	1.7	**Danville** (town) Hendricks County
118	1.7	**Hobart** (city) Lake County
118	1.7	**Logansport** (city) Cass County
118	1.7	**Madison** (city) Jefferson County
118	1.7	**Michigan City** (city) LaPorte County
118	1.7	**New Castle** (city) Henry County
126	1.8	**Brazil** (city) Clay County
126	1.8	**Goshen** (city) Elkhart County
126	1.8	**Greentown** (town) Howard County
126	1.8	**New Whiteland** (town) Johnson County
130	1.9	**Cumberland** (town) Marion County
130	1.9	**Elwood** (city) Madison County
130	1.9	**Jeffersonville** (city) Clark County
130	1.9	**Knox** (city) Starke County
130	1.9	**Kokomo** (city) Howard County
130	1.9	**Portage** (city) Porter County
130	1.9	**Princeton** (city) Gibson County
137	2.0	**De Motte** (town) Jasper County
137	2.0	**Greenfield** (city) Hancock County
137	2.0	**Hartford City** (city) Blackford County
137	2.0	**Indianapolis** (city) Marion County
137	2.0	**Lawrenceburg** (city) Dearborn County
137	2.0	**Merrillville** (town) Lake County
137	2.0	**Peru** (city) Miami County
137	2.0	**Scottsburg** (city) Scott County
137	2.0	**Seymour** (city) Jackson County
137	2.0	**Winchester** (city) Randolph County
147	2.1	**Charlestown** (city) Clark County
148	2.2	**Boonville** (city) Warrick County
148	2.2	**Shelbyville** (city) Shelby County
148	2.2	**Tell City** (city) Perry County

***Note:** This section ranks incorporated places and CDPs (Census Designated Places) with populations of 2,500 or more. Unincorporated postal areas were not considered. Please refer to the User Guide for additional information.*

Marriage Status: Widowed

Top 150 Places Ranked in *Descending* Order

State Rank	Percent	Place
1	16.3	**Monticello** (city) White County
2	12.3	**Sullivan** (city) Sullivan County
3	12.2	**Clinton** (city) Vermillion County
4	12.1	**Delphi** (city) Carroll County
5	11.8	**Lawrenceburg** (city) Dearborn County
6	11.2	**Boonville** (city) Warrick County
6	11.2	**Paoli** (town) Orange County
8	11.0	**Clarksville** (town) Clark County
9	10.8	**Portland** (city) Jay County
10	10.6	**Berne** (city) Adams County
10	10.6	**Salem** (city) Washington County
12	10.5	**Lagrange** (town) LaGrange County
13	10.4	**Mitchell** (city) Lawrence County
13	10.4	**Union City** (city) Randolph County
15	10.3	**Linton** (city) Greene County
16	10.0	**Ossian** (town) Wells County
17	9.8	**Bedford** (city) Lawrence County
17	9.8	**Mooresville** (town) Morgan County
19	9.7	**Auburn** (city) DeKalb County
19	9.7	**Tipton** (city) Tipton County
21	9.6	**Batesville** (city) Ripley County
21	9.6	**North Manchester** (town) Wabash County
23	9.5	**Alexandria** (city) Madison County
23	9.5	**Connersville** (city) Fayette County
23	9.5	**Decatur** (city) Adams County
23	9.5	**Winchester** (city) Randolph County
27	9.4	**Corydon** (town) Harrison County
28	9.2	**Attica** (city) Fountain County
28	9.2	**Greentown** (town) Howard County
28	9.2	**Rushville** (city) Rush County
28	9.2	**Washington** (city) Daviess County
32	9.1	**Bicknell** (city) Knox County
32	9.1	**Gary** (city) Lake County
32	9.1	**Rockville** (town) Parke County
32	9.1	**Tell City** (city) Perry County
36	9.0	**New Castle** (city) Henry County
37	8.9	**Knox** (city) Starke County
37	8.9	**North Vernon** (city) Jennings County
37	8.9	**Shelbyville** (city) Shelby County
40	8.8	**Fortville** (town) Hancock County
41	8.7	**Richmond** (city) Wayne County
42	8.6	**Brookville** (town) Franklin County
42	8.6	**Elwood** (city) Madison County
42	8.6	**Frankfort** (city) Clinton County
45	8.5	**Loogootee** (city) Martin County
45	8.5	**Madison** (city) Jefferson County
45	8.5	**Munster** (town) Lake County
45	8.5	**Rochester** (city) Fulton County
45	8.5	**Winfield** (town) Lake County
50	8.4	**Centerville** (town) Wayne County
50	8.4	**Crown Point** (city) Lake County
50	8.4	**Lebanon** (city) Boone County
53	8.3	**Brownstown** (town) Jackson County
53	8.3	**Hartford City** (city) Blackford County
53	8.3	**Huntingburg** (city) Dubois County
53	8.3	**Marion** (city) Grant County
53	8.3	**Seymour** (city) Jackson County
58	8.2	**Bluffton** (city) Wells County
58	8.2	**Greenfield** (city) Hancock County
60	8.1	**Franklin** (city) Johnson County
60	8.1	**Greencastle** (city) Putnam County
60	8.1	**La Porte** (city) LaPorte County
60	8.1	**Martinsville** (city) Morgan County
64	8.0	**Charlestown** (city) Clark County
64	8.0	**Kendallville** (city) Noble County
64	8.0	**Vincennes** (city) Knox County
67	7.9	**Dyer** (town) Lake County
67	7.9	**Winamac** (town) Pulaski County
69	7.8	**Whiting** (city) Lake County
70	7.7	**Mishawaka** (city) Saint Joseph County
70	7.7	**New Albany** (city) Floyd County
72	7.6	**Highland** (town) Lake County
72	7.6	**Kokomo** (city) Howard County
72	7.6	**North Terre Haute** (CDP) Vigo County
72	7.6	**Sellersburg** (town) Clark County
72	7.6	**Syracuse** (town) Kosciusko County
77	7.5	**Angola** (city) Steuben County
77	7.5	**Ellettsville** (town) Monroe County
79	7.4	**Beech Grove** (city) Marion County
79	7.4	**Greensburg** (city) Decatur County
81	7.3	**Anderson** (city) Madison County
81	7.3	**Gas City** (city) Grant County
81	7.3	**Huntington** (city) Huntington County
84	7.2	**Austin** (city) Scott County
84	7.2	**De Motte** (town) Jasper County
84	7.2	**Logansport** (city) Cass County
84	7.2	**Wabash** (city) Wabash County
88	7.1	**New Haven** (city) Allen County
89	7.0	**Danville** (town) Hendricks County
89	7.0	**Elkhart** (city) Elkhart County
89	7.0	**Evansville** (city) Vanderburgh County
89	7.0	**Portage** (city) Porter County
89	7.0	**Princeton** (city) Gibson County
94	6.9	**Hobart** (city) Lake County
94	6.9	**Peru** (city) Miami County
94	6.9	**Rensselaer** (city) Jasper County
97	6.8	**Bright** (CDP) Dearborn County
97	6.8	**Speedway** (town) Marion County
99	6.7	**Hanover** (town) Jefferson County
99	6.7	**Jasper** (city) Dubois County
99	6.7	**Lowell** (town) Lake County
99	6.7	**Merrillville** (town) Lake County
103	6.6	**East Chicago** (city) Lake County
103	6.6	**Fort Branch** (town) Gibson County
103	6.6	**Plymouth** (city) Marshall County
106	6.5	**Brazil** (city) Clay County
106	6.5	**Butler** (city) DeKalb County
106	6.5	**Goshen** (city) Elkhart County
106	6.5	**Greendale** (city) Dearborn County
106	6.5	**Schererville** (town) Lake County
106	6.5	**South Bend** (city) Saint Joseph County
112	6.4	**Columbia City** (city) Whitley County
112	6.4	**Crawfordsville** (city) Montgomery County
112	6.4	**Edinburgh** (town) Johnson County
112	6.4	**Valparaiso** (city) Porter County
116	6.3	**Chesterton** (town) Porter County
116	6.3	**Winona Lake** (town) Kosciusko County
118	6.2	**Griffith** (town) Lake County
118	6.2	**Michigan City** (city) LaPorte County
118	6.2	**Muncie** (city) Delaware County
118	6.2	**Pendleton** (town) Madison County
118	6.2	**Simonton Lake** (CDP) Elkhart County
118	6.2	**Terre Haute** (city) Vigo County
118	6.2	**Yorktown** (town) Delaware County
125	6.1	**Cicero** (town) Hamilton County
125	6.1	**Columbus** (city) Bartholomew County
125	6.1	**Garrett** (city) DeKalb County
125	6.1	**Hammond** (city) Lake County
125	6.1	**Shorewood Forest** (CDP) Porter County
130	6.0	**Jeffersonville** (city) Clark County
130	6.0	**Scottsburg** (city) Scott County
130	6.0	**Sheridan** (town) Hamilton County
133	5.9	**Brownsburg** (town) Hendricks County
133	5.9	**Fort Wayne** (city) Allen County
133	5.9	**Greenwood** (city) Johnson County
133	5.9	**Smithville-Sanders** (CDP) Monroe County
137	5.8	**Lake Station** (city) Lake County
137	5.8	**New Whiteland** (town) Johnson County
137	5.8	**Santa Claus** (town) Spencer County
137	5.8	**Warsaw** (city) Kosciusko County
141	5.7	**Highland** (CDP) Vanderburgh County
141	5.7	**Mount Vernon** (city) Posey County
141	5.7	**Plainfield** (town) Hendricks County
144	5.5	**Lakes of the Four Seasons** (CDP) Lake County
144	5.5	**Lawrence** (city) Marion County
144	5.5	**Osceola** (town) Saint Joseph County
147	5.3	**Roselawn** (CDP) Newton County
148	5.2	**Indianapolis** (city) Marion County
149	5.1	**Chandler** (town) Warrick County
149	5.1	**Country Squire Lakes** (CDP) Jennings County

Note: *This section ranks incorporated places and CDPs (Census Designated Places) with populations of 2,500 or more. Unincorporated postal areas were not considered. Please refer to the User Guide for additional information.*

Marriage Status: Widowed

Top 150 Places Ranked in *Ascending* Order

State Rank	Percent	Place
1	0.0	**McCordsville** (town) Hancock County
2	0.3	**Notre Dame** (CDP) Saint Joseph County
3	1.2	**Hidden Valley** (CDP) Dearborn County
4	1.5	**Whitestown** (town) Boone County
5	1.7	**Porter** (town) Porter County
6	2.3	**Westville** (town) LaPorte County
7	2.6	**Middlebury** (town) Elkhart County
8	2.7	**West Lafayette** (city) Tippecanoe County
9	2.9	**Ligonier** (city) Noble County
10	3.0	**Bloomington** (city) Monroe County
10	3.0	**Fishers** (city) Hamilton County
12	3.1	**Huntertown** (town) Allen County
12	3.1	**Leo-Cedarville** (town) Allen County
14	3.4	**Westfield** (city) Hamilton County
15	3.5	**Salt Creek Commons** (CDP) Porter County
15	3.5	**Whiteland** (town) Johnson County
17	3.6	**Cedar Lake** (town) Lake County
17	3.6	**Pittsboro** (town) Hendricks County
19	3.7	**Zionsville** (town) Boone County
20	3.8	**Carmel** (city) Hamilton County
20	3.8	**Heritage Lake** (CDP) Putnam County
22	3.9	**Bargersville** (town) Johnson County
23	4.0	**Bremen** (town) Marshall County
23	4.0	**Melody Hill** (CDP) Vanderburgh County
25	4.1	**Cumberland** (town) Marion County
25	4.1	**Dunlap** (CDP) Elkhart County
27	4.2	**Granger** (CDP) Saint Joseph County
27	4.2	**Nappanee** (city) Elkhart County
27	4.2	**Newburgh** (town) Warrick County
30	4.5	**Noblesville** (city) Hamilton County
31	4.6	**Aurora** (city) Dearborn County
31	4.6	**Avon** (town) Hendricks County
33	4.7	**Fairmount** (town) Grant County
33	4.7	**Hebron** (town) Porter County
35	4.8	**Saint John** (town) Lake County
36	4.9	**Georgetown** (town) Floyd County
36	4.9	**South Haven** (CDP) Porter County
38	5.0	**Upland** (town) Grant County
39	5.1	**Chandler** (town) Warrick County
39	5.1	**Country Squire Lakes** (CDP) Jennings County
39	5.1	**Lafayette** (city) Tippecanoe County
42	5.2	**Indianapolis** (city) Marion County
43	5.3	**Roselawn** (CDP) Newton County
44	5.5	**Lakes of the Four Seasons** (CDP) Lake County
44	5.5	**Lawrence** (city) Marion County
44	5.5	**Osceola** (town) Saint Joseph County
47	5.7	**Highland** (CDP) Vanderburgh County
47	5.7	**Mount Vernon** (city) Posey County
47	5.7	**Plainfield** (town) Hendricks County
50	5.8	**Lake Station** (city) Lake County
50	5.8	**New Whiteland** (town) Johnson County
50	5.8	**Santa Claus** (town) Spencer County
50	5.8	**Warsaw** (city) Kosciusko County
54	5.9	**Brownsburg** (town) Hendricks County
54	5.9	**Fort Wayne** (city) Allen County
54	5.9	**Greenwood** (city) Johnson County
54	5.9	**Smithville-Sanders** (CDP) Monroe County
58	6.0	**Jeffersonville** (city) Clark County
58	6.0	**Scottsburg** (city) Scott County
58	6.0	**Sheridan** (town) Hamilton County
61	6.1	**Cicero** (town) Hamilton County
61	6.1	**Columbus** (city) Bartholomew County
61	6.1	**Garrett** (city) DeKalb County
61	6.1	**Hammond** (city) Lake County
61	6.1	**Shorewood Forest** (CDP) Porter County
66	6.2	**Griffith** (town) Lake County
66	6.2	**Michigan City** (city) LaPorte County
66	6.2	**Muncie** (city) Delaware County
66	6.2	**Pendleton** (town) Madison County
66	6.2	**Simonton Lake** (CDP) Elkhart County
66	6.2	**Terre Haute** (city) Vigo County
66	6.2	**Yorktown** (town) Delaware County
73	6.3	**Chesterton** (town) Porter County
73	6.3	**Winona Lake** (town) Kosciusko County
75	6.4	**Columbia City** (city) Whitley County
75	6.4	**Crawfordsville** (city) Montgomery County
75	6.4	**Edinburgh** (town) Johnson County
75	6.4	**Valparaiso** (city) Porter County
79	6.5	**Brazil** (city) Clay County
79	6.5	**Butler** (city) DeKalb County
79	6.5	**Goshen** (city) Elkhart County
79	6.5	**Greendale** (city) Dearborn County
79	6.5	**Schererville** (town) Lake County
79	6.5	**South Bend** (city) Saint Joseph County
85	6.6	**East Chicago** (city) Lake County
85	6.6	**Fort Branch** (town) Gibson County
85	6.6	**Plymouth** (city) Marshall County
88	6.7	**Hanover** (town) Jefferson County
88	6.7	**Jasper** (city) Dubois County
88	6.7	**Lowell** (town) Lake County
88	6.7	**Merrillville** (town) Lake County
92	6.8	**Bright** (CDP) Dearborn County
92	6.8	**Speedway** (town) Marion County
94	6.9	**Hobart** (city) Lake County
94	6.9	**Peru** (city) Miami County
94	6.9	**Rensselaer** (city) Jasper County
97	7.0	**Danville** (town) Hendricks County
97	7.0	**Elkhart** (city) Elkhart County
97	7.0	**Evansville** (city) Vanderburgh County
97	7.0	**Portage** (city) Porter County
97	7.0	**Princeton** (city) Gibson County
102	7.1	**New Haven** (city) Allen County
103	7.2	**Austin** (city) Scott County
103	7.2	**De Motte** (town) Jasper County
103	7.2	**Logansport** (city) Cass County
103	7.2	**Wabash** (city) Wabash County
107	7.3	**Anderson** (city) Madison County
107	7.3	**Gas City** (city) Grant County
107	7.3	**Huntington** (city) Huntington County
110	7.4	**Beech Grove** (city) Marion County
110	7.4	**Greensburg** (city) Decatur County
112	7.5	**Angola** (city) Steuben County
112	7.5	**Ellettsville** (town) Monroe County
114	7.6	**Highland** (town) Lake County
114	7.6	**Kokomo** (city) Howard County
114	7.6	**North Terre Haute** (CDP) Vigo County
114	7.6	**Sellersburg** (town) Clark County
114	7.6	**Syracuse** (town) Kosciusko County
119	7.7	**Mishawaka** (city) Saint Joseph County
119	7.7	**New Albany** (city) Floyd County
121	7.8	**Whiting** (city) Lake County
122	7.9	**Dyer** (town) Lake County
122	7.9	**Winamac** (town) Pulaski County
124	8.0	**Charlestown** (city) Clark County
124	8.0	**Kendallville** (city) Noble County
124	8.0	**Vincennes** (city) Knox County
127	8.1	**Franklin** (city) Johnson County
127	8.1	**Greencastle** (city) Putnam County
127	8.1	**La Porte** (city) LaPorte County
127	8.1	**Martinsville** (city) Morgan County
131	8.2	**Bluffton** (city) Wells County
131	8.2	**Greenfield** (city) Hancock County
133	8.3	**Brownstown** (town) Jackson County
133	8.3	**Hartford City** (city) Blackford County
133	8.3	**Huntingburg** (city) Dubois County
133	8.3	**Marion** (city) Grant County
133	8.3	**Seymour** (city) Jackson County
138	8.4	**Centerville** (town) Wayne County
138	8.4	**Crown Point** (city) Lake County
138	8.4	**Lebanon** (city) Boone County
141	8.5	**Loogootee** (city) Martin County
141	8.5	**Madison** (city) Jefferson County
141	8.5	**Munster** (town) Lake County
141	8.5	**Rochester** (city) Fulton County
141	8.5	**Winfield** (town) Lake County
146	8.6	**Brookville** (town) Franklin County
146	8.6	**Elwood** (city) Madison County
146	8.6	**Frankfort** (city) Clinton County
149	8.7	**Richmond** (city) Wayne County
150	8.8	**Fortville** (town) Hancock County

Note: *This section ranks incorporated places and CDPs (Census Designated Places) with populations of 2,500 or more. Unincorporated postal areas were not considered. Please refer to the User Guide for additional information.*

Rankings

Marriage Status: Divorced

Top 150 Places Ranked in *Descending* Order

State Rank	Percent	Place
1	24.8	**Loogootee** (city) Martin County
2	24.3	**Rochester** (city) Fulton County
3	23.8	**Clinton** (city) Vermillion County
4	22.6	**Union City** (city) Randolph County
4	22.6	**Westville** (town) LaPorte County
6	22.1	**Centerville** (town) Wayne County
7	21.5	**Corydon** (town) Harrison County
8	21.4	**Knox** (city) Starke County
9	21.2	**Mitchell** (city) Lawrence County
10	21.1	**Country Squire Lakes** (CDP) Jennings County
10	21.1	**Paoli** (town) Orange County
12	21.0	**New Castle** (city) Henry County
13	20.9	**Salem** (city) Washington County
14	20.7	**Ellettsville** (town) Monroe County
15	20.6	**Lawrenceburg** (city) Dearborn County
16	20.5	**Martinsville** (city) Morgan County
16	20.5	**Sullivan** (city) Sullivan County
18	20.2	**Connersville** (city) Fayette County
19	20.1	**Syracuse** (town) Kosciusko County
20	19.9	**Bedford** (city) Lawrence County
20	19.9	**Gas City** (city) Grant County
20	19.9	**Madison** (city) Jefferson County
23	19.8	**Butler** (city) DeKalb County
24	19.3	**Kendallville** (city) Noble County
25	19.1	**Anderson** (city) Madison County
25	19.1	**North Vernon** (city) Jennings County
27	19.0	**New Whiteland** (town) Johnson County
27	19.0	**Princeton** (city) Gibson County
29	18.7	**Brownstown** (town) Jackson County
30	18.5	**Lagrange** (town) LaGrange County
31	18.4	**Decatur** (city) Adams County
32	18.0	**Rushville** (city) Rush County
33	17.8	**La Porte** (city) LaPorte County
34	17.7	**Evansville** (city) Vanderburgh County
35	17.5	**Kokomo** (city) Howard County
35	17.5	**Sheridan** (town) Hamilton County
37	17.4	**Brazil** (city) Clay County
37	17.4	**Garrett** (city) DeKalb County
37	17.4	**Michigan City** (city) LaPorte County
37	17.4	**North Terre Haute** (CDP) Vigo County
37	17.4	**Richmond** (city) Wayne County
42	17.3	**Brookville** (town) Franklin County
43	17.1	**Attica** (city) Fountain County
43	17.1	**Aurora** (city) Dearborn County
43	17.1	**Crawfordsville** (city) Montgomery County
43	17.1	**Wabash** (city) Wabash County
47	17.0	**Beech Grove** (city) Marion County
48	16.9	**Winamac** (town) Pulaski County
49	16.8	**Lebanon** (city) Boone County
49	16.8	**Rockville** (town) Parke County
51	16.7	**Clarksville** (town) Clark County
51	16.7	**Linton** (city) Greene County
51	16.7	**Marion** (city) Grant County
51	16.7	**New Albany** (city) Floyd County
51	16.7	**Simonton Lake** (CDP) Elkhart County
56	16.6	**Vincennes** (city) Knox County
57	16.5	**Charlestown** (city) Clark County
58	16.4	**Greensburg** (city) Decatur County
58	16.4	**Mishawaka** (city) Saint Joseph County
60	16.3	**Elkhart** (city) Elkhart County
60	16.3	**Peru** (city) Miami County
62	16.1	**Columbia City** (city) Whitley County
62	16.1	**Elwood** (city) Madison County
62	16.1	**Pendleton** (town) Madison County
62	16.1	**Shelbyville** (city) Shelby County
62	16.1	**Tell City** (city) Perry County
67	15.9	**Delphi** (city) Carroll County
68	15.7	**Warsaw** (city) Kosciusko County
69	15.6	**Fairmount** (town) Grant County
69	15.6	**Seymour** (city) Jackson County
71	15.5	**Greenfield** (city) Hancock County
71	15.5	**Lafayette** (city) Tippecanoe County
71	15.5	**Mount Vernon** (city) Posey County
71	15.5	**Portland** (city) Jay County
75	15.3	**Plainfield** (town) Hendricks County
76	15.2	**Sellersburg** (town) Clark County
77	15.1	**De Motte** (town) Jasper County
77	15.1	**Edinburgh** (town) Johnson County
77	15.1	**Jeffersonville** (city) Clark County
80	15.0	**Ligonier** (city) Noble County
80	15.0	**Plymouth** (city) Marshall County
80	15.0	**Whiteland** (town) Johnson County
83	14.9	**Logansport** (city) Cass County
83	14.9	**Mooresville** (town) Morgan County
83	14.9	**Terre Haute** (city) Vigo County
86	14.8	**Franklin** (city) Johnson County
86	14.8	**Speedway** (town) Marion County
88	14.7	**Boonville** (city) Warrick County
89	14.6	**Greentown** (town) Howard County
90	14.5	**New Haven** (city) Allen County
90	14.5	**Washington** (city) Daviess County
92	14.4	**Greencastle** (city) Putnam County
93	14.3	**Bicknell** (city) Knox County
93	14.3	**Gary** (city) Lake County
95	14.2	**Danville** (town) Hendricks County
96	14.1	**Alexandria** (city) Madison County
96	14.1	**Auburn** (city) DeKalb County
96	14.1	**Frankfort** (city) Clinton County
96	14.1	**Monticello** (city) White County
100	14.0	**Angola** (city) Steuben County
100	14.0	**Greendale** (city) Dearborn County
102	13.5	**Fortville** (town) Hancock County
103	13.4	**Avon** (town) Hendricks County
103	13.4	**Columbus** (city) Bartholomew County
103	13.4	**Yorktown** (town) Delaware County
106	13.3	**Merrillville** (town) Lake County
106	13.3	**Nappanee** (city) Elkhart County
108	13.2	**Bluffton** (city) Wells County
108	13.2	**Fort Wayne** (city) Allen County
108	13.2	**Greenwood** (city) Johnson County
108	13.2	**Highland** (town) Lake County
108	13.2	**Portage** (city) Porter County
113	13.1	**Huntertown** (town) Allen County
113	13.1	**Indianapolis** (city) Marion County
113	13.1	**South Bend** (city) Saint Joseph County
116	13.0	**Huntingburg** (city) Dubois County
117	12.9	**Hanover** (town) Jefferson County
117	12.9	**Huntington** (city) Huntington County
117	12.9	**Jasper** (city) Dubois County
117	12.9	**Muncie** (city) Delaware County
117	12.9	**Newburgh** (town) Warrick County
122	12.8	**Austin** (city) Scott County
123	12.7	**Bremen** (town) Marshall County
123	12.7	**Melody Hill** (CDP) Vanderburgh County
125	12.6	**Griffith** (town) Lake County
125	12.6	**Scottsburg** (city) Scott County
125	12.6	**Whitestown** (town) Boone County
128	12.5	**Fort Branch** (town) Gibson County
128	12.5	**Valparaiso** (city) Porter County
130	12.4	**Winchester** (city) Randolph County
131	12.3	**Cicero** (town) Hamilton County
131	12.3	**Rensselaer** (city) Jasper County
131	12.3	**Tipton** (city) Tipton County
134	12.2	**Hartford City** (city) Blackford County
134	12.2	**Lake Station** (city) Lake County
134	12.2	**South Haven** (CDP) Porter County
137	12.1	**Goshen** (city) Elkhart County
138	12.0	**Cedar Lake** (town) Lake County
138	12.0	**Hebron** (town) Porter County
138	12.0	**Hobart** (city) Lake County
141	11.9	**Chesterton** (town) Porter County
141	11.9	**Hammond** (city) Lake County
141	11.9	**Smithville-Sanders** (CDP) Monroe County
144	11.6	**Cumberland** (town) Marion County
144	11.6	**Noblesville** (city) Hamilton County
146	11.2	**Lawrence** (city) Marion County
147	10.8	**Chandler** (town) Warrick County
148	10.7	**Crown Point** (city) Lake County
149	10.6	**Brownsburg** (town) Hendricks County
149	10.6	**Pittsboro** (town) Hendricks County

Note: *This section ranks incorporated places and CDPs (Census Designated Places) with populations of 2,500 or more. Unincorporated postal areas were not considered. Please refer to the User Guide for additional information.*

Marriage Status: Divorced

Top 150 Places Ranked in *Ascending* Order

State Rank	Percent	Place
1	1.4	**Notre Dame** (CDP) Saint Joseph County
2	2.9	**West Lafayette** (city) Tippecanoe County
3	4.7	**Upland** (town) Grant County
4	5.5	**Granger** (CDP) Saint Joseph County
5	5.7	**Winfield** (town) Lake County
6	6.8	**Heritage Lake** (CDP) Putnam County
6	6.8	**Santa Claus** (town) Spencer County
8	6.9	**Zionsville** (town) Boone County
9	7.2	**Saint John** (town) Lake County
10	7.5	**Highland** (CDP) Vanderburgh County
11	7.7	**Leo-Cedarville** (town) Allen County
12	7.9	**Carmel** (city) Hamilton County
12	7.9	**Shorewood Forest** (CDP) Porter County
14	8.0	**Berne** (city) Adams County
15	8.1	**Middlebury** (town) Elkhart County
15	8.1	**Roselawn** (CDP) Newton County
17	8.4	**Bloomington** (city) Monroe County
18	8.5	**Dyer** (town) Lake County
19	8.6	**Hidden Valley** (CDP) Dearborn County
20	8.7	**Dunlap** (CDP) Elkhart County
20	8.7	**Winona Lake** (town) Kosciusko County
22	8.8	**Batesville** (city) Ripley County
22	8.8	**Porter** (town) Porter County
22	8.8	**Westfield** (city) Hamilton County
22	8.8	**Whiting** (city) Lake County
26	9.1	**Munster** (town) Lake County
27	9.3	**Lakes of the Four Seasons** (CDP) Lake County
27	9.3	**Ossian** (town) Wells County
27	9.3	**Salt Creek Commons** (CDP) Porter County
30	9.4	**Bargersville** (town) Johnson County
31	9.5	**Lowell** (town) Lake County
31	9.5	**Osceola** (town) Saint Joseph County
33	9.7	**Fishers** (city) Hamilton County
34	9.8	**Schererville** (town) Lake County
35	9.9	**Bright** (CDP) Dearborn County
35	9.9	**McCordsville** (town) Hancock County
35	9.9	**North Manchester** (town) Wabash County
38	10.2	**Georgetown** (town) Floyd County
39	10.5	**East Chicago** (city) Lake County
40	10.6	**Brownsburg** (town) Hendricks County
40	10.6	**Pittsboro** (town) Hendricks County
42	10.7	**Crown Point** (city) Lake County
43	10.8	**Chandler** (town) Warrick County
44	11.2	**Lawrence** (city) Marion County
45	11.6	**Cumberland** (town) Marion County
45	11.6	**Noblesville** (city) Hamilton County
47	11.9	**Chesterton** (town) Porter County
47	11.9	**Hammond** (city) Lake County
47	11.9	**Smithville-Sanders** (CDP) Monroe County
50	12.0	**Cedar Lake** (town) Lake County
50	12.0	**Hebron** (town) Porter County
50	12.0	**Hobart** (city) Lake County
53	12.1	**Goshen** (city) Elkhart County
54	12.2	**Hartford City** (city) Blackford County
54	12.2	**Lake Station** (city) Lake County
54	12.2	**South Haven** (CDP) Porter County
57	12.3	**Cicero** (town) Hamilton County
57	12.3	**Rensselaer** (city) Jasper County
57	12.3	**Tipton** (city) Tipton County
60	12.4	**Winchester** (city) Randolph County
61	12.5	**Fort Branch** (town) Gibson County
61	12.5	**Valparaiso** (city) Porter County
63	12.6	**Griffith** (town) Lake County
63	12.6	**Scottsburg** (city) Scott County
63	12.6	**Whitestown** (town) Boone County
66	12.7	**Bremen** (town) Marshall County
66	12.7	**Melody Hill** (CDP) Vanderburgh County
68	12.8	**Austin** (city) Scott County
69	12.9	**Hanover** (town) Jefferson County
69	12.9	**Huntington** (city) Huntington County
69	12.9	**Jasper** (city) Dubois County
69	12.9	**Muncie** (city) Delaware County
69	12.9	**Newburgh** (town) Warrick County
74	13.0	**Huntingburg** (city) Dubois County
75	13.1	**Huntertown** (town) Allen County
75	13.1	**Indianapolis** (city) Marion County
75	13.1	**South Bend** (city) Saint Joseph County
78	13.2	**Bluffton** (city) Wells County
78	13.2	**Fort Wayne** (city) Allen County
78	13.2	**Greenwood** (city) Johnson County
78	13.2	**Highland** (town) Lake County
78	13.2	**Portage** (city) Porter County
83	13.3	**Merrillville** (town) Lake County
83	13.3	**Nappanee** (city) Elkhart County
85	13.4	**Avon** (town) Hendricks County
85	13.4	**Columbus** (city) Bartholomew County
85	13.4	**Yorktown** (town) Delaware County
88	13.5	**Fortville** (town) Hancock County
89	14.0	**Angola** (city) Steuben County
89	14.0	**Greendale** (city) Dearborn County
91	14.1	**Alexandria** (city) Madison County
91	14.1	**Auburn** (city) DeKalb County
91	14.1	**Frankfort** (city) Clinton County
91	14.1	**Monticello** (city) White County
95	14.2	**Danville** (town) Hendricks County
96	14.3	**Bicknell** (city) Knox County
96	14.3	**Gary** (city) Lake County
98	14.4	**Greencastle** (city) Putnam County
99	14.5	**New Haven** (city) Allen County
99	14.5	**Washington** (city) Daviess County
101	14.6	**Greentown** (town) Howard County
102	14.7	**Boonville** (city) Warrick County
103	14.8	**Franklin** (city) Johnson County
103	14.8	**Speedway** (town) Marion County
105	14.9	**Logansport** (city) Cass County
105	14.9	**Mooresville** (town) Morgan County
105	14.9	**Terre Haute** (city) Vigo County
108	15.0	**Ligonier** (city) Noble County
108	15.0	**Plymouth** (city) Marshall County
108	15.0	**Whiteland** (town) Johnson County
111	15.1	**De Motte** (town) Jasper County
111	15.1	**Edinburgh** (town) Johnson County
111	15.1	**Jeffersonville** (city) Clark County
114	15.2	**Sellersburg** (town) Clark County
115	15.3	**Plainfield** (town) Hendricks County
116	15.5	**Greenfield** (city) Hancock County
116	15.5	**Lafayette** (city) Tippecanoe County
116	15.5	**Mount Vernon** (city) Posey County
116	15.5	**Portland** (city) Jay County
120	15.6	**Fairmount** (town) Grant County
120	15.6	**Seymour** (city) Jackson County
122	15.7	**Warsaw** (city) Kosciusko County
123	15.9	**Delphi** (city) Carroll County
124	16.1	**Columbia City** (city) Whitley County
124	16.1	**Elwood** (city) Madison County
124	16.1	**Pendleton** (town) Madison County
124	16.1	**Shelbyville** (city) Shelby County
124	16.1	**Tell City** (city) Perry County
129	16.3	**Elkhart** (city) Elkhart County
129	16.3	**Peru** (city) Miami County
131	16.4	**Greensburg** (city) Decatur County
131	16.4	**Mishawaka** (city) Saint Joseph County
133	16.5	**Charlestown** (city) Clark County
134	16.6	**Vincennes** (city) Knox County
135	16.7	**Clarksville** (town) Clark County
135	16.7	**Linton** (city) Greene County
135	16.7	**Marion** (city) Grant County
135	16.7	**New Albany** (city) Floyd County
135	16.7	**Simonton Lake** (CDP) Elkhart County
140	16.8	**Lebanon** (city) Boone County
140	16.8	**Rockville** (town) Parke County
142	16.9	**Winamac** (town) Pulaski County
143	17.0	**Beech Grove** (city) Marion County
144	17.1	**Attica** (city) Fountain County
144	17.1	**Aurora** (city) Dearborn County
144	17.1	**Crawfordsville** (city) Montgomery County
144	17.1	**Wabash** (city) Wabash County
148	17.3	**Brookville** (town) Franklin County
149	17.4	**Brazil** (city) Clay County
149	17.4	**Garrett** (city) DeKalb County

Note: *This section ranks incorporated places and CDPs (Census Designated Places) with populations of 2,500 or more. Unincorporated postal areas were not considered. Please refer to the User Guide for additional information.*

Foreign Born

Top 150 Places Ranked in *Descending* Order

State Rank	Percent	Place
1	24.5	**West Lafayette** (city) Tippecanoe County
2	23.8	**Ligonier** (city) Noble County
3	16.4	**Logansport** (city) Cass County
4	16.3	**Speedway** (town) Marion County
5	15.7	**East Chicago** (city) Lake County
6	15.0	**Goshen** (city) Elkhart County
7	13.5	**Frankfort** (city) Clinton County
8	13.4	**Columbus** (city) Bartholomew County
9	12.4	**Huntingburg** (city) Dubois County
10	12.2	**Elkhart** (city) Elkhart County
11	12.1	**Bloomington** (city) Monroe County
12	11.9	**Delphi** (city) Carroll County
13	11.6	**Carmel** (city) Hamilton County
14	11.3	**Hammond** (city) Lake County
15	10.7	**Munster** (town) Lake County
15	10.7	**Schererville** (town) Lake County
17	10.0	**Notre Dame** (CDP) Saint Joseph County
18	9.3	**Indianapolis** (city) Marion County
18	9.3	**Plymouth** (city) Marshall County
20	9.2	**Avon** (town) Hendricks County
21	8.9	**Fishers** (city) Hamilton County
22	8.8	**Seymour** (city) Jackson County
23	8.5	**Lagrange** (town) LaGrange County
23	8.5	**South Bend** (city) Saint Joseph County
25	8.0	**Lawrence** (city) Marion County
26	7.9	**Crown Point** (city) Lake County
26	7.9	**Granger** (CDP) Saint Joseph County
28	7.8	**Fort Wayne** (city) Allen County
28	7.8	**Greenwood** (city) Johnson County
28	7.8	**Winona Lake** (town) Kosciusko County
31	7.6	**Whiting** (city) Lake County
32	7.5	**Lakes of the Four Seasons** (CDP) Lake County
32	7.5	**Warsaw** (city) Kosciusko County
34	7.1	**Lafayette** (city) Tippecanoe County
35	7.0	**Edinburgh** (town) Johnson County
35	7.0	**Monticello** (city) White County
37	6.9	**Dyer** (town) Lake County
38	6.8	**Union City** (city) Randolph County
38	6.8	**Whitestown** (town) Boone County
40	6.7	**Plainfield** (town) Hendricks County
41	6.2	**Osceola** (town) Saint Joseph County
42	6.0	**Bremen** (town) Marshall County
42	6.0	**Cicero** (town) Hamilton County
42	6.0	**Winfield** (town) Lake County
45	5.9	**Clarksville** (town) Clark County
45	5.9	**Dunlap** (CDP) Elkhart County
45	5.9	**Highland** (town) Lake County
45	5.9	**Lake Station** (city) Lake County
45	5.9	**Shorewood Forest** (CDP) Porter County
50	5.8	**Jasper** (city) Dubois County
50	5.8	**La Porte** (city) LaPorte County
52	5.7	**Westfield** (city) Hamilton County
53	5.6	**Zionsville** (town) Boone County
54	5.4	**Mishawaka** (city) Saint Joseph County
55	5.3	**Newburgh** (town) Warrick County
55	5.3	**Portage** (city) Porter County
55	5.3	**Washington** (city) Daviess County
58	5.2	**Valparaiso** (city) Porter County
59	5.0	**Brownsburg** (town) Hendricks County
60	4.9	**Merrillville** (town) Lake County
61	4.8	**Crawfordsville** (city) Montgomery County
62	4.7	**Shelbyville** (city) Shelby County
63	4.5	**Charlestown** (city) Clark County
63	4.5	**Country Squire Lakes** (CDP) Jennings County
65	4.4	**Griffith** (town) Lake County
65	4.4	**Saint John** (town) Lake County
67	4.3	**De Motte** (town) Jasper County
68	4.0	**Chesterton** (town) Porter County
68	4.0	**Middlebury** (town) Elkhart County
70	3.9	**Noblesville** (city) Hamilton County
71	3.8	**Princeton** (city) Gibson County
72	3.7	**Salt Creek Commons** (CDP) Porter County
73	3.5	**Batesville** (city) Ripley County
73	3.5	**Michigan City** (city) LaPorte County
73	3.5	**Portland** (city) Jay County
73	3.5	**Roselawn** (CDP) Newton County
77	3.4	**Upland** (town) Grant County
78	3.3	**Jeffersonville** (city) Clark County
78	3.3	**North Manchester** (town) Wabash County
78	3.3	**Richmond** (city) Wayne County
81	3.2	**Greencastle** (city) Putnam County
81	3.2	**Huntertown** (town) Allen County
83	3.1	**Terre Haute** (city) Vigo County
84	3.0	**Anderson** (city) Madison County
84	3.0	**Kendallville** (city) Noble County
86	2.9	**Angola** (city) Steuben County
87	2.8	**Hobart** (city) Lake County
87	2.8	**McCordsville** (town) Hancock County
89	2.7	**Evansville** (city) Vanderburgh County
89	2.7	**Muncie** (city) Delaware County
91	2.6	**Bargersville** (town) Johnson County
91	2.6	**Cedar Lake** (town) Lake County
91	2.6	**Nappanee** (city) Elkhart County
91	2.6	**Simonton Lake** (CDP) Elkhart County
95	2.5	**Kokomo** (city) Howard County
95	2.5	**Leo-Cedarville** (town) Allen County
97	2.4	**Greensburg** (city) Decatur County
97	2.4	**Huntington** (city) Huntington County
99	2.3	**Hanover** (town) Jefferson County
99	2.3	**Tipton** (city) Tipton County
99	2.3	**Winamac** (town) Pulaski County
102	2.2	**Danville** (town) Hendricks County
102	2.2	**Marion** (city) Grant County
102	2.2	**Syracuse** (town) Kosciusko County
105	2.1	**Mitchell** (city) Lawrence County
106	2.0	**Franklin** (city) Johnson County
106	2.0	**Gary** (city) Lake County
106	2.0	**Greenfield** (city) Hancock County
106	2.0	**Paoli** (town) Orange County
110	1.9	**Beech Grove** (city) Marion County
110	1.9	**Bright** (CDP) Dearborn County
110	1.9	**New Albany** (city) Floyd County
113	1.8	**Cumberland** (town) Marion County
113	1.8	**Madison** (city) Jefferson County
113	1.8	**Porter** (town) Porter County
113	1.8	**Rensselaer** (city) Jasper County
117	1.7	**Bedford** (city) Lawrence County
118	1.6	**Berne** (city) Adams County
118	1.6	**Sellersburg** (town) Clark County
118	1.6	**Vincennes** (city) Knox County
121	1.5	**Austin** (city) Scott County
121	1.5	**Georgetown** (town) Floyd County
121	1.5	**Rockville** (town) Parke County
121	1.5	**Winchester** (city) Randolph County
125	1.4	**Attica** (city) Fountain County
125	1.4	**Fairmount** (town) Grant County
125	1.4	**Hartford City** (city) Blackford County
125	1.4	**Martinsville** (city) Morgan County
125	1.4	**Melody Hill** (CDP) Vanderburgh County
125	1.4	**Smithville-Sanders** (CDP) Monroe County
125	1.4	**Sullivan** (city) Sullivan County
132	1.3	**Brownstown** (town) Jackson County
132	1.3	**Lebanon** (city) Boone County
132	1.3	**Lowell** (town) Lake County
132	1.3	**South Haven** (CDP) Porter County
132	1.3	**Whiteland** (town) Johnson County
137	1.2	**Auburn** (city) DeKalb County
137	1.2	**Aurora** (city) Dearborn County
137	1.2	**Boonville** (city) Warrick County
137	1.2	**New Haven** (city) Allen County
141	1.1	**Hidden Valley** (CDP) Dearborn County
141	1.1	**New Whiteland** (town) Johnson County
141	1.1	**Peru** (city) Miami County
141	1.1	**Pittsboro** (town) Hendricks County
141	1.1	**Westville** (town) LaPorte County
146	1.0	**Columbia City** (city) Whitley County
146	1.0	**Gas City** (city) Grant County
146	1.0	**Highland** (CDP) Vanderburgh County
146	1.0	**Ossian** (town) Wells County
146	1.0	**Wabash** (city) Wabash County

Note: *This section ranks incorporated places and CDPs (Census Designated Places) with populations of 2,500 or more. Unincorporated postal areas were not considered. Please refer to the User Guide for additional information.*

Foreign Born

Top 150 Places Ranked in *Ascending* Order

State Rank	Percent	Place
1	0.0	**Centerville** (town) Wayne County
1	0.0	**Corydon** (town) Harrison County
1	0.0	**Greendale** (city) Dearborn County
1	0.0	**Lawrenceburg** (city) Dearborn County
1	0.0	**Pendleton** (town) Madison County
6	0.1	**Salem** (city) Washington County
7	0.2	**Brazil** (city) Clay County
7	0.2	**Ellettsville** (town) Monroe County
7	0.2	**Heritage Lake** (CDP) Putnam County
7	0.2	**Mooresville** (town) Morgan County
7	0.2	**North Terre Haute** (CDP) Vigo County
12	0.3	**Bicknell** (city) Knox County
12	0.3	**Butler** (city) DeKalb County
12	0.3	**Chandler** (town) Warrick County
12	0.3	**Clinton** (city) Vermillion County
12	0.3	**Greentown** (town) Howard County
12	0.3	**Linton** (city) Greene County
12	0.3	**Scottsburg** (city) Scott County
19	0.4	**Sheridan** (town) Hamilton County
20	0.5	**Brookville** (town) Franklin County
21	0.6	**Connersville** (city) Fayette County
21	0.6	**Fortville** (town) Hancock County
21	0.6	**Loogootee** (city) Martin County
21	0.6	**Yorktown** (town) Delaware County
25	0.7	**Bluffton** (city) Wells County
25	0.7	**Decatur** (city) Adams County
25	0.7	**Fort Branch** (town) Gibson County
25	0.7	**Mount Vernon** (city) Posey County
25	0.7	**North Vernon** (city) Jennings County
25	0.7	**Tell City** (city) Perry County
31	0.8	**Alexandria** (city) Madison County
31	0.8	**Garrett** (city) DeKalb County
31	0.8	**Hebron** (town) Porter County
31	0.8	**New Castle** (city) Henry County
31	0.8	**Rochester** (city) Fulton County
36	0.9	**Elwood** (city) Madison County
36	0.9	**Knox** (city) Starke County
36	0.9	**Rushville** (city) Rush County
36	0.9	**Santa Claus** (town) Spencer County
40	1.0	**Columbia City** (city) Whitley County
40	1.0	**Gas City** (city) Grant County
40	1.0	**Highland** (CDP) Vanderburgh County
40	1.0	**Ossian** (town) Wells County
40	1.0	**Wabash** (city) Wabash County
45	1.1	**Hidden Valley** (CDP) Dearborn County
45	1.1	**New Whiteland** (town) Johnson County
45	1.1	**Peru** (city) Miami County
45	1.1	**Pittsboro** (town) Hendricks County
45	1.1	**Westville** (town) LaPorte County
50	1.2	**Auburn** (city) DeKalb County
50	1.2	**Aurora** (city) Dearborn County
50	1.2	**Boonville** (city) Warrick County
50	1.2	**New Haven** (city) Allen County
54	1.3	**Brownstown** (town) Jackson County
54	1.3	**Lebanon** (city) Boone County
54	1.3	**Lowell** (town) Lake County
54	1.3	**South Haven** (CDP) Porter County
54	1.3	**Whiteland** (town) Johnson County
59	1.4	**Attica** (city) Fountain County
59	1.4	**Fairmount** (town) Grant County
59	1.4	**Hartford City** (city) Blackford County
59	1.4	**Martinsville** (city) Morgan County
59	1.4	**Melody Hill** (CDP) Vanderburgh County
59	1.4	**Smithville-Sanders** (CDP) Monroe County
59	1.4	**Sullivan** (city) Sullivan County
66	1.5	**Austin** (city) Scott County
66	1.5	**Georgetown** (town) Floyd County
66	1.5	**Rockville** (town) Parke County
66	1.5	**Winchester** (city) Randolph County
70	1.6	**Berne** (city) Adams County
70	1.6	**Sellersburg** (town) Clark County
70	1.6	**Vincennes** (city) Knox County
73	1.7	**Bedford** (city) Lawrence County
74	1.8	**Cumberland** (town) Marion County
74	1.8	**Madison** (city) Jefferson County
74	1.8	**Porter** (town) Porter County
74	1.8	**Rensselaer** (city) Jasper County
78	1.9	**Beech Grove** (city) Marion County
78	1.9	**Bright** (CDP) Dearborn County
78	1.9	**New Albany** (city) Floyd County
81	2.0	**Franklin** (city) Johnson County
81	2.0	**Gary** (city) Lake County
81	2.0	**Greenfield** (city) Hancock County
81	2.0	**Paoli** (town) Orange County
85	2.1	**Mitchell** (city) Lawrence County
86	2.2	**Danville** (town) Hendricks County
86	2.2	**Marion** (city) Grant County
86	2.2	**Syracuse** (town) Kosciusko County
89	2.3	**Hanover** (town) Jefferson County
89	2.3	**Tipton** (city) Tipton County
89	2.3	**Winamac** (town) Pulaski County
92	2.4	**Greensburg** (city) Decatur County
92	2.4	**Huntington** (city) Huntington County
94	2.5	**Kokomo** (city) Howard County
94	2.5	**Leo-Cedarville** (town) Allen County
96	2.6	**Bargersville** (town) Johnson County
96	2.6	**Cedar Lake** (town) Lake County
96	2.6	**Nappanee** (city) Elkhart County
96	2.6	**Simonton Lake** (CDP) Elkhart County
100	2.7	**Evansville** (city) Vanderburgh County
100	2.7	**Muncie** (city) Delaware County
102	2.8	**Hobart** (city) Lake County
102	2.8	**McCordsville** (town) Hancock County
104	2.9	**Angola** (city) Steuben County
105	3.0	**Anderson** (city) Madison County
105	3.0	**Kendallville** (city) Noble County
107	3.1	**Terre Haute** (city) Vigo County
108	3.2	**Greencastle** (city) Putnam County
108	3.2	**Huntertown** (town) Allen County
110	3.3	**Jeffersonville** (city) Clark County
110	3.3	**North Manchester** (town) Wabash County
110	3.3	**Richmond** (city) Wayne County
113	3.4	**Upland** (town) Grant County
114	3.5	**Batesville** (city) Ripley County
114	3.5	**Michigan City** (city) LaPorte County
114	3.5	**Portland** (city) Jay County
114	3.5	**Roselawn** (CDP) Newton County
118	3.7	**Salt Creek Commons** (CDP) Porter County
119	3.8	**Princeton** (city) Gibson County
120	3.9	**Noblesville** (city) Hamilton County
121	4.0	**Chesterton** (town) Porter County
121	4.0	**Middlebury** (town) Elkhart County
123	4.3	**De Motte** (town) Jasper County
124	4.4	**Griffith** (town) Lake County
124	4.4	**Saint John** (town) Lake County
126	4.5	**Charlestown** (city) Clark County
126	4.5	**Country Squire Lakes** (CDP) Jennings County
128	4.7	**Shelbyville** (city) Shelby County
129	4.8	**Crawfordsville** (city) Montgomery County
130	4.9	**Merrillville** (town) Lake County
131	5.0	**Brownsburg** (town) Hendricks County
132	5.2	**Valparaiso** (city) Porter County
133	5.3	**Newburgh** (town) Warrick County
133	5.3	**Portage** (city) Porter County
133	5.3	**Washington** (city) Daviess County
136	5.4	**Mishawaka** (city) Saint Joseph County
137	5.6	**Zionsville** (town) Boone County
138	5.7	**Westfield** (city) Hamilton County
139	5.8	**Jasper** (city) Dubois County
139	5.8	**La Porte** (city) LaPorte County
141	5.9	**Clarksville** (town) Clark County
141	5.9	**Dunlap** (CDP) Elkhart County
141	5.9	**Highland** (town) Lake County
141	5.9	**Lake Station** (city) Lake County
141	5.9	**Shorewood Forest** (CDP) Porter County
146	6.0	**Bremen** (town) Marshall County
146	6.0	**Cicero** (town) Hamilton County
146	6.0	**Winfield** (town) Lake County
149	6.2	**Osceola** (town) Saint Joseph County
150	6.7	**Plainfield** (town) Hendricks County

Note: *This section ranks incorporated places and CDPs (Census Designated Places) with populations of 2,500 or more. Unincorporated postal areas were not considered. Please refer to the User Guide for additional information.*

Speak English-only at Home

Top 150 Places Ranked in *Descending* Order

State Rank	Percent	Place
1	99.9	**Sullivan** (city) Sullivan County
2	99.6	**Tell City** (city) Perry County
3	99.4	**Bicknell** (city) Knox County
3	99.4	**Corydon** (town) Harrison County
3	99.4	**Salem** (city) Washington County
6	99.3	**Greentown** (town) Howard County
6	99.3	**Mooresville** (town) Morgan County
8	99.1	**Chandler** (town) Warrick County
8	99.1	**Connersville** (city) Fayette County
8	99.1	**Lawrenceburg** (city) Dearborn County
8	99.1	**Mount Vernon** (city) Posey County
8	99.1	**Pendleton** (town) Madison County
8	99.1	**Whiteland** (town) Johnson County
14	99.0	**Yorktown** (town) Delaware County
15	98.9	**Paoli** (town) Orange County
15	98.9	**Rochester** (city) Fulton County
17	98.8	**Centerville** (town) Wayne County
18	98.7	**Brownstown** (town) Jackson County
18	98.7	**Highland** (CDP) Vanderburgh County
18	98.7	**Linton** (city) Greene County
18	98.7	**North Vernon** (city) Jennings County
22	98.6	**Brookville** (town) Franklin County
22	98.6	**South Haven** (CDP) Porter County
24	98.5	**Brazil** (city) Clay County
24	98.5	**Hebron** (town) Porter County
24	98.5	**Heritage Lake** (CDP) Putnam County
24	98.5	**North Terre Haute** (CDP) Vigo County
28	98.4	**Rushville** (city) Rush County
29	98.3	**Boonville** (city) Warrick County
29	98.3	**Columbia City** (city) Whitley County
31	98.2	**Bedford** (city) Lawrence County
31	98.2	**Elwood** (city) Madison County
31	98.2	**Knox** (city) Starke County
31	98.2	**Rockville** (town) Parke County
35	98.1	**Fort Branch** (town) Gibson County
35	98.1	**Martinsville** (city) Morgan County
35	98.1	**New Castle** (city) Henry County
38	97.9	**Cumberland** (town) Marion County
39	97.8	**Fairmount** (town) Grant County
39	97.8	**Fortville** (town) Hancock County
39	97.8	**Garrett** (city) DeKalb County
39	97.8	**Peru** (city) Miami County
39	97.8	**Pittsboro** (town) Hendricks County
44	97.7	**Loogootee** (city) Martin County
44	97.7	**Winchester** (city) Randolph County
46	97.5	**Auburn** (city) DeKalb County
46	97.5	**Aurora** (city) Dearborn County
46	97.5	**Hanover** (town) Jefferson County
46	97.5	**Vincennes** (city) Knox County
50	97.4	**Butler** (city) DeKalb County
50	97.4	**New Haven** (city) Allen County
50	97.4	**Ossian** (town) Wells County
53	97.3	**Melody Hill** (CDP) Vanderburgh County
54	97.2	**Lebanon** (city) Boone County
55	97.1	**Bluffton** (city) Wells County
55	97.1	**Gas City** (city) Grant County
55	97.1	**Madison** (city) Jefferson County
58	97.0	**Bright** (CDP) Dearborn County
58	97.0	**Hartford City** (city) Blackford County
58	97.0	**Tipton** (city) Tipton County
61	96.9	**New Whiteland** (town) Johnson County
61	96.9	**Sheridan** (town) Hamilton County
63	96.8	**Attica** (city) Fountain County
63	96.8	**Beech Grove** (city) Marion County
63	96.8	**McCordsville** (town) Hancock County
66	96.6	**Greenfield** (city) Hancock County
66	96.6	**New Albany** (city) Floyd County
68	96.5	**Santa Claus** (town) Spencer County
68	96.5	**Sellersburg** (town) Clark County
70	96.4	**Austin** (city) Scott County
70	96.4	**Clinton** (city) Vermillion County
70	96.4	**Greendale** (city) Dearborn County
73	96.3	**Alexandria** (city) Madison County
74	96.2	**Evansville** (city) Vanderburgh County
74	96.2	**Franklin** (city) Johnson County
74	96.2	**Wabash** (city) Wabash County
77	96.1	**Kokomo** (city) Howard County
78	96.0	**De Motte** (town) Jasper County
78	96.0	**Westville** (town) LaPorte County
80	95.9	**Porter** (town) Porter County
81	95.8	**Danville** (town) Hendricks County
81	95.8	**Ellettsville** (town) Monroe County
81	95.8	**Hidden Valley** (CDP) Dearborn County
81	95.8	**Upland** (town) Grant County
85	95.7	**Marion** (city) Grant County
86	95.6	**Berne** (city) Adams County
86	95.6	**Greencastle** (city) Putnam County
86	95.6	**Muncie** (city) Delaware County
86	95.6	**Rensselaer** (city) Jasper County
90	95.5	**Huntington** (city) Huntington County
91	95.4	**Batesville** (city) Ripley County
91	95.4	**Georgetown** (town) Floyd County
91	95.4	**Huntertown** (town) Allen County
94	95.3	**Gary** (city) Lake County
94	95.3	**Scottsburg** (city) Scott County
94	95.3	**Winamac** (town) Pulaski County
97	95.0	**Greensburg** (city) Decatur County
97	95.0	**Lowell** (town) Lake County
97	95.0	**Mitchell** (city) Lawrence County
97	95.0	**Newburgh** (town) Warrick County
97	95.0	**Smithville-Sanders** (CDP) Monroe County
102	94.9	**Angola** (city) Steuben County
102	94.9	**Decatur** (city) Adams County
102	94.9	**Jeffersonville** (city) Clark County
102	94.9	**Terre Haute** (city) Vigo County
106	94.8	**Bargersville** (town) Johnson County
107	94.7	**Cedar Lake** (town) Lake County
107	94.7	**Richmond** (city) Wayne County
109	94.6	**Anderson** (city) Madison County
109	94.6	**Michigan City** (city) LaPorte County
109	94.6	**Simonton Lake** (CDP) Elkhart County
112	94.5	**Kendallville** (city) Noble County
113	94.4	**Country Squire Lakes** (CDP) Jennings County
113	94.4	**North Manchester** (town) Wabash County
113	94.4	**Princeton** (city) Gibson County
116	94.3	**Nappanee** (city) Elkhart County
116	94.3	**Shorewood Forest** (CDP) Porter County
118	94.2	**Charlestown** (city) Clark County
119	94.1	**Noblesville** (city) Hamilton County
120	94.0	**Chesterton** (town) Porter County
120	94.0	**Leo-Cedarville** (town) Allen County
122	93.8	**Brownsburg** (town) Hendricks County
122	93.8	**Mishawaka** (city) Saint Joseph County
124	93.7	**Syracuse** (town) Kosciusko County
125	93.5	**Hobart** (city) Lake County
125	93.5	**Zionsville** (town) Boone County
127	93.4	**Cicero** (town) Hamilton County
127	93.4	**Roselawn** (CDP) Newton County
129	93.1	**Saint John** (town) Lake County
130	92.8	**Valparaiso** (city) Porter County
131	92.7	**Whitestown** (town) Boone County
132	92.6	**Clarksville** (town) Clark County
133	92.4	**Salt Creek Commons** (CDP) Porter County
134	92.3	**Jasper** (city) Dubois County
135	92.0	**Shelbyville** (city) Shelby County
136	91.9	**Crawfordsville** (city) Montgomery County
137	91.6	**Westfield** (city) Hamilton County
138	91.4	**Portland** (city) Jay County
139	91.3	**Osceola** (town) Saint Joseph County
140	91.2	**Union City** (city) Randolph County
141	91.1	**Winfield** (town) Lake County
142	91.0	**Granger** (CDP) Saint Joseph County
143	90.8	**Dunlap** (CDP) Elkhart County
143	90.8	**Griffith** (town) Lake County
145	90.2	**Merrillville** (town) Lake County
146	90.0	**Edinburgh** (town) Johnson County
146	90.0	**Fishers** (city) Hamilton County
148	89.7	**Plainfield** (town) Hendricks County
149	89.3	**Avon** (town) Hendricks County
150	89.2	**Bremen** (town) Marshall County

Note: *This section ranks incorporated places and CDPs (Census Designated Places) with populations of 2,500 or more. Unincorporated postal areas were not considered. Please refer to the User Guide for additional information.*

Speak English Only at Home

Top 150 Places Ranked in *Ascending* Order

State Rank	Percent	Place
1	44.3	**Ligonier** (city) Noble County
2	55.1	**East Chicago** (city) Lake County
3	71.3	**West Lafayette** (city) Tippecanoe County
4	71.9	**Goshen** (city) Elkhart County
5	73.2	**Frankfort** (city) Clinton County
5	73.2	**Logansport** (city) Cass County
7	74.2	**Hammond** (city) Lake County
8	78.6	**Lake Station** (city) Lake County
9	79.2	**Plymouth** (city) Marshall County
10	79.4	**Elkhart** (city) Elkhart County
11	80.5	**Munster** (town) Lake County
11	80.5	**Speedway** (town) Marion County
13	81.0	**Whiting** (city) Lake County
14	82.1	**Lagrange** (town) LaGrange County
15	83.3	**Schererville** (town) Lake County
16	83.5	**Delphi** (city) Carroll County
17	84.9	**Bloomington** (city) Monroe County
17	84.9	**Notre Dame** (CDP) Saint Joseph County
19	85.1	**South Bend** (city) Saint Joseph County
20	85.2	**Huntingburg** (city) Dubois County
21	85.4	**Columbus** (city) Bartholomew County
22	86.2	**Monticello** (city) White County
22	86.2	**Winona Lake** (town) Kosciusko County
24	86.5	**Lawrence** (city) Marion County
25	86.7	**Indianapolis** (city) Marion County
26	86.9	**Dyer** (town) Lake County
27	87.0	**Carmel** (city) Hamilton County
27	87.0	**Washington** (city) Daviess County
29	87.2	**Middlebury** (town) Elkhart County
30	87.6	**Seymour** (city) Jackson County
30	87.6	**Warsaw** (city) Kosciusko County
32	87.8	**Crown Point** (city) Lake County
33	88.0	**Fort Wayne** (city) Allen County
34	88.1	**Lafayette** (city) Tippecanoe County
35	88.3	**Lakes of the Four Seasons** (CDP) Lake County
36	88.5	**Highland** (town) Lake County
36	88.5	**La Porte** (city) LaPorte County
38	88.6	**Greenwood** (city) Johnson County
39	89.2	**Bremen** (town) Marshall County
39	89.2	**Portage** (city) Porter County
41	89.3	**Avon** (town) Hendricks County
42	89.7	**Plainfield** (town) Hendricks County
43	90.0	**Edinburgh** (town) Johnson County
43	90.0	**Fishers** (city) Hamilton County
45	90.2	**Merrillville** (town) Lake County
46	90.8	**Dunlap** (CDP) Elkhart County
46	90.8	**Griffith** (town) Lake County
48	91.0	**Granger** (CDP) Saint Joseph County
49	91.1	**Winfield** (town) Lake County
50	91.2	**Union City** (city) Randolph County
51	91.3	**Osceola** (town) Saint Joseph County
52	91.4	**Portland** (city) Jay County
53	91.6	**Westfield** (city) Hamilton County
54	91.9	**Crawfordsville** (city) Montgomery County
55	92.0	**Shelbyville** (city) Shelby County
56	92.3	**Jasper** (city) Dubois County
57	92.4	**Salt Creek Commons** (CDP) Porter County
58	92.6	**Clarksville** (town) Clark County
59	92.7	**Whitestown** (town) Boone County
60	92.8	**Valparaiso** (city) Porter County
61	93.1	**Saint John** (town) Lake County
62	93.4	**Cicero** (town) Hamilton County
62	93.4	**Roselawn** (CDP) Newton County
64	93.5	**Hobart** (city) Lake County
64	93.5	**Zionsville** (town) Boone County
66	93.7	**Syracuse** (town) Kosciusko County
67	93.8	**Brownsburg** (town) Hendricks County
67	93.8	**Mishawaka** (city) Saint Joseph County
69	94.0	**Chesterton** (town) Porter County
69	94.0	**Leo-Cedarville** (town) Allen County
71	94.1	**Noblesville** (city) Hamilton County
72	94.2	**Charlestown** (city) Clark County
73	94.3	**Nappanee** (city) Elkhart County
73	94.3	**Shorewood Forest** (CDP) Porter County
75	94.4	**Country Squire Lakes** (CDP) Jennings County
75	94.4	**North Manchester** (town) Wabash County
75	94.4	**Princeton** (city) Gibson County
78	94.5	**Kendallville** (city) Noble County
79	94.6	**Anderson** (city) Madison County
79	94.6	**Michigan City** (city) LaPorte County
79	94.6	**Simonton Lake** (CDP) Elkhart County
82	94.7	**Cedar Lake** (town) Lake County
82	94.7	**Richmond** (city) Wayne County
84	94.8	**Bargersville** (town) Johnson County
85	94.9	**Angola** (city) Steuben County
85	94.9	**Decatur** (city) Adams County
85	94.9	**Jeffersonville** (city) Clark County
85	94.9	**Terre Haute** (city) Vigo County
89	95.0	**Greensburg** (city) Decatur County
89	95.0	**Lowell** (town) Lake County
89	95.0	**Mitchell** (city) Lawrence County
89	95.0	**Newburgh** (town) Warrick County
89	95.0	**Smithville-Sanders** (CDP) Monroe County
94	95.3	**Gary** (city) Lake County
94	95.3	**Scottsburg** (city) Scott County
94	95.3	**Winamac** (town) Pulaski County
97	95.4	**Batesville** (city) Ripley County
97	95.4	**Georgetown** (town) Floyd County
97	95.4	**Huntertown** (town) Allen County
100	95.5	**Huntington** (city) Huntington County
101	95.6	**Berne** (city) Adams County
101	95.6	**Greencastle** (city) Putnam County
101	95.6	**Muncie** (city) Delaware County
101	95.6	**Rensselaer** (city) Jasper County
105	95.7	**Marion** (city) Grant County
106	95.8	**Danville** (town) Hendricks County
106	95.8	**Ellettsville** (town) Monroe County
106	95.8	**Hidden Valley** (CDP) Dearborn County
106	95.8	**Upland** (town) Grant County
110	95.9	**Porter** (town) Porter County
111	96.0	**De Motte** (town) Jasper County
111	96.0	**Westville** (town) LaPorte County
113	96.1	**Kokomo** (city) Howard County
114	96.2	**Evansville** (city) Vanderburgh County
114	96.2	**Franklin** (city) Johnson County
114	96.2	**Wabash** (city) Wabash County
117	96.3	**Alexandria** (city) Madison County
118	96.4	**Austin** (city) Scott County
118	96.4	**Clinton** (city) Vermillion County
118	96.4	**Greendale** (city) Dearborn County
121	96.5	**Santa Claus** (town) Spencer County
121	96.5	**Sellersburg** (town) Clark County
123	96.6	**Greenfield** (city) Hancock County
123	96.6	**New Albany** (city) Floyd County
125	96.8	**Attica** (city) Fountain County
125	96.8	**Beech Grove** (city) Marion County
125	96.8	**McCordsville** (town) Hancock County
128	96.9	**New Whiteland** (town) Johnson County
128	96.9	**Sheridan** (town) Hamilton County
130	97.0	**Bright** (CDP) Dearborn County
130	97.0	**Hartford City** (city) Blackford County
130	97.0	**Tipton** (city) Tipton County
133	97.1	**Bluffton** (city) Wells County
133	97.1	**Gas City** (city) Grant County
133	97.1	**Madison** (city) Jefferson County
136	97.2	**Lebanon** (city) Boone County
137	97.3	**Melody Hill** (CDP) Vanderburgh County
138	97.4	**Butler** (city) DeKalb County
138	97.4	**New Haven** (city) Allen County
138	97.4	**Ossian** (town) Wells County
141	97.5	**Auburn** (city) DeKalb County
141	97.5	**Aurora** (city) Dearborn County
141	97.5	**Hanover** (town) Jefferson County
141	97.5	**Vincennes** (city) Knox County
145	97.7	**Loogootee** (city) Martin County
145	97.7	**Winchester** (city) Randolph County
147	97.8	**Fairmount** (town) Grant County
147	97.8	**Fortville** (town) Hancock County
147	97.8	**Garrett** (city) DeKalb County
147	97.8	**Peru** (city) Miami County

Note: *This section ranks incorporated places and CDPs (Census Designated Places) with populations of 2,500 or more. Unincorporated postal areas were not considered. Please refer to the User Guide for additional information.*

Individuals with a Disability

Top 150 Places Ranked in *Descending* Order

State Rank	Percent	Place
1	29.7	**Corydon** (town) Harrison County
2	27.6	**Sullivan** (city) Sullivan County
3	26.5	**Brookville** (town) Franklin County
4	24.5	**Mitchell** (city) Lawrence County
5	24.4	**Rochester** (city) Fulton County
6	23.0	**Brazil** (city) Clay County
7	22.9	**Clinton** (city) Vermillion County
8	22.3	**Martinsville** (city) Morgan County
8	22.3	**New Castle** (city) Henry County
10	22.2	**Bicknell** (city) Knox County
10	22.2	**Linton** (city) Greene County
12	22.0	**Marion** (city) Grant County
13	21.8	**Richmond** (city) Wayne County
14	21.5	**Hartford City** (city) Blackford County
15	21.2	**Anderson** (city) Madison County
16	21.0	**Rockville** (town) Parke County
17	20.9	**Knox** (city) Starke County
18	20.6	**Connersville** (city) Fayette County
18	20.6	**Salem** (city) Washington County
18	20.6	**Winamac** (town) Pulaski County
21	20.5	**Attica** (city) Fountain County
22	20.4	**Fort Branch** (town) Gibson County
22	20.4	**Terre Haute** (city) Vigo County
24	20.3	**North Terre Haute** (CDP) Vigo County
24	20.3	**Vincennes** (city) Knox County
26	20.1	**Columbia City** (city) Whitley County
27	19.7	**North Vernon** (city) Jennings County
28	19.5	**Austin** (city) Scott County
28	19.5	**Paoli** (town) Orange County
30	19.4	**Kendallville** (city) Noble County
30	19.4	**Washington** (city) Daviess County
32	19.2	**Bedford** (city) Lawrence County
32	19.2	**Scottsburg** (city) Scott County
34	19.1	**Country Squire Lakes** (CDP) Jennings County
34	19.1	**Elwood** (city) Madison County
36	18.8	**Kokomo** (city) Howard County
37	18.7	**Greenfield** (city) Hancock County
38	18.6	**Rensselaer** (city) Jasper County
39	18.5	**East Chicago** (city) Lake County
39	18.5	**Loogootee** (city) Martin County
41	18.4	**Decatur** (city) Adams County
42	18.3	**Gary** (city) Lake County
43	18.0	**Boonville** (city) Warrick County
43	18.0	**Madison** (city) Jefferson County
43	18.0	**Monticello** (city) White County
43	18.0	**Portland** (city) Jay County
43	18.0	**Sheridan** (town) Hamilton County
48	17.9	**Bremen** (town) Marshall County
48	17.9	**Clarksville** (town) Clark County
48	17.9	**Evansville** (city) Vanderburgh County
51	17.8	**Angola** (city) Steuben County
51	17.8	**Aurora** (city) Dearborn County
51	17.8	**Mooresville** (town) Morgan County
54	17.7	**Gas City** (city) Grant County
54	17.7	**Greencastle** (city) Putnam County
54	17.7	**Union City** (city) Randolph County
57	17.6	**Peru** (city) Miami County
58	17.5	**Ellettsville** (town) Monroe County
59	17.3	**Charlestown** (city) Clark County
60	17.1	**Muncie** (city) Delaware County
60	17.1	**Tell City** (city) Perry County
62	16.9	**Garrett** (city) DeKalb County
63	16.8	**Berne** (city) Adams County
63	16.8	**Butler** (city) DeKalb County
65	16.7	**Elkhart** (city) Elkhart County
66	16.6	**Crawfordsville** (city) Montgomery County
66	16.6	**Fairmount** (town) Grant County
68	16.5	**Huntington** (city) Huntington County
68	16.5	**Mount Vernon** (city) Posey County
70	16.4	**New Albany** (city) Floyd County
70	16.4	**Princeton** (city) Gibson County
72	16.3	**Delphi** (city) Carroll County
72	16.3	**Shelbyville** (city) Shelby County
74	16.2	**Beech Grove** (city) Marion County
74	16.2	**Fortville** (town) Hancock County
74	16.2	**Tipton** (city) Tipton County
77	16.1	**Auburn** (city) DeKalb County
77	16.1	**Plymouth** (city) Marshall County
79	16.0	**Greentown** (town) Howard County
79	16.0	**Winchester** (city) Randolph County
81	15.8	**Rushville** (city) Rush County
82	15.6	**Brownstown** (town) Jackson County
82	15.6	**Whiting** (city) Lake County
84	15.5	**Hammond** (city) Lake County
84	15.5	**Seymour** (city) Jackson County
86	15.4	**Jeffersonville** (city) Clark County
86	15.4	**South Bend** (city) Saint Joseph County
88	15.3	**Lake Station** (city) Lake County
88	15.3	**Lebanon** (city) Boone County
90	15.2	**Lafayette** (city) Tippecanoe County
90	15.2	**Logansport** (city) Cass County
92	15.1	**North Manchester** (town) Wabash County
92	15.1	**Smithville-Sanders** (CDP) Monroe County
94	15.0	**La Porte** (city) LaPorte County
94	15.0	**Lagrange** (town) LaGrange County
94	15.0	**Mishawaka** (city) Saint Joseph County
97	14.9	**Bluffton** (city) Wells County
98	14.7	**Michigan City** (city) LaPorte County
98	14.7	**Newburgh** (town) Warrick County
100	14.6	**Ossian** (town) Wells County
100	14.6	**Syracuse** (town) Kosciusko County
102	14.5	**Edinburgh** (town) Johnson County
102	14.5	**Wabash** (city) Wabash County
104	14.3	**Speedway** (town) Marion County
104	14.3	**Warsaw** (city) Kosciusko County
106	14.1	**Frankfort** (city) Clinton County
107	14.0	**Greensburg** (city) Decatur County
107	14.0	**New Haven** (city) Allen County
109	13.9	**Lawrenceburg** (city) Dearborn County
110	13.8	**Centerville** (town) Wayne County
110	13.8	**Greendale** (city) Dearborn County
112	13.7	**Danville** (town) Hendricks County
112	13.7	**Goshen** (city) Elkhart County
112	13.7	**Indianapolis** (city) Marion County
115	13.5	**Alexandria** (city) Madison County
115	13.5	**Lawrence** (city) Marion County
117	13.4	**Middlebury** (town) Elkhart County
118	13.3	**Fort Wayne** (city) Allen County
118	13.3	**Highland** (town) Lake County
118	13.3	**Merrillville** (town) Lake County
121	13.2	**Bright** (CDP) Dearborn County
121	13.2	**Griffith** (town) Lake County
121	13.2	**Hobart** (city) Lake County
121	13.2	**Plainfield** (town) Hendricks County
125	13.1	**Cicero** (town) Hamilton County
125	13.1	**Portage** (city) Porter County
125	13.1	**Simonton Lake** (CDP) Elkhart County
128	13.0	**De Motte** (town) Jasper County
129	12.9	**Heritage Lake** (CDP) Putnam County
129	12.9	**Pendleton** (town) Madison County
131	12.8	**Nappanee** (city) Elkhart County
132	12.7	**Melody Hill** (CDP) Vanderburgh County
133	12.6	**Roselawn** (CDP) Newton County
134	12.5	**Brownsburg** (town) Hendricks County
135	12.3	**Batesville** (city) Ripley County
135	12.3	**Dunlap** (CDP) Elkhart County
135	12.3	**Hanover** (town) Jefferson County
138	12.2	**Franklin** (city) Johnson County
138	12.2	**Osceola** (town) Saint Joseph County
138	12.2	**South Haven** (CDP) Porter County
141	12.1	**Highland** (CDP) Vanderburgh County
142	11.9	**Chandler** (town) Warrick County
142	11.9	**Jasper** (city) Dubois County
142	11.9	**New Whiteland** (town) Johnson County
145	11.8	**Cumberland** (town) Marion County
145	11.8	**Huntingburg** (city) Dubois County
145	11.8	**Yorktown** (town) Delaware County
148	11.7	**Columbus** (city) Bartholomew County
149	11.6	**Lowell** (town) Lake County
149	11.6	**Munster** (town) Lake County

Note: *This section ranks incorporated places and CDPs (Census Designated Places) with populations of 2,500 or more. Unincorporated postal areas were not considered. Please refer to the User Guide for additional information.*

Individuals with a Disability

Top 150 Places Ranked in *Ascending* Order

State Rank	Percent	Place
1	5.1	**Porter** (town) Porter County
2	5.4	**McCordsville** (town) Hancock County
3	5.8	**Zionsville** (town) Boone County
4	5.9	**Notre Dame** (CDP) Saint Joseph County
5	6.1	**Carmel** (city) Hamilton County
5	6.1	**Fishers** (city) Hamilton County
7	6.2	**West Lafayette** (city) Tippecanoe County
8	6.3	**Georgetown** (town) Floyd County
9	6.5	**Leo-Cedarville** (town) Allen County
10	7.0	**Whitestown** (town) Boone County
11	8.0	**Granger** (CDP) Saint Joseph County
11	8.0	**Sellersburg** (town) Clark County
13	8.2	**Hidden Valley** (CDP) Dearborn County
14	8.5	**Bargersville** (town) Johnson County
14	8.5	**Upland** (town) Grant County
16	8.6	**Shorewood Forest** (CDP) Porter County
16	8.6	**Westfield** (city) Hamilton County
18	8.7	**Avon** (town) Hendricks County
18	8.7	**Pittsboro** (town) Hendricks County
20	8.8	**Chesterton** (town) Porter County
21	9.0	**Winfield** (town) Lake County
22	9.1	**Saint John** (town) Lake County
23	9.2	**Whiteland** (town) Johnson County
24	9.4	**Westville** (town) LaPorte County
25	9.5	**Noblesville** (city) Hamilton County
26	9.6	**Huntertown** (town) Allen County
26	9.6	**Lakes of the Four Seasons** (CDP) Lake County
28	9.8	**Bloomington** (city) Monroe County
28	9.8	**Dyer** (town) Lake County
30	10.1	**Winona Lake** (town) Kosciusko County
31	10.3	**Schererville** (town) Lake County
32	10.4	**Ligonier** (city) Noble County
33	10.5	**Cedar Lake** (town) Lake County
34	10.6	**Hebron** (town) Porter County
35	10.8	**Salt Creek Commons** (CDP) Porter County
36	10.9	**Valparaiso** (city) Porter County
37	11.2	**Crown Point** (city) Lake County
37	11.2	**Santa Claus** (town) Spencer County
39	11.5	**Greenwood** (city) Johnson County
40	11.6	**Lowell** (town) Lake County
40	11.6	**Munster** (town) Lake County
42	11.7	**Columbus** (city) Bartholomew County
43	11.8	**Cumberland** (town) Marion County
43	11.8	**Huntingburg** (city) Dubois County
43	11.8	**Yorktown** (town) Delaware County
46	11.9	**Chandler** (town) Warrick County
46	11.9	**Jasper** (city) Dubois County
46	11.9	**New Whiteland** (town) Johnson County
49	12.1	**Highland** (CDP) Vanderburgh County
50	12.2	**Franklin** (city) Johnson County
50	12.2	**Osceola** (town) Saint Joseph County
50	12.2	**South Haven** (CDP) Porter County
53	12.3	**Batesville** (city) Ripley County
53	12.3	**Dunlap** (CDP) Elkhart County
53	12.3	**Hanover** (town) Jefferson County
56	12.5	**Brownsburg** (town) Hendricks County
57	12.6	**Roselawn** (CDP) Newton County
58	12.7	**Melody Hill** (CDP) Vanderburgh County
59	12.8	**Nappanee** (city) Elkhart County
60	12.9	**Heritage Lake** (CDP) Putnam County
60	12.9	**Pendleton** (town) Madison County
62	13.0	**De Motte** (town) Jasper County
63	13.1	**Cicero** (town) Hamilton County
63	13.1	**Portage** (city) Porter County
63	13.1	**Simonton Lake** (CDP) Elkhart County
66	13.2	**Bright** (CDP) Dearborn County
66	13.2	**Griffith** (town) Lake County
66	13.2	**Hobart** (city) Lake County
66	13.2	**Plainfield** (town) Hendricks County
70	13.3	**Fort Wayne** (city) Allen County
70	13.3	**Highland** (town) Lake County
70	13.3	**Merrillville** (town) Lake County
73	13.4	**Middlebury** (town) Elkhart County
74	13.5	**Alexandria** (city) Madison County
74	13.5	**Lawrence** (city) Marion County
76	13.7	**Danville** (town) Hendricks County
76	13.7	**Goshen** (city) Elkhart County
76	13.7	**Indianapolis** (city) Marion County
79	13.8	**Centerville** (town) Wayne County
79	13.8	**Greendale** (city) Dearborn County
81	13.9	**Lawrenceburg** (city) Dearborn County
82	14.0	**Greensburg** (city) Decatur County
82	14.0	**New Haven** (city) Allen County
84	14.1	**Frankfort** (city) Clinton County
85	14.3	**Speedway** (town) Marion County
85	14.3	**Warsaw** (city) Kosciusko County
87	14.5	**Edinburgh** (town) Johnson County
87	14.5	**Wabash** (city) Wabash County
89	14.6	**Ossian** (town) Wells County
89	14.6	**Syracuse** (town) Kosciusko County
91	14.7	**Michigan City** (city) LaPorte County
91	14.7	**Newburgh** (town) Warrick County
93	14.9	**Bluffton** (city) Wells County
94	15.0	**La Porte** (city) LaPorte County
94	15.0	**Lagrange** (town) LaGrange County
94	15.0	**Mishawaka** (city) Saint Joseph County
97	15.1	**North Manchester** (town) Wabash County
97	15.1	**Smithville-Sanders** (CDP) Monroe County
99	15.2	**Lafayette** (city) Tippecanoe County
99	15.2	**Logansport** (city) Cass County
101	15.3	**Lake Station** (city) Lake County
101	15.3	**Lebanon** (city) Boone County
103	15.4	**Jeffersonville** (city) Clark County
103	15.4	**South Bend** (city) Saint Joseph County
105	15.5	**Hammond** (city) Lake County
105	15.5	**Seymour** (city) Jackson County
107	15.6	**Brownstown** (town) Jackson County
107	15.6	**Whiting** (city) Lake County
109	15.8	**Rushville** (city) Rush County
110	16.0	**Greentown** (town) Howard County
110	16.0	**Winchester** (city) Randolph County
112	16.1	**Auburn** (city) DeKalb County
112	16.1	**Plymouth** (city) Marshall County
114	16.2	**Beech Grove** (city) Marion County
114	16.2	**Fortville** (town) Hancock County
114	16.2	**Tipton** (city) Tipton County
117	16.3	**Delphi** (city) Carroll County
117	16.3	**Shelbyville** (city) Shelby County
119	16.4	**New Albany** (city) Floyd County
119	16.4	**Princeton** (city) Gibson County
121	16.5	**Huntington** (city) Huntington County
121	16.5	**Mount Vernon** (city) Posey County
123	16.6	**Crawfordsville** (city) Montgomery County
123	16.6	**Fairmount** (town) Grant County
125	16.7	**Elkhart** (city) Elkhart County
126	16.8	**Berne** (city) Adams County
126	16.8	**Butler** (city) DeKalb County
128	16.9	**Garrett** (city) DeKalb County
129	17.1	**Muncie** (city) Delaware County
129	17.1	**Tell City** (city) Perry County
131	17.3	**Charlestown** (city) Clark County
132	17.5	**Ellettsville** (town) Monroe County
133	17.6	**Peru** (city) Miami County
134	17.7	**Gas City** (city) Grant County
134	17.7	**Greencastle** (city) Putnam County
134	17.7	**Union City** (city) Randolph County
137	17.8	**Angola** (city) Steuben County
137	17.8	**Aurora** (city) Dearborn County
137	17.8	**Mooresville** (town) Morgan County
140	17.9	**Bremen** (town) Marshall County
140	17.9	**Clarksville** (town) Clark County
140	17.9	**Evansville** (city) Vanderburgh County
143	18.0	**Boonville** (city) Warrick County
143	18.0	**Madison** (city) Jefferson County
143	18.0	**Monticello** (city) White County
143	18.0	**Portland** (city) Jay County
143	18.0	**Sheridan** (town) Hamilton County
148	18.3	**Gary** (city) Lake County
149	18.4	**Decatur** (city) Adams County
150	18.5	**East Chicago** (city) Lake County

***Note:** This section ranks incorporated places and CDPs (Census Designated Places) with populations of 2,500 or more. Unincorporated postal areas were not considered. Please refer to the User Guide for additional information.*

Veterans

Top 150 Places Ranked in *Descending* Order

State Rank	Percent	Place
1	14.6	**Melody Hill** (CDP) Vanderburgh County
2	13.8	**Tipton** (city) Tipton County
3	13.1	**Country Squire Lakes** (CDP) Jennings County
4	13.0	**Georgetown** (town) Floyd County
5	12.3	**South Haven** (CDP) Porter County
6	12.2	**Corydon** (town) Harrison County
7	11.7	**Smithville-Sanders** (CDP) Monroe County
8	11.6	**Rockville** (town) Parke County
9	11.2	**Centerville** (town) Wayne County
9	11.2	**Mitchell** (city) Lawrence County
11	11.1	**Fort Branch** (town) Gibson County
11	11.1	**Fortville** (town) Hancock County
11	11.1	**Loogootee** (city) Martin County
11	11.1	**Porter** (town) Porter County
15	11.0	**Salem** (city) Washington County
15	11.0	**Shorewood Forest** (CDP) Porter County
17	10.9	**Cumberland** (town) Marion County
17	10.9	**Mooresville** (town) Morgan County
17	10.9	**Pendleton** (town) Madison County
17	10.9	**Syracuse** (town) Kosciusko County
21	10.8	**De Motte** (town) Jasper County
22	10.7	**Bicknell** (city) Knox County
22	10.7	**Clarksville** (town) Clark County
22	10.7	**Greendale** (city) Dearborn County
22	10.7	**Martinsville** (city) Morgan County
22	10.7	**McCordsville** (town) Hancock County
27	10.6	**Huntertown** (town) Allen County
27	10.6	**Santa Claus** (town) Spencer County
29	10.5	**Gas City** (city) Grant County
29	10.5	**Peru** (city) Miami County
31	10.3	**Batesville** (city) Ripley County
31	10.3	**Hobart** (city) Lake County
33	10.2	**Greenfield** (city) Hancock County
33	10.2	**Hidden Valley** (CDP) Dearborn County
33	10.2	**Richmond** (city) Wayne County
36	10.1	**Kokomo** (city) Howard County
37	9.9	**Bedford** (city) Lawrence County
37	9.9	**Franklin** (city) Johnson County
37	9.9	**Sheridan** (town) Hamilton County
37	9.9	**Washington** (city) Daviess County
41	9.8	**Lagrange** (town) LaGrange County
41	9.8	**Rushville** (city) Rush County
43	9.7	**Winamac** (town) Pulaski County
44	9.6	**Brazil** (city) Clay County
44	9.6	**Connersville** (city) Fayette County
44	9.6	**Madison** (city) Jefferson County
44	9.6	**Monticello** (city) White County
44	9.6	**Tell City** (city) Perry County
49	9.4	**Brownsburg** (town) Hendricks County
49	9.4	**Hartford City** (city) Blackford County
49	9.4	**Heritage Lake** (CDP) Putnam County
52	9.3	**Beech Grove** (city) Marion County
52	9.3	**Jasper** (city) Dubois County
52	9.3	**Lawrence** (city) Marion County
52	9.3	**Rensselaer** (city) Jasper County
56	9.2	**Anderson** (city) Madison County
57	9.1	**Cicero** (town) Hamilton County
57	9.1	**Lowell** (town) Lake County
57	9.1	**Wabash** (city) Wabash County
60	9.0	**Jeffersonville** (city) Clark County
60	9.0	**New Haven** (city) Allen County
60	9.0	**Pittsboro** (town) Hendricks County
63	8.9	**Greenwood** (city) Johnson County
63	8.9	**La Porte** (city) LaPorte County
63	8.9	**Princeton** (city) Gibson County
63	8.9	**Yorktown** (town) Delaware County
67	8.8	**Lebanon** (city) Boone County
67	8.8	**North Terre Haute** (CDP) Vigo County
69	8.7	**Cedar Lake** (town) Lake County
70	8.6	**Auburn** (city) DeKalb County
70	8.6	**Butler** (city) DeKalb County
70	8.6	**Crown Point** (city) Lake County
70	8.6	**Gary** (city) Lake County
70	8.6	**Highland** (town) Lake County
70	8.6	**Merrillville** (town) Lake County
70	8.6	**Ossian** (town) Wells County
77	8.5	**Chandler** (town) Warrick County
77	8.5	**Lake Station** (city) Lake County
77	8.5	**New Albany** (city) Floyd County
77	8.5	**Plymouth** (city) Marshall County
81	8.4	**Bargersville** (town) Johnson County
81	8.4	**Chesterton** (town) Porter County
81	8.4	**Evansville** (city) Vanderburgh County
81	8.4	**Plainfield** (town) Hendricks County
81	8.4	**Rochester** (city) Fulton County
81	8.4	**Scottsburg** (city) Scott County
87	8.3	**Shelbyville** (city) Shelby County
88	8.2	**Bluffton** (city) Wells County
88	8.2	**Bright** (CDP) Dearborn County
88	8.2	**Mishawaka** (city) Saint Joseph County
88	8.2	**New Castle** (city) Henry County
88	8.2	**Saint John** (town) Lake County
88	8.2	**Vincennes** (city) Knox County
88	8.2	**Whiteland** (town) Johnson County
95	8.1	**Boonville** (city) Warrick County
96	8.0	**Avon** (town) Hendricks County
96	8.0	**Dyer** (town) Lake County
96	8.0	**Sellersburg** (town) Clark County
99	7.9	**Huntingburg** (city) Dubois County
99	7.9	**Michigan City** (city) LaPorte County
99	7.9	**Simonton Lake** (CDP) Elkhart County
102	7.8	**Seymour** (city) Jackson County
102	7.8	**Union City** (city) Randolph County
104	7.7	**Clinton** (city) Vermillion County
104	7.7	**Griffith** (town) Lake County
104	7.7	**Linton** (city) Greene County
107	7.6	**Danville** (town) Hendricks County
107	7.6	**Lafayette** (city) Tippecanoe County
107	7.6	**Middlebury** (town) Elkhart County
107	7.6	**Osceola** (town) Saint Joseph County
107	7.6	**Portland** (city) Jay County
112	7.5	**Garrett** (city) DeKalb County
112	7.5	**Terre Haute** (city) Vigo County
112	7.5	**Winona Lake** (town) Kosciusko County
115	7.4	**Huntington** (city) Huntington County
115	7.4	**Marion** (city) Grant County
115	7.4	**Paoli** (town) Orange County
115	7.4	**Sullivan** (city) Sullivan County
119	7.3	**Decatur** (city) Adams County
119	7.3	**Elwood** (city) Madison County
119	7.3	**Fort Wayne** (city) Allen County
119	7.3	**Lawrenceburg** (city) Dearborn County
123	7.2	**Noblesville** (city) Hamilton County
123	7.2	**Portage** (city) Porter County
123	7.2	**Schererville** (town) Lake County
126	7.1	**Charlestown** (city) Clark County
126	7.1	**Newburgh** (town) Warrick County
128	7.0	**Crawfordsville** (city) Montgomery County
128	7.0	**Greentown** (town) Howard County
128	7.0	**Highland** (CDP) Vanderburgh County
128	7.0	**Indianapolis** (city) Marion County
132	6.9	**Aurora** (city) Dearborn County
132	6.9	**Columbia City** (city) Whitley County
132	6.9	**Logansport** (city) Cass County
135	6.8	**Granger** (CDP) Saint Joseph County
135	6.8	**Greencastle** (city) Putnam County
135	6.8	**Hanover** (town) Jefferson County
135	6.8	**Mount Vernon** (city) Posey County
135	6.8	**Warsaw** (city) Kosciusko County
140	6.7	**Brownstown** (town) Jackson County
140	6.7	**Delphi** (city) Carroll County
140	6.7	**Hammond** (city) Lake County
140	6.7	**North Vernon** (city) Jennings County
144	6.6	**Alexandria** (city) Madison County
144	6.6	**Bremen** (town) Marshall County
144	6.6	**Dunlap** (CDP) Elkhart County
147	6.5	**Angola** (city) Steuben County
147	6.5	**Frankfort** (city) Clinton County
147	6.5	**Speedway** (town) Marion County
150	6.4	**Kendallville** (city) Noble County

Note: *This section ranks incorporated places and CDPs (Census Designated Places) with populations of 2,500 or more. Unincorporated postal areas were not considered. Please refer to the User Guide for additional information.*

Veterans

Top 150 Places Ranked in *Ascending* Order

State Rank	Percent	Place
1	1.0	**Notre Dame** (CDP) Saint Joseph County
2	2.0	**West Lafayette** (city) Tippecanoe County
3	3.1	**Upland** (town) Grant County
4	3.3	**Bloomington** (city) Monroe County
5	4.5	**Leo-Cedarville** (town) Allen County
6	4.6	**East Chicago** (city) Lake County
6	4.6	**Salt Creek Commons** (CDP) Porter County
6	4.6	**Whiting** (city) Lake County
9	4.9	**Whitestown** (town) Boone County
10	5.0	**Roselawn** (CDP) Newton County
10	5.0	**Zionsville** (town) Boone County
12	5.1	**New Whiteland** (town) Johnson County
13	5.2	**Lakes of the Four Seasons** (CDP) Lake County
14	5.4	**Carmel** (city) Hamilton County
14	5.4	**Fishers** (city) Hamilton County
16	5.5	**Fairmount** (town) Grant County
16	5.5	**Greensburg** (city) Decatur County
18	5.6	**Westfield** (city) Hamilton County
19	5.7	**Elkhart** (city) Elkhart County
19	5.7	**Westville** (town) LaPorte County
21	5.9	**Ellettsville** (town) Monroe County
21	5.9	**Hebron** (town) Porter County
23	6.0	**Attica** (city) Fountain County
23	6.0	**Berne** (city) Adams County
23	6.0	**Ligonier** (city) Noble County
26	6.1	**Columbus** (city) Bartholomew County
26	6.1	**Muncie** (city) Delaware County
26	6.1	**Nappanee** (city) Elkhart County
26	6.1	**North Manchester** (town) Wabash County
26	6.1	**Valparaiso** (city) Porter County
26	6.1	**Winfield** (town) Lake County
32	6.2	**Austin** (city) Scott County
32	6.2	**Brookville** (town) Franklin County
32	6.2	**Edinburgh** (town) Johnson County
32	6.2	**Goshen** (city) Elkhart County
32	6.2	**Knox** (city) Starke County
32	6.2	**South Bend** (city) Saint Joseph County
38	6.4	**Kendallville** (city) Noble County
38	6.4	**Munster** (town) Lake County
38	6.4	**Winchester** (city) Randolph County
41	6.5	**Angola** (city) Steuben County
41	6.5	**Frankfort** (city) Clinton County
41	6.5	**Speedway** (town) Marion County
44	6.6	**Alexandria** (city) Madison County
44	6.6	**Bremen** (town) Marshall County
44	6.6	**Dunlap** (CDP) Elkhart County
47	6.7	**Brownstown** (town) Jackson County
47	6.7	**Delphi** (city) Carroll County
47	6.7	**Hammond** (city) Lake County
47	6.7	**North Vernon** (city) Jennings County
51	6.8	**Granger** (CDP) Saint Joseph County
51	6.8	**Greencastle** (city) Putnam County
51	6.8	**Hanover** (town) Jefferson County
51	6.8	**Mount Vernon** (city) Posey County
51	6.8	**Warsaw** (city) Kosciusko County
56	6.9	**Aurora** (city) Dearborn County
56	6.9	**Columbia City** (city) Whitley County
56	6.9	**Logansport** (city) Cass County
59	7.0	**Crawfordsville** (city) Montgomery County
59	7.0	**Greentown** (town) Howard County
59	7.0	**Highland** (CDP) Vanderburgh County
59	7.0	**Indianapolis** (city) Marion County
63	7.1	**Charlestown** (city) Clark County
63	7.1	**Newburgh** (town) Warrick County
65	7.2	**Noblesville** (city) Hamilton County
65	7.2	**Portage** (city) Porter County
65	7.2	**Schererville** (town) Lake County
68	7.3	**Decatur** (city) Adams County
68	7.3	**Elwood** (city) Madison County
68	7.3	**Fort Wayne** (city) Allen County
68	7.3	**Lawrenceburg** (city) Dearborn County
72	7.4	**Huntington** (city) Huntington County
72	7.4	**Marion** (city) Grant County
72	7.4	**Paoli** (town) Orange County
72	7.4	**Sullivan** (city) Sullivan County
76	7.5	**Garrett** (city) DeKalb County
76	7.5	**Terre Haute** (city) Vigo County
76	7.5	**Winona Lake** (town) Kosciusko County
79	7.6	**Danville** (town) Hendricks County
79	7.6	**Lafayette** (city) Tippecanoe County
79	7.6	**Middlebury** (town) Elkhart County
79	7.6	**Osceola** (town) Saint Joseph County
79	7.6	**Portland** (city) Jay County
84	7.7	**Clinton** (city) Vermillion County
84	7.7	**Griffith** (town) Lake County
84	7.7	**Linton** (city) Greene County
87	7.8	**Seymour** (city) Jackson County
87	7.8	**Union City** (city) Randolph County
89	7.9	**Huntingburg** (city) Dubois County
89	7.9	**Michigan City** (city) LaPorte County
89	7.9	**Simonton Lake** (CDP) Elkhart County
92	8.0	**Avon** (town) Hendricks County
92	8.0	**Dyer** (town) Lake County
92	8.0	**Sellersburg** (town) Clark County
95	8.1	**Boonville** (city) Warrick County
96	8.2	**Bluffton** (city) Wells County
96	8.2	**Bright** (CDP) Dearborn County
96	8.2	**Mishawaka** (city) Saint Joseph County
96	8.2	**New Castle** (city) Henry County
96	8.2	**Saint John** (town) Lake County
96	8.2	**Vincennes** (city) Knox County
96	8.2	**Whiteland** (town) Johnson County
103	8.3	**Shelbyville** (city) Shelby County
104	8.4	**Bargersville** (town) Johnson County
104	8.4	**Chesterton** (town) Porter County
104	8.4	**Evansville** (city) Vanderburgh County
104	8.4	**Plainfield** (town) Hendricks County
104	8.4	**Rochester** (city) Fulton County
104	8.4	**Scottsburg** (city) Scott County
110	8.5	**Chandler** (town) Warrick County
110	8.5	**Lake Station** (city) Lake County
110	8.5	**New Albany** (city) Floyd County
110	8.5	**Plymouth** (city) Marshall County
114	8.6	**Auburn** (city) DeKalb County
114	8.6	**Butler** (city) DeKalb County
114	8.6	**Crown Point** (city) Lake County
114	8.6	**Gary** (city) Lake County
114	8.6	**Highland** (town) Lake County
114	8.6	**Merrillville** (town) Lake County
114	8.6	**Ossian** (town) Wells County
121	8.7	**Cedar Lake** (town) Lake County
122	8.8	**Lebanon** (city) Boone County
122	8.8	**North Terre Haute** (CDP) Vigo County
124	8.9	**Greenwood** (city) Johnson County
124	8.9	**La Porte** (city) LaPorte County
124	8.9	**Princeton** (city) Gibson County
124	8.9	**Yorktown** (town) Delaware County
128	9.0	**Jeffersonville** (city) Clark County
128	9.0	**New Haven** (city) Allen County
128	9.0	**Pittsboro** (town) Hendricks County
131	9.1	**Cicero** (town) Hamilton County
131	9.1	**Lowell** (town) Lake County
131	9.1	**Wabash** (city) Wabash County
134	9.2	**Anderson** (city) Madison County
135	9.3	**Beech Grove** (city) Marion County
135	9.3	**Jasper** (city) Dubois County
135	9.3	**Lawrence** (city) Marion County
135	9.3	**Rensselaer** (city) Jasper County
139	9.4	**Brownsburg** (town) Hendricks County
139	9.4	**Hartford City** (city) Blackford County
139	9.4	**Heritage Lake** (CDP) Putnam County
142	9.6	**Brazil** (city) Clay County
142	9.6	**Connersville** (city) Fayette County
142	9.6	**Madison** (city) Jefferson County
142	9.6	**Monticello** (city) White County
142	9.6	**Tell City** (city) Perry County
147	9.7	**Winamac** (town) Pulaski County
148	9.8	**Lagrange** (town) LaGrange County
148	9.8	**Rushville** (city) Rush County
150	9.9	**Bedford** (city) Lawrence County

Note: *This section ranks incorporated places and CDPs (Census Designated Places) with populations of 2,500 or more. Unincorporated postal areas were not considered. Please refer to the User Guide for additional information.*

Ancestry: German

Top 150 Places Ranked in *Descending* Order

State Rank	Percent	Place
1	50.5	**Bright** (CDP) Dearborn County
2	44.0	**Batesville** (city) Ripley County
3	43.6	**Huntingburg** (city) Dubois County
4	42.8	**Jasper** (city) Dubois County
5	42.6	**Highland** (CDP) Vanderburgh County
6	40.0	**Hidden Valley** (CDP) Dearborn County
7	38.0	**Auburn** (city) DeKalb County
8	36.7	**Aurora** (city) Dearborn County
8	36.7	**Greensburg** (city) Decatur County
10	36.5	**Winamac** (town) Pulaski County
11	35.8	**Santa Claus** (town) Spencer County
12	35.1	**Brookville** (town) Franklin County
13	34.9	**Lowell** (town) Lake County
14	34.6	**North Manchester** (town) Wabash County
15	33.2	**Greendale** (city) Dearborn County
15	33.2	**New Haven** (city) Allen County
17	33.0	**Fort Branch** (town) Gibson County
18	32.5	**Huntington** (city) Huntington County
19	31.8	**Lawrenceburg** (city) Dearborn County
20	31.2	**Shorewood Forest** (CDP) Porter County
21	30.9	**Angola** (city) Steuben County
22	30.8	**Melody Hill** (CDP) Vanderburgh County
23	30.6	**Decatur** (city) Adams County
23	30.6	**Heritage Lake** (CDP) Putnam County
25	29.8	**Lakes of the Four Seasons** (CDP) Lake County
25	29.8	**Mount Vernon** (city) Posey County
27	29.7	**Sellersburg** (town) Clark County
28	29.5	**Newburgh** (town) Warrick County
29	29.4	**La Porte** (city) LaPorte County
30	29.2	**Bluffton** (city) Wells County
30	29.2	**Tell City** (city) Perry County
32	29.0	**Cedar Lake** (town) Lake County
33	28.8	**Nappanee** (city) Elkhart County
34	28.7	**Winona Lake** (town) Kosciusko County
35	28.5	**Chesterton** (town) Porter County
36	28.4	**Upland** (town) Grant County
37	28.3	**Rensselaer** (city) Jasper County
38	28.2	**Whitestown** (town) Boone County
39	28.0	**Huntertown** (town) Allen County
39	28.0	**Valparaiso** (city) Porter County
41	27.7	**Ossian** (town) Wells County
42	27.4	**Hanover** (town) Jefferson County
43	27.1	**Smithville-Sanders** (CDP) Monroe County
44	27.0	**Fishers** (city) Hamilton County
44	27.0	**Garrett** (city) DeKalb County
46	26.8	**Bremen** (town) Marshall County
46	26.8	**Pendleton** (town) Madison County
46	26.8	**Wabash** (city) Wabash County
46	26.8	**Zionsville** (town) Boone County
50	26.7	**Berne** (city) Adams County
51	26.6	**Pittsboro** (town) Hendricks County
52	26.3	**Chandler** (town) Warrick County
53	26.1	**Fort Wayne** (city) Allen County
54	25.9	**Hebron** (town) Porter County
55	25.7	**Evansville** (city) Vanderburgh County
55	25.7	**Noblesville** (city) Hamilton County
57	25.6	**Columbia City** (city) Whitley County
58	25.4	**Lafayette** (city) Tippecanoe County
59	25.3	**Brazil** (city) Clay County
59	25.3	**Centerville** (town) Wayne County
61	25.2	**Rochester** (city) Fulton County
62	25.1	**Leo-Cedarville** (town) Allen County
63	25.0	**Avon** (town) Hendricks County
64	24.8	**Carmel** (city) Hamilton County
64	24.8	**Greentown** (town) Howard County
66	24.7	**Dunlap** (CDP) Elkhart County
67	24.6	**Granger** (CDP) Saint Joseph County
68	24.4	**Shelbyville** (city) Shelby County
69	24.3	**Simonton Lake** (CDP) Elkhart County
69	24.3	**Westfield** (city) Hamilton County
69	24.3	**Whiteland** (town) Johnson County
72	24.2	**Fairmount** (town) Grant County
72	24.2	**West Lafayette** (city) Tippecanoe County
74	24.1	**Cicero** (town) Hamilton County
75	24.0	**Paoli** (town) Orange County
76	23.9	**Butler** (city) DeKalb County
76	23.9	**Roselawn** (CDP) Newton County
76	23.9	**Rushville** (city) Rush County
79	23.8	**Ellettsville** (town) Monroe County
79	23.8	**Porter** (town) Porter County
81	23.7	**Georgetown** (town) Floyd County
81	23.7	**Knox** (city) Starke County
83	23.4	**Warsaw** (city) Kosciusko County
84	23.3	**New Albany** (city) Floyd County
84	23.3	**Winfield** (town) Lake County
86	23.1	**Yorktown** (town) Delaware County
87	22.9	**Corydon** (town) Harrison County
87	22.9	**Greenwood** (city) Johnson County
89	22.7	**Beech Grove** (city) Marion County
89	22.7	**Goshen** (city) Elkhart County
89	22.7	**Syracuse** (town) Kosciusko County
92	22.6	**Greenfield** (city) Hancock County
92	22.6	**McCordsville** (town) Hancock County
92	22.6	**Saint John** (town) Lake County
95	22.4	**Brownstown** (town) Jackson County
95	22.4	**Washington** (city) Daviess County
97	22.3	**Crown Point** (city) Lake County
97	22.3	**Hobart** (city) Lake County
99	22.2	**Tipton** (city) Tipton County
100	22.1	**Danville** (town) Hendricks County
100	22.1	**Madison** (city) Jefferson County
100	22.1	**Schererville** (town) Lake County
103	22.0	**Linton** (city) Greene County
104	21.9	**Mishawaka** (city) Saint Joseph County
104	21.9	**Osceola** (town) Saint Joseph County
106	21.8	**Griffith** (town) Lake County
106	21.8	**Winchester** (city) Randolph County
108	21.7	**Highland** (town) Lake County
109	21.6	**Bargersville** (town) Johnson County
109	21.6	**De Motte** (town) Jasper County
109	21.6	**Dyer** (town) Lake County
112	21.5	**Brownsburg** (town) Hendricks County
112	21.5	**Franklin** (city) Johnson County
112	21.5	**Seymour** (city) Jackson County
112	21.5	**Vincennes** (city) Knox County
116	21.4	**Elwood** (city) Madison County
116	21.4	**Portland** (city) Jay County
118	21.3	**Lagrange** (town) LaGrange County
119	21.2	**Delphi** (city) Carroll County
120	21.1	**Loogootee** (city) Martin County
121	20.9	**Attica** (city) Fountain County
122	20.6	**Martinsville** (city) Morgan County
122	20.6	**Middlebury** (town) Elkhart County
122	20.6	**Princeton** (city) Gibson County
122	20.6	**Union City** (city) Randolph County
126	20.4	**Marion** (city) Grant County
127	20.2	**Crawfordsville** (city) Montgomery County
127	20.2	**Jeffersonville** (city) Clark County
127	20.2	**Kendallville** (city) Noble County
127	20.2	**Plymouth** (city) Marshall County
131	20.1	**Columbus** (city) Bartholomew County
132	20.0	**Michigan City** (city) LaPorte County
132	20.0	**Notre Dame** (CDP) Saint Joseph County
134	19.9	**Bloomington** (city) Monroe County
135	19.8	**Westville** (town) LaPorte County
136	19.7	**Mooresville** (town) Morgan County
137	19.6	**Lebanon** (city) Boone County
138	19.5	**New Whiteland** (town) Johnson County
139	19.4	**Charlestown** (city) Clark County
140	19.3	**North Terre Haute** (CDP) Vigo County
141	19.2	**Logansport** (city) Cass County
141	19.2	**Speedway** (town) Marion County
143	19.1	**Kokomo** (city) Howard County
143	19.1	**South Haven** (CDP) Porter County
145	19.0	**Clarksville** (town) Clark County
146	18.6	**Terre Haute** (city) Vigo County
147	18.5	**Rockville** (town) Parke County
148	18.4	**Connersville** (city) Fayette County
149	18.3	**Cumberland** (town) Marion County
149	18.3	**Richmond** (city) Wayne County

Note: *This section ranks incorporated places and CDPs (Census Designated Places) with populations of 2,500 or more. Unincorporated postal areas were not considered. Please refer to the User Guide for additional information.*

Ancestry: English

Top 150 Places Ranked in *Descending* Order

State Rank	Percent	Place
1	20.8	**Mount Vernon** (city) Posey County
2	17.9	**Bicknell** (city) Knox County
3	16.6	**Hidden Valley** (CDP) Dearborn County
3	16.6	**Highland** (CDP) Vanderburgh County
5	16.5	**Smithville-Sanders** (CDP) Monroe County
6	15.7	**Scottsburg** (city) Scott County
7	15.5	**Boonville** (city) Warrick County
8	15.3	**Heritage Lake** (CDP) Putnam County
9	14.2	**McCordsville** (town) Hancock County
10	14.0	**Auburn** (city) DeKalb County
11	13.8	**Rockville** (town) Parke County
11	13.8	**Whitestown** (town) Boone County
13	13.7	**Greendale** (city) Dearborn County
14	13.4	**Zionsville** (town) Boone County
15	13.1	**Gas City** (city) Grant County
16	12.9	**Bargersville** (town) Johnson County
17	12.7	**Martinsville** (city) Morgan County
18	12.5	**Cumberland** (town) Marion County
18	12.5	**Madison** (city) Jefferson County
20	12.3	**Carmel** (city) Hamilton County
21	12.2	**Sullivan** (city) Sullivan County
22	12.1	**Ossian** (town) Wells County
23	12.0	**Mooresville** (town) Morgan County
24	11.8	**Lawrenceburg** (city) Dearborn County
24	11.8	**Yorktown** (town) Delaware County
26	11.7	**Rochester** (city) Fulton County
27	11.6	**New Castle** (city) Henry County
28	11.4	**Simonton Lake** (CDP) Elkhart County
29	11.3	**Clinton** (city) Vermillion County
29	11.3	**Evansville** (city) Vanderburgh County
29	11.3	**Upland** (town) Grant County
32	11.1	**Ellettsville** (town) Monroe County
32	11.1	**Monticello** (city) White County
34	10.8	**Aurora** (city) Dearborn County
34	10.8	**Bloomington** (city) Monroe County
34	10.8	**Linton** (city) Greene County
34	10.8	**North Terre Haute** (CDP) Vigo County
34	10.8	**Santa Claus** (town) Spencer County
39	10.7	**Greenwood** (city) Johnson County
40	10.6	**Angola** (city) Steuben County
40	10.6	**Greentown** (town) Howard County
42	10.3	**Pittsboro** (town) Hendricks County
42	10.3	**Sellersburg** (town) Clark County
44	10.2	**Winchester** (city) Randolph County
45	10.1	**Middlebury** (town) Elkhart County
46	10.0	**Fishers** (city) Hamilton County
46	10.0	**Greenfield** (city) Hancock County
46	10.0	**Hartford City** (city) Blackford County
46	10.0	**Lagrange** (town) LaGrange County
46	10.0	**Noblesville** (city) Hamilton County
51	9.7	**Brownsburg** (town) Hendricks County
51	9.7	**Georgetown** (town) Floyd County
53	9.6	**Avon** (town) Hendricks County
53	9.6	**Brownstown** (town) Jackson County
53	9.6	**Granger** (CDP) Saint Joseph County
53	9.6	**Lebanon** (city) Boone County
53	9.6	**Speedway** (town) Marion County
53	9.6	**Valparaiso** (city) Porter County
53	9.6	**Warsaw** (city) Kosciusko County
60	9.5	**Decatur** (city) Adams County
60	9.5	**North Manchester** (town) Wabash County
60	9.5	**Osceola** (town) Saint Joseph County
63	9.4	**Alexandria** (city) Madison County
63	9.4	**De Motte** (town) Jasper County
63	9.4	**Lowell** (town) Lake County
66	9.3	**Princeton** (city) Gibson County
66	9.3	**Westfield** (city) Hamilton County
68	9.2	**Columbia City** (city) Whitley County
68	9.2	**Columbus** (city) Bartholomew County
68	9.2	**Corydon** (town) Harrison County
71	9.1	**Bedford** (city) Lawrence County
71	9.1	**Crawfordsville** (city) Montgomery County
73	9.0	**Hanover** (town) Jefferson County
73	9.0	**Hobart** (city) Lake County
73	9.0	**New Albany** (city) Floyd County
73	9.0	**Richmond** (city) Wayne County
73	9.0	**Rushville** (city) Rush County
78	8.9	**Chandler** (town) Warrick County
78	8.9	**Huntertown** (town) Allen County
78	8.9	**Mitchell** (city) Lawrence County
78	8.9	**Winona Lake** (town) Kosciusko County
82	8.8	**Kendallville** (city) Noble County
82	8.8	**Leo-Cedarville** (town) Allen County
82	8.8	**Pendleton** (town) Madison County
82	8.8	**Winfield** (town) Lake County
86	8.7	**Jeffersonville** (city) Clark County
86	8.7	**Newburgh** (town) Warrick County
86	8.7	**Washington** (city) Daviess County
89	8.6	**Clarksville** (town) Clark County
89	8.6	**Greencastle** (city) Putnam County
89	8.6	**Whiteland** (town) Johnson County
92	8.5	**Paoli** (town) Orange County
92	8.5	**Tipton** (city) Tipton County
94	8.4	**Kokomo** (city) Howard County
94	8.4	**Lafayette** (city) Tippecanoe County
94	8.4	**Melody Hill** (CDP) Vanderburgh County
97	8.3	**Cedar Lake** (town) Lake County
97	8.3	**Plainfield** (town) Hendricks County
99	8.2	**Seymour** (city) Jackson County
100	8.1	**Charlestown** (city) Clark County
100	8.1	**Shorewood Forest** (CDP) Porter County
102	8.0	**Portland** (city) Jay County
102	8.0	**Syracuse** (town) Kosciusko County
102	8.0	**Terre Haute** (city) Vigo County
105	7.9	**Chesterton** (town) Porter County
105	7.9	**Hebron** (town) Porter County
105	7.9	**Huntington** (city) Huntington County
105	7.9	**Salem** (city) Washington County
109	7.8	**Batesville** (city) Ripley County
109	7.8	**Bluffton** (city) Wells County
109	7.8	**Brazil** (city) Clay County
109	7.8	**Bremen** (town) Marshall County
109	7.8	**Franklin** (city) Johnson County
109	7.8	**Jasper** (city) Dubois County
109	7.8	**Tell City** (city) Perry County
116	7.7	**Country Squire Lakes** (CDP) Jennings County
116	7.7	**South Haven** (CDP) Porter County
118	7.6	**Sheridan** (town) Hamilton County
119	7.5	**Saint John** (town) Lake County
120	7.4	**Delphi** (city) Carroll County
120	7.4	**West Lafayette** (city) Tippecanoe County
122	7.3	**Loogootee** (city) Martin County
123	7.2	**Knox** (city) Starke County
123	7.2	**Muncie** (city) Delaware County
125	7.1	**La Porte** (city) LaPorte County
125	7.1	**Wabash** (city) Wabash County
127	7.0	**Cicero** (town) Hamilton County
127	7.0	**Danville** (town) Hendricks County
127	7.0	**Munster** (town) Lake County
130	6.9	**Fort Branch** (town) Gibson County
130	6.9	**Shelbyville** (city) Shelby County
132	6.8	**Beech Grove** (city) Marion County
132	6.8	**Brookville** (town) Franklin County
132	6.8	**Greensburg** (city) Decatur County
132	6.8	**New Haven** (city) Allen County
136	6.7	**Edinburgh** (town) Johnson County
136	6.7	**Frankfort** (city) Clinton County
136	6.7	**Highland** (town) Lake County
139	6.6	**Bright** (CDP) Dearborn County
139	6.6	**Marion** (city) Grant County
141	6.5	**Anderson** (city) Madison County
141	6.5	**Fort Wayne** (city) Allen County
143	6.4	**Austin** (city) Scott County
143	6.4	**Lawrence** (city) Marion County
143	6.4	**Peru** (city) Miami County
146	6.3	**Berne** (city) Adams County
146	6.3	**Mishawaka** (city) Saint Joseph County
148	6.2	**Crown Point** (city) Lake County
148	6.2	**Indianapolis** (city) Marion County
148	6.2	**Nappanee** (city) Elkhart County

Note: *This section ranks incorporated places and CDPs (Census Designated Places) with populations of 2,500 or more. Unincorporated postal areas were not considered. Please refer to the User Guide for additional information.*

Ancestry: American

Top 150 Places Ranked in *Descending* Order

State Rank	Percent	Place
1	32.2	**Fortville** (town) Hancock County
2	27.3	**Sheridan** (town) Hamilton County
3	22.3	**Brownstown** (town) Jackson County
4	20.4	**Salem** (city) Washington County
5	19.3	**Bicknell** (city) Knox County
6	19.1	**Cumberland** (town) Marion County
7	18.9	**Seymour** (city) Jackson County
8	17.7	**Greensburg** (city) Decatur County
9	17.4	**Shelbyville** (city) Shelby County
10	17.1	**North Terre Haute** (CDP) Vigo County
11	16.7	**Mooresville** (town) Morgan County
12	16.5	**Huntertown** (town) Allen County
12	16.5	**Tipton** (city) Tipton County
14	16.4	**Cicero** (town) Hamilton County
15	16.3	**Country Squire Lakes** (CDP) Jennings County
16	15.9	**Brownsburg** (town) Hendricks County
17	15.8	**Greenfield** (city) Hancock County
18	15.7	**Boonville** (city) Warrick County
19	15.6	**Elwood** (city) Madison County
20	15.3	**Peru** (city) Miami County
21	15.2	**Brookville** (town) Franklin County
21	15.2	**Edinburgh** (town) Johnson County
23	15.1	**Lebanon** (city) Boone County
24	15.0	**Bargersville** (town) Johnson County
24	15.0	**Melody Hill** (CDP) Vanderburgh County
24	15.0	**Rushville** (city) Rush County
27	14.9	**Connersville** (city) Fayette County
28	14.8	**Butler** (city) DeKalb County
28	14.8	**New Castle** (city) Henry County
30	14.6	**Osceola** (town) Saint Joseph County
31	14.5	**Charlestown** (city) Clark County
32	14.4	**Alexandria** (city) Madison County
33	14.3	**North Vernon** (city) Jennings County
34	14.2	**Columbus** (city) Bartholomew County
35	14.1	**Rochester** (city) Fulton County
36	13.7	**Wabash** (city) Wabash County
37	13.4	**Westfield** (city) Hamilton County
38	13.3	**Middlebury** (town) Elkhart County
39	13.1	**Gas City** (city) Grant County
40	12.9	**Clinton** (city) Vermillion County
40	12.9	**New Whiteland** (town) Johnson County
42	12.5	**Auburn** (city) DeKalb County
42	12.5	**Bluffton** (city) Wells County
42	12.5	**Pendleton** (town) Madison County
45	12.4	**Decatur** (city) Adams County
45	12.4	**Whiteland** (town) Johnson County
47	12.2	**Yorktown** (town) Delaware County
48	12.1	**Paoli** (town) Orange County
48	12.1	**Tell City** (city) Perry County
50	12.0	**Greentown** (town) Howard County
50	12.0	**Noblesville** (city) Hamilton County
52	11.9	**Austin** (city) Scott County
53	11.8	**Simonton Lake** (CDP) Elkhart County
54	11.7	**New Haven** (city) Allen County
54	11.7	**Plainfield** (town) Hendricks County
54	11.7	**Washington** (city) Daviess County
57	11.6	**Terre Haute** (city) Vigo County
58	11.5	**Bedford** (city) Lawrence County
58	11.5	**Fort Branch** (town) Gibson County
60	11.4	**Corydon** (town) Harrison County
60	11.4	**Delphi** (city) Carroll County
60	11.4	**Kendallville** (city) Noble County
60	11.4	**Linton** (city) Greene County
64	11.3	**Danville** (town) Hendricks County
64	11.3	**Kokomo** (city) Howard County
64	11.3	**Pittsboro** (town) Hendricks County
67	11.2	**Chandler** (town) Warrick County
67	11.2	**Loogootee** (city) Martin County
67	11.2	**Monticello** (city) White County
70	11.1	**Attica** (city) Fountain County
70	11.1	**Martinsville** (city) Morgan County
72	11.0	**Princeton** (city) Gibson County
72	11.0	**Rockville** (town) Parke County
74	10.9	**Dunlap** (CDP) Elkhart County
74	10.9	**Huntington** (city) Huntington County
74	10.9	**Lawrenceburg** (city) Dearborn County
77	10.8	**Highland** (CDP) Vanderburgh County
77	10.8	**Portland** (city) Jay County
79	10.5	**Syracuse** (town) Kosciusko County
80	10.3	**Scottsburg** (city) Scott County
81	10.2	**Crawfordsville** (city) Montgomery County
81	10.2	**Franklin** (city) Johnson County
81	10.2	**Winchester** (city) Randolph County
84	10.1	**Mishawaka** (city) Saint Joseph County
84	10.1	**Santa Claus** (town) Spencer County
86	9.9	**Fishers** (city) Hamilton County
86	9.9	**North Manchester** (town) Wabash County
88	9.8	**Aurora** (city) Dearborn County
88	9.8	**Columbia City** (city) Whitley County
88	9.8	**Muncie** (city) Delaware County
88	9.8	**Smithville-Sanders** (CDP) Monroe County
92	9.7	**Logansport** (city) Cass County
93	9.6	**Carmel** (city) Hamilton County
93	9.6	**Centerville** (town) Wayne County
93	9.6	**Mitchell** (city) Lawrence County
93	9.6	**Zionsville** (town) Boone County
97	9.4	**Fairmount** (town) Grant County
97	9.4	**Mount Vernon** (city) Posey County
97	9.4	**Roselawn** (CDP) Newton County
100	9.3	**Brazil** (city) Clay County
101	9.2	**Anderson** (city) Madison County
101	9.2	**Newburgh** (town) Warrick County
103	9.1	**Hartford City** (city) Blackford County
103	9.1	**Marion** (city) Grant County
105	8.9	**Goshen** (city) Elkhart County
106	8.7	**Ellettsville** (town) Monroe County
106	8.7	**Greendale** (city) Dearborn County
106	8.7	**Warsaw** (city) Kosciusko County
109	8.6	**Bremen** (town) Marshall County
109	8.6	**Greenwood** (city) Johnson County
111	8.5	**Richmond** (city) Wayne County
112	8.4	**Clarksville** (town) Clark County
112	8.4	**Jasper** (city) Dubois County
112	8.4	**Union City** (city) Randolph County
112	8.4	**Winona Lake** (town) Kosciusko County
116	8.3	**New Albany** (city) Floyd County
117	8.1	**Bright** (CDP) Dearborn County
117	8.1	**Greencastle** (city) Putnam County
119	8.0	**Georgetown** (town) Floyd County
119	8.0	**McCordsville** (town) Hancock County
119	8.0	**Vincennes** (city) Knox County
122	7.9	**Angola** (city) Steuben County
123	7.7	**Batesville** (city) Ripley County
124	7.6	**Lawrence** (city) Marion County
125	7.5	**Knox** (city) Starke County
126	7.4	**Beech Grove** (city) Marion County
126	7.4	**Huntingburg** (city) Dubois County
126	7.4	**Ossian** (town) Wells County
126	7.4	**Sellersburg** (town) Clark County
130	7.3	**Plymouth** (city) Marshall County
130	7.3	**Sullivan** (city) Sullivan County
132	7.2	**Jeffersonville** (city) Clark County
132	7.2	**Lagrange** (town) LaGrange County
134	7.1	**Evansville** (city) Vanderburgh County
134	7.1	**Frankfort** (city) Clinton County
136	7.0	**Avon** (town) Hendricks County
136	7.0	**Granger** (CDP) Saint Joseph County
136	7.0	**Lowell** (town) Lake County
139	6.9	**Garrett** (city) DeKalb County
140	6.7	**Elkhart** (city) Elkhart County
141	6.6	**Speedway** (town) Marion County
142	6.5	**Madison** (city) Jefferson County
142	6.5	**Winamac** (town) Pulaski County
144	6.4	**Fort Wayne** (city) Allen County
144	6.4	**Rensselaer** (city) Jasper County
146	6.3	**Indianapolis** (city) Marion County
147	6.1	**Lafayette** (city) Tippecanoe County
148	6.0	**Hanover** (town) Jefferson County
148	6.0	**Heritage Lake** (CDP) Putnam County
148	6.0	**Nappanee** (city) Elkhart County

Note: *This section ranks incorporated places and CDPs (Census Designated Places) with populations of 2,500 or more. Unincorporated postal areas were not considered. Please refer to the User Guide for additional information.*

Ancestry: Irish

Top 150 Places Ranked in *Descending* Order

State Rank	Percent	Place
1	27.4	**Knox** (city) Starke County
2	25.5	**Notre Dame** (CDP) Saint Joseph County
3	25.3	**Corydon** (town) Harrison County
4	23.4	**Salt Creek Commons** (CDP) Porter County
5	22.9	**Bright** (CDP) Dearborn County
6	21.9	**Heritage Lake** (CDP) Putnam County
7	21.5	**Lowell** (town) Lake County
8	21.2	**Cedar Lake** (town) Lake County
9	20.9	**Aurora** (city) Dearborn County
10	20.3	**Hobart** (city) Lake County
11	19.7	**Lakes of the Four Seasons** (CDP) Lake County
12	19.3	**Valparaiso** (city) Porter County
13	19.1	**Loogootee** (city) Martin County
14	18.7	**Sellersburg** (town) Clark County
14	18.7	**South Haven** (CDP) Porter County
16	18.2	**Winamac** (town) Pulaski County
17	17.8	**Greendale** (city) Dearborn County
18	17.7	**North Terre Haute** (CDP) Vigo County
19	17.2	**Georgetown** (town) Floyd County
19	17.2	**Paoli** (town) Orange County
21	17.1	**Schererville** (town) Lake County
22	17.0	**Attica** (city) Fountain County
23	16.7	**Smithville-Sanders** (CDP) Monroe County
24	16.6	**Hidden Valley** (CDP) Dearborn County
25	16.4	**Saint John** (town) Lake County
26	16.2	**Dyer** (town) Lake County
26	16.2	**Melody Hill** (CDP) Vanderburgh County
28	16.0	**Pendleton** (town) Madison County
29	15.9	**Roselawn** (CDP) Newton County
30	15.6	**Chesterton** (town) Porter County
31	15.5	**Munster** (town) Lake County
32	15.3	**Westville** (town) LaPorte County
33	15.2	**Beech Grove** (city) Marion County
33	15.2	**Westfield** (city) Hamilton County
35	15.1	**Ellettsville** (town) Monroe County
36	15.0	**Linton** (city) Greene County
37	14.9	**Dunlap** (CDP) Elkhart County
37	14.9	**Highland** (CDP) Vanderburgh County
37	14.9	**Lake Station** (city) Lake County
37	14.9	**Winfield** (town) Lake County
41	14.8	**Brookville** (town) Franklin County
42	14.7	**La Porte** (city) LaPorte County
42	14.7	**Santa Claus** (town) Spencer County
42	14.7	**Yorktown** (town) Delaware County
45	14.6	**Whitestown** (town) Boone County
46	14.5	**Carmel** (city) Hamilton County
47	14.3	**Whiteland** (town) Johnson County
48	14.2	**Crawfordsville** (city) Montgomery County
49	14.1	**Fortville** (town) Hancock County
49	14.1	**Greensburg** (city) Decatur County
51	14.0	**Alexandria** (city) Madison County
52	13.9	**Jeffersonville** (city) Clark County
53	13.8	**Crown Point** (city) Lake County
53	13.8	**Highland** (town) Lake County
53	13.8	**New Albany** (city) Floyd County
53	13.8	**Rensselaer** (city) Jasper County
53	13.8	**Wabash** (city) Wabash County
53	13.8	**Winona Lake** (town) Kosciusko County
59	13.6	**Lafayette** (city) Tippecanoe County
60	13.5	**Mooresville** (town) Morgan County
61	13.4	**Bicknell** (city) Knox County
61	13.4	**Richmond** (city) Wayne County
61	13.4	**Shorewood Forest** (CDP) Porter County
64	13.3	**Cumberland** (town) Marion County
64	13.3	**Syracuse** (town) Kosciusko County
66	13.1	**Portage** (city) Porter County
67	13.0	**Avon** (town) Hendricks County
67	13.0	**Bedford** (city) Lawrence County
67	13.0	**Fort Branch** (town) Gibson County
67	13.0	**Granger** (CDP) Saint Joseph County
67	13.0	**Griffith** (town) Lake County
67	13.0	**Huntington** (city) Huntington County
67	13.0	**Pittsboro** (town) Hendricks County
67	13.0	**Upland** (town) Grant County
75	12.9	**Butler** (city) DeKalb County
76	12.8	**Madison** (city) Jefferson County
77	12.7	**Cicero** (town) Hamilton County
77	12.7	**Fairmount** (town) Grant County
77	12.7	**Newburgh** (town) Warrick County
77	12.7	**Vincennes** (city) Knox County
81	12.6	**Lawrenceburg** (city) Dearborn County
82	12.5	**Auburn** (city) DeKalb County
82	12.5	**Elwood** (city) Madison County
82	12.5	**Muncie** (city) Delaware County
82	12.5	**Osceola** (town) Saint Joseph County
82	12.5	**Salem** (city) Washington County
87	12.4	**Noblesville** (city) Hamilton County
87	12.4	**Plainfield** (town) Hendricks County
89	12.3	**Mishawaka** (city) Saint Joseph County
89	12.3	**Porter** (town) Porter County
91	12.2	**Angola** (city) Steuben County
91	12.2	**Clarksville** (town) Clark County
91	12.2	**Greenfield** (city) Hancock County
94	12.1	**Michigan City** (city) LaPorte County
94	12.1	**Warsaw** (city) Kosciusko County
96	12.0	**Fishers** (city) Hamilton County
97	11.9	**Winchester** (city) Randolph County
98	11.8	**Charlestown** (city) Clark County
98	11.8	**Scottsburg** (city) Scott County
100	11.7	**De Motte** (town) Jasper County
100	11.7	**Ossian** (town) Wells County
100	11.7	**Tell City** (city) Perry County
103	11.6	**Edinburgh** (town) Johnson County
103	11.6	**Evansville** (city) Vanderburgh County
103	11.6	**Franklin** (city) Johnson County
103	11.6	**Jasper** (city) Dubois County
107	11.5	**Batesville** (city) Ripley County
107	11.5	**Hebron** (town) Porter County
107	11.5	**Huntingburg** (city) Dubois County
110	11.4	**Garrett** (city) DeKalb County
111	11.3	**Brownsburg** (town) Hendricks County
111	11.3	**Connersville** (city) Fayette County
113	11.2	**Danville** (town) Hendricks County
113	11.2	**New Haven** (city) Allen County
115	11.1	**Brownstown** (town) Jackson County
115	11.1	**West Lafayette** (city) Tippecanoe County
117	11.0	**Anderson** (city) Madison County
117	11.0	**Frankfort** (city) Clinton County
117	11.0	**Greenwood** (city) Johnson County
117	11.0	**Hanover** (town) Jefferson County
117	11.0	**Martinsville** (city) Morgan County
117	11.0	**Shelbyville** (city) Shelby County
117	11.0	**Washington** (city) Daviess County
124	10.9	**Bloomington** (city) Monroe County
124	10.9	**Hartford City** (city) Blackford County
126	10.8	**Kokomo** (city) Howard County
126	10.8	**Lebanon** (city) Boone County
126	10.8	**Mount Vernon** (city) Posey County
126	10.8	**Whiting** (city) Lake County
126	10.8	**Zionsville** (town) Boone County
131	10.6	**Nappanee** (city) Elkhart County
132	10.5	**Bremen** (town) Marshall County
133	10.4	**Brazil** (city) Clay County
134	10.3	**New Castle** (city) Henry County
134	10.3	**Rochester** (city) Fulton County
136	10.2	**Greentown** (town) Howard County
136	10.2	**Huntertown** (town) Allen County
136	10.2	**Rushville** (city) Rush County
139	10.1	**Gas City** (city) Grant County
139	10.1	**Kendallville** (city) Noble County
139	10.1	**Terre Haute** (city) Vigo County
142	10.0	**Peru** (city) Miami County
142	10.0	**Princeton** (city) Gibson County
144	9.9	**Bargersville** (town) Johnson County
144	9.9	**Country Squire Lakes** (CDP) Jennings County
144	9.9	**Marion** (city) Grant County
144	9.9	**North Manchester** (town) Wabash County
148	9.8	**Sullivan** (city) Sullivan County
149	9.6	**Chandler** (town) Warrick County
149	9.6	**Columbus** (city) Bartholomew County

Note: *This section ranks incorporated places and CDPs (Census Designated Places) with populations of 2,500 or more. Unincorporated postal areas were not considered. Please refer to the User Guide for additional information.*

Rankings

Ancestry: Italian

Top 150 Places Ranked in *Descending* Order

State Rank	Percent	Place
1	12.2	**Notre Dame** (CDP) Saint Joseph County
1	12.2	**Shorewood Forest** (CDP) Porter County
3	11.5	**Bremen** (town) Marshall County
4	11.3	**Saint John** (town) Lake County
5	10.9	**Hebron** (town) Porter County
5	10.9	**South Haven** (CDP) Porter County
7	10.2	**Dyer** (town) Lake County
8	10.0	**Clinton** (city) Vermillion County
9	9.8	**Munster** (town) Lake County
10	9.0	**Cedar Lake** (town) Lake County
11	8.7	**Highland** (CDP) Vanderburgh County
12	8.4	**Crown Point** (city) Lake County
13	8.0	**Chandler** (town) Warrick County
14	7.9	**Lake Station** (city) Lake County
15	7.7	**Chesterton** (town) Porter County
16	7.2	**Heritage Lake** (CDP) Putnam County
16	7.2	**Schererville** (town) Lake County
18	6.8	**Cicero** (town) Hamilton County
19	6.6	**Georgetown** (town) Floyd County
20	6.3	**Valparaiso** (city) Porter County
21	6.2	**Leo-Cedarville** (town) Allen County
21	6.2	**Nappanee** (city) Elkhart County
23	5.4	**Alexandria** (city) Madison County
23	5.4	**Mitchell** (city) Lawrence County
25	5.1	**Zionsville** (town) Boone County
26	5.0	**Hobart** (city) Lake County
27	4.9	**Delphi** (city) Carroll County
27	4.9	**Lawrenceburg** (city) Dearborn County
29	4.8	**West Lafayette** (city) Tippecanoe County
30	4.5	**Noblesville** (city) Hamilton County
31	4.4	**Winfield** (town) Lake County
32	4.3	**Plainfield** (town) Hendricks County
33	4.2	**Greensburg** (city) Decatur County
33	4.2	**Newburgh** (town) Warrick County
33	4.2	**Salt Creek Commons** (CDP) Porter County
33	4.2	**Westfield** (city) Hamilton County
37	4.0	**Bloomington** (city) Monroe County
37	4.0	**Carmel** (city) Hamilton County
37	4.0	**Portage** (city) Porter County
40	3.7	**Batesville** (city) Ripley County
41	3.5	**Bedford** (city) Lawrence County
41	3.5	**Franklin** (city) Johnson County
41	3.5	**Logansport** (city) Cass County
44	3.4	**Beech Grove** (city) Marion County
44	3.4	**Brownstown** (town) Jackson County
44	3.4	**Monticello** (city) White County
44	3.4	**Paoli** (town) Orange County
48	3.2	**Warsaw** (city) Kosciusko County
49	3.1	**Hammond** (city) Lake County
49	3.1	**Jeffersonville** (city) Clark County
51	2.9	**Winchester** (city) Randolph County
52	2.8	**Westville** (town) LaPorte County
53	2.6	**Anderson** (city) Madison County
53	2.6	**Edinburgh** (town) Johnson County
53	2.6	**Madison** (city) Jefferson County
56	2.5	**Brookville** (town) Franklin County
56	2.5	**Lawrence** (city) Marion County
56	2.5	**Merrillville** (town) Lake County
56	2.5	**Rushville** (city) Rush County
60	2.3	**Kokomo** (city) Howard County
60	2.3	**Muncie** (city) Delaware County
60	2.3	**Richmond** (city) Wayne County
63	2.1	**Huntington** (city) Huntington County
64	2.0	**Marion** (city) Grant County
64	2.0	**North Manchester** (town) Wabash County

Note: *This section ranks incorporated places and CDPs (Census Designated Places) with populations of 2,500 or more. Unincorporated postal areas were not considered. Please refer to the User Guide for additional information.*

Employment: Management, Business, and Financial Occupations

Top 150 Places Ranked in *Descending* Order

State Rank	Percent	Place
1	27.7	**Zionsville** (town) Boone County
2	26.3	**Carmel** (city) Hamilton County
2	26.3	**Whitestown** (town) Boone County
4	26.0	**Fishers** (city) Hamilton County
4	26.0	**Winfield** (town) Lake County
6	24.3	**Shorewood Forest** (CDP) Porter County
7	23.9	**Bargersville** (town) Johnson County
8	22.7	**Smithville-Sanders** (CDP) Monroe County
8	22.7	**Westfield** (city) Hamilton County
10	22.4	**Munster** (town) Lake County
11	21.1	**Whiteland** (town) Johnson County
12	20.3	**Granger** (CDP) Saint Joseph County
12	20.3	**Pittsboro** (town) Hendricks County
12	20.3	**Saint John** (town) Lake County
15	20.1	**Middlebury** (town) Elkhart County
16	19.8	**Noblesville** (city) Hamilton County
17	19.6	**McCordsville** (town) Hancock County
18	19.3	**Hidden Valley** (CDP) Dearborn County
19	19.2	**Avon** (town) Hendricks County
20	18.4	**Highland** (CDP) Vanderburgh County
21	18.0	**Centerville** (town) Wayne County
22	17.8	**Columbus** (city) Bartholomew County
23	17.7	**Batesville** (city) Ripley County
24	17.5	**Winona Lake** (town) Kosciusko County
25	16.4	**Brownsburg** (town) Hendricks County
25	16.4	**Chesterton** (town) Porter County
25	16.4	**Santa Claus** (town) Spencer County
28	16.2	**Heritage Lake** (CDP) Putnam County
29	16.1	**Cumberland** (town) Marion County
30	16.0	**Schererville** (town) Lake County
31	15.7	**Crown Point** (city) Lake County
31	15.7	**Greenwood** (city) Johnson County
31	15.7	**Lawrence** (city) Marion County
34	15.5	**Sellersburg** (town) Clark County
35	15.3	**Dunlap** (CDP) Elkhart County
36	15.2	**Cedar Lake** (town) Lake County
37	15.0	**Dyer** (town) Lake County
37	15.0	**Plainfield** (town) Hendricks County
39	14.9	**Highland** (town) Lake County
39	14.9	**Huntertown** (town) Allen County
39	14.9	**Sheridan** (town) Hamilton County
42	14.7	**Valparaiso** (city) Porter County
43	14.6	**Porter** (town) Porter County
44	14.5	**Columbia City** (city) Whitley County
45	14.2	**Delphi** (city) Carroll County
45	14.2	**Greendale** (city) Dearborn County
45	14.2	**Pendleton** (town) Madison County
48	14.1	**Jeffersonville** (city) Clark County
48	14.1	**Lebanon** (city) Boone County
50	14.0	**Danville** (town) Hendricks County
50	14.0	**Indianapolis** (city) Marion County
50	14.0	**Newburgh** (town) Warrick County
53	13.8	**Lakes of the Four Seasons** (CDP) Lake County
54	13.6	**Georgetown** (town) Floyd County
54	13.6	**Mitchell** (city) Lawrence County
56	13.3	**Jasper** (city) Dubois County
56	13.3	**Lowell** (town) Lake County
56	13.3	**Simonton Lake** (CDP) Elkhart County
56	13.3	**Yorktown** (town) Delaware County
60	13.0	**Salt Creek Commons** (CDP) Porter County
60	13.0	**Upland** (town) Grant County
62	12.9	**Cicero** (town) Hamilton County
62	12.9	**Fairmount** (town) Grant County
62	12.9	**Hebron** (town) Porter County
65	12.8	**Bloomington** (city) Monroe County
65	12.8	**Melody Hill** (CDP) Vanderburgh County
65	12.8	**Ossian** (town) Wells County
65	12.8	**Tipton** (city) Tipton County
69	12.7	**Attica** (city) Fountain County
69	12.7	**Charlestown** (city) Clark County
69	12.7	**Franklin** (city) Johnson County
72	12.6	**Fortville** (town) Hancock County
72	12.6	**Linton** (city) Greene County
72	12.6	**Salem** (city) Washington County
75	12.2	**Clarksville** (town) Clark County
75	12.2	**North Manchester** (town) Wabash County
75	12.2	**Speedway** (town) Marion County
78	12.1	**Greensburg** (city) Decatur County
78	12.1	**Kendallville** (city) Noble County
80	12.0	**Auburn** (city) DeKalb County
80	12.0	**Fort Wayne** (city) Allen County
80	12.0	**Hobart** (city) Lake County
80	12.0	**Warsaw** (city) Kosciusko County
84	11.9	**Greenfield** (city) Hancock County
85	11.8	**Mount Vernon** (city) Posey County
86	11.6	**Huntingburg** (city) Dubois County
86	11.6	**Paoli** (town) Orange County
88	11.5	**Brookville** (town) Franklin County
88	11.5	**Whiting** (city) Lake County
90	11.4	**Leo-Cedarville** (town) Allen County
91	11.1	**Garrett** (city) DeKalb County
91	11.1	**Madison** (city) Jefferson County
93	11.0	**Wabash** (city) Wabash County
94	10.9	**Bright** (CDP) Dearborn County
94	10.9	**Merrillville** (town) Lake County
94	10.9	**Syracuse** (town) Kosciusko County
97	10.8	**Griffith** (town) Lake County
98	10.7	**Evansville** (city) Vanderburgh County
98	10.7	**New Albany** (city) Floyd County
100	10.6	**Lafayette** (city) Tippecanoe County
101	10.5	**Ellettsville** (town) Monroe County
101	10.5	**Scottsburg** (city) Scott County
103	10.4	**Corydon** (town) Harrison County
103	10.4	**Fort Branch** (town) Gibson County
103	10.4	**Seymour** (city) Jackson County
103	10.4	**South Haven** (CDP) Porter County
107	10.3	**Alexandria** (city) Madison County
107	10.3	**Chandler** (town) Warrick County
107	10.3	**Hanover** (town) Jefferson County
107	10.3	**Rushville** (city) Rush County
111	10.2	**Bluffton** (city) Wells County
111	10.2	**Michigan City** (city) LaPorte County
113	10.1	**Mishawaka** (city) Saint Joseph County
113	10.1	**Muncie** (city) Delaware County
113	10.1	**New Haven** (city) Allen County
113	10.1	**Rochester** (city) Fulton County
117	10.0	**Berne** (city) Adams County
118	9.9	**Nappanee** (city) Elkhart County
118	9.9	**Osceola** (town) Saint Joseph County
120	9.8	**North Vernon** (city) Jennings County
120	9.8	**Shelbyville** (city) Shelby County
120	9.8	**Vincennes** (city) Knox County
123	9.7	**South Bend** (city) Saint Joseph County
124	9.6	**Greentown** (town) Howard County
124	9.6	**Portage** (city) Porter County
126	9.5	**Beech Grove** (city) Marion County
127	9.4	**Princeton** (city) Gibson County
127	9.4	**Winamac** (town) Pulaski County
129	9.3	**Loogootee** (city) Martin County
129	9.3	**Richmond** (city) Wayne County
131	9.0	**Crawfordsville** (city) Montgomery County
131	9.0	**Washington** (city) Daviess County
133	8.9	**Brazil** (city) Clay County
133	8.9	**Terre Haute** (city) Vigo County
135	8.8	**West Lafayette** (city) Tippecanoe County
135	8.8	**Westville** (town) LaPorte County
137	8.7	**Hammond** (city) Lake County
137	8.7	**Mooresville** (town) Morgan County
139	8.6	**Bicknell** (city) Knox County
139	8.6	**Rockville** (town) Parke County
141	8.5	**Boonville** (city) Warrick County
141	8.5	**Hartford City** (city) Blackford County
141	8.5	**Martinsville** (city) Morgan County
141	8.5	**New Whiteland** (town) Johnson County
145	8.3	**Tell City** (city) Perry County
146	8.2	**Rensselaer** (city) Jasper County
146	8.2	**Winchester** (city) Randolph County
148	8.1	**Bedford** (city) Lawrence County
148	8.1	**New Castle** (city) Henry County
150	8.0	**Anderson** (city) Madison County

***Note:** This section ranks incorporated places and CDPs (Census Designated Places) with populations of 2,500 or more. Unincorporated postal areas were not considered. Please refer to the User Guide for additional information.*

Employment: Management, Business, and Financial Occupations

Top 150 Places Ranked in *Ascending* Order

State Rank	Percent	Place
1	2.4	**Clinton** (city) Vermillion County
2	2.7	**Union City** (city) Randolph County
3	3.3	**Roselawn** (CDP) Newton County
4	3.5	**Country Squire Lakes** (CDP) Jennings County
5	3.9	**Lake Station** (city) Lake County
6	4.2	**De Motte** (town) Jasper County
7	4.3	**Lawrenceburg** (city) Dearborn County
7	4.3	**Sullivan** (city) Sullivan County
9	5.0	**Peru** (city) Miami County
10	5.3	**Notre Dame** (CDP) Saint Joseph County
11	5.5	**Portland** (city) Jay County
12	5.6	**Austin** (city) Scott County
12	5.6	**Elwood** (city) Madison County
12	5.6	**Frankfort** (city) Clinton County
15	5.7	**Ligonier** (city) Noble County
16	5.8	**Monticello** (city) White County
17	5.9	**Edinburgh** (town) Johnson County
18	6.1	**Brownstown** (town) Jackson County
18	6.1	**La Porte** (city) LaPorte County
18	6.1	**Lagrange** (town) LaGrange County
21	6.2	**Knox** (city) Starke County
22	6.3	**Connersville** (city) Fayette County
23	6.5	**Logansport** (city) Cass County
23	6.5	**North Terre Haute** (CDP) Vigo County
25	6.6	**Huntington** (city) Huntington County
26	6.7	**Butler** (city) DeKalb County
26	6.7	**Elkhart** (city) Elkhart County
28	6.8	**Greencastle** (city) Putnam County
29	6.9	**Aurora** (city) Dearborn County
30	7.1	**Kokomo** (city) Howard County
31	7.2	**Decatur** (city) Adams County
32	7.4	**Angola** (city) Steuben County
33	7.5	**Marion** (city) Grant County
34	7.6	**East Chicago** (city) Lake County
34	7.6	**Gary** (city) Lake County
36	7.7	**Goshen** (city) Elkhart County
36	7.7	**Plymouth** (city) Marshall County
38	7.8	**Gas City** (city) Grant County
39	7.9	**Bremen** (town) Marshall County
40	8.0	**Anderson** (city) Madison County
41	8.1	**Bedford** (city) Lawrence County
41	8.1	**New Castle** (city) Henry County
43	8.2	**Rensselaer** (city) Jasper County
43	8.2	**Winchester** (city) Randolph County
45	8.3	**Tell City** (city) Perry County
46	8.5	**Boonville** (city) Warrick County
46	8.5	**Hartford City** (city) Blackford County
46	8.5	**Martinsville** (city) Morgan County
46	8.5	**New Whiteland** (town) Johnson County
50	8.6	**Bicknell** (city) Knox County
50	8.6	**Rockville** (town) Parke County
52	8.7	**Hammond** (city) Lake County
52	8.7	**Mooresville** (town) Morgan County
54	8.8	**West Lafayette** (city) Tippecanoe County
54	8.8	**Westville** (town) LaPorte County
56	8.9	**Brazil** (city) Clay County
56	8.9	**Terre Haute** (city) Vigo County
58	9.0	**Crawfordsville** (city) Montgomery County
58	9.0	**Washington** (city) Daviess County
60	9.3	**Loogootee** (city) Martin County
60	9.3	**Richmond** (city) Wayne County
62	9.4	**Princeton** (city) Gibson County
62	9.4	**Winamac** (town) Pulaski County
64	9.5	**Beech Grove** (city) Marion County
65	9.6	**Greentown** (town) Howard County
65	9.6	**Portage** (city) Porter County
67	9.7	**South Bend** (city) Saint Joseph County
68	9.8	**North Vernon** (city) Jennings County
68	9.8	**Shelbyville** (city) Shelby County
68	9.8	**Vincennes** (city) Knox County
71	9.9	**Nappanee** (city) Elkhart County
71	9.9	**Osceola** (town) Saint Joseph County
73	10.0	**Berne** (city) Adams County
74	10.1	**Mishawaka** (city) Saint Joseph County
74	10.1	**Muncie** (city) Delaware County
74	10.1	**New Haven** (city) Allen County
74	10.1	**Rochester** (city) Fulton County
78	10.2	**Bluffton** (city) Wells County
78	10.2	**Michigan City** (city) LaPorte County
80	10.3	**Alexandria** (city) Madison County
80	10.3	**Chandler** (town) Warrick County
80	10.3	**Hanover** (town) Jefferson County
80	10.3	**Rushville** (city) Rush County
84	10.4	**Corydon** (town) Harrison County
84	10.4	**Fort Branch** (town) Gibson County
84	10.4	**Seymour** (city) Jackson County
84	10.4	**South Haven** (CDP) Porter County
88	10.5	**Ellettsville** (town) Monroe County
88	10.5	**Scottsburg** (city) Scott County
90	10.6	**Lafayette** (city) Tippecanoe County
91	10.7	**Evansville** (city) Vanderburgh County
91	10.7	**New Albany** (city) Floyd County
93	10.8	**Griffith** (town) Lake County
94	10.9	**Bright** (CDP) Dearborn County
94	10.9	**Merrillville** (town) Lake County
94	10.9	**Syracuse** (town) Kosciusko County
97	11.0	**Wabash** (city) Wabash County
98	11.1	**Garrett** (city) DeKalb County
98	11.1	**Madison** (city) Jefferson County
100	11.4	**Leo-Cedarville** (town) Allen County
101	11.5	**Brookville** (town) Franklin County
101	11.5	**Whiting** (city) Lake County
103	11.6	**Huntingburg** (city) Dubois County
103	11.6	**Paoli** (town) Orange County
105	11.8	**Mount Vernon** (city) Posey County
106	11.9	**Greenfield** (city) Hancock County
107	12.0	**Auburn** (city) DeKalb County
107	12.0	**Fort Wayne** (city) Allen County
107	12.0	**Hobart** (city) Lake County
107	12.0	**Warsaw** (city) Kosciusko County
111	12.1	**Greensburg** (city) Decatur County
111	12.1	**Kendallville** (city) Noble County
113	12.2	**Clarksville** (town) Clark County
113	12.2	**North Manchester** (town) Wabash County
113	12.2	**Speedway** (town) Marion County
116	12.6	**Fortville** (town) Hancock County
116	12.6	**Linton** (city) Greene County
116	12.6	**Salem** (city) Washington County
119	12.7	**Attica** (city) Fountain County
119	12.7	**Charlestown** (city) Clark County
119	12.7	**Franklin** (city) Johnson County
122	12.8	**Bloomington** (city) Monroe County
122	12.8	**Melody Hill** (CDP) Vanderburgh County
122	12.8	**Ossian** (town) Wells County
122	12.8	**Tipton** (city) Tipton County
126	12.9	**Cicero** (town) Hamilton County
126	12.9	**Fairmount** (town) Grant County
126	12.9	**Hebron** (town) Porter County
129	13.0	**Salt Creek Commons** (CDP) Porter County
129	13.0	**Upland** (town) Grant County
131	13.3	**Jasper** (city) Dubois County
131	13.3	**Lowell** (town) Lake County
131	13.3	**Simonton Lake** (CDP) Elkhart County
131	13.3	**Yorktown** (town) Delaware County
135	13.6	**Georgetown** (town) Floyd County
135	13.6	**Mitchell** (city) Lawrence County
137	13.8	**Lakes of the Four Seasons** (CDP) Lake County
138	14.0	**Danville** (town) Hendricks County
138	14.0	**Indianapolis** (city) Marion County
138	14.0	**Newburgh** (town) Warrick County
141	14.1	**Jeffersonville** (city) Clark County
141	14.1	**Lebanon** (city) Boone County
143	14.2	**Delphi** (city) Carroll County
143	14.2	**Greendale** (city) Dearborn County
143	14.2	**Pendleton** (town) Madison County
146	14.5	**Columbia City** (city) Whitley County
147	14.6	**Porter** (town) Porter County
148	14.7	**Valparaiso** (city) Porter County
149	14.9	**Highland** (town) Lake County
149	14.9	**Huntertown** (town) Allen County

Note: *This section ranks incorporated places and CDPs (Census Designated Places) with populations of 2,500 or more. Unincorporated postal areas were not considered. Please refer to the User Guide for additional information.*

Employment: Computer, Engineering, and Science Occupations

Top 150 Places Ranked in *Descending* Order

State Rank	Percent	Place
1	16.8	**Columbus** (city) Bartholomew County
2	12.7	**West Lafayette** (city) Tippecanoe County
3	11.1	**Cicero** (town) Hamilton County
4	11.0	**Carmel** (city) Hamilton County
5	10.8	**Zionsville** (town) Boone County
6	10.5	**Fishers** (city) Hamilton County
7	9.4	**Westfield** (city) Hamilton County
8	8.2	**Avon** (town) Hendricks County
8	8.2	**Whitestown** (town) Boone County
10	8.1	**Bargersville** (town) Johnson County
10	8.1	**McCordsville** (town) Hancock County
10	8.1	**Upland** (town) Grant County
13	7.7	**Santa Claus** (town) Spencer County
13	7.7	**Warsaw** (city) Kosciusko County
13	7.7	**Yorktown** (town) Delaware County
16	7.4	**Newburgh** (town) Warrick County
17	7.1	**Greenwood** (city) Johnson County
18	7.0	**Bright** (CDP) Dearborn County
19	6.7	**Mount Vernon** (city) Posey County
20	6.6	**Highland** (CDP) Vanderburgh County
20	6.6	**Jasper** (city) Dubois County
20	6.6	**Notre Dame** (CDP) Saint Joseph County
20	6.6	**Plainfield** (town) Hendricks County
20	6.6	**Winona Lake** (town) Kosciusko County
25	6.5	**Angola** (city) Steuben County
25	6.5	**Noblesville** (city) Hamilton County
27	6.4	**Granger** (CDP) Saint Joseph County
28	6.1	**Batesville** (city) Ripley County
28	6.1	**Bloomington** (city) Monroe County
30	6.0	**Lawrence** (city) Marion County
30	6.0	**Saint John** (town) Lake County
32	5.9	**Greendale** (city) Dearborn County
32	5.9	**Pittsboro** (town) Hendricks County
34	5.8	**Georgetown** (town) Floyd County
34	5.8	**Speedway** (town) Marion County
36	5.7	**Lafayette** (city) Tippecanoe County
37	5.6	**Greensburg** (city) Decatur County
37	5.6	**North Manchester** (town) Wabash County
37	5.6	**Smithville-Sanders** (CDP) Monroe County
40	5.5	**Melody Hill** (CDP) Vanderburgh County
41	5.3	**Seymour** (city) Jackson County
41	5.3	**Valparaiso** (city) Porter County
43	5.2	**Bremen** (town) Marshall County
43	5.2	**Ellettsville** (town) Monroe County
45	5.1	**Cumberland** (town) Marion County
45	5.1	**Leo-Cedarville** (town) Allen County
45	5.1	**Sellersburg** (town) Clark County
45	5.1	**Tipton** (city) Tipton County
45	5.1	**Union City** (city) Randolph County
50	5.0	**Munster** (town) Lake County
50	5.0	**Pendleton** (town) Madison County
52	4.9	**Lakes of the Four Seasons** (CDP) Lake County
53	4.8	**Lawrenceburg** (city) Dearborn County
53	4.8	**Ossian** (town) Wells County
55	4.7	**Boonville** (city) Warrick County
55	4.7	**Indianapolis** (city) Marion County
57	4.6	**Fort Wayne** (city) Allen County
57	4.6	**Greenfield** (city) Hancock County
59	4.5	**Salt Creek Commons** (CDP) Porter County
60	4.4	**Cedar Lake** (town) Lake County
61	4.3	**Princeton** (city) Gibson County
62	4.2	**Kokomo** (city) Howard County
62	4.2	**Lebanon** (city) Boone County
64	4.1	**Brownsburg** (town) Hendricks County
64	4.1	**Crown Point** (city) Lake County
64	4.1	**Terre Haute** (city) Vigo County
64	4.1	**Whiteland** (town) Johnson County
68	4.0	**Hidden Valley** (CDP) Dearborn County
68	4.0	**New Albany** (city) Floyd County
68	4.0	**New Haven** (city) Allen County
68	4.0	**Rochester** (city) Fulton County
68	4.0	**Schererville** (town) Lake County
68	4.0	**Winamac** (town) Pulaski County
74	3.9	**Huntertown** (town) Allen County
74	3.9	**South Bend** (city) Saint Joseph County
76	3.8	**Danville** (town) Hendricks County
76	3.8	**Evansville** (city) Vanderburgh County
76	3.8	**Goshen** (city) Elkhart County
76	3.8	**Jeffersonville** (city) Clark County
80	3.7	**Chesterton** (town) Porter County
80	3.7	**Highland** (town) Lake County
82	3.6	**Dyer** (town) Lake County
82	3.6	**Hanover** (town) Jefferson County
82	3.6	**North Terre Haute** (CDP) Vigo County
82	3.6	**Sullivan** (city) Sullivan County
86	3.5	**Bedford** (city) Lawrence County
86	3.5	**Charlestown** (city) Clark County
86	3.5	**Hartford City** (city) Blackford County
86	3.5	**Portage** (city) Porter County
90	3.4	**Attica** (city) Fountain County
90	3.4	**Clarksville** (town) Clark County
90	3.4	**Madison** (city) Jefferson County
93	3.3	**Hobart** (city) Lake County
93	3.3	**Mishawaka** (city) Saint Joseph County
95	3.2	**Beech Grove** (city) Marion County
95	3.2	**Fortville** (town) Hancock County
95	3.2	**Greentown** (town) Howard County
95	3.2	**Linton** (city) Greene County
95	3.2	**Tell City** (city) Perry County
100	3.1	**Auburn** (city) DeKalb County
100	3.1	**Connersville** (city) Fayette County
100	3.1	**Dunlap** (CDP) Elkhart County
100	3.1	**Edinburgh** (town) Johnson County
100	3.1	**Garrett** (city) DeKalb County
100	3.1	**Griffith** (town) Lake County
100	3.1	**Osceola** (town) Saint Joseph County
107	3.0	**Clinton** (city) Vermillion County
107	3.0	**Middlebury** (town) Elkhart County
107	3.0	**Sheridan** (town) Hamilton County
110	2.9	**Aurora** (city) Dearborn County
110	2.9	**Franklin** (city) Johnson County
112	2.8	**Merrillville** (town) Lake County
112	2.8	**North Vernon** (city) Jennings County
112	2.8	**Scottsburg** (city) Scott County
112	2.8	**Syracuse** (town) Kosciusko County
116	2.7	**Chandler** (town) Warrick County
116	2.7	**La Porte** (city) LaPorte County
116	2.7	**Muncie** (city) Delaware County
116	2.7	**Nappanee** (city) Elkhart County
116	2.7	**South Haven** (CDP) Porter County
121	2.6	**Anderson** (city) Madison County
121	2.6	**Bluffton** (city) Wells County
121	2.6	**Butler** (city) DeKalb County
121	2.6	**Greencastle** (city) Putnam County
121	2.6	**Kendallville** (city) Noble County
121	2.6	**Westville** (town) LaPorte County
127	2.5	**Centerville** (town) Wayne County
127	2.5	**Elkhart** (city) Elkhart County
127	2.5	**New Whiteland** (town) Johnson County
127	2.5	**Peru** (city) Miami County
127	2.5	**Porter** (town) Porter County
127	2.5	**Richmond** (city) Wayne County
127	2.5	**Shelbyville** (city) Shelby County
127	2.5	**Shorewood Forest** (CDP) Porter County
135	2.4	**Country Squire Lakes** (CDP) Jennings County
136	2.3	**Austin** (city) Scott County
136	2.3	**De Motte** (town) Jasper County
136	2.3	**Hammond** (city) Lake County
136	2.3	**Loogootee** (city) Martin County
136	2.3	**New Castle** (city) Henry County
141	2.2	**Rockville** (town) Parke County
142	2.1	**Berne** (city) Adams County
142	2.1	**Decatur** (city) Adams County
142	2.1	**Monticello** (city) White County
142	2.1	**Simonton Lake** (CDP) Elkhart County
146	2.0	**Crawfordsville** (city) Montgomery County
146	2.0	**Lagrange** (town) LaGrange County
148	1.9	**Alexandria** (city) Madison County
148	1.9	**Brookville** (town) Franklin County
148	1.9	**Huntingburg** (city) Dubois County

Note: *This section ranks incorporated places and CDPs (Census Designated Places) with populations of 2,500 or more. Unincorporated postal areas were not considered. Please refer to the User Guide for additional information.*

Employment: Computer, Engineering, and Science Occupations

Top 150 Places Ranked in *Ascending* Order

State Rank	Percent	Place
1	0.0	**Gas City** (city) Grant County
1	0.0	**Hebron** (town) Porter County
3	0.5	**Mitchell** (city) Lawrence County
4	0.7	**Logansport** (city) Cass County
5	0.8	**Plymouth** (city) Marshall County
6	0.9	**Brazil** (city) Clay County
6	0.9	**East Chicago** (city) Lake County
6	0.9	**Wabash** (city) Wabash County
9	1.0	**Corydon** (town) Harrison County
10	1.1	**Paoli** (town) Orange County
10	1.1	**Portland** (city) Jay County
10	1.1	**Whiting** (city) Lake County
13	1.2	**Brownstown** (town) Jackson County
13	1.2	**Rushville** (city) Rush County
15	1.3	**Heritage Lake** (CDP) Putnam County
15	1.3	**Huntington** (city) Huntington County
15	1.3	**Knox** (city) Starke County
15	1.3	**Lake Station** (city) Lake County
15	1.3	**Marion** (city) Grant County
15	1.3	**Vincennes** (city) Knox County
21	1.4	**Gary** (city) Lake County
21	1.4	**Rensselaer** (city) Jasper County
21	1.4	**Washington** (city) Daviess County
24	1.5	**Bicknell** (city) Knox County
24	1.5	**Elwood** (city) Madison County
24	1.5	**Ligonier** (city) Noble County
24	1.5	**Roselawn** (CDP) Newton County
24	1.5	**Winchester** (city) Randolph County
29	1.6	**Fort Branch** (town) Gibson County
29	1.6	**Michigan City** (city) LaPorte County
29	1.6	**Mooresville** (town) Morgan County
29	1.6	**Salem** (city) Washington County
29	1.6	**Winfield** (town) Lake County
34	1.7	**Columbia City** (city) Whitley County
34	1.7	**Frankfort** (city) Clinton County
36	1.8	**Delphi** (city) Carroll County
36	1.8	**Fairmount** (town) Grant County
36	1.8	**Lowell** (town) Lake County
36	1.8	**Martinsville** (city) Morgan County
40	1.9	**Alexandria** (city) Madison County
40	1.9	**Brookville** (town) Franklin County
40	1.9	**Huntingburg** (city) Dubois County
43	2.0	**Crawfordsville** (city) Montgomery County
43	2.0	**Lagrange** (town) LaGrange County
45	2.1	**Berne** (city) Adams County
45	2.1	**Decatur** (city) Adams County
45	2.1	**Monticello** (city) White County
45	2.1	**Simonton Lake** (CDP) Elkhart County
49	2.2	**Rockville** (town) Parke County
50	2.3	**Austin** (city) Scott County
50	2.3	**De Motte** (town) Jasper County
50	2.3	**Hammond** (city) Lake County
50	2.3	**Loogootee** (city) Martin County
50	2.3	**New Castle** (city) Henry County
55	2.4	**Country Squire Lakes** (CDP) Jennings County
56	2.5	**Centerville** (town) Wayne County
56	2.5	**Elkhart** (city) Elkhart County
56	2.5	**New Whiteland** (town) Johnson County
56	2.5	**Peru** (city) Miami County
56	2.5	**Porter** (town) Porter County
56	2.5	**Richmond** (city) Wayne County
56	2.5	**Shelbyville** (city) Shelby County
56	2.5	**Shorewood Forest** (CDP) Porter County
64	2.6	**Anderson** (city) Madison County
64	2.6	**Bluffton** (city) Wells County
64	2.6	**Butler** (city) DeKalb County
64	2.6	**Greencastle** (city) Putnam County
64	2.6	**Kendallville** (city) Noble County
64	2.6	**Westville** (town) LaPorte County
70	2.7	**Chandler** (town) Warrick County
70	2.7	**La Porte** (city) LaPorte County
70	2.7	**Muncie** (city) Delaware County
70	2.7	**Nappanee** (city) Elkhart County
70	2.7	**South Haven** (CDP) Porter County
75	2.8	**Merrillville** (town) Lake County
75	2.8	**North Vernon** (city) Jennings County
75	2.8	**Scottsburg** (city) Scott County
75	2.8	**Syracuse** (town) Kosciusko County
79	2.9	**Aurora** (city) Dearborn County
79	2.9	**Franklin** (city) Johnson County
81	3.0	**Clinton** (city) Vermillion County
81	3.0	**Middlebury** (town) Elkhart County
81	3.0	**Sheridan** (town) Hamilton County
84	3.1	**Auburn** (city) DeKalb County
84	3.1	**Connersville** (city) Fayette County
84	3.1	**Dunlap** (CDP) Elkhart County
84	3.1	**Edinburgh** (town) Johnson County
84	3.1	**Garrett** (city) DeKalb County
84	3.1	**Griffith** (town) Lake County
84	3.1	**Osceola** (town) Saint Joseph County
91	3.2	**Beech Grove** (city) Marion County
91	3.2	**Fortville** (town) Hancock County
91	3.2	**Greentown** (town) Howard County
91	3.2	**Linton** (city) Greene County
91	3.2	**Tell City** (city) Perry County
96	3.3	**Hobart** (city) Lake County
96	3.3	**Mishawaka** (city) Saint Joseph County
98	3.4	**Attica** (city) Fountain County
98	3.4	**Clarksville** (town) Clark County
98	3.4	**Madison** (city) Jefferson County
101	3.5	**Bedford** (city) Lawrence County
101	3.5	**Charlestown** (city) Clark County
101	3.5	**Hartford City** (city) Blackford County
101	3.5	**Portage** (city) Porter County
105	3.6	**Dyer** (town) Lake County
105	3.6	**Hanover** (town) Jefferson County
105	3.6	**North Terre Haute** (CDP) Vigo County
105	3.6	**Sullivan** (city) Sullivan County
109	3.7	**Chesterton** (town) Porter County
109	3.7	**Highland** (town) Lake County
111	3.8	**Danville** (town) Hendricks County
111	3.8	**Evansville** (city) Vanderburgh County
111	3.8	**Goshen** (city) Elkhart County
111	3.8	**Jeffersonville** (city) Clark County
115	3.9	**Huntertown** (town) Allen County
115	3.9	**South Bend** (city) Saint Joseph County
117	4.0	**Hidden Valley** (CDP) Dearborn County
117	4.0	**New Albany** (city) Floyd County
117	4.0	**New Haven** (city) Allen County
117	4.0	**Rochester** (city) Fulton County
117	4.0	**Schererville** (town) Lake County
117	4.0	**Winamac** (town) Pulaski County
123	4.1	**Brownsburg** (town) Hendricks County
123	4.1	**Crown Point** (city) Lake County
123	4.1	**Terre Haute** (city) Vigo County
123	4.1	**Whiteland** (town) Johnson County
127	4.2	**Kokomo** (city) Howard County
127	4.2	**Lebanon** (city) Boone County
129	4.3	**Princeton** (city) Gibson County
130	4.4	**Cedar Lake** (town) Lake County
131	4.5	**Salt Creek Commons** (CDP) Porter County
132	4.6	**Fort Wayne** (city) Allen County
132	4.6	**Greenfield** (city) Hancock County
134	4.7	**Boonville** (city) Warrick County
134	4.7	**Indianapolis** (city) Marion County
136	4.8	**Lawrenceburg** (city) Dearborn County
136	4.8	**Ossian** (town) Wells County
138	4.9	**Lakes of the Four Seasons** (CDP) Lake County
139	5.0	**Munster** (town) Lake County
139	5.0	**Pendleton** (town) Madison County
141	5.1	**Cumberland** (town) Marion County
141	5.1	**Leo-Cedarville** (town) Allen County
141	5.1	**Sellersburg** (town) Clark County
141	5.1	**Tipton** (city) Tipton County
141	5.1	**Union City** (city) Randolph County
146	5.2	**Bremen** (town) Marshall County
146	5.2	**Ellettsville** (town) Monroe County
148	5.3	**Seymour** (city) Jackson County
148	5.3	**Valparaiso** (city) Porter County
150	5.5	**Melody Hill** (CDP) Vanderburgh County

Note: *This section ranks incorporated places and CDPs (Census Designated Places) with populations of 2,500 or more. Unincorporated postal areas were not considered. Please refer to the User Guide for additional information.*

Employment: Education, Legal, Community Service, Arts, and Media Occupations

Top 150 Places Ranked in *Descending* Order

State Rank	Percent	Place
1	32.4	**Notre Dame** (CDP) Saint Joseph County
2	29.4	**West Lafayette** (city) Tippecanoe County
3	25.1	**Upland** (town) Grant County
4	22.4	**Bloomington** (city) Monroe County
5	16.6	**Corydon** (town) Harrison County
6	16.0	**Valparaiso** (city) Porter County
6	16.0	**Winona Lake** (town) Kosciusko County
8	15.6	**Carmel** (city) Hamilton County
9	15.4	**Greencastle** (city) Putnam County
10	14.9	**Granger** (CDP) Saint Joseph County
11	14.4	**Zionsville** (town) Boone County
12	14.3	**Lowell** (town) Lake County
13	13.8	**Whitestown** (town) Boone County
14	13.6	**Fishers** (city) Hamilton County
15	13.5	**Berne** (city) Adams County
16	13.0	**Terre Haute** (city) Vigo County
17	12.9	**Angola** (city) Steuben County
17	12.9	**Hanover** (town) Jefferson County
17	12.9	**Heritage Lake** (CDP) Putnam County
20	12.7	**Chesterton** (town) Porter County
20	12.7	**Fortville** (town) Hancock County
20	12.7	**Hidden Valley** (CDP) Dearborn County
23	12.6	**Muncie** (city) Delaware County
24	12.5	**Batesville** (city) Ripley County
25	12.2	**McCordsville** (town) Hancock County
25	12.2	**Westfield** (city) Hamilton County
27	12.1	**Shorewood Forest** (CDP) Porter County
28	12.0	**Santa Claus** (town) Spencer County
29	11.9	**Crawfordsville** (city) Montgomery County
29	11.9	**Pendleton** (town) Madison County
29	11.9	**South Bend** (city) Saint Joseph County
32	11.6	**New Whiteland** (town) Johnson County
32	11.6	**Plainfield** (town) Hendricks County
34	11.5	**Rockville** (town) Parke County
35	11.4	**Porter** (town) Porter County
36	11.3	**Brazil** (city) Clay County
37	11.0	**Bright** (CDP) Dearborn County
37	11.0	**Dyer** (town) Lake County
39	10.8	**Gas City** (city) Grant County
40	10.7	**Munster** (town) Lake County
41	10.6	**Boonville** (city) Warrick County
41	10.6	**Crown Point** (city) Lake County
41	10.6	**Franklin** (city) Johnson County
41	10.6	**Huntertown** (town) Allen County
45	10.5	**Schererville** (town) Lake County
46	10.4	**Fort Wayne** (city) Allen County
46	10.4	**New Castle** (city) Henry County
48	10.3	**Madison** (city) Jefferson County
48	10.3	**Noblesville** (city) Hamilton County
50	10.2	**Danville** (town) Hendricks County
50	10.2	**Hobart** (city) Lake County
52	10.1	**Lawrence** (city) Marion County
52	10.1	**Marion** (city) Grant County
54	10.0	**Georgetown** (town) Floyd County
55	9.9	**Goshen** (city) Elkhart County
55	9.9	**Osceola** (town) Saint Joseph County
55	9.9	**Scottsburg** (city) Scott County
55	9.9	**Smithville-Sanders** (CDP) Monroe County
59	9.8	**Indianapolis** (city) Marion County
59	9.8	**Mishawaka** (city) Saint Joseph County
61	9.7	**Greendale** (city) Dearborn County
61	9.7	**Highland** (CDP) Vanderburgh County
61	9.7	**Nappanee** (city) Elkhart County
61	9.7	**Richmond** (city) Wayne County
61	9.7	**Saint John** (town) Lake County
66	9.6	**Auburn** (city) DeKalb County
67	9.5	**Greentown** (town) Howard County
67	9.5	**Yorktown** (town) Delaware County
69	9.4	**Plymouth** (city) Marshall County
70	9.3	**Huntington** (city) Huntington County
71	9.2	**Brownsburg** (town) Hendricks County
71	9.2	**North Manchester** (town) Wabash County
71	9.2	**Sellersburg** (town) Clark County
71	9.2	**Warsaw** (city) Kosciusko County
75	9.1	**Brownstown** (town) Jackson County
75	9.1	**Evansville** (city) Vanderburgh County
75	9.1	**Merrillville** (town) Lake County
78	9.0	**Gary** (city) Lake County
78	9.0	**Winamac** (town) Pulaski County
80	8.9	**Avon** (town) Hendricks County
80	8.9	**Delphi** (city) Carroll County
80	8.9	**Jasper** (city) Dubois County
80	8.9	**Speedway** (town) Marion County
80	8.9	**Winchester** (city) Randolph County
85	8.8	**Lafayette** (city) Tippecanoe County
85	8.8	**Lakes of the Four Seasons** (CDP) Lake County
85	8.8	**New Albany** (city) Floyd County
88	8.7	**Anderson** (city) Madison County
88	8.7	**Centerville** (town) Wayne County
88	8.7	**Ellettsville** (town) Monroe County
88	8.7	**Wabash** (city) Wabash County
92	8.5	**Cicero** (town) Hamilton County
93	8.4	**Middlebury** (town) Elkhart County
94	8.3	**Highland** (town) Lake County
94	8.3	**Mooresville** (town) Morgan County
94	8.3	**North Terre Haute** (CDP) Vigo County
94	8.3	**Pittsboro** (town) Hendricks County
98	8.2	**Mitchell** (city) Lawrence County
99	8.1	**Columbus** (city) Bartholomew County
99	8.1	**Cumberland** (town) Marion County
99	8.1	**Dunlap** (CDP) Elkhart County
99	8.1	**Rensselaer** (city) Jasper County
99	8.1	**Salem** (city) Washington County
104	8.0	**Greenfield** (city) Hancock County
104	8.0	**Jeffersonville** (city) Clark County
104	8.0	**Michigan City** (city) LaPorte County
104	8.0	**Seymour** (city) Jackson County
104	8.0	**Washington** (city) Daviess County
109	7.8	**Cedar Lake** (town) Lake County
109	7.8	**Garrett** (city) DeKalb County
109	7.8	**Hammond** (city) Lake County
109	7.8	**Rushville** (city) Rush County
113	7.7	**Kokomo** (city) Howard County
113	7.7	**Melody Hill** (CDP) Vanderburgh County
113	7.7	**Tipton** (city) Tipton County
116	7.6	**Bicknell** (city) Knox County
116	7.6	**Greenwood** (city) Johnson County
118	7.5	**Clinton** (city) Vermillion County
118	7.5	**Lebanon** (city) Boone County
118	7.5	**Linton** (city) Greene County
121	7.3	**Hartford City** (city) Blackford County
122	7.2	**Beech Grove** (city) Marion County
122	7.2	**Columbia City** (city) Whitley County
122	7.2	**Fort Branch** (town) Gibson County
122	7.2	**Peru** (city) Miami County
126	7.1	**Decatur** (city) Adams County
126	7.1	**Huntingburg** (city) Dubois County
126	7.1	**Newburgh** (town) Warrick County
126	7.1	**Vincennes** (city) Knox County
130	7.0	**East Chicago** (city) Lake County
131	6.9	**Greensburg** (city) Decatur County
131	6.9	**Portage** (city) Porter County
131	6.9	**Sheridan** (town) Hamilton County
134	6.8	**Bedford** (city) Lawrence County
134	6.8	**Lawrenceburg** (city) Dearborn County
136	6.7	**Frankfort** (city) Clinton County
137	6.6	**Attica** (city) Fountain County
137	6.6	**Simonton Lake** (CDP) Elkhart County
139	6.5	**Knox** (city) Starke County
139	6.5	**New Haven** (city) Allen County
141	6.4	**Austin** (city) Scott County
141	6.4	**Bremen** (town) Marshall County
141	6.4	**Elkhart** (city) Elkhart County
141	6.4	**Fairmount** (town) Grant County
141	6.4	**La Porte** (city) LaPorte County
146	6.3	**Rochester** (city) Fulton County
147	6.0	**Hebron** (town) Porter County
147	6.0	**Winfield** (town) Lake County
149	5.9	**Connersville** (city) Fayette County
149	5.9	**Kendallville** (city) Noble County

Note: *This section ranks incorporated places and CDPs (Census Designated Places) with populations of 2,500 or more. Unincorporated postal areas were not considered. Please refer to the User Guide for additional information.*

Employment: Education, Legal, Community Service, Arts, and Media Occupations

Top 150 Places Ranked in *Ascending* Order

State Rank	Percent	Place
1	1.2	**Ligonier** (city) Noble County
2	2.6	**Roselawn** (CDP) Newton County
3	2.9	**Edinburgh** (town) Johnson County
4	3.0	**Chandler** (town) Warrick County
4	3.0	**Country Squire Lakes** (CDP) Jennings County
4	3.0	**Salt Creek Commons** (CDP) Porter County
7	3.1	**De Motte** (town) Jasper County
8	3.3	**Elwood** (city) Madison County
9	3.5	**Lake Station** (city) Lake County
10	3.7	**Union City** (city) Randolph County
11	3.9	**Princeton** (city) Gibson County
12	4.0	**Brookville** (town) Franklin County
12	4.0	**Loogootee** (city) Martin County
14	4.1	**Westville** (town) LaPorte County
15	4.2	**Syracuse** (town) Kosciusko County
16	4.4	**Lagrange** (town) LaGrange County
16	4.4	**Mount Vernon** (city) Posey County
18	4.7	**South Haven** (CDP) Porter County
19	4.8	**Portland** (city) Jay County
20	4.9	**Clarksville** (town) Clark County
20	4.9	**Whiting** (city) Lake County
22	5.0	**Leo-Cedarville** (town) Allen County
22	5.0	**Paoli** (town) Orange County
24	5.1	**Aurora** (city) Dearborn County
24	5.1	**Bluffton** (city) Wells County
24	5.1	**Monticello** (city) White County
24	5.1	**Sullivan** (city) Sullivan County
28	5.2	**Butler** (city) DeKalb County
28	5.2	**Shelbyville** (city) Shelby County
30	5.3	**Charlestown** (city) Clark County
31	5.4	**Logansport** (city) Cass County
31	5.4	**Whiteland** (town) Johnson County
33	5.5	**Alexandria** (city) Madison County
33	5.5	**Griffith** (town) Lake County
35	5.6	**Martinsville** (city) Morgan County
35	5.6	**Tell City** (city) Perry County
37	5.7	**North Vernon** (city) Jennings County
37	5.7	**Ossian** (town) Wells County
39	5.8	**Bargersville** (town) Johnson County
40	5.9	**Connersville** (city) Fayette County
40	5.9	**Kendallville** (city) Noble County
42	6.0	**Hebron** (town) Porter County
42	6.0	**Winfield** (town) Lake County
44	6.3	**Rochester** (city) Fulton County
45	6.4	**Austin** (city) Scott County
45	6.4	**Bremen** (town) Marshall County
45	6.4	**Elkhart** (city) Elkhart County
45	6.4	**Fairmount** (town) Grant County
45	6.4	**La Porte** (city) LaPorte County
50	6.5	**Knox** (city) Starke County
50	6.5	**New Haven** (city) Allen County
52	6.6	**Attica** (city) Fountain County
52	6.6	**Simonton Lake** (CDP) Elkhart County
54	6.7	**Frankfort** (city) Clinton County
55	6.8	**Bedford** (city) Lawrence County
55	6.8	**Lawrenceburg** (city) Dearborn County
57	6.9	**Greensburg** (city) Decatur County
57	6.9	**Portage** (city) Porter County
57	6.9	**Sheridan** (town) Hamilton County
60	7.0	**East Chicago** (city) Lake County
61	7.1	**Decatur** (city) Adams County
61	7.1	**Huntingburg** (city) Dubois County
61	7.1	**Newburgh** (town) Warrick County
61	7.1	**Vincennes** (city) Knox County
65	7.2	**Beech Grove** (city) Marion County
65	7.2	**Columbia City** (city) Whitley County
65	7.2	**Fort Branch** (town) Gibson County
65	7.2	**Peru** (city) Miami County
69	7.3	**Hartford City** (city) Blackford County
70	7.5	**Clinton** (city) Vermillion County
70	7.5	**Lebanon** (city) Boone County
70	7.5	**Linton** (city) Greene County
73	7.6	**Bicknell** (city) Knox County
73	7.6	**Greenwood** (city) Johnson County
75	7.7	**Kokomo** (city) Howard County
75	7.7	**Melody Hill** (CDP) Vanderburgh County
75	7.7	**Tipton** (city) Tipton County
78	7.8	**Cedar Lake** (town) Lake County
78	7.8	**Garrett** (city) DeKalb County
78	7.8	**Hammond** (city) Lake County
78	7.8	**Rushville** (city) Rush County
82	8.0	**Greenfield** (city) Hancock County
82	8.0	**Jeffersonville** (city) Clark County
82	8.0	**Michigan City** (city) LaPorte County
82	8.0	**Seymour** (city) Jackson County
82	8.0	**Washington** (city) Daviess County
87	8.1	**Columbus** (city) Bartholomew County
87	8.1	**Cumberland** (town) Marion County
87	8.1	**Dunlap** (CDP) Elkhart County
87	8.1	**Rensselaer** (city) Jasper County
87	8.1	**Salem** (city) Washington County
92	8.2	**Mitchell** (city) Lawrence County
93	8.3	**Highland** (town) Lake County
93	8.3	**Mooresville** (town) Morgan County
93	8.3	**North Terre Haute** (CDP) Vigo County
93	8.3	**Pittsboro** (town) Hendricks County
97	8.4	**Middlebury** (town) Elkhart County
98	8.5	**Cicero** (town) Hamilton County
99	8.7	**Anderson** (city) Madison County
99	8.7	**Centerville** (town) Wayne County
99	8.7	**Ellettsville** (town) Monroe County
99	8.7	**Wabash** (city) Wabash County
103	8.8	**Lafayette** (city) Tippecanoe County
103	8.8	**Lakes of the Four Seasons** (CDP) Lake County
103	8.8	**New Albany** (city) Floyd County
106	8.9	**Avon** (town) Hendricks County
106	8.9	**Delphi** (city) Carroll County
106	8.9	**Jasper** (city) Dubois County
106	8.9	**Speedway** (town) Marion County
106	8.9	**Winchester** (city) Randolph County
111	9.0	**Gary** (city) Lake County
111	9.0	**Winamac** (town) Pulaski County
113	9.1	**Brownstown** (town) Jackson County
113	9.1	**Evansville** (city) Vanderburgh County
113	9.1	**Merrillville** (town) Lake County
116	9.2	**Brownsburg** (town) Hendricks County
116	9.2	**North Manchester** (town) Wabash County
116	9.2	**Sellersburg** (town) Clark County
116	9.2	**Warsaw** (city) Kosciusko County
120	9.3	**Huntington** (city) Huntington County
121	9.4	**Plymouth** (city) Marshall County
122	9.5	**Greentown** (town) Howard County
122	9.5	**Yorktown** (town) Delaware County
124	9.6	**Auburn** (city) DeKalb County
125	9.7	**Greendale** (city) Dearborn County
125	9.7	**Highland** (CDP) Vanderburgh County
125	9.7	**Nappanee** (city) Elkhart County
125	9.7	**Richmond** (city) Wayne County
125	9.7	**Saint John** (town) Lake County
130	9.8	**Indianapolis** (city) Marion County
130	9.8	**Mishawaka** (city) Saint Joseph County
132	9.9	**Goshen** (city) Elkhart County
132	9.9	**Osceola** (town) Saint Joseph County
132	9.9	**Scottsburg** (city) Scott County
132	9.9	**Smithville-Sanders** (CDP) Monroe County
136	10.0	**Georgetown** (town) Floyd County
137	10.1	**Lawrence** (city) Marion County
137	10.1	**Marion** (city) Grant County
139	10.2	**Danville** (town) Hendricks County
139	10.2	**Hobart** (city) Lake County
141	10.3	**Madison** (city) Jefferson County
141	10.3	**Noblesville** (city) Hamilton County
143	10.4	**Fort Wayne** (city) Allen County
143	10.4	**New Castle** (city) Henry County
145	10.5	**Schererville** (town) Lake County
146	10.6	**Boonville** (city) Warrick County
146	10.6	**Crown Point** (city) Lake County
146	10.6	**Franklin** (city) Johnson County
146	10.6	**Huntertown** (town) Allen County
150	10.7	**Munster** (town) Lake County

Note: *This section ranks incorporated places and CDPs (Census Designated Places) with populations of 2,500 or more. Unincorporated postal areas were not considered. Please refer to the User Guide for additional information.*

Employment: Healthcare Practitioners

Top 150 Places Ranked in *Descending* Order

State Rank	Percent	Place
1	15.3	**Smithville-Sanders** (CDP) Monroe County
2	13.8	**Whitestown** (town) Boone County
3	12.7	**Yorktown** (town) Delaware County
4	12.1	**Shorewood Forest** (CDP) Porter County
5	11.6	**McCordsville** (town) Hancock County
6	11.2	**Melody Hill** (CDP) Vanderburgh County
7	11.1	**Georgetown** (town) Floyd County
8	10.6	**Granger** (CDP) Saint Joseph County
8	10.6	**Saint John** (town) Lake County
10	10.4	**Munster** (town) Lake County
11	10.3	**Winfield** (town) Lake County
12	10.1	**Bremen** (town) Marshall County
13	10.0	**Highland** (CDP) Vanderburgh County
14	9.9	**Charlestown** (city) Clark County
15	9.5	**Carmel** (city) Hamilton County
15	9.5	**Huntertown** (town) Allen County
17	9.4	**Brookville** (town) Franklin County
17	9.4	**Zionsville** (town) Boone County
19	9.3	**Crown Point** (city) Lake County
20	9.2	**Avon** (town) Hendricks County
20	9.2	**Whiteland** (town) Johnson County
22	9.0	**Aurora** (city) Dearborn County
22	9.0	**Clinton** (city) Vermillion County
22	9.0	**Pittsboro** (town) Hendricks County
25	8.9	**Hebron** (town) Porter County
26	8.8	**Brownsburg** (town) Hendricks County
26	8.8	**Newburgh** (town) Warrick County
28	8.7	**Bargersville** (town) Johnson County
28	8.7	**Danville** (town) Hendricks County
28	8.7	**Fishers** (city) Hamilton County
31	8.6	**Cicero** (town) Hamilton County
32	8.5	**Alexandria** (city) Madison County
33	8.4	**Middlebury** (town) Elkhart County
34	8.3	**Corydon** (town) Harrison County
34	8.3	**Cumberland** (town) Marion County
34	8.3	**Dyer** (town) Lake County
37	8.2	**Loogootee** (city) Martin County
38	8.1	**Bedford** (city) Lawrence County
38	8.1	**Fortville** (town) Hancock County
40	8.0	**Chandler** (town) Warrick County
40	8.0	**Elwood** (city) Madison County
40	8.0	**Greenfield** (city) Hancock County
40	8.0	**Lakes of the Four Seasons** (CDP) Lake County
40	8.0	**Osceola** (town) Saint Joseph County
45	7.9	**Pendleton** (town) Madison County
45	7.9	**Santa Claus** (town) Spencer County
47	7.8	**Leo-Cedarville** (town) Allen County
47	7.8	**Westfield** (city) Hamilton County
49	7.7	**Connersville** (city) Fayette County
50	7.6	**Dunlap** (CDP) Elkhart County
50	7.6	**Schererville** (town) Lake County
52	7.5	**Centerville** (town) Wayne County
53	7.4	**Batesville** (city) Ripley County
53	7.4	**Bright** (CDP) Dearborn County
53	7.4	**Columbia City** (city) Whitley County
53	7.4	**Greendale** (city) Dearborn County
57	7.1	**Bluffton** (city) Wells County
57	7.1	**Huntingburg** (city) Dubois County
57	7.1	**Winamac** (town) Pulaski County
60	7.0	**North Manchester** (town) Wabash County
61	6.9	**New Albany** (city) Floyd County
62	6.8	**Greenwood** (city) Johnson County
62	6.8	**Heritage Lake** (CDP) Putnam County
62	6.8	**Merrillville** (town) Lake County
62	6.8	**Richmond** (city) Wayne County
66	6.7	**Noblesville** (city) Hamilton County
67	6.6	**De Motte** (town) Jasper County
67	6.6	**New Haven** (city) Allen County
69	6.5	**Plainfield** (town) Hendricks County
69	6.5	**Valparaiso** (city) Porter County
71	6.4	**Chesterton** (town) Porter County
71	6.4	**Fort Branch** (town) Gibson County
73	6.3	**Franklin** (city) Johnson County
73	6.3	**Indianapolis** (city) Marion County
73	6.3	**Westville** (town) LaPorte County
76	6.2	**Hidden Valley** (CDP) Dearborn County
76	6.2	**Hobart** (city) Lake County
76	6.2	**Porter** (town) Porter County
79	6.1	**Linton** (city) Greene County
80	6.0	**Bicknell** (city) Knox County
80	6.0	**Clarksville** (town) Clark County
80	6.0	**Kokomo** (city) Howard County
80	6.0	**Lake Station** (city) Lake County
80	6.0	**Speedway** (town) Marion County
85	5.9	**Ellettsville** (town) Monroe County
85	5.9	**Lafayette** (city) Tippecanoe County
85	5.9	**Sullivan** (city) Sullivan County
88	5.8	**Madison** (city) Jefferson County
88	5.8	**Mishawaka** (city) Saint Joseph County
90	5.7	**Lawrence** (city) Marion County
90	5.7	**Logansport** (city) Cass County
90	5.7	**Sheridan** (town) Hamilton County
90	5.7	**Vincennes** (city) Knox County
90	5.7	**Wabash** (city) Wabash County
95	5.6	**Anderson** (city) Madison County
95	5.6	**Fort Wayne** (city) Allen County
95	5.6	**Kendallville** (city) Noble County
95	5.6	**Princeton** (city) Gibson County
99	5.5	**Lebanon** (city) Boone County
100	5.4	**Highland** (town) Lake County
100	5.4	**Jeffersonville** (city) Clark County
100	5.4	**Lawrenceburg** (city) Dearborn County
100	5.4	**Marion** (city) Grant County
100	5.4	**Rensselaer** (city) Jasper County
100	5.4	**Shelbyville** (city) Shelby County
100	5.4	**Warsaw** (city) Kosciusko County
107	5.3	**Beech Grove** (city) Marion County
107	5.3	**Butler** (city) DeKalb County
107	5.3	**Columbus** (city) Bartholomew County
107	5.3	**New Castle** (city) Henry County
107	5.3	**Sellersburg** (town) Clark County
107	5.3	**South Haven** (CDP) Porter County
107	5.3	**Terre Haute** (city) Vigo County
114	5.2	**Paoli** (town) Orange County
115	5.1	**Decatur** (city) Adams County
115	5.1	**Monticello** (city) White County
115	5.1	**Mount Vernon** (city) Posey County
115	5.1	**South Bend** (city) Saint Joseph County
115	5.1	**Washington** (city) Daviess County
120	5.0	**Auburn** (city) DeKalb County
120	5.0	**Greentown** (town) Howard County
120	5.0	**Griffith** (town) Lake County
120	5.0	**Portage** (city) Porter County
124	4.9	**Evansville** (city) Vanderburgh County
124	4.9	**Hanover** (town) Jefferson County
126	4.8	**La Porte** (city) LaPorte County
126	4.8	**Muncie** (city) Delaware County
128	4.7	**Attica** (city) Fountain County
128	4.7	**Mitchell** (city) Lawrence County
130	4.6	**Gary** (city) Lake County
130	4.6	**Lowell** (town) Lake County
130	4.6	**Winchester** (city) Randolph County
133	4.5	**Salem** (city) Washington County
133	4.5	**Seymour** (city) Jackson County
133	4.5	**Union City** (city) Randolph County
136	4.4	**Berne** (city) Adams County
136	4.4	**Bloomington** (city) Monroe County
136	4.4	**Jasper** (city) Dubois County
139	4.2	**Fairmount** (town) Grant County
139	4.2	**Scottsburg** (city) Scott County
141	4.1	**Huntington** (city) Huntington County
142	4.0	**Goshen** (city) Elkhart County
142	4.0	**Portland** (city) Jay County
144	3.9	**Michigan City** (city) LaPorte County
144	3.9	**Peru** (city) Miami County
146	3.8	**Cedar Lake** (town) Lake County
147	3.7	**Austin** (city) Scott County
147	3.7	**Brownstown** (town) Jackson County
147	3.7	**Knox** (city) Starke County
150	3.6	**Brazil** (city) Clay County

Note: *This section ranks incorporated places and CDPs (Census Designated Places) with populations of 2,500 or more. Unincorporated postal areas were not considered. Please refer to the User Guide for additional information.*

Employment: Healthcare Practitioners

Top 150 Places Ranked in *Ascending* Order

State Rank	Percent	Place
1	0.4	**Notre Dame** (CDP) Saint Joseph County
2	0.6	**Ligonier** (city) Noble County
3	0.9	**Country Squire Lakes** (CDP) Jennings County
4	1.2	**Lagrange** (town) LaGrange County
5	1.3	**New Whiteland** (town) Johnson County
6	1.5	**Whiting** (city) Lake County
7	1.8	**Garrett** (city) DeKalb County
8	1.9	**Edinburgh** (town) Johnson County
9	2.2	**Nappanee** (city) Elkhart County
9	2.2	**Tell City** (city) Perry County
9	2.2	**Tipton** (city) Tipton County
12	2.3	**Ossian** (town) Wells County
12	2.3	**Upland** (town) Grant County
14	2.4	**Rochester** (city) Fulton County
15	2.5	**Mooresville** (town) Morgan County
16	2.6	**Delphi** (city) Carroll County
16	2.6	**Roselawn** (CDP) Newton County
18	2.7	**North Terre Haute** (CDP) Vigo County
18	2.7	**Rushville** (city) Rush County
20	2.8	**Boonville** (city) Warrick County
20	2.8	**Winona Lake** (town) Kosciusko County
22	2.9	**Elkhart** (city) Elkhart County
22	2.9	**Martinsville** (city) Morgan County
22	2.9	**North Vernon** (city) Jennings County
25	3.0	**Syracuse** (town) Kosciusko County
26	3.2	**Crawfordsville** (city) Montgomery County
26	3.2	**West Lafayette** (city) Tippecanoe County
28	3.3	**Greensburg** (city) Decatur County
29	3.4	**Angola** (city) Steuben County
29	3.4	**Gas City** (city) Grant County
29	3.4	**Greencastle** (city) Putnam County
29	3.4	**Hartford City** (city) Blackford County
29	3.4	**Rockville** (town) Parke County
29	3.4	**Simonton Lake** (CDP) Elkhart County
35	3.5	**East Chicago** (city) Lake County
35	3.5	**Salt Creek Commons** (CDP) Porter County
37	3.6	**Brazil** (city) Clay County
37	3.6	**Frankfort** (city) Clinton County
37	3.6	**Hammond** (city) Lake County
37	3.6	**Plymouth** (city) Marshall County
41	3.7	**Austin** (city) Scott County
41	3.7	**Brownstown** (town) Jackson County
41	3.7	**Knox** (city) Starke County
44	3.8	**Cedar Lake** (town) Lake County
45	3.9	**Michigan City** (city) LaPorte County
45	3.9	**Peru** (city) Miami County
47	4.0	**Goshen** (city) Elkhart County
47	4.0	**Portland** (city) Jay County
49	4.1	**Huntington** (city) Huntington County
50	4.2	**Fairmount** (town) Grant County
50	4.2	**Scottsburg** (city) Scott County
52	4.4	**Berne** (city) Adams County
52	4.4	**Bloomington** (city) Monroe County
52	4.4	**Jasper** (city) Dubois County
55	4.5	**Salem** (city) Washington County
55	4.5	**Seymour** (city) Jackson County
55	4.5	**Union City** (city) Randolph County
58	4.6	**Gary** (city) Lake County
58	4.6	**Lowell** (town) Lake County
58	4.6	**Winchester** (city) Randolph County
61	4.7	**Attica** (city) Fountain County
61	4.7	**Mitchell** (city) Lawrence County
63	4.8	**La Porte** (city) LaPorte County
63	4.8	**Muncie** (city) Delaware County
65	4.9	**Evansville** (city) Vanderburgh County
65	4.9	**Hanover** (town) Jefferson County
67	5.0	**Auburn** (city) DeKalb County
67	5.0	**Greentown** (town) Howard County
67	5.0	**Griffith** (town) Lake County
67	5.0	**Portage** (city) Porter County
71	5.1	**Decatur** (city) Adams County
71	5.1	**Monticello** (city) White County
71	5.1	**Mount Vernon** (city) Posey County
71	5.1	**South Bend** (city) Saint Joseph County
71	5.1	**Washington** (city) Daviess County
76	5.2	**Paoli** (town) Orange County
77	5.3	**Beech Grove** (city) Marion County
77	5.3	**Butler** (city) DeKalb County
77	5.3	**Columbus** (city) Bartholomew County
77	5.3	**New Castle** (city) Henry County
77	5.3	**Sellersburg** (town) Clark County
77	5.3	**South Haven** (CDP) Porter County
77	5.3	**Terre Haute** (city) Vigo County
84	5.4	**Highland** (town) Lake County
84	5.4	**Jeffersonville** (city) Clark County
84	5.4	**Lawrenceburg** (city) Dearborn County
84	5.4	**Marion** (city) Grant County
84	5.4	**Rensselaer** (city) Jasper County
84	5.4	**Shelbyville** (city) Shelby County
84	5.4	**Warsaw** (city) Kosciusko County
91	5.5	**Lebanon** (city) Boone County
92	5.6	**Anderson** (city) Madison County
92	5.6	**Fort Wayne** (city) Allen County
92	5.6	**Kendallville** (city) Noble County
92	5.6	**Princeton** (city) Gibson County
96	5.7	**Lawrence** (city) Marion County
96	5.7	**Logansport** (city) Cass County
96	5.7	**Sheridan** (town) Hamilton County
96	5.7	**Vincennes** (city) Knox County
96	5.7	**Wabash** (city) Wabash County
101	5.8	**Madison** (city) Jefferson County
101	5.8	**Mishawaka** (city) Saint Joseph County
103	5.9	**Ellettsville** (town) Monroe County
103	5.9	**Lafayette** (city) Tippecanoe County
103	5.9	**Sullivan** (city) Sullivan County
106	6.0	**Bicknell** (city) Knox County
106	6.0	**Clarksville** (town) Clark County
106	6.0	**Kokomo** (city) Howard County
106	6.0	**Lake Station** (city) Lake County
106	6.0	**Speedway** (town) Marion County
111	6.1	**Linton** (city) Greene County
112	6.2	**Hidden Valley** (CDP) Dearborn County
112	6.2	**Hobart** (city) Lake County
112	6.2	**Porter** (town) Porter County
115	6.3	**Franklin** (city) Johnson County
115	6.3	**Indianapolis** (city) Marion County
115	6.3	**Westville** (town) LaPorte County
118	6.4	**Chesterton** (town) Porter County
118	6.4	**Fort Branch** (town) Gibson County
120	6.5	**Plainfield** (town) Hendricks County
120	6.5	**Valparaiso** (city) Porter County
122	6.6	**De Motte** (town) Jasper County
122	6.6	**New Haven** (city) Allen County
124	6.7	**Noblesville** (city) Hamilton County
125	6.8	**Greenwood** (city) Johnson County
125	6.8	**Heritage Lake** (CDP) Putnam County
125	6.8	**Merrillville** (town) Lake County
125	6.8	**Richmond** (city) Wayne County
129	6.9	**New Albany** (city) Floyd County
130	7.0	**North Manchester** (town) Wabash County
131	7.1	**Bluffton** (city) Wells County
131	7.1	**Huntingburg** (city) Dubois County
131	7.1	**Winamac** (town) Pulaski County
134	7.4	**Batesville** (city) Ripley County
134	7.4	**Bright** (CDP) Dearborn County
134	7.4	**Columbia City** (city) Whitley County
134	7.4	**Greendale** (city) Dearborn County
138	7.5	**Centerville** (town) Wayne County
139	7.6	**Dunlap** (CDP) Elkhart County
139	7.6	**Schererville** (town) Lake County
141	7.7	**Connersville** (city) Fayette County
142	7.8	**Leo-Cedarville** (town) Allen County
142	7.8	**Westfield** (city) Hamilton County
144	7.9	**Pendleton** (town) Madison County
144	7.9	**Santa Claus** (town) Spencer County
146	8.0	**Chandler** (town) Warrick County
146	8.0	**Elwood** (city) Madison County
146	8.0	**Greenfield** (city) Hancock County
146	8.0	**Lakes of the Four Seasons** (CDP) Lake County
146	8.0	**Osceola** (town) Saint Joseph County

Note: *This section ranks incorporated places and CDPs (Census Designated Places) with populations of 2,500 or more. Unincorporated postal areas were not considered. Please refer to the User Guide for additional information.*

Employment: Service Occupations

Top 150 Places Ranked in *Descending* Order

State Rank	Percent	Place
1	29.9	**Gary** (city) Lake County
2	28.6	**Marion** (city) Grant County
3	27.9	**East Chicago** (city) Lake County
3	27.9	**Knox** (city) Starke County
5	26.8	**North Terre Haute** (CDP) Vigo County
6	26.0	**Muncie** (city) Delaware County
7	25.8	**Elwood** (city) Madison County
8	25.6	**Vincennes** (city) Knox County
8	25.6	**Winamac** (town) Pulaski County
10	25.4	**Lake Station** (city) Lake County
11	25.0	**Anderson** (city) Madison County
11	25.0	**Aurora** (city) Dearborn County
13	24.3	**Country Squire Lakes** (CDP) Jennings County
14	24.1	**Fairmount** (town) Grant County
15	23.6	**Hanover** (town) Jefferson County
15	23.6	**Michigan City** (city) LaPorte County
17	23.3	**Alexandria** (city) Madison County
18	23.2	**Terre Haute** (city) Vigo County
19	23.1	**Bicknell** (city) Knox County
19	23.1	**Brazil** (city) Clay County
21	23.0	**Bloomington** (city) Monroe County
22	22.5	**Peru** (city) Miami County
23	22.3	**Wabash** (city) Wabash County
24	22.2	**Richmond** (city) Wayne County
24	22.2	**Sheridan** (town) Hamilton County
26	22.1	**Tipton** (city) Tipton County
26	22.1	**Whiting** (city) Lake County
28	22.0	**La Porte** (city) LaPorte County
28	22.0	**Ossian** (town) Wells County
28	22.0	**Portage** (city) Porter County
31	21.9	**Rensselaer** (city) Jasper County
32	21.8	**South Bend** (city) Saint Joseph County
33	21.7	**Brookville** (town) Franklin County
34	21.6	**Mitchell** (city) Lawrence County
35	21.5	**Clarksville** (town) Clark County
36	21.4	**Paoli** (town) Orange County
37	21.3	**Tell City** (city) Perry County
38	21.2	**Hammond** (city) Lake County
38	21.2	**North Manchester** (town) Wabash County
40	21.1	**Kokomo** (city) Howard County
41	20.7	**Connersville** (city) Fayette County
41	20.7	**Greendale** (city) Dearborn County
43	20.6	**Bedford** (city) Lawrence County
43	20.6	**Martinsville** (city) Morgan County
45	20.2	**Westville** (town) LaPorte County
46	20.1	**Greencastle** (city) Putnam County
46	20.1	**Notre Dame** (CDP) Saint Joseph County
46	20.1	**Sullivan** (city) Sullivan County
49	19.9	**Bluffton** (city) Wells County
49	19.9	**Evansville** (city) Vanderburgh County
49	19.9	**Franklin** (city) Johnson County
49	19.9	**Linton** (city) Greene County
49	19.9	**Mount Vernon** (city) Posey County
49	19.9	**Syracuse** (town) Kosciusko County
55	19.7	**Middlebury** (town) Elkhart County
56	19.6	**Hebron** (town) Porter County
56	19.6	**West Lafayette** (city) Tippecanoe County
58	19.4	**Rochester** (city) Fulton County
59	19.3	**Lagrange** (town) LaGrange County
60	19.2	**Cedar Lake** (town) Lake County
60	19.2	**Edinburgh** (town) Johnson County
60	19.2	**New Castle** (city) Henry County
63	19.1	**Lafayette** (city) Tippecanoe County
63	19.1	**Madison** (city) Jefferson County
63	19.1	**Portland** (city) Jay County
66	19.0	**Hobart** (city) Lake County
66	19.0	**Mishawaka** (city) Saint Joseph County
66	19.0	**New Haven** (city) Allen County
69	18.9	**Austin** (city) Scott County
69	18.9	**Fort Branch** (town) Gibson County
69	18.9	**South Haven** (CDP) Porter County
69	18.9	**Washington** (city) Daviess County
73	18.8	**Huntington** (city) Huntington County
74	18.7	**Boonville** (city) Warrick County
74	18.7	**New Whiteland** (town) Johnson County
74	18.7	**Santa Claus** (town) Spencer County
77	18.4	**Griffith** (town) Lake County
77	18.4	**Speedway** (town) Marion County
77	18.4	**Union City** (city) Randolph County
80	18.3	**Rockville** (town) Parke County
81	18.2	**Centerville** (town) Wayne County
82	18.1	**Beech Grove** (city) Marion County
82	18.1	**Princeton** (city) Gibson County
84	17.9	**Decatur** (city) Adams County
84	17.9	**Ellettsville** (town) Monroe County
84	17.9	**Winona Lake** (town) Kosciusko County
87	17.8	**Brownsburg** (town) Hendricks County
87	17.8	**Indianapolis** (city) Marion County
89	17.7	**Loogootee** (city) Martin County
90	17.6	**Crawfordsville** (city) Montgomery County
90	17.6	**Fort Wayne** (city) Allen County
90	17.6	**Jeffersonville** (city) Clark County
93	17.4	**Merrillville** (town) Lake County
94	17.3	**New Albany** (city) Floyd County
95	17.2	**Highland** (town) Lake County
95	17.2	**Mooresville** (town) Morgan County
95	17.2	**Shelbyville** (city) Shelby County
98	17.1	**Columbia City** (city) Whitley County
98	17.1	**Lawrenceburg** (city) Dearborn County
98	17.1	**North Vernon** (city) Jennings County
101	17.0	**Danville** (town) Hendricks County
101	17.0	**Hartford City** (city) Blackford County
101	17.0	**Seymour** (city) Jackson County
104	16.9	**Logansport** (city) Cass County
104	16.9	**Salt Creek Commons** (CDP) Porter County
106	16.6	**Corydon** (town) Harrison County
107	16.5	**Angola** (city) Steuben County
107	16.5	**Elkhart** (city) Elkhart County
107	16.5	**Yorktown** (town) Delaware County
110	16.4	**Berne** (city) Adams County
110	16.4	**Chesterton** (town) Porter County
110	16.4	**Rushville** (city) Rush County
110	16.4	**Salem** (city) Washington County
114	16.3	**Greenwood** (city) Johnson County
114	16.3	**Lawrence** (city) Marion County
116	16.2	**Melody Hill** (CDP) Vanderburgh County
117	16.1	**Charlestown** (city) Clark County
117	16.1	**Frankfort** (city) Clinton County
117	16.1	**Plymouth** (city) Marshall County
120	15.9	**Brownstown** (town) Jackson County
120	15.9	**Upland** (town) Grant County
122	15.8	**Jasper** (city) Dubois County
123	15.7	**Crown Point** (city) Lake County
123	15.7	**Lebanon** (city) Boone County
123	15.7	**Simonton Lake** (CDP) Elkhart County
126	15.6	**Chandler** (town) Warrick County
127	15.5	**Shorewood Forest** (CDP) Porter County
127	15.5	**Valparaiso** (city) Porter County
129	15.3	**Auburn** (city) DeKalb County
129	15.3	**Roselawn** (CDP) Newton County
131	15.2	**Clinton** (city) Vermillion County
132	15.1	**Smithville-Sanders** (CDP) Monroe County
132	15.1	**Winchester** (city) Randolph County
134	15.0	**Goshen** (city) Elkhart County
134	15.0	**Greentown** (town) Howard County
134	15.0	**Plainfield** (town) Hendricks County
137	14.9	**Delphi** (city) Carroll County
137	14.9	**Ligonier** (city) Noble County
139	14.7	**Whitestown** (town) Boone County
140	14.6	**Greenfield** (city) Hancock County
141	14.5	**Huntertown** (town) Allen County
142	14.4	**Avon** (town) Hendricks County
142	14.4	**Greensburg** (city) Decatur County
142	14.4	**Kendallville** (city) Noble County
142	14.4	**Noblesville** (city) Hamilton County
146	14.3	**Huntingburg** (city) Dubois County
147	14.2	**Attica** (city) Fountain County
147	14.2	**Schererville** (town) Lake County
149	14.0	**Newburgh** (town) Warrick County
149	14.0	**Sellersburg** (town) Clark County

Note: *This section ranks incorporated places and CDPs (Census Designated Places) with populations of 2,500 or more. Unincorporated postal areas were not considered. Please refer to the User Guide for additional information.*

Employment: Service Occupations

Top 150 Places Ranked in *Ascending* Order

State Rank	Percent	Place
1	8.2	**Fortville** (town) Hancock County
2	8.6	**Carmel** (city) Hamilton County
3	8.9	**Osceola** (town) Saint Joseph County
4	9.0	**Dunlap** (CDP) Elkhart County
5	9.1	**Zionsville** (town) Boone County
6	9.4	**Fishers** (city) Hamilton County
7	9.7	**Butler** (city) DeKalb County
8	9.8	**Granger** (CDP) Saint Joseph County
9	10.0	**Warsaw** (city) Kosciusko County
10	10.1	**Highland** (CDP) Vanderburgh County
10	10.1	**McCordsville** (town) Hancock County
12	10.7	**Bargersville** (town) Johnson County
12	10.7	**Westfield** (city) Hamilton County
14	10.8	**De Motte** (town) Jasper County
15	11.0	**Batesville** (city) Ripley County
15	11.0	**Saint John** (town) Lake County
15	11.0	**Whiteland** (town) Johnson County
18	11.4	**Heritage Lake** (CDP) Putnam County
19	11.7	**Bremen** (town) Marshall County
20	11.9	**Porter** (town) Porter County
21	12.0	**Lakes of the Four Seasons** (CDP) Lake County
21	12.0	**Pendleton** (town) Madison County
23	12.1	**Munster** (town) Lake County
24	12.6	**Georgetown** (town) Floyd County
24	12.6	**Hidden Valley** (CDP) Dearborn County
24	12.6	**Winfield** (town) Lake County
27	12.7	**Dyer** (town) Lake County
27	12.7	**Nappanee** (city) Elkhart County
27	12.7	**Pittsboro** (town) Hendricks County
30	13.0	**Cumberland** (town) Marion County
31	13.1	**Bright** (CDP) Dearborn County
31	13.1	**Lowell** (town) Lake County
33	13.4	**Gas City** (city) Grant County
33	13.4	**Monticello** (city) White County
35	13.6	**Garrett** (city) DeKalb County
36	13.7	**Columbus** (city) Bartholomew County
36	13.7	**Leo-Cedarville** (town) Allen County
38	13.8	**Cicero** (town) Hamilton County
38	13.8	**Scottsburg** (city) Scott County
40	14.0	**Newburgh** (town) Warrick County
40	14.0	**Sellersburg** (town) Clark County
42	14.2	**Attica** (city) Fountain County
42	14.2	**Schererville** (town) Lake County
44	14.3	**Huntingburg** (city) Dubois County
45	14.4	**Avon** (town) Hendricks County
45	14.4	**Greensburg** (city) Decatur County
45	14.4	**Kendallville** (city) Noble County
45	14.4	**Noblesville** (city) Hamilton County
49	14.5	**Huntertown** (town) Allen County
50	14.6	**Greenfield** (city) Hancock County
51	14.7	**Whitestown** (town) Boone County
52	14.9	**Delphi** (city) Carroll County
52	14.9	**Ligonier** (city) Noble County
54	15.0	**Goshen** (city) Elkhart County
54	15.0	**Greentown** (town) Howard County
54	15.0	**Plainfield** (town) Hendricks County
57	15.1	**Smithville-Sanders** (CDP) Monroe County
57	15.1	**Winchester** (city) Randolph County
59	15.2	**Clinton** (city) Vermillion County
60	15.3	**Auburn** (city) DeKalb County
60	15.3	**Roselawn** (CDP) Newton County
62	15.5	**Shorewood Forest** (CDP) Porter County
62	15.5	**Valparaiso** (city) Porter County
64	15.6	**Chandler** (town) Warrick County
65	15.7	**Crown Point** (city) Lake County
65	15.7	**Lebanon** (city) Boone County
65	15.7	**Simonton Lake** (CDP) Elkhart County
68	15.8	**Jasper** (city) Dubois County
69	15.9	**Brownstown** (town) Jackson County
69	15.9	**Upland** (town) Grant County
71	16.1	**Charlestown** (city) Clark County
71	16.1	**Frankfort** (city) Clinton County
71	16.1	**Plymouth** (city) Marshall County
74	16.2	**Melody Hill** (CDP) Vanderburgh County
75	16.3	**Greenwood** (city) Johnson County
75	16.3	**Lawrence** (city) Marion County
77	16.4	**Berne** (city) Adams County
77	16.4	**Chesterton** (town) Porter County
77	16.4	**Rushville** (city) Rush County
77	16.4	**Salem** (city) Washington County
81	16.5	**Angola** (city) Steuben County
81	16.5	**Elkhart** (city) Elkhart County
81	16.5	**Yorktown** (town) Delaware County
84	16.6	**Corydon** (town) Harrison County
85	16.9	**Logansport** (city) Cass County
85	16.9	**Salt Creek Commons** (CDP) Porter County
87	17.0	**Danville** (town) Hendricks County
87	17.0	**Hartford City** (city) Blackford County
87	17.0	**Seymour** (city) Jackson County
90	17.1	**Columbia City** (city) Whitley County
90	17.1	**Lawrenceburg** (city) Dearborn County
90	17.1	**North Vernon** (city) Jennings County
93	17.2	**Highland** (town) Lake County
93	17.2	**Mooresville** (town) Morgan County
93	17.2	**Shelbyville** (city) Shelby County
96	17.3	**New Albany** (city) Floyd County
97	17.4	**Merrillville** (town) Lake County
98	17.6	**Crawfordsville** (city) Montgomery County
98	17.6	**Fort Wayne** (city) Allen County
98	17.6	**Jeffersonville** (city) Clark County
101	17.7	**Loogootee** (city) Martin County
102	17.8	**Brownsburg** (town) Hendricks County
102	17.8	**Indianapolis** (city) Marion County
104	17.9	**Decatur** (city) Adams County
104	17.9	**Ellettsville** (town) Monroe County
104	17.9	**Winona Lake** (town) Kosciusko County
107	18.1	**Beech Grove** (city) Marion County
107	18.1	**Princeton** (city) Gibson County
109	18.2	**Centerville** (town) Wayne County
110	18.3	**Rockville** (town) Parke County
111	18.4	**Griffith** (town) Lake County
111	18.4	**Speedway** (town) Marion County
111	18.4	**Union City** (city) Randolph County
114	18.7	**Boonville** (city) Warrick County
114	18.7	**New Whiteland** (town) Johnson County
114	18.7	**Santa Claus** (town) Spencer County
117	18.8	**Huntington** (city) Huntington County
118	18.9	**Austin** (city) Scott County
118	18.9	**Fort Branch** (town) Gibson County
118	18.9	**South Haven** (CDP) Porter County
118	18.9	**Washington** (city) Daviess County
122	19.0	**Hobart** (city) Lake County
122	19.0	**Mishawaka** (city) Saint Joseph County
122	19.0	**New Haven** (city) Allen County
125	19.1	**Lafayette** (city) Tippecanoe County
125	19.1	**Madison** (city) Jefferson County
125	19.1	**Portland** (city) Jay County
128	19.2	**Cedar Lake** (town) Lake County
128	19.2	**Edinburgh** (town) Johnson County
128	19.2	**New Castle** (city) Henry County
131	19.3	**Lagrange** (town) LaGrange County
132	19.4	**Rochester** (city) Fulton County
133	19.6	**Hebron** (town) Porter County
133	19.6	**West Lafayette** (city) Tippecanoe County
135	19.7	**Middlebury** (town) Elkhart County
136	19.9	**Bluffton** (city) Wells County
136	19.9	**Evansville** (city) Vanderburgh County
136	19.9	**Franklin** (city) Johnson County
136	19.9	**Linton** (city) Greene County
136	19.9	**Mount Vernon** (city) Posey County
136	19.9	**Syracuse** (town) Kosciusko County
142	20.1	**Greencastle** (city) Putnam County
142	20.1	**Notre Dame** (CDP) Saint Joseph County
142	20.1	**Sullivan** (city) Sullivan County
145	20.2	**Westville** (town) LaPorte County
146	20.6	**Bedford** (city) Lawrence County
146	20.6	**Martinsville** (city) Morgan County
148	20.7	**Connersville** (city) Fayette County
148	20.7	**Greendale** (city) Dearborn County
150	21.1	**Kokomo** (city) Howard County

Note: *This section ranks incorporated places and CDPs (Census Designated Places) with populations of 2,500 or more. Unincorporated postal areas were not considered. Please refer to the User Guide for additional information.*

Employment: Sales and Office Occupations

Top 150 Places Ranked in *Descending* Order

State Rank	Percent	Place
1	33.5	**Clinton** (city) Vermillion County
2	31.2	**Beech Grove** (city) Marion County
2	31.2	**Leo-Cedarville** (town) Allen County
4	31.0	**Pendleton** (town) Madison County
5	30.2	**Notre Dame** (CDP) Saint Joseph County
6	29.9	**De Motte** (town) Jasper County
7	29.8	**Simonton Lake** (CDP) Elkhart County
8	29.6	**Gas City** (city) Grant County
9	29.1	**Chandler** (town) Warrick County
9	29.1	**Fortville** (town) Hancock County
11	29.0	**Noblesville** (city) Hamilton County
12	28.9	**Danville** (town) Hendricks County
13	28.7	**Brownstown** (town) Jackson County
13	28.7	**Nappanee** (city) Elkhart County
15	28.6	**Sellersburg** (town) Clark County
16	28.4	**McCordsville** (town) Hancock County
17	28.2	**Ellettsville** (town) Monroe County
18	27.8	**Heritage Lake** (CDP) Putnam County
18	27.8	**Lakes of the Four Seasons** (CDP) Lake County
18	27.8	**Mitchell** (city) Lawrence County
21	27.7	**Mooresville** (town) Morgan County
22	27.4	**Cumberland** (town) Marion County
22	27.4	**New Whiteland** (town) Johnson County
24	27.2	**Griffith** (town) Lake County
24	27.2	**Lawrenceburg** (city) Dearborn County
26	27.0	**Osceola** (town) Saint Joseph County
26	27.0	**Winchester** (city) Randolph County
28	26.7	**Clarksville** (town) Clark County
29	26.6	**Greenfield** (city) Hancock County
30	26.5	**Greenwood** (city) Johnson County
30	26.5	**Whiteland** (town) Johnson County
32	26.4	**Brownsburg** (town) Hendricks County
32	26.4	**Lebanon** (city) Boone County
34	26.0	**New Albany** (city) Floyd County
34	26.0	**Rushville** (city) Rush County
36	25.9	**Jeffersonville** (city) Clark County
36	25.9	**Mishawaka** (city) Saint Joseph County
36	25.9	**Valparaiso** (city) Porter County
39	25.8	**Greendale** (city) Dearborn County
39	25.8	**Melody Hill** (CDP) Vanderburgh County
41	25.7	**Corydon** (town) Harrison County
41	25.7	**Huntertown** (town) Allen County
43	25.4	**Plainfield** (town) Hendricks County
44	25.3	**Greentown** (town) Howard County
44	25.3	**Porter** (town) Porter County
44	25.3	**Roselawn** (CDP) Newton County
47	25.2	**Fishers** (city) Hamilton County
48	25.1	**Georgetown** (town) Floyd County
49	25.0	**Indianapolis** (city) Marion County
49	25.0	**Westfield** (city) Hamilton County
51	24.9	**La Porte** (city) LaPorte County
52	24.8	**Highland** (town) Lake County
52	24.8	**Muncie** (city) Delaware County
54	24.7	**Fort Wayne** (city) Allen County
54	24.7	**Lawrence** (city) Marion County
54	24.7	**Martinsville** (city) Morgan County
54	24.7	**Merrillville** (town) Lake County
54	24.7	**Upland** (town) Grant County
54	24.7	**Yorktown** (town) Delaware County
60	24.6	**Avon** (town) Hendricks County
60	24.6	**Munster** (town) Lake County
62	24.4	**Batesville** (city) Ripley County
62	24.4	**Evansville** (city) Vanderburgh County
62	24.4	**Whiting** (city) Lake County
65	24.1	**Granger** (CDP) Saint Joseph County
65	24.1	**Jasper** (city) Dubois County
67	24.0	**New Haven** (city) Allen County
67	24.0	**Schererville** (town) Lake County
69	23.9	**Anderson** (city) Madison County
69	23.9	**Monticello** (city) White County
71	23.8	**Speedway** (town) Marion County
72	23.6	**Connersville** (city) Fayette County
72	23.6	**Hammond** (city) Lake County
72	23.6	**Winfield** (town) Lake County
75	23.5	**Highland** (CDP) Vanderburgh County
75	23.5	**Loogootee** (city) Martin County
75	23.5	**Saint John** (town) Lake County
78	23.4	**Westville** (town) LaPorte County
79	23.3	**Angola** (city) Steuben County
80	23.1	**Gary** (city) Lake County
81	23.0	**Centerville** (town) Wayne County
81	23.0	**Dunlap** (CDP) Elkhart County
81	23.0	**Ossian** (town) Wells County
81	23.0	**Terre Haute** (city) Vigo County
85	22.9	**Bright** (CDP) Dearborn County
85	22.9	**Portage** (city) Porter County
87	22.8	**Michigan City** (city) LaPorte County
87	22.8	**South Bend** (city) Saint Joseph County
89	22.7	**Boonville** (city) Warrick County
89	22.7	**Columbia City** (city) Whitley County
89	22.7	**Decatur** (city) Adams County
92	22.6	**Bedford** (city) Lawrence County
92	22.6	**Dyer** (town) Lake County
92	22.6	**Hobart** (city) Lake County
92	22.6	**Scottsburg** (city) Scott County
96	22.5	**Huntington** (city) Huntington County
96	22.5	**Marion** (city) Grant County
96	22.5	**Rockville** (town) Parke County
96	22.5	**Winona Lake** (town) Kosciusko County
100	22.4	**Bluffton** (city) Wells County
101	22.3	**Lake Station** (city) Lake County
101	22.3	**Shelbyville** (city) Shelby County
103	22.2	**New Castle** (city) Henry County
103	22.2	**Newburgh** (town) Warrick County
103	22.2	**Tell City** (city) Perry County
106	22.1	**Mount Vernon** (city) Posey County
107	22.0	**Berne** (city) Adams County
107	22.0	**Crawfordsville** (city) Montgomery County
109	21.9	**Carmel** (city) Hamilton County
109	21.9	**Lafayette** (city) Tippecanoe County
109	21.9	**Lowell** (town) Lake County
109	21.9	**South Haven** (CDP) Porter County
113	21.8	**Crown Point** (city) Lake County
114	21.7	**Richmond** (city) Wayne County
115	21.5	**Charlestown** (city) Clark County
115	21.5	**Greencastle** (city) Putnam County
115	21.5	**Shorewood Forest** (CDP) Porter County
115	21.5	**Warsaw** (city) Kosciusko County
119	21.4	**Salt Creek Commons** (CDP) Porter County
119	21.4	**Wabash** (city) Wabash County
121	21.3	**Franklin** (city) Johnson County
122	21.1	**Alexandria** (city) Madison County
122	21.1	**Brookville** (town) Franklin County
122	21.1	**Cedar Lake** (town) Lake County
122	21.1	**Edinburgh** (town) Johnson County
122	21.1	**Goshen** (city) Elkhart County
127	21.0	**Aurora** (city) Dearborn County
127	21.0	**Rochester** (city) Fulton County
129	20.9	**Seymour** (city) Jackson County
129	20.9	**Syracuse** (town) Kosciusko County
131	20.7	**Huntingburg** (city) Dubois County
131	20.7	**North Terre Haute** (CDP) Vigo County
133	20.6	**Plymouth** (city) Marshall County
133	20.6	**Salem** (city) Washington County
135	20.5	**Chesterton** (town) Porter County
135	20.5	**Kokomo** (city) Howard County
137	20.3	**Auburn** (city) DeKalb County
137	20.3	**Linton** (city) Greene County
137	20.3	**Rensselaer** (city) Jasper County
140	20.0	**Bloomington** (city) Monroe County
140	20.0	**Garrett** (city) DeKalb County
142	19.9	**Brazil** (city) Clay County
142	19.9	**Peru** (city) Miami County
144	19.8	**Middlebury** (town) Elkhart County
145	19.6	**East Chicago** (city) Lake County
145	19.6	**Hanover** (town) Jefferson County
145	19.6	**Santa Claus** (town) Spencer County
148	19.5	**Bargersville** (town) Johnson County
149	19.4	**Fairmount** (town) Grant County
150	19.3	**Washington** (city) Daviess County

***Note:** This section ranks incorporated places and CDPs (Census Designated Places) with populations of 2,500 or more. Unincorporated postal areas were not considered. Please refer to the User Guide for additional information.*

Employment: Sales and Office Occupations

Top 150 Places Ranked in *Ascending* Order

State Rank	Percent	Place
1	9.3	**Union City** (city) Randolph County
2	11.1	**Lagrange** (town) LaGrange County
3	11.4	**Winamac** (town) Pulaski County
4	11.8	**Ligonier** (city) Noble County
5	12.5	**Kendallville** (city) Noble County
6	13.4	**Bremen** (town) Marshall County
7	13.5	**Hebron** (town) Porter County
7	13.5	**Smithville-Sanders** (CDP) Monroe County
7	13.5	**Whitestown** (town) Boone County
10	14.7	**Sullivan** (city) Sullivan County
11	14.8	**Cicero** (town) Hamilton County
12	15.0	**Fort Branch** (town) Gibson County
13	15.4	**Austin** (city) Scott County
14	16.0	**Madison** (city) Jefferson County
14	16.0	**Tipton** (city) Tipton County
16	16.3	**Sheridan** (town) Hamilton County
17	16.5	**Greensburg** (city) Decatur County
18	16.7	**Portland** (city) Jay County
19	17.2	**Logansport** (city) Cass County
20	17.4	**Frankfort** (city) Clinton County
21	17.5	**Hidden Valley** (CDP) Dearborn County
22	17.7	**Columbus** (city) Bartholomew County
22	17.7	**Delphi** (city) Carroll County
22	17.7	**Princeton** (city) Gibson County
25	17.9	**Country Squire Lakes** (CDP) Jennings County
25	17.9	**North Manchester** (town) Wabash County
27	18.0	**Attica** (city) Fountain County
28	18.1	**Vincennes** (city) Knox County
29	18.2	**Pittsboro** (town) Hendricks County
30	18.3	**Bicknell** (city) Knox County
31	18.5	**Knox** (city) Starke County
31	18.5	**West Lafayette** (city) Tippecanoe County
33	18.6	**Paoli** (town) Orange County
34	18.7	**North Vernon** (city) Jennings County
35	18.8	**Elkhart** (city) Elkhart County
36	19.1	**Hartford City** (city) Blackford County
36	19.1	**Zionsville** (town) Boone County
38	19.2	**Butler** (city) DeKalb County
38	19.2	**Elwood** (city) Madison County
40	19.3	**Washington** (city) Daviess County
41	19.4	**Fairmount** (town) Grant County
42	19.5	**Bargersville** (town) Johnson County
43	19.6	**East Chicago** (city) Lake County
43	19.6	**Hanover** (town) Jefferson County
43	19.6	**Santa Claus** (town) Spencer County
46	19.8	**Middlebury** (town) Elkhart County
47	19.9	**Brazil** (city) Clay County
47	19.9	**Peru** (city) Miami County
49	20.0	**Bloomington** (city) Monroe County
49	20.0	**Garrett** (city) DeKalb County
51	20.3	**Auburn** (city) DeKalb County
51	20.3	**Linton** (city) Greene County
51	20.3	**Rensselaer** (city) Jasper County
54	20.5	**Chesterton** (town) Porter County
54	20.5	**Kokomo** (city) Howard County
56	20.6	**Plymouth** (city) Marshall County
56	20.6	**Salem** (city) Washington County
58	20.7	**Huntingburg** (city) Dubois County
58	20.7	**North Terre Haute** (CDP) Vigo County
60	20.9	**Seymour** (city) Jackson County
60	20.9	**Syracuse** (town) Kosciusko County
62	21.0	**Aurora** (city) Dearborn County
62	21.0	**Rochester** (city) Fulton County
64	21.1	**Alexandria** (city) Madison County
64	21.1	**Brookville** (town) Franklin County
64	21.1	**Cedar Lake** (town) Lake County
64	21.1	**Edinburgh** (town) Johnson County
64	21.1	**Goshen** (city) Elkhart County
69	21.3	**Franklin** (city) Johnson County
70	21.4	**Salt Creek Commons** (CDP) Porter County
70	21.4	**Wabash** (city) Wabash County
72	21.5	**Charlestown** (city) Clark County
72	21.5	**Greencastle** (city) Putnam County
72	21.5	**Shorewood Forest** (CDP) Porter County
72	21.5	**Warsaw** (city) Kosciusko County
76	21.7	**Richmond** (city) Wayne County
77	21.8	**Crown Point** (city) Lake County
78	21.9	**Carmel** (city) Hamilton County
78	21.9	**Lafayette** (city) Tippecanoe County
78	21.9	**Lowell** (town) Lake County
78	21.9	**South Haven** (CDP) Porter County
82	22.0	**Berne** (city) Adams County
82	22.0	**Crawfordsville** (city) Montgomery County
84	22.1	**Mount Vernon** (city) Posey County
85	22.2	**New Castle** (city) Henry County
85	22.2	**Newburgh** (town) Warrick County
85	22.2	**Tell City** (city) Perry County
88	22.3	**Lake Station** (city) Lake County
88	22.3	**Shelbyville** (city) Shelby County
90	22.4	**Bluffton** (city) Wells County
91	22.5	**Huntington** (city) Huntington County
91	22.5	**Marion** (city) Grant County
91	22.5	**Rockville** (town) Parke County
91	22.5	**Winona Lake** (town) Kosciusko County
95	22.6	**Bedford** (city) Lawrence County
95	22.6	**Dyer** (town) Lake County
95	22.6	**Hobart** (city) Lake County
95	22.6	**Scottsburg** (city) Scott County
99	22.7	**Boonville** (city) Warrick County
99	22.7	**Columbia City** (city) Whitley County
99	22.7	**Decatur** (city) Adams County
102	22.8	**Michigan City** (city) LaPorte County
102	22.8	**South Bend** (city) Saint Joseph County
104	22.9	**Bright** (CDP) Dearborn County
104	22.9	**Portage** (city) Porter County
106	23.0	**Centerville** (town) Wayne County
106	23.0	**Dunlap** (CDP) Elkhart County
106	23.0	**Ossian** (town) Wells County
106	23.0	**Terre Haute** (city) Vigo County
110	23.1	**Gary** (city) Lake County
111	23.3	**Angola** (city) Steuben County
112	23.4	**Westville** (town) LaPorte County
113	23.5	**Highland** (CDP) Vanderburgh County
113	23.5	**Loogootee** (city) Martin County
113	23.5	**Saint John** (town) Lake County
116	23.6	**Connersville** (city) Fayette County
116	23.6	**Hammond** (city) Lake County
116	23.6	**Winfield** (town) Lake County
119	23.8	**Speedway** (town) Marion County
120	23.9	**Anderson** (city) Madison County
120	23.9	**Monticello** (city) White County
122	24.0	**New Haven** (city) Allen County
122	24.0	**Schererville** (town) Lake County
124	24.1	**Granger** (CDP) Saint Joseph County
124	24.1	**Jasper** (city) Dubois County
126	24.4	**Batesville** (city) Ripley County
126	24.4	**Evansville** (city) Vanderburgh County
126	24.4	**Whiting** (city) Lake County
129	24.6	**Avon** (town) Hendricks County
129	24.6	**Munster** (town) Lake County
131	24.7	**Fort Wayne** (city) Allen County
131	24.7	**Lawrence** (city) Marion County
131	24.7	**Martinsville** (city) Morgan County
131	24.7	**Merrillville** (town) Lake County
131	24.7	**Upland** (town) Grant County
131	24.7	**Yorktown** (town) Delaware County
137	24.8	**Highland** (town) Lake County
137	24.8	**Muncie** (city) Delaware County
139	24.9	**La Porte** (city) LaPorte County
140	25.0	**Indianapolis** (city) Marion County
140	25.0	**Westfield** (city) Hamilton County
142	25.1	**Georgetown** (town) Floyd County
143	25.2	**Fishers** (city) Hamilton County
144	25.3	**Greentown** (town) Howard County
144	25.3	**Porter** (town) Porter County
144	25.3	**Roselawn** (CDP) Newton County
147	25.4	**Plainfield** (town) Hendricks County
148	25.7	**Corydon** (town) Harrison County
148	25.7	**Huntertown** (town) Allen County
150	25.8	**Greendale** (city) Dearborn County

***Note:** This section ranks incorporated places and CDPs (Census Designated Places) with populations of 2,500 or more. Unincorporated postal areas were not considered. Please refer to the User Guide for additional information.*

Employment: Natural Resources, Construction, and Maintenance Occupations

Top 150 Places Ranked in *Descending* Order

State Rank	Percent	Place
1	27.1	**Sullivan** (city) Sullivan County
2	24.3	**Roselawn** (CDP) Newton County
3	20.5	**De Motte** (town) Jasper County
4	18.5	**Hebron** (town) Porter County
5	17.5	**South Haven** (CDP) Porter County
6	17.1	**Monticello** (city) White County
7	16.5	**Cedar Lake** (town) Lake County
8	15.0	**Sheridan** (town) Hamilton County
9	14.9	**Attica** (city) Fountain County
9	14.9	**Delphi** (city) Carroll County
11	14.8	**Hidden Valley** (CDP) Dearborn County
12	14.3	**Alexandria** (city) Madison County
13	14.2	**Martinsville** (city) Morgan County
14	13.5	**New Whiteland** (town) Johnson County
15	13.3	**Fairmount** (town) Grant County
15	13.3	**Union City** (city) Randolph County
17	13.2	**Lake Station** (city) Lake County
18	13.1	**Westville** (town) LaPorte County
19	12.9	**Portland** (city) Jay County
20	12.5	**Heritage Lake** (CDP) Putnam County
20	12.5	**Syracuse** (town) Kosciusko County
20	12.5	**Tipton** (city) Tipton County
23	12.2	**Salt Creek Commons** (CDP) Porter County
24	12.0	**Mooresville** (town) Morgan County
24	12.0	**Newburgh** (town) Warrick County
26	11.9	**Country Squire Lakes** (CDP) Jennings County
26	11.9	**Lagrange** (town) LaGrange County
28	11.8	**Linton** (city) Greene County
29	11.7	**Bicknell** (city) Knox County
29	11.7	**Chesterton** (town) Porter County
31	11.6	**Princeton** (city) Gibson County
32	11.5	**Cicero** (town) Hamilton County
33	11.4	**Rockville** (town) Parke County
33	11.4	**Winfield** (town) Lake County
35	11.3	**Pendleton** (town) Madison County
35	11.3	**Salem** (city) Washington County
35	11.3	**Washington** (city) Daviess County
38	11.1	**Fortville** (town) Hancock County
38	11.1	**Logansport** (city) Cass County
40	11.0	**Lawrence** (city) Marion County
41	10.9	**Bedford** (city) Lawrence County
41	10.9	**Bright** (CDP) Dearborn County
41	10.9	**Lawrenceburg** (city) Dearborn County
41	10.9	**Lowell** (town) Lake County
45	10.8	**Rensselaer** (city) Jasper County
46	10.7	**Garrett** (city) DeKalb County
47	10.5	**Fort Branch** (town) Gibson County
47	10.5	**Greenfield** (city) Hancock County
47	10.5	**Shelbyville** (city) Shelby County
50	10.4	**Whiting** (city) Lake County
51	10.3	**Schererville** (town) Lake County
52	10.2	**Dyer** (town) Lake County
52	10.2	**Hammond** (city) Lake County
52	10.2	**Scottsburg** (city) Scott County
55	10.1	**Aurora** (city) Dearborn County
55	10.1	**Hartford City** (city) Blackford County
55	10.1	**Paoli** (town) Orange County
55	10.1	**Smithville-Sanders** (CDP) Monroe County
59	9.9	**Frankfort** (city) Clinton County
59	9.9	**Peru** (city) Miami County
61	9.8	**Leo-Cedarville** (town) Allen County
61	9.8	**Rochester** (city) Fulton County
63	9.7	**Boonville** (city) Warrick County
63	9.7	**Griffith** (town) Lake County
65	9.6	**Crawfordsville** (city) Montgomery County
66	9.5	**Lebanon** (city) Boone County
67	9.4	**Highland** (town) Lake County
67	9.4	**Merrillville** (town) Lake County
67	9.4	**Portage** (city) Porter County
70	9.3	**North Terre Haute** (CDP) Vigo County
71	9.2	**Franklin** (city) Johnson County
72	9.1	**Hobart** (city) Lake County
72	9.1	**Saint John** (town) Lake County
72	9.1	**Winchester** (city) Randolph County
75	9.0	**Crown Point** (city) Lake County
75	9.0	**North Vernon** (city) Jennings County
77	8.7	**Brookville** (town) Franklin County
77	8.7	**Huntington** (city) Huntington County
77	8.7	**Michigan City** (city) LaPorte County
80	8.6	**Clinton** (city) Vermillion County
80	8.6	**Goshen** (city) Elkhart County
80	8.6	**La Porte** (city) LaPorte County
83	8.5	**New Albany** (city) Floyd County
84	8.4	**Lakes of the Four Seasons** (CDP) Lake County
84	8.4	**North Manchester** (town) Wabash County
86	8.3	**East Chicago** (city) Lake County
86	8.3	**Porter** (town) Porter County
88	8.2	**Shorewood Forest** (CDP) Porter County
88	8.2	**Whiteland** (town) Johnson County
90	8.1	**Anderson** (city) Madison County
90	8.1	**Charlestown** (city) Clark County
90	8.1	**McCordsville** (town) Hancock County
93	8.0	**Georgetown** (town) Floyd County
93	8.0	**Huntingburg** (city) Dubois County
95	7.9	**Bargersville** (town) Johnson County
95	7.9	**Brownstown** (town) Jackson County
95	7.9	**Melody Hill** (CDP) Vanderburgh County
95	7.9	**Mount Vernon** (city) Posey County
99	7.8	**Greenwood** (city) Johnson County
99	7.8	**Kokomo** (city) Howard County
99	7.8	**Mitchell** (city) Lawrence County
99	7.8	**Sellersburg** (town) Clark County
103	7.7	**Brazil** (city) Clay County
103	7.7	**Cumberland** (town) Marion County
105	7.6	**Clarksville** (town) Clark County
105	7.6	**Gas City** (city) Grant County
105	7.6	**New Haven** (city) Allen County
105	7.6	**Pittsboro** (town) Hendricks County
109	7.5	**Berne** (city) Adams County
109	7.5	**Evansville** (city) Vanderburgh County
111	7.4	**Chandler** (town) Warrick County
111	7.4	**Loogootee** (city) Martin County
111	7.4	**Speedway** (town) Marion County
114	7.3	**Decatur** (city) Adams County
114	7.3	**Indianapolis** (city) Marion County
116	7.2	**Huntertown** (town) Allen County
116	7.2	**Tell City** (city) Perry County
118	7.1	**Beech Grove** (city) Marion County
118	7.1	**Lafayette** (city) Tippecanoe County
118	7.1	**New Castle** (city) Henry County
118	7.1	**Winamac** (town) Pulaski County
122	7.0	**Fort Wayne** (city) Allen County
122	7.0	**Middlebury** (town) Elkhart County
122	7.0	**Mishawaka** (city) Saint Joseph County
122	7.0	**Plainfield** (town) Hendricks County
126	6.9	**Ellettsville** (town) Monroe County
126	6.9	**Elwood** (city) Madison County
126	6.9	**Osceola** (town) Saint Joseph County
129	6.8	**Rushville** (city) Rush County
129	6.8	**Seymour** (city) Jackson County
131	6.6	**Warsaw** (city) Kosciusko County
132	6.5	**Bluffton** (city) Wells County
132	6.5	**Elkhart** (city) Elkhart County
132	6.5	**Madison** (city) Jefferson County
132	6.5	**Muncie** (city) Delaware County
136	6.4	**Connersville** (city) Fayette County
136	6.4	**Jasper** (city) Dubois County
136	6.4	**Ossian** (town) Wells County
136	6.4	**Wabash** (city) Wabash County
140	6.3	**Avon** (town) Hendricks County
140	6.3	**Bremen** (town) Marshall County
140	6.3	**Knox** (city) Starke County
140	6.3	**Terre Haute** (city) Vigo County
144	6.2	**Batesville** (city) Ripley County
144	6.2	**Columbia City** (city) Whitley County
144	6.2	**Ligonier** (city) Noble County
147	6.1	**Butler** (city) DeKalb County
148	6.0	**Brownsburg** (town) Hendricks County
149	5.9	**Danville** (town) Hendricks County
149	5.9	**Gary** (city) Lake County

Note: *This section ranks incorporated places and CDPs (Census Designated Places) with populations of 2,500 or more. Unincorporated postal areas were not considered. Please refer to the User Guide for additional information.*

Employment: Natural Resources, Construction, and Maintenance Occupations

Top 150 Places Ranked in *Ascending* Order

State Rank	Percent	Place
1	2.0	**Notre Dame** (CDP) Saint Joseph County
2	2.5	**Upland** (town) Grant County
3	2.7	**Austin** (city) Scott County
3	2.7	**Carmel** (city) Hamilton County
5	3.0	**Fishers** (city) Hamilton County
6	3.3	**Zionsville** (town) Boone County
7	3.5	**Nappanee** (city) Elkhart County
7	3.5	**Simonton Lake** (CDP) Elkhart County
7	3.5	**West Lafayette** (city) Tippecanoe County
7	3.5	**Whitestown** (town) Boone County
11	3.6	**Bloomington** (city) Monroe County
11	3.6	**Greendale** (city) Dearborn County
13	3.7	**Corydon** (town) Harrison County
14	3.8	**Centerville** (town) Wayne County
14	3.8	**Edinburgh** (town) Johnson County
16	4.4	**Auburn** (city) DeKalb County
17	4.6	**Columbus** (city) Bartholomew County
17	4.6	**Greencastle** (city) Putnam County
19	4.7	**Granger** (CDP) Saint Joseph County
19	4.7	**Greensburg** (city) Decatur County
19	4.7	**Highland** (CDP) Vanderburgh County
19	4.7	**Winona Lake** (town) Kosciusko County
23	4.8	**Plymouth** (city) Marshall County
24	5.0	**Westfield** (city) Hamilton County
25	5.1	**Vincennes** (city) Knox County
26	5.2	**Dunlap** (CDP) Elkhart County
27	5.3	**South Bend** (city) Saint Joseph County
28	5.4	**Kendallville** (city) Noble County
29	5.6	**Greentown** (town) Howard County
29	5.6	**Jeffersonville** (city) Clark County
29	5.6	**Marion** (city) Grant County
32	5.7	**Angola** (city) Steuben County
32	5.7	**Valparaiso** (city) Porter County
34	5.8	**Munster** (town) Lake County
34	5.8	**Noblesville** (city) Hamilton County
34	5.8	**Richmond** (city) Wayne County
34	5.8	**Santa Claus** (town) Spencer County
34	5.8	**Yorktown** (town) Delaware County
39	5.9	**Danville** (town) Hendricks County
39	5.9	**Gary** (city) Lake County
39	5.9	**Hanover** (town) Jefferson County
42	6.0	**Brownsburg** (town) Hendricks County
43	6.1	**Butler** (city) DeKalb County
44	6.2	**Batesville** (city) Ripley County
44	6.2	**Columbia City** (city) Whitley County
44	6.2	**Ligonier** (city) Noble County
47	6.3	**Avon** (town) Hendricks County
47	6.3	**Bremen** (town) Marshall County
47	6.3	**Knox** (city) Starke County
47	6.3	**Terre Haute** (city) Vigo County
51	6.4	**Connersville** (city) Fayette County
51	6.4	**Jasper** (city) Dubois County
51	6.4	**Ossian** (town) Wells County
51	6.4	**Wabash** (city) Wabash County
55	6.5	**Bluffton** (city) Wells County
55	6.5	**Elkhart** (city) Elkhart County
55	6.5	**Madison** (city) Jefferson County
55	6.5	**Muncie** (city) Delaware County
59	6.6	**Warsaw** (city) Kosciusko County
60	6.8	**Rushville** (city) Rush County
60	6.8	**Seymour** (city) Jackson County
62	6.9	**Ellettsville** (town) Monroe County
62	6.9	**Elwood** (city) Madison County
62	6.9	**Osceola** (town) Saint Joseph County
65	7.0	**Fort Wayne** (city) Allen County
65	7.0	**Middlebury** (town) Elkhart County
65	7.0	**Mishawaka** (city) Saint Joseph County
65	7.0	**Plainfield** (town) Hendricks County
69	7.1	**Beech Grove** (city) Marion County
69	7.1	**Lafayette** (city) Tippecanoe County
69	7.1	**New Castle** (city) Henry County
69	7.1	**Winamac** (town) Pulaski County
73	7.2	**Huntertown** (town) Allen County
73	7.2	**Tell City** (city) Perry County
75	7.3	**Decatur** (city) Adams County
75	7.3	**Indianapolis** (city) Marion County
77	7.4	**Chandler** (town) Warrick County
77	7.4	**Loogootee** (city) Martin County
77	7.4	**Speedway** (town) Marion County
80	7.5	**Berne** (city) Adams County
80	7.5	**Evansville** (city) Vanderburgh County
82	7.6	**Clarksville** (town) Clark County
82	7.6	**Gas City** (city) Grant County
82	7.6	**New Haven** (city) Allen County
82	7.6	**Pittsboro** (town) Hendricks County
86	7.7	**Brazil** (city) Clay County
86	7.7	**Cumberland** (town) Marion County
88	7.8	**Greenwood** (city) Johnson County
88	7.8	**Kokomo** (city) Howard County
88	7.8	**Mitchell** (city) Lawrence County
88	7.8	**Sellersburg** (town) Clark County
92	7.9	**Bargersville** (town) Johnson County
92	7.9	**Brownstown** (town) Jackson County
92	7.9	**Melody Hill** (CDP) Vanderburgh County
92	7.9	**Mount Vernon** (city) Posey County
96	8.0	**Georgetown** (town) Floyd County
96	8.0	**Huntingburg** (city) Dubois County
98	8.1	**Anderson** (city) Madison County
98	8.1	**Charlestown** (city) Clark County
98	8.1	**McCordsville** (town) Hancock County
101	8.2	**Shorewood Forest** (CDP) Porter County
101	8.2	**Whiteland** (town) Johnson County
103	8.3	**East Chicago** (city) Lake County
103	8.3	**Porter** (town) Porter County
105	8.4	**Lakes of the Four Seasons** (CDP) Lake County
105	8.4	**North Manchester** (town) Wabash County
107	8.5	**New Albany** (city) Floyd County
108	8.6	**Clinton** (city) Vermillion County
108	8.6	**Goshen** (city) Elkhart County
108	8.6	**La Porte** (city) LaPorte County
111	8.7	**Brookville** (town) Franklin County
111	8.7	**Huntington** (city) Huntington County
111	8.7	**Michigan City** (city) LaPorte County
114	9.0	**Crown Point** (city) Lake County
114	9.0	**North Vernon** (city) Jennings County
116	9.1	**Hobart** (city) Lake County
116	9.1	**Saint John** (town) Lake County
116	9.1	**Winchester** (city) Randolph County
119	9.2	**Franklin** (city) Johnson County
120	9.3	**North Terre Haute** (CDP) Vigo County
121	9.4	**Highland** (town) Lake County
121	9.4	**Merrillville** (town) Lake County
121	9.4	**Portage** (city) Porter County
124	9.5	**Lebanon** (city) Boone County
125	9.6	**Crawfordsville** (city) Montgomery County
126	9.7	**Boonville** (city) Warrick County
126	9.7	**Griffith** (town) Lake County
128	9.8	**Leo-Cedarville** (town) Allen County
128	9.8	**Rochester** (city) Fulton County
130	9.9	**Frankfort** (city) Clinton County
130	9.9	**Peru** (city) Miami County
132	10.1	**Aurora** (city) Dearborn County
132	10.1	**Hartford City** (city) Blackford County
132	10.1	**Paoli** (town) Orange County
132	10.1	**Smithville-Sanders** (CDP) Monroe County
136	10.2	**Dyer** (town) Lake County
136	10.2	**Hammond** (city) Lake County
136	10.2	**Scottsburg** (city) Scott County
139	10.3	**Schererville** (town) Lake County
140	10.4	**Whiting** (city) Lake County
141	10.5	**Fort Branch** (town) Gibson County
141	10.5	**Greenfield** (city) Hancock County
141	10.5	**Shelbyville** (city) Shelby County
144	10.7	**Garrett** (city) DeKalb County
145	10.8	**Rensselaer** (city) Jasper County
146	10.9	**Bedford** (city) Lawrence County
146	10.9	**Bright** (CDP) Dearborn County
146	10.9	**Lawrenceburg** (city) Dearborn County
146	10.9	**Lowell** (town) Lake County
150	11.0	**Lawrence** (city) Marion County

Note: *This section ranks incorporated places and CDPs (Census Designated Places) with populations of 2,500 or more. Unincorporated postal areas were not considered. Please refer to the User Guide for additional information.*

Employment: Production, Transportation, and Material Moving Occupations

Top 150 Places Ranked in *Descending* Order

State Rank	Percent	Place
1	58.2	**Ligonier** (city) Noble County
2	45.2	**Butler** (city) DeKalb County
3	44.9	**Austin** (city) Scott County
4	44.1	**Lagrange** (town) LaGrange County
5	43.0	**Union City** (city) Randolph County
6	42.1	**Edinburgh** (town) Johnson County
7	41.4	**Kendallville** (city) Noble County
8	39.7	**Elkhart** (city) Elkhart County
9	39.0	**Bremen** (town) Marshall County
9	39.0	**Frankfort** (city) Clinton County
11	36.9	**Plymouth** (city) Marshall County
12	36.5	**Greensburg** (city) Decatur County
12	36.5	**Logansport** (city) Cass County
14	36.0	**Country Squire Lakes** (CDP) Jennings County
15	35.8	**Portland** (city) Jay County
16	34.0	**North Vernon** (city) Jennings County
17	31.9	**Garrett** (city) DeKalb County
18	31.2	**Hartford City** (city) Blackford County
19	30.7	**Decatur** (city) Adams County
20	30.6	**Nappanee** (city) Elkhart County
21	30.4	**Auburn** (city) DeKalb County
22	30.0	**Fort Branch** (town) Gibson County
22	30.0	**Tell City** (city) Perry County
24	29.9	**Goshen** (city) Elkhart County
25	29.5	**Elwood** (city) Madison County
25	29.5	**Knox** (city) Starke County
27	29.4	**Princeton** (city) Gibson County
28	29.3	**Huntingburg** (city) Dubois County
29	29.0	**Peru** (city) Miami County
30	28.9	**Huntington** (city) Huntington County
30	28.9	**Rushville** (city) Rush County
32	28.6	**Dunlap** (CDP) Elkhart County
33	27.8	**Madison** (city) Jefferson County
34	27.7	**Monticello** (city) White County
34	27.7	**Warsaw** (city) Kosciusko County
36	27.5	**Gas City** (city) Grant County
37	27.4	**Brownstown** (town) Jackson County
37	27.4	**Loogootee** (city) Martin County
39	27.3	**Vincennes** (city) Knox County
40	27.2	**Seymour** (city) Jackson County
41	27.1	**Rochester** (city) Fulton County
41	27.1	**Shelbyville** (city) Shelby County
43	27.0	**Paoli** (town) Orange County
43	27.0	**Washington** (city) Daviess County
45	26.9	**Greentown** (town) Howard County
46	26.5	**Winamac** (town) Pulaski County
47	26.3	**Connersville** (city) Fayette County
47	26.3	**Osceola** (town) Saint Joseph County
49	26.2	**Bluffton** (city) Wells County
49	26.2	**Scottsburg** (city) Scott County
51	25.8	**Syracuse** (town) Kosciusko County
52	25.7	**Winchester** (city) Randolph County
53	25.6	**Greencastle** (city) Putnam County
54	25.5	**Kokomo** (city) Howard County
54	25.5	**Salt Creek Commons** (CDP) Porter County
54	25.5	**Simonton Lake** (CDP) Elkhart County
57	25.4	**Attica** (city) Fountain County
57	25.4	**New Castle** (city) Henry County
59	25.1	**Delphi** (city) Carroll County
59	25.1	**East Chicago** (city) Lake County
61	25.0	**Roselawn** (CDP) Newton County
62	24.9	**Salem** (city) Washington County
63	24.8	**Crawfordsville** (city) Montgomery County
64	24.7	**Brazil** (city) Clay County
65	24.6	**La Porte** (city) LaPorte County
66	24.3	**Lake Station** (city) Lake County
67	24.2	**Angola** (city) Steuben County
68	24.1	**Whiting** (city) Lake County
69	24.0	**Berne** (city) Adams County
70	23.9	**Rensselaer** (city) Jasper County
71	23.8	**Chandler** (town) Warrick County
72	23.7	**Wabash** (city) Wabash County
73	23.6	**Lawrenceburg** (city) Dearborn County
74	23.2	**Bicknell** (city) Knox County
75	23.1	**Columbia City** (city) Whitley County
76	23.0	**Ossian** (town) Wells County
77	22.9	**Charlestown** (city) Clark County
78	22.8	**De Motte** (town) Jasper County
79	22.7	**Hammond** (city) Lake County
80	22.4	**Boonville** (city) Warrick County
81	22.3	**Mount Vernon** (city) Posey County
81	22.3	**New Haven** (city) Allen County
83	22.0	**Mooresville** (town) Morgan County
83	22.0	**North Terre Haute** (CDP) Vigo County
83	22.0	**Rockville** (town) Parke County
86	21.9	**Brookville** (town) Franklin County
86	21.9	**Richmond** (city) Wayne County
88	21.6	**Martinsville** (city) Morgan County
89	21.5	**Tipton** (city) Tipton County
90	21.4	**Westville** (town) LaPorte County
91	21.1	**Michigan City** (city) LaPorte County
92	20.9	**Lafayette** (city) Tippecanoe County
93	20.8	**Clinton** (city) Vermillion County
94	20.7	**Hebron** (town) Porter County
94	20.7	**Portage** (city) Porter County
96	20.4	**Jasper** (city) Dubois County
97	20.2	**Griffith** (town) Lake County
98	20.0	**Aurora** (city) Dearborn County
98	20.0	**Lowell** (town) Lake County
100	19.9	**Porter** (town) Porter County
101	19.8	**Evansville** (city) Vanderburgh County
102	19.7	**Jeffersonville** (city) Clark County
103	19.4	**Bedford** (city) Lawrence County
103	19.4	**South Bend** (city) Saint Joseph County
105	19.2	**Hanover** (town) Jefferson County
105	19.2	**Sullivan** (city) Sullivan County
107	19.1	**Marion** (city) Grant County
108	19.0	**Mishawaka** (city) Saint Joseph County
109	18.9	**Merrillville** (town) Lake County
110	18.8	**Cicero** (town) Hamilton County
111	18.7	**Linton** (city) Greene County
112	18.6	**Gary** (city) Lake County
113	18.5	**South Haven** (CDP) Porter County
114	18.4	**Beech Grove** (city) Marion County
115	18.3	**North Manchester** (town) Wabash County
116	18.2	**Centerville** (town) Wayne County
116	18.2	**Fort Wayne** (city) Allen County
118	18.0	**Anderson** (city) Madison County
118	18.0	**Fairmount** (town) Grant County
120	17.9	**Pittsboro** (town) Hendricks County
121	17.8	**New Albany** (city) Floyd County
122	17.7	**Clarksville** (town) Clark County
122	17.7	**Corydon** (town) Harrison County
124	17.5	**Hobart** (city) Lake County
124	17.5	**Speedway** (town) Marion County
126	17.2	**Lebanon** (city) Boone County
127	17.1	**Franklin** (city) Johnson County
128	17.0	**Highland** (CDP) Vanderburgh County
129	16.8	**Bright** (CDP) Dearborn County
130	16.6	**Dyer** (town) Lake County
130	16.6	**Ellettsville** (town) Monroe County
130	16.6	**New Whiteland** (town) Johnson County
133	16.2	**Highland** (town) Lake County
133	16.2	**Lakes of the Four Seasons** (CDP) Lake County
133	16.2	**Terre Haute** (city) Vigo County
136	16.0	**Columbus** (city) Bartholomew County
136	16.0	**Leo-Cedarville** (town) Allen County
138	15.9	**Sheridan** (town) Hamilton County
139	15.7	**Greenfield** (city) Hancock County
139	15.7	**Mitchell** (city) Lawrence County
141	15.4	**Bargersville** (town) Johnson County
142	15.1	**Alexandria** (city) Madison County
142	15.1	**Fortville** (town) Hancock County
142	15.1	**Indianapolis** (city) Marion County
145	14.7	**Batesville** (city) Ripley County
146	14.5	**Newburgh** (town) Warrick County
146	14.5	**Sellersburg** (town) Clark County
148	14.4	**Whiteland** (town) Johnson County
149	14.3	**Cumberland** (town) Marion County
150	13.9	**Crown Point** (city) Lake County

Note: *This section ranks incorporated places and CDPs (Census Designated Places) with populations of 2,500 or more. Unincorporated postal areas were not considered. Please refer to the User Guide for additional information.*

Employment: Production, Transportation, and Material Moving Occupations

Top 150 Places Ranked in *Ascending* Order

State Rank	Percent	Place
1	2.0	**McCordsville** (town) Hancock County
2	3.0	**Notre Dame** (CDP) Saint Joseph County
3	3.4	**Fishers** (city) Hamilton County
4	3.8	**Shorewood Forest** (CDP) Porter County
5	4.3	**West Lafayette** (city) Tippecanoe County
6	4.5	**Carmel** (city) Hamilton County
7	6.2	**Whitestown** (town) Boone County
7	6.2	**Zionsville** (town) Boone County
9	6.7	**Pendleton** (town) Madison County
10	7.2	**Westfield** (city) Hamilton County
11	7.6	**Noblesville** (city) Hamilton County
12	7.7	**Smithville-Sanders** (CDP) Monroe County
13	7.8	**Bloomington** (city) Monroe County
14	8.3	**Upland** (town) Grant County
15	8.4	**Winfield** (town) Lake County
16	9.0	**Munster** (town) Lake County
17	9.2	**Granger** (CDP) Saint Joseph County
18	9.3	**Avon** (town) Hendricks County
19	9.8	**Saint John** (town) Lake County
19	9.8	**Yorktown** (town) Delaware County
21	10.4	**Valparaiso** (city) Porter County
22	10.6	**Lawrence** (city) Marion County
23	11.2	**Heritage Lake** (CDP) Putnam County
24	11.3	**Brownsburg** (town) Hendricks County
25	11.5	**Danville** (town) Hendricks County
26	11.8	**Santa Claus** (town) Spencer County
27	12.0	**Winona Lake** (town) Kosciusko County
28	12.1	**Cedar Lake** (town) Lake County
29	12.2	**Greenwood** (city) Johnson County
30	12.3	**Chesterton** (town) Porter County
31	12.6	**Greendale** (city) Dearborn County
31	12.6	**Muncie** (city) Delaware County
33	12.9	**Hidden Valley** (CDP) Dearborn County
33	12.9	**Melody Hill** (CDP) Vanderburgh County
33	12.9	**Plainfield** (town) Hendricks County
36	13.4	**Schererville** (town) Lake County
37	13.6	**Huntertown** (town) Allen County
37	13.6	**Middlebury** (town) Elkhart County
39	13.7	**Georgetown** (town) Floyd County
40	13.9	**Crown Point** (city) Lake County
41	14.3	**Cumberland** (town) Marion County
42	14.4	**Whiteland** (town) Johnson County
43	14.5	**Newburgh** (town) Warrick County
43	14.5	**Sellersburg** (town) Clark County
45	14.7	**Batesville** (city) Ripley County
46	15.1	**Alexandria** (city) Madison County
46	15.1	**Fortville** (town) Hancock County
46	15.1	**Indianapolis** (city) Marion County
49	15.4	**Bargersville** (town) Johnson County
50	15.7	**Greenfield** (city) Hancock County
50	15.7	**Mitchell** (city) Lawrence County
52	15.9	**Sheridan** (town) Hamilton County
53	16.0	**Columbus** (city) Bartholomew County
53	16.0	**Leo-Cedarville** (town) Allen County
55	16.2	**Highland** (town) Lake County
55	16.2	**Lakes of the Four Seasons** (CDP) Lake County
55	16.2	**Terre Haute** (city) Vigo County
58	16.6	**Dyer** (town) Lake County
58	16.6	**Ellettsville** (town) Monroe County
58	16.6	**New Whiteland** (town) Johnson County
61	16.8	**Bright** (CDP) Dearborn County
62	17.0	**Highland** (CDP) Vanderburgh County
63	17.1	**Franklin** (city) Johnson County
64	17.2	**Lebanon** (city) Boone County
65	17.5	**Hobart** (city) Lake County
65	17.5	**Speedway** (town) Marion County
67	17.7	**Clarksville** (town) Clark County
67	17.7	**Corydon** (town) Harrison County
69	17.8	**New Albany** (city) Floyd County
70	17.9	**Pittsboro** (town) Hendricks County
71	18.0	**Anderson** (city) Madison County
71	18.0	**Fairmount** (town) Grant County
73	18.2	**Centerville** (town) Wayne County
73	18.2	**Fort Wayne** (city) Allen County
75	18.3	**North Manchester** (town) Wabash County
76	18.4	**Beech Grove** (city) Marion County
77	18.5	**South Haven** (CDP) Porter County
78	18.6	**Gary** (city) Lake County
79	18.7	**Linton** (city) Greene County
80	18.8	**Cicero** (town) Hamilton County
81	18.9	**Merrillville** (town) Lake County
82	19.0	**Mishawaka** (city) Saint Joseph County
83	19.1	**Marion** (city) Grant County
84	19.2	**Hanover** (town) Jefferson County
84	19.2	**Sullivan** (city) Sullivan County
86	19.4	**Bedford** (city) Lawrence County
86	19.4	**South Bend** (city) Saint Joseph County
88	19.7	**Jeffersonville** (city) Clark County
89	19.8	**Evansville** (city) Vanderburgh County
90	19.9	**Porter** (town) Porter County
91	20.0	**Aurora** (city) Dearborn County
91	20.0	**Lowell** (town) Lake County
93	20.2	**Griffith** (town) Lake County
94	20.4	**Jasper** (city) Dubois County
95	20.7	**Hebron** (town) Porter County
95	20.7	**Portage** (city) Porter County
97	20.8	**Clinton** (city) Vermillion County
98	20.9	**Lafayette** (city) Tippecanoe County
99	21.1	**Michigan City** (city) LaPorte County
100	21.4	**Westville** (town) LaPorte County
101	21.5	**Tipton** (city) Tipton County
102	21.6	**Martinsville** (city) Morgan County
103	21.9	**Brookville** (town) Franklin County
103	21.9	**Richmond** (city) Wayne County
105	22.0	**Mooresville** (town) Morgan County
105	22.0	**North Terre Haute** (CDP) Vigo County
105	22.0	**Rockville** (town) Parke County
108	22.3	**Mount Vernon** (city) Posey County
108	22.3	**New Haven** (city) Allen County
110	22.4	**Boonville** (city) Warrick County
111	22.7	**Hammond** (city) Lake County
112	22.8	**De Motte** (town) Jasper County
113	22.9	**Charlestown** (city) Clark County
114	23.0	**Ossian** (town) Wells County
115	23.1	**Columbia City** (city) Whitley County
116	23.2	**Bicknell** (city) Knox County
117	23.6	**Lawrenceburg** (city) Dearborn County
118	23.7	**Wabash** (city) Wabash County
119	23.8	**Chandler** (town) Warrick County
120	23.9	**Rensselaer** (city) Jasper County
121	24.0	**Berne** (city) Adams County
122	24.1	**Whiting** (city) Lake County
123	24.2	**Angola** (city) Steuben County
124	24.3	**Lake Station** (city) Lake County
125	24.6	**La Porte** (city) LaPorte County
126	24.7	**Brazil** (city) Clay County
127	24.8	**Crawfordsville** (city) Montgomery County
128	24.9	**Salem** (city) Washington County
129	25.0	**Roselawn** (CDP) Newton County
130	25.1	**Delphi** (city) Carroll County
130	25.1	**East Chicago** (city) Lake County
132	25.4	**Attica** (city) Fountain County
132	25.4	**New Castle** (city) Henry County
134	25.5	**Kokomo** (city) Howard County
134	25.5	**Salt Creek Commons** (CDP) Porter County
134	25.5	**Simonton Lake** (CDP) Elkhart County
137	25.6	**Greencastle** (city) Putnam County
138	25.7	**Winchester** (city) Randolph County
139	25.8	**Syracuse** (town) Kosciusko County
140	26.2	**Bluffton** (city) Wells County
140	26.2	**Scottsburg** (city) Scott County
142	26.3	**Connersville** (city) Fayette County
142	26.3	**Osceola** (town) Saint Joseph County
144	26.5	**Winamac** (town) Pulaski County
145	26.9	**Greentown** (town) Howard County
146	27.0	**Paoli** (town) Orange County
146	27.0	**Washington** (city) Daviess County
148	27.1	**Rochester** (city) Fulton County
148	27.1	**Shelbyville** (city) Shelby County
150	27.2	**Seymour** (city) Jackson County

Note: *This section ranks incorporated places and CDPs (Census Designated Places) with populations of 2,500 or more. Unincorporated postal areas were not considered. Please refer to the User Guide for additional information.*

Per Capita Income

Top 150 Places Ranked in *Descending* Order

State Rank	Dollars	Place
1	60,565	**Zionsville** (town) Boone County
2	55,796	**Carmel** (city) Hamilton County
3	46,619	**Fishers** (city) Hamilton County
4	45,816	**Smithville-Sanders** (CDP) Monroe County
5	45,236	**Hidden Valley** (CDP) Dearborn County
6	45,210	**Shorewood Forest** (CDP) Porter County
7	45,182	**Granger** (CDP) Saint Joseph County
8	42,503	**Saint John** (town) Lake County
9	40,173	**Dyer** (town) Lake County
10	39,915	**Munster** (town) Lake County
11	39,347	**Bargersville** (town) Johnson County
12	39,294	**McCordsville** (town) Hancock County
13	38,618	**Newburgh** (town) Warrick County
14	38,314	**Winfield** (town) Lake County
15	37,855	**Westfield** (city) Hamilton County
16	36,641	**Schererville** (town) Lake County
17	36,568	**Chesterton** (town) Porter County
18	34,913	**Avon** (town) Hendricks County
19	34,910	**Noblesville** (city) Hamilton County
20	33,764	**Lakes of the Four Seasons** (CDP) Lake County
21	33,726	**Melody Hill** (CDP) Vanderburgh County
22	33,659	**Porter** (town) Porter County
23	33,636	**Crown Point** (city) Lake County
24	33,228	**Santa Claus** (town) Spencer County
25	32,690	**Brownsburg** (town) Hendricks County
26	32,307	**Whiteland** (town) Johnson County
27	32,241	**Huntertown** (town) Allen County
28	31,993	**Jasper** (city) Dubois County
29	31,895	**Columbus** (city) Bartholomew County
30	31,880	**Heritage Lake** (CDP) Putnam County
31	31,815	**Cicero** (town) Hamilton County
32	31,646	**Yorktown** (town) Delaware County
33	31,371	**Highland** (town) Lake County
34	31,059	**Highland** (CDP) Vanderburgh County
35	30,271	**Cedar Lake** (town) Lake County
36	30,212	**Greendale** (city) Dearborn County
37	30,142	**Bright** (CDP) Dearborn County
38	30,117	**Pendleton** (town) Madison County
39	29,911	**Auburn** (city) DeKalb County
40	29,667	**Georgetown** (town) Floyd County
41	29,591	**Danville** (town) Hendricks County
42	29,511	**Mount Vernon** (city) Posey County
43	29,462	**Lebanon** (city) Boone County
44	29,211	**Batesville** (city) Ripley County
45	29,067	**Valparaiso** (city) Porter County
46	29,052	**Whitestown** (town) Boone County
47	28,814	**Cumberland** (town) Marion County
48	28,647	**Leo-Cedarville** (town) Allen County
49	28,471	**Sellersburg** (town) Clark County
50	28,404	**Middlebury** (town) Elkhart County
51	28,383	**Plainfield** (town) Hendricks County
52	28,333	**Pittsboro** (town) Hendricks County
53	28,078	**Greenwood** (city) Johnson County
54	27,704	**Simonton Lake** (CDP) Elkhart County
55	27,616	**Fortville** (town) Hancock County
56	27,550	**Hobart** (city) Lake County
57	27,430	**Griffith** (town) Lake County
58	27,335	**Fort Branch** (town) Gibson County
59	27,137	**Warsaw** (city) Kosciusko County
60	26,973	**Winona Lake** (town) Kosciusko County
61	26,860	**Ellettsville** (town) Monroe County
62	26,840	**Jeffersonville** (city) Clark County
63	26,749	**Merrillville** (town) Lake County
64	26,647	**Franklin** (city) Johnson County
65	26,644	**Corydon** (town) Harrison County
66	26,397	**Lawrence** (city) Marion County
67	26,232	**Indianapolis** (city) Marion County
68	26,025	**Greenfield** (city) Hancock County
69	25,652	**Tipton** (city) Tipton County
70	25,645	**Lowell** (town) Lake County
71	25,498	**Portage** (city) Porter County
72	25,310	**Berne** (city) Adams County
73	25,266	**New Albany** (city) Floyd County
74	25,154	**Columbia City** (city) Whitley County
75	25,066	**Fort Wayne** (city) Allen County
76	25,019	**Clarksville** (town) Clark County
77	24,929	**Greensburg** (city) Decatur County
78	24,876	**Wabash** (city) Wabash County
79	24,828	**Greentown** (town) Howard County
80	24,677	**Whiting** (city) Lake County
81	24,675	**Shelbyville** (city) Shelby County
82	24,667	**Dunlap** (CDP) Elkhart County
83	24,463	**Kokomo** (city) Howard County
84	24,368	**Salt Creek Commons** (CDP) Porter County
85	24,305	**Attica** (city) Fountain County
86	24,292	**Sheridan** (town) Hamilton County
87	24,222	**South Haven** (CDP) Porter County
88	24,128	**Madison** (city) Jefferson County
89	24,117	**Lafayette** (city) Tippecanoe County
90	24,105	**Mooresville** (town) Morgan County
91	23,846	**Ossian** (town) Wells County
92	23,694	**Syracuse** (town) Kosciusko County
93	23,680	**Osceola** (town) Saint Joseph County
94	23,627	**Bedford** (city) Lawrence County
95	23,558	**North Vernon** (city) Jennings County
96	23,343	**Lawrenceburg** (city) Dearborn County
97	23,255	**Rochester** (city) Fulton County
98	23,154	**Hebron** (town) Porter County
99	23,077	**Scottsburg** (city) Scott County
100	23,041	**Bluffton** (city) Wells County
101	22,972	**Winchester** (city) Randolph County
102	22,873	**Speedway** (town) Marion County
103	22,835	**Rensselaer** (city) Jasper County
104	22,827	**Centerville** (town) Wayne County
105	22,815	**Nappanee** (city) Elkhart County
106	22,685	**Princeton** (city) Gibson County
107	22,674	**Boonville** (city) Warrick County
108	22,623	**Loogootee** (city) Martin County
109	22,375	**Evansville** (city) Vanderburgh County
110	22,152	**Tell City** (city) Perry County
111	22,146	**Decatur** (city) Adams County
112	22,124	**Mishawaka** (city) Saint Joseph County
113	22,007	**De Motte** (town) Jasper County
114	21,972	**Bloomington** (city) Monroe County
115	21,942	**Seymour** (city) Jackson County
116	21,925	**Roselawn** (CDP) Newton County
117	21,910	**Huntingburg** (city) Dubois County
118	21,870	**Delphi** (city) Carroll County
119	21,808	**Charlestown** (city) Clark County
120	21,642	**New Whiteland** (town) Johnson County
121	21,604	**Aurora** (city) Dearborn County
122	21,556	**Ligonier** (city) Noble County
123	21,523	**Rushville** (city) Rush County
124	21,450	**Goshen** (city) Elkhart County
125	21,425	**Elwood** (city) Madison County
126	21,384	**Monticello** (city) White County
127	21,340	**Lagrange** (town) LaGrange County
128	21,336	**Alexandria** (city) Madison County
129	21,278	**New Haven** (city) Allen County
130	21,120	**Winamac** (town) Pulaski County
131	21,100	**South Bend** (city) Saint Joseph County
132	21,057	**Crawfordsville** (city) Montgomery County
133	21,043	**Chandler** (town) Warrick County
134	20,972	**Mitchell** (city) Lawrence County
135	20,960	**Kendallville** (city) Noble County
136	20,907	**Richmond** (city) Wayne County
137	20,896	**Bremen** (town) Marshall County
138	20,753	**Martinsville** (city) Morgan County
139	20,716	**Linton** (city) Greene County
140	20,515	**Angola** (city) Steuben County
141	20,470	**Upland** (town) Grant County
142	20,407	**Rockville** (town) Parke County
143	20,389	**Knox** (city) Starke County
144	20,388	**Beech Grove** (city) Marion County
145	20,337	**Hammond** (city) Lake County
146	20,322	**Huntington** (city) Huntington County
147	20,321	**Connersville** (city) Fayette County
148	20,300	**Washington** (city) Daviess County
149	20,279	**Michigan City** (city) LaPorte County
150	20,240	**Butler** (city) DeKalb County

Note: *This section ranks incorporated places and CDPs (Census Designated Places) with populations of 2,500 or more. Unincorporated postal areas were not considered. Please refer to the User Guide for additional information.*

Per Capita Income

Top 150 Places Ranked in *Ascending* Order

State Rank	Dollars	Place
1	5,995	**Notre Dame** (CDP) Saint Joseph County
2	9,439	**Westville** (town) LaPorte County
3	15,159	**East Chicago** (city) Lake County
4	15,278	**Country Squire Lakes** (CDP) Jennings County
5	15,433	**Union City** (city) Randolph County
6	15,915	**Austin** (city) Scott County
7	17,198	**Hanover** (town) Jefferson County
8	17,217	**Lake Station** (city) Lake County
9	17,392	**Gary** (city) Lake County
10	17,494	**Clinton** (city) Vermillion County
11	17,631	**Marion** (city) Grant County
12	17,709	**Plymouth** (city) Marshall County
13	18,035	**Bicknell** (city) Knox County
14	18,300	**Brownstown** (town) Jackson County
15	18,426	**Elkhart** (city) Elkhart County
16	18,442	**Logansport** (city) Cass County
17	18,553	**Portland** (city) Jay County
18	18,612	**Paoli** (town) Orange County
19	18,821	**North Terre Haute** (CDP) Vigo County
20	18,875	**Brazil** (city) Clay County
21	18,890	**Sullivan** (city) Sullivan County
22	18,891	**Muncie** (city) Delaware County
23	19,143	**Garrett** (city) DeKalb County
24	19,263	**Terre Haute** (city) Vigo County
25	19,421	**West Lafayette** (city) Tippecanoe County
26	19,529	**Vincennes** (city) Knox County
27	19,532	**Fairmount** (town) Grant County
28	19,602	**Hartford City** (city) Blackford County
29	19,689	**Greencastle** (city) Putnam County
30	19,727	**Salem** (city) Washington County
31	19,852	**Brookville** (town) Franklin County
32	19,905	**Peru** (city) Miami County
33	19,924	**North Manchester** (town) Wabash County
34	19,928	**Gas City** (city) Grant County
35	19,980	**La Porte** (city) LaPorte County
36	20,057	**Frankfort** (city) Clinton County
37	20,110	**New Castle** (city) Henry County
38	20,140	**Edinburgh** (town) Johnson County
39	20,207	**Anderson** (city) Madison County
40	20,240	**Butler** (city) DeKalb County
41	20,279	**Michigan City** (city) LaPorte County
42	20,300	**Washington** (city) Daviess County
43	20,321	**Connersville** (city) Fayette County
44	20,322	**Huntington** (city) Huntington County
45	20,337	**Hammond** (city) Lake County
46	20,388	**Beech Grove** (city) Marion County
47	20,389	**Knox** (city) Starke County
48	20,407	**Rockville** (town) Parke County
49	20,470	**Upland** (town) Grant County
50	20,515	**Angola** (city) Steuben County
51	20,716	**Linton** (city) Greene County
52	20,753	**Martinsville** (city) Morgan County
53	20,896	**Bremen** (town) Marshall County
54	20,907	**Richmond** (city) Wayne County
55	20,960	**Kendallville** (city) Noble County
56	20,972	**Mitchell** (city) Lawrence County
57	21,043	**Chandler** (town) Warrick County
58	21,057	**Crawfordsville** (city) Montgomery County
59	21,100	**South Bend** (city) Saint Joseph County
60	21,120	**Winamac** (town) Pulaski County
61	21,278	**New Haven** (city) Allen County
62	21,336	**Alexandria** (city) Madison County
63	21,340	**Lagrange** (town) LaGrange County
64	21,384	**Monticello** (city) White County
65	21,425	**Elwood** (city) Madison County
66	21,450	**Goshen** (city) Elkhart County
67	21,523	**Rushville** (city) Rush County
68	21,556	**Ligonier** (city) Noble County
69	21,604	**Aurora** (city) Dearborn County
70	21,642	**New Whiteland** (town) Johnson County
71	21,808	**Charlestown** (city) Clark County
72	21,870	**Delphi** (city) Carroll County
73	21,910	**Huntingburg** (city) Dubois County
74	21,925	**Roselawn** (CDP) Newton County
75	21,942	**Seymour** (city) Jackson County
76	21,972	**Bloomington** (city) Monroe County
77	22,007	**De Motte** (town) Jasper County
78	22,124	**Mishawaka** (city) Saint Joseph County
79	22,146	**Decatur** (city) Adams County
80	22,152	**Tell City** (city) Perry County
81	22,375	**Evansville** (city) Vanderburgh County
82	22,623	**Loogootee** (city) Martin County
83	22,674	**Boonville** (city) Warrick County
84	22,685	**Princeton** (city) Gibson County
85	22,815	**Nappanee** (city) Elkhart County
86	22,827	**Centerville** (town) Wayne County
87	22,835	**Rensselaer** (city) Jasper County
88	22,873	**Speedway** (town) Marion County
89	22,972	**Winchester** (city) Randolph County
90	23,041	**Bluffton** (city) Wells County
91	23,077	**Scottsburg** (city) Scott County
92	23,154	**Hebron** (town) Porter County
93	23,255	**Rochester** (city) Fulton County
94	23,343	**Lawrenceburg** (city) Dearborn County
95	23,558	**North Vernon** (city) Jennings County
96	23,627	**Bedford** (city) Lawrence County
97	23,680	**Osceola** (town) Saint Joseph County
98	23,694	**Syracuse** (town) Kosciusko County
99	23,846	**Ossian** (town) Wells County
100	24,105	**Mooresville** (town) Morgan County
101	24,117	**Lafayette** (city) Tippecanoe County
102	24,128	**Madison** (city) Jefferson County
103	24,222	**South Haven** (CDP) Porter County
104	24,292	**Sheridan** (town) Hamilton County
105	24,305	**Attica** (city) Fountain County
106	24,368	**Salt Creek Commons** (CDP) Porter County
107	24,463	**Kokomo** (city) Howard County
108	24,667	**Dunlap** (CDP) Elkhart County
109	24,675	**Shelbyville** (city) Shelby County
110	24,677	**Whiting** (city) Lake County
111	24,828	**Greentown** (town) Howard County
112	24,876	**Wabash** (city) Wabash County
113	24,929	**Greensburg** (city) Decatur County
114	25,019	**Clarksville** (town) Clark County
115	25,066	**Fort Wayne** (city) Allen County
116	25,154	**Columbia City** (city) Whitley County
117	25,266	**New Albany** (city) Floyd County
118	25,310	**Berne** (city) Adams County
119	25,498	**Portage** (city) Porter County
120	25,645	**Lowell** (town) Lake County
121	25,652	**Tipton** (city) Tipton County
122	26,025	**Greenfield** (city) Hancock County
123	26,232	**Indianapolis** (city) Marion County
124	26,397	**Lawrence** (city) Marion County
125	26,644	**Corydon** (town) Harrison County
126	26,647	**Franklin** (city) Johnson County
127	26,749	**Merrillville** (town) Lake County
128	26,840	**Jeffersonville** (city) Clark County
129	26,860	**Ellettsville** (town) Monroe County
130	26,973	**Winona Lake** (town) Kosciusko County
131	27,137	**Warsaw** (city) Kosciusko County
132	27,335	**Fort Branch** (town) Gibson County
133	27,430	**Griffith** (town) Lake County
134	27,550	**Hobart** (city) Lake County
135	27,616	**Fortville** (town) Hancock County
136	27,704	**Simonton Lake** (CDP) Elkhart County
137	28,078	**Greenwood** (city) Johnson County
138	28,333	**Pittsboro** (town) Hendricks County
139	28,383	**Plainfield** (town) Hendricks County
140	28,404	**Middlebury** (town) Elkhart County
141	28,471	**Sellersburg** (town) Clark County
142	28,647	**Leo-Cedarville** (town) Allen County
143	28,814	**Cumberland** (town) Marion County
144	29,052	**Whitestown** (town) Boone County
145	29,067	**Valparaiso** (city) Porter County
146	29,211	**Batesville** (city) Ripley County
147	29,462	**Lebanon** (city) Boone County
148	29,511	**Mount Vernon** (city) Posey County
149	29,591	**Danville** (town) Hendricks County
150	29,667	**Georgetown** (town) Floyd County

***Note:** This section ranks incorporated places and CDPs (Census Designated Places) with populations of 2,500 or more. Unincorporated postal areas were not considered. Please refer to the User Guide for additional information.*

Median Household Income

Top 150 Places Ranked in *Descending* Order

State Rank	Dollars	Place
1	127,152	**Zionsville** (town) Boone County
2	109,201	**Carmel** (city) Hamilton County
3	103,701	**Saint John** (town) Lake County
4	102,950	**Shorewood Forest** (CDP) Porter County
5	101,979	**Hidden Valley** (CDP) Dearborn County
6	101,469	**Fishers** (city) Hamilton County
7	100,863	**McCordsville** (town) Hancock County
8	100,182	**Granger** (CDP) Saint Joseph County
9	96,272	**Winfield** (town) Lake County
10	94,519	**Porter** (town) Porter County
11	89,906	**Lakes of the Four Seasons** (CDP) Lake County
12	89,144	**Westfield** (city) Hamilton County
13	85,433	**Avon** (town) Hendricks County
14	82,500	**Georgetown** (town) Floyd County
15	81,673	**Bargersville** (town) Johnson County
16	80,690	**Smithville-Sanders** (CDP) Monroe County
17	79,167	**Dyer** (town) Lake County
18	78,469	**Melody Hill** (CDP) Vanderburgh County
19	78,251	**Munster** (town) Lake County
20	75,474	**Santa Claus** (town) Spencer County
21	74,876	**Whitestown** (town) Boone County
22	74,803	**Leo-Cedarville** (town) Allen County
23	74,681	**Noblesville** (city) Hamilton County
24	74,575	**Huntertown** (town) Allen County
25	72,955	**Pittsboro** (town) Hendricks County
26	71,742	**Highland** (CDP) Vanderburgh County
27	71,583	**Salt Creek Commons** (CDP) Porter County
28	70,702	**Cedar Lake** (town) Lake County
29	70,455	**Whiteland** (town) Johnson County
30	69,471	**Crown Point** (city) Lake County
31	68,986	**Brownsburg** (town) Hendricks County
32	68,594	**Dunlap** (CDP) Elkhart County
33	68,166	**Schererville** (town) Lake County
34	67,816	**Newburgh** (town) Warrick County
35	67,031	**Middlebury** (town) Elkhart County
36	66,861	**Chesterton** (town) Porter County
37	66,701	**Cicero** (town) Hamilton County
38	66,146	**Bright** (CDP) Dearborn County
39	65,500	**Heritage Lake** (CDP) Putnam County
40	64,074	**Danville** (town) Hendricks County
41	62,574	**Lowell** (town) Lake County
42	62,500	**Pendleton** (town) Madison County
43	62,372	**Yorktown** (town) Delaware County
44	62,345	**Highland** (town) Lake County
45	62,121	**Plainfield** (town) Hendricks County
46	61,617	**Sellersburg** (town) Clark County
47	61,533	**Fortville** (town) Hancock County
48	61,025	**Cumberland** (town) Marion County
49	60,456	**Winona Lake** (town) Kosciusko County
50	60,381	**New Whiteland** (town) Johnson County
51	60,171	**Roselawn** (CDP) Newton County
52	59,818	**Ossian** (town) Wells County
53	59,188	**Simonton Lake** (CDP) Elkhart County
54	58,366	**Hobart** (city) Lake County
55	58,083	**Osceola** (town) Saint Joseph County
56	57,625	**Whiting** (city) Lake County
57	57,535	**Columbus** (city) Bartholomew County
58	57,500	**Upland** (town) Grant County
59	57,452	**Griffith** (town) Lake County
60	56,367	**Franklin** (city) Johnson County
61	56,330	**Merrillville** (town) Lake County
62	56,302	**Greendale** (city) Dearborn County
63	55,878	**Jasper** (city) Dubois County
64	55,274	**Greenwood** (city) Johnson County
65	54,566	**Portage** (city) Porter County
66	54,375	**Hebron** (town) Porter County
67	53,750	**Mount Vernon** (city) Posey County
68	53,344	**Batesville** (city) Ripley County
69	52,861	**Jeffersonville** (city) Clark County
70	52,513	**Mooresville** (town) Morgan County
71	52,507	**Valparaiso** (city) Porter County
72	52,130	**Greenfield** (city) Hancock County
73	50,919	**Ligonier** (city) Noble County
74	50,781	**Greensburg** (city) Decatur County
75	50,375	**Alexandria** (city) Madison County
76	50,107	**Lawrence** (city) Marion County
77	50,046	**Warsaw** (city) Kosciusko County
78	49,940	**Fort Branch** (town) Gibson County
79	49,901	**South Haven** (CDP) Porter County
80	49,160	**Chandler** (town) Warrick County
81	48,984	**Huntingburg** (city) Dubois County
82	48,657	**Ellettsville** (town) Monroe County
83	48,620	**Butler** (city) DeKalb County
84	48,071	**Shelbyville** (city) Shelby County
85	47,649	**New Haven** (city) Allen County
86	47,283	**Greentown** (town) Howard County
87	47,234	**Lebanon** (city) Boone County
88	47,129	**Auburn** (city) DeKalb County
89	46,611	**Columbia City** (city) Whitley County
90	46,602	**Sheridan** (town) Hamilton County
91	46,444	**Madison** (city) Jefferson County
92	46,442	**De Motte** (town) Jasper County
93	46,401	**Berne** (city) Adams County
94	46,310	**Tipton** (city) Tipton County
95	46,146	**Nappanee** (city) Elkhart County
96	46,090	**Scottsburg** (city) Scott County
97	46,055	**Goshen** (city) Elkhart County
98	46,029	**Greencastle** (city) Putnam County
99	45,853	**Fort Wayne** (city) Allen County
100	45,775	**North Manchester** (town) Wabash County
101	45,043	**Hanover** (town) Jefferson County
102	44,709	**Indianapolis** (city) Marion County
103	44,556	**Delphi** (city) Carroll County
104	44,458	**Bremen** (town) Marshall County
105	44,427	**Hammond** (city) Lake County
106	44,145	**Corydon** (town) Harrison County
107	44,094	**Wabash** (city) Wabash County
108	43,914	**New Albany** (city) Floyd County
109	43,894	**Lafayette** (city) Tippecanoe County
110	43,664	**Seymour** (city) Jackson County
111	43,636	**Syracuse** (town) Kosciusko County
112	43,563	**Loogootee** (city) Martin County
113	42,912	**Rensselaer** (city) Jasper County
114	42,885	**Edinburgh** (town) Johnson County
115	42,872	**Clarksville** (town) Clark County
116	42,829	**Gas City** (city) Grant County
117	42,824	**Fairmount** (town) Grant County
118	42,703	**Centerville** (town) Wayne County
119	42,450	**Charlestown** (city) Clark County
120	42,415	**Winchester** (city) Randolph County
121	42,302	**Huntington** (city) Huntington County
122	42,277	**Garrett** (city) DeKalb County
123	42,200	**North Vernon** (city) Jennings County
124	42,145	**Tell City** (city) Perry County
125	42,092	**Martinsville** (city) Morgan County
126	41,982	**Frankfort** (city) Clinton County
127	41,951	**Lagrange** (town) LaGrange County
128	41,930	**Lake Station** (city) Lake County
129	41,568	**Angola** (city) Steuben County
130	41,366	**Kokomo** (city) Howard County
131	41,340	**North Terre Haute** (CDP) Vigo County
131	41,340	**Princeton** (city) Gibson County
133	41,136	**Monticello** (city) White County
134	41,019	**Boonville** (city) Warrick County
135	41,004	**Decatur** (city) Adams County
136	40,899	**Crawfordsville** (city) Montgomery County
137	40,724	**Westville** (town) LaPorte County
138	40,451	**Rochester** (city) Fulton County
139	40,194	**Bluffton** (city) Wells County
140	40,154	**Rushville** (city) Rush County
141	40,109	**Speedway** (town) Marion County
142	40,076	**Bedford** (city) Lawrence County
143	39,821	**Mishawaka** (city) Saint Joseph County
144	39,317	**Linton** (city) Greene County
145	39,301	**Brownstown** (town) Jackson County
146	38,696	**Winamac** (town) Pulaski County
147	38,631	**Michigan City** (city) LaPorte County
148	38,598	**Mitchell** (city) Lawrence County
149	37,917	**Attica** (city) Fountain County
150	37,819	**Beech Grove** (city) Marion County

Note: *This section ranks incorporated places and CDPs (Census Designated Places) with populations of 2,500 or more. Unincorporated postal areas were not considered. Please refer to the User Guide for additional information.*

Median Household Income

Top 150 Places Ranked in *Ascending* Order

State Rank	Dollars	Place
1	15,625	**Notre Dame** (CDP) Saint Joseph County
2	29,293	**Gary** (city) Lake County
3	29,344	**Sullivan** (city) Sullivan County
4	30,205	**East Chicago** (city) Lake County
5	31,230	**West Lafayette** (city) Tippecanoe County
6	31,587	**Union City** (city) Randolph County
7	32,296	**Brookville** (town) Franklin County
8	32,372	**Muncie** (city) Delaware County
9	32,472	**Country Squire Lakes** (CDP) Jennings County
10	32,879	**Marion** (city) Grant County
11	33,172	**Bloomington** (city) Monroe County
12	33,381	**Richmond** (city) Wayne County
13	33,577	**Clinton** (city) Vermillion County
14	33,709	**Knox** (city) Starke County
15	33,779	**Paoli** (town) Orange County
16	33,902	**Connersville** (city) Fayette County
17	34,483	**Salem** (city) Washington County
18	34,693	**Anderson** (city) Madison County
19	34,746	**Terre Haute** (city) Vigo County
20	34,920	**Austin** (city) Scott County
21	34,991	**Peru** (city) Miami County
22	35,042	**Brazil** (city) Clay County
23	35,603	**Logansport** (city) Cass County
24	35,713	**Plymouth** (city) Marshall County
25	35,919	**Portland** (city) Jay County
26	36,136	**Hartford City** (city) Blackford County
27	36,342	**Elwood** (city) Madison County
28	36,375	**Rockville** (town) Parke County
29	36,411	**Washington** (city) Daviess County
30	36,655	**New Castle** (city) Henry County
31	36,724	**Vincennes** (city) Knox County
32	36,734	**La Porte** (city) LaPorte County
33	36,956	**Evansville** (city) Vanderburgh County
34	37,045	**Bicknell** (city) Knox County
35	37,121	**Elkhart** (city) Elkhart County
36	37,123	**Lawrenceburg** (city) Dearborn County
37	37,232	**Kendallville** (city) Noble County
38	37,441	**South Bend** (city) Saint Joseph County
39	37,808	**Aurora** (city) Dearborn County
40	37,819	**Beech Grove** (city) Marion County
41	37,917	**Attica** (city) Fountain County
42	38,598	**Mitchell** (city) Lawrence County
43	38,631	**Michigan City** (city) LaPorte County
44	38,696	**Winamac** (town) Pulaski County
45	39,301	**Brownstown** (town) Jackson County
46	39,317	**Linton** (city) Greene County
47	39,821	**Mishawaka** (city) Saint Joseph County
48	40,076	**Bedford** (city) Lawrence County
49	40,109	**Speedway** (town) Marion County
50	40,154	**Rushville** (city) Rush County
51	40,194	**Bluffton** (city) Wells County
52	40,451	**Rochester** (city) Fulton County
53	40,724	**Westville** (town) LaPorte County
54	40,899	**Crawfordsville** (city) Montgomery County
55	41,004	**Decatur** (city) Adams County
56	41,019	**Boonville** (city) Warrick County
57	41,136	**Monticello** (city) White County
58	41,340	**North Terre Haute** (CDP) Vigo County
58	41,340	**Princeton** (city) Gibson County
60	41,366	**Kokomo** (city) Howard County
61	41,568	**Angola** (city) Steuben County
62	41,930	**Lake Station** (city) Lake County
63	41,951	**Lagrange** (town) LaGrange County
64	41,982	**Frankfort** (city) Clinton County
65	42,092	**Martinsville** (city) Morgan County
66	42,145	**Tell City** (city) Perry County
67	42,200	**North Vernon** (city) Jennings County
68	42,277	**Garrett** (city) DeKalb County
69	42,302	**Huntington** (city) Huntington County
70	42,415	**Winchester** (city) Randolph County
71	42,450	**Charlestown** (city) Clark County
72	42,703	**Centerville** (town) Wayne County
73	42,824	**Fairmount** (town) Grant County
74	42,829	**Gas City** (city) Grant County
75	42,872	**Clarksville** (town) Clark County
76	42,885	**Edinburgh** (town) Johnson County
77	42,912	**Rensselaer** (city) Jasper County
78	43,563	**Loogootee** (city) Martin County
79	43,636	**Syracuse** (town) Kosciusko County
80	43,664	**Seymour** (city) Jackson County
81	43,894	**Lafayette** (city) Tippecanoe County
82	43,914	**New Albany** (city) Floyd County
83	44,094	**Wabash** (city) Wabash County
84	44,145	**Corydon** (town) Harrison County
85	44,427	**Hammond** (city) Lake County
86	44,458	**Bremen** (town) Marshall County
87	44,556	**Delphi** (city) Carroll County
88	44,709	**Indianapolis** (city) Marion County
89	45,043	**Hanover** (town) Jefferson County
90	45,775	**North Manchester** (town) Wabash County
91	45,853	**Fort Wayne** (city) Allen County
92	46,029	**Greencastle** (city) Putnam County
93	46,055	**Goshen** (city) Elkhart County
94	46,090	**Scottsburg** (city) Scott County
95	46,146	**Nappanee** (city) Elkhart County
96	46,310	**Tipton** (city) Tipton County
97	46,401	**Berne** (city) Adams County
98	46,442	**De Motte** (town) Jasper County
99	46,444	**Madison** (city) Jefferson County
100	46,602	**Sheridan** (town) Hamilton County
101	46,611	**Columbia City** (city) Whitley County
102	47,129	**Auburn** (city) DeKalb County
103	47,234	**Lebanon** (city) Boone County
104	47,283	**Greentown** (town) Howard County
105	47,649	**New Haven** (city) Allen County
106	48,071	**Shelbyville** (city) Shelby County
107	48,620	**Butler** (city) DeKalb County
108	48,657	**Ellettsville** (town) Monroe County
109	48,984	**Huntingburg** (city) Dubois County
110	49,160	**Chandler** (town) Warrick County
111	49,901	**South Haven** (CDP) Porter County
112	49,940	**Fort Branch** (town) Gibson County
113	50,046	**Warsaw** (city) Kosciusko County
114	50,107	**Lawrence** (city) Marion County
115	50,375	**Alexandria** (city) Madison County
116	50,781	**Greensburg** (city) Decatur County
117	50,919	**Ligonier** (city) Noble County
118	52,130	**Greenfield** (city) Hancock County
119	52,507	**Valparaiso** (city) Porter County
120	52,513	**Mooresville** (town) Morgan County
121	52,861	**Jeffersonville** (city) Clark County
122	53,344	**Batesville** (city) Ripley County
123	53,750	**Mount Vernon** (city) Posey County
124	54,375	**Hebron** (town) Porter County
125	54,566	**Portage** (city) Porter County
126	55,274	**Greenwood** (city) Johnson County
127	55,878	**Jasper** (city) Dubois County
128	56,302	**Greendale** (city) Dearborn County
129	56,330	**Merrillville** (town) Lake County
130	56,367	**Franklin** (city) Johnson County
131	57,452	**Griffith** (town) Lake County
132	57,500	**Upland** (town) Grant County
133	57,535	**Columbus** (city) Bartholomew County
134	57,625	**Whiting** (city) Lake County
135	58,083	**Osceola** (town) Saint Joseph County
136	58,366	**Hobart** (city) Lake County
137	59,188	**Simonton Lake** (CDP) Elkhart County
138	59,818	**Ossian** (town) Wells County
139	60,171	**Roselawn** (CDP) Newton County
140	60,381	**New Whiteland** (town) Johnson County
141	60,456	**Winona Lake** (town) Kosciusko County
142	61,025	**Cumberland** (town) Marion County
143	61,533	**Fortville** (town) Hancock County
144	61,617	**Sellersburg** (town) Clark County
145	62,121	**Plainfield** (town) Hendricks County
146	62,345	**Highland** (town) Lake County
147	62,372	**Yorktown** (town) Delaware County
148	62,500	**Pendleton** (town) Madison County
149	62,574	**Lowell** (town) Lake County
150	64,074	**Danville** (town) Hendricks County

Note: *This section ranks incorporated places and CDPs (Census Designated Places) with populations of 2,500 or more. Unincorporated postal areas were not considered. Please refer to the User Guide for additional information.*

Average Household Income

Top 150 Places Ranked in *Descending* Order

State Rank	Dollars	Place
1	169,680	**Zionsville** (town) Boone County
2	147,771	**Carmel** (city) Hamilton County
3	137,748	**Hidden Valley** (CDP) Dearborn County
4	131,022	**Granger** (CDP) Saint Joseph County
5	128,847	**Fishers** (city) Hamilton County
6	121,622	**Saint John** (town) Lake County
7	117,726	**Winfield** (town) Lake County
8	117,556	**Shorewood Forest** (CDP) Porter County
9	111,002	**McCordsville** (town) Hancock County
10	110,158	**Bargersville** (town) Johnson County
11	108,176	**Westfield** (city) Hamilton County
12	104,417	**Dyer** (town) Lake County
13	103,690	**Porter** (town) Porter County
14	102,764	**Smithville-Sanders** (CDP) Monroe County
15	100,558	**Munster** (town) Lake County
16	98,463	**Avon** (town) Hendricks County
17	93,070	**Noblesville** (city) Hamilton County
18	92,194	**Chesterton** (town) Porter County
19	91,926	**Lakes of the Four Seasons** (CDP) Lake County
20	91,876	**Huntertown** (town) Allen County
21	90,899	**Santa Claus** (town) Spencer County
22	90,340	**Whiteland** (town) Johnson County
23	89,991	**Newburgh** (town) Warrick County
24	89,719	**Middlebury** (town) Elkhart County
25	89,007	**Schererville** (town) Lake County
26	88,421	**Georgetown** (town) Floyd County
27	88,179	**Melody Hill** (CDP) Vanderburgh County
28	86,960	**Brownsburg** (town) Hendricks County
29	86,595	**Leo-Cedarville** (town) Allen County
30	85,980	**Highland** (CDP) Vanderburgh County
31	85,043	**Cedar Lake** (town) Lake County
32	84,875	**Crown Point** (city) Lake County
33	81,702	**Pittsboro** (town) Hendricks County
34	81,234	**Heritage Lake** (CDP) Putnam County
35	81,047	**Whitestown** (town) Boone County
36	80,524	**Yorktown** (town) Delaware County
37	79,700	**Salt Creek Commons** (CDP) Porter County
38	78,572	**Bright** (CDP) Dearborn County
39	77,946	**Jasper** (city) Dubois County
40	77,192	**Upland** (town) Grant County
41	76,773	**Cicero** (town) Hamilton County
42	76,663	**Danville** (town) Hendricks County
43	76,424	**Cumberland** (town) Marion County
44	76,343	**Columbus** (city) Bartholomew County
45	75,526	**Sellersburg** (town) Clark County
46	75,217	**Winona Lake** (town) Kosciusko County
47	73,803	**Highland** (town) Lake County
48	73,581	**Plainfield** (town) Hendricks County
49	73,233	**Dunlap** (CDP) Elkhart County
50	71,869	**Pendleton** (town) Madison County
51	71,440	**Valparaiso** (city) Porter County
52	71,313	**Simonton Lake** (CDP) Elkhart County
53	70,662	**Lowell** (town) Lake County
54	70,416	**Greenwood** (city) Johnson County
55	69,730	**Batesville** (city) Ripley County
56	69,482	**Fort Branch** (town) Gibson County
57	69,317	**Greendale** (city) Dearborn County
58	68,950	**Mount Vernon** (city) Posey County
59	68,836	**Hobart** (city) Lake County
60	68,466	**Warsaw** (city) Kosciusko County
61	68,262	**Auburn** (city) DeKalb County
62	67,944	**Whiting** (city) Lake County
63	67,641	**Franklin** (city) Johnson County
64	67,290	**Griffith** (town) Lake County
65	66,598	**Fortville** (town) Hancock County
66	66,291	**Lawrence** (city) Marion County
67	65,359	**Lebanon** (city) Boone County
68	65,178	**Merrillville** (town) Lake County
69	65,161	**Jeffersonville** (city) Clark County
70	65,121	**Osceola** (town) Saint Joseph County
71	64,349	**Roselawn** (CDP) Newton County
72	63,830	**Hebron** (town) Porter County
73	63,698	**Indianapolis** (city) Marion County
74	63,385	**Ossian** (town) Wells County
75	63,023	**Ligonier** (city) Noble County
76	62,924	**Portage** (city) Porter County
77	62,629	**Huntingburg** (city) Dubois County
78	61,682	**South Haven** (CDP) Porter County
79	61,650	**Ellettsville** (town) Monroe County
80	60,942	**Fort Wayne** (city) Allen County
81	60,664	**Greenfield** (city) Hancock County
82	59,757	**Shelbyville** (city) Shelby County
83	59,595	**Tipton** (city) Tipton County
84	59,574	**Berne** (city) Adams County
85	59,478	**Greensburg** (city) Decatur County
86	59,307	**Greentown** (town) Howard County
87	59,259	**West Lafayette** (city) Tippecanoe County
88	59,141	**Nappanee** (city) Elkhart County
89	58,716	**Sheridan** (town) Hamilton County
90	58,373	**Greencastle** (city) Putnam County
91	58,181	**New Whiteland** (town) Johnson County
92	58,076	**Mooresville** (town) Morgan County
93	57,702	**Scottsburg** (city) Scott County
94	57,103	**North Vernon** (city) Jennings County
95	56,665	**Princeton** (city) Gibson County
96	56,574	**Madison** (city) Jefferson County
97	56,373	**Chandler** (town) Warrick County
98	56,220	**Centerville** (town) Wayne County
99	56,147	**New Albany** (city) Floyd County
100	56,062	**Columbia City** (city) Whitley County
101	56,054	**Butler** (city) DeKalb County
102	55,890	**Charlestown** (city) Clark County
103	55,750	**Corydon** (town) Harrison County
104	55,393	**Winchester** (city) Randolph County
105	55,375	**Goshen** (city) Elkhart County
106	55,348	**Wabash** (city) Wabash County
107	55,147	**Kokomo** (city) Howard County
108	55,113	**Bloomington** (city) Monroe County
109	55,058	**Clarksville** (town) Clark County
110	54,725	**Aurora** (city) Dearborn County
111	54,570	**Attica** (city) Fountain County
112	54,473	**Lafayette** (city) Tippecanoe County
113	54,413	**New Haven** (city) Allen County
114	54,387	**Hanover** (town) Jefferson County
115	54,230	**Rensselaer** (city) Jasper County
116	54,217	**Angola** (city) Steuben County
117	54,057	**Syracuse** (town) Kosciusko County
118	53,814	**Westville** (town) LaPorte County
119	53,796	**Hammond** (city) Lake County
120	53,725	**Seymour** (city) Jackson County
121	53,657	**Boonville** (city) Warrick County
122	53,608	**Alexandria** (city) Madison County
123	53,443	**Frankfort** (city) Clinton County
124	53,438	**Delphi** (city) Carroll County
125	53,289	**Bedford** (city) Lawrence County
126	52,946	**Bluffton** (city) Wells County
127	52,434	**South Bend** (city) Saint Joseph County
128	52,077	**Bremen** (town) Marshall County
129	52,072	**Tell City** (city) Perry County
130	51,695	**Martinsville** (city) Morgan County
131	51,578	**Lawrenceburg** (city) Dearborn County
132	51,534	**Speedway** (town) Marion County
133	51,496	**Monticello** (city) White County
134	51,370	**Huntington** (city) Huntington County
135	51,324	**De Motte** (town) Jasper County
136	50,921	**Elwood** (city) Madison County
137	50,802	**Rushville** (city) Rush County
138	50,604	**Washington** (city) Daviess County
139	50,570	**Crawfordsville** (city) Montgomery County
140	50,533	**Lagrange** (town) LaGrange County
141	50,371	**Richmond** (city) Wayne County
142	50,350	**Evansville** (city) Vanderburgh County
143	50,312	**Mishawaka** (city) Saint Joseph County
144	50,217	**Fairmount** (town) Grant County
145	50,213	**Michigan City** (city) LaPorte County
146	50,090	**Lake Station** (city) Lake County
147	50,050	**North Manchester** (town) Wabash County
148	49,968	**Loogootee** (city) Martin County
149	49,965	**Decatur** (city) Adams County
150	49,726	**Rochester** (city) Fulton County

Note: *This section ranks incorporated places and CDPs (Census Designated Places) with populations of 2,500 or more. Unincorporated postal areas were not considered. Please refer to the User Guide for additional information.*

Average Household Income

Top 150 Places Ranked in *Ascending* Order

State Rank	Dollars	Place
1	18,193	**Notre Dame** (CDP) Saint Joseph County
2	38,000	**Union City** (city) Randolph County
3	38,568	**Clinton** (city) Vermillion County
4	40,367	**East Chicago** (city) Lake County
5	40,382	**Austin** (city) Scott County
6	40,423	**Sullivan** (city) Sullivan County
7	40,504	**Country Squire Lakes** (CDP) Jennings County
8	40,917	**Gary** (city) Lake County
9	42,330	**Portland** (city) Jay County
10	43,029	**Marion** (city) Grant County
11	43,359	**Salem** (city) Washington County
12	43,790	**Brookville** (town) Franklin County
13	43,888	**Paoli** (town) Orange County
14	43,931	**Bicknell** (city) Knox County
15	44,711	**Muncie** (city) Delaware County
16	45,069	**Plymouth** (city) Marshall County
17	45,378	**Rockville** (town) Parke County
18	45,852	**Brazil** (city) Clay County
19	45,965	**Anderson** (city) Madison County
20	46,187	**Vincennes** (city) Knox County
21	46,294	**Linton** (city) Greene County
22	46,665	**Logansport** (city) Cass County
23	46,698	**Brownstown** (town) Jackson County
24	46,700	**New Castle** (city) Henry County
25	46,776	**Peru** (city) Miami County
26	46,931	**Terre Haute** (city) Vigo County
27	46,945	**Hartford City** (city) Blackford County
28	46,951	**Connersville** (city) Fayette County
29	47,042	**Elkhart** (city) Elkhart County
30	47,133	**Kendallville** (city) Noble County
31	47,451	**La Porte** (city) LaPorte County
32	48,036	**Gas City** (city) Grant County
33	48,372	**Mitchell** (city) Lawrence County
34	48,393	**Garrett** (city) DeKalb County
35	48,825	**Knox** (city) Starke County
36	49,095	**North Terre Haute** (CDP) Vigo County
37	49,446	**Beech Grove** (city) Marion County
38	49,515	**Edinburgh** (town) Johnson County
39	49,708	**Winamac** (town) Pulaski County
40	49,726	**Rochester** (city) Fulton County
41	49,965	**Decatur** (city) Adams County
42	49,968	**Loogootee** (city) Martin County
43	50,050	**North Manchester** (town) Wabash County
44	50,090	**Lake Station** (city) Lake County
45	50,213	**Michigan City** (city) LaPorte County
46	50,217	**Fairmount** (town) Grant County
47	50,312	**Mishawaka** (city) Saint Joseph County
48	50,350	**Evansville** (city) Vanderburgh County
49	50,371	**Richmond** (city) Wayne County
50	50,533	**Lagrange** (town) LaGrange County
51	50,570	**Crawfordsville** (city) Montgomery County
52	50,604	**Washington** (city) Daviess County
53	50,802	**Rushville** (city) Rush County
54	50,921	**Elwood** (city) Madison County
55	51,324	**De Motte** (town) Jasper County
56	51,370	**Huntington** (city) Huntington County
57	51,496	**Monticello** (city) White County
58	51,534	**Speedway** (town) Marion County
59	51,578	**Lawrenceburg** (city) Dearborn County
60	51,695	**Martinsville** (city) Morgan County
61	52,072	**Tell City** (city) Perry County
62	52,077	**Bremen** (town) Marshall County
63	52,434	**South Bend** (city) Saint Joseph County
64	52,946	**Bluffton** (city) Wells County
65	53,289	**Bedford** (city) Lawrence County
66	53,438	**Delphi** (city) Carroll County
67	53,443	**Frankfort** (city) Clinton County
68	53,608	**Alexandria** (city) Madison County
69	53,657	**Boonville** (city) Warrick County
70	53,725	**Seymour** (city) Jackson County
71	53,796	**Hammond** (city) Lake County
72	53,814	**Westville** (town) LaPorte County
73	54,057	**Syracuse** (town) Kosciusko County
74	54,217	**Angola** (city) Steuben County
75	54,230	**Rensselaer** (city) Jasper County
76	54,387	**Hanover** (town) Jefferson County
77	54,413	**New Haven** (city) Allen County
78	54,473	**Lafayette** (city) Tippecanoe County
79	54,570	**Attica** (city) Fountain County
80	54,725	**Aurora** (city) Dearborn County
81	55,058	**Clarksville** (town) Clark County
82	55,113	**Bloomington** (city) Monroe County
83	55,147	**Kokomo** (city) Howard County
84	55,348	**Wabash** (city) Wabash County
85	55,375	**Goshen** (city) Elkhart County
86	55,393	**Winchester** (city) Randolph County
87	55,750	**Corydon** (town) Harrison County
88	55,890	**Charlestown** (city) Clark County
89	56,054	**Butler** (city) DeKalb County
90	56,062	**Columbia City** (city) Whitley County
91	56,147	**New Albany** (city) Floyd County
92	56,220	**Centerville** (town) Wayne County
93	56,373	**Chandler** (town) Warrick County
94	56,574	**Madison** (city) Jefferson County
95	56,665	**Princeton** (city) Gibson County
96	57,103	**North Vernon** (city) Jennings County
97	57,702	**Scottsburg** (city) Scott County
98	58,076	**Mooresville** (town) Morgan County
99	58,181	**New Whiteland** (town) Johnson County
100	58,373	**Greencastle** (city) Putnam County
101	58,716	**Sheridan** (town) Hamilton County
102	59,141	**Nappanee** (city) Elkhart County
103	59,259	**West Lafayette** (city) Tippecanoe County
104	59,307	**Greentown** (town) Howard County
105	59,478	**Greensburg** (city) Decatur County
106	59,574	**Berne** (city) Adams County
107	59,595	**Tipton** (city) Tipton County
108	59,757	**Shelbyville** (city) Shelby County
109	60,664	**Greenfield** (city) Hancock County
110	60,942	**Fort Wayne** (city) Allen County
111	61,650	**Ellettsville** (town) Monroe County
112	61,682	**South Haven** (CDP) Porter County
113	62,629	**Huntingburg** (city) Dubois County
114	62,924	**Portage** (city) Porter County
115	63,023	**Ligonier** (city) Noble County
116	63,385	**Ossian** (town) Wells County
117	63,698	**Indianapolis** (city) Marion County
118	63,830	**Hebron** (town) Porter County
119	64,349	**Roselawn** (CDP) Newton County
120	65,121	**Osceola** (town) Saint Joseph County
121	65,161	**Jeffersonville** (city) Clark County
122	65,178	**Merrillville** (town) Lake County
123	65,359	**Lebanon** (city) Boone County
124	66,291	**Lawrence** (city) Marion County
125	66,598	**Fortville** (town) Hancock County
126	67,290	**Griffith** (town) Lake County
127	67,641	**Franklin** (city) Johnson County
128	67,944	**Whiting** (city) Lake County
129	68,262	**Auburn** (city) DeKalb County
130	68,466	**Warsaw** (city) Kosciusko County
131	68,836	**Hobart** (city) Lake County
132	68,950	**Mount Vernon** (city) Posey County
133	69,317	**Greendale** (city) Dearborn County
134	69,482	**Fort Branch** (town) Gibson County
135	69,730	**Batesville** (city) Ripley County
136	70,416	**Greenwood** (city) Johnson County
137	70,662	**Lowell** (town) Lake County
138	71,313	**Simonton Lake** (CDP) Elkhart County
139	71,440	**Valparaiso** (city) Porter County
140	71,869	**Pendleton** (town) Madison County
141	73,233	**Dunlap** (CDP) Elkhart County
142	73,581	**Plainfield** (town) Hendricks County
143	73,803	**Highland** (town) Lake County
144	75,217	**Winona Lake** (town) Kosciusko County
145	75,526	**Sellersburg** (town) Clark County
146	76,343	**Columbus** (city) Bartholomew County
147	76,424	**Cumberland** (town) Marion County
148	76,663	**Danville** (town) Hendricks County
149	76,773	**Cicero** (town) Hamilton County
150	77,192	**Upland** (town) Grant County

Note: *This section ranks incorporated places and CDPs (Census Designated Places) with populations of 2,500 or more. Unincorporated postal areas were not considered. Please refer to the User Guide for additional information.*

Households with Income of $100,000 or More

Top 150 Places Ranked in *Descending* Order

State Rank	Percent	Place
1	60.6	**Zionsville** (town) Boone County
2	54.7	**Carmel** (city) Hamilton County
3	53.4	**Saint John** (town) Lake County
4	52.8	**Shorewood Forest** (CDP) Porter County
5	52.0	**McCordsville** (town) Hancock County
6	51.1	**Hidden Valley** (CDP) Dearborn County
7	50.9	**Fishers** (city) Hamilton County
8	50.1	**Granger** (CDP) Saint Joseph County
9	48.4	**Winfield** (town) Lake County
10	45.4	**Porter** (town) Porter County
11	44.4	**Westfield** (city) Hamilton County
12	42.8	**Avon** (town) Hendricks County
13	40.2	**Lakes of the Four Seasons** (CDP) Lake County
14	38.6	**Bargersville** (town) Johnson County
15	38.3	**Leo-Cedarville** (town) Allen County
16	38.2	**Georgetown** (town) Floyd County
16	38.2	**Munster** (town) Lake County
18	37.3	**Dyer** (town) Lake County
18	37.3	**Middlebury** (town) Elkhart County
20	33.9	**Melody Hill** (CDP) Vanderburgh County
21	33.6	**Salt Creek Commons** (CDP) Porter County
22	33.1	**Smithville-Sanders** (CDP) Monroe County
23	33.0	**Noblesville** (city) Hamilton County
24	32.8	**Whiteland** (town) Johnson County
25	32.5	**Chesterton** (town) Porter County
25	32.5	**Schererville** (town) Lake County
27	32.0	**Santa Claus** (town) Spencer County
28	31.5	**Huntertown** (town) Allen County
29	31.0	**Brownsburg** (town) Hendricks County
30	30.3	**Crown Point** (city) Lake County
31	30.0	**Hebron** (town) Porter County
32	29.4	**Pittsboro** (town) Hendricks County
32	29.4	**Whitestown** (town) Boone County
34	28.2	**Bright** (CDP) Dearborn County
34	28.2	**Danville** (town) Hendricks County
36	27.7	**Cumberland** (town) Marion County
37	26.4	**Newburgh** (town) Warrick County
38	25.9	**Cedar Lake** (town) Lake County
38	25.9	**Winona Lake** (town) Kosciusko County
40	25.4	**Yorktown** (town) Delaware County
41	25.0	**Pendleton** (town) Madison County
41	25.0	**Plainfield** (town) Hendricks County
43	24.9	**Highland** (CDP) Vanderburgh County
43	24.9	**Whiting** (city) Lake County
45	24.8	**Highland** (town) Lake County
46	24.7	**Columbus** (city) Bartholomew County
47	24.4	**Heritage Lake** (CDP) Putnam County
48	24.1	**Cicero** (town) Hamilton County
49	23.1	**Mount Vernon** (city) Posey County
50	22.6	**Simonton Lake** (CDP) Elkhart County
51	22.5	**Franklin** (city) Johnson County
52	22.2	**Fortville** (town) Hancock County
53	22.0	**Lowell** (town) Lake County
54	21.7	**Griffith** (town) Lake County
55	21.5	**Sellersburg** (town) Clark County
56	21.1	**Valparaiso** (city) Porter County
57	21.0	**Lawrence** (city) Marion County
58	20.9	**Upland** (town) Grant County
59	20.8	**Scottsburg** (city) Scott County
60	20.7	**Hobart** (city) Lake County
61	20.4	**Greenwood** (city) Johnson County
62	20.2	**Batesville** (city) Ripley County
62	20.2	**Jasper** (city) Dubois County
64	20.1	**Dunlap** (CDP) Elkhart County
65	19.9	**Huntingburg** (city) Dubois County
66	19.2	**Portage** (city) Porter County
67	18.8	**West Lafayette** (city) Tippecanoe County
68	18.6	**Merrillville** (town) Lake County
69	18.2	**Fort Branch** (town) Gibson County
69	18.2	**Greendale** (city) Dearborn County
71	17.4	**South Haven** (CDP) Porter County
71	17.4	**Warsaw** (city) Kosciusko County
73	16.8	**Indianapolis** (city) Marion County
73	16.8	**Sheridan** (town) Hamilton County
75	16.7	**Roselawn** (CDP) Newton County
76	16.4	**Auburn** (city) DeKalb County
76	16.4	**Lebanon** (city) Boone County
76	16.4	**Madison** (city) Jefferson County
79	16.3	**Greenfield** (city) Hancock County
80	16.1	**Lawrenceburg** (city) Dearborn County
81	15.9	**Rensselaer** (city) Jasper County
82	15.8	**Jeffersonville** (city) Clark County
83	15.5	**Bloomington** (city) Monroe County
83	15.5	**Westville** (town) LaPorte County
85	15.4	**Delphi** (city) Carroll County
86	15.3	**Nappanee** (city) Elkhart County
86	15.3	**Shelbyville** (city) Shelby County
88	15.0	**Berne** (city) Adams County
88	15.0	**Ossian** (town) Wells County
90	14.6	**Charlestown** (city) Clark County
90	14.6	**Fort Wayne** (city) Allen County
92	14.1	**Mooresville** (town) Morgan County
93	14.0	**Greentown** (town) Howard County
94	13.8	**North Vernon** (city) Jennings County
94	13.8	**Osceola** (town) Saint Joseph County
96	13.6	**Ellettsville** (town) Monroe County
97	13.5	**Boonville** (city) Warrick County
98	13.4	**Corydon** (town) Harrison County
99	13.3	**New Albany** (city) Floyd County
99	13.3	**Rushville** (city) Rush County
101	13.1	**Greensburg** (city) Decatur County
102	13.0	**Centerville** (town) Wayne County
102	13.0	**Goshen** (city) Elkhart County
102	13.0	**Seymour** (city) Jackson County
102	13.0	**Washington** (city) Daviess County
106	12.8	**Attica** (city) Fountain County
106	12.8	**Kokomo** (city) Howard County
108	12.6	**Bremen** (town) Marshall County
109	12.2	**Clarksville** (town) Clark County
109	12.2	**Rochester** (city) Fulton County
111	11.8	**Aurora** (city) Dearborn County
112	11.6	**Bluffton** (city) Wells County
112	11.6	**Butler** (city) DeKalb County
114	11.5	**Angola** (city) Steuben County
114	11.5	**Columbia City** (city) Whitley County
114	11.5	**Lafayette** (city) Tippecanoe County
114	11.5	**Tell City** (city) Perry County
118	11.4	**Hammond** (city) Lake County
118	11.4	**Sullivan** (city) Sullivan County
120	11.3	**Martinsville** (city) Morgan County
120	11.3	**Speedway** (town) Marion County
122	11.2	**Frankfort** (city) Clinton County
123	11.1	**Richmond** (city) Wayne County
124	11.0	**Beech Grove** (city) Marion County
125	10.9	**Loogootee** (city) Martin County
125	10.9	**South Bend** (city) Saint Joseph County
125	10.9	**Tipton** (city) Tipton County
128	10.7	**Lagrange** (town) LaGrange County
128	10.7	**New Haven** (city) Allen County
128	10.7	**Winamac** (town) Pulaski County
131	10.5	**Bedford** (city) Lawrence County
131	10.5	**Huntington** (city) Huntington County
133	10.3	**Crawfordsville** (city) Montgomery County
134	10.0	**Hanover** (town) Jefferson County
135	9.9	**Evansville** (city) Vanderburgh County
136	9.8	**Mishawaka** (city) Saint Joseph County
137	9.7	**Elwood** (city) Madison County
137	9.7	**Greencastle** (city) Putnam County
139	9.6	**Chandler** (town) Warrick County
139	9.6	**Ligonier** (city) Noble County
141	9.5	**Michigan City** (city) LaPorte County
142	9.4	**Muncie** (city) Delaware County
142	9.4	**Winchester** (city) Randolph County
144	9.2	**Wabash** (city) Wabash County
145	9.1	**Brazil** (city) Clay County
146	9.0	**Terre Haute** (city) Vigo County
147	8.8	**Paoli** (town) Orange County
148	8.7	**Lake Station** (city) Lake County
149	8.6	**Logansport** (city) Cass County
149	8.6	**Monticello** (city) White County

Note: *This section ranks incorporated places and CDPs (Census Designated Places) with populations of 2,500 or more. Unincorporated postal areas were not considered. Please refer to the User Guide for additional information.*

Households with Income of $100,000 or More

Top 150 Places Ranked in *Ascending* Order

State Rank	Percent	Place
1	0.0	**Notre Dame** (CDP) Saint Joseph County
2	1.8	**Union City** (city) Randolph County
3	3.1	**Garrett** (city) DeKalb County
4	4.5	**Clinton** (city) Vermillion County
5	4.6	**Austin** (city) Scott County
6	5.6	**Edinburgh** (town) Johnson County
6	5.6	**North Manchester** (town) Wabash County
8	6.0	**Rockville** (town) Parke County
9	6.2	**Portland** (city) Jay County
10	6.3	**East Chicago** (city) Lake County
10	6.3	**Knox** (city) Starke County
12	6.5	**Marion** (city) Grant County
13	6.6	**New Whiteland** (town) Johnson County
14	6.8	**Gary** (city) Lake County
14	6.8	**North Terre Haute** (CDP) Vigo County
16	6.9	**New Castle** (city) Henry County
17	7.0	**Brookville** (town) Franklin County
17	7.0	**Brownstown** (town) Jackson County
19	7.1	**Gas City** (city) Grant County
19	7.1	**Peru** (city) Miami County
21	7.2	**Plymouth** (city) Marshall County
22	7.4	**Vincennes** (city) Knox County
23	7.5	**La Porte** (city) LaPorte County
23	7.5	**Salem** (city) Washington County
25	7.6	**Fairmount** (town) Grant County
26	7.7	**Bicknell** (city) Knox County
26	7.7	**Mitchell** (city) Lawrence County
28	7.8	**Hartford City** (city) Blackford County
29	7.9	**Country Squire Lakes** (CDP) Jennings County
30	8.0	**Alexandria** (city) Madison County
31	8.1	**Kendallville** (city) Noble County
31	8.1	**Linton** (city) Greene County
31	8.1	**Syracuse** (town) Kosciusko County
34	8.2	**Elkhart** (city) Elkhart County
34	8.2	**Princeton** (city) Gibson County
36	8.3	**Anderson** (city) Madison County
36	8.3	**De Motte** (town) Jasper County
38	8.4	**Decatur** (city) Adams County
39	8.5	**Connersville** (city) Fayette County
40	8.6	**Logansport** (city) Cass County
40	8.6	**Monticello** (city) White County
42	8.7	**Lake Station** (city) Lake County
43	8.8	**Paoli** (town) Orange County
44	9.0	**Terre Haute** (city) Vigo County
45	9.1	**Brazil** (city) Clay County
46	9.2	**Wabash** (city) Wabash County
47	9.4	**Muncie** (city) Delaware County
47	9.4	**Winchester** (city) Randolph County
49	9.5	**Michigan City** (city) LaPorte County
50	9.6	**Chandler** (town) Warrick County
50	9.6	**Ligonier** (city) Noble County
52	9.7	**Elwood** (city) Madison County
52	9.7	**Greencastle** (city) Putnam County
54	9.8	**Mishawaka** (city) Saint Joseph County
55	9.9	**Evansville** (city) Vanderburgh County
56	10.0	**Hanover** (town) Jefferson County
57	10.3	**Crawfordsville** (city) Montgomery County
58	10.5	**Bedford** (city) Lawrence County
58	10.5	**Huntington** (city) Huntington County
60	10.7	**Lagrange** (town) LaGrange County
60	10.7	**New Haven** (city) Allen County
60	10.7	**Winamac** (town) Pulaski County
63	10.9	**Loogootee** (city) Martin County
63	10.9	**South Bend** (city) Saint Joseph County
63	10.9	**Tipton** (city) Tipton County
66	11.0	**Beech Grove** (city) Marion County
67	11.1	**Richmond** (city) Wayne County
68	11.2	**Frankfort** (city) Clinton County
69	11.3	**Martinsville** (city) Morgan County
69	11.3	**Speedway** (town) Marion County
71	11.4	**Hammond** (city) Lake County
71	11.4	**Sullivan** (city) Sullivan County
73	11.5	**Angola** (city) Steuben County
73	11.5	**Columbia City** (city) Whitley County
73	11.5	**Lafayette** (city) Tippecanoe County
73	11.5	**Tell City** (city) Perry County
77	11.6	**Bluffton** (city) Wells County
77	11.6	**Butler** (city) DeKalb County
79	11.8	**Aurora** (city) Dearborn County
80	12.2	**Clarksville** (town) Clark County
80	12.2	**Rochester** (city) Fulton County
82	12.6	**Bremen** (town) Marshall County
83	12.8	**Attica** (city) Fountain County
83	12.8	**Kokomo** (city) Howard County
85	13.0	**Centerville** (town) Wayne County
85	13.0	**Goshen** (city) Elkhart County
85	13.0	**Seymour** (city) Jackson County
85	13.0	**Washington** (city) Daviess County
89	13.1	**Greensburg** (city) Decatur County
90	13.3	**New Albany** (city) Floyd County
90	13.3	**Rushville** (city) Rush County
92	13.4	**Corydon** (town) Harrison County
93	13.5	**Boonville** (city) Warrick County
94	13.6	**Ellettsville** (town) Monroe County
95	13.8	**North Vernon** (city) Jennings County
95	13.8	**Osceola** (town) Saint Joseph County
97	14.0	**Greentown** (town) Howard County
98	14.1	**Mooresville** (town) Morgan County
99	14.6	**Charlestown** (city) Clark County
99	14.6	**Fort Wayne** (city) Allen County
101	15.0	**Berne** (city) Adams County
101	15.0	**Ossian** (town) Wells County
103	15.3	**Nappanee** (city) Elkhart County
103	15.3	**Shelbyville** (city) Shelby County
105	15.4	**Delphi** (city) Carroll County
106	15.5	**Bloomington** (city) Monroe County
106	15.5	**Westville** (town) LaPorte County
108	15.8	**Jeffersonville** (city) Clark County
109	15.9	**Rensselaer** (city) Jasper County
110	16.1	**Lawrenceburg** (city) Dearborn County
111	16.3	**Greenfield** (city) Hancock County
112	16.4	**Auburn** (city) DeKalb County
112	16.4	**Lebanon** (city) Boone County
112	16.4	**Madison** (city) Jefferson County
115	16.7	**Roselawn** (CDP) Newton County
116	16.8	**Indianapolis** (city) Marion County
116	16.8	**Sheridan** (town) Hamilton County
118	17.4	**South Haven** (CDP) Porter County
118	17.4	**Warsaw** (city) Kosciusko County
120	18.2	**Fort Branch** (town) Gibson County
120	18.2	**Greendale** (city) Dearborn County
122	18.6	**Merrillville** (town) Lake County
123	18.8	**West Lafayette** (city) Tippecanoe County
124	19.2	**Portage** (city) Porter County
125	19.9	**Huntingburg** (city) Dubois County
126	20.1	**Dunlap** (CDP) Elkhart County
127	20.2	**Batesville** (city) Ripley County
127	20.2	**Jasper** (city) Dubois County
129	20.4	**Greenwood** (city) Johnson County
130	20.7	**Hobart** (city) Lake County
131	20.8	**Scottsburg** (city) Scott County
132	20.9	**Upland** (town) Grant County
133	21.0	**Lawrence** (city) Marion County
134	21.1	**Valparaiso** (city) Porter County
135	21.5	**Sellersburg** (town) Clark County
136	21.7	**Griffith** (town) Lake County
137	22.0	**Lowell** (town) Lake County
138	22.2	**Fortville** (town) Hancock County
139	22.5	**Franklin** (city) Johnson County
140	22.6	**Simonton Lake** (CDP) Elkhart County
141	23.1	**Mount Vernon** (city) Posey County
142	24.1	**Cicero** (town) Hamilton County
143	24.4	**Heritage Lake** (CDP) Putnam County
144	24.7	**Columbus** (city) Bartholomew County
145	24.8	**Highland** (town) Lake County
146	24.9	**Highland** (CDP) Vanderburgh County
146	24.9	**Whiting** (city) Lake County
148	25.0	**Pendleton** (town) Madison County
148	25.0	**Plainfield** (town) Hendricks County
150	25.4	**Yorktown** (town) Delaware County

***Note:** This section ranks incorporated places and CDPs (Census Designated Places) with populations of 2,500 or more. Unincorporated postal areas were not considered. Please refer to the User Guide for additional information.*

Poverty Rate

Top 150 Places Ranked in *Descending* Order

State Rank	Percent	Place
1	80.2	**Notre Dame** (CDP) Saint Joseph County
2	41.1	**West Lafayette** (city) Tippecanoe County
3	37.5	**Bloomington** (city) Monroe County
4	35.8	**Gary** (city) Lake County
5	34.6	**East Chicago** (city) Lake County
6	32.5	**Country Squire Lakes** (CDP) Jennings County
7	29.9	**Muncie** (city) Delaware County
8	28.0	**Union City** (city) Randolph County
9	26.7	**Lawrenceburg** (city) Dearborn County
10	26.4	**Marion** (city) Grant County
11	26.0	**Terre Haute** (city) Vigo County
12	25.8	**Anderson** (city) Madison County
12	25.8	**Bicknell** (city) Knox County
12	25.8	**Westville** (town) LaPorte County
15	25.5	**Austin** (city) Scott County
15	25.5	**Michigan City** (city) LaPorte County
17	25.4	**Lake Station** (city) Lake County
17	25.4	**South Bend** (city) Saint Joseph County
19	24.8	**Elkhart** (city) Elkhart County
20	24.2	**Connersville** (city) Fayette County
21	23.9	**Plymouth** (city) Marshall County
22	23.7	**Brazil** (city) Clay County
23	23.6	**Alexandria** (city) Madison County
23	23.6	**Sullivan** (city) Sullivan County
25	23.4	**Richmond** (city) Wayne County
26	23.3	**Evansville** (city) Vanderburgh County
26	23.3	**New Castle** (city) Henry County
28	22.9	**Vincennes** (city) Knox County
29	22.7	**Peru** (city) Miami County
30	22.5	**Elwood** (city) Madison County
31	22.4	**La Porte** (city) LaPorte County
32	22.2	**Hammond** (city) Lake County
33	21.8	**Loogootee** (city) Martin County
34	21.6	**Martinsville** (city) Morgan County
35	21.5	**Knox** (city) Starke County
36	21.2	**Corydon** (town) Harrison County
37	21.1	**Beech Grove** (city) Marion County
38	21.0	**Speedway** (town) Marion County
39	20.4	**Centerville** (town) Wayne County
39	20.4	**Kokomo** (city) Howard County
39	20.4	**Salem** (city) Washington County
42	20.3	**Brookville** (town) Franklin County
43	20.2	**Clinton** (city) Vermillion County
43	20.2	**Decatur** (city) Adams County
45	20.1	**Garrett** (city) DeKalb County
45	20.1	**Indianapolis** (city) Marion County
47	20.0	**Tell City** (city) Perry County
48	19.9	**Portland** (city) Jay County
48	19.9	**Winchester** (city) Randolph County
50	19.8	**North Vernon** (city) Jennings County
51	19.7	**Seymour** (city) Jackson County
52	19.6	**Rockville** (town) Parke County
53	19.2	**Madison** (city) Jefferson County
54	19.1	**Attica** (city) Fountain County
55	19.0	**Kendallville** (city) Noble County
56	18.9	**Lafayette** (city) Tippecanoe County
57	18.8	**Mishawaka** (city) Saint Joseph County
58	18.6	**Chandler** (town) Warrick County
58	18.6	**Linton** (city) Greene County
58	18.6	**North Terre Haute** (CDP) Vigo County
61	18.5	**Fairmount** (town) Grant County
61	18.5	**Rushville** (city) Rush County
63	18.4	**Simonton Lake** (CDP) Elkhart County
63	18.4	**Washington** (city) Daviess County
65	18.3	**Logansport** (city) Cass County
65	18.3	**New Albany** (city) Floyd County
67	18.0	**Huntingburg** (city) Dubois County
68	17.9	**Bedford** (city) Lawrence County
68	17.9	**Edinburgh** (town) Johnson County
68	17.9	**Winamac** (town) Pulaski County
71	17.8	**Brownstown** (town) Jackson County
71	17.8	**Fort Wayne** (city) Allen County
71	17.8	**Hanover** (town) Jefferson County
74	17.6	**Bluffton** (city) Wells County
74	17.6	**Boonville** (city) Warrick County
74	17.6	**South Haven** (CDP) Porter County
77	17.4	**Wabash** (city) Wabash County
78	17.3	**Goshen** (city) Elkhart County
78	17.3	**Hebron** (town) Porter County
78	17.3	**Upland** (town) Grant County
81	17.2	**Portage** (city) Porter County
82	16.9	**Angola** (city) Steuben County
82	16.9	**Huntington** (city) Huntington County
84	16.6	**Hartford City** (city) Blackford County
85	16.5	**Gas City** (city) Grant County
85	16.5	**Rensselaer** (city) Jasper County
87	16.4	**Paoli** (town) Orange County
88	16.3	**Frankfort** (city) Clinton County
88	16.3	**Whiting** (city) Lake County
90	16.2	**Lagrange** (town) LaGrange County
90	16.2	**Shelbyville** (city) Shelby County
92	16.0	**Delphi** (city) Carroll County
93	15.8	**Lawrence** (city) Marion County
94	15.6	**Syracuse** (town) Kosciusko County
95	15.5	**Crawfordsville** (city) Montgomery County
96	15.4	**Scottsburg** (city) Scott County
97	15.3	**Ellettsville** (town) Monroe County
98	15.0	**Mount Vernon** (city) Posey County
98	15.0	**Princeton** (city) Gibson County
100	14.7	**Columbia City** (city) Whitley County
100	14.7	**Rochester** (city) Fulton County
102	14.6	**Charlestown** (city) Clark County
103	14.5	**Aurora** (city) Dearborn County
103	14.5	**Sheridan** (town) Hamilton County
105	14.3	**Berne** (city) Adams County
106	14.1	**Bremen** (town) Marshall County
106	14.1	**Mooresville** (town) Morgan County
106	14.1	**North Manchester** (town) Wabash County
109	13.8	**Greencastle** (city) Putnam County
110	13.6	**Valparaiso** (city) Porter County
111	13.3	**Tipton** (city) Tipton County
112	13.2	**Warsaw** (city) Kosciusko County
113	13.0	**Greentown** (town) Howard County
114	12.9	**Greenfield** (city) Hancock County
115	12.6	**Winona Lake** (town) Kosciusko County
116	12.5	**Butler** (city) DeKalb County
116	12.5	**Greensburg** (city) Decatur County
118	12.3	**New Haven** (city) Allen County
119	12.2	**Columbus** (city) Bartholomew County
119	12.2	**Greenwood** (city) Johnson County
121	12.0	**Mitchell** (city) Lawrence County
122	11.7	**Auburn** (city) DeKalb County
123	11.5	**Clarksville** (town) Clark County
124	11.1	**Hobart** (city) Lake County
125	11.0	**Jasper** (city) Dubois County
126	10.9	**Merrillville** (town) Lake County
127	10.4	**Franklin** (city) Johnson County
128	10.3	**Dunlap** (CDP) Elkhart County
129	10.2	**Jeffersonville** (city) Clark County
130	10.1	**Nappanee** (city) Elkhart County
131	10.0	**Whitestown** (town) Boone County
132	9.9	**Cedar Lake** (town) Lake County
133	9.8	**Batesville** (city) Ripley County
134	9.3	**Lebanon** (city) Boone County
134	9.3	**Monticello** (city) White County
136	9.2	**Fort Branch** (town) Gibson County
137	9.1	**Lowell** (town) Lake County
138	9.0	**Highland** (CDP) Vanderburgh County
139	8.9	**Griffith** (town) Lake County
139	8.9	**Smithville-Sanders** (CDP) Monroe County
141	8.6	**Plainfield** (town) Hendricks County
142	8.5	**Ligonier** (city) Noble County
142	8.5	**Porter** (town) Porter County
142	8.5	**Sellersburg** (town) Clark County
145	8.2	**Yorktown** (town) Delaware County
146	8.1	**Chesterton** (town) Porter County
147	8.0	**Cumberland** (town) Marion County
147	8.0	**De Motte** (town) Jasper County
149	7.8	**Crown Point** (city) Lake County
149	7.8	**Roselawn** (CDP) Newton County

***Note:** This section ranks incorporated places and CDPs (Census Designated Places) with populations of 2,500 or more. Unincorporated postal areas were not considered. Please refer to the User Guide for additional information.*

Poverty Rate

Top 150 Places Ranked in *Ascending* Order

State Rank	Percent	Place
1	1.0	**Leo-Cedarville** (town) Allen County
2	1.3	**Georgetown** (town) Floyd County
3	1.6	**McCordsville** (town) Hancock County
4	2.2	**Winfield** (town) Lake County
5	2.3	**Middlebury** (town) Elkhart County
6	2.6	**Zionsville** (town) Boone County
7	3.1	**Whiteland** (town) Johnson County
8	3.2	**Saint John** (town) Lake County
9	3.3	**Fishers** (city) Hamilton County
10	3.4	**Brownsburg** (town) Hendricks County
11	3.5	**Shorewood Forest** (CDP) Porter County
12	3.6	**Dyer** (town) Lake County
13	3.7	**Carmel** (city) Hamilton County
14	4.1	**Granger** (CDP) Saint Joseph County
15	4.5	**Schererville** (town) Lake County
16	4.8	**Munster** (town) Lake County
16	4.8	**Santa Claus** (town) Spencer County
18	5.0	**Fortville** (town) Hancock County
18	5.0	**New Whiteland** (town) Johnson County
20	5.2	**Bright** (CDP) Dearborn County
20	5.2	**Pittsboro** (town) Hendricks County
22	5.4	**Avon** (town) Hendricks County
22	5.4	**Huntertown** (town) Allen County
22	5.4	**Lakes of the Four Seasons** (CDP) Lake County
22	5.4	**Pendleton** (town) Madison County
26	5.6	**Hidden Valley** (CDP) Dearborn County
27	5.9	**Cicero** (town) Hamilton County
28	6.1	**Melody Hill** (CDP) Vanderburgh County
29	6.4	**Bargersville** (town) Johnson County
30	6.5	**Noblesville** (city) Hamilton County
31	6.7	**Osceola** (town) Saint Joseph County
31	6.7	**Ossian** (town) Wells County
31	6.7	**Westfield** (city) Hamilton County
34	7.0	**Greendale** (city) Dearborn County
35	7.2	**Danville** (town) Hendricks County
36	7.3	**Newburgh** (town) Warrick County
36	7.3	**Salt Creek Commons** (CDP) Porter County
38	7.5	**Heritage Lake** (CDP) Putnam County
39	7.7	**Highland** (town) Lake County
40	7.8	**Crown Point** (city) Lake County
40	7.8	**Roselawn** (CDP) Newton County
42	8.0	**Cumberland** (town) Marion County
42	8.0	**De Motte** (town) Jasper County
44	8.1	**Chesterton** (town) Porter County
45	8.2	**Yorktown** (town) Delaware County
46	8.5	**Ligonier** (city) Noble County
46	8.5	**Porter** (town) Porter County
46	8.5	**Sellersburg** (town) Clark County
49	8.6	**Plainfield** (town) Hendricks County
50	8.9	**Griffith** (town) Lake County
50	8.9	**Smithville-Sanders** (CDP) Monroe County
52	9.0	**Highland** (CDP) Vanderburgh County
53	9.1	**Lowell** (town) Lake County
54	9.2	**Fort Branch** (town) Gibson County
55	9.3	**Lebanon** (city) Boone County
55	9.3	**Monticello** (city) White County
57	9.8	**Batesville** (city) Ripley County
58	9.9	**Cedar Lake** (town) Lake County
59	10.0	**Whitestown** (town) Boone County
60	10.1	**Nappanee** (city) Elkhart County
61	10.2	**Jeffersonville** (city) Clark County
62	10.3	**Dunlap** (CDP) Elkhart County
63	10.4	**Franklin** (city) Johnson County
64	10.9	**Merrillville** (town) Lake County
65	11.0	**Jasper** (city) Dubois County
66	11.1	**Hobart** (city) Lake County
67	11.5	**Clarksville** (town) Clark County
68	11.7	**Auburn** (city) DeKalb County
69	12.0	**Mitchell** (city) Lawrence County
70	12.2	**Columbus** (city) Bartholomew County
70	12.2	**Greenwood** (city) Johnson County
72	12.3	**New Haven** (city) Allen County
73	12.5	**Butler** (city) DeKalb County
73	12.5	**Greensburg** (city) Decatur County
75	12.6	**Winona Lake** (town) Kosciusko County
76	12.9	**Greenfield** (city) Hancock County
77	13.0	**Greentown** (town) Howard County
78	13.2	**Warsaw** (city) Kosciusko County
79	13.3	**Tipton** (city) Tipton County
80	13.6	**Valparaiso** (city) Porter County
81	13.8	**Greencastle** (city) Putnam County
82	14.1	**Bremen** (town) Marshall County
82	14.1	**Mooresville** (town) Morgan County
82	14.1	**North Manchester** (town) Wabash County
85	14.3	**Berne** (city) Adams County
86	14.5	**Aurora** (city) Dearborn County
86	14.5	**Sheridan** (town) Hamilton County
88	14.6	**Charlestown** (city) Clark County
89	14.7	**Columbia City** (city) Whitley County
89	14.7	**Rochester** (city) Fulton County
91	15.0	**Mount Vernon** (city) Posey County
91	15.0	**Princeton** (city) Gibson County
93	15.3	**Ellettsville** (town) Monroe County
94	15.4	**Scottsburg** (city) Scott County
95	15.5	**Crawfordsville** (city) Montgomery County
96	15.6	**Syracuse** (town) Kosciusko County
97	15.8	**Lawrence** (city) Marion County
98	16.0	**Delphi** (city) Carroll County
99	16.2	**Lagrange** (town) LaGrange County
99	16.2	**Shelbyville** (city) Shelby County
101	16.3	**Frankfort** (city) Clinton County
101	16.3	**Whiting** (city) Lake County
103	16.4	**Paoli** (town) Orange County
104	16.5	**Gas City** (city) Grant County
104	16.5	**Rensselaer** (city) Jasper County
106	16.6	**Hartford City** (city) Blackford County
107	16.9	**Angola** (city) Steuben County
107	16.9	**Huntington** (city) Huntington County
109	17.2	**Portage** (city) Porter County
110	17.3	**Goshen** (city) Elkhart County
110	17.3	**Hebron** (town) Porter County
110	17.3	**Upland** (town) Grant County
113	17.4	**Wabash** (city) Wabash County
114	17.6	**Bluffton** (city) Wells County
114	17.6	**Boonville** (city) Warrick County
114	17.6	**South Haven** (CDP) Porter County
117	17.8	**Brownstown** (town) Jackson County
117	17.8	**Fort Wayne** (city) Allen County
117	17.8	**Hanover** (town) Jefferson County
120	17.9	**Bedford** (city) Lawrence County
120	17.9	**Edinburgh** (town) Johnson County
120	17.9	**Winamac** (town) Pulaski County
123	18.0	**Huntingburg** (city) Dubois County
124	18.3	**Logansport** (city) Cass County
124	18.3	**New Albany** (city) Floyd County
126	18.4	**Simonton Lake** (CDP) Elkhart County
126	18.4	**Washington** (city) Daviess County
128	18.5	**Fairmount** (town) Grant County
128	18.5	**Rushville** (city) Rush County
130	18.6	**Chandler** (town) Warrick County
130	18.6	**Linton** (city) Greene County
130	18.6	**North Terre Haute** (CDP) Vigo County
133	18.8	**Mishawaka** (city) Saint Joseph County
134	18.9	**Lafayette** (city) Tippecanoe County
135	19.0	**Kendallville** (city) Noble County
136	19.1	**Attica** (city) Fountain County
137	19.2	**Madison** (city) Jefferson County
138	19.6	**Rockville** (town) Parke County
139	19.7	**Seymour** (city) Jackson County
140	19.8	**North Vernon** (city) Jennings County
141	19.9	**Portland** (city) Jay County
141	19.9	**Winchester** (city) Randolph County
143	20.0	**Tell City** (city) Perry County
144	20.1	**Garrett** (city) DeKalb County
144	20.1	**Indianapolis** (city) Marion County
146	20.2	**Clinton** (city) Vermillion County
146	20.2	**Decatur** (city) Adams County
148	20.3	**Brookville** (town) Franklin County
149	20.4	**Centerville** (town) Wayne County
149	20.4	**Kokomo** (city) Howard County

Note: *This section ranks incorporated places and CDPs (Census Designated Places) with populations of 2,500 or more. Unincorporated postal areas were not considered. Please refer to the User Guide for additional information.*

Educational Attainment: High School Diploma or Higher

Top 150 Places Ranked in *Descending* Order

State Rank	Percent	Place
1	99.4	**McCordsville** (town) Hancock County
2	97.9	**Carmel** (city) Hamilton County
3	97.8	**Zionsville** (town) Boone County
4	97.5	**Fishers** (city) Hamilton County
5	97.3	**Greendale** (city) Dearborn County
6	96.7	**Georgetown** (town) Floyd County
7	96.6	**Granger** (CDP) Saint Joseph County
7	96.6	**Shorewood Forest** (CDP) Porter County
9	96.5	**Santa Claus** (town) Spencer County
10	96.3	**Huntertown** (town) Allen County
11	96.2	**Westfield** (city) Hamilton County
12	96.1	**Notre Dame** (CDP) Saint Joseph County
12	96.1	**Saint John** (town) Lake County
14	95.9	**Heritage Lake** (CDP) Putnam County
15	95.7	**Highland** (CDP) Vanderburgh County
16	95.6	**Pittsboro** (town) Hendricks County
17	95.4	**Hidden Valley** (CDP) Dearborn County
18	95.3	**Pendleton** (town) Madison County
18	95.3	**Upland** (town) Grant County
18	95.3	**Whiteland** (town) Johnson County
18	95.3	**Yorktown** (town) Delaware County
22	95.2	**Melody Hill** (CDP) Vanderburgh County
23	94.9	**Fortville** (town) Hancock County
24	94.8	**Lakes of the Four Seasons** (CDP) Lake County
24	94.8	**Whitestown** (town) Boone County
26	94.7	**Fort Branch** (town) Gibson County
26	94.7	**Munster** (town) Lake County
26	94.7	**Valparaiso** (city) Porter County
26	94.7	**West Lafayette** (city) Tippecanoe County
30	94.6	**Noblesville** (city) Hamilton County
31	94.3	**Dyer** (town) Lake County
32	94.1	**Newburgh** (town) Warrick County
33	94.0	**Winfield** (town) Lake County
34	93.6	**Danville** (town) Hendricks County
34	93.6	**Schererville** (town) Lake County
36	93.4	**Batesville** (city) Ripley County
37	93.2	**Chesterton** (town) Porter County
38	93.1	**Highland** (town) Lake County
38	93.1	**New Whiteland** (town) Johnson County
40	93.0	**Griffith** (town) Lake County
41	92.8	**Plainfield** (town) Hendricks County
42	92.7	**Bright** (CDP) Dearborn County
42	92.7	**Brownsburg** (town) Hendricks County
42	92.7	**Cicero** (town) Hamilton County
45	92.6	**Bloomington** (city) Monroe County
46	92.5	**Avon** (town) Hendricks County
47	92.0	**Berne** (city) Adams County
47	92.0	**Leo-Cedarville** (town) Allen County
47	92.0	**Merrillville** (town) Lake County
50	91.9	**Crown Point** (city) Lake County
50	91.9	**Porter** (town) Porter County
52	91.5	**Columbus** (city) Bartholomew County
53	91.3	**Smithville-Sanders** (CDP) Monroe County
54	91.2	**Auburn** (city) DeKalb County
55	91.1	**Greenfield** (city) Hancock County
55	91.1	**Greenwood** (city) Johnson County
55	91.1	**Lowell** (town) Lake County
58	90.8	**Bluffton** (city) Wells County
59	90.7	**Jeffersonville** (city) Clark County
60	90.3	**Cedar Lake** (town) Lake County
60	90.3	**Middlebury** (town) Elkhart County
62	90.1	**Chandler** (town) Warrick County
62	90.1	**Ossian** (town) Wells County
64	90.0	**Greensburg** (city) Decatur County
65	89.9	**Hobart** (city) Lake County
66	89.6	**Hebron** (town) Porter County
67	89.5	**Dunlap** (CDP) Elkhart County
68	89.4	**Madison** (city) Jefferson County
69	89.3	**Greentown** (town) Howard County
70	89.2	**Bargersville** (town) Johnson County
70	89.2	**Mount Vernon** (city) Posey County
72	88.8	**Sellersburg** (town) Clark County
73	88.7	**New Haven** (city) Allen County
73	88.7	**Tell City** (city) Perry County
75	88.6	**Fort Wayne** (city) Allen County
75	88.6	**Franklin** (city) Johnson County
75	88.6	**South Haven** (CDP) Porter County
75	88.6	**Winamac** (town) Pulaski County
79	88.4	**Hanover** (town) Jefferson County
79	88.4	**Jasper** (city) Dubois County
81	88.3	**Cumberland** (town) Marion County
81	88.3	**North Manchester** (town) Wabash County
81	88.3	**Portage** (city) Porter County
84	88.1	**Scottsburg** (city) Scott County
85	88.0	**Centerville** (town) Wayne County
85	88.0	**Greencastle** (city) Putnam County
85	88.0	**Mishawaka** (city) Saint Joseph County
88	87.9	**Princeton** (city) Gibson County
88	87.9	**Rochester** (city) Fulton County
90	87.6	**Lafayette** (city) Tippecanoe County
90	87.6	**Whiting** (city) Lake County
90	87.6	**Winona Lake** (town) Kosciusko County
93	87.5	**Bedford** (city) Lawrence County
93	87.5	**Columbia City** (city) Whitley County
95	87.4	**Brownstown** (town) Jackson County
95	87.4	**Fairmount** (town) Grant County
97	87.3	**Salt Creek Commons** (CDP) Porter County
97	87.3	**Tipton** (city) Tipton County
99	87.2	**Angola** (city) Steuben County
100	87.1	**Lebanon** (city) Boone County
100	87.1	**Speedway** (town) Marion County
102	87.0	**De Motte** (town) Jasper County
102	87.0	**Decatur** (city) Adams County
102	87.0	**Lawrenceburg** (city) Dearborn County
105	86.9	**Evansville** (city) Vanderburgh County
105	86.9	**Garrett** (city) DeKalb County
105	86.9	**Kokomo** (city) Howard County
105	86.9	**Nappanee** (city) Elkhart County
105	86.9	**North Terre Haute** (CDP) Vigo County
110	86.8	**Beech Grove** (city) Marion County
110	86.8	**Boonville** (city) Warrick County
110	86.8	**Gas City** (city) Grant County
110	86.8	**New Castle** (city) Henry County
114	86.7	**Brazil** (city) Clay County
114	86.7	**Muncie** (city) Delaware County
114	86.7	**Sheridan** (town) Hamilton County
117	86.6	**Loogootee** (city) Martin County
118	86.5	**Ellettsville** (town) Monroe County
118	86.5	**Huntington** (city) Huntington County
118	86.5	**Wabash** (city) Wabash County
121	86.2	**Clarksville** (town) Clark County
121	86.2	**Clinton** (city) Vermillion County
123	86.1	**Mooresville** (town) Morgan County
124	86.0	**Bremen** (town) Marshall County
124	86.0	**Lawrence** (city) Marion County
126	85.9	**Crawfordsville** (city) Montgomery County
127	85.8	**Rockville** (town) Parke County
128	85.6	**Michigan City** (city) LaPorte County
128	85.6	**Monticello** (city) White County
130	85.5	**Indianapolis** (city) Marion County
131	85.4	**Attica** (city) Fountain County
132	85.2	**Aurora** (city) Dearborn County
133	85.0	**Hartford City** (city) Blackford County
133	85.0	**Terre Haute** (city) Vigo County
135	84.9	**Gary** (city) Lake County
135	84.9	**La Porte** (city) LaPorte County
135	84.9	**Roselawn** (CDP) Newton County
135	84.9	**Warsaw** (city) Kosciusko County
139	84.8	**Anderson** (city) Madison County
140	84.7	**Seymour** (city) Jackson County
141	84.6	**New Albany** (city) Floyd County
142	84.3	**Edinburgh** (town) Johnson County
142	84.3	**Kendallville** (city) Noble County
142	84.3	**Osceola** (town) Saint Joseph County
145	84.1	**Corydon** (town) Harrison County
146	83.9	**Shelbyville** (city) Shelby County
147	83.8	**Winchester** (city) Randolph County
148	83.7	**Vincennes** (city) Knox County
149	83.4	**South Bend** (city) Saint Joseph County
150	83.2	**Peru** (city) Miami County

Note: *This section ranks incorporated places and CDPs (Census Designated Places) with populations of 2,500 or more. Unincorporated postal areas were not considered. Please refer to the User Guide for additional information.*

Educational Attainment: High School Diploma or Higher

Top 150 Places Ranked in *Ascending* Order

State Rank	Percent	Place
1	60.6	**Ligonier** (city) Noble County
2	71.0	**Country Squire Lakes** (CDP) Jennings County
3	72.1	**East Chicago** (city) Lake County
4	72.4	**Austin** (city) Scott County
5	74.2	**Logansport** (city) Cass County
6	75.9	**Union City** (city) Randolph County
7	76.1	**Elkhart** (city) Elkhart County
8	76.8	**Knox** (city) Starke County
9	76.9	**Goshen** (city) Elkhart County
10	78.2	**Connersville** (city) Fayette County
11	78.8	**Lagrange** (town) LaGrange County
11	78.8	**Lake Station** (city) Lake County
13	79.0	**Huntingburg** (city) Dubois County
14	79.1	**Portland** (city) Jay County
15	79.3	**Frankfort** (city) Clinton County
16	79.5	**Delphi** (city) Carroll County
17	79.6	**Washington** (city) Daviess County
18	79.7	**Paoli** (town) Orange County
19	79.8	**Salem** (city) Washington County
19	79.8	**Westville** (town) LaPorte County
21	80.3	**Hammond** (city) Lake County
22	80.6	**Plymouth** (city) Marshall County
23	81.3	**Butler** (city) DeKalb County
23	81.3	**Mitchell** (city) Lawrence County
23	81.3	**Syracuse** (town) Kosciusko County
26	81.6	**North Vernon** (city) Jennings County
27	81.7	**Rushville** (city) Rush County
27	81.7	**Sullivan** (city) Sullivan County
29	81.9	**Charlestown** (city) Clark County
30	82.3	**Alexandria** (city) Madison County
30	82.3	**Brookville** (town) Franklin County
30	82.3	**Martinsville** (city) Morgan County
33	82.6	**Richmond** (city) Wayne County
34	82.7	**Elwood** (city) Madison County
34	82.7	**Linton** (city) Greene County
36	82.8	**Rensselaer** (city) Jasper County
37	82.9	**Marion** (city) Grant County
38	83.1	**Bicknell** (city) Knox County
38	83.1	**Simonton Lake** (CDP) Elkhart County
40	83.2	**Peru** (city) Miami County
41	83.4	**South Bend** (city) Saint Joseph County
42	83.7	**Vincennes** (city) Knox County
43	83.8	**Winchester** (city) Randolph County
44	83.9	**Shelbyville** (city) Shelby County
45	84.1	**Corydon** (town) Harrison County
46	84.3	**Edinburgh** (town) Johnson County
46	84.3	**Kendallville** (city) Noble County
46	84.3	**Osceola** (town) Saint Joseph County
49	84.6	**New Albany** (city) Floyd County
50	84.7	**Seymour** (city) Jackson County
51	84.8	**Anderson** (city) Madison County
52	84.9	**Gary** (city) Lake County
52	84.9	**La Porte** (city) LaPorte County
52	84.9	**Roselawn** (CDP) Newton County
52	84.9	**Warsaw** (city) Kosciusko County
56	85.0	**Hartford City** (city) Blackford County
56	85.0	**Terre Haute** (city) Vigo County
58	85.2	**Aurora** (city) Dearborn County
59	85.4	**Attica** (city) Fountain County
60	85.5	**Indianapolis** (city) Marion County
61	85.6	**Michigan City** (city) LaPorte County
61	85.6	**Monticello** (city) White County
63	85.8	**Rockville** (town) Parke County
64	85.9	**Crawfordsville** (city) Montgomery County
65	86.0	**Bremen** (town) Marshall County
65	86.0	**Lawrence** (city) Marion County
67	86.1	**Mooresville** (town) Morgan County
68	86.2	**Clarksville** (town) Clark County
68	86.2	**Clinton** (city) Vermillion County
70	86.5	**Ellettsville** (town) Monroe County
70	86.5	**Huntington** (city) Huntington County
70	86.5	**Wabash** (city) Wabash County
73	86.6	**Loogootee** (city) Martin County
74	86.7	**Brazil** (city) Clay County
74	86.7	**Muncie** (city) Delaware County
74	86.7	**Sheridan** (town) Hamilton County
77	86.8	**Beech Grove** (city) Marion County
77	86.8	**Boonville** (city) Warrick County
77	86.8	**Gas City** (city) Grant County
77	86.8	**New Castle** (city) Henry County
81	86.9	**Evansville** (city) Vanderburgh County
81	86.9	**Garrett** (city) DeKalb County
81	86.9	**Kokomo** (city) Howard County
81	86.9	**Nappanee** (city) Elkhart County
81	86.9	**North Terre Haute** (CDP) Vigo County
86	87.0	**De Motte** (town) Jasper County
86	87.0	**Decatur** (city) Adams County
86	87.0	**Lawrenceburg** (city) Dearborn County
89	87.1	**Lebanon** (city) Boone County
89	87.1	**Speedway** (town) Marion County
91	87.2	**Angola** (city) Steuben County
92	87.3	**Salt Creek Commons** (CDP) Porter County
92	87.3	**Tipton** (city) Tipton County
94	87.4	**Brownstown** (town) Jackson County
94	87.4	**Fairmount** (town) Grant County
96	87.5	**Bedford** (city) Lawrence County
96	87.5	**Columbia City** (city) Whitley County
98	87.6	**Lafayette** (city) Tippecanoe County
98	87.6	**Whiting** (city) Lake County
98	87.6	**Winona Lake** (town) Kosciusko County
101	87.9	**Princeton** (city) Gibson County
101	87.9	**Rochester** (city) Fulton County
103	88.0	**Centerville** (town) Wayne County
103	88.0	**Greencastle** (city) Putnam County
103	88.0	**Mishawaka** (city) Saint Joseph County
106	88.1	**Scottsburg** (city) Scott County
107	88.3	**Cumberland** (town) Marion County
107	88.3	**North Manchester** (town) Wabash County
107	88.3	**Portage** (city) Porter County
110	88.4	**Hanover** (town) Jefferson County
110	88.4	**Jasper** (city) Dubois County
112	88.6	**Fort Wayne** (city) Allen County
112	88.6	**Franklin** (city) Johnson County
112	88.6	**South Haven** (CDP) Porter County
112	88.6	**Winamac** (town) Pulaski County
116	88.7	**New Haven** (city) Allen County
116	88.7	**Tell City** (city) Perry County
118	88.8	**Sellersburg** (town) Clark County
119	89.2	**Bargersville** (town) Johnson County
119	89.2	**Mount Vernon** (city) Posey County
121	89.3	**Greentown** (town) Howard County
122	89.4	**Madison** (city) Jefferson County
123	89.5	**Dunlap** (CDP) Elkhart County
124	89.6	**Hebron** (town) Porter County
125	89.9	**Hobart** (city) Lake County
126	90.0	**Greensburg** (city) Decatur County
127	90.1	**Chandler** (town) Warrick County
127	90.1	**Ossian** (town) Wells County
129	90.3	**Cedar Lake** (town) Lake County
129	90.3	**Middlebury** (town) Elkhart County
131	90.7	**Jeffersonville** (city) Clark County
132	90.8	**Bluffton** (city) Wells County
133	91.1	**Greenfield** (city) Hancock County
133	91.1	**Greenwood** (city) Johnson County
133	91.1	**Lowell** (town) Lake County
136	91.2	**Auburn** (city) DeKalb County
137	91.3	**Smithville-Sanders** (CDP) Monroe County
138	91.5	**Columbus** (city) Bartholomew County
139	91.9	**Crown Point** (city) Lake County
139	91.9	**Porter** (town) Porter County
141	92.0	**Berne** (city) Adams County
141	92.0	**Leo-Cedarville** (town) Allen County
141	92.0	**Merrillville** (town) Lake County
144	92.5	**Avon** (town) Hendricks County
145	92.6	**Bloomington** (city) Monroe County
146	92.7	**Bright** (CDP) Dearborn County
146	92.7	**Brownsburg** (town) Hendricks County
146	92.7	**Cicero** (town) Hamilton County
149	92.8	**Plainfield** (town) Hendricks County
150	93.0	**Griffith** (town) Lake County

Note: *This section ranks incorporated places and CDPs (Census Designated Places) with populations of 2,500 or more. Unincorporated postal areas were not considered. Please refer to the User Guide for additional information.*

Educational Attainment: Bachelor's Degree or Higher

Top 150 Places Ranked in *Descending* Order

State Rank	Percent	Place
1	76.5	**Notre Dame** (CDP) Saint Joseph County
2	71.9	**West Lafayette** (city) Tippecanoe County
3	71.0	**Carmel** (city) Hamilton County
4	70.4	**Zionsville** (town) Boone County
5	65.1	**Fishers** (city) Hamilton County
6	58.3	**Whitestown** (town) Boone County
7	58.1	**McCordsville** (town) Hancock County
8	56.8	**Bloomington** (city) Monroe County
9	56.5	**Westfield** (city) Hamilton County
10	52.7	**Granger** (CDP) Saint Joseph County
11	50.7	**Upland** (town) Grant County
12	50.4	**Shorewood Forest** (CDP) Porter County
13	45.8	**Noblesville** (city) Hamilton County
14	42.7	**Munster** (town) Lake County
15	40.5	**Smithville-Sanders** (CDP) Monroe County
16	40.1	**Winona Lake** (town) Kosciusko County
17	39.9	**Columbus** (city) Bartholomew County
18	39.5	**Valparaiso** (city) Porter County
19	38.9	**Saint John** (town) Lake County
20	38.7	**Avon** (town) Hendricks County
21	37.6	**Hidden Valley** (CDP) Dearborn County
22	37.1	**Georgetown** (town) Floyd County
23	35.6	**Brownsburg** (town) Hendricks County
24	35.0	**Bargersville** (town) Johnson County
25	34.7	**Santa Claus** (town) Spencer County
26	33.5	**Pittsboro** (town) Hendricks County
27	33.3	**Crown Point** (city) Lake County
27	33.3	**Highland** (CDP) Vanderburgh County
29	32.8	**Batesville** (city) Ripley County
29	32.8	**Lawrence** (city) Marion County
31	31.9	**Porter** (town) Porter County
32	31.7	**Schererville** (town) Lake County
33	31.6	**Melody Hill** (CDP) Vanderburgh County
34	31.3	**Newburgh** (town) Warrick County
35	31.0	**Chesterton** (town) Porter County
36	30.4	**Dyer** (town) Lake County
37	30.3	**Plainfield** (town) Hendricks County
38	30.1	**Winfield** (town) Lake County
39	30.0	**Speedway** (town) Marion County
40	29.7	**Indianapolis** (city) Marion County
41	29.5	**Danville** (town) Hendricks County
42	29.4	**Greenwood** (city) Johnson County
42	29.4	**Middlebury** (town) Elkhart County
42	29.4	**North Manchester** (town) Wabash County
45	29.0	**Pendleton** (town) Madison County
46	28.9	**Huntertown** (town) Allen County
47	28.6	**Fortville** (town) Hancock County
48	28.4	**Warsaw** (city) Kosciusko County
49	28.1	**Greendale** (city) Dearborn County
50	28.0	**Yorktown** (town) Delaware County
51	27.7	**Lakes of the Four Seasons** (CDP) Lake County
52	27.6	**Whiteland** (town) Johnson County
53	26.8	**Fort Wayne** (city) Allen County
54	26.7	**Highland** (town) Lake County
54	26.7	**Leo-Cedarville** (town) Allen County
56	25.8	**Lebanon** (city) Boone County
57	25.6	**Cumberland** (town) Marion County
58	25.4	**Cicero** (town) Hamilton County
58	25.4	**Heritage Lake** (CDP) Putnam County
60	24.9	**Jasper** (city) Dubois County
61	24.8	**Ellettsville** (town) Monroe County
62	24.5	**Lafayette** (city) Tippecanoe County
63	24.3	**Mishawaka** (city) Saint Joseph County
63	24.3	**South Bend** (city) Saint Joseph County
65	24.2	**Berne** (city) Adams County
66	24.1	**Franklin** (city) Johnson County
67	23.6	**Muncie** (city) Delaware County
68	23.4	**Auburn** (city) DeKalb County
68	23.4	**Columbia City** (city) Whitley County
68	23.4	**Merrillville** (town) Lake County
71	23.1	**Angola** (city) Steuben County
71	23.1	**Sellersburg** (town) Clark County
73	22.1	**Terre Haute** (city) Vigo County
74	22.0	**Bright** (CDP) Dearborn County
75	21.9	**Corydon** (town) Harrison County
75	21.9	**Goshen** (city) Elkhart County
77	21.8	**Greenfield** (city) Hancock County
78	21.5	**Hobart** (city) Lake County
79	21.1	**Jeffersonville** (city) Clark County
80	20.7	**Evansville** (city) Vanderburgh County
81	20.6	**Cedar Lake** (town) Lake County
81	20.6	**New Albany** (city) Floyd County
81	20.6	**New Whiteland** (town) Johnson County
84	20.4	**Lowell** (town) Lake County
85	20.3	**Greensburg** (city) Decatur County
86	20.1	**Bremen** (town) Marshall County
87	19.2	**Crawfordsville** (city) Montgomery County
87	19.2	**Seymour** (city) Jackson County
87	19.2	**Simonton Lake** (CDP) Elkhart County
90	19.0	**Fort Branch** (town) Gibson County
91	18.8	**Griffith** (town) Lake County
91	18.8	**Madison** (city) Jefferson County
93	18.7	**Osceola** (town) Saint Joseph County
94	18.6	**Dunlap** (CDP) Elkhart County
95	18.2	**Brookville** (town) Franklin County
96	18.1	**Richmond** (city) Wayne County
97	17.9	**Clarksville** (town) Clark County
98	17.8	**Greencastle** (city) Putnam County
99	17.7	**Delphi** (city) Carroll County
100	17.6	**Tipton** (city) Tipton County
101	17.5	**Ossian** (town) Wells County
102	17.4	**Plymouth** (city) Marshall County
103	17.3	**Kokomo** (city) Howard County
104	17.2	**Attica** (city) Fountain County
104	17.2	**Nappanee** (city) Elkhart County
104	17.2	**Rensselaer** (city) Jasper County
107	17.0	**Shelbyville** (city) Shelby County
108	16.9	**Centerville** (town) Wayne County
109	16.6	**Bluffton** (city) Wells County
109	16.6	**Michigan City** (city) LaPorte County
111	16.2	**Greentown** (town) Howard County
111	16.2	**Mount Vernon** (city) Posey County
113	16.1	**La Porte** (city) LaPorte County
113	16.1	**New Haven** (city) Allen County
115	15.7	**Linton** (city) Greene County
115	15.7	**Portage** (city) Porter County
117	15.5	**Huntington** (city) Huntington County
117	15.5	**Tell City** (city) Perry County
119	15.4	**Washington** (city) Daviess County
120	15.2	**Huntingburg** (city) Dubois County
121	15.1	**Beech Grove** (city) Marion County
121	15.1	**Scottsburg** (city) Scott County
121	15.1	**Syracuse** (town) Kosciusko County
121	15.1	**Vincennes** (city) Knox County
125	14.9	**Boonville** (city) Warrick County
126	14.8	**Alexandria** (city) Madison County
126	14.8	**Bedford** (city) Lawrence County
126	14.8	**Brazil** (city) Clay County
129	14.7	**New Castle** (city) Henry County
130	14.5	**Anderson** (city) Madison County
130	14.5	**Rushville** (city) Rush County
130	14.5	**Winchester** (city) Randolph County
133	14.4	**Salt Creek Commons** (CDP) Porter County
134	14.3	**Hanover** (town) Jefferson County
135	14.2	**Marion** (city) Grant County
136	14.1	**Salem** (city) Washington County
137	14.0	**Hammond** (city) Lake County
137	14.0	**Rockville** (town) Parke County
139	13.7	**Charlestown** (city) Clark County
139	13.7	**Monticello** (city) White County
141	13.6	**North Terre Haute** (CDP) Vigo County
141	13.6	**Sheridan** (town) Hamilton County
141	13.6	**Winamac** (town) Pulaski County
144	13.3	**Aurora** (city) Dearborn County
144	13.3	**Whiting** (city) Lake County
146	13.2	**Hebron** (town) Porter County
147	13.1	**Elkhart** (city) Elkhart County
148	12.9	**Kendallville** (city) Noble County
149	12.8	**Gary** (city) Lake County
150	12.6	**North Vernon** (city) Jennings County

***Note:** This section ranks incorporated places and CDPs (Census Designated Places) with populations of 2,500 or more. Unincorporated postal areas were not considered. Please refer to the User Guide for additional information.*

Rankings

Educational Attainment: Bachelor's Degree or Higher

Top 150 Places Ranked in *Ascending* Order

State Rank	Percent	Place
1	1.8	**Ligonier** (city) Noble County
2	4.4	**Country Squire Lakes** (CDP) Jennings County
3	4.8	**Union City** (city) Randolph County
4	5.3	**Edinburgh** (town) Johnson County
4	5.3	**Westville** (town) LaPorte County
6	5.9	**Roselawn** (CDP) Newton County
7	6.0	**Lake Station** (city) Lake County
8	6.8	**Austin** (city) Scott County
9	7.3	**Knox** (city) Starke County
10	8.0	**Bicknell** (city) Knox County
10	8.0	**Portland** (city) Jay County
12	8.1	**Lagrange** (town) LaGrange County
13	8.3	**Paoli** (town) Orange County
14	8.6	**East Chicago** (city) Lake County
15	8.7	**Butler** (city) DeKalb County
16	9.0	**South Haven** (CDP) Porter County
17	9.5	**Connersville** (city) Fayette County
17	9.5	**De Motte** (town) Jasper County
19	9.7	**Clinton** (city) Vermillion County
20	9.9	**Hartford City** (city) Blackford County
21	10.2	**Gas City** (city) Grant County
22	10.3	**Loogootee** (city) Martin County
23	10.4	**Brownstown** (town) Jackson County
23	10.4	**Princeton** (city) Gibson County
25	10.7	**Chandler** (town) Warrick County
26	10.8	**Elwood** (city) Madison County
26	10.8	**Peru** (city) Miami County
28	10.9	**Logansport** (city) Cass County
28	10.9	**Rochester** (city) Fulton County
28	10.9	**Sullivan** (city) Sullivan County
31	11.1	**Garrett** (city) DeKalb County
32	11.2	**Decatur** (city) Adams County
32	11.2	**Lawrenceburg** (city) Dearborn County
32	11.2	**Martinsville** (city) Morgan County
32	11.2	**Mitchell** (city) Lawrence County
36	11.3	**Frankfort** (city) Clinton County
37	11.4	**Mooresville** (town) Morgan County
38	12.0	**Fairmount** (town) Grant County
39	12.3	**Wabash** (city) Wabash County
40	12.6	**North Vernon** (city) Jennings County
41	12.8	**Gary** (city) Lake County
42	12.9	**Kendallville** (city) Noble County
43	13.1	**Elkhart** (city) Elkhart County
44	13.2	**Hebron** (town) Porter County
45	13.3	**Aurora** (city) Dearborn County
45	13.3	**Whiting** (city) Lake County
47	13.6	**North Terre Haute** (CDP) Vigo County
47	13.6	**Sheridan** (town) Hamilton County
47	13.6	**Winamac** (town) Pulaski County
50	13.7	**Charlestown** (city) Clark County
50	13.7	**Monticello** (city) White County
52	14.0	**Hammond** (city) Lake County
52	14.0	**Rockville** (town) Parke County
54	14.1	**Salem** (city) Washington County
55	14.2	**Marion** (city) Grant County
56	14.3	**Hanover** (town) Jefferson County
57	14.4	**Salt Creek Commons** (CDP) Porter County
58	14.5	**Anderson** (city) Madison County
58	14.5	**Rushville** (city) Rush County
58	14.5	**Winchester** (city) Randolph County
61	14.7	**New Castle** (city) Henry County
62	14.8	**Alexandria** (city) Madison County
62	14.8	**Bedford** (city) Lawrence County
62	14.8	**Brazil** (city) Clay County
65	14.9	**Boonville** (city) Warrick County
66	15.1	**Beech Grove** (city) Marion County
66	15.1	**Scottsburg** (city) Scott County
66	15.1	**Syracuse** (town) Kosciusko County
66	15.1	**Vincennes** (city) Knox County
70	15.2	**Huntingburg** (city) Dubois County
71	15.4	**Washington** (city) Daviess County
72	15.5	**Huntington** (city) Huntington County
72	15.5	**Tell City** (city) Perry County
74	15.7	**Linton** (city) Greene County
74	15.7	**Portage** (city) Porter County
76	16.1	**La Porte** (city) LaPorte County
76	16.1	**New Haven** (city) Allen County
78	16.2	**Greentown** (town) Howard County
78	16.2	**Mount Vernon** (city) Posey County
80	16.6	**Bluffton** (city) Wells County
80	16.6	**Michigan City** (city) LaPorte County
82	16.9	**Centerville** (town) Wayne County
83	17.0	**Shelbyville** (city) Shelby County
84	17.2	**Attica** (city) Fountain County
84	17.2	**Nappanee** (city) Elkhart County
84	17.2	**Rensselaer** (city) Jasper County
87	17.3	**Kokomo** (city) Howard County
88	17.4	**Plymouth** (city) Marshall County
89	17.5	**Ossian** (town) Wells County
90	17.6	**Tipton** (city) Tipton County
91	17.7	**Delphi** (city) Carroll County
92	17.8	**Greencastle** (city) Putnam County
93	17.9	**Clarksville** (town) Clark County
94	18.1	**Richmond** (city) Wayne County
95	18.2	**Brookville** (town) Franklin County
96	18.6	**Dunlap** (CDP) Elkhart County
97	18.7	**Osceola** (town) Saint Joseph County
98	18.8	**Griffith** (town) Lake County
98	18.8	**Madison** (city) Jefferson County
100	19.0	**Fort Branch** (town) Gibson County
101	19.2	**Crawfordsville** (city) Montgomery County
101	19.2	**Seymour** (city) Jackson County
101	19.2	**Simonton Lake** (CDP) Elkhart County
104	20.1	**Bremen** (town) Marshall County
105	20.3	**Greensburg** (city) Decatur County
106	20.4	**Lowell** (town) Lake County
107	20.6	**Cedar Lake** (town) Lake County
107	20.6	**New Albany** (city) Floyd County
107	20.6	**New Whiteland** (town) Johnson County
110	20.7	**Evansville** (city) Vanderburgh County
111	21.1	**Jeffersonville** (city) Clark County
112	21.5	**Hobart** (city) Lake County
113	21.8	**Greenfield** (city) Hancock County
114	21.9	**Corydon** (town) Harrison County
114	21.9	**Goshen** (city) Elkhart County
116	22.0	**Bright** (CDP) Dearborn County
117	22.1	**Terre Haute** (city) Vigo County
118	23.1	**Angola** (city) Steuben County
118	23.1	**Sellersburg** (town) Clark County
120	23.4	**Auburn** (city) DeKalb County
120	23.4	**Columbia City** (city) Whitley County
120	23.4	**Merrillville** (town) Lake County
123	23.6	**Muncie** (city) Delaware County
124	24.1	**Franklin** (city) Johnson County
125	24.2	**Berne** (city) Adams County
126	24.3	**Mishawaka** (city) Saint Joseph County
126	24.3	**South Bend** (city) Saint Joseph County
128	24.5	**Lafayette** (city) Tippecanoe County
129	24.8	**Ellettsville** (town) Monroe County
130	24.9	**Jasper** (city) Dubois County
131	25.4	**Cicero** (town) Hamilton County
131	25.4	**Heritage Lake** (CDP) Putnam County
133	25.6	**Cumberland** (town) Marion County
134	25.8	**Lebanon** (city) Boone County
135	26.7	**Highland** (town) Lake County
135	26.7	**Leo-Cedarville** (town) Allen County
137	26.8	**Fort Wayne** (city) Allen County
138	27.6	**Whiteland** (town) Johnson County
139	27.7	**Lakes of the Four Seasons** (CDP) Lake County
140	28.0	**Yorktown** (town) Delaware County
141	28.1	**Greendale** (city) Dearborn County
142	28.4	**Warsaw** (city) Kosciusko County
143	28.6	**Fortville** (town) Hancock County
144	28.9	**Huntertown** (town) Allen County
145	29.0	**Pendleton** (town) Madison County
146	29.4	**Greenwood** (city) Johnson County
146	29.4	**Middlebury** (town) Elkhart County
146	29.4	**North Manchester** (town) Wabash County
149	29.5	**Danville** (town) Hendricks County
150	29.7	**Indianapolis** (city) Marion County

Note: *This section ranks incorporated places and CDPs (Census Designated Places) with populations of 2,500 or more. Unincorporated postal areas were not considered. Please refer to the User Guide for additional information.*

Educational Attainment: Graduate/Professional Degree or Higher

Top 150 Places Ranked in *Descending* Order

State Rank	Percent	Place
1	45.6	**West Lafayette** (city) Tippecanoe County
2	37.1	**Notre Dame** (CDP) Saint Joseph County
3	33.2	**Zionsville** (town) Boone County
4	30.6	**Bloomington** (city) Monroe County
5	29.0	**Carmel** (city) Hamilton County
6	28.7	**Upland** (town) Grant County
7	23.4	**Fishers** (city) Hamilton County
8	23.0	**Granger** (CDP) Saint Joseph County
9	20.0	**Shorewood Forest** (CDP) Porter County
10	18.8	**Whitestown** (town) Boone County
11	17.4	**Westfield** (city) Hamilton County
12	17.1	**Columbus** (city) Bartholomew County
13	16.3	**McCordsville** (town) Hancock County
14	14.9	**Munster** (town) Lake County
15	14.7	**Santa Claus** (town) Spencer County
16	14.5	**Hidden Valley** (CDP) Dearborn County
16	14.5	**North Manchester** (town) Wabash County
18	14.4	**Valparaiso** (city) Porter County
19	14.2	**Winona Lake** (town) Kosciusko County
20	14.0	**Avon** (town) Hendricks County
21	13.8	**Heritage Lake** (CDP) Putnam County
22	13.6	**Saint John** (town) Lake County
23	13.3	**Noblesville** (city) Hamilton County
24	12.8	**Highland** (CDP) Vanderburgh County
25	12.6	**Schererville** (town) Lake County
26	12.5	**Chesterton** (town) Porter County
27	12.4	**Bargersville** (town) Johnson County
28	12.2	**Huntertown** (town) Allen County
29	12.1	**Porter** (town) Porter County
30	11.8	**Melody Hill** (CDP) Vanderburgh County
31	11.5	**Brownsburg** (town) Hendricks County
32	11.4	**Pittsboro** (town) Hendricks County
32	11.4	**Smithville-Sanders** (CDP) Monroe County
34	11.3	**Pendleton** (town) Madison County
34	11.3	**Plainfield** (town) Hendricks County
34	11.3	**Speedway** (town) Marion County
37	10.7	**Batesville** (city) Ripley County
38	10.6	**Georgetown** (town) Floyd County
38	10.6	**Greendale** (city) Dearborn County
38	10.6	**Lawrence** (city) Marion County
41	10.5	**Indianapolis** (city) Marion County
41	10.5	**Muncie** (city) Delaware County
41	10.5	**Yorktown** (town) Delaware County
44	10.4	**Cicero** (town) Hamilton County
44	10.4	**Corydon** (town) Harrison County
44	10.4	**Dyer** (town) Lake County
47	10.3	**Angola** (city) Steuben County
48	10.1	**Cumberland** (town) Marion County
48	10.1	**Warsaw** (city) Kosciusko County
50	10.0	**Crown Point** (city) Lake County
50	10.0	**Goshen** (city) Elkhart County
52	9.8	**South Bend** (city) Saint Joseph County
52	9.8	**Winfield** (town) Lake County
54	9.3	**Bremen** (town) Marshall County
55	9.2	**Fort Wayne** (city) Allen County
56	9.1	**Danville** (town) Hendricks County
56	9.1	**Fortville** (town) Hancock County
58	9.0	**Tell City** (city) Perry County
58	9.0	**Terre Haute** (city) Vigo County
60	8.9	**Dunlap** (CDP) Elkhart County
60	8.9	**Middlebury** (town) Elkhart County
62	8.7	**Attica** (city) Fountain County
62	8.7	**Franklin** (city) Johnson County
62	8.7	**Newburgh** (town) Warrick County
65	8.6	**Greencastle** (city) Putnam County
66	8.4	**Lafayette** (city) Tippecanoe County
66	8.4	**Merrillville** (town) Lake County
66	8.4	**Mishawaka** (city) Saint Joseph County
69	8.1	**Greenwood** (city) Johnson County
69	8.1	**Richmond** (city) Wayne County
71	8.0	**Highland** (town) Lake County
71	8.0	**Lebanon** (city) Boone County
73	7.9	**Lowell** (town) Lake County
73	7.9	**Madison** (city) Jefferson County
75	7.8	**Berne** (city) Adams County
75	7.8	**Columbia City** (city) Whitley County
77	7.7	**Delphi** (city) Carroll County
77	7.7	**Fort Branch** (town) Gibson County
77	7.7	**Sellersburg** (town) Clark County
80	7.5	**New Albany** (city) Floyd County
81	7.1	**Lakes of the Four Seasons** (CDP) Lake County
82	7.0	**Ellettsville** (town) Monroe County
82	7.0	**Evansville** (city) Vanderburgh County
82	7.0	**Plymouth** (city) Marshall County
85	6.9	**Greenfield** (city) Hancock County
85	6.9	**Huntington** (city) Huntington County
85	6.9	**Jeffersonville** (city) Clark County
85	6.9	**Rockville** (town) Parke County
89	6.8	**Auburn** (city) DeKalb County
89	6.8	**Boonville** (city) Warrick County
89	6.8	**Bright** (CDP) Dearborn County
89	6.8	**Greensburg** (city) Decatur County
93	6.6	**Hobart** (city) Lake County
93	6.6	**Jasper** (city) Dubois County
93	6.6	**Nappanee** (city) Elkhart County
93	6.6	**Whiteland** (town) Johnson County
97	6.5	**Monticello** (city) White County
98	6.4	**Brookville** (town) Franklin County
98	6.4	**Vincennes** (city) Knox County
100	6.3	**Bluffton** (city) Wells County
100	6.3	**Cedar Lake** (town) Lake County
100	6.3	**Shelbyville** (city) Shelby County
103	6.2	**Kokomo** (city) Howard County
103	6.2	**Marion** (city) Grant County
103	6.2	**Seymour** (city) Jackson County
106	6.0	**Crawfordsville** (city) Montgomery County
106	6.0	**Greentown** (town) Howard County
106	6.0	**Osceola** (town) Saint Joseph County
109	5.8	**Michigan City** (city) LaPorte County
109	5.8	**Rensselaer** (city) Jasper County
111	5.7	**Bedford** (city) Lawrence County
111	5.7	**Linton** (city) Greene County
111	5.7	**Loogootee** (city) Martin County
114	5.6	**Huntingburg** (city) Dubois County
114	5.6	**Portage** (city) Porter County
114	5.6	**Salem** (city) Washington County
117	5.4	**Mount Vernon** (city) Posey County
118	5.3	**Hartford City** (city) Blackford County
118	5.3	**La Porte** (city) LaPorte County
120	5.2	**Centerville** (town) Wayne County
120	5.2	**Hanover** (town) Jefferson County
120	5.2	**Lawrenceburg** (city) Dearborn County
120	5.2	**Ossian** (town) Wells County
124	5.1	**New Whiteland** (town) Johnson County
124	5.1	**Simonton Lake** (CDP) Elkhart County
124	5.1	**Winchester** (city) Randolph County
127	5.0	**North Terre Haute** (CDP) Vigo County
128	4.9	**Winamac** (town) Pulaski County
129	4.8	**Anderson** (city) Madison County
129	4.8	**Beech Grove** (city) Marion County
129	4.8	**Gary** (city) Lake County
129	4.8	**Rochester** (city) Fulton County
129	4.8	**Washington** (city) Daviess County
134	4.7	**Mitchell** (city) Lawrence County
134	4.7	**North Vernon** (city) Jennings County
134	4.7	**Sullivan** (city) Sullivan County
137	4.6	**Rushville** (city) Rush County
138	4.5	**Clarksville** (town) Clark County
139	4.4	**Brownstown** (town) Jackson County
139	4.4	**Kendallville** (city) Noble County
139	4.4	**Tipton** (city) Tipton County
142	4.3	**Alexandria** (city) Madison County
142	4.3	**Elkhart** (city) Elkhart County
142	4.3	**New Castle** (city) Henry County
142	4.3	**Salt Creek Commons** (CDP) Porter County
146	4.2	**Griffith** (town) Lake County
146	4.2	**Wabash** (city) Wabash County
148	4.1	**Chandler** (town) Warrick County
148	4.1	**Charlestown** (city) Clark County
148	4.1	**New Haven** (city) Allen County

Note: *This section ranks incorporated places and CDPs (Census Designated Places) with populations of 2,500 or more. Unincorporated postal areas were not considered. Please refer to the User Guide for additional information.*

Educational Attainment: Graduate/Professional Degree or Higher

Top 150 Places Ranked in *Ascending* Order

State Rank	Percent	Place
1	0.4	**Ligonier** (city) Noble County
2	0.9	**Westville** (town) LaPorte County
3	1.4	**Austin** (city) Scott County
4	1.5	**Butler** (city) DeKalb County
5	1.6	**Country Squire Lakes** (CDP) Jennings County
6	1.8	**Edinburgh** (town) Johnson County
7	1.9	**Fairmount** (town) Grant County
8	2.1	**Lake Station** (city) Lake County
9	2.4	**Connersville** (city) Fayette County
9	2.4	**Union City** (city) Randolph County
11	2.7	**Bicknell** (city) Knox County
11	2.7	**Clinton** (city) Vermillion County
11	2.7	**De Motte** (town) Jasper County
11	2.7	**Gas City** (city) Grant County
11	2.7	**Roselawn** (CDP) Newton County
16	2.8	**Elwood** (city) Madison County
17	2.9	**East Chicago** (city) Lake County
17	2.9	**Knox** (city) Starke County
19	3.0	**Decatur** (city) Adams County
20	3.1	**Lagrange** (town) LaGrange County
20	3.1	**Mooresville** (town) Morgan County
22	3.3	**Logansport** (city) Cass County
22	3.3	**Peru** (city) Miami County
22	3.3	**Sheridan** (town) Hamilton County
22	3.3	**South Haven** (CDP) Porter County
22	3.3	**Syracuse** (town) Kosciusko County
27	3.4	**Garrett** (city) DeKalb County
27	3.4	**Martinsville** (city) Morgan County
27	3.4	**Portland** (city) Jay County
27	3.4	**Princeton** (city) Gibson County
31	3.5	**Hebron** (town) Porter County
32	3.6	**Scottsburg** (city) Scott County
33	3.7	**Aurora** (city) Dearborn County
33	3.7	**Hammond** (city) Lake County
35	3.9	**Brazil** (city) Clay County
35	3.9	**Frankfort** (city) Clinton County
35	3.9	**Paoli** (town) Orange County
38	4.0	**Leo-Cedarville** (town) Allen County
38	4.0	**Whiting** (city) Lake County
40	4.1	**Chandler** (town) Warrick County
40	4.1	**Charlestown** (city) Clark County
40	4.1	**New Haven** (city) Allen County
43	4.2	**Griffith** (town) Lake County
43	4.2	**Wabash** (city) Wabash County
45	4.3	**Alexandria** (city) Madison County
45	4.3	**Elkhart** (city) Elkhart County
45	4.3	**New Castle** (city) Henry County
45	4.3	**Salt Creek Commons** (CDP) Porter County
49	4.4	**Brownstown** (town) Jackson County
49	4.4	**Kendallville** (city) Noble County
49	4.4	**Tipton** (city) Tipton County
52	4.5	**Clarksville** (town) Clark County
53	4.6	**Rushville** (city) Rush County
54	4.7	**Mitchell** (city) Lawrence County
54	4.7	**North Vernon** (city) Jennings County
54	4.7	**Sullivan** (city) Sullivan County
57	4.8	**Anderson** (city) Madison County
57	4.8	**Beech Grove** (city) Marion County
57	4.8	**Gary** (city) Lake County
57	4.8	**Rochester** (city) Fulton County
57	4.8	**Washington** (city) Daviess County
62	4.9	**Winamac** (town) Pulaski County
63	5.0	**North Terre Haute** (CDP) Vigo County
64	5.1	**New Whiteland** (town) Johnson County
64	5.1	**Simonton Lake** (CDP) Elkhart County
64	5.1	**Winchester** (city) Randolph County
67	5.2	**Centerville** (town) Wayne County
67	5.2	**Hanover** (town) Jefferson County
67	5.2	**Lawrenceburg** (city) Dearborn County
67	5.2	**Ossian** (town) Wells County
71	5.3	**Hartford City** (city) Blackford County
71	5.3	**La Porte** (city) LaPorte County
73	5.4	**Mount Vernon** (city) Posey County
74	5.6	**Huntingburg** (city) Dubois County
74	5.6	**Portage** (city) Porter County
74	5.6	**Salem** (city) Washington County
77	5.7	**Bedford** (city) Lawrence County
77	5.7	**Linton** (city) Greene County
77	5.7	**Loogootee** (city) Martin County
80	5.8	**Michigan City** (city) LaPorte County
80	5.8	**Rensselaer** (city) Jasper County
82	6.0	**Crawfordsville** (city) Montgomery County
82	6.0	**Greentown** (town) Howard County
82	6.0	**Osceola** (town) Saint Joseph County
85	6.2	**Kokomo** (city) Howard County
85	6.2	**Marion** (city) Grant County
85	6.2	**Seymour** (city) Jackson County
88	6.3	**Bluffton** (city) Wells County
88	6.3	**Cedar Lake** (town) Lake County
88	6.3	**Shelbyville** (city) Shelby County
91	6.4	**Brookville** (town) Franklin County
91	6.4	**Vincennes** (city) Knox County
93	6.5	**Monticello** (city) White County
94	6.6	**Hobart** (city) Lake County
94	6.6	**Jasper** (city) Dubois County
94	6.6	**Nappanee** (city) Elkhart County
94	6.6	**Whiteland** (town) Johnson County
98	6.8	**Auburn** (city) DeKalb County
98	6.8	**Boonville** (city) Warrick County
98	6.8	**Bright** (CDP) Dearborn County
98	6.8	**Greensburg** (city) Decatur County
102	6.9	**Greenfield** (city) Hancock County
102	6.9	**Huntington** (city) Huntington County
102	6.9	**Jeffersonville** (city) Clark County
102	6.9	**Rockville** (town) Parke County
106	7.0	**Ellettsville** (town) Monroe County
106	7.0	**Evansville** (city) Vanderburgh County
106	7.0	**Plymouth** (city) Marshall County
109	7.1	**Lakes of the Four Seasons** (CDP) Lake County
110	7.5	**New Albany** (city) Floyd County
111	7.7	**Delphi** (city) Carroll County
111	7.7	**Fort Branch** (town) Gibson County
111	7.7	**Sellersburg** (town) Clark County
114	7.8	**Berne** (city) Adams County
114	7.8	**Columbia City** (city) Whitley County
116	7.9	**Lowell** (town) Lake County
116	7.9	**Madison** (city) Jefferson County
118	8.0	**Highland** (town) Lake County
118	8.0	**Lebanon** (city) Boone County
120	8.1	**Greenwood** (city) Johnson County
120	8.1	**Richmond** (city) Wayne County
122	8.4	**Lafayette** (city) Tippecanoe County
122	8.4	**Merrillville** (town) Lake County
122	8.4	**Mishawaka** (city) Saint Joseph County
125	8.6	**Greencastle** (city) Putnam County
126	8.7	**Attica** (city) Fountain County
126	8.7	**Franklin** (city) Johnson County
126	8.7	**Newburgh** (town) Warrick County
129	8.9	**Dunlap** (CDP) Elkhart County
129	8.9	**Middlebury** (town) Elkhart County
131	9.0	**Tell City** (city) Perry County
131	9.0	**Terre Haute** (city) Vigo County
133	9.1	**Danville** (town) Hendricks County
133	9.1	**Fortville** (town) Hancock County
135	9.2	**Fort Wayne** (city) Allen County
136	9.3	**Bremen** (town) Marshall County
137	9.8	**South Bend** (city) Saint Joseph County
137	9.8	**Winfield** (town) Lake County
139	10.0	**Crown Point** (city) Lake County
139	10.0	**Goshen** (city) Elkhart County
141	10.1	**Cumberland** (town) Marion County
141	10.1	**Warsaw** (city) Kosciusko County
143	10.3	**Angola** (city) Steuben County
144	10.4	**Cicero** (town) Hamilton County
144	10.4	**Corydon** (town) Harrison County
144	10.4	**Dyer** (town) Lake County
147	10.5	**Indianapolis** (city) Marion County
147	10.5	**Muncie** (city) Delaware County
147	10.5	**Yorktown** (town) Delaware County
150	10.6	**Georgetown** (town) Floyd County

Note: *This section ranks incorporated places and CDPs (Census Designated Places) with populations of 2,500 or more. Unincorporated postal areas were not considered. Please refer to the User Guide for additional information.*

Homeownership Rate

Top 150 Places Ranked in *Descending* Order

State Rank	Percent	Place
1	98.3	**Saint John** (town) Lake County
2	97.6	**Shorewood Forest** (CDP) Porter County
3	95.5	**Granger** (CDP) Saint Joseph County
4	94.2	**Highland** (CDP) Vanderburgh County
5	93.9	**Lakes of the Four Seasons** (CDP) Lake County
6	93.5	**Melody Hill** (CDP) Vanderburgh County
7	93.2	**Heritage Lake** (CDP) Putnam County
8	92.1	**Huntertown** (town) Allen County
9	91.0	**Dyer** (town) Lake County
10	90.4	**Roselawn** (CDP) Newton County
11	89.8	**Hidden Valley** (CDP) Dearborn County
12	89.7	**McCordsville** (town) Hancock County
13	89.2	**Santa Claus** (town) Spencer County
13	89.2	**Winfield** (town) Lake County
15	88.0	**Dunlap** (CDP) Elkhart County
16	87.9	**Leo-Cedarville** (town) Allen County
17	87.5	**Osceola** (town) Saint Joseph County
18	86.3	**Salt Creek Commons** (CDP) Porter County
19	86.2	**New Whiteland** (town) Johnson County
20	86.0	**Munster** (town) Lake County
21	85.5	**Bright** (CDP) Dearborn County
22	85.1	**Pittsboro** (town) Hendricks County
23	84.9	**Whiteland** (town) Johnson County
24	83.8	**Cicero** (town) Hamilton County
25	83.7	**Georgetown** (town) Floyd County
26	82.0	**Porter** (town) Porter County
27	81.4	**Westfield** (city) Hamilton County
28	81.3	**Yorktown** (town) Delaware County
29	81.2	**Smithville-Sanders** (CDP) Monroe County
30	81.0	**Lowell** (town) Lake County
31	80.9	**Avon** (town) Hendricks County
32	80.8	**Fishers** (city) Hamilton County
33	80.7	**Zionsville** (town) Boone County
34	80.1	**Cedar Lake** (town) Lake County
34	80.1	**Ossian** (town) Wells County
36	79.8	**Middlebury** (town) Elkhart County
37	79.0	**Crown Point** (city) Lake County
38	78.4	**Highland** (town) Lake County
39	78.2	**Greendale** (city) Dearborn County
40	78.0	**Simonton Lake** (CDP) Elkhart County
41	77.9	**Schererville** (town) Lake County
42	77.7	**Westville** (town) LaPorte County
43	77.6	**Carmel** (city) Hamilton County
44	75.8	**Whitestown** (town) Boone County
45	75.1	**Hobart** (city) Lake County
46	75.0	**Brownsburg** (town) Hendricks County
46	75.0	**Newburgh** (town) Warrick County
48	74.9	**Mitchell** (city) Lawrence County
49	74.1	**Bargersville** (town) Johnson County
50	73.7	**Country Squire Lakes** (CDP) Jennings County
51	73.6	**Centerville** (town) Wayne County
52	73.3	**Sellersburg** (town) Clark County
52	73.3	**South Haven** (CDP) Porter County
54	72.7	**Cumberland** (town) Marion County
55	72.5	**Butler** (city) DeKalb County
55	72.5	**Hartford City** (city) Blackford County
55	72.5	**Jasper** (city) Dubois County
58	72.2	**Greentown** (town) Howard County
59	71.7	**Ellettsville** (town) Monroe County
59	71.7	**Hebron** (town) Porter County
61	71.6	**New Haven** (city) Allen County
62	70.5	**Boonville** (city) Warrick County
62	70.5	**Fairmount** (town) Grant County
64	70.2	**Jeffersonville** (city) Clark County
65	69.9	**Delphi** (city) Carroll County
65	69.9	**Noblesville** (city) Hamilton County
67	69.8	**Fort Branch** (town) Gibson County
68	69.5	**Auburn** (city) DeKalb County
68	69.5	**North Terre Haute** (CDP) Vigo County
68	69.5	**Tell City** (city) Perry County
71	69.2	**Fortville** (town) Hancock County
71	69.2	**Lake Station** (city) Lake County
73	68.6	**Plainfield** (town) Hendricks County
74	68.5	**Portage** (city) Porter County
75	68.2	**Gas City** (city) Grant County
76	68.1	**Batesville** (city) Ripley County
76	68.1	**Chesterton** (town) Porter County
76	68.1	**Linton** (city) Greene County
79	67.8	**Danville** (town) Hendricks County
80	67.7	**Berne** (city) Adams County
81	67.5	**Mount Vernon** (city) Posey County
82	67.2	**Austin** (city) Scott County
83	66.9	**Mooresville** (town) Morgan County
84	66.2	**Bluffton** (city) Wells County
84	66.2	**Wabash** (city) Wabash County
86	66.1	**Monticello** (city) White County
87	65.9	**Tipton** (city) Tipton County
88	65.8	**Griffith** (town) Lake County
89	65.6	**Pendleton** (town) Madison County
90	65.5	**Alexandria** (city) Madison County
90	65.5	**Garrett** (city) DeKalb County
90	65.5	**Rochester** (city) Fulton County
90	65.5	**Rockville** (town) Parke County
94	65.4	**Lawrence** (city) Marion County
95	65.1	**Merrillville** (town) Lake County
96	64.9	**Bedford** (city) Lawrence County
97	64.8	**Huntington** (city) Huntington County
98	64.5	**Loogootee** (city) Martin County
99	64.4	**Decatur** (city) Adams County
99	64.4	**Lagrange** (town) LaGrange County
99	64.4	**Winchester** (city) Randolph County
102	64.3	**Chandler** (town) Warrick County
103	64.2	**Columbia City** (city) Whitley County
104	63.9	**Corydon** (town) Harrison County
105	63.8	**De Motte** (town) Jasper County
106	63.6	**Columbus** (city) Bartholomew County
107	63.1	**Franklin** (city) Johnson County
108	63.0	**Paoli** (town) Orange County
109	62.9	**Whiting** (city) Lake County
110	62.8	**Seymour** (city) Jackson County
110	62.8	**Washington** (city) Daviess County
112	62.5	**Elwood** (city) Madison County
112	62.5	**Frankfort** (city) Clinton County
114	62.4	**Salem** (city) Washington County
115	62.2	**Nappanee** (city) Elkhart County
115	62.2	**Winamac** (town) Pulaski County
117	62.0	**Fort Wayne** (city) Allen County
118	61.8	**Lebanon** (city) Boone County
118	61.8	**Upland** (town) Grant County
120	61.6	**Union City** (city) Randolph County
121	61.4	**Brownstown** (town) Jackson County
122	61.2	**Bicknell** (city) Knox County
123	61.1	**Peru** (city) Miami County
124	60.7	**Kokomo** (city) Howard County
125	60.6	**Huntingburg** (city) Dubois County
126	60.5	**Clarksville** (town) Clark County
127	60.0	**Ligonier** (city) Noble County
127	60.0	**Portland** (city) Jay County
129	59.9	**Scottsburg** (city) Scott County
130	59.8	**Logansport** (city) Cass County
131	59.7	**Hammond** (city) Lake County
131	59.7	**North Manchester** (town) Wabash County
133	59.3	**Charlestown** (city) Clark County
133	59.3	**Shelbyville** (city) Shelby County
133	59.3	**Winona Lake** (town) Kosciusko County
136	59.1	**Brazil** (city) Clay County
137	58.5	**Attica** (city) Fountain County
137	58.5	**Sheridan** (town) Hamilton County
139	58.4	**Madison** (city) Jefferson County
140	58.2	**Greenfield** (city) Hancock County
140	58.2	**New Castle** (city) Henry County
142	58.0	**Princeton** (city) Gibson County
143	57.8	**Clinton** (city) Vermillion County
144	57.7	**Connersville** (city) Fayette County
144	57.7	**Greensburg** (city) Decatur County
146	57.6	**Greenwood** (city) Johnson County
147	57.2	**La Porte** (city) LaPorte County
147	57.2	**South Bend** (city) Saint Joseph County
149	57.1	**Kendallville** (city) Noble County
149	57.1	**Rensselaer** (city) Jasper County

Note: *This section ranks incorporated places and CDPs (Census Designated Places) with populations of 2,500 or more. Unincorporated postal areas were not considered. Please refer to the User Guide for additional information.*

Homeownership Rate

Top 150 Places Ranked in *Ascending* Order

State Rank	Percent	Place
1	0.0	**Notre Dame** (CDP) Saint Joseph County
2	34.4	**West Lafayette** (city) Tippecanoe County
3	34.5	**Bloomington** (city) Monroe County
4	43.8	**East Chicago** (city) Lake County
5	45.7	**Speedway** (town) Marion County
6	46.6	**Lafayette** (city) Tippecanoe County
7	46.8	**Elkhart** (city) Elkhart County
8	47.1	**Aurora** (city) Dearborn County
9	48.3	**Angola** (city) Steuben County
10	49.8	**Vincennes** (city) Knox County
11	49.9	**Lawrenceburg** (city) Dearborn County
12	50.2	**Mishawaka** (city) Saint Joseph County
13	51.4	**Greencastle** (city) Putnam County
13	51.4	**Muncie** (city) Delaware County
15	51.7	**Terre Haute** (city) Vigo County
16	51.9	**North Vernon** (city) Jennings County
17	52.0	**Edinburgh** (town) Johnson County
17	52.0	**Gary** (city) Lake County
19	52.9	**Martinsville** (city) Morgan County
20	53.4	**Indianapolis** (city) Marion County
21	53.5	**Beech Grove** (city) Marion County
22	54.0	**Michigan City** (city) LaPorte County
23	54.4	**Sullivan** (city) Sullivan County
24	54.5	**Evansville** (city) Vanderburgh County
25	54.6	**Hanover** (town) Jefferson County
26	54.9	**Brookville** (town) Franklin County
27	55.2	**Knox** (city) Starke County
28	55.4	**Bremen** (town) Marshall County
28	55.4	**New Albany** (city) Floyd County
30	55.5	**Goshen** (city) Elkhart County
31	55.8	**Crawfordsville** (city) Montgomery County
32	55.9	**Marion** (city) Grant County
33	56.0	**Anderson** (city) Madison County
33	56.0	**Plymouth** (city) Marshall County
35	56.1	**Valparaiso** (city) Porter County
36	56.2	**Syracuse** (town) Kosciusko County
36	56.2	**Warsaw** (city) Kosciusko County
38	56.8	**Richmond** (city) Wayne County
39	56.9	**Rushville** (city) Rush County
40	57.1	**Kendallville** (city) Noble County
40	57.1	**Rensselaer** (city) Jasper County
42	57.2	**La Porte** (city) LaPorte County
42	57.2	**South Bend** (city) Saint Joseph County
44	57.6	**Greenwood** (city) Johnson County
45	57.7	**Connersville** (city) Fayette County
45	57.7	**Greensburg** (city) Decatur County
47	57.8	**Clinton** (city) Vermillion County
48	58.0	**Princeton** (city) Gibson County
49	58.2	**Greenfield** (city) Hancock County
49	58.2	**New Castle** (city) Henry County
51	58.4	**Madison** (city) Jefferson County
52	58.5	**Attica** (city) Fountain County
52	58.5	**Sheridan** (town) Hamilton County
54	59.1	**Brazil** (city) Clay County
55	59.3	**Charlestown** (city) Clark County
55	59.3	**Shelbyville** (city) Shelby County
55	59.3	**Winona Lake** (town) Kosciusko County
58	59.7	**Hammond** (city) Lake County
58	59.7	**North Manchester** (town) Wabash County
60	59.8	**Logansport** (city) Cass County
61	59.9	**Scottsburg** (city) Scott County
62	60.0	**Ligonier** (city) Noble County
62	60.0	**Portland** (city) Jay County
64	60.5	**Clarksville** (town) Clark County
65	60.6	**Huntingburg** (city) Dubois County
66	60.7	**Kokomo** (city) Howard County
67	61.1	**Peru** (city) Miami County
68	61.2	**Bicknell** (city) Knox County
69	61.4	**Brownstown** (town) Jackson County
70	61.6	**Union City** (city) Randolph County
71	61.8	**Lebanon** (city) Boone County
71	61.8	**Upland** (town) Grant County
73	62.0	**Fort Wayne** (city) Allen County
74	62.2	**Nappanee** (city) Elkhart County
74	62.2	**Winamac** (town) Pulaski County
76	62.4	**Salem** (city) Washington County
77	62.5	**Elwood** (city) Madison County
77	62.5	**Frankfort** (city) Clinton County
79	62.8	**Seymour** (city) Jackson County
79	62.8	**Washington** (city) Daviess County
81	62.9	**Whiting** (city) Lake County
82	63.0	**Paoli** (town) Orange County
83	63.1	**Franklin** (city) Johnson County
84	63.6	**Columbus** (city) Bartholomew County
85	63.8	**De Motte** (town) Jasper County
86	63.9	**Corydon** (town) Harrison County
87	64.2	**Columbia City** (city) Whitley County
88	64.3	**Chandler** (town) Warrick County
89	64.4	**Decatur** (city) Adams County
89	64.4	**Lagrange** (town) LaGrange County
89	64.4	**Winchester** (city) Randolph County
92	64.5	**Loogootee** (city) Martin County
93	64.8	**Huntington** (city) Huntington County
94	64.9	**Bedford** (city) Lawrence County
95	65.1	**Merrillville** (town) Lake County
96	65.4	**Lawrence** (city) Marion County
97	65.5	**Alexandria** (city) Madison County
97	65.5	**Garrett** (city) DeKalb County
97	65.5	**Rochester** (city) Fulton County
97	65.5	**Rockville** (town) Parke County
101	65.6	**Pendleton** (town) Madison County
102	65.8	**Griffith** (town) Lake County
103	65.9	**Tipton** (city) Tipton County
104	66.1	**Monticello** (city) White County
105	66.2	**Bluffton** (city) Wells County
105	66.2	**Wabash** (city) Wabash County
107	66.9	**Mooresville** (town) Morgan County
108	67.2	**Austin** (city) Scott County
109	67.5	**Mount Vernon** (city) Posey County
110	67.7	**Berne** (city) Adams County
111	67.8	**Danville** (town) Hendricks County
112	68.1	**Batesville** (city) Ripley County
112	68.1	**Chesterton** (town) Porter County
112	68.1	**Linton** (city) Greene County
115	68.2	**Gas City** (city) Grant County
116	68.5	**Portage** (city) Porter County
117	68.6	**Plainfield** (town) Hendricks County
118	69.2	**Fortville** (town) Hancock County
118	69.2	**Lake Station** (city) Lake County
120	69.5	**Auburn** (city) DeKalb County
120	69.5	**North Terre Haute** (CDP) Vigo County
120	69.5	**Tell City** (city) Perry County
123	69.8	**Fort Branch** (town) Gibson County
124	69.9	**Delphi** (city) Carroll County
124	69.9	**Noblesville** (city) Hamilton County
126	70.2	**Jeffersonville** (city) Clark County
127	70.5	**Boonville** (city) Warrick County
127	70.5	**Fairmount** (town) Grant County
129	71.6	**New Haven** (city) Allen County
130	71.7	**Ellettsville** (town) Monroe County
130	71.7	**Hebron** (town) Porter County
132	72.2	**Greentown** (town) Howard County
133	72.5	**Butler** (city) DeKalb County
133	72.5	**Hartford City** (city) Blackford County
133	72.5	**Jasper** (city) Dubois County
136	72.7	**Cumberland** (town) Marion County
137	73.3	**Sellersburg** (town) Clark County
137	73.3	**South Haven** (CDP) Porter County
139	73.6	**Centerville** (town) Wayne County
140	73.7	**Country Squire Lakes** (CDP) Jennings County
141	74.1	**Bargersville** (town) Johnson County
142	74.9	**Mitchell** (city) Lawrence County
143	75.0	**Brownsburg** (town) Hendricks County
143	75.0	**Newburgh** (town) Warrick County
145	75.1	**Hobart** (city) Lake County
146	75.8	**Whitestown** (town) Boone County
147	77.6	**Carmel** (city) Hamilton County
148	77.7	**Westville** (town) LaPorte County
149	77.9	**Schererville** (town) Lake County
150	78.0	**Simonton Lake** (CDP) Elkhart County

Note: *This section ranks incorporated places and CDPs (Census Designated Places) with populations of 2,500 or more. Unincorporated postal areas were not considered. Please refer to the User Guide for additional information.*

Median Home Value

Top 150 Places Ranked in *Descending* Order

State Rank	Dollars	Place
1	360,100	**Zionsville** (town) Boone County
2	350,300	**Shorewood Forest** (CDP) Porter County
3	320,400	**Carmel** (city) Hamilton County
4	275,200	**Winfield** (town) Lake County
5	274,300	**Saint John** (town) Lake County
6	240,100	**Fishers** (city) Hamilton County
7	232,300	**Westfield** (city) Hamilton County
8	217,700	**Munster** (town) Lake County
9	211,000	**Whitestown** (town) Boone County
10	209,800	**McCordsville** (town) Hancock County
11	206,300	**Schererville** (town) Lake County
12	203,500	**Granger** (CDP) Saint Joseph County
13	199,400	**Dyer** (town) Lake County
14	192,600	**Hidden Valley** (CDP) Dearborn County
14	192,600	**West Lafayette** (city) Tippecanoe County
16	190,000	**Leo-Cedarville** (town) Allen County
17	185,200	**Avon** (town) Hendricks County
18	184,500	**Lakes of the Four Seasons** (CDP) Lake County
19	183,700	**Noblesville** (city) Hamilton County
20	180,700	**Bargersville** (town) Johnson County
21	178,700	**Georgetown** (town) Floyd County
22	178,400	**Crown Point** (city) Lake County
23	176,300	**Bloomington** (city) Monroe County
23	176,300	**Chesterton** (town) Porter County
25	175,000	**Valparaiso** (city) Porter County
26	171,800	**Porter** (town) Porter County
27	170,100	**Cedar Lake** (town) Lake County
28	168,600	**Bright** (CDP) Dearborn County
29	167,800	**Santa Claus** (town) Spencer County
30	165,700	**Batesville** (city) Ripley County
31	165,400	**Winona Lake** (town) Kosciusko County
32	163,600	**Brownsburg** (town) Hendricks County
33	162,200	**Middlebury** (town) Elkhart County
34	159,600	**Pittsboro** (town) Hendricks County
35	158,300	**Highland** (CDP) Vanderburgh County
36	156,800	**Heritage Lake** (CDP) Putnam County
37	155,400	**Highland** (town) Lake County
38	155,100	**Plainfield** (town) Hendricks County
38	155,100	**Smithville-Sanders** (CDP) Monroe County
40	154,600	**Cumberland** (town) Marion County
40	154,600	**Simonton Lake** (CDP) Elkhart County
42	154,500	**De Motte** (town) Jasper County
42	154,500	**Huntertown** (town) Allen County
44	152,800	**Danville** (town) Hendricks County
45	152,200	**Lowell** (town) Lake County
46	151,000	**Jasper** (city) Dubois County
47	149,500	**Melody Hill** (CDP) Vanderburgh County
48	148,500	**Columbus** (city) Bartholomew County
49	144,900	**Sellersburg** (town) Clark County
50	143,700	**Newburgh** (town) Warrick County
51	143,100	**Greenwood** (city) Johnson County
52	141,000	**Portage** (city) Porter County
53	140,300	**Cicero** (town) Hamilton County
54	139,800	**Dunlap** (CDP) Elkhart County
55	136,300	**Hebron** (town) Porter County
56	135,600	**Griffith** (town) Lake County
57	134,400	**Pendleton** (town) Madison County
58	134,300	**Hobart** (city) Lake County
59	133,900	**Yorktown** (town) Delaware County
60	133,600	**Lawrence** (city) Marion County
61	133,000	**Lawrenceburg** (city) Dearborn County
62	132,800	**Upland** (town) Grant County
63	132,200	**Bremen** (town) Marshall County
64	132,000	**Greenfield** (city) Hancock County
65	128,600	**Merrillville** (town) Lake County
66	128,300	**Jeffersonville** (city) Clark County
67	127,700	**Aurora** (city) Dearborn County
68	125,600	**Salt Creek Commons** (CDP) Porter County
69	125,000	**Madison** (city) Jefferson County
70	124,900	**Greendale** (city) Dearborn County
71	124,300	**Warsaw** (city) Kosciusko County
72	123,700	**Mooresville** (town) Morgan County
73	123,500	**Indianapolis** (city) Marion County
74	123,300	**Whiting** (city) Lake County
75	123,100	**Ellettsville** (town) Monroe County
76	121,300	**Nappanee** (city) Elkhart County
77	121,000	**Whiteland** (town) Johnson County
78	120,600	**Syracuse** (town) Kosciusko County
79	120,500	**Angola** (city) Steuben County
80	120,200	**Rensselaer** (city) Jasper County
81	119,200	**Franklin** (city) Johnson County
82	119,100	**Roselawn** (CDP) Newton County
83	118,900	**Ossian** (town) Wells County
84	117,000	**Speedway** (town) Marion County
85	116,000	**Sheridan** (town) Hamilton County
86	114,700	**Fort Branch** (town) Gibson County
87	114,500	**Fortville** (town) Hancock County
88	113,800	**Lebanon** (city) Boone County
89	112,900	**Clarksville** (town) Clark County
90	112,300	**South Haven** (CDP) Porter County
91	111,300	**New Albany** (city) Floyd County
92	111,000	**Goshen** (city) Elkhart County
93	110,300	**Greensburg** (city) Decatur County
94	109,300	**Charlestown** (city) Clark County
95	109,200	**Osceola** (town) Saint Joseph County
96	108,400	**Seymour** (city) Jackson County
97	108,300	**Corydon** (town) Harrison County
98	108,000	**Brookville** (town) Franklin County
99	107,700	**Huntingburg** (city) Dubois County
100	106,500	**Fort Wayne** (city) Allen County
101	106,400	**Auburn** (city) DeKalb County
102	106,200	**Columbia City** (city) Whitley County
103	105,300	**Lafayette** (city) Tippecanoe County
104	104,400	**Brownstown** (town) Jackson County
105	103,900	**Greencastle** (city) Putnam County
106	97,500	**Mount Vernon** (city) Posey County
107	97,300	**New Haven** (city) Allen County
108	97,200	**Scottsburg** (city) Scott County
109	96,300	**Martinsville** (city) Morgan County
109	96,300	**Shelbyville** (city) Shelby County
111	96,200	**Beech Grove** (city) Marion County
112	95,300	**Greentown** (town) Howard County
113	94,900	**Bluffton** (city) Wells County
114	94,400	**New Whiteland** (town) Johnson County
115	94,000	**Decatur** (city) Adams County
116	93,700	**Monticello** (city) White County
117	93,400	**La Porte** (city) LaPorte County
118	93,300	**Mishawaka** (city) Saint Joseph County
119	93,200	**Berne** (city) Adams County
120	92,900	**Kendallville** (city) Noble County
121	91,700	**Crawfordsville** (city) Montgomery County
122	91,000	**North Manchester** (town) Wabash County
122	91,000	**Tell City** (city) Perry County
124	90,500	**North Terre Haute** (CDP) Vigo County
125	89,800	**Boonville** (city) Warrick County
126	89,700	**Evansville** (city) Vanderburgh County
127	89,200	**Plymouth** (city) Marshall County
128	89,000	**Michigan City** (city) LaPorte County
129	88,800	**Westville** (town) LaPorte County
130	87,700	**Elkhart** (city) Elkhart County
131	87,600	**Bedford** (city) Lawrence County
131	87,600	**Hammond** (city) Lake County
133	87,500	**Centerville** (town) Wayne County
134	86,600	**Tipton** (city) Tipton County
135	86,400	**Garrett** (city) DeKalb County
136	86,100	**North Vernon** (city) Jennings County
137	85,300	**Richmond** (city) Wayne County
138	85,200	**Kokomo** (city) Howard County
139	85,100	**Chandler** (town) Warrick County
140	85,000	**Edinburgh** (town) Johnson County
141	84,900	**Hanover** (town) Jefferson County
141	84,900	**Rochester** (city) Fulton County
143	84,700	**Loogootee** (city) Martin County
143	84,700	**Rushville** (city) Rush County
145	83,600	**Lagrange** (town) LaGrange County
146	82,200	**Washington** (city) Daviess County
147	82,100	**Winamac** (town) Pulaski County
148	81,700	**Salem** (city) Washington County
149	81,300	**Fairmount** (town) Grant County
150	81,100	**South Bend** (city) Saint Joseph County

Note: *This section ranks incorporated places and CDPs (Census Designated Places) with populations of 2,500 or more. Unincorporated postal areas were not considered. Please refer to the User Guide for additional information.*

Median Home Value

Top 150 Places Ranked in *Ascending* Order

State Rank	Dollars	Place
1	33,900	**Country Squire Lakes** (CDP) Jennings County
2	48,400	**Union City** (city) Randolph County
3	50,800	**Bicknell** (city) Knox County
4	55,900	**Hartford City** (city) Blackford County
5	60,400	**Peru** (city) Miami County
6	62,500	**Clinton** (city) Vermillion County
7	65,400	**Logansport** (city) Cass County
7	65,400	**Marion** (city) Grant County
9	65,700	**Linton** (city) Greene County
10	66,300	**Gary** (city) Lake County
11	66,600	**Elwood** (city) Madison County
12	68,500	**Connersville** (city) Fayette County
13	70,500	**Anderson** (city) Madison County
13	70,500	**Muncie** (city) Delaware County
15	70,900	**Portland** (city) Jay County
16	71,500	**Mitchell** (city) Lawrence County
17	71,700	**New Castle** (city) Henry County
18	72,200	**Brazil** (city) Clay County
19	72,300	**Sullivan** (city) Sullivan County
20	72,400	**Winchester** (city) Randolph County
21	72,900	**Austin** (city) Scott County
22	73,300	**East Chicago** (city) Lake County
23	73,700	**Vincennes** (city) Knox County
24	75,300	**Paoli** (town) Orange County
25	75,600	**Alexandria** (city) Madison County
25	75,600	**Rockville** (town) Parke County
27	76,600	**Knox** (city) Starke County
27	76,600	**Terre Haute** (city) Vigo County
29	77,300	**Wabash** (city) Wabash County
30	78,400	**Huntington** (city) Huntington County
31	78,500	**Butler** (city) DeKalb County
32	78,700	**Attica** (city) Fountain County
32	78,700	**Lake Station** (city) Lake County
34	79,000	**Frankfort** (city) Clinton County
35	80,300	**Delphi** (city) Carroll County
35	80,300	**Gas City** (city) Grant County
37	80,900	**Ligonier** (city) Noble County
38	81,000	**Princeton** (city) Gibson County
39	81,100	**South Bend** (city) Saint Joseph County
40	81,300	**Fairmount** (town) Grant County
41	81,700	**Salem** (city) Washington County
42	82,100	**Winamac** (town) Pulaski County
43	82,200	**Washington** (city) Daviess County
44	83,600	**Lagrange** (town) LaGrange County
45	84,700	**Loogootee** (city) Martin County
45	84,700	**Rushville** (city) Rush County
47	84,900	**Hanover** (town) Jefferson County
47	84,900	**Rochester** (city) Fulton County
49	85,000	**Edinburgh** (town) Johnson County
50	85,100	**Chandler** (town) Warrick County
51	85,200	**Kokomo** (city) Howard County
52	85,300	**Richmond** (city) Wayne County
53	86,100	**North Vernon** (city) Jennings County
54	86,400	**Garrett** (city) DeKalb County
55	86,600	**Tipton** (city) Tipton County
56	87,500	**Centerville** (town) Wayne County
57	87,600	**Bedford** (city) Lawrence County
57	87,600	**Hammond** (city) Lake County
59	87,700	**Elkhart** (city) Elkhart County
60	88,800	**Westville** (town) LaPorte County
61	89,000	**Michigan City** (city) LaPorte County
62	89,200	**Plymouth** (city) Marshall County
63	89,700	**Evansville** (city) Vanderburgh County
64	89,800	**Boonville** (city) Warrick County
65	90,500	**North Terre Haute** (CDP) Vigo County
66	91,000	**North Manchester** (town) Wabash County
66	91,000	**Tell City** (city) Perry County
68	91,700	**Crawfordsville** (city) Montgomery County
69	92,900	**Kendallville** (city) Noble County
70	93,200	**Berne** (city) Adams County
71	93,300	**Mishawaka** (city) Saint Joseph County
72	93,400	**La Porte** (city) LaPorte County
73	93,700	**Monticello** (city) White County
74	94,000	**Decatur** (city) Adams County
75	94,400	**New Whiteland** (town) Johnson County
76	94,900	**Bluffton** (city) Wells County
77	95,300	**Greentown** (town) Howard County
78	96,200	**Beech Grove** (city) Marion County
79	96,300	**Martinsville** (city) Morgan County
79	96,300	**Shelbyville** (city) Shelby County
81	97,200	**Scottsburg** (city) Scott County
82	97,300	**New Haven** (city) Allen County
83	97,500	**Mount Vernon** (city) Posey County
84	103,900	**Greencastle** (city) Putnam County
85	104,400	**Brownstown** (town) Jackson County
86	105,300	**Lafayette** (city) Tippecanoe County
87	106,200	**Columbia City** (city) Whitley County
88	106,400	**Auburn** (city) DeKalb County
89	106,500	**Fort Wayne** (city) Allen County
90	107,700	**Huntingburg** (city) Dubois County
91	108,000	**Brookville** (town) Franklin County
92	108,300	**Corydon** (town) Harrison County
93	108,400	**Seymour** (city) Jackson County
94	109,200	**Osceola** (town) Saint Joseph County
95	109,300	**Charlestown** (city) Clark County
96	110,300	**Greensburg** (city) Decatur County
97	111,000	**Goshen** (city) Elkhart County
98	111,300	**New Albany** (city) Floyd County
99	112,300	**South Haven** (CDP) Porter County
100	112,900	**Clarksville** (town) Clark County
101	113,800	**Lebanon** (city) Boone County
102	114,500	**Fortville** (town) Hancock County
103	114,700	**Fort Branch** (town) Gibson County
104	116,000	**Sheridan** (town) Hamilton County
105	117,000	**Speedway** (town) Marion County
106	118,900	**Ossian** (town) Wells County
107	119,100	**Roselawn** (CDP) Newton County
108	119,200	**Franklin** (city) Johnson County
109	120,200	**Rensselaer** (city) Jasper County
110	120,500	**Angola** (city) Steuben County
111	120,600	**Syracuse** (town) Kosciusko County
112	121,000	**Whiteland** (town) Johnson County
113	121,300	**Nappanee** (city) Elkhart County
114	123,100	**Ellettsville** (town) Monroe County
115	123,300	**Whiting** (city) Lake County
116	123,500	**Indianapolis** (city) Marion County
117	123,700	**Mooresville** (town) Morgan County
118	124,300	**Warsaw** (city) Kosciusko County
119	124,900	**Greendale** (city) Dearborn County
120	125,000	**Madison** (city) Jefferson County
121	125,600	**Salt Creek Commons** (CDP) Porter County
122	127,700	**Aurora** (city) Dearborn County
123	128,300	**Jeffersonville** (city) Clark County
124	128,600	**Merrillville** (town) Lake County
125	132,000	**Greenfield** (city) Hancock County
126	132,200	**Bremen** (town) Marshall County
127	132,800	**Upland** (town) Grant County
128	133,000	**Lawrenceburg** (city) Dearborn County
129	133,600	**Lawrence** (city) Marion County
130	133,900	**Yorktown** (town) Delaware County
131	134,300	**Hobart** (city) Lake County
132	134,400	**Pendleton** (town) Madison County
133	135,600	**Griffith** (town) Lake County
134	136,300	**Hebron** (town) Porter County
135	139,800	**Dunlap** (CDP) Elkhart County
136	140,300	**Cicero** (town) Hamilton County
137	141,000	**Portage** (city) Porter County
138	143,100	**Greenwood** (city) Johnson County
139	143,700	**Newburgh** (town) Warrick County
140	144,900	**Sellersburg** (town) Clark County
141	148,500	**Columbus** (city) Bartholomew County
142	149,500	**Melody Hill** (CDP) Vanderburgh County
143	151,000	**Jasper** (city) Dubois County
144	152,200	**Lowell** (town) Lake County
145	152,800	**Danville** (town) Hendricks County
146	154,500	**De Motte** (town) Jasper County
146	154,500	**Huntertown** (town) Allen County
148	154,600	**Cumberland** (town) Marion County
148	154,600	**Simonton Lake** (CDP) Elkhart County
150	155,100	**Plainfield** (town) Hendricks County

Note: *This section ranks incorporated places and CDPs (Census Designated Places) with populations of 2,500 or more. Unincorporated postal areas were not considered. Please refer to the User Guide for additional information.*

Median Year Structure Built

Top 150 Places Ranked in *Descending* Order

State Rank	Year	Place
1	2008	**Whitestown** (town) Boone County
2	2005	**McCordsville** (town) Hancock County
3	2004	**Huntertown** (town) Allen County
4	2003	**Bargersville** (town) Johnson County
5	2002	**Westfield** (city) Hamilton County
6	2001	**Winfield** (town) Lake County
7	2000	**Avon** (town) Hendricks County
7	2000	**Noblesville** (city) Hamilton County
7	2000	**Pittsboro** (town) Hendricks County
10	1999	**Fishers** (city) Hamilton County
10	1999	**Zionsville** (town) Boone County
12	1998	**Saint John** (town) Lake County
13	1997	**Brownsburg** (town) Hendricks County
14	1995	**Santa Claus** (town) Spencer County
15	1994	**Carmel** (city) Hamilton County
15	1994	**Heritage Lake** (CDP) Putnam County
15	1994	**Plainfield** (town) Hendricks County
18	1993	**Notre Dame** (CDP) Saint Joseph County
19	1992	**Danville** (town) Hendricks County
19	1992	**De Motte** (town) Jasper County
21	1991	**Franklin** (city) Johnson County
21	1991	**Greenwood** (city) Johnson County
21	1991	**Hidden Valley** (CDP) Dearborn County
21	1991	**Lawrence** (city) Marion County
21	1991	**Leo-Cedarville** (town) Allen County
26	1990	**Bright** (CDP) Dearborn County
26	1990	**Country Squire Lakes** (CDP) Jennings County
28	1988	**Ellettsville** (town) Monroe County
28	1988	**Greenfield** (city) Hancock County
28	1988	**Porter** (town) Porter County
31	1987	**Georgetown** (town) Floyd County
31	1987	**Granger** (CDP) Saint Joseph County
31	1987	**Schererville** (town) Lake County
34	1986	**Dyer** (town) Lake County
34	1986	**Hebron** (town) Porter County
36	1985	**Shorewood Forest** (CDP) Porter County
37	1984	**Smithville-Sanders** (CDP) Monroe County
37	1984	**Whiteland** (town) Johnson County
37	1984	**Winona Lake** (town) Kosciusko County
40	1983	**Crown Point** (city) Lake County
40	1983	**Westville** (town) LaPorte County
42	1982	**Bloomington** (city) Monroe County
42	1982	**Cumberland** (town) Marion County
42	1982	**Ossian** (town) Wells County
45	1981	**Angola** (city) Steuben County
45	1981	**Highland** (CDP) Vanderburgh County
45	1981	**West Lafayette** (city) Tippecanoe County
48	1980	**Chesterton** (town) Porter County
48	1980	**Cicero** (town) Hamilton County
48	1980	**Middlebury** (town) Elkhart County
51	1979	**Columbia City** (city) Whitley County
51	1979	**Columbus** (city) Bartholomew County
51	1979	**Goshen** (city) Elkhart County
51	1979	**Jasper** (city) Dubois County
51	1979	**Simonton Lake** (CDP) Elkhart County
56	1978	**Jeffersonville** (city) Clark County
56	1978	**Lakes of the Four Seasons** (CDP) Lake County
56	1978	**Lebanon** (city) Boone County
56	1978	**Lowell** (town) Lake County
56	1978	**Portage** (city) Porter County
56	1978	**Roselawn** (CDP) Newton County
56	1978	**Salt Creek Commons** (CDP) Porter County
63	1977	**Auburn** (city) DeKalb County
63	1977	**Mooresville** (town) Morgan County
63	1977	**Sellersburg** (town) Clark County
66	1976	**Batesville** (city) Ripley County
66	1976	**Chandler** (town) Warrick County
66	1976	**Fortville** (town) Hancock County
66	1976	**Valparaiso** (city) Porter County
66	1976	**Warsaw** (city) Kosciusko County
71	1975	**Cedar Lake** (town) Lake County
72	1974	**Bremen** (town) Marshall County
72	1974	**Lawrenceburg** (city) Dearborn County
72	1974	**Melody Hill** (CDP) Vanderburgh County
72	1974	**Merrillville** (town) Lake County
72	1974	**Mishawaka** (city) Saint Joseph County
72	1974	**Nappanee** (city) Elkhart County
72	1974	**Upland** (town) Grant County
79	1973	**Dunlap** (CDP) Elkhart County
79	1973	**Hanover** (town) Jefferson County
79	1973	**Loogootee** (city) Martin County
79	1973	**New Haven** (city) Allen County
79	1973	**Pendleton** (town) Madison County
79	1973	**Seymour** (city) Jackson County
79	1973	**Syracuse** (town) Kosciusko County
86	1972	**Greensburg** (city) Decatur County
86	1972	**Newburgh** (town) Warrick County
86	1972	**North Vernon** (city) Jennings County
89	1971	**Indianapolis** (city) Marion County
89	1971	**Lafayette** (city) Tippecanoe County
89	1971	**Munster** (town) Lake County
89	1971	**Scottsburg** (city) Scott County
89	1971	**Yorktown** (town) Delaware County
94	1970	**Clarksville** (town) Clark County
94	1970	**Fort Wayne** (city) Allen County
94	1970	**New Whiteland** (town) Johnson County
97	1969	**Brownstown** (town) Jackson County
97	1969	**Kendallville** (city) Noble County
97	1969	**Plymouth** (city) Marshall County
97	1969	**Sheridan** (town) Hamilton County
101	1968	**Austin** (city) Scott County
101	1968	**Berne** (city) Adams County
101	1968	**Bluffton** (city) Wells County
101	1968	**Gas City** (city) Grant County
105	1967	**Greentown** (town) Howard County
105	1967	**Griffith** (town) Lake County
105	1967	**Mount Vernon** (city) Posey County
105	1967	**North Terre Haute** (CDP) Vigo County
105	1967	**Shelbyville** (city) Shelby County
105	1967	**South Haven** (CDP) Porter County
111	1966	**Brookville** (town) Franklin County
111	1966	**Highland** (town) Lake County
111	1966	**Hobart** (city) Lake County
111	1966	**Mitchell** (city) Lawrence County
115	1965	**Kokomo** (city) Howard County
116	1964	**Elkhart** (city) Elkhart County
116	1964	**Linton** (city) Greene County
116	1964	**Madison** (city) Jefferson County
116	1964	**Monticello** (city) White County
116	1964	**Osceola** (town) Saint Joseph County
116	1964	**Paoli** (town) Orange County
116	1964	**Salem** (city) Washington County
123	1963	**Edinburgh** (town) Johnson County
123	1963	**Fort Branch** (town) Gibson County
123	1963	**Greencastle** (city) Putnam County
126	1962	**Alexandria** (city) Madison County
126	1962	**Charlestown** (city) Clark County
126	1962	**Hartford City** (city) Blackford County
126	1962	**New Albany** (city) Floyd County
126	1962	**Rockville** (town) Parke County
126	1962	**Speedway** (town) Marion County
132	1961	**Beech Grove** (city) Marion County
132	1961	**Fairmount** (town) Grant County
132	1961	**Michigan City** (city) LaPorte County
132	1961	**Tell City** (city) Perry County
136	1960	**Anderson** (city) Madison County
136	1960	**Centerville** (town) Wayne County
136	1960	**Corydon** (town) Harrison County
136	1960	**Crawfordsville** (city) Montgomery County
136	1960	**Greendale** (city) Dearborn County
136	1960	**Lagrange** (town) LaGrange County
136	1960	**Ligonier** (city) Noble County
136	1960	**Muncie** (city) Delaware County
136	1960	**Union City** (city) Randolph County
145	1959	**Bedford** (city) Lawrence County
145	1959	**Boonville** (city) Warrick County
145	1959	**Decatur** (city) Adams County
145	1959	**Princeton** (city) Gibson County
145	1959	**Rensselaer** (city) Jasper County
150	1958	**Evansville** (city) Vanderburgh County

***Note:** This section ranks incorporated places and CDPs (Census Designated Places) with populations of 2,500 or more. Unincorporated postal areas were not considered. Please refer to the User Guide for additional information.*

Median Year Structure Built

Top 150 Places Ranked in *Ascending* Order

State Rank	Year	Place
1	<1940	**Aurora** (city) Dearborn County
1	<1940	**Bicknell** (city) Knox County
1	<1940	**Logansport** (city) Cass County
1	<1940	**Peru** (city) Miami County
1	<1940	**Whiting** (city) Lake County
6	1941	**Clinton** (city) Vermillion County
6	1941	**Huntington** (city) Huntington County
8	1942	**East Chicago** (city) Lake County
8	1942	**Elwood** (city) Madison County
10	1948	**Winamac** (town) Pulaski County
11	1949	**Wabash** (city) Wabash County
12	1950	**Delphi** (city) Carroll County
13	1951	**Hammond** (city) Lake County
13	1951	**Rushville** (city) Rush County
13	1951	**Tipton** (city) Tipton County
16	1952	**Attica** (city) Fountain County
16	1952	**Butler** (city) DeKalb County
18	1953	**Brazil** (city) Clay County
18	1953	**Portland** (city) Jay County
18	1953	**Terre Haute** (city) Vigo County
21	1954	**Frankfort** (city) Clinton County
21	1954	**Winchester** (city) Randolph County
23	1955	**Gary** (city) Lake County
23	1955	**La Porte** (city) LaPorte County
23	1955	**South Bend** (city) Saint Joseph County
23	1955	**Sullivan** (city) Sullivan County
27	1956	**Connersville** (city) Fayette County
27	1956	**Richmond** (city) Wayne County
29	1957	**Garrett** (city) DeKalb County
29	1957	**New Castle** (city) Henry County
29	1957	**North Manchester** (town) Wabash County
29	1957	**Vincennes** (city) Knox County
29	1957	**Washington** (city) Daviess County
34	1958	**Evansville** (city) Vanderburgh County
34	1958	**Huntingburg** (city) Dubois County
34	1958	**Knox** (city) Starke County
34	1958	**Lake Station** (city) Lake County
34	1958	**Marion** (city) Grant County
34	1958	**Martinsville** (city) Morgan County
34	1958	**Rochester** (city) Fulton County
41	1959	**Bedford** (city) Lawrence County
41	1959	**Boonville** (city) Warrick County
41	1959	**Decatur** (city) Adams County
41	1959	**Princeton** (city) Gibson County
41	1959	**Rensselaer** (city) Jasper County
46	1960	**Anderson** (city) Madison County
46	1960	**Centerville** (town) Wayne County
46	1960	**Corydon** (town) Harrison County
46	1960	**Crawfordsville** (city) Montgomery County
46	1960	**Greendale** (city) Dearborn County
46	1960	**Lagrange** (town) LaGrange County
46	1960	**Ligonier** (city) Noble County
46	1960	**Muncie** (city) Delaware County
46	1960	**Union City** (city) Randolph County
55	1961	**Beech Grove** (city) Marion County
55	1961	**Fairmount** (town) Grant County
55	1961	**Michigan City** (city) LaPorte County
55	1961	**Tell City** (city) Perry County
59	1962	**Alexandria** (city) Madison County
59	1962	**Charlestown** (city) Clark County
59	1962	**Hartford City** (city) Blackford County
59	1962	**New Albany** (city) Floyd County
59	1962	**Rockville** (town) Parke County
59	1962	**Speedway** (town) Marion County
65	1963	**Edinburgh** (town) Johnson County
65	1963	**Fort Branch** (town) Gibson County
65	1963	**Greencastle** (city) Putnam County
68	1964	**Elkhart** (city) Elkhart County
68	1964	**Linton** (city) Greene County
68	1964	**Madison** (city) Jefferson County
68	1964	**Monticello** (city) White County
68	1964	**Osceola** (town) Saint Joseph County
68	1964	**Paoli** (town) Orange County
68	1964	**Salem** (city) Washington County
75	1965	**Kokomo** (city) Howard County
76	1966	**Brookville** (town) Franklin County
76	1966	**Highland** (town) Lake County
76	1966	**Hobart** (city) Lake County
76	1966	**Mitchell** (city) Lawrence County
80	1967	**Greentown** (town) Howard County
80	1967	**Griffith** (town) Lake County
80	1967	**Mount Vernon** (city) Posey County
80	1967	**North Terre Haute** (CDP) Vigo County
80	1967	**Shelbyville** (city) Shelby County
80	1967	**South Haven** (CDP) Porter County
86	1968	**Austin** (city) Scott County
86	1968	**Berne** (city) Adams County
86	1968	**Bluffton** (city) Wells County
86	1968	**Gas City** (city) Grant County
90	1969	**Brownstown** (town) Jackson County
90	1969	**Kendallville** (city) Noble County
90	1969	**Plymouth** (city) Marshall County
90	1969	**Sheridan** (town) Hamilton County
94	1970	**Clarksville** (town) Clark County
94	1970	**Fort Wayne** (city) Allen County
94	1970	**New Whiteland** (town) Johnson County
97	1971	**Indianapolis** (city) Marion County
97	1971	**Lafayette** (city) Tippecanoe County
97	1971	**Munster** (town) Lake County
97	1971	**Scottsburg** (city) Scott County
97	1971	**Yorktown** (town) Delaware County
102	1972	**Greensburg** (city) Decatur County
102	1972	**Newburgh** (town) Warrick County
102	1972	**North Vernon** (city) Jennings County
105	1973	**Dunlap** (CDP) Elkhart County
105	1973	**Hanover** (town) Jefferson County
105	1973	**Loogootee** (city) Martin County
105	1973	**New Haven** (city) Allen County
105	1973	**Pendleton** (town) Madison County
105	1973	**Seymour** (city) Jackson County
105	1973	**Syracuse** (town) Kosciusko County
112	1974	**Bremen** (town) Marshall County
112	1974	**Lawrenceburg** (city) Dearborn County
112	1974	**Melody Hill** (CDP) Vanderburgh County
112	1974	**Merrillville** (town) Lake County
112	1974	**Mishawaka** (city) Saint Joseph County
112	1974	**Nappanee** (city) Elkhart County
112	1974	**Upland** (town) Grant County
119	1975	**Cedar Lake** (town) Lake County
120	1976	**Batesville** (city) Ripley County
120	1976	**Chandler** (town) Warrick County
120	1976	**Fortville** (town) Hancock County
120	1976	**Valparaiso** (city) Porter County
120	1976	**Warsaw** (city) Kosciusko County
125	1977	**Auburn** (city) DeKalb County
125	1977	**Mooresville** (town) Morgan County
125	1977	**Sellersburg** (town) Clark County
128	1978	**Jeffersonville** (city) Clark County
128	1978	**Lakes of the Four Seasons** (CDP) Lake County
128	1978	**Lebanon** (city) Boone County
128	1978	**Lowell** (town) Lake County
128	1978	**Portage** (city) Porter County
128	1978	**Roselawn** (CDP) Newton County
128	1978	**Salt Creek Commons** (CDP) Porter County
135	1979	**Columbia City** (city) Whitley County
135	1979	**Columbus** (city) Bartholomew County
135	1979	**Goshen** (city) Elkhart County
135	1979	**Jasper** (city) Dubois County
135	1979	**Simonton Lake** (CDP) Elkhart County
140	1980	**Chesterton** (town) Porter County
140	1980	**Cicero** (town) Hamilton County
140	1980	**Middlebury** (town) Elkhart County
143	1981	**Angola** (city) Steuben County
143	1981	**Highland** (CDP) Vanderburgh County
143	1981	**West Lafayette** (city) Tippecanoe County
146	1982	**Bloomington** (city) Monroe County
146	1982	**Cumberland** (town) Marion County
146	1982	**Ossian** (town) Wells County
149	1983	**Crown Point** (city) Lake County
149	1983	**Westville** (town) LaPorte County

Note: *This section ranks incorporated places and CDPs (Census Designated Places) with populations of 2,500 or more. Unincorporated postal areas were not considered. Please refer to the User Guide for additional information.*

Homeowner Vacancy Rate

Top 150 Places Ranked in *Descending* Order

State Rank	Percent	Place
1	16.8	**Aurora** (city) Dearborn County
2	10.8	**Rockville** (town) Parke County
3	10.0	**Madison** (city) Jefferson County
4	8.8	**Smithville-Sanders** (CDP) Monroe County
5	8.4	**Monticello** (city) White County
6	8.3	**Paoli** (town) Orange County
7	7.6	**Upland** (town) Grant County
8	7.5	**Connersville** (city) Fayette County
9	6.1	**Angola** (city) Steuben County
9	6.1	**Lake Station** (city) Lake County
11	5.9	**De Motte** (town) Jasper County
12	5.8	**Westville** (town) LaPorte County
13	5.4	**Union City** (city) Randolph County
14	5.3	**New Castle** (city) Henry County
15	4.9	**Plymouth** (city) Marshall County
16	4.8	**Mitchell** (city) Lawrence County
16	4.8	**Rensselaer** (city) Jasper County
16	4.8	**Sheridan** (town) Hamilton County
19	4.7	**Brookville** (town) Franklin County
19	4.7	**Marion** (city) Grant County
21	4.4	**Rushville** (city) Rush County
22	4.3	**Brazil** (city) Clay County
22	4.3	**Wabash** (city) Wabash County
24	4.2	**Jasper** (city) Dubois County
25	4.1	**Bedford** (city) Lawrence County
25	4.1	**Butler** (city) DeKalb County
25	4.1	**Salem** (city) Washington County
28	4.0	**Scottsburg** (city) Scott County
28	4.0	**Speedway** (town) Marion County
30	3.9	**Anderson** (city) Madison County
30	3.9	**Charlestown** (city) Clark County
30	3.9	**Clarksville** (town) Clark County
30	3.9	**Elwood** (city) Madison County
30	3.9	**Princeton** (city) Gibson County
35	3.8	**Terre Haute** (city) Vigo County
36	3.7	**McCordsville** (town) Hancock County
36	3.7	**Mount Vernon** (city) Posey County
36	3.7	**Roselawn** (CDP) Newton County
39	3.6	**Auburn** (city) DeKalb County
39	3.6	**Batesville** (city) Ripley County
39	3.6	**Cedar Lake** (town) Lake County
39	3.6	**Melody Hill** (CDP) Vanderburgh County
39	3.6	**Muncie** (city) Delaware County
44	3.5	**Centerville** (town) Wayne County
44	3.5	**North Manchester** (town) Wabash County
44	3.5	**Santa Claus** (town) Spencer County
47	3.4	**Alexandria** (city) Madison County
47	3.4	**Chandler** (town) Warrick County
47	3.4	**Franklin** (city) Johnson County
47	3.4	**Greendale** (city) Dearborn County
47	3.4	**Lawrence** (city) Marion County
47	3.4	**South Haven** (CDP) Porter County
53	3.3	**Clinton** (city) Vermillion County
53	3.3	**Ellettsville** (town) Monroe County
55	3.2	**Fairmount** (town) Grant County
55	3.2	**Gary** (city) Lake County
55	3.2	**Kokomo** (city) Howard County
58	3.1	**Elkhart** (city) Elkhart County
58	3.1	**Georgetown** (town) Floyd County
58	3.1	**Ossian** (town) Wells County
58	3.1	**Richmond** (city) Wayne County
62	3.0	**Gas City** (city) Grant County
62	3.0	**Ligonier** (city) Noble County
62	3.0	**Seymour** (city) Jackson County
65	2.9	**Greentown** (town) Howard County
65	2.9	**Highland** (CDP) Vanderburgh County
65	2.9	**Portland** (city) Jay County
65	2.9	**South Bend** (city) Saint Joseph County
65	2.9	**Tipton** (city) Tipton County
65	2.9	**Whiting** (city) Lake County
71	2.8	**Cumberland** (town) Marion County
71	2.8	**Hidden Valley** (CDP) Dearborn County
73	2.6	**Loogootee** (city) Martin County
73	2.6	**Winfield** (town) Lake County
75	2.5	**Greenfield** (city) Hancock County
75	2.5	**Knox** (city) Starke County
77	2.4	**Carmel** (city) Hamilton County
77	2.4	**Hartford City** (city) Blackford County
77	2.4	**Jeffersonville** (city) Clark County
77	2.4	**New Albany** (city) Floyd County
77	2.4	**Syracuse** (town) Kosciusko County
82	2.3	**La Porte** (city) LaPorte County
82	2.3	**Linton** (city) Greene County
82	2.3	**North Terre Haute** (CDP) Vigo County
82	2.3	**Simonton Lake** (CDP) Elkhart County
86	2.2	**Evansville** (city) Vanderburgh County
86	2.2	**Peru** (city) Miami County
88	2.1	**Bremen** (town) Marshall County
88	2.1	**Crawfordsville** (city) Montgomery County
88	2.1	**East Chicago** (city) Lake County
88	2.1	**Greencastle** (city) Putnam County
88	2.1	**Hanover** (town) Jefferson County
88	2.1	**Indianapolis** (city) Marion County
88	2.1	**Michigan City** (city) LaPorte County
95	2.0	**Beech Grove** (city) Marion County
95	2.0	**Hammond** (city) Lake County
97	1.9	**Huntington** (city) Huntington County
97	1.9	**Kendallville** (city) Noble County
97	1.9	**Lafayette** (city) Tippecanoe County
97	1.9	**North Vernon** (city) Jennings County
97	1.9	**Valparaiso** (city) Porter County
97	1.9	**Vincennes** (city) Knox County
97	1.9	**Winchester** (city) Randolph County
104	1.8	**Berne** (city) Adams County
104	1.8	**Fort Wayne** (city) Allen County
104	1.8	**Goshen** (city) Elkhart County
104	1.8	**Nappanee** (city) Elkhart County
108	1.7	**Cicero** (town) Hamilton County
108	1.7	**Huntertown** (town) Allen County
108	1.7	**Mishawaka** (city) Saint Joseph County
108	1.7	**Washington** (city) Daviess County
112	1.6	**Brownstown** (town) Jackson County
112	1.6	**Highland** (town) Lake County
112	1.6	**Munster** (town) Lake County
112	1.6	**Portage** (city) Porter County
116	1.4	**Lebanon** (city) Boone County
116	1.4	**Logansport** (city) Cass County
116	1.4	**Noblesville** (city) Hamilton County
116	1.4	**Tell City** (city) Perry County
120	1.3	**Crown Point** (city) Lake County
120	1.3	**Delphi** (city) Carroll County
120	1.3	**Schererville** (town) Lake County
123	1.2	**Pittsboro** (town) Hendricks County
123	1.2	**Shelbyville** (city) Shelby County
125	1.1	**Bluffton** (city) Wells County
125	1.1	**Dyer** (town) Lake County
125	1.1	**Greenwood** (city) Johnson County
128	1.0	**Hobart** (city) Lake County
128	1.0	**Merrillville** (town) Lake County
130	0.9	**Avon** (town) Hendricks County
130	0.9	**Bloomington** (city) Monroe County
130	0.9	**Heritage Lake** (CDP) Putnam County
130	0.9	**Huntingburg** (city) Dubois County
130	0.9	**Plainfield** (town) Hendricks County
130	0.9	**Yorktown** (town) Delaware County
136	0.8	**Columbus** (city) Bartholomew County
137	0.7	**Danville** (town) Hendricks County
137	0.7	**Warsaw** (city) Kosciusko County
139	0.6	**Brownsburg** (town) Hendricks County
139	0.6	**Columbia City** (city) Whitley County
141	0.5	**Frankfort** (city) Clinton County
141	0.5	**New Haven** (city) Allen County
141	0.5	**West Lafayette** (city) Tippecanoe County
144	0.4	**Fishers** (city) Hamilton County
145	0.3	**Granger** (CDP) Saint Joseph County
145	0.3	**Westfield** (city) Hamilton County
147	0.2	**Griffith** (town) Lake County
148	0.1	**Saint John** (town) Lake County
149	0.0	**Attica** (city) Fountain County
149	0.0	**Austin** (city) Scott County

***Note:** This section ranks incorporated places and CDPs (Census Designated Places) with populations of 2,500 or more. Unincorporated postal areas were not considered. Please refer to the User Guide for additional information.*

Median Selected Monthly Owner Costs: With Mortgage

Top 150 Places Ranked in *Descending* Order

State Rank	Dollars	Place
1	2,349	**Shorewood Forest** (CDP) Porter County
2	2,192	**Zionsville** (town) Boone County
3	1,968	**Carmel** (city) Hamilton County
4	1,732	**Winfield** (town) Lake County
5	1,706	**Saint John** (town) Lake County
6	1,612	**Westfield** (city) Hamilton County
7	1,580	**Munster** (town) Lake County
8	1,579	**Fishers** (city) Hamilton County
9	1,560	**Whitestown** (town) Boone County
10	1,504	**McCordsville** (town) Hancock County
11	1,486	**Avon** (town) Hendricks County
12	1,449	**Hidden Valley** (CDP) Dearborn County
13	1,425	**Dyer** (town) Lake County
14	1,408	**Lakes of the Four Seasons** (CDP) Lake County
14	1,408	**Schererville** (town) Lake County
16	1,397	**Georgetown** (town) Floyd County
17	1,391	**Porter** (town) Porter County
18	1,384	**Crown Point** (city) Lake County
19	1,379	**Granger** (CDP) Saint Joseph County
20	1,374	**West Lafayette** (city) Tippecanoe County
21	1,372	**Bargersville** (town) Johnson County
22	1,370	**Valparaiso** (city) Porter County
23	1,366	**Noblesville** (city) Hamilton County
24	1,358	**Chesterton** (town) Porter County
25	1,341	**Danville** (town) Hendricks County
26	1,298	**Pittsboro** (town) Hendricks County
27	1,295	**Heritage Lake** (CDP) Putnam County
28	1,291	**Cedar Lake** (town) Lake County
29	1,284	**Winona Lake** (town) Kosciusko County
30	1,261	**Bright** (CDP) Dearborn County
31	1,256	**Leo-Cedarville** (town) Allen County
32	1,255	**Santa Claus** (town) Spencer County
33	1,242	**Highland** (CDP) Vanderburgh County
34	1,240	**Brownsburg** (town) Hendricks County
35	1,238	**Newburgh** (town) Warrick County
36	1,237	**Plainfield** (town) Hendricks County
37	1,236	**Portage** (city) Porter County
38	1,219	**Lowell** (town) Lake County
39	1,208	**Bloomington** (city) Monroe County
40	1,205	**Highland** (town) Lake County
41	1,204	**Batesville** (city) Ripley County
42	1,195	**Merrillville** (town) Lake County
43	1,189	**Hebron** (town) Porter County
44	1,188	**Griffith** (town) Lake County
45	1,177	**Huntertown** (town) Allen County
46	1,176	**De Motte** (town) Jasper County
47	1,170	**Whiteland** (town) Johnson County
48	1,167	**Lawrence** (city) Marion County
49	1,162	**Hobart** (city) Lake County
50	1,161	**Cumberland** (town) Marion County
51	1,160	**Melody Hill** (CDP) Vanderburgh County
52	1,158	**Middlebury** (town) Elkhart County
53	1,156	**Columbus** (city) Bartholomew County
54	1,144	**Salt Creek Commons** (CDP) Porter County
55	1,142	**South Haven** (CDP) Porter County
56	1,131	**Upland** (town) Grant County
57	1,127	**Fortville** (town) Hancock County
58	1,125	**Pendleton** (town) Madison County
59	1,124	**Indianapolis** (city) Marion County
59	1,124	**Yorktown** (town) Delaware County
61	1,120	**Smithville-Sanders** (CDP) Monroe County
62	1,115	**Greenwood** (city) Johnson County
63	1,113	**Lebanon** (city) Boone County
64	1,105	**Dunlap** (CDP) Elkhart County
65	1,104	**Franklin** (city) Johnson County
66	1,103	**Jasper** (city) Dubois County
66	1,103	**Westville** (town) LaPorte County
68	1,099	**Sellersburg** (town) Clark County
69	1,094	**Jeffersonville** (city) Clark County
70	1,093	**Whiting** (city) Lake County
71	1,070	**Cicero** (town) Hamilton County
72	1,066	**Simonton Lake** (CDP) Elkhart County
73	1,057	**Aurora** (city) Dearborn County
74	1,053	**Greenfield** (city) Hancock County
75	1,047	**Lawrenceburg** (city) Dearborn County
76	1,046	**Bremen** (town) Marshall County
77	1,041	**Shelbyville** (city) Shelby County
78	1,029	**Speedway** (town) Marion County
79	1,026	**Osceola** (town) Saint Joseph County
80	1,023	**East Chicago** (city) Lake County
81	1,022	**Charlestown** (city) Clark County
82	1,021	**Greencastle** (city) Putnam County
83	1,014	**Fort Branch** (town) Gibson County
84	1,009	**Loogootee** (city) Martin County
85	1,006	**Clarksville** (town) Clark County
86	1,005	**Mooresville** (town) Morgan County
87	1,002	**Huntingburg** (city) Dubois County
88	1,001	**Nappanee** (city) Elkhart County
89	996	**Greentown** (town) Howard County
90	992	**New Albany** (city) Floyd County
91	988	**Greendale** (city) Dearborn County
92	987	**Warsaw** (city) Kosciusko County
93	985	**Gary** (city) Lake County
94	984	**Hammond** (city) Lake County
94	984	**Madison** (city) Jefferson County
96	982	**Seymour** (city) Jackson County
97	979	**Roselawn** (CDP) Newton County
98	978	**Ellettsville** (town) Monroe County
99	974	**Columbia City** (city) Whitley County
100	973	**Martinsville** (city) Morgan County
101	970	**Scottsburg** (city) Scott County
102	968	**Edinburgh** (town) Johnson County
103	965	**Angola** (city) Steuben County
103	965	**Sheridan** (town) Hamilton County
105	961	**Goshen** (city) Elkhart County
106	958	**Alexandria** (city) Madison County
106	958	**Mount Vernon** (city) Posey County
108	953	**Fort Wayne** (city) Allen County
109	952	**Beech Grove** (city) Marion County
109	952	**Delphi** (city) Carroll County
111	951	**Brownstown** (town) Jackson County
112	950	**Country Squire Lakes** (CDP) Jennings County
113	949	**Berne** (city) Adams County
113	949	**Greensburg** (city) Decatur County
115	948	**Ligonier** (city) Noble County
116	940	**Knox** (city) Starke County
116	940	**Linton** (city) Greene County
118	939	**Lake Station** (city) Lake County
119	932	**Syracuse** (town) Kosciusko County
120	931	**Lafayette** (city) Tippecanoe County
120	931	**Mishawaka** (city) Saint Joseph County
122	929	**La Porte** (city) LaPorte County
123	927	**Boonville** (city) Warrick County
124	926	**Evansville** (city) Vanderburgh County
125	921	**New Whiteland** (town) Johnson County
126	918	**Austin** (city) Scott County
127	913	**Corydon** (town) Harrison County
128	911	**New Haven** (city) Allen County
129	909	**Frankfort** (city) Clinton County
130	908	**Rensselaer** (city) Jasper County
131	906	**Hanover** (town) Jefferson County
132	905	**South Bend** (city) Saint Joseph County
133	902	**Attica** (city) Fountain County
134	898	**Michigan City** (city) LaPorte County
134	898	**Tipton** (city) Tipton County
136	896	**Bedford** (city) Lawrence County
136	896	**North Vernon** (city) Jennings County
138	893	**Auburn** (city) DeKalb County
138	893	**Elkhart** (city) Elkhart County
140	883	**Garrett** (city) DeKalb County
141	881	**Rushville** (city) Rush County
142	880	**Richmond** (city) Wayne County
143	878	**Chandler** (town) Warrick County
144	875	**Butler** (city) DeKalb County
145	874	**Kokomo** (city) Howard County
146	872	**Washington** (city) Daviess County
147	869	**Crawfordsville** (city) Montgomery County
147	869	**Rochester** (city) Fulton County
149	868	**Salem** (city) Washington County
150	866	**Anderson** (city) Madison County

Note: *This section ranks incorporated places and CDPs (Census Designated Places) with populations of 2,500 or more. Unincorporated postal areas were not considered. Please refer to the User Guide for additional information.*

Median Selected Monthly Owner Costs: With Mortgage

Top 150 Places Ranked in *Ascending* Order

State Rank	Dollars	Place
1	716	**Bicknell** (city) Knox County
2	749	**Union City** (city) Randolph County
3	758	**Rockville** (town) Parke County
4	759	**Lagrange** (town) LaGrange County
4	759	**Sullivan** (city) Sullivan County
6	764	**Marion** (city) Grant County
7	769	**Portland** (city) Jay County
8	776	**Clinton** (city) Vermillion County
9	780	**Wabash** (city) Wabash County
10	783	**Peru** (city) Miami County
11	784	**Winchester** (city) Randolph County
12	796	**Hartford City** (city) Blackford County
13	804	**Tell City** (city) Perry County
14	808	**Vincennes** (city) Knox County
15	809	**Muncie** (city) Delaware County
16	812	**Logansport** (city) Cass County
17	817	**Kendallville** (city) Noble County
18	820	**Elwood** (city) Madison County
19	828	**Bluffton** (city) Wells County
20	834	**Huntington** (city) Huntington County
21	836	**North Terre Haute** (CDP) Vigo County
22	837	**North Manchester** (town) Wabash County
23	841	**Gas City** (city) Grant County
24	843	**Brazil** (city) Clay County
24	843	**Ossian** (town) Wells County
26	845	**New Castle** (city) Henry County
27	846	**Paoli** (town) Orange County
28	848	**Mitchell** (city) Lawrence County
29	849	**Terre Haute** (city) Vigo County
30	851	**Winamac** (town) Pulaski County
31	852	**Monticello** (city) White County
32	853	**Plymouth** (city) Marshall County
33	857	**Centerville** (town) Wayne County
33	857	**Connersville** (city) Fayette County
35	859	**Decatur** (city) Adams County
35	859	**Fairmount** (town) Grant County
37	862	**Brookville** (town) Franklin County
38	866	**Anderson** (city) Madison County
38	866	**Princeton** (city) Gibson County
40	868	**Salem** (city) Washington County
41	869	**Crawfordsville** (city) Montgomery County
41	869	**Rochester** (city) Fulton County
43	872	**Washington** (city) Daviess County
44	874	**Kokomo** (city) Howard County
45	875	**Butler** (city) DeKalb County
46	878	**Chandler** (town) Warrick County
47	880	**Richmond** (city) Wayne County
48	881	**Rushville** (city) Rush County
49	883	**Garrett** (city) DeKalb County
50	893	**Auburn** (city) DeKalb County
50	893	**Elkhart** (city) Elkhart County
52	896	**Bedford** (city) Lawrence County
52	896	**North Vernon** (city) Jennings County
54	898	**Michigan City** (city) LaPorte County
54	898	**Tipton** (city) Tipton County
56	902	**Attica** (city) Fountain County
57	905	**South Bend** (city) Saint Joseph County
58	906	**Hanover** (town) Jefferson County
59	908	**Rensselaer** (city) Jasper County
60	909	**Frankfort** (city) Clinton County
61	911	**New Haven** (city) Allen County
62	913	**Corydon** (town) Harrison County
63	918	**Austin** (city) Scott County
64	921	**New Whiteland** (town) Johnson County
65	926	**Evansville** (city) Vanderburgh County
66	927	**Boonville** (city) Warrick County
67	929	**La Porte** (city) LaPorte County
68	931	**Lafayette** (city) Tippecanoe County
68	931	**Mishawaka** (city) Saint Joseph County
70	932	**Syracuse** (town) Kosciusko County
71	939	**Lake Station** (city) Lake County
72	940	**Knox** (city) Starke County
72	940	**Linton** (city) Greene County
74	948	**Ligonier** (city) Noble County
75	949	**Berne** (city) Adams County
75	949	**Greensburg** (city) Decatur County
77	950	**Country Squire Lakes** (CDP) Jennings County
78	951	**Brownstown** (town) Jackson County
79	952	**Beech Grove** (city) Marion County
79	952	**Delphi** (city) Carroll County
81	953	**Fort Wayne** (city) Allen County
82	958	**Alexandria** (city) Madison County
82	958	**Mount Vernon** (city) Posey County
84	961	**Goshen** (city) Elkhart County
85	965	**Angola** (city) Steuben County
85	965	**Sheridan** (town) Hamilton County
87	968	**Edinburgh** (town) Johnson County
88	970	**Scottsburg** (city) Scott County
89	973	**Martinsville** (city) Morgan County
90	974	**Columbia City** (city) Whitley County
91	978	**Ellettsville** (town) Monroe County
92	979	**Roselawn** (CDP) Newton County
93	982	**Seymour** (city) Jackson County
94	984	**Hammond** (city) Lake County
94	984	**Madison** (city) Jefferson County
96	985	**Gary** (city) Lake County
97	987	**Warsaw** (city) Kosciusko County
98	988	**Greendale** (city) Dearborn County
99	992	**New Albany** (city) Floyd County
100	996	**Greentown** (town) Howard County
101	1,001	**Nappanee** (city) Elkhart County
102	1,002	**Huntingburg** (city) Dubois County
103	1,005	**Mooresville** (town) Morgan County
104	1,006	**Clarksville** (town) Clark County
105	1,009	**Loogootee** (city) Martin County
106	1,014	**Fort Branch** (town) Gibson County
107	1,021	**Greencastle** (city) Putnam County
108	1,022	**Charlestown** (city) Clark County
109	1,023	**East Chicago** (city) Lake County
110	1,026	**Osceola** (town) Saint Joseph County
111	1,029	**Speedway** (town) Marion County
112	1,041	**Shelbyville** (city) Shelby County
113	1,046	**Bremen** (town) Marshall County
114	1,047	**Lawrenceburg** (city) Dearborn County
115	1,053	**Greenfield** (city) Hancock County
116	1,057	**Aurora** (city) Dearborn County
117	1,066	**Simonton Lake** (CDP) Elkhart County
118	1,070	**Cicero** (town) Hamilton County
119	1,093	**Whiting** (city) Lake County
120	1,094	**Jeffersonville** (city) Clark County
121	1,099	**Sellersburg** (town) Clark County
122	1,103	**Jasper** (city) Dubois County
122	1,103	**Westville** (town) LaPorte County
124	1,104	**Franklin** (city) Johnson County
125	1,105	**Dunlap** (CDP) Elkhart County
126	1,113	**Lebanon** (city) Boone County
127	1,115	**Greenwood** (city) Johnson County
128	1,120	**Smithville-Sanders** (CDP) Monroe County
129	1,124	**Indianapolis** (city) Marion County
129	1,124	**Yorktown** (town) Delaware County
131	1,125	**Pendleton** (town) Madison County
132	1,127	**Fortville** (town) Hancock County
133	1,131	**Upland** (town) Grant County
134	1,142	**South Haven** (CDP) Porter County
135	1,144	**Salt Creek Commons** (CDP) Porter County
136	1,156	**Columbus** (city) Bartholomew County
137	1,158	**Middlebury** (town) Elkhart County
138	1,160	**Melody Hill** (CDP) Vanderburgh County
139	1,161	**Cumberland** (town) Marion County
140	1,162	**Hobart** (city) Lake County
141	1,167	**Lawrence** (city) Marion County
142	1,170	**Whiteland** (town) Johnson County
143	1,176	**De Motte** (town) Jasper County
144	1,177	**Huntertown** (town) Allen County
145	1,188	**Griffith** (town) Lake County
146	1,189	**Hebron** (town) Porter County
147	1,195	**Merrillville** (town) Lake County
148	1,204	**Batesville** (city) Ripley County
149	1,205	**Highland** (town) Lake County
150	1,208	**Bloomington** (city) Monroe County

Note: *This section ranks incorporated places and CDPs (Census Designated Places) with populations of 2,500 or more. Unincorporated postal areas were not considered. Please refer to the User Guide for additional information.*

Median Selected Monthly Owner Costs: Without Mortgage

Top 150 Places Ranked in *Descending* Order

State Rank	Dollars	Place
1	709	**Winfield** (town) Lake County
2	664	**Zionsville** (town) Boone County
3	587	**Carmel** (city) Hamilton County
4	582	**Shorewood Forest** (CDP) Porter County
5	571	**Saint John** (town) Lake County
6	556	**Munster** (town) Lake County
6	556	**Westfield** (city) Hamilton County
8	550	**Dyer** (town) Lake County
9	544	**Bargersville** (town) Johnson County
9	544	**Fishers** (city) Hamilton County
11	511	**Lakes of the Four Seasons** (CDP) Lake County
12	505	**Hebron** (town) Porter County
13	501	**Noblesville** (city) Hamilton County
14	494	**Chesterton** (town) Porter County
14	494	**Newburgh** (town) Warrick County
16	493	**Cumberland** (town) Marion County
17	480	**Highland** (CDP) Vanderburgh County
17	480	**Porter** (town) Porter County
19	478	**Crown Point** (city) Lake County
20	473	**Brownsburg** (town) Hendricks County
21	466	**Hidden Valley** (CDP) Dearborn County
22	465	**West Lafayette** (city) Tippecanoe County
23	462	**Pittsboro** (town) Hendricks County
23	462	**Portage** (city) Porter County
23	462	**Schererville** (town) Lake County
26	458	**Valparaiso** (city) Porter County
27	455	**Cedar Lake** (town) Lake County
27	455	**Danville** (town) Hendricks County
27	455	**Georgetown** (town) Floyd County
30	454	**Westville** (town) LaPorte County
31	453	**McCordsville** (town) Hancock County
32	452	**Avon** (town) Hendricks County
33	451	**Lebanon** (city) Boone County
34	450	**Bloomington** (city) Monroe County
35	449	**Santa Claus** (town) Spencer County
36	446	**Whitestown** (town) Boone County
37	444	**Huntertown** (town) Allen County
38	439	**Hobart** (city) Lake County
39	435	**Highland** (town) Lake County
40	432	**Greenwood** (city) Johnson County
41	431	**Bright** (CDP) Dearborn County
42	430	**Heritage Lake** (CDP) Putnam County
42	430	**Pendleton** (town) Madison County
44	429	**Granger** (CDP) Saint Joseph County
45	424	**Plainfield** (town) Hendricks County
45	424	**Salt Creek Commons** (CDP) Porter County
45	424	**Sellersburg** (town) Clark County
48	422	**Nappanee** (city) Elkhart County
48	422	**Roselawn** (CDP) Newton County
50	421	**Middlebury** (town) Elkhart County
51	420	**Lowell** (town) Lake County
52	418	**Sheridan** (town) Hamilton County
52	418	**Yorktown** (town) Delaware County
54	417	**Griffith** (town) Lake County
55	416	**Lawrence** (city) Marion County
56	413	**Ellettsville** (town) Monroe County
56	413	**Goshen** (city) Elkhart County
58	411	**Lake Station** (city) Lake County
59	409	**Indianapolis** (city) Marion County
60	407	**La Porte** (city) LaPorte County
61	402	**Merrillville** (town) Lake County
61	402	**Shelbyville** (city) Shelby County
63	401	**Columbus** (city) Bartholomew County
64	399	**Smithville-Sanders** (CDP) Monroe County
65	397	**Jasper** (city) Dubois County
66	395	**Whiteland** (town) Johnson County
67	393	**Boonville** (city) Warrick County
67	393	**Gary** (city) Lake County
67	393	**Hammond** (city) Lake County
70	392	**Clarksville** (town) Clark County
71	391	**New Whiteland** (town) Johnson County
72	389	**Greentown** (town) Howard County
73	388	**Aurora** (city) Dearborn County
73	388	**Columbia City** (city) Whitley County
75	387	**Evansville** (city) Vanderburgh County
75	387	**Jeffersonville** (city) Clark County
75	387	**Warsaw** (city) Kosciusko County
78	385	**Melody Hill** (CDP) Vanderburgh County
79	384	**Bedford** (city) Lawrence County
79	384	**Cicero** (town) Hamilton County
79	384	**Country Squire Lakes** (CDP) Jennings County
82	383	**Fairmount** (town) Grant County
82	383	**Fort Branch** (town) Gibson County
84	382	**Scottsburg** (city) Scott County
85	380	**Franklin** (city) Johnson County
85	380	**Greencastle** (city) Putnam County
87	379	**Greenfield** (city) Hancock County
87	379	**South Haven** (CDP) Porter County
87	379	**Upland** (town) Grant County
90	378	**Angola** (city) Steuben County
90	378	**New Albany** (city) Floyd County
92	374	**Martinsville** (city) Morgan County
93	371	**Whiting** (city) Lake County
94	370	**Mount Vernon** (city) Posey County
94	370	**Plymouth** (city) Marshall County
96	369	**Batesville** (city) Ripley County
97	367	**Centerville** (town) Wayne County
97	367	**Speedway** (town) Marion County
99	366	**Brookville** (town) Franklin County
99	366	**East Chicago** (city) Lake County
99	366	**Michigan City** (city) LaPorte County
102	364	**Chandler** (town) Warrick County
102	364	**De Motte** (town) Jasper County
104	363	**Connersville** (city) Fayette County
104	363	**Gas City** (city) Grant County
106	362	**Princeton** (city) Gibson County
107	361	**Beech Grove** (city) Marion County
107	361	**Charlestown** (city) Clark County
109	360	**Terre Haute** (city) Vigo County
110	359	**Syracuse** (town) Kosciusko County
111	358	**Hanover** (town) Jefferson County
111	358	**Simonton Lake** (CDP) Elkhart County
113	357	**Alexandria** (city) Madison County
114	356	**Elwood** (city) Madison County
114	356	**Garrett** (city) DeKalb County
114	356	**Mishawaka** (city) Saint Joseph County
117	354	**Huntingburg** (city) Dubois County
118	353	**Linton** (city) Greene County
118	353	**Tipton** (city) Tipton County
120	352	**Fort Wayne** (city) Allen County
121	350	**Anderson** (city) Madison County
122	349	**Brownstown** (town) Jackson County
123	348	**Edinburgh** (town) Johnson County
124	346	**Fortville** (town) Hancock County
124	346	**Leo-Cedarville** (town) Allen County
126	345	**Bluffton** (city) Wells County
126	345	**Dunlap** (CDP) Elkhart County
126	345	**Lagrange** (town) LaGrange County
126	345	**Richmond** (city) Wayne County
130	344	**Winchester** (city) Randolph County
131	343	**Washington** (city) Daviess County
132	340	**Muncie** (city) Delaware County
132	340	**Union City** (city) Randolph County
134	338	**Butler** (city) DeKalb County
135	337	**South Bend** (city) Saint Joseph County
136	336	**Elkhart** (city) Elkhart County
137	334	**Greendale** (city) Dearborn County
137	334	**Sullivan** (city) Sullivan County
139	333	**North Vernon** (city) Jennings County
140	332	**Winona Lake** (town) Kosciusko County
141	330	**Berne** (city) Adams County
142	329	**Greensburg** (city) Decatur County
143	328	**Monticello** (city) White County
144	327	**Attica** (city) Fountain County
144	327	**Paoli** (town) Orange County
146	326	**Brazil** (city) Clay County
146	326	**Tell City** (city) Perry County
148	325	**Madison** (city) Jefferson County
149	324	**Knox** (city) Starke County
149	324	**North Terre Haute** (CDP) Vigo County

***Note:** This section ranks incorporated places and CDPs (Census Designated Places) with populations of 2,500 or more. Unincorporated postal areas were not considered. Please refer to the User Guide for additional information.*

Median Selected Monthly Owner Costs: Without Mortgage

Top 150 Places Ranked in *Ascending* Order

State Rank	Dollars	Place
1	238	**Ossian** (town) Wells County
2	242	**Lawrenceburg** (city) Dearborn County
3	257	**Clinton** (city) Vermillion County
4	269	**Loogootee** (city) Martin County
5	271	**Portland** (city) Jay County
6	285	**Osceola** (town) Saint Joseph County
6	285	**Rockville** (town) Parke County
8	288	**Decatur** (city) Adams County
8	288	**Salem** (city) Washington County
10	296	**Marion** (city) Grant County
11	298	**Bremen** (town) Marshall County
12	299	**Bicknell** (city) Knox County
12	299	**Logansport** (city) Cass County
12	299	**Peru** (city) Miami County
15	302	**North Manchester** (town) Wabash County
16	304	**Crawfordsville** (city) Montgomery County
17	307	**Ligonier** (city) Noble County
18	309	**Austin** (city) Scott County
19	311	**Auburn** (city) DeKalb County
20	312	**Rensselaer** (city) Jasper County
21	313	**Delphi** (city) Carroll County
21	313	**New Castle** (city) Henry County
23	314	**Kendallville** (city) Noble County
23	314	**Mitchell** (city) Lawrence County
23	314	**Rochester** (city) Fulton County
23	314	**Rushville** (city) Rush County
27	315	**Hartford City** (city) Blackford County
27	315	**Kokomo** (city) Howard County
27	315	**Winamac** (town) Pulaski County
30	317	**Mooresville** (town) Morgan County
31	318	**Seymour** (city) Jackson County
32	319	**Huntington** (city) Huntington County
32	319	**Wabash** (city) Wabash County
34	320	**Corydon** (town) Harrison County
34	320	**New Haven** (city) Allen County
34	320	**Vincennes** (city) Knox County
37	321	**Frankfort** (city) Clinton County
37	321	**Lafayette** (city) Tippecanoe County
39	324	**Knox** (city) Starke County
39	324	**North Terre Haute** (CDP) Vigo County
41	325	**Madison** (city) Jefferson County
42	326	**Brazil** (city) Clay County
42	326	**Tell City** (city) Perry County
44	327	**Attica** (city) Fountain County
44	327	**Paoli** (town) Orange County
46	328	**Monticello** (city) White County
47	329	**Greensburg** (city) Decatur County
48	330	**Berne** (city) Adams County
49	332	**Winona Lake** (town) Kosciusko County
50	333	**North Vernon** (city) Jennings County
51	334	**Greendale** (city) Dearborn County
51	334	**Sullivan** (city) Sullivan County
53	336	**Elkhart** (city) Elkhart County
54	337	**South Bend** (city) Saint Joseph County
55	338	**Butler** (city) DeKalb County
56	340	**Muncie** (city) Delaware County
56	340	**Union City** (city) Randolph County
58	343	**Washington** (city) Daviess County
59	344	**Winchester** (city) Randolph County
60	345	**Bluffton** (city) Wells County
60	345	**Dunlap** (CDP) Elkhart County
60	345	**Lagrange** (town) LaGrange County
60	345	**Richmond** (city) Wayne County
64	346	**Fortville** (town) Hancock County
64	346	**Leo-Cedarville** (town) Allen County
66	348	**Edinburgh** (town) Johnson County
67	349	**Brownstown** (town) Jackson County
68	350	**Anderson** (city) Madison County
69	352	**Fort Wayne** (city) Allen County
70	353	**Linton** (city) Greene County
70	353	**Tipton** (city) Tipton County
72	354	**Huntingburg** (city) Dubois County
73	356	**Elwood** (city) Madison County
73	356	**Garrett** (city) DeKalb County
73	356	**Mishawaka** (city) Saint Joseph County
76	357	**Alexandria** (city) Madison County
77	358	**Hanover** (town) Jefferson County
77	358	**Simonton Lake** (CDP) Elkhart County
79	359	**Syracuse** (town) Kosciusko County
80	360	**Terre Haute** (city) Vigo County
81	361	**Beech Grove** (city) Marion County
81	361	**Charlestown** (city) Clark County
83	362	**Princeton** (city) Gibson County
84	363	**Connersville** (city) Fayette County
84	363	**Gas City** (city) Grant County
86	364	**Chandler** (town) Warrick County
86	364	**De Motte** (town) Jasper County
88	366	**Brookville** (town) Franklin County
88	366	**East Chicago** (city) Lake County
88	366	**Michigan City** (city) LaPorte County
91	367	**Centerville** (town) Wayne County
91	367	**Speedway** (town) Marion County
93	369	**Batesville** (city) Ripley County
94	370	**Mount Vernon** (city) Posey County
94	370	**Plymouth** (city) Marshall County
96	371	**Whiting** (city) Lake County
97	374	**Martinsville** (city) Morgan County
98	378	**Angola** (city) Steuben County
98	378	**New Albany** (city) Floyd County
100	379	**Greenfield** (city) Hancock County
100	379	**South Haven** (CDP) Porter County
100	379	**Upland** (town) Grant County
103	380	**Franklin** (city) Johnson County
103	380	**Greencastle** (city) Putnam County
105	382	**Scottsburg** (city) Scott County
106	383	**Fairmount** (town) Grant County
106	383	**Fort Branch** (town) Gibson County
108	384	**Bedford** (city) Lawrence County
108	384	**Cicero** (town) Hamilton County
108	384	**Country Squire Lakes** (CDP) Jennings County
111	385	**Melody Hill** (CDP) Vanderburgh County
112	387	**Evansville** (city) Vanderburgh County
112	387	**Jeffersonville** (city) Clark County
112	387	**Warsaw** (city) Kosciusko County
115	388	**Aurora** (city) Dearborn County
115	388	**Columbia City** (city) Whitley County
117	389	**Greentown** (town) Howard County
118	391	**New Whiteland** (town) Johnson County
119	392	**Clarksville** (town) Clark County
120	393	**Boonville** (city) Warrick County
120	393	**Gary** (city) Lake County
120	393	**Hammond** (city) Lake County
123	395	**Whiteland** (town) Johnson County
124	397	**Jasper** (city) Dubois County
125	399	**Smithville-Sanders** (CDP) Monroe County
126	401	**Columbus** (city) Bartholomew County
127	402	**Merrillville** (town) Lake County
127	402	**Shelbyville** (city) Shelby County
129	407	**La Porte** (city) LaPorte County
130	409	**Indianapolis** (city) Marion County
131	411	**Lake Station** (city) Lake County
132	413	**Ellettsville** (town) Monroe County
132	413	**Goshen** (city) Elkhart County
134	416	**Lawrence** (city) Marion County
135	417	**Griffith** (town) Lake County
136	418	**Sheridan** (town) Hamilton County
136	418	**Yorktown** (town) Delaware County
138	420	**Lowell** (town) Lake County
139	421	**Middlebury** (town) Elkhart County
140	422	**Nappanee** (city) Elkhart County
140	422	**Roselawn** (CDP) Newton County
142	424	**Plainfield** (town) Hendricks County
142	424	**Salt Creek Commons** (CDP) Porter County
142	424	**Sellersburg** (town) Clark County
145	429	**Granger** (CDP) Saint Joseph County
146	430	**Heritage Lake** (CDP) Putnam County
146	430	**Pendleton** (town) Madison County
148	431	**Bright** (CDP) Dearborn County
149	432	**Greenwood** (city) Johnson County
150	435	**Highland** (town) Lake County

Note: *This section ranks incorporated places and CDPs (Census Designated Places) with populations of 2,500 or more. Unincorporated postal areas were not considered. Please refer to the User Guide for additional information.*

Median Gross Rent

Top 150 Places Ranked in *Descending* Order

State Rank	Dollars	Place
1	1,472	**Granger** (CDP) Saint Joseph County
2	1,401	**Hidden Valley** (CDP) Dearborn County
3	1,345	**Melody Hill** (CDP) Vanderburgh County
4	1,332	**Whitestown** (town) Boone County
5	1,308	**Winfield** (town) Lake County
6	1,261	**New Whiteland** (town) Johnson County
7	1,255	**Porter** (town) Porter County
8	1,249	**Zionsville** (town) Boone County
9	1,193	**Lakes of the Four Seasons** (CDP) Lake County
10	1,175	**Fishers** (city) Hamilton County
11	1,162	**Westfield** (city) Hamilton County
12	1,150	**Carmel** (city) Hamilton County
13	1,091	**Highland** (CDP) Vanderburgh County
14	1,090	**McCordsville** (town) Hancock County
15	1,087	**Leo-Cedarville** (town) Allen County
16	1,086	**Smithville-Sanders** (CDP) Monroe County
17	1,072	**Munster** (town) Lake County
18	1,055	**Avon** (town) Hendricks County
19	1,032	**Brownsburg** (town) Hendricks County
20	1,026	**Merrillville** (town) Lake County
21	1,025	**Whiteland** (town) Johnson County
22	1,017	**Highland** (town) Lake County
23	999	**Dyer** (town) Lake County
24	993	**Noblesville** (city) Hamilton County
25	990	**Plainfield** (town) Hendricks County
26	989	**Crown Point** (city) Lake County
27	986	**Lowell** (town) Lake County
28	977	**Salt Creek Commons** (CDP) Porter County
29	972	**Osceola** (town) Saint Joseph County
30	968	**Huntertown** (town) Allen County
31	955	**Bargersville** (town) Johnson County
31	955	**Santa Claus** (town) Spencer County
33	950	**Pittsboro** (town) Hendricks County
34	944	**South Haven** (CDP) Porter County
35	940	**Schererville** (town) Lake County
36	936	**Sellersburg** (town) Clark County
37	907	**Lake Station** (city) Lake County
37	907	**Middlebury** (town) Elkhart County
39	903	**Greenwood** (city) Johnson County
40	897	**Valparaiso** (city) Porter County
41	888	**Bright** (CDP) Dearborn County
41	888	**Country Squire Lakes** (CDP) Jennings County
43	885	**Chesterton** (town) Porter County
44	884	**Portage** (city) Porter County
45	879	**Centerville** (town) Wayne County
46	873	**Hobart** (city) Lake County
47	865	**Roselawn** (CDP) Newton County
48	864	**Columbus** (city) Bartholomew County
49	863	**Bloomington** (city) Monroe County
50	861	**Cedar Lake** (town) Lake County
51	860	**West Lafayette** (city) Tippecanoe County
52	857	**Griffith** (town) Lake County
53	854	**Greenfield** (city) Hancock County
54	852	**Hammond** (city) Lake County
54	852	**Pendleton** (town) Madison County
56	850	**Fortville** (town) Hancock County
57	847	**Chandler** (town) Warrick County
58	842	**Saint John** (town) Lake County
59	840	**Indianapolis** (city) Marion County
60	837	**Simonton Lake** (CDP) Elkhart County
61	834	**Danville** (town) Hendricks County
62	832	**Whiting** (city) Lake County
63	824	**De Motte** (town) Jasper County
64	823	**Lawrence** (city) Marion County
65	807	**Dunlap** (CDP) Elkhart County
66	803	**Warsaw** (city) Kosciusko County
67	798	**Franklin** (city) Johnson County
68	792	**Jeffersonville** (city) Clark County
69	789	**Lafayette** (city) Tippecanoe County
70	785	**Newburgh** (town) Warrick County
71	779	**Gas City** (city) Grant County
72	770	**Mooresville** (town) Morgan County
73	769	**Alexandria** (city) Madison County
74	767	**Clarksville** (town) Clark County
74	767	**Cumberland** (town) Marion County
76	764	**Charlestown** (city) Clark County
77	763	**Brownstown** (town) Jackson County
78	760	**Hebron** (town) Porter County
79	758	**Austin** (city) Scott County
79	758	**Greensburg** (city) Decatur County
79	758	**Lebanon** (city) Boone County
82	757	**Shelbyville** (city) Shelby County
83	754	**Scottsburg** (city) Scott County
84	753	**Beech Grove** (city) Marion County
84	753	**New Albany** (city) Floyd County
86	752	**Greentown** (town) Howard County
87	751	**Gary** (city) Lake County
88	750	**New Haven** (city) Allen County
89	748	**Georgetown** (town) Floyd County
90	746	**Seymour** (city) Jackson County
91	745	**Goshen** (city) Elkhart County
92	741	**Michigan City** (city) LaPorte County
92	741	**South Bend** (city) Saint Joseph County
92	741	**Speedway** (town) Marion County
95	738	**Evansville** (city) Vanderburgh County
96	737	**Syracuse** (town) Kosciusko County
97	731	**Butler** (city) DeKalb County
98	730	**Mishawaka** (city) Saint Joseph County
99	728	**Edinburgh** (town) Johnson County
100	727	**Batesville** (city) Ripley County
100	727	**Cicero** (town) Hamilton County
102	725	**Angola** (city) Steuben County
102	725	**North Terre Haute** (CDP) Vigo County
104	724	**Anderson** (city) Madison County
105	722	**Elkhart** (city) Elkhart County
106	719	**Hanover** (town) Jefferson County
106	719	**Tipton** (city) Tipton County
108	715	**Madison** (city) Jefferson County
109	714	**Muncie** (city) Delaware County
110	712	**Rensselaer** (city) Jasper County
111	709	**North Manchester** (town) Wabash County
112	708	**Fort Wayne** (city) Allen County
113	703	**Corydon** (town) Harrison County
114	697	**Sheridan** (town) Hamilton County
114	697	**Yorktown** (town) Delaware County
116	696	**Delphi** (city) Carroll County
116	696	**Winona Lake** (town) Kosciusko County
118	694	**Ossian** (town) Wells County
118	694	**Terre Haute** (city) Vigo County
120	691	**Fort Branch** (town) Gibson County
121	689	**Greencastle** (city) Putnam County
121	689	**Martinsville** (city) Morgan County
121	689	**Mount Vernon** (city) Posey County
124	686	**Garrett** (city) DeKalb County
125	684	**Auburn** (city) DeKalb County
125	684	**Lawrenceburg** (city) Dearborn County
127	683	**Elwood** (city) Madison County
128	678	**Frankfort** (city) Clinton County
128	678	**Huntington** (city) Huntington County
130	673	**East Chicago** (city) Lake County
130	673	**Vincennes** (city) Knox County
132	672	**Kokomo** (city) Howard County
132	672	**La Porte** (city) LaPorte County
134	670	**Plymouth** (city) Marshall County
135	668	**Nappanee** (city) Elkhart County
136	663	**Monticello** (city) White County
137	662	**Connersville** (city) Fayette County
137	662	**New Castle** (city) Henry County
139	659	**Sullivan** (city) Sullivan County
140	656	**Bedford** (city) Lawrence County
140	656	**North Vernon** (city) Jennings County
142	655	**Boonville** (city) Warrick County
143	653	**Richmond** (city) Wayne County
144	651	**Kendallville** (city) Noble County
144	651	**Linton** (city) Greene County
146	650	**Attica** (city) Fountain County
146	650	**Ligonier** (city) Noble County
146	650	**Marion** (city) Grant County
149	649	**Aurora** (city) Dearborn County
149	649	**Brookville** (town) Franklin County

Note: *This section ranks incorporated places and CDPs (Census Designated Places) with populations of 2,500 or more. Unincorporated postal areas were not considered. Please refer to the User Guide for additional information.*

Median Gross Rent

Top 150 Places Ranked in *Ascending* Order

State Rank	Dollars	Place
1	477	**Clinton** (city) Vermillion County
2	480	**Berne** (city) Adams County
3	498	**Rockville** (town) Parke County
4	521	**Loogootee** (city) Martin County
5	540	**Mitchell** (city) Lawrence County
6	542	**Huntingburg** (city) Dubois County
7	543	**Fairmount** (town) Grant County
8	558	**Union City** (city) Randolph County
9	560	**Bluffton** (city) Wells County
10	563	**Jasper** (city) Dubois County
11	565	**Decatur** (city) Adams County
12	569	**Lagrange** (town) LaGrange County
13	577	**Portland** (city) Jay County
14	583	**Salem** (city) Washington County
15	590	**Bicknell** (city) Knox County
15	590	**Columbia City** (city) Whitley County
17	598	**Paoli** (town) Orange County
18	606	**Hartford City** (city) Blackford County
19	608	**Westville** (town) LaPorte County
20	611	**Tell City** (city) Perry County
21	616	**Brazil** (city) Clay County
22	622	**Washington** (city) Daviess County
23	626	**Winamac** (town) Pulaski County
24	630	**Ellettsville** (town) Monroe County
25	631	**Logansport** (city) Cass County
26	632	**Upland** (town) Grant County
27	633	**Peru** (city) Miami County
27	633	**Winchester** (city) Randolph County
29	636	**Knox** (city) Starke County
30	637	**Crawfordsville** (city) Montgomery County
30	637	**Rochester** (city) Fulton County
32	640	**Wabash** (city) Wabash County
33	644	**Princeton** (city) Gibson County
34	646	**Notre Dame** (CDP) Saint Joseph County
35	648	**Bremen** (town) Marshall County
36	649	**Aurora** (city) Dearborn County
36	649	**Brookville** (town) Franklin County
36	649	**Greendale** (city) Dearborn County
36	649	**Rushville** (city) Rush County
40	650	**Attica** (city) Fountain County
40	650	**Ligonier** (city) Noble County
40	650	**Marion** (city) Grant County
43	651	**Kendallville** (city) Noble County
43	651	**Linton** (city) Greene County
45	653	**Richmond** (city) Wayne County
46	655	**Boonville** (city) Warrick County
47	656	**Bedford** (city) Lawrence County
47	656	**North Vernon** (city) Jennings County
49	659	**Sullivan** (city) Sullivan County
50	662	**Connersville** (city) Fayette County
50	662	**New Castle** (city) Henry County
52	663	**Monticello** (city) White County
53	668	**Nappanee** (city) Elkhart County
54	670	**Plymouth** (city) Marshall County
55	672	**Kokomo** (city) Howard County
55	672	**La Porte** (city) LaPorte County
57	673	**East Chicago** (city) Lake County
57	673	**Vincennes** (city) Knox County
59	678	**Frankfort** (city) Clinton County
59	678	**Huntington** (city) Huntington County
61	683	**Elwood** (city) Madison County
62	684	**Auburn** (city) DeKalb County
62	684	**Lawrenceburg** (city) Dearborn County
64	686	**Garrett** (city) DeKalb County
65	689	**Greencastle** (city) Putnam County
65	689	**Martinsville** (city) Morgan County
65	689	**Mount Vernon** (city) Posey County
68	691	**Fort Branch** (town) Gibson County
69	694	**Ossian** (town) Wells County
69	694	**Terre Haute** (city) Vigo County
71	696	**Delphi** (city) Carroll County
71	696	**Winona Lake** (town) Kosciusko County
73	697	**Sheridan** (town) Hamilton County
73	697	**Yorktown** (town) Delaware County
75	703	**Corydon** (town) Harrison County
76	708	**Fort Wayne** (city) Allen County
77	709	**North Manchester** (town) Wabash County
78	712	**Rensselaer** (city) Jasper County
79	714	**Muncie** (city) Delaware County
80	715	**Madison** (city) Jefferson County
81	719	**Hanover** (town) Jefferson County
81	719	**Tipton** (city) Tipton County
83	722	**Elkhart** (city) Elkhart County
84	724	**Anderson** (city) Madison County
85	725	**Angola** (city) Steuben County
85	725	**North Terre Haute** (CDP) Vigo County
87	727	**Batesville** (city) Ripley County
87	727	**Cicero** (town) Hamilton County
89	728	**Edinburgh** (town) Johnson County
90	730	**Mishawaka** (city) Saint Joseph County
91	731	**Butler** (city) DeKalb County
92	737	**Syracuse** (town) Kosciusko County
93	738	**Evansville** (city) Vanderburgh County
94	741	**Michigan City** (city) LaPorte County
94	741	**South Bend** (city) Saint Joseph County
94	741	**Speedway** (town) Marion County
97	745	**Goshen** (city) Elkhart County
98	746	**Seymour** (city) Jackson County
99	748	**Georgetown** (town) Floyd County
100	750	**New Haven** (city) Allen County
101	751	**Gary** (city) Lake County
102	752	**Greentown** (town) Howard County
103	753	**Beech Grove** (city) Marion County
103	753	**New Albany** (city) Floyd County
105	754	**Scottsburg** (city) Scott County
106	757	**Shelbyville** (city) Shelby County
107	758	**Austin** (city) Scott County
107	758	**Greensburg** (city) Decatur County
107	758	**Lebanon** (city) Boone County
110	760	**Hebron** (town) Porter County
111	763	**Brownstown** (town) Jackson County
112	764	**Charlestown** (city) Clark County
113	767	**Clarksville** (town) Clark County
113	767	**Cumberland** (town) Marion County
115	769	**Alexandria** (city) Madison County
116	770	**Mooresville** (town) Morgan County
117	779	**Gas City** (city) Grant County
118	785	**Newburgh** (town) Warrick County
119	789	**Lafayette** (city) Tippecanoe County
120	792	**Jeffersonville** (city) Clark County
121	798	**Franklin** (city) Johnson County
122	803	**Warsaw** (city) Kosciusko County
123	807	**Dunlap** (CDP) Elkhart County
124	823	**Lawrence** (city) Marion County
125	824	**De Motte** (town) Jasper County
126	832	**Whiting** (city) Lake County
127	834	**Danville** (town) Hendricks County
128	837	**Simonton Lake** (CDP) Elkhart County
129	840	**Indianapolis** (city) Marion County
130	842	**Saint John** (town) Lake County
131	847	**Chandler** (town) Warrick County
132	850	**Fortville** (town) Hancock County
133	852	**Hammond** (city) Lake County
133	852	**Pendleton** (town) Madison County
135	854	**Greenfield** (city) Hancock County
136	857	**Griffith** (town) Lake County
137	860	**West Lafayette** (city) Tippecanoe County
138	861	**Cedar Lake** (town) Lake County
139	863	**Bloomington** (city) Monroe County
140	864	**Columbus** (city) Bartholomew County
141	865	**Roselawn** (CDP) Newton County
142	873	**Hobart** (city) Lake County
143	879	**Centerville** (town) Wayne County
144	884	**Portage** (city) Porter County
145	885	**Chesterton** (town) Porter County
146	888	**Bright** (CDP) Dearborn County
146	888	**Country Squire Lakes** (CDP) Jennings County
148	897	**Valparaiso** (city) Porter County
149	903	**Greenwood** (city) Johnson County
150	907	**Lake Station** (city) Lake County

Note: *This section ranks incorporated places and CDPs (Census Designated Places) with populations of 2,500 or more. Unincorporated postal areas were not considered. Please refer to the User Guide for additional information.*

Rental Vacancy Rate

Top 150 Places Ranked in *Descending* Order

State Rank	Percent	Place
1	25.1	**Whiting** (city) Lake County
2	20.9	**Ossian** (town) Wells County
3	20.0	**Winfield** (town) Lake County
4	19.8	**Butler** (city) DeKalb County
5	19.3	**Berne** (city) Adams County
6	19.2	**New Castle** (city) Henry County
7	18.0	**Richmond** (city) Wayne County
8	17.9	**Mitchell** (city) Lawrence County
9	16.5	**Greentown** (town) Howard County
10	15.7	**Centerville** (town) Wayne County
11	14.8	**Mishawaka** (city) Saint Joseph County
12	14.7	**Austin** (city) Scott County
12	14.7	**Granger** (CDP) Saint Joseph County
14	14.2	**Bicknell** (city) Knox County
14	14.2	**Rochester** (city) Fulton County
16	14.0	**Newburgh** (town) Warrick County
17	13.6	**Santa Claus** (town) Spencer County
18	13.2	**South Bend** (city) Saint Joseph County
19	13.1	**Fort Branch** (town) Gibson County
19	13.1	**Lagrange** (town) LaGrange County
21	12.8	**Pittsboro** (town) Hendricks County
22	12.6	**Connersville** (city) Fayette County
22	12.6	**Washington** (city) Daviess County
24	12.3	**Linton** (city) Greene County
25	12.1	**Pendleton** (town) Madison County
26	11.7	**Bedford** (city) Lawrence County
27	11.6	**Cedar Lake** (town) Lake County
27	11.6	**Jeffersonville** (city) Clark County
29	11.3	**Shelbyville** (city) Shelby County
29	11.3	**Syracuse** (town) Kosciusko County
31	10.8	**Fishers** (city) Hamilton County
32	10.7	**Alexandria** (city) Madison County
33	10.6	**Rushville** (city) Rush County
34	10.5	**Bluffton** (city) Wells County
35	10.3	**Clarksville** (town) Clark County
36	10.2	**Corydon** (town) Harrison County
36	10.2	**Huntingburg** (city) Dubois County
38	10.0	**Bright** (CDP) Dearborn County
38	10.0	**New Albany** (city) Floyd County
40	9.9	**Martinsville** (city) Morgan County
41	9.8	**Zionsville** (town) Boone County
42	9.6	**Brookville** (town) Franklin County
42	9.6	**Vincennes** (city) Knox County
44	9.5	**Cumberland** (town) Marion County
45	9.3	**Lebanon** (city) Boone County
46	9.0	**East Chicago** (city) Lake County
46	9.0	**Frankfort** (city) Clinton County
46	9.0	**Greendale** (city) Dearborn County
49	8.9	**Knox** (city) Starke County
50	8.8	**Gas City** (city) Grant County
51	8.7	**Crawfordsville** (city) Montgomery County
52	8.6	**Columbus** (city) Bartholomew County
52	8.6	**Nappanee** (city) Elkhart County
54	8.5	**Muncie** (city) Delaware County
54	8.5	**North Terre Haute** (CDP) Vigo County
54	8.5	**Scottsburg** (city) Scott County
54	8.5	**Winamac** (town) Pulaski County
58	8.4	**Carmel** (city) Hamilton County
58	8.4	**Gary** (city) Lake County
58	8.4	**Indianapolis** (city) Marion County
61	8.2	**Anderson** (city) Madison County
62	8.1	**Terre Haute** (city) Vigo County
63	8.0	**Lawrenceburg** (city) Dearborn County
63	8.0	**Marion** (city) Grant County
63	8.0	**Sullivan** (city) Sullivan County
66	7.9	**Rensselaer** (city) Jasper County
67	7.8	**Hanover** (town) Jefferson County
68	7.7	**Merrillville** (town) Lake County
68	7.7	**Plymouth** (city) Marshall County
70	7.6	**Elkhart** (city) Elkhart County
70	7.6	**Fort Wayne** (city) Allen County
70	7.6	**Plainfield** (town) Hendricks County
73	7.3	**Westville** (town) LaPorte County
74	7.2	**Aurora** (city) Dearborn County
74	7.2	**Georgetown** (town) Floyd County
76	7.1	**Kokomo** (city) Howard County
77	7.0	**North Vernon** (city) Jennings County
78	6.9	**Chandler** (town) Warrick County
78	6.9	**Decatur** (city) Adams County
78	6.9	**Lawrence** (city) Marion County
81	6.8	**De Motte** (town) Jasper County
81	6.8	**Greensburg** (city) Decatur County
81	6.8	**Kendallville** (city) Noble County
84	6.7	**Madison** (city) Jefferson County
85	6.6	**Evansville** (city) Vanderburgh County
86	6.5	**Greenwood** (city) Johnson County
86	6.5	**Speedway** (town) Marion County
88	6.4	**Valparaiso** (city) Porter County
89	6.2	**Garrett** (city) DeKalb County
89	6.2	**Griffith** (town) Lake County
91	6.0	**Simonton Lake** (CDP) Elkhart County
92	5.9	**Elwood** (city) Madison County
93	5.8	**Portland** (city) Jay County
93	5.8	**Wabash** (city) Wabash County
95	5.7	**Boonville** (city) Warrick County
95	5.7	**Ellettsville** (town) Monroe County
95	5.7	**Princeton** (city) Gibson County
98	5.6	**Franklin** (city) Johnson County
98	5.6	**Michigan City** (city) LaPorte County
98	5.6	**Westfield** (city) Hamilton County
101	5.5	**Goshen** (city) Elkhart County
101	5.5	**Greencastle** (city) Putnam County
101	5.5	**Hammond** (city) Lake County
104	5.4	**Mooresville** (town) Morgan County
105	5.3	**Bloomington** (city) Monroe County
105	5.3	**Salem** (city) Washington County
107	5.2	**Hobart** (city) Lake County
107	5.2	**Lafayette** (city) Tippecanoe County
107	5.2	**West Lafayette** (city) Tippecanoe County
110	5.1	**Winchester** (city) Randolph County
111	5.0	**Auburn** (city) DeKalb County
111	5.0	**La Porte** (city) LaPorte County
113	4.9	**Huntington** (city) Huntington County
113	4.9	**Mount Vernon** (city) Posey County
113	4.9	**Sellersburg** (town) Clark County
113	4.9	**Seymour** (city) Jackson County
117	4.8	**Portage** (city) Porter County
118	4.7	**Avon** (town) Hendricks County
118	4.7	**Logansport** (city) Cass County
118	4.7	**New Haven** (city) Allen County
121	4.6	**Schererville** (town) Lake County
121	4.6	**Tipton** (city) Tipton County
121	4.6	**Warsaw** (city) Kosciusko County
124	4.4	**Bargersville** (town) Johnson County
124	4.4	**Union City** (city) Randolph County
126	4.3	**Charlestown** (city) Clark County
127	4.2	**Ligonier** (city) Noble County
127	4.2	**Sheridan** (town) Hamilton County
129	4.1	**Bremen** (town) Marshall County
129	4.1	**Brownsburg** (town) Hendricks County
131	4.0	**Danville** (town) Hendricks County
131	4.0	**Upland** (town) Grant County
133	3.9	**Delphi** (city) Carroll County
134	3.8	**Batesville** (city) Ripley County
134	3.8	**Crown Point** (city) Lake County
136	3.7	**Brownstown** (town) Jackson County
137	3.4	**Jasper** (city) Dubois County
138	3.3	**Noblesville** (city) Hamilton County
139	3.2	**Hartford City** (city) Blackford County
139	3.2	**Notre Dame** (CDP) Saint Joseph County
141	3.1	**Whitestown** (town) Boone County
142	3.0	**Fairmount** (town) Grant County
143	2.9	**Attica** (city) Fountain County
144	2.7	**Edinburgh** (town) Johnson County
145	2.6	**Columbia City** (city) Whitley County
146	2.4	**Greenfield** (city) Hancock County
147	2.3	**Tell City** (city) Perry County
148	2.2	**Peru** (city) Miami County
149	1.8	**Beech Grove** (city) Marion County
150	1.6	**North Manchester** (town) Wabash County

Note: *This section ranks incorporated places and CDPs (Census Designated Places) with populations of 2,500 or more. Unincorporated postal areas were not considered. Please refer to the User Guide for additional information.*

Population with Health Insurance

Top 150 Places Ranked in *Descending* Order

State Rank	Percent	Place
1	97.9	**Bargersville** (town) Johnson County
2	97.5	**Notre Dame** (CDP) Saint Joseph County
3	97.3	**Santa Claus** (town) Spencer County
3	97.3	**Smithville-Sanders** (CDP) Monroe County
5	97.2	**Hidden Valley** (CDP) Dearborn County
6	96.9	**Leo-Cedarville** (town) Allen County
7	96.8	**Shorewood Forest** (CDP) Porter County
7	96.8	**Zionsville** (town) Boone County
9	96.7	**Pittsboro** (town) Hendricks County
10	96.5	**Carmel** (city) Hamilton County
10	96.5	**Saint John** (town) Lake County
12	96.4	**Upland** (town) Grant County
13	96.3	**Dyer** (town) Lake County
14	95.9	**Fishers** (city) Hamilton County
15	95.8	**Granger** (CDP) Saint Joseph County
15	95.8	**Huntertown** (town) Allen County
17	95.6	**Georgetown** (town) Floyd County
18	95.5	**Crown Point** (city) Lake County
18	95.5	**Whiteland** (town) Johnson County
20	95.4	**Chesterton** (town) Porter County
20	95.4	**Decatur** (city) Adams County
22	95.3	**Bright** (CDP) Dearborn County
23	95.2	**Yorktown** (town) Delaware County
24	95.1	**Munster** (town) Lake County
25	94.7	**Winfield** (town) Lake County
26	94.5	**Berne** (city) Adams County
26	94.5	**West Lafayette** (city) Tippecanoe County
28	94.3	**Lakes of the Four Seasons** (CDP) Lake County
29	94.2	**Mount Vernon** (city) Posey County
30	94.1	**Batesville** (city) Ripley County
31	93.6	**Hebron** (town) Porter County
32	93.4	**Highland** (town) Lake County
32	93.4	**Lawrenceburg** (city) Dearborn County
32	93.4	**Salt Creek Commons** (CDP) Porter County
35	93.3	**Greendale** (city) Dearborn County
35	93.3	**Westfield** (city) Hamilton County
37	93.2	**Fortville** (town) Hancock County
38	93.1	**Auburn** (city) DeKalb County
38	93.1	**Cumberland** (town) Marion County
38	93.1	**Hobart** (city) Lake County
38	93.1	**North Manchester** (town) Wabash County
38	93.1	**Plainfield** (town) Hendricks County
43	93.0	**Avon** (town) Hendricks County
44	92.9	**Alexandria** (city) Madison County
44	92.9	**Tipton** (city) Tipton County
46	92.7	**Jasper** (city) Dubois County
46	92.7	**Simonton Lake** (CDP) Elkhart County
48	92.6	**Highland** (CDP) Vanderburgh County
48	92.6	**Noblesville** (city) Hamilton County
50	92.5	**Brookville** (town) Franklin County
51	92.4	**Mooresville** (town) Morgan County
52	92.3	**Monticello** (city) White County
53	92.1	**Ellettsville** (town) Monroe County
53	92.1	**Greenfield** (city) Hancock County
53	92.1	**Griffith** (town) Lake County
56	92.0	**Fort Branch** (town) Gibson County
56	92.0	**Scottsburg** (city) Scott County
58	91.9	**Greencastle** (city) Putnam County
59	91.7	**Cedar Lake** (town) Lake County
59	91.7	**Dunlap** (CDP) Elkhart County
59	91.7	**Madison** (city) Jefferson County
59	91.7	**Salem** (city) Washington County
63	91.6	**Osceola** (town) Saint Joseph County
64	91.5	**Danville** (town) Hendricks County
65	91.4	**Columbia City** (city) Whitley County
65	91.4	**Pendleton** (town) Madison County
65	91.4	**Princeton** (city) Gibson County
65	91.4	**Schererville** (town) Lake County
69	91.3	**Corydon** (town) Harrison County
69	91.3	**New Albany** (city) Floyd County
69	91.3	**Porter** (town) Porter County
69	91.3	**Whitestown** (town) Boone County
73	91.2	**Brazil** (city) Clay County
73	91.2	**Greensburg** (city) Decatur County
73	91.2	**Lowell** (town) Lake County
76	91.1	**Brownstown** (town) Jackson County
76	91.1	**Valparaiso** (city) Porter County
78	91.0	**Brownsburg** (town) Hendricks County
79	90.9	**Franklin** (city) Johnson County
79	90.9	**Rensselaer** (city) Jasper County
81	90.8	**Bloomington** (city) Monroe County
81	90.8	**Jeffersonville** (city) Clark County
83	90.6	**Loogootee** (city) Martin County
83	90.6	**New Haven** (city) Allen County
83	90.6	**Westville** (town) LaPorte County
86	90.5	**De Motte** (town) Jasper County
86	90.5	**North Terre Haute** (CDP) Vigo County
88	90.4	**Bluffton** (city) Wells County
88	90.4	**Gas City** (city) Grant County
88	90.4	**Merrillville** (town) Lake County
88	90.4	**New Whiteland** (town) Johnson County
92	90.3	**Clinton** (city) Vermillion County
92	90.3	**Greentown** (town) Howard County
94	90.1	**Boonville** (city) Warrick County
94	90.1	**Chandler** (town) Warrick County
94	90.1	**Columbus** (city) Bartholomew County
94	90.1	**Hanover** (town) Jefferson County
94	90.1	**Winona Lake** (town) Kosciusko County
99	90.0	**Greenwood** (city) Johnson County
99	90.0	**Heritage Lake** (CDP) Putnam County
99	90.0	**McCordsville** (town) Hancock County
99	90.0	**Melody Hill** (CDP) Vanderburgh County
99	90.0	**Middlebury** (town) Elkhart County
104	89.9	**Charlestown** (city) Clark County
105	89.8	**Austin** (city) Scott County
105	89.8	**Bedford** (city) Lawrence County
105	89.8	**Lebanon** (city) Boone County
108	89.7	**Beech Grove** (city) Marion County
109	89.6	**Portage** (city) Porter County
109	89.6	**Wabash** (city) Wabash County
109	89.6	**Whiting** (city) Lake County
112	89.5	**Rockville** (town) Parke County
112	89.5	**Tell City** (city) Perry County
114	89.4	**Attica** (city) Fountain County
114	89.4	**Newburgh** (town) Warrick County
114	89.4	**Vincennes** (city) Knox County
117	89.2	**Huntington** (city) Huntington County
117	89.2	**Kokomo** (city) Howard County
119	89.1	**Seymour** (city) Jackson County
119	89.1	**Speedway** (town) Marion County
121	89.0	**Sellersburg** (town) Clark County
122	88.9	**Fairmount** (town) Grant County
122	88.9	**Muncie** (city) Delaware County
122	88.9	**Rushville** (city) Rush County
125	88.8	**Peru** (city) Miami County
126	88.7	**Ossian** (town) Wells County
127	88.5	**Roselawn** (CDP) Newton County
128	88.4	**Huntingburg** (city) Dubois County
128	88.4	**Knox** (city) Starke County
128	88.4	**Portland** (city) Jay County
128	88.4	**Terre Haute** (city) Vigo County
132	88.3	**Delphi** (city) Carroll County
132	88.3	**Evansville** (city) Vanderburgh County
132	88.3	**Fort Wayne** (city) Allen County
132	88.3	**Garrett** (city) DeKalb County
132	88.3	**Hartford City** (city) Blackford County
132	88.3	**New Castle** (city) Henry County
132	88.3	**Paoli** (town) Orange County
139	88.0	**Shelbyville** (city) Shelby County
139	88.0	**Warsaw** (city) Kosciusko County
139	88.0	**Washington** (city) Daviess County
142	87.9	**Michigan City** (city) LaPorte County
143	87.8	**Centerville** (town) Wayne County
143	87.8	**North Vernon** (city) Jennings County
145	87.7	**South Haven** (CDP) Porter County
146	87.5	**Rochester** (city) Fulton County
146	87.5	**Winamac** (town) Pulaski County
148	87.4	**Indianapolis** (city) Marion County
148	87.4	**Martinsville** (city) Morgan County
150	87.3	**Angola** (city) Steuben County

Note: *This section ranks incorporated places and CDPs (Census Designated Places) with populations of 2,500 or more. Unincorporated postal areas were not considered. Please refer to the User Guide for additional information.*

Population with Health Insurance

Top 150 Places Ranked in *Ascending* Order

State Rank	Percent	Place
1	80.0	**Sullivan** (city) Sullivan County
2	80.8	**Country Squire Lakes** (CDP) Jennings County
3	81.1	**Bicknell** (city) Knox County
4	81.3	**Butler** (city) DeKalb County
5	82.4	**Elkhart** (city) Elkhart County
6	82.6	**Goshen** (city) Elkhart County
6	82.6	**Union City** (city) Randolph County
8	82.9	**East Chicago** (city) Lake County
9	83.2	**Logansport** (city) Cass County
10	83.3	**Edinburgh** (town) Johnson County
11	83.9	**Ligonier** (city) Noble County
12	84.3	**Connersville** (city) Fayette County
13	84.6	**Sheridan** (town) Hamilton County
14	84.9	**Hammond** (city) Lake County
14	84.9	**Lake Station** (city) Lake County
16	85.0	**Cicero** (town) Hamilton County
17	85.3	**Crawfordsville** (city) Montgomery County
18	85.4	**Plymouth** (city) Marshall County
19	85.5	**Aurora** (city) Dearborn County
20	85.6	**Linton** (city) Greene County
21	85.7	**La Porte** (city) LaPorte County
21	85.7	**Syracuse** (town) Kosciusko County
23	85.9	**Mitchell** (city) Lawrence County
23	85.9	**Richmond** (city) Wayne County
25	86.0	**Nappanee** (city) Elkhart County
26	86.2	**Lagrange** (town) LaGrange County
26	86.2	**South Bend** (city) Saint Joseph County
28	86.3	**Lawrence** (city) Marion County
29	86.4	**Winchester** (city) Randolph County
30	86.6	**Elwood** (city) Madison County
31	86.7	**Lafayette** (city) Tippecanoe County
31	86.7	**Mishawaka** (city) Saint Joseph County
33	86.8	**Anderson** (city) Madison County
34	86.9	**Frankfort** (city) Clinton County
34	86.9	**Kendallville** (city) Noble County
36	87.0	**Gary** (city) Lake County
37	87.1	**Marion** (city) Grant County
38	87.2	**Bremen** (town) Marshall County
38	87.2	**Clarksville** (town) Clark County
40	87.3	**Angola** (city) Steuben County
41	87.4	**Indianapolis** (city) Marion County
41	87.4	**Martinsville** (city) Morgan County
43	87.5	**Rochester** (city) Fulton County
43	87.5	**Winamac** (town) Pulaski County
45	87.7	**South Haven** (CDP) Porter County
46	87.8	**Centerville** (town) Wayne County
46	87.8	**North Vernon** (city) Jennings County
48	87.9	**Michigan City** (city) LaPorte County
49	88.0	**Shelbyville** (city) Shelby County
49	88.0	**Warsaw** (city) Kosciusko County
49	88.0	**Washington** (city) Daviess County
52	88.3	**Delphi** (city) Carroll County
52	88.3	**Evansville** (city) Vanderburgh County
52	88.3	**Fort Wayne** (city) Allen County
52	88.3	**Garrett** (city) DeKalb County
52	88.3	**Hartford City** (city) Blackford County
52	88.3	**New Castle** (city) Henry County
52	88.3	**Paoli** (town) Orange County
59	88.4	**Huntingburg** (city) Dubois County
59	88.4	**Knox** (city) Starke County
59	88.4	**Portland** (city) Jay County
59	88.4	**Terre Haute** (city) Vigo County
63	88.5	**Roselawn** (CDP) Newton County
64	88.7	**Ossian** (town) Wells County
65	88.8	**Peru** (city) Miami County
66	88.9	**Fairmount** (town) Grant County
66	88.9	**Muncie** (city) Delaware County
66	88.9	**Rushville** (city) Rush County
69	89.0	**Sellersburg** (town) Clark County
70	89.1	**Seymour** (city) Jackson County
70	89.1	**Speedway** (town) Marion County
72	89.2	**Huntington** (city) Huntington County
72	89.2	**Kokomo** (city) Howard County
74	89.4	**Attica** (city) Fountain County
74	89.4	**Newburgh** (town) Warrick County
74	89.4	**Vincennes** (city) Knox County
77	89.5	**Rockville** (town) Parke County
77	89.5	**Tell City** (city) Perry County
79	89.6	**Portage** (city) Porter County
79	89.6	**Wabash** (city) Wabash County
79	89.6	**Whiting** (city) Lake County
82	89.7	**Beech Grove** (city) Marion County
83	89.8	**Austin** (city) Scott County
83	89.8	**Bedford** (city) Lawrence County
83	89.8	**Lebanon** (city) Boone County
86	89.9	**Charlestown** (city) Clark County
87	90.0	**Greenwood** (city) Johnson County
87	90.0	**Heritage Lake** (CDP) Putnam County
87	90.0	**McCordsville** (town) Hancock County
87	90.0	**Melody Hill** (CDP) Vanderburgh County
87	90.0	**Middlebury** (town) Elkhart County
92	90.1	**Boonville** (city) Warrick County
92	90.1	**Chandler** (town) Warrick County
92	90.1	**Columbus** (city) Bartholomew County
92	90.1	**Hanover** (town) Jefferson County
92	90.1	**Winona Lake** (town) Kosciusko County
97	90.3	**Clinton** (city) Vermillion County
97	90.3	**Greentown** (town) Howard County
99	90.4	**Bluffton** (city) Wells County
99	90.4	**Gas City** (city) Grant County
99	90.4	**Merrillville** (town) Lake County
99	90.4	**New Whiteland** (town) Johnson County
103	90.5	**De Motte** (town) Jasper County
103	90.5	**North Terre Haute** (CDP) Vigo County
105	90.6	**Loogootee** (city) Martin County
105	90.6	**New Haven** (city) Allen County
105	90.6	**Westville** (town) LaPorte County
108	90.8	**Bloomington** (city) Monroe County
108	90.8	**Jeffersonville** (city) Clark County
110	90.9	**Franklin** (city) Johnson County
110	90.9	**Rensselaer** (city) Jasper County
112	91.0	**Brownsburg** (town) Hendricks County
113	91.1	**Brownstown** (town) Jackson County
113	91.1	**Valparaiso** (city) Porter County
115	91.2	**Brazil** (city) Clay County
115	91.2	**Greensburg** (city) Decatur County
115	91.2	**Lowell** (town) Lake County
118	91.3	**Corydon** (town) Harrison County
118	91.3	**New Albany** (city) Floyd County
118	91.3	**Porter** (town) Porter County
118	91.3	**Whitestown** (town) Boone County
122	91.4	**Columbia City** (city) Whitley County
122	91.4	**Pendleton** (town) Madison County
122	91.4	**Princeton** (city) Gibson County
122	91.4	**Schererville** (town) Lake County
126	91.5	**Danville** (town) Hendricks County
127	91.6	**Osceola** (town) Saint Joseph County
128	91.7	**Cedar Lake** (town) Lake County
128	91.7	**Dunlap** (CDP) Elkhart County
128	91.7	**Madison** (city) Jefferson County
128	91.7	**Salem** (city) Washington County
132	91.9	**Greencastle** (city) Putnam County
133	92.0	**Fort Branch** (town) Gibson County
133	92.0	**Scottsburg** (city) Scott County
135	92.1	**Ellettsville** (town) Monroe County
135	92.1	**Greenfield** (city) Hancock County
135	92.1	**Griffith** (town) Lake County
138	92.3	**Monticello** (city) White County
139	92.4	**Mooresville** (town) Morgan County
140	92.5	**Brookville** (town) Franklin County
141	92.6	**Highland** (CDP) Vanderburgh County
141	92.6	**Noblesville** (city) Hamilton County
143	92.7	**Jasper** (city) Dubois County
143	92.7	**Simonton Lake** (CDP) Elkhart County
145	92.9	**Alexandria** (city) Madison County
145	92.9	**Tipton** (city) Tipton County
147	93.0	**Avon** (town) Hendricks County
148	93.1	**Auburn** (city) DeKalb County
148	93.1	**Cumberland** (town) Marion County
148	93.1	**Hobart** (city) Lake County

Note: *This section ranks incorporated places and CDPs (Census Designated Places) with populations of 2,500 or more. Unincorporated postal areas were not considered. Please refer to the User Guide for additional information.*

Population with Private Health Insurance

Top 150 Places Ranked in *Descending* Order

State Rank	Percent	Place
1	95.4	**Notre Dame** (CDP) Saint Joseph County
2	92.1	**Zionsville** (town) Boone County
3	90.5	**Fishers** (city) Hamilton County
4	89.8	**Bargersville** (town) Johnson County
5	89.7	**Saint John** (town) Lake County
6	89.6	**West Lafayette** (city) Tippecanoe County
7	89.5	**Carmel** (city) Hamilton County
8	89.1	**Georgetown** (town) Floyd County
9	88.5	**Leo-Cedarville** (town) Allen County
10	87.8	**Upland** (town) Grant County
11	87.0	**Granger** (CDP) Saint Joseph County
12	86.9	**Santa Claus** (town) Spencer County
13	86.8	**McCordsville** (town) Hancock County
14	86.3	**Westfield** (city) Hamilton County
15	85.5	**Whiteland** (town) Johnson County
16	85.4	**Fortville** (town) Hancock County
17	85.2	**Hidden Valley** (CDP) Dearborn County
18	85.1	**Munster** (town) Lake County
19	84.6	**Smithville-Sanders** (CDP) Monroe County
20	84.5	**Avon** (town) Hendricks County
20	84.5	**Chesterton** (town) Porter County
22	84.4	**Dyer** (town) Lake County
23	84.2	**Winfield** (town) Lake County
24	83.4	**Pittsboro** (town) Hendricks County
25	82.8	**Huntertown** (town) Allen County
26	82.4	**Noblesville** (city) Hamilton County
27	81.8	**Bright** (CDP) Dearborn County
27	81.8	**Yorktown** (town) Delaware County
29	81.7	**Brownsburg** (town) Hendricks County
30	81.6	**Whitestown** (town) Boone County
31	81.4	**Crown Point** (city) Lake County
32	81.3	**Highland** (CDP) Vanderburgh County
32	81.3	**Ossian** (town) Wells County
32	81.3	**Shorewood Forest** (CDP) Porter County
35	80.5	**Jasper** (city) Dubois County
35	80.5	**Lakes of the Four Seasons** (CDP) Lake County
37	80.3	**Heritage Lake** (CDP) Putnam County
38	79.8	**Pendleton** (town) Madison County
39	79.7	**Schererville** (town) Lake County
40	79.3	**Roselawn** (CDP) Newton County
41	78.9	**Highland** (town) Lake County
42	78.6	**Batesville** (city) Ripley County
43	78.5	**Cedar Lake** (town) Lake County
44	78.4	**Hebron** (town) Porter County
45	77.6	**Lowell** (town) Lake County
46	77.3	**Bloomington** (city) Monroe County
47	77.2	**Melody Hill** (CDP) Vanderburgh County
48	76.9	**Hobart** (city) Lake County
49	76.8	**Cicero** (town) Hamilton County
49	76.8	**Winona Lake** (town) Kosciusko County
51	76.7	**Dunlap** (CDP) Elkhart County
51	76.7	**Franklin** (city) Johnson County
53	76.0	**Danville** (town) Hendricks County
53	76.0	**Fort Branch** (town) Gibson County
55	75.9	**Tipton** (city) Tipton County
56	75.3	**Columbus** (city) Bartholomew County
57	75.2	**Valparaiso** (city) Porter County
58	75.1	**Plainfield** (town) Hendricks County
59	75.0	**Salt Creek Commons** (CDP) Porter County
60	74.8	**Sellersburg** (town) Clark County
61	74.7	**Mount Vernon** (city) Posey County
62	74.5	**Auburn** (city) DeKalb County
63	74.3	**Middlebury** (town) Elkhart County
64	74.1	**Chandler** (town) Warrick County
64	74.1	**Newburgh** (town) Warrick County
64	74.1	**Porter** (town) Porter County
67	74.0	**Nappanee** (city) Elkhart County
68	73.5	**Greentown** (town) Howard County
68	73.5	**Osceola** (town) Saint Joseph County
70	73.3	**De Motte** (town) Jasper County
71	73.0	**North Manchester** (town) Wabash County
72	72.6	**Cumberland** (town) Marion County
72	72.6	**Jeffersonville** (city) Clark County
74	72.5	**Hanover** (town) Jefferson County
74	72.5	**Warsaw** (city) Kosciusko County
76	72.3	**Greendale** (city) Dearborn County
77	72.2	**Greensburg** (city) Decatur County
78	72.1	**Greencastle** (city) Putnam County
78	72.1	**Lebanon** (city) Boone County
80	72.0	**Decatur** (city) Adams County
80	72.0	**Greenfield** (city) Hancock County
82	71.9	**Berne** (city) Adams County
82	71.9	**Boonville** (city) Warrick County
82	71.9	**Brownstown** (town) Jackson County
85	71.6	**Merrillville** (town) Lake County
86	71.4	**Loogootee** (city) Martin County
87	71.3	**Greenwood** (city) Johnson County
88	71.1	**Simonton Lake** (CDP) Elkhart County
89	71.0	**Ellettsville** (town) Monroe County
90	70.7	**Alexandria** (city) Madison County
91	70.4	**Portage** (city) Porter County
92	70.3	**Griffith** (town) Lake County
93	70.0	**New Whiteland** (town) Johnson County
94	69.8	**Columbia City** (city) Whitley County
95	69.7	**Delphi** (city) Carroll County
96	69.5	**Huntingburg** (city) Dubois County
97	69.1	**Westville** (town) LaPorte County
98	69.0	**Lawrenceburg** (city) Dearborn County
99	68.7	**Centerville** (town) Wayne County
99	68.7	**Mooresville** (town) Morgan County
101	68.6	**Whiting** (city) Lake County
102	68.5	**Madison** (city) Jefferson County
102	68.5	**Scottsburg** (city) Scott County
104	68.3	**New Haven** (city) Allen County
105	68.2	**Rensselaer** (city) Jasper County
106	67.9	**Gas City** (city) Grant County
106	67.9	**Rushville** (city) Rush County
108	67.8	**Princeton** (city) Gibson County
109	67.6	**New Albany** (city) Floyd County
110	67.4	**Lagrange** (town) LaGrange County
110	67.4	**South Haven** (CDP) Porter County
112	67.1	**Seymour** (city) Jackson County
112	67.1	**Winamac** (town) Pulaski County
114	67.0	**Garrett** (city) DeKalb County
115	66.9	**Attica** (city) Fountain County
115	66.9	**Shelbyville** (city) Shelby County
117	66.7	**Huntington** (city) Huntington County
117	66.7	**Sheridan** (town) Hamilton County
119	66.6	**Monticello** (city) White County
120	66.1	**Wabash** (city) Wabash County
121	65.8	**Fairmount** (town) Grant County
121	65.8	**Hartford City** (city) Blackford County
123	65.4	**Tell City** (city) Perry County
124	65.3	**Muncie** (city) Delaware County
125	65.2	**North Terre Haute** (CDP) Vigo County
126	64.9	**Corydon** (town) Harrison County
126	64.9	**Kokomo** (city) Howard County
128	64.7	**Kendallville** (city) Noble County
129	64.5	**Charlestown** (city) Clark County
129	64.5	**Mishawaka** (city) Saint Joseph County
131	64.1	**Angola** (city) Steuben County
131	64.1	**Edinburgh** (town) Johnson County
133	63.8	**Clarksville** (town) Clark County
134	63.7	**Speedway** (town) Marion County
135	63.5	**Fort Wayne** (city) Allen County
135	63.5	**Lawrence** (city) Marion County
137	63.4	**Bedford** (city) Lawrence County
137	63.4	**Rockville** (town) Parke County
139	63.3	**Austin** (city) Scott County
139	63.3	**Crawfordsville** (city) Montgomery County
141	63.2	**Bluffton** (city) Wells County
142	62.9	**Lafayette** (city) Tippecanoe County
143	62.7	**Vincennes** (city) Knox County
144	62.6	**Brazil** (city) Clay County
145	62.3	**Syracuse** (town) Kosciusko County
146	62.2	**Clinton** (city) Vermillion County
147	61.9	**Brookville** (town) Franklin County
148	61.6	**Portland** (city) Jay County
149	61.1	**Evansville** (city) Vanderburgh County
150	61.0	**Terre Haute** (city) Vigo County

Note: *This section ranks incorporated places and CDPs (Census Designated Places) with populations of 2,500 or more. Unincorporated postal areas were not considered. Please refer to the User Guide for additional information.*

Population with Private Health Insurance

Top 150 Places Ranked in *Ascending* Order

State Rank	Percent	Place
1	43.3	**Union City** (city) Randolph County
2	43.7	**Country Squire Lakes** (CDP) Jennings County
3	43.8	**East Chicago** (city) Lake County
4	44.1	**Gary** (city) Lake County
5	46.2	**Bicknell** (city) Knox County
6	49.5	**Elkhart** (city) Elkhart County
7	52.1	**Sullivan** (city) Sullivan County
8	52.3	**Knox** (city) Starke County
9	53.1	**Connersville** (city) Fayette County
9	53.1	**Plymouth** (city) Marshall County
11	53.6	**Marion** (city) Grant County
12	54.1	**Anderson** (city) Madison County
13	54.2	**Michigan City** (city) LaPorte County
14	54.5	**Richmond** (city) Wayne County
15	55.2	**Martinsville** (city) Morgan County
16	56.0	**South Bend** (city) Saint Joseph County
17	56.1	**Lake Station** (city) Lake County
18	56.4	**Aurora** (city) Dearborn County
18	56.4	**Beech Grove** (city) Marion County
20	56.6	**Washington** (city) Daviess County
21	57.0	**Peru** (city) Miami County
22	57.2	**Hammond** (city) Lake County
23	57.6	**Paoli** (town) Orange County
24	58.3	**Elwood** (city) Madison County
25	58.4	**New Castle** (city) Henry County
26	58.6	**Butler** (city) DeKalb County
26	58.6	**North Vernon** (city) Jennings County
28	58.7	**Winchester** (city) Randolph County
29	59.1	**Ligonier** (city) Noble County
29	59.1	**Mitchell** (city) Lawrence County
31	59.3	**La Porte** (city) LaPorte County
32	59.4	**Goshen** (city) Elkhart County
33	59.5	**Logansport** (city) Cass County
34	60.4	**Bremen** (town) Marshall County
34	60.4	**Frankfort** (city) Clinton County
36	60.5	**Indianapolis** (city) Marion County
36	60.5	**Rochester** (city) Fulton County
38	60.7	**Linton** (city) Greene County
39	60.9	**Salem** (city) Washington County
40	61.0	**Terre Haute** (city) Vigo County
41	61.1	**Evansville** (city) Vanderburgh County
42	61.6	**Portland** (city) Jay County
43	61.9	**Brookville** (town) Franklin County
44	62.2	**Clinton** (city) Vermillion County
45	62.3	**Syracuse** (town) Kosciusko County
46	62.6	**Brazil** (city) Clay County
47	62.7	**Vincennes** (city) Knox County
48	62.9	**Lafayette** (city) Tippecanoe County
49	63.2	**Bluffton** (city) Wells County
50	63.3	**Austin** (city) Scott County
50	63.3	**Crawfordsville** (city) Montgomery County
52	63.4	**Bedford** (city) Lawrence County
52	63.4	**Rockville** (town) Parke County
54	63.5	**Fort Wayne** (city) Allen County
54	63.5	**Lawrence** (city) Marion County
56	63.7	**Speedway** (town) Marion County
57	63.8	**Clarksville** (town) Clark County
58	64.1	**Angola** (city) Steuben County
58	64.1	**Edinburgh** (town) Johnson County
60	64.5	**Charlestown** (city) Clark County
60	64.5	**Mishawaka** (city) Saint Joseph County
62	64.7	**Kendallville** (city) Noble County
63	64.9	**Corydon** (town) Harrison County
63	64.9	**Kokomo** (city) Howard County
65	65.2	**North Terre Haute** (CDP) Vigo County
66	65.3	**Muncie** (city) Delaware County
67	65.4	**Tell City** (city) Perry County
68	65.8	**Fairmount** (town) Grant County
68	65.8	**Hartford City** (city) Blackford County
70	66.1	**Wabash** (city) Wabash County
71	66.6	**Monticello** (city) White County
72	66.7	**Huntington** (city) Huntington County
72	66.7	**Sheridan** (town) Hamilton County
74	66.9	**Attica** (city) Fountain County
74	66.9	**Shelbyville** (city) Shelby County
76	67.0	**Garrett** (city) DeKalb County
77	67.1	**Seymour** (city) Jackson County
77	67.1	**Winamac** (town) Pulaski County
79	67.4	**Lagrange** (town) LaGrange County
79	67.4	**South Haven** (CDP) Porter County
81	67.6	**New Albany** (city) Floyd County
82	67.8	**Princeton** (city) Gibson County
83	67.9	**Gas City** (city) Grant County
83	67.9	**Rushville** (city) Rush County
85	68.2	**Rensselaer** (city) Jasper County
86	68.3	**New Haven** (city) Allen County
87	68.5	**Madison** (city) Jefferson County
87	68.5	**Scottsburg** (city) Scott County
89	68.6	**Whiting** (city) Lake County
90	68.7	**Centerville** (town) Wayne County
90	68.7	**Mooresville** (town) Morgan County
92	69.0	**Lawrenceburg** (city) Dearborn County
93	69.1	**Westville** (town) LaPorte County
94	69.5	**Huntingburg** (city) Dubois County
95	69.7	**Delphi** (city) Carroll County
96	69.8	**Columbia City** (city) Whitley County
97	70.0	**New Whiteland** (town) Johnson County
98	70.3	**Griffith** (town) Lake County
99	70.4	**Portage** (city) Porter County
100	70.7	**Alexandria** (city) Madison County
101	71.0	**Ellettsville** (town) Monroe County
102	71.1	**Simonton Lake** (CDP) Elkhart County
103	71.3	**Greenwood** (city) Johnson County
104	71.4	**Loogootee** (city) Martin County
105	71.6	**Merrillville** (town) Lake County
106	71.9	**Berne** (city) Adams County
106	71.9	**Boonville** (city) Warrick County
106	71.9	**Brownstown** (town) Jackson County
109	72.0	**Decatur** (city) Adams County
109	72.0	**Greenfield** (city) Hancock County
111	72.1	**Greencastle** (city) Putnam County
111	72.1	**Lebanon** (city) Boone County
113	72.2	**Greensburg** (city) Decatur County
114	72.3	**Greendale** (city) Dearborn County
115	72.5	**Hanover** (town) Jefferson County
115	72.5	**Warsaw** (city) Kosciusko County
117	72.6	**Cumberland** (town) Marion County
117	72.6	**Jeffersonville** (city) Clark County
119	73.0	**North Manchester** (town) Wabash County
120	73.3	**De Motte** (town) Jasper County
121	73.5	**Greentown** (town) Howard County
121	73.5	**Osceola** (town) Saint Joseph County
123	74.0	**Nappanee** (city) Elkhart County
124	74.1	**Chandler** (town) Warrick County
124	74.1	**Newburgh** (town) Warrick County
124	74.1	**Porter** (town) Porter County
127	74.3	**Middlebury** (town) Elkhart County
128	74.5	**Auburn** (city) DeKalb County
129	74.7	**Mount Vernon** (city) Posey County
130	74.8	**Sellersburg** (town) Clark County
131	75.0	**Salt Creek Commons** (CDP) Porter County
132	75.1	**Plainfield** (town) Hendricks County
133	75.2	**Valparaiso** (city) Porter County
134	75.3	**Columbus** (city) Bartholomew County
135	75.9	**Tipton** (city) Tipton County
136	76.0	**Danville** (town) Hendricks County
136	76.0	**Fort Branch** (town) Gibson County
138	76.7	**Dunlap** (CDP) Elkhart County
138	76.7	**Franklin** (city) Johnson County
140	76.8	**Cicero** (town) Hamilton County
140	76.8	**Winona Lake** (town) Kosciusko County
142	76.9	**Hobart** (city) Lake County
143	77.2	**Melody Hill** (CDP) Vanderburgh County
144	77.3	**Bloomington** (city) Monroe County
145	77.6	**Lowell** (town) Lake County
146	78.4	**Hebron** (town) Porter County
147	78.5	**Cedar Lake** (town) Lake County
148	78.6	**Batesville** (city) Ripley County
149	78.9	**Highland** (town) Lake County
150	79.3	**Roselawn** (CDP) Newton County

Note: *This section ranks incorporated places and CDPs (Census Designated Places) with populations of 2,500 or more. Unincorporated postal areas were not considered. Please refer to the User Guide for additional information.*

Population with Public Health Insurance

Top 150 Places Ranked in *Descending* Order

State Rank	Percent	Place
1	55.6	**Gary** (city) Lake County
2	52.4	**Union City** (city) Randolph County
3	50.4	**Country Squire Lakes** (CDP) Jennings County
4	49.6	**Clinton** (city) Vermillion County
4	49.6	**East Chicago** (city) Lake County
6	49.0	**Knox** (city) Starke County
7	48.8	**Marion** (city) Grant County
8	47.5	**Anderson** (city) Madison County
9	47.1	**New Castle** (city) Henry County
10	47.0	**Salem** (city) Washington County
11	46.4	**Peru** (city) Miami County
12	45.8	**Beech Grove** (city) Marion County
13	45.4	**Richmond** (city) Wayne County
14	45.3	**Bicknell** (city) Knox County
15	44.7	**Brookville** (town) Franklin County
16	44.4	**Michigan City** (city) LaPorte County
17	44.3	**Connersville** (city) Fayette County
18	44.0	**Washington** (city) Daviess County
19	43.8	**Martinsville** (city) Morgan County
19	43.8	**Sullivan** (city) Sullivan County
21	43.2	**Plymouth** (city) Marshall County
22	42.6	**Winchester** (city) Randolph County
23	42.4	**Rochester** (city) Fulton County
24	42.3	**Bluffton** (city) Wells County
25	41.9	**Corydon** (town) Harrison County
25	41.9	**Elkhart** (city) Elkhart County
25	41.9	**Monticello** (city) White County
28	41.6	**Bedford** (city) Lawrence County
28	41.6	**Madison** (city) Jefferson County
30	41.5	**Kokomo** (city) Howard County
31	41.4	**Elwood** (city) Madison County
31	41.4	**Portland** (city) Jay County
33	41.3	**Brazil** (city) Clay County
34	41.1	**Linton** (city) Greene County
35	41.0	**Paoli** (town) Orange County
36	40.9	**Rockville** (town) Parke County
37	40.8	**Mitchell** (city) Lawrence County
38	40.7	**Vincennes** (city) Knox County
39	40.6	**La Porte** (city) LaPorte County
40	40.3	**Alexandria** (city) Madison County
41	40.0	**Lake Station** (city) Lake County
42	39.9	**Evansville** (city) Vanderburgh County
43	39.7	**Terre Haute** (city) Vigo County
44	39.5	**South Bend** (city) Saint Joseph County
44	39.5	**Tell City** (city) Perry County
46	39.2	**Brownstown** (town) Jackson County
46	39.2	**North Vernon** (city) Jennings County
48	38.9	**Austin** (city) Scott County
48	38.9	**Syracuse** (town) Kosciusko County
50	38.7	**North Terre Haute** (CDP) Vigo County
51	38.6	**Hartford City** (city) Blackford County
52	38.4	**Attica** (city) Fountain County
52	38.4	**Berne** (city) Adams County
54	38.1	**Aurora** (city) Dearborn County
54	38.1	**Scottsburg** (city) Scott County
56	38.0	**Boonville** (city) Warrick County
57	37.8	**Lawrenceburg** (city) Dearborn County
57	37.8	**Wabash** (city) Wabash County
59	37.7	**Frankfort** (city) Clinton County
59	37.7	**Rushville** (city) Rush County
61	37.6	**Hammond** (city) Lake County
62	37.4	**Bremen** (town) Marshall County
62	37.4	**Mooresville** (town) Morgan County
64	37.2	**Simonton Lake** (CDP) Elkhart County
65	37.1	**Columbia City** (city) Whitley County
65	37.1	**Rensselaer** (city) Jasper County
67	37.0	**Greendale** (city) Dearborn County
68	36.8	**Clarksville** (town) Clark County
68	36.8	**Gas City** (city) Grant County
68	36.8	**New Albany** (city) Floyd County
68	36.8	**Princeton** (city) Gibson County
72	36.3	**Charlestown** (city) Clark County
72	36.3	**Decatur** (city) Adams County
74	36.1	**Kendallville** (city) Noble County
75	35.9	**Indianapolis** (city) Marion County
76	35.8	**Goshen** (city) Elkhart County
77	35.6	**Speedway** (town) Marion County
78	35.1	**Delphi** (city) Carroll County
78	35.1	**Greentown** (town) Howard County
80	34.9	**Garrett** (city) DeKalb County
81	34.8	**Angola** (city) Steuben County
81	34.8	**Muncie** (city) Delaware County
81	34.8	**North Manchester** (town) Wabash County
84	34.7	**Ellettsville** (town) Monroe County
84	34.7	**Fort Wayne** (city) Allen County
84	34.7	**Greenfield** (city) Hancock County
87	34.6	**Logansport** (city) Cass County
88	34.5	**New Haven** (city) Allen County
89	34.4	**Loogootee** (city) Martin County
89	34.4	**Mount Vernon** (city) Posey County
89	34.4	**Winamac** (town) Pulaski County
92	34.1	**Crawfordsville** (city) Montgomery County
93	33.9	**Greencastle** (city) Putnam County
94	33.8	**Lafayette** (city) Tippecanoe County
95	33.6	**Mishawaka** (city) Saint Joseph County
96	33.5	**Ligonier** (city) Noble County
97	33.4	**Centerville** (town) Wayne County
97	33.4	**Huntington** (city) Huntington County
99	33.3	**De Motte** (town) Jasper County
100	33.1	**Lebanon** (city) Boone County
101	32.9	**Fairmount** (town) Grant County
101	32.9	**Highland** (CDP) Vanderburgh County
103	32.7	**Cumberland** (town) Marion County
103	32.7	**Griffith** (town) Lake County
103	32.7	**Tipton** (city) Tipton County
106	32.6	**Portage** (city) Porter County
106	32.6	**Shelbyville** (city) Shelby County
108	32.5	**Auburn** (city) DeKalb County
109	32.2	**New Whiteland** (town) Johnson County
110	32.1	**South Haven** (CDP) Porter County
111	32.0	**Whiting** (city) Lake County
112	31.9	**Seymour** (city) Jackson County
113	31.8	**Lagrange** (town) LaGrange County
113	31.8	**Lawrence** (city) Marion County
115	31.6	**Jeffersonville** (city) Clark County
116	31.2	**Fort Branch** (town) Gibson County
116	31.2	**Hobart** (city) Lake County
118	30.8	**Westville** (town) LaPorte County
119	30.6	**Greenwood** (city) Johnson County
120	30.5	**Batesville** (city) Ripley County
120	30.5	**Middlebury** (town) Elkhart County
122	30.4	**Greensburg** (city) Decatur County
123	30.2	**Merrillville** (town) Lake County
123	30.2	**Plainfield** (town) Hendricks County
125	30.1	**Edinburgh** (town) Johnson County
126	29.8	**Yorktown** (town) Delaware County
127	29.6	**Highland** (town) Lake County
128	29.5	**Crown Point** (city) Lake County
129	29.0	**Huntingburg** (city) Dubois County
130	28.9	**Hebron** (town) Porter County
130	28.9	**Newburgh** (town) Warrick County
132	28.5	**Sheridan** (town) Hamilton County
133	28.2	**Butler** (city) DeKalb County
133	28.2	**Melody Hill** (CDP) Vanderburgh County
135	28.1	**Hanover** (town) Jefferson County
136	27.8	**Chandler** (town) Warrick County
137	27.7	**Columbus** (city) Bartholomew County
138	27.5	**Bright** (CDP) Dearborn County
139	27.2	**Franklin** (city) Johnson County
140	26.9	**Hidden Valley** (CDP) Dearborn County
141	26.8	**Osceola** (town) Saint Joseph County
141	26.8	**Valparaiso** (city) Porter County
143	26.4	**Smithville-Sanders** (CDP) Monroe County
144	26.3	**Dyer** (town) Lake County
145	26.2	**Shorewood Forest** (CDP) Porter County
146	26.1	**Lakes of the Four Seasons** (CDP) Lake County
147	25.5	**Pendleton** (town) Madison County
148	25.4	**Warsaw** (city) Kosciusko County
149	25.3	**Danville** (town) Hendricks County
149	25.3	**Salt Creek Commons** (CDP) Porter County

***Note:** This section ranks incorporated places and CDPs (Census Designated Places) with populations of 2,500 or more. Unincorporated postal areas were not considered. Please refer to the User Guide for additional information.*

Population with Public Health Insurance

Top 150 Places Ranked in *Ascending* Order

State Rank	Percent	Place
1	4.3	**Notre Dame** (CDP) Saint Joseph County
2	6.4	**McCordsville** (town) Hancock County
3	11.2	**West Lafayette** (city) Tippecanoe County
4	11.5	**Fishers** (city) Hamilton County
5	12.6	**Zionsville** (town) Boone County
6	14.3	**Leo-Cedarville** (town) Allen County
7	14.5	**Georgetown** (town) Floyd County
8	14.8	**Whitestown** (town) Boone County
9	15.0	**Westfield** (city) Hamilton County
9	15.0	**Whiteland** (town) Johnson County
11	15.8	**Carmel** (city) Hamilton County
12	18.2	**Avon** (town) Hendricks County
13	18.3	**Ossian** (town) Wells County
14	18.8	**Saint John** (town) Lake County
15	19.5	**Granger** (CDP) Saint Joseph County
15	19.5	**Noblesville** (city) Hamilton County
17	19.6	**Roselawn** (CDP) Newton County
18	19.8	**Bargersville** (town) Johnson County
18	19.8	**Upland** (town) Grant County
20	20.1	**Bloomington** (city) Monroe County
20	20.1	**Fortville** (town) Hancock County
22	20.7	**Winona Lake** (town) Kosciusko County
23	21.3	**Cicero** (town) Hamilton County
24	21.5	**Winfield** (town) Lake County
25	21.8	**Brownsburg** (town) Hendricks County
26	22.5	**Cedar Lake** (town) Lake County
26	22.5	**Pittsboro** (town) Hendricks County
28	22.8	**Porter** (town) Porter County
29	23.0	**Chesterton** (town) Porter County
29	23.0	**Heritage Lake** (CDP) Putnam County
29	23.0	**Nappanee** (city) Elkhart County
32	23.1	**Munster** (town) Lake County
33	23.5	**Dunlap** (CDP) Elkhart County
34	23.7	**Huntertown** (town) Allen County
35	24.0	**Jasper** (city) Dubois County
36	24.2	**Santa Claus** (town) Spencer County
37	24.3	**Sellersburg** (town) Clark County
38	24.9	**Lowell** (town) Lake County
39	25.2	**Schererville** (town) Lake County
40	25.3	**Danville** (town) Hendricks County
40	25.3	**Salt Creek Commons** (CDP) Porter County
42	25.4	**Warsaw** (city) Kosciusko County
43	25.5	**Pendleton** (town) Madison County
44	26.1	**Lakes of the Four Seasons** (CDP) Lake County
45	26.2	**Shorewood Forest** (CDP) Porter County
46	26.3	**Dyer** (town) Lake County
47	26.4	**Smithville-Sanders** (CDP) Monroe County
48	26.8	**Osceola** (town) Saint Joseph County
48	26.8	**Valparaiso** (city) Porter County
50	26.9	**Hidden Valley** (CDP) Dearborn County
51	27.2	**Franklin** (city) Johnson County
52	27.5	**Bright** (CDP) Dearborn County
53	27.7	**Columbus** (city) Bartholomew County
54	27.8	**Chandler** (town) Warrick County
55	28.1	**Hanover** (town) Jefferson County
56	28.2	**Butler** (city) DeKalb County
56	28.2	**Melody Hill** (CDP) Vanderburgh County
58	28.5	**Sheridan** (town) Hamilton County
59	28.9	**Hebron** (town) Porter County
59	28.9	**Newburgh** (town) Warrick County
61	29.0	**Huntingburg** (city) Dubois County
62	29.5	**Crown Point** (city) Lake County
63	29.6	**Highland** (town) Lake County
64	29.8	**Yorktown** (town) Delaware County
65	30.1	**Edinburgh** (town) Johnson County
66	30.2	**Merrillville** (town) Lake County
66	30.2	**Plainfield** (town) Hendricks County
68	30.4	**Greensburg** (city) Decatur County
69	30.5	**Batesville** (city) Ripley County
69	30.5	**Middlebury** (town) Elkhart County
71	30.6	**Greenwood** (city) Johnson County
72	30.8	**Westville** (town) LaPorte County
73	31.2	**Fort Branch** (town) Gibson County
73	31.2	**Hobart** (city) Lake County
75	31.6	**Jeffersonville** (city) Clark County
76	31.8	**Lagrange** (town) LaGrange County
76	31.8	**Lawrence** (city) Marion County
78	31.9	**Seymour** (city) Jackson County
79	32.0	**Whiting** (city) Lake County
80	32.1	**South Haven** (CDP) Porter County
81	32.2	**New Whiteland** (town) Johnson County
82	32.5	**Auburn** (city) DeKalb County
83	32.6	**Portage** (city) Porter County
83	32.6	**Shelbyville** (city) Shelby County
85	32.7	**Cumberland** (town) Marion County
85	32.7	**Griffith** (town) Lake County
85	32.7	**Tipton** (city) Tipton County
88	32.9	**Fairmount** (town) Grant County
88	32.9	**Highland** (CDP) Vanderburgh County
90	33.1	**Lebanon** (city) Boone County
91	33.3	**De Motte** (town) Jasper County
92	33.4	**Centerville** (town) Wayne County
92	33.4	**Huntington** (city) Huntington County
94	33.5	**Ligonier** (city) Noble County
95	33.6	**Mishawaka** (city) Saint Joseph County
96	33.8	**Lafayette** (city) Tippecanoe County
97	33.9	**Greencastle** (city) Putnam County
98	34.1	**Crawfordsville** (city) Montgomery County
99	34.4	**Loogootee** (city) Martin County
99	34.4	**Mount Vernon** (city) Posey County
99	34.4	**Winamac** (town) Pulaski County
102	34.5	**New Haven** (city) Allen County
103	34.6	**Logansport** (city) Cass County
104	34.7	**Ellettsville** (town) Monroe County
104	34.7	**Fort Wayne** (city) Allen County
104	34.7	**Greenfield** (city) Hancock County
107	34.8	**Angola** (city) Steuben County
107	34.8	**Muncie** (city) Delaware County
107	34.8	**North Manchester** (town) Wabash County
110	34.9	**Garrett** (city) DeKalb County
111	35.1	**Delphi** (city) Carroll County
111	35.1	**Greentown** (town) Howard County
113	35.6	**Speedway** (town) Marion County
114	35.8	**Goshen** (city) Elkhart County
115	35.9	**Indianapolis** (city) Marion County
116	36.1	**Kendallville** (city) Noble County
117	36.3	**Charlestown** (city) Clark County
117	36.3	**Decatur** (city) Adams County
119	36.8	**Clarksville** (town) Clark County
119	36.8	**Gas City** (city) Grant County
119	36.8	**New Albany** (city) Floyd County
119	36.8	**Princeton** (city) Gibson County
123	37.0	**Greendale** (city) Dearborn County
124	37.1	**Columbia City** (city) Whitley County
124	37.1	**Rensselaer** (city) Jasper County
126	37.2	**Simonton Lake** (CDP) Elkhart County
127	37.4	**Bremen** (town) Marshall County
127	37.4	**Mooresville** (town) Morgan County
129	37.6	**Hammond** (city) Lake County
130	37.7	**Frankfort** (city) Clinton County
130	37.7	**Rushville** (city) Rush County
132	37.8	**Lawrenceburg** (city) Dearborn County
132	37.8	**Wabash** (city) Wabash County
134	38.0	**Boonville** (city) Warrick County
135	38.1	**Aurora** (city) Dearborn County
135	38.1	**Scottsburg** (city) Scott County
137	38.4	**Attica** (city) Fountain County
137	38.4	**Berne** (city) Adams County
139	38.6	**Hartford City** (city) Blackford County
140	38.7	**North Terre Haute** (CDP) Vigo County
141	38.9	**Austin** (city) Scott County
141	38.9	**Syracuse** (town) Kosciusko County
143	39.2	**Brownstown** (town) Jackson County
143	39.2	**North Vernon** (city) Jennings County
145	39.5	**South Bend** (city) Saint Joseph County
145	39.5	**Tell City** (city) Perry County
147	39.7	**Terre Haute** (city) Vigo County
148	39.9	**Evansville** (city) Vanderburgh County
149	40.0	**Lake Station** (city) Lake County
150	40.3	**Alexandria** (city) Madison County

Note: *This section ranks incorporated places and CDPs (Census Designated Places) with populations of 2,500 or more. Unincorporated postal areas were not considered. Please refer to the User Guide for additional information.*

Population with No Health Insurance

Top 150 Places Ranked in *Descending* Order

State Rank	Percent	Place
1	20.0	**Sullivan** (city) Sullivan County
2	19.2	**Country Squire Lakes** (CDP) Jennings County
3	18.9	**Bicknell** (city) Knox County
4	18.7	**Butler** (city) DeKalb County
5	17.6	**Elkhart** (city) Elkhart County
6	17.4	**Goshen** (city) Elkhart County
6	17.4	**Union City** (city) Randolph County
8	17.1	**East Chicago** (city) Lake County
9	16.8	**Logansport** (city) Cass County
10	16.7	**Edinburgh** (town) Johnson County
11	16.1	**Ligonier** (city) Noble County
12	15.7	**Connersville** (city) Fayette County
13	15.4	**Sheridan** (town) Hamilton County
14	15.1	**Hammond** (city) Lake County
14	15.1	**Lake Station** (city) Lake County
16	15.0	**Cicero** (town) Hamilton County
17	14.7	**Crawfordsville** (city) Montgomery County
18	14.6	**Plymouth** (city) Marshall County
19	14.5	**Aurora** (city) Dearborn County
20	14.4	**Linton** (city) Greene County
21	14.3	**La Porte** (city) LaPorte County
21	14.3	**Syracuse** (town) Kosciusko County
23	14.1	**Mitchell** (city) Lawrence County
23	14.1	**Richmond** (city) Wayne County
25	14.0	**Nappanee** (city) Elkhart County
26	13.8	**Lagrange** (town) LaGrange County
26	13.8	**South Bend** (city) Saint Joseph County
28	13.7	**Lawrence** (city) Marion County
29	13.6	**Winchester** (city) Randolph County
30	13.4	**Elwood** (city) Madison County
31	13.3	**Lafayette** (city) Tippecanoe County
31	13.3	**Mishawaka** (city) Saint Joseph County
33	13.2	**Anderson** (city) Madison County
34	13.1	**Frankfort** (city) Clinton County
34	13.1	**Kendallville** (city) Noble County
36	13.0	**Gary** (city) Lake County
37	12.9	**Marion** (city) Grant County
38	12.8	**Bremen** (town) Marshall County
38	12.8	**Clarksville** (town) Clark County
40	12.7	**Angola** (city) Steuben County
41	12.6	**Indianapolis** (city) Marion County
41	12.6	**Martinsville** (city) Morgan County
43	12.5	**Rochester** (city) Fulton County
43	12.5	**Winamac** (town) Pulaski County
45	12.3	**South Haven** (CDP) Porter County
46	12.2	**Centerville** (town) Wayne County
46	12.2	**North Vernon** (city) Jennings County
48	12.1	**Michigan City** (city) LaPorte County
49	12.0	**Shelbyville** (city) Shelby County
49	12.0	**Warsaw** (city) Kosciusko County
49	12.0	**Washington** (city) Daviess County
52	11.7	**Delphi** (city) Carroll County
52	11.7	**Evansville** (city) Vanderburgh County
52	11.7	**Fort Wayne** (city) Allen County
52	11.7	**Garrett** (city) DeKalb County
52	11.7	**Hartford City** (city) Blackford County
52	11.7	**New Castle** (city) Henry County
52	11.7	**Paoli** (town) Orange County
59	11.6	**Huntingburg** (city) Dubois County
59	11.6	**Knox** (city) Starke County
59	11.6	**Portland** (city) Jay County
59	11.6	**Terre Haute** (city) Vigo County
63	11.5	**Roselawn** (CDP) Newton County
64	11.3	**Ossian** (town) Wells County
65	11.2	**Peru** (city) Miami County
66	11.1	**Fairmount** (town) Grant County
66	11.1	**Muncie** (city) Delaware County
66	11.1	**Rushville** (city) Rush County
69	11.0	**Sellersburg** (town) Clark County
70	10.9	**Seymour** (city) Jackson County
70	10.9	**Speedway** (town) Marion County
72	10.8	**Huntington** (city) Huntington County
72	10.8	**Kokomo** (city) Howard County
74	10.6	**Attica** (city) Fountain County
74	10.6	**Newburgh** (town) Warrick County
74	10.6	**Vincennes** (city) Knox County
77	10.5	**Rockville** (town) Parke County
77	10.5	**Tell City** (city) Perry County
79	10.4	**Portage** (city) Porter County
79	10.4	**Wabash** (city) Wabash County
79	10.4	**Whiting** (city) Lake County
82	10.3	**Beech Grove** (city) Marion County
83	10.2	**Austin** (city) Scott County
83	10.2	**Bedford** (city) Lawrence County
83	10.2	**Lebanon** (city) Boone County
86	10.1	**Charlestown** (city) Clark County
87	10.0	**Greenwood** (city) Johnson County
87	10.0	**Heritage Lake** (CDP) Putnam County
87	10.0	**McCordsville** (town) Hancock County
87	10.0	**Melody Hill** (CDP) Vanderburgh County
87	10.0	**Middlebury** (town) Elkhart County
92	9.9	**Boonville** (city) Warrick County
92	9.9	**Chandler** (town) Warrick County
92	9.9	**Columbus** (city) Bartholomew County
92	9.9	**Hanover** (town) Jefferson County
92	9.9	**Winona Lake** (town) Kosciusko County
97	9.7	**Clinton** (city) Vermillion County
97	9.7	**Greentown** (town) Howard County
99	9.6	**Bluffton** (city) Wells County
99	9.6	**Gas City** (city) Grant County
99	9.6	**Merrillville** (town) Lake County
99	9.6	**New Whiteland** (town) Johnson County
103	9.5	**De Motte** (town) Jasper County
103	9.5	**North Terre Haute** (CDP) Vigo County
105	9.4	**Loogootee** (city) Martin County
105	9.4	**New Haven** (city) Allen County
105	9.4	**Westville** (town) LaPorte County
108	9.2	**Bloomington** (city) Monroe County
108	9.2	**Jeffersonville** (city) Clark County
110	9.1	**Franklin** (city) Johnson County
110	9.1	**Rensselaer** (city) Jasper County
112	9.0	**Brownsburg** (town) Hendricks County
113	8.9	**Brownstown** (town) Jackson County
113	8.9	**Valparaiso** (city) Porter County
115	8.8	**Brazil** (city) Clay County
115	8.8	**Greensburg** (city) Decatur County
115	8.8	**Lowell** (town) Lake County
118	8.7	**Corydon** (town) Harrison County
118	8.7	**New Albany** (city) Floyd County
118	8.7	**Porter** (town) Porter County
118	8.7	**Whitestown** (town) Boone County
122	8.6	**Columbia City** (city) Whitley County
122	8.6	**Pendleton** (town) Madison County
122	8.6	**Princeton** (city) Gibson County
122	8.6	**Schererville** (town) Lake County
126	8.5	**Danville** (town) Hendricks County
127	8.4	**Osceola** (town) Saint Joseph County
128	8.3	**Cedar Lake** (town) Lake County
128	8.3	**Dunlap** (CDP) Elkhart County
128	8.3	**Madison** (city) Jefferson County
128	8.3	**Salem** (city) Washington County
132	8.1	**Greencastle** (city) Putnam County
133	8.0	**Fort Branch** (town) Gibson County
133	8.0	**Scottsburg** (city) Scott County
135	7.9	**Ellettsville** (town) Monroe County
135	7.9	**Greenfield** (city) Hancock County
135	7.9	**Griffith** (town) Lake County
138	7.7	**Monticello** (city) White County
139	7.6	**Mooresville** (town) Morgan County
140	7.5	**Brookville** (town) Franklin County
141	7.4	**Highland** (CDP) Vanderburgh County
141	7.4	**Noblesville** (city) Hamilton County
143	7.3	**Jasper** (city) Dubois County
143	7.3	**Simonton Lake** (CDP) Elkhart County
145	7.1	**Alexandria** (city) Madison County
145	7.1	**Tipton** (city) Tipton County
147	7.0	**Avon** (town) Hendricks County
148	6.9	**Auburn** (city) DeKalb County
148	6.9	**Cumberland** (town) Marion County
148	6.9	**Hobart** (city) Lake County

***Note:** This section ranks incorporated places and CDPs (Census Designated Places) with populations of 2,500 or more. Unincorporated postal areas were not considered. Please refer to the User Guide for additional information.*

Population with No Health Insurance

Top 150 Places Ranked in *Ascending* Order

State Rank	Percent	Place
1	2.1	**Bargersville** (town) Johnson County
2	2.5	**Notre Dame** (CDP) Saint Joseph County
3	2.7	**Santa Claus** (town) Spencer County
3	2.7	**Smithville-Sanders** (CDP) Monroe County
5	2.8	**Hidden Valley** (CDP) Dearborn County
6	3.1	**Leo-Cedarville** (town) Allen County
7	3.2	**Shorewood Forest** (CDP) Porter County
7	3.2	**Zionsville** (town) Boone County
9	3.3	**Pittsboro** (town) Hendricks County
10	3.5	**Carmel** (city) Hamilton County
10	3.5	**Saint John** (town) Lake County
12	3.6	**Upland** (town) Grant County
13	3.7	**Dyer** (town) Lake County
14	4.1	**Fishers** (city) Hamilton County
15	4.2	**Granger** (CDP) Saint Joseph County
15	4.2	**Huntertown** (town) Allen County
17	4.4	**Georgetown** (town) Floyd County
18	4.5	**Crown Point** (city) Lake County
18	4.5	**Whiteland** (town) Johnson County
20	4.6	**Chesterton** (town) Porter County
20	4.6	**Decatur** (city) Adams County
22	4.7	**Bright** (CDP) Dearborn County
23	4.8	**Yorktown** (town) Delaware County
24	4.9	**Munster** (town) Lake County
25	5.3	**Winfield** (town) Lake County
26	5.5	**Berne** (city) Adams County
26	5.5	**West Lafayette** (city) Tippecanoe County
28	5.7	**Lakes of the Four Seasons** (CDP) Lake County
29	5.8	**Mount Vernon** (city) Posey County
30	5.9	**Batesville** (city) Ripley County
31	6.4	**Hebron** (town) Porter County
32	6.6	**Highland** (town) Lake County
32	6.6	**Lawrenceburg** (city) Dearborn County
32	6.6	**Salt Creek Commons** (CDP) Porter County
35	6.7	**Greendale** (city) Dearborn County
35	6.7	**Westfield** (city) Hamilton County
37	6.8	**Fortville** (town) Hancock County
38	6.9	**Auburn** (city) DeKalb County
38	6.9	**Cumberland** (town) Marion County
38	6.9	**Hobart** (city) Lake County
38	6.9	**North Manchester** (town) Wabash County
38	6.9	**Plainfield** (town) Hendricks County
43	7.0	**Avon** (town) Hendricks County
44	7.1	**Alexandria** (city) Madison County
44	7.1	**Tipton** (city) Tipton County
46	7.3	**Jasper** (city) Dubois County
46	7.3	**Simonton Lake** (CDP) Elkhart County
48	7.4	**Highland** (CDP) Vanderburgh County
48	7.4	**Noblesville** (city) Hamilton County
50	7.5	**Brookville** (town) Franklin County
51	7.6	**Mooresville** (town) Morgan County
52	7.7	**Monticello** (city) White County
53	7.9	**Ellettsville** (town) Monroe County
53	7.9	**Greenfield** (city) Hancock County
53	7.9	**Griffith** (town) Lake County
56	8.0	**Fort Branch** (town) Gibson County
56	8.0	**Scottsburg** (city) Scott County
58	8.1	**Greencastle** (city) Putnam County
59	8.3	**Cedar Lake** (town) Lake County
59	8.3	**Dunlap** (CDP) Elkhart County
59	8.3	**Madison** (city) Jefferson County
59	8.3	**Salem** (city) Washington County
63	8.4	**Osceola** (town) Saint Joseph County
64	8.5	**Danville** (town) Hendricks County
65	8.6	**Columbia City** (city) Whitley County
65	8.6	**Pendleton** (town) Madison County
65	8.6	**Princeton** (city) Gibson County
65	8.6	**Schererville** (town) Lake County
69	8.7	**Corydon** (town) Harrison County
69	8.7	**New Albany** (city) Floyd County
69	8.7	**Porter** (town) Porter County
69	8.7	**Whitestown** (town) Boone County
73	8.8	**Brazil** (city) Clay County
73	8.8	**Greensburg** (city) Decatur County
73	8.8	**Lowell** (town) Lake County
76	8.9	**Brownstown** (town) Jackson County
76	8.9	**Valparaiso** (city) Porter County
78	9.0	**Brownsburg** (town) Hendricks County
79	9.1	**Franklin** (city) Johnson County
79	9.1	**Rensselaer** (city) Jasper County
81	9.2	**Bloomington** (city) Monroe County
81	9.2	**Jeffersonville** (city) Clark County
83	9.4	**Loogootee** (city) Martin County
83	9.4	**New Haven** (city) Allen County
83	9.4	**Westville** (town) LaPorte County
86	9.5	**De Motte** (town) Jasper County
86	9.5	**North Terre Haute** (CDP) Vigo County
88	9.6	**Bluffton** (city) Wells County
88	9.6	**Gas City** (city) Grant County
88	9.6	**Merrillville** (town) Lake County
88	9.6	**New Whiteland** (town) Johnson County
92	9.7	**Clinton** (city) Vermillion County
92	9.7	**Greentown** (town) Howard County
94	9.9	**Boonville** (city) Warrick County
94	9.9	**Chandler** (town) Warrick County
94	9.9	**Columbus** (city) Bartholomew County
94	9.9	**Hanover** (town) Jefferson County
94	9.9	**Winona Lake** (town) Kosciusko County
99	10.0	**Greenwood** (city) Johnson County
99	10.0	**Heritage Lake** (CDP) Putnam County
99	10.0	**McCordsville** (town) Hancock County
99	10.0	**Melody Hill** (CDP) Vanderburgh County
99	10.0	**Middlebury** (town) Elkhart County
104	10.1	**Charlestown** (city) Clark County
105	10.2	**Austin** (city) Scott County
105	10.2	**Bedford** (city) Lawrence County
105	10.2	**Lebanon** (city) Boone County
108	10.3	**Beech Grove** (city) Marion County
109	10.4	**Portage** (city) Porter County
109	10.4	**Wabash** (city) Wabash County
109	10.4	**Whiting** (city) Lake County
112	10.5	**Rockville** (town) Parke County
112	10.5	**Tell City** (city) Perry County
114	10.6	**Attica** (city) Fountain County
114	10.6	**Newburgh** (town) Warrick County
114	10.6	**Vincennes** (city) Knox County
117	10.8	**Huntington** (city) Huntington County
117	10.8	**Kokomo** (city) Howard County
119	10.9	**Seymour** (city) Jackson County
119	10.9	**Speedway** (town) Marion County
121	11.0	**Sellersburg** (town) Clark County
122	11.1	**Fairmount** (town) Grant County
122	11.1	**Muncie** (city) Delaware County
122	11.1	**Rushville** (city) Rush County
125	11.2	**Peru** (city) Miami County
126	11.3	**Ossian** (town) Wells County
127	11.5	**Roselawn** (CDP) Newton County
128	11.6	**Huntingburg** (city) Dubois County
128	11.6	**Knox** (city) Starke County
128	11.6	**Portland** (city) Jay County
128	11.6	**Terre Haute** (city) Vigo County
132	11.7	**Delphi** (city) Carroll County
132	11.7	**Evansville** (city) Vanderburgh County
132	11.7	**Fort Wayne** (city) Allen County
132	11.7	**Garrett** (city) DeKalb County
132	11.7	**Hartford City** (city) Blackford County
132	11.7	**New Castle** (city) Henry County
132	11.7	**Paoli** (town) Orange County
139	12.0	**Shelbyville** (city) Shelby County
139	12.0	**Warsaw** (city) Kosciusko County
139	12.0	**Washington** (city) Daviess County
142	12.1	**Michigan City** (city) LaPorte County
143	12.2	**Centerville** (town) Wayne County
143	12.2	**North Vernon** (city) Jennings County
145	12.3	**South Haven** (CDP) Porter County
146	12.5	**Rochester** (city) Fulton County
146	12.5	**Winamac** (town) Pulaski County
148	12.6	**Indianapolis** (city) Marion County
148	12.6	**Martinsville** (city) Morgan County
150	12.7	**Angola** (city) Steuben County

Note: *This section ranks incorporated places and CDPs (Census Designated Places) with populations of 2,500 or more. Unincorporated postal areas were not considered. Please refer to the User Guide for additional information.*

Population Under 18 Years Old with No Health Insurance

Top 150 Places Ranked in *Descending* Order

State Rank	Percent	Place
1	17.3	**Ossian** (town) Wells County
2	17.2	**Rochester** (city) Fulton County
3	16.2	**Sheridan** (town) Hamilton County
4	13.5	**Country Squire Lakes** (CDP) Jennings County
5	13.2	**Warsaw** (city) Kosciusko County
6	13.1	**Cicero** (town) Hamilton County
7	13.0	**Sullivan** (city) Sullivan County
8	12.6	**Loogootee** (city) Martin County
9	12.3	**Plymouth** (city) Marshall County
10	12.2	**Angola** (city) Steuben County
11	11.7	**Butler** (city) DeKalb County
12	11.6	**Union City** (city) Randolph County
12	11.6	**Winchester** (city) Randolph County
14	11.4	**Bremen** (town) Marshall County
15	11.2	**Chandler** (town) Warrick County
15	11.2	**Sellersburg** (town) Clark County
17	11.0	**Melody Hill** (CDP) Vanderburgh County
18	10.7	**Middlebury** (town) Elkhart County
19	10.4	**Mitchell** (city) Lawrence County
19	10.4	**Shelbyville** (city) Shelby County
19	10.4	**Winamac** (town) Pulaski County
22	10.3	**Auburn** (city) DeKalb County
23	10.2	**Edinburgh** (town) Johnson County
23	10.2	**Logansport** (city) Cass County
23	10.2	**North Vernon** (city) Jennings County
26	10.1	**Bluffton** (city) Wells County
27	10.0	**Goshen** (city) Elkhart County
28	9.9	**Lebanon** (city) Boone County
29	9.7	**Columbus** (city) Bartholomew County
29	9.7	**Richmond** (city) Wayne County
31	9.4	**Nappanee** (city) Elkhart County
32	9.3	**Clarksville** (town) Clark County
33	9.0	**Centerville** (town) Wayne County
34	8.9	**Roselawn** (CDP) Newton County
35	8.8	**Syracuse** (town) Kosciusko County
36	8.7	**Schererville** (town) Lake County
37	8.6	**Crawfordsville** (city) Montgomery County
38	8.5	**Lagrange** (town) LaGrange County
39	8.4	**Brownsburg** (town) Hendricks County
40	8.3	**Rensselaer** (city) Jasper County
41	8.0	**La Porte** (city) LaPorte County
41	8.0	**Martinsville** (city) Morgan County
43	7.9	**Elkhart** (city) Elkhart County
44	7.8	**Cumberland** (town) Marion County
45	7.7	**Ellettsville** (town) Monroe County
46	7.6	**Hartford City** (city) Blackford County
46	7.6	**Highland** (CDP) Vanderburgh County
46	7.6	**Huntington** (city) Huntington County
49	7.5	**East Chicago** (city) Lake County
50	7.4	**Franklin** (city) Johnson County
50	7.4	**Whiting** (city) Lake County
52	7.2	**Lake Station** (city) Lake County
52	7.2	**Ligonier** (city) Noble County
52	7.2	**Lowell** (town) Lake County
55	7.1	**Washington** (city) Daviess County
56	7.0	**Fort Wayne** (city) Allen County
56	7.0	**Gas City** (city) Grant County
56	7.0	**Kendallville** (city) Noble County
56	7.0	**New Castle** (city) Henry County
56	7.0	**Portland** (city) Jay County
61	6.9	**Mishawaka** (city) Saint Joseph County
62	6.8	**Jeffersonville** (city) Clark County
63	6.6	**Greenfield** (city) Hancock County
63	6.6	**Merrillville** (town) Lake County
65	6.5	**Hammond** (city) Lake County
65	6.5	**Princeton** (city) Gibson County
67	6.4	**Cedar Lake** (town) Lake County
67	6.4	**Decatur** (city) Adams County
67	6.4	**Garrett** (city) DeKalb County
67	6.4	**Greenwood** (city) Johnson County
67	6.4	**McCordsville** (town) Hancock County
72	6.3	**Lawrence** (city) Marion County
72	6.3	**Paoli** (town) Orange County
74	6.2	**Bedford** (city) Lawrence County
74	6.2	**Connersville** (city) Fayette County
74	6.2	**Greensburg** (city) Decatur County
77	6.1	**Anderson** (city) Madison County
77	6.1	**Indianapolis** (city) Marion County
77	6.1	**Seymour** (city) Jackson County
80	5.8	**Bloomington** (city) Monroe County
81	5.7	**Kokomo** (city) Howard County
81	5.7	**North Manchester** (town) Wabash County
81	5.7	**Plainfield** (town) Hendricks County
81	5.7	**Terre Haute** (city) Vigo County
85	5.6	**Heritage Lake** (CDP) Putnam County
85	5.6	**Linton** (city) Greene County
85	5.6	**New Haven** (city) Allen County
85	5.6	**South Bend** (city) Saint Joseph County
89	5.5	**Boonville** (city) Warrick County
89	5.5	**De Motte** (town) Jasper County
89	5.5	**Lafayette** (city) Tippecanoe County
89	5.5	**Rushville** (city) Rush County
93	5.4	**Muncie** (city) Delaware County
93	5.4	**Simonton Lake** (CDP) Elkhart County
95	5.3	**Batesville** (city) Ripley County
95	5.3	**Huntingburg** (city) Dubois County
95	5.3	**Mooresville** (town) Morgan County
98	5.2	**Aurora** (city) Dearborn County
98	5.2	**Columbia City** (city) Whitley County
98	5.2	**Danville** (town) Hendricks County
98	5.2	**Greendale** (city) Dearborn County
102	5.1	**Michigan City** (city) LaPorte County
102	5.1	**Monticello** (city) White County
102	5.1	**West Lafayette** (city) Tippecanoe County
105	5.0	**Jasper** (city) Dubois County
105	5.0	**Marion** (city) Grant County
107	4.9	**Evansville** (city) Vanderburgh County
107	4.9	**Tell City** (city) Perry County
109	4.8	**Highland** (town) Lake County
110	4.7	**Hanover** (town) Jefferson County
110	4.7	**Winona Lake** (town) Kosciusko County
112	4.6	**Brookville** (town) Franklin County
113	4.5	**Charlestown** (city) Clark County
113	4.5	**Fairmount** (town) Grant County
113	4.5	**Noblesville** (city) Hamilton County
116	4.4	**Salem** (city) Washington County
117	4.3	**Austin** (city) Scott County
118	4.2	**Fishers** (city) Hamilton County
119	4.1	**Elwood** (city) Madison County
119	4.1	**Frankfort** (city) Clinton County
121	4.0	**Wabash** (city) Wabash County
122	3.9	**Griffith** (town) Lake County
123	3.8	**Dunlap** (CDP) Elkhart County
123	3.8	**Granger** (CDP) Saint Joseph County
125	3.7	**Beech Grove** (city) Marion County
125	3.7	**Hobart** (city) Lake County
125	3.7	**New Albany** (city) Floyd County
128	3.6	**Berne** (city) Adams County
128	3.6	**Fort Branch** (town) Gibson County
130	3.5	**Speedway** (town) Marion County
130	3.5	**Vincennes** (city) Knox County
130	3.5	**Westville** (town) LaPorte County
133	3.4	**Crown Point** (city) Lake County
133	3.4	**Gary** (city) Lake County
133	3.4	**Greencastle** (city) Putnam County
136	3.3	**Portage** (city) Porter County
136	3.3	**Westfield** (city) Hamilton County
138	3.1	**Lakes of the Four Seasons** (CDP) Lake County
139	3.0	**Pittsboro** (town) Hendricks County
139	3.0	**Valparaiso** (city) Porter County
141	2.9	**Peru** (city) Miami County
141	2.9	**South Haven** (CDP) Porter County
143	2.8	**Bright** (CDP) Dearborn County
143	2.8	**North Terre Haute** (CDP) Vigo County
145	2.7	**Brazil** (city) Clay County
145	2.7	**Delphi** (city) Carroll County
147	2.6	**Leo-Cedarville** (town) Allen County
147	2.6	**Winfield** (town) Lake County
149	2.3	**Attica** (city) Fountain County
149	2.3	**Huntertown** (town) Allen County

Note: *This section ranks incorporated places and CDPs (Census Designated Places) with populations of 2,500 or more. Unincorporated postal areas were not considered. Please refer to the User Guide for additional information.*

Population Under 18 Years Old with No Health Insurance

Top 150 Places Ranked in *Ascending* Order

State Rank	Percent	Place
1	0.0	**Alexandria** (city) Madison County
1	0.0	**Brownstown** (town) Jackson County
1	0.0	**Corydon** (town) Harrison County
1	0.0	**Fortville** (town) Hancock County
1	0.0	**Greentown** (town) Howard County
1	0.0	**Hebron** (town) Porter County
1	0.0	**Lawrenceburg** (city) Dearborn County
1	0.0	**Newburgh** (town) Warrick County
1	0.0	**Osceola** (town) Saint Joseph County
1	0.0	**Porter** (town) Porter County
1	0.0	**Rockville** (town) Parke County
1	0.0	**Santa Claus** (town) Spencer County
1	0.0	**Smithville-Sanders** (CDP) Monroe County
1	0.0	**Whiteland** (town) Johnson County
15	0.2	**Salt Creek Commons** (CDP) Porter County
16	0.6	**Bargersville** (town) Johnson County
16	0.6	**Madison** (city) Jefferson County
18	0.7	**Mount Vernon** (city) Posey County
18	0.7	**Notre Dame** (CDP) Saint Joseph County
18	0.7	**Scottsburg** (city) Scott County
21	0.8	**Munster** (town) Lake County
22	0.9	**Dyer** (town) Lake County
23	1.0	**Knox** (city) Starke County
24	1.1	**Yorktown** (town) Delaware County
25	1.3	**Upland** (town) Grant County
25	1.3	**Whitestown** (town) Boone County
27	1.4	**Shorewood Forest** (CDP) Porter County
28	1.5	**Hidden Valley** (CDP) Dearborn County
29	1.6	**Georgetown** (town) Floyd County
29	1.6	**Tipton** (city) Tipton County
31	1.8	**Avon** (town) Hendricks County
31	1.8	**Chesterton** (town) Porter County
31	1.8	**Pendleton** (town) Madison County
34	2.0	**Bicknell** (city) Knox County
34	2.0	**Carmel** (city) Hamilton County
34	2.0	**Clinton** (city) Vermillion County
34	2.0	**Zionsville** (town) Boone County
38	2.2	**New Whiteland** (town) Johnson County
38	2.2	**Saint John** (town) Lake County
40	2.3	**Attica** (city) Fountain County
40	2.3	**Huntertown** (town) Allen County
42	2.6	**Leo-Cedarville** (town) Allen County
42	2.6	**Winfield** (town) Lake County
44	2.7	**Brazil** (city) Clay County
44	2.7	**Delphi** (city) Carroll County
46	2.8	**Bright** (CDP) Dearborn County
46	2.8	**North Terre Haute** (CDP) Vigo County
48	2.9	**Peru** (city) Miami County
48	2.9	**South Haven** (CDP) Porter County
50	3.0	**Pittsboro** (town) Hendricks County
50	3.0	**Valparaiso** (city) Porter County
52	3.1	**Lakes of the Four Seasons** (CDP) Lake County
53	3.3	**Portage** (city) Porter County
53	3.3	**Westfield** (city) Hamilton County
55	3.4	**Crown Point** (city) Lake County
55	3.4	**Gary** (city) Lake County
55	3.4	**Greencastle** (city) Putnam County
58	3.5	**Speedway** (town) Marion County
58	3.5	**Vincennes** (city) Knox County
58	3.5	**Westville** (town) LaPorte County
61	3.6	**Berne** (city) Adams County
61	3.6	**Fort Branch** (town) Gibson County
63	3.7	**Beech Grove** (city) Marion County
63	3.7	**Hobart** (city) Lake County
63	3.7	**New Albany** (city) Floyd County
66	3.8	**Dunlap** (CDP) Elkhart County
66	3.8	**Granger** (CDP) Saint Joseph County
68	3.9	**Griffith** (town) Lake County
69	4.0	**Wabash** (city) Wabash County
70	4.1	**Elwood** (city) Madison County
70	4.1	**Frankfort** (city) Clinton County
72	4.2	**Fishers** (city) Hamilton County
73	4.3	**Austin** (city) Scott County
74	4.4	**Salem** (city) Washington County
75	4.5	**Charlestown** (city) Clark County
75	4.5	**Fairmount** (town) Grant County
75	4.5	**Noblesville** (city) Hamilton County
78	4.6	**Brookville** (town) Franklin County
79	4.7	**Hanover** (town) Jefferson County
79	4.7	**Winona Lake** (town) Kosciusko County
81	4.8	**Highland** (town) Lake County
82	4.9	**Evansville** (city) Vanderburgh County
82	4.9	**Tell City** (city) Perry County
84	5.0	**Jasper** (city) Dubois County
84	5.0	**Marion** (city) Grant County
86	5.1	**Michigan City** (city) LaPorte County
86	5.1	**Monticello** (city) White County
86	5.1	**West Lafayette** (city) Tippecanoe County
89	5.2	**Aurora** (city) Dearborn County
89	5.2	**Columbia City** (city) Whitley County
89	5.2	**Danville** (town) Hendricks County
89	5.2	**Greendale** (city) Dearborn County
93	5.3	**Batesville** (city) Ripley County
93	5.3	**Huntingburg** (city) Dubois County
93	5.3	**Mooresville** (town) Morgan County
96	5.4	**Muncie** (city) Delaware County
96	5.4	**Simonton Lake** (CDP) Elkhart County
98	5.5	**Boonville** (city) Warrick County
98	5.5	**De Motte** (town) Jasper County
98	5.5	**Lafayette** (city) Tippecanoe County
98	5.5	**Rushville** (city) Rush County
102	5.6	**Heritage Lake** (CDP) Putnam County
102	5.6	**Linton** (city) Greene County
102	5.6	**New Haven** (city) Allen County
102	5.6	**South Bend** (city) Saint Joseph County
106	5.7	**Kokomo** (city) Howard County
106	5.7	**North Manchester** (town) Wabash County
106	5.7	**Plainfield** (town) Hendricks County
106	5.7	**Terre Haute** (city) Vigo County
110	5.8	**Bloomington** (city) Monroe County
111	6.1	**Anderson** (city) Madison County
111	6.1	**Indianapolis** (city) Marion County
111	6.1	**Seymour** (city) Jackson County
114	6.2	**Bedford** (city) Lawrence County
114	6.2	**Connersville** (city) Fayette County
114	6.2	**Greensburg** (city) Decatur County
117	6.3	**Lawrence** (city) Marion County
117	6.3	**Paoli** (town) Orange County
119	6.4	**Cedar Lake** (town) Lake County
119	6.4	**Decatur** (city) Adams County
119	6.4	**Garrett** (city) DeKalb County
119	6.4	**Greenwood** (city) Johnson County
119	6.4	**McCordsville** (town) Hancock County
124	6.5	**Hammond** (city) Lake County
124	6.5	**Princeton** (city) Gibson County
126	6.6	**Greenfield** (city) Hancock County
126	6.6	**Merrillville** (town) Lake County
128	6.8	**Jeffersonville** (city) Clark County
129	6.9	**Mishawaka** (city) Saint Joseph County
130	7.0	**Fort Wayne** (city) Allen County
130	7.0	**Gas City** (city) Grant County
130	7.0	**Kendallville** (city) Noble County
130	7.0	**New Castle** (city) Henry County
130	7.0	**Portland** (city) Jay County
135	7.1	**Washington** (city) Daviess County
136	7.2	**Lake Station** (city) Lake County
136	7.2	**Ligonier** (city) Noble County
136	7.2	**Lowell** (town) Lake County
139	7.4	**Franklin** (city) Johnson County
139	7.4	**Whiting** (city) Lake County
141	7.5	**East Chicago** (city) Lake County
142	7.6	**Hartford City** (city) Blackford County
142	7.6	**Highland** (CDP) Vanderburgh County
142	7.6	**Huntington** (city) Huntington County
145	7.7	**Ellettsville** (town) Monroe County
146	7.8	**Cumberland** (town) Marion County
147	7.9	**Elkhart** (city) Elkhart County
148	8.0	**La Porte** (city) LaPorte County
148	8.0	**Martinsville** (city) Morgan County
150	8.3	**Rensselaer** (city) Jasper County

Note: *This section ranks incorporated places and CDPs (Census Designated Places) with populations of 2,500 or more. Unincorporated postal areas were not considered. Please refer to the User Guide for additional information.*

Commute to Work: Car

Top 150 Places Ranked in *Descending* Order

State Rank	Percent	Place
1	98.3	**Lowell** (town) Lake County
2	98.2	**Charlestown** (city) Clark County
3	97.8	**Smithville-Sanders** (CDP) Monroe County
4	97.7	**Yorktown** (town) Delaware County
5	97.6	**Greentown** (town) Howard County
5	97.6	**Heritage Lake** (CDP) Putnam County
7	97.5	**Greenfield** (city) Hancock County
7	97.5	**Lake Station** (city) Lake County
7	97.5	**Simonton Lake** (CDP) Elkhart County
10	97.3	**Chandler** (town) Warrick County
10	97.3	**Dunlap** (CDP) Elkhart County
10	97.3	**Huntertown** (town) Allen County
13	97.1	**Monticello** (city) White County
14	96.8	**Tell City** (city) Perry County
15	96.6	**Austin** (city) Scott County
15	96.6	**Loogootee** (city) Martin County
17	96.4	**Fortville** (town) Hancock County
18	96.3	**New Whiteland** (town) Johnson County
19	96.2	**Ellettsville** (town) Monroe County
19	96.2	**Sullivan** (city) Sullivan County
19	96.2	**Union City** (city) Randolph County
22	96.1	**Brazil** (city) Clay County
23	96.0	**Georgetown** (town) Floyd County
23	96.0	**Kendallville** (city) Noble County
23	96.0	**Mount Vernon** (city) Posey County
26	95.9	**Linton** (city) Greene County
26	95.9	**North Terre Haute** (CDP) Vigo County
26	95.9	**Shelbyville** (city) Shelby County
26	95.9	**Westville** (town) LaPorte County
30	95.8	**Decatur** (city) Adams County
30	95.8	**Garrett** (city) DeKalb County
30	95.8	**North Vernon** (city) Jennings County
30	95.8	**Pittsboro** (town) Hendricks County
30	95.8	**Rushville** (city) Rush County
35	95.7	**Columbia City** (city) Whitley County
35	95.7	**Osceola** (town) Saint Joseph County
37	95.6	**Sellersburg** (town) Clark County
38	95.5	**New Haven** (city) Allen County
39	95.4	**Mitchell** (city) Lawrence County
40	95.2	**Auburn** (city) DeKalb County
40	95.2	**Franklin** (city) Johnson County
40	95.2	**Salt Creek Commons** (CDP) Porter County
43	94.9	**Gas City** (city) Grant County
43	94.9	**Lebanon** (city) Boone County
43	94.9	**Whitestown** (town) Boone County
46	94.8	**Bright** (CDP) Dearborn County
46	94.8	**Frankfort** (city) Clinton County
46	94.8	**New Castle** (city) Henry County
46	94.8	**Ossian** (town) Wells County
50	94.7	**Centerville** (town) Wayne County
50	94.7	**Rensselaer** (city) Jasper County
50	94.7	**Tipton** (city) Tipton County
50	94.7	**Whiteland** (town) Johnson County
54	94.6	**Bremen** (town) Marshall County
54	94.6	**Fairmount** (town) Grant County
54	94.6	**Scottsburg** (city) Scott County
57	94.5	**Brownsburg** (town) Hendricks County
57	94.5	**Clarksville** (town) Clark County
57	94.5	**Huntingburg** (city) Dubois County
60	94.4	**Bedford** (city) Lawrence County
60	94.4	**Logansport** (city) Cass County
62	94.3	**Greensburg** (city) Decatur County
62	94.3	**Ligonier** (city) Noble County
64	94.2	**Greendale** (city) Dearborn County
64	94.2	**Nappanee** (city) Elkhart County
64	94.2	**Plymouth** (city) Marshall County
67	94.1	**Alexandria** (city) Madison County
68	94.0	**Bargersville** (town) Johnson County
68	94.0	**South Haven** (CDP) Porter County
68	94.0	**Wabash** (city) Wabash County
71	93.9	**Columbus** (city) Bartholomew County
71	93.9	**Delphi** (city) Carroll County
71	93.9	**Greenwood** (city) Johnson County
71	93.9	**Shorewood Forest** (CDP) Porter County
75	93.8	**Cumberland** (town) Marion County
75	93.8	**Rochester** (city) Fulton County
77	93.7	**Mooresville** (town) Morgan County
78	93.6	**Bluffton** (city) Wells County
78	93.6	**Kokomo** (city) Howard County
78	93.6	**Mishawaka** (city) Saint Joseph County
81	93.5	**New Albany** (city) Floyd County
81	93.5	**Santa Claus** (town) Spencer County
81	93.5	**Seymour** (city) Jackson County
84	93.4	**Hobart** (city) Lake County
84	93.4	**Newburgh** (town) Warrick County
84	93.4	**Salem** (city) Washington County
87	93.3	**Beech Grove** (city) Marion County
87	93.3	**Jasper** (city) Dubois County
87	93.3	**Porter** (town) Porter County
90	93.2	**Fort Branch** (town) Gibson County
90	93.2	**Hebron** (town) Porter County
90	93.2	**Lakes of the Four Seasons** (CDP) Lake County
90	93.2	**Winamac** (town) Pulaski County
94	93.1	**Aurora** (city) Dearborn County
94	93.1	**Connersville** (city) Fayette County
94	93.1	**Granger** (CDP) Saint Joseph County
94	93.1	**Hidden Valley** (CDP) Dearborn County
94	93.1	**Highland** (CDP) Vanderburgh County
94	93.1	**Lawrence** (city) Marion County
94	93.1	**Merrillville** (town) Lake County
94	93.1	**Paoli** (town) Orange County
94	93.1	**Sheridan** (town) Hamilton County
103	93.0	**Brookville** (town) Franklin County
103	93.0	**Cedar Lake** (town) Lake County
103	93.0	**Fort Wayne** (city) Allen County
103	93.0	**Jeffersonville** (city) Clark County
103	93.0	**Peru** (city) Miami County
103	93.0	**Warsaw** (city) Kosciusko County
109	92.9	**Hartford City** (city) Blackford County
109	92.9	**Knox** (city) Starke County
109	92.9	**Leo-Cedarville** (town) Allen County
109	92.9	**Portage** (city) Porter County
113	92.8	**Edinburgh** (town) Johnson County
114	92.7	**Berne** (city) Adams County
114	92.7	**Hammond** (city) Lake County
114	92.7	**Melody Hill** (CDP) Vanderburgh County
114	92.7	**Middlebury** (town) Elkhart County
114	92.7	**Syracuse** (town) Kosciusko County
119	92.6	**De Motte** (town) Jasper County
119	92.6	**McCordsville** (town) Hancock County
121	92.5	**Winchester** (city) Randolph County
122	92.4	**Avon** (town) Hendricks County
122	92.4	**Elwood** (city) Madison County
122	92.4	**Speedway** (town) Marion County
122	92.4	**Washington** (city) Daviess County
126	92.3	**Highland** (town) Lake County
126	92.3	**Schererville** (town) Lake County
128	92.0	**Crown Point** (city) Lake County
128	92.0	**Danville** (town) Hendricks County
128	92.0	**Dyer** (town) Lake County
128	92.0	**Winfield** (town) Lake County
132	91.9	**Evansville** (city) Vanderburgh County
132	91.9	**Plainfield** (town) Hendricks County
134	91.8	**Griffith** (town) Lake County
135	91.7	**Elkhart** (city) Elkhart County
135	91.7	**Vincennes** (city) Knox County
135	91.7	**Westfield** (city) Hamilton County
138	91.6	**Goshen** (city) Elkhart County
138	91.6	**Michigan City** (city) LaPorte County
140	91.5	**Butler** (city) DeKalb County
140	91.5	**Indianapolis** (city) Marion County
142	91.4	**Madison** (city) Jefferson County
143	91.3	**Batesville** (city) Ripley County
144	91.1	**Lawrenceburg** (city) Dearborn County
145	91.0	**Clinton** (city) Vermillion County
145	91.0	**Crawfordsville** (city) Montgomery County
145	91.0	**Huntington** (city) Huntington County
145	91.0	**La Porte** (city) LaPorte County
145	91.0	**Noblesville** (city) Hamilton County
150	90.9	**Bicknell** (city) Knox County

Note: *This section ranks incorporated places and CDPs (Census Designated Places) with populations of 2,500 or more. Unincorporated postal areas were not considered. Please refer to the User Guide for additional information.*

Rankings

Commute to Work: Car

Top 150 Places Ranked in *Ascending* Order

State Rank	Percent	Place
1	10.4	**Notre Dame** (CDP) Saint Joseph County
2	57.7	**West Lafayette** (city) Tippecanoe County
3	63.3	**Upland** (town) Grant County
4	70.8	**Greencastle** (city) Putnam County
5	72.0	**Bloomington** (city) Monroe County
6	78.7	**Hanover** (town) Jefferson County
7	83.2	**Marion** (city) Grant County
8	83.5	**Muncie** (city) Delaware County
9	85.3	**Winona Lake** (town) Kosciusko County
10	85.6	**Munster** (town) Lake County
10	85.6	**North Manchester** (town) Wabash County
12	86.2	**Valparaiso** (city) Porter County
13	86.5	**Angola** (city) Steuben County
14	86.8	**Country Squire Lakes** (CDP) Jennings County
15	87.6	**Terre Haute** (city) Vigo County
16	87.8	**Rockville** (town) Parke County
17	88.1	**Gary** (city) Lake County
18	88.2	**Richmond** (city) Wayne County
19	88.3	**Cicero** (town) Hamilton County
20	89.4	**Attica** (city) Fountain County
20	89.4	**Lafayette** (city) Tippecanoe County
20	89.4	**Roselawn** (CDP) Newton County
20	89.4	**South Bend** (city) Saint Joseph County
24	89.5	**Pendleton** (town) Madison County
24	89.5	**Zionsville** (town) Boone County
26	89.6	**Carmel** (city) Hamilton County
26	89.6	**Portland** (city) Jay County
28	89.7	**Lagrange** (town) LaGrange County
29	90.2	**Chesterton** (town) Porter County
29	90.2	**Corydon** (town) Harrison County
29	90.2	**Fishers** (city) Hamilton County
32	90.4	**East Chicago** (city) Lake County
33	90.5	**Anderson** (city) Madison County
33	90.5	**Boonville** (city) Warrick County
33	90.5	**Brownstown** (town) Jackson County
36	90.6	**Martinsville** (city) Morgan County
36	90.6	**Saint John** (town) Lake County
36	90.6	**Whiting** (city) Lake County
39	90.9	**Bicknell** (city) Knox County
39	90.9	**Princeton** (city) Gibson County
41	91.0	**Clinton** (city) Vermillion County
41	91.0	**Crawfordsville** (city) Montgomery County
41	91.0	**Huntington** (city) Huntington County
41	91.0	**La Porte** (city) LaPorte County
41	91.0	**Noblesville** (city) Hamilton County
46	91.1	**Lawrenceburg** (city) Dearborn County
47	91.3	**Batesville** (city) Ripley County
48	91.4	**Madison** (city) Jefferson County
49	91.5	**Butler** (city) DeKalb County
49	91.5	**Indianapolis** (city) Marion County
51	91.6	**Goshen** (city) Elkhart County
51	91.6	**Michigan City** (city) LaPorte County
53	91.7	**Elkhart** (city) Elkhart County
53	91.7	**Vincennes** (city) Knox County
53	91.7	**Westfield** (city) Hamilton County
56	91.8	**Griffith** (town) Lake County
57	91.9	**Evansville** (city) Vanderburgh County
57	91.9	**Plainfield** (town) Hendricks County
59	92.0	**Crown Point** (city) Lake County
59	92.0	**Danville** (town) Hendricks County
59	92.0	**Dyer** (town) Lake County
59	92.0	**Winfield** (town) Lake County
63	92.3	**Highland** (town) Lake County
63	92.3	**Schererville** (town) Lake County
65	92.4	**Avon** (town) Hendricks County
65	92.4	**Elwood** (city) Madison County
65	92.4	**Speedway** (town) Marion County
65	92.4	**Washington** (city) Daviess County
69	92.5	**Winchester** (city) Randolph County
70	92.6	**De Motte** (town) Jasper County
70	92.6	**McCordsville** (town) Hancock County
72	92.7	**Berne** (city) Adams County
72	92.7	**Hammond** (city) Lake County
72	92.7	**Melody Hill** (CDP) Vanderburgh County
72	92.7	**Middlebury** (town) Elkhart County
72	92.7	**Syracuse** (town) Kosciusko County
77	92.8	**Edinburgh** (town) Johnson County
78	92.9	**Hartford City** (city) Blackford County
78	92.9	**Knox** (city) Starke County
78	92.9	**Leo-Cedarville** (town) Allen County
78	92.9	**Portage** (city) Porter County
82	93.0	**Brookville** (town) Franklin County
82	93.0	**Cedar Lake** (town) Lake County
82	93.0	**Fort Wayne** (city) Allen County
82	93.0	**Jeffersonville** (city) Clark County
82	93.0	**Peru** (city) Miami County
82	93.0	**Warsaw** (city) Kosciusko County
88	93.1	**Aurora** (city) Dearborn County
88	93.1	**Connersville** (city) Fayette County
88	93.1	**Granger** (CDP) Saint Joseph County
88	93.1	**Hidden Valley** (CDP) Dearborn County
88	93.1	**Highland** (CDP) Vanderburgh County
88	93.1	**Lawrence** (city) Marion County
88	93.1	**Merrillville** (town) Lake County
88	93.1	**Paoli** (town) Orange County
88	93.1	**Sheridan** (town) Hamilton County
97	93.2	**Fort Branch** (town) Gibson County
97	93.2	**Hebron** (town) Porter County
97	93.2	**Lakes of the Four Seasons** (CDP) Lake County
97	93.2	**Winamac** (town) Pulaski County
101	93.3	**Beech Grove** (city) Marion County
101	93.3	**Jasper** (city) Dubois County
101	93.3	**Porter** (town) Porter County
104	93.4	**Hobart** (city) Lake County
104	93.4	**Newburgh** (town) Warrick County
104	93.4	**Salem** (city) Washington County
107	93.5	**New Albany** (city) Floyd County
107	93.5	**Santa Claus** (town) Spencer County
107	93.5	**Seymour** (city) Jackson County
110	93.6	**Bluffton** (city) Wells County
110	93.6	**Kokomo** (city) Howard County
110	93.6	**Mishawaka** (city) Saint Joseph County
113	93.7	**Mooresville** (town) Morgan County
114	93.8	**Cumberland** (town) Marion County
114	93.8	**Rochester** (city) Fulton County
116	93.9	**Columbus** (city) Bartholomew County
116	93.9	**Delphi** (city) Carroll County
116	93.9	**Greenwood** (city) Johnson County
116	93.9	**Shorewood Forest** (CDP) Porter County
120	94.0	**Bargersville** (town) Johnson County
120	94.0	**South Haven** (CDP) Porter County
120	94.0	**Wabash** (city) Wabash County
123	94.1	**Alexandria** (city) Madison County
124	94.2	**Greendale** (city) Dearborn County
124	94.2	**Nappanee** (city) Elkhart County
124	94.2	**Plymouth** (city) Marshall County
127	94.3	**Greensburg** (city) Decatur County
127	94.3	**Ligonier** (city) Noble County
129	94.4	**Bedford** (city) Lawrence County
129	94.4	**Logansport** (city) Cass County
131	94.5	**Brownsburg** (town) Hendricks County
131	94.5	**Clarksville** (town) Clark County
131	94.5	**Huntingburg** (city) Dubois County
134	94.6	**Bremen** (town) Marshall County
134	94.6	**Fairmount** (town) Grant County
134	94.6	**Scottsburg** (city) Scott County
137	94.7	**Centerville** (town) Wayne County
137	94.7	**Rensselaer** (city) Jasper County
137	94.7	**Tipton** (city) Tipton County
137	94.7	**Whiteland** (town) Johnson County
141	94.8	**Bright** (CDP) Dearborn County
141	94.8	**Frankfort** (city) Clinton County
141	94.8	**New Castle** (city) Henry County
141	94.8	**Ossian** (town) Wells County
145	94.9	**Gas City** (city) Grant County
145	94.9	**Lebanon** (city) Boone County
145	94.9	**Whitestown** (town) Boone County
148	95.2	**Auburn** (city) DeKalb County
148	95.2	**Franklin** (city) Johnson County
148	95.2	**Salt Creek Commons** (CDP) Porter County

Note: *This section ranks incorporated places and CDPs (Census Designated Places) with populations of 2,500 or more. Unincorporated postal areas were not considered. Please refer to the User Guide for additional information.*

Commute to Work: Public Transportation

Top 150 Places Ranked in *Descending* Order

State Rank	Percent	Place
1	6.7	**Bloomington** (city) Monroe County
1	6.7	**Munster** (town) Lake County
3	6.1	**West Lafayette** (city) Tippecanoe County
4	6.0	**Gary** (city) Lake County
5	3.6	**Lafayette** (city) Tippecanoe County
6	3.4	**East Chicago** (city) Lake County
7	3.3	**Saint John** (town) Lake County
8	3.2	**Muncie** (city) Delaware County
9	3.1	**Speedway** (town) Marion County
10	3.0	**Dyer** (town) Lake County
10	3.0	**Hammond** (city) Lake County
10	3.0	**Highland** (town) Lake County
13	2.9	**Griffith** (town) Lake County
14	2.8	**South Bend** (city) Saint Joseph County
15	2.6	**Clinton** (city) Vermillion County
16	2.5	**Schererville** (town) Lake County
17	2.4	**Evansville** (city) Vanderburgh County
18	2.3	**Chesterton** (town) Porter County
19	2.1	**South Haven** (CDP) Porter County
20	2.0	**Indianapolis** (city) Marion County
20	2.0	**Michigan City** (city) LaPorte County
22	1.8	**Merrillville** (town) Lake County
22	1.8	**Mishawaka** (city) Saint Joseph County
24	1.7	**Beech Grove** (city) Marion County
24	1.7	**Westville** (town) LaPorte County
26	1.6	**Boonville** (city) Warrick County
26	1.6	**Jeffersonville** (city) Clark County
26	1.6	**New Albany** (city) Floyd County
26	1.6	**Terre Haute** (city) Vigo County
26	1.6	**Whiting** (city) Lake County
31	1.4	**Crown Point** (city) Lake County
31	1.4	**Elkhart** (city) Elkhart County
31	1.4	**Shorewood Forest** (CDP) Porter County
34	1.3	**New Whiteland** (town) Johnson County
34	1.3	**Porter** (town) Porter County
34	1.3	**Valparaiso** (city) Porter County
37	1.2	**Cedar Lake** (town) Lake County
37	1.2	**Ellettsville** (town) Monroe County
37	1.2	**Salt Creek Commons** (CDP) Porter County
40	1.1	**Fort Wayne** (city) Allen County
41	1.0	**Clarksville** (town) Clark County
41	1.0	**Logansport** (city) Cass County
41	1.0	**Portage** (city) Porter County
41	1.0	**Upland** (town) Grant County
45	0.9	**Columbus** (city) Bartholomew County
45	0.9	**Greendale** (city) Dearborn County
45	0.9	**Hobart** (city) Lake County
48	0.8	**Connersville** (city) Fayette County
48	0.8	**Hanover** (town) Jefferson County
48	0.8	**Rensselaer** (city) Jasper County
51	0.7	**Attica** (city) Fountain County
51	0.7	**Butler** (city) DeKalb County
53	0.6	**Bright** (CDP) Dearborn County
53	0.6	**Goshen** (city) Elkhart County
53	0.6	**North Manchester** (town) Wabash County
53	0.6	**Richmond** (city) Wayne County
53	0.6	**Wabash** (city) Wabash County
53	0.6	**Whiteland** (town) Johnson County
59	0.5	**Columbia City** (city) Whitley County
59	0.5	**Highland** (CDP) Vanderburgh County
59	0.5	**Kokomo** (city) Howard County
59	0.5	**Marion** (city) Grant County
59	0.5	**Osceola** (town) Saint Joseph County
59	0.5	**Portland** (city) Jay County
65	0.4	**Angola** (city) Steuben County
65	0.4	**Bargersville** (town) Johnson County
65	0.4	**Fort Branch** (town) Gibson County
65	0.4	**Franklin** (city) Johnson County
65	0.4	**Greensburg** (city) Decatur County
65	0.4	**Greenwood** (city) Johnson County
65	0.4	**Lawrence** (city) Marion County
65	0.4	**Princeton** (city) Gibson County
65	0.4	**Rochester** (city) Fulton County
65	0.4	**Vincennes** (city) Knox County
65	0.4	**Winfield** (town) Lake County
65	0.4	**Winona Lake** (town) Kosciusko County
77	0.3	**Anderson** (city) Madison County
77	0.3	**Fishers** (city) Hamilton County
77	0.3	**Lake Station** (city) Lake County
77	0.3	**New Castle** (city) Henry County
77	0.3	**Washington** (city) Daviess County
82	0.2	**Carmel** (city) Hamilton County
82	0.2	**Granger** (CDP) Saint Joseph County
82	0.2	**La Porte** (city) LaPorte County
82	0.2	**Melody Hill** (CDP) Vanderburgh County
82	0.2	**Notre Dame** (CDP) Saint Joseph County
82	0.2	**Paoli** (town) Orange County
82	0.2	**Peru** (city) Miami County
82	0.2	**Pittsboro** (town) Hendricks County
82	0.2	**Plymouth** (city) Marshall County
82	0.2	**Seymour** (city) Jackson County
92	0.1	**Cumberland** (town) Marion County
92	0.1	**Jasper** (city) Dubois County
92	0.1	**Linton** (city) Greene County
92	0.1	**Madison** (city) Jefferson County
92	0.1	**New Haven** (city) Allen County
92	0.1	**Shelbyville** (city) Shelby County
92	0.1	**Zionsville** (town) Boone County
99	0.0	**Alexandria** (city) Madison County
99	0.0	**Auburn** (city) DeKalb County
99	0.0	**Aurora** (city) Dearborn County
99	0.0	**Austin** (city) Scott County
99	0.0	**Avon** (town) Hendricks County
99	0.0	**Batesville** (city) Ripley County
99	0.0	**Bedford** (city) Lawrence County
99	0.0	**Berne** (city) Adams County
99	0.0	**Bicknell** (city) Knox County
99	0.0	**Bluffton** (city) Wells County
99	0.0	**Brazil** (city) Clay County
99	0.0	**Bremen** (town) Marshall County
99	0.0	**Brookville** (town) Franklin County
99	0.0	**Brownsburg** (town) Hendricks County
99	0.0	**Brownstown** (town) Jackson County
99	0.0	**Centerville** (town) Wayne County
99	0.0	**Chandler** (town) Warrick County
99	0.0	**Charlestown** (city) Clark County
99	0.0	**Cicero** (town) Hamilton County
99	0.0	**Corydon** (town) Harrison County
99	0.0	**Country Squire Lakes** (CDP) Jennings County
99	0.0	**Crawfordsville** (city) Montgomery County
99	0.0	**Danville** (town) Hendricks County
99	0.0	**De Motte** (town) Jasper County
99	0.0	**Decatur** (city) Adams County
99	0.0	**Delphi** (city) Carroll County
99	0.0	**Dunlap** (CDP) Elkhart County
99	0.0	**Edinburgh** (town) Johnson County
99	0.0	**Elwood** (city) Madison County
99	0.0	**Fairmount** (town) Grant County
99	0.0	**Fortville** (town) Hancock County
99	0.0	**Frankfort** (city) Clinton County
99	0.0	**Garrett** (city) DeKalb County
99	0.0	**Gas City** (city) Grant County
99	0.0	**Georgetown** (town) Floyd County
99	0.0	**Greencastle** (city) Putnam County
99	0.0	**Greenfield** (city) Hancock County
99	0.0	**Greentown** (town) Howard County
99	0.0	**Hartford City** (city) Blackford County
99	0.0	**Hebron** (town) Porter County
99	0.0	**Heritage Lake** (CDP) Putnam County
99	0.0	**Hidden Valley** (CDP) Dearborn County
99	0.0	**Huntertown** (town) Allen County
99	0.0	**Huntingburg** (city) Dubois County
99	0.0	**Huntington** (city) Huntington County
99	0.0	**Kendallville** (city) Noble County
99	0.0	**Knox** (city) Starke County
99	0.0	**Lagrange** (town) LaGrange County
99	0.0	**Lakes of the Four Seasons** (CDP) Lake County
99	0.0	**Lawrenceburg** (city) Dearborn County
99	0.0	**Lebanon** (city) Boone County
99	0.0	**Leo-Cedarville** (town) Allen County

Note: *This section ranks incorporated places and CDPs (Census Designated Places) with populations of 2,500 or more. Unincorporated postal areas were not considered. Please refer to the User Guide for additional information.*

Commute to Work: Walk

Top 150 Places Ranked in *Descending* Order

State Rank	Percent	Place
1	70.5	**Notre Dame** (CDP) Saint Joseph County
2	26.6	**West Lafayette** (city) Tippecanoe County
3	24.4	**Greencastle** (city) Putnam County
4	13.7	**Hanover** (town) Jefferson County
5	13.0	**Upland** (town) Grant County
6	12.8	**Bloomington** (city) Monroe County
7	9.8	**North Manchester** (town) Wabash County
8	8.9	**Marion** (city) Grant County
9	7.8	**Lagrange** (town) LaGrange County
10	7.5	**Muncie** (city) Delaware County
11	7.4	**Winona Lake** (town) Kosciusko County
12	7.1	**Knox** (city) Starke County
13	6.6	**Lawrenceburg** (city) Dearborn County
13	6.6	**Princeton** (city) Gibson County
15	6.2	**Angola** (city) Steuben County
15	6.2	**Crawfordsville** (city) Montgomery County
17	6.1	**Huntington** (city) Huntington County
18	5.8	**Butler** (city) DeKalb County
19	5.5	**Valparaiso** (city) Porter County
20	5.4	**Terre Haute** (city) Vigo County
21	5.2	**Clinton** (city) Vermillion County
22	5.0	**Richmond** (city) Wayne County
22	5.0	**Whiting** (city) Lake County
24	4.7	**Hebron** (town) Porter County
25	4.4	**Rockville** (town) Parke County
26	4.3	**Pendleton** (town) Madison County
27	4.2	**Vincennes** (city) Knox County
27	4.2	**Washington** (city) Daviess County
29	4.1	**Attica** (city) Fountain County
30	4.0	**Brownstown** (town) Jackson County
31	3.9	**Newburgh** (town) Warrick County
32	3.8	**Anderson** (city) Madison County
32	3.8	**Brookville** (town) Franklin County
32	3.8	**Gas City** (city) Grant County
35	3.7	**Martinsville** (city) Morgan County
36	3.6	**Hartford City** (city) Blackford County
37	3.4	**La Porte** (city) LaPorte County
37	3.4	**Portland** (city) Jay County
39	3.3	**Paoli** (town) Orange County
40	3.2	**Boonville** (city) Warrick County
40	3.2	**Country Squire Lakes** (CDP) Jennings County
40	3.2	**Goshen** (city) Elkhart County
40	3.2	**Madison** (city) Jefferson County
40	3.2	**Plymouth** (city) Marshall County
45	3.1	**Michigan City** (city) LaPorte County
45	3.1	**South Bend** (city) Saint Joseph County
45	3.1	**Sullivan** (city) Sullivan County
48	3.0	**Edinburgh** (town) Johnson County
49	2.9	**Aurora** (city) Dearborn County
49	2.9	**Wabash** (city) Wabash County
49	2.9	**Winamac** (town) Pulaski County
52	2.8	**Brazil** (city) Clay County
52	2.8	**Bremen** (town) Marshall County
52	2.8	**East Chicago** (city) Lake County
55	2.7	**Elkhart** (city) Elkhart County
55	2.7	**Mitchell** (city) Lawrence County
55	2.7	**North Vernon** (city) Jennings County
55	2.7	**Peru** (city) Miami County
55	2.7	**Rensselaer** (city) Jasper County
60	2.5	**Evansville** (city) Vanderburgh County
60	2.5	**Greensburg** (city) Decatur County
60	2.5	**Union City** (city) Randolph County
63	2.4	**Bedford** (city) Lawrence County
63	2.4	**Fairmount** (town) Grant County
63	2.4	**Hammond** (city) Lake County
66	2.3	**Danville** (town) Hendricks County
66	2.3	**Lafayette** (city) Tippecanoe County
68	2.2	**Beech Grove** (city) Marion County
68	2.2	**Corydon** (town) Harrison County
68	2.2	**Kendallville** (city) Noble County
68	2.2	**Mishawaka** (city) Saint Joseph County
68	2.2	**Nappanee** (city) Elkhart County
68	2.2	**Salem** (city) Washington County
68	2.2	**Shorewood Forest** (CDP) Porter County
75	2.1	**Cicero** (town) Hamilton County
75	2.1	**Logansport** (city) Cass County
75	2.1	**Mooresville** (town) Morgan County
78	2.0	**Bluffton** (city) Wells County
78	2.0	**Gary** (city) Lake County
78	2.0	**Huntingburg** (city) Dubois County
78	2.0	**Jasper** (city) Dubois County
78	2.0	**Ligonier** (city) Noble County
78	2.0	**New Albany** (city) Floyd County
84	1.9	**Cumberland** (town) Marion County
84	1.9	**Decatur** (city) Adams County
84	1.9	**Warsaw** (city) Kosciusko County
84	1.9	**Winchester** (city) Randolph County
88	1.8	**Connersville** (city) Fayette County
88	1.8	**Indianapolis** (city) Marion County
88	1.8	**Loogootee** (city) Martin County
88	1.8	**South Haven** (CDP) Porter County
92	1.7	**Delphi** (city) Carroll County
92	1.7	**Elwood** (city) Madison County
92	1.7	**Franklin** (city) Johnson County
92	1.7	**New Castle** (city) Henry County
96	1.6	**Batesville** (city) Ripley County
96	1.6	**Ellettsville** (town) Monroe County
96	1.6	**Portage** (city) Porter County
96	1.6	**Shelbyville** (city) Shelby County
96	1.6	**Tell City** (city) Perry County
101	1.5	**Berne** (city) Adams County
101	1.5	**Crown Point** (city) Lake County
101	1.5	**Porter** (town) Porter County
104	1.4	**Chesterton** (town) Porter County
104	1.4	**Seymour** (city) Jackson County
104	1.4	**Sheridan** (town) Hamilton County
107	1.3	**Columbus** (city) Bartholomew County
108	1.2	**Fort Wayne** (city) Allen County
108	1.2	**Greentown** (town) Howard County
108	1.2	**Greenwood** (city) Johnson County
108	1.2	**Plainfield** (town) Hendricks County
108	1.2	**Scottsburg** (city) Scott County
108	1.2	**Whiteland** (town) Johnson County
114	1.1	**Bargersville** (town) Johnson County
114	1.1	**Carmel** (city) Hamilton County
114	1.1	**Cedar Lake** (town) Lake County
114	1.1	**Columbia City** (city) Whitley County
114	1.1	**De Motte** (town) Jasper County
114	1.1	**Dyer** (town) Lake County
114	1.1	**Fort Branch** (town) Gibson County
114	1.1	**Jeffersonville** (city) Clark County
114	1.1	**Kokomo** (city) Howard County
114	1.1	**Lawrence** (city) Marion County
114	1.1	**McCordsville** (town) Hancock County
114	1.1	**Mount Vernon** (city) Posey County
114	1.1	**Noblesville** (city) Hamilton County
114	1.1	**Syracuse** (town) Kosciusko County
114	1.1	**Zionsville** (town) Boone County
129	1.0	**Alexandria** (city) Madison County
129	1.0	**Bicknell** (city) Knox County
129	1.0	**Garrett** (city) DeKalb County
129	1.0	**Roselawn** (CDP) Newton County
133	0.9	**Georgetown** (town) Floyd County
133	0.9	**Greenfield** (city) Hancock County
133	0.9	**New Haven** (city) Allen County
133	0.9	**Rushville** (city) Rush County
133	0.9	**Speedway** (town) Marion County
138	0.8	**Clarksville** (town) Clark County
138	0.8	**Highland** (CDP) Vanderburgh County
138	0.8	**Highland** (town) Lake County
138	0.8	**Linton** (city) Greene County
138	0.8	**Pittsboro** (town) Hendricks County
143	0.7	**Bright** (CDP) Dearborn County
143	0.7	**Greendale** (city) Dearborn County
143	0.7	**Lake Station** (city) Lake County
143	0.7	**Westfield** (city) Hamilton County
147	0.6	**Avon** (town) Hendricks County
147	0.6	**Monticello** (city) White County
149	0.5	**Centerville** (town) Wayne County
149	0.5	**Charlestown** (city) Clark County

Note: *This section ranks incorporated places and CDPs (Census Designated Places) with populations of 2,500 or more. Unincorporated postal areas were not considered. Please refer to the User Guide for additional information.*

Commute to Work: Walk

Top 150 Places Ranked in *Ascending* Order

State Rank	Percent	Place
1	0.0	**Austin** (city) Scott County
1	0.0	**Chandler** (town) Warrick County
1	0.0	**Fortville** (town) Hancock County
1	0.0	**Heritage Lake** (CDP) Putnam County
1	0.0	**Hidden Valley** (CDP) Dearborn County
1	0.0	**Huntertown** (town) Allen County
1	0.0	**Leo-Cedarville** (town) Allen County
1	0.0	**Melody Hill** (CDP) Vanderburgh County
1	0.0	**Middlebury** (town) Elkhart County
1	0.0	**North Terre Haute** (CDP) Vigo County
1	0.0	**Ossian** (town) Wells County
1	0.0	**Rochester** (city) Fulton County
1	0.0	**Salt Creek Commons** (CDP) Porter County
1	0.0	**Simonton Lake** (CDP) Elkhart County
1	0.0	**Smithville-Sanders** (CDP) Monroe County
1	0.0	**Whitestown** (town) Boone County
1	0.0	**Winfield** (town) Lake County
18	0.2	**Saint John** (town) Lake County
18	0.2	**Schererville** (town) Lake County
18	0.2	**Sellersburg** (town) Clark County
18	0.2	**Yorktown** (town) Delaware County
22	0.3	**Auburn** (city) DeKalb County
22	0.3	**Hobart** (city) Lake County
22	0.3	**Lebanon** (city) Boone County
22	0.3	**Lowell** (town) Lake County
22	0.3	**Tipton** (city) Tipton County
22	0.3	**Westville** (town) LaPorte County
28	0.4	**Brownsburg** (town) Hendricks County
28	0.4	**Dunlap** (CDP) Elkhart County
28	0.4	**Fishers** (city) Hamilton County
28	0.4	**Granger** (CDP) Saint Joseph County
28	0.4	**Griffith** (town) Lake County
28	0.4	**Lakes of the Four Seasons** (CDP) Lake County
28	0.4	**Osceola** (town) Saint Joseph County
35	0.5	**Centerville** (town) Wayne County
35	0.5	**Charlestown** (city) Clark County
35	0.5	**Frankfort** (city) Clinton County
35	0.5	**Merrillville** (town) Lake County
35	0.5	**Munster** (town) Lake County
35	0.5	**New Whiteland** (town) Johnson County
35	0.5	**Santa Claus** (town) Spencer County
42	0.6	**Avon** (town) Hendricks County
42	0.6	**Monticello** (city) White County
44	0.7	**Bright** (CDP) Dearborn County
44	0.7	**Greendale** (city) Dearborn County
44	0.7	**Lake Station** (city) Lake County
44	0.7	**Westfield** (city) Hamilton County
48	0.8	**Clarksville** (town) Clark County
48	0.8	**Highland** (CDP) Vanderburgh County
48	0.8	**Highland** (town) Lake County
48	0.8	**Linton** (city) Greene County
48	0.8	**Pittsboro** (town) Hendricks County
53	0.9	**Georgetown** (town) Floyd County
53	0.9	**Greenfield** (city) Hancock County
53	0.9	**New Haven** (city) Allen County
53	0.9	**Rushville** (city) Rush County
53	0.9	**Speedway** (town) Marion County
58	1.0	**Alexandria** (city) Madison County
58	1.0	**Bicknell** (city) Knox County
58	1.0	**Garrett** (city) DeKalb County
58	1.0	**Roselawn** (CDP) Newton County
62	1.1	**Bargersville** (town) Johnson County
62	1.1	**Carmel** (city) Hamilton County
62	1.1	**Cedar Lake** (town) Lake County
62	1.1	**Columbia City** (city) Whitley County
62	1.1	**De Motte** (town) Jasper County
62	1.1	**Dyer** (town) Lake County
62	1.1	**Fort Branch** (town) Gibson County
62	1.1	**Jeffersonville** (city) Clark County
62	1.1	**Kokomo** (city) Howard County
62	1.1	**Lawrence** (city) Marion County
62	1.1	**McCordsville** (town) Hancock County
62	1.1	**Mount Vernon** (city) Posey County
62	1.1	**Noblesville** (city) Hamilton County
62	1.1	**Syracuse** (town) Kosciusko County
62	1.1	**Zionsville** (town) Boone County
77	1.2	**Fort Wayne** (city) Allen County
77	1.2	**Greentown** (town) Howard County
77	1.2	**Greenwood** (city) Johnson County
77	1.2	**Plainfield** (town) Hendricks County
77	1.2	**Scottsburg** (city) Scott County
77	1.2	**Whiteland** (town) Johnson County
83	1.3	**Columbus** (city) Bartholomew County
84	1.4	**Chesterton** (town) Porter County
84	1.4	**Seymour** (city) Jackson County
84	1.4	**Sheridan** (town) Hamilton County
87	1.5	**Berne** (city) Adams County
87	1.5	**Crown Point** (city) Lake County
87	1.5	**Porter** (town) Porter County
90	1.6	**Batesville** (city) Ripley County
90	1.6	**Ellettsville** (town) Monroe County
90	1.6	**Portage** (city) Porter County
90	1.6	**Shelbyville** (city) Shelby County
90	1.6	**Tell City** (city) Perry County
95	1.7	**Delphi** (city) Carroll County
95	1.7	**Elwood** (city) Madison County
95	1.7	**Franklin** (city) Johnson County
95	1.7	**New Castle** (city) Henry County
99	1.8	**Connersville** (city) Fayette County
99	1.8	**Indianapolis** (city) Marion County
99	1.8	**Loogootee** (city) Martin County
99	1.8	**South Haven** (CDP) Porter County
103	1.9	**Cumberland** (town) Marion County
103	1.9	**Decatur** (city) Adams County
103	1.9	**Warsaw** (city) Kosciusko County
103	1.9	**Winchester** (city) Randolph County
107	2.0	**Bluffton** (city) Wells County
107	2.0	**Gary** (city) Lake County
107	2.0	**Huntingburg** (city) Dubois County
107	2.0	**Jasper** (city) Dubois County
107	2.0	**Ligonier** (city) Noble County
107	2.0	**New Albany** (city) Floyd County
113	2.1	**Cicero** (town) Hamilton County
113	2.1	**Logansport** (city) Cass County
113	2.1	**Mooresville** (town) Morgan County
116	2.2	**Beech Grove** (city) Marion County
116	2.2	**Corydon** (town) Harrison County
116	2.2	**Kendallville** (city) Noble County
116	2.2	**Mishawaka** (city) Saint Joseph County
116	2.2	**Nappanee** (city) Elkhart County
116	2.2	**Salem** (city) Washington County
116	2.2	**Shorewood Forest** (CDP) Porter County
123	2.3	**Danville** (town) Hendricks County
123	2.3	**Lafayette** (city) Tippecanoe County
125	2.4	**Bedford** (city) Lawrence County
125	2.4	**Fairmount** (town) Grant County
125	2.4	**Hammond** (city) Lake County
128	2.5	**Evansville** (city) Vanderburgh County
128	2.5	**Greensburg** (city) Decatur County
128	2.5	**Union City** (city) Randolph County
131	2.7	**Elkhart** (city) Elkhart County
131	2.7	**Mitchell** (city) Lawrence County
131	2.7	**North Vernon** (city) Jennings County
131	2.7	**Peru** (city) Miami County
131	2.7	**Rensselaer** (city) Jasper County
136	2.8	**Brazil** (city) Clay County
136	2.8	**Bremen** (town) Marshall County
136	2.8	**East Chicago** (city) Lake County
139	2.9	**Aurora** (city) Dearborn County
139	2.9	**Wabash** (city) Wabash County
139	2.9	**Winamac** (town) Pulaski County
142	3.0	**Edinburgh** (town) Johnson County
143	3.1	**Michigan City** (city) LaPorte County
143	3.1	**South Bend** (city) Saint Joseph County
143	3.1	**Sullivan** (city) Sullivan County
146	3.2	**Boonville** (city) Warrick County
146	3.2	**Country Squire Lakes** (CDP) Jennings County
146	3.2	**Goshen** (city) Elkhart County
146	3.2	**Madison** (city) Jefferson County
146	3.2	**Plymouth** (city) Marshall County

Note: *This section ranks incorporated places and CDPs (Census Designated Places) with populations of 2,500 or more. Unincorporated postal areas were not considered. Please refer to the User Guide for additional information.*

Rankings

Commute to Work: Work from Home

Top 150 Places Ranked in *Descending* Order

State Rank	Percent	Place
1	19.4	**Upland** (town) Grant County
2	12.3	**Notre Dame** (CDP) Saint Joseph County
3	8.6	**Cicero** (town) Hamilton County
3	8.6	**Fishers** (city) Hamilton County
5	8.3	**Carmel** (city) Hamilton County
6	8.0	**Zionsville** (town) Boone County
7	7.6	**Corydon** (town) Harrison County
7	7.6	**Noblesville** (city) Hamilton County
9	7.3	**Middlebury** (town) Elkhart County
10	7.1	**Leo-Cedarville** (town) Allen County
11	7.0	**Melody Hill** (CDP) Vanderburgh County
12	6.6	**Westfield** (city) Hamilton County
13	6.3	**McCordsville** (town) Hancock County
14	6.1	**Avon** (town) Hendricks County
14	6.1	**Marion** (city) Grant County
14	6.1	**Winona Lake** (town) Kosciusko County
17	6.0	**Granger** (CDP) Saint Joseph County
18	5.9	**Pendleton** (town) Madison County
19	5.8	**Hidden Valley** (CDP) Dearborn County
20	5.7	**Chesterton** (town) Porter County
21	5.6	**De Motte** (town) Jasper County
22	5.4	**Rochester** (city) Fulton County
23	5.2	**Munster** (town) Lake County
23	5.2	**Ossian** (town) Wells County
23	5.2	**Plainfield** (town) Hendricks County
26	5.1	**Danville** (town) Hendricks County
26	5.1	**Martinsville** (city) Morgan County
26	5.1	**Whitestown** (town) Boone County
29	5.0	**Santa Claus** (town) Spencer County
30	4.9	**Angola** (city) Steuben County
30	4.9	**Portland** (city) Jay County
32	4.8	**Fort Branch** (town) Gibson County
32	4.8	**Valparaiso** (city) Porter County
32	4.8	**West Lafayette** (city) Tippecanoe County
32	4.8	**Winfield** (town) Lake County
36	4.7	**Batesville** (city) Ripley County
37	4.6	**Lakes of the Four Seasons** (CDP) Lake County
37	4.6	**Lawrence** (city) Marion County
37	4.6	**Saint John** (town) Lake County
40	4.5	**Bargersville** (town) Johnson County
40	4.5	**Centerville** (town) Wayne County
42	4.3	**Berne** (city) Adams County
43	4.1	**Bloomington** (city) Monroe County
43	4.1	**Hobart** (city) Lake County
43	4.1	**Jasper** (city) Dubois County
46	3.9	**Terre Haute** (city) Vigo County
47	3.8	**Cedar Lake** (town) Lake County
47	3.8	**Greenwood** (city) Johnson County
47	3.8	**Hanover** (town) Jefferson County
50	3.7	**Attica** (city) Fountain County
50	3.7	**Fort Wayne** (city) Allen County
52	3.6	**Bright** (CDP) Dearborn County
52	3.6	**Brownsburg** (town) Hendricks County
52	3.6	**Fortville** (town) Hancock County
52	3.6	**Greendale** (city) Dearborn County
52	3.6	**North Terre Haute** (CDP) Vigo County
52	3.6	**Salt Creek Commons** (CDP) Porter County
52	3.6	**Syracuse** (town) Kosciusko County
52	3.6	**Whiteland** (town) Johnson County
60	3.5	**North Manchester** (town) Wabash County
60	3.5	**Salem** (city) Washington County
62	3.4	**Huntingburg** (city) Dubois County
62	3.4	**Schererville** (town) Lake County
64	3.3	**Muncie** (city) Delaware County
64	3.3	**Paoli** (town) Orange County
66	3.2	**Georgetown** (town) Floyd County
66	3.2	**Highland** (CDP) Vanderburgh County
66	3.2	**Indianapolis** (city) Marion County
66	3.2	**Kokomo** (city) Howard County
66	3.2	**La Porte** (city) LaPorte County
66	3.2	**Rockville** (town) Parke County
72	3.1	**Anderson** (city) Madison County
72	3.1	**Crown Point** (city) Lake County
72	3.1	**Highland** (town) Lake County
72	3.1	**Jeffersonville** (city) Clark County
72	3.1	**Rushville** (city) Rush County
77	3.0	**Clarksville** (town) Clark County
77	3.0	**Greencastle** (city) Putnam County
77	3.0	**Madison** (city) Jefferson County
77	3.0	**Portage** (city) Porter County
77	3.0	**Sellersburg** (town) Clark County
77	3.0	**Tipton** (city) Tipton County
83	2.9	**Auburn** (city) DeKalb County
83	2.9	**Bluffton** (city) Wells County
83	2.9	**South Bend** (city) Saint Joseph County
83	2.9	**Warsaw** (city) Kosciusko County
83	2.9	**Winchester** (city) Randolph County
88	2.8	**Alexandria** (city) Madison County
88	2.8	**Brookville** (town) Franklin County
88	2.8	**Dyer** (town) Lake County
91	2.7	**Newburgh** (town) Warrick County
91	2.7	**Porter** (town) Porter County
93	2.6	**Boonville** (city) Warrick County
93	2.6	**Columbus** (city) Bartholomew County
93	2.6	**Elwood** (city) Madison County
93	2.6	**Griffith** (town) Lake County
93	2.6	**Huntertown** (town) Allen County
98	2.5	**Bedford** (city) Lawrence County
98	2.5	**Bremen** (town) Marshall County
98	2.5	**Cumberland** (town) Marion County
98	2.5	**Huntington** (city) Huntington County
98	2.5	**Osceola** (town) Saint Joseph County
98	2.5	**Richmond** (city) Wayne County
104	2.4	**Bicknell** (city) Knox County
104	2.4	**Country Squire Lakes** (CDP) Jennings County
104	2.4	**Delphi** (city) Carroll County
104	2.4	**Garrett** (city) DeKalb County
104	2.4	**Goshen** (city) Elkhart County
104	2.4	**Heritage Lake** (CDP) Putnam County
104	2.4	**Lafayette** (city) Tippecanoe County
104	2.4	**Lebanon** (city) Boone County
104	2.4	**Merrillville** (town) Lake County
104	2.4	**Michigan City** (city) LaPorte County
104	2.4	**Mount Vernon** (city) Posey County
104	2.4	**New Albany** (city) Floyd County
104	2.4	**New Haven** (city) Allen County
104	2.4	**Speedway** (town) Marion County
118	2.3	**Aurora** (city) Dearborn County
118	2.3	**Connersville** (city) Fayette County
118	2.3	**Greensburg** (city) Decatur County
118	2.3	**Mooresville** (town) Morgan County
118	2.3	**Sheridan** (town) Hamilton County
123	2.2	**Smithville-Sanders** (CDP) Monroe County
124	2.1	**New Castle** (city) Henry County
125	2.0	**Beech Grove** (city) Marion County
125	2.0	**Elkhart** (city) Elkhart County
125	2.0	**Mishawaka** (city) Saint Joseph County
125	2.0	**Wabash** (city) Wabash County
125	2.0	**Westville** (town) LaPorte County
125	2.0	**Winamac** (town) Pulaski County
131	1.9	**Lagrange** (town) LaGrange County
131	1.9	**Mitchell** (city) Lawrence County
131	1.9	**New Whiteland** (town) Johnson County
131	1.9	**Scottsburg** (city) Scott County
131	1.9	**Shorewood Forest** (CDP) Porter County
136	1.8	**Fairmount** (town) Grant County
136	1.8	**Franklin** (city) Johnson County
136	1.8	**Gary** (city) Lake County
139	1.7	**Butler** (city) DeKalb County
139	1.7	**Evansville** (city) Vanderburgh County
139	1.7	**Lawrenceburg** (city) Dearborn County
142	1.6	**Columbia City** (city) Whitley County
143	1.5	**Brownstown** (town) Jackson County
143	1.5	**Crawfordsville** (city) Montgomery County
143	1.5	**Dunlap** (CDP) Elkhart County
143	1.5	**Frankfort** (city) Clinton County
143	1.5	**Simonton Lake** (CDP) Elkhart County
143	1.5	**South Haven** (CDP) Porter County
149	1.4	**Decatur** (city) Adams County
149	1.4	**Greenfield** (city) Hancock County

Note: *This section ranks incorporated places and CDPs (Census Designated Places) with populations of 2,500 or more. Unincorporated postal areas were not considered. Please refer to the User Guide for additional information.*

Commute to Work: Work from Home

Top 150 Places Ranked in *Ascending* Order

State Rank	Percent	Place
1	0.0	**Greentown** (town) Howard County
1	0.0	**Knox** (city) Starke County
1	0.0	**Loogootee** (city) Martin County
4	0.4	**East Chicago** (city) Lake County
5	0.5	**Whiting** (city) Lake County
6	0.6	**Brazil** (city) Clay County
6	0.6	**Logansport** (city) Cass County
6	0.6	**Princeton** (city) Gibson County
6	0.6	**Union City** (city) Randolph County
10	0.7	**Gas City** (city) Grant County
10	0.7	**Lowell** (town) Lake County
10	0.7	**Sullivan** (city) Sullivan County
13	0.8	**Lake Station** (city) Lake County
13	0.8	**Monticello** (city) White County
13	0.8	**Yorktown** (town) Delaware County
16	0.9	**Kendallville** (city) Noble County
16	0.9	**Linton** (city) Greene County
16	0.9	**North Vernon** (city) Jennings County
16	0.9	**Vincennes** (city) Knox County
20	1.0	**Edinburgh** (town) Johnson County
20	1.0	**Ellettsville** (town) Monroe County
20	1.0	**Peru** (city) Miami County
23	1.1	**Chandler** (town) Warrick County
23	1.1	**Hebron** (town) Porter County
23	1.1	**Shelbyville** (city) Shelby County
26	1.2	**Austin** (city) Scott County
26	1.2	**Clinton** (city) Vermillion County
26	1.2	**Hammond** (city) Lake County
26	1.2	**Plymouth** (city) Marshall County
26	1.2	**Roselawn** (CDP) Newton County
31	1.3	**Charlestown** (city) Clark County
31	1.3	**Hartford City** (city) Blackford County
31	1.3	**Ligonier** (city) Noble County
31	1.3	**Nappanee** (city) Elkhart County
31	1.3	**Rensselaer** (city) Jasper County
31	1.3	**Washington** (city) Daviess County
37	1.4	**Decatur** (city) Adams County
37	1.4	**Greenfield** (city) Hancock County
37	1.4	**Pittsboro** (town) Hendricks County
37	1.4	**Seymour** (city) Jackson County
37	1.4	**Tell City** (city) Perry County
42	1.5	**Brownstown** (town) Jackson County
42	1.5	**Crawfordsville** (city) Montgomery County
42	1.5	**Dunlap** (CDP) Elkhart County
42	1.5	**Frankfort** (city) Clinton County
42	1.5	**Simonton Lake** (CDP) Elkhart County
42	1.5	**South Haven** (CDP) Porter County
48	1.6	**Columbia City** (city) Whitley County
49	1.7	**Butler** (city) DeKalb County
49	1.7	**Evansville** (city) Vanderburgh County
49	1.7	**Lawrenceburg** (city) Dearborn County
52	1.8	**Fairmount** (town) Grant County
52	1.8	**Franklin** (city) Johnson County
52	1.8	**Gary** (city) Lake County
55	1.9	**Lagrange** (town) LaGrange County
55	1.9	**Mitchell** (city) Lawrence County
55	1.9	**New Whiteland** (town) Johnson County
55	1.9	**Scottsburg** (city) Scott County
55	1.9	**Shorewood Forest** (CDP) Porter County
60	2.0	**Beech Grove** (city) Marion County
60	2.0	**Elkhart** (city) Elkhart County
60	2.0	**Mishawaka** (city) Saint Joseph County
60	2.0	**Wabash** (city) Wabash County
60	2.0	**Westville** (town) LaPorte County
60	2.0	**Winamac** (town) Pulaski County
66	2.1	**New Castle** (city) Henry County
67	2.2	**Smithville-Sanders** (CDP) Monroe County
68	2.3	**Aurora** (city) Dearborn County
68	2.3	**Connersville** (city) Fayette County
68	2.3	**Greensburg** (city) Decatur County
68	2.3	**Mooresville** (town) Morgan County
68	2.3	**Sheridan** (town) Hamilton County
73	2.4	**Bicknell** (city) Knox County
73	2.4	**Country Squire Lakes** (CDP) Jennings County
73	2.4	**Delphi** (city) Carroll County
73	2.4	**Garrett** (city) DeKalb County
73	2.4	**Goshen** (city) Elkhart County
73	2.4	**Heritage Lake** (CDP) Putnam County
73	2.4	**Lafayette** (city) Tippecanoe County
73	2.4	**Lebanon** (city) Boone County
73	2.4	**Merrillville** (town) Lake County
73	2.4	**Michigan City** (city) LaPorte County
73	2.4	**Mount Vernon** (city) Posey County
73	2.4	**New Albany** (city) Floyd County
73	2.4	**New Haven** (city) Allen County
73	2.4	**Speedway** (town) Marion County
87	2.5	**Bedford** (city) Lawrence County
87	2.5	**Bremen** (town) Marshall County
87	2.5	**Cumberland** (town) Marion County
87	2.5	**Huntington** (city) Huntington County
87	2.5	**Osceola** (town) Saint Joseph County
87	2.5	**Richmond** (city) Wayne County
93	2.6	**Boonville** (city) Warrick County
93	2.6	**Columbus** (city) Bartholomew County
93	2.6	**Elwood** (city) Madison County
93	2.6	**Griffith** (town) Lake County
93	2.6	**Huntertown** (town) Allen County
98	2.7	**Newburgh** (town) Warrick County
98	2.7	**Porter** (town) Porter County
100	2.8	**Alexandria** (city) Madison County
100	2.8	**Brookville** (town) Franklin County
100	2.8	**Dyer** (town) Lake County
103	2.9	**Auburn** (city) DeKalb County
103	2.9	**Bluffton** (city) Wells County
103	2.9	**South Bend** (city) Saint Joseph County
103	2.9	**Warsaw** (city) Kosciusko County
103	2.9	**Winchester** (city) Randolph County
108	3.0	**Clarksville** (town) Clark County
108	3.0	**Greencastle** (city) Putnam County
108	3.0	**Madison** (city) Jefferson County
108	3.0	**Portage** (city) Porter County
108	3.0	**Sellersburg** (town) Clark County
108	3.0	**Tipton** (city) Tipton County
114	3.1	**Anderson** (city) Madison County
114	3.1	**Crown Point** (city) Lake County
114	3.1	**Highland** (town) Lake County
114	3.1	**Jeffersonville** (city) Clark County
114	3.1	**Rushville** (city) Rush County
119	3.2	**Georgetown** (town) Floyd County
119	3.2	**Highland** (CDP) Vanderburgh County
119	3.2	**Indianapolis** (city) Marion County
119	3.2	**Kokomo** (city) Howard County
119	3.2	**La Porte** (city) LaPorte County
119	3.2	**Rockville** (town) Parke County
125	3.3	**Muncie** (city) Delaware County
125	3.3	**Paoli** (town) Orange County
127	3.4	**Huntingburg** (city) Dubois County
127	3.4	**Schererville** (town) Lake County
129	3.5	**North Manchester** (town) Wabash County
129	3.5	**Salem** (city) Washington County
131	3.6	**Bright** (CDP) Dearborn County
131	3.6	**Brownsburg** (town) Hendricks County
131	3.6	**Fortville** (town) Hancock County
131	3.6	**Greendale** (city) Dearborn County
131	3.6	**North Terre Haute** (CDP) Vigo County
131	3.6	**Salt Creek Commons** (CDP) Porter County
131	3.6	**Syracuse** (town) Kosciusko County
131	3.6	**Whiteland** (town) Johnson County
139	3.7	**Attica** (city) Fountain County
139	3.7	**Fort Wayne** (city) Allen County
141	3.8	**Cedar Lake** (town) Lake County
141	3.8	**Greenwood** (city) Johnson County
141	3.8	**Hanover** (town) Jefferson County
144	3.9	**Terre Haute** (city) Vigo County
145	4.1	**Bloomington** (city) Monroe County
145	4.1	**Hobart** (city) Lake County
145	4.1	**Jasper** (city) Dubois County
148	4.3	**Berne** (city) Adams County
149	4.5	**Bargersville** (town) Johnson County
149	4.5	**Centerville** (town) Wayne County

Note: *This section ranks incorporated places and CDPs (Census Designated Places) with populations of 2,500 or more. Unincorporated postal areas were not considered. Please refer to the User Guide for additional information.*

Mean Travel Time to Work

Top 150 Places Ranked in *Descending* Order

State Rank	Minutes	Place
1	36.7	**Lowell** (town) Lake County
2	36.3	**Saint John** (town) Lake County
3	36.2	**Heritage Lake** (CDP) Putnam County
4	35.4	**Lakes of the Four Seasons** (CDP) Lake County
5	34.7	**Cedar Lake** (town) Lake County
6	34.5	**Roselawn** (CDP) Newton County
7	32.0	**Pendleton** (town) Madison County
8	31.9	**McCordsville** (town) Hancock County
9	31.8	**Bright** (CDP) Dearborn County
10	31.6	**Hidden Valley** (CDP) Dearborn County
11	30.9	**Shorewood Forest** (CDP) Porter County
12	30.2	**Schererville** (town) Lake County
13	29.9	**Dyer** (town) Lake County
14	29.5	**Avon** (town) Hendricks County
15	29.3	**Hebron** (town) Porter County
16	29.2	**Munster** (town) Lake County
17	29.1	**Salt Creek Commons** (CDP) Porter County
18	28.9	**Whiting** (city) Lake County
19	28.2	**Centerville** (town) Wayne County
20	28.1	**Brownsburg** (town) Hendricks County
21	28.0	**Crown Point** (city) Lake County
22	27.8	**Georgetown** (town) Floyd County
23	27.6	**Bargersville** (town) Johnson County
23	27.6	**Salem** (city) Washington County
25	27.5	**Fishers** (city) Hamilton County
25	27.5	**Pittsboro** (town) Hendricks County
27	27.4	**Brookville** (town) Franklin County
27	27.4	**Lawrence** (city) Marion County
29	27.3	**Merrillville** (town) Lake County
29	27.3	**South Haven** (CDP) Porter County
31	27.0	**Gary** (city) Lake County
32	26.9	**Highland** (town) Lake County
32	26.9	**Sheridan** (town) Hamilton County
34	26.8	**Hobart** (city) Lake County
35	26.7	**Hammond** (city) Lake County
35	26.7	**Winfield** (town) Lake County
37	26.6	**Portage** (city) Porter County
38	26.5	**Cumberland** (town) Marion County
38	26.5	**De Motte** (town) Jasper County
38	26.5	**Lake Station** (city) Lake County
41	26.4	**Fortville** (town) Hancock County
42	26.3	**Chesterton** (town) Porter County
42	26.3	**Cicero** (town) Hamilton County
44	26.1	**Noblesville** (city) Hamilton County
44	26.1	**Santa Claus** (town) Spencer County
46	25.9	**Porter** (town) Porter County
46	25.9	**Zionsville** (town) Boone County
48	25.8	**Alexandria** (city) Madison County
49	25.7	**Griffith** (town) Lake County
49	25.7	**Huntertown** (town) Allen County
49	25.7	**Martinsville** (city) Morgan County
52	25.4	**Leo-Cedarville** (town) Allen County
53	25.3	**Greenwood** (city) Johnson County
53	25.3	**Scottsburg** (city) Scott County
53	25.3	**Smithville-Sanders** (CDP) Monroe County
56	25.0	**Charlestown** (city) Clark County
56	25.0	**Danville** (town) Hendricks County
58	24.9	**Osceola** (town) Saint Joseph County
59	24.7	**Greentown** (town) Howard County
59	24.7	**Whiteland** (town) Johnson County
61	24.5	**Greendale** (city) Dearborn County
62	24.4	**Chandler** (town) Warrick County
63	24.2	**Carmel** (city) Hamilton County
63	24.2	**Loogootee** (city) Martin County
65	24.1	**New Whiteland** (town) Johnson County
66	23.9	**New Castle** (city) Henry County
67	23.8	**Linton** (city) Greene County
67	23.8	**Westfield** (city) Hamilton County
69	23.7	**Anderson** (city) Madison County
69	23.7	**Connersville** (city) Fayette County
69	23.7	**East Chicago** (city) Lake County
72	23.5	**Bicknell** (city) Knox County
72	23.5	**Hartford City** (city) Blackford County
72	23.5	**Rushville** (city) Rush County
72	23.5	**Westville** (town) LaPorte County
76	23.3	**Butler** (city) DeKalb County
76	23.3	**Elwood** (city) Madison County
76	23.3	**Granger** (CDP) Saint Joseph County
76	23.3	**North Vernon** (city) Jennings County
80	23.1	**Franklin** (city) Johnson County
80	23.1	**Indianapolis** (city) Marion County
82	23.0	**Garrett** (city) DeKalb County
83	22.9	**Rockville** (town) Parke County
83	22.9	**Whitestown** (town) Boone County
85	22.8	**Corydon** (town) Harrison County
86	22.7	**Beech Grove** (city) Marion County
86	22.7	**Knox** (city) Starke County
86	22.7	**Union City** (city) Randolph County
89	22.5	**Delphi** (city) Carroll County
90	22.4	**Ossian** (town) Wells County
91	22.2	**Brazil** (city) Clay County
92	22.1	**Country Squire Lakes** (CDP) Jennings County
92	22.1	**Greenfield** (city) Hancock County
92	22.1	**Mitchell** (city) Lawrence County
92	22.1	**Rochester** (city) Fulton County
96	22.0	**Clinton** (city) Vermillion County
96	22.0	**Fort Branch** (town) Gibson County
96	22.0	**Lawrenceburg** (city) Dearborn County
96	22.0	**Valparaiso** (city) Porter County
100	21.9	**Lebanon** (city) Boone County
101	21.7	**Jeffersonville** (city) Clark County
101	21.7	**Nappanee** (city) Elkhart County
101	21.7	**Plainfield** (town) Hendricks County
101	21.7	**Sellersburg** (town) Clark County
105	21.6	**Attica** (city) Fountain County
105	21.6	**Batesville** (city) Ripley County
105	21.6	**Lagrange** (town) LaGrange County
108	21.5	**Mooresville** (town) Morgan County
109	21.4	**Hanover** (town) Jefferson County
110	21.2	**Speedway** (town) Marion County
110	21.2	**Tipton** (city) Tipton County
112	21.0	**Aurora** (city) Dearborn County
112	21.0	**Clarksville** (town) Clark County
114	20.9	**Dunlap** (CDP) Elkhart County
114	20.9	**Fort Wayne** (city) Allen County
114	20.9	**North Manchester** (town) Wabash County
117	20.8	**Mishawaka** (city) Saint Joseph County
118	20.7	**North Terre Haute** (CDP) Vigo County
119	20.6	**Bremen** (town) Marshall County
119	20.6	**Yorktown** (town) Delaware County
121	20.5	**Kendallville** (city) Noble County
122	20.3	**Gas City** (city) Grant County
123	20.2	**Decatur** (city) Adams County
123	20.2	**New Albany** (city) Floyd County
123	20.2	**Simonton Lake** (CDP) Elkhart County
126	20.1	**Columbia City** (city) Whitley County
126	20.1	**Frankfort** (city) Clinton County
128	20.0	**Austin** (city) Scott County
129	19.9	**New Haven** (city) Allen County
129	19.9	**Shelbyville** (city) Shelby County
129	19.9	**South Bend** (city) Saint Joseph County
132	19.8	**Fairmount** (town) Grant County
132	19.8	**Highland** (CDP) Vanderburgh County
132	19.8	**Washington** (city) Daviess County
135	19.7	**Boonville** (city) Warrick County
136	19.6	**Michigan City** (city) LaPorte County
136	19.6	**Paoli** (town) Orange County
138	19.4	**Ellettsville** (town) Monroe County
138	19.4	**Melody Hill** (CDP) Vanderburgh County
140	19.3	**La Porte** (city) LaPorte County
140	19.3	**Peru** (city) Miami County
142	19.2	**Elkhart** (city) Elkhart County
142	19.2	**Syracuse** (town) Kosciusko County
144	18.9	**Bedford** (city) Lawrence County
144	18.9	**Bluffton** (city) Wells County
144	18.9	**Muncie** (city) Delaware County
147	18.7	**Evansville** (city) Vanderburgh County
147	18.7	**Kokomo** (city) Howard County
149	18.6	**Huntingburg** (city) Dubois County
150	18.4	**Logansport** (city) Cass County

Note: *This section ranks incorporated places and CDPs (Census Designated Places) with populations of 2,500 or more. Unincorporated postal areas were not considered. Please refer to the User Guide for additional information.*

Mean Travel Time to Work

Top 150 Places Ranked in *Ascending* Order

State Rank	Minutes	Place
1	10.6	**Notre Dame** (CDP) Saint Joseph County
2	11.5	**Portland** (city) Jay County
3	13.0	**Upland** (town) Grant County
4	13.5	**Warsaw** (city) Kosciusko County
5	14.5	**Angola** (city) Steuben County
5	14.5	**Vincennes** (city) Knox County
7	15.1	**Richmond** (city) Wayne County
8	15.6	**Greencastle** (city) Putnam County
8	15.6	**Marion** (city) Grant County
8	15.6	**West Lafayette** (city) Tippecanoe County
11	16.0	**Monticello** (city) White County
12	16.1	**Bloomington** (city) Monroe County
13	16.2	**Winchester** (city) Randolph County
14	16.6	**Mount Vernon** (city) Posey County
15	16.7	**Jasper** (city) Dubois County
15	16.7	**Lafayette** (city) Tippecanoe County
15	16.7	**Wabash** (city) Wabash County
18	16.8	**Brownstown** (town) Jackson County
18	16.8	**Crawfordsville** (city) Montgomery County
18	16.8	**Winamac** (town) Pulaski County
21	17.3	**Columbus** (city) Bartholomew County
21	17.3	**Goshen** (city) Elkhart County
23	17.4	**Greensburg** (city) Decatur County
23	17.4	**Huntington** (city) Huntington County
23	17.4	**Ligonier** (city) Noble County
26	17.5	**Berne** (city) Adams County
27	17.6	**Edinburgh** (town) Johnson County
27	17.6	**Sullivan** (city) Sullivan County
27	17.6	**Winona Lake** (town) Kosciusko County
30	17.7	**Auburn** (city) DeKalb County
30	17.7	**Newburgh** (town) Warrick County
30	17.7	**Tell City** (city) Perry County
33	17.8	**Rensselaer** (city) Jasper County
33	17.8	**Seymour** (city) Jackson County
33	17.8	**Terre Haute** (city) Vigo County
36	18.0	**Madison** (city) Jefferson County
36	18.0	**Middlebury** (town) Elkhart County
38	18.2	**Princeton** (city) Gibson County
39	18.4	**Logansport** (city) Cass County
39	18.4	**Plymouth** (city) Marshall County
41	18.6	**Huntingburg** (city) Dubois County
42	18.7	**Evansville** (city) Vanderburgh County
42	18.7	**Kokomo** (city) Howard County
44	18.9	**Bedford** (city) Lawrence County
44	18.9	**Bluffton** (city) Wells County
44	18.9	**Muncie** (city) Delaware County
47	19.2	**Elkhart** (city) Elkhart County
47	19.2	**Syracuse** (town) Kosciusko County
49	19.3	**La Porte** (city) LaPorte County
49	19.3	**Peru** (city) Miami County
51	19.4	**Ellettsville** (town) Monroe County
51	19.4	**Melody Hill** (CDP) Vanderburgh County
53	19.6	**Michigan City** (city) LaPorte County
53	19.6	**Paoli** (town) Orange County
55	19.7	**Boonville** (city) Warrick County
56	19.8	**Fairmount** (town) Grant County
56	19.8	**Highland** (CDP) Vanderburgh County
56	19.8	**Washington** (city) Daviess County
59	19.9	**New Haven** (city) Allen County
59	19.9	**Shelbyville** (city) Shelby County
59	19.9	**South Bend** (city) Saint Joseph County
62	20.0	**Austin** (city) Scott County
63	20.1	**Columbia City** (city) Whitley County
63	20.1	**Frankfort** (city) Clinton County
65	20.2	**Decatur** (city) Adams County
65	20.2	**New Albany** (city) Floyd County
65	20.2	**Simonton Lake** (CDP) Elkhart County
68	20.3	**Gas City** (city) Grant County
69	20.5	**Kendallville** (city) Noble County
70	20.6	**Bremen** (town) Marshall County
70	20.6	**Yorktown** (town) Delaware County
72	20.7	**North Terre Haute** (CDP) Vigo County
73	20.8	**Mishawaka** (city) Saint Joseph County
74	20.9	**Dunlap** (CDP) Elkhart County
74	20.9	**Fort Wayne** (city) Allen County
74	20.9	**North Manchester** (town) Wabash County
77	21.0	**Aurora** (city) Dearborn County
77	21.0	**Clarksville** (town) Clark County
79	21.2	**Speedway** (town) Marion County
79	21.2	**Tipton** (city) Tipton County
81	21.4	**Hanover** (town) Jefferson County
82	21.5	**Mooresville** (town) Morgan County
83	21.6	**Attica** (city) Fountain County
83	21.6	**Batesville** (city) Ripley County
83	21.6	**Lagrange** (town) LaGrange County
86	21.7	**Jeffersonville** (city) Clark County
86	21.7	**Nappanee** (city) Elkhart County
86	21.7	**Plainfield** (town) Hendricks County
86	21.7	**Sellersburg** (town) Clark County
90	21.9	**Lebanon** (city) Boone County
91	22.0	**Clinton** (city) Vermillion County
91	22.0	**Fort Branch** (town) Gibson County
91	22.0	**Lawrenceburg** (city) Dearborn County
91	22.0	**Valparaiso** (city) Porter County
95	22.1	**Country Squire Lakes** (CDP) Jennings County
95	22.1	**Greenfield** (city) Hancock County
95	22.1	**Mitchell** (city) Lawrence County
95	22.1	**Rochester** (city) Fulton County
99	22.2	**Brazil** (city) Clay County
100	22.4	**Ossian** (town) Wells County
101	22.5	**Delphi** (city) Carroll County
102	22.7	**Beech Grove** (city) Marion County
102	22.7	**Knox** (city) Starke County
102	22.7	**Union City** (city) Randolph County
105	22.8	**Corydon** (town) Harrison County
106	22.9	**Rockville** (town) Parke County
106	22.9	**Whitestown** (town) Boone County
108	23.0	**Garrett** (city) DeKalb County
109	23.1	**Franklin** (city) Johnson County
109	23.1	**Indianapolis** (city) Marion County
111	23.3	**Butler** (city) DeKalb County
111	23.3	**Elwood** (city) Madison County
111	23.3	**Granger** (CDP) Saint Joseph County
111	23.3	**North Vernon** (city) Jennings County
115	23.5	**Bicknell** (city) Knox County
115	23.5	**Hartford City** (city) Blackford County
115	23.5	**Rushville** (city) Rush County
115	23.5	**Westville** (town) LaPorte County
119	23.7	**Anderson** (city) Madison County
119	23.7	**Connersville** (city) Fayette County
119	23.7	**East Chicago** (city) Lake County
122	23.8	**Linton** (city) Greene County
122	23.8	**Westfield** (city) Hamilton County
124	23.9	**New Castle** (city) Henry County
125	24.1	**New Whiteland** (town) Johnson County
126	24.2	**Carmel** (city) Hamilton County
126	24.2	**Loogootee** (city) Martin County
128	24.4	**Chandler** (town) Warrick County
129	24.5	**Greendale** (city) Dearborn County
130	24.7	**Greentown** (town) Howard County
130	24.7	**Whiteland** (town) Johnson County
132	24.9	**Osceola** (town) Saint Joseph County
133	25.0	**Charlestown** (city) Clark County
133	25.0	**Danville** (town) Hendricks County
135	25.3	**Greenwood** (city) Johnson County
135	25.3	**Scottsburg** (city) Scott County
135	25.3	**Smithville-Sanders** (CDP) Monroe County
138	25.4	**Leo-Cedarville** (town) Allen County
139	25.7	**Griffith** (town) Lake County
139	25.7	**Huntertown** (town) Allen County
139	25.7	**Martinsville** (city) Morgan County
142	25.8	**Alexandria** (city) Madison County
143	25.9	**Porter** (town) Porter County
143	25.9	**Zionsville** (town) Boone County
145	26.1	**Noblesville** (city) Hamilton County
145	26.1	**Santa Claus** (town) Spencer County
147	26.3	**Chesterton** (town) Porter County
147	26.3	**Cicero** (town) Hamilton County
149	26.4	**Fortville** (town) Hancock County
150	26.5	**Cumberland** (town) Marion County

***Note:** This section ranks incorporated places and CDPs (Census Designated Places) with populations of 2,500 or more. Unincorporated postal areas were not considered. Please refer to the User Guide for additional information.*

Violent Crime Rate per 10,000 Population

Top 150 Places Ranked in *Descending* Order

State Rank	Rate	Place
1	133.4	**Indianapolis** (city) Marion County
2	104.5	**South Bend** (city) Saint Joseph County
3	72.2	**Kokomo** (city) Howard County
4	69.1	**Evansville** (city) Vanderburgh County
5	68.0	**Aurora** (city) Dearborn County
6	66.6	**East Chicago** (city) Lake County
7	63.5	**Hammond** (city) Lake County
8	62.1	**Gary** (city) Lake County
9	58.5	**Lawrenceburg** (city) Dearborn County
10	56.7	**Boonville** (city) Warrick County
11	52.0	**Bloomington** (city) Monroe County
12	51.8	**Greenwood** (city) Johnson County
13	50.7	**Franklin** (city) Johnson County
14	50.4	**Lafayette** (city) Tippecanoe County
15	50.2	**Clinton** (city) Vermillion County
16	49.7	**Clarksville** (town) Clark County
17	47.5	**Crawfordsville** (city) Montgomery County
17	47.5	**La Porte** (city) LaPorte County
19	47.3	**Anderson** (city) Madison County
20	43.6	**Edinburgh** (town) Johnson County
21	43.0	**Greenfield** (city) Hancock County
22	35.9	**Fairmount** (town) Grant County
23	35.8	**Fort Wayne** (city) Allen County
24	35.7	**Muncie** (city) Delaware County
25	34.2	**Marion** (city) Grant County
26	33.7	**Seymour** (city) Jackson County
27	33.1	**Hobart** (city) Lake County
28	32.6	**Huntingburg** (city) Dubois County
29	31.3	**Speedway** (town) Marion County
30	28.3	**Cumberland** (town) Marion County
31	26.5	**Plainfield** (town) Hendricks County
32	26.3	**North Vernon** (city) Jennings County
33	24.5	**New Haven** (city) Allen County
34	23.9	**Batesville** (city) Ripley County
35	22.7	**Portland** (city) Jay County
36	22.5	**Jasper** (city) Dubois County
37	21.5	**Mishawaka** (city) Saint Joseph County
38	18.8	**Whitestown** (town) Boone County
39	18.6	**Porter** (town) Porter County
40	18.0	**Alexandria** (city) Madison County
41	15.9	**Highland** (town) Lake County
42	15.7	**Tipton** (city) Tipton County
43	15.5	**Griffith** (town) Lake County
44	14.4	**Valparaiso** (city) Porter County
45	14.3	**Elwood** (city) Madison County
46	14.1	**Jeffersonville** (city) Clark County
47	13.6	**Logansport** (city) Cass County
48	13.5	**Ellettsville** (town) Monroe County
49	13.4	**Vincennes** (city) Knox County
50	12.7	**Lake Station** (city) Lake County
51	12.1	**Bargersville** (town) Johnson County
52	11.9	**Hartford City** (city) Blackford County
53	11.2	**Knox** (city) Starke County
54	10.5	**Decatur** (city) Adams County
54	10.5	**West Lafayette** (city) Tippecanoe County
56	10.1	**Munster** (town) Lake County
57	9.5	**Frankfort** (city) Clinton County
58	8.3	**Bedford** (city) Lawrence County
59	7.9	**Sellersburg** (town) Clark County
60	7.7	**Linton** (city) Greene County
61	7.2	**Mooresville** (town) Morgan County
62	7.0	**Bluffton** (city) Wells County
63	6.9	**Gas City** (city) Grant County
64	6.8	**Tell City** (city) Perry County
65	6.0	**Plymouth** (city) Marshall County
66	5.9	**Chesterton** (town) Porter County
67	5.7	**Westfield** (city) Hamilton County
68	4.7	**Fishers** (city) Hamilton County
69	3.4	**Crown Point** (city) Lake County
70	2.5	**Dyer** (town) Lake County
71	2.3	**Ligonier** (city) Noble County
72	2.1	**Lowell** (town) Lake County
72	2.1	**Winchester** (city) Randolph County
74	1.8	**Carmel** (city) Hamilton County
75	1.6	**New Whiteland** (town) Johnson County
76	1.2	**Saint John** (town) Lake County

***Note:** This section ranks incorporated places and CDPs (Census Designated Places) with populations of 2,500 or more. Unincorporated postal areas were not considered. Please refer to the User Guide for additional information.*

Violent Crime Rate per 10,000 Population

Top 150 Places Ranked in *Ascending* Order

State Rank	Rate	Place
1	1.2	**Saint John** (town) Lake County
2	1.6	**New Whiteland** (town) Johnson County
3	1.8	**Carmel** (city) Hamilton County
4	2.1	**Lowell** (town) Lake County
4	2.1	**Winchester** (city) Randolph County
6	2.3	**Ligonier** (city) Noble County
7	2.5	**Dyer** (town) Lake County
8	3.4	**Crown Point** (city) Lake County
9	4.7	**Fishers** (city) Hamilton County
10	5.7	**Westfield** (city) Hamilton County
11	5.9	**Chesterton** (town) Porter County
12	6.0	**Plymouth** (city) Marshall County
13	6.8	**Tell City** (city) Perry County
14	6.9	**Gas City** (city) Grant County
15	7.0	**Bluffton** (city) Wells County
16	7.2	**Mooresville** (town) Morgan County
17	7.7	**Linton** (city) Greene County
18	7.9	**Sellersburg** (town) Clark County
19	8.3	**Bedford** (city) Lawrence County
20	9.5	**Frankfort** (city) Clinton County
21	10.1	**Munster** (town) Lake County
22	10.5	**Decatur** (city) Adams County
22	10.5	**West Lafayette** (city) Tippecanoe County
24	11.2	**Knox** (city) Starke County
25	11.9	**Hartford City** (city) Blackford County
26	12.1	**Bargersville** (town) Johnson County
27	12.7	**Lake Station** (city) Lake County
28	13.4	**Vincennes** (city) Knox County
29	13.5	**Ellettsville** (town) Monroe County
30	13.6	**Logansport** (city) Cass County
31	14.1	**Jeffersonville** (city) Clark County
32	14.3	**Elwood** (city) Madison County
33	14.4	**Valparaiso** (city) Porter County
34	15.5	**Griffith** (town) Lake County
35	15.7	**Tipton** (city) Tipton County
36	15.9	**Highland** (town) Lake County
37	18.0	**Alexandria** (city) Madison County
38	18.6	**Porter** (town) Porter County
39	18.8	**Whitestown** (town) Boone County
40	21.5	**Mishawaka** (city) Saint Joseph County
41	22.5	**Jasper** (city) Dubois County
42	22.7	**Portland** (city) Jay County
43	23.9	**Batesville** (city) Ripley County
44	24.5	**New Haven** (city) Allen County
45	26.3	**North Vernon** (city) Jennings County
46	26.5	**Plainfield** (town) Hendricks County
47	28.3	**Cumberland** (town) Marion County
48	31.3	**Speedway** (town) Marion County
49	32.6	**Huntingburg** (city) Dubois County
50	33.1	**Hobart** (city) Lake County
51	33.7	**Seymour** (city) Jackson County
52	34.2	**Marion** (city) Grant County
53	35.7	**Muncie** (city) Delaware County
54	35.8	**Fort Wayne** (city) Allen County
55	35.9	**Fairmount** (town) Grant County
56	43.0	**Greenfield** (city) Hancock County
57	43.6	**Edinburgh** (town) Johnson County
58	47.3	**Anderson** (city) Madison County
59	47.5	**Crawfordsville** (city) Montgomery County
59	47.5	**La Porte** (city) LaPorte County
61	49.7	**Clarksville** (town) Clark County
62	50.2	**Clinton** (city) Vermillion County
63	50.4	**Lafayette** (city) Tippecanoe County
64	50.7	**Franklin** (city) Johnson County
65	51.8	**Greenwood** (city) Johnson County
66	52.0	**Bloomington** (city) Monroe County
67	56.7	**Boonville** (city) Warrick County
68	58.5	**Lawrenceburg** (city) Dearborn County
69	62.1	**Gary** (city) Lake County
70	63.5	**Hammond** (city) Lake County
71	66.6	**East Chicago** (city) Lake County
72	68.0	**Aurora** (city) Dearborn County
73	69.1	**Evansville** (city) Vanderburgh County
74	72.2	**Kokomo** (city) Howard County
75	104.5	**South Bend** (city) Saint Joseph County
76	133.4	**Indianapolis** (city) Marion County

Note: *This section ranks incorporated places and CDPs (Census Designated Places) with populations of 2,500 or more. Unincorporated postal areas were not considered. Please refer to the User Guide for additional information.*

Property Crime Rate per 10,000 Population

Top 150 Places Ranked in *Descending* Order

State Rank	Rate	Place
1	1,073.6	**Edinburgh** (town) Johnson County
2	572.6	**Vincennes** (city) Knox County
3	547.5	**Knox** (city) Starke County
4	546.3	**Clarksville** (town) Clark County
5	500.9	**Evansville** (city) Vanderburgh County
6	500.7	**South Bend** (city) Saint Joseph County
7	460.3	**Scottsburg** (city) Scott County
8	441.2	**Indianapolis** (city) Marion County
9	440.0	**Anderson** (city) Madison County
10	416.5	**Hobart** (city) Lake County
11	412.8	**Warsaw** (city) Kosciusko County
12	410.7	**Speedway** (town) Marion County
13	409.1	**Winchester** (city) Randolph County
14	402.4	**Columbus** (city) Bartholomew County
15	396.0	**Peru** (city) Miami County
16	391.4	**Hammond** (city) Lake County
17	388.8	**Aurora** (city) Dearborn County
18	385.3	**Rushville** (city) Rush County
19	373.4	**Seymour** (city) Jackson County
20	372.9	**Logansport** (city) Cass County
21	372.4	**Marion** (city) Grant County
22	367.4	**Merrillville** (town) Lake County
23	364.9	**Lafayette** (city) Tippecanoe County
24	362.0	**Muncie** (city) Delaware County
25	351.0	**Elkhart** (city) Elkhart County
26	345.6	**East Chicago** (city) Lake County
27	340.5	**Gary** (city) Lake County
28	339.6	**Franklin** (city) Johnson County
29	336.8	**Goshen** (city) Elkhart County
30	325.6	**Highland** (town) Lake County
31	324.1	**Clinton** (city) Vermillion County
32	323.9	**Greenwood** (city) Johnson County
33	318.0	**Fort Wayne** (city) Allen County
34	315.6	**Frankfort** (city) Clinton County
35	303.6	**Bloomington** (city) Monroe County
36	302.4	**Jeffersonville** (city) Clark County
37	302.0	**Gas City** (city) Grant County
38	299.5	**Boonville** (city) Warrick County
39	289.0	**Kokomo** (city) Howard County
40	288.4	**Mooresville** (town) Morgan County
41	281.6	**Linton** (city) Greene County
42	280.1	**Lake Station** (city) Lake County
43	279.8	**Shelbyville** (city) Shelby County
44	276.2	**Cumberland** (town) Marion County
45	273.8	**Plymouth** (city) Marshall County
46	266.9	**Plainfield** (town) Hendricks County
47	263.5	**Elwood** (city) Madison County
48	260.3	**Lawrenceburg** (city) Dearborn County
49	258.9	**North Vernon** (city) Jennings County
50	256.7	**Crawfordsville** (city) Montgomery County
51	254.6	**La Porte** (city) LaPorte County
52	252.8	**Bedford** (city) Lawrence County
53	227.9	**Beech Grove** (city) Marion County
53	227.9	**Kendallville** (city) Noble County
55	219.8	**Griffith** (town) Lake County
56	216.4	**New Haven** (city) Allen County
57	212.3	**Whiting** (city) Lake County
58	201.8	**Munster** (town) Lake County
59	199.8	**Alexandria** (city) Madison County
60	188.8	**Greenfield** (city) Hancock County
61	186.2	**Whitestown** (town) Boone County
62	185.6	**Ellettsville** (town) Monroe County
63	179.0	**Tell City** (city) Perry County
64	169.3	**Bargersville** (town) Johnson County
65	161.2	**Cedar Lake** (town) Lake County
66	155.2	**Charlestown** (city) Clark County
67	151.5	**Nappanee** (city) Elkhart County
68	151.2	**Tipton** (city) Tipton County
68	151.2	**Valparaiso** (city) Porter County
70	144.7	**Batesville** (city) Ripley County
71	143.6	**Decatur** (city) Adams County
72	143.0	**Portland** (city) Jay County
73	134.2	**Bremen** (town) Marshall County
74	131.7	**Noblesville** (city) Hamilton County
75	117.6	**Danville** (town) Hendricks County
76	114.5	**Brownsburg** (town) Hendricks County
77	113.3	**Crown Point** (city) Lake County
78	102.7	**Jasper** (city) Dubois County
79	101.4	**Westfield** (city) Hamilton County
80	100.1	**West Lafayette** (city) Tippecanoe County
81	97.3	**Sellersburg** (town) Clark County
82	92.6	**Fishers** (city) Hamilton County
83	89.5	**Huntingburg** (city) Dubois County
84	86.7	**Chesterton** (town) Porter County
85	85.1	**Dyer** (town) Lake County
86	83.7	**Ligonier** (city) Noble County
87	83.5	**Saint John** (town) Lake County
88	80.5	**Porter** (town) Porter County
89	80.0	**Hartford City** (city) Blackford County
90	74.7	**Carmel** (city) Hamilton County
91	63.8	**New Whiteland** (town) Johnson County
92	38.9	**Berne** (city) Adams County
93	25.2	**Fairmount** (town) Grant County
94	6.3	**Lowell** (town) Lake County

Note: *This section ranks incorporated places and CDPs (Census Designated Places) with populations of 2,500 or more. Unincorporated postal areas were not considered. Please refer to the User Guide for additional information.*

Property Crime Rate per 10,000 Population

Top 150 Places Ranked in *Ascending* Order

State Rank	Rate	Place
1	6.3	**Lowell** (town) Lake County
2	25.2	**Fairmount** (town) Grant County
3	38.9	**Berne** (city) Adams County
4	63.8	**New Whiteland** (town) Johnson County
5	74.7	**Carmel** (city) Hamilton County
6	80.0	**Hartford City** (city) Blackford County
7	80.5	**Porter** (town) Porter County
8	83.5	**Saint John** (town) Lake County
9	83.7	**Ligonier** (city) Noble County
10	85.1	**Dyer** (town) Lake County
11	86.7	**Chesterton** (town) Porter County
12	89.5	**Huntingburg** (city) Dubois County
13	92.6	**Fishers** (city) Hamilton County
14	97.3	**Sellersburg** (town) Clark County
15	100.1	**West Lafayette** (city) Tippecanoe County
16	101.4	**Westfield** (city) Hamilton County
17	102.7	**Jasper** (city) Dubois County
18	113.3	**Crown Point** (city) Lake County
19	114.5	**Brownsburg** (town) Hendricks County
20	117.6	**Danville** (town) Hendricks County
21	131.7	**Noblesville** (city) Hamilton County
22	134.2	**Bremen** (town) Marshall County
23	143.0	**Portland** (city) Jay County
24	143.6	**Decatur** (city) Adams County
25	144.7	**Batesville** (city) Ripley County
26	151.2	**Tipton** (city) Tipton County
26	151.2	**Valparaiso** (city) Porter County
28	151.5	**Nappanee** (city) Elkhart County
29	155.2	**Charlestown** (city) Clark County
30	161.2	**Cedar Lake** (town) Lake County
31	169.3	**Bargersville** (town) Johnson County
32	179.0	**Tell City** (city) Perry County
33	185.6	**Ellettsville** (town) Monroe County
34	186.2	**Whitestown** (town) Boone County
35	188.8	**Greenfield** (city) Hancock County
36	199.8	**Alexandria** (city) Madison County
37	201.8	**Munster** (town) Lake County
38	212.3	**Whiting** (city) Lake County
39	216.4	**New Haven** (city) Allen County
40	219.8	**Griffith** (town) Lake County
41	227.9	**Beech Grove** (city) Marion County
41	227.9	**Kendallville** (city) Noble County
43	252.8	**Bedford** (city) Lawrence County
44	254.6	**La Porte** (city) LaPorte County
45	256.7	**Crawfordsville** (city) Montgomery County
46	258.9	**North Vernon** (city) Jennings County
47	260.3	**Lawrenceburg** (city) Dearborn County
48	263.5	**Elwood** (city) Madison County
49	266.9	**Plainfield** (town) Hendricks County
50	273.8	**Plymouth** (city) Marshall County
51	276.2	**Cumberland** (town) Marion County
52	279.8	**Shelbyville** (city) Shelby County
53	280.1	**Lake Station** (city) Lake County
54	281.6	**Linton** (city) Greene County
55	288.4	**Mooresville** (town) Morgan County
56	289.0	**Kokomo** (city) Howard County
57	299.5	**Boonville** (city) Warrick County
58	302.0	**Gas City** (city) Grant County
59	302.4	**Jeffersonville** (city) Clark County
60	303.6	**Bloomington** (city) Monroe County
61	315.6	**Frankfort** (city) Clinton County
62	318.0	**Fort Wayne** (city) Allen County
63	323.9	**Greenwood** (city) Johnson County
64	324.1	**Clinton** (city) Vermillion County
65	325.6	**Highland** (town) Lake County
66	336.8	**Goshen** (city) Elkhart County
67	339.6	**Franklin** (city) Johnson County
68	340.5	**Gary** (city) Lake County
69	345.6	**East Chicago** (city) Lake County
70	351.0	**Elkhart** (city) Elkhart County
71	362.0	**Muncie** (city) Delaware County
72	364.9	**Lafayette** (city) Tippecanoe County
73	367.4	**Merrillville** (town) Lake County
74	372.4	**Marion** (city) Grant County
75	372.9	**Logansport** (city) Cass County
76	373.4	**Seymour** (city) Jackson County
77	385.3	**Rushville** (city) Rush County
78	388.8	**Aurora** (city) Dearborn County
79	391.4	**Hammond** (city) Lake County
80	396.0	**Peru** (city) Miami County
81	402.4	**Columbus** (city) Bartholomew County
82	409.1	**Winchester** (city) Randolph County
83	410.7	**Speedway** (town) Marion County
84	412.8	**Warsaw** (city) Kosciusko County
85	416.5	**Hobart** (city) Lake County
86	440.0	**Anderson** (city) Madison County
87	441.2	**Indianapolis** (city) Marion County
88	460.3	**Scottsburg** (city) Scott County
89	500.7	**South Bend** (city) Saint Joseph County
90	500.9	**Evansville** (city) Vanderburgh County
91	546.3	**Clarksville** (town) Clark County
92	547.5	**Knox** (city) Starke County
93	572.6	**Vincennes** (city) Knox County
94	1,073.6	**Edinburgh** (town) Johnson County

Note: *This section ranks incorporated places and CDPs (Census Designated Places) with populations of 2,500 or more. Unincorporated postal areas were not considered. Please refer to the User Guide for additional information.*

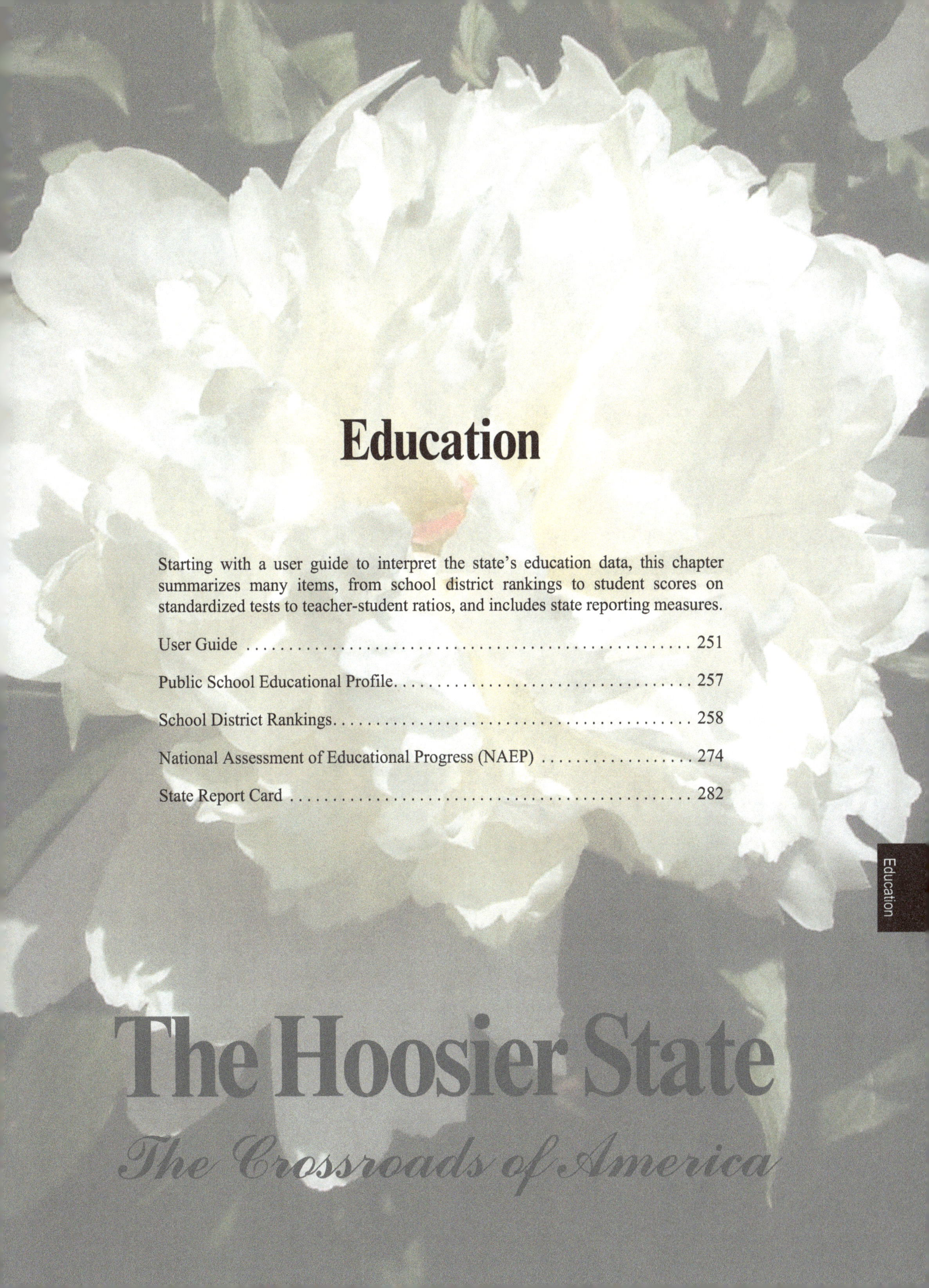

Education

Starting with a user guide to interpret the state's education data, this chapter summarizes many items, from school district rankings to student scores on standardized tests to teacher-student ratios, and includes state reporting measures.

User Guide 251

Public School Educational Profile. 257

School District Rankings. 258

National Assessment of Educational Progress (NAEP) 274

State Report Card 282

The Hoosier State

The Crossroads of America

User Guide

Public School Educational Profile

SCHOOLS

Schools: Total number of schools in the district. Figures exclude schools with the following status codes: 2 (school has closed since the time of the last report) and 6 (school is temporarily closed and may reopen within three years).
Source: U.S. Department of Education, National Center for Education Statistics, Common Core of Data, Public Elementary/Secondary School Universe Survey: School Year 2015-2016.

Instructional Level

Primary: Low grade—prekindergarten through 3; high grade—prekindergarten through 8
Middle: Low grade—4 through 7; high grade—4 through 9
High: Low grade—7 through 12; high grade—12 only
Other/Not Reported: Any configuration not falling within the previous three, including ungraded schools

Curriculum

Regular: A regular school is defined as a public elementary/secondary school that does not focus primarily on vocational, special, or alternative education.

Special Education: A special education school is defined as a public elementary/secondary school that focuses primarily on special education, including instruction for any of the following: autism, deaf-blindness, developmental delay, hearing impairment, mental retardation, multiple disabilities, orthopedic impairment, serious emotional disturbance, specific learning disability, speech or language impairment, traumatic brain injury, visual impairment, and other health impairments. These schools adapt curriculum, materials or instruction for students served.

Vocational: A vocational educational school is defined as a public elementary/secondary school that focuses primarily on providing formal preparation for semi-skilled, skilled, technical, or professional occupations for high school-aged students who have opted to develop or expand their employment opportunities, often in lieu of preparing for college entry.

Alternative: A public elementary/secondary school that addresses needs of students which typically cannot be met in a regular school; provides nontraditional education; serves as an adjunct to a regular school; and falls outside of the categories of regular, special education, or vocational education.

Type

Magnet: A special school or program designed to attract students of different racial/ethnic backgrounds for the purpose of reducing, preventing or eliminating racial isolation (50 percent or more minority enrollment); and/or to provide an academic or social focus on a particular theme (e.g., science/math, performing arts, gifted/talented, or foreign language).

Charter: A school providing free public elementary and/or secondary education to eligible students under a specific charter granted by the state legislature or other appropriate authority, and designated by such authority to be a charter school.

Title I Eligible: A school designated under appropriate state and federal regulations as being eligible for participation in programs authorized by Title I of Public Law 103-382.

School-wide Title I: A school in which all the pupils in a school are designated under appropriate state and federal regulations as being eligible for participation in programs authorized by Title I of Public Law 103-382.

STUDENTS

Students: A student is an individual for whom instruction is provided in an elementary or secondary education program that is not an adult education program and is under the jurisdiction of a school, school system, or other education institution.
Sources: U.S. Department of Education, National Center for Education Statistics, Common Core of Data, Local Education Agency (School District) Universe Survey: School Year 2015-2016; U.S. Department of Education, National Center for Education Statistics, Common Core of Data, Public Elementary/Secondary School Universe Survey: School Year 2015-2016

Gender: Percentage of male and female students.

Race/Ethnicity

White: A person having origins in any of the original peoples of Europe, North Africa, or the Middle East.
Figures include non-Hispanic whites only.

Black: A person having origins in any of the black racial groups of Africa. Figures include non-Hispanic blacks only.

Asian: A person having origins in any of the original peoples of the Far east, Southeast Asia, and the Indian subcontinent. This includes, for example, China, India, Japan, Korea, and the Philippines. Figures include non-Hispanic Asians only.

American Indian/Alaska Native: A person having origins in any of the original peoples of North America, and who maintains cultural identification through tribal affiliation or community recognition. Figures include non-Hispanic American Indian/Alaska Natives only.

Hawaiian Native/Pacific Islander: A person having origins in any of the original peoples of Hawaii, Guam, Samoa, or other Pacific Islands. Figures include non-Hispanic Hawaiian Native/Pacific Islanders only.

Two or More Races: A person identifying himself or herself as of two or more of the following race groups: White, Black, Asian, Native Hawaiian/Pacific Islander, or American Indian/Alaska Native. Some, but not all, reporting districts use this category. Figures include non-Hispanics, multiple-race students only.

Hispanic: A person of Mexican, Puerto Rican, Cuban, Central or South American, or other Spanish culture or origin, regardless of race.

Special Programs

Individual Education Program (IEP): A written instructional plan for students with disabilities designated as special education students under IDEA-Part B. The written instructional plan includes a statement of present levels of educational performance of a child; statement of annual goals, including short-term instructional objectives; statement of specific educational services to be provided and the extent to which the child will be able to participate in regular educational programs; the projected date for initiation and anticipated duration of services; the appropriate objectives, criteria and evaluation procedures; and the schedules for determining, on at least an annual basis, whether instructional objectives are being achieved. *Source: U.S. Department of Education, National Center for Education Statistics, Common Core of Data, Local Education Agency (School District) Universe Survey: School Year 2015-2016*

English Language Learner (ELL): Formerly referred to as Limited English Proficient (LEP). Students being served in appropriate programs of language assistance (e.g., English as a Second Language, High Intensity Language Training, bilingual education). Does not include pupils enrolled in a class to learn a language other than English. Also Limited-English-Proficient students are individuals who were not born in the United States or whose native language is a language other than English; or individuals who come from environments where a language other than English is dominant; or individuals who are American Indians and Alaskan Natives and who come from environments where a language other than English has had a significant impact on their level of English language proficiency; and who, by reason thereof, have sufficient difficulty speaking, reading, writing, or understanding the English language, to deny such individuals the opportunity to learn successfully in classrooms where the language of instruction is English or to participate fully in our society. *Source: U.S. Department of Education, National Center for Education Statistics, Common Core of Data, Local Education Agency (School District) Universe Survey: School Year 2015-2016*

Eligible for Free Lunch Program: The free lunch program is defined as a program under the National School Lunch Act that provides cash subsidies for free lunches to students based on family size and income criteria. *Source: U.S. Department of Education, National Center for Education Statistics, Common Core of Data, Public Elementary/Secondary School Universe Survey: School Year 2015-2016*

Eligible for Reduced-Price Lunch Program: A student who is eligible to participate in the Reduced-Price Lunch Program under the National School Lunch Act. *Source: U.S. Department of Education, National Center for Education Statistics, Common Core of Data, Public Elementary/Secondary School Universe Survey: School Year 2015-2016*

ADJUSTED COHORT GRADUATION RATE (ACGR)

The 4-year ACGR is the number of students who graduate in 4 years with a regular high school diploma divided by the number of students who form the adjusted cohort for the graduating class. From the beginning of 9th grade (or the earliest high school grade), students who are entering that grade for the first time form a cohort that is "adjusted" by adding any students who subsequently transfer into the cohort and subtracting any students who subsequently transfer out, emigrate to another country, or die. There are some differences in how states implemented the requirements for the ACGR, leading to the potential for differences across states in how the rates are calculated. This is particularly applicable to the population of children with disabilities. Black includes African American, Hispanic includes Latino, Asian/Pacific Islander includes Native Hawaiian or Other Pacific Islander, and American Indian includes Alaska Native. Race categories exclude Hispanic origin unless specified. Variances of +/- 5% from year-to-year for any subgroup over 50 in cohort size were addressed with states through ED's Coordinated Data Quality Review. With one exception, West Virginia, states provided explanations for the increase/decrease. The state comment was not accepted by the data steward (OESE) for California, Illinois, Louisiana, New Mexico, Texas, Utah and the District of Columbia. Those seven states and West Virginia received a letter from OESE to the state's Chief State School Officer outlining data quality concerns that are expected to be addressed in future submissions. *Source: EDFacts Data Groups 695 and 696, School Year 2015–16, October 25, 2017.*

STATUS DROPOUT RATE

"Status" dropouts are 16- to 24-year-olds who are not enrolled in school and who have not completed a high school program, regardless of when they left school. People who have received GED credentials are counted as high school completers. Data are based on a sample survey of the noninstitutionalized and institutionalized populations. The noninstitutionalized population includes persons living in households as well as persons living in college and university housing, military quarters, facilities for workers and religious groups, and temporary shelters for the homeless. The institutionalized population includes persons living in adult and juvenile correctional facilities, nursing facilities, and other healthcare facilities. Totals include other racial/ethnic groups not separately shown. Race categories exclude persons of Hispanic ethnicity. *Source: Trends in High School Dropout and Completion Rates in the United States: 2014, March 2018*

Note: Drop-out rates are no longer available to the general public disaggregated by grade, race/ethnicity, and gender at the school district level.

STAFF

Teachers: Teachers are defined as individuals who provide instruction to pre-kindergarten, kindergarten, grades 1 through 12, or ungraded classes, or individuals who teach in an environment other than a classroom setting, and who maintain daily student attendance records. Numbers reported are full-time equivalents (FTE). The students per teacher ratio is shown in parentheses. *Source: U.S. Department of Education, National Center for Education Statistics, Common Core of Data, Local Education Agency (School District) Universe Survey: School Year 2015-2016.*

Teacher Salary: The average classroom teacher salary in 2015-2016. *Source: National Education Association, Rankings of the States 2017 and Estimates of School Statistics 2018*

Librarians/Media Specialists: Library and media support staff are defined as staff members who render other professional library and media services; also includes library aides and those involved in library/media support. Their duties include selecting, preparing, caring for, and making available to instructional staff, equipment, films, filmstrips, transparencies, tapes, TV programs, and similar materials maintained separately or as part of an instructional materials center. Also included are activities in the audio-visual center, TV studio, related-work-study areas, and services provided by audio-visual personnel. Numbers reported are full-time equivalents (FTE). The students per librarian/media specialist ratio is shown in parentheses. *Source: U.S. Department of Education, National Center for Education Statistics, Common Core of Data, Local Education Agency (School District) Universe Survey: School Year 2015-2016.*

Guidance Counselors: Professional staff assigned specific duties and school time for any of the following activities in an elementary or secondary setting: counseling with students and parents; consulting with other staff members on learning problems; evaluating student abilities; assisting students in making educational and career choices; assisting students in personal and social development; providing referral assistance; and/or working with other staff members in planning and conducting guidance programs for students. The state applies its own standards in apportioning the aggregate of guidance counselors/directors into the elementary and secondary level components. Numbers reported are full-time equivalents (FTE). The students per guidance counselor ratio is shown in parentheses. *Source: U.S. Department of Education, National Center for Education Statistics, Common Core of Data, Local Education Agency (School District) Universe Survey: School Year 2015-2016.*

RATIOS

Number of Students per Teacher: The number of students divided by the number of teachers (FTE). See Number of Students and Number of Teachers above for more information. *Source: U.S. Department of Education, National Center for Education Statistics, Common Core of Data, Local Education Agency (School District) Universe Survey: School Year 2015-2016.*

Number of Students per Librarian: The number of students divided by the number of library and media support staff. Library and media support staff are defined as staff members who render other professional library and media services; also includes library aides and those involved in library/media support. Their duties include selecting, preparing, caring for, and making available to instructional staff, equipment, films, filmstrips, transparencies, tapes, TV programs, and similar materials maintained separately or as part of an instructional materials center. Also included are activities in the audio-visual center, TV studio, related-work-study areas, and services provided by audio-visual personnel. Numbers are based on full-time equivalents. *Source: U.S. Department of Education, National Center for Education Statistics, Common Core of Data, Local Education Agency (School District) Universe Survey: School Year 2015-2016.*

Number of Students per Counselor: The number of students divided by the number of guidance counselors. Guidance counselors are professional staff assigned specific duties and school time for any of the following activities in an elementary or secondary setting: counseling with students and parents; consulting with other staff members on learning problems; evaluating student abilities; assisting students in making educational and career choices; assisting students in personal and social development; providing referral assistance; and/or working with other staff members in planning and conducting guidance programs for students. The state applies its own standards in apportioning the aggregate of guidance counselors/directors into the elementary and secondary level components. Numbers reported are full-time equivalents. *Source: U.S. Department of Education, National Center for Education Statistics, Common Core of Data, Local Education Agency (School District) Universe Survey: School Year 2015-2016.*

FINANCES

Total Expenditures per Pupil: This is the total expenditures divided by the fall membership as reported in the state finance file. The total expenditures is the subtotal of direct state support expenditures for private schools, debt services expenditures—interest and total expenditures for education.

Total Current Expenditures per Pupil: This is the total current expenditures for public elementary and secondary education divided by the fall membership as reported in the state finance file. The expenditures for equipment, non-public education, school construction, debt financing and community services are excluded from this data item.

Instruction Expenditures per Pupil: This is the total of instructional expenditures divided by the fall membership as reported in the state finance file. Instruction expenditures are for services and materials directly related to classroom instruction and the interaction between teachers and students. Teacher salaries and benefits, textbooks, classroom supplies and extra curricular activities are included in Instruction. Expenditures for the library and in-service teacher training are reported as instruction support services. Guidance counselors and nurses are reported under student support services.

Support Services Expenditures per Pupil: This is the total of support services expenditures divided by the fall membership as reported in the state finance file.

Non-Instruction Expenditures per Pupil: This is the total for food services operations expenditures and enterprise operations expenditures divided by the fall membership as reported in the state finance file. This does not include property or community services expenditures.

Net Current Expenditures per Attendance for Title I: Net current expenditures per average daily attendance (ADA) are calculated by NCES. Net current expenditures are calculated by NCES and are equal to current expenditures minus total exclusions. Computation of ADA is defined by state laws or regulations or by NCES. Net current expenditures per ADA (or state per public expenditures—SPPE) are used to calculate allocations for certain federal education programs, including Title I, impact aid, Indian education and individuals with disabilities.

Total Revenues per Pupil: Total revenues per student are the total revenues from all sources divided by the fall membership as reported in the state finance file.

Federal Revenues per Pupil: Federal revenues per student are federal revenues divided by the fall membership as reported in the state finance file.

State Revenues per Pupil: State revenues per student are revenues received by the LEAs from the state, divided by the fall membership as reported in the state finance file.

Local Revenues per Pupil: Local revenues per student are the total of all local revenue categories divided by the fall membership as reported in the state finance file. Local revenues are raised and allocated by local governments.

Intermediate Revenue per Pupil: Intermediate revenue per pupil are intermediate sources of revenue divided by the student membership as reported on the state finance file. Intermediate sources of revenue are from educational agencies that possess independent fund-raising capabilities and that operate between the state and local government levels. *Source: U.S. Department of Education, National Center for Education Statistics, Common Core of Data (CCD), National Public Education Financial Survey (State Fiscal), 2014-15 (FY 2015) v.1a*

COLLEGE ENTRANCE EXAM SCORES

Scholastic Aptitude Test (SAT). On March 5, 2014, the College Board announced its plan to redesign the SAT in order to link the exam more closely to the work high school students encounter in the classroom. The new exam was administered for the first time in March 2016. Some of the major changes are: an emphasis on the use of evidence to support answers, a shift away from obscure vocabulary to words that students are more likely to encounter in college and career, a math section that is focused on fewer areas, a return to the 1600-point score scale, an optional essay, and the removal of penalty for wrong answers (rights-only scoring). Note: The College Board strongly discourages the comparison or ranking of states on the basis of SAT scores alone. *Source: The College Board, SAT, 2017 College-Bound Seniors, State Profile Reports*

American College Testing Program (ACT). *Source: ACT, Inc., 2017 ACT National and State Scores*

Note: n/a indicates data not available.

School District Rankings

Number of Schools: Total number of schools in the district. *Source: U.S. Department of Education, National Center for Education Statistics, Common Core of Data, Public Elementary/Secondary School Universe Survey: School Year 2015-2016.*

Number of Teachers: Teachers are defined as individuals who provide instruction to pre-kindergarten, kindergarten, grades 1 through 12, or ungraded classes, or individuals who teach in an environment other than a classroom setting, and who maintain daily student attendance records. Numbers reported are full-time equivalents (FTE). *Source: U.S. Department of Education, National Center for Education Statistics, Common Core of Data, Local Education Agency (School District) Universe Survey: School Year 2015-2016.*

Number of Students: A student is an individual for whom instruction is provided in an elementary or secondary education program that is not an adult education program and is under the jurisdiction of a school, school system, or other education institution. *Source: U.S. Department of Education, National Center for Education Statistics, Common Core of Data, Local Education Agency (School District) Universe Survey: School Year 2015-2016*

Male Students: Percentage of students who are male. *Source: U.S. Department of Education, National Center for Education Statistics, Common Core of Data, Local Education Agency (School District) Universe Survey: School Year 2015-2016*

Female Students: Percentage of students who are female. *Source: U.S. Department of Education, National Center for Education Statistics, Common Core of Data, Local Education Agency (School District) Universe Survey: School Year 2015-2016*

White Students: Percentage of students who are white (a person having origins in any of the original peoples of Europe, North Africa, or the Middle East). Figures include non-Hispanic whites only. *Source: U.S. Department of Education, National Center for Education Statistics, Common Core of Data, Local Education Agency (School District) Universe Survey: School Year 2015-2016*

Black Students: Percentage of students who are black (a person having origins in any of the black racial groups of Africa). Figures include non-Hispanic blacks only. *Source: U.S. Department of Education, National Center for Education Statistics, Common Core of Data, Local Education Agency (School District) Universe Survey: School Year 2015-2016*

Asian Students: Percentage of students who are Asian (a person having origins in any of the original peoples of the Far east, Southeast Asia, and the Indian subcontinent. This includes, for example, China, India, Japan, Korea, and the Philippines). Figures include non-Hispanic Asians only. *Source: U.S. Department of Education, National Center for Education Statistics, Common Core of Data, Local Education Agency (School District) Universe Survey: School Year 2015-2016*

American Indian/Alaska Native Students: Percentage of students who are American Indian/Alaska Native Students (a person having origins in any of the original peoples of North America, and who maintains cultural identification through tribal affiliation or community recognition). Figures include non-Hispanic American Indian/Alaska Natives only. *Source: U.S. Department of Education, National Center for Education Statistics, Common Core of Data, Local Education Agency (School District) Universe Survey: School Year 2015-2016*

Hawaiian Native/Pacific Islander Students: Percentage of students who are Hawaiian Native/Pacific Islander (a person having origins in any of the original peoples of Hawaii, Guam, Samoa, or other Pacific Islands). Figures include non-Hispanic Hawaiian Native/Pacific Islanders only. *Source: U.S. Department of Education, National Center for Education Statistics, Common Core of Data, Local Education Agency (School District) Universe Survey: School Year 2015-2016*

Students who are Two or More Races: Percentage of students who are two or more races (a person identifying himself or herself as of two or more of the following race groups: White, Black, Asian, Native Hawaiian/Pacific Islander, or American Indian/Alaska Native). Some, but not all, reporting districts use this category. Figures include non-Hispanic, multiple-race students only. *Source: U.S. Department of Education, National Center for Education Statistics, Common Core of Data, Local Education Agency (School District) Universe Survey: School Year 2015-2016*

Hispanic Students: Percentage of students who are Hispanic (a person of Mexican, Puerto Rican, Cuban, Central or South American, or other Spanish culture or origin, regardless of race). *Source: U.S. Department of Education, National Center for Education Statistics, Common Core of Data, Local Education Agency (School District) Universe Survey: School Year 2015-2016*

Individual Education Program (IEP) Students: Percentage of students who have an Individual Education Program (IEP) which is a written instructional plan for students with disabilities designated as special education students under IDEA-Part B. The written instructional plan includes a statement of present levels of educational performance of a child; statement of annual goals, including short-term instructional objectives; statement of specific educational services to be provided and the extent to which the child will be able to participate in regular educational programs; the projected date for initiation and anticipated duration of services; the appropriate objectives, criteria and evaluation procedures; and the schedules for determining, on at least an annual basis, whether instructional objectives are being achieved. *Source: U.S. Department of Education, National Center for Education Statistics, Common Core of Data, Local Education Agency (School District) Universe Survey: School Year 2015-2016*

English Language Learner (ELL) Students: Percentage of students who are English Language Learners (ELL). Formerly referred to as Limited English Proficient (LEP). Students being served in appropriate programs of language assistance (e.g., English as a Second Language, High Intensity Language Training, bilingual education). Does not include pupils enrolled in a class to learn a language other than English. Also Limited-English-Proficient students are individuals who were not born in the United States or whose native language is a language other than English; or individuals who come from environments where a language other than English is dominant; or individuals who are American Indians and Alaskan Natives and who come from environments where a language other than English has had a significant impact on their level of English language proficiency; and who, by reason thereof, have sufficient difficulty speaking, reading, writing, or understanding the English language, to deny such individuals the opportunity to learn successfully in classrooms where the language of instruction is English or to participate fully in our society. *Source: U.S. Department of Education, National Center for Education Statistics, Common Core of Data, Local Education Agency (School District) Universe Survey: School Year 2015-2016*

Students Eligible for Free Lunch Program: Percentage of students that are eligible for the free lunch program. The free lunch program is defined as a program under the National School Lunch Act that provides cash subsidies for free lunches to students based on family size and income criteria. *Source: U.S. Department of Education, National Center for Education Statistics, Common Core of Data, Public Elementary/Secondary School Universe Survey: School Year 2015-2016*

Students Eligible for Reduced-Price Lunch Program: Percentage of students that are eligible for the reduced-price lunch program. A student who is eligible to participate in the reduced-price lunch program under the National School Lunch Act. *Source: U.S. Department of Education, National Center for Education Statistics, Common Core of Data, Public Elementary/Secondary School Universe Survey: School Year 2015-2016*

Student/Teacher Ratio: The number of students divided by the number of teachers (FTE). See Number of Students and Number of Teachers above for for information. *Source: U.S. Department of Education, National Center for Education Statistics, Common Core of Data, Local Education Agency (School District) Universe Survey: School Year 2015-2016*

Student/Librarian Ratio: The number of students divided by the number of library and media support staff. Library and media support staff are defined as staff members who render other professional library and media services; also includes library aides and those involved in library/media support. Their duties include selecting, preparing, caring for, and making available to instructional staff, equipment, films, filmstrips, transparencies, tapes, TV programs, and similar materials maintained separately or as part of an instructional materials center. Also included are activities in the audio-visual center, TV studio, related-work-study areas, and services provided by audio-visual personnel. Numbers are based on full-time equivalents. *Source: U.S. Department of Education, National Center for Education Statistics, Common Core of Data, Local Education Agency (School District) Universe Survey: School Year 2015-2016.*

Student/Counselor Ratio: The number of students divided by the number of guidance counselors. Guidance counselors are professional staff assigned specific duties and school time for any of the following activities in an elementary or secondary setting: counseling with students and parents; consulting with other staff members on learning problems; evaluating student abilities; assisting students in making educational and career choices; assisting students in personal and social development; providing referral assistance; and/or working with other staff members in planning and conducting guidance programs for students. The state applies its own standards in apportioning the aggregate of guidance counselors/directors into the elementary and secondary level components. Numbers reported are full-time equivalents. *Source: U.S. Department of Education, National Center for Education Statistics, Common Core of Data, Local Education Agency (School District) Universe Survey: School Year 2015-2016.*

Current Spending per Student: Expenditure for Instruction, Support Services, and Other Elementary/Secondary Programs. Includes salaries, employee benefits, purchased services, and supplies, as well as payments made by states on behalf of school districts. Also includes transfers made by school districts into their own retirement system. Excludes expenditure for Non-Elementary/Secondary Programs, debt service, capital outlay, and transfers to other governments or school districts. This item is formally called "Current Expenditures for Public Elementary/Secondary Education."

Values shown are dollars per pupil per year. They were calculated by dividing the total dollar amounts by the fall membership. Fall membership is comprised of the total student enrollment on October 1 (or the closest school day to October 1) for all grade levels (including prekindergarten and kindergarten) and ungraded pupils. Membership includes students both present and absent on the measurement day. *Source: U.S. Department of Education, National Center for Education Statistics, Common Core of Data, School District Finance Survey (F-33), Fiscal Year 2014.*

Total General Revenue per Student: The sum of revenue contributions emerging from local, state, and federal sources as reported in the district finance file.

Values shown are dollars per pupil per year. They were calculated by dividing the total dollar amounts by the fall membership. Fall membership is comprised of the total student enrollment on October 1 (or the closest school day to October 1) for all grade levels (including prekindergarten and kindergarten) and ungraded pupils. Membership includes students both present and absent on the measurement day. *Source: U.S. Department of Education, National Center for Education Statistics, Common Core of Data, School District Finance Survey (F-33), Fiscal Year 2014.*

Long-Term Debt per Student (end of FY): Includes long-term credit obligations of the school system or its parent government and all interest-bearing short-term (repayable within 1 year) credit obligations. Excludes non-interest bearing short-term obligations, interfund obligations, amounts owed in a trust agency capacity, advances and contingent loans from other governments, and rights of individuals to benefits from school system employee retirement funds.

Values shown are dollars per pupil per year. They were calculated by dividing the total dollar amounts at the end of the fiscal year by the fall membership. Fall membership is comprised of the total student enrollment on October 1 (or the closest school day to October 1) for all grade levels (including prekindergarten and kindergarten) and ungraded pupils. Membership includes students both present and absent on the measurement day. *Source: U.S. Department of Education, National Center for Education Statistics, Common Core of Data, School District Finance Survey (F-33), Fiscal Year 2014.*

Note: n/a indicates data not available.

National Assessment of Educational Progress (NAEP)

The National Assessment of Educational Progress (NAEP), also known as "The Nation's Report Card," is the only nationally representative and continuing assessment of what America's students know and can do in various subject areas. As a result of the "No Child Left Behind" legislation, all states are required to participate in NAEP.

For more information, visit the U.S. Department of Education, National Center for Education Statistics at http://nces.ed.gov/nationsreportcard.

State Report Card

ISTEP+

ISTEP+ is an assessment that measures student achievement beginning in Grade 10. ISTEP+ assesses student achievement levels in English/Language Arts, and Mathematics according to the Indiana Academic Standards that were adopted by the Indiana State Board of Education.

IREAD-3

The Indiana Reading Evaluation and Determination (IREAD-3) assessment measures foundational reading standards to Grade 3 students each spring. Based on the Indiana Academic Standards, IREAD-3 is a summative assessment that was developed in accordance with House Enrolled Act 1367 (also known as Public Law 109 in 2010).

Public School Educational Profile

Category	Value	Category	Value
Schools *(2015-2016)*	1,922	**Status Dropout Rate** (%) *(2014)*	
Instructional Level		All Students	8.0
Primary	1,102	White	7.3
Middle	348	Black	11.0
High	378	Asian	n/a
Other/Not Reported	94	American Indian/Alaska Native	n/a
Curriculum		Hispanic	13.5
Regular	1,864	**Staff** *(2015-2016)*	
Special Education	22	Teachers (FTE)	57,676.6
Vocational	28	Average Salary in 2017 ($)	54,308
Alternative	8	Librarians/Media Specialists (FTE)	692.2
Type		Guidance Counselors (FTE)	1,963.9
Magnet	30	**Ratios** *(2015-2016)*	
Charter	89	Number of Students per Teacher	18.1 to 1
Title I Eligible	1,510	Number of Students per Librarian	1,512.1 to 1
School-wide Title I	1,219	Number of Students per Guidance Counselor	533.0 to 1
Students *(2015-2016)*	1,046,685	**Finances** *(2014-2015)*	
Gender (%)		Expenditures ($ per student)	
Male	51.3	Total Expenditures	10,946
Female	48.7	Current Expenditures	9,529
Race/Ethnicity (%)		Instruction	5,482
White, Non-Hispanic	69.3	Support Services	3,589
Black, Non-Hispanic	12.4	Non-Instruction	459
Asian, Non-Hispanic	2.2	Net Current per Attendance for Title I	9,614
American Indian/Alaska Native, Non-Hispanic	0.2	Revenue ($ per student)	
Hawaiian Native/Pacific Islander, Non-Hispanic	0.1	Total Revenue	11,568
Two or More Races, Non-Hispanic	4.7	From Federal Sources	945
Hispanic of Any Race	11.1	From State Sources	6,487
Special Programs (%)		From Local Sources	4,137
Individual Education Program (IEP)	16.4	From Intermediate Sources	14
English Language Learner (ELL)	4.8	**College Entrance Exam Scores**	
Eligible for Free Lunch Program	41.0	New SAT Test *(2017)*	
Eligible for Reduced-Price Lunch Program	7.2	Participation Rate (%)	63
Adjusted Cohort Graduation Rate (%) *(2015-2016)*		Mean Combined Score	1,074
All Students	86.8	Mean Evidence-based Reading & Writing Score	542
White, Non-Hispanic	89.5	Mean Math Score	532
Black, Non-Hispanic	73.8	ACT *(2017)*	
Asian/Pacific Islander, Non-Hispanic	89.0	Participation Rate (%)	35
American Indian/Alaska Native, Non-Hispanic	83.0	Mean Composite Score	22.6
Hispanic of Any Race	82.7	Mean English Score	22.0
Students with Disabilities	72.0	Mean Math Score	22.4
Limited English Proficient	71.0	Mean Reading Score	23.2
Economically Disadvantaged	85.0	Mean Science Score	22.3

Note: *For an explanation of data, please refer to the User Guide at the beginning of this chapter*

Number of Schools

Rank	Number	District Name	City
1	68	Indianapolis Public Schools	Indianapolis
2	50	Fort Wayne Community Schools	Fort Wayne
3	37	Evansville Vanderburgh Sch Corp	Evansville
4	36	South Bend Community Sch Corp	South Bend
5	28	Vigo County School Corp	Terre Haute
6	22	Hamilton Southeastern Schools	Fishers
6	22	Monroe County Com Sch Corp	Bloomington
8	21	Elkhart Community Schools	Elkhart
8	21	School City of Hammond	Hammond
10	20	Greater Clark County Schools	Jeffersonville
11	19	Tippecanoe School Corp	Lafayette
12	18	M S D Warren Township	Indianapolis
12	18	M S D Wayne Township	Indianapolis
14	17	Bartholomew Con School Corp	Columbus
14	17	M S D Lawrence Township	Indianapolis
14	17	Perry Township Schools	Indianapolis
14	17	Warrick County School Corp	Boonville
18	16	East Allen County Schools	New Haven
18	16	New Albany-Floyd County Con Sch	New Albany
20	15	Carmel Clay Schools	Carmel
20	15	Gary Community School Corp	Gary
20	15	North Lawrence Com Schools	Bedford
20	15	Penn-Harris-Madison Sch Corp	Mishawaka
24	14	Muncie Community Schools	Muncie
25	13	Lafayette School Corporation	Lafayette
25	13	M S D Pike Township	Indianapolis
25	13	M S D Washington Twp	Indianapolis
25	13	Michigan City Area Schools	Michigan City
29	12	Avon Community School Corp	Avon
29	12	Kokomo School Corporation	Kokomo
29	12	Valparaiso Community Schools	Valparaiso
32	11	Huntington County Com Sch Corp	Huntington
32	11	Lake Central School Corp	Saint John
32	11	Laporte Community School Corp	Laporte
32	11	Noblesville Schools	Noblesville
32	11	Northwest Allen County Schools	Fort Wayne
32	11	Portage Township Schools	Portage
32	11	Warsaw Community Schools	Warsaw
39	10	Brownsburg Community Sch Corp	Brownsburg
39	10	Clay Community Schools	Brazil
39	10	Crown Point Community Sch Corp	Crown Point
39	10	Jay School Corporation	Portland
39	10	M S D Martinsville Schools	Martinsville
39	10	Richmond Community Schools	Richmond
39	10	School City of Mishawaka	Mishawaka
46	9	Anderson Community School Corp	Anderson
46	9	Duneland School Corporation	Chesterton
46	9	Fayette County School Corp	Connersville
46	9	Franklin Township Com Sch Corp	Indianapolis
46	9	Goshen Community Schools	Goshen
46	9	Logansport Community Sch Corp	Logansport
46	9	M S D Decatur Township	Indianapolis
46	9	M S D Southwest Allen County Schls	Fort Wayne
46	9	Marion Community Schools	Marion
46	9	South Harrison Com Schools	Corydon
46	9	Westfield-Washington Schools	Westfield
57	8	Center Grove Com Sch Corp	Greenwood
57	8	Clark-Pleasant Com School Corp	Whiteland
57	8	Franklin Community School Corp	Franklin
57	8	Greenfield-Central Com Schools	Greenfield
57	8	Jennings County School Corp	North Vernon
57	8	Merrillville Community School	Merrillville
57	8	New Castle Community Sch Corp	New Castle
57	8	School City of East Chicago	East Chicago
57	8	West Clark Community Schools	Sellersburg
57	8	Zionsville Community Schools	Zionsville
67	7	Concord Community Schools	Elkhart
67	7	East Noble School Corp	Kendallville
67	7	M S D Wabash County Schools	Wabash
67	7	Middlebury Community Schools	Middlebury
67	7	Mooresville Con School Corp	Mooresville
67	7	Plainfield Community Sch Corp	Plainfield
67	7	Plymouth Community School Corp	Plymouth
67	7	Richland-Bean Blossom C S C	Ellettsville
67	7	Seymour Community Schools	Seymour
76	6	Brown County School Corporation	Nashville
76	6	Crawford County Com School Corp	Marengo
76	6	Crawfordsville Com Schools	Crawfordsville
76	6	Dekalb County Ctl United SD	Waterloo
76	6	East Porter County School Corp	Kouts
76	6	Greater Jasper Con Schs	Jasper
76	6	Greenwood Community Sch Corp	Greenwood
76	6	Lebanon Community School Corp	Lebanon
76	6	M S D Steuben County	Angola
76	6	Madison Consolidated Schools	Madison
76	6	North Spencer County Sch Corp	Lincoln City
76	6	Rush County Schools	Rushville
76	6	School City of Hobart	Hobart
76	6	School Town of Highland	Highland
76	6	School Town of Speedway	Speedway
76	6	Scott County SD 2	Scottsburg
76	6	Shelbyville Central Schools	Shelbyville
76	6	South Dearborn Com School Corp	Aurora
76	6	Spencer-Owen Community Schools	Spencer
76	6	Vincennes Community Sch Corp	Vincennes
76	6	Washington Com Schools	Washington
76	6	Whitley County Cons Schools	Columbia City
98	5	Beech Grove City Schools	Beech Grove
98	5	Blackford County Schools	Hartford City
98	5	Community Schools of Frankfort	Frankfort
98	5	Delaware Community School Corp	Muncie
98	5	Franklin County Com Sch Corp	Brookville
98	5	Frankton-Lapel Community Schools	Anderson
98	5	Greencastle Community Sch Corp	Greencastle
98	5	Griffith Public Schools	Griffith
98	5	Kankakee Valley School Corp	Wheatfield
98	5	Lakeland School Corporation	Lagrange
98	5	M S D Mount Vernon	Mount Vernon
98	5	Mississinewa Community Schl Corp	Gas City
98	5	Mt Vernon Community Sch Corp	Fortville
98	5	New Prairie United School Corp	New Carlisle
98	5	North Montgomery Com Sch Corp	Crawfordsville
98	5	North West Hendricks Schools	Lizton
98	5	Pike County School Corp	Petersburg
98	5	Randolph Central School Corp	Winchester
98	5	School Town of Munster	Munster
98	5	South Madison Com Sch Corp	Pendleton
98	5	South Montgomery Com Sch Corp	New Market
98	5	South Vermillion Com Sch Corp	Clinton
98	5	Southern Hancock Co Com Sch Corp	New Palestine
98	5	Southwest School Corp	Sullivan
98	5	Sunman-Dearborn Com Sch Corp	Saint Leon
98	5	Tri-Creek School Corporation	Lowell
98	5	Twin Lakes School Corp	Monticello
98	5	Wa-Nee Community Schools	Nappanee
98	5	Wawasee Community School Corp	Syracuse
98	5	Westview School Corporation	Topeka
128	4	Batesville Community Schl Corp	Batesville
128	4	Baugo Community Schools	Elkhart
128	4	Benton Community School Corp	Fowler
128	4	Brownstown Cnt Com Sch Corp	Brownstown
128	4	Centerville-Abington Com Schs	Centerville
128	4	Danville Community School Corp	Danville
128	4	Decatur County Com Schools	Greensburg
128	4	Elwood Community School Corp	Elwood
128	4	Fairfield Community Schools	Goshen
128	4	Hamilton Heights School Corp	Arcadia
128	4	Hanover Community School Corp	Cedar Lake
128	4	John Glenn School Corporation	Walkerton
128	4	Lake Ridge New Tech Schools	Gary
128	4	Lawrenceburg Com School Corp	Lawrenceburg
128	4	Maconaquah School Corp	Bunker Hill
128	4	Mill Creek Community Sch Corp	Clayton
128	4	Mitchell Community Schools	Mitchell
128	4	Nineveh-Hensley-Jackson United	Trafalgar
128	4	North Adams Community Schools	Decatur
128	4	North Gibson School Corp	Princeton
128	4	North Harrison Com School Corp	Ramsey
128	4	North Putnam Community Schools	Bainbridge
128	4	Northern Wells Com Schools	Ossian
128	4	Peru Community Schools	Peru
128	4	Rensselaer Central School Corp	Rensselaer
128	4	Rochester Community Sch Corp	Rochester
128	4	South Gibson School Corp	Fort Branch
128	4	Southwest Dubois County Sch Corp	Huntingburg
128	4	Switzerland County School Corp	Vevay
128	4	Tippecanoe Valley School Corp	Akron
128	4	West Noble School Corporation	Ligonier
128	4	Western School Corp	Russiaville
128	4	Whitko Community School Corp	Larwill
128	4	Yorktown Community Schools	Yorktown
162	3	Garrett-Keyser-Butler Com	Garrett
162	3	Greensburg Community Schools	Greensburg
162	3	Knox Community School Corp	Knox
162	3	Manchester Community Schools	N Manchester
162	3	Salem Community Schools	Salem
162	3	Tipton Community School Corp	Tipton
162	3	West Lafayette Com School Corp	West Lafayette
162	3	Western Boone County Com SD	Thorntown
170	2	Tell City-Troy Twp School Corp	Tell City
171	1	Hoosier Acad Virtual Charter	Indianapolis
171	1	Indiana Connections Academy	Indianapolis

Number of Teachers

Rank	Number	District Name	City
1	1,924.3	Indianapolis Public Schools	Indianapolis
2	1,668.9	Evansville Vanderburgh Sch Corp	Evansville
3	1,491.5	Fort Wayne Community Schools	Fort Wayne
4	1,020.2	Hamilton Southeastern Schools	Fishers
5	973.5	M S D Wayne Township	Indianapolis
6	845.1	South Bend Community Sch Corp	South Bend
7	828.9	Vigo County School Corp	Terre Haute
8	812.7	Carmel Clay Schools	Carmel
9	786.0	M S D Lawrence Township	Indianapolis
10	775.4	Perry Township Schools	Indianapolis
11	742.9	Elkhart Community Schools	Elkhart
12	741.4	School City of Hammond	Hammond
13	677.0	Monroe County Com Sch Corp	Bloomington
14	643.2	Tippecanoe School Corp	Lafayette
15	615.2	Bartholomew Con School Corp	Columbus
16	598.8	M S D Washington Twp	Indianapolis
17	571.5	M S D Pike Township	Indianapolis
18	563.6	New Albany-Floyd County Con Sch	New Albany
19	562.5	Warrick County School Corp	Boonville
20	559.1	M S D Warren Township	Indianapolis
21	537.0	East Allen County Schools	New Haven
22	521.0	Greater Clark County Schools	Jeffersonville
23	502.3	Penn-Harris-Madison Sch Corp	Mishawaka
24	485.6	Brownsburg Community Sch Corp	Brownsburg
25	483.0	Noblesville Schools	Noblesville
26	475.1	Lafayette School Corporation	Lafayette
27	460.7	Lake Central School Corp	Saint John
28	455.0	Anderson Community School Corp	Anderson
29	437.5	Franklin Township Com Sch Corp	Indianapolis
30	436.3	Avon Community School Corp	Avon
31	417.1	Warsaw Community Schools	Warsaw
32	414.5	Portage Township Schools	Portage
33	409.0	Crown Point Community Sch Corp	Crown Point
34	396.8	M S D Southwest Allen County Schls	Fort Wayne
35	392.0	Goshen Community Schools	Goshen
36	378.6	Northwest Allen County Schools	Fort Wayne
37	377.0	Center Grove Com Sch Corp	Greenwood
38	373.5	Kokomo School Corporation	Kokomo
38	373.5	Richmond Community Schools	Richmond
40	367.2	Laporte Community School Corp	Laporte
41	366.5	Muncie Community Schools	Muncie
42	364.9	Michigan City Area Schools	Michigan City
43	350.9	Westfield-Washington Schools	Westfield
44	350.1	Merrillville Community School	Merrillville
45	347.9	Zionsville Community Schools	Zionsville
46	330.0	M S D Decatur Township	Indianapolis
47	326.1	Huntington County Com Sch Corp	Huntington
48	317.8	Valparaiso Community Schools	Valparaiso
49	313.9	North Lawrence Com Schools	Bedford
50	303.9	Concord Community Schools	Elkhart
51	299.0	Duneland School Corporation	Chesterton
52	296.3	Clark-Pleasant Com School Corp	Whiteland
53	291.5	School City of Mishawaka	Mishawaka
54	289.7	M S D Martinsville Schools	Martinsville
55	278.3	Clay Community Schools	Brazil
56	270.0	Gary Community School Corp	Gary
57	267.0	Jennings County School Corp	North Vernon
58	258.0	Logansport Community Sch Corp	Logansport
58	258.0	School City of East Chicago	East Chicago
60	253.8	Plainfield Community Sch Corp	Plainfield
61	250.0	Greenfield-Central Com Schools	Greenfield
62	247.9	Middlebury Community Schools	Middlebury
63	247.5	West Clark Community Schools	Sellersburg
64	239.0	New Castle Community Sch Corp	New Castle
65	238.6	Franklin Community School Corp	Franklin
66	231.8	East Noble School Corp	Kendallville
67	229.0	Seymour Community Schools	Seymour
68	216.0	Shelbyville Central Schools	Shelbyville
69	214.0	Plymouth Community School Corp	Plymouth
70	209.5	Greenwood Community Sch Corp	Greenwood
71	208.6	Fayette County School Corp	Connersville
72	206.0	Jay School Corporation	Portland
73	205.0	South Madison Com Sch Corp	Pendleton
74	204.3	Marion Community Schools	Marion
75	201.5	Mt Vernon Community Sch Corp	Fortville

Note: This section only includes districts with 1,500 or more students; All categories are ranked from high to low

76	201.0	South Harrison Com Schools	Corydon
77	200.0	Mooresville Con School Corp	Mooresville
78	199.0	Kankakee Valley School Corp	Wheatfield
79	195.0	Whitley County Cons Schools	Columbia City
80	193.5	Sunman-Dearborn Com Sch Corp	Saint Leon
81	191.0	Lebanon Community School Corp	Lebanon
82	186.0	Dekalb County Ctl United SD	Waterloo
83	182.5	Community Schools of Frankfort	Frankfort
84	178.0	School City of Hobart	Hobart
85	176.4	Wawasee Community School Corp	Syracuse
86	172.0	Wa-Nee Community Schools	Nappanee
87	170.0	School Town of Highland	Highland
88	168.3	Beech Grove City Schools	Beech Grove
89	164.3	Vincennes Community Sch Corp	Vincennes
90	161.8	Decatur County Com Schools	Greensburg
91	160.0	School Town of Munster	Munster
92	158.0	Madison Consolidated Schools	Madison
93	157.5	Crawfordsville Com Schools	Crawfordsville
93	157.5	M S D Steuben County	Angola
95	154.9	Richland-Bean Blossom C S C	Ellettsville
96	150.8	Greater Jasper Con Schs	Jasper
97	150.0	Twin Lakes School Corp	Monticello
98	148.7	Western School Corp	Russiaville
99	148.3	Tri-Creek School Corporation	Lowell
100	148.0	East Porter County School Corp	Kouts
101	147.5	Frankton-Lapel Community Schools	Anderson
102	146.2	Scott County SD 2	Scottsburg
103	146.0	Rush County Schools	Rushville
104	145.0	Brown County School Corporation	Nashville
104	145.0	Franklin County Com Sch Corp	Brookville
106	143.9	Griffith Public Schools	Griffith
107	142.4	Danville Community School Corp	Danville
108	138.2	West Noble School Corporation	Ligonier
109	138.0	Southern Hancock Co Com Sch Corp	New Palestine
110	137.2	West Lafayette Com School Corp	West Lafayette
110	137.2	Westview School Corporation	Topeka
112	136.5	South Dearborn Com School Corp	Aurora
113	136.0	Delaware Community School Corp	Muncie
114	135.5	M S D Mount Vernon	Mount Vernon
115	134.6	Northern Wells Com Schools	Ossian
116	134.4	North Spencer County Sch Corp	Lincoln City
117	132.6	M S D Wabash County Schools	Wabash
117	132.6	North Gibson School Corp	Princeton
119	131.0	Mississinewa Community Schl Corp	Gas City
120	130.0	Greensburg Community Schools	Greensburg
121	129.2	Washington Com Schools	Washington
122	129.1	Lakeland School Corporation	Lagrange
123	128.7	School Town of Speedway	Speedway
124	126.7	Benton Community School Corp	Fowler
125	126.4	Pike County School Corp	Petersburg
126	126.0	Spencer-Owen Community Schools	Spencer
127	123.5	New Prairie United School Corp	New Carlisle
128	123.0	Peru Community Schools	Peru
129	122.0	Maconaquah School Corp	Bunker Hill
130	121.0	North Adams Community Schools	Decatur
131	120.8	Batesville Community Schl Corp	Batesville
132	119.7	Hamilton Heights School Corp	Arcadia
133	117.6	South Gibson School Corp	Fort Branch
134	117.0	Lawrenceburg Com School Corp	Lawrenceburg
135	116.0	Greencastle Community Sch Corp	Greencastle
136	115.8	Yorktown Community Schools	Yorktown
137	115.1	South Montgomery Com Sch Corp	New Market
138	115.0	North Montgomery Com Sch Corp	Crawfordsville
139	113.7	South Vermillion Com Sch Corp	Clinton
140	113.0	Southwest School Corp	Sullivan
140	113.0	Tippecanoe Valley School Corp	Akron
142	111.5	John Glenn School Corporation	Walkerton
143	111.4	Salem Community Schools	Salem
144	111.0	North Harrison Com School Corp	Ramsey
145	110.8	Fairfield Community Schools	Goshen
146	108.3	Garrett-Keyser-Butler Com	Garrett
147	108.0	Nineveh-Hensley-Jackson United	Trafalgar
148	106.0	Centerville-Abington Com Schs	Centerville
148	106.0	Knox Community School Corp	Knox
150	104.3	Randolph Central School Corp	Winchester
151	104.0	Tipton Community School Corp	Tipton
152	103.0	Rensselaer Central School Corp	Rensselaer
153	101.1	Rochester Community Sch Corp	Rochester
154	101.0	Lake Ridge New Tech Schools	Gary
154	101.0	Mill Creek Community Sch Corp	Clayton
156	100.0	North Putnam Community Schools	Bainbridge
157	99.5	Southwest Dubois County Sch Corp	Huntingburg
158	98.8	North West Hendricks Schools	Lizton
159	97.0	Baugo Community Schools	Elkhart
159	97.0	Hanover Community School Corp	Cedar Lake
161	93.0	Mitchell Community Schools	Mitchell
162	92.1	Switzerland County School Corp	Vevay
163	91.5	Brownstown Cnt Com Sch Corp	Brownstown
164	89.0	Tell City-Troy Twp School Corp	Tell City
165	87.6	Western Boone County Com SD	Thorntown
166	87.0	Blackford County Schools	Hartford City
167	85.9	Indiana Connections Academy	Indianapolis
168	84.9	Manchester Community Schools	N Manchester
169	82.0	Elwood Community School Corp	Elwood
170	81.1	Crawford County Com School Corp	Marengo
171	68.0	Whitko Community School Corp	Larwill
172	36.2	Hoosier Acad Virtual Charter	Indianapolis

Number of Students

Rank	Number	District Name	City
1	31,371	Indianapolis Public Schools	Indianapolis
2	30,182	Fort Wayne Community Schools	Fort Wayne
3	22,825	Evansville Vanderburgh Sch Corp	Evansville
4	21,291	Hamilton Southeastern Schools	Fishers
5	20,430	South Bend Community Sch Corp	South Bend
6	16,091	M S D Wayne Township	Indianapolis
7	15,918	Carmel Clay Schools	Carmel
8	15,675	Perry Township Schools	Indianapolis
9	15,237	Vigo County School Corp	Terre Haute
10	15,060	M S D Lawrence Township	Indianapolis
11	14,116	School City of Hammond	Hammond
12	13,949	Elkhart Community Schools	Elkhart
13	13,108	Tippecanoe School Corp	Lafayette
14	12,773	M S D Warren Township	Indianapolis
15	11,612	M S D Pike Township	Indianapolis
16	11,586	Bartholomew Con School Corp	Columbus
17	11,136	New Albany-Floyd County Con Sch	New Albany
18	11,030	Monroe County Com Sch Corp	Bloomington
19	10,888	Greater Clark County Schools	Jeffersonville
20	10,624	M S D Washington Twp	Indianapolis
21	10,310	Noblesville Schools	Noblesville
22	10,126	Warrick County School Corp	Boonville
23	9,966	Penn-Harris-Madison Sch Corp	Mishawaka
24	9,606	Lake Central School Corp	Saint John
25	9,482	Avon Community School Corp	Avon
26	9,288	Franklin Township Com Sch Corp	Indianapolis
27	9,075	East Allen County Schools	New Haven
28	8,545	Anderson Community School Corp	Anderson
29	8,477	Brownsburg Community Sch Corp	Brownsburg
30	8,369	Crown Point Community Sch Corp	Crown Point
31	7,963	Center Grove Com Sch Corp	Greenwood
32	7,791	Portage Township Schools	Portage
33	7,466	Lafayette School Corporation	Lafayette
34	7,238	Westfield-Washington Schools	Westfield
35	7,227	Northwest Allen County Schools	Fort Wayne
36	7,097	M S D Southwest Allen County Schls	Fort Wayne
37	7,059	Kokomo School Corporation	Kokomo
38	7,024	Warsaw Community Schools	Warsaw
39	6,743	Merrillville Community School	Merrillville
40	6,728	Goshen Community Schools	Goshen
41	6,725	Zionsville Community Schools	Zionsville
42	6,709	Laporte Community School Corp	Laporte
43	6,681	Clark-Pleasant Com School Corp	Whiteland
44	6,629	Gary Community School Corp	Gary
45	6,628	Muncie Community Schools	Muncie
46	6,294	M S D Decatur Township	Indianapolis
46	6,294	Valparaiso Community Schools	Valparaiso
48	6,003	Michigan City Area Schools	Michigan City
49	5,720	Duneland School Corporation	Chesterton
50	5,588	Richmond Community Schools	Richmond
51	5,471	Huntington County Com Sch Corp	Huntington
52	5,113	Plainfield Community Sch Corp	Plainfield
53	5,031	M S D Martinsville Schools	Martinsville
53	5,031	North Lawrence Com Schools	Bedford
55	4,961	School City of East Chicago	East Chicago
56	4,918	Franklin Community School Corp	Franklin
57	4,836	Concord Community Schools	Elkhart
58	4,815	Marion Community Schools	Marion
59	4,732	Seymour Community Schools	Seymour
60	4,707	School City of Mishawaka	Mishawaka
61	4,699	Greenfield-Central Com Schools	Greenfield
62	4,540	West Clark Community Schools	Sellersburg
63	4,444	Jennings County School Corp	North Vernon
64	4,340	Middlebury Community Schools	Middlebury
65	4,293	South Madison Com Sch Corp	Pendleton
66	4,289	Logansport Community Sch Corp	Logansport
67	4,242	Mooresville Con School Corp	Mooresville
68	4,192	Clay Community Schools	Brazil
69	4,107	School City of Hobart	Hobart
70	4,028	Shelbyville Central Schools	Shelbyville
71	4,014	Sunman-Dearborn Com Sch Corp	Saint Leon
72	3,861	Hoosier Acad Virtual Charter	Indianapolis
73	3,774	School Town of Munster	Munster
74	3,705	Indiana Connections Academy	Indianapolis
75	3,695	Dekalb County Ctl United SD	Waterloo
76	3,641	East Noble School Corp	Kendallville
77	3,640	Fayette County School Corp	Connersville
78	3,557	Lebanon Community School Corp	Lebanon
79	3,547	Plymouth Community School Corp	Plymouth
80	3,519	New Castle Community Sch Corp	New Castle
81	3,514	Greenwood Community Sch Corp	Greenwood
82	3,496	Jay School Corporation	Portland
83	3,477	Whitley County Cons Schools	Columbia City
84	3,467	Kankakee Valley School Corp	Wheatfield
85	3,415	Mt Vernon Community Sch Corp	Fortville
86	3,318	South Harrison Com Schools	Corydon
87	3,305	Tri-Creek School Corporation	Lowell
88	3,224	Wawasee Community School Corp	Syracuse
89	3,210	Greater Jasper Con Schs	Jasper
90	3,184	School Town of Highland	Highland
91	3,147	Community Schools of Frankfort	Frankfort
92	3,069	Southern Hancock Co Com Sch Corp	New Palestine
93	2,863	Madison Consolidated Schools	Madison
94	2,858	Wa-Nee Community Schools	Nappanee
95	2,791	Vincennes Community Sch Corp	Vincennes
96	2,778	Richland-Bean Blossom C S C	Ellettsville
97	2,749	Spencer-Owen Community Schools	Spencer
98	2,708	South Dearborn Com School Corp	Aurora
99	2,673	Franklin County Com Sch Corp	Brookville
100	2,638	M S D Steuben County	Angola
101	2,572	Washington Com Schools	Washington
102	2,543	New Prairie United School Corp	New Carlisle
103	2,539	Scott County SD 2	Scottsburg
104	2,500	Western School Corp	Russiaville
105	2,463	Danville Community School Corp	Danville
106	2,440	Delaware Community School Corp	Muncie
107	2,405	West Noble School Corporation	Ligonier
108	2,391	Maconaquah School Corp	Bunker Hill
109	2,388	Crawfordsville Com Schools	Crawfordsville
110	2,378	Greensburg Community Schools	Greensburg
111	2,363	Twin Lakes School Corp	Monticello
112	2,344	Frankton-Lapel Community Schools	Anderson
113	2,341	Griffith Public Schools	Griffith
114	2,329	Northern Wells Com Schools	Ossian
115	2,288	East Porter County School Corp	Kouts
116	2,244	Yorktown Community Schools	Yorktown
117	2,232	Lakeland School Corporation	Lagrange
118	2,210	North Harrison Com School Corp	Ramsey
119	2,209	Hamilton Heights School Corp	Arcadia
119	2,209	Rush County Schools	Rushville
121	2,200	Peru Community Schools	Peru
122	2,187	Brown County School Corporation	Nashville
123	2,181	Beech Grove City Schools	Beech Grove
124	2,160	West Lafayette Com School Corp	West Lafayette
125	2,151	Westview School Corporation	Topeka
126	2,148	Hanover Community School Corp	Cedar Lake
127	2,129	M S D Mount Vernon	Mount Vernon
128	2,125	North Gibson School Corp	Princeton
129	2,066	North Spencer County Sch Corp	Lincoln City
130	2,026	Fairfield Community Schools	Goshen
131	2,022	Mississinewa Community Schl Corp	Gas City
132	2,013	Batesville Community Schl Corp	Batesville
133	1,994	Lake Ridge New Tech Schools	Gary
134	1,973	M S D Wabash County Schools	Wabash
135	1,972	North Adams Community Schools	Decatur
136	1,960	Salem Community Schools	Salem
137	1,949	North Montgomery Com Sch Corp	Crawfordsville
138	1,944	Tippecanoe Valley School Corp	Akron
139	1,941	Pike County School Corp	Petersburg
140	1,921	Decatur County Com Schools	Greensburg
141	1,918	Greencastle Community Sch Corp	Greencastle
142	1,915	Baugo Community Schools	Elkhart
143	1,889	Knox Community School Corp	Knox
144	1,865	Blackford County Schools	Hartford City
145	1,857	Benton Community School Corp	Fowler
146	1,842	South Gibson School Corp	Fort Branch
147	1,824	Lawrenceburg Com School Corp	Lawrenceburg
147	1,824	North West Hendricks Schools	Lizton
149	1,818	South Vermillion Com Sch Corp	Clinton
150	1,816	Rochester Community Sch Corp	Rochester
151	1,812	South Montgomery Com Sch Corp	New Market
152	1,774	School Town of Speedway	Speedway
153	1,764	Mitchell Community Schools	Mitchell

Note: This section only includes districts with 1,500 or more students; All categories are ranked from high to low

154	1,748	Tipton Community School Corp	Tipton
155	1,745	Southwest Dubois County Sch Corp	Huntingburg
156	1,735	Garrett-Keyser-Butler Com	Garrett
157	1,726	Elwood Community School Corp	Elwood
158	1,702	Southwest School Corp	Sullivan
159	1,683	Crawford County Com School Corp	Marengo
160	1,678	Western Boone County Com SD	Thorntown
161	1,674	John Glenn School Corporation	Walkerton
162	1,656	Tell City-Troy Twp School Corp	Tell City
163	1,648	Nineveh-Hensley-Jackson United	Trafalgar
164	1,628	Rensselaer Central School Corp	Rensselaer
165	1,610	Mill Creek Community Sch Corp	Clayton
166	1,606	Switzerland County School Corp	Vevay
167	1,603	Whitko Community School Corp	Larwill
168	1,579	Centerville-Abington Com Schs	Centerville
169	1,566	Brownstown Cnt Com Sch Corp	Brownstown
170	1,528	North Putnam Community Schools	Bainbridge
171	1,520	Randolph Central School Corp	Winchester
172	1,519	Manchester Community Schools	N Manchester

Male Students

Rank	Percent	District Name	City
1	54.5	North Gibson School Corp	Princeton
2	54.4	Frankton-Lapel Community Schools	Anderson
3	54.0	Brownstown Cnt Com Sch Corp	Brownstown
4	53.9	South Vermillion Com Sch Corp	Clinton
4	53.9	Southwest School Corp	Sullivan
6	53.8	North West Hendricks Schools	Lizton
7	53.6	Nineveh-Hensley-Jackson United	Trafalgar
7	53.6	Switzerland County School Corp	Vevay
9	53.4	Griffith Public Schools	Griffith
10	53.2	Batesville Community Schl Corp	Batesville
11	53.1	Mill Creek Community Sch Corp	Clayton
12	52.9	School Town of Speedway	Speedway
13	52.8	Blackford County Schools	Hartford City
13	52.8	School City of Mishawaka	Mishawaka
15	52.7	Greenwood Community Sch Corp	Greenwood
15	52.7	Mississinewa Community Schl Corp	Gas City
15	52.7	Muncie Community Schools	Muncie
18	52.5	Clark-Pleasant Com School Corp	Whiteland
18	52.5	North Lawrence Com Schools	Bedford
18	52.5	Western Boone County Com SD	Thorntown
18	52.5	Whitley County Cons Schools	Columbia City
22	52.4	Mitchell Community Schools	Mitchell
22	52.4	North Montgomery Com Sch Corp	Crawfordsville
24	52.3	Anderson Community School Corp	Anderson
24	52.3	Crawford County Com School Corp	Marengo
24	52.3	Delaware Community School Corp	Muncie
24	52.3	Monroe County Com Sch Corp	Bloomington
24	52.3	Rensselaer Central School Corp	Rensselaer
24	52.3	School Town of Highland	Highland
30	52.2	Benton Community School Corp	Fowler
30	52.2	M S D Mount Vernon	Mount Vernon
30	52.2	Perry Township Schools	Indianapolis
30	52.2	Plymouth Community School Corp	Plymouth
30	52.2	Wawasee Community School Corp	Syracuse
35	52.1	Goshen Community Schools	Goshen
35	52.1	Hanover Community School Corp	Cedar Lake
35	52.1	John Glenn School Corporation	Walkerton
35	52.1	Peru Community Schools	Peru
35	52.1	South Montgomery Com Sch Corp	New Market
35	52.1	Twin Lakes School Corp	Monticello
35	52.1	Zionsville Community Schools	Zionsville
42	52.0	Brown County School Corporation	Nashville
42	52.0	Marion Community Schools	Marion
42	52.0	Portage Township Schools	Portage
42	52.0	School City of East Chicago	East Chicago
42	52.0	Tri-Creek School Corporation	Lowell
47	51.9	Concord Community Schools	Elkhart
47	51.9	Lakeland School Corporation	Lagrange
47	51.9	M S D Martinsville Schools	Martinsville
47	51.9	Seymour Community Schools	Seymour
47	51.9	South Bend Community Sch Corp	South Bend
47	51.9	Warrick County School Corp	Boonville
47	51.9	West Lafayette Com School Corp	West Lafayette
47	51.9	Westfield-Washington Schools	Westfield
55	51.8	Danville Community School Corp	Danville
55	51.8	Greencastle Community Sch Corp	Greencastle
55	51.8	M S D Lawrence Township	Indianapolis
55	51.8	Richmond Community Schools	Richmond
55	51.8	Westview School Corporation	Topeka
60	51.7	Community Schools of Frankfort	Frankfort
60	51.7	Crown Point Community Sch Corp	Crown Point
60	51.7	Fairfield Community Schools	Goshen
60	51.7	Greater Clark County Schools	Jeffersonville
60	51.7	Indianapolis Public Schools	Indianapolis
60	51.7	Logansport Community Sch Corp	Logansport
60	51.7	Michigan City Area Schools	Michigan City
60	51.7	North Spencer County Sch Corp	Lincoln City
60	51.7	Spencer-Owen Community Schools	Spencer
60	51.7	Washington Com Schools	Washington
70	51.6	Hamilton Heights School Corp	Arcadia
70	51.6	Huntington County Com Sch Corp	Huntington
70	51.6	M S D Washington Twp	Indianapolis
70	51.6	Madison Consolidated Schools	Madison
70	51.6	Northern Wells Com Schools	Ossian
70	51.6	Shelbyville Central Schools	Shelbyville
70	51.6	Southern Hancock Co Com Sch Corp	New Palestine
70	51.6	Sunman-Dearborn Com Sch Corp	Saint Leon
78	51.5	Avon Community School Corp	Avon
78	51.5	Dekalb County Ctl United SD	Waterloo
78	51.5	Duneland School Corporation	Chesterton
78	51.5	Lafayette School Corporation	Lafayette
78	51.5	M S D Warren Township	Indianapolis
78	51.5	Salem Community Schools	Salem
78	51.5	South Harrison Com Schools	Corydon
78	51.5	Vigo County School Corp	Terre Haute
78	51.5	West Clark Community Schools	Sellersburg
87	51.4	Center Grove Com Sch Corp	Greenwood
87	51.4	East Noble School Corp	Kendallville
87	51.4	Fayette County School Corp	Connersville
87	51.4	Franklin Township Com Sch Corp	Indianapolis
87	51.4	Knox Community School Corp	Knox
87	51.4	Lake Central School Corp	Saint John
87	51.4	South Dearborn Com School Corp	Aurora
87	51.4	Tipton Community School Corp	Tipton
87	51.4	Warsaw Community Schools	Warsaw
96	51.3	Decatur County Com Schools	Greensburg
96	51.3	East Allen County Schools	New Haven
96	51.3	Evansville Vanderburgh Sch Corp	Evansville
96	51.3	Greensburg Community Schools	Greensburg
96	51.3	Kankakee Valley School Corp	Wheatfield
96	51.3	Lebanon Community School Corp	Lebanon
96	51.3	M S D Decatur Township	Indianapolis
96	51.3	Penn-Harris-Madison Sch Corp	Mishawaka
96	51.3	Plainfield Community Sch Corp	Plainfield
96	51.3	Vincennes Community Sch Corp	Vincennes
106	51.2	Brownsburg Community Sch Corp	Brownsburg
106	51.2	Franklin County Com Sch Corp	Brookville
106	51.2	Greenfield-Central Com Schools	Greenfield
106	51.2	Laporte Community School Corp	Laporte
106	51.2	Mooresville Con School Corp	Mooresville
106	51.2	Mt Vernon Community Sch Corp	Fortville
106	51.2	Noblesville Schools	Noblesville
106	51.2	Pike County School Corp	Petersburg
106	51.2	Richland-Bean Blossom C S C	Ellettsville
106	51.2	Valparaiso Community Schools	Valparaiso
116	51.1	Elwood Community School Corp	Elwood
116	51.1	M S D Pike Township	Indianapolis
116	51.1	Maconaquah School Corp	Bunker Hill
116	51.1	New Prairie United School Corp	New Carlisle
120	51.0	Centerville-Abington Com Schs	Centerville
120	51.0	East Porter County School Corp	Kouts
120	51.0	Fort Wayne Community Schools	Fort Wayne
120	51.0	Jay School Corporation	Portland
120	51.0	Kokomo School Corporation	Kokomo
120	51.0	New Albany-Floyd County Con Sch	New Albany
120	51.0	School City of Hammond	Hammond
120	51.0	South Madison Com Sch Corp	Pendleton
120	51.0	Tell City-Troy Twp School Corp	Tell City
120	51.0	Tippecanoe School Corp	Lafayette
120	51.0	Whitko Community School Corp	Larwill
131	50.9	Beech Grove City Schools	Beech Grove
131	50.9	Wa-Nee Community Schools	Nappanee
133	50.8	Bartholomew Con School Corp	Columbus
133	50.8	Elkhart Community Schools	Elkhart
133	50.8	Hamilton Southeastern Schools	Fishers
133	50.8	M S D Southwest Allen County Schls	Fort Wayne
133	50.8	Manchester Community Schools	N Manchester
133	50.8	Merrillville Community School	Merrillville
133	50.8	New Castle Community Sch Corp	New Castle
133	50.8	North Harrison Com School Corp	Ramsey
133	50.8	North Putnam Community Schools	Bainbridge
133	50.8	School Town of Munster	Munster
143	50.7	Carmel Clay Schools	Carmel
143	50.7	Jennings County School Corp	North Vernon
143	50.7	Lawrenceburg Com School Corp	Lawrenceburg
143	50.7	Middlebury Community Schools	Middlebury
147	50.6	Clay Community Schools	Brazil
147	50.6	Franklin Community School Corp	Franklin
147	50.6	M S D Wabash County Schools	Wabash
150	50.5	M S D Steuben County	Angola
150	50.5	West Noble School Corporation	Ligonier
152	50.4	North Adams Community Schools	Decatur
153	50.3	Northwest Allen County Schools	Fort Wayne
154	50.2	Rush County Schools	Rushville
154	50.2	School City of Hobart	Hobart
154	50.2	Yorktown Community Schools	Yorktown
157	50.1	Greater Jasper Con Schs	Jasper
157	50.1	Randolph Central School Corp	Winchester
157	50.1	Scott County SD 2	Scottsburg
160	50.0	M S D Wayne Township	Indianapolis
161	49.8	Rochester Community Sch Corp	Rochester
162	49.7	Gary Community School Corp	Gary
163	49.6	Baugo Community Schools	Elkhart
163	49.6	Lake Ridge New Tech Schools	Gary
165	49.5	Western School Corp	Russiaville
166	49.2	Southwest Dubois County Sch Corp	Huntingburg
167	49.1	Crawfordsville Com Schools	Crawfordsville
168	49.0	Garrett-Keyser-Butler Com	Garrett
168	49.0	South Gibson School Corp	Fort Branch
170	48.9	Tippecanoe Valley School Corp	Akron
171	46.2	Hoosier Acad Virtual Charter	Indianapolis
172	43.3	Indiana Connections Academy	Indianapolis

Female Students

Rank	Percent	District Name	City
1	56.7	Indiana Connections Academy	Indianapolis
2	53.8	Hoosier Acad Virtual Charter	Indianapolis
3	51.1	Tippecanoe Valley School Corp	Akron
4	51.0	Garrett-Keyser-Butler Com	Garrett
4	51.0	South Gibson School Corp	Fort Branch
6	50.9	Crawfordsville Com Schools	Crawfordsville
7	50.8	Southwest Dubois County Sch Corp	Huntingburg
8	50.5	Western School Corp	Russiaville
9	50.4	Baugo Community Schools	Elkhart
9	50.4	Lake Ridge New Tech Schools	Gary
11	50.3	Gary Community School Corp	Gary
12	50.2	Rochester Community Sch Corp	Rochester
13	50.0	M S D Wayne Township	Indianapolis
14	49.9	Greater Jasper Con Schs	Jasper
14	49.9	Randolph Central School Corp	Winchester
14	49.9	Scott County SD 2	Scottsburg
17	49.8	Rush County Schools	Rushville
17	49.8	School City of Hobart	Hobart
17	49.8	Yorktown Community Schools	Yorktown
20	49.7	Northwest Allen County Schools	Fort Wayne
21	49.6	North Adams Community Schools	Decatur
22	49.5	M S D Steuben County	Angola
22	49.5	West Noble School Corporation	Ligonier
24	49.4	Clay Community Schools	Brazil
24	49.4	Franklin Community School Corp	Franklin
24	49.4	M S D Wabash County Schools	Wabash
27	49.3	Carmel Clay Schools	Carmel
27	49.3	Jennings County School Corp	North Vernon
27	49.3	Lawrenceburg Com School Corp	Lawrenceburg
27	49.3	Middlebury Community Schools	Middlebury
31	49.2	Bartholomew Con School Corp	Columbus
31	49.2	Elkhart Community Schools	Elkhart
31	49.2	Hamilton Southeastern Schools	Fishers
31	49.2	M S D Southwest Allen County Schls	Fort Wayne
31	49.2	Manchester Community Schools	N Manchester
31	49.2	Merrillville Community School	Merrillville
31	49.2	New Castle Community Sch Corp	New Castle
31	49.2	North Harrison Com School Corp	Ramsey
31	49.2	North Putnam Community Schools	Bainbridge
31	49.2	School Town of Munster	Munster
41	49.1	Beech Grove City Schools	Beech Grove
41	49.1	Wa-Nee Community Schools	Nappanee
43	49.0	Centerville-Abington Com Schs	Centerville
43	49.0	East Porter County School Corp	Kouts
43	49.0	Fort Wayne Community Schools	Fort Wayne
43	49.0	Jay School Corporation	Portland
43	49.0	Kokomo School Corporation	Kokomo
43	49.0	New Albany-Floyd County Con Sch	New Albany
43	49.0	School City of Hammond	Hammond
43	49.0	South Madison Com Sch Corp	Pendleton
43	49.0	Tell City-Troy Twp School Corp	Tell City
43	49.0	Tippecanoe School Corp	Lafayette
43	49.0	Whitko Community School Corp	Larwill
54	48.9	Elwood Community School Corp	Elwood

Note: This section only includes districts with 1,500 or more students; All categories are ranked from high to low

54	48.9	M S D Pike Township	Indianapolis
54	48.9	Maconaquah School Corp	Bunker Hill
54	48.9	New Prairie United School Corp	New Carlisle
58	48.8	Brownsburg Community Sch Corp	Brownsburg
58	48.8	Franklin County Com Sch Corp	Brookville
58	48.8	Greenfield-Central Com Schools	Greenfield
58	48.8	Laporte Community School Corp	Laporte
58	48.8	Mooresville Con School Corp	Mooresville
58	48.8	Mt Vernon Community Sch Corp	Fortville
58	48.8	Noblesville Schools	Noblesville
58	48.8	Pike County School Corp	Petersburg
58	48.8	Richland-Bean Blossom C S C	Ellettsville
58	48.8	Valparaiso Community Schools	Valparaiso
68	48.7	Decatur County Com Schools	Greensburg
68	48.7	East Allen County Schools	New Haven
68	48.7	Evansville Vanderburgh Sch Corp	Evansville
68	48.7	Greensburg Community Schools	Greensburg
68	48.7	Kankakee Valley School Corp	Wheatfield
68	48.7	Lebanon Community School Corp	Lebanon
68	48.7	M S D Decatur Township	Indianapolis
68	48.7	Penn-Harris-Madison Sch Corp	Mishawaka
68	48.7	Plainfield Community Sch Corp	Plainfield
68	48.7	Vincennes Community Sch Corp	Vincennes
78	48.6	Center Grove Com Sch Corp	Greenwood
78	48.6	East Noble School Corp	Kendallville
78	48.6	Fayette County School Corp	Connersville
78	48.6	Franklin Township Com Sch Corp	Indianapolis
78	48.6	Knox Community School Corp	Knox
78	48.6	Lake Central School Corp	Saint John
78	48.6	South Dearborn Com School Corp	Aurora
78	48.6	Tipton Community School Corp	Tipton
78	48.6	Warsaw Community Schools	Warsaw
87	48.5	Avon Community School Corp	Avon
87	48.5	Dekalb County Ctl United SD	Waterloo
87	48.5	Duneland School Corporation	Chesterton
87	48.5	Lafayette School Corporation	Lafayette
87	48.5	M S D Warren Township	Indianapolis
87	48.5	Salem Community Schools	Salem
87	48.5	South Harrison Com Schools	Corydon
87	48.5	Vigo County School Corp	Terre Haute
87	48.5	West Clark Community Schools	Sellersburg
96	48.4	Hamilton Heights School Corp	Arcadia
96	48.4	Huntington County Com Sch Corp	Huntington
96	48.4	M S D Washington Twp	Indianapolis
96	48.4	Madison Consolidated Schools	Madison
96	48.4	Northern Wells Com Schools	Ossian
96	48.4	Shelbyville Central Schools	Shelbyville
96	48.4	Southern Hancock Co Com Sch Corp	New Palestine
96	48.4	Sunman-Dearborn Com Sch Corp	Saint Leon
104	48.3	Community Schools of Frankfort	Frankfort
104	48.3	Crown Point Community Sch Corp	Crown Point
104	48.3	Fairfield Community Schools	Goshen
104	48.3	Greater Clark County Schools	Jeffersonville
104	48.3	Indianapolis Public Schools	Indianapolis
104	48.3	Logansport Community Sch Corp	Logansport
104	48.3	Michigan City Area Schools	Michigan City
104	48.3	North Spencer County Sch Corp	Lincoln City
104	48.3	Spencer-Owen Community Schools	Spencer
104	48.3	Washington Com Schools	Washington
114	48.2	Danville Community School Corp	Danville
114	48.2	Greencastle Community Sch Corp	Greencastle
114	48.2	M S D Lawrence Township	Indianapolis
114	48.2	Richmond Community Schools	Richmond
114	48.2	Westview School Corporation	Topeka
119	48.1	Concord Community Schools	Elkhart
119	48.1	Lakeland School Corporation	Lagrange
119	48.1	M S D Martinsville Schools	Martinsville
119	48.1	Seymour Community Schools	Seymour
119	48.1	South Bend Community Sch Corp	South Bend
119	48.1	Warrick County School Corp	Boonville
119	48.1	West Lafayette Com School Corp	West Lafayette
119	48.1	Westfield-Washington Schools	Westfield
127	48.0	Brown County School Corporation	Nashville
127	48.0	Marion Community Schools	Marion
127	48.0	Portage Township Schools	Portage
127	48.0	School City of East Chicago	East Chicago
127	48.0	Tri-Creek School Corporation	Lowell
132	47.9	Goshen Community Schools	Goshen
132	47.9	Hanover Community School Corp	Cedar Lake
132	47.9	John Glenn School Corporation	Walkerton
132	47.9	Peru Community Schools	Peru
132	47.9	South Montgomery Com Sch Corp	New Market
132	47.9	Twin Lakes School Corp	Monticello
132	47.9	Zionsville Community Schools	Zionsville
139	47.8	Benton Community School Corp	Fowler
139	47.8	M S D Mount Vernon	Mount Vernon
139	47.8	Perry Township Schools	Indianapolis
139	47.8	Plymouth Community School Corp	Plymouth
139	47.8	Wawasee Community School Corp	Syracuse
144	47.7	Anderson Community School Corp	Anderson
144	47.7	Crawford County Com School Corp	Marengo
144	47.7	Delaware Community School Corp	Muncie
144	47.7	Monroe County Com Sch Corp	Bloomington
144	47.7	Rensselaer Central School Corp	Rensselaer
144	47.7	School Town of Highland	Highland
150	47.6	Mitchell Community Schools	Mitchell
150	47.6	North Montgomery Com Sch Corp	Crawfordsville
152	47.5	Clark-Pleasant Com School Corp	Whiteland
152	47.5	North Lawrence Com Schools	Bedford
152	47.5	Western Boone County Com SD	Thorntown
152	47.5	Whitley County Cons Schools	Columbia City
156	47.3	Greenwood Community Sch Corp	Greenwood
156	47.3	Mississinewa Community Schl Corp	Gas City
156	47.3	Muncie Community Schools	Muncie
159	47.2	Blackford County Schools	Hartford City
159	47.2	School City of Mishawaka	Mishawaka
161	47.1	School Town of Speedway	Speedway
162	46.9	Mill Creek Community Sch Corp	Clayton
163	46.8	Batesville Community Schl Corp	Batesville
164	46.6	Griffith Public Schools	Griffith
165	46.4	Nineveh-Hensley-Jackson United	Trafalgar
165	46.4	Switzerland County School Corp	Vevay
167	46.2	North West Hendricks Schools	Lizton
168	46.1	South Vermillion Com Sch Corp	Clinton
168	46.1	Southwest School Corp	Sullivan
170	46.0	Brownstown Cnt Com Sch Corp	Brownstown
171	45.6	Frankton-Lapel Community Schools	Anderson
172	45.5	North Gibson School Corp	Princeton

White Students

Rank	Percent	District Name	City
1	98.2	Franklin County Com Sch Corp	Brookville
2	96.9	North Putnam Community Schools	Bainbridge
3	96.7	Decatur County Com Schools	Greensburg
4	96.3	Crawford County Com School Corp	Marengo
5	96.0	Sunman-Dearborn Com Sch Corp	Saint Leon
6	95.9	Nineveh-Hensley-Jackson United	Trafalgar
7	95.8	Pike County School Corp	Petersburg
7	95.8	Switzerland County School Corp	Vevay
9	95.6	Brownstown Cnt Com Sch Corp	Brownstown
10	95.5	South Dearborn Com School Corp	Aurora
10	95.5	South Vermillion Com Sch Corp	Clinton
12	95.3	Clay Community Schools	Brazil
12	95.3	M S D Wabash County Schools	Wabash
14	95.2	North Harrison Com School Corp	Ramsey
14	95.2	Westview School Corporation	Topeka
16	95.1	Salem Community Schools	Salem
16	95.1	Western Boone County Com SD	Thorntown
18	95.0	Spencer-Owen Community Schools	Spencer
19	94.9	Mitchell Community Schools	Mitchell
20	94.8	Mill Creek Community Sch Corp	Clayton
20	94.8	South Gibson School Corp	Fort Branch
22	94.6	North West Hendricks Schools	Lizton
22	94.6	Scott County SD 2	Scottsburg
24	94.4	M S D Martinsville Schools	Martinsville
24	94.4	Southwest School Corp	Sullivan
26	94.2	Fayette County School Corp	Connersville
27	94.0	Southern Hancock Co Com Sch Corp	New Palestine
28	93.9	Greensburg Community Schools	Greensburg
29	93.8	Brown County School Corporation	Nashville
30	93.7	Hamilton Heights School Corp	Arcadia
30	93.7	North Lawrence Com Schools	Bedford
32	93.6	Greenfield-Central Com Schools	Greenfield
32	93.6	Knox Community School Corp	Knox
34	93.5	Blackford County Schools	Hartford City
34	93.5	Whitko Community School Corp	Larwill
36	93.4	Mooresville Con School Corp	Mooresville
36	93.4	Rush County Schools	Rushville
38	93.3	Delaware Community School Corp	Muncie
39	93.2	Randolph Central School Corp	Winchester
40	93.1	Huntington County Com Sch Corp	Huntington
41	92.8	Danville Community School Corp	Danville
41	92.8	North Montgomery Com Sch Corp	Crawfordsville
43	92.6	South Montgomery Com Sch Corp	New Market
44	92.5	Tell City-Troy Twp School Corp	Tell City
45	92.4	Tipton Community School Corp	Tipton
46	92.2	Whitley County Cons Schools	Columbia City
47	92.1	Jay School Corporation	Portland
47	92.1	Jennings County School Corp	North Vernon
47	92.1	Northern Wells Com Schools	Ossian
50	92.0	Batesville Community Schl Corp	Batesville
51	91.9	Garrett-Keyser-Butler Com	Garrett
52	91.8	Dekalb County Ctl United SD	Waterloo
52	91.8	Frankton-Lapel Community Schools	Anderson
54	91.6	Centerville-Abington Com Schs	Centerville
54	91.6	Fairfield Community Schools	Goshen
56	91.5	South Madison Com Sch Corp	Pendleton
57	91.2	South Harrison Com Schools	Corydon
58	91.0	M S D Mount Vernon	Mount Vernon
59	90.9	East Noble School Corp	Kendallville
60	90.7	Greencastle Community Sch Corp	Greencastle
61	90.2	John Glenn School Corporation	Walkerton
62	90.1	New Castle Community Sch Corp	New Castle
62	90.1	Richland-Bean Blossom C S C	Ellettsville
64	90.0	Rochester Community Sch Corp	Rochester
64	90.0	West Clark Community Schools	Sellersburg
66	89.9	North Spencer County Sch Corp	Lincoln City
66	89.9	Vincennes Community Sch Corp	Vincennes
68	89.7	Lawrenceburg Com School Corp	Lawrenceburg
69	89.5	East Porter County School Corp	Kouts
70	89.1	Elwood Community School Corp	Elwood
70	89.1	Warrick County School Corp	Boonville
72	88.9	Madison Consolidated Schools	Madison
73	88.5	Manchester Community Schools	N Manchester
73	88.5	Peru Community Schools	Peru
75	88.3	Mississinewa Community Schl Corp	Gas City
76	88.2	Benton Community School Corp	Fowler
76	88.2	Center Grove Com Sch Corp	Greenwood
78	88.1	Franklin Community School Corp	Franklin
78	88.1	Rensselaer Central School Corp	Rensselaer
80	88.0	Kankakee Valley School Corp	Wheatfield
81	87.8	Lebanon Community School Corp	Lebanon
82	87.7	Yorktown Community Schools	Yorktown
83	86.4	Tri-Creek School Corporation	Lowell
84	86.2	Middlebury Community Schools	Middlebury
84	86.2	Wa-Nee Community Schools	Nappanee
86	86.1	Plainfield Community Sch Corp	Plainfield
87	86.0	Northwest Allen County Schools	Fort Wayne
88	85.6	Zionsville Community Schools	Zionsville
89	85.5	New Prairie United School Corp	New Carlisle
89	85.5	Noblesville Schools	Noblesville
91	85.2	Western School Corp	Russiaville
92	85.0	Maconaquah School Corp	Bunker Hill
93	84.9	Wawasee Community School Corp	Syracuse
94	83.9	M S D Steuben County	Angola
95	83.8	North Gibson School Corp	Princeton
96	83.7	Mt Vernon Community Sch Corp	Fortville
97	83.1	North Adams Community Schools	Decatur
98	83.0	Greater Jasper Con Schs	Jasper
99	82.8	Duneland School Corporation	Chesterton
100	82.6	Hanover Community School Corp	Cedar Lake
101	82.1	Twin Lakes School Corp	Monticello
102	81.9	Vigo County School Corp	Terre Haute
102	81.9	Westfield-Washington Schools	Westfield
104	81.5	Baugo Community Schools	Elkhart
105	81.4	Clark-Pleasant Com School Corp	Whiteland
106	81.3	M S D Southwest Allen County Schls	Fort Wayne
107	81.0	Greenwood Community Sch Corp	Greenwood
108	80.8	Tippecanoe Valley School Corp	Akron
109	80.7	Indiana Connections Academy	Indianapolis
110	80.3	Valparaiso Community Schools	Valparaiso
111	79.7	Penn-Harris-Madison Sch Corp	Mishawaka
112	79.6	Crown Point Community Sch Corp	Crown Point
113	79.5	Shelbyville Central Schools	Shelbyville
114	78.8	Lakeland School Corporation	Lagrange
115	78.7	New Albany-Floyd County Con Sch	New Albany
116	78.0	Monroe County Com Sch Corp	Bloomington
117	77.6	Hoosier Acad Virtual Charter	Indianapolis
118	77.5	School City of Mishawaka	Mishawaka
119	77.1	Brownsburg Community Sch Corp	Brownsburg
120	76.9	Beech Grove City Schools	Beech Grove
121	76.8	Franklin Township Com Sch Corp	Indianapolis
122	76.7	Laporte Community School Corp	Laporte
123	76.5	Crawfordsville Com Schools	Crawfordsville
124	75.6	Hamilton Southeastern Schools	Fishers
125	75.1	Tippecanoe School Corp	Lafayette
126	74.5	Carmel Clay Schools	Carmel
127	73.7	Warsaw Community Schools	Warsaw
128	73.6	Washington Com Schools	Washington
129	73.5	Bartholomew Con School Corp	Columbus
130	73.2	Lake Central School Corp	Saint John
131	72.7	M S D Decatur Township	Indianapolis
132	72.3	Seymour Community Schools	Seymour
133	72.0	Plymouth Community School Corp	Plymouth

Education

Note: This section only includes districts with 1,500 or more students; All categories are ranked from high to low

134	71.9	Southwest Dubois County Sch Corp	Huntingburg
135	70.7	Avon Community School Corp	Avon
136	70.3	Evansville Vanderburgh Sch Corp	Evansville
136	70.3	Richmond Community Schools	Richmond
138	68.4	Kokomo School Corporation	Kokomo
139	67.0	Muncie Community Schools	Muncie
140	66.1	School City of Hobart	Hobart
141	64.6	East Allen County Schools	New Haven
141	64.6	Greater Clark County Schools	Jeffersonville
143	63.4	Anderson Community School Corp	Anderson
144	61.8	School Town of Highland	Highland
145	60.6	Portage Township Schools	Portage
145	60.6	School Town of Munster	Munster
147	59.7	West Lafayette Com School Corp	West Lafayette
148	57.7	Marion Community Schools	Marion
149	54.9	Logansport Community Sch Corp	Logansport
150	53.8	Perry Township Schools	Indianapolis
151	50.3	Concord Community Schools	Elkhart
152	49.9	Griffith Public Schools	Griffith
152	49.9	Lafayette School Corporation	Lafayette
154	49.8	School Town of Speedway	Speedway
155	49.2	Community Schools of Frankfort	Frankfort
155	49.2	West Noble School Corporation	Ligonier
157	47.8	Michigan City Area Schools	Michigan City
158	45.5	Fort Wayne Community Schools	Fort Wayne
159	45.3	Elkhart Community Schools	Elkhart
160	42.7	Goshen Community Schools	Goshen
161	40.2	Lake Ridge New Tech Schools	Gary
162	36.5	M S D Wayne Township	Indianapolis
163	36.2	South Bend Community Sch Corp	South Bend
164	29.3	M S D Warren Township	Indianapolis
165	29.1	M S D Lawrence Township	Indianapolis
166	28.9	M S D Washington Twp	Indianapolis
167	21.9	Indianapolis Public Schools	Indianapolis
168	16.2	School City of Hammond	Hammond
169	14.4	Merrillville Community School	Merrillville
170	10.4	M S D Pike Township	Indianapolis
171	1.6	School City of East Chicago	East Chicago
172	1.4	Gary Community School Corp	Gary

Black Students

Rank	Percent	District Name	City
1	91.7	Gary Community School Corp	Gary
2	60.4	Merrillville Community School	Merrillville
3	59.0	M S D Pike Township	Indianapolis
4	50.2	School City of East Chicago	East Chicago
5	49.6	M S D Warren Township	Indianapolis
6	48.2	Indianapolis Public Schools	Indianapolis
7	42.0	M S D Lawrence Township	Indianapolis
8	40.2	M S D Washington Twp	Indianapolis
9	33.3	Michigan City Area Schools	Michigan City
10	33.2	South Bend Community Sch Corp	South Bend
11	31.9	School City of Hammond	Hammond
12	31.0	M S D Wayne Township	Indianapolis
13	27.9	Lake Ridge New Tech Schools	Gary
14	24.6	School Town of Speedway	Speedway
15	23.4	Fort Wayne Community Schools	Fort Wayne
16	20.2	Griffith Public Schools	Griffith
17	18.0	Anderson Community School Corp	Anderson
18	17.5	Muncie Community Schools	Muncie
19	17.4	Marion Community Schools	Marion
20	15.6	Lafayette School Corporation	Lafayette
21	14.7	Elkhart Community Schools	Elkhart
22	13.9	Evansville Vanderburgh Sch Corp	Evansville
23	13.8	East Allen County Schools	New Haven
23	13.8	Kokomo School Corporation	Kokomo
25	13.1	Greater Clark County Schools	Jeffersonville
26	11.1	Avon Community School Corp	Avon
27	11.0	Portage Township Schools	Portage
28	10.6	Brownsburg Community Sch Corp	Brownsburg
29	10.3	Hoosier Acad Virtual Charter	Indianapolis
29	10.3	M S D Decatur Township	Indianapolis
31	9.3	Concord Community Schools	Elkhart
32	8.5	New Albany-Floyd County Con Sch	New Albany
33	8.3	Beech Grove City Schools	Beech Grove
34	8.0	Richmond Community Schools	Richmond
35	7.3	West Lafayette Com School Corp	West Lafayette
36	7.0	Hamilton Southeastern Schools	Fishers
37	6.9	Mt Vernon Community Sch Corp	Fortville
38	6.7	School City of Hobart	Hobart
39	6.6	School City of Mishawaka	Mishawaka
40	6.4	Franklin Township Com Sch Corp	Indianapolis
41	6.3	Indiana Connections Academy	Indianapolis
41	6.3	School Town of Munster	Munster
43	6.1	Perry Township Schools	Indianapolis
44	5.3	School Town of Highland	Highland
44	5.3	Vigo County School Corp	Terre Haute
46	5.1	M S D Southwest Allen County Schls	Fort Wayne
46	5.1	Western School Corp	Russiaville
48	5.0	Lake Central School Corp	Saint John
48	5.0	Monroe County Com Sch Corp	Bloomington
50	4.9	Penn-Harris-Madison Sch Corp	Mishawaka
51	4.6	Tippecanoe School Corp	Lafayette
52	3.8	Noblesville Schools	Noblesville
52	3.8	North Gibson School Corp	Princeton
54	3.6	Carmel Clay Schools	Carmel
55	3.4	Valparaiso Community Schools	Valparaiso
56	3.2	Yorktown Community Schools	Yorktown
57	3.0	Laporte Community School Corp	Laporte
57	3.0	Westfield-Washington Schools	Westfield
59	2.8	Plainfield Community Sch Corp	Plainfield
60	2.7	Peru Community Schools	Peru
61	2.6	Clark-Pleasant Com School Corp	Whiteland
62	2.5	Maconaquah School Corp	Bunker Hill
63	2.4	Crown Point Community Sch Corp	Crown Point
63	2.4	Greenwood Community Sch Corp	Greenwood
65	2.3	Warsaw Community Schools	Warsaw
66	2.2	Goshen Community Schools	Goshen
67	2.1	Bartholomew Con School Corp	Columbus
67	2.1	Crawfordsville Com Schools	Crawfordsville
69	2.0	South Madison Com Sch Corp	Pendleton
69	2.0	Washington Com Schools	Washington
71	1.9	Baugo Community Schools	Elkhart
72	1.8	Madison Consolidated Schools	Madison
72	1.8	Northwest Allen County Schools	Fort Wayne
72	1.8	Shelbyville Central Schools	Shelbyville
72	1.8	Vincennes Community Sch Corp	Vincennes
76	1.7	Duneland School Corporation	Chesterton
77	1.6	Franklin Community School Corp	Franklin
77	1.6	Lebanon Community School Corp	Lebanon
77	1.6	M S D Mount Vernon	Mount Vernon
80	1.5	Center Grove Com Sch Corp	Greenwood
80	1.5	Delaware Community School Corp	Muncie
80	1.5	Hamilton Heights School Corp	Arcadia
80	1.5	North Adams Community Schools	Decatur
80	1.5	Zionsville Community Schools	Zionsville
85	1.4	Hanover Community School Corp	Cedar Lake
85	1.4	Mississinewa Community Schl Corp	Gas City
87	1.3	Lawrenceburg Com School Corp	Lawrenceburg
87	1.3	New Castle Community Sch Corp	New Castle
87	1.3	Warrick County School Corp	Boonville
90	1.2	Danville Community School Corp	Danville
90	1.2	Fayette County School Corp	Connersville
90	1.2	Wa-Nee Community Schools	Nappanee
93	1.1	Logansport Community Sch Corp	Logansport
93	1.1	Richland-Bean Blossom C S C	Ellettsville
93	1.1	Whitko Community School Corp	Larwill
96	1.0	Fairfield Community Schools	Goshen
96	1.0	Frankton-Lapel Community Schools	Anderson
96	1.0	Greencastle Community Sch Corp	Greencastle
99	0.9	Middlebury Community Schools	Middlebury
99	0.9	North West Hendricks Schools	Lizton
99	0.9	Rush County Schools	Rushville
102	0.8	Centerville-Abington Com Schs	Centerville
102	0.8	Community Schools of Frankfort	Frankfort
102	0.8	M S D Martinsville Schools	Martinsville
102	0.8	Manchester Community Schools	N Manchester
102	0.8	Plymouth Community School Corp	Plymouth
102	0.8	Rochester Community Sch Corp	Rochester
102	0.8	Tri-Creek School Corporation	Lowell
102	0.8	Westview School Corporation	Topeka
110	0.7	M S D Steuben County	Angola
110	0.7	Mill Creek Community Sch Corp	Clayton
110	0.7	Mooresville Con School Corp	Mooresville
110	0.7	Seymour Community Schools	Seymour
110	0.7	West Clark Community Schools	Sellersburg
115	0.6	Greenfield-Central Com Schools	Greenfield
115	0.6	Northern Wells Com Schools	Ossian
115	0.6	Randolph Central School Corp	Winchester
115	0.6	Salem Community Schools	Salem
115	0.6	Spencer-Owen Community Schools	Spencer
115	0.6	Tippecanoe Valley School Corp	Akron
121	0.5	Benton Community School Corp	Fowler
121	0.5	Brown County School Corporation	Nashville
121	0.5	John Glenn School Corporation	Walkerton
121	0.5	Lakeland School Corporation	Lagrange
121	0.5	North Montgomery Com Sch Corp	Crawfordsville
121	0.5	Pike County School Corp	Petersburg
121	0.5	Rensselaer Central School Corp	Rensselaer
121	0.5	South Gibson School Corp	Fort Branch
121	0.5	Southern Hancock Co Com Sch Corp	New Palestine
121	0.5	Tipton Community School Corp	Tipton
121	0.5	Twin Lakes School Corp	Monticello
121	0.5	Wawasee Community School Corp	Syracuse
121	0.5	Whitley County Cons Schools	Columbia City
134	0.4	Crawford County Com School Corp	Marengo
134	0.4	East Noble School Corp	Kendallville
134	0.4	East Porter County School Corp	Kouts
134	0.4	Garrett-Keyser-Butler Com	Garrett
134	0.4	Greater Jasper Con Schs	Jasper
134	0.4	Huntington County Com Sch Corp	Huntington
134	0.4	Jennings County School Corp	North Vernon
134	0.4	M S D Wabash County Schools	Wabash
134	0.4	New Prairie United School Corp	New Carlisle
134	0.4	Nineveh-Hensley-Jackson United	Trafalgar
134	0.4	North Putnam Community Schools	Bainbridge
134	0.4	Scott County SD 2	Scottsburg
134	0.4	South Harrison Com Schools	Corydon
134	0.4	Switzerland County School Corp	Vevay
134	0.4	Tell City-Troy Twp School Corp	Tell City
149	0.3	Clay Community Schools	Brazil
149	0.3	Dekalb County Ctl United SD	Waterloo
149	0.3	Elwood Community School Corp	Elwood
149	0.3	Jay School Corporation	Portland
149	0.3	Kankakee Valley School Corp	Wheatfield
149	0.3	Mitchell Community Schools	Mitchell
149	0.3	North Harrison Com School Corp	Ramsey
149	0.3	South Dearborn Com School Corp	Aurora
149	0.3	South Montgomery Com Sch Corp	New Market
158	0.2	Blackford County Schools	Hartford City
158	0.2	Brownstown Cnt Com Sch Corp	Brownstown
158	0.2	Decatur County Com Schools	Greensburg
158	0.2	Franklin County Com Sch Corp	Brookville
158	0.2	Greensburg Community Schools	Greensburg
158	0.2	North Lawrence Com Schools	Bedford
158	0.2	North Spencer County Sch Corp	Lincoln City
158	0.2	South Vermillion Com Sch Corp	Clinton
158	0.2	Southwest Dubois County Sch Corp	Huntingburg
158	0.2	Southwest School Corp	Sullivan
158	0.2	West Noble School Corporation	Ligonier
169	0.1	Batesville Community Schl Corp	Batesville
169	0.1	Knox Community School Corp	Knox
169	0.1	Sunman-Dearborn Com Sch Corp	Saint Leon
169	0.1	Western Boone County Com SD	Thorntown

Asian Students

Rank	Percent	District Name	City
1	22.3	West Lafayette Com School Corp	West Lafayette
2	20.8	Perry Township Schools	Indianapolis
3	12.9	Carmel Clay Schools	Carmel
4	8.6	East Allen County Schools	New Haven
5	7.7	School Town of Munster	Munster
6	6.2	Hamilton Southeastern Schools	Fishers
7	5.9	Penn-Harris-Madison Sch Corp	Mishawaka
8	5.8	Bartholomew Con School Corp	Columbus
9	5.7	Clark-Pleasant Com School Corp	Whiteland
10	5.4	Fort Wayne Community Schools	Fort Wayne
11	4.8	Monroe County Com Sch Corp	Bloomington
11	4.8	School Town of Speedway	Speedway
13	4.4	Avon Community School Corp	Avon
13	4.4	M S D Southwest Allen County Schls	Fort Wayne
15	4.3	Zionsville Community Schools	Zionsville
16	4.2	Franklin Township Com Sch Corp	Indianapolis
17	3.8	M S D Washington Twp	Indianapolis
18	3.4	Center Grove Com Sch Corp	Greenwood
19	3.2	Northwest Allen County Schools	Fort Wayne
20	3.0	Plainfield Community Sch Corp	Plainfield
21	2.9	Lake Central School Corp	Saint John
21	2.9	Tippecanoe School Corp	Lafayette
23	2.7	Warrick County School Corp	Boonville
24	2.5	Brownsburg Community Sch Corp	Brownsburg
24	2.5	Westfield-Washington Schools	Westfield
24	2.5	Yorktown Community Schools	Yorktown
27	2.4	Crown Point Community Sch Corp	Crown Point
28	2.3	Noblesville Schools	Noblesville
29	2.2	Logansport Community Sch Corp	Logansport
30	2.0	Valparaiso Community Schools	Valparaiso
31	1.9	Greencastle Community Sch Corp	Greencastle
31	1.9	Greenwood Community Sch Corp	Greenwood
33	1.8	M S D Pike Township	Indianapolis
33	1.8	Western School Corp	Russiaville
35	1.6	Batesville Community Schl Corp	Batesville
35	1.6	Seymour Community Schools	Seymour

Note: This section only includes districts with 1,500 or more students; All categories are ranked from high to low

35	1.6	Vigo County School Corp	Terre Haute
35	1.6	Warsaw Community Schools	Warsaw
39	1.5	New Albany-Floyd County Con Sch	New Albany
39	1.5	School Town of Highland	Highland
41	1.4	Evansville Vanderburgh Sch Corp	Evansville
41	1.4	Indiana Connections Academy	Indianapolis
41	1.4	Kokomo School Corporation	Kokomo
41	1.4	Richmond Community Schools	Richmond
45	1.3	Duneland School Corporation	Chesterton
45	1.3	Mill Creek Community Sch Corp	Clayton
45	1.3	Shelbyville Central Schools	Shelbyville
45	1.3	South Bend Community Sch Corp	South Bend
49	1.2	Concord Community Schools	Elkhart
49	1.2	Crawfordsville Com Schools	Crawfordsville
49	1.2	Franklin Community School Corp	Franklin
49	1.2	Goshen Community Schools	Goshen
49	1.2	M S D Lawrence Township	Indianapolis
49	1.2	Middlebury Community Schools	Middlebury
49	1.2	Northern Wells Com Schools	Ossian
56	1.1	Elkhart Community Schools	Elkhart
56	1.1	Madison Consolidated Schools	Madison
56	1.1	Manchester Community Schools	N Manchester
56	1.1	Merrillville Community School	Merrillville
56	1.1	Mt Vernon Community Sch Corp	Fortville
56	1.1	Tell City-Troy Twp School Corp	Tell City
62	1.0	Dekalb County Ctl United SD	Waterloo
62	1.0	Greater Clark County Schools	Jeffersonville
62	1.0	Greater Jasper Con Schs	Jasper
62	1.0	Greenfield-Central Com Schools	Greenfield
62	1.0	Maconaquah School Corp	Bunker Hill
62	1.0	South Madison Com Sch Corp	Pendleton
68	0.9	Marion Community Schools	Marion
69	0.8	Brown County School Corporation	Nashville
69	0.8	Griffith Public Schools	Griffith
69	0.8	Hanover Community School Corp	Cedar Lake
69	0.8	Lebanon Community School Corp	Lebanon
69	0.8	M S D Warren Township	Indianapolis
69	0.8	North Gibson School Corp	Princeton
69	0.8	Portage Township Schools	Portage
69	0.8	Spencer-Owen Community Schools	Spencer
77	0.7	Lakeland School Corporation	Lagrange
77	0.7	Lawrenceburg Com School Corp	Lawrenceburg
77	0.7	M S D Martinsville Schools	Martinsville
77	0.7	M S D Steuben County	Angola
77	0.7	M S D Wayne Township	Indianapolis
77	0.7	Mississinewa Community Schl Corp	Gas City
77	0.7	New Castle Community Sch Corp	New Castle
77	0.7	South Gibson School Corp	Fort Branch
77	0.7	Southern Hancock Co Com Sch Corp	New Palestine
77	0.7	Wa-Nee Community Schools	Nappanee
77	0.7	Washington Com Schools	Washington
77	0.7	West Clark Community Schools	Sellersburg
89	0.6	Baugo Community Schools	Elkhart
89	0.6	Beech Grove City Schools	Beech Grove
89	0.6	Centerville-Abington Com Schs	Centerville
89	0.6	East Noble School Corp	Kendallville
89	0.6	Greensburg Community Schools	Greensburg
89	0.6	Hoosier Acad Virtual Charter	Indianapolis
89	0.6	Indianapolis Public Schools	Indianapolis
89	0.6	Lafayette School Corporation	Lafayette
89	0.6	M S D Decatur Township	Indianapolis
89	0.6	Muncie Community Schools	Muncie
89	0.6	North Adams Community Schools	Decatur
89	0.6	North Lawrence Com Schools	Bedford
89	0.6	North Montgomery Com Sch Corp	Crawfordsville
89	0.6	North Spencer County Sch Corp	Lincoln City
89	0.6	Rush County Schools	Rushville
89	0.6	Salem Community Schools	Salem
89	0.6	Scott County SD 2	Scottsburg
89	0.6	Tipton Community School Corp	Tipton
89	0.6	Vincennes Community Sch Corp	Vincennes
89	0.6	Whitley County Cons Schools	Columbia City
109	0.5	Delaware Community School Corp	Muncie
109	0.5	Fairfield Community Schools	Goshen
109	0.5	Hamilton Heights School Corp	Arcadia
109	0.5	Huntington County Com Sch Corp	Huntington
109	0.5	M S D Wabash County Schools	Wabash
109	0.5	Peru Community Schools	Peru
109	0.5	Plymouth Community School Corp	Plymouth
109	0.5	Richland-Bean Blossom C S C	Ellettsville
109	0.5	Rochester Community Sch Corp	Rochester
109	0.5	School City of Hobart	Hobart
109	0.5	School City of Mishawaka	Mishawaka
109	0.5	South Harrison Com Schools	Corydon
109	0.5	Westview School Corporation	Topeka
122	0.4	Anderson Community School Corp	Anderson
122	0.4	Brownstown Cnt Com Sch Corp	Brownstown
122	0.4	Clay Community Schools	Brazil
122	0.4	Danville Community School Corp	Danville
122	0.4	Fayette County School Corp	Connersville
122	0.4	Franklin County Com Sch Corp	Brookville
122	0.4	Jay School Corporation	Portland
122	0.4	John Glenn School Corporation	Walkerton
122	0.4	Laporte Community School Corp	Laporte
122	0.4	M S D Mount Vernon	Mount Vernon
122	0.4	Michigan City Area Schools	Michigan City
122	0.4	Nineveh-Hensley-Jackson United	Trafalgar
122	0.4	Randolph Central School Corp	Winchester
122	0.4	South Dearborn Com School Corp	Aurora
122	0.4	Southwest Dubois County Sch Corp	Huntingburg
122	0.4	Tippecanoe Valley School Corp	Akron
122	0.4	West Noble School Corporation	Ligonier
139	0.3	Benton Community School Corp	Fowler
139	0.3	Blackford County Schools	Hartford City
139	0.3	East Porter County School Corp	Kouts
139	0.3	Garrett-Keyser-Butler Com	Garrett
139	0.3	Kankakee Valley School Corp	Wheatfield
139	0.3	Mitchell Community Schools	Mitchell
139	0.3	Mooresville Con School Corp	Mooresville
139	0.3	New Prairie United School Corp	New Carlisle
139	0.3	North Harrison Com School Corp	Ramsey
139	0.3	North West Hendricks Schools	Lizton
139	0.3	Pike County School Corp	Petersburg
139	0.3	Rensselaer Central School Corp	Rensselaer
139	0.3	South Montgomery Com Sch Corp	New Market
139	0.3	Sunman-Dearborn Com Sch Corp	Saint Leon
139	0.3	Switzerland County School Corp	Vevay
139	0.3	Tri-Creek School Corporation	Lowell
139	0.3	Twin Lakes School Corp	Monticello
139	0.3	Wawasee Community School Corp	Syracuse
139	0.3	Western Boone County Com SD	Thorntown
139	0.3	Whitko Community School Corp	Larwill
159	0.2	Community Schools of Frankfort	Frankfort
159	0.2	Crawford County Com School Corp	Marengo
159	0.2	Elwood Community School Corp	Elwood
159	0.2	Frankton-Lapel Community Schools	Anderson
159	0.2	Lake Ridge New Tech Schools	Gary
159	0.2	School City of Hammond	Hammond
165	0.1	Decatur County Com Schools	Greensburg
165	0.1	Jennings County School Corp	North Vernon
165	0.1	Knox Community School Corp	Knox
165	0.1	School City of East Chicago	East Chicago
165	0.1	South Vermillion Com Sch Corp	Clinton
165	0.1	Southwest School Corp	Sullivan
171	0.0	Gary Community School Corp	Gary
171	0.0	North Putnam Community Schools	Bainbridge

American Indian/Alaska Native Students

Rank	Percent	District Name	City
1	0.9	Peru Community Schools	Peru
2	0.7	Brown County School Corporation	Nashville
2	0.7	Maconaquah School Corp	Bunker Hill
2	0.7	Manchester Community Schools	N Manchester
5	0.6	John Glenn School Corporation	Walkerton
5	0.6	North Adams Community Schools	Decatur
7	0.5	Hanover Community School Corp	Cedar Lake
7	0.5	Hoosier Acad Virtual Charter	Indianapolis
7	0.5	Lake Central School Corp	Saint John
7	0.5	M S D Wabash County Schools	Wabash
7	0.5	Rochester Community Sch Corp	Rochester
7	0.5	School City of Mishawaka	Mishawaka
7	0.5	Southwest School Corp	Sullivan
7	0.5	Spencer-Owen Community Schools	Spencer
7	0.5	Tippecanoe Valley School Corp	Akron
7	0.5	Washington Com Schools	Washington
7	0.5	Whitley County Cons Schools	Columbia City
18	0.4	Bartholomew Con School Corp	Columbus
18	0.4	Brownstown Cnt Com Sch Corp	Brownstown
18	0.4	Fairfield Community Schools	Goshen
18	0.4	Fort Wayne Community Schools	Fort Wayne
18	0.4	Hamilton Heights School Corp	Arcadia
18	0.4	Lake Ridge New Tech Schools	Gary
18	0.4	Lakeland School Corporation	Lagrange
18	0.4	M S D Martinsville Schools	Martinsville
18	0.4	Mooresville Con School Corp	Mooresville
18	0.4	Muncie Community Schools	Muncie
18	0.4	North Lawrence Com Schools	Bedford
18	0.4	Northern Wells Com Schools	Ossian
18	0.4	Penn-Harris-Madison Sch Corp	Mishawaka
18	0.4	School City of Hobart	Hobart
18	0.4	South Bend Community Sch Corp	South Bend
18	0.4	South Harrison Com Schools	Corydon
18	0.4	Tell City-Troy Twp School Corp	Tell City
18	0.4	Western School Corp	Russiaville
36	0.3	Clay Community Schools	Brazil
36	0.3	Crown Point Community Sch Corp	Crown Point
36	0.3	Danville Community School Corp	Danville
36	0.3	Decatur County Com Schools	Greensburg
36	0.3	Delaware Community School Corp	Muncie
36	0.3	Garrett-Keyser-Butler Com	Garrett
36	0.3	Greencastle Community Sch Corp	Greencastle
36	0.3	Greenfield-Central Com Schools	Greenfield
36	0.3	Greensburg Community Schools	Greensburg
36	0.3	Griffith Public Schools	Griffith
36	0.3	Huntington County Com Sch Corp	Huntington
36	0.3	Kankakee Valley School Corp	Wheatfield
36	0.3	Knox Community School Corp	Knox
36	0.3	Lafayette School Corporation	Lafayette
36	0.3	M S D Decatur Township	Indianapolis
36	0.3	M S D Southwest Allen County Schls	Fort Wayne
36	0.3	M S D Steuben County	Angola
36	0.3	Michigan City Area Schools	Michigan City
36	0.3	Middlebury Community Schools	Middlebury
36	0.3	Monroe County Com Sch Corp	Bloomington
36	0.3	New Albany-Floyd County Con Sch	New Albany
36	0.3	Plymouth Community School Corp	Plymouth
36	0.3	Richmond Community Schools	Richmond
36	0.3	Scott County SD 2	Scottsburg
36	0.3	South Madison Com Sch Corp	Pendleton
61	0.2	Baugo Community Schools	Elkhart
61	0.2	Benton Community School Corp	Fowler
61	0.2	Brownsburg Community Sch Corp	Brownsburg
61	0.2	Center Grove Com Sch Corp	Greenwood
61	0.2	Clark-Pleasant Com School Corp	Whiteland
61	0.2	Crawfordsville Com Schools	Crawfordsville
61	0.2	Duneland School Corporation	Chesterton
61	0.2	East Allen County Schools	New Haven
61	0.2	East Porter County School Corp	Kouts
61	0.2	Evansville Vanderburgh Sch Corp	Evansville
61	0.2	Franklin Township Com Sch Corp	Indianapolis
61	0.2	Goshen Community Schools	Goshen
61	0.2	Greater Clark County Schools	Jeffersonville
61	0.2	Hamilton Southeastern Schools	Fishers
61	0.2	Indiana Connections Academy	Indianapolis
61	0.2	Jennings County School Corp	North Vernon
61	0.2	Kokomo School Corporation	Kokomo
61	0.2	Lawrenceburg Com School Corp	Lawrenceburg
61	0.2	Logansport Community Sch Corp	Logansport
61	0.2	M S D Mount Vernon	Mount Vernon
61	0.2	M S D Wayne Township	Indianapolis
61	0.2	Marion Community Schools	Marion
61	0.2	Mill Creek Community Sch Corp	Clayton
61	0.2	Mississinewa Community Schl Corp	Gas City
61	0.2	Mt Vernon Community Sch Corp	Fortville
61	0.2	New Prairie United School Corp	New Carlisle
61	0.2	Noblesville Schools	Noblesville
61	0.2	North Montgomery Com Sch Corp	Crawfordsville
61	0.2	North Putnam Community Schools	Bainbridge
61	0.2	North Spencer County Sch Corp	Lincoln City
61	0.2	Northwest Allen County Schools	Fort Wayne
61	0.2	Pike County School Corp	Petersburg
61	0.2	Portage Township Schools	Portage
61	0.2	Rensselaer Central School Corp	Rensselaer
61	0.2	Salem Community Schools	Salem
61	0.2	School Town of Highland	Highland
61	0.2	Shelbyville Central Schools	Shelbyville
61	0.2	Southern Hancock Co Com Sch Corp	New Palestine
61	0.2	Tippecanoe School Corp	Lafayette
61	0.2	Tipton Community School Corp	Tipton
61	0.2	Tri-Creek School Corporation	Lowell
61	0.2	Twin Lakes School Corp	Monticello
61	0.2	Valparaiso Community Schools	Valparaiso
61	0.2	Vigo County School Corp	Terre Haute
61	0.2	Warrick County School Corp	Boonville
61	0.2	Warsaw Community Schools	Warsaw
61	0.2	Wawasee Community School Corp	Syracuse
61	0.2	Western Boone County Com SD	Thorntown
61	0.2	Westfield-Washington Schools	Westfield
61	0.2	Yorktown Community Schools	Yorktown
61	0.2	Zionsville Community Schools	Zionsville
112	0.1	Anderson Community School Corp	Anderson
112	0.1	Avon Community School Corp	Avon
112	0.1	Blackford County Schools	Hartford City
112	0.1	Carmel Clay Schools	Carmel

Education

Note: This section only includes districts with 1,500 or more students; All categories are ranked from high to low

112	0.1	Centerville-Abington Com Schs	Centerville
112	0.1	Concord Community Schools	Elkhart
112	0.1	Crawford County Com School Corp	Marengo
112	0.1	Dekalb County Ctl United SD	Waterloo
112	0.1	East Noble School Corp	Kendallville
112	0.1	Elkhart Community Schools	Elkhart
112	0.1	Elwood Community School Corp	Elwood
112	0.1	Franklin Community School Corp	Franklin
112	0.1	Frankton-Lapel Community Schools	Anderson
112	0.1	Gary Community School Corp	Gary
112	0.1	Greater Jasper Con Schs	Jasper
112	0.1	Greenwood Community Sch Corp	Greenwood
112	0.1	Indianapolis Public Schools	Indianapolis
112	0.1	Laporte Community School Corp	Laporte
112	0.1	Lebanon Community School Corp	Lebanon
112	0.1	M S D Lawrence Township	Indianapolis
112	0.1	M S D Warren Township	Indianapolis
112	0.1	M S D Washington Twp	Indianapolis
112	0.1	Madison Consolidated Schools	Madison
112	0.1	Merrillville Community School	Merrillville
112	0.1	Mitchell Community Schools	Mitchell
112	0.1	New Castle Community Sch Corp	New Castle
112	0.1	North Harrison Com School Corp	Ramsey
112	0.1	North West Hendricks Schools	Lizton
112	0.1	Perry Township Schools	Indianapolis
112	0.1	Plainfield Community Sch Corp	Plainfield
112	0.1	Richland-Bean Blossom C S C	Ellettsville
112	0.1	Rush County Schools	Rushville
112	0.1	School City of Hammond	Hammond
112	0.1	School Town of Munster	Munster
112	0.1	School Town of Speedway	Speedway
112	0.1	Seymour Community Schools	Seymour
112	0.1	South Dearborn Com School Corp	Aurora
112	0.1	South Gibson School Corp	Fort Branch
112	0.1	South Montgomery Com Sch Corp	New Market
112	0.1	South Vermillion Com Sch Corp	Clinton
112	0.1	Southwest Dubois County Sch Corp	Huntingburg
112	0.1	Sunman-Dearborn Com Sch Corp	Saint Leon
112	0.1	Switzerland County School Corp	Vevay
112	0.1	Vincennes Community Sch Corp	Vincennes
112	0.1	Wa-Nee Community Schools	Nappanee
112	0.1	West Clark Community Schools	Sellersburg
112	0.1	Whitko Community School Corp	Larwill
159	0.0	Batesville Community Schl Corp	Batesville
159	0.0	Beech Grove City Schools	Beech Grove
159	0.0	Community Schools of Frankfort	Frankfort
159	0.0	Fayette County School Corp	Connersville
159	0.0	Franklin County Com Sch Corp	Brookville
159	0.0	Jay School Corporation	Portland
159	0.0	M S D Pike Township	Indianapolis
159	0.0	Nineveh-Hensley-Jackson United	Trafalgar
159	0.0	North Gibson School Corp	Princeton
159	0.0	Randolph Central School Corp	Winchester
159	0.0	School City of East Chicago	East Chicago
159	0.0	West Lafayette Com School Corp	West Lafayette
159	0.0	West Noble School Corporation	Ligonier
159	0.0	Westview School Corporation	Topeka

Native Hawaiian/Pacific Islander Students

Rank	Percent	District Name	City
1	1.1	Garrett-Keyser-Butler Com	Garrett
2	0.4	Evansville Vanderburgh Sch Corp	Evansville
3	0.2	Carmel Clay Schools	Carmel
3	0.2	Center Grove Com Sch Corp	Greenwood
3	0.2	Elwood Community School Corp	Elwood
3	0.2	Fort Wayne Community Schools	Fort Wayne
3	0.2	Greensburg Community Schools	Greensburg
3	0.2	North Adams Community Schools	Decatur
3	0.2	Scott County SD 2	Scottsburg
3	0.2	South Vermillion Com Sch Corp	Clinton
3	0.2	West Clark Community Schools	Sellersburg
12	0.1	Avon Community School Corp	Avon
12	0.1	Bartholomew Con School Corp	Columbus
12	0.1	Brownsburg Community Sch Corp	Brownsburg
12	0.1	Centerville-Abington Com Schs	Centerville
12	0.1	Clark-Pleasant Com School Corp	Whiteland
12	0.1	Clay Community Schools	Brazil
12	0.1	Community Schools of Frankfort	Frankfort
12	0.1	Concord Community Schools	Elkhart
12	0.1	Crawford County Com School Corp	Marengo
12	0.1	Crown Point Community Sch Corp	Crown Point
12	0.1	Delaware Community School Corp	Muncie
12	0.1	East Noble School Corp	Kendallville
12	0.1	Elkhart Community Schools	Elkhart
12	0.1	Franklin Community School Corp	Franklin
12	0.1	Franklin Township Com Sch Corp	Indianapolis
12	0.1	Greater Clark County Schools	Jeffersonville
12	0.1	Greater Jasper Con Schs	Jasper
12	0.1	Greenwood Community Sch Corp	Greenwood
12	0.1	Hamilton Southeastern Schools	Fishers
12	0.1	Hoosier Acad Virtual Charter	Indianapolis
12	0.1	Indianapolis Public Schools	Indianapolis
12	0.1	Jay School Corporation	Portland
12	0.1	Lafayette School Corporation	Lafayette
12	0.1	Lake Ridge New Tech Schools	Gary
12	0.1	Lakeland School Corporation	Lagrange
12	0.1	Laporte Community School Corp	Laporte
12	0.1	M S D Decatur Township	Indianapolis
12	0.1	M S D Lawrence Township	Indianapolis
12	0.1	M S D Martinsville Schools	Martinsville
12	0.1	M S D Southwest Allen County Schls	Fort Wayne
12	0.1	M S D Steuben County	Angola
12	0.1	M S D Warren Township	Indianapolis
12	0.1	M S D Wayne Township	Indianapolis
12	0.1	Madison Consolidated Schools	Madison
12	0.1	Middlebury Community Schools	Middlebury
12	0.1	Mill Creek Community Sch Corp	Clayton
12	0.1	Monroe County Com Sch Corp	Bloomington
12	0.1	Mt Vernon Community Sch Corp	Fortville
12	0.1	Muncie Community Schools	Muncie
12	0.1	New Albany-Floyd County Con Sch	New Albany
12	0.1	Noblesville Schools	Noblesville
12	0.1	North Lawrence Com Schools	Bedford
12	0.1	North West Hendricks Schools	Lizton
12	0.1	Northern Wells Com Schools	Ossian
12	0.1	Penn-Harris-Madison Sch Corp	Mishawaka
12	0.1	Perry Township Schools	Indianapolis
12	0.1	Richland-Bean Blossom C S C	Ellettsville
12	0.1	Rochester Community Sch Corp	Rochester
12	0.1	Salem Community Schools	Salem
12	0.1	School Town of Speedway	Speedway
12	0.1	South Bend Community Sch Corp	South Bend
12	0.1	South Gibson School Corp	Fort Branch
12	0.1	South Madison Com Sch Corp	Pendleton
12	0.1	South Montgomery Com Sch Corp	New Market
12	0.1	Sunman-Dearborn Com Sch Corp	Saint Leon
12	0.1	Tipton Community School Corp	Tipton
12	0.1	Vigo County School Corp	Terre Haute
12	0.1	Vincennes Community Sch Corp	Vincennes
12	0.1	West Noble School Corporation	Ligonier
12	0.1	Western Boone County Com SD	Thorntown
12	0.1	Westview School Corporation	Topeka
12	0.1	Whitley County Cons Schools	Columbia City
12	0.1	Zionsville Community Schools	Zionsville
75	0.0	Anderson Community School Corp	Anderson
75	0.0	Batesville Community Schl Corp	Batesville
75	0.0	Baugo Community Schools	Elkhart
75	0.0	Beech Grove City Schools	Beech Grove
75	0.0	Benton Community School Corp	Fowler
75	0.0	Blackford County Schools	Hartford City
75	0.0	Brown County School Corporation	Nashville
75	0.0	Brownstown Cnt Com Sch Corp	Brownstown
75	0.0	Crawfordsville Com Schools	Crawfordsville
75	0.0	Danville Community School Corp	Danville
75	0.0	Decatur County Com Schools	Greensburg
75	0.0	Dekalb County Ctl United SD	Waterloo
75	0.0	Duneland School Corporation	Chesterton
75	0.0	East Allen County Schools	New Haven
75	0.0	East Porter County School Corp	Kouts
75	0.0	Fairfield Community Schools	Goshen
75	0.0	Fayette County School Corp	Connersville
75	0.0	Franklin County Com Sch Corp	Brookville
75	0.0	Frankton-Lapel Community Schools	Anderson
75	0.0	Gary Community School Corp	Gary
75	0.0	Goshen Community Schools	Goshen
75	0.0	Greencastle Community Sch Corp	Greencastle
75	0.0	Greenfield-Central Com Schools	Greenfield
75	0.0	Griffith Public Schools	Griffith
75	0.0	Hamilton Heights School Corp	Arcadia
75	0.0	Hanover Community School Corp	Cedar Lake
75	0.0	Huntington County Com Sch Corp	Huntington
75	0.0	Indiana Connections Academy	Indianapolis
75	0.0	Jennings County School Corp	North Vernon
75	0.0	John Glenn School Corporation	Walkerton
75	0.0	Kankakee Valley School Corp	Wheatfield
75	0.0	Knox Community School Corp	Knox
75	0.0	Kokomo School Corporation	Kokomo
75	0.0	Lake Central School Corp	Saint John
75	0.0	Lawrenceburg Com School Corp	Lawrenceburg
75	0.0	Lebanon Community School Corp	Lebanon
75	0.0	Logansport Community Sch Corp	Logansport
75	0.0	M S D Mount Vernon	Mount Vernon
75	0.0	M S D Pike Township	Indianapolis
75	0.0	M S D Wabash County Schools	Wabash
75	0.0	M S D Washington Twp	Indianapolis
75	0.0	Maconaquah School Corp	Bunker Hill
75	0.0	Manchester Community Schools	N Manchester
75	0.0	Marion Community Schools	Marion
75	0.0	Merrillville Community School	Merrillville
75	0.0	Michigan City Area Schools	Michigan City
75	0.0	Mississinewa Community Schl Corp	Gas City
75	0.0	Mitchell Community Schools	Mitchell
75	0.0	Mooresville Con School Corp	Mooresville
75	0.0	New Castle Community Sch Corp	New Castle
75	0.0	New Prairie United School Corp	New Carlisle
75	0.0	Nineveh-Hensley-Jackson United	Trafalgar
75	0.0	North Gibson School Corp	Princeton
75	0.0	North Harrison Com School Corp	Ramsey
75	0.0	North Montgomery Com Sch Corp	Crawfordsville
75	0.0	North Putnam Community Schools	Bainbridge
75	0.0	North Spencer County Sch Corp	Lincoln City
75	0.0	Northwest Allen County Schools	Fort Wayne
75	0.0	Peru Community Schools	Peru
75	0.0	Pike County School Corp	Petersburg
75	0.0	Plainfield Community Sch Corp	Plainfield
75	0.0	Plymouth Community School Corp	Plymouth
75	0.0	Portage Township Schools	Portage
75	0.0	Randolph Central School Corp	Winchester
75	0.0	Rensselaer Central School Corp	Rensselaer
75	0.0	Richmond Community Schools	Richmond
75	0.0	Rush County Schools	Rushville
75	0.0	School City of East Chicago	East Chicago
75	0.0	School City of Hammond	Hammond
75	0.0	School City of Hobart	Hobart
75	0.0	School City of Mishawaka	Mishawaka
75	0.0	School Town of Highland	Highland
75	0.0	School Town of Munster	Munster
75	0.0	Seymour Community Schools	Seymour
75	0.0	Shelbyville Central Schools	Shelbyville
75	0.0	South Dearborn Com School Corp	Aurora
75	0.0	South Harrison Com Schools	Corydon
75	0.0	Southern Hancock Co Com Sch Corp	New Palestine
75	0.0	Southwest Dubois County Sch Corp	Huntingburg
75	0.0	Southwest School Corp	Sullivan
75	0.0	Spencer-Owen Community Schools	Spencer
75	0.0	Switzerland County School Corp	Vevay
75	0.0	Tell City-Troy Twp School Corp	Tell City
75	0.0	Tippecanoe School Corp	Lafayette
75	0.0	Tippecanoe Valley School Corp	Akron
75	0.0	Tri-Creek School Corporation	Lowell
75	0.0	Twin Lakes School Corp	Monticello
75	0.0	Valparaiso Community Schools	Valparaiso
75	0.0	Wa-Nee Community Schools	Nappanee
75	0.0	Warrick County School Corp	Boonville
75	0.0	Warsaw Community Schools	Warsaw
75	0.0	Washington Com Schools	Washington
75	0.0	Wawasee Community School Corp	Syracuse
75	0.0	West Lafayette Com School Corp	West Lafayette
75	0.0	Western School Corp	Russiaville
75	0.0	Westfield-Washington Schools	Westfield
75	0.0	Whitko Community School Corp	Larwill
75	0.0	Yorktown Community Schools	Yorktown

Students who are Two or More Races

Rank	Percent	District Name	City
1	13.7	Marion Community Schools	Marion
2	12.0	Richmond Community Schools	Richmond
3	10.8	Muncie Community Schools	Muncie
4	10.6	Kokomo School Corporation	Kokomo
5	9.6	Evansville Vanderburgh Sch Corp	Evansville
5	9.6	Michigan City Area Schools	Michigan City
7	9.4	South Bend Community Sch Corp	South Bend
8	9.3	Fort Wayne Community Schools	Fort Wayne
9	8.8	North Gibson School Corp	Princeton
10	8.4	Greater Clark County Schools	Jeffersonville
11	7.7	Anderson Community School Corp	Anderson
11	7.7	Vigo County School Corp	Terre Haute
13	7.4	Elkhart Community Schools	Elkhart
13	7.4	M S D Warren Township	Indianapolis
15	7.3	Maconaquah School Corp	Bunker Hill

Note: This section only includes districts with 1,500 or more students; All categories are ranked from high to low

16	7.1	M S D Washington Twp	Indianapolis
17	7.0	Lawrenceburg Com School Corp	Lawrenceburg
17	7.0	M S D Lawrence Township	Indianapolis
19	6.8	School City of Mishawaka	Mishawaka
20	6.7	Beech Grove City Schools	Beech Grove
20	6.7	Concord Community Schools	Elkhart
20	6.7	Monroe County Com Sch Corp	Bloomington
20	6.7	School Town of Speedway	Speedway
24	6.4	Baugo Community Schools	Elkhart
25	6.2	Lafayette School Corporation	Lafayette
26	6.1	M S D Wayne Township	Indianapolis
27	6.0	Carmel Clay Schools	Carmel
27	6.0	Lake Ridge New Tech Schools	Gary
27	6.0	M S D Pike Township	Indianapolis
27	6.0	New Albany-Floyd County Con Sch	New Albany
31	5.6	Franklin Township Com Sch Corp	Indianapolis
32	5.5	Greenwood Community Sch Corp	Greenwood
33	5.4	Avon Community School Corp	Avon
33	5.4	Merrillville Community School	Merrillville
33	5.4	Mississinewa Community Schl Corp	Gas City
36	5.3	Laporte Community School Corp	Laporte
36	5.3	M S D Decatur Township	Indianapolis
38	5.2	Clark-Pleasant Com School Corp	Whiteland
39	5.1	Centerville-Abington Com Schs	Centerville
39	5.1	Mt Vernon Community Sch Corp	Fortville
39	5.1	Perry Township Schools	Indianapolis
39	5.1	West Lafayette Com School Corp	West Lafayette
43	4.9	Hamilton Southeastern Schools	Fishers
43	4.9	Twin Lakes School Corp	Monticello
45	4.8	Brownsburg Community Sch Corp	Brownsburg
45	4.8	East Allen County Schools	New Haven
45	4.8	Indianapolis Public Schools	Indianapolis
45	4.8	Richland-Bean Blossom C S C	Ellettsville
45	4.8	Vincennes Community Sch Corp	Vincennes
50	4.7	M S D Mount Vernon	Mount Vernon
50	4.7	Portage Township Schools	Portage
50	4.7	Westfield-Washington Schools	Westfield
53	4.6	South Harrison Com Schools	Corydon
54	4.5	Western School Corp	Russiaville
55	4.4	Bartholomew Con School Corp	Columbus
55	4.4	Hoosier Acad Virtual Charter	Indianapolis
57	4.3	Indiana Connections Academy	Indianapolis
57	4.3	Lakeland School Corporation	Lagrange
57	4.3	New Castle Community Sch Corp	New Castle
57	4.3	Northwest Allen County Schools	Fort Wayne
57	4.3	Peru Community Schools	Peru
57	4.3	Zionsville Community Schools	Zionsville
63	4.2	Tippecanoe Valley School Corp	Akron
63	4.2	Warrick County School Corp	Boonville
65	4.1	Gary Community School Corp	Gary
65	4.1	School Town of Munster	Munster
65	4.1	Tippecanoe School Corp	Lafayette
65	4.1	Yorktown Community Schools	Yorktown
69	4.0	Penn-Harris-Madison Sch Corp	Mishawaka
69	4.0	School City of Hammond	Hammond
69	4.0	Seymour Community Schools	Seymour
69	4.0	Valparaiso Community Schools	Valparaiso
73	3.9	M S D Southwest Allen County Schls	Fort Wayne
73	3.9	Wa-Nee Community Schools	Nappanee
75	3.8	Dekalb County Ctl United SD	Waterloo
75	3.8	Franklin Community School Corp	Franklin
77	3.7	Frankton-Lapel Community Schools	Anderson
78	3.6	Griffith Public Schools	Griffith
78	3.6	Logansport Community Sch Corp	Logansport
78	3.6	Manchester Community Schools	N Manchester
78	3.6	Shelbyville Central Schools	Shelbyville
82	3.5	Garrett-Keyser-Butler Com	Garrett
82	3.5	Greencastle Community Sch Corp	Greencastle
82	3.5	Lebanon Community School Corp	Lebanon
82	3.5	Madison Consolidated Schools	Madison
82	3.5	Plainfield Community Sch Corp	Plainfield
82	3.5	Washington Com Schools	Washington
88	3.4	Duneland School Corporation	Chesterton
88	3.4	M S D Steuben County	Angola
88	3.4	South Montgomery Com Sch Corp	New Market
88	3.4	Tell City-Troy Twp School Corp	Tell City
92	3.3	Blackford County Schools	Hartford City
92	3.3	Danville Community School Corp	Danville
92	3.3	Elwood Community School Corp	Elwood
92	3.3	Rochester Community Sch Corp	Rochester
96	3.2	Delaware Community School Corp	Muncie
96	3.2	John Glenn School Corporation	Walkerton
96	3.2	Mooresville Con School Corp	Mooresville
99	3.1	Crawfordsville Com Schools	Crawfordsville
99	3.1	Goshen Community Schools	Goshen
99	3.1	Hanover Community School Corp	Cedar Lake
99	3.1	New Prairie United School Corp	New Carlisle
99	3.1	West Clark Community Schools	Sellersburg
104	3.0	Lake Central School Corp	Saint John
104	3.0	Rush County Schools	Rushville
104	3.0	School Town of Highland	Highland
104	3.0	South Madison Com Sch Corp	Pendleton
104	3.0	Whitley County Cons Schools	Columbia City
109	2.8	Center Grove Com Sch Corp	Greenwood
109	2.8	Greenfield-Central Com Schools	Greenfield
109	2.8	Jay School Corporation	Portland
109	2.8	School City of Hobart	Hobart
113	2.6	Fayette County School Corp	Connersville
113	2.6	Noblesville Schools	Noblesville
113	2.6	Tipton Community School Corp	Tipton
116	2.5	Crown Point Community Sch Corp	Crown Point
116	2.5	Greensburg Community Schools	Greensburg
116	2.5	Huntington County Com Sch Corp	Huntington
116	2.5	Randolph Central School Corp	Winchester
116	2.5	South Dearborn Com School Corp	Aurora
116	2.5	Wawasee Community School Corp	Syracuse
122	2.4	North Adams Community Schools	Decatur
123	2.3	Benton Community School Corp	Fowler
123	2.3	Brown County School Corporation	Nashville
123	2.3	North Lawrence Com Schools	Bedford
123	2.3	Northern Wells Com Schools	Ossian
123	2.3	Warsaw Community Schools	Warsaw
128	2.2	Mitchell Community Schools	Mitchell
129	2.1	East Porter County School Corp	Kouts
129	2.1	South Gibson School Corp	Fort Branch
129	2.1	South Vermillion Com Sch Corp	Clinton
129	2.1	Southern Hancock Co Com Sch Corp	New Palestine
129	2.1	Spencer-Owen Community Schools	Spencer
129	2.1	Tri-Creek School Corporation	Lowell
135	2.0	Jennings County School Corp	North Vernon
135	2.0	Middlebury Community Schools	Middlebury
135	2.0	North West Hendricks Schools	Lizton
135	2.0	Pike County School Corp	Petersburg
135	2.0	Sunman-Dearborn Com Sch Corp	Saint Leon
140	1.9	Crawford County Com School Corp	Marengo
140	1.9	M S D Martinsville Schools	Martinsville
140	1.9	North Montgomery Com Sch Corp	Crawfordsville
140	1.9	Southwest School Corp	Sullivan
144	1.8	Batesville Community Schl Corp	Batesville
144	1.8	Clay Community Schools	Brazil
144	1.8	North Harrison Com Sch Corp	Ramsey
144	1.8	Plymouth Community School Corp	Plymouth
144	1.8	Rensselaer Central School Corp	Rensselaer
144	1.8	Switzerland County School Corp	Vevay
150	1.7	M S D Wabash County Schools	Wabash
150	1.7	Mill Creek Community Sch Corp	Clayton
150	1.7	Nineveh-Hensley-Jackson United	Trafalgar
150	1.7	Western Boone County Com SD	Thorntown
154	1.6	North Putnam Community Schools	Bainbridge
154	1.6	Salem Community Schools	Salem
154	1.6	School City of East Chicago	East Chicago
157	1.5	Community Schools of Frankfort	Frankfort
157	1.5	East Noble School Corp	Kendallville
157	1.5	Scott County SD 2	Scottsburg
160	1.3	Brownstown Cnt Com Sch Corp	Brownstown
160	1.3	Decatur County Com Schools	Greensburg
160	1.3	Fairfield Community Schools	Goshen
160	1.3	Greater Jasper Con Schs	Jasper
160	1.3	Knox Community School Corp	Knox
165	1.2	North Spencer County Sch Corp	Lincoln City
165	1.2	Southwest Dubois County Sch Corp	Huntingburg
167	1.1	Westview School Corporation	Topeka
167	1.1	Whitko Community School Corp	Larwill
169	1.0	Hamilton Heights School Corp	Arcadia
169	1.0	Kankakee Valley School Corp	Wheatfield
171	0.9	West Noble School Corporation	Ligonier
172	0.6	Franklin County Com Sch Corp	Brookville

Hispanic Students

Rank	Percent	District Name	City
1	50.5	Goshen Community Schools	Goshen
2	49.1	West Noble School Corporation	Ligonier
3	48.3	Community Schools of Frankfort	Frankfort
4	47.6	School City of Hammond	Hammond
5	46.4	School City of East Chicago	East Chicago
6	38.0	Logansport Community Sch Corp	Logansport
7	32.2	Concord Community Schools	Elkhart
8	31.3	Elkhart Community Schools	Elkhart
9	28.3	School Town of Highland	Highland
10	27.3	Lafayette School Corporation	Lafayette
11	26.1	Southwest Dubois County Sch Corp	Huntingburg
12	25.4	M S D Wayne Township	Indianapolis
13	25.3	Griffith Public Schools	Griffith
13	25.3	Lake Ridge New Tech Schools	Gary
15	24.5	Plymouth Community School Corp	Plymouth
16	24.3	Indianapolis Public Schools	Indianapolis
17	23.4	School City of Hobart	Hobart
18	22.8	M S D Pike Township	Indianapolis
19	22.7	Portage Township Schools	Portage
20	21.2	School Town of Munster	Munster
20	21.2	Seymour Community Schools	Seymour
22	20.7	M S D Lawrence Township	Indianapolis
23	19.9	M S D Washington Twp	Indianapolis
23	19.9	Warsaw Community Schools	Warsaw
25	19.8	Washington Com Schools	Washington
26	19.5	South Bend Community Sch Corp	South Bend
27	18.6	Merrillville Community School	Merrillville
28	17.0	Crawfordsville Com Schools	Crawfordsville
29	15.8	Fort Wayne Community Schools	Fort Wayne
30	15.4	Lake Central School Corp	Saint John
31	15.3	Lakeland School Corporation	Lagrange
32	14.5	Laporte Community School Corp	Laporte
33	14.2	Greater Jasper Con Schs	Jasper
34	14.0	Perry Township Schools	Indianapolis
34	14.0	School Town of Speedway	Speedway
36	13.6	Bartholomew Con School Corp	Columbus
37	13.5	Shelbyville Central Schools	Shelbyville
37	13.5	Tippecanoe Valley School Corp	Akron
39	13.0	Tippecanoe School Corp	Lafayette
40	12.8	M S D Warren Township	Indianapolis
41	12.7	Crown Point Community Sch Corp	Crown Point
42	12.5	Greater Clark County Schools	Jeffersonville
43	12.1	Twin Lakes School Corp	Monticello
44	11.7	Hanover Community School Corp	Cedar Lake
44	11.7	North Adams Community Schools	Decatur
46	11.5	Wawasee Community School Corp	Syracuse
47	11.0	M S D Steuben County	Angola
48	10.8	M S D Decatur Township	Indianapolis
49	10.6	Duneland School Corporation	Chesterton
50	10.5	New Prairie United School Corp	New Carlisle
51	10.4	Anderson Community School Corp	Anderson
52	10.1	Kankakee Valley School Corp	Wheatfield
53	10.0	Marion Community Schools	Marion
53	10.0	Tri-Creek School Corporation	Lowell
53	10.0	Valparaiso Community Schools	Valparaiso
56	9.5	Baugo Community Schools	Elkhart
57	9.3	Middlebury Community Schools	Middlebury
58	9.1	Rensselaer Central School Corp	Rensselaer
59	9.0	Greenwood Community Sch Corp	Greenwood
60	8.7	Michigan City Area Schools	Michigan City
61	8.5	Benton Community School Corp	Fowler
62	8.2	Avon Community School Corp	Avon
63	8.0	School City of Mishawaka	Mishawaka
64	7.9	East Allen County Schools	New Haven
64	7.9	Richmond Community Schools	Richmond
66	7.8	North Spencer County Sch Corp	Lincoln City
66	7.8	Wa-Nee Community Schools	Nappanee
68	7.6	Westfield-Washington Schools	Westfield
69	7.5	Beech Grove City Schools	Beech Grove
70	7.3	East Porter County School Corp	Kouts
71	7.1	Indiana Connections Academy	Indianapolis
72	6.8	Franklin Township Com Sch Corp	Indianapolis
73	6.7	Elwood Community School Corp	Elwood
74	6.5	Hoosier Acad Virtual Charter	Indianapolis
75	6.4	East Noble School Corp	Kendallville
76	6.3	Lebanon Community School Corp	Lebanon
77	6.0	Hamilton Southeastern Schools	Fishers
78	5.7	Kokomo School Corporation	Kokomo
79	5.6	West Lafayette Com School Corp	West Lafayette
80	5.5	Noblesville Schools	Noblesville
81	5.4	Manchester Community Schools	N Manchester
82	5.3	West Clark Community Schools	Sellersburg
83	5.2	Fairfield Community Schools	Goshen
83	5.2	Jennings County School Corp	North Vernon
85	5.1	Franklin Community School Corp	Franklin
85	5.1	John Glenn School Corporation	Walkerton
85	5.1	Monroe County Com Sch Corp	Bloomington
85	5.1	Penn-Harris-Madison Sch Corp	Mishawaka
89	5.0	New Albany-Floyd County Con Sch	New Albany
90	4.9	M S D Southwest Allen County Schls	Fort Wayne
91	4.7	Brownsburg Community Sch Corp	Brownsburg
91	4.7	Clark-Pleasant Com School Corp	Whiteland
91	4.7	Rochester Community Sch Corp	Rochester

Note: This section only includes districts with 1,500 or more students; All categories are ranked from high to low

Education

94	4.6	Knox Community School Corp	Knox
95	4.5	Madison Consolidated Schools	Madison
95	4.5	Northwest Allen County Schools	Fort Wayne
97	4.4	Batesville Community Schl Corp	Batesville
97	4.4	Plainfield Community Sch Corp	Plainfield
99	4.3	Jay School Corporation	Portland
100	4.2	Evansville Vanderburgh Sch Corp	Evansville
101	4.1	Zionsville Community Schools	Zionsville
102	4.0	North Montgomery Com Sch Corp	Crawfordsville
103	3.9	Mississinewa Community Schl Corp	Gas City
104	3.8	Whitko Community School Corp	Larwill
105	3.7	Center Grove Com Sch Corp	Greenwood
105	3.7	Tipton Community School Corp	Tipton
107	3.6	Muncie Community Schools	Muncie
107	3.6	New Castle Community Sch Corp	New Castle
109	3.5	Maconaquah School Corp	Bunker Hill
110	3.4	Randolph Central School Corp	Winchester
111	3.3	Northern Wells Com Schools	Ossian
111	3.3	South Montgomery Com Sch Corp	New Market
113	3.2	Huntington County Com Sch Corp	Huntington
113	3.2	Richland-Bean Blossom C S C	Ellettsville
113	3.2	Vigo County School Corp	Terre Haute
113	3.2	Whitley County Cons Schools	Columbia City
117	3.1	Frankton-Lapel Community Schools	Anderson
117	3.1	Western School Corp	Russiaville
119	3.0	Hamilton Heights School Corp	Arcadia
119	3.0	Peru Community Schools	Peru
121	2.9	Dekalb County Ctl United SD	Waterloo
121	2.9	Mt Vernon Community Sch Corp	Fortville
121	2.9	North Gibson School Corp	Princeton
121	2.9	South Harrison Com Schools	Corydon
121	2.9	Southwest School Corp	Sullivan
126	2.8	Vincennes Community Sch Corp	Vincennes
127	2.7	Carmel Clay Schools	Carmel
127	2.7	North Lawrence Com Schools	Bedford
129	2.6	Blackford County Schools	Hartford City
129	2.6	Gary Community School Corp	Gary
129	2.6	Greencastle Community Sch Corp	Greencastle
132	2.5	Garrett-Keyser-Butler Com	Garrett
132	2.5	Scott County SD 2	Scottsburg
132	2.5	Warrick County School Corp	Boonville
135	2.4	Southern Hancock Co Com Sch Corp	New Palestine
135	2.4	Western Boone County Com SD	Thorntown
135	2.4	Yorktown Community Schools	Yorktown
138	2.3	Greensburg Community Schools	Greensburg
138	2.3	M S D Mount Vernon	Mount Vernon
138	2.3	Tell City-Troy Twp School Corp	Tell City
141	2.2	Mitchell Community Schools	Mitchell
141	2.2	North Harrison Com School Corp	Ramsey
141	2.2	Westview School Corporation	Topeka
144	2.1	Brownstown Cnt Com Sch Corp	Brownstown
144	2.1	South Madison Com Sch Corp	Pendleton
146	2.0	Mooresville Con School Corp	Mooresville
147	1.9	Clay Community Schools	Brazil
147	1.9	Danville Community School Corp	Danville
147	1.9	North West Hendricks Schools	Lizton
147	1.9	Rush County Schools	Rushville
151	1.8	Brown County School Corporation	Nashville
151	1.8	South Gibson School Corp	Fort Branch
151	1.8	South Vermillion Com Sch Corp	Clinton
154	1.7	Fayette County School Corp	Connersville
154	1.7	Greenfield-Central Com Schools	Greenfield
154	1.7	M S D Martinsville Schools	Martinsville
154	1.7	M S D Wabash County Schools	Wabash
154	1.7	Salem Community Schools	Salem
159	1.6	Centerville-Abington Com Schs	Centerville
159	1.6	Nineveh-Hensley-Jackson United	Trafalgar
159	1.6	Switzerland County School Corp	Vevay
162	1.5	Decatur County Com Schools	Greensburg
163	1.4	Sunman-Dearborn Com Sch Corp	Saint Leon
164	1.3	Pike County School Corp	Petersburg
165	1.1	Crawford County Com School Corp	Marengo
165	1.1	Delaware Community School Corp	Muncie
165	1.1	Lawrenceburg Com School Corp	Lawrenceburg
165	1.1	Mill Creek Community Sch Corp	Clayton
165	1.1	South Dearborn Com School Corp	Aurora
165	1.1	Spencer-Owen Community Schools	Spencer
171	1.0	North Putnam Community Schools	Bainbridge
172	0.6	Franklin County Com Sch Corp	Brookville

Individual Education Program Students

Rank	Percent	District Name	City
1	30.9	North Gibson School Corp	Princeton
2	28.4	Jay School Corporation	Portland
3	25.2	Salem Community Schools	Salem
4	25.1	Benton Community School Corp	Fowler
5	24.9	M S D Mount Vernon	Mount Vernon
6	24.1	Brown County School Corporation	Nashville
7	23.8	Washington Com Schools	Washington
8	23.4	South Gibson School Corp	Fort Branch
9	22.8	Beech Grove City Schools	Beech Grove
10	21.9	Muncie Community Schools	Muncie
11	21.8	Richmond Community Schools	Richmond
12	21.6	Randolph Central School Corp	Winchester
13	21.3	Pike County School Corp	Petersburg
14	21.2	Clay Community Schools	Brazil
15	21.1	Lebanon Community School Corp	Lebanon
15	21.1	Spencer-Owen Community Schools	Spencer
17	20.7	Anderson Community School Corp	Anderson
17	20.7	Crawfordsville Com Schools	Crawfordsville
17	20.7	East Noble School Corp	Kendallville
20	20.6	Mitchell Community Schools	Mitchell
20	20.6	North Montgomery Com Sch Corp	Crawfordsville
22	20.5	Crawford County Com School Corp	Marengo
22	20.5	North Harrison Com School Corp	Ramsey
22	20.5	Tippecanoe Valley School Corp	Akron
25	20.4	South Bend Community Sch Corp	South Bend
26	20.3	North Lawrence Com Schools	Bedford
27	20.1	Greenfield-Central Com Schools	Greenfield
28	20.0	Warrick County School Corp	Boonville
29	19.9	Jennings County School Corp	North Vernon
29	19.9	South Vermillion Com Sch Corp	Clinton
29	19.9	Switzerland County School Corp	Vevay
32	19.7	Vigo County School Corp	Terre Haute
33	19.6	Lafayette School Corporation	Lafayette
34	19.5	Kokomo School Corporation	Kokomo
35	19.3	Michigan City Area Schools	Michigan City
35	19.3	New Castle Community Sch Corp	New Castle
35	19.3	School City of Mishawaka	Mishawaka
38	19.1	Indianapolis Public Schools	Indianapolis
38	19.1	School City of East Chicago	East Chicago
38	19.1	Whitko Community School Corp	Larwill
41	19.0	South Montgomery Com Sch Corp	New Market
42	18.8	Decatur County Com Schools	Greensburg
42	18.8	Lawrenceburg Com School Corp	Lawrenceburg
44	18.7	New Albany-Floyd County Con Sch	New Albany
44	18.7	South Dearborn Com School Corp	Aurora
46	18.6	Richland-Bean Blossom C S C	Ellettsville
47	18.5	Lakeland School Corporation	Lagrange
48	18.2	Seymour Community Schools	Seymour
49	18.0	North Putnam Community Schools	Bainbridge
50	17.9	Vincennes Community Sch Corp	Vincennes
51	17.8	Duneland School Corporation	Chesterton
51	17.8	Greater Clark County Schools	Jeffersonville
51	17.8	Scott County SD 2	Scottsburg
51	17.8	Wawasee Community School Corp	Syracuse
55	17.7	M S D Washington Twp	Indianapolis
56	17.6	Huntington County Com Sch Corp	Huntington
56	17.6	South Madison Com Sch Corp	Pendleton
58	17.5	Evansville Vanderburgh Sch Corp	Evansville
58	17.5	Mt Vernon Community Sch Corp	Fortville
60	17.3	Fort Wayne Community Schools	Fort Wayne
60	17.3	Portage Township Schools	Portage
62	17.2	M S D Martinsville Schools	Martinsville
62	17.2	Madison Consolidated Schools	Madison
62	17.2	North Adams Community Schools	Decatur
62	17.2	Tell City-Troy Twp School Corp	Tell City
62	17.2	Whitley County Cons Schools	Columbia City
67	17.1	Franklin Township Com Sch Corp	Indianapolis
67	17.1	Frankton-Lapel Community Schools	Anderson
67	17.1	North Spencer County Sch Corp	Lincoln City
67	17.1	South Harrison Com Schools	Corydon
71	17.0	Blackford County Schools	Hartford City
72	16.9	Garrett-Keyser-Butler Com	Garrett
72	16.9	Rensselaer Central School Corp	Rensselaer
74	16.8	Delaware Community School Corp	Muncie
74	16.8	Elwood Community School Corp	Elwood
74	16.8	Greensburg Community Schools	Greensburg
74	16.8	West Clark Community Schools	Sellersburg
78	16.6	Franklin Community School Corp	Franklin
78	16.6	Maconaquah School Corp	Bunker Hill
78	16.6	Shelbyville Central Schools	Shelbyville
78	16.6	Warsaw Community Schools	Warsaw
82	16.5	Greencastle Community Sch Corp	Greencastle
82	16.5	Southern Hancock Co Com Sch Corp	New Palestine
84	16.4	Kankakee Valley School Corp	Wheatfield
85	16.3	Elkhart Community Schools	Elkhart
85	16.3	M S D Steuben County	Angola
85	16.3	M S D Warren Township	Indianapolis
85	16.3	Monroe County Com Sch Corp	Bloomington
85	16.3	Nineveh-Hensley-Jackson United	Trafalgar
90	16.2	Indiana Connections Academy	Indianapolis
90	16.2	School Town of Speedway	Speedway
90	16.2	Westfield-Washington Schools	Westfield
93	16.1	Fayette County School Corp	Connersville
93	16.1	Western Boone County Com SD	Thorntown
95	16.0	Greenwood Community Sch Corp	Greenwood
95	16.0	Mississinewa Community Schl Corp	Gas City
95	16.0	Northern Wells Com Schools	Ossian
98	15.9	Sunman-Dearborn Com Sch Corp	Saint Leon
99	15.8	Dekalb County Ctl United SD	Waterloo
99	15.8	Franklin County Com Sch Corp	Brookville
99	15.8	Tipton Community School Corp	Tipton
102	15.7	New Prairie United School Corp	New Carlisle
103	15.6	Concord Community Schools	Elkhart
103	15.6	East Porter County School Corp	Kouts
103	15.6	Hamilton Heights School Corp	Arcadia
103	15.6	Noblesville Schools	Noblesville
103	15.6	Tippecanoe School Corp	Lafayette
108	15.5	Mill Creek Community Sch Corp	Clayton
108	15.5	Penn-Harris-Madison Sch Corp	Mishawaka
108	15.5	Plainfield Community Sch Corp	Plainfield
108	15.5	Rochester Community Sch Corp	Rochester
112	15.4	Clark-Pleasant Com School Corp	Whiteland
112	15.4	Valparaiso Community Schools	Valparaiso
114	15.3	Brownstown Cnt Com Sch Corp	Brownstown
114	15.3	Rush County Schools	Rushville
116	15.1	Lake Ridge New Tech Schools	Gary
117	15.0	Peru Community Schools	Peru
118	14.9	Batesville Community Schl Corp	Batesville
119	14.8	Avon Community School Corp	Avon
119	14.8	Gary Community School Corp	Gary
119	14.8	M S D Pike Township	Indianapolis
119	14.8	Marion Community Schools	Marion
123	14.7	Mooresville Con School Corp	Mooresville
123	14.7	Perry Township Schools	Indianapolis
125	14.6	Goshen Community Schools	Goshen
126	14.5	Hoosier Acad Virtual Charter	Indianapolis
126	14.5	School City of Hammond	Hammond
126	14.5	Southwest Dubois County Sch Corp	Huntingburg
129	14.4	Center Grove Com Sch Corp	Greenwood
129	14.4	Laporte Community School Corp	Laporte
131	14.3	Griffith Public Schools	Griffith
131	14.3	M S D Lawrence Township	Indianapolis
131	14.3	Westview School Corporation	Topeka
134	14.2	M S D Decatur Township	Indianapolis
135	14.1	Manchester Community Schools	N Manchester
135	14.1	Southwest School Corp	Sullivan
137	14.0	Wa-Nee Community Schools	Nappanee
138	13.9	East Allen County Schools	New Haven
138	13.9	Lake Central School Corp	Saint John
138	13.9	M S D Wabash County Schools	Wabash
141	13.8	M S D Wayne Township	Indianapolis
141	13.8	School Town of Munster	Munster
143	13.7	Greater Jasper Con Schs	Jasper
143	13.7	Merrillville Community School	Merrillville
145	13.6	John Glenn School Corporation	Walkerton
146	13.4	Baugo Community Schools	Elkhart
146	13.4	Community Schools of Frankfort	Frankfort
148	13.3	Northwest Allen County Schools	Fort Wayne
149	13.2	Middlebury Community Schools	Middlebury
150	13.1	School City of Hobart	Hobart
151	13.0	Fairfield Community Schools	Goshen
151	13.0	Western School Corp	Russiaville
153	12.9	Bartholomew Con School Corp	Columbus
153	12.9	Zionsville Community Schools	Zionsville
155	12.7	Danville Community School Corp	Danville
156	12.6	Hanover Community School Corp	Cedar Lake
157	12.5	School Town of Highland	Highland
158	12.4	West Noble School Corporation	Ligonier
159	12.3	North West Hendricks Schools	Lizton
159	12.3	Yorktown Community Schools	Yorktown
161	12.2	Crown Point Community Sch Corp	Crown Point
161	12.2	Plymouth Community School Corp	Plymouth
163	12.1	Twin Lakes School Corp	Monticello
164	12.0	Brownsburg Community Sch Corp	Brownsburg
164	12.0	Tri-Creek School Corporation	Lowell
166	11.9	Logansport Community Sch Corp	Logansport
167	11.6	Centerville-Abington Com Schs	Centerville
168	11.5	West Lafayette Com School Corp	West Lafayette
169	11.4	Knox Community School Corp	Knox
170	10.8	Hamilton Southeastern Schools	Fishers
171	10.7	Carmel Clay Schools	Carmel

Note: This section only includes districts with 1,500 or more students; All categories are ranked from high to low

172	9.5	M S D Southwest Allen County Schls	Fort Wayne

English Language Learner Students

Rank	Percent	District Name	City
1	27.7	Westview School Corporation	Topeka
2	26.6	Community Schools of Frankfort	Frankfort
3	24.2	Logansport Community Sch Corp	Logansport
4	22.1	Goshen Community Schools	Goshen
5	21.5	West Noble School Corporation	Ligonier
6	20.0	Perry Township Schools	Indianapolis
7	18.2	Concord Community Schools	Elkhart
8	15.0	M S D Pike Township	Indianapolis
9	14.3	M S D Washington Twp	Indianapolis
10	14.0	Indianapolis Public Schools	Indianapolis
11	13.6	Elkhart Community Schools	Elkhart
12	13.5	Southwest Dubois County Sch Corp	Huntingburg
13	12.9	M S D Wayne Township	Indianapolis
14	12.3	Seymour Community Schools	Seymour
15	12.2	Fairfield Community Schools	Goshen
15	12.2	M S D Lawrence Township	Indianapolis
17	11.9	School City of Hammond	Hammond
18	11.5	Lafayette School Corporation	Lafayette
19	11.1	School City of East Chicago	East Chicago
20	11.0	School Town of Speedway	Speedway
21	9.4	Warsaw Community Schools	Warsaw
22	9.2	Plymouth Community School Corp	Plymouth
23	9.0	South Bend Community Sch Corp	South Bend
24	8.9	Washington Com Schools	Washington
25	8.6	Lakeland School Corporation	Lagrange
26	8.1	Fort Wayne Community Schools	Fort Wayne
27	7.7	Crawfordsville Com Schools	Crawfordsville
28	7.6	Bartholomew Con School Corp	Columbus
28	7.6	East Allen County Schools	New Haven
28	7.6	Middlebury Community Schools	Middlebury
31	6.7	Tippecanoe Valley School Corp	Akron
32	6.4	M S D Warren Township	Indianapolis
33	5.7	Greater Clark County Schools	Jeffersonville
34	5.5	Shelbyville Central Schools	Shelbyville
34	5.5	West Lafayette Com School Corp	West Lafayette
36	5.4	Greater Jasper Con Schs	Jasper
36	5.4	Tippecanoe School Corp	Lafayette
38	4.8	M S D Decatur Township	Indianapolis
39	4.7	Twin Lakes School Corp	Monticello
40	4.6	Wa-Nee Community Schools	Nappanee
41	4.4	Laporte Community School Corp	Laporte
42	4.2	Richmond Community Schools	Richmond
43	4.0	Baugo Community Schools	Elkhart
44	3.9	Avon Community School Corp	Avon
45	3.8	Lake Ridge New Tech Schools	Gary
45	3.8	North Spencer County Sch Corp	Lincoln City
47	3.7	Anderson Community School Corp	Anderson
47	3.7	Beech Grove City Schools	Beech Grove
49	3.6	Wawasee Community School Corp	Syracuse
50	3.5	Greenwood Community Sch Corp	Greenwood
50	3.5	M S D Steuben County	Angola
52	3.3	Valparaiso Community Schools	Valparaiso
53	3.2	East Noble School Corp	Kendallville
54	3.1	Carmel Clay Schools	Carmel
54	3.1	Clark-Pleasant Com School Corp	Whiteland
54	3.1	Kankakee Valley School Corp	Wheatfield
54	3.1	School Town of Munster	Munster
54	3.1	Westfield-Washington Schools	Westfield
59	3.0	Franklin Township Com Sch Corp	Indianapolis
60	2.9	Jay School Corporation	Portland
60	2.9	Marion Community Schools	Marion
60	2.9	Rensselaer Central School Corp	Rensselaer
63	2.8	Hamilton Southeastern Schools	Fishers
64	2.7	Monroe County Com Sch Corp	Bloomington
64	2.7	Penn-Harris-Madison Sch Corp	Mishawaka
64	2.7	West Clark Community Schools	Sellersburg
67	2.6	Manchester Community Schools	N Manchester
67	2.6	Noblesville Schools	Noblesville
69	2.5	Benton Community School Corp	Fowler
70	2.4	Evansville Vanderburgh Sch Corp	Evansville
71	2.3	Crown Point Community Sch Corp	Crown Point
71	2.3	Merrillville Community School	Merrillville
73	2.2	Lake Central School Corp	Saint John
73	2.2	New Prairie United School Corp	New Carlisle
73	2.2	School Town of Highland	Highland
76	2.0	Portage Township Schools	Portage
77	1.9	North Montgomery Com Sch Corp	Crawfordsville
78	1.8	New Albany-Floyd County Con Sch	New Albany
79	1.7	Madison Consolidated Schools	Madison
79	1.7	Plainfield Community Sch Corp	Plainfield
81	1.6	Brownsburg Community Sch Corp	Brownsburg
81	1.6	Hanover Community School Corp	Cedar Lake
81	1.6	Jennings County School Corp	North Vernon
81	1.6	Kokomo School Corporation	Kokomo
81	1.6	Lebanon Community School Corp	Lebanon
81	1.6	Northern Wells Com Schools	Ossian
81	1.6	School City of Mishawaka	Mishawaka
88	1.5	Batesville Community Schl Corp	Batesville
88	1.5	Elwood Community School Corp	Elwood
88	1.5	Michigan City Area Schools	Michigan City
88	1.5	North Gibson School Corp	Princeton
92	1.3	Franklin Community School Corp	Franklin
92	1.3	Knox Community School Corp	Knox
94	1.2	Center Grove Com Sch Corp	Greenwood
94	1.2	School City of Hobart	Hobart
94	1.2	Vigo County School Corp	Terre Haute
94	1.2	Yorktown Community Schools	Yorktown
98	1.1	Frankton-Lapel Community Schools	Anderson
98	1.1	Garrett-Keyser-Butler Com	Garrett
98	1.1	Griffith Public Schools	Griffith
98	1.1	M S D Southwest Allen County Schls	Fort Wayne
98	1.1	Northwest Allen County Schools	Fort Wayne
98	1.1	Rochester Community Sch Corp	Rochester
98	1.1	Tri-Creek School Corporation	Lowell
105	1.0	Greencastle Community Sch Corp	Greencastle
105	1.0	Hamilton Heights School Corp	Arcadia
105	1.0	Maconaquah School Corp	Bunker Hill
105	1.0	Muncie Community Schools	Muncie
105	1.0	Randolph Central School Corp	Winchester
105	1.0	Rush County Schools	Rushville
105	1.0	South Harrison Com Schools	Corydon
105	1.0	Tipton Community School Corp	Tipton
113	0.9	Blackford County Schools	Hartford City
113	0.9	John Glenn School Corporation	Walkerton
113	0.9	Mississinewa Community Schl Corp	Gas City
116	0.8	Dekalb County Ctl United SD	Waterloo
116	0.8	Duneland School Corporation	Chesterton
116	0.8	Greensburg Community Schools	Greensburg
116	0.8	Indiana Connections Academy	Indianapolis
116	0.8	M S D Wabash County Schools	Wabash
116	0.8	New Castle Community Sch Corp	New Castle
116	0.8	South Madison Com Sch Corp	Pendleton
116	0.8	Warrick County School Corp	Boonville
116	0.8	Zionsville Community Schools	Zionsville
125	0.7	Hoosier Acad Virtual Charter	Indianapolis
125	0.7	M S D Mount Vernon	Mount Vernon
125	0.7	Tell City-Troy Twp School Corp	Tell City
125	0.7	Western School Corp	Russiaville
129	0.6	Danville Community School Corp	Danville
129	0.6	East Porter County School Corp	Kouts
129	0.6	North Adams Community Schools	Decatur
129	0.6	Peru Community Schools	Peru
129	0.6	Southern Hancock Co Com Sch Corp	New Palestine
129	0.6	Sunman-Dearborn Com Sch Corp	Saint Leon
129	0.6	Whitko Community School Corp	Larwill
136	0.5	Clay Community Schools	Brazil
136	0.5	Mt Vernon Community Sch Corp	Fortville
138	0.4	Huntington County Com Sch Corp	Huntington
138	0.4	Mill Creek Community Sch Corp	Clayton
138	0.4	Richland-Bean Blossom C S C	Ellettsville
138	0.4	Salem Community Schools	Salem
138	0.4	Scott County SD 2	Scottsburg
138	0.4	Switzerland County School Corp	Vevay
138	0.4	Whitley County Cons Schools	Columbia City
145	0.3	Centerville-Abington Com Schs	Centerville
145	0.3	Crawford County Com School Corp	Marengo
145	0.3	Lawrenceburg Com School Corp	Lawrenceburg
145	0.3	Pike County School Corp	Petersburg
145	0.3	South Gibson School Corp	Fort Branch
145	0.3	Spencer-Owen Community Schools	Spencer
145	0.3	Vincennes Community Sch Corp	Vincennes
152	0.2	Brown County School Corporation	Nashville
152	0.2	Brownstown Cnt Com Sch Corp	Brownstown
152	0.2	Decatur County Com Schools	Greensburg
152	0.2	Fayette County School Corp	Connersville
152	0.2	Greenfield-Central Com Schools	Greenfield
152	0.2	M S D Martinsville Schools	Martinsville
152	0.2	Mitchell Community Schools	Mitchell
152	0.2	Mooresville Con School Corp	Mooresville
152	0.2	Nineveh-Hensley-Jackson United	Trafalgar
152	0.2	North Harrison Com School Corp	Ramsey
152	0.2	North Lawrence Com Schools	Bedford
152	0.2	North West Hendricks Schools	Lizton
152	0.2	South Montgomery Com Sch Corp	New Market
152	0.2	South Vermillion Com Sch Corp	Clinton
152	0.2	Western Boone County Com SD	Thorntown
167	0.1	Delaware Community School Corp	Muncie
167	0.1	Franklin County Com Sch Corp	Brookville
167	0.1	Gary Community School Corp	Gary
167	0.1	South Dearborn Com School Corp	Aurora
n/a	n/a	North Putnam Community Schools	Bainbridge
n/a	n/a	Southwest School Corp	Sullivan

Students Eligible for Free Lunch

Rank	Percent	District Name	City
1	83.7	School City of East Chicago	East Chicago
2	80.7	Lake Ridge New Tech Schools	Gary
3	78.3	Gary Community School Corp	Gary
4	74.1	School City of Hammond	Hammond
5	71.2	Anderson Community School Corp	Anderson
6	69.7	Marion Community Schools	Marion
7	69.3	Community Schools of Frankfort	Frankfort
8	68.5	Richmond Community Schools	Richmond
9	68.2	Muncie Community Schools	Muncie
10	68.1	Indianapolis Public Schools	Indianapolis
11	66.9	Michigan City Area Schools	Michigan City
12	66.7	M S D Wayne Township	Indianapolis
13	65.5	M S D Warren Township	Indianapolis
14	63.9	South Bend Community Sch Corp	South Bend
15	62.5	Kokomo School Corporation	Kokomo
16	59.9	Lafayette School Corporation	Lafayette
17	58.8	Beech Grove City Schools	Beech Grove
18	57.6	Elwood Community School Corp	Elwood
18	57.6	M S D Pike Township	Indianapolis
20	57.2	Washington Com Schools	Washington
21	56.8	Elkhart Community Schools	Elkhart
22	56.7	Fort Wayne Community Schools	Fort Wayne
23	56.6	M S D Lawrence Township	Indianapolis
24	56.2	School City of Mishawaka	Mishawaka
25	55.8	M S D Decatur Township	Indianapolis
26	54.5	Vincennes Community Sch Corp	Vincennes
27	54.0	Peru Community Schools	Peru
28	53.4	Perry Township Schools	Indianapolis
29	52.9	Fayette County School Corp	Connersville
29	52.9	Goshen Community Schools	Goshen
31	52.7	Crawfordsville Com Schools	Crawfordsville
32	51.3	M S D Washington Twp	Indianapolis
33	50.4	School Town of Speedway	Speedway
34	50.2	West Noble School Corporation	Ligonier
35	50.1	Merrillville Community School	Merrillville
36	49.9	Evansville Vanderburgh Sch Corp	Evansville
37	49.8	Crawford County Com School Corp	Marengo
38	49.5	Greater Clark County Schools	Jeffersonville
38	49.5	Knox Community School Corp	Knox
40	49.3	Blackford County Schools	Hartford City
41	48.8	Mississinewa Community Schl Corp	Gas City
41	48.8	Plymouth Community School Corp	Plymouth
43	48.5	New Castle Community Sch Corp	New Castle
44	48.4	Maconaquah School Corp	Bunker Hill
45	47.8	Concord Community Schools	Elkhart
46	46.8	Mitchell Community Schools	Mitchell
47	46.7	Scott County SD 2	Scottsburg
48	46.3	Logansport Community Sch Corp	Logansport
49	46.1	Jennings County School Corp	North Vernon
49	46.1	Vigo County School Corp	Terre Haute
51	45.6	South Vermillion Com Sch Corp	Clinton
52	45.2	Randolph Central School Corp	Winchester
53	44.6	Clay Community Schools	Brazil
53	44.6	Jay School Corporation	Portland
55	44.3	Seymour Community Schools	Seymour
56	43.9	Salem Community Schools	Salem
57	43.7	Shelbyville Central Schools	Shelbyville
58	43.5	Portage Township Schools	Portage
59	43.4	Tippecanoe Valley School Corp	Akron
60	43.3	Switzerland County School Corp	Vevay
61	43.2	Laporte Community School Corp	Laporte
62	42.6	East Allen County Schools	New Haven
63	42.5	Griffith Public Schools	Griffith
64	42.2	Rush County Schools	Rushville
65	42.1	Spencer-Owen Community Schools	Spencer
66	41.6	North Gibson School Corp	Princeton
67	41.4	Brown County School Corporation	Nashville
68	41.3	M S D Martinsville Schools	Martinsville
69	41.2	Rochester Community Sch Corp	Rochester
70	41.1	North Adams Community Schools	Decatur
71	40.9	Lakeland School Corporation	Lagrange
71	40.9	Madison Consolidated Schools	Madison

Note: This section only includes districts with 1,500 or more students; All categories are ranked from high to low

73	40.7	South Dearborn Com School Corp	Aurora
73	40.7	Southwest Dubois County Sch Corp	Huntingburg
75	40.6	Greensburg Community Schools	Greensburg
76	40.5	Southwest School Corp	Sullivan
77	40.4	Franklin County Com Sch Corp	Brookville
78	39.3	Benton Community School Corp	Fowler
79	38.6	Warsaw Community Schools	Warsaw
80	38.4	Greenwood Community Sch Corp	Greenwood
81	38.1	South Harrison Com Schools	Corydon
82	38.0	Rensselaer Central School Corp	Rensselaer
83	37.5	Twin Lakes School Corp	Monticello
84	36.6	East Noble School Corp	Kendallville
84	36.6	Garrett-Keyser-Butler Com	Garrett
84	36.6	North Lawrence Com Schools	Bedford
87	36.4	New Albany-Floyd County Con Sch	New Albany
88	36.3	Tell City-Troy Twp School Corp	Tell City
89	36.2	Bartholomew Con School Corp	Columbus
90	36.1	Greencastle Community Sch Corp	Greencastle
90	36.1	M S D Wabash County Schools	Wabash
92	36.0	Decatur County Com Schools	Greensburg
92	36.0	Manchester Community Schools	N Manchester
94	35.8	School City of Hobart	Hobart
95	35.4	Wawasee Community School Corp	Syracuse
96	35.1	Huntington County Com Sch Corp	Huntington
96	35.1	North Harrison Com School Corp	Ramsey
98	35.0	Whitko Community School Corp	Larwill
99	34.9	Lawrenceburg Com School Corp	Lawrenceburg
99	34.9	M S D Steuben County	Angola
101	34.6	North Putnam Community Schools	Bainbridge
102	34.1	Mooresville Con School Corp	Mooresville
103	33.8	Clark-Pleasant Com School Corp	Whiteland
103	33.8	Indiana Connections Academy	Indianapolis
105	33.4	Lebanon Community School Corp	Lebanon
105	33.4	South Montgomery Com Sch Corp	New Market
107	33.3	M S D Mount Vernon	Mount Vernon
107	33.3	Tipton Community School Corp	Tipton
109	33.2	Franklin Community School Corp	Franklin
110	32.4	Delaware Community School Corp	Muncie
111	32.2	Pike County School Corp	Petersburg
112	31.5	Kankakee Valley School Corp	Wheatfield
113	31.0	Monroe County Com Sch Corp	Bloomington
114	30.7	Dekalb County Ctl United SD	Waterloo
115	30.3	North Montgomery Com Sch Corp	Crawfordsville
116	30.1	Centerville-Abington Com Schs	Centerville
117	29.7	Richland-Bean Blossom C S C	Ellettsville
118	29.2	Baugo Community Schools	Elkhart
118	29.2	Brownstown Cnt Com Sch Corp	Brownstown
118	29.2	Tippecanoe School Corp	Lafayette
121	29.0	School Town of Highland	Highland
122	28.9	Franklin Township Com Sch Corp	Indianapolis
123	28.7	Frankton-Lapel Community Schools	Anderson
124	28.2	John Glenn School Corporation	Walkerton
124	28.2	West Clark Community Schools	Sellersburg
126	27.0	Greenfield-Central Com Schools	Greenfield
126	27.0	Western School Corp	Russiaville
126	27.0	Yorktown Community Schools	Yorktown
129	26.6	New Prairie United School Corp	New Carlisle
130	26.5	Western Boone County Com SD	Thorntown
131	25.1	Greater Jasper Con Schs	Jasper
131	25.1	South Madison Com Sch Corp	Pendleton
133	24.7	Hamilton Heights School Corp	Arcadia
134	24.6	Nineveh-Hensley-Jackson United	Trafalgar
135	23.4	Duneland School Corporation	Chesterton
136	23.1	Middlebury Community Schools	Middlebury
137	22.9	Danville Community School Corp	Danville
137	22.9	Mill Creek Community Sch Corp	Clayton
139	22.5	Northern Wells Com Schools	Ossian
140	22.3	Warrick County School Corp	Boonville
141	22.0	North Spencer County Sch Corp	Lincoln City
142	21.8	Valparaiso Community Schools	Valparaiso
143	21.3	Tri-Creek School Corporation	Lowell
144	21.1	Batesville Community Schl Corp	Batesville
144	21.1	Whitley County Cons Schools	Columbia City
146	20.6	Penn-Harris-Madison Sch Corp	Mishawaka
147	20.4	Hoosier Acad Virtual Charter	Indianapolis
148	20.3	Wa-Nee Community Schools	Nappanee
149	20.2	Avon Community School Corp	Avon
150	19.5	Mt Vernon Community Sch Corp	Fortville
151	19.4	Plainfield Community Sch Corp	Plainfield
152	19.2	Sunman-Dearborn Com Sch Corp	Saint Leon
153	19.0	South Gibson School Corp	Fort Branch
153	19.0	Westview School Corporation	Topeka
155	18.7	Hanover Community School Corp	Cedar Lake
156	18.2	Noblesville Schools	Noblesville
157	17.4	Brownsburg Community Sch Corp	Brownsburg
158	16.1	Crown Point Community Sch Corp	Crown Point
159	14.6	East Porter County School Corp	Kouts
160	14.5	North West Hendricks Schools	Lizton
160	14.5	Southern Hancock Co Com Sch Corp	New Palestine
162	14.3	Lake Central School Corp	Saint John
163	14.2	Fairfield Community Schools	Goshen
163	14.2	West Lafayette Com School Corp	West Lafayette
165	13.7	Center Grove Com Sch Corp	Greenwood
166	13.6	School Town of Munster	Munster
167	13.0	Westfield-Washington Schools	Westfield
168	10.8	M S D Southwest Allen County Schls	Fort Wayne
169	10.7	Northwest Allen County Schools	Fort Wayne
170	9.3	Hamilton Southeastern Schools	Fishers
171	6.7	Carmel Clay Schools	Carmel
172	3.1	Zionsville Community Schools	Zionsville

Students Eligible for Reduced-Price Lunch

Rank	Percent	District Name	City
1	19.8	Westview School Corporation	Topeka
2	13.1	Garrett-Keyser-Butler Com	Garrett
3	12.6	Manchester Community Schools	N Manchester
4	12.0	North Lawrence Com Schools	Bedford
5	11.7	Jennings County School Corp	North Vernon
5	11.7	Twin Lakes School Corp	Monticello
7	11.6	Wa-Nee Community Schools	Nappanee
8	11.5	Merrillville Community School	Merrillville
9	11.4	North Harrison Com School Corp	Ramsey
10	11.0	Dekalb County Ctl United SD	Waterloo
11	10.9	M S D Steuben County	Angola
11	10.9	Whitko Community School Corp	Larwill
13	10.7	Clark-Pleasant Com School Corp	Whiteland
13	10.7	Jay School Corporation	Portland
13	10.7	School City of Mishawaka	Mishawaka
13	10.7	Tippecanoe Valley School Corp	Akron
13	10.7	West Noble School Corporation	Ligonier
18	10.6	Indiana Connections Academy	Indianapolis
18	10.6	Randolph Central School Corp	Winchester
20	10.5	North Gibson School Corp	Princeton
21	10.4	Concord Community Schools	Elkhart
21	10.4	Crawford County Com School Corp	Marengo
21	10.4	Greensburg Community Schools	Greensburg
21	10.4	Mississinewa Community Schl Corp	Gas City
21	10.4	Peru Community Schools	Peru
26	10.3	Portage Township Schools	Portage
27	10.2	Brown County School Corporation	Nashville
28	10.1	Goshen Community Schools	Goshen
28	10.1	M S D Decatur Township	Indianapolis
30	9.9	Scott County SD 2	Scottsburg
31	9.8	North Adams Community Schools	Decatur
31	9.8	Plymouth Community School Corp	Plymouth
31	9.8	Wawasee Community School Corp	Syracuse
34	9.7	Beech Grove City Schools	Beech Grove
34	9.7	Rensselaer Central School Corp	Rensselaer
36	9.6	Decatur County Com Schools	Greensburg
36	9.6	Fayette County School Corp	Connersville
36	9.6	Logansport Community Sch Corp	Logansport
39	9.5	East Noble School Corp	Kendallville
39	9.5	Greencastle Community Sch Corp	Greencastle
41	9.4	John Glenn School Corporation	Walkerton
41	9.4	Lakeland School Corporation	Lagrange
41	9.4	Madison Consolidated Schools	Madison
44	9.3	Clay Community Schools	Brazil
44	9.3	Salem Community Schools	Salem
44	9.3	Switzerland County School Corp	Vevay
47	9.2	Crawfordsville Com Schools	Crawfordsville
47	9.2	Huntington County Com Sch Corp	Huntington
47	9.2	M S D Martinsville Schools	Martinsville
47	9.2	Maconaquah School Corp	Bunker Hill
47	9.2	Warsaw Community Schools	Warsaw
52	9.1	Brownstown Cnt Com Sch Corp	Brownstown
53	9.0	M S D Warren Township	Indianapolis
54	8.9	Pike County School Corp	Petersburg
55	8.8	Franklin Township Com Sch Corp	Indianapolis
56	8.7	Franklin Community School Corp	Franklin
56	8.7	South Harrison Com Schools	Corydon
56	8.7	Vigo County School Corp	Terre Haute
59	8.6	Franklin County Com Sch Corp	Brookville
60	8.5	Griffith Public Schools	Griffith
60	8.5	Middlebury Community Schools	Middlebury
62	8.4	Baugo Community Schools	Elkhart
62	8.4	Spencer-Owen Community Schools	Spencer
64	8.2	New Castle Community Sch Corp	New Castle
65	8.1	Elkhart Community Schools	Elkhart
65	8.1	Evansville Vanderburgh Sch Corp	Evansville
65	8.1	M S D Wayne Township	Indianapolis
65	8.1	Rush County Schools	Rushville
65	8.1	Seymour Community Schools	Seymour
65	8.1	Western Boone County Com SD	Thorntown
71	8.0	Greater Jasper Con Schs	Jasper
71	8.0	School City of Hobart	Hobart
73	7.9	Kokomo School Corporation	Kokomo
73	7.9	Laporte Community School Corp	Laporte
73	7.9	Lebanon Community School Corp	Lebanon
73	7.9	Richmond Community Schools	Richmond
73	7.9	Rochester Community Sch Corp	Rochester
73	7.9	West Clark Community Schools	Sellersburg
79	7.8	Danville Community School Corp	Danville
79	7.8	Fort Wayne Community Schools	Fort Wayne
79	7.8	Frankton-Lapel Community Schools	Anderson
79	7.8	Greenwood Community Sch Corp	Greenwood
79	7.8	Knox Community School Corp	Knox
79	7.8	North Montgomery Com Sch Corp	Crawfordsville
85	7.7	Centerville-Abington Com Schs	Centerville
85	7.7	Mooresville Con School Corp	Mooresville
85	7.7	New Prairie United School Corp	New Carlisle
88	7.6	East Allen County Schools	New Haven
88	7.6	North Putnam Community Schools	Bainbridge
88	7.6	Perry Township Schools	Indianapolis
88	7.6	Southwest School Corp	Sullivan
92	7.5	Bartholomew Con School Corp	Columbus
92	7.5	Nineveh-Hensley-Jackson United	Trafalgar
92	7.5	South Bend Community Sch Corp	South Bend
92	7.5	Yorktown Community Schools	Yorktown
96	7.4	Vincennes Community Sch Corp	Vincennes
96	7.4	Whitley County Cons Schools	Columbia City
98	7.3	Delaware Community School Corp	Muncie
98	7.3	M S D Lawrence Township	Indianapolis
100	7.2	Blackford County Schools	Hartford City
100	7.2	Greater Clark County Schools	Jeffersonville
100	7.2	South Vermillion Com Sch Corp	Clinton
103	7.1	Benton Community School Corp	Fowler
103	7.1	Warrick County School Corp	Boonville
105	7.0	Community Schools of Frankfort	Frankfort
106	6.9	Anderson Community School Corp	Anderson
106	6.9	Lake Ridge New Tech Schools	Gary
106	6.9	Northern Wells Com Schools	Ossian
109	6.8	Avon Community School Corp	Avon
109	6.8	Muncie Community Schools	Muncie
109	6.8	Washington Com Schools	Washington
112	6.7	Fairfield Community Schools	Goshen
112	6.7	Plainfield Community Sch Corp	Plainfield
112	6.7	Richland-Bean Blossom C S C	Ellettsville
112	6.7	School City of Hammond	Hammond
112	6.7	Tipton Community School Corp	Tipton
117	6.6	Lafayette School Corporation	Lafayette
117	6.6	South Madison Com Sch Corp	Pendleton
119	6.4	Shelbyville Central Schools	Shelbyville
119	6.4	Tippecanoe School Corp	Lafayette
121	6.3	Kankakee Valley School Corp	Wheatfield
121	6.3	M S D Wabash County Schools	Wabash
121	6.3	School Town of Speedway	Speedway
121	6.3	Southwest Dubois County Sch Corp	Huntingburg
125	6.2	Hamilton Heights School Corp	Arcadia
125	6.2	Lawrenceburg Com School Corp	Lawrenceburg
127	6.1	Brownsburg Community Sch Corp	Brownsburg
127	6.1	Elwood Community School Corp	Elwood
127	6.1	M S D Washington Twp	Indianapolis
127	6.1	Penn-Harris-Madison Sch Corp	Mishawaka
131	6.0	School Town of Highland	Highland
131	6.0	Tri-Creek School Corporation	Lowell
133	5.9	Batesville Community Schl Corp	Batesville
133	5.9	Center Grove Com Sch Corp	Greenwood
133	5.9	East Porter County School Corp	Kouts
133	5.9	M S D Mount Vernon	Mount Vernon
133	5.9	Michigan City Area Schools	Michigan City
133	5.9	New Albany-Floyd County Con Sch	New Albany
133	5.9	Tell City-Troy Twp School Corp	Tell City
140	5.7	Marion Community Schools	Marion
140	5.7	South Dearborn Com School Corp	Aurora
142	5.6	Mitchell Community Schools	Mitchell
143	5.5	Greenfield-Central Com Schools	Greenfield
143	5.5	Mt Vernon Community Sch Corp	Fortville
145	5.4	M S D Pike Township	Indianapolis
145	5.4	Valparaiso Community Schools	Valparaiso
147	5.3	Monroe County Com Sch Corp	Bloomington
147	5.3	Sunman-Dearborn Com Sch Corp	Saint Leon
149	5.2	South Gibson School Corp	Fort Branch

Note: This section only includes districts with 1,500 or more students; All categories are ranked from high to low

149	5.2	Western School Corp	Russiaville
151	5.1	Northwest Allen County Schools	Fort Wayne
152	5.0	North Spencer County Sch Corp	Lincoln City
152	5.0	Southern Hancock Co Com Sch Corp	New Palestine
154	4.9	Crown Point Community Sch Corp	Crown Point
155	4.8	Noblesville Schools	Noblesville
155	4.8	South Montgomery Com Sch Corp	New Market
157	4.6	North West Hendricks Schools	Lizton
158	4.5	School Town of Munster	Munster
159	4.4	Hanover Community School Corp	Cedar Lake
160	4.3	Mill Creek Community Sch Corp	Clayton
161	4.2	Hamilton Southeastern Schools	Fishers
161	4.2	Hoosier Acad Virtual Charter	Indianapolis
163	4.1	Lake Central School Corp	Saint John
164	4.0	Duneland School Corporation	Chesterton
164	4.0	M S D Southwest Allen County Schls	Fort Wayne
166	3.4	West Lafayette Com School Corp	West Lafayette
167	2.6	Indianapolis Public Schools	Indianapolis
167	2.6	School City of East Chicago	East Chicago
169	2.5	Westfield-Washington Schools	Westfield
170	2.3	Carmel Clay Schools	Carmel
171	1.8	Zionsville Community Schools	Zionsville
172	0.2	Gary Community School Corp	Gary

Student/Teacher Ratio

(number of students per teacher)

Rank	Number	District Name	City
1	11.9	Decatur County Com Schools	Greensburg
2	13.0	Beech Grove City Schools	Beech Grove
3	13.7	Evansville Vanderburgh Sch Corp	Evansville
4	13.8	School Town of Speedway	Speedway
5	14.6	Randolph Central School Corp	Winchester
6	14.7	Benton Community School Corp	Fowler
6	14.7	New Castle Community Sch Corp	New Castle
8	14.9	Centerville-Abington Com Schs	Centerville
8	14.9	M S D Wabash County Schools	Wabash
10	15.0	John Glenn School Corporation	Walkerton
10	15.0	Richmond Community Schools	Richmond
12	15.1	Brown County School Corporation	Nashville
12	15.1	Clay Community Schools	Brazil
12	15.1	Rush County Schools	Rushville
12	15.1	Southwest School Corp	Sullivan
16	15.2	Crawfordsville Com Schools	Crawfordsville
17	15.3	Nineveh-Hensley-Jackson United	Trafalgar
17	15.3	North Putnam Community Schools	Bainbridge
19	15.4	Mississinewa Community Schl Corp	Gas City
19	15.4	North Spencer County Sch Corp	Lincoln City
19	15.4	Pike County School Corp	Petersburg
22	15.5	East Porter County School Corp	Kouts
23	15.6	Lawrenceburg Com School Corp	Lawrenceburg
24	15.7	East Noble School Corp	Kendallville
24	15.7	Lafayette School Corporation	Lafayette
24	15.7	M S D Mount Vernon	Mount Vernon
24	15.7	South Gibson School Corp	Fort Branch
24	15.7	South Montgomery Com Sch Corp	New Market
24	15.7	West Lafayette Com School Corp	West Lafayette
24	15.7	Westview School Corporation	Topeka
31	15.8	Rensselaer Central School Corp	Rensselaer
31	15.8	Twin Lakes School Corp	Monticello
33	15.9	Concord Community Schools	Elkhart
33	15.9	Frankton-Lapel Community Schools	Anderson
33	15.9	Mill Creek Community Sch Corp	Clayton
36	16.0	Garrett-Keyser-Butler Com	Garrett
36	16.0	North Gibson School Corp	Princeton
36	16.0	North Lawrence Com Schools	Bedford
36	16.0	South Vermillion Com Sch Corp	Clinton
40	16.1	School City of Mishawaka	Mishawaka
41	16.3	Griffith Public Schools	Griffith
41	16.3	Indianapolis Public Schools	Indianapolis
41	16.3	Monroe County Com Sch Corp	Bloomington
41	16.3	North Adams Community Schools	Decatur
45	16.5	Greencastle Community Sch Corp	Greencastle
45	16.5	M S D Wayne Township	Indianapolis
45	16.5	Michigan City Area Schools	Michigan City
45	16.5	South Harrison Com Schools	Corydon
49	16.6	Jennings County School Corp	North Vernon
49	16.6	Logansport Community Sch Corp	Logansport
49	16.6	Plymouth Community School Corp	Plymouth
49	16.6	Wa-Nee Community Schools	Nappanee
53	16.7	Batesville Community Schl Corp	Batesville
53	16.7	M S D Steuben County	Angola
55	16.8	Greenwood Community Sch Corp	Greenwood
55	16.8	Huntington County Com Sch Corp	Huntington
55	16.8	Tipton Community School Corp	Tipton
55	16.8	Warsaw Community Schools	Warsaw
55	16.8	Western School Corp	Russiaville
60	16.9	East Allen County Schools	New Haven
60	16.9	Mt Vernon Community Sch Corp	Fortville
60	16.9	North Montgomery Com Sch Corp	Crawfordsville
63	17.0	Jay School Corporation	Portland
63	17.0	Vincennes Community Sch Corp	Vincennes
65	17.1	Brownstown Cnt Com Sch Corp	Brownstown
66	17.2	Community Schools of Frankfort	Frankfort
66	17.2	Goshen Community Schools	Goshen
66	17.2	Tippecanoe Valley School Corp	Akron
69	17.3	Danville Community School Corp	Danville
69	17.3	Lakeland School Corporation	Lagrange
69	17.3	Northern Wells Com Schools	Ossian
72	17.4	Kankakee Valley School Corp	Wheatfield
72	17.4	M S D Martinsville Schools	Martinsville
72	17.4	Scott County SD 2	Scottsburg
72	17.4	Switzerland County School Corp	Vevay
72	17.4	West Noble School Corporation	Ligonier
77	17.5	Brownsburg Community Sch Corp	Brownsburg
77	17.5	Fayette County School Corp	Connersville
77	17.5	Middlebury Community Schools	Middlebury
77	17.5	Southwest Dubois County Sch Corp	Huntingburg
81	17.6	Salem Community Schools	Salem
82	17.7	M S D Washington Twp	Indianapolis
83	17.8	Knox Community School Corp	Knox
83	17.8	Whitley County Cons Schools	Columbia City
85	17.9	Delaware Community School Corp	Muncie
85	17.9	M S D Southwest Allen County Schls	Fort Wayne
85	17.9	Manchester Community Schools	N Manchester
85	17.9	Peru Community Schools	Peru
85	17.9	Richland-Bean Blossom C S C	Ellettsville
90	18.0	Rochester Community Sch Corp	Rochester
90	18.0	Warrick County School Corp	Boonville
92	18.1	Madison Consolidated Schools	Madison
92	18.1	Muncie Community Schools	Muncie
94	18.3	Fairfield Community Schools	Goshen
94	18.3	Greensburg Community Schools	Greensburg
94	18.3	Laporte Community School Corp	Laporte
94	18.3	Wawasee Community School Corp	Syracuse
94	18.3	West Clark Community Schools	Sellersburg
99	18.4	Franklin County Com Sch Corp	Brookville
99	18.4	Vigo County School Corp	Terre Haute
101	18.5	Hamilton Heights School Corp	Arcadia
101	18.5	North West Hendricks Schools	Lizton
103	18.6	Lebanon Community School Corp	Lebanon
103	18.6	Shelbyville Central Schools	Shelbyville
103	18.6	Tell City-Troy Twp School Corp	Tell City
106	18.7	School Town of Highland	Highland
107	18.8	Anderson Community School Corp	Anderson
107	18.8	Bartholomew Con School Corp	Columbus
107	18.8	Elkhart Community Schools	Elkhart
107	18.8	Greenfield-Central Com Schools	Greenfield
107	18.8	Portage Township Schools	Portage
112	18.9	Kokomo School Corporation	Kokomo
113	19.0	Mitchell Community Schools	Mitchell
113	19.0	School City of Hammond	Hammond
115	19.1	Duneland School Corporation	Chesterton
115	19.1	M S D Decatur Township	Indianapolis
115	19.1	Northwest Allen County Schools	Fort Wayne
118	19.2	M S D Lawrence Township	Indianapolis
118	19.2	School City of East Chicago	East Chicago
118	19.2	Western Boone County Com SD	Thorntown
121	19.3	Merrillville Community School	Merrillville
121	19.3	Zionsville Community Schools	Zionsville
123	19.4	Yorktown Community Schools	Yorktown
124	19.6	Carmel Clay Schools	Carmel
124	19.6	Maconaquah School Corp	Bunker Hill
126	19.7	Baugo Community Schools	Elkhart
126	19.7	Lake Ridge New Tech Schools	Gary
128	19.8	New Albany-Floyd County Con Sch	New Albany
128	19.8	Penn-Harris-Madison Sch Corp	Mishawaka
128	19.8	South Dearborn Com School Corp	Aurora
128	19.8	Valparaiso Community Schools	Valparaiso
132	19.9	Dekalb County Ctl United SD	Waterloo
132	19.9	North Harrison Com School Corp	Ramsey
132	19.9	Washington Com Schools	Washington
135	20.1	Plainfield Community Sch Corp	Plainfield
136	20.2	Fort Wayne Community Schools	Fort Wayne
136	20.2	Perry Township Schools	Indianapolis
138	20.3	M S D Pike Township	Indianapolis
139	20.4	Tippecanoe School Corp	Lafayette
140	20.5	Crown Point Community Sch Corp	Crown Point
141	20.6	Franklin Community School Corp	Franklin
141	20.6	New Prairie United School Corp	New Carlisle
141	20.6	Westfield-Washington Schools	Westfield
144	20.7	Seymour Community Schools	Seymour
144	20.7	Sunman-Dearborn Com Sch Corp	Saint Leon
146	20.8	Crawford County Com School Corp	Marengo
147	20.9	Greater Clark County Schools	Jeffersonville
147	20.9	Hamilton Southeastern Schools	Fishers
147	20.9	Lake Central School Corp	Saint John
147	20.9	South Madison Com Sch Corp	Pendleton
151	21.0	Elwood Community School Corp	Elwood
152	21.1	Center Grove Com Sch Corp	Greenwood
153	21.2	Franklin Township Com Sch Corp	Indianapolis
153	21.2	Mooresville Con School Corp	Mooresville
155	21.3	Greater Jasper Con Schs	Jasper
155	21.3	Noblesville Schools	Noblesville
157	21.4	Blackford County Schools	Hartford City
158	21.7	Avon Community School Corp	Avon
159	21.8	Spencer-Owen Community Schools	Spencer
160	22.1	Hanover Community School Corp	Cedar Lake
161	22.2	Southern Hancock Co Com Sch Corp	New Palestine
162	22.3	Tri-Creek School Corporation	Lowell
163	22.6	Clark-Pleasant Com School Corp	Whiteland
164	22.8	M S D Warren Township	Indianapolis
165	23.1	School City of Hobart	Hobart
166	23.6	Marion Community Schools	Marion
166	23.6	School Town of Munster	Munster
166	23.6	Whitko Community School Corp	Larwill
169	24.2	South Bend Community Sch Corp	South Bend
170	24.6	Gary Community School Corp	Gary
171	43.2	Indiana Connections Academy	Indianapolis
172	106.7	Hoosier Acad Virtual Charter	Indianapolis

Student/Librarian Ratio

(number of students per librarian)

Rank	Number	District Name	City
1	304.0	Randolph Central School Corp	Winchester
2	368.2	Rush County Schools	Rushville
3	383.6	Greencastle Community Sch Corp	Greencastle
4	413.2	North Spencer County Sch Corp	Lincoln City
5	527.6	M S D Steuben County	Angola
6	545.7	Michigan City Area Schools	Michigan City
7	552.3	Hamilton Heights School Corp	Arcadia
8	575.3	Elwood Community School Corp	Elwood
9	581.7	Southwest Dubois County Sch Corp	Huntingburg
10	597.0	Crawfordsville Com Schools	Crawfordsville
11	608.0	Lawrenceburg Com School Corp	Lawrenceburg
12	609.5	Vigo County School Corp	Terre Haute
13	612.7	Logansport Community Sch Corp	Logansport
14	620.9	Richmond Community Schools	Richmond
15	635.6	Duneland School Corporation	Chesterton
16	653.3	Salem Community Schools	Salem
17	668.3	Franklin County Com Sch Corp	Brookville
18	671.0	Batesville Community Schl Corp	Batesville
19	720.0	West Lafayette Com School Corp	West Lafayette
20	735.3	Monroe County Com Sch Corp	Bloomington
21	736.4	Muncie Community Schools	Muncie
22	736.7	North Harrison Com School Corp	Ramsey
23	756.7	West Clark Community Schools	Sellersburg
24	776.8	Anderson Community School Corp	Anderson
25	786.8	Community Schools of Frankfort	Frankfort
26	789.5	Centerville-Abington Com Schs	Centerville
27	801.7	West Noble School Corporation	Ligonier
28	804.2	Westfield-Washington Schools	Westfield
29	824.0	Nineveh-Hensley-Jackson United	Trafalgar
30	828.6	Gary Community School Corp	Gary
31	829.4	M S D Pike Township	Indianapolis
32	830.4	School City of Hammond	Hammond
33	830.8	Indianapolis Public Schools	Indianapolis
34	852.2	Plainfield Community Sch Corp	Plainfield
35	887.0	School Town of Speedway	Speedway
36	909.0	South Vermillion Com Sch Corp	Clinton
37	937.3	Noblesville Schools	Noblesville
38	948.2	Avon Community School Corp	Avon
39	965.8	M S D Washington Twp	Indianapolis
40	972.0	Tippecanoe Valley School Corp	Akron
41	1,005.7	M S D Wayne Township	Indianapolis
42	1,013.9	Hamilton Southeastern Schools	Fishers
43	1,032.0	Franklin Township Com Sch Corp	Indianapolis
44	1,061.2	Carmel Clay Schools	Carmel
45	1,062.5	North Gibson School Corp	Princeton
46	1,064.5	M S D Mount Vernon	Mount Vernon
47	1,066.6	Lafayette School Corporation	Lafayette
48	1,165.3	Jay School Corporation	Portland

Note: This section only includes districts with 1,500 or more students; All categories are ranked from high to low

49	1,181.5	Twin Lakes School Corp	Monticello
50	1,189.0	Greensburg Community Schools	Greensburg
51	1,231.5	Danville Community School Corp	Danville
52	1,257.8	M S D Martinsville Schools	Martinsville
52	1,257.8	North Lawrence Com Schools	Bedford
54	1,341.8	Laporte Community School Corp	Laporte
55	1,397.3	Clay Community Schools	Brazil
56	1,519.0	Manchester Community Schools	N Manchester
57	1,528.0	North Putnam Community Schools	Bainbridge
58	1,566.0	Brownstown Cnt Com Sch Corp	Brownstown
59	1,573.5	M S D Decatur Township	Indianapolis
60	1,592.0	School Town of Highland	Highland
61	1,596.6	M S D Warren Township	Indianapolis
62	1,606.0	Switzerland County School Corp	Vevay
63	1,610.0	Mill Creek Community Sch Corp	Clayton
64	1,612.0	Wawasee Community School Corp	Syracuse
65	1,628.0	Rensselaer Central School Corp	Rensselaer
66	1,656.0	Tell City-Troy Twp School Corp	Tell City
67	1,659.0	South Harrison Com Schools	Corydon
68	1,674.0	John Glenn School Corporation	Walkerton
69	1,678.0	Western Boone County Com SD	Thorntown
70	1,685.8	Merrillville Community School	Merrillville
71	1,702.0	Southwest School Corp	Sullivan
72	1,735.0	Garrett-Keyser-Butler Com	Garrett
73	1,748.0	Tipton Community School Corp	Tipton
74	1,764.0	Mitchell Community Schools	Mitchell
75	1,774.3	M S D Southwest Allen County Schls	Fort Wayne
76	1,775.4	Fort Wayne Community Schools	Fort Wayne
77	1,812.0	South Montgomery Com Sch Corp	New Market
78	1,816.0	Rochester Community Sch Corp	Rochester
79	1,820.0	Fayette County School Corp	Connersville
80	1,824.0	North West Hendricks Schools	Lizton
81	1,847.5	Dekalb County Ctl United SD	Waterloo
82	1,857.0	Benton Community School Corp	Fowler
83	1,865.0	Blackford County Schools	Hartford City
84	1,882.5	M S D Lawrence Township	Indianapolis
85	1,887.0	School Town of Munster	Munster
86	1,915.0	Baugo Community Schools	Elkhart
87	1,921.0	Decatur County Com Schools	Greensburg
88	1,941.0	Pike County School Corp	Petersburg
89	1,972.0	North Adams Community Schools	Decatur
90	1,973.0	M S D Wabash County Schools	Wabash
91	1,994.0	Lake Ridge New Tech Schools	Gary
92	2,022.0	Mississinewa Community Schl Corp	Gas City
93	2,026.0	Fairfield Community Schools	Goshen
94	2,119.3	Brownsburg Community Sch Corp	Brownsburg
95	2,146.5	South Madison Com Sch Corp	Pendleton
96	2,148.0	Hanover Community School Corp	Cedar Lake
97	2,151.0	Westview School Corporation	Topeka
98	2,177.6	Greater Clark County Schools	Jeffersonville
99	2,181.0	Beech Grove City Schools	Beech Grove
100	2,200.0	Peru Community Schools	Peru
101	2,268.8	East Allen County Schools	New Haven
102	2,317.2	Bartholomew Con School Corp	Columbus
103	2,324.8	Elkhart Community Schools	Elkhart
104	2,329.0	Northern Wells Com Schools	Ossian
105	2,341.3	Warsaw Community Schools	Warsaw
106	2,391.0	Maconaquah School Corp	Bunker Hill
107	2,440.0	Delaware Community School Corp	Muncie
108	2,459.0	Franklin Community School Corp	Franklin
109	2,491.5	Penn-Harris-Madison Sch Corp	Mishawaka
110	2,500.0	Western School Corp	Russiaville
111	2,531.5	Warrick County School Corp	Boonville
112	2,543.0	New Prairie United School Corp	New Carlisle
113	2,553.8	South Bend Community Sch Corp	South Bend
114	2,572.0	Washington Com Schools	Washington
115	2,597.0	Portage Township Schools	Portage
116	2,708.0	South Dearborn Com School Corp	Aurora
117	2,735.5	Huntington County Com Sch Corp	Huntington
118	2,778.0	Richland-Bean Blossom C S C	Ellettsville
119	2,784.0	New Albany-Floyd County Con Sch	New Albany
120	2,791.0	Vincennes Community Sch Corp	Vincennes
121	2,858.0	Wa-Nee Community Schools	Nappanee
122	2,863.0	Madison Consolidated Schools	Madison
123	3,069.0	Southern Hancock Co Com Sch Corp	New Palestine
124	3,147.0	Valparaiso Community Schools	Valparaiso
125	3,224.0	Concord Community Schools	Elkhart
126	3,305.0	Tri-Creek School Corporation	Lowell
127	3,340.5	Clark-Pleasant Com School Corp	Whiteland
128	3,364.0	Goshen Community Schools	Goshen
129	3,415.0	Mt Vernon Community Sch Corp	Fortville
130	3,467.0	Kankakee Valley School Corp	Wheatfield
131	3,477.0	Whitley County Cons Schools	Columbia City
132	3,519.0	New Castle Community Sch Corp	New Castle
133	3,529.5	Kokomo School Corporation	Kokomo
134	3,547.0	Plymouth Community School Corp	Plymouth
135	3,557.0	Lebanon Community School Corp	Lebanon
136	3,918.8	Perry Township Schools	Indianapolis
137	4,014.0	Sunman-Dearborn Com Sch Corp	Saint Leon
138	4,028.0	Shelbyville Central Schools	Shelbyville
139	4,107.0	School City of Hobart	Hobart
140	4,242.0	Mooresville Con School Corp	Mooresville
141	4,340.0	Middlebury Community Schools	Middlebury
142	4,369.3	Tippecanoe School Corp	Lafayette
143	4,444.0	Jennings County School Corp	North Vernon
144	4,576.0	East Porter County School Corp	Kouts
145	4,699.0	Greenfield-Central Com Schools	Greenfield
146	4,707.0	School City of Mishawaka	Mishawaka
147	4,961.0	School City of East Chicago	East Chicago
148	5,706.3	Evansville Vanderburgh Sch Corp	Evansville
149	6,725.0	Zionsville Community Schools	Zionsville
150	7,227.0	Northwest Allen County Schools	Fort Wayne
151	7,963.0	Center Grove Com Sch Corp	Greenwood
152	8,369.0	Crown Point Community Sch Corp	Crown Point
153	9,606.0	Lake Central School Corp	Saint John
n/a	n/a	Brown County School Corporation	Nashville
n/a	n/a	Crawford County Com School Corp	Marengo
n/a	n/a	East Noble School Corp	Kendallville
n/a	n/a	Frankton-Lapel Community Schools	Anderson
n/a	n/a	Greater Jasper Con Schs	Jasper
n/a	n/a	Greenwood Community Sch Corp	Greenwood
n/a	n/a	Griffith Public Schools	Griffith
n/a	n/a	Hoosier Acad Virtual Charter	Indianapolis
n/a	n/a	Indiana Connections Academy	Indianapolis
n/a	n/a	Knox Community School Corp	Knox
n/a	n/a	Lakeland School Corporation	Lagrange
n/a	n/a	Marion Community Schools	Marion
n/a	n/a	North Montgomery Com Sch Corp	Crawfordsville
n/a	n/a	Scott County SD 2	Scottsburg
n/a	n/a	Seymour Community Schools	Seymour
n/a	n/a	South Gibson School Corp	Fort Branch
n/a	n/a	Spencer-Owen Community Schools	Spencer
n/a	n/a	Whitko Community School Corp	Larwill
n/a	n/a	Yorktown Community Schools	Yorktown

Student/Counselor Ratio

(number of students per counselor)

Rank	Number	District Name	City
1	265.3	School Town of Highland	Highland
2	276.2	Muncie Community Schools	Muncie
3	280.0	Salem Community Schools	Salem
4	281.7	North Adams Community Schools	Decatur
5	289.2	Garrett-Keyser-Butler Com	Garrett
6	301.1	Dekalb County Ctl United SD	Waterloo
7	302.0	South Montgomery Com Sch Corp	New Market
8	304.0	Randolph Central School Corp	Winchester
9	305.6	North Putnam Community Schools	Bainbridge
10	317.4	Scott County SD 2	Scottsburg
11	317.6	Wa-Nee Community Schools	Nappanee
12	323.5	Pike County School Corp	Petersburg
13	324.8	North Montgomery Com Sch Corp	Crawfordsville
14	328.5	Northwest Allen County Schools	Fort Wayne
15	328.8	M S D Wabash County Schools	Wabash
16	330.9	Fayette County School Corp	Connersville
17	331.0	East Noble School Corp	Kendallville
18	331.5	Gary Community School Corp	Gary
19	333.5	Michigan City Area Schools	Michigan City
20	337.7	Fairfield Community Schools	Goshen
21	339.1	New Prairie United School Corp	New Carlisle
22	340.7	M S D Southwest Allen County Schls	Fort Wayne
23	341.8	Jennings County School Corp	North Vernon
24	341.9	Huntington County Com Sch Corp	Huntington
25	348.0	New Albany-Floyd County Con Sch	New Albany
26	348.6	Delaware Community School Corp	Muncie
27	349.0	Southwest Dubois County Sch Corp	Huntingburg
28	349.7	Community Schools of Frankfort	Frankfort
29	351.9	Danville Community School Corp	Danville
30	352.8	Mitchell Community Schools	Mitchell
31	363.6	South Vermillion Com Sch Corp	Clinton
32	364.8	Lawrenceburg Com School Corp	Lawrenceburg
32	364.8	North West Hendricks Schools	Lizton
34	368.4	South Gibson School Corp	Fort Branch
35	368.7	South Harrison Com Schools	Corydon
36	372.7	Laporte Community School Corp	Laporte
37	373.6	Zionsville Community Schools	Zionsville
38	374.1	Middlebury Community Schools	Middlebury
39	376.9	M S D Steuben County	Angola
40	381.3	Duneland School Corporation	Chesterton
41	386.3	Whitley County Cons Schools	Columbia City
42	388.2	Northern Wells Com Schools	Ossian
43	388.8	Tippecanoe Valley School Corp	Akron
44	389.6	Portage Township Schools	Portage
45	391.5	Brownstown Cnt Com Sch Corp	Brownstown
46	394.8	Concord Community Schools	Elkhart
47	395.2	Lebanon Community School Corp	Lebanon
48	396.3	Greensburg Community Schools	Greensburg
49	398.0	Crawfordsville Com Schools	Crawfordsville
50	398.8	Lake Ridge New Tech Schools	Gary
51	400.8	West Noble School Corporation	Ligonier
52	407.0	Rensselaer Central School Corp	Rensselaer
53	409.8	Franklin Community School Corp	Franklin
54	415.2	Greencastle Community Sch Corp	Greencastle
55	420.5	Goshen Community Schools	Goshen
56	434.0	Manchester Community Schools	N Manchester
57	435.3	Vigo County School Corp	Terre Haute
58	437.4	Brown County School Corporation	Nashville
59	438.9	Evansville Vanderburgh Sch Corp	Evansville
60	440.0	Peru Community Schools	Peru
61	442.0	North Harrison Com School Corp	Ramsey
62	443.5	School Town of Speedway	Speedway
63	446.0	Sunman-Dearborn Com Sch Corp	Saint Leon
64	446.6	M S D Pike Township	Indianapolis
65	448.8	Yorktown Community Schools	Yorktown
66	452.5	Lafayette School Corporation	Lafayette
67	456.3	School City of Hobart	Hobart
68	457.4	Lake Central School Corp	Saint John
69	468.6	Noblesville Schools	Noblesville
70	468.8	Frankton-Lapel Community Schools	Anderson
71	472.3	Knox Community School Corp	Knox
72	472.6	Twin Lakes School Corp	Monticello
73	474.1	Avon Community School Corp	Avon
74	477.2	Clark-Pleasant Com School Corp	Whiteland
74	477.2	Madison Consolidated Schools	Madison
76	479.3	Westfield-Washington Schools	Westfield
77	483.9	Hamilton Southeastern Schools	Fishers
78	495.3	Kankakee Valley School Corp	Wheatfield
79	500.0	Western School Corp	Russiaville
80	502.7	New Castle Community Sch Corp	New Castle
81	503.7	Bartholomew Con School Corp	Columbus
82	504.4	West Clark Community Schools	Sellersburg
83	518.7	Merrillville Community School	Merrillville
84	520.1	Brownsburg Community Sch Corp	Brownsburg
85	524.0	Clay Community Schools	Brazil
86	531.2	M S D Washington Twp	Indianapolis
87	534.6	Franklin County Com Sch Corp	Brookville
88	536.5	Elkhart Community Schools	Elkhart
89	536.6	South Madison Com Sch Corp	Pendleton
90	536.7	Mill Creek Community Sch Corp	Clayton
91	537.3	Wawasee Community School Corp	Syracuse
92	540.0	West Lafayette Com School Corp	West Lafayette
93	545.3	Beech Grove City Schools	Beech Grove
94	546.4	Franklin Township Com Sch Corp	Indianapolis
95	549.3	Nineveh-Hensley-Jackson United	Trafalgar
96	555.6	Richland-Bean Blossom C S C	Ellettsville
97	558.0	John Glenn School Corporation	Walkerton
97	558.0	Lakeland School Corporation	Lagrange
99	558.8	Richmond Community Schools	Richmond
100	567.2	East Allen County Schools	New Haven
101	569.9	Tippecanoe School Corp	Lafayette
102	575.3	Elwood Community School Corp	Elwood
103	580.5	Monroe County Com Sch Corp	Bloomington
104	585.3	Griffith Public Schools	Griffith
105	588.4	School City of Mishawaka	Mishawaka
106	597.8	Maconaquah School Corp	Bunker Hill
107	604.9	Greater Clark County Schools	Jeffersonville
108	605.3	Rochester Community Sch Corp	Rochester
109	615.1	Indianapolis Public Schools	Indianapolis
110	617.5	Indiana Connections Academy	Indianapolis
111	619.0	Benton Community School Corp	Fowler
112	621.7	Blackford County Schools	Hartford City
113	622.9	Penn-Harris-Madison Sch Corp	Mishawaka
114	628.9	M S D Martinsville Schools	Martinsville
114	628.9	North Lawrence Com Schools	Bedford
116	629.0	School Town of Munster	Munster
117	636.7	Carmel Clay Schools	Carmel
118	638.3	Baugo Community Schools	Elkhart
119	640.3	Decatur County Com Schools	Greensburg
120	671.0	Batesville Community Schl Corp	Batesville
121	677.0	South Dearborn Com School Corp	Aurora
122	683.0	Mt Vernon Community Sch Corp	Fortville
123	688.7	North Spencer County Sch Corp	Lincoln City
124	699.3	Valparaiso Community Schools	Valparaiso
125	699.6	M S D Wayne Township	Indianapolis

Note: This section only includes districts with 1,500 or more students; All categories are ranked from high to low

126	700.5	M S D Lawrence Township	Indianapolis
127	702.8	Greenwood Community Sch Corp	Greenwood
128	707.0	Mooresville Con School Corp	Mooresville
129	708.3	North Gibson School Corp	Princeton
130	709.7	M S D Mount Vernon	Mount Vernon
131	723.9	Center Grove Com Sch Corp	Greenwood
132	730.4	Plainfield Community Sch Corp	Plainfield
133	736.3	Hamilton Heights School Corp	Arcadia
133	736.3	Rush County Schools	Rushville
135	745.7	School City of Hammond	Hammond
136	751.4	M S D Warren Township	Indianapolis
137	767.3	Southern Hancock Co Com Sch Corp	New Palestine
138	778.9	Warrick County School Corp	Boonville
139	783.2	Greenfield-Central Com Schools	Greenfield
140	789.5	Centerville-Abington Com Schs	Centerville
141	801.5	Whitko Community School Corp	Larwill
142	803.0	Switzerland County School Corp	Vevay
143	805.6	Shelbyville Central Schools	Shelbyville
144	817.2	South Bend Community Sch Corp	South Bend
145	826.3	Tri-Creek School Corporation	Lowell
146	828.0	Tell City-Troy Twp School Corp	Tell City
147	851.0	Southwest School Corp	Sullivan
148	857.8	Logansport Community Sch Corp	Logansport
149	874.0	Jay School Corporation	Portland
149	874.0	Tipton Community School Corp	Tipton
151	878.0	Warsaw Community Schools	Warsaw
152	882.4	Kokomo School Corporation	Kokomo
153	886.8	Plymouth Community School Corp	Plymouth
154	899.1	M S D Decatur Township	Indianapolis
155	914.6	Fort Wayne Community Schools	Fort Wayne
156	916.3	Spencer-Owen Community Schools	Spencer
157	979.7	Perry Township Schools	Indianapolis
158	992.2	School City of East Chicago	East Chicago
159	1,011.0	Mississinewa Community Schl Corp	Gas City
160	1,068.1	Anderson Community School Corp	Anderson
161	1,070.0	Greater Jasper Con Schs	Jasper
162	1,075.5	Westview School Corporation	Topeka
163	1,144.0	East Porter County School Corp	Kouts
164	1,195.6	Crown Point Community Sch Corp	Crown Point
165	1,286.0	Washington Com Schools	Washington
166	1,395.5	Vincennes Community Sch Corp	Vincennes
167	1,605.0	Marion Community Schools	Marion
168	1,678.0	Western Boone County Com SD	Thorntown
169	2,103.8	Crawford County Com School Corp	Marengo
170	2,148.0	Hanover Community School Corp	Cedar Lake
171	2,366.0	Seymour Community Schools	Seymour
n/a	n/a	Hoosier Acad Virtual Charter	Indianapolis

Current Expenditures per Student

Rank	Dollars	District Name	City
1	13,324	School City of East Chicago	East Chicago
2	12,827	Marion Community Schools	Marion
3	12,396	Indianapolis Public Schools	Indianapolis
4	12,249	School City of Mishawaka	Mishawaka
5	12,021	Gary Community School Corp	Gary
6	11,926	Muncie Community Schools	Muncie
7	11,833	M S D Mount Vernon	Mount Vernon
8	11,581	Logansport Community Sch Corp	Logansport
9	11,561	Lafayette School Corporation	Lafayette
10	11,522	Michigan City Area Schools	Michigan City
11	11,398	Goshen Community Schools	Goshen
12	11,367	M S D Wayne Township	Indianapolis
13	11,351	School Town of Speedway	Speedway
14	11,265	Anderson Community School Corp	Anderson
15	11,202	School City of Hammond	Hammond
16	11,172	North Adams Community Schools	Decatur
17	11,156	M S D Wabash County Schools	Wabash
18	11,082	Brown County School Corporation	Nashville
19	10,933	New Castle Community Sch Corp	New Castle
20	10,802	Crawfordsville Com Schools	Crawfordsville
21	10,723	Dekalb County Ctl United SD	Waterloo
22	10,636	Pike County School Corp	Petersburg
23	10,531	Jay School Corporation	Portland
24	10,522	M S D Pike Township	Indianapolis
25	10,447	Fayette County School Corp	Connersville
26	10,421	South Bend Community Sch Corp	South Bend
27	10,401	M S D Washington Twp	Indianapolis
28	10,335	Lebanon Community School Corp	Lebanon
29	10,219	Evansville Vanderburgh Sch Corp	Evansville
30	10,180	Fort Wayne Community Schools	Fort Wayne
31	10,173	Laporte Community School Corp	Laporte
32	10,162	Elkhart Community Schools	Elkhart
33	10,083	Benton Community School Corp	Fowler
34	10,042	Whitko Community School Corp	Larwill
35	10,039	Jennings County School Corp	North Vernon
36	10,023	Crawford County Com School Corp	Marengo
37	10,004	North Gibson School Corp	Princeton
38	9,992	West Lafayette Com School Corp	West Lafayette
39	9,936	Kokomo School Corporation	Kokomo
40	9,912	North Lawrence Com Schools	Bedford
41	9,853	Tippecanoe Valley School Corp	Akron
42	9,847	Knox Community School Corp	Knox
43	9,818	Westview School Corporation	Topeka
44	9,806	Richmond Community Schools	Richmond
45	9,751	M S D Lawrence Township	Indianapolis
46	9,724	Greater Jasper Con Schs	Jasper
47	9,720	Wawasee Community School Corp	Syracuse
48	9,709	M S D Warren Township	Indianapolis
49	9,670	South Vermillion Com Sch Corp	Clinton
50	9,660	Lake Ridge New Tech Schools	Gary
51	9,650	Switzerland County School Corp	Vevay
52	9,642	South Harrison Com Schools	Corydon
53	9,620	Randolph Central School Corp	Winchester
54	9,615	West Noble School Corporation	Ligonier
55	9,595	Warsaw Community Schools	Warsaw
56	9,588	Rush County Schools	Rushville
57	9,574	Monroe County Com Sch Corp	Bloomington
58	9,532	South Montgomery Com Sch Corp	New Market
59	9,529	Noblesville Schools	Noblesville
60	9,502	M S D Martinsville Schools	Martinsville
61	9,500	New Albany-Floyd County Con Sch	New Albany
62	9,492	North Montgomery Com Sch Corp	Crawfordsville
63	9,490	Spencer-Owen Community Schools	Spencer
64	9,480	Elwood Community School Corp	Elwood
65	9,452	M S D Decatur Township	Indianapolis
66	9,425	Lakeland School Corporation	Lagrange
67	9,406	Community Schools of Frankfort	Frankfort
68	9,372	Merrillville Community School	Merrillville
69	9,361	Greater Clark County Schools	Jeffersonville
70	9,332	Perry Township Schools	Indianapolis
71	9,316	Greensburg Community Schools	Greensburg
72	9,315	Bartholomew Con School Corp	Columbus
73	9,285	Garrett-Keyser-Butler Com	Garrett
74	9,271	East Allen County Schools	New Haven
75	9,247	Southwest Dubois County Sch Corp	Huntingburg
76	9,244	Carmel Clay Schools	Carmel
77	9,241	Blackford County Schools	Hartford City
78	9,240	Tell City-Troy Twp School Corp	Tell City
79	9,235	Westfield-Washington Schools	Westfield
80	9,206	Southwest School Corp	Sullivan
81	9,183	North Harrison Com School Corp	Ramsey
82	9,146	Clark-Pleasant Com School Corp	Whiteland
83	9,145	Clay Community Schools	Brazil
84	9,136	Plymouth Community School Corp	Plymouth
85	9,109	Beech Grove City Schools	Beech Grove
86	9,083	Decatur County Com Schools	Greensburg
87	9,067	Mitchell Community Schools	Mitchell
88	9,048	Greencastle Community Sch Corp	Greencastle
89	8,984	Brownstown Cnt Com Sch Corp	Brownstown
90	8,943	Vincennes Community Sch Corp	Vincennes
91	8,937	Western School Corp	Russiaville
92	8,901	Seymour Community Schools	Seymour
93	8,897	Scott County SD 2	Scottsburg
94	8,891	Tri-Creek School Corporation	Lowell
95	8,885	Huntington County Com Sch Corp	Huntington
96	8,857	Rochester Community Sch Corp	Rochester
97	8,845	Zionsville Community Schools	Zionsville
98	8,844	South Dearborn Com School Corp	Aurora
99	8,796	M S D Southwest Allen County Schls	Fort Wayne
100	8,785	South Gibson School Corp	Fort Branch
101	8,761	Franklin County Com Sch Corp	Brookville
102	8,748	Sunman-Dearborn Com Sch Corp	Saint Leon
102	8,748	Vigo County School Corp	Terre Haute
104	8,712	Warrick County School Corp	Boonville
105	8,685	Lawrenceburg Com School Corp	Lawrenceburg
106	8,668	Hamilton Heights School Corp	Arcadia
107	8,652	John Glenn School Corporation	Walkerton
108	8,621	Maconaquah School Corp	Bunker Hill
109	8,609	Batesville Community Schl Corp	Batesville
110	8,605	Lake Central School Corp	Saint John
111	8,601	Western Boone County Com SD	Thorntown
112	8,590	Greenwood Community Sch Corp	Greenwood
113	8,587	North Putnam Community Schools	Bainbridge
114	8,585	M S D Steuben County	Angola
115	8,579	Peru Community Schools	Peru
116	8,576	Salem Community Schools	Salem
117	8,569	Rensselaer Central School Corp	Rensselaer
118	8,557	Richland-Bean Blossom C S C	Ellettsville
119	8,522	East Noble School Corp	Kendallville
120	8,494	Wa-Nee Community Schools	Nappanee
121	8,460	School Town of Highland	Highland
122	8,454	North West Hendricks Schools	Lizton
123	8,430	Whitley County Cons Schools	Columbia City
124	8,396	Danville Community School Corp	Danville
125	8,370	Twin Lakes School Corp	Monticello
126	8,314	Delaware Community School Corp	Muncie
127	8,295	Manchester Community Schools	N Manchester
128	8,289	Avon Community School Corp	Avon
129	8,278	Mississinewa Community Schl Corp	Gas City
130	8,262	Baugo Community Schools	Elkhart
131	8,244	Franklin Community School Corp	Franklin
132	8,221	Northern Wells Com Schools	Ossian
133	8,215	Duneland School Corporation	Chesterton
134	8,197	Tippecanoe School Corp	Lafayette
135	8,191	School Town of Munster	Munster
136	8,181	Centerville-Abington Com Schs	Centerville
137	8,180	Shelbyville Central Schools	Shelbyville
138	8,117	Hamilton Southeastern Schools	Fishers
139	8,108	Franklin Township Com Sch Corp	Indianapolis
140	8,089	Crown Point Community Sch Corp	Crown Point
141	8,071	Plainfield Community Sch Corp	Plainfield
142	8,068	Fairfield Community Schools	Goshen
143	8,039	North Spencer County Sch Corp	Lincoln City
144	8,005	Nineveh-Hensley-Jackson United	Trafalgar
145	7,996	Madison Consolidated Schools	Madison
146	7,968	Center Grove Com Sch Corp	Greenwood
147	7,957	Brownsburg Community Sch Corp	Brownsburg
148	7,921	Kankakee Valley School Corp	Wheatfield
149	7,891	Middlebury Community Schools	Middlebury
150	7,886	New Prairie United School Corp	New Carlisle
151	7,875	Tipton Community School Corp	Tipton
152	7,809	School City of Hobart	Hobart
153	7,801	Concord Community Schools	Elkhart
154	7,796	Griffith Public Schools	Griffith
155	7,792	Portage Township Schools	Portage
156	7,754	Mill Creek Community Sch Corp	Clayton
157	7,752	East Porter County School Corp	Kouts
158	7,696	Mooresville Con School Corp	Mooresville
159	7,593	Hanover Community School Corp	Cedar Lake
160	7,588	West Clark Community Schools	Sellersburg
161	7,576	Greenfield-Central Com Schools	Greenfield
162	7,532	Penn-Harris-Madison Sch Corp	Mishawaka
163	7,526	Washington Com Schools	Washington
164	7,520	Northwest Allen County Schools	Fort Wayne
165	7,503	Valparaiso Community Schools	Valparaiso
166	7,385	Frankton-Lapel Community Schools	Anderson
167	7,219	Mt Vernon Community Sch Corp	Fortville
168	7,184	Southern Hancock Co Com Sch Corp	New Palestine
169	7,144	Yorktown Community Schools	Yorktown
170	7,002	South Madison Com Sch Corp	Pendleton
171	4,814	Hoosier Acad Virtual Charter	Indianapolis
172	4,763	Indiana Connections Academy	Indianapolis

Total General Revenue per Student

Rank	Dollars	District Name	City
1	15,770	Merrillville Community School	Merrillville
2	15,494	Indianapolis Public Schools	Indianapolis
3	15,061	Greater Jasper Con Schs	Jasper
3	15,061	School City of East Chicago	East Chicago
5	14,924	M S D Mount Vernon	Mount Vernon
6	14,884	Lafayette School Corporation	Lafayette
7	14,742	M S D Wayne Township	Indianapolis
8	14,707	Logansport Community Sch Corp	Logansport
9	14,676	Anderson Community School Corp	Anderson
10	14,646	Goshen Community Schools	Goshen
11	14,620	Michigan City Area Schools	Michigan City
12	14,436	Muncie Community Schools	Muncie
13	14,336	M S D Wabash County Schools	Wabash
14	14,295	Marion Community Schools	Marion
15	14,188	South Bend Community Sch Corp	South Bend
16	14,179	School City of Hammond	Hammond
17	14,175	Crawfordsville Com Schools	Crawfordsville
18	14,164	North Adams Community Schools	Decatur
19	14,151	South Montgomery Com Sch Corp	New Market
20	13,976	Laporte Community School Corp	Laporte
21	13,763	School City of Mishawaka	Mishawaka
22	13,738	North Gibson School Corp	Princeton
23	13,686	Whitko Community School Corp	Larwill
24	13,607	Lebanon Community School Corp	Lebanon
25	13,491	Lake Ridge New Tech Schools	Gary
26	13,449	Noblesville Schools	Noblesville

Note: This section only includes districts with 1,500 or more students; All categories are ranked from high to low

27	13,298	West Lafayette Com School Corp	West Lafayette
28	13,288	New Castle Community Sch Corp	New Castle
29	13,262	M S D Lawrence Township	Indianapolis
30	13,179	M S D Warren Township	Indianapolis
31	13,162	Westfield-Washington Schools	Westfield
32	13,115	Southwest School Corp	Sullivan
33	13,029	Gary Community School Corp	Gary
34	13,019	M S D Pike Township	Indianapolis
35	13,017	Wawasee Community School Corp	Syracuse
36	12,974	Southwest Dubois County Sch Corp	Huntingburg
37	12,939	Tippecanoe Valley School Corp	Akron
38	12,825	Brownstown Cnt Com Sch Corp	Brownstown
39	12,824	Zionsville Community Schools	Zionsville
40	12,821	Elkhart Community Schools	Elkhart
41	12,735	School Town of Speedway	Speedway
42	12,713	New Prairie United School Corp	New Carlisle
43	12,658	M S D Washington Twp	Indianapolis
44	12,621	Fayette County School Corp	Connersville
45	12,619	Benton Community School Corp	Fowler
46	12,593	Pike County School Corp	Petersburg
47	12,589	Lake Central School Corp	Saint John
48	12,507	M S D Decatur Township	Indianapolis
49	12,482	South Harrison Com Schools	Corydon
50	12,441	Warsaw Community Schools	Warsaw
51	12,409	Jay School Corporation	Portland
52	12,376	Duneland School Corporation	Chesterton
53	12,367	Brown County School Corporation	Nashville
54	12,350	Beech Grove City Schools	Beech Grove
55	12,336	Bartholomew Con School Corp	Columbus
56	12,304	Vincennes Community Sch Corp	Vincennes
57	12,277	North Montgomery Com Sch Corp	Crawfordsville
58	12,276	Clark-Pleasant Com School Corp	Whiteland
58	12,276	Franklin Community School Corp	Franklin
60	12,264	Monroe County Com Sch Corp	Bloomington
61	12,249	Perry Township Schools	Indianapolis
62	12,190	New Albany-Floyd County Con Sch	New Albany
63	12,146	Evansville Vanderburgh Sch Corp	Evansville
64	12,143	Plymouth Community School Corp	Plymouth
65	12,105	Tri-Creek School Corporation	Lowell
66	12,103	North West Hendricks Schools	Lizton
67	12,098	North Lawrence Com Schools	Bedford
68	12,049	Madison Consolidated Schools	Madison
69	12,016	Westview School Corporation	Topeka
70	12,015	Kokomo School Corporation	Kokomo
71	11,994	Dekalb County Ctl United SD	Waterloo
72	11,959	Mt Vernon Community Sch Corp	Fortville
73	11,951	Crown Point Community Sch Corp	Crown Point
74	11,915	Fort Wayne Community Schools	Fort Wayne
75	11,899	Tell City-Troy Twp School Corp	Tell City
76	11,897	Greater Clark County Schools	Jeffersonville
77	11,891	Tippecanoe School Corp	Lafayette
78	11,808	Wa-Nee Community Schools	Nappanee
79	11,776	Sunman-Dearborn Com Sch Corp	Saint Leon
80	11,765	Carmel Clay Schools	Carmel
81	11,763	School Town of Munster	Munster
82	11,725	M S D Steuben County	Angola
83	11,706	Greencastle Community Sch Corp	Greencastle
84	11,636	Danville Community School Corp	Danville
85	11,631	Crawford County Com School Corp	Marengo
86	11,629	Plainfield Community Sch Corp	Plainfield
87	11,625	Elwood Community School Corp	Elwood
88	11,610	Switzerland County School Corp	Vevay
89	11,605	Hamilton Heights School Corp	Arcadia
90	11,586	Maconaquah School Corp	Bunker Hill
91	11,584	Penn-Harris-Madison Sch Corp	Mishawaka
92	11,537	Garrett-Keyser-Butler Com	Garrett
93	11,518	Avon Community School Corp	Avon
94	11,513	West Noble School Corporation	Ligonier
95	11,494	East Noble School Corp	Kendallville
96	11,470	Greensburg Community Schools	Greensburg
97	11,469	Greenfield-Central Com Schools	Greenfield
98	11,441	Knox Community School Corp	Knox
99	11,432	Concord Community Schools	Elkhart
100	11,419	Randolph Central School Corp	Winchester
101	11,407	South Vermillion Com Sch Corp	Clinton
102	11,384	South Dearborn Com School Corp	Aurora
103	11,379	Western Boone County Com SD	Thorntown
104	11,365	Lawrenceburg Com School Corp	Lawrenceburg
105	11,359	South Gibson School Corp	Fort Branch
106	11,341	Franklin Township Com Sch Corp	Indianapolis
107	11,333	Community Schools of Frankfort	Frankfort
108	11,284	Seymour Community Schools	Seymour
109	11,242	Richmond Community Schools	Richmond
110	11,240	Rush County Schools	Rushville
111	11,235	Decatur County Com Schools	Greensburg
112	11,221	Hanover Community School Corp	Cedar Lake
113	11,211	Baugo Community Schools	Elkhart
114	11,205	Mitchell Community Schools	Mitchell
115	11,187	M S D Southwest Allen County Schls	Fort Wayne
116	11,182	Brownsburg Community Sch Corp	Brownsburg
117	11,162	Richland-Bean Blossom C S C	Ellettsville
118	11,153	Blackford County Schools	Hartford City
119	11,148	North Putnam Community Schools	Bainbridge
120	11,121	Lakeland School Corporation	Lagrange
121	11,108	Griffith Public Schools	Griffith
122	11,088	Spencer-Owen Community Schools	Spencer
123	11,053	Twin Lakes School Corp	Monticello
124	11,028	Rensselaer Central School Corp	Rensselaer
125	11,024	East Porter County School Corp	Kouts
126	11,020	Shelbyville Central Schools	Shelbyville
127	11,000	Jennings County School Corp	North Vernon
128	10,931	North Spencer County Sch Corp	Lincoln City
129	10,873	Salem Community Schools	Salem
130	10,872	Middlebury Community Schools	Middlebury
131	10,863	Kankakee Valley School Corp	Wheatfield
132	10,861	East Allen County Schools	New Haven
133	10,841	Franklin County Com Sch Corp	Brookville
134	10,834	School City of Hobart	Hobart
135	10,800	Rochester Community Sch Corp	Rochester
136	10,799	Valparaiso Community Schools	Valparaiso
137	10,780	North Harrison Com School Corp	Ramsey
138	10,770	Western School Corp	Russiaville
139	10,752	Portage Township Schools	Portage
140	10,746	Washington Com Schools	Washington
141	10,711	Clay Community Schools	Brazil
142	10,703	Mill Creek Community Sch Corp	Clayton
143	10,682	Whitley County Cons Schools	Columbia City
144	10,667	Scott County SD 2	Scottsburg
145	10,649	Center Grove Com Sch Corp	Greenwood
146	10,625	West Clark Community Schools	Sellersburg
147	10,614	School Town of Highland	Highland
148	10,596	Northern Wells Com Schools	Ossian
149	10,586	Huntington County Com Sch Corp	Huntington
150	10,545	John Glenn School Corporation	Walkerton
151	10,524	Nineveh-Hensley-Jackson United	Trafalgar
152	10,498	Fairfield Community Schools	Goshen
153	10,494	Delaware Community School Corp	Muncie
154	10,470	Vigo County School Corp	Terre Haute
155	10,465	Warrick County School Corp	Boonville
156	10,462	Northwest Allen County Schools	Fort Wayne
157	10,438	Hamilton Southeastern Schools	Fishers
158	10,406	M S D Martinsville Schools	Martinsville
159	10,382	Greenwood Community Sch Corp	Greenwood
160	10,353	Manchester Community Schools	N Manchester
161	10,326	Peru Community Schools	Peru
162	10,258	Batesville Community Schl Corp	Batesville
163	10,218	Southern Hancock Co Com Sch Corp	New Palestine
164	10,176	Frankton-Lapel Community Schools	Anderson
165	10,095	Tipton Community School Corp	Tipton
166	10,056	Mississinewa Community Schl Corp	Gas City
167	10,055	Centerville-Abington Com Schs	Centerville
168	9,996	South Madison Com Sch Corp	Pendleton
169	9,776	Mooresville Con School Corp	Mooresville
170	9,537	Yorktown Community Schools	Yorktown
171	6,263	Indiana Connections Academy	Indianapolis
172	5,346	Hoosier Acad Virtual Charter	Indianapolis

Long-Term Debt per Student (end of FY)

Rank	Dollars	District Name	City
1	34,941	Mt Vernon Community Sch Corp	Fortville
2	30,375	Zionsville Community Schools	Zionsville
3	29,906	Hanover Community School Corp	Cedar Lake
4	29,903	North West Hendricks Schools	Lizton
5	25,995	Avon Community School Corp	Avon
6	25,825	Franklin Community School Corp	Franklin
7	25,771	Franklin Township Com Sch Corp	Indianapolis
8	23,722	Westfield-Washington Schools	Westfield
9	22,901	Plainfield Community Sch Corp	Plainfield
10	22,765	Lake Central School Corp	Saint John
11	21,902	Tri-Creek School Corporation	Lowell
12	21,828	M S D Decatur Township	Indianapolis
13	21,439	Danville Community School Corp	Danville
14	21,382	North Gibson School Corp	Princeton
15	21,132	Whitko Community School Corp	Larwill
16	21,099	Brownsburg Community Sch Corp	Brownsburg
17	20,922	Crawfordsville Com Schools	Crawfordsville
18	20,763	Merrillville Community School	Merrillville
19	19,855	Indianapolis Public Schools	Indianapolis
20	19,320	Western Boone County Com SD	Thorntown
21	19,275	Clark-Pleasant Com School Corp	Whiteland
22	19,199	Greenfield-Central Com Schools	Greenfield
23	19,188	School Town of Munster	Munster
24	17,836	School City of Hobart	Hobart
25	17,271	Anderson Community School Corp	Anderson
26	16,761	Southwest Dubois County Sch Corp	Huntingburg
27	16,650	Middlebury Community Schools	Middlebury
28	16,590	Northwest Allen County Schools	Fort Wayne
29	16,530	M S D Wayne Township	Indianapolis
30	16,402	Sunman-Dearborn Com Sch Corp	Saint Leon
31	16,401	Griffith Public Schools	Griffith
32	16,354	Noblesville Schools	Noblesville
33	15,909	Crown Point Community Sch Corp	Crown Point
34	15,716	Hamilton Southeastern Schools	Fishers
35	15,682	Kankakee Valley School Corp	Wheatfield
36	15,557	Lake Ridge New Tech Schools	Gary
37	15,215	Tell City-Troy Twp School Corp	Tell City
38	15,153	Lebanon Community School Corp	Lebanon
39	15,073	South Gibson School Corp	Fort Branch
40	14,975	East Porter County School Corp	Kouts
41	14,302	Michigan City Area Schools	Michigan City
42	14,274	Frankton-Lapel Community Schools	Anderson
43	14,253	South Madison Com Sch Corp	Pendleton
44	14,242	West Clark Community Schools	Sellersburg
45	14,241	Concord Community Schools	Elkhart
46	13,581	Garrett-Keyser-Butler Com	Garrett
47	13,562	New Prairie United School Corp	New Carlisle
48	13,496	Southwest School Corp	Sullivan
49	13,375	Baugo Community Schools	Elkhart
50	13,349	Center Grove Com Sch Corp	Greenwood
51	13,332	Mill Creek Community Sch Corp	Clayton
52	13,263	Jay School Corporation	Portland
53	13,230	Mitchell Community Schools	Mitchell
54	13,200	South Harrison Com Schools	Corydon
55	12,993	Bartholomew Con School Corp	Columbus
56	12,886	Beech Grove City Schools	Beech Grove
57	12,816	South Dearborn Com School Corp	Aurora
58	12,638	Southern Hancock Co Com Sch Corp	New Palestine
59	12,474	School City of Hammond	Hammond
60	12,326	Northern Wells Com Schools	Ossian
61	12,183	Wawasee Community School Corp	Syracuse
62	12,096	Vincennes Community Sch Corp	Vincennes
63	11,822	Rensselaer Central School Corp	Rensselaer
64	11,807	Warsaw Community Schools	Warsaw
65	11,670	Richland-Bean Blossom C S C	Ellettsville
66	11,629	New Albany-Floyd County Con Sch	New Albany
67	11,539	Fairfield Community Schools	Goshen
68	11,509	Shelbyville Central Schools	Shelbyville
69	11,406	Community Schools of Frankfort	Frankfort
70	10,789	South Montgomery Com Sch Corp	New Market
71	10,378	Benton Community School Corp	Fowler
72	10,049	Greater Clark County Schools	Jeffersonville
73	10,015	Peru Community Schools	Peru
74	9,991	School Town of Highland	Highland
75	9,973	M S D Lawrence Township	Indianapolis
76	9,786	Washington Com Schools	Washington
77	9,785	Valparaiso Community Schools	Valparaiso
78	9,609	Randolph Central School Corp	Winchester
79	9,603	Spencer-Owen Community Schools	Spencer
80	9,310	Goshen Community Schools	Goshen
80	9,310	Tipton Community School Corp	Tipton
82	9,164	North Harrison Com School Corp	Ramsey
83	9,046	Greater Jasper Con Schs	Jasper
84	9,010	Muncie Community Schools	Muncie
85	9,006	Greencastle Community Sch Corp	Greencastle
86	8,977	Decatur County Com Schools	Greensburg
87	8,876	Elwood Community School Corp	Elwood
88	8,778	Rush County Schools	Rushville
89	8,770	Gary Community School Corp	Gary
90	8,748	John Glenn School Corporation	Walkerton
91	8,741	Carmel Clay Schools	Carmel
92	8,716	North Lawrence Com Schools	Bedford
93	8,671	Batesville Community Schl Corp	Batesville
94	8,667	Western School Corp	Russiaville
95	8,635	Monroe County Com Sch Corp	Bloomington
96	8,592	Whitley County Cons Schools	Columbia City
97	8,532	West Lafayette Com School Corp	West Lafayette
98	8,518	Crawford County Com School Corp	Marengo
99	8,460	School City of Mishawaka	Mishawaka
100	8,457	Perry Township Schools	Indianapolis
101	8,390	Pike County School Corp	Petersburg
102	8,229	North Adams Community Schools	Decatur
103	8,181	South Bend Community Sch Corp	South Bend
104	8,170	Tippecanoe School Corp	Lafayette

Note: This section only includes districts with 1,500 or more students; All categories are ranked from high to low

105	8,164	Plymouth Community School Corp	Plymouth
106	8,057	Brown County School Corporation	Nashville
107	7,961	Evansville Vanderburgh Sch Corp	Evansville
108	7,647	M S D Steuben County	Angola
109	7,571	Greensburg Community Schools	Greensburg
110	7,524	Duneland School Corporation	Chesterton
111	7,459	Lawrenceburg Com School Corp	Lawrenceburg
112	7,436	Manchester Community Schools	N Manchester
113	7,430	Tippecanoe Valley School Corp	Akron
114	7,426	Salem Community Schools	Salem
115	7,382	Westview School Corporation	Topeka
116	7,340	M S D Southwest Allen County Schls	Fort Wayne
117	7,245	Portage Township Schools	Portage
118	7,217	West Noble School Corporation	Ligonier
119	7,077	Elkhart Community Schools	Elkhart
120	6,763	North Putnam Community Schools	Bainbridge
121	6,665	Nineveh-Hensley-Jackson United	Trafalgar
122	6,552	Centerville-Abington Com Schs	Centerville
123	6,463	Knox Community School Corp	Knox
124	6,393	North Spencer County Sch Corp	Lincoln City
125	6,376	Lafayette School Corporation	Lafayette
126	6,298	Hamilton Heights School Corp	Arcadia
127	6,266	Logansport Community Sch Corp	Logansport
128	6,151	Brownstown Cnt Com Sch Corp	Brownstown
129	6,144	M S D Warren Township	Indianapolis
130	6,107	Marion Community Schools	Marion
131	6,000	Rochester Community Sch Corp	Rochester
132	5,612	Scott County SD 2	Scottsburg
133	5,589	Lakeland School Corporation	Lagrange
134	5,305	M S D Mount Vernon	Mount Vernon
135	5,275	Huntington County Com Sch Corp	Huntington
136	5,269	Penn-Harris-Madison Sch Corp	Mishawaka
137	5,107	East Noble School Corp	Kendallville
138	5,095	Fort Wayne Community Schools	Fort Wayne
139	5,025	Blackford County Schools	Hartford City
140	4,998	Wa-Nee Community Schools	Nappanee
141	4,987	Seymour Community Schools	Seymour
142	4,983	North Montgomery Com Sch Corp	Crawfordsville
143	4,925	Madison Consolidated Schools	Madison
144	4,878	Jennings County School Corp	North Vernon
145	4,747	Yorktown Community Schools	Yorktown
146	4,728	Dekalb County Ctl United SD	Waterloo
147	4,691	Mississinewa Community Schl Corp	Gas City
148	4,690	M S D Washington Twp	Indianapolis
149	4,659	Kokomo School Corporation	Kokomo
150	4,591	M S D Wabash County Schools	Wabash
151	4,501	Delaware Community School Corp	Muncie
152	4,443	Franklin County Com Sch Corp	Brookville
153	4,384	East Allen County Schools	New Haven
154	4,371	Mooresville Con School Corp	Mooresville
155	3,950	Greenwood Community Sch Corp	Greenwood
156	3,944	Fayette County School Corp	Connersville
157	3,749	Clay Community Schools	Brazil
158	3,610	Maconaquah School Corp	Bunker Hill
159	3,353	South Vermillion Com Sch Corp	Clinton
160	3,338	Laporte Community School Corp	Laporte
161	3,297	Twin Lakes School Corp	Monticello
162	3,296	Vigo County School Corp	Terre Haute
163	3,105	Richmond Community Schools	Richmond
164	3,009	School City of East Chicago	East Chicago
165	2,807	M S D Pike Township	Indianapolis
166	2,748	Switzerland County School Corp	Vevay
167	2,137	Warrick County School Corp	Boonville
168	2,012	New Castle Community Sch Corp	New Castle
169	1,188	M S D Martinsville Schools	Martinsville
170	539	School Town of Speedway	Speedway
171	0	Hoosier Acad Virtual Charter	Indianapolis
171	0	Indiana Connections Academy	Indianapolis

Note: This section only includes districts with 1,500 or more students; All categories are ranked from high to low

The Nation's Report Card

2017 Mathematics State Snapshot Report
Indiana • Grade 4 • Public Schools

Overall Results

- In 2017, the average score of fourth-grade students in Indiana was 247. This was higher than the average score of 239 for public school students in the nation.
- The average score for students in Indiana in 2017 (247) was not significantly different from their average score in 2015 (248) and was higher than their average score in 2000 (233).
- The percentage of students in Indiana who performed at or above the NAEP *Proficient* level was 48 percent in 2017. This percentage was not significantly different from that in 2015 (50 percent) and was greater than that in 2000 (30 percent).
- The percentage of students in Indiana who performed at or above the NAEP *Basic* level was 86 percent in 2017. This percentage was smaller than that in 2015 (89 percent) and was greater than that in 2000 (77 percent).

Achievement-Level Percentages and Average Score Results

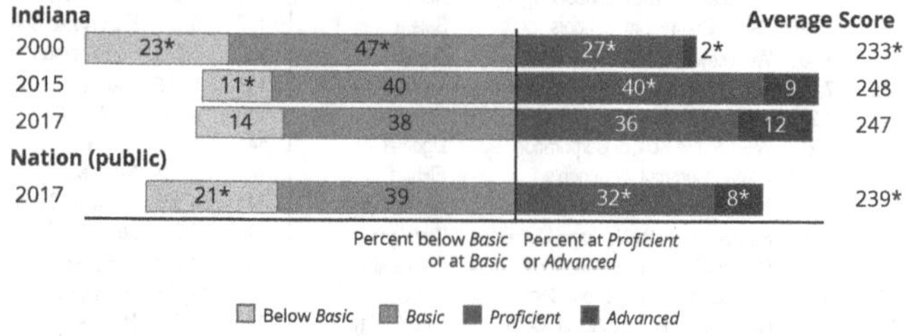

* Significantly different ($p < .05$) from state's results in 2017. Significance tests were performed using unrounded numbers.
NOTE: Detail may not sum to totals because of rounding.

Compare the Average Score in 2017 to Other States/Jurisdictions

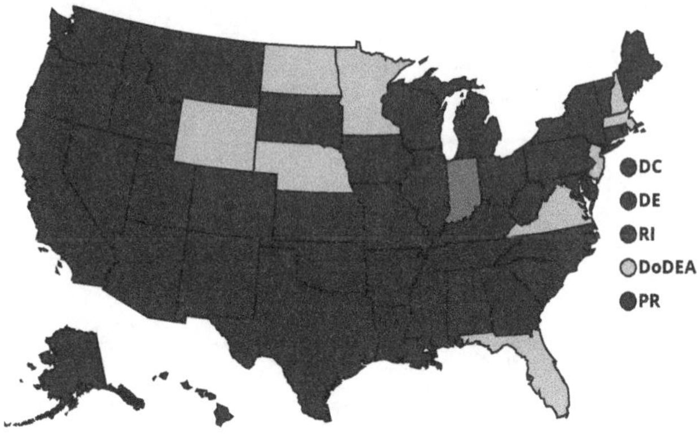

In 2017, the average score in Indiana (247) was
- lower than those in 0 states/jurisdictions
- higher than those in 42 states/jurisdictions
- not significantly different from those in 10 states/jurisdictions

DoDEA = Department of Defense Education Activity (overseas and domestic schools)

Average Scores for State/Jurisdiction and Nation (public)

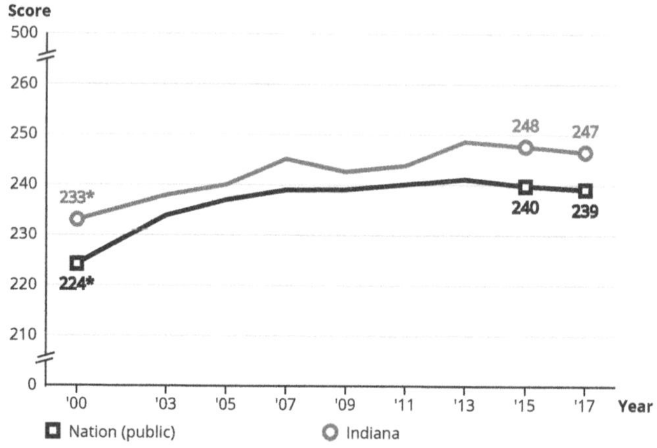

* Significantly different ($p < .05$) from 2017. Significance tests were performed using unrounded numbers.

Results for Student Groups in 2017

Reporting Groups	Percentage of students	Avg. score	Percentage at or above *Basic*	Percentage at or above *Proficient*	Percentage at *Advanced*
Race/Ethnicity					
White	70	251	90	54	14
Black	11	226	67	21	2
Hispanic	11	234	75	32	4
Asian	2	‡	‡	‡	‡
American Indian/Alaska Native	#	‡	‡	‡	‡
Native Hawaiian/Pacific Islander	#	‡	‡	‡	‡
Two or more races	5	244	82	41	12
Gender					
Male	51	248	86	50	15
Female	49	245	86	46	10
National School Lunch Program					
Eligible	49	235	78	34	5
Not eligible	49	258	93	63	20

Rounds to zero.
‡ Reporting standards not met.
NOTE: Detail may not sum to totals because of rounding, and because the "Information not available" category for the National School Lunch Program, which provides free/reduced-price lunches, is not displayed. Black includes African American and Hispanic includes Latino. Race categories exclude Hispanic origin.

Score Gaps for Student Groups

- In 2017, Black students had an average score that was 25 points lower than that for White students. This performance gap was not significantly different from that in 2000 (25 points).
- In 2017, Hispanic students had an average score that was 17 points lower than that for White students. Data are not reported for Hispanic students in 2000, because reporting standards were not met.
- In 2017, male students in Indiana had an average score that was not significantly different from that for female students.
- In 2017, students who were eligible for free/reduced-price school lunch, an indicator of low family income, had an average score that was 22 points lower than that for students who were not eligible. This performance gap was not significantly different from that in 2000 (20 points).

ies NATIONAL CENTER FOR EDUCATION STATISTICS
Institute of Education Sciences

NOTE: The NAEP mathematics scale ranges from 0 to 500. Statistical comparisons are calculated on the basis of unrounded scale scores or percentages. Read more about how to interpret NAEP results from the mathematics assessment at https://nces.ed.gov/nationsreportcard/mathematics/interpret_results.aspx.
SOURCE: U.S. Department of Education, Institute of Education Sciences, National Center for Education Statistics, National Assessment of Educational Progress (NAEP), various years, 2000-2017 Mathematics Assessments.

The Nation's Report Card

2017 Mathematics State Snapshot Report
Indiana • Grade 8 • Public Schools

Overall Results

- In 2017, the average score of eighth-grade students in Indiana was 288. This was higher than the average score of 282 for public school students in the nation.
- The average score for students in Indiana in 2017 (288) was not significantly different from their average score in 2015 (287) and was higher than their average score in 2000 (281).
- The percentage of students in Indiana who performed at or above the NAEP *Proficient* level was 38 percent in 2017. This percentage was not significantly different from that in 2015 (39 percent) and was greater than that in 2000 (29 percent).
- The percentage of students in Indiana who performed at or above the NAEP *Basic* level was 75 percent in 2017. This percentage was not significantly different from that in 2015 (77 percent) and in 2000 (74 percent).

Achievement-Level Percentages and Average Score Results

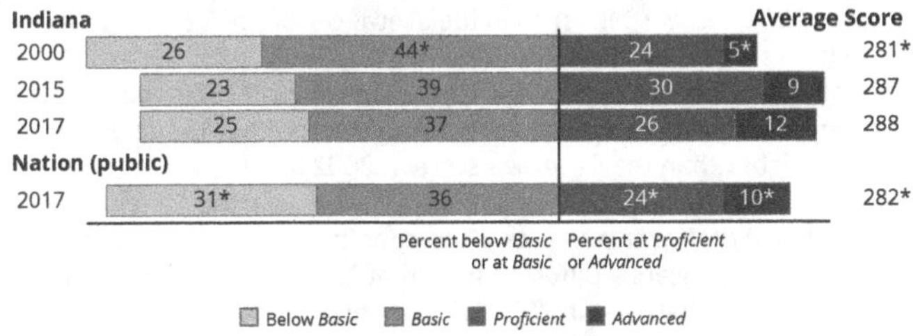

* Significantly different ($p < .05$) from state's results in 2017. Significance tests were performed using unrounded numbers.
NOTE: Detail may not sum to totals because of rounding.

Compare the Average Score in 2017 to Other States/Jurisdictions

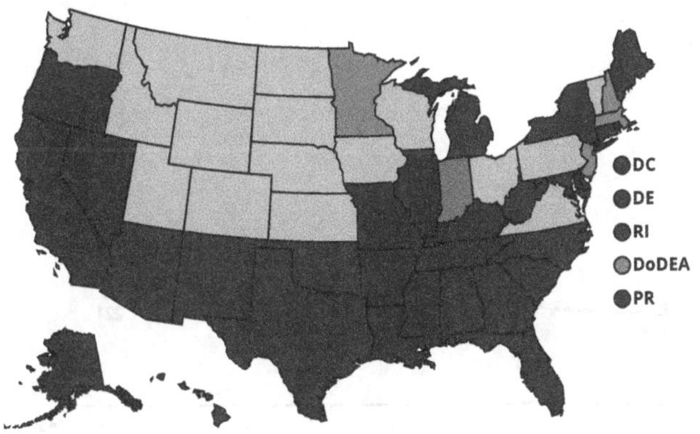

In 2017, the average score in Indiana (288) was
- lower than those in 5 states/jurisdictions
- higher than those in 31 states/jurisdictions
- not significantly different from those in 16 states/jurisdictions

DoDEA = Department of Defense Education Activity (overseas and domestic schools)

Average Scores for State/Jurisdiction and Nation (public)

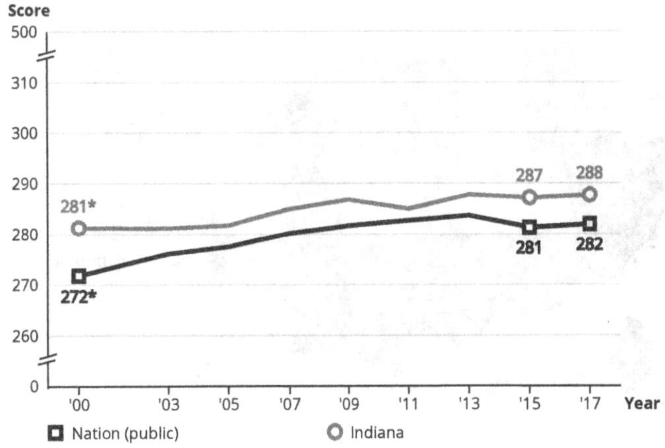

* Significantly different ($p < .05$) from 2017. Significance tests were performed using unrounded numbers.

Results for Student Groups in 2017

Reporting Groups	Percentage of students	Avg. score	Percentage at or above *Basic*	Percentage at or above *Proficient*	Percentage at *Advanced*
Race/Ethnicity					
White	73	292	79	42	13
Black	10	270	58	19	4
Hispanic	10	276	63	26	6
Asian	3	‡	‡	‡	‡
American Indian/Alaska Native	#	‡	‡	‡	‡
Native Hawaiian/Pacific Islander	#	‡	‡	‡	‡
Two or more races	4	276	60	29	6
Gender					
Male	50	287	74	38	12
Female	50	288	75	38	12
National School Lunch Program					
Eligible	43	273	62	22	4
Not eligible	56	299	85	50	18

\# Rounds to zero.
‡ Reporting standards not met.
NOTE: Detail may not sum to totals because of rounding, and because the "Information not available" category for the National School Lunch Program, which provides free/reduced-price lunches, is not displayed. Black includes African American and Hispanic includes Latino. Race categories exclude Hispanic origin.

Score Gaps for Student Groups

- In 2017, Black students had an average score that was 21 points lower than that for White students. This performance gap was not significantly different from that in 2000 (29 points).
- In 2017, Hispanic students had an average score that was 16 points lower than that for White students. Data are not reported for Hispanic students in 2000, because reporting standards were not met.
- In 2017, male students in Indiana had an average score that was not significantly different from that for female students.
- In 2017, students who were eligible for free/reduced-price school lunch, an indicator of low family income, had an average score that was 26 points lower than that for students who were not eligible. This performance gap was wider than that in 2000 (17 points).

Education

ies NATIONAL CENTER FOR EDUCATION STATISTICS Institute of Education Sciences

NOTE: The NAEP mathematics scale ranges from 0 to 500. Statistical comparisons are calculated on the basis of unrounded scale scores or percentages. Read more about how to interpret NAEP results from the mathematics assessment at https://nces.ed.gov/nationsreportcard/mathematics/interpret_results.aspx.
SOURCE: U.S. Department of Education, Institute of Education Sciences, National Center for Education Statistics, National Assessment of Educational Progress (NAEP), various years, 2000-2017 Mathematics Assessments.

The Nation's Report Card

2017 Reading State Snapshot Report
Indiana • Grade 4 • Public Schools

Overall Results

- In 2017, the average score of fourth-grade students in Indiana was 226. This was higher than the average score of 221 for public school students in the nation.
- The average score for students in Indiana in 2017 (226) was not significantly different from their average score in 2015 (227) and was higher than their average score in 2002 (222).
- The percentage of students in Indiana who performed at or above the NAEP *Proficient* level was 41 percent in 2017. This percentage was not significantly different from that in 2015 (40 percent) and was greater than that in 2002 (33 percent).
- The percentage of students in Indiana who performed at or above the NAEP *Basic* level was 73 percent in 2017. This percentage was not significantly different from that in 2015 (75 percent) and was greater than that in 2002 (68 percent).

Achievement-Level Percentages and Average Score Results

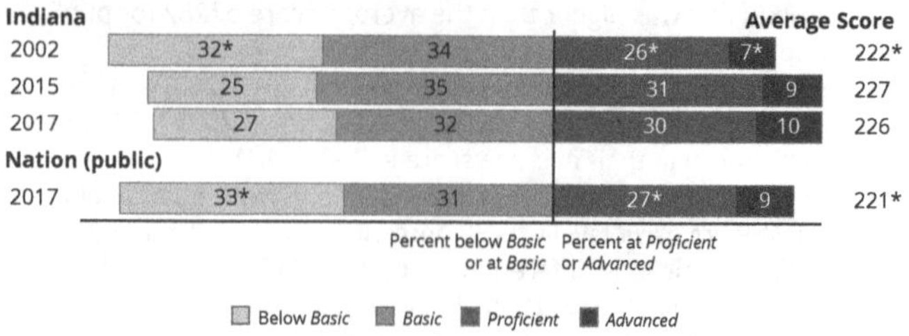

* Significantly different ($p < .05$) from state's results in 2017. Significance tests were performed using unrounded numbers.
NOTE: Detail may not sum to totals because of rounding.

Compare the Average Score in 2017 to Other States/Jurisdictions

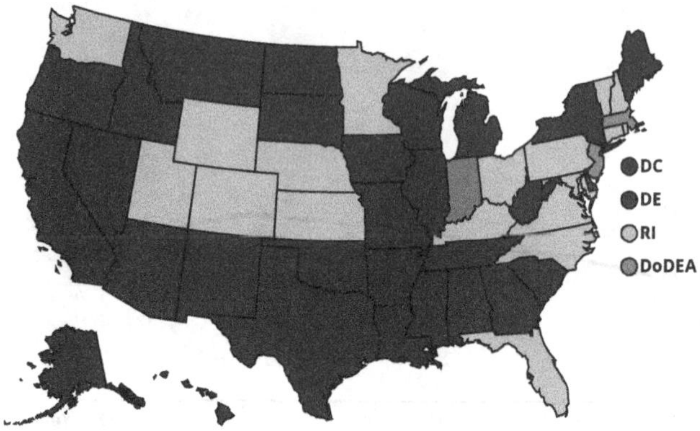

In 2017, the average score in Indiana (226) was
- lower than those in 3 states/jurisdictions
- higher than those in 30 states/jurisdictions
- not significantly different from those in 18 states/jurisdictions

DoDEA = Department of Defense Education Activity (overseas and domestic schools)

Average Scores for State/Jurisdiction and Nation (public)

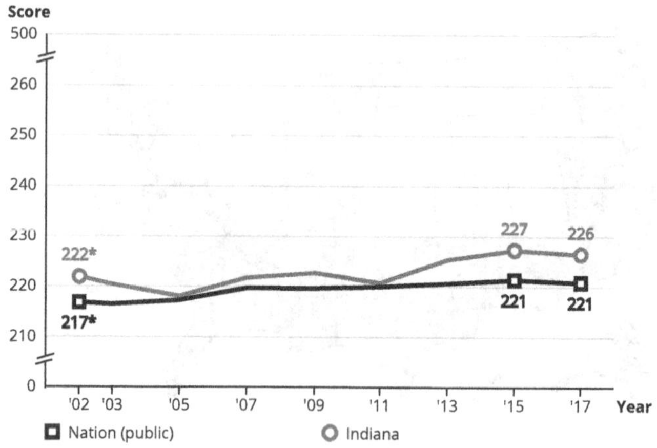

* Significantly different ($p < .05$) from 2017. Significance tests were performed using unrounded numbers.

Results for Student Groups in 2017

Reporting Groups	Percentage of students	Avg. score	Percentage at or above *Basic*	Percentage at or above *Proficient*	Percentage at *Advanced*
Race/Ethnicity					
White	71	231	78	46	12
Black	11	210	55	21	3
Hispanic	11	214	60	28	4
Asian	2	‡	‡	‡	‡
American Indian/Alaska Native	#	‡	‡	‡	‡
Native Hawaiian/Pacific Islander	#	‡	‡	‡	‡
Two or more races	4	224	70	39	11
Gender					
Male	51	224	70	39	9
Female	49	229	76	43	11
National School Lunch Program					
Eligible	49	215	62	28	4
Not eligible	49	238	84	54	17

\# Rounds to zero.
‡ Reporting standards not met.
NOTE: Detail may not sum to totals because of rounding, and because the "Information not available" category for the National School Lunch Program, which provides free/reduced-price lunches, is not displayed. Black includes African American and Hispanic includes Latino. Race categories exclude Hispanic origin.

Score Gaps for Student Groups

- In 2017, Black students had an average score that was 21 points lower than that for White students. This performance gap was not significantly different from that in 2002 (23 points).
- In 2017, Hispanic students had an average score that was 17 points lower than that for White students. This performance gap was not significantly different from that in 2002 (9 points).
- In 2017, female students in Indiana had an average score that was higher than that for male students by 5 points.
- In 2017, students who were eligible for free/reduced-price school lunch, an indicator of low family income, had an average score that was 23 points lower than that for students who were not eligible. This performance gap was not significantly different from that in 2002 (23 points).

ies NATIONAL CENTER FOR EDUCATION STATISTICS
Institute of Education Sciences

NOTE: The NAEP reading scale ranges from 0 to 500. Statistical comparisons are calculated on the basis of unrounded scale scores or percentages. Read more about how to interpret NAEP results from the reading assessment at https://nces.ed.gov/nationsreportcard/reading/interpret_results.aspx.
SOURCE: U.S. Department of Education, Institute of Education Sciences, National Center for Education Statistics, National Assessment of Educational Progress (NAEP), various years, 2002-2017 Reading Assessments.

The Nation's Report Card

2017 Reading State Snapshot Report
Indiana • Grade 8 • Public Schools

Overall Results

- In 2017, the average score of eighth-grade students in Indiana was 272. This was higher than the average score of 265 for public school students in the nation.
- The average score for students in Indiana in 2017 (272) was higher than their average score in 2015 (268) and in 2002 (265).
- The percentage of students in Indiana who performed at or above the NAEP *Proficient* level was 41 percent in 2017. This percentage was not significantly different from that in 2015 (37 percent) and was greater than that in 2002 (32 percent).
- The percentage of students in Indiana who performed at or above the NAEP *Basic* level was 82 percent in 2017. This percentage was not significantly different from that in 2015 (80 percent) and was greater than that in 2002 (77 percent).

Achievement-Level Percentages and Average Score Results

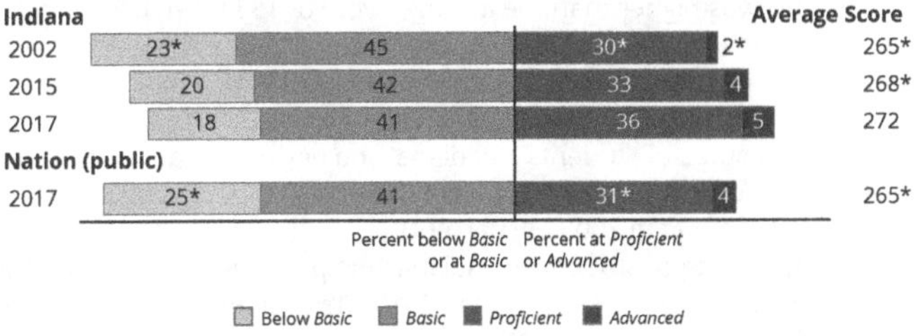

* Significantly different ($p < .05$) from state's results in 2017. Significance tests were performed using unrounded numbers.
NOTE: Detail may not sum to totals because of rounding.

Compare the Average Score in 2017 to Other States/Jurisdictions

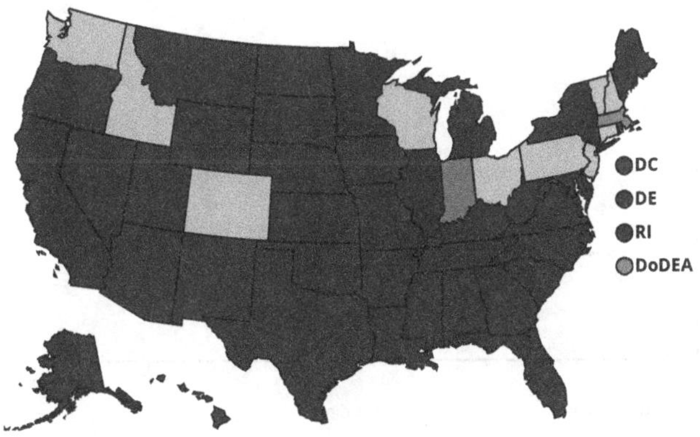

In 2017, the average score in Indiana (272) was
- lower than those in 2 states/jurisdictions
- higher than those in 39 states/jurisdictions
- not significantly different from those in 10 states/jurisdictions

DoDEA = Department of Defense Education Activity (overseas and domestic schools)

Average Scores for State/Jurisdiction and Nation (public)

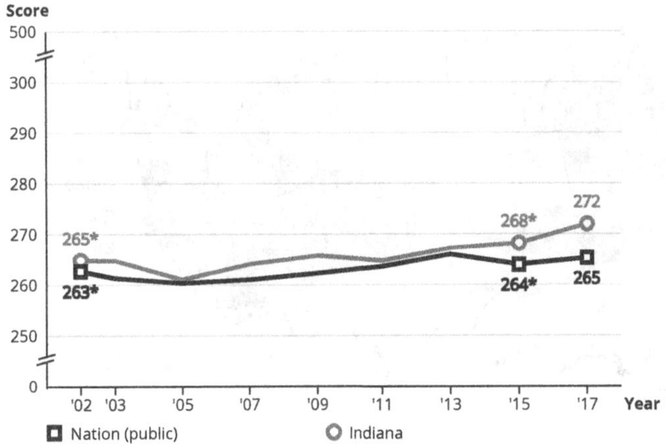

* Significantly different ($p < .05$) from 2017. Significance tests were performed using unrounded numbers.

Results for Student Groups in 2017

Reporting Groups	Percentage of students	Avg. score	Percentage at or above *Basic*	Percentage at or above *Proficient*	Percentage at *Advanced*
Race/Ethnicity					
White	73	275	85	45	5
Black	10	255	68	19	1
Hispanic	10	265	77	34	3
Asian	3	281	87	55	9
American Indian/Alaska Native	#	‡	‡	‡	‡
Native Hawaiian/Pacific Islander	#	‡	‡	‡	‡
Two or more races	4	266	77	32	5
Gender					
Male	50	267	79	36	3
Female	50	277	86	46	6
National School Lunch Program					
Eligible	44	261	73	28	2
Not eligible	55	281	90	52	7

Rounds to zero.
‡ Reporting standards not met.
NOTE: Detail may not sum to totals because of rounding, and because the "Information not available" category for the National School Lunch Program, which provides free/reduced-price lunches, is not displayed. Black includes African American and Hispanic includes Latino. Race categories exclude Hispanic origin.

Score Gaps for Student Groups

- In 2017, Black students had an average score that was 20 points lower than that for White students. This performance gap was not significantly different from that in 2002 (20 points).
- In 2017, Hispanic students had an average score that was 10 points lower than that for White students. Data are not reported for Hispanic students in 2002, because reporting standards were not met.
- In 2017, female students in Indiana had an average score that was higher than that for male students by 9 points.
- In 2017, students who were eligible for free/reduced-price school lunch, an indicator of low family income, had an average score that was 20 points lower than that for students who were not eligible. This performance gap was not significantly different from that in 2002 (16 points).

Education

ies NATIONAL CENTER FOR EDUCATION STATISTICS
Institute of Education Sciences

NOTE: The NAEP reading scale ranges from 0 to 500. Statistical comparisons are calculated on the basis of unrounded scale scores or percentages. Read more about how to interpret NAEP results from the reading assessment at https://nces.ed.gov/nationsreportcard/reading/interpret_results.aspx.
SOURCE: U.S. Department of Education, Institute of Education Sciences, National Center for Education Statistics, National Assessment of Educational Progress (NAEP), various years, 2002-2017 Reading Assessments.

The Nation's Report Card

2015 Science State Snapshot Report

Indiana • Grade 4 • Public Schools

Overall Results

- In 2015, the average score of fourth-grade students in Indiana was 159. This was higher than the average score of 153 for public school students in the nation.
- The average score for students in Indiana in 2015 (159) was higher than their average score in 2009 (153).
- The percentage of students in Indiana who performed at or above the NAEP *Proficient* level was 42 percent in 2015. This percentage was greater than that in 2009 (35 percent).
- The percentage of students in Indiana who performed at or above the NAEP *Basic* level was 83 percent in 2015. This percentage was greater than that in 2009 (78 percent).

Achievement-Level Percentages and Average Score Results

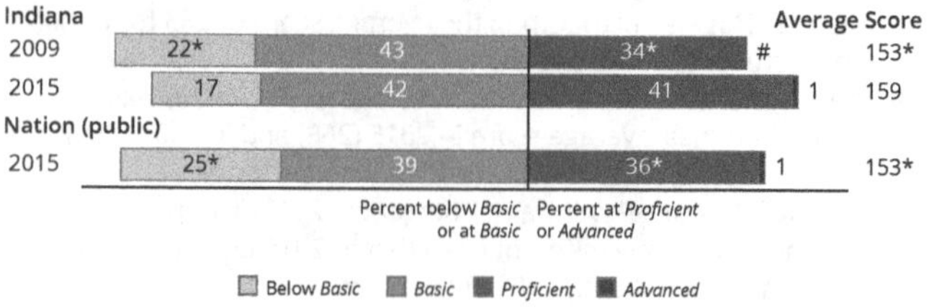

Rounds to zero.
* Significantly different ($p < .05$) from state's results in 2015. Significance tests were performed using unrounded numbers.
NOTE: Detail may not sum to totals because of rounding.

Compare the Average Score in 2015 to Other States/Jurisdictions

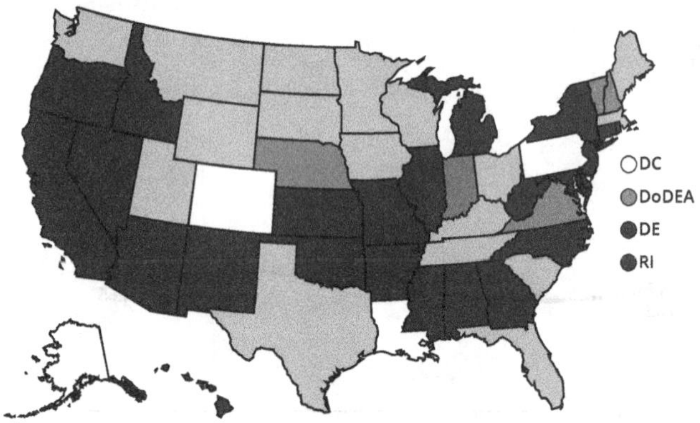

In 2015, the average score in Indiana (159) was
- lower than those in 5 states/jurisdictions
- higher than those in 24 states/jurisdictions
- not significantly different from those in 17 states/jurisdictions

- 5 states/jurisdictions did not participate in 2015

DoDEA = Department of Defense Education Activity (overseas and domestic schools)

Average Scores for State/Jurisdiction and Nation (public)

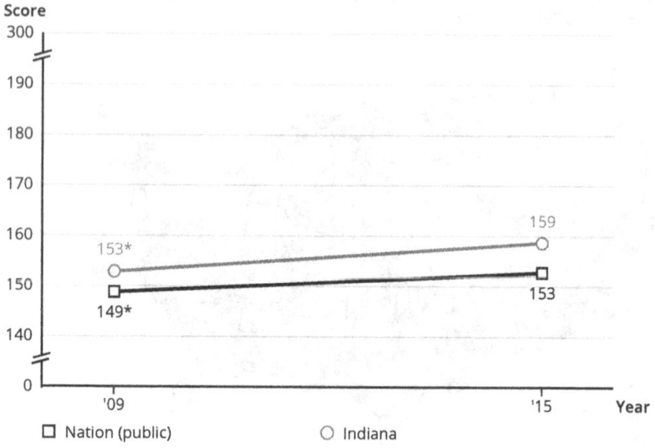

* Significantly different ($p < .05$) from 2015. Significance tests were performed using unrounded numbers.

Results for Student Groups in 2015

Reporting Groups	Percentage of students	Avg. score	Percentage at or above *Basic*	Percentage at or above *Proficient*	Percentage at *Advanced*
Race/Ethnicity					
White	69	165	90	49	1
Black	12	132	54	11	#
Hispanic	12	144	71	22	#
Asian	2	‡	‡	‡	‡
American Indian/Alaska Native	#	‡	‡	‡	‡
Native Hawaiian/Pacific Islander	#	‡	‡	‡	‡
Two or more races	5	159	86	39	#
Gender					
Male	50	160	83	43	1
Female	50	158	83	40	1
National School Lunch Program					
Eligible	50	147	74	26	#
Not eligible	49	170	93	58	1

Rounds to zero.
‡ Reporting standards not met.
NOTE: Detail may not sum to totals because of rounding, and because the "Information not available" category for the National School Lunch Program, which provides free/reduced-price lunches, is not displayed. Black includes African American and Hispanic includes Latino. Race categories exclude Hispanic origin.

Score Gaps for Student Groups

- In 2015, Black students had an average score that was 33 points lower than that for White students. This performance gap was not significantly different from that in 2009 (29 points).
- In 2015, Hispanic students had an average score that was 21 points lower than that for White students. This performance gap was not significantly different from that in 2009 (23 points).
- In 2015, male students in Indiana had an average score that was not significantly different from that for female students.
- In 2015, students who were eligible for free/reduced-price school lunch, an indicator of low family income, had an average score that was 23 points lower than that for students who were not eligible. This performance gap was not significantly different from that in 2009 (21 points).

ies NATIONAL CENTER FOR EDUCATION STATISTICS
Institute of Education Sciences

NOTE: The NAEP science scale ranges from 0 to 300. Statistical comparisons are calculated on the basis of unrounded scale scores or percentages.
SOURCE: U.S. Department of Education, Institute of Education Sciences, National Center for Education Statistics, National Assessment of Educational Progress (NAEP), 2009 and 2015 Science Assessments.

The Nation's Report Card

2015 Science State Snapshot Report
Indiana • Grade 8 • Public Schools

Overall Results

- In 2015, the average score of eighth-grade students in Indiana was 156. This was higher than the average score of 153 for public school students in the nation.
- The average score for students in Indiana in 2015 (156) was higher than their average score in 2011 (153) and in 2009 (152).
- The percentage of students in Indiana who performed at or above the NAEP *Proficient* level was 36 percent in 2015. This percentage was not significantly different from that in 2011 (33 percent) and in 2009 (32 percent).
- The percentage of students in Indiana who performed at or above the NAEP *Basic* level was 70 percent in 2015. This percentage was not significantly different from that in 2011 (67 percent) and in 2009 (67 percent).

Achievement-Level Percentages and Average Score Results

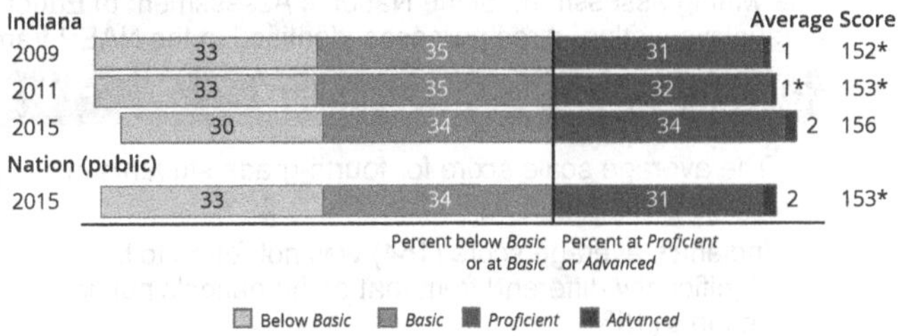

* Significantly different ($p < .05$) from state's results in 2015. Significance tests were performed using unrounded numbers.
NOTE: Detail may not sum to totals because of rounding.

Compare the Average Score in 2015 to Other States/Jurisdictions

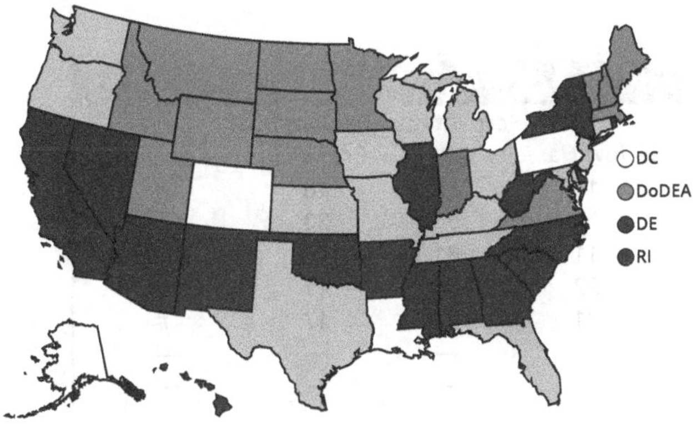

In 2015, the average score in Indiana (156) was
- lower than those in 14 states/jurisdictions
- higher than those in 17 states/jurisdictions
- not significantly different from those in 15 states/jurisdictions

- 5 states/jurisdictions did not participate in 2015

DoDEA = Department of Defense Education Activity (overseas and domestic schools)

Average Scores for State/Jurisdiction and Nation (public)

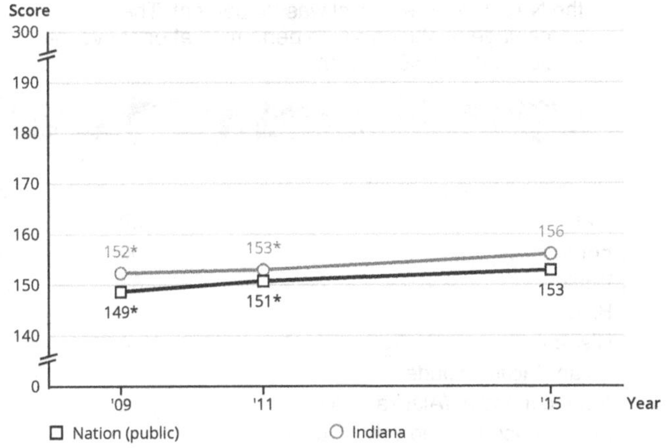

* Significantly different ($p < .05$) from 2015. Significance tests were performed using unrounded numbers.

Results for Student Groups in 2015

Reporting Groups	Percentage of students	Avg. score	Percentage at or above *Basic*	Percentage at or above *Proficient*	Percentage at *Advanced*
Race/Ethnicity					
White	73	163	79	42	3
Black	11	126	30	6	#
Hispanic	10	140	49	17	#
Asian	2	‡	‡	‡	‡
American Indian/Alaska Native	#	‡	‡	‡	‡
Native Hawaiian/Pacific Islander	#	‡	‡	‡	‡
Two or more races	4	147	59	27	1
Gender					
Male	51	160	74	41	3
Female	49	152	66	30	1
National School Lunch Program					
Eligible	50	144	56	21	#
Not eligible	50	168	84	50	4

\# Rounds to zero.
‡ Reporting standards not met.
NOTE: Detail may not sum to totals because of rounding, and because the "Information not available" category for the National School Lunch Program, which provides free/reduced-price lunches, is not displayed. Black includes African American and Hispanic includes Latino. Race categories exclude Hispanic origin.

Score Gaps for Student Groups

- In 2015, Black students had an average score that was 37 points lower than that for White students. This performance gap was not significantly different from that in 2009 (33 points).
- In 2015, Hispanic students had an average score that was 23 points lower than that for White students. This performance gap was not significantly different from that in 2009 (24 points).
- In 2015, male students in Indiana had an average score that was higher than that for female students by 8 points.
- In 2015, students who were eligible for free/reduced-price school lunch, an indicator of low family income, had an average score that was 24 points lower than that for students who were not eligible. This performance gap was not significantly different from that in 2009 (26 points).

ies NATIONAL CENTER FOR EDUCATION STATISTICS
Institute of Education Sciences

NOTE: The NAEP science scale ranges from 0 to 300. Statistical comparisons are calculated on the basis of unrounded scale scores or percentages.
SOURCE: U.S. Department of Education, Institute of Education Sciences, National Center for Education Statistics, National Assessment of Educational Progress (NAEP), various years, 2009-2015 Science Assessments.

NCES National Center for Education Statistics

The Nation's Report Card State **Writing 2002**

Indiana Grade 4 Public School

Snapshot Report

NCES 2003-532IN4

The writing assessment of the National Assessment of Educational Progress (NAEP) measures narrative, informative, and persuasive writing–three purposes identified in the NAEP framework. The NAEP writing scale ranges from 0 to 300.

Overall Writing Results for Indiana

- The average scale score for fourth-grade students in Indiana was 154.
- Indiana's average score (154) was not found to be significantly different[1] from that of the nation's public schools (153).
- Students' average scale scores in Indiana were higher than those in 24 jurisdictions[2], not significantly different from those in 16 jurisdictions, and lower than those in 7 jurisdictions.
- The percentage of students who performed at or above the NAEP *Proficient* level was 26 percent. The percentage of students who performed at or above the *Basic* level was 88 percent.

Student Percentage at Each Achievement Level

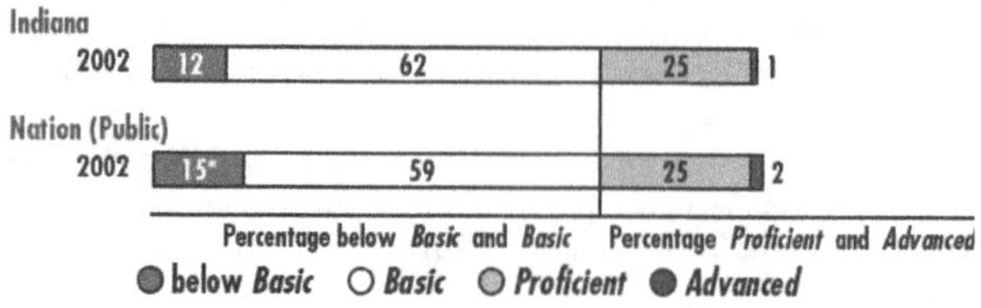

Performance of NAEP Reporting Groups in Indiana

Reporting groups	Percentage of students	Average Score	Percentage of students at Below *Basic*	*Basic*	*Proficient*	*Advanced*
Male	50	144	18	65	16	#
Female	50	163	7 ↓	58	33	3
White	80	157 ↓	11	61 ↑	27	2 ↓
Black	13	138	22	66	11	#
Hispanic	4	144	21	62	17	#
Asian/Pacific Islander	1	---	---	---	---	---
American Indian/Alaska Native	1	---	---	---	---	---
Free/reduced-priced school lunch						
Eligible	33	141	21	65	14	#
Not eligible	60	160 ↓	9	60 ↑	29 ↓	2 ↓
Information not available	7	167 ↑	6 ↓	55	37	2

Average Score Gaps Between Selected Groups

- Female students in Indiana had an average score that was higher than that of male students (19 points). This performance gap was not significantly different from that of the Nation (18 points).
- White students had an average score that was higher than that of Black students (18 points). This performance gap was not significantly different from that of the Nation (20 points).
- White students had an average score that was higher than that of Hispanic students (13 points). This performance gap was not significantly different from that of the Nation (19 points).
- Students who were not eligible for free/reduced-price school lunch had an average score that was higher than that of students who were eligible (18 points). This performance gap was not significantly different from that of the Nation (22 points).

Writing Scale Scores at Selected Percentiles

Scale Score Distribution

	25th Percentile	**50th** Percentile	**75th** Percentile
Indiana	*131* ↑	*154*	*177*
Nation (Public)	*128*	*153*	*178*

An examination of scores at different percentiles on the 0-300 NAEP writing scale at each grade indicates how well students at lower, middle, and higher levels of the distribution performed. For example, the data above shows that 75 percent of students in public schools nationally scored below *178,* while 75 percent of students in Indiana scored below *177.*

\# Percentage rounds to zero.
--- Reporting standards not met; sample size insufficient to permit a reliable estimate.
* Significantly different from Indiana.
↑ Significantly higher than, ↓ lower than appropriate subgroup in the nation (public).
[1] Comparisons (higher/lower/not different) are based on statistical tests. The .05 level was used for testing statistical significance.
[2] "Jurisdictions" includes participating states and other jurisdictions (such as Guam or the District of Columbia).
NOTE: Detail may not sum to totals because of rounding. Score gaps are calculated based on differences between unrounded average scale scores.
Visit http://nces.ed.gov/nationsreportcard/states/ for additional results and detailed information.
SOURCE: U.S. Department of Education, Institute of Education Sciences, National Center for Education Statistics, National Assessment of Educational Progress (NAEP), 2002 Writing Assessment.

ies NATIONAL CENTER FOR EDUCATION STATISTICS Institute of Education Sciences

NCES 2008-470IN8

The Nation's Report Card Writing 2007 State Snapshot Report

Indiana
Grade 8
Public Schools

The National Assessment of Educational Progress (NAEP) assesses writing for three purposes identified in the NAEP framework: narrative, informative, and persuasive. The NAEP writing scale ranges from 0 to 300.

Overall Writing Results for Indiana

- In 2007, the average scale score for eighth-grade students in Indiana was 155. This was higher than their average score in 2002 (150).[1]
- Indiana's average score (155) in 2007 was not significantly different from that of the nation's public schools (154).
- Of the 45 states and one other jurisdiction that participated in the 2007 eighth-grade assessment, students' average scale score in Indiana was higher than those in 13 jurisdictions, not significantly different from those in 21 jurisdictions, and lower than those in 11 jurisdictions.[2]
- The percentage of students in Indiana who performed at or above the NAEP *Proficient* level was 30 percent in 2007. This percentage was not significantly different from that in 2002 (26 percent).
- The percentage of students in Indiana who performed at or above the NAEP *Basic* level was 89 percent in 2007. This percentage was greater than that in 2002 (85 percent).

Percentages at NAEP Achievement Levels and Average Score

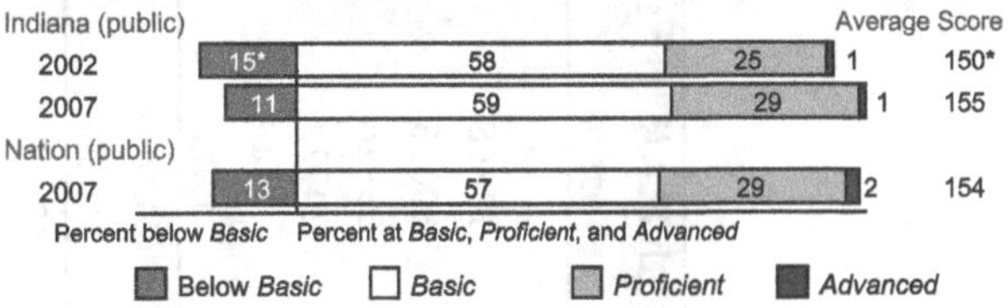

NOTE: The NAEP grade 8 writing achievement levels correspond to the following scale points: Below *Basic*, 113 or lower; *Basic*, 114–172; *Proficient*, 173–223; *Advanced*, 224 or above.

Performance of NAEP Reporting Groups in Indiana: 2007

Reporting groups	Percent of students	Average score	Percent below *Basic*	Percent of students at or above *Basic*	Percent of students at or above *Proficient*	Percent *Advanced*
Male	50	144↑	16↓	84↑	17	#
Female	50	165	5	95	42	1
White	78↓	158↑	9↓	91↑	33	1
Black	12	140↑	18↓	82↑	12	#
Hispanic	6↑	139	22	78	18	#
Asian/Pacific Islander	1	‡	‡	‡	‡	‡
American Indian/Alaska Native	#	‡	‡	‡	‡	‡
Eligible for National School Lunch Program	35↑	142	18	82	17	#
Not eligible for National School Lunch Program	65	161↑	7↓	93↑	37	1

Average Score Gaps Between Selected Groups

- In 2007, male students in Indiana had an average score that was lower than that of female students by 22 points. This performance gap was not significantly different from that of 2002 (24 points).
- In 2007, Black students had an average score that was lower than that of White students by 18 points. This performance gap was not significantly different from that of 2002 (27 points).
- In 2007, Hispanic students had an average score that was lower than that of White students by 19 points. Data are not reported for Hispanic students in 2002, because reporting standards were not met. Therefore, the performance gap results are not reported.
- In 2007, students who were eligible for free/reduced-price school lunch, an indicator of poverty, had an average score that was lower than that of students who were not eligible for free/reduced-price school lunch by 19 points. This performance gap was not significantly different from that of 2002 (17 points).
- In 2007, the score gap between students at the 75th percentile and students at the 25th percentile was 42 points. This performance gap was not significantly different from that of 2002 (47 points).

Writing Scores at Selected Percentiles in Indiana

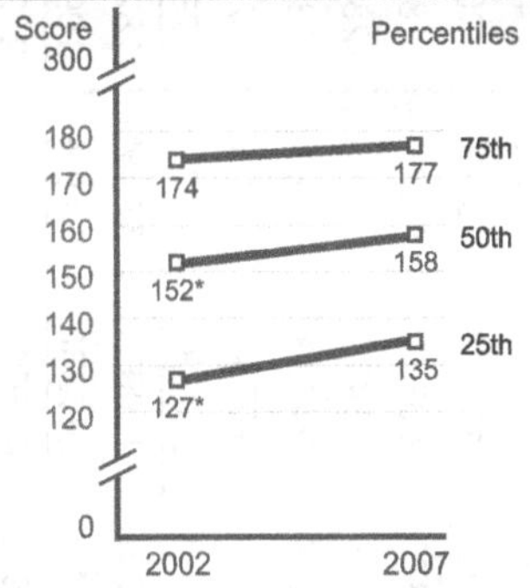

NOTE: Scores at selected percentiles on the NAEP writing scale indicate how well students at lower, middle, and higher levels performed.

Education

Rounds to zero.
‡ Reporting standards not met.
* Significantly different from 2007.
↑ Significantly higher than 2002. ↓ Significantly lower than 2002.

[1] Comparisons (higher/lower/narrower/wider/not different) are based on statistical tests. The .05 level with appropriate adjustments for multiple comparisons was used for testing statistical significance. Statistical comparisons are calculated on the basis of unrounded scale scores or percentages. Comparisons across jurisdictions and comparisons with the nation or within a jurisdiction across years may be affected by differences in exclusion rates for students with disabilities (SD) and English language learners (ELL). The exclusion rates for SD and ELL in Indiana were 3 percent and 1 percent in 2007, respectively. For more information on NAEP significance testing, see http://nces.ed.gov/nationsreportcard/writing/interpret-results.asp#statistical.

[2] "Jurisdiction" refers to states, the District of Columbia, and the Department of Defense Education Activity schools.

NOTE: Detail may not sum to totals because of rounding and because the "Information not available" category for the National School Lunch Program, which provides free and reduced-price lunches, and the "Unclassified" category for race/ethnicity are not displayed. Visit http://nces.ed.gov/nationsreportcard/states/ for additional results and detailed information.

SOURCE: U.S. Department of Education, Institute of Education Sciences, National Center for Education Statistics, National Assessment of Educational Progress (NAEP), 2002 and 2007 Writing Assessments.

ISTEP+ 2018 Grade 3-8 Final Statewide Summary

Student Demographic	ELA Pass N	ELA Test N	ELA Pass %	Math Pass N	Math Test N	Math Pass %	Both ELA/Math Pass N	Both ELA/Math Test N	Both ELA/Math Pass %
American Indian	547	918	59.6%	465	921	50.5%	392	915	42.8%
Asian	9049	11877	76.2%	9074	11912	76.2%	8099	11868	68.2%
Black	24873	60371	41.2%	18921	60561	31.2%	14899	60096	24.8%
Hispanic	33065	63470	52.1%	28927	63590	45.5%	23396	63324	36.9%
Multiracial	15059	24783	60.8%	13047	24842	52.5%	11231	24722	45.4%
Native Hawaiian or Other Pacific Islander	228	374	61.0%	213	375	56.8%	185	374	49.5%
White	239720	341389	70.2%	223403	342061	65.3%	196617	340892	57.7%
Paid meals	194276	250071	77.7%	182584	250369	72.9%	165561	249780	66.3%
Free/Reduced price meals	125793	247338	50.9%	109535	248065	44.2%	87696	246698	35.5%
General Education	300922	425604	70.7%	272065	426205	63.8%	240352	424938	56.6%
Special Education	19280	72478	26.6%	20194	72916	27.7%	12995	72206	18.0%
Non-English Language Learner	313453	473821	66.2%	285162	474779	60.1%	249002	472939	52.6%
English Language Learner	6749	24261	27.8%	7097	24342	29.2%	4345	24205	18.0%
Female	172281	246749	69.8%	143628	247012	58.1%	130514	246329	53.0%
Male	150260	256433	58.6%	150422	257250	58.5%	124305	255862	48.6%

Grade Demographic	ELA Pass N	ELA Test N	ELA Pass %	Math Pass N	Math Test N	Math Pass %	Both ELA/Math Pass N	Both ELA/Math Test N	Both ELA/Math Pass %
Grade 3	56311	83545	67.4%	49747	83954	59.3%	44302	83411	53.1%
Grade 4	54355	85250	63.8%	52074	85515	60.9%	44850	85134	52.7%
Grade 5	51490	85205	60.4%	55927	85271	65.6%	44742	85025	52.6%
Grade 6	54706	83841	65.2%	48566	83949	57.9%	42852	83689	51.2%
Grade 7	52901	82309	64.3%	41443	82469	50.3%	37236	82132	45.3%
Grade 8	52778	83032	63.6%	46293	83104	55.7%	40837	82800	49.3%

Source: Indiana Department of Education

ISTEP+ 2018 Grade 10 Final Statewide Summary

Student Demographic	ELA Pass N	ELA Test N	ELA Pass %	Math Pass N	Math Test N	Math Pass %	Both ELA/Math Pass N	Both ELA/Math Test N	Both ELA/Math Pass %
American Indian	89	162	54.9%	60	161	37.3%	54	160	33.8%
Asian	1300	1941	67.0%	1162	1942	59.8%	1032	1928	53.5%
Black	3047	9206	33.1%	1233	9226	13.4%	1071	9025	11.9%
Hispanic	4053	9041	44.8%	1927	9047	21.3%	1680	8933	18.8%
Multiracial	1942	3473	55.9%	1045	3447	30.3%	969	3411	28.4%
Native Hawaiian or Other Pacific Islander	28	55	50.9%	11	56	19.6%	10	55	18.2%
White	36781	56387	65.2%	23565	56313	41.8%	21944	55943	39.2%
Paid meals	32574	45391	71.8%	21989	45328	48.5%	20691	45112	45.9%
Free/Reduced price meals	14330	33788	42.4%	6877	33772	20.4%	5964	33300	17.9%
General Education	45245	69621	65.0%	28090	69542	40.4%	26076	69034	37.8%
Special Education	1673	9672	17.3%	780	9675	8.1%	581	9488	6.1%
Non-English Language Learner	46611	76225	61.1%	28655	76130	37.6%	26583	75504	35.2%
English Language Learner	307	3068	10.0%	215	3087	7.0%	74	3018	2.5%
Female	26054	39727	65.6%	14747	39708	37.1%	13986	39410	35.5%
Male	21186	40538	52.3%	14256	40484	35.2%	12774	40045	31.9%

Grade Demographic	ELA Pass N	ELA Test N	ELA Pass %	Math Pass N	Math Test N	Math Pass %	Both ELA/Math Pass N	Both ELA/Math Test N	Both ELA/Math Pass %
Grade 10	47240	80265	58.9%	29003	80192	36.2%	26760	79455	33.7%

Source: Indiana Department of Education

Education

SPRING & SUMMER 2018 IREAD 3 RESULTS

Student Demographic	IREAD PASS N*	IREAD TEST N	IREAD Pass %
American Indian	122	139	87.8%
Asian	1,801	2,162	83.3%
Black	7,832	10,546	74.3%
Hispanic	8,609	10,925	78.8%
Multiracial	3,835	4,389	87.4%
Native Hawaiian or Other Pacific Islander	54	63	85.7%
White	51,294	56,182	91.3%
Free/Reduced price meals	35,428	43,493	81.5%
Paid meals	36,591	38,553	94.9%
General Education	66,181	71,771	92.2%
Special Education	7,366	12,082	61.0%
English Language Learner	4,997	7,219	69.2%
Non-English Language Learner	67,383	75,313	89.5%
Female	36,914	41,475	89.0%
Male	36,633	42,931	85.3%

School Demographic	IREAD PASS N*	IREAD TEST N	IREAD Pass %
Public	67,300	77,832	86.5%
Non-Public	6,247	6,574	95.0%
Total	**73,547**	**84,406**	**87.1%**

*Totals may not match due to "Unknown" students

Students are counted in the above totals once regardless of how many times they attempted the test.

Source: Indiana Department of Education

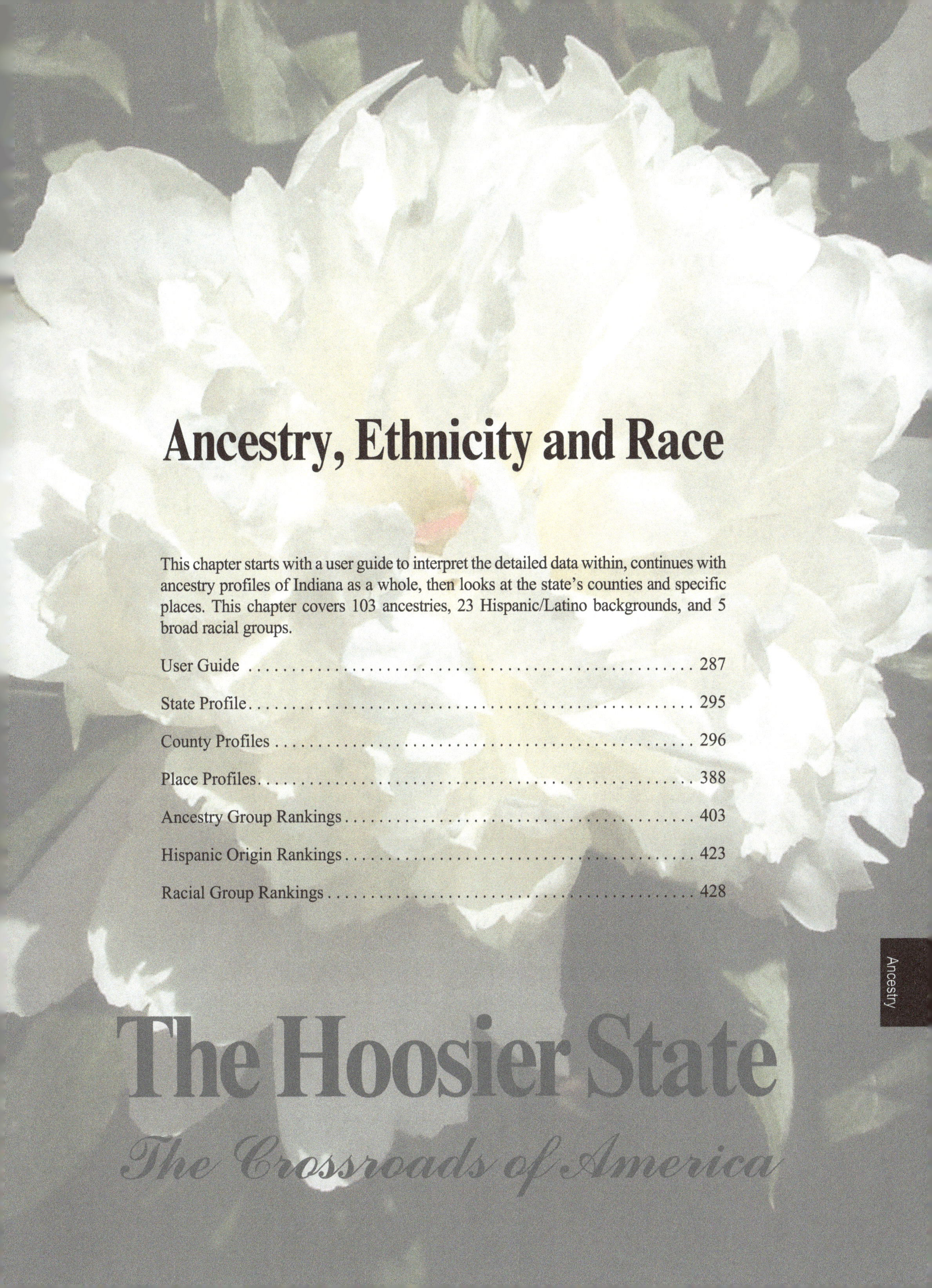

Ancestry, Ethnicity and Race

This chapter starts with a user guide to interpret the detailed data within, continues with ancestry profiles of Indiana as a whole, then looks at the state's counties and specific places. This chapter covers 103 ancestries, 23 Hispanic/Latino backgrounds, and 5 broad racial groups.

User Guide 287

State Profile 295

County Profiles 296

Place Profiles 388

Ancestry Group Rankings 403

Hispanic Origin Rankings 423

Racial Group Rankings 428

The Hoosier State

The Crossroads of America

User Guide

Places Covered

The ancestry and ethnicity profile section of this book covers the state and all counties and places with populations of 50,000 or more. Places included fall into one of the following categories:

Incorporated Places. Depending on the state, places are incorporated as either cities, towns, villages, boroughs, municipalities, independent cities, or corporations. A few municipalities have a form of government combined with another entity (e.g. county) and are listed as special cities or consolidated, unified, or metropolitan governments.

Census Designated Places (CDP). The U.S. Census Bureau defines a CDP as "a statistical entity," defined for each decennial census according to Census Bureau guidelines, comprising a densely settled concentration of population that is not within an incorporated place, but is locally identified by a name. CDPs are delineated cooperatively by state and local officials and the Census Bureau, following Census Bureau guidelines.

Minor Civil Divisions (called charter townships, districts, gores, grants, locations, plantations, purchases, reservations, towns, townships, and unorganized territories) for the states where the Census Bureau has determined that they serve as general-purpose governments. Those states are Connecticut, Maine, Massachusetts, Michigan, Minnesota, New Hampshire, New Jersey, New York, Pennsylvania, Rhode Island, Vermont, and Wisconsin. In some states incorporated municipalities are part of minor civil divisions and in some states they are independent of them.

Note: Several states have incorporated municipalities and minor civil divisions in the same county with the same name. Those communities are given separate entries (e.g. Burlington, New Jersey, in Burlington County will be listed under both the city and township of Burlington). A few states have Census Designated Places and minor civil divisions in the same county with the same name. Those communities are given separate entries (e.g. Bridgewater, Massachusetts, in Plymouth County will be listed under both the CDP and town of Bridgewater).

Source of Data

The ethnicities shown in this book were compiled from two different sources. Data for Race and Hispanic Origin was taken from Census 2010 Summary File 1 (SF1) while Ancestry data was taken from the American Community Survey (ACS) 2006-2010 Five-Year Estimate. The distinction is important because SF1 contains 100-percent data, which is the information compiled from the questions asked of all people and about every housing unit. ACS estimates are compiled from a sampling of households. The 2006-2010 Five-Year Estimate is based on data collected from January 1, 2006 to December 31, 2010.

The American Community Survey (ACS) is a relatively new survey conducted by the U.S. Census Bureau. It uses a series of monthly samples to produce annually updated data for the same small areas (census tracts and block groups) formerly surveyed via the decennial census long-form sample. While some version of this survey has been in the field since 1999, it was not fully implemented in terms of coverage until 2006. In 2005 it was expanded to cover all counties in the country and the 1-in-40 households sampling rate was first applied. The full implementation of the (household) sampling strategy for ACS entails having the survey mailed to about 250,000 households nationwide every month of every year and was begun in January 2005. In January 2006 sampling of group quarters was added to complete the sample as planned. In any given year about 2.5% (1 in 40) of U.S. households will receive the survey. Over any 5-year period about 1 in 8 households should receive the survey (as compared to about 1 in 6 that received the census long form in the 2000 census). Since receiving the survey is not the same as responding to it, the Bureau has adopted a strategy of sampling for non-response, resulting in something closer to 1 in 11 households actually participating in the survey over any 5-year period. For more information about the American Community Survey visit http://www.census.gov/acs/www.

Ancestry

Ancestry refers to a person's ethnic origin, heritage, descent, or "roots," which may reflect their place of birth or that of previous generations of their family. Some ethnic identities, such as "Egyptian" or "Polish" can be traced to geographic areas outside the United States, while other ethnicities such as "Pennsylvania German" or "Cajun" evolved in the United States.

The intent of the ancestry question in the ACS was not to measure the degree of attachment the respondent had to a particular ethnicity, but simply to establish that the respondent had a connection to and self-identified with a particular ethnic group. For example, a response of "Irish" might reflect total involvement in an Irish community or only a memory of ancestors several generations removed from the respondent.

The Census Bureau coded the responses into a numeric representation of over 1,000 categories. Responses initially were processed through an automated coding system; then, those that were not automatically assigned a code were coded by individuals trained in coding ancestry responses. The code list reflects the results of the Census Bureau's own research and consultations with many ethnic experts. Many decisions were made to determine the classification of responses. These decisions affected the grouping of the tabulated data. For example, the "Indonesian" category includes the responses of "Indonesian," "Celebesian," "Moluccan," and a number of other responses.

Ancestries Covered

Afghan
African, Sub-Saharan
- African
- Cape Verdean
- Ethiopian
- Ghanaian
- Kenyan
- Liberian
- Nigerian
- Senegalese
- Sierra Leonean
- Somalian
- South African
- Sudanese
- Ugandan
- Zimbabwean
- Other Sub-Saharan African

Albanian
Alsatian
American
Arab
- Arab
- Egyptian
- Iraqi
- Jordanian
- Lebanese
- Moroccan
- Palestinian
- Syrian
- Other Arab

Armenian
Assyrian/Chaldean/Syriac
Australian
Austrian
Basque
Belgian
Brazilian
British
Bulgarian
Cajun
Canadian
Carpatho Rusyn
Celtic
Croatian
Cypriot
Czech
Czechoslovakian
Danish
Dutch
Eastern European
English
Estonian
European
Finnish
French, ex. Basque
French Canadian
German
German Russian
Greek
Guyanese
Hungarian
Icelander
Iranian
Irish
Israeli
Italian
Latvian
Lithuanian
Luxemburger
Macedonian
Maltese
New Zealander
Northern European
Norwegian
Pennsylvania German
Polish
Portuguese
Romanian
Russian
Scandinavian
Scotch-Irish
Scottish
Serbian
Slavic
Slovak
Slovene
Soviet Union
Swedish
Swiss
Turkish
Ukrainian
Welsh
West Indian, ex. Hispanic
- Bahamian
- Barbadian
- Belizean
- Bermudan
- British West Indian
- Dutch West Indian
- Haitian
- Jamaican
- Trinidadian/Tobagonian
- U.S. Virgin Islander
- West Indian
- Other West Indian

Yugoslavian

The ancestry question allowed respondents to report one or more ancestry groups. Generally, only the first two responses reported were coded. If a response was in terms of a dual ancestry, for example, "Irish English," the person was assigned two codes, in this case one for Irish and another for English. However, in certain cases, multiple responses such as "French Canadian," "Scotch-Irish," "Greek Cypriot," and "Black Dutch" were assigned a single code reflecting their status as unique groups. If a person reported one of these unique groups in addition to another group, for example, "Scotch-Irish English," resulting in three terms, that person received one code for the unique group (Scotch-Irish) and another one for the remaining group (English). If a person reported "English Irish French," only English and Irish were coded. If there were more than two ancestries listed and one of the ancestries was a part of another, such as "German Bavarian Hawaiian," the responses were coded using the more detailed groups (Bavarian and Hawaiian).

The Census Bureau accepted "American" as a unique ethnicity if it was given alone or with one other ancestry. There were some groups such as "American Indian," "Mexican American," and "African American" that were coded and identified separately.

The ancestry question is asked for every person in the American Community Survey, regardless of age, place of birth, Hispanic origin, or race.

Although some people consider religious affiliation a component of ethnic identity, the ancestry question was not designed to collect any information concerning religion. Thus, if a religion was given as an answer to the ancestry question, it was listed in the "Other groups" category which is not shown in this book.

Ancestry should not be confused with a person's place of birth, although a person's place of birth and ancestry may be the same.

Hispanic Origin

The data on the Hispanic or Latino population were derived from answers to a Census 2010 question that was asked of all people. The terms "Spanish," "Hispanic origin," and "Latino" are used interchangeably. Some respondents identify with all three terms while others may identify with only one of these three specific terms. Hispanics or Latinos who identify with the terms "Spanish," "Hispanic," or "Latino" are those who classify themselves in one of the specific Spanish, Hispanic, or Latino categories listed on the questionnaire ("Mexican," "Puerto Rican," or "Cuban") as well as those who indicate that they are "other Spanish/Hispanic/Latino." People who do not identify with one of the specific origins listed on the questionnaire but indicate that they are "other Spanish/Hispanic/Latino" are those whose origins are from Spain, the Spanish-speaking countries of Central or South America, the Dominican Republic, or people identifying themselves generally as Spanish, Spanish-American, Hispanic, Hispano, Latino, and so on. All write-in responses to the "other Spanish/Hispanic/Latino" category were coded.

Hispanic Origins Covered

Hispanic or Latino	Salvadoran	Argentinean	Uruguayan
Central American, ex. Mexican	Other Central American	Bolivian	Venezuelan
Costa Rican	Cuban	Chilean	Other South American
Guatemalan	Dominican Republic	Colombian	Other Hispanic or Latino
Honduran	Mexican	Ecuadorian	
Nicaraguan	Puerto Rican	Paraguayan	
Panamanian	South American	Peruvian	

Origin can be viewed as the heritage, nationality group, lineage, or country of birth of the person or the person's parents or ancestors before their arrival in the United States. People who identify their origin as Hispanic, Latino, or Spanish may be of any race.

Ethnicities Based on Race

The data on race were derived from answers to the Census 2010 question on race that was asked of individuals in the United States. The Census Bureau collects racial data in accordance with guidelines provided by the U.S. Office of Management and Budget (OMB), and these data are based on self-identification.

The racial categories included in the census questionnaire generally reflect a social definition of race recognized in this country and not an attempt to define race biologically, anthropologically, or genetically. In addition, it is recognized that the categories of the race item include racial and national origin or sociocultural groups. People may choose to report more than one race to indicate their racial mixture, such as "American Indian" and "White." People who identify their origin as Hispanic, Latino, or Spanish may be of any race.

African American or Black: A person having origins in any of the Black racial groups of Africa. It includes people who indicated their race(s) as "Black, African Am., or Negro" or reported entries such as African American, Kenyan, Nigerian, or Haitian.

American Indian or Alaska Native: A person having origins in any of the original peoples of North and South America (including Central America) and who maintains tribal affiliation or community attachment. This category includes people who indicated their race(s) as "American Indian or Alaska Native" or reported their enrolled or principal tribe, such as Navajo, Blackfeet, Inupiat, Yup'ik, or Central American Indian groups or South American Indian groups.

Asian: A person having origins in any of the original peoples of the Far East, Southeast Asia, or the Indian subcontinent, including, for example, Cambodia, China, India, Japan, Korea, Malaysia, Pakistan, the Philippine Islands, Thailand, and Vietnam. It includes people who indicated their race(s) as "Asian" or reported entries such as "Asian Indian," "Chinese," "Filipino," "Korean," "Japanese," "Vietnamese," and "Other Asian" or provided other detailed Asian responses.

Racial Groups Covered

African-American/Black	Crow	Spanish American Indian	Korean
Not Hispanic	Delaware	Tlingit-Haida *(Alaska Native)*	Laotian
Hispanic	Hopi	Tohono O'Odham	Malaysian
American Indian/Alaska Native	Houma	Tsimshian *(Alaska Native)*	Nepalese
Not Hispanic	Inupiat *(Alaska Native)*	Ute	Pakistani
Hispanic	Iroquois	Yakama	Sri Lankan
Alaska Athabascan *(Ala. Nat.)*	Kiowa	Yaqui	Taiwanese
Aleut *(Alaska Native)*	Lumbee	Yuman	Thai
Apache	Menominee	Yup'ik *(Alaska Native)*	Vietnamese
Arapaho	Mexican American Indian	**Asian**	**Hawaii Native/Pacific Islander**
Blackfeet	Navajo	*Not Hispanic*	*Not Hispanic*
Canadian/French Am. Indian	Osage	*Hispanic*	*Hispanic*
Central American Indian	Ottawa	Bangladeshi	Fijian
Cherokee	Paiute	Bhutanese	Guamanian/Chamorro
Cheyenne	Pima	Burmese	Marshallese
Chickasaw	Potawatomi	Cambodian	Native Hawaiian
Chippewa	Pueblo	Chinese, ex. Taiwanese	Samoan
Choctaw	Puget Sound Salish	Filipino	Tongan
Colville	Seminole	Hmong	**White**
Comanche	Shoshone	Indian	*Not Hispanic*
Cree	Sioux	Indonesian	*Hispanic*
Creek	South American Indian	Japanese	

Native Hawaiian or Other Pacific Islander: A person having origins in any of the original peoples of Hawaii, Guam, Samoa, or other Pacific Islands. It includes people who indicated their race(s) as "Pacific Islander" or reported entries such as "Native Hawaiian," "Guamanian or Chamorro," "Samoan," and "Other Pacific Islander" or provided other detailed Pacific Islander responses.

White: A person having origins in any of the original peoples of Europe, the Middle East, or North Africa. It includes people who indicated their race(s) as "White" or reported entries such as Irish, German, Italian, Lebanese, Arab, Moroccan, or Caucasian.

Profiles

Each profile shows the name of the place, the county (if a place spans more than one county, the county that holds the majority of the population is shown), and the 2010 population (based on 100-percent data from Census 2010 Summary File 1). The rest of each profile is comprised of all 218 ethnicities grouped into three sections: ancestry; Hispanic origin; and race.

Column one displays the ancestry/Hispanic origin/race name, column two displays the number of people reporting each ancestry/Hispanic origin/race, and column three is the percent of the total population reporting each ancestry/Hispanic origin/race. The population figure shown is used to calculate the value in the "%" column for ethnicities based on race and Hispanic origin. The 2006-2010 estimated population figure from the American Community Survey (not shown) is used to calculate the value in the "%" column for all other ancestries.

For ethnicities in the ancestries group, the value in the "Number" column includes multiple ancestries reported. For example, if a person reported a multiple ancestry such as "French Danish," that response was counted twice in the tabulations, once in the French category and again in the Danish category. Thus, the sum of the counts is not the total population but the total of all responses. Numbers in parentheses indicate the number of people reporting a single ancestry. People reporting a single ancestry includes all people who reported only one ethnic group such as "German." Also included in this category are people with only a multiple-term response such as "Scotch-Irish" who are assigned a single code because they represent one distinct group. For example, the count for German would be interpreted as "The number of people who reported that German was their only ancestry."

For ethnicities based on Hispanic origin, the value in the "Number" column represents the number of people who reported being Mexican, Puerto Rican, Cuban or other Spanish/Hispanic/ Latino (all written-in responses were coded). All ethnicities based on Hispanic origin can be of any race.

For ethnicities based on race data the value in the "Number" column represents the total number of people who reported each category alone or in combination with one or more other race categories. This number represents the maximum number of people reporting and therefore the individual race categories may add up to more than the total population because people may be included in more than one category. The figures in parentheses show the number of people that reported that particular ethnicity alone, not in combination with any other race. For example, in Alabama, the entry for Korean shows 8,320 in parentheses and 10,624 in the "Number" column. This means that 8,320 people reported being Korean alone and 10,624 people reported being Korean alone or in combination with one or more other races.

Rankings

In the rankings section, each ethnicity has three tables. The first table shows the top 10 places sorted by ethnic population (based on all places, regardless of total population), the second table shows the top 10 places sorted by percent of the total population (based on all places, regardless of total population), the third table shows the top 10 places sorted by percent of the total population (based on places with total population of 50,000 or more).

Within each table, column one displays the place name, the state, and the county (if a place spans more than one county, the county that holds the majority of the population is shown). Column one in the first table displays the state only. Column two displays the number of people reporting each ancestry (includes people reporting multiple ancestries), Hispanic origin, or race (alone or in combination with any other race). Column three is the percent of the total population reporting each ancestry, Hispanic origin or race. For tables representing ethnicities based on race or Hispanic origin, the 100-percent population figure from SF1 is used to calculate the value in the "%" column. For all other ancestries, the 2006-2010 five-year estimated population figure from the American Community Survey is used to calculate the value in the "%" column.

Alphabetical Ethnicity Cross-Reference Guide

Afghan *see* Ancestry–Afghan
African *see* Ancestry–African, Sub-Saharan: African
African-American *see* Race–African-American/Black
African-American: Hispanic *see* Race–African-American/Black: Hispanic
African-American: Not Hispanic *see* Race–African-American/Black: Not Hispanic
Alaska Athabascan *see* Race–Alaska Native: Alaska Athabascan
Alaska Native *see* Race–American Indian/Alaska Native
Alaska Native: Hispanic *see* Race–American Indian/Alaska Native: Hispanic
Alaska Native: Not Hispanic *see* Race–American Indian/Alaska Native: Not Hispanic
Albanian *see* Ancestry–Albanian
Aleut *see* Race–Alaska Native: Aleut
Alsatian *see* Ancestry–Alsatian

American *see* Ancestry–American
American Indian *see* Race–American Indian/Alaska Native
American Indian: Hispanic *see* Race–American Indian/Alaska Native: Hispanic
American Indian: Not Hispanic *see* Race–American Indian/Alaska Native: Not Hispanic
Apache *see* Race–American Indian: Apache
Arab *see* Ancestry–Arab: Arab
Arab: Other *see* Ancestry–Arab: Other
Arapaho *see* Race–American Indian: Arapaho
Argentinean *see* Hispanic Origin–South American: Argentinean
Armenian *see* Ancestry–Armenian
Asian *see* Race–Asian
Asian Indian *see* Race–Asian: Indian
Asian: Hispanic *see* Race–Asian: Hispanic
Asian: Not Hispanic *see* Race–Asian: Not Hispanic
Assyrian *see* Ancestry–Assyrian/Chaldean/Syriac
Australian *see* Ancestry–Australian
Austrian *see* Ancestry–Austrian
Bahamian *see* Ancestry–West Indian: Bahamian, except Hispanic
Bangladeshi *see* Race–Asian: Bangladeshi
Barbadian *see* Ancestry–West Indian: Barbadian, except Hispanic
Basque *see* Ancestry–Basque
Belgian *see* Ancestry–Belgian
Belizean *see* Ancestry–West Indian: Belizean, except Hispanic
Bermudan *see* Ancestry–West Indian: Bermudan, except Hispanic
Bhutanese *see* Race–Asian: Bhutanese
Black *see* Race–African-American/Black
Black: Hispanic *see* Race–African-American/Black: Hispanic
Black: Not Hispanic *see* Race–African-American/Black: Not Hispanic
Blackfeet *see* Race–American Indian: Blackfeet
Bolivian *see* Hispanic Origin–South American: Bolivian
Brazilian *see* Ancestry–Brazilian
British *see* Ancestry–British
British West Indian *see* Ancestry–West Indian: British West Indian, except Hispanic
Bulgarian *see* Ancestry–Bulgarian
Burmese *see* Race–Asian: Burmese
Cajun *see* Ancestry–Cajun
Cambodian *see* Race–Asian: Cambodian
Canadian *see* Ancestry–Canadian
Canadian/French American Indian *see* Race–American Indian: Canadian/French American Indian
Cape Verdean *see* Ancestry–African, Sub-Saharan: Cape Verdean
Carpatho Rusyn *see* Ancestry–Carpatho Rusyn
Celtic *see* Ancestry–Celtic
Central American *see* Hispanic Origin–Central American, except Mexican
Central American Indian *see* Race–American Indian: Central American Indian
Central American: Other *see* Hispanic Origin–Central American: Other Central American
Chaldean *see* Ancestry–Assyrian/Chaldean/Syriac
Chamorro *see* Race–Hawaii Native/Pacific Islander: Guamanian or Chamorro
Cherokee *see* Race–American Indian: Cherokee
Cheyenne *see* Race–American Indian: Cheyenne
Chickasaw *see* Race–American Indian: Chickasaw
Chilean *see* Hispanic Origin–South American: Chilean
Chinese (except Taiwanese) *see* Race–Asian: Chinese, except Taiwanese
Chippewa *see* Race–American Indian: Chippewa
Choctaw *see* Race–American Indian: Choctaw
Colombian *see* Hispanic Origin–South American: Colombian
Colville *see* Race–American Indian: Colville
Comanche *see* Race–American Indian: Comanche
Costa Rican *see* Hispanic Origin–Central American: Costa Rican
Cree *see* Race–American Indian: Cree
Creek *see* Race–American Indian: Creek
Croatian *see* Ancestry–Croatian
Crow *see* Race–American Indian: Crow
Cuban *see* Hispanic Origin–Cuban
Cypriot *see* Ancestry–Cypriot
Czech *see* Ancestry–Czech
Czechoslovakian *see* Ancestry–Czechoslovakian
Danish *see* Ancestry–Danish
Delaware *see* Race–American Indian: Delaware
Dominican Republic *see* Hispanic Origin–Dominican Republic
Dutch *see* Ancestry–Dutch
Dutch West Indian *see* Ancestry–West Indian: Dutch West Indian, except Hispanic
Eastern European *see* Ancestry–Eastern European
Ecuadorian *see* Hispanic Origin–South American: Ecuadorian
Egyptian *see* Ancestry–Arab: Egyptian
English *see* Ancestry–English
Eskimo *see* Race–Alaska Native: Inupiat
Estonian *see* Ancestry–Estonian
Ethiopian *see* Ancestry–African, Sub-Saharan: Ethiopian
European *see* Ancestry–European
Fijian *see* Race–Hawaii Native/Pacific Islander: Fijian
Filipino *see* Race–Asian: Filipino
Finnish *see* Ancestry–Finnish
French (except Basque) *see* Ancestry–French, except Basque
French Canadian *see* Ancestry–French Canadian
German *see* Ancestry–German
German Russian *see* Ancestry–German Russian
Ghanaian *see* Ancestry–African, Sub-Saharan: Ghanaian
Greek *see* Ancestry–Greek
Guamanian *see* Race–Hawaii Native/Pacific Islander: Guamanian or Chamorro
Guatemalan *see* Hispanic Origin–Central American: Guatemalan
Guyanese *see* Ancestry–Guyanese
Haitian *see* Ancestry–West Indian: Haitian, except Hispanic
Hawaii Native *see* Race–Hawaii Native/Pacific Islander

Hawaii Native: Hispanic *see* Race–Hawaii Native/Pacific Islander: Hispanic
Hawaii Native: Not Hispanic *see* Race–Hawaii Native/Pacific Islander: Not Hispanic
Hispanic or Latino: *see* Hispanic Origin–Hispanic or Latino (of any race)
Hispanic or Latino: Other *see* Hispanic Origin–Other Hispanic or Latino
Hmong *see* Race–Asian: Hmong
Honduran *see* Hispanic Origin–Central American: Honduran
Hopi *see* Race–American Indian: Hopi
Houma *see* Race–American Indian: Houma
Hungarian *see* Ancestry–Hungarian
Icelander *see* Ancestry–Icelander
Indonesian *see* Race–Asian: Indonesian
Inupiat *see* Race–Alaska Native: Inupiat
Iranian *see* Ancestry–Iranian
Iraqi *see* Ancestry–Arab: Iraqi
Irish *see* Ancestry–Irish
Iroquois *see* Race–American Indian: Iroquois
Israeli *see* Ancestry–Israeli
Italian *see* Ancestry–Italian
Jamaican *see* Ancestry–West Indian: Jamaican, except Hispanic
Japanese *see* Race–Asian: Japanese
Jordanian *see* Ancestry–Arab: Jordanian
Kenyan *see* Ancestry–African, Sub-Saharan: Kenyan
Kiowa *see* Race–American Indian: Kiowa
Korean *see* Race–Asian: Korean
Laotian *see* Race–Asian: Laotian
Latvian *see* Ancestry–Latvian
Lebanese *see* Ancestry–Arab: Lebanese
Liberian *see* Ancestry–African, Sub-Saharan: Liberian
Lithuanian *see* Ancestry–Lithuanian
Lumbee *see* Race–American Indian: Lumbee
Luxemburger *see* Ancestry–Luxemburger
Macedonian *see* Ancestry–Macedonian
Malaysian *see* Race–Asian: Malaysian
Maltese *see* Ancestry–Maltese
Marshallese *see* Race–Hawaii Native/Pacific Islander: Marshallese
Menominee *see* Race–American Indian: Menominee
Mexican *see* Hispanic Origin–Mexican
Mexican American Indian *see* Race–American Indian: Mexican American Indian
Moroccan *see* Ancestry–Arab: Moroccan
Native Hawaiian *see* Race–Hawaii Native/Pacific Islander: Native Hawaiian
Navajo *see* Race–American Indian: Navajo
Nepalese *see* Race–Asian: Nepalese
New Zealander *see* Ancestry–New Zealander
Nicaraguan *see* Hispanic Origin–Central American: Nicaraguan
Nigerian *see* Ancestry–African, Sub-Saharan: Nigerian
Northern European *see* Ancestry–Northern European
Norwegian *see* Ancestry–Norwegian
Osage *see* Race–American Indian: Osage
Ottawa *see* Race–American Indian: Ottawa
Pacific Islander *see* Race–Hawaii Native/Pacific Islander
Pacific Islander: Hispanic *see* Race–Hawaii Native/Pacific Islander: Hispanic
Pacific Islander: Not Hispanic *see* Race–Hawaii Native/Pacific Islander: Not Hispanic
Paiute *see* Race–American Indian: Paiute
Pakistani *see* Race–Asian: Pakistani
Palestinian *see* Ancestry–Arab: Palestinian
Panamanian *see* Hispanic Origin–Central American: Panamanian
Paraguayan *see* Hispanic Origin–South American: Paraguayan
Pennsylvania German *see* Ancestry–Pennsylvania German
Peruvian *see* Hispanic Origin–South American: Peruvian
Pima *see* Race–American Indian: Pima
Polish *see* Ancestry–Polish
Portuguese *see* Ancestry–Portuguese
Potawatomi *see* Race–American Indian: Potawatomi
Pueblo *see* Race–American Indian: Pueblo
Puerto Rican *see* Hispanic Origin–Puerto Rican
Puget Sound Salish *see* Race–American Indian: Puget Sound Salish
Romanian *see* Ancestry–Romanian
Russian *see* Ancestry–Russian
Salvadoran *see* Hispanic Origin–Central American: Salvadoran
Samoan *see* Race–Hawaii Native/Pacific Islander: Samoan
Scandinavian *see* Ancestry–Scandinavian
Scotch-Irish *see* Ancestry–Scotch-Irish
Scottish *see* Ancestry–Scottish
Seminole *see* Race–American Indian: Seminole
Senegalese *see* Ancestry–African, Sub-Saharan: Senegalese
Serbian *see* Ancestry–Serbian
Shoshone *see* Race–American Indian: Shoshone
Sierra Leonean *see* Ancestry–African, Sub-Saharan: Sierra Leonean
Sioux *see* Race–American Indian: Sioux
Slavic *see* Ancestry–Slavic
Slovak *see* Ancestry–Slovak
Slovene *see* Ancestry–Slovene
Somalian *see* Ancestry–African, Sub-Saharan: Somalian
South African *see* Ancestry–African, Sub-Saharan: South African
South American *see* Hispanic Origin–South American
South American Indian *see* Race–American Indian: South American Indian
South American: Other *see* Hispanic Origin–South American: Other South American
Soviet Union *see* Ancestry–Soviet Union
Spanish American Indian *see* Race–American Indian: Spanish American Indian
Sri Lankan *see* Race–Asian: Sri Lankan
Sub-Saharan African *see* Ancestry–African, Sub-Saharan
Sub-Saharan African: Other *see* Ancestry–African, Sub-Saharan: Other
Sudanese *see* Ancestry–African, Sub-Saharan: Sudanese
Swedish *see* Ancestry–Swedish
Swiss *see* Ancestry–Swiss

Syriac *see* Ancestry–Assyrian/Chaldean/Syriac
Syrian *see* Ancestry–Arab: Syrian
Taiwanese *see* Race–Asian: Taiwanese
Thai *see* Race–Asian: Thai
Tlingit-Haida *see* Race–Alaska Native: Tlingit-Haida
Tohono O'Odham *see* Race–American Indian: Tohono O'Odham
Tongan *see* Race–Hawaii Native/Pacific Islander: Tongan
Trinidadian and Tobagonian *see* Ancestry–West Indian: Trinidadian and Tobagonian, except Hispanic
Tsimshian *see* Race–Alaska Native: Tsimshian
Turkish *see* Ancestry–Turkish
U.S. Virgin Islander *see* Ancestry–West Indian: U.S. Virgin Islander, except Hispanic
Ugandan *see* Ancestry–African, Sub-Saharan: Ugandan
Ukrainian *see* Ancestry–Ukrainian
Uruguayan *see* Hispanic Origin–South American: Uruguayan
Ute *see* Race–American Indian: Ute
Venezuelan *see* Hispanic Origin–South American: Venezuelan
Vietnamese *see* Race–Asian: Vietnamese
Welsh *see* Ancestry–Welsh
West Indian *see* Ancestry–West Indian: West Indian, except Hispanic
West Indian (except Hispanic) *see* Ancestry–West Indian, except Hispanic
West Indian: Other *see* Ancestry–West Indian: Other, except Hispanic
White *see* Race–White
White: Hispanic *see* Race–White: Hispanic
White: Not Hispanic *see* Race–White: Not Hispanic
Yakama *see* Race–American Indian: Yakama
Yaqui *see* Race–American Indian: Yaqui
Yugoslavian *see* Ancestry–Yugoslavian
Yuman *see* Race–American Indian: Yuman
Yup'ik *see* Race–Alaska Native: Yup'ik
Zimbabwean *see* Ancestry–African, Sub-Saharan: Zimbabwean

State Profile

Population: 6,483,802

Ancestry	Population	%
Afghan (242)	261	<0.01
African, Sub-Saharan (65,151)	79,021	1.23
African (56,028)	68,814	1.07
Cape Verdean (9)	28	<0.01
Ethiopian (1,265)	1,431	0.02
Ghanaian (303)	322	0.01
Kenyan (647)	663	0.01
Liberian (732)	771	0.01
Nigerian (3,000)	3,311	0.05
Senegalese (179)	193	<0.01
Sierra Leonean (0)	41	<0.01
Somalian (586)	626	0.01
South African (376)	600	0.01
Sudanese (422)	433	0.01
Ugandan (69)	109	<0.01
Zimbabwean (149)	162	<0.01
Other Sub-Saharan African (1,386)	1,517	0.02
Albanian (458)	703	0.01
Alsatian (82)	300	<0.01
American (644,285)	644,285	10.04
Arab (10,118)	15,838	0.25
Arab (2,653)	3,625	0.06
Egyptian (1,080)	1,376	0.02
Iraqi (304)	594	0.01
Jordanian (521)	596	0.01
Lebanese (2,109)	4,417	0.07
Moroccan (406)	571	0.01
Palestinian (774)	885	0.01
Syrian (839)	2,104	0.03
Other Arab (1,432)	1,670	0.03
Armenian (479)	1,080	0.02
Assyrian/Chaldean/Syriac (199)	453	0.01
Australian (687)	1,313	0.02
Austrian (2,431)	9,059	0.14
Basque (3)	81	<0.01
Belgian (4,026)	13,481	0.21
Brazilian (1,192)	1,706	0.03
British (10,920)	23,647	0.37
Bulgarian (676)	1,359	0.02
Cajun (301)	666	0.01
Canadian (4,537)	9,085	0.14
Carpatho Rusyn (24)	62	<0.01
Celtic (252)	636	0.01
Croatian (4,180)	13,306	0.21
Cypriot (88)	88	<0.01
Czech (4,832)	18,523	0.29
Czechoslovakian (2,305)	5,115	0.08
Danish (3,532)	13,281	0.21
Dutch (37,596)	144,391	2.25
Eastern European (2,179)	2,605	0.04
English (248,297)	623,154	9.71
Estonian (51)	365	0.01
European (51,753)	58,511	0.91
Finnish (1,411)	5,241	0.08
French, ex. Basque (34,177)	167,332	2.61
French Canadian (6,999)	17,621	0.27
German (740,501)	1,692,418	26.37
German Russian (34)	194	<0.01
Greek (11,608)	23,572	0.37
Guyanese (81)	158	<0.01
Hungarian (12,566)	38,908	0.61
Icelander (146)	292	<0.01
Iranian (1,687)	2,332	0.04
Irish (234,713)	827,853	12.90
Israeli (343)	483	0.01
Italian (64,626)	185,128	2.88
Latvian (814)	1,490	0.02
Lithuanian (4,371)	11,699	0.18
Luxemburger (94)	591	0.01
Macedonian (3,873)	5,064	0.08
Maltese (43)	197	<0.01
New Zealander (221)	318	<0.01
Northern European (3,042)	3,363	0.05
Norwegian (10,599)	36,566	0.57
Pennsylvania German (10,066)	13,018	0.20
Polish (76,354)	210,729	3.28
Portuguese (1,567)	4,720	0.07
Romanian (4,190)	8,644	0.13
Russian (9,274)	25,824	0.40
Scandinavian (2,637)	6,406	0.10
Scotch-Irish (38,900)	95,439	1.49
Scottish (42,470)	123,773	1.93
Serbian (6,179)	11,326	0.18
Slavic (922)	2,352	0.04
Slovak (7,358)	21,051	0.33
Slovene (996)	2,873	0.04
Soviet Union (0)	0	<0.01
Swedish (16,589)	65,409	1.02
Swiss (14,649)	44,777	0.70
Turkish (1,124)	1,592	0.02
Ukrainian (4,411)	9,005	0.14
Welsh (9,294)	38,925	0.61
West Indian, ex. Hispanic (3,921)	6,151	0.10
Bahamian (68)	109	<0.01
Barbadian (41)	97	<0.01
Belizean (79)	147	<0.01
Bermudan (42)	42	<0.01
British West Indian (212)	347	0.01
Dutch West Indian (51)	294	<0.01
Haitian (1,290)	1,721	0.03
Jamaican (1,605)	2,228	0.03
Trinidadian/Tobagonian (156)	233	<0.01
U.S. Virgin Islander (8)	8	<0.01
West Indian (290)	804	0.01
Other West Indian (79)	121	<0.01
Yugoslavian (4,274)	6,328	0.10

Hispanic Origin	Population	%
Hispanic or Latino (of any race)	389,707	6.01
Central American, ex. Mexican	22,093	0.34
Costa Rican	592	0.01
Guatemalan	5,933	0.09
Honduran	5,345	0.08
Nicaraguan	1,431	0.02
Panamanian	1,218	0.02
Salvadoran	7,401	0.11
Other Central American	173	<0.01
Cuban	4,042	0.06
Dominican Republic	2,340	0.04
Mexican	295,373	4.56
Puerto Rican	30,304	0.47
South American	10,032	0.15
Argentinean	1,027	0.02
Bolivian	425	0.01
Chilean	647	0.01
Colombian	2,854	0.04
Ecuadorian	1,092	0.02
Paraguayan	88	<0.01
Peruvian	2,225	0.03
Uruguayan	150	<0.01
Venezuelan	1,440	0.02
Other South American	84	<0.01
Other Hispanic or Latino	25,523	0.39

Race*	Population	%
African-American/Black (591,397)	654,415	10.09
Not Hispanic (582,140)	638,353	9.85
Hispanic (9,257)	16,062	0.25
American Indian/Alaska Native (18,462)	49,738	0.77
Not Hispanic (14,165)	41,469	0.64
Hispanic (4,297)	8,269	0.13
Alaska Athabascan *(Ala. Nat.)* (23)	36	<0.01
Aleut *(Alaska Native)* (40)	55	<0.01
Apache (277)	824	0.01
Arapaho (20)	43	<0.01
Blackfeet (375)	2,065	0.03
Canadian/French Am. Ind. (101)	248	<0.01
Central American Ind. (87)	152	<0.01
Cherokee (3,036)	12,583	0.19
Cheyenne (43)	157	<0.01
Chickasaw (83)	195	<0.01
Chippewa (618)	1,208	0.02
Choctaw (323)	852	0.01
Colville (11)	14	<0.01
Comanche (64)	142	<0.01
Cree (38)	115	<0.01
Creek (186)	375	0.01
Crow (36)	122	<0.01
Delaware (77)	196	<0.01
Hopi (20)	60	<0.01
Houma (29)	43	<0.01
Inupiat *(Alaska Native)* (42)	95	<0.01
Iroquois (255)	640	0.01
Kiowa (24)	35	<0.01
Lumbee (101)	189	<0.01
Menominee (40)	71	<0.01
Mexican American Ind. (938)	1,441	0.02
Navajo (230)	547	0.01
Osage (39)	114	<0.01
Ottawa (82)	164	<0.01
Paiute (18)	36	<0.01
Pima (12)	24	<0.01
Potawatomi (368)	724	0.01
Pueblo (62)	132	<0.01
Puget Sound Salish (13)	19	<0.01
Seminole (27)	149	<0.01
Shoshone (26)	75	<0.01
Sioux (508)	1,340	0.02
South American Ind. (99)	257	<0.01
Spanish American Ind. (91)	137	<0.01
Tlingit-Haida *(Alaska Native)* (43)	65	<0.01
Tohono O'Odham (11)	26	<0.01
Tsimshian *(Alaska Native)* (3)	5	<0.01
Ute (33)	56	<0.01
Yakama (5)	7	<0.01
Yaqui (22)	50	<0.01
Yuman (8)	13	<0.01
Yup'ik *(Alaska Native)* (21)	29	<0.01
Asian (102,474)	126,750	1.95
Not Hispanic (101,444)	123,750	1.91
Hispanic (1,030)	3,000	0.05
Bangladeshi (480)	539	0.01
Bhutanese (1)	3	<0.01
Burmese (7,523)	7,868	0.12
Cambodian (816)	1,019	0.02
Chinese, ex. Taiwanese (21,100)	24,468	0.38
Filipino (10,652)	16,988	0.26
Hmong (175)	218	<0.01
Indian (27,598)	30,947	0.48
Indonesian (547)	823	0.01
Japanese (4,896)	8,437	0.13
Korean (10,322)	13,685	0.21
Laotian (1,129)	1,466	0.02
Malaysian (332)	471	0.01
Nepalese (253)	278	<0.01
Pakistani (2,685)	3,098	0.05
Sri Lankan (331)	372	0.01
Taiwanese (1,387)	1,646	0.03
Thai (1,432)	2,176	0.03
Vietnamese (6,845)	8,175	0.13
Hawaii Native/Pacific Islander (2,348)	6,385	0.10
Not Hispanic (1,853)	5,116	0.08
Hispanic (495)	1,269	0.02
Fijian (15)	35	<0.01
Guamanian/Chamorro (636)	1,113	0.02
Marshallese (71)	82	<0.01
Native Hawaiian (728)	2,223	0.03
Samoan (326)	830	0.01
Tongan (60)	114	<0.01
White (5,467,906)	5,583,367	86.11
Not Hispanic (5,286,453)	5,377,916	82.94
Hispanic (181,453)	205,451	3.17

*Notes: † The Census 2010 population figure is used to calculate the percentages in the Hispanic Origin and Race categories. Ancestry percentages are based on the 2006-2010 American Community Survey population (not shown); ‡ Numbers in parentheses indicate the number of people reporting a single ancestry; * Numbers in parentheses indicate the number of persons reporting this race alone, not in combination with any other race; Please refer to the Explanation of Data for more information.*

County Profiles

Adams County

Population: 34,387

Ancestry	Population	%
Afghan (0)	0	<0.01
African, Sub-Saharan (0)	2	0.01
African (0)	2	0.01
Cape Verdean (0)	0	<0.01
Ethiopian (0)	0	<0.01
Ghanaian (0)	0	<0.01
Kenyan (0)	0	<0.01
Liberian (0)	0	<0.01
Nigerian (0)	0	<0.01
Senegalese (0)	0	<0.01
Sierra Leonean (0)	0	<0.01
Somalian (0)	0	<0.01
South African (0)	0	<0.01
Sudanese (0)	0	<0.01
Ugandan (0)	0	<0.01
Zimbabwean (0)	0	<0.01
Other Sub-Saharan African (0)	0	<0.01
Albanian (0)	0	<0.01
Alsatian (0)	0	<0.01
American (2,706)	2,706	7.92
Arab (67)	67	0.20
Arab (40)	40	0.12
Egyptian (0)	0	<0.01
Iraqi (0)	0	<0.01
Jordanian (0)	0	<0.01
Lebanese (0)	0	<0.01
Moroccan (0)	0	<0.01
Palestinian (0)	0	<0.01
Syrian (0)	0	<0.01
Other Arab (27)	27	0.08
Armenian (0)	0	<0.01
Assyrian/Chaldean/Syriac (0)	0	<0.01
Australian (0)	0	<0.01
Austrian (0)	0	<0.01
Basque (0)	0	<0.01
Belgian (0)	6	0.02
Brazilian (0)	0	<0.01
British (30)	120	0.35
Bulgarian (0)	0	<0.01
Cajun (0)	0	<0.01
Canadian (0)	0	<0.01
Carpatho Rusyn (0)	0	<0.01
Celtic (0)	0	<0.01
Croatian (0)	0	<0.01
Cypriot (0)	0	<0.01
Czech (22)	85	0.25
Czechoslovakian (0)	0	<0.01
Danish (9)	13	0.04
Dutch (124)	414	1.21
Eastern European (0)	0	<0.01
English (876)	2,362	6.91
Estonian (0)	0	<0.01
European (151)	179	0.52
Finnish (0)	0	<0.01
French, ex. Basque (151)	869	2.54
French Canadian (8)	15	0.04
German (8,189)	14,656	42.90
German Russian (0)	0	<0.01
Greek (0)	0	<0.01
Guyanese (0)	0	<0.01
Hungarian (0)	112	0.33
Icelander (0)	0	<0.01
Iranian (0)	0	<0.01
Irish (747)	2,818	8.25
Israeli (0)	0	<0.01
Italian (97)	295	0.86
Latvian (0)	0	<0.01
Lithuanian (0)	21	0.06
Luxemburger (0)	0	<0.01
Macedonian (0)	0	<0.01
Maltese (0)	0	<0.01
New Zealander (0)	0	<0.01
Northern European (0)	0	<0.01
Norwegian (17)	132	0.39
Pennsylvania German (355)	422	1.24
Polish (153)	288	0.84
Portuguese (0)	19	0.06
Romanian (0)	13	0.04
Russian (11)	19	0.06
Scandinavian (12)	12	0.04
Scotch-Irish (95)	297	0.87
Scottish (177)	298	0.87
Serbian (0)	4	0.01
Slavic (0)	0	<0.01
Slovak (0)	0	<0.01
Slovene (0)	0	<0.01
Soviet Union (0)	0	<0.01
Swedish (73)	184	0.54
Swiss (2,133)	4,826	14.13
Turkish (0)	0	<0.01
Ukrainian (0)	0	<0.01
Welsh (5)	32	0.09
West Indian, ex. Hispanic (0)	0	<0.01
Bahamian (0)	0	<0.01
Barbadian (0)	0	<0.01
Belizean (0)	0	<0.01
Bermudan (0)	0	<0.01
British West Indian (0)	0	<0.01
Dutch West Indian (0)	0	<0.01
Haitian (0)	0	<0.01
Jamaican (0)	0	<0.01
Trinidadian/Tobagonian (0)	0	<0.01
U.S. Virgin Islander (0)	0	<0.01
West Indian (0)	0	<0.01
Other West Indian (0)	0	<0.01
Yugoslavian (0)	19	0.06

Hispanic Origin	Population	%
Hispanic or Latino (of any race)	1,412	4.11
Central American, ex. Mexican	27	0.08
Costa Rican	2	0.01
Guatemalan	8	0.02
Honduran	7	0.02
Nicaraguan	3	0.01
Panamanian	0	<0.01
Salvadoran	7	0.02
Other Central American	0	<0.01
Cuban	1	<0.01
Dominican Republic	1	<0.01
Mexican	1,229	3.57
Puerto Rican	36	0.10
South American	5	0.01
Argentinean	0	<0.01
Bolivian	0	<0.01
Chilean	0	<0.01
Colombian	2	0.01
Ecuadorian	1	<0.01
Paraguayan	0	<0.01
Peruvian	2	0.01
Uruguayan	0	<0.01
Venezuelan	0	<0.01
Other South American	0	<0.01
Other Hispanic or Latino	113	0.33

Race*	Population	%
African-American/Black (107)	190	0.55
Not Hispanic (102)	171	0.50
Hispanic (5)	19	0.06
American Indian/Alaska Native (71)	160	0.47
Not Hispanic (60)	139	0.40
Hispanic (11)	21	0.06
Alaska Athabascan *(Ala. Nat.)* (0)	0	<0.01
Aleut *(Alaska Native)* (0)	0	<0.01
Apache (1)	1	<0.01
Arapaho (0)	0	<0.01
Blackfeet (1)	11	0.03
Canadian/French Am. Ind. (0)	0	<0.01
Central American Ind. (0)	0	<0.01
Cherokee (13)	38	0.11
Cheyenne (0)	2	0.01
Chickasaw (0)	0	<0.01
Chippewa (0)	1	<0.01
Choctaw (0)	0	<0.01
Colville (0)	0	<0.01
Comanche (0)	0	<0.01
Cree (0)	0	<0.01
Creek (1)	2	0.01
Crow (0)	0	<0.01
Delaware (0)	0	<0.01
Hopi (0)	0	<0.01
Houma (0)	0	<0.01
Inupiat *(Alaska Native)* (0)	0	<0.01
Iroquois (0)	0	<0.01
Kiowa (0)	0	<0.01
Lumbee (1)	4	0.01
Menominee (1)	1	<0.01
Mexican American Ind. (2)	5	0.01
Navajo (0)	1	<0.01
Osage (0)	0	<0.01
Ottawa (6)	8	0.02
Paiute (0)	0	<0.01
Pima (0)	0	<0.01
Potawatomi (0)	0	<0.01
Pueblo (0)	0	<0.01
Puget Sound Salish (0)	0	<0.01
Seminole (0)	0	<0.01
Shoshone (0)	0	<0.01
Sioux (0)	2	0.01
South American Ind. (0)	0	<0.01
Spanish American Ind. (0)	0	<0.01
Tlingit-Haida *(Alaska Native)* (1)	1	<0.01
Tohono O'Odham (0)	0	<0.01
Tsimshian *(Alaska Native)* (0)	0	<0.01
Ute (0)	0	<0.01
Yakama (0)	0	<0.01
Yaqui (0)	0	<0.01
Yuman (0)	0	<0.01
Yup'ik *(Alaska Native)* (0)	0	<0.01
Asian (78)	119	0.35
Not Hispanic (78)	118	0.34
Hispanic (0)	1	<0.01
Bangladeshi (0)	0	<0.01
Bhutanese (0)	0	<0.01
Burmese (0)	0	<0.01
Cambodian (2)	2	0.01
Chinese, ex. Taiwanese (33)	37	0.11
Filipino (8)	11	0.03
Hmong (0)	0	<0.01
Indian (11)	15	0.04
Indonesian (0)	0	<0.01
Japanese (10)	20	0.06
Korean (12)	25	0.07
Laotian (0)	1	<0.01
Malaysian (0)	0	<0.01
Nepalese (0)	0	<0.01
Pakistani (0)	1	<0.01
Sri Lankan (0)	0	<0.01
Taiwanese (0)	0	<0.01
Thai (1)	1	<0.01
Vietnamese (0)	1	<0.01
Hawaii Native/Pacific Islander (7)	16	0.05
Not Hispanic (7)	14	0.04
Hispanic (0)	2	0.01
Fijian (0)	0	<0.01
Guamanian/Chamorro (4)	7	0.02
Marshallese (0)	0	<0.01
Native Hawaiian (2)	3	0.01
Samoan (1)	1	<0.01
Tongan (0)	0	<0.01
White (33,349)	33,642	97.83
Not Hispanic (32,521)	32,712	95.13
Hispanic (828)	930	2.70

*Notes: † The Census 2010 population figure is used to calculate the percentages in the Hispanic Origin and Race categories. Ancestry percentages are based on the 2006-2010 American Community Survey population (not shown); ‡ Numbers in parentheses indicate the number of people reporting a single ancestry; * Numbers in parentheses indicate the number of persons reporting this race alone, not in combination with any other race; Please refer to the Explanation of Data for more information.*

Allen County

Population: 355,329

Ancestry	Population	%
Afghan (20)	20	0.01
African, Sub-Saharan (13,880)	14,109	4.02
African (13,341)	13,561	3.86
Cape Verdean (0)	0	<0.01
Ethiopian (47)	47	0.01
Ghanaian (0)	0	<0.01
Kenyan (38)	38	0.01
Liberian (0)	0	<0.01
Nigerian (179)	179	0.05
Senegalese (0)	0	<0.01
Sierra Leonean (0)	0	<0.01
Somalian (68)	68	0.02
South African (43)	52	0.01
Sudanese (0)	0	<0.01
Ugandan (0)	0	<0.01
Zimbabwean (0)	0	<0.01
Other Sub-Saharan African (164)	164	0.05
Albanian (33)	33	0.01
Alsatian (8)	8	<0.01
American (37,575)	37,575	10.70
Arab (572)	850	0.24
Arab (207)	222	0.06
Egyptian (25)	79	0.02
Iraqi (44)	54	0.02
Jordanian (10)	10	<0.01
Lebanese (168)	304	0.09
Moroccan (10)	10	<0.01
Palestinian (24)	24	0.01
Syrian (63)	126	0.04
Other Arab (21)	21	0.01
Armenian (81)	111	0.03
Assyrian/Chaldean/Syriac (10)	10	<0.01
Australian (27)	54	0.02
Austrian (180)	417	0.12
Basque (0)	0	<0.01
Belgian (54)	361	0.10
Brazilian (0)	21	0.01
British (497)	1,044	0.30
Bulgarian (204)	240	0.07
Cajun (0)	0	<0.01
Canadian (374)	823	0.23
Carpatho Rusyn (0)	0	<0.01
Celtic (8)	39	0.01
Croatian (161)	285	0.08
Cypriot (0)	0	<0.01
Czech (323)	1,167	0.33
Czechoslovakian (77)	163	0.05
Danish (231)	818	0.23
Dutch (1,406)	5,546	1.58
Eastern European (119)	128	0.04
English (9,653)	28,287	8.05
Estonian (0)	12	<0.01
European (2,248)	2,447	0.70
Finnish (44)	387	0.11
French, ex. Basque (2,975)	14,701	4.18
French Canadian (406)	1,101	0.31
German (58,425)	117,343	33.40
German Russian (0)	0	<0.01
Greek (490)	980	0.28
Guyanese (0)	0	<0.01
Hungarian (461)	1,535	0.44
Icelander (0)	16	<0.01
Iranian (32)	32	0.01
Irish (11,114)	40,071	11.41
Israeli (34)	34	0.01
Italian (3,789)	10,076	2.87
Latvian (70)	86	0.02
Lithuanian (74)	368	0.10
Luxemburger (0)	36	0.01
Macedonian (393)	718	0.20
Maltese (0)	16	<0.01
New Zealander (0)	11	<0.01
Northern European (136)	136	0.04
Norwegian (639)	2,413	0.69
Pennsylvania German (592)	702	0.20
Polish (2,538)	8,297	2.36
Portuguese (175)	337	0.10
Romanian (267)	564	0.16
Russian (555)	1,249	0.36
Scandinavian (227)	562	0.16
Scotch-Irish (1,495)	4,257	1.21
Scottish (1,887)	6,619	1.88
Serbian (0)	93	0.03
Slavic (59)	104	0.03
Slovak (208)	604	0.17
Slovene (34)	71	0.02
Soviet Union (0)	0	<0.01
Swedish (613)	3,110	0.89
Swiss (953)	3,644	1.04
Turkish (46)	46	0.01
Ukrainian (257)	583	0.17
Welsh (366)	1,757	0.50
West Indian, ex. Hispanic (573)	671	0.19
Bahamian (0)	0	<0.01
Barbadian (0)	0	<0.01
Belizean (0)	0	<0.01
Bermudan (0)	0	<0.01
British West Indian (74)	74	0.02
Dutch West Indian (0)	0	<0.01
Haitian (346)	377	0.11
Jamaican (147)	196	0.06
Trinidadian/Tobagonian (0)	0	<0.01
U.S. Virgin Islander (0)	0	<0.01
West Indian (6)	24	0.01
Other West Indian (0)	0	<0.01
Yugoslavian (1,518)	1,589	0.45

Hispanic Origin	Population	%
Hispanic or Latino (of any race)	23,093	6.50
Central American, ex. Mexican	1,489	0.42
Costa Rican	39	0.01
Guatemalan	809	0.23
Honduran	148	0.04
Nicaraguan	42	0.01
Panamanian	56	0.02
Salvadoran	385	0.11
Other Central American	10	<0.01
Cuban	226	0.06
Dominican Republic	86	0.02
Mexican	17,596	4.95
Puerto Rican	1,119	0.31
South American	785	0.22
Argentinean	46	0.01
Bolivian	25	0.01
Chilean	19	0.01
Colombian	299	0.08
Ecuadorian	172	0.05
Paraguayan	6	<0.01
Peruvian	149	0.04
Uruguayan	11	<0.01
Venezuelan	57	0.02
Other South American	1	<0.01
Other Hispanic or Latino	1,792	0.50

Race*	Population	%
African-American/Black (41,618)	47,666	13.41
Not Hispanic (40,998)	46,357	13.05
Hispanic (620)	1,309	0.37
American Indian/Alaska Native (1,246)	3,335	0.94
Not Hispanic (987)	2,735	0.77
Hispanic (259)	600	0.17
Alaska Athabascan *(Ala. Nat.)* (4)	4	<0.01
Aleut *(Alaska Native)* (1)	1	<0.01
Apache (19)	51	0.01
Arapaho (2)	3	<0.01
Blackfeet (26)	133	0.04
Canadian/French Am. Ind. (2)	6	<0.01
Central American Ind. (5)	12	<0.01
Cherokee (164)	615	0.17
Cheyenne (2)	8	<0.01
Chickasaw (5)	13	<0.01
Chippewa (46)	87	0.02
Choctaw (22)	68	0.02
Colville (0)	0	<0.01
Comanche (3)	10	<0.01
Cree (1)	9	<0.01
Creek (12)	30	0.01
Crow (1)	12	<0.01
Delaware (1)	12	<0.01
Hopi (2)	7	<0.01
Houma (0)	3	<0.01
Inupiat *(Alaska Native)* (3)	3	<0.01
Iroquois (32)	61	0.02
Kiowa (3)	3	<0.01
Lumbee (1)	4	<0.01
Menominee (0)	1	<0.01
Mexican American Ind. (59)	88	0.02
Navajo (12)	32	0.01
Osage (3)	6	<0.01
Ottawa (11)	17	<0.01
Paiute (0)	1	<0.01
Pima (4)	7	<0.01
Potawatomi (11)	30	0.01
Pueblo (2)	7	<0.01
Puget Sound Salish (0)	0	<0.01
Seminole (1)	12	<0.01
Shoshone (0)	0	<0.01
Sioux (23)	77	0.02
South American Ind. (4)	10	<0.01
Spanish American Ind. (2)	3	<0.01
Tlingit-Haida *(Alaska Native)* (2)	5	<0.01
Tohono O'Odham (0)	0	<0.01
Tsimshian *(Alaska Native)* (0)	0	<0.01
Ute (1)	2	<0.01
Yakama (0)	0	<0.01
Yaqui (4)	7	<0.01
Yuman (0)	0	<0.01
Yup'ik *(Alaska Native)* (1)	2	<0.01
Asian (9,721)	11,438	3.22
Not Hispanic (9,611)	11,184	3.15
Hispanic (110)	254	0.07
Bangladeshi (45)	48	0.01
Bhutanese (0)	0	<0.01
Burmese (3,676)	3,846	1.08
Cambodian (45)	60	0.02
Chinese, ex. Taiwanese (686)	877	0.25
Filipino (679)	1,066	0.30
Hmong (0)	0	<0.01
Indian (1,560)	1,862	0.52
Indonesian (24)	36	0.01
Japanese (183)	346	0.10
Korean (397)	603	0.17
Laotian (347)	439	0.12
Malaysian (19)	44	0.01
Nepalese (10)	11	<0.01
Pakistani (174)	243	0.07
Sri Lankan (31)	37	0.01
Taiwanese (41)	57	0.02
Thai (154)	235	0.07
Vietnamese (1,014)	1,156	0.33
Hawaii Native/Pacific Islander (189)	454	0.13
Not Hispanic (119)	334	0.09
Hispanic (70)	120	0.03
Fijian (2)	2	<0.01
Guamanian/Chamorro (71)	112	0.03
Marshallese (2)	2	<0.01
Native Hawaiian (61)	162	0.05
Samoan (15)	50	0.01
Tongan (0)	1	<0.01
White (281,653)	291,063	81.91
Not Hispanic (271,789)	279,219	78.58
Hispanic (9,864)	11,844	3.33

*Notes: † The Census 2010 population figure is used to calculate the percentages in the Hispanic Origin and Race categories. Ancestry percentages are based on the 2006-2010 American Community Survey population (not shown); ‡ Numbers in parentheses indicate the number of people reporting a single ancestry; * Numbers in parentheses indicate the number of persons reporting this race alone, not in combination with any other race; Please refer to the Explanation of Data for more information.*

Bartholomew County

Population: 76,794

Ancestry	Population	%
Afghan (0)	0	<0.01
African, Sub-Saharan (33)	132	0.17
African (5)	34	0.04
Cape Verdean (0)	0	<0.01
Ethiopian (0)	0	<0.01
Ghanaian (10)	10	0.01
Kenyan (0)	0	<0.01
Liberian (0)	0	<0.01
Nigerian (18)	88	0.12
Senegalese (0)	0	<0.01
Sierra Leonean (0)	0	<0.01
Somalian (0)	0	<0.01
South African (0)	0	<0.01
Sudanese (0)	0	<0.01
Ugandan (0)	0	<0.01
Zimbabwean (0)	0	<0.01
Other Sub-Saharan African (0)	0	<0.01
Albanian (0)	0	<0.01
Alsatian (0)	0	<0.01
American (8,145)	8,145	10.74
Arab (59)	109	0.14
Arab (0)	11	0.01
Egyptian (20)	39	0.05
Iraqi (0)	0	<0.01
Jordanian (0)	0	<0.01
Lebanese (0)	20	0.03
Moroccan (39)	39	0.05
Palestinian (0)	0	<0.01
Syrian (0)	0	<0.01
Other Arab (0)	0	<0.01
Armenian (20)	28	0.04
Assyrian/Chaldean/Syriac (0)	0	<0.01
Australian (0)	0	<0.01
Austrian (0)	26	0.03
Basque (0)	0	<0.01
Belgian (9)	20	0.03
Brazilian (23)	23	0.03
British (336)	620	0.82
Bulgarian (0)	8	0.01
Cajun (36)	36	0.05
Canadian (28)	101	0.13
Carpatho Rusyn (0)	0	<0.01
Celtic (0)	0	<0.01
Croatian (86)	124	0.16
Cypriot (0)	0	<0.01
Czech (50)	270	0.36
Czechoslovakian (16)	116	0.15
Danish (81)	313	0.41
Dutch (422)	1,313	1.73
Eastern European (0)	0	<0.01
English (3,715)	9,397	12.39
Estonian (0)	0	<0.01
European (675)	793	1.05
Finnish (30)	61	0.08
French, ex. Basque (511)	1,903	2.51
French Canadian (110)	179	0.24
German (10,414)	21,608	28.49
German Russian (0)	0	<0.01
Greek (73)	129	0.17
Guyanese (0)	0	<0.01
Hungarian (91)	181	0.24
Icelander (0)	0	<0.01
Iranian (0)	0	<0.01
Irish (2,883)	9,281	12.24
Israeli (0)	0	<0.01
Italian (655)	1,675	2.21
Latvian (0)	0	<0.01
Lithuanian (0)	33	0.04
Luxemburger (0)	0	<0.01
Macedonian (0)	8	0.01
Maltese (0)	0	<0.01
New Zealander (0)	0	<0.01
Northern European (17)	17	0.02
Norwegian (138)	656	0.86
Pennsylvania German (42)	54	0.07
Polish (362)	1,523	2.01
Portuguese (13)	13	0.02
Romanian (189)	189	0.25
Russian (43)	221	0.29
Scandinavian (108)	247	0.33
Scotch-Irish (676)	1,789	2.36
Scottish (727)	2,450	3.23
Serbian (0)	11	0.01
Slavic (0)	0	<0.01
Slovak (11)	52	0.07
Slovene (8)	21	0.03
Soviet Union (0)	0	<0.01
Swedish (127)	467	0.62
Swiss (130)	420	0.55
Turkish (0)	0	<0.01
Ukrainian (13)	44	0.06
Welsh (91)	638	0.84
West Indian, ex. Hispanic (42)	53	0.07
Bahamian (0)	0	<0.01
Barbadian (0)	0	<0.01
Belizean (0)	0	<0.01
Bermudan (0)	0	<0.01
British West Indian (0)	0	<0.01
Dutch West Indian (0)	0	<0.01
Haitian (24)	24	0.03
Jamaican (0)	11	0.01
Trinidadian/Tobagonian (0)	0	<0.01
U.S. Virgin Islander (0)	0	<0.01
West Indian (10)	10	0.01
Other West Indian (8)	8	0.01
Yugoslavian (42)	45	0.06

Hispanic Origin	Population	%
Hispanic or Latino (of any race)	4,762	6.20
Central American, ex. Mexican	202	0.26
Costa Rican	5	0.01
Guatemalan	111	0.14
Honduran	32	0.04
Nicaraguan	2	<0.01
Panamanian	5	0.01
Salvadoran	41	0.05
Other Central American	6	0.01
Cuban	21	0.03
Dominican Republic	9	0.01
Mexican	3,985	5.19
Puerto Rican	198	0.26
South American	92	0.12
Argentinean	18	0.02
Bolivian	2	<0.01
Chilean	10	0.01
Colombian	22	0.03
Ecuadorian	10	0.01
Paraguayan	0	<0.01
Peruvian	12	0.02
Uruguayan	3	<0.01
Venezuelan	15	0.02
Other South American	0	<0.01
Other Hispanic or Latino	255	0.33

Race*	Population	%
African-American/Black (1,420)	1,937	2.52
Not Hispanic (1,360)	1,841	2.40
Hispanic (60)	96	0.13
American Indian/Alaska Native (209)	522	0.68
Not Hispanic (145)	417	0.54
Hispanic (64)	105	0.14
Alaska Athabascan *(Ala. Nat.)* (0)	0	<0.01
Aleut *(Alaska Native)* (0)	0	<0.01
Apache (2)	9	0.01
Arapaho (1)	1	<0.01
Blackfeet (2)	25	0.03
Canadian/French Am. Ind. (0)	1	<0.01
Central American Ind. (5)	8	0.01
Cherokee (24)	146	0.19
Cheyenne (0)	3	<0.01
Chickasaw (0)	1	<0.01
Chippewa (5)	5	0.01
Choctaw (3)	7	0.01
Colville (0)	0	<0.01
Comanche (0)	0	<0.01
Cree (0)	0	<0.01
Creek (0)	0	<0.01
Crow (0)	1	<0.01
Delaware (0)	1	<0.01
Hopi (1)	1	<0.01
Houma (0)	0	<0.01
Inupiat *(Alaska Native)* (1)	1	<0.01
Iroquois (2)	4	0.01
Kiowa (0)	0	<0.01
Lumbee (0)	0	<0.01
Menominee (0)	1	<0.01
Mexican American Ind. (10)	19	0.02
Navajo (11)	22	0.03
Osage (0)	0	<0.01
Ottawa (2)	3	<0.01
Paiute (0)	0	<0.01
Pima (0)	0	<0.01
Potawatomi (5)	5	0.01
Pueblo (1)	1	<0.01
Puget Sound Salish (0)	0	<0.01
Seminole (1)	1	<0.01
Shoshone (0)	0	<0.01
Sioux (5)	10	0.01
South American Ind. (0)	1	<0.01
Spanish American Ind. (0)	0	<0.01
Tlingit-Haida *(Alaska Native)* (0)	0	<0.01
Tohono O'Odham (0)	0	<0.01
Tsimshian *(Alaska Native)* (0)	0	<0.01
Ute (6)	6	0.01
Yakama (0)	0	<0.01
Yaqui (0)	1	<0.01
Yuman (0)	0	<0.01
Yup'ik *(Alaska Native)* (0)	0	<0.01
Asian (2,632)	2,846	3.71
Not Hispanic (2,622)	2,814	3.66
Hispanic (10)	32	0.04
Bangladeshi (16)	17	0.02
Bhutanese (0)	0	<0.01
Burmese (0)	0	<0.01
Cambodian (0)	0	<0.01
Chinese, ex. Taiwanese (414)	460	0.60
Filipino (71)	117	0.15
Hmong (4)	4	0.01
Indian (1,379)	1,425	1.86
Indonesian (12)	16	0.02
Japanese (391)	437	0.57
Korean (70)	101	0.13
Laotian (12)	15	0.02
Malaysian (6)	11	0.01
Nepalese (3)	3	<0.01
Pakistani (15)	17	0.02
Sri Lankan (4)	4	0.01
Taiwanese (28)	32	0.04
Thai (15)	28	0.04
Vietnamese (131)	146	0.19
Hawaii Native/Pacific Islander (48)	128	0.17
Not Hispanic (37)	106	0.14
Hispanic (11)	22	0.03
Fijian (0)	0	<0.01
Guamanian/Chamorro (13)	30	0.04
Marshallese (0)	0	<0.01
Native Hawaiian (21)	62	0.08
Samoan (7)	9	0.01
Tongan (1)	2	<0.01
White (68,824)	69,950	91.09
Not Hispanic (66,817)	67,711	88.17
Hispanic (2,007)	2,239	2.92

*Notes: † The Census 2010 population figure is used to calculate the percentages in the Hispanic Origin and Race categories. Ancestry percentages are based on the 2006-2010 American Community Survey population (not shown); ‡ Numbers in parentheses indicate the number of people reporting a single ancestry; * Numbers in parentheses indicate the number of persons reporting this race alone, not in combination with any other race; Please refer to the Explanation of Data for more information.*

Benton County

Population: 8,854

Ancestry	Population	%
Afghan (0)	0	<0.01
African, Sub-Saharan (7)	7	0.08
African (0)	0	<0.01
Cape Verdean (0)	0	<0.01
Ethiopian (0)	0	<0.01
Ghanaian (0)	0	<0.01
Kenyan (0)	0	<0.01
Liberian (0)	0	<0.01
Nigerian (0)	0	<0.01
Senegalese (0)	0	<0.01
Sierra Leonean (0)	0	<0.01
Somalian (0)	0	<0.01
South African (7)	7	0.08
Sudanese (0)	0	<0.01
Ugandan (0)	0	<0.01
Zimbabwean (0)	0	<0.01
Other Sub-Saharan African (0)	0	<0.01
Albanian (0)	0	<0.01
Alsatian (0)	0	<0.01
American (999)	999	11.33
Arab (0)	0	<0.01
Arab (0)	0	<0.01
Egyptian (0)	0	<0.01
Iraqi (0)	0	<0.01
Jordanian (0)	0	<0.01
Lebanese (0)	0	<0.01
Moroccan (0)	0	<0.01
Palestinian (0)	0	<0.01
Syrian (0)	0	<0.01
Other Arab (0)	0	<0.01
Armenian (0)	0	<0.01
Assyrian/Chaldean/Syriac (0)	0	<0.01
Australian (0)	0	<0.01
Austrian (13)	45	0.51
Basque (0)	0	<0.01
Belgian (0)	4	0.05
Brazilian (0)	0	<0.01
British (7)	22	0.25
Bulgarian (0)	0	<0.01
Cajun (0)	0	<0.01
Canadian (1)	1	0.01
Carpatho Rusyn (0)	0	<0.01
Celtic (0)	0	<0.01
Croatian (0)	0	<0.01
Cypriot (0)	0	<0.01
Czech (0)	9	0.10
Czechoslovakian (0)	0	<0.01
Danish (0)	9	0.10
Dutch (74)	261	2.96
Eastern European (0)	0	<0.01
English (314)	763	8.65
Estonian (0)	0	<0.01
European (44)	62	0.70
Finnish (0)	38	0.43
French, ex. Basque (73)	429	4.86
French Canadian (21)	30	0.34
German (1,188)	2,854	32.36
German Russian (0)	0	<0.01
Greek (16)	16	0.18
Guyanese (0)	0	<0.01
Hungarian (3)	3	0.03
Icelander (0)	0	<0.01
Iranian (0)	0	<0.01
Irish (370)	1,495	16.95
Israeli (0)	0	<0.01
Italian (31)	102	1.16
Latvian (0)	0	<0.01
Lithuanian (5)	8	0.09
Luxemburger (0)	0	<0.01
Macedonian (0)	0	<0.01
Maltese (0)	0	<0.01
New Zealander (0)	0	<0.01
Northern European (0)	0	<0.01
Norwegian (24)	71	0.80
Pennsylvania German (0)	0	<0.01
Polish (67)	189	2.14
Portuguese (0)	0	<0.01
Romanian (0)	0	<0.01
Russian (0)	8	0.09
Scandinavian (22)	34	0.39
Scotch-Irish (41)	158	1.79
Scottish (76)	140	1.59
Serbian (0)	0	<0.01
Slavic (0)	0	<0.01
Slovak (0)	0	<0.01
Slovene (0)	0	<0.01
Soviet Union (0)	0	<0.01
Swedish (70)	149	1.69
Swiss (0)	17	0.19
Turkish (0)	0	<0.01
Ukrainian (0)	0	<0.01
Welsh (0)	15	0.17
West Indian, ex. Hispanic (0)	0	<0.01
Bahamian (0)	0	<0.01
Barbadian (0)	0	<0.01
Belizean (0)	0	<0.01
Bermudan (0)	0	<0.01
British West Indian (0)	0	<0.01
Dutch West Indian (0)	0	<0.01
Haitian (0)	0	<0.01
Jamaican (0)	0	<0.01
Trinidadian/Tobagonian (0)	0	<0.01
U.S. Virgin Islander (0)	0	<0.01
West Indian (0)	0	<0.01
Other West Indian (0)	0	<0.01
Yugoslavian (0)	0	<0.01

Hispanic Origin	Population	%
Hispanic or Latino (of any race)	431	4.87
Central American, ex. Mexican	6	0.07
Costa Rican	0	<0.01
Guatemalan	0	<0.01
Honduran	0	<0.01
Nicaraguan	0	<0.01
Panamanian	0	<0.01
Salvadoran	2	0.02
Other Central American	4	0.05
Cuban	9	0.10
Dominican Republic	0	<0.01
Mexican	378	4.27
Puerto Rican	7	0.08
South American	5	0.06
Argentinean	0	<0.01
Bolivian	0	<0.01
Chilean	4	0.05
Colombian	1	0.01
Ecuadorian	0	<0.01
Paraguayan	0	<0.01
Peruvian	0	<0.01
Uruguayan	0	<0.01
Venezuelan	0	<0.01
Other South American	0	<0.01
Other Hispanic or Latino	26	0.29

Race*	Population	%
African-American/Black (42)	78	0.88
Not Hispanic (36)	64	0.72
Hispanic (6)	14	0.16
American Indian/Alaska Native (11)	38	0.43
Not Hispanic (11)	36	0.41
Hispanic (0)	2	0.02
Alaska Athabascan *(Ala. Nat.)* (0)	0	<0.01
Aleut *(Alaska Native)* (0)	0	<0.01
Apache (0)	0	<0.01
Arapaho (0)	0	<0.01
Blackfeet (0)	1	0.01
Canadian/French Am. Ind. (0)	0	<0.01
Central American Ind. (0)	0	<0.01
Cherokee (10)	18	0.20
Cheyenne (0)	0	<0.01
Chickasaw (0)	0	<0.01
Chippewa (0)	0	<0.01
Choctaw (0)	0	<0.01
Colville (0)	0	<0.01
Comanche (0)	0	<0.01
Cree (0)	1	0.01
Creek (0)	0	<0.01
Crow (0)	0	<0.01
Delaware (0)	0	<0.01
Hopi (0)	0	<0.01
Houma (0)	0	<0.01
Inupiat *(Alaska Native)* (0)	0	<0.01
Iroquois (1)	1	0.01
Kiowa (0)	0	<0.01
Lumbee (0)	0	<0.01
Menominee (0)	0	<0.01
Mexican American Ind. (0)	1	0.01
Navajo (0)	0	<0.01
Osage (0)	0	<0.01
Ottawa (0)	0	<0.01
Paiute (0)	0	<0.01
Pima (0)	0	<0.01
Potawatomi (0)	0	<0.01
Pueblo (0)	0	<0.01
Puget Sound Salish (0)	0	<0.01
Seminole (0)	1	0.01
Shoshone (0)	0	<0.01
Sioux (0)	2	0.02
South American Ind. (0)	0	<0.01
Spanish American Ind. (0)	0	<0.01
Tlingit-Haida *(Alaska Native)* (0)	0	<0.01
Tohono O'Odham (0)	0	<0.01
Tsimshian *(Alaska Native)* (0)	0	<0.01
Ute (0)	0	<0.01
Yakama (0)	0	<0.01
Yaqui (0)	0	<0.01
Yuman (0)	0	<0.01
Yup'ik *(Alaska Native)* (0)	0	<0.01
Asian (15)	22	0.25
Not Hispanic (15)	22	0.25
Hispanic (0)	0	<0.01
Bangladeshi (0)	0	<0.01
Bhutanese (0)	0	<0.01
Burmese (0)	0	<0.01
Cambodian (0)	0	<0.01
Chinese, ex. Taiwanese (7)	7	0.08
Filipino (2)	3	0.03
Hmong (0)	0	<0.01
Indian (4)	9	0.10
Indonesian (0)	0	<0.01
Japanese (0)	0	<0.01
Korean (1)	2	0.02
Laotian (0)	0	<0.01
Malaysian (0)	0	<0.01
Nepalese (0)	0	<0.01
Pakistani (0)	0	<0.01
Sri Lankan (0)	0	<0.01
Taiwanese (0)	0	<0.01
Thai (0)	0	<0.01
Vietnamese (0)	0	<0.01
Hawaii Native/Pacific Islander (3)	3	0.03
Not Hispanic (3)	3	0.03
Hispanic (0)	0	<0.01
Fijian (0)	0	<0.01
Guamanian/Chamorro (2)	2	0.02
Marshallese (0)	0	<0.01
Native Hawaiian (0)	0	<0.01
Samoan (0)	1	0.01
Tongan (0)	0	<0.01
White (8,489)	8,586	96.97
Not Hispanic (8,298)	8,355	94.36
Hispanic (191)	231	2.61

*Notes: † The Census 2010 population figure is used to calculate the percentages in the Hispanic Origin and Race categories. Ancestry percentages are based on the 2006-2010 American Community Survey population (not shown); ‡ Numbers in parentheses indicate the number of people reporting a single ancestry; * Numbers in parentheses indicate the number of persons reporting this race alone, not in combination with any other race; Please refer to the Explanation of Data for more information.*

Blackford County

Population: 12,766

Ancestry	Population	%
Afghan (0)	0	<0.01
African, Sub-Saharan (0)	0	<0.01
African (0)	0	<0.01
Cape Verdean (0)	0	<0.01
Ethiopian (0)	0	<0.01
Ghanaian (0)	0	<0.01
Kenyan (0)	0	<0.01
Liberian (0)	0	<0.01
Nigerian (0)	0	<0.01
Senegalese (0)	0	<0.01
Sierra Leonean (0)	0	<0.01
Somalian (0)	0	<0.01
South African (0)	0	<0.01
Sudanese (0)	0	<0.01
Ugandan (0)	0	<0.01
Zimbabwean (0)	0	<0.01
Other Sub-Saharan African (0)	0	<0.01
Albanian (0)	0	<0.01
Alsatian (0)	0	<0.01
American (1,514)	1,514	11.68
Arab (0)	0	<0.01
Arab (0)	0	<0.01
Egyptian (0)	0	<0.01
Iraqi (0)	0	<0.01
Jordanian (0)	0	<0.01
Lebanese (0)	0	<0.01
Moroccan (0)	0	<0.01
Palestinian (0)	0	<0.01
Syrian (0)	0	<0.01
Other Arab (0)	0	<0.01
Armenian (0)	0	<0.01
Assyrian/Chaldean/Syriac (0)	0	<0.01
Australian (0)	0	<0.01
Austrian (0)	0	<0.01
Basque (0)	0	<0.01
Belgian (0)	0	<0.01
Brazilian (0)	0	<0.01
British (30)	112	0.86
Bulgarian (0)	0	<0.01
Cajun (0)	0	<0.01
Canadian (0)	28	0.22
Carpatho Rusyn (0)	0	<0.01
Celtic (0)	0	<0.01
Croatian (0)	0	<0.01
Cypriot (0)	0	<0.01
Czech (0)	35	0.27
Czechoslovakian (0)	0	<0.01
Danish (0)	0	<0.01
Dutch (189)	534	4.12
Eastern European (0)	0	<0.01
English (917)	1,760	13.58
Estonian (0)	0	<0.01
European (104)	115	0.89
Finnish (6)	13	0.10
French, ex. Basque (31)	252	1.94
French Canadian (29)	129	1.00
German (2,153)	3,992	30.80
German Russian (0)	0	<0.01
Greek (0)	10	0.08
Guyanese (0)	0	<0.01
Hungarian (22)	22	0.17
Icelander (0)	0	<0.01
Iranian (0)	0	<0.01
Irish (483)	2,170	16.74
Israeli (0)	0	<0.01
Italian (39)	183	1.41
Latvian (0)	0	<0.01
Lithuanian (0)	0	<0.01
Luxemburger (0)	0	<0.01
Macedonian (0)	0	<0.01
Maltese (0)	0	<0.01
New Zealander (0)	0	<0.01
Northern European (0)	0	<0.01
Norwegian (19)	19	0.15
Pennsylvania German (16)	16	0.12
Polish (31)	104	0.80
Portuguese (0)	0	<0.01
Romanian (0)	0	<0.01
Russian (2)	2	0.02
Scandinavian (0)	0	<0.01
Scotch-Irish (79)	183	1.41
Scottish (39)	132	1.02
Serbian (0)	0	<0.01
Slavic (0)	0	<0.01
Slovak (0)	12	0.09
Slovene (0)	0	<0.01
Soviet Union (0)	0	<0.01
Swedish (9)	48	0.37
Swiss (11)	78	0.60
Turkish (0)	0	<0.01
Ukrainian (0)	19	0.15
Welsh (6)	162	1.25
West Indian, ex. Hispanic (0)	0	<0.01
Bahamian (0)	0	<0.01
Barbadian (0)	0	<0.01
Belizean (0)	0	<0.01
Bermudan (0)	0	<0.01
British West Indian (0)	0	<0.01
Dutch West Indian (0)	0	<0.01
Haitian (0)	0	<0.01
Jamaican (0)	0	<0.01
Trinidadian/Tobagonian (0)	0	<0.01
U.S. Virgin Islander (0)	0	<0.01
West Indian (0)	0	<0.01
Other West Indian (0)	0	<0.01
Yugoslavian (0)	0	<0.01

Hispanic Origin	Population	%
Hispanic or Latino (of any race)	117	0.92
Central American, ex. Mexican	2	0.02
Costa Rican	0	<0.01
Guatemalan	2	0.02
Honduran	0	<0.01
Nicaraguan	0	<0.01
Panamanian	0	<0.01
Salvadoran	0	<0.01
Other Central American	0	<0.01
Cuban	1	0.01
Dominican Republic	0	<0.01
Mexican	90	0.70
Puerto Rican	8	0.06
South American	0	<0.01
Argentinean	0	<0.01
Bolivian	0	<0.01
Chilean	0	<0.01
Colombian	0	<0.01
Ecuadorian	0	<0.01
Paraguayan	0	<0.01
Peruvian	0	<0.01
Uruguayan	0	<0.01
Venezuelan	0	<0.01
Other South American	0	<0.01
Other Hispanic or Latino	16	0.13

Race*	Population	%
African-American/Black (49)	95	0.74
Not Hispanic (48)	93	0.73
Hispanic (1)	2	0.02
American Indian/Alaska Native (22)	100	0.78
Not Hispanic (22)	96	0.75
Hispanic (0)	4	0.03
Alaska Athabascan *(Ala. Nat.)* (0)	0	<0.01
Aleut *(Alaska Native)* (0)	0	<0.01
Apache (1)	1	0.01
Arapaho (0)	0	<0.01
Blackfeet (0)	5	0.04
Canadian/French Am. Ind. (0)	0	<0.01
Central American Ind. (0)	0	<0.01
Cherokee (1)	20	0.16
Cheyenne (0)	1	0.01
Chickasaw (0)	0	<0.01
Chippewa (0)	0	<0.01
Choctaw (0)	0	<0.01
Colville (0)	0	<0.01
Comanche (0)	0	<0.01
Cree (0)	1	0.01
Creek (0)	0	<0.01
Crow (0)	0	<0.01
Delaware (0)	0	<0.01
Hopi (0)	0	<0.01
Houma (0)	0	<0.01
Inupiat *(Alaska Native)* (0)	1	0.01
Iroquois (1)	5	0.04
Kiowa (0)	0	<0.01
Lumbee (2)	2	0.02
Menominee (1)	1	0.01
Mexican American Ind. (0)	0	<0.01
Navajo (0)	0	<0.01
Osage (0)	0	<0.01
Ottawa (1)	2	0.02
Paiute (0)	0	<0.01
Pima (0)	0	<0.01
Potawatomi (0)	0	<0.01
Pueblo (0)	2	0.02
Puget Sound Salish (0)	0	<0.01
Seminole (0)	0	<0.01
Shoshone (2)	2	0.02
Sioux (1)	5	0.04
South American Ind. (0)	0	<0.01
Spanish American Ind. (0)	0	<0.01
Tlingit-Haida *(Alaska Native)* (0)	0	<0.01
Tohono O'Odham (0)	0	<0.01
Tsimshian *(Alaska Native)* (0)	0	<0.01
Ute (0)	0	<0.01
Yakama (0)	0	<0.01
Yaqui (0)	0	<0.01
Yuman (0)	0	<0.01
Yup'ik *(Alaska Native)* (0)	0	<0.01
Asian (19)	39	0.31
Not Hispanic (19)	39	0.31
Hispanic (0)	0	<0.01
Bangladeshi (0)	0	<0.01
Bhutanese (0)	0	<0.01
Burmese (0)	0	<0.01
Cambodian (0)	0	<0.01
Chinese, ex. Taiwanese (4)	4	0.03
Filipino (4)	15	0.12
Hmong (0)	0	<0.01
Indian (2)	6	0.05
Indonesian (0)	0	<0.01
Japanese (1)	2	0.02
Korean (4)	8	0.06
Laotian (0)	0	<0.01
Malaysian (0)	0	<0.01
Nepalese (0)	0	<0.01
Pakistani (0)	0	<0.01
Sri Lankan (0)	0	<0.01
Taiwanese (0)	0	<0.01
Thai (0)	0	<0.01
Vietnamese (2)	2	0.02
Hawaii Native/Pacific Islander (4)	13	0.10
Not Hispanic (4)	12	0.09
Hispanic (0)	1	0.01
Fijian (0)	0	<0.01
Guamanian/Chamorro (0)	0	<0.01
Marshallese (0)	0	<0.01
Native Hawaiian (3)	9	0.07
Samoan (1)	4	0.03
Tongan (0)	0	<0.01
White (12,470)	12,629	98.93
Not Hispanic (12,403)	12,545	98.27
Hispanic (67)	84	0.66

*Notes: † The Census 2010 population figure is used to calculate the percentages in the Hispanic Origin and Race categories. Ancestry percentages are based on the 2006-2010 American Community Survey population (not shown); ‡ Numbers in parentheses indicate the number of people reporting a single ancestry; * Numbers in parentheses indicate the number of persons reporting this race alone, not in combination with any other race; Please refer to the Explanation of Data for more information.*

Boone County

Population: 56,640

Ancestry	Population	%
Afghan (0)	0	<0.01
African, Sub-Saharan (81)	113	0.21
African (0)	32	0.06
Cape Verdean (0)	0	<0.01
Ethiopian (12)	12	0.02
Ghanaian (0)	0	<0.01
Kenyan (0)	0	<0.01
Liberian (0)	0	<0.01
Nigerian (0)	0	<0.01
Senegalese (0)	0	<0.01
Sierra Leonean (0)	0	<0.01
Somalian (69)	69	0.13
South African (0)	0	<0.01
Sudanese (0)	0	<0.01
Ugandan (0)	0	<0.01
Zimbabwean (0)	0	<0.01
Other Sub-Saharan African (0)	0	<0.01
Albanian (13)	13	0.02
Alsatian (0)	0	<0.01
American (4,933)	4,933	9.00
Arab (53)	174	0.32
Arab (0)	0	<0.01
Egyptian (27)	38	0.07
Iraqi (0)	0	<0.01
Jordanian (0)	0	<0.01
Lebanese (0)	45	0.08
Moroccan (0)	0	<0.01
Palestinian (0)	0	<0.01
Syrian (0)	65	0.12
Other Arab (26)	26	0.05
Armenian (0)	0	<0.01
Assyrian/Chaldean/Syriac (0)	0	<0.01
Australian (0)	0	<0.01
Austrian (10)	74	0.14
Basque (0)	10	0.02
Belgian (59)	102	0.19
Brazilian (0)	0	<0.01
British (243)	329	0.60
Bulgarian (0)	54	0.10
Cajun (0)	0	<0.01
Canadian (108)	169	0.31
Carpatho Rusyn (0)	0	<0.01
Celtic (0)	17	0.03
Croatian (9)	95	0.17
Cypriot (0)	0	<0.01
Czech (41)	194	0.35
Czechoslovakian (99)	99	0.18
Danish (46)	173	0.32
Dutch (328)	1,300	2.37
Eastern European (33)	71	0.13
English (5,917)	10,595	19.34
Estonian (0)	0	<0.01
European (877)	976	1.78
Finnish (41)	104	0.19
French, ex. Basque (310)	1,843	3.36
French Canadian (87)	178	0.32
German (6,755)	15,863	28.95
German Russian (0)	0	<0.01
Greek (144)	217	0.40
Guyanese (0)	0	<0.01
Hungarian (48)	262	0.48
Icelander (0)	0	<0.01
Iranian (52)	66	0.12
Irish (2,326)	7,740	14.13
Israeli (0)	0	<0.01
Italian (718)	2,000	3.65
Latvian (0)	0	<0.01
Lithuanian (12)	104	0.19
Luxemburger (0)	11	0.02
Macedonian (2)	10	0.02
Maltese (0)	0	<0.01
New Zealander (13)	13	0.02
Northern European (58)	58	0.11
Norwegian (104)	294	0.54
Pennsylvania German (21)	42	0.08
Polish (486)	1,107	2.02
Portuguese (62)	62	0.11
Romanian (20)	83	0.15
Russian (77)	344	0.63
Scandinavian (0)	10	0.02
Scotch-Irish (527)	923	1.68
Scottish (756)	1,623	2.96
Serbian (0)	42	0.08
Slavic (105)	119	0.22
Slovak (144)	286	0.52
Slovene (18)	63	0.11
Soviet Union (0)	0	<0.01
Swedish (164)	464	0.85
Swiss (30)	182	0.33
Turkish (0)	0	<0.01
Ukrainian (97)	206	0.38
Welsh (75)	250	0.46
West Indian, ex. Hispanic (0)	14	0.03
Bahamian (0)	0	<0.01
Barbadian (0)	0	<0.01
Belizean (0)	0	<0.01
Bermudan (0)	0	<0.01
British West Indian (0)	0	<0.01
Dutch West Indian (0)	14	0.03
Haitian (0)	0	<0.01
Jamaican (0)	0	<0.01
Trinidadian/Tobagonian (0)	0	<0.01
U.S. Virgin Islander (0)	0	<0.01
West Indian (0)	0	<0.01
Other West Indian (0)	0	<0.01
Yugoslavian (55)	55	0.10

Hispanic Origin	Population	%
Hispanic or Latino (of any race)	1,270	2.24
Central American, ex. Mexican	107	0.19
Costa Rican	5	0.01
Guatemalan	40	0.07
Honduran	27	0.05
Nicaraguan	6	0.01
Panamanian	14	0.02
Salvadoran	14	0.02
Other Central American	1	<0.01
Cuban	35	0.06
Dominican Republic	16	0.03
Mexican	741	1.31
Puerto Rican	135	0.24
South American	120	0.21
Argentinean	19	0.03
Bolivian	7	0.01
Chilean	6	0.01
Colombian	52	0.09
Ecuadorian	14	0.02
Paraguayan	1	<0.01
Peruvian	10	0.02
Uruguayan	1	<0.01
Venezuelan	10	0.02
Other South American	0	<0.01
Other Hispanic or Latino	116	0.20

Race*	Population	%
African-American/Black (495)	741	1.31
Not Hispanic (484)	706	1.25
Hispanic (11)	35	0.06
American Indian/Alaska Native (103)	305	0.54
Not Hispanic (91)	283	0.50
Hispanic (12)	22	0.04
Alaska Athabascan *(Ala. Nat.)* (0)	0	<0.01
Aleut *(Alaska Native)* (0)	0	<0.01
Apache (0)	3	0.01
Arapaho (0)	0	<0.01
Blackfeet (4)	10	0.02
Canadian/French Am. Ind. (0)	1	<0.01
Central American Ind. (0)	0	<0.01
Cherokee (19)	76	0.13
Cheyenne (1)	2	<0.01
Chickasaw (1)	2	<0.01
Chippewa (0)	4	0.01
Choctaw (5)	7	0.01
Colville (0)	0	<0.01
Comanche (0)	1	<0.01
Cree (0)	0	<0.01
Creek (0)	1	<0.01
Crow (0)	1	<0.01
Delaware (3)	3	0.01
Hopi (0)	0	<0.01
Houma (0)	0	<0.01
Inupiat *(Alaska Native)* (0)	2	<0.01
Iroquois (3)	7	0.01
Kiowa (4)	4	0.01
Lumbee (2)	4	0.01
Menominee (0)	0	<0.01
Mexican American Ind. (0)	1	<0.01
Navajo (3)	5	0.01
Osage (0)	1	<0.01
Ottawa (0)	1	<0.01
Paiute (2)	4	0.01
Pima (0)	0	<0.01
Potawatomi (0)	3	0.01
Pueblo (3)	3	0.01
Puget Sound Salish (0)	0	<0.01
Seminole (0)	1	<0.01
Shoshone (0)	0	<0.01
Sioux (4)	9	0.02
South American Ind. (0)	5	0.01
Spanish American Ind. (0)	0	<0.01
Tlingit-Haida *(Alaska Native)* (0)	0	<0.01
Tohono O'Odham (0)	0	<0.01
Tsimshian *(Alaska Native)* (0)	0	<0.01
Ute (0)	0	<0.01
Yakama (0)	0	<0.01
Yaqui (0)	0	<0.01
Yuman (0)	0	<0.01
Yup'ik *(Alaska Native)* (0)	0	<0.01
Asian (942)	1,214	2.14
Not Hispanic (941)	1,201	2.12
Hispanic (1)	13	0.02
Bangladeshi (2)	5	0.01
Bhutanese (0)	0	<0.01
Burmese (0)	1	<0.01
Cambodian (1)	1	<0.01
Chinese, ex. Taiwanese (329)	362	0.64
Filipino (73)	140	0.25
Hmong (8)	12	0.02
Indian (216)	257	0.45
Indonesian (1)	5	0.01
Japanese (38)	82	0.14
Korean (71)	122	0.22
Laotian (3)	3	0.01
Malaysian (1)	1	<0.01
Nepalese (0)	0	<0.01
Pakistani (50)	54	0.10
Sri Lankan (3)	3	0.01
Taiwanese (21)	24	0.04
Thai (11)	14	0.02
Vietnamese (68)	80	0.14
Hawaii Native/Pacific Islander (11)	30	0.05
Not Hispanic (10)	28	0.05
Hispanic (1)	2	<0.01
Fijian (0)	0	<0.01
Guamanian/Chamorro (1)	3	0.01
Marshallese (0)	0	<0.01
Native Hawaiian (1)	6	0.01
Samoan (1)	3	0.01
Tongan (0)	0	<0.01
White (53,953)	54,685	96.55
Not Hispanic (53,151)	53,789	94.97
Hispanic (802)	896	1.58

*Notes: † The Census 2010 population figure is used to calculate the percentages in the Hispanic Origin and Race categories. Ancestry percentages are based on the 2006-2010 American Community Survey population (not shown); ‡ Numbers in parentheses indicate the number of people reporting a single ancestry; * Numbers in parentheses indicate the number of persons reporting this race alone, not in combination with any other race; Please refer to the Explanation of Data for more information.*

Brown County

Population: 15,242

Ancestry	Population	%
Afghan (0)	0	<0.01
African, Sub-Saharan (0)	23	0.15
African (0)	23	0.15
Cape Verdean (0)	0	<0.01
Ethiopian (0)	0	<0.01
Ghanaian (0)	0	<0.01
Kenyan (0)	0	<0.01
Liberian (0)	0	<0.01
Nigerian (0)	0	<0.01
Senegalese (0)	0	<0.01
Sierra Leonean (0)	0	<0.01
Somalian (0)	0	<0.01
South African (0)	0	<0.01
Sudanese (0)	0	<0.01
Ugandan (0)	0	<0.01
Zimbabwean (0)	0	<0.01
Other Sub-Saharan African (0)	0	<0.01
Albanian (0)	0	<0.01
Alsatian (0)	0	<0.01
American (1,719)	1,719	11.26
Arab (0)	0	<0.01
Arab (0)	0	<0.01
Egyptian (0)	0	<0.01
Iraqi (0)	0	<0.01
Jordanian (0)	0	<0.01
Lebanese (0)	0	<0.01
Moroccan (0)	0	<0.01
Palestinian (0)	0	<0.01
Syrian (0)	0	<0.01
Other Arab (0)	0	<0.01
Armenian (0)	0	<0.01
Assyrian/Chaldean/Syriac (0)	0	<0.01
Australian (0)	0	<0.01
Austrian (0)	3	0.02
Basque (0)	0	<0.01
Belgian (0)	58	0.38
Brazilian (0)	0	<0.01
British (73)	148	0.97
Bulgarian (0)	0	<0.01
Cajun (0)	0	<0.01
Canadian (11)	31	0.20
Carpatho Rusyn (0)	0	<0.01
Celtic (0)	0	<0.01
Croatian (0)	0	<0.01
Cypriot (0)	0	<0.01
Czech (9)	9	0.06
Czechoslovakian (5)	5	0.03
Danish (0)	12	0.08
Dutch (40)	396	2.59
Eastern European (18)	18	0.12
English (758)	1,764	11.55
Estonian (0)	0	<0.01
European (234)	283	1.85
Finnish (0)	0	<0.01
French, ex. Basque (114)	330	2.16
French Canadian (28)	40	0.26
German (1,793)	4,159	27.23
German Russian (0)	0	<0.01
Greek (25)	136	0.89
Guyanese (0)	0	<0.01
Hungarian (13)	95	0.62
Icelander (0)	0	<0.01
Iranian (0)	0	<0.01
Irish (520)	2,000	13.10
Israeli (0)	0	<0.01
Italian (186)	358	2.34
Latvian (0)	0	<0.01
Lithuanian (0)	0	<0.01
Luxemburger (0)	0	<0.01
Macedonian (0)	0	<0.01
Maltese (0)	0	<0.01
New Zealander (0)	0	<0.01
Northern European (0)	23	0.15
Norwegian (27)	78	0.51
Pennsylvania German (0)	0	<0.01
Polish (109)	347	2.27
Portuguese (0)	0	<0.01
Romanian (13)	47	0.31
Russian (0)	62	0.41
Scandinavian (0)	0	<0.01
Scotch-Irish (102)	291	1.91
Scottish (266)	474	3.10
Serbian (0)	0	<0.01
Slavic (0)	0	<0.01
Slovak (18)	67	0.44
Slovene (0)	0	<0.01
Soviet Union (0)	0	<0.01
Swedish (12)	93	0.61
Swiss (9)	9	0.06
Turkish (0)	0	<0.01
Ukrainian (0)	0	<0.01
Welsh (11)	112	0.73
West Indian, ex. Hispanic (0)	0	<0.01
Bahamian (0)	0	<0.01
Barbadian (0)	0	<0.01
Belizean (0)	0	<0.01
Bermudan (0)	0	<0.01
British West Indian (0)	0	<0.01
Dutch West Indian (0)	0	<0.01
Haitian (0)	0	<0.01
Jamaican (0)	0	<0.01
Trinidadian/Tobagonian (0)	0	<0.01
U.S. Virgin Islander (0)	0	<0.01
West Indian (0)	0	<0.01
Other West Indian (0)	0	<0.01
Yugoslavian (0)	41	0.27

Hispanic Origin	Population	%
Hispanic or Latino (of any race)	178	1.17
Central American, ex. Mexican	12	0.08
Costa Rican	0	<0.01
Guatemalan	6	0.04
Honduran	5	0.03
Nicaraguan	0	<0.01
Panamanian	1	0.01
Salvadoran	0	<0.01
Other Central American	0	<0.01
Cuban	8	0.05
Dominican Republic	0	<0.01
Mexican	129	0.85
Puerto Rican	6	0.04
South American	4	0.03
Argentinean	1	0.01
Bolivian	0	<0.01
Chilean	0	<0.01
Colombian	1	0.01
Ecuadorian	0	<0.01
Paraguayan	1	0.01
Peruvian	0	<0.01
Uruguayan	0	<0.01
Venezuelan	1	0.01
Other South American	0	<0.01
Other Hispanic or Latino	19	0.12

Race*	Population	%
African-American/Black (53)	85	0.56
Not Hispanic (53)	85	0.56
Hispanic (0)	0	<0.01
American Indian/Alaska Native (50)	147	0.96
Not Hispanic (47)	128	0.84
Hispanic (3)	19	0.12
Alaska Athabascan *(Ala. Nat.)* (0)	0	<0.01
Aleut *(Alaska Native)* (0)	0	<0.01
Apache (0)	4	0.03
Arapaho (0)	0	<0.01
Blackfeet (0)	8	0.05
Canadian/French Am. Ind. (0)	0	<0.01
Central American Ind. (0)	0	<0.01
Cherokee (3)	38	0.25
Cheyenne (0)	0	<0.01
Chickasaw (0)	0	<0.01
Chippewa (2)	4	0.03
Choctaw (0)	1	0.01
Colville (0)	0	<0.01
Comanche (0)	0	<0.01
Cree (0)	0	<0.01
Creek (0)	0	<0.01
Crow (0)	0	<0.01
Delaware (0)	0	<0.01
Hopi (0)	0	<0.01
Houma (0)	0	<0.01
Inupiat *(Alaska Native)* (0)	0	<0.01
Iroquois (0)	0	<0.01
Kiowa (0)	0	<0.01
Lumbee (0)	0	<0.01
Menominee (0)	0	<0.01
Mexican American Ind. (0)	0	<0.01
Navajo (0)	0	<0.01
Osage (0)	0	<0.01
Ottawa (0)	0	<0.01
Paiute (0)	0	<0.01
Pima (0)	0	<0.01
Potawatomi (1)	1	0.01
Pueblo (2)	2	0.01
Puget Sound Salish (0)	0	<0.01
Seminole (0)	0	<0.01
Shoshone (0)	0	<0.01
Sioux (5)	11	0.07
South American Ind. (0)	0	<0.01
Spanish American Ind. (0)	0	<0.01
Tlingit-Haida *(Alaska Native)* (0)	0	<0.01
Tohono O'Odham (1)	1	0.01
Tsimshian *(Alaska Native)* (0)	0	<0.01
Ute (0)	7	0.05
Yakama (0)	0	<0.01
Yaqui (0)	0	<0.01
Yuman (0)	0	<0.01
Yup'ik *(Alaska Native)* (0)	0	<0.01
Asian (44)	78	0.51
Not Hispanic (44)	77	0.51
Hispanic (0)	1	0.01
Bangladeshi (0)	0	<0.01
Bhutanese (0)	0	<0.01
Burmese (0)	0	<0.01
Cambodian (0)	0	<0.01
Chinese, ex. Taiwanese (11)	12	0.08
Filipino (17)	29	0.19
Hmong (0)	0	<0.01
Indian (1)	5	0.03
Indonesian (0)	0	<0.01
Japanese (1)	7	0.05
Korean (4)	9	0.06
Laotian (0)	0	<0.01
Malaysian (1)	1	0.01
Nepalese (0)	0	<0.01
Pakistani (0)	0	<0.01
Sri Lankan (0)	0	<0.01
Taiwanese (1)	1	0.01
Thai (4)	6	0.04
Vietnamese (0)	3	0.02
Hawaii Native/Pacific Islander (1)	8	0.05
Not Hispanic (1)	8	0.05
Hispanic (0)	0	<0.01
Fijian (0)	0	<0.01
Guamanian/Chamorro (1)	2	0.01
Marshallese (0)	0	<0.01
Native Hawaiian (0)	1	0.01
Samoan (0)	0	<0.01
Tongan (0)	0	<0.01
White (14,874)	15,040	98.67
Not Hispanic (14,761)	14,900	97.76
Hispanic (113)	140	0.92

*Notes: † The Census 2010 population figure is used to calculate the percentages in the Hispanic Origin and Race categories. Ancestry percentages are based on the 2006-2010 American Community Survey population (not shown); ‡ Numbers in parentheses indicate the number of people reporting a single ancestry; * Numbers in parentheses indicate the number of persons reporting this race alone, not in combination with any other race; Please refer to the Explanation of Data for more information.*

Carroll County

Population: 20,155

Ancestry	Population	%
Afghan (0)	0	<0.01
African, Sub-Saharan (0)	0	<0.01
African (0)	0	<0.01
Cape Verdean (0)	0	<0.01
Ethiopian (0)	0	<0.01
Ghanaian (0)	0	<0.01
Kenyan (0)	0	<0.01
Liberian (0)	0	<0.01
Nigerian (0)	0	<0.01
Senegalese (0)	0	<0.01
Sierra Leonean (0)	0	<0.01
Somalian (0)	0	<0.01
South African (0)	0	<0.01
Sudanese (0)	0	<0.01
Ugandan (0)	0	<0.01
Zimbabwean (0)	0	<0.01
Other Sub-Saharan African (0)	0	<0.01
Albanian (0)	0	<0.01
Alsatian (0)	0	<0.01
American (2,964)	2,964	14.72
Arab (31)	90	0.45
Arab (31)	90	0.45
Egyptian (0)	0	<0.01
Iraqi (0)	0	<0.01
Jordanian (0)	0	<0.01
Lebanese (0)	0	<0.01
Moroccan (0)	0	<0.01
Palestinian (0)	0	<0.01
Syrian (0)	0	<0.01
Other Arab (0)	0	<0.01
Armenian (0)	0	<0.01
Assyrian/Chaldean/Syriac (0)	0	<0.01
Australian (8)	8	0.04
Austrian (0)	0	<0.01
Basque (0)	0	<0.01
Belgian (0)	25	0.12
Brazilian (0)	0	<0.01
British (20)	40	0.20
Bulgarian (0)	18	0.09
Cajun (0)	0	<0.01
Canadian (0)	0	<0.01
Carpatho Rusyn (0)	0	<0.01
Celtic (23)	23	0.11
Croatian (0)	8	0.04
Cypriot (0)	0	<0.01
Czech (15)	30	0.15
Czechoslovakian (29)	64	0.32
Danish (14)	26	0.13
Dutch (100)	555	2.76
Eastern European (21)	21	0.10
English (799)	1,779	8.84
Estonian (0)	0	<0.01
European (46)	46	0.23
Finnish (0)	0	<0.01
French, ex. Basque (107)	401	1.99
French Canadian (12)	32	0.16
German (2,761)	5,987	29.73
German Russian (0)	0	<0.01
Greek (27)	27	0.13
Guyanese (0)	0	<0.01
Hungarian (13)	52	0.26
Icelander (0)	0	<0.01
Iranian (0)	0	<0.01
Irish (770)	2,543	12.63
Israeli (0)	0	<0.01
Italian (149)	480	2.38
Latvian (0)	0	<0.01
Lithuanian (9)	36	0.18
Luxemburger (0)	0	<0.01
Macedonian (0)	0	<0.01
Maltese (0)	0	<0.01
New Zealander (0)	0	<0.01
Northern European (0)	0	<0.01
Norwegian (49)	122	0.61
Pennsylvania German (61)	72	0.36
Polish (150)	383	1.90
Portuguese (30)	63	0.31
Romanian (10)	10	0.05
Russian (0)	13	0.06
Scandinavian (12)	12	0.06
Scotch-Irish (161)	267	1.33
Scottish (183)	578	2.87
Serbian (0)	0	<0.01
Slavic (0)	0	<0.01
Slovak (19)	32	0.16
Slovene (6)	6	0.03
Soviet Union (0)	0	<0.01
Swedish (131)	382	1.90
Swiss (6)	64	0.32
Turkish (0)	0	<0.01
Ukrainian (11)	11	0.05
Welsh (7)	85	0.42
West Indian, ex. Hispanic (0)	0	<0.01
Bahamian (0)	0	<0.01
Barbadian (0)	0	<0.01
Belizean (0)	0	<0.01
Bermudan (0)	0	<0.01
British West Indian (0)	0	<0.01
Dutch West Indian (0)	0	<0.01
Haitian (0)	0	<0.01
Jamaican (0)	0	<0.01
Trinidadian/Tobagonian (0)	0	<0.01
U.S. Virgin Islander (0)	0	<0.01
West Indian (0)	0	<0.01
Other West Indian (0)	0	<0.01
Yugoslavian (0)	0	<0.01

Hispanic Origin	Population	%
Hispanic or Latino (of any race)	711	3.53
Central American, ex. Mexican	80	0.40
Costa Rican	1	<0.01
Guatemalan	35	0.17
Honduran	6	0.03
Nicaraguan	0	<0.01
Panamanian	0	<0.01
Salvadoran	38	0.19
Other Central American	0	<0.01
Cuban	17	0.08
Dominican Republic	0	<0.01
Mexican	546	2.71
Puerto Rican	21	0.10
South American	6	0.03
Argentinean	0	<0.01
Bolivian	0	<0.01
Chilean	0	<0.01
Colombian	3	0.01
Ecuadorian	0	<0.01
Paraguayan	0	<0.01
Peruvian	1	<0.01
Uruguayan	2	0.01
Venezuelan	0	<0.01
Other South American	0	<0.01
Other Hispanic or Latino	41	0.20

Race*	Population	%
African-American/Black (48)	111	0.55
Not Hispanic (42)	101	0.50
Hispanic (6)	10	0.05
American Indian/Alaska Native (38)	112	0.56
Not Hispanic (33)	85	0.42
Hispanic (5)	27	0.13
Alaska Athabascan *(Ala. Nat.)* (0)	0	<0.01
Aleut *(Alaska Native)* (0)	0	<0.01
Apache (2)	4	0.02
Arapaho (0)	0	<0.01
Blackfeet (0)	1	<0.01
Canadian/French Am. Ind. (1)	8	0.04
Central American Ind. (0)	0	<0.01
Cherokee (12)	32	0.16
Cheyenne (0)	0	<0.01
Chickasaw (0)	0	<0.01
Chippewa (0)	1	<0.01
Choctaw (2)	2	0.01
Colville (0)	0	<0.01
Comanche (0)	0	<0.01
Cree (0)	0	<0.01
Creek (0)	0	<0.01
Crow (0)	2	0.01
Delaware (0)	0	<0.01
Hopi (0)	0	<0.01
Houma (0)	0	<0.01
Inupiat *(Alaska Native)* (0)	0	<0.01
Iroquois (0)	1	<0.01
Kiowa (0)	0	<0.01
Lumbee (0)	0	<0.01
Menominee (0)	0	<0.01
Mexican American Ind. (1)	11	0.05
Navajo (0)	0	<0.01
Osage (0)	0	<0.01
Ottawa (1)	1	<0.01
Paiute (0)	0	<0.01
Pima (0)	0	<0.01
Potawatomi (1)	2	0.01
Pueblo (0)	0	<0.01
Puget Sound Salish (0)	0	<0.01
Seminole (0)	0	<0.01
Shoshone (0)	0	<0.01
Sioux (1)	6	0.03
South American Ind. (0)	0	<0.01
Spanish American Ind. (0)	0	<0.01
Tlingit-Haida *(Alaska Native)* (0)	0	<0.01
Tohono O'Odham (0)	0	<0.01
Tsimshian *(Alaska Native)* (0)	0	<0.01
Ute (0)	0	<0.01
Yakama (0)	0	<0.01
Yaqui (0)	0	<0.01
Yuman (0)	0	<0.01
Yup'ik *(Alaska Native)* (0)	0	<0.01
Asian (21)	52	0.26
Not Hispanic (20)	51	0.25
Hispanic (1)	1	<0.01
Bangladeshi (0)	0	<0.01
Bhutanese (0)	0	<0.01
Burmese (0)	0	<0.01
Cambodian (0)	0	<0.01
Chinese, ex. Taiwanese (8)	12	0.06
Filipino (6)	17	0.08
Hmong (0)	0	<0.01
Indian (1)	4	0.02
Indonesian (0)	1	<0.01
Japanese (1)	8	0.04
Korean (1)	6	0.03
Laotian (1)	1	<0.01
Malaysian (0)	0	<0.01
Nepalese (0)	0	<0.01
Pakistani (0)	0	<0.01
Sri Lankan (0)	0	<0.01
Taiwanese (0)	1	<0.01
Thai (1)	1	<0.01
Vietnamese (0)	1	<0.01
Hawaii Native/Pacific Islander (1)	8	0.04
Not Hispanic (1)	6	0.03
Hispanic (0)	2	0.01
Fijian (0)	0	<0.01
Guamanian/Chamorro (0)	1	<0.01
Marshallese (0)	0	<0.01
Native Hawaiian (0)	5	0.02
Samoan (0)	1	<0.01
Tongan (0)	0	<0.01
White (19,500)	19,687	97.68
Not Hispanic (19,188)	19,332	95.92
Hispanic (312)	355	1.76

*Notes: † The Census 2010 population figure is used to calculate the percentages in the Hispanic Origin and Race categories. Ancestry percentages are based on the 2006-2010 American Community Survey population (not shown); ‡ Numbers in parentheses indicate the number of people reporting a single ancestry; * Numbers in parentheses indicate the number of persons reporting this race alone, not in combination with any other race; Please refer to the Explanation of Data for more information.*

Cass County

Population: 38,966

Ancestry	Population	%
Afghan (0)	0	<0.01
African, Sub-Saharan (66)	70	0.18
African (66)	70	0.18
Cape Verdean (0)	0	<0.01
Ethiopian (0)	0	<0.01
Ghanaian (0)	0	<0.01
Kenyan (0)	0	<0.01
Liberian (0)	0	<0.01
Nigerian (0)	0	<0.01
Senegalese (0)	0	<0.01
Sierra Leonean (0)	0	<0.01
Somalian (0)	0	<0.01
South African (0)	0	<0.01
Sudanese (0)	0	<0.01
Ugandan (0)	0	<0.01
Zimbabwean (0)	0	<0.01
Other Sub-Saharan African (0)	0	<0.01
Albanian (0)	0	<0.01
Alsatian (0)	0	<0.01
American (5,862)	5,862	15.01
Arab (0)	0	<0.01
Arab (0)	0	<0.01
Egyptian (0)	0	<0.01
Iraqi (0)	0	<0.01
Jordanian (0)	0	<0.01
Lebanese (0)	0	<0.01
Moroccan (0)	0	<0.01
Palestinian (0)	0	<0.01
Syrian (0)	0	<0.01
Other Arab (0)	0	<0.01
Armenian (0)	0	<0.01
Assyrian/Chaldean/Syriac (0)	0	<0.01
Australian (0)	12	0.03
Austrian (0)	13	0.03
Basque (0)	0	<0.01
Belgian (0)	22	0.06
Brazilian (0)	0	<0.01
British (4)	38	0.10
Bulgarian (0)	0	<0.01
Cajun (0)	0	<0.01
Canadian (11)	63	0.16
Carpatho Rusyn (0)	0	<0.01
Celtic (0)	0	<0.01
Croatian (0)	9	0.02
Cypriot (0)	0	<0.01
Czech (18)	89	0.23
Czechoslovakian (26)	26	0.07
Danish (19)	144	0.37
Dutch (148)	839	2.15
Eastern European (0)	11	0.03
English (1,315)	3,523	9.02
Estonian (0)	0	<0.01
European (145)	157	0.40
Finnish (16)	16	0.04
French, ex. Basque (135)	823	2.11
French Canadian (12)	61	0.16
German (4,131)	9,358	23.96
German Russian (0)	0	<0.01
Greek (33)	64	0.16
Guyanese (0)	0	<0.01
Hungarian (14)	93	0.24
Icelander (0)	0	<0.01
Iranian (0)	0	<0.01
Irish (1,310)	4,619	11.83
Israeli (0)	0	<0.01
Italian (613)	1,328	3.40
Latvian (0)	0	<0.01
Lithuanian (14)	17	0.04
Luxemburger (0)	0	<0.01
Macedonian (0)	0	<0.01
Maltese (0)	0	<0.01
New Zealander (0)	0	<0.01
Northern European (13)	13	0.03
Norwegian (35)	79	0.20
Pennsylvania German (9)	23	0.06
Polish (301)	842	2.16
Portuguese (0)	0	<0.01
Romanian (0)	0	<0.01
Russian (19)	33	0.08
Scandinavian (32)	40	0.10
Scotch-Irish (159)	278	0.71
Scottish (79)	303	0.78
Serbian (52)	52	0.13
Slavic (0)	0	<0.01
Slovak (26)	31	0.08
Slovene (0)	0	<0.01
Soviet Union (0)	0	<0.01
Swedish (132)	423	1.08
Swiss (40)	105	0.27
Turkish (0)	0	<0.01
Ukrainian (14)	31	0.08
Welsh (72)	216	0.55
West Indian, ex. Hispanic (0)	0	<0.01
Bahamian (0)	0	<0.01
Barbadian (0)	0	<0.01
Belizean (0)	0	<0.01
Bermudan (0)	0	<0.01
British West Indian (0)	0	<0.01
Dutch West Indian (0)	0	<0.01
Haitian (0)	0	<0.01
Jamaican (0)	0	<0.01
Trinidadian/Tobagonian (0)	0	<0.01
U.S. Virgin Islander (0)	0	<0.01
West Indian (0)	0	<0.01
Other West Indian (0)	0	<0.01
Yugoslavian (0)	0	<0.01

Hispanic Origin	Population	%
Hispanic or Latino (of any race)	4,897	12.57
Central American, ex. Mexican	699	1.79
Costa Rican	0	<0.01
Guatemalan	430	1.10
Honduran	75	0.19
Nicaraguan	12	0.03
Panamanian	2	0.01
Salvadoran	180	0.46
Other Central American	0	<0.01
Cuban	66	0.17
Dominican Republic	50	0.13
Mexican	3,571	9.16
Puerto Rican	90	0.23
South American	73	0.19
Argentinean	4	0.01
Bolivian	0	<0.01
Chilean	0	<0.01
Colombian	7	0.02
Ecuadorian	13	0.03
Paraguayan	0	<0.01
Peruvian	47	0.12
Uruguayan	0	<0.01
Venezuelan	2	0.01
Other South American	0	<0.01
Other Hispanic or Latino	348	0.89

Race*	Population	%
African-American/Black (578)	787	2.02
Not Hispanic (519)	703	1.80
Hispanic (59)	84	0.22
American Indian/Alaska Native (199)	351	0.90
Not Hispanic (100)	227	0.58
Hispanic (99)	124	0.32
Alaska Athabascan *(Ala. Nat.)* (0)	0	<0.01
Aleut *(Alaska Native)* (1)	1	<0.01
Apache (6)	6	0.02
Arapaho (0)	1	<0.01
Blackfeet (0)	0	<0.01
Canadian/French Am. Ind. (1)	3	0.01
Central American Ind. (30)	30	0.08
Cherokee (15)	52	0.13
Cheyenne (0)	4	0.01
Chickasaw (0)	0	<0.01
Chippewa (5)	6	0.02
Choctaw (3)	4	0.01
Colville (0)	0	<0.01
Comanche (0)	0	<0.01
Cree (3)	3	0.01
Creek (0)	1	<0.01
Crow (0)	6	0.02
Delaware (0)	0	<0.01
Hopi (0)	0	<0.01
Houma (0)	0	<0.01
Inupiat *(Alaska Native)* (0)	0	<0.01
Iroquois (2)	5	0.01
Kiowa (0)	0	<0.01
Lumbee (0)	0	<0.01
Menominee (0)	0	<0.01
Mexican American Ind. (20)	32	0.08
Navajo (1)	1	<0.01
Osage (0)	4	0.01
Ottawa (0)	0	<0.01
Paiute (0)	0	<0.01
Pima (0)	0	<0.01
Potawatomi (0)	3	0.01
Pueblo (0)	0	<0.01
Puget Sound Salish (0)	0	<0.01
Seminole (0)	0	<0.01
Shoshone (0)	0	<0.01
Sioux (7)	15	0.04
South American Ind. (0)	0	<0.01
Spanish American Ind. (0)	0	<0.01
Tlingit-Haida *(Alaska Native)* (1)	2	0.01
Tohono O'Odham (0)	0	<0.01
Tsimshian *(Alaska Native)* (0)	0	<0.01
Ute (0)	0	<0.01
Yakama (0)	0	<0.01
Yaqui (0)	0	<0.01
Yuman (0)	0	<0.01
Yup'ik *(Alaska Native)* (0)	0	<0.01
Asian (419)	497	1.28
Not Hispanic (407)	465	1.19
Hispanic (12)	32	0.08
Bangladeshi (0)	0	<0.01
Bhutanese (0)	0	<0.01
Burmese (142)	144	0.37
Cambodian (0)	0	<0.01
Chinese, ex. Taiwanese (38)	46	0.12
Filipino (53)	74	0.19
Hmong (0)	0	<0.01
Indian (27)	35	0.09
Indonesian (1)	1	<0.01
Japanese (10)	21	0.05
Korean (3)	8	0.02
Laotian (55)	64	0.16
Malaysian (0)	0	<0.01
Nepalese (0)	0	<0.01
Pakistani (0)	3	0.01
Sri Lankan (0)	0	<0.01
Taiwanese (2)	3	0.01
Thai (13)	14	0.04
Vietnamese (39)	40	0.10
Hawaii Native/Pacific Islander (30)	45	0.12
Not Hispanic (3)	10	0.03
Hispanic (27)	35	0.09
Fijian (0)	0	<0.01
Guamanian/Chamorro (19)	22	0.06
Marshallese (0)	0	<0.01
Native Hawaiian (7)	11	0.03
Samoan (0)	0	<0.01
Tongan (0)	5	0.01
White (34,385)	34,942	89.67
Not Hispanic (32,624)	32,974	84.62
Hispanic (1,761)	1,968	5.05

*Notes: † The Census 2010 population figure is used to calculate the percentages in the Hispanic Origin and Race categories. Ancestry percentages are based on the 2006-2010 American Community Survey population (not shown); ‡ Numbers in parentheses indicate the number of people reporting a single ancestry; * Numbers in parentheses indicate the number of persons reporting this race alone, not in combination with any other race; Please refer to the Explanation of Data for more information.*

Clark County

Population: 110,232

Ancestry	Population	%
Afghan (0)	0	<0.01
African, Sub-Saharan (121)	166	0.15
African (73)	106	0.10
Cape Verdean (0)	0	<0.01
Ethiopian (0)	0	<0.01
Ghanaian (0)	0	<0.01
Kenyan (0)	0	<0.01
Liberian (0)	0	<0.01
Nigerian (0)	0	<0.01
Senegalese (0)	0	<0.01
Sierra Leonean (0)	0	<0.01
Somalian (0)	0	<0.01
South African (48)	60	0.06
Sudanese (0)	0	<0.01
Ugandan (0)	0	<0.01
Zimbabwean (0)	0	<0.01
Other Sub-Saharan African (0)	0	<0.01
Albanian (0)	0	<0.01
Alsatian (0)	0	<0.01
American (13,939)	13,939	12.98
Arab (31)	54	0.05
Arab (0)	0	<0.01
Egyptian (0)	0	<0.01
Iraqi (0)	0	<0.01
Jordanian (0)	0	<0.01
Lebanese (19)	42	0.04
Moroccan (12)	12	0.01
Palestinian (0)	0	<0.01
Syrian (0)	0	<0.01
Other Arab (0)	0	<0.01
Armenian (0)	0	<0.01
Assyrian/Chaldean/Syriac (0)	0	<0.01
Australian (14)	14	0.01
Austrian (0)	20	0.02
Basque (0)	0	<0.01
Belgian (42)	91	0.08
Brazilian (95)	95	0.09
British (218)	329	0.31
Bulgarian (0)	0	<0.01
Cajun (20)	84	0.08
Canadian (17)	73	0.07
Carpatho Rusyn (0)	0	<0.01
Celtic (8)	25	0.02
Croatian (236)	264	0.25
Cypriot (0)	0	<0.01
Czech (43)	143	0.13
Czechoslovakian (30)	41	0.04
Danish (14)	147	0.14
Dutch (294)	1,774	1.65
Eastern European (0)	0	<0.01
English (4,820)	10,538	9.81
Estonian (0)	0	<0.01
European (601)	668	0.62
Finnish (2)	5	<0.01
French, ex. Basque (569)	2,795	2.60
French Canadian (183)	293	0.27
German (11,509)	26,105	24.31
German Russian (0)	0	<0.01
Greek (35)	99	0.09
Guyanese (0)	0	<0.01
Hungarian (106)	227	0.21
Icelander (17)	25	0.02
Iranian (0)	19	0.02
Irish (5,085)	16,094	14.99
Israeli (0)	0	<0.01
Italian (865)	2,483	2.31
Latvian (0)	0	<0.01
Lithuanian (19)	35	0.03
Luxemburger (0)	0	<0.01
Macedonian (0)	0	<0.01
Maltese (0)	0	<0.01
New Zealander (0)	33	0.03
Northern European (0)	0	<0.01
Norwegian (61)	255	0.24
Pennsylvania German (0)	50	0.05
Polish (420)	1,122	1.04
Portuguese (26)	130	0.12
Romanian (85)	96	0.09
Russian (38)	261	0.24
Scandinavian (39)	64	0.06
Scotch-Irish (719)	1,670	1.56
Scottish (896)	2,140	1.99
Serbian (40)	40	0.04
Slavic (0)	0	<0.01
Slovak (48)	99	0.09
Slovene (11)	37	0.03
Soviet Union (0)	0	<0.01
Swedish (121)	371	0.35
Swiss (49)	315	0.29
Turkish (0)	0	<0.01
Ukrainian (0)	12	0.01
Welsh (57)	439	0.41
West Indian, ex. Hispanic (18)	37	0.03
Bahamian (0)	0	<0.01
Barbadian (0)	0	<0.01
Belizean (0)	0	<0.01
Bermudan (0)	0	<0.01
British West Indian (0)	0	<0.01
Dutch West Indian (0)	0	<0.01
Haitian (13)	32	0.03
Jamaican (5)	5	<0.01
Trinidadian/Tobagonian (0)	0	<0.01
U.S. Virgin Islander (0)	0	<0.01
West Indian (0)	0	<0.01
Other West Indian (0)	0	<0.01
Yugoslavian (17)	29	0.03

Hispanic Origin	Population	%
Hispanic or Latino (of any race)	5,350	4.85
Central American, ex. Mexican	362	0.33
Costa Rican	14	0.01
Guatemalan	64	0.06
Honduran	116	0.11
Nicaraguan	14	0.01
Panamanian	23	0.02
Salvadoran	131	0.12
Other Central American	0	<0.01
Cuban	127	0.12
Dominican Republic	15	0.01
Mexican	3,970	3.60
Puerto Rican	361	0.33
South American	115	0.10
Argentinean	17	0.02
Bolivian	9	0.01
Chilean	2	<0.01
Colombian	23	0.02
Ecuadorian	26	0.02
Paraguayan	0	<0.01
Peruvian	21	0.02
Uruguayan	0	<0.01
Venezuelan	17	0.02
Other South American	0	<0.01
Other Hispanic or Latino	400	0.36

Race*	Population	%
African-American/Black (7,661)	9,134	8.29
Not Hispanic (7,541)	8,927	8.10
Hispanic (120)	207	0.19
American Indian/Alaska Native (303)	844	0.77
Not Hispanic (255)	745	0.68
Hispanic (48)	99	0.09
Alaska Athabascan *(Ala. Nat.)* (0)	0	<0.01
Aleut *(Alaska Native)* (0)	0	<0.01
Apache (7)	14	0.01
Arapaho (0)	0	<0.01
Blackfeet (11)	23	0.02
Canadian/French Am. Ind. (4)	5	<0.01
Central American Ind. (0)	0	<0.01
Cherokee (67)	277	0.25
Cheyenne (0)	1	<0.01
Chickasaw (2)	9	0.01
Chippewa (5)	12	0.01
Choctaw (11)	30	0.03
Colville (0)	0	<0.01
Comanche (1)	2	<0.01
Cree (0)	0	<0.01
Creek (8)	12	0.01
Crow (0)	0	<0.01
Delaware (1)	4	<0.01
Hopi (0)	0	<0.01
Houma (4)	4	<0.01
Inupiat *(Alaska Native)* (4)	4	<0.01
Iroquois (4)	12	0.01
Kiowa (0)	0	<0.01
Lumbee (3)	3	<0.01
Menominee (0)	1	<0.01
Mexican American Ind. (23)	26	0.02
Navajo (6)	8	0.01
Osage (1)	2	<0.01
Ottawa (0)	4	<0.01
Paiute (0)	0	<0.01
Pima (3)	3	<0.01
Potawatomi (3)	5	<0.01
Pueblo (0)	0	<0.01
Puget Sound Salish (0)	0	<0.01
Seminole (3)	3	<0.01
Shoshone (0)	2	<0.01
Sioux (8)	20	0.02
South American Ind. (0)	1	<0.01
Spanish American Ind. (0)	0	<0.01
Tlingit-Haida *(Alaska Native)* (0)	0	<0.01
Tohono O'Odham (0)	0	<0.01
Tsimshian *(Alaska Native)* (0)	0	<0.01
Ute (0)	0	<0.01
Yakama (0)	0	<0.01
Yaqui (0)	0	<0.01
Yuman (0)	0	<0.01
Yup'ik *(Alaska Native)* (0)	0	<0.01
Asian (875)	1,228	1.11
Not Hispanic (858)	1,186	1.08
Hispanic (17)	42	0.04
Bangladeshi (0)	1	<0.01
Bhutanese (0)	0	<0.01
Burmese (6)	6	0.01
Cambodian (16)	17	0.02
Chinese, ex. Taiwanese (117)	151	0.14
Filipino (182)	290	0.26
Hmong (0)	0	<0.01
Indian (171)	220	0.20
Indonesian (2)	7	0.01
Japanese (62)	104	0.09
Korean (93)	156	0.14
Laotian (6)	10	0.01
Malaysian (1)	1	<0.01
Nepalese (0)	0	<0.01
Pakistani (24)	27	0.02
Sri Lankan (5)	5	<0.01
Taiwanese (23)	26	0.02
Thai (19)	33	0.03
Vietnamese (57)	69	0.06
Hawaii Native/Pacific Islander (53)	154	0.14
Not Hispanic (43)	141	0.13
Hispanic (10)	13	0.01
Fijian (0)	0	<0.01
Guamanian/Chamorro (27)	47	0.04
Marshallese (0)	0	<0.01
Native Hawaiian (14)	56	0.05
Samoan (5)	11	0.01
Tongan (0)	0	<0.01
White (95,961)	98,242	89.12
Not Hispanic (93,887)	95,860	86.96
Hispanic (2,074)	2,382	2.16

*Notes: † The Census 2010 population figure is used to calculate the percentages in the Hispanic Origin and Race categories. Ancestry percentages are based on the 2006-2010 American Community Survey population (not shown); ‡ Numbers in parentheses indicate the number of people reporting a single ancestry; * Numbers in parentheses indicate the number of persons reporting this race alone, not in combination with any other race; Please refer to the Explanation of Data for more information.*

Clay County

Population: 26,890

Ancestry	Population	%
Afghan (0)	0	<0.01
African, Sub-Saharan (0)	41	0.15
African (0)	41	0.15
Cape Verdean (0)	0	<0.01
Ethiopian (0)	0	<0.01
Ghanaian (0)	0	<0.01
Kenyan (0)	0	<0.01
Liberian (0)	0	<0.01
Nigerian (0)	0	<0.01
Senegalese (0)	0	<0.01
Sierra Leonean (0)	0	<0.01
Somalian (0)	0	<0.01
South African (0)	0	<0.01
Sudanese (0)	0	<0.01
Ugandan (0)	0	<0.01
Zimbabwean (0)	0	<0.01
Other Sub-Saharan African (0)	0	<0.01
Albanian (0)	0	<0.01
Alsatian (0)	0	<0.01
American (5,442)	5,442	20.17
Arab (4)	17	0.06
Arab (0)	0	<0.01
Egyptian (4)	4	0.01
Iraqi (0)	0	<0.01
Jordanian (0)	0	<0.01
Lebanese (0)	0	<0.01
Moroccan (0)	0	<0.01
Palestinian (0)	0	<0.01
Syrian (0)	13	0.05
Other Arab (0)	0	<0.01
Armenian (0)	0	<0.01
Assyrian/Chaldean/Syriac (0)	0	<0.01
Australian (0)	0	<0.01
Austrian (10)	62	0.23
Basque (0)	0	<0.01
Belgian (2)	55	0.20
Brazilian (0)	0	<0.01
British (47)	219	0.81
Bulgarian (0)	14	0.05
Cajun (0)	0	<0.01
Canadian (55)	71	0.26
Carpatho Rusyn (0)	0	<0.01
Celtic (0)	0	<0.01
Croatian (4)	20	0.07
Cypriot (0)	0	<0.01
Czech (0)	7	0.03
Czechoslovakian (0)	0	<0.01
Danish (2)	15	0.06
Dutch (63)	670	2.48
Eastern European (0)	0	<0.01
English (1,207)	2,980	11.04
Estonian (0)	0	<0.01
European (208)	208	0.77
Finnish (26)	43	0.16
French, ex. Basque (158)	1,070	3.97
French Canadian (0)	44	0.16
German (2,902)	7,877	29.19
German Russian (0)	0	<0.01
Greek (0)	0	<0.01
Guyanese (0)	0	<0.01
Hungarian (0)	27	0.10
Icelander (0)	0	<0.01
Iranian (0)	0	<0.01
Irish (787)	3,444	12.76
Israeli (0)	0	<0.01
Italian (135)	561	2.08
Latvian (11)	11	0.04
Lithuanian (11)	14	0.05
Luxemburger (0)	0	<0.01
Macedonian (0)	0	<0.01
Maltese (0)	0	<0.01
New Zealander (0)	0	<0.01
Northern European (0)	0	<0.01
Norwegian (6)	41	0.15
Pennsylvania German (0)	0	<0.01
Polish (118)	358	1.33
Portuguese (25)	25	0.09
Romanian (0)	0	<0.01
Russian (29)	75	0.28
Scandinavian (18)	18	0.07
Scotch-Irish (200)	441	1.63
Scottish (133)	545	2.02
Serbian (0)	23	0.09
Slavic (0)	24	0.09
Slovak (9)	37	0.14
Slovene (0)	0	<0.01
Soviet Union (0)	0	<0.01
Swedish (7)	78	0.29
Swiss (12)	112	0.42
Turkish (19)	39	0.14
Ukrainian (0)	0	<0.01
Welsh (56)	350	1.30
West Indian, ex. Hispanic (0)	0	<0.01
Bahamian (0)	0	<0.01
Barbadian (0)	0	<0.01
Belizean (0)	0	<0.01
Bermudan (0)	0	<0.01
British West Indian (0)	0	<0.01
Dutch West Indian (0)	0	<0.01
Haitian (0)	0	<0.01
Jamaican (0)	0	<0.01
Trinidadian/Tobagonian (0)	0	<0.01
U.S. Virgin Islander (0)	0	<0.01
West Indian (0)	0	<0.01
Other West Indian (0)	0	<0.01
Yugoslavian (0)	23	0.09

Hispanic Origin	Population	%
Hispanic or Latino (of any race)	307	1.14
Central American, ex. Mexican	9	0.03
Costa Rican	1	<0.01
Guatemalan	5	0.02
Honduran	1	<0.01
Nicaraguan	0	<0.01
Panamanian	2	0.01
Salvadoran	0	<0.01
Other Central American	0	<0.01
Cuban	5	0.02
Dominican Republic	0	<0.01
Mexican	214	0.80
Puerto Rican	21	0.08
South American	9	0.03
Argentinean	0	<0.01
Bolivian	0	<0.01
Chilean	0	<0.01
Colombian	9	0.03
Ecuadorian	0	<0.01
Paraguayan	0	<0.01
Peruvian	0	<0.01
Uruguayan	0	<0.01
Venezuelan	0	<0.01
Other South American	0	<0.01
Other Hispanic or Latino	49	0.18

Race*	Population	%
African-American/Black (87)	183	0.68
Not Hispanic (85)	177	0.66
Hispanic (2)	6	0.02
American Indian/Alaska Native (59)	156	0.58
Not Hispanic (57)	151	0.56
Hispanic (2)	5	0.02
Alaska Athabascan *(Ala. Nat.)* (0)	0	<0.01
Aleut *(Alaska Native)* (0)	0	<0.01
Apache (0)	0	<0.01
Arapaho (0)	0	<0.01
Blackfeet (0)	12	0.04
Canadian/French Am. Ind. (0)	0	<0.01
Central American Ind. (0)	0	<0.01
Cherokee (15)	53	0.20
Cheyenne (0)	6	0.02
Chickasaw (0)	1	<0.01
Chippewa (0)	0	<0.01
Choctaw (0)	1	<0.01
Colville (0)	0	<0.01
Comanche (0)	0	<0.01
Cree (1)	1	<0.01
Creek (0)	1	<0.01
Crow (1)	3	0.01
Delaware (0)	0	<0.01
Hopi (0)	0	<0.01
Houma (0)	0	<0.01
Inupiat *(Alaska Native)* (1)	2	0.01
Iroquois (0)	0	<0.01
Kiowa (0)	0	<0.01
Lumbee (0)	2	0.01
Menominee (0)	0	<0.01
Mexican American Ind. (1)	1	<0.01
Navajo (5)	8	0.03
Osage (0)	0	<0.01
Ottawa (0)	0	<0.01
Paiute (0)	0	<0.01
Pima (0)	0	<0.01
Potawatomi (0)	0	<0.01
Pueblo (0)	0	<0.01
Puget Sound Salish (0)	0	<0.01
Seminole (0)	0	<0.01
Shoshone (0)	0	<0.01
Sioux (2)	8	0.03
South American Ind. (0)	0	<0.01
Spanish American Ind. (0)	0	<0.01
Tlingit-Haida *(Alaska Native)* (0)	0	<0.01
Tohono O'Odham (0)	0	<0.01
Tsimshian *(Alaska Native)* (0)	0	<0.01
Ute (0)	0	<0.01
Yakama (0)	0	<0.01
Yaqui (0)	0	<0.01
Yuman (0)	0	<0.01
Yup'ik *(Alaska Native)* (0)	0	<0.01
Asian (60)	85	0.32
Not Hispanic (60)	85	0.32
Hispanic (0)	0	<0.01
Bangladeshi (0)	0	<0.01
Bhutanese (0)	0	<0.01
Burmese (0)	0	<0.01
Cambodian (0)	0	<0.01
Chinese, ex. Taiwanese (12)	13	0.05
Filipino (9)	13	0.05
Hmong (0)	0	<0.01
Indian (20)	27	0.10
Indonesian (0)	0	<0.01
Japanese (1)	4	0.01
Korean (6)	9	0.03
Laotian (0)	0	<0.01
Malaysian (0)	0	<0.01
Nepalese (0)	0	<0.01
Pakistani (0)	0	<0.01
Sri Lankan (0)	0	<0.01
Taiwanese (0)	0	<0.01
Thai (3)	4	0.01
Vietnamese (6)	6	0.02
Hawaii Native/Pacific Islander (8)	15	0.06
Not Hispanic (8)	15	0.06
Hispanic (0)	0	<0.01
Fijian (0)	0	<0.01
Guamanian/Chamorro (0)	0	<0.01
Marshallese (0)	0	<0.01
Native Hawaiian (7)	13	0.05
Samoan (0)	2	0.01
Tongan (0)	0	<0.01
White (26,303)	26,539	98.69
Not Hispanic (26,146)	26,362	98.04
Hispanic (157)	177	0.66

*Notes: † The Census 2010 population figure is used to calculate the percentages in the Hispanic Origin and Race categories. Ancestry percentages are based on the 2006-2010 American Community Survey population (not shown); ‡ Numbers in parentheses indicate the number of people reporting a single ancestry; * Numbers in parentheses indicate the number of persons reporting this race alone, not in combination with any other race; Please refer to the Explanation of Data for more information.*

Clinton County

Population: 33,224

Ancestry	Population	%
Afghan (0)	0	<0.01
African, Sub-Saharan (12)	12	0.04
African (12)	12	0.04
Cape Verdean (0)	0	<0.01
Ethiopian (0)	0	<0.01
Ghanaian (0)	0	<0.01
Kenyan (0)	0	<0.01
Liberian (0)	0	<0.01
Nigerian (0)	0	<0.01
Senegalese (0)	0	<0.01
Sierra Leonean (0)	0	<0.01
Somalian (0)	0	<0.01
South African (0)	0	<0.01
Sudanese (0)	0	<0.01
Ugandan (0)	0	<0.01
Zimbabwean (0)	0	<0.01
Other Sub-Saharan African (0)	0	<0.01
Albanian (0)	3	0.01
Alsatian (0)	0	<0.01
American (3,678)	3,678	11.06
Arab (9)	39	0.12
Arab (0)	0	<0.01
Egyptian (0)	0	<0.01
Iraqi (0)	0	<0.01
Jordanian (0)	0	<0.01
Lebanese (0)	0	<0.01
Moroccan (0)	0	<0.01
Palestinian (0)	0	<0.01
Syrian (9)	39	0.12
Other Arab (0)	0	<0.01
Armenian (0)	0	<0.01
Assyrian/Chaldean/Syriac (0)	0	<0.01
Australian (0)	0	<0.01
Austrian (0)	17	0.05
Basque (0)	0	<0.01
Belgian (27)	104	0.31
Brazilian (0)	0	<0.01
British (12)	45	0.14
Bulgarian (0)	0	<0.01
Cajun (0)	0	<0.01
Canadian (16)	16	0.05
Carpatho Rusyn (0)	0	<0.01
Celtic (0)	0	<0.01
Croatian (11)	66	0.20
Cypriot (0)	0	<0.01
Czech (26)	30	0.09
Czechoslovakian (0)	0	<0.01
Danish (17)	80	0.24
Dutch (201)	848	2.55
Eastern European (0)	0	<0.01
English (1,469)	3,188	9.58
Estonian (0)	0	<0.01
European (243)	312	0.94
Finnish (0)	12	0.04
French, ex. Basque (204)	684	2.06
French Canadian (17)	17	0.05
German (3,236)	7,465	22.44
German Russian (0)	0	<0.01
Greek (0)	109	0.33
Guyanese (0)	0	<0.01
Hungarian (24)	84	0.25
Icelander (0)	0	<0.01
Iranian (0)	0	<0.01
Irish (1,057)	3,413	10.26
Israeli (0)	0	<0.01
Italian (158)	460	1.38
Latvian (0)	0	<0.01
Lithuanian (9)	13	0.04
Luxemburger (0)	0	<0.01
Macedonian (0)	0	<0.01
Maltese (0)	0	<0.01
New Zealander (22)	22	0.07
Northern European (3)	3	0.01
Norwegian (39)	154	0.46
Pennsylvania German (38)	50	0.15
Polish (215)	450	1.35
Portuguese (0)	0	<0.01
Romanian (10)	18	0.05
Russian (0)	0	<0.01
Scandinavian (38)	38	0.11
Scotch-Irish (129)	324	0.97
Scottish (551)	899	2.70
Serbian (63)	162	0.49
Slavic (0)	0	<0.01
Slovak (0)	3	0.01
Slovene (0)	0	<0.01
Soviet Union (0)	0	<0.01
Swedish (72)	392	1.18
Swiss (5)	73	0.22
Turkish (0)	0	<0.01
Ukrainian (26)	26	0.08
Welsh (57)	222	0.67
West Indian, ex. Hispanic (0)	0	<0.01
Bahamian (0)	0	<0.01
Barbadian (0)	0	<0.01
Belizean (0)	0	<0.01
Bermudan (0)	0	<0.01
British West Indian (0)	0	<0.01
Dutch West Indian (0)	0	<0.01
Haitian (0)	0	<0.01
Jamaican (0)	0	<0.01
Trinidadian/Tobagonian (0)	0	<0.01
U.S. Virgin Islander (0)	0	<0.01
West Indian (0)	0	<0.01
Other West Indian (0)	0	<0.01
Yugoslavian (30)	30	0.09

Hispanic Origin	Population	%
Hispanic or Latino (of any race)	4,395	13.23
Central American, ex. Mexican	121	0.36
Costa Rican	1	<0.01
Guatemalan	55	0.17
Honduran	9	0.03
Nicaraguan	9	0.03
Panamanian	2	0.01
Salvadoran	45	0.14
Other Central American	0	<0.01
Cuban	4	0.01
Dominican Republic	0	<0.01
Mexican	3,958	11.91
Puerto Rican	53	0.16
South American	14	0.04
Argentinean	4	0.01
Bolivian	0	<0.01
Chilean	0	<0.01
Colombian	9	0.03
Ecuadorian	0	<0.01
Paraguayan	0	<0.01
Peruvian	1	<0.01
Uruguayan	0	<0.01
Venezuelan	0	<0.01
Other South American	0	<0.01
Other Hispanic or Latino	245	0.74

Race*	Population	%
African-American/Black (142)	229	0.69
Not Hispanic (138)	205	0.62
Hispanic (4)	24	0.07
American Indian/Alaska Native (83)	212	0.64
Not Hispanic (44)	143	0.43
Hispanic (39)	69	0.21
Alaska Athabascan *(Ala. Nat.)* (0)	0	<0.01
Aleut *(Alaska Native)* (0)	0	<0.01
Apache (2)	2	0.01
Arapaho (0)	0	<0.01
Blackfeet (2)	7	0.02
Canadian/French Am. Ind. (0)	0	<0.01
Central American Ind. (0)	0	<0.01
Cherokee (13)	59	0.18
Cheyenne (0)	1	<0.01
Chickasaw (1)	1	<0.01
Chippewa (2)	5	0.02
Choctaw (3)	4	0.01
Colville (0)	0	<0.01
Comanche (0)	0	<0.01
Cree (1)	1	<0.01
Creek (0)	0	<0.01
Crow (0)	0	<0.01
Delaware (0)	0	<0.01
Hopi (0)	0	<0.01
Houma (0)	0	<0.01
Inupiat *(Alaska Native)* (3)	4	0.01
Iroquois (0)	3	0.01
Kiowa (0)	0	<0.01
Lumbee (0)	0	<0.01
Menominee (0)	0	<0.01
Mexican American Ind. (6)	10	0.03
Navajo (0)	0	<0.01
Osage (0)	0	<0.01
Ottawa (1)	1	<0.01
Paiute (1)	1	<0.01
Pima (0)	0	<0.01
Potawatomi (0)	1	<0.01
Pueblo (0)	0	<0.01
Puget Sound Salish (0)	0	<0.01
Seminole (0)	0	<0.01
Shoshone (0)	0	<0.01
Sioux (1)	1	<0.01
South American Ind. (0)	1	<0.01
Spanish American Ind. (2)	2	0.01
Tlingit-Haida *(Alaska Native)* (0)	0	<0.01
Tohono O'Odham (0)	0	<0.01
Tsimshian *(Alaska Native)* (0)	0	<0.01
Ute (0)	0	<0.01
Yakama (0)	0	<0.01
Yaqui (0)	0	<0.01
Yuman (0)	0	<0.01
Yup'ik *(Alaska Native)* (0)	0	<0.01
Asian (72)	124	0.37
Not Hispanic (65)	95	0.29
Hispanic (7)	29	0.09
Bangladeshi (0)	0	<0.01
Bhutanese (0)	0	<0.01
Burmese (0)	0	<0.01
Cambodian (0)	0	<0.01
Chinese, ex. Taiwanese (12)	15	0.05
Filipino (23)	42	0.13
Hmong (0)	0	<0.01
Indian (10)	13	0.04
Indonesian (1)	1	<0.01
Japanese (6)	13	0.04
Korean (13)	16	0.05
Laotian (0)	1	<0.01
Malaysian (0)	0	<0.01
Nepalese (0)	0	<0.01
Pakistani (0)	0	<0.01
Sri Lankan (0)	0	<0.01
Taiwanese (0)	0	<0.01
Thai (1)	5	0.02
Vietnamese (2)	4	0.01
Hawaii Native/Pacific Islander (3)	25	0.08
Not Hispanic (3)	13	0.04
Hispanic (0)	12	0.04
Fijian (0)	0	<0.01
Guamanian/Chamorro (0)	1	<0.01
Marshallese (0)	0	<0.01
Native Hawaiian (2)	8	0.02
Samoan (1)	3	0.01
Tongan (0)	0	<0.01
White (30,232)	30,625	92.18
Not Hispanic (28,349)	28,552	85.94
Hispanic (1,883)	2,073	6.24

*Notes: † The Census 2010 population figure is used to calculate the percentages in the Hispanic Origin and Race categories. Ancestry percentages are based on the 2006-2010 American Community Survey population (not shown); ‡ Numbers in parentheses indicate the number of people reporting a single ancestry; * Numbers in parentheses indicate the number of persons reporting this race alone, not in combination with any other race; Please refer to the Explanation of Data for more information.*

Crawford County

Population: 10,713

Ancestry	Population	%
Afghan (0)	0	<0.01
African, Sub-Saharan (0)	0	<0.01
African (0)	0	<0.01
Cape Verdean (0)	0	<0.01
Ethiopian (0)	0	<0.01
Ghanaian (0)	0	<0.01
Kenyan (0)	0	<0.01
Liberian (0)	0	<0.01
Nigerian (0)	0	<0.01
Senegalese (0)	0	<0.01
Sierra Leonean (0)	0	<0.01
Somalian (0)	0	<0.01
South African (0)	0	<0.01
Sudanese (0)	0	<0.01
Ugandan (0)	0	<0.01
Zimbabwean (0)	0	<0.01
Other Sub-Saharan African (0)	0	<0.01
Albanian (0)	0	<0.01
Alsatian (0)	0	<0.01
American (1,454)	1,454	13.43
Arab (0)	0	<0.01
Arab (0)	0	<0.01
Egyptian (0)	0	<0.01
Iraqi (0)	0	<0.01
Jordanian (0)	0	<0.01
Lebanese (0)	0	<0.01
Moroccan (0)	0	<0.01
Palestinian (0)	0	<0.01
Syrian (0)	0	<0.01
Other Arab (0)	0	<0.01
Armenian (0)	0	<0.01
Assyrian/Chaldean/Syriac (0)	0	<0.01
Australian (0)	0	<0.01
Austrian (3)	25	0.23
Basque (0)	0	<0.01
Belgian (0)	0	<0.01
Brazilian (0)	0	<0.01
British (5)	17	0.16
Bulgarian (0)	0	<0.01
Cajun (0)	0	<0.01
Canadian (0)	0	<0.01
Carpatho Rusyn (0)	0	<0.01
Celtic (0)	0	<0.01
Croatian (0)	3	0.03
Cypriot (0)	0	<0.01
Czech (0)	0	<0.01
Czechoslovakian (0)	0	<0.01
Danish (72)	72	0.67
Dutch (29)	283	2.61
Eastern European (0)	0	<0.01
English (449)	940	8.68
Estonian (0)	0	<0.01
European (198)	228	2.11
Finnish (0)	0	<0.01
French, ex. Basque (58)	251	2.32
French Canadian (33)	80	0.74
German (965)	2,577	23.81
German Russian (0)	0	<0.01
Greek (24)	62	0.57
Guyanese (0)	0	<0.01
Hungarian (0)	26	0.24
Icelander (0)	0	<0.01
Iranian (0)	0	<0.01
Irish (564)	1,881	17.38
Israeli (0)	0	<0.01
Italian (20)	70	0.65
Latvian (0)	0	<0.01
Lithuanian (0)	0	<0.01
Luxemburger (0)	0	<0.01
Macedonian (0)	0	<0.01
Maltese (0)	0	<0.01
New Zealander (0)	0	<0.01
Northern European (0)	0	<0.01
Norwegian (8)	8	0.07
Pennsylvania German (0)	0	<0.01
Polish (22)	70	0.65
Portuguese (10)	12	0.11
Romanian (0)	0	<0.01
Russian (85)	88	0.81
Scandinavian (0)	0	<0.01
Scotch-Irish (88)	176	1.63
Scottish (48)	326	3.01
Serbian (0)	0	<0.01
Slavic (0)	0	<0.01
Slovak (0)	6	0.06
Slovene (0)	0	<0.01
Soviet Union (0)	0	<0.01
Swedish (22)	198	1.83
Swiss (16)	44	0.41
Turkish (0)	0	<0.01
Ukrainian (0)	0	<0.01
Welsh (8)	40	0.37
West Indian, ex. Hispanic (0)	0	<0.01
Bahamian (0)	0	<0.01
Barbadian (0)	0	<0.01
Belizean (0)	0	<0.01
Bermudan (0)	0	<0.01
British West Indian (0)	0	<0.01
Dutch West Indian (0)	0	<0.01
Haitian (0)	0	<0.01
Jamaican (0)	0	<0.01
Trinidadian/Tobagonian (0)	0	<0.01
U.S. Virgin Islander (0)	0	<0.01
West Indian (0)	0	<0.01
Other West Indian (0)	0	<0.01
Yugoslavian (0)	0	<0.01

Hispanic Origin	Population	%
Hispanic or Latino (of any race)	126	1.18
Central American, ex. Mexican	10	0.09
Costa Rican	0	<0.01
Guatemalan	4	0.04
Honduran	4	0.04
Nicaraguan	0	<0.01
Panamanian	2	0.02
Salvadoran	0	<0.01
Other Central American	0	<0.01
Cuban	0	<0.01
Dominican Republic	0	<0.01
Mexican	70	0.65
Puerto Rican	18	0.17
South American	3	0.03
Argentinean	0	<0.01
Bolivian	0	<0.01
Chilean	0	<0.01
Colombian	0	<0.01
Ecuadorian	1	0.01
Paraguayan	0	<0.01
Peruvian	2	0.02
Uruguayan	0	<0.01
Venezuelan	0	<0.01
Other South American	0	<0.01
Other Hispanic or Latino	25	0.23

Race*	Population	%
African-American/Black (24)	47	0.44
Not Hispanic (21)	42	0.39
Hispanic (3)	5	0.05
American Indian/Alaska Native (43)	103	0.96
Not Hispanic (40)	99	0.92
Hispanic (3)	4	0.04
Alaska Athabascan *(Ala. Nat.)* (0)	0	<0.01
Aleut *(Alaska Native)* (0)	0	<0.01
Apache (0)	3	0.03
Arapaho (0)	0	<0.01
Blackfeet (0)	1	0.01
Canadian/French Am. Ind. (1)	1	0.01
Central American Ind. (0)	0	<0.01
Cherokee (9)	42	0.39
Cheyenne (0)	0	<0.01
Chickasaw (0)	1	0.01
Chippewa (1)	2	0.02
Choctaw (0)	0	<0.01
Colville (0)	0	<0.01
Comanche (0)	0	<0.01
Cree (0)	0	<0.01
Creek (0)	1	0.01
Crow (0)	0	<0.01
Delaware (0)	0	<0.01
Hopi (0)	0	<0.01
Houma (0)	0	<0.01
Inupiat *(Alaska Native)* (0)	0	<0.01
Iroquois (1)	1	0.01
Kiowa (0)	0	<0.01
Lumbee (0)	0	<0.01
Menominee (1)	1	0.01
Mexican American Ind. (0)	0	<0.01
Navajo (0)	3	0.03
Osage (0)	5	0.05
Ottawa (0)	0	<0.01
Paiute (0)	0	<0.01
Pima (0)	0	<0.01
Potawatomi (0)	0	<0.01
Pueblo (0)	3	0.03
Puget Sound Salish (0)	0	<0.01
Seminole (1)	5	0.05
Shoshone (0)	0	<0.01
Sioux (0)	2	0.02
South American Ind. (0)	0	<0.01
Spanish American Ind. (0)	0	<0.01
Tlingit-Haida *(Alaska Native)* (0)	0	<0.01
Tohono O'Odham (0)	0	<0.01
Tsimshian *(Alaska Native)* (0)	0	<0.01
Ute (0)	0	<0.01
Yakama (0)	0	<0.01
Yaqui (0)	0	<0.01
Yuman (0)	0	<0.01
Yup'ik *(Alaska Native)* (0)	0	<0.01
Asian (20)	36	0.34
Not Hispanic (20)	36	0.34
Hispanic (0)	0	<0.01
Bangladeshi (0)	0	<0.01
Bhutanese (0)	0	<0.01
Burmese (0)	0	<0.01
Cambodian (0)	0	<0.01
Chinese, ex. Taiwanese (3)	5	0.05
Filipino (11)	14	0.13
Hmong (0)	0	<0.01
Indian (2)	5	0.05
Indonesian (0)	0	<0.01
Japanese (1)	4	0.04
Korean (0)	0	<0.01
Laotian (0)	0	<0.01
Malaysian (0)	0	<0.01
Nepalese (0)	0	<0.01
Pakistani (0)	0	<0.01
Sri Lankan (0)	0	<0.01
Taiwanese (0)	0	<0.01
Thai (0)	8	0.07
Vietnamese (1)	1	0.01
Hawaii Native/Pacific Islander (9)	13	0.12
Not Hispanic (9)	12	0.11
Hispanic (0)	1	0.01
Fijian (0)	0	<0.01
Guamanian/Chamorro (0)	2	0.02
Marshallese (0)	0	<0.01
Native Hawaiian (8)	8	0.07
Samoan (0)	0	<0.01
Tongan (0)	0	<0.01
White (10,438)	10,556	98.53
Not Hispanic (10,390)	10,492	97.94
Hispanic (48)	64	0.60

*Notes: † The Census 2010 population figure is used to calculate the percentages in the Hispanic Origin and Race categories. Ancestry percentages are based on the 2006-2010 American Community Survey population (not shown); ‡ Numbers in parentheses indicate the number of people reporting a single ancestry; * Numbers in parentheses indicate the number of persons reporting this race alone, not in combination with any other race; Please refer to the Explanation of Data for more information.*

Daviess County

Population: 31,648

Ancestry	Population	%
Afghan (0)	0	<0.01
African, Sub-Saharan (0)	0	<0.01
African (0)	0	<0.01
Cape Verdean (0)	0	<0.01
Ethiopian (0)	0	<0.01
Ghanaian (0)	0	<0.01
Kenyan (0)	0	<0.01
Liberian (0)	0	<0.01
Nigerian (0)	0	<0.01
Senegalese (0)	0	<0.01
Sierra Leonean (0)	0	<0.01
Somalian (0)	0	<0.01
South African (0)	0	<0.01
Sudanese (0)	0	<0.01
Ugandan (0)	0	<0.01
Zimbabwean (0)	0	<0.01
Other Sub-Saharan African (0)	0	<0.01
Albanian (0)	0	<0.01
Alsatian (0)	0	<0.01
American (3,345)	3,345	10.77
Arab (0)	0	<0.01
Arab (0)	0	<0.01
Egyptian (0)	0	<0.01
Iraqi (0)	0	<0.01
Jordanian (0)	0	<0.01
Lebanese (0)	0	<0.01
Moroccan (0)	0	<0.01
Palestinian (0)	0	<0.01
Syrian (0)	0	<0.01
Other Arab (0)	0	<0.01
Armenian (0)	0	<0.01
Assyrian/Chaldean/Syriac (0)	0	<0.01
Australian (0)	0	<0.01
Austrian (56)	71	0.23
Basque (0)	0	<0.01
Belgian (0)	0	<0.01
Brazilian (0)	0	<0.01
British (25)	67	0.22
Bulgarian (0)	0	<0.01
Cajun (0)	0	<0.01
Canadian (28)	28	0.09
Carpatho Rusyn (0)	0	<0.01
Celtic (0)	0	<0.01
Croatian (0)	0	<0.01
Cypriot (0)	0	<0.01
Czech (9)	27	0.09
Czechoslovakian (0)	0	<0.01
Danish (0)	107	0.34
Dutch (137)	465	1.50
Eastern European (0)	0	<0.01
English (1,595)	3,282	10.57
Estonian (0)	0	<0.01
European (126)	126	0.41
Finnish (0)	0	<0.01
French, ex. Basque (193)	1,010	3.25
French Canadian (118)	120	0.39
German (6,043)	9,761	31.44
German Russian (0)	0	<0.01
Greek (9)	19	0.06
Guyanese (0)	0	<0.01
Hungarian (0)	31	0.10
Icelander (0)	0	<0.01
Iranian (0)	0	<0.01
Irish (1,363)	4,056	13.06
Israeli (0)	0	<0.01
Italian (188)	335	1.08
Latvian (0)	0	<0.01
Lithuanian (0)	0	<0.01
Luxemburger (0)	0	<0.01
Macedonian (0)	0	<0.01
Maltese (0)	0	<0.01
New Zealander (0)	0	<0.01
Northern European (34)	34	0.11
Norwegian (11)	117	0.38
Pennsylvania German (545)	545	1.76
Polish (76)	190	0.61
Portuguese (0)	0	<0.01
Romanian (0)	6	0.02
Russian (0)	0	<0.01
Scandinavian (0)	0	<0.01
Scotch-Irish (551)	776	2.50
Scottish (63)	307	0.99
Serbian (0)	11	0.04
Slavic (0)	15	0.05
Slovak (0)	0	<0.01
Slovene (0)	0	<0.01
Soviet Union (0)	0	<0.01
Swedish (178)	607	1.96
Swiss (238)	359	1.16
Turkish (0)	0	<0.01
Ukrainian (0)	0	<0.01
Welsh (64)	105	0.34
West Indian, ex. Hispanic (0)	63	0.20
Bahamian (0)	0	<0.01
Barbadian (0)	0	<0.01
Belizean (0)	0	<0.01
Bermudan (0)	0	<0.01
British West Indian (0)	0	<0.01
Dutch West Indian (0)	0	<0.01
Haitian (0)	0	<0.01
Jamaican (0)	63	0.20
Trinidadian/Tobagonian (0)	0	<0.01
U.S. Virgin Islander (0)	0	<0.01
West Indian (0)	0	<0.01
Other West Indian (0)	0	<0.01
Yugoslavian (0)	0	<0.01

Hispanic Origin	Population	%
Hispanic or Latino (of any race)	1,314	4.15
Central American, ex. Mexican	265	0.84
Costa Rican	1	<0.01
Guatemalan	75	0.24
Honduran	14	0.04
Nicaraguan	4	0.01
Panamanian	1	<0.01
Salvadoran	169	0.53
Other Central American	1	<0.01
Cuban	9	0.03
Dominican Republic	6	0.02
Mexican	917	2.90
Puerto Rican	42	0.13
South American	15	0.05
Argentinean	0	<0.01
Bolivian	0	<0.01
Chilean	0	<0.01
Colombian	3	0.01
Ecuadorian	1	<0.01
Paraguayan	0	<0.01
Peruvian	11	0.03
Uruguayan	0	<0.01
Venezuelan	0	<0.01
Other South American	0	<0.01
Other Hispanic or Latino	60	0.19

Race*	Population	%
African-American/Black (172)	311	0.98
Not Hispanic (165)	292	0.92
Hispanic (7)	19	0.06
American Indian/Alaska Native (71)	142	0.45
Not Hispanic (62)	117	0.37
Hispanic (9)	25	0.08
Alaska Athabascan *(Ala. Nat.)* (0)	0	<0.01
Aleut *(Alaska Native)* (0)	0	<0.01
Apache (4)	5	0.02
Arapaho (0)	0	<0.01
Blackfeet (0)	0	<0.01
Canadian/French Am. Ind. (0)	0	<0.01
Central American Ind. (0)	0	<0.01
Cherokee (15)	36	0.11
Cheyenne (0)	0	<0.01
Chickasaw (0)	0	<0.01
Chippewa (1)	2	0.01
Choctaw (3)	9	0.03
Colville (0)	0	<0.01
Comanche (0)	1	<0.01
Cree (0)	0	<0.01
Creek (0)	0	<0.01
Crow (0)	0	<0.01
Delaware (0)	0	<0.01
Hopi (0)	0	<0.01
Houma (0)	0	<0.01
Inupiat *(Alaska Native)* (0)	0	<0.01
Iroquois (1)	2	0.01
Kiowa (0)	0	<0.01
Lumbee (1)	2	0.01
Menominee (0)	0	<0.01
Mexican American Ind. (2)	3	0.01
Navajo (6)	6	0.02
Osage (0)	0	<0.01
Ottawa (0)	0	<0.01
Paiute (0)	0	<0.01
Pima (0)	0	<0.01
Potawatomi (0)	0	<0.01
Pueblo (0)	0	<0.01
Puget Sound Salish (0)	0	<0.01
Seminole (0)	0	<0.01
Shoshone (0)	0	<0.01
Sioux (5)	5	0.02
South American Ind. (1)	1	<0.01
Spanish American Ind. (0)	0	<0.01
Tlingit-Haida *(Alaska Native)* (0)	0	<0.01
Tohono O'Odham (0)	0	<0.01
Tsimshian *(Alaska Native)* (0)	0	<0.01
Ute (0)	0	<0.01
Yakama (0)	0	<0.01
Yaqui (0)	0	<0.01
Yuman (0)	0	<0.01
Yup'ik *(Alaska Native)* (3)	3	0.01
Asian (161)	195	0.62
Not Hispanic (161)	195	0.62
Hispanic (0)	0	<0.01
Bangladeshi (0)	0	<0.01
Bhutanese (0)	0	<0.01
Burmese (79)	80	0.25
Cambodian (0)	0	<0.01
Chinese, ex. Taiwanese (15)	17	0.05
Filipino (21)	35	0.11
Hmong (0)	0	<0.01
Indian (10)	13	0.04
Indonesian (0)	0	<0.01
Japanese (7)	18	0.06
Korean (9)	13	0.04
Laotian (0)	0	<0.01
Malaysian (0)	1	<0.01
Nepalese (0)	0	<0.01
Pakistani (9)	9	0.03
Sri Lankan (0)	0	<0.01
Taiwanese (1)	1	<0.01
Thai (2)	2	0.01
Vietnamese (4)	4	0.01
Hawaii Native/Pacific Islander (8)	21	0.07
Not Hispanic (6)	18	0.06
Hispanic (2)	3	0.01
Fijian (0)	0	<0.01
Guamanian/Chamorro (1)	1	<0.01
Marshallese (0)	0	<0.01
Native Hawaiian (5)	13	0.04
Samoan (0)	0	<0.01
Tongan (0)	0	<0.01
White (30,077)	30,395	96.04
Not Hispanic (29,696)	29,921	94.54
Hispanic (381)	474	1.50

*Notes: † The Census 2010 population figure is used to calculate the percentages in the Hispanic Origin and Race categories. Ancestry percentages are based on the 2006-2010 American Community Survey population (not shown); ‡ Numbers in parentheses indicate the number of people reporting a single ancestry; * Numbers in parentheses indicate the number of persons reporting this race alone, not in combination with any other race; Please refer to the Explanation of Data for more information.*

DeKalb County

Population: 42,223

Ancestry	Population	%
Afghan (0)	0	<0.01
African, Sub-Saharan (0)	0	<0.01
African (0)	0	<0.01
Cape Verdean (0)	0	<0.01
Ethiopian (0)	0	<0.01
Ghanaian (0)	0	<0.01
Kenyan (0)	0	<0.01
Liberian (0)	0	<0.01
Nigerian (0)	0	<0.01
Senegalese (0)	0	<0.01
Sierra Leonean (0)	0	<0.01
Somalian (0)	0	<0.01
South African (0)	0	<0.01
Sudanese (0)	0	<0.01
Ugandan (0)	0	<0.01
Zimbabwean (0)	0	<0.01
Other Sub-Saharan African (0)	0	<0.01
Albanian (0)	0	<0.01
Alsatian (0)	12	0.03
American (4,559)	4,559	10.86
Arab (0)	16	0.04
Arab (0)	0	<0.01
Egyptian (0)	0	<0.01
Iraqi (0)	0	<0.01
Jordanian (0)	0	<0.01
Lebanese (0)	16	0.04
Moroccan (0)	0	<0.01
Palestinian (0)	0	<0.01
Syrian (0)	0	<0.01
Other Arab (0)	0	<0.01
Armenian (0)	0	<0.01
Assyrian/Chaldean/Syriac (0)	0	<0.01
Australian (10)	41	0.10
Austrian (0)	0	<0.01
Basque (0)	0	<0.01
Belgian (46)	233	0.56
Brazilian (0)	0	<0.01
British (36)	83	0.20
Bulgarian (0)	0	<0.01
Cajun (0)	0	<0.01
Canadian (16)	20	0.05
Carpatho Rusyn (0)	0	<0.01
Celtic (0)	0	<0.01
Croatian (9)	23	0.05
Cypriot (0)	0	<0.01
Czech (21)	45	0.11
Czechoslovakian (15)	44	0.10
Danish (2)	33	0.08
Dutch (208)	1,078	2.57
Eastern European (0)	0	<0.01
English (1,250)	3,814	9.09
Estonian (0)	0	<0.01
European (276)	315	0.75
Finnish (9)	19	0.05
French, ex. Basque (191)	1,666	3.97
French Canadian (44)	113	0.27
German (7,441)	15,242	36.32
German Russian (0)	0	<0.01
Greek (25)	32	0.08
Guyanese (0)	0	<0.01
Hungarian (13)	116	0.28
Icelander (0)	0	<0.01
Iranian (0)	0	<0.01
Irish (1,085)	4,517	10.76
Israeli (0)	0	<0.01
Italian (389)	1,155	2.75
Latvian (0)	0	<0.01
Lithuanian (0)	0	<0.01
Luxemburger (0)	0	<0.01
Macedonian (0)	0	<0.01
Maltese (0)	0	<0.01
New Zealander (0)	0	<0.01
Northern European (0)	0	<0.01
Norwegian (20)	219	0.52
Pennsylvania German (66)	190	0.45
Polish (548)	1,695	4.04
Portuguese (9)	20	0.05
Romanian (22)	32	0.08
Russian (38)	86	0.20
Scandinavian (12)	12	0.03
Scotch-Irish (162)	495	1.18
Scottish (238)	929	2.21
Serbian (0)	0	<0.01
Slavic (0)	0	<0.01
Slovak (43)	138	0.33
Slovene (0)	12	0.03
Soviet Union (0)	0	<0.01
Swedish (65)	446	1.06
Swiss (154)	662	1.58
Turkish (0)	0	<0.01
Ukrainian (57)	145	0.35
Welsh (27)	206	0.49
West Indian, ex. Hispanic (0)	0	<0.01
Bahamian (0)	0	<0.01
Barbadian (0)	0	<0.01
Belizean (0)	0	<0.01
Bermudan (0)	0	<0.01
British West Indian (0)	0	<0.01
Dutch West Indian (0)	0	<0.01
Haitian (0)	0	<0.01
Jamaican (0)	0	<0.01
Trinidadian/Tobagonian (0)	0	<0.01
U.S. Virgin Islander (0)	0	<0.01
West Indian (0)	0	<0.01
Other West Indian (0)	0	<0.01
Yugoslavian (0)	17	0.04

Hispanic Origin	Population	%
Hispanic or Latino (of any race)	1,031	2.44
Central American, ex. Mexican	34	0.08
Costa Rican	2	<0.01
Guatemalan	16	0.04
Honduran	7	0.02
Nicaraguan	2	<0.01
Panamanian	0	<0.01
Salvadoran	7	0.02
Other Central American	0	<0.01
Cuban	8	0.02
Dominican Republic	1	<0.01
Mexican	838	1.98
Puerto Rican	51	0.12
South American	19	0.04
Argentinean	0	<0.01
Bolivian	1	<0.01
Chilean	3	0.01
Colombian	5	0.01
Ecuadorian	2	<0.01
Paraguayan	0	<0.01
Peruvian	1	<0.01
Uruguayan	6	0.01
Venezuelan	1	<0.01
Other South American	0	<0.01
Other Hispanic or Latino	80	0.19

Race*	Population	%
African-American/Black (148)	298	0.71
Not Hispanic (141)	275	0.65
Hispanic (7)	23	0.05
American Indian/Alaska Native (99)	258	0.61
Not Hispanic (84)	221	0.52
Hispanic (15)	37	0.09
Alaska Athabascan *(Ala. Nat.)* (0)	0	<0.01
Aleut *(Alaska Native)* (1)	1	<0.01
Apache (0)	10	0.02
Arapaho (0)	0	<0.01
Blackfeet (5)	15	0.04
Canadian/French Am. Ind. (0)	0	<0.01
Central American Ind. (1)	1	<0.01
Cherokee (26)	62	0.15
Cheyenne (1)	1	<0.01
Chickasaw (0)	0	<0.01
Chippewa (7)	10	0.02
Choctaw (3)	5	0.01
Colville (0)	0	<0.01
Comanche (0)	0	<0.01
Cree (0)	0	<0.01
Creek (0)	0	<0.01
Crow (0)	0	<0.01
Delaware (0)	0	<0.01
Hopi (0)	0	<0.01
Houma (0)	0	<0.01
Inupiat *(Alaska Native)* (0)	0	<0.01
Iroquois (4)	7	0.02
Kiowa (0)	0	<0.01
Lumbee (1)	1	<0.01
Menominee (0)	0	<0.01
Mexican American Ind. (2)	5	0.01
Navajo (0)	3	0.01
Osage (0)	0	<0.01
Ottawa (1)	1	<0.01
Paiute (0)	0	<0.01
Pima (0)	0	<0.01
Potawatomi (4)	6	0.01
Pueblo (0)	0	<0.01
Puget Sound Salish (0)	0	<0.01
Seminole (0)	0	<0.01
Shoshone (0)	1	<0.01
Sioux (1)	6	0.01
South American Ind. (0)	0	<0.01
Spanish American Ind. (0)	0	<0.01
Tlingit-Haida *(Alaska Native)* (0)	0	<0.01
Tohono O'Odham (0)	0	<0.01
Tsimshian *(Alaska Native)* (0)	0	<0.01
Ute (0)	0	<0.01
Yakama (0)	0	<0.01
Yaqui (0)	0	<0.01
Yuman (0)	0	<0.01
Yup'ik *(Alaska Native)* (0)	0	<0.01
Asian (192)	264	0.63
Not Hispanic (186)	245	0.58
Hispanic (6)	19	0.04
Bangladeshi (0)	0	<0.01
Bhutanese (0)	0	<0.01
Burmese (0)	0	<0.01
Cambodian (10)	13	0.03
Chinese, ex. Taiwanese (29)	34	0.08
Filipino (45)	64	0.15
Hmong (0)	0	<0.01
Indian (35)	35	0.08
Indonesian (1)	1	<0.01
Japanese (9)	19	0.04
Korean (13)	17	0.04
Laotian (1)	1	<0.01
Malaysian (0)	0	<0.01
Nepalese (0)	0	<0.01
Pakistani (3)	10	0.02
Sri Lankan (0)	0	<0.01
Taiwanese (0)	0	<0.01
Thai (8)	8	0.02
Vietnamese (27)	45	0.11
Hawaii Native/Pacific Islander (17)	39	0.09
Not Hispanic (17)	34	0.08
Hispanic (0)	5	0.01
Fijian (0)	0	<0.01
Guamanian/Chamorro (8)	18	0.04
Marshallese (0)	0	<0.01
Native Hawaiian (2)	13	0.03
Samoan (0)	0	<0.01
Tongan (0)	0	<0.01
White (40,931)	41,392	98.03
Not Hispanic (40,406)	40,737	96.48
Hispanic (525)	655	1.55

*Notes: † The Census 2010 population figure is used to calculate the percentages in the Hispanic Origin and Race categories. Ancestry percentages are based on the 2006-2010 American Community Survey population (not shown); ‡ Numbers in parentheses indicate the number of people reporting a single ancestry; * Numbers in parentheses indicate the number of persons reporting this race alone, not in combination with any other race; Please refer to the Explanation of Data for more information.*

Dearborn County

Population: 50,047

Ancestry	Population	%
Afghan (0)	0	<0.01
African, Sub-Saharan (0)	37	0.07
African (0)	37	0.07
Cape Verdean (0)	0	<0.01
Ethiopian (0)	0	<0.01
Ghanaian (0)	0	<0.01
Kenyan (0)	0	<0.01
Liberian (0)	0	<0.01
Nigerian (0)	0	<0.01
Senegalese (0)	0	<0.01
Sierra Leonean (0)	0	<0.01
Somalian (0)	0	<0.01
South African (0)	0	<0.01
Sudanese (0)	0	<0.01
Ugandan (0)	0	<0.01
Zimbabwean (0)	0	<0.01
Other Sub-Saharan African (0)	0	<0.01
Albanian (0)	0	<0.01
Alsatian (0)	53	0.11
American (3,843)	3,843	7.75
Arab (31)	60	0.12
Arab (0)	0	<0.01
Egyptian (0)	0	<0.01
Iraqi (0)	0	<0.01
Jordanian (0)	0	<0.01
Lebanese (17)	46	0.09
Moroccan (14)	14	0.03
Palestinian (0)	0	<0.01
Syrian (0)	0	<0.01
Other Arab (0)	0	<0.01
Armenian (0)	0	<0.01
Assyrian/Chaldean/Syriac (0)	0	<0.01
Australian (0)	0	<0.01
Austrian (26)	160	0.32
Basque (0)	0	<0.01
Belgian (0)	13	0.03
Brazilian (0)	0	<0.01
British (46)	70	0.14
Bulgarian (0)	0	<0.01
Cajun (22)	22	0.04
Canadian (17)	34	0.07
Carpatho Rusyn (0)	0	<0.01
Celtic (0)	0	<0.01
Croatian (0)	10	0.02
Cypriot (0)	0	<0.01
Czech (12)	57	0.11
Czechoslovakian (23)	31	0.06
Danish (13)	123	0.25
Dutch (84)	1,060	2.14
Eastern European (0)	0	<0.01
English (1,503)	5,667	11.43
Estonian (0)	0	<0.01
European (625)	636	1.28
Finnish (15)	182	0.37
French, ex. Basque (257)	1,528	3.08
French Canadian (35)	89	0.18
German (10,530)	23,046	46.48
German Russian (0)	0	<0.01
Greek (22)	201	0.41
Guyanese (0)	0	<0.01
Hungarian (25)	144	0.29
Icelander (0)	0	<0.01
Iranian (0)	0	<0.01
Irish (2,500)	9,509	19.18
Israeli (0)	0	<0.01
Italian (577)	1,814	3.66
Latvian (0)	0	<0.01
Lithuanian (44)	54	0.11
Luxemburger (0)	0	<0.01
Macedonian (0)	0	<0.01
Maltese (0)	0	<0.01
New Zealander (0)	0	<0.01
Northern European (0)	0	<0.01
Norwegian (14)	131	0.26
Pennsylvania German (11)	11	0.02
Polish (109)	641	1.29
Portuguese (0)	30	0.06
Romanian (10)	110	0.22
Russian (111)	268	0.54
Scandinavian (22)	33	0.07
Scotch-Irish (304)	716	1.44
Scottish (283)	675	1.36
Serbian (0)	0	<0.01
Slavic (0)	9	0.02
Slovak (0)	0	<0.01
Slovene (0)	42	0.08
Soviet Union (0)	0	<0.01
Swedish (37)	162	0.33
Swiss (32)	112	0.23
Turkish (0)	0	<0.01
Ukrainian (18)	35	0.07
Welsh (60)	255	0.51
West Indian, ex. Hispanic (0)	0	<0.01
Bahamian (0)	0	<0.01
Barbadian (0)	0	<0.01
Belizean (0)	0	<0.01
Bermudan (0)	0	<0.01
British West Indian (0)	0	<0.01
Dutch West Indian (0)	0	<0.01
Haitian (0)	0	<0.01
Jamaican (0)	0	<0.01
Trinidadian/Tobagonian (0)	0	<0.01
U.S. Virgin Islander (0)	0	<0.01
West Indian (0)	0	<0.01
Other West Indian (0)	0	<0.01
Yugoslavian (13)	13	0.03

Hispanic Origin	Population	%
Hispanic or Latino (of any race)	502	1.00
Central American, ex. Mexican	39	0.08
Costa Rican	4	0.01
Guatemalan	19	0.04
Honduran	10	0.02
Nicaraguan	0	<0.01
Panamanian	1	<0.01
Salvadoran	5	0.01
Other Central American	0	<0.01
Cuban	9	0.02
Dominican Republic	15	0.03
Mexican	292	0.58
Puerto Rican	49	0.10
South American	35	0.07
Argentinean	2	<0.01
Bolivian	0	<0.01
Chilean	4	0.01
Colombian	11	0.02
Ecuadorian	1	<0.01
Paraguayan	4	0.01
Peruvian	4	0.01
Uruguayan	0	<0.01
Venezuelan	6	0.01
Other South American	3	0.01
Other Hispanic or Latino	63	0.13

Race*	Population	%
African-American/Black (300)	492	0.98
Not Hispanic (291)	481	0.96
Hispanic (9)	11	0.02
American Indian/Alaska Native (87)	249	0.50
Not Hispanic (79)	225	0.45
Hispanic (8)	24	0.05
Alaska Athabascan *(Ala. Nat.)* (0)	0	<0.01
Aleut *(Alaska Native)* (0)	0	<0.01
Apache (1)	6	0.01
Arapaho (0)	0	<0.01
Blackfeet (5)	14	0.03
Canadian/French Am. Ind. (0)	1	<0.01
Central American Ind. (0)	0	<0.01
Cherokee (19)	75	0.15
Cheyenne (0)	0	<0.01
Chickasaw (0)	0	<0.01
Chippewa (5)	5	0.01
Choctaw (2)	6	0.01
Colville (0)	0	<0.01
Comanche (1)	1	<0.01
Cree (1)	1	<0.01
Creek (2)	2	<0.01
Crow (0)	0	<0.01
Delaware (0)	0	<0.01
Hopi (0)	0	<0.01
Houma (0)	0	<0.01
Inupiat *(Alaska Native)* (2)	2	<0.01
Iroquois (0)	1	<0.01
Kiowa (0)	0	<0.01
Lumbee (1)	1	<0.01
Menominee (0)	0	<0.01
Mexican American Ind. (4)	4	0.01
Navajo (0)	3	0.01
Osage (0)	0	<0.01
Ottawa (0)	0	<0.01
Paiute (0)	0	<0.01
Pima (2)	2	<0.01
Potawatomi (0)	1	<0.01
Pueblo (0)	0	<0.01
Puget Sound Salish (0)	0	<0.01
Seminole (0)	0	<0.01
Shoshone (0)	0	<0.01
Sioux (1)	8	0.02
South American Ind. (0)	0	<0.01
Spanish American Ind. (1)	1	<0.01
Tlingit-Haida *(Alaska Native)* (1)	3	0.01
Tohono O'Odham (0)	0	<0.01
Tsimshian *(Alaska Native)* (0)	0	<0.01
Ute (0)	0	<0.01
Yakama (0)	0	<0.01
Yaqui (0)	0	<0.01
Yuman (0)	0	<0.01
Yup'ik *(Alaska Native)* (0)	0	<0.01
Asian (189)	286	0.57
Not Hispanic (187)	282	0.56
Hispanic (2)	4	0.01
Bangladeshi (0)	0	<0.01
Bhutanese (0)	0	<0.01
Burmese (0)	0	<0.01
Cambodian (1)	1	<0.01
Chinese, ex. Taiwanese (29)	35	0.07
Filipino (50)	92	0.18
Hmong (0)	0	<0.01
Indian (25)	32	0.06
Indonesian (0)	0	<0.01
Japanese (18)	28	0.06
Korean (18)	32	0.06
Laotian (0)	0	<0.01
Malaysian (0)	0	<0.01
Nepalese (0)	0	<0.01
Pakistani (1)	1	<0.01
Sri Lankan (0)	0	<0.01
Taiwanese (2)	2	<0.01
Thai (4)	7	0.01
Vietnamese (33)	42	0.08
Hawaii Native/Pacific Islander (26)	44	0.09
Not Hispanic (24)	40	0.08
Hispanic (2)	4	0.01
Fijian (0)	0	<0.01
Guamanian/Chamorro (5)	7	0.01
Marshallese (1)	1	<0.01
Native Hawaiian (6)	13	0.03
Samoan (6)	7	0.01
Tongan (0)	0	<0.01
White (48,780)	49,247	98.40
Not Hispanic (48,486)	48,894	97.70
Hispanic (294)	353	0.71

*Notes: † The Census 2010 population figure is used to calculate the percentages in the Hispanic Origin and Race categories. Ancestry percentages are based on the 2006-2010 American Community Survey population (not shown); ‡ Numbers in parentheses indicate the number of people reporting a single ancestry; * Numbers in parentheses indicate the number of persons reporting this race alone, not in combination with any other race; Please refer to the Explanation of Data for more information.*

Decatur County

Population: 25,740

Ancestry	Population	%
Afghan (0)	0	<0.01
African, Sub-Saharan (0)	0	<0.01
African (0)	0	<0.01
Cape Verdean (0)	0	<0.01
Ethiopian (0)	0	<0.01
Ghanaian (0)	0	<0.01
Kenyan (0)	0	<0.01
Liberian (0)	0	<0.01
Nigerian (0)	0	<0.01
Senegalese (0)	0	<0.01
Sierra Leonean (0)	0	<0.01
Somalian (0)	0	<0.01
South African (0)	0	<0.01
Sudanese (0)	0	<0.01
Ugandan (0)	0	<0.01
Zimbabwean (0)	0	<0.01
Other Sub-Saharan African (0)	0	<0.01
Albanian (0)	0	<0.01
Alsatian (0)	0	<0.01
American (4,383)	4,383	17.13
Arab (16)	64	0.25
Arab (0)	0	<0.01
Egyptian (0)	0	<0.01
Iraqi (0)	0	<0.01
Jordanian (0)	0	<0.01
Lebanese (16)	64	0.25
Moroccan (0)	0	<0.01
Palestinian (0)	0	<0.01
Syrian (0)	0	<0.01
Other Arab (0)	0	<0.01
Armenian (0)	0	<0.01
Assyrian/Chaldean/Syriac (0)	0	<0.01
Australian (0)	0	<0.01
Austrian (0)	0	<0.01
Basque (0)	0	<0.01
Belgian (0)	0	<0.01
Brazilian (0)	0	<0.01
British (49)	208	0.81
Bulgarian (0)	0	<0.01
Cajun (0)	0	<0.01
Canadian (8)	8	0.03
Carpatho Rusyn (0)	0	<0.01
Celtic (0)	0	<0.01
Croatian (0)	61	0.24
Cypriot (0)	0	<0.01
Czech (0)	33	0.13
Czechoslovakian (0)	0	<0.01
Danish (0)	15	0.06
Dutch (96)	459	1.79
Eastern European (0)	0	<0.01
English (1,148)	2,400	9.38
Estonian (0)	0	<0.01
European (86)	95	0.37
Finnish (0)	30	0.12
French, ex. Basque (42)	497	1.94
French Canadian (3)	21	0.08
German (4,867)	7,607	29.73
German Russian (0)	0	<0.01
Greek (20)	20	0.08
Guyanese (0)	0	<0.01
Hungarian (15)	15	0.06
Icelander (0)	0	<0.01
Iranian (0)	0	<0.01
Irish (1,094)	2,596	10.15
Israeli (0)	0	<0.01
Italian (191)	408	1.59
Latvian (0)	0	<0.01
Lithuanian (0)	0	<0.01
Luxemburger (0)	0	<0.01
Macedonian (0)	0	<0.01
Maltese (0)	0	<0.01
New Zealander (0)	0	<0.01
Northern European (38)	38	0.15
Norwegian (75)	138	0.54
Pennsylvania German (9)	9	0.04
Polish (60)	135	0.53
Portuguese (0)	0	<0.01
Romanian (0)	8	0.03
Russian (13)	32	0.13
Scandinavian (0)	0	<0.01
Scotch-Irish (106)	388	1.52
Scottish (57)	248	0.97
Serbian (0)	0	<0.01
Slavic (0)	0	<0.01
Slovak (5)	5	0.02
Slovene (0)	0	<0.01
Soviet Union (0)	0	<0.01
Swedish (31)	114	0.45
Swiss (4)	18	0.07
Turkish (0)	0	<0.01
Ukrainian (0)	0	<0.01
Welsh (53)	125	0.49
West Indian, ex. Hispanic (0)	0	<0.01
Bahamian (0)	0	<0.01
Barbadian (0)	0	<0.01
Belizean (0)	0	<0.01
Bermudan (0)	0	<0.01
British West Indian (0)	0	<0.01
Dutch West Indian (0)	0	<0.01
Haitian (0)	0	<0.01
Jamaican (0)	0	<0.01
Trinidadian/Tobagonian (0)	0	<0.01
U.S. Virgin Islander (0)	0	<0.01
West Indian (0)	0	<0.01
Other West Indian (0)	0	<0.01
Yugoslavian (0)	0	<0.01

Hispanic Origin	Population	%
Hispanic or Latino (of any race)	426	1.66
Central American, ex. Mexican	17	0.07
Costa Rican	0	<0.01
Guatemalan	12	0.05
Honduran	2	0.01
Nicaraguan	0	<0.01
Panamanian	3	0.01
Salvadoran	0	<0.01
Other Central American	0	<0.01
Cuban	6	0.02
Dominican Republic	6	0.02
Mexican	304	1.18
Puerto Rican	20	0.08
South American	13	0.05
Argentinean	0	<0.01
Bolivian	0	<0.01
Chilean	0	<0.01
Colombian	10	0.04
Ecuadorian	0	<0.01
Paraguayan	0	<0.01
Peruvian	1	<0.01
Uruguayan	0	<0.01
Venezuelan	2	0.01
Other South American	0	<0.01
Other Hispanic or Latino	60	0.23

Race*	Population	%
African-American/Black (82)	139	0.54
Not Hispanic (76)	128	0.50
Hispanic (6)	11	0.04
American Indian/Alaska Native (39)	140	0.54
Not Hispanic (36)	130	0.51
Hispanic (3)	10	0.04
Alaska Athabascan *(Ala. Nat.)* (0)	0	<0.01
Aleut *(Alaska Native)* (0)	0	<0.01
Apache (2)	5	0.02
Arapaho (0)	0	<0.01
Blackfeet (5)	16	0.06
Canadian/French Am. Ind. (0)	0	<0.01
Central American Ind. (0)	0	<0.01
Cherokee (12)	51	0.20
Cheyenne (0)	0	<0.01
Chickasaw (1)	1	<0.01
Chippewa (0)	1	<0.01
Choctaw (0)	0	<0.01
Colville (0)	0	<0.01
Comanche (0)	0	<0.01
Cree (0)	0	<0.01
Creek (0)	0	<0.01
Crow (0)	0	<0.01
Delaware (0)	0	<0.01
Hopi (0)	0	<0.01
Houma (0)	0	<0.01
Inupiat *(Alaska Native)* (0)	0	<0.01
Iroquois (1)	6	0.02
Kiowa (1)	1	<0.01
Lumbee (0)	0	<0.01
Menominee (0)	0	<0.01
Mexican American Ind. (0)	2	0.01
Navajo (0)	0	<0.01
Osage (0)	0	<0.01
Ottawa (0)	0	<0.01
Paiute (0)	0	<0.01
Pima (0)	0	<0.01
Potawatomi (2)	2	0.01
Pueblo (0)	0	<0.01
Puget Sound Salish (0)	0	<0.01
Seminole (0)	0	<0.01
Shoshone (0)	0	<0.01
Sioux (1)	1	<0.01
South American Ind. (0)	0	<0.01
Spanish American Ind. (0)	0	<0.01
Tlingit-Haida *(Alaska Native)* (0)	0	<0.01
Tohono O'Odham (0)	0	<0.01
Tsimshian *(Alaska Native)* (0)	0	<0.01
Ute (0)	0	<0.01
Yakama (0)	0	<0.01
Yaqui (1)	1	<0.01
Yuman (0)	0	<0.01
Yup'ik *(Alaska Native)* (0)	0	<0.01
Asian (186)	228	0.89
Not Hispanic (178)	217	0.84
Hispanic (8)	11	0.04
Bangladeshi (0)	0	<0.01
Bhutanese (0)	0	<0.01
Burmese (0)	0	<0.01
Cambodian (0)	0	<0.01
Chinese, ex. Taiwanese (21)	35	0.14
Filipino (44)	62	0.24
Hmong (0)	0	<0.01
Indian (37)	42	0.16
Indonesian (3)	3	0.01
Japanese (46)	52	0.20
Korean (12)	23	0.09
Laotian (0)	0	<0.01
Malaysian (0)	0	<0.01
Nepalese (0)	0	<0.01
Pakistani (0)	0	<0.01
Sri Lankan (0)	0	<0.01
Taiwanese (0)	0	<0.01
Thai (1)	3	0.01
Vietnamese (12)	14	0.05
Hawaii Native/Pacific Islander (7)	15	0.06
Not Hispanic (7)	15	0.06
Hispanic (0)	0	<0.01
Fijian (0)	0	<0.01
Guamanian/Chamorro (0)	5	0.02
Marshallese (0)	0	<0.01
Native Hawaiian (7)	7	0.03
Samoan (0)	0	<0.01
Tongan (0)	0	<0.01
White (25,053)	25,270	98.17
Not Hispanic (24,796)	24,987	97.07
Hispanic (257)	283	1.10

*Notes: † The Census 2010 population figure is used to calculate the percentages in the Hispanic Origin and Race categories. Ancestry percentages are based on the 2006-2010 American Community Survey population (not shown); ‡ Numbers in parentheses indicate the number of people reporting a single ancestry; * Numbers in parentheses indicate the number of persons reporting this race alone, not in combination with any other race; Please refer to the Explanation of Data for more information.*

Delaware County

Population: 117,671

Ancestry	Population	%
Afghan (57)	57	0.05
African, Sub-Saharan (681)	888	0.76
African (559)	750	0.64
Cape Verdean (0)	0	<0.01
Ethiopian (0)	0	<0.01
Ghanaian (0)	0	<0.01
Kenyan (14)	14	0.01
Liberian (0)	0	<0.01
Nigerian (0)	0	<0.01
Senegalese (0)	0	<0.01
Sierra Leonean (0)	0	<0.01
Somalian (0)	0	<0.01
South African (0)	16	0.01
Sudanese (0)	0	<0.01
Ugandan (0)	0	<0.01
Zimbabwean (0)	0	<0.01
Other Sub-Saharan African (108)	108	0.09
Albanian (57)	57	0.05
Alsatian (0)	22	0.02
American (12,465)	12,465	10.62
Arab (20)	308	0.26
Arab (0)	84	0.07
Egyptian (0)	14	0.01
Iraqi (0)	14	0.01
Jordanian (0)	0	<0.01
Lebanese (0)	0	<0.01
Moroccan (0)	13	0.01
Palestinian (20)	20	0.02
Syrian (0)	145	0.12
Other Arab (0)	18	0.02
Armenian (0)	0	<0.01
Assyrian/Chaldean/Syriac (0)	0	<0.01
Australian (14)	42	0.04
Austrian (27)	97	0.08
Basque (0)	0	<0.01
Belgian (0)	120	0.10
Brazilian (0)	0	<0.01
British (280)	528	0.45
Bulgarian (9)	27	0.02
Cajun (0)	0	<0.01
Canadian (151)	236	0.20
Carpatho Rusyn (0)	0	<0.01
Celtic (10)	10	0.01
Croatian (0)	103	0.09
Cypriot (0)	0	<0.01
Czech (110)	134	0.11
Czechoslovakian (0)	0	<0.01
Danish (66)	176	0.15
Dutch (573)	2,448	2.09
Eastern European (0)	14	0.01
English (4,920)	12,070	10.29
Estonian (0)	0	<0.01
European (1,015)	1,091	0.93
Finnish (26)	59	0.05
French, ex. Basque (507)	2,992	2.55
French Canadian (34)	94	0.08
German (11,023)	26,947	22.96
German Russian (0)	0	<0.01
Greek (193)	317	0.27
Guyanese (0)	0	<0.01
Hungarian (114)	260	0.22
Icelander (0)	0	<0.01
Iranian (72)	78	0.07
Irish (4,908)	16,641	14.18
Israeli (24)	35	0.03
Italian (1,127)	2,615	2.23
Latvian (0)	9	0.01
Lithuanian (77)	99	0.08
Luxemburger (0)	32	0.03
Macedonian (12)	33	0.03
Maltese (0)	0	<0.01
New Zealander (0)	18	0.02
Northern European (17)	17	0.01
Norwegian (120)	575	0.49
Pennsylvania German (34)	73	0.06
Polish (560)	1,704	1.45
Portuguese (0)	19	0.02
Romanian (52)	157	0.13
Russian (96)	284	0.24
Scandinavian (0)	74	0.06
Scotch-Irish (707)	1,477	1.26
Scottish (789)	2,382	2.03
Serbian (0)	15	0.01
Slavic (22)	22	0.02
Slovak (30)	118	0.10
Slovene (0)	0	<0.01
Soviet Union (0)	0	<0.01
Swedish (297)	860	0.73
Swiss (146)	495	0.42
Turkish (34)	34	0.03
Ukrainian (18)	48	0.04
Welsh (207)	744	0.63
West Indian, ex. Hispanic (41)	41	0.03
Bahamian (0)	0	<0.01
Barbadian (28)	28	0.02
Belizean (0)	0	<0.01
Bermudan (0)	0	<0.01
British West Indian (0)	0	<0.01
Dutch West Indian (0)	0	<0.01
Haitian (0)	0	<0.01
Jamaican (13)	13	0.01
Trinidadian/Tobagonian (0)	0	<0.01
U.S. Virgin Islander (0)	0	<0.01
West Indian (0)	0	<0.01
Other West Indian (0)	0	<0.01
Yugoslavian (12)	27	0.02

Hispanic Origin	Population	%
Hispanic or Latino (of any race)	2,088	1.77
Central American, ex. Mexican	86	0.07
Costa Rican	5	<0.01
Guatemalan	20	0.02
Honduran	15	0.01
Nicaraguan	7	0.01
Panamanian	25	0.02
Salvadoran	11	0.01
Other Central American	3	<0.01
Cuban	47	0.04
Dominican Republic	28	0.02
Mexican	1,409	1.20
Puerto Rican	166	0.14
South American	87	0.07
Argentinean	12	0.01
Bolivian	9	0.01
Chilean	14	0.01
Colombian	12	0.01
Ecuadorian	2	<0.01
Paraguayan	1	<0.01
Peruvian	18	0.02
Uruguayan	2	<0.01
Venezuelan	13	0.01
Other South American	4	<0.01
Other Hispanic or Latino	265	0.23

Race*	Population	%
African-American/Black (8,146)	9,525	8.09
Not Hispanic (8,051)	9,346	7.94
Hispanic (95)	179	0.15
American Indian/Alaska Native (302)	921	0.78
Not Hispanic (255)	822	0.70
Hispanic (47)	99	0.08
Alaska Athabascan *(Ala. Nat.)* (0)	2	<0.01
Aleut *(Alaska Native)* (0)	0	<0.01
Apache (4)	19	0.02
Arapaho (0)	1	<0.01
Blackfeet (7)	50	0.04
Canadian/French Am. Ind. (3)	3	<0.01
Central American Ind. (1)	1	<0.01
Cherokee (80)	296	0.25
Cheyenne (0)	0	<0.01
Chickasaw (1)	1	<0.01
Chippewa (2)	8	0.01
Choctaw (1)	3	<0.01
Colville (0)	0	<0.01
Comanche (0)	0	<0.01
Cree (1)	5	<0.01
Creek (0)	3	<0.01
Crow (4)	4	<0.01
Delaware (0)	7	0.01
Hopi (0)	0	<0.01
Houma (0)	0	<0.01
Inupiat *(Alaska Native)* (0)	0	<0.01
Iroquois (6)	8	0.01
Kiowa (0)	0	<0.01
Lumbee (3)	3	<0.01
Menominee (1)	1	<0.01
Mexican American Ind. (16)	18	0.02
Navajo (4)	8	0.01
Osage (0)	1	<0.01
Ottawa (0)	1	<0.01
Paiute (0)	0	<0.01
Pima (0)	0	<0.01
Potawatomi (5)	5	<0.01
Pueblo (0)	1	<0.01
Puget Sound Salish (1)	1	<0.01
Seminole (1)	2	<0.01
Shoshone (0)	6	0.01
Sioux (8)	20	0.02
South American Ind. (2)	4	<0.01
Spanish American Ind. (3)	3	<0.01
Tlingit-Haida *(Alaska Native)* (5)	7	0.01
Tohono O'Odham (0)	0	<0.01
Tsimshian *(Alaska Native)* (0)	0	<0.01
Ute (0)	0	<0.01
Yakama (0)	0	<0.01
Yaqui (0)	0	<0.01
Yuman (0)	0	<0.01
Yup'ik *(Alaska Native)* (0)	0	<0.01
Asian (1,144)	1,577	1.34
Not Hispanic (1,128)	1,541	1.31
Hispanic (16)	36	0.03
Bangladeshi (23)	25	0.02
Bhutanese (0)	0	<0.01
Burmese (2)	2	<0.01
Cambodian (0)	0	<0.01
Chinese, ex. Taiwanese (301)	343	0.29
Filipino (132)	226	0.19
Hmong (2)	2	<0.01
Indian (289)	347	0.29
Indonesian (2)	3	<0.01
Japanese (64)	128	0.11
Korean (142)	195	0.17
Laotian (2)	6	0.01
Malaysian (3)	5	<0.01
Nepalese (10)	13	0.01
Pakistani (22)	25	0.02
Sri Lankan (4)	4	<0.01
Taiwanese (23)	26	0.02
Thai (14)	26	0.02
Vietnamese (68)	81	0.07
Hawaii Native/Pacific Islander (60)	188	0.16
Not Hispanic (56)	175	0.15
Hispanic (4)	13	0.01
Fijian (0)	1	<0.01
Guamanian/Chamorro (7)	17	0.01
Marshallese (0)	0	<0.01
Native Hawaiian (22)	69	0.06
Samoan (13)	31	0.03
Tongan (1)	3	<0.01
White (104,872)	107,158	91.07
Not Hispanic (103,721)	105,750	89.87
Hispanic (1,151)	1,408	1.20

*Notes: † The Census 2010 population figure is used to calculate the percentages in the Hispanic Origin and Race categories. Ancestry percentages are based on the 2006-2010 American Community Survey population (not shown); ‡ Numbers in parentheses indicate the number of people reporting a single ancestry; * Numbers in parentheses indicate the number of persons reporting this race alone, not in combination with any other race; Please refer to the Explanation of Data for more information.*

Dubois County

Population: 41,889

Ancestry	Population	%
Afghan (0)	0	<0.01
African, Sub-Saharan (15)	48	0.11
African (15)	48	0.11
Cape Verdean (0)	0	<0.01
Ethiopian (0)	0	<0.01
Ghanaian (0)	0	<0.01
Kenyan (0)	0	<0.01
Liberian (0)	0	<0.01
Nigerian (0)	0	<0.01
Senegalese (0)	0	<0.01
Sierra Leonean (0)	0	<0.01
Somalian (0)	0	<0.01
South African (0)	0	<0.01
Sudanese (0)	0	<0.01
Ugandan (0)	0	<0.01
Zimbabwean (0)	0	<0.01
Other Sub-Saharan African (0)	0	<0.01
Albanian (0)	0	<0.01
Alsatian (0)	0	<0.01
American (3,742)	3,742	8.95
Arab (43)	43	0.10
Arab (0)	0	<0.01
Egyptian (0)	0	<0.01
Iraqi (0)	0	<0.01
Jordanian (0)	0	<0.01
Lebanese (0)	0	<0.01
Moroccan (0)	0	<0.01
Palestinian (0)	0	<0.01
Syrian (0)	0	<0.01
Other Arab (43)	43	0.10
Armenian (0)	0	<0.01
Assyrian/Chaldean/Syriac (0)	0	<0.01
Australian (0)	0	<0.01
Austrian (0)	8	0.02
Basque (0)	0	<0.01
Belgian (0)	17	0.04
Brazilian (0)	0	<0.01
British (16)	45	0.11
Bulgarian (0)	0	<0.01
Cajun (0)	11	0.03
Canadian (28)	28	0.07
Carpatho Rusyn (0)	0	<0.01
Celtic (0)	0	<0.01
Croatian (42)	42	0.10
Cypriot (0)	0	<0.01
Czech (0)	0	<0.01
Czechoslovakian (7)	19	0.05
Danish (0)	21	0.05
Dutch (102)	597	1.43
Eastern European (14)	14	0.03
English (1,346)	2,809	6.72
Estonian (0)	0	<0.01
European (281)	315	0.75
Finnish (0)	0	<0.01
French, ex. Basque (208)	904	2.16
French Canadian (0)	110	0.26
German (19,473)	24,267	58.04
German Russian (0)	0	<0.01
Greek (51)	59	0.14
Guyanese (0)	0	<0.01
Hungarian (23)	28	0.07
Icelander (0)	0	<0.01
Iranian (0)	0	<0.01
Irish (1,006)	3,394	8.12
Israeli (0)	0	<0.01
Italian (156)	419	1.00
Latvian (0)	0	<0.01
Lithuanian (0)	0	<0.01
Luxemburger (0)	0	<0.01
Macedonian (0)	0	<0.01
Maltese (0)	9	0.02
New Zealander (0)	0	<0.01
Northern European (49)	49	0.12
Norwegian (24)	137	0.33
Pennsylvania German (0)	0	<0.01
Polish (36)	205	0.49
Portuguese (0)	28	0.07
Romanian (0)	0	<0.01
Russian (16)	80	0.19
Scandinavian (0)	0	<0.01
Scotch-Irish (183)	426	1.02
Scottish (62)	330	0.79
Serbian (17)	17	0.04
Slavic (0)	0	<0.01
Slovak (0)	17	0.04
Slovene (0)	0	<0.01
Soviet Union (0)	0	<0.01
Swedish (56)	272	0.65
Swiss (100)	327	0.78
Turkish (0)	0	<0.01
Ukrainian (0)	0	<0.01
Welsh (13)	55	0.13
West Indian, ex. Hispanic (36)	47	0.11
Bahamian (0)	0	<0.01
Barbadian (0)	0	<0.01
Belizean (0)	0	<0.01
Bermudan (0)	0	<0.01
British West Indian (0)	0	<0.01
Dutch West Indian (0)	0	<0.01
Haitian (0)	0	<0.01
Jamaican (36)	47	0.11
Trinidadian/Tobagonian (0)	0	<0.01
U.S. Virgin Islander (0)	0	<0.01
West Indian (0)	0	<0.01
Other West Indian (0)	0	<0.01
Yugoslavian (0)	0	<0.01

Hispanic Origin	Population	%
Hispanic or Latino (of any race)	2,521	6.02
Central American, ex. Mexican	932	2.22
Costa Rican	0	<0.01
Guatemalan	62	0.15
Honduran	44	0.11
Nicaraguan	0	<0.01
Panamanian	4	0.01
Salvadoran	822	1.96
Other Central American	0	<0.01
Cuban	24	0.06
Dominican Republic	1	<0.01
Mexican	1,212	2.89
Puerto Rican	50	0.12
South American	36	0.09
Argentinean	1	<0.01
Bolivian	1	<0.01
Chilean	2	<0.01
Colombian	12	0.03
Ecuadorian	3	0.01
Paraguayan	0	<0.01
Peruvian	16	0.04
Uruguayan	0	<0.01
Venezuelan	1	<0.01
Other South American	0	<0.01
Other Hispanic or Latino	266	0.64

Race*	Population	%
African-American/Black (122)	216	0.52
Not Hispanic (109)	177	0.42
Hispanic (13)	39	0.09
American Indian/Alaska Native (66)	147	0.35
Not Hispanic (51)	128	0.31
Hispanic (15)	19	0.05
Alaska Athabascan *(Ala. Nat.)* (0)	0	<0.01
Aleut *(Alaska Native)* (0)	0	<0.01
Apache (0)	0	<0.01
Arapaho (3)	3	0.01
Blackfeet (0)	2	<0.01
Canadian/French Am. Ind. (0)	0	<0.01
Central American Ind. (1)	1	<0.01
Cherokee (4)	33	0.08
Cheyenne (0)	0	<0.01
Chickasaw (1)	1	<0.01
Chippewa (1)	1	<0.01
Choctaw (5)	5	0.01
Colville (0)	0	<0.01
Comanche (0)	1	<0.01
Cree (0)	0	<0.01
Creek (3)	8	0.02
Crow (0)	0	<0.01
Delaware (0)	0	<0.01
Hopi (0)	0	<0.01
Houma (0)	0	<0.01
Inupiat *(Alaska Native)* (1)	1	<0.01
Iroquois (1)	1	<0.01
Kiowa (0)	0	<0.01
Lumbee (0)	0	<0.01
Menominee (0)	0	<0.01
Mexican American Ind. (2)	2	<0.01
Navajo (1)	2	<0.01
Osage (0)	0	<0.01
Ottawa (0)	0	<0.01
Paiute (0)	0	<0.01
Pima (0)	0	<0.01
Potawatomi (0)	0	<0.01
Pueblo (0)	0	<0.01
Puget Sound Salish (0)	0	<0.01
Seminole (0)	0	<0.01
Shoshone (0)	0	<0.01
Sioux (1)	8	0.02
South American Ind. (0)	0	<0.01
Spanish American Ind. (0)	0	<0.01
Tlingit-Haida *(Alaska Native)* (0)	0	<0.01
Tohono O'Odham (0)	0	<0.01
Tsimshian *(Alaska Native)* (0)	0	<0.01
Ute (0)	0	<0.01
Yakama (0)	0	<0.01
Yaqui (0)	0	<0.01
Yuman (0)	0	<0.01
Yup'ik *(Alaska Native)* (0)	0	<0.01
Asian (189)	246	0.59
Not Hispanic (189)	241	0.58
Hispanic (0)	5	0.01
Bangladeshi (0)	0	<0.01
Bhutanese (0)	0	<0.01
Burmese (0)	0	<0.01
Cambodian (0)	0	<0.01
Chinese, ex. Taiwanese (42)	46	0.11
Filipino (26)	57	0.14
Hmong (0)	0	<0.01
Indian (72)	83	0.20
Indonesian (1)	1	<0.01
Japanese (5)	11	0.03
Korean (8)	8	0.02
Laotian (0)	0	<0.01
Malaysian (1)	1	<0.01
Nepalese (0)	0	<0.01
Pakistani (0)	0	<0.01
Sri Lankan (0)	0	<0.01
Taiwanese (0)	1	<0.01
Thai (2)	2	<0.01
Vietnamese (25)	25	0.06
Hawaii Native/Pacific Islander (11)	32	0.08
Not Hispanic (5)	13	0.03
Hispanic (6)	19	0.05
Fijian (0)	0	<0.01
Guamanian/Chamorro (5)	6	0.01
Marshallese (0)	0	<0.01
Native Hawaiian (5)	8	0.02
Samoan (0)	0	<0.01
Tongan (0)	0	<0.01
White (39,839)	40,176	95.91
Not Hispanic (38,791)	38,991	93.08
Hispanic (1,048)	1,185	2.83

*Notes: † The Census 2010 population figure is used to calculate the percentages in the Hispanic Origin and Race categories. Ancestry percentages are based on the 2006-2010 American Community Survey population (not shown); ‡ Numbers in parentheses indicate the number of people reporting a single ancestry; * Numbers in parentheses indicate the number of persons reporting this race alone, not in combination with any other race; Please refer to the Explanation of Data for more information.*

Elkhart County

Population: 197,559

Ancestry	Population	%
Afghan (0)	0	<0.01
African, Sub-Saharan (433)	555	0.28
African (310)	380	0.19
Cape Verdean (0)	0	<0.01
Ethiopian (7)	7	<0.01
Ghanaian (0)	0	<0.01
Kenyan (100)	100	0.05
Liberian (0)	0	<0.01
Nigerian (0)	0	<0.01
Senegalese (16)	16	0.01
Sierra Leonean (0)	9	<0.01
Somalian (0)	0	<0.01
South African (0)	0	<0.01
Sudanese (0)	0	<0.01
Ugandan (0)	0	<0.01
Zimbabwean (0)	13	0.01
Other Sub-Saharan African (0)	30	0.02
Albanian (0)	0	<0.01
Alsatian (0)	24	0.01
American (14,962)	14,962	7.60
Arab (202)	259	0.13
Arab (23)	23	0.01
Egyptian (0)	0	<0.01
Iraqi (11)	11	0.01
Jordanian (0)	0	<0.01
Lebanese (9)	51	0.03
Moroccan (16)	16	0.01
Palestinian (0)	0	<0.01
Syrian (40)	55	0.03
Other Arab (103)	103	0.05
Armenian (0)	0	<0.01
Assyrian/Chaldean/Syriac (0)	0	<0.01
Australian (0)	0	<0.01
Austrian (15)	263	0.13
Basque (0)	0	<0.01
Belgian (219)	547	0.28
Brazilian (89)	151	0.08
British (212)	414	0.21
Bulgarian (0)	0	<0.01
Cajun (64)	64	0.03
Canadian (119)	319	0.16
Carpatho Rusyn (0)	0	<0.01
Celtic (0)	0	<0.01
Croatian (12)	43	0.02
Cypriot (0)	0	<0.01
Czech (295)	911	0.46
Czechoslovakian (55)	55	0.03
Danish (112)	406	0.21
Dutch (2,047)	6,429	3.27
Eastern European (35)	35	0.02
English (5,739)	14,886	7.56
Estonian (0)	0	<0.01
European (1,759)	1,842	0.94
Finnish (50)	174	0.09
French, ex. Basque (588)	4,474	2.27
French Canadian (269)	780	0.40
German (24,238)	55,836	28.36
German Russian (0)	47	0.02
Greek (91)	381	0.19
Guyanese (10)	10	0.01
Hungarian (281)	1,307	0.66
Icelander (0)	0	<0.01
Iranian (0)	0	<0.01
Irish (5,104)	20,060	10.19
Israeli (0)	0	<0.01
Italian (2,143)	5,372	2.73
Latvian (17)	17	0.01
Lithuanian (82)	132	0.07
Luxemburger (0)	0	<0.01
Macedonian (0)	0	<0.01
Maltese (0)	0	<0.01
New Zealander (0)	0	<0.01
Northern European (54)	54	0.03
Norwegian (263)	1,166	0.59
Pennsylvania German (2,244)	2,673	1.36
Polish (1,563)	5,788	2.94
Portuguese (85)	111	0.06
Romanian (38)	114	0.06
Russian (371)	873	0.44
Scandinavian (119)	150	0.08
Scotch-Irish (1,010)	2,457	1.25
Scottish (862)	2,628	1.33
Serbian (24)	24	0.01
Slavic (16)	26	0.01
Slovak (22)	75	0.04
Slovene (30)	71	0.04
Soviet Union (0)	0	<0.01
Swedish (980)	2,441	1.24
Swiss (1,495)	6,590	3.35
Turkish (0)	10	0.01
Ukrainian (556)	764	0.39
Welsh (208)	1,017	0.52
West Indian, ex. Hispanic (278)	278	0.14
Bahamian (0)	0	<0.01
Barbadian (0)	0	<0.01
Belizean (0)	0	<0.01
Bermudan (0)	0	<0.01
British West Indian (0)	0	<0.01
Dutch West Indian (14)	14	0.01
Haitian (93)	93	0.05
Jamaican (171)	171	0.09
Trinidadian/Tobagonian (0)	0	<0.01
U.S. Virgin Islander (0)	0	<0.01
West Indian (0)	0	<0.01
Other West Indian (0)	0	<0.01
Yugoslavian (12)	50	0.03

Hispanic Origin	Population	%
Hispanic or Latino (of any race)	27,886	14.12
Central American, ex. Mexican	1,736	0.88
Costa Rican	21	0.01
Guatemalan	270	0.14
Honduran	699	0.35
Nicaraguan	36	0.02
Panamanian	30	0.02
Salvadoran	665	0.34
Other Central American	15	0.01
Cuban	105	0.05
Dominican Republic	57	0.03
Mexican	22,867	11.57
Puerto Rican	1,176	0.60
South American	407	0.21
Argentinean	23	0.01
Bolivian	74	0.04
Chilean	21	0.01
Colombian	82	0.04
Ecuadorian	50	0.03
Paraguayan	7	<0.01
Peruvian	45	0.02
Uruguayan	20	0.01
Venezuelan	79	0.04
Other South American	6	<0.01
Other Hispanic or Latino	1,538	0.78

Race*	Population	%
African-American/Black (11,307)	13,745	6.96
Not Hispanic (10,989)	13,153	6.66
Hispanic (318)	592	0.30
American Indian/Alaska Native (747)	1,830	0.93
Not Hispanic (434)	1,299	0.66
Hispanic (313)	531	0.27
Alaska Athabascan *(Ala. Nat.)* (0)	0	<0.01
Aleut *(Alaska Native)* (1)	1	<0.01
Apache (6)	22	0.01
Arapaho (0)	2	<0.01
Blackfeet (13)	77	0.04
Canadian/French Am. Ind. (1)	9	<0.01
Central American Ind. (1)	4	<0.01
Cherokee (88)	351	0.18
Cheyenne (1)	5	<0.01
Chickasaw (4)	9	<0.01
Chippewa (19)	52	0.03
Choctaw (15)	31	0.02
Colville (0)	0	<0.01
Comanche (7)	12	0.01
Cree (1)	6	<0.01
Creek (0)	4	<0.01
Crow (1)	7	<0.01
Delaware (0)	5	<0.01
Hopi (0)	0	<0.01
Houma (0)	0	<0.01
Inupiat *(Alaska Native)* (0)	0	<0.01
Iroquois (9)	19	0.01
Kiowa (0)	0	<0.01
Lumbee (7)	8	<0.01
Menominee (1)	1	<0.01
Mexican American Ind. (83)	134	0.07
Navajo (11)	20	0.01
Osage (0)	2	<0.01
Ottawa (7)	13	0.01
Paiute (0)	4	<0.01
Pima (0)	0	<0.01
Potawatomi (31)	69	0.03
Pueblo (1)	6	<0.01
Puget Sound Salish (0)	0	<0.01
Seminole (3)	9	<0.01
Shoshone (0)	2	<0.01
Sioux (18)	54	0.03
South American Ind. (4)	11	0.01
Spanish American Ind. (7)	8	<0.01
Tlingit-Haida *(Alaska Native)* (1)	1	<0.01
Tohono O'Odham (0)	1	<0.01
Tsimshian *(Alaska Native)* (1)	1	<0.01
Ute (0)	0	<0.01
Yakama (0)	0	<0.01
Yaqui (0)	3	<0.01
Yuman (0)	0	<0.01
Yup'ik *(Alaska Native)* (3)	3	<0.01
Asian (1,915)	2,597	1.31
Not Hispanic (1,879)	2,496	1.26
Hispanic (36)	101	0.05
Bangladeshi (15)	16	0.01
Bhutanese (0)	0	<0.01
Burmese (1)	6	<0.01
Cambodian (214)	263	0.13
Chinese, ex. Taiwanese (239)	317	0.16
Filipino (178)	307	0.16
Hmong (1)	4	<0.01
Indian (371)	468	0.24
Indonesian (11)	43	0.02
Japanese (56)	130	0.07
Korean (156)	250	0.13
Laotian (292)	355	0.18
Malaysian (3)	7	<0.01
Nepalese (11)	13	0.01
Pakistani (27)	41	0.02
Sri Lankan (17)	17	0.01
Taiwanese (9)	9	<0.01
Thai (27)	47	0.02
Vietnamese (153)	214	0.11
Hawaii Native/Pacific Islander (81)	208	0.11
Not Hispanic (60)	148	0.07
Hispanic (21)	60	0.03
Fijian (1)	2	<0.01
Guamanian/Chamorro (22)	45	0.02
Marshallese (5)	8	<0.01
Native Hawaiian (13)	53	0.03
Samoan (10)	24	0.01
Tongan (6)	6	<0.01
White (163,792)	168,311	85.20
Not Hispanic (152,555)	155,820	78.87
Hispanic (11,237)	12,491	6.32

*Notes: † The Census 2010 population figure is used to calculate the percentages in the Hispanic Origin and Race categories. Ancestry percentages are based on the 2006-2010 American Community Survey population (not shown); ‡ Numbers in parentheses indicate the number of people reporting a single ancestry; * Numbers in parentheses indicate the number of persons reporting this race alone, not in combination with any other race; Please refer to the Explanation of Data for more information.*

Fayette County

Population: 24,277

Ancestry	Population	%
Afghan (0)	0	<0.01
African, Sub-Saharan (25)	25	0.10
African (25)	25	0.10
Cape Verdean (0)	0	<0.01
Ethiopian (0)	0	<0.01
Ghanaian (0)	0	<0.01
Kenyan (0)	0	<0.01
Liberian (0)	0	<0.01
Nigerian (0)	0	<0.01
Senegalese (0)	0	<0.01
Sierra Leonean (0)	0	<0.01
Somalian (0)	0	<0.01
South African (0)	0	<0.01
Sudanese (0)	0	<0.01
Ugandan (0)	0	<0.01
Zimbabwean (0)	0	<0.01
Other Sub-Saharan African (0)	0	<0.01
Albanian (0)	0	<0.01
Alsatian (0)	0	<0.01
American (3,695)	3,695	15.16
Arab (7)	7	0.03
Arab (0)	0	<0.01
Egyptian (0)	0	<0.01
Iraqi (0)	0	<0.01
Jordanian (0)	0	<0.01
Lebanese (7)	7	0.03
Moroccan (0)	0	<0.01
Palestinian (0)	0	<0.01
Syrian (0)	0	<0.01
Other Arab (0)	0	<0.01
Armenian (0)	0	<0.01
Assyrian/Chaldean/Syriac (0)	0	<0.01
Australian (0)	0	<0.01
Austrian (0)	0	<0.01
Basque (0)	0	<0.01
Belgian (0)	0	<0.01
Brazilian (0)	0	<0.01
British (50)	73	0.30
Bulgarian (0)	0	<0.01
Cajun (0)	0	<0.01
Canadian (16)	16	0.07
Carpatho Rusyn (0)	0	<0.01
Celtic (0)	0	<0.01
Croatian (0)	0	<0.01
Cypriot (0)	0	<0.01
Czech (6)	6	0.02
Czechoslovakian (0)	0	<0.01
Danish (0)	0	<0.01
Dutch (54)	298	1.22
Eastern European (0)	0	<0.01
English (1,152)	1,989	8.16
Estonian (0)	0	<0.01
European (66)	100	0.41
Finnish (0)	19	0.08
French, ex. Basque (118)	358	1.47
French Canadian (0)	0	<0.01
German (2,516)	4,991	20.48
German Russian (0)	0	<0.01
Greek (32)	32	0.13
Guyanese (0)	0	<0.01
Hungarian (27)	50	0.21
Icelander (0)	0	<0.01
Iranian (0)	0	<0.01
Irish (1,030)	2,887	11.85
Israeli (0)	0	<0.01
Italian (105)	248	1.02
Latvian (0)	0	<0.01
Lithuanian (26)	26	0.11
Luxemburger (0)	0	<0.01
Macedonian (0)	0	<0.01
Maltese (0)	0	<0.01
New Zealander (0)	0	<0.01
Northern European (0)	0	<0.01
Norwegian (11)	57	0.23
Pennsylvania German (11)	19	0.08
Polish (59)	150	0.62
Portuguese (0)	0	<0.01
Romanian (0)	0	<0.01
Russian (0)	0	<0.01
Scandinavian (0)	18	0.07
Scotch-Irish (185)	393	1.61
Scottish (252)	351	1.44
Serbian (0)	0	<0.01
Slavic (0)	0	<0.01
Slovak (8)	52	0.21
Slovene (0)	0	<0.01
Soviet Union (0)	0	<0.01
Swedish (7)	49	0.20
Swiss (7)	7	0.03
Turkish (0)	0	<0.01
Ukrainian (0)	0	<0.01
Welsh (21)	62	0.25
West Indian, ex. Hispanic (0)	11	0.05
Bahamian (0)	0	<0.01
Barbadian (0)	0	<0.01
Belizean (0)	0	<0.01
Bermudan (0)	0	<0.01
British West Indian (0)	0	<0.01
Dutch West Indian (0)	11	0.05
Haitian (0)	0	<0.01
Jamaican (0)	0	<0.01
Trinidadian/Tobagonian (0)	0	<0.01
U.S. Virgin Islander (0)	0	<0.01
West Indian (0)	0	<0.01
Other West Indian (0)	0	<0.01
Yugoslavian (0)	0	<0.01

Hispanic Origin	Population	%
Hispanic or Latino (of any race)	223	0.92
Central American, ex. Mexican	14	0.06
Costa Rican	0	<0.01
Guatemalan	7	0.03
Honduran	3	0.01
Nicaraguan	0	<0.01
Panamanian	3	0.01
Salvadoran	1	<0.01
Other Central American	0	<0.01
Cuban	6	0.02
Dominican Republic	0	<0.01
Mexican	127	0.52
Puerto Rican	23	0.09
South American	16	0.07
Argentinean	5	0.02
Bolivian	0	<0.01
Chilean	0	<0.01
Colombian	0	<0.01
Ecuadorian	0	<0.01
Paraguayan	0	<0.01
Peruvian	4	0.02
Uruguayan	0	<0.01
Venezuelan	7	0.03
Other South American	0	<0.01
Other Hispanic or Latino	37	0.15

Race*	Population	%
African-American/Black (322)	428	1.76
Not Hispanic (318)	423	1.74
Hispanic (4)	5	0.02
American Indian/Alaska Native (32)	126	0.52
Not Hispanic (30)	124	0.51
Hispanic (2)	2	0.01
Alaska Athabascan *(Ala. Nat.)* (0)	0	<0.01
Aleut *(Alaska Native)* (0)	0	<0.01
Apache (0)	1	<0.01
Arapaho (0)	0	<0.01
Blackfeet (0)	0	<0.01
Canadian/French Am. Ind. (0)	0	<0.01
Central American Ind. (0)	0	<0.01
Cherokee (6)	41	0.17
Cheyenne (0)	0	<0.01
Chickasaw (0)	0	<0.01
Chippewa (0)	1	<0.01
Choctaw (0)	0	<0.01
Colville (0)	0	<0.01
Comanche (0)	0	<0.01
Cree (0)	0	<0.01
Creek (0)	3	0.01
Crow (0)	0	<0.01
Delaware (2)	2	0.01
Hopi (0)	0	<0.01
Houma (0)	0	<0.01
Inupiat *(Alaska Native)* (0)	0	<0.01
Iroquois (0)	3	0.01
Kiowa (0)	0	<0.01
Lumbee (0)	0	<0.01
Menominee (0)	0	<0.01
Mexican American Ind. (2)	2	0.01
Navajo (1)	1	<0.01
Osage (0)	0	<0.01
Ottawa (0)	0	<0.01
Paiute (0)	0	<0.01
Pima (0)	0	<0.01
Potawatomi (0)	0	<0.01
Pueblo (0)	0	<0.01
Puget Sound Salish (0)	0	<0.01
Seminole (0)	0	<0.01
Shoshone (1)	1	<0.01
Sioux (0)	5	0.02
South American Ind. (0)	0	<0.01
Spanish American Ind. (0)	0	<0.01
Tlingit-Haida *(Alaska Native)* (0)	0	<0.01
Tohono O'Odham (0)	0	<0.01
Tsimshian *(Alaska Native)* (0)	0	<0.01
Ute (0)	0	<0.01
Yakama (0)	0	<0.01
Yaqui (0)	0	<0.01
Yuman (0)	0	<0.01
Yup'ik *(Alaska Native)* (0)	0	<0.01
Asian (81)	101	0.42
Not Hispanic (79)	98	0.40
Hispanic (2)	3	0.01
Bangladeshi (0)	0	<0.01
Bhutanese (0)	0	<0.01
Burmese (0)	0	<0.01
Cambodian (1)	1	<0.01
Chinese, ex. Taiwanese (15)	16	0.07
Filipino (20)	23	0.09
Hmong (0)	0	<0.01
Indian (20)	22	0.09
Indonesian (4)	4	0.02
Japanese (3)	5	0.02
Korean (7)	12	0.05
Laotian (0)	0	<0.01
Malaysian (0)	0	<0.01
Nepalese (0)	0	<0.01
Pakistani (1)	1	<0.01
Sri Lankan (0)	0	<0.01
Taiwanese (0)	0	<0.01
Thai (0)	0	<0.01
Vietnamese (8)	10	0.04
Hawaii Native/Pacific Islander (0)	7	0.03
Not Hispanic (0)	7	0.03
Hispanic (0)	0	<0.01
Fijian (0)	0	<0.01
Guamanian/Chamorro (0)	0	<0.01
Marshallese (0)	0	<0.01
Native Hawaiian (0)	5	0.02
Samoan (0)	0	<0.01
Tongan (0)	0	<0.01
White (23,532)	23,765	97.89
Not Hispanic (23,392)	23,609	97.25
Hispanic (140)	156	0.64

*Notes: † The Census 2010 population figure is used to calculate the percentages in the Hispanic Origin and Race categories. Ancestry percentages are based on the 2006-2010 American Community Survey population (not shown); ‡ Numbers in parentheses indicate the number of people reporting a single ancestry; * Numbers in parentheses indicate the number of persons reporting this race alone, not in combination with any other race; Please refer to the Explanation of Data for more information.*

Floyd County

Population: 74,578

Ancestry	Population	%
Afghan (0)	0	<0.01
African, Sub-Saharan (40)	61	0.08
African (40)	61	0.08
Cape Verdean (0)	0	<0.01
Ethiopian (0)	0	<0.01
Ghanaian (0)	0	<0.01
Kenyan (0)	0	<0.01
Liberian (0)	0	<0.01
Nigerian (0)	0	<0.01
Senegalese (0)	0	<0.01
Sierra Leonean (0)	0	<0.01
Somalian (0)	0	<0.01
South African (0)	0	<0.01
Sudanese (0)	0	<0.01
Ugandan (0)	0	<0.01
Zimbabwean (0)	0	<0.01
Other Sub-Saharan African (0)	0	<0.01
Albanian (0)	0	<0.01
Alsatian (4)	4	0.01
American (7,820)	7,820	10.63
Arab (34)	66	0.09
Arab (0)	0	<0.01
Egyptian (0)	0	<0.01
Iraqi (10)	10	0.01
Jordanian (0)	0	<0.01
Lebanese (11)	43	0.06
Moroccan (0)	0	<0.01
Palestinian (13)	13	0.02
Syrian (0)	0	<0.01
Other Arab (0)	0	<0.01
Armenian (0)	8	0.01
Assyrian/Chaldean/Syriac (0)	0	<0.01
Australian (0)	0	<0.01
Austrian (34)	45	0.06
Basque (0)	17	0.02
Belgian (16)	65	0.09
Brazilian (0)	0	<0.01
British (109)	295	0.40
Bulgarian (0)	7	0.01
Cajun (0)	0	<0.01
Canadian (51)	79	0.11
Carpatho Rusyn (0)	0	<0.01
Celtic (0)	14	0.02
Croatian (33)	66	0.09
Cypriot (0)	0	<0.01
Czech (25)	44	0.06
Czechoslovakian (0)	8	0.01
Danish (18)	58	0.08
Dutch (253)	1,193	1.62
Eastern European (0)	0	<0.01
English (3,186)	8,122	11.04
Estonian (0)	0	<0.01
European (872)	951	1.29
Finnish (9)	76	0.10
French, ex. Basque (529)	2,728	3.71
French Canadian (68)	119	0.16
German (9,945)	21,642	29.41
German Russian (0)	0	<0.01
Greek (54)	141	0.19
Guyanese (0)	0	<0.01
Hungarian (14)	134	0.18
Icelander (0)	0	<0.01
Iranian (0)	0	<0.01
Irish (3,515)	11,068	15.04
Israeli (0)	0	<0.01
Italian (542)	1,490	2.02
Latvian (14)	39	0.05
Lithuanian (23)	57	0.08
Luxemburger (0)	0	<0.01
Macedonian (0)	0	<0.01
Maltese (0)	0	<0.01
New Zealander (0)	0	<0.01
Northern European (8)	8	0.01
Norwegian (136)	361	0.49
Pennsylvania German (11)	11	0.01
Polish (138)	570	0.77
Portuguese (0)	81	0.11
Romanian (0)	60	0.08
Russian (55)	148	0.20
Scandinavian (19)	19	0.03
Scotch-Irish (471)	1,332	1.81
Scottish (598)	1,651	2.24
Serbian (0)	0	<0.01
Slavic (0)	11	0.01
Slovak (18)	122	0.17
Slovene (15)	53	0.07
Soviet Union (0)	0	<0.01
Swedish (86)	279	0.38
Swiss (96)	452	0.61
Turkish (0)	0	<0.01
Ukrainian (0)	28	0.04
Welsh (203)	556	0.76
West Indian, ex. Hispanic (0)	0	<0.01
Bahamian (0)	0	<0.01
Barbadian (0)	0	<0.01
Belizean (0)	0	<0.01
Bermudan (0)	0	<0.01
British West Indian (0)	0	<0.01
Dutch West Indian (0)	0	<0.01
Haitian (0)	0	<0.01
Jamaican (0)	0	<0.01
Trinidadian/Tobagonian (0)	0	<0.01
U.S. Virgin Islander (0)	0	<0.01
West Indian (0)	0	<0.01
Other West Indian (0)	0	<0.01
Yugoslavian (0)	0	<0.01

Hispanic Origin	Population	%
Hispanic or Latino (of any race)	1,972	2.64
Central American, ex. Mexican	137	0.18
Costa Rican	2	<0.01
Guatemalan	50	0.07
Honduran	37	0.05
Nicaraguan	2	<0.01
Panamanian	24	0.03
Salvadoran	21	0.03
Other Central American	1	<0.01
Cuban	47	0.06
Dominican Republic	5	0.01
Mexican	1,372	1.84
Puerto Rican	167	0.22
South American	75	0.10
Argentinean	2	<0.01
Bolivian	3	<0.01
Chilean	4	0.01
Colombian	27	0.04
Ecuadorian	22	0.03
Paraguayan	1	<0.01
Peruvian	10	0.01
Uruguayan	0	<0.01
Venezuelan	6	0.01
Other South American	0	<0.01
Other Hispanic or Latino	169	0.23

Race*	Population	%
African-American/Black (3,873)	4,753	6.37
Not Hispanic (3,822)	4,660	6.25
Hispanic (51)	93	0.12
American Indian/Alaska Native (168)	531	0.71
Not Hispanic (146)	478	0.64
Hispanic (22)	53	0.07
Alaska Athabascan *(Ala. Nat.)* (0)	1	<0.01
Aleut *(Alaska Native)* (5)	6	0.01
Apache (4)	7	0.01
Arapaho (0)	0	<0.01
Blackfeet (2)	16	0.02
Canadian/French Am. Ind. (0)	0	<0.01
Central American Ind. (3)	4	0.01
Cherokee (47)	208	0.28
Cheyenne (0)	1	<0.01
Chickasaw (2)	4	0.01
Chippewa (8)	12	0.02
Choctaw (10)	17	0.02
Colville (0)	0	<0.01
Comanche (0)	0	<0.01
Cree (0)	0	<0.01
Creek (1)	4	0.01
Crow (0)	0	<0.01
Delaware (0)	0	<0.01
Hopi (0)	0	<0.01
Houma (0)	0	<0.01
Inupiat *(Alaska Native)* (0)	0	<0.01
Iroquois (0)	5	0.01
Kiowa (0)	0	<0.01
Lumbee (2)	2	<0.01
Menominee (0)	0	<0.01
Mexican American Ind. (6)	7	0.01
Navajo (0)	4	0.01
Osage (0)	0	<0.01
Ottawa (3)	3	<0.01
Paiute (0)	0	<0.01
Pima (0)	1	<0.01
Potawatomi (1)	2	<0.01
Pueblo (0)	0	<0.01
Puget Sound Salish (0)	0	<0.01
Seminole (0)	3	<0.01
Shoshone (1)	1	<0.01
Sioux (4)	12	0.02
South American Ind. (1)	1	<0.01
Spanish American Ind. (0)	0	<0.01
Tlingit-Haida *(Alaska Native)* (0)	1	<0.01
Tohono O'Odham (0)	0	<0.01
Tsimshian *(Alaska Native)* (0)	0	<0.01
Ute (1)	1	<0.01
Yakama (0)	0	<0.01
Yaqui (0)	0	<0.01
Yuman (0)	0	<0.01
Yup'ik *(Alaska Native)* (0)	0	<0.01
Asian (704)	965	1.29
Not Hispanic (694)	947	1.27
Hispanic (10)	18	0.02
Bangladeshi (0)	0	<0.01
Bhutanese (0)	0	<0.01
Burmese (0)	0	<0.01
Cambodian (34)	44	0.06
Chinese, ex. Taiwanese (127)	160	0.21
Filipino (127)	198	0.27
Hmong (1)	4	0.01
Indian (143)	167	0.22
Indonesian (0)	2	<0.01
Japanese (72)	117	0.16
Korean (67)	114	0.15
Laotian (3)	4	0.01
Malaysian (0)	0	<0.01
Nepalese (0)	0	<0.01
Pakistani (43)	43	0.06
Sri Lankan (1)	3	<0.01
Taiwanese (7)	9	0.01
Thai (8)	15	0.02
Vietnamese (31)	39	0.05
Hawaii Native/Pacific Islander (16)	55	0.07
Not Hispanic (16)	48	0.06
Hispanic (0)	7	0.01
Fijian (0)	0	<0.01
Guamanian/Chamorro (2)	8	0.01
Marshallese (0)	0	<0.01
Native Hawaiian (8)	21	0.03
Samoan (1)	8	0.01
Tongan (0)	0	<0.01
White (67,408)	68,838	92.30
Not Hispanic (66,505)	67,736	90.83
Hispanic (903)	1,102	1.48

*Notes: † The Census 2010 population figure is used to calculate the percentages in the Hispanic Origin and Race categories. Ancestry percentages are based on the 2006-2010 American Community Survey population (not shown); ‡ Numbers in parentheses indicate the number of people reporting a single ancestry; * Numbers in parentheses indicate the number of persons reporting this race alone, not in combination with any other race; Please refer to the Explanation of Data for more information.*

Fountain County

Population: 17,240

Ancestry	Population	%
Afghan (0)	0	<0.01
African, Sub-Saharan (20)	20	0.12
African (0)	0	<0.01
Cape Verdean (0)	0	<0.01
Ethiopian (20)	20	0.12
Ghanaian (0)	0	<0.01
Kenyan (0)	0	<0.01
Liberian (0)	0	<0.01
Nigerian (0)	0	<0.01
Senegalese (0)	0	<0.01
Sierra Leonean (0)	0	<0.01
Somalian (0)	0	<0.01
South African (0)	0	<0.01
Sudanese (0)	0	<0.01
Ugandan (0)	0	<0.01
Zimbabwean (0)	0	<0.01
Other Sub-Saharan African (0)	0	<0.01
Albanian (0)	0	<0.01
Alsatian (0)	0	<0.01
American (2,482)	2,482	14.32
Arab (6)	15	0.09
Arab (0)	0	<0.01
Egyptian (0)	0	<0.01
Iraqi (0)	0	<0.01
Jordanian (0)	0	<0.01
Lebanese (0)	0	<0.01
Moroccan (0)	9	0.05
Palestinian (0)	0	<0.01
Syrian (6)	6	0.03
Other Arab (0)	0	<0.01
Armenian (0)	0	<0.01
Assyrian/Chaldean/Syriac (0)	0	<0.01
Australian (0)	0	<0.01
Austrian (8)	8	0.05
Basque (0)	0	<0.01
Belgian (13)	72	0.42
Brazilian (0)	0	<0.01
British (33)	71	0.41
Bulgarian (0)	0	<0.01
Cajun (0)	0	<0.01
Canadian (0)	5	0.03
Carpatho Rusyn (0)	0	<0.01
Celtic (0)	0	<0.01
Croatian (0)	0	<0.01
Cypriot (0)	0	<0.01
Czech (0)	40	0.23
Czechoslovakian (4)	4	0.02
Danish (8)	15	0.09
Dutch (127)	582	3.36
Eastern European (0)	0	<0.01
English (943)	2,168	12.51
Estonian (0)	0	<0.01
European (186)	212	1.22
Finnish (0)	0	<0.01
French, ex. Basque (175)	436	2.52
French Canadian (40)	82	0.47
German (1,147)	3,742	21.59
German Russian (0)	0	<0.01
Greek (0)	0	<0.01
Guyanese (0)	0	<0.01
Hungarian (0)	64	0.37
Icelander (0)	0	<0.01
Iranian (0)	0	<0.01
Irish (626)	2,497	14.41
Israeli (0)	0	<0.01
Italian (86)	240	1.38
Latvian (12)	12	0.07
Lithuanian (36)	50	0.29
Luxemburger (0)	0	<0.01
Macedonian (0)	0	<0.01
Maltese (0)	0	<0.01
New Zealander (0)	0	<0.01
Northern European (0)	0	<0.01
Norwegian (7)	26	0.15
Pennsylvania German (8)	16	0.09
Polish (47)	214	1.23
Portuguese (0)	0	<0.01
Romanian (0)	0	<0.01
Russian (0)	13	0.08
Scandinavian (3)	3	0.02
Scotch-Irish (138)	443	2.56
Scottish (169)	326	1.88
Serbian (0)	0	<0.01
Slavic (0)	0	<0.01
Slovak (0)	7	0.04
Slovene (0)	0	<0.01
Soviet Union (0)	0	<0.01
Swedish (64)	306	1.77
Swiss (0)	22	0.13
Turkish (0)	0	<0.01
Ukrainian (20)	20	0.12
Welsh (12)	126	0.73
West Indian, ex. Hispanic (0)	13	0.08
Bahamian (0)	0	<0.01
Barbadian (0)	0	<0.01
Belizean (0)	0	<0.01
Bermudan (0)	0	<0.01
British West Indian (0)	0	<0.01
Dutch West Indian (0)	13	0.08
Haitian (0)	0	<0.01
Jamaican (0)	0	<0.01
Trinidadian/Tobagonian (0)	0	<0.01
U.S. Virgin Islander (0)	0	<0.01
West Indian (0)	0	<0.01
Other West Indian (0)	0	<0.01
Yugoslavian (0)	0	<0.01

Hispanic Origin	Population	%
Hispanic or Latino (of any race)	373	2.16
Central American, ex. Mexican	15	0.09
Costa Rican	0	<0.01
Guatemalan	2	0.01
Honduran	11	0.06
Nicaraguan	0	<0.01
Panamanian	2	0.01
Salvadoran	0	<0.01
Other Central American	0	<0.01
Cuban	1	0.01
Dominican Republic	0	<0.01
Mexican	314	1.82
Puerto Rican	12	0.07
South American	6	0.03
Argentinean	0	<0.01
Bolivian	0	<0.01
Chilean	0	<0.01
Colombian	2	0.01
Ecuadorian	0	<0.01
Paraguayan	0	<0.01
Peruvian	4	0.02
Uruguayan	0	<0.01
Venezuelan	0	<0.01
Other South American	0	<0.01
Other Hispanic or Latino	25	0.15

Race*	Population	%
African-American/Black (28)	67	0.39
Not Hispanic (26)	62	0.36
Hispanic (2)	5	0.03
American Indian/Alaska Native (54)	132	0.77
Not Hispanic (48)	125	0.73
Hispanic (6)	7	0.04
Alaska Athabascan *(Ala. Nat.)* (0)	0	<0.01
Aleut *(Alaska Native)* (0)	0	<0.01
Apache (0)	2	0.01
Arapaho (0)	0	<0.01
Blackfeet (0)	6	0.03
Canadian/French Am. Ind. (0)	0	<0.01
Central American Ind. (1)	1	0.01
Cherokee (19)	61	0.35
Cheyenne (0)	0	<0.01
Chickasaw (1)	1	0.01
Chippewa (9)	11	0.06
Choctaw (4)	6	0.03
Colville (0)	0	<0.01
Comanche (0)	0	<0.01
Cree (0)	0	<0.01
Creek (0)	0	<0.01
Crow (0)	0	<0.01
Delaware (0)	0	<0.01
Hopi (0)	0	<0.01
Houma (0)	0	<0.01
Inupiat *(Alaska Native)* (3)	3	0.02
Iroquois (1)	1	0.01
Kiowa (0)	0	<0.01
Lumbee (0)	0	<0.01
Menominee (0)	0	<0.01
Mexican American Ind. (0)	2	0.01
Navajo (0)	0	<0.01
Osage (0)	0	<0.01
Ottawa (2)	2	0.01
Paiute (0)	0	<0.01
Pima (0)	0	<0.01
Potawatomi (3)	3	0.02
Pueblo (0)	0	<0.01
Puget Sound Salish (0)	0	<0.01
Seminole (0)	0	<0.01
Shoshone (0)	0	<0.01
Sioux (0)	1	0.01
South American Ind. (1)	1	0.01
Spanish American Ind. (0)	0	<0.01
Tlingit-Haida *(Alaska Native)* (0)	0	<0.01
Tohono O'Odham (0)	0	<0.01
Tsimshian *(Alaska Native)* (0)	0	<0.01
Ute (0)	0	<0.01
Yakama (0)	0	<0.01
Yaqui (0)	0	<0.01
Yuman (0)	0	<0.01
Yup'ik *(Alaska Native)* (0)	0	<0.01
Asian (35)	70	0.41
Not Hispanic (35)	69	0.40
Hispanic (0)	1	0.01
Bangladeshi (0)	0	<0.01
Bhutanese (0)	0	<0.01
Burmese (0)	0	<0.01
Cambodian (0)	0	<0.01
Chinese, ex. Taiwanese (10)	14	0.08
Filipino (10)	25	0.15
Hmong (0)	0	<0.01
Indian (4)	7	0.04
Indonesian (0)	0	<0.01
Japanese (4)	15	0.09
Korean (3)	12	0.07
Laotian (1)	1	0.01
Malaysian (0)	0	<0.01
Nepalese (0)	0	<0.01
Pakistani (0)	0	<0.01
Sri Lankan (0)	0	<0.01
Taiwanese (0)	0	<0.01
Thai (1)	1	0.01
Vietnamese (0)	0	<0.01
Hawaii Native/Pacific Islander (1)	8	0.05
Not Hispanic (1)	7	0.04
Hispanic (0)	1	0.01
Fijian (0)	0	<0.01
Guamanian/Chamorro (0)	1	0.01
Marshallese (0)	0	<0.01
Native Hawaiian (1)	4	0.02
Samoan (0)	0	<0.01
Tongan (0)	0	<0.01
White (16,802)	16,973	98.45
Not Hispanic (16,598)	16,748	97.15
Hispanic (204)	225	1.31

*Notes: † The Census 2010 population figure is used to calculate the percentages in the Hispanic Origin and Race categories. Ancestry percentages are based on the 2006-2010 American Community Survey population (not shown); ‡ Numbers in parentheses indicate the number of people reporting a single ancestry; * Numbers in parentheses indicate the number of persons reporting this race alone, not in combination with any other race; Please refer to the Explanation of Data for more information.*

Franklin County

Population: 23,087

Ancestry	Population	%
Afghan (0)	0	<0.01
African, Sub-Saharan (0)	0	<0.01
African (0)	0	<0.01
Cape Verdean (0)	0	<0.01
Ethiopian (0)	0	<0.01
Ghanaian (0)	0	<0.01
Kenyan (0)	0	<0.01
Liberian (0)	0	<0.01
Nigerian (0)	0	<0.01
Senegalese (0)	0	<0.01
Sierra Leonean (0)	0	<0.01
Somalian (0)	0	<0.01
South African (0)	0	<0.01
Sudanese (0)	0	<0.01
Ugandan (0)	0	<0.01
Zimbabwean (0)	0	<0.01
Other Sub-Saharan African (0)	0	<0.01
Albanian (0)	0	<0.01
Alsatian (0)	15	0.06
American (3,410)	3,410	14.70
Arab (0)	31	0.13
Arab (0)	0	<0.01
Egyptian (0)	0	<0.01
Iraqi (0)	0	<0.01
Jordanian (0)	0	<0.01
Lebanese (0)	0	<0.01
Moroccan (0)	0	<0.01
Palestinian (0)	0	<0.01
Syrian (0)	31	0.13
Other Arab (0)	0	<0.01
Armenian (0)	0	<0.01
Assyrian/Chaldean/Syriac (0)	0	<0.01
Australian (0)	0	<0.01
Austrian (28)	53	0.23
Basque (0)	0	<0.01
Belgian (11)	11	0.05
Brazilian (14)	14	0.06
British (12)	59	0.25
Bulgarian (0)	0	<0.01
Cajun (0)	0	<0.01
Canadian (16)	29	0.13
Carpatho Rusyn (0)	0	<0.01
Celtic (0)	0	<0.01
Croatian (10)	31	0.13
Cypriot (0)	0	<0.01
Czech (0)	0	<0.01
Czechoslovakian (0)	0	<0.01
Danish (0)	62	0.27
Dutch (18)	253	1.09
Eastern European (2)	2	0.01
English (832)	2,208	9.52
Estonian (0)	0	<0.01
European (98)	98	0.42
Finnish (24)	27	0.12
French, ex. Basque (90)	461	1.99
French Canadian (12)	21	0.09
German (6,045)	9,354	40.33
German Russian (0)	0	<0.01
Greek (0)	0	<0.01
Guyanese (0)	0	<0.01
Hungarian (87)	127	0.55
Icelander (0)	0	<0.01
Iranian (0)	0	<0.01
Irish (787)	3,045	13.13
Israeli (0)	0	<0.01
Italian (110)	400	1.72
Latvian (0)	0	<0.01
Lithuanian (8)	8	0.03
Luxemburger (0)	10	0.04
Macedonian (0)	0	<0.01
Maltese (0)	0	<0.01
New Zealander (0)	0	<0.01
Northern European (19)	19	0.08
Norwegian (7)	53	0.23
Pennsylvania German (8)	8	0.03
Polish (41)	202	0.87
Portuguese (0)	0	<0.01
Romanian (0)	19	0.08
Russian (86)	189	0.81
Scandinavian (0)	0	<0.01
Scotch-Irish (107)	198	0.85
Scottish (230)	387	1.67
Serbian (0)	0	<0.01
Slavic (0)	0	<0.01
Slovak (0)	0	<0.01
Slovene (0)	8	0.03
Soviet Union (0)	0	<0.01
Swedish (12)	210	0.91
Swiss (19)	57	0.25
Turkish (0)	0	<0.01
Ukrainian (11)	22	0.09
Welsh (8)	99	0.43
West Indian, ex. Hispanic (0)	0	<0.01
Bahamian (0)	0	<0.01
Barbadian (0)	0	<0.01
Belizean (0)	0	<0.01
Bermudan (0)	0	<0.01
British West Indian (0)	0	<0.01
Dutch West Indian (0)	0	<0.01
Haitian (0)	0	<0.01
Jamaican (0)	0	<0.01
Trinidadian/Tobagonian (0)	0	<0.01
U.S. Virgin Islander (0)	0	<0.01
West Indian (0)	0	<0.01
Other West Indian (0)	0	<0.01
Yugoslavian (9)	9	0.04

Hispanic Origin	Population	%
Hispanic or Latino (of any race)	210	0.91
Central American, ex. Mexican	26	0.11
Costa Rican	2	0.01
Guatemalan	7	0.03
Honduran	7	0.03
Nicaraguan	0	<0.01
Panamanian	2	0.01
Salvadoran	8	0.03
Other Central American	0	<0.01
Cuban	4	0.02
Dominican Republic	3	0.01
Mexican	140	0.61
Puerto Rican	18	0.08
South American	5	0.02
Argentinean	0	<0.01
Bolivian	0	<0.01
Chilean	0	<0.01
Colombian	0	<0.01
Ecuadorian	1	<0.01
Paraguayan	0	<0.01
Peruvian	4	0.02
Uruguayan	0	<0.01
Venezuelan	0	<0.01
Other South American	0	<0.01
Other Hispanic or Latino	14	0.06

Race*	Population	%
African-American/Black (37)	79	0.34
Not Hispanic (34)	69	0.30
Hispanic (3)	10	0.04
American Indian/Alaska Native (34)	129	0.56
Not Hispanic (27)	115	0.50
Hispanic (7)	14	0.06
Alaska Athabascan *(Ala. Nat.)* (0)	0	<0.01
Aleut *(Alaska Native)* (0)	0	<0.01
Apache (0)	0	<0.01
Arapaho (0)	0	<0.01
Blackfeet (1)	7	0.03
Canadian/French Am. Ind. (0)	0	<0.01
Central American Ind. (0)	0	<0.01
Cherokee (12)	55	0.24
Cheyenne (0)	0	<0.01
Chickasaw (0)	0	<0.01
Chippewa (1)	1	<0.01
Choctaw (0)	1	<0.01
Colville (0)	0	<0.01
Comanche (0)	0	<0.01
Cree (0)	0	<0.01
Creek (0)	0	<0.01
Crow (0)	0	<0.01
Delaware (0)	0	<0.01
Hopi (0)	0	<0.01
Houma (0)	0	<0.01
Inupiat *(Alaska Native)* (0)	0	<0.01
Iroquois (4)	7	0.03
Kiowa (1)	1	<0.01
Lumbee (0)	0	<0.01
Menominee (0)	0	<0.01
Mexican American Ind. (2)	2	0.01
Navajo (2)	2	0.01
Osage (0)	0	<0.01
Ottawa (0)	0	<0.01
Paiute (0)	0	<0.01
Pima (1)	2	0.01
Potawatomi (0)	0	<0.01
Pueblo (0)	0	<0.01
Puget Sound Salish (0)	0	<0.01
Seminole (0)	0	<0.01
Shoshone (0)	1	<0.01
Sioux (0)	0	<0.01
South American Ind. (0)	0	<0.01
Spanish American Ind. (1)	1	<0.01
Tlingit-Haida *(Alaska Native)* (0)	0	<0.01
Tohono O'Odham (0)	0	<0.01
Tsimshian *(Alaska Native)* (0)	0	<0.01
Ute (0)	0	<0.01
Yakama (0)	0	<0.01
Yaqui (0)	0	<0.01
Yuman (0)	0	<0.01
Yup'ik *(Alaska Native)* (0)	0	<0.01
Asian (55)	82	0.36
Not Hispanic (55)	82	0.36
Hispanic (0)	0	<0.01
Bangladeshi (0)	0	<0.01
Bhutanese (0)	0	<0.01
Burmese (0)	0	<0.01
Cambodian (1)	3	0.01
Chinese, ex. Taiwanese (19)	29	0.13
Filipino (19)	32	0.14
Hmong (0)	0	<0.01
Indian (5)	7	0.03
Indonesian (0)	0	<0.01
Japanese (2)	2	0.01
Korean (5)	5	0.02
Laotian (0)	0	<0.01
Malaysian (0)	1	<0.01
Nepalese (0)	0	<0.01
Pakistani (0)	0	<0.01
Sri Lankan (0)	0	<0.01
Taiwanese (0)	0	<0.01
Thai (0)	0	<0.01
Vietnamese (4)	4	0.02
Hawaii Native/Pacific Islander (2)	14	0.06
Not Hispanic (2)	14	0.06
Hispanic (0)	0	<0.01
Fijian (0)	0	<0.01
Guamanian/Chamorro (1)	1	<0.01
Marshallese (0)	0	<0.01
Native Hawaiian (1)	6	0.03
Samoan (0)	1	<0.01
Tongan (0)	0	<0.01
White (22,703)	22,877	99.09
Not Hispanic (22,600)	22,748	98.53
Hispanic (103)	129	0.56

*Notes: † The Census 2010 population figure is used to calculate the percentages in the Hispanic Origin and Race categories. Ancestry percentages are based on the 2006-2010 American Community Survey population (not shown); ‡ Numbers in parentheses indicate the number of people reporting a single ancestry; * Numbers in parentheses indicate the number of persons reporting this race alone, not in combination with any other race; Please refer to the Explanation of Data for more information.*

Fulton County

Population: 20,836

Ancestry	Population	%
Afghan (0)	0	<0.01
African, Sub-Saharan (0)	25	0.12
African (0)	9	0.04
Cape Verdean (0)	0	<0.01
Ethiopian (0)	0	<0.01
Ghanaian (0)	0	<0.01
Kenyan (0)	0	<0.01
Liberian (0)	0	<0.01
Nigerian (0)	0	<0.01
Senegalese (0)	0	<0.01
Sierra Leonean (0)	0	<0.01
Somalian (0)	0	<0.01
South African (0)	16	0.08
Sudanese (0)	0	<0.01
Ugandan (0)	0	<0.01
Zimbabwean (0)	0	<0.01
Other Sub-Saharan African (0)	0	<0.01
Albanian (40)	40	0.19
Alsatian (0)	0	<0.01
American (3,922)	3,922	18.96
Arab (0)	0	<0.01
Arab (0)	0	<0.01
Egyptian (0)	0	<0.01
Iraqi (0)	0	<0.01
Jordanian (0)	0	<0.01
Lebanese (0)	0	<0.01
Moroccan (0)	0	<0.01
Palestinian (0)	0	<0.01
Syrian (0)	0	<0.01
Other Arab (0)	0	<0.01
Armenian (0)	0	<0.01
Assyrian/Chaldean/Syriac (0)	0	<0.01
Australian (0)	0	<0.01
Austrian (0)	14	0.07
Basque (0)	0	<0.01
Belgian (8)	8	0.04
Brazilian (0)	0	<0.01
British (26)	42	0.20
Bulgarian (0)	0	<0.01
Cajun (0)	0	<0.01
Canadian (4)	7	0.03
Carpatho Rusyn (0)	0	<0.01
Celtic (0)	0	<0.01
Croatian (11)	66	0.32
Cypriot (0)	0	<0.01
Czech (0)	69	0.33
Czechoslovakian (30)	30	0.15
Danish (8)	19	0.09
Dutch (122)	545	2.63
Eastern European (0)	0	<0.01
English (950)	2,061	9.96
Estonian (0)	0	<0.01
European (108)	108	0.52
Finnish (0)	0	<0.01
French, ex. Basque (79)	400	1.93
French Canadian (34)	41	0.20
German (3,052)	5,940	28.72
German Russian (0)	0	<0.01
Greek (0)	26	0.13
Guyanese (0)	0	<0.01
Hungarian (26)	55	0.27
Icelander (0)	0	<0.01
Iranian (0)	0	<0.01
Irish (665)	2,250	10.88
Israeli (0)	0	<0.01
Italian (87)	485	2.34
Latvian (3)	3	0.01
Lithuanian (28)	68	0.33
Luxemburger (0)	0	<0.01
Macedonian (0)	0	<0.01
Maltese (0)	0	<0.01
New Zealander (0)	0	<0.01
Northern European (0)	0	<0.01
Norwegian (109)	183	0.88
Pennsylvania German (100)	143	0.69
Polish (120)	347	1.68
Portuguese (10)	17	0.08
Romanian (0)	11	0.05
Russian (31)	42	0.20
Scandinavian (9)	18	0.09
Scotch-Irish (104)	273	1.32
Scottish (111)	297	1.44
Serbian (13)	13	0.06
Slavic (0)	0	<0.01
Slovak (0)	0	<0.01
Slovene (0)	76	0.37
Soviet Union (0)	0	<0.01
Swedish (55)	158	0.76
Swiss (0)	7	0.03
Turkish (0)	0	<0.01
Ukrainian (0)	0	<0.01
Welsh (6)	119	0.58
West Indian, ex. Hispanic (0)	0	<0.01
Bahamian (0)	0	<0.01
Barbadian (0)	0	<0.01
Belizean (0)	0	<0.01
Bermudan (0)	0	<0.01
British West Indian (0)	0	<0.01
Dutch West Indian (0)	0	<0.01
Haitian (0)	0	<0.01
Jamaican (0)	0	<0.01
Trinidadian/Tobagonian (0)	0	<0.01
U.S. Virgin Islander (0)	0	<0.01
West Indian (0)	0	<0.01
Other West Indian (0)	0	<0.01
Yugoslavian (24)	39	0.19

Hispanic Origin	Population	%
Hispanic or Latino (of any race)	882	4.23
Central American, ex. Mexican	10	0.05
Costa Rican	1	<0.01
Guatemalan	1	<0.01
Honduran	1	<0.01
Nicaraguan	2	0.01
Panamanian	5	0.02
Salvadoran	0	<0.01
Other Central American	0	<0.01
Cuban	5	0.02
Dominican Republic	4	0.02
Mexican	763	3.66
Puerto Rican	41	0.20
South American	10	0.05
Argentinean	0	<0.01
Bolivian	0	<0.01
Chilean	0	<0.01
Colombian	0	<0.01
Ecuadorian	2	0.01
Paraguayan	0	<0.01
Peruvian	8	0.04
Uruguayan	0	<0.01
Venezuelan	0	<0.01
Other South American	0	<0.01
Other Hispanic or Latino	49	0.24

Race*	Population	%
African-American/Black (150)	244	1.17
Not Hispanic (144)	231	1.11
Hispanic (6)	13	0.06
American Indian/Alaska Native (96)	181	0.87
Not Hispanic (73)	153	0.73
Hispanic (23)	28	0.13
Alaska Athabascan *(Ala. Nat.)* (1)	1	<0.01
Aleut *(Alaska Native)* (0)	0	<0.01
Apache (1)	1	<0.01
Arapaho (0)	0	<0.01
Blackfeet (2)	11	0.05
Canadian/French Am. Ind. (0)	2	0.01
Central American Ind. (0)	0	<0.01
Cherokee (16)	42	0.20
Cheyenne (2)	2	0.01
Chickasaw (0)	0	<0.01
Chippewa (4)	4	0.02
Choctaw (2)	2	0.01
Colville (0)	0	<0.01
Comanche (0)	0	<0.01
Cree (0)	0	<0.01
Creek (0)	0	<0.01
Crow (0)	0	<0.01
Delaware (0)	0	<0.01
Hopi (0)	0	<0.01
Houma (0)	0	<0.01
Inupiat *(Alaska Native)* (1)	1	<0.01
Iroquois (2)	2	0.01
Kiowa (2)	2	0.01
Lumbee (0)	0	<0.01
Menominee (0)	0	<0.01
Mexican American Ind. (0)	0	<0.01
Navajo (0)	0	<0.01
Osage (0)	0	<0.01
Ottawa (0)	0	<0.01
Paiute (0)	0	<0.01
Pima (0)	0	<0.01
Potawatomi (0)	3	0.01
Pueblo (0)	0	<0.01
Puget Sound Salish (0)	0	<0.01
Seminole (0)	0	<0.01
Shoshone (0)	0	<0.01
Sioux (1)	2	0.01
South American Ind. (0)	0	<0.01
Spanish American Ind. (0)	0	<0.01
Tlingit-Haida *(Alaska Native)* (0)	0	<0.01
Tohono O'Odham (0)	0	<0.01
Tsimshian *(Alaska Native)* (0)	0	<0.01
Ute (0)	0	<0.01
Yakama (0)	0	<0.01
Yaqui (0)	0	<0.01
Yuman (0)	0	<0.01
Yup'ik *(Alaska Native)* (0)	0	<0.01
Asian (101)	129	0.62
Not Hispanic (101)	125	0.60
Hispanic (0)	4	0.02
Bangladeshi (0)	0	<0.01
Bhutanese (0)	0	<0.01
Burmese (0)	0	<0.01
Cambodian (0)	0	<0.01
Chinese, ex. Taiwanese (38)	42	0.20
Filipino (25)	39	0.19
Hmong (0)	0	<0.01
Indian (12)	15	0.07
Indonesian (1)	1	<0.01
Japanese (2)	3	0.01
Korean (12)	14	0.07
Laotian (2)	4	0.02
Malaysian (0)	0	<0.01
Nepalese (0)	0	<0.01
Pakistani (4)	4	0.02
Sri Lankan (0)	0	<0.01
Taiwanese (1)	1	<0.01
Thai (0)	0	<0.01
Vietnamese (1)	3	0.01
Hawaii Native/Pacific Islander (5)	9	0.04
Not Hispanic (5)	9	0.04
Hispanic (0)	0	<0.01
Fijian (0)	0	<0.01
Guamanian/Chamorro (0)	0	<0.01
Marshallese (0)	0	<0.01
Native Hawaiian (2)	6	0.03
Samoan (0)	0	<0.01
Tongan (0)	0	<0.01
White (19,800)	20,019	96.08
Not Hispanic (19,438)	19,616	94.14
Hispanic (362)	403	1.93

*Notes: † The Census 2010 population figure is used to calculate the percentages in the Hispanic Origin and Race categories. Ancestry percentages are based on the 2006-2010 American Community Survey population (not shown); ‡ Numbers in parentheses indicate the number of people reporting a single ancestry; * Numbers in parentheses indicate the number of persons reporting this race alone, not in combination with any other race; Please refer to the Explanation of Data for more information.*

Gibson County

Population: 33,503

Ancestry	Population	%
Afghan (0)	0	<0.01
African, Sub-Saharan (16)	47	0.14
African (0)	31	0.09
Cape Verdean (0)	0	<0.01
Ethiopian (16)	16	0.05
Ghanaian (0)	0	<0.01
Kenyan (0)	0	<0.01
Liberian (0)	0	<0.01
Nigerian (0)	0	<0.01
Senegalese (0)	0	<0.01
Sierra Leonean (0)	0	<0.01
Somalian (0)	0	<0.01
South African (0)	0	<0.01
Sudanese (0)	0	<0.01
Ugandan (0)	0	<0.01
Zimbabwean (0)	0	<0.01
Other Sub-Saharan African (0)	0	<0.01
Albanian (0)	0	<0.01
Alsatian (0)	0	<0.01
American (8,119)	8,119	24.32
Arab (19)	19	0.06
Arab (19)	19	0.06
Egyptian (0)	0	<0.01
Iraqi (0)	0	<0.01
Jordanian (0)	0	<0.01
Lebanese (0)	0	<0.01
Moroccan (0)	0	<0.01
Palestinian (0)	0	<0.01
Syrian (0)	0	<0.01
Other Arab (0)	0	<0.01
Armenian (0)	0	<0.01
Assyrian/Chaldean/Syriac (0)	0	<0.01
Australian (0)	124	0.37
Austrian (26)	26	0.08
Basque (0)	0	<0.01
Belgian (0)	27	0.08
Brazilian (0)	0	<0.01
British (53)	89	0.27
Bulgarian (0)	0	<0.01
Cajun (0)	0	<0.01
Canadian (0)	6	0.02
Carpatho Rusyn (0)	0	<0.01
Celtic (0)	0	<0.01
Croatian (5)	5	0.01
Cypriot (0)	0	<0.01
Czech (3)	50	0.15
Czechoslovakian (0)	0	<0.01
Danish (44)	46	0.14
Dutch (145)	645	1.93
Eastern European (0)	4	0.01
English (1,984)	3,899	11.68
Estonian (0)	0	<0.01
European (132)	132	0.40
Finnish (0)	0	<0.01
French, ex. Basque (421)	1,217	3.65
French Canadian (41)	57	0.17
German (4,779)	9,440	28.28
German Russian (0)	0	<0.01
Greek (0)	104	0.31
Guyanese (0)	0	<0.01
Hungarian (12)	18	0.05
Icelander (0)	0	<0.01
Iranian (0)	0	<0.01
Irish (1,282)	4,383	13.13
Israeli (0)	0	<0.01
Italian (216)	688	2.06
Latvian (0)	0	<0.01
Lithuanian (0)	0	<0.01
Luxemburger (0)	0	<0.01
Macedonian (0)	0	<0.01
Maltese (0)	0	<0.01
New Zealander (0)	35	0.10
Northern European (0)	0	<0.01
Norwegian (13)	79	0.24
Pennsylvania German (0)	9	0.03
Polish (147)	379	1.14
Portuguese (0)	100	0.30
Romanian (5)	5	0.01
Russian (0)	33	0.10
Scandinavian (18)	36	0.11
Scotch-Irish (244)	886	2.65
Scottish (100)	314	0.94
Serbian (0)	0	<0.01
Slavic (0)	0	<0.01
Slovak (0)	0	<0.01
Slovene (0)	0	<0.01
Soviet Union (0)	0	<0.01
Swedish (78)	339	1.02
Swiss (0)	36	0.11
Turkish (0)	0	<0.01
Ukrainian (0)	100	0.30
Welsh (72)	124	0.37
West Indian, ex. Hispanic (6)	6	0.02
Bahamian (0)	0	<0.01
Barbadian (0)	0	<0.01
Belizean (0)	0	<0.01
Bermudan (0)	0	<0.01
British West Indian (0)	0	<0.01
Dutch West Indian (0)	0	<0.01
Haitian (0)	0	<0.01
Jamaican (6)	6	0.02
Trinidadian/Tobagonian (0)	0	<0.01
U.S. Virgin Islander (0)	0	<0.01
West Indian (0)	0	<0.01
Other West Indian (0)	0	<0.01
Yugoslavian (0)	0	<0.01

Hispanic Origin	Population	%
Hispanic or Latino (of any race)	441	1.32
Central American, ex. Mexican	38	0.11
Costa Rican	2	0.01
Guatemalan	9	0.03
Honduran	0	<0.01
Nicaraguan	2	0.01
Panamanian	10	0.03
Salvadoran	15	0.04
Other Central American	0	<0.01
Cuban	9	0.03
Dominican Republic	5	0.01
Mexican	277	0.83
Puerto Rican	39	0.12
South American	32	0.10
Argentinean	3	0.01
Bolivian	0	<0.01
Chilean	0	<0.01
Colombian	8	0.02
Ecuadorian	1	<0.01
Paraguayan	0	<0.01
Peruvian	3	0.01
Uruguayan	0	<0.01
Venezuelan	17	0.05
Other South American	0	<0.01
Other Hispanic or Latino	41	0.12

Race*	Population	%
African-American/Black (597)	913	2.73
Not Hispanic (589)	892	2.66
Hispanic (8)	21	0.06
American Indian/Alaska Native (72)	239	0.71
Not Hispanic (59)	208	0.62
Hispanic (13)	31	0.09
Alaska Athabascan *(Ala. Nat.)* (0)	0	<0.01
Aleut *(Alaska Native)* (0)	0	<0.01
Apache (1)	5	0.01
Arapaho (0)	0	<0.01
Blackfeet (2)	22	0.07
Canadian/French Am. Ind. (0)	4	0.01
Central American Ind. (0)	0	<0.01
Cherokee (14)	79	0.24
Cheyenne (0)	0	<0.01
Chickasaw (6)	6	0.02
Chippewa (2)	3	0.01
Choctaw (2)	4	0.01
Colville (0)	0	<0.01
Comanche (1)	1	<0.01
Cree (0)	0	<0.01
Creek (0)	1	<0.01
Crow (0)	1	<0.01
Delaware (1)	2	0.01
Hopi (0)	0	<0.01
Houma (0)	0	<0.01
Inupiat *(Alaska Native)* (0)	0	<0.01
Iroquois (0)	0	<0.01
Kiowa (0)	0	<0.01
Lumbee (0)	0	<0.01
Menominee (0)	0	<0.01
Mexican American Ind. (3)	5	0.01
Navajo (2)	7	0.02
Osage (0)	0	<0.01
Ottawa (0)	0	<0.01
Paiute (0)	0	<0.01
Pima (0)	0	<0.01
Potawatomi (0)	1	<0.01
Pueblo (0)	0	<0.01
Puget Sound Salish (0)	0	<0.01
Seminole (0)	0	<0.01
Shoshone (0)	0	<0.01
Sioux (3)	6	0.02
South American Ind. (0)	0	<0.01
Spanish American Ind. (0)	0	<0.01
Tlingit-Haida *(Alaska Native)* (0)	0	<0.01
Tohono O'Odham (0)	0	<0.01
Tsimshian *(Alaska Native)* (0)	0	<0.01
Ute (0)	0	<0.01
Yakama (0)	0	<0.01
Yaqui (0)	0	<0.01
Yuman (0)	0	<0.01
Yup'ik *(Alaska Native)* (0)	0	<0.01
Asian (156)	211	0.63
Not Hispanic (155)	209	0.62
Hispanic (1)	2	0.01
Bangladeshi (0)	0	<0.01
Bhutanese (0)	0	<0.01
Burmese (0)	0	<0.01
Cambodian (0)	0	<0.01
Chinese, ex. Taiwanese (21)	22	0.07
Filipino (30)	47	0.14
Hmong (14)	14	0.04
Indian (50)	51	0.15
Indonesian (0)	0	<0.01
Japanese (14)	27	0.08
Korean (6)	17	0.05
Laotian (0)	0	<0.01
Malaysian (0)	0	<0.01
Nepalese (2)	3	0.01
Pakistani (0)	0	<0.01
Sri Lankan (0)	0	<0.01
Taiwanese (0)	2	0.01
Thai (6)	8	0.02
Vietnamese (11)	15	0.04
Hawaii Native/Pacific Islander (3)	9	0.03
Not Hispanic (2)	7	0.02
Hispanic (1)	2	0.01
Fijian (1)	2	0.01
Guamanian/Chamorro (1)	1	<0.01
Marshallese (0)	0	<0.01
Native Hawaiian (1)	1	<0.01
Samoan (0)	0	<0.01
Tongan (0)	0	<0.01
White (31,986)	32,500	97.01
Not Hispanic (31,752)	32,210	96.14
Hispanic (234)	290	0.87

*Notes: † The Census 2010 population figure is used to calculate the percentages in the Hispanic Origin and Race categories. Ancestry percentages are based on the 2006-2010 American Community Survey population (not shown); ‡ Numbers in parentheses indicate the number of people reporting a single ancestry; * Numbers in parentheses indicate the number of persons reporting this race alone, not in combination with any other race; Please refer to the Explanation of Data for more information.*

Grant County

Population: 70,061

Ancestry	Population	%
Afghan (0)	0	<0.01
African, Sub-Saharan (111)	153	0.22
African (111)	153	0.22
Cape Verdean (0)	0	<0.01
Ethiopian (0)	0	<0.01
Ghanaian (0)	0	<0.01
Kenyan (0)	0	<0.01
Liberian (0)	0	<0.01
Nigerian (0)	0	<0.01
Senegalese (0)	0	<0.01
Sierra Leonean (0)	0	<0.01
Somalian (0)	0	<0.01
South African (0)	0	<0.01
Sudanese (0)	0	<0.01
Ugandan (0)	0	<0.01
Zimbabwean (0)	0	<0.01
Other Sub-Saharan African (0)	0	<0.01
Albanian (0)	0	<0.01
Alsatian (0)	0	<0.01
American (8,708)	8,708	12.41
Arab (34)	58	0.08
Arab (0)	0	<0.01
Egyptian (0)	0	<0.01
Iraqi (0)	0	<0.01
Jordanian (0)	0	<0.01
Lebanese (0)	16	0.02
Moroccan (12)	12	0.02
Palestinian (0)	0	<0.01
Syrian (22)	30	0.04
Other Arab (0)	0	<0.01
Armenian (0)	0	<0.01
Assyrian/Chaldean/Syriac (0)	2	<0.01
Australian (0)	14	0.02
Austrian (42)	45	0.06
Basque (0)	0	<0.01
Belgian (41)	123	0.18
Brazilian (0)	0	<0.01
British (200)	293	0.42
Bulgarian (0)	0	<0.01
Cajun (0)	0	<0.01
Canadian (33)	81	0.12
Carpatho Rusyn (0)	0	<0.01
Celtic (0)	0	<0.01
Croatian (0)	13	0.02
Cypriot (0)	0	<0.01
Czech (24)	50	0.07
Czechoslovakian (0)	27	0.04
Danish (9)	35	0.05
Dutch (226)	1,352	1.93
Eastern European (14)	37	0.05
English (3,162)	6,288	8.96
Estonian (0)	0	<0.01
European (384)	444	0.63
Finnish (4)	27	0.04
French, ex. Basque (315)	1,293	1.84
French Canadian (40)	61	0.09
German (6,141)	13,704	19.53
German Russian (8)	8	0.01
Greek (102)	155	0.22
Guyanese (0)	0	<0.01
Hungarian (17)	110	0.16
Icelander (13)	13	0.02
Iranian (41)	41	0.06
Irish (2,378)	7,039	10.03
Israeli (0)	0	<0.01
Italian (579)	1,186	1.69
Latvian (0)	13	0.02
Lithuanian (9)	16	0.02
Luxemburger (0)	0	<0.01
Macedonian (0)	0	<0.01
Maltese (0)	0	<0.01
New Zealander (0)	0	<0.01
Northern European (26)	26	0.04
Norwegian (122)	258	0.37
Pennsylvania German (18)	49	0.07
Polish (211)	749	1.07
Portuguese (41)	41	0.06
Romanian (12)	15	0.02
Russian (22)	61	0.09
Scandinavian (28)	54	0.08
Scotch-Irish (578)	892	1.27
Scottish (529)	1,245	1.77
Serbian (0)	0	<0.01
Slavic (0)	0	<0.01
Slovak (64)	141	0.20
Slovene (0)	0	<0.01
Soviet Union (0)	0	<0.01
Swedish (223)	641	0.91
Swiss (34)	189	0.27
Turkish (0)	0	<0.01
Ukrainian (12)	12	0.02
Welsh (154)	520	0.74
West Indian, ex. Hispanic (21)	72	0.10
Bahamian (0)	0	<0.01
Barbadian (0)	0	<0.01
Belizean (0)	0	<0.01
Bermudan (0)	0	<0.01
British West Indian (0)	0	<0.01
Dutch West Indian (0)	51	0.07
Haitian (0)	0	<0.01
Jamaican (0)	0	<0.01
Trinidadian/Tobagonian (0)	0	<0.01
U.S. Virgin Islander (0)	0	<0.01
West Indian (0)	0	<0.01
Other West Indian (21)	21	0.03
Yugoslavian (48)	48	0.07

Hispanic Origin	Population	%
Hispanic or Latino (of any race)	2,517	3.59
Central American, ex. Mexican	50	0.07
Costa Rican	4	0.01
Guatemalan	14	0.02
Honduran	11	0.02
Nicaraguan	7	0.01
Panamanian	6	0.01
Salvadoran	8	0.01
Other Central American	0	<0.01
Cuban	41	0.06
Dominican Republic	4	0.01
Mexican	1,962	2.80
Puerto Rican	145	0.21
South American	52	0.07
Argentinean	2	<0.01
Bolivian	5	0.01
Chilean	4	0.01
Colombian	9	0.01
Ecuadorian	10	0.01
Paraguayan	0	<0.01
Peruvian	8	0.01
Uruguayan	1	<0.01
Venezuelan	11	0.02
Other South American	2	<0.01
Other Hispanic or Latino	263	0.38

Race*	Population	%
African-American/Black (4,888)	5,917	8.45
Not Hispanic (4,805)	5,747	8.20
Hispanic (83)	170	0.24
American Indian/Alaska Native (234)	580	0.83
Not Hispanic (218)	528	0.75
Hispanic (16)	52	0.07
Alaska Athabascan *(Ala. Nat.)* (0)	0	<0.01
Aleut *(Alaska Native)* (0)	0	<0.01
Apache (2)	19	0.03
Arapaho (0)	0	<0.01
Blackfeet (1)	25	0.04
Canadian/French Am. Ind. (2)	2	<0.01
Central American Ind. (1)	3	<0.01
Cherokee (49)	158	0.23
Cheyenne (1)	2	<0.01
Chickasaw (1)	4	0.01
Chippewa (7)	14	0.02
Choctaw (10)	18	0.03
Colville (0)	0	<0.01
Comanche (1)	1	<0.01
Cree (0)	0	<0.01
Creek (0)	1	<0.01
Crow (1)	4	0.01
Delaware (0)	4	0.01
Hopi (1)	1	<0.01
Houma (0)	0	<0.01
Inupiat *(Alaska Native)* (0)	0	<0.01
Iroquois (0)	3	<0.01
Kiowa (0)	0	<0.01
Lumbee (1)	6	0.01
Menominee (0)	0	<0.01
Mexican American Ind. (5)	5	0.01
Navajo (4)	5	0.01
Osage (0)	1	<0.01
Ottawa (0)	0	<0.01
Paiute (0)	0	<0.01
Pima (0)	0	<0.01
Potawatomi (4)	4	0.01
Pueblo (1)	1	<0.01
Puget Sound Salish (0)	0	<0.01
Seminole (0)	0	<0.01
Shoshone (0)	0	<0.01
Sioux (1)	11	0.02
South American Ind. (0)	0	<0.01
Spanish American Ind. (1)	1	<0.01
Tlingit-Haida *(Alaska Native)* (0)	0	<0.01
Tohono O'Odham (0)	0	<0.01
Tsimshian *(Alaska Native)* (0)	0	<0.01
Ute (0)	0	<0.01
Yakama (0)	0	<0.01
Yaqui (0)	0	<0.01
Yuman (0)	0	<0.01
Yup'ik *(Alaska Native)* (0)	0	<0.01
Asian (411)	615	0.88
Not Hispanic (408)	594	0.85
Hispanic (3)	21	0.03
Bangladeshi (0)	0	<0.01
Bhutanese (0)	0	<0.01
Burmese (0)	0	<0.01
Cambodian (7)	7	0.01
Chinese, ex. Taiwanese (69)	106	0.15
Filipino (105)	148	0.21
Hmong (0)	0	<0.01
Indian (93)	105	0.15
Indonesian (0)	2	<0.01
Japanese (14)	56	0.08
Korean (55)	98	0.14
Laotian (0)	0	<0.01
Malaysian (0)	0	<0.01
Nepalese (0)	0	<0.01
Pakistani (7)	8	0.01
Sri Lankan (4)	6	0.01
Taiwanese (0)	1	<0.01
Thai (6)	11	0.02
Vietnamese (39)	50	0.07
Hawaii Native/Pacific Islander (17)	61	0.09
Not Hispanic (14)	48	0.07
Hispanic (3)	13	0.02
Fijian (0)	7	0.01
Guamanian/Chamorro (1)	4	0.01
Marshallese (0)	0	<0.01
Native Hawaiian (5)	20	0.03
Samoan (6)	15	0.02
Tongan (0)	0	<0.01
White (61,811)	63,396	90.49
Not Hispanic (60,633)	61,954	88.43
Hispanic (1,178)	1,442	2.06

*Notes: † The Census 2010 population figure is used to calculate the percentages in the Hispanic Origin and Race categories. Ancestry percentages are based on the 2006-2010 American Community Survey population (not shown); ‡ Numbers in parentheses indicate the number of people reporting a single ancestry; * Numbers in parentheses indicate the number of persons reporting this race alone, not in combination with any other race; Please refer to the Explanation of Data for more information.*

Greene County

Population: 33,165

Ancestry	Population	%
Afghan (0)	0	<0.01
African, Sub-Saharan (0)	53	0.16
African (0)	53	0.16
Cape Verdean (0)	0	<0.01
Ethiopian (0)	0	<0.01
Ghanaian (0)	0	<0.01
Kenyan (0)	0	<0.01
Liberian (0)	0	<0.01
Nigerian (0)	0	<0.01
Senegalese (0)	0	<0.01
Sierra Leonean (0)	0	<0.01
Somalian (0)	0	<0.01
South African (0)	0	<0.01
Sudanese (0)	0	<0.01
Ugandan (0)	0	<0.01
Zimbabwean (0)	0	<0.01
Other Sub-Saharan African (0)	0	<0.01
Albanian (0)	0	<0.01
Alsatian (0)	0	<0.01
American (4,269)	4,269	12.90
Arab (18)	18	0.05
Arab (0)	0	<0.01
Egyptian (0)	0	<0.01
Iraqi (0)	0	<0.01
Jordanian (0)	0	<0.01
Lebanese (18)	18	0.05
Moroccan (0)	0	<0.01
Palestinian (0)	0	<0.01
Syrian (0)	0	<0.01
Other Arab (0)	0	<0.01
Armenian (0)	0	<0.01
Assyrian/Chaldean/Syriac (0)	0	<0.01
Australian (0)	0	<0.01
Austrian (0)	51	0.15
Basque (0)	0	<0.01
Belgian (9)	31	0.09
Brazilian (0)	0	<0.01
British (43)	289	0.87
Bulgarian (0)	0	<0.01
Cajun (0)	0	<0.01
Canadian (10)	18	0.05
Carpatho Rusyn (0)	0	<0.01
Celtic (0)	10	0.03
Croatian (0)	16	0.05
Cypriot (12)	12	0.04
Czech (33)	44	0.13
Czechoslovakian (6)	6	0.02
Danish (48)	116	0.35
Dutch (168)	1,040	3.14
Eastern European (0)	0	<0.01
English (1,524)	3,696	11.17
Estonian (0)	0	<0.01
European (37)	143	0.43
Finnish (17)	30	0.09
French, ex. Basque (213)	1,195	3.61
French Canadian (22)	49	0.15
German (2,525)	8,429	25.48
German Russian (0)	0	<0.01
Greek (59)	86	0.26
Guyanese (0)	0	<0.01
Hungarian (0)	64	0.19
Icelander (0)	0	<0.01
Iranian (0)	0	<0.01
Irish (1,146)	5,543	16.75
Israeli (0)	0	<0.01
Italian (123)	461	1.39
Latvian (0)	0	<0.01
Lithuanian (10)	15	0.05
Luxemburger (0)	0	<0.01
Macedonian (0)	0	<0.01
Maltese (0)	0	<0.01
New Zealander (0)	0	<0.01
Northern European (22)	22	0.07
Norwegian (34)	133	0.40
Pennsylvania German (68)	73	0.22
Polish (78)	285	0.86
Portuguese (11)	263	0.79
Romanian (0)	0	<0.01
Russian (33)	106	0.32
Scandinavian (0)	19	0.06
Scotch-Irish (181)	492	1.49
Scottish (349)	671	2.03
Serbian (0)	0	<0.01
Slavic (0)	0	<0.01
Slovak (10)	31	0.09
Slovene (0)	8	0.02
Soviet Union (0)	0	<0.01
Swedish (177)	432	1.31
Swiss (58)	162	0.49
Turkish (0)	7	0.02
Ukrainian (0)	0	<0.01
Welsh (98)	389	1.18
West Indian, ex. Hispanic (0)	5	0.02
Bahamian (0)	0	<0.01
Barbadian (0)	0	<0.01
Belizean (0)	0	<0.01
Bermudan (0)	0	<0.01
British West Indian (0)	0	<0.01
Dutch West Indian (0)	0	<0.01
Haitian (0)	0	<0.01
Jamaican (0)	0	<0.01
Trinidadian/Tobagonian (0)	0	<0.01
U.S. Virgin Islander (0)	0	<0.01
West Indian (0)	5	0.02
Other West Indian (0)	0	<0.01
Yugoslavian (0)	0	<0.01

Hispanic Origin	Population	%
Hispanic or Latino (of any race)	322	0.97
Central American, ex. Mexican	11	0.03
Costa Rican	1	<0.01
Guatemalan	3	0.01
Honduran	4	0.01
Nicaraguan	0	<0.01
Panamanian	2	0.01
Salvadoran	1	<0.01
Other Central American	0	<0.01
Cuban	15	0.05
Dominican Republic	0	<0.01
Mexican	206	0.62
Puerto Rican	41	0.12
South American	19	0.06
Argentinean	4	0.01
Bolivian	0	<0.01
Chilean	4	0.01
Colombian	8	0.02
Ecuadorian	0	<0.01
Paraguayan	0	<0.01
Peruvian	2	0.01
Uruguayan	0	<0.01
Venezuelan	1	<0.01
Other South American	0	<0.01
Other Hispanic or Latino	30	0.09

Race*	Population	%
African-American/Black (49)	111	0.33
Not Hispanic (49)	104	0.31
Hispanic (0)	7	0.02
American Indian/Alaska Native (93)	232	0.70
Not Hispanic (82)	214	0.65
Hispanic (11)	18	0.05
Alaska Athabascan *(Ala. Nat.)* (0)	0	<0.01
Aleut *(Alaska Native)* (0)	0	<0.01
Apache (3)	3	0.01
Arapaho (0)	0	<0.01
Blackfeet (0)	5	0.02
Canadian/French Am. Ind. (0)	0	<0.01
Central American Ind. (0)	0	<0.01
Cherokee (20)	75	0.23
Cheyenne (0)	0	<0.01
Chickasaw (0)	0	<0.01
Chippewa (1)	6	0.02
Choctaw (2)	4	0.01
Colville (0)	0	<0.01
Comanche (0)	0	<0.01
Cree (0)	0	<0.01
Creek (11)	11	0.03
Crow (0)	0	<0.01
Delaware (0)	0	<0.01
Hopi (0)	0	<0.01
Houma (0)	0	<0.01
Inupiat *(Alaska Native)* (0)	0	<0.01
Iroquois (2)	5	0.02
Kiowa (0)	0	<0.01
Lumbee (1)	1	<0.01
Menominee (0)	0	<0.01
Mexican American Ind. (0)	1	<0.01
Navajo (6)	9	0.03
Osage (2)	4	0.01
Ottawa (1)	1	<0.01
Paiute (0)	0	<0.01
Pima (1)	1	<0.01
Potawatomi (1)	1	<0.01
Pueblo (0)	0	<0.01
Puget Sound Salish (0)	0	<0.01
Seminole (0)	3	0.01
Shoshone (0)	0	<0.01
Sioux (5)	10	0.03
South American Ind. (0)	1	<0.01
Spanish American Ind. (0)	0	<0.01
Tlingit-Haida *(Alaska Native)* (0)	0	<0.01
Tohono O'Odham (0)	0	<0.01
Tsimshian *(Alaska Native)* (0)	0	<0.01
Ute (0)	0	<0.01
Yakama (0)	0	<0.01
Yaqui (0)	0	<0.01
Yuman (0)	0	<0.01
Yup'ik *(Alaska Native)* (0)	0	<0.01
Asian (96)	148	0.45
Not Hispanic (96)	147	0.44
Hispanic (0)	1	<0.01
Bangladeshi (0)	0	<0.01
Bhutanese (0)	0	<0.01
Burmese (0)	0	<0.01
Cambodian (0)	0	<0.01
Chinese, ex. Taiwanese (25)	29	0.09
Filipino (26)	49	0.15
Hmong (0)	0	<0.01
Indian (14)	23	0.07
Indonesian (2)	2	0.01
Japanese (5)	7	0.02
Korean (7)	9	0.03
Laotian (0)	0	<0.01
Malaysian (0)	0	<0.01
Nepalese (0)	0	<0.01
Pakistani (0)	0	<0.01
Sri Lankan (0)	0	<0.01
Taiwanese (0)	1	<0.01
Thai (9)	11	0.03
Vietnamese (7)	8	0.02
Hawaii Native/Pacific Islander (4)	15	0.05
Not Hispanic (4)	14	0.04
Hispanic (0)	1	<0.01
Fijian (0)	0	<0.01
Guamanian/Chamorro (2)	2	0.01
Marshallese (0)	0	<0.01
Native Hawaiian (1)	3	0.01
Samoan (1)	2	0.01
Tongan (0)	0	<0.01
White (32,548)	32,819	98.96
Not Hispanic (32,343)	32,581	98.24
Hispanic (205)	238	0.72

*Notes: † The Census 2010 population figure is used to calculate the percentages in the Hispanic Origin and Race categories. Ancestry percentages are based on the 2006-2010 American Community Survey population (not shown); ‡ Numbers in parentheses indicate the number of people reporting a single ancestry; * Numbers in parentheses indicate the number of persons reporting this race alone, not in combination with any other race; Please refer to the Explanation of Data for more information.*

Hamilton County

Population: 274,569

Ancestry	Population	%
Afghan (33)	52	0.02
African, Sub-Saharan (512)	865	0.33
African (292)	491	0.19
Cape Verdean (0)	0	<0.01
Ethiopian (12)	12	<0.01
Ghanaian (0)	0	<0.01
Kenyan (57)	57	0.02
Liberian (0)	0	<0.01
Nigerian (79)	79	0.03
Senegalese (13)	13	<0.01
Sierra Leonean (0)	0	<0.01
Somalian (0)	0	<0.01
South African (13)	147	0.06
Sudanese (0)	11	<0.01
Ugandan (0)	0	<0.01
Zimbabwean (0)	0	<0.01
Other Sub-Saharan African (46)	55	0.02
Albanian (40)	50	0.02
Alsatian (0)	0	<0.01
American (20,130)	20,130	7.71
Arab (929)	1,516	0.58
Arab (293)	472	0.18
Egyptian (313)	342	0.13
Iraqi (0)	14	0.01
Jordanian (33)	45	0.02
Lebanese (126)	351	0.13
Moroccan (25)	48	0.02
Palestinian (24)	24	0.01
Syrian (43)	105	0.04
Other Arab (72)	115	0.04
Armenian (10)	31	0.01
Assyrian/Chaldean/Syriac (0)	0	<0.01
Australian (45)	92	0.04
Austrian (132)	463	0.18
Basque (0)	0	<0.01
Belgian (188)	853	0.33
Brazilian (88)	113	0.04
British (949)	1,717	0.66
Bulgarian (29)	68	0.03
Cajun (0)	22	0.01
Canadian (254)	569	0.22
Carpatho Rusyn (0)	16	0.01
Celtic (39)	54	0.02
Croatian (59)	420	0.16
Cypriot (0)	0	<0.01
Czech (244)	1,135	0.43
Czechoslovakian (222)	345	0.13
Danish (351)	1,114	0.43
Dutch (1,397)	6,141	2.35
Eastern European (375)	436	0.17
English (11,345)	34,092	13.05
Estonian (0)	13	<0.01
European (4,212)	4,815	1.84
Finnish (125)	304	0.12
French, ex. Basque (1,492)	8,233	3.15
French Canadian (420)	997	0.38
German (28,858)	75,694	28.97
German Russian (0)	0	<0.01
Greek (609)	1,579	0.60
Guyanese (0)	0	<0.01
Hungarian (313)	1,807	0.69
Icelander (0)	12	<0.01
Iranian (420)	565	0.22
Irish (10,366)	38,147	14.60
Israeli (21)	21	0.01
Italian (4,036)	12,040	4.61
Latvian (313)	439	0.17
Lithuanian (147)	488	0.19
Luxemburger (0)	22	0.01
Macedonian (67)	139	0.05
Maltese (0)	0	<0.01
New Zealander (14)	14	0.01
Northern European (153)	153	0.06
Norwegian (870)	3,017	1.15
Pennsylvania German (109)	189	0.07
Polish (2,509)	9,200	3.52
Portuguese (124)	368	0.14
Romanian (295)	476	0.18
Russian (1,243)	2,517	0.96
Scandinavian (237)	459	0.18
Scotch-Irish (1,543)	4,467	1.71
Scottish (2,503)	8,076	3.09
Serbian (74)	250	0.10
Slavic (12)	50	0.02
Slovak (234)	698	0.27
Slovene (89)	259	0.10
Soviet Union (0)	0	<0.01
Swedish (792)	4,394	1.68
Swiss (356)	1,505	0.58
Turkish (95)	121	0.05
Ukrainian (424)	901	0.34
Welsh (751)	2,739	1.05
West Indian, ex. Hispanic (150)	231	0.09
Bahamian (0)	0	<0.01
Barbadian (0)	0	<0.01
Belizean (11)	31	0.01
Bermudan (19)	19	0.01
British West Indian (13)	13	<0.01
Dutch West Indian (0)	0	<0.01
Haitian (12)	28	0.01
Jamaican (70)	115	0.04
Trinidadian/Tobagonian (13)	13	<0.01
U.S. Virgin Islander (0)	0	<0.01
West Indian (12)	12	<0.01
Other West Indian (0)	0	<0.01
Yugoslavian (273)	338	0.13

Hispanic Origin	Population	%
Hispanic or Latino (of any race)	9,426	3.43
Central American, ex. Mexican	796	0.29
Costa Rican	40	0.01
Guatemalan	269	0.10
Honduran	94	0.03
Nicaraguan	60	0.02
Panamanian	98	0.04
Salvadoran	220	0.08
Other Central American	15	0.01
Cuban	272	0.10
Dominican Republic	147	0.05
Mexican	5,449	1.98
Puerto Rican	885	0.32
South American	1,071	0.39
Argentinean	99	0.04
Bolivian	36	0.01
Chilean	59	0.02
Colombian	362	0.13
Ecuadorian	33	0.01
Paraguayan	9	<0.01
Peruvian	178	0.06
Uruguayan	12	<0.01
Venezuelan	273	0.10
Other South American	10	<0.01
Other Hispanic or Latino	806	0.29

Race*	Population	%
African-American/Black (9,603)	11,401	4.15
Not Hispanic (9,395)	11,044	4.02
Hispanic (208)	357	0.13
American Indian/Alaska Native (529)	1,309	0.48
Not Hispanic (437)	1,130	0.41
Hispanic (92)	179	0.07
Alaska Athabascan *(Ala. Nat.)* (0)	0	<0.01
Aleut *(Alaska Native)* (1)	1	<0.01
Apache (24)	35	0.01
Arapaho (0)	0	<0.01
Blackfeet (17)	50	0.02
Canadian/French Am. Ind. (1)	1	<0.01
Central American Ind. (1)	4	<0.01
Cherokee (80)	256	0.09
Cheyenne (0)	0	<0.01
Chickasaw (0)	1	<0.01
Chippewa (26)	45	0.02
Choctaw (7)	26	0.01
Colville (0)	0	<0.01
Comanche (0)	3	<0.01
Cree (3)	4	<0.01
Creek (5)	11	<0.01
Crow (2)	2	<0.01
Delaware (0)	3	<0.01
Hopi (2)	4	<0.01
Houma (0)	0	<0.01
Inupiat *(Alaska Native)* (2)	3	<0.01
Iroquois (5)	15	0.01
Kiowa (2)	2	<0.01
Lumbee (7)	8	<0.01
Menominee (1)	2	<0.01
Mexican American Ind. (42)	55	0.02
Navajo (12)	17	0.01
Osage (4)	10	<0.01
Ottawa (2)	6	<0.01
Paiute (2)	3	<0.01
Pima (0)	0	<0.01
Potawatomi (12)	23	0.01
Pueblo (0)	1	<0.01
Puget Sound Salish (0)	0	<0.01
Seminole (0)	3	<0.01
Shoshone (0)	1	<0.01
Sioux (17)	26	0.01
South American Ind. (2)	13	<0.01
Spanish American Ind. (2)	5	<0.01
Tlingit-Haida *(Alaska Native)* (1)	1	<0.01
Tohono O'Odham (0)	0	<0.01
Tsimshian *(Alaska Native)* (0)	2	<0.01
Ute (2)	3	<0.01
Yakama (0)	0	<0.01
Yaqui (2)	3	<0.01
Yuman (0)	0	<0.01
Yup'ik *(Alaska Native)* (0)	1	<0.01
Asian (13,175)	15,326	5.58
Not Hispanic (13,122)	15,185	5.53
Hispanic (53)	141	0.05
Bangladeshi (77)	83	0.03
Bhutanese (1)	3	<0.01
Burmese (4)	16	0.01
Cambodian (103)	120	0.04
Chinese, ex. Taiwanese (3,567)	3,954	1.44
Filipino (734)	1,189	0.43
Hmong (102)	113	0.04
Indian (4,541)	4,889	1.78
Indonesian (102)	126	0.05
Japanese (650)	938	0.34
Korean (1,248)	1,565	0.57
Laotian (36)	51	0.02
Malaysian (21)	33	0.01
Nepalese (35)	35	0.01
Pakistani (413)	457	0.17
Sri Lankan (52)	58	0.02
Taiwanese (200)	237	0.09
Thai (72)	137	0.05
Vietnamese (839)	974	0.35
Hawaii Native/Pacific Islander (97)	264	0.10
Not Hispanic (72)	215	0.08
Hispanic (25)	49	0.02
Fijian (0)	0	<0.01
Guamanian/Chamorro (14)	33	0.01
Marshallese (1)	1	<0.01
Native Hawaiian (48)	113	0.04
Samoan (14)	41	0.01
Tongan (4)	7	<0.01
White (242,985)	247,416	90.11
Not Hispanic (237,317)	241,153	87.83
Hispanic (5,668)	6,263	2.28

*Notes: † The Census 2010 population figure is used to calculate the percentages in the Hispanic Origin and Race categories. Ancestry percentages are based on the 2006-2010 American Community Survey population (not shown); ‡ Numbers in parentheses indicate the number of people reporting a single ancestry; * Numbers in parentheses indicate the number of persons reporting this race alone, not in combination with any other race; Please refer to the Explanation of Data for more information.*

Hancock County

Population: 70,002

Ancestry	Population	%
Afghan (0)	0	<0.01
African, Sub-Saharan (11)	110	0.16
African (0)	6	0.01
Cape Verdean (0)	0	<0.01
Ethiopian (0)	93	0.14
Ghanaian (0)	0	<0.01
Kenyan (11)	11	0.02
Liberian (0)	0	<0.01
Nigerian (0)	0	<0.01
Senegalese (0)	0	<0.01
Sierra Leonean (0)	0	<0.01
Somalian (0)	0	<0.01
South African (0)	0	<0.01
Sudanese (0)	0	<0.01
Ugandan (0)	0	<0.01
Zimbabwean (0)	0	<0.01
Other Sub-Saharan African (0)	0	<0.01
Albanian (0)	0	<0.01
Alsatian (0)	3	<0.01
American (8,011)	8,011	11.78
Arab (25)	50	0.07
Arab (6)	6	0.01
Egyptian (17)	17	0.02
Iraqi (0)	0	<0.01
Jordanian (0)	0	<0.01
Lebanese (0)	25	0.04
Moroccan (0)	0	<0.01
Palestinian (2)	2	<0.01
Syrian (0)	0	<0.01
Other Arab (0)	0	<0.01
Armenian (0)	0	<0.01
Assyrian/Chaldean/Syriac (0)	0	<0.01
Australian (34)	34	0.05
Austrian (0)	104	0.15
Basque (0)	0	<0.01
Belgian (0)	17	0.02
Brazilian (0)	0	<0.01
British (145)	421	0.62
Bulgarian (12)	12	0.02
Cajun (0)	0	<0.01
Canadian (63)	184	0.27
Carpatho Rusyn (0)	0	<0.01
Celtic (0)	12	0.02
Croatian (10)	12	0.02
Cypriot (0)	0	<0.01
Czech (34)	71	0.10
Czechoslovakian (17)	59	0.09
Danish (0)	72	0.11
Dutch (525)	1,448	2.13
Eastern European (41)	41	0.06
English (3,875)	8,036	11.82
Estonian (0)	0	<0.01
European (574)	583	0.86
Finnish (6)	46	0.07
French, ex. Basque (378)	1,556	2.29
French Canadian (153)	229	0.34
German (8,009)	17,832	26.22
German Russian (0)	0	<0.01
Greek (76)	120	0.18
Guyanese (0)	0	<0.01
Hungarian (35)	201	0.30
Icelander (0)	0	<0.01
Iranian (0)	25	0.04
Irish (3,413)	9,434	13.87
Israeli (0)	0	<0.01
Italian (456)	1,510	2.22
Latvian (0)	0	<0.01
Lithuanian (14)	67	0.10
Luxemburger (0)	11	0.02
Macedonian (0)	0	<0.01
Maltese (0)	12	0.02
New Zealander (0)	0	<0.01
Northern European (89)	89	0.13
Norwegian (58)	284	0.42
Pennsylvania German (15)	17	0.02
Polish (309)	950	1.40
Portuguese (30)	91	0.13
Romanian (78)	100	0.15
Russian (112)	264	0.39
Scandinavian (19)	56	0.08
Scotch-Irish (516)	985	1.45
Scottish (647)	1,351	1.99
Serbian (0)	2	<0.01
Slavic (7)	20	0.03
Slovak (0)	38	0.06
Slovene (0)	12	0.02
Soviet Union (0)	0	<0.01
Swedish (138)	385	0.57
Swiss (10)	185	0.27
Turkish (119)	119	0.17
Ukrainian (86)	166	0.24
Welsh (95)	565	0.83
West Indian, ex. Hispanic (14)	14	0.02
Bahamian (0)	0	<0.01
Barbadian (0)	0	<0.01
Belizean (0)	0	<0.01
Bermudan (14)	14	0.02
British West Indian (0)	0	<0.01
Dutch West Indian (0)	0	<0.01
Haitian (0)	0	<0.01
Jamaican (0)	0	<0.01
Trinidadian/Tobagonian (0)	0	<0.01
U.S. Virgin Islander (0)	0	<0.01
West Indian (0)	0	<0.01
Other West Indian (0)	0	<0.01
Yugoslavian (28)	28	0.04

Hispanic Origin	Population	%
Hispanic or Latino (of any race)	1,216	1.74
Central American, ex. Mexican	60	0.09
Costa Rican	7	0.01
Guatemalan	16	0.02
Honduran	9	0.01
Nicaraguan	2	<0.01
Panamanian	10	0.01
Salvadoran	16	0.02
Other Central American	0	<0.01
Cuban	41	0.06
Dominican Republic	21	0.03
Mexican	768	1.10
Puerto Rican	155	0.22
South American	60	0.09
Argentinean	5	0.01
Bolivian	7	0.01
Chilean	3	<0.01
Colombian	7	0.01
Ecuadorian	3	<0.01
Paraguayan	0	<0.01
Peruvian	15	0.02
Uruguayan	0	<0.01
Venezuelan	20	0.03
Other South American	0	<0.01
Other Hispanic or Latino	111	0.16

Race*	Population	%
African-American/Black (1,452)	1,758	2.51
Not Hispanic (1,420)	1,702	2.43
Hispanic (32)	56	0.08
American Indian/Alaska Native (154)	443	0.63
Not Hispanic (136)	392	0.56
Hispanic (18)	51	0.07
Alaska Athabascan *(Ala. Nat.)* (0)	0	<0.01
Aleut *(Alaska Native)* (2)	7	0.01
Apache (4)	8	0.01
Arapaho (2)	4	0.01
Blackfeet (5)	19	0.03
Canadian/French Am. Ind. (0)	0	<0.01
Central American Ind. (0)	0	<0.01
Cherokee (16)	112	0.16
Cheyenne (0)	1	<0.01
Chickasaw (1)	1	<0.01
Chippewa (4)	6	0.01
Choctaw (7)	14	0.02
Colville (0)	0	<0.01
Comanche (0)	1	<0.01
Cree (0)	0	<0.01
Creek (2)	2	<0.01
Crow (5)	5	0.01
Delaware (3)	6	0.01
Hopi (0)	1	<0.01
Houma (1)	1	<0.01
Inupiat *(Alaska Native)* (0)	0	<0.01
Iroquois (2)	8	0.01
Kiowa (0)	0	<0.01
Lumbee (3)	3	<0.01
Menominee (0)	0	<0.01
Mexican American Ind. (6)	6	0.01
Navajo (0)	0	<0.01
Osage (0)	0	<0.01
Ottawa (0)	0	<0.01
Paiute (0)	0	<0.01
Pima (0)	1	<0.01
Potawatomi (3)	4	0.01
Pueblo (0)	0	<0.01
Puget Sound Salish (0)	0	<0.01
Seminole (0)	0	<0.01
Shoshone (0)	0	<0.01
Sioux (6)	18	0.03
South American Ind. (0)	3	<0.01
Spanish American Ind. (0)	0	<0.01
Tlingit-Haida *(Alaska Native)* (0)	0	<0.01
Tohono O'Odham (0)	0	<0.01
Tsimshian *(Alaska Native)* (0)	0	<0.01
Ute (1)	1	<0.01
Yakama (0)	0	<0.01
Yaqui (1)	2	<0.01
Yuman (0)	0	<0.01
Yup'ik *(Alaska Native)* (0)	0	<0.01
Asian (558)	796	1.14
Not Hispanic (554)	787	1.12
Hispanic (4)	9	0.01
Bangladeshi (0)	2	<0.01
Bhutanese (0)	0	<0.01
Burmese (0)	0	<0.01
Cambodian (1)	6	0.01
Chinese, ex. Taiwanese (79)	102	0.15
Filipino (106)	183	0.26
Hmong (0)	0	<0.01
Indian (114)	147	0.21
Indonesian (2)	2	<0.01
Japanese (42)	81	0.12
Korean (89)	134	0.19
Laotian (7)	8	0.01
Malaysian (0)	0	<0.01
Nepalese (0)	0	<0.01
Pakistani (6)	11	0.02
Sri Lankan (0)	0	<0.01
Taiwanese (6)	6	0.01
Thai (13)	19	0.03
Vietnamese (54)	63	0.09
Hawaii Native/Pacific Islander (20)	35	0.05
Not Hispanic (14)	26	0.04
Hispanic (6)	9	0.01
Fijian (0)	0	<0.01
Guamanian/Chamorro (11)	11	0.02
Marshallese (1)	1	<0.01
Native Hawaiian (4)	11	0.02
Samoan (3)	3	<0.01
Tongan (0)	0	<0.01
White (66,644)	67,458	96.37
Not Hispanic (65,859)	66,557	95.08
Hispanic (785)	901	1.29

*Notes: † The Census 2010 population figure is used to calculate the percentages in the Hispanic Origin and Race categories. Ancestry percentages are based on the 2006-2010 American Community Survey population (not shown); ‡ Numbers in parentheses indicate the number of people reporting a single ancestry; * Numbers in parentheses indicate the number of persons reporting this race alone, not in combination with any other race; Please refer to the Explanation of Data for more information.*

Harrison County

Population: 39,364

Ancestry	Population	%
Afghan (0)	0	<0.01
African, Sub-Saharan (0)	5	0.01
African (0)	5	0.01
Cape Verdean (0)	0	<0.01
Ethiopian (0)	0	<0.01
Ghanaian (0)	0	<0.01
Kenyan (0)	0	<0.01
Liberian (0)	0	<0.01
Nigerian (0)	0	<0.01
Senegalese (0)	0	<0.01
Sierra Leonean (0)	0	<0.01
Somalian (0)	0	<0.01
South African (0)	0	<0.01
Sudanese (0)	0	<0.01
Ugandan (0)	0	<0.01
Zimbabwean (0)	0	<0.01
Other Sub-Saharan African (0)	0	<0.01
Albanian (0)	0	<0.01
Alsatian (0)	0	<0.01
American (6,364)	6,364	16.48
Arab (0)	0	<0.01
Arab (0)	0	<0.01
Egyptian (0)	0	<0.01
Iraqi (0)	0	<0.01
Jordanian (0)	0	<0.01
Lebanese (0)	0	<0.01
Moroccan (0)	0	<0.01
Palestinian (0)	0	<0.01
Syrian (0)	0	<0.01
Other Arab (0)	0	<0.01
Armenian (0)	0	<0.01
Assyrian/Chaldean/Syriac (0)	0	<0.01
Australian (0)	0	<0.01
Austrian (0)	22	0.06
Basque (0)	0	<0.01
Belgian (0)	15	0.04
Brazilian (0)	0	<0.01
British (28)	150	0.39
Bulgarian (0)	0	<0.01
Cajun (15)	15	0.04
Canadian (3)	14	0.04
Carpatho Rusyn (0)	0	<0.01
Celtic (0)	0	<0.01
Croatian (0)	0	<0.01
Cypriot (0)	0	<0.01
Czech (0)	26	0.07
Czechoslovakian (0)	0	<0.01
Danish (70)	101	0.26
Dutch (58)	331	0.86
Eastern European (0)	10	0.03
English (2,195)	4,943	12.80
Estonian (0)	0	<0.01
European (433)	441	1.14
Finnish (0)	42	0.11
French, ex. Basque (194)	1,332	3.45
French Canadian (16)	38	0.10
German (5,776)	12,024	31.14
German Russian (0)	0	<0.01
Greek (16)	95	0.25
Guyanese (0)	0	<0.01
Hungarian (79)	156	0.40
Icelander (0)	0	<0.01
Iranian (0)	0	<0.01
Irish (1,678)	4,952	12.82
Israeli (0)	0	<0.01
Italian (140)	643	1.67
Latvian (0)	0	<0.01
Lithuanian (28)	28	0.07
Luxemburger (0)	0	<0.01
Macedonian (0)	0	<0.01
Maltese (0)	0	<0.01
New Zealander (0)	0	<0.01
Northern European (0)	0	<0.01
Norwegian (42)	207	0.54
Pennsylvania German (0)	0	<0.01
Polish (71)	410	1.06
Portuguese (0)	30	0.08
Romanian (0)	0	<0.01
Russian (0)	12	0.03
Scandinavian (13)	54	0.14
Scotch-Irish (204)	572	1.48
Scottish (325)	890	2.30
Serbian (0)	0	<0.01
Slavic (11)	11	0.03
Slovak (0)	37	0.10
Slovene (0)	0	<0.01
Soviet Union (0)	0	<0.01
Swedish (17)	271	0.70
Swiss (0)	145	0.38
Turkish (0)	0	<0.01
Ukrainian (0)	15	0.04
Welsh (86)	190	0.49
West Indian, ex. Hispanic (0)	0	<0.01
Bahamian (0)	0	<0.01
Barbadian (0)	0	<0.01
Belizean (0)	0	<0.01
Bermudan (0)	0	<0.01
British West Indian (0)	0	<0.01
Dutch West Indian (0)	0	<0.01
Haitian (0)	0	<0.01
Jamaican (0)	0	<0.01
Trinidadian/Tobagonian (0)	0	<0.01
U.S. Virgin Islander (0)	0	<0.01
West Indian (0)	0	<0.01
Other West Indian (0)	0	<0.01
Yugoslavian (0)	0	<0.01

Hispanic Origin	Population	%
Hispanic or Latino (of any race)	581	1.48
Central American, ex. Mexican	24	0.06
Costa Rican	0	<0.01
Guatemalan	15	0.04
Honduran	4	0.01
Nicaraguan	1	<0.01
Panamanian	3	0.01
Salvadoran	1	<0.01
Other Central American	0	<0.01
Cuban	17	0.04
Dominican Republic	3	0.01
Mexican	412	1.05
Puerto Rican	34	0.09
South American	18	0.05
Argentinean	0	<0.01
Bolivian	0	<0.01
Chilean	0	<0.01
Colombian	3	0.01
Ecuadorian	4	0.01
Paraguayan	0	<0.01
Peruvian	8	0.02
Uruguayan	0	<0.01
Venezuelan	3	0.01
Other South American	0	<0.01
Other Hispanic or Latino	73	0.19

Race*	Population	%
African-American/Black (178)	299	0.76
Not Hispanic (167)	284	0.72
Hispanic (11)	15	0.04
American Indian/Alaska Native (88)	251	0.64
Not Hispanic (84)	243	0.62
Hispanic (4)	8	0.02
Alaska Athabascan *(Ala. Nat.)* (0)	0	<0.01
Aleut *(Alaska Native)* (0)	0	<0.01
Apache (0)	2	0.01
Arapaho (0)	0	<0.01
Blackfeet (2)	7	0.02
Canadian/French Am. Ind. (0)	0	<0.01
Central American Ind. (0)	0	<0.01
Cherokee (23)	84	0.21
Cheyenne (0)	0	<0.01
Chickasaw (1)	2	0.01
Chippewa (9)	11	0.03
Choctaw (2)	6	0.02
Colville (0)	0	<0.01
Comanche (0)	0	<0.01
Cree (0)	5	0.01
Creek (1)	1	<0.01
Crow (0)	0	<0.01
Delaware (0)	0	<0.01
Hopi (0)	0	<0.01
Houma (0)	1	<0.01
Inupiat *(Alaska Native)* (0)	1	<0.01
Iroquois (1)	8	0.02
Kiowa (0)	0	<0.01
Lumbee (0)	0	<0.01
Menominee (0)	0	<0.01
Mexican American Ind. (0)	1	<0.01
Navajo (3)	5	0.01
Osage (3)	3	0.01
Ottawa (0)	0	<0.01
Paiute (0)	0	<0.01
Pima (0)	1	<0.01
Potawatomi (0)	0	<0.01
Pueblo (0)	0	<0.01
Puget Sound Salish (0)	0	<0.01
Seminole (0)	0	<0.01
Shoshone (0)	2	0.01
Sioux (2)	5	0.01
South American Ind. (0)	0	<0.01
Spanish American Ind. (0)	0	<0.01
Tlingit-Haida *(Alaska Native)* (0)	0	<0.01
Tohono O'Odham (0)	0	<0.01
Tsimshian *(Alaska Native)* (0)	0	<0.01
Ute (0)	0	<0.01
Yakama (0)	0	<0.01
Yaqui (0)	0	<0.01
Yuman (0)	0	<0.01
Yup'ik *(Alaska Native)* (0)	0	<0.01
Asian (155)	228	0.58
Not Hispanic (153)	222	0.56
Hispanic (2)	6	0.02
Bangladeshi (0)	0	<0.01
Bhutanese (0)	0	<0.01
Burmese (0)	0	<0.01
Cambodian (13)	13	0.03
Chinese, ex. Taiwanese (23)	30	0.08
Filipino (42)	61	0.15
Hmong (0)	0	<0.01
Indian (24)	37	0.09
Indonesian (2)	4	0.01
Japanese (13)	30	0.08
Korean (16)	27	0.07
Laotian (1)	1	<0.01
Malaysian (2)	4	0.01
Nepalese (0)	0	<0.01
Pakistani (0)	0	<0.01
Sri Lankan (0)	0	<0.01
Taiwanese (0)	0	<0.01
Thai (3)	4	0.01
Vietnamese (3)	6	0.02
Hawaii Native/Pacific Islander (11)	35	0.09
Not Hispanic (9)	31	0.08
Hispanic (2)	4	0.01
Fijian (0)	0	<0.01
Guamanian/Chamorro (2)	3	0.01
Marshallese (1)	1	<0.01
Native Hawaiian (4)	18	0.05
Samoan (1)	7	0.02
Tongan (0)	0	<0.01
White (38,341)	38,711	98.34
Not Hispanic (37,984)	38,330	97.37
Hispanic (357)	381	0.97

*Notes: † The Census 2010 population figure is used to calculate the percentages in the Hispanic Origin and Race categories. Ancestry percentages are based on the 2006-2010 American Community Survey population (not shown); ‡ Numbers in parentheses indicate the number of people reporting a single ancestry; * Numbers in parentheses indicate the number of persons reporting this race alone, not in combination with any other race; Please refer to the Explanation of Data for more information.*

Hendricks County

Population: 145,448

Ancestry	Population	%
Afghan (0)	0	<0.01
African, Sub-Saharan (771)	852	0.61
African (342)	414	0.30
Cape Verdean (0)	0	<0.01
Ethiopian (222)	227	0.16
Ghanaian (0)	0	<0.01
Kenyan (9)	9	0.01
Liberian (0)	0	<0.01
Nigerian (178)	178	0.13
Senegalese (0)	0	<0.01
Sierra Leonean (0)	0	<0.01
Somalian (0)	0	<0.01
South African (0)	0	<0.01
Sudanese (0)	0	<0.01
Ugandan (0)	0	<0.01
Zimbabwean (0)	0	<0.01
Other Sub-Saharan African (20)	24	0.02
Albanian (0)	0	<0.01
Alsatian (0)	0	<0.01
American (13,161)	13,161	9.40
Arab (278)	493	0.35
Arab (105)	105	0.07
Egyptian (0)	8	0.01
Iraqi (0)	0	<0.01
Jordanian (11)	34	0.02
Lebanese (14)	114	0.08
Moroccan (9)	9	0.01
Palestinian (0)	0	<0.01
Syrian (118)	202	0.14
Other Arab (21)	21	0.01
Armenian (0)	41	0.03
Assyrian/Chaldean/Syriac (0)	0	<0.01
Australian (37)	46	0.03
Austrian (52)	187	0.13
Basque (0)	0	<0.01
Belgian (78)	276	0.20
Brazilian (149)	178	0.13
British (301)	641	0.46
Bulgarian (10)	21	0.01
Cajun (13)	23	0.02
Canadian (86)	97	0.07
Carpatho Rusyn (0)	0	<0.01
Celtic (15)	36	0.03
Croatian (81)	94	0.07
Cypriot (0)	0	<0.01
Czech (62)	434	0.31
Czechoslovakian (35)	94	0.07
Danish (144)	406	0.29
Dutch (651)	2,584	1.85
Eastern European (0)	0	<0.01
English (12,097)	22,690	16.20
Estonian (0)	0	<0.01
European (1,380)	1,495	1.07
Finnish (25)	189	0.13
French, ex. Basque (970)	3,793	2.71
French Canadian (233)	668	0.48
German (16,426)	39,646	28.31
German Russian (0)	0	<0.01
Greek (261)	550	0.39
Guyanese (13)	18	0.01
Hungarian (228)	392	0.28
Icelander (10)	31	0.02
Iranian (38)	38	0.03
Irish (7,226)	21,306	15.22
Israeli (0)	0	<0.01
Italian (1,531)	4,460	3.19
Latvian (40)	126	0.09
Lithuanian (99)	336	0.24
Luxemburger (0)	0	<0.01
Macedonian (50)	71	0.05
Maltese (0)	11	0.01
New Zealander (0)	0	<0.01
Northern European (122)	148	0.11
Norwegian (425)	1,048	0.75
Pennsylvania German (83)	91	0.06
Polish (880)	2,693	1.92
Portuguese (89)	219	0.16
Romanian (131)	285	0.20
Russian (243)	750	0.54
Scandinavian (49)	240	0.17
Scotch-Irish (1,537)	2,756	1.97
Scottish (1,356)	4,228	3.02
Serbian (103)	156	0.11
Slavic (68)	137	0.10
Slovak (189)	404	0.29
Slovene (33)	129	0.09
Soviet Union (0)	0	<0.01
Swedish (238)	1,343	0.96
Swiss (161)	403	0.29
Turkish (0)	11	0.01
Ukrainian (41)	86	0.06
Welsh (171)	987	0.70
West Indian, ex. Hispanic (159)	314	0.22
Bahamian (13)	13	0.01
Barbadian (0)	0	<0.01
Belizean (0)	0	<0.01
Bermudan (0)	0	<0.01
British West Indian (100)	150	0.11
Dutch West Indian (0)	0	<0.01
Haitian (32)	46	0.03
Jamaican (0)	0	<0.01
Trinidadian/Tobagonian (14)	14	0.01
U.S. Virgin Islander (0)	0	<0.01
West Indian (0)	91	0.06
Other West Indian (0)	0	<0.01
Yugoslavian (125)	178	0.13

Hispanic Origin	Population	%
Hispanic or Latino (of any race)	4,379	3.01
Central American, ex. Mexican	483	0.33
Costa Rican	33	0.02
Guatemalan	101	0.07
Honduran	103	0.07
Nicaraguan	38	0.03
Panamanian	38	0.03
Salvadoran	165	0.11
Other Central American	5	<0.01
Cuban	84	0.06
Dominican Republic	120	0.08
Mexican	2,479	1.70
Puerto Rican	422	0.29
South American	417	0.29
Argentinean	23	0.02
Bolivian	8	0.01
Chilean	39	0.03
Colombian	79	0.05
Ecuadorian	47	0.03
Paraguayan	0	<0.01
Peruvian	168	0.12
Uruguayan	3	<0.01
Venezuelan	49	0.03
Other South American	1	<0.01
Other Hispanic or Latino	374	0.26

Race*	Population	%
African-American/Black (7,084)	8,091	5.56
Not Hispanic (6,988)	7,929	5.45
Hispanic (96)	162	0.11
American Indian/Alaska Native (293)	777	0.53
Not Hispanic (231)	667	0.46
Hispanic (62)	110	0.08
Alaska Athabascan *(Ala. Nat.)* (0)	2	<0.01
Aleut *(Alaska Native)* (0)	0	<0.01
Apache (3)	10	0.01
Arapaho (0)	0	<0.01
Blackfeet (4)	26	0.02
Canadian/French Am. Ind. (4)	4	<0.01
Central American Ind. (4)	8	0.01
Cherokee (46)	186	0.13
Cheyenne (2)	2	<0.01
Chickasaw (7)	9	0.01
Chippewa (6)	14	0.01
Choctaw (5)	15	0.01
Colville (0)	0	<0.01
Comanche (0)	0	<0.01
Cree (2)	4	<0.01
Creek (0)	2	<0.01
Crow (0)	0	<0.01
Delaware (3)	9	0.01
Hopi (0)	4	<0.01
Houma (0)	2	<0.01
Inupiat *(Alaska Native)* (0)	0	<0.01
Iroquois (6)	12	0.01
Kiowa (1)	1	<0.01
Lumbee (1)	1	<0.01
Menominee (0)	0	<0.01
Mexican American Ind. (13)	20	0.01
Navajo (2)	6	<0.01
Osage (0)	0	<0.01
Ottawa (0)	0	<0.01
Paiute (0)	0	<0.01
Pima (0)	0	<0.01
Potawatomi (4)	11	0.01
Pueblo (2)	4	<0.01
Puget Sound Salish (0)	0	<0.01
Seminole (0)	2	<0.01
Shoshone (0)	0	<0.01
Sioux (11)	22	0.02
South American Ind. (6)	7	<0.01
Spanish American Ind. (3)	3	<0.01
Tlingit-Haida *(Alaska Native)* (0)	0	<0.01
Tohono O'Odham (0)	0	<0.01
Tsimshian *(Alaska Native)* (0)	0	<0.01
Ute (1)	3	<0.01
Yakama (1)	1	<0.01
Yaqui (1)	1	<0.01
Yuman (2)	2	<0.01
Yup'ik *(Alaska Native)* (0)	0	<0.01
Asian (3,028)	3,757	2.58
Not Hispanic (2,984)	3,657	2.51
Hispanic (44)	100	0.07
Bangladeshi (17)	17	0.01
Bhutanese (0)	0	<0.01
Burmese (6)	6	<0.01
Cambodian (16)	16	0.01
Chinese, ex. Taiwanese (317)	391	0.27
Filipino (442)	680	0.47
Hmong (0)	0	<0.01
Indian (1,205)	1,325	0.91
Indonesian (19)	37	0.03
Japanese (113)	203	0.14
Korean (152)	267	0.18
Laotian (12)	22	0.02
Malaysian (6)	9	0.01
Nepalese (4)	4	<0.01
Pakistani (217)	240	0.17
Sri Lankan (2)	2	<0.01
Taiwanese (34)	40	0.03
Thai (28)	52	0.04
Vietnamese (316)	351	0.24
Hawaii Native/Pacific Islander (59)	170	0.12
Not Hispanic (47)	141	0.10
Hispanic (12)	29	0.02
Fijian (1)	1	<0.01
Guamanian/Chamorro (21)	29	0.02
Marshallese (0)	0	<0.01
Native Hawaiian (22)	72	0.05
Samoan (10)	19	0.01
Tongan (0)	0	<0.01
White (131,117)	133,198	91.58
Not Hispanic (128,664)	130,451	89.69
Hispanic (2,453)	2,747	1.89

*Notes: † The Census 2010 population figure is used to calculate the percentages in the Hispanic Origin and Race categories. Ancestry percentages are based on the 2006-2010 American Community Survey population (not shown); ‡ Numbers in parentheses indicate the number of people reporting a single ancestry; * Numbers in parentheses indicate the number of persons reporting this race alone, not in combination with any other race; Please refer to the Explanation of Data for more information.*

Henry County

Population: 49,462

Ancestry	Population	%
Afghan (0)	0	<0.01
African, Sub-Saharan (169)	186	0.38
African (169)	186	0.38
Cape Verdean (0)	0	<0.01
Ethiopian (0)	0	<0.01
Ghanaian (0)	0	<0.01
Kenyan (0)	0	<0.01
Liberian (0)	0	<0.01
Nigerian (0)	0	<0.01
Senegalese (0)	0	<0.01
Sierra Leonean (0)	0	<0.01
Somalian (0)	0	<0.01
South African (0)	0	<0.01
Sudanese (0)	0	<0.01
Ugandan (0)	0	<0.01
Zimbabwean (0)	0	<0.01
Other Sub-Saharan African (0)	0	<0.01
Albanian (0)	0	<0.01
Alsatian (0)	0	<0.01
American (6,509)	6,509	13.31
Arab (16)	34	0.07
Arab (16)	16	0.03
Egyptian (0)	0	<0.01
Iraqi (0)	0	<0.01
Jordanian (0)	0	<0.01
Lebanese (0)	0	<0.01
Moroccan (0)	18	0.04
Palestinian (0)	0	<0.01
Syrian (0)	0	<0.01
Other Arab (0)	0	<0.01
Armenian (0)	0	<0.01
Assyrian/Chaldean/Syriac (0)	0	<0.01
Australian (0)	0	<0.01
Austrian (0)	111	0.23
Basque (0)	0	<0.01
Belgian (0)	16	0.03
Brazilian (0)	0	<0.01
British (113)	134	0.27
Bulgarian (0)	0	<0.01
Cajun (0)	0	<0.01
Canadian (25)	39	0.08
Carpatho Rusyn (0)	0	<0.01
Celtic (0)	0	<0.01
Croatian (17)	63	0.13
Cypriot (0)	0	<0.01
Czech (0)	48	0.10
Czechoslovakian (50)	63	0.13
Danish (17)	88	0.18
Dutch (261)	997	2.04
Eastern European (0)	0	<0.01
English (2,484)	4,466	9.13
Estonian (0)	0	<0.01
European (365)	378	0.77
Finnish (0)	16	0.03
French, ex. Basque (361)	1,123	2.30
French Canadian (41)	42	0.09
German (4,692)	9,750	19.93
German Russian (0)	0	<0.01
Greek (154)	171	0.35
Guyanese (0)	0	<0.01
Hungarian (55)	102	0.21
Icelander (0)	0	<0.01
Iranian (0)	0	<0.01
Irish (2,011)	5,789	11.83
Israeli (0)	0	<0.01
Italian (255)	583	1.19
Latvian (0)	0	<0.01
Lithuanian (0)	2	<0.01
Luxemburger (0)	0	<0.01
Macedonian (0)	0	<0.01
Maltese (0)	0	<0.01
New Zealander (0)	0	<0.01
Northern European (88)	88	0.18
Norwegian (27)	155	0.32
Pennsylvania German (55)	55	0.11
Polish (145)	326	0.67
Portuguese (35)	44	0.09
Romanian (0)	10	0.02
Russian (8)	38	0.08
Scandinavian (18)	96	0.20
Scotch-Irish (356)	542	1.11
Scottish (384)	884	1.81
Serbian (0)	0	<0.01
Slavic (0)	0	<0.01
Slovak (0)	19	0.04
Slovene (0)	0	<0.01
Soviet Union (0)	0	<0.01
Swedish (60)	119	0.24
Swiss (57)	128	0.26
Turkish (0)	0	<0.01
Ukrainian (0)	0	<0.01
Welsh (28)	141	0.29
West Indian, ex. Hispanic (18)	29	0.06
Bahamian (0)	0	<0.01
Barbadian (0)	0	<0.01
Belizean (0)	0	<0.01
Bermudan (0)	0	<0.01
British West Indian (0)	0	<0.01
Dutch West Indian (0)	11	0.02
Haitian (0)	0	<0.01
Jamaican (0)	0	<0.01
Trinidadian/Tobagonian (0)	0	<0.01
U.S. Virgin Islander (0)	0	<0.01
West Indian (18)	18	0.04
Other West Indian (0)	0	<0.01
Yugoslavian (4)	4	0.01

Hispanic Origin	Population	%
Hispanic or Latino (of any race)	691	1.40
Central American, ex. Mexican	24	0.05
Costa Rican	0	<0.01
Guatemalan	5	0.01
Honduran	6	0.01
Nicaraguan	1	<0.01
Panamanian	2	<0.01
Salvadoran	10	0.02
Other Central American	0	<0.01
Cuban	39	0.08
Dominican Republic	2	<0.01
Mexican	474	0.96
Puerto Rican	45	0.09
South American	14	0.03
Argentinean	0	<0.01
Bolivian	0	<0.01
Chilean	1	<0.01
Colombian	6	0.01
Ecuadorian	0	<0.01
Paraguayan	0	<0.01
Peruvian	4	0.01
Uruguayan	0	<0.01
Venezuelan	3	0.01
Other South American	0	<0.01
Other Hispanic or Latino	93	0.19

Race*	Population	%
African-American/Black (1,070)	1,326	2.68
Not Hispanic (1,064)	1,295	2.62
Hispanic (6)	31	0.06
American Indian/Alaska Native (72)	310	0.63
Not Hispanic (63)	285	0.58
Hispanic (9)	25	0.05
Alaska Athabascan *(Ala. Nat.)* (0)	0	<0.01
Aleut *(Alaska Native)* (0)	0	<0.01
Apache (0)	4	0.01
Arapaho (0)	0	<0.01
Blackfeet (6)	19	0.04
Canadian/French Am. Ind. (1)	2	<0.01
Central American Ind. (0)	0	<0.01
Cherokee (12)	89	0.18
Cheyenne (0)	0	<0.01
Chickasaw (0)	0	<0.01
Chippewa (2)	5	0.01
Choctaw (1)	4	0.01
Colville (0)	0	<0.01
Comanche (0)	0	<0.01
Cree (0)	0	<0.01
Creek (2)	2	<0.01
Crow (0)	0	<0.01
Delaware (0)	0	<0.01
Hopi (1)	2	<0.01
Houma (0)	0	<0.01
Inupiat *(Alaska Native)* (0)	0	<0.01
Iroquois (0)	0	<0.01
Kiowa (0)	0	<0.01
Lumbee (0)	0	<0.01
Menominee (0)	0	<0.01
Mexican American Ind. (2)	2	<0.01
Navajo (1)	1	<0.01
Osage (0)	0	<0.01
Ottawa (0)	1	<0.01
Paiute (0)	0	<0.01
Pima (0)	0	<0.01
Potawatomi (0)	0	<0.01
Pueblo (0)	0	<0.01
Puget Sound Salish (0)	0	<0.01
Seminole (0)	2	<0.01
Shoshone (0)	0	<0.01
Sioux (2)	6	0.01
South American Ind. (1)	1	<0.01
Spanish American Ind. (0)	0	<0.01
Tlingit-Haida *(Alaska Native)* (0)	0	<0.01
Tohono O'Odham (0)	0	<0.01
Tsimshian *(Alaska Native)* (0)	0	<0.01
Ute (1)	1	<0.01
Yakama (0)	0	<0.01
Yaqui (0)	0	<0.01
Yuman (0)	0	<0.01
Yup'ik *(Alaska Native)* (0)	0	<0.01
Asian (156)	255	0.52
Not Hispanic (154)	248	0.50
Hispanic (2)	7	0.01
Bangladeshi (0)	0	<0.01
Bhutanese (0)	0	<0.01
Burmese (0)	0	<0.01
Cambodian (0)	0	<0.01
Chinese, ex. Taiwanese (31)	50	0.10
Filipino (18)	53	0.11
Hmong (0)	0	<0.01
Indian (42)	53	0.11
Indonesian (3)	3	0.01
Japanese (15)	31	0.06
Korean (13)	22	0.04
Laotian (0)	1	<0.01
Malaysian (2)	5	0.01
Nepalese (0)	0	<0.01
Pakistani (3)	3	0.01
Sri Lankan (0)	0	<0.01
Taiwanese (0)	0	<0.01
Thai (4)	4	0.01
Vietnamese (18)	22	0.04
Hawaii Native/Pacific Islander (5)	26	0.05
Not Hispanic (5)	24	0.05
Hispanic (0)	2	<0.01
Fijian (0)	0	<0.01
Guamanian/Chamorro (1)	1	<0.01
Marshallese (0)	0	<0.01
Native Hawaiian (3)	18	0.04
Samoan (0)	6	0.01
Tongan (0)	0	<0.01
White (47,351)	47,916	96.87
Not Hispanic (46,933)	47,429	95.89
Hispanic (418)	487	0.98

*Notes: † The Census 2010 population figure is used to calculate the percentages in the Hispanic Origin and Race categories. Ancestry percentages are based on the 2006-2010 American Community Survey population (not shown); ‡ Numbers in parentheses indicate the number of people reporting a single ancestry; * Numbers in parentheses indicate the number of persons reporting this race alone, not in combination with any other race; Please refer to the Explanation of Data for more information.*

Howard County

Population: 82,752

Ancestry	Population	%
Afghan (0)	0	<0.01
African, Sub-Saharan (90)	326	0.39
African (90)	326	0.39
Cape Verdean (0)	0	<0.01
Ethiopian (0)	0	<0.01
Ghanaian (0)	0	<0.01
Kenyan (0)	0	<0.01
Liberian (0)	0	<0.01
Nigerian (0)	0	<0.01
Senegalese (0)	0	<0.01
Sierra Leonean (0)	0	<0.01
Somalian (0)	0	<0.01
South African (0)	0	<0.01
Sudanese (0)	0	<0.01
Ugandan (0)	0	<0.01
Zimbabwean (0)	0	<0.01
Other Sub-Saharan African (0)	0	<0.01
Albanian (0)	11	0.01
Alsatian (5)	5	0.01
American (12,747)	12,747	15.30
Arab (36)	98	0.12
Arab (0)	25	0.03
Egyptian (0)	0	<0.01
Iraqi (0)	0	<0.01
Jordanian (0)	0	<0.01
Lebanese (24)	52	0.06
Moroccan (0)	0	<0.01
Palestinian (12)	12	0.01
Syrian (0)	9	0.01
Other Arab (0)	0	<0.01
Armenian (0)	0	<0.01
Assyrian/Chaldean/Syriac (0)	0	<0.01
Australian (10)	17	0.02
Austrian (15)	65	0.08
Basque (0)	0	<0.01
Belgian (0)	73	0.09
Brazilian (9)	9	0.01
British (189)	335	0.40
Bulgarian (0)	0	<0.01
Cajun (0)	18	0.02
Canadian (24)	74	0.09
Carpatho Rusyn (0)	0	<0.01
Celtic (0)	0	<0.01
Croatian (0)	7	0.01
Cypriot (0)	0	<0.01
Czech (57)	123	0.15
Czechoslovakian (13)	47	0.06
Danish (13)	58	0.07
Dutch (268)	1,877	2.25
Eastern European (0)	0	<0.01
English (4,070)	8,975	10.77
Estonian (0)	0	<0.01
European (529)	663	0.80
Finnish (0)	59	0.07
French, ex. Basque (360)	1,675	2.01
French Canadian (116)	442	0.53
German (7,665)	18,627	22.35
German Russian (0)	0	<0.01
Greek (210)	328	0.39
Guyanese (37)	37	0.04
Hungarian (114)	273	0.33
Icelander (0)	13	0.02
Iranian (0)	0	<0.01
Irish (2,507)	8,466	10.16
Israeli (0)	0	<0.01
Italian (733)	1,872	2.25
Latvian (0)	0	<0.01
Lithuanian (45)	74	0.09
Luxemburger (0)	0	<0.01
Macedonian (0)	0	<0.01
Maltese (0)	0	<0.01
New Zealander (0)	0	<0.01
Northern European (34)	34	0.04
Norwegian (288)	608	0.73
Pennsylvania German (68)	99	0.12
Polish (623)	1,589	1.91
Portuguese (22)	75	0.09
Romanian (122)	224	0.27
Russian (64)	92	0.11
Scandinavian (7)	42	0.05
Scotch-Irish (555)	1,130	1.36
Scottish (392)	1,270	1.52
Serbian (0)	21	0.03
Slavic (0)	0	<0.01
Slovak (40)	115	0.14
Slovene (8)	8	0.01
Soviet Union (0)	0	<0.01
Swedish (210)	793	0.95
Swiss (76)	293	0.35
Turkish (0)	0	<0.01
Ukrainian (47)	70	0.08
Welsh (72)	459	0.55
West Indian, ex. Hispanic (10)	21	0.03
Bahamian (0)	0	<0.01
Barbadian (0)	0	<0.01
Belizean (0)	0	<0.01
Bermudan (0)	0	<0.01
British West Indian (10)	10	0.01
Dutch West Indian (0)	0	<0.01
Haitian (0)	0	<0.01
Jamaican (0)	11	0.01
Trinidadian/Tobagonian (0)	0	<0.01
U.S. Virgin Islander (0)	0	<0.01
West Indian (0)	0	<0.01
Other West Indian (0)	0	<0.01
Yugoslavian (40)	40	0.05

Hispanic Origin	Population	%
Hispanic or Latino (of any race)	2,203	2.66
Central American, ex. Mexican	66	0.08
Costa Rican	4	<0.01
Guatemalan	21	0.03
Honduran	17	0.02
Nicaraguan	2	<0.01
Panamanian	8	0.01
Salvadoran	14	0.02
Other Central American	0	<0.01
Cuban	31	0.04
Dominican Republic	2	<0.01
Mexican	1,552	1.88
Puerto Rican	212	0.26
South American	53	0.06
Argentinean	0	<0.01
Bolivian	3	<0.01
Chilean	14	0.02
Colombian	20	0.02
Ecuadorian	1	<0.01
Paraguayan	0	<0.01
Peruvian	5	0.01
Uruguayan	0	<0.01
Venezuelan	9	0.01
Other South American	1	<0.01
Other Hispanic or Latino	287	0.35

Race*	Population	%
African-American/Black (5,680)	6,891	8.33
Not Hispanic (5,585)	6,701	8.10
Hispanic (95)	190	0.23
American Indian/Alaska Native (286)	782	0.94
Not Hispanic (246)	692	0.84
Hispanic (40)	90	0.11
Alaska Athabascan *(Ala. Nat.)* (0)	0	<0.01
Aleut *(Alaska Native)* (0)	0	<0.01
Apache (2)	8	0.01
Arapaho (1)	1	<0.01
Blackfeet (10)	24	0.03
Canadian/French Am. Ind. (0)	1	<0.01
Central American Ind. (0)	0	<0.01
Cherokee (55)	227	0.27
Cheyenne (0)	0	<0.01
Chickasaw (0)	0	<0.01
Chippewa (16)	30	0.04
Choctaw (9)	17	0.02
Colville (2)	2	<0.01
Comanche (0)	2	<0.01
Cree (0)	7	0.01
Creek (4)	6	0.01
Crow (1)	1	<0.01
Delaware (0)	0	<0.01
Hopi (1)	2	<0.01
Houma (0)	0	<0.01
Inupiat *(Alaska Native)* (0)	3	<0.01
Iroquois (4)	8	0.01
Kiowa (0)	0	<0.01
Lumbee (0)	3	<0.01
Menominee (0)	0	<0.01
Mexican American Ind. (8)	18	0.02
Navajo (1)	5	0.01
Osage (1)	4	<0.01
Ottawa (0)	0	<0.01
Paiute (1)	1	<0.01
Pima (0)	0	<0.01
Potawatomi (1)	3	<0.01
Pueblo (0)	2	<0.01
Puget Sound Salish (0)	0	<0.01
Seminole (0)	3	<0.01
Shoshone (4)	4	<0.01
Sioux (10)	26	0.03
South American Ind. (2)	2	<0.01
Spanish American Ind. (2)	2	<0.01
Tlingit-Haida *(Alaska Native)* (1)	1	<0.01
Tohono O'Odham (0)	0	<0.01
Tsimshian *(Alaska Native)* (0)	0	<0.01
Ute (0)	1	<0.01
Yakama (0)	0	<0.01
Yaqui (0)	0	<0.01
Yuman (0)	0	<0.01
Yup'ik *(Alaska Native)* (0)	0	<0.01
Asian (740)	1,020	1.23
Not Hispanic (737)	992	1.20
Hispanic (3)	28	0.03
Bangladeshi (5)	5	0.01
Bhutanese (0)	0	<0.01
Burmese (0)	0	<0.01
Cambodian (0)	0	<0.01
Chinese, ex. Taiwanese (176)	217	0.26
Filipino (149)	205	0.25
Hmong (5)	5	0.01
Indian (156)	196	0.24
Indonesian (0)	3	<0.01
Japanese (22)	78	0.09
Korean (51)	103	0.12
Laotian (0)	0	<0.01
Malaysian (1)	4	<0.01
Nepalese (1)	1	<0.01
Pakistani (16)	17	0.02
Sri Lankan (8)	8	0.01
Taiwanese (7)	14	0.02
Thai (11)	19	0.02
Vietnamese (105)	123	0.15
Hawaii Native/Pacific Islander (20)	70	0.08
Not Hispanic (13)	59	0.07
Hispanic (7)	11	0.01
Fijian (0)	0	<0.01
Guamanian/Chamorro (8)	10	0.01
Marshallese (0)	0	<0.01
Native Hawaiian (6)	29	0.04
Samoan (5)	18	0.02
Tongan (0)	0	<0.01
White (73,284)	75,188	90.86
Not Hispanic (72,091)	73,744	89.11
Hispanic (1,193)	1,444	1.74

*Notes: † The Census 2010 population figure is used to calculate the percentages in the Hispanic Origin and Race categories. Ancestry percentages are based on the 2006-2010 American Community Survey population (not shown); ‡ Numbers in parentheses indicate the number of people reporting a single ancestry; * Numbers in parentheses indicate the number of persons reporting this race alone, not in combination with any other race; Please refer to the Explanation of Data for more information.*

Huntington County

Population: 37,124

Ancestry	Population	%
Afghan (0)	0	<0.01
African, Sub-Saharan (0)	0	<0.01
African (0)	0	<0.01
Cape Verdean (0)	0	<0.01
Ethiopian (0)	0	<0.01
Ghanaian (0)	0	<0.01
Kenyan (0)	0	<0.01
Liberian (0)	0	<0.01
Nigerian (0)	0	<0.01
Senegalese (0)	0	<0.01
Sierra Leonean (0)	0	<0.01
Somalian (0)	0	<0.01
South African (0)	0	<0.01
Sudanese (0)	0	<0.01
Ugandan (0)	0	<0.01
Zimbabwean (0)	0	<0.01
Other Sub-Saharan African (0)	0	<0.01
Albanian (0)	0	<0.01
Alsatian (0)	0	<0.01
American (4,815)	4,815	12.90
Arab (20)	20	0.05
Arab (0)	0	<0.01
Egyptian (11)	11	0.03
Iraqi (0)	0	<0.01
Jordanian (0)	0	<0.01
Lebanese (9)	9	0.02
Moroccan (0)	0	<0.01
Palestinian (0)	0	<0.01
Syrian (0)	0	<0.01
Other Arab (0)	0	<0.01
Armenian (0)	0	<0.01
Assyrian/Chaldean/Syriac (0)	0	<0.01
Australian (0)	0	<0.01
Austrian (3)	19	0.05
Basque (0)	0	<0.01
Belgian (102)	126	0.34
Brazilian (0)	0	<0.01
British (38)	109	0.29
Bulgarian (0)	0	<0.01
Cajun (0)	0	<0.01
Canadian (45)	50	0.13
Carpatho Rusyn (0)	0	<0.01
Celtic (0)	0	<0.01
Croatian (15)	25	0.07
Cypriot (0)	0	<0.01
Czech (25)	105	0.28
Czechoslovakian (11)	41	0.11
Danish (11)	86	0.23
Dutch (272)	936	2.51
Eastern European (0)	0	<0.01
English (1,986)	4,525	12.12
Estonian (0)	0	<0.01
European (310)	316	0.85
Finnish (0)	8	0.02
French, ex. Basque (272)	1,299	3.48
French Canadian (55)	153	0.41
German (6,921)	14,143	37.90
German Russian (0)	0	<0.01
Greek (32)	53	0.14
Guyanese (0)	0	<0.01
Hungarian (3)	42	0.11
Icelander (0)	0	<0.01
Iranian (0)	0	<0.01
Irish (1,416)	5,560	14.90
Israeli (0)	0	<0.01
Italian (250)	745	2.00
Latvian (0)	0	<0.01
Lithuanian (11)	93	0.25
Luxemburger (0)	0	<0.01
Macedonian (0)	0	<0.01
Maltese (0)	8	0.02
New Zealander (0)	0	<0.01
Northern European (0)	0	<0.01
Norwegian (121)	298	0.80
Pennsylvania German (13)	23	0.06
Polish (158)	664	1.78
Portuguese (0)	0	<0.01
Romanian (0)	13	0.03
Russian (9)	72	0.19
Scandinavian (29)	33	0.09
Scotch-Irish (150)	395	1.06
Scottish (221)	646	1.73
Serbian (0)	0	<0.01
Slavic (0)	0	<0.01
Slovak (8)	27	0.07
Slovene (0)	0	<0.01
Soviet Union (0)	0	<0.01
Swedish (134)	376	1.01
Swiss (64)	238	0.64
Turkish (0)	13	0.03
Ukrainian (31)	62	0.17
Welsh (50)	192	0.51
West Indian, ex. Hispanic (0)	0	<0.01
Bahamian (0)	0	<0.01
Barbadian (0)	0	<0.01
Belizean (0)	0	<0.01
Bermudan (0)	0	<0.01
British West Indian (0)	0	<0.01
Dutch West Indian (0)	0	<0.01
Haitian (0)	0	<0.01
Jamaican (0)	0	<0.01
Trinidadian/Tobagonian (0)	0	<0.01
U.S. Virgin Islander (0)	0	<0.01
West Indian (0)	0	<0.01
Other West Indian (0)	0	<0.01
Yugoslavian (5)	5	0.01

Hispanic Origin	Population	%
Hispanic or Latino (of any race)	631	1.70
Central American, ex. Mexican	30	0.08
Costa Rican	0	<0.01
Guatemalan	19	0.05
Honduran	5	0.01
Nicaraguan	0	<0.01
Panamanian	1	<0.01
Salvadoran	5	0.01
Other Central American	0	<0.01
Cuban	7	0.02
Dominican Republic	1	<0.01
Mexican	455	1.23
Puerto Rican	46	0.12
South American	13	0.04
Argentinean	1	<0.01
Bolivian	0	<0.01
Chilean	4	0.01
Colombian	2	0.01
Ecuadorian	3	0.01
Paraguayan	0	<0.01
Peruvian	2	0.01
Uruguayan	0	<0.01
Venezuelan	1	<0.01
Other South American	0	<0.01
Other Hispanic or Latino	79	0.21

Race*	Population	%
African-American/Black (160)	295	0.79
Not Hispanic (155)	286	0.77
Hispanic (5)	9	0.02
American Indian/Alaska Native (140)	291	0.78
Not Hispanic (124)	257	0.69
Hispanic (16)	34	0.09
Alaska Athabascan *(Ala. Nat.)* (0)	0	<0.01
Aleut *(Alaska Native)* (0)	0	<0.01
Apache (3)	5	0.01
Arapaho (0)	0	<0.01
Blackfeet (1)	8	0.02
Canadian/French Am. Ind. (0)	0	<0.01
Central American Ind. (1)	1	<0.01
Cherokee (30)	64	0.17
Cheyenne (0)	0	<0.01
Chickasaw (0)	0	<0.01
Chippewa (1)	2	0.01
Choctaw (0)	0	<0.01
Colville (0)	0	<0.01
Comanche (0)	0	<0.01
Cree (0)	0	<0.01
Creek (1)	1	<0.01
Crow (0)	1	<0.01
Delaware (3)	3	0.01
Hopi (0)	0	<0.01
Houma (0)	0	<0.01
Inupiat *(Alaska Native)* (0)	0	<0.01
Iroquois (0)	1	<0.01
Kiowa (0)	0	<0.01
Lumbee (0)	1	<0.01
Menominee (0)	0	<0.01
Mexican American Ind. (5)	5	0.01
Navajo (0)	1	<0.01
Osage (0)	3	0.01
Ottawa (4)	6	0.02
Paiute (0)	0	<0.01
Pima (0)	0	<0.01
Potawatomi (1)	1	<0.01
Pueblo (5)	5	0.01
Puget Sound Salish (3)	3	0.01
Seminole (0)	0	<0.01
Shoshone (0)	0	<0.01
Sioux (2)	4	0.01
South American Ind. (0)	0	<0.01
Spanish American Ind. (0)	1	<0.01
Tlingit-Haida *(Alaska Native)* (0)	0	<0.01
Tohono O'Odham (0)	0	<0.01
Tsimshian *(Alaska Native)* (0)	0	<0.01
Ute (0)	0	<0.01
Yakama (0)	0	<0.01
Yaqui (0)	0	<0.01
Yuman (0)	0	<0.01
Yup'ik *(Alaska Native)* (0)	0	<0.01
Asian (167)	243	0.65
Not Hispanic (167)	234	0.63
Hispanic (0)	9	0.02
Bangladeshi (0)	0	<0.01
Bhutanese (0)	0	<0.01
Burmese (2)	2	0.01
Cambodian (9)	9	0.02
Chinese, ex. Taiwanese (40)	51	0.14
Filipino (19)	36	0.10
Hmong (0)	0	<0.01
Indian (43)	49	0.13
Indonesian (0)	0	<0.01
Japanese (16)	31	0.08
Korean (21)	43	0.12
Laotian (0)	0	<0.01
Malaysian (1)	2	0.01
Nepalese (0)	0	<0.01
Pakistani (0)	1	<0.01
Sri Lankan (0)	0	<0.01
Taiwanese (1)	3	0.01
Thai (1)	5	0.01
Vietnamese (3)	6	0.02
Hawaii Native/Pacific Islander (8)	18	0.05
Not Hispanic (6)	15	0.04
Hispanic (2)	3	0.01
Fijian (0)	0	<0.01
Guamanian/Chamorro (4)	6	0.02
Marshallese (0)	0	<0.01
Native Hawaiian (1)	6	0.02
Samoan (1)	2	0.01
Tongan (0)	0	<0.01
White (36,062)	36,463	98.22
Not Hispanic (35,692)	36,016	97.02
Hispanic (370)	447	1.20

*Notes: † The Census 2010 population figure is used to calculate the percentages in the Hispanic Origin and Race categories. Ancestry percentages are based on the 2006-2010 American Community Survey population (not shown); ‡ Numbers in parentheses indicate the number of people reporting a single ancestry; * Numbers in parentheses indicate the number of persons reporting this race alone, not in combination with any other race; Please refer to the Explanation of Data for more information.*

Jackson County

Population: 42,376

Ancestry	Population	%
Afghan (0)	0	<0.01
African, Sub-Saharan (0)	0	<0.01
African (0)	0	<0.01
Cape Verdean (0)	0	<0.01
Ethiopian (0)	0	<0.01
Ghanaian (0)	0	<0.01
Kenyan (0)	0	<0.01
Liberian (0)	0	<0.01
Nigerian (0)	0	<0.01
Senegalese (0)	0	<0.01
Sierra Leonean (0)	0	<0.01
Somalian (0)	0	<0.01
South African (0)	0	<0.01
Sudanese (0)	0	<0.01
Ugandan (0)	0	<0.01
Zimbabwean (0)	0	<0.01
Other Sub-Saharan African (0)	0	<0.01
Albanian (0)	0	<0.01
Alsatian (0)	0	<0.01
American (5,488)	5,488	13.10
Arab (0)	47	0.11
Arab (0)	0	<0.01
Egyptian (0)	42	0.10
Iraqi (0)	0	<0.01
Jordanian (0)	0	<0.01
Lebanese (0)	5	0.01
Moroccan (0)	0	<0.01
Palestinian (0)	0	<0.01
Syrian (0)	0	<0.01
Other Arab (0)	0	<0.01
Armenian (3)	3	0.01
Assyrian/Chaldean/Syriac (0)	0	<0.01
Australian (0)	9	0.02
Austrian (0)	11	0.03
Basque (0)	0	<0.01
Belgian (0)	4	0.01
Brazilian (0)	0	<0.01
British (19)	75	0.18
Bulgarian (0)	0	<0.01
Cajun (15)	15	0.04
Canadian (0)	0	<0.01
Carpatho Rusyn (0)	0	<0.01
Celtic (0)	0	<0.01
Croatian (0)	0	<0.01
Cypriot (0)	0	<0.01
Czech (0)	0	<0.01
Czechoslovakian (78)	78	0.19
Danish (141)	141	0.34
Dutch (96)	923	2.20
Eastern European (0)	3	0.01
English (1,647)	3,842	9.17
Estonian (0)	0	<0.01
European (180)	186	0.44
Finnish (0)	19	0.05
French, ex. Basque (206)	946	2.26
French Canadian (62)	131	0.31
German (6,586)	12,053	28.76
German Russian (0)	0	<0.01
Greek (69)	91	0.22
Guyanese (0)	0	<0.01
Hungarian (9)	21	0.05
Icelander (0)	0	<0.01
Iranian (0)	0	<0.01
Irish (1,075)	5,351	12.77
Israeli (0)	0	<0.01
Italian (224)	507	1.21
Latvian (0)	0	<0.01
Lithuanian (0)	0	<0.01
Luxemburger (0)	0	<0.01
Macedonian (0)	0	<0.01
Maltese (0)	0	<0.01
New Zealander (0)	0	<0.01
Northern European (0)	0	<0.01
Norwegian (18)	95	0.23
Pennsylvania German (0)	0	<0.01

Polish (34)	205	0.49
Portuguese (0)	66	0.16
Romanian (0)	0	<0.01
Russian (0)	11	0.03
Scandinavian (0)	23	0.05
Scotch-Irish (192)	551	1.31
Scottish (551)	959	2.29
Serbian (0)	9	0.02
Slavic (0)	0	<0.01
Slovak (0)	26	0.06
Slovene (0)	0	<0.01
Soviet Union (0)	0	<0.01
Swedish (76)	122	0.29
Swiss (12)	17	0.04
Turkish (33)	62	0.15
Ukrainian (0)	26	0.06
Welsh (47)	245	0.58
West Indian, ex. Hispanic (0)	0	<0.01
Bahamian (0)	0	<0.01
Barbadian (0)	0	<0.01
Belizean (0)	0	<0.01
Bermudan (0)	0	<0.01
British West Indian (0)	0	<0.01
Dutch West Indian (0)	0	<0.01
Haitian (0)	0	<0.01
Jamaican (0)	0	<0.01
Trinidadian/Tobagonian (0)	0	<0.01
U.S. Virgin Islander (0)	0	<0.01
West Indian (0)	0	<0.01
Other West Indian (0)	0	<0.01
Yugoslavian (0)	6	0.01

Hispanic Origin	Population	%
Hispanic or Latino (of any race)	2,410	5.69
Central American, ex. Mexican	127	0.30
Costa Rican	2	<0.01
Guatemalan	41	0.10
Honduran	52	0.12
Nicaraguan	6	0.01
Panamanian	18	0.04
Salvadoran	8	0.02
Other Central American	0	<0.01
Cuban	7	0.02
Dominican Republic	3	0.01
Mexican	1,942	4.58
Puerto Rican	79	0.19
South American	11	0.03
Argentinean	0	<0.01
Bolivian	0	<0.01
Chilean	2	<0.01
Colombian	1	<0.01
Ecuadorian	5	0.01
Paraguayan	0	<0.01
Peruvian	1	<0.01
Uruguayan	0	<0.01
Venezuelan	2	<0.01
Other South American	0	<0.01
Other Hispanic or Latino	241	0.57

Race*	Population	%
African-American/Black (282)	439	1.04
Not Hispanic (265)	410	0.97
Hispanic (17)	29	0.07
American Indian/Alaska Native (89)	295	0.70
Not Hispanic (82)	265	0.63
Hispanic (7)	30	0.07
Alaska Athabascan *(Ala. Nat.)* (0)	0	<0.01
Aleut *(Alaska Native)* (0)	0	<0.01
Apache (1)	2	<0.01
Arapaho (0)	0	<0.01
Blackfeet (5)	11	0.03
Canadian/French Am. Ind. (0)	0	<0.01
Central American Ind. (1)	4	0.01
Cherokee (27)	118	0.28
Cheyenne (1)	1	<0.01
Chickasaw (0)	0	<0.01
Chippewa (2)	3	0.01
Choctaw (3)	9	0.02
Colville (0)	0	<0.01
Comanche (0)	1	<0.01
Cree (0)	0	<0.01
Creek (1)	1	<0.01
Crow (0)	1	<0.01
Delaware (0)	0	<0.01
Hopi (0)	0	<0.01
Houma (0)	0	<0.01
Inupiat *(Alaska Native)* (0)	4	0.01
Iroquois (1)	2	<0.01
Kiowa (0)	1	<0.01
Lumbee (0)	0	<0.01
Menominee (0)	0	<0.01
Mexican American Ind. (0)	1	<0.01
Navajo (0)	0	<0.01
Osage (0)	0	<0.01
Ottawa (0)	0	<0.01
Paiute (0)	0	<0.01
Pima (0)	0	<0.01
Potawatomi (1)	1	<0.01
Pueblo (0)	0	<0.01
Puget Sound Salish (0)	0	<0.01
Seminole (0)	0	<0.01
Shoshone (0)	0	<0.01
Sioux (4)	7	0.02
South American Ind. (0)	0	<0.01
Spanish American Ind. (0)	0	<0.01
Tlingit-Haida *(Alaska Native)* (0)	0	<0.01
Tohono O'Odham (0)	0	<0.01
Tsimshian *(Alaska Native)* (0)	0	<0.01
Ute (0)	0	<0.01
Yakama (0)	0	<0.01
Yaqui (0)	0	<0.01
Yuman (0)	0	<0.01
Yup'ik *(Alaska Native)* (0)	0	<0.01
Asian (359)	427	1.01
Not Hispanic (356)	420	0.99
Hispanic (3)	7	0.02
Bangladeshi (0)	0	<0.01
Bhutanese (0)	0	<0.01
Burmese (0)	0	<0.01
Cambodian (0)	0	<0.01
Chinese, ex. Taiwanese (33)	36	0.08
Filipino (52)	81	0.19
Hmong (1)	3	0.01
Indian (50)	58	0.14
Indonesian (3)	8	0.02
Japanese (145)	158	0.37
Korean (16)	23	0.05
Laotian (0)	0	<0.01
Malaysian (1)	1	<0.01
Nepalese (1)	1	<0.01
Pakistani (10)	11	0.03
Sri Lankan (0)	0	<0.01
Taiwanese (0)	0	<0.01
Thai (6)	6	0.01
Vietnamese (35)	40	0.09
Hawaii Native/Pacific Islander (27)	47	0.11
Not Hispanic (18)	35	0.08
Hispanic (9)	12	0.03
Fijian (0)	0	<0.01
Guamanian/Chamorro (16)	20	0.05
Marshallese (0)	0	<0.01
Native Hawaiian (11)	21	0.05
Samoan (0)	1	<0.01
Tongan (0)	0	<0.01
White (40,044)	40,573	95.75
Not Hispanic (38,826)	39,210	92.53
Hispanic (1,218)	1,363	3.22

*Notes: † The Census 2010 population figure is used to calculate the percentages in the Hispanic Origin and Race categories. Ancestry percentages are based on the 2006-2010 American Community Survey population (not shown); ‡ Numbers in parentheses indicate the number of people reporting a single ancestry; * Numbers in parentheses indicate the number of persons reporting this race alone, not in combination with any other race; Please refer to the Explanation of Data for more information.*

Jasper County

Population: 33,478

Ancestry	Population	%
Afghan (0)	0	<0.01
African, Sub-Saharan (16)	16	0.05
African (16)	16	0.05
Cape Verdean (0)	0	<0.01
Ethiopian (0)	0	<0.01
Ghanaian (0)	0	<0.01
Kenyan (0)	0	<0.01
Liberian (0)	0	<0.01
Nigerian (0)	0	<0.01
Senegalese (0)	0	<0.01
Sierra Leonean (0)	0	<0.01
Somalian (0)	0	<0.01
South African (0)	0	<0.01
Sudanese (0)	0	<0.01
Ugandan (0)	0	<0.01
Zimbabwean (0)	0	<0.01
Other Sub-Saharan African (0)	0	<0.01
Albanian (0)	0	<0.01
Alsatian (0)	0	<0.01
American (2,281)	2,281	6.90
Arab (0)	0	<0.01
Arab (0)	0	<0.01
Egyptian (0)	0	<0.01
Iraqi (0)	0	<0.01
Jordanian (0)	0	<0.01
Lebanese (0)	0	<0.01
Moroccan (0)	0	<0.01
Palestinian (0)	0	<0.01
Syrian (0)	0	<0.01
Other Arab (0)	0	<0.01
Armenian (0)	0	<0.01
Assyrian/Chaldean/Syriac (0)	7	0.02
Australian (0)	0	<0.01
Austrian (21)	40	0.12
Basque (0)	0	<0.01
Belgian (0)	16	0.05
Brazilian (0)	0	<0.01
British (28)	50	0.15
Bulgarian (0)	0	<0.01
Cajun (0)	0	<0.01
Canadian (9)	9	0.03
Carpatho Rusyn (0)	0	<0.01
Celtic (0)	0	<0.01
Croatian (36)	171	0.52
Cypriot (0)	0	<0.01
Czech (103)	225	0.68
Czechoslovakian (0)	77	0.23
Danish (0)	48	0.15
Dutch (1,680)	3,174	9.60
Eastern European (11)	11	0.03
English (799)	3,076	9.31
Estonian (0)	0	<0.01
European (208)	305	0.92
Finnish (0)	70	0.21
French, ex. Basque (187)	916	2.77
French Canadian (35)	132	0.40
German (2,624)	9,110	27.56
German Russian (0)	0	<0.01
Greek (100)	151	0.46
Guyanese (0)	0	<0.01
Hungarian (97)	365	1.10
Icelander (0)	0	<0.01
Iranian (0)	0	<0.01
Irish (1,233)	5,461	16.52
Israeli (0)	0	<0.01
Italian (156)	813	2.46
Latvian (0)	0	<0.01
Lithuanian (43)	120	0.36
Luxemburger (0)	0	<0.01
Macedonian (5)	5	0.02
Maltese (0)	0	<0.01
New Zealander (0)	0	<0.01
Northern European (0)	0	<0.01
Norwegian (74)	247	0.75
Pennsylvania German (13)	34	0.10
Polish (774)	1,994	6.03
Portuguese (0)	14	0.04
Romanian (23)	98	0.30
Russian (27)	108	0.33
Scandinavian (23)	50	0.15
Scotch-Irish (197)	538	1.63
Scottish (233)	731	2.21
Serbian (94)	260	0.79
Slavic (0)	10	0.03
Slovak (46)	255	0.77
Slovene (0)	16	0.05
Soviet Union (0)	0	<0.01
Swedish (108)	618	1.87
Swiss (4)	68	0.21
Turkish (0)	0	<0.01
Ukrainian (49)	62	0.19
Welsh (20)	191	0.58
West Indian, ex. Hispanic (0)	0	<0.01
Bahamian (0)	0	<0.01
Barbadian (0)	0	<0.01
Belizean (0)	0	<0.01
Bermudan (0)	0	<0.01
British West Indian (0)	0	<0.01
Dutch West Indian (0)	0	<0.01
Haitian (0)	0	<0.01
Jamaican (0)	0	<0.01
Trinidadian/Tobagonian (0)	0	<0.01
U.S. Virgin Islander (0)	0	<0.01
West Indian (0)	0	<0.01
Other West Indian (0)	0	<0.01
Yugoslavian (0)	0	<0.01

Hispanic Origin	Population	%
Hispanic or Latino (of any race)	1,823	5.45
Central American, ex. Mexican	60	0.18
Costa Rican	4	0.01
Guatemalan	15	0.04
Honduran	36	0.11
Nicaraguan	2	0.01
Panamanian	0	<0.01
Salvadoran	3	0.01
Other Central American	0	<0.01
Cuban	20	0.06
Dominican Republic	0	<0.01
Mexican	1,517	4.53
Puerto Rican	99	0.30
South American	14	0.04
Argentinean	2	0.01
Bolivian	2	0.01
Chilean	1	<0.01
Colombian	2	0.01
Ecuadorian	1	<0.01
Paraguayan	0	<0.01
Peruvian	6	0.02
Uruguayan	0	<0.01
Venezuelan	0	<0.01
Other South American	0	<0.01
Other Hispanic or Latino	113	0.34

Race*	Population	%
African-American/Black (212)	310	0.93
Not Hispanic (208)	298	0.89
Hispanic (4)	12	0.04
American Indian/Alaska Native (68)	191	0.57
Not Hispanic (53)	157	0.47
Hispanic (15)	34	0.10
Alaska Athabascan *(Ala. Nat.)* (0)	0	<0.01
Aleut *(Alaska Native)* (0)	0	<0.01
Apache (3)	9	0.03
Arapaho (0)	0	<0.01
Blackfeet (3)	6	0.02
Canadian/French Am. Ind. (0)	0	<0.01
Central American Ind. (0)	0	<0.01
Cherokee (13)	49	0.15
Cheyenne (0)	0	<0.01
Chickasaw (0)	0	<0.01
Chippewa (2)	4	0.01
Choctaw (3)	9	0.03
Colville (0)	0	<0.01
Comanche (0)	1	<0.01
Cree (0)	0	<0.01
Creek (1)	1	<0.01
Crow (0)	0	<0.01
Delaware (0)	0	<0.01
Hopi (0)	0	<0.01
Houma (0)	0	<0.01
Inupiat *(Alaska Native)* (0)	0	<0.01
Iroquois (0)	1	<0.01
Kiowa (0)	0	<0.01
Lumbee (0)	0	<0.01
Menominee (0)	0	<0.01
Mexican American Ind. (1)	2	0.01
Navajo (0)	1	<0.01
Osage (0)	0	<0.01
Ottawa (0)	0	<0.01
Paiute (0)	0	<0.01
Pima (0)	0	<0.01
Potawatomi (1)	1	<0.01
Pueblo (0)	1	<0.01
Puget Sound Salish (0)	0	<0.01
Seminole (0)	1	<0.01
Shoshone (0)	0	<0.01
Sioux (2)	5	0.01
South American Ind. (2)	2	0.01
Spanish American Ind. (0)	0	<0.01
Tlingit-Haida *(Alaska Native)* (0)	0	<0.01
Tohono O'Odham (0)	0	<0.01
Tsimshian *(Alaska Native)* (0)	0	<0.01
Ute (0)	0	<0.01
Yakama (0)	0	<0.01
Yaqui (0)	0	<0.01
Yuman (0)	0	<0.01
Yup'ik *(Alaska Native)* (0)	0	<0.01
Asian (133)	194	0.58
Not Hispanic (123)	179	0.53
Hispanic (10)	15	0.04
Bangladeshi (0)	0	<0.01
Bhutanese (0)	0	<0.01
Burmese (0)	0	<0.01
Cambodian (0)	0	<0.01
Chinese, ex. Taiwanese (23)	32	0.10
Filipino (49)	68	0.20
Hmong (0)	0	<0.01
Indian (27)	35	0.10
Indonesian (1)	3	0.01
Japanese (4)	23	0.07
Korean (12)	14	0.04
Laotian (0)	0	<0.01
Malaysian (0)	0	<0.01
Nepalese (0)	0	<0.01
Pakistani (0)	2	0.01
Sri Lankan (0)	0	<0.01
Taiwanese (0)	0	<0.01
Thai (4)	4	0.01
Vietnamese (2)	5	0.01
Hawaii Native/Pacific Islander (11)	29	0.09
Not Hispanic (9)	27	0.08
Hispanic (2)	2	0.01
Fijian (0)	0	<0.01
Guamanian/Chamorro (6)	6	0.02
Marshallese (0)	0	<0.01
Native Hawaiian (1)	12	0.04
Samoan (0)	3	0.01
Tongan (3)	4	0.01
White (32,056)	32,375	96.71
Not Hispanic (30,988)	31,235	93.30
Hispanic (1,068)	1,140	3.41

*Notes: † The Census 2010 population figure is used to calculate the percentages in the Hispanic Origin and Race categories. Ancestry percentages are based on the 2006-2010 American Community Survey population (not shown); ‡ Numbers in parentheses indicate the number of people reporting a single ancestry; * Numbers in parentheses indicate the number of persons reporting this race alone, not in combination with any other race; Please refer to the Explanation of Data for more information.*

Jay County

Population: 21,253

Ancestry	Population	%
Afghan (0)	0	<0.01
African, Sub-Saharan (0)	0	<0.01
African (0)	0	<0.01
Cape Verdean (0)	0	<0.01
Ethiopian (0)	0	<0.01
Ghanaian (0)	0	<0.01
Kenyan (0)	0	<0.01
Liberian (0)	0	<0.01
Nigerian (0)	0	<0.01
Senegalese (0)	0	<0.01
Sierra Leonean (0)	0	<0.01
Somalian (0)	0	<0.01
South African (0)	0	<0.01
Sudanese (0)	0	<0.01
Ugandan (0)	0	<0.01
Zimbabwean (0)	0	<0.01
Other Sub-Saharan African (0)	0	<0.01
Albanian (0)	0	<0.01
Alsatian (17)	17	0.08
American (2,803)	2,803	13.07
Arab (0)	0	<0.01
Arab (0)	0	<0.01
Egyptian (0)	0	<0.01
Iraqi (0)	0	<0.01
Jordanian (0)	0	<0.01
Lebanese (0)	0	<0.01
Moroccan (0)	0	<0.01
Palestinian (0)	0	<0.01
Syrian (0)	0	<0.01
Other Arab (0)	0	<0.01
Armenian (0)	0	<0.01
Assyrian/Chaldean/Syriac (0)	0	<0.01
Australian (0)	0	<0.01
Austrian (0)	0	<0.01
Basque (0)	0	<0.01
Belgian (18)	133	0.62
Brazilian (0)	0	<0.01
British (3)	69	0.32
Bulgarian (0)	24	0.11
Cajun (0)	0	<0.01
Canadian (0)	0	<0.01
Carpatho Rusyn (0)	0	<0.01
Celtic (0)	0	<0.01
Croatian (0)	0	<0.01
Cypriot (0)	0	<0.01
Czech (0)	0	<0.01
Czechoslovakian (5)	5	0.02
Danish (12)	47	0.22
Dutch (68)	357	1.67
Eastern European (0)	0	<0.01
English (1,384)	2,503	11.67
Estonian (0)	0	<0.01
European (45)	49	0.23
Finnish (13)	13	0.06
French, ex. Basque (36)	289	1.35
French Canadian (92)	127	0.59
German (4,242)	7,321	34.14
German Russian (0)	0	<0.01
Greek (0)	17	0.08
Guyanese (0)	0	<0.01
Hungarian (8)	37	0.17
Icelander (0)	0	<0.01
Iranian (0)	0	<0.01
Irish (615)	2,486	11.59
Israeli (0)	0	<0.01
Italian (110)	260	1.21
Latvian (9)	9	0.04
Lithuanian (0)	0	<0.01
Luxemburger (0)	0	<0.01
Macedonian (0)	0	<0.01
Maltese (0)	0	<0.01
New Zealander (0)	0	<0.01
Northern European (0)	0	<0.01
Norwegian (22)	51	0.24
Pennsylvania German (41)	66	0.31
Polish (30)	80	0.37
Portuguese (72)	72	0.34
Romanian (0)	0	<0.01
Russian (0)	4	0.02
Scandinavian (0)	0	<0.01
Scotch-Irish (109)	156	0.73
Scottish (87)	269	1.25
Serbian (0)	0	<0.01
Slavic (0)	0	<0.01
Slovak (0)	0	<0.01
Slovene (0)	0	<0.01
Soviet Union (0)	0	<0.01
Swedish (44)	117	0.55
Swiss (152)	405	1.89
Turkish (0)	0	<0.01
Ukrainian (0)	0	<0.01
Welsh (45)	293	1.37
West Indian, ex. Hispanic (0)	0	<0.01
Bahamian (0)	0	<0.01
Barbadian (0)	0	<0.01
Belizean (0)	0	<0.01
Bermudan (0)	0	<0.01
British West Indian (0)	0	<0.01
Dutch West Indian (0)	0	<0.01
Haitian (0)	0	<0.01
Jamaican (0)	0	<0.01
Trinidadian/Tobagonian (0)	0	<0.01
U.S. Virgin Islander (0)	0	<0.01
West Indian (0)	0	<0.01
Other West Indian (0)	0	<0.01
Yugoslavian (0)	0	<0.01

Hispanic Origin	Population	%
Hispanic or Latino (of any race)	577	2.71
Central American, ex. Mexican	12	0.06
Costa Rican	1	<0.01
Guatemalan	4	0.02
Honduran	4	0.02
Nicaraguan	0	<0.01
Panamanian	2	0.01
Salvadoran	1	<0.01
Other Central American	0	<0.01
Cuban	2	0.01
Dominican Republic	0	<0.01
Mexican	503	2.37
Puerto Rican	7	0.03
South American	3	0.01
Argentinean	0	<0.01
Bolivian	0	<0.01
Chilean	0	<0.01
Colombian	2	0.01
Ecuadorian	0	<0.01
Paraguayan	1	<0.01
Peruvian	0	<0.01
Uruguayan	0	<0.01
Venezuelan	0	<0.01
Other South American	0	<0.01
Other Hispanic or Latino	50	0.24

Race*	Population	%
African-American/Black (60)	102	0.48
Not Hispanic (58)	98	0.46
Hispanic (2)	4	0.02
American Indian/Alaska Native (23)	98	0.46
Not Hispanic (21)	95	0.45
Hispanic (2)	3	0.01
Alaska Athabascan *(Ala. Nat.)* (0)	0	<0.01
Aleut *(Alaska Native)* (0)	0	<0.01
Apache (0)	0	<0.01
Arapaho (0)	0	<0.01
Blackfeet (0)	1	<0.01
Canadian/French Am. Ind. (0)	1	<0.01
Central American Ind. (2)	2	0.01
Cherokee (7)	35	0.16
Cheyenne (0)	0	<0.01
Chickasaw (0)	1	<0.01
Chippewa (0)	0	<0.01
Choctaw (1)	1	<0.01
Colville (0)	0	<0.01
Comanche (0)	0	<0.01
Cree (0)	0	<0.01
Creek (2)	2	0.01
Crow (0)	1	<0.01
Delaware (0)	0	<0.01
Hopi (0)	0	<0.01
Houma (0)	0	<0.01
Inupiat *(Alaska Native)* (0)	0	<0.01
Iroquois (0)	1	<0.01
Kiowa (0)	0	<0.01
Lumbee (0)	0	<0.01
Menominee (0)	0	<0.01
Mexican American Ind. (0)	1	<0.01
Navajo (0)	0	<0.01
Osage (0)	0	<0.01
Ottawa (0)	0	<0.01
Paiute (0)	0	<0.01
Pima (0)	0	<0.01
Potawatomi (0)	0	<0.01
Pueblo (0)	0	<0.01
Puget Sound Salish (0)	0	<0.01
Seminole (1)	1	<0.01
Shoshone (0)	0	<0.01
Sioux (1)	1	<0.01
South American Ind. (0)	1	<0.01
Spanish American Ind. (0)	0	<0.01
Tlingit-Haida *(Alaska Native)* (0)	0	<0.01
Tohono O'Odham (0)	0	<0.01
Tsimshian *(Alaska Native)* (0)	0	<0.01
Ute (0)	0	<0.01
Yakama (0)	0	<0.01
Yaqui (0)	0	<0.01
Yuman (0)	0	<0.01
Yup'ik *(Alaska Native)* (0)	0	<0.01
Asian (78)	122	0.57
Not Hispanic (77)	118	0.56
Hispanic (1)	4	0.02
Bangladeshi (0)	0	<0.01
Bhutanese (0)	0	<0.01
Burmese (0)	0	<0.01
Cambodian (4)	4	0.02
Chinese, ex. Taiwanese (5)	6	0.03
Filipino (22)	37	0.17
Hmong (0)	0	<0.01
Indian (12)	14	0.07
Indonesian (0)	0	<0.01
Japanese (27)	46	0.22
Korean (2)	6	0.03
Laotian (0)	0	<0.01
Malaysian (0)	0	<0.01
Nepalese (0)	0	<0.01
Pakistani (0)	0	<0.01
Sri Lankan (0)	0	<0.01
Taiwanese (0)	0	<0.01
Thai (2)	2	0.01
Vietnamese (3)	3	0.01
Hawaii Native/Pacific Islander (0)	8	0.04
Not Hispanic (0)	7	0.03
Hispanic (0)	1	<0.01
Fijian (0)	0	<0.01
Guamanian/Chamorro (0)	2	0.01
Marshallese (0)	0	<0.01
Native Hawaiian (0)	2	0.01
Samoan (0)	1	<0.01
Tongan (0)	0	<0.01
White (20,619)	20,804	97.89
Not Hispanic (20,356)	20,502	96.47
Hispanic (263)	302	1.42

*Notes: † The Census 2010 population figure is used to calculate the percentages in the Hispanic Origin and Race categories. Ancestry percentages are based on the 2006-2010 American Community Survey population (not shown); ‡ Numbers in parentheses indicate the number of people reporting a single ancestry; * Numbers in parentheses indicate the number of persons reporting this race alone, not in combination with any other race; Please refer to the Explanation of Data for more information.*

Jefferson County

Population: 32,428

Ancestry	Population	%
Afghan (12)	12	0.04
African, Sub-Saharan (0)	43	0.13
African (0)	43	0.13
Cape Verdean (0)	0	<0.01
Ethiopian (0)	0	<0.01
Ghanaian (0)	0	<0.01
Kenyan (0)	0	<0.01
Liberian (0)	0	<0.01
Nigerian (0)	0	<0.01
Senegalese (0)	0	<0.01
Sierra Leonean (0)	0	<0.01
Somalian (0)	0	<0.01
South African (0)	0	<0.01
Sudanese (0)	0	<0.01
Ugandan (0)	0	<0.01
Zimbabwean (0)	0	<0.01
Other Sub-Saharan African (0)	0	<0.01
Albanian (0)	0	<0.01
Alsatian (0)	0	<0.01
American (4,982)	4,982	15.38
Arab (25)	25	0.08
Arab (10)	10	0.03
Egyptian (0)	0	<0.01
Iraqi (0)	0	<0.01
Jordanian (0)	0	<0.01
Lebanese (0)	0	<0.01
Moroccan (0)	0	<0.01
Palestinian (0)	0	<0.01
Syrian (15)	15	0.05
Other Arab (0)	0	<0.01
Armenian (15)	15	0.05
Assyrian/Chaldean/Syriac (0)	0	<0.01
Australian (0)	0	<0.01
Austrian (0)	27	0.08
Basque (0)	0	<0.01
Belgian (45)	61	0.19
Brazilian (0)	0	<0.01
British (20)	123	0.38
Bulgarian (0)	0	<0.01
Cajun (0)	0	<0.01
Canadian (8)	8	0.02
Carpatho Rusyn (0)	0	<0.01
Celtic (44)	71	0.22
Croatian (7)	65	0.20
Cypriot (0)	0	<0.01
Czech (0)	11	0.03
Czechoslovakian (0)	0	<0.01
Danish (0)	92	0.28
Dutch (77)	531	1.64
Eastern European (0)	0	<0.01
English (1,900)	3,641	11.24
Estonian (0)	0	<0.01
European (259)	274	0.85
Finnish (0)	0	<0.01
French, ex. Basque (222)	871	2.69
French Canadian (57)	119	0.37
German (3,292)	7,622	23.53
German Russian (0)	0	<0.01
Greek (24)	86	0.27
Guyanese (0)	0	<0.01
Hungarian (31)	194	0.60
Icelander (0)	0	<0.01
Iranian (0)	0	<0.01
Irish (1,254)	4,191	12.94
Israeli (0)	0	<0.01
Italian (195)	621	1.92
Latvian (0)	0	<0.01
Lithuanian (18)	18	0.06
Luxemburger (0)	0	<0.01
Macedonian (25)	25	0.08
Maltese (0)	0	<0.01
New Zealander (0)	0	<0.01
Northern European (12)	28	0.09
Norwegian (59)	100	0.31
Pennsylvania German (23)	23	0.07
Polish (67)	457	1.41
Portuguese (0)	17	0.05
Romanian (0)	0	<0.01
Russian (0)	75	0.23
Scandinavian (18)	28	0.09
Scotch-Irish (445)	886	2.74
Scottish (356)	788	2.43
Serbian (0)	19	0.06
Slavic (0)	12	0.04
Slovak (0)	95	0.29
Slovene (0)	0	<0.01
Soviet Union (0)	0	<0.01
Swedish (80)	204	0.63
Swiss (39)	252	0.78
Turkish (0)	0	<0.01
Ukrainian (17)	34	0.10
Welsh (71)	273	0.84
West Indian, ex. Hispanic (0)	0	<0.01
Bahamian (0)	0	<0.01
Barbadian (0)	0	<0.01
Belizean (0)	0	<0.01
Bermudan (0)	0	<0.01
British West Indian (0)	0	<0.01
Dutch West Indian (0)	0	<0.01
Haitian (0)	0	<0.01
Jamaican (0)	0	<0.01
Trinidadian/Tobagonian (0)	0	<0.01
U.S. Virgin Islander (0)	0	<0.01
West Indian (0)	0	<0.01
Other West Indian (0)	0	<0.01
Yugoslavian (34)	34	0.10

Hispanic Origin	Population	%
Hispanic or Latino (of any race)	755	2.33
Central American, ex. Mexican	55	0.17
Costa Rican	0	<0.01
Guatemalan	5	0.02
Honduran	44	0.14
Nicaraguan	0	<0.01
Panamanian	2	0.01
Salvadoran	4	0.01
Other Central American	0	<0.01
Cuban	12	0.04
Dominican Republic	0	<0.01
Mexican	564	1.74
Puerto Rican	50	0.15
South American	25	0.08
Argentinean	2	0.01
Bolivian	3	0.01
Chilean	2	0.01
Colombian	8	0.02
Ecuadorian	5	0.02
Paraguayan	0	<0.01
Peruvian	2	0.01
Uruguayan	0	<0.01
Venezuelan	3	0.01
Other South American	0	<0.01
Other Hispanic or Latino	49	0.15

Race*	Population	%
African-American/Black (542)	743	2.29
Not Hispanic (530)	725	2.24
Hispanic (12)	18	0.06
American Indian/Alaska Native (69)	195	0.60
Not Hispanic (59)	179	0.55
Hispanic (10)	16	0.05
Alaska Athabascan *(Ala. Nat.)* (0)	0	<0.01
Aleut *(Alaska Native)* (0)	0	<0.01
Apache (0)	4	0.01
Arapaho (0)	0	<0.01
Blackfeet (4)	12	0.04
Canadian/French Am. Ind. (0)	1	<0.01
Central American Ind. (0)	0	<0.01
Cherokee (21)	63	0.19
Cheyenne (0)	0	<0.01
Chickasaw (1)	1	<0.01
Chippewa (5)	5	0.02
Choctaw (2)	2	0.01
Colville (0)	0	<0.01
Comanche (0)	0	<0.01
Cree (0)	0	<0.01
Creek (0)	2	0.01
Crow (0)	0	<0.01
Delaware (0)	1	<0.01
Hopi (0)	0	<0.01
Houma (0)	0	<0.01
Inupiat *(Alaska Native)* (1)	3	0.01
Iroquois (1)	5	0.02
Kiowa (0)	0	<0.01
Lumbee (0)	0	<0.01
Menominee (0)	0	<0.01
Mexican American Ind. (1)	1	<0.01
Navajo (1)	1	<0.01
Osage (0)	0	<0.01
Ottawa (0)	0	<0.01
Paiute (0)	1	<0.01
Pima (0)	0	<0.01
Potawatomi (2)	2	0.01
Pueblo (0)	0	<0.01
Puget Sound Salish (0)	1	<0.01
Seminole (0)	0	<0.01
Shoshone (0)	0	<0.01
Sioux (1)	11	0.03
South American Ind. (0)	0	<0.01
Spanish American Ind. (0)	0	<0.01
Tlingit-Haida *(Alaska Native)* (0)	0	<0.01
Tohono O'Odham (0)	0	<0.01
Tsimshian *(Alaska Native)* (0)	0	<0.01
Ute (0)	0	<0.01
Yakama (0)	0	<0.01
Yaqui (0)	0	<0.01
Yuman (0)	0	<0.01
Yup'ik *(Alaska Native)* (0)	0	<0.01
Asian (211)	279	0.86
Not Hispanic (211)	276	0.85
Hispanic (0)	3	0.01
Bangladeshi (0)	0	<0.01
Bhutanese (0)	0	<0.01
Burmese (0)	0	<0.01
Cambodian (0)	0	<0.01
Chinese, ex. Taiwanese (64)	69	0.21
Filipino (42)	72	0.22
Hmong (0)	2	0.01
Indian (33)	43	0.13
Indonesian (4)	4	0.01
Japanese (39)	47	0.14
Korean (12)	20	0.06
Laotian (0)	0	<0.01
Malaysian (0)	0	<0.01
Nepalese (0)	0	<0.01
Pakistani (3)	3	0.01
Sri Lankan (0)	0	<0.01
Taiwanese (0)	0	<0.01
Thai (2)	3	0.01
Vietnamese (6)	9	0.03
Hawaii Native/Pacific Islander (6)	19	0.06
Not Hispanic (5)	16	0.05
Hispanic (1)	3	0.01
Fijian (0)	0	<0.01
Guamanian/Chamorro (1)	4	0.01
Marshallese (0)	0	<0.01
Native Hawaiian (3)	7	0.02
Samoan (1)	2	0.01
Tongan (0)	0	<0.01
White (30,876)	31,283	96.47
Not Hispanic (30,463)	30,829	95.07
Hispanic (413)	454	1.40

*Notes: † The Census 2010 population figure is used to calculate the percentages in the Hispanic Origin and Race categories. Ancestry percentages are based on the 2006-2010 American Community Survey population (not shown); ‡ Numbers in parentheses indicate the number of people reporting a single ancestry; * Numbers in parentheses indicate the number of persons reporting this race alone, not in combination with any other race; Please refer to the Explanation of Data for more information.*

Jennings County

Population: 28,525

Ancestry	Population	%
Afghan (0)	0	<0.01
African, Sub-Saharan (51)	51	0.18
African (51)	51	0.18
Cape Verdean (0)	0	<0.01
Ethiopian (0)	0	<0.01
Ghanaian (0)	0	<0.01
Kenyan (0)	0	<0.01
Liberian (0)	0	<0.01
Nigerian (0)	0	<0.01
Senegalese (0)	0	<0.01
Sierra Leonean (0)	0	<0.01
Somalian (0)	0	<0.01
South African (0)	0	<0.01
Sudanese (0)	0	<0.01
Ugandan (0)	0	<0.01
Zimbabwean (0)	0	<0.01
Other Sub-Saharan African (0)	0	<0.01
Albanian (0)	0	<0.01
Alsatian (0)	0	<0.01
American (4,191)	4,191	14.72
Arab (91)	110	0.39
Arab (84)	84	0.30
Egyptian (0)	0	<0.01
Iraqi (0)	0	<0.01
Jordanian (0)	0	<0.01
Lebanese (7)	26	0.09
Moroccan (0)	0	<0.01
Palestinian (0)	0	<0.01
Syrian (0)	0	<0.01
Other Arab (0)	0	<0.01
Armenian (0)	0	<0.01
Assyrian/Chaldean/Syriac (0)	0	<0.01
Australian (0)	109	0.38
Austrian (11)	29	0.10
Basque (0)	0	<0.01
Belgian (0)	25	0.09
Brazilian (0)	0	<0.01
British (13)	49	0.17
Bulgarian (0)	0	<0.01
Cajun (0)	0	<0.01
Canadian (84)	138	0.48
Carpatho Rusyn (0)	0	<0.01
Celtic (0)	0	<0.01
Croatian (0)	0	<0.01
Cypriot (0)	0	<0.01
Czech (0)	16	0.06
Czechoslovakian (9)	21	0.07
Danish (0)	0	<0.01
Dutch (43)	399	1.40
Eastern European (0)	0	<0.01
English (1,050)	2,036	7.15
Estonian (0)	0	<0.01
European (163)	163	0.57
Finnish (0)	21	0.07
French, ex. Basque (93)	479	1.68
French Canadian (0)	0	<0.01
German (3,063)	7,449	26.16
German Russian (0)	0	<0.01
Greek (0)	0	<0.01
Guyanese (0)	0	<0.01
Hungarian (29)	47	0.17
Icelander (0)	0	<0.01
Iranian (0)	0	<0.01
Irish (1,240)	4,631	16.27
Israeli (0)	0	<0.01
Italian (47)	301	1.06
Latvian (0)	0	<0.01
Lithuanian (0)	0	<0.01
Luxemburger (0)	0	<0.01
Macedonian (0)	0	<0.01
Maltese (0)	0	<0.01
New Zealander (0)	0	<0.01
Northern European (0)	0	<0.01
Norwegian (33)	347	1.22
Pennsylvania German (0)	65	0.23
Polish (9)	65	0.23
Portuguese (0)	22	0.08
Romanian (9)	9	0.03
Russian (0)	35	0.12
Scandinavian (0)	0	<0.01
Scotch-Irish (133)	452	1.59
Scottish (236)	343	1.20
Serbian (0)	0	<0.01
Slavic (0)	0	<0.01
Slovak (0)	0	<0.01
Slovene (0)	0	<0.01
Soviet Union (0)	0	<0.01
Swedish (24)	119	0.42
Swiss (12)	23	0.08
Turkish (0)	0	<0.01
Ukrainian (0)	0	<0.01
Welsh (21)	47	0.17
West Indian, ex. Hispanic (10)	19	0.07
Bahamian (0)	0	<0.01
Barbadian (0)	0	<0.01
Belizean (0)	0	<0.01
Bermudan (0)	0	<0.01
British West Indian (0)	0	<0.01
Dutch West Indian (0)	0	<0.01
Haitian (0)	0	<0.01
Jamaican (0)	9	0.03
Trinidadian/Tobagonian (0)	0	<0.01
U.S. Virgin Islander (0)	0	<0.01
West Indian (10)	10	0.04
Other West Indian (0)	0	<0.01
Yugoslavian (0)	0	<0.01

Hispanic Origin	Population	%
Hispanic or Latino (of any race)	571	2.00
Central American, ex. Mexican	27	0.09
Costa Rican	1	<0.01
Guatemalan	6	0.02
Honduran	6	0.02
Nicaraguan	5	0.02
Panamanian	3	0.01
Salvadoran	6	0.02
Other Central American	0	<0.01
Cuban	6	0.02
Dominican Republic	1	<0.01
Mexican	464	1.63
Puerto Rican	17	0.06
South American	9	0.03
Argentinean	0	<0.01
Bolivian	0	<0.01
Chilean	1	<0.01
Colombian	7	0.02
Ecuadorian	0	<0.01
Paraguayan	0	<0.01
Peruvian	1	<0.01
Uruguayan	0	<0.01
Venezuelan	0	<0.01
Other South American	0	<0.01
Other Hispanic or Latino	47	0.16

Race*	Population	%
African-American/Black (216)	327	1.15
Not Hispanic (206)	314	1.10
Hispanic (10)	13	0.05
American Indian/Alaska Native (30)	166	0.58
Not Hispanic (30)	162	0.57
Hispanic (0)	4	0.01
Alaska Athabascan *(Ala. Nat.)* (3)	3	0.01
Aleut *(Alaska Native)* (0)	0	<0.01
Apache (0)	2	0.01
Arapaho (0)	1	<0.01
Blackfeet (0)	14	0.05
Canadian/French Am. Ind. (1)	1	<0.01
Central American Ind. (0)	0	<0.01
Cherokee (7)	76	0.27
Cheyenne (1)	1	<0.01
Chickasaw (0)	1	<0.01
Chippewa (2)	2	0.01
Choctaw (0)	2	0.01
Colville (0)	0	<0.01
Comanche (0)	0	<0.01
Cree (0)	6	0.02
Creek (0)	1	<0.01
Crow (0)	0	<0.01
Delaware (0)	2	0.01
Hopi (0)	0	<0.01
Houma (0)	0	<0.01
Inupiat *(Alaska Native)* (0)	0	<0.01
Iroquois (0)	0	<0.01
Kiowa (0)	0	<0.01
Lumbee (0)	0	<0.01
Menominee (0)	0	<0.01
Mexican American Ind. (0)	0	<0.01
Navajo (0)	6	0.02
Osage (0)	0	<0.01
Ottawa (0)	0	<0.01
Paiute (0)	0	<0.01
Pima (0)	0	<0.01
Potawatomi (0)	1	<0.01
Pueblo (0)	0	<0.01
Puget Sound Salish (0)	0	<0.01
Seminole (0)	0	<0.01
Shoshone (0)	0	<0.01
Sioux (4)	6	0.02
South American Ind. (0)	0	<0.01
Spanish American Ind. (0)	0	<0.01
Tlingit-Haida *(Alaska Native)* (0)	0	<0.01
Tohono O'Odham (0)	0	<0.01
Tsimshian *(Alaska Native)* (0)	0	<0.01
Ute (0)	0	<0.01
Yakama (0)	0	<0.01
Yaqui (0)	0	<0.01
Yuman (0)	0	<0.01
Yup'ik *(Alaska Native)* (0)	0	<0.01
Asian (62)	107	0.38
Not Hispanic (62)	107	0.38
Hispanic (0)	0	<0.01
Bangladeshi (0)	0	<0.01
Bhutanese (0)	0	<0.01
Burmese (0)	0	<0.01
Cambodian (3)	3	0.01
Chinese, ex. Taiwanese (6)	10	0.04
Filipino (10)	19	0.07
Hmong (0)	0	<0.01
Indian (9)	16	0.06
Indonesian (0)	0	<0.01
Japanese (16)	29	0.10
Korean (8)	17	0.06
Laotian (0)	0	<0.01
Malaysian (0)	0	<0.01
Nepalese (0)	0	<0.01
Pakistani (1)	1	<0.01
Sri Lankan (0)	0	<0.01
Taiwanese (0)	0	<0.01
Thai (3)	3	0.01
Vietnamese (5)	5	0.02
Hawaii Native/Pacific Islander (0)	5	0.02
Not Hispanic (0)	3	0.01
Hispanic (0)	2	0.01
Fijian (0)	0	<0.01
Guamanian/Chamorro (0)	1	<0.01
Marshallese (0)	0	<0.01
Native Hawaiian (0)	2	0.01
Samoan (0)	0	<0.01
Tongan (0)	0	<0.01
White (27,611)	27,929	97.91
Not Hispanic (27,361)	27,630	96.86
Hispanic (250)	299	1.05

*Notes: † The Census 2010 population figure is used to calculate the percentages in the Hispanic Origin and Race categories. Ancestry percentages are based on the 2006-2010 American Community Survey population (not shown); ‡ Numbers in parentheses indicate the number of people reporting a single ancestry; * Numbers in parentheses indicate the number of persons reporting this race alone, not in combination with any other race; Please refer to the Explanation of Data for more information.*

Johnson County

Population: 139,654

Ancestry	Population	%
Afghan (0)	0	<0.01
African, Sub-Saharan (105)	105	0.08
African (33)	33	0.02
Cape Verdean (0)	0	<0.01
Ethiopian (0)	0	<0.01
Ghanaian (46)	46	0.03
Kenyan (26)	26	0.02
Liberian (0)	0	<0.01
Nigerian (0)	0	<0.01
Senegalese (0)	0	<0.01
Sierra Leonean (0)	0	<0.01
Somalian (0)	0	<0.01
South African (0)	0	<0.01
Sudanese (0)	0	<0.01
Ugandan (0)	0	<0.01
Zimbabwean (0)	0	<0.01
Other Sub-Saharan African (0)	0	<0.01
Albanian (14)	37	0.03
Alsatian (0)	0	<0.01
American (13,982)	13,982	10.28
Arab (262)	345	0.25
Arab (65)	83	0.06
Egyptian (0)	0	<0.01
Iraqi (0)	0	<0.01
Jordanian (101)	101	0.07
Lebanese (30)	77	0.06
Moroccan (24)	24	0.02
Palestinian (0)	0	<0.01
Syrian (0)	0	<0.01
Other Arab (42)	60	0.04
Armenian (0)	0	<0.01
Assyrian/Chaldean/Syriac (0)	0	<0.01
Australian (3)	3	<0.01
Austrian (18)	123	0.09
Basque (0)	0	<0.01
Belgian (21)	85	0.06
Brazilian (0)	0	<0.01
British (391)	1,089	0.80
Bulgarian (49)	49	0.04
Cajun (0)	83	0.06
Canadian (77)	287	0.21
Carpatho Rusyn (0)	0	<0.01
Celtic (0)	20	0.01
Croatian (58)	220	0.16
Cypriot (0)	0	<0.01
Czech (60)	210	0.15
Czechoslovakian (28)	40	0.03
Danish (79)	239	0.18
Dutch (978)	3,206	2.36
Eastern European (66)	66	0.05
English (6,193)	15,677	11.53
Estonian (0)	17	0.01
European (1,400)	1,600	1.18
Finnish (77)	244	0.18
French, ex. Basque (813)	3,000	2.21
French Canadian (290)	564	0.41
German (16,159)	38,193	28.08
German Russian (0)	9	0.01
Greek (90)	390	0.29
Guyanese (0)	0	<0.01
Hungarian (179)	694	0.51
Icelander (0)	0	<0.01
Iranian (79)	110	0.08
Irish (6,701)	21,347	15.70
Israeli (0)	0	<0.01
Italian (1,629)	4,981	3.66
Latvian (10)	10	0.01
Lithuanian (0)	61	0.04
Luxemburger (0)	0	<0.01
Macedonian (65)	65	0.05
Maltese (0)	0	<0.01
New Zealander (24)	24	0.02
Northern European (93)	114	0.08
Norwegian (353)	903	0.66
Pennsylvania German (70)	80	0.06
Polish (828)	2,800	2.06
Portuguese (17)	121	0.09
Romanian (76)	189	0.14
Russian (192)	477	0.35
Scandinavian (43)	70	0.05
Scotch-Irish (941)	2,434	1.79
Scottish (1,328)	3,328	2.45
Serbian (15)	32	0.02
Slavic (15)	33	0.02
Slovak (99)	191	0.14
Slovene (64)	118	0.09
Soviet Union (0)	0	<0.01
Swedish (222)	1,194	0.88
Swiss (265)	584	0.43
Turkish (36)	36	0.03
Ukrainian (56)	98	0.07
Welsh (163)	849	0.62
West Indian, ex. Hispanic (27)	36	0.03
Bahamian (0)	0	<0.01
Barbadian (0)	0	<0.01
Belizean (0)	0	<0.01
Bermudan (0)	0	<0.01
British West Indian (0)	0	<0.01
Dutch West Indian (0)	0	<0.01
Haitian (0)	0	<0.01
Jamaican (27)	36	0.03
Trinidadian/Tobagonian (0)	0	<0.01
U.S. Virgin Islander (0)	0	<0.01
West Indian (0)	0	<0.01
Other West Indian (0)	0	<0.01
Yugoslavian (36)	40	0.03

Hispanic Origin	Population	%
Hispanic or Latino (of any race)	4,270	3.06
Central American, ex. Mexican	201	0.14
Costa Rican	10	0.01
Guatemalan	48	0.03
Honduran	61	0.04
Nicaraguan	13	0.01
Panamanian	29	0.02
Salvadoran	37	0.03
Other Central American	3	<0.01
Cuban	56	0.04
Dominican Republic	32	0.02
Mexican	3,168	2.27
Puerto Rican	354	0.25
South American	185	0.13
Argentinean	16	0.01
Bolivian	9	0.01
Chilean	9	0.01
Colombian	47	0.03
Ecuadorian	6	<0.01
Paraguayan	4	<0.01
Peruvian	57	0.04
Uruguayan	0	<0.01
Venezuelan	36	0.03
Other South American	1	<0.01
Other Hispanic or Latino	274	0.20

Race*	Population	%
African-American/Black (1,578)	2,365	1.69
Not Hispanic (1,536)	2,260	1.62
Hispanic (42)	105	0.08
American Indian/Alaska Native (315)	878	0.63
Not Hispanic (252)	756	0.54
Hispanic (63)	122	0.09
Alaska Athabascan *(Ala. Nat.)* (0)	1	<0.01
Aleut *(Alaska Native)* (0)	2	<0.01
Apache (6)	17	0.01
Arapaho (0)	0	<0.01
Blackfeet (10)	35	0.03
Canadian/French Am. Ind. (0)	0	<0.01
Central American Ind. (0)	1	<0.01
Cherokee (61)	258	0.18
Cheyenne (1)	3	<0.01
Chickasaw (1)	5	<0.01
Chippewa (2)	20	0.01
Choctaw (13)	25	0.02
Colville (0)	1	<0.01
Comanche (0)	3	<0.01
Cree (0)	0	<0.01
Creek (5)	12	0.01
Crow (3)	10	0.01
Delaware (0)	0	<0.01
Hopi (0)	1	<0.01
Houma (0)	0	<0.01
Inupiat *(Alaska Native)* (0)	0	<0.01
Iroquois (4)	8	0.01
Kiowa (0)	0	<0.01
Lumbee (0)	4	<0.01
Menominee (0)	0	<0.01
Mexican American Ind. (13)	24	0.02
Navajo (5)	8	0.01
Osage (0)	0	<0.01
Ottawa (0)	6	<0.01
Paiute (0)	0	<0.01
Pima (0)	0	<0.01
Potawatomi (5)	5	<0.01
Pueblo (3)	6	<0.01
Puget Sound Salish (0)	0	<0.01
Seminole (0)	0	<0.01
Shoshone (0)	1	<0.01
Sioux (11)	24	0.02
South American Ind. (1)	1	<0.01
Spanish American Ind. (0)	0	<0.01
Tlingit-Haida *(Alaska Native)* (0)	0	<0.01
Tohono O'Odham (0)	6	<0.01
Tsimshian *(Alaska Native)* (0)	0	<0.01
Ute (0)	0	<0.01
Yakama (0)	0	<0.01
Yaqui (1)	1	<0.01
Yuman (0)	0	<0.01
Yup'ik *(Alaska Native)* (1)	1	<0.01
Asian (2,744)	3,360	2.41
Not Hispanic (2,716)	3,303	2.37
Hispanic (28)	57	0.04
Bangladeshi (1)	2	<0.01
Bhutanese (0)	0	<0.01
Burmese (5)	5	<0.01
Cambodian (6)	10	0.01
Chinese, ex. Taiwanese (310)	368	0.26
Filipino (235)	435	0.31
Hmong (3)	3	<0.01
Indian (1,613)	1,738	1.24
Indonesian (10)	15	0.01
Japanese (163)	267	0.19
Korean (124)	182	0.13
Laotian (1)	2	<0.01
Malaysian (2)	2	<0.01
Nepalese (9)	9	0.01
Pakistani (24)	28	0.02
Sri Lankan (5)	5	<0.01
Taiwanese (13)	15	0.01
Thai (18)	32	0.02
Vietnamese (133)	161	0.12
Hawaii Native/Pacific Islander (46)	140	0.10
Not Hispanic (46)	119	0.09
Hispanic (0)	21	0.02
Fijian (0)	0	<0.01
Guamanian/Chamorro (3)	16	0.01
Marshallese (0)	0	<0.01
Native Hawaiian (14)	48	0.03
Samoan (7)	15	0.01
Tongan (0)	0	<0.01
White (131,140)	133,110	95.31
Not Hispanic (128,903)	130,545	93.48
Hispanic (2,237)	2,565	1.84

*Notes: † The Census 2010 population figure is used to calculate the percentages in the Hispanic Origin and Race categories. Ancestry percentages are based on the 2006-2010 American Community Survey population (not shown); ‡ Numbers in parentheses indicate the number of people reporting a single ancestry; * Numbers in parentheses indicate the number of persons reporting this race alone, not in combination with any other race; Please refer to the Explanation of Data for more information.*

Knox County

Population: 38,440

Ancestry	Population	%
Afghan (0)	0	<0.01
African, Sub-Saharan (0)	4	0.01
African (0)	4	0.01
Cape Verdean (0)	0	<0.01
Ethiopian (0)	0	<0.01
Ghanaian (0)	0	<0.01
Kenyan (0)	0	<0.01
Liberian (0)	0	<0.01
Nigerian (0)	0	<0.01
Senegalese (0)	0	<0.01
Sierra Leonean (0)	0	<0.01
Somalian (0)	0	<0.01
South African (0)	0	<0.01
Sudanese (0)	0	<0.01
Ugandan (0)	0	<0.01
Zimbabwean (0)	0	<0.01
Other Sub-Saharan African (0)	0	<0.01
Albanian (0)	0	<0.01
Alsatian (0)	0	<0.01
American (7,662)	7,662	19.94
Arab (12)	12	0.03
Arab (0)	0	<0.01
Egyptian (0)	0	<0.01
Iraqi (0)	0	<0.01
Jordanian (0)	0	<0.01
Lebanese (0)	0	<0.01
Moroccan (0)	0	<0.01
Palestinian (0)	0	<0.01
Syrian (12)	12	0.03
Other Arab (0)	0	<0.01
Armenian (0)	0	<0.01
Assyrian/Chaldean/Syriac (0)	0	<0.01
Australian (0)	0	<0.01
Austrian (0)	54	0.14
Basque (0)	0	<0.01
Belgian (57)	105	0.27
Brazilian (0)	0	<0.01
British (68)	113	0.29
Bulgarian (0)	0	<0.01
Cajun (0)	0	<0.01
Canadian (18)	54	0.14
Carpatho Rusyn (0)	0	<0.01
Celtic (0)	0	<0.01
Croatian (0)	14	0.04
Cypriot (0)	0	<0.01
Czech (0)	35	0.09
Czechoslovakian (0)	49	0.13
Danish (14)	73	0.19
Dutch (62)	467	1.22
Eastern European (0)	0	<0.01
English (1,791)	3,502	9.11
Estonian (0)	0	<0.01
European (130)	169	0.44
Finnish (0)	6	0.02
French, ex. Basque (640)	2,181	5.68
French Canadian (10)	58	0.15
German (4,962)	10,340	26.91
German Russian (0)	0	<0.01
Greek (78)	118	0.31
Guyanese (0)	0	<0.01
Hungarian (36)	128	0.33
Icelander (0)	0	<0.01
Iranian (0)	0	<0.01
Irish (1,408)	4,980	12.96
Israeli (0)	0	<0.01
Italian (249)	825	2.15
Latvian (0)	0	<0.01
Lithuanian (0)	65	0.17
Luxemburger (0)	0	<0.01
Macedonian (0)	0	<0.01
Maltese (0)	0	<0.01
New Zealander (0)	0	<0.01
Northern European (0)	0	<0.01
Norwegian (73)	191	0.50
Pennsylvania German (0)	21	0.05
Polish (249)	347	0.90
Portuguese (0)	0	<0.01
Romanian (0)	0	<0.01
Russian (45)	55	0.14
Scandinavian (12)	12	0.03
Scotch-Irish (305)	581	1.51
Scottish (251)	572	1.49
Serbian (34)	34	0.09
Slavic (0)	0	<0.01
Slovak (0)	0	<0.01
Slovene (0)	0	<0.01
Soviet Union (0)	0	<0.01
Swedish (16)	98	0.26
Swiss (39)	60	0.16
Turkish (0)	0	<0.01
Ukrainian (0)	14	0.04
Welsh (30)	223	0.58
West Indian, ex. Hispanic (34)	34	0.09
Bahamian (34)	34	0.09
Barbadian (0)	0	<0.01
Belizean (0)	0	<0.01
Bermudan (0)	0	<0.01
British West Indian (0)	0	<0.01
Dutch West Indian (0)	0	<0.01
Haitian (0)	0	<0.01
Jamaican (0)	0	<0.01
Trinidadian/Tobagonian (0)	0	<0.01
U.S. Virgin Islander (0)	0	<0.01
West Indian (0)	0	<0.01
Other West Indian (0)	0	<0.01
Yugoslavian (0)	0	<0.01

Hispanic Origin	Population	%
Hispanic or Latino (of any race)	590	1.53
Central American, ex. Mexican	30	0.08
Costa Rican	8	0.02
Guatemalan	11	0.03
Honduran	7	0.02
Nicaraguan	1	<0.01
Panamanian	0	<0.01
Salvadoran	3	0.01
Other Central American	0	<0.01
Cuban	8	0.02
Dominican Republic	0	<0.01
Mexican	421	1.10
Puerto Rican	55	0.14
South American	21	0.05
Argentinean	1	<0.01
Bolivian	1	<0.01
Chilean	0	<0.01
Colombian	7	0.02
Ecuadorian	5	0.01
Paraguayan	0	<0.01
Peruvian	1	<0.01
Uruguayan	1	<0.01
Venezuelan	4	0.01
Other South American	1	<0.01
Other Hispanic or Latino	55	0.14

Race*	Population	%
African-American/Black (1,009)	1,220	3.17
Not Hispanic (994)	1,191	3.10
Hispanic (15)	29	0.08
American Indian/Alaska Native (73)	222	0.58
Not Hispanic (64)	207	0.54
Hispanic (9)	15	0.04
Alaska Athabascan *(Ala. Nat.)* (0)	0	<0.01
Aleut *(Alaska Native)* (0)	0	<0.01
Apache (0)	1	<0.01
Arapaho (0)	2	0.01
Blackfeet (2)	12	0.03
Canadian/French Am. Ind. (0)	5	0.01
Central American Ind. (0)	0	<0.01
Cherokee (18)	67	0.17
Cheyenne (4)	6	0.02
Chickasaw (0)	1	<0.01
Chippewa (3)	7	0.02
Choctaw (2)	2	0.01
Colville (0)	0	<0.01
Comanche (0)	0	<0.01
Cree (0)	0	<0.01
Creek (2)	2	0.01
Crow (0)	1	<0.01
Delaware (0)	0	<0.01
Hopi (0)	0	<0.01
Houma (0)	0	<0.01
Inupiat *(Alaska Native)* (0)	0	<0.01
Iroquois (0)	1	<0.01
Kiowa (0)	0	<0.01
Lumbee (0)	0	<0.01
Menominee (1)	1	<0.01
Mexican American Ind. (4)	5	0.01
Navajo (0)	4	0.01
Osage (1)	3	0.01
Ottawa (0)	0	<0.01
Paiute (0)	0	<0.01
Pima (0)	0	<0.01
Potawatomi (0)	1	<0.01
Pueblo (0)	0	<0.01
Puget Sound Salish (0)	0	<0.01
Seminole (0)	0	<0.01
Shoshone (0)	0	<0.01
Sioux (1)	5	0.01
South American Ind. (1)	1	<0.01
Spanish American Ind. (0)	0	<0.01
Tlingit-Haida *(Alaska Native)* (0)	0	<0.01
Tohono O'Odham (0)	1	<0.01
Tsimshian *(Alaska Native)* (0)	0	<0.01
Ute (0)	0	<0.01
Yakama (0)	0	<0.01
Yaqui (0)	0	<0.01
Yuman (0)	0	<0.01
Yup'ik *(Alaska Native)* (0)	0	<0.01
Asian (215)	281	0.73
Not Hispanic (214)	277	0.72
Hispanic (1)	4	0.01
Bangladeshi (0)	0	<0.01
Bhutanese (0)	0	<0.01
Burmese (10)	10	0.03
Cambodian (1)	3	0.01
Chinese, ex. Taiwanese (31)	41	0.11
Filipino (49)	67	0.17
Hmong (0)	0	<0.01
Indian (30)	34	0.09
Indonesian (0)	0	<0.01
Japanese (21)	36	0.09
Korean (44)	54	0.14
Laotian (0)	0	<0.01
Malaysian (2)	2	0.01
Nepalese (0)	0	<0.01
Pakistani (1)	1	<0.01
Sri Lankan (0)	0	<0.01
Taiwanese (3)	3	0.01
Thai (5)	7	0.02
Vietnamese (12)	14	0.04
Hawaii Native/Pacific Islander (11)	24	0.06
Not Hispanic (11)	24	0.06
Hispanic (0)	0	<0.01
Fijian (0)	0	<0.01
Guamanian/Chamorro (1)	3	0.01
Marshallese (0)	0	<0.01
Native Hawaiian (8)	15	0.04
Samoan (0)	2	0.01
Tongan (0)	0	<0.01
White (36,475)	36,919	96.04
Not Hispanic (36,154)	36,531	95.03
Hispanic (321)	388	1.01

*Notes: † The Census 2010 population figure is used to calculate the percentages in the Hispanic Origin and Race categories. Ancestry percentages are based on the 2006-2010 American Community Survey population (not shown); ‡ Numbers in parentheses indicate the number of people reporting a single ancestry; * Numbers in parentheses indicate the number of persons reporting this race alone, not in combination with any other race; Please refer to the Explanation of Data for more information.*

Kosciusko County

Population: 77,358

Ancestry	Population	%
Afghan (0)	0	<0.01
African, Sub-Saharan (74)	121	0.16
African (15)	62	0.08
Cape Verdean (0)	0	<0.01
Ethiopian (0)	0	<0.01
Ghanaian (0)	0	<0.01
Kenyan (0)	0	<0.01
Liberian (0)	0	<0.01
Nigerian (0)	0	<0.01
Senegalese (0)	0	<0.01
Sierra Leonean (0)	0	<0.01
Somalian (0)	0	<0.01
South African (59)	59	0.08
Sudanese (0)	0	<0.01
Ugandan (0)	0	<0.01
Zimbabwean (0)	0	<0.01
Other Sub-Saharan African (0)	0	<0.01
Albanian (0)	0	<0.01
Alsatian (0)	0	<0.01
American (6,279)	6,279	8.16
Arab (52)	81	0.11
Arab (0)	0	<0.01
Egyptian (0)	0	<0.01
Iraqi (0)	0	<0.01
Jordanian (21)	21	0.03
Lebanese (31)	49	0.06
Moroccan (0)	0	<0.01
Palestinian (0)	0	<0.01
Syrian (0)	0	<0.01
Other Arab (0)	11	0.01
Armenian (0)	15	0.02
Assyrian/Chaldean/Syriac (0)	0	<0.01
Australian (0)	8	0.01
Austrian (59)	90	0.12
Basque (0)	0	<0.01
Belgian (36)	188	0.24
Brazilian (0)	0	<0.01
British (98)	109	0.14
Bulgarian (11)	11	0.01
Cajun (0)	0	<0.01
Canadian (38)	74	0.10
Carpatho Rusyn (0)	13	0.02
Celtic (0)	0	<0.01
Croatian (0)	24	0.03
Cypriot (0)	0	<0.01
Czech (12)	31	0.04
Czechoslovakian (19)	19	0.02
Danish (15)	83	0.11
Dutch (660)	2,983	3.87
Eastern European (30)	30	0.04
English (3,275)	8,348	10.84
Estonian (0)	0	<0.01
European (592)	612	0.79
Finnish (12)	33	0.04
French, ex. Basque (297)	2,131	2.77
French Canadian (127)	248	0.32
German (11,595)	25,753	33.45
German Russian (0)	0	<0.01
Greek (175)	439	0.57
Guyanese (0)	0	<0.01
Hungarian (135)	364	0.47
Icelander (9)	9	0.01
Iranian (0)	0	<0.01
Irish (2,722)	8,867	11.52
Israeli (0)	0	<0.01
Italian (796)	1,855	2.41
Latvian (0)	8	0.01
Lithuanian (91)	114	0.15
Luxemburger (0)	0	<0.01
Macedonian (0)	0	<0.01
Maltese (0)	0	<0.01
New Zealander (0)	0	<0.01
Northern European (12)	12	0.02
Norwegian (145)	485	0.63
Pennsylvania German (336)	445	0.58
Polish (494)	1,845	2.40
Portuguese (23)	69	0.09
Romanian (0)	15	0.02
Russian (12)	119	0.15
Scandinavian (0)	49	0.06
Scotch-Irish (242)	784	1.02
Scottish (478)	1,343	1.74
Serbian (2)	41	0.05
Slavic (0)	0	<0.01
Slovak (3)	44	0.06
Slovene (11)	11	0.01
Soviet Union (0)	0	<0.01
Swedish (130)	547	0.71
Swiss (386)	1,393	1.81
Turkish (0)	0	<0.01
Ukrainian (18)	45	0.06
Welsh (248)	864	1.12
West Indian, ex. Hispanic (0)	0	<0.01
Bahamian (0)	0	<0.01
Barbadian (0)	0	<0.01
Belizean (0)	0	<0.01
Bermudan (0)	0	<0.01
British West Indian (0)	0	<0.01
Dutch West Indian (0)	0	<0.01
Haitian (0)	0	<0.01
Jamaican (0)	0	<0.01
Trinidadian/Tobagonian (0)	0	<0.01
U.S. Virgin Islander (0)	0	<0.01
West Indian (0)	0	<0.01
Other West Indian (0)	0	<0.01
Yugoslavian (10)	23	0.03

Hispanic Origin	Population	%
Hispanic or Latino (of any race)	5,634	7.28
Central American, ex. Mexican	137	0.18
Costa Rican	5	0.01
Guatemalan	55	0.07
Honduran	47	0.06
Nicaraguan	5	0.01
Panamanian	13	0.02
Salvadoran	12	0.02
Other Central American	0	<0.01
Cuban	16	0.02
Dominican Republic	7	0.01
Mexican	4,942	6.39
Puerto Rican	118	0.15
South American	106	0.14
Argentinean	30	0.04
Bolivian	0	<0.01
Chilean	4	0.01
Colombian	37	0.05
Ecuadorian	10	0.01
Paraguayan	0	<0.01
Peruvian	18	0.02
Uruguayan	0	<0.01
Venezuelan	3	<0.01
Other South American	4	0.01
Other Hispanic or Latino	308	0.40

Race*	Population	%
African-American/Black (572)	871	1.13
Not Hispanic (542)	816	1.05
Hispanic (30)	55	0.07
American Indian/Alaska Native (232)	525	0.68
Not Hispanic (178)	450	0.58
Hispanic (54)	75	0.10
Alaska Athabascan *(Ala. Nat.)* (0)	0	<0.01
Aleut *(Alaska Native)* (1)	1	<0.01
Apache (6)	10	0.01
Arapaho (0)	0	<0.01
Blackfeet (5)	27	0.03
Canadian/French Am. Ind. (0)	0	<0.01
Central American Ind. (0)	0	<0.01
Cherokee (41)	119	0.15
Cheyenne (0)	0	<0.01
Chickasaw (0)	2	<0.01
Chippewa (12)	22	0.03
Choctaw (9)	15	0.02
Colville (0)	0	<0.01
Comanche (2)	2	<0.01
Cree (0)	0	<0.01
Creek (3)	6	0.01
Crow (0)	2	<0.01
Delaware (0)	0	<0.01
Hopi (0)	0	<0.01
Houma (0)	0	<0.01
Inupiat *(Alaska Native)* (1)	1	<0.01
Iroquois (0)	6	0.01
Kiowa (0)	0	<0.01
Lumbee (0)	0	<0.01
Menominee (1)	3	<0.01
Mexican American Ind. (14)	14	0.02
Navajo (6)	8	0.01
Osage (0)	0	<0.01
Ottawa (1)	1	<0.01
Paiute (1)	1	<0.01
Pima (0)	0	<0.01
Potawatomi (7)	12	0.02
Pueblo (1)	1	<0.01
Puget Sound Salish (0)	0	<0.01
Seminole (0)	1	<0.01
Shoshone (0)	0	<0.01
Sioux (3)	9	0.01
South American Ind. (2)	6	0.01
Spanish American Ind. (2)	2	<0.01
Tlingit-Haida *(Alaska Native)* (0)	0	<0.01
Tohono O'Odham (0)	0	<0.01
Tsimshian *(Alaska Native)* (0)	0	<0.01
Ute (0)	0	<0.01
Yakama (1)	2	<0.01
Yaqui (0)	0	<0.01
Yuman (0)	0	<0.01
Yup'ik *(Alaska Native)* (0)	0	<0.01
Asian (650)	832	1.08
Not Hispanic (642)	815	1.05
Hispanic (8)	17	0.02
Bangladeshi (0)	0	<0.01
Bhutanese (0)	0	<0.01
Burmese (0)	1	<0.01
Cambodian (25)	33	0.04
Chinese, ex. Taiwanese (149)	180	0.23
Filipino (87)	132	0.17
Hmong (0)	0	<0.01
Indian (224)	236	0.31
Indonesian (1)	1	<0.01
Japanese (19)	50	0.06
Korean (52)	82	0.11
Laotian (20)	24	0.03
Malaysian (0)	0	<0.01
Nepalese (4)	4	0.01
Pakistani (7)	9	0.01
Sri Lankan (0)	0	<0.01
Taiwanese (0)	0	<0.01
Thai (18)	21	0.03
Vietnamese (35)	53	0.07
Hawaii Native/Pacific Islander (19)	55	0.07
Not Hispanic (19)	48	0.06
Hispanic (0)	7	0.01
Fijian (0)	0	<0.01
Guamanian/Chamorro (4)	14	0.02
Marshallese (0)	0	<0.01
Native Hawaiian (5)	24	0.03
Samoan (5)	5	0.01
Tongan (0)	0	<0.01
White (72,188)	73,202	94.63
Not Hispanic (69,531)	70,242	90.80
Hispanic (2,657)	2,960	3.83

*Notes: † The Census 2010 population figure is used to calculate the percentages in the Hispanic Origin and Race categories. Ancestry percentages are based on the 2006-2010 American Community Survey population (not shown); ‡ Numbers in parentheses indicate the number of people reporting a single ancestry; * Numbers in parentheses indicate the number of persons reporting this race alone, not in combination with any other race; Please refer to the Explanation of Data for more information.*

LaGrange County

Population: 37,128

Ancestry	Population	%
Afghan (0)	0	<0.01
African, Sub-Saharan (3)	3	0.01
African (0)	0	<0.01
Cape Verdean (0)	0	<0.01
Ethiopian (3)	3	0.01
Ghanaian (0)	0	<0.01
Kenyan (0)	0	<0.01
Liberian (0)	0	<0.01
Nigerian (0)	0	<0.01
Senegalese (0)	0	<0.01
Sierra Leonean (0)	0	<0.01
Somalian (0)	0	<0.01
South African (0)	0	<0.01
Sudanese (0)	0	<0.01
Ugandan (0)	0	<0.01
Zimbabwean (0)	0	<0.01
Other Sub-Saharan African (0)	0	<0.01
Albanian (0)	0	<0.01
Alsatian (0)	0	<0.01
American (4,915)	4,915	13.29
Arab (38)	38	0.10
Arab (0)	0	<0.01
Egyptian (0)	0	<0.01
Iraqi (0)	0	<0.01
Jordanian (0)	0	<0.01
Lebanese (0)	0	<0.01
Moroccan (0)	0	<0.01
Palestinian (0)	0	<0.01
Syrian (0)	0	<0.01
Other Arab (38)	38	0.10
Armenian (0)	0	<0.01
Assyrian/Chaldean/Syriac (0)	0	<0.01
Australian (0)	0	<0.01
Austrian (0)	9	0.02
Basque (0)	0	<0.01
Belgian (0)	0	<0.01
Brazilian (0)	0	<0.01
British (0)	0	<0.01
Bulgarian (0)	0	<0.01
Cajun (0)	0	<0.01
Canadian (0)	9	0.02
Carpatho Rusyn (0)	0	<0.01
Celtic (0)	0	<0.01
Croatian (0)	0	<0.01
Cypriot (0)	0	<0.01
Czech (12)	12	0.03
Czechoslovakian (0)	9	0.02
Danish (9)	53	0.14
Dutch (383)	850	2.30
Eastern European (0)	0	<0.01
English (1,188)	2,364	6.39
Estonian (0)	0	<0.01
European (348)	377	1.02
Finnish (27)	50	0.14
French, ex. Basque (92)	734	1.98
French Canadian (8)	115	0.31
German (7,663)	13,346	36.07
German Russian (0)	0	<0.01
Greek (36)	50	0.14
Guyanese (0)	0	<0.01
Hungarian (44)	76	0.21
Icelander (0)	0	<0.01
Iranian (0)	0	<0.01
Irish (478)	2,377	6.43
Israeli (0)	0	<0.01
Italian (252)	409	1.11
Latvian (0)	0	<0.01
Lithuanian (0)	7	0.02
Luxemburger (0)	0	<0.01
Macedonian (0)	0	<0.01
Maltese (0)	0	<0.01
New Zealander (0)	0	<0.01
Northern European (0)	0	<0.01
Norwegian (0)	46	0.12
Pennsylvania German (1,342)	1,373	3.71
Polish (174)	553	1.49
Portuguese (0)	0	<0.01
Romanian (0)	13	0.04
Russian (10)	10	0.03
Scandinavian (5)	14	0.04
Scotch-Irish (173)	365	0.99
Scottish (109)	393	1.06
Serbian (0)	0	<0.01
Slavic (0)	22	0.06
Slovak (0)	20	0.05
Slovene (0)	0	<0.01
Soviet Union (0)	0	<0.01
Swedish (190)	397	1.07
Swiss (2,569)	4,215	11.39
Turkish (0)	0	<0.01
Ukrainian (8)	8	0.02
Welsh (10)	82	0.22
West Indian, ex. Hispanic (0)	0	<0.01
Bahamian (0)	0	<0.01
Barbadian (0)	0	<0.01
Belizean (0)	0	<0.01
Bermudan (0)	0	<0.01
British West Indian (0)	0	<0.01
Dutch West Indian (0)	0	<0.01
Haitian (0)	0	<0.01
Jamaican (0)	0	<0.01
Trinidadian/Tobagonian (0)	0	<0.01
U.S. Virgin Islander (0)	0	<0.01
West Indian (0)	0	<0.01
Other West Indian (0)	0	<0.01
Yugoslavian (0)	0	<0.01

Hispanic Origin	Population	%
Hispanic or Latino (of any race)	1,317	3.55
Central American, ex. Mexican	28	0.08
Costa Rican	0	<0.01
Guatemalan	2	0.01
Honduran	1	<0.01
Nicaraguan	0	<0.01
Panamanian	3	0.01
Salvadoran	21	0.06
Other Central American	1	<0.01
Cuban	5	0.01
Dominican Republic	0	<0.01
Mexican	1,197	3.22
Puerto Rican	27	0.07
South American	12	0.03
Argentinean	0	<0.01
Bolivian	5	0.01
Chilean	0	<0.01
Colombian	0	<0.01
Ecuadorian	3	0.01
Paraguayan	3	0.01
Peruvian	1	<0.01
Uruguayan	0	<0.01
Venezuelan	0	<0.01
Other South American	0	<0.01
Other Hispanic or Latino	48	0.13

Race*	Population	%
African-American/Black (117)	182	0.49
Not Hispanic (109)	161	0.43
Hispanic (8)	21	0.06
American Indian/Alaska Native (71)	176	0.47
Not Hispanic (65)	165	0.44
Hispanic (6)	11	0.03
Alaska Athabascan *(Ala. Nat.)* (0)	0	<0.01
Aleut *(Alaska Native)* (1)	1	<0.01
Apache (0)	0	<0.01
Arapaho (0)	0	<0.01
Blackfeet (1)	2	0.01
Canadian/French Am. Ind. (0)	1	<0.01
Central American Ind. (0)	0	<0.01
Cherokee (19)	51	0.14
Cheyenne (0)	0	<0.01
Chickasaw (0)	0	<0.01
Chippewa (9)	13	0.04
Choctaw (0)	0	<0.01
Colville (0)	0	<0.01
Comanche (0)	0	<0.01
Cree (0)	1	<0.01
Creek (0)	0	<0.01
Crow (0)	0	<0.01
Delaware (0)	0	<0.01
Hopi (0)	0	<0.01
Houma (0)	0	<0.01
Inupiat *(Alaska Native)* (0)	0	<0.01
Iroquois (0)	1	<0.01
Kiowa (0)	0	<0.01
Lumbee (0)	0	<0.01
Menominee (0)	0	<0.01
Mexican American Ind. (0)	0	<0.01
Navajo (1)	7	0.02
Osage (0)	0	<0.01
Ottawa (1)	3	0.01
Paiute (0)	0	<0.01
Pima (0)	0	<0.01
Potawatomi (6)	10	0.03
Pueblo (1)	1	<0.01
Puget Sound Salish (0)	0	<0.01
Seminole (0)	1	<0.01
Shoshone (0)	0	<0.01
Sioux (2)	6	0.02
South American Ind. (0)	0	<0.01
Spanish American Ind. (0)	0	<0.01
Tlingit-Haida *(Alaska Native)* (0)	0	<0.01
Tohono O'Odham (0)	1	<0.01
Tsimshian *(Alaska Native)* (0)	0	<0.01
Ute (0)	0	<0.01
Yakama (0)	0	<0.01
Yaqui (0)	0	<0.01
Yuman (0)	0	<0.01
Yup'ik *(Alaska Native)* (0)	0	<0.01
Asian (118)	196	0.53
Not Hispanic (118)	186	0.50
Hispanic (0)	10	0.03
Bangladeshi (0)	0	<0.01
Bhutanese (0)	0	<0.01
Burmese (7)	7	0.02
Cambodian (0)	0	<0.01
Chinese, ex. Taiwanese (42)	51	0.14
Filipino (20)	24	0.06
Hmong (0)	0	<0.01
Indian (10)	26	0.07
Indonesian (0)	0	<0.01
Japanese (3)	9	0.02
Korean (12)	20	0.05
Laotian (0)	1	<0.01
Malaysian (0)	0	<0.01
Nepalese (0)	0	<0.01
Pakistani (0)	0	<0.01
Sri Lankan (0)	0	<0.01
Taiwanese (0)	2	0.01
Thai (4)	4	0.01
Vietnamese (12)	22	0.06
Hawaii Native/Pacific Islander (2)	10	0.03
Not Hispanic (1)	7	0.02
Hispanic (1)	3	0.01
Fijian (0)	0	<0.01
Guamanian/Chamorro (2)	3	0.01
Marshallese (0)	0	<0.01
Native Hawaiian (0)	5	0.01
Samoan (0)	0	<0.01
Tongan (0)	0	<0.01
White (35,874)	36,168	97.41
Not Hispanic (35,290)	35,507	95.63
Hispanic (584)	661	1.78

*Notes: † The Census 2010 population figure is used to calculate the percentages in the Hispanic Origin and Race categories. Ancestry percentages are based on the 2006-2010 American Community Survey population (not shown); ‡ Numbers in parentheses indicate the number of people reporting a single ancestry; * Numbers in parentheses indicate the number of persons reporting this race alone, not in combination with any other race; Please refer to the Explanation of Data for more information.*

LaPorte County

Population: 111,467

Ancestry	Population	%
Afghan (0)	0	<0.01
African, Sub-Saharan (1,031)	1,164	1.05
African (1,015)	1,148	1.03
Cape Verdean (0)	0	<0.01
Ethiopian (8)	8	0.01
Ghanaian (0)	0	<0.01
Kenyan (0)	0	<0.01
Liberian (0)	0	<0.01
Nigerian (8)	8	0.01
Senegalese (0)	0	<0.01
Sierra Leonean (0)	0	<0.01
Somalian (0)	0	<0.01
South African (0)	0	<0.01
Sudanese (0)	0	<0.01
Ugandan (0)	0	<0.01
Zimbabwean (0)	0	<0.01
Other Sub-Saharan African (0)	0	<0.01
Albanian (26)	42	0.04
Alsatian (0)	0	<0.01
American (6,496)	6,496	5.86
Arab (388)	627	0.57
Arab (8)	30	0.03
Egyptian (0)	0	<0.01
Iraqi (0)	0	<0.01
Jordanian (0)	0	<0.01
Lebanese (348)	555	0.50
Moroccan (15)	15	0.01
Palestinian (7)	7	0.01
Syrian (10)	20	0.02
Other Arab (0)	0	<0.01
Armenian (21)	36	0.03
Assyrian/Chaldean/Syriac (0)	18	0.02
Australian (5)	5	<0.01
Austrian (46)	222	0.20
Basque (0)	0	<0.01
Belgian (73)	225	0.20
Brazilian (0)	0	<0.01
British (137)	336	0.30
Bulgarian (0)	0	<0.01
Cajun (0)	0	<0.01
Canadian (74)	129	0.12
Carpatho Rusyn (0)	0	<0.01
Celtic (11)	14	0.01
Croatian (39)	136	0.12
Cypriot (0)	0	<0.01
Czech (132)	940	0.85
Czechoslovakian (101)	152	0.14
Danish (51)	325	0.29
Dutch (662)	2,757	2.49
Eastern European (23)	23	0.02
English (2,406)	9,237	8.33
Estonian (0)	0	<0.01
European (947)	1,001	0.90
Finnish (33)	115	0.10
French, ex. Basque (422)	2,330	2.10
French Canadian (190)	412	0.37
German (12,739)	34,098	30.74
German Russian (0)	0	<0.01
Greek (160)	366	0.33
Guyanese (0)	0	<0.01
Hungarian (301)	1,270	1.14
Icelander (0)	5	<0.01
Iranian (60)	60	0.05
Irish (4,123)	17,004	15.33
Israeli (0)	0	<0.01
Italian (920)	3,794	3.42
Latvian (0)	17	0.02
Lithuanian (197)	606	0.55
Luxemburger (10)	10	0.01
Macedonian (0)	0	<0.01
Maltese (0)	0	<0.01
New Zealander (0)	0	<0.01
Northern European (24)	24	0.02
Norwegian (257)	691	0.62
Pennsylvania German (36)	87	0.08
Polish (5,037)	12,809	11.55
Portuguese (7)	69	0.06
Romanian (33)	159	0.14
Russian (149)	490	0.44
Scandinavian (71)	201	0.18
Scotch-Irish (327)	1,160	1.05
Scottish (486)	1,879	1.69
Serbian (45)	155	0.14
Slavic (42)	134	0.12
Slovak (127)	338	0.30
Slovene (53)	99	0.09
Soviet Union (0)	0	<0.01
Swedish (804)	2,892	2.61
Swiss (93)	401	0.36
Turkish (0)	0	<0.01
Ukrainian (88)	135	0.12
Welsh (90)	436	0.39
West Indian, ex. Hispanic (68)	76	0.07
Bahamian (0)	0	<0.01
Barbadian (0)	0	<0.01
Belizean (0)	0	<0.01
Bermudan (9)	9	0.01
British West Indian (0)	0	<0.01
Dutch West Indian (0)	0	<0.01
Haitian (28)	28	0.03
Jamaican (31)	39	0.04
Trinidadian/Tobagonian (0)	0	<0.01
U.S. Virgin Islander (0)	0	<0.01
West Indian (0)	0	<0.01
Other West Indian (0)	0	<0.01
Yugoslavian (3)	42	0.04

Hispanic Origin	Population	%
Hispanic or Latino (of any race)	6,093	5.47
Central American, ex. Mexican	109	0.10
Costa Rican	3	<0.01
Guatemalan	33	0.03
Honduran	10	0.01
Nicaraguan	20	0.02
Panamanian	24	0.02
Salvadoran	19	0.02
Other Central American	0	<0.01
Cuban	65	0.06
Dominican Republic	6	0.01
Mexican	4,997	4.48
Puerto Rican	498	0.45
South American	65	0.06
Argentinean	5	<0.01
Bolivian	2	<0.01
Chilean	1	<0.01
Colombian	24	0.02
Ecuadorian	3	<0.01
Paraguayan	0	<0.01
Peruvian	23	0.02
Uruguayan	2	<0.01
Venezuelan	2	<0.01
Other South American	3	<0.01
Other Hispanic or Latino	353	0.32

Race*	Population	%
African-American/Black (12,001)	13,400	12.02
Not Hispanic (11,835)	13,082	11.74
Hispanic (166)	318	0.29
American Indian/Alaska Native (306)	886	0.79
Not Hispanic (246)	750	0.67
Hispanic (60)	136	0.12
Alaska Athabascan *(Ala. Nat.)* (1)	1	<0.01
Aleut *(Alaska Native)* (1)	1	<0.01
Apache (6)	28	0.03
Arapaho (0)	0	<0.01
Blackfeet (5)	66	0.06
Canadian/French Am. Ind. (1)	4	<0.01
Central American Ind. (0)	0	<0.01
Cherokee (51)	245	0.22
Cheyenne (0)	3	<0.01
Chickasaw (3)	9	0.01
Chippewa (19)	38	0.03
Choctaw (3)	7	0.01
Colville (1)	1	<0.01
Comanche (1)	1	<0.01
Cree (0)	0	<0.01
Creek (4)	5	<0.01
Crow (0)	2	<0.01
Delaware (0)	1	<0.01
Hopi (0)	1	<0.01
Houma (0)	0	<0.01
Inupiat *(Alaska Native)* (0)	0	<0.01
Iroquois (1)	12	0.01
Kiowa (0)	0	<0.01
Lumbee (0)	0	<0.01
Menominee (3)	4	<0.01
Mexican American Ind. (15)	23	0.02
Navajo (5)	15	0.01
Osage (0)	0	<0.01
Ottawa (1)	1	<0.01
Paiute (0)	0	<0.01
Pima (0)	0	<0.01
Potawatomi (7)	17	0.02
Pueblo (0)	0	<0.01
Puget Sound Salish (0)	0	<0.01
Seminole (0)	0	<0.01
Shoshone (0)	2	<0.01
Sioux (9)	31	0.03
South American Ind. (1)	2	<0.01
Spanish American Ind. (1)	1	<0.01
Tlingit-Haida *(Alaska Native)* (0)	0	<0.01
Tohono O'Odham (1)	1	<0.01
Tsimshian *(Alaska Native)* (0)	0	<0.01
Ute (0)	0	<0.01
Yakama (0)	0	<0.01
Yaqui (0)	0	<0.01
Yuman (0)	0	<0.01
Yup'ik *(Alaska Native)* (0)	0	<0.01
Asian (583)	883	0.79
Not Hispanic (570)	828	0.74
Hispanic (13)	55	0.05
Bangladeshi (0)	0	<0.01
Bhutanese (0)	0	<0.01
Burmese (0)	0	<0.01
Cambodian (3)	3	<0.01
Chinese, ex. Taiwanese (114)	137	0.12
Filipino (119)	203	0.18
Hmong (0)	0	<0.01
Indian (161)	203	0.18
Indonesian (2)	5	<0.01
Japanese (30)	84	0.08
Korean (57)	88	0.08
Laotian (1)	1	<0.01
Malaysian (0)	0	<0.01
Nepalese (0)	0	<0.01
Pakistani (15)	20	0.02
Sri Lankan (4)	5	<0.01
Taiwanese (5)	7	0.01
Thai (11)	16	0.01
Vietnamese (42)	52	0.05
Hawaii Native/Pacific Islander (21)	77	0.07
Not Hispanic (13)	55	0.05
Hispanic (8)	22	0.02
Fijian (0)	0	<0.01
Guamanian/Chamorro (3)	5	<0.01
Marshallese (0)	0	<0.01
Native Hawaiian (7)	31	0.03
Samoan (6)	14	0.01
Tongan (0)	2	<0.01
White (93,787)	96,128	86.24
Not Hispanic (90,695)	92,503	82.99
Hispanic (3,092)	3,625	3.25

*Notes: † The Census 2010 population figure is used to calculate the percentages in the Hispanic Origin and Race categories. Ancestry percentages are based on the 2006-2010 American Community Survey population (not shown); ‡ Numbers in parentheses indicate the number of people reporting a single ancestry; * Numbers in parentheses indicate the number of persons reporting this race alone, not in combination with any other race; Please refer to the Explanation of Data for more information.*

Lake County

Population: 496,005

Ancestry	Population	%
Afghan (3)	3	<0.01
African, Sub-Saharan (4,161)	4,695	0.95
African (3,731)	4,119	0.83
Cape Verdean (9)	28	0.01
Ethiopian (171)	171	0.03
Ghanaian (28)	40	0.01
Kenyan (0)	0	<0.01
Liberian (0)	11	<0.01
Nigerian (179)	270	0.05
Senegalese (0)	0	<0.01
Sierra Leonean (0)	0	<0.01
Somalian (0)	0	<0.01
South African (43)	43	0.01
Sudanese (0)	0	<0.01
Ugandan (0)	0	<0.01
Zimbabwean (0)	0	<0.01
Other Sub-Saharan African (0)	13	<0.01
Albanian (31)	113	0.02
Alsatian (0)	18	<0.01
American (18,230)	18,230	3.69
Arab (1,852)	2,164	0.44
Arab (643)	753	0.15
Egyptian (294)	294	0.06
Iraqi (0)	0	<0.01
Jordanian (104)	104	0.02
Lebanese (105)	170	0.03
Moroccan (27)	57	0.01
Palestinian (475)	545	0.11
Syrian (142)	162	0.03
Other Arab (62)	79	0.02
Armenian (67)	104	0.02
Assyrian/Chaldean/Syriac (89)	99	0.02
Australian (39)	56	0.01
Austrian (154)	761	0.15
Basque (0)	0	<0.01
Belgian (121)	529	0.11
Brazilian (58)	80	0.02
British (271)	596	0.12
Bulgarian (134)	204	0.04
Cajun (0)	0	<0.01
Canadian (121)	447	0.09
Carpatho Rusyn (24)	33	0.01
Celtic (0)	7	<0.01
Croatian (1,920)	6,296	1.27
Cypriot (0)	0	<0.01
Czech (699)	2,416	0.49
Czechoslovakian (330)	845	0.17
Danish (179)	1,008	0.20
Dutch (5,546)	14,612	2.96
Eastern European (369)	412	0.08
English (7,382)	26,727	5.41
Estonian (0)	51	0.01
European (1,875)	2,139	0.43
Finnish (81)	403	0.08
French, ex. Basque (1,095)	8,687	1.76
French Canadian (266)	1,263	0.26
German (22,632)	79,686	16.12
German Russian (0)	0	<0.01
Greek (3,437)	5,765	1.17
Guyanese (14)	14	<0.01
Hungarian (2,159)	6,256	1.27
Icelander (14)	28	0.01
Iranian (0)	9	<0.01
Irish (12,098)	54,906	11.11
Israeli (0)	0	<0.01
Italian (7,796)	23,510	4.76
Latvian (0)	118	0.02
Lithuanian (1,156)	3,170	0.64
Luxemburger (0)	19	<0.01
Macedonian (2,383)	2,623	0.53
Maltese (10)	58	0.01
New Zealander (0)	0	<0.01
Northern European (225)	243	0.05
Norwegian (628)	2,635	0.53
Pennsylvania German (63)	281	0.06
Polish (18,732)	47,271	9.56
Portuguese (41)	191	0.04
Romanian (684)	1,504	0.30
Russian (956)	2,898	0.59
Scandinavian (37)	306	0.06
Scotch-Irish (1,452)	4,669	0.94
Scottish (1,170)	5,537	1.12
Serbian (3,318)	5,406	1.09
Slavic (164)	312	0.06
Slovak (3,772)	9,890	2.00
Slovene (123)	262	0.05
Soviet Union (0)	0	<0.01
Swedish (1,440)	7,763	1.57
Swiss (123)	755	0.15
Turkish (141)	176	0.04
Ukrainian (616)	1,355	0.27
Welsh (438)	1,892	0.38
West Indian, ex. Hispanic (377)	710	0.14
Bahamian (0)	14	<0.01
Barbadian (0)	0	<0.01
Belizean (31)	31	0.01
Bermudan (0)	0	<0.01
British West Indian (0)	64	0.01
Dutch West Indian (0)	0	<0.01
Haitian (42)	100	0.02
Jamaican (254)	353	0.07
Trinidadian/Tobagonian (18)	18	<0.01
U.S. Virgin Islander (0)	0	<0.01
West Indian (7)	105	0.02
Other West Indian (25)	25	0.01
Yugoslavian (404)	753	0.15

Hispanic Origin	Population	%
Hispanic or Latino (of any race)	82,663	16.67
Central American, ex. Mexican	1,194	0.24
Costa Rican	34	0.01
Guatemalan	390	0.08
Honduran	265	0.05
Nicaraguan	92	0.02
Panamanian	78	0.02
Salvadoran	325	0.07
Other Central American	10	<0.01
Cuban	467	0.09
Dominican Republic	125	0.03
Mexican	64,912	13.09
Puerto Rican	11,991	2.42
South American	719	0.14
Argentinean	103	0.02
Bolivian	24	<0.01
Chilean	36	0.01
Colombian	185	0.04
Ecuadorian	143	0.03
Paraguayan	4	<0.01
Peruvian	170	0.03
Uruguayan	19	<0.01
Venezuelan	33	0.01
Other South American	2	<0.01
Other Hispanic or Latino	3,255	0.66

Race*	Population	%
African-American/Black (128,263)	133,434	26.90
Not Hispanic (125,506)	129,279	26.06
Hispanic (2,757)	4,155	0.84
American Indian/Alaska Native (1,628)	4,217	0.85
Not Hispanic (913)	2,839	0.57
Hispanic (715)	1,378	0.28
Alaska Athabascan *(Ala. Nat.)* (3)	8	<0.01
Aleut *(Alaska Native)* (1)	1	<0.01
Apache (32)	87	0.02
Arapaho (1)	8	<0.01
Blackfeet (26)	155	0.03
Canadian/French Am. Ind. (10)	24	<0.01
Central American Ind. (5)	10	<0.01
Cherokee (158)	872	0.18
Cheyenne (1)	9	<0.01
Chickasaw (4)	13	<0.01
Chippewa (50)	113	0.02
Choctaw (13)	72	0.01
Colville (0)	0	<0.01
Comanche (3)	8	<0.01
Cree (4)	11	<0.01
Creek (25)	56	0.01
Crow (2)	8	<0.01
Delaware (2)	12	<0.01
Hopi (1)	2	<0.01
Houma (5)	6	<0.01
Inupiat *(Alaska Native)* (2)	11	<0.01
Iroquois (21)	52	0.01
Kiowa (2)	3	<0.01
Lumbee (8)	13	<0.01
Menominee (4)	20	<0.01
Mexican American Ind. (124)	203	0.04
Navajo (12)	39	0.01
Osage (3)	5	<0.01
Ottawa (2)	10	<0.01
Paiute (3)	4	<0.01
Pima (1)	3	<0.01
Potawatomi (12)	29	0.01
Pueblo (4)	6	<0.01
Puget Sound Salish (0)	2	<0.01
Seminole (0)	19	<0.01
Shoshone (8)	11	<0.01
Sioux (41)	105	0.02
South American Ind. (15)	51	0.01
Spanish American Ind. (5)	9	<0.01
Tlingit-Haida *(Alaska Native)* (10)	13	<0.01
Tohono O'Odham (1)	1	<0.01
Tsimshian *(Alaska Native)* (1)	1	<0.01
Ute (6)	7	<0.01
Yakama (0)	0	<0.01
Yaqui (4)	6	<0.01
Yuman (0)	0	<0.01
Yup'ik *(Alaska Native)* (0)	2	<0.01
Asian (6,142)	7,952	1.60
Not Hispanic (5,981)	7,441	1.50
Hispanic (161)	511	0.10
Bangladeshi (34)	39	0.01
Bhutanese (0)	0	<0.01
Burmese (5)	5	<0.01
Cambodian (25)	30	0.01
Chinese, ex. Taiwanese (1,038)	1,278	0.26
Filipino (1,464)	2,054	0.41
Hmong (4)	5	<0.01
Indian (1,899)	2,115	0.43
Indonesian (23)	41	0.01
Japanese (123)	335	0.07
Korean (514)	704	0.14
Laotian (17)	20	<0.01
Malaysian (5)	13	<0.01
Nepalese (14)	15	<0.01
Pakistani (320)	364	0.07
Sri Lankan (4)	4	<0.01
Taiwanese (36)	44	0.01
Thai (126)	194	0.04
Vietnamese (280)	367	0.07
Hawaii Native/Pacific Islander (108)	408	0.08
Not Hispanic (63)	256	0.05
Hispanic (45)	152	0.03
Fijian (1)	5	<0.01
Guamanian/Chamorro (15)	55	0.01
Marshallese (0)	0	<0.01
Native Hawaiian (47)	112	0.02
Samoan (18)	71	0.01
Tongan (0)	0	<0.01
White (319,412)	329,031	66.34
Not Hispanic (274,162)	279,401	56.33
Hispanic (45,250)	49,630	10.01

*Notes: † The Census 2010 population figure is used to calculate the percentages in the Hispanic Origin and Race categories. Ancestry percentages are based on the 2006-2010 American Community Survey population (not shown); ‡ Numbers in parentheses indicate the number of people reporting a single ancestry; * Numbers in parentheses indicate the number of persons reporting this race alone, not in combination with any other race; Please refer to the Explanation of Data for more information.*

Lawrence County

Population: 46,134

Ancestry	Population	%
Afghan (0)	0	<0.01
African, Sub-Saharan (0)	0	<0.01
African (0)	0	<0.01
Cape Verdean (0)	0	<0.01
Ethiopian (0)	0	<0.01
Ghanaian (0)	0	<0.01
Kenyan (0)	0	<0.01
Liberian (0)	0	<0.01
Nigerian (0)	0	<0.01
Senegalese (0)	0	<0.01
Sierra Leonean (0)	0	<0.01
Somalian (0)	0	<0.01
South African (0)	0	<0.01
Sudanese (0)	0	<0.01
Ugandan (0)	0	<0.01
Zimbabwean (0)	0	<0.01
Other Sub-Saharan African (0)	0	<0.01
Albanian (0)	0	<0.01
Alsatian (0)	0	<0.01
American (6,069)	6,069	13.14
Arab (11)	11	0.02
Arab (1)	1	<0.01
Egyptian (10)	10	0.02
Iraqi (0)	0	<0.01
Jordanian (0)	0	<0.01
Lebanese (0)	0	<0.01
Moroccan (0)	0	<0.01
Palestinian (0)	0	<0.01
Syrian (0)	0	<0.01
Other Arab (0)	0	<0.01
Armenian (0)	0	<0.01
Assyrian/Chaldean/Syriac (0)	0	<0.01
Australian (0)	0	<0.01
Austrian (21)	67	0.15
Basque (0)	0	<0.01
Belgian (11)	11	0.02
Brazilian (10)	10	0.02
British (33)	64	0.14
Bulgarian (0)	0	<0.01
Cajun (0)	0	<0.01
Canadian (49)	67	0.15
Carpatho Rusyn (0)	0	<0.01
Celtic (3)	3	0.01
Croatian (0)	36	0.08
Cypriot (0)	0	<0.01
Czech (0)	37	0.08
Czechoslovakian (0)	0	<0.01
Danish (58)	105	0.23
Dutch (163)	593	1.28
Eastern European (9)	9	0.02
English (2,075)	4,826	10.45
Estonian (0)	0	<0.01
European (302)	403	0.87
Finnish (0)	57	0.12
French, ex. Basque (300)	1,128	2.44
French Canadian (158)	202	0.44
German (3,506)	8,521	18.45
German Russian (0)	0	<0.01
Greek (16)	57	0.12
Guyanese (0)	0	<0.01
Hungarian (59)	112	0.24
Icelander (0)	0	<0.01
Iranian (0)	0	<0.01
Irish (2,296)	6,726	14.56
Israeli (0)	0	<0.01
Italian (457)	1,098	2.38
Latvian (0)	0	<0.01
Lithuanian (28)	37	0.08
Luxemburger (0)	0	<0.01
Macedonian (0)	0	<0.01
Maltese (0)	0	<0.01
New Zealander (0)	0	<0.01
Northern European (0)	0	<0.01
Norwegian (56)	133	0.29
Pennsylvania German (103)	103	0.22
Polish (135)	325	0.70
Portuguese (0)	0	<0.01
Romanian (51)	100	0.22
Russian (28)	83	0.18
Scandinavian (4)	75	0.16
Scotch-Irish (441)	946	2.05
Scottish (395)	1,344	2.91
Serbian (0)	0	<0.01
Slavic (0)	0	<0.01
Slovak (10)	38	0.08
Slovene (0)	0	<0.01
Soviet Union (0)	0	<0.01
Swedish (44)	249	0.54
Swiss (0)	6	0.01
Turkish (0)	0	<0.01
Ukrainian (0)	0	<0.01
Welsh (153)	291	0.63
West Indian, ex. Hispanic (11)	73	0.16
Bahamian (0)	0	<0.01
Barbadian (0)	0	<0.01
Belizean (0)	0	<0.01
Bermudan (0)	0	<0.01
British West Indian (0)	0	<0.01
Dutch West Indian (11)	58	0.13
Haitian (0)	15	0.03
Jamaican (0)	0	<0.01
Trinidadian/Tobagonian (0)	0	<0.01
U.S. Virgin Islander (0)	0	<0.01
West Indian (0)	0	<0.01
Other West Indian (0)	0	<0.01
Yugoslavian (9)	9	0.02

Hispanic Origin	Population	%
Hispanic or Latino (of any race)	545	1.18
Central American, ex. Mexican	20	0.04
Costa Rican	10	0.02
Guatemalan	3	0.01
Honduran	1	<0.01
Nicaraguan	2	<0.01
Panamanian	1	<0.01
Salvadoran	3	0.01
Other Central American	0	<0.01
Cuban	18	0.04
Dominican Republic	3	0.01
Mexican	364	0.79
Puerto Rican	45	0.10
South American	21	0.05
Argentinean	0	<0.01
Bolivian	3	0.01
Chilean	0	<0.01
Colombian	11	0.02
Ecuadorian	0	<0.01
Paraguayan	0	<0.01
Peruvian	4	0.01
Uruguayan	0	<0.01
Venezuelan	2	<0.01
Other South American	1	<0.01
Other Hispanic or Latino	74	0.16

Race*	Population	%
African-American/Black (186)	301	0.65
Not Hispanic (181)	293	0.64
Hispanic (5)	8	0.02
American Indian/Alaska Native (158)	418	0.91
Not Hispanic (148)	393	0.85
Hispanic (10)	25	0.05
Alaska Athabascan *(Ala. Nat.)* (0)	0	<0.01
Aleut *(Alaska Native)* (0)	0	<0.01
Apache (0)	4	0.01
Arapaho (0)	0	<0.01
Blackfeet (1)	7	0.02
Canadian/French Am. Ind. (1)	3	0.01
Central American Ind. (0)	1	<0.01
Cherokee (48)	147	0.32
Cheyenne (1)	1	<0.01
Chickasaw (1)	1	<0.01
Chippewa (9)	11	0.02
Choctaw (2)	9	0.02
Colville (0)	0	<0.01
Comanche (0)	0	<0.01
Cree (0)	0	<0.01
Creek (1)	2	<0.01
Crow (0)	0	<0.01
Delaware (1)	1	<0.01
Hopi (0)	0	<0.01
Houma (0)	0	<0.01
Inupiat *(Alaska Native)* (0)	0	<0.01
Iroquois (6)	8	0.02
Kiowa (0)	0	<0.01
Lumbee (6)	11	0.02
Menominee (0)	0	<0.01
Mexican American Ind. (3)	3	0.01
Navajo (1)	7	0.02
Osage (0)	0	<0.01
Ottawa (0)	0	<0.01
Paiute (0)	0	<0.01
Pima (0)	0	<0.01
Potawatomi (1)	1	<0.01
Pueblo (0)	0	<0.01
Puget Sound Salish (0)	1	<0.01
Seminole (0)	0	<0.01
Shoshone (0)	0	<0.01
Sioux (7)	18	0.04
South American Ind. (1)	1	<0.01
Spanish American Ind. (3)	3	0.01
Tlingit-Haida *(Alaska Native)* (0)	0	<0.01
Tohono O'Odham (0)	0	<0.01
Tsimshian *(Alaska Native)* (0)	0	<0.01
Ute (1)	1	<0.01
Yakama (0)	0	<0.01
Yaqui (0)	0	<0.01
Yuman (0)	0	<0.01
Yup'ik *(Alaska Native)* (0)	0	<0.01
Asian (224)	315	0.68
Not Hispanic (224)	300	0.65
Hispanic (0)	15	0.03
Bangladeshi (0)	0	<0.01
Bhutanese (0)	0	<0.01
Burmese (0)	0	<0.01
Cambodian (0)	0	<0.01
Chinese, ex. Taiwanese (51)	63	0.14
Filipino (57)	108	0.23
Hmong (0)	0	<0.01
Indian (58)	66	0.14
Indonesian (0)	0	<0.01
Japanese (9)	21	0.05
Korean (15)	19	0.04
Laotian (0)	0	<0.01
Malaysian (0)	0	<0.01
Nepalese (0)	0	<0.01
Pakistani (0)	0	<0.01
Sri Lankan (0)	0	<0.01
Taiwanese (1)	4	0.01
Thai (3)	5	0.01
Vietnamese (24)	27	0.06
Hawaii Native/Pacific Islander (14)	32	0.07
Not Hispanic (9)	25	0.05
Hispanic (5)	7	0.02
Fijian (0)	0	<0.01
Guamanian/Chamorro (9)	13	0.03
Marshallese (0)	0	<0.01
Native Hawaiian (3)	5	0.01
Samoan (0)	2	<0.01
Tongan (0)	0	<0.01
White (44,905)	45,406	98.42
Not Hispanic (44,562)	45,003	97.55
Hispanic (343)	403	0.87

*Notes: † The Census 2010 population figure is used to calculate the percentages in the Hispanic Origin and Race categories. Ancestry percentages are based on the 2006-2010 American Community Survey population (not shown); ‡ Numbers in parentheses indicate the number of people reporting a single ancestry; * Numbers in parentheses indicate the number of persons reporting this race alone, not in combination with any other race; Please refer to the Explanation of Data for more information.*

Madison County

Population: 131,636

Ancestry	Population	%
Afghan (0)	0	<0.01
African, Sub-Saharan (735)	768	0.58
African (630)	663	0.50
Cape Verdean (0)	0	<0.01
Ethiopian (18)	18	0.01
Ghanaian (0)	0	<0.01
Kenyan (43)	43	0.03
Liberian (0)	0	<0.01
Nigerian (0)	0	<0.01
Senegalese (0)	0	<0.01
Sierra Leonean (0)	0	<0.01
Somalian (0)	0	<0.01
South African (0)	0	<0.01
Sudanese (18)	18	0.01
Ugandan (0)	0	<0.01
Zimbabwean (0)	0	<0.01
Other Sub-Saharan African (26)	26	0.02
Albanian (0)	0	<0.01
Alsatian (0)	0	<0.01
American (16,493)	16,493	12.55
Arab (30)	71	0.05
Arab (0)	0	<0.01
Egyptian (0)	0	<0.01
Iraqi (0)	0	<0.01
Jordanian (0)	0	<0.01
Lebanese (12)	41	0.03
Moroccan (18)	30	0.02
Palestinian (0)	0	<0.01
Syrian (0)	0	<0.01
Other Arab (0)	0	<0.01
Armenian (0)	0	<0.01
Assyrian/Chaldean/Syriac (0)	0	<0.01
Australian (12)	12	0.01
Austrian (85)	230	0.17
Basque (0)	0	<0.01
Belgian (5)	60	0.05
Brazilian (0)	0	<0.01
British (224)	469	0.36
Bulgarian (24)	24	0.02
Cajun (31)	44	0.03
Canadian (96)	125	0.10
Carpatho Rusyn (0)	0	<0.01
Celtic (0)	12	0.01
Croatian (9)	133	0.10
Cypriot (0)	0	<0.01
Czech (57)	196	0.15
Czechoslovakian (13)	56	0.04
Danish (28)	148	0.11
Dutch (753)	3,039	2.31
Eastern European (51)	51	0.04
English (6,450)	13,634	10.37
Estonian (0)	0	<0.01
European (947)	1,060	0.81
Finnish (13)	121	0.09
French, ex. Basque (1,072)	3,068	2.33
French Canadian (158)	266	0.20
German (12,897)	28,231	21.48
German Russian (0)	0	<0.01
Greek (221)	300	0.23
Guyanese (0)	0	<0.01
Hungarian (65)	197	0.15
Icelander (0)	0	<0.01
Iranian (11)	11	0.01
Irish (4,927)	15,124	11.51
Israeli (0)	0	<0.01
Italian (921)	2,169	1.65
Latvian (8)	8	0.01
Lithuanian (6)	17	0.01
Luxemburger (0)	6	<0.01
Macedonian (15)	15	0.01
Maltese (0)	0	<0.01
New Zealander (0)	0	<0.01
Northern European (90)	107	0.08
Norwegian (114)	353	0.27
Pennsylvania German (28)	40	0.03
Polish (618)	1,642	1.25
Portuguese (36)	136	0.10
Romanian (84)	108	0.08
Russian (76)	194	0.15
Scandinavian (15)	162	0.12
Scotch-Irish (729)	1,856	1.41
Scottish (1,189)	2,721	2.07
Serbian (78)	90	0.07
Slavic (13)	26	0.02
Slovak (39)	69	0.05
Slovene (0)	23	0.02
Soviet Union (0)	0	<0.01
Swedish (364)	903	0.69
Swiss (79)	401	0.31
Turkish (35)	113	0.09
Ukrainian (9)	84	0.06
Welsh (314)	923	0.70
West Indian, ex. Hispanic (42)	56	0.04
Bahamian (0)	0	<0.01
Barbadian (0)	0	<0.01
Belizean (0)	0	<0.01
Bermudan (0)	0	<0.01
British West Indian (0)	0	<0.01
Dutch West Indian (0)	0	<0.01
Haitian (0)	0	<0.01
Jamaican (29)	29	0.02
Trinidadian/Tobagonian (0)	0	<0.01
U.S. Virgin Islander (0)	0	<0.01
West Indian (0)	0	<0.01
Other West Indian (13)	27	0.02
Yugoslavian (8)	40	0.03

Hispanic Origin	Population	%
Hispanic or Latino (of any race)	4,189	3.18
Central American, ex. Mexican	175	0.13
Costa Rican	1	<0.01
Guatemalan	81	0.06
Honduran	30	0.02
Nicaraguan	19	0.01
Panamanian	6	<0.01
Salvadoran	38	0.03
Other Central American	0	<0.01
Cuban	48	0.04
Dominican Republic	23	0.02
Mexican	3,302	2.51
Puerto Rican	202	0.15
South American	73	0.06
Argentinean	12	0.01
Bolivian	3	<0.01
Chilean	7	0.01
Colombian	30	0.02
Ecuadorian	8	0.01
Paraguayan	0	<0.01
Peruvian	7	0.01
Uruguayan	0	<0.01
Venezuelan	5	<0.01
Other South American	1	<0.01
Other Hispanic or Latino	366	0.28

Race*	Population	%
African-American/Black (10,963)	12,333	9.37
Not Hispanic (10,887)	12,168	9.24
Hispanic (76)	165	0.13
American Indian/Alaska Native (320)	907	0.69
Not Hispanic (253)	784	0.60
Hispanic (67)	123	0.09
Alaska Athabascan *(Ala. Nat.)* (0)	0	<0.01
Aleut *(Alaska Native)* (0)	0	<0.01
Apache (11)	16	0.01
Arapaho (0)	0	<0.01
Blackfeet (2)	41	0.03
Canadian/French Am. Ind. (5)	7	0.01
Central American Ind. (0)	7	0.01
Cherokee (78)	249	0.19
Cheyenne (2)	9	0.01
Chickasaw (0)	1	<0.01
Chippewa (6)	9	0.01
Choctaw (8)	19	0.01
Colville (0)	0	<0.01
Comanche (0)	0	<0.01
Cree (0)	0	<0.01
Creek (2)	4	<0.01
Crow (0)	0	<0.01
Delaware (0)	9	0.01
Hopi (0)	1	<0.01
Houma (0)	0	<0.01
Inupiat *(Alaska Native)* (2)	6	<0.01
Iroquois (0)	8	0.01
Kiowa (1)	1	<0.01
Lumbee (1)	1	<0.01
Menominee (0)	2	<0.01
Mexican American Ind. (21)	35	0.03
Navajo (2)	11	0.01
Osage (2)	3	<0.01
Ottawa (0)	0	<0.01
Paiute (0)	0	<0.01
Pima (0)	0	<0.01
Potawatomi (3)	7	0.01
Pueblo (0)	0	<0.01
Puget Sound Salish (0)	0	<0.01
Seminole (0)	3	<0.01
Shoshone (0)	1	<0.01
Sioux (10)	22	0.02
South American Ind. (0)	6	<0.01
Spanish American Ind. (2)	4	<0.01
Tlingit-Haida *(Alaska Native)* (0)	0	<0.01
Tohono O'Odham (0)	0	<0.01
Tsimshian *(Alaska Native)* (0)	0	<0.01
Ute (4)	4	<0.01
Yakama (0)	0	<0.01
Yaqui (0)	0	<0.01
Yuman (0)	0	<0.01
Yup'ik *(Alaska Native)* (0)	0	<0.01
Asian (553)	851	0.65
Not Hispanic (547)	815	0.62
Hispanic (6)	36	0.03
Bangladeshi (5)	5	<0.01
Bhutanese (0)	0	<0.01
Burmese (0)	0	<0.01
Cambodian (0)	0	<0.01
Chinese, ex. Taiwanese (122)	153	0.12
Filipino (98)	180	0.14
Hmong (0)	0	<0.01
Indian (84)	108	0.08
Indonesian (7)	7	0.01
Japanese (53)	123	0.09
Korean (58)	112	0.09
Laotian (1)	5	<0.01
Malaysian (1)	1	<0.01
Nepalese (0)	0	<0.01
Pakistani (7)	7	0.01
Sri Lankan (0)	0	<0.01
Taiwanese (1)	4	<0.01
Thai (18)	25	0.02
Vietnamese (48)	71	0.05
Hawaii Native/Pacific Islander (45)	106	0.08
Not Hispanic (41)	85	0.06
Hispanic (4)	21	0.02
Fijian (0)	0	<0.01
Guamanian/Chamorro (7)	16	0.01
Marshallese (0)	0	<0.01
Native Hawaiian (13)	47	0.04
Samoan (12)	17	0.01
Tongan (2)	5	<0.01
White (115,452)	117,627	89.36
Not Hispanic (113,577)	115,443	87.70
Hispanic (1,875)	2,184	1.66

*Notes: † The Census 2010 population figure is used to calculate the percentages in the Hispanic Origin and Race categories. Ancestry percentages are based on the 2006-2010 American Community Survey population (not shown); ‡ Numbers in parentheses indicate the number of people reporting a single ancestry; * Numbers in parentheses indicate the number of persons reporting this race alone, not in combination with any other race; Please refer to the Explanation of Data for more information.*

Marion County

Population: 903,393

Ancestry	Population	%
Afghan (29)	29	<0.01
African, Sub-Saharan (36,354)	46,331	5.20
African (31,078)	40,758	4.57
Cape Verdean (0)	0	<0.01
Ethiopian (469)	489	0.05
Ghanaian (154)	154	0.02
Kenyan (85)	85	0.01
Liberian (687)	687	0.08
Nigerian (1,976)	2,117	0.24
Senegalese (150)	150	0.02
Sierra Leonean (0)	0	<0.01
Somalian (432)	464	0.05
South African (20)	43	<0.01
Sudanese (376)	376	0.04
Ugandan (14)	54	0.01
Zimbabwean (149)	149	0.02
Other Sub-Saharan African (764)	805	0.09
Albanian (51)	108	0.01
Alsatian (0)	12	<0.01
American (58,784)	58,784	6.60
Arab (1,866)	2,962	0.33
Arab (445)	610	0.07
Egyptian (147)	158	0.02
Iraqi (132)	192	0.02
Jordanian (152)	182	0.02
Lebanese (444)	892	0.10
Moroccan (96)	141	0.02
Palestinian (12)	45	0.01
Syrian (79)	274	0.03
Other Arab (359)	468	0.05
Armenian (34)	162	0.02
Assyrian/Chaldean/Syriac (44)	54	0.01
Australian (198)	269	0.03
Austrian (359)	1,206	0.14
Basque (0)	0	<0.01
Belgian (291)	896	0.10
Brazilian (158)	303	0.03
British (1,883)	3,902	0.44
Bulgarian (18)	80	0.01
Cajun (29)	52	0.01
Canadian (749)	1,489	0.17
Carpatho Rusyn (0)	0	<0.01
Celtic (15)	23	<0.01
Croatian (130)	477	0.05
Cypriot (0)	0	<0.01
Czech (427)	1,642	0.18
Czechoslovakian (229)	479	0.05
Danish (528)	1,777	0.20
Dutch (3,129)	13,035	1.46
Eastern European (312)	348	0.04
English (27,379)	75,268	8.45
Estonian (27)	113	0.01
European (8,667)	10,318	1.16
Finnish (213)	505	0.06
French, ex. Basque (3,707)	17,752	1.99
French Canadian (652)	1,747	0.20
German (64,968)	168,045	18.86
German Russian (22)	22	<0.01
Greek (1,310)	2,786	0.31
Guyanese (0)	0	<0.01
Hungarian (967)	3,106	0.35
Icelander (0)	0	<0.01
Iranian (349)	515	0.06
Irish (32,321)	105,245	11.81
Israeli (55)	107	0.01
Italian (8,233)	23,155	2.60
Latvian (158)	291	0.03
Lithuanian (325)	1,236	0.14
Luxemburger (34)	110	0.01
Macedonian (199)	381	0.04
Maltese (22)	56	0.01
New Zealander (54)	54	0.01
Northern European (657)	688	0.08
Norwegian (1,065)	4,086	0.46
Pennsylvania German (339)	438	0.05
Polish (4,171)	13,696	1.54
Portuguese (159)	545	0.06
Romanian (659)	1,037	0.12
Russian (1,431)	3,445	0.39
Scandinavian (609)	1,225	0.14
Scotch-Irish (5,607)	12,209	1.37
Scottish (5,392)	15,696	1.76
Serbian (259)	778	0.09
Slavic (134)	489	0.05
Slovak (397)	1,138	0.13
Slovene (221)	549	0.06
Soviet Union (0)	0	<0.01
Swedish (1,561)	6,274	0.70
Swiss (582)	2,601	0.29
Turkish (160)	263	0.03
Ukrainian (482)	914	0.10
Welsh (1,418)	5,354	0.60
West Indian, ex. Hispanic (1,343)	2,084	0.23
Bahamian (8)	8	<0.01
Barbadian (13)	55	0.01
Belizean (28)	76	0.01
Bermudan (0)	0	<0.01
British West Indian (0)	13	<0.01
Dutch West Indian (0)	38	<0.01
Haitian (569)	810	0.09
Jamaican (545)	627	0.07
Trinidadian/Tobagonian (72)	110	0.01
U.S. Virgin Islander (0)	0	<0.01
West Indian (96)	335	0.04
Other West Indian (12)	12	<0.01
Yugoslavian (356)	567	0.06

Hispanic Origin	Population	%
Hispanic or Latino (of any race)	84,466	9.35
Central American, ex. Mexican	8,394	0.93
Costa Rican	131	0.01
Guatemalan	1,787	0.20
Honduran	2,530	0.28
Nicaraguan	739	0.08
Panamanian	324	0.04
Salvadoran	2,814	0.31
Other Central American	69	0.01
Cuban	829	0.09
Dominican Republic	1,189	0.13
Mexican	61,972	6.86
Puerto Rican	3,880	0.43
South American	2,298	0.25
Argentinean	217	0.02
Bolivian	51	0.01
Chilean	90	0.01
Colombian	643	0.07
Ecuadorian	187	0.02
Paraguayan	13	<0.01
Peruvian	684	0.08
Uruguayan	32	<0.01
Venezuelan	359	0.04
Other South American	22	<0.01
Other Hispanic or Latino	5,904	0.65

Race*	Population	%
African-American/Black (240,975)	256,418	28.38
Not Hispanic (238,454)	252,235	27.92
Hispanic (2,521)	4,183	0.46
American Indian/Alaska Native (2,901)	8,132	0.90
Not Hispanic (1,954)	6,488	0.72
Hispanic (947)	1,644	0.18
Alaska Athabascan *(Ala. Nat.)* (2)	3	<0.01
Aleut *(Alaska Native)* (12)	14	<0.01
Apache (46)	115	0.01
Arapaho (5)	5	<0.01
Blackfeet (67)	387	0.04
Canadian/French Am. Ind. (10)	27	<0.01
Central American Ind. (8)	13	<0.01
Cherokee (421)	1,851	0.20
Cheyenne (1)	20	<0.01
Chickasaw (6)	12	<0.01
Chippewa (80)	154	0.02
Choctaw (28)	112	0.01
Colville (4)	4	<0.01
Comanche (11)	31	<0.01
Cree (0)	14	<0.01
Creek (19)	36	<0.01
Crow (1)	11	<0.01
Delaware (15)	34	<0.01
Hopi (4)	13	<0.01
Houma (3)	3	<0.01
Inupiat *(Alaska Native)* (9)	20	<0.01
Iroquois (40)	107	0.01
Kiowa (3)	6	<0.01
Lumbee (12)	23	<0.01
Menominee (4)	5	<0.01
Mexican American Ind. (199)	284	0.03
Navajo (42)	104	0.01
Osage (4)	15	<0.01
Ottawa (3)	15	<0.01
Paiute (0)	5	<0.01
Pima (0)	1	<0.01
Potawatomi (58)	95	0.01
Pueblo (11)	31	<0.01
Puget Sound Salish (0)	0	<0.01
Seminole (2)	17	<0.01
Shoshone (2)	12	<0.01
Sioux (65)	225	0.02
South American Ind. (15)	41	<0.01
Spanish American Ind. (31)	38	<0.01
Tlingit-Haida *(Alaska Native)* (4)	6	<0.01
Tohono O'Odham (1)	2	<0.01
Tsimshian *(Alaska Native)* (1)	1	<0.01
Ute (2)	5	<0.01
Yakama (0)	1	<0.01
Yaqui (3)	5	<0.01
Yuman (2)	4	<0.01
Yup'ik *(Alaska Native)* (0)	2	<0.01
Asian (18,314)	22,872	2.53
Not Hispanic (18,119)	22,304	2.47
Hispanic (195)	568	0.06
Bangladeshi (125)	138	0.02
Bhutanese (0)	0	<0.01
Burmese (3,525)	3,671	0.41
Cambodian (102)	139	0.02
Chinese, ex. Taiwanese (2,851)	3,455	0.38
Filipino (1,826)	2,930	0.32
Hmong (15)	24	<0.01
Indian (4,901)	5,565	0.62
Indonesian (80)	149	0.02
Japanese (567)	1,234	0.14
Korean (1,255)	1,903	0.21
Laotian (120)	147	0.02
Malaysian (29)	46	0.01
Nepalese (54)	56	0.01
Pakistani (574)	655	0.07
Sri Lankan (37)	45	<0.01
Taiwanese (154)	178	0.02
Thai (258)	394	0.04
Vietnamese (1,210)	1,438	0.16
Hawaii Native/Pacific Islander (458)	1,258	0.14
Not Hispanic (333)	924	0.10
Hispanic (125)	334	0.04
Fijian (3)	7	<0.01
Guamanian/Chamorro (154)	252	0.03
Marshallese (1)	1	<0.01
Native Hawaiian (137)	401	0.04
Samoan (84)	164	0.02
Tongan (5)	10	<0.01
White (566,853)	588,637	65.16
Not Hispanic (537,905)	555,252	61.46
Hispanic (28,948)	33,385	3.70

*Notes: † The Census 2010 population figure is used to calculate the percentages in the Hispanic Origin and Race categories. Ancestry percentages are based on the 2006-2010 American Community Survey population (not shown); ‡ Numbers in parentheses indicate the number of people reporting a single ancestry; * Numbers in parentheses indicate the number of persons reporting this race alone, not in combination with any other race; Please refer to the Explanation of Data for more information.*

Marshall County

Population: 47,051

Ancestry	Population	%
Afghan (0)	0	<0.01
African, Sub-Saharan (29)	29	0.06
African (0)	0	<0.01
Cape Verdean (0)	0	<0.01
Ethiopian (0)	0	<0.01
Ghanaian (0)	0	<0.01
Kenyan (0)	0	<0.01
Liberian (0)	0	<0.01
Nigerian (29)	29	0.06
Senegalese (0)	0	<0.01
Sierra Leonean (0)	0	<0.01
Somalian (0)	0	<0.01
South African (0)	0	<0.01
Sudanese (0)	0	<0.01
Ugandan (0)	0	<0.01
Zimbabwean (0)	0	<0.01
Other Sub-Saharan African (0)	0	<0.01
Albanian (0)	0	<0.01
Alsatian (0)	4	0.01
American (4,404)	4,404	9.38
Arab (3)	124	0.26
Arab (0)	0	<0.01
Egyptian (0)	12	0.03
Iraqi (0)	0	<0.01
Jordanian (0)	0	<0.01
Lebanese (3)	3	0.01
Moroccan (0)	0	<0.01
Palestinian (0)	0	<0.01
Syrian (0)	109	0.23
Other Arab (0)	0	<0.01
Armenian (0)	0	<0.01
Assyrian/Chaldean/Syriac (0)	29	0.06
Australian (0)	0	<0.01
Austrian (69)	69	0.15
Basque (0)	0	<0.01
Belgian (52)	181	0.39
Brazilian (0)	0	<0.01
British (56)	83	0.18
Bulgarian (0)	14	0.03
Cajun (0)	0	<0.01
Canadian (11)	38	0.08
Carpatho Rusyn (0)	0	<0.01
Celtic (0)	0	<0.01
Croatian (23)	62	0.13
Cypriot (0)	0	<0.01
Czech (104)	369	0.79
Czechoslovakian (23)	79	0.17
Danish (35)	70	0.15
Dutch (218)	1,220	2.60
Eastern European (20)	20	0.04
English (1,198)	4,012	8.54
Estonian (0)	7	0.01
European (541)	566	1.20
Finnish (0)	3	0.01
French, ex. Basque (206)	981	2.09
French Canadian (9)	89	0.19
German (8,027)	16,645	35.43
German Russian (0)	0	<0.01
Greek (75)	232	0.49
Guyanese (0)	0	<0.01
Hungarian (118)	293	0.62
Icelander (0)	0	<0.01
Iranian (19)	30	0.06
Irish (1,370)	5,238	11.15
Israeli (0)	0	<0.01
Italian (332)	1,265	2.69
Latvian (4)	4	0.01
Lithuanian (75)	111	0.24
Luxemburger (10)	10	0.02
Macedonian (0)	0	<0.01
Maltese (0)	0	<0.01
New Zealander (0)	0	<0.01
Northern European (16)	16	0.03
Norwegian (39)	197	0.42
Pennsylvania German (398)	476	1.01
Polish (746)	2,260	4.81
Portuguese (23)	93	0.20
Romanian (114)	225	0.48
Russian (17)	130	0.28
Scandinavian (10)	67	0.14
Scotch-Irish (161)	653	1.39
Scottish (343)	735	1.56
Serbian (331)	347	0.74
Slavic (0)	26	0.06
Slovak (14)	21	0.04
Slovene (4)	4	0.01
Soviet Union (0)	0	<0.01
Swedish (195)	680	1.45
Swiss (151)	689	1.47
Turkish (16)	16	0.03
Ukrainian (55)	80	0.17
Welsh (0)	119	0.25
West Indian, ex. Hispanic (24)	24	0.05
Bahamian (0)	0	<0.01
Barbadian (0)	0	<0.01
Belizean (0)	0	<0.01
Bermudan (0)	0	<0.01
British West Indian (0)	0	<0.01
Dutch West Indian (0)	0	<0.01
Haitian (16)	16	0.03
Jamaican (8)	8	0.02
Trinidadian/Tobagonian (0)	0	<0.01
U.S. Virgin Islander (0)	0	<0.01
West Indian (0)	0	<0.01
Other West Indian (0)	0	<0.01
Yugoslavian (27)	27	0.06

Hispanic Origin	Population	%
Hispanic or Latino (of any race)	3,971	8.44
Central American, ex. Mexican	320	0.68
Costa Rican	1	<0.01
Guatemalan	26	0.06
Honduran	284	0.60
Nicaraguan	1	<0.01
Panamanian	1	<0.01
Salvadoran	7	0.01
Other Central American	0	<0.01
Cuban	16	0.03
Dominican Republic	11	0.02
Mexican	3,078	6.54
Puerto Rican	97	0.21
South American	37	0.08
Argentinean	0	<0.01
Bolivian	3	0.01
Chilean	6	0.01
Colombian	9	0.02
Ecuadorian	1	<0.01
Paraguayan	1	<0.01
Peruvian	12	0.03
Uruguayan	0	<0.01
Venezuelan	0	<0.01
Other South American	5	0.01
Other Hispanic or Latino	412	0.88

Race*	Population	%
African-American/Black (220)	446	0.95
Not Hispanic (196)	391	0.83
Hispanic (24)	55	0.12
American Indian/Alaska Native (116)	352	0.75
Not Hispanic (80)	296	0.63
Hispanic (36)	56	0.12
Alaska Athabascan *(Ala. Nat.)* (0)	0	<0.01
Aleut *(Alaska Native)* (1)	1	<0.01
Apache (0)	3	0.01
Arapaho (0)	0	<0.01
Blackfeet (2)	18	0.04
Canadian/French Am. Ind. (6)	14	0.03
Central American Ind. (0)	3	0.01
Cherokee (18)	86	0.18
Cheyenne (0)	2	<0.01
Chickasaw (0)	0	<0.01
Chippewa (4)	6	0.01
Choctaw (0)	2	<0.01
Colville (0)	0	<0.01
Comanche (0)	0	<0.01
Cree (0)	3	0.01
Creek (0)	2	<0.01
Crow (0)	1	<0.01
Delaware (2)	2	<0.01
Hopi (0)	0	<0.01
Houma (0)	0	<0.01
Inupiat *(Alaska Native)* (0)	0	<0.01
Iroquois (2)	5	0.01
Kiowa (0)	0	<0.01
Lumbee (0)	0	<0.01
Menominee (0)	0	<0.01
Mexican American Ind. (4)	11	0.02
Navajo (1)	4	0.01
Osage (0)	1	<0.01
Ottawa (0)	0	<0.01
Paiute (0)	0	<0.01
Pima (0)	0	<0.01
Potawatomi (2)	10	0.02
Pueblo (2)	2	<0.01
Puget Sound Salish (0)	0	<0.01
Seminole (0)	1	<0.01
Shoshone (3)	3	0.01
Sioux (1)	5	0.01
South American Ind. (0)	0	<0.01
Spanish American Ind. (0)	0	<0.01
Tlingit-Haida *(Alaska Native)* (0)	0	<0.01
Tohono O'Odham (0)	0	<0.01
Tsimshian *(Alaska Native)* (0)	0	<0.01
Ute (0)	0	<0.01
Yakama (0)	0	<0.01
Yaqui (0)	1	<0.01
Yuman (0)	0	<0.01
Yup'ik *(Alaska Native)* (0)	0	<0.01
Asian (215)	306	0.65
Not Hispanic (210)	291	0.62
Hispanic (5)	15	0.03
Bangladeshi (0)	0	<0.01
Bhutanese (0)	0	<0.01
Burmese (0)	0	<0.01
Cambodian (1)	1	<0.01
Chinese, ex. Taiwanese (46)	48	0.10
Filipino (43)	69	0.15
Hmong (0)	0	<0.01
Indian (17)	29	0.06
Indonesian (3)	5	0.01
Japanese (5)	29	0.06
Korean (21)	42	0.09
Laotian (14)	21	0.04
Malaysian (0)	0	<0.01
Nepalese (0)	0	<0.01
Pakistani (7)	7	0.01
Sri Lankan (1)	1	<0.01
Taiwanese (2)	2	<0.01
Thai (15)	23	0.05
Vietnamese (29)	32	0.07
Hawaii Native/Pacific Islander (7)	12	0.03
Not Hispanic (2)	7	0.01
Hispanic (5)	5	0.01
Fijian (0)	1	<0.01
Guamanian/Chamorro (2)	2	<0.01
Marshallese (0)	0	<0.01
Native Hawaiian (2)	5	0.01
Samoan (0)	0	<0.01
Tongan (0)	0	<0.01
White (44,000)	44,694	94.99
Not Hispanic (42,098)	42,569	90.47
Hispanic (1,902)	2,125	4.52

*Notes: † The Census 2010 population figure is used to calculate the percentages in the Hispanic Origin and Race categories. Ancestry percentages are based on the 2006-2010 American Community Survey population (not shown); ‡ Numbers in parentheses indicate the number of people reporting a single ancestry; * Numbers in parentheses indicate the number of persons reporting this race alone, not in combination with any other race; Please refer to the Explanation of Data for more information.*

Martin County

Population: 10,334

Ancestry	Population	%
Afghan (0)	0	<0.01
African, Sub-Saharan (0)	0	<0.01
African (0)	0	<0.01
Cape Verdean (0)	0	<0.01
Ethiopian (0)	0	<0.01
Ghanaian (0)	0	<0.01
Kenyan (0)	0	<0.01
Liberian (0)	0	<0.01
Nigerian (0)	0	<0.01
Senegalese (0)	0	<0.01
Sierra Leonean (0)	0	<0.01
Somalian (0)	0	<0.01
South African (0)	0	<0.01
Sudanese (0)	0	<0.01
Ugandan (0)	0	<0.01
Zimbabwean (0)	0	<0.01
Other Sub-Saharan African (0)	0	<0.01
Albanian (0)	0	<0.01
Alsatian (0)	0	<0.01
American (1,307)	1,307	12.66
Arab (0)	0	<0.01
Arab (0)	0	<0.01
Egyptian (0)	0	<0.01
Iraqi (0)	0	<0.01
Jordanian (0)	0	<0.01
Lebanese (0)	0	<0.01
Moroccan (0)	0	<0.01
Palestinian (0)	0	<0.01
Syrian (0)	0	<0.01
Other Arab (0)	0	<0.01
Armenian (0)	0	<0.01
Assyrian/Chaldean/Syriac (0)	0	<0.01
Australian (0)	0	<0.01
Austrian (0)	0	<0.01
Basque (0)	0	<0.01
Belgian (0)	8	0.08
Brazilian (0)	0	<0.01
British (33)	33	0.32
Bulgarian (0)	0	<0.01
Cajun (0)	0	<0.01
Canadian (0)	0	<0.01
Carpatho Rusyn (0)	0	<0.01
Celtic (0)	0	<0.01
Croatian (0)	0	<0.01
Cypriot (0)	0	<0.01
Czech (0)	0	<0.01
Czechoslovakian (0)	0	<0.01
Danish (0)	0	<0.01
Dutch (2)	56	0.54
Eastern European (0)	0	<0.01
English (907)	1,539	14.91
Estonian (0)	0	<0.01
European (0)	0	<0.01
Finnish (0)	0	<0.01
French, ex. Basque (32)	208	2.01
French Canadian (0)	0	<0.01
German (1,657)	2,873	27.83
German Russian (0)	0	<0.01
Greek (0)	0	<0.01
Guyanese (0)	0	<0.01
Hungarian (0)	16	0.15
Icelander (0)	0	<0.01
Iranian (0)	0	<0.01
Irish (757)	1,982	19.20
Israeli (0)	0	<0.01
Italian (0)	18	0.17
Latvian (0)	0	<0.01
Lithuanian (0)	0	<0.01
Luxemburger (0)	0	<0.01
Macedonian (0)	0	<0.01
Maltese (0)	0	<0.01
New Zealander (0)	0	<0.01
Northern European (0)	0	<0.01
Norwegian (0)	41	0.40
Pennsylvania German (63)	63	0.61
Polish (50)	65	0.63
Portuguese (0)	0	<0.01
Romanian (0)	0	<0.01
Russian (10)	37	0.36
Scandinavian (0)	0	<0.01
Scotch-Irish (55)	137	1.33
Scottish (35)	66	0.64
Serbian (0)	0	<0.01
Slavic (0)	9	0.09
Slovak (0)	0	<0.01
Slovene (0)	0	<0.01
Soviet Union (0)	0	<0.01
Swedish (0)	6	0.06
Swiss (0)	21	0.20
Turkish (0)	0	<0.01
Ukrainian (0)	0	<0.01
Welsh (0)	0	<0.01
West Indian, ex. Hispanic (0)	0	<0.01
Bahamian (0)	0	<0.01
Barbadian (0)	0	<0.01
Belizean (0)	0	<0.01
Bermudan (0)	0	<0.01
British West Indian (0)	0	<0.01
Dutch West Indian (0)	0	<0.01
Haitian (0)	0	<0.01
Jamaican (0)	0	<0.01
Trinidadian/Tobagonian (0)	0	<0.01
U.S. Virgin Islander (0)	0	<0.01
West Indian (0)	0	<0.01
Other West Indian (0)	0	<0.01
Yugoslavian (0)	0	<0.01

Hispanic Origin	Population	%
Hispanic or Latino (of any race)	70	0.68
Central American, ex. Mexican	3	0.03
Costa Rican	0	<0.01
Guatemalan	3	0.03
Honduran	0	<0.01
Nicaraguan	0	<0.01
Panamanian	0	<0.01
Salvadoran	0	<0.01
Other Central American	0	<0.01
Cuban	3	0.03
Dominican Republic	0	<0.01
Mexican	55	0.53
Puerto Rican	2	0.02
South American	1	0.01
Argentinean	0	<0.01
Bolivian	0	<0.01
Chilean	0	<0.01
Colombian	1	0.01
Ecuadorian	0	<0.01
Paraguayan	0	<0.01
Peruvian	0	<0.01
Uruguayan	0	<0.01
Venezuelan	0	<0.01
Other South American	0	<0.01
Other Hispanic or Latino	6	0.06

Race*	Population	%
African-American/Black (10)	40	0.39
Not Hispanic (10)	36	0.35
Hispanic (0)	4	0.04
American Indian/Alaska Native (30)	63	0.61
Not Hispanic (26)	56	0.54
Hispanic (4)	7	0.07
Alaska Athabascan *(Ala. Nat.)* (0)	0	<0.01
Aleut *(Alaska Native)* (0)	0	<0.01
Apache (0)	1	0.01
Arapaho (0)	0	<0.01
Blackfeet (1)	2	0.02
Canadian/French Am. Ind. (0)	1	0.01
Central American Ind. (0)	0	<0.01
Cherokee (12)	26	0.25
Cheyenne (0)	0	<0.01
Chickasaw (0)	0	<0.01
Chippewa (0)	0	<0.01
Choctaw (0)	0	<0.01
Colville (0)	0	<0.01
Comanche (0)	0	<0.01
Cree (0)	0	<0.01
Creek (0)	0	<0.01
Crow (0)	0	<0.01
Delaware (0)	0	<0.01
Hopi (0)	1	0.01
Houma (0)	0	<0.01
Inupiat *(Alaska Native)* (0)	0	<0.01
Iroquois (0)	2	0.02
Kiowa (0)	0	<0.01
Lumbee (0)	0	<0.01
Menominee (0)	0	<0.01
Mexican American Ind. (3)	3	0.03
Navajo (0)	0	<0.01
Osage (0)	0	<0.01
Ottawa (0)	0	<0.01
Paiute (0)	0	<0.01
Pima (0)	0	<0.01
Potawatomi (0)	1	0.01
Pueblo (0)	0	<0.01
Puget Sound Salish (0)	0	<0.01
Seminole (0)	0	<0.01
Shoshone (0)	0	<0.01
Sioux (2)	2	0.02
South American Ind. (0)	0	<0.01
Spanish American Ind. (0)	0	<0.01
Tlingit-Haida *(Alaska Native)* (0)	0	<0.01
Tohono O'Odham (0)	0	<0.01
Tsimshian *(Alaska Native)* (0)	0	<0.01
Ute (0)	0	<0.01
Yakama (0)	0	<0.01
Yaqui (0)	1	0.01
Yuman (0)	0	<0.01
Yup'ik *(Alaska Native)* (0)	0	<0.01
Asian (29)	41	0.40
Not Hispanic (29)	41	0.40
Hispanic (0)	0	<0.01
Bangladeshi (0)	0	<0.01
Bhutanese (0)	0	<0.01
Burmese (0)	0	<0.01
Cambodian (0)	0	<0.01
Chinese, ex. Taiwanese (9)	9	0.09
Filipino (10)	15	0.15
Hmong (0)	0	<0.01
Indian (0)	4	0.04
Indonesian (0)	0	<0.01
Japanese (4)	4	0.04
Korean (3)	6	0.06
Laotian (0)	0	<0.01
Malaysian (0)	0	<0.01
Nepalese (0)	0	<0.01
Pakistani (0)	0	<0.01
Sri Lankan (0)	0	<0.01
Taiwanese (0)	0	<0.01
Thai (1)	1	0.01
Vietnamese (0)	0	<0.01
Hawaii Native/Pacific Islander (0)	2	0.02
Not Hispanic (0)	2	0.02
Hispanic (0)	0	<0.01
Fijian (0)	0	<0.01
Guamanian/Chamorro (0)	0	<0.01
Marshallese (0)	0	<0.01
Native Hawaiian (0)	0	<0.01
Samoan (0)	0	<0.01
Tongan (0)	0	<0.01
White (10,164)	10,237	99.06
Not Hispanic (10,125)	10,193	98.64
Hispanic (39)	44	0.43

*Notes: † The Census 2010 population figure is used to calculate the percentages in the Hispanic Origin and Race categories. Ancestry percentages are based on the 2006-2010 American Community Survey population (not shown); ‡ Numbers in parentheses indicate the number of people reporting a single ancestry; * Numbers in parentheses indicate the number of persons reporting this race alone, not in combination with any other race; Please refer to the Explanation of Data for more information.*

Miami County

Population: 36,903

Ancestry	Population	%
Afghan (0)	0	<0.01
African, Sub-Saharan (77)	77	0.21
African (69)	69	0.18
Cape Verdean (0)	0	<0.01
Ethiopian (0)	0	<0.01
Ghanaian (0)	0	<0.01
Kenyan (0)	0	<0.01
Liberian (0)	0	<0.01
Nigerian (0)	0	<0.01
Senegalese (0)	0	<0.01
Sierra Leonean (0)	0	<0.01
Somalian (0)	0	<0.01
South African (8)	8	0.02
Sudanese (0)	0	<0.01
Ugandan (0)	0	<0.01
Zimbabwean (0)	0	<0.01
Other Sub-Saharan African (0)	0	<0.01
Albanian (0)	0	<0.01
Alsatian (0)	0	<0.01
American (6,467)	6,467	17.33
Arab (36)	36	0.10
Arab (0)	0	<0.01
Egyptian (0)	0	<0.01
Iraqi (0)	0	<0.01
Jordanian (0)	0	<0.01
Lebanese (27)	27	0.07
Moroccan (0)	0	<0.01
Palestinian (0)	0	<0.01
Syrian (9)	9	0.02
Other Arab (0)	0	<0.01
Armenian (11)	11	0.03
Assyrian/Chaldean/Syriac (0)	0	<0.01
Australian (6)	6	0.02
Austrian (13)	24	0.06
Basque (0)	0	<0.01
Belgian (0)	20	0.05
Brazilian (0)	0	<0.01
British (17)	49	0.13
Bulgarian (0)	4	0.01
Cajun (0)	0	<0.01
Canadian (25)	60	0.16
Carpatho Rusyn (0)	0	<0.01
Celtic (0)	0	<0.01
Croatian (21)	32	0.09
Cypriot (0)	0	<0.01
Czech (19)	148	0.40
Czechoslovakian (0)	0	<0.01
Danish (0)	97	0.26
Dutch (248)	933	2.50
Eastern European (0)	0	<0.01
English (1,159)	3,121	8.37
Estonian (0)	0	<0.01
European (439)	508	1.36
Finnish (0)	77	0.21
French, ex. Basque (82)	626	1.68
French Canadian (109)	219	0.59
German (4,894)	10,153	27.21
German Russian (4)	4	0.01
Greek (4)	69	0.18
Guyanese (0)	0	<0.01
Hungarian (58)	136	0.36
Icelander (0)	0	<0.01
Iranian (0)	0	<0.01
Irish (1,271)	4,473	11.99
Israeli (0)	0	<0.01
Italian (620)	951	2.55
Latvian (0)	0	<0.01
Lithuanian (18)	63	0.17
Luxemburger (0)	0	<0.01
Macedonian (0)	0	<0.01
Maltese (0)	0	<0.01
New Zealander (0)	0	<0.01
Northern European (8)	8	0.02
Norwegian (35)	94	0.25
Pennsylvania German (99)	139	0.37
Polish (148)	668	1.79
Portuguese (0)	19	0.05
Romanian (0)	26	0.07
Russian (0)	80	0.21
Scandinavian (0)	7	0.02
Scotch-Irish (95)	360	0.96
Scottish (241)	642	1.72
Serbian (0)	0	<0.01
Slavic (0)	0	<0.01
Slovak (34)	74	0.20
Slovene (0)	0	<0.01
Soviet Union (0)	0	<0.01
Swedish (140)	324	0.87
Swiss (146)	221	0.59
Turkish (0)	0	<0.01
Ukrainian (44)	53	0.14
Welsh (53)	173	0.46
West Indian, ex. Hispanic (9)	9	0.02
Bahamian (0)	0	<0.01
Barbadian (0)	0	<0.01
Belizean (0)	0	<0.01
Bermudan (0)	0	<0.01
British West Indian (0)	0	<0.01
Dutch West Indian (0)	0	<0.01
Haitian (0)	0	<0.01
Jamaican (9)	9	0.02
Trinidadian/Tobagonian (0)	0	<0.01
U.S. Virgin Islander (0)	0	<0.01
West Indian (0)	0	<0.01
Other West Indian (0)	0	<0.01
Yugoslavian (0)	5	0.01

Hispanic Origin	Population	%
Hispanic or Latino (of any race)	906	2.46
Central American, ex. Mexican	35	0.09
Costa Rican	0	<0.01
Guatemalan	7	0.02
Honduran	17	0.05
Nicaraguan	2	0.01
Panamanian	2	0.01
Salvadoran	7	0.02
Other Central American	0	<0.01
Cuban	18	0.05
Dominican Republic	0	<0.01
Mexican	695	1.88
Puerto Rican	89	0.24
South American	10	0.03
Argentinean	1	<0.01
Bolivian	1	<0.01
Chilean	0	<0.01
Colombian	1	<0.01
Ecuadorian	0	<0.01
Paraguayan	0	<0.01
Peruvian	3	0.01
Uruguayan	1	<0.01
Venezuelan	3	0.01
Other South American	0	<0.01
Other Hispanic or Latino	59	0.16

Race*	Population	%
African-American/Black (1,673)	1,941	5.26
Not Hispanic (1,649)	1,893	5.13
Hispanic (24)	48	0.13
American Indian/Alaska Native (335)	592	1.60
Not Hispanic (309)	551	1.49
Hispanic (26)	41	0.11
Alaska Athabascan *(Ala. Nat.)* (0)	0	<0.01
Aleut *(Alaska Native)* (0)	0	<0.01
Apache (0)	3	0.01
Arapaho (0)	0	<0.01
Blackfeet (5)	14	0.04
Canadian/French Am. Ind. (0)	1	<0.01
Central American Ind. (0)	0	<0.01
Cherokee (23)	72	0.20
Cheyenne (1)	1	<0.01
Chickasaw (3)	3	0.01
Chippewa (10)	18	0.05
Choctaw (8)	9	0.02
Colville (0)	0	<0.01
Comanche (3)	3	0.01
Cree (1)	1	<0.01
Creek (0)	0	<0.01
Crow (0)	0	<0.01
Delaware (0)	0	<0.01
Hopi (0)	0	<0.01
Houma (0)	0	<0.01
Inupiat *(Alaska Native)* (0)	0	<0.01
Iroquois (5)	8	0.02
Kiowa (0)	0	<0.01
Lumbee (0)	0	<0.01
Menominee (0)	0	<0.01
Mexican American Ind. (5)	6	0.02
Navajo (5)	6	0.02
Osage (0)	0	<0.01
Ottawa (0)	0	<0.01
Paiute (0)	0	<0.01
Pima (0)	0	<0.01
Potawatomi (3)	6	0.02
Pueblo (0)	1	<0.01
Puget Sound Salish (0)	0	<0.01
Seminole (0)	1	<0.01
Shoshone (0)	0	<0.01
Sioux (0)	4	0.01
South American Ind. (3)	4	0.01
Spanish American Ind. (0)	0	<0.01
Tlingit-Haida *(Alaska Native)* (0)	0	<0.01
Tohono O'Odham (0)	0	<0.01
Tsimshian *(Alaska Native)* (0)	0	<0.01
Ute (1)	2	0.01
Yakama (0)	0	<0.01
Yaqui (0)	0	<0.01
Yuman (0)	0	<0.01
Yup'ik *(Alaska Native)* (0)	0	<0.01
Asian (129)	219	0.59
Not Hispanic (128)	215	0.58
Hispanic (1)	4	0.01
Bangladeshi (0)	0	<0.01
Bhutanese (0)	0	<0.01
Burmese (0)	0	<0.01
Cambodian (1)	1	<0.01
Chinese, ex. Taiwanese (39)	46	0.12
Filipino (28)	57	0.15
Hmong (0)	0	<0.01
Indian (10)	17	0.05
Indonesian (2)	3	0.01
Japanese (13)	28	0.08
Korean (14)	42	0.11
Laotian (0)	0	<0.01
Malaysian (0)	0	<0.01
Nepalese (0)	0	<0.01
Pakistani (0)	0	<0.01
Sri Lankan (0)	0	<0.01
Taiwanese (1)	2	0.01
Thai (9)	13	0.04
Vietnamese (2)	7	0.02
Hawaii Native/Pacific Islander (8)	30	0.08
Not Hispanic (8)	23	0.06
Hispanic (0)	7	0.02
Fijian (0)	0	<0.01
Guamanian/Chamorro (0)	2	0.01
Marshallese (1)	1	<0.01
Native Hawaiian (6)	23	0.06
Samoan (1)	1	<0.01
Tongan (0)	0	<0.01
White (33,876)	34,512	93.52
Not Hispanic (33,307)	33,868	91.78
Hispanic (569)	644	1.75

*Notes: † The Census 2010 population figure is used to calculate the percentages in the Hispanic Origin and Race categories. Ancestry percentages are based on the 2006-2010 American Community Survey population (not shown); ‡ Numbers in parentheses indicate the number of people reporting a single ancestry; * Numbers in parentheses indicate the number of persons reporting this race alone, not in combination with any other race; Please refer to the Explanation of Data for more information.*

Monroe County

Population: 137,974

Ancestry	Population	%
Afghan (59)	59	0.04
African, Sub-Saharan (554)	680	0.51
African (445)	567	0.42
Cape Verdean (0)	0	<0.01
Ethiopian (32)	33	0.02
Ghanaian (0)	0	<0.01
Kenyan (0)	0	<0.01
Liberian (0)	0	<0.01
Nigerian (14)	14	0.01
Senegalese (0)	0	<0.01
Sierra Leonean (0)	0	<0.01
Somalian (0)	0	<0.01
South African (63)	63	0.05
Sudanese (0)	0	<0.01
Ugandan (0)	0	<0.01
Zimbabwean (0)	0	<0.01
Other Sub-Saharan African (0)	3	<0.01
Albanian (20)	20	0.01
Alsatian (0)	19	0.01
American (10,838)	10,838	8.06
Arab (408)	623	0.46
Arab (187)	196	0.15
Egyptian (8)	21	0.02
Iraqi (30)	30	0.02
Jordanian (0)	10	0.01
Lebanese (67)	180	0.13
Moroccan (27)	27	0.02
Palestinian (0)	8	0.01
Syrian (13)	75	0.06
Other Arab (76)	76	0.06
Armenian (14)	37	0.03
Assyrian/Chaldean/Syriac (0)	0	<0.01
Australian (25)	53	0.04
Austrian (115)	577	0.43
Basque (0)	49	0.04
Belgian (53)	285	0.21
Brazilian (103)	132	0.10
British (278)	1,053	0.78
Bulgarian (29)	29	0.02
Cajun (16)	32	0.02
Canadian (145)	266	0.20
Carpatho Rusyn (0)	0	<0.01
Celtic (0)	0	<0.01
Croatian (48)	185	0.14
Cypriot (0)	0	<0.01
Czech (173)	852	0.63
Czechoslovakian (21)	186	0.14
Danish (155)	464	0.35
Dutch (1,078)	3,442	2.56
Eastern European (296)	354	0.26
English (5,578)	15,851	11.79
Estonian (0)	27	0.02
European (2,220)	2,518	1.87
Finnish (12)	66	0.05
French, ex. Basque (921)	4,080	3.03
French Canadian (185)	477	0.35
German (10,605)	33,322	24.79
German Russian (0)	0	<0.01
Greek (265)	656	0.49
Guyanese (0)	0	<0.01
Hungarian (228)	977	0.73
Icelander (21)	41	0.03
Iranian (187)	209	0.16
Irish (5,191)	18,106	13.47
Israeli (91)	168	0.12
Italian (1,545)	5,397	4.01
Latvian (10)	10	0.01
Lithuanian (105)	406	0.30
Luxemburger (0)	66	0.05
Macedonian (48)	62	0.05
Maltese (0)	0	<0.01
New Zealander (0)	0	<0.01
Northern European (118)	154	0.11
Norwegian (459)	1,703	1.27
Pennsylvania German (71)	123	0.09
Polish (1,312)	4,992	3.71
Portuguese (18)	87	0.06
Romanian (110)	320	0.24
Russian (573)	1,627	1.21
Scandinavian (88)	268	0.20
Scotch-Irish (1,432)	3,759	2.80
Scottish (1,032)	3,952	2.94
Serbian (61)	174	0.13
Slavic (0)	23	0.02
Slovak (55)	247	0.18
Slovene (19)	96	0.07
Soviet Union (0)	0	<0.01
Swedish (421)	1,891	1.41
Swiss (143)	663	0.49
Turkish (111)	111	0.08
Ukrainian (164)	350	0.26
Welsh (299)	1,280	0.95
West Indian, ex. Hispanic (85)	137	0.10
Bahamian (0)	0	<0.01
Barbadian (0)	0	<0.01
Belizean (0)	0	<0.01
Bermudan (0)	0	<0.01
British West Indian (0)	0	<0.01
Dutch West Indian (0)	36	0.03
Haitian (0)	0	<0.01
Jamaican (72)	72	0.05
Trinidadian/Tobagonian (0)	0	<0.01
U.S. Virgin Islander (0)	0	<0.01
West Indian (13)	29	0.02
Other West Indian (0)	0	<0.01
Yugoslavian (17)	50	0.04

Hispanic Origin	Population	%
Hispanic or Latino (of any race)	4,029	2.92
Central American, ex. Mexican	245	0.18
Costa Rican	43	0.03
Guatemalan	48	0.03
Honduran	38	0.03
Nicaraguan	34	0.02
Panamanian	34	0.02
Salvadoran	44	0.03
Other Central American	4	<0.01
Cuban	157	0.11
Dominican Republic	55	0.04
Mexican	2,249	1.63
Puerto Rican	449	0.33
South American	435	0.32
Argentinean	65	0.05
Bolivian	11	0.01
Chilean	51	0.04
Colombian	108	0.08
Ecuadorian	42	0.03
Paraguayan	6	<0.01
Peruvian	76	0.06
Uruguayan	7	0.01
Venezuelan	69	0.05
Other South American	0	<0.01
Other Hispanic or Latino	439	0.32

Race*	Population	%
African-American/Black (4,491)	5,857	4.25
Not Hispanic (4,363)	5,617	4.07
Hispanic (128)	240	0.17
American Indian/Alaska Native (353)	1,141	0.83
Not Hispanic (288)	955	0.69
Hispanic (65)	186	0.13
Alaska Athabascan *(Ala. Nat.)* (1)	1	<0.01
Aleut *(Alaska Native)* (0)	2	<0.01
Apache (5)	15	0.01
Arapaho (2)	2	<0.01
Blackfeet (0)	52	0.04
Canadian/French Am. Ind. (3)	6	<0.01
Central American Ind. (3)	7	0.01
Cherokee (61)	281	0.20
Cheyenne (0)	0	<0.01
Chickasaw (5)	5	<0.01
Chippewa (14)	35	0.03
Choctaw (9)	24	0.02
Colville (1)	1	<0.01
Comanche (0)	0	<0.01
Cree (0)	1	<0.01
Creek (7)	8	0.01
Crow (1)	2	<0.01
Delaware (7)	11	0.01
Hopi (1)	2	<0.01
Houma (0)	0	<0.01
Inupiat *(Alaska Native)* (0)	3	<0.01
Iroquois (8)	17	0.01
Kiowa (0)	0	<0.01
Lumbee (4)	9	0.01
Menominee (1)	2	<0.01
Mexican American Ind. (9)	23	0.02
Navajo (9)	15	0.01
Osage (0)	2	<0.01
Ottawa (1)	1	<0.01
Paiute (0)	0	<0.01
Pima (0)	0	<0.01
Potawatomi (3)	12	0.01
Pueblo (1)	4	<0.01
Puget Sound Salish (5)	5	<0.01
Seminole (2)	5	<0.01
Shoshone (0)	1	<0.01
Sioux (11)	28	0.02
South American Ind. (2)	7	0.01
Spanish American Ind. (3)	21	0.02
Tlingit-Haida *(Alaska Native)* (1)	2	<0.01
Tohono O'Odham (3)	8	0.01
Tsimshian *(Alaska Native)* (0)	0	<0.01
Ute (0)	0	<0.01
Yakama (3)	3	<0.01
Yaqui (0)	0	<0.01
Yuman (0)	0	<0.01
Yup'ik *(Alaska Native)* (0)	1	<0.01
Asian (7,214)	8,487	6.15
Not Hispanic (7,190)	8,402	6.09
Hispanic (24)	85	0.06
Bangladeshi (24)	33	0.02
Bhutanese (0)	0	<0.01
Burmese (23)	24	0.02
Cambodian (6)	10	0.01
Chinese, ex. Taiwanese (2,196)	2,472	1.79
Filipino (300)	548	0.40
Hmong (5)	6	<0.01
Indian (1,393)	1,553	1.13
Indonesian (80)	93	0.07
Japanese (288)	486	0.35
Korean (1,850)	2,001	1.45
Laotian (7)	11	0.01
Malaysian (50)	60	0.04
Nepalese (21)	21	0.02
Pakistani (96)	112	0.08
Sri Lankan (38)	40	0.03
Taiwanese (252)	282	0.20
Thai (96)	121	0.09
Vietnamese (204)	262	0.19
Hawaii Native/Pacific Islander (62)	167	0.12
Not Hispanic (56)	138	0.10
Hispanic (6)	29	0.02
Fijian (1)	1	<0.01
Guamanian/Chamorro (12)	26	0.02
Marshallese (0)	0	<0.01
Native Hawaiian (20)	54	0.04
Samoan (6)	21	0.02
Tongan (0)	0	<0.01
White (121,109)	124,277	90.07
Not Hispanic (118,837)	121,628	88.15
Hispanic (2,272)	2,649	1.92

*Notes: † The Census 2010 population figure is used to calculate the percentages in the Hispanic Origin and Race categories. Ancestry percentages are based on the 2006-2010 American Community Survey population (not shown); ‡ Numbers in parentheses indicate the number of people reporting a single ancestry; * Numbers in parentheses indicate the number of persons reporting this race alone, not in combination with any other race; Please refer to the Explanation of Data for more information.*

Montgomery County

Population: 38,124

Ancestry	Population	%
Afghan (0)	0	<0.01
African, Sub-Saharan (0)	0	<0.01
African (0)	0	<0.01
Cape Verdean (0)	0	<0.01
Ethiopian (0)	0	<0.01
Ghanaian (0)	0	<0.01
Kenyan (0)	0	<0.01
Liberian (0)	0	<0.01
Nigerian (0)	0	<0.01
Senegalese (0)	0	<0.01
Sierra Leonean (0)	0	<0.01
Somalian (0)	0	<0.01
South African (0)	0	<0.01
Sudanese (0)	0	<0.01
Ugandan (0)	0	<0.01
Zimbabwean (0)	0	<0.01
Other Sub-Saharan African (0)	0	<0.01
Albanian (34)	34	0.09
Alsatian (0)	0	<0.01
American (6,304)	6,304	16.53
Arab (3)	8	0.02
Arab (0)	0	<0.01
Egyptian (0)	0	<0.01
Iraqi (0)	0	<0.01
Jordanian (0)	0	<0.01
Lebanese (3)	8	0.02
Moroccan (0)	0	<0.01
Palestinian (0)	0	<0.01
Syrian (0)	0	<0.01
Other Arab (0)	0	<0.01
Armenian (0)	0	<0.01
Assyrian/Chaldean/Syriac (0)	0	<0.01
Australian (0)	0	<0.01
Austrian (0)	0	<0.01
Basque (0)	0	<0.01
Belgian (6)	6	0.02
Brazilian (0)	0	<0.01
British (30)	80	0.21
Bulgarian (0)	0	<0.01
Cajun (11)	11	0.03
Canadian (23)	34	0.09
Carpatho Rusyn (0)	0	<0.01
Celtic (0)	0	<0.01
Croatian (41)	95	0.25
Cypriot (0)	0	<0.01
Czech (4)	20	0.05
Czechoslovakian (37)	74	0.19
Danish (0)	17	0.04
Dutch (186)	1,044	2.74
Eastern European (0)	0	<0.01
English (2,222)	4,610	12.09
Estonian (0)	0	<0.01
European (175)	193	0.51
Finnish (0)	68	0.18
French, ex. Basque (189)	686	1.80
French Canadian (12)	88	0.23
German (3,226)	8,601	22.55
German Russian (0)	0	<0.01
Greek (25)	44	0.12
Guyanese (0)	0	<0.01
Hungarian (0)	0	<0.01
Icelander (0)	0	<0.01
Iranian (0)	0	<0.01
Irish (1,442)	5,508	14.44
Israeli (0)	0	<0.01
Italian (406)	854	2.24
Latvian (0)	13	0.03
Lithuanian (0)	50	0.13
Luxemburger (0)	0	<0.01
Macedonian (0)	0	<0.01
Maltese (0)	0	<0.01
New Zealander (0)	0	<0.01
Northern European (0)	0	<0.01
Norwegian (25)	159	0.42
Pennsylvania German (0)	4	0.01
Polish (85)	389	1.02
Portuguese (0)	8	0.02
Romanian (45)	91	0.24
Russian (0)	0	<0.01
Scandinavian (31)	48	0.13
Scotch-Irish (272)	678	1.78
Scottish (454)	959	2.51
Serbian (0)	0	<0.01
Slavic (0)	6	0.02
Slovak (22)	50	0.13
Slovene (0)	11	0.03
Soviet Union (0)	0	<0.01
Swedish (65)	348	0.91
Swiss (9)	152	0.40
Turkish (0)	0	<0.01
Ukrainian (48)	68	0.18
Welsh (105)	252	0.66
West Indian, ex. Hispanic (0)	0	<0.01
Bahamian (0)	0	<0.01
Barbadian (0)	0	<0.01
Belizean (0)	0	<0.01
Bermudan (0)	0	<0.01
British West Indian (0)	0	<0.01
Dutch West Indian (0)	0	<0.01
Haitian (0)	0	<0.01
Jamaican (0)	0	<0.01
Trinidadian/Tobagonian (0)	0	<0.01
U.S. Virgin Islander (0)	0	<0.01
West Indian (0)	0	<0.01
Other West Indian (0)	0	<0.01
Yugoslavian (0)	0	<0.01

Hispanic Origin	Population	%
Hispanic or Latino (of any race)	1,739	4.56
Central American, ex. Mexican	57	0.15
Costa Rican	1	<0.01
Guatemalan	45	0.12
Honduran	6	0.02
Nicaraguan	0	<0.01
Panamanian	0	<0.01
Salvadoran	5	0.01
Other Central American	0	<0.01
Cuban	11	0.03
Dominican Republic	0	<0.01
Mexican	1,523	3.99
Puerto Rican	36	0.09
South American	37	0.10
Argentinean	6	0.02
Bolivian	1	<0.01
Chilean	5	0.01
Colombian	15	0.04
Ecuadorian	1	<0.01
Paraguayan	0	<0.01
Peruvian	8	0.02
Uruguayan	0	<0.01
Venezuelan	1	<0.01
Other South American	0	<0.01
Other Hispanic or Latino	75	0.20

Race*	Population	%
African-American/Black (327)	496	1.30
Not Hispanic (307)	469	1.23
Hispanic (20)	27	0.07
American Indian/Alaska Native (98)	259	0.68
Not Hispanic (72)	213	0.56
Hispanic (26)	46	0.12
Alaska Athabascan *(Ala. Nat.)* (0)	0	<0.01
Aleut *(Alaska Native)* (0)	0	<0.01
Apache (0)	6	0.02
Arapaho (0)	0	<0.01
Blackfeet (3)	7	0.02
Canadian/French Am. Ind. (0)	0	<0.01
Central American Ind. (0)	0	<0.01
Cherokee (18)	73	0.19
Cheyenne (1)	1	<0.01
Chickasaw (0)	0	<0.01
Chippewa (0)	0	<0.01
Choctaw (5)	11	0.03
Colville (0)	0	<0.01
Comanche (0)	0	<0.01
Cree (0)	0	<0.01
Creek (0)	0	<0.01
Crow (1)	1	<0.01
Delaware (0)	0	<0.01
Hopi (0)	0	<0.01
Houma (0)	0	<0.01
Inupiat *(Alaska Native)* (0)	0	<0.01
Iroquois (3)	7	0.02
Kiowa (1)	2	0.01
Lumbee (0)	0	<0.01
Menominee (0)	0	<0.01
Mexican American Ind. (5)	8	0.02
Navajo (0)	3	0.01
Osage (0)	0	<0.01
Ottawa (1)	1	<0.01
Paiute (0)	0	<0.01
Pima (0)	0	<0.01
Potawatomi (0)	0	<0.01
Pueblo (4)	4	0.01
Puget Sound Salish (0)	0	<0.01
Seminole (2)	2	0.01
Shoshone (0)	0	<0.01
Sioux (4)	9	0.02
South American Ind. (0)	0	<0.01
Spanish American Ind. (1)	3	0.01
Tlingit-Haida *(Alaska Native)* (0)	0	<0.01
Tohono O'Odham (0)	0	<0.01
Tsimshian *(Alaska Native)* (0)	0	<0.01
Ute (2)	2	0.01
Yakama (0)	0	<0.01
Yaqui (0)	0	<0.01
Yuman (0)	0	<0.01
Yup'ik *(Alaska Native)* (0)	0	<0.01
Asian (213)	287	0.75
Not Hispanic (209)	281	0.74
Hispanic (4)	6	0.02
Bangladeshi (5)	5	0.01
Bhutanese (0)	0	<0.01
Burmese (0)	0	<0.01
Cambodian (0)	0	<0.01
Chinese, ex. Taiwanese (62)	71	0.19
Filipino (27)	59	0.15
Hmong (0)	0	<0.01
Indian (57)	59	0.15
Indonesian (0)	0	<0.01
Japanese (20)	36	0.09
Korean (20)	32	0.08
Laotian (0)	0	<0.01
Malaysian (0)	1	<0.01
Nepalese (1)	1	<0.01
Pakistani (1)	1	<0.01
Sri Lankan (0)	0	<0.01
Taiwanese (1)	1	<0.01
Thai (1)	1	<0.01
Vietnamese (14)	15	0.04
Hawaii Native/Pacific Islander (6)	25	0.07
Not Hispanic (6)	22	0.06
Hispanic (0)	3	0.01
Fijian (0)	0	<0.01
Guamanian/Chamorro (0)	3	0.01
Marshallese (0)	0	<0.01
Native Hawaiian (4)	8	0.02
Samoan (1)	5	0.01
Tongan (0)	0	<0.01
White (36,309)	36,764	96.43
Not Hispanic (35,374)	35,752	93.78
Hispanic (935)	1,012	2.65

*Notes: † The Census 2010 population figure is used to calculate the percentages in the Hispanic Origin and Race categories. Ancestry percentages are based on the 2006-2010 American Community Survey population (not shown); ‡ Numbers in parentheses indicate the number of people reporting a single ancestry; * Numbers in parentheses indicate the number of persons reporting this race alone, not in combination with any other race; Please refer to the Explanation of Data for more information.*

Morgan County

Population: 68,894

Ancestry	Population	%
Afghan (0)	0	<0.01
African, Sub-Saharan (25)	79	0.12
African (25)	79	0.12
Cape Verdean (0)	0	<0.01
Ethiopian (0)	0	<0.01
Ghanaian (0)	0	<0.01
Kenyan (0)	0	<0.01
Liberian (0)	0	<0.01
Nigerian (0)	0	<0.01
Senegalese (0)	0	<0.01
Sierra Leonean (0)	0	<0.01
Somalian (0)	0	<0.01
South African (0)	0	<0.01
Sudanese (0)	0	<0.01
Ugandan (0)	0	<0.01
Zimbabwean (0)	0	<0.01
Other Sub-Saharan African (0)	0	<0.01
Albanian (0)	0	<0.01
Alsatian (0)	0	<0.01
American (9,793)	9,793	14.26
Arab (34)	50	0.07
Arab (0)	0	<0.01
Egyptian (0)	0	<0.01
Iraqi (0)	0	<0.01
Jordanian (16)	16	0.02
Lebanese (18)	34	0.05
Moroccan (0)	0	<0.01
Palestinian (0)	0	<0.01
Syrian (0)	0	<0.01
Other Arab (0)	0	<0.01
Armenian (0)	0	<0.01
Assyrian/Chaldean/Syriac (0)	0	<0.01
Australian (0)	0	<0.01
Austrian (16)	26	0.04
Basque (0)	0	<0.01
Belgian (0)	41	0.06
Brazilian (0)	0	<0.01
British (112)	286	0.42
Bulgarian (0)	0	<0.01
Cajun (0)	0	<0.01
Canadian (16)	43	0.06
Carpatho Rusyn (0)	0	<0.01
Celtic (0)	0	<0.01
Croatian (0)	5	0.01
Cypriot (0)	0	<0.01
Czech (11)	119	0.17
Czechoslovakian (48)	91	0.13
Danish (10)	45	0.07
Dutch (304)	1,510	2.20
Eastern European (0)	0	<0.01
English (4,750)	9,130	13.30
Estonian (0)	0	<0.01
European (524)	663	0.97
Finnish (15)	66	0.10
French, ex. Basque (341)	1,662	2.42
French Canadian (103)	118	0.17
German (6,614)	17,306	25.21
German Russian (0)	0	<0.01
Greek (43)	218	0.32
Guyanese (0)	0	<0.01
Hungarian (107)	254	0.37
Icelander (0)	0	<0.01
Iranian (0)	0	<0.01
Irish (3,575)	10,663	15.53
Israeli (0)	0	<0.01
Italian (556)	1,340	1.95
Latvian (0)	0	<0.01
Lithuanian (3)	3	<0.01
Luxemburger (0)	0	<0.01
Macedonian (0)	0	<0.01
Maltese (0)	0	<0.01
New Zealander (0)	0	<0.01
Northern European (23)	35	0.05
Norwegian (52)	325	0.47
Pennsylvania German (0)	26	0.04
Polish (290)	880	1.28
Portuguese (17)	40	0.06
Romanian (29)	90	0.13
Russian (23)	61	0.09
Scandinavian (0)	102	0.15
Scotch-Irish (429)	1,276	1.86
Scottish (583)	2,018	2.94
Serbian (0)	0	<0.01
Slavic (0)	12	0.02
Slovak (21)	53	0.08
Slovene (36)	142	0.21
Soviet Union (0)	0	<0.01
Swedish (62)	431	0.63
Swiss (208)	307	0.45
Turkish (0)	0	<0.01
Ukrainian (9)	37	0.05
Welsh (111)	408	0.59
West Indian, ex. Hispanic (0)	0	<0.01
Bahamian (0)	0	<0.01
Barbadian (0)	0	<0.01
Belizean (0)	0	<0.01
Bermudan (0)	0	<0.01
British West Indian (0)	0	<0.01
Dutch West Indian (0)	0	<0.01
Haitian (0)	0	<0.01
Jamaican (0)	0	<0.01
Trinidadian/Tobagonian (0)	0	<0.01
U.S. Virgin Islander (0)	0	<0.01
West Indian (0)	0	<0.01
Other West Indian (0)	0	<0.01
Yugoslavian (0)	23	0.03

Hispanic Origin	Population	%
Hispanic or Latino (of any race)	820	1.19
Central American, ex. Mexican	51	0.07
Costa Rican	8	0.01
Guatemalan	19	0.03
Honduran	5	0.01
Nicaraguan	4	0.01
Panamanian	14	0.02
Salvadoran	1	<0.01
Other Central American	0	<0.01
Cuban	30	0.04
Dominican Republic	6	0.01
Mexican	529	0.77
Puerto Rican	71	0.10
South American	38	0.06
Argentinean	5	0.01
Bolivian	2	<0.01
Chilean	1	<0.01
Colombian	12	0.02
Ecuadorian	2	<0.01
Paraguayan	0	<0.01
Peruvian	14	0.02
Uruguayan	0	<0.01
Venezuelan	2	<0.01
Other South American	0	<0.01
Other Hispanic or Latino	95	0.14

Race*	Population	%
African-American/Black (176)	396	0.57
Not Hispanic (175)	388	0.56
Hispanic (1)	8	0.01
American Indian/Alaska Native (200)	506	0.73
Not Hispanic (177)	472	0.69
Hispanic (23)	34	0.05
Alaska Athabascan *(Ala. Nat.)* (0)	0	<0.01
Aleut *(Alaska Native)* (0)	0	<0.01
Apache (0)	3	<0.01
Arapaho (1)	1	<0.01
Blackfeet (2)	7	0.01
Canadian/French Am. Ind. (3)	3	<0.01
Central American Ind. (2)	2	<0.01
Cherokee (54)	186	0.27
Cheyenne (0)	0	<0.01
Chickasaw (3)	3	<0.01
Chippewa (4)	11	0.02
Choctaw (3)	10	0.01
Colville (0)	0	<0.01
Comanche (5)	6	0.01
Cree (0)	0	<0.01
Creek (4)	5	0.01
Crow (0)	2	<0.01
Delaware (2)	2	<0.01
Hopi (0)	1	<0.01
Houma (0)	3	<0.01
Inupiat *(Alaska Native)* (2)	2	<0.01
Iroquois (1)	1	<0.01
Kiowa (1)	1	<0.01
Lumbee (6)	6	0.01
Menominee (0)	0	<0.01
Mexican American Ind. (5)	6	0.01
Navajo (2)	4	0.01
Osage (0)	0	<0.01
Ottawa (1)	1	<0.01
Paiute (1)	2	<0.01
Pima (0)	0	<0.01
Potawatomi (0)	0	<0.01
Pueblo (0)	0	<0.01
Puget Sound Salish (0)	0	<0.01
Seminole (0)	0	<0.01
Shoshone (0)	1	<0.01
Sioux (6)	24	0.03
South American Ind. (0)	1	<0.01
Spanish American Ind. (0)	0	<0.01
Tlingit-Haida *(Alaska Native)* (0)	0	<0.01
Tohono O'Odham (0)	0	<0.01
Tsimshian *(Alaska Native)* (0)	0	<0.01
Ute (0)	0	<0.01
Yakama (0)	0	<0.01
Yaqui (0)	0	<0.01
Yuman (0)	0	<0.01
Yup'ik *(Alaska Native)* (0)	0	<0.01
Asian (248)	377	0.55
Not Hispanic (241)	369	0.54
Hispanic (7)	8	0.01
Bangladeshi (0)	0	<0.01
Bhutanese (0)	0	<0.01
Burmese (0)	0	<0.01
Cambodian (3)	3	<0.01
Chinese, ex. Taiwanese (69)	81	0.12
Filipino (61)	98	0.14
Hmong (0)	0	<0.01
Indian (30)	45	0.07
Indonesian (0)	0	<0.01
Japanese (13)	34	0.05
Korean (25)	43	0.06
Laotian (1)	4	0.01
Malaysian (1)	1	<0.01
Nepalese (0)	0	<0.01
Pakistani (0)	1	<0.01
Sri Lankan (0)	0	<0.01
Taiwanese (3)	11	0.02
Thai (6)	10	0.01
Vietnamese (17)	24	0.03
Hawaii Native/Pacific Islander (19)	44	0.06
Not Hispanic (19)	44	0.06
Hispanic (0)	0	<0.01
Fijian (0)	0	<0.01
Guamanian/Chamorro (1)	9	0.01
Marshallese (0)	0	<0.01
Native Hawaiian (2)	8	0.01
Samoan (0)	8	0.01
Tongan (0)	0	<0.01
White (67,307)	68,005	98.71
Not Hispanic (66,782)	67,418	97.86
Hispanic (525)	587	0.85

*Notes: † The Census 2010 population figure is used to calculate the percentages in the Hispanic Origin and Race categories. Ancestry percentages are based on the 2006-2010 American Community Survey population (not shown); ‡ Numbers in parentheses indicate the number of people reporting a single ancestry; * Numbers in parentheses indicate the number of persons reporting this race alone, not in combination with any other race; Please refer to the Explanation of Data for more information.*

Newton County

Population: 14,244

Ancestry	Population	%
Afghan (0)	0	<0.01
African, Sub-Saharan (33)	33	0.23
African (33)	33	0.23
Cape Verdean (0)	0	<0.01
Ethiopian (0)	0	<0.01
Ghanaian (0)	0	<0.01
Kenyan (0)	0	<0.01
Liberian (0)	0	<0.01
Nigerian (0)	0	<0.01
Senegalese (0)	0	<0.01
Sierra Leonean (0)	0	<0.01
Somalian (0)	0	<0.01
South African (0)	0	<0.01
Sudanese (0)	0	<0.01
Ugandan (0)	0	<0.01
Zimbabwean (0)	0	<0.01
Other Sub-Saharan African (0)	0	<0.01
Albanian (0)	0	<0.01
Alsatian (0)	0	<0.01
American (929)	929	6.50
Arab (8)	18	0.13
Arab (0)	0	<0.01
Egyptian (0)	0	<0.01
Iraqi (0)	0	<0.01
Jordanian (0)	0	<0.01
Lebanese (8)	8	0.06
Moroccan (0)	0	<0.01
Palestinian (0)	0	<0.01
Syrian (0)	10	0.07
Other Arab (0)	0	<0.01
Armenian (0)	0	<0.01
Assyrian/Chaldean/Syriac (0)	0	<0.01
Australian (4)	4	0.03
Austrian (25)	96	0.67
Basque (0)	0	<0.01
Belgian (0)	0	<0.01
Brazilian (0)	0	<0.01
British (0)	0	<0.01
Bulgarian (0)	3	0.02
Cajun (0)	0	<0.01
Canadian (3)	3	0.02
Carpatho Rusyn (0)	0	<0.01
Celtic (0)	0	<0.01
Croatian (28)	124	0.87
Cypriot (0)	0	<0.01
Czech (5)	149	1.04
Czechoslovakian (0)	13	0.09
Danish (23)	53	0.37
Dutch (273)	1,082	7.57
Eastern European (8)	8	0.06
English (598)	1,571	10.99
Estonian (0)	0	<0.01
European (141)	141	0.99
Finnish (24)	47	0.33
French, ex. Basque (112)	741	5.18
French Canadian (47)	118	0.83
German (1,384)	4,351	30.43
German Russian (0)	0	<0.01
Greek (16)	22	0.15
Guyanese (0)	0	<0.01
Hungarian (55)	86	0.60
Icelander (0)	0	<0.01
Iranian (0)	0	<0.01
Irish (452)	2,418	16.91
Israeli (0)	0	<0.01
Italian (144)	566	3.96
Latvian (0)	6	0.04
Lithuanian (4)	4	0.03
Luxemburger (0)	5	0.03
Macedonian (0)	0	<0.01
Maltese (0)	0	<0.01
New Zealander (0)	0	<0.01
Northern European (9)	9	0.06
Norwegian (4)	121	0.85
Pennsylvania German (6)	15	0.10
Polish (449)	1,152	8.06
Portuguese (3)	3	0.02
Romanian (41)	41	0.29
Russian (0)	90	0.63
Scandinavian (0)	0	<0.01
Scotch-Irish (107)	282	1.97
Scottish (72)	249	1.74
Serbian (13)	21	0.15
Slavic (0)	0	<0.01
Slovak (24)	71	0.50
Slovene (0)	0	<0.01
Soviet Union (0)	0	<0.01
Swedish (56)	284	1.99
Swiss (0)	13	0.09
Turkish (0)	0	<0.01
Ukrainian (0)	0	<0.01
Welsh (36)	82	0.57
West Indian, ex. Hispanic (0)	0	<0.01
Bahamian (0)	0	<0.01
Barbadian (0)	0	<0.01
Belizean (0)	0	<0.01
Bermudan (0)	0	<0.01
British West Indian (0)	0	<0.01
Dutch West Indian (0)	0	<0.01
Haitian (0)	0	<0.01
Jamaican (0)	0	<0.01
Trinidadian/Tobagonian (0)	0	<0.01
U.S. Virgin Islander (0)	0	<0.01
West Indian (0)	0	<0.01
Other West Indian (0)	0	<0.01
Yugoslavian (0)	0	<0.01

Hispanic Origin	Population	%
Hispanic or Latino (of any race)	717	5.03
Central American, ex. Mexican	70	0.49
Costa Rican	0	<0.01
Guatemalan	5	0.04
Honduran	1	0.01
Nicaraguan	0	<0.01
Panamanian	0	<0.01
Salvadoran	64	0.45
Other Central American	0	<0.01
Cuban	2	0.01
Dominican Republic	0	<0.01
Mexican	536	3.76
Puerto Rican	33	0.23
South American	5	0.04
Argentinean	0	<0.01
Bolivian	0	<0.01
Chilean	1	0.01
Colombian	0	<0.01
Ecuadorian	0	<0.01
Paraguayan	0	<0.01
Peruvian	0	<0.01
Uruguayan	0	<0.01
Venezuelan	4	0.03
Other South American	0	<0.01
Other Hispanic or Latino	71	0.50

Race*	Population	%
African-American/Black (56)	91	0.64
Not Hispanic (53)	82	0.58
Hispanic (3)	9	0.06
American Indian/Alaska Native (42)	102	0.72
Not Hispanic (33)	84	0.59
Hispanic (9)	18	0.13
Alaska Athabascan *(Ala. Nat.)* (0)	0	<0.01
Aleut *(Alaska Native)* (0)	0	<0.01
Apache (0)	2	0.01
Arapaho (0)	0	<0.01
Blackfeet (0)	2	0.01
Canadian/French Am. Ind. (0)	0	<0.01
Central American Ind. (0)	0	<0.01
Cherokee (4)	21	0.15
Cheyenne (0)	1	0.01
Chickasaw (0)	0	<0.01
Chippewa (5)	11	0.08
Choctaw (0)	0	<0.01
Colville (0)	0	<0.01
Comanche (0)	0	<0.01
Cree (0)	0	<0.01
Creek (0)	3	0.02
Crow (1)	1	0.01
Delaware (0)	0	<0.01
Hopi (0)	0	<0.01
Houma (0)	0	<0.01
Inupiat *(Alaska Native)* (0)	0	<0.01
Iroquois (0)	3	0.02
Kiowa (0)	0	<0.01
Lumbee (0)	0	<0.01
Menominee (0)	0	<0.01
Mexican American Ind. (0)	2	0.01
Navajo (0)	0	<0.01
Osage (0)	0	<0.01
Ottawa (0)	0	<0.01
Paiute (0)	0	<0.01
Pima (0)	0	<0.01
Potawatomi (0)	2	0.01
Pueblo (0)	0	<0.01
Puget Sound Salish (0)	0	<0.01
Seminole (0)	1	0.01
Shoshone (0)	0	<0.01
Sioux (0)	4	0.03
South American Ind. (0)	0	<0.01
Spanish American Ind. (0)	0	<0.01
Tlingit-Haida *(Alaska Native)* (0)	0	<0.01
Tohono O'Odham (0)	0	<0.01
Tsimshian *(Alaska Native)* (0)	0	<0.01
Ute (0)	0	<0.01
Yakama (0)	0	<0.01
Yaqui (0)	0	<0.01
Yuman (0)	0	<0.01
Yup'ik *(Alaska Native)* (0)	0	<0.01
Asian (38)	51	0.36
Not Hispanic (38)	50	0.35
Hispanic (0)	1	0.01
Bangladeshi (0)	0	<0.01
Bhutanese (0)	0	<0.01
Burmese (0)	0	<0.01
Cambodian (0)	0	<0.01
Chinese, ex. Taiwanese (10)	13	0.09
Filipino (13)	20	0.14
Hmong (0)	0	<0.01
Indian (4)	5	0.04
Indonesian (0)	0	<0.01
Japanese (1)	1	0.01
Korean (6)	8	0.06
Laotian (0)	0	<0.01
Malaysian (0)	0	<0.01
Nepalese (0)	0	<0.01
Pakistani (0)	0	<0.01
Sri Lankan (0)	0	<0.01
Taiwanese (0)	0	<0.01
Thai (1)	1	0.01
Vietnamese (3)	3	0.02
Hawaii Native/Pacific Islander (2)	5	0.04
Not Hispanic (2)	5	0.04
Hispanic (0)	0	<0.01
Fijian (0)	0	<0.01
Guamanian/Chamorro (0)	0	<0.01
Marshallese (0)	0	<0.01
Native Hawaiian (0)	0	<0.01
Samoan (0)	0	<0.01
Tongan (0)	0	<0.01
White (13,700)	13,846	97.21
Not Hispanic (13,296)	13,391	94.01
Hispanic (404)	455	3.19

*Notes: † The Census 2010 population figure is used to calculate the percentages in the Hispanic Origin and Race categories. Ancestry percentages are based on the 2006-2010 American Community Survey population (not shown); ‡ Numbers in parentheses indicate the number of people reporting a single ancestry; * Numbers in parentheses indicate the number of persons reporting this race alone, not in combination with any other race; Please refer to the Explanation of Data for more information.*

Noble County

Population: 47,536

Ancestry	Population	%
Afghan (0)	0	<0.01
African, Sub-Saharan (32)	40	0.08
African (0)	0	<0.01
Cape Verdean (0)	0	<0.01
Ethiopian (0)	0	<0.01
Ghanaian (0)	0	<0.01
Kenyan (0)	0	<0.01
Liberian (0)	0	<0.01
Nigerian (0)	0	<0.01
Senegalese (0)	0	<0.01
Sierra Leonean (0)	0	<0.01
Somalian (0)	0	<0.01
South African (32)	40	0.08
Sudanese (0)	0	<0.01
Ugandan (0)	0	<0.01
Zimbabwean (0)	0	<0.01
Other Sub-Saharan African (0)	0	<0.01
Albanian (0)	0	<0.01
Alsatian (0)	0	<0.01
American (5,294)	5,294	11.14
Arab (16)	35	0.07
Arab (0)	0	<0.01
Egyptian (0)	19	0.04
Iraqi (0)	0	<0.01
Jordanian (0)	0	<0.01
Lebanese (16)	16	0.03
Moroccan (0)	0	<0.01
Palestinian (0)	0	<0.01
Syrian (0)	0	<0.01
Other Arab (0)	0	<0.01
Armenian (0)	0	<0.01
Assyrian/Chaldean/Syriac (0)	0	<0.01
Australian (0)	0	<0.01
Austrian (9)	45	0.09
Basque (0)	0	<0.01
Belgian (17)	160	0.34
Brazilian (0)	0	<0.01
British (61)	133	0.28
Bulgarian (0)	0	<0.01
Cajun (0)	0	<0.01
Canadian (82)	110	0.23
Carpatho Rusyn (0)	0	<0.01
Celtic (0)	0	<0.01
Croatian (0)	0	<0.01
Cypriot (0)	0	<0.01
Czech (56)	89	0.19
Czechoslovakian (0)	0	<0.01
Danish (0)	104	0.22
Dutch (408)	1,136	2.39
Eastern European (2)	2	<0.01
English (1,450)	4,033	8.49
Estonian (0)	0	<0.01
European (282)	289	0.61
Finnish (0)	0	<0.01
French, ex. Basque (291)	1,493	3.14
French Canadian (70)	112	0.24
German (7,671)	15,283	32.17
German Russian (0)	88	0.19
Greek (16)	72	0.15
Guyanese (0)	0	<0.01
Hungarian (52)	118	0.25
Icelander (0)	0	<0.01
Iranian (0)	0	<0.01
Irish (1,419)	4,657	9.80
Israeli (0)	0	<0.01
Italian (175)	770	1.62
Latvian (0)	0	<0.01
Lithuanian (13)	24	0.05
Luxemburger (0)	0	<0.01
Macedonian (0)	0	<0.01
Maltese (0)	0	<0.01
New Zealander (0)	0	<0.01
Northern European (0)	0	<0.01
Norwegian (68)	265	0.56
Pennsylvania German (430)	490	1.03
Polish (495)	1,055	2.22
Portuguese (0)	0	<0.01
Romanian (7)	11	0.02
Russian (31)	31	0.07
Scandinavian (35)	35	0.07
Scotch-Irish (183)	619	1.30
Scottish (157)	889	1.87
Serbian (0)	0	<0.01
Slavic (0)	0	<0.01
Slovak (0)	82	0.17
Slovene (0)	0	<0.01
Soviet Union (0)	0	<0.01
Swedish (157)	526	1.11
Swiss (156)	293	0.62
Turkish (0)	0	<0.01
Ukrainian (0)	0	<0.01
Welsh (16)	148	0.31
West Indian, ex. Hispanic (0)	75	0.16
Bahamian (0)	0	<0.01
Barbadian (0)	0	<0.01
Belizean (0)	0	<0.01
Bermudan (0)	0	<0.01
British West Indian (0)	0	<0.01
Dutch West Indian (0)	0	<0.01
Haitian (0)	0	<0.01
Jamaican (0)	75	0.16
Trinidadian/Tobagonian (0)	0	<0.01
U.S. Virgin Islander (0)	0	<0.01
West Indian (0)	0	<0.01
Other West Indian (0)	0	<0.01
Yugoslavian (14)	59	0.12

Hispanic Origin	Population	%
Hispanic or Latino (of any race)	4,567	9.61
Central American, ex. Mexican	54	0.11
Costa Rican	0	<0.01
Guatemalan	20	0.04
Honduran	18	0.04
Nicaraguan	0	<0.01
Panamanian	0	<0.01
Salvadoran	16	0.03
Other Central American	0	<0.01
Cuban	5	0.01
Dominican Republic	3	0.01
Mexican	4,297	9.04
Puerto Rican	38	0.08
South American	13	0.03
Argentinean	0	<0.01
Bolivian	0	<0.01
Chilean	0	<0.01
Colombian	4	0.01
Ecuadorian	2	<0.01
Paraguayan	0	<0.01
Peruvian	6	0.01
Uruguayan	0	<0.01
Venezuelan	1	<0.01
Other South American	0	<0.01
Other Hispanic or Latino	157	0.33

Race*	Population	%
African-American/Black (185)	335	0.70
Not Hispanic (170)	309	0.65
Hispanic (15)	26	0.05
American Indian/Alaska Native (102)	290	0.61
Not Hispanic (90)	254	0.53
Hispanic (12)	36	0.08
Alaska Athabascan *(Ala. Nat.)* (0)	0	<0.01
Aleut *(Alaska Native)* (1)	1	<0.01
Apache (0)	2	<0.01
Arapaho (0)	0	<0.01
Blackfeet (2)	7	0.01
Canadian/French Am. Ind. (0)	2	<0.01
Central American Ind. (0)	0	<0.01
Cherokee (18)	83	0.17
Cheyenne (0)	0	<0.01
Chickasaw (0)	0	<0.01
Chippewa (8)	12	0.03
Choctaw (0)	1	<0.01
Colville (0)	0	<0.01
Comanche (0)	0	<0.01
Cree (0)	0	<0.01
Creek (0)	0	<0.01
Crow (5)	5	0.01
Delaware (0)	1	<0.01
Hopi (0)	0	<0.01
Houma (0)	0	<0.01
Inupiat *(Alaska Native)* (0)	0	<0.01
Iroquois (2)	6	0.01
Kiowa (0)	0	<0.01
Lumbee (0)	0	<0.01
Menominee (1)	1	<0.01
Mexican American Ind. (5)	10	0.02
Navajo (5)	6	0.01
Osage (0)	1	<0.01
Ottawa (0)	0	<0.01
Paiute (0)	0	<0.01
Pima (0)	0	<0.01
Potawatomi (0)	1	<0.01
Pueblo (0)	0	<0.01
Puget Sound Salish (0)	0	<0.01
Seminole (0)	0	<0.01
Shoshone (0)	0	<0.01
Sioux (10)	17	0.04
South American Ind. (1)	1	<0.01
Spanish American Ind. (0)	0	<0.01
Tlingit-Haida *(Alaska Native)* (2)	2	<0.01
Tohono O'Odham (0)	0	<0.01
Tsimshian *(Alaska Native)* (0)	0	<0.01
Ute (0)	0	<0.01
Yakama (0)	0	<0.01
Yaqui (0)	0	<0.01
Yuman (0)	0	<0.01
Yup'ik *(Alaska Native)* (0)	0	<0.01
Asian (176)	267	0.56
Not Hispanic (174)	258	0.54
Hispanic (2)	9	0.02
Bangladeshi (0)	0	<0.01
Bhutanese (0)	0	<0.01
Burmese (0)	0	<0.01
Cambodian (7)	7	0.01
Chinese, ex. Taiwanese (31)	36	0.08
Filipino (40)	78	0.16
Hmong (0)	0	<0.01
Indian (24)	33	0.07
Indonesian (0)	0	<0.01
Japanese (7)	13	0.03
Korean (14)	18	0.04
Laotian (11)	11	0.02
Malaysian (0)	0	<0.01
Nepalese (0)	0	<0.01
Pakistani (5)	5	0.01
Sri Lankan (1)	1	<0.01
Taiwanese (0)	0	<0.01
Thai (5)	6	0.01
Vietnamese (28)	47	0.10
Hawaii Native/Pacific Islander (6)	30	0.06
Not Hispanic (5)	24	0.05
Hispanic (1)	6	0.01
Fijian (0)	0	<0.01
Guamanian/Chamorro (2)	4	0.01
Marshallese (0)	0	<0.01
Native Hawaiian (2)	14	0.03
Samoan (0)	0	<0.01
Tongan (0)	0	<0.01
White (43,970)	44,565	93.75
Not Hispanic (42,104)	42,498	89.40
Hispanic (1,866)	2,067	4.35

*Notes: † The Census 2010 population figure is used to calculate the percentages in the Hispanic Origin and Race categories. Ancestry percentages are based on the 2006-2010 American Community Survey population (not shown); ‡ Numbers in parentheses indicate the number of people reporting a single ancestry; * Numbers in parentheses indicate the number of persons reporting this race alone, not in combination with any other race; Please refer to the Explanation of Data for more information.*

Ohio County

Population: 6,128

Ancestry	Population	%
Afghan (0)	0	<0.01
African, Sub-Saharan (0)	0	<0.01
African (0)	0	<0.01
Cape Verdean (0)	0	<0.01
Ethiopian (0)	0	<0.01
Ghanaian (0)	0	<0.01
Kenyan (0)	0	<0.01
Liberian (0)	0	<0.01
Nigerian (0)	0	<0.01
Senegalese (0)	0	<0.01
Sierra Leonean (0)	0	<0.01
Somalian (0)	0	<0.01
South African (0)	0	<0.01
Sudanese (0)	0	<0.01
Ugandan (0)	0	<0.01
Zimbabwean (0)	0	<0.01
Other Sub-Saharan African (0)	0	<0.01
Albanian (0)	0	<0.01
Alsatian (0)	0	<0.01
American (742)	742	12.23
Arab (0)	0	<0.01
Arab (0)	0	<0.01
Egyptian (0)	0	<0.01
Iraqi (0)	0	<0.01
Jordanian (0)	0	<0.01
Lebanese (0)	0	<0.01
Moroccan (0)	0	<0.01
Palestinian (0)	0	<0.01
Syrian (0)	0	<0.01
Other Arab (0)	0	<0.01
Armenian (0)	0	<0.01
Assyrian/Chaldean/Syriac (0)	0	<0.01
Australian (0)	0	<0.01
Austrian (0)	0	<0.01
Basque (0)	0	<0.01
Belgian (0)	26	0.43
Brazilian (0)	0	<0.01
British (18)	18	0.30
Bulgarian (0)	0	<0.01
Cajun (0)	0	<0.01
Canadian (0)	0	<0.01
Carpatho Rusyn (0)	0	<0.01
Celtic (0)	0	<0.01
Croatian (0)	0	<0.01
Cypriot (0)	0	<0.01
Czech (0)	0	<0.01
Czechoslovakian (0)	0	<0.01
Danish (0)	0	<0.01
Dutch (26)	60	0.99
Eastern European (0)	0	<0.01
English (221)	443	7.30
Estonian (0)	0	<0.01
European (62)	62	1.02
Finnish (0)	0	<0.01
French, ex. Basque (53)	137	2.26
French Canadian (6)	40	0.66
German (1,078)	2,031	33.48
German Russian (0)	0	<0.01
Greek (0)	0	<0.01
Guyanese (0)	0	<0.01
Hungarian (53)	82	1.35
Icelander (0)	0	<0.01
Iranian (0)	0	<0.01
Irish (268)	764	12.59
Israeli (0)	0	<0.01
Italian (93)	263	4.33
Latvian (0)	0	<0.01
Lithuanian (0)	0	<0.01
Luxemburger (0)	0	<0.01
Macedonian (0)	0	<0.01
Maltese (0)	0	<0.01
New Zealander (0)	0	<0.01
Northern European (0)	0	<0.01
Norwegian (0)	0	<0.01
Pennsylvania German (0)	0	<0.01
Polish (109)	118	1.94
Portuguese (0)	3	0.05
Romanian (0)	3	0.05
Russian (0)	0	<0.01
Scandinavian (0)	6	0.10
Scotch-Irish (16)	72	1.19
Scottish (53)	95	1.57
Serbian (0)	0	<0.01
Slavic (0)	0	<0.01
Slovak (5)	12	0.20
Slovene (0)	0	<0.01
Soviet Union (0)	0	<0.01
Swedish (0)	3	0.05
Swiss (0)	0	<0.01
Turkish (0)	0	<0.01
Ukrainian (0)	0	<0.01
Welsh (0)	0	<0.01
West Indian, ex. Hispanic (0)	0	<0.01
Bahamian (0)	0	<0.01
Barbadian (0)	0	<0.01
Belizean (0)	0	<0.01
Bermudan (0)	0	<0.01
British West Indian (0)	0	<0.01
Dutch West Indian (0)	0	<0.01
Haitian (0)	0	<0.01
Jamaican (0)	0	<0.01
Trinidadian/Tobagonian (0)	0	<0.01
U.S. Virgin Islander (0)	0	<0.01
West Indian (0)	0	<0.01
Other West Indian (0)	0	<0.01
Yugoslavian (0)	0	<0.01

Hispanic Origin	Population	%
Hispanic or Latino (of any race)	69	1.13
Central American, ex. Mexican	7	0.11
Costa Rican	0	<0.01
Guatemalan	5	0.08
Honduran	1	0.02
Nicaraguan	1	0.02
Panamanian	0	<0.01
Salvadoran	0	<0.01
Other Central American	0	<0.01
Cuban	1	0.02
Dominican Republic	0	<0.01
Mexican	48	0.78
Puerto Rican	2	0.03
South American	2	0.03
Argentinean	1	0.02
Bolivian	0	<0.01
Chilean	0	<0.01
Colombian	0	<0.01
Ecuadorian	0	<0.01
Paraguayan	0	<0.01
Peruvian	1	0.02
Uruguayan	0	<0.01
Venezuelan	0	<0.01
Other South American	0	<0.01
Other Hispanic or Latino	9	0.15

Race*	Population	%
African-American/Black (22)	31	0.51
Not Hispanic (21)	30	0.49
Hispanic (1)	1	0.02
American Indian/Alaska Native (12)	34	0.55
Not Hispanic (11)	33	0.54
Hispanic (1)	1	0.02
Alaska Athabascan *(Ala. Nat.)* (0)	0	<0.01
Aleut *(Alaska Native)* (0)	0	<0.01
Apache (0)	0	<0.01
Arapaho (0)	0	<0.01
Blackfeet (0)	0	<0.01
Canadian/French Am. Ind. (0)	0	<0.01
Central American Ind. (0)	0	<0.01
Cherokee (2)	14	0.23
Cheyenne (0)	0	<0.01
Chickasaw (0)	0	<0.01
Chippewa (0)	0	<0.01
Choctaw (0)	1	0.02
Colville (0)	0	<0.01
Comanche (0)	0	<0.01
Cree (0)	0	<0.01
Creek (0)	0	<0.01
Crow (0)	0	<0.01
Delaware (3)	7	0.11
Hopi (0)	0	<0.01
Houma (0)	0	<0.01
Inupiat *(Alaska Native)* (0)	0	<0.01
Iroquois (0)	0	<0.01
Kiowa (0)	0	<0.01
Lumbee (0)	0	<0.01
Menominee (0)	0	<0.01
Mexican American Ind. (0)	0	<0.01
Navajo (0)	0	<0.01
Osage (0)	0	<0.01
Ottawa (0)	0	<0.01
Paiute (0)	0	<0.01
Pima (0)	0	<0.01
Potawatomi (0)	0	<0.01
Pueblo (0)	0	<0.01
Puget Sound Salish (0)	0	<0.01
Seminole (0)	0	<0.01
Shoshone (0)	0	<0.01
Sioux (0)	0	<0.01
South American Ind. (0)	0	<0.01
Spanish American Ind. (0)	0	<0.01
Tlingit-Haida *(Alaska Native)* (0)	0	<0.01
Tohono O'Odham (0)	0	<0.01
Tsimshian *(Alaska Native)* (0)	0	<0.01
Ute (0)	0	<0.01
Yakama (0)	0	<0.01
Yaqui (0)	0	<0.01
Yuman (0)	0	<0.01
Yup'ik *(Alaska Native)* (0)	0	<0.01
Asian (19)	25	0.41
Not Hispanic (19)	25	0.41
Hispanic (0)	0	<0.01
Bangladeshi (0)	0	<0.01
Bhutanese (0)	0	<0.01
Burmese (0)	0	<0.01
Cambodian (0)	0	<0.01
Chinese, ex. Taiwanese (6)	6	0.10
Filipino (7)	7	0.11
Hmong (0)	0	<0.01
Indian (0)	0	<0.01
Indonesian (0)	0	<0.01
Japanese (1)	6	0.10
Korean (1)	1	0.02
Laotian (0)	0	<0.01
Malaysian (0)	0	<0.01
Nepalese (0)	0	<0.01
Pakistani (0)	0	<0.01
Sri Lankan (0)	0	<0.01
Taiwanese (0)	0	<0.01
Thai (1)	1	0.02
Vietnamese (3)	3	0.05
Hawaii Native/Pacific Islander (0)	0	<0.01
Not Hispanic (0)	0	<0.01
Hispanic (0)	0	<0.01
Fijian (0)	0	<0.01
Guamanian/Chamorro (0)	0	<0.01
Marshallese (0)	0	<0.01
Native Hawaiian (0)	0	<0.01
Samoan (0)	0	<0.01
Tongan (0)	0	<0.01
White (6,012)	6,056	98.83
Not Hispanic (5,967)	6,005	97.99
Hispanic (45)	51	0.83

*Notes: † The Census 2010 population figure is used to calculate the percentages in the Hispanic Origin and Race categories. Ancestry percentages are based on the 2006-2010 American Community Survey population (not shown); ‡ Numbers in parentheses indicate the number of people reporting a single ancestry; * Numbers in parentheses indicate the number of persons reporting this race alone, not in combination with any other race; Please refer to the Explanation of Data for more information.*

Orange County

Population: 19,840

Ancestry	Population	%
Afghan (0)	0	<0.01
African, Sub-Saharan (10)	10	0.05
African (10)	10	0.05
Cape Verdean (0)	0	<0.01
Ethiopian (0)	0	<0.01
Ghanaian (0)	0	<0.01
Kenyan (0)	0	<0.01
Liberian (0)	0	<0.01
Nigerian (0)	0	<0.01
Senegalese (0)	0	<0.01
Sierra Leonean (0)	0	<0.01
Somalian (0)	0	<0.01
South African (0)	0	<0.01
Sudanese (0)	0	<0.01
Ugandan (0)	0	<0.01
Zimbabwean (0)	0	<0.01
Other Sub-Saharan African (0)	0	<0.01
Albanian (0)	0	<0.01
Alsatian (0)	0	<0.01
American (2,390)	2,390	12.06
Arab (0)	0	<0.01
Arab (0)	0	<0.01
Egyptian (0)	0	<0.01
Iraqi (0)	0	<0.01
Jordanian (0)	0	<0.01
Lebanese (0)	0	<0.01
Moroccan (0)	0	<0.01
Palestinian (0)	0	<0.01
Syrian (0)	0	<0.01
Other Arab (0)	0	<0.01
Armenian (0)	0	<0.01
Assyrian/Chaldean/Syriac (0)	0	<0.01
Australian (0)	0	<0.01
Austrian (0)	0	<0.01
Basque (0)	0	<0.01
Belgian (0)	0	<0.01
Brazilian (0)	0	<0.01
British (41)	53	0.27
Bulgarian (0)	0	<0.01
Cajun (0)	34	0.17
Canadian (0)	0	<0.01
Carpatho Rusyn (0)	0	<0.01
Celtic (0)	5	0.03
Croatian (0)	0	<0.01
Cypriot (0)	0	<0.01
Czech (8)	18	0.09
Czechoslovakian (0)	0	<0.01
Danish (12)	12	0.06
Dutch (79)	341	1.72
Eastern European (0)	0	<0.01
English (1,068)	1,929	9.73
Estonian (0)	0	<0.01
European (148)	154	0.78
Finnish (0)	11	0.06
French, ex. Basque (70)	370	1.87
French Canadian (18)	18	0.09
German (1,681)	3,731	18.82
German Russian (0)	0	<0.01
Greek (0)	8	0.04
Guyanese (0)	0	<0.01
Hungarian (0)	51	0.26
Icelander (0)	0	<0.01
Iranian (0)	0	<0.01
Irish (919)	2,449	12.36
Israeli (0)	0	<0.01
Italian (70)	229	1.16
Latvian (0)	0	<0.01
Lithuanian (0)	0	<0.01
Luxemburger (0)	0	<0.01
Macedonian (0)	0	<0.01
Maltese (0)	0	<0.01
New Zealander (0)	0	<0.01
Northern European (0)	0	<0.01
Norwegian (37)	49	0.25
Pennsylvania German (856)	913	4.61
Polish (102)	142	0.72
Portuguese (0)	0	<0.01
Romanian (7)	28	0.14
Russian (0)	27	0.14
Scandinavian (0)	0	<0.01
Scotch-Irish (164)	338	1.71
Scottish (166)	304	1.53
Serbian (0)	0	<0.01
Slavic (0)	0	<0.01
Slovak (0)	32	0.16
Slovene (0)	0	<0.01
Soviet Union (0)	0	<0.01
Swedish (15)	76	0.38
Swiss (32)	109	0.55
Turkish (0)	0	<0.01
Ukrainian (0)	0	<0.01
Welsh (47)	107	0.54
West Indian, ex. Hispanic (37)	84	0.42
Bahamian (0)	0	<0.01
Barbadian (0)	0	<0.01
Belizean (0)	0	<0.01
Bermudan (0)	0	<0.01
British West Indian (0)	0	<0.01
Dutch West Indian (0)	0	<0.01
Haitian (0)	0	<0.01
Jamaican (37)	84	0.42
Trinidadian/Tobagonian (0)	0	<0.01
U.S. Virgin Islander (0)	0	<0.01
West Indian (0)	0	<0.01
Other West Indian (0)	0	<0.01
Yugoslavian (0)	0	<0.01

Hispanic Origin	Population	%
Hispanic or Latino (of any race)	194	0.98
Central American, ex. Mexican	8	0.04
Costa Rican	2	0.01
Guatemalan	3	0.02
Honduran	0	<0.01
Nicaraguan	1	0.01
Panamanian	2	0.01
Salvadoran	0	<0.01
Other Central American	0	<0.01
Cuban	3	0.02
Dominican Republic	1	0.01
Mexican	139	0.70
Puerto Rican	20	0.10
South American	7	0.04
Argentinean	0	<0.01
Bolivian	0	<0.01
Chilean	0	<0.01
Colombian	4	0.02
Ecuadorian	3	0.02
Paraguayan	0	<0.01
Peruvian	0	<0.01
Uruguayan	0	<0.01
Venezuelan	0	<0.01
Other South American	0	<0.01
Other Hispanic or Latino	16	0.08

Race*	Population	%
African-American/Black (170)	242	1.22
Not Hispanic (168)	237	1.19
Hispanic (2)	5	0.03
American Indian/Alaska Native (62)	187	0.94
Not Hispanic (52)	172	0.87
Hispanic (10)	15	0.08
Alaska Athabascan *(Ala. Nat.)* (0)	0	<0.01
Aleut *(Alaska Native)* (0)	0	<0.01
Apache (1)	2	0.01
Arapaho (0)	0	<0.01
Blackfeet (0)	3	0.02
Canadian/French Am. Ind. (1)	1	0.01
Central American Ind. (0)	0	<0.01
Cherokee (14)	72	0.36
Cheyenne (0)	0	<0.01
Chickasaw (0)	3	0.02
Chippewa (1)	5	0.03
Choctaw (1)	6	0.03
Colville (0)	0	<0.01
Comanche (0)	3	0.02
Cree (0)	0	<0.01
Creek (1)	1	0.01
Crow (0)	0	<0.01
Delaware (1)	1	0.01
Hopi (0)	0	<0.01
Houma (0)	0	<0.01
Inupiat *(Alaska Native)* (0)	0	<0.01
Iroquois (0)	0	<0.01
Kiowa (0)	0	<0.01
Lumbee (0)	1	0.01
Menominee (0)	0	<0.01
Mexican American Ind. (0)	1	0.01
Navajo (0)	0	<0.01
Osage (0)	0	<0.01
Ottawa (0)	1	0.01
Paiute (0)	0	<0.01
Pima (0)	0	<0.01
Potawatomi (0)	1	0.01
Pueblo (0)	0	<0.01
Puget Sound Salish (0)	0	<0.01
Seminole (0)	2	0.01
Shoshone (0)	0	<0.01
Sioux (0)	6	0.03
South American Ind. (0)	0	<0.01
Spanish American Ind. (0)	0	<0.01
Tlingit-Haida *(Alaska Native)* (1)	1	0.01
Tohono O'Odham (0)	0	<0.01
Tsimshian *(Alaska Native)* (0)	0	<0.01
Ute (0)	0	<0.01
Yakama (0)	0	<0.01
Yaqui (1)	3	0.02
Yuman (0)	0	<0.01
Yup'ik *(Alaska Native)* (0)	0	<0.01
Asian (62)	85	0.43
Not Hispanic (61)	84	0.42
Hispanic (1)	1	0.01
Bangladeshi (0)	0	<0.01
Bhutanese (0)	0	<0.01
Burmese (0)	0	<0.01
Cambodian (0)	0	<0.01
Chinese, ex. Taiwanese (11)	13	0.07
Filipino (33)	42	0.21
Hmong (0)	0	<0.01
Indian (12)	17	0.09
Indonesian (0)	1	0.01
Japanese (0)	3	0.02
Korean (2)	4	0.02
Laotian (0)	0	<0.01
Malaysian (0)	0	<0.01
Nepalese (0)	0	<0.01
Pakistani (2)	2	0.01
Sri Lankan (0)	0	<0.01
Taiwanese (0)	1	0.01
Thai (1)	1	0.01
Vietnamese (1)	1	0.01
Hawaii Native/Pacific Islander (2)	7	0.04
Not Hispanic (2)	7	0.04
Hispanic (0)	0	<0.01
Fijian (0)	0	<0.01
Guamanian/Chamorro (1)	1	0.01
Marshallese (0)	0	<0.01
Native Hawaiian (1)	4	0.02
Samoan (0)	1	0.01
Tongan (0)	0	<0.01
White (19,245)	19,476	98.17
Not Hispanic (19,144)	19,353	97.55
Hispanic (101)	123	0.62

*Notes: † The Census 2010 population figure is used to calculate the percentages in the Hispanic Origin and Race categories. Ancestry percentages are based on the 2006-2010 American Community Survey population (not shown); ‡ Numbers in parentheses indicate the number of people reporting a single ancestry; * Numbers in parentheses indicate the number of persons reporting this race alone, not in combination with any other race; Please refer to the Explanation of Data for more information.*

Owen County

Population: 21,575

Ancestry	Population	%
Afghan (0)	0	<0.01
African, Sub-Saharan (0)	0	<0.01
African (0)	0	<0.01
Cape Verdean (0)	0	<0.01
Ethiopian (0)	0	<0.01
Ghanaian (0)	0	<0.01
Kenyan (0)	0	<0.01
Liberian (0)	0	<0.01
Nigerian (0)	0	<0.01
Senegalese (0)	0	<0.01
Sierra Leonean (0)	0	<0.01
Somalian (0)	0	<0.01
South African (0)	0	<0.01
Sudanese (0)	0	<0.01
Ugandan (0)	0	<0.01
Zimbabwean (0)	0	<0.01
Other Sub-Saharan African (0)	0	<0.01
Albanian (0)	0	<0.01
Alsatian (0)	0	<0.01
American (1,817)	1,817	8.36
Arab (3)	16	0.07
Arab (0)	0	<0.01
Egyptian (0)	0	<0.01
Iraqi (0)	0	<0.01
Jordanian (0)	0	<0.01
Lebanese (0)	0	<0.01
Moroccan (3)	3	0.01
Palestinian (0)	0	<0.01
Syrian (0)	13	0.06
Other Arab (0)	0	<0.01
Armenian (0)	0	<0.01
Assyrian/Chaldean/Syriac (0)	0	<0.01
Australian (0)	0	<0.01
Austrian (0)	18	0.08
Basque (0)	0	<0.01
Belgian (0)	0	<0.01
Brazilian (0)	0	<0.01
British (32)	45	0.21
Bulgarian (0)	0	<0.01
Cajun (0)	7	0.03
Canadian (0)	0	<0.01
Carpatho Rusyn (0)	0	<0.01
Celtic (0)	0	<0.01
Croatian (0)	0	<0.01
Cypriot (0)	0	<0.01
Czech (0)	9	0.04
Czechoslovakian (0)	10	0.05
Danish (0)	16	0.07
Dutch (84)	448	2.06
Eastern European (0)	0	<0.01
English (602)	1,927	8.87
Estonian (0)	0	<0.01
European (120)	166	0.76
Finnish (0)	0	<0.01
French, ex. Basque (100)	414	1.90
French Canadian (14)	33	0.15
German (2,612)	6,233	28.67
German Russian (0)	0	<0.01
Greek (27)	67	0.31
Guyanese (0)	0	<0.01
Hungarian (46)	122	0.56
Icelander (0)	0	<0.01
Iranian (0)	0	<0.01
Irish (1,110)	4,506	20.73
Israeli (0)	0	<0.01
Italian (74)	241	1.11
Latvian (7)	7	0.03
Lithuanian (0)	19	0.09
Luxemburger (0)	0	<0.01
Macedonian (0)	0	<0.01
Maltese (0)	0	<0.01
New Zealander (0)	0	<0.01
Northern European (0)	0	<0.01
Norwegian (0)	6	0.03
Pennsylvania German (53)	53	0.24
Polish (108)	268	1.23
Portuguese (0)	11	0.05
Romanian (0)	3	0.01
Russian (29)	88	0.40
Scandinavian (0)	19	0.09
Scotch-Irish (124)	317	1.46
Scottish (157)	486	2.24
Serbian (0)	0	<0.01
Slavic (0)	7	0.03
Slovak (17)	17	0.08
Slovene (0)	0	<0.01
Soviet Union (0)	0	<0.01
Swedish (149)	202	0.93
Swiss (0)	58	0.27
Turkish (0)	0	<0.01
Ukrainian (0)	0	<0.01
Welsh (0)	61	0.28
West Indian, ex. Hispanic (0)	0	<0.01
Bahamian (0)	0	<0.01
Barbadian (0)	0	<0.01
Belizean (0)	0	<0.01
Bermudan (0)	0	<0.01
British West Indian (0)	0	<0.01
Dutch West Indian (0)	0	<0.01
Haitian (0)	0	<0.01
Jamaican (0)	0	<0.01
Trinidadian/Tobagonian (0)	0	<0.01
U.S. Virgin Islander (0)	0	<0.01
West Indian (0)	0	<0.01
Other West Indian (0)	0	<0.01
Yugoslavian (24)	38	0.17

Hispanic Origin	Population	%
Hispanic or Latino (of any race)	198	0.92
Central American, ex. Mexican	4	0.02
Costa Rican	0	<0.01
Guatemalan	2	0.01
Honduran	0	<0.01
Nicaraguan	1	<0.01
Panamanian	1	<0.01
Salvadoran	0	<0.01
Other Central American	0	<0.01
Cuban	3	0.01
Dominican Republic	0	<0.01
Mexican	133	0.62
Puerto Rican	18	0.08
South American	9	0.04
Argentinean	2	0.01
Bolivian	0	<0.01
Chilean	0	<0.01
Colombian	4	0.02
Ecuadorian	0	<0.01
Paraguayan	0	<0.01
Peruvian	0	<0.01
Uruguayan	0	<0.01
Venezuelan	3	0.01
Other South American	0	<0.01
Other Hispanic or Latino	31	0.14

Race*	Population	%
African-American/Black (65)	116	0.54
Not Hispanic (65)	116	0.54
Hispanic (0)	0	<0.01
American Indian/Alaska Native (75)	172	0.80
Not Hispanic (72)	167	0.77
Hispanic (3)	5	0.02
Alaska Athabascan *(Ala. Nat.)* (0)	0	<0.01
Aleut *(Alaska Native)* (0)	0	<0.01
Apache (0)	0	<0.01
Arapaho (0)	0	<0.01
Blackfeet (2)	15	0.07
Canadian/French Am. Ind. (0)	0	<0.01
Central American Ind. (0)	1	<0.01
Cherokee (21)	55	0.25
Cheyenne (0)	0	<0.01
Chickasaw (1)	3	0.01
Chippewa (7)	8	0.04
Choctaw (2)	4	0.02
Colville (0)	0	<0.01
Comanche (0)	0	<0.01
Cree (3)	5	0.02
Creek (4)	4	0.02
Crow (0)	4	0.02
Delaware (0)	1	<0.01
Hopi (0)	0	<0.01
Houma (0)	0	<0.01
Inupiat *(Alaska Native)* (0)	1	<0.01
Iroquois (0)	3	0.01
Kiowa (0)	0	<0.01
Lumbee (0)	1	<0.01
Menominee (0)	0	<0.01
Mexican American Ind. (1)	1	<0.01
Navajo (0)	0	<0.01
Osage (0)	1	<0.01
Ottawa (0)	0	<0.01
Paiute (0)	0	<0.01
Pima (0)	0	<0.01
Potawatomi (0)	0	<0.01
Pueblo (1)	1	<0.01
Puget Sound Salish (0)	0	<0.01
Seminole (0)	0	<0.01
Shoshone (0)	1	<0.01
Sioux (1)	7	0.03
South American Ind. (0)	0	<0.01
Spanish American Ind. (0)	0	<0.01
Tlingit-Haida *(Alaska Native)* (0)	0	<0.01
Tohono O'Odham (0)	0	<0.01
Tsimshian *(Alaska Native)* (0)	0	<0.01
Ute (0)	0	<0.01
Yakama (0)	0	<0.01
Yaqui (0)	0	<0.01
Yuman (0)	0	<0.01
Yup'ik *(Alaska Native)* (0)	0	<0.01
Asian (66)	108	0.50
Not Hispanic (65)	107	0.50
Hispanic (1)	1	<0.01
Bangladeshi (0)	0	<0.01
Bhutanese (0)	0	<0.01
Burmese (0)	0	<0.01
Cambodian (0)	0	<0.01
Chinese, ex. Taiwanese (13)	14	0.06
Filipino (21)	36	0.17
Hmong (0)	0	<0.01
Indian (9)	16	0.07
Indonesian (0)	0	<0.01
Japanese (6)	13	0.06
Korean (5)	14	0.06
Laotian (1)	1	<0.01
Malaysian (0)	0	<0.01
Nepalese (0)	0	<0.01
Pakistani (2)	2	0.01
Sri Lankan (0)	0	<0.01
Taiwanese (0)	3	0.01
Thai (2)	2	0.01
Vietnamese (2)	3	0.01
Hawaii Native/Pacific Islander (1)	6	0.03
Not Hispanic (1)	6	0.03
Hispanic (0)	0	<0.01
Fijian (0)	0	<0.01
Guamanian/Chamorro (0)	0	<0.01
Marshallese (0)	0	<0.01
Native Hawaiian (1)	5	0.02
Samoan (0)	0	<0.01
Tongan (0)	0	<0.01
White (21,129)	21,315	98.79
Not Hispanic (20,983)	21,157	98.06
Hispanic (146)	158	0.73

*Notes: † The Census 2010 population figure is used to calculate the percentages in the Hispanic Origin and Race categories. Ancestry percentages are based on the 2006-2010 American Community Survey population (not shown); ‡ Numbers in parentheses indicate the number of people reporting a single ancestry; * Numbers in parentheses indicate the number of persons reporting this race alone, not in combination with any other race; Please refer to the Explanation of Data for more information.*

Parke County

Population: 17,339

Ancestry	Population	%
Afghan (0)	0	<0.01
African, Sub-Saharan (12)	21	0.12
African (12)	21	0.12
Cape Verdean (0)	0	<0.01
Ethiopian (0)	0	<0.01
Ghanaian (0)	0	<0.01
Kenyan (0)	0	<0.01
Liberian (0)	0	<0.01
Nigerian (0)	0	<0.01
Senegalese (0)	0	<0.01
Sierra Leonean (0)	0	<0.01
Somalian (0)	0	<0.01
South African (0)	0	<0.01
Sudanese (0)	0	<0.01
Ugandan (0)	0	<0.01
Zimbabwean (0)	0	<0.01
Other Sub-Saharan African (0)	0	<0.01
Albanian (0)	0	<0.01
Alsatian (0)	0	<0.01
American (4,820)	4,820	27.71
Arab (56)	56	0.32
Arab (0)	0	<0.01
Egyptian (0)	0	<0.01
Iraqi (0)	0	<0.01
Jordanian (0)	0	<0.01
Lebanese (0)	0	<0.01
Moroccan (0)	0	<0.01
Palestinian (0)	0	<0.01
Syrian (56)	56	0.32
Other Arab (0)	0	<0.01
Armenian (0)	0	<0.01
Assyrian/Chaldean/Syriac (0)	0	<0.01
Australian (0)	0	<0.01
Austrian (0)	21	0.12
Basque (0)	0	<0.01
Belgian (0)	0	<0.01
Brazilian (0)	0	<0.01
British (4)	31	0.18
Bulgarian (0)	0	<0.01
Cajun (0)	0	<0.01
Canadian (46)	46	0.26
Carpatho Rusyn (0)	0	<0.01
Celtic (0)	13	0.07
Croatian (16)	16	0.09
Cypriot (0)	0	<0.01
Czech (5)	14	0.08
Czechoslovakian (0)	0	<0.01
Danish (25)	25	0.14
Dutch (116)	533	3.06
Eastern European (0)	0	<0.01
English (842)	1,749	10.06
Estonian (0)	0	<0.01
European (33)	33	0.19
Finnish (0)	0	<0.01
French, ex. Basque (74)	403	2.32
French Canadian (0)	0	<0.01
German (2,135)	4,115	23.66
German Russian (0)	0	<0.01
Greek (0)	27	0.16
Guyanese (0)	0	<0.01
Hungarian (71)	94	0.54
Icelander (0)	0	<0.01
Iranian (0)	0	<0.01
Irish (653)	1,859	10.69
Israeli (0)	0	<0.01
Italian (156)	262	1.51
Latvian (0)	0	<0.01
Lithuanian (14)	27	0.16
Luxemburger (0)	0	<0.01
Macedonian (0)	0	<0.01
Maltese (0)	0	<0.01
New Zealander (0)	0	<0.01
Northern European (38)	38	0.22
Norwegian (7)	61	0.35
Pennsylvania German (109)	109	0.63
Polish (68)	159	0.91
Portuguese (19)	19	0.11
Romanian (0)	39	0.22
Russian (9)	14	0.08
Scandinavian (8)	8	0.05
Scotch-Irish (89)	220	1.26
Scottish (132)	322	1.85
Serbian (9)	9	0.05
Slavic (0)	12	0.07
Slovak (0)	20	0.11
Slovene (0)	0	<0.01
Soviet Union (0)	0	<0.01
Swedish (27)	91	0.52
Swiss (225)	242	1.39
Turkish (13)	13	0.07
Ukrainian (14)	14	0.08
Welsh (173)	217	1.25
West Indian, ex. Hispanic (0)	0	<0.01
Bahamian (0)	0	<0.01
Barbadian (0)	0	<0.01
Belizean (0)	0	<0.01
Bermudan (0)	0	<0.01
British West Indian (0)	0	<0.01
Dutch West Indian (0)	0	<0.01
Haitian (0)	0	<0.01
Jamaican (0)	0	<0.01
Trinidadian/Tobagonian (0)	0	<0.01
U.S. Virgin Islander (0)	0	<0.01
West Indian (0)	0	<0.01
Other West Indian (0)	0	<0.01
Yugoslavian (0)	0	<0.01

Hispanic Origin	Population	%
Hispanic or Latino (of any race)	215	1.24
Central American, ex. Mexican	1	0.01
Costa Rican	0	<0.01
Guatemalan	0	<0.01
Honduran	1	0.01
Nicaraguan	0	<0.01
Panamanian	0	<0.01
Salvadoran	0	<0.01
Other Central American	0	<0.01
Cuban	1	0.01
Dominican Republic	0	<0.01
Mexican	184	1.06
Puerto Rican	11	0.06
South American	1	0.01
Argentinean	0	<0.01
Bolivian	0	<0.01
Chilean	0	<0.01
Colombian	0	<0.01
Ecuadorian	0	<0.01
Paraguayan	0	<0.01
Peruvian	0	<0.01
Uruguayan	0	<0.01
Venezuelan	1	0.01
Other South American	0	<0.01
Other Hispanic or Latino	17	0.10

Race*	Population	%
African-American/Black (397)	436	2.51
Not Hispanic (391)	429	2.47
Hispanic (6)	7	0.04
American Indian/Alaska Native (64)	108	0.62
Not Hispanic (53)	96	0.55
Hispanic (11)	12	0.07
Alaska Athabascan *(Ala. Nat.)* (0)	0	<0.01
Aleut *(Alaska Native)* (0)	1	0.01
Apache (1)	2	0.01
Arapaho (0)	0	<0.01
Blackfeet (2)	2	0.01
Canadian/French Am. Ind. (0)	1	0.01
Central American Ind. (0)	0	<0.01
Cherokee (14)	31	0.18
Cheyenne (0)	0	<0.01
Chickasaw (0)	0	<0.01
Chippewa (1)	1	0.01
Choctaw (0)	2	0.01
Colville (0)	0	<0.01
Comanche (0)	0	<0.01
Cree (0)	0	<0.01
Creek (0)	0	<0.01
Crow (0)	0	<0.01
Delaware (0)	0	<0.01
Hopi (0)	0	<0.01
Houma (0)	0	<0.01
Inupiat *(Alaska Native)* (0)	0	<0.01
Iroquois (0)	2	0.01
Kiowa (0)	0	<0.01
Lumbee (1)	1	0.01
Menominee (0)	0	<0.01
Mexican American Ind. (1)	2	0.01
Navajo (2)	2	0.01
Osage (0)	0	<0.01
Ottawa (0)	0	<0.01
Paiute (0)	0	<0.01
Pima (0)	0	<0.01
Potawatomi (4)	4	0.02
Pueblo (0)	0	<0.01
Puget Sound Salish (0)	0	<0.01
Seminole (0)	0	<0.01
Shoshone (0)	0	<0.01
Sioux (0)	0	<0.01
South American Ind. (0)	0	<0.01
Spanish American Ind. (1)	1	0.01
Tlingit-Haida *(Alaska Native)* (0)	0	<0.01
Tohono O'Odham (0)	0	<0.01
Tsimshian *(Alaska Native)* (0)	0	<0.01
Ute (0)	0	<0.01
Yakama (0)	0	<0.01
Yaqui (0)	0	<0.01
Yuman (0)	0	<0.01
Yup'ik *(Alaska Native)* (0)	0	<0.01
Asian (34)	44	0.25
Not Hispanic (33)	42	0.24
Hispanic (1)	2	0.01
Bangladeshi (0)	0	<0.01
Bhutanese (0)	0	<0.01
Burmese (0)	0	<0.01
Cambodian (0)	0	<0.01
Chinese, ex. Taiwanese (5)	6	0.03
Filipino (8)	11	0.06
Hmong (0)	0	<0.01
Indian (2)	2	0.01
Indonesian (0)	0	<0.01
Japanese (6)	10	0.06
Korean (8)	9	0.05
Laotian (0)	0	<0.01
Malaysian (0)	0	<0.01
Nepalese (0)	0	<0.01
Pakistani (0)	0	<0.01
Sri Lankan (0)	0	<0.01
Taiwanese (0)	0	<0.01
Thai (1)	1	0.01
Vietnamese (2)	3	0.02
Hawaii Native/Pacific Islander (4)	5	0.03
Not Hispanic (4)	5	0.03
Hispanic (0)	0	<0.01
Fijian (1)	1	0.01
Guamanian/Chamorro (0)	0	<0.01
Marshallese (0)	0	<0.01
Native Hawaiian (1)	1	0.01
Samoan (0)	0	<0.01
Tongan (0)	0	<0.01
White (16,671)	16,767	96.70
Not Hispanic (16,545)	16,635	95.94
Hispanic (126)	132	0.76

*Notes: † The Census 2010 population figure is used to calculate the percentages in the Hispanic Origin and Race categories. Ancestry percentages are based on the 2006-2010 American Community Survey population (not shown); ‡ Numbers in parentheses indicate the number of people reporting a single ancestry; * Numbers in parentheses indicate the number of persons reporting this race alone, not in combination with any other race; Please refer to the Explanation of Data for more information.*

Perry County

Population: 19,338

Ancestry	Population	%
Afghan (0)	0	<0.01
African, Sub-Saharan (0)	4	0.02
African (0)	4	0.02
Cape Verdean (0)	0	<0.01
Ethiopian (0)	0	<0.01
Ghanaian (0)	0	<0.01
Kenyan (0)	0	<0.01
Liberian (0)	0	<0.01
Nigerian (0)	0	<0.01
Senegalese (0)	0	<0.01
Sierra Leonean (0)	0	<0.01
Somalian (0)	0	<0.01
South African (0)	0	<0.01
Sudanese (0)	0	<0.01
Ugandan (0)	0	<0.01
Zimbabwean (0)	0	<0.01
Other Sub-Saharan African (0)	0	<0.01
Albanian (0)	0	<0.01
Alsatian (0)	0	<0.01
American (2,237)	2,237	11.58
Arab (0)	9	0.05
Arab (0)	0	<0.01
Egyptian (0)	0	<0.01
Iraqi (0)	0	<0.01
Jordanian (0)	0	<0.01
Lebanese (0)	0	<0.01
Moroccan (0)	0	<0.01
Palestinian (0)	0	<0.01
Syrian (0)	9	0.05
Other Arab (0)	0	<0.01
Armenian (0)	0	<0.01
Assyrian/Chaldean/Syriac (0)	0	<0.01
Australian (0)	0	<0.01
Austrian (0)	0	<0.01
Basque (0)	0	<0.01
Belgian (93)	360	1.86
Brazilian (0)	0	<0.01
British (13)	86	0.45
Bulgarian (0)	11	0.06
Cajun (0)	0	<0.01
Canadian (12)	12	0.06
Carpatho Rusyn (0)	0	<0.01
Celtic (2)	2	0.01
Croatian (0)	0	<0.01
Cypriot (0)	0	<0.01
Czech (0)	26	0.13
Czechoslovakian (0)	0	<0.01
Danish (0)	0	<0.01
Dutch (3)	247	1.28
Eastern European (0)	0	<0.01
English (831)	1,679	8.69
Estonian (0)	0	<0.01
European (109)	109	0.56
Finnish (0)	0	<0.01
French, ex. Basque (304)	1,216	6.30
French Canadian (0)	4	0.02
German (3,720)	7,309	37.84
German Russian (0)	0	<0.01
Greek (0)	0	<0.01
Guyanese (0)	0	<0.01
Hungarian (0)	0	<0.01
Icelander (0)	0	<0.01
Iranian (0)	0	<0.01
Irish (888)	2,779	14.39
Israeli (0)	0	<0.01
Italian (95)	220	1.14
Latvian (0)	0	<0.01
Lithuanian (0)	0	<0.01
Luxemburger (0)	0	<0.01
Macedonian (0)	0	<0.01
Maltese (0)	0	<0.01
New Zealander (0)	0	<0.01
Northern European (0)	0	<0.01
Norwegian (12)	12	0.06
Pennsylvania German (0)	10	0.05
Polish (99)	231	1.20
Portuguese (0)	0	<0.01
Romanian (0)	0	<0.01
Russian (8)	16	0.08
Scandinavian (0)	0	<0.01
Scotch-Irish (36)	198	1.03
Scottish (45)	254	1.31
Serbian (0)	0	<0.01
Slavic (0)	8	0.04
Slovak (0)	0	<0.01
Slovene (0)	0	<0.01
Soviet Union (0)	0	<0.01
Swedish (0)	77	0.40
Swiss (113)	320	1.66
Turkish (0)	0	<0.01
Ukrainian (0)	0	<0.01
Welsh (49)	135	0.70
West Indian, ex. Hispanic (5)	10	0.05
Bahamian (0)	0	<0.01
Barbadian (0)	0	<0.01
Belizean (0)	0	<0.01
Bermudan (0)	0	<0.01
British West Indian (0)	0	<0.01
Dutch West Indian (0)	0	<0.01
Haitian (0)	0	<0.01
Jamaican (0)	5	0.03
Trinidadian/Tobagonian (0)	0	<0.01
U.S. Virgin Islander (0)	0	<0.01
West Indian (5)	5	0.03
Other West Indian (0)	0	<0.01
Yugoslavian (0)	0	<0.01

Hispanic Origin	Population	%
Hispanic or Latino (of any race)	192	0.99
Central American, ex. Mexican	7	0.04
Costa Rican	0	<0.01
Guatemalan	0	<0.01
Honduran	2	0.01
Nicaraguan	0	<0.01
Panamanian	0	<0.01
Salvadoran	5	0.03
Other Central American	0	<0.01
Cuban	0	<0.01
Dominican Republic	0	<0.01
Mexican	142	0.73
Puerto Rican	17	0.09
South American	2	0.01
Argentinean	0	<0.01
Bolivian	1	0.01
Chilean	0	<0.01
Colombian	0	<0.01
Ecuadorian	0	<0.01
Paraguayan	0	<0.01
Peruvian	1	0.01
Uruguayan	0	<0.01
Venezuelan	0	<0.01
Other South American	0	<0.01
Other Hispanic or Latino	24	0.12

Race*	Population	%
African-American/Black (471)	515	2.66
Not Hispanic (469)	510	2.64
Hispanic (2)	5	0.03
American Indian/Alaska Native (36)	94	0.49
Not Hispanic (34)	90	0.47
Hispanic (2)	4	0.02
Alaska Athabascan *(Ala. Nat.)* (0)	0	<0.01
Aleut *(Alaska Native)* (2)	2	0.01
Apache (3)	3	0.02
Arapaho (0)	0	<0.01
Blackfeet (1)	2	0.01
Canadian/French Am. Ind. (0)	0	<0.01
Central American Ind. (0)	0	<0.01
Cherokee (3)	28	0.14
Cheyenne (0)	0	<0.01
Chickasaw (0)	0	<0.01
Chippewa (3)	6	0.03
Choctaw (1)	1	0.01
Colville (0)	0	<0.01
Comanche (0)	0	<0.01
Cree (0)	0	<0.01
Creek (3)	3	0.02
Crow (0)	1	0.01
Delaware (0)	0	<0.01
Hopi (0)	0	<0.01
Houma (0)	0	<0.01
Inupiat *(Alaska Native)* (0)	0	<0.01
Iroquois (2)	2	0.01
Kiowa (0)	0	<0.01
Lumbee (1)	1	0.01
Menominee (0)	0	<0.01
Mexican American Ind. (0)	0	<0.01
Navajo (0)	0	<0.01
Osage (0)	0	<0.01
Ottawa (0)	0	<0.01
Paiute (0)	0	<0.01
Pima (0)	0	<0.01
Potawatomi (1)	1	0.01
Pueblo (0)	0	<0.01
Puget Sound Salish (0)	0	<0.01
Seminole (0)	0	<0.01
Shoshone (4)	4	0.02
Sioux (0)	2	0.01
South American Ind. (1)	1	0.01
Spanish American Ind. (0)	0	<0.01
Tlingit-Haida *(Alaska Native)* (0)	0	<0.01
Tohono O'Odham (0)	0	<0.01
Tsimshian *(Alaska Native)* (0)	0	<0.01
Ute (0)	0	<0.01
Yakama (0)	0	<0.01
Yaqui (0)	0	<0.01
Yuman (0)	0	<0.01
Yup'ik *(Alaska Native)* (0)	0	<0.01
Asian (69)	95	0.49
Not Hispanic (69)	95	0.49
Hispanic (0)	0	<0.01
Bangladeshi (0)	0	<0.01
Bhutanese (0)	0	<0.01
Burmese (0)	0	<0.01
Cambodian (0)	0	<0.01
Chinese, ex. Taiwanese (16)	17	0.09
Filipino (12)	20	0.10
Hmong (0)	0	<0.01
Indian (11)	12	0.06
Indonesian (1)	2	0.01
Japanese (20)	24	0.12
Korean (5)	9	0.05
Laotian (0)	0	<0.01
Malaysian (0)	0	<0.01
Nepalese (0)	0	<0.01
Pakistani (3)	3	0.02
Sri Lankan (0)	0	<0.01
Taiwanese (0)	0	<0.01
Thai (1)	1	0.01
Vietnamese (0)	0	<0.01
Hawaii Native/Pacific Islander (4)	6	0.03
Not Hispanic (4)	6	0.03
Hispanic (0)	0	<0.01
Fijian (0)	0	<0.01
Guamanian/Chamorro (1)	1	0.01
Marshallese (0)	0	<0.01
Native Hawaiian (3)	3	0.02
Samoan (0)	1	0.01
Tongan (0)	0	<0.01
White (18,557)	18,700	96.70
Not Hispanic (18,428)	18,553	95.94
Hispanic (129)	147	0.76

*Notes: † The Census 2010 population figure is used to calculate the percentages in the Hispanic Origin and Race categories. Ancestry percentages are based on the 2006-2010 American Community Survey population (not shown); ‡ Numbers in parentheses indicate the number of people reporting a single ancestry; * Numbers in parentheses indicate the number of persons reporting this race alone, not in combination with any other race; Please refer to the Explanation of Data for more information.*

Pike County

Population: 12,845

Ancestry	Population	%
Afghan (0)	0	<0.01
African, Sub-Saharan (0)	0	<0.01
African (0)	0	<0.01
Cape Verdean (0)	0	<0.01
Ethiopian (0)	0	<0.01
Ghanaian (0)	0	<0.01
Kenyan (0)	0	<0.01
Liberian (0)	0	<0.01
Nigerian (0)	0	<0.01
Senegalese (0)	0	<0.01
Sierra Leonean (0)	0	<0.01
Somalian (0)	0	<0.01
South African (0)	0	<0.01
Sudanese (0)	0	<0.01
Ugandan (0)	0	<0.01
Zimbabwean (0)	0	<0.01
Other Sub-Saharan African (0)	0	<0.01
Albanian (0)	0	<0.01
Alsatian (0)	0	<0.01
American (3,325)	3,325	25.67
Arab (0)	0	<0.01
Arab (0)	0	<0.01
Egyptian (0)	0	<0.01
Iraqi (0)	0	<0.01
Jordanian (0)	0	<0.01
Lebanese (0)	0	<0.01
Moroccan (0)	0	<0.01
Palestinian (0)	0	<0.01
Syrian (0)	0	<0.01
Other Arab (0)	0	<0.01
Armenian (0)	0	<0.01
Assyrian/Chaldean/Syriac (0)	0	<0.01
Australian (0)	2	0.02
Austrian (0)	0	<0.01
Basque (0)	0	<0.01
Belgian (0)	0	<0.01
Brazilian (0)	0	<0.01
British (64)	99	0.76
Bulgarian (0)	0	<0.01
Cajun (0)	0	<0.01
Canadian (0)	0	<0.01
Carpatho Rusyn (0)	0	<0.01
Celtic (0)	0	<0.01
Croatian (0)	3	0.02
Cypriot (0)	0	<0.01
Czech (0)	3	0.02
Czechoslovakian (0)	0	<0.01
Danish (0)	35	0.27
Dutch (22)	119	0.92
Eastern European (9)	9	0.07
English (698)	1,473	11.37
Estonian (0)	0	<0.01
European (92)	151	1.17
Finnish (0)	0	<0.01
French, ex. Basque (62)	431	3.33
French Canadian (16)	23	0.18
German (1,781)	3,248	25.07
German Russian (0)	0	<0.01
Greek (0)	0	<0.01
Guyanese (0)	0	<0.01
Hungarian (0)	20	0.15
Icelander (0)	0	<0.01
Iranian (0)	0	<0.01
Irish (608)	2,052	15.84
Israeli (0)	0	<0.01
Italian (7)	75	0.58
Latvian (0)	0	<0.01
Lithuanian (0)	0	<0.01
Luxemburger (0)	0	<0.01
Macedonian (0)	0	<0.01
Maltese (0)	0	<0.01
New Zealander (0)	0	<0.01
Northern European (0)	0	<0.01
Norwegian (14)	14	0.11
Pennsylvania German (0)	0	<0.01
Polish (45)	112	0.86
Portuguese (25)	40	0.31
Romanian (0)	0	<0.01
Russian (25)	52	0.40
Scandinavian (0)	0	<0.01
Scotch-Irish (165)	220	1.70
Scottish (69)	162	1.25
Serbian (0)	0	<0.01
Slavic (0)	0	<0.01
Slovak (0)	0	<0.01
Slovene (0)	0	<0.01
Soviet Union (0)	0	<0.01
Swedish (19)	39	0.30
Swiss (0)	6	0.05
Turkish (0)	0	<0.01
Ukrainian (10)	10	0.08
Welsh (0)	84	0.65
West Indian, ex. Hispanic (0)	0	<0.01
Bahamian (0)	0	<0.01
Barbadian (0)	0	<0.01
Belizean (0)	0	<0.01
Bermudan (0)	0	<0.01
British West Indian (0)	0	<0.01
Dutch West Indian (0)	0	<0.01
Haitian (0)	0	<0.01
Jamaican (0)	0	<0.01
Trinidadian/Tobagonian (0)	0	<0.01
U.S. Virgin Islander (0)	0	<0.01
West Indian (0)	0	<0.01
Other West Indian (0)	0	<0.01
Yugoslavian (0)	0	<0.01

Hispanic Origin	Population	%
Hispanic or Latino (of any race)	120	0.93
Central American, ex. Mexican	12	0.09
Costa Rican	1	0.01
Guatemalan	6	0.05
Honduran	1	0.01
Nicaraguan	0	<0.01
Panamanian	0	<0.01
Salvadoran	4	0.03
Other Central American	0	<0.01
Cuban	2	0.02
Dominican Republic	1	0.01
Mexican	69	0.54
Puerto Rican	19	0.15
South American	3	0.02
Argentinean	0	<0.01
Bolivian	0	<0.01
Chilean	0	<0.01
Colombian	2	0.02
Ecuadorian	0	<0.01
Paraguayan	0	<0.01
Peruvian	1	0.01
Uruguayan	0	<0.01
Venezuelan	0	<0.01
Other South American	0	<0.01
Other Hispanic or Latino	14	0.11

Race*	Population	%
African-American/Black (39)	62	0.48
Not Hispanic (38)	60	0.47
Hispanic (1)	2	0.02
American Indian/Alaska Native (27)	69	0.54
Not Hispanic (25)	66	0.51
Hispanic (2)	3	0.02
Alaska Athabascan *(Ala. Nat.)* (0)	0	<0.01
Aleut *(Alaska Native)* (0)	0	<0.01
Apache (2)	2	0.02
Arapaho (0)	0	<0.01
Blackfeet (1)	8	0.06
Canadian/French Am. Ind. (0)	0	<0.01
Central American Ind. (0)	0	<0.01
Cherokee (3)	19	0.15
Cheyenne (0)	0	<0.01
Chickasaw (0)	0	<0.01
Chippewa (0)	0	<0.01
Choctaw (6)	7	0.05
Colville (0)	0	<0.01
Comanche (0)	0	<0.01
Cree (0)	0	<0.01
Creek (0)	0	<0.01
Crow (0)	0	<0.01
Delaware (0)	0	<0.01
Hopi (0)	0	<0.01
Houma (0)	0	<0.01
Inupiat *(Alaska Native)* (0)	0	<0.01
Iroquois (3)	3	0.02
Kiowa (0)	0	<0.01
Lumbee (0)	0	<0.01
Menominee (0)	0	<0.01
Mexican American Ind. (0)	0	<0.01
Navajo (1)	1	0.01
Osage (0)	0	<0.01
Ottawa (0)	0	<0.01
Paiute (0)	0	<0.01
Pima (0)	0	<0.01
Potawatomi (0)	0	<0.01
Pueblo (0)	0	<0.01
Puget Sound Salish (0)	0	<0.01
Seminole (0)	0	<0.01
Shoshone (0)	0	<0.01
Sioux (1)	2	0.02
South American Ind. (0)	0	<0.01
Spanish American Ind. (0)	0	<0.01
Tlingit-Haida *(Alaska Native)* (0)	0	<0.01
Tohono O'Odham (0)	0	<0.01
Tsimshian *(Alaska Native)* (0)	0	<0.01
Ute (0)	0	<0.01
Yakama (0)	0	<0.01
Yaqui (0)	0	<0.01
Yuman (0)	0	<0.01
Yup'ik *(Alaska Native)* (0)	0	<0.01
Asian (25)	43	0.33
Not Hispanic (25)	43	0.33
Hispanic (0)	0	<0.01
Bangladeshi (0)	0	<0.01
Bhutanese (0)	0	<0.01
Burmese (0)	0	<0.01
Cambodian (0)	0	<0.01
Chinese, ex. Taiwanese (7)	8	0.06
Filipino (9)	18	0.14
Hmong (0)	0	<0.01
Indian (4)	7	0.05
Indonesian (0)	0	<0.01
Japanese (1)	1	0.01
Korean (2)	2	0.02
Laotian (0)	0	<0.01
Malaysian (0)	0	<0.01
Nepalese (0)	0	<0.01
Pakistani (0)	0	<0.01
Sri Lankan (0)	0	<0.01
Taiwanese (0)	0	<0.01
Thai (1)	1	0.01
Vietnamese (1)	1	0.01
Hawaii Native/Pacific Islander (4)	8	0.06
Not Hispanic (3)	7	0.05
Hispanic (1)	1	0.01
Fijian (0)	0	<0.01
Guamanian/Chamorro (1)	1	0.01
Marshallese (0)	0	<0.01
Native Hawaiian (2)	4	0.03
Samoan (0)	0	<0.01
Tongan (0)	0	<0.01
White (12,610)	12,708	98.93
Not Hispanic (12,544)	12,622	98.26
Hispanic (66)	86	0.67

*Notes: † The Census 2010 population figure is used to calculate the percentages in the Hispanic Origin and Race categories. Ancestry percentages are based on the 2006-2010 American Community Survey population (not shown); ‡ Numbers in parentheses indicate the number of people reporting a single ancestry; * Numbers in parentheses indicate the number of persons reporting this race alone, not in combination with any other race; Please refer to the Explanation of Data for more information.*

Porter County

Population: 164,343

Ancestry	Population	%
Afghan (13)	13	0.01
African, Sub-Saharan (408)	525	0.32
African (389)	499	0.31
Cape Verdean (0)	0	<0.01
Ethiopian (0)	0	<0.01
Ghanaian (0)	7	<0.01
Kenyan (0)	0	<0.01
Liberian (0)	0	<0.01
Nigerian (0)	0	<0.01
Senegalese (0)	0	<0.01
Sierra Leonean (0)	0	<0.01
Somalian (0)	0	<0.01
South African (0)	0	<0.01
Sudanese (19)	19	0.01
Ugandan (0)	0	<0.01
Zimbabwean (0)	0	<0.01
Other Sub-Saharan African (0)	0	<0.01
Albanian (0)	21	0.01
Alsatian (48)	59	0.04
American (9,144)	9,144	5.64
Arab (266)	428	0.26
Arab (75)	120	0.07
Egyptian (0)	8	<0.01
Iraqi (0)	0	<0.01
Jordanian (28)	28	0.02
Lebanese (107)	178	0.11
Moroccan (0)	0	<0.01
Palestinian (0)	0	<0.01
Syrian (44)	80	0.05
Other Arab (12)	14	0.01
Armenian (61)	244	0.15
Assyrian/Chaldean/Syriac (48)	110	0.07
Australian (13)	24	0.01
Austrian (151)	524	0.32
Basque (3)	3	<0.01
Belgian (39)	152	0.09
Brazilian (38)	42	0.03
British (150)	376	0.23
Bulgarian (12)	26	0.02
Cajun (15)	25	0.02
Canadian (160)	420	0.26
Carpatho Rusyn (0)	0	<0.01
Celtic (0)	17	0.01
Croatian (723)	1,989	1.23
Cypriot (7)	7	<0.01
Czech (342)	1,147	0.71
Czechoslovakian (125)	403	0.25
Danish (152)	620	0.38
Dutch (1,229)	4,652	2.87
Eastern European (79)	91	0.06
English (3,833)	15,704	9.69
Estonian (0)	0	<0.01
European (1,356)	1,511	0.93
Finnish (51)	189	0.12
French, ex. Basque (745)	4,574	2.82
French Canadian (394)	961	0.59
German (15,720)	47,080	29.06
German Russian (0)	0	<0.01
Greek (1,225)	2,145	1.32
Guyanese (0)	0	<0.01
Hungarian (929)	2,850	1.76
Icelander (18)	18	0.01
Iranian (44)	143	0.09
Irish (7,617)	30,032	18.54
Israeli (5)	5	<0.01
Italian (2,981)	9,415	5.81
Latvian (0)	16	0.01
Lithuanian (862)	1,338	0.83
Luxemburger (3)	44	0.03
Macedonian (483)	668	0.41
Maltese (0)	0	<0.01
New Zealander (0)	0	<0.01
Northern European (138)	138	0.09
Norwegian (601)	1,823	1.13
Pennsylvania German (15)	106	0.07
Polish (5,895)	16,382	10.11
Portuguese (0)	0	<0.01
Romanian (225)	688	0.42
Russian (235)	1,703	1.05
Scandinavian (69)	126	0.08
Scotch-Irish (1,176)	2,783	1.72
Scottish (1,063)	3,644	2.25
Serbian (888)	1,781	1.10
Slavic (144)	328	0.20
Slovak (1,039)	3,403	2.10
Slovene (74)	342	0.21
Soviet Union (0)	0	<0.01
Swedish (1,022)	4,337	2.68
Swiss (73)	445	0.27
Turkish (0)	0	<0.01
Ukrainian (262)	645	0.40
Welsh (205)	1,320	0.81
West Indian, ex. Hispanic (30)	86	0.05
Bahamian (0)	0	<0.01
Barbadian (0)	0	<0.01
Belizean (0)	0	<0.01
Bermudan (0)	0	<0.01
British West Indian (0)	0	<0.01
Dutch West Indian (0)	6	<0.01
Haitian (0)	0	<0.01
Jamaican (10)	10	0.01
Trinidadian/Tobagonian (0)	13	0.01
U.S. Virgin Islander (0)	0	<0.01
West Indian (20)	57	0.04
Other West Indian (0)	0	<0.01
Yugoslavian (92)	200	0.12

Hispanic Origin	Population	%
Hispanic or Latino (of any race)	13,933	8.48
Central American, ex. Mexican	216	0.13
Costa Rican	12	0.01
Guatemalan	107	0.07
Honduran	24	0.01
Nicaraguan	10	0.01
Panamanian	34	0.02
Salvadoran	25	0.02
Other Central American	4	<0.01
Cuban	123	0.07
Dominican Republic	33	0.02
Mexican	9,521	5.79
Puerto Rican	2,893	1.76
South American	306	0.19
Argentinean	63	0.04
Bolivian	32	0.02
Chilean	48	0.03
Colombian	37	0.02
Ecuadorian	30	0.02
Paraguayan	3	<0.01
Peruvian	67	0.04
Uruguayan	1	<0.01
Venezuelan	22	0.01
Other South American	3	<0.01
Other Hispanic or Latino	841	0.51

Race*	Population	%
African-American/Black (4,894)	5,884	3.58
Not Hispanic (4,649)	5,438	3.31
Hispanic (245)	446	0.27
American Indian/Alaska Native (494)	1,340	0.82
Not Hispanic (349)	1,023	0.62
Hispanic (145)	317	0.19
Alaska Athabascan *(Ala. Nat.)* (1)	1	<0.01
Aleut *(Alaska Native)* (0)	0	<0.01
Apache (4)	22	0.01
Arapaho (0)	0	<0.01
Blackfeet (9)	69	0.04
Canadian/French Am. Ind. (5)	7	<0.01
Central American Ind. (2)	5	<0.01
Cherokee (76)	341	0.21
Cheyenne (0)	1	<0.01
Chickasaw (1)	2	<0.01
Chippewa (42)	81	0.05
Choctaw (4)	16	0.01
Colville (0)	0	<0.01
Comanche (1)	2	<0.01
Cree (2)	2	<0.01
Creek (6)	24	0.01
Crow (0)	0	<0.01
Delaware (1)	4	<0.01
Hopi (0)	2	<0.01
Houma (2)	2	<0.01
Inupiat *(Alaska Native)* (0)	0	<0.01
Iroquois (9)	24	0.01
Kiowa (0)	1	<0.01
Lumbee (0)	0	<0.01
Menominee (1)	5	<0.01
Mexican American Ind. (23)	46	0.03
Navajo (7)	25	0.02
Osage (0)	7	<0.01
Ottawa (2)	3	<0.01
Paiute (0)	0	<0.01
Pima (0)	0	<0.01
Potawatomi (8)	19	0.01
Pueblo (5)	6	<0.01
Puget Sound Salish (0)	0	<0.01
Seminole (1)	5	<0.01
Shoshone (0)	3	<0.01
Sioux (24)	52	0.03
South American Ind. (11)	18	0.01
Spanish American Ind. (1)	2	<0.01
Tlingit-Haida *(Alaska Native)* (1)	1	<0.01
Tohono O'Odham (4)	4	<0.01
Tsimshian *(Alaska Native)* (0)	0	<0.01
Ute (2)	2	<0.01
Yakama (0)	0	<0.01
Yaqui (1)	6	<0.01
Yuman (0)	0	<0.01
Yup'ik *(Alaska Native)* (2)	2	<0.01
Asian (1,994)	2,690	1.64
Not Hispanic (1,960)	2,562	1.56
Hispanic (34)	128	0.08
Bangladeshi (3)	3	<0.01
Bhutanese (0)	0	<0.01
Burmese (1)	1	<0.01
Cambodian (7)	8	<0.01
Chinese, ex. Taiwanese (474)	572	0.35
Filipino (382)	593	0.36
Hmong (0)	0	<0.01
Indian (487)	568	0.35
Indonesian (2)	3	<0.01
Japanese (77)	196	0.12
Korean (156)	254	0.15
Laotian (17)	22	0.01
Malaysian (0)	1	<0.01
Nepalese (0)	0	<0.01
Pakistani (85)	95	0.06
Sri Lankan (7)	11	0.01
Taiwanese (13)	21	0.01
Thai (57)	93	0.06
Vietnamese (150)	178	0.11
Hawaii Native/Pacific Islander (36)	127	0.08
Not Hispanic (31)	107	0.07
Hispanic (5)	20	0.01
Fijian (0)	0	<0.01
Guamanian/Chamorro (17)	23	0.01
Marshallese (1)	1	<0.01
Native Hawaiian (4)	34	0.02
Samoan (5)	10	0.01
Tongan (0)	4	<0.01
White (149,995)	152,894	93.03
Not Hispanic (141,243)	143,149	87.10
Hispanic (8,752)	9,745	5.93

*Notes: † The Census 2010 population figure is used to calculate the percentages in the Hispanic Origin and Race categories. Ancestry percentages are based on the 2006-2010 American Community Survey population (not shown); ‡ Numbers in parentheses indicate the number of people reporting a single ancestry; * Numbers in parentheses indicate the number of persons reporting this race alone, not in combination with any other race; Please refer to the Explanation of Data for more information.*

Posey County

Population: 25,910

Ancestry	Population	%
Afghan (0)	0	<0.01
African, Sub-Saharan (0)	0	<0.01
African (0)	0	<0.01
Cape Verdean (0)	0	<0.01
Ethiopian (0)	0	<0.01
Ghanaian (0)	0	<0.01
Kenyan (0)	0	<0.01
Liberian (0)	0	<0.01
Nigerian (0)	0	<0.01
Senegalese (0)	0	<0.01
Sierra Leonean (0)	0	<0.01
Somalian (0)	0	<0.01
South African (0)	0	<0.01
Sudanese (0)	0	<0.01
Ugandan (0)	0	<0.01
Zimbabwean (0)	0	<0.01
Other Sub-Saharan African (0)	0	<0.01
Albanian (0)	0	<0.01
Alsatian (0)	0	<0.01
American (3,553)	3,553	13.61
Arab (0)	0	<0.01
Arab (0)	0	<0.01
Egyptian (0)	0	<0.01
Iraqi (0)	0	<0.01
Jordanian (0)	0	<0.01
Lebanese (0)	0	<0.01
Moroccan (0)	0	<0.01
Palestinian (0)	0	<0.01
Syrian (0)	0	<0.01
Other Arab (0)	0	<0.01
Armenian (0)	0	<0.01
Assyrian/Chaldean/Syriac (0)	0	<0.01
Australian (0)	0	<0.01
Austrian (0)	0	<0.01
Basque (0)	0	<0.01
Belgian (0)	3	0.01
Brazilian (0)	0	<0.01
British (22)	38	0.15
Bulgarian (0)	0	<0.01
Cajun (0)	0	<0.01
Canadian (36)	46	0.18
Carpatho Rusyn (0)	0	<0.01
Celtic (0)	0	<0.01
Croatian (0)	0	<0.01
Cypriot (0)	0	<0.01
Czech (0)	168	0.64
Czechoslovakian (12)	12	0.05
Danish (0)	10	0.04
Dutch (63)	293	1.12
Eastern European (0)	0	<0.01
English (1,195)	2,921	11.19
Estonian (0)	0	<0.01
European (36)	77	0.30
Finnish (17)	67	0.26
French, ex. Basque (182)	606	2.32
French Canadian (0)	12	0.05
German (6,955)	11,392	43.65
German Russian (0)	0	<0.01
Greek (17)	72	0.28
Guyanese (0)	0	<0.01
Hungarian (0)	35	0.13
Icelander (0)	0	<0.01
Iranian (0)	0	<0.01
Irish (893)	3,028	11.60
Israeli (38)	38	0.15
Italian (58)	436	1.67
Latvian (0)	0	<0.01
Lithuanian (0)	5	0.02
Luxemburger (0)	0	<0.01
Macedonian (0)	0	<0.01
Maltese (0)	0	<0.01
New Zealander (0)	0	<0.01
Northern European (5)	5	0.02
Norwegian (7)	124	0.48
Pennsylvania German (0)	0	<0.01
Polish (64)	224	0.86
Portuguese (0)	0	<0.01
Romanian (0)	0	<0.01
Russian (112)	136	0.52
Scandinavian (0)	6	0.02
Scotch-Irish (141)	438	1.68
Scottish (83)	452	1.73
Serbian (0)	0	<0.01
Slavic (0)	8	0.03
Slovak (0)	13	0.05
Slovene (0)	0	<0.01
Soviet Union (0)	0	<0.01
Swedish (1)	29	0.11
Swiss (22)	139	0.53
Turkish (0)	0	<0.01
Ukrainian (21)	21	0.08
Welsh (63)	140	0.54
West Indian, ex. Hispanic (0)	0	<0.01
Bahamian (0)	0	<0.01
Barbadian (0)	0	<0.01
Belizean (0)	0	<0.01
Bermudan (0)	0	<0.01
British West Indian (0)	0	<0.01
Dutch West Indian (0)	0	<0.01
Haitian (0)	0	<0.01
Jamaican (0)	0	<0.01
Trinidadian/Tobagonian (0)	0	<0.01
U.S. Virgin Islander (0)	0	<0.01
West Indian (0)	0	<0.01
Other West Indian (0)	0	<0.01
Yugoslavian (0)	0	<0.01

Hispanic Origin	Population	%
Hispanic or Latino (of any race)	248	0.96
Central American, ex. Mexican	8	0.03
Costa Rican	1	<0.01
Guatemalan	5	0.02
Honduran	0	<0.01
Nicaraguan	0	<0.01
Panamanian	0	<0.01
Salvadoran	2	0.01
Other Central American	0	<0.01
Cuban	9	0.03
Dominican Republic	3	0.01
Mexican	143	0.55
Puerto Rican	39	0.15
South American	23	0.09
Argentinean	5	0.02
Bolivian	2	0.01
Chilean	2	0.01
Colombian	3	0.01
Ecuadorian	5	0.02
Paraguayan	0	<0.01
Peruvian	1	<0.01
Uruguayan	0	<0.01
Venezuelan	5	0.02
Other South American	0	<0.01
Other Hispanic or Latino	23	0.09

Race*	Population	%
African-American/Black (233)	388	1.50
Not Hispanic (230)	383	1.48
Hispanic (3)	5	0.02
American Indian/Alaska Native (48)	144	0.56
Not Hispanic (42)	138	0.53
Hispanic (6)	6	0.02
Alaska Athabascan *(Ala. Nat.)* (0)	0	<0.01
Aleut *(Alaska Native)* (0)	0	<0.01
Apache (1)	1	<0.01
Arapaho (0)	0	<0.01
Blackfeet (4)	4	0.02
Canadian/French Am. Ind. (2)	2	0.01
Central American Ind. (0)	0	<0.01
Cherokee (9)	46	0.18
Cheyenne (0)	0	<0.01
Chickasaw (1)	1	<0.01
Chippewa (2)	3	0.01
Choctaw (0)	0	<0.01
Colville (0)	0	<0.01
Comanche (0)	4	0.02
Cree (0)	0	<0.01
Creek (0)	1	<0.01
Crow (0)	0	<0.01
Delaware (6)	6	0.02
Hopi (0)	0	<0.01
Houma (0)	0	<0.01
Inupiat *(Alaska Native)* (0)	0	<0.01
Iroquois (0)	1	<0.01
Kiowa (0)	0	<0.01
Lumbee (2)	2	0.01
Menominee (0)	0	<0.01
Mexican American Ind. (3)	3	0.01
Navajo (1)	1	<0.01
Osage (0)	1	<0.01
Ottawa (0)	0	<0.01
Paiute (0)	0	<0.01
Pima (0)	0	<0.01
Potawatomi (1)	4	0.02
Pueblo (0)	0	<0.01
Puget Sound Salish (0)	0	<0.01
Seminole (0)	0	<0.01
Shoshone (0)	0	<0.01
Sioux (0)	1	<0.01
South American Ind. (0)	0	<0.01
Spanish American Ind. (1)	1	<0.01
Tlingit-Haida *(Alaska Native)* (0)	0	<0.01
Tohono O'Odham (0)	0	<0.01
Tsimshian *(Alaska Native)* (0)	0	<0.01
Ute (0)	0	<0.01
Yakama (0)	0	<0.01
Yaqui (0)	0	<0.01
Yuman (0)	0	<0.01
Yup'ik *(Alaska Native)* (0)	0	<0.01
Asian (70)	98	0.38
Not Hispanic (70)	96	0.37
Hispanic (0)	2	0.01
Bangladeshi (0)	0	<0.01
Bhutanese (0)	0	<0.01
Burmese (0)	0	<0.01
Cambodian (0)	0	<0.01
Chinese, ex. Taiwanese (25)	25	0.10
Filipino (6)	8	0.03
Hmong (0)	0	<0.01
Indian (17)	24	0.09
Indonesian (0)	0	<0.01
Japanese (3)	6	0.02
Korean (8)	17	0.07
Laotian (0)	0	<0.01
Malaysian (0)	0	<0.01
Nepalese (0)	0	<0.01
Pakistani (0)	0	<0.01
Sri Lankan (0)	0	<0.01
Taiwanese (1)	1	<0.01
Thai (4)	10	0.04
Vietnamese (6)	6	0.02
Hawaii Native/Pacific Islander (4)	8	0.03
Not Hispanic (4)	8	0.03
Hispanic (0)	0	<0.01
Fijian (0)	0	<0.01
Guamanian/Chamorro (3)	5	0.02
Marshallese (0)	0	<0.01
Native Hawaiian (0)	1	<0.01
Samoan (0)	0	<0.01
Tongan (0)	0	<0.01
White (25,185)	25,455	98.24
Not Hispanic (25,046)	25,294	97.62
Hispanic (139)	161	0.62

*Notes: † The Census 2010 population figure is used to calculate the percentages in the Hispanic Origin and Race categories. Ancestry percentages are based on the 2006-2010 American Community Survey population (not shown); ‡ Numbers in parentheses indicate the number of people reporting a single ancestry; * Numbers in parentheses indicate the number of persons reporting this race alone, not in combination with any other race; Please refer to the Explanation of Data for more information.*

Pulaski County

Population: 13,402

Ancestry	Population	%
Afghan (0)	0	<0.01
African, Sub-Saharan (0)	0	<0.01
African (0)	0	<0.01
Cape Verdean (0)	0	<0.01
Ethiopian (0)	0	<0.01
Ghanaian (0)	0	<0.01
Kenyan (0)	0	<0.01
Liberian (0)	0	<0.01
Nigerian (0)	0	<0.01
Senegalese (0)	0	<0.01
Sierra Leonean (0)	0	<0.01
Somalian (0)	0	<0.01
South African (0)	0	<0.01
Sudanese (0)	0	<0.01
Ugandan (0)	0	<0.01
Zimbabwean (0)	0	<0.01
Other Sub-Saharan African (0)	0	<0.01
Albanian (0)	0	<0.01
Alsatian (0)	0	<0.01
American (1,115)	1,115	8.20
Arab (0)	0	<0.01
Arab (0)	0	<0.01
Egyptian (0)	0	<0.01
Iraqi (0)	0	<0.01
Jordanian (0)	0	<0.01
Lebanese (0)	0	<0.01
Moroccan (0)	0	<0.01
Palestinian (0)	0	<0.01
Syrian (0)	0	<0.01
Other Arab (0)	0	<0.01
Armenian (0)	0	<0.01
Assyrian/Chaldean/Syriac (0)	0	<0.01
Australian (0)	0	<0.01
Austrian (4)	15	0.11
Basque (0)	0	<0.01
Belgian (0)	8	0.06
Brazilian (0)	0	<0.01
British (0)	25	0.18
Bulgarian (0)	0	<0.01
Cajun (0)	0	<0.01
Canadian (0)	0	<0.01
Carpatho Rusyn (0)	0	<0.01
Celtic (0)	0	<0.01
Croatian (16)	37	0.27
Cypriot (0)	0	<0.01
Czech (14)	103	0.76
Czechoslovakian (9)	34	0.25
Danish (24)	40	0.29
Dutch (72)	280	2.06
Eastern European (0)	0	<0.01
English (432)	1,173	8.63
Estonian (0)	0	<0.01
European (6)	83	0.61
Finnish (0)	8	0.06
French, ex. Basque (80)	302	2.22
French Canadian (0)	9	0.07
German (2,138)	4,404	32.39
German Russian (0)	0	<0.01
Greek (36)	50	0.37
Guyanese (0)	0	<0.01
Hungarian (27)	87	0.64
Icelander (0)	0	<0.01
Iranian (0)	0	<0.01
Irish (360)	1,656	12.18
Israeli (0)	0	<0.01
Italian (148)	261	1.92
Latvian (0)	0	<0.01
Lithuanian (96)	183	1.35
Luxemburger (0)	11	0.08
Macedonian (0)	0	<0.01
Maltese (0)	0	<0.01
New Zealander (0)	0	<0.01
Northern European (0)	0	<0.01
Norwegian (90)	176	1.29
Pennsylvania German (4)	4	0.03
Polish (203)	531	3.91
Portuguese (0)	0	<0.01
Romanian (0)	28	0.21
Russian (0)	60	0.44
Scandinavian (0)	0	<0.01
Scotch-Irish (103)	166	1.22
Scottish (24)	112	0.82
Serbian (8)	10	0.07
Slavic (0)	0	<0.01
Slovak (0)	11	0.08
Slovene (0)	0	<0.01
Soviet Union (0)	0	<0.01
Swedish (68)	165	1.21
Swiss (8)	211	1.55
Turkish (0)	0	<0.01
Ukrainian (0)	0	<0.01
Welsh (20)	117	0.86
West Indian, ex. Hispanic (0)	0	<0.01
Bahamian (0)	0	<0.01
Barbadian (0)	0	<0.01
Belizean (0)	0	<0.01
Bermudan (0)	0	<0.01
British West Indian (0)	0	<0.01
Dutch West Indian (0)	0	<0.01
Haitian (0)	0	<0.01
Jamaican (0)	0	<0.01
Trinidadian/Tobagonian (0)	0	<0.01
U.S. Virgin Islander (0)	0	<0.01
West Indian (0)	0	<0.01
Other West Indian (0)	0	<0.01
Yugoslavian (24)	24	0.18

Hispanic Origin	Population	%
Hispanic or Latino (of any race)	325	2.43
Central American, ex. Mexican	19	0.14
Costa Rican	0	<0.01
Guatemalan	0	<0.01
Honduran	0	<0.01
Nicaraguan	0	<0.01
Panamanian	0	<0.01
Salvadoran	19	0.14
Other Central American	0	<0.01
Cuban	2	0.01
Dominican Republic	0	<0.01
Mexican	261	1.95
Puerto Rican	19	0.14
South American	1	0.01
Argentinean	0	<0.01
Bolivian	0	<0.01
Chilean	0	<0.01
Colombian	0	<0.01
Ecuadorian	1	0.01
Paraguayan	0	<0.01
Peruvian	0	<0.01
Uruguayan	0	<0.01
Venezuelan	0	<0.01
Other South American	0	<0.01
Other Hispanic or Latino	23	0.17

Race*	Population	%
African-American/Black (88)	104	0.78
Not Hispanic (87)	102	0.76
Hispanic (1)	2	0.01
American Indian/Alaska Native (40)	109	0.81
Not Hispanic (38)	100	0.75
Hispanic (2)	9	0.07
Alaska Athabascan *(Ala. Nat.)* (0)	0	<0.01
Aleut *(Alaska Native)* (0)	0	<0.01
Apache (1)	4	0.03
Arapaho (0)	0	<0.01
Blackfeet (0)	4	0.03
Canadian/French Am. Ind. (0)	0	<0.01
Central American Ind. (0)	0	<0.01
Cherokee (12)	25	0.19
Cheyenne (0)	0	<0.01
Chickasaw (0)	0	<0.01
Chippewa (0)	8	0.06
Choctaw (0)	1	0.01
Colville (0)	0	<0.01
Comanche (2)	5	0.04
Cree (0)	0	<0.01
Creek (2)	2	0.01
Crow (0)	0	<0.01
Delaware (1)	1	0.01
Hopi (0)	0	<0.01
Houma (0)	0	<0.01
Inupiat *(Alaska Native)* (0)	0	<0.01
Iroquois (0)	0	<0.01
Kiowa (0)	0	<0.01
Lumbee (0)	0	<0.01
Menominee (0)	0	<0.01
Mexican American Ind. (1)	2	0.01
Navajo (1)	1	0.01
Osage (0)	3	0.02
Ottawa (0)	0	<0.01
Paiute (0)	0	<0.01
Pima (0)	0	<0.01
Potawatomi (0)	0	<0.01
Pueblo (0)	0	<0.01
Puget Sound Salish (0)	0	<0.01
Seminole (0)	0	<0.01
Shoshone (0)	0	<0.01
Sioux (0)	1	0.01
South American Ind. (0)	0	<0.01
Spanish American Ind. (0)	0	<0.01
Tlingit-Haida *(Alaska Native)* (0)	0	<0.01
Tohono O'Odham (0)	0	<0.01
Tsimshian *(Alaska Native)* (0)	0	<0.01
Ute (0)	4	0.03
Yakama (0)	0	<0.01
Yaqui (0)	0	<0.01
Yuman (0)	0	<0.01
Yup'ik *(Alaska Native)* (0)	0	<0.01
Asian (29)	50	0.37
Not Hispanic (27)	45	0.34
Hispanic (2)	5	0.04
Bangladeshi (0)	0	<0.01
Bhutanese (0)	0	<0.01
Burmese (0)	0	<0.01
Cambodian (0)	0	<0.01
Chinese, ex. Taiwanese (10)	10	0.07
Filipino (13)	26	0.19
Hmong (0)	0	<0.01
Indian (1)	5	0.04
Indonesian (0)	0	<0.01
Japanese (2)	3	0.02
Korean (1)	3	0.02
Laotian (0)	0	<0.01
Malaysian (0)	0	<0.01
Nepalese (0)	0	<0.01
Pakistani (0)	0	<0.01
Sri Lankan (0)	0	<0.01
Taiwanese (0)	0	<0.01
Thai (0)	1	0.01
Vietnamese (0)	0	<0.01
Hawaii Native/Pacific Islander (3)	4	0.03
Not Hispanic (3)	3	0.02
Hispanic (0)	1	0.01
Fijian (0)	0	<0.01
Guamanian/Chamorro (0)	0	<0.01
Marshallese (0)	0	<0.01
Native Hawaiian (1)	2	0.01
Samoan (0)	0	<0.01
Tongan (0)	0	<0.01
White (13,025)	13,159	98.19
Not Hispanic (12,823)	12,922	96.42
Hispanic (202)	237	1.77

*Notes: † The Census 2010 population figure is used to calculate the percentages in the Hispanic Origin and Race categories. Ancestry percentages are based on the 2006-2010 American Community Survey population (not shown); ‡ Numbers in parentheses indicate the number of people reporting a single ancestry; * Numbers in parentheses indicate the number of persons reporting this race alone, not in combination with any other race; Please refer to the Explanation of Data for more information.*

Putnam County

Population: 37,963

Ancestry	Population	%
Afghan (0)	0	<0.01
African, Sub-Saharan (167)	251	0.66
African (125)	195	0.51
Cape Verdean (0)	0	<0.01
Ethiopian (0)	0	<0.01
Ghanaian (14)	14	0.04
Kenyan (0)	0	<0.01
Liberian (0)	0	<0.01
Nigerian (14)	14	0.04
Senegalese (0)	14	0.04
Sierra Leonean (0)	0	<0.01
Somalian (0)	0	<0.01
South African (14)	14	0.04
Sudanese (0)	0	<0.01
Ugandan (0)	0	<0.01
Zimbabwean (0)	0	<0.01
Other Sub-Saharan African (0)	0	<0.01
Albanian (0)	0	<0.01
Alsatian (0)	0	<0.01
American (5,804)	5,804	15.25
Arab (86)	148	0.39
Arab (76)	110	0.29
Egyptian (0)	0	<0.01
Iraqi (0)	0	<0.01
Jordanian (0)	0	<0.01
Lebanese (10)	20	0.05
Moroccan (0)	0	<0.01
Palestinian (0)	0	<0.01
Syrian (0)	18	0.05
Other Arab (0)	0	<0.01
Armenian (0)	0	<0.01
Assyrian/Chaldean/Syriac (0)	0	<0.01
Australian (0)	43	0.11
Austrian (0)	49	0.13
Basque (0)	0	<0.01
Belgian (0)	26	0.07
Brazilian (0)	0	<0.01
British (38)	50	0.13
Bulgarian (0)	116	0.30
Cajun (0)	0	<0.01
Canadian (24)	89	0.23
Carpatho Rusyn (0)	0	<0.01
Celtic (15)	24	0.06
Croatian (0)	13	0.03
Cypriot (0)	0	<0.01
Czech (30)	163	0.43
Czechoslovakian (39)	91	0.24
Danish (0)	20	0.05
Dutch (140)	1,194	3.14
Eastern European (0)	0	<0.01
English (2,464)	4,786	12.58
Estonian (0)	0	<0.01
European (401)	401	1.05
Finnish (0)	0	<0.01
French, ex. Basque (150)	1,071	2.81
French Canadian (43)	117	0.31
German (3,897)	8,993	23.64
German Russian (0)	0	<0.01
Greek (13)	63	0.17
Guyanese (0)	0	<0.01
Hungarian (149)	158	0.42
Icelander (0)	0	<0.01
Iranian (0)	0	<0.01
Irish (1,213)	4,826	12.68
Israeli (19)	19	0.05
Italian (414)	972	2.55
Latvian (11)	11	0.03
Lithuanian (0)	0	<0.01
Luxemburger (0)	0	<0.01
Macedonian (8)	8	0.02
Maltese (0)	0	<0.01
New Zealander (0)	0	<0.01
Northern European (23)	78	0.21
Norwegian (74)	248	0.65
Pennsylvania German (16)	70	0.18
Polish (109)	581	1.53
Portuguese (25)	25	0.07
Romanian (0)	0	<0.01
Russian (14)	20	0.05
Scandinavian (31)	52	0.14
Scotch-Irish (489)	994	2.61
Scottish (448)	879	2.31
Serbian (0)	23	0.06
Slavic (12)	33	0.09
Slovak (53)	53	0.14
Slovene (25)	25	0.07
Soviet Union (0)	0	<0.01
Swedish (57)	307	0.81
Swiss (67)	185	0.49
Turkish (3)	3	0.01
Ukrainian (2)	29	0.08
Welsh (69)	350	0.92
West Indian, ex. Hispanic (9)	18	0.05
Bahamian (0)	0	<0.01
Barbadian (0)	0	<0.01
Belizean (0)	0	<0.01
Bermudan (0)	0	<0.01
British West Indian (0)	0	<0.01
Dutch West Indian (0)	0	<0.01
Haitian (9)	9	0.02
Jamaican (0)	9	0.02
Trinidadian/Tobagonian (0)	0	<0.01
U.S. Virgin Islander (0)	0	<0.01
West Indian (0)	0	<0.01
Other West Indian (0)	0	<0.01
Yugoslavian (2)	101	0.27

Hispanic Origin	Population	%
Hispanic or Latino (of any race)	587	1.55
Central American, ex. Mexican	40	0.11
Costa Rican	4	0.01
Guatemalan	8	0.02
Honduran	8	0.02
Nicaraguan	6	0.02
Panamanian	6	0.02
Salvadoran	8	0.02
Other Central American	0	<0.01
Cuban	9	0.02
Dominican Republic	1	<0.01
Mexican	394	1.04
Puerto Rican	68	0.18
South American	23	0.06
Argentinean	1	<0.01
Bolivian	0	<0.01
Chilean	4	0.01
Colombian	7	0.02
Ecuadorian	0	<0.01
Paraguayan	1	<0.01
Peruvian	7	0.02
Uruguayan	0	<0.01
Venezuelan	3	0.01
Other South American	0	<0.01
Other Hispanic or Latino	52	0.14

Race*	Population	%
African-American/Black (1,505)	1,648	4.34
Not Hispanic (1,485)	1,624	4.28
Hispanic (20)	24	0.06
American Indian/Alaska Native (98)	247	0.65
Not Hispanic (90)	219	0.58
Hispanic (8)	28	0.07
Alaska Athabascan *(Ala. Nat.)* (0)	0	<0.01
Aleut *(Alaska Native)* (0)	0	<0.01
Apache (3)	12	0.03
Arapaho (0)	1	<0.01
Blackfeet (6)	15	0.04
Canadian/French Am. Ind. (0)	0	<0.01
Central American Ind. (1)	1	<0.01
Cherokee (18)	69	0.18
Cheyenne (0)	0	<0.01
Chickasaw (2)	6	0.02
Chippewa (1)	1	<0.01
Choctaw (1)	3	0.01
Colville (0)	2	0.01
Comanche (0)	0	<0.01
Cree (0)	0	<0.01
Creek (3)	4	0.01
Crow (0)	2	0.01
Delaware (2)	3	0.01
Hopi (0)	0	<0.01
Houma (0)	0	<0.01
Inupiat *(Alaska Native)* (0)	0	<0.01
Iroquois (1)	2	0.01
Kiowa (0)	0	<0.01
Lumbee (0)	0	<0.01
Menominee (0)	0	<0.01
Mexican American Ind. (0)	0	<0.01
Navajo (1)	9	0.02
Osage (0)	1	<0.01
Ottawa (0)	0	<0.01
Paiute (0)	0	<0.01
Pima (0)	0	<0.01
Potawatomi (0)	0	<0.01
Pueblo (0)	0	<0.01
Puget Sound Salish (0)	0	<0.01
Seminole (0)	1	<0.01
Shoshone (0)	0	<0.01
Sioux (4)	6	0.02
South American Ind. (1)	1	<0.01
Spanish American Ind. (0)	0	<0.01
Tlingit-Haida *(Alaska Native)* (0)	0	<0.01
Tohono O'Odham (0)	0	<0.01
Tsimshian *(Alaska Native)* (0)	0	<0.01
Ute (0)	0	<0.01
Yakama (0)	0	<0.01
Yaqui (0)	0	<0.01
Yuman (0)	0	<0.01
Yup'ik *(Alaska Native)* (4)	4	0.01
Asian (279)	362	0.95
Not Hispanic (273)	347	0.91
Hispanic (6)	15	0.04
Bangladeshi (0)	0	<0.01
Bhutanese (0)	0	<0.01
Burmese (0)	0	<0.01
Cambodian (0)	0	<0.01
Chinese, ex. Taiwanese (72)	85	0.22
Filipino (29)	46	0.12
Hmong (0)	0	<0.01
Indian (30)	43	0.11
Indonesian (1)	3	0.01
Japanese (76)	93	0.24
Korean (23)	43	0.11
Laotian (3)	6	0.02
Malaysian (0)	1	<0.01
Nepalese (0)	0	<0.01
Pakistani (4)	4	0.01
Sri Lankan (0)	0	<0.01
Taiwanese (0)	0	<0.01
Thai (3)	5	0.01
Vietnamese (19)	28	0.07
Hawaii Native/Pacific Islander (14)	38	0.10
Not Hispanic (10)	30	0.08
Hispanic (4)	8	0.02
Fijian (0)	0	<0.01
Guamanian/Chamorro (0)	0	<0.01
Marshallese (0)	0	<0.01
Native Hawaiian (7)	21	0.06
Samoan (1)	5	0.01
Tongan (0)	0	<0.01
White (35,449)	35,844	94.42
Not Hispanic (35,128)	35,474	93.44
Hispanic (321)	370	0.97

*Notes: † The Census 2010 population figure is used to calculate the percentages in the Hispanic Origin and Race categories. Ancestry percentages are based on the 2006-2010 American Community Survey population (not shown); ‡ Numbers in parentheses indicate the number of people reporting a single ancestry; * Numbers in parentheses indicate the number of persons reporting this race alone, not in combination with any other race; Please refer to the Explanation of Data for more information.*

Randolph County

Population: 26,171

Ancestry	Population	%
Afghan (0)	0	<0.01
African, Sub-Saharan (26)	26	0.10
African (0)	0	<0.01
Cape Verdean (0)	0	<0.01
Ethiopian (0)	0	<0.01
Ghanaian (0)	0	<0.01
Kenyan (0)	0	<0.01
Liberian (0)	0	<0.01
Nigerian (0)	0	<0.01
Senegalese (0)	0	<0.01
Sierra Leonean (0)	0	<0.01
Somalian (0)	0	<0.01
South African (26)	26	0.10
Sudanese (0)	0	<0.01
Ugandan (0)	0	<0.01
Zimbabwean (0)	0	<0.01
Other Sub-Saharan African (0)	0	<0.01
Albanian (0)	0	<0.01
Alsatian (0)	0	<0.01
American (3,020)	3,020	11.50
Arab (0)	0	<0.01
Arab (0)	0	<0.01
Egyptian (0)	0	<0.01
Iraqi (0)	0	<0.01
Jordanian (0)	0	<0.01
Lebanese (0)	0	<0.01
Moroccan (0)	0	<0.01
Palestinian (0)	0	<0.01
Syrian (0)	0	<0.01
Other Arab (0)	0	<0.01
Armenian (0)	8	0.03
Assyrian/Chaldean/Syriac (0)	0	<0.01
Australian (0)	0	<0.01
Austrian (0)	0	<0.01
Basque (0)	0	<0.01
Belgian (3)	11	0.04
Brazilian (0)	0	<0.01
British (29)	36	0.14
Bulgarian (0)	0	<0.01
Cajun (0)	0	<0.01
Canadian (3)	8	0.03
Carpatho Rusyn (0)	0	<0.01
Celtic (0)	0	<0.01
Croatian (0)	0	<0.01
Cypriot (0)	0	<0.01
Czech (17)	17	0.06
Czechoslovakian (0)	27	0.10
Danish (22)	43	0.16
Dutch (127)	620	2.36
Eastern European (0)	0	<0.01
English (1,603)	2,985	11.37
Estonian (0)	0	<0.01
European (109)	109	0.42
Finnish (5)	11	0.04
French, ex. Basque (83)	536	2.04
French Canadian (7)	19	0.07
German (2,854)	6,229	23.72
German Russian (0)	0	<0.01
Greek (4)	4	0.02
Guyanese (0)	0	<0.01
Hungarian (0)	32	0.12
Icelander (0)	0	<0.01
Iranian (0)	0	<0.01
Irish (1,347)	3,656	13.92
Israeli (0)	0	<0.01
Italian (157)	512	1.95
Latvian (0)	0	<0.01
Lithuanian (0)	17	0.06
Luxemburger (0)	0	<0.01
Macedonian (5)	5	0.02
Maltese (0)	0	<0.01
New Zealander (0)	0	<0.01
Northern European (0)	0	<0.01
Norwegian (19)	39	0.15
Pennsylvania German (81)	133	0.51
Polish (107)	263	1.00
Portuguese (0)	9	0.03
Romanian (0)	8	0.03
Russian (5)	5	0.02
Scandinavian (0)	3	0.01
Scotch-Irish (160)	355	1.35
Scottish (239)	459	1.75
Serbian (0)	0	<0.01
Slavic (0)	0	<0.01
Slovak (16)	16	0.06
Slovene (0)	0	<0.01
Soviet Union (0)	0	<0.01
Swedish (23)	70	0.27
Swiss (28)	130	0.50
Turkish (0)	0	<0.01
Ukrainian (10)	42	0.16
Welsh (43)	84	0.32
West Indian, ex. Hispanic (0)	0	<0.01
Bahamian (0)	0	<0.01
Barbadian (0)	0	<0.01
Belizean (0)	0	<0.01
Bermudan (0)	0	<0.01
British West Indian (0)	0	<0.01
Dutch West Indian (0)	0	<0.01
Haitian (0)	0	<0.01
Jamaican (0)	0	<0.01
Trinidadian/Tobagonian (0)	0	<0.01
U.S. Virgin Islander (0)	0	<0.01
West Indian (0)	0	<0.01
Other West Indian (0)	0	<0.01
Yugoslavian (3)	12	0.05

Hispanic Origin	Population	%
Hispanic or Latino (of any race)	790	3.02
Central American, ex. Mexican	25	0.10
Costa Rican	0	<0.01
Guatemalan	19	0.07
Honduran	4	0.02
Nicaraguan	1	<0.01
Panamanian	1	<0.01
Salvadoran	0	<0.01
Other Central American	0	<0.01
Cuban	14	0.05
Dominican Republic	1	<0.01
Mexican	680	2.60
Puerto Rican	14	0.05
South American	3	0.01
Argentinean	0	<0.01
Bolivian	0	<0.01
Chilean	2	0.01
Colombian	1	<0.01
Ecuadorian	0	<0.01
Paraguayan	0	<0.01
Peruvian	0	<0.01
Uruguayan	0	<0.01
Venezuelan	0	<0.01
Other South American	0	<0.01
Other Hispanic or Latino	53	0.20

Race*	Population	%
African-American/Black (117)	221	0.84
Not Hispanic (114)	204	0.78
Hispanic (3)	17	0.06
American Indian/Alaska Native (89)	182	0.70
Not Hispanic (83)	169	0.65
Hispanic (6)	13	0.05
Alaska Athabascan *(Ala. Nat.)* (0)	0	<0.01
Aleut *(Alaska Native)* (0)	0	<0.01
Apache (0)	0	<0.01
Arapaho (0)	0	<0.01
Blackfeet (3)	8	0.03
Canadian/French Am. Ind. (0)	0	<0.01
Central American Ind. (0)	0	<0.01
Cherokee (30)	67	0.26
Cheyenne (0)	3	0.01
Chickasaw (1)	1	<0.01
Chippewa (5)	5	0.02
Choctaw (0)	0	<0.01
Colville (0)	0	<0.01
Comanche (0)	0	<0.01
Cree (1)	1	<0.01
Creek (1)	1	<0.01
Crow (0)	0	<0.01
Delaware (0)	1	<0.01
Hopi (0)	0	<0.01
Houma (0)	0	<0.01
Inupiat *(Alaska Native)* (0)	0	<0.01
Iroquois (0)	0	<0.01
Kiowa (0)	0	<0.01
Lumbee (2)	4	0.02
Menominee (0)	0	<0.01
Mexican American Ind. (1)	1	<0.01
Navajo (0)	0	<0.01
Osage (0)	1	<0.01
Ottawa (2)	2	0.01
Paiute (0)	0	<0.01
Pima (0)	0	<0.01
Potawatomi (2)	3	0.01
Pueblo (0)	0	<0.01
Puget Sound Salish (0)	0	<0.01
Seminole (0)	0	<0.01
Shoshone (0)	0	<0.01
Sioux (3)	3	0.01
South American Ind. (1)	1	<0.01
Spanish American Ind. (0)	0	<0.01
Tlingit-Haida *(Alaska Native)* (1)	1	<0.01
Tohono O'Odham (0)	0	<0.01
Tsimshian *(Alaska Native)* (0)	0	<0.01
Ute (0)	0	<0.01
Yakama (0)	0	<0.01
Yaqui (0)	0	<0.01
Yuman (0)	0	<0.01
Yup'ik *(Alaska Native)* (0)	0	<0.01
Asian (61)	108	0.41
Not Hispanic (57)	101	0.39
Hispanic (4)	7	0.03
Bangladeshi (0)	0	<0.01
Bhutanese (0)	0	<0.01
Burmese (0)	0	<0.01
Cambodian (0)	0	<0.01
Chinese, ex. Taiwanese (11)	12	0.05
Filipino (11)	24	0.09
Hmong (0)	0	<0.01
Indian (10)	19	0.07
Indonesian (0)	0	<0.01
Japanese (5)	14	0.05
Korean (6)	15	0.06
Laotian (0)	0	<0.01
Malaysian (0)	0	<0.01
Nepalese (0)	0	<0.01
Pakistani (3)	3	0.01
Sri Lankan (0)	0	<0.01
Taiwanese (0)	0	<0.01
Thai (7)	12	0.05
Vietnamese (2)	2	0.01
Hawaii Native/Pacific Islander (8)	19	0.07
Not Hispanic (8)	18	0.07
Hispanic (0)	1	<0.01
Fijian (0)	0	<0.01
Guamanian/Chamorro (4)	4	0.02
Marshallese (0)	0	<0.01
Native Hawaiian (0)	9	0.03
Samoan (0)	0	<0.01
Tongan (0)	0	<0.01
White (25,158)	25,422	97.14
Not Hispanic (24,895)	25,100	95.91
Hispanic (263)	322	1.23

*Notes: † The Census 2010 population figure is used to calculate the percentages in the Hispanic Origin and Race categories. Ancestry percentages are based on the 2006-2010 American Community Survey population (not shown); ‡ Numbers in parentheses indicate the number of people reporting a single ancestry; * Numbers in parentheses indicate the number of persons reporting this race alone, not in combination with any other race; Please refer to the Explanation of Data for more information.*

Ripley County

Population: 28,818

Ancestry	Population	%
Afghan (0)	0	<0.01
African, Sub-Saharan (0)	13	0.05
African (0)	5	0.02
Cape Verdean (0)	0	<0.01
Ethiopian (0)	0	<0.01
Ghanaian (0)	0	<0.01
Kenyan (0)	0	<0.01
Liberian (0)	0	<0.01
Nigerian (0)	0	<0.01
Senegalese (0)	0	<0.01
Sierra Leonean (0)	0	<0.01
Somalian (0)	8	0.03
South African (0)	0	<0.01
Sudanese (0)	0	<0.01
Ugandan (0)	0	<0.01
Zimbabwean (0)	0	<0.01
Other Sub-Saharan African (0)	0	<0.01
Albanian (0)	0	<0.01
Alsatian (0)	0	<0.01
American (4,046)	4,046	14.16
Arab (100)	103	0.36
Arab (0)	0	<0.01
Egyptian (62)	62	0.22
Iraqi (35)	35	0.12
Jordanian (0)	0	<0.01
Lebanese (3)	6	0.02
Moroccan (0)	0	<0.01
Palestinian (0)	0	<0.01
Syrian (0)	0	<0.01
Other Arab (0)	0	<0.01
Armenian (0)	0	<0.01
Assyrian/Chaldean/Syriac (0)	0	<0.01
Australian (0)	0	<0.01
Austrian (0)	31	0.11
Basque (0)	0	<0.01
Belgian (29)	57	0.20
Brazilian (0)	0	<0.01
British (27)	42	0.15
Bulgarian (0)	13	0.05
Cajun (0)	0	<0.01
Canadian (47)	77	0.27
Carpatho Rusyn (0)	0	<0.01
Celtic (0)	0	<0.01
Croatian (0)	8	0.03
Cypriot (0)	0	<0.01
Czech (14)	14	0.05
Czechoslovakian (0)	0	<0.01
Danish (7)	7	0.02
Dutch (98)	504	1.76
Eastern European (7)	7	0.02
English (990)	2,480	8.68
Estonian (0)	0	<0.01
European (115)	115	0.40
Finnish (0)	0	<0.01
French, ex. Basque (65)	534	1.87
French Canadian (11)	74	0.26
German (7,279)	12,391	43.37
German Russian (0)	0	<0.01
Greek (3)	9	0.03
Guyanese (0)	0	<0.01
Hungarian (13)	47	0.16
Icelander (0)	0	<0.01
Iranian (0)	0	<0.01
Irish (1,007)	3,984	13.94
Israeli (0)	0	<0.01
Italian (211)	823	2.88
Latvian (0)	0	<0.01
Lithuanian (0)	0	<0.01
Luxemburger (0)	18	0.06
Macedonian (0)	0	<0.01
Maltese (0)	0	<0.01
New Zealander (0)	0	<0.01
Northern European (0)	0	<0.01
Norwegian (67)	92	0.32
Pennsylvania German (0)	10	0.04
Polish (65)	201	0.70
Portuguese (0)	13	0.05
Romanian (14)	31	0.11
Russian (6)	24	0.08
Scandinavian (0)	0	<0.01
Scotch-Irish (210)	386	1.35
Scottish (84)	373	1.31
Serbian (70)	96	0.34
Slavic (0)	0	<0.01
Slovak (0)	13	0.05
Slovene (0)	0	<0.01
Soviet Union (0)	0	<0.01
Swedish (0)	94	0.33
Swiss (21)	96	0.34
Turkish (13)	13	0.05
Ukrainian (11)	11	0.04
Welsh (24)	101	0.35
West Indian, ex. Hispanic (0)	0	<0.01
Bahamian (0)	0	<0.01
Barbadian (0)	0	<0.01
Belizean (0)	0	<0.01
Bermudan (0)	0	<0.01
British West Indian (0)	0	<0.01
Dutch West Indian (0)	0	<0.01
Haitian (0)	0	<0.01
Jamaican (0)	0	<0.01
Trinidadian/Tobagonian (0)	0	<0.01
U.S. Virgin Islander (0)	0	<0.01
West Indian (0)	0	<0.01
Other West Indian (0)	0	<0.01
Yugoslavian (6)	6	0.02

Hispanic Origin	Population	%
Hispanic or Latino (of any race)	445	1.54
Central American, ex. Mexican	31	0.11
Costa Rican	0	<0.01
Guatemalan	14	0.05
Honduran	9	0.03
Nicaraguan	0	<0.01
Panamanian	0	<0.01
Salvadoran	8	0.03
Other Central American	0	<0.01
Cuban	3	0.01
Dominican Republic	2	0.01
Mexican	351	1.22
Puerto Rican	20	0.07
South American	7	0.02
Argentinean	0	<0.01
Bolivian	0	<0.01
Chilean	0	<0.01
Colombian	2	0.01
Ecuadorian	1	<0.01
Paraguayan	0	<0.01
Peruvian	1	<0.01
Uruguayan	1	<0.01
Venezuelan	2	0.01
Other South American	0	<0.01
Other Hispanic or Latino	31	0.11

Race*	Population	%
African-American/Black (69)	129	0.45
Not Hispanic (67)	118	0.41
Hispanic (2)	11	0.04
American Indian/Alaska Native (51)	199	0.69
Not Hispanic (37)	171	0.59
Hispanic (14)	28	0.10
Alaska Athabascan *(Ala. Nat.)* (0)	0	<0.01
Aleut *(Alaska Native)* (0)	0	<0.01
Apache (0)	2	0.01
Arapaho (0)	0	<0.01
Blackfeet (0)	4	0.01
Canadian/French Am. Ind. (0)	1	<0.01
Central American Ind. (0)	0	<0.01
Cherokee (3)	46	0.16
Cheyenne (0)	2	0.01
Chickasaw (0)	0	<0.01
Chippewa (1)	2	0.01
Choctaw (0)	0	<0.01
Colville (0)	0	<0.01
Comanche (0)	0	<0.01
Cree (0)	0	<0.01
Creek (0)	0	<0.01
Crow (0)	0	<0.01
Delaware (0)	0	<0.01
Hopi (0)	0	<0.01
Houma (0)	0	<0.01
Inupiat *(Alaska Native)* (0)	0	<0.01
Iroquois (5)	8	0.03
Kiowa (0)	0	<0.01
Lumbee (0)	0	<0.01
Menominee (0)	0	<0.01
Mexican American Ind. (5)	5	0.02
Navajo (0)	0	<0.01
Osage (0)	0	<0.01
Ottawa (0)	0	<0.01
Paiute (0)	0	<0.01
Pima (0)	0	<0.01
Potawatomi (4)	4	0.01
Pueblo (0)	0	<0.01
Puget Sound Salish (0)	1	<0.01
Seminole (0)	0	<0.01
Shoshone (0)	0	<0.01
Sioux (0)	1	<0.01
South American Ind. (0)	0	<0.01
Spanish American Ind. (0)	0	<0.01
Tlingit-Haida *(Alaska Native)* (1)	1	<0.01
Tohono O'Odham (0)	0	<0.01
Tsimshian *(Alaska Native)* (0)	0	<0.01
Ute (0)	0	<0.01
Yakama (0)	0	<0.01
Yaqui (0)	0	<0.01
Yuman (0)	0	<0.01
Yup'ik *(Alaska Native)* (0)	0	<0.01
Asian (146)	190	0.66
Not Hispanic (146)	183	0.64
Hispanic (0)	7	0.02
Bangladeshi (0)	0	<0.01
Bhutanese (0)	0	<0.01
Burmese (0)	0	<0.01
Cambodian (0)	0	<0.01
Chinese, ex. Taiwanese (24)	25	0.09
Filipino (19)	38	0.13
Hmong (0)	0	<0.01
Indian (86)	91	0.32
Indonesian (0)	0	<0.01
Japanese (8)	17	0.06
Korean (6)	8	0.03
Laotian (0)	0	<0.01
Malaysian (0)	0	<0.01
Nepalese (0)	0	<0.01
Pakistani (0)	1	<0.01
Sri Lankan (0)	0	<0.01
Taiwanese (2)	3	0.01
Thai (1)	1	<0.01
Vietnamese (0)	0	<0.01
Hawaii Native/Pacific Islander (4)	11	0.04
Not Hispanic (3)	9	0.03
Hispanic (1)	2	0.01
Fijian (0)	0	<0.01
Guamanian/Chamorro (1)	1	<0.01
Marshallese (0)	0	<0.01
Native Hawaiian (2)	3	0.01
Samoan (0)	4	0.01
Tongan (1)	1	<0.01
White (28,132)	28,386	98.50
Not Hispanic (27,879)	28,099	97.51
Hispanic (253)	287	1.00

*Notes: † The Census 2010 population figure is used to calculate the percentages in the Hispanic Origin and Race categories. Ancestry percentages are based on the 2006-2010 American Community Survey population (not shown); ‡ Numbers in parentheses indicate the number of people reporting a single ancestry; * Numbers in parentheses indicate the number of persons reporting this race alone, not in combination with any other race; Please refer to the Explanation of Data for more information.*

Rush County

Population: 17,392

Ancestry	Population	%
Afghan (0)	0	<0.01
African, Sub-Saharan (0)	0	<0.01
African (0)	0	<0.01
Cape Verdean (0)	0	<0.01
Ethiopian (0)	0	<0.01
Ghanaian (0)	0	<0.01
Kenyan (0)	0	<0.01
Liberian (0)	0	<0.01
Nigerian (0)	0	<0.01
Senegalese (0)	0	<0.01
Sierra Leonean (0)	0	<0.01
Somalian (0)	0	<0.01
South African (0)	0	<0.01
Sudanese (0)	0	<0.01
Ugandan (0)	0	<0.01
Zimbabwean (0)	0	<0.01
Other Sub-Saharan African (0)	0	<0.01
Albanian (0)	0	<0.01
Alsatian (0)	0	<0.01
American (2,956)	2,956	16.83
Arab (0)	0	<0.01
Arab (0)	0	<0.01
Egyptian (0)	0	<0.01
Iraqi (0)	0	<0.01
Jordanian (0)	0	<0.01
Lebanese (0)	0	<0.01
Moroccan (0)	0	<0.01
Palestinian (0)	0	<0.01
Syrian (0)	0	<0.01
Other Arab (0)	0	<0.01
Armenian (0)	0	<0.01
Assyrian/Chaldean/Syriac (0)	0	<0.01
Australian (0)	0	<0.01
Austrian (2)	2	0.01
Basque (0)	0	<0.01
Belgian (0)	29	0.17
Brazilian (0)	0	<0.01
British (0)	0	<0.01
Bulgarian (0)	0	<0.01
Cajun (3)	3	0.02
Canadian (0)	0	<0.01
Carpatho Rusyn (0)	0	<0.01
Celtic (0)	0	<0.01
Croatian (0)	0	<0.01
Cypriot (0)	0	<0.01
Czech (0)	8	0.05
Czechoslovakian (0)	0	<0.01
Danish (0)	0	<0.01
Dutch (148)	414	2.36
Eastern European (0)	0	<0.01
English (1,233)	2,089	11.89
Estonian (0)	0	<0.01
European (186)	194	1.10
Finnish (0)	0	<0.01
French, ex. Basque (81)	238	1.35
French Canadian (0)	0	<0.01
German (2,018)	4,105	23.37
German Russian (0)	0	<0.01
Greek (0)	33	0.19
Guyanese (0)	0	<0.01
Hungarian (8)	36	0.20
Icelander (0)	0	<0.01
Iranian (0)	0	<0.01
Irish (823)	2,106	11.99
Israeli (0)	0	<0.01
Italian (78)	104	0.59
Latvian (0)	0	<0.01
Lithuanian (12)	12	0.07
Luxemburger (0)	0	<0.01
Macedonian (0)	0	<0.01
Maltese (0)	0	<0.01
New Zealander (0)	0	<0.01
Northern European (0)	0	<0.01
Norwegian (14)	41	0.23
Pennsylvania German (0)	0	<0.01
Polish (72)	187	1.06
Portuguese (0)	0	<0.01
Romanian (0)	35	0.20
Russian (16)	26	0.15
Scandinavian (21)	21	0.12
Scotch-Irish (158)	233	1.33
Scottish (207)	354	2.02
Serbian (0)	0	<0.01
Slavic (0)	0	<0.01
Slovak (0)	0	<0.01
Slovene (0)	0	<0.01
Soviet Union (0)	0	<0.01
Swedish (0)	134	0.76
Swiss (67)	67	0.38
Turkish (0)	0	<0.01
Ukrainian (0)	0	<0.01
Welsh (3)	113	0.64
West Indian, ex. Hispanic (0)	0	<0.01
Bahamian (0)	0	<0.01
Barbadian (0)	0	<0.01
Belizean (0)	0	<0.01
Bermudan (0)	0	<0.01
British West Indian (0)	0	<0.01
Dutch West Indian (0)	0	<0.01
Haitian (0)	0	<0.01
Jamaican (0)	0	<0.01
Trinidadian/Tobagonian (0)	0	<0.01
U.S. Virgin Islander (0)	0	<0.01
West Indian (0)	0	<0.01
Other West Indian (0)	0	<0.01
Yugoslavian (0)	0	<0.01

Hispanic Origin	Population	%
Hispanic or Latino (of any race)	190	1.09
Central American, ex. Mexican	5	0.03
Costa Rican	0	<0.01
Guatemalan	4	0.02
Honduran	1	0.01
Nicaraguan	0	<0.01
Panamanian	0	<0.01
Salvadoran	0	<0.01
Other Central American	0	<0.01
Cuban	8	0.05
Dominican Republic	0	<0.01
Mexican	142	0.82
Puerto Rican	11	0.06
South American	2	0.01
Argentinean	0	<0.01
Bolivian	0	<0.01
Chilean	0	<0.01
Colombian	0	<0.01
Ecuadorian	1	0.01
Paraguayan	0	<0.01
Peruvian	0	<0.01
Uruguayan	0	<0.01
Venezuelan	1	0.01
Other South American	0	<0.01
Other Hispanic or Latino	22	0.13

Race*	Population	%
African-American/Black (132)	210	1.21
Not Hispanic (129)	204	1.17
Hispanic (3)	6	0.03
American Indian/Alaska Native (32)	82	0.47
Not Hispanic (32)	80	0.46
Hispanic (0)	2	0.01
Alaska Athabascan *(Ala. Nat.)* (0)	0	<0.01
Aleut *(Alaska Native)* (0)	0	<0.01
Apache (0)	0	<0.01
Arapaho (0)	0	<0.01
Blackfeet (0)	3	0.02
Canadian/French Am. Ind. (0)	0	<0.01
Central American Ind. (0)	0	<0.01
Cherokee (3)	24	0.14
Cheyenne (0)	0	<0.01
Chickasaw (0)	0	<0.01
Chippewa (0)	0	<0.01
Choctaw (0)	1	0.01
Colville (0)	0	<0.01
Comanche (0)	0	<0.01
Cree (0)	0	<0.01
Creek (0)	0	<0.01
Crow (0)	0	<0.01
Delaware (6)	6	0.03
Hopi (0)	0	<0.01
Houma (0)	0	<0.01
Inupiat *(Alaska Native)* (0)	0	<0.01
Iroquois (0)	0	<0.01
Kiowa (0)	0	<0.01
Lumbee (0)	0	<0.01
Menominee (0)	0	<0.01
Mexican American Ind. (0)	1	0.01
Navajo (0)	0	<0.01
Osage (0)	0	<0.01
Ottawa (0)	0	<0.01
Paiute (0)	0	<0.01
Pima (0)	0	<0.01
Potawatomi (1)	1	0.01
Pueblo (0)	0	<0.01
Puget Sound Salish (0)	0	<0.01
Seminole (0)	0	<0.01
Shoshone (0)	0	<0.01
Sioux (2)	2	0.01
South American Ind. (0)	0	<0.01
Spanish American Ind. (0)	0	<0.01
Tlingit-Haida *(Alaska Native)* (2)	2	0.01
Tohono O'Odham (0)	0	<0.01
Tsimshian *(Alaska Native)* (0)	0	<0.01
Ute (0)	0	<0.01
Yakama (0)	0	<0.01
Yaqui (0)	0	<0.01
Yuman (0)	0	<0.01
Yup'ik *(Alaska Native)* (1)	1	0.01
Asian (57)	66	0.38
Not Hispanic (57)	66	0.38
Hispanic (0)	0	<0.01
Bangladeshi (0)	0	<0.01
Bhutanese (0)	0	<0.01
Burmese (0)	0	<0.01
Cambodian (0)	1	0.01
Chinese, ex. Taiwanese (12)	12	0.07
Filipino (12)	13	0.07
Hmong (0)	0	<0.01
Indian (6)	7	0.04
Indonesian (0)	0	<0.01
Japanese (13)	16	0.09
Korean (12)	13	0.07
Laotian (0)	0	<0.01
Malaysian (0)	0	<0.01
Nepalese (0)	0	<0.01
Pakistani (1)	1	0.01
Sri Lankan (0)	0	<0.01
Taiwanese (0)	0	<0.01
Thai (0)	0	<0.01
Vietnamese (1)	2	0.01
Hawaii Native/Pacific Islander (4)	8	0.05
Not Hispanic (3)	6	0.03
Hispanic (1)	2	0.01
Fijian (0)	0	<0.01
Guamanian/Chamorro (1)	1	0.01
Marshallese (0)	0	<0.01
Native Hawaiian (0)	3	0.02
Samoan (1)	1	0.01
Tongan (0)	0	<0.01
White (16,945)	17,074	98.17
Not Hispanic (16,839)	16,954	97.48
Hispanic (106)	120	0.69

*Notes: † The Census 2010 population figure is used to calculate the percentages in the Hispanic Origin and Race categories. Ancestry percentages are based on the 2006-2010 American Community Survey population (not shown); ‡ Numbers in parentheses indicate the number of people reporting a single ancestry; * Numbers in parentheses indicate the number of persons reporting this race alone, not in combination with any other race; Please refer to the Explanation of Data for more information.*

Scott County

Population: 24,181

Ancestry	Population	%
Afghan (0)	0	<0.01
African, Sub-Saharan (15)	59	0.24
African (0)	44	0.18
Cape Verdean (0)	0	<0.01
Ethiopian (0)	0	<0.01
Ghanaian (0)	0	<0.01
Kenyan (0)	0	<0.01
Liberian (0)	0	<0.01
Nigerian (0)	0	<0.01
Senegalese (0)	0	<0.01
Sierra Leonean (0)	0	<0.01
Somalian (0)	0	<0.01
South African (0)	0	<0.01
Sudanese (0)	0	<0.01
Ugandan (0)	0	<0.01
Zimbabwean (0)	0	<0.01
Other Sub-Saharan African (15)	15	0.06
Albanian (0)	0	<0.01
Alsatian (0)	0	<0.01
American (4,841)	4,841	20.08
Arab (0)	0	<0.01
Arab (0)	0	<0.01
Egyptian (0)	0	<0.01
Iraqi (0)	0	<0.01
Jordanian (0)	0	<0.01
Lebanese (0)	0	<0.01
Moroccan (0)	0	<0.01
Palestinian (0)	0	<0.01
Syrian (0)	0	<0.01
Other Arab (0)	0	<0.01
Armenian (0)	0	<0.01
Assyrian/Chaldean/Syriac (0)	0	<0.01
Australian (0)	0	<0.01
Austrian (14)	42	0.17
Basque (0)	0	<0.01
Belgian (0)	0	<0.01
Brazilian (0)	0	<0.01
British (23)	23	0.10
Bulgarian (0)	0	<0.01
Cajun (0)	0	<0.01
Canadian (9)	9	0.04
Carpatho Rusyn (0)	0	<0.01
Celtic (0)	0	<0.01
Croatian (21)	67	0.28
Cypriot (0)	0	<0.01
Czech (28)	43	0.18
Czechoslovakian (11)	11	0.05
Danish (0)	15	0.06
Dutch (162)	331	1.37
Eastern European (0)	0	<0.01
English (1,519)	2,418	10.03
Estonian (0)	0	<0.01
European (15)	38	0.16
Finnish (0)	41	0.17
French, ex. Basque (173)	536	2.22
French Canadian (0)	9	0.04
German (1,824)	3,752	15.56
German Russian (0)	0	<0.01
Greek (0)	49	0.20
Guyanese (0)	0	<0.01
Hungarian (13)	13	0.05
Icelander (5)	5	0.02
Iranian (0)	0	<0.01
Irish (1,336)	2,862	11.87
Israeli (0)	0	<0.01
Italian (323)	531	2.20
Latvian (0)	0	<0.01
Lithuanian (0)	0	<0.01
Luxemburger (0)	0	<0.01
Macedonian (0)	0	<0.01
Maltese (0)	0	<0.01
New Zealander (0)	0	<0.01
Northern European (11)	11	0.05
Norwegian (85)	117	0.49
Pennsylvania German (0)	11	0.05
Polish (56)	206	0.85
Portuguese (0)	0	<0.01
Romanian (0)	0	<0.01
Russian (0)	0	<0.01
Scandinavian (0)	9	0.04
Scotch-Irish (319)	493	2.04
Scottish (307)	612	2.54
Serbian (0)	0	<0.01
Slavic (15)	38	0.16
Slovak (8)	8	0.03
Slovene (0)	0	<0.01
Soviet Union (0)	0	<0.01
Swedish (39)	204	0.85
Swiss (0)	0	<0.01
Turkish (0)	0	<0.01
Ukrainian (0)	0	<0.01
Welsh (72)	134	0.56
West Indian, ex. Hispanic (0)	0	<0.01
Bahamian (0)	0	<0.01
Barbadian (0)	0	<0.01
Belizean (0)	0	<0.01
Bermudan (0)	0	<0.01
British West Indian (0)	0	<0.01
Dutch West Indian (0)	0	<0.01
Haitian (0)	0	<0.01
Jamaican (0)	0	<0.01
Trinidadian/Tobagonian (0)	0	<0.01
U.S. Virgin Islander (0)	0	<0.01
West Indian (0)	0	<0.01
Other West Indian (0)	0	<0.01
Yugoslavian (0)	0	<0.01

Hispanic Origin	Population	%
Hispanic or Latino (of any race)	354	1.46
Central American, ex. Mexican	8	0.03
Costa Rican	0	<0.01
Guatemalan	0	<0.01
Honduran	2	0.01
Nicaraguan	0	<0.01
Panamanian	2	0.01
Salvadoran	4	0.02
Other Central American	0	<0.01
Cuban	1	<0.01
Dominican Republic	1	<0.01
Mexican	267	1.10
Puerto Rican	21	0.09
South American	6	0.02
Argentinean	0	<0.01
Bolivian	1	<0.01
Chilean	0	<0.01
Colombian	3	0.01
Ecuadorian	2	0.01
Paraguayan	0	<0.01
Peruvian	0	<0.01
Uruguayan	0	<0.01
Venezuelan	0	<0.01
Other South American	0	<0.01
Other Hispanic or Latino	50	0.21

Race*	Population	%
African-American/Black (57)	106	0.44
Not Hispanic (52)	98	0.41
Hispanic (5)	8	0.03
American Indian/Alaska Native (46)	112	0.46
Not Hispanic (43)	100	0.41
Hispanic (3)	12	0.05
Alaska Athabascan *(Ala. Nat.)* (0)	0	<0.01
Aleut *(Alaska Native)* (0)	0	<0.01
Apache (1)	4	0.02
Arapaho (0)	3	0.01
Blackfeet (5)	7	0.03
Canadian/French Am. Ind. (0)	0	<0.01
Central American Ind. (0)	0	<0.01
Cherokee (15)	45	0.19
Cheyenne (0)	4	0.02
Chickasaw (0)	0	<0.01
Chippewa (1)	1	<0.01
Choctaw (0)	0	<0.01
Colville (0)	0	<0.01
Comanche (1)	1	<0.01
Cree (0)	0	<0.01
Creek (0)	1	<0.01
Crow (1)	1	<0.01
Delaware (0)	0	<0.01
Hopi (0)	0	<0.01
Houma (0)	0	<0.01
Inupiat *(Alaska Native)* (0)	0	<0.01
Iroquois (0)	0	<0.01
Kiowa (0)	0	<0.01
Lumbee (0)	0	<0.01
Menominee (0)	0	<0.01
Mexican American Ind. (0)	0	<0.01
Navajo (0)	0	<0.01
Osage (0)	0	<0.01
Ottawa (0)	0	<0.01
Paiute (0)	0	<0.01
Pima (0)	0	<0.01
Potawatomi (4)	10	0.04
Pueblo (0)	0	<0.01
Puget Sound Salish (0)	0	<0.01
Seminole (0)	1	<0.01
Shoshone (0)	0	<0.01
Sioux (2)	2	0.01
South American Ind. (0)	0	<0.01
Spanish American Ind. (0)	0	<0.01
Tlingit-Haida *(Alaska Native)* (0)	0	<0.01
Tohono O'Odham (0)	0	<0.01
Tsimshian *(Alaska Native)* (0)	0	<0.01
Ute (0)	0	<0.01
Yakama (0)	0	<0.01
Yaqui (0)	0	<0.01
Yuman (0)	0	<0.01
Yup'ik *(Alaska Native)* (0)	0	<0.01
Asian (108)	140	0.58
Not Hispanic (104)	131	0.54
Hispanic (4)	9	0.04
Bangladeshi (0)	0	<0.01
Bhutanese (0)	0	<0.01
Burmese (0)	0	<0.01
Cambodian (0)	0	<0.01
Chinese, ex. Taiwanese (14)	16	0.07
Filipino (38)	41	0.17
Hmong (0)	2	0.01
Indian (20)	28	0.12
Indonesian (0)	2	0.01
Japanese (18)	20	0.08
Korean (15)	21	0.09
Laotian (0)	0	<0.01
Malaysian (0)	0	<0.01
Nepalese (0)	0	<0.01
Pakistani (0)	2	0.01
Sri Lankan (0)	0	<0.01
Taiwanese (0)	0	<0.01
Thai (1)	2	0.01
Vietnamese (1)	5	0.02
Hawaii Native/Pacific Islander (14)	21	0.09
Not Hispanic (14)	21	0.09
Hispanic (0)	0	<0.01
Fijian (0)	0	<0.01
Guamanian/Chamorro (6)	6	0.02
Marshallese (0)	0	<0.01
Native Hawaiian (5)	7	0.03
Samoan (3)	3	0.01
Tongan (0)	0	<0.01
White (23,667)	23,838	98.58
Not Hispanic (23,471)	23,603	97.61
Hispanic (196)	235	0.97

*Notes: † The Census 2010 population figure is used to calculate the percentages in the Hispanic Origin and Race categories. Ancestry percentages are based on the 2006-2010 American Community Survey population (not shown); ‡ Numbers in parentheses indicate the number of people reporting a single ancestry; * Numbers in parentheses indicate the number of persons reporting this race alone, not in combination with any other race; Please refer to the Explanation of Data for more information.*

Shelby County

Population: 44,436

Ancestry	Population	%
Afghan (0)	0	<0.01
African, Sub-Saharan (0)	0	<0.01
African (0)	0	<0.01
Cape Verdean (0)	0	<0.01
Ethiopian (0)	0	<0.01
Ghanaian (0)	0	<0.01
Kenyan (0)	0	<0.01
Liberian (0)	0	<0.01
Nigerian (0)	0	<0.01
Senegalese (0)	0	<0.01
Sierra Leonean (0)	0	<0.01
Somalian (0)	0	<0.01
South African (0)	0	<0.01
Sudanese (0)	0	<0.01
Ugandan (0)	0	<0.01
Zimbabwean (0)	0	<0.01
Other Sub-Saharan African (0)	0	<0.01
Albanian (0)	0	<0.01
Alsatian (0)	0	<0.01
American (5,789)	5,789	13.09
Arab (14)	47	0.11
Arab (0)	0	<0.01
Egyptian (0)	0	<0.01
Iraqi (0)	0	<0.01
Jordanian (0)	0	<0.01
Lebanese (0)	12	0.03
Moroccan (0)	0	<0.01
Palestinian (0)	0	<0.01
Syrian (14)	35	0.08
Other Arab (0)	0	<0.01
Armenian (11)	11	0.02
Assyrian/Chaldean/Syriac (0)	0	<0.01
Australian (13)	13	0.03
Austrian (10)	20	0.05
Basque (0)	0	<0.01
Belgian (0)	48	0.11
Brazilian (0)	0	<0.01
British (124)	246	0.56
Bulgarian (0)	0	<0.01
Cajun (0)	0	<0.01
Canadian (43)	69	0.16
Carpatho Rusyn (0)	0	<0.01
Celtic (0)	0	<0.01
Croatian (0)	0	<0.01
Cypriot (0)	0	<0.01
Czech (34)	34	0.08
Czechoslovakian (0)	0	<0.01
Danish (0)	23	0.05
Dutch (174)	899	2.03
Eastern European (0)	0	<0.01
English (2,010)	3,980	9.00
Estonian (0)	0	<0.01
European (237)	249	0.56
Finnish (0)	34	0.08
French, ex. Basque (317)	867	1.96
French Canadian (21)	58	0.13
German (6,717)	12,619	28.53
German Russian (0)	0	<0.01
Greek (0)	52	0.12
Guyanese (0)	0	<0.01
Hungarian (17)	33	0.07
Icelander (0)	0	<0.01
Iranian (0)	0	<0.01
Irish (1,991)	5,388	12.18
Israeli (35)	35	0.08
Italian (268)	599	1.35
Latvian (0)	11	0.02
Lithuanian (13)	13	0.03
Luxemburger (0)	0	<0.01
Macedonian (0)	0	<0.01
Maltese (0)	0	<0.01
New Zealander (0)	0	<0.01
Northern European (0)	0	<0.01
Norwegian (44)	44	0.10
Pennsylvania German (12)	40	0.09
Polish (130)	477	1.08
Portuguese (0)	0	<0.01
Romanian (0)	27	0.06
Russian (44)	100	0.23
Scandinavian (31)	48	0.11
Scotch-Irish (360)	642	1.45
Scottish (256)	823	1.86
Serbian (0)	17	0.04
Slavic (0)	0	<0.01
Slovak (9)	9	0.02
Slovene (0)	10	0.02
Soviet Union (0)	0	<0.01
Swedish (53)	347	0.78
Swiss (47)	159	0.36
Turkish (0)	0	<0.01
Ukrainian (14)	20	0.05
Welsh (100)	276	0.62
West Indian, ex. Hispanic (0)	0	<0.01
Bahamian (0)	0	<0.01
Barbadian (0)	0	<0.01
Belizean (0)	0	<0.01
Bermudan (0)	0	<0.01
British West Indian (0)	0	<0.01
Dutch West Indian (0)	0	<0.01
Haitian (0)	0	<0.01
Jamaican (0)	0	<0.01
Trinidadian/Tobagonian (0)	0	<0.01
U.S. Virgin Islander (0)	0	<0.01
West Indian (0)	0	<0.01
Other West Indian (0)	0	<0.01
Yugoslavian (0)	8	0.02

Hispanic Origin	Population	%
Hispanic or Latino (of any race)	1,647	3.71
Central American, ex. Mexican	49	0.11
Costa Rican	1	<0.01
Guatemalan	19	0.04
Honduran	14	0.03
Nicaraguan	6	0.01
Panamanian	3	0.01
Salvadoran	5	0.01
Other Central American	1	<0.01
Cuban	6	0.01
Dominican Republic	14	0.03
Mexican	1,413	3.18
Puerto Rican	45	0.10
South American	43	0.10
Argentinean	1	<0.01
Bolivian	2	<0.01
Chilean	2	<0.01
Colombian	6	0.01
Ecuadorian	1	<0.01
Paraguayan	0	<0.01
Peruvian	30	0.07
Uruguayan	0	<0.01
Venezuelan	1	<0.01
Other South American	0	<0.01
Other Hispanic or Latino	77	0.17

Race*	Population	%
African-American/Black (455)	646	1.45
Not Hispanic (428)	608	1.37
Hispanic (27)	38	0.09
American Indian/Alaska Native (95)	241	0.54
Not Hispanic (85)	208	0.47
Hispanic (10)	33	0.07
Alaska Athabascan *(Ala. Nat.)* (0)	0	<0.01
Aleut *(Alaska Native)* (0)	0	<0.01
Apache (3)	3	0.01
Arapaho (0)	0	<0.01
Blackfeet (1)	5	0.01
Canadian/French Am. Ind. (1)	1	<0.01
Central American Ind. (0)	0	<0.01
Cherokee (33)	88	0.20
Cheyenne (0)	1	<0.01
Chickasaw (0)	0	<0.01
Chippewa (5)	5	0.01
Choctaw (0)	3	0.01
Colville (0)	0	<0.01
Comanche (1)	1	<0.01
Cree (0)	0	<0.01
Creek (0)	0	<0.01
Crow (0)	0	<0.01
Delaware (1)	1	<0.01
Hopi (0)	0	<0.01
Houma (0)	0	<0.01
Inupiat *(Alaska Native)* (0)	0	<0.01
Iroquois (1)	1	<0.01
Kiowa (0)	0	<0.01
Lumbee (1)	1	<0.01
Menominee (0)	0	<0.01
Mexican American Ind. (3)	6	0.01
Navajo (0)	0	<0.01
Osage (0)	0	<0.01
Ottawa (0)	0	<0.01
Paiute (1)	1	<0.01
Pima (0)	0	<0.01
Potawatomi (2)	2	<0.01
Pueblo (0)	1	<0.01
Puget Sound Salish (0)	0	<0.01
Seminole (0)	3	0.01
Shoshone (0)	0	<0.01
Sioux (7)	12	0.03
South American Ind. (0)	1	<0.01
Spanish American Ind. (0)	0	<0.01
Tlingit-Haida *(Alaska Native)* (0)	0	<0.01
Tohono O'Odham (0)	0	<0.01
Tsimshian *(Alaska Native)* (0)	0	<0.01
Ute (0)	0	<0.01
Yakama (0)	0	<0.01
Yaqui (0)	0	<0.01
Yuman (0)	0	<0.01
Yup'ik *(Alaska Native)* (0)	0	<0.01
Asian (244)	336	0.76
Not Hispanic (242)	318	0.72
Hispanic (2)	18	0.04
Bangladeshi (0)	0	<0.01
Bhutanese (0)	0	<0.01
Burmese (0)	0	<0.01
Cambodian (4)	4	0.01
Chinese, ex. Taiwanese (42)	51	0.11
Filipino (33)	70	0.16
Hmong (1)	1	<0.01
Indian (18)	23	0.05
Indonesian (0)	0	<0.01
Japanese (102)	118	0.27
Korean (20)	38	0.09
Laotian (0)	0	<0.01
Malaysian (0)	2	<0.01
Nepalese (0)	0	<0.01
Pakistani (2)	2	<0.01
Sri Lankan (0)	0	<0.01
Taiwanese (0)	0	<0.01
Thai (4)	4	0.01
Vietnamese (1)	6	0.01
Hawaii Native/Pacific Islander (13)	34	0.08
Not Hispanic (7)	23	0.05
Hispanic (6)	11	0.02
Fijian (0)	1	<0.01
Guamanian/Chamorro (9)	11	0.02
Marshallese (0)	0	<0.01
Native Hawaiian (3)	10	0.02
Samoan (0)	2	<0.01
Tongan (1)	1	<0.01
White (42,402)	42,899	96.54
Not Hispanic (41,622)	42,004	94.53
Hispanic (780)	895	2.01

*Notes: † The Census 2010 population figure is used to calculate the percentages in the Hispanic Origin and Race categories. Ancestry percentages are based on the 2006-2010 American Community Survey population (not shown); ‡ Numbers in parentheses indicate the number of people reporting a single ancestry; * Numbers in parentheses indicate the number of persons reporting this race alone, not in combination with any other race; Please refer to the Explanation of Data for more information.*

Spencer County

Population: 20,952

Ancestry	Population	%
Afghan (0)	0	<0.01
African, Sub-Saharan (0)	0	<0.01
African (0)	0	<0.01
Cape Verdean (0)	0	<0.01
Ethiopian (0)	0	<0.01
Ghanaian (0)	0	<0.01
Kenyan (0)	0	<0.01
Liberian (0)	0	<0.01
Nigerian (0)	0	<0.01
Senegalese (0)	0	<0.01
Sierra Leonean (0)	0	<0.01
Somalian (0)	0	<0.01
South African (0)	0	<0.01
Sudanese (0)	0	<0.01
Ugandan (0)	0	<0.01
Zimbabwean (0)	0	<0.01
Other Sub-Saharan African (0)	0	<0.01
Albanian (0)	0	<0.01
Alsatian (0)	0	<0.01
American (2,337)	2,337	11.14
Arab (0)	0	<0.01
Arab (0)	0	<0.01
Egyptian (0)	0	<0.01
Iraqi (0)	0	<0.01
Jordanian (0)	0	<0.01
Lebanese (0)	0	<0.01
Moroccan (0)	0	<0.01
Palestinian (0)	0	<0.01
Syrian (0)	0	<0.01
Other Arab (0)	0	<0.01
Armenian (0)	0	<0.01
Assyrian/Chaldean/Syriac (0)	0	<0.01
Australian (0)	0	<0.01
Austrian (0)	5	0.02
Basque (0)	2	0.01
Belgian (20)	61	0.29
Brazilian (0)	0	<0.01
British (8)	35	0.17
Bulgarian (0)	0	<0.01
Cajun (0)	0	<0.01
Canadian (41)	41	0.20
Carpatho Rusyn (0)	0	<0.01
Celtic (0)	0	<0.01
Croatian (0)	0	<0.01
Cypriot (0)	0	<0.01
Czech (40)	104	0.50
Czechoslovakian (0)	7	0.03
Danish (0)	33	0.16
Dutch (58)	475	2.26
Eastern European (0)	0	<0.01
English (1,039)	2,633	12.55
Estonian (0)	0	<0.01
European (15)	26	0.12
Finnish (0)	0	<0.01
French, ex. Basque (192)	828	3.95
French Canadian (0)	8	0.04
German (5,956)	9,861	47.01
German Russian (0)	0	<0.01
Greek (0)	11	0.05
Guyanese (0)	0	<0.01
Hungarian (0)	8	0.04
Icelander (0)	0	<0.01
Iranian (0)	0	<0.01
Irish (945)	3,446	16.43
Israeli (0)	0	<0.01
Italian (39)	217	1.03
Latvian (0)	0	<0.01
Lithuanian (0)	0	<0.01
Luxemburger (0)	0	<0.01
Macedonian (0)	0	<0.01
Maltese (0)	5	0.02
New Zealander (0)	0	<0.01
Northern European (0)	0	<0.01
Norwegian (20)	56	0.27
Pennsylvania German (0)	8	0.04
Polish (27)	171	0.82
Portuguese (0)	7	0.03
Romanian (8)	22	0.10
Russian (19)	39	0.19
Scandinavian (0)	0	<0.01
Scotch-Irish (90)	343	1.64
Scottish (96)	367	1.75
Serbian (0)	0	<0.01
Slavic (0)	0	<0.01
Slovak (0)	0	<0.01
Slovene (0)	0	<0.01
Soviet Union (0)	0	<0.01
Swedish (0)	57	0.27
Swiss (40)	89	0.42
Turkish (0)	0	<0.01
Ukrainian (5)	11	0.05
Welsh (55)	137	0.65
West Indian, ex. Hispanic (0)	0	<0.01
Bahamian (0)	0	<0.01
Barbadian (0)	0	<0.01
Belizean (0)	0	<0.01
Bermudan (0)	0	<0.01
British West Indian (0)	0	<0.01
Dutch West Indian (0)	0	<0.01
Haitian (0)	0	<0.01
Jamaican (0)	0	<0.01
Trinidadian/Tobagonian (0)	0	<0.01
U.S. Virgin Islander (0)	0	<0.01
West Indian (0)	0	<0.01
Other West Indian (0)	0	<0.01
Yugoslavian (9)	12	0.06

Hispanic Origin	Population	%
Hispanic or Latino (of any race)	517	2.47
Central American, ex. Mexican	40	0.19
Costa Rican	0	<0.01
Guatemalan	23	0.11
Honduran	0	<0.01
Nicaraguan	0	<0.01
Panamanian	1	<0.01
Salvadoran	16	0.08
Other Central American	0	<0.01
Cuban	2	0.01
Dominican Republic	0	<0.01
Mexican	426	2.03
Puerto Rican	23	0.11
South American	3	0.01
Argentinean	0	<0.01
Bolivian	0	<0.01
Chilean	0	<0.01
Colombian	3	0.01
Ecuadorian	0	<0.01
Paraguayan	0	<0.01
Peruvian	0	<0.01
Uruguayan	0	<0.01
Venezuelan	0	<0.01
Other South American	0	<0.01
Other Hispanic or Latino	23	0.11

Race*	Population	%
African-American/Black (96)	166	0.79
Not Hispanic (96)	154	0.74
Hispanic (0)	12	0.06
American Indian/Alaska Native (41)	93	0.44
Not Hispanic (38)	85	0.41
Hispanic (3)	8	0.04
Alaska Athabascan *(Ala. Nat.)* (0)	0	<0.01
Aleut *(Alaska Native)* (0)	0	<0.01
Apache (1)	1	<0.01
Arapaho (0)	0	<0.01
Blackfeet (0)	4	0.02
Canadian/French Am. Ind. (0)	0	<0.01
Central American Ind. (0)	0	<0.01
Cherokee (8)	27	0.13
Cheyenne (0)	0	<0.01
Chickasaw (1)	1	<0.01
Chippewa (5)	7	0.03
Choctaw (0)	0	<0.01
Colville (0)	0	<0.01
Comanche (1)	1	<0.01
Cree (0)	0	<0.01
Creek (0)	3	0.01
Crow (0)	0	<0.01
Delaware (1)	1	<0.01
Hopi (0)	0	<0.01
Houma (0)	0	<0.01
Inupiat *(Alaska Native)* (0)	0	<0.01
Iroquois (1)	5	0.02
Kiowa (0)	0	<0.01
Lumbee (0)	2	0.01
Menominee (0)	0	<0.01
Mexican American Ind. (0)	3	0.01
Navajo (0)	0	<0.01
Osage (0)	0	<0.01
Ottawa (0)	0	<0.01
Paiute (0)	0	<0.01
Pima (0)	0	<0.01
Potawatomi (0)	1	<0.01
Pueblo (0)	0	<0.01
Puget Sound Salish (0)	0	<0.01
Seminole (0)	0	<0.01
Shoshone (0)	0	<0.01
Sioux (0)	1	<0.01
South American Ind. (0)	0	<0.01
Spanish American Ind. (0)	0	<0.01
Tlingit-Haida *(Alaska Native)* (0)	0	<0.01
Tohono O'Odham (0)	0	<0.01
Tsimshian *(Alaska Native)* (0)	0	<0.01
Ute (0)	0	<0.01
Yakama (0)	0	<0.01
Yaqui (0)	0	<0.01
Yuman (0)	0	<0.01
Yup'ik *(Alaska Native)* (0)	0	<0.01
Asian (72)	91	0.43
Not Hispanic (69)	83	0.40
Hispanic (3)	8	0.04
Bangladeshi (0)	0	<0.01
Bhutanese (0)	0	<0.01
Burmese (0)	0	<0.01
Cambodian (0)	0	<0.01
Chinese, ex. Taiwanese (14)	14	0.07
Filipino (23)	29	0.14
Hmong (0)	0	<0.01
Indian (10)	13	0.06
Indonesian (0)	0	<0.01
Japanese (4)	10	0.05
Korean (12)	16	0.08
Laotian (0)	0	<0.01
Malaysian (0)	0	<0.01
Nepalese (0)	0	<0.01
Pakistani (0)	0	<0.01
Sri Lankan (0)	0	<0.01
Taiwanese (0)	0	<0.01
Thai (4)	4	0.02
Vietnamese (2)	4	0.02
Hawaii Native/Pacific Islander (0)	2	0.01
Not Hispanic (0)	2	0.01
Hispanic (0)	0	<0.01
Fijian (0)	0	<0.01
Guamanian/Chamorro (0)	0	<0.01
Marshallese (0)	0	<0.01
Native Hawaiian (0)	1	<0.01
Samoan (0)	1	<0.01
Tongan (0)	0	<0.01
White (20,295)	20,452	97.61
Not Hispanic (20,101)	20,221	96.51
Hispanic (194)	231	1.10

*Notes: † The Census 2010 population figure is used to calculate the percentages in the Hispanic Origin and Race categories. Ancestry percentages are based on the 2006-2010 American Community Survey population (not shown); ‡ Numbers in parentheses indicate the number of people reporting a single ancestry; * Numbers in parentheses indicate the number of persons reporting this race alone, not in combination with any other race; Please refer to the Explanation of Data for more information.*

St. Joseph County

Population: 266,931

Ancestry	Population	%
Afghan (0)	0	<0.01
African, Sub-Saharan (1,951)	2,311	0.87
African (1,405)	1,676	0.63
Cape Verdean (0)	0	<0.01
Ethiopian (117)	130	0.05
Ghanaian (51)	51	0.02
Kenyan (202)	218	0.08
Liberian (13)	41	0.02
Nigerian (26)	26	0.01
Senegalese (0)	0	<0.01
Sierra Leonean (0)	32	0.01
Somalian (0)	0	<0.01
South African (0)	0	<0.01
Sudanese (0)	0	<0.01
Ugandan (8)	8	<0.01
Zimbabwean (0)	0	<0.01
Other Sub-Saharan African (129)	129	0.05
Albanian (9)	22	0.01
Alsatian (0)	12	<0.01
American (12,056)	12,056	4.52
Arab (727)	1,372	0.51
Arab (114)	177	0.07
Egyptian (15)	15	0.01
Iraqi (23)	213	0.08
Jordanian (0)	0	<0.01
Lebanese (225)	541	0.20
Moroccan (0)	6	<0.01
Palestinian (119)	119	0.04
Syrian (28)	98	0.04
Other Arab (203)	203	0.08
Armenian (8)	84	0.03
Assyrian/Chaldean/Syriac (0)	65	0.02
Australian (14)	21	0.01
Austrian (233)	1,075	0.40
Basque (0)	0	<0.01
Belgian (1,903)	5,196	1.95
Brazilian (94)	191	0.07
British (396)	1,048	0.39
Bulgarian (22)	60	0.02
Cajun (0)	21	0.01
Canadian (185)	432	0.16
Carpatho Rusyn (0)	0	<0.01
Celtic (42)	117	0.04
Croatian (83)	531	0.20
Cypriot (8)	8	<0.01
Czech (167)	992	0.37
Czechoslovakian (90)	221	0.08
Danish (161)	817	0.31
Dutch (1,193)	7,104	2.67
Eastern European (102)	155	0.06
English (6,156)	22,539	8.46
Estonian (16)	61	0.02
European (2,257)	2,495	0.94
Finnish (82)	344	0.13
French, ex. Basque (1,130)	7,792	2.92
French Canadian (298)	1,298	0.49
German (20,852)	67,432	25.30
German Russian (0)	10	<0.01
Greek (331)	1,145	0.43
Guyanese (0)	0	<0.01
Hungarian (3,146)	8,972	3.37
Icelander (13)	13	<0.01
Iranian (97)	146	0.05
Irish (9,304)	41,235	15.47
Israeli (0)	0	<0.01
Italian (3,413)	12,012	4.51
Latvian (10)	22	0.01
Lithuanian (148)	656	0.25
Luxemburger (16)	55	0.02
Macedonian (0)	96	0.04
Maltese (0)	0	<0.01
New Zealander (0)	0	<0.01
Northern European (204)	244	0.09
Norwegian (605)	2,350	0.88
Pennsylvania German (204)	499	0.19
Polish (14,234)	31,955	11.99
Portuguese (86)	405	0.15
Romanian (182)	265	0.10
Russian (448)	1,628	0.61
Scandinavian (152)	402	0.15
Scotch-Irish (1,280)	3,995	1.50
Scottish (1,023)	4,114	1.54
Serbian (201)	437	0.16
Slavic (23)	69	0.03
Slovak (104)	391	0.15
Slovene (37)	127	0.05
Soviet Union (0)	0	<0.01
Swedish (1,330)	5,105	1.92
Swiss (381)	1,502	0.56
Turkish (58)	135	0.05
Ukrainian (129)	424	0.16
Welsh (262)	1,380	0.52
West Indian, ex. Hispanic (202)	289	0.11
Bahamian (0)	9	<0.01
Barbadian (0)	0	<0.01
Belizean (0)	0	<0.01
Bermudan (0)	0	<0.01
British West Indian (15)	15	0.01
Dutch West Indian (11)	11	<0.01
Haitian (0)	0	<0.01
Jamaican (81)	136	0.05
Trinidadian/Tobagonian (39)	52	0.02
U.S. Virgin Islander (0)	0	<0.01
West Indian (56)	66	0.02
Other West Indian (0)	0	<0.01
Yugoslavian (816)	1,000	0.38

Hispanic Origin	Population	%
Hispanic or Latino (of any race)	19,395	7.27
Central American, ex. Mexican	626	0.23
Costa Rican	31	0.01
Guatemalan	142	0.05
Honduran	121	0.05
Nicaraguan	87	0.03
Panamanian	62	0.02
Salvadoran	176	0.07
Other Central American	7	<0.01
Cuban	259	0.10
Dominican Republic	80	0.03
Mexican	15,338	5.75
Puerto Rican	1,074	0.40
South American	632	0.24
Argentinean	57	0.02
Bolivian	15	0.01
Chilean	67	0.03
Colombian	148	0.06
Ecuadorian	94	0.04
Paraguayan	15	0.01
Peruvian	66	0.02
Uruguayan	14	0.01
Venezuelan	153	0.06
Other South American	3	<0.01
Other Hispanic or Latino	1,386	0.52

Race*	Population	%
African-American/Black (33,958)	38,255	14.33
Not Hispanic (33,407)	37,205	13.94
Hispanic (551)	1,050	0.39
American Indian/Alaska Native (1,030)	2,825	1.06
Not Hispanic (791)	2,345	0.88
Hispanic (239)	480	0.18
Alaska Athabascan *(Ala. Nat.)* (0)	0	<0.01
Aleut *(Alaska Native)* (2)	3	<0.01
Apache (9)	38	0.01
Arapaho (1)	2	<0.01
Blackfeet (19)	122	0.05
Canadian/French Am. Ind. (13)	35	0.01
Central American Ind. (3)	8	<0.01
Cherokee (125)	609	0.23
Cheyenne (2)	3	<0.01
Chickasaw (6)	19	0.01
Chippewa (31)	84	0.03
Choctaw (14)	49	0.02
Colville (1)	1	<0.01
Comanche (4)	5	<0.01
Cree (1)	6	<0.01
Creek (11)	21	0.01
Crow (2)	4	<0.01
Delaware (2)	11	<0.01
Hopi (1)	2	<0.01
Houma (2)	2	<0.01
Inupiat *(Alaska Native)* (0)	3	<0.01
Iroquois (5)	19	0.01
Kiowa (0)	0	<0.01
Lumbee (6)	16	0.01
Menominee (4)	4	<0.01
Mexican American Ind. (56)	88	0.03
Navajo (2)	12	<0.01
Osage (1)	2	<0.01
Ottawa (3)	13	<0.01
Paiute (3)	4	<0.01
Pima (0)	0	<0.01
Potawatomi (109)	212	0.08
Pueblo (1)	5	<0.01
Puget Sound Salish (1)	2	<0.01
Seminole (0)	7	<0.01
Shoshone (0)	1	<0.01
Sioux (16)	39	0.01
South American Ind. (7)	20	0.01
Spanish American Ind. (8)	11	<0.01
Tlingit-Haida *(Alaska Native)* (5)	6	<0.01
Tohono O'Odham (0)	0	<0.01
Tsimshian *(Alaska Native)* (0)	0	<0.01
Ute (0)	1	<0.01
Yakama (0)	0	<0.01
Yaqui (1)	2	<0.01
Yuman (0)	0	<0.01
Yup'ik *(Alaska Native)* (4)	4	<0.01
Asian (5,036)	6,342	2.38
Not Hispanic (4,985)	6,168	2.31
Hispanic (51)	174	0.07
Bangladeshi (10)	13	<0.01
Bhutanese (0)	0	<0.01
Burmese (5)	5	<0.01
Cambodian (115)	134	0.05
Chinese, ex. Taiwanese (1,272)	1,538	0.58
Filipino (507)	853	0.32
Hmong (2)	4	<0.01
Indian (1,127)	1,293	0.48
Indonesian (28)	36	0.01
Japanese (179)	350	0.13
Korean (631)	814	0.30
Laotian (81)	112	0.04
Malaysian (4)	5	<0.01
Nepalese (6)	7	<0.01
Pakistani (158)	172	0.06
Sri Lankan (27)	31	0.01
Taiwanese (59)	68	0.03
Thai (62)	94	0.04
Vietnamese (581)	652	0.24
Hawaii Native/Pacific Islander (194)	428	0.16
Not Hispanic (180)	381	0.14
Hispanic (14)	47	0.02
Fijian (0)	0	<0.01
Guamanian/Chamorro (26)	50	0.02
Marshallese (2)	2	<0.01
Native Hawaiian (39)	118	0.04
Samoan (43)	107	0.04
Tongan (34)	58	0.02
White (209,972)	216,802	81.22
Not Hispanic (201,701)	207,214	77.63
Hispanic (8,271)	9,588	3.59

*Notes: † The Census 2010 population figure is used to calculate the percentages in the Hispanic Origin and Race categories. Ancestry percentages are based on the 2006-2010 American Community Survey population (not shown); ‡ Numbers in parentheses indicate the number of people reporting a single ancestry; * Numbers in parentheses indicate the number of persons reporting this race alone, not in combination with any other race; Please refer to the Explanation of Data for more information.*

Starke County

Population: 23,363

Ancestry	Population	%
Afghan (0)	0	<0.01
African, Sub-Saharan (5)	5	0.02
African (5)	5	0.02
Cape Verdean (0)	0	<0.01
Ethiopian (0)	0	<0.01
Ghanaian (0)	0	<0.01
Kenyan (0)	0	<0.01
Liberian (0)	0	<0.01
Nigerian (0)	0	<0.01
Senegalese (0)	0	<0.01
Sierra Leonean (0)	0	<0.01
Somalian (0)	0	<0.01
South African (0)	0	<0.01
Sudanese (0)	0	<0.01
Ugandan (0)	0	<0.01
Zimbabwean (0)	0	<0.01
Other Sub-Saharan African (0)	0	<0.01
Albanian (0)	0	<0.01
Alsatian (0)	0	<0.01
American (2,038)	2,038	8.73
Arab (12)	18	0.08
Arab (12)	12	0.05
Egyptian (0)	0	<0.01
Iraqi (0)	0	<0.01
Jordanian (0)	0	<0.01
Lebanese (0)	6	0.03
Moroccan (0)	0	<0.01
Palestinian (0)	0	<0.01
Syrian (0)	0	<0.01
Other Arab (0)	0	<0.01
Armenian (19)	19	0.08
Assyrian/Chaldean/Syriac (0)	0	<0.01
Australian (0)	0	<0.01
Austrian (4)	15	0.06
Basque (0)	0	<0.01
Belgian (0)	17	0.07
Brazilian (0)	0	<0.01
British (18)	18	0.08
Bulgarian (20)	20	0.09
Cajun (0)	0	<0.01
Canadian (3)	12	0.05
Carpatho Rusyn (0)	0	<0.01
Celtic (0)	0	<0.01
Croatian (3)	20	0.09
Cypriot (0)	0	<0.01
Czech (136)	421	1.80
Czechoslovakian (36)	46	0.20
Danish (8)	73	0.31
Dutch (140)	633	2.71
Eastern European (0)	0	<0.01
English (808)	2,067	8.85
Estonian (0)	0	<0.01
European (166)	172	0.74
Finnish (0)	12	0.05
French, ex. Basque (119)	782	3.35
French Canadian (11)	77	0.33
German (2,476)	6,355	27.22
German Russian (0)	0	<0.01
Greek (70)	102	0.44
Guyanese (0)	0	<0.01
Hungarian (60)	178	0.76
Icelander (0)	0	<0.01
Iranian (0)	0	<0.01
Irish (977)	3,799	16.27
Israeli (0)	0	<0.01
Italian (392)	913	3.91
Latvian (0)	0	<0.01
Lithuanian (91)	178	0.76
Luxemburger (12)	14	0.06
Macedonian (0)	0	<0.01
Maltese (0)	0	<0.01
New Zealander (0)	0	<0.01
Northern European (2)	2	0.01
Norwegian (59)	270	1.16
Pennsylvania German (38)	96	0.41
Polish (912)	1,621	6.94
Portuguese (0)	0	<0.01
Romanian (0)	76	0.33
Russian (13)	107	0.46
Scandinavian (15)	33	0.14
Scotch-Irish (86)	338	1.45
Scottish (272)	629	2.69
Serbian (73)	128	0.55
Slavic (0)	35	0.15
Slovak (11)	108	0.46
Slovene (0)	0	<0.01
Soviet Union (0)	0	<0.01
Swedish (157)	436	1.87
Swiss (0)	16	0.07
Turkish (0)	0	<0.01
Ukrainian (7)	22	0.09
Welsh (0)	113	0.48
West Indian, ex. Hispanic (0)	0	<0.01
Bahamian (0)	0	<0.01
Barbadian (0)	0	<0.01
Belizean (0)	0	<0.01
Bermudan (0)	0	<0.01
British West Indian (0)	0	<0.01
Dutch West Indian (0)	0	<0.01
Haitian (0)	0	<0.01
Jamaican (0)	0	<0.01
Trinidadian/Tobagonian (0)	0	<0.01
U.S. Virgin Islander (0)	0	<0.01
West Indian (0)	0	<0.01
Other West Indian (0)	0	<0.01
Yugoslavian (0)	24	0.10

Hispanic Origin	Population	%
Hispanic or Latino (of any race)	766	3.28
Central American, ex. Mexican	9	0.04
Costa Rican	2	0.01
Guatemalan	6	0.03
Honduran	0	<0.01
Nicaraguan	0	<0.01
Panamanian	0	<0.01
Salvadoran	1	<0.01
Other Central American	0	<0.01
Cuban	7	0.03
Dominican Republic	1	<0.01
Mexican	544	2.33
Puerto Rican	106	0.45
South American	7	0.03
Argentinean	0	<0.01
Bolivian	0	<0.01
Chilean	4	0.02
Colombian	2	0.01
Ecuadorian	0	<0.01
Paraguayan	0	<0.01
Peruvian	1	<0.01
Uruguayan	0	<0.01
Venezuelan	0	<0.01
Other South American	0	<0.01
Other Hispanic or Latino	92	0.39

Race*	Population	%
African-American/Black (66)	132	0.56
Not Hispanic (63)	124	0.53
Hispanic (3)	8	0.03
American Indian/Alaska Native (76)	209	0.89
Not Hispanic (61)	181	0.77
Hispanic (15)	28	0.12
Alaska Athabascan *(Ala. Nat.)* (0)	0	<0.01
Aleut *(Alaska Native)* (0)	0	<0.01
Apache (2)	9	0.04
Arapaho (0)	0	<0.01
Blackfeet (2)	10	0.04
Canadian/French Am. Ind. (5)	12	0.05
Central American Ind. (0)	0	<0.01
Cherokee (8)	44	0.19
Cheyenne (3)	3	0.01
Chickasaw (0)	0	<0.01
Chippewa (4)	11	0.05
Choctaw (0)	0	<0.01
Colville (0)	0	<0.01
Comanche (0)	1	<0.01
Cree (2)	3	0.01
Creek (0)	0	<0.01
Crow (0)	0	<0.01
Delaware (0)	0	<0.01
Hopi (0)	0	<0.01
Houma (0)	0	<0.01
Inupiat *(Alaska Native)* (0)	0	<0.01
Iroquois (2)	2	0.01
Kiowa (0)	0	<0.01
Lumbee (0)	0	<0.01
Menominee (8)	8	0.03
Mexican American Ind. (0)	5	0.02
Navajo (0)	0	<0.01
Osage (2)	2	0.01
Ottawa (2)	7	0.03
Paiute (0)	0	<0.01
Pima (0)	0	<0.01
Potawatomi (4)	6	0.03
Pueblo (0)	0	<0.01
Puget Sound Salish (0)	0	<0.01
Seminole (0)	0	<0.01
Shoshone (0)	2	0.01
Sioux (1)	6	0.03
South American Ind. (0)	0	<0.01
Spanish American Ind. (0)	0	<0.01
Tlingit-Haida *(Alaska Native)* (0)	0	<0.01
Tohono O'Odham (0)	0	<0.01
Tsimshian *(Alaska Native)* (0)	0	<0.01
Ute (0)	0	<0.01
Yakama (0)	0	<0.01
Yaqui (0)	0	<0.01
Yuman (0)	0	<0.01
Yup'ik *(Alaska Native)* (0)	0	<0.01
Asian (41)	75	0.32
Not Hispanic (41)	72	0.31
Hispanic (0)	3	0.01
Bangladeshi (0)	0	<0.01
Bhutanese (0)	0	<0.01
Burmese (0)	0	<0.01
Cambodian (0)	0	<0.01
Chinese, ex. Taiwanese (8)	9	0.04
Filipino (12)	27	0.12
Hmong (0)	0	<0.01
Indian (6)	11	0.05
Indonesian (0)	0	<0.01
Japanese (5)	14	0.06
Korean (7)	13	0.06
Laotian (0)	0	<0.01
Malaysian (0)	0	<0.01
Nepalese (0)	0	<0.01
Pakistani (0)	1	<0.01
Sri Lankan (0)	0	<0.01
Taiwanese (0)	0	<0.01
Thai (1)	1	<0.01
Vietnamese (1)	1	<0.01
Hawaii Native/Pacific Islander (0)	2	0.01
Not Hispanic (0)	2	0.01
Hispanic (0)	0	<0.01
Fijian (0)	0	<0.01
Guamanian/Chamorro (0)	1	<0.01
Marshallese (0)	0	<0.01
Native Hawaiian (0)	1	<0.01
Samoan (0)	0	<0.01
Tongan (0)	0	<0.01
White (22,683)	22,970	98.32
Not Hispanic (22,212)	22,426	95.99
Hispanic (471)	544	2.33

*Notes: † The Census 2010 population figure is used to calculate the percentages in the Hispanic Origin and Race categories. Ancestry percentages are based on the 2006-2010 American Community Survey population (not shown); ‡ Numbers in parentheses indicate the number of people reporting a single ancestry; * Numbers in parentheses indicate the number of persons reporting this race alone, not in combination with any other race; Please refer to the Explanation of Data for more information.*

Steuben County

Population: 34,185

Ancestry	Population	%
Afghan (0)	0	<0.01
African, Sub-Saharan (11)	14	0.04
African (11)	11	0.03
Cape Verdean (0)	0	<0.01
Ethiopian (0)	0	<0.01
Ghanaian (0)	0	<0.01
Kenyan (0)	0	<0.01
Liberian (0)	0	<0.01
Nigerian (0)	0	<0.01
Senegalese (0)	0	<0.01
Sierra Leonean (0)	0	<0.01
Somalian (0)	0	<0.01
South African (0)	3	0.01
Sudanese (0)	0	<0.01
Ugandan (0)	0	<0.01
Zimbabwean (0)	0	<0.01
Other Sub-Saharan African (0)	0	<0.01
Albanian (0)	0	<0.01
Alsatian (0)	0	<0.01
American (2,789)	2,789	8.18
Arab (14)	18	0.05
Arab (0)	0	<0.01
Egyptian (0)	0	<0.01
Iraqi (3)	3	0.01
Jordanian (0)	0	<0.01
Lebanese (11)	11	0.03
Moroccan (0)	0	<0.01
Palestinian (0)	0	<0.01
Syrian (0)	4	0.01
Other Arab (0)	0	<0.01
Armenian (0)	0	<0.01
Assyrian/Chaldean/Syriac (0)	0	<0.01
Australian (0)	0	<0.01
Austrian (46)	82	0.24
Basque (0)	0	<0.01
Belgian (10)	19	0.06
Brazilian (0)	0	<0.01
British (33)	65	0.19
Bulgarian (0)	0	<0.01
Cajun (0)	0	<0.01
Canadian (105)	139	0.41
Carpatho Rusyn (0)	0	<0.01
Celtic (0)	0	<0.01
Croatian (0)	26	0.08
Cypriot (0)	0	<0.01
Czech (37)	246	0.72
Czechoslovakian (4)	80	0.23
Danish (8)	45	0.13
Dutch (258)	1,012	2.97
Eastern European (0)	0	<0.01
English (1,336)	4,294	12.60
Estonian (0)	0	<0.01
European (147)	149	0.44
Finnish (0)	3	0.01
French, ex. Basque (127)	1,173	3.44
French Canadian (54)	109	0.32
German (6,144)	12,899	37.84
German Russian (0)	0	<0.01
Greek (94)	162	0.48
Guyanese (0)	0	<0.01
Hungarian (50)	175	0.51
Icelander (0)	0	<0.01
Iranian (0)	0	<0.01
Irish (871)	3,573	10.48
Israeli (0)	0	<0.01
Italian (505)	1,449	4.25
Latvian (2)	2	0.01
Lithuanian (18)	26	0.08
Luxemburger (0)	12	0.04
Macedonian (11)	11	0.03
Maltese (0)	0	<0.01
New Zealander (0)	0	<0.01
Northern European (20)	20	0.06
Norwegian (59)	307	0.90
Pennsylvania German (33)	51	0.15
Polish (389)	1,207	3.54
Portuguese (11)	11	0.03
Romanian (37)	37	0.11
Russian (17)	94	0.28
Scandinavian (11)	22	0.06
Scotch-Irish (226)	571	1.67
Scottish (219)	562	1.65
Serbian (0)	0	<0.01
Slavic (0)	0	<0.01
Slovak (12)	49	0.14
Slovene (0)	10	0.03
Soviet Union (0)	0	<0.01
Swedish (93)	373	1.09
Swiss (81)	351	1.03
Turkish (0)	0	<0.01
Ukrainian (0)	25	0.07
Welsh (43)	309	0.91
West Indian, ex. Hispanic (0)	0	<0.01
Bahamian (0)	0	<0.01
Barbadian (0)	0	<0.01
Belizean (0)	0	<0.01
Bermudan (0)	0	<0.01
British West Indian (0)	0	<0.01
Dutch West Indian (0)	0	<0.01
Haitian (0)	0	<0.01
Jamaican (0)	0	<0.01
Trinidadian/Tobagonian (0)	0	<0.01
U.S. Virgin Islander (0)	0	<0.01
West Indian (0)	0	<0.01
Other West Indian (0)	0	<0.01
Yugoslavian (28)	130	0.38

Hispanic Origin	Population	%
Hispanic or Latino (of any race)	982	2.87
Central American, ex. Mexican	26	0.08
Costa Rican	3	0.01
Guatemalan	3	0.01
Honduran	1	<0.01
Nicaraguan	0	<0.01
Panamanian	1	<0.01
Salvadoran	18	0.05
Other Central American	0	<0.01
Cuban	4	0.01
Dominican Republic	0	<0.01
Mexican	774	2.26
Puerto Rican	83	0.24
South American	16	0.05
Argentinean	3	0.01
Bolivian	1	<0.01
Chilean	1	<0.01
Colombian	4	0.01
Ecuadorian	2	0.01
Paraguayan	0	<0.01
Peruvian	2	0.01
Uruguayan	1	<0.01
Venezuelan	2	0.01
Other South American	0	<0.01
Other Hispanic or Latino	79	0.23

Race*	Population	%
African-American/Black (179)	275	0.80
Not Hispanic (155)	243	0.71
Hispanic (24)	32	0.09
American Indian/Alaska Native (93)	206	0.60
Not Hispanic (81)	191	0.56
Hispanic (12)	15	0.04
Alaska Athabascan *(Ala. Nat.)* (0)	0	<0.01
Aleut *(Alaska Native)* (0)	0	<0.01
Apache (0)	1	<0.01
Arapaho (0)	0	<0.01
Blackfeet (0)	5	0.01
Canadian/French Am. Ind. (0)	1	<0.01
Central American Ind. (0)	0	<0.01
Cherokee (19)	46	0.13
Cheyenne (0)	3	0.01
Chickasaw (0)	1	<0.01
Chippewa (4)	9	0.03
Choctaw (1)	6	0.02
Colville (0)	0	<0.01
Comanche (0)	0	<0.01
Cree (0)	0	<0.01
Creek (0)	0	<0.01
Crow (1)	1	<0.01
Delaware (0)	0	<0.01
Hopi (0)	3	0.01
Houma (0)	0	<0.01
Inupiat *(Alaska Native)* (0)	0	<0.01
Iroquois (4)	7	0.02
Kiowa (0)	0	<0.01
Lumbee (0)	0	<0.01
Menominee (0)	0	<0.01
Mexican American Ind. (3)	3	0.01
Navajo (3)	6	0.02
Osage (0)	1	<0.01
Ottawa (3)	6	0.02
Paiute (0)	0	<0.01
Pima (0)	0	<0.01
Potawatomi (0)	2	0.01
Pueblo (0)	0	<0.01
Puget Sound Salish (0)	0	<0.01
Seminole (0)	0	<0.01
Shoshone (0)	1	<0.01
Sioux (0)	3	0.01
South American Ind. (1)	1	<0.01
Spanish American Ind. (0)	0	<0.01
Tlingit-Haida *(Alaska Native)* (0)	0	<0.01
Tohono O'Odham (0)	0	<0.01
Tsimshian *(Alaska Native)* (0)	0	<0.01
Ute (1)	1	<0.01
Yakama (0)	0	<0.01
Yaqui (0)	0	<0.01
Yuman (0)	0	<0.01
Yup'ik *(Alaska Native)* (0)	0	<0.01
Asian (167)	248	0.73
Not Hispanic (162)	241	0.70
Hispanic (5)	7	0.02
Bangladeshi (1)	1	<0.01
Bhutanese (0)	0	<0.01
Burmese (0)	0	<0.01
Cambodian (0)	0	<0.01
Chinese, ex. Taiwanese (29)	33	0.10
Filipino (31)	55	0.16
Hmong (0)	0	<0.01
Indian (33)	49	0.14
Indonesian (0)	0	<0.01
Japanese (8)	16	0.05
Korean (29)	41	0.12
Laotian (0)	0	<0.01
Malaysian (2)	3	0.01
Nepalese (4)	4	0.01
Pakistani (12)	13	0.04
Sri Lankan (0)	0	<0.01
Taiwanese (2)	3	0.01
Thai (10)	12	0.04
Vietnamese (2)	3	0.01
Hawaii Native/Pacific Islander (11)	18	0.05
Not Hispanic (6)	12	0.04
Hispanic (5)	6	0.02
Fijian (0)	0	<0.01
Guamanian/Chamorro (6)	7	0.02
Marshallese (0)	0	<0.01
Native Hawaiian (3)	7	0.02
Samoan (0)	0	<0.01
Tongan (0)	0	<0.01
White (33,098)	33,400	97.70
Not Hispanic (32,513)	32,778	95.88
Hispanic (585)	622	1.82

*Notes: † The Census 2010 population figure is used to calculate the percentages in the Hispanic Origin and Race categories. Ancestry percentages are based on the 2006-2010 American Community Survey population (not shown); ‡ Numbers in parentheses indicate the number of people reporting a single ancestry; * Numbers in parentheses indicate the number of persons reporting this race alone, not in combination with any other race; Please refer to the Explanation of Data for more information.*

Sullivan County

Population: 21,475

Ancestry	Population	%
Afghan (0)	0	<0.01
African, Sub-Saharan (158)	176	0.82
African (140)	158	0.73
Cape Verdean (0)	0	<0.01
Ethiopian (0)	0	<0.01
Ghanaian (0)	0	<0.01
Kenyan (0)	0	<0.01
Liberian (0)	0	<0.01
Nigerian (0)	0	<0.01
Senegalese (0)	0	<0.01
Sierra Leonean (0)	0	<0.01
Somalian (0)	0	<0.01
South African (0)	0	<0.01
Sudanese (0)	0	<0.01
Ugandan (0)	0	<0.01
Zimbabwean (0)	0	<0.01
Other Sub-Saharan African (18)	18	0.08
Albanian (0)	0	<0.01
Alsatian (0)	0	<0.01
American (4,259)	4,259	19.79
Arab (17)	35	0.16
Arab (0)	0	<0.01
Egyptian (0)	0	<0.01
Iraqi (0)	0	<0.01
Jordanian (0)	0	<0.01
Lebanese (0)	0	<0.01
Moroccan (17)	26	0.12
Palestinian (0)	0	<0.01
Syrian (0)	0	<0.01
Other Arab (0)	9	0.04
Armenian (0)	0	<0.01
Assyrian/Chaldean/Syriac (0)	0	<0.01
Australian (0)	0	<0.01
Austrian (0)	10	0.05
Basque (0)	0	<0.01
Belgian (28)	31	0.14
Brazilian (0)	0	<0.01
British (8)	16	0.07
Bulgarian (0)	0	<0.01
Cajun (0)	0	<0.01
Canadian (0)	0	<0.01
Carpatho Rusyn (0)	0	<0.01
Celtic (2)	7	0.03
Croatian (0)	0	<0.01
Cypriot (0)	0	<0.01
Czech (22)	137	0.64
Czechoslovakian (16)	16	0.07
Danish (0)	0	<0.01
Dutch (111)	473	2.20
Eastern European (0)	0	<0.01
English (1,135)	2,083	9.68
Estonian (0)	0	<0.01
European (101)	114	0.53
Finnish (0)	0	<0.01
French, ex. Basque (211)	537	2.50
French Canadian (14)	34	0.16
German (1,960)	4,475	20.79
German Russian (0)	0	<0.01
Greek (11)	18	0.08
Guyanese (0)	0	<0.01
Hungarian (20)	52	0.24
Icelander (0)	0	<0.01
Iranian (0)	0	<0.01
Irish (697)	2,223	10.33
Israeli (0)	0	<0.01
Italian (114)	316	1.47
Latvian (0)	0	<0.01
Lithuanian (14)	19	0.09
Luxemburger (0)	0	<0.01
Macedonian (0)	0	<0.01
Maltese (0)	0	<0.01
New Zealander (0)	0	<0.01
Northern European (0)	0	<0.01
Norwegian (21)	30	0.14
Pennsylvania German (15)	15	0.07
Polish (149)	420	1.95
Portuguese (0)	0	<0.01
Romanian (0)	0	<0.01
Russian (21)	34	0.16
Scandinavian (0)	0	<0.01
Scotch-Irish (146)	440	2.04
Scottish (58)	332	1.54
Serbian (0)	0	<0.01
Slavic (0)	0	<0.01
Slovak (2)	4	0.02
Slovene (0)	0	<0.01
Soviet Union (0)	0	<0.01
Swedish (4)	89	0.41
Swiss (0)	124	0.58
Turkish (0)	0	<0.01
Ukrainian (0)	6	0.03
Welsh (5)	122	0.57
West Indian, ex. Hispanic (0)	0	<0.01
Bahamian (0)	0	<0.01
Barbadian (0)	0	<0.01
Belizean (0)	0	<0.01
Bermudan (0)	0	<0.01
British West Indian (0)	0	<0.01
Dutch West Indian (0)	0	<0.01
Haitian (0)	0	<0.01
Jamaican (0)	0	<0.01
Trinidadian/Tobagonian (0)	0	<0.01
U.S. Virgin Islander (0)	0	<0.01
West Indian (0)	0	<0.01
Other West Indian (0)	0	<0.01
Yugoslavian (15)	15	0.07

Hispanic Origin	Population	%
Hispanic or Latino (of any race)	294	1.37
Central American, ex. Mexican	9	0.04
Costa Rican	0	<0.01
Guatemalan	3	0.01
Honduran	3	0.01
Nicaraguan	0	<0.01
Panamanian	2	0.01
Salvadoran	1	<0.01
Other Central American	0	<0.01
Cuban	10	0.05
Dominican Republic	1	<0.01
Mexican	205	0.95
Puerto Rican	21	0.10
South American	6	0.03
Argentinean	0	<0.01
Bolivian	0	<0.01
Chilean	2	0.01
Colombian	4	0.02
Ecuadorian	0	<0.01
Paraguayan	0	<0.01
Peruvian	0	<0.01
Uruguayan	0	<0.01
Venezuelan	0	<0.01
Other South American	0	<0.01
Other Hispanic or Latino	42	0.20

Race*	Population	%
African-American/Black (961)	1,024	4.77
Not Hispanic (946)	1,007	4.69
Hispanic (15)	17	0.08
American Indian/Alaska Native (58)	170	0.79
Not Hispanic (53)	159	0.74
Hispanic (5)	11	0.05
Alaska Athabascan *(Ala. Nat.)* (0)	0	<0.01
Aleut *(Alaska Native)* (0)	0	<0.01
Apache (1)	4	0.02
Arapaho (0)	1	<0.01
Blackfeet (4)	10	0.05
Canadian/French Am. Ind. (1)	1	<0.01
Central American Ind. (0)	0	<0.01
Cherokee (11)	47	0.22
Cheyenne (0)	0	<0.01
Chickasaw (0)	1	<0.01
Chippewa (1)	6	0.03
Choctaw (0)	0	<0.01
Colville (0)	0	<0.01
Comanche (0)	0	<0.01
Cree (0)	0	<0.01
Creek (4)	4	0.02
Crow (0)	0	<0.01
Delaware (0)	0	<0.01
Hopi (0)	0	<0.01
Houma (0)	0	<0.01
Inupiat *(Alaska Native)* (0)	0	<0.01
Iroquois (2)	6	0.03
Kiowa (0)	0	<0.01
Lumbee (1)	1	<0.01
Menominee (0)	0	<0.01
Mexican American Ind. (1)	2	0.01
Navajo (2)	3	0.01
Osage (1)	1	<0.01
Ottawa (1)	1	<0.01
Paiute (0)	0	<0.01
Pima (0)	0	<0.01
Potawatomi (0)	1	<0.01
Pueblo (0)	1	<0.01
Puget Sound Salish (0)	0	<0.01
Seminole (0)	0	<0.01
Shoshone (0)	0	<0.01
Sioux (1)	1	<0.01
South American Ind. (0)	0	<0.01
Spanish American Ind. (1)	1	<0.01
Tlingit-Haida *(Alaska Native)* (0)	0	<0.01
Tohono O'Odham (0)	0	<0.01
Tsimshian *(Alaska Native)* (0)	0	<0.01
Ute (0)	0	<0.01
Yakama (0)	0	<0.01
Yaqui (0)	0	<0.01
Yuman (0)	0	<0.01
Yup'ik *(Alaska Native)* (1)	2	0.01
Asian (40)	76	0.35
Not Hispanic (39)	72	0.34
Hispanic (1)	4	0.02
Bangladeshi (0)	0	<0.01
Bhutanese (0)	0	<0.01
Burmese (0)	0	<0.01
Cambodian (0)	0	<0.01
Chinese, ex. Taiwanese (5)	5	0.02
Filipino (8)	16	0.07
Hmong (0)	0	<0.01
Indian (18)	27	0.13
Indonesian (0)	0	<0.01
Japanese (1)	11	0.05
Korean (2)	6	0.03
Laotian (1)	2	0.01
Malaysian (0)	0	<0.01
Nepalese (0)	0	<0.01
Pakistani (1)	3	0.01
Sri Lankan (0)	0	<0.01
Taiwanese (0)	0	<0.01
Thai (0)	2	0.01
Vietnamese (2)	3	0.01
Hawaii Native/Pacific Islander (1)	2	0.01
Not Hispanic (1)	2	0.01
Hispanic (0)	0	<0.01
Fijian (0)	0	<0.01
Guamanian/Chamorro (0)	0	<0.01
Marshallese (0)	0	<0.01
Native Hawaiian (1)	2	0.01
Samoan (0)	0	<0.01
Tongan (0)	0	<0.01
White (20,132)	20,347	94.75
Not Hispanic (19,930)	20,130	93.74
Hispanic (202)	217	1.01

*Notes: † The Census 2010 population figure is used to calculate the percentages in the Hispanic Origin and Race categories. Ancestry percentages are based on the 2006-2010 American Community Survey population (not shown); ‡ Numbers in parentheses indicate the number of people reporting a single ancestry; * Numbers in parentheses indicate the number of persons reporting this race alone, not in combination with any other race; Please refer to the Explanation of Data for more information.*

Switzerland County

Population: 10,613

Ancestry	Population	%
Afghan (0)	0	<0.01
African, Sub-Saharan (0)	0	<0.01
African (0)	0	<0.01
Cape Verdean (0)	0	<0.01
Ethiopian (0)	0	<0.01
Ghanaian (0)	0	<0.01
Kenyan (0)	0	<0.01
Liberian (0)	0	<0.01
Nigerian (0)	0	<0.01
Senegalese (0)	0	<0.01
Sierra Leonean (0)	0	<0.01
Somalian (0)	0	<0.01
South African (0)	0	<0.01
Sudanese (0)	0	<0.01
Ugandan (0)	0	<0.01
Zimbabwean (0)	0	<0.01
Other Sub-Saharan African (0)	0	<0.01
Albanian (0)	0	<0.01
Alsatian (0)	0	<0.01
American (1,670)	1,670	16.07
Arab (9)	12	0.12
Arab (0)	0	<0.01
Egyptian (9)	9	0.09
Iraqi (0)	0	<0.01
Jordanian (0)	0	<0.01
Lebanese (0)	3	0.03
Moroccan (0)	0	<0.01
Palestinian (0)	0	<0.01
Syrian (0)	0	<0.01
Other Arab (0)	0	<0.01
Armenian (0)	0	<0.01
Assyrian/Chaldean/Syriac (0)	0	<0.01
Australian (34)	34	0.33
Austrian (0)	16	0.15
Basque (0)	0	<0.01
Belgian (0)	0	<0.01
Brazilian (0)	0	<0.01
British (0)	0	<0.01
Bulgarian (0)	0	<0.01
Cajun (0)	0	<0.01
Canadian (0)	0	<0.01
Carpatho Rusyn (0)	0	<0.01
Celtic (0)	0	<0.01
Croatian (0)	0	<0.01
Cypriot (0)	0	<0.01
Czech (3)	58	0.56
Czechoslovakian (0)	0	<0.01
Danish (0)	23	0.22
Dutch (10)	135	1.30
Eastern European (0)	0	<0.01
English (447)	1,049	10.09
Estonian (0)	0	<0.01
European (0)	0	<0.01
Finnish (0)	0	<0.01
French, ex. Basque (24)	151	1.45
French Canadian (0)	20	0.19
German (940)	2,635	25.35
German Russian (0)	0	<0.01
Greek (12)	55	0.53
Guyanese (0)	0	<0.01
Hungarian (3)	8	0.08
Icelander (0)	0	<0.01
Iranian (0)	0	<0.01
Irish (509)	1,372	13.20
Israeli (0)	0	<0.01
Italian (16)	176	1.69
Latvian (0)	0	<0.01
Lithuanian (0)	0	<0.01
Luxemburger (0)	0	<0.01
Macedonian (0)	0	<0.01
Maltese (0)	0	<0.01
New Zealander (0)	0	<0.01
Northern European (51)	51	0.49
Norwegian (0)	52	0.50
Pennsylvania German (5)	5	0.05
Polish (20)	147	1.41
Portuguese (0)	0	<0.01
Romanian (0)	0	<0.01
Russian (0)	4	0.04
Scandinavian (0)	0	<0.01
Scotch-Irish (89)	348	3.35
Scottish (132)	278	2.67
Serbian (0)	0	<0.01
Slavic (0)	0	<0.01
Slovak (0)	4	0.04
Slovene (0)	0	<0.01
Soviet Union (0)	0	<0.01
Swedish (0)	37	0.36
Swiss (14)	120	1.15
Turkish (0)	0	<0.01
Ukrainian (0)	0	<0.01
Welsh (85)	100	0.96
West Indian, ex. Hispanic (3)	3	0.03
Bahamian (0)	0	<0.01
Barbadian (0)	0	<0.01
Belizean (0)	0	<0.01
Bermudan (0)	0	<0.01
British West Indian (0)	0	<0.01
Dutch West Indian (0)	0	<0.01
Haitian (0)	0	<0.01
Jamaican (3)	3	0.03
Trinidadian/Tobagonian (0)	0	<0.01
U.S. Virgin Islander (0)	0	<0.01
West Indian (0)	0	<0.01
Other West Indian (0)	0	<0.01
Yugoslavian (0)	121	1.16

Hispanic Origin	Population	%
Hispanic or Latino (of any race)	147	1.39
Central American, ex. Mexican	7	0.07
Costa Rican	0	<0.01
Guatemalan	4	0.04
Honduran	2	0.02
Nicaraguan	0	<0.01
Panamanian	1	0.01
Salvadoran	0	<0.01
Other Central American	0	<0.01
Cuban	5	0.05
Dominican Republic	0	<0.01
Mexican	113	1.06
Puerto Rican	9	0.08
South American	1	0.01
Argentinean	0	<0.01
Bolivian	0	<0.01
Chilean	0	<0.01
Colombian	0	<0.01
Ecuadorian	0	<0.01
Paraguayan	0	<0.01
Peruvian	1	0.01
Uruguayan	0	<0.01
Venezuelan	0	<0.01
Other South American	0	<0.01
Other Hispanic or Latino	12	0.11

Race*	Population	%
African-American/Black (32)	56	0.53
Not Hispanic (31)	54	0.51
Hispanic (1)	2	0.02
American Indian/Alaska Native (18)	62	0.58
Not Hispanic (16)	56	0.53
Hispanic (2)	6	0.06
Alaska Athabascan *(Ala. Nat.)* (0)	0	<0.01
Aleut *(Alaska Native)* (0)	0	<0.01
Apache (1)	1	0.01
Arapaho (0)	0	<0.01
Blackfeet (0)	5	0.05
Canadian/French Am. Ind. (0)	0	<0.01
Central American Ind. (0)	0	<0.01
Cherokee (4)	21	0.20
Cheyenne (0)	0	<0.01
Chickasaw (0)	1	0.01
Chippewa (1)	2	0.02
Choctaw (1)	1	0.01
Colville (0)	0	<0.01
Comanche (0)	0	<0.01
Cree (0)	0	<0.01
Creek (0)	0	<0.01
Crow (0)	0	<0.01
Delaware (0)	0	<0.01
Hopi (0)	0	<0.01
Houma (0)	0	<0.01
Inupiat *(Alaska Native)* (0)	0	<0.01
Iroquois (1)	1	0.01
Kiowa (0)	0	<0.01
Lumbee (0)	0	<0.01
Menominee (0)	0	<0.01
Mexican American Ind. (1)	1	0.01
Navajo (0)	0	<0.01
Osage (0)	0	<0.01
Ottawa (0)	0	<0.01
Paiute (0)	0	<0.01
Pima (0)	0	<0.01
Potawatomi (0)	0	<0.01
Pueblo (0)	0	<0.01
Puget Sound Salish (0)	0	<0.01
Seminole (1)	8	0.08
Shoshone (0)	0	<0.01
Sioux (0)	1	0.01
South American Ind. (0)	0	<0.01
Spanish American Ind. (0)	0	<0.01
Tlingit-Haida *(Alaska Native)* (0)	0	<0.01
Tohono O'Odham (0)	0	<0.01
Tsimshian *(Alaska Native)* (0)	0	<0.01
Ute (0)	0	<0.01
Yakama (0)	0	<0.01
Yaqui (0)	0	<0.01
Yuman (0)	0	<0.01
Yup'ik *(Alaska Native)* (0)	0	<0.01
Asian (18)	23	0.22
Not Hispanic (18)	23	0.22
Hispanic (0)	0	<0.01
Bangladeshi (0)	0	<0.01
Bhutanese (0)	0	<0.01
Burmese (0)	0	<0.01
Cambodian (1)	1	0.01
Chinese, ex. Taiwanese (0)	0	<0.01
Filipino (2)	2	0.02
Hmong (0)	0	<0.01
Indian (9)	13	0.12
Indonesian (0)	0	<0.01
Japanese (0)	0	<0.01
Korean (2)	2	0.02
Laotian (0)	0	<0.01
Malaysian (0)	0	<0.01
Nepalese (0)	0	<0.01
Pakistani (0)	0	<0.01
Sri Lankan (0)	0	<0.01
Taiwanese (1)	1	0.01
Thai (2)	3	0.03
Vietnamese (0)	0	<0.01
Hawaii Native/Pacific Islander (2)	5	0.05
Not Hispanic (2)	3	0.03
Hispanic (0)	2	0.02
Fijian (0)	0	<0.01
Guamanian/Chamorro (0)	0	<0.01
Marshallese (0)	0	<0.01
Native Hawaiian (2)	3	0.03
Samoan (0)	0	<0.01
Tongan (0)	0	<0.01
White (10,381)	10,460	98.56
Not Hispanic (10,318)	10,387	97.87
Hispanic (63)	73	0.69

*Notes: † The Census 2010 population figure is used to calculate the percentages in the Hispanic Origin and Race categories. Ancestry percentages are based on the 2006-2010 American Community Survey population (not shown); ‡ Numbers in parentheses indicate the number of people reporting a single ancestry; * Numbers in parentheses indicate the number of persons reporting this race alone, not in combination with any other race; Please refer to the Explanation of Data for more information.*

Tippecanoe County

Population: 172,780

Ancestry	Population	%
Afghan (16)	16	0.01
African, Sub-Saharan (614)	719	0.43
African (250)	324	0.19
Cape Verdean (0)	0	<0.01
Ethiopian (72)	72	0.04
Ghanaian (0)	0	<0.01
Kenyan (62)	62	0.04
Liberian (32)	32	0.02
Nigerian (101)	101	0.06
Senegalese (0)	0	<0.01
Sierra Leonean (0)	0	<0.01
Somalian (0)	0	<0.01
South African (0)	0	<0.01
Sudanese (9)	9	0.01
Ugandan (0)	0	<0.01
Zimbabwean (0)	0	<0.01
Other Sub-Saharan African (88)	119	0.07
Albanian (90)	90	0.05
Alsatian (0)	0	<0.01
American (10,255)	10,255	6.08
Arab (281)	478	0.28
Arab (46)	92	0.05
Egyptian (65)	103	0.06
Iraqi (0)	0	<0.01
Jordanian (24)	24	0.01
Lebanese (59)	140	0.08
Moroccan (42)	42	0.02
Palestinian (0)	0	<0.01
Syrian (0)	21	0.01
Other Arab (45)	56	0.03
Armenian (20)	20	0.01
Assyrian/Chaldean/Syriac (8)	59	0.03
Australian (80)	96	0.06
Austrian (85)	310	0.18
Basque (0)	0	<0.01
Belgian (72)	356	0.21
Brazilian (149)	183	0.11
British (487)	1,072	0.64
Bulgarian (26)	51	0.03
Cajun (11)	22	0.01
Canadian (80)	254	0.15
Carpatho Rusyn (0)	0	<0.01
Celtic (0)	23	0.01
Croatian (10)	261	0.15
Cypriot (61)	61	0.04
Czech (220)	597	0.35
Czechoslovakian (17)	70	0.04
Danish (99)	444	0.26
Dutch (1,714)	5,265	3.12
Eastern European (47)	77	0.05
English (6,797)	18,157	10.77
Estonian (8)	8	<0.01
European (1,712)	1,938	1.15
Finnish (93)	174	0.10
French, ex. Basque (1,102)	5,699	3.38
French Canadian (139)	398	0.24
German (16,261)	46,342	27.48
German Russian (0)	0	<0.01
Greek (289)	482	0.29
Guyanese (0)	0	<0.01
Hungarian (257)	842	0.50
Icelander (0)	18	0.01
Iranian (42)	47	0.03
Irish (6,393)	23,518	13.95
Israeli (0)	0	<0.01
Italian (2,306)	6,187	3.67
Latvian (15)	33	0.02
Lithuanian (28)	244	0.14
Luxemburger (0)	58	0.03
Macedonian (9)	9	0.01
Maltese (0)	0	<0.01
New Zealander (94)	94	0.06
Northern European (111)	111	0.07
Norwegian (289)	1,212	0.72
Pennsylvania German (52)	135	0.08
Polish (1,698)	5,824	3.45
Portuguese (27)	105	0.06
Romanian (117)	229	0.14
Russian (567)	1,438	0.85
Scandinavian (32)	122	0.07
Scotch-Irish (1,018)	2,944	1.75
Scottish (1,400)	3,847	2.28
Serbian (55)	135	0.08
Slavic (0)	38	0.02
Slovak (72)	205	0.12
Slovene (23)	36	0.02
Soviet Union (0)	0	<0.01
Swedish (468)	2,125	1.26
Swiss (340)	1,084	0.64
Turkish (164)	164	0.10
Ukrainian (45)	227	0.13
Welsh (249)	1,360	0.81
West Indian, ex. Hispanic (80)	147	0.09
Bahamian (13)	13	0.01
Barbadian (0)	0	<0.01
Belizean (0)	0	<0.01
Bermudan (0)	0	<0.01
British West Indian (0)	8	<0.01
Dutch West Indian (0)	8	<0.01
Haitian (7)	17	0.01
Jamaican (22)	36	0.02
Trinidadian/Tobagonian (0)	13	0.01
U.S. Virgin Islander (8)	8	<0.01
West Indian (30)	30	0.02
Other West Indian (0)	14	0.01
Yugoslavian (40)	95	0.06

Hispanic Origin	Population	%
Hispanic or Latino (of any race)	12,947	7.49
Central American, ex. Mexican	587	0.34
Costa Rican	39	0.02
Guatemalan	143	0.08
Honduran	50	0.03
Nicaraguan	55	0.03
Panamanian	92	0.05
Salvadoran	208	0.12
Other Central American	0	<0.01
Cuban	163	0.09
Dominican Republic	68	0.04
Mexican	10,271	5.94
Puerto Rican	581	0.34
South American	575	0.33
Argentinean	106	0.06
Bolivian	33	0.02
Chilean	40	0.02
Colombian	209	0.12
Ecuadorian	64	0.04
Paraguayan	2	<0.01
Peruvian	71	0.04
Uruguayan	8	<0.01
Venezuelan	39	0.02
Other South American	3	<0.01
Other Hispanic or Latino	702	0.41

Race*	Population	%
African-American/Black (6,913)	8,421	4.87
Not Hispanic (6,731)	8,044	4.66
Hispanic (182)	377	0.22
American Indian/Alaska Native (453)	1,261	0.73
Not Hispanic (349)	1,064	0.62
Hispanic (104)	197	0.11
Alaska Athabascan *(Ala. Nat.)* (5)	5	<0.01
Aleut *(Alaska Native)* (1)	2	<0.01
Apache (4)	19	0.01
Arapaho (0)	0	<0.01
Blackfeet (7)	39	0.02
Canadian/French Am. Ind. (2)	5	<0.01
Central American Ind. (1)	1	<0.01
Cherokee (72)	337	0.20
Cheyenne (2)	8	<0.01
Chickasaw (4)	7	<0.01
Chippewa (20)	28	0.02
Choctaw (8)	21	0.01
Colville (0)	0	<0.01
Comanche (2)	4	<0.01
Cree (2)	2	<0.01
Creek (4)	18	0.01
Crow (2)	3	<0.01
Delaware (1)	5	<0.01
Hopi (1)	1	<0.01
Houma (6)	6	<0.01
Inupiat *(Alaska Native)* (3)	8	<0.01
Iroquois (10)	20	0.01
Kiowa (0)	0	<0.01
Lumbee (7)	9	0.01
Menominee (1)	1	<0.01
Mexican American Ind. (30)	36	0.02
Navajo (0)	5	<0.01
Osage (2)	5	<0.01
Ottawa (11)	14	0.01
Paiute (1)	1	<0.01
Pima (0)	0	<0.01
Potawatomi (3)	16	0.01
Pueblo (1)	3	<0.01
Puget Sound Salish (1)	1	<0.01
Seminole (3)	8	<0.01
Shoshone (0)	0	<0.01
Sioux (15)	36	0.02
South American Ind. (2)	12	0.01
Spanish American Ind. (0)	0	<0.01
Tlingit-Haida *(Alaska Native)* (0)	5	<0.01
Tohono O'Odham (0)	0	<0.01
Tsimshian *(Alaska Native)* (0)	0	<0.01
Ute (0)	1	<0.01
Yakama (0)	0	<0.01
Yaqui (1)	1	<0.01
Yuman (0)	1	<0.01
Yup'ik *(Alaska Native)* (1)	1	<0.01
Asian (10,730)	11,876	6.87
Not Hispanic (10,679)	11,745	6.80
Hispanic (51)	131	0.08
Bangladeshi (53)	60	0.03
Bhutanese (0)	0	<0.01
Burmese (13)	17	0.01
Cambodian (6)	10	0.01
Chinese, ex. Taiwanese (3,657)	3,941	2.28
Filipino (363)	611	0.35
Hmong (1)	1	<0.01
Indian (2,713)	2,858	1.65
Indonesian (85)	99	0.06
Japanese (425)	578	0.33
Korean (1,918)	2,090	1.21
Laotian (16)	29	0.02
Malaysian (149)	169	0.10
Nepalese (21)	22	0.01
Pakistani (198)	220	0.13
Sri Lankan (72)	73	0.04
Taiwanese (353)	405	0.23
Thai (117)	152	0.09
Vietnamese (302)	363	0.21
Hawaii Native/Pacific Islander (50)	187	0.11
Not Hispanic (41)	157	0.09
Hispanic (9)	30	0.02
Fijian (3)	3	<0.01
Guamanian/Chamorro (21)	33	0.02
Marshallese (0)	0	<0.01
Native Hawaiian (14)	55	0.03
Samoan (3)	23	0.01
Tongan (2)	3	<0.01
White (145,190)	148,641	86.03
Not Hispanic (138,855)	141,569	81.94
Hispanic (6,335)	7,072	4.09

*Notes: † The Census 2010 population figure is used to calculate the percentages in the Hispanic Origin and Race categories. Ancestry percentages are based on the 2006-2010 American Community Survey population (not shown); ‡ Numbers in parentheses indicate the number of people reporting a single ancestry; * Numbers in parentheses indicate the number of persons reporting this race alone, not in combination with any other race; Please refer to the Explanation of Data for more information.*

Tipton County

Population: 15,936

Ancestry	Population	%
Afghan (0)	0	<0.01
African, Sub-Saharan (0)	3	0.02
African (0)	3	0.02
Cape Verdean (0)	0	<0.01
Ethiopian (0)	0	<0.01
Ghanaian (0)	0	<0.01
Kenyan (0)	0	<0.01
Liberian (0)	0	<0.01
Nigerian (0)	0	<0.01
Senegalese (0)	0	<0.01
Sierra Leonean (0)	0	<0.01
Somalian (0)	0	<0.01
South African (0)	0	<0.01
Sudanese (0)	0	<0.01
Ugandan (0)	0	<0.01
Zimbabwean (0)	0	<0.01
Other Sub-Saharan African (0)	0	<0.01
Albanian (0)	9	0.06
Alsatian (0)	0	<0.01
American (2,345)	2,345	14.54
Arab (0)	16	0.10
Arab (0)	0	<0.01
Egyptian (0)	0	<0.01
Iraqi (0)	0	<0.01
Jordanian (0)	0	<0.01
Lebanese (0)	16	0.10
Moroccan (0)	0	<0.01
Palestinian (0)	0	<0.01
Syrian (0)	0	<0.01
Other Arab (0)	0	<0.01
Armenian (0)	0	<0.01
Assyrian/Chaldean/Syriac (0)	0	<0.01
Australian (0)	0	<0.01
Austrian (23)	23	0.14
Basque (0)	0	<0.01
Belgian (0)	0	<0.01
Brazilian (0)	0	<0.01
British (37)	72	0.45
Bulgarian (0)	0	<0.01
Cajun (0)	0	<0.01
Canadian (0)	3	0.02
Carpatho Rusyn (0)	0	<0.01
Celtic (0)	0	<0.01
Croatian (0)	5	0.03
Cypriot (0)	0	<0.01
Czech (0)	16	0.10
Czechoslovakian (0)	0	<0.01
Danish (18)	43	0.27
Dutch (159)	384	2.38
Eastern European (0)	0	<0.01
English (859)	1,988	12.32
Estonian (0)	0	<0.01
European (69)	78	0.48
Finnish (0)	0	<0.01
French, ex. Basque (70)	352	2.18
French Canadian (14)	42	0.26
German (2,062)	4,602	28.53
German Russian (0)	0	<0.01
Greek (41)	41	0.25
Guyanese (0)	0	<0.01
Hungarian (19)	134	0.83
Icelander (0)	0	<0.01
Iranian (0)	0	<0.01
Irish (366)	1,551	9.61
Israeli (0)	0	<0.01
Italian (31)	231	1.43
Latvian (0)	0	<0.01
Lithuanian (0)	0	<0.01
Luxemburger (0)	0	<0.01
Macedonian (0)	0	<0.01
Maltese (0)	0	<0.01
New Zealander (0)	0	<0.01
Northern European (0)	0	<0.01
Norwegian (12)	115	0.71
Pennsylvania German (2)	2	0.01
Polish (58)	202	1.25
Portuguese (10)	10	0.06
Romanian (0)	0	<0.01
Russian (21)	27	0.17
Scandinavian (0)	2	0.01
Scotch-Irish (158)	360	2.23
Scottish (116)	477	2.96
Serbian (0)	0	<0.01
Slavic (0)	0	<0.01
Slovak (23)	23	0.14
Slovene (0)	0	<0.01
Soviet Union (0)	0	<0.01
Swedish (20)	94	0.58
Swiss (18)	44	0.27
Turkish (0)	0	<0.01
Ukrainian (6)	6	0.04
Welsh (10)	13	0.08
West Indian, ex. Hispanic (0)	0	<0.01
Bahamian (0)	0	<0.01
Barbadian (0)	0	<0.01
Belizean (0)	0	<0.01
Bermudan (0)	0	<0.01
British West Indian (0)	0	<0.01
Dutch West Indian (0)	0	<0.01
Haitian (0)	0	<0.01
Jamaican (0)	0	<0.01
Trinidadian/Tobagonian (0)	0	<0.01
U.S. Virgin Islander (0)	0	<0.01
West Indian (0)	0	<0.01
Other West Indian (0)	0	<0.01
Yugoslavian (12)	12	0.07

Hispanic Origin	Population	%
Hispanic or Latino (of any race)	346	2.17
Central American, ex. Mexican	6	0.04
Costa Rican	0	<0.01
Guatemalan	1	0.01
Honduran	0	<0.01
Nicaraguan	0	<0.01
Panamanian	1	0.01
Salvadoran	4	0.03
Other Central American	0	<0.01
Cuban	5	0.03
Dominican Republic	0	<0.01
Mexican	280	1.76
Puerto Rican	12	0.08
South American	6	0.04
Argentinean	0	<0.01
Bolivian	0	<0.01
Chilean	0	<0.01
Colombian	2	0.01
Ecuadorian	0	<0.01
Paraguayan	0	<0.01
Peruvian	0	<0.01
Uruguayan	0	<0.01
Venezuelan	4	0.03
Other South American	0	<0.01
Other Hispanic or Latino	37	0.23

Race*	Population	%
African-American/Black (29)	77	0.48
Not Hispanic (28)	74	0.46
Hispanic (1)	3	0.02
American Indian/Alaska Native (23)	66	0.41
Not Hispanic (20)	57	0.36
Hispanic (3)	9	0.06
Alaska Athabascan *(Ala. Nat.)* (0)	0	<0.01
Aleut *(Alaska Native)* (0)	0	<0.01
Apache (0)	0	<0.01
Arapaho (0)	0	<0.01
Blackfeet (3)	4	0.03
Canadian/French Am. Ind. (0)	0	<0.01
Central American Ind. (0)	0	<0.01
Cherokee (0)	18	0.11
Cheyenne (0)	0	<0.01
Chickasaw (0)	0	<0.01
Chippewa (0)	0	<0.01
Choctaw (0)	0	<0.01
Colville (1)	1	0.01
Comanche (3)	5	0.03
Cree (0)	0	<0.01
Creek (0)	0	<0.01
Crow (0)	0	<0.01
Delaware (0)	0	<0.01
Hopi (0)	0	<0.01
Houma (0)	0	<0.01
Inupiat *(Alaska Native)* (0)	0	<0.01
Iroquois (0)	0	<0.01
Kiowa (0)	0	<0.01
Lumbee (0)	0	<0.01
Menominee (0)	0	<0.01
Mexican American Ind. (0)	0	<0.01
Navajo (0)	0	<0.01
Osage (0)	0	<0.01
Ottawa (1)	3	0.02
Paiute (0)	0	<0.01
Pima (0)	0	<0.01
Potawatomi (0)	0	<0.01
Pueblo (0)	0	<0.01
Puget Sound Salish (0)	0	<0.01
Seminole (0)	0	<0.01
Shoshone (0)	0	<0.01
Sioux (3)	3	0.02
South American Ind. (0)	0	<0.01
Spanish American Ind. (0)	0	<0.01
Tlingit-Haida *(Alaska Native)* (0)	0	<0.01
Tohono O'Odham (0)	0	<0.01
Tsimshian *(Alaska Native)* (0)	0	<0.01
Ute (0)	0	<0.01
Yakama (0)	0	<0.01
Yaqui (0)	0	<0.01
Yuman (0)	0	<0.01
Yup'ik *(Alaska Native)* (0)	0	<0.01
Asian (65)	88	0.55
Not Hispanic (64)	83	0.52
Hispanic (1)	5	0.03
Bangladeshi (0)	0	<0.01
Bhutanese (0)	0	<0.01
Burmese (0)	0	<0.01
Cambodian (0)	0	<0.01
Chinese, ex. Taiwanese (9)	12	0.08
Filipino (7)	14	0.09
Hmong (0)	0	<0.01
Indian (17)	24	0.15
Indonesian (0)	0	<0.01
Japanese (4)	7	0.04
Korean (10)	13	0.08
Laotian (0)	0	<0.01
Malaysian (0)	0	<0.01
Nepalese (0)	0	<0.01
Pakistani (1)	1	0.01
Sri Lankan (0)	0	<0.01
Taiwanese (1)	1	0.01
Thai (1)	2	0.01
Vietnamese (9)	9	0.06
Hawaii Native/Pacific Islander (5)	15	0.09
Not Hispanic (5)	15	0.09
Hispanic (0)	0	<0.01
Fijian (0)	0	<0.01
Guamanian/Chamorro (0)	0	<0.01
Marshallese (0)	0	<0.01
Native Hawaiian (4)	11	0.07
Samoan (0)	1	0.01
Tongan (0)	0	<0.01
White (15,551)	15,705	98.55
Not Hispanic (15,355)	15,469	97.07
Hispanic (196)	236	1.48

*Notes: † The Census 2010 population figure is used to calculate the percentages in the Hispanic Origin and Race categories. Ancestry percentages are based on the 2006-2010 American Community Survey population (not shown); ‡ Numbers in parentheses indicate the number of people reporting a single ancestry; * Numbers in parentheses indicate the number of persons reporting this race alone, not in combination with any other race; Please refer to the Explanation of Data for more information.*

Union County

Population: 7,516

Ancestry	Population	%
Afghan (0)	0	<0.01
African, Sub-Saharan (0)	0	<0.01
African (0)	0	<0.01
Cape Verdean (0)	0	<0.01
Ethiopian (0)	0	<0.01
Ghanaian (0)	0	<0.01
Kenyan (0)	0	<0.01
Liberian (0)	0	<0.01
Nigerian (0)	0	<0.01
Senegalese (0)	0	<0.01
Sierra Leonean (0)	0	<0.01
Somalian (0)	0	<0.01
South African (0)	0	<0.01
Sudanese (0)	0	<0.01
Ugandan (0)	0	<0.01
Zimbabwean (0)	0	<0.01
Other Sub-Saharan African (0)	0	<0.01
Albanian (0)	0	<0.01
Alsatian (0)	0	<0.01
American (865)	865	11.59
Arab (0)	0	<0.01
Arab (0)	0	<0.01
Egyptian (0)	0	<0.01
Iraqi (0)	0	<0.01
Jordanian (0)	0	<0.01
Lebanese (0)	0	<0.01
Moroccan (0)	0	<0.01
Palestinian (0)	0	<0.01
Syrian (0)	0	<0.01
Other Arab (0)	0	<0.01
Armenian (0)	0	<0.01
Assyrian/Chaldean/Syriac (0)	0	<0.01
Australian (0)	0	<0.01
Austrian (0)	9	0.12
Basque (0)	0	<0.01
Belgian (0)	0	<0.01
Brazilian (0)	0	<0.01
British (0)	18	0.24
Bulgarian (0)	0	<0.01
Cajun (0)	0	<0.01
Canadian (0)	0	<0.01
Carpatho Rusyn (0)	0	<0.01
Celtic (0)	0	<0.01
Croatian (0)	0	<0.01
Cypriot (0)	0	<0.01
Czech (0)	0	<0.01
Czechoslovakian (0)	0	<0.01
Danish (0)	0	<0.01
Dutch (68)	197	2.64
Eastern European (0)	0	<0.01
English (400)	900	12.06
Estonian (0)	0	<0.01
European (25)	25	0.33
Finnish (0)	14	0.19
French, ex. Basque (4)	102	1.37
French Canadian (15)	19	0.25
German (917)	1,954	26.18
German Russian (0)	0	<0.01
Greek (0)	0	<0.01
Guyanese (0)	0	<0.01
Hungarian (0)	0	<0.01
Icelander (0)	0	<0.01
Iranian (0)	0	<0.01
Irish (391)	1,197	16.04
Israeli (0)	0	<0.01
Italian (63)	256	3.43
Latvian (0)	0	<0.01
Lithuanian (0)	0	<0.01
Luxemburger (0)	0	<0.01
Macedonian (0)	0	<0.01
Maltese (0)	0	<0.01
New Zealander (0)	0	<0.01
Northern European (0)	0	<0.01
Norwegian (3)	12	0.16
Pennsylvania German (0)	0	<0.01
Polish (37)	62	0.83
Portuguese (0)	0	<0.01
Romanian (0)	12	0.16
Russian (0)	18	0.24
Scandinavian (5)	9	0.12
Scotch-Irish (90)	137	1.84
Scottish (52)	173	2.32
Serbian (0)	0	<0.01
Slavic (0)	0	<0.01
Slovak (0)	13	0.17
Slovene (8)	8	0.11
Soviet Union (0)	0	<0.01
Swedish (0)	3	0.04
Swiss (12)	42	0.56
Turkish (0)	0	<0.01
Ukrainian (0)	0	<0.01
Welsh (33)	36	0.48
West Indian, ex. Hispanic (0)	0	<0.01
Bahamian (0)	0	<0.01
Barbadian (0)	0	<0.01
Belizean (0)	0	<0.01
Bermudan (0)	0	<0.01
British West Indian (0)	0	<0.01
Dutch West Indian (0)	0	<0.01
Haitian (0)	0	<0.01
Jamaican (0)	0	<0.01
Trinidadian/Tobagonian (0)	0	<0.01
U.S. Virgin Islander (0)	0	<0.01
West Indian (0)	0	<0.01
Other West Indian (0)	0	<0.01
Yugoslavian (0)	0	<0.01

Hispanic Origin	Population	%
Hispanic or Latino (of any race)	82	1.09
Central American, ex. Mexican	6	0.08
Costa Rican	0	<0.01
Guatemalan	5	0.07
Honduran	0	<0.01
Nicaraguan	0	<0.01
Panamanian	1	0.01
Salvadoran	0	<0.01
Other Central American	0	<0.01
Cuban	0	<0.01
Dominican Republic	6	0.08
Mexican	51	0.68
Puerto Rican	4	0.05
South American	1	0.01
Argentinean	0	<0.01
Bolivian	0	<0.01
Chilean	0	<0.01
Colombian	1	0.01
Ecuadorian	0	<0.01
Paraguayan	0	<0.01
Peruvian	0	<0.01
Uruguayan	0	<0.01
Venezuelan	0	<0.01
Other South American	0	<0.01
Other Hispanic or Latino	14	0.19

Race*	Population	%
African-American/Black (33)	47	0.63
Not Hispanic (33)	47	0.63
Hispanic (0)	0	<0.01
American Indian/Alaska Native (23)	59	0.78
Not Hispanic (19)	53	0.71
Hispanic (4)	6	0.08
Alaska Athabascan *(Ala. Nat.)* (0)	0	<0.01
Aleut *(Alaska Native)* (0)	0	<0.01
Apache (0)	1	0.01
Arapaho (0)	0	<0.01
Blackfeet (1)	4	0.05
Canadian/French Am. Ind. (0)	0	<0.01
Central American Ind. (0)	0	<0.01
Cherokee (3)	22	0.29
Cheyenne (0)	0	<0.01
Chickasaw (0)	0	<0.01
Chippewa (0)	0	<0.01
Choctaw (5)	7	0.09
Colville (0)	0	<0.01
Comanche (0)	1	0.01
Cree (0)	0	<0.01
Creek (0)	0	<0.01
Crow (0)	0	<0.01
Delaware (0)	1	0.01
Hopi (0)	0	<0.01
Houma (0)	0	<0.01
Inupiat *(Alaska Native)* (0)	0	<0.01
Iroquois (0)	0	<0.01
Kiowa (0)	0	<0.01
Lumbee (0)	0	<0.01
Menominee (0)	0	<0.01
Mexican American Ind. (1)	1	0.01
Navajo (3)	3	0.04
Osage (0)	0	<0.01
Ottawa (0)	0	<0.01
Paiute (0)	0	<0.01
Pima (0)	0	<0.01
Potawatomi (0)	0	<0.01
Pueblo (0)	0	<0.01
Puget Sound Salish (0)	0	<0.01
Seminole (0)	0	<0.01
Shoshone (0)	0	<0.01
Sioux (0)	1	0.01
South American Ind. (0)	0	<0.01
Spanish American Ind. (0)	0	<0.01
Tlingit-Haida *(Alaska Native)* (0)	0	<0.01
Tohono O'Odham (0)	0	<0.01
Tsimshian *(Alaska Native)* (0)	0	<0.01
Ute (0)	0	<0.01
Yakama (0)	0	<0.01
Yaqui (0)	1	0.01
Yuman (0)	0	<0.01
Yup'ik *(Alaska Native)* (0)	0	<0.01
Asian (19)	40	0.53
Not Hispanic (19)	40	0.53
Hispanic (0)	0	<0.01
Bangladeshi (0)	0	<0.01
Bhutanese (0)	0	<0.01
Burmese (0)	0	<0.01
Cambodian (0)	0	<0.01
Chinese, ex. Taiwanese (1)	2	0.03
Filipino (6)	22	0.29
Hmong (0)	0	<0.01
Indian (7)	9	0.12
Indonesian (0)	0	<0.01
Japanese (1)	3	0.04
Korean (2)	2	0.03
Laotian (0)	0	<0.01
Malaysian (0)	0	<0.01
Nepalese (0)	0	<0.01
Pakistani (0)	0	<0.01
Sri Lankan (0)	0	<0.01
Taiwanese (0)	0	<0.01
Thai (0)	0	<0.01
Vietnamese (0)	2	0.03
Hawaii Native/Pacific Islander (6)	13	0.17
Not Hispanic (6)	13	0.17
Hispanic (0)	0	<0.01
Fijian (0)	0	<0.01
Guamanian/Chamorro (0)	0	<0.01
Marshallese (0)	0	<0.01
Native Hawaiian (6)	12	0.16
Samoan (0)	0	<0.01
Tongan (0)	0	<0.01
White (7,331)	7,408	98.56
Not Hispanic (7,280)	7,352	97.82
Hispanic (51)	56	0.75

*Notes: † The Census 2010 population figure is used to calculate the percentages in the Hispanic Origin and Race categories. Ancestry percentages are based on the 2006-2010 American Community Survey population (not shown); ‡ Numbers in parentheses indicate the number of people reporting a single ancestry; * Numbers in parentheses indicate the number of persons reporting this race alone, not in combination with any other race; Please refer to the Explanation of Data for more information.*

Vanderburgh County

Population: 179,703

Ancestry	Population	%
Afghan (0)	0	<0.01
African, Sub-Saharan (169)	291	0.16
African (101)	180	0.10
Cape Verdean (0)	0	<0.01
Ethiopian (38)	72	0.04
Ghanaian (0)	0	<0.01
Kenyan (0)	0	<0.01
Liberian (0)	0	<0.01
Nigerian (8)	17	0.01
Senegalese (0)	0	<0.01
Sierra Leonean (0)	0	<0.01
Somalian (0)	0	<0.01
South African (0)	0	<0.01
Sudanese (0)	0	<0.01
Ugandan (14)	14	0.01
Zimbabwean (0)	0	<0.01
Other Sub-Saharan African (8)	8	<0.01
Albanian (0)	0	<0.01
Alsatian (0)	13	0.01
American (32,701)	32,701	18.34
Arab (116)	189	0.11
Arab (20)	55	0.03
Egyptian (0)	0	<0.01
Iraqi (16)	16	0.01
Jordanian (15)	15	0.01
Lebanese (24)	51	0.03
Moroccan (0)	0	<0.01
Palestinian (30)	30	0.02
Syrian (0)	11	0.01
Other Arab (11)	11	0.01
Armenian (70)	78	0.04
Assyrian/Chaldean/Syriac (0)	0	<0.01
Australian (39)	39	0.02
Austrian (15)	189	0.11
Basque (0)	0	<0.01
Belgian (0)	75	0.04
Brazilian (62)	62	0.03
British (377)	676	0.38
Bulgarian (12)	24	0.01
Cajun (0)	12	0.01
Canadian (150)	201	0.11
Carpatho Rusyn (0)	0	<0.01
Celtic (15)	38	0.02
Croatian (38)	95	0.05
Cypriot (0)	0	<0.01
Czech (55)	306	0.17
Czechoslovakian (84)	202	0.11
Danish (21)	217	0.12
Dutch (662)	2,816	1.58
Eastern European (13)	27	0.02
English (6,870)	16,696	9.36
Estonian (0)	3	<0.01
European (1,067)	1,215	0.68
Finnish (31)	93	0.05
French, ex. Basque (1,257)	4,630	2.60
French Canadian (174)	323	0.18
German (32,284)	57,653	32.34
German Russian (0)	0	<0.01
Greek (136)	296	0.17
Guyanese (0)	49	0.03
Hungarian (56)	284	0.16
Icelander (19)	19	0.01
Iranian (20)	20	0.01
Irish (5,702)	20,941	11.74
Israeli (0)	0	<0.01
Italian (928)	3,274	1.84
Latvian (12)	12	0.01
Lithuanian (23)	187	0.10
Luxemburger (0)	0	<0.01
Macedonian (0)	0	<0.01
Maltese (0)	0	<0.01
New Zealander (0)	0	<0.01
Northern European (40)	57	0.03
Norwegian (307)	903	0.51
Pennsylvania German (86)	111	0.06
Polish (868)	2,648	1.49
Portuguese (89)	121	0.07
Romanian (0)	10	0.01
Russian (347)	736	0.41
Scandinavian (19)	29	0.02
Scotch-Irish (971)	2,757	1.55
Scottish (1,164)	2,907	1.63
Serbian (27)	27	0.02
Slavic (0)	11	0.01
Slovak (63)	221	0.12
Slovene (0)	0	<0.01
Soviet Union (0)	0	<0.01
Swedish (324)	747	0.42
Swiss (44)	455	0.26
Turkish (11)	25	0.01
Ukrainian (215)	304	0.17
Welsh (142)	658	0.37
West Indian, ex. Hispanic (63)	111	0.06
Bahamian (0)	0	<0.01
Barbadian (0)	0	<0.01
Belizean (9)	9	0.01
Bermudan (0)	0	<0.01
British West Indian (0)	0	<0.01
Dutch West Indian (0)	0	<0.01
Haitian (31)	58	0.03
Jamaican (23)	44	0.02
Trinidadian/Tobagonian (0)	0	<0.01
U.S. Virgin Islander (0)	0	<0.01
West Indian (0)	0	<0.01
Other West Indian (0)	0	<0.01
Yugoslavian (0)	24	0.01

Hispanic Origin	Population	%
Hispanic or Latino (of any race)	3,873	2.16
Central American, ex. Mexican	299	0.17
Costa Rican	20	0.01
Guatemalan	66	0.04
Honduran	49	0.03
Nicaraguan	49	0.03
Panamanian	31	0.02
Salvadoran	76	0.04
Other Central American	8	<0.01
Cuban	99	0.06
Dominican Republic	29	0.02
Mexican	2,521	1.40
Puerto Rican	328	0.18
South American	173	0.10
Argentinean	9	0.01
Bolivian	18	0.01
Chilean	14	0.01
Colombian	42	0.02
Ecuadorian	10	0.01
Paraguayan	2	<0.01
Peruvian	47	0.03
Uruguayan	1	<0.01
Venezuelan	29	0.02
Other South American	1	<0.01
Other Hispanic or Latino	424	0.24

Race*	Population	%
African-American/Black (16,347)	19,012	10.58
Not Hispanic (16,228)	18,759	10.44
Hispanic (119)	253	0.14
American Indian/Alaska Native (399)	1,168	0.65
Not Hispanic (345)	1,060	0.59
Hispanic (54)	108	0.06
Alaska Athabascan *(Ala. Nat.)* (0)	1	<0.01
Aleut *(Alaska Native)* (0)	0	<0.01
Apache (6)	25	0.01
Arapaho (1)	1	<0.01
Blackfeet (8)	57	0.03
Canadian/French Am. Ind. (1)	2	<0.01
Central American Ind. (2)	2	<0.01
Cherokee (86)	364	0.20
Cheyenne (4)	11	0.01
Chickasaw (1)	4	<0.01
Chippewa (12)	22	0.01
Choctaw (7)	20	0.01
Colville (1)	1	<0.01
Comanche (0)	2	<0.01
Cree (0)	2	<0.01
Creek (1)	1	<0.01
Crow (0)	2	<0.01
Delaware (4)	6	<0.01
Hopi (0)	1	<0.01
Houma (2)	4	<0.01
Inupiat *(Alaska Native)* (0)	1	<0.01
Iroquois (4)	16	0.01
Kiowa (0)	1	<0.01
Lumbee (5)	16	0.01
Menominee (0)	0	<0.01
Mexican American Ind. (8)	10	0.01
Navajo (5)	13	0.01
Osage (2)	2	<0.01
Ottawa (0)	0	<0.01
Paiute (0)	0	<0.01
Pima (0)	0	<0.01
Potawatomi (0)	3	<0.01
Pueblo (1)	3	<0.01
Puget Sound Salish (0)	0	<0.01
Seminole (1)	3	<0.01
Shoshone (0)	6	<0.01
Sioux (33)	65	0.04
South American Ind. (3)	6	<0.01
Spanish American Ind. (1)	1	<0.01
Tlingit-Haida *(Alaska Native)* (1)	1	<0.01
Tohono O'Odham (0)	0	<0.01
Tsimshian *(Alaska Native)* (0)	0	<0.01
Ute (0)	0	<0.01
Yakama (0)	0	<0.01
Yaqui (0)	1	<0.01
Yuman (0)	0	<0.01
Yup'ik *(Alaska Native)* (0)	0	<0.01
Asian (2,003)	2,666	1.48
Not Hispanic (1,986)	2,616	1.46
Hispanic (17)	50	0.03
Bangladeshi (7)	7	<0.01
Bhutanese (0)	0	<0.01
Burmese (3)	5	<0.01
Cambodian (4)	9	0.01
Chinese, ex. Taiwanese (482)	573	0.32
Filipino (246)	396	0.22
Hmong (0)	0	<0.01
Indian (484)	566	0.31
Indonesian (8)	15	0.01
Japanese (171)	266	0.15
Korean (184)	290	0.16
Laotian (5)	13	0.01
Malaysian (15)	19	0.01
Nepalese (15)	26	0.01
Pakistani (5)	12	0.01
Sri Lankan (1)	3	<0.01
Taiwanese (8)	12	0.01
Thai (32)	62	0.03
Vietnamese (277)	330	0.18
Hawaii Native/Pacific Islander (104)	237	0.13
Not Hispanic (89)	201	0.11
Hispanic (15)	36	0.02
Fijian (0)	0	<0.01
Guamanian/Chamorro (24)	40	0.02
Marshallese (51)	56	0.03
Native Hawaiian (14)	71	0.04
Samoan (5)	24	0.01
Tongan (0)	0	<0.01
White (154,882)	158,732	88.33
Not Hispanic (153,080)	156,600	87.14
Hispanic (1,802)	2,132	1.19

*Notes: † The Census 2010 population figure is used to calculate the percentages in the Hispanic Origin and Race categories. Ancestry percentages are based on the 2006-2010 American Community Survey population (not shown); ‡ Numbers in parentheses indicate the number of people reporting a single ancestry; * Numbers in parentheses indicate the number of persons reporting this race alone, not in combination with any other race; Please refer to the Explanation of Data for more information.*

Vermillion County

Population: 16,212

Ancestry	Population	%
Afghan (0)	0	<0.01
African, Sub-Saharan (0)	0	<0.01
African (0)	0	<0.01
Cape Verdean (0)	0	<0.01
Ethiopian (0)	0	<0.01
Ghanaian (0)	0	<0.01
Kenyan (0)	0	<0.01
Liberian (0)	0	<0.01
Nigerian (0)	0	<0.01
Senegalese (0)	0	<0.01
Sierra Leonean (0)	0	<0.01
Somalian (0)	0	<0.01
South African (0)	0	<0.01
Sudanese (0)	0	<0.01
Ugandan (0)	0	<0.01
Zimbabwean (0)	0	<0.01
Other Sub-Saharan African (0)	0	<0.01
Albanian (0)	0	<0.01
Alsatian (0)	0	<0.01
American (4,058)	4,058	24.73
Arab (12)	58	0.35
Arab (0)	0	<0.01
Egyptian (0)	0	<0.01
Iraqi (0)	0	<0.01
Jordanian (0)	0	<0.01
Lebanese (0)	0	<0.01
Moroccan (0)	0	<0.01
Palestinian (0)	0	<0.01
Syrian (0)	46	0.28
Other Arab (12)	12	0.07
Armenian (0)	0	<0.01
Assyrian/Chaldean/Syriac (0)	0	<0.01
Australian (0)	0	<0.01
Austrian (2)	7	0.04
Basque (0)	0	<0.01
Belgian (17)	58	0.35
Brazilian (0)	0	<0.01
British (27)	66	0.40
Bulgarian (0)	0	<0.01
Cajun (0)	0	<0.01
Canadian (5)	5	0.03
Carpatho Rusyn (0)	0	<0.01
Celtic (0)	0	<0.01
Croatian (0)	0	<0.01
Cypriot (0)	0	<0.01
Czech (19)	82	0.50
Czechoslovakian (0)	25	0.15
Danish (3)	12	0.07
Dutch (21)	429	2.61
Eastern European (0)	0	<0.01
English (836)	1,604	9.77
Estonian (0)	0	<0.01
European (232)	240	1.46
Finnish (0)	12	0.07
French, ex. Basque (106)	456	2.78
French Canadian (9)	16	0.10
German (1,506)	3,203	19.52
German Russian (0)	0	<0.01
Greek (16)	53	0.32
Guyanese (0)	0	<0.01
Hungarian (70)	141	0.86
Icelander (0)	0	<0.01
Iranian (0)	0	<0.01
Irish (546)	1,802	10.98
Israeli (0)	0	<0.01
Italian (746)	1,301	7.93
Latvian (0)	0	<0.01
Lithuanian (25)	67	0.41
Luxemburger (0)	2	0.01
Macedonian (0)	0	<0.01
Maltese (0)	0	<0.01
New Zealander (0)	0	<0.01
Northern European (0)	0	<0.01
Norwegian (13)	45	0.27
Pennsylvania German (5)	8	0.05
Polish (61)	218	1.33
Portuguese (26)	37	0.23
Romanian (17)	21	0.13
Russian (0)	14	0.09
Scandinavian (11)	11	0.07
Scotch-Irish (122)	234	1.43
Scottish (105)	382	2.33
Serbian (27)	90	0.55
Slavic (10)	10	0.06
Slovak (2)	2	0.01
Slovene (3)	3	0.02
Soviet Union (0)	0	<0.01
Swedish (28)	187	1.14
Swiss (3)	20	0.12
Turkish (0)	16	0.10
Ukrainian (0)	0	<0.01
Welsh (27)	208	1.27
West Indian, ex. Hispanic (0)	0	<0.01
Bahamian (0)	0	<0.01
Barbadian (0)	0	<0.01
Belizean (0)	0	<0.01
Bermudan (0)	0	<0.01
British West Indian (0)	0	<0.01
Dutch West Indian (0)	0	<0.01
Haitian (0)	0	<0.01
Jamaican (0)	0	<0.01
Trinidadian/Tobagonian (0)	0	<0.01
U.S. Virgin Islander (0)	0	<0.01
West Indian (0)	0	<0.01
Other West Indian (0)	0	<0.01
Yugoslavian (0)	56	0.34

Hispanic Origin	Population	%
Hispanic or Latino (of any race)	130	0.80
Central American, ex. Mexican	3	0.02
Costa Rican	0	<0.01
Guatemalan	1	0.01
Honduran	0	<0.01
Nicaraguan	0	<0.01
Panamanian	2	0.01
Salvadoran	0	<0.01
Other Central American	0	<0.01
Cuban	3	0.02
Dominican Republic	0	<0.01
Mexican	83	0.51
Puerto Rican	19	0.12
South American	2	0.01
Argentinean	1	0.01
Bolivian	0	<0.01
Chilean	0	<0.01
Colombian	0	<0.01
Ecuadorian	0	<0.01
Paraguayan	0	<0.01
Peruvian	0	<0.01
Uruguayan	0	<0.01
Venezuelan	0	<0.01
Other South American	1	0.01
Other Hispanic or Latino	20	0.12

Race*	Population	%
African-American/Black (24)	68	0.42
Not Hispanic (21)	63	0.39
Hispanic (3)	5	0.03
American Indian/Alaska Native (37)	92	0.57
Not Hispanic (29)	82	0.51
Hispanic (8)	10	0.06
Alaska Athabascan *(Ala. Nat.)* (0)	0	<0.01
Aleut *(Alaska Native)* (0)	0	<0.01
Apache (1)	3	0.02
Arapaho (0)	0	<0.01
Blackfeet (0)	2	0.01
Canadian/French Am. Ind. (0)	0	<0.01
Central American Ind. (0)	0	<0.01
Cherokee (12)	35	0.22
Cheyenne (0)	1	0.01
Chickasaw (0)	0	<0.01
Chippewa (1)	2	0.01
Choctaw (0)	4	0.02
Colville (0)	0	<0.01
Comanche (0)	0	<0.01
Cree (0)	0	<0.01
Creek (0)	0	<0.01
Crow (0)	0	<0.01
Delaware (0)	0	<0.01
Hopi (0)	0	<0.01
Houma (0)	0	<0.01
Inupiat *(Alaska Native)* (0)	0	<0.01
Iroquois (0)	0	<0.01
Kiowa (0)	0	<0.01
Lumbee (0)	0	<0.01
Menominee (0)	0	<0.01
Mexican American Ind. (0)	0	<0.01
Navajo (2)	2	0.01
Osage (1)	1	0.01
Ottawa (0)	0	<0.01
Paiute (0)	0	<0.01
Pima (0)	0	<0.01
Potawatomi (0)	1	0.01
Pueblo (0)	0	<0.01
Puget Sound Salish (0)	0	<0.01
Seminole (0)	0	<0.01
Shoshone (0)	0	<0.01
Sioux (2)	3	0.02
South American Ind. (0)	0	<0.01
Spanish American Ind. (0)	0	<0.01
Tlingit-Haida *(Alaska Native)* (0)	0	<0.01
Tohono O'Odham (0)	0	<0.01
Tsimshian *(Alaska Native)* (0)	0	<0.01
Ute (0)	0	<0.01
Yakama (0)	0	<0.01
Yaqui (0)	0	<0.01
Yuman (0)	0	<0.01
Yup'ik *(Alaska Native)* (0)	0	<0.01
Asian (31)	57	0.35
Not Hispanic (31)	57	0.35
Hispanic (0)	0	<0.01
Bangladeshi (0)	0	<0.01
Bhutanese (0)	0	<0.01
Burmese (0)	0	<0.01
Cambodian (0)	0	<0.01
Chinese, ex. Taiwanese (10)	10	0.06
Filipino (5)	18	0.11
Hmong (0)	0	<0.01
Indian (2)	5	0.03
Indonesian (0)	0	<0.01
Japanese (2)	10	0.06
Korean (3)	8	0.05
Laotian (0)	0	<0.01
Malaysian (0)	0	<0.01
Nepalese (0)	0	<0.01
Pakistani (0)	0	<0.01
Sri Lankan (0)	0	<0.01
Taiwanese (0)	0	<0.01
Thai (4)	5	0.03
Vietnamese (2)	2	0.01
Hawaii Native/Pacific Islander (5)	16	0.10
Not Hispanic (5)	16	0.10
Hispanic (0)	0	<0.01
Fijian (0)	0	<0.01
Guamanian/Chamorro (1)	3	0.02
Marshallese (0)	0	<0.01
Native Hawaiian (2)	7	0.04
Samoan (1)	3	0.02
Tongan (0)	0	<0.01
White (15,932)	16,064	99.09
Not Hispanic (15,862)	15,985	98.60
Hispanic (70)	79	0.49

*Notes: † The Census 2010 population figure is used to calculate the percentages in the Hispanic Origin and Race categories. Ancestry percentages are based on the 2006-2010 American Community Survey population (not shown); ‡ Numbers in parentheses indicate the number of people reporting a single ancestry; * Numbers in parentheses indicate the number of persons reporting this race alone, not in combination with any other race; Please refer to the Explanation of Data for more information.*

Vigo County

Population: 107,848

Ancestry	Population	%
Afghan (0)	0	<0.01
African, Sub-Saharan (879)	1,024	0.96
African (757)	902	0.84
Cape Verdean (0)	0	<0.01
Ethiopian (0)	0	<0.01
Ghanaian (0)	0	<0.01
Kenyan (0)	0	<0.01
Liberian (0)	0	<0.01
Nigerian (100)	100	0.09
Senegalese (0)	0	<0.01
Sierra Leonean (0)	0	<0.01
Somalian (6)	6	0.01
South African (0)	0	<0.01
Sudanese (0)	0	<0.01
Ugandan (16)	16	0.01
Zimbabwean (0)	0	<0.01
Other Sub-Saharan African (0)	0	<0.01
Albanian (0)	0	<0.01
Alsatian (0)	0	<0.01
American (21,645)	21,645	20.20
Arab (560)	632	0.59
Arab (127)	136	0.13
Egyptian (0)	0	<0.01
Iraqi (0)	0	<0.01
Jordanian (6)	6	0.01
Lebanese (75)	75	0.07
Moroccan (0)	0	<0.01
Palestinian (0)	0	<0.01
Syrian (100)	163	0.15
Other Arab (252)	252	0.24
Armenian (0)	0	<0.01
Assyrian/Chaldean/Syriac (0)	0	<0.01
Australian (0)	0	<0.01
Austrian (36)	190	0.18
Basque (0)	0	<0.01
Belgian (35)	112	0.10
Brazilian (0)	0	<0.01
British (326)	551	0.51
Bulgarian (22)	64	0.06
Cajun (0)	0	<0.01
Canadian (71)	100	0.09
Carpatho Rusyn (0)	0	<0.01
Celtic (0)	0	<0.01
Croatian (51)	85	0.08
Cypriot (0)	0	<0.01
Czech (106)	382	0.36
Czechoslovakian (69)	89	0.08
Danish (41)	81	0.08
Dutch (544)	2,378	2.22
Eastern European (36)	36	0.03
English (4,354)	11,058	10.32
Estonian (0)	53	0.05
European (935)	1,075	1.00
Finnish (32)	56	0.05
French, ex. Basque (963)	3,480	3.25
French Canadian (75)	160	0.15
German (9,794)	24,242	22.62
German Russian (0)	0	<0.01
Greek (40)	92	0.09
Guyanese (0)	0	<0.01
Hungarian (178)	708	0.66
Icelander (0)	13	0.01
Iranian (0)	2	<0.01
Irish (3,683)	13,045	12.17
Israeli (13)	13	0.01
Italian (1,585)	3,352	3.13
Latvian (69)	118	0.11
Lithuanian (59)	227	0.21
Luxemburger (0)	8	0.01
Macedonian (0)	0	<0.01
Maltese (0)	0	<0.01
New Zealander (0)	0	<0.01
Northern European (8)	11	0.01
Norwegian (218)	513	0.48
Pennsylvania German (14)	51	0.05
Polish (516)	1,905	1.78
Portuguese (0)	12	0.01
Romanian (235)	320	0.30
Russian (35)	301	0.28
Scandinavian (41)	50	0.05
Scotch-Irish (618)	1,739	1.62
Scottish (759)	2,295	2.14
Serbian (24)	98	0.09
Slavic (0)	43	0.04
Slovak (68)	247	0.23
Slovene (37)	37	0.03
Soviet Union (0)	0	<0.01
Swedish (232)	782	0.73
Swiss (65)	246	0.23
Turkish (8)	23	0.02
Ukrainian (133)	133	0.12
Welsh (220)	1,081	1.01
West Indian, ex. Hispanic (27)	32	0.03
Bahamian (0)	0	<0.01
Barbadian (0)	0	<0.01
Belizean (0)	0	<0.01
Bermudan (0)	0	<0.01
British West Indian (0)	0	<0.01
Dutch West Indian (0)	5	<0.01
Haitian (27)	27	0.03
Jamaican (0)	0	<0.01
Trinidadian/Tobagonian (0)	0	<0.01
U.S. Virgin Islander (0)	0	<0.01
West Indian (0)	0	<0.01
Other West Indian (0)	0	<0.01
Yugoslavian (27)	55	0.05

Hispanic Origin	Population	%
Hispanic or Latino (of any race)	2,469	2.29
Central American, ex. Mexican	79	0.07
Costa Rican	5	<0.01
Guatemalan	25	0.02
Honduran	23	0.02
Nicaraguan	2	<0.01
Panamanian	11	0.01
Salvadoran	13	0.01
Other Central American	0	<0.01
Cuban	58	0.05
Dominican Republic	16	0.01
Mexican	1,881	1.74
Puerto Rican	188	0.17
South American	92	0.09
Argentinean	15	0.01
Bolivian	6	0.01
Chilean	8	0.01
Colombian	33	0.03
Ecuadorian	6	0.01
Paraguayan	3	<0.01
Peruvian	8	0.01
Uruguayan	0	<0.01
Venezuelan	13	0.01
Other South American	0	<0.01
Other Hispanic or Latino	155	0.14

Race*	Population	%
African-American/Black (7,437)	8,887	8.24
Not Hispanic (7,371)	8,749	8.11
Hispanic (66)	138	0.13
American Indian/Alaska Native (364)	948	0.88
Not Hispanic (321)	866	0.80
Hispanic (43)	82	0.08
Alaska Athabascan *(Ala. Nat.)* (2)	2	<0.01
Aleut *(Alaska Native)* (0)	0	<0.01
Apache (3)	21	0.02
Arapaho (0)	0	<0.01
Blackfeet (3)	39	0.04
Canadian/French Am. Ind. (1)	2	<0.01
Central American Ind. (1)	1	<0.01
Cherokee (52)	233	0.22
Cheyenne (1)	7	0.01
Chickasaw (0)	4	<0.01
Chippewa (9)	14	0.01
Choctaw (3)	9	0.01
Colville (0)	0	<0.01
Comanche (1)	4	<0.01
Cree (8)	9	0.01
Creek (7)	8	0.01
Crow (0)	1	<0.01
Delaware (2)	3	<0.01
Hopi (2)	2	<0.01
Houma (2)	2	<0.01
Inupiat *(Alaska Native)* (0)	0	<0.01
Iroquois (2)	9	0.01
Kiowa (2)	2	<0.01
Lumbee (0)	2	<0.01
Menominee (2)	2	<0.01
Mexican American Ind. (17)	25	0.02
Navajo (1)	7	0.01
Osage (4)	4	<0.01
Ottawa (1)	1	<0.01
Paiute (0)	0	<0.01
Pima (0)	0	<0.01
Potawatomi (13)	15	0.01
Pueblo (0)	0	<0.01
Puget Sound Salish (0)	0	<0.01
Seminole (0)	2	<0.01
Shoshone (1)	2	<0.01
Sioux (18)	43	0.04
South American Ind. (1)	1	<0.01
Spanish American Ind. (0)	0	<0.01
Tlingit-Haida *(Alaska Native)* (0)	1	<0.01
Tohono O'Odham (0)	0	<0.01
Tsimshian *(Alaska Native)* (0)	0	<0.01
Ute (1)	1	<0.01
Yakama (0)	0	<0.01
Yaqui (0)	3	<0.01
Yuman (2)	2	<0.01
Yup'ik *(Alaska Native)* (0)	0	<0.01
Asian (1,781)	2,173	2.01
Not Hispanic (1,777)	2,159	2.00
Hispanic (4)	14	0.01
Bangladeshi (12)	12	0.01
Bhutanese (0)	0	<0.01
Burmese (0)	0	<0.01
Cambodian (1)	1	<0.01
Chinese, ex. Taiwanese (346)	395	0.37
Filipino (277)	368	0.34
Hmong (6)	8	0.01
Indian (553)	605	0.56
Indonesian (7)	10	0.01
Japanese (123)	204	0.19
Korean (182)	230	0.21
Laotian (0)	5	<0.01
Malaysian (3)	14	0.01
Nepalese (15)	15	0.01
Pakistani (17)	24	0.02
Sri Lankan (0)	1	<0.01
Taiwanese (57)	62	0.06
Thai (15)	17	0.02
Vietnamese (95)	113	0.10
Hawaii Native/Pacific Islander (36)	112	0.10
Not Hispanic (32)	106	0.10
Hispanic (4)	6	0.01
Fijian (0)	0	<0.01
Guamanian/Chamorro (9)	12	0.01
Marshallese (1)	4	<0.01
Native Hawaiian (15)	64	0.06
Samoan (5)	16	0.01
Tongan (0)	2	<0.01
White (95,207)	97,436	90.35
Not Hispanic (93,550)	95,591	88.63
Hispanic (1,657)	1,845	1.71

*Notes: † The Census 2010 population figure is used to calculate the percentages in the Hispanic Origin and Race categories. Ancestry percentages are based on the 2006-2010 American Community Survey population (not shown); ‡ Numbers in parentheses indicate the number of people reporting a single ancestry; * Numbers in parentheses indicate the number of persons reporting this race alone, not in combination with any other race; Please refer to the Explanation of Data for more information.*

Ancestry

Wabash County

Population: 32,888

Ancestry	Population	%
Afghan (0)	0	<0.01
African, Sub-Saharan (67)	73	0.22
African (39)	45	0.14
Cape Verdean (0)	0	<0.01
Ethiopian (0)	0	<0.01
Ghanaian (0)	0	<0.01
Kenyan (0)	0	<0.01
Liberian (0)	0	<0.01
Nigerian (0)	0	<0.01
Senegalese (0)	0	<0.01
Sierra Leonean (0)	0	<0.01
Somalian (11)	11	0.03
South African (0)	0	<0.01
Sudanese (0)	0	<0.01
Ugandan (17)	17	0.05
Zimbabwean (0)	0	<0.01
Other Sub-Saharan African (0)	0	<0.01
Albanian (0)	0	<0.01
Alsatian (0)	0	<0.01
American (6,017)	6,017	18.11
Arab (0)	0	<0.01
Arab (0)	0	<0.01
Egyptian (0)	0	<0.01
Iraqi (0)	0	<0.01
Jordanian (0)	0	<0.01
Lebanese (0)	0	<0.01
Moroccan (0)	0	<0.01
Palestinian (0)	0	<0.01
Syrian (0)	0	<0.01
Other Arab (0)	0	<0.01
Armenian (0)	0	<0.01
Assyrian/Chaldean/Syriac (0)	0	<0.01
Australian (0)	0	<0.01
Austrian (27)	41	0.12
Basque (0)	0	<0.01
Belgian (11)	41	0.12
Brazilian (0)	0	<0.01
British (30)	128	0.39
Bulgarian (18)	18	0.05
Cajun (0)	0	<0.01
Canadian (21)	29	0.09
Carpatho Rusyn (0)	0	<0.01
Celtic (0)	0	<0.01
Croatian (0)	13	0.04
Cypriot (0)	0	<0.01
Czech (53)	58	0.17
Czechoslovakian (40)	40	0.12
Danish (7)	18	0.05
Dutch (267)	928	2.79
Eastern European (0)	0	<0.01
English (1,313)	3,342	10.06
Estonian (0)	0	<0.01
European (187)	192	0.58
Finnish (0)	0	<0.01
French, ex. Basque (173)	712	2.14
French Canadian (24)	35	0.11
German (5,604)	10,394	31.28
German Russian (0)	0	<0.01
Greek (9)	20	0.06
Guyanese (0)	0	<0.01
Hungarian (27)	45	0.14
Icelander (0)	0	<0.01
Iranian (0)	0	<0.01
Irish (1,038)	3,323	10.00
Israeli (0)	0	<0.01
Italian (180)	450	1.35
Latvian (0)	0	<0.01
Lithuanian (0)	0	<0.01
Luxemburger (0)	0	<0.01
Macedonian (0)	0	<0.01
Maltese (0)	0	<0.01
New Zealander (0)	0	<0.01
Northern European (39)	39	0.12
Norwegian (76)	99	0.30
Pennsylvania German (63)	76	0.23
Polish (157)	344	1.04
Portuguese (0)	0	<0.01
Romanian (0)	0	<0.01
Russian (0)	7	0.02
Scandinavian (0)	37	0.11
Scotch-Irish (196)	451	1.36
Scottish (172)	574	1.73
Serbian (4)	12	0.04
Slavic (0)	0	<0.01
Slovak (9)	36	0.11
Slovene (0)	0	<0.01
Soviet Union (0)	0	<0.01
Swedish (66)	141	0.42
Swiss (66)	146	0.44
Turkish (0)	0	<0.01
Ukrainian (25)	25	0.08
Welsh (26)	206	0.62
West Indian, ex. Hispanic (32)	32	0.10
Bahamian (0)	0	<0.01
Barbadian (0)	0	<0.01
Belizean (0)	0	<0.01
Bermudan (0)	0	<0.01
British West Indian (0)	0	<0.01
Dutch West Indian (15)	15	0.05
Haitian (10)	10	0.03
Jamaican (0)	0	<0.01
Trinidadian/Tobagonian (0)	0	<0.01
U.S. Virgin Islander (0)	0	<0.01
West Indian (7)	7	0.02
Other West Indian (0)	0	<0.01
Yugoslavian (0)	0	<0.01

Hispanic Origin	Population	%
Hispanic or Latino (of any race)	697	2.12
Central American, ex. Mexican	13	0.04
Costa Rican	1	<0.01
Guatemalan	10	0.03
Honduran	1	<0.01
Nicaraguan	0	<0.01
Panamanian	0	<0.01
Salvadoran	1	<0.01
Other Central American	0	<0.01
Cuban	8	0.02
Dominican Republic	0	<0.01
Mexican	584	1.78
Puerto Rican	29	0.09
South American	15	0.05
Argentinean	0	<0.01
Bolivian	2	0.01
Chilean	0	<0.01
Colombian	8	0.02
Ecuadorian	0	<0.01
Paraguayan	0	<0.01
Peruvian	1	<0.01
Uruguayan	0	<0.01
Venezuelan	4	0.01
Other South American	0	<0.01
Other Hispanic or Latino	48	0.15

Race*	Population	%
African-American/Black (163)	272	0.83
Not Hispanic (155)	258	0.78
Hispanic (8)	14	0.04
American Indian/Alaska Native (217)	396	1.20
Not Hispanic (211)	377	1.15
Hispanic (6)	19	0.06
Alaska Athabascan *(Ala. Nat.)* (0)	0	<0.01
Aleut *(Alaska Native)* (0)	0	<0.01
Apache (3)	3	0.01
Arapaho (0)	0	<0.01
Blackfeet (1)	8	0.02
Canadian/French Am. Ind. (0)	1	<0.01
Central American Ind. (1)	1	<0.01
Cherokee (21)	69	0.21
Cheyenne (0)	0	<0.01
Chickasaw (0)	0	<0.01
Chippewa (2)	2	0.01
Choctaw (6)	7	0.02
Colville (0)	0	<0.01
Comanche (1)	1	<0.01
Cree (0)	0	<0.01
Creek (3)	3	0.01
Crow (0)	1	<0.01
Delaware (0)	0	<0.01
Hopi (0)	0	<0.01
Houma (1)	3	0.01
Inupiat *(Alaska Native)* (0)	0	<0.01
Iroquois (2)	4	0.01
Kiowa (0)	2	0.01
Lumbee (0)	0	<0.01
Menominee (1)	1	<0.01
Mexican American Ind. (2)	5	0.02
Navajo (1)	3	0.01
Osage (1)	2	0.01
Ottawa (0)	0	<0.01
Paiute (0)	0	<0.01
Pima (0)	0	<0.01
Potawatomi (0)	2	0.01
Pueblo (2)	2	0.01
Puget Sound Salish (0)	0	<0.01
Seminole (0)	0	<0.01
Shoshone (0)	0	<0.01
Sioux (4)	6	0.02
South American Ind. (0)	2	0.01
Spanish American Ind. (0)	0	<0.01
Tlingit-Haida *(Alaska Native)* (0)	0	<0.01
Tohono O'Odham (0)	0	<0.01
Tsimshian *(Alaska Native)* (0)	0	<0.01
Ute (0)	0	<0.01
Yakama (0)	0	<0.01
Yaqui (0)	0	<0.01
Yuman (0)	2	0.01
Yup'ik *(Alaska Native)* (0)	0	<0.01
Asian (138)	179	0.54
Not Hispanic (134)	172	0.52
Hispanic (4)	7	0.02
Bangladeshi (0)	0	<0.01
Bhutanese (0)	0	<0.01
Burmese (3)	3	0.01
Cambodian (7)	7	0.02
Chinese, ex. Taiwanese (18)	19	0.06
Filipino (23)	37	0.11
Hmong (0)	0	<0.01
Indian (32)	36	0.11
Indonesian (0)	0	<0.01
Japanese (12)	18	0.05
Korean (18)	22	0.07
Laotian (12)	15	0.05
Malaysian (0)	0	<0.01
Nepalese (0)	0	<0.01
Pakistani (0)	0	<0.01
Sri Lankan (1)	1	<0.01
Taiwanese (4)	4	0.01
Thai (4)	4	0.01
Vietnamese (3)	8	0.02
Hawaii Native/Pacific Islander (6)	17	0.05
Not Hispanic (6)	15	0.05
Hispanic (0)	2	0.01
Fijian (0)	0	<0.01
Guamanian/Chamorro (2)	4	0.01
Marshallese (1)	1	<0.01
Native Hawaiian (1)	2	0.01
Samoan (2)	5	0.02
Tongan (0)	0	<0.01
White (31,764)	32,112	97.64
Not Hispanic (31,369)	31,668	96.29
Hispanic (395)	444	1.35

*Notes: † The Census 2010 population figure is used to calculate the percentages in the Hispanic Origin and Race categories. Ancestry percentages are based on the 2006-2010 American Community Survey population (not shown); ‡ Numbers in parentheses indicate the number of people reporting a single ancestry; * Numbers in parentheses indicate the number of persons reporting this race alone, not in combination with any other race; Please refer to the Explanation of Data for more information.*

Warren County

Population: 8,508

Ancestry	Population	%
Afghan (0)	0	<0.01
African, Sub-Saharan (0)	0	<0.01
African (0)	0	<0.01
Cape Verdean (0)	0	<0.01
Ethiopian (0)	0	<0.01
Ghanaian (0)	0	<0.01
Kenyan (0)	0	<0.01
Liberian (0)	0	<0.01
Nigerian (0)	0	<0.01
Senegalese (0)	0	<0.01
Sierra Leonean (0)	0	<0.01
Somalian (0)	0	<0.01
South African (0)	0	<0.01
Sudanese (0)	0	<0.01
Ugandan (0)	0	<0.01
Zimbabwean (0)	0	<0.01
Other Sub-Saharan African (0)	0	<0.01
Albanian (0)	0	<0.01
Alsatian (0)	0	<0.01
American (789)	789	9.21
Arab (0)	0	<0.01
Arab (0)	0	<0.01
Egyptian (0)	0	<0.01
Iraqi (0)	0	<0.01
Jordanian (0)	0	<0.01
Lebanese (0)	0	<0.01
Moroccan (0)	0	<0.01
Palestinian (0)	0	<0.01
Syrian (0)	0	<0.01
Other Arab (0)	0	<0.01
Armenian (0)	0	<0.01
Assyrian/Chaldean/Syriac (0)	0	<0.01
Australian (3)	3	0.04
Austrian (0)	9	0.11
Basque (0)	0	<0.01
Belgian (0)	12	0.14
Brazilian (0)	0	<0.01
British (0)	14	0.16
Bulgarian (0)	0	<0.01
Cajun (0)	0	<0.01
Canadian (12)	15	0.18
Carpatho Rusyn (0)	0	<0.01
Celtic (0)	0	<0.01
Croatian (0)	0	<0.01
Cypriot (0)	0	<0.01
Czech (2)	4	0.05
Czechoslovakian (0)	0	<0.01
Danish (0)	48	0.56
Dutch (72)	398	4.65
Eastern European (0)	0	<0.01
English (471)	968	11.30
Estonian (0)	0	<0.01
European (27)	64	0.75
Finnish (0)	0	<0.01
French, ex. Basque (36)	202	2.36
French Canadian (7)	7	0.08
German (902)	2,368	27.65
German Russian (0)	0	<0.01
Greek (0)	0	<0.01
Guyanese (0)	0	<0.01
Hungarian (0)	0	<0.01
Icelander (0)	0	<0.01
Iranian (0)	0	<0.01
Irish (158)	934	10.91
Israeli (0)	0	<0.01
Italian (16)	85	0.99
Latvian (0)	0	<0.01
Lithuanian (3)	3	0.04
Luxemburger (0)	0	<0.01
Macedonian (0)	0	<0.01
Maltese (0)	0	<0.01
New Zealander (0)	0	<0.01
Northern European (9)	15	0.18
Norwegian (15)	36	0.42
Pennsylvania German (0)	0	<0.01
Polish (103)	177	2.07
Portuguese (26)	26	0.30
Romanian (0)	0	<0.01
Russian (0)	0	<0.01
Scandinavian (0)	0	<0.01
Scotch-Irish (99)	141	1.65
Scottish (141)	264	3.08
Serbian (0)	0	<0.01
Slavic (0)	0	<0.01
Slovak (0)	0	<0.01
Slovene (0)	0	<0.01
Soviet Union (0)	0	<0.01
Swedish (65)	202	2.36
Swiss (10)	11	0.13
Turkish (0)	0	<0.01
Ukrainian (0)	0	<0.01
Welsh (1)	54	0.63
West Indian, ex. Hispanic (0)	0	<0.01
Bahamian (0)	0	<0.01
Barbadian (0)	0	<0.01
Belizean (0)	0	<0.01
Bermudan (0)	0	<0.01
British West Indian (0)	0	<0.01
Dutch West Indian (0)	0	<0.01
Haitian (0)	0	<0.01
Jamaican (0)	0	<0.01
Trinidadian/Tobagonian (0)	0	<0.01
U.S. Virgin Islander (0)	0	<0.01
West Indian (0)	0	<0.01
Other West Indian (0)	0	<0.01
Yugoslavian (0)	0	<0.01

Hispanic Origin	Population	%
Hispanic or Latino (of any race)	70	0.82
Central American, ex. Mexican	0	<0.01
Costa Rican	0	<0.01
Guatemalan	0	<0.01
Honduran	0	<0.01
Nicaraguan	0	<0.01
Panamanian	0	<0.01
Salvadoran	0	<0.01
Other Central American	0	<0.01
Cuban	1	0.01
Dominican Republic	0	<0.01
Mexican	47	0.55
Puerto Rican	7	0.08
South American	5	0.06
Argentinean	0	<0.01
Bolivian	0	<0.01
Chilean	0	<0.01
Colombian	3	0.04
Ecuadorian	0	<0.01
Paraguayan	0	<0.01
Peruvian	0	<0.01
Uruguayan	0	<0.01
Venezuelan	0	<0.01
Other South American	2	0.02
Other Hispanic or Latino	10	0.12

Race*	Population	%
African-American/Black (11)	27	0.32
Not Hispanic (10)	26	0.31
Hispanic (1)	1	0.01
American Indian/Alaska Native (13)	35	0.41
Not Hispanic (13)	35	0.41
Hispanic (0)	0	<0.01
Alaska Athabascan *(Ala. Nat.)* (0)	0	<0.01
Aleut *(Alaska Native)* (4)	4	0.05
Apache (0)	0	<0.01
Arapaho (0)	0	<0.01
Blackfeet (0)	0	<0.01
Canadian/French Am. Ind. (0)	0	<0.01
Central American Ind. (0)	0	<0.01
Cherokee (5)	19	0.22
Cheyenne (0)	0	<0.01
Chickasaw (0)	0	<0.01
Chippewa (0)	0	<0.01
Choctaw (0)	0	<0.01
Colville (0)	0	<0.01
Comanche (0)	0	<0.01
Cree (0)	0	<0.01
Creek (0)	0	<0.01
Crow (0)	0	<0.01
Delaware (0)	0	<0.01
Hopi (0)	0	<0.01
Houma (0)	0	<0.01
Inupiat *(Alaska Native)* (1)	1	0.01
Iroquois (0)	0	<0.01
Kiowa (0)	0	<0.01
Lumbee (0)	0	<0.01
Menominee (0)	0	<0.01
Mexican American Ind. (0)	0	<0.01
Navajo (0)	0	<0.01
Osage (0)	2	0.02
Ottawa (0)	0	<0.01
Paiute (0)	0	<0.01
Pima (0)	0	<0.01
Potawatomi (0)	0	<0.01
Pueblo (0)	0	<0.01
Puget Sound Salish (0)	0	<0.01
Seminole (0)	0	<0.01
Shoshone (0)	0	<0.01
Sioux (0)	0	<0.01
South American Ind. (0)	0	<0.01
Spanish American Ind. (0)	0	<0.01
Tlingit-Haida *(Alaska Native)* (0)	0	<0.01
Tohono O'Odham (0)	0	<0.01
Tsimshian *(Alaska Native)* (0)	0	<0.01
Ute (0)	0	<0.01
Yakama (0)	0	<0.01
Yaqui (0)	0	<0.01
Yuman (0)	0	<0.01
Yup'ik *(Alaska Native)* (0)	0	<0.01
Asian (36)	48	0.56
Not Hispanic (36)	47	0.55
Hispanic (0)	1	0.01
Bangladeshi (0)	0	<0.01
Bhutanese (0)	0	<0.01
Burmese (0)	0	<0.01
Cambodian (0)	0	<0.01
Chinese, ex. Taiwanese (2)	2	0.02
Filipino (11)	15	0.18
Hmong (0)	0	<0.01
Indian (8)	10	0.12
Indonesian (0)	0	<0.01
Japanese (4)	5	0.06
Korean (0)	2	0.02
Laotian (0)	0	<0.01
Malaysian (0)	0	<0.01
Nepalese (0)	0	<0.01
Pakistani (0)	0	<0.01
Sri Lankan (0)	0	<0.01
Taiwanese (0)	0	<0.01
Thai (4)	5	0.06
Vietnamese (6)	6	0.07
Hawaii Native/Pacific Islander (6)	7	0.08
Not Hispanic (6)	7	0.08
Hispanic (0)	0	<0.01
Fijian (0)	0	<0.01
Guamanian/Chamorro (0)	0	<0.01
Marshallese (0)	0	<0.01
Native Hawaiian (2)	2	0.02
Samoan (4)	4	0.05
Tongan (0)	0	<0.01
White (8,363)	8,420	98.97
Not Hispanic (8,321)	8,369	98.37
Hispanic (42)	51	0.60

*Notes: † The Census 2010 population figure is used to calculate the percentages in the Hispanic Origin and Race categories. Ancestry percentages are based on the 2006-2010 American Community Survey population (not shown); ‡ Numbers in parentheses indicate the number of people reporting a single ancestry; * Numbers in parentheses indicate the number of persons reporting this race alone, not in combination with any other race; Please refer to the Explanation of Data for more information.*

Warrick County

Population: 59,689

Ancestry	Population	%
Afghan (0)	0	<0.01
African, Sub-Saharan (112)	130	0.22
African (21)	39	0.07
Cape Verdean (0)	0	<0.01
Ethiopian (0)	0	<0.01
Ghanaian (0)	0	<0.01
Kenyan (0)	0	<0.01
Liberian (0)	0	<0.01
Nigerian (91)	91	0.16
Senegalese (0)	0	<0.01
Sierra Leonean (0)	0	<0.01
Somalian (0)	0	<0.01
South African (0)	0	<0.01
Sudanese (0)	0	<0.01
Ugandan (0)	0	<0.01
Zimbabwean (0)	0	<0.01
Other Sub-Saharan African (0)	0	<0.01
Albanian (0)	0	<0.01
Alsatian (0)	0	<0.01
American (7,842)	7,842	13.43
Arab (80)	102	0.17
Arab (0)	0	<0.01
Egyptian (53)	53	0.09
Iraqi (0)	0	<0.01
Jordanian (0)	0	<0.01
Lebanese (17)	17	0.03
Moroccan (0)	0	<0.01
Palestinian (0)	0	<0.01
Syrian (10)	32	0.05
Other Arab (0)	0	<0.01
Armenian (0)	0	<0.01
Assyrian/Chaldean/Syriac (0)	0	<0.01
Australian (0)	0	<0.01
Austrian (37)	49	0.08
Basque (0)	0	<0.01
Belgian (13)	136	0.23
Brazilian (39)	85	0.15
British (82)	210	0.36
Bulgarian (15)	45	0.08
Cajun (0)	0	<0.01
Canadian (82)	91	0.16
Carpatho Rusyn (0)	0	<0.01
Celtic (0)	0	<0.01
Croatian (5)	5	0.01
Cypriot (0)	0	<0.01
Czech (35)	110	0.19
Czechoslovakian (9)	32	0.05
Danish (0)	141	0.24
Dutch (212)	1,030	1.76
Eastern European (0)	0	<0.01
English (2,828)	7,311	12.52
Estonian (0)	0	<0.01
European (436)	501	0.86
Finnish (23)	51	0.09
French, ex. Basque (385)	2,146	3.68
French Canadian (52)	109	0.19
German (10,375)	20,598	35.27
German Russian (0)	0	<0.01
Greek (27)	27	0.05
Guyanese (0)	0	<0.01
Hungarian (23)	160	0.27
Icelander (0)	0	<0.01
Iranian (20)	62	0.11
Irish (2,323)	9,014	15.44
Israeli (8)	8	0.01
Italian (283)	1,227	2.10
Latvian (0)	0	<0.01
Lithuanian (5)	31	0.05
Luxemburger (9)	9	0.02
Macedonian (0)	0	<0.01
Maltese (0)	0	<0.01
New Zealander (0)	0	<0.01
Northern European (0)	0	<0.01
Norwegian (50)	208	0.36
Pennsylvania German (0)	22	0.04
Polish (598)	1,145	1.96
Portuguese (0)	11	0.02
Romanian (12)	25	0.04
Russian (164)	211	0.36
Scandinavian (9)	59	0.10
Scotch-Irish (342)	843	1.44
Scottish (520)	1,857	3.18
Serbian (105)	105	0.18
Slavic (0)	0	<0.01
Slovak (0)	63	0.11
Slovene (0)	0	<0.01
Soviet Union (0)	0	<0.01
Swedish (81)	306	0.52
Swiss (50)	129	0.22
Turkish (0)	0	<0.01
Ukrainian (60)	184	0.32
Welsh (72)	370	0.63
West Indian, ex. Hispanic (0)	18	0.03
Bahamian (0)	18	0.03
Barbadian (0)	0	<0.01
Belizean (0)	0	<0.01
Bermudan (0)	0	<0.01
British West Indian (0)	0	<0.01
Dutch West Indian (0)	0	<0.01
Haitian (0)	0	<0.01
Jamaican (0)	0	<0.01
Trinidadian/Tobagonian (0)	0	<0.01
U.S. Virgin Islander (0)	0	<0.01
West Indian (0)	0	<0.01
Other West Indian (0)	0	<0.01
Yugoslavian (0)	0	<0.01

Hispanic Origin	Population	%
Hispanic or Latino (of any race)	946	1.58
Central American, ex. Mexican	60	0.10
Costa Rican	5	0.01
Guatemalan	23	0.04
Honduran	7	0.01
Nicaraguan	6	0.01
Panamanian	5	0.01
Salvadoran	14	0.02
Other Central American	0	<0.01
Cuban	28	0.05
Dominican Republic	6	0.01
Mexican	536	0.90
Puerto Rican	105	0.18
South American	86	0.14
Argentinean	3	0.01
Bolivian	0	<0.01
Chilean	11	0.02
Colombian	23	0.04
Ecuadorian	9	0.02
Paraguayan	0	<0.01
Peruvian	23	0.04
Uruguayan	0	<0.01
Venezuelan	17	0.03
Other South American	0	<0.01
Other Hispanic or Latino	125	0.21

Race*	Population	%
African-American/Black (803)	1,148	1.92
Not Hispanic (780)	1,102	1.85
Hispanic (23)	46	0.08
American Indian/Alaska Native (124)	361	0.60
Not Hispanic (98)	330	0.55
Hispanic (26)	31	0.05
Alaska Athabascan *(Ala. Nat.)* (0)	0	<0.01
Aleut *(Alaska Native)* (1)	1	<0.01
Apache (1)	3	0.01
Arapaho (0)	0	<0.01
Blackfeet (2)	9	0.02
Canadian/French Am. Ind. (2)	9	0.02
Central American Ind. (0)	2	<0.01
Cherokee (30)	128	0.21
Cheyenne (0)	1	<0.01
Chickasaw (3)	4	0.01
Chippewa (2)	6	0.01
Choctaw (9)	12	0.02
Colville (0)	0	<0.01
Comanche (1)	2	<0.01
Cree (0)	0	<0.01
Creek (1)	2	<0.01
Crow (0)	3	0.01
Delaware (0)	0	<0.01
Hopi (1)	2	<0.01
Houma (0)	0	<0.01
Inupiat *(Alaska Native)* (0)	0	<0.01
Iroquois (3)	6	0.01
Kiowa (0)	0	<0.01
Lumbee (0)	0	<0.01
Menominee (0)	0	<0.01
Mexican American Ind. (7)	8	0.01
Navajo (1)	5	0.01
Osage (0)	0	<0.01
Ottawa (0)	0	<0.01
Paiute (0)	0	<0.01
Pima (0)	0	<0.01
Potawatomi (5)	6	0.01
Pueblo (0)	3	0.01
Puget Sound Salish (0)	0	<0.01
Seminole (3)	4	0.01
Shoshone (0)	0	<0.01
Sioux (2)	2	<0.01
South American Ind. (0)	0	<0.01
Spanish American Ind. (0)	0	<0.01
Tlingit-Haida *(Alaska Native)* (1)	1	<0.01
Tohono O'Odham (0)	0	<0.01
Tsimshian *(Alaska Native)* (0)	0	<0.01
Ute (0)	0	<0.01
Yakama (0)	0	<0.01
Yaqui (1)	1	<0.01
Yuman (0)	0	<0.01
Yup'ik *(Alaska Native)* (0)	0	<0.01
Asian (960)	1,178	1.97
Not Hispanic (957)	1,169	1.96
Hispanic (3)	9	0.02
Bangladeshi (0)	2	<0.01
Bhutanese (0)	0	<0.01
Burmese (4)	4	0.01
Cambodian (1)	1	<0.01
Chinese, ex. Taiwanese (121)	145	0.24
Filipino (132)	212	0.36
Hmong (0)	0	<0.01
Indian (354)	383	0.64
Indonesian (2)	6	0.01
Japanese (67)	100	0.17
Korean (67)	89	0.15
Laotian (0)	0	<0.01
Malaysian (0)	0	<0.01
Nepalese (11)	12	0.02
Pakistani (64)	68	0.11
Sri Lankan (0)	1	<0.01
Taiwanese (3)	4	0.01
Thai (12)	17	0.03
Vietnamese (85)	99	0.17
Hawaii Native/Pacific Islander (18)	35	0.06
Not Hispanic (18)	33	0.06
Hispanic (0)	2	<0.01
Fijian (1)	1	<0.01
Guamanian/Chamorro (5)	8	0.01
Marshallese (2)	2	<0.01
Native Hawaiian (6)	15	0.03
Samoan (1)	2	<0.01
Tongan (0)	0	<0.01
White (56,700)	57,454	96.26
Not Hispanic (56,095)	56,799	95.16
Hispanic (605)	655	1.10

*Notes: † The Census 2010 population figure is used to calculate the percentages in the Hispanic Origin and Race categories. Ancestry percentages are based on the 2006-2010 American Community Survey population (not shown); ‡ Numbers in parentheses indicate the number of people reporting a single ancestry; * Numbers in parentheses indicate the number of persons reporting this race alone, not in combination with any other race; Please refer to the Explanation of Data for more information.*

Washington County

Population: 28,262

Ancestry	Population	%
Afghan (0)	0	<0.01
African, Sub-Saharan (0)	0	<0.01
African (0)	0	<0.01
Cape Verdean (0)	0	<0.01
Ethiopian (0)	0	<0.01
Ghanaian (0)	0	<0.01
Kenyan (0)	0	<0.01
Liberian (0)	0	<0.01
Nigerian (0)	0	<0.01
Senegalese (0)	0	<0.01
Sierra Leonean (0)	0	<0.01
Somalian (0)	0	<0.01
South African (0)	0	<0.01
Sudanese (0)	0	<0.01
Ugandan (0)	0	<0.01
Zimbabwean (0)	0	<0.01
Other Sub-Saharan African (0)	0	<0.01
Albanian (0)	0	<0.01
Alsatian (0)	0	<0.01
American (4,023)	4,023	14.25
Arab (0)	18	0.06
Arab (0)	0	<0.01
Egyptian (0)	18	0.06
Iraqi (0)	0	<0.01
Jordanian (0)	0	<0.01
Lebanese (0)	0	<0.01
Moroccan (0)	0	<0.01
Palestinian (0)	0	<0.01
Syrian (0)	0	<0.01
Other Arab (0)	0	<0.01
Armenian (0)	0	<0.01
Assyrian/Chaldean/Syriac (0)	0	<0.01
Australian (0)	0	<0.01
Austrian (0)	0	<0.01
Basque (0)	0	<0.01
Belgian (0)	2	0.01
Brazilian (0)	0	<0.01
British (40)	64	0.23
Bulgarian (0)	0	<0.01
Cajun (0)	10	0.04
Canadian (11)	11	0.04
Carpatho Rusyn (0)	0	<0.01
Celtic (0)	0	<0.01
Croatian (0)	0	<0.01
Cypriot (0)	0	<0.01
Czech (0)	0	<0.01
Czechoslovakian (5)	5	0.02
Danish (9)	16	0.06
Dutch (293)	577	2.04
Eastern European (7)	14	0.05
English (1,504)	2,714	9.62
Estonian (0)	0	<0.01
European (116)	116	0.41
Finnish (25)	25	0.09
French, ex. Basque (97)	637	2.26
French Canadian (0)	30	0.11
German (3,234)	7,109	25.19
German Russian (0)	0	<0.01
Greek (12)	20	0.07
Guyanese (0)	0	<0.01
Hungarian (10)	10	0.04
Icelander (0)	0	<0.01
Iranian (0)	0	<0.01
Irish (1,401)	3,854	13.65
Israeli (0)	0	<0.01
Italian (114)	290	1.03
Latvian (0)	0	<0.01
Lithuanian (0)	0	<0.01
Luxemburger (0)	0	<0.01
Macedonian (0)	0	<0.01
Maltese (0)	0	<0.01
New Zealander (0)	0	<0.01
Northern European (0)	0	<0.01
Norwegian (2)	4	0.01
Pennsylvania German (167)	167	0.59
Polish (37)	146	0.52
Portuguese (0)	0	<0.01
Romanian (0)	8	0.03
Russian (22)	111	0.39
Scandinavian (0)	38	0.13
Scotch-Irish (224)	581	2.06
Scottish (299)	572	2.03
Serbian (0)	0	<0.01
Slavic (0)	0	<0.01
Slovak (0)	0	<0.01
Slovene (0)	0	<0.01
Soviet Union (0)	0	<0.01
Swedish (32)	97	0.34
Swiss (36)	135	0.48
Turkish (0)	0	<0.01
Ukrainian (0)	0	<0.01
Welsh (16)	242	0.86
West Indian, ex. Hispanic (0)	0	<0.01
Bahamian (0)	0	<0.01
Barbadian (0)	0	<0.01
Belizean (0)	0	<0.01
Bermudan (0)	0	<0.01
British West Indian (0)	0	<0.01
Dutch West Indian (0)	0	<0.01
Haitian (0)	0	<0.01
Jamaican (0)	0	<0.01
Trinidadian/Tobagonian (0)	0	<0.01
U.S. Virgin Islander (0)	0	<0.01
West Indian (0)	0	<0.01
Other West Indian (0)	0	<0.01
Yugoslavian (0)	0	<0.01

Hispanic Origin	Population	%
Hispanic or Latino (of any race)	304	1.08
Central American, ex. Mexican	5	0.02
Costa Rican	0	<0.01
Guatemalan	1	<0.01
Honduran	0	<0.01
Nicaraguan	0	<0.01
Panamanian	0	<0.01
Salvadoran	3	0.01
Other Central American	1	<0.01
Cuban	8	0.03
Dominican Republic	0	<0.01
Mexican	215	0.76
Puerto Rican	39	0.14
South American	4	0.01
Argentinean	0	<0.01
Bolivian	0	<0.01
Chilean	0	<0.01
Colombian	0	<0.01
Ecuadorian	0	<0.01
Paraguayan	0	<0.01
Peruvian	4	0.01
Uruguayan	0	<0.01
Venezuelan	0	<0.01
Other South American	0	<0.01
Other Hispanic or Latino	33	0.12

Race*	Population	%
African-American/Black (64)	111	0.39
Not Hispanic (63)	106	0.38
Hispanic (1)	5	0.02
American Indian/Alaska Native (62)	188	0.67
Not Hispanic (45)	159	0.56
Hispanic (17)	29	0.10
Alaska Athabascan *(Ala. Nat.)* (0)	0	<0.01
Aleut *(Alaska Native)* (0)	0	<0.01
Apache (2)	12	0.04
Arapaho (0)	0	<0.01
Blackfeet (1)	3	0.01
Canadian/French Am. Ind. (2)	3	0.01
Central American Ind. (0)	0	<0.01
Cherokee (14)	72	0.25
Cheyenne (2)	3	0.01
Chickasaw (0)	5	0.02
Chippewa (0)	1	<0.01
Choctaw (1)	5	0.02
Colville (0)	0	<0.01
Comanche (2)	3	0.01
Cree (0)	0	<0.01
Creek (0)	0	<0.01
Crow (0)	0	<0.01
Delaware (0)	1	<0.01
Hopi (0)	0	<0.01
Houma (0)	0	<0.01
Inupiat *(Alaska Native)* (0)	0	<0.01
Iroquois (0)	1	<0.01
Kiowa (0)	1	<0.01
Lumbee (0)	0	<0.01
Menominee (0)	0	<0.01
Mexican American Ind. (0)	1	<0.01
Navajo (1)	1	<0.01
Osage (0)	1	<0.01
Ottawa (1)	1	<0.01
Paiute (0)	0	<0.01
Pima (0)	0	<0.01
Potawatomi (0)	0	<0.01
Pueblo (0)	0	<0.01
Puget Sound Salish (2)	2	0.01
Seminole (0)	0	<0.01
Shoshone (0)	0	<0.01
Sioux (4)	9	0.03
South American Ind. (0)	0	<0.01
Spanish American Ind. (0)	0	<0.01
Tlingit-Haida *(Alaska Native)* (0)	0	<0.01
Tohono O'Odham (0)	0	<0.01
Tsimshian *(Alaska Native)* (0)	0	<0.01
Ute (0)	0	<0.01
Yakama (0)	0	<0.01
Yaqui (0)	0	<0.01
Yuman (0)	0	<0.01
Yup'ik *(Alaska Native)* (0)	0	<0.01
Asian (86)	128	0.45
Not Hispanic (86)	125	0.44
Hispanic (0)	3	0.01
Bangladeshi (0)	0	<0.01
Bhutanese (0)	0	<0.01
Burmese (0)	0	<0.01
Cambodian (1)	2	0.01
Chinese, ex. Taiwanese (14)	17	0.06
Filipino (24)	51	0.18
Hmong (0)	0	<0.01
Indian (2)	5	0.02
Indonesian (0)	0	<0.01
Japanese (11)	16	0.06
Korean (4)	5	0.02
Laotian (0)	0	<0.01
Malaysian (0)	0	<0.01
Nepalese (0)	0	<0.01
Pakistani (0)	0	<0.01
Sri Lankan (0)	0	<0.01
Taiwanese (0)	0	<0.01
Thai (10)	16	0.06
Vietnamese (10)	11	0.04
Hawaii Native/Pacific Islander (2)	6	0.02
Not Hispanic (2)	6	0.02
Hispanic (0)	0	<0.01
Fijian (0)	0	<0.01
Guamanian/Chamorro (0)	0	<0.01
Marshallese (0)	0	<0.01
Native Hawaiian (1)	2	0.01
Samoan (0)	0	<0.01
Tongan (0)	0	<0.01
White (27,714)	27,954	98.91
Not Hispanic (27,539)	27,736	98.14
Hispanic (175)	218	0.77

*Notes: † The Census 2010 population figure is used to calculate the percentages in the Hispanic Origin and Race categories. Ancestry percentages are based on the 2006-2010 American Community Survey population (not shown); ‡ Numbers in parentheses indicate the number of people reporting a single ancestry; * Numbers in parentheses indicate the number of persons reporting this race alone, not in combination with any other race; Please refer to the Explanation of Data for more information.*

Wayne County

Population: 68,917

Ancestry	Population	%
Afghan (0)	0	<0.01
African, Sub-Saharan (172)	195	0.28
African (172)	192	0.28
Cape Verdean (0)	0	<0.01
Ethiopian (0)	0	<0.01
Ghanaian (0)	0	<0.01
Kenyan (0)	0	<0.01
Liberian (0)	0	<0.01
Nigerian (0)	0	<0.01
Senegalese (0)	0	<0.01
Sierra Leonean (0)	0	<0.01
Somalian (0)	0	<0.01
South African (0)	3	<0.01
Sudanese (0)	0	<0.01
Ugandan (0)	0	<0.01
Zimbabwean (0)	0	<0.01
Other Sub-Saharan African (0)	0	<0.01
Albanian (0)	0	<0.01
Alsatian (0)	0	<0.01
American (7,563)	7,563	10.93
Arab (33)	33	0.05
Arab (0)	0	<0.01
Egyptian (0)	0	<0.01
Iraqi (0)	0	<0.01
Jordanian (0)	0	<0.01
Lebanese (17)	17	0.02
Moroccan (0)	0	<0.01
Palestinian (9)	9	0.01
Syrian (0)	0	<0.01
Other Arab (7)	7	0.01
Armenian (14)	14	0.02
Assyrian/Chaldean/Syriac (0)	0	<0.01
Australian (0)	0	<0.01
Austrian (0)	11	0.02
Basque (0)	0	<0.01
Belgian (0)	40	0.06
Brazilian (0)	0	<0.01
British (114)	288	0.42
Bulgarian (0)	0	<0.01
Cajun (0)	0	<0.01
Canadian (106)	139	0.20
Carpatho Rusyn (0)	0	<0.01
Celtic (0)	0	<0.01
Croatian (15)	21	0.03
Cypriot (0)	0	<0.01
Czech (15)	64	0.09
Czechoslovakian (0)	6	0.01
Danish (28)	118	0.17
Dutch (414)	1,908	2.76
Eastern European (10)	10	0.01
English (3,421)	7,639	11.04
Estonian (0)	0	<0.01
European (741)	782	1.13
Finnish (0)	0	<0.01
French, ex. Basque (255)	1,119	1.62
French Canadian (16)	65	0.09
German (7,720)	16,908	24.44
German Russian (0)	6	0.01
Greek (90)	131	0.19
Guyanese (7)	30	0.04
Hungarian (108)	233	0.34
Icelander (0)	0	<0.01
Iranian (104)	104	0.15
Irish (2,655)	8,196	11.85
Israeli (0)	0	<0.01
Italian (993)	2,010	2.91
Latvian (9)	9	0.01
Lithuanian (16)	24	0.03
Luxemburger (0)	12	0.02
Macedonian (93)	93	0.13
Maltese (11)	22	0.03
New Zealander (0)	0	<0.01
Northern European (41)	41	0.06
Norwegian (43)	272	0.39
Pennsylvania German (79)	95	0.14
Polish (215)	760	1.10
Portuguese (10)	32	0.05
Romanian (0)	0	<0.01
Russian (93)	143	0.21
Scandinavian (19)	19	0.03
Scotch-Irish (532)	1,333	1.93
Scottish (456)	1,247	1.80
Serbian (19)	19	0.03
Slavic (16)	16	0.02
Slovak (16)	27	0.04
Slovene (6)	13	0.02
Soviet Union (0)	0	<0.01
Swedish (143)	297	0.43
Swiss (148)	278	0.40
Turkish (0)	13	0.02
Ukrainian (24)	30	0.04
Welsh (92)	372	0.54
West Indian, ex. Hispanic (18)	21	0.03
Bahamian (0)	0	<0.01
Barbadian (0)	0	<0.01
Belizean (0)	0	<0.01
Bermudan (0)	0	<0.01
British West Indian (0)	0	<0.01
Dutch West Indian (0)	3	<0.01
Haitian (12)	12	0.02
Jamaican (6)	6	0.01
Trinidadian/Tobagonian (0)	0	<0.01
U.S. Virgin Islander (0)	0	<0.01
West Indian (0)	0	<0.01
Other West Indian (0)	0	<0.01
Yugoslavian (0)	23	0.03

Hispanic Origin	Population	%
Hispanic or Latino (of any race)	1,804	2.62
Central American, ex. Mexican	64	0.09
Costa Rican	2	<0.01
Guatemalan	19	0.03
Honduran	14	0.02
Nicaraguan	2	<0.01
Panamanian	13	0.02
Salvadoran	10	0.01
Other Central American	4	0.01
Cuban	38	0.06
Dominican Republic	4	0.01
Mexican	1,278	1.85
Puerto Rican	182	0.26
South American	98	0.14
Argentinean	3	<0.01
Bolivian	1	<0.01
Chilean	8	0.01
Colombian	32	0.05
Ecuadorian	13	0.02
Paraguayan	0	<0.01
Peruvian	33	0.05
Uruguayan	1	<0.01
Venezuelan	6	0.01
Other South American	1	<0.01
Other Hispanic or Latino	140	0.20

Race*	Population	%
African-American/Black (3,418)	4,558	6.61
Not Hispanic (3,349)	4,451	6.46
Hispanic (69)	107	0.16
American Indian/Alaska Native (171)	629	0.91
Not Hispanic (140)	566	0.82
Hispanic (31)	63	0.09
Alaska Athabascan *(Ala. Nat.)* (0)	0	<0.01
Aleut *(Alaska Native)* (0)	0	<0.01
Apache (1)	9	0.01
Arapaho (0)	0	<0.01
Blackfeet (4)	29	0.04
Canadian/French Am. Ind. (0)	3	<0.01
Central American Ind. (0)	2	<0.01
Cherokee (43)	187	0.27
Cheyenne (0)	0	<0.01
Chickasaw (0)	6	0.01
Chippewa (7)	14	0.02
Choctaw (1)	4	0.01
Colville (0)	0	<0.01
Comanche (3)	3	<0.01
Cree (0)	0	<0.01
Creek (0)	2	<0.01
Crow (0)	1	<0.01
Delaware (0)	0	<0.01
Hopi (1)	3	<0.01
Houma (1)	1	<0.01
Inupiat *(Alaska Native)* (0)	0	<0.01
Iroquois (6)	10	0.01
Kiowa (0)	0	<0.01
Lumbee (1)	5	0.01
Menominee (2)	2	<0.01
Mexican American Ind. (11)	17	0.02
Navajo (2)	7	0.01
Osage (0)	0	<0.01
Ottawa (0)	0	<0.01
Paiute (2)	2	<0.01
Pima (0)	2	<0.01
Potawatomi (1)	4	0.01
Pueblo (1)	2	<0.01
Puget Sound Salish (0)	0	<0.01
Seminole (1)	2	<0.01
Shoshone (0)	0	<0.01
Sioux (1)	9	0.01
South American Ind. (3)	3	<0.01
Spanish American Ind. (5)	8	0.01
Tlingit-Haida *(Alaska Native)* (0)	0	<0.01
Tohono O'Odham (0)	0	<0.01
Tsimshian *(Alaska Native)* (0)	0	<0.01
Ute (0)	0	<0.01
Yakama (0)	0	<0.01
Yaqui (0)	0	<0.01
Yuman (0)	0	<0.01
Yup'ik *(Alaska Native)* (0)	0	<0.01
Asian (527)	734	1.07
Not Hispanic (522)	721	1.05
Hispanic (5)	13	0.02
Bangladeshi (0)	0	<0.01
Bhutanese (0)	0	<0.01
Burmese (0)	0	<0.01
Cambodian (4)	12	0.02
Chinese, ex. Taiwanese (78)	88	0.13
Filipino (104)	159	0.23
Hmong (0)	0	<0.01
Indian (130)	145	0.21
Indonesian (2)	5	0.01
Japanese (55)	81	0.12
Korean (31)	48	0.07
Laotian (18)	23	0.03
Malaysian (0)	0	<0.01
Nepalese (1)	2	<0.01
Pakistani (12)	12	0.02
Sri Lankan (1)	2	<0.01
Taiwanese (3)	4	0.01
Thai (6)	7	0.01
Vietnamese (36)	45	0.07
Hawaii Native/Pacific Islander (49)	138	0.20
Not Hispanic (44)	130	0.19
Hispanic (5)	8	0.01
Fijian (0)	0	<0.01
Guamanian/Chamorro (4)	4	0.01
Marshallese (0)	0	<0.01
Native Hawaiian (8)	28	0.04
Samoan (2)	3	<0.01
Tongan (0)	0	<0.01
White (62,140)	63,798	92.57
Not Hispanic (61,322)	62,805	91.13
Hispanic (818)	993	1.44

*Notes: † The Census 2010 population figure is used to calculate the percentages in the Hispanic Origin and Race categories. Ancestry percentages are based on the 2006-2010 American Community Survey population (not shown); ‡ Numbers in parentheses indicate the number of people reporting a single ancestry; * Numbers in parentheses indicate the number of persons reporting this race alone, not in combination with any other race; Please refer to the Explanation of Data for more information.*

Wells County

Population: 27,636

Ancestry	Population	%
Afghan (0)	0	<0.01
African, Sub-Saharan (0)	0	<0.01
African (0)	0	<0.01
Cape Verdean (0)	0	<0.01
Ethiopian (0)	0	<0.01
Ghanaian (0)	0	<0.01
Kenyan (0)	0	<0.01
Liberian (0)	0	<0.01
Nigerian (0)	0	<0.01
Senegalese (0)	0	<0.01
Sierra Leonean (0)	0	<0.01
Somalian (0)	0	<0.01
South African (0)	0	<0.01
Sudanese (0)	0	<0.01
Ugandan (0)	0	<0.01
Zimbabwean (0)	0	<0.01
Other Sub-Saharan African (0)	0	<0.01
Albanian (0)	0	<0.01
Alsatian (0)	0	<0.01
American (2,856)	2,856	10.29
Arab (0)	0	<0.01
Arab (0)	0	<0.01
Egyptian (0)	0	<0.01
Iraqi (0)	0	<0.01
Jordanian (0)	0	<0.01
Lebanese (0)	0	<0.01
Moroccan (0)	0	<0.01
Palestinian (0)	0	<0.01
Syrian (0)	0	<0.01
Other Arab (0)	0	<0.01
Armenian (0)	0	<0.01
Assyrian/Chaldean/Syriac (0)	0	<0.01
Australian (0)	0	<0.01
Austrian (28)	28	0.10
Basque (0)	0	<0.01
Belgian (8)	25	0.09
Brazilian (0)	0	<0.01
British (35)	71	0.26
Bulgarian (0)	0	<0.01
Cajun (0)	0	<0.01
Canadian (6)	6	0.02
Carpatho Rusyn (0)	0	<0.01
Celtic (0)	0	<0.01
Croatian (0)	0	<0.01
Cypriot (0)	0	<0.01
Czech (9)	9	0.03
Czechoslovakian (0)	0	<0.01
Danish (30)	58	0.21
Dutch (174)	726	2.62
Eastern European (0)	0	<0.01
English (1,819)	3,418	12.32
Estonian (0)	0	<0.01
European (130)	132	0.48
Finnish (47)	94	0.34
French, ex. Basque (151)	1,027	3.70
French Canadian (143)	225	0.81
German (5,702)	10,646	38.37
German Russian (0)	0	<0.01
Greek (14)	14	0.05
Guyanese (0)	0	<0.01
Hungarian (41)	66	0.24
Icelander (0)	0	<0.01
Iranian (0)	0	<0.01
Irish (821)	3,009	10.85
Israeli (0)	0	<0.01
Italian (160)	589	2.12
Latvian (0)	0	<0.01
Lithuanian (9)	9	0.03
Luxemburger (0)	0	<0.01
Macedonian (0)	0	<0.01
Maltese (0)	0	<0.01
New Zealander (0)	0	<0.01
Northern European (5)	5	0.02
Norwegian (24)	46	0.17
Pennsylvania German (37)	37	0.13
Polish (120)	439	1.58
Portuguese (0)	0	<0.01
Romanian (0)	0	<0.01
Russian (7)	31	0.11
Scandinavian (14)	30	0.11
Scotch-Irish (92)	159	0.57
Scottish (184)	423	1.52
Serbian (13)	13	0.05
Slavic (0)	0	<0.01
Slovak (9)	33	0.12
Slovene (0)	0	<0.01
Soviet Union (0)	0	<0.01
Swedish (21)	54	0.19
Swiss (864)	1,426	5.14
Turkish (0)	0	<0.01
Ukrainian (16)	23	0.08
Welsh (19)	152	0.55
West Indian, ex. Hispanic (0)	0	<0.01
Bahamian (0)	0	<0.01
Barbadian (0)	0	<0.01
Belizean (0)	0	<0.01
Bermudan (0)	0	<0.01
British West Indian (0)	0	<0.01
Dutch West Indian (0)	0	<0.01
Haitian (0)	0	<0.01
Jamaican (0)	0	<0.01
Trinidadian/Tobagonian (0)	0	<0.01
U.S. Virgin Islander (0)	0	<0.01
West Indian (0)	0	<0.01
Other West Indian (0)	0	<0.01
Yugoslavian (3)	6	0.02

Hispanic Origin	Population	%
Hispanic or Latino (of any race)	564	2.04
Central American, ex. Mexican	22	0.08
Costa Rican	2	0.01
Guatemalan	4	0.01
Honduran	2	0.01
Nicaraguan	0	<0.01
Panamanian	5	0.02
Salvadoran	9	0.03
Other Central American	0	<0.01
Cuban	2	0.01
Dominican Republic	0	<0.01
Mexican	424	1.53
Puerto Rican	46	0.17
South American	21	0.08
Argentinean	0	<0.01
Bolivian	0	<0.01
Chilean	0	<0.01
Colombian	17	0.06
Ecuadorian	3	0.01
Paraguayan	0	<0.01
Peruvian	1	<0.01
Uruguayan	0	<0.01
Venezuelan	0	<0.01
Other South American	0	<0.01
Other Hispanic or Latino	49	0.18

Race*	Population	%
African-American/Black (96)	187	0.68
Not Hispanic (89)	165	0.60
Hispanic (7)	22	0.08
American Indian/Alaska Native (76)	181	0.65
Not Hispanic (71)	161	0.58
Hispanic (5)	20	0.07
Alaska Athabascan *(Ala. Nat.)* (0)	0	<0.01
Aleut *(Alaska Native)* (0)	0	<0.01
Apache (0)	0	<0.01
Arapaho (0)	0	<0.01
Blackfeet (4)	8	0.03
Canadian/French Am. Ind. (0)	0	<0.01
Central American Ind. (0)	0	<0.01
Cherokee (21)	60	0.22
Cheyenne (1)	2	0.01
Chickasaw (0)	0	<0.01
Chippewa (1)	1	<0.01
Choctaw (0)	1	<0.01
Colville (0)	0	<0.01
Comanche (0)	0	<0.01
Cree (0)	0	<0.01
Creek (2)	8	0.03
Crow (0)	0	<0.01
Delaware (0)	0	<0.01
Hopi (0)	0	<0.01
Houma (0)	0	<0.01
Inupiat *(Alaska Native)* (0)	0	<0.01
Iroquois (1)	2	0.01
Kiowa (0)	0	<0.01
Lumbee (0)	0	<0.01
Menominee (0)	0	<0.01
Mexican American Ind. (2)	2	0.01
Navajo (0)	0	<0.01
Osage (0)	0	<0.01
Ottawa (2)	2	0.01
Paiute (0)	0	<0.01
Pima (0)	0	<0.01
Potawatomi (0)	0	<0.01
Pueblo (1)	1	<0.01
Puget Sound Salish (0)	0	<0.01
Seminole (0)	0	<0.01
Shoshone (0)	0	<0.01
Sioux (11)	13	0.05
South American Ind. (0)	1	<0.01
Spanish American Ind. (0)	0	<0.01
Tlingit-Haida *(Alaska Native)* (0)	0	<0.01
Tohono O'Odham (0)	0	<0.01
Tsimshian *(Alaska Native)* (0)	0	<0.01
Ute (0)	0	<0.01
Yakama (0)	0	<0.01
Yaqui (0)	0	<0.01
Yuman (2)	2	0.01
Yup'ik *(Alaska Native)* (0)	0	<0.01
Asian (107)	141	0.51
Not Hispanic (102)	136	0.49
Hispanic (5)	5	0.02
Bangladeshi (0)	0	<0.01
Bhutanese (0)	0	<0.01
Burmese (0)	0	<0.01
Cambodian (4)	6	0.02
Chinese, ex. Taiwanese (33)	33	0.12
Filipino (25)	33	0.12
Hmong (0)	1	<0.01
Indian (0)	5	0.02
Indonesian (0)	0	<0.01
Japanese (5)	5	0.02
Korean (20)	25	0.09
Laotian (0)	1	<0.01
Malaysian (0)	0	<0.01
Nepalese (0)	0	<0.01
Pakistani (0)	0	<0.01
Sri Lankan (0)	0	<0.01
Taiwanese (1)	1	<0.01
Thai (5)	7	0.03
Vietnamese (5)	5	0.02
Hawaii Native/Pacific Islander (3)	9	0.03
Not Hispanic (3)	9	0.03
Hispanic (0)	0	<0.01
Fijian (0)	0	<0.01
Guamanian/Chamorro (1)	2	0.01
Marshallese (0)	0	<0.01
Native Hawaiian (1)	1	<0.01
Samoan (0)	0	<0.01
Tongan (0)	0	<0.01
White (26,902)	27,132	98.18
Not Hispanic (26,604)	26,796	96.96
Hispanic (298)	336	1.22

*Notes: † The Census 2010 population figure is used to calculate the percentages in the Hispanic Origin and Race categories. Ancestry percentages are based on the 2006-2010 American Community Survey population (not shown); ‡ Numbers in parentheses indicate the number of people reporting a single ancestry; * Numbers in parentheses indicate the number of persons reporting this race alone, not in combination with any other race; Please refer to the Explanation of Data for more information.*

White County

Population: 24,643

Ancestry	Population	%
Afghan (0)	0	<0.01
African, Sub-Saharan (0)	0	<0.01
African (0)	0	<0.01
Cape Verdean (0)	0	<0.01
Ethiopian (0)	0	<0.01
Ghanaian (0)	0	<0.01
Kenyan (0)	0	<0.01
Liberian (0)	0	<0.01
Nigerian (0)	0	<0.01
Senegalese (0)	0	<0.01
Sierra Leonean (0)	0	<0.01
Somalian (0)	0	<0.01
South African (0)	0	<0.01
Sudanese (0)	0	<0.01
Ugandan (0)	0	<0.01
Zimbabwean (0)	0	<0.01
Other Sub-Saharan African (0)	0	<0.01
Albanian (0)	0	<0.01
Alsatian (0)	0	<0.01
American (2,068)	2,068	8.36
Arab (0)	5	0.02
Arab (0)	3	0.01
Egyptian (0)	0	<0.01
Iraqi (0)	0	<0.01
Jordanian (0)	0	<0.01
Lebanese (0)	2	0.01
Moroccan (0)	0	<0.01
Palestinian (0)	0	<0.01
Syrian (0)	0	<0.01
Other Arab (0)	0	<0.01
Armenian (0)	0	<0.01
Assyrian/Chaldean/Syriac (0)	0	<0.01
Australian (0)	0	<0.01
Austrian (13)	25	0.10
Basque (0)	0	<0.01
Belgian (0)	24	0.10
Brazilian (0)	0	<0.01
British (40)	45	0.18
Bulgarian (0)	0	<0.01
Cajun (0)	0	<0.01
Canadian (21)	107	0.43
Carpatho Rusyn (0)	0	<0.01
Celtic (0)	0	<0.01
Croatian (28)	59	0.24
Cypriot (0)	0	<0.01
Czech (36)	106	0.43
Czechoslovakian (14)	14	0.06
Danish (35)	121	0.49
Dutch (261)	985	3.98
Eastern European (0)	0	<0.01
English (839)	2,392	9.67
Estonian (0)	0	<0.01
European (61)	147	0.59
Finnish (0)	9	0.04
French, ex. Basque (247)	683	2.76
French Canadian (7)	84	0.34
German (2,961)	6,687	27.04
German Russian (0)	0	<0.01
Greek (9)	18	0.07
Guyanese (0)	0	<0.01
Hungarian (48)	83	0.34
Icelander (0)	0	<0.01
Iranian (0)	0	<0.01
Irish (923)	3,284	13.28
Israeli (0)	0	<0.01
Italian (133)	576	2.33
Latvian (0)	0	<0.01
Lithuanian (13)	29	0.12
Luxemburger (0)	0	<0.01
Macedonian (0)	8	0.03
Maltese (0)	0	<0.01
New Zealander (0)	0	<0.01
Northern European (30)	30	0.12
Norwegian (54)	98	0.40
Pennsylvania German (12)	18	0.07
Polish (343)	1,061	4.29
Portuguese (0)	8	0.03
Romanian (0)	0	<0.01
Russian (0)	86	0.35
Scandinavian (11)	11	0.04
Scotch-Irish (176)	401	1.62
Scottish (174)	488	1.97
Serbian (20)	24	0.10
Slavic (12)	12	0.05
Slovak (3)	43	0.17
Slovene (0)	9	0.04
Soviet Union (0)	0	<0.01
Swedish (129)	425	1.72
Swiss (18)	57	0.23
Turkish (9)	10	0.04
Ukrainian (0)	24	0.10
Welsh (81)	121	0.49
West Indian, ex. Hispanic (0)	0	<0.01
Bahamian (0)	0	<0.01
Barbadian (0)	0	<0.01
Belizean (0)	0	<0.01
Bermudan (0)	0	<0.01
British West Indian (0)	0	<0.01
Dutch West Indian (0)	0	<0.01
Haitian (0)	0	<0.01
Jamaican (0)	0	<0.01
Trinidadian/Tobagonian (0)	0	<0.01
U.S. Virgin Islander (0)	0	<0.01
West Indian (0)	0	<0.01
Other West Indian (0)	0	<0.01
Yugoslavian (0)	0	<0.01

Hispanic Origin	Population	%
Hispanic or Latino (of any race)	1,746	7.09
Central American, ex. Mexican	349	1.42
Costa Rican	0	<0.01
Guatemalan	12	0.05
Honduran	8	0.03
Nicaraguan	5	0.02
Panamanian	2	0.01
Salvadoran	322	1.31
Other Central American	0	<0.01
Cuban	6	0.02
Dominican Republic	0	<0.01
Mexican	1,225	4.97
Puerto Rican	48	0.19
South American	4	0.02
Argentinean	0	<0.01
Bolivian	0	<0.01
Chilean	0	<0.01
Colombian	2	0.01
Ecuadorian	0	<0.01
Paraguayan	0	<0.01
Peruvian	0	<0.01
Uruguayan	0	<0.01
Venezuelan	0	<0.01
Other South American	2	0.01
Other Hispanic or Latino	114	0.46

Race*	Population	%
African-American/Black (68)	126	0.51
Not Hispanic (51)	104	0.42
Hispanic (17)	22	0.09
American Indian/Alaska Native (71)	214	0.87
Not Hispanic (52)	172	0.70
Hispanic (19)	42	0.17
Alaska Athabascan *(Ala. Nat.)* (0)	0	<0.01
Aleut *(Alaska Native)* (0)	0	<0.01
Apache (1)	10	0.04
Arapaho (0)	0	<0.01
Blackfeet (2)	10	0.04
Canadian/French Am. Ind. (4)	5	0.02
Central American Ind. (0)	0	<0.01
Cherokee (7)	73	0.30
Cheyenne (4)	4	0.02
Chickasaw (0)	0	<0.01
Chippewa (3)	3	0.01
Choctaw (0)	2	0.01
Colville (0)	0	<0.01
Comanche (0)	0	<0.01
Cree (0)	0	<0.01
Creek (4)	6	0.02
Crow (0)	0	<0.01
Delaware (0)	0	<0.01
Hopi (0)	0	<0.01
Houma (0)	0	<0.01
Inupiat *(Alaska Native)* (0)	0	<0.01
Iroquois (1)	1	<0.01
Kiowa (0)	0	<0.01
Lumbee (0)	1	<0.01
Menominee (0)	0	<0.01
Mexican American Ind. (1)	1	<0.01
Navajo (0)	3	0.01
Osage (0)	0	<0.01
Ottawa (0)	0	<0.01
Paiute (0)	1	<0.01
Pima (0)	0	<0.01
Potawatomi (0)	1	<0.01
Pueblo (0)	0	<0.01
Puget Sound Salish (0)	0	<0.01
Seminole (0)	0	<0.01
Shoshone (0)	0	<0.01
Sioux (1)	5	0.02
South American Ind. (0)	0	<0.01
Spanish American Ind. (0)	0	<0.01
Tlingit-Haida *(Alaska Native)* (0)	0	<0.01
Tohono O'Odham (0)	0	<0.01
Tsimshian *(Alaska Native)* (0)	0	<0.01
Ute (0)	0	<0.01
Yakama (0)	0	<0.01
Yaqui (0)	0	<0.01
Yuman (0)	0	<0.01
Yup'ik *(Alaska Native)* (0)	0	<0.01
Asian (89)	140	0.57
Not Hispanic (83)	131	0.53
Hispanic (6)	9	0.04
Bangladeshi (0)	0	<0.01
Bhutanese (0)	0	<0.01
Burmese (0)	0	<0.01
Cambodian (0)	0	<0.01
Chinese, ex. Taiwanese (17)	24	0.10
Filipino (30)	47	0.19
Hmong (0)	0	<0.01
Indian (4)	5	0.02
Indonesian (1)	1	<0.01
Japanese (5)	24	0.10
Korean (6)	12	0.05
Laotian (0)	0	<0.01
Malaysian (0)	0	<0.01
Nepalese (0)	0	<0.01
Pakistani (8)	9	0.04
Sri Lankan (0)	0	<0.01
Taiwanese (0)	0	<0.01
Thai (2)	2	0.01
Vietnamese (11)	11	0.04
Hawaii Native/Pacific Islander (5)	18	0.07
Not Hispanic (4)	17	0.07
Hispanic (1)	1	<0.01
Fijian (0)	0	<0.01
Guamanian/Chamorro (1)	1	<0.01
Marshallese (0)	0	<0.01
Native Hawaiian (0)	8	0.03
Samoan (1)	2	0.01
Tongan (0)	0	<0.01
White (23,132)	23,471	95.24
Not Hispanic (22,470)	22,696	92.10
Hispanic (662)	775	3.14

*Notes: † The Census 2010 population figure is used to calculate the percentages in the Hispanic Origin and Race categories. Ancestry percentages are based on the 2006-2010 American Community Survey population (not shown); ‡ Numbers in parentheses indicate the number of people reporting a single ancestry; * Numbers in parentheses indicate the number of persons reporting this race alone, not in combination with any other race; Please refer to the Explanation of Data for more information.*

Whitley County

Population: 33,292

Ancestry	Population	%
Afghan (0)	0	<0.01
African, Sub-Saharan (1)	1	<0.01
African (0)	0	<0.01
Cape Verdean (0)	0	<0.01
Ethiopian (1)	1	<0.01
Ghanaian (0)	0	<0.01
Kenyan (0)	0	<0.01
Liberian (0)	0	<0.01
Nigerian (0)	0	<0.01
Senegalese (0)	0	<0.01
Sierra Leonean (0)	0	<0.01
Somalian (0)	0	<0.01
South African (0)	0	<0.01
Sudanese (0)	0	<0.01
Ugandan (0)	0	<0.01
Zimbabwean (0)	0	<0.01
Other Sub-Saharan African (0)	0	<0.01
Albanian (0)	0	<0.01
Alsatian (0)	0	<0.01
American (4,128)	4,128	12.51
Arab (37)	83	0.25
Arab (0)	40	0.12
Egyptian (0)	0	<0.01
Iraqi (0)	2	0.01
Jordanian (0)	0	<0.01
Lebanese (4)	8	0.02
Moroccan (0)	0	<0.01
Palestinian (27)	27	0.08
Syrian (6)	6	0.02
Other Arab (0)	0	<0.01
Armenian (0)	0	<0.01
Assyrian/Chaldean/Syriac (0)	0	<0.01
Australian (0)	6	0.02
Austrian (0)	23	0.07
Basque (0)	0	<0.01
Belgian (15)	26	0.08
Brazilian (14)	14	0.04
British (27)	45	0.14
Bulgarian (0)	0	<0.01
Cajun (0)	0	<0.01
Canadian (12)	17	0.05
Carpatho Rusyn (0)	0	<0.01
Celtic (0)	0	<0.01
Croatian (0)	3	0.01
Cypriot (0)	0	<0.01
Czech (4)	27	0.08
Czechoslovakian (14)	14	0.04
Danish (46)	139	0.42
Dutch (195)	763	2.31
Eastern European (0)	0	<0.01
English (1,248)	3,056	9.26
Estonian (0)	0	<0.01
European (291)	291	0.88
Finnish (10)	23	0.07
French, ex. Basque (284)	1,079	3.27
French Canadian (37)	55	0.17
German (6,903)	12,613	38.23
German Russian (0)	0	<0.01
Greek (39)	59	0.18
Guyanese (0)	0	<0.01
Hungarian (111)	187	0.57
Icelander (7)	13	0.04
Iranian (0)	0	<0.01
Irish (887)	4,141	12.55
Israeli (0)	0	<0.01
Italian (238)	575	1.74
Latvian (0)	0	<0.01
Lithuanian (0)	11	0.03
Luxemburger (0)	0	<0.01
Macedonian (0)	11	0.03
Maltese (0)	0	<0.01
New Zealander (0)	0	<0.01
Northern European (0)	0	<0.01
Norwegian (116)	252	0.76
Pennsylvania German (37)	37	0.11
Polish (193)	479	1.45
Portuguese (0)	45	0.14
Romanian (12)	28	0.08
Russian (7)	129	0.39
Scandinavian (27)	39	0.12
Scotch-Irish (245)	573	1.74
Scottish (279)	628	1.90
Serbian (0)	0	<0.01
Slavic (22)	22	0.07
Slovak (0)	0	<0.01
Slovene (0)	46	0.14
Soviet Union (0)	0	<0.01
Swedish (236)	334	1.01
Swiss (87)	514	1.56
Turkish (0)	0	<0.01
Ukrainian (0)	0	<0.01
Welsh (30)	134	0.41
West Indian, ex. Hispanic (19)	47	0.14
Bahamian (0)	0	<0.01
Barbadian (0)	14	0.04
Belizean (0)	0	<0.01
Bermudan (0)	0	<0.01
British West Indian (0)	0	<0.01
Dutch West Indian (0)	0	<0.01
Haitian (19)	19	0.06
Jamaican (0)	0	<0.01
Trinidadian/Tobagonian (0)	0	<0.01
U.S. Virgin Islander (0)	0	<0.01
West Indian (0)	0	<0.01
Other West Indian (0)	14	0.04
Yugoslavian (0)	61	0.18

Hispanic Origin	Population	%
Hispanic or Latino (of any race)	515	1.55
Central American, ex. Mexican	20	0.06
Costa Rican	1	<0.01
Guatemalan	14	0.04
Honduran	1	<0.01
Nicaraguan	0	<0.01
Panamanian	0	<0.01
Salvadoran	4	0.01
Other Central American	0	<0.01
Cuban	3	0.01
Dominican Republic	0	<0.01
Mexican	397	1.19
Puerto Rican	34	0.10
South American	5	0.02
Argentinean	1	<0.01
Bolivian	0	<0.01
Chilean	0	<0.01
Colombian	2	0.01
Ecuadorian	0	<0.01
Paraguayan	0	<0.01
Peruvian	0	<0.01
Uruguayan	0	<0.01
Venezuelan	2	0.01
Other South American	0	<0.01
Other Hispanic or Latino	56	0.17

Race*	Population	%
African-American/Black (99)	199	0.60
Not Hispanic (96)	189	0.57
Hispanic (3)	10	0.03
American Indian/Alaska Native (92)	259	0.78
Not Hispanic (76)	230	0.69
Hispanic (16)	29	0.09
Alaska Athabascan *(Ala. Nat.)* (0)	0	<0.01
Aleut *(Alaska Native)* (0)	0	<0.01
Apache (1)	2	0.01
Arapaho (0)	0	<0.01
Blackfeet (0)	7	0.02
Canadian/French Am. Ind. (0)	1	<0.01
Central American Ind. (0)	0	<0.01
Cherokee (7)	67	0.20
Cheyenne (0)	0	<0.01
Chickasaw (0)	0	<0.01
Chippewa (3)	5	0.02
Choctaw (1)	1	<0.01
Colville (0)	0	<0.01
Comanche (2)	2	0.01
Cree (0)	0	<0.01
Creek (0)	0	<0.01
Crow (0)	0	<0.01
Delaware (0)	0	<0.01
Hopi (0)	0	<0.01
Houma (0)	0	<0.01
Inupiat *(Alaska Native)* (0)	0	<0.01
Iroquois (0)	2	0.01
Kiowa (0)	0	<0.01
Lumbee (0)	0	<0.01
Menominee (0)	0	<0.01
Mexican American Ind. (4)	7	0.02
Navajo (3)	4	0.01
Osage (1)	1	<0.01
Ottawa (0)	0	<0.01
Paiute (0)	0	<0.01
Pima (0)	0	<0.01
Potawatomi (2)	2	0.01
Pueblo (5)	9	0.03
Puget Sound Salish (0)	0	<0.01
Seminole (0)	0	<0.01
Shoshone (0)	0	<0.01
Sioux (1)	5	0.02
South American Ind. (0)	1	<0.01
Spanish American Ind. (1)	1	<0.01
Tlingit-Haida *(Alaska Native)* (0)	0	<0.01
Tohono O'Odham (0)	0	<0.01
Tsimshian *(Alaska Native)* (0)	0	<0.01
Ute (0)	0	<0.01
Yakama (0)	0	<0.01
Yaqui (0)	0	<0.01
Yuman (0)	0	<0.01
Yup'ik *(Alaska Native)* (0)	0	<0.01
Asian (105)	184	0.55
Not Hispanic (105)	183	0.55
Hispanic (0)	1	<0.01
Bangladeshi (0)	0	<0.01
Bhutanese (0)	0	<0.01
Burmese (1)	1	<0.01
Cambodian (0)	0	<0.01
Chinese, ex. Taiwanese (34)	40	0.12
Filipino (25)	34	0.10
Hmong (0)	0	<0.01
Indian (21)	25	0.08
Indonesian (0)	2	0.01
Japanese (9)	28	0.08
Korean (5)	25	0.08
Laotian (1)	2	0.01
Malaysian (0)	0	<0.01
Nepalese (0)	0	<0.01
Pakistani (1)	5	0.02
Sri Lankan (1)	1	<0.01
Taiwanese (0)	0	<0.01
Thai (3)	7	0.02
Vietnamese (2)	5	0.02
Hawaii Native/Pacific Islander (7)	28	0.08
Not Hispanic (7)	27	0.08
Hispanic (0)	1	<0.01
Fijian (0)	0	<0.01
Guamanian/Chamorro (0)	0	<0.01
Marshallese (0)	0	<0.01
Native Hawaiian (1)	9	0.03
Samoan (6)	11	0.03
Tongan (0)	0	<0.01
White (32,479)	32,852	98.68
Not Hispanic (32,147)	32,466	97.52
Hispanic (332)	386	1.16

*Notes: † The Census 2010 population figure is used to calculate the percentages in the Hispanic Origin and Race categories. Ancestry percentages are based on the 2006-2010 American Community Survey population (not shown); ‡ Numbers in parentheses indicate the number of people reporting a single ancestry; * Numbers in parentheses indicate the number of persons reporting this race alone, not in combination with any other race; Please refer to the Explanation of Data for more information.*

Place Profiles

Anderson

Place Type: City
County: Madison
Population: 56,129

Ancestry	Population	%
Afghan (0)	0	<0.01
African, Sub-Saharan (628)	648	1.14
African (523)	543	0.96
Cape Verdean (0)	0	<0.01
Ethiopian (18)	18	0.03
Ghanaian (0)	0	<0.01
Kenyan (43)	43	0.08
Liberian (0)	0	<0.01
Nigerian (0)	0	<0.01
Senegalese (0)	0	<0.01
Sierra Leonean (0)	0	<0.01
Somalian (0)	0	<0.01
South African (0)	0	<0.01
Sudanese (18)	18	0.03
Ugandan (0)	0	<0.01
Zimbabwean (0)	0	<0.01
Other Sub-Saharan African (26)	26	0.05
Albanian (0)	0	<0.01
Alsatian (0)	0	<0.01
American (5,914)	5,914	10.42
Arab (12)	24	0.04
Arab (0)	0	<0.01
Egyptian (0)	0	<0.01
Iraqi (0)	0	<0.01
Jordanian (0)	0	<0.01
Lebanese (0)	0	<0.01
Moroccan (12)	24	0.04
Palestinian (0)	0	<0.01
Syrian (0)	0	<0.01
Other Arab (0)	0	<0.01
Armenian (0)	0	<0.01
Assyrian/Chaldean/Syriac (0)	0	<0.01
Australian (12)	12	0.02
Austrian (44)	103	0.18
Basque (0)	0	<0.01
Belgian (0)	23	0.04
Brazilian (0)	0	<0.01
British (73)	153	0.27
Bulgarian (0)	0	<0.01
Cajun (0)	0	<0.01
Canadian (21)	50	0.09
Carpatho Rusyn (0)	0	<0.01
Celtic (0)	12	0.02
Croatian (9)	59	0.10
Cypriot (0)	0	<0.01
Czech (25)	45	0.08
Czechoslovakian (12)	12	0.02
Danish (0)	33	0.06
Dutch (429)	1,593	2.81
Eastern European (0)	0	<0.01
English (2,333)	4,934	8.69
Estonian (0)	0	<0.01
European (290)	313	0.55
Finnish (13)	35	0.06
French, ex. Basque (493)	1,268	2.23
French Canadian (18)	66	0.12
German (4,469)	10,377	18.28
German Russian (0)	0	<0.01
Greek (82)	126	0.22
Guyanese (0)	0	<0.01
Hungarian (41)	83	0.15
Icelander (0)	0	<0.01
Iranian (0)	0	<0.01
Irish (1,989)	6,464	11.39
Israeli (0)	0	<0.01
Italian (364)	869	1.53
Latvian (0)	0	<0.01
Lithuanian (0)	0	<0.01
Luxemburger (0)	6	0.01
Macedonian (0)	0	<0.01
Maltese (0)	0	<0.01
New Zealander (0)	0	<0.01
Northern European (0)	0	<0.01
Norwegian (62)	167	0.29
Pennsylvania German (0)	12	0.02
Polish (295)	917	1.62
Portuguese (21)	26	0.05
Romanian (17)	17	0.03
Russian (21)	61	0.11
Scandinavian (0)	75	0.13
Scotch-Irish (302)	792	1.40
Scottish (453)	861	1.52
Serbian (0)	12	0.02
Slavic (0)	13	0.02
Slovak (23)	23	0.04
Slovene (0)	9	0.02
Soviet Union (0)	0	<0.01
Swedish (160)	302	0.53
Swiss (30)	113	0.20
Turkish (10)	33	0.06
Ukrainian (0)	22	0.04
Welsh (94)	399	0.70
West Indian, ex. Hispanic (42)	56	0.10
Bahamian (0)	0	<0.01
Barbadian (0)	0	<0.01
Belizean (0)	0	<0.01
Bermudan (0)	0	<0.01
British West Indian (0)	0	<0.01
Dutch West Indian (0)	0	<0.01
Haitian (0)	0	<0.01
Jamaican (29)	29	0.05
Trinidadian/Tobagonian (0)	0	<0.01
U.S. Virgin Islander (0)	0	<0.01
West Indian (0)	0	<0.01
Other West Indian (13)	27	0.05
Yugoslavian (0)	12	0.02

Hispanic Origin	Population	%
Hispanic or Latino (of any race)	2,719	4.84
Central American, ex. Mexican	115	0.20
Costa Rican	1	<0.01
Guatemalan	59	0.11
Honduran	16	0.03
Nicaraguan	19	0.03
Panamanian	1	<0.01
Salvadoran	19	0.03
Other Central American	0	<0.01
Cuban	26	0.05
Dominican Republic	15	0.03
Mexican	2,199	3.92
Puerto Rican	118	0.21
South American	23	0.04
Argentinean	3	0.01
Bolivian	3	0.01
Chilean	3	0.01
Colombian	6	0.01
Ecuadorian	2	<0.01
Paraguayan	0	<0.01
Peruvian	3	0.01
Uruguayan	0	<0.01
Venezuelan	3	0.01
Other South American	0	<0.01
Other Hispanic or Latino	223	0.40

Race*	Population	%
African-American/Black (8,532)	9,500	16.93
Not Hispanic (8,470)	9,376	16.70
Hispanic (62)	124	0.22
American Indian/Alaska Native (185)	528	0.94
Not Hispanic (134)	432	0.77
Hispanic (51)	96	0.17
Alaska Athabascan *(Ala. Nat.)* (0)	0	<0.01
Aleut *(Alaska Native)* (0)	0	<0.01
Apache (7)	9	0.02
Arapaho (0)	0	<0.01
Blackfeet (1)	32	0.06
Canadian/French Am. Ind. (0)	1	<0.01
Central American Ind. (0)	7	0.01
Cherokee (44)	127	0.23
Cheyenne (1)	4	0.01
Chickasaw (0)	1	<0.01
Chippewa (3)	6	0.01
Choctaw (5)	10	0.02
Colville (0)	0	<0.01
Comanche (0)	0	<0.01
Cree (0)	0	<0.01
Creek (2)	3	0.01
Crow (0)	0	<0.01
Delaware (0)	6	0.01
Hopi (0)	1	<0.01
Houma (0)	0	<0.01
Inupiat *(Alaska Native)* (0)	1	<0.01
Iroquois (0)	7	0.01
Kiowa (1)	1	<0.01
Lumbee (0)	0	<0.01
Menominee (0)	0	<0.01
Mexican American Ind. (16)	30	0.05
Navajo (2)	11	0.02
Osage (2)	2	<0.01
Ottawa (0)	0	<0.01
Paiute (0)	0	<0.01
Pima (0)	0	<0.01
Potawatomi (3)	7	0.01
Pueblo (0)	0	<0.01
Puget Sound Salish (0)	0	<0.01
Seminole (0)	2	<0.01
Shoshone (0)	1	<0.01
Sioux (3)	11	0.02
South American Ind. (0)	0	<0.01
Spanish American Ind. (1)	2	<0.01
Tlingit-Haida *(Alaska Native)* (0)	0	<0.01
Tohono O'Odham (0)	0	<0.01
Tsimshian *(Alaska Native)* (0)	0	<0.01
Ute (4)	4	0.01
Yakama (0)	0	<0.01
Yaqui (0)	0	<0.01
Yuman (0)	0	<0.01
Yup'ik *(Alaska Native)* (0)	0	<0.01
Asian (265)	401	0.71
Not Hispanic (264)	383	0.68
Hispanic (1)	18	0.03
Bangladeshi (0)	0	<0.01
Bhutanese (0)	0	<0.01
Burmese (0)	0	<0.01
Cambodian (0)	0	<0.01
Chinese, ex. Taiwanese (46)	58	0.10
Filipino (50)	76	0.14
Hmong (0)	0	<0.01
Indian (39)	53	0.09
Indonesian (0)	0	<0.01
Japanese (19)	57	0.10
Korean (32)	58	0.10
Laotian (0)	2	<0.01
Malaysian (1)	1	<0.01
Nepalese (0)	0	<0.01
Pakistani (1)	1	<0.01
Sri Lankan (0)	0	<0.01
Taiwanese (0)	2	<0.01
Thai (7)	11	0.02
Vietnamese (37)	46	0.08
Hawaii Native/Pacific Islander (25)	54	0.10
Not Hispanic (22)	43	0.08
Hispanic (3)	11	0.02
Fijian (0)	0	<0.01
Guamanian/Chamorro (5)	8	0.01
Marshallese (0)	0	<0.01
Native Hawaiian (5)	22	0.04
Samoan (8)	11	0.02
Tongan (0)	0	<0.01
White (44,204)	45,548	81.15
Not Hispanic (43,181)	44,327	78.97
Hispanic (1,023)	1,221	2.18

*Notes: † The Census 2010 population figure is used to calculate the percentages in the Hispanic Origin and Race categories. Ancestry percentages are based on the 2006-2010 American Community Survey population (not shown); ‡ Numbers in parentheses indicate the number of people reporting a single ancestry; * Numbers in parentheses indicate the number of persons reporting this race alone, not in combination with any other race; Please refer to the Explanation of Data for more information.*

Bloomington

Place Type: City
County: Monroe
Population: 80,405

Ancestry	Population	%
Afghan (59)	59	0.08
African, Sub-Saharan (498)	593	0.76
African (417)	508	0.65
Cape Verdean (0)	0	<0.01
Ethiopian (4)	5	0.01
Ghanaian (0)	0	<0.01
Kenyan (0)	0	<0.01
Liberian (0)	0	<0.01
Nigerian (14)	14	0.02
Senegalese (0)	0	<0.01
Sierra Leonean (0)	0	<0.01
Somalian (0)	0	<0.01
South African (63)	63	0.08
Sudanese (0)	0	<0.01
Ugandan (0)	0	<0.01
Zimbabwean (0)	0	<0.01
Other Sub-Saharan African (0)	3	<0.01
Albanian (20)	20	0.03
Alsatian (0)	19	0.02
American (3,411)	3,411	4.35
Arab (363)	548	0.70
Arab (187)	187	0.24
Egyptian (8)	21	0.03
Iraqi (30)	30	0.04
Jordanian (0)	10	0.01
Lebanese (67)	167	0.21
Moroccan (27)	27	0.03
Palestinian (0)	0	<0.01
Syrian (13)	75	0.10
Other Arab (31)	31	0.04
Armenian (14)	37	0.05
Assyrian/Chaldean/Syriac (0)	0	<0.01
Australian (18)	46	0.06
Austrian (70)	439	0.56
Basque (0)	0	<0.01
Belgian (23)	155	0.20
Brazilian (40)	69	0.09
British (181)	729	0.93
Bulgarian (29)	29	0.04
Cajun (0)	0	<0.01
Canadian (71)	138	0.18
Carpatho Rusyn (0)	0	<0.01
Celtic (0)	0	<0.01
Croatian (48)	171	0.22
Cypriot (0)	0	<0.01
Czech (129)	478	0.61
Czechoslovakian (19)	85	0.11
Danish (127)	353	0.45
Dutch (483)	1,696	2.16
Eastern European (296)	354	0.45
English (2,870)	8,739	11.13
Estonian (0)	15	0.02
European (1,245)	1,404	1.79
Finnish (12)	42	0.05
French, ex. Basque (581)	2,654	3.38
French Canadian (73)	305	0.39
German (5,754)	19,499	24.84
German Russian (0)	0	<0.01
Greek (227)	551	0.70
Guyanese (0)	0	<0.01
Hungarian (165)	767	0.98
Icelander (21)	41	0.05
Iranian (187)	201	0.26
Irish (3,083)	10,941	13.94
Israeli (91)	168	0.21
Italian (1,043)	3,669	4.67
Latvian (10)	10	0.01
Lithuanian (82)	362	0.46
Luxemburger (0)	0	<0.01
Macedonian (48)	62	0.08
Maltese (0)	0	<0.01
New Zealander (0)	0	<0.01
Northern European (62)	98	0.12
Norwegian (240)	1,150	1.47
Pennsylvania German (21)	58	0.07
Polish (952)	3,792	4.83
Portuguese (9)	52	0.07
Romanian (110)	270	0.34
Russian (341)	1,268	1.62
Scandinavian (25)	161	0.21
Scotch-Irish (826)	2,163	2.76
Scottish (576)	2,274	2.90
Serbian (49)	155	0.20
Slavic (0)	23	0.03
Slovak (37)	194	0.25
Slovene (10)	65	0.08
Soviet Union (0)	0	<0.01
Swedish (305)	1,462	1.86
Swiss (98)	457	0.58
Turkish (111)	111	0.14
Ukrainian (122)	232	0.30
Welsh (171)	840	1.07
West Indian, ex. Hispanic (57)	96	0.12
Bahamian (0)	0	<0.01
Barbadian (0)	0	<0.01
Belizean (0)	0	<0.01
Bermudan (0)	0	<0.01
British West Indian (0)	0	<0.01
Dutch West Indian (0)	23	0.03
Haitian (0)	0	<0.01
Jamaican (57)	57	0.07
Trinidadian/Tobagonian (0)	0	<0.01
U.S. Virgin Islander (0)	0	<0.01
West Indian (0)	16	0.02
Other West Indian (0)	0	<0.01
Yugoslavian (17)	50	0.06

Hispanic Origin	Population	%
Hispanic or Latino (of any race)	2,823	3.51
Central American, ex. Mexican	165	0.21
Costa Rican	21	0.03
Guatemalan	38	0.05
Honduran	21	0.03
Nicaraguan	28	0.03
Panamanian	22	0.03
Salvadoran	31	0.04
Other Central American	4	<0.01
Cuban	126	0.16
Dominican Republic	43	0.05
Mexican	1,506	1.87
Puerto Rican	348	0.43
South American	349	0.43
Argentinean	57	0.07
Bolivian	11	0.01
Chilean	36	0.04
Colombian	85	0.11
Ecuadorian	30	0.04
Paraguayan	5	0.01
Peruvian	67	0.08
Uruguayan	5	0.01
Venezuelan	53	0.07
Other South American	0	<0.01
Other Hispanic or Latino	286	0.36

Race*	Population	%
African-American/Black (3,671)	4,618	5.74
Not Hispanic (3,562)	4,423	5.50
Hispanic (109)	195	0.24
American Indian/Alaska Native (214)	699	0.87
Not Hispanic (176)	591	0.74
Hispanic (38)	108	0.13
Alaska Athabascan *(Ala. Nat.)* (1)	1	<0.01
Aleut *(Alaska Native)* (0)	2	<0.01
Apache (4)	11	0.01
Arapaho (0)	0	<0.01
Blackfeet (0)	26	0.03
Canadian/French Am. Ind. (0)	1	<0.01
Central American Ind. (1)	2	<0.01
Cherokee (37)	161	0.20
Cheyenne (0)	0	<0.01
Chickasaw (2)	2	<0.01
Chippewa (10)	21	0.03
Choctaw (8)	19	0.02
Colville (0)	0	<0.01
Comanche (0)	0	<0.01
Cree (0)	1	<0.01
Creek (4)	5	0.01
Crow (0)	0	<0.01
Delaware (5)	8	0.01
Hopi (1)	2	<0.01
Houma (0)	0	<0.01
Inupiat *(Alaska Native)* (0)	3	<0.01
Iroquois (5)	9	0.01
Kiowa (0)	0	<0.01
Lumbee (4)	4	<0.01
Menominee (1)	2	<0.01
Mexican American Ind. (6)	14	0.02
Navajo (3)	9	0.01
Osage (0)	2	<0.01
Ottawa (1)	1	<0.01
Paiute (0)	0	<0.01
Pima (0)	0	<0.01
Potawatomi (3)	10	0.01
Pueblo (0)	3	<0.01
Puget Sound Salish (5)	5	0.01
Seminole (0)	3	<0.01
Shoshone (0)	1	<0.01
Sioux (9)	24	0.03
South American Ind. (2)	4	<0.01
Spanish American Ind. (3)	21	0.03
Tlingit-Haida *(Alaska Native)* (0)	1	<0.01
Tohono O'Odham (3)	8	0.01
Tsimshian *(Alaska Native)* (0)	0	<0.01
Ute (0)	0	<0.01
Yakama (3)	3	<0.01
Yaqui (0)	0	<0.01
Yuman (0)	0	<0.01
Yup'ik *(Alaska Native)* (0)	1	<0.01
Asian (6,399)	7,368	9.16
Not Hispanic (6,378)	7,298	9.08
Hispanic (21)	70	0.09
Bangladeshi (21)	27	0.03
Bhutanese (0)	0	<0.01
Burmese (17)	18	0.02
Cambodian (5)	9	0.01
Chinese, ex. Taiwanese (2,004)	2,230	2.77
Filipino (161)	312	0.39
Hmong (4)	5	0.01
Indian (1,263)	1,390	1.73
Indonesian (71)	78	0.10
Japanese (242)	395	0.49
Korean (1,696)	1,807	2.25
Laotian (6)	8	0.01
Malaysian (49)	59	0.07
Nepalese (19)	19	0.02
Pakistani (76)	87	0.11
Sri Lankan (38)	40	0.05
Taiwanese (235)	260	0.32
Thai (83)	103	0.13
Vietnamese (168)	203	0.25
Hawaii Native/Pacific Islander (42)	120	0.15
Not Hispanic (37)	95	0.12
Hispanic (5)	25	0.03
Fijian (1)	1	<0.01
Guamanian/Chamorro (11)	24	0.03
Marshallese (0)	0	<0.01
Native Hawaiian (11)	37	0.05
Samoan (6)	16	0.02
Tongan (0)	0	<0.01
White (66,751)	68,936	85.74
Not Hispanic (65,189)	67,128	83.49
Hispanic (1,562)	1,808	2.25

*Notes: † The Census 2010 population figure is used to calculate the percentages in the Hispanic Origin and Race categories. Ancestry percentages are based on the 2006-2010 American Community Survey population (not shown); ‡ Numbers in parentheses indicate the number of people reporting a single ancestry; * Numbers in parentheses indicate the number of persons reporting this race alone, not in combination with any other race; Please refer to the Explanation of Data for more information.*

Carmel

Place Type: City
County: Hamilton
Population: 79,191

Ancestry	Population	%
Afghan (18)	37	0.05
African, Sub-Saharan (83)	255	0.33
African (58)	95	0.12
Cape Verdean (0)	0	<0.01
Ethiopian (12)	12	0.02
Ghanaian (0)	0	<0.01
Kenyan (0)	0	<0.01
Liberian (0)	0	<0.01
Nigerian (0)	0	<0.01
Senegalese (0)	0	<0.01
Sierra Leonean (0)	0	<0.01
Somalian (0)	0	<0.01
South African (13)	137	0.18
Sudanese (0)	11	0.01
Ugandan (0)	0	<0.01
Zimbabwean (0)	0	<0.01
Other Sub-Saharan African (0)	0	<0.01
Albanian (0)	0	<0.01
Alsatian (0)	0	<0.01
American (4,712)	4,712	6.14
Arab (378)	563	0.73
Arab (86)	101	0.13
Egyptian (164)	164	0.21
Iraqi (0)	0	<0.01
Jordanian (8)	8	0.01
Lebanese (40)	160	0.21
Moroccan (13)	36	0.05
Palestinian (24)	24	0.03
Syrian (0)	0	<0.01
Other Arab (43)	70	0.09
Armenian (0)	21	0.03
Assyrian/Chaldean/Syriac (0)	0	<0.01
Australian (31)	42	0.05
Austrian (32)	161	0.21
Basque (0)	0	<0.01
Belgian (26)	352	0.46
Brazilian (0)	11	0.01
British (449)	626	0.82
Bulgarian (0)	16	0.02
Cajun (0)	0	<0.01
Canadian (77)	166	0.22
Carpatho Rusyn (0)	16	0.02
Celtic (14)	14	0.02
Croatian (23)	175	0.23
Cypriot (0)	0	<0.01
Czech (33)	336	0.44
Czechoslovakian (60)	115	0.15
Danish (161)	597	0.78
Dutch (320)	1,777	2.31
Eastern European (149)	164	0.21
English (3,161)	11,352	14.79
Estonian (0)	13	0.02
European (1,056)	1,241	1.62
Finnish (14)	70	0.09
French, ex. Basque (305)	2,214	2.88
French Canadian (128)	225	0.29
German (7,760)	21,955	28.60
German Russian (0)	0	<0.01
Greek (192)	485	0.63
Guyanese (0)	0	<0.01
Hungarian (86)	504	0.66
Icelander (0)	12	0.02
Iranian (203)	253	0.33
Irish (3,191)	12,211	15.91
Israeli (0)	0	<0.01
Italian (1,290)	3,728	4.86
Latvian (129)	129	0.17
Lithuanian (57)	120	0.16
Luxemburger (0)	22	0.03
Macedonian (55)	104	0.14
Maltese (0)	0	<0.01
New Zealander (0)	0	<0.01
Northern European (105)	105	0.14
Norwegian (335)	995	1.30
Pennsylvania German (15)	42	0.05
Polish (680)	3,117	4.06
Portuguese (22)	112	0.15
Romanian (112)	200	0.26
Russian (676)	1,522	1.98
Scandinavian (74)	90	0.12
Scotch-Irish (468)	1,430	1.86
Scottish (684)	2,632	3.43
Serbian (21)	40	0.05
Slavic (0)	0	<0.01
Slovak (103)	356	0.46
Slovene (17)	109	0.14
Soviet Union (0)	0	<0.01
Swedish (222)	1,414	1.84
Swiss (49)	431	0.56
Turkish (69)	69	0.09
Ukrainian (161)	271	0.35
Welsh (83)	628	0.82
West Indian, ex. Hispanic (39)	55	0.07
Bahamian (0)	0	<0.01
Barbadian (0)	0	<0.01
Belizean (0)	0	<0.01
Bermudan (0)	0	<0.01
British West Indian (0)	0	<0.01
Dutch West Indian (0)	0	<0.01
Haitian (0)	16	0.02
Jamaican (39)	39	0.05
Trinidadian/Tobagonian (0)	0	<0.01
U.S. Virgin Islander (0)	0	<0.01
West Indian (0)	0	<0.01
Other West Indian (0)	0	<0.01
Yugoslavian (51)	67	0.09

Hispanic Origin	Population	%
Hispanic or Latino (of any race)	2,009	2.54
Central American, ex. Mexican	181	0.23
Costa Rican	8	0.01
Guatemalan	87	0.11
Honduran	9	0.01
Nicaraguan	20	0.03
Panamanian	28	0.04
Salvadoran	28	0.04
Other Central American	1	<0.01
Cuban	101	0.13
Dominican Republic	40	0.05
Mexican	944	1.19
Puerto Rican	226	0.29
South American	310	0.39
Argentinean	38	0.05
Bolivian	12	0.02
Chilean	22	0.03
Colombian	125	0.16
Ecuadorian	17	0.02
Paraguayan	3	<0.01
Peruvian	49	0.06
Uruguayan	3	<0.01
Venezuelan	40	0.05
Other South American	1	<0.01
Other Hispanic or Latino	207	0.26

Race*	Population	%
African-American/Black (2,354)	2,767	3.49
Not Hispanic (2,299)	2,674	3.38
Hispanic (55)	93	0.12
American Indian/Alaska Native (130)	354	0.45
Not Hispanic (104)	304	0.38
Hispanic (26)	50	0.06
Alaska Athabascan *(Ala. Nat.)* (0)	0	<0.01
Aleut *(Alaska Native)* (0)	0	<0.01
Apache (6)	6	0.01
Arapaho (0)	0	<0.01
Blackfeet (4)	16	0.02
Canadian/French Am. Ind. (0)	0	<0.01
Central American Ind. (1)	2	<0.01
Cherokee (17)	57	0.07
Cheyenne (0)	0	<0.01
Chickasaw (0)	0	<0.01
Chippewa (4)	6	0.01
Choctaw (5)	11	0.01
Colville (0)	0	<0.01
Comanche (0)	3	<0.01
Cree (3)	3	<0.01
Creek (0)	1	<0.01
Crow (1)	1	<0.01
Delaware (0)	0	<0.01
Hopi (2)	4	0.01
Houma (0)	0	<0.01
Inupiat *(Alaska Native)* (1)	1	<0.01
Iroquois (1)	8	0.01
Kiowa (0)	0	<0.01
Lumbee (2)	2	<0.01
Menominee (0)	0	<0.01
Mexican American Ind. (16)	21	0.03
Navajo (1)	4	0.01
Osage (3)	3	<0.01
Ottawa (1)	5	0.01
Paiute (0)	0	<0.01
Pima (0)	0	<0.01
Potawatomi (3)	11	0.01
Pueblo (0)	0	<0.01
Puget Sound Salish (0)	0	<0.01
Seminole (0)	1	<0.01
Shoshone (0)	0	<0.01
Sioux (3)	5	0.01
South American Ind. (1)	1	<0.01
Spanish American Ind. (2)	2	<0.01
Tlingit-Haida *(Alaska Native)* (0)	0	<0.01
Tohono O'Odham (0)	0	<0.01
Tsimshian *(Alaska Native)* (0)	0	<0.01
Ute (0)	1	<0.01
Yakama (0)	0	<0.01
Yaqui (2)	2	<0.01
Yuman (0)	0	<0.01
Yup'ik *(Alaska Native)* (0)	1	<0.01
Asian (7,009)	7,838	9.90
Not Hispanic (6,988)	7,790	9.84
Hispanic (21)	48	0.06
Bangladeshi (34)	35	0.04
Bhutanese (0)	0	<0.01
Burmese (1)	8	0.01
Cambodian (17)	22	0.03
Chinese, ex. Taiwanese (2,557)	2,754	3.48
Filipino (265)	411	0.52
Hmong (27)	27	0.03
Indian (2,384)	2,526	3.19
Indonesian (32)	41	0.05
Japanese (320)	415	0.52
Korean (583)	684	0.86
Laotian (9)	9	0.01
Malaysian (7)	17	0.02
Nepalese (12)	12	0.02
Pakistani (186)	211	0.27
Sri Lankan (30)	35	0.04
Taiwanese (145)	177	0.22
Thai (24)	42	0.05
Vietnamese (236)	279	0.35
Hawaii Native/Pacific Islander (20)	87	0.11
Not Hispanic (17)	77	0.10
Hispanic (3)	10	0.01
Fijian (0)	0	<0.01
Guamanian/Chamorro (5)	11	0.01
Marshallese (0)	0	<0.01
Native Hawaiian (8)	33	0.04
Samoan (5)	16	0.02
Tongan (0)	0	<0.01
White (67,654)	68,938	87.05
Not Hispanic (66,295)	67,446	85.17
Hispanic (1,359)	1,492	1.88

*Notes: † The Census 2010 population figure is used to calculate the percentages in the Hispanic Origin and Race categories. Ancestry percentages are based on the 2006-2010 American Community Survey population (not shown); ‡ Numbers in parentheses indicate the number of people reporting a single ancestry; * Numbers in parentheses indicate the number of persons reporting this race alone, not in combination with any other race; Please refer to the Explanation of Data for more information.*

Elkhart

Place Type: City
County: Elkhart
Population: 50,949

Ancestry	Population	%
Afghan (0)	0	<0.01
African, Sub-Saharan (296)	409	0.79
African (235)	305	0.59
Cape Verdean (0)	0	<0.01
Ethiopian (0)	0	<0.01
Ghanaian (0)	0	<0.01
Kenyan (61)	61	0.12
Liberian (0)	0	<0.01
Nigerian (0)	0	<0.01
Senegalese (0)	0	<0.01
Sierra Leonean (0)	0	<0.01
Somalian (0)	0	<0.01
South African (0)	0	<0.01
Sudanese (0)	0	<0.01
Ugandan (0)	0	<0.01
Zimbabwean (0)	13	0.03
Other Sub-Saharan African (0)	30	0.06
Albanian (0)	0	<0.01
Alsatian (0)	0	<0.01
American (2,012)	2,012	3.88
Arab (109)	109	0.21
Arab (23)	23	0.04
Egyptian (0)	0	<0.01
Iraqi (0)	0	<0.01
Jordanian (0)	0	<0.01
Lebanese (9)	9	0.02
Moroccan (16)	16	0.03
Palestinian (0)	0	<0.01
Syrian (0)	0	<0.01
Other Arab (61)	61	0.12
Armenian (0)	0	<0.01
Assyrian/Chaldean/Syriac (0)	0	<0.01
Australian (0)	0	<0.01
Austrian (0)	38	0.07
Basque (0)	0	<0.01
Belgian (18)	123	0.24
Brazilian (30)	92	0.18
British (41)	111	0.21
Bulgarian (0)	0	<0.01
Cajun (0)	0	<0.01
Canadian (15)	79	0.15
Carpatho Rusyn (0)	0	<0.01
Celtic (0)	0	<0.01
Croatian (0)	17	0.03
Cypriot (0)	0	<0.01
Czech (106)	195	0.38
Czechoslovakian (14)	14	0.03
Danish (21)	53	0.10
Dutch (374)	1,346	2.60
Eastern European (9)	9	0.02
English (1,054)	3,278	6.32
Estonian (0)	0	<0.01
European (207)	207	0.40
Finnish (34)	48	0.09
French, ex. Basque (155)	1,022	1.97
French Canadian (35)	203	0.39
German (3,461)	9,960	19.21
German Russian (0)	0	<0.01
Greek (51)	82	0.16
Guyanese (0)	0	<0.01
Hungarian (111)	258	0.50
Icelander (0)	0	<0.01
Iranian (0)	0	<0.01
Irish (1,183)	5,091	9.82
Israeli (0)	0	<0.01
Italian (711)	1,611	3.11
Latvian (11)	11	0.02
Lithuanian (21)	21	0.04
Luxemburger (0)	0	<0.01
Macedonian (0)	0	<0.01
Maltese (0)	0	<0.01
New Zealander (0)	0	<0.01
Northern European (26)	26	0.05
Norwegian (55)	299	0.58
Pennsylvania German (226)	347	0.67
Polish (487)	1,234	2.38
Portuguese (42)	42	0.08
Romanian (11)	40	0.08
Russian (27)	162	0.31
Scandinavian (60)	60	0.12
Scotch-Irish (331)	647	1.25
Scottish (137)	679	1.31
Serbian (0)	0	<0.01
Slavic (0)	0	<0.01
Slovak (0)	11	0.02
Slovene (18)	18	0.03
Soviet Union (0)	0	<0.01
Swedish (105)	422	0.81
Swiss (64)	504	0.97
Turkish (0)	0	<0.01
Ukrainian (29)	39	0.08
Welsh (44)	213	0.41
West Indian, ex. Hispanic (121)	121	0.23
Bahamian (0)	0	<0.01
Barbadian (0)	0	<0.01
Belizean (0)	0	<0.01
Bermudan (0)	0	<0.01
British West Indian (0)	0	<0.01
Dutch West Indian (0)	0	<0.01
Haitian (0)	0	<0.01
Jamaican (121)	121	0.23
Trinidadian/Tobagonian (0)	0	<0.01
U.S. Virgin Islander (0)	0	<0.01
West Indian (0)	0	<0.01
Other West Indian (0)	0	<0.01
Yugoslavian (0)	0	<0.01

Hispanic Origin	Population	%
Hispanic or Latino (of any race)	11,451	22.48
Central American, ex. Mexican	912	1.79
Costa Rican	1	<0.01
Guatemalan	93	0.18
Honduran	390	0.77
Nicaraguan	14	0.03
Panamanian	2	<0.01
Salvadoran	400	0.79
Other Central American	12	0.02
Cuban	26	0.05
Dominican Republic	19	0.04
Mexican	9,313	18.28
Puerto Rican	392	0.77
South American	121	0.24
Argentinean	10	0.02
Bolivian	29	0.06
Chilean	6	0.01
Colombian	24	0.05
Ecuadorian	7	0.01
Paraguayan	2	<0.01
Peruvian	20	0.04
Uruguayan	1	<0.01
Venezuelan	22	0.04
Other South American	0	<0.01
Other Hispanic or Latino	668	1.31

Race*	Population	%
African-American/Black (7,862)	9,108	17.88
Not Hispanic (7,705)	8,843	17.36
Hispanic (157)	265	0.52
American Indian/Alaska Native (290)	706	1.39
Not Hispanic (154)	482	0.95
Hispanic (136)	224	0.44
Alaska Athabascan *(Ala. Nat.)* (0)	0	<0.01
Aleut *(Alaska Native)* (0)	0	<0.01
Apache (0)	5	0.01
Arapaho (0)	0	<0.01
Blackfeet (5)	31	0.06
Canadian/French Am. Ind. (0)	5	0.01
Central American Ind. (1)	4	0.01
Cherokee (28)	120	0.24
Cheyenne (0)	3	0.01
Chickasaw (2)	2	<0.01
Chippewa (4)	14	0.03
Choctaw (4)	12	0.02
Colville (0)	0	<0.01
Comanche (2)	2	<0.01
Cree (1)	4	0.01
Creek (0)	4	0.01
Crow (0)	4	0.01
Delaware (0)	0	<0.01
Hopi (0)	0	<0.01
Houma (0)	0	<0.01
Inupiat *(Alaska Native)* (0)	0	<0.01
Iroquois (3)	5	0.01
Kiowa (0)	0	<0.01
Lumbee (7)	8	0.02
Menominee (0)	0	<0.01
Mexican American Ind. (32)	55	0.11
Navajo (3)	7	0.01
Osage (0)	0	<0.01
Ottawa (4)	6	0.01
Paiute (0)	3	0.01
Pima (0)	0	<0.01
Potawatomi (14)	28	0.05
Pueblo (0)	0	<0.01
Puget Sound Salish (0)	0	<0.01
Seminole (0)	0	<0.01
Shoshone (0)	0	<0.01
Sioux (7)	21	0.04
South American Ind. (3)	4	0.01
Spanish American Ind. (2)	3	0.01
Tlingit-Haida *(Alaska Native)* (0)	0	<0.01
Tohono O'Odham (0)	0	<0.01
Tsimshian *(Alaska Native)* (0)	0	<0.01
Ute (0)	0	<0.01
Yakama (0)	0	<0.01
Yaqui (0)	0	<0.01
Yuman (0)	0	<0.01
Yup'ik *(Alaska Native)* (0)	0	<0.01
Asian (452)	660	1.30
Not Hispanic (430)	625	1.23
Hispanic (22)	35	0.07
Bangladeshi (3)	3	0.01
Bhutanese (0)	0	<0.01
Burmese (0)	0	<0.01
Cambodian (49)	66	0.13
Chinese, ex. Taiwanese (43)	77	0.15
Filipino (46)	76	0.15
Hmong (0)	0	<0.01
Indian (93)	115	0.23
Indonesian (1)	8	0.02
Japanese (10)	32	0.06
Korean (37)	60	0.12
Laotian (87)	115	0.23
Malaysian (0)	1	<0.01
Nepalese (0)	0	<0.01
Pakistani (9)	15	0.03
Sri Lankan (4)	4	0.01
Taiwanese (1)	1	<0.01
Thai (11)	22	0.04
Vietnamese (12)	24	0.05
Hawaii Native/Pacific Islander (33)	71	0.14
Not Hispanic (20)	44	0.09
Hispanic (13)	27	0.05
Fijian (0)	0	<0.01
Guamanian/Chamorro (11)	17	0.03
Marshallese (1)	1	<0.01
Native Hawaiian (6)	19	0.04
Samoan (5)	8	0.02
Tongan (6)	6	0.01
White (33,672)	35,539	69.75
Not Hispanic (29,565)	30,987	60.82
Hispanic (4,107)	4,552	8.93

*Notes: † The Census 2010 population figure is used to calculate the percentages in the Hispanic Origin and Race categories. Ancestry percentages are based on the 2006-2010 American Community Survey population (not shown); ‡ Numbers in parentheses indicate the number of people reporting a single ancestry; * Numbers in parentheses indicate the number of persons reporting this race alone, not in combination with any other race; Please refer to the Explanation of Data for more information.*

Evansville

Place Type: City
County: Vanderburgh
Population: 117,429

Ancestry	Population	%
Afghan (0)	0	<0.01
African, Sub-Saharan (120)	233	0.20
African (90)	160	0.14
Cape Verdean (0)	0	<0.01
Ethiopian (0)	34	0.03
Ghanaian (0)	0	<0.01
Kenyan (0)	0	<0.01
Liberian (0)	0	<0.01
Nigerian (8)	17	0.01
Senegalese (0)	0	<0.01
Sierra Leonean (0)	0	<0.01
Somalian (0)	0	<0.01
South African (0)	0	<0.01
Sudanese (0)	0	<0.01
Ugandan (14)	14	0.01
Zimbabwean (0)	0	<0.01
Other Sub-Saharan African (8)	8	0.01
Albanian (0)	0	<0.01
Alsatian (0)	0	<0.01
American (23,162)	23,162	19.60
Arab (79)	117	0.10
Arab (7)	7	0.01
Egyptian (0)	0	<0.01
Iraqi (16)	16	0.01
Jordanian (15)	15	0.01
Lebanese (0)	27	0.02
Moroccan (0)	0	<0.01
Palestinian (30)	30	0.03
Syrian (0)	11	0.01
Other Arab (11)	11	0.01
Armenian (70)	78	0.07
Assyrian/Chaldean/Syriac (0)	0	<0.01
Australian (39)	39	0.03
Austrian (9)	109	0.09
Basque (0)	0	<0.01
Belgian (0)	75	0.06
Brazilian (62)	62	0.05
British (257)	446	0.38
Bulgarian (0)	0	<0.01
Cajun (0)	12	0.01
Canadian (61)	71	0.06
Carpatho Rusyn (0)	0	<0.01
Celtic (0)	23	0.02
Croatian (0)	47	0.04
Cypriot (0)	0	<0.01
Czech (39)	152	0.13
Czechoslovakian (44)	73	0.06
Danish (8)	133	0.11
Dutch (466)	1,856	1.57
Eastern European (0)	14	0.01
English (4,204)	9,922	8.40
Estonian (0)	0	<0.01
European (672)	768	0.65
Finnish (18)	80	0.07
French, ex. Basque (892)	2,952	2.50
French Canadian (99)	110	0.09
German (18,318)	33,828	28.62
German Russian (0)	0	<0.01
Greek (52)	135	0.11
Guyanese (0)	49	0.04
Hungarian (56)	136	0.12
Icelander (0)	0	<0.01
Iranian (20)	20	0.02
Irish (3,732)	14,073	11.91
Israeli (0)	0	<0.01
Italian (622)	2,111	1.79
Latvian (12)	12	0.01
Lithuanian (0)	83	0.07
Luxemburger (0)	0	<0.01
Macedonian (0)	0	<0.01
Maltese (0)	0	<0.01
New Zealander (0)	0	<0.01
Northern European (17)	34	0.03
Norwegian (132)	375	0.32
Pennsylvania German (21)	33	0.03
Polish (462)	1,485	1.26
Portuguese (63)	95	0.08
Romanian (0)	10	0.01
Russian (177)	381	0.32
Scandinavian (17)	25	0.02
Scotch-Irish (666)	1,964	1.66
Scottish (823)	2,023	1.71
Serbian (13)	13	0.01
Slavic (0)	11	0.01
Slovak (55)	157	0.13
Slovene (0)	0	<0.01
Soviet Union (0)	0	<0.01
Swedish (203)	477	0.40
Swiss (11)	216	0.18
Turkish (11)	25	0.02
Ukrainian (129)	129	0.11
Welsh (82)	380	0.32
West Indian, ex. Hispanic (23)	55	0.05
Bahamian (0)	0	<0.01
Barbadian (0)	0	<0.01
Belizean (0)	0	<0.01
Bermudan (0)	0	<0.01
British West Indian (0)	0	<0.01
Dutch West Indian (0)	0	<0.01
Haitian (0)	11	0.01
Jamaican (23)	44	0.04
Trinidadian/Tobagonian (0)	0	<0.01
U.S. Virgin Islander (0)	0	<0.01
West Indian (0)	0	<0.01
Other West Indian (0)	0	<0.01
Yugoslavian (0)	0	<0.01

Hispanic Origin	Population	%
Hispanic or Latino (of any race)	3,014	2.57
Central American, ex. Mexican	178	0.15
Costa Rican	7	0.01
Guatemalan	31	0.03
Honduran	31	0.03
Nicaraguan	35	0.03
Panamanian	24	0.02
Salvadoran	45	0.04
Other Central American	5	<0.01
Cuban	64	0.05
Dominican Republic	24	0.02
Mexican	2,073	1.77
Puerto Rican	245	0.21
South American	118	0.10
Argentinean	9	0.01
Bolivian	4	<0.01
Chilean	4	<0.01
Colombian	32	0.03
Ecuadorian	9	0.01
Paraguayan	2	<0.01
Peruvian	33	0.03
Uruguayan	0	<0.01
Venezuelan	24	0.02
Other South American	1	<0.01
Other Hispanic or Latino	312	0.27

Race*	Population	%
African-American/Black (14,766)	17,089	14.55
Not Hispanic (14,672)	16,871	14.37
Hispanic (94)	218	0.19
American Indian/Alaska Native (312)	916	0.78
Not Hispanic (269)	831	0.71
Hispanic (43)	85	0.07
Alaska Athabascan *(Ala. Nat.)* (0)	1	<0.01
Aleut *(Alaska Native)* (0)	0	<0.01
Apache (6)	23	0.02
Arapaho (1)	1	<0.01
Blackfeet (5)	39	0.03
Canadian/French Am. Ind. (1)	2	<0.01
Central American Ind. (1)	1	<0.01
Cherokee (71)	283	0.24
Cheyenne (4)	11	0.01
Chickasaw (1)	3	<0.01
Chippewa (12)	18	0.02
Choctaw (5)	16	0.01
Colville (1)	1	<0.01
Comanche (0)	2	<0.01
Cree (0)	2	<0.01
Creek (0)	0	<0.01
Crow (0)	1	<0.01
Delaware (4)	6	0.01
Hopi (0)	1	<0.01
Houma (2)	4	<0.01
Inupiat *(Alaska Native)* (0)	1	<0.01
Iroquois (3)	14	0.01
Kiowa (0)	1	<0.01
Lumbee (1)	11	0.01
Menominee (0)	0	<0.01
Mexican American Ind. (5)	7	0.01
Navajo (3)	10	0.01
Osage (2)	2	<0.01
Ottawa (0)	0	<0.01
Paiute (0)	0	<0.01
Pima (0)	0	<0.01
Potawatomi (0)	1	<0.01
Pueblo (1)	3	<0.01
Puget Sound Salish (0)	0	<0.01
Seminole (1)	3	<0.01
Shoshone (0)	0	<0.01
Sioux (25)	52	0.04
South American Ind. (2)	4	<0.01
Spanish American Ind. (1)	1	<0.01
Tlingit-Haida *(Alaska Native)* (0)	0	<0.01
Tohono O'Odham (0)	0	<0.01
Tsimshian *(Alaska Native)* (0)	0	<0.01
Ute (0)	0	<0.01
Yakama (0)	0	<0.01
Yaqui (0)	1	<0.01
Yuman (0)	0	<0.01
Yup'ik *(Alaska Native)* (0)	0	<0.01
Asian (1,160)	1,578	1.34
Not Hispanic (1,149)	1,544	1.31
Hispanic (11)	34	0.03
Bangladeshi (6)	6	0.01
Bhutanese (0)	0	<0.01
Burmese (1)	1	<0.01
Cambodian (2)	3	<0.01
Chinese, ex. Taiwanese (254)	319	0.27
Filipino (161)	248	0.21
Hmong (0)	0	<0.01
Indian (307)	369	0.31
Indonesian (6)	12	0.01
Japanese (69)	135	0.11
Korean (102)	162	0.14
Laotian (2)	2	<0.01
Malaysian (13)	17	0.01
Nepalese (14)	23	0.02
Pakistani (5)	10	0.01
Sri Lankan (0)	0	<0.01
Taiwanese (6)	10	0.01
Thai (23)	40	0.03
Vietnamese (155)	194	0.17
Hawaii Native/Pacific Islander (84)	176	0.15
Not Hispanic (72)	150	0.13
Hispanic (12)	26	0.02
Fijian (0)	0	<0.01
Guamanian/Chamorro (18)	30	0.03
Marshallese (44)	49	0.04
Native Hawaiian (12)	49	0.04
Samoan (5)	20	0.02
Tongan (0)	0	<0.01
White (96,266)	99,372	84.62
Not Hispanic (94,961)	97,793	83.28
Hispanic (1,305)	1,579	1.34

*Notes: † The Census 2010 population figure is used to calculate the percentages in the Hispanic Origin and Race categories. Ancestry percentages are based on the 2006-2010 American Community Survey population (not shown); ‡ Numbers in parentheses indicate the number of people reporting a single ancestry; * Numbers in parentheses indicate the number of persons reporting this race alone, not in combination with any other race; Please refer to the Explanation of Data for more information.*

Fishers

Place Type: Town
County: Hamilton
Population: 76,794

Ancestry	Population	%
Afghan (15)	15	0.02
African, Sub-Saharan (240)	258	0.36
African (102)	111	0.15
Cape Verdean (0)	0	<0.01
Ethiopian (0)	0	<0.01
Ghanaian (0)	0	<0.01
Kenyan (0)	0	<0.01
Liberian (0)	0	<0.01
Nigerian (79)	79	0.11
Senegalese (13)	13	0.02
Sierra Leonean (0)	0	<0.01
Somalian (0)	0	<0.01
South African (0)	0	<0.01
Sudanese (0)	0	<0.01
Ugandan (0)	0	<0.01
Zimbabwean (0)	0	<0.01
Other Sub-Saharan African (46)	55	0.08
Albanian (0)	10	0.01
Alsatian (0)	0	<0.01
American (3,929)	3,929	5.48
Arab (450)	580	0.81
Arab (207)	235	0.33
Egyptian (113)	125	0.17
Iraqi (0)	0	<0.01
Jordanian (25)	37	0.05
Lebanese (73)	135	0.19
Moroccan (0)	0	<0.01
Palestinian (0)	0	<0.01
Syrian (32)	32	0.04
Other Arab (0)	16	0.02
Armenian (10)	10	0.01
Assyrian/Chaldean/Syriac (0)	0	<0.01
Australian (0)	36	0.05
Austrian (46)	233	0.32
Basque (0)	0	<0.01
Belgian (74)	165	0.23
Brazilian (10)	24	0.03
British (228)	451	0.63
Bulgarian (0)	0	<0.01
Cajun (0)	22	0.03
Canadian (95)	195	0.27
Carpatho Rusyn (0)	0	<0.01
Celtic (14)	14	0.02
Croatian (19)	84	0.12
Cypriot (0)	0	<0.01
Czech (105)	513	0.72
Czechoslovakian (27)	41	0.06
Danish (129)	282	0.39
Dutch (353)	1,512	2.11
Eastern European (75)	75	0.10
English (3,213)	9,173	12.79
Estonian (0)	0	<0.01
European (1,290)	1,428	1.99
Finnish (13)	83	0.12
French, ex. Basque (468)	2,611	3.64
French Canadian (108)	382	0.53
German (8,414)	20,883	29.11
German Russian (0)	0	<0.01
Greek (206)	637	0.89
Guyanese (0)	0	<0.01
Hungarian (127)	463	0.65
Icelander (0)	0	<0.01
Iranian (161)	181	0.25
Irish (3,090)	10,537	14.69
Israeli (21)	21	0.03
Italian (1,156)	3,343	4.66
Latvian (13)	13	0.02
Lithuanian (24)	166	0.23
Luxemburger (0)	0	<0.01
Macedonian (0)	10	0.01
Maltese (0)	0	<0.01
New Zealander (14)	14	0.02
Northern European (24)	24	0.03
Norwegian (335)	843	1.17
Pennsylvania German (12)	27	0.04
Polish (774)	2,912	4.06
Portuguese (59)	185	0.26
Romanian (85)	109	0.15
Russian (142)	350	0.49
Scandinavian (97)	183	0.26
Scotch-Irish (518)	1,293	1.80
Scottish (656)	2,188	3.05
Serbian (29)	47	0.07
Slavic (12)	50	0.07
Slovak (36)	63	0.09
Slovene (48)	54	0.08
Soviet Union (0)	0	<0.01
Swedish (283)	1,288	1.80
Swiss (143)	576	0.80
Turkish (0)	0	<0.01
Ukrainian (39)	97	0.14
Welsh (393)	930	1.30
West Indian, ex. Hispanic (13)	58	0.08
Bahamian (0)	0	<0.01
Barbadian (0)	0	<0.01
Belizean (0)	0	<0.01
Bermudan (0)	0	<0.01
British West Indian (13)	13	0.02
Dutch West Indian (0)	0	<0.01
Haitian (0)	0	<0.01
Jamaican (0)	45	0.06
Trinidadian/Tobagonian (0)	0	<0.01
U.S. Virgin Islander (0)	0	<0.01
West Indian (0)	0	<0.01
Other West Indian (0)	0	<0.01
Yugoslavian (90)	133	0.19

Hispanic Origin	Population	%
Hispanic or Latino (of any race)	2,638	3.44
Central American, ex. Mexican	162	0.21
Costa Rican	9	0.01
Guatemalan	54	0.07
Honduran	16	0.02
Nicaraguan	13	0.02
Panamanian	39	0.05
Salvadoran	28	0.04
Other Central American	3	<0.01
Cuban	90	0.12
Dominican Republic	46	0.06
Mexican	1,389	1.81
Puerto Rican	349	0.45
South American	359	0.47
Argentinean	29	0.04
Bolivian	5	0.01
Chilean	15	0.02
Colombian	127	0.17
Ecuadorian	9	0.01
Paraguayan	3	<0.01
Peruvian	62	0.08
Uruguayan	7	0.01
Venezuelan	93	0.12
Other South American	9	0.01
Other Hispanic or Latino	243	0.32

Race*	Population	%
African-American/Black (4,299)	4,958	6.46
Not Hispanic (4,228)	4,837	6.30
Hispanic (71)	121	0.16
American Indian/Alaska Native (126)	302	0.39
Not Hispanic (109)	267	0.35
Hispanic (17)	35	0.05
Alaska Athabascan *(Ala. Nat.)* (0)	0	<0.01
Aleut *(Alaska Native)* (0)	0	<0.01
Apache (4)	9	0.01
Arapaho (0)	0	<0.01
Blackfeet (2)	4	0.01
Canadian/French Am. Ind. (0)	0	<0.01
Central American Ind. (0)	1	<0.01
Cherokee (20)	61	0.08
Cheyenne (0)	0	<0.01
Chickasaw (0)	1	<0.01
Chippewa (5)	9	0.01
Choctaw (0)	6	0.01
Colville (0)	0	<0.01
Comanche (0)	0	<0.01
Cree (0)	1	<0.01
Creek (1)	1	<0.01
Crow (0)	0	<0.01
Delaware (0)	2	<0.01
Hopi (0)	0	<0.01
Houma (0)	0	<0.01
Inupiat *(Alaska Native)* (0)	0	<0.01
Iroquois (3)	6	0.01
Kiowa (1)	1	<0.01
Lumbee (5)	6	0.01
Menominee (1)	2	<0.01
Mexican American Ind. (3)	3	<0.01
Navajo (0)	2	<0.01
Osage (0)	0	<0.01
Ottawa (1)	1	<0.01
Paiute (2)	3	<0.01
Pima (0)	0	<0.01
Potawatomi (6)	7	0.01
Pueblo (0)	1	<0.01
Puget Sound Salish (0)	0	<0.01
Seminole (0)	0	<0.01
Shoshone (0)	0	<0.01
Sioux (7)	9	0.01
South American Ind. (0)	10	0.01
Spanish American Ind. (0)	0	<0.01
Tlingit-Haida *(Alaska Native)* (1)	1	<0.01
Tohono O'Odham (0)	0	<0.01
Tsimshian *(Alaska Native)* (0)	0	<0.01
Ute (0)	0	<0.01
Yakama (0)	0	<0.01
Yaqui (0)	0	<0.01
Yuman (0)	0	<0.01
Yup'ik *(Alaska Native)* (0)	0	<0.01
Asian (4,188)	4,930	6.42
Not Hispanic (4,174)	4,883	6.36
Hispanic (14)	47	0.06
Bangladeshi (31)	35	0.05
Bhutanese (1)	3	<0.01
Burmese (2)	6	0.01
Cambodian (9)	14	0.02
Chinese, ex. Taiwanese (703)	818	1.07
Filipino (241)	391	0.51
Hmong (11)	11	0.01
Indian (1,639)	1,785	2.32
Indonesian (46)	53	0.07
Japanese (220)	316	0.41
Korean (457)	575	0.75
Laotian (19)	25	0.03
Malaysian (8)	10	0.01
Nepalese (18)	18	0.02
Pakistani (177)	189	0.25
Sri Lankan (10)	11	0.01
Taiwanese (40)	45	0.06
Thai (24)	47	0.06
Vietnamese (383)	439	0.57
Hawaii Native/Pacific Islander (19)	58	0.08
Not Hispanic (14)	46	0.06
Hispanic (5)	12	0.02
Fijian (0)	0	<0.01
Guamanian/Chamorro (3)	6	0.01
Marshallese (0)	0	<0.01
Native Hawaiian (5)	16	0.02
Samoan (4)	11	0.01
Tongan (3)	6	0.01
White (65,754)	67,165	87.46
Not Hispanic (64,058)	65,289	85.02
Hispanic (1,696)	1,876	2.44

*Notes: † The Census 2010 population figure is used to calculate the percentages in the Hispanic Origin and Race categories. Ancestry percentages are based on the 2006-2010 American Community Survey population (not shown); ‡ Numbers in parentheses indicate the number of people reporting a single ancestry; * Numbers in parentheses indicate the number of persons reporting this race alone, not in combination with any other race; Please refer to the Explanation of Data for more information.*

Fort Wayne

Place Type: City
County: Allen
Population: 253,691

Ancestry	Population	%
Afghan (20)	20	0.01
African, Sub-Saharan (13,049)	13,249	5.22
African (12,562)	12,753	5.03
Cape Verdean (0)	0	<0.01
Ethiopian (47)	47	0.02
Ghanaian (0)	0	<0.01
Kenyan (27)	27	0.01
Liberian (0)	0	<0.01
Nigerian (138)	138	0.05
Senegalese (0)	0	<0.01
Sierra Leonean (0)	0	<0.01
Somalian (68)	68	0.03
South African (43)	52	0.02
Sudanese (0)	0	<0.01
Ugandan (0)	0	<0.01
Zimbabwean (0)	0	<0.01
Other Sub-Saharan African (164)	164	0.06
Albanian (33)	33	0.01
Alsatian (8)	8	<0.01
American (25,688)	25,688	10.12
Arab (475)	664	0.26
Arab (207)	222	0.09
Egyptian (8)	8	<0.01
Iraqi (44)	54	0.02
Jordanian (10)	10	<0.01
Lebanese (121)	235	0.09
Moroccan (10)	10	<0.01
Palestinian (0)	0	<0.01
Syrian (54)	104	0.04
Other Arab (21)	21	0.01
Armenian (81)	81	0.03
Assyrian/Chaldean/Syriac (10)	10	<0.01
Australian (27)	54	0.02
Austrian (105)	250	0.10
Basque (0)	0	<0.01
Belgian (27)	220	0.09
Brazilian (0)	21	0.01
British (375)	767	0.30
Bulgarian (126)	156	0.06
Cajun (0)	0	<0.01
Canadian (295)	681	0.27
Carpatho Rusyn (0)	0	<0.01
Celtic (8)	30	0.01
Croatian (150)	244	0.10
Cypriot (0)	0	<0.01
Czech (224)	837	0.33
Czechoslovakian (53)	130	0.05
Danish (182)	601	0.24
Dutch (872)	3,612	1.42
Eastern European (101)	110	0.04
English (6,224)	19,734	7.78
Estonian (0)	12	<0.01
European (1,501)	1,608	0.63
Finnish (18)	185	0.07
French, ex. Basque (1,952)	9,917	3.91
French Canadian (321)	813	0.32
German (36,666)	76,622	30.20
German Russian (0)	0	<0.01
Greek (380)	732	0.29
Guyanese (0)	0	<0.01
Hungarian (350)	1,122	0.44
Icelander (0)	9	<0.01
Iranian (8)	8	<0.01
Irish (8,309)	28,352	11.17
Israeli (34)	34	0.01
Italian (2,543)	6,703	2.64
Latvian (70)	70	0.03
Lithuanian (39)	278	0.11
Luxemburger (0)	36	0.01
Macedonian (328)	580	0.23
Maltese (0)	0	<0.01
New Zealander (0)	11	<0.01
Northern European (96)	96	0.04
Norwegian (393)	1,488	0.59
Pennsylvania German (190)	255	0.10
Polish (1,714)	5,438	2.14
Portuguese (175)	324	0.13
Romanian (184)	387	0.15
Russian (344)	913	0.36
Scandinavian (153)	269	0.11
Scotch-Irish (998)	3,125	1.23
Scottish (1,270)	4,615	1.82
Serbian (0)	75	0.03
Slavic (47)	92	0.04
Slovak (196)	468	0.18
Slovene (0)	37	0.01
Soviet Union (0)	0	<0.01
Swedish (460)	1,940	0.76
Swiss (615)	2,499	0.98
Turkish (46)	46	0.02
Ukrainian (155)	293	0.12
Welsh (248)	1,388	0.55
West Indian, ex. Hispanic (567)	665	0.26
Bahamian (0)	0	<0.01
Barbadian (0)	0	<0.01
Belizean (0)	0	<0.01
Bermudan (0)	0	<0.01
British West Indian (74)	74	0.03
Dutch West Indian (0)	0	<0.01
Haitian (346)	377	0.15
Jamaican (147)	196	0.08
Trinidadian/Tobagonian (0)	0	<0.01
U.S. Virgin Islander (0)	0	<0.01
West Indian (0)	18	0.01
Other West Indian (0)	0	<0.01
Yugoslavian (1,385)	1,443	0.57

Hispanic Origin	Population	%
Hispanic or Latino (of any race)	20,200	7.96
Central American, ex. Mexican	1,346	0.53
Costa Rican	38	0.01
Guatemalan	729	0.29
Honduran	129	0.05
Nicaraguan	37	0.01
Panamanian	38	0.01
Salvadoran	369	0.15
Other Central American	6	<0.01
Cuban	174	0.07
Dominican Republic	72	0.03
Mexican	15,545	6.13
Puerto Rican	939	0.37
South American	651	0.26
Argentinean	36	0.01
Bolivian	15	0.01
Chilean	18	0.01
Colombian	235	0.09
Ecuadorian	159	0.06
Paraguayan	4	<0.01
Peruvian	128	0.05
Uruguayan	10	<0.01
Venezuelan	45	0.02
Other South American	1	<0.01
Other Hispanic or Latino	1,473	0.58

Race*	Population	%
African-American/Black (39,085)	44,499	17.54
Not Hispanic (38,514)	43,301	17.07
Hispanic (571)	1,198	0.47
American Indian/Alaska Native (939)	2,669	1.05
Not Hispanic (730)	2,172	0.86
Hispanic (209)	497	0.20
Alaska Athabascan *(Ala. Nat.)* (4)	4	<0.01
Aleut *(Alaska Native)* (1)	1	<0.01
Apache (15)	43	0.02
Arapaho (2)	3	<0.01
Blackfeet (18)	110	0.04
Canadian/French Am. Ind. (2)	4	<0.01
Central American Ind. (5)	11	<0.01
Cherokee (126)	481	0.19
Cheyenne (2)	6	<0.01
Chickasaw (5)	13	0.01
Chippewa (28)	63	0.02
Choctaw (19)	55	0.02
Colville (0)	0	<0.01
Comanche (3)	4	<0.01
Cree (1)	9	<0.01
Creek (6)	18	0.01
Crow (1)	12	<0.01
Delaware (1)	12	<0.01
Hopi (2)	7	<0.01
Houma (0)	3	<0.01
Inupiat *(Alaska Native)* (3)	3	<0.01
Iroquois (20)	41	0.02
Kiowa (3)	3	<0.01
Lumbee (1)	2	<0.01
Menominee (0)	1	<0.01
Mexican American Ind. (42)	67	0.03
Navajo (8)	26	0.01
Osage (1)	1	<0.01
Ottawa (9)	15	0.01
Paiute (0)	1	<0.01
Pima (4)	7	<0.01
Potawatomi (7)	26	0.01
Pueblo (2)	7	<0.01
Puget Sound Salish (0)	0	<0.01
Seminole (0)	11	<0.01
Shoshone (0)	0	<0.01
Sioux (21)	68	0.03
South American Ind. (4)	9	<0.01
Spanish American Ind. (2)	3	<0.01
Tlingit-Haida *(Alaska Native)* (2)	4	<0.01
Tohono O'Odham (0)	0	<0.01
Tsimshian *(Alaska Native)* (0)	0	<0.01
Ute (1)	2	<0.01
Yakama (0)	0	<0.01
Yaqui (3)	5	<0.01
Yuman (0)	0	<0.01
Yup'ik *(Alaska Native)* (1)	2	<0.01
Asian (8,379)	9,768	3.85
Not Hispanic (8,279)	9,548	3.76
Hispanic (100)	220	0.09
Bangladeshi (37)	40	0.02
Bhutanese (0)	0	<0.01
Burmese (3,653)	3,819	1.51
Cambodian (38)	46	0.02
Chinese, ex. Taiwanese (493)	643	0.25
Filipino (520)	823	0.32
Hmong (0)	0	<0.01
Indian (1,183)	1,426	0.56
Indonesian (18)	26	0.01
Japanese (128)	252	0.10
Korean (313)	474	0.19
Laotian (290)	369	0.15
Malaysian (19)	41	0.02
Nepalese (10)	11	<0.01
Pakistani (114)	161	0.06
Sri Lankan (17)	19	0.01
Taiwanese (33)	47	0.02
Thai (132)	202	0.08
Vietnamese (818)	939	0.37
Hawaii Native/Pacific Islander (154)	354	0.14
Not Hispanic (91)	249	0.10
Hispanic (63)	105	0.04
Fijian (2)	2	<0.01
Guamanian/Chamorro (67)	102	0.04
Marshallese (1)	1	<0.01
Native Hawaiian (41)	119	0.05
Samoan (13)	38	0.01
Tongan (0)	1	<0.01
White (186,763)	194,759	76.77
Not Hispanic (178,436)	184,757	72.83
Hispanic (8,327)	10,002	3.94

*Notes: † The Census 2010 population figure is used to calculate the percentages in the Hispanic Origin and Race categories. Ancestry percentages are based on the 2006-2010 American Community Survey population (not shown); ‡ Numbers in parentheses indicate the number of people reporting a single ancestry; * Numbers in parentheses indicate the number of persons reporting this race alone, not in combination with any other race; Please refer to the Explanation of Data for more information.*

Gary

Place Type: City
County: Lake
Population: 80,294

Ancestry	Population	%
Afghan (0)	0	<0.01
African, Sub-Saharan (1,504)	1,824	2.16
African (1,278)	1,527	1.81
Cape Verdean (0)	0	<0.01
Ethiopian (121)	121	0.14
Ghanaian (10)	10	0.01
Kenyan (0)	0	<0.01
Liberian (0)	11	0.01
Nigerian (95)	155	0.18
Senegalese (0)	0	<0.01
Sierra Leonean (0)	0	<0.01
Somalian (0)	0	<0.01
South African (0)	0	<0.01
Sudanese (0)	0	<0.01
Ugandan (0)	0	<0.01
Zimbabwean (0)	0	<0.01
Other Sub-Saharan African (0)	0	<0.01
Albanian (0)	0	<0.01
Alsatian (0)	0	<0.01
American (1,013)	1,013	1.20
Arab (18)	18	0.02
Arab (0)	0	<0.01
Egyptian (0)	0	<0.01
Iraqi (0)	0	<0.01
Jordanian (0)	0	<0.01
Lebanese (0)	0	<0.01
Moroccan (18)	18	0.02
Palestinian (0)	0	<0.01
Syrian (0)	0	<0.01
Other Arab (0)	0	<0.01
Armenian (0)	0	<0.01
Assyrian/Chaldean/Syriac (0)	0	<0.01
Australian (0)	0	<0.01
Austrian (0)	30	0.04
Basque (0)	0	<0.01
Belgian (12)	43	0.05
Brazilian (21)	30	0.04
British (26)	68	0.08
Bulgarian (0)	0	<0.01
Cajun (0)	0	<0.01
Canadian (0)	19	0.02
Carpatho Rusyn (0)	0	<0.01
Celtic (0)	0	<0.01
Croatian (100)	187	0.22
Cypriot (0)	0	<0.01
Czech (24)	24	0.03
Czechoslovakian (0)	0	<0.01
Danish (0)	29	0.03
Dutch (71)	315	0.37
Eastern European (37)	37	0.04
English (724)	1,454	1.72
Estonian (0)	0	<0.01
European (42)	42	0.05
Finnish (7)	7	0.01
French, ex. Basque (15)	207	0.25
French Canadian (10)	19	0.02
German (600)	2,519	2.98
German Russian (0)	0	<0.01
Greek (89)	164	0.19
Guyanese (0)	0	<0.01
Hungarian (65)	167	0.20
Icelander (0)	0	<0.01
Iranian (0)	0	<0.01
Irish (730)	2,537	3.01
Israeli (0)	0	<0.01
Italian (152)	530	0.63
Latvian (0)	0	<0.01
Lithuanian (46)	162	0.19
Luxemburger (0)	0	<0.01
Macedonian (0)	0	<0.01
Maltese (10)	10	0.01
New Zealander (0)	0	<0.01
Northern European (0)	0	<0.01
Norwegian (16)	194	0.23
Pennsylvania German (0)	0	<0.01
Polish (375)	1,164	1.38
Portuguese (0)	0	<0.01
Romanian (0)	9	0.01
Russian (0)	46	0.05
Scandinavian (0)	0	<0.01
Scotch-Irish (34)	169	0.20
Scottish (67)	204	0.24
Serbian (9)	9	0.01
Slavic (0)	12	0.01
Slovak (43)	209	0.25
Slovene (0)	0	<0.01
Soviet Union (0)	0	<0.01
Swedish (27)	98	0.12
Swiss (0)	24	0.03
Turkish (12)	12	0.01
Ukrainian (20)	31	0.04
Welsh (0)	90	0.11
West Indian, ex. Hispanic (198)	265	0.31
Bahamian (0)	0	<0.01
Barbadian (0)	0	<0.01
Belizean (0)	0	<0.01
Bermudan (0)	0	<0.01
British West Indian (0)	0	<0.01
Dutch West Indian (0)	0	<0.01
Haitian (0)	14	0.02
Jamaican (173)	192	0.23
Trinidadian/Tobagonian (0)	0	<0.01
U.S. Virgin Islander (0)	0	<0.01
West Indian (0)	34	0.04
Other West Indian (25)	25	0.03
Yugoslavian (17)	24	0.03

Hispanic Origin	Population	%
Hispanic or Latino (of any race)	4,128	5.14
Central American, ex. Mexican	47	0.06
Costa Rican	0	<0.01
Guatemalan	19	0.02
Honduran	12	0.01
Nicaraguan	2	<0.01
Panamanian	9	0.01
Salvadoran	5	0.01
Other Central American	0	<0.01
Cuban	61	0.08
Dominican Republic	24	0.03
Mexican	2,553	3.18
Puerto Rican	1,223	1.52
South American	14	0.02
Argentinean	1	<0.01
Bolivian	1	<0.01
Chilean	1	<0.01
Colombian	8	0.01
Ecuadorian	0	<0.01
Paraguayan	0	<0.01
Peruvian	2	<0.01
Uruguayan	0	<0.01
Venezuelan	1	<0.01
Other South American	0	<0.01
Other Hispanic or Latino	206	0.26

Race*	Population	%
African-American/Black (68,107)	69,508	86.57
Not Hispanic (67,363)	68,449	85.25
Hispanic (744)	1,059	1.32
American Indian/Alaska Native (241)	760	0.95
Not Hispanic (197)	659	0.82
Hispanic (44)	101	0.13
Alaska Athabascan *(Ala. Nat.)* (0)	0	<0.01
Aleut *(Alaska Native)* (0)	0	<0.01
Apache (9)	16	0.02
Arapaho (0)	0	<0.01
Blackfeet (5)	43	0.05
Canadian/French Am. Ind. (0)	1	<0.01
Central American Ind. (2)	3	<0.01
Cherokee (12)	153	0.19
Cheyenne (0)	0	<0.01
Chickasaw (0)	4	<0.01
Chippewa (5)	11	0.01
Choctaw (3)	27	0.03
Colville (0)	0	<0.01
Comanche (1)	2	<0.01
Cree (4)	7	0.01
Creek (2)	20	0.02
Crow (0)	0	<0.01
Delaware (0)	2	<0.01
Hopi (0)	0	<0.01
Houma (4)	4	<0.01
Inupiat *(Alaska Native)* (0)	0	<0.01
Iroquois (2)	5	0.01
Kiowa (0)	0	<0.01
Lumbee (3)	3	<0.01
Menominee (1)	6	0.01
Mexican American Ind. (6)	15	0.02
Navajo (1)	6	0.01
Osage (0)	0	<0.01
Ottawa (0)	0	<0.01
Paiute (0)	1	<0.01
Pima (0)	0	<0.01
Potawatomi (1)	1	<0.01
Pueblo (0)	0	<0.01
Puget Sound Salish (0)	0	<0.01
Seminole (0)	12	0.01
Shoshone (0)	0	<0.01
Sioux (4)	17	0.02
South American Ind. (1)	3	<0.01
Spanish American Ind. (0)	0	<0.01
Tlingit-Haida *(Alaska Native)* (0)	0	<0.01
Tohono O'Odham (0)	0	<0.01
Tsimshian *(Alaska Native)* (0)	0	<0.01
Ute (0)	0	<0.01
Yakama (0)	0	<0.01
Yaqui (0)	0	<0.01
Yuman (0)	0	<0.01
Yup'ik *(Alaska Native)* (0)	0	<0.01
Asian (164)	345	0.43
Not Hispanic (156)	309	0.38
Hispanic (8)	36	0.04
Bangladeshi (0)	1	<0.01
Bhutanese (0)	0	<0.01
Burmese (0)	0	<0.01
Cambodian (7)	7	0.01
Chinese, ex. Taiwanese (23)	86	0.11
Filipino (42)	75	0.09
Hmong (0)	0	<0.01
Indian (23)	52	0.06
Indonesian (0)	0	<0.01
Japanese (11)	34	0.04
Korean (24)	42	0.05
Laotian (6)	6	0.01
Malaysian (0)	0	<0.01
Nepalese (0)	0	<0.01
Pakistani (6)	9	0.01
Sri Lankan (0)	0	<0.01
Taiwanese (0)	0	<0.01
Thai (2)	4	<0.01
Vietnamese (7)	19	0.02
Hawaii Native/Pacific Islander (8)	46	0.06
Not Hispanic (5)	32	0.04
Hispanic (3)	14	0.02
Fijian (0)	0	<0.01
Guamanian/Chamorro (1)	6	0.01
Marshallese (0)	0	<0.01
Native Hawaiian (1)	4	<0.01
Samoan (3)	15	0.02
Tongan (0)	0	<0.01
White (8,619)	9,685	12.06
Not Hispanic (7,151)	7,969	9.92
Hispanic (1,468)	1,716	2.14

*Notes: † The Census 2010 population figure is used to calculate the percentages in the Hispanic Origin and Race categories. Ancestry percentages are based on the 2006-2010 American Community Survey population (not shown); ‡ Numbers in parentheses indicate the number of people reporting a single ancestry; * Numbers in parentheses indicate the number of persons reporting this race alone, not in combination with any other race; Please refer to the Explanation of Data for more information.*

Hammond

Place Type: City
County: Lake
Population: 80,830

Ancestry	Population	%
Afghan (0)	0	<0.01
African, Sub-Saharan (354)	421	0.52
African (354)	398	0.49
Cape Verdean (0)	0	<0.01
Ethiopian (0)	0	<0.01
Ghanaian (0)	0	<0.01
Kenyan (0)	0	<0.01
Liberian (0)	0	<0.01
Nigerian (0)	10	0.01
Senegalese (0)	0	<0.01
Sierra Leonean (0)	0	<0.01
Somalian (0)	0	<0.01
South African (0)	0	<0.01
Sudanese (0)	0	<0.01
Ugandan (0)	0	<0.01
Zimbabwean (0)	0	<0.01
Other Sub-Saharan African (0)	13	0.02
Albanian (0)	61	0.08
Alsatian (0)	18	0.02
American (2,149)	2,149	2.64
Arab (180)	272	0.33
Arab (52)	144	0.18
Egyptian (83)	83	0.10
Iraqi (0)	0	<0.01
Jordanian (30)	30	0.04
Lebanese (0)	0	<0.01
Moroccan (0)	0	<0.01
Palestinian (0)	0	<0.01
Syrian (0)	0	<0.01
Other Arab (15)	15	0.02
Armenian (18)	27	0.03
Assyrian/Chaldean/Syriac (7)	7	0.01
Australian (21)	21	0.03
Austrian (8)	59	0.07
Basque (0)	0	<0.01
Belgian (12)	27	0.03
Brazilian (0)	13	0.02
British (30)	79	0.10
Bulgarian (0)	0	<0.01
Cajun (0)	0	<0.01
Canadian (10)	55	0.07
Carpatho Rusyn (0)	0	<0.01
Celtic (0)	7	0.01
Croatian (230)	908	1.12
Cypriot (0)	0	<0.01
Czech (94)	369	0.45
Czechoslovakian (61)	101	0.12
Danish (12)	85	0.10
Dutch (205)	1,088	1.34
Eastern European (180)	180	0.22
English (879)	3,228	3.97
Estonian (0)	18	0.02
European (122)	150	0.18
Finnish (25)	153	0.19
French, ex. Basque (215)	1,407	1.73
French Canadian (103)	345	0.42
German (2,610)	9,601	11.81
German Russian (0)	0	<0.01
Greek (438)	881	1.08
Guyanese (14)	14	0.02
Hungarian (298)	827	1.02
Icelander (0)	0	<0.01
Iranian (0)	0	<0.01
Irish (1,741)	8,337	10.25
Israeli (0)	0	<0.01
Italian (835)	2,841	3.49
Latvian (0)	0	<0.01
Lithuanian (107)	242	0.30
Luxemburger (0)	0	<0.01
Macedonian (0)	9	0.01
Maltese (0)	0	<0.01
New Zealander (0)	0	<0.01
Northern European (49)	49	0.06
Norwegian (77)	322	0.40
Pennsylvania German (18)	76	0.09
Polish (3,706)	7,497	9.22
Portuguese (0)	64	0.08
Romanian (16)	77	0.09
Russian (89)	275	0.34
Scandinavian (17)	65	0.08
Scotch-Irish (223)	574	0.71
Scottish (30)	627	0.77
Serbian (228)	572	0.70
Slavic (0)	22	0.03
Slovak (705)	1,791	2.20
Slovene (0)	0	<0.01
Soviet Union (0)	0	<0.01
Swedish (222)	1,016	1.25
Swiss (12)	81	0.10
Turkish (0)	8	0.01
Ukrainian (129)	244	0.30
Welsh (59)	241	0.30
West Indian, ex. Hispanic (42)	135	0.17
Bahamian (0)	0	<0.01
Barbadian (0)	0	<0.01
Belizean (0)	0	<0.01
Bermudan (0)	0	<0.01
British West Indian (0)	0	<0.01
Dutch West Indian (0)	0	<0.01
Haitian (42)	86	0.11
Jamaican (0)	49	0.06
Trinidadian/Tobagonian (0)	0	<0.01
U.S. Virgin Islander (0)	0	<0.01
West Indian (0)	0	<0.01
Other West Indian (0)	0	<0.01
Yugoslavian (0)	0	<0.01

Hispanic Origin	Population	%
Hispanic or Latino (of any race)	27,563	34.10
Central American, ex. Mexican	526	0.65
Costa Rican	18	0.02
Guatemalan	172	0.21
Honduran	117	0.14
Nicaraguan	19	0.02
Panamanian	21	0.03
Salvadoran	174	0.22
Other Central American	5	0.01
Cuban	140	0.17
Dominican Republic	10	0.01
Mexican	22,684	28.06
Puerto Rican	3,081	3.81
South American	141	0.17
Argentinean	29	0.04
Bolivian	0	<0.01
Chilean	5	0.01
Colombian	36	0.04
Ecuadorian	12	0.01
Paraguayan	1	<0.01
Peruvian	40	0.05
Uruguayan	6	0.01
Venezuelan	12	0.01
Other South American	0	<0.01
Other Hispanic or Latino	981	1.21

Race*	Population	%
African-American/Black (18,224)	19,336	23.92
Not Hispanic (17,568)	18,369	22.73
Hispanic (656)	967	1.20
American Indian/Alaska Native (411)	930	1.15
Not Hispanic (145)	489	0.60
Hispanic (266)	441	0.55
Alaska Athabascan *(Ala. Nat.)* (0)	0	<0.01
Aleut *(Alaska Native)* (0)	0	<0.01
Apache (5)	19	0.02
Arapaho (1)	1	<0.01
Blackfeet (7)	24	0.03
Canadian/French Am. Ind. (1)	1	<0.01
Central American Ind. (0)	0	<0.01
Cherokee (40)	182	0.23
Cheyenne (0)	0	<0.01
Chickasaw (0)	2	<0.01
Chippewa (6)	21	0.03
Choctaw (4)	18	0.02
Colville (0)	0	<0.01
Comanche (1)	3	<0.01
Cree (0)	0	<0.01
Creek (8)	10	0.01
Crow (1)	4	<0.01
Delaware (0)	0	<0.01
Hopi (0)	0	<0.01
Houma (0)	0	<0.01
Inupiat *(Alaska Native)* (0)	0	<0.01
Iroquois (1)	6	0.01
Kiowa (0)	0	<0.01
Lumbee (0)	0	<0.01
Menominee (0)	1	<0.01
Mexican American Ind. (44)	69	0.09
Navajo (1)	4	<0.01
Osage (0)	0	<0.01
Ottawa (2)	3	<0.01
Paiute (0)	0	<0.01
Pima (0)	0	<0.01
Potawatomi (1)	6	0.01
Pueblo (0)	0	<0.01
Puget Sound Salish (0)	2	<0.01
Seminole (0)	3	<0.01
Shoshone (6)	6	0.01
Sioux (7)	12	0.01
South American Ind. (2)	9	0.01
Spanish American Ind. (3)	3	<0.01
Tlingit-Haida *(Alaska Native)* (0)	0	<0.01
Tohono O'Odham (0)	0	<0.01
Tsimshian *(Alaska Native)* (0)	0	<0.01
Ute (6)	7	0.01
Yakama (0)	0	<0.01
Yaqui (3)	3	<0.01
Yuman (0)	0	<0.01
Yup'ik *(Alaska Native)* (0)	0	<0.01
Asian (804)	1,059	1.31
Not Hispanic (753)	931	1.15
Hispanic (51)	128	0.16
Bangladeshi (1)	2	<0.01
Bhutanese (0)	0	<0.01
Burmese (0)	0	<0.01
Cambodian (5)	5	0.01
Chinese, ex. Taiwanese (385)	422	0.52
Filipino (126)	203	0.25
Hmong (0)	0	<0.01
Indian (118)	135	0.17
Indonesian (2)	4	<0.01
Japanese (11)	54	0.07
Korean (34)	55	0.07
Laotian (0)	0	<0.01
Malaysian (0)	0	<0.01
Nepalese (1)	1	<0.01
Pakistani (40)	44	0.05
Sri Lankan (1)	1	<0.01
Taiwanese (3)	3	<0.01
Thai (12)	19	0.02
Vietnamese (35)	48	0.06
Hawaii Native/Pacific Islander (24)	97	0.12
Not Hispanic (9)	47	0.06
Hispanic (15)	50	0.06
Fijian (0)	1	<0.01
Guamanian/Chamorro (4)	9	0.01
Marshallese (0)	0	<0.01
Native Hawaiian (8)	30	0.04
Samoan (8)	21	0.03
Tongan (0)	0	<0.01
White (47,984)	50,206	62.11
Not Hispanic (33,534)	34,532	42.72
Hispanic (14,450)	15,674	19.39

*Notes: † The Census 2010 population figure is used to calculate the percentages in the Hispanic Origin and Race categories. Ancestry percentages are based on the 2006-2010 American Community Survey population (not shown); ‡ Numbers in parentheses indicate the number of people reporting a single ancestry; * Numbers in parentheses indicate the number of persons reporting this race alone, not in combination with any other race; Please refer to the Explanation of Data for more information.*

Indianapolis

Place Type: City
County: Marion
Population: 820,445

Ancestry	Population	%
Afghan (29)	29	<0.01
African, Sub-Saharan (34,151)	43,672	5.39
African (29,012)	38,288	4.73
Cape Verdean (0)	0	<0.01
Ethiopian (443)	443	0.05
Ghanaian (154)	154	0.02
Kenyan (63)	63	0.01
Liberian (687)	687	0.08
Nigerian (1,907)	2,048	0.25
Senegalese (150)	150	0.02
Sierra Leonean (0)	0	<0.01
Somalian (432)	432	0.05
South African (20)	43	0.01
Sudanese (376)	376	0.05
Ugandan (14)	54	0.01
Zimbabwean (149)	149	0.02
Other Sub-Saharan African (744)	785	0.10
Albanian (51)	105	0.01
Alsatian (0)	12	<0.01
American (52,433)	52,433	6.47
Arab (1,818)	2,776	0.34
Arab (433)	542	0.07
Egyptian (147)	158	0.02
Iraqi (132)	192	0.02
Jordanian (152)	182	0.02
Lebanese (410)	826	0.10
Moroccan (96)	141	0.02
Palestinian (12)	45	0.01
Syrian (77)	239	0.03
Other Arab (359)	451	0.06
Armenian (34)	158	0.02
Assyrian/Chaldean/Syriac (44)	44	0.01
Australian (189)	258	0.03
Austrian (325)	1,084	0.13
Basque (0)	0	<0.01
Belgian (276)	866	0.11
Brazilian (121)	259	0.03
British (1,698)	3,547	0.44
Bulgarian (18)	80	0.01
Cajun (29)	52	0.01
Canadian (702)	1,392	0.17
Carpatho Rusyn (0)	0	<0.01
Celtic (0)	8	<0.01
Croatian (94)	412	0.05
Cypriot (0)	0	<0.01
Czech (366)	1,484	0.18
Czechoslovakian (226)	393	0.05
Danish (513)	1,483	0.18
Dutch (2,739)	11,553	1.43
Eastern European (299)	332	0.04
English (24,751)	67,644	8.35
Estonian (15)	99	0.01
European (7,714)	9,215	1.14
Finnish (177)	436	0.05
French, ex. Basque (3,373)	15,735	1.94
French Canadian (515)	1,565	0.19
German (58,139)	149,656	18.48
German Russian (11)	11	<0.01
Greek (1,089)	2,372	0.29
Guyanese (0)	0	<0.01
Hungarian (951)	2,960	0.37
Icelander (0)	0	<0.01
Iranian (325)	455	0.06
Irish (29,177)	93,959	11.60
Israeli (55)	107	0.01
Italian (7,266)	20,396	2.52
Latvian (142)	275	0.03
Lithuanian (298)	1,175	0.15
Luxemburger (34)	97	0.01
Macedonian (127)	265	0.03
Maltese (22)	56	0.01
New Zealander (35)	35	<0.01
Northern European (560)	584	0.07
Norwegian (967)	3,636	0.45
Pennsylvania German (256)	355	0.04
Polish (3,961)	12,731	1.57
Portuguese (86)	414	0.05
Romanian (629)	1,001	0.12
Russian (1,361)	3,280	0.41
Scandinavian (590)	1,199	0.15
Scotch-Irish (5,103)	10,956	1.35
Scottish (4,801)	14,050	1.73
Serbian (258)	777	0.10
Slavic (134)	455	0.06
Slovak (344)	1,058	0.13
Slovene (203)	497	0.06
Soviet Union (0)	0	<0.01
Swedish (1,395)	5,593	0.69
Swiss (481)	2,276	0.28
Turkish (160)	243	0.03
Ukrainian (395)	792	0.10
Welsh (1,266)	4,603	0.57
West Indian, ex. Hispanic (1,133)	1,846	0.23
Bahamian (8)	8	<0.01
Barbadian (13)	55	0.01
Belizean (28)	51	0.01
Bermudan (0)	0	<0.01
British West Indian (0)	13	<0.01
Dutch West Indian (0)	38	<0.01
Haitian (394)	635	0.08
Jamaican (510)	589	0.07
Trinidadian/Tobagonian (72)	110	0.01
U.S. Virgin Islander (0)	0	<0.01
West Indian (96)	335	0.04
Other West Indian (12)	12	<0.01
Yugoslavian (327)	531	0.07

Hispanic Origin	Population	%
Hispanic or Latino (of any race)	77,352	9.43
Central American, ex. Mexican	7,746	0.94
Costa Rican	125	0.02
Guatemalan	1,616	0.20
Honduran	2,302	0.28
Nicaraguan	668	0.08
Panamanian	274	0.03
Salvadoran	2,695	0.33
Other Central American	66	0.01
Cuban	739	0.09
Dominican Republic	1,124	0.14
Mexican	56,771	6.92
Puerto Rican	3,431	0.42
South American	2,068	0.25
Argentinean	207	0.03
Bolivian	47	0.01
Chilean	83	0.01
Colombian	587	0.07
Ecuadorian	160	0.02
Paraguayan	11	<0.01
Peruvian	611	0.07
Uruguayan	29	<0.01
Venezuelan	314	0.04
Other South American	19	<0.01
Other Hispanic or Latino	5,473	0.67

Race*	Population	%
African-American/Black (225,355)	239,354	29.17
Not Hispanic (223,053)	235,521	28.71
Hispanic (2,302)	3,833	0.47
American Indian/Alaska Native (2,611)	7,323	0.89
Not Hispanic (1,760)	5,844	0.71
Hispanic (851)	1,479	0.18
Alaska Athabascan *(Ala. Nat.)* (2)	3	<0.01
Aleut *(Alaska Native)* (12)	14	<0.01
Apache (43)	98	0.01
Arapaho (4)	4	<0.01
Blackfeet (63)	354	0.04
Canadian/French Am. Ind. (10)	22	<0.01
Central American Ind. (6)	11	<0.01
Cherokee (378)	1,682	0.21
Cheyenne (1)	18	<0.01
Chickasaw (6)	12	<0.01
Chippewa (64)	134	0.02
Choctaw (26)	99	0.01
Colville (0)	0	<0.01
Comanche (11)	28	<0.01
Cree (0)	13	<0.01
Creek (14)	31	<0.01
Crow (1)	11	<0.01
Delaware (8)	27	<0.01
Hopi (4)	13	<0.01
Houma (3)	3	<0.01
Inupiat *(Alaska Native)* (9)	20	<0.01
Iroquois (33)	96	0.01
Kiowa (2)	5	<0.01
Lumbee (8)	17	<0.01
Menominee (4)	5	<0.01
Mexican American Ind. (187)	263	0.03
Navajo (40)	100	0.01
Osage (4)	15	<0.01
Ottawa (3)	15	<0.01
Paiute (0)	5	<0.01
Pima (0)	1	<0.01
Potawatomi (54)	88	0.01
Pueblo (10)	26	<0.01
Puget Sound Salish (0)	0	<0.01
Seminole (2)	17	<0.01
Shoshone (2)	7	<0.01
Sioux (55)	201	0.02
South American Ind. (14)	39	<0.01
Spanish American Ind. (19)	23	<0.01
Tlingit-Haida *(Alaska Native)* (4)	6	<0.01
Tohono O'Odham (1)	2	<0.01
Tsimshian *(Alaska Native)* (1)	1	<0.01
Ute (2)	4	<0.01
Yakama (0)	1	<0.01
Yaqui (3)	5	<0.01
Yuman (2)	4	<0.01
Yup'ik *(Alaska Native)* (0)	2	<0.01
Asian (17,236)	21,294	2.60
Not Hispanic (17,053)	20,777	2.53
Hispanic (183)	517	0.06
Bangladeshi (115)	128	0.02
Bhutanese (0)	0	<0.01
Burmese (3,476)	3,622	0.44
Cambodian (85)	118	0.01
Chinese, ex. Taiwanese (2,666)	3,197	0.39
Filipino (1,628)	2,608	0.32
Hmong (15)	24	<0.01
Indian (4,739)	5,358	0.65
Indonesian (76)	142	0.02
Japanese (517)	1,094	0.13
Korean (1,043)	1,558	0.19
Laotian (115)	142	0.02
Malaysian (29)	44	0.01
Nepalese (45)	46	0.01
Pakistani (544)	625	0.08
Sri Lankan (34)	42	0.01
Taiwanese (144)	160	0.02
Thai (226)	352	0.04
Vietnamese (1,138)	1,347	0.16
Hawaii Native/Pacific Islander (384)	1,129	0.14
Not Hispanic (274)	820	0.10
Hispanic (110)	309	0.04
Fijian (3)	5	<0.01
Guamanian/Chamorro (128)	216	0.03
Marshallese (0)	0	<0.01
Native Hawaiian (114)	361	0.04
Samoan (71)	145	0.02
Tongan (5)	10	<0.01
White (507,005)	526,672	64.19
Not Hispanic (480,960)	496,520	60.52
Hispanic (26,045)	30,152	3.68

*Notes: † The Census 2010 population figure is used to calculate the percentages in the Hispanic Origin and Race categories. Ancestry percentages are based on the 2006-2010 American Community Survey population (not shown); ‡ Numbers in parentheses indicate the number of people reporting a single ancestry; * Numbers in parentheses indicate the number of persons reporting this race alone, not in combination with any other race; Please refer to the Explanation of Data for more information.*

Lafayette

Place Type: City
County: Tippecanoe
Population: 67,140

Ancestry	Population	%
Afghan (0)	0	<0.01
African, Sub-Saharan (177)	247	0.37
African (66)	105	0.16
Cape Verdean (0)	0	<0.01
Ethiopian (0)	0	<0.01
Ghanaian (0)	0	<0.01
Kenyan (33)	33	0.05
Liberian (32)	32	0.05
Nigerian (23)	23	0.03
Senegalese (0)	0	<0.01
Sierra Leonean (0)	0	<0.01
Somalian (0)	0	<0.01
South African (0)	0	<0.01
Sudanese (0)	0	<0.01
Ugandan (0)	0	<0.01
Zimbabwean (0)	0	<0.01
Other Sub-Saharan African (23)	54	0.08
Albanian (0)	0	<0.01
Alsatian (0)	0	<0.01
American (4,832)	4,832	7.30
Arab (14)	25	0.04
Arab (0)	0	<0.01
Egyptian (0)	0	<0.01
Iraqi (0)	0	<0.01
Jordanian (0)	0	<0.01
Lebanese (14)	14	0.02
Moroccan (0)	0	<0.01
Palestinian (0)	0	<0.01
Syrian (0)	0	<0.01
Other Arab (0)	11	0.02
Armenian (0)	0	<0.01
Assyrian/Chaldean/Syriac (8)	30	0.05
Australian (0)	0	<0.01
Austrian (6)	79	0.12
Basque (0)	0	<0.01
Belgian (20)	100	0.15
Brazilian (8)	31	0.05
British (163)	331	0.50
Bulgarian (0)	0	<0.01
Cajun (11)	22	0.03
Canadian (34)	34	0.05
Carpatho Rusyn (0)	0	<0.01
Celtic (0)	0	<0.01
Croatian (0)	33	0.05
Cypriot (0)	0	<0.01
Czech (40)	84	0.13
Czechoslovakian (0)	36	0.05
Danish (9)	74	0.11
Dutch (663)	2,127	3.22
Eastern European (29)	40	0.06
English (2,659)	6,889	10.41
Estonian (0)	0	<0.01
European (543)	672	1.02
Finnish (40)	63	0.10
French, ex. Basque (322)	1,964	2.97
French Canadian (110)	177	0.27
German (6,095)	16,791	25.38
German Russian (0)	0	<0.01
Greek (94)	147	0.22
Guyanese (0)	0	<0.01
Hungarian (132)	247	0.37
Icelander (0)	0	<0.01
Iranian (0)	0	<0.01
Irish (2,843)	10,032	15.17
Israeli (0)	0	<0.01
Italian (789)	1,624	2.46
Latvian (0)	0	<0.01
Lithuanian (11)	45	0.07
Luxemburger (0)	45	0.07
Macedonian (0)	0	<0.01
Maltese (0)	0	<0.01
New Zealander (68)	68	0.10
Northern European (77)	77	0.12
Norwegian (35)	249	0.38
Pennsylvania German (0)	61	0.09
Polish (693)	1,900	2.87
Portuguese (27)	27	0.04
Romanian (28)	61	0.09
Russian (84)	391	0.59
Scandinavian (26)	36	0.05
Scotch-Irish (519)	1,115	1.69
Scottish (610)	1,572	2.38
Serbian (0)	0	<0.01
Slavic (0)	27	0.04
Slovak (23)	44	0.07
Slovene (0)	0	<0.01
Soviet Union (0)	0	<0.01
Swedish (80)	556	0.84
Swiss (78)	302	0.46
Turkish (49)	49	0.07
Ukrainian (45)	94	0.14
Welsh (88)	360	0.54
West Indian, ex. Hispanic (8)	26	0.04
Bahamian (0)	0	<0.01
Barbadian (0)	0	<0.01
Belizean (0)	0	<0.01
Bermudan (0)	0	<0.01
British West Indian (0)	0	<0.01
Dutch West Indian (0)	8	0.01
Haitian (0)	10	0.02
Jamaican (0)	0	<0.01
Trinidadian/Tobagonian (0)	0	<0.01
U.S. Virgin Islander (8)	8	0.01
West Indian (0)	0	<0.01
Other West Indian (0)	0	<0.01
Yugoslavian (0)	0	<0.01

Hispanic Origin	Population	%
Hispanic or Latino (of any race)	8,107	12.07
Central American, ex. Mexican	283	0.42
Costa Rican	12	0.02
Guatemalan	81	0.12
Honduran	10	0.01
Nicaraguan	16	0.02
Panamanian	26	0.04
Salvadoran	138	0.21
Other Central American	0	<0.01
Cuban	78	0.12
Dominican Republic	33	0.05
Mexican	6,965	10.37
Puerto Rican	253	0.38
South American	130	0.19
Argentinean	16	0.02
Bolivian	12	0.02
Chilean	13	0.02
Colombian	39	0.06
Ecuadorian	23	0.03
Paraguayan	0	<0.01
Peruvian	18	0.03
Uruguayan	0	<0.01
Venezuelan	9	0.01
Other South American	0	<0.01
Other Hispanic or Latino	365	0.54

Race*	Population	%
African-American/Black (4,164)	4,987	7.43
Not Hispanic (4,050)	4,752	7.08
Hispanic (114)	235	0.35
American Indian/Alaska Native (245)	672	1.00
Not Hispanic (171)	544	0.81
Hispanic (74)	128	0.19
Alaska Athabascan *(Ala. Nat.)* (4)	4	0.01
Aleut *(Alaska Native)* (1)	2	<0.01
Apache (2)	12	0.02
Arapaho (0)	0	<0.01
Blackfeet (6)	27	0.04
Canadian/French Am. Ind. (2)	3	<0.01
Central American Ind. (0)	0	<0.01
Cherokee (39)	195	0.29
Cheyenne (1)	4	0.01
Chickasaw (0)	3	<0.01
Chippewa (8)	12	0.02
Choctaw (7)	9	0.01
Colville (0)	0	<0.01
Comanche (1)	3	<0.01
Cree (1)	1	<0.01
Creek (0)	4	0.01
Crow (2)	2	<0.01
Delaware (1)	3	<0.01
Hopi (0)	0	<0.01
Houma (6)	6	0.01
Inupiat *(Alaska Native)* (1)	1	<0.01
Iroquois (8)	14	0.02
Kiowa (0)	0	<0.01
Lumbee (5)	5	0.01
Menominee (0)	0	<0.01
Mexican American Ind. (23)	24	0.04
Navajo (0)	2	<0.01
Osage (0)	0	<0.01
Ottawa (4)	5	0.01
Paiute (0)	0	<0.01
Pima (0)	0	<0.01
Potawatomi (1)	6	0.01
Pueblo (0)	0	<0.01
Puget Sound Salish (0)	0	<0.01
Seminole (0)	5	0.01
Shoshone (0)	0	<0.01
Sioux (12)	23	0.03
South American Ind. (0)	7	0.01
Spanish American Ind. (0)	0	<0.01
Tlingit-Haida *(Alaska Native)* (0)	5	0.01
Tohono O'Odham (0)	0	<0.01
Tsimshian *(Alaska Native)* (0)	0	<0.01
Ute (0)	1	<0.01
Yakama (0)	0	<0.01
Yaqui (1)	1	<0.01
Yuman (0)	1	<0.01
Yup'ik *(Alaska Native)* (0)	0	<0.01
Asian (925)	1,224	1.82
Not Hispanic (908)	1,160	1.73
Hispanic (17)	64	0.10
Bangladeshi (5)	5	0.01
Bhutanese (0)	0	<0.01
Burmese (6)	8	0.01
Cambodian (1)	1	<0.01
Chinese, ex. Taiwanese (188)	226	0.34
Filipino (111)	200	0.30
Hmong (0)	0	<0.01
Indian (196)	225	0.34
Indonesian (9)	9	0.01
Japanese (71)	107	0.16
Korean (190)	239	0.36
Laotian (6)	11	0.02
Malaysian (3)	4	0.01
Nepalese (3)	3	<0.01
Pakistani (10)	13	0.02
Sri Lankan (0)	0	<0.01
Taiwanese (19)	20	0.03
Thai (12)	25	0.04
Vietnamese (63)	79	0.12
Hawaii Native/Pacific Islander (20)	73	0.11
Not Hispanic (14)	55	0.08
Hispanic (6)	18	0.03
Fijian (0)	0	<0.01
Guamanian/Chamorro (17)	20	0.03
Marshallese (0)	0	<0.01
Native Hawaiian (3)	18	0.03
Samoan (0)	13	0.02
Tongan (0)	1	<0.01
White (56,108)	57,759	86.03
Not Hispanic (52,557)	53,754	80.06
Hispanic (3,551)	4,005	5.97

*Notes: † The Census 2010 population figure is used to calculate the percentages in the Hispanic Origin and Race categories. Ancestry percentages are based on the 2006-2010 American Community Survey population (not shown); ‡ Numbers in parentheses indicate the number of people reporting a single ancestry; * Numbers in parentheses indicate the number of persons reporting this race alone, not in combination with any other race; Please refer to the Explanation of Data for more information.*

Muncie

Place Type: City
County: Delaware
Population: 70,085

Ancestry	Population	%
Afghan (0)	0	<0.01
African, Sub-Saharan (668)	875	1.25
African (546)	737	1.05
Cape Verdean (0)	0	<0.01
Ethiopian (0)	0	<0.01
Ghanaian (0)	0	<0.01
Kenyan (14)	14	0.02
Liberian (0)	0	<0.01
Nigerian (0)	0	<0.01
Senegalese (0)	0	<0.01
Sierra Leonean (0)	0	<0.01
Somalian (0)	0	<0.01
South African (0)	16	0.02
Sudanese (0)	0	<0.01
Ugandan (0)	0	<0.01
Zimbabwean (0)	0	<0.01
Other Sub-Saharan African (108)	108	0.15
Albanian (57)	57	0.08
Alsatian (0)	22	0.03
American (6,079)	6,079	8.68
Arab (7)	204	0.29
Arab (0)	84	0.12
Egyptian (0)	14	0.02
Iraqi (0)	14	0.02
Jordanian (0)	0	<0.01
Lebanese (0)	0	<0.01
Moroccan (0)	13	0.02
Palestinian (7)	7	0.01
Syrian (0)	66	0.09
Other Arab (0)	6	0.01
Armenian (0)	0	<0.01
Assyrian/Chaldean/Syriac (0)	0	<0.01
Australian (14)	27	0.04
Austrian (9)	45	0.06
Basque (0)	0	<0.01
Belgian (0)	110	0.16
Brazilian (0)	0	<0.01
British (225)	372	0.53
Bulgarian (9)	9	0.01
Cajun (0)	0	<0.01
Canadian (125)	194	0.28
Carpatho Rusyn (0)	0	<0.01
Celtic (10)	10	0.01
Croatian (0)	103	0.15
Cypriot (0)	0	<0.01
Czech (63)	87	0.12
Czechoslovakian (0)	0	<0.01
Danish (36)	119	0.17
Dutch (245)	1,417	2.02
Eastern European (0)	0	<0.01
English (2,398)	6,521	9.31
Estonian (0)	0	<0.01
European (449)	525	0.75
Finnish (26)	42	0.06
French, ex. Basque (286)	1,865	2.66
French Canadian (26)	64	0.09
German (5,967)	14,993	21.41
German Russian (0)	0	<0.01
Greek (143)	214	0.31
Guyanese (0)	0	<0.01
Hungarian (78)	175	0.25
Icelander (0)	0	<0.01
Iranian (72)	78	0.11
Irish (2,747)	9,462	13.51
Israeli (13)	24	0.03
Italian (867)	1,965	2.81
Latvian (0)	9	0.01
Lithuanian (64)	77	0.11
Luxemburger (0)	32	0.05
Macedonian (12)	23	0.03
Maltese (0)	0	<0.01
New Zealander (0)	18	0.03
Northern European (17)	17	0.02
Norwegian (47)	422	0.60
Pennsylvania German (0)	14	0.02
Polish (413)	1,148	1.64
Portuguese (0)	12	0.02
Romanian (40)	59	0.08
Russian (59)	162	0.23
Scandinavian (0)	14	0.02
Scotch-Irish (395)	930	1.33
Scottish (318)	1,264	1.81
Serbian (0)	15	0.02
Slavic (22)	22	0.03
Slovak (30)	118	0.17
Slovene (0)	0	<0.01
Soviet Union (0)	0	<0.01
Swedish (144)	494	0.71
Swiss (84)	326	0.47
Turkish (34)	34	0.05
Ukrainian (0)	30	0.04
Welsh (78)	511	0.73
West Indian, ex. Hispanic (41)	41	0.06
Bahamian (0)	0	<0.01
Barbadian (28)	28	0.04
Belizean (0)	0	<0.01
Bermudan (0)	0	<0.01
British West Indian (0)	0	<0.01
Dutch West Indian (0)	0	<0.01
Haitian (0)	0	<0.01
Jamaican (13)	13	0.02
Trinidadian/Tobagonian (0)	0	<0.01
U.S. Virgin Islander (0)	0	<0.01
West Indian (0)	0	<0.01
Other West Indian (0)	0	<0.01
Yugoslavian (12)	27	0.04

Hispanic Origin	Population	%
Hispanic or Latino (of any race)	1,579	2.25
Central American, ex. Mexican	62	0.09
Costa Rican	5	0.01
Guatemalan	9	0.01
Honduran	12	0.02
Nicaraguan	3	<0.01
Panamanian	21	0.03
Salvadoran	11	0.02
Other Central American	1	<0.01
Cuban	38	0.05
Dominican Republic	21	0.03
Mexican	1,061	1.51
Puerto Rican	133	0.19
South American	63	0.09
Argentinean	7	0.01
Bolivian	5	0.01
Chilean	11	0.02
Colombian	6	0.01
Ecuadorian	2	<0.01
Paraguayan	1	<0.01
Peruvian	12	0.02
Uruguayan	2	<0.01
Venezuelan	13	0.02
Other South American	4	0.01
Other Hispanic or Latino	201	0.29

Race*	Population	%
African-American/Black (7,655)	8,829	12.60
Not Hispanic (7,569)	8,664	12.36
Hispanic (86)	165	0.24
American Indian/Alaska Native (203)	650	0.93
Not Hispanic (174)	577	0.82
Hispanic (29)	73	0.10
Alaska Athabascan *(Ala. Nat.)* (0)	0	<0.01
Aleut *(Alaska Native)* (0)	0	<0.01
Apache (0)	12	0.02
Arapaho (0)	1	<0.01
Blackfeet (5)	42	0.06
Canadian/French Am. Ind. (0)	0	<0.01
Central American Ind. (0)	0	<0.01
Cherokee (51)	182	0.26
Cheyenne (0)	0	<0.01
Chickasaw (0)	0	<0.01
Chippewa (2)	5	0.01
Choctaw (1)	3	<0.01
Colville (0)	0	<0.01
Comanche (0)	0	<0.01
Cree (1)	5	0.01
Creek (0)	2	<0.01
Crow (2)	2	<0.01
Delaware (0)	2	<0.01
Hopi (0)	0	<0.01
Houma (0)	0	<0.01
Inupiat *(Alaska Native)* (0)	0	<0.01
Iroquois (5)	7	0.01
Kiowa (0)	0	<0.01
Lumbee (3)	3	<0.01
Menominee (1)	1	<0.01
Mexican American Ind. (9)	11	0.02
Navajo (4)	7	0.01
Osage (0)	1	<0.01
Ottawa (0)	0	<0.01
Paiute (0)	0	<0.01
Pima (0)	0	<0.01
Potawatomi (5)	5	0.01
Pueblo (0)	1	<0.01
Puget Sound Salish (1)	1	<0.01
Seminole (1)	2	<0.01
Shoshone (0)	6	0.01
Sioux (8)	20	0.03
South American Ind. (2)	4	0.01
Spanish American Ind. (2)	2	<0.01
Tlingit-Haida *(Alaska Native)* (0)	0	<0.01
Tohono O'Odham (0)	0	<0.01
Tsimshian *(Alaska Native)* (0)	0	<0.01
Ute (0)	0	<0.01
Yakama (0)	0	<0.01
Yaqui (0)	0	<0.01
Yuman (0)	0	<0.01
Yup'ik *(Alaska Native)* (0)	0	<0.01
Asian (849)	1,173	1.67
Not Hispanic (839)	1,143	1.63
Hispanic (10)	30	0.04
Bangladeshi (21)	23	0.03
Bhutanese (0)	0	<0.01
Burmese (2)	2	<0.01
Cambodian (0)	0	<0.01
Chinese, ex. Taiwanese (250)	282	0.40
Filipino (74)	143	0.20
Hmong (2)	2	<0.01
Indian (196)	248	0.35
Indonesian (2)	2	<0.01
Japanese (48)	86	0.12
Korean (111)	142	0.20
Laotian (2)	3	<0.01
Malaysian (1)	3	<0.01
Nepalese (10)	13	0.02
Pakistani (12)	14	0.02
Sri Lankan (4)	4	0.01
Taiwanese (22)	25	0.04
Thai (9)	16	0.02
Vietnamese (51)	62	0.09
Hawaii Native/Pacific Islander (42)	138	0.20
Not Hispanic (39)	126	0.18
Hispanic (3)	12	0.02
Fijian (0)	1	<0.01
Guamanian/Chamorro (3)	12	0.02
Marshallese (0)	0	<0.01
Native Hawaiian (15)	44	0.06
Samoan (9)	19	0.03
Tongan (1)	3	<0.01
White (58,853)	60,636	86.52
Not Hispanic (58,018)	59,588	85.02
Hispanic (835)	1,048	1.50

*Notes: † The Census 2010 population figure is used to calculate the percentages in the Hispanic Origin and Race categories. Ancestry percentages are based on the 2006-2010 American Community Survey population (not shown); ‡ Numbers in parentheses indicate the number of people reporting a single ancestry; * Numbers in parentheses indicate the number of persons reporting this race alone, not in combination with any other race; Please refer to the Explanation of Data for more information.*

Noblesville

Place Type: City
County: Hamilton
Population: 51,969

Ancestry	Population	%
Afghan (0)	0	<0.01
African, Sub-Saharan (155)	278	0.57
African (98)	221	0.45
Cape Verdean (0)	0	<0.01
Ethiopian (0)	0	<0.01
Ghanaian (0)	0	<0.01
Kenyan (57)	57	0.12
Liberian (0)	0	<0.01
Nigerian (0)	0	<0.01
Senegalese (0)	0	<0.01
Sierra Leonean (0)	0	<0.01
Somalian (0)	0	<0.01
South African (0)	0	<0.01
Sudanese (0)	0	<0.01
Ugandan (0)	0	<0.01
Zimbabwean (0)	0	<0.01
Other Sub-Saharan African (0)	0	<0.01
Albanian (40)	40	0.08
Alsatian (0)	0	<0.01
American (4,429)	4,429	9.09
Arab (55)	183	0.38
Arab (0)	113	0.23
Egyptian (30)	30	0.06
Iraqi (0)	0	<0.01
Jordanian (0)	0	<0.01
Lebanese (13)	18	0.04
Moroccan (12)	12	0.02
Palestinian (0)	0	<0.01
Syrian (0)	10	0.02
Other Arab (0)	0	<0.01
Armenian (0)	0	<0.01
Assyrian/Chaldean/Syriac (0)	0	<0.01
Australian (14)	14	0.03
Austrian (25)	25	0.05
Basque (0)	0	<0.01
Belgian (32)	247	0.51
Brazilian (28)	28	0.06
British (102)	213	0.44
Bulgarian (29)	41	0.08
Cajun (0)	0	<0.01
Canadian (32)	57	0.12
Carpatho Rusyn (0)	0	<0.01
Celtic (0)	15	0.03
Croatian (17)	56	0.11
Cypriot (0)	0	<0.01
Czech (68)	109	0.22
Czechoslovakian (84)	108	0.22
Danish (24)	71	0.15
Dutch (352)	1,089	2.24
Eastern European (126)	126	0.26
English (1,576)	5,811	11.93
Estonian (0)	0	<0.01
European (875)	1,091	2.24
Finnish (53)	67	0.14
French, ex. Basque (320)	1,734	3.56
French Canadian (90)	186	0.38
German (5,244)	13,766	28.26
German Russian (0)	0	<0.01
Greek (100)	174	0.36
Guyanese (0)	0	<0.01
Hungarian (60)	207	0.42
Icelander (0)	0	<0.01
Iranian (56)	131	0.27
Irish (1,929)	7,262	14.91
Israeli (0)	0	<0.01
Italian (726)	2,728	5.60
Latvian (41)	167	0.34
Lithuanian (9)	46	0.09
Luxemburger (0)	0	<0.01
Macedonian (12)	25	0.05
Maltese (0)	0	<0.01
New Zealander (0)	0	<0.01
Northern European (24)	24	0.05
Norwegian (100)	621	1.27
Pennsylvania German (69)	83	0.17
Polish (653)	1,516	3.11
Portuguese (27)	27	0.06
Romanian (33)	62	0.13
Russian (142)	216	0.44
Scandinavian (14)	83	0.17
Scotch-Irish (220)	817	1.68
Scottish (383)	1,261	2.59
Serbian (24)	70	0.14
Slavic (0)	0	<0.01
Slovak (45)	139	0.29
Slovene (12)	12	0.02
Soviet Union (0)	0	<0.01
Swedish (132)	695	1.43
Swiss (41)	212	0.44
Turkish (26)	52	0.11
Ukrainian (191)	436	0.90
Welsh (132)	497	1.02
West Indian, ex. Hispanic (75)	75	0.15
Bahamian (0)	0	<0.01
Barbadian (0)	0	<0.01
Belizean (0)	0	<0.01
Bermudan (19)	19	0.04
British West Indian (0)	0	<0.01
Dutch West Indian (0)	0	<0.01
Haitian (12)	12	0.02
Jamaican (31)	31	0.06
Trinidadian/Tobagonian (13)	13	0.03
U.S. Virgin Islander (0)	0	<0.01
West Indian (0)	0	<0.01
Other West Indian (0)	0	<0.01
Yugoslavian (121)	121	0.25

Hispanic Origin	Population	%
Hispanic or Latino (of any race)	2,209	4.25
Central American, ex. Mexican	244	0.47
Costa Rican	19	0.04
Guatemalan	59	0.11
Honduran	31	0.06
Nicaraguan	14	0.03
Panamanian	10	0.02
Salvadoran	111	0.21
Other Central American	0	<0.01
Cuban	43	0.08
Dominican Republic	40	0.08
Mexican	1,245	2.40
Puerto Rican	210	0.40
South American	253	0.49
Argentinean	19	0.04
Bolivian	11	0.02
Chilean	11	0.02
Colombian	68	0.13
Ecuadorian	4	0.01
Paraguayan	0	<0.01
Peruvian	41	0.08
Uruguayan	2	<0.01
Venezuelan	97	0.19
Other South American	0	<0.01
Other Hispanic or Latino	174	0.33

Race*	Population	%
African-American/Black (1,896)	2,300	4.43
Not Hispanic (1,840)	2,196	4.23
Hispanic (56)	104	0.20
American Indian/Alaska Native (109)	281	0.54
Not Hispanic (87)	243	0.47
Hispanic (22)	38	0.07
Alaska Athabascan *(Ala. Nat.)* (0)	0	<0.01
Aleut *(Alaska Native)* (0)	0	<0.01
Apache (0)	5	0.01
Arapaho (0)	0	<0.01
Blackfeet (6)	16	0.03
Canadian/French Am. Ind. (0)	0	<0.01
Central American Ind. (0)	0	<0.01
Cherokee (13)	58	0.11
Cheyenne (0)	0	<0.01
Chickasaw (0)	0	<0.01
Chippewa (10)	18	0.03
Choctaw (1)	5	0.01
Colville (0)	0	<0.01
Comanche (0)	0	<0.01
Cree (0)	0	<0.01
Creek (4)	8	0.02
Crow (1)	1	<0.01
Delaware (0)	0	<0.01
Hopi (0)	0	<0.01
Houma (0)	0	<0.01
Inupiat *(Alaska Native)* (0)	1	<0.01
Iroquois (0)	0	<0.01
Kiowa (0)	0	<0.01
Lumbee (0)	0	<0.01
Menominee (0)	0	<0.01
Mexican American Ind. (9)	10	0.02
Navajo (5)	5	0.01
Osage (1)	1	<0.01
Ottawa (0)	0	<0.01
Paiute (0)	0	<0.01
Pima (0)	0	<0.01
Potawatomi (1)	1	<0.01
Pueblo (0)	0	<0.01
Puget Sound Salish (0)	0	<0.01
Seminole (0)	1	<0.01
Shoshone (0)	1	<0.01
Sioux (6)	11	0.02
South American Ind. (1)	2	<0.01
Spanish American Ind. (0)	0	<0.01
Tlingit-Haida *(Alaska Native)* (0)	0	<0.01
Tohono O'Odham (0)	0	<0.01
Tsimshian *(Alaska Native)* (0)	0	<0.01
Ute (2)	2	<0.01
Yakama (0)	0	<0.01
Yaqui (0)	1	<0.01
Yuman (0)	0	<0.01
Yup'ik *(Alaska Native)* (0)	0	<0.01
Asian (874)	1,149	2.21
Not Hispanic (864)	1,128	2.17
Hispanic (10)	21	0.04
Bangladeshi (12)	12	0.02
Bhutanese (0)	0	<0.01
Burmese (0)	0	<0.01
Cambodian (21)	26	0.05
Chinese, ex. Taiwanese (125)	157	0.30
Filipino (114)	198	0.38
Hmong (12)	14	0.03
Indian (241)	262	0.50
Indonesian (12)	15	0.03
Japanese (43)	86	0.17
Korean (94)	143	0.28
Laotian (4)	13	0.03
Malaysian (5)	5	0.01
Nepalese (0)	0	<0.01
Pakistani (11)	12	0.02
Sri Lankan (7)	7	0.01
Taiwanese (2)	2	<0.01
Thai (12)	24	0.05
Vietnamese (123)	139	0.27
Hawaii Native/Pacific Islander (35)	80	0.15
Not Hispanic (24)	61	0.12
Hispanic (11)	19	0.04
Fijian (0)	0	<0.01
Guamanian/Chamorro (2)	7	0.01
Marshallese (1)	1	<0.01
Native Hawaiian (27)	51	0.10
Samoan (3)	11	0.02
Tongan (1)	1	<0.01
White (47,333)	48,170	92.69
Not Hispanic (46,089)	46,797	90.05
Hispanic (1,244)	1,373	2.64

*Notes: † The Census 2010 population figure is used to calculate the percentages in the Hispanic Origin and Race categories. Ancestry percentages are based on the 2006-2010 American Community Survey population (not shown); ‡ Numbers in parentheses indicate the number of people reporting a single ancestry; * Numbers in parentheses indicate the number of persons reporting this race alone, not in combination with any other race; Please refer to the Explanation of Data for more information.*

South Bend

Place Type: City
County: St. Joseph
Population: 101,168

Ancestry	Population	%
Afghan (0)	0	<0.01
African, Sub-Saharan (979)	1,287	1.26
African (699)	952	0.93
Cape Verdean (0)	0	<0.01
Ethiopian (0)	0	<0.01
Ghanaian (0)	0	<0.01
Kenyan (202)	218	0.21
Liberian (0)	28	0.03
Nigerian (0)	0	<0.01
Senegalese (0)	0	<0.01
Sierra Leonean (0)	11	0.01
Somalian (0)	0	<0.01
South African (0)	0	<0.01
Sudanese (0)	0	<0.01
Ugandan (0)	0	<0.01
Zimbabwean (0)	0	<0.01
Other Sub-Saharan African (78)	78	0.08
Albanian (0)	0	<0.01
Alsatian (0)	0	<0.01
American (3,845)	3,845	3.77
Arab (72)	131	0.13
Arab (27)	27	0.03
Egyptian (0)	0	<0.01
Iraqi (23)	33	0.03
Jordanian (0)	0	<0.01
Lebanese (9)	33	0.03
Moroccan (0)	6	0.01
Palestinian (0)	0	<0.01
Syrian (0)	19	0.02
Other Arab (13)	13	0.01
Armenian (8)	44	0.04
Assyrian/Chaldean/Syriac (0)	0	<0.01
Australian (0)	0	<0.01
Austrian (89)	275	0.27
Basque (0)	0	<0.01
Belgian (397)	871	0.85
Brazilian (10)	50	0.05
British (158)	336	0.33
Bulgarian (22)	47	0.05
Cajun (0)	0	<0.01
Canadian (66)	126	0.12
Carpatho Rusyn (0)	0	<0.01
Celtic (10)	10	0.01
Croatian (23)	295	0.29
Cypriot (0)	0	<0.01
Czech (35)	264	0.26
Czechoslovakian (42)	84	0.08
Danish (20)	88	0.09
Dutch (249)	2,222	2.18
Eastern European (13)	66	0.06
English (1,797)	6,318	6.19
Estonian (0)	8	0.01
European (680)	796	0.78
Finnish (33)	93	0.09
French, ex. Basque (209)	2,323	2.28
French Canadian (84)	422	0.41
German (5,733)	19,199	18.81
German Russian (0)	0	<0.01
Greek (89)	308	0.30
Guyanese (0)	0	<0.01
Hungarian (1,068)	2,904	2.85
Icelander (0)	0	<0.01
Iranian (13)	13	0.01
Irish (2,788)	12,089	11.84
Israeli (0)	0	<0.01
Italian (1,079)	3,341	3.27
Latvian (10)	10	0.01
Lithuanian (55)	176	0.17
Luxemburger (13)	13	0.01
Macedonian (0)	0	<0.01
Maltese (0)	0	<0.01
New Zealander (0)	0	<0.01
Northern European (62)	62	0.06
Norwegian (116)	459	0.45
Pennsylvania German (48)	140	0.14
Polish (4,876)	10,370	10.16
Portuguese (23)	54	0.05
Romanian (68)	88	0.09
Russian (238)	730	0.72
Scandinavian (35)	150	0.15
Scotch-Irish (314)	1,065	1.04
Scottish (213)	1,319	1.29
Serbian (71)	165	0.16
Slavic (10)	10	0.01
Slovak (42)	131	0.13
Slovene (0)	9	0.01
Soviet Union (0)	0	<0.01
Swedish (291)	1,638	1.60
Swiss (141)	343	0.34
Turkish (50)	104	0.10
Ukrainian (58)	214	0.21
Welsh (92)	372	0.36
West Indian, ex. Hispanic (98)	117	0.11
Bahamian (0)	9	0.01
Barbadian (0)	0	<0.01
Belizean (0)	0	<0.01
Bermudan (0)	0	<0.01
British West Indian (15)	15	0.01
Dutch West Indian (11)	11	0.01
Haitian (0)	0	<0.01
Jamaican (12)	12	0.01
Trinidadian/Tobagonian (39)	39	0.04
U.S. Virgin Islander (0)	0	<0.01
West Indian (21)	31	0.03
Other West Indian (0)	0	<0.01
Yugoslavian (364)	514	0.50

Hispanic Origin	Population	%
Hispanic or Latino (of any race)	13,116	12.96
Central American, ex. Mexican	292	0.29
Costa Rican	7	0.01
Guatemalan	66	0.07
Honduran	49	0.05
Nicaraguan	46	0.05
Panamanian	21	0.02
Salvadoran	98	0.10
Other Central American	5	<0.01
Cuban	111	0.11
Dominican Republic	42	0.04
Mexican	11,025	10.90
Puerto Rican	525	0.52
South American	275	0.27
Argentinean	33	0.03
Bolivian	10	0.01
Chilean	27	0.03
Colombian	53	0.05
Ecuadorian	47	0.05
Paraguayan	10	0.01
Peruvian	17	0.02
Uruguayan	5	<0.01
Venezuelan	73	0.07
Other South American	0	<0.01
Other Hispanic or Latino	846	0.84

Race*	Population	%
African-American/Black (26,906)	29,667	29.32
Not Hispanic (26,496)	28,893	28.56
Hispanic (410)	774	0.77
American Indian/Alaska Native (478)	1,334	1.32
Not Hispanic (310)	1,029	1.02
Hispanic (168)	305	0.30
Alaska Athabascan *(Ala. Nat.)* (0)	0	<0.01
Aleut *(Alaska Native)* (0)	0	<0.01
Apache (6)	29	0.03
Arapaho (0)	1	<0.01
Blackfeet (14)	74	0.07
Canadian/French Am. Ind. (1)	5	<0.01
Central American Ind. (3)	8	0.01
Cherokee (54)	281	0.28
Cheyenne (0)	1	<0.01
Chickasaw (3)	6	0.01
Chippewa (12)	29	0.03
Choctaw (5)	23	0.02
Colville (1)	1	<0.01
Comanche (0)	1	<0.01
Cree (0)	1	<0.01
Creek (0)	4	<0.01
Crow (0)	0	<0.01
Delaware (1)	1	<0.01
Hopi (0)	0	<0.01
Houma (0)	0	<0.01
Inupiat *(Alaska Native)* (0)	1	<0.01
Iroquois (0)	4	<0.01
Kiowa (0)	0	<0.01
Lumbee (4)	10	0.01
Menominee (1)	1	<0.01
Mexican American Ind. (31)	54	0.05
Navajo (1)	8	0.01
Osage (0)	0	<0.01
Ottawa (0)	3	<0.01
Paiute (3)	3	<0.01
Pima (0)	0	<0.01
Potawatomi (38)	74	0.07
Pueblo (0)	4	<0.01
Puget Sound Salish (0)	0	<0.01
Seminole (0)	5	<0.01
Shoshone (0)	1	<0.01
Sioux (4)	9	0.01
South American Ind. (2)	3	<0.01
Spanish American Ind. (8)	11	0.01
Tlingit-Haida *(Alaska Native)* (3)	4	<0.01
Tohono O'Odham (0)	0	<0.01
Tsimshian *(Alaska Native)* (0)	0	<0.01
Ute (0)	0	<0.01
Yakama (0)	0	<0.01
Yaqui (0)	0	<0.01
Yuman (0)	0	<0.01
Yup'ik *(Alaska Native)* (0)	0	<0.01
Asian (1,318)	1,824	1.80
Not Hispanic (1,295)	1,742	1.72
Hispanic (23)	82	0.08
Bangladeshi (1)	2	<0.01
Bhutanese (0)	0	<0.01
Burmese (0)	0	<0.01
Cambodian (76)	80	0.08
Chinese, ex. Taiwanese (258)	360	0.36
Filipino (205)	345	0.34
Hmong (2)	2	<0.01
Indian (211)	266	0.26
Indonesian (11)	14	0.01
Japanese (44)	102	0.10
Korean (107)	164	0.16
Laotian (34)	53	0.05
Malaysian (2)	3	<0.01
Nepalese (3)	4	<0.01
Pakistani (12)	16	0.02
Sri Lankan (8)	9	0.01
Taiwanese (17)	19	0.02
Thai (24)	37	0.04
Vietnamese (242)	267	0.26
Hawaii Native/Pacific Islander (64)	185	0.18
Not Hispanic (55)	156	0.15
Hispanic (9)	29	0.03
Fijian (0)	0	<0.01
Guamanian/Chamorro (12)	20	0.02
Marshallese (0)	0	<0.01
Native Hawaiian (17)	55	0.05
Samoan (17)	55	0.05
Tongan (11)	20	0.02
White (61,199)	64,797	64.05
Not Hispanic (56,474)	59,298	58.61
Hispanic (4,725)	5,499	5.44

*Notes: † The Census 2010 population figure is used to calculate the percentages in the Hispanic Origin and Race categories. Ancestry percentages are based on the 2006-2010 American Community Survey population (not shown); ‡ Numbers in parentheses indicate the number of people reporting a single ancestry; * Numbers in parentheses indicate the number of persons reporting this race alone, not in combination with any other race; Please refer to the Explanation of Data for more information.*

Terre Haute

Place Type: City
County: Vigo
Population: 60,785

Ancestry	Population	%
Afghan (0)	0	<0.01
African, Sub-Saharan (691)	806	1.33
African (685)	800	1.32
Cape Verdean (0)	0	<0.01
Ethiopian (0)	0	<0.01
Ghanaian (0)	0	<0.01
Kenyan (0)	0	<0.01
Liberian (0)	0	<0.01
Nigerian (0)	0	<0.01
Senegalese (0)	0	<0.01
Sierra Leonean (0)	0	<0.01
Somalian (6)	6	0.01
South African (0)	0	<0.01
Sudanese (0)	0	<0.01
Ugandan (0)	0	<0.01
Zimbabwean (0)	0	<0.01
Other Sub-Saharan African (0)	0	<0.01
Albanian (0)	0	<0.01
Alsatian (0)	0	<0.01
American (11,657)	11,657	19.29
Arab (453)	525	0.87
Arab (108)	117	0.19
Egyptian (0)	0	<0.01
Iraqi (0)	0	<0.01
Jordanian (6)	6	0.01
Lebanese (24)	24	0.04
Moroccan (0)	0	<0.01
Palestinian (0)	0	<0.01
Syrian (74)	137	0.23
Other Arab (241)	241	0.40
Armenian (0)	0	<0.01
Assyrian/Chaldean/Syriac (0)	0	<0.01
Australian (0)	0	<0.01
Austrian (25)	85	0.14
Basque (0)	0	<0.01
Belgian (35)	75	0.12
Brazilian (0)	0	<0.01
British (90)	153	0.25
Bulgarian (0)	0	<0.01
Cajun (0)	0	<0.01
Canadian (33)	62	0.10
Carpatho Rusyn (0)	0	<0.01
Celtic (0)	0	<0.01
Croatian (51)	85	0.14
Cypriot (0)	0	<0.01
Czech (69)	232	0.38
Czechoslovakian (43)	53	0.09
Danish (38)	75	0.12
Dutch (335)	1,355	2.24
Eastern European (26)	26	0.04
English (2,093)	5,550	9.18
Estonian (0)	53	0.09
European (396)	484	0.80
Finnish (32)	32	0.05
French, ex. Basque (487)	1,765	2.92
French Canadian (31)	85	0.14
German (5,115)	13,440	22.24
German Russian (0)	0	<0.01
Greek (15)	52	0.09
Guyanese (0)	0	<0.01
Hungarian (135)	438	0.72
Icelander (0)	13	0.02
Iranian (0)	0	<0.01
Irish (2,031)	7,200	11.91
Israeli (13)	13	0.02
Italian (848)	1,814	3.00
Latvian (69)	118	0.20
Lithuanian (33)	110	0.18
Luxemburger (0)	0	<0.01
Macedonian (0)	0	<0.01
Maltese (0)	0	<0.01
New Zealander (0)	0	<0.01
Northern European (0)	3	<0.01
Norwegian (51)	196	0.32
Pennsylvania German (2)	15	0.02
Polish (251)	1,184	1.96
Portuguese (0)	0	<0.01
Romanian (178)	263	0.44
Russian (7)	256	0.42
Scandinavian (41)	50	0.08
Scotch-Irish (308)	884	1.46
Scottish (348)	1,286	2.13
Serbian (24)	66	0.11
Slavic (0)	32	0.05
Slovak (22)	60	0.10
Slovene (16)	16	0.03
Soviet Union (0)	0	<0.01
Swedish (86)	475	0.79
Swiss (42)	165	0.27
Turkish (8)	23	0.04
Ukrainian (20)	20	0.03
Welsh (122)	591	0.98
West Indian, ex. Hispanic (27)	27	0.04
Bahamian (0)	0	<0.01
Barbadian (0)	0	<0.01
Belizean (0)	0	<0.01
Bermudan (0)	0	<0.01
British West Indian (0)	0	<0.01
Dutch West Indian (0)	0	<0.01
Haitian (27)	27	0.04
Jamaican (0)	0	<0.01
Trinidadian/Tobagonian (0)	0	<0.01
U.S. Virgin Islander (0)	0	<0.01
West Indian (0)	0	<0.01
Other West Indian (0)	0	<0.01
Yugoslavian (27)	55	0.09

Hispanic Origin	Population	%
Hispanic or Latino (of any race)	1,893	3.11
Central American, ex. Mexican	63	0.10
Costa Rican	3	<0.01
Guatemalan	16	0.03
Honduran	22	0.04
Nicaraguan	2	<0.01
Panamanian	8	0.01
Salvadoran	12	0.02
Other Central American	0	<0.01
Cuban	46	0.08
Dominican Republic	10	0.02
Mexican	1,469	2.42
Puerto Rican	140	0.23
South American	70	0.12
Argentinean	12	0.02
Bolivian	6	0.01
Chilean	6	0.01
Colombian	28	0.05
Ecuadorian	4	0.01
Paraguayan	0	<0.01
Peruvian	5	0.01
Uruguayan	0	<0.01
Venezuelan	9	0.01
Other South American	0	<0.01
Other Hispanic or Latino	95	0.16

Race*	Population	%
African-American/Black (6,644)	7,819	12.86
Not Hispanic (6,587)	7,705	12.68
Hispanic (57)	114	0.19
American Indian/Alaska Native (259)	685	1.13
Not Hispanic (231)	632	1.04
Hispanic (28)	53	0.09
Alaska Athabascan *(Ala. Nat.)* (0)	0	<0.01
Aleut *(Alaska Native)* (0)	0	<0.01
Apache (1)	8	0.01
Arapaho (0)	0	<0.01
Blackfeet (2)	24	0.04
Canadian/French Am. Ind. (1)	1	<0.01
Central American Ind. (0)	0	<0.01
Cherokee (34)	159	0.26
Cheyenne (0)	6	0.01
Chickasaw (0)	4	0.01
Chippewa (2)	3	<0.01
Choctaw (3)	9	0.01
Colville (0)	0	<0.01
Comanche (0)	2	<0.01
Cree (8)	9	0.01
Creek (7)	8	0.01
Crow (0)	0	<0.01
Delaware (0)	1	<0.01
Hopi (0)	0	<0.01
Houma (2)	2	<0.01
Inupiat *(Alaska Native)* (0)	0	<0.01
Iroquois (0)	4	0.01
Kiowa (2)	2	<0.01
Lumbee (0)	2	<0.01
Menominee (1)	1	<0.01
Mexican American Ind. (13)	20	0.03
Navajo (1)	6	0.01
Osage (1)	1	<0.01
Ottawa (0)	0	<0.01
Paiute (0)	0	<0.01
Pima (0)	0	<0.01
Potawatomi (5)	6	0.01
Pueblo (0)	0	<0.01
Puget Sound Salish (0)	0	<0.01
Seminole (0)	1	<0.01
Shoshone (0)	0	<0.01
Sioux (15)	34	0.06
South American Ind. (0)	0	<0.01
Spanish American Ind. (0)	0	<0.01
Tlingit-Haida *(Alaska Native)* (0)	1	<0.01
Tohono O'Odham (0)	0	<0.01
Tsimshian *(Alaska Native)* (0)	0	<0.01
Ute (1)	1	<0.01
Yakama (0)	0	<0.01
Yaqui (0)	3	<0.01
Yuman (0)	0	<0.01
Yup'ik *(Alaska Native)* (0)	0	<0.01
Asian (879)	1,092	1.80
Not Hispanic (876)	1,081	1.78
Hispanic (3)	11	0.02
Bangladeshi (2)	2	<0.01
Bhutanese (0)	0	<0.01
Burmese (0)	0	<0.01
Cambodian (1)	1	<0.01
Chinese, ex. Taiwanese (222)	254	0.42
Filipino (104)	159	0.26
Hmong (5)	7	0.01
Indian (213)	242	0.40
Indonesian (2)	5	0.01
Japanese (65)	112	0.18
Korean (118)	141	0.23
Laotian (0)	0	<0.01
Malaysian (1)	9	0.01
Nepalese (5)	5	0.01
Pakistani (2)	6	0.01
Sri Lankan (0)	1	<0.01
Taiwanese (52)	55	0.09
Thai (7)	9	0.01
Vietnamese (28)	41	0.07
Hawaii Native/Pacific Islander (26)	79	0.13
Not Hispanic (22)	73	0.12
Hispanic (4)	6	0.01
Fijian (0)	0	<0.01
Guamanian/Chamorro (8)	11	0.02
Marshallese (0)	0	<0.01
Native Hawaiian (10)	44	0.07
Samoan (2)	13	0.02
Tongan (0)	2	<0.01
White (50,750)	52,377	86.17
Not Hispanic (49,456)	50,949	83.82
Hispanic (1,294)	1,428	2.35

*Notes: † The Census 2010 population figure is used to calculate the percentages in the Hispanic Origin and Race categories. Ancestry percentages are based on the 2006-2010 American Community Survey population (not shown); ‡ Numbers in parentheses indicate the number of people reporting a single ancestry; * Numbers in parentheses indicate the number of persons reporting this race alone, not in combination with any other race; Please refer to the Explanation of Data for more information.*

Ancestry Group Rankings

Afghan

Top 10 Places Sorted by Population
Based on all places, regardless of total population

Place	Population	%
Bloomington (city) Monroe County	59	0.08
York (town) Delaware County	57	0.62
Carmel (city) Hamilton County	37	0.05
Indianapolis (city) Marion County	29	<0.01
Fort Wayne (city) Allen County	20	0.01
Fishers (town) Hamilton County	15	0.02
Portage (city) Porter County	13	0.04
Hanover (town) Jefferson County	12	0.36
Munster (town) Lake County	3	0.01
Aberdeen (cdp) Porter County	0	0.00

Top 10 Places Sorted by Percent of Total Population
Based on all places, regardless of total population

Place	Population	%
York (town) Delaware County	57	0.62
Hanover (town) Jefferson County	12	0.36
Bloomington (city) Monroe County	59	0.08
Carmel (city) Hamilton County	37	0.05
Portage (city) Porter County	13	0.04
Fishers (town) Hamilton County	15	0.02
Fort Wayne (city) Allen County	20	0.01
Munster (town) Lake County	3	0.01
Indianapolis (city) Marion County	29	<0.01
Aberdeen (cdp) Porter County	0	0.00

Top 10 Places Sorted by Percent of Total Population
Based on places with total population of 50,000 or more

Place	Population	%
Bloomington (city) Monroe County	59	0.08
Carmel (city) Hamilton County	37	0.05
Fishers (town) Hamilton County	15	0.02
Fort Wayne (city) Allen County	20	0.01
Indianapolis (city) Marion County	29	<0.01
Anderson (city) Madison County	0	0.00
Elkhart (city) Elkhart County	0	0.00
Evansville (city) Vanderburgh County	0	0.00
Gary (city) Lake County	0	0.00
Hammond (city) Lake County	0	0.00

African, Sub-Saharan

Top 10 Places Sorted by Population
Based on all places, regardless of total population

Place	Population	%
Indianapolis (city) Marion County	43,672	5.39
Fort Wayne (city) Allen County	13,249	5.22
Gary (city) Lake County	1,824	2.16
Lawrence (city) Marion County	1,653	3.72
South Bend (city) St. Joseph County	1,287	1.26
Merrillville (town) Lake County	902	2.62
Muncie (city) Delaware County	875	1.25
Terre Haute (city) Vigo County	806	1.33
Speedway (town) Marion County	709	5.94
Anderson (city) Madison County	648	1.14

Top 10 Places Sorted by Percent of Total Population
Based on all places, regardless of total population

Place	Population	%
Warren Park (town) Marion County	130	9.37
Spring Grove (town) Wayne County	25	7.16
Harmony (town) Clay County	41	6.44
Speedway (town) Marion County	709	5.94
Greenville (town) Floyd County	31	5.48
Indianapolis (city) Marion County	43,672	5.39
Fort Wayne (city) Allen County	13,249	5.22
Stilesville (town) Hendricks County	15	5.21
Hunter (town) Allen County	224	4.76
Lawrence (city) Marion County	1,653	3.72

Top 10 Places Sorted by Percent of Total Population
Based on places with total population of 50,000 or more

Place	Population	%
Indianapolis (city) Marion County	43,672	5.39
Fort Wayne (city) Allen County	13,249	5.22
Gary (city) Lake County	1,824	2.16
Terre Haute (city) Vigo County	806	1.33
South Bend (city) St. Joseph County	1,287	1.26
Muncie (city) Delaware County	875	1.25
Anderson (city) Madison County	648	1.14
Elkhart (city) Elkhart County	409	0.79
Bloomington (city) Monroe County	593	0.76
Hammond (city) Lake County	421	0.52

African, Sub-Saharan: African

Top 10 Places Sorted by Population
Based on all places, regardless of total population

Place	Population	%
Indianapolis (city) Marion County	38,288	4.73
Fort Wayne (city) Allen County	12,753	5.03
Lawrence (city) Marion County	1,595	3.59
Gary (city) Lake County	1,527	1.81
South Bend (city) St. Joseph County	952	0.93
Merrillville (town) Lake County	867	2.52
Terre Haute (city) Vigo County	800	1.32
Muncie (city) Delaware County	737	1.05
Michigan City (city) LaPorte County	629	1.99
East Chicago (city) Lake County	595	1.97

Top 10 Places Sorted by Percent of Total Population
Based on all places, regardless of total population

Place	Population	%
Warren Park (town) Marion County	130	9.37
Spring Grove (town) Wayne County	25	7.16
Harmony (town) Clay County	41	6.44
Greenville (town) Floyd County	31	5.48
Stilesville (town) Hendricks County	15	5.21
Fort Wayne (city) Allen County	12,753	5.03
Speedway (town) Marion County	581	4.87
Hunter (town) Allen County	224	4.76
Indianapolis (city) Marion County	38,288	4.73
Lawrence (city) Marion County	1,595	3.59

Top 10 Places Sorted by Percent of Total Population
Based on places with total population of 50,000 or more

Place	Population	%
Fort Wayne (city) Allen County	12,753	5.03
Indianapolis (city) Marion County	38,288	4.73
Gary (city) Lake County	1,527	1.81
Terre Haute (city) Vigo County	800	1.32
Muncie (city) Delaware County	737	1.05
Anderson (city) Madison County	543	0.96
South Bend (city) St. Joseph County	952	0.93
Bloomington (city) Monroe County	508	0.65
Elkhart (city) Elkhart County	305	0.59
Hammond (city) Lake County	398	0.49

African, Sub-Saharan: Cape Verdean

Top 10 Places Sorted by Population
Based on all places, regardless of total population

Place	Population	%
Dyer (town) Lake County	28	0.18
Aberdeen (cdp) Porter County	0	0.00
Advance (town) Boone County	0	0.00
Akron (town) Fulton County	0	0.00
Alamo (town) Montgomery County	0	0.00
Albany (town) Delaware County	0	0.00
Albion (town) Noble County	0	0.00
Alexandria (city) Madison County	0	0.00
Alfordsville (town) Daviess County	0	0.00
Alton (town) Crawford County	0	0.00

Top 10 Places Sorted by Percent of Total Population
Based on all places, regardless of total population

Place	Population	%
Dyer (town) Lake County	28	0.18
Aberdeen (cdp) Porter County	0	0.00
Advance (town) Boone County	0	0.00
Akron (town) Fulton County	0	0.00
Alamo (town) Montgomery County	0	0.00
Albany (town) Delaware County	0	0.00
Albion (town) Noble County	0	0.00
Alexandria (city) Madison County	0	0.00
Alfordsville (town) Daviess County	0	0.00
Alton (town) Crawford County	0	0.00

Top 10 Places Sorted by Percent of Total Population
Based on places with total population of 50,000 or more

Place	Population	%
Anderson (city) Madison County	0	0.00
Bloomington (city) Monroe County	0	0.00
Carmel (city) Hamilton County	0	0.00
Elkhart (city) Elkhart County	0	0.00
Evansville (city) Vanderburgh County	0	0.00
Fishers (town) Hamilton County	0	0.00
Fort Wayne (city) Allen County	0	0.00
Gary (city) Lake County	0	0.00
Hammond (city) Lake County	0	0.00
Indianapolis (city) Marion County	0	0.00

African, Sub-Saharan: Ethiopian

Top 10 Places Sorted by Population
Based on all places, regardless of total population

Place	Population	%
Indianapolis (city) Marion County	443	0.05
Gary (city) Lake County	121	0.14
Plainfield (town) Hendricks County	82	0.31
Fort Wayne (city) Allen County	47	0.02
Speedway (town) Marion County	46	0.39
Purdue University (cdp) Tippecanoe County	46	0.35
Evansville (city) Vanderburgh County	34	0.03
Hobart (city) Lake County	30	0.11
West Lafayette (city) Tippecanoe County	26	0.09
Anderson (city) Madison County	18	0.03

Top 10 Places Sorted by Percent of Total Population
Based on all places, regardless of total population

Place	Population	%
Speedway (town) Marion County	46	0.39
Purdue University (cdp) Tippecanoe County	46	0.35
Plainfield (town) Hendricks County	82	0.31
Notre Dame (cdp) St. Joseph County	13	0.17
Gary (city) Lake County	121	0.14
Hobart (city) Lake County	30	0.11
West Lafayette (city) Tippecanoe County	26	0.09
Indianapolis (city) Marion County	443	0.05
Crown Point (city) Lake County	13	0.05
Evansville (city) Vanderburgh County	34	0.03

Top 10 Places Sorted by Percent of Total Population
Based on places with total population of 50,000 or more

Place	Population	%
Gary (city) Lake County	121	0.14
Indianapolis (city) Marion County	443	0.05
Evansville (city) Vanderburgh County	34	0.03
Anderson (city) Madison County	18	0.03
Fort Wayne (city) Allen County	47	0.02
Carmel (city) Hamilton County	12	0.02
Bloomington (city) Monroe County	5	0.01
Elkhart (city) Elkhart County	0	0.00
Fishers (town) Hamilton County	0	0.00
Hammond (city) Lake County	0	0.00

African, Sub-Saharan: Ghanaian

Top 10 Places Sorted by Population

Based on all places, regardless of total population

Place	Population	%
Indianapolis (city) Marion County	154	0.02
Mishawaka (city) St. Joseph County	51	0.11
Franklin (city) Johnson County	46	0.20
Merrillville (town) Lake County	18	0.05
Greencastle (city) Putnam County	14	0.14
Schererville (town) Lake County	12	0.04
Columbus (city) Bartholomew County	10	0.02
Gary (city) Lake County	10	0.01
Valparaiso (city) Porter County	7	0.02
Aberdeen (cdp) Porter County	0	0.00

Top 10 Places Sorted by Percent of Total Population

Based on all places, regardless of total population

Place	Population	%
Franklin (city) Johnson County	46	0.20
Greencastle (city) Putnam County	14	0.14
Mishawaka (city) St. Joseph County	51	0.11
Merrillville (town) Lake County	18	0.05
Schererville (town) Lake County	12	0.04
Indianapolis (city) Marion County	154	0.02
Columbus (city) Bartholomew County	10	0.02
Valparaiso (city) Porter County	7	0.02
Gary (city) Lake County	10	0.01
Aberdeen (cdp) Porter County	0	0.00

Top 10 Places Sorted by Percent of Total Population

Based on places with total population of 50,000 or more

Place	Population	%
Indianapolis (city) Marion County	154	0.02
Gary (city) Lake County	10	0.01
Anderson (city) Madison County	0	0.00
Bloomington (city) Monroe County	0	0.00
Carmel (city) Hamilton County	0	0.00
Elkhart (city) Elkhart County	0	0.00
Evansville (city) Vanderburgh County	0	0.00
Fishers (town) Hamilton County	0	0.00
Fort Wayne (city) Allen County	0	0.00
Hammond (city) Lake County	0	0.00

African, Sub-Saharan: Kenyan

Top 10 Places Sorted by Population

Based on all places, regardless of total population

Place	Population	%
South Bend (city) St. Joseph County	218	0.21
Indianapolis (city) Marion County	63	0.01
Elkhart (city) Elkhart County	61	0.12
Noblesville (city) Hamilton County	57	0.12
Anderson (city) Madison County	43	0.08
Goshen (city) Elkhart County	35	0.11
Lafayette (city) Tippecanoe County	33	0.05
West Lafayette (city) Tippecanoe County	29	0.10
Fort Wayne (city) Allen County	27	0.01
Greenwood (city) Johnson County	26	0.05

Top 10 Places Sorted by Percent of Total Population

Based on all places, regardless of total population

Place	Population	%
Bristol (town) Elkhart County	4	0.24
South Bend (city) St. Joseph County	218	0.21
Speedway (town) Marion County	22	0.18
Elkhart (city) Elkhart County	61	0.12
Noblesville (city) Hamilton County	57	0.12
Goshen (city) Elkhart County	35	0.11
West Lafayette (city) Tippecanoe County	29	0.10
Anderson (city) Madison County	43	0.08
Lafayette (city) Tippecanoe County	33	0.05
Greenwood (city) Johnson County	26	0.05

Top 10 Places Sorted by Percent of Total Population

Based on places with total population of 50,000 or more

Place	Population	%
South Bend (city) St. Joseph County	218	0.21
Elkhart (city) Elkhart County	61	0.12
Anderson (city) Madison County	43	0.08
Lafayette (city) Tippecanoe County	33	0.05
Muncie (city) Delaware County	14	0.02
Indianapolis (city) Marion County	63	0.01
Fort Wayne (city) Allen County	27	0.01
Bloomington (city) Monroe County	0	0.00
Carmel (city) Hamilton County	0	0.00
Evansville (city) Vanderburgh County	0	0.00

African, Sub-Saharan: Liberian

Top 10 Places Sorted by Population

Based on all places, regardless of total population

Place	Population	%
Indianapolis (city) Marion County	687	0.08
Lafayette (city) Tippecanoe County	32	0.05
South Bend (city) St. Joseph County	28	0.03
Notre Dame (cdp) St. Joseph County	13	0.17
Gary (city) Lake County	11	0.01
Aberdeen (cdp) Porter County	0	0.00
Advance (town) Boone County	0	0.00
Akron (town) Fulton County	0	0.00
Alamo (town) Montgomery County	0	0.00
Albany (town) Delaware County	0	0.00

Top 10 Places Sorted by Percent of Total Population

Based on all places, regardless of total population

Place	Population	%
Notre Dame (cdp) St. Joseph County	13	0.17
Indianapolis (city) Marion County	687	0.08
Lafayette (city) Tippecanoe County	32	0.05
South Bend (city) St. Joseph County	28	0.03
Gary (city) Lake County	11	0.01
Aberdeen (cdp) Porter County	0	0.00
Advance (town) Boone County	0	0.00
Akron (town) Fulton County	0	0.00
Alamo (town) Montgomery County	0	0.00
Albany (town) Delaware County	0	0.00

Top 10 Places Sorted by Percent of Total Population

Based on places with total population of 50,000 or more

Place	Population	%
Indianapolis (city) Marion County	687	0.08
Lafayette (city) Tippecanoe County	32	0.05
South Bend (city) St. Joseph County	28	0.03
Gary (city) Lake County	11	0.01
Anderson (city) Madison County	0	0.00
Bloomington (city) Monroe County	0	0.00
Carmel (city) Hamilton County	0	0.00
Elkhart (city) Elkhart County	0	0.00
Evansville (city) Vanderburgh County	0	0.00
Fishers (town) Hamilton County	0	0.00

African, Sub-Saharan: Nigerian

Top 10 Places Sorted by Population

Based on all places, regardless of total population

Place	Population	%
Indianapolis (city) Marion County	2,048	0.25
Gary (city) Lake County	155	0.18
Fort Wayne (city) Allen County	138	0.05
Crown Point (city) Lake County	95	0.36
Plainfield (town) Hendricks County	84	0.32
Fishers (town) Hamilton County	79	0.11
West Lafayette (city) Tippecanoe County	49	0.17
Speedway (town) Marion County	40	0.34
Avon (town) Hendricks County	28	0.24
Notre Dame (cdp) St. Joseph County	26	0.35

Top 10 Places Sorted by Percent of Total Population

Based on all places, regardless of total population

Place	Population	%
Rocky Ripple (town) Marion County	3	0.47
Crown Point (city) Lake County	95	0.36
Notre Dame (cdp) St. Joseph County	26	0.35
Speedway (town) Marion County	40	0.34
Plainfield (town) Hendricks County	84	0.32
Indianapolis (city) Marion County	2,048	0.25
Avon (town) Hendricks County	28	0.24
Gary (city) Lake County	155	0.18
Purdue University (cdp) Tippecanoe County	23	0.18
West Lafayette (city) Tippecanoe County	49	0.17

Top 10 Places Sorted by Percent of Total Population

Based on places with total population of 50,000 or more

Place	Population	%
Indianapolis (city) Marion County	2,048	0.25
Gary (city) Lake County	155	0.18
Fishers (town) Hamilton County	79	0.11
Fort Wayne (city) Allen County	138	0.05
Lafayette (city) Tippecanoe County	23	0.03
Bloomington (city) Monroe County	14	0.02
Evansville (city) Vanderburgh County	17	0.01
Hammond (city) Lake County	10	0.01
Anderson (city) Madison County	0	0.00
Carmel (city) Hamilton County	0	0.00

African, Sub-Saharan: Senegalese

Top 10 Places Sorted by Population

Based on all places, regardless of total population

Place	Population	%
Indianapolis (city) Marion County	150	0.02
Greencastle (city) Putnam County	14	0.14
Fishers (town) Hamilton County	13	0.02
Aberdeen (cdp) Porter County	0	0.00
Advance (town) Boone County	0	0.00
Akron (town) Fulton County	0	0.00
Alamo (town) Montgomery County	0	0.00
Albany (town) Delaware County	0	0.00
Albion (town) Noble County	0	0.00
Alexandria (city) Madison County	0	0.00

Top 10 Places Sorted by Percent of Total Population

Based on all places, regardless of total population

Place	Population	%
Greencastle (city) Putnam County	14	0.14
Indianapolis (city) Marion County	150	0.02
Fishers (town) Hamilton County	13	0.02
Aberdeen (cdp) Porter County	0	0.00
Advance (town) Boone County	0	0.00
Akron (town) Fulton County	0	0.00
Alamo (town) Montgomery County	0	0.00
Albany (town) Delaware County	0	0.00
Albion (town) Noble County	0	0.00
Alexandria (city) Madison County	0	0.00

Top 10 Places Sorted by Percent of Total Population

Based on places with total population of 50,000 or more

Place	Population	%
Indianapolis (city) Marion County	150	0.02
Fishers (town) Hamilton County	13	0.02
Anderson (city) Madison County	0	0.00
Bloomington (city) Monroe County	0	0.00
Carmel (city) Hamilton County	0	0.00
Elkhart (city) Elkhart County	0	0.00
Evansville (city) Vanderburgh County	0	0.00
Fort Wayne (city) Allen County	0	0.00
Gary (city) Lake County	0	0.00
Hammond (city) Lake County	0	0.00

African, Sub-Saharan: Sierra Leonean

Top 10 Places Sorted by Population

Based on all places, regardless of total population

Place	Population	%
Mishawaka (city) St. Joseph County	21	0.04
South Bend (city) St. Joseph County	11	0.01
Goshen (city) Elkhart County	9	0.03
Aberdeen (cdp) Porter County	0	0.00
Advance (town) Boone County	0	0.00
Akron (town) Fulton County	0	0.00
Alamo (town) Montgomery County	0	0.00
Albany (town) Delaware County	0	0.00
Albion (town) Noble County	0	0.00
Alexandria (city) Madison County	0	0.00

Top 10 Places Sorted by Percent of Total Population

Based on all places, regardless of total population

Place	Population	%
Mishawaka (city) St. Joseph County	21	0.04
Goshen (city) Elkhart County	9	0.03
South Bend (city) St. Joseph County	11	0.01

Aberdeen (cdp) Porter County	0	0.00
Advance (town) Boone County	0	0.00
Akron (town) Fulton County	0	0.00
Alamo (town) Montgomery County	0	0.00
Albany (town) Delaware County	0	0.00
Albion (town) Noble County	0	0.00
Alexandria (city) Madison County	0	0.00

Top 10 Places Sorted by Percent of Total Population
Based on places with total population of 50,000 or more

Place	Population	%
South Bend (city) St. Joseph County	11	0.01
Anderson (city) Madison County	0	0.00
Bloomington (city) Monroe County	0	0.00
Carmel (city) Hamilton County	0	0.00
Elkhart (city) Elkhart County	0	0.00
Evansville (city) Vanderburgh County	0	0.00
Fishers (town) Hamilton County	0	0.00
Fort Wayne (city) Allen County	0	0.00
Gary (city) Lake County	0	0.00
Hammond (city) Lake County	0	0.00

African, Sub-Saharan: Somalian

Top 10 Places Sorted by Population
Based on all places, regardless of total population

Place	Population	%
Indianapolis (city) Marion County	432	0.05
Fort Wayne (city) Allen County	68	0.03
Lawrence (city) Marion County	32	0.07
North Manchester (town) Wabash County	11	0.18
Terre Haute (city) Vigo County	6	0.01
Aberdeen (cdp) Porter County	0	0.00
Advance (town) Boone County	0	0.00
Akron (town) Fulton County	0	0.00
Alamo (town) Montgomery County	0	0.00
Albany (town) Delaware County	0	0.00

Top 10 Places Sorted by Percent of Total Population
Based on all places, regardless of total population

Place	Population	%
North Manchester (town) Wabash County	11	0.18
Lawrence (city) Marion County	32	0.07
Indianapolis (city) Marion County	432	0.05
Fort Wayne (city) Allen County	68	0.03
Terre Haute (city) Vigo County	6	0.01
Aberdeen (cdp) Porter County	0	0.00
Advance (town) Boone County	0	0.00
Akron (town) Fulton County	0	0.00
Alamo (town) Montgomery County	0	0.00
Albany (town) Delaware County	0	0.00

Top 10 Places Sorted by Percent of Total Population
Based on places with total population of 50,000 or more

Place	Population	%
Indianapolis (city) Marion County	432	0.05
Fort Wayne (city) Allen County	68	0.03
Terre Haute (city) Vigo County	6	0.01
Anderson (city) Madison County	0	0.00
Bloomington (city) Monroe County	0	0.00
Carmel (city) Hamilton County	0	0.00
Elkhart (city) Elkhart County	0	0.00
Evansville (city) Vanderburgh County	0	0.00
Fishers (town) Hamilton County	0	0.00
Gary (city) Lake County	0	0.00

African, Sub-Saharan: South African

Top 10 Places Sorted by Population
Based on all places, regardless of total population

Place	Population	%
Carmel (city) Hamilton County	137	0.18
Bloomington (city) Monroe County	63	0.08
Fort Wayne (city) Allen County	52	0.02
Schererville (town) Lake County	43	0.15
Indianapolis (city) Marion County	43	0.01
Ligonier (city) Noble County	40	0.93
Warsaw (city) Kosciusko County	16	0.12
Muncie (city) Delaware County	16	0.02
Greencastle (city) Putnam County	14	0.14
Westfield (town) Hamilton County	10	0.04

Top 10 Places Sorted by Percent of Total Population
Based on all places, regardless of total population

Place	Population	%
Ligonier (city) Noble County	40	0.93
Clear Lake (town) Steuben County	3	0.70
Otterbein (town) Benton County	7	0.62
Fountain City (town) Wayne County	3	0.42
Carmel (city) Hamilton County	137	0.18
Schererville (town) Lake County	43	0.15
Greencastle (city) Putnam County	14	0.14
Warsaw (city) Kosciusko County	16	0.12
Bloomington (city) Monroe County	63	0.08
Peru (city) Miami County	8	0.07

Top 10 Places Sorted by Percent of Total Population
Based on places with total population of 50,000 or more

Place	Population	%
Carmel (city) Hamilton County	137	0.18
Bloomington (city) Monroe County	63	0.08
Fort Wayne (city) Allen County	52	0.02
Muncie (city) Delaware County	16	0.02
Indianapolis (city) Marion County	43	0.01
Anderson (city) Madison County	0	0.00
Elkhart (city) Elkhart County	0	0.00
Evansville (city) Vanderburgh County	0	0.00
Fishers (town) Hamilton County	0	0.00
Gary (city) Lake County	0	0.00

African, Sub-Saharan: Sudanese

Top 10 Places Sorted by Population
Based on all places, regardless of total population

Place	Population	%
Indianapolis (city) Marion County	376	0.05
Chesterton (town) Porter County	19	0.14
Anderson (city) Madison County	18	0.03
Carmel (city) Hamilton County	11	0.01
West Lafayette (city) Tippecanoe County	9	0.03
Aberdeen (cdp) Porter County	0	0.00
Advance (town) Boone County	0	0.00
Akron (town) Fulton County	0	0.00
Alamo (town) Montgomery County	0	0.00
Albany (town) Delaware County	0	0.00

Top 10 Places Sorted by Percent of Total Population
Based on all places, regardless of total population

Place	Population	%
Chesterton (town) Porter County	19	0.14
Indianapolis (city) Marion County	376	0.05
Anderson (city) Madison County	18	0.03
West Lafayette (city) Tippecanoe County	9	0.03
Carmel (city) Hamilton County	11	0.01
Aberdeen (cdp) Porter County	0	0.00
Advance (town) Boone County	0	0.00
Akron (town) Fulton County	0	0.00
Alamo (town) Montgomery County	0	0.00
Albany (town) Delaware County	0	0.00

Top 10 Places Sorted by Percent of Total Population
Based on places with total population of 50,000 or more

Place	Population	%
Indianapolis (city) Marion County	376	0.05
Anderson (city) Madison County	18	0.03
Carmel (city) Hamilton County	11	0.01
Bloomington (city) Monroe County	0	0.00
Elkhart (city) Elkhart County	0	0.00
Evansville (city) Vanderburgh County	0	0.00
Fishers (town) Hamilton County	0	0.00
Fort Wayne (city) Allen County	0	0.00
Gary (city) Lake County	0	0.00
Hammond (city) Lake County	0	0.00

African, Sub-Saharan: Ugandan

Top 10 Places Sorted by Population
Based on all places, regardless of total population

Place	Population	%
Indianapolis (city) Marion County	54	0.01
North Manchester (town) Wabash County	17	0.28
St. Mary of the Woods (cdp) Vigo County	16	1.44
Evansville (city) Vanderburgh County	14	0.01
Mishawaka (city) St. Joseph County	8	0.02
Aberdeen (cdp) Porter County	0	0.00
Advance (town) Boone County	0	0.00
Akron (town) Fulton County	0	0.00
Alamo (town) Montgomery County	0	0.00
Albany (town) Delaware County	0	0.00

Top 10 Places Sorted by Percent of Total Population
Based on all places, regardless of total population

Place	Population	%
St. Mary of the Woods (cdp) Vigo County	16	1.44
North Manchester (town) Wabash County	17	0.28
Mishawaka (city) St. Joseph County	8	0.02
Indianapolis (city) Marion County	54	0.01
Evansville (city) Vanderburgh County	14	0.01
Aberdeen (cdp) Porter County	0	0.00
Advance (town) Boone County	0	0.00
Akron (town) Fulton County	0	0.00
Alamo (town) Montgomery County	0	0.00
Albany (town) Delaware County	0	0.00

Top 10 Places Sorted by Percent of Total Population
Based on places with total population of 50,000 or more

Place	Population	%
Indianapolis (city) Marion County	54	0.01
Evansville (city) Vanderburgh County	14	0.01
Anderson (city) Madison County	0	0.00
Bloomington (city) Monroe County	0	0.00
Carmel (city) Hamilton County	0	0.00
Elkhart (city) Elkhart County	0	0.00
Fishers (town) Hamilton County	0	0.00
Fort Wayne (city) Allen County	0	0.00
Gary (city) Lake County	0	0.00
Hammond (city) Lake County	0	0.00

African, Sub-Saharan: Zimbabwean

Top 10 Places Sorted by Population
Based on all places, regardless of total population

Place	Population	%
Indianapolis (city) Marion County	149	0.02
Elkhart (city) Elkhart County	13	0.03
Aberdeen (cdp) Porter County	0	0.00
Advance (town) Boone County	0	0.00
Akron (town) Fulton County	0	0.00
Alamo (town) Montgomery County	0	0.00
Albany (town) Delaware County	0	0.00
Albion (town) Noble County	0	0.00
Alexandria (city) Madison County	0	0.00
Alfordsville (town) Daviess County	0	0.00

Top 10 Places Sorted by Percent of Total Population
Based on all places, regardless of total population

Place	Population	%
Elkhart (city) Elkhart County	13	0.03
Indianapolis (city) Marion County	149	0.02
Aberdeen (cdp) Porter County	0	0.00
Advance (town) Boone County	0	0.00
Akron (town) Fulton County	0	0.00
Alamo (town) Montgomery County	0	0.00
Albany (town) Delaware County	0	0.00
Albion (town) Noble County	0	0.00
Alexandria (city) Madison County	0	0.00
Alfordsville (town) Daviess County	0	0.00

Top 10 Places Sorted by Percent of Total Population
Based on places with total population of 50,000 or more

Place	Population	%
Elkhart (city) Elkhart County	13	0.03
Indianapolis (city) Marion County	149	0.02
Anderson (city) Madison County	0	0.00
Bloomington (city) Monroe County	0	0.00
Carmel (city) Hamilton County	0	0.00
Evansville (city) Vanderburgh County	0	0.00
Fishers (town) Hamilton County	0	0.00
Fort Wayne (city) Allen County	0	0.00
Gary (city) Lake County	0	0.00
Hammond (city) Lake County	0	0.00

African, Sub-Saharan: Other

Top 10 Places Sorted by Population
Based on all places, regardless of total population

Place	Population	%
Indianapolis (city) Marion County	785	0.10
Fort Wayne (city) Allen County	164	0.06
Muncie (city) Delaware County	108	0.15
South Bend (city) St. Joseph County	78	0.08
West Lafayette (city) Tippecanoe County	65	0.22
Fishers (town) Hamilton County	55	0.08
Lafayette (city) Tippecanoe County	54	0.08
Granger (cdp) St. Joseph County	38	0.13
Elkhart (city) Elkhart County	30	0.06
Anderson (city) Madison County	26	0.05

Top 10 Places Sorted by Percent of Total Population
Based on all places, regardless of total population

Place	Population	%
Austin (city) Scott County	15	0.37
West Lafayette (city) Tippecanoe County	65	0.22
Speedway (town) Marion County	20	0.17
Notre Dame (cdp) St. Joseph County	13	0.17
Muncie (city) Delaware County	108	0.15
Granger (cdp) St. Joseph County	38	0.13
Indianapolis (city) Marion County	785	0.10
South Bend (city) St. Joseph County	78	0.08
Fishers (town) Hamilton County	55	0.08
Lafayette (city) Tippecanoe County	54	0.08

Top 10 Places Sorted by Percent of Total Population
Based on places with total population of 50,000 or more

Place	Population	%
Muncie (city) Delaware County	108	0.15
Indianapolis (city) Marion County	785	0.10
South Bend (city) St. Joseph County	78	0.08
Fishers (town) Hamilton County	55	0.08
Lafayette (city) Tippecanoe County	54	0.08
Fort Wayne (city) Allen County	164	0.06
Elkhart (city) Elkhart County	30	0.06
Anderson (city) Madison County	26	0.05
Hammond (city) Lake County	13	0.02
Evansville (city) Vanderburgh County	8	0.01

Albanian

Top 10 Places Sorted by Population
Based on all places, regardless of total population

Place	Population	%
Indianapolis (city) Marion County	105	0.01
West Lafayette (city) Tippecanoe County	80	0.27
Hammond (city) Lake County	61	0.08
Muncie (city) Delaware County	57	0.08
Noblesville (city) Hamilton County	40	0.08
Greenwood (city) Johnson County	37	0.08
Crawfordsville (city) Montgomery County	34	0.21
Fort Wayne (city) Allen County	33	0.01
Michigan City (city) LaPorte County	26	0.08
Bloomington (city) Monroe County	20	0.03

Top 10 Places Sorted by Percent of Total Population
Based on all places, regardless of total population

Place	Population	%
West Lafayette (city) Tippecanoe County	80	0.27
Ogden Dunes (town) Porter County	3	0.24
Crawfordsville (city) Montgomery County	34	0.21
Rossville (town) Clinton County	3	0.21
Winfield (town) Lake County	7	0.18
Meridian Hills (town) Marion County	3	0.18
Notre Dame (cdp) St. Joseph County	13	0.17
Cedar Lake (town) Lake County	14	0.13
Hammond (city) Lake County	61	0.08
Muncie (city) Delaware County	57	0.08

Top 10 Places Sorted by Percent of Total Population
Based on places with total population of 50,000 or more

Place	Population	%
Hammond (city) Lake County	61	0.08
Muncie (city) Delaware County	57	0.08
Bloomington (city) Monroe County	20	0.03
Indianapolis (city) Marion County	105	0.01
Fort Wayne (city) Allen County	33	0.01
Fishers (town) Hamilton County	10	0.01
Anderson (city) Madison County	0	0.00
Carmel (city) Hamilton County	0	0.00
Elkhart (city) Elkhart County	0	0.00
Evansville (city) Vanderburgh County	0	0.00

Alsatian

Top 10 Places Sorted by Population
Based on all places, regardless of total population

Place	Population	%
Greendale (city) Dearborn County	53	1.16
Aberdeen (cdp) Porter County	48	2.20
Goshen (city) Elkhart County	24	0.08
Muncie (city) Delaware County	22	0.03
Bloomington (city) Monroe County	19	0.02
Hammond (city) Lake County	18	0.02
Auburn (city) DeKalb County	12	0.10
Mishawaka (city) St. Joseph County	12	0.03
Indianapolis (city) Marion County	12	<0.01
Portage (city) Porter County	11	0.03

Top 10 Places Sorted by Percent of Total Population
Based on all places, regardless of total population

Place	Population	%
Aberdeen (cdp) Porter County	48	2.20
Greendale (city) Dearborn County	53	1.16
Shirley (town) Hancock County	3	0.40
Argos (town) Marshall County	4	0.25
George (town) Floyd County	4	0.15
Auburn (city) DeKalb County	12	0.10
Goshen (city) Elkhart County	24	0.08
Muncie (city) Delaware County	22	0.03
Mishawaka (city) St. Joseph County	12	0.03
Portage (city) Porter County	11	0.03

Top 10 Places Sorted by Percent of Total Population
Based on places with total population of 50,000 or more

Place	Population	%
Muncie (city) Delaware County	22	0.03
Bloomington (city) Monroe County	19	0.02
Hammond (city) Lake County	18	0.02
Indianapolis (city) Marion County	12	<0.01
Fort Wayne (city) Allen County	8	<0.01
Anderson (city) Madison County	0	0.00
Carmel (city) Hamilton County	0	0.00
Elkhart (city) Elkhart County	0	0.00
Evansville (city) Vanderburgh County	0	0.00
Fishers (town) Hamilton County	0	0.00

American

Top 10 Places Sorted by Population
Based on all places, regardless of total population

Place	Population	%
Indianapolis (city) Marion County	52,433	6.47
Fort Wayne (city) Allen County	25,688	10.12
Evansville (city) Vanderburgh County	23,162	19.60
Terre Haute (city) Vigo County	11,657	19.29
Kokomo (city) Howard County	6,617	14.42
Muncie (city) Delaware County	6,079	8.68
Anderson (city) Madison County	5,914	10.42
Jeffersonville (city) Clark County	5,374	12.75
Lafayette (city) Tippecanoe County	4,832	7.30
Carmel (city) Hamilton County	4,712	6.14

Top 10 Places Sorted by Percent of Total Population
Based on all places, regardless of total population

Place	Population	%
Williams (cdp) Lawrence County	173	81.60
Marshall (town) Parke County	169	65.25
Jalapa (cdp) Grant County	122	61.62
Mecca (town) Parke County	207	57.66
St. Bernice (cdp) Vermillion County	350	53.52
Montezuma (town) Parke County	392	50.84
Freelandville (cdp) Knox County	195	47.68
Staunton (town) Clay County	308	46.46
Bloomingdale (town) Parke County	153	43.22
Decker (town) Knox County	84	42.86

Top 10 Places Sorted by Percent of Total Population
Based on places with total population of 50,000 or more

Place	Population	%
Evansville (city) Vanderburgh County	23,162	19.60
Terre Haute (city) Vigo County	11,657	19.29
Anderson (city) Madison County	5,914	10.42
Fort Wayne (city) Allen County	25,688	10.12
Muncie (city) Delaware County	6,079	8.68
Lafayette (city) Tippecanoe County	4,832	7.30
Indianapolis (city) Marion County	52,433	6.47
Carmel (city) Hamilton County	4,712	6.14
Fishers (town) Hamilton County	3,929	5.48
Bloomington (city) Monroe County	3,411	4.35

Arab: Total

Top 10 Places Sorted by Population
Based on all places, regardless of total population

Place	Population	%
Indianapolis (city) Marion County	2,776	0.34
Schererville (town) Lake County	668	2.35
Fort Wayne (city) Allen County	664	0.26
Fishers (town) Hamilton County	580	0.81
Carmel (city) Hamilton County	563	0.73
Bloomington (city) Monroe County	548	0.70
Terre Haute (city) Vigo County	525	0.87
Mishawaka (city) St. Joseph County	475	0.99
Highland (town) Lake County	337	1.42
Michigan City (city) LaPorte County	330	1.04

Top 10 Places Sorted by Percent of Total Population
Based on all places, regardless of total population

Place	Population	%
Pottawattamie Park (town) LaPorte County	26	13.13
Versailles (town) Ripley County	97	5.50
Riley (town) Vigo County	11	5.07
Shorewood Forest (cdp) Porter County	127	4.21
Topeka (town) LaGrange County	38	3.02
Campbellsburg (town) Washington County	18	2.86
Dune Acres (town) Porter County	7	2.67
Schererville (town) Lake County	668	2.35
Long Beach (town) LaPorte County	32	2.19
Perrysville (town) Vermillion County	12	2.11

Top 10 Places Sorted by Percent of Total Population
Based on places with total population of 50,000 or more

Place	Population	%
Terre Haute (city) Vigo County	525	0.87
Fishers (town) Hamilton County	580	0.81
Carmel (city) Hamilton County	563	0.73
Bloomington (city) Monroe County	548	0.70
Indianapolis (city) Marion County	2,776	0.34
Hammond (city) Lake County	272	0.33
Muncie (city) Delaware County	204	0.29
Fort Wayne (city) Allen County	664	0.26
Elkhart (city) Elkhart County	109	0.21
South Bend (city) St. Joseph County	131	0.13

Arab: Arab

Top 10 Places Sorted by Population
Based on all places, regardless of total population

Place	Population	%
Indianapolis (city) Marion County	542	0.07
Highland (town) Lake County	326	1.37
Fishers (town) Hamilton County	235	0.33
Fort Wayne (city) Allen County	222	0.09
Schererville (town) Lake County	216	0.76
Bloomington (city) Monroe County	187	0.24
Hammond (city) Lake County	144	0.18
Terre Haute (city) Vigo County	117	0.19
Mishawaka (city) St. Joseph County	116	0.24
Noblesville (city) Hamilton County	113	0.23

Top 10 Places Sorted by Percent of Total Population
Based on all places, regardless of total population

Place	Population	%
Edinburgh (town) Johnson County	65	1.66
Shorewood Forest (cdp) Porter County	50	1.66
Highland (town) Lake County	326	1.37

Please refer to the Explanation of Data in the front of the book for more detailed information.

Burns Harbor (town) Porter County	12	0.96
Greencastle (city) Putnam County	91	0.88
Highland (cdp) Vanderburgh County	35	0.83
Oakland City (city) Gibson County	19	0.81
Avon (town) Hendricks County	92	0.79
Schererville (town) Lake County	216	0.76
Koontz Lake (cdp) Starke County	12	0.74

Top 10 Places Sorted by Percent of Total Population

Based on places with total population of 50,000 or more

Place	Population	%
Fishers (town) Hamilton County	235	0.33
Bloomington (city) Monroe County	187	0.24
Terre Haute (city) Vigo County	117	0.19
Hammond (city) Lake County	144	0.18
Carmel (city) Hamilton County	101	0.13
Muncie (city) Delaware County	84	0.12
Fort Wayne (city) Allen County	222	0.09
Indianapolis (city) Marion County	542	0.07
Elkhart (city) Elkhart County	23	0.04
South Bend (city) St. Joseph County	27	0.03

Arab: Egyptian

Top 10 Places Sorted by Population

Based on all places, regardless of total population

Place	Population	%
Carmel (city) Hamilton County	164	0.21
Schererville (town) Lake County	159	0.56
Indianapolis (city) Marion County	158	0.02
Fishers (town) Hamilton County	125	0.17
Hammond (city) Lake County	83	0.10
New Haven (city) Allen County	71	0.51
Versailles (town) Ripley County	62	3.52
Dyer (town) Lake County	52	0.33
Seymour (city) Jackson County	42	0.23
Lebanon (city) Boone County	38	0.24

Top 10 Places Sorted by Percent of Total Population

Based on all places, regardless of total population

Place	Population	%
Versailles (town) Ripley County	62	3.52
Campbellsburg (town) Washington County	18	2.86
Avilla (town) Noble County	19	0.86
Schererville (town) Lake County	159	0.56
New Haven (city) Allen County	71	0.51
Vevay (town) Switzerland County	9	0.45
Dyer (town) Lake County	52	0.33
Lebanon (city) Boone County	38	0.24
Seymour (city) Jackson County	42	0.23
Mitchell (city) Lawrence County	10	0.22

Top 10 Places Sorted by Percent of Total Population

Based on places with total population of 50,000 or more

Place	Population	%
Carmel (city) Hamilton County	164	0.21
Fishers (town) Hamilton County	125	0.17
Hammond (city) Lake County	83	0.10
Bloomington (city) Monroe County	21	0.03
Indianapolis (city) Marion County	158	0.02
Muncie (city) Delaware County	14	0.02
Fort Wayne (city) Allen County	8	<0.01
Anderson (city) Madison County	0	0.00
Elkhart (city) Elkhart County	0	0.00
Evansville (city) Vanderburgh County	0	0.00

Arab: Iraqi

Top 10 Places Sorted by Population

Based on all places, regardless of total population

Place	Population	%
Indianapolis (city) Marion County	192	0.02
Fort Wayne (city) Allen County	54	0.02
Mishawaka (city) St. Joseph County	45	0.09
Versailles (town) Ripley County	35	1.99
South Bend (city) St. Joseph County	33	0.03
Bloomington (city) Monroe County	30	0.04
Evansville (city) Vanderburgh County	16	0.01
Westfield (town) Hamilton County	14	0.05
Muncie (city) Delaware County	14	0.02
Hamilton (town) Steuben County	3	0.19

Top 10 Places Sorted by Percent of Total Population

Based on all places, regardless of total population

Place	Population	%
Versailles (town) Ripley County	35	1.99
Hamilton (town) Steuben County	3	0.19
Churubusco (town) Whitley County	2	0.10
Mishawaka (city) St. Joseph County	45	0.09
Westfield (town) Hamilton County	14	0.05
Bloomington (city) Monroe County	30	0.04
South Bend (city) St. Joseph County	33	0.03
Indianapolis (city) Marion County	192	0.02
Fort Wayne (city) Allen County	54	0.02
Muncie (city) Delaware County	14	0.02

Top 10 Places Sorted by Percent of Total Population

Based on places with total population of 50,000 or more

Place	Population	%
Bloomington (city) Monroe County	30	0.04
South Bend (city) St. Joseph County	33	0.03
Indianapolis (city) Marion County	192	0.02
Fort Wayne (city) Allen County	54	0.02
Muncie (city) Delaware County	14	0.02
Evansville (city) Vanderburgh County	16	0.01
Anderson (city) Madison County	0	0.00
Carmel (city) Hamilton County	0	0.00
Elkhart (city) Elkhart County	0	0.00
Fishers (town) Hamilton County	0	0.00

Arab: Jordanian

Top 10 Places Sorted by Population

Based on all places, regardless of total population

Place	Population	%
Indianapolis (city) Marion County	182	0.02
Greenwood (city) Johnson County	101	0.21
Fishers (town) Hamilton County	37	0.05
Brownsburg (town) Hendricks County	34	0.17
Hammond (city) Lake County	30	0.04
Portage (city) Porter County	28	0.08
Dyer (town) Lake County	25	0.16
Lake Station (city) Lake County	18	0.14
Evansville (city) Vanderburgh County	15	0.01
Purdue University (cdp) Tippecanoe County	13	0.10

Top 10 Places Sorted by Percent of Total Population

Based on all places, regardless of total population

Place	Population	%
Greenwood (city) Johnson County	101	0.21
Brownsburg (town) Hendricks County	34	0.17
Dyer (town) Lake County	25	0.16
Lake Station (city) Lake County	18	0.14
Purdue University (cdp) Tippecanoe County	13	0.10
Portage (city) Porter County	28	0.08
Munster (town) Lake County	13	0.06
Fishers (town) Hamilton County	37	0.05
Hammond (city) Lake County	30	0.04
West Lafayette (city) Tippecanoe County	11	0.04

Top 10 Places Sorted by Percent of Total Population

Based on places with total population of 50,000 or more

Place	Population	%
Fishers (town) Hamilton County	37	0.05
Hammond (city) Lake County	30	0.04
Indianapolis (city) Marion County	182	0.02
Evansville (city) Vanderburgh County	15	0.01
Bloomington (city) Monroe County	10	0.01
Carmel (city) Hamilton County	8	0.01
Terre Haute (city) Vigo County	6	0.01
Fort Wayne (city) Allen County	10	<0.01
Anderson (city) Madison County	0	0.00
Elkhart (city) Elkhart County	0	0.00

Arab: Lebanese

Top 10 Places Sorted by Population

Based on all places, regardless of total population

Place	Population	%
Indianapolis (city) Marion County	826	0.10
Michigan City (city) LaPorte County	288	0.91
Fort Wayne (city) Allen County	235	0.09
Granger (cdp) St. Joseph County	227	0.80
Bloomington (city) Monroe County	167	0.21
Mishawaka (city) St. Joseph County	166	0.35
Carmel (city) Hamilton County	160	0.21
Fishers (town) Hamilton County	135	0.19
Valparaiso (city) Porter County	57	0.18
Notre Dame (cdp) St. Joseph County	52	0.70

Top 10 Places Sorted by Percent of Total Population

Based on all places, regardless of total population

Place	Population	%
Pottawattamie Park (town) LaPorte County	26	13.13
Dune Acres (town) Porter County	7	2.67
Long Beach (town) LaPorte County	32	2.19
Trail Creek (town) LaPorte County	39	1.97
Hebron (town) Porter County	40	1.14
New Ross (town) Montgomery County	3	1.00
Michigan City (city) LaPorte County	288	0.91
Simonton Lake (cdp) Elkhart County	42	0.83
Granger (cdp) St. Joseph County	227	0.80
Meridian Hills (town) Marion County	12	0.74

Top 10 Places Sorted by Percent of Total Population

Based on places with total population of 50,000 or more

Place	Population	%
Bloomington (city) Monroe County	167	0.21
Carmel (city) Hamilton County	160	0.21
Fishers (town) Hamilton County	135	0.19
Indianapolis (city) Marion County	826	0.10
Fort Wayne (city) Allen County	235	0.09
Terre Haute (city) Vigo County	24	0.04
South Bend (city) St. Joseph County	33	0.03
Evansville (city) Vanderburgh County	27	0.02
Lafayette (city) Tippecanoe County	14	0.02
Elkhart (city) Elkhart County	9	0.02

Arab: Moroccan

Top 10 Places Sorted by Population

Based on all places, regardless of total population

Place	Population	%
Indianapolis (city) Marion County	141	0.02
Columbus (city) Bartholomew County	39	0.09
Carmel (city) Hamilton County	36	0.05
Dyer (town) Lake County	30	0.19
Bloomington (city) Monroe County	27	0.03
Franklin (city) Johnson County	24	0.11
Anderson (city) Madison County	24	0.04
Gary (city) Lake County	18	0.02
Elkhart (city) Elkhart County	16	0.03
Bright (cdp) Dearborn County	14	0.27

Top 10 Places Sorted by Percent of Total Population

Based on all places, regardless of total population

Place	Population	%
Gosport (town) Owen County	3	0.31
Bright (cdp) Dearborn County	14	0.27
Gas City (city) Grant County	12	0.20
Dyer (town) Lake County	30	0.19
Franklin (city) Johnson County	24	0.11
Columbus (city) Bartholomew County	39	0.09
Carmel (city) Hamilton County	36	0.05
Anderson (city) Madison County	24	0.04
Bloomington (city) Monroe County	27	0.03
Elkhart (city) Elkhart County	16	0.03

Top 10 Places Sorted by Percent of Total Population

Based on places with total population of 50,000 or more

Place	Population	%
Carmel (city) Hamilton County	36	0.05
Anderson (city) Madison County	24	0.04
Bloomington (city) Monroe County	27	0.03
Elkhart (city) Elkhart County	16	0.03
Indianapolis (city) Marion County	141	0.02
Gary (city) Lake County	18	0.02
Muncie (city) Delaware County	13	0.02
South Bend (city) St. Joseph County	6	0.01
Fort Wayne (city) Allen County	10	<0.01
Evansville (city) Vanderburgh County	0	0.00

Arab: Palestinian

Top 10 Places Sorted by Population
Based on all places, regardless of total population

Place	Population	%
Schererville (town) Lake County	293	1.03
Mishawaka (city) St. Joseph County	119	0.25
Munster (town) Lake County	96	0.41
Crown Point (city) Lake County	71	0.27
Indianapolis (city) Marion County	45	0.01
St. John (town) Lake County	43	0.31
Evansville (city) Vanderburgh County	30	0.03
Columbia City (city) Whitley County	27	0.33
Dyer (town) Lake County	24	0.15
Carmel (city) Hamilton County	24	0.03

Top 10 Places Sorted by Percent of Total Population
Based on all places, regardless of total population

Place	Population	%
Schererville (town) Lake County	293	1.03
Munster (town) Lake County	96	0.41
Columbia City (city) Whitley County	27	0.33
St. John (town) Lake County	43	0.31
Crown Point (city) Lake County	71	0.27
Mishawaka (city) St. Joseph County	119	0.25
Dyer (town) Lake County	24	0.15
New Palestine (town) Hancock County	2	0.09
East Chicago (city) Lake County	18	0.06
New Albany (city) Floyd County	13	0.04

Top 10 Places Sorted by Percent of Total Population
Based on places with total population of 50,000 or more

Place	Population	%
Evansville (city) Vanderburgh County	30	0.03
Carmel (city) Hamilton County	24	0.03
Indianapolis (city) Marion County	45	0.01
Muncie (city) Delaware County	7	0.01
Anderson (city) Madison County	0	0.00
Bloomington (city) Monroe County	0	0.00
Elkhart (city) Elkhart County	0	0.00
Fishers (town) Hamilton County	0	0.00
Fort Wayne (city) Allen County	0	0.00
Gary (city) Lake County	0	0.00

Arab: Syrian

Top 10 Places Sorted by Population
Based on all places, regardless of total population

Place	Population	%
Indianapolis (city) Marion County	239	0.03
Terre Haute (city) Vigo County	137	0.23
Fort Wayne (city) Allen County	104	0.04
Shorewood Forest (cdp) Porter County	77	2.55
Bloomington (city) Monroe County	75	0.10
Merrillville (town) Lake County	66	0.19
Muncie (city) Delaware County	66	0.09
Plainfield (town) Hendricks County	54	0.20
Shelbyville (city) Shelby County	35	0.19
Munster (town) Lake County	35	0.15

Top 10 Places Sorted by Percent of Total Population
Based on all places, regardless of total population

Place	Population	%
Shorewood Forest (cdp) Porter County	77	2.55
Whites (town) Boone County	33	1.72
Knightsville (town) Clay County	13	1.47
Morocco (town) Newton County	10	1.14
Meridian Hills (town) Marion County	17	1.04
Converse (town) Miami County	9	0.69
Rossville (town) Clinton County	9	0.62
Dunlap (cdp) Elkhart County	23	0.40
Fairview Park (town) Vermillion County	5	0.37
Tri-Lakes (cdp) Whitley County	6	0.36

Top 10 Places Sorted by Percent of Total Population
Based on places with total population of 50,000 or more

Place	Population	%
Terre Haute (city) Vigo County	137	0.23
Bloomington (city) Monroe County	75	0.10
Muncie (city) Delaware County	66	0.09
Fort Wayne (city) Allen County	104	0.04
Fishers (town) Hamilton County	32	0.04
Indianapolis (city) Marion County	239	0.03
South Bend (city) St. Joseph County	19	0.02
Evansville (city) Vanderburgh County	11	0.01
Anderson (city) Madison County	0	0.00
Carmel (city) Hamilton County	0	0.00

Arab: Other

Top 10 Places Sorted by Population
Based on all places, regardless of total population

Place	Population	%
Indianapolis (city) Marion County	451	0.06
Terre Haute (city) Vigo County	241	0.40
Granger (cdp) St. Joseph County	73	0.26
Carmel (city) Hamilton County	70	0.09
Elkhart (city) Elkhart County	61	0.12
Greenwood (city) Johnson County	60	0.13
Jasper (city) Dubois County	43	0.30
Topeka (town) LaGrange County	38	3.02
Dyer (town) Lake County	35	0.22
Bloomington (city) Monroe County	31	0.04

Top 10 Places Sorted by Percent of Total Population
Based on all places, regardless of total population

Place	Population	%
Riley (town) Vigo County	11	5.07
Topeka (town) LaGrange County	38	3.02
Perrysville (town) Vermillion County	12	2.11
Berne (city) Adams County	18	0.44
Terre Haute (city) Vigo County	241	0.40
Jasper (city) Dubois County	43	0.30
Granger (cdp) St. Joseph County	73	0.26
Dyer (town) Lake County	35	0.22
Greenwood (city) Johnson County	60	0.13
Griffith (town) Lake County	22	0.13

Top 10 Places Sorted by Percent of Total Population
Based on places with total population of 50,000 or more

Place	Population	%
Terre Haute (city) Vigo County	241	0.40
Elkhart (city) Elkhart County	61	0.12
Carmel (city) Hamilton County	70	0.09
Indianapolis (city) Marion County	451	0.06
Bloomington (city) Monroe County	31	0.04
Fishers (town) Hamilton County	16	0.02
Hammond (city) Lake County	15	0.02
Lafayette (city) Tippecanoe County	11	0.02
Fort Wayne (city) Allen County	21	0.01
South Bend (city) St. Joseph County	13	0.01

Armenian

Top 10 Places Sorted by Population
Based on all places, regardless of total population

Place	Population	%
Chesterton (town) Porter County	207	1.57
Indianapolis (city) Marion County	158	0.02
Fort Wayne (city) Allen County	81	0.03
Evansville (city) Vanderburgh County	78	0.07
South Bend (city) St. Joseph County	44	0.04
Bloomington (city) Monroe County	37	0.05
La Porte (city) LaPorte County	36	0.16
Notre Dame (cdp) St. Joseph County	28	0.38
Columbus (city) Bartholomew County	28	0.06
Hammond (city) Lake County	27	0.03

Top 10 Places Sorted by Percent of Total Population
Based on all places, regardless of total population

Place	Population	%
Chesterton (town) Porter County	207	1.57
Rocky Ripple (town) Marion County	4	0.62
Notre Dame (cdp) St. Joseph County	28	0.38
Porter (town) Porter County	9	0.18
Crothersville (town) Jackson County	3	0.17
La Porte (city) LaPorte County	36	0.16
Madison (city) Jefferson County	15	0.13
Peru (city) Miami County	11	0.10
Schererville (town) Lake County	25	0.09
Crown Point (city) Lake County	24	0.09

Top 10 Places Sorted by Percent of Total Population
Based on places with total population of 50,000 or more

Place	Population	%
Evansville (city) Vanderburgh County	78	0.07
Bloomington (city) Monroe County	37	0.05
South Bend (city) St. Joseph County	44	0.04
Fort Wayne (city) Allen County	81	0.03
Hammond (city) Lake County	27	0.03
Carmel (city) Hamilton County	21	0.03
Indianapolis (city) Marion County	158	0.02
Fishers (town) Hamilton County	10	0.01
Anderson (city) Madison County	0	0.00
Elkhart (city) Elkhart County	0	0.00

Assyrian/Chaldean/Syriac

Top 10 Places Sorted by Population
Based on all places, regardless of total population

Place	Population	%
Aberdeen (cdp) Porter County	61	2.79
Mishawaka (city) St. Joseph County	52	0.11
Indianapolis (city) Marion County	44	0.01
Hobart (city) Lake County	42	0.15
Lafayette (city) Tippecanoe County	30	0.05
Merrillville (town) Lake County	21	0.06
Valparaiso (city) Porter County	20	0.06
Schererville (town) Lake County	19	0.07
Michigan City (city) LaPorte County	18	0.06
West Lafayette (city) Tippecanoe County	15	0.05

Top 10 Places Sorted by Percent of Total Population
Based on all places, regardless of total population

Place	Population	%
Aberdeen (cdp) Porter County	61	2.79
Notre Dame (cdp) St. Joseph County	13	0.17
Hobart (city) Lake County	42	0.15
Jonesboro (city) Grant County	2	0.13
Mishawaka (city) St. Joseph County	52	0.11
Purdue University (cdp) Tippecanoe County	14	0.11
Schererville (town) Lake County	19	0.07
Merrillville (town) Lake County	21	0.06
Valparaiso (city) Porter County	20	0.06
Michigan City (city) LaPorte County	18	0.06

Top 10 Places Sorted by Percent of Total Population
Based on places with total population of 50,000 or more

Place	Population	%
Lafayette (city) Tippecanoe County	30	0.05
Indianapolis (city) Marion County	44	0.01
Hammond (city) Lake County	7	0.01
Fort Wayne (city) Allen County	10	<0.01
Anderson (city) Madison County	0	0.00
Bloomington (city) Monroe County	0	0.00
Carmel (city) Hamilton County	0	0.00
Elkhart (city) Elkhart County	0	0.00
Evansville (city) Vanderburgh County	0	0.00
Fishers (town) Hamilton County	0	0.00

Australian

Top 10 Places Sorted by Population
Based on all places, regardless of total population

Place	Population	%
Indianapolis (city) Marion County	258	0.03
Princeton (city) Gibson County	124	1.44
North Vernon (city) Jennings County	109	1.71
Purdue University (cdp) Tippecanoe County	89	0.69
Fort Wayne (city) Allen County	54	0.02
Bloomington (city) Monroe County	46	0.06
Carmel (city) Hamilton County	42	0.05
Evansville (city) Vanderburgh County	39	0.03
Fishers (town) Hamilton County	36	0.05
Muncie (city) Delaware County	27	0.04

Top 10 Places Sorted by Percent of Total Population
Based on all places, regardless of total population

Place	Population	%
North Vernon (city) Jennings County	109	1.71
Princeton (city) Gibson County	124	1.44
Pine Village (town) Warren County	3	1.35

Spurgeon (town) Pike County	2	1.25
Ashley (town) DeKalb County	10	0.91
Purdue University (cdp) Tippecanoe County	89	0.69
Russellville (town) Putnam County	2	0.68
Spring Lake (town) Hancock County	2	0.68
Southport (city) Marion County	9	0.57
Morocco (town) Newton County	4	0.46

Top 10 Places Sorted by Percent of Total Population

Based on places with total population of 50,000 or more

Place	Population	%
Bloomington (city) Monroe County	46	0.06
Carmel (city) Hamilton County	42	0.05
Fishers (town) Hamilton County	36	0.05
Muncie (city) Delaware County	27	0.04
Indianapolis (city) Marion County	258	0.03
Evansville (city) Vanderburgh County	39	0.03
Hammond (city) Lake County	21	0.03
Fort Wayne (city) Allen County	54	0.02
Anderson (city) Madison County	12	0.02
Elkhart (city) Elkhart County	0	0.00

Austrian

Top 10 Places Sorted by Population

Based on all places, regardless of total population

Place	Population	%
Indianapolis (city) Marion County	1,084	0.13
Bloomington (city) Monroe County	439	0.56
South Bend (city) St. Joseph County	275	0.27
Fort Wayne (city) Allen County	250	0.10
Fishers (town) Hamilton County	233	0.32
Granger (cdp) St. Joseph County	219	0.77
Valparaiso (city) Porter County	192	0.62
Mishawaka (city) St. Joseph County	183	0.38
Carmel (city) Hamilton County	161	0.21
West Lafayette (city) Tippecanoe County	146	0.50

Top 10 Places Sorted by Percent of Total Population

Based on all places, regardless of total population

Place	Population	%
Uniondale (town) Wells County	12	6.78
North Crows Nest (town) Marion County	2	4.76
North Salem (town) Hendricks County	17	4.53
Aberdeen (cdp) Porter County	81	3.71
Dayton (town) Tippecanoe County	24	2.51
Spring Hill (town) Marion County	2	2.38
Dillsboro (town) Dearborn County	29	2.16
Indian Village (town) St. Joseph County	2	2.04
Kennard (town) Henry County	10	2.00
Chalmers (town) White County	9	1.72

Top 10 Places Sorted by Percent of Total Population

Based on places with total population of 50,000 or more

Place	Population	%
Bloomington (city) Monroe County	439	0.56
Fishers (town) Hamilton County	233	0.32
South Bend (city) St. Joseph County	275	0.27
Carmel (city) Hamilton County	161	0.21
Anderson (city) Madison County	103	0.18
Terre Haute (city) Vigo County	85	0.14
Indianapolis (city) Marion County	1,084	0.13
Lafayette (city) Tippecanoe County	79	0.12
Fort Wayne (city) Allen County	250	0.10
Evansville (city) Vanderburgh County	109	0.09

Basque

Top 10 Places Sorted by Population

Based on all places, regardless of total population

Place	Population	%
New Albany (city) Floyd County	17	0.05
Lebanon (city) Boone County	10	0.06
Ogden Dunes (town) Porter County	3	0.24
Gentryville (town) Spencer County	2	0.90
Aberdeen (cdp) Porter County	0	0.00
Advance (town) Boone County	0	0.00
Akron (town) Fulton County	0	0.00
Alamo (town) Montgomery County	0	0.00
Albany (town) Delaware County	0	0.00
Albion (town) Noble County	0	0.00

Top 10 Places Sorted by Percent of Total Population

Based on all places, regardless of total population

Place	Population	%
Gentryville (town) Spencer County	2	0.90
Ogden Dunes (town) Porter County	3	0.24
Lebanon (city) Boone County	10	0.06
New Albany (city) Floyd County	17	0.05
Aberdeen (cdp) Porter County	0	0.00
Advance (town) Boone County	0	0.00
Akron (town) Fulton County	0	0.00
Alamo (town) Montgomery County	0	0.00
Albany (town) Delaware County	0	0.00
Albion (town) Noble County	0	0.00

Top 10 Places Sorted by Percent of Total Population

Based on places with total population of 50,000 or more

Place	Population	%
Anderson (city) Madison County	0	0.00
Bloomington (city) Monroe County	0	0.00
Carmel (city) Hamilton County	0	0.00
Elkhart (city) Elkhart County	0	0.00
Evansville (city) Vanderburgh County	0	0.00
Fishers (town) Hamilton County	0	0.00
Fort Wayne (city) Allen County	0	0.00
Gary (city) Lake County	0	0.00
Hammond (city) Lake County	0	0.00
Indianapolis (city) Marion County	0	0.00

Belgian

Top 10 Places Sorted by Population

Based on all places, regardless of total population

Place	Population	%
Mishawaka (city) St. Joseph County	1,831	3.82
South Bend (city) St. Joseph County	871	0.85
Indianapolis (city) Marion County	866	0.11
Carmel (city) Hamilton County	352	0.46
Granger (cdp) St. Joseph County	347	1.22
Noblesville (city) Hamilton County	247	0.51
Fort Wayne (city) Allen County	220	0.09
Fishers (town) Hamilton County	165	0.23
Bloomington (city) Monroe County	155	0.20
Tell City (city) Perry County	144	1.95

Top 10 Places Sorted by Percent of Total Population

Based on all places, regardless of total population

Place	Population	%
Mishawaka (city) St. Joseph County	1,831	3.82
Albion (town) Noble County	75	2.76
Osceola (town) St. Joseph County	62	2.62
Schneider (town) Lake County	6	2.35
Hudson Lake (cdp) LaPorte County	29	2.16
Indian Village (town) St. Joseph County	2	2.04
Pierceton (town) Kosciusko County	20	1.97
Tell City (city) Perry County	144	1.95
Shelby (cdp) Lake County	7	1.92
Troy (town) Perry County	8	1.82

Top 10 Places Sorted by Percent of Total Population

Based on places with total population of 50,000 or more

Place	Population	%
South Bend (city) St. Joseph County	871	0.85
Carmel (city) Hamilton County	352	0.46
Elkhart (city) Elkhart County	123	0.24
Fishers (town) Hamilton County	165	0.23
Bloomington (city) Monroe County	155	0.20
Muncie (city) Delaware County	110	0.16
Lafayette (city) Tippecanoe County	100	0.15
Terre Haute (city) Vigo County	75	0.12
Indianapolis (city) Marion County	866	0.11
Fort Wayne (city) Allen County	220	0.09

Brazilian

Top 10 Places Sorted by Population

Based on all places, regardless of total population

Place	Population	%
Indianapolis (city) Marion County	259	0.03
Plainfield (town) Hendricks County	149	0.56
West Lafayette (city) Tippecanoe County	104	0.35
Clarksville (town) Clark County	95	0.41
Elkhart (city) Elkhart County	92	0.18
Bloomington (city) Monroe County	69	0.09
Evansville (city) Vanderburgh County	62	0.05
Goshen (city) Elkhart County	59	0.19
Westfield (town) Hamilton County	50	0.18
South Bend (city) St. Joseph County	50	0.05

Top 10 Places Sorted by Percent of Total Population

Based on all places, regardless of total population

Place	Population	%
Plainfield (town) Hendricks County	149	0.56
Meridian Hills (town) Marion County	7	0.43
Clarksville (town) Clark County	95	0.41
West Lafayette (city) Tippecanoe County	104	0.35
Notre Dame (cdp) St. Joseph County	24	0.32
Chesterton (town) Porter County	38	0.29
Kouts (town) Porter County	4	0.22
Goshen (city) Elkhart County	59	0.19
Elkhart (city) Elkhart County	92	0.18
Westfield (town) Hamilton County	50	0.18

Top 10 Places Sorted by Percent of Total Population

Based on places with total population of 50,000 or more

Place	Population	%
Elkhart (city) Elkhart County	92	0.18
Bloomington (city) Monroe County	69	0.09
Evansville (city) Vanderburgh County	62	0.05
South Bend (city) St. Joseph County	50	0.05
Lafayette (city) Tippecanoe County	31	0.05
Gary (city) Lake County	30	0.04
Indianapolis (city) Marion County	259	0.03
Fishers (town) Hamilton County	24	0.03
Hammond (city) Lake County	13	0.02
Fort Wayne (city) Allen County	21	0.01

British

Top 10 Places Sorted by Population

Based on all places, regardless of total population

Place	Population	%
Indianapolis (city) Marion County	3,547	0.44
Fort Wayne (city) Allen County	767	0.30
Bloomington (city) Monroe County	729	0.93
Carmel (city) Hamilton County	626	0.82
Fishers (town) Hamilton County	451	0.63
Evansville (city) Vanderburgh County	446	0.38
Muncie (city) Delaware County	372	0.53
South Bend (city) St. Joseph County	336	0.33
Lafayette (city) Tippecanoe County	331	0.50
Greenwood (city) Johnson County	323	0.68

Top 10 Places Sorted by Percent of Total Population

Based on all places, regardless of total population

Place	Population	%
Clarksburg (cdp) Decatur County	60	49.18
Medaryville (town) Pulaski County	25	5.02
Laconia (town) Harrison County	2	5.00
Carbon (town) Clay County	15	4.66
Mount Auburn (town) Wayne County	7	4.61
Dune Acres (town) Porter County	12	4.58
Chrisney (town) Spencer County	26	4.13
Vallonia (cdp) Jackson County	16	3.40
Woodlawn Heights (town) Madison County	3	3.23
Kimmell (cdp) Noble County	9	2.55

Top 10 Places Sorted by Percent of Total Population

Based on places with total population of 50,000 or more

Place	Population	%
Bloomington (city) Monroe County	729	0.93
Carmel (city) Hamilton County	626	0.82
Fishers (town) Hamilton County	451	0.63
Muncie (city) Delaware County	372	0.53
Lafayette (city) Tippecanoe County	331	0.50
Indianapolis (city) Marion County	3,547	0.44
Evansville (city) Vanderburgh County	446	0.38
South Bend (city) St. Joseph County	336	0.33
Fort Wayne (city) Allen County	767	0.30
Anderson (city) Madison County	153	0.27

Bulgarian

Top 10 Places Sorted by Population
Based on all places, regardless of total population

Place	Population	%
Fort Wayne (city) Allen County	156	0.06
Indianapolis (city) Marion County	80	0.01
Highland (town) Lake County	57	0.24
Munster (town) Lake County	55	0.24
Lebanon (city) Boone County	54	0.34
Merrillville (town) Lake County	50	0.15
South Bend (city) St. Joseph County	47	0.05
Noblesville (city) Hamilton County	41	0.08
West Lafayette (city) Tippecanoe County	38	0.13
Bloomington (city) Monroe County	29	0.04

Top 10 Places Sorted by Percent of Total Population
Based on all places, regardless of total population

Place	Population	%
Arcadia (town) Hamilton County	11	0.74
Melody Hill (cdp) Vanderburgh County	24	0.69
North Terre Haute (cdp) Vigo County	24	0.52
Hope (town) Bartholomew County	8	0.43
Portland (city) Jay County	24	0.37
Lebanon (city) Boone County	54	0.34
North Manchester (town) Wabash County	18	0.30
Bremen (town) Marshall County	14	0.30
Highland (town) Lake County	57	0.24
Munster (town) Lake County	55	0.24

Top 10 Places Sorted by Percent of Total Population
Based on places with total population of 50,000 or more

Place	Population	%
Fort Wayne (city) Allen County	156	0.06
South Bend (city) St. Joseph County	47	0.05
Bloomington (city) Monroe County	29	0.04
Carmel (city) Hamilton County	16	0.02
Indianapolis (city) Marion County	80	0.01
Muncie (city) Delaware County	9	0.01
Anderson (city) Madison County	0	0.00
Elkhart (city) Elkhart County	0	0.00
Evansville (city) Vanderburgh County	0	0.00
Fishers (town) Hamilton County	0	0.00

Cajun

Top 10 Places Sorted by Population
Based on all places, regardless of total population

Place	Population	%
Greenwood (city) Johnson County	72	0.15
Clarksville (town) Clark County	55	0.24
Indianapolis (city) Marion County	52	0.01
Columbus (city) Bartholomew County	36	0.08
Jeffersonville (city) Clark County	29	0.07
Portage (city) Porter County	25	0.07
Plainfield (town) Hendricks County	23	0.09
Lawrenceburg (city) Dearborn County	22	0.44
Fishers (town) Hamilton County	22	0.03
Lafayette (city) Tippecanoe County	22	0.03

Top 10 Places Sorted by Percent of Total Population
Based on all places, regardless of total population

Place	Population	%
Lawrenceburg (city) Dearborn County	22	0.44
Carthage (town) Rush County	3	0.40
Clarksville (town) Clark County	55	0.24
Ingalls (town) Madison County	4	0.21
Huntingburg (city) Dubois County	11	0.19
Salem (city) Washington County	10	0.16
Greenwood (city) Johnson County	72	0.15
Plainfield (town) Hendricks County	23	0.09
Columbus (city) Bartholomew County	36	0.08
Jeffersonville (city) Clark County	29	0.07

Top 10 Places Sorted by Percent of Total Population
Based on places with total population of 50,000 or more

Place	Population	%
Fishers (town) Hamilton County	22	0.03
Lafayette (city) Tippecanoe County	22	0.03
Indianapolis (city) Marion County	52	0.01
Evansville (city) Vanderburgh County	12	0.01
Anderson (city) Madison County	0	0.00
Bloomington (city) Monroe County	0	0.00
Carmel (city) Hamilton County	0	0.00
Elkhart (city) Elkhart County	0	0.00
Fort Wayne (city) Allen County	0	0.00
Gary (city) Lake County	0	0.00

Canadian

Top 10 Places Sorted by Population
Based on all places, regardless of total population

Place	Population	%
Indianapolis (city) Marion County	1,392	0.17
Fort Wayne (city) Allen County	681	0.27
Granger (cdp) St. Joseph County	201	0.71
Fishers (town) Hamilton County	195	0.27
Muncie (city) Delaware County	194	0.28
Greenwood (city) Johnson County	181	0.38
Carmel (city) Hamilton County	166	0.22
Cumberland (town) Marion County	149	2.58
Bloomington (city) Monroe County	138	0.18
South Bend (city) St. Joseph County	126	0.12

Top 10 Places Sorted by Percent of Total Population
Based on all places, regardless of total population

Place	Population	%
Buffalo (cdp) White County	74	10.72
Buck Creek (cdp) Tippecanoe County	30	8.57
Sidney (town) Kosciusko County	4	3.85
Napoleon (town) Ripley County	6	3.16
Cumberland (town) Marion County	149	2.58
State Line City (town) Warren County	3	2.46
La Fontaine (town) Wabash County	17	2.39
Fillmore (town) Putnam County	10	2.23
New Paris (cdp) Elkhart County	28	2.14
Switz City (town) Greene County	8	1.99

Top 10 Places Sorted by Percent of Total Population
Based on places with total population of 50,000 or more

Place	Population	%
Muncie (city) Delaware County	194	0.28
Fort Wayne (city) Allen County	681	0.27
Fishers (town) Hamilton County	195	0.27
Carmel (city) Hamilton County	166	0.22
Bloomington (city) Monroe County	138	0.18
Indianapolis (city) Marion County	1,392	0.17
Elkhart (city) Elkhart County	79	0.15
South Bend (city) St. Joseph County	126	0.12
Terre Haute (city) Vigo County	62	0.10
Anderson (city) Madison County	50	0.09

Carpatho Rusyn

Top 10 Places Sorted by Population
Based on all places, regardless of total population

Place	Population	%
Carmel (city) Hamilton County	16	0.02
Schererville (town) Lake County	13	0.05
Munster (town) Lake County	11	0.05
St. John (town) Lake County	9	0.07
Aberdeen (cdp) Porter County	0	0.00
Advance (town) Boone County	0	0.00
Akron (town) Fulton County	0	0.00
Alamo (town) Montgomery County	0	0.00
Albany (town) Delaware County	0	0.00
Albion (town) Noble County	0	0.00

Top 10 Places Sorted by Percent of Total Population
Based on all places, regardless of total population

Place	Population	%
St. John (town) Lake County	9	0.07
Schererville (town) Lake County	13	0.05
Munster (town) Lake County	11	0.05
Carmel (city) Hamilton County	16	0.02
Aberdeen (cdp) Porter County	0	0.00
Advance (town) Boone County	0	0.00
Akron (town) Fulton County	0	0.00
Alamo (town) Montgomery County	0	0.00
Albany (town) Delaware County	0	0.00
Albion (town) Noble County	0	0.00

Top 10 Places Sorted by Percent of Total Population
Based on places with total population of 50,000 or more

Place	Population	%
Carmel (city) Hamilton County	16	0.02
Anderson (city) Madison County	0	0.00
Bloomington (city) Monroe County	0	0.00
Elkhart (city) Elkhart County	0	0.00
Evansville (city) Vanderburgh County	0	0.00
Fishers (town) Hamilton County	0	0.00
Fort Wayne (city) Allen County	0	0.00
Gary (city) Lake County	0	0.00
Hammond (city) Lake County	0	0.00
Indianapolis (city) Marion County	0	0.00

Celtic

Top 10 Places Sorted by Population
Based on all places, regardless of total population

Place	Population	%
Fort Wayne (city) Allen County	30	0.01
Jeffersonville (city) Clark County	25	0.06
Evansville (city) Vanderburgh County	23	0.02
Plainfield (town) Hendricks County	21	0.08
Franklin (city) Johnson County	17	0.08
Mishawaka (city) St. Joseph County	16	0.03
Highland (cdp) Vanderburgh County	15	0.36
Greencastle (city) Putnam County	15	0.14
Brownsburg (town) Hendricks County	15	0.07
Lawrence (city) Marion County	15	0.03

Top 10 Places Sorted by Percent of Total Population
Based on all places, regardless of total population

Place	Population	%
Worthington (town) Greene County	10	0.51
Rockville (town) Parke County	13	0.49
Shelburn (town) Sullivan County	7	0.47
Highland (cdp) Vanderburgh County	15	0.36
Wanatah (town) LaPorte County	3	0.28
Orleans (town) Orange County	5	0.26
Princes Lakes (town) Johnson County	3	0.26
Burns Harbor (town) Porter County	3	0.24
Oolitic (town) Lawrence County	3	0.22
Cannelton (city) Perry County	2	0.15

Top 10 Places Sorted by Percent of Total Population
Based on places with total population of 50,000 or more

Place	Population	%
Evansville (city) Vanderburgh County	23	0.02
Carmel (city) Hamilton County	14	0.02
Fishers (town) Hamilton County	14	0.02
Anderson (city) Madison County	12	0.02
Fort Wayne (city) Allen County	30	0.01
Muncie (city) Delaware County	10	0.01
South Bend (city) St. Joseph County	10	0.01
Hammond (city) Lake County	7	0.01
Indianapolis (city) Marion County	8	<0.01
Bloomington (city) Monroe County	0	0.00

Croatian

Top 10 Places Sorted by Population
Based on all places, regardless of total population

Place	Population	%
Hammond (city) Lake County	908	1.12
Schererville (town) Lake County	664	2.33
Highland (town) Lake County	663	2.80
Crown Point (city) Lake County	585	2.24
Munster (town) Lake County	516	2.22
Hobart (city) Lake County	483	1.70
Indianapolis (city) Marion County	412	0.05
Merrillville (town) Lake County	359	1.04
St. John (town) Lake County	328	2.39
Portage (city) Porter County	297	0.82

Top 10 Places Sorted by Percent of Total Population
Based on all places, regardless of total population

Place	Population	%
Lake Santee (cdp) Decatur County	61	9.52
Montmorenci (cdp) Tippecanoe County	11	6.51
Aberdeen (cdp) Porter County	118	5.40

Ogden Dunes (town) Porter County	51	4.16
Schneider (town) Lake County	10	3.92
La Crosse (town) LaPorte County	22	3.74
Salt Creek Commons (cdp) Porter County	76	3.46
Hebron (town) Porter County	119	3.39
Harmony (town) Clay County	20	3.14
Lakes of the Four Seasons (cdp) Lake County	216	2.86

Top 10 Places Sorted by Percent of Total Population

Based on places with total population of 50,000 or more

Place	Population	%
Hammond (city) Lake County	908	1.12
South Bend (city) St. Joseph County	295	0.29
Carmel (city) Hamilton County	175	0.23
Gary (city) Lake County	187	0.22
Bloomington (city) Monroe County	171	0.22
Muncie (city) Delaware County	103	0.15
Terre Haute (city) Vigo County	85	0.14
Fishers (town) Hamilton County	84	0.12
Fort Wayne (city) Allen County	244	0.10
Anderson (city) Madison County	59	0.10

Cypriot

Top 10 Places Sorted by Population

Based on all places, regardless of total population

Place	Population	%
West Lafayette (city) Tippecanoe County	61	0.21
Aberdeen (cdp) Porter County	0	0.00
Advance (town) Boone County	0	0.00
Akron (town) Fulton County	0	0.00
Alamo (town) Montgomery County	0	0.00
Albany (town) Delaware County	0	0.00
Albion (town) Noble County	0	0.00
Alexandria (city) Madison County	0	0.00
Alfordsville (town) Daviess County	0	0.00
Alton (town) Crawford County	0	0.00

Top 10 Places Sorted by Percent of Total Population

Based on all places, regardless of total population

Place	Population	%
West Lafayette (city) Tippecanoe County	61	0.21
Aberdeen (cdp) Porter County	0	0.00
Advance (town) Boone County	0	0.00
Akron (town) Fulton County	0	0.00
Alamo (town) Montgomery County	0	0.00
Albany (town) Delaware County	0	0.00
Albion (town) Noble County	0	0.00
Alexandria (city) Madison County	0	0.00
Alfordsville (town) Daviess County	0	0.00
Alton (town) Crawford County	0	0.00

Top 10 Places Sorted by Percent of Total Population

Based on places with total population of 50,000 or more

Place	Population	%
Anderson (city) Madison County	0	0.00
Bloomington (city) Monroe County	0	0.00
Carmel (city) Hamilton County	0	0.00
Elkhart (city) Elkhart County	0	0.00
Evansville (city) Vanderburgh County	0	0.00
Fishers (town) Hamilton County	0	0.00
Fort Wayne (city) Allen County	0	0.00
Gary (city) Lake County	0	0.00
Hammond (city) Lake County	0	0.00
Indianapolis (city) Marion County	0	0.00

Czech

Top 10 Places Sorted by Population

Based on all places, regardless of total population

Place	Population	%
Indianapolis (city) Marion County	1,484	0.18
Fort Wayne (city) Allen County	837	0.33
Fishers (town) Hamilton County	513	0.72
Bloomington (city) Monroe County	478	0.61
Hammond (city) Lake County	369	0.45
Crown Point (city) Lake County	361	1.38
West Lafayette (city) Tippecanoe County	342	1.17
Carmel (city) Hamilton County	336	0.44
Valparaiso (city) Porter County	288	0.93
South Bend (city) St. Joseph County	264	0.26

Top 10 Places Sorted by Percent of Total Population

Based on all places, regardless of total population

Place	Population	%
San Pierre (cdp) Starke County	12	13.33
Wolcott (town) White County	40	3.66
Kingsbury (town) LaPorte County	8	3.56
Dune Acres (town) Porter County	9	3.44
Long Beach (town) LaPorte County	50	3.42
North Judson (town) Starke County	54	3.12
Trail Creek (town) LaPorte County	61	3.09
Ogden Dunes (town) Porter County	36	2.94
Roseland (town) St. Joseph County	35	2.93
Culver (town) Marshall County	38	2.63

Top 10 Places Sorted by Percent of Total Population

Based on places with total population of 50,000 or more

Place	Population	%
Fishers (town) Hamilton County	513	0.72
Bloomington (city) Monroe County	478	0.61
Hammond (city) Lake County	369	0.45
Carmel (city) Hamilton County	336	0.44
Terre Haute (city) Vigo County	232	0.38
Elkhart (city) Elkhart County	195	0.38
Fort Wayne (city) Allen County	837	0.33
South Bend (city) St. Joseph County	264	0.26
Indianapolis (city) Marion County	1,484	0.18
Evansville (city) Vanderburgh County	152	0.13

Czechoslovakian

Top 10 Places Sorted by Population

Based on all places, regardless of total population

Place	Population	%
Indianapolis (city) Marion County	393	0.05
Hobart (city) Lake County	178	0.63
Fort Wayne (city) Allen County	130	0.05
Carmel (city) Hamilton County	115	0.15
Noblesville (city) Hamilton County	108	0.22
Portage (city) Porter County	104	0.29
Hammond (city) Lake County	101	0.12
Bloomington (city) Monroe County	85	0.11
South Bend (city) St. Joseph County	84	0.08
Chesterton (town) Porter County	83	0.63

Top 10 Places Sorted by Percent of Total Population

Based on all places, regardless of total population

Place	Population	%
Medaryville (town) Pulaski County	34	6.83
North Salem (town) Hendricks County	7	1.87
Orland (town) Steuben County	11	1.79
Roanoke (town) Huntington County	30	1.66
Cloverdale (town) Putnam County	30	1.28
Hamlet (town) Starke County	10	1.21
Shorewood Forest (cdp) Porter County	30	1.00
Delphi (city) Carroll County	29	0.93
St. Mary of the Woods (cdp) Vigo County	10	0.90
Grabill (town) Allen County	8	0.80

Top 10 Places Sorted by Percent of Total Population

Based on places with total population of 50,000 or more

Place	Population	%
Carmel (city) Hamilton County	115	0.15
Hammond (city) Lake County	101	0.12
Bloomington (city) Monroe County	85	0.11
Terre Haute (city) Vigo County	53	0.09
South Bend (city) St. Joseph County	84	0.08
Evansville (city) Vanderburgh County	73	0.06
Fishers (town) Hamilton County	41	0.06
Indianapolis (city) Marion County	393	0.05
Fort Wayne (city) Allen County	130	0.05
Lafayette (city) Tippecanoe County	36	0.05

Danish

Top 10 Places Sorted by Population

Based on all places, regardless of total population

Place	Population	%
Indianapolis (city) Marion County	1,483	0.18
Fort Wayne (city) Allen County	601	0.24
Carmel (city) Hamilton County	597	0.78
Bloomington (city) Monroe County	353	0.45
Fishers (town) Hamilton County	282	0.39
Valparaiso (city) Porter County	278	0.90
Mishawaka (city) St. Joseph County	245	0.51
Columbus (city) Bartholomew County	222	0.51
Hobart (city) Lake County	169	0.60
Granger (cdp) St. Joseph County	165	0.58

Top 10 Places Sorted by Percent of Total Population

Based on all places, regardless of total population

Place	Population	%
Mexico (cdp) Miami County	36	5.14
Kirklin (town) Clinton County	42	4.60
Spring Hill (town) Marion County	3	3.57
Dayton (town) Tippecanoe County	25	2.61
North Webster (town) Kosciusko County	29	2.50
Kentland (town) Newton County	44	2.20
James (town) Boone County	19	2.13
Hidden Valley (cdp) Dearborn County	107	2.11
Ulen (town) Boone County	3	2.10
Hamlet (town) Starke County	16	1.93

Top 10 Places Sorted by Percent of Total Population

Based on places with total population of 50,000 or more

Place	Population	%
Carmel (city) Hamilton County	597	0.78
Bloomington (city) Monroe County	353	0.45
Fishers (town) Hamilton County	282	0.39
Fort Wayne (city) Allen County	601	0.24
Indianapolis (city) Marion County	1,483	0.18
Muncie (city) Delaware County	119	0.17
Terre Haute (city) Vigo County	75	0.12
Evansville (city) Vanderburgh County	133	0.11
Lafayette (city) Tippecanoe County	74	0.11
Hammond (city) Lake County	85	0.10

Dutch

Top 10 Places Sorted by Population

Based on all places, regardless of total population

Place	Population	%
Indianapolis (city) Marion County	11,553	1.43
Fort Wayne (city) Allen County	3,612	1.42
South Bend (city) St. Joseph County	2,222	2.18
Lafayette (city) Tippecanoe County	2,127	3.22
Evansville (city) Vanderburgh County	1,856	1.57
Carmel (city) Hamilton County	1,777	2.31
Highland (town) Lake County	1,729	7.29
Bloomington (city) Monroe County	1,696	2.16
Anderson (city) Madison County	1,593	2.81
Fishers (town) Hamilton County	1,512	2.11

Top 10 Places Sorted by Percent of Total Population

Based on all places, regardless of total population

Place	Population	%
Monterey (town) Pulaski County	37	19.79
Orland (town) Steuben County	99	16.15
Shepardsville (cdp) Vigo County	10	16.13
New Trenton (cdp) Franklin County	72	16.00
De Motte (town) Jasper County	591	15.82
Bryant (town) Jay County	45	15.00
Lake Village (cdp) Newton County	93	14.05
Merom (town) Sullivan County	24	12.97
San Pierre (cdp) Starke County	11	12.22
Yeoman (town) Carroll County	8	11.94

Top 10 Places Sorted by Percent of Total Population

Based on places with total population of 50,000 or more

Place	Population	%
Lafayette (city) Tippecanoe County	2,127	3.22
Anderson (city) Madison County	1,593	2.81
Elkhart (city) Elkhart County	1,346	2.60
Carmel (city) Hamilton County	1,777	2.31
Terre Haute (city) Vigo County	1,355	2.24
South Bend (city) St. Joseph County	2,222	2.18
Bloomington (city) Monroe County	1,696	2.16
Fishers (town) Hamilton County	1,512	2.11
Muncie (city) Delaware County	1,417	2.02
Evansville (city) Vanderburgh County	1,856	1.57

Eastern European

Top 10 Places Sorted by Population

Based on all places, regardless of total population

Place	Population	%
Bloomington (city) Monroe County	354	0.45
Indianapolis (city) Marion County	332	0.04
Hammond (city) Lake County	180	0.22
Carmel (city) Hamilton County	164	0.21
Noblesville (city) Hamilton County	126	0.26
Fort Wayne (city) Allen County	110	0.04
Hobart (city) Lake County	78	0.27
Fishers (town) Hamilton County	75	0.10
South Bend (city) St. Joseph County	66	0.06
Zionsville (town) Boone County	63	0.47

Top 10 Places Sorted by Percent of Total Population

Based on all places, regardless of total population

Place	Population	%
River Forest (town) Madison County	7	18.92
Burlington (town) Carroll County	21	2.94
Williams Creek (town) Marion County	4	1.00
Edinburgh (town) Johnson County	37	0.95
Bargersville (town) Johnson County	29	0.75
Meridian Hills (town) Marion County	12	0.74
Zionsville (town) Boone County	63	0.47
Bloomington (city) Monroe County	354	0.45
Whites (town) Boone County	8	0.42
Versailles (town) Ripley County	7	0.40

Top 10 Places Sorted by Percent of Total Population

Based on places with total population of 50,000 or more

Place	Population	%
Bloomington (city) Monroe County	354	0.45
Hammond (city) Lake County	180	0.22
Carmel (city) Hamilton County	164	0.21
Fishers (town) Hamilton County	75	0.10
South Bend (city) St. Joseph County	66	0.06
Lafayette (city) Tippecanoe County	40	0.06
Indianapolis (city) Marion County	332	0.04
Fort Wayne (city) Allen County	110	0.04
Gary (city) Lake County	37	0.04
Terre Haute (city) Vigo County	26	0.04

English

Top 10 Places Sorted by Population

Based on all places, regardless of total population

Place	Population	%
Indianapolis (city) Marion County	67,644	8.35
Fort Wayne (city) Allen County	19,734	7.78
Carmel (city) Hamilton County	11,352	14.79
Evansville (city) Vanderburgh County	9,922	8.40
Fishers (town) Hamilton County	9,173	12.79
Bloomington (city) Monroe County	8,739	11.13
Lafayette (city) Tippecanoe County	6,889	10.41
Muncie (city) Delaware County	6,521	9.31
South Bend (city) St. Joseph County	6,318	6.19
Noblesville (city) Hamilton County	5,811	11.93

Top 10 Places Sorted by Percent of Total Population

Based on all places, regardless of total population

Place	Population	%
Scotland (cdp) Greene County	11	100.00
New Amsterdam (town) Harrison County	6	100.00
Emison (cdp) Knox County	47	60.26
New Goshen (cdp) Vigo County	116	52.02
Toad Hop (cdp) Vigo County	24	47.06
Tennyson (town) Warrick County	127	39.56
Richland (town) Spencer County	154	37.56
Alfordsville (town) Daviess County	49	35.25
Amo (town) Hendricks County	178	34.36
Patriot (town) Switzerland County	93	34.19

Top 10 Places Sorted by Percent of Total Population

Based on places with total population of 50,000 or more

Place	Population	%
Carmel (city) Hamilton County	11,352	14.79
Fishers (town) Hamilton County	9,173	12.79
Bloomington (city) Monroe County	8,739	11.13
Lafayette (city) Tippecanoe County	6,889	10.41
Muncie (city) Delaware County	6,521	9.31
Terre Haute (city) Vigo County	5,550	9.18
Anderson (city) Madison County	4,934	8.69
Evansville (city) Vanderburgh County	9,922	8.40
Indianapolis (city) Marion County	67,644	8.35
Fort Wayne (city) Allen County	19,734	7.78

Estonian

Top 10 Places Sorted by Population

Based on all places, regardless of total population

Place	Population	%
Indianapolis (city) Marion County	99	0.01
Terre Haute (city) Vigo County	53	0.09
Mishawaka (city) St. Joseph County	37	0.08
Munster (town) Lake County	33	0.14
Hammond (city) Lake County	18	0.02
Franklin (city) Johnson County	17	0.08
Bloomington (city) Monroe County	15	0.02
Carmel (city) Hamilton County	13	0.02
Warren Park (town) Marion County	12	0.87
Fort Wayne (city) Allen County	12	<0.01

Top 10 Places Sorted by Percent of Total Population

Based on all places, regardless of total population

Place	Population	%
Crows Nest (town) Marion County	2	2.41
Warren Park (town) Marion County	12	0.87
Darmstadt (town) Vanderburgh County	3	0.23
New Carlisle (town) St. Joseph County	4	0.22
Munster (town) Lake County	33	0.14
Terre Haute (city) Vigo County	53	0.09
Mishawaka (city) St. Joseph County	37	0.08
Franklin (city) Johnson County	17	0.08
West Lafayette (city) Tippecanoe County	8	0.03
Hammond (city) Lake County	18	0.02

Top 10 Places Sorted by Percent of Total Population

Based on places with total population of 50,000 or more

Place	Population	%
Terre Haute (city) Vigo County	53	0.09
Hammond (city) Lake County	18	0.02
Bloomington (city) Monroe County	15	0.02
Carmel (city) Hamilton County	13	0.02
Indianapolis (city) Marion County	99	0.01
South Bend (city) St. Joseph County	8	0.01
Fort Wayne (city) Allen County	12	<0.01
Anderson (city) Madison County	0	0.00
Elkhart (city) Elkhart County	0	0.00
Evansville (city) Vanderburgh County	0	0.00

European

Top 10 Places Sorted by Population

Based on all places, regardless of total population

Place	Population	%
Indianapolis (city) Marion County	9,215	1.14
Fort Wayne (city) Allen County	1,608	0.63
Fishers (town) Hamilton County	1,428	1.99
Bloomington (city) Monroe County	1,404	1.79
Carmel (city) Hamilton County	1,241	1.62
Noblesville (city) Hamilton County	1,091	2.24
South Bend (city) St. Joseph County	796	0.78
Evansville (city) Vanderburgh County	768	0.65
Granger (cdp) St. Joseph County	756	2.67
Lafayette (city) Tippecanoe County	672	1.02

Top 10 Places Sorted by Percent of Total Population

Based on all places, regardless of total population

Place	Population	%
Williams (cdp) Lawrence County	24	11.32
Crandall (town) Harrison County	11	10.19
Ulen (town) Boone County	14	9.79
Metamora (cdp) Franklin County	8	9.52
Homecroft (town) Marion County	41	7.04
Cedar Grove (town) Franklin County	8	7.02
Cadiz (town) Henry County	8	6.78
St. Bernice (cdp) Vermillion County	44	6.73
Galena (cdp) Floyd County	116	6.17
Larwill (town) Whitley County	15	5.54

Top 10 Places Sorted by Percent of Total Population

Based on places with total population of 50,000 or more

Place	Population	%
Fishers (town) Hamilton County	1,428	1.99
Bloomington (city) Monroe County	1,404	1.79
Carmel (city) Hamilton County	1,241	1.62
Indianapolis (city) Marion County	9,215	1.14
Lafayette (city) Tippecanoe County	672	1.02
Terre Haute (city) Vigo County	484	0.80
South Bend (city) St. Joseph County	796	0.78
Muncie (city) Delaware County	525	0.75
Evansville (city) Vanderburgh County	768	0.65
Fort Wayne (city) Allen County	1,608	0.63

Finnish

Top 10 Places Sorted by Population

Based on all places, regardless of total population

Place	Population	%
Indianapolis (city) Marion County	436	0.05
Fort Wayne (city) Allen County	185	0.07
Hammond (city) Lake County	153	0.19
Lawrenceburg (city) Dearborn County	137	2.74
Granger (cdp) St. Joseph County	122	0.43
Portage (city) Porter County	104	0.29
South Bend (city) St. Joseph County	93	0.09
Fishers (town) Hamilton County	83	0.12
Greenwood (city) Johnson County	80	0.17
Evansville (city) Vanderburgh County	80	0.07

Top 10 Places Sorted by Percent of Total Population

Based on all places, regardless of total population

Place	Population	%
Poseyville (town) Posey County	67	6.18
Lawrenceburg (city) Dearborn County	137	2.74
Cedar Grove (town) Franklin County	3	2.63
Michiana Shores (town) LaPorte County	9	2.19
De Motte (town) Jasper County	70	1.87
Galena (cdp) Floyd County	35	1.86
Dana (town) Vermillion County	9	1.77
Fowler (town) Benton County	38	1.65
Sandborn (town) Knox County	6	1.55
Ossian (town) Wells County	47	1.33

Top 10 Places Sorted by Percent of Total Population

Based on places with total population of 50,000 or more

Place	Population	%
Hammond (city) Lake County	153	0.19
Fishers (town) Hamilton County	83	0.12
Lafayette (city) Tippecanoe County	63	0.10
South Bend (city) St. Joseph County	93	0.09
Carmel (city) Hamilton County	70	0.09
Elkhart (city) Elkhart County	48	0.09
Fort Wayne (city) Allen County	185	0.07
Evansville (city) Vanderburgh County	80	0.07
Muncie (city) Delaware County	42	0.06
Anderson (city) Madison County	35	0.06

French, except Basque

Top 10 Places Sorted by Population

Based on all places, regardless of total population

Place	Population	%
Indianapolis (city) Marion County	15,735	1.94
Fort Wayne (city) Allen County	9,917	3.91
Evansville (city) Vanderburgh County	2,952	2.50
Bloomington (city) Monroe County	2,654	3.38
Fishers (town) Hamilton County	2,611	3.64
South Bend (city) St. Joseph County	2,323	2.28
Carmel (city) Hamilton County	2,214	2.88
Lafayette (city) Tippecanoe County	1,964	2.97
Muncie (city) Delaware County	1,865	2.66
Mishawaka (city) St. Joseph County	1,835	3.83

Top 10 Places Sorted by Percent of Total Population

Based on all places, regardless of total population

Place	Population	%
Raglesville (cdp) Daviess County	44	84.62
Griffin (town) Posey County	83	34.30
Stockwell (cdp) Tippecanoe County	152	24.68

Collegeville (cdp) Jasper County	10	20.83
West Point (cdp) Tippecanoe County	94	16.46
Alton (town) Crawford County	13	15.29
Colburn (cdp) Tippecanoe County	15	14.02
Zanesville (town) Wells County	105	13.98
New Goshen (cdp) Vigo County	30	13.45
Blountsville (town) Henry County	12	12.12

Top 10 Places Sorted by Percent of Total Population
Based on places with total population of 50,000 or more

Place	Population	%
Fort Wayne (city) Allen County	9,917	3.91
Fishers (town) Hamilton County	2,611	3.64
Bloomington (city) Monroe County	2,654	3.38
Lafayette (city) Tippecanoe County	1,964	2.97
Terre Haute (city) Vigo County	1,765	2.92
Carmel (city) Hamilton County	2,214	2.88
Muncie (city) Delaware County	1,865	2.66
Evansville (city) Vanderburgh County	2,952	2.50
South Bend (city) St. Joseph County	2,323	2.28
Anderson (city) Madison County	1,268	2.23

French Canadian

Top 10 Places Sorted by Population
Based on all places, regardless of total population

Place	Population	%
Indianapolis (city) Marion County	1,565	0.19
Fort Wayne (city) Allen County	813	0.32
South Bend (city) St. Joseph County	422	0.41
Fishers (town) Hamilton County	382	0.53
Hammond (city) Lake County	345	0.42
Kokomo (city) Howard County	324	0.71
Bloomington (city) Monroe County	305	0.39
Greenwood (city) Johnson County	302	0.63
Mishawaka (city) St. Joseph County	278	0.58
Portage (city) Porter County	226	0.62

Top 10 Places Sorted by Percent of Total Population
Based on all places, regardless of total population

Place	Population	%
Howe (cdp) LaGrange County	87	12.79
Country Club Heights (town) Madison County	5	9.80
Pierceton (town) Kosciusko County	40	3.93
Campbellsburg (town) Washington County	23	3.66
Roseland (town) St. Joseph County	39	3.26
Andrews (town) Huntington County	43	3.25
Woodlawn Heights (town) Madison County	3	3.23
Waveland (town) Montgomery County	12	3.10
New (town) Fountain County	4	2.96
Smithville-Sanders (cdp) Monroe County	55	2.20

Top 10 Places Sorted by Percent of Total Population
Based on places with total population of 50,000 or more

Place	Population	%
Fishers (town) Hamilton County	382	0.53
Hammond (city) Lake County	345	0.42
South Bend (city) St. Joseph County	422	0.41
Bloomington (city) Monroe County	305	0.39
Elkhart (city) Elkhart County	203	0.39
Fort Wayne (city) Allen County	813	0.32
Carmel (city) Hamilton County	225	0.29
Lafayette (city) Tippecanoe County	177	0.27
Indianapolis (city) Marion County	1,565	0.19
Terre Haute (city) Vigo County	85	0.14

German

Top 10 Places Sorted by Population
Based on all places, regardless of total population

Place	Population	%
Indianapolis (city) Marion County	149,656	18.48
Fort Wayne (city) Allen County	76,622	30.20
Evansville (city) Vanderburgh County	33,828	28.62
Carmel (city) Hamilton County	21,955	28.60
Fishers (town) Hamilton County	20,883	29.11
Bloomington (city) Monroe County	19,499	24.84
South Bend (city) St. Joseph County	19,199	18.81
Lafayette (city) Tippecanoe County	16,791	25.38
Muncie (city) Delaware County	14,993	21.41
Noblesville (city) Hamilton County	13,766	28.26

Top 10 Places Sorted by Percent of Total Population
Based on all places, regardless of total population

Place	Population	%
Oldenburg (town) Franklin County	485	79.64
St. Meinrad (cdp) Spencer County	266	78.93
Dubois (cdp) Dubois County	204	72.86
Cedar Grove (town) Franklin County	82	71.93
Ferdinand (town) Dubois County	1,534	71.12
Clarksburg (cdp) Decatur County	85	69.67
Shelby (cdp) Lake County	245	67.31
Cannelburg (town) Daviess County	97	66.90
Parkers Settlement (cdp) Posey County	496	65.01
St. Leon (town) Dearborn County	523	63.55

Top 10 Places Sorted by Percent of Total Population
Based on places with total population of 50,000 or more

Place	Population	%
Fort Wayne (city) Allen County	76,622	30.20
Fishers (town) Hamilton County	20,883	29.11
Evansville (city) Vanderburgh County	33,828	28.62
Carmel (city) Hamilton County	21,955	28.60
Lafayette (city) Tippecanoe County	16,791	25.38
Bloomington (city) Monroe County	19,499	24.84
Terre Haute (city) Vigo County	13,440	22.24
Muncie (city) Delaware County	14,993	21.41
Elkhart (city) Elkhart County	9,960	19.21
South Bend (city) St. Joseph County	19,199	18.81

German Russian

Top 10 Places Sorted by Population
Based on all places, regardless of total population

Place	Population	%
Simonton Lake (cdp) Elkhart County	47	0.93
Lawrence (city) Marion County	11	0.02
Indianapolis (city) Marion County	11	<0.01
Mishawaka (city) St. Joseph County	10	0.02
Van Buren (town) Grant County	8	0.91
Hagers (town) Wayne County	6	0.36
Grissom AFB (cdp) Miami County	4	0.22
Aberdeen (cdp) Porter County	0	0.00
Advance (town) Boone County	0	0.00
Akron (town) Fulton County	0	0.00

Top 10 Places Sorted by Percent of Total Population
Based on all places, regardless of total population

Place	Population	%
Simonton Lake (cdp) Elkhart County	47	0.93
Van Buren (town) Grant County	8	0.91
Hagers (town) Wayne County	6	0.36
Grissom AFB (cdp) Miami County	4	0.22
Lawrence (city) Marion County	11	0.02
Mishawaka (city) St. Joseph County	10	0.02
Indianapolis (city) Marion County	11	<0.01
Aberdeen (cdp) Porter County	0	0.00
Advance (town) Boone County	0	0.00
Akron (town) Fulton County	0	0.00

Top 10 Places Sorted by Percent of Total Population
Based on places with total population of 50,000 or more

Place	Population	%
Indianapolis (city) Marion County	11	<0.01
Anderson (city) Madison County	0	0.00
Bloomington (city) Monroe County	0	0.00
Carmel (city) Hamilton County	0	0.00
Elkhart (city) Elkhart County	0	0.00
Evansville (city) Vanderburgh County	0	0.00
Fishers (town) Hamilton County	0	0.00
Fort Wayne (city) Allen County	0	0.00
Gary (city) Lake County	0	0.00
Hammond (city) Lake County	0	0.00

Greek

Top 10 Places Sorted by Population
Based on all places, regardless of total population

Place	Population	%
Indianapolis (city) Marion County	2,372	0.29
Hammond (city) Lake County	881	1.08
Munster (town) Lake County	784	3.37
Fort Wayne (city) Allen County	732	0.29
Crown Point (city) Lake County	661	2.53
Fishers (town) Hamilton County	637	0.89
Schererville (town) Lake County	571	2.01
Bloomington (city) Monroe County	551	0.70
Portage (city) Porter County	528	1.45
Carmel (city) Hamilton County	485	0.63

Top 10 Places Sorted by Percent of Total Population
Based on all places, regardless of total population

Place	Population	%
Shorewood Forest (cdp) Porter County	320	10.61
Manilla (cdp) Rush County	33	10.28
Rocky Ripple (town) Marion County	49	7.61
Bethany (town) Morgan County	9	7.03
River Forest (town) Madison County	2	5.41
Morris (town) Shelby County	40	3.88
Munster (town) Lake County	784	3.37
Ogden Dunes (town) Porter County	37	3.02
Michigan (town) Clinton County	14	2.90
Homecroft (town) Marion County	16	2.75

Top 10 Places Sorted by Percent of Total Population
Based on places with total population of 50,000 or more

Place	Population	%
Hammond (city) Lake County	881	1.08
Fishers (town) Hamilton County	637	0.89
Bloomington (city) Monroe County	551	0.70
Carmel (city) Hamilton County	485	0.63
Muncie (city) Delaware County	214	0.31
South Bend (city) St. Joseph County	308	0.30
Indianapolis (city) Marion County	2,372	0.29
Fort Wayne (city) Allen County	732	0.29
Lafayette (city) Tippecanoe County	147	0.22
Anderson (city) Madison County	126	0.22

Guyanese

Top 10 Places Sorted by Population
Based on all places, regardless of total population

Place	Population	%
Evansville (city) Vanderburgh County	49	0.04
Richmond (city) Wayne County	30	0.08
Hammond (city) Lake County	14	0.02
Goshen (city) Elkhart County	10	0.03
Aberdeen (cdp) Porter County	0	0.00
Advance (town) Boone County	0	0.00
Akron (town) Fulton County	0	0.00
Alamo (town) Montgomery County	0	0.00
Albany (town) Delaware County	0	0.00
Albion (town) Noble County	0	0.00

Top 10 Places Sorted by Percent of Total Population
Based on all places, regardless of total population

Place	Population	%
Richmond (city) Wayne County	30	0.08
Evansville (city) Vanderburgh County	49	0.04
Goshen (city) Elkhart County	10	0.03
Hammond (city) Lake County	14	0.02
Aberdeen (cdp) Porter County	0	0.00
Advance (town) Boone County	0	0.00
Akron (town) Fulton County	0	0.00
Alamo (town) Montgomery County	0	0.00
Albany (town) Delaware County	0	0.00
Albion (town) Noble County	0	0.00

Top 10 Places Sorted by Percent of Total Population
Based on places with total population of 50,000 or more

Place	Population	%
Evansville (city) Vanderburgh County	49	0.04
Hammond (city) Lake County	14	0.02
Anderson (city) Madison County	0	0.00
Bloomington (city) Monroe County	0	0.00
Carmel (city) Hamilton County	0	0.00
Elkhart (city) Elkhart County	0	0.00
Fishers (town) Hamilton County	0	0.00
Fort Wayne (city) Allen County	0	0.00
Gary (city) Lake County	0	0.00
Indianapolis (city) Marion County	0	0.00

Hungarian

Top 10 Places Sorted by Population

Based on all places, regardless of total population

Place	Population	%
Indianapolis (city) Marion County	2,960	0.37
South Bend (city) St. Joseph County	2,904	2.85
Mishawaka (city) St. Joseph County	1,337	2.79
Fort Wayne (city) Allen County	1,122	0.44
Hammond (city) Lake County	827	1.02
Bloomington (city) Monroe County	767	0.98
Valparaiso (city) Porter County	744	2.40
Highland (town) Lake County	707	2.98
Portage (city) Porter County	668	1.84
Granger (cdp) St. Joseph County	655	2.31

Top 10 Places Sorted by Percent of Total Population

Based on all places, regardless of total population

Place	Population	%
Tri-Lakes (cdp) Whitley County	122	7.40
Aberdeen (cdp) Porter County	132	6.04
Roseland (town) St. Joseph County	72	6.03
Lake Village (cdp) Newton County	33	4.98
Trail Creek (town) LaPorte County	94	4.75
Hudson Lake (cdp) LaPorte County	59	4.39
New Carlisle (town) St. Joseph County	76	4.13
Hanna (cdp) LaPorte County	19	4.09
Walkerton (town) St. Joseph County	90	3.92
North Webster (town) Kosciusko County	45	3.88

Top 10 Places Sorted by Percent of Total Population

Based on places with total population of 50,000 or more

Place	Population	%
South Bend (city) St. Joseph County	2,904	2.85
Hammond (city) Lake County	827	1.02
Bloomington (city) Monroe County	767	0.98
Terre Haute (city) Vigo County	438	0.72
Carmel (city) Hamilton County	504	0.66
Fishers (town) Hamilton County	463	0.65
Elkhart (city) Elkhart County	258	0.50
Fort Wayne (city) Allen County	1,122	0.44
Indianapolis (city) Marion County	2,960	0.37
Lafayette (city) Tippecanoe County	247	0.37

Icelander

Top 10 Places Sorted by Population

Based on all places, regardless of total population

Place	Population	%
Bloomington (city) Monroe County	41	0.05
Plainfield (town) Hendricks County	31	0.12
Charlestown (city) Clark County	25	0.33
Purdue University (cdp) Tippecanoe County	18	0.14
Valparaiso (city) Porter County	18	0.06
South Whitley (town) Whitley County	13	0.64
Upland (town) Grant County	13	0.32
Notre Dame (cdp) St. Joseph County	13	0.17
Terre Haute (city) Vigo County	13	0.02
Carmel (city) Hamilton County	12	0.02

Top 10 Places Sorted by Percent of Total Population

Based on all places, regardless of total population

Place	Population	%
South Whitley (town) Whitley County	13	0.64
Charlestown (city) Clark County	25	0.33
Upland (town) Grant County	13	0.32
Notre Dame (cdp) St. Joseph County	13	0.17
Purdue University (cdp) Tippecanoe County	18	0.14
Plainfield (town) Hendricks County	31	0.12
Austin (city) Scott County	5	0.12
Valparaiso (city) Porter County	18	0.06
Bloomington (city) Monroe County	41	0.05
New Haven (city) Allen County	7	0.05

Top 10 Places Sorted by Percent of Total Population

Based on places with total population of 50,000 or more

Place	Population	%
Bloomington (city) Monroe County	41	0.05
Terre Haute (city) Vigo County	13	0.02
Carmel (city) Hamilton County	12	0.02
Fort Wayne (city) Allen County	9	<0.01
Anderson (city) Madison County	0	0.00
Elkhart (city) Elkhart County	0	0.00
Evansville (city) Vanderburgh County	0	0.00
Fishers (town) Hamilton County	0	0.00
Gary (city) Lake County	0	0.00
Hammond (city) Lake County	0	0.00

Iranian

Top 10 Places Sorted by Population

Based on all places, regardless of total population

Place	Population	%
Indianapolis (city) Marion County	455	0.06
Carmel (city) Hamilton County	253	0.33
Bloomington (city) Monroe County	201	0.26
Fishers (town) Hamilton County	181	0.25
Noblesville (city) Hamilton County	131	0.27
Granger (cdp) St. Joseph County	124	0.44
Portage (city) Porter County	99	0.27
Muncie (city) Delaware County	78	0.11
Whiteland (town) Johnson County	68	1.61
Michigan City (city) LaPorte County	44	0.14

Top 10 Places Sorted by Percent of Total Population

Based on all places, regardless of total population

Place	Population	%
Williams Creek (town) Marion County	10	2.50
Burns Harbor (town) Porter County	31	2.48
Spring Hill (town) Marion County	2	2.38
Whiteland (town) Johnson County	68	1.61
Wynnedale (town) Marion County	3	1.28
Riley (town) Vigo County	2	0.92
McCordsville (town) Hancock County	25	0.60
Granger (cdp) St. Joseph County	124	0.44
Bremen (town) Marshall County	19	0.41
Carmel (city) Hamilton County	253	0.33

Top 10 Places Sorted by Percent of Total Population

Based on places with total population of 50,000 or more

Place	Population	%
Carmel (city) Hamilton County	253	0.33
Bloomington (city) Monroe County	201	0.26
Fishers (town) Hamilton County	181	0.25
Muncie (city) Delaware County	78	0.11
Indianapolis (city) Marion County	455	0.06
Evansville (city) Vanderburgh County	20	0.02
South Bend (city) St. Joseph County	13	0.01
Fort Wayne (city) Allen County	8	<0.01
Anderson (city) Madison County	0	0.00
Elkhart (city) Elkhart County	0	0.00

Irish

Top 10 Places Sorted by Population

Based on all places, regardless of total population

Place	Population	%
Indianapolis (city) Marion County	93,959	11.60
Fort Wayne (city) Allen County	28,352	11.17
Evansville (city) Vanderburgh County	14,073	11.91
Carmel (city) Hamilton County	12,211	15.91
South Bend (city) St. Joseph County	12,089	11.84
Bloomington (city) Monroe County	10,941	13.94
Fishers (town) Hamilton County	10,537	14.69
Lafayette (city) Tippecanoe County	10,032	15.17
Muncie (city) Delaware County	9,462	13.51
Hammond (city) Lake County	8,337	10.25

Top 10 Places Sorted by Percent of Total Population

Based on all places, regardless of total population

Place	Population	%
Fish Lake (cdp) LaPorte County	405	45.25
Alton (town) Crawford County	38	44.71
Hayden (cdp) Jennings County	336	44.27
Painted Hills (cdp) Morgan County	187	42.60
Salamonia (town) Jay County	92	42.59
East Enterprise (cdp) Switzerland County	109	39.78
New Goshen (cdp) Vigo County	88	39.46
Notre Dame (cdp) St. Joseph County	2,794	37.61
Buffalo (cdp) White County	243	35.22
Yeoman (town) Carroll County	23	34.33

Top 10 Places Sorted by Percent of Total Population

Based on places with total population of 50,000 or more

Place	Population	%
Carmel (city) Hamilton County	12,211	15.91
Lafayette (city) Tippecanoe County	10,032	15.17
Fishers (town) Hamilton County	10,537	14.69
Bloomington (city) Monroe County	10,941	13.94
Muncie (city) Delaware County	9,462	13.51
Evansville (city) Vanderburgh County	14,073	11.91
Terre Haute (city) Vigo County	7,200	11.91
South Bend (city) St. Joseph County	12,089	11.84
Indianapolis (city) Marion County	93,959	11.60
Anderson (city) Madison County	6,464	11.39

Israeli

Top 10 Places Sorted by Population

Based on all places, regardless of total population

Place	Population	%
Bloomington (city) Monroe County	168	0.21
Indianapolis (city) Marion County	107	0.01
Mount Vernon (city) Posey County	38	0.56
Fort Wayne (city) Allen County	34	0.01
Muncie (city) Delaware County	24	0.03
Fishers (town) Hamilton County	21	0.03
Terre Haute (city) Vigo County	13	0.02
York (town) Delaware County	11	0.12
Portage (city) Porter County	5	0.01
Aberdeen (cdp) Porter County	0	0.00

Top 10 Places Sorted by Percent of Total Population

Based on all places, regardless of total population

Place	Population	%
Mount Vernon (city) Posey County	38	0.56
Bloomington (city) Monroe County	168	0.21
York (town) Delaware County	11	0.12
Muncie (city) Delaware County	24	0.03
Fishers (town) Hamilton County	21	0.03
Terre Haute (city) Vigo County	13	0.02
Indianapolis (city) Marion County	107	0.01
Fort Wayne (city) Allen County	34	0.01
Portage (city) Porter County	5	0.01
Aberdeen (cdp) Porter County	0	0.00

Top 10 Places Sorted by Percent of Total Population

Based on places with total population of 50,000 or more

Place	Population	%
Bloomington (city) Monroe County	168	0.21
Muncie (city) Delaware County	24	0.03
Fishers (town) Hamilton County	21	0.03
Terre Haute (city) Vigo County	13	0.02
Indianapolis (city) Marion County	107	0.01
Fort Wayne (city) Allen County	34	0.01
Anderson (city) Madison County	0	0.00
Carmel (city) Hamilton County	0	0.00
Elkhart (city) Elkhart County	0	0.00
Evansville (city) Vanderburgh County	0	0.00

Italian

Top 10 Places Sorted by Population

Based on all places, regardless of total population

Place	Population	%
Indianapolis (city) Marion County	20,396	2.52
Fort Wayne (city) Allen County	6,703	2.64
Carmel (city) Hamilton County	3,728	4.86
Bloomington (city) Monroe County	3,669	4.67
Fishers (town) Hamilton County	3,343	4.66
South Bend (city) St. Joseph County	3,341	3.27
Hammond (city) Lake County	2,841	3.49
Noblesville (city) Hamilton County	2,728	5.60
Mishawaka (city) St. Joseph County	2,342	4.89
Schererville (town) Lake County	2,160	7.58

Top 10 Places Sorted by Percent of Total Population

Based on all places, regardless of total population

Place	Population	%
Deputy (cdp) Jefferson County	16	59.26
Buck Creek (cdp) Tippecanoe County	119	34.00
Stockwell (cdp) Tippecanoe County	181	29.38

San Pierre (cdp) Starke County	21	23.33
East Enterprise (cdp) Switzerland County	51	18.61
Avoca (cdp) Lawrence County	97	18.44
Blanford (cdp) Vermillion County	63	18.16
Bass Lake (cdp) Starke County	234	16.49
Notre Dame (cdp) St. Joseph County	1,191	16.03
New Goshen (cdp) Vigo County	34	15.25

Top 10 Places Sorted by Percent of Total Population
Based on places with total population of 50,000 or more

Place	Population	%
Carmel (city) Hamilton County	3,728	4.86
Bloomington (city) Monroe County	3,669	4.67
Fishers (town) Hamilton County	3,343	4.66
Hammond (city) Lake County	2,841	3.49
South Bend (city) St. Joseph County	3,341	3.27
Elkhart (city) Elkhart County	1,611	3.11
Terre Haute (city) Vigo County	1,814	3.00
Muncie (city) Delaware County	1,965	2.81
Fort Wayne (city) Allen County	6,703	2.64
Indianapolis (city) Marion County	20,396	2.52

Latvian

Top 10 Places Sorted by Population
Based on all places, regardless of total population

Place	Population	%
Indianapolis (city) Marion County	275	0.03
Noblesville (city) Hamilton County	167	0.34
Carmel (city) Hamilton County	129	0.17
Terre Haute (city) Vigo County	118	0.20
Fort Wayne (city) Allen County	70	0.03
Lake Dalecarlia (cdp) Lake County	47	3.10
Westfield (town) Hamilton County	39	0.14
Griffith (town) Lake County	38	0.22
Munster (town) Lake County	23	0.10
West Lafayette (city) Tippecanoe County	18	0.06

Top 10 Places Sorted by Percent of Total Population
Based on all places, regardless of total population

Place	Population	%
Lake Dalecarlia (cdp) Lake County	47	3.10
Long Beach (town) LaPorte County	11	0.75
Kewanna (town) Fulton County	3	0.53
Frankton (town) Madison County	8	0.41
Attica (city) Fountain County	12	0.37
Bristol (town) Elkhart County	6	0.37
Noblesville (city) Hamilton County	167	0.34
Upland (town) Grant County	13	0.32
Rocky Ripple (town) Marion County	2	0.31
Kentland (town) Newton County	6	0.30

Top 10 Places Sorted by Percent of Total Population
Based on places with total population of 50,000 or more

Place	Population	%
Terre Haute (city) Vigo County	118	0.20
Carmel (city) Hamilton County	129	0.17
Indianapolis (city) Marion County	275	0.03
Fort Wayne (city) Allen County	70	0.03
Fishers (town) Hamilton County	13	0.02
Elkhart (city) Elkhart County	11	0.02
Evansville (city) Vanderburgh County	12	0.01
Bloomington (city) Monroe County	10	0.01
South Bend (city) St. Joseph County	10	0.01
Muncie (city) Delaware County	9	0.01

Lithuanian

Top 10 Places Sorted by Population
Based on all places, regardless of total population

Place	Population	%
Indianapolis (city) Marion County	1,175	0.15
Bloomington (city) Monroe County	362	0.46
Fort Wayne (city) Allen County	278	0.11
Munster (town) Lake County	274	1.18
Valparaiso (city) Porter County	271	0.87
Lakes of the Four Seasons (cdp) Lake County	265	3.51
Schererville (town) Lake County	263	0.92
Highland (town) Lake County	258	1.09
St. John (town) Lake County	242	1.76
Hammond (city) Lake County	242	0.30

Top 10 Places Sorted by Percent of Total Population
Based on all places, regardless of total population

Place	Population	%
Beverly Shores (town) Porter County	144	21.30
Michiana Shores (town) LaPorte County	36	8.76
Dune Acres (town) Porter County	14	5.34
Lakes of the Four Seasons (cdp) Lake County	265	3.51
Star City (cdp) Pulaski County	9	2.94
Monterey (town) Pulaski County	5	2.67
Francesville (town) Pulaski County	20	2.22
Hudson Lake (cdp) LaPorte County	29	2.16
Town of Pines (town) Porter County	15	2.14
Lake Dalecarlia (cdp) Lake County	28	1.85

Top 10 Places Sorted by Percent of Total Population
Based on places with total population of 50,000 or more

Place	Population	%
Bloomington (city) Monroe County	362	0.46
Hammond (city) Lake County	242	0.30
Fishers (town) Hamilton County	166	0.23
Gary (city) Lake County	162	0.19
Terre Haute (city) Vigo County	110	0.18
South Bend (city) St. Joseph County	176	0.17
Carmel (city) Hamilton County	120	0.16
Indianapolis (city) Marion County	1,175	0.15
Fort Wayne (city) Allen County	278	0.11
Muncie (city) Delaware County	77	0.11

Luxemburger

Top 10 Places Sorted by Population
Based on all places, regardless of total population

Place	Population	%
Indianapolis (city) Marion County	97	0.01
Lafayette (city) Tippecanoe County	45	0.07
Fort Wayne (city) Allen County	36	0.01
Muncie (city) Delaware County	32	0.05
Granger (cdp) St. Joseph County	26	0.09
Carmel (city) Hamilton County	22	0.03
Batesville (city) Ripley County	18	0.28
Purdue University (cdp) Tippecanoe County	13	0.10
South Bend (city) St. Joseph County	13	0.01
Lawrence (city) Marion County	12	0.03

Top 10 Places Sorted by Percent of Total Population
Based on all places, regardless of total population

Place	Population	%
Beverly Shores (town) Porter County	5	0.74
St. Mary of the Woods (cdp) Vigo County	8	0.72
Koontz Lake (cdp) Starke County	10	0.62
Morocco (town) Newton County	5	0.57
Wynnedale (town) Marion County	1	0.43
Batesville (city) Ripley County	18	0.28
Roseland (town) St. Joseph County	3	0.25
Ogden Dunes (town) Porter County	3	0.24
Fairview Park (town) Vermillion County	2	0.15
North Judson (town) Starke County	2	0.12

Top 10 Places Sorted by Percent of Total Population
Based on places with total population of 50,000 or more

Place	Population	%
Lafayette (city) Tippecanoe County	45	0.07
Muncie (city) Delaware County	32	0.05
Carmel (city) Hamilton County	22	0.03
Indianapolis (city) Marion County	97	0.01
Fort Wayne (city) Allen County	36	0.01
South Bend (city) St. Joseph County	13	0.01
Anderson (city) Madison County	6	0.01
Bloomington (city) Monroe County	0	0.00
Elkhart (city) Elkhart County	0	0.00
Evansville (city) Vanderburgh County	0	0.00

Macedonian

Top 10 Places Sorted by Population
Based on all places, regardless of total population

Place	Population	%
Crown Point (city) Lake County	901	3.46
Fort Wayne (city) Allen County	580	0.23
Schererville (town) Lake County	401	1.41
Winfield (town) Lake County	385	9.73
Indianapolis (city) Marion County	265	0.03
Hobart (city) Lake County	221	0.78
Portage (city) Porter County	181	0.50
Wheeler (cdp) Porter County	172	38.22
Merrillville (town) Lake County	158	0.46
Munster (town) Lake County	145	0.62

Top 10 Places Sorted by Percent of Total Population
Based on all places, regardless of total population

Place	Population	%
Wheeler (cdp) Porter County	172	38.22
Winfield (town) Lake County	385	9.73
Shorewood Forest (cdp) Porter County	118	3.91
Crown Point (city) Lake County	901	3.46
Schererville (town) Lake County	401	1.41
Lakes of the Four Seasons (cdp) Lake County	79	1.05
St. John (town) Lake County	109	0.79
Hobart (city) Lake County	221	0.78
Dune Acres (town) Porter County	2	0.76
Beverly Shores (town) Porter County	5	0.74

Top 10 Places Sorted by Percent of Total Population
Based on places with total population of 50,000 or more

Place	Population	%
Fort Wayne (city) Allen County	580	0.23
Carmel (city) Hamilton County	104	0.14
Bloomington (city) Monroe County	62	0.08
Indianapolis (city) Marion County	265	0.03
Muncie (city) Delaware County	23	0.03
Fishers (town) Hamilton County	10	0.01
Hammond (city) Lake County	9	0.01
Anderson (city) Madison County	0	0.00
Elkhart (city) Elkhart County	0	0.00
Evansville (city) Vanderburgh County	0	0.00

Maltese

Top 10 Places Sorted by Population
Based on all places, regardless of total population

Place	Population	%
Indianapolis (city) Marion County	56	0.01
Crown Point (city) Lake County	48	0.18
Richmond (city) Wayne County	22	0.06
Leo-Cedarville (town) Allen County	16	0.46
Gary (city) Lake County	10	0.01
Jasper (city) Dubois County	9	0.06
Roanoke (town) Huntington County	8	0.44
Santa Claus (town) Spencer County	5	0.19
Aberdeen (cdp) Porter County	0	0.00
Advance (town) Boone County	0	0.00

Top 10 Places Sorted by Percent of Total Population
Based on all places, regardless of total population

Place	Population	%
Leo-Cedarville (town) Allen County	16	0.46
Roanoke (town) Huntington County	8	0.44
Santa Claus (town) Spencer County	5	0.19
Crown Point (city) Lake County	48	0.18
Richmond (city) Wayne County	22	0.06
Jasper (city) Dubois County	9	0.06
Indianapolis (city) Marion County	56	0.01
Gary (city) Lake County	10	0.01
Aberdeen (cdp) Porter County	0	0.00
Advance (town) Boone County	0	0.00

Top 10 Places Sorted by Percent of Total Population
Based on places with total population of 50,000 or more

Place	Population	%
Indianapolis (city) Marion County	56	0.01
Gary (city) Lake County	10	0.01
Anderson (city) Madison County	0	0.00
Bloomington (city) Monroe County	0	0.00
Carmel (city) Hamilton County	0	0.00
Elkhart (city) Elkhart County	0	0.00
Evansville (city) Vanderburgh County	0	0.00
Fishers (town) Hamilton County	0	0.00
Fort Wayne (city) Allen County	0	0.00
Hammond (city) Lake County	0	0.00

New Zealander

Top 10 Places Sorted by Population

Based on all places, regardless of total population

Place	Population	%
Lafayette (city) Tippecanoe County	68	0.10
Princeton (city) Gibson County	35	0.41
Indianapolis (city) Marion County	35	<0.01
West Lafayette (city) Tippecanoe County	26	0.09
Speedway (town) Marion County	19	0.16
Muncie (city) Delaware County	18	0.03
Fishers (town) Hamilton County	14	0.02
Zionsville (town) Boone County	13	0.10
Fort Wayne (city) Allen County	11	<0.01
Aberdeen (cdp) Porter County	0	0.00

Top 10 Places Sorted by Percent of Total Population

Based on all places, regardless of total population

Place	Population	%
Princeton (city) Gibson County	35	0.41
Speedway (town) Marion County	19	0.16
Lafayette (city) Tippecanoe County	68	0.10
Zionsville (town) Boone County	13	0.10
West Lafayette (city) Tippecanoe County	26	0.09
Muncie (city) Delaware County	18	0.03
Fishers (town) Hamilton County	14	0.02
Indianapolis (city) Marion County	35	<0.01
Fort Wayne (city) Allen County	11	<0.01
Aberdeen (cdp) Porter County	0	0.00

Top 10 Places Sorted by Percent of Total Population

Based on places with total population of 50,000 or more

Place	Population	%
Lafayette (city) Tippecanoe County	68	0.10
Muncie (city) Delaware County	18	0.03
Fishers (town) Hamilton County	14	0.02
Indianapolis (city) Marion County	35	<0.01
Fort Wayne (city) Allen County	11	<0.01
Anderson (city) Madison County	0	0.00
Bloomington (city) Monroe County	0	0.00
Carmel (city) Hamilton County	0	0.00
Elkhart (city) Elkhart County	0	0.00
Evansville (city) Vanderburgh County	0	0.00

Northern European

Top 10 Places Sorted by Population

Based on all places, regardless of total population

Place	Population	%
Indianapolis (city) Marion County	584	0.07
Carmel (city) Hamilton County	105	0.14
Bloomington (city) Monroe County	98	0.12
Fort Wayne (city) Allen County	96	0.04
Granger (cdp) St. Joseph County	85	0.30
Pendleton (town) Madison County	82	1.86
Lawrence (city) Marion County	80	0.18
Lafayette (city) Tippecanoe County	77	0.12
Mishawaka (city) St. Joseph County	73	0.15
South Haven (cdp) Porter County	72	1.35

Top 10 Places Sorted by Percent of Total Population

Based on all places, regardless of total population

Place	Population	%
Indian Village (town) St. Joseph County	4	4.08
Poneto (town) Wells County	5	2.54
Fontanet (cdp) Vigo County	8	2.09
Greens Fork (town) Wayne County	8	1.92
Pendleton (town) Madison County	82	1.86
Ogden Dunes (town) Porter County	20	1.63
Meridian Hills (town) Marion County	24	1.47
Heritage Lake (cdp) Putnam County	38	1.46
South Haven (cdp) Porter County	72	1.35
Millersburg (town) Elkhart County	12	1.32

Top 10 Places Sorted by Percent of Total Population

Based on places with total population of 50,000 or more

Place	Population	%
Carmel (city) Hamilton County	105	0.14
Bloomington (city) Monroe County	98	0.12
Lafayette (city) Tippecanoe County	77	0.12
Indianapolis (city) Marion County	584	0.07
South Bend (city) St. Joseph County	62	0.06
Hammond (city) Lake County	49	0.06
Elkhart (city) Elkhart County	26	0.05
Fort Wayne (city) Allen County	96	0.04
Evansville (city) Vanderburgh County	34	0.03
Fishers (town) Hamilton County	24	0.03

Norwegian

Top 10 Places Sorted by Population

Based on all places, regardless of total population

Place	Population	%
Indianapolis (city) Marion County	3,636	0.45
Fort Wayne (city) Allen County	1,488	0.59
Bloomington (city) Monroe County	1,150	1.47
Carmel (city) Hamilton County	995	1.30
Fishers (town) Hamilton County	843	1.17
Noblesville (city) Hamilton County	621	1.27
Granger (cdp) St. Joseph County	587	2.07
South Bend (city) St. Joseph County	459	0.45
Mishawaka (city) St. Joseph County	428	0.89
Muncie (city) Delaware County	422	0.60

Top 10 Places Sorted by Percent of Total Population

Based on all places, regardless of total population

Place	Population	%
Spring Hill (town) Marion County	5	5.95
Hebron (town) Porter County	162	4.62
Ogden Dunes (town) Porter County	52	4.24
Dune Acres (town) Porter County	10	3.82
Wingate (town) Montgomery County	8	3.64
Springport (town) Henry County	6	3.59
Williams Creek (town) Marion County	14	3.50
Marshall (town) Parke County	9	3.47
Roanoke (town) Huntington County	61	3.38
Winfield (town) Lake County	121	3.06

Top 10 Places Sorted by Percent of Total Population

Based on places with total population of 50,000 or more

Place	Population	%
Bloomington (city) Monroe County	1,150	1.47
Carmel (city) Hamilton County	995	1.30
Fishers (town) Hamilton County	843	1.17
Muncie (city) Delaware County	422	0.60
Fort Wayne (city) Allen County	1,488	0.59
Elkhart (city) Elkhart County	299	0.58
Indianapolis (city) Marion County	3,636	0.45
South Bend (city) St. Joseph County	459	0.45
Hammond (city) Lake County	322	0.40
Lafayette (city) Tippecanoe County	249	0.38

Pennsylvania German

Top 10 Places Sorted by Population

Based on all places, regardless of total population

Place	Population	%
Indianapolis (city) Marion County	355	0.04
Elkhart (city) Elkhart County	347	0.67
Fort Wayne (city) Allen County	255	0.10
Goshen (city) Elkhart County	215	0.69
South Bend (city) St. Joseph County	140	0.14
Mishawaka (city) St. Joseph County	129	0.27
Auburn (city) DeKalb County	85	0.68
Noblesville (city) Hamilton County	83	0.17
Lawrence (city) Marion County	77	0.17
New Paris (cdp) Elkhart County	76	5.80

Top 10 Places Sorted by Percent of Total Population

Based on all places, regardless of total population

Place	Population	%
Burns City (cdp) Martin County	63	43.45
Kingsbury (town) LaPorte County	19	8.44
New Paris (cdp) Elkhart County	76	5.80
Burket (town) Kosciusko County	5	2.69
Lagrange (town) LaGrange County	73	2.66
Hamlet (town) Starke County	21	2.54
Culver (town) Marshall County	31	2.15
Topeka (town) LaGrange County	24	1.91
North Liberty (town) St. Joseph County	26	1.66
Henryville (cdp) Clark County	36	1.64

Top 10 Places Sorted by Percent of Total Population

Based on places with total population of 50,000 or more

Place	Population	%
Elkhart (city) Elkhart County	347	0.67
South Bend (city) St. Joseph County	140	0.14
Fort Wayne (city) Allen County	255	0.10
Hammond (city) Lake County	76	0.09
Lafayette (city) Tippecanoe County	61	0.09
Bloomington (city) Monroe County	58	0.07
Carmel (city) Hamilton County	42	0.05
Indianapolis (city) Marion County	355	0.04
Fishers (town) Hamilton County	27	0.04
Evansville (city) Vanderburgh County	33	0.03

Polish

Top 10 Places Sorted by Population

Based on all places, regardless of total population

Place	Population	%
Indianapolis (city) Marion County	12,731	1.57
South Bend (city) St. Joseph County	10,370	10.16
Hammond (city) Lake County	7,497	9.22
Fort Wayne (city) Allen County	5,438	2.14
Schererville (town) Lake County	4,977	17.48
Mishawaka (city) St. Joseph County	4,612	9.63
Highland (town) Lake County	3,947	16.65
Munster (town) Lake County	3,822	16.44
Bloomington (city) Monroe County	3,792	4.83
Portage (city) Porter County	3,667	10.10

Top 10 Places Sorted by Percent of Total Population

Based on all places, regardless of total population

Place	Population	%
Lake Village (cdp) Newton County	171	25.83
Trail Creek (town) LaPorte County	376	19.02
Shorewood Forest (cdp) Porter County	537	17.81
Schererville (town) Lake County	4,977	17.48
St. John (town) Lake County	2,401	17.48
Lakes of the Four Seasons (cdp) Lake County	1,298	17.20
Highland (town) Lake County	3,947	16.65
Munster (town) Lake County	3,822	16.44
Dyer (town) Lake County	2,496	15.64
Whiting (city) Lake County	781	15.55

Top 10 Places Sorted by Percent of Total Population

Based on places with total population of 50,000 or more

Place	Population	%
South Bend (city) St. Joseph County	10,370	10.16
Hammond (city) Lake County	7,497	9.22
Bloomington (city) Monroe County	3,792	4.83
Carmel (city) Hamilton County	3,117	4.06
Fishers (town) Hamilton County	2,912	4.06
Lafayette (city) Tippecanoe County	1,900	2.87
Elkhart (city) Elkhart County	1,234	2.38
Fort Wayne (city) Allen County	5,438	2.14
Terre Haute (city) Vigo County	1,184	1.96
Muncie (city) Delaware County	1,148	1.64

Portuguese

Top 10 Places Sorted by Population

Based on all places, regardless of total population

Place	Population	%
Indianapolis (city) Marion County	414	0.05
Fort Wayne (city) Allen County	324	0.13
Fishers (town) Hamilton County	185	0.26
Granger (cdp) St. Joseph County	128	0.45
Carmel (city) Hamilton County	112	0.15
Lawrence (city) Marion County	108	0.24
Princeton (city) Gibson County	100	1.16
Evansville (city) Vanderburgh County	95	0.08
Plymouth (city) Marshall County	85	0.85
Greenwood (city) Johnson County	83	0.17

Top 10 Places Sorted by Percent of Total Population

Based on all places, regardless of total population

Place	Population	%
Kingsbury (town) LaPorte County	7	3.11
Rocky Ripple (town) Marion County	14	2.17
Leesburg (town) Kosciusko County	15	2.10

Kewanna (town) Fulton County	10	1.76
Orestes (town) Madison County	4	1.40
Princeton (city) Gibson County	100	1.16
Portland (city) Jay County	72	1.11
Plymouth (city) Marshall County	85	0.85
Ingalls (town) Madison County	14	0.74
Flora (town) Carroll County	13	0.61

Top 10 Places Sorted by Percent of Total Population
Based on places with total population of 50,000 or more

Place	Population	%
Fishers (town) Hamilton County	185	0.26
Carmel (city) Hamilton County	112	0.15
Fort Wayne (city) Allen County	324	0.13
Evansville (city) Vanderburgh County	95	0.08
Hammond (city) Lake County	64	0.08
Elkhart (city) Elkhart County	42	0.08
Bloomington (city) Monroe County	52	0.07
Indianapolis (city) Marion County	414	0.05
South Bend (city) St. Joseph County	54	0.05
Anderson (city) Madison County	26	0.05

Romanian

Top 10 Places Sorted by Population
Based on all places, regardless of total population

Place	Population	%
Indianapolis (city) Marion County	1,001	0.12
Fort Wayne (city) Allen County	387	0.15
Schererville (town) Lake County	368	1.29
Bloomington (city) Monroe County	270	0.34
Terre Haute (city) Vigo County	263	0.44
Portage (city) Porter County	233	0.64
Highland (town) Lake County	211	0.89
Carmel (city) Hamilton County	200	0.26
Columbus (city) Bartholomew County	176	0.41
Munster (town) Lake County	153	0.66

Top 10 Places Sorted by Percent of Total Population
Based on all places, regardless of total population

Place	Population	%
Moores Hill (town) Dearborn County	52	6.54
Avoca (cdp) Lawrence County	34	6.46
New Trenton (cdp) Franklin County	19	4.22
Medaryville (town) Pulaski County	19	3.82
Rosedale (town) Parke County	31	3.55
Eaton (town) Delaware County	66	3.50
Rolling Prairie (cdp) LaPorte County	10	2.38
Kouts (town) Porter County	27	1.47
Stilesville (town) Hendricks County	4	1.39
Beverly Shores (town) Porter County	9	1.33

Top 10 Places Sorted by Percent of Total Population
Based on places with total population of 50,000 or more

Place	Population	%
Terre Haute (city) Vigo County	263	0.44
Bloomington (city) Monroe County	270	0.34
Carmel (city) Hamilton County	200	0.26
Fort Wayne (city) Allen County	387	0.15
Fishers (town) Hamilton County	109	0.15
Indianapolis (city) Marion County	1,001	0.12
South Bend (city) St. Joseph County	88	0.09
Hammond (city) Lake County	77	0.09
Lafayette (city) Tippecanoe County	61	0.09
Muncie (city) Delaware County	59	0.08

Russian

Top 10 Places Sorted by Population
Based on all places, regardless of total population

Place	Population	%
Indianapolis (city) Marion County	3,280	0.41
Carmel (city) Hamilton County	1,522	1.98
Bloomington (city) Monroe County	1,268	1.62
Fort Wayne (city) Allen County	913	0.36
South Bend (city) St. Joseph County	730	0.72
West Lafayette (city) Tippecanoe County	545	1.86
Lafayette (city) Tippecanoe County	391	0.59
Evansville (city) Vanderburgh County	381	0.32
Portage (city) Porter County	364	1.00
Fishers (town) Hamilton County	350	0.49

Top 10 Places Sorted by Percent of Total Population
Based on all places, regardless of total population

Place	Population	%
La Paz (town) Marshall County	30	6.05
Orland (town) Steuben County	37	6.04
Brookville (town) Franklin County	155	5.78
Ulen (town) Boone County	7	4.90
Crane (town) Martin County	14	4.76
New Trenton (cdp) Franklin County	19	4.22
Shorewood Forest (cdp) Porter County	114	3.78
Russellville (town) Putnam County	11	3.77
Salt Creek Commons (cdp) Porter County	72	3.28
Beverly Shores (town) Porter County	22	3.25

Top 10 Places Sorted by Percent of Total Population
Based on places with total population of 50,000 or more

Place	Population	%
Carmel (city) Hamilton County	1,522	1.98
Bloomington (city) Monroe County	1,268	1.62
South Bend (city) St. Joseph County	730	0.72
Lafayette (city) Tippecanoe County	391	0.59
Fishers (town) Hamilton County	350	0.49
Terre Haute (city) Vigo County	256	0.42
Indianapolis (city) Marion County	3,280	0.41
Fort Wayne (city) Allen County	913	0.36
Hammond (city) Lake County	275	0.34
Evansville (city) Vanderburgh County	381	0.32

Scandinavian

Top 10 Places Sorted by Population
Based on all places, regardless of total population

Place	Population	%
Indianapolis (city) Marion County	1,199	0.15
Fort Wayne (city) Allen County	269	0.11
Columbus (city) Bartholomew County	229	0.53
Fishers (town) Hamilton County	183	0.26
Bloomington (city) Monroe County	161	0.21
South Bend (city) St. Joseph County	150	0.15
Carmel (city) Hamilton County	90	0.12
Dyer (town) Lake County	85	0.53
Noblesville (city) Hamilton County	83	0.17
Westfield (town) Hamilton County	82	0.30

Top 10 Places Sorted by Percent of Total Population
Based on all places, regardless of total population

Place	Population	%
Fulton (town) Fulton County	18	10.00
Argos (town) Marshall County	47	2.99
Leo-Cedarville (town) Allen County	67	1.93
Dayton (town) Tippecanoe County	18	1.88
Hudson (town) Steuben County	11	1.78
Oakland City (city) Gibson County	36	1.53
Carthage (town) Rush County	11	1.45
Beverly Shores (town) Porter County	8	1.18
Corydon (town) Harrison County	36	1.17
Dune Acres (town) Porter County	3	1.15

Top 10 Places Sorted by Percent of Total Population
Based on places with total population of 50,000 or more

Place	Population	%
Fishers (town) Hamilton County	183	0.26
Bloomington (city) Monroe County	161	0.21
Indianapolis (city) Marion County	1,199	0.15
South Bend (city) St. Joseph County	150	0.15
Anderson (city) Madison County	75	0.13
Carmel (city) Hamilton County	90	0.12
Elkhart (city) Elkhart County	60	0.12
Fort Wayne (city) Allen County	269	0.11
Hammond (city) Lake County	65	0.08
Terre Haute (city) Vigo County	50	0.08

Scotch-Irish

Top 10 Places Sorted by Population
Based on all places, regardless of total population

Place	Population	%
Indianapolis (city) Marion County	10,956	1.35
Fort Wayne (city) Allen County	3,125	1.23
Bloomington (city) Monroe County	2,163	2.76
Evansville (city) Vanderburgh County	1,964	1.66
Carmel (city) Hamilton County	1,430	1.86
Fishers (town) Hamilton County	1,293	1.80
Lafayette (city) Tippecanoe County	1,115	1.69
Columbus (city) Bartholomew County	1,110	2.56
South Bend (city) St. Joseph County	1,065	1.04
Muncie (city) Delaware County	930	1.33

Top 10 Places Sorted by Percent of Total Population
Based on all places, regardless of total population

Place	Population	%
Kent (cdp) Jefferson County	50	26.04
North Crows Nest (town) Marion County	7	16.67
Scipio (cdp) Jennings County	27	13.11
Straughn (town) Henry County	25	12.14
Cannelburg (town) Daviess County	15	10.34
Clarksburg (cdp) Decatur County	12	9.84
Freelandville (cdp) Knox County	40	9.78
Tri-Lakes (cdp) Whitley County	161	9.76
Hamlet (town) Starke County	80	9.66
Brooksburg (town) Jefferson County	7	8.14

Top 10 Places Sorted by Percent of Total Population
Based on places with total population of 50,000 or more

Place	Population	%
Bloomington (city) Monroe County	2,163	2.76
Carmel (city) Hamilton County	1,430	1.86
Fishers (town) Hamilton County	1,293	1.80
Lafayette (city) Tippecanoe County	1,115	1.69
Evansville (city) Vanderburgh County	1,964	1.66
Terre Haute (city) Vigo County	884	1.46
Anderson (city) Madison County	792	1.40
Indianapolis (city) Marion County	10,956	1.35
Muncie (city) Delaware County	930	1.33
Elkhart (city) Elkhart County	647	1.25

Scottish

Top 10 Places Sorted by Population
Based on all places, regardless of total population

Place	Population	%
Indianapolis (city) Marion County	14,050	1.73
Fort Wayne (city) Allen County	4,615	1.82
Carmel (city) Hamilton County	2,632	3.43
Bloomington (city) Monroe County	2,274	2.90
Fishers (town) Hamilton County	2,188	3.05
Evansville (city) Vanderburgh County	2,023	1.71
Lafayette (city) Tippecanoe County	1,572	2.38
Columbus (city) Bartholomew County	1,401	3.23
South Bend (city) St. Joseph County	1,319	1.29
Terre Haute (city) Vigo County	1,286	2.13

Top 10 Places Sorted by Percent of Total Population
Based on all places, regardless of total population

Place	Population	%
Collegeville (cdp) Jasper County	22	45.83
Colburn (cdp) Tippecanoe County	39	36.45
Shepardsville (cdp) Vigo County	11	17.74
Sulphur Springs (town) Henry County	42	14.38
Sims (cdp) Grant County	29	14.08
Kimmell (cdp) Noble County	47	13.31
Orestes (town) Madison County	33	11.54
Arlington (cdp) Rush County	41	10.85
Leesburg (town) Kosciusko County	72	10.07
Gaston (town) Delaware County	82	10.04

Top 10 Places Sorted by Percent of Total Population
Based on places with total population of 50,000 or more

Place	Population	%
Carmel (city) Hamilton County	2,632	3.43
Fishers (town) Hamilton County	2,188	3.05
Bloomington (city) Monroe County	2,274	2.90
Lafayette (city) Tippecanoe County	1,572	2.38
Terre Haute (city) Vigo County	1,286	2.13
Fort Wayne (city) Allen County	4,615	1.82
Muncie (city) Delaware County	1,264	1.81
Indianapolis (city) Marion County	14,050	1.73
Evansville (city) Vanderburgh County	2,023	1.71
Anderson (city) Madison County	861	1.52

Serbian

Top 10 Places Sorted by Population
Based on all places, regardless of total population

Place	Population	%
Munster (town) Lake County	984	4.23
Schererville (town) Lake County	859	3.02
Indianapolis (city) Marion County	777	0.10
Hobart (city) Lake County	614	2.16
Hammond (city) Lake County	572	0.70
St. John (town) Lake County	439	3.20
Valparaiso (city) Porter County	421	1.36
Crown Point (city) Lake County	337	1.29
Portage (city) Porter County	268	0.74
Highland (town) Lake County	259	1.09

Top 10 Places Sorted by Percent of Total Population
Based on all places, regardless of total population

Place	Population	%
Shorewood Forest (cdp) Porter County	139	4.61
Munster (town) Lake County	984	4.23
Reynolds (town) White County	20	3.29
St. John (town) Lake County	439	3.20
Pottawattamie Park (town) LaPorte County	6	3.03
Schererville (town) Lake County	859	3.02
Blanford (cdp) Vermillion County	10	2.88
North Crows Nest (town) Marion County	1	2.38
Hobart (city) Lake County	614	2.16
Whiting (city) Lake County	98	1.95

Top 10 Places Sorted by Percent of Total Population
Based on places with total population of 50,000 or more

Place	Population	%
Hammond (city) Lake County	572	0.70
Bloomington (city) Monroe County	155	0.20
South Bend (city) St. Joseph County	165	0.16
Terre Haute (city) Vigo County	66	0.11
Indianapolis (city) Marion County	777	0.10
Fishers (town) Hamilton County	47	0.07
Carmel (city) Hamilton County	40	0.05
Fort Wayne (city) Allen County	75	0.03
Muncie (city) Delaware County	15	0.02
Anderson (city) Madison County	12	0.02

Slavic

Top 10 Places Sorted by Population
Based on all places, regardless of total population

Place	Population	%
Indianapolis (city) Marion County	455	0.06
Zionsville (town) Boone County	119	0.89
Fort Wayne (city) Allen County	92	0.04
Valparaiso (city) Porter County	82	0.26
Schererville (town) Lake County	67	0.24
Shorewood Forest (cdp) Porter County	62	2.06
Fishers (town) Hamilton County	50	0.07
Chesterton (town) Porter County	42	0.32
Portage (city) Porter County	42	0.12
Highland (town) Lake County	40	0.17

Top 10 Places Sorted by Percent of Total Population
Based on all places, regardless of total population

Place	Population	%
Long Beach (town) LaPorte County	32	2.19
Shorewood Forest (cdp) Porter County	62	2.06
Rocky Ripple (town) Marion County	8	1.24
Dayton (town) Tippecanoe County	11	1.15
Zionsville (town) Boone County	119	0.89
Hebron (town) Porter County	29	0.83
Lagrange (town) LaGrange County	22	0.80
Remington (town) Jasper County	10	0.78
Scottsburg (city) Scott County	38	0.57
Ogden Dunes (town) Porter County	6	0.49

Top 10 Places Sorted by Percent of Total Population
Based on places with total population of 50,000 or more

Place	Population	%
Fishers (town) Hamilton County	50	0.07
Indianapolis (city) Marion County	455	0.06
Terre Haute (city) Vigo County	32	0.05
Fort Wayne (city) Allen County	92	0.04
Lafayette (city) Tippecanoe County	27	0.04
Bloomington (city) Monroe County	23	0.03
Hammond (city) Lake County	22	0.03
Muncie (city) Delaware County	22	0.03
Anderson (city) Madison County	13	0.02
Gary (city) Lake County	12	0.01

Slovak

Top 10 Places Sorted by Population
Based on all places, regardless of total population

Place	Population	%
Hammond (city) Lake County	1,791	2.20
Indianapolis (city) Marion County	1,058	0.13
Schererville (town) Lake County	1,051	3.69
Highland (town) Lake County	896	3.78
Munster (town) Lake County	814	3.50
Portage (city) Porter County	766	2.11
Hobart (city) Lake County	689	2.43
Whiting (city) Lake County	584	11.63
Merrillville (town) Lake County	576	1.67
Valparaiso (city) Porter County	530	1.71

Top 10 Places Sorted by Percent of Total Population
Based on all places, regardless of total population

Place	Population	%
Whiting (city) Lake County	584	11.63
Mexico (cdp) Miami County	66	9.43
Alton (town) Crawford County	6	7.06
Hebron (town) Porter County	174	4.96
Highland (town) Lake County	896	3.78
Schererville (town) Lake County	1,051	3.69
Ogden Dunes (town) Porter County	45	3.67
Munster (town) Lake County	814	3.50
St. John (town) Lake County	425	3.09
Pottawattamie Park (town) LaPorte County	6	3.03

Top 10 Places Sorted by Percent of Total Population
Based on places with total population of 50,000 or more

Place	Population	%
Hammond (city) Lake County	1,791	2.20
Carmel (city) Hamilton County	356	0.46
Gary (city) Lake County	209	0.25
Bloomington (city) Monroe County	194	0.25
Fort Wayne (city) Allen County	468	0.18
Muncie (city) Delaware County	118	0.17
Indianapolis (city) Marion County	1,058	0.13
Evansville (city) Vanderburgh County	157	0.13
South Bend (city) St. Joseph County	131	0.13
Terre Haute (city) Vigo County	60	0.10

Slovene

Top 10 Places Sorted by Population
Based on all places, regardless of total population

Place	Population	%
Indianapolis (city) Marion County	497	0.06
Portage (city) Porter County	218	0.60
Carmel (city) Hamilton County	109	0.14
Westfield (town) Hamilton County	84	0.30
Greenwood (city) Johnson County	75	0.16
Bloomington (city) Monroe County	65	0.08
Dyer (town) Lake County	64	0.40
Granger (cdp) St. Joseph County	59	0.21
Fishers (town) Hamilton County	54	0.08
Munster (town) Lake County	51	0.22

Top 10 Places Sorted by Percent of Total Population
Based on all places, regardless of total population

Place	Population	%
Clermont (town) Marion County	34	2.47
Dune Acres (town) Porter County	3	1.15
Indian Village (town) St. Joseph County	1	1.02
Westville (town) LaPorte County	42	0.74
Porter (town) Porter County	36	0.73
Portage (city) Porter County	218	0.60
Columbia City (city) Whitley County	46	0.56
Lakes of the Four Seasons (cdp) Lake County	40	0.53
Dyer (town) Lake County	64	0.40
Ogden Dunes (town) Porter County	4	0.33

Top 10 Places Sorted by Percent of Total Population
Based on places with total population of 50,000 or more

Place	Population	%
Carmel (city) Hamilton County	109	0.14
Bloomington (city) Monroe County	65	0.08
Fishers (town) Hamilton County	54	0.08
Indianapolis (city) Marion County	497	0.06
Elkhart (city) Elkhart County	18	0.03
Terre Haute (city) Vigo County	16	0.03
Anderson (city) Madison County	9	0.02
Fort Wayne (city) Allen County	37	0.01
South Bend (city) St. Joseph County	9	0.01
Evansville (city) Vanderburgh County	0	0.00

Soviet Union

Top 10 Places Sorted by Population
Based on all places, regardless of total population

Place	Population	%
Aberdeen (cdp) Porter County	0	0.00
Advance (town) Boone County	0	0.00
Akron (town) Fulton County	0	0.00
Alamo (town) Montgomery County	0	0.00
Albany (town) Delaware County	0	0.00
Albion (town) Noble County	0	0.00
Alexandria (city) Madison County	0	0.00
Alfordsville (town) Daviess County	0	0.00
Alton (town) Crawford County	0	0.00
Altona (town) DeKalb County	0	0.00

Top 10 Places Sorted by Percent of Total Population
Based on all places, regardless of total population

Place	Population	%
Aberdeen (cdp) Porter County	0	0.00
Advance (town) Boone County	0	0.00
Akron (town) Fulton County	0	0.00
Alamo (town) Montgomery County	0	0.00
Albany (town) Delaware County	0	0.00
Albion (town) Noble County	0	0.00
Alexandria (city) Madison County	0	0.00
Alfordsville (town) Daviess County	0	0.00
Alton (town) Crawford County	0	0.00
Altona (town) DeKalb County	0	0.00

Top 10 Places Sorted by Percent of Total Population
Based on places with total population of 50,000 or more

Place	Population	%
Anderson (city) Madison County	0	0.00
Bloomington (city) Monroe County	0	0.00
Carmel (city) Hamilton County	0	0.00
Elkhart (city) Elkhart County	0	0.00
Evansville (city) Vanderburgh County	0	0.00
Fishers (town) Hamilton County	0	0.00
Fort Wayne (city) Allen County	0	0.00
Gary (city) Lake County	0	0.00
Hammond (city) Lake County	0	0.00
Indianapolis (city) Marion County	0	0.00

Swedish

Top 10 Places Sorted by Population
Based on all places, regardless of total population

Place	Population	%
Indianapolis (city) Marion County	5,593	0.69
Fort Wayne (city) Allen County	1,940	0.76
South Bend (city) St. Joseph County	1,638	1.60
Bloomington (city) Monroe County	1,462	1.86
Carmel (city) Hamilton County	1,414	1.84
Fishers (town) Hamilton County	1,288	1.80
Mishawaka (city) St. Joseph County	1,045	2.18
Hammond (city) Lake County	1,016	1.25
Valparaiso (city) Porter County	906	2.92
Portage (city) Porter County	786	2.17

Top 10 Places Sorted by Percent of Total Population
Based on all places, regardless of total population

Place	Population	%
Point Isabel (cdp) Grant County	9	16.67
State Line City (town) Warren County	17	13.93
Spring Lake (town) Hancock County	35	11.82

Shelby (cdp) Lake County	36	9.89
Fish Lake (cdp) LaPorte County	68	7.60
Spring Hill (town) Marion County	6	7.14
Winfield (town) Lake County	258	6.52
Koontz Lake (cdp) Starke County	99	6.10
New Carlisle (town) St. Joseph County	102	5.54
Morocco (town) Newton County	48	5.47

Top 10 Places Sorted by Percent of Total Population

Based on places with total population of 50,000 or more

Place	Population	%
Bloomington (city) Monroe County	1,462	1.86
Carmel (city) Hamilton County	1,414	1.84
Fishers (town) Hamilton County	1,288	1.80
South Bend (city) St. Joseph County	1,638	1.60
Hammond (city) Lake County	1,016	1.25
Lafayette (city) Tippecanoe County	556	0.84
Elkhart (city) Elkhart County	422	0.81
Terre Haute (city) Vigo County	475	0.79
Fort Wayne (city) Allen County	1,940	0.76
Muncie (city) Delaware County	494	0.71

Swiss

Top 10 Places Sorted by Population

Based on all places, regardless of total population

Place	Population	%
Fort Wayne (city) Allen County	2,499	0.98
Indianapolis (city) Marion County	2,276	0.28
Goshen (city) Elkhart County	1,482	4.74
Berne (city) Adams County	1,005	24.67
Fishers (town) Hamilton County	576	0.80
Bluffton (city) Wells County	526	5.52
Elkhart (city) Elkhart County	504	0.97
Bloomington (city) Monroe County	457	0.58
Carmel (city) Hamilton County	431	0.56
South Bend (city) St. Joseph County	343	0.34

Top 10 Places Sorted by Percent of Total Population

Based on all places, regardless of total population

Place	Population	%
Berne (city) Adams County	1,005	24.67
Bryant (town) Jay County	46	15.33
Monroe (town) Adams County	137	15.02
Wakarusa (town) Elkhart County	162	8.86
Vera Cruz (town) Wells County	14	7.73
Geneva (town) Adams County	86	7.00
Waterloo (town) DeKalb County	127	5.82
Bluffton (city) Wells County	526	5.52
Topeka (town) LaGrange County	68	5.41
Shipshewana (town) LaGrange County	32	5.36

Top 10 Places Sorted by Percent of Total Population

Based on places with total population of 50,000 or more

Place	Population	%
Fort Wayne (city) Allen County	2,499	0.98
Elkhart (city) Elkhart County	504	0.97
Fishers (town) Hamilton County	576	0.80
Bloomington (city) Monroe County	457	0.58
Carmel (city) Hamilton County	431	0.56
Muncie (city) Delaware County	326	0.47
Lafayette (city) Tippecanoe County	302	0.46
South Bend (city) St. Joseph County	343	0.34
Indianapolis (city) Marion County	2,276	0.28
Terre Haute (city) Vigo County	165	0.27

Turkish

Top 10 Places Sorted by Population

Based on all places, regardless of total population

Place	Population	%
Indianapolis (city) Marion County	243	0.03
Bloomington (city) Monroe County	111	0.14
South Bend (city) St. Joseph County	104	0.10
West Lafayette (city) Tippecanoe County	99	0.34
Elwood (city) Madison County	73	0.82
Carmel (city) Hamilton County	69	0.09
Noblesville (city) Hamilton County	52	0.11
Lafayette (city) Tippecanoe County	49	0.07
Fort Wayne (city) Allen County	46	0.02
Franklin (city) Johnson County	36	0.16

Top 10 Places Sorted by Percent of Total Population

Based on all places, regardless of total population

Place	Population	%
Universal (town) Vermillion County	13	3.40
Idaville (cdp) White County	9	1.77
Harmony (town) Clay County	11	1.73
Elwood (city) Madison County	73	0.82
Roseland (town) St. Joseph County	8	0.67
Fillmore (town) Putnam County	3	0.67
Dana (town) Vermillion County	3	0.59
West Lafayette (city) Tippecanoe County	99	0.34
Jasonville (city) Greene County	7	0.30
Meridian Hills (town) Marion County	3	0.18

Top 10 Places Sorted by Percent of Total Population

Based on places with total population of 50,000 or more

Place	Population	%
Bloomington (city) Monroe County	111	0.14
South Bend (city) St. Joseph County	104	0.10
Carmel (city) Hamilton County	69	0.09
Lafayette (city) Tippecanoe County	49	0.07
Anderson (city) Madison County	33	0.06
Muncie (city) Delaware County	34	0.05
Terre Haute (city) Vigo County	23	0.04
Indianapolis (city) Marion County	243	0.03
Fort Wayne (city) Allen County	46	0.02
Evansville (city) Vanderburgh County	25	0.02

Ukrainian

Top 10 Places Sorted by Population

Based on all places, regardless of total population

Place	Population	%
Indianapolis (city) Marion County	792	0.10
Noblesville (city) Hamilton County	436	0.90
Fort Wayne (city) Allen County	293	0.12
Carmel (city) Hamilton County	271	0.35
Hammond (city) Lake County	244	0.30
Bloomington (city) Monroe County	232	0.30
South Bend (city) St. Joseph County	214	0.21
Hobart (city) Lake County	157	0.55
Highland (town) Lake County	155	0.65
Portage (city) Porter County	145	0.40

Top 10 Places Sorted by Percent of Total Population

Based on all places, regardless of total population

Place	Population	%
Darlington (town) Montgomery County	29	3.36
Kingman (town) Fountain County	20	3.32
Bourbon (town) Marshall County	41	2.28
New Paris (cdp) Elkhart County	28	2.14
Melody Hill (cdp) Vanderburgh County	73	2.11
Lake Santee (cdp) Decatur County	11	1.72
Shelby (cdp) Lake County	6	1.65
Milford (town) Kosciusko County	25	1.59
Dunlap (cdp) Elkhart County	91	1.57
Otwell (cdp) Pike County	10	1.47

Top 10 Places Sorted by Percent of Total Population

Based on places with total population of 50,000 or more

Place	Population	%
Carmel (city) Hamilton County	271	0.35
Hammond (city) Lake County	244	0.30
Bloomington (city) Monroe County	232	0.30
South Bend (city) St. Joseph County	214	0.21
Fishers (town) Hamilton County	97	0.14
Lafayette (city) Tippecanoe County	94	0.14
Fort Wayne (city) Allen County	293	0.12
Evansville (city) Vanderburgh County	129	0.11
Indianapolis (city) Marion County	792	0.10
Elkhart (city) Elkhart County	39	0.08

Welsh

Top 10 Places Sorted by Population

Based on all places, regardless of total population

Place	Population	%
Indianapolis (city) Marion County	4,603	0.57
Fort Wayne (city) Allen County	1,388	0.55
Fishers (town) Hamilton County	930	1.30
Bloomington (city) Monroe County	840	1.07
Carmel (city) Hamilton County	628	0.82
Terre Haute (city) Vigo County	591	0.98
Muncie (city) Delaware County	511	0.73
Noblesville (city) Hamilton County	497	1.02
Lawrence (city) Marion County	454	1.02
Greenwood (city) Johnson County	412	0.87

Top 10 Places Sorted by Percent of Total Population

Based on all places, regardless of total population

Place	Population	%
Saratoga (town) Randolph County	31	16.49
Ragsdale (cdp) Knox County	16	14.41
Newport (town) Vermillion County	39	10.18
Jalapa (cdp) Grant County	16	8.08
Pennville (town) Jay County	58	7.86
Westphalia (cdp) Knox County	10	6.99
Fowlerton (town) Grant County	18	6.84
Pottawattamie Park (town) LaPorte County	11	5.56
Chrisney (town) Spencer County	32	5.09
Dublin (town) Wayne County	29	5.04

Top 10 Places Sorted by Percent of Total Population

Based on places with total population of 50,000 or more

Place	Population	%
Fishers (town) Hamilton County	930	1.30
Bloomington (city) Monroe County	840	1.07
Terre Haute (city) Vigo County	591	0.98
Carmel (city) Hamilton County	628	0.82
Muncie (city) Delaware County	511	0.73
Anderson (city) Madison County	399	0.70
Indianapolis (city) Marion County	4,603	0.57
Fort Wayne (city) Allen County	1,388	0.55
Lafayette (city) Tippecanoe County	360	0.54
Elkhart (city) Elkhart County	213	0.41

West Indian, excluding Hispanic

Top 10 Places Sorted by Population

Based on all places, regardless of total population

Place	Population	%
Indianapolis (city) Marion County	1,846	0.23
Fort Wayne (city) Allen County	665	0.26
Gary (city) Lake County	265	0.31
Cumberland (town) Marion County	175	3.03
East Chicago (city) Lake County	146	0.48
Hammond (city) Lake County	135	0.17
Elkhart (city) Elkhart County	121	0.23
South Bend (city) St. Joseph County	117	0.11
Bloomington (city) Monroe County	96	0.12
French Lick (town) Orange County	84	4.37

Top 10 Places Sorted by Percent of Total Population

Based on all places, regardless of total population

Place	Population	%
French Lick (town) Orange County	84	4.37
Oolitic (town) Lawrence County	47	3.45
Cumberland (town) Marion County	175	3.03
Ligonier (city) Noble County	75	1.75
Tri-Lakes (cdp) Whitley County	28	1.70
Avon (town) Hendricks County	77	0.66
Utica (town) Clark County	5	0.56
Washington (city) Daviess County	63	0.55
Newburgh (town) Warrick County	18	0.55
Green (town) Howard County	11	0.55

Top 10 Places Sorted by Percent of Total Population

Based on places with total population of 50,000 or more

Place	Population	%
Gary (city) Lake County	265	0.31
Fort Wayne (city) Allen County	665	0.26
Indianapolis (city) Marion County	1,846	0.23
Elkhart (city) Elkhart County	121	0.23
Hammond (city) Lake County	135	0.17
Bloomington (city) Monroe County	96	0.12
South Bend (city) St. Joseph County	117	0.11
Anderson (city) Madison County	56	0.10
Fishers (town) Hamilton County	58	0.08
Carmel (city) Hamilton County	55	0.07

West Indian: Bahamian, excluding Hispanic

Top 10 Places Sorted by Population
Based on all places, regardless of total population

Place	Population	%
Vincennes (city) Knox County	34	0.19
Newburgh (town) Warrick County	18	0.55
Crown Point (city) Lake County	14	0.05
Purdue University (cdp) Tippecanoe County	13	0.10
South Bend (city) St. Joseph County	9	0.01
Indianapolis (city) Marion County	8	<0.01
Aberdeen (cdp) Porter County	0	0.00
Advance (town) Boone County	0	0.00
Akron (town) Fulton County	0	0.00
Alamo (town) Montgomery County	0	0.00

Top 10 Places Sorted by Percent of Total Population
Based on all places, regardless of total population

Place	Population	%
Newburgh (town) Warrick County	18	0.55
Vincennes (city) Knox County	34	0.19
Purdue University (cdp) Tippecanoe County	13	0.10
Crown Point (city) Lake County	14	0.05
South Bend (city) St. Joseph County	9	0.01
Indianapolis (city) Marion County	8	<0.01
Aberdeen (cdp) Porter County	0	0.00
Advance (town) Boone County	0	0.00
Akron (town) Fulton County	0	0.00
Alamo (town) Montgomery County	0	0.00

Top 10 Places Sorted by Percent of Total Population
Based on places with total population of 50,000 or more

Place	Population	%
South Bend (city) St. Joseph County	9	0.01
Indianapolis (city) Marion County	8	<0.01
Anderson (city) Madison County	0	0.00
Bloomington (city) Monroe County	0	0.00
Carmel (city) Hamilton County	0	0.00
Elkhart (city) Elkhart County	0	0.00
Evansville (city) Vanderburgh County	0	0.00
Fishers (town) Hamilton County	0	0.00
Fort Wayne (city) Allen County	0	0.00
Gary (city) Lake County	0	0.00

West Indian: Barbadian, excluding Hispanic

Top 10 Places Sorted by Population
Based on all places, regardless of total population

Place	Population	%
Indianapolis (city) Marion County	55	0.01
Muncie (city) Delaware County	28	0.04
Tri-Lakes (cdp) Whitley County	14	0.85
Aberdeen (cdp) Porter County	0	0.00
Advance (town) Boone County	0	0.00
Akron (town) Fulton County	0	0.00
Alamo (town) Montgomery County	0	0.00
Albany (town) Delaware County	0	0.00
Albion (town) Noble County	0	0.00
Alexandria (city) Madison County	0	0.00

Top 10 Places Sorted by Percent of Total Population
Based on all places, regardless of total population

Place	Population	%
Tri-Lakes (cdp) Whitley County	14	0.85
Muncie (city) Delaware County	28	0.04
Indianapolis (city) Marion County	55	0.01
Aberdeen (cdp) Porter County	0	0.00
Advance (town) Boone County	0	0.00
Akron (town) Fulton County	0	0.00
Alamo (town) Montgomery County	0	0.00
Albany (town) Delaware County	0	0.00
Albion (town) Noble County	0	0.00
Alexandria (city) Madison County	0	0.00

Top 10 Places Sorted by Percent of Total Population
Based on places with total population of 50,000 or more

Place	Population	%
Muncie (city) Delaware County	28	0.04
Indianapolis (city) Marion County	55	0.01
Anderson (city) Madison County	0	0.00
Bloomington (city) Monroe County	0	0.00
Carmel (city) Hamilton County	0	0.00
Elkhart (city) Elkhart County	0	0.00
Evansville (city) Vanderburgh County	0	0.00
Fishers (town) Hamilton County	0	0.00
Fort Wayne (city) Allen County	0	0.00
Gary (city) Lake County	0	0.00

West Indian: Belizean, excluding Hispanic

Top 10 Places Sorted by Population
Based on all places, regardless of total population

Place	Population	%
Indianapolis (city) Marion County	51	0.01
Munster (town) Lake County	31	0.13
Westfield (town) Hamilton County	31	0.11
Lawrence (city) Marion County	25	0.06
Aberdeen (cdp) Porter County	0	0.00
Advance (town) Boone County	0	0.00
Akron (town) Fulton County	0	0.00
Alamo (town) Montgomery County	0	0.00
Albany (town) Delaware County	0	0.00
Albion (town) Noble County	0	0.00

Top 10 Places Sorted by Percent of Total Population
Based on all places, regardless of total population

Place	Population	%
Munster (town) Lake County	31	0.13
Westfield (town) Hamilton County	31	0.11
Lawrence (city) Marion County	25	0.06
Indianapolis (city) Marion County	51	0.01
Aberdeen (cdp) Porter County	0	0.00
Advance (town) Boone County	0	0.00
Akron (town) Fulton County	0	0.00
Alamo (town) Montgomery County	0	0.00
Albany (town) Delaware County	0	0.00
Albion (town) Noble County	0	0.00

Top 10 Places Sorted by Percent of Total Population
Based on places with total population of 50,000 or more

Place	Population	%
Indianapolis (city) Marion County	51	0.01
Anderson (city) Madison County	0	0.00
Bloomington (city) Monroe County	0	0.00
Carmel (city) Hamilton County	0	0.00
Elkhart (city) Elkhart County	0	0.00
Evansville (city) Vanderburgh County	0	0.00
Fishers (town) Hamilton County	0	0.00
Fort Wayne (city) Allen County	0	0.00
Gary (city) Lake County	0	0.00
Hammond (city) Lake County	0	0.00

West Indian: Bermudan, excluding Hispanic

Top 10 Places Sorted by Population
Based on all places, regardless of total population

Place	Population	%
Noblesville (city) Hamilton County	19	0.04
Michigan City (city) LaPorte County	9	0.03
Aberdeen (cdp) Porter County	0	0.00
Advance (town) Boone County	0	0.00
Akron (town) Fulton County	0	0.00
Alamo (town) Montgomery County	0	0.00
Albany (town) Delaware County	0	0.00
Albion (town) Noble County	0	0.00
Alexandria (city) Madison County	0	0.00
Alfordsville (town) Daviess County	0	0.00

Top 10 Places Sorted by Percent of Total Population
Based on all places, regardless of total population

Place	Population	%
Noblesville (city) Hamilton County	19	0.04
Michigan City (city) LaPorte County	9	0.03
Aberdeen (cdp) Porter County	0	0.00
Advance (town) Boone County	0	0.00
Akron (town) Fulton County	0	0.00
Alamo (town) Montgomery County	0	0.00
Albany (town) Delaware County	0	0.00
Albion (town) Noble County	0	0.00
Alexandria (city) Madison County	0	0.00
Alfordsville (town) Daviess County	0	0.00

Top 10 Places Sorted by Percent of Total Population
Based on places with total population of 50,000 or more

Place	Population	%
Anderson (city) Madison County	0	0.00
Bloomington (city) Monroe County	0	0.00
Carmel (city) Hamilton County	0	0.00
Elkhart (city) Elkhart County	0	0.00
Evansville (city) Vanderburgh County	0	0.00
Fishers (town) Hamilton County	0	0.00
Fort Wayne (city) Allen County	0	0.00
Gary (city) Lake County	0	0.00
Hammond (city) Lake County	0	0.00
Indianapolis (city) Marion County	0	0.00

West Indian: British West Indian, excluding Hispanic

Top 10 Places Sorted by Population
Based on all places, regardless of total population

Place	Population	%
Avon (town) Hendricks County	77	0.66
Fort Wayne (city) Allen County	74	0.03
East Chicago (city) Lake County	64	0.21
South Bend (city) St. Joseph County	15	0.01
Fishers (town) Hamilton County	13	0.02
Indianapolis (city) Marion County	13	<0.01
Kokomo (city) Howard County	10	0.02
Purdue University (cdp) Tippecanoe County	8	0.06
Aberdeen (cdp) Porter County	0	0.00
Advance (town) Boone County	0	0.00

Top 10 Places Sorted by Percent of Total Population
Based on all places, regardless of total population

Place	Population	%
Avon (town) Hendricks County	77	0.66
East Chicago (city) Lake County	64	0.21
Purdue University (cdp) Tippecanoe County	8	0.06
Fort Wayne (city) Allen County	74	0.03
Fishers (town) Hamilton County	13	0.02
Kokomo (city) Howard County	10	0.02
South Bend (city) St. Joseph County	15	0.01
Indianapolis (city) Marion County	13	<0.01
Aberdeen (cdp) Porter County	0	0.00
Advance (town) Boone County	0	0.00

Top 10 Places Sorted by Percent of Total Population
Based on places with total population of 50,000 or more

Place	Population	%
Fort Wayne (city) Allen County	74	0.03
Fishers (town) Hamilton County	13	0.02
South Bend (city) St. Joseph County	15	0.01
Indianapolis (city) Marion County	13	<0.01
Anderson (city) Madison County	0	0.00
Bloomington (city) Monroe County	0	0.00
Carmel (city) Hamilton County	0	0.00
Elkhart (city) Elkhart County	0	0.00
Evansville (city) Vanderburgh County	0	0.00
Gary (city) Lake County	0	0.00

West Indian: Dutch West Indian, excluding Hispanic

Top 10 Places Sorted by Population
Based on all places, regardless of total population

Place	Population	%
Oolitic (town) Lawrence County	47	3.45
Indianapolis (city) Marion County	38	<0.01
Bloomington (city) Monroe County	23	0.03
Marion (city) Grant County	19	0.06
Lebanon (city) Boone County	14	0.09
Attica (city) Fountain County	13	0.40
Bedford (city) Lawrence County	11	0.08
Connersville (city) Fayette County	11	0.08
New Castle (city) Henry County	11	0.06
South Bend (city) St. Joseph County	11	0.01

Please refer to the Explanation of Data in the front of the book for more detailed information.

Top 10 Places Sorted by Percent of Total Population
Based on all places, regardless of total population

Place	Population	%
Oolitic (town) Lawrence County	47	3.45
Burns Harbor (town) Porter County	6	0.48
Attica (city) Fountain County	13	0.40
West Terre Haute (town) Vigo County	5	0.27
Lebanon (city) Boone County	14	0.09
Bedford (city) Lawrence County	11	0.08
Connersville (city) Fayette County	11	0.08
Marion (city) Grant County	19	0.06
New Castle (city) Henry County	11	0.06
Bloomington (city) Monroe County	23	0.03

Top 10 Places Sorted by Percent of Total Population
Based on places with total population of 50,000 or more

Place	Population	%
Bloomington (city) Monroe County	23	0.03
South Bend (city) St. Joseph County	11	0.01
Lafayette (city) Tippecanoe County	8	0.01
Indianapolis (city) Marion County	38	<0.01
Anderson (city) Madison County	0	0.00
Carmel (city) Hamilton County	0	0.00
Elkhart (city) Elkhart County	0	0.00
Evansville (city) Vanderburgh County	0	0.00
Fishers (town) Hamilton County	0	0.00
Fort Wayne (city) Allen County	0	0.00

West Indian: Haitian, excluding Hispanic

Top 10 Places Sorted by Population
Based on all places, regardless of total population

Place	Population	%
Indianapolis (city) Marion County	635	0.08
Fort Wayne (city) Allen County	377	0.15
Cumberland (town) Marion County	175	3.03
Hammond (city) Lake County	86	0.11
Jeffersonville (city) Clark County	32	0.08
Terre Haute (city) Vigo County	27	0.04
Bremen (town) Marshall County	16	0.35
Carmel (city) Hamilton County	16	0.02
La Porte (city) LaPorte County	15	0.07
Goshen (city) Elkhart County	14	0.04

Top 10 Places Sorted by Percent of Total Population
Based on all places, regardless of total population

Place	Population	%
Cumberland (town) Marion County	175	3.03
Bremen (town) Marshall County	16	0.35
North Manchester (town) Wabash County	10	0.17
Fort Wayne (city) Allen County	377	0.15
Hammond (city) Lake County	86	0.11
Indianapolis (city) Marion County	635	0.08
Jeffersonville (city) Clark County	32	0.08
La Porte (city) LaPorte County	15	0.07
Purdue University (cdp) Tippecanoe County	7	0.05
Terre Haute (city) Vigo County	27	0.04

Top 10 Places Sorted by Percent of Total Population
Based on places with total population of 50,000 or more

Place	Population	%
Fort Wayne (city) Allen County	377	0.15
Hammond (city) Lake County	86	0.11
Indianapolis (city) Marion County	635	0.08
Terre Haute (city) Vigo County	27	0.04
Carmel (city) Hamilton County	16	0.02
Gary (city) Lake County	14	0.02
Lafayette (city) Tippecanoe County	10	0.02
Evansville (city) Vanderburgh County	11	0.01
Anderson (city) Madison County	0	0.00
Bloomington (city) Monroe County	0	0.00

West Indian: Jamaican, excluding Hispanic

Top 10 Places Sorted by Population
Based on all places, regardless of total population

Place	Population	%
Indianapolis (city) Marion County	589	0.07
Fort Wayne (city) Allen County	196	0.08
Gary (city) Lake County	192	0.23
Elkhart (city) Elkhart County	121	0.23
French Lick (town) Orange County	84	4.37
Granger (cdp) St. Joseph County	79	0.28
Ligonier (city) Noble County	75	1.75
Washington (city) Daviess County	63	0.55
Bloomington (city) Monroe County	57	0.07
Hammond (city) Lake County	49	0.06

Top 10 Places Sorted by Percent of Total Population
Based on all places, regardless of total population

Place	Population	%
French Lick (town) Orange County	84	4.37
Ligonier (city) Noble County	75	1.75
Utica (town) Clark County	5	0.56
Washington (city) Daviess County	63	0.55
Green (town) Howard County	11	0.55
Jasper (city) Dubois County	47	0.32
Granger (cdp) St. Joseph County	79	0.28
Gary (city) Lake County	192	0.23
Elkhart (city) Elkhart County	121	0.23
Purdue University (cdp) Tippecanoe County	27	0.21

Top 10 Places Sorted by Percent of Total Population
Based on places with total population of 50,000 or more

Place	Population	%
Gary (city) Lake County	192	0.23
Elkhart (city) Elkhart County	121	0.23
Fort Wayne (city) Allen County	196	0.08
Indianapolis (city) Marion County	589	0.07
Bloomington (city) Monroe County	57	0.07
Hammond (city) Lake County	49	0.06
Fishers (town) Hamilton County	45	0.06
Carmel (city) Hamilton County	39	0.05
Anderson (city) Madison County	29	0.05
Evansville (city) Vanderburgh County	44	0.04

West Indian: Trinidadian and Tobagonian, excluding Hispanic

Top 10 Places Sorted by Population
Based on all places, regardless of total population

Place	Population	%
Indianapolis (city) Marion County	110	0.01
South Bend (city) St. Joseph County	39	0.04
East Chicago (city) Lake County	18	0.06
Notre Dame (cdp) St. Joseph County	13	0.17
Portage (city) Porter County	13	0.04
West Lafayette (city) Tippecanoe County	13	0.04
Noblesville (city) Hamilton County	13	0.03
Aberdeen (cdp) Porter County	0	0.00
Advance (town) Boone County	0	0.00
Akron (town) Fulton County	0	0.00

Top 10 Places Sorted by Percent of Total Population
Based on all places, regardless of total population

Place	Population	%
Notre Dame (cdp) St. Joseph County	13	0.17
East Chicago (city) Lake County	18	0.06
South Bend (city) St. Joseph County	39	0.04
Portage (city) Porter County	13	0.04
West Lafayette (city) Tippecanoe County	13	0.04
Noblesville (city) Hamilton County	13	0.03
Indianapolis (city) Marion County	110	0.01
Aberdeen (cdp) Porter County	0	0.00
Advance (town) Boone County	0	0.00
Akron (town) Fulton County	0	0.00

Top 10 Places Sorted by Percent of Total Population
Based on places with total population of 50,000 or more

Place	Population	%
South Bend (city) St. Joseph County	39	0.04
Indianapolis (city) Marion County	110	0.01
Anderson (city) Madison County	0	0.00
Bloomington (city) Monroe County	0	0.00
Carmel (city) Hamilton County	0	0.00
Elkhart (city) Elkhart County	0	0.00
Evansville (city) Vanderburgh County	0	0.00
Fishers (town) Hamilton County	0	0.00
Fort Wayne (city) Allen County	0	0.00
Gary (city) Lake County	0	0.00

West Indian: U.S. Virgin Islander, excluding Hispanic

Top 10 Places Sorted by Population
Based on all places, regardless of total population

Place	Population	%
Lafayette (city) Tippecanoe County	8	0.01
Aberdeen (cdp) Porter County	0	0.00
Advance (town) Boone County	0	0.00
Akron (town) Fulton County	0	0.00
Alamo (town) Montgomery County	0	0.00
Albany (town) Delaware County	0	0.00
Albion (town) Noble County	0	0.00
Alexandria (city) Madison County	0	0.00
Alfordsville (town) Daviess County	0	0.00
Alton (town) Crawford County	0	0.00

Top 10 Places Sorted by Percent of Total Population
Based on all places, regardless of total population

Place	Population	%
Lafayette (city) Tippecanoe County	8	0.01
Aberdeen (cdp) Porter County	0	0.00
Advance (town) Boone County	0	0.00
Akron (town) Fulton County	0	0.00
Alamo (town) Montgomery County	0	0.00
Albany (town) Delaware County	0	0.00
Albion (town) Noble County	0	0.00
Alexandria (city) Madison County	0	0.00
Alfordsville (town) Daviess County	0	0.00
Alton (town) Crawford County	0	0.00

Top 10 Places Sorted by Percent of Total Population
Based on places with total population of 50,000 or more

Place	Population	%
Lafayette (city) Tippecanoe County	8	0.01
Anderson (city) Madison County	0	0.00
Bloomington (city) Monroe County	0	0.00
Carmel (city) Hamilton County	0	0.00
Elkhart (city) Elkhart County	0	0.00
Evansville (city) Vanderburgh County	0	0.00
Fishers (town) Hamilton County	0	0.00
Fort Wayne (city) Allen County	0	0.00
Gary (city) Lake County	0	0.00
Hammond (city) Lake County	0	0.00

West Indian: West Indian, excluding Hispanic

Top 10 Places Sorted by Population
Based on all places, regardless of total population

Place	Population	%
Indianapolis (city) Marion County	335	0.04
East Chicago (city) Lake County	64	0.21
Mishawaka (city) St. Joseph County	35	0.07
Gary (city) Lake County	34	0.04
South Bend (city) St. Joseph County	31	0.03
Valparaiso (city) Porter County	23	0.07
Fort Wayne (city) Allen County	18	0.01
Bloomington (city) Monroe County	16	0.02
Westfield (town) Hamilton County	12	0.04
Columbus (city) Bartholomew County	10	0.02

Top 10 Places Sorted by Percent of Total Population
Based on all places, regardless of total population

Place	Population	%
Jasonville (city) Greene County	5	0.22
East Chicago (city) Lake County	64	0.21
North Manchester (town) Wabash County	7	0.12
Mishawaka (city) St. Joseph County	35	0.07
Valparaiso (city) Porter County	23	0.07
Tell City (city) Perry County	5	0.07
Indianapolis (city) Marion County	335	0.04
Gary (city) Lake County	34	0.04
Westfield (town) Hamilton County	12	0.04
South Bend (city) St. Joseph County	31	0.03

Top 10 Places Sorted by Percent of Total Population
Based on places with total population of 50,000 or more

Place	Population	%
Indianapolis (city) Marion County	335	0.04

Ancestry

Gary (city) Lake County	34	0.04
South Bend (city) St. Joseph County	31	0.03
Bloomington (city) Monroe County	16	0.02
Fort Wayne (city) Allen County	18	0.01
Anderson (city) Madison County	0	0.00
Carmel (city) Hamilton County	0	0.00
Elkhart (city) Elkhart County	0	0.00
Evansville (city) Vanderburgh County	0	0.00
Fishers (town) Hamilton County	0	0.00

West Indian: Other, excluding Hispanic

Top 10 Places Sorted by Population

Based on all places, regardless of total population

Place	Population	%
Anderson (city) Madison County	27	0.05
Gary (city) Lake County	25	0.03
Marion (city) Grant County	21	0.07
Tri-Lakes (cdp) Whitley County	14	0.85
Purdue University (cdp) Tippecanoe County	14	0.11
Indianapolis (city) Marion County	12	<0.01
Columbus (city) Bartholomew County	8	0.02
Aberdeen (cdp) Porter County	0	0.00
Advance (town) Boone County	0	0.00
Akron (town) Fulton County	0	0.00

Top 10 Places Sorted by Percent of Total Population

Based on all places, regardless of total population

Place	Population	%
Tri-Lakes (cdp) Whitley County	14	0.85
Purdue University (cdp) Tippecanoe County	14	0.11
Marion (city) Grant County	21	0.07
Anderson (city) Madison County	27	0.05
Gary (city) Lake County	25	0.03
Columbus (city) Bartholomew County	8	0.02
Indianapolis (city) Marion County	12	<0.01
Aberdeen (cdp) Porter County	0	0.00
Advance (town) Boone County	0	0.00
Akron (town) Fulton County	0	0.00

Top 10 Places Sorted by Percent of Total Population

Based on places with total population of 50,000 or more

Place	Population	%
Anderson (city) Madison County	27	0.05
Gary (city) Lake County	25	0.03
Indianapolis (city) Marion County	12	<0.01
Bloomington (city) Monroe County	0	0.00
Carmel (city) Hamilton County	0	0.00
Elkhart (city) Elkhart County	0	0.00
Evansville (city) Vanderburgh County	0	0.00
Fishers (town) Hamilton County	0	0.00
Fort Wayne (city) Allen County	0	0.00
Hammond (city) Lake County	0	0.00

Yugoslavian

Top 10 Places Sorted by Population

Based on all places, regardless of total population

Place	Population	%
Fort Wayne (city) Allen County	1,443	0.57
Indianapolis (city) Marion County	531	0.07
South Bend (city) St. Joseph County	514	0.50
Mishawaka (city) St. Joseph County	446	0.93
Fishers (town) Hamilton County	133	0.19
Dyer (town) Lake County	127	0.80
Noblesville (city) Hamilton County	121	0.25
Brownsburg (town) Hendricks County	119	0.58
Schererville (town) Lake County	110	0.39
Munster (town) Lake County	81	0.35

Top 10 Places Sorted by Percent of Total Population

Based on all places, regardless of total population

Place	Population	%
Gosport (town) Owen County	24	2.48
Springport (town) Henry County	4	2.40
Zanesville (town) Wells County	13	1.73
Town of Pines (town) Porter County	10	1.43
Arcadia (town) Hamilton County	17	1.14
Hanover (town) Jefferson County	34	1.01
Mishawaka (city) St. Joseph County	446	0.93
Winamac (town) Pulaski County	24	0.90
North Webster (town) Kosciusko County	10	0.86
Dyer (town) Lake County	127	0.80

Top 10 Places Sorted by Percent of Total Population

Based on places with total population of 50,000 or more

Place	Population	%
Fort Wayne (city) Allen County	1,443	0.57
South Bend (city) St. Joseph County	514	0.50
Fishers (town) Hamilton County	133	0.19
Carmel (city) Hamilton County	67	0.09
Terre Haute (city) Vigo County	55	0.09
Indianapolis (city) Marion County	531	0.07
Bloomington (city) Monroe County	50	0.06
Muncie (city) Delaware County	27	0.04
Gary (city) Lake County	24	0.03
Anderson (city) Madison County	12	0.02

Hispanic Origin Rankings

Hispanic or Latino (of any race)

Top 10 Places Sorted by Population
Based on all places, regardless of total population

Place	Population	%
Indianapolis (city) Marion County	77,352	9.43
Hammond (city) Lake County	27,563	34.10
Fort Wayne (city) Allen County	20,200	7.96
East Chicago (city) Lake County	15,105	50.86
South Bend (city) St. Joseph County	13,116	12.96
Elkhart (city) Elkhart County	11,451	22.48
Goshen (city) Elkhart County	8,903	28.07
Lafayette (city) Tippecanoe County	8,107	12.07
Portage (city) Porter County	6,044	16.41
Lawrence (city) Marion County	5,155	11.21

Top 10 Places Sorted by Percent of Total Population
Based on all places, regardless of total population

Place	Population	%
Ligonier (city) Noble County	2,270	51.53
East Chicago (city) Lake County	15,105	50.86
Ambia (town) Benton County	104	43.51
Whiting (city) Lake County	2,036	40.74
Hammond (city) Lake County	27,563	34.10
Akron (town) Fulton County	351	30.08
Monon (town) White County	505	28.42
Goshen (city) Elkhart County	8,903	28.07
Lake Station (city) Lake County	3,517	27.97
New Chicago (town) Lake County	558	27.42

Top 10 Places Sorted by Percent of Total Population
Based on places with total population of 50,000 or more

Place	Population	%
Hammond (city) Lake County	27,563	34.10
Elkhart (city) Elkhart County	11,451	22.48
South Bend (city) St. Joseph County	13,116	12.96
Lafayette (city) Tippecanoe County	8,107	12.07
Indianapolis (city) Marion County	77,352	9.43
Fort Wayne (city) Allen County	20,200	7.96
Gary (city) Lake County	4,128	5.14
Anderson (city) Madison County	2,719	4.84
Noblesville (city) Hamilton County	2,209	4.25
Bloomington (city) Monroe County	2,823	3.51

Central American, excluding Mexican

Top 10 Places Sorted by Population
Based on all places, regardless of total population

Place	Population	%
Indianapolis (city) Marion County	7,746	0.94
Fort Wayne (city) Allen County	1,346	0.53
Elkhart (city) Elkhart County	912	1.79
Logansport (city) Cass County	641	3.48
Huntingburg (city) Dubois County	533	8.80
Hammond (city) Lake County	526	0.65
Lawrence (city) Marion County	481	1.05
Jasper (city) Dubois County	342	2.27
Goshen (city) Elkhart County	310	0.98
South Bend (city) St. Joseph County	292	0.29

Top 10 Places Sorted by Percent of Total Population
Based on all places, regardless of total population

Place	Population	%
Monon (town) White County	261	14.69
Huntingburg (city) Dubois County	533	8.80
Alton (town) Crawford County	2	3.64
Logansport (city) Cass County	641	3.48
Jonesville (town) Bartholomew County	6	3.39
Brook (town) Newton County	29	2.91
Sidney (town) Kosciusko County	2	2.41
Jasper (city) Dubois County	342	2.27
Washington (city) Daviess County	237	2.06
Plymouth (city) Marshall County	206	2.05

Top 10 Places Sorted by Percent of Total Population
Based on places with total population of 50,000 or more

Place	Population	%
Elkhart (city) Elkhart County	912	1.79
Indianapolis (city) Marion County	7,746	0.94
Hammond (city) Lake County	526	0.65
Fort Wayne (city) Allen County	1,346	0.53
Noblesville (city) Hamilton County	244	0.47
Lafayette (city) Tippecanoe County	283	0.42
South Bend (city) St. Joseph County	292	0.29
Carmel (city) Hamilton County	181	0.23
Bloomington (city) Monroe County	165	0.21
Fishers (town) Hamilton County	162	0.21

Central American: Costa Rican

Top 10 Places Sorted by Population
Based on all places, regardless of total population

Place	Population	%
Indianapolis (city) Marion County	125	0.02
Fort Wayne (city) Allen County	38	0.01
Bloomington (city) Monroe County	21	0.03
Noblesville (city) Hamilton County	19	0.04
Hammond (city) Lake County	18	0.02
Goshen (city) Elkhart County	14	0.04
Purdue University (cdp) Tippecanoe County	12	0.10
Lafayette (city) Tippecanoe County	12	0.02
Plainfield (town) Hendricks County	11	0.04
West Lafayette (city) Tippecanoe County	10	0.03

Top 10 Places Sorted by Percent of Total Population
Based on all places, regardless of total population

Place	Population	%
Fillmore (town) Putnam County	3	0.56
Tecumseh (cdp) Vigo County	2	0.30
Otwell (cdp) Pike County	1	0.23
Wilkinson (town) Hancock County	1	0.22
Bicknell (city) Knox County	5	0.17
Brooklyn (town) Morgan County	2	0.13
Koontz Lake (cdp) Starke County	2	0.13
Shirley (town) Hancock County	1	0.12
Melody Hill (cdp) Vanderburgh County	4	0.11
Purdue University (cdp) Tippecanoe County	12	0.10

Top 10 Places Sorted by Percent of Total Population
Based on places with total population of 50,000 or more

Place	Population	%
Noblesville (city) Hamilton County	19	0.04
Bloomington (city) Monroe County	21	0.03
Indianapolis (city) Marion County	125	0.02
Hammond (city) Lake County	18	0.02
Lafayette (city) Tippecanoe County	12	0.02
Fort Wayne (city) Allen County	38	0.01
Fishers (town) Hamilton County	9	0.01
Carmel (city) Hamilton County	8	0.01
Evansville (city) Vanderburgh County	7	0.01
South Bend (city) St. Joseph County	7	0.01

Central American: Guatemalan

Top 10 Places Sorted by Population
Based on all places, regardless of total population

Place	Population	%
Indianapolis (city) Marion County	1,616	0.20
Fort Wayne (city) Allen County	729	0.29
Logansport (city) Cass County	412	2.24
Hammond (city) Lake County	172	0.21
Lawrence (city) Marion County	140	0.30
Elkhart (city) Elkhart County	93	0.18
Carmel (city) Hamilton County	87	0.11
Columbus (city) Bartholomew County	82	0.19
Lafayette (city) Tippecanoe County	81	0.12
Goshen (city) Elkhart County	71	0.22

Top 10 Places Sorted by Percent of Total Population
Based on all places, regardless of total population

Place	Population	%
Logansport (city) Cass County	412	2.24
Williams Creek (town) Marion County	3	0.74
Mentone (town) Kosciusko County	7	0.70
Delphi (city) Carroll County	20	0.69
Dale (town) Spencer County	11	0.69
West College Corner (town) Union County	4	0.59
Washington (city) Daviess County	66	0.57
Bourbon (town) Marshall County	8	0.44
Pennville (town) Jay County	3	0.43
Wynnedale (town) Marion County	1	0.43

Top 10 Places Sorted by Percent of Total Population
Based on places with total population of 50,000 or more

Place	Population	%
Fort Wayne (city) Allen County	729	0.29
Hammond (city) Lake County	172	0.21
Indianapolis (city) Marion County	1,616	0.20
Elkhart (city) Elkhart County	93	0.18
Lafayette (city) Tippecanoe County	81	0.12
Carmel (city) Hamilton County	87	0.11
Anderson (city) Madison County	59	0.11
Noblesville (city) Hamilton County	59	0.11
South Bend (city) St. Joseph County	66	0.07
Fishers (town) Hamilton County	54	0.07

Central American: Honduran

Top 10 Places Sorted by Population
Based on all places, regardless of total population

Place	Population	%
Indianapolis (city) Marion County	2,302	0.28
Elkhart (city) Elkhart County	390	0.77
Plymouth (city) Marshall County	199	1.98
Lawrence (city) Marion County	161	0.35
Fort Wayne (city) Allen County	129	0.05
Goshen (city) Elkhart County	124	0.39
Hammond (city) Lake County	117	0.14
Logansport (city) Cass County	54	0.29
Plainfield (town) Hendricks County	52	0.19
South Bend (city) St. Joseph County	49	0.05

Top 10 Places Sorted by Percent of Total Population
Based on all places, regardless of total population

Place	Population	%
Alton (town) Crawford County	2	3.64
Plymouth (city) Marshall County	199	1.98
Dupont (town) Jefferson County	6	1.77
Dubois (cdp) Dubois County	8	1.64
Stilesville (town) Hendricks County	4	1.27
Roseland (town) St. Joseph County	7	1.11
Bourbon (town) Marshall County	15	0.83
Bremen (town) Marshall County	37	0.81
Elkhart (city) Elkhart County	390	0.77
Holland (town) Dubois County	4	0.64

Top 10 Places Sorted by Percent of Total Population
Based on places with total population of 50,000 or more

Place	Population	%
Elkhart (city) Elkhart County	390	0.77
Indianapolis (city) Marion County	2,302	0.28
Hammond (city) Lake County	117	0.14
Noblesville (city) Hamilton County	31	0.06
Fort Wayne (city) Allen County	129	0.05
South Bend (city) St. Joseph County	49	0.05
Terre Haute (city) Vigo County	22	0.04
Evansville (city) Vanderburgh County	31	0.03
Bloomington (city) Monroe County	21	0.03
Anderson (city) Madison County	16	0.03

Central American: Nicaraguan

Top 10 Places Sorted by Population
Based on all places, regardless of total population

Place	Population	%
Indianapolis (city) Marion County	668	0.08
Lawrence (city) Marion County	67	0.15
South Bend (city) St. Joseph County	46	0.05
Fort Wayne (city) Allen County	37	0.01
Evansville (city) Vanderburgh County	35	0.03
Bloomington (city) Monroe County	28	0.03
Carmel (city) Hamilton County	20	0.03
Anderson (city) Madison County	19	0.03
Hammond (city) Lake County	19	0.02
Merrillville (town) Lake County	17	0.05

Top 10 Places Sorted by Percent of Total Population
Based on all places, regardless of total population

Place	Population	%
Royal Center (town) Cass County	3	0.35
Geneva (town) Adams County	3	0.23
Reynolds (town) White County	1	0.19
Lawrence (city) Marion County	67	0.15
Patoka (town) Gibson County	1	0.14
Notre Dame (cdp) St. Joseph County	8	0.13
Milford (town) Kosciusko County	2	0.13
Sheridan (town) Hamilton County	3	0.11
Hagers (town) Wayne County	2	0.11
Indianapolis (city) Marion County	668	0.08

Top 10 Places Sorted by Percent of Total Population
Based on places with total population of 50,000 or more

Place	Population	%
Indianapolis (city) Marion County	668	0.08
South Bend (city) St. Joseph County	46	0.05
Evansville (city) Vanderburgh County	35	0.03
Bloomington (city) Monroe County	28	0.03
Carmel (city) Hamilton County	20	0.03
Anderson (city) Madison County	19	0.03
Elkhart (city) Elkhart County	14	0.03
Noblesville (city) Hamilton County	14	0.03
Hammond (city) Lake County	19	0.02
Lafayette (city) Tippecanoe County	16	0.02

Central American: Panamanian

Top 10 Places Sorted by Population
Based on all places, regardless of total population

Place	Population	%
Indianapolis (city) Marion County	274	0.03
Fishers (town) Hamilton County	39	0.05
Fort Wayne (city) Allen County	38	0.01
West Lafayette (city) Tippecanoe County	28	0.09
Carmel (city) Hamilton County	28	0.04
Lafayette (city) Tippecanoe County	26	0.04
Lawrence (city) Marion County	25	0.05
Evansville (city) Vanderburgh County	24	0.02
Bloomington (city) Monroe County	22	0.03
Hammond (city) Lake County	21	0.03

Top 10 Places Sorted by Percent of Total Population
Based on all places, regardless of total population

Place	Population	%
Sidney (town) Kosciusko County	2	2.41
Lake Santee (cdp) Decatur County	3	0.37
Ogden Dunes (town) Porter County	4	0.36
Bristol (town) Elkhart County	4	0.25
Arcadia (town) Hamilton County	4	0.24
Notre Dame (cdp) St. Joseph County	11	0.18
Akron (town) Fulton County	2	0.17
Speedway (town) Marion County	19	0.16
Dana (town) Vermillion County	1	0.16
Purdue University (cdp) Tippecanoe County	17	0.14

Top 10 Places Sorted by Percent of Total Population
Based on places with total population of 50,000 or more

Place	Population	%
Fishers (town) Hamilton County	39	0.05
Carmel (city) Hamilton County	28	0.04
Lafayette (city) Tippecanoe County	26	0.04
Indianapolis (city) Marion County	274	0.03
Bloomington (city) Monroe County	22	0.03
Hammond (city) Lake County	21	0.03
Muncie (city) Delaware County	21	0.03
Evansville (city) Vanderburgh County	24	0.02
South Bend (city) St. Joseph County	21	0.02
Noblesville (city) Hamilton County	10	0.02

Central American: Salvadoran

Top 10 Places Sorted by Population
Based on all places, regardless of total population

Place	Population	%
Indianapolis (city) Marion County	2,695	0.33
Huntingburg (city) Dubois County	498	8.22
Elkhart (city) Elkhart County	400	0.79
Fort Wayne (city) Allen County	369	0.15
Jasper (city) Dubois County	290	1.93
Monon (town) White County	248	13.96
Hammond (city) Lake County	174	0.22
Logansport (city) Cass County	166	0.90
Washington (city) Daviess County	154	1.34
Lafayette (city) Tippecanoe County	138	0.21

Top 10 Places Sorted by Percent of Total Population
Based on all places, regardless of total population

Place	Population	%
Monon (town) White County	248	13.96
Huntingburg (city) Dubois County	498	8.22
Jonesville (town) Bartholomew County	6	3.39
Brook (town) Newton County	29	2.91
Jasper (city) Dubois County	290	1.93
Chalmers (town) White County	7	1.38
Washington (city) Daviess County	154	1.34
Idaville (cdp) White County	6	1.30
Stinesville (town) Monroe County	2	1.01
Logansport (city) Cass County	166	0.90

Top 10 Places Sorted by Percent of Total Population
Based on places with total population of 50,000 or more

Place	Population	%
Elkhart (city) Elkhart County	400	0.79
Indianapolis (city) Marion County	2,695	0.33
Hammond (city) Lake County	174	0.22
Lafayette (city) Tippecanoe County	138	0.21
Noblesville (city) Hamilton County	111	0.21
Fort Wayne (city) Allen County	369	0.15
South Bend (city) St. Joseph County	98	0.10
Evansville (city) Vanderburgh County	45	0.04
Bloomington (city) Monroe County	31	0.04
Carmel (city) Hamilton County	28	0.04

Central American: Other Central American

Top 10 Places Sorted by Population
Based on all places, regardless of total population

Place	Population	%
Indianapolis (city) Marion County	66	0.01
Elkhart (city) Elkhart County	12	0.02
Westfield (town) Hamilton County	11	0.04
Columbus (city) Bartholomew County	6	0.01
Fort Wayne (city) Allen County	6	<0.01
Hammond (city) Lake County	5	0.01
Evansville (city) Vanderburgh County	5	<0.01
South Bend (city) St. Joseph County	5	<0.01
Fowler (town) Benton County	4	0.17
East Chicago (city) Lake County	4	0.01

Top 10 Places Sorted by Percent of Total Population
Based on all places, regardless of total population

Place	Population	%
Fowler (town) Benton County	4	0.17
Westfield (town) Hamilton County	11	0.04
Osceola (town) St. Joseph County	1	0.04
Elkhart (city) Elkhart County	12	0.02
Avon (town) Hendricks County	3	0.02
Notre Dame (cdp) St. Joseph County	1	0.02
Indianapolis (city) Marion County	66	0.01
Columbus (city) Bartholomew County	6	0.01
Hammond (city) Lake County	5	0.01
East Chicago (city) Lake County	4	0.01

Top 10 Places Sorted by Percent of Total Population
Based on places with total population of 50,000 or more

Place	Population	%
Elkhart (city) Elkhart County	12	0.02
Indianapolis (city) Marion County	66	0.01
Hammond (city) Lake County	5	0.01
Fort Wayne (city) Allen County	6	<0.01
Evansville (city) Vanderburgh County	5	<0.01
South Bend (city) St. Joseph County	5	<0.01
Bloomington (city) Monroe County	4	<0.01
Fishers (town) Hamilton County	3	<0.01
Carmel (city) Hamilton County	1	<0.01
Muncie (city) Delaware County	1	<0.01

Cuban

Top 10 Places Sorted by Population
Based on all places, regardless of total population

Place	Population	%
Indianapolis (city) Marion County	739	0.09
Fort Wayne (city) Allen County	174	0.07
Hammond (city) Lake County	140	0.17
Bloomington (city) Monroe County	126	0.16
South Bend (city) St. Joseph County	111	0.11
Carmel (city) Hamilton County	101	0.13
Fishers (town) Hamilton County	90	0.12
Lafayette (city) Tippecanoe County	78	0.12
Jeffersonville (city) Clark County	72	0.16
Evansville (city) Vanderburgh County	64	0.05

Top 10 Places Sorted by Percent of Total Population
Based on all places, regardless of total population

Place	Population	%
Economy (town) Wayne County	4	2.14
Sidney (town) Kosciusko County	1	1.20
Modoc (town) Randolph County	2	1.02
Notre Dame (cdp) St. Joseph County	55	0.92
Collegeville (cdp) Jasper County	2	0.61
Hayden (cdp) Jennings County	3	0.58
Lewisville (town) Henry County	2	0.55
Hudson Lake (cdp) LaPorte County	7	0.54
New Salisbury (cdp) Harrison County	3	0.49
Shelburn (town) Sullivan County	6	0.48

Top 10 Places Sorted by Percent of Total Population
Based on places with total population of 50,000 or more

Place	Population	%
Hammond (city) Lake County	140	0.17
Bloomington (city) Monroe County	126	0.16
Carmel (city) Hamilton County	101	0.13
Fishers (town) Hamilton County	90	0.12
Lafayette (city) Tippecanoe County	78	0.12
South Bend (city) St. Joseph County	111	0.11
Indianapolis (city) Marion County	739	0.09
Gary (city) Lake County	61	0.08
Terre Haute (city) Vigo County	46	0.08
Noblesville (city) Hamilton County	43	0.08

Dominican Republic

Top 10 Places Sorted by Population
Based on all places, regardless of total population

Place	Population	%
Indianapolis (city) Marion County	1,124	0.14
Fort Wayne (city) Allen County	72	0.03
Fishers (town) Hamilton County	46	0.06
Bloomington (city) Monroe County	43	0.05
Logansport (city) Cass County	42	0.23
South Bend (city) St. Joseph County	42	0.04
Noblesville (city) Hamilton County	40	0.08
Carmel (city) Hamilton County	40	0.05
Lafayette (city) Tippecanoe County	33	0.05
Speedway (town) Marion County	32	0.27

Top 10 Places Sorted by Percent of Total Population
Based on all places, regardless of total population

Place	Population	%
Painted Hills (cdp) Morgan County	2	0.30
Liberty (town) Union County	6	0.28
Speedway (town) Marion County	32	0.27

Logansport (city) Cass County	42	0.23
Crothersville (town) Jackson County	3	0.19
Avon (town) Hendricks County	23	0.18
Fortville (town) Hancock County	7	0.18
Akron (town) Fulton County	2	0.17
Indianapolis (city) Marion County	1,124	0.14
Brownsburg (town) Hendricks County	23	0.11

Top 10 Places Sorted by Percent of Total Population

Based on places with total population of 50,000 or more

Place	Population	%
Indianapolis (city) Marion County	1,124	0.14
Noblesville (city) Hamilton County	40	0.08
Fishers (town) Hamilton County	46	0.06
Bloomington (city) Monroe County	43	0.05
Carmel (city) Hamilton County	40	0.05
Lafayette (city) Tippecanoe County	33	0.05
South Bend (city) St. Joseph County	42	0.04
Elkhart (city) Elkhart County	19	0.04
Fort Wayne (city) Allen County	72	0.03
Gary (city) Lake County	24	0.03

Mexican

Top 10 Places Sorted by Population

Based on all places, regardless of total population

Place	Population	%
Indianapolis (city) Marion County	56,771	6.92
Hammond (city) Lake County	22,684	28.06
Fort Wayne (city) Allen County	15,545	6.13
East Chicago (city) Lake County	11,819	39.80
South Bend (city) St. Joseph County	11,025	10.90
Elkhart (city) Elkhart County	9,313	18.28
Goshen (city) Elkhart County	7,781	24.53
Lafayette (city) Tippecanoe County	6,965	10.37
Portage (city) Porter County	4,011	10.89
Lawrence (city) Marion County	3,827	8.32

Top 10 Places Sorted by Percent of Total Population

Based on all places, regardless of total population

Place	Population	%
Ligonier (city) Noble County	2,185	49.60
Ambia (town) Benton County	104	43.51
East Chicago (city) Lake County	11,819	39.80
Whiting (city) Lake County	1,765	35.32
Akron (town) Fulton County	342	29.31
Hammond (city) Lake County	22,684	28.06
Goshen (city) Elkhart County	7,781	24.53
Frankfort (city) Clinton County	3,693	22.49
New Chicago (town) Lake County	427	20.98
Lake Station (city) Lake County	2,522	20.06

Top 10 Places Sorted by Percent of Total Population

Based on places with total population of 50,000 or more

Place	Population	%
Hammond (city) Lake County	22,684	28.06
Elkhart (city) Elkhart County	9,313	18.28
South Bend (city) St. Joseph County	11,025	10.90
Lafayette (city) Tippecanoe County	6,965	10.37
Indianapolis (city) Marion County	56,771	6.92
Fort Wayne (city) Allen County	15,545	6.13
Anderson (city) Madison County	2,199	3.92
Gary (city) Lake County	2,553	3.18
Terre Haute (city) Vigo County	1,469	2.42
Noblesville (city) Hamilton County	1,245	2.40

Puerto Rican

Top 10 Places Sorted by Population

Based on all places, regardless of total population

Place	Population	%
Indianapolis (city) Marion County	3,431	0.42
Hammond (city) Lake County	3,081	3.81
East Chicago (city) Lake County	2,528	8.51
Portage (city) Porter County	1,608	4.37
Gary (city) Lake County	1,223	1.52
Fort Wayne (city) Allen County	939	0.37
Hobart (city) Lake County	850	2.93
Lake Station (city) Lake County	843	6.71
Merrillville (town) Lake County	817	2.32
South Bend (city) St. Joseph County	525	0.52

Top 10 Places Sorted by Percent of Total Population

Based on all places, regardless of total population

Place	Population	%
East Chicago (city) Lake County	2,528	8.51
Lake Station (city) Lake County	843	6.71
New Chicago (town) Lake County	98	4.82
Portage (city) Porter County	1,608	4.37
Hammond (city) Lake County	3,081	3.81
Whiting (city) Lake County	163	3.26
Monterey (town) Pulaski County	7	3.21
Hobart (city) Lake County	850	2.93
Cadiz (town) Henry County	4	2.67
Crandall (town) Harrison County	4	2.63

Top 10 Places Sorted by Percent of Total Population

Based on places with total population of 50,000 or more

Place	Population	%
Hammond (city) Lake County	3,081	3.81
Gary (city) Lake County	1,223	1.52
Elkhart (city) Elkhart County	392	0.77
South Bend (city) St. Joseph County	525	0.52
Fishers (town) Hamilton County	349	0.45
Bloomington (city) Monroe County	348	0.43
Indianapolis (city) Marion County	3,431	0.42
Noblesville (city) Hamilton County	210	0.40
Lafayette (city) Tippecanoe County	253	0.38
Fort Wayne (city) Allen County	939	0.37

South American

Top 10 Places Sorted by Population

Based on all places, regardless of total population

Place	Population	%
Indianapolis (city) Marion County	2,068	0.25
Fort Wayne (city) Allen County	651	0.26
Fishers (town) Hamilton County	359	0.47
Bloomington (city) Monroe County	349	0.43
Carmel (city) Hamilton County	310	0.39
South Bend (city) St. Joseph County	275	0.27
Noblesville (city) Hamilton County	253	0.49
West Lafayette (city) Tippecanoe County	241	0.81
Lawrence (city) Marion County	164	0.36
Hammond (city) Lake County	141	0.17

Top 10 Places Sorted by Percent of Total Population

Based on all places, regardless of total population

Place	Population	%
Woodlawn Heights (town) Madison County	1	1.27
Notre Dame (cdp) St. Joseph County	70	1.17
Beverly Shores (town) Porter County	6	0.98
Oakland City (city) Gibson County	21	0.86
Mount Ayr (town) Newton County	1	0.82
West Lafayette (city) Tippecanoe County	241	0.81
Carbon (town) Clay County	3	0.76
Purdue University (cdp) Tippecanoe County	87	0.71
Meridian Hills (town) Marion County	9	0.56
Dune Acres (town) Porter County	1	0.55

Top 10 Places Sorted by Percent of Total Population

Based on places with total population of 50,000 or more

Place	Population	%
Noblesville (city) Hamilton County	253	0.49
Fishers (town) Hamilton County	359	0.47
Bloomington (city) Monroe County	349	0.43
Carmel (city) Hamilton County	310	0.39
South Bend (city) St. Joseph County	275	0.27
Fort Wayne (city) Allen County	651	0.26
Indianapolis (city) Marion County	2,068	0.25
Elkhart (city) Elkhart County	121	0.24
Lafayette (city) Tippecanoe County	130	0.19
Hammond (city) Lake County	141	0.17

South American: Argentinean

Top 10 Places Sorted by Population

Based on all places, regardless of total population

Place	Population	%
Indianapolis (city) Marion County	207	0.03
Bloomington (city) Monroe County	57	0.07
West Lafayette (city) Tippecanoe County	53	0.18
Carmel (city) Hamilton County	38	0.05
Fort Wayne (city) Allen County	36	0.01
South Bend (city) St. Joseph County	33	0.03
Fishers (town) Hamilton County	29	0.04
Hammond (city) Lake County	29	0.04
Noblesville (city) Hamilton County	19	0.04
Columbus (city) Bartholomew County	16	0.04

Top 10 Places Sorted by Percent of Total Population

Based on all places, regardless of total population

Place	Population	%
Dune Acres (town) Porter County	1	0.55
Battle Ground (town) Tippecanoe County	4	0.30
Michigan (town) Clinton County	1	0.21
West Lafayette (city) Tippecanoe County	53	0.18
Winona Lake (town) Kosciusko County	9	0.18
Memphis (cdp) Clark County	1	0.14
Wheatfield (town) Jasper County	1	0.12
Charlestown (city) Clark County	8	0.11
Hebron (town) Porter County	4	0.11
Purdue University (cdp) Tippecanoe County	12	0.10

Top 10 Places Sorted by Percent of Total Population

Based on places with total population of 50,000 or more

Place	Population	%
Bloomington (city) Monroe County	57	0.07
Carmel (city) Hamilton County	38	0.05
Fishers (town) Hamilton County	29	0.04
Hammond (city) Lake County	29	0.04
Noblesville (city) Hamilton County	19	0.04
Indianapolis (city) Marion County	207	0.03
South Bend (city) St. Joseph County	33	0.03
Lafayette (city) Tippecanoe County	16	0.02
Terre Haute (city) Vigo County	12	0.02
Elkhart (city) Elkhart County	10	0.02

South American: Bolivian

Top 10 Places Sorted by Population

Based on all places, regardless of total population

Place	Population	%
Indianapolis (city) Marion County	47	0.01
Goshen (city) Elkhart County	29	0.09
Elkhart (city) Elkhart County	29	0.06
West Lafayette (city) Tippecanoe County	17	0.06
Portage (city) Porter County	17	0.05
Fort Wayne (city) Allen County	15	0.01
Schererville (town) Lake County	13	0.04
Carmel (city) Hamilton County	12	0.02
Lafayette (city) Tippecanoe County	12	0.02
Noblesville (city) Hamilton County	11	0.02

Top 10 Places Sorted by Percent of Total Population

Based on all places, regardless of total population

Place	Population	%
Topeka (town) LaGrange County	5	0.43
Somerset (cdp) Wabash County	1	0.25
Hudson Lake (cdp) LaPorte County	2	0.15
Whites (town) Boone County	3	0.10
Goshen (city) Elkhart County	29	0.09
Highland (cdp) Vanderburgh County	4	0.09
Upland (town) Grant County	3	0.08
Charlestown (city) Clark County	5	0.07
Elkhart (city) Elkhart County	29	0.06
West Lafayette (city) Tippecanoe County	17	0.06

Top 10 Places Sorted by Percent of Total Population

Based on places with total population of 50,000 or more

Place	Population	%
Elkhart (city) Elkhart County	29	0.06
Carmel (city) Hamilton County	12	0.02
Lafayette (city) Tippecanoe County	12	0.02
Noblesville (city) Hamilton County	11	0.02
Indianapolis (city) Marion County	47	0.01
Fort Wayne (city) Allen County	15	0.01
Bloomington (city) Monroe County	11	0.01
South Bend (city) St. Joseph County	10	0.01
Terre Haute (city) Vigo County	6	0.01
Fishers (town) Hamilton County	5	0.01

South American: Chilean

Top 10 Places Sorted by Population

Based on all places, regardless of total population

Place	Population	%
Indianapolis (city) Marion County	83	0.01
Bloomington (city) Monroe County	36	0.04
Valparaiso (city) Porter County	30	0.09
South Bend (city) St. Joseph County	27	0.03
Carmel (city) Hamilton County	22	0.03
Fort Wayne (city) Allen County	18	0.01
West Lafayette (city) Tippecanoe County	15	0.05
Fishers (town) Hamilton County	15	0.02
Lafayette (city) Tippecanoe County	13	0.02
Brownsburg (town) Hendricks County	12	0.06

Top 10 Places Sorted by Percent of Total Population

Based on all places, regardless of total population

Place	Population	%
Woodlawn Heights (town) Madison County	1	1.27
Beverly Shores (town) Porter County	6	0.98
Mount Ayr (town) Newton County	1	0.82
Landess (cdp) Grant County	1	0.53
Roseland (town) St. Joseph County	2	0.32
St. Leon (town) Dearborn County	2	0.29
Homecroft (town) Marion County	2	0.28
New Market (town) Montgomery County	1	0.16
St. Mary of the Woods (cdp) Vigo County	1	0.13
Clayton (town) Hendricks County	1	0.10

Top 10 Places Sorted by Percent of Total Population

Based on places with total population of 50,000 or more

Place	Population	%
Bloomington (city) Monroe County	36	0.04
South Bend (city) St. Joseph County	27	0.03
Carmel (city) Hamilton County	22	0.03
Fishers (town) Hamilton County	15	0.02
Lafayette (city) Tippecanoe County	13	0.02
Muncie (city) Delaware County	11	0.02
Noblesville (city) Hamilton County	11	0.02
Indianapolis (city) Marion County	83	0.01
Fort Wayne (city) Allen County	18	0.01
Elkhart (city) Elkhart County	6	0.01

South American: Colombian

Top 10 Places Sorted by Population

Based on all places, regardless of total population

Place	Population	%
Indianapolis (city) Marion County	587	0.07
Fort Wayne (city) Allen County	235	0.09
Fishers (town) Hamilton County	127	0.17
Carmel (city) Hamilton County	125	0.16
West Lafayette (city) Tippecanoe County	94	0.32
Bloomington (city) Monroe County	85	0.11
Noblesville (city) Hamilton County	68	0.13
South Bend (city) St. Joseph County	53	0.05
Lawrence (city) Marion County	41	0.09
Lafayette (city) Tippecanoe County	39	0.06

Top 10 Places Sorted by Percent of Total Population

Based on all places, regardless of total population

Place	Population	%
Carbon (town) Clay County	3	0.76
Notre Dame (cdp) St. Joseph County	27	0.45
Avoca (cdp) Lawrence County	2	0.34
Ingalls (town) Madison County	8	0.33
West Lafayette (city) Tippecanoe County	94	0.32
Uniondale (town) Wells County	1	0.32
Meridian Hills (town) Marion County	5	0.31
Whites (town) Boone County	8	0.28
Bargersville (town) Johnson County	10	0.25
Purdue University (cdp) Tippecanoe County	29	0.24

Top 10 Places Sorted by Percent of Total Population

Based on places with total population of 50,000 or more

Place	Population	%
Fishers (town) Hamilton County	127	0.17
Carmel (city) Hamilton County	125	0.16
Noblesville (city) Hamilton County	68	0.13
Bloomington (city) Monroe County	85	0.11
Fort Wayne (city) Allen County	235	0.09
Indianapolis (city) Marion County	587	0.07
Lafayette (city) Tippecanoe County	39	0.06
South Bend (city) St. Joseph County	53	0.05
Terre Haute (city) Vigo County	28	0.05
Elkhart (city) Elkhart County	24	0.05

South American: Ecuadorian

Top 10 Places Sorted by Population

Based on all places, regardless of total population

Place	Population	%
Indianapolis (city) Marion County	160	0.02
Fort Wayne (city) Allen County	159	0.06
South Bend (city) St. Joseph County	47	0.05
Bloomington (city) Monroe County	30	0.04
Munster (town) Lake County	24	0.10
Lafayette (city) Tippecanoe County	23	0.03
Notre Dame (cdp) St. Joseph County	21	0.35
Dyer (town) Lake County	18	0.11
Merrillville (town) Lake County	18	0.05
Lawrence (city) Marion County	18	0.04

Top 10 Places Sorted by Percent of Total Population

Based on all places, regardless of total population

Place	Population	%
Notre Dame (cdp) St. Joseph County	21	0.35
Whiting (city) Lake County	11	0.22
New Chicago (town) Lake County	3	0.15
Dyer (town) Lake County	18	0.11
Sellersburg (town) Clark County	7	0.11
Munster (town) Lake County	24	0.10
Newburgh (town) Warrick County	3	0.09
Upland (town) Grant County	3	0.08
Purdue University (cdp) Tippecanoe County	9	0.07
Hamilton (town) Steuben County	1	0.07

Top 10 Places Sorted by Percent of Total Population

Based on places with total population of 50,000 or more

Place	Population	%
Fort Wayne (city) Allen County	159	0.06
South Bend (city) St. Joseph County	47	0.05
Bloomington (city) Monroe County	30	0.04
Lafayette (city) Tippecanoe County	23	0.03
Indianapolis (city) Marion County	160	0.02
Carmel (city) Hamilton County	17	0.02
Hammond (city) Lake County	12	0.01
Evansville (city) Vanderburgh County	9	0.01
Fishers (town) Hamilton County	9	0.01
Elkhart (city) Elkhart County	7	0.01

South American: Paraguayan

Top 10 Places Sorted by Population

Based on all places, regardless of total population

Place	Population	%
Indianapolis (city) Marion County	11	<0.01
South Bend (city) St. Joseph County	10	0.01
Bloomington (city) Monroe County	5	0.01
Hidden Valley (cdp) Dearborn County	4	0.07
Granger (cdp) St. Joseph County	4	0.01
Fort Wayne (city) Allen County	4	<0.01
Goshen (city) Elkhart County	3	0.01
Carmel (city) Hamilton County	3	<0.01
Fishers (town) Hamilton County	3	<0.01
Aberdeen (cdp) Porter County	2	0.11

Top 10 Places Sorted by Percent of Total Population

Based on all places, regardless of total population

Place	Population	%
Nashville (town) Brown County	1	0.12
Aberdeen (cdp) Porter County	2	0.11
Hidden Valley (cdp) Dearborn County	4	0.07
Purdue University (cdp) Tippecanoe County	2	0.02
South Bend (city) St. Joseph County	10	0.01
Bloomington (city) Monroe County	5	0.01
Granger (cdp) St. Joseph County	4	0.01
Goshen (city) Elkhart County	3	0.01
St. John (town) Lake County	2	0.01
Greencastle (city) Putnam County	1	0.01

Top 10 Places Sorted by Percent of Total Population

Based on places with total population of 50,000 or more

Place	Population	%
South Bend (city) St. Joseph County	10	0.01
Bloomington (city) Monroe County	5	0.01
Indianapolis (city) Marion County	11	<0.01
Fort Wayne (city) Allen County	4	<0.01
Carmel (city) Hamilton County	3	<0.01
Fishers (town) Hamilton County	3	<0.01
Elkhart (city) Elkhart County	2	<0.01
Evansville (city) Vanderburgh County	2	<0.01
Hammond (city) Lake County	1	<0.01
Muncie (city) Delaware County	1	<0.01

South American: Peruvian

Top 10 Places Sorted by Population

Based on all places, regardless of total population

Place	Population	%
Indianapolis (city) Marion County	611	0.07
Fort Wayne (city) Allen County	128	0.05
Bloomington (city) Monroe County	67	0.08
Plainfield (town) Hendricks County	63	0.23
Fishers (town) Hamilton County	62	0.08
Carmel (city) Hamilton County	49	0.06
Lawrence (city) Marion County	46	0.10
Logansport (city) Cass County	45	0.24
Noblesville (city) Hamilton County	41	0.08
Hammond (city) Lake County	40	0.05

Top 10 Places Sorted by Percent of Total Population

Based on all places, regardless of total population

Place	Population	%
Van Bibber Lake (cdp) Putnam County	2	0.41
Burns Harbor (town) Porter County	4	0.35
Meridian Hills (town) Marion County	4	0.25
Logansport (city) Cass County	45	0.24
Plainfield (town) Hendricks County	63	0.23
Huntingburg (city) Dubois County	12	0.20
Corydon (town) Harrison County	6	0.19
Ferdinand (town) Dubois County	4	0.19
Newburgh (town) Warrick County	6	0.18
Pittsboro (town) Hendricks County	5	0.17

Top 10 Places Sorted by Percent of Total Population

Based on places with total population of 50,000 or more

Place	Population	%
Bloomington (city) Monroe County	67	0.08
Fishers (town) Hamilton County	62	0.08
Noblesville (city) Hamilton County	41	0.08
Indianapolis (city) Marion County	611	0.07
Carmel (city) Hamilton County	49	0.06
Fort Wayne (city) Allen County	128	0.05
Hammond (city) Lake County	40	0.05
Elkhart (city) Elkhart County	20	0.04
Evansville (city) Vanderburgh County	33	0.03
Lafayette (city) Tippecanoe County	18	0.03

South American: Uruguayan

Top 10 Places Sorted by Population

Based on all places, regardless of total population

Place	Population	%
Indianapolis (city) Marion County	29	<0.01
Fort Wayne (city) Allen County	10	<0.01
East Chicago (city) Lake County	7	0.02
Fishers (town) Hamilton County	7	0.01
Hammond (city) Lake County	6	0.01
Mishawaka (city) St. Joseph County	6	0.01
Bloomington (city) Monroe County	5	0.01
South Bend (city) St. Joseph County	5	<0.01
West Lafayette (city) Tippecanoe County	4	0.01
Avon (town) Hendricks County	3	0.02

Top 10 Places Sorted by Percent of Total Population

Based on all places, regardless of total population

Place	Population	%
Napoleon (town) Ripley County	1	0.43
Flora (town) Carroll County	2	0.10
New Paris (cdp) Elkhart County	1	0.07

Whiting (city) Lake County	2	0.04
Notre Dame (cdp) St. Joseph County	2	0.03
East Chicago (city) Lake County	7	0.02
Avon (town) Hendricks County	3	0.02
Ellettsville (town) Monroe County	1	0.02
Grissom AFB (cdp) Miami County	1	0.02
Fishers (town) Hamilton County	7	0.01

Top 10 Places Sorted by Percent of Total Population

Based on places with total population of 50,000 or more

Place	Population	%
Fishers (town) Hamilton County	7	0.01
Hammond (city) Lake County	6	0.01
Bloomington (city) Monroe County	5	0.01
Indianapolis (city) Marion County	29	<0.01
Fort Wayne (city) Allen County	10	<0.01
South Bend (city) St. Joseph County	5	<0.01
Carmel (city) Hamilton County	3	<0.01
Muncie (city) Delaware County	2	<0.01
Noblesville (city) Hamilton County	2	<0.01
Elkhart (city) Elkhart County	1	<0.01

South American: Venezuelan

Top 10 Places Sorted by Population

Based on all places, regardless of total population

Place	Population	%
Indianapolis (city) Marion County	314	0.04
Noblesville (city) Hamilton County	97	0.19
Fishers (town) Hamilton County	93	0.12
South Bend (city) St. Joseph County	73	0.07
Bloomington (city) Monroe County	53	0.07
Fort Wayne (city) Allen County	45	0.02
Lawrence (city) Marion County	40	0.09
Carmel (city) Hamilton County	40	0.05
Mishawaka (city) St. Joseph County	36	0.07
Westfield (town) Hamilton County	35	0.12

Top 10 Places Sorted by Percent of Total Population

Based on all places, regardless of total population

Place	Population	%
Oakland City (city) Gibson County	17	0.70
Switz City (town) Greene County	1	0.34
Clear Lake (town) Steuben County	1	0.29
Kentland (town) Newton County	4	0.23
Noblesville (city) Hamilton County	97	0.19
Notre Dame (cdp) St. Joseph County	8	0.13
McCordsville (town) Hancock County	6	0.13
Utica (town) Clark County	1	0.13
Fishers (town) Hamilton County	93	0.12
Westfield (town) Hamilton County	35	0.12

Top 10 Places Sorted by Percent of Total Population

Based on places with total population of 50,000 or more

Place	Population	%
Noblesville (city) Hamilton County	97	0.19
Fishers (town) Hamilton County	93	0.12
South Bend (city) St. Joseph County	73	0.07
Bloomington (city) Monroe County	53	0.07
Carmel (city) Hamilton County	40	0.05
Indianapolis (city) Marion County	314	0.04
Elkhart (city) Elkhart County	22	0.04
Fort Wayne (city) Allen County	45	0.02
Evansville (city) Vanderburgh County	24	0.02
Muncie (city) Delaware County	13	0.02

South American: Other South American

Top 10 Places Sorted by Population

Based on all places, regardless of total population

Place	Population	%
Indianapolis (city) Marion County	19	<0.01
Fishers (town) Hamilton County	9	0.01
Bremen (town) Marshall County	5	0.11
Muncie (city) Delaware County	4	0.01
Hidden Valley (cdp) Dearborn County	3	0.06
La Porte (city) LaPorte County	3	0.01
Mishawaka (city) St. Joseph County	3	0.01
Reynolds (town) White County	2	0.38
Mentone (town) Kosciusko County	2	0.20
Marion (city) Grant County	2	0.01

Top 10 Places Sorted by Percent of Total Population

Based on all places, regardless of total population

Place	Population	%
Reynolds (town) White County	2	0.38
Mentone (town) Kosciusko County	2	0.20
Bremen (town) Marshall County	5	0.11
Hidden Valley (cdp) Dearborn County	3	0.06
Bristol (town) Elkhart County	1	0.06
Edinburgh (town) Johnson County	1	0.02
Porter (town) Porter County	1	0.02
Fishers (town) Hamilton County	9	0.01
Muncie (city) Delaware County	4	0.01
La Porte (city) LaPorte County	3	0.01

Top 10 Places Sorted by Percent of Total Population

Based on places with total population of 50,000 or more

Place	Population	%
Fishers (town) Hamilton County	9	0.01
Muncie (city) Delaware County	4	0.01
Indianapolis (city) Marion County	19	<0.01
Carmel (city) Hamilton County	1	<0.01
Evansville (city) Vanderburgh County	1	<0.01
Fort Wayne (city) Allen County	1	<0.01
Anderson (city) Madison County	0	0.00
Bloomington (city) Monroe County	0	0.00
Elkhart (city) Elkhart County	0	0.00
Gary (city) Lake County	0	0.00

Other Hispanic or Latino

Top 10 Places Sorted by Population

Based on all places, regardless of total population

Place	Population	%
Indianapolis (city) Marion County	5,473	0.67
Fort Wayne (city) Allen County	1,473	0.58
Hammond (city) Lake County	981	1.21
South Bend (city) St. Joseph County	846	0.84
Elkhart (city) Elkhart County	668	1.31
East Chicago (city) Lake County	483	1.63
Lafayette (city) Tippecanoe County	365	0.54
Goshen (city) Elkhart County	340	1.07
Evansville (city) Vanderburgh County	312	0.27
Bloomington (city) Monroe County	286	0.36

Top 10 Places Sorted by Percent of Total Population

Based on all places, regardless of total population

Place	Population	%
Plymouth (city) Marshall County	221	2.20
Monon (town) White County	36	2.03
Windfall City (town) Tipton County	14	1.98
Hamlet (town) Starke County	14	1.75
Bremen (town) Marshall County	78	1.70
East Chicago (city) Lake County	483	1.63
Logansport (city) Cass County	265	1.44
Frankfort (city) Clinton County	235	1.43
Boswell (town) Benton County	11	1.41
Crows Nest (town) Marion County	1	1.37

Top 10 Places Sorted by Percent of Total Population

Based on places with total population of 50,000 or more

Place	Population	%
Elkhart (city) Elkhart County	668	1.31
Hammond (city) Lake County	981	1.21
South Bend (city) St. Joseph County	846	0.84
Indianapolis (city) Marion County	5,473	0.67
Fort Wayne (city) Allen County	1,473	0.58
Lafayette (city) Tippecanoe County	365	0.54
Anderson (city) Madison County	223	0.40
Bloomington (city) Monroe County	286	0.36
Noblesville (city) Hamilton County	174	0.33
Fishers (town) Hamilton County	243	0.32

Racial Group Rankings

African-American/Black

Top 10 Places Sorted by Population

Based on all places, regardless of total population

Place	Population	%
Indianapolis (city) Marion County	239,354	29.17
Gary (city) Lake County	69,508	86.57
Fort Wayne (city) Allen County	44,499	17.54
South Bend (city) St. Joseph County	29,667	29.32
Hammond (city) Lake County	19,336	23.92
Evansville (city) Vanderburgh County	17,089	14.55
Merrillville (town) Lake County	16,337	46.35
East Chicago (city) Lake County	13,135	44.23
Lawrence (city) Marion County	12,900	28.04
Michigan City (city) LaPorte County	9,686	30.77

Top 10 Places Sorted by Percent of Total Population

Based on all places, regardless of total population

Place	Population	%
Gary (city) Lake County	69,508	86.57
Merrillville (town) Lake County	16,337	46.35
East Chicago (city) Lake County	13,135	44.23
Wynnedale (town) Marion County	83	35.93
Michigan City (city) LaPorte County	9,686	30.77
South Bend (city) St. Joseph County	29,667	29.32
Indianapolis (city) Marion County	239,354	29.17
Lawrence (city) Marion County	12,900	28.04
Westville (town) LaPorte County	1,486	25.39
Hammond (city) Lake County	19,336	23.92

Top 10 Places Sorted by Percent of Total Population

Based on places with total population of 50,000 or more

Place	Population	%
Gary (city) Lake County	69,508	86.57
South Bend (city) St. Joseph County	29,667	29.32
Indianapolis (city) Marion County	239,354	29.17
Hammond (city) Lake County	19,336	23.92
Elkhart (city) Elkhart County	9,108	17.88
Fort Wayne (city) Allen County	44,499	17.54
Anderson (city) Madison County	9,500	16.93
Evansville (city) Vanderburgh County	17,089	14.55
Terre Haute (city) Vigo County	7,819	12.86
Muncie (city) Delaware County	8,829	12.60

African-American/Black: Not Hispanic

Top 10 Places Sorted by Population

Based on all places, regardless of total population

Place	Population	%
Indianapolis (city) Marion County	235,521	28.71
Gary (city) Lake County	68,449	85.25
Fort Wayne (city) Allen County	43,301	17.07
South Bend (city) St. Joseph County	28,893	28.56
Hammond (city) Lake County	18,369	22.73
Evansville (city) Vanderburgh County	16,871	14.37
Merrillville (town) Lake County	15,889	45.08
Lawrence (city) Marion County	12,650	27.50
East Chicago (city) Lake County	12,330	41.52
Michigan City (city) LaPorte County	9,477	30.11

Top 10 Places Sorted by Percent of Total Population

Based on all places, regardless of total population

Place	Population	%
Gary (city) Lake County	68,449	85.25
Merrillville (town) Lake County	15,889	45.08
East Chicago (city) Lake County	12,330	41.52
Wynnedale (town) Marion County	83	35.93
Michigan City (city) LaPorte County	9,477	30.11
Indianapolis (city) Marion County	235,521	28.71
South Bend (city) St. Joseph County	28,893	28.56
Lawrence (city) Marion County	12,650	27.50
Westville (town) LaPorte County	1,481	25.30
Grissom AFB (cdp) Miami County	1,286	23.23

Top 10 Places Sorted by Percent of Total Population

Based on places with total population of 50,000 or more

Place	Population	%
Gary (city) Lake County	68,449	85.25
Indianapolis (city) Marion County	235,521	28.71
South Bend (city) St. Joseph County	28,893	28.56
Hammond (city) Lake County	18,369	22.73
Elkhart (city) Elkhart County	8,843	17.36
Fort Wayne (city) Allen County	43,301	17.07
Anderson (city) Madison County	9,376	16.70
Evansville (city) Vanderburgh County	16,871	14.37
Terre Haute (city) Vigo County	7,705	12.68
Muncie (city) Delaware County	8,664	12.36

African-American/Black: Hispanic

Top 10 Places Sorted by Population

Based on all places, regardless of total population

Place	Population	%
Indianapolis (city) Marion County	3,833	0.47
Fort Wayne (city) Allen County	1,198	0.47
Gary (city) Lake County	1,059	1.32
Hammond (city) Lake County	967	1.20
East Chicago (city) Lake County	805	2.71
South Bend (city) St. Joseph County	774	0.77
Merrillville (town) Lake County	448	1.27
Elkhart (city) Elkhart County	265	0.52
Lawrence (city) Marion County	250	0.54
Lafayette (city) Tippecanoe County	235	0.35

Top 10 Places Sorted by Percent of Total Population

Based on all places, regardless of total population

Place	Population	%
East Chicago (city) Lake County	805	2.71
Gary (city) Lake County	1,059	1.32
Merrillville (town) Lake County	448	1.27
Leavenworth (town) Crawford County	3	1.26
Hammond (city) Lake County	967	1.20
Lake Station (city) Lake County	139	1.11
Whiting (city) Lake County	52	1.04
Elizabeth (town) Bartholomew County	5	0.99
Kewanna (town) Fulton County	6	0.98
Wheeler (cdp) Porter County	4	0.90

Top 10 Places Sorted by Percent of Total Population

Based on places with total population of 50,000 or more

Place	Population	%
Gary (city) Lake County	1,059	1.32
Hammond (city) Lake County	967	1.20
South Bend (city) St. Joseph County	774	0.77
Elkhart (city) Elkhart County	265	0.52
Indianapolis (city) Marion County	3,833	0.47
Fort Wayne (city) Allen County	1,198	0.47
Lafayette (city) Tippecanoe County	235	0.35
Bloomington (city) Monroe County	195	0.24
Muncie (city) Delaware County	165	0.24
Anderson (city) Madison County	124	0.22

American Indian/Alaska Native

Top 10 Places Sorted by Population

Based on all places, regardless of total population

Place	Population	%
Indianapolis (city) Marion County	7,323	0.89
Fort Wayne (city) Allen County	2,669	1.05
South Bend (city) St. Joseph County	1,334	1.32
Hammond (city) Lake County	930	1.15
Evansville (city) Vanderburgh County	916	0.78
Gary (city) Lake County	760	0.95
Elkhart (city) Elkhart County	706	1.39
Bloomington (city) Monroe County	699	0.87
Terre Haute (city) Vigo County	685	1.13
Lafayette (city) Tippecanoe County	672	1.00

Top 10 Places Sorted by Percent of Total Population

Based on all places, regardless of total population

Place	Population	%
Fredericksburg (town) Washington County	6	7.06
Canaan (cdp) Jefferson County	4	4.44
Dunreith (town) Henry County	6	3.39
Jonesville (town) Bartholomew County	6	3.39
Burket (town) Kosciusko County	6	3.08
Alamo (town) Montgomery County	2	3.03
Coalmont (cdp) Clay County	12	2.99
Wheeler (cdp) Porter County	13	2.93
Springport (town) Henry County	4	2.68
Lagro (town) Wabash County	11	2.65

Top 10 Places Sorted by Percent of Total Population

Based on places with total population of 50,000 or more

Place	Population	%
Elkhart (city) Elkhart County	706	1.39
South Bend (city) St. Joseph County	1,334	1.32
Hammond (city) Lake County	930	1.15
Terre Haute (city) Vigo County	685	1.13
Fort Wayne (city) Allen County	2,669	1.05
Lafayette (city) Tippecanoe County	672	1.00
Gary (city) Lake County	760	0.95
Anderson (city) Madison County	528	0.94
Muncie (city) Delaware County	650	0.93
Indianapolis (city) Marion County	7,323	0.89

American Indian/Alaska Native: Not Hispanic

Top 10 Places Sorted by Population

Based on all places, regardless of total population

Place	Population	%
Indianapolis (city) Marion County	5,844	0.71
Fort Wayne (city) Allen County	2,172	0.86
South Bend (city) St. Joseph County	1,029	1.02
Evansville (city) Vanderburgh County	831	0.71
Gary (city) Lake County	659	0.82
Terre Haute (city) Vigo County	632	1.04
Bloomington (city) Monroe County	591	0.74
Muncie (city) Delaware County	577	0.82
Lafayette (city) Tippecanoe County	544	0.81
Mishawaka (city) St. Joseph County	489	1.01

Top 10 Places Sorted by Percent of Total Population

Based on all places, regardless of total population

Place	Population	%
Canaan (cdp) Jefferson County	4	4.44
Dunreith (town) Henry County	6	3.39
Jonesville (town) Bartholomew County	6	3.39
Alamo (town) Montgomery County	2	3.03
Coalmont (cdp) Clay County	12	2.99
Wheeler (cdp) Porter County	13	2.93
Springport (town) Henry County	4	2.68
Lagro (town) Wabash County	11	2.65
Losantville (town) Randolph County	6	2.53
Bethany (town) Morgan County	2	2.47

Top 10 Places Sorted by Percent of Total Population

Based on places with total population of 50,000 or more

Place	Population	%
Terre Haute (city) Vigo County	632	1.04
South Bend (city) St. Joseph County	1,029	1.02
Elkhart (city) Elkhart County	482	0.95
Fort Wayne (city) Allen County	2,172	0.86
Gary (city) Lake County	659	0.82
Muncie (city) Delaware County	577	0.82
Lafayette (city) Tippecanoe County	544	0.81
Anderson (city) Madison County	432	0.77
Bloomington (city) Monroe County	591	0.74
Indianapolis (city) Marion County	5,844	0.71

American Indian/Alaska Native: Hispanic

Top 10 Places Sorted by Population
Based on all places, regardless of total population

Place	Population	%
Indianapolis (city) Marion County	1,479	0.18
Fort Wayne (city) Allen County	497	0.20
Hammond (city) Lake County	441	0.55
South Bend (city) St. Joseph County	305	0.30
Elkhart (city) Elkhart County	224	0.44
East Chicago (city) Lake County	209	0.70
Goshen (city) Elkhart County	137	0.43
Lafayette (city) Tippecanoe County	128	0.19
Lawrence (city) Marion County	118	0.26
Logansport (city) Cass County	111	0.60

Top 10 Places Sorted by Percent of Total Population
Based on all places, regardless of total population

Place	Population	%
Fredericksburg (town) Washington County	4	4.71
Burket (town) Kosciusko County	5	2.56
Akron (town) Fulton County	20	1.71
Mount Ayr (town) Newton County	2	1.64
Reynolds (town) White County	8	1.50
Schneider (town) Lake County	3	1.08
Linden (town) Montgomery County	8	1.05
Whiting (city) Lake County	48	0.96
Francisco (town) Gibson County	4	0.85
New Chicago (town) Lake County	17	0.84

Top 10 Places Sorted by Percent of Total Population
Based on places with total population of 50,000 or more

Place	Population	%
Hammond (city) Lake County	441	0.55
Elkhart (city) Elkhart County	224	0.44
South Bend (city) St. Joseph County	305	0.30
Fort Wayne (city) Allen County	497	0.20
Lafayette (city) Tippecanoe County	128	0.19
Indianapolis (city) Marion County	1,479	0.18
Anderson (city) Madison County	96	0.17
Bloomington (city) Monroe County	108	0.13
Gary (city) Lake County	101	0.13
Muncie (city) Delaware County	73	0.10

Alaska Native: Alaska Athabascan

Top 10 Places Sorted by Population
Based on all places, regardless of total population

Place	Population	%
Cedar Lake (town) Lake County	5	0.04
Lafayette (city) Tippecanoe County	4	0.01
Fort Wayne (city) Allen County	4	<0.01
North Vernon (city) Jennings County	3	0.04
Indianapolis (city) Marion County	3	<0.01
West Terre Haute (town) Vigo County	2	0.09
Brownsburg (town) Hendricks County	2	0.01
Chesterton (town) Porter County	1	0.01
Bloomington (city) Monroe County	1	<0.01
Evansville (city) Vanderburgh County	1	<0.01

Top 10 Places Sorted by Percent of Total Population
Based on all places, regardless of total population

Place	Population	%
West Terre Haute (town) Vigo County	2	0.09
Cedar Lake (town) Lake County	5	0.04
North Vernon (city) Jennings County	3	0.04
Lafayette (city) Tippecanoe County	4	0.01
Brownsburg (town) Hendricks County	2	0.01
Chesterton (town) Porter County	1	0.01
Fort Wayne (city) Allen County	4	<0.01
Indianapolis (city) Marion County	3	<0.01
Bloomington (city) Monroe County	1	<0.01
Evansville (city) Vanderburgh County	1	<0.01

Top 10 Places Sorted by Percent of Total Population
Based on places with total population of 50,000 or more

Place	Population	%
Lafayette (city) Tippecanoe County	4	0.01
Fort Wayne (city) Allen County	4	<0.01
Indianapolis (city) Marion County	3	<0.01
Bloomington (city) Monroe County	1	<0.01
Evansville (city) Vanderburgh County	1	<0.01
Anderson (city) Madison County	0	0.00
Carmel (city) Hamilton County	0	0.00
Elkhart (city) Elkhart County	0	0.00
Fishers (town) Hamilton County	0	0.00
Gary (city) Lake County	0	0.00

Alaska Native: Aleut

Top 10 Places Sorted by Population
Based on all places, regardless of total population

Place	Population	%
Indianapolis (city) Marion County	14	<0.01
Cannelton (city) Perry County	2	0.13
Bloomington (city) Monroe County	2	<0.01
Greenwood (city) Johnson County	2	<0.01
Lafayette (city) Tippecanoe County	2	<0.01
La Paz (town) Marshall County	1	0.18
Rockville (town) Parke County	1	0.04
Auburn (city) DeKalb County	1	0.01
Logansport (city) Cass County	1	0.01
Fort Wayne (city) Allen County	1	<0.01

Top 10 Places Sorted by Percent of Total Population
Based on all places, regardless of total population

Place	Population	%
La Paz (town) Marshall County	1	0.18
Cannelton (city) Perry County	2	0.13
Rockville (town) Parke County	1	0.04
Auburn (city) DeKalb County	1	0.01
Logansport (city) Cass County	1	0.01
Indianapolis (city) Marion County	14	<0.01
Bloomington (city) Monroe County	2	<0.01
Greenwood (city) Johnson County	2	<0.01
Lafayette (city) Tippecanoe County	2	<0.01
Fort Wayne (city) Allen County	1	<0.01

Top 10 Places Sorted by Percent of Total Population
Based on places with total population of 50,000 or more

Place	Population	%
Indianapolis (city) Marion County	14	<0.01
Bloomington (city) Monroe County	2	<0.01
Lafayette (city) Tippecanoe County	2	<0.01
Fort Wayne (city) Allen County	1	<0.01
Anderson (city) Madison County	0	0.00
Carmel (city) Hamilton County	0	0.00
Elkhart (city) Elkhart County	0	0.00
Evansville (city) Vanderburgh County	0	0.00
Fishers (town) Hamilton County	0	0.00
Gary (city) Lake County	0	0.00

American Indian: Apache

Top 10 Places Sorted by Population
Based on all places, regardless of total population

Place	Population	%
Indianapolis (city) Marion County	98	0.01
Fort Wayne (city) Allen County	43	0.02
South Bend (city) St. Joseph County	29	0.03
Evansville (city) Vanderburgh County	23	0.02
Hammond (city) Lake County	19	0.02
Michigan City (city) LaPorte County	17	0.05
Gary (city) Lake County	16	0.02
Lawrence (city) Marion County	12	0.03
Lafayette (city) Tippecanoe County	12	0.02
Muncie (city) Delaware County	12	0.02

Top 10 Places Sorted by Percent of Total Population
Based on all places, regardless of total population

Place	Population	%
Fredericksburg (town) Washington County	6	7.06
Canaan (cdp) Jefferson County	4	4.44
Economy (town) Wayne County	1	0.53
Perrysville (town) Vermillion County	2	0.44
Lyons (town) Greene County	3	0.40
Shirley (town) Hancock County	3	0.36
Swayzee (town) Grant County	3	0.31
Sheridan (town) Hamilton County	8	0.30
St. Leon (town) Dearborn County	2	0.29
Jonesboro (city) Grant County	5	0.28

Top 10 Places Sorted by Percent of Total Population
Based on places with total population of 50,000 or more

Place	Population	%
South Bend (city) St. Joseph County	29	0.03
Fort Wayne (city) Allen County	43	0.02
Evansville (city) Vanderburgh County	23	0.02
Hammond (city) Lake County	19	0.02
Gary (city) Lake County	16	0.02
Lafayette (city) Tippecanoe County	12	0.02
Muncie (city) Delaware County	12	0.02
Anderson (city) Madison County	9	0.02
Indianapolis (city) Marion County	98	0.01
Bloomington (city) Monroe County	11	0.01

American Indian: Arapaho

Top 10 Places Sorted by Population
Based on all places, regardless of total population

Place	Population	%
Indianapolis (city) Marion County	4	<0.01
New Palestine (town) Hancock County	3	0.15
Austin (city) Scott County	3	0.07
Jasper (city) Dubois County	3	0.02
East Chicago (city) Lake County	3	0.01
Fort Wayne (city) Allen County	3	<0.01
Wheatland (town) Knox County	2	0.42
Highland (town) Lake County	2	0.01
Roachdale (town) Putnam County	1	0.11
Shelburn (town) Sullivan County	1	0.08

Top 10 Places Sorted by Percent of Total Population
Based on all places, regardless of total population

Place	Population	%
Wheatland (town) Knox County	2	0.42
New Palestine (town) Hancock County	3	0.15
Roachdale (town) Putnam County	1	0.11
Shelburn (town) Sullivan County	1	0.08
Austin (city) Scott County	3	0.07
Country Squire Lakes (cdp) Jennings County	1	0.03
Smithville-Sanders (cdp) Monroe County	1	0.03
Jasper (city) Dubois County	3	0.02
East Chicago (city) Lake County	3	0.01
Highland (town) Lake County	2	0.01

Top 10 Places Sorted by Percent of Total Population
Based on places with total population of 50,000 or more

Place	Population	%
Indianapolis (city) Marion County	4	<0.01
Fort Wayne (city) Allen County	3	<0.01
Evansville (city) Vanderburgh County	1	<0.01
Hammond (city) Lake County	1	<0.01
Muncie (city) Delaware County	1	<0.01
South Bend (city) St. Joseph County	1	<0.01
Anderson (city) Madison County	0	0.00
Bloomington (city) Monroe County	0	0.00
Carmel (city) Hamilton County	0	0.00
Elkhart (city) Elkhart County	0	0.00

American Indian: Blackfeet

Top 10 Places Sorted by Population
Based on all places, regardless of total population

Place	Population	%
Indianapolis (city) Marion County	354	0.04
Fort Wayne (city) Allen County	110	0.04
South Bend (city) St. Joseph County	74	0.07
Gary (city) Lake County	43	0.05
Muncie (city) Delaware County	42	0.06
Evansville (city) Vanderburgh County	39	0.03
Portage (city) Porter County	35	0.10
Anderson (city) Madison County	32	0.06
Elkhart (city) Elkhart County	31	0.06
Michigan City (city) LaPorte County	28	0.09

Top 10 Places Sorted by Percent of Total Population
Based on all places, regardless of total population

Place	Population	%
Burnettsville (town) White County	2	0.58
Lynnville (town) Warrick County	5	0.56
Laketon (cdp) Wabash County	3	0.48

Waveland (town) Montgomery County	2	0.48
Spurgeon (town) Pike County	1	0.48
Carlisle (town) Sullivan County	3	0.43
Decker (town) Knox County	1	0.40
Hayden (cdp) Jennings County	2	0.38
Manilla (cdp) Rush County	1	0.37
Roachdale (town) Putnam County	3	0.32

Top 10 Places Sorted by Percent of Total Population
Based on places with total population of 50,000 or more

Place	Population	%
South Bend (city) St. Joseph County	74	0.07
Muncie (city) Delaware County	42	0.06
Anderson (city) Madison County	32	0.06
Elkhart (city) Elkhart County	31	0.06
Gary (city) Lake County	43	0.05
Indianapolis (city) Marion County	354	0.04
Fort Wayne (city) Allen County	110	0.04
Lafayette (city) Tippecanoe County	27	0.04
Terre Haute (city) Vigo County	24	0.04
Evansville (city) Vanderburgh County	39	0.03

American Indian: Canadian/French American Indian

Top 10 Places Sorted by Population
Based on all places, regardless of total population

Place	Population	%
Indianapolis (city) Marion County	22	<0.01
Granger (cdp) St. Joseph County	12	0.04
Walkerton (town) St. Joseph County	10	0.47
Koontz Lake (cdp) Starke County	7	0.45
East Chicago (city) Lake County	6	0.02
Vincennes (city) Knox County	5	0.03
Schererville (town) Lake County	5	0.02
Elkhart (city) Elkhart County	5	0.01
Jeffersonville (city) Clark County	5	0.01
South Bend (city) St. Joseph County	5	<0.01

Top 10 Places Sorted by Percent of Total Population
Based on all places, regardless of total population

Place	Population	%
Hamlet (town) Starke County	4	0.50
Walkerton (town) St. Joseph County	10	0.47
Koontz Lake (cdp) Starke County	7	0.45
Butlerville (cdp) Jennings County	1	0.35
Camden (town) Carroll County	2	0.33
Markleville (town) Madison County	1	0.19
Chandler (town) Warrick County	4	0.14
Ingalls (town) Madison County	3	0.13
Lakeville (town) St. Joseph County	1	0.13
Shirley (town) Hancock County	1	0.12

Top 10 Places Sorted by Percent of Total Population
Based on places with total population of 50,000 or more

Place	Population	%
Elkhart (city) Elkhart County	5	0.01
Indianapolis (city) Marion County	22	<0.01
South Bend (city) St. Joseph County	5	<0.01
Fort Wayne (city) Allen County	4	<0.01
Lafayette (city) Tippecanoe County	3	<0.01
Evansville (city) Vanderburgh County	2	<0.01
Anderson (city) Madison County	1	<0.01
Bloomington (city) Monroe County	1	<0.01
Gary (city) Lake County	1	<0.01
Hammond (city) Lake County	1	<0.01

American Indian: Central American Indian

Top 10 Places Sorted by Population
Based on all places, regardless of total population

Place	Population	%
Logansport (city) Cass County	27	0.15
Fort Wayne (city) Allen County	11	<0.01
Indianapolis (city) Marion County	11	<0.01
Columbus (city) Bartholomew County	8	0.02
South Bend (city) St. Joseph County	8	0.01
Anderson (city) Madison County	7	0.01
Pittsboro (town) Hendricks County	4	0.14
Seymour (city) Jackson County	4	0.02
Elkhart (city) Elkhart County	4	0.01
Merrillville (town) Lake County	4	0.01

Top 10 Places Sorted by Percent of Total Population
Based on all places, regardless of total population

Place	Population	%
Bourbon (town) Marshall County	3	0.17
Rocky Ripple (town) Marion County	1	0.17
Logansport (city) Cass County	27	0.15
Pittsboro (town) Hendricks County	4	0.14
Newburgh (town) Warrick County	2	0.06
Gas City (city) Grant County	3	0.05
Columbus (city) Bartholomew County	8	0.02
Seymour (city) Jackson County	4	0.02
Avon (town) Hendricks County	2	0.02
Huntingburg (city) Dubois County	1	0.02

Top 10 Places Sorted by Percent of Total Population
Based on places with total population of 50,000 or more

Place	Population	%
South Bend (city) St. Joseph County	8	0.01
Anderson (city) Madison County	7	0.01
Elkhart (city) Elkhart County	4	0.01
Fort Wayne (city) Allen County	11	<0.01
Indianapolis (city) Marion County	11	<0.01
Gary (city) Lake County	3	<0.01
Bloomington (city) Monroe County	2	<0.01
Carmel (city) Hamilton County	2	<0.01
Evansville (city) Vanderburgh County	1	<0.01
Fishers (town) Hamilton County	1	<0.01

American Indian: Cherokee

Top 10 Places Sorted by Population
Based on all places, regardless of total population

Place	Population	%
Indianapolis (city) Marion County	1,682	0.21
Fort Wayne (city) Allen County	481	0.19
Evansville (city) Vanderburgh County	283	0.24
South Bend (city) St. Joseph County	281	0.28
Lafayette (city) Tippecanoe County	195	0.29
Muncie (city) Delaware County	182	0.26
Hammond (city) Lake County	182	0.23
Bloomington (city) Monroe County	161	0.20
Terre Haute (city) Vigo County	159	0.26
Gary (city) Lake County	153	0.19

Top 10 Places Sorted by Percent of Total Population
Based on all places, regardless of total population

Place	Population	%
Fredericksburg (town) Washington County	6	7.06
Deputy (cdp) Jefferson County	2	2.33
Springport (town) Henry County	3	2.01
Medora (town) Jackson County	13	1.88
Wheeler (cdp) Porter County	8	1.81
Losantville (town) Randolph County	4	1.69
Jonesville (town) Bartholomew County	3	1.69
Andrews (town) Huntington County	15	1.31
Vera Cruz (town) Wells County	1	1.25
Bethany (town) Morgan County	1	1.23

Top 10 Places Sorted by Percent of Total Population
Based on places with total population of 50,000 or more

Place	Population	%
Lafayette (city) Tippecanoe County	195	0.29
South Bend (city) St. Joseph County	281	0.28
Muncie (city) Delaware County	182	0.26
Terre Haute (city) Vigo County	159	0.26
Evansville (city) Vanderburgh County	283	0.24
Elkhart (city) Elkhart County	120	0.24
Hammond (city) Lake County	182	0.23
Anderson (city) Madison County	127	0.23
Indianapolis (city) Marion County	1,682	0.21
Bloomington (city) Monroe County	161	0.20

American Indian: Cheyenne

Top 10 Places Sorted by Population
Based on all places, regardless of total population

Place	Population	%
Indianapolis (city) Marion County	18	<0.01
Evansville (city) Vanderburgh County	11	0.01
Terre Haute (city) Vigo County	6	0.01
Fort Wayne (city) Allen County	6	<0.01
Elwood (city) Madison County	5	0.06
Vincennes (city) Knox County	5	0.03
Monticello (city) White County	4	0.07
Logansport (city) Cass County	4	0.02
Anderson (city) Madison County	4	0.01
Lafayette (city) Tippecanoe County	4	0.01

Top 10 Places Sorted by Percent of Total Population
Based on all places, regardless of total population

Place	Population	%
Holton (town) Ripley County	2	0.42
Universal (town) Vermillion County	1	0.28
Geneva (town) Adams County	2	0.15
Monticello (city) White County	4	0.07
Elwood (city) Madison County	5	0.06
Vincennes (city) Knox County	5	0.03
Bicknell (city) Knox County	1	0.03
Country Squire Lakes (cdp) Jennings County	1	0.03
Union City (city) Randolph County	1	0.03
Logansport (city) Cass County	4	0.02

Top 10 Places Sorted by Percent of Total Population
Based on places with total population of 50,000 or more

Place	Population	%
Evansville (city) Vanderburgh County	11	0.01
Terre Haute (city) Vigo County	6	0.01
Anderson (city) Madison County	4	0.01
Lafayette (city) Tippecanoe County	4	0.01
Elkhart (city) Elkhart County	3	0.01
Indianapolis (city) Marion County	18	<0.01
Fort Wayne (city) Allen County	6	<0.01
South Bend (city) St. Joseph County	1	<0.01
Bloomington (city) Monroe County	0	0.00
Carmel (city) Hamilton County	0	0.00

American Indian: Chickasaw

Top 10 Places Sorted by Population
Based on all places, regardless of total population

Place	Population	%
Fort Wayne (city) Allen County	13	0.01
Indianapolis (city) Marion County	12	<0.01
Jeffersonville (city) Clark County	8	0.02
Mishawaka (city) St. Joseph County	7	0.01
South Bend (city) St. Joseph County	6	0.01
Boonville (city) Warrick County	4	0.06
New Albany (city) Floyd County	4	0.01
Terre Haute (city) Vigo County	4	0.01
Gary (city) Lake County	4	<0.01
Bunker Hill (town) Miami County	3	0.34

Top 10 Places Sorted by Percent of Total Population
Based on all places, regardless of total population

Place	Population	%
Bunker Hill (town) Miami County	3	0.34
Richland (town) Spencer County	1	0.24
Cynthiana (town) Posey County	1	0.18
Rolling Prairie (cdp) LaPorte County	1	0.17
Fountain City (town) Wayne County	1	0.13
Centerville (town) Wayne County	3	0.12
Paoli (town) Orange County	3	0.08
Boonville (city) Warrick County	4	0.06
Vevay (town) Switzerland County	1	0.06
Hope (town) Bartholomew County	1	0.05

Top 10 Places Sorted by Percent of Total Population
Based on places with total population of 50,000 or more

Place	Population	%
Fort Wayne (city) Allen County	13	0.01
South Bend (city) St. Joseph County	6	0.01
Terre Haute (city) Vigo County	4	0.01
Indianapolis (city) Marion County	12	<0.01
Gary (city) Lake County	4	<0.01
Evansville (city) Vanderburgh County	3	<0.01
Lafayette (city) Tippecanoe County	3	<0.01
Bloomington (city) Monroe County	2	<0.01
Elkhart (city) Elkhart County	2	<0.01
Hammond (city) Lake County	2	<0.01

American Indian: Chippewa

Top 10 Places Sorted by Population

Based on all places, regardless of total population

Place	Population	%
Indianapolis (city) Marion County	134	0.02
Fort Wayne (city) Allen County	63	0.02
South Bend (city) St. Joseph County	29	0.03
Portage (city) Porter County	26	0.07
Bloomington (city) Monroe County	21	0.03
Hammond (city) Lake County	21	0.03
Kokomo (city) Howard County	19	0.04
Noblesville (city) Hamilton County	18	0.03
Evansville (city) Vanderburgh County	18	0.02
Elkhart (city) Elkhart County	14	0.03

Top 10 Places Sorted by Percent of Total Population

Based on all places, regardless of total population

Place	Population	%
Gentryville (town) Spencer County	4	1.49
Schneider (town) Lake County	3	1.08
San Pierre (cdp) Starke County	1	0.69
Ogden Dunes (town) Porter County	5	0.45
Clifford (town) Bartholomew County	1	0.43
Shelburn (town) Sullivan County	5	0.40
Switz City (town) Greene County	1	0.34
Rocky Ripple (town) Marion County	2	0.33
Collegeville (cdp) Jasper County	1	0.30
Burns Harbor (town) Porter County	3	0.26

Top 10 Places Sorted by Percent of Total Population

Based on places with total population of 50,000 or more

Place	Population	%
South Bend (city) St. Joseph County	29	0.03
Bloomington (city) Monroe County	21	0.03
Hammond (city) Lake County	21	0.03
Noblesville (city) Hamilton County	18	0.03
Elkhart (city) Elkhart County	14	0.03
Indianapolis (city) Marion County	134	0.02
Fort Wayne (city) Allen County	63	0.02
Evansville (city) Vanderburgh County	18	0.02
Lafayette (city) Tippecanoe County	12	0.02
Gary (city) Lake County	11	0.01

American Indian: Choctaw

Top 10 Places Sorted by Population

Based on all places, regardless of total population

Place	Population	%
Indianapolis (city) Marion County	99	0.01
Fort Wayne (city) Allen County	55	0.02
Gary (city) Lake County	27	0.03
South Bend (city) St. Joseph County	23	0.02
Bloomington (city) Monroe County	19	0.02
Hammond (city) Lake County	18	0.02
Jeffersonville (city) Clark County	16	0.04
Evansville (city) Vanderburgh County	16	0.01
Elkhart (city) Elkhart County	12	0.02
New Albany (city) Floyd County	11	0.03

Top 10 Places Sorted by Percent of Total Population

Based on all places, regardless of total population

Place	Population	%
Cedar Grove (town) Franklin County	1	0.64
Memphis (cdp) Clark County	4	0.58
Ashley (town) DeKalb County	3	0.31
Mecca (town) Parke County	1	0.30
Mount Summit (town) Henry County	1	0.28
Waldron (cdp) Shelby County	2	0.25
Lagro (town) Wabash County	1	0.24
Palmyra (town) Harrison County	2	0.22
Hayden (cdp) Jennings County	1	0.19
Bargersville (town) Johnson County	7	0.17

Top 10 Places Sorted by Percent of Total Population

Based on places with total population of 50,000 or more

Place	Population	%
Gary (city) Lake County	27	0.03
Fort Wayne (city) Allen County	55	0.02
South Bend (city) St. Joseph County	23	0.02
Bloomington (city) Monroe County	19	0.02
Hammond (city) Lake County	18	0.02
Elkhart (city) Elkhart County	12	0.02
Anderson (city) Madison County	10	0.02
Indianapolis (city) Marion County	99	0.01
Evansville (city) Vanderburgh County	16	0.01
Carmel (city) Hamilton County	11	0.01

American Indian: Colville

Top 10 Places Sorted by Population

Based on all places, regardless of total population

Place	Population	%
Speedway (town) Marion County	4	0.03
Heritage Lake (cdp) Putnam County	2	0.07
Kokomo (city) Howard County	2	<0.01
Evansville (city) Vanderburgh County	1	<0.01
South Bend (city) St. Joseph County	1	<0.01
Aberdeen (cdp) Porter County	0	0.00
Advance (town) Boone County	0	0.00
Akron (town) Fulton County	0	0.00
Alamo (town) Montgomery County	0	0.00
Albany (town) Delaware County	0	0.00

Top 10 Places Sorted by Percent of Total Population

Based on all places, regardless of total population

Place	Population	%
Heritage Lake (cdp) Putnam County	2	0.07
Speedway (town) Marion County	4	0.03
Kokomo (city) Howard County	2	<0.01
Evansville (city) Vanderburgh County	1	<0.01
South Bend (city) St. Joseph County	1	<0.01
Aberdeen (cdp) Porter County	0	0.00
Advance (town) Boone County	0	0.00
Akron (town) Fulton County	0	0.00
Alamo (town) Montgomery County	0	0.00
Albany (town) Delaware County	0	0.00

Top 10 Places Sorted by Percent of Total Population

Based on places with total population of 50,000 or more

Place	Population	%
Evansville (city) Vanderburgh County	1	<0.01
South Bend (city) St. Joseph County	1	<0.01
Anderson (city) Madison County	0	0.00
Bloomington (city) Monroe County	0	0.00
Carmel (city) Hamilton County	0	0.00
Elkhart (city) Elkhart County	0	0.00
Fishers (town) Hamilton County	0	0.00
Fort Wayne (city) Allen County	0	0.00
Gary (city) Lake County	0	0.00
Hammond (city) Lake County	0	0.00

American Indian: Comanche

Top 10 Places Sorted by Population

Based on all places, regardless of total population

Place	Population	%
Indianapolis (city) Marion County	28	<0.01
Mooresville (town) Morgan County	4	0.04
Fort Wayne (city) Allen County	4	<0.01
Hunter (town) Allen County	3	0.06
Greenwood (city) Johnson County	3	0.01
Lawrence (city) Marion County	3	0.01
Carmel (city) Hamilton County	3	<0.01
Hammond (city) Lake County	3	<0.01
Lafayette (city) Tippecanoe County	3	<0.01
Etna Green (town) Kosciusko County	2	0.34

Top 10 Places Sorted by Percent of Total Population

Based on all places, regardless of total population

Place	Population	%
Etna Green (town) Kosciusko County	2	0.34
Francesville (town) Pulaski County	2	0.23
Medaryville (town) Pulaski County	1	0.16
Roseland (town) St. Joseph County	1	0.16
West College Corner (town) Union County	1	0.15
Bristol (town) Elkhart County	2	0.12
Hunter (town) Allen County	3	0.06
Crothersville (town) Jackson County	1	0.06
Mooresville (town) Morgan County	4	0.04
Fairmount (town) Grant County	1	0.03

Top 10 Places Sorted by Percent of Total Population

Based on places with total population of 50,000 or more

Place	Population	%
Indianapolis (city) Marion County	28	<0.01
Fort Wayne (city) Allen County	4	<0.01
Carmel (city) Hamilton County	3	<0.01
Hammond (city) Lake County	3	<0.01
Lafayette (city) Tippecanoe County	3	<0.01
Elkhart (city) Elkhart County	2	<0.01
Evansville (city) Vanderburgh County	2	<0.01
Gary (city) Lake County	2	<0.01
Terre Haute (city) Vigo County	2	<0.01
South Bend (city) St. Joseph County	1	<0.01

American Indian: Cree

Top 10 Places Sorted by Population

Based on all places, regardless of total population

Place	Population	%
Indianapolis (city) Marion County	13	<0.01
Terre Haute (city) Vigo County	9	0.01
Fort Wayne (city) Allen County	9	<0.01
Gary (city) Lake County	7	0.01
Muncie (city) Delaware County	5	0.01
Elkhart (city) Elkhart County	4	0.01
Plymouth (city) Marshall County	3	0.03
Plainfield (town) Hendricks County	3	0.01
Carmel (city) Hamilton County	3	<0.01
Logansport (city) Cass County	2	0.01

Top 10 Places Sorted by Percent of Total Population

Based on all places, regardless of total population

Place	Population	%
Losantville (town) Randolph County	1	0.42
Boswell (town) Benton County	1	0.13
Mulberry (town) Clinton County	1	0.08
Warren Park (town) Marion County	1	0.07
Plymouth (city) Marshall County	3	0.03
Middlebury (town) Elkhart County	1	0.03
Greendale (city) Dearborn County	1	0.02
Hartford City (city) Blackford County	1	0.02
Terre Haute (city) Vigo County	9	0.01
Gary (city) Lake County	7	0.01

Top 10 Places Sorted by Percent of Total Population

Based on places with total population of 50,000 or more

Place	Population	%
Terre Haute (city) Vigo County	9	0.01
Gary (city) Lake County	7	0.01
Muncie (city) Delaware County	5	0.01
Elkhart (city) Elkhart County	4	0.01
Indianapolis (city) Marion County	13	<0.01
Fort Wayne (city) Allen County	9	<0.01
Carmel (city) Hamilton County	3	<0.01
Evansville (city) Vanderburgh County	2	<0.01
Bloomington (city) Monroe County	1	<0.01
Fishers (town) Hamilton County	1	<0.01

American Indian: Creek

Top 10 Places Sorted by Population

Based on all places, regardless of total population

Place	Population	%
Indianapolis (city) Marion County	31	<0.01
Gary (city) Lake County	20	0.02
Fort Wayne (city) Allen County	18	0.01
Hammond (city) Lake County	10	0.01
Jeffersonville (city) Clark County	9	0.02
Valparaiso (city) Porter County	8	0.03
Noblesville (city) Hamilton County	8	0.02
Portage (city) Porter County	8	0.02
Terre Haute (city) Vigo County	8	0.01
Lake Station (city) Lake County	7	0.06

Top 10 Places Sorted by Percent of Total Population

Based on all places, regardless of total population

Place	Population	%
Laketon (cdp) Wabash County	3	0.48
Grandview (town) Spencer County	3	0.40
Holland (town) Dubois County	2	0.32

Roseland (town) St. Joseph County	2	0.32
Michiana Shores (town) LaPorte County	1	0.32
Ferdinand (town) Dubois County	5	0.23
Cannelton (city) Perry County	3	0.19
Monticello (city) White County	6	0.11
Brook (town) Newton County	1	0.10
Green (town) Howard County	2	0.08

Top 10 Places Sorted by Percent of Total Population

Based on places with total population of 50,000 or more

Place	Population	%
Gary (city) Lake County	20	0.02
Noblesville (city) Hamilton County	8	0.02
Fort Wayne (city) Allen County	18	0.01
Hammond (city) Lake County	10	0.01
Terre Haute (city) Vigo County	8	0.01
Bloomington (city) Monroe County	5	0.01
Elkhart (city) Elkhart County	4	0.01
Lafayette (city) Tippecanoe County	4	0.01
Anderson (city) Madison County	3	0.01
Indianapolis (city) Marion County	31	<0.01

American Indian: Crow

Top 10 Places Sorted by Population

Based on all places, regardless of total population

Place	Population	%
Fort Wayne (city) Allen County	12	<0.01
Indianapolis (city) Marion County	11	<0.01
Franklin (city) Johnson County	6	0.03
Ligonier (city) Noble County	5	0.11
Galveston (town) Cass County	4	0.31
Greenfield (city) Hancock County	4	0.02
Elkhart (city) Elkhart County	4	0.01
Hammond (city) Lake County	4	<0.01
Marion (city) Grant County	3	0.01
Bargersville (town) Johnson County	2	0.05

Top 10 Places Sorted by Percent of Total Population

Based on all places, regardless of total population

Place	Population	%
Galveston (town) Cass County	4	0.31
Coalmont (cdp) Clay County	1	0.25
Ligonier (city) Noble County	5	0.11
Bargersville (town) Johnson County	2	0.05
New Palestine (town) Hancock County	1	0.05
Franklin (city) Johnson County	6	0.03
Delphi (city) Carroll County	1	0.03
Greenfield (city) Hancock County	4	0.02
Bremen (town) Marshall County	1	0.02
Gas City (city) Grant County	1	0.02

Top 10 Places Sorted by Percent of Total Population

Based on places with total population of 50,000 or more

Place	Population	%
Elkhart (city) Elkhart County	4	0.01
Fort Wayne (city) Allen County	12	<0.01
Indianapolis (city) Marion County	11	<0.01
Hammond (city) Lake County	4	<0.01
Lafayette (city) Tippecanoe County	2	<0.01
Muncie (city) Delaware County	2	<0.01
Carmel (city) Hamilton County	1	<0.01
Evansville (city) Vanderburgh County	1	<0.01
Noblesville (city) Hamilton County	1	<0.01
Anderson (city) Madison County	0	0.00

American Indian: Delaware

Top 10 Places Sorted by Population

Based on all places, regardless of total population

Place	Population	%
Indianapolis (city) Marion County	27	<0.01
Fort Wayne (city) Allen County	12	<0.01
Bloomington (city) Monroe County	8	0.01
Milroy (cdp) Rush County	6	0.99
Anderson (city) Madison County	6	0.01
Evansville (city) Vanderburgh County	6	0.01
Mishawaka (city) St. Joseph County	6	0.01
Mount Vernon (city) Posey County	4	0.06
Goshen (city) Elkhart County	4	0.01
Clermont (town) Marion County	3	0.22

Top 10 Places Sorted by Percent of Total Population

Based on all places, regardless of total population

Place	Population	%
Milroy (cdp) Rush County	6	0.99
Fontanet (cdp) Vigo County	1	0.24
Richland (town) Spencer County	1	0.24
Clermont (town) Marion County	3	0.22
West Baden Springs (town) Orange County	1	0.17
Patoka (town) Gibson County	1	0.14
Argos (town) Marshall County	2	0.12
Eaton (town) Delaware County	2	0.11
Francesville (town) Pulaski County	1	0.11
Gaston (town) Delaware County	1	0.11

Top 10 Places Sorted by Percent of Total Population

Based on places with total population of 50,000 or more

Place	Population	%
Bloomington (city) Monroe County	8	0.01
Anderson (city) Madison County	6	0.01
Evansville (city) Vanderburgh County	6	0.01
Indianapolis (city) Marion County	27	<0.01
Fort Wayne (city) Allen County	12	<0.01
Lafayette (city) Tippecanoe County	3	<0.01
Fishers (town) Hamilton County	2	<0.01
Gary (city) Lake County	2	<0.01
Muncie (city) Delaware County	2	<0.01
South Bend (city) St. Joseph County	1	<0.01

American Indian: Hopi

Top 10 Places Sorted by Population

Based on all places, regardless of total population

Place	Population	%
Indianapolis (city) Marion County	13	<0.01
Fort Wayne (city) Allen County	7	<0.01
North Salem (town) Hendricks County	4	0.77
Carmel (city) Hamilton County	4	0.01
Richmond (city) Wayne County	3	0.01
Portage (city) Porter County	2	0.01
Bloomington (city) Monroe County	2	<0.01
Kokomo (city) Howard County	2	<0.01
Griffith (town) Lake County	1	0.01
Anderson (city) Madison County	1	<0.01

Top 10 Places Sorted by Percent of Total Population

Based on all places, regardless of total population

Place	Population	%
North Salem (town) Hendricks County	4	0.77
Carmel (city) Hamilton County	4	0.01
Richmond (city) Wayne County	3	0.01
Portage (city) Porter County	2	0.01
Griffith (town) Lake County	1	0.01
Indianapolis (city) Marion County	13	<0.01
Fort Wayne (city) Allen County	7	<0.01
Bloomington (city) Monroe County	2	<0.01
Kokomo (city) Howard County	2	<0.01
Anderson (city) Madison County	1	<0.01

Top 10 Places Sorted by Percent of Total Population

Based on places with total population of 50,000 or more

Place	Population	%
Carmel (city) Hamilton County	4	0.01
Indianapolis (city) Marion County	13	<0.01
Fort Wayne (city) Allen County	7	<0.01
Bloomington (city) Monroe County	2	<0.01
Anderson (city) Madison County	1	<0.01
Evansville (city) Vanderburgh County	1	<0.01
Elkhart (city) Elkhart County	0	0.00
Fishers (town) Hamilton County	0	0.00
Gary (city) Lake County	0	0.00
Hammond (city) Lake County	0	0.00

American Indian: Houma

Top 10 Places Sorted by Population

Based on all places, regardless of total population

Place	Population	%
Lafayette (city) Tippecanoe County	6	0.01
Charlestown (city) Clark County	4	0.05
Evansville (city) Vanderburgh County	4	<0.01
Gary (city) Lake County	4	<0.01
La Fontaine (town) Wabash County	3	0.34
Martinsville (city) Morgan County	3	0.03
Fort Wayne (city) Allen County	3	<0.01
Indianapolis (city) Marion County	3	<0.01
East Chicago (city) Lake County	2	0.01
Portage (city) Porter County	2	0.01

Top 10 Places Sorted by Percent of Total Population

Based on all places, regardless of total population

Place	Population	%
La Fontaine (town) Wabash County	3	0.34
Charlestown (city) Clark County	4	0.05
Martinsville (city) Morgan County	3	0.03
Corydon (town) Harrison County	1	0.03
Lafayette (city) Tippecanoe County	6	0.01
East Chicago (city) Lake County	2	0.01
Portage (city) Porter County	2	0.01
Evansville (city) Vanderburgh County	4	<0.01
Gary (city) Lake County	4	<0.01
Fort Wayne (city) Allen County	3	<0.01

Top 10 Places Sorted by Percent of Total Population

Based on places with total population of 50,000 or more

Place	Population	%
Lafayette (city) Tippecanoe County	6	0.01
Evansville (city) Vanderburgh County	4	<0.01
Gary (city) Lake County	4	<0.01
Fort Wayne (city) Allen County	3	<0.01
Indianapolis (city) Marion County	3	<0.01
Terre Haute (city) Vigo County	2	<0.01
Anderson (city) Madison County	0	0.00
Bloomington (city) Monroe County	0	0.00
Carmel (city) Hamilton County	0	0.00
Elkhart (city) Elkhart County	0	0.00

Alaska Native: Inupiat (Eskimo)

Top 10 Places Sorted by Population

Based on all places, regardless of total population

Place	Population	%
Indianapolis (city) Marion County	20	<0.01
Merrillville (town) Lake County	8	0.02
Frankfort (city) Clinton County	4	0.02
Jeffersonville (city) Clark County	4	0.01
Vallonia (cdp) Jackson County	3	0.89
Hillsboro (town) Fountain County	3	0.56
Pendleton (town) Madison County	3	0.07
Madison (city) Jefferson County	3	0.03
Bloomington (city) Monroe County	3	<0.01
Fort Wayne (city) Allen County	3	<0.01

Top 10 Places Sorted by Percent of Total Population

Based on all places, regardless of total population

Place	Population	%
Vallonia (cdp) Jackson County	3	0.89
Hillsboro (town) Fountain County	3	0.56
Pendleton (town) Madison County	3	0.07
Montpelier (city) Blackford County	1	0.06
Madison (city) Jefferson County	3	0.03
Browns (town) Jackson County	1	0.03
Merrillville (town) Lake County	8	0.02
Frankfort (city) Clinton County	4	0.02
Lowell (town) Lake County	2	0.02
Mooresville (town) Morgan County	2	0.02

Top 10 Places Sorted by Percent of Total Population

Based on places with total population of 50,000 or more

Place	Population	%
Indianapolis (city) Marion County	20	<0.01
Bloomington (city) Monroe County	3	<0.01
Fort Wayne (city) Allen County	3	<0.01
Anderson (city) Madison County	1	<0.01
Carmel (city) Hamilton County	1	<0.01
Evansville (city) Vanderburgh County	1	<0.01
Lafayette (city) Tippecanoe County	1	<0.01
Noblesville (city) Hamilton County	1	<0.01
South Bend (city) St. Joseph County	1	<0.01
Elkhart (city) Elkhart County	0	0.00

American Indian: Iroquois

Top 10 Places Sorted by Population

Based on all places, regardless of total population

Place	Population	%
Indianapolis (city) Marion County	96	0.01
Fort Wayne (city) Allen County	41	0.02
Lafayette (city) Tippecanoe County	14	0.02
Evansville (city) Vanderburgh County	14	0.01
Lawrence (city) Marion County	10	0.02
Bloomington (city) Monroe County	9	0.01
Greenwood (city) Johnson County	8	0.02
Richmond (city) Wayne County	8	0.02
Carmel (city) Hamilton County	8	0.01
Lake Station (city) Lake County	7	0.06

Top 10 Places Sorted by Percent of Total Population

Based on all places, regardless of total population

Place	Population	%
Laurel (town) Franklin County	4	0.78
Grandview (town) Spencer County	4	0.53
Altona (town) DeKalb County	1	0.51
Fish Lake (cdp) LaPorte County	3	0.30
Mulberry (town) Clinton County	3	0.24
Wheeler (cdp) Porter County	1	0.23
Reynolds (town) White County	1	0.19
Medora (town) Jackson County	1	0.14
Town of Pines (town) Porter County	1	0.14
Fountain City (town) Wayne County	1	0.13

Top 10 Places Sorted by Percent of Total Population

Based on places with total population of 50,000 or more

Place	Population	%
Fort Wayne (city) Allen County	41	0.02
Lafayette (city) Tippecanoe County	14	0.02
Indianapolis (city) Marion County	96	0.01
Evansville (city) Vanderburgh County	14	0.01
Bloomington (city) Monroe County	9	0.01
Carmel (city) Hamilton County	8	0.01
Anderson (city) Madison County	7	0.01
Muncie (city) Delaware County	7	0.01
Fishers (town) Hamilton County	6	0.01
Hammond (city) Lake County	6	0.01

American Indian: Kiowa

Top 10 Places Sorted by Population

Based on all places, regardless of total population

Place	Population	%
Indianapolis (city) Marion County	5	<0.01
Fort Wayne (city) Allen County	3	<0.01
Wabash (city) Wabash County	2	0.02
Crawfordsville (city) Montgomery County	2	0.01
Hobart (city) Lake County	2	0.01
Terre Haute (city) Vigo County	2	<0.01
Spring Hill (town) Marion County	1	1.02
Hebron (town) Porter County	1	0.03
Salem (city) Washington County	1	0.02
Greensburg (city) Decatur County	1	0.01

Top 10 Places Sorted by Percent of Total Population

Based on all places, regardless of total population

Place	Population	%
Spring Hill (town) Marion County	1	1.02
Hebron (town) Porter County	1	0.03
Wabash (city) Wabash County	2	0.02
Salem (city) Washington County	1	0.02
Crawfordsville (city) Montgomery County	2	0.01
Hobart (city) Lake County	2	0.01
Greensburg (city) Decatur County	1	0.01
Seymour (city) Jackson County	1	0.01
Indianapolis (city) Marion County	5	<0.01
Fort Wayne (city) Allen County	3	<0.01

Top 10 Places Sorted by Percent of Total Population

Based on places with total population of 50,000 or more

Place	Population	%
Indianapolis (city) Marion County	5	<0.01
Fort Wayne (city) Allen County	3	<0.01
Terre Haute (city) Vigo County	2	<0.01
Anderson (city) Madison County	1	<0.01
Evansville (city) Vanderburgh County	1	<0.01
Fishers (town) Hamilton County	1	<0.01
Bloomington (city) Monroe County	0	0.00
Carmel (city) Hamilton County	0	0.00
Elkhart (city) Elkhart County	0	0.00
Gary (city) Lake County	0	0.00

American Indian: Lumbee

Top 10 Places Sorted by Population

Based on all places, regardless of total population

Place	Population	%
Indianapolis (city) Marion County	17	<0.01
Evansville (city) Vanderburgh County	11	0.01
Bedford (city) Lawrence County	10	0.07
South Bend (city) St. Joseph County	10	0.01
Elkhart (city) Elkhart County	8	0.02
Marion (city) Grant County	6	0.02
Fishers (town) Hamilton County	6	0.01
Lafayette (city) Tippecanoe County	5	0.01
New Whiteland (town) Johnson County	4	0.07
Bloomington (city) Monroe County	4	<0.01

Top 10 Places Sorted by Percent of Total Population

Based on all places, regardless of total population

Place	Population	%
Hatfield (cdp) Spencer County	2	0.25
Clay City (town) Clay County	2	0.23
Poseyville (town) Posey County	2	0.19
Stockwell (cdp) Tippecanoe County	1	0.18
Farmland (town) Randolph County	2	0.15
Parker City (town) Randolph County	2	0.14
Dillsboro (town) Dearborn County	1	0.08
Bedford (city) Lawrence County	10	0.07
New Whiteland (town) Johnson County	4	0.07
Cumberland (town) Marion County	2	0.04

Top 10 Places Sorted by Percent of Total Population

Based on places with total population of 50,000 or more

Place	Population	%
Elkhart (city) Elkhart County	8	0.02
Evansville (city) Vanderburgh County	11	0.01
South Bend (city) St. Joseph County	10	0.01
Fishers (town) Hamilton County	6	0.01
Lafayette (city) Tippecanoe County	5	0.01
Indianapolis (city) Marion County	17	<0.01
Bloomington (city) Monroe County	4	<0.01
Gary (city) Lake County	3	<0.01
Muncie (city) Delaware County	3	<0.01
Carmel (city) Hamilton County	2	<0.01

American Indian: Menominee

Top 10 Places Sorted by Population

Based on all places, regardless of total population

Place	Population	%
Gary (city) Lake County	6	0.01
Indianapolis (city) Marion County	5	<0.01
Whiting (city) Lake County	3	0.06
Elwood (city) Madison County	2	0.02
Hobart (city) Lake County	2	0.01
Munster (town) Lake County	2	0.01
Bloomington (city) Monroe County	2	<0.01
Fishers (town) Hamilton County	2	<0.01
Mishawaka (city) St. Joseph County	2	<0.01
English (town) Crawford County	1	0.16

Top 10 Places Sorted by Percent of Total Population

Based on all places, regardless of total population

Place	Population	%
English (town) Crawford County	1	0.16
Geneva (town) Adams County	1	0.08
Hudson Lake (cdp) LaPorte County	1	0.08
Kingsford Heights (town) LaPorte County	1	0.07
Whiting (city) Lake County	3	0.06
Montpelier (city) Blackford County	1	0.06
Elwood (city) Madison County	2	0.02
Gary (city) Lake County	6	0.01
Hobart (city) Lake County	2	0.01
Munster (town) Lake County	2	0.01

Top 10 Places Sorted by Percent of Total Population

Based on places with total population of 50,000 or more

Place	Population	%
Gary (city) Lake County	6	0.01
Indianapolis (city) Marion County	5	<0.01
Bloomington (city) Monroe County	2	<0.01
Fishers (town) Hamilton County	2	<0.01
Fort Wayne (city) Allen County	1	<0.01
Hammond (city) Lake County	1	<0.01
Muncie (city) Delaware County	1	<0.01
South Bend (city) St. Joseph County	1	<0.01
Terre Haute (city) Vigo County	1	<0.01
Anderson (city) Madison County	0	0.00

American Indian: Mexican American Indian

Top 10 Places Sorted by Population

Based on all places, regardless of total population

Place	Population	%
Indianapolis (city) Marion County	263	0.03
Hammond (city) Lake County	69	0.09
Fort Wayne (city) Allen County	67	0.03
Elkhart (city) Elkhart County	55	0.11
South Bend (city) St. Joseph County	54	0.05
East Chicago (city) Lake County	48	0.16
Goshen (city) Elkhart County	35	0.11
Logansport (city) Cass County	32	0.17
Anderson (city) Madison County	30	0.05
Lafayette (city) Tippecanoe County	24	0.04

Top 10 Places Sorted by Percent of Total Population

Based on all places, regardless of total population

Place	Population	%
Millersburg (town) Elkhart County	5	0.55
Burket (town) Kosciusko County	1	0.51
Delphi (city) Carroll County	11	0.38
Somerset (cdp) Wabash County	1	0.25
New Chicago (town) Lake County	4	0.20
Kingman (town) Fountain County	1	0.20
Dale (town) Spencer County	3	0.19
Logansport (city) Cass County	32	0.17
Bargersville (town) Johnson County	7	0.17
Rocky Ripple (town) Marion County	1	0.17

Top 10 Places Sorted by Percent of Total Population

Based on places with total population of 50,000 or more

Place	Population	%
Elkhart (city) Elkhart County	55	0.11
Hammond (city) Lake County	69	0.09
South Bend (city) St. Joseph County	54	0.05
Anderson (city) Madison County	30	0.05
Lafayette (city) Tippecanoe County	24	0.04
Indianapolis (city) Marion County	263	0.03
Fort Wayne (city) Allen County	67	0.03
Carmel (city) Hamilton County	21	0.03
Terre Haute (city) Vigo County	20	0.03
Gary (city) Lake County	15	0.02

American Indian: Navajo

Top 10 Places Sorted by Population

Based on all places, regardless of total population

Place	Population	%
Indianapolis (city) Marion County	100	0.01
Fort Wayne (city) Allen County	26	0.01
Valparaiso (city) Porter County	12	0.04
Anderson (city) Madison County	11	0.02
Evansville (city) Vanderburgh County	10	0.01
Bloomington (city) Monroe County	9	0.01
South Bend (city) St. Joseph County	8	0.01
Richmond (city) Wayne County	7	0.02
Elkhart (city) Elkhart County	7	0.01
Muncie (city) Delaware County	7	0.01

Top 10 Places Sorted by Percent of Total Population

Based on all places, regardless of total population

Place	Population	%
Patoka (town) Gibson County	6	0.82
Coalmont (cdp) Clay County	3	0.75

Elizabeth (town) Harrison County	1	0.62
Odon (town) Daviess County	6	0.44
Kingsbury (town) LaPorte County	1	0.41
Dana (town) Vermillion County	2	0.33
New Salisbury (cdp) Harrison County	2	0.33
Burns Harbor (town) Porter County	3	0.26
Hope (town) Bartholomew County	5	0.24
Clay City (town) Clay County	2	0.23

Top 10 Places Sorted by Percent of Total Population

Based on places with total population of 50,000 or more

Place	Population	%
Anderson (city) Madison County	11	0.02
Indianapolis (city) Marion County	100	0.01
Fort Wayne (city) Allen County	26	0.01
Evansville (city) Vanderburgh County	10	0.01
Bloomington (city) Monroe County	9	0.01
South Bend (city) St. Joseph County	8	0.01
Elkhart (city) Elkhart County	7	0.01
Muncie (city) Delaware County	7	0.01
Gary (city) Lake County	6	0.01
Terre Haute (city) Vigo County	6	0.01

American Indian: Osage

Top 10 Places Sorted by Population

Based on all places, regardless of total population

Place	Population	%
Indianapolis (city) Marion County	15	<0.01
New Haven (city) Allen County	5	0.03
Portage (city) Porter County	5	0.01
Indian Heights (cdp) Howard County	4	0.13
North Terre Haute (cdp) Vigo County	3	0.07
Huntington (city) Huntington County	3	0.02
St. John (town) Lake County	3	0.02
Westfield (town) Hamilton County	3	0.01
Carmel (city) Hamilton County	3	<0.01
Linton (city) Greene County	2	0.04

Top 10 Places Sorted by Percent of Total Population

Based on all places, regardless of total population

Place	Population	%
Medaryville (town) Pulaski County	1	0.16
Indian Heights (cdp) Howard County	4	0.13
Ridgeville (town) Randolph County	1	0.12
Bass Lake (cdp) Starke County	1	0.08
Sweetser (town) Grant County	1	0.08
North Terre Haute (cdp) Vigo County	3	0.07
Fairview Park (town) Vermillion County	1	0.07
Shadeland (town) Tippecanoe County	1	0.06
Cloverdale (town) Putnam County	1	0.05
Linton (city) Greene County	2	0.04

Top 10 Places Sorted by Percent of Total Population

Based on places with total population of 50,000 or more

Place	Population	%
Indianapolis (city) Marion County	15	<0.01
Carmel (city) Hamilton County	3	<0.01
Anderson (city) Madison County	2	<0.01
Bloomington (city) Monroe County	2	<0.01
Evansville (city) Vanderburgh County	2	<0.01
Fort Wayne (city) Allen County	1	<0.01
Muncie (city) Delaware County	1	<0.01
Noblesville (city) Hamilton County	1	<0.01
Terre Haute (city) Vigo County	1	<0.01
Elkhart (city) Elkhart County	0	0.00

American Indian: Ottawa

Top 10 Places Sorted by Population

Based on all places, regardless of total population

Place	Population	%
Fort Wayne (city) Allen County	15	0.01
Indianapolis (city) Marion County	15	<0.01
Elkhart (city) Elkhart County	6	0.01
Mishawaka (city) St. Joseph County	6	0.01
North Judson (town) Starke County	5	0.28
Carmel (city) Hamilton County	5	0.01
Lafayette (city) Tippecanoe County	5	0.01
Edinburgh (town) Johnson County	4	0.09
Jeffersonville (city) Clark County	4	0.01
George (town) Floyd County	3	0.10

Top 10 Places Sorted by Percent of Total Population

Based on all places, regardless of total population

Place	Population	%
Switz City (town) Greene County	1	0.34
North Judson (town) Starke County	5	0.28
Wolcottville (town) Noble County	2	0.20
Warren (town) Huntington County	2	0.16
George (town) Floyd County	3	0.10
Edinburgh (town) Johnson County	4	0.09
Daleville (town) Delaware County	1	0.06
New Carlisle (town) St. Joseph County	1	0.05
Winchester (city) Randolph County	2	0.04
Butler (city) DeKalb County	1	0.04

Top 10 Places Sorted by Percent of Total Population

Based on places with total population of 50,000 or more

Place	Population	%
Fort Wayne (city) Allen County	15	0.01
Elkhart (city) Elkhart County	6	0.01
Carmel (city) Hamilton County	5	0.01
Lafayette (city) Tippecanoe County	5	0.01
Indianapolis (city) Marion County	15	<0.01
Hammond (city) Lake County	3	<0.01
South Bend (city) St. Joseph County	3	<0.01
Bloomington (city) Monroe County	1	<0.01
Fishers (town) Hamilton County	1	<0.01
Anderson (city) Madison County	0	0.00

American Indian: Paiute

Top 10 Places Sorted by Population

Based on all places, regardless of total population

Place	Population	%
Indianapolis (city) Marion County	5	<0.01
Lebanon (city) Boone County	4	0.03
Elkhart (city) Elkhart County	3	0.01
Schererville (town) Lake County	3	0.01
Fishers (town) Hamilton County	3	<0.01
South Bend (city) St. Joseph County	3	<0.01
Dayton (town) Tippecanoe County	1	0.07
Notre Dame (cdp) St. Joseph County	1	0.02
Madison (city) Jefferson County	1	0.01
Fort Wayne (city) Allen County	1	<0.01

Top 10 Places Sorted by Percent of Total Population

Based on all places, regardless of total population

Place	Population	%
Dayton (town) Tippecanoe County	1	0.07
Lebanon (city) Boone County	4	0.03
Notre Dame (cdp) St. Joseph County	1	0.02
Elkhart (city) Elkhart County	3	0.01
Schererville (town) Lake County	3	0.01
Madison (city) Jefferson County	1	0.01
Indianapolis (city) Marion County	5	<0.01
Fishers (town) Hamilton County	3	<0.01
South Bend (city) St. Joseph County	3	<0.01
Fort Wayne (city) Allen County	1	<0.01

Top 10 Places Sorted by Percent of Total Population

Based on places with total population of 50,000 or more

Place	Population	%
Elkhart (city) Elkhart County	3	0.01
Indianapolis (city) Marion County	5	<0.01
Fishers (town) Hamilton County	3	<0.01
South Bend (city) St. Joseph County	3	<0.01
Fort Wayne (city) Allen County	1	<0.01
Gary (city) Lake County	1	<0.01
Anderson (city) Madison County	0	0.00
Bloomington (city) Monroe County	0	0.00
Carmel (city) Hamilton County	0	0.00
Evansville (city) Vanderburgh County	0	0.00

American Indian: Pima

Top 10 Places Sorted by Population

Based on all places, regardless of total population

Place	Population	%
Fort Wayne (city) Allen County	7	<0.01
Cedar Lake (town) Lake County	3	0.03
Clarksville (town) Clark County	3	0.01
Richmond (city) Wayne County	2	0.01
Linton (city) Greene County	1	0.02
Greenfield (city) Hancock County	1	<0.01
Indianapolis (city) Marion County	1	<0.01
Aberdeen (cdp) Porter County	0	0.00
Advance (town) Boone County	0	0.00
Akron (town) Fulton County	0	0.00

Top 10 Places Sorted by Percent of Total Population

Based on all places, regardless of total population

Place	Population	%
Cedar Lake (town) Lake County	3	0.03
Linton (city) Greene County	1	0.02
Clarksville (town) Clark County	3	0.01
Richmond (city) Wayne County	2	0.01
Fort Wayne (city) Allen County	7	<0.01
Greenfield (city) Hancock County	1	<0.01
Indianapolis (city) Marion County	1	<0.01
Aberdeen (cdp) Porter County	0	0.00
Advance (town) Boone County	0	0.00
Akron (town) Fulton County	0	0.00

Top 10 Places Sorted by Percent of Total Population

Based on places with total population of 50,000 or more

Place	Population	%
Fort Wayne (city) Allen County	7	<0.01
Indianapolis (city) Marion County	1	<0.01
Anderson (city) Madison County	0	0.00
Bloomington (city) Monroe County	0	0.00
Carmel (city) Hamilton County	0	0.00
Elkhart (city) Elkhart County	0	0.00
Evansville (city) Vanderburgh County	0	0.00
Fishers (town) Hamilton County	0	0.00
Gary (city) Lake County	0	0.00
Hammond (city) Lake County	0	0.00

American Indian: Potawatomi

Top 10 Places Sorted by Population

Based on all places, regardless of total population

Place	Population	%
Indianapolis (city) Marion County	88	0.01
South Bend (city) St. Joseph County	74	0.07
Mishawaka (city) St. Joseph County	58	0.12
Elkhart (city) Elkhart County	28	0.05
Fort Wayne (city) Allen County	26	0.01
Granger (cdp) St. Joseph County	16	0.05
Carmel (city) Hamilton County	11	0.01
Valparaiso (city) Porter County	10	0.03
Bloomington (city) Monroe County	10	0.01
Anderson (city) Madison County	7	0.01

Top 10 Places Sorted by Percent of Total Population

Based on all places, regardless of total population

Place	Population	%
Bass Lake (cdp) Starke County	4	0.33
Fountain City (town) Wayne County	2	0.25
Hanna (cdp) LaPorte County	1	0.22
New Carlisle (town) St. Joseph County	4	0.21
Wakarusa (town) Elkhart County	3	0.17
Morris (town) Shelby County	2	0.16
Farmland (town) Randolph County	2	0.15
Hudson Lake (cdp) LaPorte County	2	0.15
Darmstadt (town) Vanderburgh County	2	0.14
Kingsford Heights (town) LaPorte County	2	0.14

Top 10 Places Sorted by Percent of Total Population

Based on places with total population of 50,000 or more

Place	Population	%
South Bend (city) St. Joseph County	74	0.07
Elkhart (city) Elkhart County	28	0.05
Indianapolis (city) Marion County	88	0.01
Fort Wayne (city) Allen County	26	0.01
Carmel (city) Hamilton County	11	0.01
Bloomington (city) Monroe County	10	0.01
Anderson (city) Madison County	7	0.01
Fishers (town) Hamilton County	7	0.01
Hammond (city) Lake County	6	0.01
Lafayette (city) Tippecanoe County	6	0.01

American Indian: Pueblo

Top 10 Places Sorted by Population

Based on all places, regardless of total population

Place	Population	%
Indianapolis (city) Marion County	26	<0.01
Fort Wayne (city) Allen County	7	<0.01
Goshen (city) Elkhart County	6	0.02
Lawrence (city) Marion County	5	0.01
South Bend (city) St. Joseph County	4	<0.01
Crawfordsville (city) Montgomery County	3	0.02
Portage (city) Porter County	3	0.01
West Lafayette (city) Tippecanoe County	3	0.01
Bloomington (city) Monroe County	3	<0.01
Evansville (city) Vanderburgh County	3	<0.01

Top 10 Places Sorted by Percent of Total Population

Based on all places, regardless of total population

Place	Population	%
Argos (town) Marshall County	2	0.12
Hartford City (city) Blackford County	2	0.03
Goshen (city) Elkhart County	6	0.02
Crawfordsville (city) Montgomery County	3	0.02
Danville (town) Hendricks County	2	0.02
Lake Station (city) Lake County	2	0.02
Wabash (city) Wabash County	2	0.02
Edinburgh (town) Johnson County	1	0.02
Rensselaer (city) Jasper County	1	0.02
Winona Lake (town) Kosciusko County	1	0.02

Top 10 Places Sorted by Percent of Total Population

Based on places with total population of 50,000 or more

Place	Population	%
Indianapolis (city) Marion County	26	<0.01
Fort Wayne (city) Allen County	7	<0.01
South Bend (city) St. Joseph County	4	<0.01
Bloomington (city) Monroe County	3	<0.01
Evansville (city) Vanderburgh County	3	<0.01
Fishers (town) Hamilton County	1	<0.01
Muncie (city) Delaware County	1	<0.01
Anderson (city) Madison County	0	0.00
Carmel (city) Hamilton County	0	0.00
Elkhart (city) Elkhart County	0	0.00

American Indian: Puget Sound Salish

Top 10 Places Sorted by Population

Based on all places, regardless of total population

Place	Population	%
Bloomington (city) Monroe County	5	0.01
Hammond (city) Lake County	2	<0.01
Mishawaka (city) St. Joseph County	2	<0.01
Muncie (city) Delaware County	1	<0.01
Aberdeen (cdp) Porter County	0	0.00
Advance (town) Boone County	0	0.00
Akron (town) Fulton County	0	0.00
Alamo (town) Montgomery County	0	0.00
Albany (town) Delaware County	0	0.00
Albion (town) Noble County	0	0.00

Top 10 Places Sorted by Percent of Total Population

Based on all places, regardless of total population

Place	Population	%
Bloomington (city) Monroe County	5	0.01
Hammond (city) Lake County	2	<0.01
Mishawaka (city) St. Joseph County	2	<0.01
Muncie (city) Delaware County	1	<0.01
Aberdeen (cdp) Porter County	0	0.00
Advance (town) Boone County	0	0.00
Akron (town) Fulton County	0	0.00
Alamo (town) Montgomery County	0	0.00
Albany (town) Delaware County	0	0.00
Albion (town) Noble County	0	0.00

Top 10 Places Sorted by Percent of Total Population

Based on places with total population of 50,000 or more

Place	Population	%
Bloomington (city) Monroe County	5	0.01
Hammond (city) Lake County	2	<0.01
Muncie (city) Delaware County	1	<0.01
Anderson (city) Madison County	0	0.00
Carmel (city) Hamilton County	0	0.00
Elkhart (city) Elkhart County	0	0.00
Evansville (city) Vanderburgh County	0	0.00
Fishers (town) Hamilton County	0	0.00
Fort Wayne (city) Allen County	0	0.00
Gary (city) Lake County	0	0.00

American Indian: Seminole

Top 10 Places Sorted by Population

Based on all places, regardless of total population

Place	Population	%
Indianapolis (city) Marion County	17	<0.01
Gary (city) Lake County	12	0.01
Fort Wayne (city) Allen County	11	<0.01
Lafayette (city) Tippecanoe County	5	0.01
South Bend (city) St. Joseph County	5	<0.01
Linton (city) Greene County	3	0.06
Kokomo (city) Howard County	3	0.01
New Albany (city) Floyd County	3	0.01
Valparaiso (city) Porter County	3	0.01
Bloomington (city) Monroe County	3	<0.01

Top 10 Places Sorted by Percent of Total Population

Based on all places, regardless of total population

Place	Population	%
Boswell (town) Benton County	1	0.13
Orleans (town) Orange County	2	0.09
Topeka (town) LaGrange County	1	0.09
Linton (city) Greene County	3	0.06
Wakarusa (town) Elkhart County	1	0.06
Boonville (city) Warrick County	1	0.02
Grissom AFB (cdp) Miami County	1	0.02
Hunter (town) Allen County	1	0.02
Rensselaer (city) Jasper County	1	0.02
Gary (city) Lake County	12	0.01

Top 10 Places Sorted by Percent of Total Population

Based on places with total population of 50,000 or more

Place	Population	%
Gary (city) Lake County	12	0.01
Lafayette (city) Tippecanoe County	5	0.01
Indianapolis (city) Marion County	17	<0.01
Fort Wayne (city) Allen County	11	<0.01
South Bend (city) St. Joseph County	5	<0.01
Bloomington (city) Monroe County	3	<0.01
Evansville (city) Vanderburgh County	3	<0.01
Hammond (city) Lake County	3	<0.01
Anderson (city) Madison County	2	<0.01
Muncie (city) Delaware County	2	<0.01

American Indian: Shoshone

Top 10 Places Sorted by Population

Based on all places, regardless of total population

Place	Population	%
Indianapolis (city) Marion County	7	<0.01
Hammond (city) Lake County	6	0.01
Muncie (city) Delaware County	6	0.01
Tell City (city) Perry County	4	0.06
Cumberland (town) Marion County	3	0.06
Lanesville (town) Harrison County	2	0.35
St. Mary of the Woods (cdp) Vigo County	2	0.25
Lake Dalecarlia (cdp) Lake County	2	0.15
Michigan City (city) LaPorte County	2	0.01
Greenville (town) Floyd County	1	0.17

Top 10 Places Sorted by Percent of Total Population

Based on all places, regardless of total population

Place	Population	%
Lanesville (town) Harrison County	2	0.35
St. Mary of the Woods (cdp) Vigo County	2	0.25
Greenville (town) Floyd County	1	0.17
Lake Dalecarlia (cdp) Lake County	2	0.15
Tell City (city) Perry County	4	0.06
Cumberland (town) Marion County	3	0.06
Hammond (city) Lake County	6	0.01
Muncie (city) Delaware County	6	0.01
Michigan City (city) LaPorte County	2	0.01
Beech Grove (city) Marion County	1	0.01

Top 10 Places Sorted by Percent of Total Population

Based on places with total population of 50,000 or more

Place	Population	%
Hammond (city) Lake County	6	0.01
Muncie (city) Delaware County	6	0.01
Indianapolis (city) Marion County	7	<0.01
Anderson (city) Madison County	1	<0.01
Bloomington (city) Monroe County	1	<0.01
Noblesville (city) Hamilton County	1	<0.01
South Bend (city) St. Joseph County	1	<0.01
Carmel (city) Hamilton County	0	0.00
Elkhart (city) Elkhart County	0	0.00
Evansville (city) Vanderburgh County	0	0.00

American Indian: Sioux

Top 10 Places Sorted by Population

Based on all places, regardless of total population

Place	Population	%
Indianapolis (city) Marion County	201	0.02
Fort Wayne (city) Allen County	68	0.03
Evansville (city) Vanderburgh County	52	0.04
Terre Haute (city) Vigo County	34	0.06
Bloomington (city) Monroe County	24	0.03
Lafayette (city) Tippecanoe County	23	0.03
Elkhart (city) Elkhart County	21	0.04
Muncie (city) Delaware County	20	0.03
Kokomo (city) Howard County	18	0.04
Gary (city) Lake County	17	0.02

Top 10 Places Sorted by Percent of Total Population

Based on all places, regardless of total population

Place	Population	%
San Pierre (cdp) Starke County	1	0.69
Wheeler (cdp) Porter County	3	0.68
Salamonia (town) Jay County	1	0.64
Shelby (cdp) Lake County	3	0.56
Colburn (cdp) Tippecanoe County	1	0.52
Trafalgar (town) Johnson County	5	0.45
Manilla (cdp) Rush County	1	0.37
Royal Center (town) Cass County	3	0.35
Campbellsburg (town) Washington County	2	0.34
Palmyra (town) Harrison County	3	0.32

Top 10 Places Sorted by Percent of Total Population

Based on places with total population of 50,000 or more

Place	Population	%
Terre Haute (city) Vigo County	34	0.06
Evansville (city) Vanderburgh County	52	0.04
Elkhart (city) Elkhart County	21	0.04
Fort Wayne (city) Allen County	68	0.03
Bloomington (city) Monroe County	24	0.03
Lafayette (city) Tippecanoe County	23	0.03
Muncie (city) Delaware County	20	0.03
Indianapolis (city) Marion County	201	0.02
Gary (city) Lake County	17	0.02
Anderson (city) Madison County	11	0.02

American Indian: South American Indian

Top 10 Places Sorted by Population

Based on all places, regardless of total population

Place	Population	%
Indianapolis (city) Marion County	39	<0.01
East Chicago (city) Lake County	18	0.06
Fishers (town) Hamilton County	10	0.01
Hammond (city) Lake County	9	0.01
Fort Wayne (city) Allen County	9	<0.01
Portage (city) Porter County	7	0.02
Lafayette (city) Tippecanoe County	7	0.01
Goshen (city) Elkhart County	6	0.02
Ingalls (town) Madison County	5	0.21
Pittsboro (town) Hendricks County	5	0.17

Top 10 Places Sorted by Percent of Total Population

Based on all places, regardless of total population

Place	Population	%
Ingalls (town) Madison County	5	0.21
Mentone (town) Kosciusko County	2	0.20
Pittsboro (town) Hendricks County	5	0.17

Rocky Ripple (town) Marion County	1	0.17
Seelyville (town) Vigo County	1	0.10
Burns Harbor (town) Porter County	1	0.09
Fortville (town) Hancock County	3	0.08
Farmland (town) Randolph County	1	0.08
Hamilton (town) Steuben County	1	0.07
East Chicago (city) Lake County	18	0.06

Top 10 Places Sorted by Percent of Total Population

Based on places with total population of 50,000 or more

Place	Population	%
Fishers (town) Hamilton County	10	0.01
Hammond (city) Lake County	9	0.01
Lafayette (city) Tippecanoe County	7	0.01
Elkhart (city) Elkhart County	4	0.01
Muncie (city) Delaware County	4	0.01
Indianapolis (city) Marion County	39	<0.01
Fort Wayne (city) Allen County	9	<0.01
Bloomington (city) Monroe County	4	<0.01
Evansville (city) Vanderburgh County	4	<0.01
Gary (city) Lake County	3	<0.01

American Indian: Spanish American Indian

Top 10 Places Sorted by Population

Based on all places, regardless of total population

Place	Population	%
Indianapolis (city) Marion County	23	<0.01
Bloomington (city) Monroe County	21	0.03
South Bend (city) St. Joseph County	11	0.01
Lawrence (city) Marion County	9	0.02
Richmond (city) Wayne County	8	0.02
Cumberland (town) Marion County	6	0.12
Goshen (city) Elkhart County	5	0.02
Schererville (town) Lake County	4	0.01
Waveland (town) Montgomery County	3	0.71
Elkhart (city) Elkhart County	3	0.01

Top 10 Places Sorted by Percent of Total Population

Based on all places, regardless of total population

Place	Population	%
Waveland (town) Montgomery County	3	0.71
Cumberland (town) Marion County	6	0.12
Selma (town) Delaware County	1	0.12
Bloomington (city) Monroe County	21	0.03
Lawrence (city) Marion County	9	0.02
Richmond (city) Wayne County	8	0.02
Goshen (city) Elkhart County	5	0.02
Gas City (city) Grant County	1	0.02
Lawrenceburg (city) Dearborn County	1	0.02
Sullivan (city) Sullivan County	1	0.02

Top 10 Places Sorted by Percent of Total Population

Based on places with total population of 50,000 or more

Place	Population	%
Bloomington (city) Monroe County	21	0.03
South Bend (city) St. Joseph County	11	0.01
Elkhart (city) Elkhart County	3	0.01
Indianapolis (city) Marion County	23	<0.01
Fort Wayne (city) Allen County	3	<0.01
Hammond (city) Lake County	3	<0.01
Anderson (city) Madison County	2	<0.01
Carmel (city) Hamilton County	2	<0.01
Muncie (city) Delaware County	2	<0.01
Evansville (city) Vanderburgh County	1	<0.01

Alaska Native: Tlingit-Haida

Top 10 Places Sorted by Population

Based on all places, regardless of total population

Place	Population	%
Indianapolis (city) Marion County	6	<0.01
Highland (town) Lake County	5	0.02
Lafayette (city) Tippecanoe County	5	0.01
Fort Wayne (city) Allen County	4	<0.01
South Bend (city) St. Joseph County	4	<0.01
Winfield (town) Lake County	2	0.05
Greendale (city) Dearborn County	2	0.04
Roseland (town) St. Joseph County	1	0.16
Walton (town) Cass County	1	0.10
French Lick (town) Orange County	1	0.06

Top 10 Places Sorted by Percent of Total Population

Based on all places, regardless of total population

Place	Population	%
Roseland (town) St. Joseph County	1	0.16
Walton (town) Cass County	1	0.10
French Lick (town) Orange County	1	0.06
Winfield (town) Lake County	2	0.05
Greendale (city) Dearborn County	2	0.04
Melody Hill (cdp) Vanderburgh County	1	0.03
Union City (city) Randolph County	1	0.03
Highland (town) Lake County	5	0.02
Hunter (town) Allen County	1	0.02
Lawrenceburg (city) Dearborn County	1	0.02

Top 10 Places Sorted by Percent of Total Population

Based on places with total population of 50,000 or more

Place	Population	%
Lafayette (city) Tippecanoe County	5	0.01
Indianapolis (city) Marion County	6	<0.01
Fort Wayne (city) Allen County	4	<0.01
South Bend (city) St. Joseph County	4	<0.01
Bloomington (city) Monroe County	1	<0.01
Fishers (town) Hamilton County	1	<0.01
Terre Haute (city) Vigo County	1	<0.01
Anderson (city) Madison County	0	0.00
Carmel (city) Hamilton County	0	0.00
Elkhart (city) Elkhart County	0	0.00

American Indian: Tohono O'Odham

Top 10 Places Sorted by Population

Based on all places, regardless of total population

Place	Population	%
Bloomington (city) Monroe County	8	0.01
Whiteland (town) Johnson County	3	0.07
Valparaiso (city) Porter County	3	0.01
Greenwood (city) Johnson County	2	<0.01
Indianapolis (city) Marion County	2	<0.01
Lagrange (town) LaGrange County	1	0.04
Dunlap (cdp) Elkhart County	1	0.02
Vincennes (city) Knox County	1	0.01
Franklin (city) Johnson County	1	<0.01
La Porte (city) LaPorte County	1	<0.01

Top 10 Places Sorted by Percent of Total Population

Based on all places, regardless of total population

Place	Population	%
Whiteland (town) Johnson County	3	0.07
Lagrange (town) LaGrange County	1	0.04
Dunlap (cdp) Elkhart County	1	0.02
Bloomington (city) Monroe County	8	0.01
Valparaiso (city) Porter County	3	0.01
Vincennes (city) Knox County	1	0.01
Greenwood (city) Johnson County	2	<0.01
Indianapolis (city) Marion County	2	<0.01
Franklin (city) Johnson County	1	<0.01
La Porte (city) LaPorte County	1	<0.01

Top 10 Places Sorted by Percent of Total Population

Based on places with total population of 50,000 or more

Place	Population	%
Bloomington (city) Monroe County	8	0.01
Indianapolis (city) Marion County	2	<0.01
Anderson (city) Madison County	0	0.00
Carmel (city) Hamilton County	0	0.00
Elkhart (city) Elkhart County	0	0.00
Evansville (city) Vanderburgh County	0	0.00
Fishers (town) Hamilton County	0	0.00
Fort Wayne (city) Allen County	0	0.00
Gary (city) Lake County	0	0.00
Hammond (city) Lake County	0	0.00

Alaska Native: Tsimshian

Top 10 Places Sorted by Population

Based on all places, regardless of total population

Place	Population	%
Cicero (town) Hamilton County	2	0.04
Indianapolis (city) Marion County	1	<0.01
Schererville (town) Lake County	1	<0.01
Aberdeen (cdp) Porter County	0	0.00
Advance (town) Boone County	0	0.00
Akron (town) Fulton County	0	0.00
Alamo (town) Montgomery County	0	0.00
Albany (town) Delaware County	0	0.00
Albion (town) Noble County	0	0.00
Alexandria (city) Madison County	0	0.00

Top 10 Places Sorted by Percent of Total Population

Based on all places, regardless of total population

Place	Population	%
Cicero (town) Hamilton County	2	0.04
Indianapolis (city) Marion County	1	<0.01
Schererville (town) Lake County	1	<0.01
Aberdeen (cdp) Porter County	0	0.00
Advance (town) Boone County	0	0.00
Akron (town) Fulton County	0	0.00
Alamo (town) Montgomery County	0	0.00
Albany (town) Delaware County	0	0.00
Albion (town) Noble County	0	0.00
Alexandria (city) Madison County	0	0.00

Top 10 Places Sorted by Percent of Total Population

Based on places with total population of 50,000 or more

Place	Population	%
Indianapolis (city) Marion County	1	<0.01
Anderson (city) Madison County	0	0.00
Bloomington (city) Monroe County	0	0.00
Carmel (city) Hamilton County	0	0.00
Elkhart (city) Elkhart County	0	0.00
Evansville (city) Vanderburgh County	0	0.00
Fishers (town) Hamilton County	0	0.00
Fort Wayne (city) Allen County	0	0.00
Gary (city) Lake County	0	0.00
Hammond (city) Lake County	0	0.00

American Indian: Ute

Top 10 Places Sorted by Population

Based on all places, regardless of total population

Place	Population	%
Hammond (city) Lake County	7	0.01
Winamac (town) Pulaski County	4	0.16
Anderson (city) Madison County	4	0.01
Indianapolis (city) Marion County	4	<0.01
Plainfield (town) Hendricks County	3	0.01
Fort Wayne (city) Allen County	2	<0.01
Noblesville (city) Hamilton County	2	<0.01
Fortville (town) Hancock County	1	0.03
Bedford (city) Lawrence County	1	0.01
Chesterton (town) Porter County	1	0.01

Top 10 Places Sorted by Percent of Total Population

Based on all places, regardless of total population

Place	Population	%
Winamac (town) Pulaski County	4	0.16
Fortville (town) Hancock County	1	0.03
Hammond (city) Lake County	7	0.01
Anderson (city) Madison County	4	0.01
Plainfield (town) Hendricks County	3	0.01
Bedford (city) Lawrence County	1	0.01
Chesterton (town) Porter County	1	0.01
New Castle (city) Henry County	1	0.01
Peru (city) Miami County	1	0.01
Speedway (town) Marion County	1	0.01

Top 10 Places Sorted by Percent of Total Population

Based on places with total population of 50,000 or more

Place	Population	%
Hammond (city) Lake County	7	0.01
Anderson (city) Madison County	4	0.01
Indianapolis (city) Marion County	4	<0.01
Fort Wayne (city) Allen County	2	<0.01
Noblesville (city) Hamilton County	2	<0.01
Carmel (city) Hamilton County	1	<0.01
Lafayette (city) Tippecanoe County	1	<0.01
Terre Haute (city) Vigo County	1	<0.01
Bloomington (city) Monroe County	0	0.00
Elkhart (city) Elkhart County	0	0.00

American Indian: Yakama

Top 10 Places Sorted by Population
Based on all places, regardless of total population

Place	Population	%
Bloomington (city) Monroe County	3	<0.01
Mentone (town) Kosciusko County	1	0.10
Avon (town) Hendricks County	1	0.01
Warsaw (city) Kosciusko County	1	0.01
Indianapolis (city) Marion County	1	<0.01
Aberdeen (cdp) Porter County	0	0.00
Advance (town) Boone County	0	0.00
Akron (town) Fulton County	0	0.00
Alamo (town) Montgomery County	0	0.00
Albany (town) Delaware County	0	0.00

Top 10 Places Sorted by Percent of Total Population
Based on all places, regardless of total population

Place	Population	%
Mentone (town) Kosciusko County	1	0.10
Avon (town) Hendricks County	1	0.01
Warsaw (city) Kosciusko County	1	0.01
Bloomington (city) Monroe County	3	<0.01
Indianapolis (city) Marion County	1	<0.01
Aberdeen (cdp) Porter County	0	0.00
Advance (town) Boone County	0	0.00
Akron (town) Fulton County	0	0.00
Alamo (town) Montgomery County	0	0.00
Albany (town) Delaware County	0	0.00

Top 10 Places Sorted by Percent of Total Population
Based on places with total population of 50,000 or more

Place	Population	%
Bloomington (city) Monroe County	3	<0.01
Indianapolis (city) Marion County	1	<0.01
Anderson (city) Madison County	0	0.00
Carmel (city) Hamilton County	0	0.00
Elkhart (city) Elkhart County	0	0.00
Evansville (city) Vanderburgh County	0	0.00
Fishers (town) Hamilton County	0	0.00
Fort Wayne (city) Allen County	0	0.00
Gary (city) Lake County	0	0.00
Hammond (city) Lake County	0	0.00

American Indian: Yaqui

Top 10 Places Sorted by Population
Based on all places, regardless of total population

Place	Population	%
Valparaiso (city) Porter County	5	0.02
Fort Wayne (city) Allen County	5	<0.01
Indianapolis (city) Marion County	5	<0.01
Hammond (city) Lake County	3	<0.01
Terre Haute (city) Vigo County	3	<0.01
Hunter (town) Allen County	2	0.04
Carmel (city) Hamilton County	2	<0.01
Liberty (town) Union County	1	0.05
Greensburg (city) Decatur County	1	0.01
Lake Station (city) Lake County	1	0.01

Top 10 Places Sorted by Percent of Total Population
Based on all places, regardless of total population

Place	Population	%
Liberty (town) Union County	1	0.05
Hunter (town) Allen County	2	0.04
Valparaiso (city) Porter County	5	0.02
Greensburg (city) Decatur County	1	0.01
Lake Station (city) Lake County	1	0.01
Fort Wayne (city) Allen County	5	<0.01
Indianapolis (city) Marion County	5	<0.01
Hammond (city) Lake County	3	<0.01
Terre Haute (city) Vigo County	3	<0.01
Carmel (city) Hamilton County	2	<0.01

Top 10 Places Sorted by Percent of Total Population
Based on places with total population of 50,000 or more

Place	Population	%
Fort Wayne (city) Allen County	5	<0.01
Indianapolis (city) Marion County	5	<0.01
Hammond (city) Lake County	3	<0.01
Terre Haute (city) Vigo County	3	<0.01
Carmel (city) Hamilton County	2	<0.01
Evansville (city) Vanderburgh County	1	<0.01
Lafayette (city) Tippecanoe County	1	<0.01
Noblesville (city) Hamilton County	1	<0.01
Anderson (city) Madison County	0	0.00
Bloomington (city) Monroe County	0	0.00

American Indian: Yuman

Top 10 Places Sorted by Population
Based on all places, regardless of total population

Place	Population	%
Indianapolis (city) Marion County	4	<0.01
Amo (town) Hendricks County	2	0.50
Wabash (city) Wabash County	2	0.02
Lafayette (city) Tippecanoe County	1	<0.01
Aberdeen (cdp) Porter County	0	0.00
Advance (town) Boone County	0	0.00
Akron (town) Fulton County	0	0.00
Alamo (town) Montgomery County	0	0.00
Albany (town) Delaware County	0	0.00
Albion (town) Noble County	0	0.00

Top 10 Places Sorted by Percent of Total Population
Based on all places, regardless of total population

Place	Population	%
Amo (town) Hendricks County	2	0.50
Wabash (city) Wabash County	2	0.02
Indianapolis (city) Marion County	4	<0.01
Lafayette (city) Tippecanoe County	1	<0.01
Aberdeen (cdp) Porter County	0	0.00
Advance (town) Boone County	0	0.00
Akron (town) Fulton County	0	0.00
Alamo (town) Montgomery County	0	0.00
Albany (town) Delaware County	0	0.00
Albion (town) Noble County	0	0.00

Top 10 Places Sorted by Percent of Total Population
Based on places with total population of 50,000 or more

Place	Population	%
Indianapolis (city) Marion County	4	<0.01
Lafayette (city) Tippecanoe County	1	<0.01
Anderson (city) Madison County	0	0.00
Bloomington (city) Monroe County	0	0.00
Carmel (city) Hamilton County	0	0.00
Elkhart (city) Elkhart County	0	0.00
Evansville (city) Vanderburgh County	0	0.00
Fishers (town) Hamilton County	0	0.00
Fort Wayne (city) Allen County	0	0.00
Gary (city) Lake County	0	0.00

Alaska Native: Yup'ik

Top 10 Places Sorted by Population
Based on all places, regardless of total population

Place	Population	%
North Liberty (town) St. Joseph County	3	0.16
Washington (city) Daviess County	3	0.03
Goshen (city) Elkhart County	3	0.01
Fort Wayne (city) Allen County	2	<0.01
Indianapolis (city) Marion County	2	<0.01
Edinburgh (town) Johnson County	1	0.02
Porter (town) Porter County	1	0.02
Rushville (city) Rush County	1	0.02
St. John (town) Lake County	1	0.01
Bloomington (city) Monroe County	1	<0.01

Top 10 Places Sorted by Percent of Total Population
Based on all places, regardless of total population

Place	Population	%
North Liberty (town) St. Joseph County	3	0.16
Washington (city) Daviess County	3	0.03
Edinburgh (town) Johnson County	1	0.02
Porter (town) Porter County	1	0.02
Rushville (city) Rush County	1	0.02
Goshen (city) Elkhart County	3	0.01
St. John (town) Lake County	1	0.01
Fort Wayne (city) Allen County	2	<0.01
Indianapolis (city) Marion County	2	<0.01
Bloomington (city) Monroe County	1	<0.01

Top 10 Places Sorted by Percent of Total Population
Based on places with total population of 50,000 or more

Place	Population	%
Fort Wayne (city) Allen County	2	<0.01
Indianapolis (city) Marion County	2	<0.01
Bloomington (city) Monroe County	1	<0.01
Carmel (city) Hamilton County	1	<0.01
Anderson (city) Madison County	0	0.00
Elkhart (city) Elkhart County	0	0.00
Evansville (city) Vanderburgh County	0	0.00
Fishers (town) Hamilton County	0	0.00
Gary (city) Lake County	0	0.00
Hammond (city) Lake County	0	0.00

Asian

Top 10 Places Sorted by Population
Based on all places, regardless of total population

Place	Population	%
Indianapolis (city) Marion County	21,294	2.60
Fort Wayne (city) Allen County	9,768	3.85
Carmel (city) Hamilton County	7,838	9.90
Bloomington (city) Monroe County	7,368	9.16
West Lafayette (city) Tippecanoe County	5,498	18.58
Fishers (town) Hamilton County	4,930	6.42
Purdue University (cdp) Tippecanoe County	2,973	24.40
Columbus (city) Bartholomew County	2,625	5.96
Greenwood (city) Johnson County	2,170	4.36
South Bend (city) St. Joseph County	1,824	1.80

Top 10 Places Sorted by Percent of Total Population
Based on all places, regardless of total population

Place	Population	%
Purdue University (cdp) Tippecanoe County	2,973	24.40
West Lafayette (city) Tippecanoe County	5,498	18.58
Notre Dame (cdp) St. Joseph County	592	9.91
Carmel (city) Hamilton County	7,838	9.90
Bloomington (city) Monroe County	7,368	9.16
Munster (town) Lake County	1,536	6.51
Fishers (town) Hamilton County	4,930	6.42
Columbus (city) Bartholomew County	2,625	5.96
Roseland (town) St. Joseph County	36	5.71
Granger (cdp) St. Joseph County	1,608	5.28

Top 10 Places Sorted by Percent of Total Population
Based on places with total population of 50,000 or more

Place	Population	%
Carmel (city) Hamilton County	7,838	9.90
Bloomington (city) Monroe County	7,368	9.16
Fishers (town) Hamilton County	4,930	6.42
Fort Wayne (city) Allen County	9,768	3.85
Indianapolis (city) Marion County	21,294	2.60
Noblesville (city) Hamilton County	1,149	2.21
Lafayette (city) Tippecanoe County	1,224	1.82
South Bend (city) St. Joseph County	1,824	1.80
Terre Haute (city) Vigo County	1,092	1.80
Muncie (city) Delaware County	1,173	1.67

Asian: Not Hispanic

Top 10 Places Sorted by Population
Based on all places, regardless of total population

Place	Population	%
Indianapolis (city) Marion County	20,777	2.53
Fort Wayne (city) Allen County	9,548	3.76
Carmel (city) Hamilton County	7,790	9.84
Bloomington (city) Monroe County	7,298	9.08
West Lafayette (city) Tippecanoe County	5,477	18.51
Fishers (town) Hamilton County	4,883	6.36
Purdue University (cdp) Tippecanoe County	2,951	24.22
Columbus (city) Bartholomew County	2,607	5.92
Greenwood (city) Johnson County	2,153	4.32
South Bend (city) St. Joseph County	1,742	1.72

Top 10 Places Sorted by Percent of Total Population
Based on all places, regardless of total population

Place	Population	%
Purdue University (cdp) Tippecanoe County	2,951	24.22
West Lafayette (city) Tippecanoe County	5,477	18.51
Carmel (city) Hamilton County	7,790	9.84

Notre Dame (cdp) St. Joseph County	568	9.51
Bloomington (city) Monroe County	7,298	9.08
Munster (town) Lake County	1,514	6.41
Fishers (town) Hamilton County	4,883	6.36
Columbus (city) Bartholomew County	2,607	5.92
Roseland (town) St. Joseph County	36	5.71
Granger (cdp) St. Joseph County	1,594	5.23

Top 10 Places Sorted by Percent of Total Population

Based on places with total population of 50,000 or more

Place	Population	%
Carmel (city) Hamilton County	7,790	9.84
Bloomington (city) Monroe County	7,298	9.08
Fishers (town) Hamilton County	4,883	6.36
Fort Wayne (city) Allen County	9,548	3.76
Indianapolis (city) Marion County	20,777	2.53
Noblesville (city) Hamilton County	1,128	2.17
Terre Haute (city) Vigo County	1,081	1.78
Lafayette (city) Tippecanoe County	1,160	1.73
South Bend (city) St. Joseph County	1,742	1.72
Muncie (city) Delaware County	1,143	1.63

Asian: Hispanic

Top 10 Places Sorted by Population

Based on all places, regardless of total population

Place	Population	%
Indianapolis (city) Marion County	517	0.06
Fort Wayne (city) Allen County	220	0.09
Hammond (city) Lake County	128	0.16
South Bend (city) St. Joseph County	82	0.08
Bloomington (city) Monroe County	70	0.09
Lafayette (city) Tippecanoe County	64	0.10
Carmel (city) Hamilton County	48	0.06
Fishers (town) Hamilton County	47	0.06
Hobart (city) Lake County	41	0.14
Portage (city) Porter County	41	0.11

Top 10 Places Sorted by Percent of Total Population

Based on all places, regardless of total population

Place	Population	%
Kingsford Heights (town) LaPorte County	7	0.49
Dale (town) Spencer County	7	0.44
Montmorenci (cdp) Tippecanoe County	1	0.41
Notre Dame (cdp) St. Joseph County	24	0.40
Corunna (town) DeKalb County	1	0.39
Whiting (city) Lake County	15	0.30
Lynn (town) Randolph County	3	0.27
Utica (town) Clark County	2	0.26
Williams Creek (town) Marion County	1	0.25
Garrett (city) DeKalb County	15	0.24

Top 10 Places Sorted by Percent of Total Population

Based on places with total population of 50,000 or more

Place	Population	%
Hammond (city) Lake County	128	0.16
Lafayette (city) Tippecanoe County	64	0.10
Fort Wayne (city) Allen County	220	0.09
Bloomington (city) Monroe County	70	0.09
South Bend (city) St. Joseph County	82	0.08
Elkhart (city) Elkhart County	35	0.07
Indianapolis (city) Marion County	517	0.06
Carmel (city) Hamilton County	48	0.06
Fishers (town) Hamilton County	47	0.06
Gary (city) Lake County	36	0.04

Asian: Bangladeshi

Top 10 Places Sorted by Population

Based on all places, regardless of total population

Place	Population	%
Indianapolis (city) Marion County	128	0.02
Fort Wayne (city) Allen County	40	0.02
Fishers (town) Hamilton County	35	0.05
Carmel (city) Hamilton County	35	0.04
Purdue University (cdp) Tippecanoe County	31	0.25
Bloomington (city) Monroe County	27	0.03
Muncie (city) Delaware County	23	0.03
West Lafayette (city) Tippecanoe County	21	0.07
Columbus (city) Bartholomew County	17	0.04
Munster (town) Lake County	13	0.06

Top 10 Places Sorted by Percent of Total Population

Based on all places, regardless of total population

Place	Population	%
Purdue University (cdp) Tippecanoe County	31	0.25
West Lafayette (city) Tippecanoe County	21	0.07
Munster (town) Lake County	13	0.06
Fishers (town) Hamilton County	35	0.05
Dyer (town) Lake County	9	0.05
Carmel (city) Hamilton County	35	0.04
Columbus (city) Bartholomew County	17	0.04
Hunter (town) Allen County	2	0.04
McCordsville (town) Hancock County	2	0.04
Bloomington (city) Monroe County	27	0.03

Top 10 Places Sorted by Percent of Total Population

Based on places with total population of 50,000 or more

Place	Population	%
Fishers (town) Hamilton County	35	0.05
Carmel (city) Hamilton County	35	0.04
Bloomington (city) Monroe County	27	0.03
Muncie (city) Delaware County	23	0.03
Indianapolis (city) Marion County	128	0.02
Fort Wayne (city) Allen County	40	0.02
Noblesville (city) Hamilton County	12	0.02
Evansville (city) Vanderburgh County	6	0.01
Lafayette (city) Tippecanoe County	5	0.01
Elkhart (city) Elkhart County	3	0.01

Asian: Bhutanese

Top 10 Places Sorted by Population

Based on all places, regardless of total population

Place	Population	%
Fishers (town) Hamilton County	3	<0.01
Aberdeen (cdp) Porter County	0	0.00
Advance (town) Boone County	0	0.00
Akron (town) Fulton County	0	0.00
Alamo (town) Montgomery County	0	0.00
Albany (town) Delaware County	0	0.00
Albion (town) Noble County	0	0.00
Alexandria (city) Madison County	0	0.00
Alfordsville (town) Daviess County	0	0.00
Alton (town) Crawford County	0	0.00

Top 10 Places Sorted by Percent of Total Population

Based on all places, regardless of total population

Place	Population	%
Fishers (town) Hamilton County	3	<0.01
Aberdeen (cdp) Porter County	0	0.00
Advance (town) Boone County	0	0.00
Akron (town) Fulton County	0	0.00
Alamo (town) Montgomery County	0	0.00
Albany (town) Delaware County	0	0.00
Albion (town) Noble County	0	0.00
Alexandria (city) Madison County	0	0.00
Alfordsville (town) Daviess County	0	0.00
Alton (town) Crawford County	0	0.00

Top 10 Places Sorted by Percent of Total Population

Based on places with total population of 50,000 or more

Place	Population	%
Fishers (town) Hamilton County	3	<0.01
Anderson (city) Madison County	0	0.00
Bloomington (city) Monroe County	0	0.00
Carmel (city) Hamilton County	0	0.00
Elkhart (city) Elkhart County	0	0.00
Evansville (city) Vanderburgh County	0	0.00
Fort Wayne (city) Allen County	0	0.00
Gary (city) Lake County	0	0.00
Hammond (city) Lake County	0	0.00
Indianapolis (city) Marion County	0	0.00

Asian: Burmese

Top 10 Places Sorted by Population

Based on all places, regardless of total population

Place	Population	%
Fort Wayne (city) Allen County	3,819	1.51
Indianapolis (city) Marion County	3,622	0.44
Logansport (city) Cass County	144	0.78
Washington (city) Daviess County	80	0.70
Speedway (town) Marion County	42	0.36
Bloomington (city) Monroe County	18	0.02
Carmel (city) Hamilton County	8	0.01
Lafayette (city) Tippecanoe County	8	0.01
Southport (city) Marion County	7	0.41
Topeka (town) LaGrange County	6	0.52

Top 10 Places Sorted by Percent of Total Population

Based on all places, regardless of total population

Place	Population	%
Fort Wayne (city) Allen County	3,819	1.51
Logansport (city) Cass County	144	0.78
Washington (city) Daviess County	80	0.70
Topeka (town) LaGrange County	6	0.52
Indianapolis (city) Marion County	3,622	0.44
Southport (city) Marion County	7	0.41
Speedway (town) Marion County	42	0.36
Melody Hill (cdp) Vanderburgh County	2	0.06
Churubusco (town) Whitley County	1	0.06
Roanoke (town) Huntington County	1	0.06

Top 10 Places Sorted by Percent of Total Population

Based on places with total population of 50,000 or more

Place	Population	%
Fort Wayne (city) Allen County	3,819	1.51
Indianapolis (city) Marion County	3,622	0.44
Bloomington (city) Monroe County	18	0.02
Carmel (city) Hamilton County	8	0.01
Lafayette (city) Tippecanoe County	8	0.01
Fishers (town) Hamilton County	6	0.01
Muncie (city) Delaware County	2	<0.01
Evansville (city) Vanderburgh County	1	<0.01
Anderson (city) Madison County	0	0.00
Elkhart (city) Elkhart County	0	0.00

Asian: Cambodian

Top 10 Places Sorted by Population

Based on all places, regardless of total population

Place	Population	%
Indianapolis (city) Marion County	118	0.01
South Bend (city) St. Joseph County	80	0.08
Goshen (city) Elkhart County	71	0.22
Elkhart (city) Elkhart County	66	0.13
Westfield (town) Hamilton County	58	0.19
Fort Wayne (city) Allen County	46	0.02
Mishawaka (city) St. Joseph County	32	0.07
Noblesville (city) Hamilton County	26	0.05
Carmel (city) Hamilton County	22	0.03
Lawrence (city) Marion County	14	0.03

Top 10 Places Sorted by Percent of Total Population

Based on all places, regardless of total population

Place	Population	%
Corunna (town) DeKalb County	3	1.18
Bristol (town) Elkhart County	9	0.56
Amboy (town) Miami County	1	0.26
Goshen (city) Elkhart County	71	0.22
Westfield (town) Hamilton County	58	0.19
Dunlap (cdp) Elkhart County	9	0.14
Warren Park (town) Marion County	2	0.14
Elkhart (city) Elkhart County	66	0.13
McCordsville (town) Hancock County	6	0.13
Brookville (town) Franklin County	3	0.12

Top 10 Places Sorted by Percent of Total Population

Based on places with total population of 50,000 or more

Place	Population	%
Elkhart (city) Elkhart County	66	0.13
South Bend (city) St. Joseph County	80	0.08
Noblesville (city) Hamilton County	26	0.05
Carmel (city) Hamilton County	22	0.03
Fort Wayne (city) Allen County	46	0.02
Fishers (town) Hamilton County	14	0.02
Indianapolis (city) Marion County	118	0.01
Bloomington (city) Monroe County	9	0.01
Gary (city) Lake County	7	0.01
Hammond (city) Lake County	5	0.01

Asian: Chinese, except Taiwanese

Top 10 Places Sorted by Population
Based on all places, regardless of total population

Place	Population	%
Indianapolis (city) Marion County	3,197	0.39
Carmel (city) Hamilton County	2,754	3.48
Bloomington (city) Monroe County	2,230	2.77
West Lafayette (city) Tippecanoe County	1,852	6.26
Purdue University (cdp) Tippecanoe County	1,285	10.55
Fishers (town) Hamilton County	818	1.07
Fort Wayne (city) Allen County	643	0.25
Columbus (city) Bartholomew County	422	0.96
Hammond (city) Lake County	422	0.52
Granger (cdp) St. Joseph County	420	1.38

Top 10 Places Sorted by Percent of Total Population
Based on all places, regardless of total population

Place	Population	%
Purdue University (cdp) Tippecanoe County	1,285	10.55
West Lafayette (city) Tippecanoe County	1,852	6.26
Carmel (city) Hamilton County	2,754	3.48
Notre Dame (cdp) St. Joseph County	208	3.48
Bloomington (city) Monroe County	2,230	2.77
Howe (cdp) LaGrange County	19	2.35
New Ross (town) Montgomery County	7	2.02
Roseland (town) St. Joseph County	11	1.75
Granger (cdp) St. Joseph County	420	1.38
St. Mary of the Woods (cdp) Vigo County	11	1.38

Top 10 Places Sorted by Percent of Total Population
Based on places with total population of 50,000 or more

Place	Population	%
Carmel (city) Hamilton County	2,754	3.48
Bloomington (city) Monroe County	2,230	2.77
Fishers (town) Hamilton County	818	1.07
Hammond (city) Lake County	422	0.52
Terre Haute (city) Vigo County	254	0.42
Muncie (city) Delaware County	282	0.40
Indianapolis (city) Marion County	3,197	0.39
South Bend (city) St. Joseph County	360	0.36
Lafayette (city) Tippecanoe County	226	0.34
Noblesville (city) Hamilton County	157	0.30

Asian: Filipino

Top 10 Places Sorted by Population
Based on all places, regardless of total population

Place	Population	%
Indianapolis (city) Marion County	2,608	0.32
Fort Wayne (city) Allen County	823	0.32
Carmel (city) Hamilton County	411	0.52
Fishers (town) Hamilton County	391	0.51
South Bend (city) St. Joseph County	345	0.34
Bloomington (city) Monroe County	312	0.39
Munster (town) Lake County	268	1.14
Merrillville (town) Lake County	254	0.72
Evansville (city) Vanderburgh County	248	0.21
Greenwood (city) Johnson County	213	0.43

Top 10 Places Sorted by Percent of Total Population
Based on all places, regardless of total population

Place	Population	%
Blountsville (town) Henry County	3	2.24
Shorewood Forest (cdp) Porter County	45	1.66
Notre Dame (cdp) St. Joseph County	86	1.44
Winfield (town) Lake County	57	1.30
McCordsville (town) Hancock County	62	1.29
Munster (town) Lake County	268	1.14
Salt Creek Commons (cdp) Porter County	24	1.13
Crane (town) Martin County	2	1.09
Dyer (town) Lake County	175	1.07
Bruceville (town) Knox County	5	1.05

Top 10 Places Sorted by Percent of Total Population
Based on places with total population of 50,000 or more

Place	Population	%
Carmel (city) Hamilton County	411	0.52
Fishers (town) Hamilton County	391	0.51
Bloomington (city) Monroe County	312	0.39
Noblesville (city) Hamilton County	198	0.38
South Bend (city) St. Joseph County	345	0.34
Indianapolis (city) Marion County	2,608	0.32
Fort Wayne (city) Allen County	823	0.32
Lafayette (city) Tippecanoe County	200	0.30
Terre Haute (city) Vigo County	159	0.26
Hammond (city) Lake County	203	0.25

Asian: Hmong

Top 10 Places Sorted by Population
Based on all places, regardless of total population

Place	Population	%
Westfield (town) Hamilton County	52	0.17
Carmel (city) Hamilton County	27	0.03
Indianapolis (city) Marion County	24	<0.01
Fort Branch (town) Gibson County	14	0.51
Noblesville (city) Hamilton County	14	0.03
Fishers (town) Hamilton County	11	0.01
Terre Haute (city) Vigo County	7	0.01
Bloomington (city) Monroe County	5	0.01
Lebanon (city) Boone County	4	0.03
Columbus (city) Bartholomew County	4	0.01

Top 10 Places Sorted by Percent of Total Population
Based on all places, regardless of total population

Place	Population	%
Fort Branch (town) Gibson County	14	0.51
Westfield (town) Hamilton County	52	0.17
Hanover (town) Jefferson County	2	0.06
Austin (city) Scott County	2	0.05
Carmel (city) Hamilton County	27	0.03
Noblesville (city) Hamilton County	14	0.03
Lebanon (city) Boone County	4	0.03
Cicero (town) Hamilton County	1	0.02
Fishers (town) Hamilton County	11	0.01
Terre Haute (city) Vigo County	7	0.01

Top 10 Places Sorted by Percent of Total Population
Based on places with total population of 50,000 or more

Place	Population	%
Carmel (city) Hamilton County	27	0.03
Noblesville (city) Hamilton County	14	0.03
Fishers (town) Hamilton County	11	0.01
Terre Haute (city) Vigo County	7	0.01
Bloomington (city) Monroe County	5	0.01
Indianapolis (city) Marion County	24	<0.01
Muncie (city) Delaware County	2	<0.01
South Bend (city) St. Joseph County	2	<0.01
Anderson (city) Madison County	0	0.00
Elkhart (city) Elkhart County	0	0.00

Asian: Indian

Top 10 Places Sorted by Population
Based on all places, regardless of total population

Place	Population	%
Indianapolis (city) Marion County	5,358	0.65
Carmel (city) Hamilton County	2,526	3.19
Fishers (town) Hamilton County	1,785	2.32
West Lafayette (city) Tippecanoe County	1,624	5.49
Fort Wayne (city) Allen County	1,426	0.56
Bloomington (city) Monroe County	1,390	1.73
Columbus (city) Bartholomew County	1,381	3.13
Greenwood (city) Johnson County	1,381	2.77
Munster (town) Lake County	718	3.04
Purdue University (cdp) Tippecanoe County	616	5.06

Top 10 Places Sorted by Percent of Total Population
Based on all places, regardless of total population

Place	Population	%
West Lafayette (city) Tippecanoe County	1,624	5.49
Purdue University (cdp) Tippecanoe County	616	5.06
Carmel (city) Hamilton County	2,526	3.19
Columbus (city) Bartholomew County	1,381	3.13
Munster (town) Lake County	718	3.04
Greenwood (city) Johnson County	1,381	2.77
Fishers (town) Hamilton County	1,785	2.32
Plainfield (town) Hendricks County	595	2.15
Laconia (town) Harrison County	1	2.00
Bloomington (city) Monroe County	1,390	1.73

Top 10 Places Sorted by Percent of Total Population
Based on places with total population of 50,000 or more

Place	Population	%
Carmel (city) Hamilton County	2,526	3.19
Fishers (town) Hamilton County	1,785	2.32
Bloomington (city) Monroe County	1,390	1.73
Indianapolis (city) Marion County	5,358	0.65
Fort Wayne (city) Allen County	1,426	0.56
Noblesville (city) Hamilton County	262	0.50
Terre Haute (city) Vigo County	242	0.40
Muncie (city) Delaware County	248	0.35
Lafayette (city) Tippecanoe County	225	0.34
Evansville (city) Vanderburgh County	369	0.31

Asian: Indonesian

Top 10 Places Sorted by Population
Based on all places, regardless of total population

Place	Population	%
Indianapolis (city) Marion County	142	0.02
Bloomington (city) Monroe County	78	0.10
Fishers (town) Hamilton County	53	0.07
West Lafayette (city) Tippecanoe County	49	0.17
Carmel (city) Hamilton County	41	0.05
Fort Wayne (city) Allen County	26	0.01
Purdue University (cdp) Tippecanoe County	23	0.19
Goshen (city) Elkhart County	17	0.05
Noblesville (city) Hamilton County	15	0.03
Plainfield (town) Hendricks County	14	0.05

Top 10 Places Sorted by Percent of Total Population
Based on all places, regardless of total population

Place	Population	%
Utica (town) Clark County	3	0.39
Pittsboro (town) Hendricks County	8	0.27
Fountain City (town) Wayne County	2	0.25
Purdue University (cdp) Tippecanoe County	23	0.19
West Lafayette (city) Tippecanoe County	49	0.17
Middle (town) Henry County	3	0.13
Bloomington (city) Monroe County	78	0.10
Fishers (town) Hamilton County	53	0.07
Notre Dame (cdp) St. Joseph County	4	0.07
Corydon (town) Harrison County	2	0.06

Top 10 Places Sorted by Percent of Total Population
Based on places with total population of 50,000 or more

Place	Population	%
Bloomington (city) Monroe County	78	0.10
Fishers (town) Hamilton County	53	0.07
Carmel (city) Hamilton County	41	0.05
Noblesville (city) Hamilton County	15	0.03
Indianapolis (city) Marion County	142	0.02
Elkhart (city) Elkhart County	8	0.02
Fort Wayne (city) Allen County	26	0.01
South Bend (city) St. Joseph County	14	0.01
Evansville (city) Vanderburgh County	12	0.01
Lafayette (city) Tippecanoe County	9	0.01

Asian: Japanese

Top 10 Places Sorted by Population
Based on all places, regardless of total population

Place	Population	%
Indianapolis (city) Marion County	1,094	0.13
Carmel (city) Hamilton County	415	0.52
Columbus (city) Bartholomew County	402	0.91
Bloomington (city) Monroe County	395	0.49
Fishers (town) Hamilton County	316	0.41
Fort Wayne (city) Allen County	252	0.10
West Lafayette (city) Tippecanoe County	206	0.70
Evansville (city) Vanderburgh County	135	0.11
Terre Haute (city) Vigo County	112	0.18
Lafayette (city) Tippecanoe County	107	0.16

Top 10 Places Sorted by Percent of Total Population
Based on all places, regardless of total population

Place	Population	%
Dunreith (town) Henry County	5	2.82
Onward (town) Cass County	2	2.00
Roseland (town) St. Joseph County	8	1.27

Spring Hill (town) Marion County	1	1.02
Columbus (city) Bartholomew County	402	0.91
St. Joe (town) DeKalb County	4	0.87
Elnora (town) Daviess County	5	0.78
Greencastle (city) Putnam County	77	0.75
Indian Village (town) St. Joseph County	1	0.75
West Lafayette (city) Tippecanoe County	206	0.70

Top 10 Places Sorted by Percent of Total Population

Based on places with total population of 50,000 or more

Place	Population	%
Carmel (city) Hamilton County	415	0.52
Bloomington (city) Monroe County	395	0.49
Fishers (town) Hamilton County	316	0.41
Terre Haute (city) Vigo County	112	0.18
Noblesville (city) Hamilton County	86	0.17
Lafayette (city) Tippecanoe County	107	0.16
Indianapolis (city) Marion County	1,094	0.13
Muncie (city) Delaware County	86	0.12
Evansville (city) Vanderburgh County	135	0.11
Fort Wayne (city) Allen County	252	0.10

Asian: Korean

Top 10 Places Sorted by Population

Based on all places, regardless of total population

Place	Population	%
Bloomington (city) Monroe County	1,807	2.25
Indianapolis (city) Marion County	1,558	0.19
West Lafayette (city) Tippecanoe County	894	3.02
Carmel (city) Hamilton County	684	0.86
Fishers (town) Hamilton County	575	0.75
Purdue University (cdp) Tippecanoe County	542	4.45
Fort Wayne (city) Allen County	474	0.19
Lawrence (city) Marion County	283	0.62
Lafayette (city) Tippecanoe County	239	0.36
Granger (cdp) St. Joseph County	223	0.73

Top 10 Places Sorted by Percent of Total Population

Based on all places, regardless of total population

Place	Population	%
Purdue University (cdp) Tippecanoe County	542	4.45
West Lafayette (city) Tippecanoe County	894	3.02
Bloomington (city) Monroe County	1,807	2.25
Notre Dame (cdp) St. Joseph County	132	2.21
Wynnedale (town) Marion County	4	1.73
Dune Acres (town) Porter County	2	1.10
Schneider (town) Lake County	3	1.08
Freetown (cdp) Jackson County	4	1.04
Utica (town) Clark County	8	1.03
Mackey (town) Gibson County	1	0.94

Top 10 Places Sorted by Percent of Total Population

Based on places with total population of 50,000 or more

Place	Population	%
Bloomington (city) Monroe County	1,807	2.25
Carmel (city) Hamilton County	684	0.86
Fishers (town) Hamilton County	575	0.75
Lafayette (city) Tippecanoe County	239	0.36
Noblesville (city) Hamilton County	143	0.28
Terre Haute (city) Vigo County	141	0.23
Muncie (city) Delaware County	142	0.20
Indianapolis (city) Marion County	1,558	0.19
Fort Wayne (city) Allen County	474	0.19
South Bend (city) St. Joseph County	164	0.16

Asian: Laotian

Top 10 Places Sorted by Population

Based on all places, regardless of total population

Place	Population	%
Fort Wayne (city) Allen County	369	0.15
Indianapolis (city) Marion County	142	0.02
Elkhart (city) Elkhart County	115	0.23
South Bend (city) St. Joseph County	53	0.05
Logansport (city) Cass County	43	0.23
Simonton Lake (cdp) Elkhart County	26	0.56
Fishers (town) Hamilton County	25	0.03
Goshen (city) Elkhart County	23	0.07
Mishawaka (city) St. Joseph County	19	0.04
Granger (cdp) St. Joseph County	18	0.06

Top 10 Places Sorted by Percent of Total Population

Based on all places, regardless of total population

Place	Population	%
Leesburg (town) Kosciusko County	11	1.98
Tecumseh (cdp) Vigo County	5	0.78
Wakarusa (town) Elkhart County	13	0.74
Simonton Lake (cdp) Elkhart County	26	0.56
Bristol (town) Elkhart County	9	0.56
Salt Creek Commons (cdp) Porter County	6	0.28
Dunlap (cdp) Elkhart County	16	0.26
Elkhart (city) Elkhart County	115	0.23
Logansport (city) Cass County	43	0.23
Hunter (town) Allen County	10	0.21

Top 10 Places Sorted by Percent of Total Population

Based on places with total population of 50,000 or more

Place	Population	%
Elkhart (city) Elkhart County	115	0.23
Fort Wayne (city) Allen County	369	0.15
South Bend (city) St. Joseph County	53	0.05
Fishers (town) Hamilton County	25	0.03
Noblesville (city) Hamilton County	13	0.03
Indianapolis (city) Marion County	142	0.02
Lafayette (city) Tippecanoe County	11	0.02
Carmel (city) Hamilton County	9	0.01
Bloomington (city) Monroe County	8	0.01
Gary (city) Lake County	6	0.01

Asian: Malaysian

Top 10 Places Sorted by Population

Based on all places, regardless of total population

Place	Population	%
West Lafayette (city) Tippecanoe County	135	0.46
Bloomington (city) Monroe County	59	0.07
Indianapolis (city) Marion County	44	0.01
Fort Wayne (city) Allen County	41	0.02
Purdue University (cdp) Tippecanoe County	19	0.16
Carmel (city) Hamilton County	17	0.02
Evansville (city) Vanderburgh County	17	0.01
Fishers (town) Hamilton County	10	0.01
Terre Haute (city) Vigo County	9	0.01
Columbus (city) Bartholomew County	6	0.01

Top 10 Places Sorted by Percent of Total Population

Based on all places, regardless of total population

Place	Population	%
West Lafayette (city) Tippecanoe County	135	0.46
Purdue University (cdp) Tippecanoe County	19	0.16
Grabill (town) Allen County	1	0.09
Warren (town) Huntington County	1	0.08
Bloomington (city) Monroe County	59	0.07
North Terre Haute (cdp) Vigo County	3	0.07
Dyer (town) Lake County	5	0.03
Angola (city) Steuben County	3	0.03
Fort Wayne (city) Allen County	41	0.02
Carmel (city) Hamilton County	17	0.02

Top 10 Places Sorted by Percent of Total Population

Based on places with total population of 50,000 or more

Place	Population	%
Bloomington (city) Monroe County	59	0.07
Fort Wayne (city) Allen County	41	0.02
Carmel (city) Hamilton County	17	0.02
Indianapolis (city) Marion County	44	0.01
Evansville (city) Vanderburgh County	17	0.01
Fishers (town) Hamilton County	10	0.01
Terre Haute (city) Vigo County	9	0.01
Noblesville (city) Hamilton County	5	0.01
Lafayette (city) Tippecanoe County	4	0.01
Muncie (city) Delaware County	3	<0.01

Asian: Nepalese

Top 10 Places Sorted by Population

Based on all places, regardless of total population

Place	Population	%
Indianapolis (city) Marion County	46	0.01
Evansville (city) Vanderburgh County	23	0.02
Bloomington (city) Monroe County	19	0.02
Fishers (town) Hamilton County	18	0.02
Munster (town) Lake County	14	0.06
Muncie (city) Delaware County	13	0.02
Carmel (city) Hamilton County	12	0.02
Purdue University (cdp) Tippecanoe County	11	0.09
Fort Wayne (city) Allen County	11	<0.01
Goshen (city) Elkhart County	10	0.03

Top 10 Places Sorted by Percent of Total Population

Based on all places, regardless of total population

Place	Population	%
Mackey (town) Gibson County	1	0.94
North Liberty (town) St. Joseph County	2	0.11
Purdue University (cdp) Tippecanoe County	11	0.09
Oakland City (city) Gibson County	2	0.08
Munster (town) Lake County	14	0.06
Angola (city) Steuben County	4	0.05
Goshen (city) Elkhart County	10	0.03
West Lafayette (city) Tippecanoe County	8	0.03
Warsaw (city) Kosciusko County	4	0.03
Evansville (city) Vanderburgh County	23	0.02

Top 10 Places Sorted by Percent of Total Population

Based on places with total population of 50,000 or more

Place	Population	%
Evansville (city) Vanderburgh County	23	0.02
Bloomington (city) Monroe County	19	0.02
Fishers (town) Hamilton County	18	0.02
Muncie (city) Delaware County	13	0.02
Carmel (city) Hamilton County	12	0.02
Indianapolis (city) Marion County	46	0.01
Terre Haute (city) Vigo County	5	0.01
Fort Wayne (city) Allen County	11	<0.01
South Bend (city) St. Joseph County	4	<0.01
Lafayette (city) Tippecanoe County	3	<0.01

Asian: Pakistani

Top 10 Places Sorted by Population

Based on all places, regardless of total population

Place	Population	%
Indianapolis (city) Marion County	625	0.08
Carmel (city) Hamilton County	211	0.27
Fishers (town) Hamilton County	189	0.25
Fort Wayne (city) Allen County	161	0.06
Plainfield (town) Hendricks County	103	0.37
Purdue University (cdp) Tippecanoe County	93	0.76
Granger (cdp) St. Joseph County	91	0.30
Bloomington (city) Monroe County	87	0.11
West Lafayette (city) Tippecanoe County	74	0.25
Schererville (town) Lake County	64	0.22

Top 10 Places Sorted by Percent of Total Population

Based on all places, regardless of total population

Place	Population	%
Plainville (town) Daviess County	4	0.84
Purdue University (cdp) Tippecanoe County	93	0.76
Dune Acres (town) Porter County	1	0.55
Aberdeen (cdp) Porter County	9	0.48
Avon (town) Hendricks County	53	0.43
Pottawattamie Park (town) LaPorte County	1	0.43
Plainfield (town) Hendricks County	103	0.37
Beverly Shores (town) Porter County	2	0.33
Winfield (town) Lake County	14	0.32
Granger (cdp) St. Joseph County	91	0.30

Top 10 Places Sorted by Percent of Total Population

Based on places with total population of 50,000 or more

Place	Population	%
Carmel (city) Hamilton County	211	0.27
Fishers (town) Hamilton County	189	0.25
Bloomington (city) Monroe County	87	0.11
Indianapolis (city) Marion County	625	0.08
Fort Wayne (city) Allen County	161	0.06
Hammond (city) Lake County	44	0.05
Elkhart (city) Elkhart County	15	0.03
South Bend (city) St. Joseph County	16	0.02
Muncie (city) Delaware County	14	0.02
Lafayette (city) Tippecanoe County	13	0.02

Asian: Sri Lankan

Top 10 Places Sorted by Population
Based on all places, regardless of total population

Place	Population	%
Indianapolis (city) Marion County	42	0.01
West Lafayette (city) Tippecanoe County	40	0.14
Bloomington (city) Monroe County	40	0.05
Carmel (city) Hamilton County	35	0.04
Fort Wayne (city) Allen County	19	0.01
Purdue University (cdp) Tippecanoe County	18	0.15
Fishers (town) Hamilton County	11	0.01
Goshen (city) Elkhart County	10	0.03
Granger (cdp) St. Joseph County	9	0.03
South Bend (city) St. Joseph County	9	0.01

Top 10 Places Sorted by Percent of Total Population
Based on all places, regardless of total population

Place	Population	%
Green (town) Howard County	4	0.17
Purdue University (cdp) Tippecanoe County	18	0.15
West Lafayette (city) Tippecanoe County	40	0.14
Notre Dame (cdp) St. Joseph County	7	0.12
Whites (town) Boone County	2	0.07
Churubusco (town) Whitley County	1	0.06
Bloomington (city) Monroe County	40	0.05
Carmel (city) Hamilton County	35	0.04
Goshen (city) Elkhart County	10	0.03
Granger (cdp) St. Joseph County	9	0.03

Top 10 Places Sorted by Percent of Total Population
Based on places with total population of 50,000 or more

Place	Population	%
Bloomington (city) Monroe County	40	0.05
Carmel (city) Hamilton County	35	0.04
Indianapolis (city) Marion County	42	0.01
Fort Wayne (city) Allen County	19	0.01
Fishers (town) Hamilton County	11	0.01
South Bend (city) St. Joseph County	9	0.01
Noblesville (city) Hamilton County	7	0.01
Elkhart (city) Elkhart County	4	0.01
Muncie (city) Delaware County	4	0.01
Hammond (city) Lake County	1	<0.01

Asian: Taiwanese

Top 10 Places Sorted by Population
Based on all places, regardless of total population

Place	Population	%
Bloomington (city) Monroe County	260	0.32
West Lafayette (city) Tippecanoe County	211	0.71
Carmel (city) Hamilton County	177	0.22
Indianapolis (city) Marion County	160	0.02
Purdue University (cdp) Tippecanoe County	118	0.97
Terre Haute (city) Vigo County	55	0.09
Fort Wayne (city) Allen County	47	0.02
Fishers (town) Hamilton County	45	0.06
Columbus (city) Bartholomew County	30	0.07
Muncie (city) Delaware County	25	0.04

Top 10 Places Sorted by Percent of Total Population
Based on all places, regardless of total population

Place	Population	%
Purdue University (cdp) Tippecanoe County	118	0.97
West Lafayette (city) Tippecanoe County	211	0.71
St. Mary of the Woods (cdp) Vigo County	4	0.50
Williams Creek (town) Marion County	2	0.49
Lagro (town) Wabash County	2	0.48
Bloomington (city) Monroe County	260	0.32
Spring Grove (town) Wayne County	1	0.29
Somerset (cdp) Wabash County	1	0.25
Gosport (town) Owen County	2	0.24
Americus (cdp) Tippecanoe County	1	0.24

Top 10 Places Sorted by Percent of Total Population
Based on places with total population of 50,000 or more

Place	Population	%
Bloomington (city) Monroe County	260	0.32
Carmel (city) Hamilton County	177	0.22
Terre Haute (city) Vigo County	55	0.09
Fishers (town) Hamilton County	45	0.06
Muncie (city) Delaware County	25	0.04
Lafayette (city) Tippecanoe County	20	0.03
Indianapolis (city) Marion County	160	0.02
Fort Wayne (city) Allen County	47	0.02
South Bend (city) St. Joseph County	19	0.02
Evansville (city) Vanderburgh County	10	0.01

Asian: Thai

Top 10 Places Sorted by Population
Based on all places, regardless of total population

Place	Population	%
Indianapolis (city) Marion County	352	0.04
Fort Wayne (city) Allen County	202	0.08
Bloomington (city) Monroe County	103	0.13
West Lafayette (city) Tippecanoe County	65	0.22
Fishers (town) Hamilton County	47	0.06
Carmel (city) Hamilton County	42	0.05
Evansville (city) Vanderburgh County	40	0.03
Crown Point (city) Lake County	37	0.14
South Bend (city) St. Joseph County	37	0.04
Purdue University (cdp) Tippecanoe County	32	0.26

Top 10 Places Sorted by Percent of Total Population
Based on all places, regardless of total population

Place	Population	%
Little York (town) Washington County	4	2.08
Cynthiana (town) Posey County	3	0.55
Mill (town) Crawford County	4	0.49
Pine Village (town) Warren County	1	0.46
Ogden Dunes (town) Porter County	5	0.45
Shorewood Forest (cdp) Porter County	11	0.41
Uniondale (town) Wells County	1	0.32
Purdue University (cdp) Tippecanoe County	32	0.26
Henryville (cdp) Clark County	5	0.26
Lake Santee (cdp) Decatur County	2	0.24

Top 10 Places Sorted by Percent of Total Population
Based on places with total population of 50,000 or more

Place	Population	%
Bloomington (city) Monroe County	103	0.13
Fort Wayne (city) Allen County	202	0.08
Fishers (town) Hamilton County	47	0.06
Carmel (city) Hamilton County	42	0.05
Noblesville (city) Hamilton County	24	0.05
Indianapolis (city) Marion County	352	0.04
South Bend (city) St. Joseph County	37	0.04
Lafayette (city) Tippecanoe County	25	0.04
Elkhart (city) Elkhart County	22	0.04
Evansville (city) Vanderburgh County	40	0.03

Asian: Vietnamese

Top 10 Places Sorted by Population
Based on all places, regardless of total population

Place	Population	%
Indianapolis (city) Marion County	1,347	0.16
Fort Wayne (city) Allen County	939	0.37
Fishers (town) Hamilton County	439	0.57
Carmel (city) Hamilton County	279	0.35
South Bend (city) St. Joseph County	267	0.26
Bloomington (city) Monroe County	203	0.25
Evansville (city) Vanderburgh County	194	0.17
Noblesville (city) Hamilton County	139	0.27
Mishawaka (city) St. Joseph County	120	0.25
Columbus (city) Bartholomew County	118	0.27

Top 10 Places Sorted by Percent of Total Population
Based on all places, regardless of total population

Place	Population	%
Hunter (town) Allen County	48	1.00
Roseland (town) St. Joseph County	6	0.95
Shamrock Lakes (town) Blackford County	2	0.87
Notre Dame (cdp) St. Joseph County	48	0.80
Fishers (town) Hamilton County	439	0.57
Middlebury (town) Elkhart County	19	0.56
Garrett (city) DeKalb County	29	0.46
Purdue University (cdp) Tippecanoe County	50	0.41
Wolcottville (town) Noble County	4	0.40
Centerville (town) Wayne County	10	0.39

Top 10 Places Sorted by Percent of Total Population
Based on places with total population of 50,000 or more

Place	Population	%
Fishers (town) Hamilton County	439	0.57
Fort Wayne (city) Allen County	939	0.37
Carmel (city) Hamilton County	279	0.35
Noblesville (city) Hamilton County	139	0.27
South Bend (city) St. Joseph County	267	0.26
Bloomington (city) Monroe County	203	0.25
Evansville (city) Vanderburgh County	194	0.17
Indianapolis (city) Marion County	1,347	0.16
Lafayette (city) Tippecanoe County	79	0.12
Muncie (city) Delaware County	62	0.09

Hawaii Native/Pacific Islander

Top 10 Places Sorted by Population
Based on all places, regardless of total population

Place	Population	%
Indianapolis (city) Marion County	1,129	0.14
Fort Wayne (city) Allen County	354	0.14
South Bend (city) St. Joseph County	185	0.18
Evansville (city) Vanderburgh County	176	0.15
Muncie (city) Delaware County	138	0.20
Bloomington (city) Monroe County	120	0.15
Richmond (city) Wayne County	118	0.32
Hammond (city) Lake County	97	0.12
Lawrence (city) Marion County	94	0.20
Carmel (city) Hamilton County	87	0.11

Top 10 Places Sorted by Percent of Total Population
Based on all places, regardless of total population

Place	Population	%
Bethany (town) Morgan County	2	2.47
Mount Etna (town) Huntington County	2	2.13
Leavenworth (town) Crawford County	5	2.10
Modoc (town) Randolph County	4	2.04
Russellville (town) Putnam County	3	0.84
Medora (town) Jackson County	5	0.72
Beverly Shores (town) Porter County	4	0.65
Collegeville (cdp) Jasper County	2	0.61
Newberry (town) Greene County	1	0.52
New Goshen (cdp) Vigo County	2	0.51

Top 10 Places Sorted by Percent of Total Population
Based on places with total population of 50,000 or more

Place	Population	%
Muncie (city) Delaware County	138	0.20
South Bend (city) St. Joseph County	185	0.18
Evansville (city) Vanderburgh County	176	0.15
Bloomington (city) Monroe County	120	0.15
Noblesville (city) Hamilton County	80	0.15
Indianapolis (city) Marion County	1,129	0.14
Fort Wayne (city) Allen County	354	0.14
Elkhart (city) Elkhart County	71	0.14
Terre Haute (city) Vigo County	79	0.13
Hammond (city) Lake County	97	0.12

Hawaii Native/Pacific Islander: Not Hispanic

Top 10 Places Sorted by Population
Based on all places, regardless of total population

Place	Population	%
Indianapolis (city) Marion County	820	0.10
Fort Wayne (city) Allen County	249	0.10
South Bend (city) St. Joseph County	156	0.15
Evansville (city) Vanderburgh County	150	0.13
Muncie (city) Delaware County	126	0.18
Richmond (city) Wayne County	110	0.30
Bloomington (city) Monroe County	95	0.12
Lawrence (city) Marion County	80	0.17
Mishawaka (city) St. Joseph County	79	0.16
Carmel (city) Hamilton County	77	0.10

Top 10 Places Sorted by Percent of Total Population
Based on all places, regardless of total population

Place	Population	%
Bethany (town) Morgan County	2	2.47
Mount Etna (town) Huntington County	2	2.13

Modoc (town) Randolph County	4	2.04
Leavenworth (town) Crawford County	4	1.68
Russellville (town) Putnam County	3	0.84
Medora (town) Jackson County	5	0.72
Beverly Shores (town) Porter County	4	0.65
Collegeville (cdp) Jasper County	2	0.61
Newberry (town) Greene County	1	0.52
New Goshen (cdp) Vigo County	2	0.51

Top 10 Places Sorted by Percent of Total Population
Based on places with total population of 50,000 or more

Place	Population	%
Muncie (city) Delaware County	126	0.18
South Bend (city) St. Joseph County	156	0.15
Evansville (city) Vanderburgh County	150	0.13
Bloomington (city) Monroe County	95	0.12
Terre Haute (city) Vigo County	73	0.12
Noblesville (city) Hamilton County	61	0.12
Indianapolis (city) Marion County	820	0.10
Fort Wayne (city) Allen County	249	0.10
Carmel (city) Hamilton County	77	0.10
Elkhart (city) Elkhart County	44	0.09

Hawaii Native/Pacific Islander: Hispanic

Top 10 Places Sorted by Population
Based on all places, regardless of total population

Place	Population	%
Indianapolis (city) Marion County	309	0.04
Fort Wayne (city) Allen County	105	0.04
Hammond (city) Lake County	50	0.06
South Bend (city) St. Joseph County	29	0.03
Elkhart (city) Elkhart County	27	0.05
Evansville (city) Vanderburgh County	26	0.02
Logansport (city) Cass County	25	0.14
Bloomington (city) Monroe County	25	0.03
Noblesville (city) Hamilton County	19	0.04
Lafayette (city) Tippecanoe County	18	0.03

Top 10 Places Sorted by Percent of Total Population
Based on all places, regardless of total population

Place	Population	%
Leavenworth (town) Crawford County	1	0.42
Corunna (town) DeKalb County	1	0.39
New Chicago (town) Lake County	5	0.25
Wheeler (cdp) Porter County	1	0.23
Huntingburg (city) Dubois County	12	0.20
Whiting (city) Lake County	8	0.16
Logansport (city) Cass County	25	0.14
Pennville (town) Jay County	1	0.14
Bunker Hill (town) Miami County	1	0.11
Burns Harbor (town) Porter County	1	0.09

Top 10 Places Sorted by Percent of Total Population
Based on places with total population of 50,000 or more

Place	Population	%
Hammond (city) Lake County	50	0.06
Elkhart (city) Elkhart County	27	0.05
Indianapolis (city) Marion County	309	0.04
Fort Wayne (city) Allen County	105	0.04
Noblesville (city) Hamilton County	19	0.04
South Bend (city) St. Joseph County	29	0.03
Bloomington (city) Monroe County	25	0.03
Lafayette (city) Tippecanoe County	18	0.03
Evansville (city) Vanderburgh County	26	0.02
Gary (city) Lake County	14	0.02

Hawaii Native/Pacific Islander: Fijian

Top 10 Places Sorted by Population
Based on all places, regardless of total population

Place	Population	%
Marion (city) Grant County	6	0.02
Indianapolis (city) Marion County	5	<0.01
East Chicago (city) Lake County	3	0.01
Princeton (city) Gibson County	2	0.02
Beech Grove (city) Marion County	2	0.01
Fort Wayne (city) Allen County	2	<0.01
Shelbyville (city) Shelby County	1	0.01
Bloomington (city) Monroe County	1	<0.01
Hammond (city) Lake County	1	<0.01
Muncie (city) Delaware County	1	<0.01

Top 10 Places Sorted by Percent of Total Population
Based on all places, regardless of total population

Place	Population	%
Marion (city) Grant County	6	0.02
Princeton (city) Gibson County	2	0.02
East Chicago (city) Lake County	3	0.01
Beech Grove (city) Marion County	2	0.01
Shelbyville (city) Shelby County	1	0.01
Indianapolis (city) Marion County	5	<0.01
Fort Wayne (city) Allen County	2	<0.01
Bloomington (city) Monroe County	1	<0.01
Hammond (city) Lake County	1	<0.01
Muncie (city) Delaware County	1	<0.01

Top 10 Places Sorted by Percent of Total Population
Based on places with total population of 50,000 or more

Place	Population	%
Indianapolis (city) Marion County	5	<0.01
Fort Wayne (city) Allen County	2	<0.01
Bloomington (city) Monroe County	1	<0.01
Hammond (city) Lake County	1	<0.01
Muncie (city) Delaware County	1	<0.01
Anderson (city) Madison County	0	0.00
Carmel (city) Hamilton County	0	0.00
Elkhart (city) Elkhart County	0	0.00
Evansville (city) Vanderburgh County	0	0.00
Fishers (town) Hamilton County	0	0.00

Hawaii Native/Pacific Islander: Guamanian or Chamorro

Top 10 Places Sorted by Population
Based on all places, regardless of total population

Place	Population	%
Indianapolis (city) Marion County	216	0.03
Fort Wayne (city) Allen County	102	0.04
Evansville (city) Vanderburgh County	30	0.03
Lawrence (city) Marion County	28	0.06
Bloomington (city) Monroe County	24	0.03
Lafayette (city) Tippecanoe County	20	0.03
South Bend (city) St. Joseph County	20	0.02
Jeffersonville (city) Clark County	18	0.04
Seymour (city) Jackson County	17	0.10
Elkhart (city) Elkhart County	17	0.03

Top 10 Places Sorted by Percent of Total Population
Based on all places, regardless of total population

Place	Population	%
Corunna (town) DeKalb County	1	0.39
Edwardsport (town) Knox County	1	0.33
Medora (town) Jackson County	2	0.29
Wheeler (cdp) Porter County	1	0.23
Bruceville (town) Knox County	1	0.21
Etna Green (town) Kosciusko County	1	0.17
Roseland (town) St. Joseph County	1	0.16
St. Bernice (cdp) Vermillion County	1	0.15
Fairview Park (town) Vermillion County	2	0.14
Colfax (town) Clinton County	1	0.14

Top 10 Places Sorted by Percent of Total Population
Based on places with total population of 50,000 or more

Place	Population	%
Fort Wayne (city) Allen County	102	0.04
Indianapolis (city) Marion County	216	0.03
Evansville (city) Vanderburgh County	30	0.03
Bloomington (city) Monroe County	24	0.03
Lafayette (city) Tippecanoe County	20	0.03
Elkhart (city) Elkhart County	17	0.03
South Bend (city) St. Joseph County	20	0.02
Muncie (city) Delaware County	12	0.02
Terre Haute (city) Vigo County	11	0.02
Carmel (city) Hamilton County	11	0.01

Hawaii Native/Pacific Islander: Marshallese

Top 10 Places Sorted by Population
Based on all places, regardless of total population

Place	Population	%
Evansville (city) Vanderburgh County	49	0.04
Goshen (city) Elkhart County	4	0.01
Nappanee (city) Elkhart County	3	0.05
Granger (cdp) St. Joseph County	2	0.01
North Manchester (town) Wabash County	1	0.02
Peru (city) Miami County	1	0.01
Elkhart (city) Elkhart County	1	<0.01
Fort Wayne (city) Allen County	1	<0.01
Lawrence (city) Marion County	1	<0.01
Noblesville (city) Hamilton County	1	<0.01

Top 10 Places Sorted by Percent of Total Population
Based on all places, regardless of total population

Place	Population	%
Nappanee (city) Elkhart County	3	0.05
Evansville (city) Vanderburgh County	49	0.04
North Manchester (town) Wabash County	1	0.02
Goshen (city) Elkhart County	4	0.01
Granger (cdp) St. Joseph County	2	0.01
Peru (city) Miami County	1	0.01
Elkhart (city) Elkhart County	1	<0.01
Fort Wayne (city) Allen County	1	<0.01
Lawrence (city) Marion County	1	<0.01
Noblesville (city) Hamilton County	1	<0.01

Top 10 Places Sorted by Percent of Total Population
Based on places with total population of 50,000 or more

Place	Population	%
Evansville (city) Vanderburgh County	49	0.04
Elkhart (city) Elkhart County	1	<0.01
Fort Wayne (city) Allen County	1	<0.01
Noblesville (city) Hamilton County	1	<0.01
Anderson (city) Madison County	0	0.00
Bloomington (city) Monroe County	0	0.00
Carmel (city) Hamilton County	0	0.00
Fishers (town) Hamilton County	0	0.00
Gary (city) Lake County	0	0.00
Hammond (city) Lake County	0	0.00

Hawaii Native/Pacific Islander: Native Hawaiian

Top 10 Places Sorted by Population
Based on all places, regardless of total population

Place	Population	%
Indianapolis (city) Marion County	361	0.04
Fort Wayne (city) Allen County	119	0.05
South Bend (city) St. Joseph County	55	0.05
Noblesville (city) Hamilton County	51	0.10
Columbus (city) Bartholomew County	50	0.11
Evansville (city) Vanderburgh County	49	0.04
Terre Haute (city) Vigo County	44	0.07
Muncie (city) Delaware County	44	0.06
Bloomington (city) Monroe County	37	0.05
Carmel (city) Hamilton County	33	0.04

Top 10 Places Sorted by Percent of Total Population
Based on all places, regardless of total population

Place	Population	%
Leavenworth (town) Crawford County	4	1.68
Beverly Shores (town) Porter County	4	0.65
Medora (town) Jackson County	4	0.58
Stinesville (town) Monroe County	1	0.51
Marengo (town) Crawford County	4	0.48
Bunker Hill (town) Miami County	4	0.45
West College Corner (town) Union County	3	0.44
Elizabeth (town) Bartholomew County	2	0.40
Dublin (town) Wayne County	3	0.38
Edgewood (town) Madison County	7	0.37

Top 10 Places Sorted by Percent of Total Population
Based on places with total population of 50,000 or more

Place	Population	%
Noblesville (city) Hamilton County	51	0.10

Terre Haute (city) Vigo County	44	0.07
Muncie (city) Delaware County	44	0.06
Fort Wayne (city) Allen County	119	0.05
South Bend (city) St. Joseph County	55	0.05
Bloomington (city) Monroe County	37	0.05
Indianapolis (city) Marion County	361	0.04
Evansville (city) Vanderburgh County	49	0.04
Carmel (city) Hamilton County	33	0.04
Hammond (city) Lake County	30	0.04

Hawaii Native/Pacific Islander: Samoan

Top 10 Places Sorted by Population
Based on all places, regardless of total population

Place	Population	%
Indianapolis (city) Marion County	145	0.02
South Bend (city) St. Joseph County	55	0.05
Fort Wayne (city) Allen County	38	0.01
Hammond (city) Lake County	21	0.03
Evansville (city) Vanderburgh County	20	0.02
Muncie (city) Delaware County	19	0.03
Lawrence (city) Marion County	18	0.04
Granger (cdp) St. Joseph County	16	0.05
Bloomington (city) Monroe County	16	0.02
Carmel (city) Hamilton County	16	0.02

Top 10 Places Sorted by Percent of Total Population
Based on all places, regardless of total population

Place	Population	%
Bethany (town) Morgan County	2	2.47
Newberry (town) Greene County	1	0.52
New Goshen (cdp) Vigo County	2	0.51
Dillsboro (town) Dearborn County	6	0.45
Arlington (cdp) Rush County	1	0.23
Eaton (town) Delaware County	4	0.22
Idaville (cdp) White County	1	0.22
Williamsport (town) Warren County	4	0.21
Woodburn (city) Allen County	3	0.20
Wanatah (town) LaPorte County	2	0.19

Top 10 Places Sorted by Percent of Total Population
Based on places with total population of 50,000 or more

Place	Population	%
South Bend (city) St. Joseph County	55	0.05
Hammond (city) Lake County	21	0.03
Muncie (city) Delaware County	19	0.03
Indianapolis (city) Marion County	145	0.02
Evansville (city) Vanderburgh County	20	0.02
Bloomington (city) Monroe County	16	0.02
Carmel (city) Hamilton County	16	0.02
Gary (city) Lake County	15	0.02
Lafayette (city) Tippecanoe County	13	0.02
Terre Haute (city) Vigo County	13	0.02

Hawaii Native/Pacific Islander: Tongan

Top 10 Places Sorted by Population
Based on all places, regardless of total population

Place	Population	%
South Bend (city) St. Joseph County	20	0.02
Osceola (town) St. Joseph County	10	0.41
Indianapolis (city) Marion County	10	<0.01
Mishawaka (city) St. Joseph County	8	0.02
Elkhart (city) Elkhart County	6	0.01
Fishers (town) Hamilton County	6	0.01
Elwood (city) Madison County	5	0.06
Logansport (city) Cass County	5	0.03
Kouts (town) Porter County	4	0.21
Muncie (city) Delaware County	3	<0.01

Top 10 Places Sorted by Percent of Total Population
Based on all places, regardless of total population

Place	Population	%
Osceola (town) St. Joseph County	10	0.41
Wheatfield (town) Jasper County	2	0.23
Kouts (town) Porter County	4	0.21
Elwood (city) Madison County	5	0.06
Logansport (city) Cass County	5	0.03
Rensselaer (city) Jasper County	2	0.03
South Bend (city) St. Joseph County	20	0.02
Mishawaka (city) St. Joseph County	8	0.02
Batesville (city) Ripley County	1	0.02
Elkhart (city) Elkhart County	6	0.01

Top 10 Places Sorted by Percent of Total Population
Based on places with total population of 50,000 or more

Place	Population	%
South Bend (city) St. Joseph County	20	0.02
Elkhart (city) Elkhart County	6	0.01
Fishers (town) Hamilton County	6	0.01
Indianapolis (city) Marion County	10	<0.01
Muncie (city) Delaware County	3	<0.01
Terre Haute (city) Vigo County	2	<0.01
Fort Wayne (city) Allen County	1	<0.01
Lafayette (city) Tippecanoe County	1	<0.01
Noblesville (city) Hamilton County	1	<0.01
Anderson (city) Madison County	0	0.00

White

Top 10 Places Sorted by Population
Based on all places, regardless of total population

Place	Population	%
Indianapolis (city) Marion County	526,672	64.19
Fort Wayne (city) Allen County	194,759	76.77
Evansville (city) Vanderburgh County	99,372	84.62
Carmel (city) Hamilton County	68,938	87.05
Bloomington (city) Monroe County	68,936	85.74
Fishers (town) Hamilton County	67,165	87.46
South Bend (city) St. Joseph County	64,797	64.05
Muncie (city) Delaware County	60,636	86.52
Lafayette (city) Tippecanoe County	57,759	86.03
Terre Haute (city) Vigo County	52,377	86.17

Top 10 Places Sorted by Percent of Total Population
Based on all places, regardless of total population

Place	Population	%
Dugger (town) Sullivan County	920	100.00
Newport (town) Vermillion County	515	100.00
Wilkinson (town) Hancock County	449	100.00
Troy (town) Perry County	385	100.00
Mooreland (town) Henry County	375	100.00
Lewisville (town) Henry County	366	100.00
Star City (cdp) Pulaski County	344	100.00
Montgomery (town) Daviess County	343	100.00
Blanford (cdp) Vermillion County	342	100.00
Larwill (town) Whitley County	283	100.00

Top 10 Places Sorted by Percent of Total Population
Based on places with total population of 50,000 or more

Place	Population	%
Noblesville (city) Hamilton County	48,170	92.69
Fishers (town) Hamilton County	67,165	87.46
Carmel (city) Hamilton County	68,938	87.05
Muncie (city) Delaware County	60,636	86.52
Terre Haute (city) Vigo County	52,377	86.17
Lafayette (city) Tippecanoe County	57,759	86.03
Bloomington (city) Monroe County	68,936	85.74
Evansville (city) Vanderburgh County	99,372	84.62
Anderson (city) Madison County	45,548	81.15
Fort Wayne (city) Allen County	194,759	76.77

White: Not Hispanic

Top 10 Places Sorted by Population
Based on all places, regardless of total population

Place	Population	%
Indianapolis (city) Marion County	496,520	60.52
Fort Wayne (city) Allen County	184,757	72.83
Evansville (city) Vanderburgh County	97,793	83.28
Carmel (city) Hamilton County	67,446	85.17
Bloomington (city) Monroe County	67,128	83.49
Fishers (town) Hamilton County	65,289	85.02
Muncie (city) Delaware County	59,588	85.02
South Bend (city) St. Joseph County	59,298	58.61
Lafayette (city) Tippecanoe County	53,754	80.06
Terre Haute (city) Vigo County	50,949	83.82

Top 10 Places Sorted by Percent of Total Population
Based on all places, regardless of total population

Place	Population	%
Newport (town) Vermillion County	515	100.00
Blanford (cdp) Vermillion County	342	100.00
Larwill (town) Whitley County	283	100.00
Wingate (town) Montgomery County	263	100.00
Buck Creek (cdp) Tippecanoe County	207	100.00
Westphalia (cdp) Knox County	202	100.00
Cedar Grove (town) Franklin County	156	100.00
Clarksburg (cdp) Decatur County	149	100.00
Springport (town) Henry County	149	100.00
Yeoman (town) Carroll County	139	100.00

Top 10 Places Sorted by Percent of Total Population
Based on places with total population of 50,000 or more

Place	Population	%
Noblesville (city) Hamilton County	46,797	90.05
Carmel (city) Hamilton County	67,446	85.17
Fishers (town) Hamilton County	65,289	85.02
Muncie (city) Delaware County	59,588	85.02
Terre Haute (city) Vigo County	50,949	83.82
Bloomington (city) Monroe County	67,128	83.49
Evansville (city) Vanderburgh County	97,793	83.28
Lafayette (city) Tippecanoe County	53,754	80.06
Anderson (city) Madison County	44,327	78.97
Fort Wayne (city) Allen County	184,757	72.83

White: Hispanic

Top 10 Places Sorted by Population
Based on all places, regardless of total population

Place	Population	%
Indianapolis (city) Marion County	30,152	3.68
Hammond (city) Lake County	15,674	19.39
Fort Wayne (city) Allen County	10,002	3.94
East Chicago (city) Lake County	8,852	29.81
South Bend (city) St. Joseph County	5,499	5.44
Elkhart (city) Elkhart County	4,552	8.93
Goshen (city) Elkhart County	4,029	12.70
Lafayette (city) Tippecanoe County	4,005	5.97
Portage (city) Porter County	3,928	10.67
Hobart (city) Lake County	2,732	9.40

Top 10 Places Sorted by Percent of Total Population
Based on all places, regardless of total population

Place	Population	%
East Chicago (city) Lake County	8,852	29.81
Ligonier (city) Noble County	1,084	24.61
Whiting (city) Lake County	1,166	23.33
Ambia (town) Benton County	55	23.01
Hammond (city) Lake County	15,674	19.39
New Chicago (town) Lake County	327	16.07
Lake Station (city) Lake County	1,914	15.22
Goshen (city) Elkhart County	4,029	12.70
Frankfort (city) Clinton County	1,888	11.50
Plymouth (city) Marshall County	1,104	11.00

Top 10 Places Sorted by Percent of Total Population
Based on places with total population of 50,000 or more

Place	Population	%
Hammond (city) Lake County	15,674	19.39
Elkhart (city) Elkhart County	4,552	8.93
Lafayette (city) Tippecanoe County	4,005	5.97
South Bend (city) St. Joseph County	5,499	5.44
Fort Wayne (city) Allen County	10,002	3.94
Indianapolis (city) Marion County	30,152	3.68
Noblesville (city) Hamilton County	1,373	2.64
Fishers (town) Hamilton County	1,876	2.44
Terre Haute (city) Vigo County	1,428	2.35
Bloomington (city) Monroe County	1,808	2.25

Profiles

This chapter begins with a detailed user guide to help with interpreting the individual county and place profiles that follow. Each profile—all 876 of them—is a concise snapshot of the data culled from census data and the previous subject-driven chapters. They are arranged alphabetically by county, then by place.

User Guide 447

Core Based Statistical Areas (CBSAs) and Counties 460

County and Place Profiles 461

The Hoosier State

The Crossroads of America

Profiles

User Guide

Places Covered

All 92 counties.

567 incorporated municipalities. Includes 119 cities, 447 towns, and one consolidated city-county.

112 Census Designated Places (CDP). The U.S. Bureau of the Census defines a CDP as "a statistical entity, defined for each decennial census according to Census Bureau guidelines, comprising a densely settled concentration of population that is not within an incorporated place, but is locally identified by a name. CDPs are delineated cooperatively by state and local officials and the Census Bureau, following Census Bureau guidelines."

105 unincorporated communities. The communities included have statistics for their ZIP Code Tabulation Area (ZCTA) available from the Census Bureau. They are referred to as "postal areas." A ZCTA is a statistical entity developed by the Census Bureau to approximate the delivery area for a US Postal Service 5-digit or 3-digit ZIP Code in the US and Puerto Rico. A ZCTA is an aggregation of census blocks that have the same predominant ZIP Code associated with the mailing addresses in the Census Bureau's Master Address File. Thus, the Postal Service's delivery areas have been adjusted to encompass whole census blocks so that the Census Bureau can tabulate census data for the ZCTAs. ZCTAs do not include all ZIP Codes used for mail delivery and therefore do not precisely depict the area within which mail deliveries associated with that ZIP Code occur. Additionally, some areas that are known by a unique name, although they are part of a larger incorporated place, are also included as "postal areas."

For a more in-depth discussion of geographic areas, please refer to the Census Bureau's Geographic Areas Reference Manual at http://www.census.gov/geo/www/garm.html.

IMPORTANT NOTES

- Since the last decennial census, the U.S. Census replaced the long-form sample with the American Community Survey (ACS), which uses a series of monthly samples to produce annually updated estimates for the same areas. ACS estimates are based on data from a sample of housing units and people in the population, not the full population. ACS sampling error (uncertainty of data) is greater for those areas with smaller populations.

- *Profiles of Indiana* uses the term "community" to refer to all places except counties. The term "county" is used to refer to counties and county-equivalents. All places are defined as of the 2010 Census.

- If a community spans multiple counties, the community will be shown in the county that contains its largest population.

- In each community profile, only school districts that have schools that are physically located within the community are shown. In addition, statistics for each school district cover the entire district, regardless of the physical location of the schools within the district.

- Special care should be taken when interpreting certain statistics for communities containing large colleges or universities. College students were counted as residents of the area in which they were living while attending college (as they have been since the 1950 census). One effect this may have is skewing the figures for population, income, housing, and educational attainment.

- Some information (e.g. income) is available for both counties and individual communities. Other information is available for just counties (e.g. election results), or just individual communities (e.g. crime rates).

County Profiles

PHYSICAL AND GEOGRAPHICAL CHARACTERISTICS

Physical Location: Describes the physical location of the county. *Source: Columbia University Press, The Columbia Gazetteer of North America and original research.*

Land and Water Area: Land and water area in square miles. *Source: U.S. Census Bureau, Census 2010*

Latitude and Longitude: Latitude and longitude in degrees. *Source: U.S. Census Bureau, Census 2010*

Time Zone: Lists the time zone. *Source: Original research*

Year Organized: Year the county government was organized. *Source: National Association of Counties*

County Seat: Lists the county seat. If a county has more than one seat, then both are listed. *Source: National Association of Counties*

Metropolitan Area: Indicates the metropolitan area the county is located in. Also lists all the component counties of that metropolitan area. The Office of Management and Budget (OMB) defines metropolitan and micropolitan statistical areas. The most current definitions are as of September 2018. *Source: U.S. Census Bureau*

Climate: Includes all weather stations located within the county. Indicates the station name and elevation as well as the monthly average high and low temperatures, average precipitation, and average snowfall. The period of record is generally 1980-2009, however, certain weather stations contain averages going back as far as 1900. *Source: Grey House Publishing, Weather America: A Thirty-Year Summary of Statistical Weather Data and Rankings, 2010*

DEMOGRAPHICS

Population: Current population. *Source: U.S. Census Bureau, American Community Survey, 2013-2017 Five-Year Estimates*

Population Growth: The increase or decrease in population since 2000. *Source: U.S. Census Bureau, Census 2000; U.S. Census Bureau, American Community Survey, 2013-2017 Five-Year Estimates*

Population Density: Total current population divided by the land area in square miles. *Source: U.S. Census Bureau, Census 2010; U.S. Census Bureau, American Community Survey, 2013-2017 Five-Year Estimates*

Race/Hispanic Origin: Figures include the U.S. Census Bureau categories of White alone; Black/African American alone; Asian alone; American Indian/Alaska Native alone; Native Hawaiian/Other Pacific Islander alone; two or more races; and Hispanic of any race. Alone refers to the fact that these figures are not in combination with any other race. *Source: U.S. Census Bureau, American Community Survey, 2013-2017 Five-Year Estimates*

The concept of race, as used by the Census Bureau, reflects self-identification by people according to the race or races with which they most closely identify. These categories are socio-political constructs and should not be interpreted as being scientific or anthropological in nature. Furthermore, the race categories include both racial and national-origin groups.

- **White.** A person having origins in any of the original peoples of Europe, the Middle East, or North Africa. It includes people who indicated their race(s) as "White" or reported entries such as Irish, German, Italian, Lebanese, Arab, Moroccan, or Caucasian.
- **Black/African American.** A person having origins in any of the Black racial groups of Africa. It includes people who indicated their race(s) as "Black, African Am., or Negro" or reported entries such as African American, Kenyan, Nigerian, or Haitian.
- **Asian.** A person having origins in any of the original peoples of the Far East, Southeast Asia, or the Indian subcontinent, including, for example, Cambodia, China, India, Japan, Korea, Malaysia, Pakistan, the Philippine Islands, Thailand, and Vietnam. It includes people who indicated their race(s) as "Asian" or reported entries such as "Asian Indian," "Chinese," "Filipino," "Korean," "Japanese," "Vietnamese," and "Other Asian" or provided other detailed Asian responses.
- **American Indian/Alaska Native.** A person having origins in any of the original peoples of North and South America (including Central America) and who maintains tribal affiliation or community attachment. This category includes people who indicated their race(s) as "American Indian or Alaska Native" or reported their enrolled or principal tribe, such as Navajo, Blackfeet, Inupiat, Yup'ik, or Central American Indian groups or South American Indian groups.
- **Native Hawaiian/Other Pacific Islander.** A person having origins in any of the original peoples of Hawaii, Guam, Samoa, or other Pacific Islands. It includes people who indicated their race(s) as "Pacific Islander" or reported entries such as "Native Hawaiian," "Guamanian or Chamorro," "Samoan," and "Other Pacific Islander" or provided other detailed Pacific Islander responses.
- **Two or More Races.** People may choose to provide two or more races either by checking two or more race response check boxes, by providing multiple responses, or by some combination of check boxes and other responses. The race response categories shown on the questionnaire are collapsed into the five minimum race groups identified by OMB, and the Census Bureau's "Some Other Race" category.
- **Hispanic.** The data on the Hispanic or Latino population were derived from answers to a question that was asked of all people. The terms "Spanish," "Hispanic origin," and "Latino" are used interchangeably. Some respondents identify with all three terms while others may identify with only one of these three specific terms. Hispanics or Latinos who identify with the terms "Spanish," "Hispanic," or "Latino" are those who classify themselves in one of the specific Spanish, Hispanic, or Latino categories listed on the questionnaire ("Mexican," "Puerto Rican," or "Cuban") as well as those who indicate that they are "other Spanish/Hispanic/Latino." People who do not identify with one of the specific origins listed on the questionnaire but indicate that they are "other Spanish/Hispanic/Latino" are those whose origins are from Spain, the Spanish-speaking countries of Central or South America, the Dominican Republic, or people identifying themselves generally as Spanish, Spanish-American, Hispanic, Hispano, Latino, and so on. All write-in responses to the "other Spanish/Hispanic/Latino" category were coded. Origin can be viewed as the heritage, nationality group, lineage, or country of birth of the person or the person's parents or ancestors before their arrival in the United States. People who identify their origin as Spanish, Hispanic, or Latino may be of any race.

Average Household Size: Number of persons in the average household. *Source: U.S. Census Bureau, American Community Survey, 2013-2017 Five-Year Estimates*

Median Age: Median age of the population. *Source: U.S. Census Bureau, American Community Survey, 2013-2017 Five-Year Estimates*

Age Under 18: Percent of the total population under 18 years old. *Source: U.S. Census Bureau, American Community Survey, 2013-2017 Five-Year Estimates*

Age 65 and Over: Percent of the total population age 65 and over. *Source: U.S. Census Bureau, American Community Survey, 2013-2017 Five-Year Estimates*

Males per 100 Females: Number of males per 100 females. *Source: U.S. Census Bureau, American Community Survey, 2013-2017 Five-Year Estimates*

Marital Status: Percentage of population never married, now married, separated, widowed, or divorced. *Source: U.S. Census Bureau, American Community Survey, 2013-2017 Five-Year Estimates*

The marital status classification refers to the status at the time of enumeration. Data on marital status are tabulated only for the population 15 years old and over. Each person was asked whether they were "Now married," "Widowed," "Separated," "Divorced," or "Never married." Couples who live together (for example, people in common-law marriages) were able to report the marital status they considered to be the most appropriate.

- **Never married.** Never married includes all people who have never been married, including people whose only marriage(s) was annulled.
- **Now married.** All people whose current marriage has not ended by widowhood or divorce. This category includes people defined as "separated."
- **Separated.** Includes people legally separated or otherwise absent from their spouse because of marital discord. Those without a final divorce decree are classified as "separated." This category also includes people who have been deserted or who have parted because they no longer want to live together, but who have not obtained a divorce.
- **Widowed.** This category includes widows and widowers who have not remarried.
- **Divorced.** This category includes people who are legally divorced and who have not remarried.

Foreign Born: Percentage of population who were not U.S. citizens at birth. Foreign-born people are those who indicated they were either a U.S. citizen by naturalization or they were not a citizen of the United States. *Source: U.S. Census Bureau, American Community Survey, 2013-2017 Five-Year Estimates*

Speak English Only: Percent of population that reported speaking only English at home. *Source: U.S. Census Bureau, American Community Survey, 2013-2017 Five-Year Estimates*

With Disability: Percent of the civilian noninstitutionalized population that reported having a disability. Disability status is determined from from six types of difficulty: vision, hearing, cognitive, ambulatory, self-care, and independent living. For children under 5 years old, hearing and vision difficulty are used to determine disability status. For children between the ages of 5 and 14, disability status is determined from hearing, vision, cognitive, ambulatory, and self-care difficulties. For people aged 15 years and older, they are considered to have a disability if they have difficulty with any one of the six difficulty types. *Source: U.S. Census Bureau, American Community Survey, 2013-2017 Five-Year Estimates*

Veterans: Percent of the civilian population 18 years and over who have served (even for a short time), but are not currently serving, on active duty in the U.S. Army, Navy, Air Force, Marine Corps, or the Coast Guard, or who served in the U.S. Merchant Marine during World War II. People who served in the National Guard or Reserves are classified as veterans only if they were ever called or ordered to active duty, not counting the 4-6 months for initial training or yearly summer camps. All other civilians are classified as nonveterans. Note: While it is possible for 17 year olds to be veterans of the Armed Forces, ACS data products are restricted to the population 18 years and older. *Source: U.S. Census Bureau, American Community Survey, 2013-2017 Five-Year Estimates*

Ancestry: Largest ancestry groups reported (up to five). The data includes persons who report multiple ancestries. For example, if a person reported being Irish and Italian, they would be included in both categories. Thus, the sum of the percentages may be greater than 100%. *Source: U.S. Census Bureau, American Community Survey, 2013-2017 Five-Year Estimates*

The data represent self-classification by people according to the ancestry group or groups with which they most closely identify. Ancestry refers to a person's ethnic origin or descent, "roots," heritage, or the place of birth of the person, the person's parents, or their ancestors before their arrival in the United States. Some ethnic identities, such as Egyptian or Polish, can be traced to geographic areas outside the United States, while other ethnicities such as Pennsylvania German or Cajun evolved in the United States.

The ancestry question was intended to provide data for groups that were not included in the Hispanic origin and race questions. Therefore, although data on all groups are collected, the ancestry data shown in these tabulations are for non-Hispanic and non-race groups. *See* Race/Hispanic Origin for information on Hispanic and race groups.

RELIGION

Religion: Lists the largest religious groups (up to six) based on the number of adherents divided by the population of the county. Adherents are defined as "all members, including full members, their children and the estimated number of other regular participants who are not considered as communicant, confirmed or full members." *Source: American Religious Bodies, 2010 U.S. Religion Census: Religious Congregations & Membership Study*

ECONOMY

Unemployment Rate: Unemployment rate as of November 2018. Includes all civilians age 16 or over who were unemployed and looking for work. *Source: U.S. Department of Labor, Bureau of Labor Statistics, Local Area Unemployment Statistics*

Leading Industries: Lists the three leading industries (excluding government) based on the number of establishments. *Source: U.S. Census Bureau, County Business Patterns 2016*

Farms: The total number of farms and the total acreage they occupy. *Source: U.S. Department of Agriculture, National Agricultural Statistics Service, 2012 Census of Agriculture*

Company Size: The numbers of companies at various employee headcounts. Includes private employers only. *Source: U.S. Census Bureau, County Business Patterns 2016*

- **Employ 1,000 or more persons.** The numbers of companies that employ 1,000 or more persons.
- **Employ 500-999 persons.** The numbers of companies that employ 500 to 999 persons.
- **Employ 100-499 persons.** The numbers of companies that employ 100 to 499 persons.
- **Employ 1-99 persons.** The numbers of companies that employ 1 to 99 persons.

Business Ownership: Number of businesses that are majority-owned by women or various minority groups. *Source: U.S. Census Bureau, 2012 Economic Census, Survey of Business Owners*

- **Women-Owned.** Number of businesses that are majority-owned by a woman. Majority ownership is defined as having 51 percent or more of the stock or equity in the business.
- **Black-Owned.** Number of businesses that are majority-owned by a Black or African American person(s). Majority ownership is defined as having 51 percent or more of the stock or equity in the business. Black or African American is defined as a person having origins in any of the black racial groups of Africa, including those who consider themselves to be "Haitian."
- **Asian-Owned.** Number of businesses that are majority-owned by an Asian person(s). Majority ownership is defined as having 51 percent or more of the stock or equity in the business.
- **American Indian/Alaska Native-Owned.** Number of businesses that are majority-owned by an American Indian or Alaska Native person(s). Majority ownership is defined as having 51 percent or more of the stock or equity in the business.
- **Hispanic-Owned.** Number of businesses that are majority-owned by a person(s) of Hispanic or Latino origin. Majority ownership is defined as having 51 percent or more of the stock or equity in the business. Hispanic or Latino origin is defined as a person of Cuban, Mexican, Puerto Rican, South or Central American, or other Spanish culture or origin, regardless of race.

EMPLOYMENT

Employment by Occupation: Percentage of the employed civilian population 16 years and over in management, professional, service, sales, farming, construction, and production occupations. *Source: U.S. Census Bureau, American Community Survey, 2013-2017 Five-Year Estimates*

- Management, business, and financial occupations include:
  - Management
  - Business and financial operations
- Computer, engineering, and science occupations include:
  - Computer and mathematical
  - Architecture and engineering
  - Life, physical, and social science
- Education, legal, community service, arts, and media occupations include:
  - Community and social service
  - Legal
  - Education, training, and library
  - Arts, design, entertainment, sports, and media
- Healthcare practitioners and technical occupations include:
  - Health diagnosing and treating practitioners
  - Health technologists and technicians
- Service occupations include:
  - Healthcare support
  - Protective services:
  - Fire fighting and prevention, and other protective service workers including supervisors
  - Law enforcement workers including supervisors

Food preparation and serving related
Building and grounds cleaning and maintenance
Personal care and service

- Sales and office occupations include:
  Sales and related
  Office and administrative support

- Natural resources, construction, and maintenance occupations include:
  Farming, fishing, and forestry
  Construction and extraction
  Installation, maintenance, and repair

- Production, transportation, and material moving occupations include:
  Production
  Transportation
  Material moving

INCOME

Per Capita Income: Per capita income is the mean income computed for every man, woman, and child in a particular group. It is derived by dividing the total income of a particular group by the total population in that group. Per capita income is rounded to the nearest whole dollar. *Source: U.S. Census Bureau, American Community Survey, 2013-2017 Five-Year Estimates*

Median Household Income: Includes the income of the householder and all other individuals 15 years old and over in the household, whether they are related to the householder or not. The median divides the income distribution into two equal parts: one-half of the cases falling below the median income and one-half above the median. For households, the median income is based on the distribution of the total number of households including those with no income. Median income for households is computed on the basis of a standard distribution and is rounded to the nearest whole dollar. *Source: U.S. Census Bureau, American Community Survey, 2013-2017 Five-Year Estimates*

Average Household Income: Average household income is obtained by dividing total household income by the total number of households. *Source: U.S. Census Bureau, American Community Survey, 2013-2017 Five-Year Estimates*

Percent of Households with Income of $100,000 or more: Percent of households with income of $100,000 or more. *Source: U.S. Census Bureau, American Community Survey, 2013-2017 Five-Year Estimates*

Poverty Rate: Percentage of population with income below the poverty level. Based on individuals for whom poverty status is determined. Poverty status was determined for all people except institutionalized people, people in military group quarters, people in college dormitories, and unrelated individuals under 15 years old. *Source: U.S. Census Bureau, American Community Survey, 2013-2017 Five-Year Estimates*

EDUCATIONAL ATTAINMENT

Figures show the percent of population age 25 and over with the following levels of educational attainment. *Source: U.S. Census Bureau, American Community Survey, 2013-2017 Five-Year Estimates*

- **High school diploma or higher.** Includes people whose highest degree is a high school diploma or its equivalent (GED), people who attended college but did not receive a degree, and people who received a college, university, or professional degree.

- **Bachelor's degree or higher.** Includes people who received a bachelor's, master's, doctorate, or professional degree.

- **Graduate/professional degree or higher.** Includes people who received a master's, doctorate, or professional degree.

HOUSING

Homeownership Rate: Percentage of housing units that are owner-occupied. *Source: U.S. Census Bureau, American Community Survey, 2013-2017 Five-Year Estimates*

Median Home Value: Median value in dollars of all owner-occupied housing units as reported by the owner. *Source: U.S. Census Bureau, American Community Survey, 2013-2017 Five-Year Estimates*

Median Year Structure Built: Year structure built refers to when the building was first constructed, not when it was remodeled, added to, or converted. For mobile homes, houseboats, RVs, etc, the manufacturer's model year was assumed to be the year built. The data relate to the number of units built during the specified periods that were still in existence at the time of enumeration. *Source: U.S. Census Bureau, American Community Survey, 2013-2017 Five-Year Estimates*

Homeowner Vacancy Rate: Proportion of the homeowner inventory that is vacant "for sale." It is computed by dividing the number of vacant units "for sale only" by the sum of the owner-occupied units, vacant units that are "for sale only," and vacant units that have been sold but not yet occupied, and then multiplying by 100. This measure is rounded to the nearest tenth. *Source: U.S. Census Bureau, American Community Survey, 2013-2017 Five-Year Estimates*

Median Selected Monthly Owner Costs: Selected monthly owner costs are the sum of payments for mortgages, deeds of trust, contracts to purchase, or similar debts on the property (including payments for the first mortgage, second mortgages,

home equity loans, and other junior mortgages); real estate taxes; fire, hazard, and flood insurance on the property; utilities (electricity, gas, and water and sewer); and fuels (oil, coal, kerosene, wood, etc.). It also includes, where appropriate, the monthly condominium fee for condominiums and mobile home costs (personal property taxes, site rent, registration fees, and license fees). Selected monthly owner costs were tabulated for all owner-occupied units, and are shown separately for units "with a mortgage" and for units "not mortgaged."
Source: U.S. Census Bureau, American Community Survey, 2013-2017 Five-Year Estimates

Median Gross Rent: Median monthly gross rent in dollars on specified renter-occupied and specified vacant-for-rent units. Specified renter-occupied and specified vacant-for-rent units exclude 1-family houses on 10 acres or more. Gross rent is the contract rent plus the estimated average monthly cost of utilities (electricity, gas, and water and sewer) and fuels (oil, coal, kerosene, wood, etc.) if these are paid by the renter (or paid for the renter by someone else). Gross rent is intended to eliminate differentials that result from varying practices with respect to the inclusion of utilities and fuels as part of the rental payment. Contract rent is the monthly rent agreed to or contracted for, regardless of any furnishings, utilities, fees, meals, or services that may be included. For vacant units, it is the monthly rent asked for the rental unit at the time of enumeration. *Source: U.S. Census Bureau, American Community Survey, 2013-2017 Five-Year Estimates*

Rental Vacancy Rate: Proportion of the rental inventory that is vacant "for rent." It is computed by dividing the number of vacant units "for rent" by the sum of the renter-occupied units, vacant units that are "for rent," and vacant units that have been rented but not yet occupied, and then multiplying by 100. This measure is rounded to the nearest tenth. *Source: U.S. Census Bureau, American Community Survey, 2013-2017 Five-Year Estimates*

VITAL STATISTICS

Birth Rate: Estimated number of births per 10,000 population in 2017. *Source: U.S. Census Bureau, Annual Components of Population Change, July 1, 2010 - July 1, 2017*

Death Rate: Estimated number of deaths per 10,000 population in 2017. *Source: U.S. Census Bureau, Annual Components of Population Change, July 1, 2010 - July 1, 2017*

Age-adjusted Cancer Mortality Rate: Number of age-adjusted deaths from cancer per 100,000 population in 2017. Cancer is defined as International Classification of Disease (ICD) codes C00–D48.9 Neoplasms. *Source: Centers for Disease Control, CDC Wonder, 2017*

Age-adjusted death rates are weighted averages of the age-specific death rates, where the weights represent a fixed population by age. They are used because the rates of almost all causes of death vary by age. Age adjustment is a technique for "removing" the effects of age from crude rates, so as to allow meaningful comparisons across populations with different underlying age structures. For example, comparing the crude rate of heart disease in Virginia to that of California is misleading, because the relatively older population in Virginia will lead to a higher crude death rate, even if the age-specific rates of heart disease in Virginia and California are the same. For such a comparison, age-adjusted rates would be preferable. Age-adjusted rates should be viewed as relative indexes rather than as direct or actual measures of mortality risk.

Death rates based on counts of twenty or less (≤ 20) are flagged as "Unreliable". Death rates based on fewer than three years of data for counties with populations of less than 100,000 in the 2000 Census counts, are also flagged as "Unreliable" if the number of deaths is five or less (≤ 5).

HEALTH INSURANCE

Health insurance coverage in the ACS and other Census Bureau surveys define coverage to include plans and programs that provide comprehensive health coverage. Plans that provide insurance for specific conditions or situations such as cancer and long-term care policies are not considered coverage. Likewise, other types of insurance like dental, vision, life, and disability insurance are not considered health insurance coverage.

For reporting purposes, the Census Bureau broadly classifies health insurance coverage as private health insurance or public coverage. Private health insurance is a plan provided through an employer or union, a plan purchased by an individual from a private company, or TRICARE or other military health care. Public health coverage includes the federal programs Medicare, Medicaid, and VA Health Care (provided through the Department of Veterans Affairs); the Children's Health Insurance Program (CHIP); and individual state health plans. The types of health insurance are not mutually exclusive; people may be covered by more than one at the same time. People who had no reported health coverage, or those whose only health coverage was Indian Health Service, were considered uninsured. *Source: U.S. Census Bureau, American Community Survey, 2013-2017 Five-Year Estimates*

- **Have Insurance:** Percent of the civilian noninstitutionalized population with any type of comprehensive health insurance.

- **Have Private Insurance.** Percent of the civilian noninstitutionalized population with private health insurance. A person may report that they have both public and private health insurance, thus, the sum of the percentages may be greater than 100%.

- **Have Public Insurance.** Percent of the civilian noninstitutionalized population with public health insurance. A person may report that they have both public and private health insurance, thus, the sum of the percentages may be greater than 100%.

- **Do Not Have Insurance.** Percent of the civilian noninstitutionalized population with no health insurance.

- **Children Under 19 With No Insurance.** Percent of the civilian noninstitutionalized population under age 19 with no health insurance.

HEALTH CARE

Number of physicians, hospital beds and hospital admission per 10,000 population. *Source: Area Health Resource File (AHRF) 2017-2018. U.S. Department of Health and Human Services, Health Resources and Services Administration, Bureau of Health Professions, Rockville, MD.*

- **Number of Physicians.** The number of active, non-federal physicians (MDs and DOs) per 10,000 population in 2016.

- **Number of Dentists.** The number of dentists per 10,000 population in 2017.

- **Number of Hospital Beds.** The number of hospital beds per 10,000 population in 2016.

- **Number of Hospital Admissions.** The number of hospital admissions per 10,000 population in 2016.

AIR QUALITY INDEX

The percentage of days in 2017 the AQI fell into the Good (0-50), Moderate (51-100), Unhealthy for Sensitive Groups (101-150), Unhealthy (151-200), Very Unhealthy (201-300), and Hazardous (300+) ranges. If a range does not appear, its value is zero. Data covers January 2017 through December 2017 and only includes counties for which air quality data was available for 100 days or more. *Source: AirData: Access to Air Pollution Data, U.S. Environmental Protection Agency, Office of Air and Radiation*

The AQI is an index for reporting daily air quality. It tells you how clean or polluted your air is, and what associated health concerns you should be aware of. The AQI focuses on health effects that can happen within a few hours or days after breathing polluted air. EPA uses the AQI for five major air pollutants regulated by the Clean Air Act: ground-level ozone, particulate matter, carbon monoxide, sulfur dioxide, and nitrogen dioxide. For each of these pollutants, EPA has established national air quality standards to protect against harmful health effects.

The AQI runs from 0 to 500. The higher the AQI value, the greater the level of air pollution and the greater the health danger. For example, an AQI value of 50 represents good air quality and little potential to affect public health, while an AQI value over 300 represents hazardous air quality. An AQI value of 100 generally corresponds to the national air quality standard for the pollutant, which is the level EPA has set to protect public health. So, AQI values below 100 are generally thought of as satisfactory. When AQI values are above 100, air quality is considered to be unhealthy—at first for certain sensitive groups of people, then for everyone as AQI values get higher. Each category corresponds to a different level of health concern. For example, when the AQI for a pollutant is between 51 and 100, the health concern is "Moderate." Here are the six levels of health concern and what they mean:

- "Good" The AQI value for your community is between 0 and 50. Air quality is considered satisfactory and air pollution poses little or no risk.

- "Moderate" The AQI for your community is between 51 and 100. Air quality is acceptable; however, for some pollutants there may be a moderate health concern for a very small number of individuals. For example, people who are unusually sensitive to ozone may experience respiratory symptoms.

- "Unhealthy for Sensitive Groups" Certain groups of people are particularly sensitive to the harmful effects of certain air pollutants. This means they are likely to be affected at lower levels than the general public. For example, children and adults who are active outdoors and people with respiratory disease are at greater risk from exposure to ozone, while people with heart disease are at greater risk from carbon monoxide. Some people may be sensitive to more than one pollutant. When AQI values are between 101 and 150, members of sensitive groups may experience health effects. The general public is not likely to be affected when the AQI is in this range.

- "Unhealthy" AQI values are between 151 and 200. Everyone may begin to experience health effects. Members of sensitive groups may experience more serious health effects.

- "Very Unhealthy" AQI values between 201 and 300 trigger a health alert, meaning everyone may experience more serious health effects.

- "Hazardous" AQI values over 300 trigger health warnings of emergency conditions. The entire population is more likely to be affected.

TRANSPORTATION

Commute to Work: Percentage of workers 16 years old and over that use the following means of transportation to commute to work: car; public transportation; walk; work from home. The means of transportation data for some areas may show workers using modes of public transportation that are not available in those areas (e.g. subway or elevated riders in a metropolitan area where there actually is no subway or elevated service). This result is largely due to people who worked during the reference week at a location that was different from their usual place of work (such as people away from home on business in an area where subway service was available) and people who used more than one means of transportation each day but whose principal means was unavailable where they lived (e.g. residents of non-metropolitan areas who drove to the fringe of a metropolitan area and took the commuter railroad most of the distance to work). *Source: U.S. Census Bureau, American Community Survey, 2013-2017 Five-Year Estimates*

Mean Travel Time to Work: Mean travel time to work for workers 16 years old and over. Travel time to work refers to the total number of minutes that it usually took the person to get from home to work each day during the reference week. The elapsed time includes time spent waiting for public transportation, picking up passengers in carpools, and time spent in other activities related to getting to work. *Source: U.S. Census Bureau, American Community Survey, 2013-2017 Five-Year Estimates*

PRESIDENTIAL ELECTION

2016 Presidential election results. *Source: Dave Leip's Atlas of U.S. Presidential Elections*

NATIONAL AND STATE PARKS

Lists National/State parks located in the area. *Source: U.S. Geological Survey, Geographic Names Information System*

ADDITIONAL INFORMATION CONTACTS

General telephone number and website address (if available) of local government.

Community Profiles

PHYSICAL AND GEOGRAPHICAL CHARACTERISTICS

Place Type: Lists the type of place (city, town, village, borough, Census-Designated Place (CDP), township, charter township, plantation, gore, district, grant, location, purchase, municipality, reservation, unorganized territory, or unincorporated postal area). *Source: U.S. Census Bureau, American Community Survey, 2013-2017 Five-Year Estimates and U.S. Postal Service, City State File*

ZCTA: *This only appears within unincorporated postal areas.* The statistics that follow cover the corresponding ZIP Code Tabulation Area (ZCTA). A ZCTA is a statistical entity developed by the Census Bureau to approximate the delivery area for a US Postal Service 5-digit or 3-digit ZIP Code in the US and Puerto Rico. A ZCTA is an aggregation of census blocks that have the same predominant ZIP Code associated with the mailing addresses in the Census Bureau's Master Address File. Thus, the Postal Service's delivery areas have been adjusted to encompass whole census blocks so that the Census Bureau can tabulate census data for the ZCTAs. ZCTAs do not include all ZIP Codes used for mail delivery and therefore do not precisely depict the area within which mail deliveries associated with that ZIP Code occur. Additionally, some areas that are known by a unique name, although they are part of a larger incorporated place, are also included as "postal areas."

Land and Water Area: Land and water area in square miles. *Source: U.S. Census Bureau, Census 2010*

Latitude and Longitude: Latitude and longitude in degrees. *Source: U.S. Census Bureau, Census 2010*

Elevation: Elevation in feet. *Source: U.S. Geological Survey, Geographic Names Information System (GNIS)*

DEMOGRAPHICS

Population: Current population. *Source: U.S. Census Bureau, American Community Survey, 2013-2017 Five-Year Estimates*

Population Growth: The increase or decrease in population since 2000. *Source: U.S. Census Bureau, Census 2000; U.S. Census Bureau, American Community Survey, 2013-2017 Five-Year Estimates*

Population Density: Total current population divided by the land area in square miles. *Source: U.S. Census Bureau, Census 2010; U.S. Census Bureau, American Community Survey, 2013-2017 Five-Year Estimates*

Race/Hispanic Origin: Figures include the U.S. Census Bureau categories of White alone; Black/African American alone; Asian alone; American Indian/Alaska Native alone; Native Hawaiian/Other Pacific Islander alone; two or more races; and Hispanic of any race. Alone refers to the fact that these figures are not in combination with any other race. *Source: U.S. Census Bureau, American Community Survey, 2013-2017 Five-Year Estimates*

The concept of race, as used by the Census Bureau, reflects self-identification by people according to the race or races with which they most closely identify. These categories are socio-political constructs and should not be interpreted as being scientific or anthropological in nature. Furthermore, the race categories include both racial and national-origin groups.

- **White.** A person having origins in any of the original peoples of Europe, the Middle East, or North Africa. It includes people who indicated their race(s) as "White" or reported entries such as Irish, German, Italian, Lebanese, Arab, Moroccan, or Caucasian.
- **Black/African American.** A person having origins in any of the Black racial groups of Africa. It includes people who indicated their race(s) as "Black, African Am., or

Negro" or reported entries such as African American, Kenyan, Nigerian, or Haitian.

- **Asian.** A person having origins in any of the original peoples of the Far East, Southeast Asia, or the Indian subcontinent, including, for example, Cambodia, China, India, Japan, Korea, Malaysia, Pakistan, the Philippine Islands, Thailand, and Vietnam. It includes people who indicated their race(s) as "Asian" or reported entries such as "Asian Indian," "Chinese," "Filipino," "Korean," "Japanese," "Vietnamese," and "Other Asian" or provided other detailed Asian responses.

- **American Indian/Alaska Native.** A person having origins in any of the original peoples of North and South America (including Central America) and who maintains tribal affiliation or community attachment. This category includes people who indicated their race(s) as "American Indian or Alaska Native" or reported their enrolled or principal tribe, such as Navajo, Blackfeet, Inupiat, Yup'ik, or Central American Indian groups or South American Indian groups.

- **Native Hawaiian/Other Pacific Islander.** A person having origins in any of the original peoples of Hawaii, Guam, Samoa, or other Pacific Islands. It includes people who indicated their race(s) as "Pacific Islander" or reported entries such as "Native Hawaiian," "Guamanian or Chamorro," "Samoan," and "Other Pacific Islander" or provided other detailed Pacific Islander responses.

- **Two or More Races.** People may choose to provide two or more races either by checking two or more race response check boxes, by providing multiple responses, or by some combination of check boxes and other responses. The race response categories shown on the questionnaire are collapsed into the five minimum race groups identified by OMB, and the Census Bureau's "Some Other Race" category.

- **Hispanic.** The data on the Hispanic or Latino population were derived from answers to a question that was asked of all people. The terms "Spanish," "Hispanic origin," and "Latino" are used interchangeably. Some respondents identify with all three terms while others may identify with only one of these three specific terms. Hispanics or Latinos who identify with the terms "Spanish," "Hispanic," or "Latino" are those who classify themselves in one of the specific Spanish, Hispanic, or Latino categories listed on the questionnaire ("Mexican," "Puerto Rican," or "Cuban") as well as those who indicate that they are "other Spanish/Hispanic/Latino." People who do not identify with one of the specific origins listed on the questionnaire but indicate that they are "other Spanish/Hispanic/Latino" are those whose origins are from Spain, the Spanish-speaking countries of Central or South America, the Dominican Republic, or people identifying themselves generally as Spanish, Spanish-American, Hispanic, Hispano, Latino, and so on. All write-in responses to the "other Spanish/Hispanic/Latino" category were coded. Origin can be viewed as the heritage, nationality group, lineage, or country of birth of the person or the person's parents or ancestors before their arrival in the United States. People who identify their origin as Spanish, Hispanic, or Latino may be of any race.

Average Household Size: Number of persons in the average household. *Source: U.S. Census Bureau, American Community Survey, 2013-2017 Five-Year Estimates*

Median Age: Median age of the population. *Source: U.S. Census Bureau, American Community Survey, 2013-2017 Five-Year Estimates*

Age Under 18: Percent of the total population under 18 years old. *Source: U.S. Census Bureau, American Community Survey, 2013-2017 Five-Year Estimates*

Age 65 and Over: Percent of the total population age 65 and over. *Source: U.S. Census Bureau, American Community Survey, 2013-2017 Five-Year Estimates*

Males per 100 Females: Number of males per 100 females. *Source: U.S. Census Bureau, American Community Survey, 2013-2017 Five-Year Estimates*

Marital Status: Percentage of population never married, now married, separated, widowed, or divorced. *Source: U.S. Census Bureau, American Community Survey, 2013-2017 Five-Year Estimates*

The marital status classification refers to the status at the time of enumeration. Data on marital status are tabulated only for the population 15 years old and over. Each person was asked whether they were "Now married," "Widowed," "Separated," "Divorced," or "Never married." Couples who live together (for example, people in common-law marriages) were able to report the marital status they considered to be the most appropriate.

- **Never married.** Never married includes all people who have never been married, including people whose only marriage(s) was annulled.

- **Now married.** All people whose current marriage has not ended by widowhood or divorce. This category includes people defined as "separated."

- **Separated.** Includes people legally separated or otherwise absent from their spouse because of marital discord. Those without a final divorce decree are classified as "separated." This category also includes people who have been deserted or who have parted because they no longer want to live together, but who have not obtained a divorce.

- **Widowed**. This category includes widows and widowers who have not remarried.
- **Divorced.** This category includes people who are legally divorced and who have not remarried.

Foreign Born: Percentage of population who were not U.S. citizens at birth. Foreign-born people are those who indicated they were either a U.S. citizen by naturalization or they were not a citizen of the United States. *Source: U.S. Census Bureau, American Community Survey, 2013-2017 Five-Year Estimates*

Speak English Only: Percent of population that reported speaking only English at home. *Source: U.S. Census Bureau, American Community Survey, 2013-2017 Five-Year Estimates*

With Disability: Percent of the civilian noninstitutionalized population that reported having a disability. Disability status is determined from from six types of difficulty: vision, hearing, cognitive, ambulatory, self-care, and independent living. For children under 5 years old, hearing and vision difficulty are used to determine disability status. For children between the ages of 5 and 14, disability status is determined from hearing, vision, cognitive, ambulatory, and self-care difficulties. For people aged 15 years and older, they are considered to have a disability if they have difficulty with any one of the six difficulty types. *Source: U.S. Census Bureau, American Community Survey, 2013-2017 Five-Year Estimates*

Veterans: Percent of the civilian population 18 years and over who have served (even for a short time), but are not currently serving, on active duty in the U.S. Army, Navy, Air Force, Marine Corps, or the Coast Guard, or who served in the U.S. Merchant Marine during World War II. People who served in the National Guard or Reserves are classified as veterans only if they were ever called or ordered to active duty, not counting the 4-6 months for initial training or yearly summer camps. All other civilians are classified as nonveterans. Note: While it is possible for 17 year olds to be veterans of the Armed Forces, ACS data products are restricted to the population 18 years and older. *Source: U.S. Census Bureau, American Community Survey, 2013-2017 Five-Year Estimates*

Ancestry: Largest ancestry groups reported (up to five). The data includes persons who report multiple ancestries. For example, if a person reported being Irish and Italian, they would be included in both categories. Thus, the sum of the percentages may be greater than 100%. *Source: U.S. Census Bureau, American Community Survey, 2013-2017 Five-Year Estimates*

The data represent self-classification by people according to the ancestry group or groups with which they most closely identify. Ancestry refers to a person's ethnic origin or descent, "roots," heritage, or the place of birth of the person, the person's parents, or their ancestors before their arrival in the United States. Some ethnic identities, such as Egyptian or Polish, can be traced to geographic areas outside the United States, while other ethnicities such as Pennsylvania German or Cajun evolved in the United States.

The ancestry question was intended to provide data for groups that were not included in the Hispanic origin and race questions. Therefore, although data on all groups are collected, the ancestry data shown in these tabulations are for non-Hispanic and non-race groups. *See* Race/Hispanic Origin for information on Hispanic and race groups.

EMPLOYMENT

Employment by Occupation: Percentage of the employed civilian population 16 years and over in management, professional, service, sales, farming, construction, and production occupations. *Source: U.S. Census Bureau, American Community Survey, 2013-2017 Five-Year Estimates*

- Management, business, and financial occupations include:
  - Management
  - Business and financial operations
- Computer, engineering, and science occupations include:
  - Computer and mathematical
  - Architecture and engineering
  - Life, physical, and social science
- Education, legal, community service, arts, and media occupations include:
  - Community and social service
  - Legal
  - Education, training, and library
  - Arts, design, entertainment, sports, and media
- Healthcare practitioners and technical occupations include:
  - Health diagnosing and treating practitioners and other technical
  - Health technologists and technicians
- Service occupations include:
  - Healthcare support
  - Protective service occupations:
    - Fire fighting and prevention, and other protective service workers including supervisors
    - Law enforcement workers including supervisors
  - Food preparation and serving related occupations
  - Building and grounds cleaning and maintenance
  - Personal care and service
- Sales and office occupations include:
  - Sales and related
  - Office and administrative support
- Natural resources, construction, and maintenance occupations include:
  - Farming, fishing, and forestry

Construction and extraction
Installation, maintenance, and repair

- Production, transportation, and material moving occupations include:
  Production
  Transportation
  Material moving

INCOME

Per Capita Income: Per capita income is the mean income computed for every man, woman, and child in a particular group. It is derived by dividing the total income of a particular group by the total population in that group. Per capita income is rounded to the nearest whole dollar. *Source: U.S. Census Bureau, American Community Survey, 2013-2017 Five-Year Estimates*

Median Household Income: Includes the income of the householder and all other individuals 15 years old and over in the household, whether they are related to the householder or not. The median divides the income distribution into two equal parts: one-half of the cases falling below the median income and one-half above the median. For households, the median income is based on the distribution of the total number of households including those with no income. Median income for households is computed on the basis of a standard distribution and is rounded to the nearest whole dollar. *Source: U.S. Census Bureau, American Community Survey, 2013-2017 Five-Year Estimates*

Average Household Income: Average household income is obtained by dividing total household income by the total number of households. *Source: U.S. Census Bureau, American Community Survey, 2013-2017 Five-Year Estimates*

Percent of Households with Income of $100,000 or more: Percent of households with income of $100,000 or more. *Source: U.S. Census Bureau, American Community Survey, 2013-2017 Five-Year Estimates*

Poverty Rate: Percentage of population with income below the poverty level. Based on individuals for whom poverty status is determined. Poverty status was determined for all people except institutionalized people, people in military group quarters, people in college dormitories, and unrelated individuals under 15 years old. *Source: U.S. Census Bureau, American Community Survey, 2013-2017 Five-Year Estimates*

EDUCATIONAL ATTAINMENT

Figures show the percent of population age 25 and over with the following levels of educational attainment. *Source: U.S. Census Bureau, American Community Survey, 2013-2017 Five-Year Estimates*

- **High school diploma or higher.** Includes people whose highest degree is a high school diploma or its equivalent (GED), people who attended college but did not receive a degree, and people who received a college, university, or professional degree.

- **Bachelor's degree or higher.** Includes people who received a bachelor's, master's, doctorate, or professional degree.

- **Graduate/professional degree or higher.** Includes people who received a master's, doctorate, or professional degree.

SCHOOL DISTRICTS

Lists the name of each school district, the grade range (PK=pre-kindergarten; KG=kindergarten), the student enrollment, and the district headquarters' phone number. In each community profile, only school districts that have schools that are physically located within the community are shown. In addition, statistics for each school district cover the entire district, regardless of the physical location of the schools within the district. *Source: U.S. Department of Education, National Center for Educational Statistics, Directory of Public Elementary and Secondary Education Agencies, 2016-17*

COLLEGES

Four-year Colleges: Lists the name of each four-year college, the type of institution (private or public; for-profit or non-profit; religious affiliation; historically black), the total estimated student enrollment in Fall 2017, the general telephone number, and the annual tuition and fees for full-time, first-time undergraduate students (in-state and out-of-state). *Source: U.S. Department of Education, National Center for Educational Statistics, IPEDS College Data, 2017-18*

Two-year Colleges: Lists the name of each two-year college, the type of institution (private or public; for-profit or non-profit; religious affiliation; historically black), the total estimated student enrollment in Fall 2017, the general telephone number, and the annual tuition and fees for full-time, first-time undergraduate students (in-state and out-of-state). *Source: U.S. Department of Education, National Center for Educational Statistics, IPEDS College Data, 2017-18*

Vocational/Technical Schools: Lists the name of each vocational/technical school, the type of institution (private or public; for-profit or non-profit; religious affiliation; historically black), the total estimated student enrollment in Fall 2017, the general telephone number, and the annual tuition and fees for full-time students. *Source: U.S. Department of Education, National Center for Educational Statistics, IPEDS College Data, 2017-18*

HOUSING

Homeownership Rate: Percentage of housing units that are owner-occupied. *Source: U.S. Census Bureau, American Community Survey, 2013-2017 Five-Year Estimates*

Median Home Value: Median value in dollars of all owner-occupied housing units as reported by the owner. *Source: U.S. Census Bureau, American Community Survey, 2013-2017 Five-Year Estimates*

Median Year Structure Built: Year structure built refers to when the building was first constructed, not when it was remodeled, added to, or converted. For mobile homes, houseboats, RVs, etc, the manufacturer's model year was assumed to be the year built. The data relate to the number of units built during the specified periods that were still in existence at the time of enumeration. *Source: U.S. Census Bureau, American Community Survey, 2013-2017 Five-Year Estimates*

Homeowner Vacancy Rate: Proportion of the homeowner inventory that is vacant "for sale." It is computed by dividing the number of vacant units "for sale only" by the sum of the owner-occupied units, vacant units that are "for sale only," and vacant units that have been sold but not yet occupied, and then multiplying by 100. This measure is rounded to the nearest tenth. *Source: U.S. Census Bureau, American Community Survey, 2013-2017 Five-Year Estimates*

Median Selected Monthly Owner Costs: Selected monthly owner costs are the sum of payments for mortgages, deeds of trust, contracts to purchase, or similar debts on the property (including payments for the first mortgage, second mortgages, home equity loans, and other junior mortgages); real estate taxes; fire, hazard, and flood insurance on the property; utilities (electricity, gas, and water and sewer); and fuels (oil, coal, kerosene, wood, etc.). It also includes, where appropriate, the monthly condominium fee for condominiums and mobile home costs (personal property taxes, site rent, registration fees, and license fees). Selected monthly owner costs were tabulated for all owner-occupied units, and are shown separately for units "with a mortgage" and for units "not mortgaged." *Source: U.S. Census Bureau, American Community Survey, 2013-2017 Five-Year Estimates*

Median Gross Rent: Median monthly gross rent in dollars on specified renter-occupied and specified vacant-for-rent units. Specified renter-occupied and specified vacant-for-rent units exclude 1-family houses on 10 acres or more. Gross rent is the contract rent plus the estimated average monthly cost of utilities (electricity, gas, and water and sewer) and fuels (oil, coal, kerosene, wood, etc.) if these are paid by the renter (or paid for the renter by someone else). Gross rent is intended to eliminate differentials that result from varying practices with respect to the inclusion of utilities and fuels as part of the rental payment. Contract rent is the monthly rent agreed to or contracted for, regardless of any furnishings, utilities, fees, meals, or services that may be included. For vacant units, it is the monthly rent asked for the rental unit at the time of enumeration. *Source: U.S. Census Bureau, American Community Survey, 2013-2017 Five-Year Estimates*

Rental Vacancy Rate: Proportion of the rental inventory that is vacant "for rent." It is computed by dividing the number of vacant units "for rent" by the sum of the renter-occupied units, vacant units that are "for rent," and vacant units that have been rented but not yet occupied, and then multiplying by 100. This measure is rounded to the nearest tenth. *Source: U.S. Census Bureau, American Community Survey, 2013-2017 Five-Year Estimates*

HEALTH INSURANCE

Health insurance coverage in the ACS and other Census Bureau surveys define coverage to include plans and programs that provide comprehensive health coverage. Plans that provide insurance for specific conditions or situations such as cancer and long-term care policies are not considered coverage. Likewise, other types of insurance like dental, vision, life, and disability insurance are not considered health insurance coverage.

For reporting purposes, the Census Bureau broadly classifies health insurance coverage as private health insurance or public coverage. Private health insurance is a plan provided through an employer or union, a plan purchased by an individual from a private company, or TRICARE or other military health care. Public health coverage includes the federal programs Medicare, Medicaid, and VA Health Care (provided through the Department of Veterans Affairs); the Children's Health Insurance Program (CHIP); and individual state health plans. The types of health insurance are not mutually exclusive; people may be covered by more than one at the same time. People who had no reported health coverage, or those whose only health coverage was Indian Health Service, were considered uninsured. *Source: U.S. Census Bureau, American Community Survey, 2013-2017 Five-Year Estimates*

- **Have Insurance:** Percent of the civilian noninstitutionalized population with any type of comprehensive health insurance.
- **Have Private Insurance.** Percent of the civilian noninstitutionalized population with private health insurance. A person may report that they have both public and private health insurance, thus, the sum of the percentages may be greater than 100%.
- **Have Public Insurance.** Percent of the civilian noninstitutionalized population with public health insurance. A person may report that they have both public and private health insurance, thus, the sum of the percentages may be greater than 100%.
- **Do Not Have Insurance.** Percent of the civilian noninstitutionalized population with no health insurance.

- **Children Under 19 With No Insurance.** Percent of the civilian noninstitutionalized population under age 19 with no health insurance.

SAFETY

Violent Crime Rate: Number of violent crimes reported per 10,000 population. Violent crimes include murder, forcible rape, robbery, and aggravated assault. Statistics include the revised definition of forcible rate if available. Otherwise statistics using the legacy definition are used. *Source: Federal Bureau of Investigation, Uniform Crime Reports 2017*

Property Crime Rate: Number of property crimes reported per 10,000 population. Property crimes include burglary, larceny-theft, and motor vehicle theft. *Source: Federal Bureau of Investigation, Uniform Crime Reports 2017*

TRANSPORTATION

Commute to Work: Percentage of workers 16 years old and over that use the following means of transportation to commute to work: car; public transportation; walk; work from home. The means of transportation data for some areas may show workers using modes of public transportation that are not available in those areas (e.g. subway or elevated riders in a metropolitan area where there actually is no subway or elevated service). This result is largely due to people who worked during the reference week at a location that was different from their usual place of work (such as people away from home on business in an area where subway service was available) and people who used more than one means of transportation each day but whose principal means was unavailable where they lived (e.g. residents of non-metropolitan areas who drove to the fringe of a metropolitan area and took the commuter railroad most of the distance to work). *Source: U.S. Census Bureau, American Community Survey, 2013-2017 Five-Year Estimates*

Mean Travel Time to Work: Mean travel time to work for workers 16 years old and over. Travel time to work refers to the total number of minutes that it usually took the person to get from home to work each day during the reference week. The elapsed time includes time spent waiting for public transportation, picking up passengers in carpools, and time spent in other activities related to getting to work. *Source: U.S. Census Bureau, American Community Survey, 2013-2017 Five-Year Estimates*

Amtrak: Indicates if Amtrak rail or bus service is available. Please note that the cities being served continually change. *Source: National Railroad Passenger Corporation, Amtrak National Timetable, 2019*

AIRPORTS

Lists the local airport(s) along with type of service and hub size. *Source: U.S. Department of Transportation, Bureau of Transportation Statistics*

ADDITIONAL INFORMATION CONTACTS

General telephone number and website address (if available) of local government.

INDIANA - Core Based Statistical Areas (CBSAs) and Counties

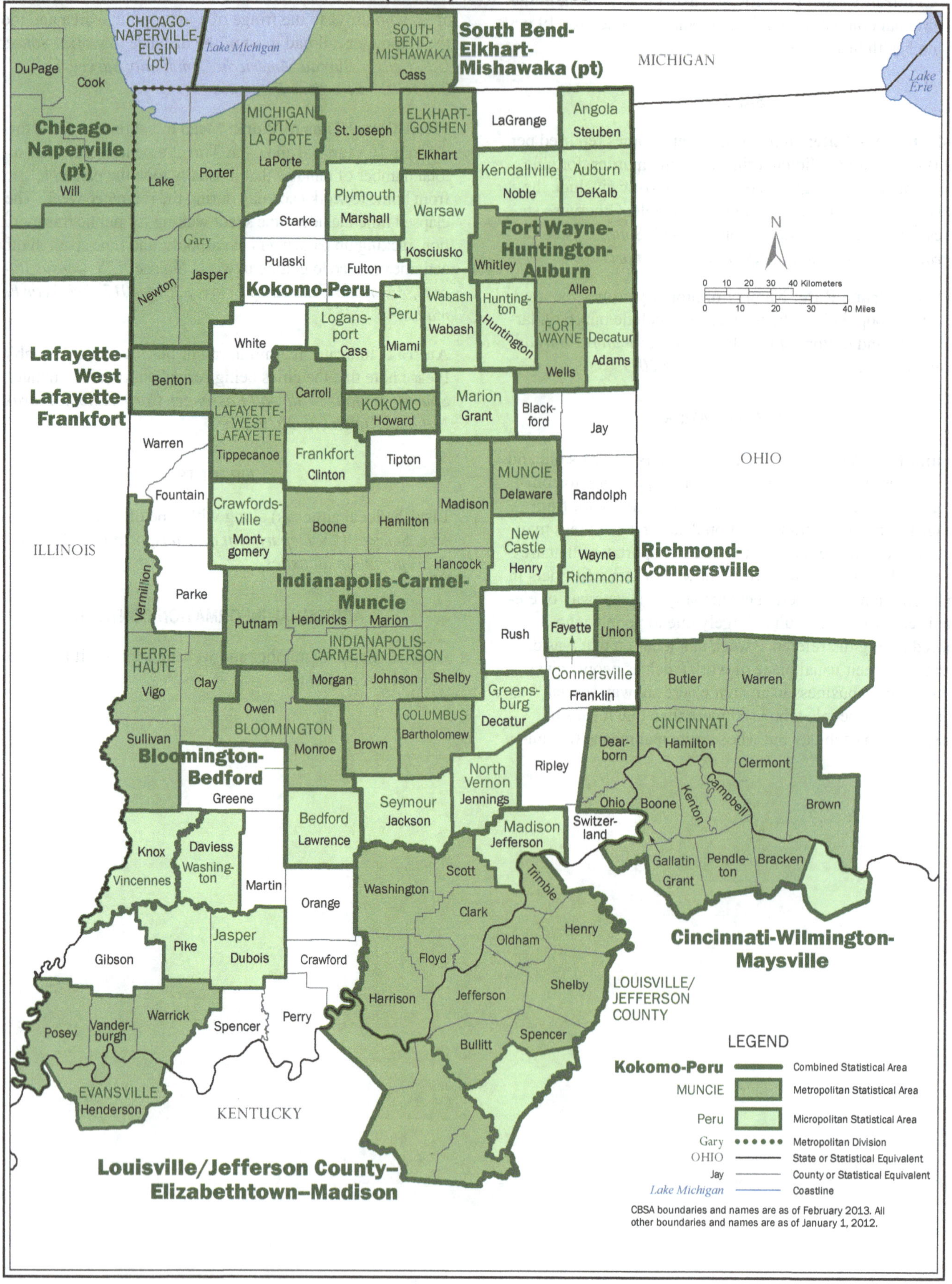

Adams County

Located in eastern Indiana; bounded on the east by Ohio. Covers a land area of 339.028 square miles, a water area of 0.938 square miles, and is located in the Eastern Time Zone at 40.75° N. Lat., 84.94° W. Long. The county was founded in 1835. County seat is Decatur.

Adams County is part of the Decatur, IN Micropolitan Statistical Area. The entire metro area includes: Adams County, IN

Weather Station: Berne — Elevation: 859 feet

	Jan	Feb	Mar	Apr	May	Jun	Jul	Aug	Sep	Oct	Nov	Dec
High	34	37	48	61	72	81	85	83	77	64	50	37
Low	19	21	30	40	51	61	65	63	55	44	34	24
Precip	2.4	2.3	2.8	3.8	3.9	4.3	4.4	3.6	2.8	2.9	3.1	2.8
Snow	8.2	7.3	4.1	0.8	0.0	0.0	0.0	0.0	0.0	0.3	1.6	5.9

High and Low temperatures in degrees Fahrenheit; Precipitation and Snow in inches

Population: 35,018; Growth (since 2000): 4.1%; Density: 103.3 persons per square mile; Race: 96.9% White, 0.9% Black/African American, 0.4% Asian, 0.0% American Indian/Alaska Native, 0.0% Native Hawaiian/Other Pacific Islander, 0.4% two or more races, 4.4% Hispanic of any race; Average household size: 2.77; Median age: 33.3; Age under 18: 31.2%; Age 65 and over: 14.8%; Males per 100 females: 97.8; Marriage status: 25.6% never married, 56.9% now married, 1.2% separated, 7.3% widowed, 10.2% divorced; Foreign born: 0.9%; Speak English only: 85.9%; With disability: 12.8%; Veterans: 6.8%; Ancestry: 29.2% German, 13.0% American, 8.1% Swiss, 6.0% Irish, 5.5% English
Religion: Six largest groups: 24.4% European Free-Church, 11.7% Lutheran, 10.5% Catholicism, 7.8% Non-denominational Protestant, 7.0% Methodist/Pietist, 5.9% Holiness
Economy: Unemployment rate: 2.8%; Leading industries: 18.3 % retail trade; 15.6 % other services (except public administration); 10.0 % construction; Farms: 1,476 totaling 210,227 acres; Company size: 0 employ 1,000 or more persons, 2 employ 500 to 999 persons, 19 employ 100 to 499 persons, 702 employ less than 100 persons; Business ownership: 859 women-owned, n/a Black-owned, 80 Hispanic-owned, n/a Asian-owned, n/a American Indian/Alaska Native-owned
Employment: 9.0% management, business, and financial, 2.6% computer, engineering, and science, 7.5% education, legal, community service, arts, and media, 5.0% healthcare practitioners, 15.9% service, 19.6% sales and office, 13.9% natural resources, construction, and maintenance, 26.3% production, transportation, and material moving
Income: Per capita: $21,534; Median household: $48,290; Average household: $60,175; Households with income of $100,000 or more: 13.5%; Poverty rate: 18.9%
Educational Attainment: High school diploma or higher: 83.6%; Bachelor's degree or higher: 14.9%; Graduate/professional degree or higher: 4.8%
Housing: Homeownership rate: 76.2%; Median home value: $118,900; Median year structure built: 1964; Homeowner vacancy rate: 0.6%; Median selected monthly owner costs: $940 with a mortgage, $329 without a mortgage; Median gross rent: $588 per month; Rental vacancy rate: 9.5%
Vital Statistics: Birth rate: 187.7 per 10,000 population; Death rate: 69.9 per 10,000 population; Age-adjusted cancer mortality rate: 159.4 deaths per 100,000 population
Health Insurance: 79.0% have insurance; 63.6% have private insurance; 27.8% have public insurance; 21.0% do not have insurance; 31.4% of children under 18 do not have insurance
Health Care: Physicians: 4.8 per 10,000 population; Dentists: 3.9 per 10,000 population; Hospital beds: 67.8 per 10,000 population; Hospital admissions: 518.3 per 10,000 population
Transportation: Commute: 91.0% car, 0.0% public transportation, 2.6% walk, 4.5% work from home; Mean travel time to work: 22.8 minutes
2016 Presidential Election: 73.1% Trump, 21.3% Clinton, 4.5% Johnson, 0.2% Stein
National and State Parks: Limberlost State Memorial
Additional Information Contacts
Adams Government .... (219) 724-5300
http://www.co.adams.in.us

Adams County Communities

BERNE (city). Covers a land area of 2.078 square miles and a water area of <.001 square miles. Located at 40.66° N. Lat; 84.96° W. Long. Elevation is 846 feet.
History: Mennonite immigrants from Berne, Switzerland, settled here in 1852 and named Berne for their former home. The Mennonite Book Concern was established here in 1882.
Population: 4,002; Growth (since 2000): -3.6%; Density: 1,926.2 persons per square mile; Race: 94.9% White, 2.8% Black/African American, 1.3% Asian, 0.0% American Indian/Alaska Native, 0.0% Native Hawaiian/Other Pacific Islander, 0.0% Two or more races, 1.7% Hispanic of any race; Average household size: 2.30; Median age: 43.9; Age under 18: 20.3%; Age 65 and over: 24.6%; Males per 100 females: 85.6; Marriage status: 25.7% never married, 55.7% now married, 1.2% separated, 10.6% widowed, 8.0% divorced; Foreign born: 1.6%; Speak English only: 95.6%; With disability: 16.8%; Veterans: 6.0%; Ancestry: 26.7% German, 17.3% Swiss, 8.8% Irish, 6.3% English, 4.5% American
Employment: 10.0% management, business, and financial, 2.1% computer, engineering, and science, 13.5% education, legal, community service, arts, and media, 4.4% healthcare practitioners, 16.4% service, 22.0% sales and office, 7.5% natural resources, construction, and maintenance, 24.0% production, transportation, and material moving
Income: Per capita: $25,310; Median household: $46,401; Average household: $59,574; Households with income of $100,000 or more: 15.0%; Poverty rate: 14.3%
Educational Attainment: High school diploma or higher: 92.0%; Bachelor's degree or higher: 24.2%; Graduate/professional degree or higher: 7.8%

School District(s)

South Adams Schools (PK-12)
Enrollment: 1,307 .... (260) 589-3133
Housing: Homeownership rate: 67.7%; Median home value: $93,200; Median year structure built: 1968; Homeowner vacancy rate: 1.8%; Median selected monthly owner costs: $949 with a mortgage, $330 without a mortgage; Median gross rent: $480 per month; Rental vacancy rate: 19.3%
Health Insurance: 94.5% have insurance; 71.9% have private insurance; 38.4% have public insurance; 5.5% do not have insurance; 3.6% of children under 18 do not have insurance
Safety: Violent crime rate: n/a per 10,000 population; Property crime rate: 38.9 per 10,000 population
Newspapers: Berne Tri-Weekly News (weekly circulation 2,500)
Transportation: Commute: 92.7% car, 0.0% public transportation, 1.5% walk, 4.3% work from home; Mean travel time to work: 17.5 minutes
Additional Information Contacts
City of Berne .... (260) 589-8526
http://www.cityofberne.com

DECATUR (city). County seat. Covers a land area of 5.777 square miles and a water area of 0.006 square miles. Located at 40.83° N. Lat; 84.93° W. Long. Elevation is 801 feet.
History: Decatur was named for Stephen Decatur, American naval hero. Novelist Gene Stratton Porter (1868-1924) lived here for three years.
Population: 9,502; Growth (since 2000): -0.3%; Density: 1,644.7 persons per square mile; Race: 94.3% White, 2.2% Black/African American, 0.4% Asian, 0.2% American Indian/Alaska Native, 0.0% Native Hawaiian/Other Pacific Islander, 0.5% Two or more races, 7.6% Hispanic of any race; Average household size: 2.26; Median age: 38.7; Age under 18: 24.3%; Age 65 and over: 15.5%; Males per 100 females: 93.8; Marriage status: 26.9% never married, 45.2% now married, 1.0% separated, 9.5% widowed, 18.4% divorced; Foreign born: 0.7%; Speak English only: 94.9%; With disability: 18.4%; Veterans: 7.3%; Ancestry: 30.6% German, 12.4% American, 9.5% English, 7.5% Irish, 2.8% Swiss
Employment: 7.2% management, business, and financial, 2.1% computer, engineering, and science, 7.1% education, legal, community service, arts, and media, 5.1% healthcare practitioners, 17.9% service, 22.7% sales and office, 7.3% natural resources, construction, and maintenance, 30.7% production, transportation, and material moving
Income: Per capita: $22,146; Median household: $41,004; Average household: $49,965; Households with income of $100,000 or more: 8.4%; Poverty rate: 20.2%
Educational Attainment: High school diploma or higher: 87.0%; Bachelor's degree or higher: 11.2%; Graduate/professional degree or higher: 3.0%

School District(s)

North Adams Community Schools (PK-12)
Enrollment: 1,959 . . . . (260) 724-7146

Housing: Homeownership rate: 64.4%; Median home value: $94,000; Median year structure built: 1959; Homeowner vacancy rate: 0.0%; Median selected monthly owner costs: $859 with a mortgage, $288 without a mortgage; Median gross rent: $565 per month; Rental vacancy rate: 6.9%
Health Insurance: 95.4% have insurance; 72.0% have private insurance; 36.3% have public insurance; 4.6% do not have insurance; 6.4% of children under 18 do not have insurance
Hospitals: Adams Memorial Hospital (87 beds)
Safety: Violent crime rate: 10.5 per 10,000 population; Property crime rate: 143.6 per 10,000 population
Newspapers: Decatur Daily Democrat (daily circulation 5,100)
Transportation: Commute: 95.8% car, 0.0% public transportation, 1.9% walk, 1.4% work from home; Mean travel time to work: 20.2 minutes
Additional Information Contacts
City of Decatur. . . . . (260) 724-7171
http://www.decaturin.org

GENEVA (town). Covers a land area of 1.087 square miles and a water area of 0.140 square miles. Located at 40.60° N. Lat; 84.96° W. Long. Elevation is 846 feet.
History: Geneva was the home of novelist Gene Stratton Porter from 1893 to 1913. Her books were set in the Limberlost Swamps here.
Population: 1,366; Growth (since 2000): -0.1%; Density: 1,257.2 persons per square mile; Race: 93.7% White, 0.0% Black/African American, 1.2% Asian, 0.0% American Indian/Alaska Native, 0.0% Native Hawaiian/Other Pacific Islander, 3.5% Two or more races, 11.8% Hispanic of any race; Average household size: 2.30; Median age: 44.1; Age under 18: 20.5%; Age 65 and over: 16.7%; Males per 100 females: 93.9; Marriage status: 28.0% never married, 51.3% now married, 1.5% separated, 7.6% widowed, 13.0% divorced; Foreign born: 6.1%; Speak English only: 89.6%; With disability: 19.8%; Veterans: 7.7%; Ancestry: 19.6% German, 13.1% Irish, 9.6% American, 5.6% Swiss, 2.6% English
Employment: 8.2% management, business, and financial, 2.2% computer, engineering, and science, 4.8% education, legal, community service, arts, and media, 6.8% healthcare practitioners, 18.2% service, 18.1% sales and office, 4.1% natural resources, construction, and maintenance, 37.6% production, transportation, and material moving
Income: Per capita: $22,079; Median household: $35,852; Average household: $52,101; Households with income of $100,000 or more: 7.4%; Poverty rate: 18.1%
Educational Attainment: High school diploma or higher: 83.3%; Bachelor's degree or higher: 12.3%; Graduate/professional degree or higher: 3.4%
Housing: Homeownership rate: 65.6%; Median home value: $83,700; Median year structure built: 1960; Homeowner vacancy rate: 0.0%; Median selected monthly owner costs: $784 with a mortgage, $328 without a mortgage; Median gross rent: $559 per month; Rental vacancy rate: 15.9%
Health Insurance: 90.0% have insurance; 60.2% have private insurance; 46.9% have public insurance; 10.0% do not have insurance; 5.4% of children under 18 do not have insurance
Transportation: Commute: 82.9% car, 0.0% public transportation, 10.2% walk, 2.2% work from home; Mean travel time to work: 15.5 minutes

MONROE (town). Covers a land area of 0.630 square miles and a water area of 0 square miles. Located at 40.75° N. Lat; 84.94° W. Long. Elevation is 823 feet.
Population: 874; Growth (since 2000): 19.1%; Density: 1,386.9 persons per square mile; Race: 98.9% White, 0.0% Black/African American, 0.5% Asian, 0.1% American Indian/Alaska Native, 0.0% Native Hawaiian/Other Pacific Islander, 0.5% Two or more races, 3.4% Hispanic of any race; Average household size: 2.78; Median age: 36.4; Age under 18: 31.1%; Age 65 and over: 19.5%; Males per 100 females: 89.6; Marriage status: 20.9% never married, 64.9% now married, 0.0% separated, 5.0% widowed, 9.1% divorced; Foreign born: 0.1%; Speak English only: 97.4%; With disability: 12.6%; Veterans: 5.8%; Ancestry: 34.6% German, 12.0% American, 7.1% Irish, 5.5% Swiss, 4.1% English
Employment: 7.5% management, business, and financial, 4.8% computer, engineering, and science, 12.8% education, legal, community service, arts, and media, 5.3% healthcare practitioners, 13.3% service, 21.5% sales and office, 10.6% natural resources, construction, and maintenance, 24.2% production, transportation, and material moving
Income: Per capita: $21,590; Median household: $53,611; Average household: $59,153; Households with income of $100,000 or more: 9.5%; Poverty rate: 4.8%
Educational Attainment: High school diploma or higher: 96.1%; Bachelor's degree or higher: 22.8%; Graduate/professional degree or higher: 10.9%

School District(s)

Adams Central Community Schools (PK-12)
Enrollment: 1,047 . . . . (260) 692-6193

Housing: Homeownership rate: 83.8%; Median home value: $111,500; Median year structure built: 1960; Homeowner vacancy rate: 1.8%; Median selected monthly owner costs: $963 with a mortgage, $339 without a mortgage; Median gross rent: $777 per month; Rental vacancy rate: 0.0%
Health Insurance: 96.6% have insurance; 86.3% have private insurance; 26.9% have public insurance; 3.4% do not have insurance; 0.0% of children under 18 do not have insurance
Transportation: Commute: 91.1% car, 0.0% public transportation, 7.6% walk, 1.2% work from home; Mean travel time to work: 21.7 minutes

Allen County

Located in northeastern Indiana; bounded on the east by Ohio; crossed by the Saint Joseph, Saint Marys, and Maumee Rivers. Covers a land area of 657.308 square miles, a water area of 2.714 square miles, and is located in the Eastern Time Zone at 41.09° N. Lat., 85.07° W. Long. The county was founded in 1823. County seat is Fort Wayne.

Allen County is part of the Fort Wayne, IN Metropolitan Statistical Area. The entire metro area includes: Allen County, IN; Wells County, IN; Whitley County, IN

Weather Station: Fort Wayne Baer Field — Elevation: 791 feet

	Jan	Feb	Mar	Apr	May	Jun	Jul	Aug	Sep	Oct	Nov	Dec
High	32	36	48	61	72	81	84	82	76	63	50	36
Low	18	21	29	39	49	59	63	61	53	42	33	23
Precip	2.3	2.1	2.8	3.5	4.1	4.2	4.3	3.7	2.8	2.9	3.0	2.8
Snow	10.2	7.8	4.1	1.1	tr	tr	tr	tr	tr	0.4	2.0	8.2

High and Low temperatures in degrees Fahrenheit; Precipitation and Snow in inches

Population: 367,747; Growth (since 2000): 10.8%; Density: 559.5 persons per square mile; Race: 79.5% White, 11.4% Black/African American, 3.5% Asian, 0.2% American Indian/Alaska Native, 0.0% Native Hawaiian/Other Pacific Islander, 3.5% two or more races, 7.2% Hispanic of any race; Average household size: 2.54; Median age: 35.7; Age under 18: 26.1%; Age 65 and over: 13.5%; Males per 100 females: 95.1; Marriage status: 31.8% never married, 50.4% now married, 1.2% separated, 5.7% widowed, 12.1% divorced; Foreign born: 6.4%; Speak English only: 89.6%; With disability: 12.4%; Veterans: 7.4%; Ancestry: 28.7% German, 9.5% Irish, 7.4% American, 6.9% English, 3.5% French
Religion: Six largest groups: 16.0% Catholicism, 9.2% Lutheran, 7.3% Non-denominational Protestant, 6.5% Baptist, 4.7% Methodist/Pietist, 3.6% Holiness
Economy: Unemployment rate: 3.2%; Leading industries: 13.8 % retail trade; 11.3 % health care and social assistance; 10.5 % other services (except public administration); Farms: 1,725 totaling 270,808 acres; Company size: 9 employ 1,000 or more persons, 14 employ 500 to 999 persons, 273 employ 100 to 499 persons, 8,834 employ less than 100 persons; Business ownership: 9,538 women-owned, 2,601 Black-owned, 871 Hispanic-owned, 1,027 Asian-owned, 204 American Indian/Alaska Native-owned
Employment: 12.6% management, business, and financial, 4.5% computer, engineering, and science, 10.2% education, legal, community service, arts, and media, 6.3% healthcare practitioners, 16.5% service, 24.3% sales and office, 7.6% natural resources, construction, and maintenance, 17.9% production, transportation, and material moving
Income: Per capita: $26,932; Median household: $51,091; Average household: $67,755; Households with income of $100,000 or more: 18.1%; Poverty rate: 14.7%
Educational Attainment: High school diploma or higher: 89.4%; Bachelor's degree or higher: 27.5%; Graduate/professional degree or higher: 9.5%
Housing: Homeownership rate: 68.3%; Median home value: $119,400; Median year structure built: 1973; Homeowner vacancy rate: 1.5%; Median selected monthly owner costs: $1,013 with a mortgage, $362 without a mortgage; Median gross rent: $719 per month; Rental vacancy rate: 7.5%

Vital Statistics: Birth rate: 140.4 per 10,000 population; Death rate: 82.3 per 10,000 population; Age-adjusted cancer mortality rate: 171.2 deaths per 100,000 population
Health Insurance: 89.2% have insurance; 67.6% have private insurance; 31.7% have public insurance; 10.8% do not have insurance; 7.5% of children under 18 do not have insurance
Health Care: Physicians: 28.1 per 10,000 population; Dentists: 6.4 per 10,000 population; Hospital beds: 47.5 per 10,000 population; Hospital admissions: 2,088.9 per 10,000 population
Air Quality Index (AQI): Percent of Days: 76.4% good, 23.3% moderate, 0.3% unhealthy for sensitive individuals, 0.0% unhealthy, 0.0% very unhealthy; Annual median: 42; Annual maximum: 105
Transportation: Commute: 93.0% car, 0.8% public transportation, 1.2% walk, 4.0% work from home; Mean travel time to work: 21.3 minutes
2016 Presidential Election: 56.5% Trump, 37.3% Clinton, 4.6% Johnson, 0.5% Stein
Additional Information Contacts
Allen Government . . . . (219) 449-3155
http://www.allencounty.us

Allen County Communities

ARCOLA (unincorporated postal area)
ZCTA: 46704
Covers a land area of 0.020 square miles and a water area of 0 square miles. Located at 41.10° N. Lat; 85.29° W. Long. Elevation is 843 feet.
Population: 32; Growth (since 2000): n/a; Density: 1,581.4 persons per square mile; Race: 100.0% White, 0.0% Black/African American, 0.0% Asian, 0.0% American Indian/Alaska Native, 0.0% Native Hawaiian/Other Pacific Islander, 0.0% Two or more races, 0.0% Hispanic of any race; Average household size: 2.67; Median age: 27.2; Age under 18: 28.1%; Age 65 and over: 0.0%; Males per 100 females: 114.3; Marriage status: 69.6% never married, 0.0% now married, 0.0% separated, 0.0% widowed, 30.4% divorced; Foreign born: 15.6%; Speak English only: 84.4%; With disability: 0.0%; Veterans: 0.0%; Ancestry: 15.6% Ukrainian
Employment: 0.0% management, business, and financial, 21.7% computer, engineering, and science, 0.0% education, legal, community service, arts, and media, 0.0% healthcare practitioners, 0.0% service, 47.8% sales and office, 30.4% natural resources, construction, and maintenance, 0.0% production, transportation, and material moving
Income: Per capita: $17,325; Median household: n/a; Average household: n/a; Households with income of $100,000 or more: n/a; Poverty rate: 15.6%
Educational Attainment: High school diploma or higher: 100.0%; Bachelor's degree or higher: 69.6%; Graduate/professional degree or higher: n/a

School District(s)
Northwest Allen County Schools (PK-12)
Enrollment: 7,459 . . . . (260) 637-3155
Housing: Homeownership rate: 100.0%; Median home value: n/a; Median year structure built: n/a; Homeowner vacancy rate: 0.0%; Median selected monthly owner costs: $0 with a mortgage, $0 without a mortgage; Median gross rent: n/a per month; Rental vacancy rate: 0.0%
Health Insurance: 78.1% have insurance; 78.1% have private insurance; 0.0% have public insurance; 21.9% do not have insurance; 0.0% of children under 18 do not have insurance
Transportation: Commute: 100.0% car, 0.0% public transportation, 0.0% walk, 0.0% work from home; Mean travel time to work: 0.0 minutes

FORT WAYNE (city). County seat. Covers a land area of 110.618 square miles and a water area of 0.214 square miles. Located at 41.09° N. Lat; 85.14° W. Long. Elevation is 810 feet.
History: The first fort at the site of Fort Wayne was Fort Miami, established in the 1680's by the French. Another stockade was built by Anthony Wayne in 1794. By 1819 a trading post and gristmill were started and more settlers appeared. When Allen County was organized in 1824, Fort Wayne was named as county seat. It was incorporated in 1829. The building of the Wabash & Erie Canal between 1832 and 1840 was a boost for Fort Wayne's economy. Fort Wayne may have claims to the first baseball game played under the lights at its League Park, where in 1883 an arc-lighting system illuminated the field for a game between a professional team from Quincy, Illinois, and a team of students from a Fort Wayne college.

Population: 262,450; Growth (since 2000): 27.6%; Density: 2,372.6 persons per square mile; Race: 74.2% White, 15.0% Black/African American, 4.3% Asian, 0.2% American Indian/Alaska Native, 0.1% Native Hawaiian/Other Pacific Islander, 4.2% Two or more races, 8.7% Hispanic of any race; Average household size: 2.46; Median age: 34.9; Age under 18: 25.7%; Age 65 and over: 13.4%; Males per 100 females: 93.8; Marriage status: 34.8% never married, 46.2% now married, 1.4% separated, 5.9% widowed, 13.2% divorced; Foreign born: 7.8%; Speak English only: 88.0%; With disability: 13.3%; Veterans: 7.3%; Ancestry: 26.1% German, 9.5% Irish, 6.5% English, 6.4% American, 3.2% French
Employment: 12.0% management, business, and financial, 4.6% computer, engineering, and science, 10.4% education, legal, community service, arts, and media, 5.6% healthcare practitioners, 17.6% service, 24.7% sales and office, 7.0% natural resources, construction, and maintenance, 18.2% production, transportation, and material moving
Income: Per capita: $25,066; Median household: $45,853; Average household: $60,942; Households with income of $100,000 or more: 14.6%; Poverty rate: 17.8%
Educational Attainment: High school diploma or higher: 88.6%; Bachelor's degree or higher: 26.8%; Graduate/professional degree or higher: 9.2%

School District(s)
East Allen County Schools (PK-12)
Enrollment: 9,116 . . . . (260) 446-0100
Fort Wayne Community Schools (PK-12)
Enrollment: 30,150 . . . . (260) 467-2025
M S D Southwest Allen County Schls (PK-12)
Enrollment: 7,193 . . . . (260) 431-2010
Northwest Allen County Schools (PK-12)
Enrollment: 7,459 . . . . (260) 637-3155
Smith Academy For Excellence (04-12)
Enrollment: 72. . . . . (260) 749-5832
Thurgood Marshall Leadership Acad (KG-08)
Enrollment: 158. . . . . (312) 226-3355
Timothy L Johnson Academy (KG-06)
Enrollment: 316. . . . . (260) 441-8727

Four-year College(s)
Brown Mackie College-Fort Wayne (Private, For-profit)
Enrollment: n/a . . . . (260) 484-4400
Concordia Theological Seminary (Private, Not-for-profit, Lutheran Church - Missouri Synod)
Enrollment: 290. . . . . (260) 452-2100
Indiana Institute of Technology (Private, Not-for-profit)
Enrollment: 7,871 . . . . (800) 937-2448
Tuition: In-state $26,370; Out-of-state $26,370
Indiana University-Purdue University-Fort Wayne (Public)
Enrollment: 10,414 . . . . (260) 481-6100
Tuition: In-state $8,330; Out-of-state $20,005
International Business College-Fort Wayne (Private, For-profit)
Enrollment: 244. . . . . (260) 459-4500
Tuition: In-state $13,960; Out-of-state $13,960
Trine University-Regional/Non-Traditional Campuses (Private, Not-for-profit)
Enrollment: 711. . . . . (260) 483-4949
Tuition: In-state $10,832; Out-of-state $10,832
University of Saint Francis-Fort Wayne (Private, Not-for-profit, Roman Catholic)
Enrollment: 2,322 . . . . (260) 399-7700
Tuition: In-state $29,430; Out-of-state $29,430

Two-year College(s)
Ross Medical Education Center-Fort Wayne (Private, For-profit)
Enrollment: 123. . . . . (260) 471-4840

Vocational/Technical School(s)
Ravenscroft Beauty College (Private, For-profit)
Enrollment: 159. . . . . (260) 486-8868
Tuition: $14,350
Rudae's School of Beauty Culture-Ft Wayne (Private, For-profit)
Enrollment: 135. . . . . (260) 483-2466
Tuition: $15,630
Housing: Homeownership rate: 62.0%; Median home value: $106,500; Median year structure built: 1970; Homeowner vacancy rate: 1.8%; Median selected monthly owner costs: $953 with a mortgage, $352 without a mortgage; Median gross rent: $708 per month; Rental vacancy rate: 7.6%

Health Insurance: 88.3% have insurance; 63.5% have private insurance; 34.7% have public insurance; 11.7% do not have insurance; 7.0% of children under 18 do not have insurance
Hospitals: Dupont Hospital (131 beds); Lutheran Hospital of Indiana (435 beds); Orthopaedic Hospital at Parkview North (37 beds); Parkview Regional Medical Center (656 beds); Saint Joseph Hospital (191 beds); The Orthopaedic Hospital of Lutheran Health Network (39 beds)
Safety: Violent crime rate: 35.8 per 10,000 population; Property crime rate: 318.0 per 10,000 population
Newspapers: Fort Wayne Ink (weekly circulation 25,000); Fort Wayne Reader (weekly circulation 25,000); Journal Gazette (daily circulation 49,000); News-Sentinel (daily circulation 27,300); Waynedale News (weekly circulation 10,000)
Transportation: Commute: 93.0% car, 1.1% public transportation, 1.2% walk, 3.7% work from home; Mean travel time to work: 20.9 minutes
Airports: Fort Wayne International (primary service/non-hub)
Additional Information Contacts
City of Fort Wayne. . . . . (260) 427-1221
http://www.cityoffortwayne.org

GRABILL (town). Covers a land area of 0.602 square miles and a water area of 0 square miles. Located at 41.21° N. Lat; 84.97° W. Long. Elevation is 817 feet.
Population: 1,471; Growth (since 2000): 32.2%; Density: 2,441.9 persons per square mile; Race: 95.4% White, 1.0% Black/African American, 0.3% Asian, 0.0% American Indian/Alaska Native, 0.0% Native Hawaiian/Other Pacific Islander, 2.9% Two or more races, 2.6% Hispanic of any race; Average household size: 2.54; Median age: 34.7; Age under 18: 26.4%; Age 65 and over: 11.1%; Males per 100 females: 92.9; Marriage status: 19.6% never married, 61.1% now married, 1.1% separated, 3.9% widowed, 15.3% divorced; Foreign born: 0.2%; Speak English only: 99.5%; With disability: 13.7%; Veterans: 10.1%; Ancestry: 40.0% German, 12.0% American, 8.8% Irish, 5.0% English, 3.2% Swiss
Employment: 10.0% management, business, and financial, 4.0% computer, engineering, and science, 6.5% education, legal, community service, arts, and media, 3.9% healthcare practitioners, 19.6% service, 25.4% sales and office, 7.9% natural resources, construction, and maintenance, 22.7% production, transportation, and material moving
Income: Per capita: $24,826; Median household: $50,167; Average household: $62,518; Households with income of $100,000 or more: 14.8%; Poverty rate: 17.5%
Educational Attainment: High school diploma or higher: 96.8%; Bachelor's degree or higher: 17.3%; Graduate/professional degree or higher: 3.8%
Housing: Homeownership rate: 82.7%; Median home value: $102,800; Median year structure built: 1981; Homeowner vacancy rate: 0.0%; Median selected monthly owner costs: $920 with a mortgage, $264 without a mortgage; Median gross rent: $644 per month; Rental vacancy rate: 9.1%
Health Insurance: 87.2% have insurance; 71.5% have private insurance; 26.1% have public insurance; 12.8% do not have insurance; 16.4% of children under 18 do not have insurance
Newspapers: East Allen Courier (weekly circulation 7,200)
Transportation: Commute: 90.7% car, 0.0% public transportation, 2.0% walk, 5.3% work from home; Mean travel time to work: 23.3 minutes
Additional Information Contacts
Town of Grabill . . . . (260) 627-5227
http://grabill.net

HARLAN (CDP). Covers a land area of 3.104 square miles and a water area of 0 square miles. Located at 41.20° N. Lat; 84.92° W. Long. Elevation is 784 feet.
Population: 1,649; Growth (since 2000): n/a; Density: 531.2 persons per square mile; Race: 99.5% White, 0.5% Black/African American, 0.0% Asian, 0.0% American Indian/Alaska Native, 0.0% Native Hawaiian/Other Pacific Islander, 0.0% Two or more races, 1.0% Hispanic of any race; Average household size: 2.99; Median age: 31.6; Age under 18: 35.6%; Age 65 and over: 13.7%; Males per 100 females: 100.0; Marriage status: 27.6% never married, 57.2% now married, 2.9% separated, 3.2% widowed, 12.0% divorced; Foreign born: 0.0%; Speak English only: 97.1%; With disability: 12.5%; Veterans: 10.1%; Ancestry: 33.5% German, 13.3% Pennsylvania German, 11.8% American, 9.3% English, 7.6% French
Employment: 15.9% management, business, and financial, 3.7% computer, engineering, and science, 6.2% education, legal, community service, arts, and media, 4.2% healthcare practitioners, 8.3% service, 27.5% sales and office, 12.1% natural resources, construction, and maintenance, 22.1% production, transportation, and material moving
Income: Per capita: $22,678; Median household: $59,255; Average household: $66,111; Households with income of $100,000 or more: 14.7%; Poverty rate: 6.0%
Educational Attainment: High school diploma or higher: 71.7%; Bachelor's degree or higher: 15.6%; Graduate/professional degree or higher: 1.9%
Housing: Homeownership rate: 79.3%; Median home value: $107,700; Median year structure built: 1982; Homeowner vacancy rate: 0.0%; Median selected monthly owner costs: $1,048 with a mortgage, $275 without a mortgage; Median gross rent: $637 per month; Rental vacancy rate: 0.0%
Health Insurance: 79.4% have insurance; 66.5% have private insurance; 23.6% have public insurance; 20.6% do not have insurance; 32.4% of children under 18 do not have insurance
Transportation: Commute: 81.3% car, 1.2% public transportation, 5.7% walk, 11.7% work from home; Mean travel time to work: 23.1 minutes

HOAGLAND (CDP). Covers a land area of 3.398 square miles and a water area of 0 square miles. Located at 40.95° N. Lat; 85.00° W. Long. Elevation is 823 feet.
Population: 888; Growth (since 2000): n/a; Density: 261.3 persons per square mile; Race: 98.4% White, 0.0% Black/African American, 0.0% Asian, 0.0% American Indian/Alaska Native, 0.0% Native Hawaiian/Other Pacific Islander, 1.6% Two or more races, 2.3% Hispanic of any race; Average household size: 2.47; Median age: 41.3; Age under 18: 21.7%; Age 65 and over: 18.9%; Males per 100 females: 96.9; Marriage status: 31.1% never married, 49.5% now married, 0.7% separated, 13.7% widowed, 5.6% divorced; Foreign born: 0.0%; Speak English only: 99.0%; With disability: 12.3%; Veterans: 3.6%; Ancestry: 37.7% German, 11.8% American, 8.8% English, 5.5% Dutch, 4.4% French
Employment: 5.0% management, business, and financial, 1.8% computer, engineering, and science, 2.0% education, legal, community service, arts, and media, 5.2% healthcare practitioners, 14.0% service, 33.3% sales and office, 13.8% natural resources, construction, and maintenance, 24.9% production, transportation, and material moving
Income: Per capita: $34,768; Median household: $47,039; Average household: $84,839; Households with income of $100,000 or more: 14.2%; Poverty rate: 7.2%
Educational Attainment: High school diploma or higher: 97.2%; Bachelor's degree or higher: 19.6%; Graduate/professional degree or higher: 2.5%
Housing: Homeownership rate: 89.4%; Median home value: $116,300; Median year structure built: 1957; Homeowner vacancy rate: 4.5%; Median selected monthly owner costs: $925 with a mortgage, $381 without a mortgage; Median gross rent: $860 per month; Rental vacancy rate: 0.0%
Health Insurance: 95.6% have insurance; 79.5% have private insurance; 30.0% have public insurance; 4.4% do not have insurance; 0.0% of children under 18 do not have insurance
Transportation: Commute: 100.0% car, 0.0% public transportation, 0.0% walk, 0.0% work from home; Mean travel time to work: 27.0 minutes

HUNTERTOWN (town). Covers a land area of 3.802 square miles and a water area of 0.010 square miles. Located at 41.21° N. Lat; 85.17° W. Long. Elevation is 833 feet.
History: Settled 1830s.
Population: 6,857; Growth (since 2000): 287.2%; Density: 1,803.4 persons per square mile; Race: 88.5% White, 3.5% Black/African American, 2.7% Asian, 0.2% American Indian/Alaska Native, 0.0% Native Hawaiian/Other Pacific Islander, 5.1% Two or more races, 3.7% Hispanic of any race; Average household size: 2.84; Median age: 35.3; Age under 18: 30.2%; Age 65 and over: 12.3%; Males per 100 females: 96.7; Marriage status: 24.1% never married, 59.7% now married, 0.5% separated, 3.1% widowed, 13.1% divorced; Foreign born: 3.2%; Speak English only: 95.4%; With disability: 9.6%; Veterans: 10.6%; Ancestry: 28.0% German, 16.5% American, 10.2% Irish, 8.9% English, 5.1% French
Employment: 14.9% management, business, and financial, 3.9% computer, engineering, and science, 10.6% education, legal, community service, arts, and media, 9.5% healthcare practitioners, 14.5% service, 25.7% sales and office, 7.2% natural resources, construction, and maintenance, 13.6% production, transportation, and material moving
Income: Per capita: $32,241; Median household: $74,575; Average household: $91,876; Households with income of $100,000 or more: 31.5%; Poverty rate: 5.4%

Educational Attainment: High school diploma or higher: 96.3%; Bachelor's degree or higher: 28.9%; Graduate/professional degree or higher: 12.2%

School District(s)

Northwest Allen County Schools (PK-12)
Enrollment: 7,459 . . . . (260) 637-3155

Housing: Homeownership rate: 92.1%; Median home value: $154,500; Median year structure built: 2004; Homeowner vacancy rate: 1.7%; Median selected monthly owner costs: $1,177 with a mortgage, $444 without a mortgage; Median gross rent: $968 per month; Rental vacancy rate: 0.0%
Health Insurance: 95.8% have insurance; 82.8% have private insurance; 23.7% have public insurance; 4.2% do not have insurance; 2.3% of children under 18 do not have insurance
Newspapers: Northwest News (weekly circulation 1,500)
Transportation: Commute: 97.3% car, 0.0% public transportation, 0.0% walk, 2.6% work from home; Mean travel time to work: 25.7 minutes

Additional Information Contacts

Town of Huntertown . . . . (260) 637-5058
http://www.huntertown.org

LEO-CEDARVILLE (town). Covers a land area of 3.713 square miles and a water area of 0.136 square miles. Located at 41.22° N. Lat; 85.02° W. Long. Elevation is 797 feet.
History: Leo-Cedarville was formed by the incorporation of the villages of Leo and Cedarville into a town in the mid-1990s in a defensive move against the rapidly expanding Fort Wayne, whose city limits currently sit five miles from the town.
Population: 3,735; Growth (since 2000): 34.3%; Density: 1,005.8 persons per square mile; Race: 94.6% White, 0.0% Black/African American, 0.0% Asian, 0.0% American Indian/Alaska Native, 0.0% Native Hawaiian/Other Pacific Islander, 1.2% Two or more races, 5.5% Hispanic of any race; Average household size: 3.04; Median age: 37.1; Age under 18: 31.5%; Age 65 and over: 10.6%; Males per 100 females: 99.4; Marriage status: 29.8% never married, 59.5% now married, 0.0% separated, 3.1% widowed, 7.7% divorced; Foreign born: 2.5%; Speak English only: 94.0%; With disability: 6.5%; Veterans: 4.5%; Ancestry: 25.1% German, 8.8% English, 8.6% Irish, 6.2% Italian, 4.8% Dutch
Employment: 11.4% management, business, and financial, 5.1% computer, engineering, and science, 5.0% education, legal, community service, arts, and media, 7.8% healthcare practitioners, 13.7% service, 31.2% sales and office, 9.8% natural resources, construction, and maintenance, 16.0% production, transportation, and material moving
Income: Per capita: $28,647; Median household: $74,803; Average household: $86,595; Households with income of $100,000 or more: 38.3%; Poverty rate: 1.0%
Educational Attainment: High school diploma or higher: 92.0%; Bachelor's degree or higher: 26.7%; Graduate/professional degree or higher: 4.0%

School District(s)

East Allen County Schools (PK-12)
Enrollment: 9,116 . . . . (260) 446-0100

Housing: Homeownership rate: 87.9%; Median home value: $190,000; Median year structure built: 1991; Homeowner vacancy rate: 0.0%; Median selected monthly owner costs: $1,256 with a mortgage, $346 without a mortgage; Median gross rent: $1,087 per month; Rental vacancy rate: 0.0%
Health Insurance: 96.9% have insurance; 88.5% have private insurance; 14.3% have public insurance; 3.1% do not have insurance; 2.6% of children under 18 do not have insurance
Transportation: Commute: 92.9% car, 0.0% public transportation, 0.0% walk, 7.1% work from home; Mean travel time to work: 25.4 minutes

Additional Information Contacts

Town of Leo-Cedarville . . . . (260) 627-6321
http://www.leocedarville.com

MONROEVILLE (town). Covers a land area of 0.744 square miles and a water area of 0 square miles. Located at 40.97° N. Lat; 84.87° W. Long. Elevation is 791 feet.
History: Settled 1841, incorporated 1865.
Population: 1,197; Growth (since 2000): -3.2%; Density: 1,608.2 persons per square mile; Race: 97.7% White, 0.0% Black/African American, 0.2% Asian, 0.2% American Indian/Alaska Native, 0.0% Native Hawaiian/Other Pacific Islander, 2.0% Two or more races, 4.2% Hispanic of any race; Average household size: 2.25; Median age: 42.9; Age under 18: 19.6%; Age 65 and over: 17.5%; Males per 100 females: 89.1; Marriage status: 27.8% never married, 50.4% now married, 2.4% separated, 14.0% widowed, 7.8% divorced; Foreign born: 0.2%; Speak English only: 96.7%; With disability: 16.3%; Veterans: 8.3%; Ancestry: 32.7% German, 12.9% Irish, 10.9% American, 6.0% French, 4.6% English
Employment: 4.2% management, business, and financial, 3.1% computer, engineering, and science, 5.1% education, legal, community service, arts, and media, 5.4% healthcare practitioners, 12.1% service, 25.5% sales and office, 8.8% natural resources, construction, and maintenance, 35.8% production, transportation, and material moving
Income: Per capita: $22,806; Median household: $45,000; Average household: $51,547; Households with income of $100,000 or more: 7.7%; Poverty rate: 8.1%
Educational Attainment: High school diploma or higher: 91.3%; Bachelor's degree or higher: 10.2%; Graduate/professional degree or higher: 4.1%

School District(s)

East Allen County Schools (PK-12)
Enrollment: 9,116 . . . . (260) 446-0100

Housing: Homeownership rate: 81.7%; Median home value: $80,600; Median year structure built: 1954; Homeowner vacancy rate: 0.0%; Median selected monthly owner costs: $840 with a mortgage, $318 without a mortgage; Median gross rent: $588 per month; Rental vacancy rate: 9.8%
Health Insurance: 89.4% have insurance; 69.1% have private insurance; 35.4% have public insurance; 10.6% do not have insurance; 1.3% of children under 18 do not have insurance
Newspapers: The Monroeville News (weekly circulation 1,200)
Transportation: Commute: 94.9% car, 0.0% public transportation, 0.9% walk, 2.6% work from home; Mean travel time to work: 21.1 minutes

NEW HAVEN (city). Covers a land area of 9.867 square miles and a water area of 0.005 square miles. Located at 41.06° N. Lat; 85.03° W. Long. Elevation is 758 feet.
History: New Haven was settled when the Wabash & Erie Canal was built. Its first residents, who came from New England, named it for the city in Connecticut.
Population: 15,895; Growth (since 2000): 28.1%; Density: 1,610.9 persons per square mile; Race: 95.1% White, 2.6% Black/African American, 0.3% Asian, 0.1% American Indian/Alaska Native, 0.0% Native Hawaiian/Other Pacific Islander, 1.3% Two or more races, 5.7% Hispanic of any race; Average household size: 2.60; Median age: 35.1; Age under 18: 26.3%; Age 65 and over: 14.8%; Males per 100 females: 92.7; Marriage status: 27.2% never married, 51.2% now married, 1.1% separated, 7.1% widowed, 14.5% divorced; Foreign born: 1.2%; Speak English only: 97.4%; With disability: 14.0%; Veterans: 9.0%; Ancestry: 33.2% German, 11.7% American, 11.2% Irish, 6.8% English, 3.8% French
Employment: 10.1% management, business, and financial, 4.0% computer, engineering, and science, 6.5% education, legal, community service, arts, and media, 6.6% healthcare practitioners, 19.0% service, 24.0% sales and office, 7.6% natural resources, construction, and maintenance, 22.3% production, transportation, and material moving
Income: Per capita: $21,278; Median household: $47,649; Average household: $54,413; Households with income of $100,000 or more: 10.7%; Poverty rate: 12.3%
Educational Attainment: High school diploma or higher: 88.7%; Bachelor's degree or higher: 16.1%; Graduate/professional degree or higher: 4.1%

School District(s)

East Allen County Schools (PK-12)
Enrollment: 9,116 . . . . (260) 446-0100

Housing: Homeownership rate: 71.6%; Median home value: $97,300; Median year structure built: 1973; Homeowner vacancy rate: 0.5%; Median selected monthly owner costs: $911 with a mortgage, $320 without a mortgage; Median gross rent: $750 per month; Rental vacancy rate: 4.7%
Health Insurance: 90.6% have insurance; 68.3% have private insurance; 34.5% have public insurance; 9.4% do not have insurance; 5.6% of children under 18 do not have insurance
Safety: Violent crime rate: 24.5 per 10,000 population; Property crime rate: 216.4 per 10,000 population
Transportation: Commute: 95.5% car, 0.1% public transportation, 0.9% walk, 2.4% work from home; Mean travel time to work: 19.9 minutes

Additional Information Contacts

City of New Haven. . . . . (260) 748-7000
http://www.newhavenin.org

SPENCERVILLE (unincorporated postal area)
ZCTA: 46788

Covers a land area of 35.517 square miles and a water area of 0.335 square miles. Located at 41.27° N. Lat; 84.91° W. Long..

Population: 3,614; Growth (since 2000): 27.5%; Density: 101.8 persons per square mile; Race: 96.1% White, 0.5% Black/African American, 0.0% Asian, 0.0% American Indian/Alaska Native, 0.0% Native Hawaiian/Other Pacific Islander, 3.5% Two or more races, 4.3% Hispanic of any race; Average household size: 3.13; Median age: 35.3; Age under 18: 34.1%; Age 65 and over: 10.9%; Males per 100 females: 108.4; Marriage status: 18.0% never married, 63.2% now married, 0.4% separated, 5.7% widowed, 13.1% divorced; Foreign born: 1.8%; Speak English only: 87.0%; With disability: 9.1%; Veterans: 10.2%; Ancestry: 38.4% German, 9.5% American, 7.3% European, 6.3% Pennsylvania German, 5.0% English

Employment: 17.4% management, business, and financial, 3.5% computer, engineering, and science, 10.0% education, legal, community service, arts, and media, 7.0% healthcare practitioners, 8.1% service, 13.8% sales and office, 21.6% natural resources, construction, and maintenance, 18.6% production, transportation, and material moving

Income: Per capita: $25,164; Median household: $61,528; Average household: $77,307; Households with income of $100,000 or more: 21.4%; Poverty rate: 16.7%

Educational Attainment: High school diploma or higher: 83.2%; Bachelor's degree or higher: 16.6%; Graduate/professional degree or higher: 5.3%

Housing: Homeownership rate: 89.7%; Median home value: $170,000; Median year structure built: 1977; Homeowner vacancy rate: 0.0%; Median selected monthly owner costs: $1,127 with a mortgage, $384 without a mortgage; Median gross rent: $770 per month; Rental vacancy rate: 5.6%

Health Insurance: 71.9% have insurance; 58.4% have private insurance; 22.5% have public insurance; 28.1% do not have insurance; 37.1% of children under 18 do not have insurance

Transportation: Commute: 82.0% car, 1.9% public transportation, 2.7% walk, 11.8% work from home; Mean travel time to work: 21.9 minutes

WOODBURN (city). Covers a land area of 0.931 square miles and a water area of 0 square miles. Located at 41.13° N. Lat; 84.86° W. Long. Elevation is 748 feet.

History: Laid out 1865. Until 1936, called Shirley City.

Population: 1,651; Growth (since 2000): 4.6%; Density: 1,773.7 persons per square mile; Race: 97.9% White, 0.0% Black/African American, 0.0% Asian, 0.0% American Indian/Alaska Native, 0.0% Native Hawaiian/Other Pacific Islander, 2.1% Two or more races, 2.1% Hispanic of any race; Average household size: 2.62; Median age: 38.4; Age under 18: 24.0%; Age 65 and over: 12.6%; Males per 100 females: 103.8; Marriage status: 30.5% never married, 52.1% now married, 1.3% separated, 5.0% widowed, 12.4% divorced; Foreign born: 0.7%; Speak English only: 98.5%; With disability: 14.4%; Veterans: 10.5%; Ancestry: 40.3% German, 13.0% American, 11.0% Irish, 7.8% English, 6.1% French

Employment: 9.4% management, business, and financial, 1.8% computer, engineering, and science, 9.7% education, legal, community service, arts, and media, 8.1% healthcare practitioners, 15.2% service, 17.8% sales and office, 8.7% natural resources, construction, and maintenance, 29.4% production, transportation, and material moving

Income: Per capita: $26,327; Median household: $60,625; Average household: $66,707; Households with income of $100,000 or more: 15.9%; Poverty rate: 4.0%

Educational Attainment: High school diploma or higher: 90.1%; Bachelor's degree or higher: 15.5%; Graduate/professional degree or higher: 6.0%

School District(s)

East Allen County Schools (PK-12)
Enrollment: 9,116 . . . . (260) 446-0100

Housing: Homeownership rate: 87.8%; Median home value: $85,100; Median year structure built: 1976; Homeowner vacancy rate: 3.0%; Median selected monthly owner costs: $886 with a mortgage, $332 without a mortgage; Median gross rent: $821 per month; Rental vacancy rate: 18.1%

Health Insurance: 86.5% have insurance; 68.7% have private insurance; 27.1% have public insurance; 13.5% do not have insurance; 21.0% of children under 18 do not have insurance

Transportation: Commute: 93.2% car, 0.0% public transportation, 0.3% walk, 5.5% work from home; Mean travel time to work: 21.7 minutes

YODER (unincorporated postal area)
ZCTA: 46798

Covers a land area of 20.604 square miles and a water area of <.001 square miles. Located at 40.94° N. Lat; 85.21° W. Long. Elevation is 810 feet.

Population: 1,559; Growth (since 2000): -16.7%; Density: 75.7 persons per square mile; Race: 96.2% White, 0.0% Black/African American, 0.7% Asian, 0.0% American Indian/Alaska Native, 0.0% Native Hawaiian/Other Pacific Islander, 3.1% Two or more races, 0.0% Hispanic of any race; Average household size: 2.48; Median age: 48.4; Age under 18: 16.3%; Age 65 and over: 16.9%; Males per 100 females: 103.1; Marriage status: 23.5% never married, 60.0% now married, 0.0% separated, 7.4% widowed, 9.1% divorced; Foreign born: 0.3%; Speak English only: 99.8%; With disability: 17.0%; Veterans: 9.1%; Ancestry: 35.8% German, 8.1% French, 6.9% American, 5.7% English, 5.5% Irish

Employment: 10.4% management, business, and financial, 3.3% computer, engineering, and science, 9.0% education, legal, community service, arts, and media, 8.2% healthcare practitioners, 13.3% service, 23.5% sales and office, 7.7% natural resources, construction, and maintenance, 24.6% production, transportation, and material moving

Income: Per capita: $33,036; Median household: $59,432; Average household: $80,626; Households with income of $100,000 or more: 22.8%; Poverty rate: 3.7%

Educational Attainment: High school diploma or higher: 85.5%; Bachelor's degree or higher: 17.0%; Graduate/professional degree or higher: 4.1%

Housing: Homeownership rate: 92.7%; Median home value: $131,500; Median year structure built: 1975; Homeowner vacancy rate: 0.0%; Median selected monthly owner costs: $1,030 with a mortgage, $451 without a mortgage; Median gross rent: $738 per month; Rental vacancy rate: 0.0%

Health Insurance: 93.8% have insurance; 70.8% have private insurance; 38.6% have public insurance; 6.2% do not have insurance; 0.0% of children under 18 do not have insurance

Transportation: Commute: 94.6% car, 0.0% public transportation, 0.0% walk, 5.4% work from home; Mean travel time to work: 22.1 minutes

Bartholomew County

Located in south central Indiana; drained by the East Fork of the White River. Covers a land area of 406.908 square miles, a water area of 2.617 square miles, and is located in the Eastern Time Zone at 39.21° N. Lat., 85.90° W. Long. The county was founded in 1821. County seat is Columbus.

Bartholomew County is part of the Columbus, IN Metropolitan Statistical Area. The entire metro area includes: Bartholomew County, IN

Weather Station: Columbus Elevation: 621 feet

	Jan	Feb	Mar	Apr	May	Jun	Jul	Aug	Sep	Oct	Nov	Dec
High	38	42	52	64	74	82	85	85	78	67	54	41
Low	21	23	31	42	52	62	65	63	55	43	34	25
Precip	2.9	2.6	3.7	4.5	5.3	3.9	4.1	3.7	3.1	3.2	3.7	3.5
Snow	5.1	3.5	2.1	0.1	tr	0.0	0.0	0.0	0.0	0.1	0.1	3.4

High and Low temperatures in degrees Fahrenheit; Precipitation and Snow in inches

Population: 81,024; Growth (since 2000): 13.4%; Density: 199.1 persons per square mile; Race: 85.5% White, 1.9% Black/African American, 6.3% Asian, 0.2% American Indian/Alaska Native, 0.1% Native Hawaiian/Other Pacific Islander, 1.9% two or more races, 6.5% Hispanic of any race; Average household size: 2.54; Median age: 38.1; Age under 18: 24.0%; Age 65 and over: 15.4%; Males per 100 females: 97.6; Marriage status: 25.6% never married, 54.8% now married, 1.5% separated, 6.2% widowed, 13.3% divorced; Foreign born: 10.1%; Speak English only: 88.6%; With disability: 11.8%; Veterans: 6.5%; Ancestry: 20.2% German, 17.0% American, 9.5% English, 9.2% Irish, 1.8% European

Religion: Six largest groups: 15.1% Baptist, 8.9% Lutheran, 6.0% Catholicism, 6.0% Methodist/Pietist, 5.1% Non-denominational Protestant, 2.1% Holiness

Economy: Unemployment rate: 2.7%; Leading industries: 16.8 % retail trade; 12.3 % health care and social assistance; 9.6 % accommodation and food services; Farms: 623 totaling 171,601 acres; Company size: 8 employ 1,000 or more persons, 7 employ 500 to 999 persons, 60 employ 100 to 499 persons, 1,760 employ less than 100 persons; Business ownership: 1,507 women-owned, 69 Black-owned, 71 Hispanic-owned, 162 Asian-owned, n/a American Indian/Alaska Native-owned

Employment: 16.3% management, business, and financial, 12.2% computer, engineering, and science, 7.4% education, legal, community service, arts, and media, 4.8% healthcare practitioners, 14.4% service, 18.9% sales and office, 6.4% natural resources, construction, and maintenance, 19.5% production, transportation, and material moving
Income: Per capita: $29,955; Median household: $57,331; Average household: $74,096; Households with income of $100,000 or more: 23.2%; Poverty rate: 12.4%
Educational Attainment: High school diploma or higher: 90.2%; Bachelor's degree or higher: 31.2%; Graduate/professional degree or higher: 12.7%
Housing: Homeownership rate: 71.0%; Median home value: $139,400; Median year structure built: 1976; Homeowner vacancy rate: 1.2%; Median selected monthly owner costs: $1,141 with a mortgage, $409 without a mortgage; Median gross rent: $854 per month; Rental vacancy rate: 7.6%
Vital Statistics: Birth rate: 135.2 per 10,000 population; Death rate: 85.3 per 10,000 population; Age-adjusted cancer mortality rate: 158.8 deaths per 100,000 population
Health Insurance: 89.8% have insurance; 74.1% have private insurance; 29.0% have public insurance; 10.2% do not have insurance; 10.0% of children under 18 do not have insurance
Health Care: Physicians: 21.4 per 10,000 population; Dentists: 7.1 per 10,000 population; Hospital beds: 24.2 per 10,000 population; Hospital admissions: 1,094.5 per 10,000 population
Air Quality Index (AQI): Percent of Days: 86.3% good, 13.7% moderate, 0.0% unhealthy for sensitive individuals, 0.0% unhealthy, 0.0% very unhealthy; Annual median: 38; Annual maximum: 93
Transportation: Commute: 93.7% car, 0.6% public transportation, 1.3% walk, 2.7% work from home; Mean travel time to work: 19.6 minutes
2016 Presidential Election: 63.1% Trump, 30.1% Clinton, 5.8% Johnson, 0.2% Stein
Additional Information Contacts
Bartholomew Government. . . . . (812) 376-2510
http://www.bartholomewco.com

Bartholomew County Communities

CLIFFORD (town). Covers a land area of 0.105 square miles and a water area of 0 square miles. Located at 39.28° N. Lat; 85.87° W. Long. Elevation is 659 feet.
Population: 188; Growth (since 2000): -35.4%; Density: 1,784.5 persons per square mile; Race: 98.9% White, 0.0% Black/African American, 1.1% Asian, 0.0% American Indian/Alaska Native, 0.0% Native Hawaiian/Other Pacific Islander, 0.0% Two or more races, 3.7% Hispanic of any race; Average household size: 2.44; Median age: 37.5; Age under 18: 21.3%; Age 65 and over: 15.4%; Males per 100 females: 119.8; Marriage status: 30.7% never married, 44.0% now married, 2.0% separated, 10.0% widowed, 15.3% divorced; Foreign born: 3.2%; Speak English only: 94.4%; With disability: 10.6%; Veterans: 10.8%; Ancestry: 50.0% American, 13.3% German, 12.2% Irish, 9.0% English, 3.2% Dutch
Employment: 0.0% management, business, and financial, 1.0% computer, engineering, and science, 11.7% education, legal, community service, arts, and media, 0.0% healthcare practitioners, 16.5% service, 30.1% sales and office, 11.7% natural resources, construction, and maintenance, 29.1% production, transportation, and material moving
Income: Per capita: $54,504; Median household: $47,321; Average household: $130,926; Households with income of $100,000 or more: 16.9%; Poverty rate: 16.0%
Educational Attainment: High school diploma or higher: 90.3%; Bachelor's degree or higher: 10.5%; Graduate/professional degree or higher: n/a
Housing: Homeownership rate: 54.5%; Median home value: $67,800; Median year structure built: 1962; Homeowner vacancy rate: 0.0%; Median selected monthly owner costs: $775 with a mortgage, $313 without a mortgage; Median gross rent: $786 per month; Rental vacancy rate: 22.2%
Health Insurance: 88.8% have insurance; 64.4% have private insurance; 38.3% have public insurance; 11.2% do not have insurance; 0.0% of children under 18 do not have insurance
Transportation: Commute: 100.0% car, 0.0% public transportation, 0.0% walk, 0.0% work from home; Mean travel time to work: 26.0 minutes

COLUMBUS (city). County seat. Covers a land area of 27.497 square miles and a water area of 0.386 square miles. Located at 39.21° N. Lat; 85.92° W. Long. Elevation is 627 feet.
History: Columbus was settled by General John Tipton, John Lindsay, and Luke Bonesteel in 1820, and was called Tiptonia. In 1821 General Tipton offered land for a county seat if the new town were named for him. The county commissioners accepted the land, but named the town Columbus.
Population: 46,926; Growth (since 2000): 20.1%; Density: 1,706.6 persons per square mile; Race: 81.4% White, 2.5% Black/African American, 10.4% Asian, 0.2% American Indian/Alaska Native, 0.1% Native Hawaiian/Other Pacific Islander, 2.1% Two or more races, 5.7% Hispanic of any race; Average household size: 2.44; Median age: 36.2; Age under 18: 24.3%; Age 65 and over: 15.0%; Males per 100 females: 93.9; Marriage status: 28.0% never married, 52.5% now married, 1.7% separated, 6.1% widowed, 13.4% divorced; Foreign born: 13.4%; Speak English only: 85.4%; With disability: 11.7%; Veterans: 6.1%; Ancestry: 20.1% German, 14.2% American, 9.6% Irish, 9.2% English, 2.0% French
Employment: 17.8% management, business, and financial, 16.8% computer, engineering, and science, 8.1% education, legal, community service, arts, and media, 5.3% healthcare practitioners, 13.7% service, 17.7% sales and office, 4.6% natural resources, construction, and maintenance, 16.0% production, transportation, and material moving
Income: Per capita: $31,895; Median household: $57,535; Average household: $76,343; Households with income of $100,000 or more: 24.7%; Poverty rate: 12.2%
Educational Attainment: High school diploma or higher: 91.5%; Bachelor's degree or higher: 39.9%; Graduate/professional degree or higher: 17.1%

School District(s)

Bartholomew Con School Corp (PK-12)
Enrollment: 11,498 . . . . (812) 376-4220
Housing: Homeownership rate: 63.6%; Median home value: $148,500; Median year structure built: 1979; Homeowner vacancy rate: 0.8%; Median selected monthly owner costs: $1,156 with a mortgage, $401 without a mortgage; Median gross rent: $864 per month; Rental vacancy rate: 8.6%
Health Insurance: 90.1% have insurance; 75.3% have private insurance; 27.7% have public insurance; 9.9% do not have insurance; 9.7% of children under 18 do not have insurance
Hospitals: Columbus Regional Hospital (225 beds)
Safety: Violent crime rate: n/a per 10,000 population; Property crime rate: 402.4 per 10,000 population
Newspapers: The Republic (daily circulation 21,200)
Transportation: Commute: 93.9% car, 0.9% public transportation, 1.3% walk, 2.6% work from home; Mean travel time to work: 17.3 minutes
Airports: Columbus Municipal (general aviation)
Additional Information Contacts
City of Columbus . . . . (812) 376-2510
http://www.columbus.in.gov

ELIZABETHTOWN (town). Covers a land area of 0.253 square miles and a water area of 0 square miles. Located at 39.14° N. Lat; 85.81° W. Long. Elevation is 636 feet.
Population: 517; Growth (since 2000): 32.2%; Density: 2,040.9 persons per square mile; Race: 91.3% White, 2.1% Black/African American, 0.0% Asian, 0.0% American Indian/Alaska Native, 0.0% Native Hawaiian/Other Pacific Islander, 1.0% Two or more races, 2.9% Hispanic of any race; Average household size: 3.21; Median age: 26.0; Age under 18: 36.0%; Age 65 and over: 4.3%; Males per 100 females: 96.9; Marriage status: 40.2% never married, 36.1% now married, 5.7% separated, 4.6% widowed, 19.0% divorced; Foreign born: 2.5%; Speak English only: 91.6%; With disability: 9.1%; Veterans: 7.3%; Ancestry: 29.2% American, 9.9% German, 8.5% English, 7.0% Italian, 3.3% Irish
Employment: 5.1% management, business, and financial, 0.5% computer, engineering, and science, 1.4% education, legal, community service, arts, and media, 1.4% healthcare practitioners, 22.7% service, 18.5% sales and office, 2.3% natural resources, construction, and maintenance, 48.1% production, transportation, and material moving
Income: Per capita: $13,428; Median household: $40,781; Average household: $41,440; Households with income of $100,000 or more: 4.3%; Poverty rate: 35.3%
Educational Attainment: High school diploma or higher: 77.2%; Bachelor's degree or higher: 2.2%; Graduate/professional degree or higher: 1.1%
Housing: Homeownership rate: 60.9%; Median home value: $71,900; Median year structure built: 1972; Homeowner vacancy rate: 3.7%; Median

selected monthly owner costs: $945 with a mortgage, $348 without a mortgage; Median gross rent: $687 per month; Rental vacancy rate: 4.3%
Health Insurance: 81.0% have insurance; 48.0% have private insurance; 37.7% have public insurance; 19.0% do not have insurance; 13.3% of children under 18 do not have insurance
Transportation: Commute: 96.7% car, 0.0% public transportation, 0.0% walk, 0.0% work from home; Mean travel time to work: 22.9 minutes

HARTSVILLE (town). Covers a land area of 0.344 square miles and a water area of 0 square miles. Located at 39.27° N. Lat; 85.70° W. Long. Elevation is 758 feet.
History: Hartsville was the first location of Hartsville College, founded in 1850 by the United Brethren denomination but moved to Huntington in 1898.
Population: 421; Growth (since 2000): 12.0%; Density: 1,224.5 persons per square mile; Race: 98.6% White, 0.0% Black/African American, 0.0% Asian, 0.0% American Indian/Alaska Native, 0.0% Native Hawaiian/Other Pacific Islander, 1.4% Two or more races, 0.0% Hispanic of any race; Average household size: 2.79; Median age: 35.3; Age under 18: 30.2%; Age 65 and over: 9.7%; Males per 100 females: 88.5; Marriage status: 29.0% never married, 46.3% now married, 0.6% separated, 5.2% widowed, 19.5% divorced; Foreign born: 1.0%; Speak English only: 99.5%; With disability: 7.8%; Veterans: 7.1%; Ancestry: 24.5% German, 22.6% American, 17.1% Irish, 5.5% English, 4.0% European
Employment: 6.6% management, business, and financial, 3.6% computer, engineering, and science, 7.8% education, legal, community service, arts, and media, 12.0% healthcare practitioners, 12.0% service, 12.0% sales and office, 10.2% natural resources, construction, and maintenance, 35.9% production, transportation, and material moving
Income: Per capita: $20,517; Median household: $50,625; Average household: $52,975; Households with income of $100,000 or more: 7.2%; Poverty rate: 16.1%
Educational Attainment: High school diploma or higher: 88.8%; Bachelor's degree or higher: 13.5%; Graduate/professional degree or higher: 1.1%
Housing: Homeownership rate: 80.1%; Median home value: $87,400; Median year structure built: Before 1940; Homeowner vacancy rate: 0.0%; Median selected monthly owner costs: $884 with a mortgage, $425 without a mortgage; Median gross rent: $933 per month; Rental vacancy rate: 0.0%
Health Insurance: 91.2% have insurance; 70.3% have private insurance; 32.1% have public insurance; 8.8% do not have insurance; 13.8% of children under 18 do not have insurance
Transportation: Commute: 92.6% car, 0.0% public transportation, 4.9% walk, 1.8% work from home; Mean travel time to work: 26.0 minutes

HOPE (town). Covers a land area of 0.951 square miles and a water area of 0 square miles. Located at 39.30° N. Lat; 85.77° W. Long. Elevation is 715 feet.
Population: 2,400; Growth (since 2000): 12.1%; Density: 2,524.0 persons per square mile; Race: 96.2% White, 0.4% Black/African American, 0.0% Asian, 0.0% American Indian/Alaska Native, 0.0% Native Hawaiian/Other Pacific Islander, 3.0% Two or more races, 1.1% Hispanic of any race; Average household size: 2.84; Median age: 33.3; Age under 18: 27.2%; Age 65 and over: 12.6%; Males per 100 females: 99.4; Marriage status: 23.8% never married, 54.5% now married, 0.9% separated, 6.5% widowed, 15.2% divorced; Foreign born: 0.7%; Speak English only: 99.3%; With disability: 13.1%; Veterans: 11.6%; Ancestry: 28.8% American, 19.9% German, 7.9% Irish, 6.5% English, 3.2% French
Employment: 10.3% management, business, and financial, 2.9% computer, engineering, and science, 5.3% education, legal, community service, arts, and media, 3.1% healthcare practitioners, 22.8% service, 27.7% sales and office, 6.7% natural resources, construction, and maintenance, 21.3% production, transportation, and material moving
Income: Per capita: $19,914; Median household: $47,083; Average household: $51,669; Households with income of $100,000 or more: 6.0%; Poverty rate: 9.2%
Educational Attainment: High school diploma or higher: 91.6%; Bachelor's degree or higher: 12.6%; Graduate/professional degree or higher: 3.8%

School District(s)

Flat Rock-Hawcreek School Corp (KG-12)
Enrollment: 848 . . . . (812) 546-2000

Housing: Homeownership rate: 75.7%; Median home value: $74,800; Median year structure built: 1959; Homeowner vacancy rate: 6.0%; Median selected monthly owner costs: $855 with a mortgage, $326 without a mortgage; Median gross rent: $796 per month; Rental vacancy rate: 0.0%
Health Insurance: 92.8% have insurance; 75.9% have private insurance; 30.4% have public insurance; 7.2% do not have insurance; 3.7% of children under 18 do not have insurance
Newspapers: Star Journal (weekly circulation 1,000)
Transportation: Commute: 90.6% car, 0.0% public transportation, 2.4% walk, 4.0% work from home; Mean travel time to work: 24.3 minutes
Additional Information Contacts
Town of Hope . . . . (812) 546-4673
http://www.hopechamber.com

JONESVILLE (town). Covers a land area of 0.128 square miles and a water area of 0 square miles. Located at 39.06° N. Lat; 85.89° W. Long. Elevation is 594 feet.
History: Laid out 1851.
Population: 210; Growth (since 2000): -4.5%; Density: 1,639.8 persons per square mile; Race: 98.1% White, 0.0% Black/African American, 0.0% Asian, 0.0% American Indian/Alaska Native, 0.0% Native Hawaiian/Other Pacific Islander, 1.9% Two or more races, 11.9% Hispanic of any race; Average household size: 2.88; Median age: 41.7; Age under 18: 24.8%; Age 65 and over: 15.2%; Males per 100 females: 101.1; Marriage status: 20.3% never married, 57.0% now married, 0.0% separated, 9.9% widowed, 12.8% divorced; Foreign born: 1.0%; Speak English only: 99.0%; With disability: 10.0%; Veterans: 3.2%; Ancestry: 25.2% German, 22.4% American, 5.2% Irish, 3.8% English, 3.8% European
Employment: 9.0% management, business, and financial, 0.0% computer, engineering, and science, 12.4% education, legal, community service, arts, and media, 2.2% healthcare practitioners, 7.9% service, 27.0% sales and office, 21.3% natural resources, construction, and maintenance, 20.2% production, transportation, and material moving
Income: Per capita: $22,926; Median household: $54,375; Average household: $62,582; Households with income of $100,000 or more: 16.4%; Poverty rate: 20.5%
Educational Attainment: High school diploma or higher: 87.0%; Bachelor's degree or higher: 11.0%; Graduate/professional degree or higher: 5.5%
Housing: Homeownership rate: 83.6%; Median home value: $80,600; Median year structure built: 1958; Homeowner vacancy rate: 4.7%; Median selected monthly owner costs: $859 with a mortgage, $275 without a mortgage; Median gross rent: n/a per month; Rental vacancy rate: 0.0%
Health Insurance: 92.9% have insurance; 74.8% have private insurance; 28.6% have public insurance; 7.1% do not have insurance; 14.5% of children under 18 do not have insurance
Transportation: Commute: 84.3% car, 0.0% public transportation, 2.2% walk, 6.7% work from home; Mean travel time to work: 23.1 minutes

TAYLORSVILLE (CDP). Covers a land area of 1.064 square miles and a water area of 0 square miles. Located at 39.30° N. Lat; 85.95° W. Long. Elevation is 653 feet.
History: Laid out 1849.
Population: 1,045; Growth (since 2000): 11.6%; Density: 981.9 persons per square mile; Race: 100.0% White, 0.0% Black/African American, 0.0% Asian, 0.0% American Indian/Alaska Native, 0.0% Native Hawaiian/Other Pacific Islander, 0.0% Two or more races, 6.2% Hispanic of any race; Average household size: 3.43; Median age: 35.1; Age under 18: 31.2%; Age 65 and over: 10.9%; Males per 100 females: 98.5; Marriage status: 27.1% never married, 60.2% now married, 0.0% separated, 2.2% widowed, 10.5% divorced; Foreign born: 0.0%; Speak English only: 100.0%; With disability: 11.3%; Veterans: 4.9%; Ancestry: 50.1% German, 14.4% English, 13.0% American, 10.0% Irish, 5.9% Swiss
Employment: 12.7% management, business, and financial, 14.2% computer, engineering, and science, 6.5% education, legal, community service, arts, and media, 0.0% healthcare practitioners, 6.0% service, 25.4% sales and office, 15.5% natural resources, construction, and maintenance, 19.6% production, transportation, and material moving
Income: Per capita: $21,636; Median household: $82,829; Average household: $73,301; Households with income of $100,000 or more: 30.5%; Poverty rate: 7.5%
Educational Attainment: High school diploma or higher: 92.6%; Bachelor's degree or higher: 9.0%; Graduate/professional degree or higher: 3.6%

School District(s)

Bartholomew Con School Corp (PK-12)
Enrollment: 11,498 . . . . (812) 376-4220

Housing: Homeownership rate: 88.2%; Median home value: $107,700; Median year structure built: 1961; Homeowner vacancy rate: 0.0%; Median selected monthly owner costs: $1,201 with a mortgage, $290 without a mortgage; Median gross rent: n/a per month; Rental vacancy rate: 0.0%
Health Insurance: 100.0% have insurance; 86.3% have private insurance; 23.0% have public insurance; 0.0% do not have insurance; 0.0% of children under 18 do not have insurance
Transportation: Commute: 96.4% car, 0.0% public transportation, 0.0% walk, 3.6% work from home; Mean travel time to work: 16.8 minutes

Benton County

Located in western Indiana; bounded on the west by Illinois. Covers a land area of 406.417 square miles, a water area of 0.091 square miles, and is located in the Eastern Time Zone at 40.61° N. Lat., 87.32° W. Long. The county was founded in 1840. County seat is Fowler.

Benton County is part of the Lafayette-West Lafayette, IN Metropolitan Statistical Area. The entire metro area includes: Benton County, IN; Carroll County, IN; Tippecanoe County, IN

Population: 8,685; Growth (since 2000): -7.8%; Density: 21.4 persons per square mile; Race: 97.7% White, 0.9% Black/African American, 0.2% Asian, 0.0% American Indian/Alaska Native, 0.0% Native Hawaiian/Other Pacific Islander, 1.0% two or more races, 5.1% Hispanic of any race; Average household size: 2.52; Median age: 40.9; Age under 18: 25.0%; Age 65 and over: 17.0%; Males per 100 females: 98.1; Marriage status: 26.1% never married, 52.8% now married, 1.2% separated, 6.6% widowed, 14.5% divorced; Foreign born: 1.9%; Speak English only: 95.5%; With disability: 18.5%; Veterans: 7.2%; Ancestry: 28.0% German, 13.3% Irish, 8.9% American, 5.8% English, 5.2% French
Religion: Five largest groups: 33.7% Methodist/Pietist, 30.6% Catholicism, 11.6% Baptist, 1.7% Presbyterian-Reformed, 1.2% Holiness
Economy: Unemployment rate: 3.4%; Leading industries: 16.1 % retail trade; 13.2 % transportation and warehousing; 12.1 % other services (except public administration); Farms: 381 totaling 254,245 acres; Company size: 0 employ 1,000 or more persons, 0 employ 500 to 999 persons, 1 employs 100 to 499 persons, 173 employ less than 100 persons; Business ownership: 211 women-owned, n/a Black-owned, n/a Hispanic-owned, 27 Asian-owned, n/a American Indian/Alaska Native-owned
Employment: 12.4% management, business, and financial, 3.0% computer, engineering, and science, 6.3% education, legal, community service, arts, and media, 3.4% healthcare practitioners, 12.9% service, 24.5% sales and office, 14.1% natural resources, construction, and maintenance, 23.3% production, transportation, and material moving
Income: Per capita: $23,652; Median household: $49,183; Average household: $58,906; Households with income of $100,000 or more: 14.4%; Poverty rate: 14.9%
Educational Attainment: High school diploma or higher: 89.5%; Bachelor's degree or higher: 16.8%; Graduate/professional degree or higher: 4.0%
Housing: Homeownership rate: 73.9%; Median home value: $84,900; Median year structure built: 1953; Homeowner vacancy rate: 3.4%; Median selected monthly owner costs: $925 with a mortgage, $372 without a mortgage; Median gross rent: $707 per month; Rental vacancy rate: 2.1%
Vital Statistics: Birth rate: 123.1 per 10,000 population; Death rate: 92.9 per 10,000 population; Age-adjusted cancer mortality rate: Unreliable deaths per 100,000 population
Health Insurance: 88.2% have insurance; 63.3% have private insurance; 38.7% have public insurance; 11.8% do not have insurance; 8.5% of children under 18 do not have insurance
Health Care: Physicians: 1.2 per 10,000 population; Dentists: 4.6 per 10,000 population; Hospital beds: 0.0 per 10,000 population; Hospital admissions: 0.0 per 10,000 population
Transportation: Commute: 89.7% car, 0.6% public transportation, 3.0% walk, 6.0% work from home; Mean travel time to work: 26.3 minutes
2016 Presidential Election: 69.9% Trump, 23.3% Clinton, 5.8% Johnson, 0.2% Stein
Additional Information Contacts
Benton Government .... (765) 884-0930
http://www.bentoncounty.in.gov

Benton County Communities

AMBIA (town). Covers a land area of 0.148 square miles and a water area of 0 square miles. Located at 40.49° N. Lat; 87.52° W. Long. Elevation is 735 feet.
Population: 252; Growth (since 2000): 27.9%; Density: 1,702.8 persons per square mile; Race: 96.0% White, 0.0% Black/African American, 0.0% Asian, 0.0% American Indian/Alaska Native, 0.0% Native Hawaiian/Other Pacific Islander, 2.0% Two or more races, 39.3% Hispanic of any race; Average household size: 3.50; Median age: 25.5; Age under 18: 39.3%; Age 65 and over: 4.4%; Males per 100 females: 102.5; Marriage status: 26.1% never married, 55.0% now married, 0.6% separated, 5.6% widowed, 13.3% divorced; Foreign born: 12.7%; Speak English only: 57.7%; With disability: 9.1%; Veterans: 3.9%; Ancestry: 21.0% German, 13.5% Irish, 10.3% Hungarian, 7.9% Turkish, 3.2% Dutch
Employment: 6.8% management, business, and financial, 3.9% computer, engineering, and science, 5.8% education, legal, community service, arts, and media, 2.9% healthcare practitioners, 14.6% service, 22.3% sales and office, 26.2% natural resources, construction, and maintenance, 17.5% production, transportation, and material moving
Income: Per capita: $15,319; Median household: $43,333; Average household: $53,006; Households with income of $100,000 or more: 11.1%; Poverty rate: 4.4%
Educational Attainment: High school diploma or higher: 78.1%; Bachelor's degree or higher: 6.3%; Graduate/professional degree or higher: n/a
Housing: Homeownership rate: 68.1%; Median home value: $41,300; Median year structure built: Before 1940; Homeowner vacancy rate: 0.0%; Median selected monthly owner costs: $707 with a mortgage, $420 without a mortgage; Median gross rent: $810 per month; Rental vacancy rate: 0.0%
Health Insurance: 74.2% have insurance; 49.6% have private insurance; 37.3% have public insurance; 25.8% do not have insurance; 18.2% of children under 18 do not have insurance
Transportation: Commute: 92.2% car, 0.0% public transportation, 1.0% walk, 5.8% work from home; Mean travel time to work: 28.6 minutes

BOSWELL (town). Covers a land area of 0.927 square miles and a water area of 0 square miles. Located at 40.52° N. Lat; 87.37° W. Long. Elevation is 755 feet.
Population: 732; Growth (since 2000): -11.5%; Density: 790.0 persons per square mile; Race: 92.8% White, 2.9% Black/African American, 0.8% Asian, 0.0% American Indian/Alaska Native, 0.0% Native Hawaiian/Other Pacific Islander, 3.6% Two or more races, 14.6% Hispanic of any race; Average household size: 2.35; Median age: 44.2; Age under 18: 21.2%; Age 65 and over: 18.3%; Males per 100 females: 92.1; Marriage status: 31.2% never married, 46.7% now married, 0.3% separated, 6.8% widowed, 15.3% divorced; Foreign born: 4.0%; Speak English only: 88.0%; With disability: 25.4%; Veterans: 6.8%; Ancestry: 21.9% German, 14.5% Irish, 8.5% American, 5.6% French, 5.5% English
Employment: 16.5% management, business, and financial, 2.7% computer, engineering, and science, 4.9% education, legal, community service, arts, and media, 1.8% healthcare practitioners, 13.1% service, 11.9% sales and office, 8.2% natural resources, construction, and maintenance, 40.9% production, transportation, and material moving
Income: Per capita: $20,080; Median household: $37,333; Average household: $46,425; Households with income of $100,000 or more: 7.3%; Poverty rate: 19.9%
Educational Attainment: High school diploma or higher: 81.3%; Bachelor's degree or higher: 8.2%; Graduate/professional degree or higher: 2.7%

School District(s)
Benton Community School Corp (PK-12)
Enrollment: 1,897 .... (765) 884-0850
Housing: Homeownership rate: 74.4%; Median home value: $58,600; Median year structure built: 1950; Homeowner vacancy rate: 4.7%; Median selected monthly owner costs: $715 with a mortgage, $355 without a mortgage; Median gross rent: $625 per month; Rental vacancy rate: 0.0%
Health Insurance: 80.6% have insurance; 52.9% have private insurance; 43.4% have public insurance; 19.4% do not have insurance; 19.9% of children under 18 do not have insurance
Transportation: Commute: 96.5% car, 0.0% public transportation, 0.0% walk, 2.8% work from home; Mean travel time to work: 24.4 minutes

EARL PARK (town). Covers a land area of 0.941 square miles and a water area of 0 square miles. Located at 40.69° N. Lat; 87.42° W. Long. Elevation is 810 feet.
History: Laid out 1872.
Population: 402; Growth (since 2000): -17.1%; Density: 427.2 persons per square mile; Race: 99.0% White, 0.0% Black/African American, 0.0% Asian, 0.0% American Indian/Alaska Native, 0.0% Native Hawaiian/Other Pacific Islander, 1.0% Two or more races, 4.2% Hispanic of any race; Average household size: 2.50; Median age: 41.8; Age under 18: 20.9%; Age 65 and over: 15.4%; Males per 100 females: 113.5; Marriage status: 32.3% never married, 44.9% now married, 2.7% separated, 4.8% widowed, 18.0% divorced; Foreign born: 1.0%; Speak English only: 99.5%; With disability: 32.6%; Veterans: 9.1%; Ancestry: 28.4% German, 20.9% Irish, 8.5% Swedish, 6.0% French, 5.7% English
Employment: 13.0% management, business, and financial, 2.2% computer, engineering, and science, 3.2% education, legal, community service, arts, and media, 2.7% healthcare practitioners, 17.3% service, 20.5% sales and office, 18.9% natural resources, construction, and maintenance, 22.2% production, transportation, and material moving
Income: Per capita: $22,988; Median household: $44,531; Average household: $55,365; Households with income of $100,000 or more: 10.8%; Poverty rate: 19.3%
Educational Attainment: High school diploma or higher: 89.5%; Bachelor's degree or higher: 11.5%; Graduate/professional degree or higher: 2.8%
Housing: Homeownership rate: 85.5%; Median home value: $58,400; Median year structure built: Before 1940; Homeowner vacancy rate: 3.4%; Median selected monthly owner costs: $863 with a mortgage, $284 without a mortgage; Median gross rent: $667 per month; Rental vacancy rate: 0.0%
Health Insurance: 89.8% have insurance; 57.5% have private insurance; 48.5% have public insurance; 10.2% do not have insurance; 9.5% of children under 18 do not have insurance
Transportation: Commute: 80.7% car, 4.5% public transportation, 9.1% walk, 5.7% work from home; Mean travel time to work: 30.0 minutes

FOWLER (town). County seat. Covers a land area of 1.397 square miles and a water area of 0.006 square miles. Located at 40.62° N. Lat; 87.32° W. Long. Elevation is 823 feet.
History: Laid out 1872.
Population: 2,272; Growth (since 2000): -5.9%; Density: 1,626.6 persons per square mile; Race: 96.5% White, 2.0% Black/African American, 0.0% Asian, 0.0% American Indian/Alaska Native, 0.0% Native Hawaiian/Other Pacific Islander, 0.8% Two or more races, 2.0% Hispanic of any race; Average household size: 2.30; Median age: 42.8; Age under 18: 24.0%; Age 65 and over: 22.8%; Males per 100 females: 92.0; Marriage status: 32.0% never married, 39.9% now married, 2.2% separated, 10.8% widowed, 17.3% divorced; Foreign born: 1.3%; Speak English only: 97.5%; With disability: 19.9%; Veterans: 7.8%; Ancestry: 32.8% German, 13.6% Irish, 8.3% American, 6.9% French, 5.2% English
Employment: 5.5% management, business, and financial, 2.4% computer, engineering, and science, 7.4% education, legal, community service, arts, and media, 3.8% healthcare practitioners, 17.3% service, 32.9% sales and office, 7.2% natural resources, construction, and maintenance, 23.7% production, transportation, and material moving
Income: Per capita: $21,808; Median household: $40,156; Average household: $49,587; Households with income of $100,000 or more: 6.9%; Poverty rate: 17.4%
Educational Attainment: High school diploma or higher: 88.0%; Bachelor's degree or higher: 16.0%; Graduate/professional degree or higher: 6.0%
Housing: Homeownership rate: 69.1%; Median home value: $76,600; Median year structure built: 1957; Homeowner vacancy rate: 4.5%; Median selected monthly owner costs: $901 with a mortgage, $334 without a mortgage; Median gross rent: $609 per month; Rental vacancy rate: 1.7%
Health Insurance: 90.3% have insurance; 63.4% have private insurance; 44.4% have public insurance; 9.7% do not have insurance; 0.0% of children under 18 do not have insurance
Newspapers: Benton Review (weekly circulation 3,000)
Transportation: Commute: 93.5% car, 0.0% public transportation, 2.6% walk, 3.1% work from home; Mean travel time to work: 23.7 minutes
Additional Information Contacts
Town of Fowler . . . . (765) 742-4044
http://www.lafayettechamber.com

OTTERBEIN (town). Covers a land area of 0.611 square miles and a water area of 0 square miles. Located at 40.49° N. Lat; 87.09° W. Long. Elevation is 709 feet.
History: Laid out 1872.
Population: 1,220; Growth (since 2000): -7.0%; Density: 1,998.3 persons per square mile; Race: 96.9% White, 0.0% Black/African American, 0.7% Asian, 0.0% American Indian/Alaska Native, 0.0% Native Hawaiian/Other Pacific Islander, 1.8% Two or more races, 5.9% Hispanic of any race; Average household size: 2.54; Median age: 32.3; Age under 18: 27.1%; Age 65 and over: 12.0%; Males per 100 females: 96.9; Marriage status: 27.7% never married, 48.2% now married, 0.0% separated, 4.3% widowed, 19.8% divorced; Foreign born: 1.6%; Speak English only: 93.7%; With disability: 20.4%; Veterans: 9.0%; Ancestry: 26.9% German, 21.9% Irish, 8.0% English, 3.8% American, 3.5% Italian
Employment: 6.9% management, business, and financial, 4.6% computer, engineering, and science, 7.0% education, legal, community service, arts, and media, 1.0% healthcare practitioners, 18.4% service, 32.8% sales and office, 15.3% natural resources, construction, and maintenance, 13.9% production, transportation, and material moving
Income: Per capita: $20,716; Median household: $40,398; Average household: $51,980; Households with income of $100,000 or more: 11.4%; Poverty rate: 21.3%
Educational Attainment: High school diploma or higher: 89.0%; Bachelor's degree or higher: 15.5%; Graduate/professional degree or higher: 2.8%

School District(s)

Benton Community School Corp (PK-12)
Enrollment: 1,897 . . . . (765) 884-0850
Housing: Homeownership rate: 57.6%; Median home value: $85,600; Median year structure built: 1957; Homeowner vacancy rate: 8.3%; Median selected monthly owner costs: $1,041 with a mortgage, $334 without a mortgage; Median gross rent: $791 per month; Rental vacancy rate: 3.2%
Health Insurance: 93.8% have insurance; 64.8% have private insurance; 41.1% have public insurance; 6.2% do not have insurance; 0.0% of children under 18 do not have insurance
Transportation: Commute: 96.9% car, 0.0% public transportation, 1.0% walk, 2.1% work from home; Mean travel time to work: 23.4 minutes

OXFORD (town). Covers a land area of 0.541 square miles and a water area of 0 square miles. Located at 40.52° N. Lat; 87.25° W. Long. Elevation is 741 feet.
History: In 1896 in Oxford a racehorse named Dan Patch was born, and brought a measure of fame to the town for the records he set. For a time, Oxford was the seat of Benton County.
Population: 1,169; Growth (since 2000): -8.0%; Density: 2,161.3 persons per square mile; Race: 99.6% White, 0.0% Black/African American, 0.0% Asian, 0.0% American Indian/Alaska Native, 0.0% Native Hawaiian/Other Pacific Islander, 0.3% Two or more races, 0.2% Hispanic of any race; Average household size: 2.47; Median age: 44.7; Age under 18: 21.5%; Age 65 and over: 18.2%; Males per 100 females: 95.3; Marriage status: 28.1% never married, 52.5% now married, 0.3% separated, 4.4% widowed, 14.9% divorced; Foreign born: 0.8%; Speak English only: 99.7%; With disability: 18.1%; Veterans: 7.7%; Ancestry: 19.2% German, 13.5% American, 11.5% Irish, 8.6% English, 3.3% French
Employment: 8.6% management, business, and financial, 2.6% computer, engineering, and science, 5.7% education, legal, community service, arts, and media, 4.3% healthcare practitioners, 15.2% service, 24.5% sales and office, 13.2% natural resources, construction, and maintenance, 26.0% production, transportation, and material moving
Income: Per capita: $23,622; Median household: $52,866; Average household: $56,775; Households with income of $100,000 or more: 10.1%; Poverty rate: 8.3%
Educational Attainment: High school diploma or higher: 89.1%; Bachelor's degree or higher: 16.5%; Graduate/professional degree or higher: 3.2%

School District(s)

Benton Community School Corp (PK-12)
Enrollment: 1,897 . . . . (765) 884-0850
Housing: Homeownership rate: 73.0%; Median home value: $73,000; Median year structure built: 1956; Homeowner vacancy rate: 2.2%; Median selected monthly owner costs: $824 with a mortgage, $338 without a mortgage; Median gross rent: $735 per month; Rental vacancy rate: 5.2%
Health Insurance: 92.7% have insurance; 73.0% have private insurance; 32.6% have public insurance; 7.3% do not have insurance; 3.8% of children under 18 do not have insurance

Transportation: Commute: 92.6% car, 0.9% public transportation, 1.8% walk, 3.9% work from home; Mean travel time to work: 28.7 minutes

Blackford County

Located in eastern Indiana; drained by the Salamonie River. Covers a land area of 165.080 square miles, a water area of 0.503 square miles, and is located in the Eastern Time Zone at 40.47° N. Lat., 85.32° W. Long. The county was founded in 1838. County seat is Hartford City.

Weather Station: Hartford City 4 ESE Elevation: 941 feet

	Jan	Feb	Mar	Apr	May	Jun	Jul	Aug	Sep	Oct	Nov	Dec
High	32	37	48	61	71	80	83	82	76	64	51	37
Low	17	21	29	40	51	60	63	62	54	42	34	22
Precip	2.3	2.1	2.8	3.5	4.2	4.1	4.2	4.1	3.0	2.7	3.3	2.9
Snow	8.4	7.1	3.9	0.9	0.0	0.0	0.0	0.0	0.0	0.4	1.5	7.0

High and Low temperatures in degrees Fahrenheit; Precipitation and Snow in inches

Population: 12,214; Growth (since 2000): -13.1%; Density: 74.0 persons per square mile; Race: 97.4% White, 0.2% Black/African American, 0.5% Asian, 0.2% American Indian/Alaska Native, 0.0% Native Hawaiian/Other Pacific Islander, 1.7% two or more races, 1.5% Hispanic of any race; Average household size: 2.32; Median age: 43.7; Age under 18: 21.8%; Age 65 and over: 20.1%; Males per 100 females: 97.2; Marriage status: 22.6% never married, 55.8% now married, 1.4% separated, 8.7% widowed, 13.0% divorced; Foreign born: 1.6%; Speak English only: 97.2%; With disability: 20.3%; Veterans: 9.7%; Ancestry: 17.2% German, 10.9% American, 10.1% Irish, 8.5% English, 2.5% French

Religion: Six largest groups: 7.5% Methodist/Pietist, 6.9% Baptist, 4.9% Holiness, 3.2% Non-denominational Protestant, 3.1% Catholicism, 2.5% Lutheran

Economy: Unemployment rate: 4.3%; Leading industries: 16.0 % other services (except public administration); 13.1 % retail trade; 12.7 % health care and social assistance; Farms: 263 totaling 88,010 acres; Company size: 0 employ 1,000 or more persons, 0 employ 500 to 999 persons, 6 employ 100 to 499 persons, 231 employs less than 100 persons; Business ownership: 145 women-owned, n/a Black-owned, n/a Hispanic-owned, n/a Asian-owned, n/a American Indian/Alaska Native-owned

Employment: 8.5% management, business, and financial, 2.7% computer, engineering, and science, 7.5% education, legal, community service, arts, and media, 4.1% healthcare practitioners, 14.4% service, 21.2% sales and office, 10.7% natural resources, construction, and maintenance, 31.0% production, transportation, and material moving

Income: Per capita: $22,328; Median household: $40,622; Average household: $52,253; Households with income of $100,000 or more: 9.3%; Poverty rate: 12.8%

Educational Attainment: High school diploma or higher: 87.7%; Bachelor's degree or higher: 11.1%; Graduate/professional degree or higher: 5.3%

Housing: Homeownership rate: 76.4%; Median home value: $68,500; Median year structure built: 1961; Homeowner vacancy rate: 2.9%; Median selected monthly owner costs: $843 with a mortgage, $325 without a mortgage; Median gross rent: $614 per month; Rental vacancy rate: 7.2%

Vital Statistics: Birth rate: 97.7 per 10,000 population; Death rate: 136.9 per 10,000 population; Age-adjusted cancer mortality rate: 244.2 deaths per 100,000 population

Health Insurance: 89.4% have insurance; 66.6% have private insurance; 39.3% have public insurance; 10.6% do not have insurance; 6.3% of children under 18 do not have insurance

Health Care: Physicians: 7.5 per 10,000 population; Dentists: 1.7 per 10,000 population; Hospital beds: 12.4 per 10,000 population; Hospital admissions: 365.2 per 10,000 population

Transportation: Commute: 93.2% car, 0.5% public transportation, 2.7% walk, 2.3% work from home; Mean travel time to work: 23.5 minutes

2016 Presidential Election: 69.2% Trump, 25.7% Clinton, 4.8% Johnson, 0.3% Stein

Additional Information Contacts

Blackford Government. . . . . (765) 348-1620
http://www.blackfordcounty.com

Blackford County Communities

HARTFORD CITY (city). County seat. Covers a land area of 3.875 square miles and a water area of 0.021 square miles. Located at 40.45° N. Lat; 85.37° W. Long. Elevation is 919 feet.

History: Settled 1832, laid out 1839.

Population: 6,002; Growth (since 2000): -13.4%; Density: 1,548.8 persons per square mile; Race: 97.0% White, 0.0% Black/African American, 0.4% Asian, 0.2% American Indian/Alaska Native, 0.0% Native Hawaiian/Other Pacific Islander, 2.4% Two or more races, 2.5% Hispanic of any race; Average household size: 2.34; Median age: 40.3; Age under 18: 23.8%; Age 65 and over: 17.3%; Males per 100 females: 90.7; Marriage status: 24.7% never married, 54.8% now married, 2.0% separated, 8.3% widowed, 12.2% divorced; Foreign born: 1.4%; Speak English only: 97.0%; With disability: 21.5%; Veterans: 9.4%; Ancestry: 17.5% German, 10.9% Irish, 10.0% English, 9.1% American, 2.6% French

Employment: 8.5% management, business, and financial, 3.5% computer, engineering, and science, 7.3% education, legal, community service, arts, and media, 3.4% healthcare practitioners, 17.0% service, 19.1% sales and office, 10.1% natural resources, construction, and maintenance, 31.2% production, transportation, and material moving

Income: Per capita: $19,602; Median household: $36,136; Average household: $46,945; Households with income of $100,000 or more: 7.8%; Poverty rate: 16.6%

Educational Attainment: High school diploma or higher: 85.0%; Bachelor's degree or higher: 9.9%; Graduate/professional degree or higher: 5.3%

School District(s)

Blackford County Schools (KG-12)
Enrollment: 1,872 . . . . (765) 348-7550

Housing: Homeownership rate: 72.5%; Median home value: $55,900; Median year structure built: 1962; Homeowner vacancy rate: 2.4%; Median selected monthly owner costs: $796 with a mortgage, $315 without a mortgage; Median gross rent: $606 per month; Rental vacancy rate: 3.2%

Health Insurance: 88.3% have insurance; 65.8% have private insurance; 38.6% have public insurance; 11.7% do not have insurance; 7.6% of children under 18 do not have insurance

Hospitals: Indiana University Health Blackford Hospital (15 beds)

Safety: Violent crime rate: 11.9 per 10,000 population; Property crime rate: 80.0 per 10,000 population

Newspapers: News-Times (daily circulation 1,500)

Transportation: Commute: 92.9% car, 0.0% public transportation, 3.6% walk, 1.3% work from home; Mean travel time to work: 23.5 minutes

Additional Information Contacts

City of Hartford City. . . . . (765) 348-1872
http://www.hartfordcity.net

MONTPELIER (city). Covers a land area of 1.542 square miles and a water area of 0 square miles. Located at 40.55° N. Lat; 85.29° W. Long. Elevation is 869 feet.

History: Settled 1836, laid out 1837, incorporated 1937.

Population: 1,701; Growth (since 2000): -11.8%; Density: 1,103.4 persons per square mile; Race: 94.2% White, 0.0% Black/African American, 1.9% Asian, 0.8% American Indian/Alaska Native, 0.0% Native Hawaiian/Other Pacific Islander, 3.1% Two or more races, 0.7% Hispanic of any race; Average household size: 2.27; Median age: 41.8; Age under 18: 24.2%; Age 65 and over: 17.6%; Males per 100 females: 100.6; Marriage status: 27.6% never married, 42.4% now married, 3.1% separated, 9.9% widowed, 20.1% divorced; Foreign born: 2.7%; Speak English only: 97.3%; With disability: 21.8%; Veterans: 9.8%; Ancestry: 20.9% German, 15.7% Irish, 12.3% American, 6.0% English, 3.8% European

Employment: 4.3% management, business, and financial, 0.6% computer, engineering, and science, 3.2% education, legal, community service, arts, and media, 4.3% healthcare practitioners, 15.6% service, 19.5% sales and office, 17.7% natural resources, construction, and maintenance, 34.8% production, transportation, and material moving

Income: Per capita: $17,207; Median household: $33,576; Average household: $39,663; Households with income of $100,000 or more: 3.9%; Poverty rate: 11.7%

Educational Attainment: High school diploma or higher: 82.7%; Bachelor's degree or higher: 6.4%; Graduate/professional degree or higher: 0.3%

School District(s)

Blackford County Schools (KG-12)
Enrollment: 1,872 . . . . (765) 348-7550

Housing: Homeownership rate: 59.5%; Median home value: $51,500; Median year structure built: 1944; Homeowner vacancy rate: 7.1%; Median selected monthly owner costs: $778 with a mortgage, $321 without a mortgage; Median gross rent: $585 per month; Rental vacancy rate: 9.6%
Health Insurance: 84.4% have insurance; 56.5% have private insurance; 44.5% have public insurance; 15.6% do not have insurance; 5.4% of children under 18 do not have insurance
Transportation: Commute: 92.5% car, 0.0% public transportation, 3.9% walk, 1.6% work from home; Mean travel time to work: 21.2 minutes

SHAMROCK LAKES (town). Covers a land area of 0.263 square miles and a water area of 0.056 square miles. Located at 40.41° N. Lat; 85.43° W. Long. Elevation is 889 feet.
Population: 272; Growth (since 2000): 61.9%; Density: 1,033.8 persons per square mile; Race: 97.4% White, 0.0% Black/African American, 0.0% Asian, 0.0% American Indian/Alaska Native, 0.0% Native Hawaiian/Other Pacific Islander, 1.8% Two or more races, 0.0% Hispanic of any race; Average household size: 2.43; Median age: 47.0; Age under 18: 22.4%; Age 65 and over: 22.8%; Males per 100 females: 94.1; Marriage status: 16.6% never married, 68.6% now married, 2.2% separated, 3.6% widowed, 11.2% divorced; Foreign born: 0.0%; Speak English only: 100.0%; With disability: 8.5%; Veterans: 9.0%; Ancestry: 14.0% American, 10.3% German, 7.0% Irish, 5.1% English, 3.3% French
Employment: 10.5% management, business, and financial, 2.4% computer, engineering, and science, 6.5% education, legal, community service, arts, and media, 1.6% healthcare practitioners, 6.5% service, 33.9% sales and office, 12.1% natural resources, construction, and maintenance, 26.6% production, transportation, and material moving
Income: Per capita: $30,188; Median household: $53,333; Average household: $71,918; Households with income of $100,000 or more: 27.7%; Poverty rate: 14.0%
Educational Attainment: High school diploma or higher: 96.4%; Bachelor's degree or higher: 18.3%; Graduate/professional degree or higher: 8.6%
Housing: Homeownership rate: 88.4%; Median home value: $131,300; Median year structure built: 1970; Homeowner vacancy rate: 0.0%; Median selected monthly owner costs: $1,240 with a mortgage, $313 without a mortgage; Median gross rent: $1,102 per month; Rental vacancy rate: 0.0%
Health Insurance: 90.1% have insurance; 70.6% have private insurance; 40.1% have public insurance; 9.9% do not have insurance; 13.8% of children under 18 do not have insurance
Transportation: Commute: 97.5% car, 0.0% public transportation, 0.0% walk, 2.5% work from home; Mean travel time to work: 27.7 minutes

Boone County

Located in central Indiana; drained by Sugar and Raccoon Creeks and the Eel River. Covers a land area of 422.913 square miles, a water area of 0.339 square miles, and is located in the Eastern Time Zone at 40.05° N. Lat., 86.47° W. Long. The county was founded in 1830. County seat is Lebanon.

Boone County is part of the Indianapolis-Carmel-Anderson, IN Metropolitan Statistical Area. The entire metro area includes: Boone County, IN; Brown County, IN; Hamilton County, IN; Hancock County, IN; Hendricks County, IN; Johnson County, IN; Madison County, IN; Marion County, IN; Morgan County, IN; Putnam County, IN; Shelby County, IN

Weather Station: Whitestown   Elevation: 935 feet

	Jan	Feb	Mar	Apr	May	Jun	Jul	Aug	Sep	Oct	Nov	Dec
High	35	40	51	64	74	83	86	84	79	66	52	39
Low	19	22	31	41	51	60	64	62	54	43	34	24
Precip	2.7	2.6	3.4	3.9	4.8	4.1	4.3	3.3	3.4	3.1	3.7	3.3
Snow	8.0	6.4	2.4	0.3	0.0	0.0	0.0	0.0	0.0	0.3	0.7	5.8

High and Low temperatures in degrees Fahrenheit; Precipitation and Snow in inches

Population: 63,013; Growth (since 2000): 36.7%; Density: 149.0 persons per square mile; Race: 93.7% White, 1.6% Black/African American, 2.6% Asian, 0.2% American Indian/Alaska Native, 0.0% Native Hawaiian/Other Pacific Islander, 1.6% two or more races, 2.7% Hispanic of any race; Average household size: 2.57; Median age: 38.4; Age under 18: 26.9%; Age 65 and over: 12.6%; Males per 100 females: 96.8; Marriage status: 22.3% never married, 62.5% now married, 0.7% separated, 5.0% widowed, 10.2% divorced; Foreign born: 3.6%; Speak English only: 95.4%; With disability: 9.7%; Veterans: 6.9%; Ancestry: 23.7% German, 12.8% American, 12.0% English, 11.2% Irish, 3.2% Italian
Religion: Six largest groups: 16.5% Catholicism, 15.5% Baptist, 7.8% Non-denominational Protestant, 6.6% Methodist/Pietist, 5.3% Presbyterian-Reformed, 2.8% Lutheran
Economy: Unemployment rate: 2.8%; Leading industries: 11.9 % professional, scientific, and technical services; 11.4 % retail trade; 9.6 % construction; Farms: 607 totaling 221,703 acres; Company size: 1 employs 1,000 or more persons, 2 employ 500 to 999 persons, 27 employ 100 to 499 persons, 1,426 employ less than 100 persons; Business ownership: 2,024 women-owned, 60 Black-owned, 40 Hispanic-owned, 53 Asian-owned, n/a American Indian/Alaska Native-owned
Employment: 21.5% management, business, and financial, 7.4% computer, engineering, and science, 11.3% education, legal, community service, arts, and media, 8.0% healthcare practitioners, 12.4% service, 20.8% sales and office, 7.1% natural resources, construction, and maintenance, 11.6% production, transportation, and material moving
Income: Per capita: $42,844; Median household: $75,591; Average household: $111,176; Households with income of $100,000 or more: 37.6%; Poverty rate: 6.1%
Educational Attainment: High school diploma or higher: 93.7%; Bachelor's degree or higher: 47.2%; Graduate/professional degree or higher: 19.2%
Housing: Homeownership rate: 75.8%; Median home value: $207,500; Median year structure built: 1991; Homeowner vacancy rate: 0.7%; Median selected monthly owner costs: $1,564 with a mortgage, $526 without a mortgage; Median gross rent: $888 per month; Rental vacancy rate: 8.1%
Vital Statistics: Birth rate: 122.0 per 10,000 population; Death rate: 71.8 per 10,000 population; Age-adjusted cancer mortality rate: 160.6 deaths per 100,000 population
Health Insurance: 93.5% have insurance; 82.4% have private insurance; 21.9% have public insurance; 6.5% do not have insurance; 4.6% of children under 18 do not have insurance
Health Care: Physicians: 84.7 per 10,000 population; Dentists: 4.7 per 10,000 population; Hospital beds: 10.9 per 10,000 population; Hospital admissions: 432.4 per 10,000 population
Air Quality Index (AQI): Percent of Days: 89.4% good, 10.2% moderate, 0.4% unhealthy for sensitive individuals, 0.0% unhealthy, 0.0% very unhealthy; Annual median: 39; Annual maximum: 101
Transportation: Commute: 92.3% car, 0.1% public transportation, 0.9% walk, 5.4% work from home; Mean travel time to work: 24.9 minutes
2016 Presidential Election: 60.4% Trump, 31.3% Clinton, 6.8% Johnson, 0.2% Stein

Additional Information Contacts

Boone Government . . . . (765) 482-2940
http://www.boonecounty.in.gov

Boone County Communities

ADVANCE (town). Covers a land area of 0.622 square miles and a water area of 0 square miles. Located at 40.00° N. Lat; 86.62° W. Long. Elevation is 932 feet.
Population: 409; Growth (since 2000): -27.2%; Density: 657.2 persons per square mile; Race: 98.8% White, 0.0% Black/African American, 1.2% Asian, 0.0% American Indian/Alaska Native, 0.0% Native Hawaiian/Other Pacific Islander, 0.0% Two or more races, 0.7% Hispanic of any race; Average household size: 2.62; Median age: 45.8; Age under 18: 21.0%; Age 65 and over: 14.4%; Males per 100 females: 107.4; Marriage status: 19.8% never married, 57.3% now married, 0.3% separated, 6.7% widowed, 16.2% divorced; Foreign born: 1.2%; Speak English only: 99.2%; With disability: 24.7%; Veterans: 9.0%; Ancestry: 22.7% German, 21.8% American, 19.3% Irish, 4.4% English, 2.9% Scottish
Employment: 7.4% management, business, and financial, 2.6% computer, engineering, and science, 5.8% education, legal, community service, arts, and media, 6.3% healthcare practitioners, 12.7% service, 32.3% sales and office, 12.7% natural resources, construction, and maintenance, 20.1% production, transportation, and material moving
Income: Per capita: $22,280; Median household: $52,083; Average household: $59,131; Households with income of $100,000 or more: 9.6%; Poverty rate: 22.2%
Educational Attainment: High school diploma or higher: 87.4%; Bachelor's degree or higher: 8.1%; Graduate/professional degree or higher: n/a

Housing: Homeownership rate: 84.6%; Median home value: $101,600; Median year structure built: 1965; Homeowner vacancy rate: 2.9%; Median selected monthly owner costs: $1,155 with a mortgage, $489 without a mortgage; Median gross rent: $680 per month; Rental vacancy rate: 25.0%
Health Insurance: 96.1% have insurance; 69.7% have private insurance; 38.9% have public insurance; 3.9% do not have insurance; 0.0% of children under 18 do not have insurance
Transportation: Commute: 94.1% car, 0.0% public transportation, 2.7% walk, 1.1% work from home; Mean travel time to work: 25.9 minutes

JAMESTOWN (town). Covers a land area of 0.876 square miles and a water area of 0 square miles. Located at 39.93° N. Lat; 86.63° W. Long. Elevation is 955 feet.
History: Jamestown developed as a stop on the stagecoach route, and later as a station on the New York Central Railroad.
Population: 1,044; Growth (since 2000): 17.8%; Density: 1,192.2 persons per square mile; Race: 99.6% White, 0.0% Black/African American, 0.0% Asian, 0.0% American Indian/Alaska Native, 0.0% Native Hawaiian/Other Pacific Islander, 0.4% Two or more races, 0.3% Hispanic of any race; Average household size: 2.46; Median age: 40.1; Age under 18: 24.9%; Age 65 and over: 13.3%; Males per 100 females: 87.8; Marriage status: 26.1% never married, 53.1% now married, 4.0% separated, 6.2% widowed, 14.6% divorced; Foreign born: 0.4%; Speak English only: 99.0%; With disability: 12.0%; Veterans: 6.4%; Ancestry: 26.0% American, 11.7% English, 10.2% Irish, 10.0% German, 4.5% Scottish
Employment: 13.7% management, business, and financial, 3.3% computer, engineering, and science, 10.6% education, legal, community service, arts, and media, 4.5% healthcare practitioners, 19.2% service, 20.5% sales and office, 11.0% natural resources, construction, and maintenance, 17.2% production, transportation, and material moving
Income: Per capita: $30,187; Median household: $50,833; Average household: $72,967; Households with income of $100,000 or more: 17.6%; Poverty rate: 17.2%
Educational Attainment: High school diploma or higher: 92.7%; Bachelor's degree or higher: 24.6%; Graduate/professional degree or higher: 7.6%

School District(s)

Western Boone Co Com Sch Dist (PK-12)
Enrollment: 1,670 . . . . (765) 482-6333
Housing: Homeownership rate: 63.0%; Median home value: $117,600; Median year structure built: 1961; Homeowner vacancy rate: 6.3%; Median selected monthly owner costs: $1,027 with a mortgage, $475 without a mortgage; Median gross rent: $810 per month; Rental vacancy rate: 6.0%
Health Insurance: 89.8% have insurance; 65.3% have private insurance; 34.8% have public insurance; 10.2% do not have insurance; 12.3% of children under 18 do not have insurance
Transportation: Commute: 93.8% car, 0.0% public transportation, 5.6% walk, 0.6% work from home; Mean travel time to work: 29.7 minutes

LEBANON (city). County seat. Covers a land area of 15.555 square miles and a water area of 0.016 square miles. Located at 40.03° N. Lat; 86.46° W. Long. Elevation is 942 feet.
History: Named for the Biblical mountain of cedars, although the trees in the area are primarily hickory trees. Lebanon received its biblical name because the forests surrounding it reminded one of its founders of the Cedars of Lebanon. Lebanon was the home of Samuel M. Ralston (1857-1925), governor of Indiana and U.S. senator.
Population: 15,710; Growth (since 2000): 10.5%; Density: 1,010.0 persons per square mile; Race: 95.7% White, 1.2% Black/African American, 0.0% Asian, 0.0% American Indian/Alaska Native, 0.0% Native Hawaiian/Other Pacific Islander, 2.9% Two or more races, 4.0% Hispanic of any race; Average household size: 2.18; Median age: 40.5; Age under 18: 21.1%; Age 65 and over: 15.9%; Males per 100 females: 92.2; Marriage status: 26.9% never married, 47.9% now married, 1.2% separated, 8.4% widowed, 16.8% divorced; Foreign born: 1.3%; Speak English only: 97.2%; With disability: 15.3%; Veterans: 8.8%; Ancestry: 19.6% German, 15.1% American, 10.8% Irish, 9.6% English, 3.6% Scottish
Employment: 14.1% management, business, and financial, 4.2% computer, engineering, and science, 7.5% education, legal, community service, arts, and media, 5.5% healthcare practitioners, 15.7% service, 26.4% sales and office, 9.5% natural resources, construction, and maintenance, 17.2% production, transportation, and material moving
Income: Per capita: $29,462; Median household: $47,234; Average household: $65,359; Households with income of $100,000 or more: 16.4%; Poverty rate: 9.3%
Educational Attainment: High school diploma or higher: 87.1%; Bachelor's degree or higher: 25.8%; Graduate/professional degree or higher: 8.0%

School District(s)

Lebanon Community School Corp (KG-12)
Enrollment: 3,463 . . . . (765) 482-0380
Housing: Homeownership rate: 61.8%; Median home value: $113,800; Median year structure built: 1978; Homeowner vacancy rate: 1.4%; Median selected monthly owner costs: $1,113 with a mortgage, $451 without a mortgage; Median gross rent: $758 per month; Rental vacancy rate: 9.3%
Health Insurance: 89.8% have insurance; 72.1% have private insurance; 33.1% have public insurance; 10.2% do not have insurance; 9.9% of children under 18 do not have insurance
Hospitals: Witham Health Services (80 beds)
Newspapers: Sun Times (weekly circulation 7,000); The Reporter (daily circulation 5,300)
Transportation: Commute: 94.9% car, 0.0% public transportation, 0.3% walk, 2.4% work from home; Mean travel time to work: 21.9 minutes
Additional Information Contacts
City of Lebanon . . . . (765) 482-1218
http://www.cityoflebanon.org

THORNTOWN (town). Covers a land area of 0.603 square miles and a water area of 0 square miles. Located at 40.13° N. Lat; 86.61° W. Long. Elevation is 853 feet.
History: Thorntown was called Keewaskee, meaning "place of thorns," when a trading post was established here by Jesuit missionaries. Thorntown was platted in 1829 by Cornelius Westfall.
Population: 1,459; Growth (since 2000): -6.6%; Density: 2,421.0 persons per square mile; Race: 96.9% White, 0.0% Black/African American, 0.7% Asian, 0.0% American Indian/Alaska Native, 0.0% Native Hawaiian/Other Pacific Islander, 1.3% Two or more races, 3.4% Hispanic of any race; Average household size: 2.60; Median age: 37.3; Age under 18: 26.1%; Age 65 and over: 15.9%; Males per 100 females: 91.4; Marriage status: 23.0% never married, 56.1% now married, 1.4% separated, 7.8% widowed, 13.1% divorced; Foreign born: 2.9%; Speak English only: 95.0%; With disability: 18.0%; Veterans: 8.7%; Ancestry: 17.3% German, 16.2% Irish, 15.3% American, 9.4% English, 2.1% French
Employment: 6.3% management, business, and financial, 2.7% computer, engineering, and science, 5.3% education, legal, community service, arts, and media, 5.9% healthcare practitioners, 23.7% service, 14.5% sales and office, 4.4% natural resources, construction, and maintenance, 37.2% production, transportation, and material moving
Income: Per capita: $22,732; Median household: $50,114; Average household: $59,679; Households with income of $100,000 or more: 11.3%; Poverty rate: 14.8%
Educational Attainment: High school diploma or higher: 83.5%; Bachelor's degree or higher: 12.4%; Graduate/professional degree or higher: 3.8%

School District(s)

Western Boone Co Com Sch Dist (PK-12)
Enrollment: 1,670 . . . . (765) 482-6333
Housing: Homeownership rate: 67.1%; Median home value: $90,800; Median year structure built: 1962; Homeowner vacancy rate: 5.5%; Median selected monthly owner costs: $992 with a mortgage, $342 without a mortgage; Median gross rent: $748 per month; Rental vacancy rate: 7.0%
Health Insurance: 83.4% have insurance; 62.7% have private insurance; 37.5% have public insurance; 16.6% do not have insurance; 18.6% of children under 18 do not have insurance
Transportation: Commute: 92.6% car, 0.5% public transportation, 3.9% walk, 3.0% work from home; Mean travel time to work: 25.2 minutes

ULEN (town). Covers a land area of 0.063 square miles and a water area of 0 square miles. Located at 40.06° N. Lat; 86.46° W. Long. Elevation is 945 feet.
Population: 183; Growth (since 2000): 48.8%; Density: 2,908.5 persons per square mile; Race: 99.5% White, 0.0% Black/African American, 0.0% Asian, 0.0% American Indian/Alaska Native, 0.0% Native Hawaiian/Other Pacific Islander, 0.5% Two or more races, 1.6% Hispanic of any race; Average household size: 2.51; Median age: 50.8; Age under 18: 21.3%; Age 65 and over: 26.8%; Males per 100 females: 105.3; Marriage status: 15.1% never married, 73.0% now married, 0.0% separated, 5.9%

widowed, 5.9% divorced; Foreign born: 0.0%; Speak English only: 98.9%; With disability: 14.2%; Veterans: 11.1%; Ancestry: 23.0% English, 15.8% German, 12.0% American, 8.7% Scottish, 6.6% French
Employment: 17.0% management, business, and financial, 12.8% computer, engineering, and science, 25.5% education, legal, community service, arts, and media, 4.3% healthcare practitioners, 9.6% service, 24.5% sales and office, 0.0% natural resources, construction, and maintenance, 6.4% production, transportation, and material moving
Income: Per capita: $55,584; Median household: $111,875; Average household: $134,292; Households with income of $100,000 or more: 64.4%; Poverty rate: 1.6%
Educational Attainment: High school diploma or higher: 97.0%; Bachelor's degree or higher: 56.1%; Graduate/professional degree or higher: 24.2%
Housing: Homeownership rate: 97.3%; Median home value: $244,300; Median year structure built: 1951; Homeowner vacancy rate: 0.0%; Median selected monthly owner costs: $1,813 with a mortgage, $556 without a mortgage; Median gross rent: n/a per month; Rental vacancy rate: 0.0%
Health Insurance: 96.7% have insurance; 85.2% have private insurance; 26.8% have public insurance; 3.3% do not have insurance; 6.4% of children under 18 do not have insurance
Transportation: Commute: 95.7% car, 0.0% public transportation, 0.0% walk, 4.3% work from home; Mean travel time to work: 23.9 minutes

WHITESTOWN (town). Covers a land area of 10.458 square miles and a water area of 0 square miles. Located at 39.96° N. Lat; 86.37° W. Long. Elevation is 938 feet.
History: Laid out 1851.
Population: 6,487; Growth (since 2000): 1,277.3%; Density: 620.3 persons per square mile; Race: 86.4% White, 6.4% Black/African American, 5.0% Asian, 1.0% American Indian/Alaska Native, 0.0% Native Hawaiian/Other Pacific Islander, 0.9% Two or more races, 4.1% Hispanic of any race; Average household size: 2.81; Median age: 29.8; Age under 18: 35.1%; Age 65 and over: 5.3%; Males per 100 females: 101.9; Marriage status: 20.8% never married, 65.1% now married, 1.4% separated, 1.5% widowed, 12.6% divorced; Foreign born: 6.8%; Speak English only: 92.7%; With disability: 7.0%; Veterans: 4.9%; Ancestry: 28.2% German, 14.6% Irish, 13.8% English, 5.6% American, 3.7% African
Employment: 26.3% management, business, and financial, 8.2% computer, engineering, and science, 13.8% education, legal, community service, arts, and media, 13.8% healthcare practitioners, 14.7% service, 13.5% sales and office, 3.5% natural resources, construction, and maintenance, 6.2% production, transportation, and material moving
Income: Per capita: $29,052; Median household: $74,876; Average household: $81,047; Households with income of $100,000 or more: 29.4%; Poverty rate: 10.0%
Educational Attainment: High school diploma or higher: 94.8%; Bachelor's degree or higher: 58.3%; Graduate/professional degree or higher: 18.8%

School District(s)

Zionsville Community Schools (PK-12)
Enrollment: 6,933 . . . . (317) 873-2858
Housing: Homeownership rate: 75.8%; Median home value: $211,000; Median year structure built: 2008; Homeowner vacancy rate: 0.0%; Median selected monthly owner costs: $1,560 with a mortgage, $446 without a mortgage; Median gross rent: $1,332 per month; Rental vacancy rate: 3.1%
Health Insurance: 91.3% have insurance; 81.6% have private insurance; 14.8% have public insurance; 8.7% do not have insurance; 1.3% of children under 18 do not have insurance
Safety: Violent crime rate: 18.8 per 10,000 population; Property crime rate: 186.2 per 10,000 population
Transportation: Commute: 94.9% car, 0.0% public transportation, 0.0% walk, 5.1% work from home; Mean travel time to work: 22.9 minutes

ZIONSVILLE (town). Covers a land area of 10.257 square miles and a water area of 0.038 square miles. Located at 39.96° N. Lat; 86.27° W. Long. Elevation is 843 feet.
History: On his way to his inauguration in Washington in 1861, Abraham Lincoln spoke from the back of a train in Zionsville, saying, "I would like to spend more time here, but there is an event to take place in Washington which cannot start until I get there."
Population: 25,810; Growth (since 2000): 194.1%; Density: 2,516.4 persons per square mile; Race: 91.5% White, 1.6% Black/African American, 5.0% Asian, 0.1% American Indian/Alaska Native, 0.0% Native Hawaiian/Other Pacific Islander, 1.5% Two or more races, 2.5% Hispanic of any race; Average household size: 2.79; Median age: 38.1; Age under 18: 29.9%; Age 65 and over: 10.0%; Males per 100 females: 94.9; Marriage status: 21.3% never married, 68.2% now married, 0.3% separated, 3.7% widowed, 6.9% divorced; Foreign born: 5.6%; Speak English only: 93.5%; With disability: 5.8%; Veterans: 5.0%; Ancestry: 26.8% German, 13.4% English, 10.8% Irish, 9.6% American, 5.1% Italian
Employment: 27.7% management, business, and financial, 10.8% computer, engineering, and science, 14.4% education, legal, community service, arts, and media, 9.4% healthcare practitioners, 9.1% service, 19.1% sales and office, 3.3% natural resources, construction, and maintenance, 6.2% production, transportation, and material moving
Income: Per capita: $60,565; Median household: $127,152; Average household: $169,680; Households with income of $100,000 or more: 60.6%; Poverty rate: 2.6%
Educational Attainment: High school diploma or higher: 97.8%; Bachelor's degree or higher: 70.4%; Graduate/professional degree or higher: 33.2%

School District(s)

Zionsville Community Schools (PK-12)
Enrollment: 6,933 . . . . (317) 873-2858
Housing: Homeownership rate: 80.7%; Median home value: $360,100; Median year structure built: 1999; Homeowner vacancy rate: 0.0%; Median selected monthly owner costs: $2,192 with a mortgage, $664 without a mortgage; Median gross rent: $1,249 per month; Rental vacancy rate: 9.8%
Health Insurance: 96.8% have insurance; 92.1% have private insurance; 12.6% have public insurance; 3.2% do not have insurance; 2.0% of children under 18 do not have insurance
Newspapers: Zionsville Times Sentinel (weekly circulation 4,200)
Transportation: Commute: 89.5% car, 0.1% public transportation, 1.1% walk, 8.0% work from home; Mean travel time to work: 25.9 minutes
Airports: Indianapolis Executive (general aviation)
Additional Information Contacts
Town of Zionsville . . . . (317) 873-5410
http://www.zionsville-in.gov

Brown County

Located in south central Indiana; drained by Salt Creek and its north fork. Covers a land area of 311.981 square miles, a water area of 4.650 square miles, and is located in the Eastern Time Zone at 39.19° N. Lat., 86.24° W. Long. The county was founded in 1836. County seat is Nashville.

Brown County is part of the Indianapolis-Carmel-Anderson, IN Metropolitan Statistical Area. The entire metro area includes: Boone County, IN; Brown County, IN; Hamilton County, IN; Hancock County, IN; Hendricks County, IN; Johnson County, IN; Madison County, IN; Marion County, IN; Morgan County, IN; Putnam County, IN; Shelby County, IN

Population: 15,007; Growth (since 2000): 0.3%; Density: 48.1 persons per square mile; Race: 96.9% White, 0.5% Black/African American, 0.8% Asian, 0.0% American Indian/Alaska Native, 0.0% Native Hawaiian/Other Pacific Islander, 1.5% two or more races, 1.6% Hispanic of any race; Average household size: 2.47; Median age: 49.3; Age under 18: 18.5%; Age 65 and over: 23.0%; Males per 100 females: 98.5; Marriage status: 20.7% never married, 58.8% now married, 1.3% separated, 8.7% widowed, 11.8% divorced; Foreign born: 1.9%; Speak English only: 98.5%; With disability: 12.7%; Veterans: 13.7%; Ancestry: 21.2% German, 11.6% Irish, 11.6% American, 10.2% English, 4.2% Scottish
Religion: Six largest groups: 8.7% Baptist, 4.9% Catholicism, 3.3% Non-denominational Protestant, 3.1% Methodist/Pietist, 1.9% Holiness, 0.4% Presbyterian-Reformed
Economy: Unemployment rate: 3.2%; Leading industries: 20.6 % retail trade; 13.1 % construction; 11.7 % accommodation and food services; Farms: 173 totaling 14,590 acres; Company size: 0 employ 1,000 or more persons, 0 employ 500 to 999 persons, 2 employ 100 to 499 persons, 348 employ less than 100 persons; Business ownership: 665 women-owned, n/a Black-owned, n/a Hispanic-owned, n/a Asian-owned, n/a American Indian/Alaska Native-owned
Employment: 12.0% management, business, and financial, 3.3% computer, engineering, and science, 11.3% education, legal, community service, arts, and media, 6.7% healthcare practitioners, 15.2% service, 24.5% sales and office, 11.5% natural resources, construction, and maintenance, 15.4% production, transportation, and material moving

Income: Per capita: $31,365; Median household: $59,292; Average household: $76,047; Households with income of $100,000 or more: 23.3%; Poverty rate: 10.6%
Educational Attainment: High school diploma or higher: 90.0%; Bachelor's degree or higher: 25.5%; Graduate/professional degree or higher: 12.8%
Housing: Homeownership rate: 83.5%; Median home value: $174,800; Median year structure built: 1983; Homeowner vacancy rate: 2.9%; Median selected monthly owner costs: $1,299 with a mortgage, $455 without a mortgage; Median gross rent: $886 per month; Rental vacancy rate: 7.5%
Vital Statistics: Birth rate: 80.5 per 10,000 population; Death rate: 91.8 per 10,000 population; Age-adjusted cancer mortality rate: 177.6 deaths per 100,000 population
Health Insurance: 89.9% have insurance; 67.5% have private insurance; 38.6% have public insurance; 10.1% do not have insurance; 2.5% of children under 18 do not have insurance
Health Care: Physicians: 8.7 per 10,000 population; Dentists: 1.3 per 10,000 population; Hospital beds: 0.0 per 10,000 population; Hospital admissions: 0.0 per 10,000 population
Air Quality Index (AQI): Percent of Days: 88.8% good, 11.2% moderate, 0.0% unhealthy for sensitive individuals, 0.0% unhealthy, 0.0% very unhealthy; Annual median: 39; Annual maximum: 90
Transportation: Commute: 93.9% car, 0.2% public transportation, 1.1% walk, 4.5% work from home; Mean travel time to work: 33.3 minutes
2016 Presidential Election: 63.1% Trump, 31.7% Clinton, 4.7% Johnson, 0.4% Stein
National and State Parks: Brown County State Park; Middle Fork State Wildlife Refuge; TC Steele State Memorial; Yellowwood State Forest
Additional Information Contacts
Brown Government . . . . (812) 988-7064
http://www.browncounty-in.gov

Brown County Communities

CORDRY SWEETWATER LAKES (CDP). Covers a land area of 2.755 square miles and a water area of 0.644 square miles. Located at 39.31° N. Lat; 86.12° W. Long. Elevation is 919 feet.
Population: 1,108; Growth (since 2000): n/a; Density: 402.2 persons per square mile; Race: 96.7% White, 0.0% Black/African American, 0.0% Asian, 0.0% American Indian/Alaska Native, 0.0% Native Hawaiian/Other Pacific Islander, 3.3% Two or more races, 0.0% Hispanic of any race; Average household size: 2.29; Median age: 60.9; Age under 18: 13.3%; Age 65 and over: 38.4%; Males per 100 females: 100.0; Marriage status: 13.4% never married, 67.8% now married, 0.0% separated, 6.0% widowed, 12.7% divorced; Foreign born: 1.1%; Speak English only: 100.0%; With disability: 8.8%; Veterans: 21.6%; Ancestry: 19.0% German, 17.6% English, 17.1% American, 9.3% Irish, 6.9% Polish
Employment: 6.6% management, business, and financial, 4.1% computer, engineering, and science, 14.9% education, legal, community service, arts, and media, 7.1% healthcare practitioners, 14.4% service, 28.0% sales and office, 19.3% natural resources, construction, and maintenance, 5.6% production, transportation, and material moving
Income: Per capita: $48,516; Median household: $69,013; Average household: $107,069; Households with income of $100,000 or more: 42.7%; Poverty rate: 3.4%
Educational Attainment: High school diploma or higher: 87.7%; Bachelor's degree or higher: 39.3%; Graduate/professional degree or higher: 18.1%
Housing: Homeownership rate: 94.0%; Median home value: $282,400; Median year structure built: 1981; Homeowner vacancy rate: 7.7%; Median selected monthly owner costs: $1,633 with a mortgage, $552 without a mortgage; Median gross rent: n/a per month; Rental vacancy rate: 0.0%
Health Insurance: 95.1% have insurance; 74.0% have private insurance; 44.9% have public insurance; 4.9% do not have insurance; 0.0% of children under 18 do not have insurance
Transportation: Commute: 100.0% car, 0.0% public transportation, 0.0% walk, 0.0% work from home; Mean travel time to work: 42.1 minutes

NASHVILLE (town). County seat. Covers a land area of 1.011 square miles and a water area of 0.005 square miles. Located at 39.21° N. Lat; 86.24° W. Long. Elevation is 594 feet.
History: Local tradition in Nashville tells of the Liars' Bench on the courthouse lawn which accommodated six tellers of tall and unlikely tales. When a bigger and better story was told by someone standing, one of the seated liars would be pushed off the end of the bench to make room for the bigger liar.
Population: 1,219; Growth (since 2000): 47.8%; Density: 1,206.2 persons per square mile; Race: 91.6% White, 2.9% Black/African American, 0.0% Asian, 0.0% American Indian/Alaska Native, 0.0% Native Hawaiian/Other Pacific Islander, 3.9% Two or more races, 4.9% Hispanic of any race; Average household size: 2.02; Median age: 55.4; Age under 18: 16.9%; Age 65 and over: 32.8%; Males per 100 females: 69.4; Marriage status: 23.4% never married, 45.4% now married, 1.2% separated, 12.2% widowed, 19.0% divorced; Foreign born: 3.3%; Speak English only: 94.7%; With disability: 13.3%; Veterans: 8.4%; Ancestry: 24.9% German, 11.6% Irish, 11.4% English, 7.3% American, 6.3% Polish
Employment: 17.6% management, business, and financial, 3.8% computer, engineering, and science, 18.1% education, legal, community service, arts, and media, 3.7% healthcare practitioners, 25.2% service, 17.6% sales and office, 4.6% natural resources, construction, and maintenance, 9.3% production, transportation, and material moving
Income: Per capita: $28,244; Median household: $44,167; Average household: $58,204; Households with income of $100,000 or more: 14.0%; Poverty rate: 18.9%
Educational Attainment: High school diploma or higher: 92.0%; Bachelor's degree or higher: 30.7%; Graduate/professional degree or higher: 19.0%

School District(s)
Brown County School Corporation (PK-12)
Enrollment: 2,107 . . . . (812) 988-6601
Housing: Homeownership rate: 45.5%; Median home value: $164,500; Median year structure built: 1970; Homeowner vacancy rate: 3.0%; Median selected monthly owner costs: $1,272 with a mortgage, $372 without a mortgage; Median gross rent: $813 per month; Rental vacancy rate: 5.5%
Health Insurance: 84.0% have insurance; 67.0% have private insurance; 34.8% have public insurance; 16.0% do not have insurance; 4.4% of children under 18 do not have insurance
Newspapers: Brown County Democrat (weekly circulation 4,400)
Transportation: Commute: 81.8% car, 0.0% public transportation, 10.9% walk, 6.8% work from home; Mean travel time to work: 20.1 minutes

NINEVEH (unincorporated postal area)
ZCTA: 46164
Covers a land area of 23.488 square miles and a water area of 0.928 square miles. Located at 39.32° N. Lat; 86.11° W. Long..
Population: 4,127; Growth (since 2000): -0.1%; Density: 175.7 persons per square mile; Race: 97.2% White, 0.2% Black/African American, 0.0% Asian, 0.0% American Indian/Alaska Native, 0.0% Native Hawaiian/Other Pacific Islander, 2.0% Two or more races, 1.2% Hispanic of any race; Average household size: 2.50; Median age: 46.7; Age under 18: 17.6%; Age 65 and over: 20.9%; Males per 100 females: 100.8; Marriage status: 22.0% never married, 60.5% now married, 0.7% separated, 4.7% widowed, 12.8% divorced; Foreign born: 0.6%; Speak English only: 98.8%; With disability: 12.0%; Veterans: 13.7%; Ancestry: 18.4% German, 14.4% Irish, 14.1% English, 12.7% American, 5.2% French
Employment: 8.0% management, business, and financial, 9.4% computer, engineering, and science, 10.2% education, legal, community service, arts, and media, 6.3% healthcare practitioners, 17.7% service, 20.8% sales and office, 16.9% natural resources, construction, and maintenance, 10.7% production, transportation, and material moving
Income: Per capita: $34,737; Median household: $67,846; Average household: $85,275; Households with income of $100,000 or more: 27.3%; Poverty rate: 13.6%
Educational Attainment: High school diploma or higher: 89.5%; Bachelor's degree or higher: 24.9%; Graduate/professional degree or higher: 9.0%

School District(s)
Brown County School Corporation (PK-12)
Enrollment: 2,107 . . . . (812) 988-6601
Housing: Homeownership rate: 88.7%; Median home value: $159,100; Median year structure built: 1978; Homeowner vacancy rate: 3.3%; Median selected monthly owner costs: $1,261 with a mortgage, $500 without a mortgage; Median gross rent: $885 per month; Rental vacancy rate: 1.6%
Health Insurance: 90.2% have insurance; 70.9% have private insurance; 35.2% have public insurance; 9.8% do not have insurance; 3.0% of children under 18 do not have insurance

Transportation: Commute: 98.3% car, 0.0% public transportation, 1.1% walk, 0.4% work from home; Mean travel time to work: 35.3 minutes

Carroll County

Located in northwest central Indiana; crossed by the Wabash River; drained by the Tippecanoe River. Covers a land area of 372.224 square miles, a water area of 2.795 square miles, and is located in the Eastern Time Zone at 40.58° N. Lat., 86.57° W. Long. The county was founded in 1828. County seat is Delphi.

Carroll County is part of the Lafayette-West Lafayette, IN Metropolitan Statistical Area. The entire metro area includes: Benton County, IN; Carroll County, IN; Tippecanoe County, IN

Weather Station: Delphi 3 S Elevation: 670 feet

	Jan	Feb	Mar	Apr	May	Jun	Jul	Aug	Sep	Oct	Nov	Dec
High	35	39	51	64	74	83	85	84	78	66	52	38
Low	19	22	31	41	51	60	63	61	53	43	35	24
Precip	2.2	2.1	2.8	3.5	4.4	4.0	4.6	3.7	2.7	3.0	3.1	2.6
Snow	5.6	4.8	2.4	0.6	tr	0.0	0.0	0.0	0.0	0.2	0.5	4.6

High and Low temperatures in degrees Fahrenheit; Precipitation and Snow in inches

Population: 19,994; Growth (since 2000): -0.8%; Density: 53.7 persons per square mile; Race: 96.3% White, 0.5% Black/African American, 0.1% Asian, 0.3% American Indian/Alaska Native, 0.0% Native Hawaiian/Other Pacific Islander, 1.2% two or more races, 3.9% Hispanic of any race; Average household size: 2.54; Median age: 42.3; Age under 18: 23.0%; Age 65 and over: 18.3%; Males per 100 females: 100.4; Marriage status: 23.2% never married, 59.4% now married, 0.5% separated, 5.9% widowed, 11.4% divorced; Foreign born: 2.7%; Speak English only: 96.3%; With disability: 15.3%; Veterans: 9.7%; Ancestry: 21.4% German, 12.2% American, 11.8% Irish, 9.1% English, 3.0% Dutch

Religion: Six largest groups: 9.3% Catholicism, 8.7% Baptist, 7.2% Methodist/Pietist, 3.2% Pentecostal, 2.9% Presbyterian-Reformed, 2.8% Non-denominational Protestant

Economy: Unemployment rate: 3.5%; Leading industries: 18.4 % construction; 13.8 % retail trade; 11.4 % other services (except public administration); Farms: 491 totaling 204,090 acres; Company size: 1 employs 1,000 or more persons, 0 employ 500 to 999 persons, 1 employs 100 to 499 persons, 383 employ less than 100 persons; Business ownership: 262 women-owned, n/a Black-owned, 28 Hispanic-owned, n/a Asian-owned, n/a American Indian/Alaska Native-owned

Employment: 11.6% management, business, and financial, 2.3% computer, engineering, and science, 7.3% education, legal, community service, arts, and media, 5.1% healthcare practitioners, 14.7% service, 19.6% sales and office, 13.1% natural resources, construction, and maintenance, 26.3% production, transportation, and material moving

Income: Per capita: $26,589; Median household: $56,188; Average household: $66,571; Households with income of $100,000 or more: 20.6%; Poverty rate: 10.2%

Educational Attainment: High school diploma or higher: 88.6%; Bachelor's degree or higher: 16.2%; Graduate/professional degree or higher: 5.2%

Housing: Homeownership rate: 81.7%; Median home value: $124,100; Median year structure built: 1961; Homeowner vacancy rate: 1.2%; Median selected monthly owner costs: $1,001 with a mortgage, $362 without a mortgage; Median gross rent: $680 per month; Rental vacancy rate: 5.1%

Vital Statistics: Birth rate: 94.8 per 10,000 population; Death rate: 93.8 per 10,000 population; Age-adjusted cancer mortality rate: 115.5 deaths per 100,000 population

Health Insurance: 89.1% have insurance; 73.1% have private insurance; 30.8% have public insurance; 10.9% do not have insurance; 10.6% of children under 18 do not have insurance

Health Care: Physicians: 1.5 per 10,000 population; Dentists: 4.0 per 10,000 population; Hospital beds: 0.0 per 10,000 population; Hospital admissions: 0.0 per 10,000 population

Air Quality Index (AQI): Percent of Days: 90.5% good, 9.5% moderate, 0.0% unhealthy for sensitive individuals, 0.0% unhealthy, 0.0% very unhealthy; Annual median: 39; Annual maximum: 77

Transportation: Commute: 93.5% car, 0.1% public transportation, 1.3% walk, 4.1% work from home; Mean travel time to work: 28.4 minutes

2016 Presidential Election: 72.6% Trump, 21.9% Clinton, 5.1% Johnson, 0.3% Stein

Additional Information Contacts

Carroll Government. . . . . (765) 564-3172
http://www.carrollcountygovernment.org

Carroll County Communities

BRINGHURST (unincorporated postal area)
ZCTA: 46913

Covers a land area of 32.901 square miles and a water area of 0 square miles. Located at 40.50° N. Lat; 86.50° W. Long. Elevation is 722 feet.

Population: 1,204; Growth (since 2000): -12.7%; Density: 36.6 persons per square mile; Race: 98.6% White, 0.0% Black/African American, 0.0% Asian, 0.0% American Indian/Alaska Native, 0.0% Native Hawaiian/Other Pacific Islander, 1.4% Two or more races, 1.4% Hispanic of any race; Average household size: 2.75; Median age: 48.3; Age under 18: 20.4%; Age 65 and over: 17.4%; Males per 100 females: 113.7; Marriage status: 16.4% never married, 75.5% now married, 0.0% separated, 2.4% widowed, 5.7% divorced; Foreign born: 0.0%; Speak English only: 99.1%; With disability: 15.3%; Veterans: 9.2%; Ancestry: 26.2% German, 18.9% Irish, 18.8% American, 11.5% English, 8.6% Polish

Employment: 8.3% management, business, and financial, 3.3% computer, engineering, and science, 9.3% education, legal, community service, arts, and media, 9.6% healthcare practitioners, 5.2% service, 18.2% sales and office, 22.2% natural resources, construction, and maintenance, 23.9% production, transportation, and material moving

Income: Per capita: $30,117; Median household: $65,833; Average household: $81,600; Households with income of $100,000 or more: 30.8%; Poverty rate: 3.6%

Educational Attainment: High school diploma or higher: 93.9%; Bachelor's degree or higher: 17.2%; Graduate/professional degree or higher: 6.1%

Housing: Homeownership rate: 90.9%; Median home value: $137,900; Median year structure built: 1949; Homeowner vacancy rate: 0.0%; Median selected monthly owner costs: $1,265 with a mortgage, $369 without a mortgage; Median gross rent: $623 per month; Rental vacancy rate: 0.0%

Health Insurance: 95.3% have insurance; 88.7% have private insurance; 22.3% have public insurance; 4.7% do not have insurance; 5.5% of children under 18 do not have insurance

Transportation: Commute: 97.5% car, 0.0% public transportation, 0.3% walk, 2.2% work from home; Mean travel time to work: 29.1 minutes

BURLINGTON (town). Covers a land area of 0.596 square miles and a water area of 0 square miles. Located at 40.48° N. Lat; 86.39° W. Long. Elevation is 784 feet.

History: Burlington was founded in 1832 as a stagecoach and tavern stop on the Michigan Road. It was named for Wyandotte Chief Burlington.

Population: 549; Growth (since 2000): 23.6%; Density: 921.3 persons per square mile; Race: 100.0% White, 0.0% Black/African American, 0.0% Asian, 0.0% American Indian/Alaska Native, 0.0% Native Hawaiian/Other Pacific Islander, 0.0% Two or more races, 0.0% Hispanic of any race; Average household size: 2.28; Median age: 43.3; Age under 18: 22.8%; Age 65 and over: 19.5%; Males per 100 females: 84.4; Marriage status: 19.8% never married, 54.7% now married, 0.5% separated, 8.3% widowed, 17.1% divorced; Foreign born: 0.4%; Speak English only: 100.0%; With disability: 14.6%; Veterans: 11.6%; Ancestry: 30.8% German, 15.8% American, 10.9% Irish, 9.7% English, 8.9% French

Employment: 11.6% management, business, and financial, 1.5% computer, engineering, and science, 4.5% education, legal, community service, arts, and media, 9.7% healthcare practitioners, 9.7% service, 27.3% sales and office, 17.6% natural resources, construction, and maintenance, 18.0% production, transportation, and material moving

Income: Per capita: $27,017; Median household: $56,094; Average household: $60,411; Households with income of $100,000 or more: 14.9%; Poverty rate: 3.8%

Educational Attainment: High school diploma or higher: 98.3%; Bachelor's degree or higher: 17.8%; Graduate/professional degree or higher: 5.0%

Housing: Homeownership rate: 80.5%; Median home value: $105,100; Median year structure built: 1955; Homeowner vacancy rate: 0.0%; Median selected monthly owner costs: $819 with a mortgage, $292 without a mortgage; Median gross rent: $550 per month; Rental vacancy rate: 0.0%

Health Insurance: 94.0% have insurance; 81.1% have private insurance; 29.3% have public insurance; 6.0% do not have insurance; 0.0% of children under 18 do not have insurance

Transportation: Commute: 97.7% car, 0.0% public transportation, 1.2% walk, 0.8% work from home; Mean travel time to work: 28.0 minutes

CAMDEN (town). Covers a land area of 0.261 square miles and a water area of <.001 square miles. Located at 40.61° N. Lat; 86.54° W. Long. Elevation is 669 feet.
Population: 632; Growth (since 2000): 8.6%; Density: 2,420.4 persons per square mile; Race: 93.0% White, 0.0% Black/African American, 0.0% Asian, 0.0% American Indian/Alaska Native, 0.6% Native Hawaiian/Other Pacific Islander, 6.3% Two or more races, 1.1% Hispanic of any race; Average household size: 2.61; Median age: 36.3; Age under 18: 26.4%; Age 65 and over: 10.8%; Males per 100 females: 90.9; Marriage status: 26.8% never married, 51.5% now married, 0.0% separated, 8.5% widowed, 13.3% divorced; Foreign born: 1.1%; Speak English only: 96.6%; With disability: 21.4%; Veterans: 6.7%; Ancestry: 18.7% German, 10.3% American, 9.8% Irish, 3.2% English, 2.4% Dutch
Employment: 8.2% management, business, and financial, 1.3% computer, engineering, and science, 7.6% education, legal, community service, arts, and media, 4.4% healthcare practitioners, 16.5% service, 15.2% sales and office, 8.2% natural resources, construction, and maintenance, 38.6% production, transportation, and material moving
Income: Per capita: $21,280; Median household: $50,714; Average household: $54,359; Households with income of $100,000 or more: 15.7%; Poverty rate: 12.3%
Educational Attainment: High school diploma or higher: 92.5%; Bachelor's degree or higher: 9.0%; Graduate/professional degree or higher: 3.2%
Housing: Homeownership rate: 71.1%; Median home value: $80,900; Median year structure built: 1951; Homeowner vacancy rate: 5.8%; Median selected monthly owner costs: $991 with a mortgage, $300 without a mortgage; Median gross rent: $596 per month; Rental vacancy rate: 6.7%
Health Insurance: 94.1% have insurance; 75.6% have private insurance; 27.8% have public insurance; 5.9% do not have insurance; 0.0% of children under 18 do not have insurance
Transportation: Commute: 95.2% car, 0.0% public transportation, 2.9% walk, 0.6% work from home; Mean travel time to work: 29.4 minutes

CUTLER (unincorporated postal area)
ZCTA: 46920
Covers a land area of 31.474 square miles and a water area of 0 square miles. Located at 40.46° N. Lat; 86.49° W. Long. Elevation is 745 feet.
Population: 1,143; Growth (since 2000): -23.1%; Density: 36.3 persons per square mile; Race: 98.9% White, 0.0% Black/African American, 0.0% Asian, 0.0% American Indian/Alaska Native, 0.0% Native Hawaiian/Other Pacific Islander, 0.0% Two or more races, 0.0% Hispanic of any race; Average household size: 2.62; Median age: 39.5; Age under 18: 24.5%; Age 65 and over: 14.4%; Males per 100 females: 106.9; Marriage status: 18.7% never married, 74.7% now married, 0.0% separated, 1.0% widowed, 5.6% divorced; Foreign born: 0.8%; Speak English only: 97.8%; With disability: 14.2%; Veterans: 12.5%; Ancestry: 18.6% German, 9.0% American, 8.6% Irish, 6.8% English, 2.4% Czech
Employment: 6.8% management, business, and financial, 5.3% computer, engineering, and science, 8.5% education, legal, community service, arts, and media, 5.2% healthcare practitioners, 3.4% service, 17.3% sales and office, 14.1% natural resources, construction, and maintenance, 39.5% production, transportation, and material moving
Income: Per capita: $27,766; Median household: $61,761; Average household: $71,563; Households with income of $100,000 or more: 24.7%; Poverty rate: 7.8%
Educational Attainment: High school diploma or higher: 88.2%; Bachelor's degree or higher: 17.2%; Graduate/professional degree or higher: 4.8%
Housing: Homeownership rate: 96.8%; Median home value: $123,200; Median year structure built: 1972; Homeowner vacancy rate: 0.0%; Median selected monthly owner costs: $1,268 with a mortgage, $457 without a mortgage; Median gross rent: n/a per month; Rental vacancy rate: 0.0%
Health Insurance: 92.1% have insurance; 82.1% have private insurance; 20.0% have public insurance; 7.9% do not have insurance; 7.1% of children under 18 do not have insurance
Transportation: Commute: 92.7% car, 0.0% public transportation, 1.4% walk, 5.9% work from home; Mean travel time to work: 34.6 minutes

DELPHI (city). County seat. Covers a land area of 2.726 square miles and a water area of 0 square miles. Located at 40.58° N. Lat; 86.67° W. Long. Elevation is 568 feet.
History: Delphi was named by Samuel Milroy (1780-1845), a member of the State Constitutional Convention of 1816, who sold the first town lots in 1828. Poet James Whitcomb Riley was a resident here.
Population: 3,057; Growth (since 2000): 1.4%; Density: 1,121.5 persons per square mile; Race: 90.1% White, 1.2% Black/African American, 0.0% Asian, 0.9% American Indian/Alaska Native, 0.0% Native Hawaiian/Other Pacific Islander, 0.9% Two or more races, 18.8% Hispanic of any race; Average household size: 2.51; Median age: 39.4; Age under 18: 23.1%; Age 65 and over: 20.8%; Males per 100 females: 91.8; Marriage status: 27.4% never married, 44.6% now married, 1.6% separated, 12.1% widowed, 15.9% divorced; Foreign born: 11.9%; Speak English only: 83.5%; With disability: 16.3%; Veterans: 6.7%; Ancestry: 21.2% German, 11.4% American, 9.1% Irish, 7.4% English, 4.9% Italian
Employment: 14.2% management, business, and financial, 1.8% computer, engineering, and science, 8.9% education, legal, community service, arts, and media, 2.6% healthcare practitioners, 14.9% service, 17.7% sales and office, 14.9% natural resources, construction, and maintenance, 25.1% production, transportation, and material moving
Income: Per capita: $21,870; Median household: $44,556; Average household: $53,438; Households with income of $100,000 or more: 15.4%; Poverty rate: 16.0%
Educational Attainment: High school diploma or higher: 79.5%; Bachelor's degree or higher: 17.7%; Graduate/professional degree or higher: 7.7%

School District(s)

Delphi Community School Corp (PK-12)
Enrollment: 1,477 .... (765) 564-2100
Housing: Homeownership rate: 69.9%; Median home value: $80,300; Median year structure built: 1950; Homeowner vacancy rate: 1.3%; Median selected monthly owner costs: $952 with a mortgage, $313 without a mortgage; Median gross rent: $696 per month; Rental vacancy rate: 3.9%
Health Insurance: 88.3% have insurance; 69.7% have private insurance; 35.1% have public insurance; 11.7% do not have insurance; 2.7% of children under 18 do not have insurance
Transportation: Commute: 93.9% car, 0.0% public transportation, 1.7% walk, 2.4% work from home; Mean travel time to work: 22.5 minutes
Additional Information Contacts
City of Delphi.. (765) 564-2097
http://www.cityofdelphi.org

FLORA (town). Covers a land area of 1.058 square miles and a water area of 0 square miles. Located at 40.55° N. Lat; 86.52° W. Long. Elevation is 705 feet.
History: Laid out 1872, incorporated 1898.
Population: 1,957; Growth (since 2000): -12.1%; Density: 1,849.5 persons per square mile; Race: 99.0% White, 0.8% Black/African American, 0.0% Asian, 0.0% American Indian/Alaska Native, 0.0% Native Hawaiian/Other Pacific Islander, 0.2% Two or more races, 0.8% Hispanic of any race; Average household size: 2.48; Median age: 37.7; Age under 18: 23.7%; Age 65 and over: 18.0%; Males per 100 females: 87.8; Marriage status: 20.9% never married, 58.2% now married, 0.4% separated, 6.5% widowed, 14.5% divorced; Foreign born: 0.9%; Speak English only: 98.6%; With disability: 14.6%; Veterans: 12.5%; Ancestry: 17.3% German, 14.8% Irish, 14.3% American, 10.1% English, 4.2% Polish
Employment: 7.9% management, business, and financial, 1.1% computer, engineering, and science, 5.7% education, legal, community service, arts, and media, 4.4% healthcare practitioners, 16.5% service, 23.1% sales and office, 8.7% natural resources, construction, and maintenance, 32.7% production, transportation, and material moving
Income: Per capita: $21,707; Median household: $47,778; Average household: $53,797; Households with income of $100,000 or more: 8.7%; Poverty rate: 14.2%
Educational Attainment: High school diploma or higher: 89.9%; Bachelor's degree or higher: 14.3%; Graduate/professional degree or higher: 4.2%

School District(s)

Carroll Consolidated School Corp (PK-12)
Enrollment: 1,111 .... (574) 967-4113
Housing: Homeownership rate: 71.4%; Median home value: $82,400; Median year structure built: 1954; Homeowner vacancy rate: 2.2%; Median selected monthly owner costs: $796 with a mortgage, $336 without a mortgage; Median gross rent: $578 per month; Rental vacancy rate: 20.7%

Health Insurance: 84.6% have insurance; 64.8% have private insurance; 36.4% have public insurance; 15.4% do not have insurance; 8.2% of children under 18 do not have insurance
Newspapers: Carroll County Comet (weekly circulation 5,000)
Transportation: Commute: 96.3% car, 0.0% public transportation, 3.7% walk, 0.0% work from home; Mean travel time to work: 31.1 minutes
Additional Information Contacts
Town of Flora . . . . (574) 967-4844
http://www.townofflora.org

YEOMAN (town). Covers a land area of 0.122 square miles and a water area of 0 square miles. Located at 40.67° N. Lat; 86.72° W. Long. Elevation is 663 feet.
History: Laid out 1880.
Population: 117; Growth (since 2000): 21.9%; Density: 961.0 persons per square mile; Race: 98.3% White, 0.9% Black/African American, 0.0% Asian, 0.0% American Indian/Alaska Native, 0.0% Native Hawaiian/Other Pacific Islander, 0.9% Two or more races, 1.7% Hispanic of any race; Average household size: 2.29; Median age: 39.2; Age under 18: 23.1%; Age 65 and over: 12.8%; Males per 100 females: 98.6; Marriage status: 35.1% never married, 36.2% now married, 1.1% separated, 6.4% widowed, 22.3% divorced; Foreign born: 0.0%; Speak English only: 98.1%; With disability: 4.3%; Veterans: 7.8%; Ancestry: 17.1% German, 5.1% English, 3.4% Irish, 2.6% American, 1.7% Dutch
Employment: 9.5% management, business, and financial, 9.5% computer, engineering, and science, 0.0% education, legal, community service, arts, and media, 9.5% healthcare practitioners, 28.6% service, 7.9% sales and office, 9.5% natural resources, construction, and maintenance, 25.4% production, transportation, and material moving
Income: Per capita: $28,738; Median household: $52,083; Average household: $66,135; Households with income of $100,000 or more: 25.5%; Poverty rate: 11.1%
Educational Attainment: High school diploma or higher: 81.7%; Bachelor's degree or higher: 14.6%; Graduate/professional degree or higher: 8.5%
Housing: Homeownership rate: 82.4%; Median home value: $84,300; Median year structure built: 1944; Homeowner vacancy rate: 0.0%; Median selected monthly owner costs: $820 with a mortgage, $283 without a mortgage; Median gross rent: $665 per month; Rental vacancy rate: 0.0%
Health Insurance: 93.2% have insurance; 71.8% have private insurance; 35.9% have public insurance; 6.8% do not have insurance; 0.0% of children under 18 do not have insurance
Transportation: Commute: 93.4% car, 0.0% public transportation, 0.0% walk, 6.6% work from home; Mean travel time to work: 26.8 minutes

Cass County

Located in north central Indiana; intersected by the Wabash River; drained by the Eel River and Deer Creek. Covers a land area of 412.155 square miles, a water area of 2.693 square miles, and is located in the Eastern Time Zone at 40.75° N. Lat., 86.36° W. Long. The county was founded in 1828. County seat is Logansport.

Cass County is part of the Logansport, IN Micropolitan Statistical Area. The entire metro area includes: Cass County, IN

Population: 38,248; Growth (since 2000): -6.6%; Density: 92.8 persons per square mile; Race: 83.3% White, 1.4% Black/African American, 1.6% Asian, 0.4% American Indian/Alaska Native, 0.1% Native Hawaiian/Other Pacific Islander, 2.6% two or more races, 14.6% Hispanic of any race; Average household size: 2.50; Median age: 40.5; Age under 18: 23.7%; Age 65 and over: 16.8%; Males per 100 females: 99.9; Marriage status: 27.3% never married, 53.2% now married, 1.4% separated, 6.9% widowed, 12.6% divorced; Foreign born: 9.1%; Speak English only: 84.7%; With disability: 15.3%; Veterans: 8.8%; Ancestry: 22.1% German, 12.7% American, 9.6% Irish, 6.6% English, 3.0% Italian
Religion: Six largest groups: 11.8% Catholicism, 8.1% Methodist/Pietist, 7.3% Baptist, 4.7% Non-denominational Protestant, 3.4% Pentecostal, 2.6% Holiness
Economy: Unemployment rate: 4.7%; Leading industries: 17.0 % retail trade; 13.9 % other services (except public administration); 10.4 % accommodation and food services; Farms: 688 totaling 200,257 acres; Company size: 1 employs 1,000 or more persons, 2 employ 500 to 999 persons, 21 employs 100 to 499 persons, 680 employ less than 100 persons; Business ownership: 743 women-owned, n/a Black-owned, 67 Hispanic-owned, n/a Asian-owned, n/a American Indian/Alaska Native-owned
Employment: 9.6% management, business, and financial, 1.5% computer, engineering, and science, 6.5% education, legal, community service, arts, and media, 5.8% healthcare practitioners, 17.2% service, 18.6% sales and office, 11.0% natural resources, construction, and maintenance, 29.8% production, transportation, and material moving
Income: Per capita: $23,592; Median household: $45,558; Average household: $59,232; Households with income of $100,000 or more: 13.2%; Poverty rate: 13.9%
Educational Attainment: High school diploma or higher: 83.1%; Bachelor's degree or higher: 13.4%; Graduate/professional degree or higher: 4.4%
Housing: Homeownership rate: 73.8%; Median home value: $84,100; Median year structure built: 1951; Homeowner vacancy rate: 1.9%; Median selected monthly owner costs: $876 with a mortgage, $335 without a mortgage; Median gross rent: $640 per month; Rental vacancy rate: 4.9%
Vital Statistics: Birth rate: 124.5 per 10,000 population; Death rate: 107.6 per 10,000 population; Age-adjusted cancer mortality rate: 179.7 deaths per 100,000 population
Health Insurance: 88.1% have insurance; 68.6% have private insurance; 33.4% have public insurance; 11.9% do not have insurance; 7.4% of children under 18 do not have insurance
Health Care: Physicians: 11.0 per 10,000 population; Dentists: 2.4 per 10,000 population; Hospital beds: 66.6 per 10,000 population; Hospital admissions: 590.1 per 10,000 population
Transportation: Commute: 94.3% car, 0.6% public transportation, 1.5% walk, 2.2% work from home; Mean travel time to work: 20.6 minutes
2016 Presidential Election: 68.3% Trump, 26.5% Clinton, 4.8% Johnson, 0.3% Stein
Additional Information Contacts
Cass Government . . . . (219) 753-7720
http://www.co.cass.in.us

Cass County Communities

GALVESTON (town). Covers a land area of 0.525 square miles and a water area of 0 square miles. Located at 40.58° N. Lat; 86.19° W. Long. Elevation is 801 feet.
Population: 1,177; Growth (since 2000): -23.2%; Density: 2,242.5 persons per square mile; Race: 96.1% White, 0.0% Black/African American, 0.0% Asian, 2.5% American Indian/Alaska Native, 0.0% Native Hawaiian/Other Pacific Islander, 1.2% Two or more races, 1.3% Hispanic of any race; Average household size: 2.25; Median age: 42.7; Age under 18: 25.7%; Age 65 and over: 20.0%; Males per 100 females: 94.2; Marriage status: 18.5% never married, 56.4% now married, 2.6% separated, 5.7% widowed, 19.5% divorced; Foreign born: 0.3%; Speak English only: 98.1%; With disability: 15.6%; Veterans: 12.2%; Ancestry: 23.7% German, 15.1% American, 14.3% Irish, 8.5% English, 2.2% Polish
Employment: 4.4% management, business, and financial, 2.3% computer, engineering, and science, 8.7% education, legal, community service, arts, and media, 9.1% healthcare practitioners, 18.0% service, 19.9% sales and office, 2.0% natural resources, construction, and maintenance, 35.6% production, transportation, and material moving
Income: Per capita: $24,968; Median household: $46,563; Average household: $55,193; Households with income of $100,000 or more: 10.4%; Poverty rate: 11.2%
Educational Attainment: High school diploma or higher: 94.9%; Bachelor's degree or higher: 15.8%; Graduate/professional degree or higher: 5.5%

School District(s)
Southeastern School Corp (KG-12)
Enrollment: 1,320 . . . . (574) 626-2525
Housing: Homeownership rate: 81.5%; Median home value: $91,600; Median year structure built: 1959; Homeowner vacancy rate: 3.3%; Median selected monthly owner costs: $958 with a mortgage, $382 without a mortgage; Median gross rent: $729 per month; Rental vacancy rate: 19.8%
Health Insurance: 94.2% have insurance; 75.8% have private insurance; 34.2% have public insurance; 5.8% do not have insurance; 5.1% of children under 18 do not have insurance
Transportation: Commute: 91.5% car, 0.0% public transportation, 1.9% walk, 2.1% work from home; Mean travel time to work: 23.7 minutes

LOGANSPORT (city). County seat. Covers a land area of 8.748 square miles and a water area of 0.222 square miles. Located at 40.75° N. Lat; 86.36° W. Long. Elevation is 640 feet.

History: Logansport began as a trading post situated at the junction of the Wabash and Eel Rivers. The first permanent settler was Alexander Chamberlain, who built the Log Pioneer Inn in 1828.

Population: 18,169; Growth (since 2000): -7.7%; Density: 2,077.0 persons per square mile; Race: 71.0% White, 2.2% Black/African American, 2.2% Asian, 0.3% American Indian/Alaska Native, 0.2% Native Hawaiian/Other Pacific Islander, 4.0% Two or more races, 27.0% Hispanic of any race; Average household size: 2.55; Median age: 35.4; Age under 18: 26.0%; Age 65 and over: 14.3%; Males per 100 females: 97.2; Marriage status: 33.3% never married, 44.6% now married, 1.7% separated, 7.2% widowed, 14.9% divorced; Foreign born: 16.4%; Speak English only: 73.2%; With disability: 15.2%; Veterans: 6.9%; Ancestry: 19.2% German, 9.7% American, 7.4% Irish, 5.4% English, 3.5% Italian

Employment: 6.5% management, business, and financial, 0.7% computer, engineering, and science, 5.4% education, legal, community service, arts, and media, 5.7% healthcare practitioners, 16.9% service, 17.2% sales and office, 11.1% natural resources, construction, and maintenance, 36.5% production, transportation, and material moving

Income: Per capita: $18,442; Median household: $35,603; Average household: $46,665; Households with income of $100,000 or more: 8.6%; Poverty rate: 18.3%

Educational Attainment: High school diploma or higher: 74.2%; Bachelor's degree or higher: 10.9%; Graduate/professional degree or higher: 3.3%

School District(s)

Indiana Department Of Corrections (07-12)
Enrollment: 391 . . . . (317) 233-3111

Logansport Community Sch Corp (PK-12)
Enrollment: 4,292 . . . . (574) 722-2911

Housing: Homeownership rate: 59.8%; Median home value: $65,400; Median year structure built: Before 1940; Homeowner vacancy rate: 1.4%; Median selected monthly owner costs: $812 with a mortgage, $299 without a mortgage; Median gross rent: $631 per month; Rental vacancy rate: 4.7%

Health Insurance: 83.2% have insurance; 59.5% have private insurance; 34.6% have public insurance; 16.8% do not have insurance; 10.2% of children under 18 do not have insurance

Hospitals: Memorial Hospital (104 beds)

Safety: Violent crime rate: 13.6 per 10,000 population; Property crime rate: 372.9 per 10,000 population

Newspapers: Pharos-Tribune (daily circulation 9,300)

Transportation: Commute: 94.4% car, 1.0% public transportation, 2.1% walk, 0.6% work from home; Mean travel time to work: 18.4 minutes

Additional Information Contacts

City of Logansport . . . . (574) 753-4745
http://www.cityoflogansport.org

LUCERNE (unincorporated postal area)
ZCTA: 46950

Covers a land area of 28.105 square miles and a water area of 0.002 square miles. Located at 40.89° N. Lat; 86.36° W. Long. Elevation is 801 feet.

Population: 726; Growth (since 2000): 9.2%; Density: 25.8 persons per square mile; Race: 99.0% White, 1.0% Black/African American, 0.0% Asian, 0.0% American Indian/Alaska Native, 0.0% Native Hawaiian/Other Pacific Islander, 0.0% Two or more races, 0.0% Hispanic of any race; Average household size: 2.61; Median age: 46.0; Age under 18: 24.8%; Age 65 and over: 23.6%; Males per 100 females: 96.6; Marriage status: 25.1% never married, 62.2% now married, 0.0% separated, 8.3% widowed, 4.4% divorced; Foreign born: 0.0%; Speak English only: 98.0%; With disability: 25.2%; Veterans: 11.4%; Ancestry: 27.5% American, 25.9% Irish, 24.7% German, 7.6% English, 4.0% Italian

Employment: 5.6% management, business, and financial, 2.5% computer, engineering, and science, 7.7% education, legal, community service, arts, and media, 0.0% healthcare practitioners, 26.1% service, 13.7% sales and office, 7.7% natural resources, construction, and maintenance, 36.6% production, transportation, and material moving

Income: Per capita: $21,864; Median household: $50,375; Average household: $56,109; Households with income of $100,000 or more: 10.1%; Poverty rate: 5.8%

Educational Attainment: High school diploma or higher: 97.0%; Bachelor's degree or higher: 15.7%; Graduate/professional degree or higher: 2.1%

Housing: Homeownership rate: 88.1%; Median home value: $87,900; Median year structure built: 1953; Homeowner vacancy rate: 0.0%; Median selected monthly owner costs: $850 with a mortgage, $306 without a mortgage; Median gross rent: $731 per month; Rental vacancy rate: 0.0%

Health Insurance: 90.9% have insurance; 74.5% have private insurance; 39.7% have public insurance; 9.1% do not have insurance; 0.0% of children under 18 do not have insurance

Transportation: Commute: 94.2% car, 0.0% public transportation, 0.0% walk, 5.8% work from home; Mean travel time to work: 23.1 minutes

NEW WAVERLY (unincorporated postal area)
ZCTA: 46961

Covers a land area of 0.484 square miles and a water area of 0 square miles. Located at 40.77° N. Lat; 86.19° W. Long. Elevation is 682 feet.

Population: 137; Growth (since 2000): 71.3%; Density: 282.9 persons per square mile; Race: 100.0% White, 0.0% Black/African American, 0.0% Asian, 0.0% American Indian/Alaska Native, 0.0% Native Hawaiian/Other Pacific Islander, 0.0% Two or more races, 0.0% Hispanic of any race; Average household size: 1.51; Median age: 35.8; Age under 18: 9.5%; Age 65 and over: 7.3%; Males per 100 females: 125.0; Marriage status: 54.6% never married, 22.3% now married, 0.0% separated, 7.7% widowed, 15.4% divorced; Foreign born: 0.0%; Speak English only: 100.0%; With disability: 0.0%; Veterans: 0.0%; Ancestry: 12.4% German, 12.4% Irish

Employment: 0.0% management, business, and financial, 0.0% computer, engineering, and science, 0.0% education, legal, community service, arts, and media, 24.8% healthcare practitioners, 0.0% service, 33.3% sales and office, 5.7% natural resources, construction, and maintenance, 36.2% production, transportation, and material moving

Income: Per capita: $26,478; Median household: $31,743; Average household: $39,864; Households with income of $100,000 or more: 6.6%; Poverty rate: 7.3%

Educational Attainment: High school diploma or higher: 90.6%; Bachelor's degree or higher: 5.7%; Graduate/professional degree or higher: n/a

Housing: Homeownership rate: 68.1%; Median home value: n/a; Median year structure built: Before 1940; Homeowner vacancy rate: 0.0%; Median selected monthly owner costs: $0 with a mortgage, $0 without a mortgage; Median gross rent: n/a per month; Rental vacancy rate: 0.0%

Health Insurance: 86.9% have insurance; 86.9% have private insurance; 7.3% have public insurance; 13.1% do not have insurance; 0.0% of children under 18 do not have insurance

Transportation: Commute: 100.0% car, 0.0% public transportation, 0.0% walk, 0.0% work from home; Mean travel time to work: 13.5 minutes

ONWARD (town). Covers a land area of 0.099 square miles and a water area of 0 square miles. Located at 40.69° N. Lat; 86.20° W. Long. Elevation is 768 feet.

Population: 115; Growth (since 2000): 42.0%; Density: 1,166.4 persons per square mile; Race: 98.3% White, 0.0% Black/African American, 0.0% Asian, 0.0% American Indian/Alaska Native, 0.0% Native Hawaiian/Other Pacific Islander, 1.7% Two or more races, 0.0% Hispanic of any race; Average household size: 2.17; Median age: 45.9; Age under 18: 17.4%; Age 65 and over: 23.5%; Males per 100 females: 104.1; Marriage status: 23.8% never married, 64.4% now married, 0.0% separated, 5.9% widowed, 5.9% divorced; Foreign born: 0.0%; Speak English only: 95.5%; With disability: 17.4%; Veterans: 18.9%; Ancestry: 24.3% German, 7.0% American, 6.1% English, 4.3% French, 3.5% Irish

Employment: 2.3% management, business, and financial, 0.0% computer, engineering, and science, 0.0% education, legal, community service, arts, and media, 0.0% healthcare practitioners, 18.6% service, 30.2% sales and office, 16.3% natural resources, construction, and maintenance, 32.6% production, transportation, and material moving

Income: Per capita: $18,470; Median household: $29,583; Average household: $38,147; Households with income of $100,000 or more: 1.9%; Poverty rate: 20.9%

Educational Attainment: High school diploma or higher: 94.3%; Bachelor's degree or higher: 8.0%; Graduate/professional degree or higher: n/a

Housing: Homeownership rate: 62.3%; Median home value: n/a; Median year structure built: Before 1940; Homeowner vacancy rate: 0.0%; Median selected monthly owner costs: $850 with a mortgage, $313 without a mortgage; Median gross rent: $506 per month; Rental vacancy rate: 0.0%
Health Insurance: 85.2% have insurance; 50.4% have private insurance; 46.1% have public insurance; 14.8% do not have insurance; 9.5% of children under 18 do not have insurance
Transportation: Commute: 95.1% car, 0.0% public transportation, 2.4% walk, 0.0% work from home; Mean travel time to work: 21.0 minutes

ROYAL CENTER (town). Covers a land area of 0.596 square miles and a water area of 0 square miles. Located at 40.86° N. Lat; 86.50° W. Long. Elevation is 735 feet.
History: Laid out 1846.
Population: 904; Growth (since 2000): 8.7%; Density: 1,518.0 persons per square mile; Race: 92.1% White, 0.9% Black/African American, 0.4% Asian, 1.0% American Indian/Alaska Native, 0.0% Native Hawaiian/Other Pacific Islander, 2.4% Two or more races, 4.1% Hispanic of any race; Average household size: 2.46; Median age: 34.9; Age under 18: 26.9%; Age 65 and over: 17.1%; Males per 100 females: 99.8; Marriage status: 24.7% never married, 50.5% now married, 0.3% separated, 8.3% widowed, 16.5% divorced; Foreign born: 1.1%; Speak English only: 98.7%; With disability: 12.1%; Veterans: 10.9%; Ancestry: 26.7% German, 15.7% American, 10.3% Irish, 5.4% English, 4.3% Swedish
Employment: 11.2% management, business, and financial, 2.0% computer, engineering, and science, 6.0% education, legal, community service, arts, and media, 5.7% healthcare practitioners, 14.2% service, 25.9% sales and office, 8.7% natural resources, construction, and maintenance, 26.4% production, transportation, and material moving
Income: Per capita: $19,408; Median household: $45,089; Average household: $47,762; Households with income of $100,000 or more: 7.1%; Poverty rate: 18.8%
Educational Attainment: High school diploma or higher: 91.5%; Bachelor's degree or higher: 12.2%; Graduate/professional degree or higher: 4.4%

School District(s)

Pioneer Regional School Corp (PK-12)
Enrollment: 942 . . . . (574) 643-2605
Housing: Homeownership rate: 83.1%; Median home value: $71,300; Median year structure built: 1949; Homeowner vacancy rate: 6.6%; Median selected monthly owner costs: $799 with a mortgage, $330 without a mortgage; Median gross rent: $670 per month; Rental vacancy rate: 16.2%
Health Insurance: 88.4% have insurance; 62.9% have private insurance; 37.9% have public insurance; 11.6% do not have insurance; 14.2% of children under 18 do not have insurance
Newspapers: Royal Centre Record (weekly circulation 1,000)
Transportation: Commute: 98.5% car, 0.0% public transportation, 0.5% walk, 0.0% work from home; Mean travel time to work: 24.9 minutes

TWELVE MILE (unincorporated postal area)
ZCTA: 46988

Covers a land area of 26.403 square miles and a water area of 0.029 square miles. Located at 40.88° N. Lat; 86.23° W. Long. Elevation is 794 feet.
Population: 1,028; Growth (since 2000): -6.9%; Density: 38.9 persons per square mile; Race: 98.4% White, 0.0% Black/African American, 0.0% Asian, 0.0% American Indian/Alaska Native, 0.0% Native Hawaiian/Other Pacific Islander, 1.6% Two or more races, 0.0% Hispanic of any race; Average household size: 2.81; Median age: 40.2; Age under 18: 26.1%; Age 65 and over: 18.3%; Males per 100 females: 99.8; Marriage status: 28.4% never married, 53.2% now married, 0.0% separated, 3.4% widowed, 15.0% divorced; Foreign born: 0.0%; Speak English only: 93.8%; With disability: 5.6%; Veterans: 5.3%; Ancestry: 34.4% German, 10.1% American, 9.6% English, 7.0% Irish, 4.1% Polish
Employment: 7.5% management, business, and financial, 0.0% computer, engineering, and science, 5.2% education, legal, community service, arts, and media, 8.7% healthcare practitioners, 20.0% service, 29.7% sales and office, 17.9% natural resources, construction, and maintenance, 11.0% production, transportation, and material moving
Income: Per capita: $39,333; Median household: $48,600; Average household: $108,502; Households with income of $100,000 or more: 12.3%; Poverty rate: 17.7%
Educational Attainment: High school diploma or higher: 86.9%; Bachelor's degree or higher: 11.0%; Graduate/professional degree or higher: 4.4%

Housing: Homeownership rate: 81.1%; Median home value: $85,900; Median year structure built: 1955; Homeowner vacancy rate: 0.0%; Median selected monthly owner costs: $978 with a mortgage, $467 without a mortgage; Median gross rent: $653 per month; Rental vacancy rate: 0.0%
Health Insurance: 83.3% have insurance; 63.1% have private insurance; 39.1% have public insurance; 16.7% do not have insurance; 3.4% of children under 18 do not have insurance
Transportation: Commute: 87.3% car, 0.0% public transportation, 0.0% walk, 12.7% work from home; Mean travel time to work: 28.5 minutes

WALTON (town). Covers a land area of 0.426 square miles and a water area of 0 square miles. Located at 40.66° N. Lat; 86.24° W. Long. Elevation is 771 feet.
History: Laid out 1852.
Population: 1,281; Growth (since 2000): 19.8%; Density: 3,005.0 persons per square mile; Race: 86.6% White, 0.0% Black/African American, 1.0% Asian, 0.0% American Indian/Alaska Native, 0.0% Native Hawaiian/Other Pacific Islander, 0.2% Two or more races, 18.5% Hispanic of any race; Average household size: 2.72; Median age: 32.2; Age under 18: 26.1%; Age 65 and over: 12.3%; Males per 100 females: 87.3; Marriage status: 24.0% never married, 57.5% now married, 0.5% separated, 6.0% widowed, 12.5% divorced; Foreign born: 13.6%; Speak English only: 79.1%; With disability: 10.6%; Veterans: 5.9%; Ancestry: 19.1% German, 17.7% Irish, 11.9% American, 7.4% English, 3.3% French
Employment: 14.6% management, business, and financial, 1.8% computer, engineering, and science, 9.5% education, legal, community service, arts, and media, 1.8% healthcare practitioners, 24.0% service, 14.9% sales and office, 13.0% natural resources, construction, and maintenance, 20.5% production, transportation, and material moving
Income: Per capita: $20,470; Median household: $43,438; Average household: $54,792; Households with income of $100,000 or more: 15.1%; Poverty rate: 9.2%
Educational Attainment: High school diploma or higher: 84.9%; Bachelor's degree or higher: 13.4%; Graduate/professional degree or higher: 5.3%

School District(s)

Southeastern School Corp (KG-12)
Enrollment: 1,320 . . . . (574) 626-2525
Housing: Homeownership rate: 68.2%; Median home value: $73,400; Median year structure built: 1954; Homeowner vacancy rate: 1.8%; Median selected monthly owner costs: $775 with a mortgage, $338 without a mortgage; Median gross rent: $665 per month; Rental vacancy rate: 0.0%
Health Insurance: 93.1% have insurance; 70.0% have private insurance; 35.3% have public insurance; 6.9% do not have insurance; 5.1% of children under 18 do not have insurance
Transportation: Commute: 95.6% car, 0.0% public transportation, 2.7% walk, 0.9% work from home; Mean travel time to work: 19.2 minutes

YOUNG AMERICA (unincorporated postal area)
ZCTA: 46998

Covers a land area of 0.082 square miles and a water area of 0 square miles. Located at 40.57° N. Lat; 86.35° W. Long. Elevation is 768 feet.
Population: 133; Growth (since 2000): 15.7%; Density: 1,628.4 persons per square mile; Race: 100.0% White, 0.0% Black/African American, 0.0% Asian, 0.0% American Indian/Alaska Native, 0.0% Native Hawaiian/Other Pacific Islander, 0.0% Two or more races, 0.0% Hispanic of any race; Average household size: 2.42; Median age: 51.2; Age under 18: 5.3%; Age 65 and over: 0.0%; Males per 100 females: 72.3; Marriage status: 0.0% never married, 81.7% now married, 0.0% separated, 4.8% widowed, 13.5% divorced; Foreign born: 0.0%; Speak English only: 94.0%; With disability: 12.0%; Veterans: 13.5%; Ancestry: 24.1% German, 15.8% English, 6.8% Polish, 6.0% Irish
Employment: 23.4% management, business, and financial, 0.0% computer, engineering, and science, 8.5% education, legal, community service, arts, and media, 0.0% healthcare practitioners, 0.0% service, 24.5% sales and office, 23.4% natural resources, construction, and maintenance, 20.2% production, transportation, and material moving
Income: Per capita: $24,809; Median household: $59,034; Average household: $57,064; Households with income of $100,000 or more: n/a; Poverty rate: 6.8%
Educational Attainment: High school diploma or higher: 82.5%; Bachelor's degree or higher: n/a; Graduate/professional degree or higher: n/a

Housing: Homeownership rate: 85.5%; Median home value: $45,700; Median year structure built: Before 1940; Homeowner vacancy rate: 0.0%; Median selected monthly owner costs: $0 with a mortgage, $0 without a mortgage; Median gross rent: n/a per month; Rental vacancy rate: 0.0%
Health Insurance: 100.0% have insurance; 82.0% have private insurance; 22.6% have public insurance; 0.0% do not have insurance; 0.0% of children under 18 do not have insurance
Transportation: Commute: 76.6% car, 0.0% public transportation, 0.0% walk, 23.4% work from home; Mean travel time to work: 0.0 minutes

Clark County

Located in southeastern Indiana; bounded on the southeast by the Ohio River and the Kentucky border; drained by Silver Creek. Covers a land area of 372.855 square miles, a water area of 3.596 square miles, and is located in the Eastern Time Zone at 38.48° N. Lat., 85.71° W. Long. The county was founded in 1801. County seat is Jeffersonville.

Clark County is part of the Louisville/Jefferson County, KY-IN Metropolitan Statistical Area. The entire metro area includes: Clark County, IN; Floyd County, IN; Harrison County, IN; Scott County, IN; Washington County, IN; Bullitt County, KY; Henry County, KY; Jefferson County, KY; Oldham County, KY; Shelby County, KY; Spencer County, KY; Trimble County, KY

Population: 114,893; Growth (since 2000): 19.1%; Density: 308.1 persons per square mile; Race: 88.3% White, 6.7% Black/African American, 0.8% Asian, 0.1% American Indian/Alaska Native, 0.0% Native Hawaiian/Other Pacific Islander, 3.4% two or more races, 5.3% Hispanic of any race; Average household size: 2.59; Median age: 38.8; Age under 18: 22.9%; Age 65 and over: 14.5%; Males per 100 females: 96.0; Marriage status: 28.1% never married, 49.9% now married, 2.1% separated, 7.0% widowed, 15.1% divorced; Foreign born: 3.3%; Speak English only: 95.3%; With disability: 14.8%; Veterans: 9.5%; Ancestry: 21.1% German, 13.6% Irish, 9.2% American, 9.1% English, 2.7% French
Religion: Six largest groups: 13.2% Baptist, 9.2% Catholicism, 5.6% Non-denominational Protestant, 3.3% Methodist/Pietist, 0.8% Presbyterian-Reformed, 0.6% Holiness
Economy: Unemployment rate: 3.6%; Leading industries: 17.1 % retail trade; 10.2 % construction; 10.2 % health care and social assistance; Farms: 515 totaling 78,545 acres; Company size: 4 employ 1,000 or more persons, 1 employs 500 to 999 persons, 84 employ 100 to 499 persons, 2,347 employ less than 100 persons; Business ownership: 2,705 women-owned, 316 Black-owned, 174 Hispanic-owned, 126 Asian-owned, 50 American Indian/Alaska Native-owned
Employment: 14.0% management, business, and financial, 3.8% computer, engineering, and science, 7.0% education, legal, community service, arts, and media, 6.3% healthcare practitioners, 16.9% service, 25.5% sales and office, 7.6% natural resources, construction, and maintenance, 18.8% production, transportation, and material moving
Income: Per capita: $26,875; Median household: $52,834; Average household: $66,583; Households with income of $100,000 or more: 18.3%; Poverty rate: 9.7%
Educational Attainment: High school diploma or higher: 88.5%; Bachelor's degree or higher: 20.0%; Graduate/professional degree or higher: 6.1%
Housing: Homeownership rate: 71.4%; Median home value: $131,500; Median year structure built: 1977; Homeowner vacancy rate: 2.6%; Median selected monthly owner costs: $1,099 with a mortgage, $391 without a mortgage; Median gross rent: $797 per month; Rental vacancy rate: 9.3%
Vital Statistics: Birth rate: 125.1 per 10,000 population; Death rate: 97.7 per 10,000 population; Age-adjusted cancer mortality rate: 183.2 deaths per 100,000 population
Health Insurance: 89.9% have insurance; 71.6% have private insurance; 31.5% have public insurance; 10.1% do not have insurance; 7.5% of children under 18 do not have insurance
Health Care: Physicians: 13.7 per 10,000 population; Dentists: 3.4 per 10,000 population; Hospital beds: 27.5 per 10,000 population; Hospital admissions: 1,248.8 per 10,000 population
Air Quality Index (AQI): Percent of Days: 84.1% good, 15.7% moderate, 0.3% unhealthy for sensitive individuals, 0.0% unhealthy, 0.0% very unhealthy; Annual median: 38; Annual maximum: 101
Transportation: Commute: 94.0% car, 0.9% public transportation, 0.9% walk, 3.3% work from home; Mean travel time to work: 24.0 minutes
2016 Presidential Election: 58.0% Trump, 36.3% Clinton, 4.4% Johnson, 0.0% Stein
National and State Parks: Deam Lake State Recreation Area; Falls of the Ohio State Park
Additional Information Contacts
Clark Government . . . . (812) 285-6200
http://www.clarkcountyconnect.net

Clark County Communities

BORDEN (town). Covers a land area of 1.392 square miles and a water area of <.001 square miles. Located at 38.47° N. Lat; 85.95° W. Long. Elevation is 561 feet.
Population: 1,108; Growth (since 2000): 35.5%; Density: 796.1 persons per square mile; Race: 98.8% White, 0.3% Black/African American, 0.0% Asian, 0.0% American Indian/Alaska Native, 0.0% Native Hawaiian/Other Pacific Islander, 0.9% Two or more races, 0.0% Hispanic of any race; Average household size: 2.90; Median age: 30.4; Age under 18: 31.8%; Age 65 and over: 10.1%; Males per 100 females: 94.2; Marriage status: 26.1% never married, 55.2% now married, 1.6% separated, 7.7% widowed, 11.0% divorced; Foreign born: 0.8%; Speak English only: 100.0%; With disability: 8.4%; Veterans: 10.4%; Ancestry: 26.3% Irish, 24.8% German, 6.0% English, 5.3% American, 2.5% French
Employment: 7.6% management, business, and financial, 2.6% computer, engineering, and science, 6.3% education, legal, community service, arts, and media, 4.5% healthcare practitioners, 19.2% service, 26.8% sales and office, 12.7% natural resources, construction, and maintenance, 20.3% production, transportation, and material moving
Income: Per capita: $22,388; Median household: $47,083; Average household: $61,658; Households with income of $100,000 or more: 13.1%; Poverty rate: 16.0%
Educational Attainment: High school diploma or higher: 91.6%; Bachelor's degree or higher: 14.9%; Graduate/professional degree or higher: 3.7%

School District(s)

West Clark Community Schools (PK-12)
Enrollment: 4,723 . . . . (812) 246-3375
Housing: Homeownership rate: 78.5%; Median home value: $109,000; Median year structure built: 1982; Homeowner vacancy rate: 4.9%; Median selected monthly owner costs: $969 with a mortgage, $385 without a mortgage; Median gross rent: $783 per month; Rental vacancy rate: 10.9%
Health Insurance: 94.9% have insurance; 67.3% have private insurance; 36.2% have public insurance; 5.1% do not have insurance; 1.4% of children under 18 do not have insurance
Transportation: Commute: 97.8% car, 0.0% public transportation, 0.0% walk, 1.9% work from home; Mean travel time to work: 29.4 minutes

CHARLESTOWN (city). Covers a land area of 11.446 square miles and a water area of 0.039 square miles. Located at 38.43° N. Lat; 85.67° W. Long. Elevation is 591 feet.
History: Charleston was platted in 1808, and served as the seat of Clark County from 1811 to 1878. In 1940 the E.I. du Pont de Nemours Company built a plant here, followed by the Goodyear Tire and Rubber Company's plant.
Population: 8,079; Growth (since 2000): 34.8%; Density: 705.8 persons per square mile; Race: 90.6% White, 1.9% Black/African American, 0.5% Asian, 0.0% American Indian/Alaska Native, 0.0% Native Hawaiian/Other Pacific Islander, 3.7% Two or more races, 7.6% Hispanic of any race; Average household size: 2.71; Median age: 36.1; Age under 18: 26.4%; Age 65 and over: 10.0%; Males per 100 females: 90.5; Marriage status: 28.6% never married, 46.8% now married, 2.1% separated, 8.0% widowed, 16.5% divorced; Foreign born: 4.5%; Speak English only: 94.2%; With disability: 17.3%; Veterans: 7.1%; Ancestry: 19.4% German, 14.5% American, 11.8% Irish, 8.1% English, 7.3% French
Employment: 12.7% management, business, and financial, 3.5% computer, engineering, and science, 5.3% education, legal, community service, arts, and media, 9.9% healthcare practitioners, 16.1% service, 21.5% sales and office, 8.1% natural resources, construction, and maintenance, 22.9% production, transportation, and material moving
Income: Per capita: $21,808; Median household: $42,450; Average household: $55,890; Households with income of $100,000 or more: 14.6%; Poverty rate: 14.6%
Educational Attainment: High school diploma or higher: 81.9%; Bachelor's degree or higher: 13.7%; Graduate/professional degree or higher: 4.1%

School District(s)

Greater Clark County Schools (PK-12)
Enrollment: 10,946 .... (812) 283-0701

Housing: Homeownership rate: 59.3%; Median home value: $109,300; Median year structure built: 1962; Homeowner vacancy rate: 3.9%; Median selected monthly owner costs: $1,022 with a mortgage, $361 without a mortgage; Median gross rent: $764 per month; Rental vacancy rate: 4.3%

Health Insurance: 89.9% have insurance; 64.5% have private insurance; 36.3% have public insurance; 10.1% do not have insurance; 4.5% of children under 18 do not have insurance

Hospitals: Saint Catherine Regional Hospital (96 beds)

Safety: Violent crime rate: n/a per 10,000 population; Property crime rate: 155.2 per 10,000 population

Newspapers: The Leader (weekly circulation 13,000)

Transportation: Commute: 98.2% car, 0.0% public transportation, 0.5% walk, 1.3% work from home; Mean travel time to work: 25.0 minutes

Additional Information Contacts

City of Charlestown .... (812) 256-3422
http://www.cityofcharlestown.com

CLARKSVILLE (town). Covers a land area of 9.973 square miles and a water area of 0.203 square miles. Located at 38.32° N. Lat; 85.77° W. Long. Elevation is 456 feet.

History: Named for General George Rogers Clark, who founded the town in 1784. Clarksville was founded in 1784 by George Rogers Clark on land given to Clark by the State of Virginia in reward for his military service. Clarksville was the site of the duel between Henry Clay and Humphrey Marshall in which each was wounded.

Population: 21,228; Growth (since 2000): -0.8%; Density: 2,128.5 persons per square mile; Race: 89.6% White, 4.1% Black/African American, 1.6% Asian, 0.2% American Indian/Alaska Native, 0.0% Native Hawaiian/Other Pacific Islander, 3.6% Two or more races, 7.9% Hispanic of any race; Average household size: 2.38; Median age: 41.5; Age under 18: 19.0%; Age 65 and over: 18.2%; Males per 100 females: 92.4; Marriage status: 28.0% never married, 44.3% now married, 2.5% separated, 11.0% widowed, 16.7% divorced; Foreign born: 5.9%; Speak English only: 92.6%; With disability: 17.9%; Veterans: 10.7%; Ancestry: 19.0% German, 12.2% Irish, 8.6% English, 8.4% American, 3.8% French

Employment: 12.2% management, business, and financial, 3.4% computer, engineering, and science, 4.9% education, legal, community service, arts, and media, 6.0% healthcare practitioners, 21.5% service, 26.7% sales and office, 7.6% natural resources, construction, and maintenance, 17.7% production, transportation, and material moving

Income: Per capita: $25,019; Median household: $42,872; Average household: $55,058; Households with income of $100,000 or more: 12.2%; Poverty rate: 11.5%

Educational Attainment: High school diploma or higher: 86.2%; Bachelor's degree or higher: 17.9%; Graduate/professional degree or higher: 4.5%

School District(s)

Clarksville Community School Corp (PK-12)
Enrollment: 1,329 .... (812) 282-7753
Greater Clark County Schools (PK-12)
Enrollment: 10,946 .... (812) 283-0701

Two-year College(s)

PJ's College of Cosmetology-Clarksville (Private, For-profit)
Enrollment: 103 .... (812) 285-8805

Housing: Homeownership rate: 60.5%; Median home value: $112,900; Median year structure built: 1970; Homeowner vacancy rate: 3.9%; Median selected monthly owner costs: $1,006 with a mortgage, $392 without a mortgage; Median gross rent: $767 per month; Rental vacancy rate: 10.3%

Health Insurance: 87.2% have insurance; 63.8% have private insurance; 36.8% have public insurance; 12.8% do not have insurance; 9.3% of children under 18 do not have insurance

Hospitals: Kentuckiana Medical Center (34 beds)

Safety: Violent crime rate: 49.7 per 10,000 population; Property crime rate: 546.3 per 10,000 population

Transportation: Commute: 94.5% car, 1.0% public transportation, 0.8% walk, 3.0% work from home; Mean travel time to work: 21.0 minutes

Additional Information Contacts

Town of Clarksville .... (812) 283-1500
http://town.clarksville.in.us

HENRYVILLE (CDP). Covers a land area of 2.847 square miles and a water area of 0.003 square miles. Located at 38.54° N. Lat; 85.77° W. Long. Elevation is 518 feet.

Population: 1,949; Growth (since 2000): 26.1%; Density: 684.6 persons per square mile; Race: 100.0% White, 0.0% Black/African American, 0.0% Asian, 0.0% American Indian/Alaska Native, 0.0% Native Hawaiian/Other Pacific Islander, 0.0% Two or more races, 0.0% Hispanic of any race; Average household size: 2.58; Median age: 33.8; Age under 18: 27.7%; Age 65 and over: 10.7%; Males per 100 females: 97.2; Marriage status: 22.5% never married, 48.7% now married, 4.4% separated, 3.4% widowed, 25.4% divorced; Foreign born: 0.6%; Speak English only: 100.0%; With disability: 11.7%; Veterans: 18.2%; Ancestry: 15.3% Irish, 12.5% German, 12.1% American, 11.6% English, 4.6% Dutch

Employment: 11.2% management, business, and financial, 3.9% computer, engineering, and science, 4.9% education, legal, community service, arts, and media, 8.6% healthcare practitioners, 18.2% service, 25.3% sales and office, 15.1% natural resources, construction, and maintenance, 12.8% production, transportation, and material moving

Income: Per capita: $25,325; Median household: $59,297; Average household: $63,999; Households with income of $100,000 or more: 9.0%; Poverty rate: 5.5%

Educational Attainment: High school diploma or higher: 89.9%; Bachelor's degree or higher: 15.7%; Graduate/professional degree or higher: 4.7%

School District(s)

West Clark Community Schools (PK-12)
Enrollment: 4,723 .... (812) 246-3375

Housing: Homeownership rate: 70.2%; Median home value: $140,700; Median year structure built: 1986; Homeowner vacancy rate: 4.9%; Median selected monthly owner costs: $1,193 with a mortgage, $370 without a mortgage; Median gross rent: $736 per month; Rental vacancy rate: 10.0%

Health Insurance: 90.4% have insurance; 77.3% have private insurance; 23.8% have public insurance; 9.6% do not have insurance; 19.2% of children under 18 do not have insurance

Transportation: Commute: 86.9% car, 0.0% public transportation, 1.1% walk, 10.1% work from home; Mean travel time to work: 27.2 minutes

JEFFERSONVILLE (city). County seat. Covers a land area of 34.064 square miles and a water area of 0.294 square miles. Located at 38.33° N. Lat; 85.70° W. Long. Elevation is 446 feet.

History: Jeffersonville was platted in 1802 and named by William Henry Harrison for Thomas Jefferson, who had suggested the plan. The Howard Shipyards were founded in 1834 and influenced the economy of Jeffersonville for a century. The city sustained heavy damage in the 1937 flooding of the Ohio River.

Population: 46,840; Growth (since 2000): 71.2%; Density: 1,375.0 persons per square mile; Race: 80.4% White, 13.7% Black/African American, 0.9% Asian, 0.1% American Indian/Alaska Native, 0.0% Native Hawaiian/Other Pacific Islander, 4.6% Two or more races, 5.2% Hispanic of any race; Average household size: 2.54; Median age: 38.2; Age under 18: 22.9%; Age 65 and over: 14.5%; Males per 100 females: 95.4; Marriage status: 31.2% never married, 47.7% now married, 1.9% separated, 6.0% widowed, 15.1% divorced; Foreign born: 3.3%; Speak English only: 94.9%; With disability: 15.4%; Veterans: 9.0%; Ancestry: 20.2% German, 13.9% Irish, 8.7% English, 7.2% American, 3.1% Italian

Employment: 14.1% management, business, and financial, 3.8% computer, engineering, and science, 8.0% education, legal, community service, arts, and media, 5.4% healthcare practitioners, 17.6% service, 25.9% sales and office, 5.6% natural resources, construction, and maintenance, 19.7% production, transportation, and material moving

Income: Per capita: $26,840; Median household: $52,861; Average household: $65,161; Households with income of $100,000 or more: 15.8%; Poverty rate: 10.2%

Educational Attainment: High school diploma or higher: 90.7%; Bachelor's degree or higher: 21.1%; Graduate/professional degree or higher: 6.9%

School District(s)

Greater Clark County Schools (PK-12)
Enrollment: 10,946 .... (812) 283-0701

Four-year College(s)

Mid-America College of Funeral Service (Private, Not-for-profit)
Enrollment: 101 .... (812) 288-8878
Tuition: In-state $11,900; Out-of-state $11,900
Ottawa University-Jeffersonville (Private, Not-for-profit, American Baptist)
Enrollment: 83 .... (812) 280-7271

Vocational/Technical School(s)
Ideal Beauty Academy (Private, For-profit)
Enrollment: 6 .... (812) 282-1371
Tuition: $12,968
Housing: Homeownership rate: 70.2%; Median home value: $128,300; Median year structure built: 1978; Homeowner vacancy rate: 2.4%; Median selected monthly owner costs: $1,094 with a mortgage, $387 without a mortgage; Median gross rent: $792 per month; Rental vacancy rate: 11.6%
Health Insurance: 90.8% have insurance; 72.6% have private insurance; 31.6% have public insurance; 9.2% do not have insurance; 6.8% of children under 18 do not have insurance
Hospitals: Clark Memorial Hospital (241 beds)
Safety: Violent crime rate: 14.1 per 10,000 population; Property crime rate: 302.4 per 10,000 population
Newspapers: Evening News (daily circulation 7,200)
Transportation: Commute: 93.0% car, 1.6% public transportation, 1.1% walk, 3.1% work from home; Mean travel time to work: 21.7 minutes
Airports: Clark Regional (general aviation)
Additional Information Contacts
City of Jeffersonville .... (812) 285-6427
http://www.cityofjeff.net

MARYSVILLE (unincorporated postal area)
ZCTA: 47141
Covers a land area of 34.119 square miles and a water area of 0.156 square miles. Located at 38.55° N. Lat; 85.61° W. Long. Elevation is 712 feet.
Population: 1,650; Growth (since 2000): 16.7%; Density: 48.4 persons per square mile; Race: 100.0% White, 0.0% Black/African American, 0.0% Asian, 0.0% American Indian/Alaska Native, 0.0% Native Hawaiian/Other Pacific Islander, 0.0% Two or more races, 17.3% Hispanic of any race; Average household size: 3.04; Median age: 36.5; Age under 18: 27.7%; Age 65 and over: 16.4%; Males per 100 females: 101.0; Marriage status: 27.4% never married, 52.8% now married, 0.0% separated, 3.7% widowed, 16.1% divorced; Foreign born: 2.4%; Speak English only: 92.0%; With disability: 14.4%; Veterans: 10.7%; Ancestry: 15.0% Irish, 10.5% German, 10.1% English, 8.0% American, 5.7% Polish
Employment: 8.2% management, business, and financial, 5.4% computer, engineering, and science, 4.0% education, legal, community service, arts, and media, 9.3% healthcare practitioners, 9.3% service, 24.7% sales and office, 22.1% natural resources, construction, and maintenance, 17.1% production, transportation, and material moving
Income: Per capita: $20,985; Median household: $48,698; Average household: $61,791; Households with income of $100,000 or more: 13.2%; Poverty rate: 6.1%
Educational Attainment: High school diploma or higher: 72.1%; Bachelor's degree or higher: 14.4%; Graduate/professional degree or higher: 2.8%
Housing: Homeownership rate: 89.7%; Median home value: $156,000; Median year structure built: 1990; Homeowner vacancy rate: 0.0%; Median selected monthly owner costs: $1,132 with a mortgage, $547 without a mortgage; Median gross rent: $727 per month; Rental vacancy rate: 0.0%
Health Insurance: 85.9% have insurance; 60.0% have private insurance; 50.9% have public insurance; 14.1% do not have insurance; 13.3% of children under 18 do not have insurance
Transportation: Commute: 94.7% car, 0.0% public transportation, 3.4% walk, 1.8% work from home; Mean travel time to work: 33.8 minutes

MEMPHIS (CDP).
Covers a land area of 2.598 square miles and a water area of 0.023 square miles. Located at 38.49° N. Lat; 85.77° W. Long. Elevation is 486 feet.
Population: 941; Growth (since 2000): 135.3%; Density: 362.3 persons per square mile; Race: 100.0% White, 0.0% Black/African American, 0.0% Asian, 0.0% American Indian/Alaska Native, 0.0% Native Hawaiian/Other Pacific Islander, 0.0% Two or more races, 0.0% Hispanic of any race; Average household size: 2.87; Median age: 34.2; Age under 18: 28.8%; Age 65 and over: 6.7%; Males per 100 females: 92.0; Marriage status: 28.6% never married, 65.1% now married, 0.0% separated, 3.1% widowed, 3.2% divorced; Foreign born: 0.0%; Speak English only: 100.0%; With disability: 5.8%; Veterans: 5.7%; Ancestry: 43.8% German, 10.5% Irish, 6.5% American, 3.6% Scotch-Irish, 3.4% French
Employment: 10.3% management, business, and financial, 14.9% computer, engineering, and science, 4.2% education, legal, community service, arts, and media, 20.4% healthcare practitioners, 11.3% service, 5.5% sales and office, 13.7% natural resources, construction, and maintenance, 19.8% production, transportation, and material moving
Income: Per capita: $29,429; Median household: $71,875; Average household: $78,449; Households with income of $100,000 or more: 25.9%; Poverty rate: 5.1%
Educational Attainment: High school diploma or higher: 95.9%; Bachelor's degree or higher: 19.5%; Graduate/professional degree or higher: 2.2%
Housing: Homeownership rate: 90.9%; Median home value: $145,900; Median year structure built: 2001; Homeowner vacancy rate: 0.0%; Median selected monthly owner costs: $989 with a mortgage, $410 without a mortgage; Median gross rent: n/a per month; Rental vacancy rate: 26.8%
Health Insurance: 88.1% have insurance; 79.2% have private insurance; 15.8% have public insurance; 11.9% do not have insurance; 0.0% of children under 18 do not have insurance
Transportation: Commute: 97.7% car, 0.0% public transportation, 0.0% walk, 2.3% work from home; Mean travel time to work: 29.9 minutes

NABB (unincorporated postal area)
ZCTA: 47147
Covers a land area of 27.811 square miles and a water area of 0.074 square miles. Located at 38.59° N. Lat; 85.55° W. Long..
Population: 1,183; Growth (since 2000): 11.4%; Density: 42.5 persons per square mile; Race: 100.0% White, 0.0% Black/African American, 0.0% Asian, 0.0% American Indian/Alaska Native, 0.0% Native Hawaiian/Other Pacific Islander, 0.0% Two or more races, 0.0% Hispanic of any race; Average household size: 3.27; Median age: 35.3; Age under 18: 34.5%; Age 65 and over: 12.3%; Males per 100 females: 96.9; Marriage status: 23.8% never married, 63.2% now married, 1.1% separated, 3.7% widowed, 9.4% divorced; Foreign born: 0.0%; Speak English only: 100.0%; With disability: 5.3%; Veterans: 11.4%; Ancestry: 18.6% American, 8.7% German, 3.9% Dutch, 3.0% Irish, 1.7% Greek
Employment: 15.2% management, business, and financial, 0.0% computer, engineering, and science, 4.4% education, legal, community service, arts, and media, 9.6% healthcare practitioners, 14.0% service, 26.3% sales and office, 15.4% natural resources, construction, and maintenance, 15.2% production, transportation, and material moving
Income: Per capita: $23,890; Median household: $54,167; Average household: $73,464; Households with income of $100,000 or more: 30.9%; Poverty rate: 14.8%
Educational Attainment: High school diploma or higher: 94.8%; Bachelor's degree or higher: 11.2%; Graduate/professional degree or higher: 6.4%
Housing: Homeownership rate: 76.5%; Median home value: $152,600; Median year structure built: 1960; Homeowner vacancy rate: 0.0%; Median selected monthly owner costs: $1,004 with a mortgage, $385 without a mortgage; Median gross rent: $787 per month; Rental vacancy rate: 0.0%
Health Insurance: 89.0% have insurance; 53.5% have private insurance; 46.2% have public insurance; 11.0% do not have insurance; 0.0% of children under 18 do not have insurance
Transportation: Commute: 96.5% car, 0.0% public transportation, 0.0% walk, 3.5% work from home; Mean travel time to work: 35.1 minutes

NEW WASHINGTON (CDP).
Covers a land area of 5.207 square miles and a water area of 0.015 square miles. Located at 38.57° N. Lat; 85.56° W. Long. Elevation is 718 feet.
Population: 531; Growth (since 2000): -2.9%; Density: 102.0 persons per square mile; Race: 100.0% White, 0.0% Black/African American, 0.0% Asian, 0.0% American Indian/Alaska Native, 0.0% Native Hawaiian/Other Pacific Islander, 0.0% Two or more races, 0.0% Hispanic of any race; Average household size: 2.93; Median age: 35.1; Age under 18: 28.1%; Age 65 and over: 10.0%; Males per 100 females: 84.4; Marriage status: 19.7% never married, 73.4% now married, 4.6% separated, 4.6% widowed, 2.3% divorced; Foreign born: 0.0%; Speak English only: 100.0%; With disability: 8.5%; Veterans: 3.4%; Ancestry: 21.1% American, 10.9% German, 6.8% English, 4.3% Irish, 1.7% British
Employment: 9.0% management, business, and financial, 0.0% computer, engineering, and science, 5.6% education, legal, community service, arts, and media, 5.2% healthcare practitioners, 38.2% service, 19.8% sales and office, 8.3% natural resources, construction, and maintenance, 13.9% production, transportation, and material moving

Income: Per capita: $21,970; Median household: $63,839; Average household: $63,860; Households with income of $100,000 or more: 11.6%; Poverty rate: n/a
Educational Attainment: High school diploma or higher: 100.0%; Bachelor's degree or higher: 26.4%; Graduate/professional degree or higher: 2.1%

School District(s)

Greater Clark County Schools (PK-12)
Enrollment: 10,946 . . . . (812) 283-0701
Housing: Homeownership rate: 69.6%; Median home value: $139,600; Median year structure built: 1963; Homeowner vacancy rate: 0.0%; Median selected monthly owner costs: $969 with a mortgage, $360 without a mortgage; Median gross rent: $759 per month; Rental vacancy rate: 0.0%
Health Insurance: 90.0% have insurance; 72.5% have private insurance; 25.8% have public insurance; 10.0% do not have insurance; 0.0% of children under 18 do not have insurance
Transportation: Commute: 98.6% car, 0.0% public transportation, 0.0% walk, 1.4% work from home; Mean travel time to work: 32.5 minutes

OTISCO (unincorporated postal area)
ZCTA: 47163
Covers a land area of 20.827 square miles and a water area of 0.136 square miles. Located at 38.53° N. Lat; 85.67° W. Long. Elevation is 673 feet.
Population: 2,046; Growth (since 2000): 18.1%; Density: 98.2 persons per square mile; Race: 99.4% White, 0.6% Black/African American, 0.0% Asian, 0.0% American Indian/Alaska Native, 0.0% Native Hawaiian/Other Pacific Islander, 0.0% Two or more races, 0.0% Hispanic of any race; Average household size: 2.87; Median age: 44.2; Age under 18: 28.2%; Age 65 and over: 15.1%; Males per 100 females: 105.4; Marriage status: 24.8% never married, 60.2% now married, 0.0% separated, 3.2% widowed, 11.9% divorced; Foreign born: 0.8%; Speak English only: 100.0%; With disability: 12.3%; Veterans: 8.4%; Ancestry: 18.2% American, 17.0% German, 9.8% Irish, 4.5% Italian, 4.0% English
Employment: 9.7% management, business, and financial, 8.2% computer, engineering, and science, 0.0% education, legal, community service, arts, and media, 2.4% healthcare practitioners, 15.9% service, 35.8% sales and office, 14.6% natural resources, construction, and maintenance, 13.5% production, transportation, and material moving
Income: Per capita: $29,413; Median household: $61,875; Average household: $83,389; Households with income of $100,000 or more: 26.1%; Poverty rate: 5.4%
Educational Attainment: High school diploma or higher: 82.6%; Bachelor's degree or higher: 15.5%; Graduate/professional degree or higher: 3.3%
Housing: Homeownership rate: 94.0%; Median home value: $138,600; Median year structure built: 1992; Homeowner vacancy rate: 0.0%; Median selected monthly owner costs: $1,106 with a mortgage, $445 without a mortgage; Median gross rent: n/a per month; Rental vacancy rate: 0.0%
Health Insurance: 91.4% have insurance; 75.2% have private insurance; 29.1% have public insurance; 8.6% do not have insurance; 17.1% of children under 18 do not have insurance
Transportation: Commute: 94.9% car, 0.0% public transportation, 0.0% walk, 3.8% work from home; Mean travel time to work: 34.6 minutes

SELLERSBURG (town). Covers a land area of 3.943 square miles and a water area of 0.030 square miles. Located at 38.39° N. Lat; 85.76° W. Long. Elevation is 486 feet.
History: Laid out 1846.
Population: 8,806; Growth (since 2000): 45.1%; Density: 2,233.5 persons per square mile; Race: 93.2% White, 1.1% Black/African American, 0.2% Asian, 0.0% American Indian/Alaska Native, 0.0% Native Hawaiian/Other Pacific Islander, 3.2% Two or more races, 4.0% Hispanic of any race; Average household size: 2.76; Median age: 36.1; Age under 18: 27.5%; Age 65 and over: 12.5%; Males per 100 females: 94.4; Marriage status: 24.8% never married, 52.4% now married, 4.3% separated, 7.6% widowed, 15.2% divorced; Foreign born: 1.6%; Speak English only: 96.5%; With disability: 8.0%; Veterans: 8.0%; Ancestry: 29.7% German, 18.7% Irish, 10.3% English, 7.4% American, 1.7% Scottish
Employment: 15.5% management, business, and financial, 5.1% computer, engineering, and science, 9.2% education, legal, community service, arts, and media, 5.3% healthcare practitioners, 14.0% service, 28.6% sales and office, 7.8% natural resources, construction, and maintenance, 14.5% production, transportation, and material moving
Income: Per capita: $28,471; Median household: $61,617; Average household: $75,526; Households with income of $100,000 or more: 21.5%; Poverty rate: 8.5%
Educational Attainment: High school diploma or higher: 88.8%; Bachelor's degree or higher: 23.1%; Graduate/professional degree or higher: 7.7%

School District(s)

Rock Creek Community Academy (KG-12)
Enrollment: 507 . . . . (812) 246-9271
West Clark Community Schools (PK-12)
Enrollment: 4,723 . . . . (812) 246-3375
Housing: Homeownership rate: 73.3%; Median home value: $144,900; Median year structure built: 1977; Homeowner vacancy rate: 0.0%; Median selected monthly owner costs: $1,099 with a mortgage, $424 without a mortgage; Median gross rent: $936 per month; Rental vacancy rate: 4.9%
Health Insurance: 89.0% have insurance; 74.8% have private insurance; 24.3% have public insurance; 11.0% do not have insurance; 11.2% of children under 18 do not have insurance
Safety: Violent crime rate: 7.9 per 10,000 population; Property crime rate: 97.3 per 10,000 population
Transportation: Commute: 95.6% car, 0.0% public transportation, 0.2% walk, 3.0% work from home; Mean travel time to work: 21.7 minutes
Additional Information Contacts
Town of Sellersburg . . . . (812) 246-7049
http://www.sellersburg.org

UTICA (town). Covers a land area of 1.266 square miles and a water area of 0.178 square miles. Located at 38.34° N. Lat; 85.66° W. Long. Elevation is 443 feet.
History: Laid out 1816.
Population: 637; Growth (since 2000): 7.8%; Density: 503.1 persons per square mile; Race: 95.4% White, 1.4% Black/African American, 0.3% Asian, 0.6% American Indian/Alaska Native, 0.0% Native Hawaiian/Other Pacific Islander, 2.2% Two or more races, 3.8% Hispanic of any race; Average household size: 2.39; Median age: 39.9; Age under 18: 22.9%; Age 65 and over: 18.7%; Males per 100 females: 91.1; Marriage status: 24.1% never married, 52.1% now married, 0.6% separated, 6.1% widowed, 17.7% divorced; Foreign born: 1.6%; Speak English only: 97.1%; With disability: 18.1%; Veterans: 10.4%; Ancestry: 25.4% German, 14.4% Irish, 7.2% English, 7.1% American, 1.7% French
Employment: 12.5% management, business, and financial, 0.7% computer, engineering, and science, 6.6% education, legal, community service, arts, and media, 7.6% healthcare practitioners, 13.2% service, 24.0% sales and office, 13.5% natural resources, construction, and maintenance, 21.9% production, transportation, and material moving
Income: Per capita: $28,258; Median household: $49,145; Average household: $64,907; Households with income of $100,000 or more: 17.2%; Poverty rate: 3.8%
Educational Attainment: High school diploma or higher: 87.3%; Bachelor's degree or higher: 18.6%; Graduate/professional degree or higher: 6.8%
Housing: Homeownership rate: 84.3%; Median home value: $122,100; Median year structure built: 1994; Homeowner vacancy rate: 0.4%; Median selected monthly owner costs: $1,044 with a mortgage, $373 without a mortgage; Median gross rent: $870 per month; Rental vacancy rate: 17.5%
Health Insurance: 91.7% have insurance; 73.3% have private insurance; 30.5% have public insurance; 8.3% do not have insurance; 10.3% of children under 18 do not have insurance
Transportation: Commute: 99.3% car, 0.0% public transportation, 0.0% walk, 0.7% work from home; Mean travel time to work: 27.9 minutes

Clay County

Located in western Indiana; drained by the Eel River and Small Birch Creek. Covers a land area of 357.542 square miles, a water area of 2.780 square miles, and is located in the Eastern Time Zone at 39.39° N. Lat., 87.12° W. Long. The county was founded in 1825. County seat is Brazil.

Clay County is part of the Terre Haute, IN Metropolitan Statistical Area. The entire metro area includes: Clay County, IN; Sullivan County, IN; Vermillion County, IN; Vigo County, IN

Population: 26,375; Growth (since 2000): -0.7%; Density: 73.8 persons per square mile; Race: 97.4% White, 0.4% Black/African American, 0.3% Asian, 0.1% American Indian/Alaska Native, 0.0% Native Hawaiian/Other

Pacific Islander, 1.6% two or more races, 1.3% Hispanic of any race; Average household size: 2.43; Median age: 40.9; Age under 18: 23.1%; Age 65 and over: 16.8%; Males per 100 females: 96.9; Marriage status: 21.2% never married, 59.5% now married, 1.5% separated, 6.6% widowed, 12.6% divorced; Foreign born: 0.8%; Speak English only: 97.9%; With disability: 19.2%; Veterans: 8.3%; Ancestry: 25.2% German, 10.2% American, 10.1% Irish, 8.5% English, 2.9% Scottish
Religion: Six largest groups: 13.9% Non-denominational Protestant, 11.6% Baptist, 7.8% Methodist/Pietist, 3.6% Presbyterian-Reformed, 2.3% Holiness, 1.5% Pentecostal
Economy: Unemployment rate: 4.0%; Leading industries: 16.9 % retail trade; 15.9 % other services (except public administration); 11.3 % construction; Farms: 579 totaling 162,883 acres; Company size: 1 employs 1,000 or more persons, 0 employ 500 to 999 persons, 6 employ 100 to 499 persons, 472 employ less than 100 persons; Business ownership: 506 women-owned, n/a Black-owned, n/a Hispanic-owned, n/a Asian-owned, n/a American Indian/Alaska Native-owned
Employment: 10.0% management, business, and financial, 2.9% computer, engineering, and science, 10.7% education, legal, community service, arts, and media, 5.7% healthcare practitioners, 18.8% service, 20.6% sales and office, 9.4% natural resources, construction, and maintenance, 21.8% production, transportation, and material moving
Income: Per capita: $24,339; Median household: $50,924; Average household: $60,074; Households with income of $100,000 or more: 16.1%; Poverty rate: 13.9%
Educational Attainment: High school diploma or higher: 90.7%; Bachelor's degree or higher: 16.6%; Graduate/professional degree or higher: 5.5%
Housing: Homeownership rate: 76.7%; Median home value: $96,000; Median year structure built: 1966; Homeowner vacancy rate: 2.3%; Median selected monthly owner costs: $980 with a mortgage, $361 without a mortgage; Median gross rent: $650 per month; Rental vacancy rate: 2.8%
Vital Statistics: Birth rate: 124.4 per 10,000 population; Death rate: 109.9 per 10,000 population; Age-adjusted cancer mortality rate: 183.5 deaths per 100,000 population
Health Insurance: 92.5% have insurance; 70.8% have private insurance; 34.6% have public insurance; 7.5% do not have insurance; 3.1% of children under 18 do not have insurance
Health Care: Physicians: 7.3 per 10,000 population; Dentists: 2.3 per 10,000 population; Hospital beds: 9.5 per 10,000 population; Hospital admissions: 178.6 per 10,000 population
Transportation: Commute: 94.9% car, 0.0% public transportation, 1.8% walk, 2.2% work from home; Mean travel time to work: 26.2 minutes
2016 Presidential Election: 75.3% Trump, 20.3% Clinton, 3.8% Johnson, 0.1% Stein
National and State Parks: Shakamak State Park
Additional Information Contacts
Clay Government . . . . (812) 448-9025
http://www.claycountyin.gov

Clay County Communities

BRAZIL (city). County seat. Covers a land area of 3.027 square miles and a water area of 0.028 square miles. Located at 39.52° N. Lat; 87.12° W. Long. Elevation is 653 feet.
History: Brazil's development was based on its coal mines and clay plants, which manufactured glazed building bricks and tiles. Brazil was named for the country in South America, the name suggested by resident William Stewart who had just read a magazine article about Brazil.
Population: 8,384; Growth (since 2000): 2.4%; Density: 2,769.7 persons per square mile; Race: 95.4% White, 0.8% Black/African American, 0.0% Asian, 0.1% American Indian/Alaska Native, 0.0% Native Hawaiian/Other Pacific Islander, 3.1% Two or more races, 1.3% Hispanic of any race; Average household size: 2.35; Median age: 35.1; Age under 18: 26.5%; Age 65 and over: 14.3%; Males per 100 females: 92.3; Marriage status: 28.4% never married, 47.7% now married, 1.8% separated, 6.5% widowed, 17.4% divorced; Foreign born: 0.2%; Speak English only: 98.5%; With disability: 23.0%; Veterans: 9.6%; Ancestry: 25.3% German, 10.4% Irish, 9.3% American, 7.8% English, 3.4% Dutch
Employment: 8.9% management, business, and financial, 0.9% computer, engineering, and science, 11.3% education, legal, community service, arts, and media, 3.6% healthcare practitioners, 23.1% service, 19.9% sales and office, 7.7% natural resources, construction, and maintenance, 24.7% production, transportation, and material moving
Income: Per capita: $18,875; Median household: $35,042; Average household: $45,852; Households with income of $100,000 or more: 9.1%; Poverty rate: 23.7%
Educational Attainment: High school diploma or higher: 86.7%; Bachelor's degree or higher: 14.8%; Graduate/professional degree or higher: 3.9%

School District(s)

Clay Community Schools (PK-12)
Enrollment: 4,125 . . . . (812) 443-4461
Housing: Homeownership rate: 59.1%; Median home value: $72,200; Median year structure built: 1953; Homeowner vacancy rate: 4.3%; Median selected monthly owner costs: $843 with a mortgage, $326 without a mortgage; Median gross rent: $616 per month; Rental vacancy rate: 0.0%
Health Insurance: 91.2% have insurance; 62.6% have private insurance; 41.3% have public insurance; 8.8% do not have insurance; 2.7% of children under 18 do not have insurance
Hospitals: Saint Vincent Clay Hospital (58 beds)
Newspapers: Brazil Times (daily circulation 4,600)
Transportation: Commute: 96.1% car, 0.0% public transportation, 2.8% walk, 0.6% work from home; Mean travel time to work: 22.2 minutes
Additional Information Contacts
City of Brazil . . . . (812) 443-2221
http://brazil.in.gov

CARBON (town). Covers a land area of 0.159 square miles and a water area of 0 square miles. Located at 39.60° N. Lat; 87.11° W. Long. Elevation is 692 feet.
Population: 503; Growth (since 2000): 50.6%; Density: 3,159.2 persons per square mile; Race: 99.8% White, 0.0% Black/African American, 0.0% Asian, 0.0% American Indian/Alaska Native, 0.0% Native Hawaiian/Other Pacific Islander, 0.2% Two or more races, 0.0% Hispanic of any race; Average household size: 2.84; Median age: 32.5; Age under 18: 30.8%; Age 65 and over: 8.5%; Males per 100 females: 102.6; Marriage status: 32.2% never married, 47.5% now married, 1.8% separated, 7.7% widowed, 12.7% divorced; Foreign born: 0.0%; Speak English only: 100.0%; With disability: 21.3%; Veterans: 4.0%; Ancestry: 20.5% German, 15.1% American, 10.9% Irish, 6.0% English, 2.0% Danish
Employment: 8.9% management, business, and financial, 2.5% computer, engineering, and science, 1.3% education, legal, community service, arts, and media, 5.1% healthcare practitioners, 21.9% service, 12.7% sales and office, 2.5% natural resources, construction, and maintenance, 45.1% production, transportation, and material moving
Income: Per capita: $17,092; Median household: $43,281; Average household: $49,527; Households with income of $100,000 or more: 5.6%; Poverty rate: 26.9%
Educational Attainment: High school diploma or higher: 89.6%; Bachelor's degree or higher: 5.1%; Graduate/professional degree or higher: 0.7%
Housing: Homeownership rate: 81.4%; Median home value: $61,900; Median year structure built: 1950; Homeowner vacancy rate: 0.0%; Median selected monthly owner costs: $765 with a mortgage, $341 without a mortgage; Median gross rent: $813 per month; Rental vacancy rate: 0.0%
Health Insurance: 89.3% have insurance; 60.4% have private insurance; 37.6% have public insurance; 10.7% do not have insurance; 0.0% of children under 18 do not have insurance
Transportation: Commute: 98.3% car, 0.0% public transportation, 1.3% walk, 0.4% work from home; Mean travel time to work: 27.2 minutes

CENTER POINT (town). Covers a land area of 0.740 square miles and a water area of 0.022 square miles. Located at 39.42° N. Lat; 87.08° W. Long. Elevation is 656 feet.
Population: 258; Growth (since 2000): -11.6%; Density: 348.6 persons per square mile; Race: 98.4% White, 0.0% Black/African American, 1.6% Asian, 0.0% American Indian/Alaska Native, 0.0% Native Hawaiian/Other Pacific Islander, 0.0% Two or more races, 0.0% Hispanic of any race; Average household size: 2.19; Median age: 37.7; Age under 18: 24.0%; Age 65 and over: 20.9%; Males per 100 females: 83.3; Marriage status: 12.9% never married, 58.4% now married, 2.5% separated, 8.9% widowed, 19.8% divorced; Foreign born: 1.6%; Speak English only: 93.5%; With disability: 19.4%; Veterans: 7.7%; Ancestry: 32.6% German, 11.2% American, 6.6% Irish, 4.7% English, 3.5% French
Employment: 0.9% management, business, and financial, 4.5% computer, engineering, and science, 1.8% education, legal, community service, arts, and media, 6.4% healthcare practitioners, 30.9% service, 20.0% sales and

office, 11.8% natural resources, construction, and maintenance, 23.6% production, transportation, and material moving
Income: Per capita: $21,579; Median household: $48,214; Average household: $48,394; Households with income of $100,000 or more: 6.8%; Poverty rate: 19.2%
Educational Attainment: High school diploma or higher: 83.8%; Bachelor's degree or higher: 11.2%; Graduate/professional degree or higher: 3.9%
Housing: Homeownership rate: 66.9%; Median home value: $71,500; Median year structure built: 1967; Homeowner vacancy rate: 16.8%; Median selected monthly owner costs: $747 with a mortgage, $314 without a mortgage; Median gross rent: $654 per month; Rental vacancy rate: 0.0%
Health Insurance: 91.1% have insurance; 72.9% have private insurance; 33.3% have public insurance; 8.9% do not have insurance; 13.4% of children under 18 do not have insurance
Transportation: Commute: 96.3% car, 0.0% public transportation, 1.9% walk, 1.9% work from home; Mean travel time to work: 26.1 minutes

CENTERPOINT (unincorporated postal area)

ZCTA: 47840

Covers a land area of 53.117 square miles and a water area of 0.550 square miles. Located at 39.41° N. Lat; 87.06° W. Long..
Population: 1,839; Growth (since 2000): 9.6%; Density: 34.6 persons per square mile; Race: 99.8% White, 0.0% Black/African American, 0.2% Asian, 0.0% American Indian/Alaska Native, 0.0% Native Hawaiian/Other Pacific Islander, 0.0% Two or more races, 0.0% Hispanic of any race; Average household size: 2.71; Median age: 33.2; Age under 18: 33.1%; Age 65 and over: 12.1%; Males per 100 females: 98.7; Marriage status: 14.9% never married, 68.9% now married, 0.4% separated, 5.1% widowed, 11.1% divorced; Foreign born: 0.2%; Speak English only: 99.1%; With disability: 12.2%; Veterans: 6.7%; Ancestry: 41.2% German, 13.6% American, 10.1% Irish, 9.3% English, 5.2% Scottish
Employment: 11.3% management, business, and financial, 1.7% computer, engineering, and science, 6.9% education, legal, community service, arts, and media, 4.5% healthcare practitioners, 20.6% service, 23.1% sales and office, 12.0% natural resources, construction, and maintenance, 19.9% production, transportation, and material moving
Income: Per capita: $22,878; Median household: $62,386; Average household: $62,958; Households with income of $100,000 or more: 13.4%; Poverty rate: 6.9%
Educational Attainment: High school diploma or higher: 90.6%; Bachelor's degree or higher: 24.8%; Graduate/professional degree or higher: 5.5%
Housing: Homeownership rate: 81.6%; Median home value: $127,900; Median year structure built: 1975; Homeowner vacancy rate: 2.8%; Median selected monthly owner costs: $1,045 with a mortgage, $377 without a mortgage; Median gross rent: $645 per month; Rental vacancy rate: 0.0%
Health Insurance: 90.2% have insurance; 76.2% have private insurance; 22.5% have public insurance; 9.8% do not have insurance; 7.2% of children under 18 do not have insurance
Transportation: Commute: 98.2% car, 0.0% public transportation, 0.3% walk, 1.5% work from home; Mean travel time to work: 36.9 minutes

CLAY CITY (town).
Covers a land area of 0.540 square miles and a water area of 0 square miles. Located at 39.28° N. Lat; 87.11° W. Long. Elevation is 594 feet.
History: Settled 1873, incorporated 1888.
Population: 771; Growth (since 2000): -24.3%; Density: 1,427.1 persons per square mile; Race: 99.5% White, 0.0% Black/African American, 0.5% Asian, 0.0% American Indian/Alaska Native, 0.0% Native Hawaiian/Other Pacific Islander, 0.0% Two or more races, 0.0% Hispanic of any race; Average household size: 2.11; Median age: 43.5; Age under 18: 20.0%; Age 65 and over: 24.4%; Males per 100 females: 80.5; Marriage status: 19.7% never married, 54.8% now married, 2.1% separated, 12.1% widowed, 13.4% divorced; Foreign born: 1.2%; Speak English only: 98.2%; With disability: 22.8%; Veterans: 9.7%; Ancestry: 35.8% German, 13.0% Irish, 12.2% English, 9.3% American, 2.6% Dutch
Employment: 6.4% management, business, and financial, 1.2% computer, engineering, and science, 11.6% education, legal, community service, arts, and media, 14.5% healthcare practitioners, 20.9% service, 18.6% sales and office, 7.3% natural resources, construction, and maintenance, 19.5% production, transportation, and material moving
Income: Per capita: $19,689; Median household: $36,750; Average household: $42,943; Households with income of $100,000 or more: 3.8%; Poverty rate: 14.4%
Educational Attainment: High school diploma or higher: 88.7%; Bachelor's degree or higher: 12.9%; Graduate/professional degree or higher: 2.2%

School District(s)

Clay Community Schools (PK-12)
Enrollment: 4,125 . . . . (812) 443-4461
Housing: Homeownership rate: 59.2%; Median home value: $70,700; Median year structure built: 1947; Homeowner vacancy rate: 2.3%; Median selected monthly owner costs: $780 with a mortgage, $361 without a mortgage; Median gross rent: $585 per month; Rental vacancy rate: 2.6%
Health Insurance: 87.3% have insurance; 64.6% have private insurance; 39.6% have public insurance; 12.7% do not have insurance; 14.5% of children under 18 do not have insurance
Newspapers: Clay City News (weekly circulation 2,000)
Transportation: Commute: 97.3% car, 0.9% public transportation, 0.0% walk, 0.9% work from home; Mean travel time to work: 29.6 minutes
Additional Information Contacts
Town of Clay City . . . . (812) 939-2345
http://www.claycity.net

COALMONT (CDP).
Covers a land area of 1.501 square miles and a water area of 0.003 square miles. Located at 39.19° N. Lat; 87.22° W. Long. Elevation is 630 feet.
Population: 190; Growth (since 2000): n/a; Density: 126.6 persons per square mile; Race: 92.1% White, 0.0% Black/African American, 0.0% Asian, 1.6% American Indian/Alaska Native, 0.0% Native Hawaiian/Other Pacific Islander, 6.3% Two or more races, 0.0% Hispanic of any race; Average household size: 1.73; Median age: 48.0; Age under 18: 13.7%; Age 65 and over: 13.7%; Males per 100 females: 103.0; Marriage status: 16.4% never married, 37.3% now married, 0.0% separated, 3.4% widowed, 42.9% divorced; Foreign born: 0.0%; Speak English only: 100.0%; With disability: 41.6%; Veterans: 0.0%; Ancestry: 21.1% English, 8.9% American, 6.8% German, 4.7% Irish, 3.2% Dutch
Employment: 8.0% management, business, and financial, 0.0% computer, engineering, and science, 0.0% education, legal, community service, arts, and media, 0.0% healthcare practitioners, 65.3% service, 0.0% sales and office, 9.3% natural resources, construction, and maintenance, 17.3% production, transportation, and material moving
Income: Per capita: $16,794; Median household: $28,438; Average household: $29,785; Households with income of $100,000 or more: n/a; Poverty rate: 20.5%
Educational Attainment: High school diploma or higher: 85.8%; Bachelor's degree or higher: n/a; Graduate/professional degree or higher: n/a
Housing: Homeownership rate: 80.0%; Median home value: n/a; Median year structure built: 1964; Homeowner vacancy rate: 0.0%; Median selected monthly owner costs: $683 with a mortgage, $248 without a mortgage; Median gross rent: n/a per month; Rental vacancy rate: 0.0%
Health Insurance: 100.0% have insurance; 56.3% have private insurance; 58.9% have public insurance; 0.0% do not have insurance; 0.0% of children under 18 do not have insurance
Transportation: Commute: 100.0% car, 0.0% public transportation, 0.0% walk, 0.0% work from home; Mean travel time to work: 0.0 minutes

CORY (unincorporated postal area)

ZCTA: 47846

Covers a land area of 31.521 square miles and a water area of 0.157 square miles. Located at 39.38° N. Lat; 87.19° W. Long. Elevation is 630 feet.
Population: 444; Growth (since 2000): -38.8%; Density: 14.1 persons per square mile; Race: 100.0% White, 0.0% Black/African American, 0.0% Asian, 0.0% American Indian/Alaska Native, 0.0% Native Hawaiian/Other Pacific Islander, 0.0% Two or more races, 5.0% Hispanic of any race; Average household size: 2.51; Median age: 48.1; Age under 18: 23.4%; Age 65 and over: 21.8%; Males per 100 females: 98.8; Marriage status: 15.2% never married, 72.7% now married, 1.9% separated, 6.4% widowed, 5.8% divorced; Foreign born: 0.0%; Speak English only: 100.0%; With disability: 16.0%; Veterans: 10.6%; Ancestry: 24.1% German, 16.0% American, 12.8% Irish, 9.9% European, 1.6% French
Employment: 9.3% management, business, and financial, 5.9% computer, engineering, and science, 11.7% education, legal, community

service, arts, and media, 8.3% healthcare practitioners, 20.5% service, 14.1% sales and office, 15.6% natural resources, construction, and maintenance, 14.6% production, transportation, and material moving
Income: Per capita: $25,701; Median household: $56,172; Average household: $63,683; Households with income of $100,000 or more: 8.4%; Poverty rate: n/a
Educational Attainment: High school diploma or higher: 95.3%; Bachelor's degree or higher: 28.9%; Graduate/professional degree or higher: 11.6%
Housing: Homeownership rate: 88.1%; Median home value: $88,200; Median year structure built: 1958; Homeowner vacancy rate: 13.8%; Median selected monthly owner costs: $1,071 with a mortgage, $336 without a mortgage; Median gross rent: $425 per month; Rental vacancy rate: 0.0%
Health Insurance: 98.2% have insurance; 80.2% have private insurance; 31.1% have public insurance; 1.8% do not have insurance; 0.0% of children under 18 do not have insurance
Transportation: Commute: 89.3% car, 0.0% public transportation, 3.4% walk, 4.9% work from home; Mean travel time to work: 26.8 minutes

HARMONY (town). Covers a land area of 0.745 square miles and a water area of 0 square miles. Located at 39.53° N. Lat; 87.07° W. Long. Elevation is 659 feet.
History: Harmony was once a prosperous coal-mining town.
Population: 716; Growth (since 2000): 21.6%; Density: 961.2 persons per square mile; Race: 98.9% White, 0.0% Black/African American, 0.0% Asian, 0.4% American Indian/Alaska Native, 0.0% Native Hawaiian/Other Pacific Islander, 0.7% Two or more races, 0.7% Hispanic of any race; Average household size: 2.17; Median age: 42.7; Age under 18: 17.7%; Age 65 and over: 15.9%; Males per 100 females: 82.7; Marriage status: 27.6% never married, 54.5% now married, 0.0% separated, 6.3% widowed, 11.6% divorced; Foreign born: 0.0%; Speak English only: 100.0%; With disability: 18.3%; Veterans: 6.6%; Ancestry: 26.3% German, 11.7% English, 11.7% Irish, 11.6% American, 10.1% French
Employment: 15.4% management, business, and financial, 1.4% computer, engineering, and science, 5.2% education, legal, community service, arts, and media, 8.7% healthcare practitioners, 16.3% service, 22.2% sales and office, 4.0% natural resources, construction, and maintenance, 26.7% production, transportation, and material moving
Income: Per capita: $26,520; Median household: $52,500; Average household: $56,843; Households with income of $100,000 or more: 15.5%; Poverty rate: 3.9%
Educational Attainment: High school diploma or higher: 88.5%; Bachelor's degree or higher: 10.4%; Graduate/professional degree or higher: 0.7%
Housing: Homeownership rate: 73.3%; Median home value: $84,900; Median year structure built: 1960; Homeowner vacancy rate: 0.0%; Median selected monthly owner costs: $886 with a mortgage, $363 without a mortgage; Median gross rent: $629 per month; Rental vacancy rate: 4.3%
Health Insurance: 95.1% have insurance; 75.3% have private insurance; 34.9% have public insurance; 4.9% do not have insurance; 0.0% of children under 18 do not have insurance
Transportation: Commute: 96.5% car, 0.0% public transportation, 0.0% walk, 3.5% work from home; Mean travel time to work: 21.2 minutes

KNIGHTSVILLE (town). Covers a land area of 1.038 square miles and a water area of 0 square miles. Located at 39.53° N. Lat; 87.09° W. Long. Elevation is 669 feet.
Population: 684; Growth (since 2000): 9.6%; Density: 658.8 persons per square mile; Race: 96.5% White, 1.0% Black/African American, 0.6% Asian, 0.0% American Indian/Alaska Native, 0.0% Native Hawaiian/Other Pacific Islander, 1.3% Two or more races, 0.6% Hispanic of any race; Average household size: 2.14; Median age: 52.1; Age under 18: 15.2%; Age 65 and over: 30.0%; Males per 100 females: 100.5; Marriage status: 13.7% never married, 44.4% now married, 0.7% separated, 19.1% widowed, 22.8% divorced; Foreign born: 1.9%; Speak English only: 99.5%; With disability: 19.5%; Veterans: 15.2%; Ancestry: 16.7% German, 12.3% English, 10.1% American, 8.3% Irish, 3.5% Scotch-Irish
Employment: 1.4% management, business, and financial, 4.7% computer, engineering, and science, 9.5% education, legal, community service, arts, and media, 1.0% healthcare practitioners, 19.3% service, 21.6% sales and office, 4.4% natural resources, construction, and maintenance, 38.2% production, transportation, and material moving
Income: Per capita: $24,885; Median household: $51,688; Average household: $55,192; Households with income of $100,000 or more: 6.3%; Poverty rate: 9.4%
Educational Attainment: High school diploma or higher: 87.1%; Bachelor's degree or higher: 10.3%; Graduate/professional degree or higher: 3.6%
Housing: Homeownership rate: 81.5%; Median home value: $72,500; Median year structure built: 1951; Homeowner vacancy rate: 0.0%; Median selected monthly owner costs: $788 with a mortgage, $338 without a mortgage; Median gross rent: $763 per month; Rental vacancy rate: 9.1%
Health Insurance: 89.0% have insurance; 70.5% have private insurance; 36.0% have public insurance; 11.0% do not have insurance; 6.7% of children under 18 do not have insurance
Transportation: Commute: 95.6% car, 0.0% public transportation, 4.4% walk, 0.0% work from home; Mean travel time to work: 22.9 minutes

STAUNTON (town). Covers a land area of 0.345 square miles and a water area of 0 square miles. Located at 39.49° N. Lat; 87.19° W. Long. Elevation is 646 feet.
History: Founded 1851.
Population: 544; Growth (since 2000): -1.1%; Density: 1,579.0 persons per square mile; Race: 100.0% White, 0.0% Black/African American, 0.0% Asian, 0.0% American Indian/Alaska Native, 0.0% Native Hawaiian/Other Pacific Islander, 0.0% Two or more races, 1.3% Hispanic of any race; Average household size: 2.69; Median age: 38.9; Age under 18: 24.3%; Age 65 and over: 13.4%; Males per 100 females: 100.8; Marriage status: 26.1% never married, 59.2% now married, 0.9% separated, 4.1% widowed, 10.6% divorced; Foreign born: 0.0%; Speak English only: 100.0%; With disability: 17.1%; Veterans: 8.7%; Ancestry: 36.9% German, 21.3% Irish, 6.6% English, 5.3% American, 4.2% French
Employment: 1.6% management, business, and financial, 0.4% computer, engineering, and science, 4.4% education, legal, community service, arts, and media, 4.4% healthcare practitioners, 33.2% service, 11.6% sales and office, 9.6% natural resources, construction, and maintenance, 34.8% production, transportation, and material moving
Income: Per capita: $20,034; Median household: $50,714; Average household: $53,659; Households with income of $100,000 or more: 11.4%; Poverty rate: 10.1%
Educational Attainment: High school diploma or higher: 88.7%; Bachelor's degree or higher: 4.9%; Graduate/professional degree or higher: 0.6%
Housing: Homeownership rate: 67.3%; Median home value: $68,600; Median year structure built: 1972; Homeowner vacancy rate: 2.9%; Median selected monthly owner costs: $893 with a mortgage, $283 without a mortgage; Median gross rent: $718 per month; Rental vacancy rate: 0.0%
Health Insurance: 84.6% have insurance; 55.7% have private insurance; 37.3% have public insurance; 15.4% do not have insurance; 4.0% of children under 18 do not have insurance
Transportation: Commute: 97.2% car, 0.0% public transportation, 1.6% walk, 0.8% work from home; Mean travel time to work: 27.5 minutes

Clinton County

Located in central Indiana; drained by Sugar Creek. Covers a land area of 405.070 square miles, a water area of 0.178 square miles, and is located in the Eastern Time Zone at 40.31° N. Lat., 86.48° W. Long. The county was founded in 1830. County seat is Frankfort.

Clinton County is part of the Frankfort, IN Micropolitan Statistical Area. The entire metro area includes: Clinton County, IN

Weather Station: Frankfort Disposal Plant — Elevation: 834 feet

	Jan	Feb	Mar	Apr	May	Jun	Jul	Aug	Sep	Oct	Nov	Dec
High	34	38	49	62	72	81	84	82	77	64	51	37
Low	19	22	30	40	50	60	63	62	54	43	34	23
Precip	2.3	2.2	3.0	3.7	4.3	4.4	4.3	3.9	3.0	3.1	3.5	2.9
Snow	7.5	6.1	2.7	0.4	tr	0.0	0.0	0.0	0.0	0.4	0.5	5.0

High and Low temperatures in degrees Fahrenheit; Precipitation and Snow in inches

Population: 32,455; Growth (since 2000): -4.2%; Density: 80.1 persons per square mile; Race: 94.9% White, 0.9% Black/African American, 0.3% Asian, 0.2% American Indian/Alaska Native, 0.1% Native Hawaiian/Other Pacific Islander, 1.0% two or more races, 15.2% Hispanic of any race; Average household size: 2.66; Median age: 38.2; Age under 18: 26.3%; Age 65 and over: 15.7%; Males per 100 females: 97.8; Marriage status: 24.6% never married, 56.2% now married, 1.9% separated, 7.0%

widowed, 12.2% divorced; Foreign born: 7.2%; Speak English only: 85.7%; With disability: 13.8%; Veterans: 6.9%; Ancestry: 21.0% German, 11.7% Irish, 10.6% American, 7.6% English, 2.2% Dutch
Religion: Six largest groups: 15.5% Catholicism, 12.9% Baptist, 6.9% Methodist/Pietist, 2.5% Holiness, 2.2% Presbyterian-Reformed, 1.6% Non-denominational Protestant
Economy: Unemployment rate: 3.1%; Leading industries: 16.3 % retail trade; 14.0 % other services (except public administration); 10.0 % construction; Farms: 597 totaling 223,428 acres; Company size: 0 employ 1,000 or more persons, 3 employ 500 to 999 persons, 13 employ 100 to 499 persons, 584 employ less than 100 persons; Business ownership: 644 women-owned, n/a Black-owned, 66 Hispanic-owned, n/a Asian-owned, n/a American Indian/Alaska Native-owned
Employment: 9.8% management, business, and financial, 2.9% computer, engineering, and science, 6.8% education, legal, community service, arts, and media, 4.7% healthcare practitioners, 14.5% service, 18.4% sales and office, 10.2% natural resources, construction, and maintenance, 32.7% production, transportation, and material moving
Income: Per capita: $23,722; Median household: $51,659; Average household: $63,223; Households with income of $100,000 or more: 17.3%; Poverty rate: 13.3%
Educational Attainment: High school diploma or higher: 86.2%; Bachelor's degree or higher: 15.7%; Graduate/professional degree or higher: 4.9%
Housing: Homeownership rate: 71.5%; Median home value: $103,700; Median year structure built: 1956; Homeowner vacancy rate: 1.7%; Median selected monthly owner costs: $1,022 with a mortgage, $356 without a mortgage; Median gross rent: $704 per month; Rental vacancy rate: 7.3%
Vital Statistics: Birth rate: 141.1 per 10,000 population; Death rate: 98.7 per 10,000 population; Age-adjusted cancer mortality rate: 191.6 deaths per 100,000 population
Health Insurance: 88.6% have insurance; 68.3% have private insurance; 32.7% have public insurance; 11.4% do not have insurance; 7.5% of children under 18 do not have insurance
Health Care: Physicians: 4.6 per 10,000 population; Dentists: 4.3 per 10,000 population; Hospital beds: 7.7 per 10,000 population; Hospital admissions: 182.5 per 10,000 population
Transportation: Commute: 92.4% car, 0.1% public transportation, 1.2% walk, 4.0% work from home; Mean travel time to work: 23.0 minutes
2016 Presidential Election: 71.5% Trump, 23.6% Clinton, 4.6% Johnson, 0.3% Stein

Additional Information Contacts
Clinton Government .... (765) 654-5715
http://www.clintonco.com

Clinton County Communities

COLFAX (town). Covers a land area of 0.363 square miles and a water area of 0 square miles. Located at 40.19° N. Lat; 86.67° W. Long. Elevation is 846 feet.
Population: 693; Growth (since 2000): -9.8%; Density: 1,907.2 persons per square mile; Race: 99.6% White, 0.0% Black/African American, 0.0% Asian, 0.0% American Indian/Alaska Native, 0.0% Native Hawaiian/Other Pacific Islander, 0.4% Two or more races, 0.0% Hispanic of any race; Average household size: 2.68; Median age: 39.9; Age under 18: 26.6%; Age 65 and over: 17.0%; Males per 100 females: 89.3; Marriage status: 23.1% never married, 56.0% now married, 2.0% separated, 5.2% widowed, 15.7% divorced; Foreign born: 0.1%; Speak English only: 99.7%; With disability: 20.9%; Veterans: 5.1%; Ancestry: 35.2% German, 21.6% Irish, 16.9% American, 11.3% English, 4.0% French
Employment: 10.7% management, business, and financial, 1.5% computer, engineering, and science, 8.1% education, legal, community service, arts, and media, 4.4% healthcare practitioners, 3.7% service, 18.0% sales and office, 14.3% natural resources, construction, and maintenance, 39.3% production, transportation, and material moving
Income: Per capita: $19,093; Median household: $41,125; Average household: $50,395; Households with income of $100,000 or more: 11.5%; Poverty rate: 18.5%
Educational Attainment: High school diploma or higher: 82.8%; Bachelor's degree or higher: 9.3%; Graduate/professional degree or higher: 3.2%
Housing: Homeownership rate: 73.0%; Median home value: $71,900; Median year structure built: 1952; Homeowner vacancy rate: 0.0%; Median selected monthly owner costs: $927 with a mortgage, $402 without a mortgage; Median gross rent: $751 per month; Rental vacancy rate: 10.3%
Health Insurance: 91.2% have insurance; 61.9% have private insurance; 42.1% have public insurance; 8.8% do not have insurance; 3.3% of children under 18 do not have insurance
Transportation: Commute: 91.4% car, 0.0% public transportation, 3.8% walk, 1.5% work from home; Mean travel time to work: 24.7 minutes

FOREST (unincorporated postal area)
ZCTA: 46039
Covers a land area of 27.071 square miles and a water area of 0 square miles. Located at 40.37° N. Lat; 86.31° W. Long. Elevation is 883 feet.
Population: 555; Growth (since 2000): -33.8%; Density: 20.5 persons per square mile; Race: 100.0% White, 0.0% Black/African American, 0.0% Asian, 0.0% American Indian/Alaska Native, 0.0% Native Hawaiian/Other Pacific Islander, 0.0% Two or more races, 0.0% Hispanic of any race; Average household size: 2.41; Median age: 58.1; Age under 18: 12.4%; Age 65 and over: 36.9%; Males per 100 females: 102.4; Marriage status: 16.8% never married, 68.0% now married, 0.0% separated, 8.6% widowed, 6.6% divorced; Foreign born: 0.0%; Speak English only: 100.0%; With disability: 20.9%; Veterans: 5.3%; Ancestry: 33.0% German, 18.4% Irish, 16.2% American, 10.6% English, 6.7% Dutch
Employment: 25.2% management, business, and financial, 6.8% computer, engineering, and science, 11.2% education, legal, community service, arts, and media, 0.0% healthcare practitioners, 8.8% service, 14.4% sales and office, 15.6% natural resources, construction, and maintenance, 18.0% production, transportation, and material moving
Income: Per capita: $26,002; Median household: $63,333; Average household: $60,570; Households with income of $100,000 or more: 17.4%; Poverty rate: 9.5%
Educational Attainment: High school diploma or higher: 100.0%; Bachelor's degree or higher: 17.5%; Graduate/professional degree or higher: 7.6%
Housing: Homeownership rate: 83.9%; Median home value: $108,200; Median year structure built: 1966; Homeowner vacancy rate: 0.0%; Median selected monthly owner costs: $769 with a mortgage, $0 without a mortgage; Median gross rent: $855 per month; Rental vacancy rate: 0.0%
Health Insurance: 90.8% have insurance; 67.2% have private insurance; 42.7% have public insurance; 9.2% do not have insurance; 27.5% of children under 18 do not have insurance
Transportation: Commute: 85.2% car, 0.0% public transportation, 0.0% walk, 14.8% work from home; Mean travel time to work: 28.6 minutes

FRANKFORT (city). County seat. Covers a land area of 6.311 square miles and a water area of 0 square miles. Located at 40.28° N. Lat; 86.51° W. Long. Elevation is 850 feet.
History: Frankfort was named for Frankfurt am Main, Germany, the home of the grandfather of the Pence brothers who owned the land on which the city was founded. Frankfort developed as the county seat of Clinton County.
Population: 16,226; Growth (since 2000): -2.6%; Density: 2,570.9 persons per square mile; Race: 91.9% White, 1.7% Black/African American, 0.2% Asian, 0.3% American Indian/Alaska Native, 0.1% Native Hawaiian/Other Pacific Islander, 1.0% Two or more races, 27.8% Hispanic of any race; Average household size: 2.68; Median age: 34.0; Age under 18: 28.6%; Age 65 and over: 14.8%; Males per 100 females: 97.1; Marriage status: 28.0% never married, 49.3% now married, 3.1% separated, 8.6% widowed, 14.1% divorced; Foreign born: 13.5%; Speak English only: 73.2%; With disability: 14.1%; Veterans: 6.5%; Ancestry: 14.2% German, 11.0% Irish, 7.1% American, 6.7% English, 1.8% Scotch-Irish
Employment: 5.6% management, business, and financial, 1.7% computer, engineering, and science, 6.7% education, legal, community service, arts, and media, 3.6% healthcare practitioners, 16.1% service, 17.4% sales and office, 9.9% natural resources, construction, and maintenance, 39.0% production, transportation, and material moving
Income: Per capita: $20,057; Median household: $41,982; Average household: $53,443; Households with income of $100,000 or more: 11.2%; Poverty rate: 16.3%
Educational Attainment: High school diploma or higher: 79.3%; Bachelor's degree or higher: 11.3%; Graduate/professional degree or higher: 3.9%

School District(s)
Clinton Prairie School Corporation (PK-12)
Enrollment: 1,252 .... (765) 659-1339

Community Schools Of Frankfort (PK-12)
Enrollment: 3,187 . . . . (765) 654-5585
Community Schools Of Frankfort (PK-12)
Enrollment: 3,187 . . . . (765) 654-5585

Housing: Homeownership rate: 62.5%; Median home value: $79,000; Median year structure built: 1954; Homeowner vacancy rate: 0.5%; Median selected monthly owner costs: $909 with a mortgage, $321 without a mortgage; Median gross rent: $678 per month; Rental vacancy rate: 9.0%
Health Insurance: 86.9% have insurance; 60.4% have private insurance; 37.7% have public insurance; 13.1% do not have insurance; 4.1% of children under 18 do not have insurance
Hospitals: Saint Vincent Frankfort Hospital (25 beds)
Safety: Violent crime rate: 9.5 per 10,000 population; Property crime rate: 315.6 per 10,000 population
Newspapers: Frankfort Times (weekly circulation 2,600); The Times (daily circulation 6,200)
Transportation: Commute: 94.8% car, 0.0% public transportation, 0.5% walk, 1.5% work from home; Mean travel time to work: 20.1 minutes
Airports: Frankfort Municipal (general aviation)
Additional Information Contacts
City of Frankfort. . . . . (765) 654-5715
http://frankfort-in.gov

KIRKLIN (town). Covers a land area of 0.341 square miles and a water area of 0 square miles. Located at 40.19° N. Lat; 86.36° W. Long. Elevation is 919 feet.
History: Kirklin was established at the junction of the Michigan Road with a state road. Nathan Kirklin bought the land here in 1828 and built a tavern.
Population: 886; Growth (since 2000): 15.7%; Density: 2,595.4 persons per square mile; Race: 96.4% White, 0.9% Black/African American, 1.8% Asian, 0.2% American Indian/Alaska Native, 0.0% Native Hawaiian/Other Pacific Islander, 0.7% Two or more races, 1.4% Hispanic of any race; Average household size: 2.63; Median age: 36.8; Age under 18: 28.3%; Age 65 and over: 8.8%; Males per 100 females: 98.5; Marriage status: 26.1% never married, 47.9% now married, 0.6% separated, 4.7% widowed, 21.4% divorced; Foreign born: 1.8%; Speak English only: 96.6%; With disability: 15.9%; Veterans: 5.0%; Ancestry: 27.8% German, 13.0% Irish, 7.7% American, 6.0% Scotch-Irish, 5.3% English
Employment: 12.6% management, business, and financial, 2.3% computer, engineering, and science, 2.1% education, legal, community service, arts, and media, 8.5% healthcare practitioners, 18.3% service, 22.2% sales and office, 12.4% natural resources, construction, and maintenance, 21.6% production, transportation, and material moving
Income: Per capita: $20,088; Median household: $46,719; Average household: $52,110; Households with income of $100,000 or more: 11.0%; Poverty rate: 26.8%
Educational Attainment: High school diploma or higher: 86.9%; Bachelor's degree or higher: 16.9%; Graduate/professional degree or higher: 3.6%
Housing: Homeownership rate: 64.7%; Median home value: $74,700; Median year structure built: 1952; Homeowner vacancy rate: 2.7%; Median selected monthly owner costs: $976 with a mortgage, $475 without a mortgage; Median gross rent: $768 per month; Rental vacancy rate: 2.5%
Health Insurance: 73.5% have insurance; 59.0% have private insurance; 21.6% have public insurance; 26.5% do not have insurance; 37.5% of children under 18 do not have insurance
Transportation: Commute: 85.0% car, 0.0% public transportation, 7.8% walk, 6.2% work from home; Mean travel time to work: 27.8 minutes

MICHIGANTOWN (town). Covers a land area of 0.264 square miles and a water area of 0 square miles. Located at 40.33° N. Lat; 86.39° W. Long. Elevation is 876 feet.
History: Michigantown was founded in 1830 and named for the Michigan Road, for which it served as a stage stop.
Population: 483; Growth (since 2000): 19.0%; Density: 1,827.5 persons per square mile; Race: 97.7% White, 0.0% Black/African American, 0.0% Asian, 0.0% American Indian/Alaska Native, 0.0% Native Hawaiian/Other Pacific Islander, 2.1% Two or more races, 0.8% Hispanic of any race; Average household size: 2.71; Median age: 35.8; Age under 18: 29.4%; Age 65 and over: 12.6%; Males per 100 females: 92.2; Marriage status: 21.7% never married, 56.1% now married, 3.9% separated, 8.1% widowed, 14.2% divorced; Foreign born: 0.2%; Speak English only: 99.3%; With disability: 17.4%; Veterans: 7.0%; Ancestry: 17.4% German, 14.5% Irish, 14.1% American, 7.2% English, 3.3% Dutch
Employment: 3.8% management, business, and financial, 1.9% computer, engineering, and science, 5.8% education, legal, community service, arts, and media, 4.8% healthcare practitioners, 8.2% service, 18.8% sales and office, 19.7% natural resources, construction, and maintenance, 37.0% production, transportation, and material moving
Income: Per capita: $21,819; Median household: $53,750; Average household: $58,856; Households with income of $100,000 or more: 16.3%; Poverty rate: 10.3%
Educational Attainment: High school diploma or higher: 92.3%; Bachelor's degree or higher: 8.4%; Graduate/professional degree or higher: 1.9%

School District(s)

Clinton Central School Corporation (KG-12)
Enrollment: 987. . . . . (765) 249-2515
Housing: Homeownership rate: 52.8%; Median home value: $89,200; Median year structure built: 1945; Homeowner vacancy rate: 1.1%; Median selected monthly owner costs: $986 with a mortgage, $325 without a mortgage; Median gross rent: $793 per month; Rental vacancy rate: 8.7%
Health Insurance: 88.2% have insurance; 71.8% have private insurance; 34.8% have public insurance; 11.8% do not have insurance; 11.7% of children under 18 do not have insurance
Transportation: Commute: 88.0% car, 0.0% public transportation, 7.1% walk, 3.8% work from home; Mean travel time to work: 26.8 minutes

MULBERRY (town). Covers a land area of 0.589 square miles and a water area of 0 square miles. Located at 40.35° N. Lat; 86.67° W. Long. Elevation is 784 feet.
History: Laid out 1858.
Population: 1,313; Growth (since 2000): -5.3%; Density: 2,227.5 persons per square mile; Race: 98.0% White, 0.8% Black/African American, 0.3% Asian, 0.0% American Indian/Alaska Native, 0.0% Native Hawaiian/Other Pacific Islander, 0.1% Two or more races, 4.0% Hispanic of any race; Average household size: 2.56; Median age: 39.4; Age under 18: 23.1%; Age 65 and over: 25.3%; Males per 100 females: 80.4; Marriage status: 19.8% never married, 53.0% now married, 0.9% separated, 17.0% widowed, 10.2% divorced; Foreign born: 2.3%; Speak English only: 95.9%; With disability: 12.2%; Veterans: 11.8%; Ancestry: 28.5% German, 13.1% Irish, 9.7% American, 8.0% English, 2.8% Dutch
Employment: 4.7% management, business, and financial, 5.8% computer, engineering, and science, 7.1% education, legal, community service, arts, and media, 6.0% healthcare practitioners, 18.1% service, 22.8% sales and office, 6.7% natural resources, construction, and maintenance, 28.8% production, transportation, and material moving
Income: Per capita: $24,980; Median household: $56,200; Average household: $64,997; Households with income of $100,000 or more: 13.8%; Poverty rate: 6.8%
Educational Attainment: High school diploma or higher: 87.6%; Bachelor's degree or higher: 17.1%; Graduate/professional degree or higher: 2.5%
Housing: Homeownership rate: 66.0%; Median home value: $98,500; Median year structure built: 1941; Homeowner vacancy rate: 2.9%; Median selected monthly owner costs: $1,057 with a mortgage, $355 without a mortgage; Median gross rent: $713 per month; Rental vacancy rate: 0.0%
Health Insurance: 92.5% have insurance; 77.0% have private insurance; 32.7% have public insurance; 7.5% do not have insurance; 6.8% of children under 18 do not have insurance
Transportation: Commute: 89.3% car, 1.9% public transportation, 3.1% walk, 4.0% work from home; Mean travel time to work: 24.6 minutes

ROSSVILLE (town). Covers a land area of 0.525 square miles and a water area of 0 square miles. Located at 40.42° N. Lat; 86.60° W. Long. Elevation is 725 feet.
History: Laid out 1834.
Population: 1,629; Growth (since 2000): 7.7%; Density: 3,104.0 persons per square mile; Race: 99.0% White, 0.0% Black/African American, 0.5% Asian, 0.0% American Indian/Alaska Native, 0.1% Native Hawaiian/Other Pacific Islander, 0.2% Two or more races, 4.7% Hispanic of any race; Average household size: 2.53; Median age: 39.6; Age under 18: 27.8%; Age 65 and over: 22.0%; Males per 100 females: 83.5; Marriage status: 21.3% never married, 54.7% now married, 1.3% separated, 10.3% widowed, 13.7% divorced; Foreign born: 0.9%; Speak English only: 96.3%; With disability: 15.0%; Veterans: 7.1%; Ancestry: 33.4% German, 10.1% English, 8.9% American, 8.4% Irish, 2.6% Polish
Employment: 8.8% management, business, and financial, 3.0% computer, engineering, and science, 7.7% education, legal, community service, arts,

and media, 3.6% healthcare practitioners, 18.1% service, 22.9% sales and office, 13.4% natural resources, construction, and maintenance, 22.5% production, transportation, and material moving
Income: Per capita: $21,246; Median household: $47,772; Average household: $54,065; Households with income of $100,000 or more: 10.0%; Poverty rate: 13.8%
Educational Attainment: High school diploma or higher: 90.5%; Bachelor's degree or higher: 16.2%; Graduate/professional degree or higher: 4.8%

School District(s)

Rossville Con School District (KG-12)
Enrollment: 869. . . . . (765) 379-2990
Housing: Homeownership rate: 64.7%; Median home value: $121,100; Median year structure built: 1973; Homeowner vacancy rate: 2.7%; Median selected monthly owner costs: $994 with a mortgage, $423 without a mortgage; Median gross rent: $794 per month; Rental vacancy rate: 3.8%
Health Insurance: 92.6% have insurance; 71.6% have private insurance; 34.3% have public insurance; 7.4% do not have insurance; 6.1% of children under 18 do not have insurance
Transportation: Commute: 93.9% car, 0.6% public transportation, 1.8% walk, 3.3% work from home; Mean travel time to work: 26.6 minutes

Crawford County

Located in southern Indiana; bounded on the south by the Ohio River and the Kentucky border; drained by the Blue and Little Blue Rivers. Covers a land area of 305.643 square miles, a water area of 3.076 square miles, and is located in the Eastern Time Zone at 38.29° N. Lat., 86.44° W. Long. The county was founded in 1818. County seat is English.

Weather Station: English 4 S Elevation: 509 feet

	Jan	Feb	Mar	Apr	May	Jun	Jul	Aug	Sep	Oct	Nov	Dec
High	42	48	58	68	77	84	88	87	81	70	58	45
Low	22	25	32	41	50	59	63	61	53	41	34	25
Precip	3.5	3.5	4.5	4.5	5.7	4.5	4.0	3.3	3.6	3.5	4.2	3.9
Snow	1.0	na	0.1	tr	0.0	0.0	0.0	0.0	0.0	tr	tr	2.0

High and Low temperatures in degrees Fahrenheit; Precipitation and Snow in inches

Population: 10,598; Growth (since 2000): -1.3%; Density: 34.7 persons per square mile; Race: 97.3% White, 0.2% Black/African American, 0.1% Asian, 0.8% American Indian/Alaska Native, 0.0% Native Hawaiian/Other Pacific Islander, 1.6% two or more races, 1.5% Hispanic of any race; Average household size: 2.62; Median age: 43.7; Age under 18: 22.1%; Age 65 and over: 18.3%; Males per 100 females: 103.0; Marriage status: 24.2% never married, 53.0% now married, 2.2% separated, 8.4% widowed, 14.4% divorced; Foreign born: 0.3%; Speak English only: 98.7%; With disability: 20.1%; Veterans: 10.3%; Ancestry: 24.9% German, 14.4% Irish, 12.3% English, 9.5% American, 2.5% French
Religion: Six largest groups: 15.2% Baptist, 6.0% Non-denominational Protestant, 5.2% Methodist/Pietist, 3.2% Latter-day Saints, 2.6% Holiness, 1.8% Catholicism
Economy: Unemployment rate: 4.7%; Leading industries: 16.8 % retail trade; 13.7 % health care and social assistance; 13.0 % accommodation and food services; Farms: 338 totaling 46,404 acres; Company size: 0 employ 1,000 or more persons, 0 employ 500 to 999 persons, 2 employ 100 to 499 persons, 129 employ less than 100 persons; Business ownership: 165 women-owned, n/a Black-owned, n/a Hispanic-owned, n/a Asian-owned, n/a American Indian/Alaska Native-owned
Employment: 7.6% management, business, and financial, 2.9% computer, engineering, and science, 6.2% education, legal, community service, arts, and media, 4.8% healthcare practitioners, 20.7% service, 16.8% sales and office, 11.6% natural resources, construction, and maintenance, 29.4% production, transportation, and material moving
Income: Per capita: $19,424; Median household: $40,067; Average household: $47,303; Households with income of $100,000 or more: 7.6%; Poverty rate: 17.8%
Educational Attainment: High school diploma or higher: 81.9%; Bachelor's degree or higher: 10.4%; Graduate/professional degree or higher: 3.9%
Housing: Homeownership rate: 83.2%; Median home value: $86,700; Median year structure built: 1985; Homeowner vacancy rate: 0.0%; Median selected monthly owner costs: $887 with a mortgage, $363 without a mortgage; Median gross rent: $562 per month; Rental vacancy rate: 8.5%
Vital Statistics: Birth rate: 106.9 per 10,000 population; Death rate: 108.8 per 10,000 population; Age-adjusted cancer mortality rate: 191.7 deaths per 100,000 population
Health Insurance: 92.0% have insurance; 65.6% have private insurance; 38.9% have public insurance; 8.0% do not have insurance; 4.4% of children under 18 do not have insurance
Health Care: Physicians: 0.0 per 10,000 population; Dentists: 0.9 per 10,000 population; Hospital beds: 0.0 per 10,000 population; Hospital admissions: 0.0 per 10,000 population
Transportation: Commute: 95.0% car, 0.3% public transportation, 1.0% walk, 2.6% work from home; Mean travel time to work: 32.7 minutes
2016 Presidential Election: 65.6% Trump, 28.8% Clinton, 5.6% Johnson, 0.0% Stein
National and State Parks: Hilands Overlook State Park
Additional Information Contacts
Crawford Government. . . . . (812) 338-2565

Crawford County Communities

ALTON (town). Covers a land area of 0.172 square miles and a water area of 0.018 square miles. Located at 38.12° N. Lat; 86.42° W. Long. Elevation is 427 feet.
Population: 39; Growth (since 2000): -26.4%; Density: 226.8 persons per square mile; Race: 100.0% White, 0.0% Black/African American, 0.0% Asian, 0.0% American Indian/Alaska Native, 0.0% Native Hawaiian/Other Pacific Islander, 0.0% Two or more races, 0.0% Hispanic of any race; Average household size: 2.44; Median age: 53.1; Age under 18: 0.0%; Age 65 and over: 20.5%; Males per 100 females: 129.2; Marriage status: 25.6% never married, 46.2% now married, 0.0% separated, 7.7% widowed, 20.5% divorced; Foreign born: 0.0%; Speak English only: 100.0%; With disability: 35.9%; Veterans: 10.3%; Ancestry: 15.4% American, 10.3% German, 5.1% Danish
Employment: 6.7% management, business, and financial, 0.0% computer, engineering, and science, 0.0% education, legal, community service, arts, and media, 0.0% healthcare practitioners, 0.0% service, 53.3% sales and office, 40.0% natural resources, construction, and maintenance, 0.0% production, transportation, and material moving
Income: Per capita: $22,646; Median household: $45,625; Average household: $50,613; Households with income of $100,000 or more: 25.0%; Poverty rate: 15.4%
Educational Attainment: High school diploma or higher: 82.4%; Bachelor's degree or higher: 23.5%; Graduate/professional degree or higher: n/a
Housing: Homeownership rate: 93.8%; Median home value: $48,300; Median year structure built: Before 1940; Homeowner vacancy rate: 0.0%; Median selected monthly owner costs: $567 with a mortgage, $354 without a mortgage; Median gross rent: n/a per month; Rental vacancy rate: 0.0%
Health Insurance: 89.7% have insurance; 41.0% have private insurance; 61.5% have public insurance; 10.3% do not have insurance; 0.0% of children under 18 do not have insurance
Transportation: Commute: 100.0% car, 0.0% public transportation, 0.0% walk, 0.0% work from home; Mean travel time to work: 0.0 minutes

ECKERTY (unincorporated postal area)
ZCTA: 47116
Covers a land area of 30.021 square miles and a water area of 0.662 square miles. Located at 38.32° N. Lat; 86.62° W. Long. Elevation is 745 feet.
Population: 578; Growth (since 2000): -32.3%; Density: 19.3 persons per square mile; Race: 100.0% White, 0.0% Black/African American, 0.0% Asian, 0.0% American Indian/Alaska Native, 0.0% Native Hawaiian/Other Pacific Islander, 0.0% Two or more races, 0.0% Hispanic of any race; Average household size: 2.40; Median age: 53.3; Age under 18: 17.5%; Age 65 and over: 21.3%; Males per 100 females: 111.3; Marriage status: 23.7% never married, 64.1% now married, 0.0% separated, 3.8% widowed, 8.4% divorced; Foreign born: 0.0%; Speak English only: 100.0%; With disability: 19.2%; Veterans: 6.1%; Ancestry: 41.9% German, 23.5% American, 21.6% English, 1.7% Norwegian, 1.7% Welsh
Employment: 8.1% management, business, and financial, 11.5% computer, engineering, and science, 8.8% education, legal, community service, arts, and media, 0.0% healthcare practitioners, 6.9% service, 21.2% sales and office, 3.5% natural resources, construction, and maintenance, 40.0% production, transportation, and material moving

Income: Per capita: $20,884; Median household: $47,625; Average household: $45,927; Households with income of $100,000 or more: n/a; Poverty rate: 8.0%
Educational Attainment: High school diploma or higher: 84.2%; Bachelor's degree or higher: 2.0%; Graduate/professional degree or higher: n/a

School District(s)

Crawford County Community Sch Corp (PK-12)
Enrollment: 1,631 . . . . (812) 365-2135

Housing: Homeownership rate: 100.0%; Median home value: $67,900; Median year structure built: 1981; Homeowner vacancy rate: 0.0%; Median selected monthly owner costs: $837 with a mortgage, $311 without a mortgage; Median gross rent: n/a per month; Rental vacancy rate: 0.0%
Health Insurance: 91.5% have insurance; 74.9% have private insurance; 25.4% have public insurance; 8.5% do not have insurance; 0.0% of children under 18 do not have insurance
Transportation: Commute: 93.8% car, 0.0% public transportation, 0.0% walk, 0.0% work from home; Mean travel time to work: 28.6 minutes

ENGLISH (town). County seat. Covers a land area of 3.044 square miles and a water area of 0 square miles. Located at 38.34° N. Lat; 86.46° W. Long. Elevation is 505 feet.
History: The town of English was laid out in 1839, and grew when it became the county seat in 1893. The town was named for William Hayden English, a U.S. congressman from Indiana.
Population: 680; Growth (since 2000): 1.0%; Density: 223.4 persons per square mile; Race: 94.6% White, 0.6% Black/African American, 0.0% Asian, 0.6% American Indian/Alaska Native, 0.0% Native Hawaiian/Other Pacific Islander, 4.3% Two or more races, 1.5% Hispanic of any race; Average household size: 2.23; Median age: 39.6; Age under 18: 25.0%; Age 65 and over: 17.5%; Males per 100 females: 89.7; Marriage status: 29.0% never married, 44.6% now married, 1.3% separated, 8.4% widowed, 18.0% divorced; Foreign born: 0.4%; Speak English only: 98.2%; With disability: 29.7%; Veterans: 5.9%; Ancestry: 18.5% American, 17.9% German, 12.2% Irish, 7.9% English, 3.5% Scottish
Employment: 3.3% management, business, and financial, 2.0% computer, engineering, and science, 1.6% education, legal, community service, arts, and media, 2.9% healthcare practitioners, 27.5% service, 17.2% sales and office, 20.1% natural resources, construction, and maintenance, 25.4% production, transportation, and material moving
Income: Per capita: $16,055; Median household: $20,795; Average household: $34,879; Households with income of $100,000 or more: 4.0%; Poverty rate: 35.8%
Educational Attainment: High school diploma or higher: 73.7%; Bachelor's degree or higher: 4.6%; Graduate/professional degree or higher: 1.5%
Housing: Homeownership rate: 53.9%; Median home value: $65,000; Median year structure built: 1977; Homeowner vacancy rate: 0.0%; Median selected monthly owner costs: $875 with a mortgage, $275 without a mortgage; Median gross rent: $372 per month; Rental vacancy rate: 4.9%
Health Insurance: 82.6% have insurance; 39.1% have private insurance; 52.5% have public insurance; 17.4% do not have insurance; 10.3% of children under 18 do not have insurance
Transportation: Commute: 90.7% car, 0.0% public transportation, 3.4% walk, 5.9% work from home; Mean travel time to work: 30.9 minutes

GRANTSBURG (unincorporated postal area)
ZCTA: 47123
Covers a land area of 7.400 square miles and a water area of 0 square miles. Located at 38.27° N. Lat; 86.48° W. Long. Elevation is 614 feet.
Population: 74; Growth (since 2000): 146.7%; Density: 10.0 persons per square mile; Race: 100.0% White, 0.0% Black/African American, 0.0% Asian, 0.0% American Indian/Alaska Native, 0.0% Native Hawaiian/Other Pacific Islander, 0.0% Two or more races, 0.0% Hispanic of any race; Average household size: 2.00; Median age: 67.4; Age under 18: 0.0%; Age 65 and over: 60.8%; Males per 100 females: 94.8; Marriage status: 0.0% never married, 100.0% now married, 0.0% separated, 0.0% widowed, 0.0% divorced; Foreign born: 0.0%; Speak English only: 100.0%; With disability: 20.3%; Veterans: 25.7%; Ancestry: 39.2% Irish, 25.7% Russian, 24.3% German
Employment: 0.0% management, business, and financial, 0.0% computer, engineering, and science, 0.0% education, legal, community service, arts, and media, 0.0% healthcare practitioners, 0.0% service, 0.0% sales and office, 0.0% natural resources, construction, and maintenance, 100.0% production, transportation, and material moving
Income: Per capita: $19,349; Median household: n/a; Average household: n/a; Households with income of $100,000 or more: n/a; Poverty rate: 20.3%
Educational Attainment: High school diploma or higher: 85.1%; Bachelor's degree or higher: 50.0%; Graduate/professional degree or higher: n/a
Housing: Homeownership rate: 100.0%; Median home value: n/a; Median year structure built: 1984; Homeowner vacancy rate: 0.0%; Median selected monthly owner costs: $0 with a mortgage, $0 without a mortgage; Median gross rent: n/a per month; Rental vacancy rate: 0.0%
Health Insurance: 100.0% have insurance; 50.0% have private insurance; 70.3% have public insurance; 0.0% do not have insurance; 0.0% of children under 18 do not have insurance
Transportation: Commute: 100.0% car, 0.0% public transportation, 0.0% walk, 0.0% work from home; Mean travel time to work: 0.0 minutes

LEAVENWORTH (town). Covers a land area of 0.822 square miles and a water area of 0.048 square miles. Located at 38.20° N. Lat; 86.35° W. Long. Elevation is 659 feet.
History: Leavenworth was founded in 1818 and served as Crawford County's seat from 1843 to 1893. A boat-building industry was established in 1830 by David Lyon, and Leavenworth became a shipping point on the Ohio River. The 1937 flooding of the Ohio River destroyed most of the town, which was rebuilt on the hills behind the original site.
Population: 355; Growth (since 2000): 0.6%; Density: 431.7 persons per square mile; Race: 92.7% White, 3.4% Black/African American, 0.0% Asian, 0.0% American Indian/Alaska Native, 0.0% Native Hawaiian/Other Pacific Islander, 3.9% Two or more races, 0.3% Hispanic of any race; Average household size: 2.35; Median age: 43.8; Age under 18: 22.5%; Age 65 and over: 30.7%; Males per 100 females: 68.8; Marriage status: 22.3% never married, 34.9% now married, 2.5% separated, 19.1% widowed, 23.7% divorced; Foreign born: 0.3%; Speak English only: 97.4%; With disability: 20.6%; Veterans: 9.5%; Ancestry: 21.1% German, 20.8% Irish, 16.6% English, 7.0% American, 3.7% French
Employment: 5.5% management, business, and financial, 2.8% computer, engineering, and science, 4.6% education, legal, community service, arts, and media, 0.9% healthcare practitioners, 24.8% service, 12.8% sales and office, 20.2% natural resources, construction, and maintenance, 28.4% production, transportation, and material moving
Income: Per capita: $19,264; Median household: $38,750; Average household: $40,402; Households with income of $100,000 or more: 7.1%; Poverty rate: 28.4%
Educational Attainment: High school diploma or higher: 81.0%; Bachelor's degree or higher: 12.3%; Graduate/professional degree or higher: 3.6%

School District(s)

Crawford County Community Sch Corp (PK-12)
Enrollment: 1,631 . . . . (812) 365-2135

Housing: Homeownership rate: 65.9%; Median home value: $59,300; Median year structure built: 1943; Homeowner vacancy rate: 0.0%; Median selected monthly owner costs: $633 with a mortgage, $354 without a mortgage; Median gross rent: $459 per month; Rental vacancy rate: 6.5%
Health Insurance: 90.2% have insurance; 63.2% have private insurance; 39.5% have public insurance; 9.8% do not have insurance; 2.5% of children under 18 do not have insurance
Transportation: Commute: 100.0% car, 0.0% public transportation, 0.0% walk, 0.0% work from home; Mean travel time to work: 25.1 minutes

MARENGO (town). Covers a land area of 0.774 square miles and a water area of 0 square miles. Located at 38.37° N. Lat; 86.34° W. Long. Elevation is 597 feet.
History: Marengo grew as a resort village in an area of coldwater springs and caves. Quarrying was an early industry.
Population: 793; Growth (since 2000): -4.3%; Density: 1,024.0 persons per square mile; Race: 95.1% White, 0.6% Black/African American, 1.8% Asian, 1.3% American Indian/Alaska Native, 0.0% Native Hawaiian/Other Pacific Islander, 1.3% Two or more races, 5.8% Hispanic of any race; Average household size: 2.63; Median age: 39.9; Age under 18: 23.7%; Age 65 and over: 17.5%; Males per 100 females: 91.7; Marriage status: 19.2% never married, 42.9% now married, 1.7% separated, 10.1% widowed, 27.7% divorced; Foreign born: 1.4%; Speak English only: 98.7%; With disability: 29.1%; Veterans: 9.3%; Ancestry: 16.6% German, 14.1% Irish, 9.1% American, 7.7% English, 5.0% French

Employment: 8.7% management, business, and financial, 1.0% computer, engineering, and science, 7.0% education, legal, community service, arts, and media, 0.7% healthcare practitioners, 14.4% service, 28.8% sales and office, 9.4% natural resources, construction, and maintenance, 30.1% production, transportation, and material moving
Income: Per capita: $14,962; Median household: $26,731; Average household: $36,061; Households with income of $100,000 or more: 2.7%; Poverty rate: 31.7%
Educational Attainment: High school diploma or higher: 74.3%; Bachelor's degree or higher: 6.3%; Graduate/professional degree or higher: 2.0%

School District(s)

Crawford County Community Sch Corp (PK-12)
Enrollment: 1,631 .... (812) 365-2135
Housing: Homeownership rate: 57.3%; Median home value: $70,900; Median year structure built: 1979; Homeowner vacancy rate: 0.0%; Median selected monthly owner costs: $771 with a mortgage, $348 without a mortgage; Median gross rent: $560 per month; Rental vacancy rate: 9.0%
Health Insurance: 83.9% have insurance; 44.5% have private insurance; 49.6% have public insurance; 16.1% do not have insurance; 9.7% of children under 18 do not have insurance
Transportation: Commute: 97.0% car, 0.0% public transportation, 3.0% walk, 0.0% work from home; Mean travel time to work: 30.4 minutes

MILLTOWN (town). Covers a land area of 1.412 square miles and a water area of 0 square miles. Located at 38.34° N. Lat; 86.27° W. Long. Elevation is 620 feet.
Population: 897; Growth (since 2000): -3.8%; Density: 635.1 persons per square mile; Race: 98.4% White, 0.0% Black/African American, 0.0% Asian, 0.0% American Indian/Alaska Native, 0.0% Native Hawaiian/Other Pacific Islander, 1.6% Two or more races, 0.0% Hispanic of any race; Average household size: 2.31; Median age: 42.5; Age under 18: 24.1%; Age 65 and over: 20.7%; Males per 100 females: 92.9; Marriage status: 23.2% never married, 52.9% now married, 1.6% separated, 4.4% widowed, 19.5% divorced; Foreign born: 0.0%; Speak English only: 98.0%; With disability: 29.0%; Veterans: 14.2%; Ancestry: 20.6% German, 16.2% English, 13.7% American, 10.8% Irish, 5.2% Dutch
Employment: 5.0% management, business, and financial, 3.4% computer, engineering, and science, 11.2% education, legal, community service, arts, and media, 3.4% healthcare practitioners, 16.5% service, 22.4% sales and office, 12.1% natural resources, construction, and maintenance, 26.1% production, transportation, and material moving
Income: Per capita: $19,219; Median household: $30,583; Average household: $40,898; Households with income of $100,000 or more: 5.9%; Poverty rate: 14.3%
Educational Attainment: High school diploma or higher: 77.8%; Bachelor's degree or higher: 13.6%; Graduate/professional degree or higher: 4.6%

School District(s)

Crawford County Community Sch Corp (PK-12)
Enrollment: 1,631 .... (812) 365-2135
Housing: Homeownership rate: 68.1%; Median home value: $84,500; Median year structure built: 1963; Homeowner vacancy rate: 0.0%; Median selected monthly owner costs: $788 with a mortgage, $333 without a mortgage; Median gross rent: $572 per month; Rental vacancy rate: 4.6%
Health Insurance: 87.9% have insurance; 60.0% have private insurance; 42.4% have public insurance; 12.1% do not have insurance; 8.8% of children under 18 do not have insurance
Transportation: Commute: 91.7% car, 0.0% public transportation, 3.7% walk, 4.6% work from home; Mean travel time to work: 33.4 minutes

TASWELL (unincorporated postal area)
ZCTA: 47175
Covers a land area of 22.449 square miles and a water area of 2.067 square miles. Located at 38.38° N. Lat; 86.57° W. Long. Elevation is 778 feet.
Population: 852; Growth (since 2000): 4.0%; Density: 38.0 persons per square mile; Race: 96.8% White, 0.0% Black/African American, 0.0% Asian, 1.6% American Indian/Alaska Native, 0.0% Native Hawaiian/Other Pacific Islander, 1.5% Two or more races, 4.7% Hispanic of any race; Average household size: 2.28; Median age: 49.9; Age under 18: 28.3%; Age 65 and over: 20.3%; Males per 100 females: 110.9; Marriage status: 20.8% never married, 40.5% now married, 11.4% separated, 14.6% widowed, 24.1% divorced; Foreign born: 0.0%; Speak English only: 98.3%; With disability: 22.9%; Veterans: 17.3%; Ancestry: 20.1% Irish, 14.0% German, 8.5% English, 5.8% American, 2.1% European
Employment: 6.3% management, business, and financial, 4.0% computer, engineering, and science, 6.0% education, legal, community service, arts, and media, 2.6% healthcare practitioners, 3.4% service, 18.1% sales and office, 17.2% natural resources, construction, and maintenance, 42.4% production, transportation, and material moving
Income: Per capita: $20,348; Median household: $32,108; Average household: $45,438; Households with income of $100,000 or more: 6.2%; Poverty rate: 7.4%
Educational Attainment: High school diploma or higher: 87.5%; Bachelor's degree or higher: 8.2%; Graduate/professional degree or higher: 6.4%
Housing: Homeownership rate: 93.0%; Median home value: $75,400; Median year structure built: 1986; Homeowner vacancy rate: 0.0%; Median selected monthly owner costs: $706 with a mortgage, $334 without a mortgage; Median gross rent: n/a per month; Rental vacancy rate: 0.0%
Health Insurance: 97.7% have insurance; 66.9% have private insurance; 35.1% have public insurance; 2.3% do not have insurance; 4.9% of children under 18 do not have insurance
Transportation: Commute: 100.0% car, 0.0% public transportation, 0.0% walk, 0.0% work from home; Mean travel time to work: 45.1 minutes

Daviess County

Located in southwestern Indiana; bounded on the south by the East Fork of the White River, on the west by the West Fork of the White River. Covers a land area of 429.487 square miles, a water area of 7.387 square miles, and is located in the Eastern Time Zone at 38.70° N. Lat., 87.08° W. Long. The county was founded in 1816. County seat is Washington.

Daviess County is part of the Washington, IN Micropolitan Statistical Area. The entire metro area includes: Daviess County, IN

Weather Station: Washington Elevation: 524 feet

	Jan	Feb	Mar	Apr	May	Jun	Jul	Aug	Sep	Oct	Nov	Dec
High	40	45	56	68	77	85	88	87	80	69	56	43
Low	25	27	36	45	55	64	67	66	58	47	38	28
Precip	3.1	2.9	4.2	4.4	5.8	4.4	4.7	3.2	3.3	3.8	4.3	3.6
Snow	3.1	2.7	1.3	0.1	tr	0.0	0.0	0.0	0.0	0.1	0.1	2.6

High and Low temperatures in degrees Fahrenheit; Precipitation and Snow in inches

Population: 32,777; Growth (since 2000): 9.9%; Density: 76.3 persons per square mile; Race: 95.2% White, 1.8% Black/African American, 0.2% Asian, 0.0% American Indian/Alaska Native, 0.0% Native Hawaiian/Other Pacific Islander, 1.0% two or more races, 4.8% Hispanic of any race; Average household size: 2.80; Median age: 34.6; Age under 18: 29.1%; Age 65 and over: 14.8%; Males per 100 females: 99.3; Marriage status: 25.4% never married, 57.1% now married, 1.1% separated, 6.2% widowed, 11.3% divorced; Foreign born: 2.4%; Speak English only: 82.9%; With disability: 14.2%; Veterans: 8.4%; Ancestry: 22.3% German, 12.3% American, 8.8% Irish, 7.9% English, 3.1% Swiss
Religion: Six largest groups: 16.7% European Free-Church, 15.9% Baptist, 8.5% Catholicism, 6.3% Methodist/Pietist, 3.6% Non-denominational Protestant, 1.9% Holiness
Economy: Unemployment rate: 2.9%; Leading industries: 21.3 % construction; 13.2 % retail trade; 11.3 % other services (except public administration); Farms: 1,325 totaling 225,156 acres; Company size: 0 employ 1,000 or more persons, 2 employ 500 to 999 persons, 8 employ 100 to 499 persons, 887 employ less than 100 persons; Business ownership: 605 women-owned, n/a Black-owned, 25 Hispanic-owned, n/a Asian-owned, n/a American Indian/Alaska Native-owned
Employment: 10.6% management, business, and financial, 2.3% computer, engineering, and science, 7.1% education, legal, community service, arts, and media, 5.0% healthcare practitioners, 15.4% service, 19.3% sales and office, 17.4% natural resources, construction, and maintenance, 22.9% production, transportation, and material moving
Income: Per capita: $21,794; Median household: $48,355; Average household: $61,292; Households with income of $100,000 or more: 17.8%; Poverty rate: 13.0%
Educational Attainment: High school diploma or higher: 74.1%; Bachelor's degree or higher: 14.2%; Graduate/professional degree or higher: 4.9%

Housing: Homeownership rate: 73.8%; Median home value: $115,400; Median year structure built: 1973; Homeowner vacancy rate: 0.9%; Median selected monthly owner costs: $974 with a mortgage, $348 without a mortgage; Median gross rent: $641 per month; Rental vacancy rate: 8.7%
Vital Statistics: Birth rate: 157.9 per 10,000 population; Death rate: 96.0 per 10,000 population; Age-adjusted cancer mortality rate: 159.8 deaths per 100,000 population
Health Insurance: 77.4% have insurance; 57.0% have private insurance; 30.7% have public insurance; 22.6% do not have insurance; 30.3% of children under 18 do not have insurance
Health Care: Physicians: 9.4 per 10,000 population; Dentists: 2.7 per 10,000 population; Hospital beds: 14.5 per 10,000 population; Hospital admissions: 696.1 per 10,000 population
Air Quality Index (AQI): Percent of Days: 100.0% good, 0.0% moderate, 0.0% unhealthy for sensitive individuals, 0.0% unhealthy, 0.0% very unhealthy; Annual median: 4; Annual maximum: 27
Transportation: Commute: 91.7% car, 0.3% public transportation, 2.9% walk, 2.3% work from home; Mean travel time to work: 25.5 minutes
2016 Presidential Election: 79.0% Trump, 16.6% Clinton, 3.6% Johnson, 0.2% Stein
National and State Parks: Glendale State Fish and Wildlife Area
Additional Information Contacts
Daviess Government. . . . . (812) 254-5262
http://www.daviess.org

Daviess County Communities

ALFORDSVILLE (town). Covers a land area of 0.068 square miles and a water area of <.001 square miles. Located at 38.56° N. Lat; 86.95° W. Long. Elevation is 512 feet.
History: Laid out 1845.
Population: 58; Growth (since 2000): -48.2%; Density: 858.4 persons per square mile; Race: 100.0% White, 0.0% Black/African American, 0.0% Asian, 0.0% American Indian/Alaska Native, 0.0% Native Hawaiian/Other Pacific Islander, 0.0% Two or more races, 0.0% Hispanic of any race; Average household size: 2.07; Median age: 60.4; Age under 18: 12.1%; Age 65 and over: 39.7%; Males per 100 females: 110.4; Marriage status: 19.3% never married, 73.7% now married, 0.0% separated, 3.5% widowed, 3.5% divorced; Foreign born: 0.0%; Speak English only: 100.0%; With disability: 36.2%; Veterans: 5.9%; Ancestry: 39.7% American, 32.8% German, 8.6% Irish, 3.4% French, 3.4% Slovak
Employment: 0.0% management, business, and financial, 0.0% computer, engineering, and science, 0.0% education, legal, community service, arts, and media, 0.0% healthcare practitioners, 0.0% service, 35.7% sales and office, 7.1% natural resources, construction, and maintenance, 57.1% production, transportation, and material moving
Income: Per capita: $21,866; Median household: $31,250; Average household: $42,539; Households with income of $100,000 or more: n/a; Poverty rate: 1.7%
Educational Attainment: High school diploma or higher: 84.3%; Bachelor's degree or higher: n/a; Graduate/professional degree or higher: n/a
Housing: Homeownership rate: 82.1%; Median home value: $73,600; Median year structure built: Before 1940; Homeowner vacancy rate: 8.0%; Median selected monthly owner costs: $788 with a mortgage, $450 without a mortgage; Median gross rent: n/a per month; Rental vacancy rate: 0.0%
Health Insurance: 98.3% have insurance; 60.3% have private insurance; 72.4% have public insurance; 1.7% do not have insurance; 0.0% of children under 18 do not have insurance
Transportation: Commute: 100.0% car, 0.0% public transportation, 0.0% walk, 0.0% work from home; Mean travel time to work: 31.4 minutes

CANNELBURG (town). Covers a land area of 0.189 square miles and a water area of 0 square miles. Located at 38.67° N. Lat; 87.00° W. Long. Elevation is 528 feet.
Population: 175; Growth (since 2000): 25.0%; Density: 926.1 persons per square mile; Race: 100.0% White, 0.0% Black/African American, 0.0% Asian, 0.0% American Indian/Alaska Native, 0.0% Native Hawaiian/Other Pacific Islander, 0.0% Two or more races, 0.0% Hispanic of any race; Average household size: 2.78; Median age: 35.3; Age under 18: 22.3%; Age 65 and over: 14.3%; Males per 100 females: 114.3; Marriage status: 21.3% never married, 63.1% now married, 0.0% separated, 6.4% widowed, 9.2% divorced; Foreign born: 0.0%; Speak English only: 93.1%; With disability: 10.3%; Veterans: 5.9%; Ancestry: 29.7% American, 15.4% German, 8.0% English, 5.7% Irish, 4.0% Swiss
Employment: 1.2% management, business, and financial, 5.9% computer, engineering, and science, 5.9% education, legal, community service, arts, and media, 5.9% healthcare practitioners, 17.6% service, 22.4% sales and office, 9.4% natural resources, construction, and maintenance, 31.8% production, transportation, and material moving
Income: Per capita: $24,225; Median household: $61,875; Average household: $66,268; Households with income of $100,000 or more: 22.3%; Poverty rate: 11.4%
Educational Attainment: High school diploma or higher: 63.3%; Bachelor's degree or higher: 5.8%; Graduate/professional degree or higher: 1.7%
Housing: Homeownership rate: 95.2%; Median home value: $132,700; Median year structure built: 1983; Homeowner vacancy rate: 0.0%; Median selected monthly owner costs: $1,042 with a mortgage, $321 without a mortgage; Median gross rent: n/a per month; Rental vacancy rate: 0.0%
Health Insurance: 72.0% have insurance; 53.1% have private insurance; 34.3% have public insurance; 28.0% do not have insurance; 25.6% of children under 18 do not have insurance
Transportation: Commute: 87.1% car, 0.0% public transportation, 9.4% walk, 3.5% work from home; Mean travel time to work: 22.9 minutes

ELNORA (town). Covers a land area of 0.948 square miles and a water area of 0 square miles. Located at 38.88° N. Lat; 87.08° W. Long. Elevation is 479 feet.
Population: 617; Growth (since 2000): -14.4%; Density: 651.0 persons per square mile; Race: 98.4% White, 0.0% Black/African American, 0.0% Asian, 0.0% American Indian/Alaska Native, 0.0% Native Hawaiian/Other Pacific Islander, 1.6% Two or more races, 1.0% Hispanic of any race; Average household size: 2.32; Median age: 42.0; Age under 18: 19.8%; Age 65 and over: 20.4%; Males per 100 females: 87.1; Marriage status: 27.2% never married, 48.6% now married, 0.0% separated, 9.4% widowed, 14.8% divorced; Foreign born: 0.0%; Speak English only: 95.9%; With disability: 25.9%; Veterans: 11.1%; Ancestry: 22.7% German, 15.4% American, 9.2% Irish, 7.9% English, 4.7% Scottish
Employment: 12.4% management, business, and financial, 4.1% computer, engineering, and science, 0.8% education, legal, community service, arts, and media, 2.5% healthcare practitioners, 22.0% service, 27.8% sales and office, 5.8% natural resources, construction, and maintenance, 24.5% production, transportation, and material moving
Income: Per capita: $19,947; Median household: $30,875; Average household: $47,080; Households with income of $100,000 or more: 14.7%; Poverty rate: 22.6%
Educational Attainment: High school diploma or higher: 81.1%; Bachelor's degree or higher: 11.2%; Graduate/professional degree or higher: 5.1%

School District(s)

North Daviess Com Schools (KG-12)
Enrollment: 1,024 . . . . (812) 636-8000
Housing: Homeownership rate: 77.4%; Median home value: $62,100; Median year structure built: 1954; Homeowner vacancy rate: 1.4%; Median selected monthly owner costs: $783 with a mortgage, $285 without a mortgage; Median gross rent: $650 per month; Rental vacancy rate: 0.0%
Health Insurance: 81.5% have insurance; 52.7% have private insurance; 46.5% have public insurance; 18.5% do not have insurance; 11.5% of children under 18 do not have insurance
Transportation: Commute: 96.6% car, 0.0% public transportation, 2.5% walk, 0.0% work from home; Mean travel time to work: 26.7 minutes

MONTGOMERY (town). Covers a land area of 0.241 square miles and a water area of 0.002 square miles. Located at 38.67° N. Lat; 87.05° W. Long. Elevation is 528 feet.
History: Montgomery grew up around St. Peter's Church which was founded in 1818.
Population: 341; Growth (since 2000): -7.3%; Density: 1,412.2 persons per square mile; Race: 100.0% White, 0.0% Black/African American, 0.0% Asian, 0.0% American Indian/Alaska Native, 0.0% Native Hawaiian/Other Pacific Islander, 0.0% Two or more races, 1.8% Hispanic of any race; Average household size: 2.35; Median age: 43.5; Age under 18: 20.8%; Age 65 and over: 15.2%; Males per 100 females: 101.8; Marriage status: 27.8% never married, 59.0% now married, 0.0% separated, 3.1% widowed, 10.1% divorced; Foreign born: 0.0%; Speak English only: 98.5%; With disability: 15.0%; Veterans: 4.1%; Ancestry: 30.2% German, 12.9% Irish, 9.7% English, 9.1% American, 5.6% Swiss
Employment: 5.0% management, business, and financial, 4.0% computer, engineering, and science, 5.5% education, legal, community service, arts,

and media, 2.0% healthcare practitioners, 17.5% service, 31.0% sales and office, 12.0% natural resources, construction, and maintenance, 23.0% production, transportation, and material moving
Income: Per capita: $24,448; Median household: $43,068; Average household: $55,326; Households with income of $100,000 or more: 11.8%; Poverty rate: 8.5%
Educational Attainment: High school diploma or higher: 78.8%; Bachelor's degree or higher: 14.4%; Graduate/professional degree or higher: 5.2%

School District(s)

Barr-Reeve Community Schools Inc (KG-12)
Enrollment: 708 . . . . (812) 486-3220

Housing: Homeownership rate: 64.8%; Median home value: $113,300; Median year structure built: 1970; Homeowner vacancy rate: 0.0%; Median selected monthly owner costs: $856 with a mortgage, $280 without a mortgage; Median gross rent: $619 per month; Rental vacancy rate: 5.6%
Health Insurance: 94.4% have insurance; 80.9% have private insurance; 31.4% have public insurance; 5.6% do not have insurance; 5.3% of children under 18 do not have insurance
Transportation: Commute: 95.4% car, 0.0% public transportation, 0.5% walk, 3.1% work from home; Mean travel time to work: 22.7 minutes

ODON (town). Covers a land area of 0.954 square miles and a water area of 0.009 square miles. Located at 38.84° N. Lat; 86.99° W. Long. Elevation is 548 feet.
History: Odon grew as a farm town on a site at a spring where George Rogers Clark and his soldiers stopped for water and to hunt buffalo.
Population: 1,501; Growth (since 2000): 9.1%; Density: 1,573.8 persons per square mile; Race: 97.1% White, 0.0% Black/African American, 2.0% Asian, 0.0% American Indian/Alaska Native, 0.0% Native Hawaiian/Other Pacific Islander, 0.9% Two or more races, 0.2% Hispanic of any race; Average household size: 2.11; Median age: 44.5; Age under 18: 23.2%; Age 65 and over: 29.6%; Males per 100 females: 84.0; Marriage status: 20.5% never married, 48.5% now married, 1.9% separated, 13.6% widowed, 17.4% divorced; Foreign born: 2.5%; Speak English only: 96.1%; With disability: 23.7%; Veterans: 12.8%; Ancestry: 14.1% German, 12.1% American, 9.5% Irish, 7.5% English, 2.0% Scottish
Employment: 11.1% management, business, and financial, 1.7% computer, engineering, and science, 6.9% education, legal, community service, arts, and media, 9.4% healthcare practitioners, 16.9% service, 17.8% sales and office, 9.0% natural resources, construction, and maintenance, 27.2% production, transportation, and material moving
Income: Per capita: $19,807; Median household: $30,524; Average household: $43,632; Households with income of $100,000 or more: 9.0%; Poverty rate: 23.2%
Educational Attainment: High school diploma or higher: 88.1%; Bachelor's degree or higher: 11.9%; Graduate/professional degree or higher: 6.2%
Housing: Homeownership rate: 55.0%; Median home value: $78,600; Median year structure built: 1969; Homeowner vacancy rate: 0.0%; Median selected monthly owner costs: $761 with a mortgage, $337 without a mortgage; Median gross rent: $596 per month; Rental vacancy rate: 2.5%
Health Insurance: 95.2% have insurance; 67.7% have private insurance; 47.1% have public insurance; 4.8% do not have insurance; 0.0% of children under 18 do not have insurance
Newspapers: The Journal (weekly circulation 2,800)
Transportation: Commute: 91.6% car, 0.0% public transportation, 5.3% walk, 3.1% work from home; Mean travel time to work: 23.0 minutes

PLAINVILLE (town). Covers a land area of 0.351 square miles and a water area of 0 square miles. Located at 38.80° N. Lat; 87.15° W. Long. Elevation is 469 feet.
Population: 447; Growth (since 2000): -12.9%; Density: 1,274.2 persons per square mile; Race: 100.0% White, 0.0% Black/African American, 0.0% Asian, 0.0% American Indian/Alaska Native, 0.0% Native Hawaiian/Other Pacific Islander, 0.0% Two or more races, 0.0% Hispanic of any race; Average household size: 2.15; Median age: 52.0; Age under 18: 18.1%; Age 65 and over: 28.2%; Males per 100 females: 100.8; Marriage status: 11.9% never married, 59.7% now married, 0.0% separated, 10.6% widowed, 17.8% divorced; Foreign born: 0.0%; Speak English only: 100.0%; With disability: 27.5%; Veterans: 16.9%; Ancestry: 20.4% American, 17.4% German, 9.8% English, 9.8% Irish, 9.2% French
Employment: 9.1% management, business, and financial, 1.5% computer, engineering, and science, 4.5% education, legal, community service, arts, and media, 5.1% healthcare practitioners, 21.7% service, 18.2% sales and office, 10.6% natural resources, construction, and maintenance, 29.3% production, transportation, and material moving
Income: Per capita: $21,316; Median household: $37,738; Average household: $44,820; Households with income of $100,000 or more: 7.8%; Poverty rate: 11.4%
Educational Attainment: High school diploma or higher: 79.3%; Bachelor's degree or higher: 7.2%; Graduate/professional degree or higher: 5.7%
Housing: Homeownership rate: 74.0%; Median home value: $63,600; Median year structure built: 1948; Homeowner vacancy rate: 2.4%; Median selected monthly owner costs: $763 with a mortgage, $301 without a mortgage; Median gross rent: $429 per month; Rental vacancy rate: 6.9%
Health Insurance: 85.5% have insurance; 68.5% have private insurance; 40.5% have public insurance; 14.5% do not have insurance; 9.8% of children under 18 do not have insurance
Transportation: Commute: 97.9% car, 0.0% public transportation, 2.1% walk, 0.0% work from home; Mean travel time to work: 20.9 minutes

RAGLESVILLE (CDP). Covers a land area of 0.854 square miles and a water area of 0.003 square miles. Located at 38.80° N. Lat; 86.96° W. Long. Elevation is 614 feet.
Population: 24; Growth (since 2000): n/a; Density: 28.1 persons per square mile; Race: 100.0% White, 0.0% Black/African American, 0.0% Asian, 0.0% American Indian/Alaska Native, 0.0% Native Hawaiian/Other Pacific Islander, 0.0% Two or more races, 0.0% Hispanic of any race; Average household size: 0.00; Median age: n/a; Age under 18: 0.0%; Age 65 and over: 0.0%; Males per 100 females: 116.9; Marriage status: 0.0% never married, 100.0% now married, 100.0% separated, 0.0% widowed, 0.0% divorced; Foreign born: 0.0%; Speak English only: 100.0%; With disability: 0.0%; Veterans: 0.0%; Ancestry: 100.0% English
Employment: 0.0% management, business, and financial, 0.0% computer, engineering, and science, 0.0% education, legal, community service, arts, and media, 0.0% healthcare practitioners, 0.0% service, 100.0% sales and office, 0.0% natural resources, construction, and maintenance, 0.0% production, transportation, and material moving
Income: Per capita: n/a; Median household: n/a; Average household: n/a; Households with income of $100,000 or more: n/a; Poverty rate: n/a
Educational Attainment: High school diploma or higher: n/a; Bachelor's degree or higher: n/a; Graduate/professional degree or higher: n/a
Housing: Homeownership rate: 100.0%; Median home value: n/a; Median year structure built: n/a; Homeowner vacancy rate: 0.0%; Median selected monthly owner costs: n/a with a mortgage, n/a without a mortgage; Median gross rent: n/a per month; Rental vacancy rate: 0.0%
Health Insurance: 0.0% have insurance; 0.0% have private insurance; 0.0% have public insurance; 100.0% do not have insurance; 0.0% of children under 18 do not have insurance
Transportation: Commute: 100.0% car, 0.0% public transportation, 0.0% walk, 0.0% work from home; Mean travel time to work: 0.0 minutes

WASHINGTON (city). County seat. Covers a land area of 4.731 square miles and a water area of 0.037 square miles. Located at 38.66° N. Lat; 87.17° W. Long. Elevation is 502 feet.
History: Washington was founded by Emmanuel Van Trees, who settled here in 1817 on the site where Fort Flora had been built in 1805. The town developed around the Baltimore & Ohio Railroad shops, and became a trading and industrial center.
Population: 11,999; Growth (since 2000): 5.4%; Density: 2,536.5 persons per square mile; Race: 88.8% White, 4.6% Black/African American, 0.2% Asian, 0.1% American Indian/Alaska Native, 0.1% Native Hawaiian/Other Pacific Islander, 1.6% Two or more races, 12.5% Hispanic of any race; Average household size: 2.49; Median age: 37.0; Age under 18: 26.0%; Age 65 and over: 17.2%; Males per 100 females: 92.9; Marriage status: 30.0% never married, 46.2% now married, 1.4% separated, 9.2% widowed, 14.5% divorced; Foreign born: 5.3%; Speak English only: 87.0%; With disability: 19.4%; Veterans: 9.9%; Ancestry: 22.4% German, 11.7% American, 11.0% Irish, 8.7% English, 2.5% French
Employment: 9.0% management, business, and financial, 1.4% computer, engineering, and science, 8.0% education, legal, community service, arts, and media, 5.1% healthcare practitioners, 18.9% service, 19.3% sales and office, 11.3% natural resources, construction, and maintenance, 27.0% production, transportation, and material moving
Income: Per capita: $20,300; Median household: $36,411; Average household: $50,604; Households with income of $100,000 or more: 13.0%; Poverty rate: 18.4%

Educational Attainment: High school diploma or higher: 79.6%; Bachelor's degree or higher: 15.4%; Graduate/professional degree or higher: 4.8%

School District(s)

Washington Community Schools (KG-12)
Enrollment: 2,682 . . . . (812) 254-5536

Housing: Homeownership rate: 62.8%; Median home value: $82,200; Median year structure built: 1957; Homeowner vacancy rate: 1.7%; Median selected monthly owner costs: $872 with a mortgage, $343 without a mortgage; Median gross rent: $622 per month; Rental vacancy rate: 12.6%
Health Insurance: 88.0% have insurance; 56.6% have private insurance; 44.0% have public insurance; 12.0% do not have insurance; 7.1% of children under 18 do not have insurance
Hospitals: Daviess Community Hospital (120 beds)
Newspapers: Washington Times-Herald (daily circulation 8,800)
Transportation: Commute: 92.4% car, 0.3% public transportation, 4.2% walk, 1.3% work from home; Mean travel time to work: 19.8 minutes
Additional Information Contacts
City of Washington . . . . (812) 254-6143
http://www.washingtonin.us

Dearborn County

Located in southeastern Indiana; bounded on the east by Ohio, and on the southeast by the Ohio River and the Kentucky border; drained by the Whitewater River. Covers a land area of 305.034 square miles, a water area of 2.382 square miles, and is located in the Eastern Time Zone at 39.15° N. Lat., 84.97° W. Long. The county was founded in 1803. County seat is Lawrenceburg.

Dearborn County is part of the Cincinnati, OH-KY-IN Metropolitan Statistical Area. The entire metro area includes: Dearborn County, IN; Ohio County, IN; Union County, IN; Boone County, KY; Bracken County, KY; Campbell County, KY; Gallatin County, KY; Grant County, KY; Kenton County, KY; Pendleton County, KY; Brown County, OH; Butler County, OH; Clermont County, OH; Hamilton County, OH; Warren County, OH

Population: 49,564; Growth (since 2000): 7.5%; Density: 162.5 persons per square mile; Race: 97.1% White, 0.8% Black/African American, 0.4% Asian, 0.2% American Indian/Alaska Native, 0.0% Native Hawaiian/Other Pacific Islander, 0.8% two or more races, 1.2% Hispanic of any race; Average household size: 2.62; Median age: 42.7; Age under 18: 23.3%; Age 65 and over: 15.9%; Males per 100 females: 98.8; Marriage status: 24.9% never married, 57.5% now married, 1.2% separated, 6.2% widowed, 11.5% divorced; Foreign born: 1.2%; Speak English only: 97.8%; With disability: 12.1%; Veterans: 9.1%; Ancestry: 39.6% German, 16.6% Irish, 10.7% English, 9.7% American, 3.0% Italian
Religion: Six largest groups: 18.6% Catholicism, 8.5% Baptist, 5.2% Lutheran, 3.8% Methodist/Pietist, 1.9% Non-denominational Protestant, 0.9% Presbyterian-Reformed
Economy: Unemployment rate: 3.6%; Leading industries: 15.8 % retail trade; 14.8 % health care and social assistance; 12.2 % construction; Farms: 561 totaling 56,573 acres; Company size: 0 employ 1,000 or more persons, 4 employ 500 to 999 persons, 12 employ 100 to 499 persons, 901 employs less than 100 persons; Business ownership: 1,375 women-owned, n/a Black-owned, 27 Hispanic-owned, 28 Asian-owned, n/a American Indian/Alaska Native-owned
Employment: 12.4% management, business, and financial, 4.3% computer, engineering, and science, 8.3% education, legal, community service, arts, and media, 6.5% healthcare practitioners, 17.7% service, 21.8% sales and office, 11.5% natural resources, construction, and maintenance, 17.5% production, transportation, and material moving
Income: Per capita: $30,228; Median household: $62,905; Average household: $78,572; Households with income of $100,000 or more: 26.5%; Poverty rate: 10.1%
Educational Attainment: High school diploma or higher: 90.8%; Bachelor's degree or higher: 21.7%; Graduate/professional degree or higher: 7.4%
Housing: Homeownership rate: 79.1%; Median home value: $160,800; Median year structure built: 1978; Homeowner vacancy rate: 2.9%; Median selected monthly owner costs: $1,227 with a mortgage, $421 without a mortgage; Median gross rent: $735 per month; Rental vacancy rate: 7.5%
Vital Statistics: Birth rate: 105.3 per 10,000 population; Death rate: 88.5 per 10,000 population; Age-adjusted cancer mortality rate: 180.2 deaths per 100,000 population
Health Insurance: 92.7% have insurance; 75.0% have private insurance; 31.2% have public insurance; 7.3% do not have insurance; 5.2% of children under 18 do not have insurance
Health Care: Physicians: 11.5 per 10,000 population; Dentists: 1.8 per 10,000 population; Hospital beds: 21.0 per 10,000 population; Hospital admissions: 923.0 per 10,000 population
Transportation: Commute: 93.7% car, 0.4% public transportation, 1.6% walk, 3.4% work from home; Mean travel time to work: 28.7 minutes
2016 Presidential Election: 75.5% Trump, 20.4% Clinton, 3.8% Johnson, 0.2% Stein
Additional Information Contacts
Dearborn Government. . . . . (812) 537-8867
http://www.dearborncounty.org

Dearborn County Communities

AURORA (city). Covers a land area of 2.761 square miles and a water area of 0.327 square miles. Located at 39.07° N. Lat; 84.90° W. Long. Elevation is 486 feet.
History: Aurora was founded in 1819 along the Ohio River. Judge Jesse Holman of the Indiana Supreme Court suggested that the town be named for the goddess of the dawn. Aurora was severely damaged in the 1937 flood of the Ohio River.
Population: 3,770; Growth (since 2000): -4.9%; Density: 1,365.7 persons per square mile; Race: 97.2% White, 0.0% Black/African American, 2.8% Asian, 0.0% American Indian/Alaska Native, 0.0% Native Hawaiian/Other Pacific Islander, 0.0% Two or more races, 0.0% Hispanic of any race; Average household size: 2.54; Median age: 36.0; Age under 18: 25.3%; Age 65 and over: 13.9%; Males per 100 females: 97.4; Marriage status: 27.5% never married, 50.8% now married, 1.6% separated, 4.6% widowed, 17.1% divorced; Foreign born: 1.2%; Speak English only: 97.5%; With disability: 17.8%; Veterans: 6.9%; Ancestry: 36.7% German, 20.9% Irish, 10.8% English, 9.8% American, 3.1% French
Employment: 6.9% management, business, and financial, 2.9% computer, engineering, and science, 5.1% education, legal, community service, arts, and media, 9.0% healthcare practitioners, 25.0% service, 21.0% sales and office, 10.1% natural resources, construction, and maintenance, 20.0% production, transportation, and material moving
Income: Per capita: $21,604; Median household: $37,808; Average household: $54,725; Households with income of $100,000 or more: 11.8%; Poverty rate: 14.5%
Educational Attainment: High school diploma or higher: 85.2%; Bachelor's degree or higher: 13.3%; Graduate/professional degree or higher: 3.7%

School District(s)

South Dearborn Community Sch Corp (PK-12)
Enrollment: 2,638 . . . . (812) 926-2090

Housing: Homeownership rate: 47.1%; Median home value: $127,700; Median year structure built: Before 1940; Homeowner vacancy rate: 16.8%; Median selected monthly owner costs: $1,057 with a mortgage, $388 without a mortgage; Median gross rent: $649 per month; Rental vacancy rate: 7.2%
Health Insurance: 85.5% have insurance; 56.4% have private insurance; 38.1% have public insurance; 14.5% do not have insurance; 5.2% of children under 18 do not have insurance
Safety: Violent crime rate: 68.0 per 10,000 population; Property crime rate: 388.8 per 10,000 population
Transportation: Commute: 93.1% car, 0.0% public transportation, 2.9% walk, 2.3% work from home; Mean travel time to work: 21.0 minutes
Additional Information Contacts
City of Aurora . . . . (812) 926-1777
http://www.aurora.in.us

BRIGHT (CDP). Covers a land area of 12.548 square miles and a water area of 0.018 square miles. Located at 39.22° N. Lat; 84.86° W. Long. Elevation is 922 feet.
History: Bright is a community in Dearborn County, which was formed in 1803. It was named for Dr. Henry Dearborn (DR), an officer in the Revolutionary War and the War of 1812.
Population: 5,326; Growth (since 2000): -1.5%; Density: 424.4 persons per square mile; Race: 97.7% White, 0.0% Black/African American, 0.0% Asian, 0.0% American Indian/Alaska Native, 0.0% Native Hawaiian/Other Pacific Islander, 1.7% Two or more races, 1.0% Hispanic of any race; Average household size: 2.67; Median age: 43.2; Age under 18: 22.7%; Age 65 and over: 15.1%; Males per 100 females: 98.3; Marriage status:

30.7% never married, 52.6% now married, 0.3% separated, 6.8% widowed, 9.9% divorced; Foreign born: 1.9%; Speak English only: 97.0%; With disability: 13.2%; Veterans: 8.2%; Ancestry: 50.5% German, 22.9% Irish, 8.1% American, 6.6% English, 5.6% French
Employment: 10.9% management, business, and financial, 7.0% computer, engineering, and science, 11.0% education, legal, community service, arts, and media, 7.4% healthcare practitioners, 13.1% service, 22.9% sales and office, 10.9% natural resources, construction, and maintenance, 16.8% production, transportation, and material moving
Income: Per capita: $30,142; Median household: $66,146; Average household: $78,572; Households with income of $100,000 or more: 28.2%; Poverty rate: 5.2%
Educational Attainment: High school diploma or higher: 92.7%; Bachelor's degree or higher: 22.0%; Graduate/professional degree or higher: 6.8%
Housing: Homeownership rate: 85.5%; Median home value: $168,600; Median year structure built: 1990; Homeowner vacancy rate: 0.0%; Median selected monthly owner costs: $1,261 with a mortgage, $431 without a mortgage; Median gross rent: $888 per month; Rental vacancy rate: 10.0%
Health Insurance: 95.3% have insurance; 81.8% have private insurance; 27.5% have public insurance; 4.7% do not have insurance; 2.8% of children under 18 do not have insurance
Transportation: Commute: 94.8% car, 0.6% public transportation, 0.7% walk, 3.6% work from home; Mean travel time to work: 31.8 minutes

---

DILLSBORO (town). Covers a land area of 1.000 square miles and a water area of 0 square miles. Located at 39.02° N. Lat; 85.06° W. Long. Elevation is 869 feet.
Population: 1,624; Growth (since 2000): 13.1%; Density: 1,623.5 persons per square mile; Race: 98.2% White, 1.4% Black/African American, 0.0% Asian, 0.0% American Indian/Alaska Native, 0.0% Native Hawaiian/Other Pacific Islander, 0.0% Two or more races, 0.6% Hispanic of any race; Average household size: 2.69; Median age: 33.0; Age under 18: 26.0%; Age 65 and over: 18.8%; Males per 100 females: 80.5; Marriage status: 27.1% never married, 48.5% now married, 2.1% separated, 14.1% widowed, 10.3% divorced; Foreign born: 2.3%; Speak English only: 98.8%; With disability: 11.7%; Veterans: 10.8%; Ancestry: 26.4% German, 18.5% Irish, 9.1% English, 7.5% American, 5.0% Italian
Employment: 7.7% management, business, and financial, 3.2% computer, engineering, and science, 5.7% education, legal, community service, arts, and media, 2.5% healthcare practitioners, 25.7% service, 25.9% sales and office, 12.1% natural resources, construction, and maintenance, 17.2% production, transportation, and material moving
Income: Per capita: $18,644; Median household: $39,348; Average household: $49,046; Households with income of $100,000 or more: 12.5%; Poverty rate: 24.3%
Educational Attainment: High school diploma or higher: 83.7%; Bachelor's degree or higher: 5.9%; Graduate/professional degree or higher: 2.7%

School District(s)

South Dearborn Community Sch Corp (PK-12)
Enrollment: 2,638 . . . . (812) 926-2090
Housing: Homeownership rate: 48.4%; Median home value: $111,500; Median year structure built: 1971; Homeowner vacancy rate: 0.0%; Median selected monthly owner costs: $1,037 with a mortgage, $428 without a mortgage; Median gross rent: $722 per month; Rental vacancy rate: 17.9%
Health Insurance: 83.3% have insurance; 59.5% have private insurance; 37.2% have public insurance; 16.7% do not have insurance; 9.5% of children under 18 do not have insurance
Transportation: Commute: 86.8% car, 0.0% public transportation, 2.9% walk, 4.1% work from home; Mean travel time to work: 31.2 minutes

---

GREENDALE (city). Covers a land area of 5.712 square miles and a water area of 0.075 square miles. Located at 39.15° N. Lat; 84.83° W. Long. Elevation is 528 feet.
History: Greendale became associated with the distilling of whiskey in 1809, when the local manufacture of distilled liquors began. The Joseph E. Seagram Company purchased a plant in Greendale in 1933.
Population: 4,537; Growth (since 2000): 5.6%; Density: 794.2 persons per square mile; Race: 96.4% White, 2.0% Black/African American, 0.0% Asian, 0.0% American Indian/Alaska Native, 0.0% Native Hawaiian/Other Pacific Islander, 0.0% Two or more races, 2.0% Hispanic of any race; Average household size: 2.33; Median age: 39.7; Age under 18: 20.9%; Age 65 and over: 17.8%; Males per 100 females: 91.6; Marriage status: 26.2% never married, 53.2% now married, 2.4% separated, 6.5% widowed, 14.0% divorced; Foreign born: 0.0%; Speak English only: 96.4%; With disability: 13.8%; Veterans: 10.7%; Ancestry: 33.2% German, 17.8% Irish, 13.7% English, 8.7% American, 3.5% French
Employment: 14.2% management, business, and financial, 5.9% computer, engineering, and science, 9.7% education, legal, community service, arts, and media, 7.4% healthcare practitioners, 20.7% service, 25.8% sales and office, 3.6% natural resources, construction, and maintenance, 12.6% production, transportation, and material moving
Income: Per capita: $30,212; Median household: $56,302; Average household: $69,317; Households with income of $100,000 or more: 18.2%; Poverty rate: 7.0%
Educational Attainment: High school diploma or higher: 97.3%; Bachelor's degree or higher: 28.1%; Graduate/professional degree or higher: 10.6%
Housing: Homeownership rate: 78.2%; Median home value: $124,900; Median year structure built: 1960; Homeowner vacancy rate: 3.4%; Median selected monthly owner costs: $988 with a mortgage, $334 without a mortgage; Median gross rent: $649 per month; Rental vacancy rate: 9.0%
Health Insurance: 93.3% have insurance; 72.3% have private insurance; 37.0% have public insurance; 6.7% do not have insurance; 5.2% of children under 18 do not have insurance
Transportation: Commute: 94.2% car, 0.9% public transportation, 0.7% walk, 3.6% work from home; Mean travel time to work: 24.5 minutes
Additional Information Contacts
City of Greendale . . . . (812) 537-9219
http://cityofgreendale.net

GUILFORD (unincorporated postal area)
ZCTA: 47022
Covers a land area of 34.003 square miles and a water area of 0 square miles. Located at 39.20° N. Lat; 84.95° W. Long. Elevation is 499 feet.
Population: 3,266; Growth (since 2000): 7.3%; Density: 96.1 persons per square mile; Race: 94.3% White, 2.1% Black/African American, 0.0% Asian, 0.0% American Indian/Alaska Native, 0.0% Native Hawaiian/Other Pacific Islander, 1.3% Two or more races, 1.3% Hispanic of any race; Average household size: 2.87; Median age: 41.6; Age under 18: 28.1%; Age 65 and over: 17.8%; Males per 100 females: 104.8; Marriage status: 13.6% never married, 70.0% now married, 1.0% separated, 6.7% widowed, 9.7% divorced; Foreign born: 1.9%; Speak English only: 98.4%; With disability: 9.5%; Veterans: 7.5%; Ancestry: 50.6% German, 22.7% Irish, 11.5% English, 5.3% American, 4.9% Italian
Employment: 17.7% management, business, and financial, 1.5% computer, engineering, and science, 8.4% education, legal, community service, arts, and media, 5.8% healthcare practitioners, 9.2% service, 21.0% sales and office, 12.9% natural resources, construction, and maintenance, 23.5% production, transportation, and material moving
Income: Per capita: $30,203; Median household: $69,470; Average household: $84,436; Households with income of $100,000 or more: 29.6%; Poverty rate: 9.1%
Educational Attainment: High school diploma or higher: 90.1%; Bachelor's degree or higher: 32.9%; Graduate/professional degree or higher: 9.2%
Housing: Homeownership rate: 92.4%; Median home value: $211,900; Median year structure built: 1987; Homeowner vacancy rate: 0.4%; Median selected monthly owner costs: $1,505 with a mortgage, $488 without a mortgage; Median gross rent: $769 per month; Rental vacancy rate: 0.0%
Health Insurance: 97.8% have insurance; 81.5% have private insurance; 28.4% have public insurance; 2.2% do not have insurance; 1.5% of children under 18 do not have insurance
Transportation: Commute: 94.8% car, 1.2% public transportation, 1.1% walk, 2.9% work from home; Mean travel time to work: 35.0 minutes

---

HIDDEN VALLEY (CDP). Covers a land area of 4.138 square miles and a water area of 0.270 square miles. Located at 39.17° N. Lat; 84.84° W. Long. Elevation is 548 feet.
History: The community of Hidden Valley and lake of the same name was built by James Jacob Rupel, legendary land developer. Active in the Greater Dayton area and Indiana for over 50 years and the former owner of Centre City Offices and the Carillon House in Downtown Dayton.
Population: 5,344; Growth (since 2000): 21.0%; Density: 1,291.4 persons per square mile; Race: 97.3% White, 0.0% Black/African American, 0.0% Asian, 0.9% American Indian/Alaska Native, 0.0% Native Hawaiian/Other Pacific Islander, 1.1% Two or more races, 4.1% Hispanic of any race;

Average household size: 3.07; Median age: 43.8; Age under 18: 28.1%; Age 65 and over: 17.4%; Males per 100 females: 101.4; Marriage status: 23.1% never married, 67.1% now married, 0.7% separated, 1.2% widowed, 8.6% divorced; Foreign born: 1.1%; Speak English only: 95.8%; With disability: 8.2%; Veterans: 10.2%; Ancestry: 40.0% German, 16.6% English, 16.6% Irish, 5.1% American, 5.1% Polish
Employment: 19.3% management, business, and financial, 4.0% computer, engineering, and science, 12.7% education, legal, community service, arts, and media, 6.2% healthcare practitioners, 12.6% service, 17.5% sales and office, 14.8% natural resources, construction, and maintenance, 12.9% production, transportation, and material moving
Income: Per capita: $45,236; Median household: $101,979; Average household: $137,748; Households with income of $100,000 or more: 51.1%; Poverty rate: 5.6%
Educational Attainment: High school diploma or higher: 95.4%; Bachelor's degree or higher: 37.6%; Graduate/professional degree or higher: 14.5%
Housing: Homeownership rate: 89.8%; Median home value: $192,600; Median year structure built: 1991; Homeowner vacancy rate: 2.8%; Median selected monthly owner costs: $1,449 with a mortgage, $466 without a mortgage; Median gross rent: $1,401 per month; Rental vacancy rate: 0.0%
Health Insurance: 97.2% have insurance; 85.2% have private insurance; 26.9% have public insurance; 2.8% do not have insurance; 1.5% of children under 18 do not have insurance
Transportation: Commute: 93.1% car, 0.0% public transportation, 0.0% walk, 5.8% work from home; Mean travel time to work: 31.6 minutes

LAWRENCEBURG (city). County seat. Covers a land area of 4.941 square miles and a water area of 0.270 square miles. Located at 39.10° N. Lat; 84.87° W. Long. Elevation is 479 feet.
History: Lawrenceburg was founded in 1801 by Captain Samuel C. Vance. It developed as a port on the Ohio River. In 1937 the river flooded the town, reaching a crest of 82.6 feet. Lawrenceburg was the site of the church where Henry Ward Beecher was pastor in 1837.
Population: 4,981; Growth (since 2000): 6.3%; Density: 1,008.1 persons per square mile; Race: 96.4% White, 2.9% Black/African American, 0.0% Asian, 0.0% American Indian/Alaska Native, 0.0% Native Hawaiian/Other Pacific Islander, 0.2% Two or more races, 0.6% Hispanic of any race; Average household size: 2.14; Median age: 43.4; Age under 18: 21.1%; Age 65 and over: 15.9%; Males per 100 females: 96.3; Marriage status: 33.2% never married, 34.4% now married, 2.0% separated, 11.8% widowed, 20.6% divorced; Foreign born: 0.0%; Speak English only: 99.1%; With disability: 13.9%; Veterans: 7.3%; Ancestry: 31.8% German, 12.6% Irish, 11.8% English, 10.9% American, 4.9% Italian
Employment: 4.3% management, business, and financial, 4.8% computer, engineering, and science, 6.8% education, legal, community service, arts, and media, 5.4% healthcare practitioners, 17.1% service, 27.2% sales and office, 10.9% natural resources, construction, and maintenance, 23.6% production, transportation, and material moving
Income: Per capita: $23,343; Median household: $37,123; Average household: $51,578; Households with income of $100,000 or more: 16.1%; Poverty rate: 26.7%
Educational Attainment: High school diploma or higher: 87.0%; Bachelor's degree or higher: 11.2%; Graduate/professional degree or higher: 5.2%

School District(s)

Lawrenceburg Community School Corp (PK-12)
Enrollment: 1,799 . . . . (812) 537-7201
Sunman-Dearborn Com Sch Corp (KG-12)
Enrollment: 3,977 . . . . (812) 623-2291

Housing: Homeownership rate: 49.9%; Median home value: $133,000; Median year structure built: 1974; Homeowner vacancy rate: 0.0%; Median selected monthly owner costs: $1,047 with a mortgage, $242 without a mortgage; Median gross rent: $684 per month; Rental vacancy rate: 8.0%
Health Insurance: 93.4% have insurance; 69.0% have private insurance; 37.8% have public insurance; 6.6% do not have insurance; 0.0% of children under 18 do not have insurance
Hospitals: Dearborn County Hospital (144 beds)
Safety: Violent crime rate: 58.5 per 10,000 population; Property crime rate: 260.3 per 10,000 population
Newspapers: Register Publications (weekly circulation 14,000)
Transportation: Commute: 91.1% car, 0.0% public transportation, 6.6% walk, 1.7% work from home; Mean travel time to work: 22.0 minutes
Additional Information Contacts
City of Lawrenceburg . . . . (812) 532-3573
http://www.lawrenceburg-in.com

MOORES HILL (town). Covers a land area of 0.539 square miles and a water area of 0 square miles. Located at 39.11° N. Lat; 85.09° W. Long. Elevation is 991 feet.
History: Laid out 1838.
Population: 642; Growth (since 2000): 1.1%; Density: 1,191.7 persons per square mile; Race: 96.6% White, 0.0% Black/African American, 0.0% Asian, 0.0% American Indian/Alaska Native, 0.0% Native Hawaiian/Other Pacific Islander, 3.4% Two or more races, 0.0% Hispanic of any race; Average household size: 2.84; Median age: 35.5; Age under 18: 28.7%; Age 65 and over: 8.9%; Males per 100 females: 90.1; Marriage status: 30.5% never married, 50.3% now married, 2.0% separated, 6.9% widowed, 12.3% divorced; Foreign born: 0.6%; Speak English only: 99.2%; With disability: 9.7%; Veterans: 10.9%; Ancestry: 16.8% Irish, 12.8% German, 11.8% English, 5.8% Scottish, 2.5% French
Employment: 10.8% management, business, and financial, 0.0% computer, engineering, and science, 1.0% education, legal, community service, arts, and media, 0.0% healthcare practitioners, 28.5% service, 11.1% sales and office, 16.3% natural resources, construction, and maintenance, 32.3% production, transportation, and material moving
Income: Per capita: $16,692; Median household: $42,143; Average household: $47,081; Households with income of $100,000 or more: 8.4%; Poverty rate: 24.3%
Educational Attainment: High school diploma or higher: 84.9%; Bachelor's degree or higher: 3.3%; Graduate/professional degree or higher: 2.0%

School District(s)

South Dearborn Community Sch Corp (PK-12)
Enrollment: 2,638 . . . . (812) 926-2090

Housing: Homeownership rate: 81.9%; Median home value: $73,900; Median year structure built: 1964; Homeowner vacancy rate: 0.0%; Median selected monthly owner costs: $849 with a mortgage, $404 without a mortgage; Median gross rent: $926 per month; Rental vacancy rate: 14.6%
Health Insurance: 89.9% have insurance; 64.8% have private insurance; 36.0% have public insurance; 10.1% do not have insurance; 0.0% of children under 18 do not have insurance
Transportation: Commute: 91.3% car, 0.0% public transportation, 0.7% walk, 5.2% work from home; Mean travel time to work: 27.3 minutes

SAINT LEON (town). Covers a land area of 6.982 square miles and a water area of 0.009 square miles. Located at 39.30° N. Lat; 84.97° W. Long. Elevation is 1,010 feet.
Population: 592; Growth (since 2000): 53.0%; Density: 84.8 persons per square mile; Race: 98.8% White, 0.0% Black/African American, 0.0% Asian, 0.0% American Indian/Alaska Native, 0.0% Native Hawaiian/Other Pacific Islander, 0.0% Two or more races, 2.5% Hispanic of any race; Average household size: 2.60; Median age: 40.0; Age under 18: 21.5%; Age 65 and over: 21.8%; Males per 100 females: 100.0; Marriage status: 20.8% never married, 65.5% now married, 0.0% separated, 7.6% widowed, 6.1% divorced; Foreign born: 2.5%; Speak English only: 97.8%; With disability: 11.1%; Veterans: 9.0%; Ancestry: 64.4% German, 13.0% Irish, 7.6% English, 5.2% American, 2.5% Dutch
Employment: 11.6% management, business, and financial, 0.4% computer, engineering, and science, 12.3% education, legal, community service, arts, and media, 5.8% healthcare practitioners, 17.7% service, 19.9% sales and office, 13.4% natural resources, construction, and maintenance, 19.1% production, transportation, and material moving
Income: Per capita: $25,250; Median household: $50,000; Average household: $62,915; Households with income of $100,000 or more: 19.3%; Poverty rate: 8.3%
Educational Attainment: High school diploma or higher: 89.8%; Bachelor's degree or higher: 19.4%; Graduate/professional degree or higher: 7.6%

School District(s)

Sunman-Dearborn Com Sch Corp (KG-12)
Enrollment: 3,977 . . . . (812) 623-2291

Housing: Homeownership rate: 74.6%; Median home value: $183,900; Median year structure built: 1978; Homeowner vacancy rate: 4.0%; Median selected monthly owner costs: $1,701 with a mortgage, $464 without a mortgage; Median gross rent: $773 per month; Rental vacancy rate: 10.8%
Health Insurance: 96.5% have insurance; 81.3% have private insurance; 33.8% have public insurance; 3.5% do not have insurance; 1.4% of children under 18 do not have insurance

Transportation: Commute: 96.0% car, 0.0% public transportation, 0.7% walk, 3.3% work from home; Mean travel time to work: 29.1 minutes

WEST HARRISON (town). Covers a land area of 0.215 square miles and a water area of 0.008 square miles. Located at 39.26° N. Lat; 84.82° W. Long. Elevation is 518 feet.
History: West Harrison was founded in 1813. General John Hunt Morgan and his Confederate cavalry raided West Harrison in 1863 before moving on to Ohio.
Population: 263; Growth (since 2000): -7.4%; Density: 1,220.7 persons per square mile; Race: 100.0% White, 0.0% Black/African American, 0.0% Asian, 0.0% American Indian/Alaska Native, 0.0% Native Hawaiian/Other Pacific Islander, 0.0% Two or more races, 1.1% Hispanic of any race; Average household size: 2.07; Median age: 32.6; Age under 18: 25.9%; Age 65 and over: 15.6%; Males per 100 females: 110.9; Marriage status: 32.0% never married, 41.3% now married, 5.8% separated, 8.3% widowed, 18.4% divorced; Foreign born: 0.0%; Speak English only: 97.0%; With disability: 21.3%; Veterans: 12.3%; Ancestry: 38.8% German, 10.6% Irish, 5.7% English, 4.6% American, 3.8% Hungarian
Employment: 3.8% management, business, and financial, 0.0% computer, engineering, and science, 0.0% education, legal, community service, arts, and media, 3.8% healthcare practitioners, 20.0% service, 27.7% sales and office, 16.2% natural resources, construction, and maintenance, 28.5% production, transportation, and material moving
Income: Per capita: $21,435; Median household: $30,313; Average household: $43,609; Households with income of $100,000 or more: 3.2%; Poverty rate: 23.1%
Educational Attainment: High school diploma or higher: 76.2%; Bachelor's degree or higher: 2.4%; Graduate/professional degree or higher: n/a

School District(s)

Sunman-Dearborn Com Sch Corp (KG-12)
Enrollment: 3,977 . . . . (812) 623-2291

Housing: Homeownership rate: 51.2%; Median home value: $83,000; Median year structure built: 1943; Homeowner vacancy rate: 0.0%; Median selected monthly owner costs: $900 with a mortgage, $438 without a mortgage; Median gross rent: $588 per month; Rental vacancy rate: 16.2%
Health Insurance: 82.1% have insurance; 56.7% have private insurance; 35.4% have public insurance; 17.9% do not have insurance; 8.8% of children under 18 do not have insurance
Transportation: Commute: 82.3% car, 0.0% public transportation, 17.7% walk, 0.0% work from home; Mean travel time to work: 16.2 minutes

Decatur County

Located in southeast central Indiana; drained by Flatrock, Small Duck, Clifty, and Sand Creeks. Covers a land area of 372.568 square miles, a water area of 0.755 square miles, and is located in the Eastern Time Zone at 39.31° N. Lat., 85.50° W. Long. The county was founded in 1821. County seat is Greensburg.

Decatur County is part of the Greensburg, IN Micropolitan Statistical Area. The entire metro area includes: Decatur County, IN

Weather Station: Greensburg Elevation: 935 feet

	Jan	Feb	Mar	Apr	May	Jun	Jul	Aug	Sep	Oct	Nov	Dec
High	36	40	51	63	73	82	85	84	77	65	52	40
Low	21	24	32	43	53	62	66	64	56	44	35	25
Precip	2.9	2.5	3.7	4.4	5.5	4.5	4.0	3.9	3.1	3.2	3.7	3.4
Snow	5.5	3.8	2.2	0.3	tr	0.0	0.0	0.0	0.0	0.2	0.2	4.2

High and Low temperatures in degrees Fahrenheit; Precipitation and Snow in inches

Population: 26,480; Growth (since 2000): 7.8%; Density: 71.1 persons per square mile; Race: 96.1% White, 0.7% Black/African American, 1.6% Asian, 0.4% American Indian/Alaska Native, 0.0% Native Hawaiian/Other Pacific Islander, 0.9% two or more races, 1.9% Hispanic of any race; Average household size: 2.52; Median age: 38.8; Age under 18: 24.6%; Age 65 and over: 15.8%; Males per 100 females: 98.2; Marriage status: 25.6% never married, 55.4% now married, 1.0% separated, 5.6% widowed, 13.4% divorced; Foreign born: 1.7%; Speak English only: 95.8%; With disability: 14.2%; Veterans: 6.7%; Ancestry: 32.9% German, 16.8% American, 11.3% Irish, 7.5% English, 3.3% Italian
Religion: Six largest groups: 25.3% Catholicism, 18.7% Baptist, 4.9% Methodist/Pietist, 3.1% Non-denominational Protestant, 2.7% Holiness, 1.4% Presbyterian-Reformed
Economy: Unemployment rate: 3.1%; Leading industries: 17.9 % retail trade; 10.7 % other services (except public administration); 10.6 % construction; Farms: 610 totaling 186,528 acres; Company size: 1 employs 1,000 or more persons, 2 employ 500 to 999 persons, 13 employ 100 to 499 persons, 609 employ less than 100 persons; Business ownership: 684 women-owned, n/a Black-owned, 41 Hispanic-owned, n/a Asian-owned, n/a American Indian/Alaska Native-owned
Employment: 13.2% management, business, and financial, 3.9% computer, engineering, and science, 7.7% education, legal, community service, arts, and media, 5.2% healthcare practitioners, 15.2% service, 15.6% sales and office, 9.5% natural resources, construction, and maintenance, 29.7% production, transportation, and material moving
Income: Per capita: $25,548; Median household: $52,270; Average household: $64,519; Households with income of $100,000 or more: 16.8%; Poverty rate: 11.4%
Educational Attainment: High school diploma or higher: 89.6%; Bachelor's degree or higher: 19.7%; Graduate/professional degree or higher: 6.9%
Housing: Homeownership rate: 69.4%; Median home value: $121,800; Median year structure built: 1972; Homeowner vacancy rate: 0.1%; Median selected monthly owner costs: $1,007 with a mortgage, $362 without a mortgage; Median gross rent: $767 per month; Rental vacancy rate: 4.9%
Vital Statistics: Birth rate: 131.3 per 10,000 population; Death rate: 101.7 per 10,000 population; Age-adjusted cancer mortality rate: 179.0 deaths per 100,000 population
Health Insurance: 90.3% have insurance; 72.8% have private insurance; 29.4% have public insurance; 9.7% do not have insurance; 7.6% of children under 18 do not have insurance
Health Care: Physicians: 9.0 per 10,000 population; Dentists: 3.0 per 10,000 population; Hospital beds: 148.3 per 10,000 population; Hospital admissions: 585.6 per 10,000 population
Transportation: Commute: 93.4% car, 0.6% public transportation, 2.0% walk, 3.1% work from home; Mean travel time to work: 21.4 minutes
2016 Presidential Election: 76.0% Trump, 19.0% Clinton, 4.4% Johnson, 0.2% Stein
National and State Parks: Greenburg Reservoir State Fishing Area
Additional Information Contacts
Decatur Government. . . . . (812) 663-2570
http://www.decaturcounty.in.gov

Decatur County Communities

CLARKSBURG (CDP). Covers a land area of 0.479 square miles and a water area of 0 square miles. Located at 39.44° N. Lat; 85.35° W. Long. Elevation is 1,053 feet.
Population: 184; Growth (since 2000): n/a; Density: 384.1 persons per square mile; Race: 100.0% White, 0.0% Black/African American, 0.0% Asian, 0.0% American Indian/Alaska Native, 0.0% Native Hawaiian/Other Pacific Islander, 0.0% Two or more races, 0.0% Hispanic of any race; Average household size: 1.77; Median age: 24.8; Age under 18: 17.4%; Age 65 and over: 7.1%; Males per 100 females: 119.1; Marriage status: 53.7% never married, 15.4% now married, 0.0% separated, 0.0% widowed, 30.9% divorced; Foreign born: 0.0%; Speak English only: 100.0%; With disability: 6.5%; Veterans: 0.0%; Ancestry: 41.8% German, 31.0% American, 5.4% Italian
Employment: 0.0% management, business, and financial, 0.0% computer, engineering, and science, 0.0% education, legal, community service, arts, and media, 23.0% healthcare practitioners, 40.8% service, 8.6% sales and office, 27.6% natural resources, construction, and maintenance, 0.0% production, transportation, and material moving
Income: Per capita: $24,323; Median household: $45,417; Average household: $44,463; Households with income of $100,000 or more: n/a; Poverty rate: 22.8%
Educational Attainment: High school diploma or higher: 30.7%; Bachelor's degree or higher: n/a; Graduate/professional degree or higher: n/a
Housing: Homeownership rate: 50.0%; Median home value: n/a; Median year structure built: 1940; Homeowner vacancy rate: 0.0%; Median selected monthly owner costs: n/a with a mortgage, n/a without a mortgage; Median gross rent: n/a per month; Rental vacancy rate: 0.0%
Health Insurance: 71.7% have insurance; 48.9% have private insurance; 29.9% have public insurance; 28.3% do not have insurance; 0.0% of children under 18 do not have insurance
Transportation: Commute: 88.4% car, 0.0% public transportation, 0.0% walk, 11.6% work from home; Mean travel time to work: 0.0 minutes

GREENSBURG (city). County seat. Covers a land area of 9.270 square miles and a water area of 0.045 square miles. Located at 39.35° N. Lat; 85.50° W. Long. Elevation is 958 feet.
History: Greensburg developed as a residential center.
Population: 12,056; Growth (since 2000): 17.5%; Density: 1,300.6 persons per square mile; Race: 94.6% White, 1.1% Black/African American, 2.8% Asian, 0.0% American Indian/Alaska Native, 0.0% Native Hawaiian/Other Pacific Islander, 0.7% Two or more races, 2.0% Hispanic of any race; Average household size: 2.36; Median age: 37.0; Age under 18: 25.2%; Age 65 and over: 15.5%; Males per 100 females: 91.9; Marriage status: 28.2% never married, 48.0% now married, 1.2% separated, 7.4% widowed, 16.4% divorced; Foreign born: 2.4%; Speak English only: 95.0%; With disability: 14.0%; Veterans: 5.5%; Ancestry: 36.7% German, 17.7% American, 14.1% Irish, 6.8% English, 4.2% Italian
Employment: 12.1% management, business, and financial, 5.6% computer, engineering, and science, 6.9% education, legal, community service, arts, and media, 3.3% healthcare practitioners, 14.4% service, 16.5% sales and office, 4.7% natural resources, construction, and maintenance, 36.5% production, transportation, and material moving
Income: Per capita: $24,929; Median household: $50,781; Average household: $59,478; Households with income of $100,000 or more: 13.1%; Poverty rate: 12.5%
Educational Attainment: High school diploma or higher: 90.0%; Bachelor's degree or higher: 20.3%; Graduate/professional degree or higher: 6.8%

School District(s)

Decatur County Community Schools (PK-12)
Enrollment: 1,875 .... (812) 663-4595
Greensburg Community Schools (PK-12)
Enrollment: 2,373 .... (812) 663-4774

Housing: Homeownership rate: 57.7%; Median home value: $110,300; Median year structure built: 1972; Homeowner vacancy rate: 0.0%; Median selected monthly owner costs: $949 with a mortgage, $329 without a mortgage; Median gross rent: $758 per month; Rental vacancy rate: 6.8%
Health Insurance: 91.2% have insurance; 72.2% have private insurance; 30.4% have public insurance; 8.8% do not have insurance; 6.2% of children under 18 do not have insurance
Hospitals: Decatur County Memorial Hospital (115 beds)
Newspapers: Greensburg Daily News (daily circulation 5,600); Greensburg Times (weekly circulation 700)
Transportation: Commute: 94.3% car, 0.4% public transportation, 2.5% walk, 2.3% work from home; Mean travel time to work: 17.4 minutes

Additional Information Contacts

City of Greensburg .... (812) 663-8582
http://www.cityofgreensburg.com

LAKE SANTEE (CDP). Covers a land area of 2.467 square miles and a water area of 0.356 square miles. Located at 39.41° N. Lat; 85.31° W. Long.
Population: 902; Growth (since 2000): n/a; Density: 365.7 persons per square mile; Race: 100.0% White, 0.0% Black/African American, 0.0% Asian, 0.0% American Indian/Alaska Native, 0.0% Native Hawaiian/Other Pacific Islander, 0.0% Two or more races, 0.0% Hispanic of any race; Average household size: 2.51; Median age: 47.1; Age under 18: 25.8%; Age 65 and over: 21.3%; Males per 100 females: 101.5; Marriage status: 12.3% never married, 66.2% now married, 1.7% separated, 9.4% widowed, 12.1% divorced; Foreign born: 0.0%; Speak English only: 100.0%; With disability: 13.3%; Veterans: 5.7%; Ancestry: 36.5% German, 26.3% American, 8.5% European, 7.5% English, 6.3% Irish
Employment: 19.1% management, business, and financial, 3.4% computer, engineering, and science, 6.3% education, legal, community service, arts, and media, 10.4% healthcare practitioners, 0.0% service, 26.1% sales and office, 14.7% natural resources, construction, and maintenance, 20.0% production, transportation, and material moving
Income: Per capita: $47,344; Median household: $64,635; Average household: $116,527; Households with income of $100,000 or more: 36.8%; Poverty rate: n/a
Educational Attainment: High school diploma or higher: 98.3%; Bachelor's degree or higher: 28.2%; Graduate/professional degree or higher: 13.1%
Housing: Homeownership rate: 96.4%; Median home value: $126,100; Median year structure built: 1982; Homeowner vacancy rate: 0.0%; Median selected monthly owner costs: $1,233 with a mortgage, $498 without a mortgage; Median gross rent: n/a per month; Rental vacancy rate: 0.0%
Health Insurance: 95.0% have insurance; 89.0% have private insurance; 22.5% have public insurance; 5.0% do not have insurance; 6.4% of children under 18 do not have insurance
Transportation: Commute: 95.4% car, 0.0% public transportation, 0.0% walk, 4.6% work from home; Mean travel time to work: 27.1 minutes

MILLHOUSEN (town). Covers a land area of 1.010 square miles and a water area of 0 square miles. Located at 39.21° N. Lat; 85.44° W. Long. Elevation is 896 feet.
History: Settled 1838, plotted 1858.
Population: 139; Growth (since 2000): 2.2%; Density: 137.6 persons per square mile; Race: 98.6% White, 0.0% Black/African American, 0.0% Asian, 0.0% American Indian/Alaska Native, 0.0% Native Hawaiian/Other Pacific Islander, 1.4% Two or more races, 0.0% Hispanic of any race; Average household size: 2.78; Median age: 37.8; Age under 18: 20.9%; Age 65 and over: 12.2%; Males per 100 females: 98.4; Marriage status: 22.4% never married, 62.9% now married, 0.0% separated, 6.0% widowed, 8.6% divorced; Foreign born: 0.0%; Speak English only: 100.0%; With disability: 18.0%; Veterans: 4.5%; Ancestry: 54.0% German, 25.9% American, 7.9% Irish, 4.3% French, 2.2% English
Employment: 16.5% management, business, and financial, 7.6% computer, engineering, and science, 2.5% education, legal, community service, arts, and media, 8.9% healthcare practitioners, 15.2% service, 21.5% sales and office, 6.3% natural resources, construction, and maintenance, 21.5% production, transportation, and material moving
Income: Per capita: $29,040; Median household: $63,750; Average household: $73,890; Households with income of $100,000 or more: 36.0%; Poverty rate: 0.7%
Educational Attainment: High school diploma or higher: 93.8%; Bachelor's degree or higher: 11.5%; Graduate/professional degree or higher: 2.1%
Housing: Homeownership rate: 94.0%; Median home value: $104,200; Median year structure built: 1943; Homeowner vacancy rate: 0.0%; Median selected monthly owner costs: $875 with a mortgage, $350 without a mortgage; Median gross rent: n/a per month; Rental vacancy rate: 0.0%
Health Insurance: 94.2% have insurance; 84.2% have private insurance; 19.4% have public insurance; 5.8% do not have insurance; 0.0% of children under 18 do not have insurance
Transportation: Commute: 100.0% car, 0.0% public transportation, 0.0% walk, 0.0% work from home; Mean travel time to work: 38.2 minutes

NEW POINT (town). Covers a land area of 0.217 square miles and a water area of 0 square miles. Located at 39.31° N. Lat; 85.33° W. Long. Elevation is 974 feet.
Population: 292; Growth (since 2000): 0.7%; Density: 1,342.6 persons per square mile; Race: 95.5% White, 1.4% Black/African American, 0.0% Asian, 0.0% American Indian/Alaska Native, 0.0% Native Hawaiian/Other Pacific Islander, 3.1% Two or more races, 2.1% Hispanic of any race; Average household size: 2.65; Median age: 37.5; Age under 18: 28.4%; Age 65 and over: 15.1%; Males per 100 females: 105.6; Marriage status: 26.0% never married, 51.6% now married, 1.3% separated, 8.1% widowed, 14.3% divorced; Foreign born: 0.0%; Speak English only: 97.4%; With disability: 22.3%; Veterans: 11.0%; Ancestry: 30.8% German, 15.4% Irish, 12.7% American, 12.0% English, 4.1% Dutch
Employment: 9.9% management, business, and financial, 0.0% computer, engineering, and science, 0.8% education, legal, community service, arts, and media, 1.7% healthcare practitioners, 19.0% service, 11.6% sales and office, 13.2% natural resources, construction, and maintenance, 43.8% production, transportation, and material moving
Income: Per capita: $18,157; Median household: $40,000; Average household: $47,325; Households with income of $100,000 or more: 7.3%; Poverty rate: 10.6%
Educational Attainment: High school diploma or higher: 77.4%; Bachelor's degree or higher: 3.6%; Graduate/professional degree or higher: 0.5%
Housing: Homeownership rate: 79.1%; Median home value: $91,300; Median year structure built: 1950; Homeowner vacancy rate: 0.0%; Median selected monthly owner costs: $1,089 with a mortgage, $385 without a mortgage; Median gross rent: $920 per month; Rental vacancy rate: 0.0%
Health Insurance: 86.6% have insurance; 57.2% have private insurance; 45.9% have public insurance; 13.4% do not have insurance; 11.6% of children under 18 do not have insurance
Transportation: Commute: 92.4% car, 0.0% public transportation, 1.7% walk, 0.8% work from home; Mean travel time to work: 19.5 minutes

SAINT PAUL (town). Covers a land area of 0.312 square miles and a water area of 0 square miles. Located at 39.43° N. Lat; 85.63° W. Long. Elevation is 856 feet.
Population: 1,139; Growth (since 2000): 11.4%; Density: 3,646.8 persons per square mile; Race: 96.8% White, 2.8% Black/African American, 0.0% Asian, 0.0% American Indian/Alaska Native, 0.0% Native Hawaiian/Other Pacific Islander, 0.0% Two or more races, 0.4% Hispanic of any race; Average household size: 2.62; Median age: 33.7; Age under 18: 25.6%; Age 65 and over: 11.2%; Males per 100 females: 97.1; Marriage status: 35.7% never married, 46.6% now married, 1.1% separated, 6.2% widowed, 11.5% divorced; Foreign born: 0.0%; Speak English only: 98.7%; With disability: 15.4%; Veterans: 7.8%; Ancestry: 23.4% American, 23.1% German, 14.0% Irish, 10.4% English, 3.4% European
Employment: 4.4% management, business, and financial, 2.1% computer, engineering, and science, 1.4% education, legal, community service, arts, and media, 3.5% healthcare practitioners, 17.7% service, 18.6% sales and office, 10.9% natural resources, construction, and maintenance, 41.5% production, transportation, and material moving
Income: Per capita: $20,738; Median household: $47,188; Average household: $52,917; Households with income of $100,000 or more: 9.2%; Poverty rate: 18.3%
Educational Attainment: High school diploma or higher: 81.3%; Bachelor's degree or higher: 8.6%; Graduate/professional degree or higher: 1.9%
Housing: Homeownership rate: 67.4%; Median home value: $80,300; Median year structure built: 1961; Homeowner vacancy rate: 4.6%; Median selected monthly owner costs: $839 with a mortgage, $375 without a mortgage; Median gross rent: $832 per month; Rental vacancy rate: 0.0%
Health Insurance: 91.0% have insurance; 70.7% have private insurance; 31.1% have public insurance; 9.0% do not have insurance; 0.0% of children under 18 do not have insurance
Transportation: Commute: 96.4% car, 0.0% public transportation, 1.1% walk, 1.8% work from home; Mean travel time to work: 23.9 minutes

WESTPORT (town). Covers a land area of 1.320 square miles and a water area of 0.013 square miles. Located at 39.18° N. Lat; 85.58° W. Long. Elevation is 814 feet.
History: Laid out 1836.
Population: 1,315; Growth (since 2000): -13.2%; Density: 996.4 persons per square mile; Race: 96.9% White, 0.0% Black/African American, 2.0% Asian, 0.0% American Indian/Alaska Native, 0.0% Native Hawaiian/Other Pacific Islander, 1.1% Two or more races, 3.0% Hispanic of any race; Average household size: 2.34; Median age: 42.9; Age under 18: 22.1%; Age 65 and over: 20.2%; Males per 100 females: 94.2; Marriage status: 18.9% never married, 57.0% now married, 2.2% separated, 7.5% widowed, 16.5% divorced; Foreign born: 2.4%; Speak English only: 96.6%; With disability: 20.3%; Veterans: 8.4%; Ancestry: 24.6% German, 19.6% American, 7.8% English, 5.2% Irish, 3.0% Scottish
Employment: 5.7% management, business, and financial, 1.7% computer, engineering, and science, 6.4% education, legal, community service, arts, and media, 10.1% healthcare practitioners, 16.6% service, 19.6% sales and office, 9.7% natural resources, construction, and maintenance, 30.2% production, transportation, and material moving
Income: Per capita: $24,091; Median household: $44,615; Average household: $56,816; Households with income of $100,000 or more: 7.7%; Poverty rate: 7.5%
Educational Attainment: High school diploma or higher: 90.2%; Bachelor's degree or higher: 10.3%; Graduate/professional degree or higher: 3.2%
Housing: Homeownership rate: 61.9%; Median home value: $93,000; Median year structure built: 1966; Homeowner vacancy rate: 0.0%; Median selected monthly owner costs: $813 with a mortgage, $365 without a mortgage; Median gross rent: $683 per month; Rental vacancy rate: 5.3%
Health Insurance: 89.6% have insurance; 69.0% have private insurance; 35.1% have public insurance; 10.4% do not have insurance; 12.5% of children under 18 do not have insurance
Transportation: Commute: 90.4% car, 0.0% public transportation, 3.8% walk, 1.9% work from home; Mean travel time to work: 24.6 minutes

DeKalb County

Located in northeastern Indiana; bounded on the east by Ohio; drained by the Saint Joseph River and Cedar and Fish Creeks. Covers a land area of 362.824 square miles, a water area of 1.026 square miles, and is located in the Eastern Time Zone at 41.40° N. Lat., 85.00° W. Long. The county was founded in 1835. County seat is Auburn.

DeKalb County is part of the Auburn, IN Micropolitan Statistical Area. The entire metro area includes: DeKalb County, IN

Population: 42,524; Growth (since 2000): 5.6%; Density: 117.2 persons per square mile; Race: 97.2% White, 0.3% Black/African American, 0.3% Asian, 0.1% American Indian/Alaska Native, 0.0% Native Hawaiian/Other Pacific Islander, 1.8% two or more races, 2.8% Hispanic of any race; Average household size: 2.58; Median age: 39.1; Age under 18: 24.8%; Age 65 and over: 15.1%; Males per 100 females: 98.4; Marriage status: 27.1% never married, 52.2% now married, 1.1% separated, 6.8% widowed, 13.9% divorced; Foreign born: 1.4%; Speak English only: 97.1%; With disability: 15.1%; Veterans: 8.4%; Ancestry: 33.4% German, 11.3% American, 10.3% Irish, 9.6% English, 6.3% European
Religion: Six largest groups: 12.5% Catholicism, 6.6% Baptist, 5.9% Methodist/Pietist, 5.7% Holiness, 3.5% Non-denominational Protestant, 3.0% Lutheran
Economy: Unemployment rate: 3.0%; Leading industries: 12.6 % manufacturing; 11.8 % other services (except public administration); 11.0 % construction; Farms: 924 totaling 160,894 acres; Company size: 0 employ 1,000 or more persons, 4 employ 500 to 999 persons, 38 employ 100 to 499 persons, 935 employ less than 100 persons; Business ownership: 879 women-owned, n/a Black-owned, n/a Hispanic-owned, n/a Asian-owned, n/a American Indian/Alaska Native-owned
Employment: 12.3% management, business, and financial, 4.0% computer, engineering, and science, 7.9% education, legal, community service, arts, and media, 4.1% healthcare practitioners, 13.2% service, 19.6% sales and office, 9.1% natural resources, construction, and maintenance, 29.8% production, transportation, and material moving
Income: Per capita: $26,057; Median household: $51,374; Average household: $65,907; Households with income of $100,000 or more: 15.8%; Poverty rate: 12.5%
Educational Attainment: High school diploma or higher: 89.7%; Bachelor's degree or higher: 17.8%; Graduate/professional degree or higher: 5.5%
Housing: Homeownership rate: 76.5%; Median home value: $113,600; Median year structure built: 1973; Homeowner vacancy rate: 2.1%; Median selected monthly owner costs: $969 with a mortgage, $357 without a mortgage; Median gross rent: $695 per month; Rental vacancy rate: 9.0%
Vital Statistics: Birth rate: 120.9 per 10,000 population; Death rate: 93.8 per 10,000 population; Age-adjusted cancer mortality rate: 178.7 deaths per 100,000 population
Health Insurance: 89.5% have insurance; 71.4% have private insurance; 30.9% have public insurance; 10.5% do not have insurance; 10.2% of children under 18 do not have insurance
Health Care: Physicians: 7.7 per 10,000 population; Dentists: 4.7 per 10,000 population; Hospital beds: 16.9 per 10,000 population; Hospital admissions: 653.4 per 10,000 population
Transportation: Commute: 94.8% car, 0.1% public transportation, 1.1% walk, 2.9% work from home; Mean travel time to work: 20.7 minutes
2016 Presidential Election: 71.3% Trump, 23.3% Clinton, 4.9% Johnson, 0.4% Stein
Additional Information Contacts
DeKalb Government . . . . (219) 925-2362
http://www.co.dekalb.in.us

DeKalb County Communities

ALTONA (town). Covers a land area of 0.217 square miles and a water area of 0 square miles. Located at 41.35° N. Lat; 85.15° W. Long. Elevation is 899 feet.
Population: 323; Growth (since 2000): 63.1%; Density: 1,486.1 persons per square mile; Race: 96.3% White, 0.0% Black/African American, 0.0% Asian, 0.0% American Indian/Alaska Native, 0.0% Native Hawaiian/Other Pacific Islander, 3.7% Two or more races, 1.5% Hispanic of any race; Average household size: 3.55; Median age: 37.6; Age under 18: 31.6%; Age 65 and over: 7.1%; Males per 100 females: 107.4; Marriage status: 34.4% never married, 48.4% now married, 1.2% separated, 5.3% widowed, 11.9% divorced; Foreign born: 0.0%; Speak English only: 99.3%; With disability: 14.9%; Veterans: 7.7%; Ancestry: 22.6% American, 20.1% European, 12.4% German, 4.3% English, 3.7% Irish
Employment: 7.9% management, business, and financial, 2.2% computer, engineering, and science, 14.4% education, legal, community service, arts,

and media, 4.3% healthcare practitioners, 9.4% service, 20.1% sales and office, 3.6% natural resources, construction, and maintenance, 38.1% production, transportation, and material moving
Income: Per capita: $19,102; Median household: $49,375; Average household: $62,284; Households with income of $100,000 or more: 20.9%; Poverty rate: 17.4%
Educational Attainment: High school diploma or higher: 86.3%; Bachelor's degree or higher: 4.3%; Graduate/professional degree or higher: 0.5%
Housing: Homeownership rate: 68.1%; Median home value: $65,000; Median year structure built: Before 1940; Homeowner vacancy rate: 7.5%; Median selected monthly owner costs: $728 with a mortgage, $405 without a mortgage; Median gross rent: $992 per month; Rental vacancy rate: 0.0%
Health Insurance: 87.9% have insurance; 62.8% have private insurance; 36.8% have public insurance; 12.1% do not have insurance; 4.7% of children under 18 do not have insurance
Transportation: Commute: 93.6% car, 0.0% public transportation, 4.8% walk, 1.6% work from home; Mean travel time to work: 21.9 minutes

ASHLEY (town). Covers a land area of 1.808 square miles and a water area of 0 square miles. Located at 41.52° N. Lat; 85.06° W. Long. Elevation is 1,010 feet.
Population: 1,062; Growth (since 2000): 5.1%; Density: 587.4 persons per square mile; Race: 97.5% White, 0.3% Black/African American, 0.0% Asian, 0.0% American Indian/Alaska Native, 0.0% Native Hawaiian/Other Pacific Islander, 1.8% Two or more races, 0.8% Hispanic of any race; Average household size: 2.44; Median age: 32.9; Age under 18: 28.4%; Age 65 and over: 12.7%; Males per 100 females: 103.5; Marriage status: 31.0% never married, 45.6% now married, 6.1% separated, 7.4% widowed, 15.9% divorced; Foreign born: 0.2%; Speak English only: 99.6%; With disability: 21.6%; Veterans: 10.5%; Ancestry: 30.5% German, 9.5% European, 8.9% American, 8.1% Irish, 7.3% English
Employment: 8.4% management, business, and financial, 4.5% computer, engineering, and science, 3.1% education, legal, community service, arts, and media, 1.9% healthcare practitioners, 16.3% service, 16.3% sales and office, 10.1% natural resources, construction, and maintenance, 39.5% production, transportation, and material moving
Income: Per capita: $20,252; Median household: $41,544; Average household: $47,974; Households with income of $100,000 or more: 6.2%; Poverty rate: 22.2%
Educational Attainment: High school diploma or higher: 86.3%; Bachelor's degree or higher: 5.3%; Graduate/professional degree or higher: 0.6%

School District(s)

Dekalb Co Ctl United Sch Dist (PK-12)
Enrollment: 3,776 . . . . (260) 920-1011
Housing: Homeownership rate: 58.9%; Median home value: $79,000; Median year structure built: 1969; Homeowner vacancy rate: 3.8%; Median selected monthly owner costs: $798 with a mortgage, $340 without a mortgage; Median gross rent: $394 per month; Rental vacancy rate: 14.0%
Health Insurance: 90.9% have insurance; 64.2% have private insurance; 39.1% have public insurance; 9.1% do not have insurance; 6.2% of children under 18 do not have insurance
Transportation: Commute: 96.9% car, 0.0% public transportation, 0.4% walk, 0.0% work from home; Mean travel time to work: 19.6 minutes
Additional Information Contacts
Town of Ashley . . . . (260) 587-3982
http://www.ashley.in.gov

AUBURN (city). County seat. Covers a land area of 7.104 square miles and a water area of 0 square miles. Located at 41.37° N. Lat; 85.05° W. Long. Elevation is 866 feet.
History: Auburn developed as a trading center for the surrounding farmlands, and as the seat of DeKalb County.
Population: 13,004; Growth (since 2000): 7.7%; Density: 1,830.4 persons per square mile; Race: 99.0% White, 0.3% Black/African American, 0.2% Asian, 0.0% American Indian/Alaska Native, 0.0% Native Hawaiian/Other Pacific Islander, 0.5% Two or more races, 1.9% Hispanic of any race; Average household size: 2.31; Median age: 39.8; Age under 18: 23.2%; Age 65 and over: 17.7%; Males per 100 females: 92.8; Marriage status: 30.2% never married, 45.9% now married, 0.7% separated, 9.7% widowed, 14.1% divorced; Foreign born: 1.2%; Speak English only: 97.5%; With disability: 16.1%; Veterans: 8.6%; Ancestry: 38.0% German, 14.0% English, 12.5% Irish, 12.5% American, 4.2% European
Employment: 12.0% management, business, and financial, 3.1% computer, engineering, and science, 9.6% education, legal, community service, arts, and media, 5.0% healthcare practitioners, 15.3% service, 20.3% sales and office, 4.4% natural resources, construction, and maintenance, 30.4% production, transportation, and material moving
Income: Per capita: $29,911; Median household: $47,129; Average household: $68,262; Households with income of $100,000 or more: 16.4%; Poverty rate: 11.7%
Educational Attainment: High school diploma or higher: 91.2%; Bachelor's degree or higher: 23.4%; Graduate/professional degree or higher: 6.8%

School District(s)

Dekalb Co Ctl United Sch Dist (PK-12)
Enrollment: 3,776 . . . . (260) 920-1011
Housing: Homeownership rate: 69.5%; Median home value: $106,400; Median year structure built: 1977; Homeowner vacancy rate: 3.6%; Median selected monthly owner costs: $893 with a mortgage, $311 without a mortgage; Median gross rent: $684 per month; Rental vacancy rate: 5.0%
Health Insurance: 93.1% have insurance; 74.5% have private insurance; 32.5% have public insurance; 6.9% do not have insurance; 10.3% of children under 18 do not have insurance
Hospitals: Dekalb Health (47 beds)
Newspapers: Evening Star (daily circulation 6,800)
Transportation: Commute: 95.2% car, 0.0% public transportation, 0.3% walk, 2.9% work from home; Mean travel time to work: 17.7 minutes
Additional Information Contacts
City of Auburn . . . . (260) 925-6450
http://www.ci.auburn.in.us

BUTLER (city). Covers a land area of 2.093 square miles and a water area of 0 square miles. Located at 41.43° N. Lat; 84.87° W. Long. Elevation is 866 feet.
Population: 2,763; Growth (since 2000): 1.4%; Density: 1,320.0 persons per square mile; Race: 95.7% White, 0.3% Black/African American, 0.0% Asian, 0.0% American Indian/Alaska Native, 0.0% Native Hawaiian/Other Pacific Islander, 2.5% Two or more races, 2.8% Hispanic of any race; Average household size: 2.85; Median age: 32.9; Age under 18: 24.0%; Age 65 and over: 11.6%; Males per 100 females: 99.4; Marriage status: 35.8% never married, 37.9% now married, 1.1% separated, 6.5% widowed, 19.8% divorced; Foreign born: 0.3%; Speak English only: 97.4%; With disability: 16.8%; Veterans: 8.6%; Ancestry: 23.9% German, 14.8% American, 13.6% European, 12.9% Irish, 3.9% Dutch
Employment: 6.7% management, business, and financial, 2.6% computer, engineering, and science, 5.2% education, legal, community service, arts, and media, 5.3% healthcare practitioners, 9.7% service, 19.2% sales and office, 6.1% natural resources, construction, and maintenance, 45.2% production, transportation, and material moving
Income: Per capita: $20,240; Median household: $48,620; Average household: $56,054; Households with income of $100,000 or more: 11.6%; Poverty rate: 12.5%
Educational Attainment: High school diploma or higher: 81.3%; Bachelor's degree or higher: 8.7%; Graduate/professional degree or higher: 1.5%

School District(s)

Dekalb Co Eastern Com Sch Dist (PK-12)
Enrollment: 1,332 . . . . (260) 868-2125
Housing: Homeownership rate: 72.5%; Median home value: $78,500; Median year structure built: 1952; Homeowner vacancy rate: 4.1%; Median selected monthly owner costs: $875 with a mortgage, $338 without a mortgage; Median gross rent: $731 per month; Rental vacancy rate: 19.8%
Health Insurance: 81.3% have insurance; 58.6% have private insurance; 28.2% have public insurance; 18.7% do not have insurance; 11.7% of children under 18 do not have insurance
Newspapers: Butler Bulletin (weekly circulation 1,000)
Transportation: Commute: 91.5% car, 0.7% public transportation, 5.8% walk, 1.7% work from home; Mean travel time to work: 23.3 minutes
Additional Information Contacts
City of Butler . . . . (260) 868-5200
http://www.butler.in.us

CORUNNA (town). Covers a land area of 0.173 square miles and a water area of 0 square miles. Located at 41.44° N. Lat; 85.14° W. Long. Elevation is 974 feet.
Population: 290; Growth (since 2000): 14.2%; Density: 1,675.3 persons per square mile; Race: 93.8% White, 1.0% Black/African American, 0.0%

Asian, 0.0% American Indian/Alaska Native, 0.0% Native Hawaiian/Other Pacific Islander, 5.2% Two or more races, 0.3% Hispanic of any race; Average household size: 2.87; Median age: 34.6; Age under 18: 30.0%; Age 65 and over: 14.8%; Males per 100 females: 96.9; Marriage status: 35.9% never married, 30.3% now married, 3.4% separated, 9.8% widowed, 23.9% divorced; Foreign born: 0.0%; Speak English only: 100.0%; With disability: 20.3%; Veterans: 9.4%; Ancestry: 15.5% German, 13.4% American, 11.0% European, 6.6% English, 4.1% Irish
Employment: 3.9% management, business, and financial, 0.8% computer, engineering, and science, 2.4% education, legal, community service, arts, and media, 0.0% healthcare practitioners, 11.8% service, 19.7% sales and office, 7.9% natural resources, construction, and maintenance, 53.5% production, transportation, and material moving
Income: Per capita: $14,593; Median household: $31,875; Average household: $37,684; Households with income of $100,000 or more: 4.0%; Poverty rate: 26.6%
Educational Attainment: High school diploma or higher: 79.5%; Bachelor's degree or higher: 8.0%; Graduate/professional degree or higher: 0.6%
Housing: Homeownership rate: 80.2%; Median home value: $52,300; Median year structure built: Before 1940; Homeowner vacancy rate: 0.0%; Median selected monthly owner costs: $773 with a mortgage, $439 without a mortgage; Median gross rent: $775 per month; Rental vacancy rate: 0.0%
Health Insurance: 84.5% have insurance; 48.6% have private insurance; 44.1% have public insurance; 15.5% do not have insurance; 6.2% of children under 18 do not have insurance
Transportation: Commute: 99.2% car, 0.0% public transportation, 0.0% walk, 0.0% work from home; Mean travel time to work: 18.5 minutes

GARRETT (city). Covers a land area of 3.851 square miles and a water area of 0 square miles. Located at 41.35° N. Lat; 85.12° W. Long. Elevation is 883 feet.
History: Garrett developed around the Baltimore & Ohio Railroad shops and roundhouse, and served the surrounding farms.
Population: 6,762; Growth (since 2000): 16.5%; Density: 1,756.1 persons per square mile; Race: 97.8% White, 0.3% Black/African American, 0.1% Asian, 0.0% American Indian/Alaska Native, 0.0% Native Hawaiian/Other Pacific Islander, 1.5% Two or more races, 2.2% Hispanic of any race; Average household size: 2.56; Median age: 36.2; Age under 18: 26.5%; Age 65 and over: 13.3%; Males per 100 females: 92.1; Marriage status: 31.1% never married, 45.4% now married, 0.9% separated, 6.1% widowed, 17.4% divorced; Foreign born: 0.8%; Speak English only: 97.8%; With disability: 16.9%; Veterans: 7.5%; Ancestry: 27.0% German, 11.4% Irish, 6.9% American, 6.1% English, 6.0% European
Employment: 11.1% management, business, and financial, 3.1% computer, engineering, and science, 7.8% education, legal, community service, arts, and media, 1.8% healthcare practitioners, 13.6% service, 20.0% sales and office, 10.7% natural resources, construction, and maintenance, 31.9% production, transportation, and material moving
Income: Per capita: $19,143; Median household: $42,277; Average household: $48,393; Households with income of $100,000 or more: 3.1%; Poverty rate: 20.1%
Educational Attainment: High school diploma or higher: 86.9%; Bachelor's degree or higher: 11.1%; Graduate/professional degree or higher: 3.4%

School District(s)

Garrett-Keyser-Butler Com Sch Corp (PK-12)
Enrollment: 1,705 .... (260) 357-3185
Housing: Homeownership rate: 65.5%; Median home value: $86,400; Median year structure built: 1957; Homeowner vacancy rate: 0.0%; Median selected monthly owner costs: $883 with a mortgage, $356 without a mortgage; Median gross rent: $686 per month; Rental vacancy rate: 6.2%
Health Insurance: 88.3% have insurance; 67.0% have private insurance; 34.9% have public insurance; 11.7% do not have insurance; 6.4% of children under 18 do not have insurance
Newspapers: Garrett Clipper (weekly circulation 1,800)
Transportation: Commute: 95.8% car, 0.0% public transportation, 1.0% walk, 2.4% work from home; Mean travel time to work: 23.0 minutes
Additional Information Contacts
City of Garrett .... (260) 357-4151
http://www.garrettindiana.us

SAINT JOE (town). Covers a land area of 0.273 square miles and a water area of 0 square miles. Located at 41.31° N. Lat; 84.90° W. Long. Elevation is 820 feet.
Population: 393; Growth (since 2000): -17.8%; Density: 1,437.0 persons per square mile; Race: 89.3% White, 0.0% Black/African American, 0.3% Asian, 1.3% American Indian/Alaska Native, 0.0% Native Hawaiian/Other Pacific Islander, 7.1% Two or more races, 2.3% Hispanic of any race; Average household size: 3.14; Median age: 30.1; Age under 18: 31.8%; Age 65 and over: 6.1%; Males per 100 females: 103.5; Marriage status: 26.8% never married, 50.4% now married, 1.8% separated, 6.0% widowed, 16.9% divorced; Foreign born: 2.3%; Speak English only: 98.3%; With disability: 13.2%; Veterans: 4.9%; Ancestry: 37.7% German, 12.5% American, 12.5% Irish, 6.4% English, 4.1% Scotch-Irish
Employment: 3.8% management, business, and financial, 4.4% computer, engineering, and science, 1.1% education, legal, community service, arts, and media, 6.6% healthcare practitioners, 13.7% service, 16.5% sales and office, 21.4% natural resources, construction, and maintenance, 32.4% production, transportation, and material moving
Income: Per capita: $17,131; Median household: $52,188; Average household: $51,199; Households with income of $100,000 or more: 8.0%; Poverty rate: 13.7%
Educational Attainment: High school diploma or higher: 91.3%; Bachelor's degree or higher: 4.8%; Graduate/professional degree or higher: 1.0%

School District(s)

Dekalb Co Eastern Com Sch Dist (PK-12)
Enrollment: 1,332 .... (260) 868-2125
Housing: Homeownership rate: 76.8%; Median home value: $66,000; Median year structure built: Before 1940; Homeowner vacancy rate: 1.0%; Median selected monthly owner costs: $838 with a mortgage, $368 without a mortgage; Median gross rent: $675 per month; Rental vacancy rate: 38.3%
Health Insurance: 84.2% have insurance; 58.5% have private insurance; 31.0% have public insurance; 15.8% do not have insurance; 12.0% of children under 18 do not have insurance
Transportation: Commute: 92.1% car, 0.0% public transportation, 3.9% walk, 1.7% work from home; Mean travel time to work: 24.2 minutes

WATERLOO (town). Covers a land area of 1.739 square miles and a water area of 0 square miles. Located at 41.43° N. Lat; 85.03° W. Long. Elevation is 906 feet.
Population: 2,227; Growth (since 2000): 1.2%; Density: 1,280.7 persons per square mile; Race: 95.7% White, 0.0% Black/African American, 1.4% Asian, 0.1% American Indian/Alaska Native, 0.0% Native Hawaiian/Other Pacific Islander, 1.5% Two or more races, 5.6% Hispanic of any race; Average household size: 2.67; Median age: 33.3; Age under 18: 32.3%; Age 65 and over: 9.0%; Males per 100 females: 102.3; Marriage status: 24.0% never married, 56.1% now married, 1.0% separated, 2.4% widowed, 17.6% divorced; Foreign born: 3.8%; Speak English only: 95.1%; With disability: 22.3%; Veterans: 10.2%; Ancestry: 31.0% German, 10.3% English, 9.6% Irish, 7.2% French, 6.1% American
Employment: 11.0% management, business, and financial, 3.2% computer, engineering, and science, 7.6% education, legal, community service, arts, and media, 6.6% healthcare practitioners, 8.6% service, 15.3% sales and office, 7.4% natural resources, construction, and maintenance, 40.4% production, transportation, and material moving
Income: Per capita: $19,301; Median household: $47,708; Average household: $50,695; Households with income of $100,000 or more: 4.9%; Poverty rate: 12.3%
Educational Attainment: High school diploma or higher: 88.1%; Bachelor's degree or higher: 13.9%; Graduate/professional degree or higher: 6.7%

School District(s)

Dekalb Co Ctl United Sch Dist (PK-12)
Enrollment: 3,776 .... (260) 920-1011
Housing: Homeownership rate: 73.5%; Median home value: $72,700; Median year structure built: 1960; Homeowner vacancy rate: 3.4%; Median selected monthly owner costs: $920 with a mortgage, $369 without a mortgage; Median gross rent: $727 per month; Rental vacancy rate: 14.7%
Health Insurance: 93.8% have insurance; 71.8% have private insurance; 33.4% have public insurance; 6.2% do not have insurance; 0.0% of children under 18 do not have insurance
Safety: Violent crime rate: 44.4 per 10,000 population; Property crime rate: 293.3 per 10,000 population

Transportation: Commute: 97.2% car, 0.0% public transportation, 1.9% walk, 0.0% work from home; Mean travel time to work: 19.3 minutes; Amtrak: Train service available.
Additional Information Contacts
Town of Waterloo .... (260) 837-7428
http://mywaterlooindiana.com

Delaware County

Located in eastern Indiana; drained by the Mississinewa River and the West Fork of the White River. Covers a land area of 392.124 square miles, a water area of 3.785 square miles, and is located in the Eastern Time Zone at 40.23° N. Lat., 85.40° W. Long. The county was founded in 1827. County seat is Muncie.

Delaware County is part of the Muncie, IN Metropolitan Statistical Area. The entire metro area includes: Delaware County, IN

Weather Station: Muncie Delaware Cnty Elevation: 978 feet

	Jan	Feb	Mar	Apr	May	Jun	Jul	Aug	Sep	Oct	Nov	Dec
High	33	38	48	61	72	81	85	83	77	64	51	38
Low	17	21	29	39	51	60	64	61	53	42	33	22
Precip	1.9	2.1	2.9	3.5	4.6	4.5	4.6	3.1	3.3	2.7	3.5	2.9
Snow	7.5	6.0	2.7	0.5	tr	0.0	0.0	0.0	0.0	0.3	1.0	6.1

High and Low temperatures in degrees Fahrenheit; Precipitation and Snow in inches

Population: 115,938; Growth (since 2000): -2.4%; Density: 295.7 persons per square mile; Race: 88.5% White, 7.3% Black/African American, 1.3% Asian, 0.1% American Indian/Alaska Native, 0.1% Native Hawaiian/Other Pacific Islander, 2.2% two or more races, 2.3% Hispanic of any race; Average household size: 2.35; Median age: 35.4; Age under 18: 18.9%; Age 65 and over: 16.3%; Males per 100 females: 92.7; Marriage status: 38.1% never married, 42.9% now married, 1.2% separated, 6.7% widowed, 12.2% divorced; Foreign born: 2.2%; Speak English only: 96.5%; With disability: 16.3%; Veterans: 7.0%; Ancestry: 18.7% German, 12.0% Irish, 11.4% American, 8.7% English, 2.0% Italian
Religion: Six largest groups: 5.5% Methodist/Pietist, 4.9% Baptist, 4.8% Non-denominational Protestant, 3.7% Holiness, 3.5% Catholicism, 2.0% Presbyterian-Reformed
Economy: Unemployment rate: 4.2%; Leading industries: 17.7 % retail trade; 16.3 % health care and social assistance; 11.9 % other services (except public administration); Farms: 610 totaling 175,266 acres; Company size: 2 employ 1,000 or more persons, 1 employs 500 to 999 persons, 59 employ 100 to 499 persons, 2,373 employ less than 100 persons; Business ownership: 2,237 women-owned, 264 Black-owned, 47 Hispanic-owned, 111 Asian-owned, n/a American Indian/Alaska Native-owned
Employment: 11.7% management, business, and financial, 3.2% computer, engineering, and science, 11.3% education, legal, community service, arts, and media, 6.2% healthcare practitioners, 21.6% service, 24.1% sales and office, 8.0% natural resources, construction, and maintenance, 13.9% production, transportation, and material moving
Income: Per capita: $23,271; Median household: $41,208; Average household: $56,758; Households with income of $100,000 or more: 13.9%; Poverty rate: 21.2%
Educational Attainment: High school diploma or higher: 89.5%; Bachelor's degree or higher: 23.9%; Graduate/professional degree or higher: 10.1%
Housing: Homeownership rate: 64.2%; Median home value: $88,600; Median year structure built: 1964; Homeowner vacancy rate: 2.1%; Median selected monthly owner costs: $902 with a mortgage, $364 without a mortgage; Median gross rent: $708 per month; Rental vacancy rate: 7.5%
Vital Statistics: Birth rate: 101.4 per 10,000 population; Death rate: 102.5 per 10,000 population; Age-adjusted cancer mortality rate: 173.4 deaths per 100,000 population
Health Insurance: 90.1% have insurance; 69.9% have private insurance; 33.5% have public insurance; 9.9% do not have insurance; 4.7% of children under 18 do not have insurance
Health Care: Physicians: 28.2 per 10,000 population; Dentists: 5.7 per 10,000 population; Hospital beds: 32.1 per 10,000 population; Hospital admissions: 1,397.0 per 10,000 population
Air Quality Index (AQI): Percent of Days: 85.0% good, 14.6% moderate, 0.4% unhealthy for sensitive individuals, 0.0% unhealthy, 0.0% very unhealthy; Annual median: 39; Annual maximum: 112
Transportation: Commute: 88.1% car, 1.9% public transportation, 4.7% walk, 3.4% work from home; Mean travel time to work: 20.6 minutes
2016 Presidential Election: 53.3% Trump, 39.9% Clinton, 5.2% Johnson, 0.6% Stein
Additional Information Contacts
Delaware Government .... (765) 747-7726
http://www.co.delaware.in.us

Delaware County Communities

ALBANY (town). Covers a land area of 1.752 square miles and a water area of 0.007 square miles. Located at 40.31° N. Lat; 85.23° W. Long. Elevation is 938 feet.
Population: 2,083; Growth (since 2000): -12.0%; Density: 1,188.7 persons per square mile; Race: 95.2% White, 0.0% Black/African American, 0.0% Asian, 0.0% American Indian/Alaska Native, 0.0% Native Hawaiian/Other Pacific Islander, 4.8% Two or more races, 2.1% Hispanic of any race; Average household size: 2.19; Median age: 44.0; Age under 18: 18.0%; Age 65 and over: 20.7%; Males per 100 females: 90.4; Marriage status: 21.2% never married, 57.0% now married, 3.1% separated, 10.0% widowed, 11.8% divorced; Foreign born: 1.6%; Speak English only: 99.1%; With disability: 16.2%; Veterans: 10.1%; Ancestry: 16.2% German, 15.9% Irish, 13.1% American, 10.7% English, 3.2% Scotch-Irish
Employment: 14.9% management, business, and financial, 1.2% computer, engineering, and science, 6.1% education, legal, community service, arts, and media, 6.6% healthcare practitioners, 18.8% service, 20.0% sales and office, 9.0% natural resources, construction, and maintenance, 23.5% production, transportation, and material moving
Income: Per capita: $24,209; Median household: $50,330; Average household: $53,828; Households with income of $100,000 or more: 10.7%; Poverty rate: 7.4%
Educational Attainment: High school diploma or higher: 94.8%; Bachelor's degree or higher: 16.7%; Graduate/professional degree or higher: 5.0%

School District(s)

Delaware Community School Corp (PK-12)
Enrollment: 2,463 .... (765) 284-5074
Housing: Homeownership rate: 67.7%; Median home value: $72,000; Median year structure built: 1954; Homeowner vacancy rate: 0.0%; Median selected monthly owner costs: $854 with a mortgage, $352 without a mortgage; Median gross rent: $520 per month; Rental vacancy rate: 18.0%
Health Insurance: 86.9% have insurance; 69.3% have private insurance; 32.6% have public insurance; 13.1% do not have insurance; 9.7% of children under 18 do not have insurance
Transportation: Commute: 93.6% car, 0.0% public transportation, 1.3% walk, 5.1% work from home; Mean travel time to work: 23.7 minutes
Additional Information Contacts
Town of Albany .... (765) 288-6681
http://www.muncie.com/Chamber-of-Commerce.aspx

DALEVILLE (town). Covers a land area of 2.051 square miles and a water area of 0.022 square miles. Located at 40.12° N. Lat; 85.56° W. Long. Elevation is 912 feet.
History: When Daleville was platted in 1838, it was expected that a canal would be built here. Instead, the railroad came in 1852.
Population: 1,595; Growth (since 2000): -3.8%; Density: 777.8 persons per square mile; Race: 95.7% White, 1.6% Black/African American, 1.1% Asian, 0.0% American Indian/Alaska Native, 0.0% Native Hawaiian/Other Pacific Islander, 1.6% Two or more races, 1.5% Hispanic of any race; Average household size: 2.42; Median age: 40.2; Age under 18: 18.6%; Age 65 and over: 16.2%; Males per 100 females: 91.7; Marriage status: 27.4% never married, 48.7% now married, 0.8% separated, 7.4% widowed, 16.5% divorced; Foreign born: 1.6%; Speak English only: 99.0%; With disability: 18.5%; Veterans: 8.6%; Ancestry: 25.1% German, 13.9% American, 12.4% Irish, 7.6% English, 2.9% Scottish
Employment: 10.8% management, business, and financial, 3.4% computer, engineering, and science, 11.6% education, legal, community service, arts, and media, 10.7% healthcare practitioners, 14.1% service, 23.8% sales and office, 9.2% natural resources, construction, and maintenance, 16.3% production, transportation, and material moving
Income: Per capita: $25,306; Median household: $45,366; Average household: $60,201; Households with income of $100,000 or more: 10.8%; Poverty rate: 11.9%
Educational Attainment: High school diploma or higher: 91.8%; Bachelor's degree or higher: 16.4%; Graduate/professional degree or higher: 4.5%

School District(s)

Daleville Community Schools (PK-12)
Enrollment: 569 . . . . (765) 378-3329

Housing: Homeownership rate: 68.9%; Median home value: $77,800; Median year structure built: 1960; Homeowner vacancy rate: 4.1%; Median selected monthly owner costs: $864 with a mortgage, $375 without a mortgage; Median gross rent: $748 per month; Rental vacancy rate: 0.0%
Health Insurance: 86.7% have insurance; 71.9% have private insurance; 31.4% have public insurance; 13.3% do not have insurance; 9.1% of children under 18 do not have insurance
Transportation: Commute: 97.3% car, 0.0% public transportation, 0.0% walk, 2.3% work from home; Mean travel time to work: 24.1 minutes

EATON (town). Covers a land area of 3.698 square miles and a water area of 0.063 square miles. Located at 40.32° N. Lat; 85.36° W. Long. Elevation is 909 feet.
Population: 1,845; Growth (since 2000): 15.1%; Density: 498.9 persons per square mile; Race: 97.8% White, 0.6% Black/African American, 0.3% Asian, 0.8% American Indian/Alaska Native, 0.0% Native Hawaiian/Other Pacific Islander, 0.5% Two or more races, 0.0% Hispanic of any race; Average household size: 2.50; Median age: 36.7; Age under 18: 26.9%; Age 65 and over: 16.2%; Males per 100 females: 104.6; Marriage status: 26.2% never married, 51.7% now married, 1.5% separated, 6.7% widowed, 15.5% divorced; Foreign born: 0.4%; Speak English only: 97.8%; With disability: 17.2%; Veterans: 9.8%; Ancestry: 21.8% German, 12.9% American, 12.0% Irish, 6.7% English, 1.5% European
Employment: 6.5% management, business, and financial, 2.0% computer, engineering, and science, 6.5% education, legal, community service, arts, and media, 9.7% healthcare practitioners, 13.9% service, 23.6% sales and office, 12.3% natural resources, construction, and maintenance, 25.5% production, transportation, and material moving
Income: Per capita: $21,146; Median household: $40,750; Average household: $53,414; Households with income of $100,000 or more: 11.5%; Poverty rate: 19.0%
Educational Attainment: High school diploma or higher: 90.1%; Bachelor's degree or higher: 12.1%; Graduate/professional degree or higher: 4.4%

School District(s)

Delaware Community School Corp (PK-12)
Enrollment: 2,463 . . . . (765) 284-5074

Housing: Homeownership rate: 66.6%; Median home value: $62,900; Median year structure built: 1960; Homeowner vacancy rate: 4.0%; Median selected monthly owner costs: $768 with a mortgage, $325 without a mortgage; Median gross rent: $786 per month; Rental vacancy rate: 3.5%
Health Insurance: 87.2% have insurance; 66.1% have private insurance; 36.3% have public insurance; 12.8% do not have insurance; 5.2% of children under 18 do not have insurance
Transportation: Commute: 98.8% car, 0.4% public transportation, 0.4% walk, 0.4% work from home; Mean travel time to work: 23.1 minutes

GASTON (town). Covers a land area of 0.351 square miles and a water area of 0 square miles. Located at 40.31° N. Lat; 85.50° W. Long. Elevation is 896 feet.
Population: 893; Growth (since 2000): -11.6%; Density: 2,546.2 persons per square mile; Race: 97.8% White, 0.3% Black/African American, 0.7% Asian, 0.0% American Indian/Alaska Native, 0.0% Native Hawaiian/Other Pacific Islander, 0.9% Two or more races, 0.7% Hispanic of any race; Average household size: 2.41; Median age: 41.2; Age under 18: 23.7%; Age 65 and over: 15.2%; Males per 100 females: 92.3; Marriage status: 23.9% never married, 52.2% now married, 2.4% separated, 6.4% widowed, 17.5% divorced; Foreign born: 1.2%; Speak English only: 98.7%; With disability: 16.0%; Veterans: 7.2%; Ancestry: 16.5% German, 14.0% Irish, 12.9% American, 7.7% English, 3.0% Scottish
Employment: 7.7% management, business, and financial, 1.8% computer, engineering, and science, 6.4% education, legal, community service, arts, and media, 7.7% healthcare practitioners, 21.0% service, 26.0% sales and office, 14.1% natural resources, construction, and maintenance, 15.3% production, transportation, and material moving
Income: Per capita: $19,233; Median household: $40,952; Average household: $46,314; Households with income of $100,000 or more: 6.8%; Poverty rate: 17.4%
Educational Attainment: High school diploma or higher: 87.1%; Bachelor's degree or higher: 14.4%; Graduate/professional degree or higher: 6.1%

School District(s)

Wes-del Community Schools (KG-12)
Enrollment: 717 . . . . (765) 358-4006

Housing: Homeownership rate: 84.1%; Median home value: $54,400; Median year structure built: 1957; Homeowner vacancy rate: 2.2%; Median selected monthly owner costs: $736 with a mortgage, $377 without a mortgage; Median gross rent: $613 per month; Rental vacancy rate: 0.0%
Health Insurance: 87.6% have insurance; 62.6% have private insurance; 39.1% have public insurance; 12.4% do not have insurance; 3.7% of children under 18 do not have insurance
Transportation: Commute: 96.6% car, 0.0% public transportation, 2.8% walk, 0.0% work from home; Mean travel time to work: 22.6 minutes

MUNCIE (city). County seat. Covers a land area of 27.196 square miles and a water area of 0.192 square miles. Located at 40.20° N. Lat; 85.39° W. Long. Elevation is 951 feet.
History: A railroad station and some factories were the impetus for the growth of Muncie, which was platted in 1827 and called Munseytown. Incorporation as a town came in 1847, and by 1865 Muncie was declared a city. About 1887 natural gas wells began to bring many new industries to Muncie. One of these was the Ball Brothers Company, producers of canning jars.
Population: 69,237; Growth (since 2000): 2.7%; Density: 2,545.8 persons per square mile; Race: 83.0% White, 11.6% Black/African American, 1.6% Asian, 0.1% American Indian/Alaska Native, 0.1% Native Hawaiian/Other Pacific Islander, 2.9% Two or more races, 3.1% Hispanic of any race; Average household size: 2.25; Median age: 28.8; Age under 18: 16.8%; Age 65 and over: 13.9%; Males per 100 females: 90.6; Marriage status: 48.4% never married, 32.5% now married, 1.3% separated, 6.2% widowed, 12.9% divorced; Foreign born: 2.7%; Speak English only: 95.6%; With disability: 17.1%; Veterans: 6.1%; Ancestry: 17.8% German, 12.5% Irish, 9.8% American, 7.2% English, 2.3% Italian
Employment: 10.1% management, business, and financial, 2.7% computer, engineering, and science, 12.6% education, legal, community service, arts, and media, 4.8% healthcare practitioners, 26.0% service, 24.8% sales and office, 6.5% natural resources, construction, and maintenance, 12.6% production, transportation, and material moving
Income: Per capita: $18,891; Median household: $32,372; Average household: $44,711; Households with income of $100,000 or more: 9.4%; Poverty rate: 29.9%
Educational Attainment: High school diploma or higher: 86.7%; Bachelor's degree or higher: 23.6%; Graduate/professional degree or higher: 10.5%

School District(s)

Burris Laboratory School (KG-12)
Enrollment: 644 . . . . (765) 285-8488
Cowan Community School Corp (PK-12)
Enrollment: 575 . . . . (765) 289-4866
Delaware Community School Corp (PK-12)
Enrollment: 2,463 . . . . (765) 284-5074
Indiana Acad For Sci Math & Humanities (10-12)
Enrollment: 330 . . . . (765) 285-8102
Inspire Academy - A Sch Of Inquiry (KG-08)
Enrollment: 174 . . . . (765) 216-7980
Muncie Community Schools (PK-12)
Enrollment: 6,598 . . . . (765) 747-5205

Four-year College(s)

Ball State University (Public)
Enrollment: 22,513 . . . . (765) 289-1241
Tuition: In-state $9,774; Out-of-state $25,942

Two-year College(s)

Ross Medical Education Center-Muncie (Private, For-profit)
Enrollment: 88 . . . . (765) 282-1950

Housing: Homeownership rate: 51.4%; Median home value: $70,500; Median year structure built: 1960; Homeowner vacancy rate: 3.6%; Median selected monthly owner costs: $809 with a mortgage, $340 without a mortgage; Median gross rent: $714 per month; Rental vacancy rate: 8.5%
Health Insurance: 88.9% have insurance; 65.3% have private insurance; 34.8% have public insurance; 11.1% do not have insurance; 5.4% of children under 18 do not have insurance
Hospitals: Indiana University Health Ball Memorial Hospital (350 beds)
Safety: Violent crime rate: 35.7 per 10,000 population; Property crime rate: 362.0 per 10,000 population
Newspapers: Star-Press (daily circulation 32,000)

Transportation: Commute: 83.5% car, 3.2% public transportation, 7.5% walk, 3.3% work from home; Mean travel time to work: 18.9 minutes
Airports: Delaware County Regional (general aviation)
Additional Information Contacts
City of Muncie . . . . (765) 747-4831
http://www.cityofmuncie.com

OAKVILLE (unincorporated postal area)
ZCTA: 47367

Covers a land area of 0.720 square miles and a water area of 0 square miles. Located at 40.08° N. Lat; 85.39° W. Long. Elevation is 1,010 feet.
Population: 26; Growth (since 2000): n/a; Density: 36.1 persons per square mile; Race: 100.0% White, 0.0% Black/African American, 0.0% Asian, 0.0% American Indian/Alaska Native, 0.0% Native Hawaiian/Other Pacific Islander, 0.0% Two or more races, 0.0% Hispanic of any race; Average household size: 2.00; Median age: n/a; Age under 18: 0.0%; Age 65 and over: 50.0%; Males per 100 females: 99.0; Marriage status: 50.0% never married, 0.0% now married, 0.0% separated, 0.0% widowed, 50.0% divorced; Foreign born: 0.0%; Speak English only: 100.0%; With disability: 0.0%; Veterans: 0.0%; Ancestry: 50.0% English, 50.0% European
Employment: 0.0% management, business, and financial, 0.0% computer, engineering, and science, 100.0% education, legal, community service, arts, and media, 0.0% healthcare practitioners, 0.0% service, 0.0% sales and office, 0.0% natural resources, construction, and maintenance, 0.0% production, transportation, and material moving
Income: Per capita: n/a; Median household: n/a; Average household: n/a; Households with income of $100,000 or more: n/a; Poverty rate: n/a
Educational Attainment: High school diploma or higher: 100.0%; Bachelor's degree or higher: 100.0%; Graduate/professional degree or higher: 100.0%
Housing: Homeownership rate: 100.0%; Median home value: n/a; Median year structure built: n/a; Homeowner vacancy rate: 0.0%; Median selected monthly owner costs: $0 with a mortgage, $0 without a mortgage; Median gross rent: n/a per month; Rental vacancy rate: 0.0%
Health Insurance: 100.0% have insurance; 100.0% have private insurance; 50.0% have public insurance; 0.0% do not have insurance; 0.0% of children under 18 do not have insurance
Transportation: Commute: 0.0% car, 0.0% public transportation, 0.0% walk, 100.0% work from home; Mean travel time to work: 0.0 minutes

SELMA (town). Covers a land area of 0.909 square miles and a water area of 0.002 square miles. Located at 40.19° N. Lat; 85.27° W. Long. Elevation is 1,004 feet.
Population: 773; Growth (since 2000): -12.2%; Density: 850.1 persons per square mile; Race: 98.1% White, 0.3% Black/African American, 0.0% Asian, 0.1% American Indian/Alaska Native, 0.0% Native Hawaiian/Other Pacific Islander, 1.3% Two or more races, 6.3% Hispanic of any race; Average household size: 2.53; Median age: 42.2; Age under 18: 21.7%; Age 65 and over: 13.7%; Males per 100 females: 89.5; Marriage status: 29.1% never married, 49.6% now married, 0.9% separated, 7.1% widowed, 14.1% divorced; Foreign born: 0.3%; Speak English only: 99.5%; With disability: 20.3%; Veterans: 14.4%; Ancestry: 16.7% German, 14.1% American, 13.5% English, 8.7% Irish, 2.3% Scottish
Employment: 9.5% management, business, and financial, 0.3% computer, engineering, and science, 11.2% education, legal, community service, arts, and media, 2.6% healthcare practitioners, 18.7% service, 25.3% sales and office, 17.2% natural resources, construction, and maintenance, 15.2% production, transportation, and material moving
Income: Per capita: $21,867; Median household: $44,853; Average household: $55,417; Households with income of $100,000 or more: 12.9%; Poverty rate: 13.5%
Educational Attainment: High school diploma or higher: 90.7%; Bachelor's degree or higher: 14.0%; Graduate/professional degree or higher: 1.7%

School District(s)
Liberty-Perry Community Sch Corp (KG-12)
Enrollment: 928. . . . . (765) 282-5615
Housing: Homeownership rate: 74.2%; Median home value: $77,300; Median year structure built: 1957; Homeowner vacancy rate: 0.0%; Median selected monthly owner costs: $922 with a mortgage, $367 without a mortgage; Median gross rent: $589 per month; Rental vacancy rate: 0.0%
Health Insurance: 89.9% have insurance; 63.1% have private insurance; 39.1% have public insurance; 10.1% do not have insurance; 3.4% of children under 18 do not have insurance
Transportation: Commute: 96.5% car, 1.2% public transportation, 1.2% walk, 0.6% work from home; Mean travel time to work: 22.4 minutes

YORKTOWN (town). Covers a land area of 8.779 square miles and a water area of 0.083 square miles. Located at 40.19° N. Lat; 85.47° W. Long. Elevation is 915 feet.
Population: 11,200; Growth (since 2000): 134.1%; Density: 1,275.8 persons per square mile; Race: 94.6% White, 2.8% Black/African American, 0.0% Asian, 0.0% American Indian/Alaska Native, 0.0% Native Hawaiian/Other Pacific Islander, 1.9% Two or more races, 0.0% Hispanic of any race; Average household size: 2.54; Median age: 40.2; Age under 18: 24.8%; Age 65 and over: 16.8%; Males per 100 females: 90.5; Marriage status: 21.5% never married, 58.9% now married, 1.1% separated, 6.2% widowed, 13.4% divorced; Foreign born: 0.6%; Speak English only: 99.0%; With disability: 11.8%; Veterans: 8.9%; Ancestry: 23.1% German, 14.7% Irish, 12.2% American, 11.8% English, 2.9% Scottish
Employment: 13.3% management, business, and financial, 7.7% computer, engineering, and science, 9.5% education, legal, community service, arts, and media, 12.7% healthcare practitioners, 16.5% service, 24.7% sales and office, 5.8% natural resources, construction, and maintenance, 9.8% production, transportation, and material moving
Income: Per capita: $31,646; Median household: $62,372; Average household: $80,524; Households with income of $100,000 or more: 25.4%; Poverty rate: 8.2%
Educational Attainment: High school diploma or higher: 95.3%; Bachelor's degree or higher: 28.0%; Graduate/professional degree or higher: 10.5%

School District(s)
Yorktown Community Schools (PK-12)
Enrollment: 2,232 . . . . (765) 759-2720
Housing: Homeownership rate: 81.3%; Median home value: $133,900; Median year structure built: 1971; Homeowner vacancy rate: 0.9%; Median selected monthly owner costs: $1,124 with a mortgage, $418 without a mortgage; Median gross rent: $697 per month; Rental vacancy rate: 0.0%
Health Insurance: 95.2% have insurance; 81.8% have private insurance; 29.8% have public insurance; 4.8% do not have insurance; 1.1% of children under 18 do not have insurance
Transportation: Commute: 97.7% car, 0.0% public transportation, 0.2% walk, 0.8% work from home; Mean travel time to work: 20.6 minutes
Additional Information Contacts
Town of Yorktown . . . . (765) 759-4002
http://www.yorktownindiana.org

Dubois County

Located in southwestern Indiana; bounded on the north by the East Fork of the White River; drained by the Patoka River. Covers a land area of 427.269 square miles, a water area of 8.064 square miles, and is located in the Eastern Time Zone at 38.37° N. Lat., 86.87° W. Long. The county was founded in 1817. County seat is Jasper.

Dubois County is part of the Jasper, IN Micropolitan Statistical Area. The entire metro area includes: Dubois County, IN; Pike County, IN

Weather Station: Dubois S Ind Forage Frm   Elevation: 689 feet

	Jan	Feb	Mar	Apr	May	Jun	Jul	Aug	Sep	Oct	Nov	Dec
High	40	44	54	65	75	83	86	86	79	68	56	43
Low	22	24	33	43	53	62	65	64	56	44	36	25
Precip	3.3	3.0	4.2	4.6	5.8	4.3	4.3	3.2	3.9	3.7	4.0	3.7
Snow	2.4	2.7	1.6	tr	0.0	0.0	0.0	0.0	0.0	0.2	tr	2.3

High and Low temperatures in degrees Fahrenheit; Precipitation and Snow in inches

Population: 42,379; Growth (since 2000): 6.8%; Density: 99.2 persons per square mile; Race: 94.2% White, 0.6% Black/African American, 0.6% Asian, 0.2% American Indian/Alaska Native, 0.0% Native Hawaiian/Other Pacific Islander, 0.9% two or more races, 7.1% Hispanic of any race; Average household size: 2.51; Median age: 40.2; Age under 18: 24.5%; Age 65 and over: 16.1%; Males per 100 females: 97.0; Marriage status: 25.9% never married, 57.5% now married, 0.6% separated, 6.4% widowed, 10.2% divorced; Foreign born: 4.3%; Speak English only: 93.7%; With disability: 10.9%; Veterans: 7.8%; Ancestry: 51.7% German, 8.4% American, 8.3% Irish, 5.7% English, 1.9% French

Religion: Six largest groups: 52.5% Catholicism, 5.8% Lutheran, 4.2% Baptist, 4.0% Methodist/Pietist, 3.7% Presbyterian-Reformed, 1.9% Non-denominational Protestant
Economy: Unemployment rate: 2.7%; Leading industries: 17.9 % retail trade; 11.2 % construction; 10.3 % health care and social assistance; Farms: 720 totaling 174,877 acres; Company size: 3 employ 1,000 or more persons, 5 employ 500 to 999 persons, 38 employ 100 to 499 persons, 1,236 employ less than 100 persons; Business ownership: 1,039 women-owned, n/a Black-owned, 43 Hispanic-owned, 64 Asian-owned, n/a American Indian/Alaska Native-owned
Employment: 12.6% management, business, and financial, 5.2% computer, engineering, and science, 8.3% education, legal, community service, arts, and media, 5.5% healthcare practitioners, 14.9% service, 21.0% sales and office, 9.7% natural resources, construction, and maintenance, 22.7% production, transportation, and material moving
Income: Per capita: $28,302; Median household: $57,307; Average household: $72,255; Households with income of $100,000 or more: 21.0%; Poverty rate: 10.0%
Educational Attainment: High school diploma or higher: 88.5%; Bachelor's degree or higher: 21.4%; Graduate/professional degree or higher: 6.0%
Housing: Homeownership rate: 77.0%; Median home value: $146,000; Median year structure built: 1977; Homeowner vacancy rate: 2.0%; Median selected monthly owner costs: $1,087 with a mortgage, $379 without a mortgage; Median gross rent: $586 per month; Rental vacancy rate: 5.0%
Vital Statistics: Birth rate: 133.9 per 10,000 population; Death rate: 94.2 per 10,000 population; Age-adjusted cancer mortality rate: 156.6 deaths per 100,000 population
Health Insurance: 93.5% have insurance; 81.2% have private insurance; 23.5% have public insurance; 6.5% do not have insurance; 3.7% of children under 18 do not have insurance
Health Care: Physicians: 21.7 per 10,000 population; Dentists: 6.6 per 10,000 population; Hospital beds: 33.7 per 10,000 population; Hospital admissions: 1,330.3 per 10,000 population
Air Quality Index (AQI): Percent of Days: 87.5% good, 12.5% moderate, 0.0% unhealthy for sensitive individuals, 0.0% unhealthy, 0.0% very unhealthy; Annual median: 32; Annual maximum: 69
Transportation: Commute: 93.8% car, 0.1% public transportation, 1.5% walk, 4.3% work from home; Mean travel time to work: 19.1 minutes
2016 Presidential Election: 66.5% Trump, 26.8% Clinton, 5.8% Johnson, 0.2% Stein
National and State Parks: Lick Fork State Recreation Area
Additional Information Contacts
Dubois Government .... (812) 481-7000
http://www.duboiscountyin.org

Dubois County Communities

BIRDSEYE (town). Covers a land area of 0.637 square miles and a water area of <.001 square miles. Located at 38.31° N. Lat; 86.70° W. Long. Elevation is 722 feet.
History: Laid out 1880.
Population: 468; Growth (since 2000): 0.6%; Density: 734.3 persons per square mile; Race: 100.0% White, 0.0% Black/African American, 0.0% Asian, 0.0% American Indian/Alaska Native, 0.0% Native Hawaiian/Other Pacific Islander, 0.0% Two or more races, 2.6% Hispanic of any race; Average household size: 2.52; Median age: 32.5; Age under 18: 27.8%; Age 65 and over: 14.7%; Males per 100 females: 88.2; Marriage status: 21.3% never married, 59.8% now married, 1.4% separated, 8.6% widowed, 10.3% divorced; Foreign born: 0.0%; Speak English only: 99.5%; With disability: 15.2%; Veterans: 6.8%; Ancestry: 41.7% German, 8.5% American, 8.5% Irish, 5.1% English, 3.2% French
Employment: 5.4% management, business, and financial, 3.2% computer, engineering, and science, 0.0% education, legal, community service, arts, and media, 2.2% healthcare practitioners, 17.3% service, 28.6% sales and office, 4.3% natural resources, construction, and maintenance, 38.9% production, transportation, and material moving
Income: Per capita: $18,784; Median household: $34,722; Average household: $44,242; Households with income of $100,000 or more: 3.2%; Poverty rate: 24.4%
Educational Attainment: High school diploma or higher: 81.7%; Bachelor's degree or higher: 6.8%; Graduate/professional degree or higher: 1.1%

School District(s)
Southeast Dubois Co Sch Corp (PK-12)
Enrollment: 1,225 .... (812) 817-0900
Housing: Homeownership rate: 66.7%; Median home value: $80,800; Median year structure built: 1973; Homeowner vacancy rate: 3.1%; Median selected monthly owner costs: $771 with a mortgage, $347 without a mortgage; Median gross rent: $563 per month; Rental vacancy rate: 6.1%
Health Insurance: 88.9% have insurance; 69.7% have private insurance; 32.7% have public insurance; 11.1% do not have insurance; 0.7% of children under 18 do not have insurance
Transportation: Commute: 95.7% car, 0.0% public transportation, 0.0% walk, 4.3% work from home; Mean travel time to work: 30.0 minutes

CELESTINE (unincorporated postal area)
ZCTA: 47521
Covers a land area of 18.851 square miles and a water area of 3.197 square miles. Located at 38.40° N. Lat; 86.72° W. Long. Elevation is 594 feet.
Population: 728; Growth (since 2000): -8.7%; Density: 38.6 persons per square mile; Race: 100.0% White, 0.0% Black/African American, 0.0% Asian, 0.0% American Indian/Alaska Native, 0.0% Native Hawaiian/Other Pacific Islander, 0.0% Two or more races, 0.0% Hispanic of any race; Average household size: 2.85; Median age: 25.9; Age under 18: 28.6%; Age 65 and over: 7.3%; Males per 100 females: 97.7; Marriage status: 39.1% never married, 55.5% now married, 0.0% separated, 2.3% widowed, 3.1% divorced; Foreign born: 0.0%; Speak English only: 98.3%; With disability: 4.8%; Veterans: 2.1%; Ancestry: 69.0% German, 1.6% American, 1.6% Irish, 1.6% Scottish
Employment: 11.9% management, business, and financial, 6.1% computer, engineering, and science, 5.1% education, legal, community service, arts, and media, 9.3% healthcare practitioners, 2.8% service, 24.0% sales and office, 26.8% natural resources, construction, and maintenance, 14.0% production, transportation, and material moving
Income: Per capita: $27,921; Median household: $77,991; Average household: $79,712; Households with income of $100,000 or more: 27.9%; Poverty rate: n/a
Educational Attainment: High school diploma or higher: 90.7%; Bachelor's degree or higher: 24.4%; Graduate/professional degree or higher: 13.7%

School District(s)
Northeast Dubois Co Sch Corp (PK-12)
Enrollment: 903 .... (812) 678-2781
Housing: Homeownership rate: 92.9%; Median home value: $162,900; Median year structure built: 1991; Homeowner vacancy rate: 0.0%; Median selected monthly owner costs: $1,138 with a mortgage, $342 without a mortgage; Median gross rent: n/a per month; Rental vacancy rate: 0.0%
Health Insurance: 96.7% have insurance; 89.7% have private insurance; 10.3% have public insurance; 3.3% do not have insurance; 0.0% of children under 18 do not have insurance
Transportation: Commute: 92.3% car, 0.0% public transportation, 0.0% walk, 7.7% work from home; Mean travel time to work: 27.4 minutes

DUBOIS (CDP). Covers a land area of 1.573 square miles and a water area of 0.025 square miles. Located at 38.45° N. Lat; 86.80° W. Long. Elevation is 505 feet.
Population: 173; Growth (since 2000): n/a; Density: 110.0 persons per square mile; Race: 100.0% White, 0.0% Black/African American, 0.0% Asian, 0.0% American Indian/Alaska Native, 0.0% Native Hawaiian/Other Pacific Islander, 0.0% Two or more races, 0.0% Hispanic of any race; Average household size: 1.38; Median age: 51.1; Age under 18: 5.8%; Age 65 and over: 30.6%; Males per 100 females: 103.3; Marriage status: 42.2% never married, 34.7% now married, 15.0% separated, 23.1% widowed, 0.0% divorced; Foreign born: 0.0%; Speak English only: 89.6%; With disability: 30.1%; Veterans: 0.0%; Ancestry: 27.2% German, 14.5% American, 8.7% English
Employment: 10.5% management, business, and financial, 0.0% computer, engineering, and science, 17.1% education, legal, community service, arts, and media, 0.0% healthcare practitioners, 0.0% service, 5.7% sales and office, 11.4% natural resources, construction, and maintenance, 55.2% production, transportation, and material moving
Income: Per capita: $23,717; Median household: n/a; Average household: $32,083; Households with income of $100,000 or more: n/a; Poverty rate: 30.1%

Educational Attainment: High school diploma or higher: 69.2%; Bachelor's degree or higher: 14.3%; Graduate/professional degree or higher: n/a

School District(s)

Northeast Dubois Co Sch Corp (PK-12)
Enrollment: 903 . . . . (812) 678-2781

Housing: Homeownership rate: 54.4%; Median home value: $107,700; Median year structure built: 1972; Homeowner vacancy rate: 0.0%; Median selected monthly owner costs: $936 with a mortgage, $239 without a mortgage; Median gross rent: n/a per month; Rental vacancy rate: 0.0%
Health Insurance: 96.5% have insurance; 65.9% have private insurance; 45.7% have public insurance; 3.5% do not have insurance; 0.0% of children under 18 do not have insurance
Transportation: Commute: 100.0% car, 0.0% public transportation, 0.0% walk, 0.0% work from home; Mean travel time to work: 0.0 minutes

FERDINAND (town). Covers a land area of 2.271 square miles and a water area of 0.038 square miles. Located at 38.23° N. Lat; 86.86° W. Long. Elevation is 538 feet.
History: Ferdinand was settled by German Catholics. It was the southern terminus of the Ferdinand Railroad, the shortest steam line in Indiana, with one locomotive making the eight-mile trip north to Huntingburg twice a day.
Population: 2,001; Growth (since 2000): -12.1%; Density: 881.0 persons per square mile; Race: 99.6% White, 0.0% Black/African American, 0.0% Asian, 0.0% American Indian/Alaska Native, 0.0% Native Hawaiian/Other Pacific Islander, 0.4% Two or more races, 0.3% Hispanic of any race; Average household size: 2.22; Median age: 49.5; Age under 18: 17.1%; Age 65 and over: 29.4%; Males per 100 females: 80.1; Marriage status: 23.7% never married, 56.7% now married, 0.8% separated, 11.2% widowed, 8.4% divorced; Foreign born: 0.1%; Speak English only: 97.8%; With disability: 15.0%; Veterans: 7.4%; Ancestry: 59.8% German, 6.6% English, 5.4% American, 4.4% Irish, 2.4% French
Employment: 11.6% management, business, and financial, 4.1% computer, engineering, and science, 10.1% education, legal, community service, arts, and media, 5.5% healthcare practitioners, 14.4% service, 19.2% sales and office, 12.5% natural resources, construction, and maintenance, 22.6% production, transportation, and material moving
Income: Per capita: $28,099; Median household: $59,375; Average household: $67,053; Households with income of $100,000 or more: 18.5%; Poverty rate: 6.8%
Educational Attainment: High school diploma or higher: 86.9%; Bachelor's degree or higher: 23.4%; Graduate/professional degree or higher: 10.1%

School District(s)

North Spencer County Sch Corp (PK-12)
Enrollment: 2,087 . . . . (812) 937-2400
Southeast Dubois Co Sch Corp (PK-12)
Enrollment: 1,225 . . . . (812) 817-0900

Housing: Homeownership rate: 74.0%; Median home value: $139,200; Median year structure built: 1967; Homeowner vacancy rate: 3.8%; Median selected monthly owner costs: $1,045 with a mortgage, $383 without a mortgage; Median gross rent: $675 per month; Rental vacancy rate: 0.0%
Health Insurance: 98.3% have insurance; 83.0% have private insurance; 31.4% have public insurance; 1.7% do not have insurance; 0.8% of children under 18 do not have insurance
Newspapers: Ferdinand News (weekly circulation 3,100)
Transportation: Commute: 94.9% car, 0.0% public transportation, 2.4% walk, 2.7% work from home; Mean travel time to work: 20.6 minutes
Additional Information Contacts
Town of Ferdinand . . . . (812) 367-2280
http://www.ferdinandindiana.org

HOLLAND (town). Covers a land area of 0.315 square miles and a water area of 0.001 square miles. Located at 38.25° N. Lat; 87.04° W. Long. Elevation is 528 feet.
Population: 734; Growth (since 2000): 5.6%; Density: 2,333.6 persons per square mile; Race: 98.6% White, 0.0% Black/African American, 1.4% Asian, 0.0% American Indian/Alaska Native, 0.0% Native Hawaiian/Other Pacific Islander, 0.0% Two or more races, 1.5% Hispanic of any race; Average household size: 2.50; Median age: 34.9; Age under 18: 31.7%; Age 65 and over: 10.1%; Males per 100 females: 93.2; Marriage status: 27.2% never married, 54.3% now married, 0.7% separated, 5.6% widowed, 12.9% divorced; Foreign born: 0.7%; Speak English only: 98.1%; With disability: 14.0%; Veterans: 10.4%; Ancestry: 59.1% German, 12.1% Irish, 11.2% English, 7.1% American, 3.7% French

Employment: 5.4% management, business, and financial, 3.7% computer, engineering, and science, 9.3% education, legal, community service, arts, and media, 2.8% healthcare practitioners, 20.1% service, 17.0% sales and office, 3.4% natural resources, construction, and maintenance, 38.2% production, transportation, and material moving
Income: Per capita: $18,542; Median household: $47,885; Average household: $47,278; Households with income of $100,000 or more: 4.3%; Poverty rate: 19.2%
Educational Attainment: High school diploma or higher: 91.7%; Bachelor's degree or higher: 16.2%; Graduate/professional degree or higher: 4.5%

School District(s)

Southwest Dubois Co Sch Corp (PK-12)
Enrollment: 1,727 . . . . (812) 683-3971

Housing: Homeownership rate: 64.3%; Median home value: $84,500; Median year structure built: 1968; Homeowner vacancy rate: 0.0%; Median selected monthly owner costs: $809 with a mortgage, $358 without a mortgage; Median gross rent: $341 per month; Rental vacancy rate: 3.7%
Health Insurance: 90.3% have insurance; 76.7% have private insurance; 23.3% have public insurance; 9.7% do not have insurance; 0.4% of children under 18 do not have insurance
Transportation: Commute: 93.8% car, 0.3% public transportation, 1.7% walk, 4.2% work from home; Mean travel time to work: 25.1 minutes

HUNTINGBURG (city). Covers a land area of 5.061 square miles and a water area of 0.213 square miles. Located at 38.30° N. Lat; 86.96° W. Long. Elevation is 489 feet.
History: Huntingburg, settled by German immigrants, developed around clay mines and poettery works.
Population: 6,633; Growth (since 2000): 18.5%; Density: 1,310.5 persons per square mile; Race: 79.5% White, 1.5% Black/African American, 1.7% Asian, 1.0% American Indian/Alaska Native, 0.0% Native Hawaiian/Other Pacific Islander, 2.9% Two or more races, 24.1% Hispanic of any race; Average household size: 2.73; Median age: 32.6; Age under 18: 31.8%; Age 65 and over: 14.2%; Males per 100 females: 91.2; Marriage status: 27.5% never married, 51.2% now married, 1.1% separated, 8.3% widowed, 13.0% divorced; Foreign born: 12.4%; Speak English only: 85.2%; With disability: 11.8%; Veterans: 7.9%; Ancestry: 43.6% German, 11.5% Irish, 7.4% American, 4.5% English, 2.0% French
Employment: 11.6% management, business, and financial, 1.9% computer, engineering, and science, 7.1% education, legal, community service, arts, and media, 7.1% healthcare practitioners, 14.3% service, 20.7% sales and office, 8.0% natural resources, construction, and maintenance, 29.3% production, transportation, and material moving
Income: Per capita: $21,910; Median household: $48,984; Average household: $62,629; Households with income of $100,000 or more: 19.9%; Poverty rate: 18.0%
Educational Attainment: High school diploma or higher: 79.0%; Bachelor's degree or higher: 15.2%; Graduate/professional degree or higher: 5.6%

School District(s)

Southeast Dubois Co Sch Corp (PK-12)
Enrollment: 1,225 . . . . (812) 817-0900
Southwest Dubois Co Sch Corp (PK-12)
Enrollment: 1,727 . . . . (812) 683-3971

Housing: Homeownership rate: 60.6%; Median home value: $107,700; Median year structure built: 1958; Homeowner vacancy rate: 0.9%; Median selected monthly owner costs: $1,002 with a mortgage, $354 without a mortgage; Median gross rent: $542 per month; Rental vacancy rate: 10.2%
Health Insurance: 88.4% have insurance; 69.5% have private insurance; 29.0% have public insurance; 11.6% do not have insurance; 5.3% of children under 18 do not have insurance
Safety: Violent crime rate: 32.6 per 10,000 population; Property crime rate: 89.5 per 10,000 population
Newspapers: Huntingburg Press (weekly circulation 2,000)
Transportation: Commute: 94.5% car, 0.0% public transportation, 2.0% walk, 3.4% work from home; Mean travel time to work: 18.6 minutes
Airports: Huntingburg (general aviation)
Additional Information Contacts
City of Huntingburg . . . . (812) 683-2211
http://www.huntingburg-in.gov

JASPER (city). County seat. Covers a land area of 13.105 square miles and a water area of 0.091 square miles. Located at 38.39° N. Lat; 86.94° W. Long. Elevation is 466 feet.

History: Jasper was settled by German Catholics in 1838, on a site where a town had been founded about 20 years earlier. An early industry was desk manufacturing.

Population: 15,716; Growth (since 2000): 29.9%; Density: 1,199.3 persons per square mile; Race: 94.6% White, 0.9% Black/African American, 0.8% Asian, 0.0% American Indian/Alaska Native, 0.0% Native Hawaiian/Other Pacific Islander, 0.3% Two or more races, 8.1% Hispanic of any race; Average household size: 2.37; Median age: 40.0; Age under 18: 23.4%; Age 65 and over: 17.2%; Males per 100 females: 96.7; Marriage status: 27.1% never married, 53.3% now married, 0.8% separated, 6.7% widowed, 12.9% divorced; Foreign born: 5.8%; Speak English only: 92.3%; With disability: 11.9%; Veterans: 9.3%; Ancestry: 42.8% German, 11.6% Irish, 8.4% American, 7.8% English, 1.9% Dutch

Employment: 13.3% management, business, and financial, 6.6% computer, engineering, and science, 8.9% education, legal, community service, arts, and media, 4.4% healthcare practitioners, 15.8% service, 24.1% sales and office, 6.4% natural resources, construction, and maintenance, 20.4% production, transportation, and material moving

Income: Per capita: $31,993; Median household: $55,878; Average household: $77,946; Households with income of $100,000 or more: 20.2%; Poverty rate: 11.0%

Educational Attainment: High school diploma or higher: 88.4%; Bachelor's degree or higher: 24.9%; Graduate/professional degree or higher: 6.6%

School District(s)

Greater Jasper Consolidated Schs (PK-12)
Enrollment: 3,129 . . . . (812) 482-1801

Housing: Homeownership rate: 72.5%; Median home value: $151,000; Median year structure built: 1979; Homeowner vacancy rate: 4.2%; Median selected monthly owner costs: $1,103 with a mortgage, $397 without a mortgage; Median gross rent: $563 per month; Rental vacancy rate: 3.4%

Health Insurance: 92.7% have insurance; 80.5% have private insurance; 24.0% have public insurance; 7.3% do not have insurance; 5.0% of children under 18 do not have insurance

Hospitals: Memorial Hospital & Health Care Center (131 beds)

Safety: Violent crime rate: 22.5 per 10,000 population; Property crime rate: 102.7 per 10,000 population

Newspapers: The Herald (daily circulation 12,600)

Transportation: Commute: 93.3% car, 0.1% public transportation, 2.0% walk, 4.1% work from home; Mean travel time to work: 16.7 minutes

Additional Information Contacts

City of Jasper . . . . (812) 482-6944
http://www.jasperindiana.gov

SAINT ANTHONY (unincorporated postal area)
ZCTA: 47575

Covers a land area of 21.176 square miles and a water area of 0.180 square miles. Located at 38.32° N. Lat; 86.80° W. Long. Elevation is 545 feet.

Population: 1,113; Growth (since 2000): 14.7%; Density: 52.6 persons per square mile; Race: 100.0% White, 0.0% Black/African American, 0.0% Asian, 0.0% American Indian/Alaska Native, 0.0% Native Hawaiian/Other Pacific Islander, 0.0% Two or more races, 0.0% Hispanic of any race; Average household size: 2.49; Median age: 39.3; Age under 18: 13.6%; Age 65 and over: 3.2%; Males per 100 females: 98.0; Marriage status: 33.5% never married, 53.1% now married, 0.0% separated, 3.6% widowed, 9.8% divorced; Foreign born: 0.0%; Speak English only: 100.0%; With disability: 3.1%; Veterans: 3.1%; Ancestry: 64.3% German, 4.3% French, 2.9% American, 2.0% Hungarian

Employment: 14.8% management, business, and financial, 1.3% computer, engineering, and science, 4.1% education, legal, community service, arts, and media, 8.6% healthcare practitioners, 12.9% service, 17.0% sales and office, 9.0% natural resources, construction, and maintenance, 32.3% production, transportation, and material moving

Income: Per capita: $30,490; Median household: $66,971; Average household: $72,502; Households with income of $100,000 or more: 20.2%; Poverty rate: 15.6%

Educational Attainment: High school diploma or higher: 94.6%; Bachelor's degree or higher: 19.1%; Graduate/professional degree or higher: n/a

Housing: Homeownership rate: 72.7%; Median home value: $201,400; Median year structure built: 1984; Homeowner vacancy rate: 0.0%; Median selected monthly owner costs: $1,247 with a mortgage, $442 without a mortgage; Median gross rent: $655 per month; Rental vacancy rate: 0.0%

Health Insurance: 84.4% have insurance; 77.4% have private insurance; 7.8% have public insurance; 15.6% do not have insurance; 28.5% of children under 18 do not have insurance

Transportation: Commute: 93.3% car, 0.0% public transportation, 0.0% walk, 6.7% work from home; Mean travel time to work: 20.7 minutes

SCHNELLVILLE (unincorporated postal area)
ZCTA: 47580

Covers a land area of 5.015 square miles and a water area of 0.013 square miles. Located at 38.36° N. Lat; 86.77° W. Long. Elevation is 653 feet.

Population: 367; Growth (since 2000): 115.9%; Density: 73.2 persons per square mile; Race: 100.0% White, 0.0% Black/African American, 0.0% Asian, 0.0% American Indian/Alaska Native, 0.0% Native Hawaiian/Other Pacific Islander, 0.0% Two or more races, 0.0% Hispanic of any race; Average household size: 3.08; Median age: 32.2; Age under 18: 19.9%; Age 65 and over: 3.5%; Males per 100 females: 112.5; Marriage status: 27.6% never married, 72.4% now married, 0.0% separated, 0.0% widowed, 0.0% divorced; Foreign born: 0.0%; Speak English only: 88.4%; With disability: 5.7%; Veterans: 9.2%; Ancestry: 49.0% German, 9.5% Italian, 6.0% European, 3.0% French

Employment: 14.9% management, business, and financial, 0.0% computer, engineering, and science, 3.9% education, legal, community service, arts, and media, 2.5% healthcare practitioners, 14.2% service, 19.2% sales and office, 9.6% natural resources, construction, and maintenance, 35.6% production, transportation, and material moving

Income: Per capita: $27,474; Median household: $80,673; Average household: $82,059; Households with income of $100,000 or more: 42.0%; Poverty rate: n/a

Educational Attainment: High school diploma or higher: 93.9%; Bachelor's degree or higher: 7.0%; Graduate/professional degree or higher: n/a

Housing: Homeownership rate: 100.0%; Median home value: $205,400; Median year structure built: 1993; Homeowner vacancy rate: 0.0%; Median selected monthly owner costs: $1,053 with a mortgage, $511 without a mortgage; Median gross rent: n/a per month; Rental vacancy rate: 0.0%

Health Insurance: 100.0% have insurance; 100.0% have private insurance; 3.5% have public insurance; 0.0% do not have insurance; 0.0% of children under 18 do not have insurance

Transportation: Commute: 97.5% car, 0.0% public transportation, 0.0% walk, 2.5% work from home; Mean travel time to work: 25.4 minutes

Elkhart County

Located in northern Indiana; bounded on the north by Michigan; drained by the Elkhart and Saint Joseph Rivers. Covers a land area of 463.170 square miles, a water area of 4.800 square miles, and is located in the Eastern Time Zone at 41.60° N. Lat., 85.86° W. Long. The county was founded in 1830. County seat is Goshen.

Elkhart County is part of the Elkhart-Goshen, IN Metropolitan Statistical Area. The entire metro area includes: Elkhart County, IN

Weather Station: Goshen College Elevation: 875 feet

	Jan	Feb	Mar	Apr	May	Jun	Jul	Aug	Sep	Oct	Nov	Dec
High	32	36	47	61	72	81	84	82	75	63	49	36
Low	18	21	29	39	49	59	63	61	54	43	34	23
Precip	2.2	2.1	2.5	3.5	3.9	4.0	4.3	4.2	3.5	3.2	3.0	2.7
Snow	10.9	9.0	5.0	1.3	tr	0.0	0.0	0.0	0.0	0.4	3.1	10.6

High and Low temperatures in degrees Fahrenheit; Precipitation and Snow in inches

Population: 202,924; Growth (since 2000): 11.0%; Density: 438.1 persons per square mile; Race: 87.6% White, 5.5% Black/African American, 1.0% Asian, 0.2% American Indian/Alaska Native, 0.1% Native Hawaiian/Other Pacific Islander, 3.1% two or more races, 15.4% Hispanic of any race; Average household size: 2.78; Median age: 35.4; Age under 18: 27.9%; Age 65 and over: 13.6%; Males per 100 females: 97.4; Marriage status: 29.0% never married, 53.8% now married, 1.7% separated, 5.4% widowed, 11.8% divorced; Foreign born: 8.0%; Speak English only: 81.4%; With disability: 13.2%; Veterans: 6.2%; Ancestry: 23.0% German, 9.9% American, 8.7% Irish, 5.8% English, 2.9% Swiss

Religion: Six largest groups: 10.4% European Free-Church, 6.9% Non-denominational Protestant, 6.3% Holiness, 5.4% Catholicism, 4.8% Methodist/Pietist, 2.3% Baptist
Economy: Unemployment rate: 3.0%; Leading industries: 16.4 % manufacturing; 14.2 % retail trade; 11.0 % other services (except public administration); Farms: 1,724 totaling 172,847 acres; Company size: 7 employ 1,000 or more persons, 14 employ 500 to 999 persons, 234 employ 100 to 499 persons, 4,601 employs less than 100 persons; Business ownership: 4,573 women-owned, 561 Black-owned, 422 Hispanic-owned, 296 Asian-owned, 59 American Indian/Alaska Native-owned
Employment: 10.5% management, business, and financial, 3.0% computer, engineering, and science, 7.8% education, legal, community service, arts, and media, 4.2% healthcare practitioners, 14.2% service, 21.6% sales and office, 7.3% natural resources, construction, and maintenance, 31.5% production, transportation, and material moving
Income: Per capita: $23,817; Median household: $52,449; Average household: $65,663; Households with income of $100,000 or more: 17.1%; Poverty rate: 13.8%
Educational Attainment: High school diploma or higher: 80.8%; Bachelor's degree or higher: 18.7%; Graduate/professional degree or higher: 6.5%
Housing: Homeownership rate: 68.6%; Median home value: $130,800; Median year structure built: 1976; Homeowner vacancy rate: 1.9%; Median selected monthly owner costs: $1,032 with a mortgage, $361 without a mortgage; Median gross rent: $747 per month; Rental vacancy rate: 6.8%
Vital Statistics: Birth rate: 153.4 per 10,000 population; Death rate: 79.1 per 10,000 population; Age-adjusted cancer mortality rate: 164.6 deaths per 100,000 population
Health Insurance: 83.1% have insurance; 62.1% have private insurance; 31.2% have public insurance; 16.9% do not have insurance; 15.2% of children under 18 do not have insurance
Health Care: Physicians: 14.9 per 10,000 population; Dentists: 3.8 per 10,000 population; Hospital beds: 19.8 per 10,000 population; Hospital admissions: 820.3 per 10,000 population
Air Quality Index (AQI): Percent of Days: 82.5% good, 17.3% moderate, 0.3% unhealthy for sensitive individuals, 0.0% unhealthy, 0.0% very unhealthy; Annual median: 38; Annual maximum: 105
Transportation: Commute: 91.7% car, 0.4% public transportation, 1.7% walk, 3.5% work from home; Mean travel time to work: 19.4 minutes
2016 Presidential Election: 63.2% Trump, 31.3% Clinton, 4.1% Johnson, 0.3% Stein
Additional Information Contacts
Elkhart Government . . . . (574) 535-6743
http://www.elkhartcountyindiana.com

Elkhart County Communities

BRISTOL (town). Covers a land area of 3.694 square miles and a water area of 0.130 square miles. Located at 41.72° N. Lat; 85.83° W. Long. Elevation is 774 feet.
Population: 1,706; Growth (since 2000): 23.4%; Density: 461.9 persons per square mile; Race: 91.5% White, 3.0% Black/African American, 1.1% Asian, 0.0% American Indian/Alaska Native, 0.0% Native Hawaiian/Other Pacific Islander, 3.2% Two or more races, 7.6% Hispanic of any race; Average household size: 2.47; Median age: 42.5; Age under 18: 23.9%; Age 65 and over: 18.7%; Males per 100 females: 98.5; Marriage status: 31.0% never married, 48.1% now married, 1.7% separated, 6.3% widowed, 14.6% divorced; Foreign born: 4.8%; Speak English only: 91.7%; With disability: 14.2%; Veterans: 12.4%; Ancestry: 20.3% German, 15.7% American, 10.2% Irish, 7.6% English, 6.4% Polish
Employment: 10.5% management, business, and financial, 2.3% computer, engineering, and science, 10.6% education, legal, community service, arts, and media, 2.8% healthcare practitioners, 14.3% service, 17.0% sales and office, 6.9% natural resources, construction, and maintenance, 35.7% production, transportation, and material moving
Income: Per capita: $27,031; Median household: $46,368; Average household: $66,784; Households with income of $100,000 or more: 14.1%; Poverty rate: 15.1%
Educational Attainment: High school diploma or higher: 89.3%; Bachelor's degree or higher: 15.3%; Graduate/professional degree or higher: 6.8%

School District(s)

Elkhart Community Schools (PK-12)
Enrollment: 13,952 . . . . (574) 262-5516
Middlebury Community Schools (KG-12)
Enrollment: 4,312 . . . . (574) 825-9425
Housing: Homeownership rate: 65.1%; Median home value: $139,400; Median year structure built: 1970; Homeowner vacancy rate: 7.5%; Median selected monthly owner costs: $1,021 with a mortgage, $386 without a mortgage; Median gross rent: $718 per month; Rental vacancy rate: 14.7%
Health Insurance: 88.3% have insurance; 69.0% have private insurance; 35.5% have public insurance; 11.7% do not have insurance; 1.9% of children under 18 do not have insurance
Transportation: Commute: 89.6% car, 0.0% public transportation, 3.3% walk, 4.5% work from home; Mean travel time to work: 26.0 minutes

DUNLAP (CDP). Covers a land area of 4.900 square miles and a water area of 0.010 square miles. Located at 41.63° N. Lat; 85.92° W. Long. Elevation is 778 feet.
Population: 6,110; Growth (since 2000): 3.8%; Density: 1,246.8 persons per square mile; Race: 89.7% White, 6.1% Black/African American, 0.7% Asian, 0.5% American Indian/Alaska Native, 0.0% Native Hawaiian/Other Pacific Islander, 2.6% Two or more races, 7.9% Hispanic of any race; Average household size: 3.01; Median age: 37.2; Age under 18: 27.1%; Age 65 and over: 12.2%; Males per 100 females: 97.1; Marriage status: 27.0% never married, 60.2% now married, 2.9% separated, 4.1% widowed, 8.7% divorced; Foreign born: 5.9%; Speak English only: 90.8%; With disability: 12.3%; Veterans: 6.6%; Ancestry: 24.7% German, 14.9% Irish, 10.9% American, 4.6% English, 4.5% Polish
Employment: 15.3% management, business, and financial, 3.1% computer, engineering, and science, 8.1% education, legal, community service, arts, and media, 7.6% healthcare practitioners, 9.0% service, 23.0% sales and office, 5.2% natural resources, construction, and maintenance, 28.6% production, transportation, and material moving
Income: Per capita: $24,667; Median household: $68,594; Average household: $73,233; Households with income of $100,000 or more: 20.1%; Poverty rate: 10.3%
Educational Attainment: High school diploma or higher: 89.5%; Bachelor's degree or higher: 18.6%; Graduate/professional degree or higher: 8.9%
Housing: Homeownership rate: 88.0%; Median home value: $139,800; Median year structure built: 1973; Homeowner vacancy rate: 0.0%; Median selected monthly owner costs: $1,105 with a mortgage, $345 without a mortgage; Median gross rent: $807 per month; Rental vacancy rate: 0.0%
Health Insurance: 91.7% have insurance; 76.7% have private insurance; 23.5% have public insurance; 8.3% do not have insurance; 3.8% of children under 18 do not have insurance
Transportation: Commute: 97.3% car, 0.0% public transportation, 0.4% walk, 1.5% work from home; Mean travel time to work: 20.9 minutes

ELKHART (city). Covers a land area of 23.453 square miles and a water area of 0.967 square miles. Located at 41.69° N. Lat; 85.97° W. Long. Elevation is 751 feet.
History: Elkhart was named for an island, thought by some to be shaped like an elk's heart, at the place where two rivers meet. The town was platted in 1832 by Dr. Havilah Beardsley. Elkhart grew when the Michigan Southern Railway Company built its shops here in 1870. It was incorporated in 1873. The musical instrument company begun here in 1875 by Charles G. Conn became the largest band instrument manufacturer in the world.
Population: 52,662; Growth (since 2000): 1.5%; Density: 2,245.4 persons per square mile; Race: 74.5% White, 14.9% Black/African American, 1.7% Asian, 0.2% American Indian/Alaska Native, 0.1% Native Hawaiian/Other Pacific Islander, 3.4% Two or more races, 23.0% Hispanic of any race; Average household size: 2.61; Median age: 33.4; Age under 18: 27.5%; Age 65 and over: 12.4%; Males per 100 females: 93.0; Marriage status: 36.4% never married, 40.3% now married, 2.7% separated, 7.0% widowed, 16.3% divorced; Foreign born: 12.2%; Speak English only: 79.4%; With disability: 16.7%; Veterans: 5.7%; Ancestry: 16.4% German, 8.1% Irish, 6.7% American, 4.8% English, 2.9% European
Employment: 6.7% management, business, and financial, 2.5% computer, engineering, and science, 6.4% education, legal, community service, arts, and media, 2.9% healthcare practitioners, 16.5% service, 18.8% sales and office, 6.5% natural resources, construction, and maintenance, 39.7% production, transportation, and material moving
Income: Per capita: $18,426; Median household: $37,121; Average household: $47,042; Households with income of $100,000 or more: 8.2%; Poverty rate: 24.8%

Educational Attainment: High school diploma or higher: 76.1%; Bachelor's degree or higher: 13.1%; Graduate/professional degree or higher: 4.3%

School District(s)

Baugo Community Schools (KG-12)
Enrollment: 1,825 . . . . (574) 293-8583
Concord Community Schools (PK-12)
Enrollment: 4,819 . . . . (574) 875-5161
Elkhart Community Schools (PK-12)
Enrollment: 13,952 . . . . (574) 262-5516

Four-year College(s)

Anabaptist Mennonite Biblical Seminary (Private, Not-for-profit, Mennonite Church)
Enrollment: 103. . . . . (574) 295-3726

Housing: Homeownership rate: 46.8%; Median home value: $87,700; Median year structure built: 1964; Homeowner vacancy rate: 3.1%; Median selected monthly owner costs: $893 with a mortgage, $336 without a mortgage; Median gross rent: $722 per month; Rental vacancy rate: 7.6%
Health Insurance: 82.4% have insurance; 49.5% have private insurance; 41.9% have public insurance; 17.6% do not have insurance; 7.9% of children under 18 do not have insurance
Hospitals: Elkhart General Hospital (365 beds)
Safety: Violent crime rate: n/a per 10,000 population; Property crime rate: 351.0 per 10,000 population
Newspapers: Elkhart Truth (daily circulation 29,000)
Transportation: Commute: 91.7% car, 1.4% public transportation, 2.7% walk, 2.0% work from home; Mean travel time to work: 19.2 minutes; Amtrak: Train service available.
Airports: Elkhart Municipal (general aviation)
Additional Information Contacts
City of Elkhart . . . . (574) 522-5272
http://www.elkhartindiana.org

GOSHEN (city). County seat. Covers a land area of 16.229 square miles and a water area of 0.355 square miles. Located at 41.57° N. Lat; 85.83° W. Long. Elevation is 801 feet.
History: Goshen was established by Mennonite settlers, who in 1894 founded Elkhart Academy which became Goshen College.
Population: 33,583; Growth (since 2000): 14.3%; Density: 2,069.3 persons per square mile; Race: 88.7% White, 2.8% Black/African American, 1.3% Asian, 0.1% American Indian/Alaska Native, 0.0% Native Hawaiian/Other Pacific Islander, 3.5% Two or more races, 30.0% Hispanic of any race; Average household size: 2.59; Median age: 35.6; Age under 18: 26.2%; Age 65 and over: 17.2%; Males per 100 females: 95.5; Marriage status: 32.2% never married, 49.2% now married, 1.8% separated, 6.5% widowed, 12.1% divorced; Foreign born: 15.0%; Speak English only: 71.9%; With disability: 13.7%; Veterans: 6.2%; Ancestry: 22.7% German, 8.9% American, 7.2% Irish, 4.7% English, 4.4% Swiss
Employment: 7.7% management, business, and financial, 3.8% computer, engineering, and science, 9.9% education, legal, community service, arts, and media, 4.0% healthcare practitioners, 15.0% service, 21.1% sales and office, 8.6% natural resources, construction, and maintenance, 29.9% production, transportation, and material moving
Income: Per capita: $21,450; Median household: $46,055; Average household: $55,375; Households with income of $100,000 or more: 13.0%; Poverty rate: 17.3%
Educational Attainment: High school diploma or higher: 76.9%; Bachelor's degree or higher: 21.9%; Graduate/professional degree or higher: 10.0%

School District(s)

Fairfield Community Schools (KG-12)
Enrollment: 2,051 . . . . (574) 831-2188
Goshen Community Schools (PK-12)
Enrollment: 6,801 . . . . (574) 533-8631
Middlebury Community Schools (KG-12)
Enrollment: 4,312 . . . . (574) 825-9425

Four-year College(s)

Goshen College (Private, Not-for-profit, Mennonite Church)
Enrollment: 950. . . . . (574) 535-7000
Tuition: In-state $33,200; Out-of-state $33,200

Housing: Homeownership rate: 55.5%; Median home value: $111,000; Median year structure built: 1979; Homeowner vacancy rate: 1.8%; Median selected monthly owner costs: $961 with a mortgage, $413 without a mortgage; Median gross rent: $745 per month; Rental vacancy rate: 5.5%
Health Insurance: 82.6% have insurance; 59.4% have private insurance; 35.8% have public insurance; 17.4% do not have insurance; 10.0% of children under 18 do not have insurance
Hospitals: IU Health Goshen Hospital (115 beds)
Safety: Violent crime rate: n/a per 10,000 population; Property crime rate: 336.8 per 10,000 population
Newspapers: Goshen News (daily circulation 16,100)
Transportation: Commute: 91.6% car, 0.6% public transportation, 3.2% walk, 2.4% work from home; Mean travel time to work: 17.3 minutes
Airports: Goshen Municipal (general aviation)
Additional Information Contacts
City of Goshen. . . . . (574) 533-8625
http://www.goshenindiana.org

MIDDLEBURY (town). Covers a land area of 3.755 square miles and a water area of 0.022 square miles. Located at 41.67° N. Lat; 85.71° W. Long. Elevation is 837 feet.
History: Laid out 1835.
Population: 3,535; Growth (since 2000): 19.6%; Density: 941.3 persons per square mile; Race: 90.9% White, 1.4% Black/African American, 0.0% Asian, 0.0% American Indian/Alaska Native, 0.0% Native Hawaiian/Other Pacific Islander, 6.9% Two or more races, 11.8% Hispanic of any race; Average household size: 3.16; Median age: 34.4; Age under 18: 30.1%; Age 65 and over: 14.4%; Males per 100 females: 94.6; Marriage status: 18.3% never married, 71.0% now married, 0.0% separated, 2.6% widowed, 8.1% divorced; Foreign born: 4.0%; Speak English only: 87.2%; With disability: 13.4%; Veterans: 7.6%; Ancestry: 20.6% German, 13.3% American, 10.4% Dutch, 10.1% English, 5.6% Irish
Employment: 20.1% management, business, and financial, 3.0% computer, engineering, and science, 8.4% education, legal, community service, arts, and media, 8.4% healthcare practitioners, 19.7% service, 19.8% sales and office, 7.0% natural resources, construction, and maintenance, 13.6% production, transportation, and material moving
Income: Per capita: $28,404; Median household: $67,031; Average household: $89,719; Households with income of $100,000 or more: 37.3%; Poverty rate: 2.3%
Educational Attainment: High school diploma or higher: 90.3%; Bachelor's degree or higher: 29.4%; Graduate/professional degree or higher: 8.9%

School District(s)

Middlebury Community Schools (KG-12)
Enrollment: 4,312 . . . . (574) 825-9425

Housing: Homeownership rate: 79.8%; Median home value: $162,200; Median year structure built: 1980; Homeowner vacancy rate: 0.0%; Median selected monthly owner costs: $1,158 with a mortgage, $421 without a mortgage; Median gross rent: $907 per month; Rental vacancy rate: 0.0%
Health Insurance: 90.0% have insurance; 74.3% have private insurance; 30.5% have public insurance; 10.0% do not have insurance; 10.7% of children under 18 do not have insurance
Transportation: Commute: 92.7% car, 0.0% public transportation, 0.0% walk, 7.3% work from home; Mean travel time to work: 18.0 minutes
Additional Information Contacts
Town of Middlebury. . . . . (574) 825-1499
http://www.middleburyin.org/publishsite/index.cfm

MILLERSBURG (town). Covers a land area of 0.544 square miles and a water area of 0 square miles. Located at 41.53° N. Lat; 85.70° W. Long. Elevation is 886 feet.
History: Laid out 1855.
Population: 891; Growth (since 2000): 2.6%; Density: 1,637.9 persons per square mile; Race: 94.7% White, 0.3% Black/African American, 0.0% Asian, 0.6% American Indian/Alaska Native, 0.0% Native Hawaiian/Other Pacific Islander, 2.9% Two or more races, 2.7% Hispanic of any race; Average household size: 2.79; Median age: 28.1; Age under 18: 29.2%; Age 65 and over: 8.5%; Males per 100 females: 104.3; Marriage status: 27.2% never married, 57.0% now married, 0.9% separated, 4.0% widowed, 11.8% divorced; Foreign born: 2.4%; Speak English only: 89.0%; With disability: 12.0%; Veterans: 8.2%; Ancestry: 32.3% German, 12.1% Irish, 8.5% English, 7.3% American, 4.3% Swiss
Employment: 7.3% management, business, and financial, 3.0% computer, engineering, and science, 2.8% education, legal, community service, arts, and media, 1.2% healthcare practitioners, 15.4% service, 26.7% sales and office, 8.1% natural resources, construction, and maintenance, 35.6% production, transportation, and material moving

Income: Per capita: $22,129; Median household: $56,641; Average household: $59,678; Households with income of $100,000 or more: 11.6%; Poverty rate: 9.3%
Educational Attainment: High school diploma or higher: 80.5%; Bachelor's degree or higher: 6.8%; Graduate/professional degree or higher: 0.8%

School District(s)

Fairfield Community Schools (KG-12)
Enrollment: 2,051 .... (574) 831-2188
Housing: Homeownership rate: 57.7%; Median home value: $94,700; Median year structure built: 1960; Homeowner vacancy rate: 0.0%; Median selected monthly owner costs: $894 with a mortgage, $325 without a mortgage; Median gross rent: $818 per month; Rental vacancy rate: 4.3%
Health Insurance: 89.5% have insurance; 75.4% have private insurance; 23.3% have public insurance; 10.5% do not have insurance; 5.0% of children under 18 do not have insurance
Transportation: Commute: 95.3% car, 0.0% public transportation, 1.6% walk, 1.0% work from home; Mean travel time to work: 18.2 minutes

NAPPANEE (city). Covers a land area of 4.149 square miles and a water area of 0 square miles. Located at 41.45° N. Lat; 86.00° W. Long. Elevation is 876 feet.
History: Nappanee grew up along the Baltimore & Ohio Railroad. Furniture manufacturing was an early industry in Nappanee, which was platted in 1874.
Population: 6,927; Growth (since 2000): 3.2%; Density: 1,669.7 persons per square mile; Race: 95.1% White, 2.5% Black/African American, 1.0% Asian, 0.0% American Indian/Alaska Native, 0.2% Native Hawaiian/Other Pacific Islander, 1.2% Two or more races, 7.3% Hispanic of any race; Average household size: 2.62; Median age: 32.1; Age under 18: 29.4%; Age 65 and over: 11.9%; Males per 100 females: 95.5; Marriage status: 23.3% never married, 59.1% now married, 5.0% separated, 4.2% widowed, 13.3% divorced; Foreign born: 2.6%; Speak English only: 94.3%; With disability: 12.8%; Veterans: 6.1%; Ancestry: 28.8% German, 10.6% Irish, 6.2% English, 6.2% Italian, 6.0% American
Employment: 9.9% management, business, and financial, 2.7% computer, engineering, and science, 9.7% education, legal, community service, arts, and media, 2.2% healthcare practitioners, 12.7% service, 28.7% sales and office, 3.5% natural resources, construction, and maintenance, 30.6% production, transportation, and material moving
Income: Per capita: $22,815; Median household: $46,146; Average household: $59,141; Households with income of $100,000 or more: 15.3%; Poverty rate: 10.1%
Educational Attainment: High school diploma or higher: 86.9%; Bachelor's degree or higher: 17.2%; Graduate/professional degree or higher: 6.6%

School District(s)

Wa-nee Community Schools (KG-12)
Enrollment: 2,849 .... (574) 773-3131
Housing: Homeownership rate: 62.2%; Median home value: $121,300; Median year structure built: 1974; Homeowner vacancy rate: 1.8%; Median selected monthly owner costs: $1,001 with a mortgage, $422 without a mortgage; Median gross rent: $668 per month; Rental vacancy rate: 8.6%
Health Insurance: 86.0% have insurance; 74.0% have private insurance; 23.0% have public insurance; 14.0% do not have insurance; 9.4% of children under 18 do not have insurance
Safety: Violent crime rate: n/a per 10,000 population; Property crime rate: 151.5 per 10,000 population
Transportation: Commute: 94.2% car, 0.0% public transportation, 2.2% walk, 1.3% work from home; Mean travel time to work: 21.7 minutes
Additional Information Contacts
City of Nappanee................................ (574) 773-2112
http://www.nappanee.org

NEW PARIS (CDP). Covers a land area of 1.333 square miles and a water area of 0 square miles. Located at 41.50° N. Lat; 85.82° W. Long. Elevation is 820 feet.
History: Laid out 1838.
Population: 1,456; Growth (since 2000): 44.7%; Density: 1,092.6 persons per square mile; Race: 99.5% White, 0.0% Black/African American, 0.5% Asian, 0.0% American Indian/Alaska Native, 0.0% Native Hawaiian/Other Pacific Islander, 0.0% Two or more races, 15.2% Hispanic of any race; Average household size: 2.62; Median age: 36.2; Age under 18: 26.6%; Age 65 and over: 9.1%; Males per 100 females: 99.2; Marriage status: 30.0% never married, 60.1% now married, 4.9% separated, 3.4% widowed, 6.5% divorced; Foreign born: 3.4%; Speak English only: 92.6%; With disability: 17.4%; Veterans: 6.0%; Ancestry: 31.7% German, 13.0% American, 6.3% English, 4.4% Swiss, 4.3% Italian
Employment: 7.0% management, business, and financial, 1.5% computer, engineering, and science, 5.7% education, legal, community service, arts, and media, 2.6% healthcare practitioners, 16.4% service, 25.2% sales and office, 4.6% natural resources, construction, and maintenance, 37.1% production, transportation, and material moving
Income: Per capita: $20,878; Median household: $39,583; Average household: $53,559; Households with income of $100,000 or more: 6.3%; Poverty rate: 3.4%
Educational Attainment: High school diploma or higher: 87.8%; Bachelor's degree or higher: 8.6%; Graduate/professional degree or higher: 0.9%

School District(s)

Fairfield Community Schools (KG-12)
Enrollment: 2,051 .... (574) 831-2188
Housing: Homeownership rate: 84.4%; Median home value: $112,400; Median year structure built: 1968; Homeowner vacancy rate: 4.9%; Median selected monthly owner costs: $869 with a mortgage, $277 without a mortgage; Median gross rent: $642 per month; Rental vacancy rate: 0.0%
Health Insurance: 83.8% have insurance; 72.4% have private insurance; 19.2% have public insurance; 16.2% do not have insurance; 18.6% of children under 18 do not have insurance
Transportation: Commute: 72.7% car, 0.0% public transportation, 5.1% walk, 17.5% work from home; Mean travel time to work: 15.2 minutes

SIMONTON LAKE (CDP). Covers a land area of 3.564 square miles and a water area of 0.471 square miles. Located at 41.75° N. Lat; 85.97° W. Long. Elevation is 784 feet.
Population: 4,615; Growth (since 2000): 13.9%; Density: 1,295.0 persons per square mile; Race: 86.5% White, 9.1% Black/African American, 2.5% Asian, 0.0% American Indian/Alaska Native, 0.0% Native Hawaiian/Other Pacific Islander, 1.8% Two or more races, 4.2% Hispanic of any race; Average household size: 2.59; Median age: 41.8; Age under 18: 24.7%; Age 65 and over: 17.6%; Males per 100 females: 96.7; Marriage status: 25.7% never married, 51.3% now married, 0.2% separated, 6.2% widowed, 16.7% divorced; Foreign born: 2.6%; Speak English only: 94.6%; With disability: 13.1%; Veterans: 7.9%; Ancestry: 24.3% German, 11.8% American, 11.4% English, 7.9% Irish, 3.6% Swedish
Employment: 13.3% management, business, and financial, 2.1% computer, engineering, and science, 6.6% education, legal, community service, arts, and media, 3.4% healthcare practitioners, 15.7% service, 29.8% sales and office, 3.5% natural resources, construction, and maintenance, 25.5% production, transportation, and material moving
Income: Per capita: $27,704; Median household: $59,188; Average household: $71,313; Households with income of $100,000 or more: 22.6%; Poverty rate: 18.4%
Educational Attainment: High school diploma or higher: 83.1%; Bachelor's degree or higher: 19.2%; Graduate/professional degree or higher: 5.1%
Housing: Homeownership rate: 78.0%; Median home value: $154,600; Median year structure built: 1979; Homeowner vacancy rate: 2.3%; Median selected monthly owner costs: $1,066 with a mortgage, $358 without a mortgage; Median gross rent: $837 per month; Rental vacancy rate: 6.0%
Health Insurance: 92.7% have insurance; 71.1% have private insurance; 37.2% have public insurance; 7.3% do not have insurance; 5.4% of children under 18 do not have insurance
Transportation: Commute: 97.5% car, 0.0% public transportation, 0.0% walk, 1.5% work from home; Mean travel time to work: 20.2 minutes

WAKARUSA (town). Covers a land area of 2.204 square miles and a water area of 0.077 square miles. Located at 41.53° N. Lat; 86.01° W. Long. Elevation is 846 feet.
History: Laid out 1852.
Population: 1,938; Growth (since 2000): 19.8%; Density: 879.3 persons per square mile; Race: 95.0% White, 1.3% Black/African American, 2.7% Asian, 0.0% American Indian/Alaska Native, 0.0% Native Hawaiian/Other Pacific Islander, 0.9% Two or more races, 2.8% Hispanic of any race; Average household size: 2.80; Median age: 37.9; Age under 18: 26.0%; Age 65 and over: 20.0%; Males per 100 females: 84.5; Marriage status: 24.2% never married, 57.8% now married, 0.7% separated, 10.8% widowed, 7.2% divorced; Foreign born: 3.0%; Speak English only: 91.4%; With disability: 11.9%; Veterans: 6.2%; Ancestry: 27.9% German, 6.9% American, 6.7% European, 5.7% English, 5.5% Irish

Employment: 14.3% management, business, and financial, 4.6% computer, engineering, and science, 11.0% education, legal, community service, arts, and media, 10.2% healthcare practitioners, 15.3% service, 17.4% sales and office, 9.7% natural resources, construction, and maintenance, 17.4% production, transportation, and material moving
Income: Per capita: $28,350; Median household: $57,426; Average household: $81,808; Households with income of $100,000 or more: 19.2%; Poverty rate: 7.4%
Educational Attainment: High school diploma or higher: 86.2%; Bachelor's degree or higher: 27.6%; Graduate/professional degree or higher: 7.0%

School District(s)

Penn-Harris-Madison School Corp (PK-12)
Enrollment: 10,051 . . . . (574) 259-7941
Wa-nee Community Schools (KG-12)
Enrollment: 2,849 . . . . (574) 773-3131

Housing: Homeownership rate: 77.1%; Median home value: $133,300; Median year structure built: 1962; Homeowner vacancy rate: 0.0%; Median selected monthly owner costs: $1,077 with a mortgage, $409 without a mortgage; Median gross rent: $732 per month; Rental vacancy rate: 0.0%
Health Insurance: 89.4% have insurance; 76.3% have private insurance; 21.8% have public insurance; 10.6% do not have insurance; 8.7% of children under 18 do not have insurance
Newspapers: Wakarusa Tribune (weekly circulation 1,400)
Transportation: Commute: 88.1% car, 0.0% public transportation, 5.3% walk, 5.4% work from home; Mean travel time to work: 20.1 minutes

Fayette County

Located in eastern Indiana; drained by the Whitewater River. Covers a land area of 215.014 square miles, a water area of 0.148 square miles, and is located in the Eastern Time Zone at 39.64° N. Lat., 85.19° W. Long. The county was founded in 1818. County seat is Connersville.

Fayette County is part of the Connersville, IN Micropolitan Statistical Area. The entire metro area includes: Fayette County, IN

Population: 23,426; Growth (since 2000): -8.4%; Density: 109.0 persons per square mile; Race: 96.2% White, 2.5% Black/African American, 0.1% Asian, 0.0% American Indian/Alaska Native, 0.0% Native Hawaiian/Other Pacific Islander, 0.5% two or more races, 1.0% Hispanic of any race; Average household size: 2.44; Median age: 42.4; Age under 18: 22.2%; Age 65 and over: 18.8%; Males per 100 females: 96.0; Marriage status: 23.4% never married, 52.4% now married, 1.3% separated, 7.4% widowed, 16.8% divorced; Foreign born: 0.6%; Speak English only: 98.8%; With disability: 17.9%; Veterans: 9.8%; Ancestry: 19.1% German, 15.3% American, 11.3% Irish, 7.7% English, 2.8% Scottish
Religion: Six largest groups: 12.7% Non-denominational Protestant, 10.1% Baptist, 8.5% Catholicism, 5.5% Methodist/Pietist, 2.4% Holiness, 1.3% Latter-day Saints
Economy: Unemployment rate: 4.9%; Leading industries: 14.9 % retail trade; 14.7 % other services (except public administration); 12.2 % health care and social assistance; Farms: 347 totaling 78,242 acres; Company size: 0 employ 1,000 or more persons, 1 employs 500 to 999 persons, 8 employ 100 to 499 persons, 441 employs less than 100 persons; Business ownership: 435 women-owned, n/a Black-owned, n/a Hispanic-owned, 32 Asian-owned, n/a American Indian/Alaska Native-owned
Employment: 8.5% management, business, and financial, 2.5% computer, engineering, and science, 5.9% education, legal, community service, arts, and media, 7.6% healthcare practitioners, 18.5% service, 22.5% sales and office, 8.8% natural resources, construction, and maintenance, 25.7% production, transportation, and material moving
Income: Per capita: $22,428; Median household: $41,476; Average household: $54,206; Households with income of $100,000 or more: 11.4%; Poverty rate: 18.2%
Educational Attainment: High school diploma or higher: 82.0%; Bachelor's degree or higher: 11.1%; Graduate/professional degree or higher: 3.6%
Housing: Homeownership rate: 68.8%; Median home value: $81,400; Median year structure built: 1963; Homeowner vacancy rate: 4.2%; Median selected monthly owner costs: $902 with a mortgage, $368 without a mortgage; Median gross rent: $680 per month; Rental vacancy rate: 10.9%
Vital Statistics: Birth rate: 103.0 per 10,000 population; Death rate: 122.4 per 10,000 population; Age-adjusted cancer mortality rate: 201.6 deaths per 100,000 population
Health Insurance: 87.6% have insurance; 61.0% have private insurance; 39.8% have public insurance; 12.4% do not have insurance; 4.8% of children under 18 do not have insurance
Health Care: Physicians: 8.6 per 10,000 population; Dentists: 3.9 per 10,000 population; Hospital beds: 32.2 per 10,000 population; Hospital admissions: 702.2 per 10,000 population
Transportation: Commute: 93.5% car, 0.4% public transportation, 1.3% walk, 3.4% work from home; Mean travel time to work: 26.1 minutes
2016 Presidential Election: 71.8% Trump, 23.6% Clinton, 4.6% Johnson, 0.0% Stein
Additional Information Contacts
Fayette Government . . . . (765) 825-8987
http://www.co.fayette.in.us

Fayette County Communities

CONNERSVILLE (city). County seat. Covers a land area of 7.745 square miles and a water area of 0.015 square miles. Located at 39.66° N. Lat; 85.14° W. Long. Elevation is 823 feet.
History: Settlement at Connersville began in 1808 when John Conner established a fur-trading post here. He founded the town of Connersville in 1813 and served as its first sheriff, in addition to operating the gristmill, sawmill, tavern, and store.
Population: 13,022; Growth (since 2000): -15.5%; Density: 1,681.4 persons per square mile; Race: 94.8% White, 3.8% Black/African American, 0.2% Asian, 0.0% American Indian/Alaska Native, 0.0% Native Hawaiian/Other Pacific Islander, 0.3% Two or more races, 1.5% Hispanic of any race; Average household size: 2.33; Median age: 41.7; Age under 18: 21.4%; Age 65 and over: 20.2%; Males per 100 females: 91.0; Marriage status: 26.2% never married, 44.1% now married, 1.4% separated, 9.5% widowed, 20.2% divorced; Foreign born: 0.6%; Speak English only: 99.1%; With disability: 20.6%; Veterans: 9.6%; Ancestry: 18.4% German, 14.9% American, 11.3% Irish, 5.8% English, 2.4% French
Employment: 6.3% management, business, and financial, 3.1% computer, engineering, and science, 5.9% education, legal, community service, arts, and media, 7.7% healthcare practitioners, 20.7% service, 23.6% sales and office, 6.4% natural resources, construction, and maintenance, 26.3% production, transportation, and material moving
Income: Per capita: $20,321; Median household: $33,902; Average household: $46,951; Households with income of $100,000 or more: 8.5%; Poverty rate: 24.2%
Educational Attainment: High school diploma or higher: 78.2%; Bachelor's degree or higher: 9.5%; Graduate/professional degree or higher: 2.4%

School District(s)

Fayette County School Corporation (PK-12)
Enrollment: 3,618 . . . . (765) 825-2178

Housing: Homeownership rate: 57.7%; Median home value: $68,500; Median year structure built: 1956; Homeowner vacancy rate: 7.5%; Median selected monthly owner costs: $857 with a mortgage, $363 without a mortgage; Median gross rent: $662 per month; Rental vacancy rate: 12.6%
Health Insurance: 84.3% have insurance; 53.1% have private insurance; 44.3% have public insurance; 15.7% do not have insurance; 6.2% of children under 18 do not have insurance
Hospitals: Fayette Regional Health System (140 beds)
Newspapers: Connersville News-Examiner (daily circulation 6,500)
Transportation: Commute: 93.1% car, 0.8% public transportation, 1.8% walk, 2.3% work from home; Mean travel time to work: 23.7 minutes; Amtrak: Train service available.

Floyd County

Located in southern Indiana; hilly region, bounded on the south by the Ohio River and the Kentucky border; drained by tributaries of the Ohio River. Covers a land area of 147.935 square miles, a water area of 1.023 square miles, and is located in the Eastern Time Zone at 38.32° N. Lat., 85.91° W. Long. The county was founded in 1819. County seat is New Albany.

Floyd County is part of the Louisville/Jefferson County, KY-IN Metropolitan Statistical Area. The entire metro area includes: Clark County, IN; Floyd County, IN; Harrison County, IN; Scott County, IN; Washington County, IN; Bullitt County, KY; Henry County, KY; Jefferson County, KY; Oldham County, KY; Shelby County, KY; Spencer County, KY; Trimble County, KY

Population: 76,481; Growth (since 2000): 8.0%; Density: 517.0 persons per square mile; Race: 90.3% White, 5.3% Black/African American, 1.1% Asian, 0.5% American Indian/Alaska Native, 0.0% Native Hawaiian/Other Pacific Islander, 2.1% two or more races, 3.1% Hispanic of any race; Average household size: 2.59; Median age: 39.9; Age under 18: 23.1%; Age 65 and over: 14.8%; Males per 100 females: 94.0; Marriage status: 29.3% never married, 51.5% now married, 1.6% separated, 6.5% widowed, 12.7% divorced; Foreign born: 2.2%; Speak English only: 96.7%; With disability: 13.3%; Veterans: 8.8%; Ancestry: 26.1% German, 13.5% Irish, 9.6% English, 9.5% American, 3.6% French
Religion: Six largest groups: 22.8% Baptist, 16.4% Catholicism, 6.4% Methodist/Pietist, 3.4% Non-denominational Protestant, 2.2% Holiness, 2.0% Lutheran
Economy: Unemployment rate: 3.5%; Leading industries: 13.5 % health care and social assistance; 11.4 % professional, scientific, and technical services; 10.9 % retail trade; Farms: 277 totaling 21,463 acres; Company size: 2 employ 1,000 or more persons, 1 employs 500 to 999 persons, 42 employ 100 to 499 persons, 1,737 employ less than 100 persons; Business ownership: 2,254 women-owned, 167 Black-owned, 33 Hispanic-owned, 81 Asian-owned, n/a American Indian/Alaska Native-owned
Employment: 15.3% management, business, and financial, 4.5% computer, engineering, and science, 9.3% education, legal, community service, arts, and media, 7.5% healthcare practitioners, 14.5% service, 25.1% sales and office, 8.1% natural resources, construction, and maintenance, 15.6% production, transportation, and material moving
Income: Per capita: $30,663; Median household: $59,451; Average household: $76,967; Households with income of $100,000 or more: 24.9%; Poverty rate: 10.8%
Educational Attainment: High school diploma or higher: 89.4%; Bachelor's degree or higher: 28.4%; Graduate/professional degree or higher: 10.6%
Housing: Homeownership rate: 72.3%; Median home value: $159,700; Median year structure built: 1974; Homeowner vacancy rate: 2.1%; Median selected monthly owner costs: $1,238 with a mortgage, $433 without a mortgage; Median gross rent: $767 per month; Rental vacancy rate: 8.9%
Vital Statistics: Birth rate: 118.1 per 10,000 population; Death rate: 97.1 per 10,000 population; Age-adjusted cancer mortality rate: 169.5 deaths per 100,000 population
Health Insurance: 93.2% have insurance; 76.8% have private insurance; 28.9% have public insurance; 6.8% do not have insurance; 4.1% of children under 18 do not have insurance
Health Care: Physicians: 22.4 per 10,000 population; Dentists: 6.7 per 10,000 population; Hospital beds: 41.4 per 10,000 population; Hospital admissions: 1,876.8 per 10,000 population
Air Quality Index (AQI): Percent of Days: 71.8% good, 26.8% moderate, 1.4% unhealthy for sensitive individuals, 0.0% unhealthy, 0.0% very unhealthy; Annual median: 41; Annual maximum: 115
Transportation: Commute: 93.9% car, 0.9% public transportation, 1.0% walk, 3.9% work from home; Mean travel time to work: 22.6 minutes
2016 Presidential Election: 56.6% Trump, 36.9% Clinton, 4.9% Johnson, 0.4% Stein
Additional Information Contacts
Floyd Government. . . . . (812) 948-5466
http://www.floydcounty.in.gov

Floyd County Communities

FLOYDS KNOBS (unincorporated postal area)
ZCTA: 47119
Covers a land area of 43.110 square miles and a water area of 0.257 square miles. Located at 38.37° N. Lat; 85.88° W. Long. Elevation is 771 feet.
Population: 11,410; Growth (since 2000): 16.7%; Density: 264.7 persons per square mile; Race: 97.3% White, 0.6% Black/African American, 0.8% Asian, 0.0% American Indian/Alaska Native, 0.0% Native Hawaiian/Other Pacific Islander, 1.0% Two or more races, 0.7% Hispanic of any race; Average household size: 2.79; Median age: 42.7; Age under 18: 24.2%; Age 65 and over: 14.5%; Males per 100 females: 98.5; Marriage status: 24.6% never married, 63.8% now married, 0.2% separated, 5.2% widowed, 6.4% divorced; Foreign born: 0.8%; Speak English only: 99.0%; With disability: 9.9%; Veterans: 10.3%; Ancestry: 33.9% German, 13.0% Irish, 12.1% American, 11.6% English, 5.2% French
Employment: 24.5% management, business, and financial, 5.9% computer, engineering, and science, 9.3% education, legal, community service, arts, and media, 7.0% healthcare practitioners, 10.5% service, 24.3% sales and office, 6.7% natural resources, construction, and maintenance, 11.9% production, transportation, and material moving
Income: Per capita: $44,732; Median household: $87,674; Average household: $124,621; Households with income of $100,000 or more: 42.1%; Poverty rate: 2.5%
Educational Attainment: High school diploma or higher: 96.2%; Bachelor's degree or higher: 41.3%; Graduate/professional degree or higher: 16.7%

School District(s)

New Albany-Floyd Co Con Sch (PK-12)
Enrollment: 11,033 . . . . (812) 949-4200
New Albany-Floyd Co Con Sch (PK-12)
Enrollment: 11,033 . . . . (812) 949-4200
Housing: Homeownership rate: 94.9%; Median home value: $243,900; Median year structure built: 1983; Homeowner vacancy rate: 2.6%; Median selected monthly owner costs: $1,678 with a mortgage, $477 without a mortgage; Median gross rent: $852 per month; Rental vacancy rate: 5.0%
Health Insurance: 96.3% have insurance; 89.4% have private insurance; 19.9% have public insurance; 3.7% do not have insurance; 3.4% of children under 18 do not have insurance
Transportation: Commute: 92.5% car, 0.3% public transportation, 0.0% walk, 7.2% work from home; Mean travel time to work: 23.3 minutes

GALENA (CDP). Covers a land area of 2.671 square miles and a water area of 0.008 square miles. Located at 38.36° N. Lat; 85.94° W. Long. Elevation is 810 feet.
History: Galena was laid out in 1836, when it was called Germantown for the German immigrants who settled here. The Galena Mill, built in 1857, was a steam-powered flour mill.
Population: 1,819; Growth (since 2000): -0.7%; Density: 681.1 persons per square mile; Race: 99.2% White, 0.0% Black/African American, 0.8% Asian, 0.0% American Indian/Alaska Native, 0.0% Native Hawaiian/Other Pacific Islander, 0.0% Two or more races, 0.0% Hispanic of any race; Average household size: 3.40; Median age: 38.0; Age under 18: 37.5%; Age 65 and over: 9.6%; Males per 100 females: 95.3; Marriage status: 24.4% never married, 59.7% now married, 0.5% separated, 10.7% widowed, 5.3% divorced; Foreign born: 1.4%; Speak English only: 99.4%; With disability: 14.6%; Veterans: 8.9%; Ancestry: 22.3% American, 18.0% German, 7.5% Irish, 4.3% English, 3.3% Italian
Employment: 15.1% management, business, and financial, 2.5% computer, engineering, and science, 11.4% education, legal, community service, arts, and media, 6.7% healthcare practitioners, 10.6% service, 32.2% sales and office, 9.7% natural resources, construction, and maintenance, 11.8% production, transportation, and material moving
Income: Per capita: $28,608; Median household: $72,552; Average household: $93,456; Households with income of $100,000 or more: 27.1%; Poverty rate: 0.9%
Educational Attainment: High school diploma or higher: 93.2%; Bachelor's degree or higher: 32.8%; Graduate/professional degree or higher: 7.7%
Housing: Homeownership rate: 85.8%; Median home value: $167,300; Median year structure built: 1979; Homeowner vacancy rate: 0.0%; Median selected monthly owner costs: $1,303 with a mortgage, $451 without a mortgage; Median gross rent: $1,139 per month; Rental vacancy rate: 5.0%
Health Insurance: 92.9% have insurance; 86.1% have private insurance; 15.8% have public insurance; 7.1% do not have insurance; 4.0% of children under 18 do not have insurance
Transportation: Commute: 96.5% car, 0.0% public transportation, 0.0% walk, 3.5% work from home; Mean travel time to work: 21.5 minutes

GEORGETOWN (town). Covers a land area of 2.049 square miles and a water area of 0.018 square miles. Located at 38.30° N. Lat; 85.96° W. Long. Elevation is 722 feet.
Population: 3,187; Growth (since 2000): 43.1%; Density: 1,555.3 persons per square mile; Race: 94.9% White, 0.2% Black/African American, 1.0% Asian, 0.0% American Indian/Alaska Native, 0.0% Native Hawaiian/Other Pacific Islander, 1.9% Two or more races, 2.8% Hispanic of any race; Average household size: 3.10; Median age: 33.5; Age under 18: 34.0%; Age 65 and over: 9.3%; Males per 100 females: 93.4; Marriage status: 22.2% never married, 62.7% now married, 1.3% separated, 4.9%

widowed, 10.2% divorced; Foreign born: 1.5%; Speak English only: 95.4%; With disability: 6.3%; Veterans: 13.0%; Ancestry: 23.7% German, 17.2% Irish, 9.7% English, 8.0% American, 6.6% Italian
Employment: 13.6% management, business, and financial, 5.8% computer, engineering, and science, 10.0% education, legal, community service, arts, and media, 11.1% healthcare practitioners, 12.6% service, 25.1% sales and office, 8.0% natural resources, construction, and maintenance, 13.7% production, transportation, and material moving
Income: Per capita: $29,667; Median household: $82,500; Average household: $88,421; Households with income of $100,000 or more: 38.2%; Poverty rate: 1.3%
Educational Attainment: High school diploma or higher: 96.7%; Bachelor's degree or higher: 37.1%; Graduate/professional degree or higher: 10.6%

School District(s)

New Albany-Floyd Co Con Sch (PK-12)
Enrollment: 11,033 . . . . (812) 949-4200
Housing: Homeownership rate: 83.7%; Median home value: $178,700; Median year structure built: 1987; Homeowner vacancy rate: 3.1%; Median selected monthly owner costs: $1,397 with a mortgage, $455 without a mortgage; Median gross rent: $748 per month; Rental vacancy rate: 7.2%
Health Insurance: 95.6% have insurance; 89.1% have private insurance; 14.5% have public insurance; 4.4% do not have insurance; 1.6% of children under 18 do not have insurance
Transportation: Commute: 96.0% car, 0.0% public transportation, 0.9% walk, 3.2% work from home; Mean travel time to work: 27.8 minutes
Additional Information Contacts
Town of Georgetown . . . . (812) 951-3012
http://georgetown.in.gov

GREENVILLE (town). Covers a land area of 0.780 square miles and a water area of <.001 square miles. Located at 38.37° N. Lat; 85.98° W. Long. Elevation is 827 feet.
History: Greenville was settled in 1807 and laid out in 1816 as a station on the Old Stage Road. A ready supply of white-oak timber led to the town becoming a center for the production of barrels, wine kegs, and wooden clocks.
Population: 696; Growth (since 2000): 17.8%; Density: 892.7 persons per square mile; Race: 98.1% White, 0.0% Black/African American, 0.0% Asian, 1.6% American Indian/Alaska Native, 0.0% Native Hawaiian/Other Pacific Islander, 0.3% Two or more races, 0.1% Hispanic of any race; Average household size: 2.90; Median age: 37.2; Age under 18: 23.7%; Age 65 and over: 10.1%; Males per 100 females: 104.5; Marriage status: 29.6% never married, 51.9% now married, 0.3% separated, 3.5% widowed, 15.0% divorced; Foreign born: 0.1%; Speak English only: 98.2%; With disability: 12.2%; Veterans: 5.1%; Ancestry: 28.6% German, 23.1% Irish, 9.2% English, 6.5% Italian, 4.9% French
Employment: 7.0% management, business, and financial, 5.5% computer, engineering, and science, 5.8% education, legal, community service, arts, and media, 5.8% healthcare practitioners, 16.8% service, 33.3% sales and office, 11.3% natural resources, construction, and maintenance, 14.5% production, transportation, and material moving
Income: Per capita: $27,920; Median household: $62,353; Average household: $74,096; Households with income of $100,000 or more: 21.7%; Poverty rate: 6.5%
Educational Attainment: High school diploma or higher: 96.5%; Bachelor's degree or higher: 20.2%; Graduate/professional degree or higher: 3.8%

School District(s)

New Albany-Floyd Co Con Sch (PK-12)
Enrollment: 11,033 . . . . (812) 949-4200
Housing: Homeownership rate: 84.2%; Median home value: $139,700; Median year structure built: 1968; Homeowner vacancy rate: 0.0%; Median selected monthly owner costs: $1,004 with a mortgage, $388 without a mortgage; Median gross rent: $676 per month; Rental vacancy rate: 13.6%
Health Insurance: 92.7% have insurance; 78.0% have private insurance; 22.7% have public insurance; 7.3% do not have insurance; 0.0% of children under 18 do not have insurance
Transportation: Commute: 90.1% car, 0.0% public transportation, 0.0% walk, 9.9% work from home; Mean travel time to work: 30.3 minutes

NEW ALBANY (city). County seat. Covers a land area of 14.939 square miles and a water area of 0.171 square miles. Located at 38.31° N. Lat; 85.83° W. Long. Elevation is 449 feet.
History: New Albany began as a river town, utilizing its location on the Ohio River for shipping and industry. The town was platted in 1813 by three brothers from New York, who named it for the capital of their former home state. New Albany received its city charter in 1838. Shipyards here built many vessels in the mid-1800's, including the "Robert E. Lee" built in 1866 for Captain John W. Cannon.
Population: 36,548; Growth (since 2000): -2.8%; Density: 2,446.6 persons per square mile; Race: 85.4% White, 9.2% Black/African American, 0.7% Asian, 0.4% American Indian/Alaska Native, 0.0% Native Hawaiian/Other Pacific Islander, 2.8% Two or more races, 4.4% Hispanic of any race; Average household size: 2.33; Median age: 38.2; Age under 18: 20.7%; Age 65 and over: 15.3%; Males per 100 females: 90.5; Marriage status: 34.0% never married, 41.6% now married, 2.4% separated, 7.7% widowed, 16.7% divorced; Foreign born: 1.9%; Speak English only: 96.6%; With disability: 16.4%; Veterans: 8.5%; Ancestry: 23.3% German, 13.8% Irish, 9.0% English, 8.3% American, 3.0% French
Employment: 10.7% management, business, and financial, 4.0% computer, engineering, and science, 8.8% education, legal, community service, arts, and media, 6.9% healthcare practitioners, 17.3% service, 26.0% sales and office, 8.5% natural resources, construction, and maintenance, 17.8% production, transportation, and material moving
Income: Per capita: $25,266; Median household: $43,914; Average household: $56,147; Households with income of $100,000 or more: 13.3%; Poverty rate: 18.3%
Educational Attainment: High school diploma or higher: 84.6%; Bachelor's degree or higher: 20.6%; Graduate/professional degree or higher: 7.5%

School District(s)

Community Montessori Inc (KG-12)
Enrollment: 542 . . . . (812) 948-1000
New Albany-Floyd Co Con Sch (PK-12)
Enrollment: 11,033 . . . . (812) 949-4200

Four-year College(s)

Indiana University-Southeast (Public)
Enrollment: 5,238 . . . . (812) 941-2333
Tuition: In-state $7,207; Out-of-state $19,038
Housing: Homeownership rate: 55.4%; Median home value: $111,300; Median year structure built: 1962; Homeowner vacancy rate: 2.4%; Median selected monthly owner costs: $992 with a mortgage, $378 without a mortgage; Median gross rent: $753 per month; Rental vacancy rate: 10.0%
Health Insurance: 91.3% have insurance; 67.6% have private insurance; 36.8% have public insurance; 8.7% do not have insurance; 3.7% of children under 18 do not have insurance
Hospitals: Floyd Memorial Hospital & Health Services (245 beds); Physicians' Medical Center
Newspapers: Tribune (daily circulation 12,200)
Transportation: Commute: 93.5% car, 1.6% public transportation, 2.0% walk, 2.4% work from home; Mean travel time to work: 20.2 minutes
Additional Information Contacts
City of New Albany . . . . (812) 948-5333
http://www.cityofnewalbany.com

Fountain County

Located in western Indiana; bounded on the west and north by the Wabash River; drained by Coal Creek. Covers a land area of 395.656 square miles, a water area of 2.224 square miles, and is located in the Eastern Time Zone at 40.12° N. Lat., 87.23° W. Long. The county was founded in 1825. County seat is Covington.
Population: 16,620; Growth (since 2000): -7.4%; Density: 42.0 persons per square mile; Race: 97.6% White, 0.4% Black/African American, 0.1% Asian, 0.3% American Indian/Alaska Native, 0.0% Native Hawaiian/Other Pacific Islander, 1.4% two or more races, 2.4% Hispanic of any race; Average household size: 2.35; Median age: 43.0; Age under 18: 22.5%; Age 65 and over: 19.3%; Males per 100 females: 98.0; Marriage status: 22.1% never married, 55.6% now married, 1.5% separated, 7.5% widowed, 14.8% divorced; Foreign born: 1.0%; Speak English only: 97.5%; With disability: 18.1%; Veterans: 7.9%; Ancestry: 24.9% German, 14.3% Irish, 11.2% American, 8.6% English, 2.6% French

Religion: Six largest groups: 11.1% Baptist, 4.4% Holiness, 4.2% Non-denominational Protestant, 3.7% Methodist/Pietist, 3.5% Catholicism, 2.5% Pentecostal
Economy: Unemployment rate: 3.8%; Leading industries: 20.1 % retail trade; 15.2 % other services (except public administration); 10.9 % accommodation and food services; Farms: 460 totaling 214,412 acres; Company size: 0 employ 1,000 or more persons, 1 employs 500 to 999 persons, 5 employ 100 to 499 persons, 297 employ less than 100 persons; Business ownership: 368 women-owned, n/a Black-owned, n/a Hispanic-owned, n/a Asian-owned, n/a American Indian/Alaska Native-owned
Employment: 10.8% management, business, and financial, 3.3% computer, engineering, and science, 7.0% education, legal, community service, arts, and media, 5.3% healthcare practitioners, 13.5% service, 17.5% sales and office, 12.0% natural resources, construction, and maintenance, 30.6% production, transportation, and material moving
Income: Per capita: $25,383; Median household: $46,669; Average household: $61,360; Households with income of $100,000 or more: 15.7%; Poverty rate: 12.6%
Educational Attainment: High school diploma or higher: 88.5%; Bachelor's degree or higher: 14.4%; Graduate/professional degree or higher: 5.0%
Housing: Homeownership rate: 74.0%; Median home value: $93,500; Median year structure built: 1963; Homeowner vacancy rate: 1.1%; Median selected monthly owner costs: $934 with a mortgage, $344 without a mortgage; Median gross rent: $633 per month; Rental vacancy rate: 5.1%
Vital Statistics: Birth rate: 124.2 per 10,000 population; Death rate: 113.3 per 10,000 population; Age-adjusted cancer mortality rate: 162.9 deaths per 100,000 population
Health Insurance: 91.0% have insurance; 72.2% have private insurance; 36.1% have public insurance; 9.0% do not have insurance; 5.9% of children under 18 do not have insurance
Health Care: Physicians: 3.0 per 10,000 population; Dentists: 2.4 per 10,000 population; Hospital beds: 0.0 per 10,000 population; Hospital admissions: 0.0 per 10,000 population
Transportation: Commute: 92.1% car, 0.5% public transportation, 2.9% walk, 3.3% work from home; Mean travel time to work: 25.4 minutes
2016 Presidential Election: 75.1% Trump, 19.6% Clinton, 4.5% Johnson, 0.1% Stein
National and State Parks: Shades State Park
Additional Information Contacts
Fountain Government . . . . (765) 793-2243
http://www.co.fountain.in.us

Fountain County Communities

ATTICA (city). Covers a land area of 1.600 square miles and a water area of 0 square miles. Located at 40.29° N. Lat; 87.24° W. Long. Elevation is 541 feet.
History: Attica developed in the late 1840's when the Wabash & Erie Canal was extended here. A prominent resident of Attica was Dr. John Evans (1814-1897), a physician who later served as Territorial Governor of Colorado and as a U.S. senator.
Population: 3,246; Growth (since 2000): -7.0%; Density: 2,029.0 persons per square mile; Race: 97.7% White, 0.5% Black/African American, 0.3% Asian, 0.4% American Indian/Alaska Native, 0.0% Native Hawaiian/Other Pacific Islander, 0.6% Two or more races, 3.8% Hispanic of any race; Average household size: 2.22; Median age: 40.5; Age under 18: 20.4%; Age 65 and over: 17.5%; Males per 100 females: 95.7; Marriage status: 26.8% never married, 46.8% now married, 2.9% separated, 9.2% widowed, 17.1% divorced; Foreign born: 1.4%; Speak English only: 96.8%; With disability: 20.5%; Veterans: 6.0%; Ancestry: 20.9% German, 17.0% Irish, 11.1% American, 6.0% English, 3.9% French
Employment: 12.7% management, business, and financial, 3.4% computer, engineering, and science, 6.6% education, legal, community service, arts, and media, 4.7% healthcare practitioners, 14.2% service, 18.0% sales and office, 14.9% natural resources, construction, and maintenance, 25.4% production, transportation, and material moving
Income: Per capita: $24,305; Median household: $37,917; Average household: $54,570; Households with income of $100,000 or more: 12.8%; Poverty rate: 19.1%
Educational Attainment: High school diploma or higher: 85.4%; Bachelor's degree or higher: 17.2%; Graduate/professional degree or higher: 8.7%

School District(s)
Attica Consolidated School Corp (PK-12)
Enrollment: 709. . . . . (765) 762-7000
Housing: Homeownership rate: 58.5%; Median home value: $78,700; Median year structure built: 1952; Homeowner vacancy rate: 0.0%; Median selected monthly owner costs: $902 with a mortgage, $327 without a mortgage; Median gross rent: $650 per month; Rental vacancy rate: 2.9%
Health Insurance: 89.4% have insurance; 66.9% have private insurance; 38.4% have public insurance; 10.6% do not have insurance; 2.3% of children under 18 do not have insurance
Newspapers: Fountain County Neighbor (weekly circulation 2,200)
Transportation: Commute: 89.4% car, 0.7% public transportation, 4.1% walk, 3.7% work from home; Mean travel time to work: 21.6 minutes
Additional Information Contacts
City of Attica . . . . (765) 761-7074
http://www.wcchamber.net; http://www.atticaonline.com

COVINGTON (city). County seat. Covers a land area of 1.176 square miles and a water area of 0 square miles. Located at 40.14° N. Lat; 87.39° W. Long. Elevation is 564 feet.
History: Covington was laid out in 1826 along the east bank of the Wabash River. A prominent resident was Edward A. Hannegan (1807-1859), U.S. senator and minister to Prussia, where he is said to have dazzled the court. Back home, Hannegan's bid for the presidency was ended when he stabbed his brother-in-law to death.
Population: 2,365; Growth (since 2000): -7.8%; Density: 2,011.2 persons per square mile; Race: 97.7% White, 1.8% Black/African American, 0.3% Asian, 0.0% American Indian/Alaska Native, 0.0% Native Hawaiian/Other Pacific Islander, 0.3% Two or more races, 0.4% Hispanic of any race; Average household size: 2.09; Median age: 46.1; Age under 18: 18.2%; Age 65 and over: 26.7%; Males per 100 females: 88.1; Marriage status: 19.7% never married, 54.4% now married, 1.4% separated, 9.8% widowed, 16.2% divorced; Foreign born: 0.5%; Speak English only: 99.1%; With disability: 19.5%; Veterans: 9.0%; Ancestry: 24.0% German, 14.8% English, 11.2% American, 10.9% Irish, 5.2% Italian
Employment: 11.4% management, business, and financial, 4.9% computer, engineering, and science, 13.9% education, legal, community service, arts, and media, 5.8% healthcare practitioners, 11.9% service, 23.5% sales and office, 6.8% natural resources, construction, and maintenance, 21.8% production, transportation, and material moving
Income: Per capita: $30,977; Median household: $45,521; Average household: $67,827; Households with income of $100,000 or more: 16.7%; Poverty rate: 10.7%
Educational Attainment: High school diploma or higher: 91.6%; Bachelor's degree or higher: 18.1%; Graduate/professional degree or higher: 7.5%

School District(s)
Covington Community School Corp (PK-12)
Enrollment: 905. . . . . (765) 793-4877
Housing: Homeownership rate: 68.0%; Median home value: $94,700; Median year structure built: 1964; Homeowner vacancy rate: 1.7%; Median selected monthly owner costs: $965 with a mortgage, $333 without a mortgage; Median gross rent: $616 per month; Rental vacancy rate: 0.0%
Health Insurance: 94.0% have insurance; 74.7% have private insurance; 39.1% have public insurance; 6.0% do not have insurance; 0.6% of children under 18 do not have insurance
Transportation: Commute: 89.1% car, 0.0% public transportation, 4.2% walk, 6.7% work from home; Mean travel time to work: 21.8 minutes
Additional Information Contacts
City of Covington. . . . . (765) 761-7074
http://www.wcchamber.net

HILLSBORO (town). Covers a land area of 0.313 square miles and a water area of 0 square miles. Located at 40.11° N. Lat; 87.16° W. Long. Elevation is 709 feet.
History: Early industry in Hillsboro was based on the clay soil used in the manufacture of tiles and bricks.
Population: 578; Growth (since 2000): 18.2%; Density: 1,845.6 persons per square mile; Race: 96.9% White, 0.0% Black/African American, 0.0% Asian, 1.4% American Indian/Alaska Native, 0.0% Native Hawaiian/Other Pacific Islander, 1.7% Two or more races, 0.5% Hispanic of any race; Average household size: 2.43; Median age: 36.9; Age under 18: 29.2%; Age 65 and over: 17.6%; Males per 100 females: 94.9; Marriage status: 22.1% never married, 60.9% now married, 2.0% separated, 6.3% widowed, 10.7% divorced; Foreign born: 0.5%; Speak English only: 99.1%;

With disability: 12.3%; Veterans: 9.5%; Ancestry: 24.4% German, 14.7% English, 11.4% Irish, 11.1% American, 3.6% French
Employment: 6.4% management, business, and financial, 3.4% computer, engineering, and science, 6.8% education, legal, community service, arts, and media, 6.4% healthcare practitioners, 9.4% service, 25.1% sales and office, 15.3% natural resources, construction, and maintenance, 27.2% production, transportation, and material moving
Income: Per capita: $24,802; Median household: $43,382; Average household: $61,267; Households with income of $100,000 or more: 14.3%; Poverty rate: 13.7%
Educational Attainment: High school diploma or higher: 91.7%; Bachelor's degree or higher: 9.6%; Graduate/professional degree or higher: 1.6%
Housing: Homeownership rate: 79.4%; Median home value: $73,000; Median year structure built: 1947; Homeowner vacancy rate: 3.9%; Median selected monthly owner costs: $869 with a mortgage, $368 without a mortgage; Median gross rent: $773 per month; Rental vacancy rate: 0.0%
Health Insurance: 92.7% have insurance; 71.3% have private insurance; 33.7% have public insurance; 7.3% do not have insurance; 5.2% of children under 18 do not have insurance
Transportation: Commute: 96.4% car, 0.0% public transportation, 1.3% walk, 0.0% work from home; Mean travel time to work: 27.4 minutes

KINGMAN (town). Covers a land area of 0.818 square miles and a water area of 0 square miles. Located at 39.97° N. Lat; 87.28° W. Long. Elevation is 702 feet.
Population: 570; Growth (since 2000): 5.9%; Density: 697.1 persons per square mile; Race: 96.7% White, 0.4% Black/African American, 0.0% Asian, 0.0% American Indian/Alaska Native, 0.0% Native Hawaiian/Other Pacific Islander, 3.0% Two or more races, 5.6% Hispanic of any race; Average household size: 2.36; Median age: 35.5; Age under 18: 25.3%; Age 65 and over: 11.8%; Males per 100 females: 99.6; Marriage status: 28.1% never married, 55.5% now married, 0.9% separated, 3.7% widowed, 12.7% divorced; Foreign born: 1.4%; Speak English only: 98.7%; With disability: 26.0%; Veterans: 9.2%; Ancestry: 19.5% German, 16.3% Irish, 5.1% English, 4.9% American, 3.0% European
Employment: 0.8% management, business, and financial, 5.3% computer, engineering, and science, 0.0% education, legal, community service, arts, and media, 5.0% healthcare practitioners, 23.7% service, 13.7% sales and office, 12.2% natural resources, construction, and maintenance, 39.3% production, transportation, and material moving
Income: Per capita: $18,525; Median household: $37,031; Average household: $46,974; Households with income of $100,000 or more: 12.2%; Poverty rate: 18.5%
Educational Attainment: High school diploma or higher: 74.7%; Bachelor's degree or higher: 7.0%; Graduate/professional degree or higher: 1.0%
Housing: Homeownership rate: 45.6%; Median home value: $82,100; Median year structure built: 1960; Homeowner vacancy rate: 6.1%; Median selected monthly owner costs: $1,021 with a mortgage, $341 without a mortgage; Median gross rent: $676 per month; Rental vacancy rate: 14.0%
Health Insurance: 87.0% have insurance; 60.7% have private insurance; 41.6% have public insurance; 13.0% do not have insurance; 4.0% of children under 18 do not have insurance
Transportation: Commute: 98.4% car, 0.8% public transportation, 0.8% walk, 0.0% work from home; Mean travel time to work: 31.7 minutes

MELLOTT (town). Covers a land area of 0.171 square miles and a water area of 0 square miles. Located at 40.16° N. Lat; 87.15° W. Long. Elevation is 705 feet.
Population: 192; Growth (since 2000): -7.2%; Density: 1,123.6 persons per square mile; Race: 99.5% White, 0.0% Black/African American, 0.0% Asian, 0.0% American Indian/Alaska Native, 0.0% Native Hawaiian/Other Pacific Islander, 0.5% Two or more races, 12.0% Hispanic of any race; Average household size: 2.56; Median age: 40.0; Age under 18: 26.6%; Age 65 and over: 20.8%; Males per 100 females: 84.1; Marriage status: 20.1% never married, 57.8% now married, 0.0% separated, 9.7% widowed, 12.3% divorced; Foreign born: 1.6%; Speak English only: 100.0%; With disability: 16.7%; Veterans: 7.1%; Ancestry: 30.2% German, 21.9% Irish, 11.5% American, 4.7% British, 4.7% Dutch
Employment: 8.0% management, business, and financial, 0.0% computer, engineering, and science, 2.7% education, legal, community service, arts, and media, 9.3% healthcare practitioners, 17.3% service, 20.0% sales and office, 13.3% natural resources, construction, and maintenance, 29.3% production, transportation, and material moving
Income: Per capita: $18,223; Median household: $36,250; Average household: $46,429; Households with income of $100,000 or more: 10.7%; Poverty rate: 11.5%
Educational Attainment: High school diploma or higher: 82.8%; Bachelor's degree or higher: n/a; Graduate/professional degree or higher: n/a
Housing: Homeownership rate: 81.3%; Median home value: $61,400; Median year structure built: 1968; Homeowner vacancy rate: 7.6%; Median selected monthly owner costs: $750 with a mortgage, $286 without a mortgage; Median gross rent: $595 per month; Rental vacancy rate: 17.6%
Health Insurance: 82.8% have insurance; 70.8% have private insurance; 28.1% have public insurance; 17.2% do not have insurance; 11.1% of children under 18 do not have insurance
Transportation: Commute: 98.6% car, 0.0% public transportation, 0.0% walk, 1.4% work from home; Mean travel time to work: 29.9 minutes

NEWTOWN (town). Covers a land area of 0.504 square miles and a water area of 0 square miles. Located at 40.20° N. Lat; 87.15° W. Long. Elevation is 709 feet.
Population: 279; Growth (since 2000): 72.2%; Density: 553.1 persons per square mile; Race: 96.4% White, 0.0% Black/African American, 0.0% Asian, 2.5% American Indian/Alaska Native, 0.0% Native Hawaiian/Other Pacific Islander, 1.1% Two or more races, 6.8% Hispanic of any race; Average household size: 2.68; Median age: 41.6; Age under 18: 25.8%; Age 65 and over: 10.4%; Males per 100 females: 128.6; Marriage status: 20.6% never married, 59.2% now married, 2.2% separated, 2.2% widowed, 17.9% divorced; Foreign born: 3.2%; Speak English only: 94.9%; With disability: 12.9%; Veterans: 8.2%; Ancestry: 34.8% German, 18.3% Irish, 9.0% English, 8.6% Scottish, 6.8% Dutch
Employment: 2.8% management, business, and financial, 4.9% computer, engineering, and science, 5.6% education, legal, community service, arts, and media, 4.2% healthcare practitioners, 12.5% service, 9.0% sales and office, 12.5% natural resources, construction, and maintenance, 48.6% production, transportation, and material moving
Income: Per capita: $26,971; Median household: $58,750; Average household: $70,097; Households with income of $100,000 or more: 16.4%; Poverty rate: 14.2%
Educational Attainment: High school diploma or higher: 90.6%; Bachelor's degree or higher: 12.5%; Graduate/professional degree or higher: 7.3%
Housing: Homeownership rate: 73.1%; Median home value: $70,600; Median year structure built: 1960; Homeowner vacancy rate: 0.0%; Median selected monthly owner costs: $808 with a mortgage, $230 without a mortgage; Median gross rent: $800 per month; Rental vacancy rate: 0.0%
Health Insurance: 83.5% have insurance; 64.9% have private insurance; 25.8% have public insurance; 16.5% do not have insurance; 19.2% of children under 18 do not have insurance
Transportation: Commute: 97.8% car, 0.0% public transportation, 0.0% walk, 0.0% work from home; Mean travel time to work: 28.1 minutes

VEEDERSBURG (town). Covers a land area of 2.717 square miles and a water area of 0 square miles. Located at 40.11° N. Lat; 87.26° W. Long. Elevation is 633 feet.
History: Veedersburg was a brick manufacturing center. The Veedersburg Paver Company furnished the brick for paving the Indianapolis Motor Speedway.
Population: 2,214; Growth (since 2000): -3.7%; Density: 815.0 persons per square mile; Race: 94.0% White, 0.0% Black/African American, 0.0% Asian, 0.6% American Indian/Alaska Native, 0.0% Native Hawaiian/Other Pacific Islander, 4.1% Two or more races, 2.7% Hispanic of any race; Average household size: 2.33; Median age: 43.0; Age under 18: 22.5%; Age 65 and over: 15.3%; Males per 100 females: 94.5; Marriage status: 26.0% never married, 47.6% now married, 1.7% separated, 6.3% widowed, 20.1% divorced; Foreign born: 2.2%; Speak English only: 95.6%; With disability: 21.1%; Veterans: 4.4%; Ancestry: 19.2% German, 12.2% Irish, 10.9% American, 5.6% English, 5.1% French
Employment: 7.8% management, business, and financial, 2.2% computer, engineering, and science, 2.2% education, legal, community service, arts, and media, 3.9% healthcare practitioners, 7.7% service, 19.5% sales and office, 10.2% natural resources, construction, and maintenance, 46.5% production, transportation, and material moving
Income: Per capita: $22,025; Median household: $46,713; Average household: $51,865; Households with income of $100,000 or more: 11.7%; Poverty rate: 17.3%

Educational Attainment: High school diploma or higher: 84.0%; Bachelor's degree or higher: 7.8%; Graduate/professional degree or higher: 2.9%

School District(s)

Southeast Fountain School Corp (PK-12)
Enrollment: 1,070 .... (765) 294-2254

Housing: Homeownership rate: 74.3%; Median home value: $71,400; Median year structure built: 1960; Homeowner vacancy rate: 0.7%; Median selected monthly owner costs: $791 with a mortgage, $340 without a mortgage; Median gross rent: $605 per month; Rental vacancy rate: 12.2%
Health Insurance: 90.9% have insurance; 71.8% have private insurance; 32.6% have public insurance; 9.1% do not have insurance; 8.2% of children under 18 do not have insurance
Transportation: Commute: 93.1% car, 0.4% public transportation, 3.2% walk, 2.7% work from home; Mean travel time to work: 22.0 minutes
Additional Information Contacts
Town of Veedersburg .... (765) 362-6800
http://www.crawfordsvillechamber.com

WALLACE (town). Covers a land area of 0.085 square miles and a water area of 0 square miles. Located at 39.99° N. Lat; 87.15° W. Long. Elevation is 702 feet.
History: Laid out 1832.
Population: 106; Growth (since 2000): 6.0%; Density: 1,242.8 persons per square mile; Race: 100.0% White, 0.0% Black/African American, 0.0% Asian, 0.0% American Indian/Alaska Native, 0.0% Native Hawaiian/Other Pacific Islander, 0.0% Two or more races, 0.0% Hispanic of any race; Average household size: 2.08; Median age: 35.3; Age under 18: 25.5%; Age 65 and over: 16.0%; Males per 100 females: 94.4; Marriage status: 26.5% never married, 44.6% now married, 0.0% separated, 14.5% widowed, 14.5% divorced; Foreign born: 1.9%; Speak English only: 96.2%; With disability: 38.7%; Veterans: 5.1%; Ancestry: 36.8% German, 14.2% Irish, 10.4% English, 8.5% American, 1.9% British
Employment: 7.1% management, business, and financial, 0.0% computer, engineering, and science, 3.6% education, legal, community service, arts, and media, 3.6% healthcare practitioners, 10.7% service, 16.1% sales and office, 16.1% natural resources, construction, and maintenance, 42.9% production, transportation, and material moving
Income: Per capita: $21,271; Median household: $36,250; Average household: $43,127; Households with income of $100,000 or more: n/a; Poverty rate: 11.7%
Educational Attainment: High school diploma or higher: 76.2%; Bachelor's degree or higher: 17.5%; Graduate/professional degree or higher: 3.2%
Housing: Homeownership rate: 72.5%; Median home value: $66,300; Median year structure built: Before 1940; Homeowner vacancy rate: 0.0%; Median selected monthly owner costs: $600 with a mortgage, $475 without a mortgage; Median gross rent: n/a per month; Rental vacancy rate: 0.0%
Health Insurance: 83.0% have insurance; 55.7% have private insurance; 37.7% have public insurance; 17.0% do not have insurance; 0.0% of children under 18 do not have insurance
Transportation: Commute: 98.0% car, 0.0% public transportation, 2.0% walk, 0.0% work from home; Mean travel time to work: 28.0 minutes

Franklin County

Located in southeastern Indiana; bounded on the east by Ohio; drained by the Whitewater River and its East Fork. Covers a land area of 384.430 square miles, a water area of 6.620 square miles, and is located in the Eastern Time Zone at 39.41° N. Lat., 85.07° W. Long. The county was founded in 1810. County seat is Brookville.

Weather Station: Brookville		Elevation: 629 feet

	Jan	Feb	Mar	Apr	May	Jun	Jul	Aug	Sep	Oct	Nov	Dec
High	38	42	53	65	75	83	87	86	80	67	55	41
Low	20	22	29	40	50	59	63	62	53	41	33	24
Precip	3.0	2.6	3.6	4.1	5.1	3.7	4.4	3.4	2.6	3.2	3.6	3.4
Snow	4.2	4.0	1.5	0.1	tr	0.0	0.0	0.0	0.0	0.1	0.6	3.7

High and Low temperatures in degrees Fahrenheit; Precipitation and Snow in inches

Population: 22,835; Growth (since 2000): 3.1%; Density: 59.4 persons per square mile; Race: 99.0% White, 0.2% Black/African American, 0.3% Asian, 0.0% American Indian/Alaska Native, 0.0% Native Hawaiian/Other Pacific Islander, 0.4% two or more races, 1.1% Hispanic of any race; Average household size: 2.56; Median age: 42.3; Age under 18: 24.1%; Age 65 and over: 16.5%; Males per 100 females: 99.9; Marriage status: 23.4% never married, 62.3% now married, 0.6% separated, 4.7% widowed, 9.6% divorced; Foreign born: 0.7%; Speak English only: 98.7%; With disability: 13.2%; Veterans: 7.7%; Ancestry: 37.6% German, 13.7% Irish, 12.8% American, 7.8% English, 2.7% Italian
Religion: Six largest groups: 20.5% Catholicism, 9.1% Baptist, 4.3% Methodist/Pietist, 4.0% Presbyterian-Reformed, 2.5% Lutheran, 1.3% Non-denominational Protestant
Economy: Unemployment rate: 3.7%; Leading industries: 14.6 % other services (except public administration); 14.4 % retail trade; 13.3 % health care and social assistance; Farms: 727 totaling 124,960 acres; Company size: 0 employ 1,000 or more persons, 0 employ 500 to 999 persons, 6 employ 100 to 499 persons, 431 employs less than 100 persons; Business ownership: 637 women-owned, n/a Black-owned, n/a Hispanic-owned, n/a Asian-owned, n/a American Indian/Alaska Native-owned
Employment: 14.2% management, business, and financial, 2.9% computer, engineering, and science, 7.1% education, legal, community service, arts, and media, 7.4% healthcare practitioners, 15.6% service, 18.8% sales and office, 12.9% natural resources, construction, and maintenance, 21.1% production, transportation, and material moving
Income: Per capita: $26,267; Median household: $55,588; Average household: $67,451; Households with income of $100,000 or more: 20.1%; Poverty rate: 9.9%
Educational Attainment: High school diploma or higher: 87.6%; Bachelor's degree or higher: 19.7%; Graduate/professional degree or higher: 6.8%
Housing: Homeownership rate: 80.3%; Median home value: $152,200; Median year structure built: 1977; Homeowner vacancy rate: 2.9%; Median selected monthly owner costs: $1,161 with a mortgage, $381 without a mortgage; Median gross rent: $668 per month; Rental vacancy rate: 5.1%
Vital Statistics: Birth rate: 95.5 per 10,000 population; Death rate: 89.3 per 10,000 population; Age-adjusted cancer mortality rate: 206.7 deaths per 100,000 population
Health Insurance: 93.1% have insurance; 75.1% have private insurance; 29.6% have public insurance; 6.9% do not have insurance; 5.9% of children under 18 do not have insurance
Health Care: Physicians: 15.8 per 10,000 population; Dentists: 6.2 per 10,000 population; Hospital beds: 0.0 per 10,000 population; Hospital admissions: 0.0 per 10,000 population
Transportation: Commute: 94.5% car, 0.1% public transportation, 0.6% walk, 4.0% work from home; Mean travel time to work: 30.1 minutes
2016 Presidential Election: 78.7% Trump, 17.9% Clinton, 3.3% Johnson, 0.1% Stein
National and State Parks: Mounds State Recreation Area
Additional Information Contacts
Franklin Government.............................. (765) 647-4985
http://www.franklincounty.in.gov

Franklin County Communities

BATH (unincorporated postal area)
ZCTA: 47010
Covers a land area of 10.764 square miles and a water area of 0.043 square miles. Located at 39.50° N. Lat; 84.85° W. Long. Elevation is 1,010 feet.
Population: 335; Growth (since 2000): -16.0%; Density: 31.1 persons per square mile; Race: 100.0% White, 0.0% Black/African American, 0.0% Asian, 0.0% American Indian/Alaska Native, 0.0% Native Hawaiian/Other Pacific Islander, 0.0% Two or more races, 0.0% Hispanic of any race; Average household size: 2.26; Median age: 47.1; Age under 18: 16.1%; Age 65 and over: 17.6%; Males per 100 females: 112.5; Marriage status: 48.4% never married, 48.4% now married, 0.0% separated, 0.0% widowed, 3.2% divorced; Foreign born: 0.0%; Speak English only: 96.4%; With disability: 3.3%; Veterans: 3.6%; Ancestry: 52.2% Irish, 43.9% German, 23.0% American, 5.7% European, 3.6% English
Employment: 0.0% management, business, and financial, 5.8% computer, engineering, and science, 6.4% education, legal, community service, arts, and media, 0.0% healthcare practitioners, 24.4% service, 27.6% sales and office, 5.8% natural resources, construction, and maintenance, 30.1% production, transportation, and material moving
Income: Per capita: $22,995; Median household: n/a; Average household: $51,628; Households with income of $100,000 or more: 23.6%; Poverty rate: 21.2%

Educational Attainment: High school diploma or higher: 100.0%; Bachelor's degree or higher: 8.8%; Graduate/professional degree or higher: 4.6%
Housing: Homeownership rate: 56.1%; Median home value: $185,400; Median year structure built: 1969; Homeowner vacancy rate: 0.0%; Median selected monthly owner costs: $1,596 with a mortgage, $0 without a mortgage; Median gross rent: n/a per month; Rental vacancy rate: 0.0%
Health Insurance: 92.8% have insurance; 34.6% have private insurance; 67.2% have public insurance; 7.2% do not have insurance; 0.0% of children under 18 do not have insurance
Transportation: Commute: 100.0% car, 0.0% public transportation, 0.0% walk, 0.0% work from home; Mean travel time to work: 0.0 minutes

BROOKVILLE (town). County seat. Covers a land area of 1.498 square miles and a water area of 0.043 square miles. Located at 39.42° N. Lat; 85.01° W. Long. Elevation is 666 feet.
History: Brookville was laid out in 1808 on a site selected by Amos Butler and Jesse Brooks Thomas. They called their settlement Brooksville in honor of Thomas' mother, whose maiden name was Brooks. The "s" was removed when Franklin County was organized a few years later and Brookville became the county seat. Thomas became a U.S. senator from Illinois and was instrumental in the Missouri Compromise of 1820.
Population: 2,543; Growth (since 2000): -4.1%; Density: 1,697.1 persons per square mile; Race: 100.0% White, 0.0% Black/African American, 0.0% Asian, 0.0% American Indian/Alaska Native, 0.0% Native Hawaiian/Other Pacific Islander, 0.0% Two or more races, 4.2% Hispanic of any race; Average household size: 2.22; Median age: 40.8; Age under 18: 22.1%; Age 65 and over: 20.3%; Males per 100 females: 87.8; Marriage status: 25.0% never married, 49.1% now married, 0.2% separated, 8.6% widowed, 17.3% divorced; Foreign born: 0.5%; Speak English only: 98.6%; With disability: 26.5%; Veterans: 6.2%; Ancestry: 35.1% German, 15.2% American, 14.8% Irish, 6.8% English, 2.5% Italian
Employment: 11.5% management, business, and financial, 1.9% computer, engineering, and science, 4.0% education, legal, community service, arts, and media, 9.4% healthcare practitioners, 21.7% service, 21.1% sales and office, 8.7% natural resources, construction, and maintenance, 21.9% production, transportation, and material moving
Income: Per capita: $19,852; Median household: $32,296; Average household: $43,790; Households with income of $100,000 or more: 7.0%; Poverty rate: 20.3%
Educational Attainment: High school diploma or higher: 82.3%; Bachelor's degree or higher: 18.2%; Graduate/professional degree or higher: 6.4%

School District(s)
Franklin County Community Sch Corp (PK-12)
Enrollment: 2,601 . . . . (765) 647-4128
Housing: Homeownership rate: 54.9%; Median home value: $108,000; Median year structure built: 1966; Homeowner vacancy rate: 4.7%; Median selected monthly owner costs: $862 with a mortgage, $366 without a mortgage; Median gross rent: $649 per month; Rental vacancy rate: 9.6%
Health Insurance: 92.5% have insurance; 61.9% have private insurance; 44.7% have public insurance; 7.5% do not have insurance; 4.6% of children under 18 do not have insurance
Newspapers: Brookville American-Democrat (weekly circulation 1,200)
Transportation: Commute: 93.0% car, 0.0% public transportation, 3.8% walk, 2.8% work from home; Mean travel time to work: 27.4 minutes
Additional Information Contacts
Town of Brookville . . . . (866) 647-6555
http://www.franklincountyin.com

CEDAR GROVE (town). Covers a land area of 0.150 square miles and a water area of <.001 square miles. Located at 39.36° N. Lat; 84.94° W. Long. Elevation is 600 feet.
Population: 216; Growth (since 2000): 16.8%; Density: 1,440.4 persons per square mile; Race: 99.1% White, 0.0% Black/African American, 0.0% Asian, 0.0% American Indian/Alaska Native, 0.0% Native Hawaiian/Other Pacific Islander, 0.9% Two or more races, 0.5% Hispanic of any race; Average household size: 2.18; Median age: 44.0; Age under 18: 20.8%; Age 65 and over: 16.7%; Males per 100 females: 90.2; Marriage status: 30.4% never married, 47.0% now married, 0.0% separated, 6.1% widowed, 16.6% divorced; Foreign born: 0.0%; Speak English only: 99.5%; With disability: 20.4%; Veterans: 3.5%; Ancestry: 52.8% German, 24.1% Irish, 4.2% American, 3.7% English, 3.2% Lithuanian
Employment: 17.5% management, business, and financial, 2.9% computer, engineering, and science, 3.9% education, legal, community service, arts, and media, 0.0% healthcare practitioners, 20.4% service, 16.5% sales and office, 16.5% natural resources, construction, and maintenance, 22.3% production, transportation, and material moving
Income: Per capita: $35,732; Median household: $49,375; Average household: $77,170; Households with income of $100,000 or more: 22.2%; Poverty rate: 18.5%
Educational Attainment: High school diploma or higher: 84.8%; Bachelor's degree or higher: 15.2%; Graduate/professional degree or higher: n/a

School District(s)
Franklin County Community Sch Corp (PK-12)
Enrollment: 2,601 . . . . (765) 647-4128
Housing: Homeownership rate: 61.6%; Median home value: $112,500; Median year structure built: Before 1940; Homeowner vacancy rate: 0.0%; Median selected monthly owner costs: $875 with a mortgage, $290 without a mortgage; Median gross rent: $673 per month; Rental vacancy rate: 0.0%
Health Insurance: 87.5% have insurance; 66.2% have private insurance; 35.6% have public insurance; 12.5% do not have insurance; 15.6% of children under 18 do not have insurance
Transportation: Commute: 92.2% car, 0.0% public transportation, 3.9% walk, 3.9% work from home; Mean travel time to work: 28.1 minutes

LAUREL (town). Covers a land area of 0.241 square miles and a water area of <.001 square miles. Located at 39.50° N. Lat; 85.19° W. Long. Elevation is 728 feet.
History: Laurel was founded in 1836 by James Conwell, who named it for Laurel, Delaware. It began as a farming community, becoming a mill town and shipping center during the canal period.
Population: 444; Growth (since 2000): -23.3%; Density: 1,840.3 persons per square mile; Race: 100.0% White, 0.0% Black/African American, 0.0% Asian, 0.0% American Indian/Alaska Native, 0.0% Native Hawaiian/Other Pacific Islander, 0.0% Two or more races, 0.0% Hispanic of any race; Average household size: 2.66; Median age: 28.5; Age under 18: 28.6%; Age 65 and over: 11.3%; Males per 100 females: 104.0; Marriage status: 32.0% never married, 41.9% now married, 1.8% separated, 9.1% widowed, 17.0% divorced; Foreign born: 0.0%; Speak English only: 99.0%; With disability: 15.8%; Veterans: 7.6%; Ancestry: 14.6% Irish, 10.6% German, 9.2% American, 2.3% English, 1.4% Scotch-Irish
Employment: 6.1% management, business, and financial, 0.0% computer, engineering, and science, 8.8% education, legal, community service, arts, and media, 6.1% healthcare practitioners, 8.2% service, 16.3% sales and office, 21.8% natural resources, construction, and maintenance, 32.7% production, transportation, and material moving
Income: Per capita: $14,061; Median household: $32,054; Average household: $36,550; Households with income of $100,000 or more: 2.4%; Poverty rate: 33.6%
Educational Attainment: High school diploma or higher: 72.8%; Bachelor's degree or higher: 4.2%; Graduate/professional degree or higher: 0.4%

School District(s)
Franklin County Community Sch Corp (PK-12)
Enrollment: 2,601 . . . . (765) 647-4128
Housing: Homeownership rate: 57.5%; Median home value: $57,500; Median year structure built: 1942; Homeowner vacancy rate: 6.5%; Median selected monthly owner costs: $730 with a mortgage, $333 without a mortgage; Median gross rent: $581 per month; Rental vacancy rate: 13.4%
Health Insurance: 79.5% have insurance; 38.7% have private insurance; 51.8% have public insurance; 20.5% do not have insurance; 15.6% of children under 18 do not have insurance
Transportation: Commute: 90.2% car, 0.0% public transportation, 1.4% walk, 0.0% work from home; Mean travel time to work: 36.3 minutes

METAMORA (CDP). Covers a land area of 0.336 square miles and a water area of 0 square miles. Located at 39.45° N. Lat; 85.14° W. Long. Elevation is 718 feet.
Population: 207; Growth (since 2000): n/a; Density: 616.4 persons per square mile; Race: 100.0% White, 0.0% Black/African American, 0.0% Asian, 0.0% American Indian/Alaska Native, 0.0% Native Hawaiian/Other Pacific Islander, 0.0% Two or more races, 0.0% Hispanic of any race; Average household size: 2.01; Median age: 55.0; Age under 18: 10.1%; Age 65 and over: 16.9%; Males per 100 females: 72.5; Marriage status: 16.9% never married, 62.3% now married, 0.0% separated, 12.6%

widowed, 8.2% divorced; Foreign born: 0.0%; Speak English only: 100.0%; With disability: 33.8%; Veterans: 4.3%; Ancestry: 50.7% German, 34.3% Polish, 20.3% American, 15.5% Scottish, 3.9% English
Employment: 11.9% management, business, and financial, 0.0% computer, engineering, and science, 0.0% education, legal, community service, arts, and media, 0.0% healthcare practitioners, 28.4% service, 38.8% sales and office, 0.0% natural resources, construction, and maintenance, 20.9% production, transportation, and material moving
Income: Per capita: $14,073; Median household: $26,836; Average household: $28,524; Households with income of $100,000 or more: n/a; Poverty rate: 8.7%
Educational Attainment: High school diploma or higher: 69.4%; Bachelor's degree or higher: n/a; Graduate/professional degree or higher: n/a
Housing: Homeownership rate: 59.2%; Median home value: $128,400; Median year structure built: 1966; Homeowner vacancy rate: 0.0%; Median selected monthly owner costs: $759 with a mortgage, n/a without a mortgage; Median gross rent: n/a per month; Rental vacancy rate: 0.0%
Health Insurance: 100.0% have insurance; 58.9% have private insurance; 49.8% have public insurance; 0.0% do not have insurance; 0.0% of children under 18 do not have insurance
Transportation: Commute: 79.1% car, 20.9% public transportation, 0.0% walk, 0.0% work from home; Mean travel time to work: 0.0 minutes

MOUNT CARMEL (town). Covers a land area of 0.045 square miles and a water area of 0 square miles. Located at 39.41° N. Lat; 84.88° W. Long. Elevation is 1,020 feet.
Population: 43; Growth (since 2000): -59.4%; Density: 947.8 persons per square mile; Race: 97.7% White, 0.0% Black/African American, 0.0% Asian, 0.0% American Indian/Alaska Native, 0.0% Native Hawaiian/Other Pacific Islander, 2.3% Two or more races, 0.0% Hispanic of any race; Average household size: 2.69; Median age: 27.5; Age under 18: 32.6%; Age 65 and over: 4.7%; Males per 100 females: 83.0; Marriage status: 31.3% never married, 46.9% now married, 0.0% separated, 9.4% widowed, 12.5% divorced; Foreign born: 0.0%; Speak English only: 100.0%; With disability: 25.6%; Veterans: 24.1%; Ancestry: 39.5% German, 7.0% American, 7.0% Norwegian, 4.7% Irish, 2.3% Bermudan
Employment: 0.0% management, business, and financial, 0.0% computer, engineering, and science, 11.8% education, legal, community service, arts, and media, 0.0% healthcare practitioners, 29.4% service, 0.0% sales and office, 0.0% natural resources, construction, and maintenance, 58.8% production, transportation, and material moving
Income: Per capita: $11,251; Median household: $35,500; Average household: $32,600; Households with income of $100,000 or more: n/a; Poverty rate: 23.3%
Educational Attainment: High school diploma or higher: 65.2%; Bachelor's degree or higher: n/a; Graduate/professional degree or higher: n/a
Housing: Homeownership rate: 62.5%; Median home value: $67,500; Median year structure built: Before 1940; Homeowner vacancy rate: 0.0%; Median selected monthly owner costs: $1,063 with a mortgage, n/a without a mortgage; Median gross rent: $550 per month; Rental vacancy rate: 0.0%
Health Insurance: 86.0% have insurance; 69.8% have private insurance; 39.5% have public insurance; 14.0% do not have insurance; 0.0% of children under 18 do not have insurance
Transportation: Commute: 94.1% car, 0.0% public transportation, 0.0% walk, 0.0% work from home; Mean travel time to work: 37.6 minutes

NEW TRENTON (CDP). Covers a land area of 0.441 square miles and a water area of 0 square miles. Located at 39.31° N. Lat; 84.90° W. Long. Elevation is 614 feet.
Population: 331; Growth (since 2000): n/a; Density: 750.1 persons per square mile; Race: 100.0% White, 0.0% Black/African American, 0.0% Asian, 0.0% American Indian/Alaska Native, 0.0% Native Hawaiian/Other Pacific Islander, 0.0% Two or more races, 0.0% Hispanic of any race; Average household size: 1.82; Median age: 58.3; Age under 18: 4.8%; Age 65 and over: 38.4%; Males per 100 females: 93.8; Marriage status: 11.8% never married, 71.9% now married, 0.0% separated, 0.0% widowed, 16.3% divorced; Foreign born: 0.0%; Speak English only: 100.0%; With disability: 54.4%; Veterans: 7.3%; Ancestry: 38.4% English, 18.7% American, 13.3% German, 6.3% Dutch, 6.3% Irish
Employment: 0.0% management, business, and financial, 0.0% computer, engineering, and science, 0.0% education, legal, community service, arts, and media, 19.3% healthcare practitioners, 0.0% service, 14.7% sales and office, 19.3% natural resources, construction, and maintenance, 46.8% production, transportation, and material moving
Income: Per capita: $17,922; Median household: n/a; Average household: $33,059; Households with income of $100,000 or more: n/a; Poverty rate: 61.6%
Educational Attainment: High school diploma or higher: 33.7%; Bachelor's degree or higher: n/a; Graduate/professional degree or higher: n/a
Housing: Homeownership rate: 100.0%; Median home value: n/a; Median year structure built: 1972; Homeowner vacancy rate: 0.0%; Median selected monthly owner costs: n/a with a mortgage, $364 without a mortgage; Median gross rent: n/a per month; Rental vacancy rate: 0.0%
Health Insurance: 100.0% have insurance; 32.9% have private insurance; 67.1% have public insurance; 0.0% do not have insurance; 0.0% of children under 18 do not have insurance
Transportation: Commute: 100.0% car, 0.0% public transportation, 0.0% walk, 0.0% work from home; Mean travel time to work: 0.0 minutes

OLDENBURG (town). Covers a land area of 0.434 square miles and a water area of 0.002 square miles. Located at 39.34° N. Lat; 85.20° W. Long. Elevation is 889 feet.
History: Oldenburg was founded in 1837 by German immigrants. It was once a brick manufacturing center.
Population: 641; Growth (since 2000): -0.9%; Density: 1,478.2 persons per square mile; Race: 99.1% White, 0.0% Black/African American, 0.0% Asian, 0.9% American Indian/Alaska Native, 0.0% Native Hawaiian/Other Pacific Islander, 0.0% Two or more races, 0.9% Hispanic of any race; Average household size: 2.45; Median age: 50.8; Age under 18: 20.9%; Age 65 and over: 32.0%; Males per 100 females: 64.8; Marriage status: 32.9% never married, 49.3% now married, 3.3% separated, 10.6% widowed, 7.2% divorced; Foreign born: 0.3%; Speak English only: 99.3%; With disability: 20.1%; Veterans: 3.6%; Ancestry: 58.0% German, 7.6% Irish, 7.0% American, 6.6% English, 4.1% French
Employment: 14.1% management, business, and financial, 5.4% computer, engineering, and science, 12.6% education, legal, community service, arts, and media, 2.9% healthcare practitioners, 14.8% service, 13.0% sales and office, 8.3% natural resources, construction, and maintenance, 28.9% production, transportation, and material moving
Income: Per capita: $24,657; Median household: $56,818; Average household: $68,683; Households with income of $100,000 or more: 22.4%; Poverty rate: 21.7%
Educational Attainment: High school diploma or higher: 92.6%; Bachelor's degree or higher: 42.3%; Graduate/professional degree or higher: 17.4%
Housing: Homeownership rate: 70.1%; Median home value: $164,200; Median year structure built: 1951; Homeowner vacancy rate: 4.5%; Median selected monthly owner costs: $1,250 with a mortgage, $392 without a mortgage; Median gross rent: $548 per month; Rental vacancy rate: 20.0%
Health Insurance: 92.6% have insurance; 75.6% have private insurance; 39.0% have public insurance; 7.4% do not have insurance; 5.1% of children under 18 do not have insurance
Transportation: Commute: 86.4% car, 0.0% public transportation, 7.1% walk, 3.9% work from home; Mean travel time to work: 17.8 minutes

Fulton County

Located in northern Indiana; drained by the Tippecanoe River. Covers a land area of 368.388 square miles, a water area of 2.877 square miles, and is located in the Eastern Time Zone at 41.05° N. Lat., 86.27° W. Long. The county was founded in 1835. County seat is Rochester.

Weather Station: Rochester — Elevation: 770 feet

	Jan	Feb	Mar	Apr	May	Jun	Jul	Aug	Sep	Oct	Nov	Dec
High	32	36	47	60	71	80	83	82	75	62	49	36
Low	17	19	28	38	49	59	62	61	52	41	32	21
Precip	2.5	2.0	2.6	3.8	4.5	3.9	4.6	4.0	3.2	3.3	3.4	2.8
Snow	10.9	8.2	3.2	0.9	0.0	0.0	0.0	0.0	0.0	0.3	1.4	7.1

High and Low temperatures in degrees Fahrenheit; Precipitation and Snow in inches

Population: 20,296; Growth (since 2000): -1.0%; Density: 55.1 persons per square mile; Race: 94.5% White, 1.0% Black/African American, 0.4% Asian, 0.5% American Indian/Alaska Native, 0.1% Native Hawaiian/Other Pacific Islander, 1.0% two or more races, 5.0% Hispanic of any race; Average household size: 2.53; Median age: 41.9; Age under 18: 23.8%; Age 65 and over: 18.2%; Males per 100 females: 98.9; Marriage status:

22.8% never married, 53.9% now married, 1.4% separated, 7.2% widowed, 16.0% divorced; Foreign born: 2.8%; Speak English only: 93.6%; With disability: 17.9%; Veterans: 9.2%; Ancestry: 27.9% German, 11.0% American, 10.3% Irish, 8.2% English, 3.0% Dutch
Religion: Six largest groups: 8.7% Methodist/Pietist, 6.5% Baptist, 5.4% Catholicism, 4.9% Non-denominational Protestant, 3.3% Holiness, 2.1% Pentecostal
Economy: Unemployment rate: 3.6%; Leading industries: 16.8 % retail trade; 14.8 % other services (except public administration); 10.0 % accommodation and food services; Farms: 653 totaling 188,411 acres; Company size: 0 employ 1,000 or more persons, 0 employ 500 to 999 persons, 10 employ 100 to 499 persons, 442 employ less than 100 persons; Business ownership: 435 women-owned, n/a Black-owned, n/a Hispanic-owned, n/a Asian-owned, n/a American Indian/Alaska Native-owned
Employment: 11.0% management, business, and financial, 2.8% computer, engineering, and science, 5.8% education, legal, community service, arts, and media, 3.5% healthcare practitioners, 15.2% service, 19.6% sales and office, 11.3% natural resources, construction, and maintenance, 30.8% production, transportation, and material moving
Income: Per capita: $23,557; Median household: $47,108; Average household: $57,635; Households with income of $100,000 or more: 11.8%; Poverty rate: 13.3%
Educational Attainment: High school diploma or higher: 86.0%; Bachelor's degree or higher: 12.8%; Graduate/professional degree or higher: 4.5%
Housing: Homeownership rate: 77.4%; Median home value: $93,600; Median year structure built: 1965; Homeowner vacancy rate: 1.9%; Median selected monthly owner costs: $912 with a mortgage, $355 without a mortgage; Median gross rent: $639 per month; Rental vacancy rate: 10.2%
Vital Statistics: Birth rate: 124.6 per 10,000 population; Death rate: 100.7 per 10,000 population; Age-adjusted cancer mortality rate: 198.5 deaths per 100,000 population
Health Insurance: 88.4% have insurance; 67.7% have private insurance; 34.4% have public insurance; 11.6% do not have insurance; 16.6% of children under 18 do not have insurance
Health Care: Physicians: 10.4 per 10,000 population; Dentists: 5.0 per 10,000 population; Hospital beds: 12.4 per 10,000 population; Hospital admissions: 506.5 per 10,000 population
Transportation: Commute: 92.2% car, 0.1% public transportation, 1.1% walk, 4.6% work from home; Mean travel time to work: 22.8 minutes
2016 Presidential Election: 71.2% Trump, 23.2% Clinton, 4.8% Johnson, 0.0% Stein
Additional Information Contacts
Fulton Government . . . . (574) 223-2912
http://www.co.fulton.in.us

Fulton County Communities

AKRON (town). Covers a land area of 0.457 square miles and a water area of 0 square miles. Located at 41.04° N. Lat; 86.02° W. Long. Elevation is 853 feet.
Population: 1,388; Growth (since 2000): 29.0%; Density: 3,036.7 persons per square mile; Race: 84.9% White, 0.0% Black/African American, 0.0% Asian, 0.5% American Indian/Alaska Native, 0.0% Native Hawaiian/Other Pacific Islander, 0.0% Two or more races, 21.9% Hispanic of any race; Average household size: 3.29; Median age: 30.3; Age under 18: 32.6%; Age 65 and over: 7.6%; Males per 100 females: 95.5; Marriage status: 24.9% never married, 59.1% now married, 1.3% separated, 2.7% widowed, 13.4% divorced; Foreign born: 12.3%; Speak English only: 77.4%; With disability: 9.9%; Veterans: 2.7%; Ancestry: 18.8% German, 12.8% Irish, 8.4% American, 3.2% English, 1.2% Norwegian
Employment: 8.1% management, business, and financial, 2.8% computer, engineering, and science, 5.9% education, legal, community service, arts, and media, 5.3% healthcare practitioners, 11.1% service, 16.0% sales and office, 6.2% natural resources, construction, and maintenance, 44.6% production, transportation, and material moving
Income: Per capita: $19,059; Median household: $46,548; Average household: $59,962; Households with income of $100,000 or more: 14.7%; Poverty rate: 15.7%
Educational Attainment: High school diploma or higher: 73.4%; Bachelor's degree or higher: 12.5%; Graduate/professional degree or higher: 7.6%

School District(s)
Tippecanoe Valley School Corp (KG-12)
Enrollment: 1,909 . . . . (574) 598-2759
Tippecanoe Valley School Corp (KG-12)
Enrollment: 1,909 . . . . (574) 598-2759
Housing: Homeownership rate: 63.7%; Median home value: $82,200; Median year structure built: 1952; Homeowner vacancy rate: 3.2%; Median selected monthly owner costs: $869 with a mortgage, $344 without a mortgage; Median gross rent: $656 per month; Rental vacancy rate: 14.4%
Health Insurance: 88.7% have insurance; 62.5% have private insurance; 33.5% have public insurance; 11.3% do not have insurance; 5.6% of children under 18 do not have insurance
Transportation: Commute: 94.7% car, 0.0% public transportation, 2.9% walk, 1.6% work from home; Mean travel time to work: 27.1 minutes

FULTON (town). Covers a land area of 0.178 square miles and a water area of 0 square miles. Located at 40.95° N. Lat; 86.26° W. Long. Elevation is 794 feet.
Population: 420; Growth (since 2000): 28.8%; Density: 2,364.6 persons per square mile; Race: 96.4% White, 0.5% Black/African American, 0.0% Asian, 0.5% American Indian/Alaska Native, 0.0% Native Hawaiian/Other Pacific Islander, 2.4% Two or more races, 1.9% Hispanic of any race; Average household size: 2.86; Median age: 35.9; Age under 18: 30.0%; Age 65 and over: 15.2%; Males per 100 females: 103.0; Marriage status: 30.1% never married, 49.8% now married, 6.3% separated, 5.6% widowed, 14.4% divorced; Foreign born: 0.0%; Speak English only: 98.8%; With disability: 14.0%; Veterans: 16.0%; Ancestry: 22.4% German, 14.3% American, 11.4% Irish, 7.1% English, 3.6% Italian
Employment: 1.2% management, business, and financial, 0.0% computer, engineering, and science, 8.3% education, legal, community service, arts, and media, 1.2% healthcare practitioners, 21.3% service, 8.3% sales and office, 20.7% natural resources, construction, and maintenance, 39.1% production, transportation, and material moving
Income: Per capita: $17,598; Median household: $45,163; Average household: $47,684; Households with income of $100,000 or more: 6.8%; Poverty rate: 17.4%
Educational Attainment: High school diploma or higher: 92.5%; Bachelor's degree or higher: 6.3%; Graduate/professional degree or higher: 1.6%

School District(s)
Caston School Corporation (PK-12)
Enrollment: 665. . . . . (574) 857-2035
Housing: Homeownership rate: 72.8%; Median home value: $62,100; Median year structure built: Before 1940; Homeowner vacancy rate: 7.8%; Median selected monthly owner costs: $690 with a mortgage, $327 without a mortgage; Median gross rent: $771 per month; Rental vacancy rate: 0.0%
Health Insurance: 79.0% have insurance; 48.1% have private insurance; 43.8% have public insurance; 21.0% do not have insurance; 11.5% of children under 18 do not have insurance
Transportation: Commute: 98.8% car, 0.0% public transportation, 0.0% walk, 1.2% work from home; Mean travel time to work: 24.7 minutes

KEWANNA (town). Covers a land area of 0.531 square miles and a water area of 0 square miles. Located at 41.02° N. Lat; 86.41° W. Long. Elevation is 784 feet.
Population: 580; Growth (since 2000): -5.5%; Density: 1,093.3 persons per square mile; Race: 99.3% White, 0.0% Black/African American, 0.0% Asian, 0.0% American Indian/Alaska Native, 0.0% Native Hawaiian/Other Pacific Islander, 0.7% Two or more races, 0.5% Hispanic of any race; Average household size: 2.18; Median age: 49.3; Age under 18: 18.1%; Age 65 and over: 21.0%; Males per 100 females: 92.8; Marriage status: 30.6% never married, 43.7% now married, 3.8% separated, 6.4% widowed, 19.3% divorced; Foreign born: 0.0%; Speak English only: 99.1%; With disability: 27.1%; Veterans: 6.3%; Ancestry: 27.8% German, 16.9% American, 9.0% Irish, 7.1% English, 6.7% Dutch
Employment: 2.1% management, business, and financial, 2.1% computer, engineering, and science, 8.5% education, legal, community service, arts, and media, 2.1% healthcare practitioners, 11.9% service, 20.9% sales and office, 7.2% natural resources, construction, and maintenance, 45.1% production, transportation, and material moving
Income: Per capita: $16,879; Median household: $30,000; Average household: $34,517; Households with income of $100,000 or more: n/a; Poverty rate: 22.9%

Educational Attainment: High school diploma or higher: 83.0%; Bachelor's degree or higher: 10.0%; Graduate/professional degree or higher: 2.7%
Housing: Homeownership rate: 77.1%; Median home value: $47,600; Median year structure built: 1955; Homeowner vacancy rate: 5.8%; Median selected monthly owner costs: $795 with a mortgage, $261 without a mortgage; Median gross rent: $515 per month; Rental vacancy rate: 23.8%
Health Insurance: 84.8% have insurance; 55.7% have private insurance; 42.9% have public insurance; 15.2% do not have insurance; 25.7% of children under 18 do not have insurance
Newspapers: The Observer (weekly circulation 600)
Transportation: Commute: 87.9% car, 0.0% public transportation, 6.9% walk, 0.0% work from home; Mean travel time to work: 18.6 minutes

ROCHESTER (city). County seat. Covers a land area of 4.691 square miles and a water area of 1.111 square miles. Located at 41.06° N. Lat; 86.20° W. Long. Elevation is 781 feet.
History: Rochester was founded in 1831 as a trading post, and became a resort town on Lake Manitou.
Population: 6,059; Growth (since 2000): -5.5%; Density: 1,291.7 persons per square mile; Race: 97.5% White, 0.4% Black/African American, 0.3% Asian, 1.2% American Indian/Alaska Native, 0.0% Native Hawaiian/Other Pacific Islander, 0.5% Two or more races, 2.8% Hispanic of any race; Average household size: 2.23; Median age: 44.0; Age under 18: 20.6%; Age 65 and over: 21.4%; Males per 100 females: 91.9; Marriage status: 24.8% never married, 42.5% now married, 0.4% separated, 8.5% widowed, 24.3% divorced; Foreign born: 0.8%; Speak English only: 98.9%; With disability: 24.4%; Veterans: 8.4%; Ancestry: 25.2% German, 14.1% American, 11.7% English, 10.3% Irish, 4.1% Polish
Employment: 10.1% management, business, and financial, 4.0% computer, engineering, and science, 6.3% education, legal, community service, arts, and media, 2.4% healthcare practitioners, 19.4% service, 21.0% sales and office, 9.8% natural resources, construction, and maintenance, 27.1% production, transportation, and material moving
Income: Per capita: $23,255; Median household: $40,451; Average household: $49,726; Households with income of $100,000 or more: 12.2%; Poverty rate: 14.7%
Educational Attainment: High school diploma or higher: 87.9%; Bachelor's degree or higher: 10.9%; Graduate/professional degree or higher: 4.8%

School District(s)

Rochester Community School Corp (PK-12)
Enrollment: 1,805 . . . . (574) 223-2159
Housing: Homeownership rate: 65.5%; Median home value: $84,900; Median year structure built: 1958; Homeowner vacancy rate: 0.0%; Median selected monthly owner costs: $869 with a mortgage, $314 without a mortgage; Median gross rent: $637 per month; Rental vacancy rate: 14.2%
Health Insurance: 87.5% have insurance; 60.5% have private insurance; 42.4% have public insurance; 12.5% do not have insurance; 17.2% of children under 18 do not have insurance
Hospitals: Woodlawn Hospital
Newspapers: Rochester Sentinel (daily circulation 3,800)
Transportation: Commute: 93.8% car, 0.4% public transportation, 0.0% walk, 5.4% work from home; Mean travel time to work: 22.1 minutes
Airports: Fulton County (general aviation)
Additional Information Contacts
City of Rochester. (574) 223-2510
http://www.rochester.in.us

Gibson County

Located in southwestern Indiana; bounded on the west by the Wabash River and the Illinois border, and on the north by the White River; also drained by the Patoka and Black Rivers. Covers a land area of 487.486 square miles, a water area of 11.679 square miles, and is located in the Central Time Zone at 38.32° N. Lat., 87.58° W. Long. The county was founded in 1813. County seat is Princeton.

Weather Station: Princeton 1 W Elevation: 479 feet

	Jan	Feb	Mar	Apr	May	Jun	Jul	Aug	Sep	Oct	Nov	Dec
High	39	44	55	66	76	85	88	87	80	68	54	42
Low	23	27	35	45	55	64	68	66	58	46	37	27
Precip	3.1	3.0	4.5	4.4	5.9	3.9	4.2	3.7	3.8	3.8	4.4	3.7
Snow	3.0	3.5	0.8	0.1	0.0	0.0	0.0	0.0	0.0	0.1	0.2	3.3

High and Low temperatures in degrees Fahrenheit; Precipitation and Snow in inches

Population: 33,596; Growth (since 2000): 3.4%; Density: 68.9 persons per square mile; Race: 95.0% White, 2.0% Black/African American, 0.3% Asian, 0.1% American Indian/Alaska Native, 0.0% Native Hawaiian/Other Pacific Islander, 1.8% two or more races, 1.5% Hispanic of any race; Average household size: 2.46; Median age: 40.5; Age under 18: 23.5%; Age 65 and over: 16.4%; Males per 100 females: 97.9; Marriage status: 25.0% never married, 55.6% now married, 1.0% separated, 6.1% widowed, 13.3% divorced; Foreign born: 1.5%; Speak English only: 97.5%; With disability: 15.1%; Veterans: 7.9%; Ancestry: 28.3% German, 11.2% Irish, 10.7% American, 9.0% English, 2.2% French
Religion: Six largest groups: 18.6% Catholicism, 7.2% Methodist/Pietist, 3.8% Holiness, 3.6% Pentecostal, 2.8% Non-denominational Protestant, 2.8% Baptist
Economy: Unemployment rate: 2.8%; Leading industries: 16.3 % retail trade; 13.5 % other services (except public administration); 10.2 % health care and social assistance; Farms: 589 totaling 268,146 acres; Company size: 1 employs 1,000 or more persons, 3 employ 500 to 999 persons, 23 employ 100 to 499 persons, 686 employ less than 100 persons; Business ownership: 569 women-owned, n/a Black-owned, n/a Hispanic-owned, 28 Asian-owned, n/a American Indian/Alaska Native-owned
Employment: 11.4% management, business, and financial, 3.4% computer, engineering, and science, 5.7% education, legal, community service, arts, and media, 6.2% healthcare practitioners, 15.6% service, 18.9% sales and office, 12.5% natural resources, construction, and maintenance, 26.3% production, transportation, and material moving
Income: Per capita: $27,342; Median household: $51,149; Average household: $68,400; Households with income of $100,000 or more: 19.1%; Poverty rate: 10.7%
Educational Attainment: High school diploma or higher: 90.8%; Bachelor's degree or higher: 16.8%; Graduate/professional degree or higher: 5.5%
Housing: Homeownership rate: 77.3%; Median home value: $105,700; Median year structure built: 1970; Homeowner vacancy rate: 1.0%; Median selected monthly owner costs: $976 with a mortgage, $366 without a mortgage; Median gross rent: $671 per month; Rental vacancy rate: 6.5%
Vital Statistics: Birth rate: 113.2 per 10,000 population; Death rate: 113.5 per 10,000 population; Age-adjusted cancer mortality rate: 146.9 deaths per 100,000 population
Health Insurance: 91.8% have insurance; 74.9% have private insurance; 29.5% have public insurance; 8.2% do not have insurance; 5.2% of children under 18 do not have insurance
Health Care: Physicians: 6.6 per 10,000 population; Dentists: 5.4 per 10,000 population; Hospital beds: 20.8 per 10,000 population; Hospital admissions: 137.3 per 10,000 population
Air Quality Index (AQI): Percent of Days: 96.4% good, 3.6% moderate, 0.0% unhealthy for sensitive individuals, 0.0% unhealthy, 0.0% very unhealthy; Annual median: 1; Annual maximum: 86
Transportation: Commute: 93.9% car, 0.2% public transportation, 2.6% walk, 2.3% work from home; Mean travel time to work: 21.5 minutes
2016 Presidential Election: 71.6% Trump, 24.0% Clinton, 4.3% Johnson, 0.1% Stein
Additional Information Contacts
Gibson Government . . . . (812) 385-5286
http://www.gibsoncounty-in.gov

Gibson County Communities

FORT BRANCH (town). Covers a land area of 1.097 square miles and a water area of 0.011 square miles. Located at 38.25° N. Lat; 87.57° W. Long. Elevation is 449 feet.
History: The town of Fort Branch was named for Old Fort Branch, built in 1811.
Population: 2,957; Growth (since 2000): 27.5%; Density: 2,695.5 persons per square mile; Race: 93.1% White, 0.3% Black/African American, 0.7% Asian, 0.2% American Indian/Alaska Native, 0.0% Native Hawaiian/Other Pacific Islander, 5.5% Two or more races, 0.5% Hispanic of any race; Average household size: 2.59; Median age: 41.9; Age under 18: 21.9%; Age 65 and over: 17.6%; Males per 100 females: 99.4; Marriage status: 26.4% never married, 54.6% now married, 0.4% separated, 6.6% widowed, 12.5% divorced; Foreign born: 0.7%; Speak English only: 98.1%; With disability: 20.4%; Veterans: 11.1%; Ancestry: 33.0% German, 13.0% Irish, 11.5% American, 6.9% English, 3.1% Canadian
Employment: 10.4% management, business, and financial, 1.6% computer, engineering, and science, 7.2% education, legal, community service, arts, and media, 6.4% healthcare practitioners, 18.9% service,

15.0% sales and office, 10.5% natural resources, construction, and maintenance, 30.0% production, transportation, and material moving
Income: Per capita: $27,335; Median household: $49,940; Average household: $69,482; Households with income of $100,000 or more: 18.2%; Poverty rate: 9.2%
Educational Attainment: High school diploma or higher: 94.7%; Bachelor's degree or higher: 19.0%; Graduate/professional degree or higher: 7.7%

School District(s)

South Gibson School Corporation (KG-12)
Enrollment: 1,839 . . . . (812) 753-4230
Housing: Homeownership rate: 69.8%; Median home value: $114,700; Median year structure built: 1963; Homeowner vacancy rate: 0.0%; Median selected monthly owner costs: $1,014 with a mortgage, $383 without a mortgage; Median gross rent: $691 per month; Rental vacancy rate: 13.1%
Health Insurance: 92.0% have insurance; 76.0% have private insurance; 31.2% have public insurance; 8.0% do not have insurance; 3.6% of children under 18 do not have insurance
Newspapers: South Gibson Star Times (weekly circulation 5,100)
Transportation: Commute: 93.2% car, 0.4% public transportation, 1.1% walk, 4.8% work from home; Mean travel time to work: 22.0 minutes
Additional Information Contacts
Town of Fort Branch . . . . (812) 385-2134
http://www.gibsoncountychamber.org

FRANCISCO (town). Covers a land area of 0.495 square miles and a water area of 0.004 square miles. Located at 38.33° N. Lat; 87.45° W. Long. Elevation is 469 feet.
History: Francisco developed when the Wabash & Erie Canal was built, and was named for a Spanish laborer on the canal.
Population: 546; Growth (since 2000): 0.6%; Density: 1,102.0 persons per square mile; Race: 97.4% White, 0.0% Black/African American, 0.0% Asian, 0.0% American Indian/Alaska Native, 0.0% Native Hawaiian/Other Pacific Islander, 2.6% Two or more races, 0.0% Hispanic of any race; Average household size: 2.46; Median age: 42.1; Age under 18: 25.3%; Age 65 and over: 14.7%; Males per 100 females: 91.4; Marriage status: 26.6% never married, 49.4% now married, 0.7% separated, 5.1% widowed, 18.8% divorced; Foreign born: 0.5%; Speak English only: 98.5%; With disability: 16.5%; Veterans: 13.0%; Ancestry: 23.6% German, 10.4% American, 9.5% English, 6.8% Irish, 2.6% Dutch
Employment: 7.3% management, business, and financial, 0.8% computer, engineering, and science, 3.8% education, legal, community service, arts, and media, 0.0% healthcare practitioners, 24.9% service, 22.2% sales and office, 8.0% natural resources, construction, and maintenance, 33.0% production, transportation, and material moving
Income: Per capita: $18,367; Median household: $37,917; Average household: $44,204; Households with income of $100,000 or more: 5.9%; Poverty rate: 15.1%
Educational Attainment: High school diploma or higher: 87.6%; Bachelor's degree or higher: 1.8%; Graduate/professional degree or higher: n/a

School District(s)

East Gibson School Corporation (PK-12)
Enrollment: 988 . . . . (812) 749-4755
Housing: Homeownership rate: 75.7%; Median home value: $62,500; Median year structure built: 1955; Homeowner vacancy rate: 5.5%; Median selected monthly owner costs: $845 with a mortgage, $393 without a mortgage; Median gross rent: $833 per month; Rental vacancy rate: 0.0%
Health Insurance: 87.9% have insurance; 66.8% have private insurance; 32.6% have public insurance; 12.1% do not have insurance; 8.2% of children under 18 do not have insurance
Transportation: Commute: 97.7% car, 0.0% public transportation, 1.1% walk, 0.8% work from home; Mean travel time to work: 22.0 minutes

HAUBSTADT (town). Covers a land area of 0.704 square miles and a water area of 0.007 square miles. Located at 38.20° N. Lat; 87.58° W. Long. Elevation is 472 feet.
Population: 1,471; Growth (since 2000): -3.8%; Density: 2,089.5 persons per square mile; Race: 98.8% White, 0.4% Black/African American, 0.0% Asian, 0.0% American Indian/Alaska Native, 0.0% Native Hawaiian/Other Pacific Islander, 0.3% Two or more races, 0.7% Hispanic of any race; Average household size: 2.34; Median age: 37.0; Age under 18: 22.9%; Age 65 and over: 15.9%; Males per 100 females: 101.4; Marriage status: 22.6% never married, 58.6% now married, 0.2% separated, 8.6% widowed, 10.2% divorced; Foreign born: 0.2%; Speak English only: 99.5%; With disability: 12.5%; Veterans: 4.2%; Ancestry: 44.5% German, 8.8% American, 5.9% Irish, 5.0% English, 1.8% Czech
Employment: 10.6% management, business, and financial, 2.1% computer, engineering, and science, 9.4% education, legal, community service, arts, and media, 7.4% healthcare practitioners, 11.5% service, 21.6% sales and office, 12.6% natural resources, construction, and maintenance, 24.8% production, transportation, and material moving
Income: Per capita: $30,253; Median household: $63,056; Average household: $71,630; Households with income of $100,000 or more: 26.9%; Poverty rate: 6.5%
Educational Attainment: High school diploma or higher: 94.5%; Bachelor's degree or higher: 19.0%; Graduate/professional degree or higher: 7.0%

School District(s)

South Gibson School Corporation (KG-12)
Enrollment: 1,839 . . . . (812) 753-4230
Housing: Homeownership rate: 79.0%; Median home value: $158,200; Median year structure built: 1975; Homeowner vacancy rate: 1.9%; Median selected monthly owner costs: $1,132 with a mortgage, $439 without a mortgage; Median gross rent: $580 per month; Rental vacancy rate: 0.0%
Health Insurance: 96.7% have insurance; 89.0% have private insurance; 21.3% have public insurance; 3.3% do not have insurance; 2.3% of children under 18 do not have insurance
Transportation: Commute: 94.2% car, 0.0% public transportation, 1.8% walk, 4.0% work from home; Mean travel time to work: 22.7 minutes

HAZLETON (town). Covers a land area of 0.333 square miles and a water area of <.001 square miles. Located at 38.49° N. Lat; 87.54° W. Long. Elevation is 453 feet.
History: Also spelled Hazelton.
Population: 339; Growth (since 2000): 17.7%; Density: 1,017.7 persons per square mile; Race: 93.2% White, 0.3% Black/African American, 0.0% Asian, 2.9% American Indian/Alaska Native, 0.0% Native Hawaiian/Other Pacific Islander, 3.5% Two or more races, 1.2% Hispanic of any race; Average household size: 2.20; Median age: 43.0; Age under 18: 23.6%; Age 65 and over: 18.3%; Males per 100 females: 100.8; Marriage status: 14.1% never married, 63.0% now married, 1.9% separated, 7.8% widowed, 15.2% divorced; Foreign born: 0.0%; Speak English only: 99.1%; With disability: 18.6%; Veterans: 16.6%; Ancestry: 29.8% German, 15.0% Irish, 11.5% American, 8.3% English, 5.9% French
Employment: 5.1% management, business, and financial, 0.0% computer, engineering, and science, 5.7% education, legal, community service, arts, and media, 7.0% healthcare practitioners, 10.8% service, 17.7% sales and office, 19.0% natural resources, construction, and maintenance, 34.8% production, transportation, and material moving
Income: Per capita: $29,756; Median household: $45,833; Average household: $65,991; Households with income of $100,000 or more: 12.3%; Poverty rate: 10.6%
Educational Attainment: High school diploma or higher: 92.7%; Bachelor's degree or higher: 7.3%; Graduate/professional degree or higher: 2.0%
Housing: Homeownership rate: 96.8%; Median home value: $50,800; Median year structure built: 1944; Homeowner vacancy rate: 0.0%; Median selected monthly owner costs: $782 with a mortgage, $333 without a mortgage; Median gross rent: n/a per month; Rental vacancy rate: 0.0%
Health Insurance: 95.9% have insurance; 77.3% have private insurance; 33.3% have public insurance; 4.1% do not have insurance; 0.0% of children under 18 do not have insurance
Transportation: Commute: 88.2% car, 0.0% public transportation, 5.9% walk, 0.0% work from home; Mean travel time to work: 29.9 minutes

MACKEY (town). Covers a land area of 0.086 square miles and a water area of 0 square miles. Located at 38.25° N. Lat; 87.39° W. Long. Elevation is 449 feet.
Population: 90; Growth (since 2000): -36.6%; Density: 1,042.6 persons per square mile; Race: 100.0% White, 0.0% Black/African American, 0.0% Asian, 0.0% American Indian/Alaska Native, 0.0% Native Hawaiian/Other Pacific Islander, 0.0% Two or more races, 0.0% Hispanic of any race; Average household size: 2.20; Median age: 39.5; Age under 18: 16.7%; Age 65 and over: 10.0%; Males per 100 females: 103.8; Marriage status: 33.8% never married, 37.5% now married, 0.0% separated, 6.3% widowed, 22.5% divorced; Foreign born: 0.0%; Speak English only: 100.0%; With disability: 10.0%; Veterans: 17.3%; Ancestry: 37.8% Irish, 27.8% German, 18.9% French, 12.2% American, 6.7% European

Employment: 2.3% management, business, and financial, 7.0% computer, engineering, and science, 7.0% education, legal, community service, arts, and media, 9.3% healthcare practitioners, 34.9% service, 16.3% sales and office, 9.3% natural resources, construction, and maintenance, 14.0% production, transportation, and material moving
Income: Per capita: $20,607; Median household: $30,938; Average household: $45,944; Households with income of $100,000 or more: 17.1%; Poverty rate: 35.6%
Educational Attainment: High school diploma or higher: 88.7%; Bachelor's degree or higher: 19.4%; Graduate/professional degree or higher: 6.5%

School District(s)

East Gibson School Corporation (PK-12)
Enrollment: 988 . . . . (812) 749-4755

Housing: Homeownership rate: 61.0%; Median home value: $97,500; Median year structure built: 1949; Homeowner vacancy rate: 0.0%; Median selected monthly owner costs: $775 with a mortgage, $429 without a mortgage; Median gross rent: $933 per month; Rental vacancy rate: 5.9%
Health Insurance: 93.3% have insurance; 86.7% have private insurance; 13.3% have public insurance; 6.7% do not have insurance; 0.0% of children under 18 do not have insurance
Transportation: Commute: 88.4% car, 0.0% public transportation, 2.3% walk, 4.7% work from home; Mean travel time to work: 22.6 minutes

OAKLAND CITY (city). Covers a land area of 1.131 square miles and a water area of 0.002 square miles. Located at 38.34° N. Lat; 87.35° W. Long. Elevation is 463 feet.
History: Oakland City developed around Oakland City College, established by the Baptist church in 1891.
Population: 2,374; Growth (since 2000): -8.3%; Density: 2,099.3 persons per square mile; Race: 96.9% White, 1.3% Black/African American, 0.1% Asian, 0.5% American Indian/Alaska Native, 0.0% Native Hawaiian/Other Pacific Islander, 0.1% Two or more races, 2.4% Hispanic of any race; Average household size: 1.99; Median age: 48.4; Age under 18: 15.2%; Age 65 and over: 23.3%; Males per 100 females: 89.5; Marriage status: 30.6% never married, 41.7% now married, 2.0% separated, 10.3% widowed, 17.4% divorced; Foreign born: 1.1%; Speak English only: 98.5%; With disability: 23.7%; Veterans: 9.2%; Ancestry: 23.2% German, 19.3% Irish, 13.0% American, 7.8% English, 4.7% French
Employment: 8.3% management, business, and financial, 0.7% computer, engineering, and science, 6.1% education, legal, community service, arts, and media, 6.2% healthcare practitioners, 16.1% service, 20.0% sales and office, 14.2% natural resources, construction, and maintenance, 28.3% production, transportation, and material moving
Income: Per capita: $22,757; Median household: $38,750; Average household: $49,358; Households with income of $100,000 or more: 8.2%; Poverty rate: 9.0%
Educational Attainment: High school diploma or higher: 78.5%; Bachelor's degree or higher: 15.9%; Graduate/professional degree or higher: 5.7%

School District(s)

East Gibson School Corporation (PK-12)
Enrollment: 988 . . . . (812) 749-4755

Four-year College(s)

Oakland City University (Private, Not-for-profit, General Baptist)
Enrollment: 1,303 . . . . (812) 749-4781
Tuition: In-state $23,700; Out-of-state $23,700

Housing: Homeownership rate: 65.6%; Median home value: $66,100; Median year structure built: 1963; Homeowner vacancy rate: 0.0%; Median selected monthly owner costs: $834 with a mortgage, $366 without a mortgage; Median gross rent: $695 per month; Rental vacancy rate: 5.3%
Health Insurance: 88.4% have insurance; 66.2% have private insurance; 40.1% have public insurance; 11.6% do not have insurance; 2.9% of children under 18 do not have insurance
Transportation: Commute: 90.1% car, 0.4% public transportation, 7.9% walk, 0.5% work from home; Mean travel time to work: 20.6 minutes
Additional Information Contacts
City of Oakland City. . . . . (812) 385-2134
http://www.gibsoncountychamber.org

OWENSVILLE (town). Covers a land area of 0.589 square miles and a water area of 0 square miles. Located at 38.27° N. Lat; 87.69° W. Long. Elevation is 509 feet.
History: Laid out 1817; incorporated 1881.
Population: 1,291; Growth (since 2000): -2.3%; Density: 2,192.8 persons per square mile; Race: 94.3% White, 0.7% Black/African American, 1.4% Asian, 0.0% American Indian/Alaska Native, 0.0% Native Hawaiian/Other Pacific Islander, 2.6% Two or more races, 0.9% Hispanic of any race; Average household size: 2.49; Median age: 42.7; Age under 18: 19.7%; Age 65 and over: 24.1%; Males per 100 females: 90.5; Marriage status: 25.9% never married, 53.1% now married, 0.9% separated, 10.4% widowed, 10.7% divorced; Foreign born: 1.5%; Speak English only: 98.8%; With disability: 18.2%; Veterans: 10.6%; Ancestry: 22.5% German, 11.5% American, 9.8% Irish, 6.7% English, 4.3% Italian
Employment: 9.9% management, business, and financial, 1.0% computer, engineering, and science, 1.9% education, legal, community service, arts, and media, 3.9% healthcare practitioners, 17.8% service, 20.9% sales and office, 8.9% natural resources, construction, and maintenance, 35.7% production, transportation, and material moving
Income: Per capita: $19,056; Median household: $41,078; Average household: $48,144; Households with income of $100,000 or more: 9.3%; Poverty rate: 14.3%
Educational Attainment: High school diploma or higher: 89.2%; Bachelor's degree or higher: 9.2%; Graduate/professional degree or higher: 4.1%

School District(s)

South Gibson School Corporation (KG-12)
Enrollment: 1,839 . . . . (812) 753-4230

Housing: Homeownership rate: 74.4%; Median home value: $85,500; Median year structure built: 1967; Homeowner vacancy rate: 2.1%; Median selected monthly owner costs: $876 with a mortgage, $385 without a mortgage; Median gross rent: $589 per month; Rental vacancy rate: 29.2%
Health Insurance: 93.5% have insurance; 67.2% have private insurance; 42.8% have public insurance; 6.5% do not have insurance; 2.6% of children under 18 do not have insurance
Transportation: Commute: 96.1% car, 0.7% public transportation, 1.2% walk, 2.0% work from home; Mean travel time to work: 24.9 minutes

PATOKA (town). Covers a land area of 1.121 square miles and a water area of 0.019 square miles. Located at 38.40° N. Lat; 87.59° W. Long. Elevation is 436 feet.
History: Patoka was settled in 1789 on the Patoka River, and platted in 1813. It was a stagecoach stop on the Vincennes-Evansville line. The name is of Indian origin meaning "logs on the bottom."
Population: 1,205; Growth (since 2000): 60.9%; Density: 1,074.9 persons per square mile; Race: 95.2% White, 1.5% Black/African American, 0.3% Asian, 0.0% American Indian/Alaska Native, 0.0% Native Hawaiian/Other Pacific Islander, 3.0% Two or more races, 2.1% Hispanic of any race; Average household size: 2.50; Median age: 32.0; Age under 18: 28.1%; Age 65 and over: 12.1%; Males per 100 females: 114.9; Marriage status: 41.3% never married, 31.5% now married, 0.8% separated, 4.1% widowed, 23.1% divorced; Foreign born: 0.3%; Speak English only: 99.2%; With disability: 16.4%; Veterans: 9.1%; Ancestry: 29.0% Irish, 24.9% German, 9.3% English, 8.8% American, 1.4% Scotch-Irish
Employment: 12.6% management, business, and financial, 2.4% computer, engineering, and science, 5.3% education, legal, community service, arts, and media, 1.8% healthcare practitioners, 18.7% service, 18.1% sales and office, 14.9% natural resources, construction, and maintenance, 26.4% production, transportation, and material moving
Income: Per capita: $20,433; Median household: $38,571; Average household: $51,322; Households with income of $100,000 or more: 9.9%; Poverty rate: 17.8%
Educational Attainment: High school diploma or higher: 87.4%; Bachelor's degree or higher: 12.7%; Graduate/professional degree or higher: 2.2%
Housing: Homeownership rate: 85.7%; Median home value: $52,100; Median year structure built: 1974; Homeowner vacancy rate: 0.0%; Median selected monthly owner costs: $803 with a mortgage, $298 without a mortgage; Median gross rent: $688 per month; Rental vacancy rate: 0.0%
Health Insurance: 87.9% have insurance; 60.0% have private insurance; 35.4% have public insurance; 12.1% do not have insurance; 2.0% of children under 18 do not have insurance
Transportation: Commute: 99.5% car, 0.0% public transportation, 0.0% walk, 0.5% work from home; Mean travel time to work: 17.0 minutes

PRINCETON (city). County seat. Covers a land area of 5.070 square miles and a water area of 0.005 square miles. Located at 38.36° N. Lat; 87.58° W. Long. Elevation is 499 feet.
History: Princeton was founded in 1814 and named for Captain William Prince. An early industry was Evans Mill, a wool-carding mill which had Abraham Lincoln as a customer in 1827.
Population: 8,573; Growth (since 2000): 4.9%; Density: 1,690.9 persons per square mile; Race: 88.5% White, 6.2% Black/African American, 0.3% Asian, 0.0% American Indian/Alaska Native, 0.0% Native Hawaiian/Other Pacific Islander, 3.1% Two or more races, 3.0% Hispanic of any race; Average household size: 2.38; Median age: 36.3; Age under 18: 25.3%; Age 65 and over: 16.8%; Males per 100 females: 91.1; Marriage status: 30.6% never married, 43.4% now married, 1.9% separated, 7.0% widowed, 19.0% divorced; Foreign born: 3.8%; Speak English only: 94.4%; With disability: 16.4%; Veterans: 8.9%; Ancestry: 20.6% German, 11.0% American, 10.0% Irish, 9.3% English, 3.0% Polish
Employment: 9.4% management, business, and financial, 4.3% computer, engineering, and science, 3.9% education, legal, community service, arts, and media, 5.6% healthcare practitioners, 18.1% service, 17.7% sales and office, 11.6% natural resources, construction, and maintenance, 29.4% production, transportation, and material moving
Income: Per capita: $22,685; Median household: $41,340; Average household: $56,665; Households with income of $100,000 or more: 8.2%; Poverty rate: 15.0%
Educational Attainment: High school diploma or higher: 87.9%; Bachelor's degree or higher: 10.4%; Graduate/professional degree or higher: 3.4%

School District(s)

North Gibson School Corp (PK-12)
Enrollment: 2,111 . . . . (812) 385-4851
Housing: Homeownership rate: 58.0%; Median home value: $81,000; Median year structure built: 1959; Homeowner vacancy rate: 3.9%; Median selected monthly owner costs: $866 with a mortgage, $362 without a mortgage; Median gross rent: $644 per month; Rental vacancy rate: 5.7%
Health Insurance: 91.4% have insurance; 67.8% have private insurance; 36.8% have public insurance; 8.6% do not have insurance; 6.5% of children under 18 do not have insurance
Hospitals: Gibson General Hospital (109 beds)
Newspapers: Oakland City Journal (weekly circulation 800); Princeton Daily Clarion (daily circulation 6,300)
Transportation: Commute: 90.9% car, 0.4% public transportation, 6.6% walk, 0.6% work from home; Mean travel time to work: 18.2 minutes
Additional Information Contacts
City of Princeton . . . . (812) 385-2134
http://www.gibsoncountychamber.org

SOMERVILLE (town). Covers a land area of 0.315 square miles and a water area of 0.002 square miles. Located at 38.28° N. Lat; 87.38° W. Long. Elevation is 469 feet.
Population: 251; Growth (since 2000): -19.6%; Density: 797.1 persons per square mile; Race: 97.6% White, 2.4% Black/African American, 0.0% Asian, 0.0% American Indian/Alaska Native, 0.0% Native Hawaiian/Other Pacific Islander, 0.0% Two or more races, 0.0% Hispanic of any race; Average household size: 2.70; Median age: 37.6; Age under 18: 29.1%; Age 65 and over: 13.1%; Males per 100 females: 103.5; Marriage status: 24.2% never married, 63.2% now married, 0.0% separated, 4.7% widowed, 7.9% divorced; Foreign born: 0.0%; Speak English only: 100.0%; With disability: 19.5%; Veterans: 11.2%; Ancestry: 45.4% German, 17.9% Irish, 13.9% American, 10.8% French, 9.2% English
Employment: 7.0% management, business, and financial, 7.9% computer, engineering, and science, 9.6% education, legal, community service, arts, and media, 7.9% healthcare practitioners, 9.6% service, 11.4% sales and office, 18.4% natural resources, construction, and maintenance, 28.1% production, transportation, and material moving
Income: Per capita: $23,124; Median household: $61,042; Average household: $62,339; Households with income of $100,000 or more: 16.1%; Poverty rate: 0.8%
Educational Attainment: High school diploma or higher: 85.0%; Bachelor's degree or higher: 15.0%; Graduate/professional degree or higher: 4.8%
Housing: Homeownership rate: 80.6%; Median home value: $81,900; Median year structure built: 1960; Homeowner vacancy rate: 0.0%; Median selected monthly owner costs: $905 with a mortgage, $241 without a mortgage; Median gross rent: $785 per month; Rental vacancy rate: 0.0%
Health Insurance: 96.8% have insurance; 82.5% have private insurance; 28.7% have public insurance; 3.2% do not have insurance; 0.0% of children under 18 do not have insurance
Transportation: Commute: 90.4% car, 0.0% public transportation, 0.0% walk, 7.9% work from home; Mean travel time to work: 31.4 minutes

Grant County

Located in east central Indiana; drained by the Mississinewa River. Covers a land area of 414.074 square miles, a water area of 0.824 square miles, and is located in the Eastern Time Zone at 40.52° N. Lat., 85.65° W. Long. The county was founded in 1831. County seat is Marion.

Grant County is part of the Marion, IN Micropolitan Statistical Area. The entire metro area includes: Grant County, IN

Weather Station: Marion 2 N Elevation: 790 feet

	Jan	Feb	Mar	Apr	May	Jun	Jul	Aug	Sep	Oct	Nov	Dec
High	33	37	48	61	72	81	84	82	77	64	51	37
Low	18	20	28	38	49	59	63	61	53	42	33	23
Precip	2.4	2.3	3.0	3.7	4.8	3.8	4.7	3.7	2.9	3.1	3.3	3.0
Snow	7.5	6.9	3.2	0.6	0.0	0.0	0.0	0.0	0.0	0.4	0.9	5.4

High and Low temperatures in degrees Fahrenheit; Precipitation and Snow in inches

Population: 67,615; Growth (since 2000): -7.9%; Density: 163.3 persons per square mile; Race: 88.0% White, 7.5% Black/African American, 0.9% Asian, 0.2% American Indian/Alaska Native, 0.0% Native Hawaiian/Other Pacific Islander, 2.8% two or more races, 4.1% Hispanic of any race; Average household size: 2.39; Median age: 39.9; Age under 18: 20.8%; Age 65 and over: 18.0%; Males per 100 females: 92.6; Marriage status: 31.2% never married, 47.6% now married, 1.2% separated, 7.3% widowed, 13.8% divorced; Foreign born: 1.5%; Speak English only: 96.9%; With disability: 18.6%; Veterans: 8.4%; Ancestry: 19.9% German, 10.6% American, 10.4% Irish, 8.1% English, 2.2% Dutch
Religion: Six largest groups: 8.9% Methodist/Pietist, 8.8% Holiness, 6.7% Baptist, 6.3% Non-denominational Protestant, 3.3% Catholicism, 1.6% European Free-Church
Economy: Unemployment rate: 4.3%; Leading industries: 17.7 % retail trade; 14.9 % other services (except public administration); 13.0 % health care and social assistance; Farms: 500 totaling 183,380 acres; Company size: 5 employ 1,000 or more persons, 3 employ 500 to 999 persons, 32 employ 100 to 499 persons, 1,236 employ less than 100 persons; Business ownership: 1,302 women-owned, 233 Black-owned, 92 Hispanic-owned, 48 Asian-owned, 38 American Indian/Alaska Native-owned
Employment: 9.3% management, business, and financial, 1.7% computer, engineering, and science, 10.7% education, legal, community service, arts, and media, 6.3% healthcare practitioners, 20.6% service, 23.1% sales and office, 7.7% natural resources, construction, and maintenance, 20.5% production, transportation, and material moving
Income: Per capita: $21,024; Median household: $42,046; Average household: $52,631; Households with income of $100,000 or more: 10.9%; Poverty rate: 19.1%
Educational Attainment: High school diploma or higher: 87.0%; Bachelor's degree or higher: 17.1%; Graduate/professional degree or higher: 6.7%
Housing: Homeownership rate: 68.4%; Median home value: $87,600; Median year structure built: 1964; Homeowner vacancy rate: 3.8%; Median selected monthly owner costs: $890 with a mortgage, $330 without a mortgage; Median gross rent: $676 per month; Rental vacancy rate: 6.6%
Vital Statistics: Birth rate: 110.5 per 10,000 population; Death rate: 119.6 per 10,000 population; Age-adjusted cancer mortality rate: 198.8 deaths per 100,000 population
Health Insurance: 89.8% have insurance; 64.3% have private insurance; 41.1% have public insurance; 10.2% do not have insurance; 4.7% of children under 18 do not have insurance
Health Care: Physicians: 12.9 per 10,000 population; Dentists: 5.7 per 10,000 population; Hospital beds: 19.6 per 10,000 population; Hospital admissions: 894.0 per 10,000 population
Transportation: Commute: 88.5% car, 0.3% public transportation, 5.1% walk, 5.0% work from home; Mean travel time to work: 18.3 minutes
2016 Presidential Election: 66.5% Trump, 27.4% Clinton, 4.7% Johnson, 0.2% Stein
Additional Information Contacts
Grant Government. . . . . (765) 668-8871
http://www.grantcounty.net

Grant County Communities

FAIRMOUNT (town). Covers a land area of 1.583 square miles and a water area of 0 square miles. Located at 40.42° N. Lat; 85.65° W. Long. Elevation is 873 feet.
History: Fairmount developed around the Wesleyan Camp Meeting Grounds, site of state and national conferences of the Methodist Church.
Population: 2,976; Growth (since 2000): -0.5%; Density: 1,880.3 persons per square mile; Race: 98.3% White, 0.0% Black/African American, 1.4% Asian, 0.0% American Indian/Alaska Native, 0.0% Native Hawaiian/Other Pacific Islander, 0.3% Two or more races, 4.7% Hispanic of any race; Average household size: 2.66; Median age: 37.9; Age under 18: 27.2%; Age 65 and over: 15.6%; Males per 100 females: 94.3; Marriage status: 27.7% never married, 52.0% now married, 2.5% separated, 4.7% widowed, 15.6% divorced; Foreign born: 1.4%; Speak English only: 97.8%; With disability: 16.6%; Veterans: 5.5%; Ancestry: 24.2% German, 12.7% Irish, 9.4% American, 4.1% French, 3.8% English
Employment: 12.9% management, business, and financial, 1.8% computer, engineering, and science, 6.4% education, legal, community service, arts, and media, 4.2% healthcare practitioners, 24.1% service, 19.4% sales and office, 13.3% natural resources, construction, and maintenance, 18.0% production, transportation, and material moving
Income: Per capita: $19,532; Median household: $42,824; Average household: $50,217; Households with income of $100,000 or more: 7.6%; Poverty rate: 18.5%
Educational Attainment: High school diploma or higher: 87.4%; Bachelor's degree or higher: 12.0%; Graduate/professional degree or higher: 1.9%

School District(s)

Madison-Grant United School Corp (PK-12)
Enrollment: 1,291 .... (765) 948-4143
Housing: Homeownership rate: 70.5%; Median home value: $81,300; Median year structure built: 1961; Homeowner vacancy rate: 3.2%; Median selected monthly owner costs: $859 with a mortgage, $383 without a mortgage; Median gross rent: $543 per month; Rental vacancy rate: 3.0%
Health Insurance: 88.9% have insurance; 65.8% have private insurance; 32.9% have public insurance; 11.1% do not have insurance; 4.5% of children under 18 do not have insurance
Safety: Violent crime rate: 35.9 per 10,000 population; Property crime rate: 25.2 per 10,000 population
Newspapers: Fairmount News Sun (weekly circulation 4,400)
Transportation: Commute: 94.6% car, 0.0% public transportation, 2.4% walk, 1.8% work from home; Mean travel time to work: 19.8 minutes
Additional Information Contacts
Town of Fairmount .... (765) 664-5107
http://marionchamber.org

FOWLERTON (town). Covers a land area of 0.196 square miles and a water area of 0 square miles. Located at 40.41° N. Lat; 85.57° W. Long. Elevation is 883 feet.
Population: 304; Growth (since 2000): 2.0%; Density: 1,554.3 persons per square mile; Race: 97.7% White, 0.0% Black/African American, 2.3% Asian, 0.0% American Indian/Alaska Native, 0.0% Native Hawaiian/Other Pacific Islander, 0.0% Two or more races, 0.0% Hispanic of any race; Average household size: 3.04; Median age: 32.0; Age under 18: 24.3%; Age 65 and over: 19.4%; Males per 100 females: 103.9; Marriage status: 20.7% never married, 48.5% now married, 1.7% separated, 12.2% widowed, 18.6% divorced; Foreign born: 2.3%; Speak English only: 96.8%; With disability: 21.4%; Veterans: 6.5%; Ancestry: 16.8% American, 10.9% German, 7.6% Irish, 3.9% Dutch, 2.3% Scottish
Employment: 3.4% management, business, and financial, 13.7% computer, engineering, and science, 2.6% education, legal, community service, arts, and media, 9.4% healthcare practitioners, 22.2% service, 11.1% sales and office, 13.7% natural resources, construction, and maintenance, 23.9% production, transportation, and material moving
Income: Per capita: $15,367; Median household: $41,111; Average household: $43,340; Households with income of $100,000 or more: 4.0%; Poverty rate: 17.1%
Educational Attainment: High school diploma or higher: 84.1%; Bachelor's degree or higher: 7.7%; Graduate/professional degree or higher: 1.0%
Housing: Homeownership rate: 68.0%; Median home value: $71,100; Median year structure built: 1983; Homeowner vacancy rate: 26.1%; Median selected monthly owner costs: $665 with a mortgage, $300 without a mortgage; Median gross rent: $670 per month; Rental vacancy rate: 13.5%
Health Insurance: 89.8% have insurance; 55.6% have private insurance; 53.0% have public insurance; 10.2% do not have insurance; 13.0% of children under 18 do not have insurance
Transportation: Commute: 98.2% car, 0.0% public transportation, 0.0% walk, 0.0% work from home; Mean travel time to work: 23.6 minutes

GAS CITY (city). Covers a land area of 4.556 square miles and a water area of 0 square miles. Located at 40.49° N. Lat; 85.60° W. Long. Elevation is 856 feet.
History: Natural gas was discovered here in 1887, giving brief fortune to Gas City. The Owens-Illinois Glass Company Plant was founded here during the gas boom.
Population: 5,920; Growth (since 2000): -0.3%; Density: 1,299.3 persons per square mile; Race: 91.1% White, 1.5% Black/African American, 0.5% Asian, 0.0% American Indian/Alaska Native, 0.0% Native Hawaiian/Other Pacific Islander, 5.5% Two or more races, 5.9% Hispanic of any race; Average household size: 2.37; Median age: 40.8; Age under 18: 24.9%; Age 65 and over: 17.5%; Males per 100 females: 93.0; Marriage status: 25.1% never married, 47.7% now married, 0.9% separated, 7.3% widowed, 19.9% divorced; Foreign born: 1.0%; Speak English only: 97.1%; With disability: 17.7%; Veterans: 10.5%; Ancestry: 13.8% German, 13.1% English, 13.1% American, 10.1% Irish, 2.6% Dutch
Employment: 7.8% management, business, and financial, 0.0% computer, engineering, and science, 10.8% education, legal, community service, arts, and media, 3.4% healthcare practitioners, 13.4% service, 29.6% sales and office, 7.6% natural resources, construction, and maintenance, 27.5% production, transportation, and material moving
Income: Per capita: $19,928; Median household: $42,829; Average household: $48,036; Households with income of $100,000 or more: 7.1%; Poverty rate: 16.5%
Educational Attainment: High school diploma or higher: 86.8%; Bachelor's degree or higher: 10.2%; Graduate/professional degree or higher: 2.7%

School District(s)

Mississinewa Community School Corp (PK-12)
Enrollment: 1,948 .... (765) 674-8528
Housing: Homeownership rate: 68.2%; Median home value: $80,300; Median year structure built: 1968; Homeowner vacancy rate: 3.0%; Median selected monthly owner costs: $841 with a mortgage, $363 without a mortgage; Median gross rent: $779 per month; Rental vacancy rate: 8.8%
Health Insurance: 90.4% have insurance; 67.9% have private insurance; 36.8% have public insurance; 9.6% do not have insurance; 7.0% of children under 18 do not have insurance
Safety: Violent crime rate: 6.9 per 10,000 population; Property crime rate: 302.0 per 10,000 population
Newspapers: Indiana Newspaper Group (weekly circulation 5,000)
Transportation: Commute: 94.9% car, 0.0% public transportation, 3.8% walk, 0.7% work from home; Mean travel time to work: 20.3 minutes
Additional Information Contacts
City of Gas City .... (765) 677-3079
http://www.gascityindiana.com

HERBST (CDP). Covers a land area of 1.305 square miles and a water area of 0 square miles. Located at 40.51° N. Lat; 85.78° W. Long. Elevation is 856 feet.
Population: 33; Growth (since 2000): n/a; Density: 25.3 persons per square mile; Race: 100.0% White, 0.0% Black/African American, 0.0% Asian, 0.0% American Indian/Alaska Native, 0.0% Native Hawaiian/Other Pacific Islander, 0.0% Two or more races, 0.0% Hispanic of any race; Average household size: 1.27; Median age: 57.8; Age under 18: 0.0%; Age 65 and over: 24.2%; Males per 100 females: 96.5; Marriage status: 0.0% never married, 45.5% now married, 0.0% separated, 27.3% widowed, 27.3% divorced; Foreign born: 0.0%; Speak English only: 100.0%; With disability: 0.0%; Veterans: 0.0%; Ancestry: 45.5% English, 27.3% German, 27.3% Irish, 21.2% French
Employment: 0.0% management, business, and financial, 0.0% computer, engineering, and science, 0.0% education, legal, community service, arts, and media, 0.0% healthcare practitioners, 36.0% service, 64.0% sales and office, 0.0% natural resources, construction, and maintenance, 0.0% production, transportation, and material moving
Income: Per capita: $26,342; Median household: $41,250; Average household: $34,004; Households with income of $100,000 or more: n/a; Poverty rate: n/a

Educational Attainment: High school diploma or higher: 100.0%; Bachelor's degree or higher: 45.5%; Graduate/professional degree or higher: 21.2%
Housing: Homeownership rate: 65.4%; Median home value: n/a; Median year structure built: 1996; Homeowner vacancy rate: 0.0%; Median selected monthly owner costs: n/a with a mortgage, n/a without a mortgage; Median gross rent: n/a per month; Rental vacancy rate: 0.0%
Health Insurance: 100.0% have insurance; 75.8% have private insurance; 51.5% have public insurance; 0.0% do not have insurance; 0.0% of children under 18 do not have insurance
Transportation: Commute: 100.0% car, 0.0% public transportation, 0.0% walk, 0.0% work from home; Mean travel time to work: 13.6 minutes

JALAPA (CDP). Covers a land area of 3.177 square miles and a water area of 0 square miles. Located at 40.63° N. Lat; 85.75° W. Long. Elevation is 817 feet.
Population: 248; Growth (since 2000): n/a; Density: 78.1 persons per square mile; Race: 100.0% White, 0.0% Black/African American, 0.0% Asian, 0.0% American Indian/Alaska Native, 0.0% Native Hawaiian/Other Pacific Islander, 0.0% Two or more races, 0.0% Hispanic of any race; Average household size: 2.36; Median age: 52.4; Age under 18: 0.0%; Age 65 and over: 0.0%; Males per 100 females: 92.1; Marriage status: 6.9% never married, 87.9% now married, 0.0% separated, 0.0% widowed, 5.2% divorced; Foreign born: 0.0%; Speak English only: 100.0%; With disability: 0.0%; Veterans: 0.0%; Ancestry: 21.0% American, 19.8% Irish, 3.6% British, 3.6% German
Employment: 8.0% management, business, and financial, 0.0% computer, engineering, and science, 7.6% education, legal, community service, arts, and media, 0.0% healthcare practitioners, 0.0% service, 4.0% sales and office, 7.6% natural resources, construction, and maintenance, 72.9% production, transportation, and material moving
Income: Per capita: $36,128; Median household: $74,519; Average household: $81,727; Households with income of $100,000 or more: 8.6%; Poverty rate: n/a
Educational Attainment: High school diploma or higher: 94.4%; Bachelor's degree or higher: n/a; Graduate/professional degree or higher: n/a
Housing: Homeownership rate: 100.0%; Median home value: $419,200; Median year structure built: 2000; Homeowner vacancy rate: 0.0%; Median selected monthly owner costs: n/a with a mortgage, $833 without a mortgage; Median gross rent: n/a per month; Rental vacancy rate: 0.0%
Health Insurance: 100.0% have insurance; 100.0% have private insurance; 0.0% have public insurance; 0.0% do not have insurance; 0.0% of children under 18 do not have insurance
Transportation: Commute: 100.0% car, 0.0% public transportation, 0.0% walk, 0.0% work from home; Mean travel time to work: 0.0 minutes

JONESBORO (city). Covers a land area of 0.891 square miles and a water area of 0 square miles. Located at 40.48° N. Lat; 85.63° W. Long. Elevation is 853 feet.
History: Jonesboro was founded in 1837 by Obadiah Jones. Its location on the Mississinewa River made it a trading center.
Population: 1,364; Growth (since 2000): -27.7%; Density: 1,531.4 persons per square mile; Race: 97.1% White, 0.9% Black/African American, 0.0% Asian, 0.0% American Indian/Alaska Native, 0.0% Native Hawaiian/Other Pacific Islander, 2.1% Two or more races, 2.1% Hispanic of any race; Average household size: 2.29; Median age: 44.4; Age under 18: 21.5%; Age 65 and over: 17.2%; Males per 100 females: 94.2; Marriage status: 22.9% never married, 48.4% now married, 2.8% separated, 11.3% widowed, 17.4% divorced; Foreign born: 0.5%; Speak English only: 97.9%; With disability: 19.2%; Veterans: 8.9%; Ancestry: 18.8% German, 10.8% Irish, 9.8% English, 8.3% American, 3.4% Dutch
Employment: 5.2% management, business, and financial, 3.3% computer, engineering, and science, 5.5% education, legal, community service, arts, and media, 8.6% healthcare practitioners, 16.3% service, 23.1% sales and office, 8.0% natural resources, construction, and maintenance, 30.1% production, transportation, and material moving
Income: Per capita: $19,998; Median household: $36,905; Average household: $45,189; Households with income of $100,000 or more: 5.9%; Poverty rate: 18.3%
Educational Attainment: High school diploma or higher: 82.7%; Bachelor's degree or higher: 11.7%; Graduate/professional degree or higher: 3.4%

School District(s)
Mississinewa Community School Corp (PK-12)
Enrollment: 1,948 . . . . (765) 674-8528
Housing: Homeownership rate: 76.0%; Median home value: $64,400; Median year structure built: 1954; Homeowner vacancy rate: 5.3%; Median selected monthly owner costs: $813 with a mortgage, $345 without a mortgage; Median gross rent: $743 per month; Rental vacancy rate: 9.0%
Health Insurance: 87.8% have insurance; 60.4% have private insurance; 42.7% have public insurance; 12.2% do not have insurance; 6.6% of children under 18 do not have insurance
Transportation: Commute: 98.8% car, 0.0% public transportation, 0.7% walk, 0.5% work from home; Mean travel time to work: 17.0 minutes

LANDESS (CDP). Covers a land area of 1.392 square miles and a water area of 0 square miles. Located at 40.61° N. Lat; 85.56° W. Long. Elevation is 869 feet.
Population: 102; Growth (since 2000): n/a; Density: 73.3 persons per square mile; Race: 100.0% White, 0.0% Black/African American, 0.0% Asian, 0.0% American Indian/Alaska Native, 0.0% Native Hawaiian/Other Pacific Islander, 0.0% Two or more races, 0.0% Hispanic of any race; Average household size: 2.55; Median age: 37.7; Age under 18: 28.4%; Age 65 and over: 7.8%; Males per 100 females: 126.5; Marriage status: 0.0% never married, 90.4% now married, 0.0% separated, 9.6% widowed, 0.0% divorced; Foreign born: 0.0%; Speak English only: 100.0%; With disability: 14.7%; Veterans: 11.0%; Ancestry: 35.3% Irish, 14.7% American, 9.8% English, 7.8% German
Employment: 0.0% management, business, and financial, 0.0% computer, engineering, and science, 16.0% education, legal, community service, arts, and media, 0.0% healthcare practitioners, 20.0% service, 30.0% sales and office, 14.0% natural resources, construction, and maintenance, 20.0% production, transportation, and material moving
Income: Per capita: $22,822; Median household: $50,938; Average household: $58,615; Households with income of $100,000 or more: 20.0%; Poverty rate: 6.9%
Educational Attainment: High school diploma or higher: 90.4%; Bachelor's degree or higher: 45.2%; Graduate/professional degree or higher: 24.7%
Housing: Homeownership rate: 100.0%; Median home value: $66,000; Median year structure built: 1965; Homeowner vacancy rate: 0.0%; Median selected monthly owner costs: $1,138 with a mortgage, n/a without a mortgage; Median gross rent: n/a per month; Rental vacancy rate: 0.0%
Health Insurance: 92.2% have insurance; 84.3% have private insurance; 7.8% have public insurance; 7.8% do not have insurance; 0.0% of children under 18 do not have insurance
Transportation: Commute: 100.0% car, 0.0% public transportation, 0.0% walk, 0.0% work from home; Mean travel time to work: 17.8 minutes

MARION (city). County seat. Covers a land area of 15.711 square miles and a water area of 0.084 square miles. Located at 40.55° N. Lat; 85.66° W. Long. Elevation is 814 feet.
History: The first settlers came to Marion in 1826. The town was laid out in 1831 and named for General Francis Marion, cavalry officer in the American Revolution. Marion grew rapidly when natural gas and oil were discovered here in the 1880's, but the boom was short-lived. Diversified industry replaced the oil wells.
Population: 28,490; Growth (since 2000): -9.0%; Density: 1,813.4 persons per square mile; Race: 77.6% White, 15.9% Black/African American, 1.4% Asian, 0.1% American Indian/Alaska Native, 0.0% Native Hawaiian/Other Pacific Islander, 4.0% Two or more races, 5.7% Hispanic of any race; Average household size: 2.26; Median age: 35.1; Age under 18: 20.1%; Age 65 and over: 16.7%; Males per 100 females: 88.8; Marriage status: 39.2% never married, 35.8% now married, 1.5% separated, 8.3% widowed, 16.7% divorced; Foreign born: 2.2%; Speak English only: 95.7%; With disability: 22.0%; Veterans: 7.4%; Ancestry: 20.4% German, 9.9% Irish, 9.1% American, 6.6% English, 2.0% Italian
Employment: 7.5% management, business, and financial, 1.3% computer, engineering, and science, 10.1% education, legal, community service, arts, and media, 5.4% healthcare practitioners, 28.6% service, 22.5% sales and office, 5.6% natural resources, construction, and maintenance, 19.1% production, transportation, and material moving
Income: Per capita: $17,631; Median household: $32,879; Average household: $43,029; Households with income of $100,000 or more: 6.5%; Poverty rate: 26.4%

Educational Attainment: High school diploma or higher: 82.9%; Bachelor's degree or higher: 14.2%; Graduate/professional degree or higher: 6.2%

School District(s)

Dr Robert H Faulkner Academy (KG-06)
Enrollment: 120 . . . . (765) 662-9910
Eastbrook Community Sch Corp (PK-12)
Enrollment: 1,415 . . . . (765) 664-0624
Marion Community Schools (PK-12)
Enrollment: 5,014 . . . . (765) 662-2546

Four-year College(s)

Indiana Wesleyan University-Marion (Private, Not-for-profit, Wesleyan)
Enrollment: 3,072 . . . . (765) 674-6901
Tuition: In-state $25,980; Out-of-state $25,980
Indiana Wesleyan University-National & Global (Private, Not-for-profit, Wesleyan)
Enrollment: 10,778 . . . . (765) 677-2870
Tuition: In-state $9,645; Out-of-state $9,645

Housing: Homeownership rate: 55.9%; Median home value: $65,400; Median year structure built: 1958; Homeowner vacancy rate: 4.7%; Median selected monthly owner costs: $764 with a mortgage, $296 without a mortgage; Median gross rent: $650 per month; Rental vacancy rate: 8.0%
Health Insurance: 87.1% have insurance; 53.6% have private insurance; 48.8% have public insurance; 12.9% do not have insurance; 5.0% of children under 18 do not have insurance
Hospitals: Marion General Hospital (191 beds); VA Northern Indiana Healthcare System - Marion
Safety: Violent crime rate: 34.2 per 10,000 population; Property crime rate: 372.4 per 10,000 population
Newspapers: Chronicle-Tribune (daily circulation 17,100)
Transportation: Commute: 83.2% car, 0.5% public transportation, 8.9% walk, 6.1% work from home; Mean travel time to work: 15.6 minutes
Airports: Marion Municipal (general aviation)
Additional Information Contacts
City of Marion . . . . (765) 662-9931
http://www.marionindiana.us

MATTHEWS (town). Covers a land area of 0.352 square miles and a water area of 0 square miles. Located at 40.39° N. Lat; 85.50° W. Long. Elevation is 879 feet.
History: Matthews was established in 1833 with a gristmill, sawmill, blacksmith shop, and general store.
Population: 645; Growth (since 2000): 8.4%; Density: 1,830.4 persons per square mile; Race: 100.0% White, 0.0% Black/African American, 0.0% Asian, 0.0% American Indian/Alaska Native, 0.0% Native Hawaiian/Other Pacific Islander, 0.0% Two or more races, 0.0% Hispanic of any race; Average household size: 2.48; Median age: 43.2; Age under 18: 21.4%; Age 65 and over: 17.2%; Males per 100 females: 95.4; Marriage status: 22.2% never married, 49.1% now married, 0.4% separated, 8.3% widowed, 20.5% divorced; Foreign born: 0.0%; Speak English only: 100.0%; With disability: 27.8%; Veterans: 7.3%; Ancestry: 26.8% German, 13.5% Irish, 8.7% English, 6.5% American, 6.4% Dutch
Employment: 2.4% management, business, and financial, 0.0% computer, engineering, and science, 4.9% education, legal, community service, arts, and media, 10.9% healthcare practitioners, 25.9% service, 14.2% sales and office, 4.5% natural resources, construction, and maintenance, 37.2% production, transportation, and material moving
Income: Per capita: $17,486; Median household: $42,000; Average household: $43,378; Households with income of $100,000 or more: 2.7%; Poverty rate: 20.8%
Educational Attainment: High school diploma or higher: 82.5%; Bachelor's degree or higher: 4.1%; Graduate/professional degree or higher: 0.6%
Housing: Homeownership rate: 74.6%; Median home value: $64,000; Median year structure built: 1954; Homeowner vacancy rate: 0.0%; Median selected monthly owner costs: $723 with a mortgage, $298 without a mortgage; Median gross rent: $539 per month; Rental vacancy rate: 0.0%
Health Insurance: 90.2% have insurance; 69.0% have private insurance; 36.3% have public insurance; 9.8% do not have insurance; 5.1% of children under 18 do not have insurance
Transportation: Commute: 100.0% car, 0.0% public transportation, 0.0% walk, 0.0% work from home; Mean travel time to work: 28.7 minutes

MIER (CDP). Covers a land area of 0.239 square miles and a water area of 0 square miles. Located at 40.57° N. Lat; 85.82° W. Long. Elevation is 823 feet.
Population: 78; Growth (since 2000): n/a; Density: 326.0 persons per square mile; Race: 100.0% White, 0.0% Black/African American, 0.0% Asian, 0.0% American Indian/Alaska Native, 0.0% Native Hawaiian/Other Pacific Islander, 0.0% Two or more races, 0.0% Hispanic of any race; Average household size: 1.73; Median age: 68.6; Age under 18: 0.0%; Age 65 and over: 61.5%; Males per 100 females: 129.4; Marriage status: 0.0% never married, 80.8% now married, 0.0% separated, 0.0% widowed, 19.2% divorced; Foreign born: 0.0%; Speak English only: 100.0%; With disability: 41.0%; Veterans: 20.5%; Ancestry: 61.5% German, 57.7% English, 19.2% Welsh
Employment: 100.0% management, business, and financial, 0.0% computer, engineering, and science, 0.0% education, legal, community service, arts, and media, 0.0% healthcare practitioners, 0.0% service, 0.0% sales and office, 0.0% natural resources, construction, and maintenance, 0.0% production, transportation, and material moving
Income: Per capita: $40,568; Median household: $63,750; Average household: $66,967; Households with income of $100,000 or more: n/a; Poverty rate: n/a
Educational Attainment: High school diploma or higher: 100.0%; Bachelor's degree or higher: 39.7%; Graduate/professional degree or higher: 39.7%
Housing: Homeownership rate: 66.7%; Median home value: n/a; Median year structure built: Before 1940; Homeowner vacancy rate: 0.0%; Median selected monthly owner costs: n/a with a mortgage, n/a without a mortgage; Median gross rent: n/a per month; Rental vacancy rate: 0.0%
Health Insurance: 100.0% have insurance; 80.8% have private insurance; 61.5% have public insurance; 0.0% do not have insurance; 0.0% of children under 18 do not have insurance
Transportation: Commute: 100.0% car, 0.0% public transportation, 0.0% walk, 0.0% work from home; Mean travel time to work: 0.0 minutes

POINT ISABEL (CDP). Covers a land area of 3.401 square miles and a water area of 0 square miles. Located at 40.42° N. Lat; 85.82° W. Long. Elevation is 883 feet.
Population: 95; Growth (since 2000): n/a; Density: 27.9 persons per square mile; Race: 100.0% White, 0.0% Black/African American, 0.0% Asian, 0.0% American Indian/Alaska Native, 0.0% Native Hawaiian/Other Pacific Islander, 0.0% Two or more races, 0.0% Hispanic of any race; Average household size: 2.79; Median age: 51.8; Age under 18: 0.0%; Age 65 and over: 27.4%; Males per 100 females: 97.8; Marriage status: 26.3% never married, 55.8% now married, 0.0% separated, 8.4% widowed, 9.5% divorced; Foreign born: 0.0%; Speak English only: 100.0%; With disability: 27.4%; Veterans: 12.6%; Ancestry: 49.5% German, 40.0% American, 28.4% Irish, 22.1% English, 9.5% Italian
Employment: 0.0% management, business, and financial, 0.0% computer, engineering, and science, 0.0% education, legal, community service, arts, and media, 0.0% healthcare practitioners, 0.0% service, 0.0% sales and office, 66.7% natural resources, construction, and maintenance, 33.3% production, transportation, and material moving
Income: Per capita: $25,592; Median household: n/a; Average household: $69,582; Households with income of $100,000 or more: 26.5%; Poverty rate: n/a
Educational Attainment: High school diploma or higher: 100.0%; Bachelor's degree or higher: 11.0%; Graduate/professional degree or higher: n/a
Housing: Homeownership rate: 100.0%; Median home value: $108,000; Median year structure built: Before 1940; Homeowner vacancy rate: 0.0%; Median selected monthly owner costs: n/a with a mortgage, n/a without a mortgage; Median gross rent: n/a per month; Rental vacancy rate: 0.0%
Health Insurance: 100.0% have insurance; 60.0% have private insurance; 40.0% have public insurance; 0.0% do not have insurance; 0.0% of children under 18 do not have insurance
Transportation: Commute: 100.0% car, 0.0% public transportation, 0.0% walk, 0.0% work from home; Mean travel time to work: 17.4 minutes

SIMS (CDP). Covers a land area of 0.998 square miles and a water area of 0 square miles. Located at 40.50° N. Lat; 85.85° W. Long. Elevation is 860 feet.
Population: 166; Growth (since 2000): n/a; Density: 166.4 persons per square mile; Race: 100.0% White, 0.0% Black/African American, 0.0% Asian, 0.0% American Indian/Alaska Native, 0.0% Native Hawaiian/Other Pacific Islander, 0.0% Two or more races, 9.6% Hispanic of any race;

Average household size: 2.05; Median age: 44.6; Age under 18: 12.7%; Age 65 and over: 0.0%; Males per 100 females: 113.7; Marriage status: 20.0% never married, 47.6% now married, 0.0% separated, 25.5% widowed, 6.9% divorced; Foreign born: 0.0%; Speak English only: 100.0%; With disability: 31.9%; Veterans: 6.2%; Ancestry: 19.9% American, 6.0% German, 5.4% English, 5.4% Scotch-Irish
Employment: 0.0% management, business, and financial, 0.0% computer, engineering, and science, 0.0% education, legal, community service, arts, and media, 29.1% healthcare practitioners, 41.8% service, 14.5% sales and office, 0.0% natural resources, construction, and maintenance, 14.5% production, transportation, and material moving
Income: Per capita: $16,670; Median household: n/a; Average household: $31,080; Households with income of $100,000 or more: n/a; Poverty rate: 23.9%
Educational Attainment: High school diploma or higher: 100.0%; Bachelor's degree or higher: 7.8%; Graduate/professional degree or higher: 7.8%
Housing: Homeownership rate: 54.3%; Median home value: n/a; Median year structure built: 1976; Homeowner vacancy rate: 0.0%; Median selected monthly owner costs: $1,234 with a mortgage, n/a without a mortgage; Median gross rent: n/a per month; Rental vacancy rate: 0.0%
Health Insurance: 94.0% have insurance; 51.8% have private insurance; 47.0% have public insurance; 6.0% do not have insurance; 0.0% of children under 18 do not have insurance
Transportation: Commute: 81.8% car, 0.0% public transportation, 0.0% walk, 0.0% work from home; Mean travel time to work: 0.0 minutes

SWAYZEE (town). Covers a land area of 0.469 square miles and a water area of 0 square miles. Located at 40.51° N. Lat; 85.82° W. Long. Elevation is 863 feet.
Population: 953; Growth (since 2000): -5.7%; Density: 2,033.7 persons per square mile; Race: 95.3% White, 1.5% Black/African American, 0.5% Asian, 2.3% American Indian/Alaska Native, 0.0% Native Hawaiian/Other Pacific Islander, 0.4% Two or more races, 0.3% Hispanic of any race; Average household size: 2.35; Median age: 41.5; Age under 18: 25.2%; Age 65 and over: 22.7%; Males per 100 females: 94.6; Marriage status: 13.4% never married, 68.2% now married, 0.8% separated, 7.1% widowed, 11.3% divorced; Foreign born: 1.0%; Speak English only: 98.3%; With disability: 15.4%; Veterans: 11.1%; Ancestry: 23.0% German, 12.1% Irish, 10.9% American, 10.7% English, 2.7% European
Employment: 11.8% management, business, and financial, 1.3% computer, engineering, and science, 12.8% education, legal, community service, arts, and media, 8.7% healthcare practitioners, 12.6% service, 22.8% sales and office, 12.3% natural resources, construction, and maintenance, 17.7% production, transportation, and material moving
Income: Per capita: $23,740; Median household: $51,458; Average household: $56,420; Households with income of $100,000 or more: 14.5%; Poverty rate: 5.7%
Educational Attainment: High school diploma or higher: 92.2%; Bachelor's degree or higher: 20.1%; Graduate/professional degree or higher: 8.8%

School District(s)

Oak Hill United School Corp (PK-12)
Enrollment: 1,304 . . . . (765) 395-3341
Housing: Homeownership rate: 88.2%; Median home value: $86,300; Median year structure built: 1953; Homeowner vacancy rate: 4.8%; Median selected monthly owner costs: $932 with a mortgage, $324 without a mortgage; Median gross rent: $738 per month; Rental vacancy rate: 12.5%
Health Insurance: 92.1% have insurance; 74.7% have private insurance; 37.7% have public insurance; 7.9% do not have insurance; 5.5% of children under 18 do not have insurance
Transportation: Commute: 97.1% car, 0.0% public transportation, 0.0% walk, 2.9% work from home; Mean travel time to work: 24.6 minutes

SWEETSER (town). Covers a land area of 1.014 square miles and a water area of 0.003 square miles. Located at 40.57° N. Lat; 85.77° W. Long. Elevation is 850 feet.
History: Laid out 1871.
Population: 1,412; Growth (since 2000): 55.8%; Density: 1,392.0 persons per square mile; Race: 97.9% White, 0.6% Black/African American, 0.0% Asian, 0.0% American Indian/Alaska Native, 0.0% Native Hawaiian/Other Pacific Islander, 1.4% Two or more races, 10.1% Hispanic of any race; Average household size: 2.36; Median age: 42.0; Age under 18: 23.0%; Age 65 and over: 20.7%; Males per 100 females: 91.1; Marriage status: 19.7% never married, 58.6% now married, 1.2% separated, 7.8% widowed, 13.9% divorced; Foreign born: 0.3%; Speak English only: 96.4%; With disability: 11.2%; Veterans: 9.5%; Ancestry: 19.5% German, 13.5% English, 10.1% American, 8.9% Irish, 3.8% Italian
Employment: 16.6% management, business, and financial, 0.5% computer, engineering, and science, 6.8% education, legal, community service, arts, and media, 7.7% healthcare practitioners, 17.7% service, 18.6% sales and office, 7.1% natural resources, construction, and maintenance, 25.1% production, transportation, and material moving
Income: Per capita: $25,512; Median household: $55,337; Average household: $59,984; Households with income of $100,000 or more: 15.0%; Poverty rate: 12.3%
Educational Attainment: High school diploma or higher: 93.2%; Bachelor's degree or higher: 18.2%; Graduate/professional degree or higher: 5.1%

School District(s)

Oak Hill United School Corp (PK-12)
Enrollment: 1,304 . . . . (765) 395-3341
Housing: Homeownership rate: 78.0%; Median home value: $104,700; Median year structure built: 1972; Homeowner vacancy rate: 1.1%; Median selected monthly owner costs: $932 with a mortgage, $353 without a mortgage; Median gross rent: $693 per month; Rental vacancy rate: 0.0%
Health Insurance: 92.5% have insurance; 74.9% have private insurance; 36.5% have public insurance; 7.5% do not have insurance; 3.7% of children under 18 do not have insurance
Transportation: Commute: 98.4% car, 0.0% public transportation, 0.0% walk, 0.6% work from home; Mean travel time to work: 19.7 minutes

UPLAND (town). Covers a land area of 3.138 square miles and a water area of 0.012 square miles. Located at 40.46° N. Lat; 85.50° W. Long. Elevation is 935 feet.
History: Upland was laid out in 1867 when the railroad arrived and a sawmill was built. Many of the early settlers were Quakers.
Population: 3,642; Growth (since 2000): -4.2%; Density: 1,160.6 persons per square mile; Race: 93.7% White, 1.0% Black/African American, 2.1% Asian, 0.8% American Indian/Alaska Native, 0.0% Native Hawaiian/Other Pacific Islander, 1.9% Two or more races, 0.9% Hispanic of any race; Average household size: 2.56; Median age: 22.2; Age under 18: 14.1%; Age 65 and over: 10.3%; Males per 100 females: 91.2; Marriage status: 57.4% never married, 32.9% now married, 0.2% separated, 5.0% widowed, 4.7% divorced; Foreign born: 3.4%; Speak English only: 95.8%; With disability: 8.5%; Veterans: 3.1%; Ancestry: 28.4% German, 13.0% Irish, 11.3% English, 5.0% Dutch, 3.8% American
Employment: 13.0% management, business, and financial, 8.1% computer, engineering, and science, 25.1% education, legal, community service, arts, and media, 2.3% healthcare practitioners, 15.9% service, 24.7% sales and office, 2.5% natural resources, construction, and maintenance, 8.3% production, transportation, and material moving
Income: Per capita: $20,470; Median household: $57,500; Average household: $77,192; Households with income of $100,000 or more: 20.9%; Poverty rate: 17.3%
Educational Attainment: High school diploma or higher: 95.3%; Bachelor's degree or higher: 50.7%; Graduate/professional degree or higher: 28.7%

School District(s)

Eastbrook Community Sch Corp (PK-12)
Enrollment: 1,415 . . . . (765) 664-0624

Four-year College(s)

Taylor University (Private, Not-for-profit, Interdenominational)
Enrollment: 2,145 . . . . (765) 998-2751
Tuition: In-state $32,885; Out-of-state $32,885
Housing: Homeownership rate: 61.8%; Median home value: $132,800; Median year structure built: 1974; Homeowner vacancy rate: 7.6%; Median selected monthly owner costs: $1,131 with a mortgage, $379 without a mortgage; Median gross rent: $632 per month; Rental vacancy rate: 4.0%
Health Insurance: 96.4% have insurance; 87.8% have private insurance; 19.8% have public insurance; 3.6% do not have insurance; 1.3% of children under 18 do not have insurance
Transportation: Commute: 63.3% car, 1.0% public transportation, 13.0% walk, 19.4% work from home; Mean travel time to work: 13.0 minutes
Additional Information Contacts
Town of Upland . . . . (765) 998-7439
http://upland.in.gov

VAN BUREN (town). Covers a land area of 0.584 square miles and a water area of 0 square miles. Located at 40.62° N. Lat; 85.50° W. Long. Elevation is 850 feet.

Population: 834; Growth (since 2000): -10.8%; Density: 1,428.5 persons per square mile; Race: 98.9% White, 0.0% Black/African American, 0.0% Asian, 0.6% American Indian/Alaska Native, 0.0% Native Hawaiian/Other Pacific Islander, 0.5% Two or more races, 0.0% Hispanic of any race; Average household size: 2.47; Median age: 41.7; Age under 18: 19.9%; Age 65 and over: 19.7%; Males per 100 females: 88.6; Marriage status: 27.3% never married, 43.3% now married, 0.5% separated, 7.1% widowed, 22.3% divorced; Foreign born: 0.0%; Speak English only: 99.8%; With disability: 20.9%; Veterans: 11.8%; Ancestry: 18.2% German, 11.8% Irish, 10.9% American, 10.1% English, 2.6% Scottish

Employment: 8.2% management, business, and financial, 1.3% computer, engineering, and science, 4.3% education, legal, community service, arts, and media, 7.2% healthcare practitioners, 22.3% service, 24.0% sales and office, 8.2% natural resources, construction, and maintenance, 24.6% production, transportation, and material moving

Income: Per capita: $20,771; Median household: $43,839; Average household: $50,655; Households with income of $100,000 or more: 6.9%; Poverty rate: 19.5%

Educational Attainment: High school diploma or higher: 88.3%; Bachelor's degree or higher: 12.4%; Graduate/professional degree or higher: 4.7%

School District(s)

Eastbrook Community Sch Corp (PK-12)
Enrollment: 1,415 . . . . (765) 664-0624

Housing: Homeownership rate: 69.7%; Median home value: $62,400; Median year structure built: 1955; Homeowner vacancy rate: 8.9%; Median selected monthly owner costs: $756 with a mortgage, $346 without a mortgage; Median gross rent: $725 per month; Rental vacancy rate: 0.0%

Health Insurance: 85.7% have insurance; 60.2% have private insurance; 44.0% have public insurance; 14.3% do not have insurance; 3.6% of children under 18 do not have insurance

Transportation: Commute: 94.5% car, 0.0% public transportation, 1.6% walk, 1.3% work from home; Mean travel time to work: 22.4 minutes

Greene County

Located in southwestern Indiana; drained by the West Fork of White River and the Eel River. Covers a land area of 542.495 square miles, a water area of 3.423 square miles, and is located in the Eastern Time Zone at 39.05° N. Lat., 87.01° W. Long. The county was founded in 1821. County seat is Bloomfield.

Population: 32,431; Growth (since 2000): -2.2%; Density: 59.8 persons per square mile; Race: 97.9% White, 0.3% Black/African American, 0.4% Asian, 0.0% American Indian/Alaska Native, 0.0% Native Hawaiian/Other Pacific Islander, 1.2% two or more races, 1.3% Hispanic of any race; Average household size: 2.54; Median age: 42.8; Age under 18: 22.4%; Age 65 and over: 18.5%; Males per 100 females: 99.7; Marriage status: 21.1% never married, 55.9% now married, 1.3% separated, 7.5% widowed, 15.4% divorced; Foreign born: 0.5%; Speak English only: 98.7%; With disability: 18.4%; Veterans: 8.3%; Ancestry: 20.4% German, 13.6% Irish, 12.3% American, 10.7% English, 3.0% Dutch

Religion: Six largest groups: 14.2% Baptist, 6.6% Non-denominational Protestant, 4.7% Methodist/Pietist, 4.1% Pentecostal, 2.6% Presbyterian-Reformed, 2.2% Catholicism

Economy: Unemployment rate: 4.9%; Leading industries: 16.8 % retail trade; 14.7 % other services (except public administration); 11.9 % construction; Farms: 810 totaling 181,086 acres; Company size: 0 employ 1,000 or more persons, 0 employ 500 to 999 persons, 4 employ 100 to 499 persons, 560 employ less than 100 persons; Business ownership: 624 women-owned, 28 Black-owned, 44 Hispanic-owned, n/a Asian-owned, n/a American Indian/Alaska Native-owned

Employment: 12.7% management, business, and financial, 4.9% computer, engineering, and science, 6.4% education, legal, community service, arts, and media, 5.2% healthcare practitioners, 18.7% service, 22.4% sales and office, 12.2% natural resources, construction, and maintenance, 17.4% production, transportation, and material moving

Income: Per capita: $24,744; Median household: $49,648; Average household: $60,655; Households with income of $100,000 or more: 14.1%; Poverty rate: 12.9%

Educational Attainment: High school diploma or higher: 87.0%; Bachelor's degree or higher: 14.5%; Graduate/professional degree or higher: 5.2%

Housing: Homeownership rate: 79.7%; Median home value: $95,900; Median year structure built: 1976; Homeowner vacancy rate: 3.3%; Median selected monthly owner costs: $997 with a mortgage, $385 without a mortgage; Median gross rent: $604 per month; Rental vacancy rate: 9.5%

Vital Statistics: Birth rate: 102.6 per 10,000 population; Death rate: 126.5 per 10,000 population; Age-adjusted cancer mortality rate: 218.4 deaths per 100,000 population

Health Insurance: 90.1% have insurance; 70.2% have private insurance; 36.8% have public insurance; 9.9% do not have insurance; 5.2% of children under 18 do not have insurance

Health Care: Physicians: 5.9 per 10,000 population; Dentists: 4.4 per 10,000 population; Hospital beds: 17.7 per 10,000 population; Hospital admissions: 684.3 per 10,000 population

Air Quality Index (AQI): Percent of Days: 82.3% good, 17.4% moderate, 0.4% unhealthy for sensitive individuals, 0.0% unhealthy, 0.0% very unhealthy; Annual median: 42; Annual maximum: 101

Transportation: Commute: 96.8% car, 0.1% public transportation, 1.4% walk, 0.7% work from home; Mean travel time to work: 28.7 minutes

2016 Presidential Election: 74.1% Trump, 21.1% Clinton, 4.0% Johnson, 0.3% Stein

Additional Information Contacts

Greene Government . . . . (812) 384-8532
http://www.co.greene.in.us

Greene County Communities

BLOOMFIELD (town). County seat. Covers a land area of 1.377 square miles and a water area of 0 square miles. Located at 39.03° N. Lat; 86.94° W. Long. Elevation is 607 feet.

Population: 2,327; Growth (since 2000): -8.5%; Density: 1,689.9 persons per square mile; Race: 94.8% White, 0.3% Black/African American, 0.0% Asian, 0.0% American Indian/Alaska Native, 0.0% Native Hawaiian/Other Pacific Islander, 4.6% Two or more races, 4.4% Hispanic of any race; Average household size: 2.22; Median age: 45.2; Age under 18: 23.0%; Age 65 and over: 21.1%; Males per 100 females: 88.2; Marriage status: 26.1% never married, 38.0% now married, 0.6% separated, 9.9% widowed, 26.0% divorced; Foreign born: 0.3%; Speak English only: 99.0%; With disability: 19.5%; Veterans: 10.0%; Ancestry: 19.1% Irish, 18.1% German, 13.7% English, 11.0% American, 4.1% Scottish

Employment: 17.6% management, business, and financial, 9.7% computer, engineering, and science, 6.4% education, legal, community service, arts, and media, 1.7% healthcare practitioners, 19.6% service, 22.8% sales and office, 8.9% natural resources, construction, and maintenance, 13.3% production, transportation, and material moving

Income: Per capita: $22,636; Median household: $35,746; Average household: $48,216; Households with income of $100,000 or more: 9.5%; Poverty rate: 17.4%

Educational Attainment: High school diploma or higher: 81.4%; Bachelor's degree or higher: 13.0%; Graduate/professional degree or higher: 3.2%

School District(s)

Bloomfield School District (PK-12)
Enrollment: 883 . . . . (812) 384-4507

Eastern Greene Schools (PK-12)
Enrollment: 1,197 . . . . (812) 825-5722

Housing: Homeownership rate: 62.0%; Median home value: $80,900; Median year structure built: 1959; Homeowner vacancy rate: 3.9%; Median selected monthly owner costs: $903 with a mortgage, $317 without a mortgage; Median gross rent: $463 per month; Rental vacancy rate: 11.6%

Health Insurance: 89.1% have insurance; 60.9% have private insurance; 44.2% have public insurance; 10.9% do not have insurance; 6.1% of children under 18 do not have insurance

Transportation: Commute: 96.9% car, 0.0% public transportation, 1.3% walk, 1.4% work from home; Mean travel time to work: 26.3 minutes

Additional Information Contacts

Town of Bloomfield . . . . (812) 384-4378
http://www.bloomfieldin.com

JASONVILLE (city). Covers a land area of 1.309 square miles and a water area of <.001 square miles. Located at 39.16° N. Lat; 87.20° W. Long. Elevation is 633 feet.

History: Laid out 1859.

Population: 1,851; Growth (since 2000): -25.7%; Density: 1,413.9 persons per square mile; Race: 100.0% White, 0.0% Black/African American, 0.0% Asian, 0.0% American Indian/Alaska Native, 0.0% Native Hawaiian/Other Pacific Islander, 0.0% Two or more races, 5.0% Hispanic of any race; Average household size: 2.78; Median age: 35.6; Age under 18: 26.5%; Age 65 and over: 17.6%; Males per 100 females: 90.2; Marriage status: 23.0% never married, 51.4% now married, 3.3% separated, 8.4% widowed, 17.3% divorced; Foreign born: 0.6%; Speak English only: 100.0%; With disability: 18.8%; Veterans: 8.1%; Ancestry: 14.0% German, 13.2% English, 12.0% American, 7.5% Irish, 2.5% French
Employment: 6.2% management, business, and financial, 3.1% computer, engineering, and science, 8.3% education, legal, community service, arts, and media, 7.1% healthcare practitioners, 20.3% service, 17.5% sales and office, 11.1% natural resources, construction, and maintenance, 26.5% production, transportation, and material moving
Income: Per capita: $17,135; Median household: $32,215; Average household: $43,885; Households with income of $100,000 or more: 3.9%; Poverty rate: 19.5%
Educational Attainment: High school diploma or higher: 82.5%; Bachelor's degree or higher: 10.6%; Graduate/professional degree or higher: 3.8%

School District(s)

M S D Shakamak Schools (PK-12)
Enrollment: 847 . . . . (812) 665-3550
Housing: Homeownership rate: 65.6%; Median home value: $45,300; Median year structure built: 1971; Homeowner vacancy rate: 2.4%; Median selected monthly owner costs: $769 with a mortgage, $276 without a mortgage; Median gross rent: $592 per month; Rental vacancy rate: 10.1%
Health Insurance: 92.8% have insurance; 68.4% have private insurance; 38.5% have public insurance; 7.2% do not have insurance; 0.8% of children under 18 do not have insurance
Transportation: Commute: 95.1% car, 0.0% public transportation, 3.7% walk, 0.0% work from home; Mean travel time to work: 29.8 minutes
Additional Information Contacts
City of Jasonville . . . . (812) 665-3622
http://www.gojasonville.com/Home/contact-us-city-public-offices.php

LINTON (city). Covers a land area of 3.022 square miles and a water area of 0 square miles. Located at 39.04° N. Lat; 87.16° W. Long. Elevation is 531 feet.
History: Linton developed as a coal-mining town.
Population: 5,288; Growth (since 2000): -8.4%; Density: 1,750.1 persons per square mile; Race: 98.0% White, 0.7% Black/African American, 0.0% Asian, 0.0% American Indian/Alaska Native, 0.3% Native Hawaiian/Other Pacific Islander, 1.1% Two or more races, 1.0% Hispanic of any race; Average household size: 2.33; Median age: 42.6; Age under 18: 21.7%; Age 65 and over: 20.3%; Males per 100 females: 91.1; Marriage status: 22.6% never married, 50.3% now married, 1.1% separated, 10.3% widowed, 16.7% divorced; Foreign born: 0.3%; Speak English only: 98.7%; With disability: 22.2%; Veterans: 7.7%; Ancestry: 22.0% German, 15.0% Irish, 11.4% American, 10.8% English, 8.8% Dutch
Employment: 12.6% management, business, and financial, 3.2% computer, engineering, and science, 7.5% education, legal, community service, arts, and media, 6.1% healthcare practitioners, 19.9% service, 20.3% sales and office, 11.8% natural resources, construction, and maintenance, 18.7% production, transportation, and material moving
Income: Per capita: $20,716; Median household: $39,317; Average household: $46,294; Households with income of $100,000 or more: 8.1%; Poverty rate: 18.6%
Educational Attainment: High school diploma or higher: 82.7%; Bachelor's degree or higher: 15.7%; Graduate/professional degree or higher: 5.7%

School District(s)

Greene-Sullivan Sp Ed Coop (KG-12)
Enrollment: n/a . . . . (812) 847-8497
Linton-Stockton School Corporation (PK-12)
Enrollment: 1,227 . . . . (812) 847-6020
Housing: Homeownership rate: 68.1%; Median home value: $65,700; Median year structure built: 1964; Homeowner vacancy rate: 2.3%; Median selected monthly owner costs: $940 with a mortgage, $353 without a mortgage; Median gross rent: $651 per month; Rental vacancy rate: 12.3%
Health Insurance: 85.6% have insurance; 60.7% have private insurance; 41.1% have public insurance; 14.4% do not have insurance; 5.6% of children under 18 do not have insurance
Hospitals: Greene County General Hospital (76 beds)
Safety: Violent crime rate: 7.7 per 10,000 population; Property crime rate: 281.6 per 10,000 population
Newspapers: Greene Co. Daily World (daily circulation 3,000)
Transportation: Commute: 95.9% car, 0.1% public transportation, 0.8% walk, 0.9% work from home; Mean travel time to work: 23.8 minutes
Additional Information Contacts
City of Linton . . . . (812) 847-4846
http://www.lintonchamber.org

LYONS (town). Covers a land area of 0.866 square miles and a water area of 0 square miles. Located at 38.99° N. Lat; 87.08° W. Long. Elevation is 531 feet.
Population: 674; Growth (since 2000): -9.9%; Density: 777.9 persons per square mile; Race: 95.1% White, 2.2% Black/African American, 1.2% Asian, 0.0% American Indian/Alaska Native, 0.0% Native Hawaiian/Other Pacific Islander, 0.0% Two or more races, 5.3% Hispanic of any race; Average household size: 2.58; Median age: 43.4; Age under 18: 18.2%; Age 65 and over: 26.1%; Males per 100 females: 96.8; Marriage status: 26.5% never married, 49.7% now married, 3.8% separated, 9.1% widowed, 14.7% divorced; Foreign born: 1.2%; Speak English only: 97.6%; With disability: 19.0%; Veterans: 9.1%; Ancestry: 17.1% German, 11.7% American, 8.5% Irish, 7.4% English, 2.8% European
Employment: 12.1% management, business, and financial, 4.2% computer, engineering, and science, 4.6% education, legal, community service, arts, and media, 4.2% healthcare practitioners, 29.2% service, 10.8% sales and office, 20.4% natural resources, construction, and maintenance, 14.6% production, transportation, and material moving
Income: Per capita: $18,905; Median household: $40,833; Average household: $48,115; Households with income of $100,000 or more: 8.4%; Poverty rate: 31.7%
Educational Attainment: High school diploma or higher: 80.7%; Bachelor's degree or higher: 7.8%; Graduate/professional degree or higher: 2.8%

School District(s)

White River Valley School District (PK-12)
Enrollment: 918 . . . . (812) 659-1424
Housing: Homeownership rate: 68.6%; Median home value: $62,000; Median year structure built: 1974; Homeowner vacancy rate: 7.2%; Median selected monthly owner costs: $855 with a mortgage, $287 without a mortgage; Median gross rent: $656 per month; Rental vacancy rate: 3.3%
Health Insurance: 85.4% have insurance; 60.6% have private insurance; 41.5% have public insurance; 14.6% do not have insurance; 26.1% of children under 18 do not have insurance
Transportation: Commute: 88.5% car, 1.3% public transportation, 10.2% walk, 0.0% work from home; Mean travel time to work: 21.6 minutes

NEWBERRY (town). Covers a land area of 0.493 square miles and a water area of 0 square miles. Located at 38.92° N. Lat; 87.02° W. Long. Elevation is 548 feet.
History: Laid out 1822.
Population: 188; Growth (since 2000): -8.7%; Density: 381.4 persons per square mile; Race: 92.0% White, 0.0% Black/African American, 0.0% Asian, 2.7% American Indian/Alaska Native, 0.0% Native Hawaiian/Other Pacific Islander, 5.3% Two or more races, 0.5% Hispanic of any race; Average household size: 2.65; Median age: 41.2; Age under 18: 24.5%; Age 65 and over: 23.9%; Males per 100 females: 96.9; Marriage status: 11.3% never married, 66.2% now married, 1.4% separated, 7.7% widowed, 14.8% divorced; Foreign born: 0.0%; Speak English only: 98.8%; With disability: 19.7%; Veterans: 2.1%; Ancestry: 37.2% German, 10.1% Irish, 8.0% American, 5.3% Scottish, 4.8% English
Employment: 19.2% management, business, and financial, 2.6% computer, engineering, and science, 2.6% education, legal, community service, arts, and media, 0.0% healthcare practitioners, 20.5% service, 7.7% sales and office, 37.2% natural resources, construction, and maintenance, 10.3% production, transportation, and material moving
Income: Per capita: $19,149; Median household: $45,938; Average household: $47,238; Households with income of $100,000 or more: 12.7%; Poverty rate: 16.0%
Educational Attainment: High school diploma or higher: 81.7%; Bachelor's degree or higher: 3.3%; Graduate/professional degree or higher: 1.7%
Housing: Homeownership rate: 90.1%; Median home value: $64,000; Median year structure built: 1954; Homeowner vacancy rate: 0.0%; Median selected monthly owner costs: $729 with a mortgage, $220 without a mortgage; Median gross rent: $494 per month; Rental vacancy rate: 0.0%

Health Insurance: 92.0% have insurance; 69.1% have private insurance; 51.1% have public insurance; 8.0% do not have insurance; 14.3% of children under 18 do not have insurance
Transportation: Commute: 98.7% car, 0.0% public transportation, 0.0% walk, 0.0% work from home; Mean travel time to work: 25.6 minutes

OWENSBURG (CDP). Covers a land area of 5.919 square miles and a water area of 0.008 square miles. Located at 38.93° N. Lat; 86.72° W. Long. Elevation is 643 feet.
Population: 536; Growth (since 2000): n/a; Density: 90.5 persons per square mile; Race: 98.5% White, 0.0% Black/African American, 0.0% Asian, 0.0% American Indian/Alaska Native, 0.0% Native Hawaiian/Other Pacific Islander, 1.5% Two or more races, 0.0% Hispanic of any race; Average household size: 2.78; Median age: 36.6; Age under 18: 26.3%; Age 65 and over: 16.6%; Males per 100 females: 116.0; Marriage status: 10.6% never married, 81.8% now married, 0.0% separated, 5.4% widowed, 2.1% divorced; Foreign born: 0.0%; Speak English only: 100.0%; With disability: 12.7%; Veterans: 12.4%; Ancestry: 23.9% German, 16.6% English, 16.0% Irish, 8.0% American, 7.1% Lithuanian
Employment: 23.4% management, business, and financial, 0.0% computer, engineering, and science, 5.8% education, legal, community service, arts, and media, 13.0% healthcare practitioners, 14.9% service, 19.5% sales and office, 7.1% natural resources, construction, and maintenance, 16.2% production, transportation, and material moving
Income: Per capita: $18,860; Median household: $38,750; Average household: $51,937; Households with income of $100,000 or more: 9.8%; Poverty rate: 8.0%
Educational Attainment: High school diploma or higher: 88.9%; Bachelor's degree or higher: 12.4%; Graduate/professional degree or higher: n/a
Housing: Homeownership rate: 88.6%; Median home value: $74,700; Median year structure built: 1982; Homeowner vacancy rate: 0.0%; Median selected monthly owner costs: $1,164 with a mortgage, $291 without a mortgage; Median gross rent: n/a per month; Rental vacancy rate: 0.0%
Health Insurance: 96.8% have insurance; 81.2% have private insurance; 38.2% have public insurance; 3.2% do not have insurance; 0.0% of children under 18 do not have insurance
Transportation: Commute: 100.0% car, 0.0% public transportation, 0.0% walk, 0.0% work from home; Mean travel time to work: 32.9 minutes

SCOTLAND (CDP). Covers a land area of 0.576 square miles and a water area of 0 square miles. Located at 38.91° N. Lat; 86.90° W. Long. Elevation is 614 feet.
Population: 146; Growth (since 2000): n/a; Density: 253.3 persons per square mile; Race: 79.5% White, 0.0% Black/African American, 7.5% Asian, 0.0% American Indian/Alaska Native, 0.0% Native Hawaiian/Other Pacific Islander, 13.0% Two or more races, 0.0% Hispanic of any race; Average household size: 2.70; Median age: 39.3; Age under 18: 42.5%; Age 65 and over: 6.2%; Males per 100 females: 94.2; Marriage status: 27.0% never married, 51.3% now married, 0.0% separated, 0.0% widowed, 21.7% divorced; Foreign born: 7.5%; Speak English only: 92.5%; With disability: 6.8%; Veterans: 22.6%; Ancestry: 26.0% English, 6.2% French
Employment: 15.8% management, business, and financial, 0.0% computer, engineering, and science, 0.0% education, legal, community service, arts, and media, 0.0% healthcare practitioners, 12.3% service, 19.3% sales and office, 15.8% natural resources, construction, and maintenance, 36.8% production, transportation, and material moving
Income: Per capita: $24,588; Median household: $52,778; Average household: $66,046; Households with income of $100,000 or more: 35.2%; Poverty rate: n/a
Educational Attainment: High school diploma or higher: 100.0%; Bachelor's degree or higher: 10.7%; Graduate/professional degree or higher: n/a
Housing: Homeownership rate: 81.5%; Median home value: $72,100; Median year structure built: 1954; Homeowner vacancy rate: 0.0%; Median selected monthly owner costs: $805 with a mortgage, n/a without a mortgage; Median gross rent: n/a per month; Rental vacancy rate: 0.0%
Health Insurance: 95.2% have insurance; 74.0% have private insurance; 34.9% have public insurance; 4.8% do not have insurance; 0.0% of children under 18 do not have insurance
Transportation: Commute: 100.0% car, 0.0% public transportation, 0.0% walk, 0.0% work from home; Mean travel time to work: 0.0 minutes

SOLSBERRY (unincorporated postal area)
ZCTA: 47459
Covers a land area of 58.367 square miles and a water area of 0 square miles. Located at 39.11° N. Lat; 86.75° W. Long. Elevation is 778 feet.
Population: 4,070; Growth (since 2000): 17.1%; Density: 69.7 persons per square mile; Race: 99.8% White, 0.2% Black/African American, 0.0% Asian, 0.0% American Indian/Alaska Native, 0.0% Native Hawaiian/Other Pacific Islander, 0.0% Two or more races, 0.0% Hispanic of any race; Average household size: 2.83; Median age: 39.2; Age under 18: 27.4%; Age 65 and over: 12.6%; Males per 100 females: 101.5; Marriage status: 19.7% never married, 62.4% now married, 1.3% separated, 5.0% widowed, 13.0% divorced; Foreign born: 0.0%; Speak English only: 99.4%; With disability: 15.0%; Veterans: 7.0%; Ancestry: 19.6% German, 12.4% English, 12.2% American, 10.9% Irish, 3.1% Polish
Employment: 13.9% management, business, and financial, 2.8% computer, engineering, and science, 1.5% education, legal, community service, arts, and media, 6.8% healthcare practitioners, 26.4% service, 22.6% sales and office, 13.4% natural resources, construction, and maintenance, 12.7% production, transportation, and material moving
Income: Per capita: $22,797; Median household: $53,500; Average household: $62,121; Households with income of $100,000 or more: 15.7%; Poverty rate: 13.0%
Educational Attainment: High school diploma or higher: 83.9%; Bachelor's degree or higher: 11.2%; Graduate/professional degree or higher: 3.6%
Housing: Homeownership rate: 86.7%; Median home value: $129,300; Median year structure built: 1992; Homeowner vacancy rate: 5.0%; Median selected monthly owner costs: $1,067 with a mortgage, $373 without a mortgage; Median gross rent: $758 per month; Rental vacancy rate: 0.0%
Health Insurance: 90.9% have insurance; 69.3% have private insurance; 33.8% have public insurance; 9.1% do not have insurance; 3.2% of children under 18 do not have insurance
Transportation: Commute: 99.2% car, 0.0% public transportation, 0.0% walk, 0.8% work from home; Mean travel time to work: 28.4 minutes

SWITZ CITY (town). Covers a land area of 0.225 square miles and a water area of 0 square miles. Located at 39.03° N. Lat; 87.05° W. Long. Elevation is 525 feet.
History: Switz City grew up around the nearby strip-mining coal fields.
Population: 233; Growth (since 2000): -25.1%; Density: 1,034.8 persons per square mile; Race: 91.0% White, 0.9% Black/African American, 0.0% Asian, 0.0% American Indian/Alaska Native, 0.0% Native Hawaiian/Other Pacific Islander, 8.2% Two or more races, 0.0% Hispanic of any race; Average household size: 2.20; Median age: 34.4; Age under 18: 30.5%; Age 65 and over: 16.7%; Males per 100 females: 99.3; Marriage status: 31.1% never married, 49.2% now married, 2.2% separated, 7.1% widowed, 12.6% divorced; Foreign born: 0.0%; Speak English only: 100.0%; With disability: 21.9%; Veterans: 4.3%; Ancestry: 18.0% German, 12.0% Irish, 11.2% American, 9.9% English, 1.3% Dutch
Employment: 12.7% management, business, and financial, 1.3% computer, engineering, and science, 5.1% education, legal, community service, arts, and media, 10.1% healthcare practitioners, 15.2% service, 27.8% sales and office, 8.9% natural resources, construction, and maintenance, 19.0% production, transportation, and material moving
Income: Per capita: $14,903; Median household: $22,500; Average household: $32,781; Households with income of $100,000 or more: 3.8%; Poverty rate: 44.2%
Educational Attainment: High school diploma or higher: 79.9%; Bachelor's degree or higher: 13.4%; Graduate/professional degree or higher: 5.4%

School District(s)

White River Valley School District (PK-12)
Enrollment: 918. . . . . (812) 659-1424
Housing: Homeownership rate: 61.3%; Median home value: $71,800; Median year structure built: 1959; Homeowner vacancy rate: 5.8%; Median selected monthly owner costs: $813 with a mortgage, $317 without a mortgage; Median gross rent: $563 per month; Rental vacancy rate: 4.4%
Health Insurance: 93.1% have insurance; 54.5% have private insurance; 52.4% have public insurance; 6.9% do not have insurance; 0.0% of children under 18 do not have insurance
Transportation: Commute: 98.7% car, 0.0% public transportation, 1.3% walk, 0.0% work from home; Mean travel time to work: 20.8 minutes

WORTHINGTON (town). Covers a land area of 0.808 square miles and a water area of 0 square miles. Located at 39.12° N. Lat; 86.98° W. Long. Elevation is 515 feet.
History: Laid out 1849.
Population: 1,252; Growth (since 2000): -15.5%; Density: 1,549.3 persons per square mile; Race: 97.4% White, 0.0% Black/African American, 0.2% Asian, 0.3% American Indian/Alaska Native, 0.0% Native Hawaiian/Other Pacific Islander, 0.0% Two or more races, 3.1% Hispanic of any race; Average household size: 2.09; Median age: 50.2; Age under 18: 19.2%; Age 65 and over: 21.9%; Males per 100 females: 91.7; Marriage status: 20.6% never married, 48.7% now married, 1.9% separated, 10.6% widowed, 20.1% divorced; Foreign born: 1.2%; Speak English only: 96.8%; With disability: 27.1%; Veterans: 9.9%; Ancestry: 29.3% German, 17.7% Irish, 14.9% English, 9.3% American, 3.4% Dutch
Employment: 5.5% management, business, and financial, 4.0% computer, engineering, and science, 6.9% education, legal, community service, arts, and media, 2.3% healthcare practitioners, 20.3% service, 19.3% sales and office, 18.2% natural resources, construction, and maintenance, 23.5% production, transportation, and material moving
Income: Per capita: $20,700; Median household: $35,104; Average household: $41,217; Households with income of $100,000 or more: 4.6%; Poverty rate: 25.7%
Educational Attainment: High school diploma or higher: 82.6%; Bachelor's degree or higher: 8.5%; Graduate/professional degree or higher: 3.5%

School District(s)

White River Valley School District (PK-12)
Enrollment: 918 . . . . (812) 659-1424
Housing: Homeownership rate: 71.2%; Median home value: $64,800; Median year structure built: 1954; Homeowner vacancy rate: 2.7%; Median selected monthly owner costs: $752 with a mortgage, $279 without a mortgage; Median gross rent: $383 per month; Rental vacancy rate: 10.8%
Health Insurance: 91.8% have insurance; 53.2% have private insurance; 56.8% have public insurance; 8.2% do not have insurance; 4.9% of children under 18 do not have insurance
Transportation: Commute: 96.1% car, 0.0% public transportation, 0.0% walk, 1.4% work from home; Mean travel time to work: 34.3 minutes

Hamilton County

Located in central Indiana; drained by the West Fork of the White River, and by several creeks. Covers a land area of 394.267 square miles, a water area of 8.170 square miles, and is located in the Eastern Time Zone at 40.05° N. Lat., 86.02° W. Long. The county was founded in 1823. County seat is Noblesville.

Hamilton County is part of the Indianapolis-Carmel-Anderson, IN Metropolitan Statistical Area. The entire metro area includes: Boone County, IN; Brown County, IN; Hamilton County, IN; Hancock County, IN; Hendricks County, IN; Johnson County, IN; Madison County, IN; Marion County, IN; Morgan County, IN; Putnam County, IN; Shelby County, IN

Population: 309,687; Growth (since 2000): 69.5%; Density: 785.5 persons per square mile; Race: 87.4% White, 3.6% Black/African American, 5.8% Asian, 0.1% American Indian/Alaska Native, 0.0% Native Hawaiian/Other Pacific Islander, 2.2% two or more races, 3.8% Hispanic of any race; Average household size: 2.70; Median age: 36.6; Age under 18: 28.2%; Age 65 and over: 11.0%; Males per 100 females: 95.3; Marriage status: 24.2% never married, 62.4% now married, 0.9% separated, 3.8% widowed, 9.6% divorced; Foreign born: 7.6%; Speak English only: 90.8%; With disability: 7.7%; Veterans: 6.1%; Ancestry: 25.3% German, 13.3% Irish, 11.8% American, 10.4% English, 3.8% Italian
Religion: Six largest groups: 14.7% Catholicism, 7.7% Non-denominational Protestant, 6.2% Methodist/Pietist, 4.4% Baptist, 3.2% Lutheran, 1.1% Presbyterian-Reformed
Economy: Unemployment rate: 2.9%; Leading industries: 16.5 % professional, scientific, and technical services; 12.2 % health care and social assistance; 10.3 % retail trade; Farms: 598 totaling 130,854 acres; Company size: 7 employ 1,000 or more persons, 13 employ 500 to 999 persons, 217 employ 100 to 499 persons, 8,419 employ less than 100 persons; Business ownership: 9,487 women-owned, 651 Black-owned, 414 Hispanic-owned, 1,715 Asian-owned, 168 American Indian/Alaska Native-owned
Employment: 23.2% management, business, and financial, 9.3% computer, engineering, and science, 12.7% education, legal, community service, arts, and media, 8.1% healthcare practitioners, 11.1% service, 24.7% sales and office, 5.0% natural resources, construction, and maintenance, 6.0% production, transportation, and material moving
Income: Per capita: $44,443; Median household: $90,582; Average household: $119,393; Households with income of $100,000 or more: 45.1%; Poverty rate: 5.0%
Educational Attainment: High school diploma or higher: 96.2%; Bachelor's degree or higher: 57.5%; Graduate/professional degree or higher: 20.7%
Housing: Homeownership rate: 78.0%; Median home value: $240,000; Median year structure built: 1996; Homeowner vacancy rate: 1.3%; Median selected monthly owner costs: $1,584 with a mortgage, $531 without a mortgage; Median gross rent: $1,103 per month; Rental vacancy rate: 7.0%
Vital Statistics: Birth rate: 120.5 per 10,000 population; Death rate: 53.9 per 10,000 population; Age-adjusted cancer mortality rate: 132.5 deaths per 100,000 population
Health Insurance: 94.3% have insurance; 86.7% have private insurance; 16.2% have public insurance; 5.7% do not have insurance; 4.2% of children under 18 do not have insurance
Health Care: Physicians: 59.4 per 10,000 population; Dentists: 7.4 per 10,000 population; Hospital beds: 17.6 per 10,000 population; Hospital admissions: 728.8 per 10,000 population
Air Quality Index (AQI): Percent of Days: 82.7% good, 16.7% moderate, 0.5% unhealthy for sensitive individuals, 0.0% unhealthy, 0.0% very unhealthy; Annual median: 40; Annual maximum: 105
Transportation: Commute: 90.4% car, 0.2% public transportation, 0.8% walk, 7.9% work from home; Mean travel time to work: 25.5 minutes
2016 Presidential Election: 56.0% Trump, 36.7% Clinton, 5.8% Johnson, 0.2% Stein
Additional Information Contacts
Hamilton Government . . . . (317) 776-9719
http://www.hamiltoncounty.in.gov

Hamilton County Communities

ARCADIA (town). Covers a land area of 0.558 square miles and a water area of 0 square miles. Located at 40.17° N. Lat; 86.02° W. Long. Elevation is 856 feet.
Population: 1,302; Growth (since 2000): -25.5%; Density: 2,334.6 persons per square mile; Race: 98.3% White, 0.3% Black/African American, 1.0% Asian, 0.0% American Indian/Alaska Native, 0.0% Native Hawaiian/Other Pacific Islander, 0.4% Two or more races, 0.0% Hispanic of any race; Average household size: 2.41; Median age: 38.2; Age under 18: 27.7%; Age 65 and over: 18.8%; Males per 100 females: 99.5; Marriage status: 21.5% never married, 56.2% now married, 0.9% separated, 8.2% widowed, 14.1% divorced; Foreign born: 1.0%; Speak English only: 99.4%; With disability: 18.3%; Veterans: 8.3%; Ancestry: 27.1% German, 18.7% American, 13.7% Irish, 5.0% English, 2.3% Dutch
Employment: 11.0% management, business, and financial, 1.2% computer, engineering, and science, 6.7% education, legal, community service, arts, and media, 5.3% healthcare practitioners, 22.4% service, 29.3% sales and office, 10.7% natural resources, construction, and maintenance, 13.3% production, transportation, and material moving
Income: Per capita: $21,325; Median household: $45,139; Average household: $50,984; Households with income of $100,000 or more: 8.5%; Poverty rate: 16.9%
Educational Attainment: High school diploma or higher: 90.4%; Bachelor's degree or higher: 14.0%; Graduate/professional degree or higher: 4.3%

School District(s)

Hamilton Heights School Corp (PK-12)
Enrollment: 2,213 . . . . (317) 984-3538
Housing: Homeownership rate: 77.1%; Median home value: $104,500; Median year structure built: 1943; Homeowner vacancy rate: 1.6%; Median selected monthly owner costs: $978 with a mortgage, $431 without a mortgage; Median gross rent: $619 per month; Rental vacancy rate: 22.3%
Health Insurance: 84.2% have insurance; 69.8% have private insurance; 33.2% have public insurance; 15.8% do not have insurance; 8.9% of children under 18 do not have insurance
Transportation: Commute: 94.8% car, 0.0% public transportation, 0.5% walk, 4.7% work from home; Mean travel time to work: 30.4 minutes

ATLANTA (town). Covers a land area of 0.302 square miles and a water area of 0 square miles. Located at 40.21° N. Lat; 86.03° W. Long. Elevation is 863 feet.
Population: 881; Growth (since 2000): 15.8%; Density: 2,921.7 persons per square mile; Race: 96.7% White, 0.2% Black/African American, 0.0% Asian, 0.0% American Indian/Alaska Native, 0.0% Native Hawaiian/Other Pacific Islander, 0.7% Two or more races, 3.5% Hispanic of any race; Average household size: 2.80; Median age: 35.9; Age under 18: 27.2%; Age 65 and over: 14.3%; Males per 100 females: 95.9; Marriage status: 23.2% never married, 60.6% now married, 2.1% separated, 3.1% widowed, 13.1% divorced; Foreign born: 1.5%; Speak English only: 98.5%; With disability: 18.4%; Veterans: 15.9%; Ancestry: 21.2% American, 20.4% German, 9.6% Irish, 6.1% English, 3.7% French
Employment: 5.1% management, business, and financial, 2.4% computer, engineering, and science, 4.0% education, legal, community service, arts, and media, 5.1% healthcare practitioners, 26.3% service, 20.1% sales and office, 20.5% natural resources, construction, and maintenance, 16.6% production, transportation, and material moving
Income: Per capita: $24,140; Median household: $60,329; Average household: $65,440; Households with income of $100,000 or more: 16.0%; Poverty rate: 6.1%
Educational Attainment: High school diploma or higher: 86.5%; Bachelor's degree or higher: 4.2%; Graduate/professional degree or higher: 1.4%
Housing: Homeownership rate: 87.3%; Median home value: $94,000; Median year structure built: Before 1940; Homeowner vacancy rate: 1.9%; Median selected monthly owner costs: $1,051 with a mortgage, $388 without a mortgage; Median gross rent: $755 per month; Rental vacancy rate: 0.0%
Health Insurance: 88.0% have insurance; 67.4% have private insurance; 39.3% have public insurance; 12.0% do not have insurance; 11.5% of children under 18 do not have insurance
Transportation: Commute: 95.1% car, 0.0% public transportation, 1.1% walk, 0.7% work from home; Mean travel time to work: 29.6 minutes

CARMEL (city). Covers a land area of 47.463 square miles and a water area of 1.085 square miles. Located at 39.97° N. Lat; 86.15° W. Long. Elevation is 853 feet.
Population: 88,595; Growth (since 2000): 134.8%; Density: 1,866.6 persons per square mile; Race: 84.0% White, 2.5% Black/African American, 10.3% Asian, 0.3% American Indian/Alaska Native, 0.0% Native Hawaiian/Other Pacific Islander, 2.2% Two or more races, 3.2% Hispanic of any race; Average household size: 2.66; Median age: 39.5; Age under 18: 26.8%; Age 65 and over: 12.9%; Males per 100 females: 95.1; Marriage status: 23.9% never married, 64.4% now married, 0.5% separated, 3.8% widowed, 7.9% divorced; Foreign born: 11.6%; Speak English only: 87.0%; With disability: 6.1%; Veterans: 5.4%; Ancestry: 24.8% German, 14.5% Irish, 12.3% English, 9.6% American, 4.0% Italian
Employment: 26.3% management, business, and financial, 11.0% computer, engineering, and science, 15.6% education, legal, community service, arts, and media, 9.5% healthcare practitioners, 8.6% service, 21.9% sales and office, 2.7% natural resources, construction, and maintenance, 4.5% production, transportation, and material moving
Income: Per capita: $55,796; Median household: $109,201; Average household: $147,771; Households with income of $100,000 or more: 54.7%; Poverty rate: 3.7%
Educational Attainment: High school diploma or higher: 97.9%; Bachelor's degree or higher: 71.0%; Graduate/professional degree or higher: 29.0%

School District(s)

Carmel Clay Schools (PK-12)
Enrollment: 16,035 . . . . (317) 844-9961
Options Charter School - Carmel (09-12)
Enrollment: 176. . . . . (317) 815-2098

Housing: Homeownership rate: 77.6%; Median home value: $320,400; Median year structure built: 1994; Homeowner vacancy rate: 2.4%; Median selected monthly owner costs: $1,968 with a mortgage, $587 without a mortgage; Median gross rent: $1,150 per month; Rental vacancy rate: 8.4%
Health Insurance: 96.5% have insurance; 89.5% have private insurance; 15.8% have public insurance; 3.5% do not have insurance; 2.0% of children under 18 do not have insurance
Hospitals: Franciscan Saint Francis Health - Carmel; Indiana University Health North Hospital; Saint Vincent Carmel Hospital (100 beds)
Safety: Violent crime rate: 1.8 per 10,000 population; Property crime rate: 74.7 per 10,000 population
Transportation: Commute: 89.6% car, 0.2% public transportation, 1.1% walk, 8.3% work from home; Mean travel time to work: 24.2 minutes
Additional Information Contacts
City of Carmel . . . . (317) 571-2400
http://www.carmel.in.gov

CICERO (town). Covers a land area of 1.708 square miles and a water area of 0.412 square miles. Located at 40.12° N. Lat; 86.03° W. Long. Elevation is 833 feet.
History: Cicero, named for a Delaware chief, grew around a Seventh-Day Adventist academy nearby.
Population: 4,880; Growth (since 2000): 13.4%; Density: 2,857.1 persons per square mile; Race: 99.7% White, 0.0% Black/African American, 0.3% Asian, 0.0% American Indian/Alaska Native, 0.0% Native Hawaiian/Other Pacific Islander, 0.0% Two or more races, 5.0% Hispanic of any race; Average household size: 2.47; Median age: 42.2; Age under 18: 20.7%; Age 65 and over: 15.3%; Males per 100 females: 97.0; Marriage status: 22.0% never married, 59.6% now married, 2.4% separated, 6.1% widowed, 12.3% divorced; Foreign born: 6.0%; Speak English only: 93.4%; With disability: 13.1%; Veterans: 9.1%; Ancestry: 24.1% German, 16.4% American, 12.7% Irish, 7.0% English, 6.8% Italian
Employment: 12.9% management, business, and financial, 11.1% computer, engineering, and science, 8.5% education, legal, community service, arts, and media, 8.6% healthcare practitioners, 13.8% service, 14.8% sales and office, 11.5% natural resources, construction, and maintenance, 18.8% production, transportation, and material moving
Income: Per capita: $31,815; Median household: $66,701; Average household: $76,773; Households with income of $100,000 or more: 24.1%; Poverty rate: 5.9%
Educational Attainment: High school diploma or higher: 92.7%; Bachelor's degree or higher: 25.4%; Graduate/professional degree or higher: 10.4%
Housing: Homeownership rate: 83.8%; Median home value: $140,300; Median year structure built: 1980; Homeowner vacancy rate: 1.7%; Median selected monthly owner costs: $1,070 with a mortgage, $384 without a mortgage; Median gross rent: $727 per month; Rental vacancy rate: 0.0%
Health Insurance: 85.0% have insurance; 76.8% have private insurance; 21.3% have public insurance; 15.0% do not have insurance; 13.1% of children under 18 do not have insurance
Transportation: Commute: 88.3% car, 0.0% public transportation, 2.1% walk, 8.6% work from home; Mean travel time to work: 26.3 minutes
Additional Information Contacts
Town of Cicero . . . . (317) 984-4900
http://www.ciceroin.org

FISHERS (city). Covers a land area of 33.585 square miles and a water area of 2.249 square miles. Located at 39.96° N. Lat; 85.97° W. Long. Elevation is 817 feet.
Population: 87,557; Growth (since 2000): 131.4%; Density: 2,607.0 persons per square mile; Race: 84.0% White, 5.6% Black/African American, 6.8% Asian, 0.0% American Indian/Alaska Native, 0.0% Native Hawaiian/Other Pacific Islander, 2.8% Two or more races, 3.8% Hispanic of any race; Average household size: 2.78; Median age: 35.2; Age under 18: 30.9%; Age 65 and over: 8.0%; Males per 100 females: 94.5; Marriage status: 24.0% never married, 63.4% now married, 1.1% separated, 3.0% widowed, 9.7% divorced; Foreign born: 8.9%; Speak English only: 90.0%; With disability: 6.1%; Veterans: 5.4%; Ancestry: 27.0% German, 12.0% Irish, 10.0% English, 9.9% American, 5.2% Polish
Employment: 26.0% management, business, and financial, 10.5% computer, engineering, and science, 13.6% education, legal, community service, arts, and media, 8.7% healthcare practitioners, 9.4% service, 25.2% sales and office, 3.0% natural resources, construction, and maintenance, 3.4% production, transportation, and material moving
Income: Per capita: $46,619; Median household: $101,469; Average household: $128,847; Households with income of $100,000 or more: 50.9%; Poverty rate: 3.3%
Educational Attainment: High school diploma or higher: 97.5%; Bachelor's degree or higher: 65.1%; Graduate/professional degree or higher: 23.4%

School District(s)

Hamilton Southeastern Schools (PK-12)
Enrollment: 21,545 . . . . (317) 594-4100

Housing: Homeownership rate: 80.8%; Median home value: $240,100; Median year structure built: 1999; Homeowner vacancy rate: 0.4%; Median selected monthly owner costs: $1,579 with a mortgage, $544 without a mortgage; Median gross rent: $1,175 per month; Rental vacancy rate: 10.8%
Health Insurance: 95.9% have insurance; 90.5% have private insurance; 11.5% have public insurance; 4.1% do not have insurance; 4.2% of children under 18 do not have insurance
Hospitals: Saint Vincent Fishers Hospital
Safety: Violent crime rate: 4.7 per 10,000 population; Property crime rate: 92.6 per 10,000 population
Transportation: Commute: 90.2% car, 0.3% public transportation, 0.4% walk, 8.6% work from home; Mean travel time to work: 27.5 minutes
Airports: Indianapolis Metropolitan (general aviation)
Additional Information Contacts
Town of Fishers. . . . . (317) 595-3140
http://www.fishers.in.us

NOBLESVILLE (city). County seat. Covers a land area of 31.374 square miles and a water area of 1.415 square miles. Located at 40.04° N. Lat; 86.01° W. Long. Elevation is 764 feet.
History: Named for James Noble, first U.S. Senator from Indiana. Noblesville was founded in 1823 by William Conner who had built a trading post nearby in 1818. Noblesville became the seat of Hamilton County, and Conner became a state senator.
Population: 59,807; Growth (since 2000): 109.2%; Density: 1,906.2 persons per square mile; Race: 89.7% White, 4.0% Black/African American, 2.5% Asian, 0.1% American Indian/Alaska Native, 0.0% Native Hawaiian/Other Pacific Islander, 2.8% Two or more races, 4.5% Hispanic of any race; Average household size: 2.67; Median age: 33.5; Age under 18: 28.3%; Age 65 and over: 10.8%; Males per 100 females: 93.8; Marriage status: 25.9% never married, 57.9% now married, 1.3% separated, 4.5% widowed, 11.6% divorced; Foreign born: 3.9%; Speak English only: 94.1%; With disability: 9.5%; Veterans: 7.2%; Ancestry: 25.7% German, 12.4% Irish, 12.0% American, 10.0% English, 4.5% Italian
Employment: 19.8% management, business, and financial, 6.5% computer, engineering, and science, 10.3% education, legal, community service, arts, and media, 6.7% healthcare practitioners, 14.4% service, 29.0% sales and office, 5.8% natural resources, construction, and maintenance, 7.6% production, transportation, and material moving
Income: Per capita: $34,910; Median household: $74,681; Average household: $93,070; Households with income of $100,000 or more: 33.0%; Poverty rate: 6.5%
Educational Attainment: High school diploma or higher: 94.6%; Bachelor's degree or higher: 45.8%; Graduate/professional degree or higher: 13.3%

School District(s)
Excel Center - Noblesville (09-12)
Enrollment: 198. . . . . (317) 524-3925
Hamilton Southeastern Schools (PK-12)
Enrollment: 21,545 . . . . (317) 594-4100
Noblesville Schools (PK-12)
Enrollment: 10,557 . . . . (317) 773-3171
Options Charter School Noblesville (06-12)
Enrollment: 204. . . . . (317) 773-8659

Vocational/Technical School(s)
Hair Fashions By Kaye Beauty College-Noblesville (Private, For-profit)
Enrollment: n/a . . . . (317) 773-6189
Tuition: $15,000

Housing: Homeownership rate: 69.9%; Median home value: $183,700; Median year structure built: 2000; Homeowner vacancy rate: 1.4%; Median selected monthly owner costs: $1,366 with a mortgage, $501 without a mortgage; Median gross rent: $993 per month; Rental vacancy rate: 3.3%
Health Insurance: 92.6% have insurance; 82.4% have private insurance; 19.5% have public insurance; 7.4% do not have insurance; 4.5% of children under 18 do not have insurance
Hospitals: Riverview Hospital (161 beds)
Safety: Violent crime rate: n/a per 10,000 population; Property crime rate: 131.7 per 10,000 population
Newspapers: Noblesville Daily Times (daily circulation 6,000)
Transportation: Commute: 91.0% car, 0.0% public transportation, 1.1% walk, 7.6% work from home; Mean travel time to work: 26.1 minutes
Additional Information Contacts
City of Noblesville . . . . (317) 776-6328
http://www.cityofnoblesville.org

SHERIDAN (town). Covers a land area of 2.137 square miles and a water area of 0.004 square miles. Located at 40.13° N. Lat; 86.22° W. Long. Elevation is 948 feet.
History: Laid out 1860.
Population: 2,828; Growth (since 2000): 12.2%; Density: 1,323.3 persons per square mile; Race: 98.5% White, 0.1% Black/African American, 0.2% Asian, 0.0% American Indian/Alaska Native, 0.0% Native Hawaiian/Other Pacific Islander, 1.0% Two or more races, 1.8% Hispanic of any race; Average household size: 2.43; Median age: 34.9; Age under 18: 29.1%; Age 65 and over: 15.7%; Males per 100 females: 100.2; Marriage status: 27.7% never married, 48.8% now married, 2.5% separated, 6.0% widowed, 17.5% divorced; Foreign born: 0.4%; Speak English only: 96.9%; With disability: 18.0%; Veterans: 9.9%; Ancestry: 27.3% American, 9.5% Irish, 8.4% German, 7.6% English, 4.2% Dutch
Employment: 14.9% management, business, and financial, 3.0% computer, engineering, and science, 6.9% education, legal, community service, arts, and media, 5.7% healthcare practitioners, 22.2% service, 16.3% sales and office, 15.0% natural resources, construction, and maintenance, 15.9% production, transportation, and material moving
Income: Per capita: $24,292; Median household: $46,602; Average household: $58,716; Households with income of $100,000 or more: 16.8%; Poverty rate: 14.5%
Educational Attainment: High school diploma or higher: 86.7%; Bachelor's degree or higher: 13.6%; Graduate/professional degree or higher: 3.3%

School District(s)
Sheridan Community Schools (PK-12)
Enrollment: 1,009 . . . . (317) 758-4172

Housing: Homeownership rate: 58.5%; Median home value: $116,000; Median year structure built: 1969; Homeowner vacancy rate: 4.8%; Median selected monthly owner costs: $965 with a mortgage, $418 without a mortgage; Median gross rent: $697 per month; Rental vacancy rate: 4.2%
Health Insurance: 84.6% have insurance; 66.7% have private insurance; 28.5% have public insurance; 15.4% do not have insurance; 16.2% of children under 18 do not have insurance
Transportation: Commute: 93.1% car, 0.0% public transportation, 1.4% walk, 2.3% work from home; Mean travel time to work: 26.9 minutes
Additional Information Contacts
Town of Sheridan . . . . (317) 758-5293
http://www.sheridan.org

WESTFIELD (city). Covers a land area of 26.838 square miles and a water area of 0.241 square miles. Located at 40.03° N. Lat; 86.16° W. Long. Elevation is 886 feet.
History: Westfield was founded in 1834 by a group of Quakers, and was an important station on the Underground Railroad for slaves fleeing to the north.
Population: 35,956; Growth (since 2000): 286.9%; Density: 1,339.7 persons per square mile; Race: 89.9% White, 3.9% Black/African American, 3.1% Asian, 0.0% American Indian/Alaska Native, 0.0% Native Hawaiian/Other Pacific Islander, 1.4% Two or more races, 4.7% Hispanic of any race; Average household size: 2.86; Median age: 34.5; Age under 18: 31.0%; Age 65 and over: 8.4%; Males per 100 females: 95.7; Marriage status: 24.8% never married, 63.0% now married, 0.7% separated, 3.4% widowed, 8.8% divorced; Foreign born: 5.7%; Speak English only: 91.6%; With disability: 8.6%; Veterans: 5.6%; Ancestry: 24.3% German, 15.2% Irish, 13.4% American, 9.3% English, 4.2% Italian
Employment: 22.7% management, business, and financial, 9.4% computer, engineering, and science, 12.2% education, legal, community service, arts, and media, 7.8% healthcare practitioners, 10.7% service, 25.0% sales and office, 5.0% natural resources, construction, and maintenance, 7.2% production, transportation, and material moving
Income: Per capita: $37,855; Median household: $89,144; Average household: $108,176; Households with income of $100,000 or more: 44.4%; Poverty rate: 6.7%
Educational Attainment: High school diploma or higher: 96.2%; Bachelor's degree or higher: 56.5%; Graduate/professional degree or higher: 17.4%

School District(s)
Westfield-Washington Schools (PK-12)
Enrollment: 7,594 . . . . (317) 867-8000

Housing: Homeownership rate: 81.4%; Median home value: $232,300; Median year structure built: 2002; Homeowner vacancy rate: 0.3%; Median selected monthly owner costs: $1,612 with a mortgage, $556 without a

mortgage; Median gross rent: $1,162 per month; Rental vacancy rate: 5.6%
Health Insurance: 93.3% have insurance; 86.3% have private insurance; 15.0% have public insurance; 6.7% do not have insurance; 3.3% of children under 18 do not have insurance
Safety: Violent crime rate: 5.7 per 10,000 population; Property crime rate: 101.4 per 10,000 population
Transportation: Commute: 91.7% car, 0.0% public transportation, 0.7% walk, 6.6% work from home; Mean travel time to work: 23.8 minutes
Additional Information Contacts
Town of Westfield . . . . (317) 804-3020
http://www.westfield.in.gov

Hancock County

Located in central Indiana; drained by the Big Blue River and by Sugar and Brandywine Creeks. Covers a land area of 306.016 square miles, a water area of 1.009 square miles, and is located in the Eastern Time Zone at 39.82° N. Lat., 85.77° W. Long. The county was founded in 1827. County seat is Greenfield.

Hancock County is part of the Indianapolis-Carmel-Anderson, IN Metropolitan Statistical Area. The entire metro area includes: Boone County, IN; Brown County, IN; Hamilton County, IN; Hancock County, IN; Hendricks County, IN; Johnson County, IN; Madison County, IN; Marion County, IN; Morgan County, IN; Putnam County, IN; Shelby County, IN

Weather Station: Greenfield Elevation: 865 feet

	Jan	Feb	Mar	Apr	May	Jun	Jul	Aug	Sep	Oct	Nov	Dec
High	35	39	50	62	72	81	85	84	78	65	52	38
Low	19	21	30	41	52	61	64	63	55	43	34	23
Precip	2.7	2.4	3.6	4.3	5.5	4.6	5.1	3.9	3.5	3.4	3.8	3.2
Snow	5.8	3.5	1.7	0.2	0.0	0.0	0.0	0.0	0.0	0.1	0.6	3.9

High and Low temperatures in degrees Fahrenheit; Precipitation and Snow in inches

Population: 72,776; Growth (since 2000): 31.4%; Density: 237.8 persons per square mile; Race: 95.1% White, 1.9% Black/African American, 0.8% Asian, 0.1% American Indian/Alaska Native, 0.0% Native Hawaiian/Other Pacific Islander, 2.0% two or more races, 2.2% Hispanic of any race; Average household size: 2.62; Median age: 40.2; Age under 18: 24.0%; Age 65 and over: 15.2%; Males per 100 females: 96.5; Marriage status: 23.9% never married, 60.0% now married, 1.1% separated, 5.2% widowed, 10.9% divorced; Foreign born: 2.1%; Speak English only: 97.3%; With disability: 13.3%; Veterans: 10.9%; Ancestry: 22.2% German, 16.1% American, 12.9% Irish, 10.0% English, 2.4% Scottish
Religion: Six largest groups: 10.7% Non-denominational Protestant, 8.2% Baptist, 6.6% Catholicism, 6.3% Methodist/Pietist, 2.7% Lutheran, 2.1% Holiness
Economy: Unemployment rate: 3.1%; Leading industries: 15.9 % construction; 11.9 % other services (except public administration); 11.7 % retail trade; Farms: 604 totaling 165,861 acres; Company size: 0 employ 1,000 or more persons, 5 employ 500 to 999 persons, 22 employ 100 to 499 persons, 1,379 employ less than 100 persons; Business ownership: 1,647 women-owned, 49 Black-owned, 66 Hispanic-owned, 123 Asian-owned, 29 American Indian/Alaska Native-owned
Employment: 15.5% management, business, and financial, 5.5% computer, engineering, and science, 9.7% education, legal, community service, arts, and media, 7.7% healthcare practitioners, 14.2% service, 25.1% sales and office, 10.5% natural resources, construction, and maintenance, 11.9% production, transportation, and material moving
Income: Per capita: $31,428; Median household: $70,973; Average household: $81,179; Households with income of $100,000 or more: 29.6%; Poverty rate: 7.0%
Educational Attainment: High school diploma or higher: 93.9%; Bachelor's degree or higher: 30.1%; Graduate/professional degree or higher: 9.9%
Housing: Homeownership rate: 77.5%; Median home value: $161,800; Median year structure built: 1988; Homeowner vacancy rate: 1.6%; Median selected monthly owner costs: $1,250 with a mortgage, $442 without a mortgage; Median gross rent: $868 per month; Rental vacancy rate: 4.0%
Vital Statistics: Birth rate: 113.0 per 10,000 population; Death rate: 80.8 per 10,000 population; Age-adjusted cancer mortality rate: 164.9 deaths per 100,000 population
Health Insurance: 92.7% have insurance; 81.2% have private insurance; 25.0% have public insurance; 7.3% do not have insurance; 6.1% of children under 18 do not have insurance
Health Care: Physicians: 23.9 per 10,000 population; Dentists: 3.7 per 10,000 population; Hospital beds: 9.2 per 10,000 population; Hospital admissions: 430.1 per 10,000 population
Transportation: Commute: 94.1% car, 0.1% public transportation, 0.9% walk, 4.3% work from home; Mean travel time to work: 26.1 minutes
2016 Presidential Election: 68.7% Trump, 24.4% Clinton, 5.7% Johnson, 0.2% Stein
Additional Information Contacts
Hancock Government . . . . (317) 462-1102
http://www.hancockcoingov.org

Hancock County Communities

CHARLOTTESVILLE (unincorporated postal area)
ZCTA: 46117
Covers a land area of 11.790 square miles and a water area of 0.022 square miles. Located at 39.81° N. Lat; 85.62° W. Long. Elevation is 942 feet.
Population: 736; Growth (since 2000): 11.2%; Density: 62.4 persons per square mile; Race: 93.5% White, 0.0% Black/African American, 0.0% Asian, 0.0% American Indian/Alaska Native, 0.0% Native Hawaiian/Other Pacific Islander, 6.5% Two or more races, 0.0% Hispanic of any race; Average household size: 2.93; Median age: 45.3; Age under 18: 33.0%; Age 65 and over: 12.2%; Males per 100 females: 96.8; Marriage status: 21.5% never married, 67.6% now married, 0.0% separated, 3.7% widowed, 7.2% divorced; Foreign born: 0.0%; Speak English only: 100.0%; With disability: 1.6%; Veterans: 5.5%; Ancestry: 37.5% German, 33.7% Welsh, 19.7% American, 10.3% Irish, 1.5% Italian
Employment: 30.6% management, business, and financial, 3.0% computer, engineering, and science, 2.7% education, legal, community service, arts, and media, 6.6% healthcare practitioners, 6.8% service, 26.0% sales and office, 3.3% natural resources, construction, and maintenance, 21.0% production, transportation, and material moving
Income: Per capita: $26,331; Median household: $70,536; Average household: $75,284; Households with income of $100,000 or more: 11.2%; Poverty rate: n/a
Educational Attainment: High school diploma or higher: 100.0%; Bachelor's degree or higher: 28.9%; Graduate/professional degree or higher: 13.2%

School District(s)

Eastern Hancock Co Com Sch Corp (PK-12)
Enrollment: 1,042 . . . . (317) 467-0064
Housing: Homeownership rate: 86.5%; Median home value: $151,500; Median year structure built: 1976; Homeowner vacancy rate: 0.0%; Median selected monthly owner costs: $1,188 with a mortgage, $446 without a mortgage; Median gross rent: n/a per month; Rental vacancy rate: 0.0%
Health Insurance: 66.6% have insurance; 58.3% have private insurance; 17.0% have public insurance; 33.4% do not have insurance; 71.0% of children under 18 do not have insurance
Transportation: Commute: 72.7% car, 0.0% public transportation, 0.0% walk, 0.0% work from home; Mean travel time to work: 20.6 minutes

FORTVILLE (town). Covers a land area of 2.976 square miles and a water area of 0.007 square miles. Located at 39.92° N. Lat; 85.85° W. Long. Elevation is 856 feet.
History: Fortville was founded in 1849 by Cephas Fort.
Population: 4,323; Growth (since 2000): 25.5%; Density: 1,452.4 persons per square mile; Race: 92.3% White, 2.2% Black/African American, 0.0% Asian, 0.0% American Indian/Alaska Native, 0.0% Native Hawaiian/Other Pacific Islander, 5.6% Two or more races, 0.0% Hispanic of any race; Average household size: 2.49; Median age: 38.8; Age under 18: 21.8%; Age 65 and over: 12.9%; Males per 100 females: 94.5; Marriage status: 22.8% never married, 54.9% now married, 2.5% separated, 8.8% widowed, 13.5% divorced; Foreign born: 0.6%; Speak English only: 97.8%; With disability: 16.2%; Veterans: 11.1%; Ancestry: 32.2% American, 15.1% German, 14.1% Irish, 5.0% European, 2.8% English
Employment: 12.6% management, business, and financial, 3.2% computer, engineering, and science, 12.7% education, legal, community service, arts, and media, 8.1% healthcare practitioners, 8.2% service, 29.1% sales and office, 11.1% natural resources, construction, and maintenance, 15.1% production, transportation, and material moving

Income: Per capita: $27,616; Median household: $61,533; Average household: $66,598; Households with income of $100,000 or more: 22.2%; Poverty rate: 5.0%
Educational Attainment: High school diploma or higher: 94.9%; Bachelor's degree or higher: 28.6%; Graduate/professional degree or higher: 9.1%

School District(s)

Mt Vernon Community School Corp (PK-12)
Enrollment: 3,544 . . . . (317) 485-3100
Housing: Homeownership rate: 69.2%; Median home value: $114,500; Median year structure built: 1976; Homeowner vacancy rate: 0.0%; Median selected monthly owner costs: $1,127 with a mortgage, $346 without a mortgage; Median gross rent: $850 per month; Rental vacancy rate: 0.0%
Health Insurance: 93.2% have insurance; 85.4% have private insurance; 20.1% have public insurance; 6.8% do not have insurance; 0.0% of children under 18 do not have insurance
Transportation: Commute: 96.4% car, 0.0% public transportation, 0.0% walk, 3.6% work from home; Mean travel time to work: 26.4 minutes
Additional Information Contacts
Town of Fortville . . . . (317) 485-4044
http://www.fortvilleindiana.org

GREENFIELD (city). County seat. Covers a land area of 12.551 square miles and a water area of 0.112 square miles. Located at 39.79° N. Lat; 85.77° W. Long. Elevation is 883 feet.
History: Named for John Green, an early settler. Greenfield was the birthplace in 1849 of poet James Whitcomb Riley. An early industry here was tomato canning.
Population: 21,565; Growth (since 2000): 47.7%; Density: 1,718.2 persons per square mile; Race: 97.0% White, 0.9% Black/African American, 1.3% Asian, 0.0% American Indian/Alaska Native, 0.1% Native Hawaiian/Other Pacific Islander, 0.6% Two or more races, 2.0% Hispanic of any race; Average household size: 2.35; Median age: 39.2; Age under 18: 23.1%; Age 65 and over: 18.2%; Males per 100 females: 92.7; Marriage status: 24.0% never married, 52.3% now married, 2.0% separated, 8.2% widowed, 15.5% divorced; Foreign born: 2.0%; Speak English only: 96.6%; With disability: 18.7%; Veterans: 10.2%; Ancestry: 22.6% German, 15.8% American, 12.2% Irish, 10.0% English, 2.6% Scottish
Employment: 11.9% management, business, and financial, 4.6% computer, engineering, and science, 8.0% education, legal, community service, arts, and media, 8.0% healthcare practitioners, 14.6% service, 26.6% sales and office, 10.5% natural resources, construction, and maintenance, 15.7% production, transportation, and material moving
Income: Per capita: $26,025; Median household: $52,130; Average household: $60,664; Households with income of $100,000 or more: 16.3%; Poverty rate: 12.9%
Educational Attainment: High school diploma or higher: 91.1%; Bachelor's degree or higher: 21.8%; Graduate/professional degree or higher: 6.9%

School District(s)

Greenfield-Central Com Schools (PK-12)
Enrollment: 4,623 . . . . (317) 462-4434
Mt Vernon Community School Corp (PK-12)
Enrollment: 3,544 . . . . (317) 485-3100
Southern Hancock Co Com Sch Corp (PK-12)
Enrollment: 3,114 . . . . (317) 861-4463
Housing: Homeownership rate: 58.2%; Median home value: $132,000; Median year structure built: 1988; Homeowner vacancy rate: 2.5%; Median selected monthly owner costs: $1,053 with a mortgage, $379 without a mortgage; Median gross rent: $854 per month; Rental vacancy rate: 2.4%
Health Insurance: 92.1% have insurance; 72.0% have private insurance; 34.7% have public insurance; 7.9% do not have insurance; 6.6% of children under 18 do not have insurance
Hospitals: Hancock Regional Hospital (94 beds)
Safety: Violent crime rate: 43.0 per 10,000 population; Property crime rate: 188.8 per 10,000 population
Newspapers: Daily Reporter (daily circulation 11,400)
Transportation: Commute: 97.5% car, 0.0% public transportation, 0.9% walk, 1.4% work from home; Mean travel time to work: 22.1 minutes
Additional Information Contacts
City of Greenfield. . . . . (317) 477-4300
http://www.greenfieldin.org

MCCORDSVILLE (town). Covers a land area of 4.701 square miles and a water area of 0.009 square miles. Located at 39.90° N. Lat; 85.93° W. Long. Elevation is 850 feet.
History: Laid out 1865.
Population: 6,116; Growth (since 2000): 439.3%; Density: 1,301.0 persons per square mile; Race: 87.9% White, 4.7% Black/African American, 0.0% Asian, 0.0% American Indian/Alaska Native, 0.0% Native Hawaiian/Other Pacific Islander, 7.4% Two or more races, 6.8% Hispanic of any race; Average household size: 2.92; Median age: 31.9; Age under 18: 27.8%; Age 65 and over: 4.6%; Males per 100 females: 93.8; Marriage status: 27.1% never married, 62.9% now married, 0.0% separated, 0.0% widowed, 9.9% divorced; Foreign born: 2.8%; Speak English only: 96.8%; With disability: 5.4%; Veterans: 10.7%; Ancestry: 22.6% German, 14.2% English, 10.9% Polish, 8.8% Irish, 8.0% American
Employment: 19.6% management, business, and financial, 8.1% computer, engineering, and science, 12.2% education, legal, community service, arts, and media, 11.6% healthcare practitioners, 10.1% service, 28.4% sales and office, 8.1% natural resources, construction, and maintenance, 2.0% production, transportation, and material moving
Income: Per capita: $39,294; Median household: $100,863; Average household: $111,002; Households with income of $100,000 or more: 52.0%; Poverty rate: 1.6%
Educational Attainment: High school diploma or higher: 99.4%; Bachelor's degree or higher: 58.1%; Graduate/professional degree or higher: 16.3%

School District(s)

Geist Montessori Academy (KG-08)
Enrollment: 376. . . . . (317) 335-1158
Mt Vernon Community School Corp (PK-12)
Enrollment: 3,544 . . . . (317) 485-3100
Housing: Homeownership rate: 89.7%; Median home value: $209,800; Median year structure built: 2005; Homeowner vacancy rate: 3.7%; Median selected monthly owner costs: $1,504 with a mortgage, $453 without a mortgage; Median gross rent: $1,090 per month; Rental vacancy rate: 0.0%
Health Insurance: 90.0% have insurance; 86.8% have private insurance; 6.4% have public insurance; 10.0% do not have insurance; 6.4% of children under 18 do not have insurance
Transportation: Commute: 92.6% car, 0.0% public transportation, 1.1% walk, 6.3% work from home; Mean travel time to work: 31.9 minutes
Airports: Indianapolis Regional (general aviation)

NEW PALESTINE (town). Covers a land area of 1.092 square miles and a water area of 0.005 square miles. Located at 39.73° N. Lat; 85.89° W. Long. Elevation is 837 feet.
History: Laid out 1838.
Population: 2,142; Growth (since 2000): 69.5%; Density: 1,961.5 persons per square mile; Race: 98.9% White, 0.0% Black/African American, 0.5% Asian, 0.0% American Indian/Alaska Native, 0.0% Native Hawaiian/Other Pacific Islander, 0.6% Two or more races, 0.1% Hispanic of any race; Average household size: 2.71; Median age: 36.9; Age under 18: 28.0%; Age 65 and over: 12.9%; Males per 100 females: 99.3; Marriage status: 23.5% never married, 58.2% now married, 0.0% separated, 6.5% widowed, 11.8% divorced; Foreign born: 0.7%; Speak English only: 99.4%; With disability: 10.8%; Veterans: 6.2%; Ancestry: 21.3% German, 18.6% American, 12.3% Irish, 6.7% English, 4.1% Italian
Employment: 22.7% management, business, and financial, 5.8% computer, engineering, and science, 8.4% education, legal, community service, arts, and media, 10.5% healthcare practitioners, 17.9% service, 17.3% sales and office, 6.6% natural resources, construction, and maintenance, 10.9% production, transportation, and material moving
Income: Per capita: $33,001; Median household: $74,750; Average household: $89,366; Households with income of $100,000 or more: 30.3%; Poverty rate: 7.8%
Educational Attainment: High school diploma or higher: 95.4%; Bachelor's degree or higher: 35.1%; Graduate/professional degree or higher: 10.2%

School District(s)

Southern Hancock Co Com Sch Corp (PK-12)
Enrollment: 3,114 . . . . (317) 861-4463
Housing: Homeownership rate: 88.9%; Median home value: $184,200; Median year structure built: 1996; Homeowner vacancy rate: 0.0%; Median selected monthly owner costs: $1,450 with a mortgage, $418 without a mortgage; Median gross rent: $900 per month; Rental vacancy rate: 23.4%

Health Insurance: 95.3% have insurance; 81.4% have private insurance; 24.8% have public insurance; 4.7% do not have insurance; 1.9% of children under 18 do not have insurance
Newspapers: New Palestine Press (weekly circulation 3,000)
Transportation: Commute: 92.4% car, 0.0% public transportation, 0.0% walk, 7.0% work from home; Mean travel time to work: 31.7 minutes

SHIRLEY (town). Covers a land area of 0.344 square miles and a water area of 0 square miles. Located at 39.89° N. Lat; 85.58° W. Long. Elevation is 1,027 feet.
Population: 804; Growth (since 2000): -0.2%; Density: 2,335.5 persons per square mile; Race: 94.5% White, 0.0% Black/African American, 0.0% Asian, 0.0% American Indian/Alaska Native, 0.0% Native Hawaiian/Other Pacific Islander, 5.5% Two or more races, 0.4% Hispanic of any race; Average household size: 2.69; Median age: 36.3; Age under 18: 28.6%; Age 65 and over: 9.7%; Males per 100 females: 97.1; Marriage status: 30.2% never married, 49.4% now married, 1.3% separated, 8.1% widowed, 12.2% divorced; Foreign born: 0.2%; Speak English only: 98.8%; With disability: 21.4%; Veterans: 6.3%; Ancestry: 21.5% American, 9.8% German, 9.5% Irish, 6.3% English, 2.4% African
Employment: 6.7% management, business, and financial, 2.3% computer, engineering, and science, 2.6% education, legal, community service, arts, and media, 4.4% healthcare practitioners, 20.9% service, 18.0% sales and office, 23.8% natural resources, construction, and maintenance, 21.2% production, transportation, and material moving
Income: Per capita: $19,940; Median household: $44,554; Average household: $52,439; Households with income of $100,000 or more: 13.7%; Poverty rate: 14.1%
Educational Attainment: High school diploma or higher: 85.3%; Bachelor's degree or higher: 6.5%; Graduate/professional degree or higher: 1.2%
Housing: Homeownership rate: 75.3%; Median home value: $71,600; Median year structure built: 1941; Homeowner vacancy rate: 4.9%; Median selected monthly owner costs: $781 with a mortgage, $344 without a mortgage; Median gross rent: $720 per month; Rental vacancy rate: 0.0%
Health Insurance: 92.2% have insurance; 60.2% have private insurance; 43.0% have public insurance; 7.8% do not have insurance; 2.0% of children under 18 do not have insurance
Transportation: Commute: 96.5% car, 0.0% public transportation, 0.0% walk, 3.5% work from home; Mean travel time to work: 30.2 minutes

SPRING LAKE (town). Covers a land area of 0.153 square miles and a water area of 0.011 square miles. Located at 39.78° N. Lat; 85.85° W. Long. Elevation is 850 feet.
History: Settled 1884, laid out 1912.
Population: 267; Growth (since 2000): 1.9%; Density: 1,749.0 persons per square mile; Race: 99.3% White, 0.7% Black/African American, 0.0% Asian, 0.0% American Indian/Alaska Native, 0.0% Native Hawaiian/Other Pacific Islander, 0.0% Two or more races, 0.0% Hispanic of any race; Average household size: 2.50; Median age: 48.8; Age under 18: 18.7%; Age 65 and over: 20.2%; Males per 100 females: 111.7; Marriage status: 21.0% never married, 63.9% now married, 0.9% separated, 6.9% widowed, 8.2% divorced; Foreign born: 0.7%; Speak English only: 98.8%; With disability: 15.7%; Veterans: 17.5%; Ancestry: 19.9% German, 16.1% American, 13.5% English, 11.6% Irish, 4.1% Italian
Employment: 10.8% management, business, and financial, 2.5% computer, engineering, and science, 5.0% education, legal, community service, arts, and media, 3.3% healthcare practitioners, 16.7% service, 37.5% sales and office, 18.3% natural resources, construction, and maintenance, 5.8% production, transportation, and material moving
Income: Per capita: $32,369; Median household: $62,750; Average household: $80,807; Households with income of $100,000 or more: 10.3%; Poverty rate: 14.2%
Educational Attainment: High school diploma or higher: 94.1%; Bachelor's degree or higher: 9.8%; Graduate/professional degree or higher: 1.5%
Housing: Homeownership rate: 94.4%; Median home value: $126,400; Median year structure built: 1954; Homeowner vacancy rate: 1.9%; Median selected monthly owner costs: $950 with a mortgage, $283 without a mortgage; Median gross rent: n/a per month; Rental vacancy rate: 0.0%
Health Insurance: 92.1% have insurance; 67.8% have private insurance; 36.7% have public insurance; 7.9% do not have insurance; 0.0% of children under 18 do not have insurance
Transportation: Commute: 99.2% car, 0.0% public transportation, 0.0% walk, 0.0% work from home; Mean travel time to work: 27.1 minutes

WILKINSON (town). Covers a land area of 0.232 square miles and a water area of 0 square miles. Located at 39.89° N. Lat; 85.61° W. Long. Elevation is 1,001 feet.
History: Laid out 1883.
Population: 373; Growth (since 2000): 4.8%; Density: 1,607.1 persons per square mile; Race: 99.7% White, 0.0% Black/African American, 0.0% Asian, 0.0% American Indian/Alaska Native, 0.0% Native Hawaiian/Other Pacific Islander, 0.3% Two or more races, 1.1% Hispanic of any race; Average household size: 2.63; Median age: 42.3; Age under 18: 23.6%; Age 65 and over: 14.2%; Males per 100 females: 106.9; Marriage status: 24.5% never married, 56.1% now married, 1.3% separated, 6.1% widowed, 13.2% divorced; Foreign born: 0.0%; Speak English only: 98.9%; With disability: 12.6%; Veterans: 11.2%; Ancestry: 20.6% German, 17.7% American, 11.3% English, 7.0% Irish, 2.1% Italian
Employment: 7.8% management, business, and financial, 6.8% computer, engineering, and science, 12.7% education, legal, community service, arts, and media, 4.4% healthcare practitioners, 24.4% service, 19.0% sales and office, 12.2% natural resources, construction, and maintenance, 12.7% production, transportation, and material moving
Income: Per capita: $26,945; Median household: $68,214; Average household: $69,846; Households with income of $100,000 or more: 19.7%; Poverty rate: 8.0%
Educational Attainment: High school diploma or higher: 90.7%; Bachelor's degree or higher: 19.0%; Graduate/professional degree or higher: 4.9%
Housing: Homeownership rate: 80.3%; Median home value: $92,200; Median year structure built: 1941; Homeowner vacancy rate: 0.0%; Median selected monthly owner costs: $758 with a mortgage, $338 without a mortgage; Median gross rent: $917 per month; Rental vacancy rate: 0.0%
Health Insurance: 86.6% have insurance; 78.3% have private insurance; 23.1% have public insurance; 13.4% do not have insurance; 17.3% of children under 18 do not have insurance
Transportation: Commute: 96.1% car, 0.0% public transportation, 2.5% walk, 1.5% work from home; Mean travel time to work: 32.4 minutes

Harrison County

Located in southern Indiana; bounded on the east, south, and southwest by the Ohio River and the Kentucky border, and on the west by the Blue River. Covers a land area of 484.516 square miles, a water area of 2.005 square miles, and is located in the Eastern Time Zone at 38.19° N. Lat., 86.10° W. Long. The county was founded in 1808. County seat is Corydon.

Harrison County is part of the Louisville/Jefferson County, KY-IN Metropolitan Statistical Area. The entire metro area includes: Clark County, IN; Floyd County, IN; Harrison County, IN; Scott County, IN; Washington County, IN; Bullitt County, KY; Henry County, KY; Jefferson County, KY; Oldham County, KY; Shelby County, KY; Spencer County, KY; Trimble County, KY

Population: 39,450; Growth (since 2000): 14.9%; Density: 81.4 persons per square mile; Race: 96.8% White, 0.2% Black/African American, 0.4% Asian, 0.6% American Indian/Alaska Native, 0.0% Native Hawaiian/Other Pacific Islander, 1.3% two or more races, 1.7% Hispanic of any race; Average household size: 2.66; Median age: 42.7; Age under 18: 22.6%; Age 65 and over: 16.6%; Males per 100 females: 100.0; Marriage status: 24.0% never married, 54.5% now married, 1.1% separated, 6.3% widowed, 15.3% divorced; Foreign born: 1.0%; Speak English only: 98.0%; With disability: 18.3%; Veterans: 9.5%; Ancestry: 27.5% German, 15.2% American, 11.9% Irish, 9.7% English, 2.8% French
Religion: Six largest groups: 11.3% Catholicism, 10.9% Methodist/Pietist, 8.3% Baptist, 2.5% Non-denominational Protestant, 2.5% Lutheran, 1.5% Pentecostal
Economy: Unemployment rate: 3.5%; Leading industries: 16.5 % retail trade; 12.9 % construction; 11.9 % health care and social assistance; Farms: 967 totaling 134,995 acres; Company size: 1 employs 1,000 or more persons, 1 employs 500 to 999 persons, 9 employ 100 to 499 persons, 661 employs less than 100 persons; Business ownership: 937 women-owned, n/a Black-owned, 67 Hispanic-owned, 36 Asian-owned, 38 American Indian/Alaska Native-owned
Employment: 11.3% management, business, and financial, 3.2% computer, engineering, and science, 7.9% education, legal, community service, arts, and media, 6.7% healthcare practitioners, 16.6% service, 23.4% sales and office, 10.1% natural resources, construction, and maintenance, 20.9% production, transportation, and material moving

Income: Per capita: $25,993; Median household: $53,897; Average household: $66,445; Households with income of $100,000 or more: 18.1%; Poverty rate: 12.9%
Educational Attainment: High school diploma or higher: 89.2%; Bachelor's degree or higher: 16.6%; Graduate/professional degree or higher: 6.1%
Housing: Homeownership rate: 82.6%; Median home value: $136,400; Median year structure built: 1981; Homeowner vacancy rate: 1.7%; Median selected monthly owner costs: $1,061 with a mortgage, $386 without a mortgage; Median gross rent: $696 per month; Rental vacancy rate: 3.6%
Vital Statistics: Birth rate: 111.8 per 10,000 population; Death rate: 87.2 per 10,000 population; Age-adjusted cancer mortality rate: 164.7 deaths per 100,000 population
Health Insurance: 92.2% have insurance; 74.3% have private insurance; 32.2% have public insurance; 7.8% do not have insurance; 4.9% of children under 18 do not have insurance
Health Care: Physicians: 8.1 per 10,000 population; Dentists: 4.5 per 10,000 population; Hospital beds: 6.3 per 10,000 population; Hospital admissions: 293.4 per 10,000 population
Transportation: Commute: 94.0% car, 0.1% public transportation, 1.2% walk, 3.8% work from home; Mean travel time to work: 29.4 minutes
2016 Presidential Election: 69.7% Trump, 25.8% Clinton, 4.1% Johnson, 0.3% Stein
Additional Information Contacts
Harrison Government . . . . (812) 738-8241
http://www.harrisoncounty.in.gov

Harrison County Communities

CENTRAL (unincorporated postal area)
ZCTA: 47110

Covers a land area of 5.799 square miles and a water area of 0 square miles. Located at 38.10° N. Lat; 86.19° W. Long. Elevation is 699 feet.
Population: 701; Growth (since 2000): n/a; Density: 120.9 persons per square mile; Race: 100.0% White, 0.0% Black/African American, 0.0% Asian, 0.0% American Indian/Alaska Native, 0.0% Native Hawaiian/Other Pacific Islander, 0.0% Two or more races, 0.0% Hispanic of any race; Average household size: 4.30; Median age: 30.6; Age under 18: 28.5%; Age 65 and over: 11.3%; Males per 100 females: 102.3; Marriage status: 23.5% never married, 52.7% now married, 0.0% separated, 2.6% widowed, 21.2% divorced; Foreign born: 0.0%; Speak English only: 97.6%; With disability: 35.8%; Veterans: 5.4%; Ancestry: 44.4% German, 24.3% American, 18.7% Irish
Employment: 0.0% management, business, and financial, 0.0% computer, engineering, and science, 0.0% education, legal, community service, arts, and media, 7.1% healthcare practitioners, 46.0% service, 5.2% sales and office, 23.0% natural resources, construction, and maintenance, 18.7% production, transportation, and material moving
Income: Per capita: $15,149; Median household: $61,583; Average household: $62,231; Households with income of $100,000 or more: n/a; Poverty rate: 7.1%
Educational Attainment: High school diploma or higher: 91.9%; Bachelor's degree or higher: n/a; Graduate/professional degree or higher: n/a

School District(s)
South Harrison Com Schools (PK-12)
Enrollment: 3,347 . . . . (812) 738-2168
Housing: Homeownership rate: 100.0%; Median home value: $120,700; Median year structure built: 1985; Homeowner vacancy rate: 0.0%; Median selected monthly owner costs: $1,135 with a mortgage, $0 without a mortgage; Median gross rent: n/a per month; Rental vacancy rate: 0.0%
Health Insurance: 77.3% have insurance; 42.1% have private insurance; 48.1% have public insurance; 22.7% do not have insurance; 12.9% of children under 18 do not have insurance
Transportation: Commute: 100.0% car, 0.0% public transportation, 0.0% walk, 0.0% work from home; Mean travel time to work: 37.3 minutes

CORYDON (town). County seat. Covers a land area of 1.649 square miles and a water area of 0 square miles. Located at 38.21° N. Lat; 86.13° W. Long. Elevation is 587 feet.
History: Corydon was named by General William Henry Harrison, who owned the land on which the town was platted. Harrison chose the name for the young shepherd in the song "Pastoral Elegy," a favorite of the day. Corydon served as the capital of Indiana for a time, and was the site of the only Civil War battle fought in Indiana. The Battle of Corydon occurred in 1863, when General John Hunt Morgan and his Confederate troops crossed the Ohio River and invaded the town.
Population: 3,116; Growth (since 2000): 14.8%; Density: 1,889.2 persons per square mile; Race: 98.6% White, 0.1% Black/African American, 0.0% Asian, 0.0% American Indian/Alaska Native, 0.0% Native Hawaiian/Other Pacific Islander, 1.3% Two or more races, 0.0% Hispanic of any race; Average household size: 2.11; Median age: 47.1; Age under 18: 16.5%; Age 65 and over: 19.2%; Males per 100 females: 84.0; Marriage status: 23.9% never married, 45.2% now married, 1.5% separated, 9.4% widowed, 21.5% divorced; Foreign born: 0.0%; Speak English only: 99.4%; With disability: 29.7%; Veterans: 12.2%; Ancestry: 25.3% Irish, 22.9% German, 11.4% American, 9.2% English, 2.7% Polish
Employment: 10.4% management, business, and financial, 1.0% computer, engineering, and science, 16.6% education, legal, community service, arts, and media, 8.3% healthcare practitioners, 16.6% service, 25.7% sales and office, 3.7% natural resources, construction, and maintenance, 17.7% production, transportation, and material moving
Income: Per capita: $26,644; Median household: $44,145; Average household: $55,750; Households with income of $100,000 or more: 13.4%; Poverty rate: 21.2%
Educational Attainment: High school diploma or higher: 84.1%; Bachelor's degree or higher: 21.9%; Graduate/professional degree or higher: 10.4%

School District(s)
South Harrison Com Schools (PK-12)
Enrollment: 3,347 . . . . (812) 738-2168
Housing: Homeownership rate: 63.9%; Median home value: $108,300; Median year structure built: 1960; Homeowner vacancy rate: 0.0%; Median selected monthly owner costs: $913 with a mortgage, $320 without a mortgage; Median gross rent: $703 per month; Rental vacancy rate: 10.2%
Health Insurance: 91.3% have insurance; 64.9% have private insurance; 41.9% have public insurance; 8.7% do not have insurance; 0.0% of children under 18 do not have insurance
Hospitals: Harrison County Hospital (68 beds)
Newspapers: Clarion News & Corydon Democrat (weekly circulation 15,000)
Transportation: Commute: 90.2% car, 0.0% public transportation, 2.2% walk, 7.6% work from home; Mean travel time to work: 22.8 minutes
Additional Information Contacts
Town of Corydon. . . . . (812) 738-2138
http://www.thisisindiana.org

CRANDALL (town). Covers a land area of 0.102 square miles and a water area of 0 square miles. Located at 38.29° N. Lat; 86.07° W. Long. Elevation is 653 feet.
Population: 169; Growth (since 2000): 29.0%; Density: 1,659.4 persons per square mile; Race: 100.0% White, 0.0% Black/African American, 0.0% Asian, 0.0% American Indian/Alaska Native, 0.0% Native Hawaiian/Other Pacific Islander, 0.0% Two or more races, 0.0% Hispanic of any race; Average household size: 2.82; Median age: 30.3; Age under 18: 42.6%; Age 65 and over: 17.8%; Males per 100 females: 100.0; Marriage status: 23.4% never married, 62.6% now married, 2.8% separated, 4.7% widowed, 9.3% divorced; Foreign born: 0.0%; Speak English only: 99.3%; With disability: 13.0%; Veterans: 11.3%; Ancestry: 33.7% German, 16.0% American, 4.1% English, 4.1% Irish, 3.0% Scottish
Employment: 8.8% management, business, and financial, 14.0% computer, engineering, and science, 7.0% education, legal, community service, arts, and media, 8.8% healthcare practitioners, 28.1% service, 14.0% sales and office, 1.8% natural resources, construction, and maintenance, 17.5% production, transportation, and material moving
Income: Per capita: $19,328; Median household: $34,500; Average household: $53,990; Households with income of $100,000 or more: 11.7%; Poverty rate: 23.1%
Educational Attainment: High school diploma or higher: 83.9%; Bachelor's degree or higher: 21.5%; Graduate/professional degree or higher: 6.5%
Housing: Homeownership rate: 78.3%; Median home value: $85,000; Median year structure built: Before 1940; Homeowner vacancy rate: 7.8%; Median selected monthly owner costs: $792 with a mortgage, $350 without a mortgage; Median gross rent: $900 per month; Rental vacancy rate: 0.0%

Health Insurance: 84.6% have insurance; 69.8% have private insurance; 28.4% have public insurance; 15.4% do not have insurance; 12.5% of children under 18 do not have insurance
Transportation: Commute: 93.0% car, 0.0% public transportation, 0.0% walk, 7.0% work from home; Mean travel time to work: 30.8 minutes

DEPAUW (unincorporated postal area)
ZCTA: 47115

Covers a land area of 56.975 square miles and a water area of 0.216 square miles. Located at 38.35° N. Lat; 86.21° W. Long. Elevation is 650 feet.

Population: 2,572; Growth (since 2000): 9.4%; Density: 45.1 persons per square mile; Race: 98.1% White, 0.3% Black/African American, 0.0% Asian, 0.0% American Indian/Alaska Native, 0.0% Native Hawaiian/Other Pacific Islander, 1.6% Two or more races, 2.4% Hispanic of any race; Average household size: 2.77; Median age: 50.2; Age under 18: 17.5%; Age 65 and over: 21.2%; Males per 100 females: 102.3; Marriage status: 21.1% never married, 65.5% now married, 0.8% separated, 4.7% widowed, 8.7% divorced; Foreign born: 2.4%; Speak English only: 97.6%; With disability: 27.3%; Veterans: 10.0%; Ancestry: 20.5% German, 14.9% American, 10.8% European, 9.9% Irish, 8.1% English

Employment: 12.1% management, business, and financial, 3.7% computer, engineering, and science, 13.8% education, legal, community service, arts, and media, 7.7% healthcare practitioners, 19.8% service, 23.2% sales and office, 5.8% natural resources, construction, and maintenance, 13.8% production, transportation, and material moving

Income: Per capita: $22,743; Median household: $40,701; Average household: $60,585; Households with income of $100,000 or more: 13.1%; Poverty rate: 15.3%

Educational Attainment: High school diploma or higher: 83.0%; Bachelor's degree or higher: 15.9%; Graduate/professional degree or higher: 6.2%

Housing: Homeownership rate: 85.9%; Median home value: $126,900; Median year structure built: 1973; Homeowner vacancy rate: 10.5%; Median selected monthly owner costs: $969 with a mortgage, $440 without a mortgage; Median gross rent: $516 per month; Rental vacancy rate: 4.6%

Health Insurance: 91.3% have insurance; 74.1% have private insurance; 36.8% have public insurance; 8.7% do not have insurance; 8.3% of children under 18 do not have insurance

Transportation: Commute: 96.0% car, 0.0% public transportation, 0.0% walk, 4.0% work from home; Mean travel time to work: 36.3 minutes

ELIZABETH (town). Covers a land area of 0.165 square miles and a water area of 0 square miles. Located at 38.12° N. Lat; 85.97° W. Long. Elevation is 728 feet.
Population: 189; Growth (since 2000): 38.0%; Density: 1,143.0 persons per square mile; Race: 95.2% White, 0.0% Black/African American, 0.0% Asian, 0.0% American Indian/Alaska Native, 0.0% Native Hawaiian/Other Pacific Islander, 4.8% Two or more races, 0.0% Hispanic of any race; Average household size: 2.74; Median age: 35.9; Age under 18: 26.5%; Age 65 and over: 14.3%; Males per 100 females: 97.6; Marriage status: 29.0% never married, 57.9% now married, 0.0% separated, 4.8% widowed, 8.3% divorced; Foreign born: 1.1%; Speak English only: 97.6%; With disability: 17.5%; Veterans: 7.9%; Ancestry: 27.0% German, 16.9% Irish, 13.8% American, 11.1% English, 2.6% Norwegian
Employment: 10.5% management, business, and financial, 1.2% computer, engineering, and science, 10.5% education, legal, community service, arts, and media, 1.2% healthcare practitioners, 19.8% service, 20.9% sales and office, 12.8% natural resources, construction, and maintenance, 23.3% production, transportation, and material moving
Income: Per capita: $22,176; Median household: $44,583; Average household: $62,620; Households with income of $100,000 or more: 14.4%; Poverty rate: 7.9%
Educational Attainment: High school diploma or higher: 93.0%; Bachelor's degree or higher: 15.6%; Graduate/professional degree or higher: 2.3%

School District(s)

South Harrison Com Schools (PK-12)
Enrollment: 3,347 . . . . (812) 738-2168

Housing: Homeownership rate: 75.4%; Median home value: $100,000; Median year structure built: 1953; Homeowner vacancy rate: 0.0%; Median selected monthly owner costs: $1,014 with a mortgage, $254 without a mortgage; Median gross rent: $792 per month; Rental vacancy rate: 19.0%

Health Insurance: 89.4% have insurance; 69.8% have private insurance; 32.3% have public insurance; 10.6% do not have insurance; 2.0% of children under 18 do not have insurance
Transportation: Commute: 88.4% car, 11.6% public transportation, 0.0% walk, 0.0% work from home; Mean travel time to work: 34.9 minutes

LACONIA (town). Covers a land area of 0.050 square miles and a water area of 0 square miles. Located at 38.03° N. Lat; 86.09° W. Long. Elevation is 663 feet.
History: Laid out 1816.
Population: 36; Growth (since 2000): 24.1%; Density: 725.3 persons per square mile; Race: 100.0% White, 0.0% Black/African American, 0.0% Asian, 0.0% American Indian/Alaska Native, 0.0% Native Hawaiian/Other Pacific Islander, 0.0% Two or more races, 8.3% Hispanic of any race; Average household size: 2.40; Median age: 58.0; Age under 18: 8.3%; Age 65 and over: 16.7%; Males per 100 females: 92.3; Marriage status: 3.0% never married, 51.5% now married, 0.0% separated, 6.1% widowed, 39.4% divorced; Foreign born: 0.0%; Speak English only: 100.0%; With disability: 44.4%; Veterans: 24.2%; Ancestry: 25.0% American, 13.9% Scottish, 8.3% German, 8.3% Scotch-Irish, 2.8% Dutch
Employment: 10.0% management, business, and financial, 0.0% computer, engineering, and science, 0.0% education, legal, community service, arts, and media, 0.0% healthcare practitioners, 10.0% service, 30.0% sales and office, 20.0% natural resources, construction, and maintenance, 30.0% production, transportation, and material moving
Income: Per capita: $19,667; Median household: $43,125; Average household: $43,267; Households with income of $100,000 or more: n/a; Poverty rate: 25.0%
Educational Attainment: High school diploma or higher: 73.3%; Bachelor's degree or higher: n/a; Graduate/professional degree or higher: n/a
Housing: Homeownership rate: 66.7%; Median home value: $80,000; Median year structure built: Before 1940; Homeowner vacancy rate: 0.0%; Median selected monthly owner costs: $750 with a mortgage, $450 without a mortgage; Median gross rent: $542 per month; Rental vacancy rate: 0.0%
Health Insurance: 88.9% have insurance; 41.7% have private insurance; 58.3% have public insurance; 11.1% do not have insurance; 0.0% of children under 18 do not have insurance
Transportation: Commute: 50.0% car, 0.0% public transportation, 0.0% walk, 50.0% work from home; Mean travel time to work: 0.0 minutes

LANESVILLE (town). Covers a land area of 0.523 square miles and a water area of 0 square miles. Located at 38.23° N. Lat; 85.99° W. Long. Elevation is 699 feet.
History: Lanesville was settled in 1792 as a stage stop and trading center for surrounding farms. It was platted in 1817, and named for General Lane, a surveyor who was an early resident.
Population: 683; Growth (since 2000): 11.2%; Density: 1,306.1 persons per square mile; Race: 94.3% White, 3.1% Black/African American, 0.0% Asian, 0.0% American Indian/Alaska Native, 0.0% Native Hawaiian/Other Pacific Islander, 2.6% Two or more races, 0.0% Hispanic of any race; Average household size: 2.59; Median age: 38.8; Age under 18: 21.8%; Age 65 and over: 20.4%; Males per 100 females: 93.8; Marriage status: 29.4% never married, 52.9% now married, 1.7% separated, 5.0% widowed, 12.7% divorced; Foreign born: 0.3%; Speak English only: 99.0%; With disability: 12.6%; Veterans: 9.6%; Ancestry: 33.5% German, 16.1% Irish, 13.5% American, 8.2% English, 6.9% French
Employment: 12.9% management, business, and financial, 4.9% computer, engineering, and science, 5.2% education, legal, community service, arts, and media, 8.0% healthcare practitioners, 20.1% service, 23.0% sales and office, 12.1% natural resources, construction, and maintenance, 13.8% production, transportation, and material moving
Income: Per capita: $26,933; Median household: $52,813; Average household: $64,963; Households with income of $100,000 or more: 18.2%; Poverty rate: 4.1%
Educational Attainment: High school diploma or higher: 96.6%; Bachelor's degree or higher: 23.4%; Graduate/professional degree or higher: 4.0%

School District(s)

Lanesville Community School Corp (PK-12)
Enrollment: 524. . . . . (812) 952-2555

Housing: Homeownership rate: 72.3%; Median home value: $127,100; Median year structure built: 1966; Homeowner vacancy rate: 3.0%; Median

selected monthly owner costs: $1,054 with a mortgage, $417 without a mortgage; Median gross rent: $713 per month; Rental vacancy rate: 7.6%
Health Insurance: 90.8% have insurance; 81.1% have private insurance; 26.4% have public insurance; 9.2% do not have insurance; 4.0% of children under 18 do not have insurance
Transportation: Commute: 90.9% car, 0.0% public transportation, 6.1% walk, 2.0% work from home; Mean travel time to work: 30.1 minutes

MAUCKPORT (town). Covers a land area of 0.189 square miles and a water area of 0.013 square miles. Located at 38.02° N. Lat; 86.20° W. Long. Elevation is 440 feet.
Population: 61; Growth (since 2000): -26.5%; Density: 322.8 persons per square mile; Race: 100.0% White, 0.0% Black/African American, 0.0% Asian, 0.0% American Indian/Alaska Native, 0.0% Native Hawaiian/Other Pacific Islander, 0.0% Two or more races, 0.0% Hispanic of any race; Average household size: 2.35; Median age: 35.3; Age under 18: 23.0%; Age 65 and over: 18.0%; Males per 100 females: 102.5; Marriage status: 47.3% never married, 34.5% now married, 9.1% separated, 3.6% widowed, 14.5% divorced; Foreign born: 0.0%; Speak English only: 100.0%; With disability: 21.3%; Veterans: 10.6%; Ancestry: 47.5% German, 9.8% American, 9.8% Irish, 4.9% English, 3.3% French
Employment: 3.2% management, business, and financial, 0.0% computer, engineering, and science, 0.0% education, legal, community service, arts, and media, 16.1% healthcare practitioners, 38.7% service, 25.8% sales and office, 16.1% natural resources, construction, and maintenance, 0.0% production, transportation, and material moving
Income: Per capita: $22,877; Median household: $36,250; Average household: $51,988; Households with income of $100,000 or more: 15.3%; Poverty rate: 1.7%
Educational Attainment: High school diploma or higher: 82.9%; Bachelor's degree or higher: 5.7%; Graduate/professional degree or higher: n/a
Housing: Homeownership rate: 88.5%; Median home value: $63,800; Median year structure built: Before 1940; Homeowner vacancy rate: 0.0%; Median selected monthly owner costs: $781 with a mortgage, $333 without a mortgage; Median gross rent: n/a per month; Rental vacancy rate: 0.0%
Health Insurance: 72.1% have insurance; 49.2% have private insurance; 26.2% have public insurance; 27.9% do not have insurance; 31.3% of children under 18 do not have insurance
Transportation: Commute: 86.2% car, 0.0% public transportation, 13.8% walk, 0.0% work from home; Mean travel time to work: 32.9 minutes

NEW AMSTERDAM (town). Covers a land area of 0.080 square miles and a water area of 0.024 square miles. Located at 38.10° N. Lat; 86.27° W. Long. Elevation is 449 feet.
Population: 20; Growth (since 2000): 1,900.0%; Density: 248.6 persons per square mile; Race: 90.0% White, 0.0% Black/African American, 0.0% Asian, 10.0% American Indian/Alaska Native, 0.0% Native Hawaiian/Other Pacific Islander, 0.0% Two or more races, 0.0% Hispanic of any race; Average household size: 2.86; Median age: 62.5; Age under 18: 10.0%; Age 65 and over: 50.0%; Males per 100 females: 125.0; Marriage status: 31.6% never married, 57.9% now married, 0.0% separated, 10.5% widowed, 0.0% divorced; Foreign born: 0.0%; Speak English only: 100.0%; With disability: 35.0%; Veterans: 0.0%; Ancestry: 70.0% German, 25.0% Irish, 20.0% Scotch-Irish
Employment: 0.0% management, business, and financial, 0.0% computer, engineering, and science, 0.0% education, legal, community service, arts, and media, 0.0% healthcare practitioners, 20.0% service, 40.0% sales and office, 0.0% natural resources, construction, and maintenance, 40.0% production, transportation, and material moving
Income: Per capita: $27,390; Median household: $87,813; Average household: $74,943; Households with income of $100,000 or more: n/a; Poverty rate: n/a
Educational Attainment: High school diploma or higher: 88.9%; Bachelor's degree or higher: 5.6%; Graduate/professional degree or higher: n/a
Housing: Homeownership rate: 100.0%; Median home value: n/a; Median year structure built: 2006; Homeowner vacancy rate: 36.4%; Median selected monthly owner costs: n/a with a mortgage, n/a without a mortgage; Median gross rent: n/a per month; Rental vacancy rate: 0.0%
Health Insurance: 85.0% have insurance; 50.0% have private insurance; 85.0% have public insurance; 15.0% do not have insurance; 0.0% of children under 18 do not have insurance
Transportation: Commute: 100.0% car, 0.0% public transportation, 0.0% walk, 0.0% work from home; Mean travel time to work: 0.0 minutes

NEW MIDDLETOWN (town). Covers a land area of 0.041 square miles and a water area of 0 square miles. Located at 38.16° N. Lat; 86.05° W. Long. Elevation is 702 feet.
Population: 42; Growth (since 2000): -45.5%; Density: 1,021.4 persons per square mile; Race: 76.2% White, 23.8% Black/African American, 0.0% Asian, 0.0% American Indian/Alaska Native, 0.0% Native Hawaiian/Other Pacific Islander, 0.0% Two or more races, 0.0% Hispanic of any race; Average household size: 2.33; Median age: 54.8; Age under 18: 11.9%; Age 65 and over: 26.2%; Males per 100 females: 121.4; Marriage status: 10.8% never married, 35.1% now married, 0.0% separated, 18.9% widowed, 35.1% divorced; Foreign born: 0.0%; Speak English only: 100.0%; With disability: 9.5%; Veterans: 29.7%; Ancestry: 42.9% Irish, 26.2% German, 9.5% English, 7.1% Austrian, 4.8% American
Employment: 5.0% management, business, and financial, 0.0% computer, engineering, and science, 5.0% education, legal, community service, arts, and media, 25.0% healthcare practitioners, 0.0% service, 30.0% sales and office, 10.0% natural resources, construction, and maintenance, 25.0% production, transportation, and material moving
Income: Per capita: $22,619; Median household: n/a; Average household: $38,200; Households with income of $100,000 or more: n/a; Poverty rate: 2.6%
Educational Attainment: High school diploma or higher: 96.7%; Bachelor's degree or higher: 16.7%; Graduate/professional degree or higher: 3.3%

School District(s)

South Harrison Com Schools (PK-12)
Enrollment: 3,347 . . . . (812) 738-2168

Housing: Homeownership rate: 38.9%; Median home value: n/a; Median year structure built: Before 1940; Homeowner vacancy rate: 56.3%; Median selected monthly owner costs: $925 with a mortgage, n/a without a mortgage; Median gross rent: n/a per month; Rental vacancy rate: 0.0%
Health Insurance: 97.6% have insurance; 54.8% have private insurance; 42.9% have public insurance; 2.4% do not have insurance; 0.0% of children under 18 do not have insurance
Transportation: Commute: 95.0% car, 0.0% public transportation, 0.0% walk, 5.0% work from home; Mean travel time to work: 38.4 minutes

NEW SALISBURY (CDP). Covers a land area of 1.978 square miles and a water area of 0 square miles. Located at 38.31° N. Lat; 86.10° W. Long. Elevation is 728 feet.
Population: 555; Growth (since 2000): n/a; Density: 280.7 persons per square mile; Race: 100.0% White, 0.0% Black/African American, 0.0% Asian, 0.0% American Indian/Alaska Native, 0.0% Native Hawaiian/Other Pacific Islander, 0.0% Two or more races, 0.0% Hispanic of any race; Average household size: 2.75; Median age: 52.3; Age under 18: 17.7%; Age 65 and over: 35.3%; Males per 100 females: 100.3; Marriage status: 16.0% never married, 69.2% now married, 0.0% separated, 11.0% widowed, 3.8% divorced; Foreign born: 0.0%; Speak English only: 100.0%; With disability: 23.8%; Veterans: 11.2%; Ancestry: 14.6% American, 13.9% English, 6.7% Irish, 6.5% European, 3.1% German
Employment: 40.8% management, business, and financial, 0.0% computer, engineering, and science, 0.0% education, legal, community service, arts, and media, 0.0% healthcare practitioners, 15.0% service, 16.7% sales and office, 27.5% natural resources, construction, and maintenance, 0.0% production, transportation, and material moving
Income: Per capita: $22,618; Median household: $35,313; Average household: $59,370; Households with income of $100,000 or more: 16.3%; Poverty rate: 16.8%
Educational Attainment: High school diploma or higher: 90.2%; Bachelor's degree or higher: 16.4%; Graduate/professional degree or higher: 7.7%
Housing: Homeownership rate: 100.0%; Median home value: $146,700; Median year structure built: 1973; Homeowner vacancy rate: 0.0%; Median selected monthly owner costs: $956 with a mortgage, $413 without a mortgage; Median gross rent: n/a per month; Rental vacancy rate: 0.0%
Health Insurance: 100.0% have insurance; 93.7% have private insurance; 39.1% have public insurance; 0.0% do not have insurance; 0.0% of children under 18 do not have insurance
Transportation: Commute: 100.0% car, 0.0% public transportation, 0.0% walk, 0.0% work from home; Mean travel time to work: 0.0 minutes

PALMYRA (town). Covers a land area of 1.238 square miles and a water area of 0.042 square miles. Located at 38.41° N. Lat; 86.11° W. Long. Elevation is 771 feet.
History: Palmyra was founded in 1810 as a farming village.

Population: 1,268; Growth (since 2000): 100.3%; Density: 1,024.2 persons per square mile; Race: 97.2% White, 0.5% Black/African American, 0.0% Asian, 0.0% American Indian/Alaska Native, 0.0% Native Hawaiian/Other Pacific Islander, 2.2% Two or more races, 0.7% Hispanic of any race; Average household size: 2.37; Median age: 38.1; Age under 18: 30.7%; Age 65 and over: 19.0%; Males per 100 females: 92.1; Marriage status: 22.3% never married, 41.0% now married, 1.6% separated, 11.2% widowed, 25.5% divorced; Foreign born: 1.3%; Speak English only: 98.5%; With disability: 17.7%; Veterans: 13.2%; Ancestry: 27.4% German, 13.1% American, 9.0% English, 8.7% Irish, 3.2% French
Employment: 10.9% management, business, and financial, 8.2% computer, engineering, and science, 3.8% education, legal, community service, arts, and media, 5.2% healthcare practitioners, 18.2% service, 23.3% sales and office, 15.1% natural resources, construction, and maintenance, 15.3% production, transportation, and material moving
Income: Per capita: $20,788; Median household: $31,951; Average household: $47,981; Households with income of $100,000 or more: 9.3%; Poverty rate: 18.8%
Educational Attainment: High school diploma or higher: 93.6%; Bachelor's degree or higher: 9.9%; Graduate/professional degree or higher: 3.5%

School District(s)

North Harrison Com School Corp (PK-12)
Enrollment: 2,237 . . . . (812) 347-2407

Housing: Homeownership rate: 55.4%; Median home value: $112,900; Median year structure built: 1976; Homeowner vacancy rate: 0.0%; Median selected monthly owner costs: $983 with a mortgage, $400 without a mortgage; Median gross rent: $596 per month; Rental vacancy rate: 0.0%
Health Insurance: 89.0% have insurance; 56.4% have private insurance; 46.1% have public insurance; 11.0% do not have insurance; 6.4% of children under 18 do not have insurance
Transportation: Commute: 95.3% car, 0.0% public transportation, 1.5% walk, 3.2% work from home; Mean travel time to work: 37.1 minutes

RAMSEY (unincorporated postal area)

ZCTA: 47166

Covers a land area of 12.842 square miles and a water area of 0 square miles. Located at 38.31° N. Lat; 86.17° W. Long. Elevation is 705 feet.
Population: 1,364; Growth (since 2000): 9.6%; Density: 106.2 persons per square mile; Race: 96.8% White, 0.0% Black/African American, 1.8% Asian, 0.0% American Indian/Alaska Native, 0.0% Native Hawaiian/Other Pacific Islander, 1.3% Two or more races, 0.0% Hispanic of any race; Average household size: 2.64; Median age: 43.1; Age under 18: 17.7%; Age 65 and over: 21.4%; Males per 100 females: 99.4; Marriage status: 29.4% never married, 49.1% now married, 0.0% separated, 6.3% widowed, 15.3% divorced; Foreign born: 1.8%; Speak English only: 98.9%; With disability: 11.6%; Veterans: 5.0%; Ancestry: 38.0% German, 9.0% English, 7.6% French, 7.2% Irish, 6.6% American
Employment: 7.7% management, business, and financial, 1.7% computer, engineering, and science, 6.9% education, legal, community service, arts, and media, 1.6% healthcare practitioners, 28.0% service, 21.1% sales and office, 13.2% natural resources, construction, and maintenance, 19.8% production, transportation, and material moving
Income: Per capita: $24,416; Median household: $41,750; Average household: $62,735; Households with income of $100,000 or more: 18.2%; Poverty rate: 19.4%
Educational Attainment: High school diploma or higher: 87.9%; Bachelor's degree or higher: 8.6%; Graduate/professional degree or higher: 2.1%

School District(s)

North Harrison Com School Corp (PK-12)
Enrollment: 2,237 . . . . (812) 347-2407

Housing: Homeownership rate: 89.3%; Median home value: $106,600; Median year structure built: 1979; Homeowner vacancy rate: 0.0%; Median selected monthly owner costs: $958 with a mortgage, $404 without a mortgage; Median gross rent: n/a per month; Rental vacancy rate: 0.0%
Health Insurance: 87.1% have insurance; 78.2% have private insurance; 23.0% have public insurance; 12.9% do not have insurance; 11.6% of children under 18 do not have insurance
Transportation: Commute: 100.0% car, 0.0% public transportation, 0.0% walk, 0.0% work from home; Mean travel time to work: 29.9 minutes

Hendricks County

Located in central Indiana; drained by the Eel and Whitelick Rivers and Mill Creek. Covers a land area of 406.911 square miles, a water area of 1.866 square miles, and is located in the Eastern Time Zone at 39.77° N. Lat., 86.51° W. Long. The county was founded in 1823. County seat is Danville.

Hendricks County is part of the Indianapolis-Carmel-Anderson, IN Metropolitan Statistical Area. The entire metro area includes: Boone County, IN; Brown County, IN; Hamilton County, IN; Hancock County, IN; Hendricks County, IN; Johnson County, IN; Madison County, IN; Marion County, IN; Morgan County, IN; Putnam County, IN; Shelby County, IN

Population: 158,170; Growth (since 2000): 52.0%; Density: 388.7 persons per square mile; Race: 88.2% White, 6.3% Black/African American, 2.6% Asian, 0.2% American Indian/Alaska Native, 0.0% Native Hawaiian/Other Pacific Islander, 1.7% two or more races, 3.6% Hispanic of any race; Average household size: 2.72; Median age: 37.6; Age under 18: 25.8%; Age 65 and over: 12.7%; Males per 100 females: 99.4; Marriage status: 24.6% never married, 58.6% now married, 1.3% separated, 5.1% widowed, 11.7% divorced; Foreign born: 4.8%; Speak English only: 93.9%; With disability: 11.4%; Veterans: 8.6%; Ancestry: 22.4% German, 12.1% American, 11.6% Irish, 8.7% English, 3.4% Italian
Religion: Six largest groups: 13.5% Baptist, 7.5% Catholicism, 6.4% Non-denominational Protestant, 5.2% Methodist/Pietist, 1.8% Lutheran, 1.5% Latter-day Saints
Economy: Unemployment rate: 3.0%; Leading industries: 13.4 % retail trade; 10.9 % health care and social assistance; 10.8 % construction; Farms: 694 totaling 218,398 acres; Company size: 3 employ 1,000 or more persons, 7 employ 500 to 999 persons, 104 employ 100 to 499 persons, 3,087 employ less than 100 persons; Business ownership: 3,878 women-owned, 332 Black-owned, 183 Hispanic-owned, 434 Asian-owned, 46 American Indian/Alaska Native-owned
Employment: 16.2% management, business, and financial, 6.2% computer, engineering, and science, 10.1% education, legal, community service, arts, and media, 7.8% healthcare practitioners, 14.5% service, 24.4% sales and office, 7.8% natural resources, construction, and maintenance, 13.0% production, transportation, and material moving
Income: Per capita: $33,031; Median household: $74,245; Average household: $88,986; Households with income of $100,000 or more: 33.8%; Poverty rate: 5.1%
Educational Attainment: High school diploma or higher: 93.6%; Bachelor's degree or higher: 35.3%; Graduate/professional degree or higher: 11.8%
Housing: Homeownership rate: 78.7%; Median home value: $171,600; Median year structure built: 1995; Homeowner vacancy rate: 0.7%; Median selected monthly owner costs: $1,346 with a mortgage, $461 without a mortgage; Median gross rent: $1,026 per month; Rental vacancy rate: 5.4%
Vital Statistics: Birth rate: 109.0 per 10,000 population; Death rate: 64.8 per 10,000 population; Age-adjusted cancer mortality rate: 150.6 deaths per 100,000 population
Health Insurance: 93.1% have insurance; 82.3% have private insurance; 21.8% have public insurance; 6.9% do not have insurance; 5.8% of children under 18 do not have insurance
Health Care: Physicians: 17.3 per 10,000 population; Dentists: 4.9 per 10,000 population; Hospital beds: 15.8 per 10,000 population; Hospital admissions: 770.1 per 10,000 population
Air Quality Index (AQI): Percent of Days: 91.7% good, 8.3% moderate, 0.0% unhealthy for sensitive individuals, 0.0% unhealthy, 0.0% very unhealthy; Annual median: 38; Annual maximum: 93
Transportation: Commute: 93.8% car, 0.1% public transportation, 0.8% walk, 4.3% work from home; Mean travel time to work: 27.0 minutes
2016 Presidential Election: 63.4% Trump, 29.7% Clinton, 5.7% Johnson, 0.3% Stein

Additional Information Contacts

Hendricks Government . . . . (317) 745-9221
http://www.co.hendricks.in.us

Hendricks County Communities

AMO (town). Covers a land area of 0.633 square miles and a water area of 0 square miles. Located at 39.69° N. Lat; 86.61° W. Long. Elevation is 820 feet.
Population: 595; Growth (since 2000): 43.7%; Density: 940.4 persons per square mile; Race: 99.2% White, 0.0% Black/African American, 0.0% Asian, 0.0% American Indian/Alaska Native, 0.0% Native Hawaiian/Other Pacific Islander, 0.8% Two or more races, 0.0% Hispanic of any race; Average household size: 3.16; Median age: 35.7; Age under 18: 23.4%; Age 65 and over: 12.1%; Males per 100 females: 99.5; Marriage status: 21.8% never married, 61.7% now married, 2.5% separated, 1.1% widowed, 15.5% divorced; Foreign born: 0.0%; Speak English only: 99.3%; With disability: 13.6%; Veterans: 7.9%; Ancestry: 19.2% American, 15.3% German, 12.6% Irish, 10.8% English, 8.2% Italian
Employment: 9.1% management, business, and financial, 1.9% computer, engineering, and science, 7.9% education, legal, community service, arts, and media, 2.8% healthcare practitioners, 17.3% service, 24.2% sales and office, 15.1% natural resources, construction, and maintenance, 21.7% production, transportation, and material moving
Income: Per capita: $24,717; Median household: $71,500; Average household: $76,164; Households with income of $100,000 or more: 16.5%; Poverty rate: 12.4%
Educational Attainment: High school diploma or higher: 82.2%; Bachelor's degree or higher: 14.9%; Graduate/professional degree or higher: 0.8%

School District(s)

Mill Creek Community Sch Corp (PK-12)
Enrollment: 1,552 . . . . (317) 539-9200
Housing: Homeownership rate: 66.0%; Median home value: $125,700; Median year structure built: Before 1940; Homeowner vacancy rate: 0.0%; Median selected monthly owner costs: $1,064 with a mortgage, $350 without a mortgage; Median gross rent: $982 per month; Rental vacancy rate: 0.0%
Health Insurance: 92.6% have insurance; 78.8% have private insurance; 25.0% have public insurance; 7.4% do not have insurance; 3.3% of children under 18 do not have insurance
Transportation: Commute: 92.0% car, 0.0% public transportation, 7.6% walk, 0.0% work from home; Mean travel time to work: 30.7 minutes

AVON (town). Covers a land area of 14.241 square miles and a water area of 0.102 square miles. Located at 39.77° N. Lat; 86.38° W. Long. Elevation is 833 feet.
History: Avon was incorporated in 1995. Previous town names included Hampton, White Lick, Smootsdale and New Philadelphia. The name Avon was placed on a sign by the railroad company.
Population: 16,479; Growth (since 2000): 163.7%; Density: 1,157.2 persons per square mile; Race: 84.0% White, 7.4% Black/African American, 3.0% Asian, 0.4% American Indian/Alaska Native, 0.0% Native Hawaiian/Other Pacific Islander, 4.6% Two or more races, 8.6% Hispanic of any race; Average household size: 2.91; Median age: 35.3; Age under 18: 27.6%; Age 65 and over: 10.9%; Males per 100 females: 93.4; Marriage status: 25.2% never married, 56.7% now married, 1.2% separated, 4.6% widowed, 13.4% divorced; Foreign born: 9.2%; Speak English only: 89.3%; With disability: 8.7%; Veterans: 8.0%; Ancestry: 25.0% German, 13.0% Irish, 9.6% English, 7.0% American, 3.1% French
Employment: 19.2% management, business, and financial, 8.2% computer, engineering, and science, 8.9% education, legal, community service, arts, and media, 9.2% healthcare practitioners, 14.4% service, 24.6% sales and office, 6.3% natural resources, construction, and maintenance, 9.3% production, transportation, and material moving
Income: Per capita: $34,913; Median household: $85,433; Average household: $98,463; Households with income of $100,000 or more: 42.8%; Poverty rate: 5.4%
Educational Attainment: High school diploma or higher: 92.5%; Bachelor's degree or higher: 38.7%; Graduate/professional degree or higher: 14.0%

School District(s)

Avon Community School Corp (PK-12)
Enrollment: 9,627 . . . . (317) 544-6000
Housing: Homeownership rate: 80.9%; Median home value: $185,200; Median year structure built: 2000; Homeowner vacancy rate: 0.9%; Median selected monthly owner costs: $1,486 with a mortgage, $452 without a mortgage; Median gross rent: $1,055 per month; Rental vacancy rate: 4.7%
Health Insurance: 93.0% have insurance; 84.5% have private insurance; 18.2% have public insurance; 7.0% do not have insurance; 1.8% of children under 18 do not have insurance
Hospitals: IU Health West Hospital
Newspapers: Hendricks Co Flyer (weekly circulation 83,000)
Transportation: Commute: 92.4% car, 0.0% public transportation, 0.6% walk, 6.1% work from home; Mean travel time to work: 29.5 minutes
Additional Information Contacts
Town of Avon . . . . (317) 272-0948
http://www.avongov.org

BROWNSBURG (town). Covers a land area of 11.076 square miles and a water area of 0.076 square miles. Located at 39.84° N. Lat; 86.39° W. Long. Elevation is 883 feet.
History: Brownsburg's first settler was James B. Brown, a Kentucky native, who settled in Brown Township in 1824. At the time the area was dense and unbroken wilderness with only hunters and trappers in the area.
Population: 24,625; Growth (since 2000): 69.6%; Density: 2,223.3 persons per square mile; Race: 91.5% White, 3.6% Black/African American, 2.6% Asian, 0.3% American Indian/Alaska Native, 0.0% Native Hawaiian/Other Pacific Islander, 0.8% Two or more races, 3.1% Hispanic of any race; Average household size: 2.69; Median age: 37.3; Age under 18: 24.3%; Age 65 and over: 13.3%; Males per 100 females: 92.2; Marriage status: 23.2% never married, 60.3% now married, 2.7% separated, 5.9% widowed, 10.6% divorced; Foreign born: 5.0%; Speak English only: 93.8%; With disability: 12.5%; Veterans: 9.4%; Ancestry: 21.5% German, 15.9% American, 11.3% Irish, 9.7% English, 3.2% French
Employment: 16.4% management, business, and financial, 4.1% computer, engineering, and science, 9.2% education, legal, community service, arts, and media, 8.8% healthcare practitioners, 17.8% service, 26.4% sales and office, 6.0% natural resources, construction, and maintenance, 11.3% production, transportation, and material moving
Income: Per capita: $32,690; Median household: $68,986; Average household: $86,960; Households with income of $100,000 or more: 31.0%; Poverty rate: 3.4%
Educational Attainment: High school diploma or higher: 92.7%; Bachelor's degree or higher: 35.6%; Graduate/professional degree or higher: 11.5%

School District(s)

Brownsburg Community School Corp (PK-12)
Enrollment: 8,719 . . . . (317) 852-5726

Vocational/Technical School(s)

Avant Gard The School (Private, For-profit)
Enrollment: n/a . . . . (317) 272-1212
Tuition: $14,130
Midwest Technical Institute (Private, For-profit)
Enrollment: n/a . . . . (317) 456-4710
Housing: Homeownership rate: 75.0%; Median home value: $163,600; Median year structure built: 1997; Homeowner vacancy rate: 0.6%; Median selected monthly owner costs: $1,240 with a mortgage, $473 without a mortgage; Median gross rent: $1,032 per month; Rental vacancy rate: 4.1%
Health Insurance: 91.0% have insurance; 81.7% have private insurance; 21.8% have public insurance; 9.0% do not have insurance; 8.4% of children under 18 do not have insurance
Safety: Violent crime rate: n/a per 10,000 population; Property crime rate: 114.5 per 10,000 population
Transportation: Commute: 94.5% car, 0.0% public transportation, 0.4% walk, 3.6% work from home; Mean travel time to work: 28.1 minutes
Additional Information Contacts
Town of Brownsburg . . . . (317) 852-1120
http://www.brownsburg.org

CLAYTON (town). Covers a land area of 0.763 square miles and a water area of 0 square miles. Located at 39.69° N. Lat; 86.52° W. Long. Elevation is 876 feet.
Population: 998; Growth (since 2000): 44.0%; Density: 1,308.7 persons per square mile; Race: 99.5% White, 0.0% Black/African American, 0.0% Asian, 0.0% American Indian/Alaska Native, 0.0% Native Hawaiian/Other Pacific Islander, 0.5% Two or more races, 1.6% Hispanic of any race; Average household size: 2.73; Median age: 36.1; Age under 18: 26.6%; Age 65 and over: 7.8%; Males per 100 females: 105.9; Marriage status: 26.7% never married, 57.9% now married, 0.4% separated, 5.1%

widowed, 10.3% divorced; Foreign born: 0.4%; Speak English only: 99.4%; With disability: 15.1%; Veterans: 8.5%; Ancestry: 22.9% German, 16.0% American, 15.0% English, 9.1% Irish, 6.8% Dutch
Employment: 13.5% management, business, and financial, 3.2% computer, engineering, and science, 8.6% education, legal, community service, arts, and media, 3.2% healthcare practitioners, 17.8% service, 20.6% sales and office, 13.1% natural resources, construction, and maintenance, 20.2% production, transportation, and material moving
Income: Per capita: $25,382; Median household: $58,125; Average household: $68,228; Households with income of $100,000 or more: 14.3%; Poverty rate: 6.7%
Educational Attainment: High school diploma or higher: 93.8%; Bachelor's degree or higher: 16.7%; Graduate/professional degree or higher: 5.1%

School District(s)

Mill Creek Community Sch Corp (PK-12)
Enrollment: 1,552 . . . . (317) 539-9200
Housing: Homeownership rate: 69.0%; Median home value: $131,300; Median year structure built: 1957; Homeowner vacancy rate: 2.6%; Median selected monthly owner costs: $1,169 with a mortgage, $395 without a mortgage; Median gross rent: $725 per month; Rental vacancy rate: 0.0%
Health Insurance: 86.6% have insurance; 72.8% have private insurance; 22.4% have public insurance; 13.4% do not have insurance; 16.0% of children under 18 do not have insurance
Transportation: Commute: 92.1% car, 0.0% public transportation, 3.7% walk, 1.7% work from home; Mean travel time to work: 27.1 minutes

COATESVILLE (town). Covers a land area of 0.653 square miles and a water area of 0.012 square miles. Located at 39.69° N. Lat; 86.67° W. Long. Elevation is 883 feet.
Population: 621; Growth (since 2000): 20.3%; Density: 950.4 persons per square mile; Race: 98.6% White, 0.0% Black/African American, 0.0% Asian, 0.0% American Indian/Alaska Native, 0.0% Native Hawaiian/Other Pacific Islander, 1.4% Two or more races, 0.0% Hispanic of any race; Average household size: 2.94; Median age: 38.2; Age under 18: 25.9%; Age 65 and over: 13.8%; Males per 100 females: 97.4; Marriage status: 27.5% never married, 57.4% now married, 4.5% separated, 5.7% widowed, 9.4% divorced; Foreign born: 0.0%; Speak English only: 98.4%; With disability: 17.1%; Veterans: 7.0%; Ancestry: 17.9% German, 13.4% Irish, 13.0% American, 7.9% English, 2.9% Scottish
Employment: 13.4% management, business, and financial, 2.7% computer, engineering, and science, 1.9% education, legal, community service, arts, and media, 3.4% healthcare practitioners, 21.5% service, 24.5% sales and office, 17.2% natural resources, construction, and maintenance, 15.3% production, transportation, and material moving
Income: Per capita: $25,929; Median household: $42,404; Average household: $74,384; Households with income of $100,000 or more: 19.3%; Poverty rate: 13.7%
Educational Attainment: High school diploma or higher: 79.9%; Bachelor's degree or higher: 17.1%; Graduate/professional degree or higher: 1.5%
Housing: Homeownership rate: 89.6%; Median home value: $102,200; Median year structure built: 1948; Homeowner vacancy rate: 3.0%; Median selected monthly owner costs: $957 with a mortgage, $345 without a mortgage; Median gross rent: $713 per month; Rental vacancy rate: 0.0%
Health Insurance: 84.7% have insurance; 62.3% have private insurance; 35.3% have public insurance; 15.3% do not have insurance; 15.6% of children under 18 do not have insurance
Transportation: Commute: 91.2% car, 2.3% public transportation, 0.0% walk, 5.0% work from home; Mean travel time to work: 31.2 minutes

DANVILLE (town). County seat. Covers a land area of 6.930 square miles and a water area of 0.046 square miles. Located at 39.76° N. Lat; 86.51° W. Long. Elevation is 955 feet.
History: Danville was settled in 1824 by Daniel Clark, a justice of the peace, for whom the town was named. In 1878 citizens of Danville carried off the desks, bookcases, and books of Central Normal College at Ladoga, and re-established it in Danville.
Population: 9,598; Growth (since 2000): 49.5%; Density: 1,385.0 persons per square mile; Race: 95.7% White, 2.0% Black/African American, 1.8% Asian, 0.0% American Indian/Alaska Native, 0.0% Native Hawaiian/Other Pacific Islander, 0.5% Two or more races, 1.1% Hispanic of any race; Average household size: 2.66; Median age: 37.8; Age under 18: 26.8%; Age 65 and over: 15.5%; Males per 100 females: 94.1; Marriage status: 24.9% never married, 54.0% now married, 1.7% separated, 7.0% widowed, 14.2% divorced; Foreign born: 2.2%; Speak English only: 95.8%; With disability: 13.7%; Veterans: 7.6%; Ancestry: 22.1% German, 11.3% American, 11.2% Irish, 7.0% English, 4.1% Scottish
Employment: 14.0% management, business, and financial, 3.8% computer, engineering, and science, 10.2% education, legal, community service, arts, and media, 8.7% healthcare practitioners, 17.0% service, 28.9% sales and office, 5.9% natural resources, construction, and maintenance, 11.5% production, transportation, and material moving
Income: Per capita: $29,591; Median household: $64,074; Average household: $76,663; Households with income of $100,000 or more: 28.2%; Poverty rate: 7.2%
Educational Attainment: High school diploma or higher: 93.6%; Bachelor's degree or higher: 29.5%; Graduate/professional degree or higher: 9.1%

School District(s)

Danville Community School Corp (PK-12)
Enrollment: 2,435 . . . . (317) 745-2212
Housing: Homeownership rate: 67.8%; Median home value: $152,800; Median year structure built: 1992; Homeowner vacancy rate: 0.7%; Median selected monthly owner costs: $1,341 with a mortgage, $455 without a mortgage; Median gross rent: $834 per month; Rental vacancy rate: 4.0%
Health Insurance: 91.5% have insurance; 76.0% have private insurance; 25.3% have public insurance; 8.5% do not have insurance; 5.2% of children under 18 do not have insurance
Hospitals: Hendricks Regional Health (141 beds)
Safety: Violent crime rate: n/a per 10,000 population; Property crime rate: 117.6 per 10,000 population
Newspapers: Danville Republican (weekly circulation 1,600)
Transportation: Commute: 92.0% car, 0.0% public transportation, 2.3% walk, 5.1% work from home; Mean travel time to work: 25.0 minutes
Additional Information Contacts
Town of Danville . . . . (317) 745-4180
http://www.danvilleindiana.org

LIZTON (town). Covers a land area of 0.574 square miles and a water area of 0 square miles. Located at 39.88° N. Lat; 86.54° W. Long. Elevation is 958 feet.
History: The area in which Lizton was established in 1851 was swamp land, but a drainage system converted it into fertile farm land. James Whitcomb Riley wrote about Lizton in his poem, "The Lizton Humorist."
Population: 485; Growth (since 2000): 30.4%; Density: 845.4 persons per square mile; Race: 99.0% White, 0.0% Black/African American, 0.0% Asian, 0.0% American Indian/Alaska Native, 0.0% Native Hawaiian/Other Pacific Islander, 1.0% Two or more races, 0.0% Hispanic of any race; Average household size: 2.57; Median age: 33.1; Age under 18: 26.6%; Age 65 and over: 4.9%; Males per 100 females: 113.1; Marriage status: 30.1% never married, 50.8% now married, 3.8% separated, 2.7% widowed, 16.4% divorced; Foreign born: 0.0%; Speak English only: 100.0%; With disability: 8.5%; Veterans: 9.0%; Ancestry: 22.5% American, 15.1% German, 9.9% Irish, 9.1% English, 3.3% Norwegian
Employment: 14.2% management, business, and financial, 4.5% computer, engineering, and science, 2.4% education, legal, community service, arts, and media, 6.5% healthcare practitioners, 13.8% service, 25.6% sales and office, 22.4% natural resources, construction, and maintenance, 10.6% production, transportation, and material moving
Income: Per capita: $24,548; Median household: $60,089; Average household: $61,176; Households with income of $100,000 or more: 21.7%; Poverty rate: 20.6%
Educational Attainment: High school diploma or higher: 96.0%; Bachelor's degree or higher: 26.9%; Graduate/professional degree or higher: 4.0%

School District(s)

North West Hendricks Schools (PK-12)
Enrollment: 1,786 . . . . (317) 994-4100
Housing: Homeownership rate: 50.8%; Median home value: $143,200; Median year structure built: 1973; Homeowner vacancy rate: 10.3%; Median selected monthly owner costs: $1,133 with a mortgage, $563 without a mortgage; Median gross rent: $828 per month; Rental vacancy rate: 19.1%
Health Insurance: 91.1% have insurance; 77.3% have private insurance; 18.4% have public insurance; 8.9% do not have insurance; 1.5% of children under 18 do not have insurance
Transportation: Commute: 91.4% car, 0.0% public transportation, 2.9% walk, 5.7% work from home; Mean travel time to work: 24.7 minutes

NORTH SALEM (town). Covers a land area of 0.260 square miles and a water area of 0 square miles. Located at 39.86° N. Lat; 86.64° W. Long. Elevation is 896 feet.

History: Laid out 1835.

Population: 491; Growth (since 2000): -16.9%; Density: 1,888.1 persons per square mile; Race: 96.3% White, 0.0% Black/African American, 0.0% Asian, 0.0% American Indian/Alaska Native, 0.0% Native Hawaiian/Other Pacific Islander, 3.7% Two or more races, 1.4% Hispanic of any race; Average household size: 2.38; Median age: 43.3; Age under 18: 17.3%; Age 65 and over: 21.2%; Males per 100 females: 101.6; Marriage status: 25.5% never married, 57.1% now married, 0.0% separated, 5.1% widowed, 12.3% divorced; Foreign born: 1.4%; Speak English only: 98.1%; With disability: 24.8%; Veterans: 7.1%; Ancestry: 22.8% American, 20.4% German, 15.1% Irish, 6.7% English, 4.9% Romanian

Employment: 10.7% management, business, and financial, 7.0% computer, engineering, and science, 8.4% education, legal, community service, arts, and media, 5.6% healthcare practitioners, 15.0% service, 18.7% sales and office, 8.9% natural resources, construction, and maintenance, 25.7% production, transportation, and material moving

Income: Per capita: $20,819; Median household: $41,413; Average household: $48,705; Households with income of $100,000 or more: 13.1%; Poverty rate: 9.8%

Educational Attainment: High school diploma or higher: 83.3%; Bachelor's degree or higher: 6.2%; Graduate/professional degree or higher: n/a

School District(s)

North West Hendricks Schools (PK-12)
Enrollment: 1,786 . . . . (317) 994-4100

Housing: Homeownership rate: 68.4%; Median home value: $110,400; Median year structure built: Before 1940; Homeowner vacancy rate: 8.4%; Median selected monthly owner costs: $933 with a mortgage, $463 without a mortgage; Median gross rent: $747 per month; Rental vacancy rate: 10.1%

Health Insurance: 86.4% have insurance; 65.8% have private insurance; 34.8% have public insurance; 13.6% do not have insurance; 0.0% of children under 18 do not have insurance

Transportation: Commute: 86.3% car, 0.0% public transportation, 4.4% walk, 9.3% work from home; Mean travel time to work: 29.2 minutes

PITTSBORO (town). Covers a land area of 2.951 square miles and a water area of 0 square miles. Located at 39.87° N. Lat; 86.46° W. Long. Elevation is 942 feet.

Population: 3,224; Growth (since 2000): 103.0%; Density: 1,092.5 persons per square mile; Race: 93.9% White, 3.3% Black/African American, 0.0% Asian, 0.0% American Indian/Alaska Native, 0.0% Native Hawaiian/Other Pacific Islander, 2.3% Two or more races, 4.2% Hispanic of any race; Average household size: 2.95; Median age: 34.1; Age under 18: 30.9%; Age 65 and over: 11.8%; Males per 100 females: 93.9; Marriage status: 19.4% never married, 66.3% now married, 0.8% separated, 3.6% widowed, 10.6% divorced; Foreign born: 1.1%; Speak English only: 97.8%; With disability: 8.7%; Veterans: 9.0%; Ancestry: 26.6% German, 13.0% Irish, 11.3% American, 10.3% English, 3.5% Dutch

Employment: 20.3% management, business, and financial, 5.9% computer, engineering, and science, 8.3% education, legal, community service, arts, and media, 9.0% healthcare practitioners, 12.7% service, 18.2% sales and office, 7.6% natural resources, construction, and maintenance, 17.9% production, transportation, and material moving

Income: Per capita: $28,333; Median household: $72,955; Average household: $81,702; Households with income of $100,000 or more: 29.4%; Poverty rate: 5.2%

Educational Attainment: High school diploma or higher: 95.6%; Bachelor's degree or higher: 33.5%; Graduate/professional degree or higher: 11.4%

School District(s)

North West Hendricks Schools (PK-12)
Enrollment: 1,786 . . . . (317) 994-4100

Housing: Homeownership rate: 85.1%; Median home value: $159,600; Median year structure built: 2000; Homeowner vacancy rate: 1.2%; Median selected monthly owner costs: $1,298 with a mortgage, $462 without a mortgage; Median gross rent: $950 per month; Rental vacancy rate: 12.8%

Health Insurance: 96.7% have insurance; 83.4% have private insurance; 22.5% have public insurance; 3.3% do not have insurance; 3.0% of children under 18 do not have insurance

Transportation: Commute: 95.8% car, 0.2% public transportation, 0.8% walk, 1.4% work from home; Mean travel time to work: 27.5 minutes

Additional Information Contacts

Town of Pittsboro . . . . (317) 892-3326
http://www.townofpittsboro.org

PLAINFIELD (town). Covers a land area of 22.274 square miles and a water area of 0.109 square miles. Located at 39.70° N. Lat; 86.37° W. Long. Elevation is 732 feet.

History: Named by Quaker settlers, "the plain people". Plainfield, which called itself the Village of Friendly Folk, developed as the headquarters of the Society of Friends. It was in Plainfield in 1842 that Martin Van Buren, campaigning for the 1844 election, was dumped into a mudhole when his carriage was purposely upset by residents who wanted him to pay attention to the need for road improvements.

Population: 31,012; Growth (since 2000): 68.6%; Density: 1,392.3 persons per square mile; Race: 84.1% White, 9.0% Black/African American, 3.8% Asian, 0.1% American Indian/Alaska Native, 0.0% Native Hawaiian/Other Pacific Islander, 1.3% Two or more races, 4.7% Hispanic of any race; Average household size: 2.51; Median age: 37.7; Age under 18: 24.2%; Age 65 and over: 13.1%; Males per 100 females: 111.7; Marriage status: 29.9% never married, 49.1% now married, 1.3% separated, 5.7% widowed, 15.3% divorced; Foreign born: 6.7%; Speak English only: 89.7%; With disability: 13.2%; Veterans: 8.4%; Ancestry: 18.1% German, 12.4% Irish, 11.7% American, 8.3% English, 4.3% Italian

Employment: 15.0% management, business, and financial, 6.6% computer, engineering, and science, 11.6% education, legal, community service, arts, and media, 6.5% healthcare practitioners, 15.0% service, 25.4% sales and office, 7.0% natural resources, construction, and maintenance, 12.9% production, transportation, and material moving

Income: Per capita: $28,383; Median household: $62,121; Average household: $73,581; Households with income of $100,000 or more: 25.0%; Poverty rate: 8.6%

Educational Attainment: High school diploma or higher: 92.8%; Bachelor's degree or higher: 30.3%; Graduate/professional degree or higher: 11.3%

School District(s)

Plainfield Community School Corp (PK-12)
Enrollment: 5,265 . . . . (317) 839-2578

Housing: Homeownership rate: 68.6%; Median home value: $155,100; Median year structure built: 1994; Homeowner vacancy rate: 0.9%; Median selected monthly owner costs: $1,237 with a mortgage, $424 without a mortgage; Median gross rent: $990 per month; Rental vacancy rate: 7.6%

Health Insurance: 93.1% have insurance; 75.1% have private insurance; 30.2% have public insurance; 6.9% do not have insurance; 5.7% of children under 18 do not have insurance

Safety: Violent crime rate: 26.5 per 10,000 population; Property crime rate: 266.9 per 10,000 population

Transportation: Commute: 91.9% car, 0.0% public transportation, 1.2% walk, 5.2% work from home; Mean travel time to work: 21.7 minutes

Additional Information Contacts

Town of Plainfield . . . . (317) 839-2561
http://townofplainfield.com

STILESVILLE (town). Covers a land area of 0.373 square miles and a water area of 0.006 square miles. Located at 39.64° N. Lat; 86.63° W. Long. Elevation is 804 feet.

History: Laid out 1828.

Population: 245; Growth (since 2000): -6.1%; Density: 657.1 persons per square mile; Race: 95.1% White, 0.0% Black/African American, 0.0% Asian, 0.0% American Indian/Alaska Native, 0.0% Native Hawaiian/Other Pacific Islander, 4.9% Two or more races, 0.0% Hispanic of any race; Average household size: 2.17; Median age: 52.6; Age under 18: 15.5%; Age 65 and over: 27.3%; Males per 100 females: 96.3; Marriage status: 18.4% never married, 55.8% now married, 2.3% separated, 9.7% widowed, 16.1% divorced; Foreign born: 0.0%; Speak English only: 99.2%; With disability: 16.3%; Veterans: 10.6%; Ancestry: 22.0% German, 16.3% American, 8.2% English, 7.8% European, 3.7% Irish

Employment: 16.4% management, business, and financial, 3.4% computer, engineering, and science, 4.3% education, legal, community service, arts, and media, 5.2% healthcare practitioners, 15.5% service, 18.1% sales and office, 10.3% natural resources, construction, and maintenance, 26.7% production, transportation, and material moving

Income: Per capita: $26,528; Median household: $35,313; Average household: $52,624; Households with income of $100,000 or more: 17.7%; Poverty rate: 9.0%

Educational Attainment: High school diploma or higher: 91.2%; Bachelor's degree or higher: 7.8%; Graduate/professional degree or higher: 2.1%
Housing: Homeownership rate: 80.5%; Median home value: $104,000; Median year structure built: 1956; Homeowner vacancy rate: 5.2%; Median selected monthly owner costs: $796 with a mortgage, $400 without a mortgage; Median gross rent: $875 per month; Rental vacancy rate: 24.1%
Health Insurance: 91.0% have insurance; 70.2% have private insurance; 44.1% have public insurance; 9.0% do not have insurance; 10.5% of children under 18 do not have insurance
Transportation: Commute: 98.2% car, 0.0% public transportation, 0.0% walk, 1.8% work from home; Mean travel time to work: 31.4 minutes

Henry County

Located in eastern Indiana; drained by the Big Blue River, Flatrock and Fall Creeks. Covers a land area of 391.876 square miles, a water area of 2.956 square miles, and is located in the Eastern Time Zone at 39.93° N. Lat., 85.40° W. Long. The county was founded in 1821. County seat is New Castle.

Henry County is part of the New Castle, IN Micropolitan Statistical Area. The entire metro area includes: Henry County, IN

Weather Station: New Castle 4 N — Elevation: 1,064 feet

	Jan	Feb	Mar	Apr	May	Jun	Jul	Aug	Sep	Oct	Nov	Dec
High	34	37	48	61	71	80	83	82	76	64	51	37
Low	18	20	28	38	49	58	61	60	52	41	33	22
Precip	2.5	2.3	3.0	4.0	5.1	4.5	5.0	3.4	2.9	3.1	3.5	2.9
Snow	6.3	4.4	1.8	0.2	tr	0.0	0.0	0.0	0.0	tr	0.7	4.7

High and Low temperatures in degrees Fahrenheit; Precipitation and Snow in inches

Population: 48,649; Growth (since 2000): 0.3%; Density: 124.1 persons per square mile; Race: 95.0% White, 2.3% Black/African American, 0.5% Asian, 0.3% American Indian/Alaska Native, 0.0% Native Hawaiian/Other Pacific Islander, 1.6% two or more races, 1.7% Hispanic of any race; Average household size: 2.50; Median age: 42.2; Age under 18: 20.8%; Age 65 and over: 18.0%; Males per 100 females: 102.9; Marriage status: 28.0% never married, 48.7% now married, 1.4% separated, 6.9% widowed, 16.4% divorced; Foreign born: 0.7%; Speak English only: 98.2%; With disability: 17.3%; Veterans: 8.7%; Ancestry: 16.1% German, 15.9% American, 10.1% Irish, 9.6% English, 1.4% Dutch
Religion: Six largest groups: 14.2% Baptist, 6.7% Holiness, 5.4% Non-denominational Protestant, 4.2% Methodist/Pietist, 2.3% Pentecostal, 2.1% European Free-Church
Economy: Unemployment rate: 3.8%; Leading industries: 16.8 % retail trade; 14.1 % health care and social assistance; 13.8 % other services (except public administration); Farms: 702 totaling 176,451 acres; Company size: 0 employ 1,000 or more persons, 3 employ 500 to 999 persons, 11 employs 100 to 499 persons, 814 employ less than 100 persons; Business ownership: 834 women-owned, n/a Black-owned, 33 Hispanic-owned, 56 Asian-owned, n/a American Indian/Alaska Native-owned
Employment: 11.1% management, business, and financial, 2.3% computer, engineering, and science, 9.3% education, legal, community service, arts, and media, 6.2% healthcare practitioners, 17.9% service, 23.5% sales and office, 9.3% natural resources, construction, and maintenance, 20.5% production, transportation, and material moving
Income: Per capita: $23,293; Median household: $46,131; Average household: $59,367; Households with income of $100,000 or more: 13.2%; Poverty rate: 16.1%
Educational Attainment: High school diploma or higher: 88.7%; Bachelor's degree or higher: 16.5%; Graduate/professional degree or higher: 5.5%
Housing: Homeownership rate: 73.1%; Median home value: $94,800; Median year structure built: 1961; Homeowner vacancy rate: 3.5%; Median selected monthly owner costs: $968 with a mortgage, $346 without a mortgage; Median gross rent: $687 per month; Rental vacancy rate: 15.7%
Vital Statistics: Birth rate: 96.1 per 10,000 population; Death rate: 113.0 per 10,000 population; Age-adjusted cancer mortality rate: 215.5 deaths per 100,000 population
Health Insurance: 90.1% have insurance; 67.5% have private insurance; 39.1% have public insurance; 9.9% do not have insurance; 5.3% of children under 18 do not have insurance
Health Care: Physicians: 9.5 per 10,000 population; Dentists: 3.7 per 10,000 population; Hospital beds: 18.6 per 10,000 population; Hospital admissions: 445.0 per 10,000 population
Air Quality Index (AQI): Percent of Days: 90.0% good, 10.0% moderate, 0.0% unhealthy for sensitive individuals, 0.0% unhealthy, 0.0% very unhealthy; Annual median: 28; Annual maximum: 62
Transportation: Commute: 93.7% car, 0.2% public transportation, 1.3% walk, 3.9% work from home; Mean travel time to work: 26.8 minutes
2016 Presidential Election: 68.9% Trump, 25.4% Clinton, 5.2% Johnson, 0.3% Stein
Additional Information Contacts
Henry Government . . . . (765) 529-6401
http://www.henryco.net

Henry County Communities

BLOUNTSVILLE (town). Covers a land area of 0.112 square miles and a water area of 0.001 square miles. Located at 40.06° N. Lat; 85.24° W. Long. Elevation is 1,093 feet.
Population: 101; Growth (since 2000): -39.2%; Density: 899.7 persons per square mile; Race: 100.0% White, 0.0% Black/African American, 0.0% Asian, 0.0% American Indian/Alaska Native, 0.0% Native Hawaiian/Other Pacific Islander, 0.0% Two or more races, 0.0% Hispanic of any race; Average household size: 2.30; Median age: 42.4; Age under 18: 20.8%; Age 65 and over: 18.8%; Males per 100 females: 78.7; Marriage status: 12.3% never married, 59.3% now married, 1.2% separated, 4.9% widowed, 23.5% divorced; Foreign born: 0.0%; Speak English only: 100.0%; With disability: 25.7%; Veterans: 8.8%; Ancestry: 17.8% American, 5.9% English, 5.9% French, 4.0% German, 4.0% Irish
Employment: 5.1% management, business, and financial, 0.0% computer, engineering, and science, 5.1% education, legal, community service, arts, and media, 2.6% healthcare practitioners, 23.1% service, 25.6% sales and office, 2.6% natural resources, construction, and maintenance, 35.9% production, transportation, and material moving
Income: Per capita: $16,194; Median household: $38,500; Average household: $36,627; Households with income of $100,000 or more: n/a; Poverty rate: 9.1%
Educational Attainment: High school diploma or higher: 75.3%; Bachelor's degree or higher: 5.2%; Graduate/professional degree or higher: 1.3%
Housing: Homeownership rate: 90.9%; Median home value: $55,000; Median year structure built: Before 1940; Homeowner vacancy rate: 0.0%; Median selected monthly owner costs: $588 with a mortgage, $292 without a mortgage; Median gross rent: n/a per month; Rental vacancy rate: 55.6%
Health Insurance: 80.2% have insurance; 53.5% have private insurance; 38.6% have public insurance; 19.8% do not have insurance; 23.8% of children under 18 do not have insurance
Transportation: Commute: 94.9% car, 0.0% public transportation, 0.0% walk, 0.0% work from home; Mean travel time to work: 29.2 minutes

CADIZ (town). Covers a land area of 0.160 square miles and a water area of 0 square miles. Located at 39.95° N. Lat; 85.49° W. Long. Elevation is 1,093 feet.
Population: 231; Growth (since 2000): 43.5%; Density: 1,447.8 persons per square mile; Race: 94.8% White, 1.7% Black/African American, 0.0% Asian, 0.0% American Indian/Alaska Native, 0.0% Native Hawaiian/Other Pacific Islander, 3.5% Two or more races, 0.0% Hispanic of any race; Average household size: 3.73; Median age: 24.4; Age under 18: 44.6%; Age 65 and over: 6.1%; Males per 100 females: 94.8; Marriage status: 30.6% never married, 54.8% now married, 0.0% separated, 3.8% widowed, 10.8% divorced; Foreign born: 0.0%; Speak English only: 100.0%; With disability: 6.1%; Veterans: 5.5%; Ancestry: 18.6% German, 5.2% English, 5.2% European, 5.2% French, 3.0% Irish
Employment: 11.0% management, business, and financial, 2.4% computer, engineering, and science, 7.3% education, legal, community service, arts, and media, 1.2% healthcare practitioners, 17.1% service, 22.0% sales and office, 9.8% natural resources, construction, and maintenance, 29.3% production, transportation, and material moving
Income: Per capita: $14,525; Median household: $45,625; Average household: $47,645; Households with income of $100,000 or more: 6.5%; Poverty rate: 34.2%
Educational Attainment: High school diploma or higher: 80.4%; Bachelor's degree or higher: 16.1%; Graduate/professional degree or higher: 3.6%

Housing: Homeownership rate: 77.4%; Median home value: $74,600; Median year structure built: Before 1940; Homeowner vacancy rate: 0.0%; Median selected monthly owner costs: $685 with a mortgage, $279 without a mortgage; Median gross rent: $581 per month; Rental vacancy rate: 0.0%
Health Insurance: 83.1% have insurance; 56.7% have private insurance; 32.5% have public insurance; 16.9% do not have insurance; 18.0% of children under 18 do not have insurance
Transportation: Commute: 98.8% car, 0.0% public transportation, 0.0% walk, 1.2% work from home; Mean travel time to work: 21.0 minutes

DUNREITH (town). Covers a land area of 0.128 square miles and a water area of 0 square miles. Located at 39.80° N. Lat; 85.44° W. Long. Elevation is 1,043 feet.
History: Dunreith developed around the Pennsylvania Railroad station.
Population: 151; Growth (since 2000): -17.9%; Density: 1,183.0 persons per square mile; Race: 96.7% White, 0.0% Black/African American, 0.0% Asian, 0.0% American Indian/Alaska Native, 0.0% Native Hawaiian/Other Pacific Islander, 1.3% Two or more races, 4.0% Hispanic of any race; Average household size: 2.56; Median age: 29.9; Age under 18: 28.5%; Age 65 and over: 19.9%; Males per 100 females: 90.3; Marriage status: 27.9% never married, 48.6% now married, 4.5% separated, 9.0% widowed, 14.4% divorced; Foreign born: 3.3%; Speak English only: 95.4%; With disability: 18.5%; Veterans: 14.8%; Ancestry: 11.9% German, 9.9% American, 9.3% Irish, 4.0% European, 2.6% English
Employment: 4.7% management, business, and financial, 0.0% computer, engineering, and science, 6.3% education, legal, community service, arts, and media, 7.8% healthcare practitioners, 25.0% service, 15.6% sales and office, 12.5% natural resources, construction, and maintenance, 28.1% production, transportation, and material moving
Income: Per capita: $18,789; Median household: $46,250; Average household: $45,937; Households with income of $100,000 or more: 5.1%; Poverty rate: 6.8%
Educational Attainment: High school diploma or higher: 86.8%; Bachelor's degree or higher: 5.5%; Graduate/professional degree or higher: 4.4%
Housing: Homeownership rate: 81.4%; Median home value: $71,100; Median year structure built: 1952; Homeowner vacancy rate: 0.0%; Median selected monthly owner costs: $940 with a mortgage, $325 without a mortgage; Median gross rent: $663 per month; Rental vacancy rate: 21.4%
Health Insurance: 88.7% have insurance; 64.2% have private insurance; 37.7% have public insurance; 11.3% do not have insurance; 6.5% of children under 18 do not have insurance
Transportation: Commute: 93.8% car, 0.0% public transportation, 0.0% walk, 4.7% work from home; Mean travel time to work: 27.7 minutes

GREENSBORO (town). Covers a land area of 0.110 square miles and a water area of 0 square miles. Located at 39.88° N. Lat; 85.46° W. Long. Elevation is 981 feet.
Population: 148; Growth (since 2000): -14.9%; Density: 1,345.5 persons per square mile; Race: 99.3% White, 0.0% Black/African American, 0.0% Asian, 0.7% American Indian/Alaska Native, 0.0% Native Hawaiian/Other Pacific Islander, 0.0% Two or more races, 0.0% Hispanic of any race; Average household size: 2.96; Median age: 23.5; Age under 18: 45.9%; Age 65 and over: 7.4%; Males per 100 females: 107.2; Marriage status: 30.8% never married, 45.1% now married, 0.0% separated, 7.7% widowed, 16.5% divorced; Foreign born: 0.0%; Speak English only: 100.0%; With disability: 8.8%; Veterans: 3.8%; Ancestry: 9.5% Irish, 6.8% American, 4.7% German, 1.4% English, 1.4% Welsh
Employment: 4.3% management, business, and financial, 0.0% computer, engineering, and science, 0.0% education, legal, community service, arts, and media, 32.6% healthcare practitioners, 8.7% service, 30.4% sales and office, 8.7% natural resources, construction, and maintenance, 15.2% production, transportation, and material moving
Income: Per capita: $12,476; Median household: $33,750; Average household: $36,602; Households with income of $100,000 or more: 2.0%; Poverty rate: 25.7%
Educational Attainment: High school diploma or higher: 90.4%; Bachelor's degree or higher: 6.8%; Graduate/professional degree or higher: 1.4%
Housing: Homeownership rate: 76.0%; Median home value: $58,600; Median year structure built: Before 1940; Homeowner vacancy rate: 9.5%; Median selected monthly owner costs: $643 with a mortgage, $400 without a mortgage; Median gross rent: $1,063 per month; Rental vacancy rate: 0.0%

Health Insurance: 81.8% have insurance; 65.5% have private insurance; 23.6% have public insurance; 18.2% do not have insurance; 22.1% of children under 18 do not have insurance
Transportation: Commute: 100.0% car, 0.0% public transportation, 0.0% walk, 0.0% work from home; Mean travel time to work: 28.6 minutes

KENNARD (town). Covers a land area of 0.421 square miles and a water area of <.001 square miles. Located at 39.91° N. Lat; 85.52° W. Long. Elevation is 1,040 feet.
Population: 604; Growth (since 2000): 32.7%; Density: 1,435.2 persons per square mile; Race: 78.8% White, 3.1% Black/African American, 0.0% Asian, 0.0% American Indian/Alaska Native, 0.0% Native Hawaiian/Other Pacific Islander, 18.0% Two or more races, 7.3% Hispanic of any race; Average household size: 4.03; Median age: 27.6; Age under 18: 37.1%; Age 65 and over: 5.8%; Males per 100 females: 104.8; Marriage status: 26.7% never married, 60.3% now married, 1.0% separated, 2.0% widowed, 11.0% divorced; Foreign born: 1.7%; Speak English only: 99.4%; With disability: 9.4%; Veterans: 6.1%; Ancestry: 18.9% Irish, 17.9% American, 12.6% German, 3.8% English, 3.1% Scottish
Employment: 9.6% management, business, and financial, 0.0% computer, engineering, and science, 7.0% education, legal, community service, arts, and media, 6.1% healthcare practitioners, 16.6% service, 24.9% sales and office, 12.7% natural resources, construction, and maintenance, 23.1% production, transportation, and material moving
Income: Per capita: $13,841; Median household: $51,429; Average household: $52,655; Households with income of $100,000 or more: 4.6%; Poverty rate: 23.6%
Educational Attainment: High school diploma or higher: 85.1%; Bachelor's degree or higher: 8.6%; Graduate/professional degree or higher: 1.1%
Housing: Homeownership rate: 80.7%; Median home value: $76,400; Median year structure built: Before 1940; Homeowner vacancy rate: 0.8%; Median selected monthly owner costs: $830 with a mortgage, $371 without a mortgage; Median gross rent: $738 per month; Rental vacancy rate: 0.0%
Health Insurance: 90.2% have insurance; 50.5% have private insurance; 47.4% have public insurance; 9.8% do not have insurance; 0.4% of children under 18 do not have insurance
Transportation: Commute: 95.0% car, 2.3% public transportation, 0.0% walk, 2.7% work from home; Mean travel time to work: 34.1 minutes

KNIGHTSTOWN (town). Covers a land area of 1.029 square miles and a water area of 0.010 square miles. Located at 39.80° N. Lat; 85.53° W. Long. Elevation is 932 feet.
History: Knightstown was named for John Knight, an engineer who was involved in the construction of the National Road here.
Population: 2,103; Growth (since 2000): -2.1%; Density: 2,043.3 persons per square mile; Race: 98.6% White, 0.5% Black/African American, 0.0% Asian, 0.0% American Indian/Alaska Native, 0.0% Native Hawaiian/Other Pacific Islander, 0.9% Two or more races, 1.9% Hispanic of any race; Average household size: 2.51; Median age: 30.0; Age under 18: 28.7%; Age 65 and over: 11.9%; Males per 100 females: 91.4; Marriage status: 37.0% never married, 38.7% now married, 1.0% separated, 8.8% widowed, 15.5% divorced; Foreign born: 0.0%; Speak English only: 98.6%; With disability: 17.2%; Veterans: 8.0%; Ancestry: 17.1% German, 10.4% English, 9.4% American, 9.3% Irish, 2.5% Dutch
Employment: 10.1% management, business, and financial, 2.4% computer, engineering, and science, 7.8% education, legal, community service, arts, and media, 8.2% healthcare practitioners, 19.3% service, 26.0% sales and office, 5.2% natural resources, construction, and maintenance, 20.9% production, transportation, and material moving
Income: Per capita: $20,618; Median household: $44,279; Average household: $50,226; Households with income of $100,000 or more: 7.4%; Poverty rate: 19.8%
Educational Attainment: High school diploma or higher: 89.8%; Bachelor's degree or higher: 16.8%; Graduate/professional degree or higher: 7.2%

School District(s)

C A Beard Memorial School Corp (PK-12)
Enrollment: 1,317 . . . . (765) 345-5101

Housing: Homeownership rate: 58.7%; Median home value: $74,600; Median year structure built: Before 1940; Homeowner vacancy rate: 7.0%; Median selected monthly owner costs: $879 with a mortgage, $367 without a mortgage; Median gross rent: $668 per month; Rental vacancy rate: 18.0%

Health Insurance: 94.2% have insurance; 71.8% have private insurance; 33.7% have public insurance; 5.8% do not have insurance; 1.3% of children under 18 do not have insurance
Newspapers: Knightstown Banner (weekly circulation 2,000)
Transportation: Commute: 96.3% car, 0.0% public transportation, 1.8% walk, 1.1% work from home; Mean travel time to work: 26.9 minutes

LEWISVILLE (town). Covers a land area of 0.253 square miles and a water area of 0 square miles. Located at 39.81° N. Lat; 85.35° W. Long. Elevation is 1,053 feet.
History: Laid out 1829.
Population: 396; Growth (since 2000): 0.3%; Density: 1,562.2 persons per square mile; Race: 97.5% White, 0.5% Black/African American, 0.0% Asian, 0.0% American Indian/Alaska Native, 0.0% Native Hawaiian/Other Pacific Islander, 1.0% Two or more races, 5.6% Hispanic of any race; Average household size: 2.93; Median age: 38.1; Age under 18: 28.8%; Age 65 and over: 14.6%; Males per 100 females: 87.7; Marriage status: 22.3% never married, 60.7% now married, 1.0% separated, 8.7% widowed, 8.3% divorced; Foreign born: 0.0%; Speak English only: 98.1%; With disability: 23.0%; Veterans: 10.6%; Ancestry: 18.9% German, 18.4% Irish, 14.1% American, 10.1% English, 3.5% Italian
Employment: 7.0% management, business, and financial, 2.8% computer, engineering, and science, 4.2% education, legal, community service, arts, and media, 6.3% healthcare practitioners, 15.4% service, 19.6% sales and office, 9.8% natural resources, construction, and maintenance, 35.0% production, transportation, and material moving
Income: Per capita: $18,280; Median household: $44,306; Average household: $52,280; Households with income of $100,000 or more: 10.3%; Poverty rate: 16.2%
Educational Attainment: High school diploma or higher: 86.2%; Bachelor's degree or higher: 10.7%; Graduate/professional degree or higher: 3.1%
Housing: Homeownership rate: 68.9%; Median home value: $66,900; Median year structure built: Before 1940; Homeowner vacancy rate: 3.1%; Median selected monthly owner costs: $833 with a mortgage, $418 without a mortgage; Median gross rent: $855 per month; Rental vacancy rate: 0.0%
Health Insurance: 91.7% have insurance; 61.4% have private insurance; 43.9% have public insurance; 8.3% do not have insurance; 0.0% of children under 18 do not have insurance
Transportation: Commute: 94.2% car, 0.0% public transportation, 2.2% walk, 2.2% work from home; Mean travel time to work: 22.7 minutes

MIDDLETOWN (town). Covers a land area of 1.156 square miles and a water area of 0.002 square miles. Located at 40.06° N. Lat; 85.54° W. Long. Elevation is 978 feet.
History: Laid out 1829.
Population: 2,485; Growth (since 2000): -0.1%; Density: 2,149.0 persons per square mile; Race: 97.3% White, 0.5% Black/African American, 1.1% Asian, 0.0% American Indian/Alaska Native, 0.0% Native Hawaiian/Other Pacific Islander, 0.5% Two or more races, 2.4% Hispanic of any race; Average household size: 2.36; Median age: 37.2; Age under 18: 23.3%; Age 65 and over: 14.6%; Males per 100 females: 88.0; Marriage status: 34.3% never married, 42.0% now married, 1.7% separated, 6.6% widowed, 17.0% divorced; Foreign born: 0.4%; Speak English only: 97.7%; With disability: 12.0%; Veterans: 5.6%; Ancestry: 15.7% American, 13.9% German, 11.2% Irish, 5.1% English, 2.4% British
Employment: 7.7% management, business, and financial, 3.1% computer, engineering, and science, 8.4% education, legal, community service, arts, and media, 1.6% healthcare practitioners, 23.4% service, 23.3% sales and office, 11.3% natural resources, construction, and maintenance, 21.3% production, transportation, and material moving
Income: Per capita: $21,108; Median household: $43,500; Average household: $50,146; Households with income of $100,000 or more: 7.9%; Poverty rate: 23.0%
Educational Attainment: High school diploma or higher: 87.6%; Bachelor's degree or higher: 14.8%; Graduate/professional degree or higher: 2.8%

School District(s)

Shenandoah School Corporation (PK-12)
Enrollment: 1,262 . . . . (765) 354-2266
Housing: Homeownership rate: 63.9%; Median home value: $72,300; Median year structure built: 1958; Homeowner vacancy rate: 0.0%; Median selected monthly owner costs: $839 with a mortgage, $391 without a mortgage; Median gross rent: $709 per month; Rental vacancy rate: 0.0%
Health Insurance: 82.5% have insurance; 60.3% have private insurance; 37.1% have public insurance; 17.5% do not have insurance; 12.6% of children under 18 do not have insurance
Newspapers: Middletown News (weekly circulation 2,000)
Transportation: Commute: 90.9% car, 0.5% public transportation, 5.4% walk, 1.0% work from home; Mean travel time to work: 28.2 minutes
Additional Information Contacts
Town of Middletown . . . . (765) 354-2268
http://www.middletownin.com

MOORELAND (town). Covers a land area of 0.144 square miles and a water area of 0 square miles. Located at 40.00° N. Lat; 85.25° W. Long. Elevation is 1,122 feet.
History: Mooreland was named for early settler Philip Moore.
Population: 287; Growth (since 2000): -27.0%; Density: 1,996.9 persons per square mile; Race: 95.5% White, 4.5% Black/African American, 0.0% Asian, 0.0% American Indian/Alaska Native, 0.0% Native Hawaiian/Other Pacific Islander, 0.0% Two or more races, 1.0% Hispanic of any race; Average household size: 2.66; Median age: 37.6; Age under 18: 28.2%; Age 65 and over: 14.3%; Males per 100 females: 82.0; Marriage status: 37.2% never married, 40.7% now married, 1.7% separated, 8.2% widowed, 13.9% divorced; Foreign born: 1.4%; Speak English only: 99.6%; With disability: 18.5%; Veterans: 4.4%; Ancestry: 16.0% American, 14.3% German, 11.5% Irish, 9.4% English, 2.1% Italian
Employment: 0.9% management, business, and financial, 0.0% computer, engineering, and science, 5.2% education, legal, community service, arts, and media, 5.2% healthcare practitioners, 36.5% service, 29.6% sales and office, 6.1% natural resources, construction, and maintenance, 16.5% production, transportation, and material moving
Income: Per capita: $14,961; Median household: $24,444; Average household: $38,167; Households with income of $100,000 or more: 7.4%; Poverty rate: 30.2%
Educational Attainment: High school diploma or higher: 84.3%; Bachelor's degree or higher: 6.2%; Graduate/professional degree or higher: 2.2%
Housing: Homeownership rate: 69.4%; Median home value: $62,800; Median year structure built: 1942; Homeowner vacancy rate: 0.0%; Median selected monthly owner costs: $731 with a mortgage, $375 without a mortgage; Median gross rent: $663 per month; Rental vacancy rate: 26.7%
Health Insurance: 90.6% have insurance; 48.1% have private insurance; 50.2% have public insurance; 9.4% do not have insurance; 0.0% of children under 18 do not have insurance
Transportation: Commute: 97.4% car, 0.0% public transportation, 0.9% walk, 0.9% work from home; Mean travel time to work: 28.5 minutes

MOUNT SUMMIT (town). Covers a land area of 0.189 square miles and a water area of 0 square miles. Located at 40.00° N. Lat; 85.39° W. Long. Elevation is 1,093 feet.
History: Mount Summit is at one of the highest elevations in Henry County.
Population: 566; Growth (since 2000): 80.8%; Density: 2,998.8 persons per square mile; Race: 97.7% White, 0.0% Black/African American, 0.0% Asian, 0.0% American Indian/Alaska Native, 0.0% Native Hawaiian/Other Pacific Islander, 0.2% Two or more races, 6.5% Hispanic of any race; Average household size: 2.50; Median age: 40.9; Age under 18: 24.4%; Age 65 and over: 16.6%; Males per 100 females: 102.3; Marriage status: 32.4% never married, 44.6% now married, 2.0% separated, 5.1% widowed, 17.9% divorced; Foreign born: 0.0%; Speak English only: 98.9%; With disability: 10.1%; Veterans: 4.2%; Ancestry: 24.0% German, 20.7% Irish, 13.3% American, 3.7% English, 3.5% Italian
Employment: 9.3% management, business, and financial, 0.7% computer, engineering, and science, 6.8% education, legal, community service, arts, and media, 5.7% healthcare practitioners, 14.3% service, 28.2% sales and office, 13.9% natural resources, construction, and maintenance, 21.1% production, transportation, and material moving
Income: Per capita: $23,554; Median household: $54,107; Average household: $58,368; Households with income of $100,000 or more: 16.8%; Poverty rate: 16.1%
Educational Attainment: High school diploma or higher: 90.4%; Bachelor's degree or higher: 16.8%; Graduate/professional degree or higher: 7.5%
Housing: Homeownership rate: 84.5%; Median home value: $80,700; Median year structure built: 1952; Homeowner vacancy rate: 2.6%; Median selected monthly owner costs: $912 with a mortgage, $432 without a mortgage; Median gross rent: $647 per month; Rental vacancy rate: 22.0%

Health Insurance: 88.9% have insurance; 64.7% have private insurance; 38.7% have public insurance; 11.1% do not have insurance; 9.4% of children under 18 do not have insurance
Transportation: Commute: 88.9% car, 0.0% public transportation, 0.4% walk, 10.8% work from home; Mean travel time to work: 28.1 minutes

NEW CASTLE (city). County seat. Covers a land area of 7.295 square miles and a water area of 0.021 square miles. Located at 39.92° N. Lat; 85.37° W. Long. Elevation is 1,063 feet.
History: New Castle was the birthplace in 1867 of Wilbur Wright, who with his brother Orville flew the first heavier-than-air craft in 1903 in North Carolina. New Castle developed as an industrial city.
Population: 17,476; Growth (since 2000): -1.7%; Density: 2,395.7 persons per square mile; Race: 95.7% White, 1.5% Black/African American, 0.7% Asian, 0.1% American Indian/Alaska Native, 0.0% Native Hawaiian/Other Pacific Islander, 1.6% Two or more races, 1.5% Hispanic of any race; Average household size: 2.38; Median age: 40.8; Age under 18: 22.6%; Age 65 and over: 18.0%; Males per 100 females: 87.6; Marriage status: 28.6% never married, 41.4% now married, 1.7% separated, 9.0% widowed, 21.0% divorced; Foreign born: 0.8%; Speak English only: 98.1%; With disability: 22.3%; Veterans: 8.2%; Ancestry: 14.8% American, 14.8% German, 11.6% English, 10.3% Irish, 1.8% Dutch
Employment: 8.1% management, business, and financial, 2.3% computer, engineering, and science, 10.4% education, legal, community service, arts, and media, 5.3% healthcare practitioners, 19.2% service, 22.2% sales and office, 7.1% natural resources, construction, and maintenance, 25.4% production, transportation, and material moving
Income: Per capita: $20,110; Median household: $36,655; Average household: $46,700; Households with income of $100,000 or more: 6.9%; Poverty rate: 23.3%
Educational Attainment: High school diploma or higher: 86.8%; Bachelor's degree or higher: 14.7%; Graduate/professional degree or higher: 4.3%

School District(s)

Blue River Valley Schools (PK-12)
Enrollment: 634. . . . . (765) 836-4816
New Castle Community School Corp (PK-12)
Enrollment: 3,459 . . . . (765) 521-7201

Housing: Homeownership rate: 58.2%; Median home value: $71,700; Median year structure built: 1957; Homeowner vacancy rate: 5.3%; Median selected monthly owner costs: $845 with a mortgage, $313 without a mortgage; Median gross rent: $662 per month; Rental vacancy rate: 19.2%
Health Insurance: 88.3% have insurance; 58.4% have private insurance; 47.1% have public insurance; 11.7% do not have insurance; 7.0% of children under 18 do not have insurance
Hospitals: Henry County Memorial Hospital (107 beds)
Newspapers: Courier-Times (daily circulation 9,200)
Transportation: Commute: 94.8% car, 0.3% public transportation, 1.7% walk, 2.1% work from home; Mean travel time to work: 23.9 minutes
Airports: New Castle-Henry Co Municipal (general aviation)
Additional Information Contacts
City of New Castle. . . . . (765) 521-6803
http://www.cityofnewcastle.net

SPICELAND (town). Covers a land area of 0.503 square miles and a water area of 0 square miles. Located at 39.84° N. Lat; 85.44° W. Long. Elevation is 1,050 feet.
History: Spiceland was settled in 1828 by a group of Quakers from North Carolina. From Spiceland Academy, founded in 1834, came historian Charles Austin Beard.
Population: 736; Growth (since 2000): -8.8%; Density: 1,463.7 persons per square mile; Race: 98.2% White, 0.0% Black/African American, 0.8% Asian, 0.0% American Indian/Alaska Native, 0.3% Native Hawaiian/Other Pacific Islander, 0.7% Two or more races, 0.0% Hispanic of any race; Average household size: 2.38; Median age: 44.2; Age under 18: 21.9%; Age 65 and over: 19.7%; Males per 100 females: 96.0; Marriage status: 25.7% never married, 54.6% now married, 0.8% separated, 5.8% widowed, 13.9% divorced; Foreign born: 1.1%; Speak English only: 98.2%; With disability: 21.7%; Veterans: 10.3%; Ancestry: 15.2% German, 12.9% Irish, 12.8% English, 9.8% American, 1.9% Polish
Employment: 4.5% management, business, and financial, 3.5% computer, engineering, and science, 7.4% education, legal, community service, arts, and media, 3.2% healthcare practitioners, 15.8% service, 26.4% sales and office, 9.6% natural resources, construction, and maintenance, 29.6% production, transportation, and material moving
Income: Per capita: $21,928; Median household: $47,917; Average household: $51,181; Households with income of $100,000 or more: 5.1%; Poverty rate: 15.1%
Educational Attainment: High school diploma or higher: 95.5%; Bachelor's degree or higher: 16.3%; Graduate/professional degree or higher: 5.1%
Housing: Homeownership rate: 72.2%; Median home value: $81,300; Median year structure built: Before 1940; Homeowner vacancy rate: 0.0%; Median selected monthly owner costs: $826 with a mortgage, $363 without a mortgage; Median gross rent: $709 per month; Rental vacancy rate: 0.0%
Health Insurance: 88.3% have insurance; 69.6% have private insurance; 35.7% have public insurance; 11.7% do not have insurance; 8.5% of children under 18 do not have insurance
Transportation: Commute: 90.9% car, 0.0% public transportation, 1.6% walk, 7.4% work from home; Mean travel time to work: 25.6 minutes

SPRINGPORT (town). Covers a land area of 0.120 square miles and a water area of 0 square miles. Located at 40.05° N. Lat; 85.39° W. Long. Elevation is 1,063 feet.
Population: 136; Growth (since 2000): -21.8%; Density: 1,131.7 persons per square mile; Race: 98.5% White, 0.0% Black/African American, 0.0% Asian, 1.5% American Indian/Alaska Native, 0.0% Native Hawaiian/Other Pacific Islander, 0.0% Two or more races, 0.0% Hispanic of any race; Average household size: 2.00; Median age: 47.0; Age under 18: 10.3%; Age 65 and over: 31.6%; Males per 100 females: 75.3; Marriage status: 22.4% never married, 49.6% now married, 1.6% separated, 8.0% widowed, 20.0% divorced; Foreign born: 0.0%; Speak English only: 100.0%; With disability: 29.4%; Veterans: 13.9%; Ancestry: 15.4% German, 14.0% American, 14.0% English, 11.0% Irish, 9.6% Scotch-Irish
Employment: 5.4% management, business, and financial, 0.0% computer, engineering, and science, 19.6% education, legal, community service, arts, and media, 0.0% healthcare practitioners, 8.9% service, 21.4% sales and office, 17.9% natural resources, construction, and maintenance, 26.8% production, transportation, and material moving
Income: Per capita: $23,469; Median household: $43,750; Average household: $45,859; Households with income of $100,000 or more: 5.9%; Poverty rate: 5.1%
Educational Attainment: High school diploma or higher: 91.5%; Bachelor's degree or higher: 14.2%; Graduate/professional degree or higher: 9.4%
Housing: Homeownership rate: 89.7%; Median home value: $74,200; Median year structure built: Before 1940; Homeowner vacancy rate: 15.3%; Median selected monthly owner costs: $731 with a mortgage, $283 without a mortgage; Median gross rent: $638 per month; Rental vacancy rate: 0.0%
Health Insurance: 90.4% have insurance; 75.0% have private insurance; 47.8% have public insurance; 9.6% do not have insurance; 0.0% of children under 18 do not have insurance
Transportation: Commute: 91.1% car, 0.0% public transportation, 0.0% walk, 3.6% work from home; Mean travel time to work: 32.5 minutes

STRAUGHN (town). Covers a land area of 0.141 square miles and a water area of 0 square miles. Located at 39.81° N. Lat; 85.29° W. Long. Elevation is 1,079 feet.
Population: 283; Growth (since 2000): 7.6%; Density: 2,010.0 persons per square mile; Race: 98.2% White, 0.0% Black/African American, 0.0% Asian, 0.0% American Indian/Alaska Native, 1.1% Native Hawaiian/Other Pacific Islander, 0.7% Two or more races, 1.1% Hispanic of any race; Average household size: 3.14; Median age: 31.5; Age under 18: 33.6%; Age 65 and over: 11.7%; Males per 100 females: 77.6; Marriage status: 23.7% never married, 62.9% now married, 2.1% separated, 5.2% widowed, 8.2% divorced; Foreign born: 0.0%; Speak English only: 99.2%; With disability: 9.5%; Veterans: 9.6%; Ancestry: 11.3% German, 11.3% Irish, 10.2% American, 9.9% Polish, 3.9% English
Employment: 14.3% management, business, and financial, 0.0% computer, engineering, and science, 7.6% education, legal, community service, arts, and media, 5.0% healthcare practitioners, 29.4% service, 17.6% sales and office, 10.9% natural resources, construction, and maintenance, 15.1% production, transportation, and material moving
Income: Per capita: $15,698; Median household: $41,250; Average household: $47,569; Households with income of $100,000 or more: 5.5%; Poverty rate: 33.6%

Educational Attainment: High school diploma or higher: 79.9%; Bachelor's degree or higher: 7.3%; Graduate/professional degree or higher: 3.0%

School District(s)

South Henry School Corp (PK-12)
Enrollment: 677. . . . . (765) 987-7882

Housing: Homeownership rate: 76.7%; Median home value: $49,000; Median year structure built: 1942; Homeowner vacancy rate: 0.0%; Median selected monthly owner costs: $762 with a mortgage, $306 without a mortgage; Median gross rent: $829 per month; Rental vacancy rate: 0.0%
Health Insurance: 87.6% have insurance; 58.3% have private insurance; 37.5% have public insurance; 12.4% do not have insurance; 0.0% of children under 18 do not have insurance
Transportation: Commute: 99.1% car, 0.9% public transportation, 0.0% walk, 0.0% work from home; Mean travel time to work: 30.8 minutes

SULPHUR SPRINGS (town). Covers a land area of 0.693 square miles and a water area of <.001 square miles. Located at 40.00° N. Lat; 85.43° W. Long. Elevation is 1,063 feet.
History: Laid out 1853.
Population: 338; Growth (since 2000): -2.3%; Density: 487.6 persons per square mile; Race: 98.5% White, 0.9% Black/African American, 0.3% Asian, 0.0% American Indian/Alaska Native, 0.0% Native Hawaiian/Other Pacific Islander, 0.3% Two or more races, 0.9% Hispanic of any race; Average household size: 2.84; Median age: 33.8; Age under 18: 18.6%; Age 65 and over: 16.0%; Males per 100 females: 96.6; Marriage status: 29.9% never married, 47.9% now married, 0.0% separated, 8.8% widowed, 13.4% divorced; Foreign born: 0.6%; Speak English only: 96.5%; With disability: 14.5%; Veterans: 12.4%; Ancestry: 23.1% German, 15.1% American, 9.8% English, 6.8% European, 6.5% Scottish
Employment: 4.8% management, business, and financial, 0.0% computer, engineering, and science, 4.2% education, legal, community service, arts, and media, 7.1% healthcare practitioners, 19.6% service, 25.0% sales and office, 14.3% natural resources, construction, and maintenance, 25.0% production, transportation, and material moving
Income: Per capita: $18,853; Median household: $44,583; Average household: $49,964; Households with income of $100,000 or more: 5.9%; Poverty rate: 21.1%
Educational Attainment: High school diploma or higher: 94.3%; Bachelor's degree or higher: 12.0%; Graduate/professional degree or higher: 2.4%
Housing: Homeownership rate: 79.0%; Median home value: $85,600; Median year structure built: 1952; Homeowner vacancy rate: 17.5%; Median selected monthly owner costs: $906 with a mortgage, $325 without a mortgage; Median gross rent: $658 per month; Rental vacancy rate: 13.8%
Health Insurance: 87.9% have insurance; 64.5% have private insurance; 35.5% have public insurance; 12.1% do not have insurance; 6.0% of children under 18 do not have insurance
Transportation: Commute: 93.3% car, 0.0% public transportation, 4.8% walk, 0.0% work from home; Mean travel time to work: 25.8 minutes

Howard County

Located in central Indiana; drained by Wildcat Creek. Covers a land area of 293.057 square miles, a water area of 0.865 square miles, and is located in the Eastern Time Zone at 40.48° N. Lat., 86.11° W. Long. The county was founded in 1844. County seat is Kokomo.

Howard County is part of the Kokomo, IN Metropolitan Statistical Area. The entire metro area includes: Howard County, IN

Weather Station: Kokomo 3 WSW   Elevation: 819 feet

	Jan	Feb	Mar	Apr	May	Jun	Jul	Aug	Sep	Oct	Nov	Dec
High	32	36	48	61	71	81	84	82	77	64	50	36
Low	16	19	27	38	49	59	62	60	52	41	32	21
Precip	2.6	2.5	3.0	3.9	4.5	4.4	4.8	4.0	3.5	3.3	3.6	3.2
Snow	11.1	10.4	5.2	1.1	tr	0.0	0.0	0.0	0.0	0.4	1.3	8.8

High and Low temperatures in degrees Fahrenheit; Precipitation and Snow in inches

Population: 82,457; Growth (since 2000): -3.0%; Density: 281.4 persons per square mile; Race: 87.8% White, 7.3% Black/African American, 1.3% Asian, 0.4% American Indian/Alaska Native, 0.0% Native Hawaiian/Other Pacific Islander, 2.3% two or more races, 3.2% Hispanic of any race; Average household size: 2.36; Median age: 41.5; Age under 18: 22.9%; Age 65 and over: 18.2%; Males per 100 females: 92.6; Marriage status: 24.6% never married, 53.5% now married, 1.6% separated, 6.9% widowed, 15.0% divorced; Foreign born: 2.0%; Speak English only: 96.9%; With disability: 17.5%; Veterans: 10.2%; Ancestry: 20.3% German, 12.2% American, 11.0% Irish, 9.2% English, 2.4% Italian
Religion: Six largest groups: 15.4% Non-denominational Protestant, 9.6% Baptist, 6.3% Catholicism, 6.0% Methodist/Pietist, 3.1% Holiness, 2.8% Pentecostal
Economy: Unemployment rate: 8.3%; Leading industries: 19.3 % retail trade; 13.6 % health care and social assistance; 13.5 % other services (except public administration); Farms: 476 totaling 144,191 acres; Company size: 3 employ 1,000 or more persons, 6 employ 500 to 999 persons, 22 employ 100 to 499 persons, 1,745 employ less than 100 persons; Business ownership: 1,610 women-owned, 174 Black-owned, 28 Hispanic-owned, 119 Asian-owned, 30 American Indian/Alaska Native-owned
Employment: 9.2% management, business, and financial, 4.8% computer, engineering, and science, 8.3% education, legal, community service, arts, and media, 6.5% healthcare practitioners, 18.7% service, 20.9% sales and office, 8.0% natural resources, construction, and maintenance, 23.7% production, transportation, and material moving
Income: Per capita: $26,294; Median household: $47,958; Average household: $61,956; Households with income of $100,000 or more: 16.8%; Poverty rate: 16.5%
Educational Attainment: High school diploma or higher: 88.9%; Bachelor's degree or higher: 20.4%; Graduate/professional degree or higher: 7.2%
Housing: Homeownership rate: 68.3%; Median home value: $101,300; Median year structure built: 1967; Homeowner vacancy rate: 2.6%; Median selected monthly owner costs: $947 with a mortgage, $321 without a mortgage; Median gross rent: $678 per month; Rental vacancy rate: 7.3%
Vital Statistics: Birth rate: 117.0 per 10,000 population; Death rate: 113.6 per 10,000 population; Age-adjusted cancer mortality rate: 180.7 deaths per 100,000 population
Health Insurance: 90.6% have insurance; 70.5% have private insurance; 37.3% have public insurance; 9.4% do not have insurance; 5.0% of children under 18 do not have insurance
Health Care: Physicians: 17.1 per 10,000 population; Dentists: 8.6 per 10,000 population; Hospital beds: 38.6 per 10,000 population; Hospital admissions: 1,227.1 per 10,000 population
Air Quality Index (AQI): Percent of Days: 85.7% good, 14.3% moderate, 0.0% unhealthy for sensitive individuals, 0.0% unhealthy, 0.0% very unhealthy; Annual median: 34; Annual maximum: 80
Transportation: Commute: 94.2% car, 0.3% public transportation, 1.0% walk, 3.2% work from home; Mean travel time to work: 19.9 minutes
2016 Presidential Election: 63.4% Trump, 30.0% Clinton, 5.0% Johnson, 0.2% Stein

Additional Information Contacts

Howard Government. . . . . (765) 456-2234
http://www.co.howard.in.us

Howard County Communities

GREENTOWN (town). Covers a land area of 1.366 square miles and a water area of 0 square miles. Located at 40.48° N. Lat; 85.96° W. Long. Elevation is 837 feet.
History: Greentown was named for Miami Chief Green. It was founded in 1848 by English, German, Scotch, and Dutch immigrants who received the land from the U.S. government.
Population: 2,626; Growth (since 2000): 3.1%; Density: 1,922.9 persons per square mile; Race: 98.3% White, 0.2% Black/African American, 0.3% Asian, 0.0% American Indian/Alaska Native, 0.0% Native Hawaiian/Other Pacific Islander, 1.2% Two or more races, 1.7% Hispanic of any race; Average household size: 2.37; Median age: 39.6; Age under 18: 26.1%; Age 65 and over: 19.2%; Males per 100 females: 85.2; Marriage status: 22.4% never married, 53.8% now married, 1.8% separated, 9.2% widowed, 14.6% divorced; Foreign born: 0.3%; Speak English only: 99.3%; With disability: 16.0%; Veterans: 7.0%; Ancestry: 24.8% German, 12.0% American, 10.6% English, 10.2% Irish, 4.6% Dutch
Employment: 9.6% management, business, and financial, 3.2% computer, engineering, and science, 9.5% education, legal, community service, arts, and media, 5.0% healthcare practitioners, 15.0% service, 25.3% sales and office, 5.6% natural resources, construction, and maintenance, 26.9% production, transportation, and material moving

Income: Per capita: $24,828; Median household: $47,283; Average household: $59,307; Households with income of $100,000 or more: 14.0%; Poverty rate: 13.0%
Educational Attainment: High school diploma or higher: 89.3%; Bachelor's degree or higher: 16.2%; Graduate/professional degree or higher: 6.0%

School District(s)

Eastern Howard School Corporation (PK-12)
Enrollment: 1,071 . . . . (765) 628-3391

Housing: Homeownership rate: 72.2%; Median home value: $95,300; Median year structure built: 1967; Homeowner vacancy rate: 2.9%; Median selected monthly owner costs: $996 with a mortgage, $389 without a mortgage; Median gross rent: $752 per month; Rental vacancy rate: 16.5%
Health Insurance: 90.3% have insurance; 73.5% have private insurance; 35.1% have public insurance; 9.7% do not have insurance; 0.0% of children under 18 do not have insurance
Transportation: Commute: 97.6% car, 0.0% public transportation, 1.2% walk, 0.0% work from home; Mean travel time to work: 24.7 minutes
Additional Information Contacts
Town of Greentown . . . . (765) 610-8461
http://www.greentownindiana.org

KOKOMO (city). County seat. Covers a land area of 18.497 square miles and a water area of 0.059 square miles. Located at 40.48° N. Lat; 86.13° W. Long. Elevation is 810 feet.
History: Kokomo was platted in 1844. The coming of the railroad in 1853 and the discovery of natural gas in 1886 brought growth to the town. Kokomo was named for a Miami chief.
Population: 57,941; Growth (since 2000): 25.7%; Density: 3,132.5 persons per square mile; Race: 84.3% White, 10.0% Black/African American, 1.6% Asian, 0.4% American Indian/Alaska Native, 0.1% Native Hawaiian/Other Pacific Islander, 2.6% Two or more races, 3.8% Hispanic of any race; Average household size: 2.25; Median age: 39.9; Age under 18: 22.5%; Age 65 and over: 18.0%; Males per 100 females: 88.0; Marriage status: 26.8% never married, 48.2% now married, 1.9% separated, 7.6% widowed, 17.5% divorced; Foreign born: 2.5%; Speak English only: 96.1%; With disability: 18.8%; Veterans: 10.1%; Ancestry: 19.1% German, 11.3% American, 10.8% Irish, 8.4% English, 2.3% Italian
Employment: 7.1% management, business, and financial, 4.2% computer, engineering, and science, 7.7% education, legal, community service, arts, and media, 6.0% healthcare practitioners, 21.1% service, 20.5% sales and office, 7.8% natural resources, construction, and maintenance, 25.5% production, transportation, and material moving
Income: Per capita: $24,463; Median household: $41,366; Average household: $55,147; Households with income of $100,000 or more: 12.8%; Poverty rate: 20.4%
Educational Attainment: High school diploma or higher: 86.9%; Bachelor's degree or higher: 17.3%; Graduate/professional degree or higher: 6.2%

School District(s)

Excel Center - Kokomo (11-12)
Enrollment: 359. . . . . (317) 524-3642
Kokomo School Corporation (PK-12)
Enrollment: 7,058 . . . . (765) 455-8000
Northwestern School Corp (PK-12)
Enrollment: 1,446 . . . . (765) 452-3060
Taylor Community School Corp (PK-12)
Enrollment: 1,410 . . . . (765) 453-3035

Four-year College(s)

Indiana University-Kokomo (Public)
Enrollment: 3,029 . . . . (765) 453-2000
Tuition: In-state $7,207; Out-of-state $19,038

Two-year College(s)

Ross Medical Education Center-Kokomo (Private, For-profit)
Enrollment: 91. . . . . (765) 453-4864

Vocational/Technical School(s)

Rudae's School of Beauty Culture-Kokomo (Private, For-profit)
Enrollment: 13. . . . . (800) 878-9744
Tuition: $15,630
Summit Salon Academy-Kokomo (Private, For-profit)
Enrollment: 86. . . . . (765) 454-9840
Tuition: $15,350

Housing: Homeownership rate: 60.7%; Median home value: $85,200; Median year structure built: 1965; Homeowner vacancy rate: 3.2%; Median selected monthly owner costs: $874 with a mortgage, $315 without a mortgage; Median gross rent: $672 per month; Rental vacancy rate: 7.1%
Health Insurance: 89.2% have insurance; 64.9% have private insurance; 41.5% have public insurance; 10.8% do not have insurance; 5.7% of children under 18 do not have insurance
Hospitals: Community Howard Regional Health (150 beds); Saint Joseph Hospital & Health Center (156 beds)
Safety: Violent crime rate: 72.2 per 10,000 population; Property crime rate: 289.0 per 10,000 population
Newspapers: Kokomo Herald (weekly circulation 500); Kokomo Perspective (weekly circulation 31,000); Kokomo Tribune (daily circulation 20,900)
Transportation: Commute: 93.6% car, 0.5% public transportation, 1.1% walk, 3.2% work from home; Mean travel time to work: 18.7 minutes
Airports: Kokomo Municipal (general aviation)
Additional Information Contacts
City of Kokomo . . . . (765) 456-7370
http://www.cityofkokomo.org

RUSSIAVILLE (town). Covers a land area of 0.806 square miles and a water area of 0 square miles. Located at 40.42° N. Lat; 86.27° W. Long. Elevation is 846 feet.
History: Laid out 1845.
Population: 1,076; Growth (since 2000): -1.5%; Density: 1,334.6 persons per square mile; Race: 97.7% White, 0.0% Black/African American, 0.2% Asian, 0.1% American Indian/Alaska Native, 0.2% Native Hawaiian/Other Pacific Islander, 1.8% Two or more races, 1.6% Hispanic of any race; Average household size: 2.30; Median age: 38.0; Age under 18: 26.0%; Age 65 and over: 12.4%; Males per 100 females: 96.4; Marriage status: 18.1% never married, 59.1% now married, 0.0% separated, 4.4% widowed, 18.4% divorced; Foreign born: 0.6%; Speak English only: 99.6%; With disability: 18.4%; Veterans: 8.0%; Ancestry: 24.0% German, 16.5% Irish, 15.9% English, 7.1% American, 4.1% Italian
Employment: 9.9% management, business, and financial, 8.5% computer, engineering, and science, 5.1% education, legal, community service, arts, and media, 12.1% healthcare practitioners, 13.4% service, 17.0% sales and office, 5.1% natural resources, construction, and maintenance, 28.9% production, transportation, and material moving
Income: Per capita: $28,218; Median household: $51,250; Average household: $63,809; Households with income of $100,000 or more: 16.3%; Poverty rate: 9.4%
Educational Attainment: High school diploma or higher: 94.7%; Bachelor's degree or higher: 21.0%; Graduate/professional degree or higher: 5.2%

School District(s)

Western School Corporation (PK-12)
Enrollment: 2,358 . . . . (765) 883-5576

Housing: Homeownership rate: 71.3%; Median home value: $100,700; Median year structure built: 1969; Homeowner vacancy rate: 0.9%; Median selected monthly owner costs: $936 with a mortgage, $284 without a mortgage; Median gross rent: $650 per month; Rental vacancy rate: 5.6%
Health Insurance: 90.9% have insurance; 78.3% have private insurance; 27.6% have public insurance; 9.1% do not have insurance; 3.2% of children under 18 do not have insurance
Transportation: Commute: 94.1% car, 0.0% public transportation, 2.0% walk, 0.6% work from home; Mean travel time to work: 31.2 minutes

Huntington County

Located in northeast central Indiana; drained by the Wabash, Salamonie, and Little Rivers. Covers a land area of 382.651 square miles, a water area of 5.071 square miles, and is located in the Eastern Time Zone at 40.83° N. Lat., 85.48° W. Long. The county was founded in 1832. County seat is Huntington.

Huntington County is part of the Huntington, IN Micropolitan Statistical Area. The entire metro area includes: Huntington County, IN

Weather Station: Huntington Elevation: 725 feet

	Jan	Feb	Mar	Apr	May	Jun	Jul	Aug	Sep	Oct	Nov	Dec
High	33	37	48	61	72	82	85	84	77	64	50	37
Low	17	19	27	38	48	58	62	61	52	40	32	22
Precip	2.3	2.0	2.6	3.5	4.3	4.2	4.1	3.7	3.0	3.1	3.0	2.7
Snow	9.7	7.1	3.2	0.8	0.0	0.0	0.0	0.0	0.0	0.2	1.0	7.3

High and Low temperatures in degrees Fahrenheit; Precipitation and Snow in inches

Population: 36,520; Growth (since 2000): -4.1%; Density: 95.4 persons per square mile; Race: 96.5% White, 0.9% Black/African American, 0.8% Asian, 0.3% American Indian/Alaska Native, 0.0% Native Hawaiian/Other Pacific Islander, 0.9% two or more races, 2.2% Hispanic of any race; Average household size: 2.40; Median age: 40.3; Age under 18: 22.0%; Age 65 and over: 16.2%; Males per 100 females: 96.6; Marriage status: 25.0% never married, 57.9% now married, 0.9% separated, 6.3% widowed, 10.8% divorced; Foreign born: 1.5%; Speak English only: 97.0%; With disability: 14.4%; Veterans: 8.1%; Ancestry: 32.8% German, 12.0% American, 11.6% Irish, 7.9% English, 1.9% Scottish
Religion: Six largest groups: 13.1% Catholicism, 9.9% Methodist/Pietist, 9.4% Holiness, 5.4% Baptist, 4.5% Non-denominational Protestant, 2.1% Lutheran
Economy: Unemployment rate: 3.8%; Leading industries: 15.6 % retail trade; 14.2 % other services (except public administration); 9.9 % accommodation and food services; Farms: 695 totaling 188,848 acres; Company size: 0 employ 1,000 or more persons, 2 employ 500 to 999 persons, 20 employ 100 to 499 persons, 844 employ less than 100 persons; Business ownership: 743 women-owned, n/a Black-owned, n/a Hispanic-owned, n/a Asian-owned, n/a American Indian/Alaska Native-owned
Employment: 11.0% management, business, and financial, 2.5% computer, engineering, and science, 9.2% education, legal, community service, arts, and media, 4.8% healthcare practitioners, 16.6% service, 21.5% sales and office, 9.1% natural resources, construction, and maintenance, 25.4% production, transportation, and material moving
Income: Per capita: $24,222; Median household: $50,063; Average household: $59,849; Households with income of $100,000 or more: 15.6%; Poverty rate: 11.6%
Educational Attainment: High school diploma or higher: 90.5%; Bachelor's degree or higher: 18.1%; Graduate/professional degree or higher: 7.0%
Housing: Homeownership rate: 76.3%; Median home value: $102,700; Median year structure built: 1955; Homeowner vacancy rate: 1.3%; Median selected monthly owner costs: $941 with a mortgage, $370 without a mortgage; Median gross rent: $690 per month; Rental vacancy rate: 5.9%
Vital Statistics: Birth rate: 115.6 per 10,000 population; Death rate: 106.2 per 10,000 population; Age-adjusted cancer mortality rate: 174.8 deaths per 100,000 population
Health Insurance: 90.6% have insurance; 72.8% have private insurance; 30.5% have public insurance; 9.4% do not have insurance; 8.3% of children under 18 do not have insurance
Health Care: Physicians: 12.9 per 10,000 population; Dentists: 4.1 per 10,000 population; Hospital beds: 9.9 per 10,000 population; Hospital admissions: 460.8 per 10,000 population
Air Quality Index (AQI): Percent of Days: 92.7% good, 7.3% moderate, 0.0% unhealthy for sensitive individuals, 0.0% unhealthy, 0.0% very unhealthy; Annual median: 39; Annual maximum: 100
Transportation: Commute: 92.4% car, 0.3% public transportation, 3.5% walk, 3.4% work from home; Mean travel time to work: 20.2 minutes
2016 Presidential Election: 72.0% Trump, 21.7% Clinton, 5.1% Johnson, 0.2% Stein
National and State Parks: Kil-So-Quah State Recreation Area; Little Turtle State Recreation Area; Markle State Recreation Area; Mount Etna State Recreation Area
Additional Information Contacts
Huntington Government . . . . (219) 358-4822
http://www.huntington.in.us

Huntington County Communities

ANDREWS (town). Covers a land area of 0.645 square miles and a water area of 0.007 square miles. Located at 40.86° N. Lat; 85.60° W. Long. Elevation is 715 feet.
History: Andrews was the birthplace of educator Ellwood Patterson Cubberley who graduated from Indiana University in 1891 and went on to be president of Vincennes University and instrumental in the early days of Stanford University.
Population: 961; Growth (since 2000): -25.5%; Density: 1,489.0 persons per square mile; Race: 95.5% White, 0.0% Black/African American, 0.5% Asian, 2.1% American Indian/Alaska Native, 0.0% Native Hawaiian/Other Pacific Islander, 1.9% Two or more races, 0.7% Hispanic of any race; Average household size: 2.20; Median age: 43.6; Age under 18: 19.3%; Age 65 and over: 14.6%; Males per 100 females: 104.4; Marriage status: 20.3% never married, 55.9% now married, 3.9% separated, 6.8% widowed, 17.1% divorced; Foreign born: 2.2%; Speak English only: 95.3%; With disability: 20.2%; Veterans: 11.7%; Ancestry: 26.0% German, 18.5% American, 7.3% English, 7.2% Irish, 2.3% Italian
Employment: 3.9% management, business, and financial, 2.3% computer, engineering, and science, 4.4% education, legal, community service, arts, and media, 4.2% healthcare practitioners, 16.9% service, 11.7% sales and office, 9.4% natural resources, construction, and maintenance, 47.3% production, transportation, and material moving
Income: Per capita: $18,596; Median household: $37,344; Average household: $39,942; Households with income of $100,000 or more: 3.7%; Poverty rate: 24.1%
Educational Attainment: High school diploma or higher: 86.1%; Bachelor's degree or higher: 5.0%; Graduate/professional degree or higher: 2.6%

School District(s)

Huntington Co Com Sch Corp (PK-12)
Enrollment: 5,404 . . . . (260) 356-8312
Housing: Homeownership rate: 65.7%; Median home value: $54,300; Median year structure built: Before 1940; Homeowner vacancy rate: 0.0%; Median selected monthly owner costs: $670 with a mortgage, $357 without a mortgage; Median gross rent: $639 per month; Rental vacancy rate: 18.9%
Health Insurance: 86.5% have insurance; 50.4% have private insurance; 51.6% have public insurance; 13.5% do not have insurance; 6.8% of children under 18 do not have insurance
Transportation: Commute: 96.8% car, 0.0% public transportation, 1.6% walk, 0.8% work from home; Mean travel time to work: 24.3 minutes
Additional Information Contacts
Town of Andrews. . . . . (260) 356-5300
http://huntingtoncountychamber.com

HUNTINGTON (city). County seat. Covers a land area of 8.707 square miles and a water area of 0.134 square miles. Located at 40.88° N. Lat; 85.51° W. Long. Elevation is 748 feet.
History: Huntington was named in 1831 for Samuel Huntington, a member of the first Continental Congress. Previous to that the community was known as Wepecheange, meaning "place of flints." Huntington was the home of John R. Kissinger, on whom Dr. Walter Reed experimented with yellow fever tests in 1900 in Cuba.
Population: 17,214; Growth (since 2000): -1.4%; Density: 1,977.0 persons per square mile; Race: 95.0% White, 1.5% Black/African American, 1.6% Asian, 0.2% American Indian/Alaska Native, 0.0% Native Hawaiian/Other Pacific Islander, 1.0% Two or more races, 3.2% Hispanic of any race; Average household size: 2.39; Median age: 35.7; Age under 18: 22.4%; Age 65 and over: 14.4%; Males per 100 females: 91.3; Marriage status: 33.7% never married, 46.1% now married, 1.1% separated, 7.3% widowed, 12.9% divorced; Foreign born: 2.4%; Speak English only: 95.5%; With disability: 16.5%; Veterans: 7.4%; Ancestry: 32.5% German, 13.0% Irish, 10.9% American, 7.9% English, 2.1% Italian
Employment: 6.6% management, business, and financial, 1.3% computer, engineering, and science, 9.3% education, legal, community service, arts, and media, 4.1% healthcare practitioners, 18.8% service, 22.5% sales and office, 8.7% natural resources, construction, and maintenance, 28.9% production, transportation, and material moving
Income: Per capita: $20,322; Median household: $42,302; Average household: $51,370; Households with income of $100,000 or more: 10.5%; Poverty rate: 16.9%
Educational Attainment: High school diploma or higher: 86.5%; Bachelor's degree or higher: 15.5%; Graduate/professional degree or higher: 6.9%

School District(s)

Huntington Co Com Sch Corp (PK-12)
Enrollment: 5,404 . . . . (260) 356-8312

Four-year College(s)

Huntington University (Private, Not-for-profit, United Brethren Church)
Enrollment: 1,321 . . . . (260) 356-6000
Tuition: In-state $25,540; Out-of-state $25,540
Housing: Homeownership rate: 64.8%; Median home value: $78,400; Median year structure built: 1941; Homeowner vacancy rate: 1.9%; Median selected monthly owner costs: $834 with a mortgage, $319 without a mortgage; Median gross rent: $678 per month; Rental vacancy rate: 4.9%
Health Insurance: 89.2% have insurance; 66.7% have private insurance; 33.4% have public insurance; 10.8% do not have insurance; 7.6% of children under 18 do not have insurance
Hospitals: Parkview Huntington Hospital (36 beds)

Newspapers: Huntington County TAB (weekly circulation 15,500); Huntington Herald-Press (daily circulation 6,400)
Transportation: Commute: 91.0% car, 0.0% public transportation, 6.1% walk, 2.5% work from home; Mean travel time to work: 17.4 minutes
Additional Information Contacts
City of Huntington . . . . (260) 356-1400
http://www.huntington.in.us

MARKLE (town). Covers a land area of 1.222 square miles and a water area of 0.049 square miles. Located at 40.83° N. Lat; 85.34° W. Long. Elevation is 781 feet.
Population: 1,311; Growth (since 2000): 19.0%; Density: 1,073.1 persons per square mile; Race: 98.3% White, 0.4% Black/African American, 0.0% Asian, 0.4% American Indian/Alaska Native, 0.0% Native Hawaiian/Other Pacific Islander, 0.9% Two or more races, 1.8% Hispanic of any race; Average household size: 2.33; Median age: 38.1; Age under 18: 21.2%; Age 65 and over: 18.2%; Males per 100 females: 91.8; Marriage status: 24.0% never married, 55.5% now married, 0.3% separated, 9.4% widowed, 11.1% divorced; Foreign born: 0.7%; Speak English only: 99.4%; With disability: 12.3%; Veterans: 8.4%; Ancestry: 31.7% German, 12.9% American, 8.5% English, 8.5% Irish, 3.5% French
Employment: 11.1% management, business, and financial, 2.2% computer, engineering, and science, 7.8% education, legal, community service, arts, and media, 5.0% healthcare practitioners, 12.2% service, 19.3% sales and office, 10.0% natural resources, construction, and maintenance, 32.2% production, transportation, and material moving
Income: Per capita: $25,028; Median household: $50,000; Average household: $60,360; Households with income of $100,000 or more: 11.4%; Poverty rate: 15.6%
Educational Attainment: High school diploma or higher: 92.6%; Bachelor's degree or higher: 15.3%; Graduate/professional degree or higher: 2.4%
Housing: Homeownership rate: 71.1%; Median home value: $85,800; Median year structure built: 1954; Homeowner vacancy rate: 0.0%; Median selected monthly owner costs: $820 with a mortgage, $340 without a mortgage; Median gross rent: $653 per month; Rental vacancy rate: 9.8%
Health Insurance: 95.0% have insurance; 76.7% have private insurance; 29.4% have public insurance; 5.0% do not have insurance; 0.0% of children under 18 do not have insurance
Transportation: Commute: 90.6% car, 0.0% public transportation, 3.9% walk, 5.5% work from home; Mean travel time to work: 19.0 minutes

MOUNT ETNA (town). Covers a land area of 0.082 square miles and a water area of <.001 square miles. Located at 40.74° N. Lat; 85.56° W. Long. Elevation is 810 feet.
History: Mount Etna was founded in 1839, and named for Mt. Etna in Sicily.
Population: 107; Growth (since 2000): -2.7%; Density: 1,305.7 persons per square mile; Race: 100.0% White, 0.0% Black/African American, 0.0% Asian, 0.0% American Indian/Alaska Native, 0.0% Native Hawaiian/Other Pacific Islander, 0.0% Two or more races, 0.9% Hispanic of any race; Average household size: 2.18; Median age: 51.8; Age under 18: 10.3%; Age 65 and over: 13.1%; Males per 100 females: 113.6; Marriage status: 14.1% never married, 76.8% now married, 2.0% separated, 3.0% widowed, 6.1% divorced; Foreign born: 0.0%; Speak English only: 99.0%; With disability: 16.8%; Veterans: 5.2%; Ancestry: 33.6% German, 20.6% Irish, 13.1% American, 11.2% Italian, 9.3% English
Employment: 20.3% management, business, and financial, 0.0% computer, engineering, and science, 4.7% education, legal, community service, arts, and media, 0.0% healthcare practitioners, 26.6% service, 21.9% sales and office, 10.9% natural resources, construction, and maintenance, 15.6% production, transportation, and material moving
Income: Per capita: $22,521; Median household: $41,250; Average household: $49,035; Households with income of $100,000 or more: n/a; Poverty rate: 0.9%
Educational Attainment: High school diploma or higher: 88.2%; Bachelor's degree or higher: 12.9%; Graduate/professional degree or higher: n/a
Housing: Homeownership rate: 85.7%; Median home value: $67,500; Median year structure built: Before 1940; Homeowner vacancy rate: 0.0%; Median selected monthly owner costs: $900 with a mortgage, $375 without a mortgage; Median gross rent: n/a per month; Rental vacancy rate: 0.0%
Health Insurance: 98.1% have insurance; 89.7% have private insurance; 24.3% have public insurance; 1.9% do not have insurance; 8.3% of children under 18 do not have insurance
Transportation: Commute: 96.9% car, 0.0% public transportation, 0.0% walk, 3.1% work from home; Mean travel time to work: 26.0 minutes

ROANOKE (town). Covers a land area of 1.197 square miles and a water area of 0.006 square miles. Located at 40.96° N. Lat; 85.38° W. Long. Elevation is 758 feet.
History: Roanoke was known for the Roanoke Classical Seminary founded in 1861 by Frederick S. Reefy. The emphasis in culture provided by the seminary gave Roanoke the reputation as the Athens of Indiana.
Population: 1,751; Growth (since 2000): 17.1%; Density: 1,462.7 persons per square mile; Race: 99.4% White, 0.2% Black/African American, 0.0% Asian, 0.0% American Indian/Alaska Native, 0.0% Native Hawaiian/Other Pacific Islander, 0.4% Two or more races, 1.1% Hispanic of any race; Average household size: 2.44; Median age: 35.9; Age under 18: 26.2%; Age 65 and over: 14.0%; Males per 100 females: 94.6; Marriage status: 24.1% never married, 60.3% now married, 0.5% separated, 4.0% widowed, 11.5% divorced; Foreign born: 0.8%; Speak English only: 98.4%; With disability: 8.6%; Veterans: 6.9%; Ancestry: 32.8% German, 14.3% Irish, 12.8% English, 10.7% American, 4.4% Scottish
Employment: 17.1% management, business, and financial, 7.9% computer, engineering, and science, 10.1% education, legal, community service, arts, and media, 9.6% healthcare practitioners, 15.9% service, 19.6% sales and office, 5.3% natural resources, construction, and maintenance, 14.6% production, transportation, and material moving
Income: Per capita: $26,914; Median household: $60,500; Average household: $67,117; Households with income of $100,000 or more: 17.1%; Poverty rate: 5.7%
Educational Attainment: High school diploma or higher: 96.4%; Bachelor's degree or higher: 33.0%; Graduate/professional degree or higher: 9.5%

School District(s)
Huntington Co Com Sch Corp (PK-12)
Enrollment: 5,404 . . . . (260) 356-8312
M S D Southwest Allen County Schls (PK-12)
Enrollment: 7,193 . . . . (260) 431-2010
Housing: Homeownership rate: 80.3%; Median home value: $119,700; Median year structure built: 1985; Homeowner vacancy rate: 0.0%; Median selected monthly owner costs: $1,005 with a mortgage, $359 without a mortgage; Median gross rent: $588 per month; Rental vacancy rate: 14.0%
Health Insurance: 93.3% have insurance; 86.1% have private insurance; 19.6% have public insurance; 6.7% do not have insurance; 8.8% of children under 18 do not have insurance
Transportation: Commute: 94.2% car, 0.0% public transportation, 1.9% walk, 2.6% work from home; Mean travel time to work: 23.5 minutes

WARREN (town). Covers a land area of 1.143 square miles and a water area of 0.005 square miles. Located at 40.69° N. Lat; 85.42° W. Long. Elevation is 827 feet.
History: Laid out 1836.
Population: 1,309; Growth (since 2000): 2.9%; Density: 1,145.3 persons per square mile; Race: 99.5% White, 0.0% Black/African American, 0.0% Asian, 0.5% American Indian/Alaska Native, 0.0% Native Hawaiian/Other Pacific Islander, 0.0% Two or more races, 0.5% Hispanic of any race; Average household size: 2.19; Median age: 43.3; Age under 18: 16.4%; Age 65 and over: 21.7%; Males per 100 females: 97.6; Marriage status: 21.5% never married, 54.3% now married, 0.3% separated, 9.9% widowed, 14.2% divorced; Foreign born: 0.0%; Speak English only: 98.2%; With disability: 18.1%; Veterans: 7.4%; Ancestry: 30.6% German, 17.6% American, 13.7% English, 7.9% Irish, 3.5% Scottish
Employment: 11.6% management, business, and financial, 2.2% computer, engineering, and science, 9.8% education, legal, community service, arts, and media, 1.5% healthcare practitioners, 24.8% service, 13.7% sales and office, 9.8% natural resources, construction, and maintenance, 26.5% production, transportation, and material moving
Income: Per capita: $26,015; Median household: $44,607; Average household: $55,137; Households with income of $100,000 or more: 8.3%; Poverty rate: 7.0%
Educational Attainment: High school diploma or higher: 93.2%; Bachelor's degree or higher: 11.8%; Graduate/professional degree or higher: 5.0%

School District(s)
Huntington Co Com Sch Corp (PK-12)
Enrollment: 5,404 . . . . (260) 356-8312
Housing: Homeownership rate: 61.8%; Median home value: $75,700; Median year structure built: 1950; Homeowner vacancy rate: 7.7%; Median

selected monthly owner costs: $765 with a mortgage, $338 without a mortgage; Median gross rent: $926 per month; Rental vacancy rate: 4.6%
Health Insurance: 83.5% have insurance; 70.4% have private insurance; 29.9% have public insurance; 16.5% do not have insurance; 14.1% of children under 18 do not have insurance
Newspapers: Warren Weekly (weekly circulation 3,200)
Transportation: Commute: 92.2% car, 0.0% public transportation, 4.3% walk, 1.0% work from home; Mean travel time to work: 22.1 minutes

Jackson County

Located in southern Indiana; bounded on the south by the Muscatatuck River; drained by the East Fork of the White River. Covers a land area of 509.312 square miles, a water area of 4.601 square miles, and is located in the Eastern Time Zone at 38.91° N. Lat., 86.04° W. Long. The county was founded in 1815. County seat is Brownstown.

Jackson County is part of the Seymour, IN Micropolitan Statistical Area. The entire metro area includes: Jackson County, IN

Weather Station: Seymour 2 N Elevation: 569 feet

	Jan	Feb	Mar	Apr	May	Jun	Jul	Aug	Sep	Oct	Nov	Dec
High	38	42	53	64	74	82	85	84	78	67	54	41
Low	21	23	31	41	51	61	64	62	53	41	33	24
Precip	3.2	2.8	3.9	4.7	5.5	4.2	4.3	4.5	3.2	3.8	3.8	3.6
Snow	3.0	3.1	2.0	tr	0.0	0.0	0.0	0.0	0.0	0.2	0.1	1.9

High and Low temperatures in degrees Fahrenheit; Precipitation and Snow in inches

Population: 43,779; Growth (since 2000): 5.9%; Density: 86.0 persons per square mile; Race: 92.0% White, 1.1% Black/African American, 1.9% Asian, 0.4% American Indian/Alaska Native, 0.0% Native Hawaiian/Other Pacific Islander, 1.1% two or more races, 6.4% Hispanic of any race; Average household size: 2.60; Median age: 38.2; Age under 18: 24.5%; Age 65 and over: 15.5%; Males per 100 females: 99.1; Marriage status: 22.9% never married, 55.7% now married, 1.5% separated, 7.1% widowed, 14.3% divorced; Foreign born: 5.0%; Speak English only: 93.3%; With disability: 14.1%; Veterans: 6.8%; Ancestry: 22.4% German, 20.8% American, 8.4% English, 8.1% Irish, 1.8% Scottish
Religion: Six largest groups: 20.2% Baptist, 19.8% Lutheran, 5.1% Holiness, 3.5% Catholicism, 3.3% Methodist/Pietist, 2.6% Non-denominational Protestant
Economy: Unemployment rate: 3.1%; Leading industries: 18.4 % retail trade; 12.3 % other services (except public administration); 10.3 % health care and social assistance; Farms: 744 totaling 183,878 acres; Company size: 2 employ 1,000 or more persons, 5 employ 500 to 999 persons, 24 employ 100 to 499 persons, 955 employ less than 100 persons; Business ownership: 653 women-owned, n/a Black-owned, n/a Hispanic-owned, 49 Asian-owned, n/a American Indian/Alaska Native-owned
Employment: 12.0% management, business, and financial, 3.9% computer, engineering, and science, 7.5% education, legal, community service, arts, and media, 4.3% healthcare practitioners, 15.6% service, 22.9% sales and office, 9.0% natural resources, construction, and maintenance, 24.7% production, transportation, and material moving
Income: Per capita: $23,260; Median household: $49,080; Average household: $59,406; Households with income of $100,000 or more: 16.0%; Poverty rate: 15.6%
Educational Attainment: High school diploma or higher: 86.9%; Bachelor's degree or higher: 15.9%; Graduate/professional degree or higher: 5.3%
Housing: Homeownership rate: 72.7%; Median home value: $114,600; Median year structure built: 1975; Homeowner vacancy rate: 2.7%; Median selected monthly owner costs: $1,026 with a mortgage, $347 without a mortgage; Median gross rent: $729 per month; Rental vacancy rate: 3.9%
Vital Statistics: Birth rate: 130.8 per 10,000 population; Death rate: 101.9 per 10,000 population; Age-adjusted cancer mortality rate: 213.4 deaths per 100,000 population
Health Insurance: 89.7% have insurance; 70.7% have private insurance; 31.4% have public insurance; 10.3% do not have insurance; 5.4% of children under 18 do not have insurance
Health Care: Physicians: 13.7 per 10,000 population; Dentists: 5.9 per 10,000 population; Hospital beds: 21.2 per 10,000 population; Hospital admissions: 648.7 per 10,000 population
Air Quality Index (AQI): Percent of Days: 91.2% good, 8.8% moderate, 0.0% unhealthy for sensitive individuals, 0.0% unhealthy, 0.0% very unhealthy; Annual median: 40; Annual maximum: 93
Transportation: Commute: 93.7% car, 0.4% public transportation, 1.6% walk, 1.9% work from home; Mean travel time to work: 20.5 minutes
2016 Presidential Election: 72.8% Trump, 21.8% Clinton, 4.7% Johnson, 0.2% Stein
National and State Parks: Muscatatuck National Wildlife Refuge; Starve Hollow State Beach
Additional Information Contacts
Jackson Government . . . . (812) 358-6116
http://www.jacksoncounty.in.gov

Jackson County Communities

BROWNSTOWN (town). County seat. Covers a land area of 1.588 square miles and a water area of 0.006 square miles. Located at 38.88° N. Lat; 86.05° W. Long. Elevation is 623 feet.
History: Brownstown was founded in 1816 as a farm town and seat of Jackson County.
Population: 2,952; Growth (since 2000): -0.9%; Density: 1,858.9 persons per square mile; Race: 98.9% White, 0.2% Black/African American, 0.0% Asian, 0.0% American Indian/Alaska Native, 0.0% Native Hawaiian/Other Pacific Islander, 0.9% Two or more races, 0.9% Hispanic of any race; Average household size: 2.60; Median age: 36.2; Age under 18: 27.0%; Age 65 and over: 15.7%; Males per 100 females: 93.1; Marriage status: 27.5% never married, 45.4% now married, 0.5% separated, 8.3% widowed, 18.7% divorced; Foreign born: 1.3%; Speak English only: 98.7%; With disability: 15.6%; Veterans: 6.7%; Ancestry: 22.4% German, 22.3% American, 11.1% Irish, 9.6% English, 3.4% Italian
Employment: 6.1% management, business, and financial, 1.2% computer, engineering, and science, 9.1% education, legal, community service, arts, and media, 3.7% healthcare practitioners, 15.9% service, 28.7% sales and office, 7.9% natural resources, construction, and maintenance, 27.4% production, transportation, and material moving
Income: Per capita: $18,300; Median household: $39,301; Average household: $46,698; Households with income of $100,000 or more: 7.0%; Poverty rate: 17.8%
Educational Attainment: High school diploma or higher: 87.4%; Bachelor's degree or higher: 10.4%; Graduate/professional degree or higher: 4.4%

School District(s)
Brownstown Cnt Com Sch Corp (PK-12)
Enrollment: 1,501 . . . . (812) 358-4271
Housing: Homeownership rate: 61.4%; Median home value: $104,400; Median year structure built: 1969; Homeowner vacancy rate: 1.6%; Median selected monthly owner costs: $951 with a mortgage, $349 without a mortgage; Median gross rent: $763 per month; Rental vacancy rate: 3.7%
Health Insurance: 91.1% have insurance; 71.9% have private insurance; 39.2% have public insurance; 8.9% do not have insurance; 0.0% of children under 18 do not have insurance
Newspapers: Jackson County Banner (weekly circulation 3,000)
Transportation: Commute: 90.5% car, 0.0% public transportation, 4.0% walk, 1.5% work from home; Mean travel time to work: 16.8 minutes
Additional Information Contacts
Town of Brownstown. . . . . (812) 358-2930
http://www.brownstownchamber.org

CROTHERSVILLE (town). Covers a land area of 1.142 square miles and a water area of 0 square miles. Located at 38.79° N. Lat; 85.84° W. Long. Elevation is 558 feet.
Population: 1,633; Growth (since 2000): 4.0%; Density: 1,430.2 persons per square mile; Race: 98.0% White, 0.0% Black/African American, 0.0% Asian, 0.4% American Indian/Alaska Native, 0.0% Native Hawaiian/Other Pacific Islander, 0.9% Two or more races, 1.7% Hispanic of any race; Average household size: 2.63; Median age: 36.0; Age under 18: 27.2%; Age 65 and over: 13.5%; Males per 100 females: 94.7; Marriage status: 27.2% never married, 51.5% now married, 1.5% separated, 4.7% widowed, 16.6% divorced; Foreign born: 0.0%; Speak English only: 99.7%; With disability: 15.0%; Veterans: 6.6%; Ancestry: 15.8% American, 14.0% German, 10.8% Irish, 9.9% English, 1.0% French
Employment: 9.3% management, business, and financial, 1.3% computer, engineering, and science, 9.9% education, legal, community service, arts, and media, 3.7% healthcare practitioners, 15.4% service, 13.2% sales and office, 5.9% natural resources, construction, and maintenance, 41.4% production, transportation, and material moving

Income: Per capita: $23,182; Median household: $50,208; Average household: $57,739; Households with income of $100,000 or more: 11.3%; Poverty rate: 14.5%
Educational Attainment: High school diploma or higher: 91.1%; Bachelor's degree or higher: 6.1%; Graduate/professional degree or higher: 1.6%

School District(s)

Crothersville Community Schools (PK-12)
Enrollment: 540. . . . . (812) 793-2601
Housing: Homeownership rate: 70.8%; Median home value: $80,200; Median year structure built: 1962; Homeowner vacancy rate: 6.5%; Median selected monthly owner costs: $894 with a mortgage, $316 without a mortgage; Median gross rent: $632 per month; Rental vacancy rate: 2.7%
Health Insurance: 91.4% have insurance; 68.8% have private insurance; 33.3% have public insurance; 8.6% do not have insurance; 5.1% of children under 18 do not have insurance
Newspapers: Crothersville Times (weekly circulation 2,300)
Transportation: Commute: 91.7% car, 0.0% public transportation, 2.0% walk, 2.7% work from home; Mean travel time to work: 24.9 minutes

FREETOWN (CDP). Covers a land area of 0.724 square miles and a water area of 0.003 square miles. Located at 38.98° N. Lat; 86.13° W. Long. Elevation is 650 feet.
Population: 320; Growth (since 2000): n/a; Density: 441.9 persons per square mile; Race: 100.0% White, 0.0% Black/African American, 0.0% Asian, 0.0% American Indian/Alaska Native, 0.0% Native Hawaiian/Other Pacific Islander, 0.0% Two or more races, 0.0% Hispanic of any race; Average household size: 2.81; Median age: 32.3; Age under 18: 40.9%; Age 65 and over: 16.3%; Males per 100 females: 94.4; Marriage status: 18.1% never married, 46.2% now married, 0.0% separated, 7.1% widowed, 28.6% divorced; Foreign born: 0.0%; Speak English only: 100.0%; With disability: 11.3%; Veterans: 0.0%; Ancestry: 12.8% American
Employment: 0.0% management, business, and financial, 19.8% computer, engineering, and science, 0.0% education, legal, community service, arts, and media, 0.0% healthcare practitioners, 14.0% service, 55.8% sales and office, 0.0% natural resources, construction, and maintenance, 10.5% production, transportation, and material moving
Income: Per capita: $16,158; Median household: $48,625; Average household: $46,589; Households with income of $100,000 or more: n/a; Poverty rate: 3.4%
Educational Attainment: High school diploma or higher: 63.4%; Bachelor's degree or higher: n/a; Graduate/professional degree or higher: n/a
Housing: Homeownership rate: 82.5%; Median home value: n/a; Median year structure built: 1976; Homeowner vacancy rate: 0.0%; Median selected monthly owner costs: $862 with a mortgage, n/a without a mortgage; Median gross rent: n/a per month; Rental vacancy rate: 0.0%
Health Insurance: 92.8% have insurance; 87.8% have private insurance; 16.3% have public insurance; 7.2% do not have insurance; 0.0% of children under 18 do not have insurance
Transportation: Commute: 100.0% car, 0.0% public transportation, 0.0% walk, 0.0% work from home; Mean travel time to work: 0.0 minutes

MEDORA (town). Covers a land area of 0.329 square miles and a water area of 0.002 square miles. Located at 38.82° N. Lat; 86.17° W. Long. Elevation is 528 feet.
Population: 621; Growth (since 2000): 9.9%; Density: 1,887.0 persons per square mile; Race: 97.4% White, 0.0% Black/African American, 0.0% Asian, 1.4% American Indian/Alaska Native, 0.0% Native Hawaiian/Other Pacific Islander, 1.1% Two or more races, 0.3% Hispanic of any race; Average household size: 2.59; Median age: 36.4; Age under 18: 26.9%; Age 65 and over: 15.0%; Males per 100 females: 99.1; Marriage status: 19.3% never married, 49.7% now married, 1.4% separated, 10.0% widowed, 21.0% divorced; Foreign born: 0.0%; Speak English only: 100.0%; With disability: 15.8%; Veterans: 8.6%; Ancestry: 27.7% American, 14.3% Irish, 11.8% German, 8.2% English, 2.6% Scotch-Irish
Employment: 6.6% management, business, and financial, 0.0% computer, engineering, and science, 5.8% education, legal, community service, arts, and media, 4.6% healthcare practitioners, 5.8% service, 18.9% sales and office, 12.7% natural resources, construction, and maintenance, 45.6% production, transportation, and material moving
Income: Per capita: $16,363; Median household: $30,000; Average household: $40,969; Households with income of $100,000 or more: 5.0%; Poverty rate: 31.9%
Educational Attainment: High school diploma or higher: 79.2%; Bachelor's degree or higher: 4.4%; Graduate/professional degree or higher: 2.5%

School District(s)

Medora Community School Corp (PK-12)
Enrollment: 224. . . . . (812) 966-2210
Housing: Homeownership rate: 80.4%; Median home value: $45,500; Median year structure built: 1964; Homeowner vacancy rate: 1.0%; Median selected monthly owner costs: $715 with a mortgage, $306 without a mortgage; Median gross rent: $677 per month; Rental vacancy rate: 26.0%
Health Insurance: 87.3% have insurance; 63.6% have private insurance; 39.9% have public insurance; 12.7% do not have insurance; 3.4% of children under 18 do not have insurance
Transportation: Commute: 87.6% car, 0.0% public transportation, 6.6% walk, 2.3% work from home; Mean travel time to work: 28.8 minutes

NORMAN (unincorporated postal area)
ZCTA: 47264
Covers a land area of 98.863 square miles and a water area of 0.287 square miles. Located at 38.97° N. Lat; 86.25° W. Long. Elevation is 869 feet.
Population: 1,440; Growth (since 2000): 0.8%; Density: 14.6 persons per square mile; Race: 100.0% White, 0.0% Black/African American, 0.0% Asian, 0.0% American Indian/Alaska Native, 0.0% Native Hawaiian/Other Pacific Islander, 0.0% Two or more races, 0.0% Hispanic of any race; Average household size: 2.74; Median age: 51.1; Age under 18: 15.1%; Age 65 and over: 20.5%; Males per 100 females: 106.4; Marriage status: 24.3% never married, 61.4% now married, 0.0% separated, 5.1% widowed, 9.1% divorced; Foreign born: 7.8%; Speak English only: 100.0%; With disability: 14.8%; Veterans: 7.7%; Ancestry: 36.7% German, 25.8% American, 5.6% French, 5.5% Irish, 5.2% Russian
Employment: 20.4% management, business, and financial, 8.7% computer, engineering, and science, 3.8% education, legal, community service, arts, and media, 3.3% healthcare practitioners, 25.6% service, 8.1% sales and office, 3.8% natural resources, construction, and maintenance, 26.3% production, transportation, and material moving
Income: Per capita: $23,867; Median household: $52,750; Average household: $62,899; Households with income of $100,000 or more: 24.8%; Poverty rate: 12.8%
Educational Attainment: High school diploma or higher: 86.9%; Bachelor's degree or higher: 11.1%; Graduate/professional degree or higher: 1.2%
Housing: Homeownership rate: 89.2%; Median home value: $133,100; Median year structure built: 1991; Homeowner vacancy rate: 0.0%; Median selected monthly owner costs: $1,098 with a mortgage, $369 without a mortgage; Median gross rent: n/a per month; Rental vacancy rate: 0.0%
Health Insurance: 82.3% have insurance; 73.8% have private insurance; 28.3% have public insurance; 17.7% do not have insurance; 38.2% of children under 18 do not have insurance
Transportation: Commute: 94.1% car, 0.0% public transportation, 4.1% walk, 1.7% work from home; Mean travel time to work: 37.9 minutes

SEYMOUR (city). Covers a land area of 11.422 square miles and a water area of 0.005 square miles. Located at 38.94° N. Lat; 85.89° W. Long. Elevation is 600 feet.
History: Seymour developed as a factory town at the junction of three railroads.
Population: 19,225; Growth (since 2000): 6.2%; Density: 1,683.1 persons per square mile; Race: 85.0% White, 1.9% Black/African American, 3.3% Asian, 0.2% American Indian/Alaska Native, 0.0% Native Hawaiian/Other Pacific Islander, 1.6% Two or more races, 11.9% Hispanic of any race; Average household size: 2.48; Median age: 36.8; Age under 18: 26.0%; Age 65 and over: 14.5%; Males per 100 females: 95.1; Marriage status: 22.5% never married, 53.6% now married, 2.0% separated, 8.3% widowed, 15.6% divorced; Foreign born: 8.8%; Speak English only: 87.6%; With disability: 15.5%; Veterans: 7.8%; Ancestry: 21.5% German, 18.9% American, 8.2% Irish, 8.2% English, 2.1% Scottish
Employment: 10.4% management, business, and financial, 5.3% computer, engineering, and science, 8.0% education, legal, community service, arts, and media, 4.5% healthcare practitioners, 17.0% service, 20.9% sales and office, 6.8% natural resources, construction, and maintenance, 27.2% production, transportation, and material moving

Income: Per capita: $21,942; Median household: $43,664; Average household: $53,725; Households with income of $100,000 or more: 13.0%; Poverty rate: 19.7%
Educational Attainment: High school diploma or higher: 84.7%; Bachelor's degree or higher: 19.2%; Graduate/professional degree or higher: 6.2%

School District(s)

Seymour Community Schools (PK-12)
Enrollment: 4,757 . . . . (812) 522-3340
Housing: Homeownership rate: 62.8%; Median home value: $108,400; Median year structure built: 1973; Homeowner vacancy rate: 3.0%; Median selected monthly owner costs: $982 with a mortgage, $318 without a mortgage; Median gross rent: $746 per month; Rental vacancy rate: 4.9%
Health Insurance: 89.1% have insurance; 67.1% have private insurance; 31.9% have public insurance; 10.9% do not have insurance; 6.1% of children under 18 do not have insurance
Hospitals: Schneck Medical Center (166 beds)
Safety: Violent crime rate: 33.7 per 10,000 population; Property crime rate: 373.4 per 10,000 population
Newspapers: The Tribune (daily circulation 8,900)
Transportation: Commute: 93.5% car, 0.2% public transportation, 1.4% walk, 1.4% work from home; Mean travel time to work: 17.8 minutes
Airports: Freeman Municipal (general aviation)
Additional Information Contacts
City of Seymour. . . . . (812) 522-4020
http://www.seymourcity.com

VALLONIA (CDP). Covers a land area of 0.761 square miles and a water area of <.001 square miles. Located at 38.85° N. Lat; 86.10° W. Long. Elevation is 535 feet.
Population: 277; Growth (since 2000): n/a; Density: 363.8 persons per square mile; Race: 100.0% White, 0.0% Black/African American, 0.0% Asian, 0.0% American Indian/Alaska Native, 0.0% Native Hawaiian/Other Pacific Islander, 0.0% Two or more races, 0.0% Hispanic of any race; Average household size: 2.07; Median age: 53.5; Age under 18: 0.0%; Age 65 and over: 22.7%; Males per 100 females: 108.7; Marriage status: 18.4% never married, 43.3% now married, 0.0% separated, 0.0% widowed, 38.3% divorced; Foreign born: 0.0%; Speak English only: 94.6%; With disability: 15.9%; Veterans: 6.9%; Ancestry: 45.5% German, 10.1% American, 5.8% English, 3.2% Irish, 3.2% Scottish
Employment: 39.4% management, business, and financial, 0.0% computer, engineering, and science, 5.3% education, legal, community service, arts, and media, 0.0% healthcare practitioners, 11.2% service, 25.9% sales and office, 10.6% natural resources, construction, and maintenance, 7.6% production, transportation, and material moving
Income: Per capita: $31,646; Median household: $31,500; Average household: $61,622; Households with income of $100,000 or more: 25.4%; Poverty rate: n/a
Educational Attainment: High school diploma or higher: 65.2%; Bachelor's degree or higher: 14.2%; Graduate/professional degree or higher: 2.4%
Housing: Homeownership rate: 85.8%; Median home value: $101,500; Median year structure built: 1971; Homeowner vacancy rate: 0.0%; Median selected monthly owner costs: $894 with a mortgage, $385 without a mortgage; Median gross rent: n/a per month; Rental vacancy rate: 0.0%
Health Insurance: 93.1% have insurance; 73.3% have private insurance; 39.7% have public insurance; 6.9% do not have insurance; 0.0% of children under 18 do not have insurance
Transportation: Commute: 87.6% car, 0.0% public transportation, 0.0% walk, 12.4% work from home; Mean travel time to work: 23.1 minutes

Jasper County

Located in northwestern Indiana; bounded on the north by the Kankakee River; drained by the Iroquois River. Covers a land area of 559.625 square miles, a water area of 1.761 square miles, and is located in the Central Time Zone at 41.02° N. Lat., 87.12° W. Long. The county was founded in 1835. County seat is Rensselaer.

Jasper County is part of the Chicago-Naperville-Elgin, IL-IN-WI Metropolitan Statistical Area. The entire metro area includes: Chicago-Naperville-Arlington Heights, IL Metropolitan Division (Cook County, IL; DuPage County, IL; Grundy County, IL; Kendall County, IL; McHenry County, IL; Will County, IL); Elgin, IL Metropolitan Division (DeKalb County, IL; Kane County, IL); Gary, IN Metropolitan Division (Jasper County, IN; Lake County, IN; Newton County, IN; Porter County, IN); Lake County-Kenosha County, IL-WI Metropolitan Division (Lake County, IL; Kenosha County, WI)

Weather Station: Rensselaer		Elevation: 649 feet

	Jan	Feb	Mar	Apr	May	Jun	Jul	Aug	Sep	Oct	Nov	Dec
High	32	36	47	61	72	81	84	82	76	63	49	36
Low	16	19	29	40	50	60	64	62	53	41	33	21
Precip	2.3	1.9	2.9	3.6	4.4	4.1	4.6	3.5	3.2	3.5	3.3	2.7
Snow	9.0	6.6	2.7	0.3	0.0	0.0	0.0	0.0	0.0	0.1	0.5	5.5

High and Low temperatures in degrees Fahrenheit; Precipitation and Snow in inches

Population: 33,448; Growth (since 2000): 11.3%; Density: 59.8 persons per square mile; Race: 95.0% White, 0.7% Black/African American, 0.4% Asian, 0.1% American Indian/Alaska Native, 0.0% Native Hawaiian/Other Pacific Islander, 1.6% two or more races, 5.9% Hispanic of any race; Average household size: 2.66; Median age: 39.0; Age under 18: 24.1%; Age 65 and over: 16.3%; Males per 100 females: 99.1; Marriage status: 27.9% never married, 54.9% now married, 1.1% separated, 5.8% widowed, 11.3% divorced; Foreign born: 2.6%; Speak English only: 95.0%; With disability: 14.4%; Veterans: 8.6%; Ancestry: 26.9% German, 14.5% Irish, 9.7% Dutch, 7.1% English, 7.1% Polish
Religion: Six largest groups: 13.0% Catholicism, 8.0% Presbyterian-Reformed, 5.6% Baptist, 4.4% Methodist/Pietist, 3.2% Non-denominational Protestant, 2.4% Lutheran
Economy: Unemployment rate: 3.7%; Leading industries: 16.5 % retail trade; 11.9 % other services (except public administration); 10.9 % construction; Farms: 615 totaling 282,831 acres; Company size: 0 employ 1,000 or more persons, 0 employ 500 to 999 persons, 18 employ 100 to 499 persons, 733 employ less than 100 persons; Business ownership: 685 women-owned, n/a Black-owned, n/a Hispanic-owned, n/a Asian-owned, 25 American Indian/Alaska Native-owned
Employment: 10.3% management, business, and financial, 2.0% computer, engineering, and science, 7.4% education, legal, community service, arts, and media, 5.6% healthcare practitioners, 15.8% service, 20.7% sales and office, 16.8% natural resources, construction, and maintenance, 21.4% production, transportation, and material moving
Income: Per capita: $24,953; Median household: $56,574; Average household: $65,974; Households with income of $100,000 or more: 18.3%; Poverty rate: 9.0%
Educational Attainment: High school diploma or higher: 87.7%; Bachelor's degree or higher: 14.9%; Graduate/professional degree or higher: 5.3%
Housing: Homeownership rate: 76.4%; Median home value: $153,200; Median year structure built: 1978; Homeowner vacancy rate: 2.3%; Median selected monthly owner costs: $1,105 with a mortgage, $358 without a mortgage; Median gross rent: $764 per month; Rental vacancy rate: 6.8%
Vital Statistics: Birth rate: 114.2 per 10,000 population; Death rate: 95.7 per 10,000 population; Age-adjusted cancer mortality rate: 159.3 deaths per 100,000 population
Health Insurance: 92.0% have insurance; 74.3% have private insurance; 31.6% have public insurance; 8.0% do not have insurance; 5.6% of children under 18 do not have insurance
Health Care: Physicians: 3.6 per 10,000 population; Dentists: 3.0 per 10,000 population; Hospital beds: 13.8 per 10,000 population; Hospital admissions: 213.8 per 10,000 population
Transportation: Commute: 93.6% car, 0.5% public transportation, 1.9% walk, 3.1% work from home; Mean travel time to work: 27.0 minutes
2016 Presidential Election: 70.1% Trump, 24.9% Clinton, 4.6% Johnson, 0.2% Stein
Additional Information Contacts
Jasper Government. . . . . (219) 866-4926
http://www.jaspercountyin.gov

Jasper County Communities

COLLEGEVILLE (CDP). Covers a land area of 1.132 square miles and a water area of 0 square miles. Located at 40.91° N. Lat; 87.16° W. Long. Elevation is 666 feet.
History: Seat of St. Joseph's College.
Population: 598; Growth (since 2000): -30.9%; Density: 528.1 persons per square mile; Race: 89.6% White, 7.4% Black/African American, 0.5% Asian, 0.0% American Indian/Alaska Native, 0.0% Native Hawaiian/Other Pacific Islander, 1.7% Two or more races, 3.8% Hispanic of any race; Average household size: 1.50; Median age: 20.3; Age under 18: 0.0%; Age 65 and over: 1.3%; Males per 100 females: 226.7; Marriage status:

96.0% never married, 2.7% now married, 0.0% separated, 1.3% widowed, 0.0% divorced; Foreign born: 0.0%; Speak English only: 98.5%; With disability: 5.5%; Veterans: 0.0%; Ancestry: 24.4% Irish, 20.4% German, 16.7% Polish, 5.0% Dutch, 4.7% English

Employment: 10.3% management, business, and financial, 2.9% computer, engineering, and science, 11.4% education, legal, community service, arts, and media, 0.0% healthcare practitioners, 27.5% service, 33.0% sales and office, 11.4% natural resources, construction, and maintenance, 3.7% production, transportation, and material moving

Income: Per capita: $6,480; Median household: n/a; Average household: n/a; Households with income of $100,000 or more: n/a; Poverty rate: n/a

Educational Attainment: High school diploma or higher: 100.0%; Bachelor's degree or higher: n/a; Graduate/professional degree or higher: n/a

Housing: Homeownership rate: 100.0%; Median home value: n/a; Median year structure built: n/a; Homeowner vacancy rate: 0.0%; Median selected monthly owner costs: n/a with a mortgage, n/a without a mortgage; Median gross rent: n/a per month; Rental vacancy rate: 0.0%

Health Insurance: 91.3% have insurance; 90.5% have private insurance; 2.2% have public insurance; 8.7% do not have insurance; 0.0% of children under 18 do not have insurance

Transportation: Commute: 62.8% car, 0.0% public transportation, 37.2% walk, 0.0% work from home; Mean travel time to work: 9.7 minutes

---

DE MOTTE (town). Covers a land area of 3.609 square miles and a water area of 0.003 square miles. Located at 41.20° N. Lat; 87.20° W. Long. Elevation is 669 feet.

Population: 3,992; Growth (since 2000): 23.4%; Density: 1,106.2 persons per square mile; Race: 95.1% White, 0.0% Black/African American, 0.7% Asian, 0.0% American Indian/Alaska Native, 0.0% Native Hawaiian/Other Pacific Islander, 1.0% Two or more races, 6.1% Hispanic of any race; Average household size: 2.42; Median age: 38.5; Age under 18: 25.9%; Age 65 and over: 20.5%; Males per 100 females: 87.1; Marriage status: 32.5% never married, 45.1% now married, 2.0% separated, 7.2% widowed, 15.1% divorced; Foreign born: 4.3%; Speak English only: 96.0%; With disability: 13.0%; Veterans: 10.8%; Ancestry: 21.6% German, 16.0% Dutch, 11.7% Irish, 10.4% Polish, 9.4% English

Employment: 4.2% management, business, and financial, 2.3% computer, engineering, and science, 3.1% education, legal, community service, arts, and media, 6.6% healthcare practitioners, 10.8% service, 29.9% sales and office, 20.5% natural resources, construction, and maintenance, 22.8% production, transportation, and material moving

Income: Per capita: $22,007; Median household: $46,442; Average household: $51,324; Households with income of $100,000 or more: 8.3%; Poverty rate: 8.0%

Educational Attainment: High school diploma or higher: 87.0%; Bachelor's degree or higher: 9.5%; Graduate/professional degree or higher: 2.7%

School District(s)

Kankakee Valley School Corp (PK-12)
Enrollment: 3,415 . . . . (219) 987-4711
North Newton School Corp (PK-12)
Enrollment: 1,439 . . . . (219) 285-2228

Housing: Homeownership rate: 63.8%; Median home value: $154,500; Median year structure built: 1992; Homeowner vacancy rate: 5.9%; Median selected monthly owner costs: $1,176 with a mortgage, $364 without a mortgage; Median gross rent: $824 per month; Rental vacancy rate: 6.8%

Health Insurance: 90.5% have insurance; 73.3% have private insurance; 33.3% have public insurance; 9.5% do not have insurance; 5.5% of children under 18 do not have insurance

Newspapers: Kankakee Valley Post News (weekly circulation 3,300)

Transportation: Commute: 92.6% car, 0.0% public transportation, 1.1% walk, 5.6% work from home; Mean travel time to work: 26.5 minutes

Additional Information Contacts

Town of De Motte . . . . (219) 987-3831
http://www.townofdemotte.com

FAIR OAKS (unincorporated postal area)
ZCTA: 47943

Covers a land area of 62.697 square miles and a water area of 0.057 square miles. Located at 41.06° N. Lat; 87.27° W. Long. Elevation is 702 feet.

Population: 1,004; Growth (since 2000): 31.6%; Density: 16.0 persons per square mile; Race: 85.3% White, 0.0% Black/African American, 0.0% Asian, 0.0% American Indian/Alaska Native, 0.0% Native Hawaiian/Other Pacific Islander, 0.0% Two or more races, 32.7% Hispanic of any race; Average household size: 3.18; Median age: 29.0; Age under 18: 23.9%; Age 65 and over: 4.3%; Males per 100 females: 116.2; Marriage status: 21.4% never married, 73.7% now married, 0.0% separated, 0.0% widowed, 4.9% divorced; Foreign born: 6.9%; Speak English only: 77.8%; With disability: 2.4%; Veterans: 8.6%; Ancestry: 34.4% German, 17.0% Slovak, 8.6% French Canadian, 5.4% Dutch, 2.2% Welsh

Employment: 2.5% management, business, and financial, 0.0% computer, engineering, and science, 3.1% education, legal, community service, arts, and media, 15.9% healthcare practitioners, 3.1% service, 17.9% sales and office, 28.5% natural resources, construction, and maintenance, 28.9% production, transportation, and material moving

Income: Per capita: $23,204; Median household: $76,250; Average household: $73,945; Households with income of $100,000 or more: 14.2%; Poverty rate: 2.7%

Educational Attainment: High school diploma or higher: 87.7%; Bachelor's degree or higher: 26.9%; Graduate/professional degree or higher: 20.6%

Housing: Homeownership rate: 23.7%; Median home value: $170,200; Median year structure built: 1999; Homeowner vacancy rate: 0.0%; Median selected monthly owner costs: $0 with a mortgage, $556 without a mortgage; Median gross rent: $968 per month; Rental vacancy rate: 0.0%

Health Insurance: 89.7% have insurance; 82.6% have private insurance; 10.8% have public insurance; 10.3% do not have insurance; 23.8% of children under 18 do not have insurance

Transportation: Commute: 97.5% car, 0.0% public transportation, 0.0% walk, 2.5% work from home; Mean travel time to work: 33.6 minutes

---

REMINGTON (town). Covers a land area of 1.018 square miles and a water area of 0 square miles. Located at 40.77° N. Lat; 87.15° W. Long. Elevation is 735 feet.

History: Laid out 1860.

Population: 1,287; Growth (since 2000): -2.7%; Density: 1,264.1 persons per square mile; Race: 97.4% White, 0.4% Black/African American, 0.9% Asian, 0.0% American Indian/Alaska Native, 0.0% Native Hawaiian/Other Pacific Islander, 1.4% Two or more races, 0.8% Hispanic of any race; Average household size: 2.27; Median age: 45.7; Age under 18: 20.5%; Age 65 and over: 18.3%; Males per 100 females: 95.2; Marriage status: 23.8% never married, 56.5% now married, 1.9% separated, 6.5% widowed, 13.1% divorced; Foreign born: 0.3%; Speak English only: 99.8%; With disability: 16.2%; Veterans: 10.2%; Ancestry: 24.3% German, 11.7% American, 9.0% Irish, 8.7% Dutch, 8.7% English

Employment: 7.2% management, business, and financial, 1.8% computer, engineering, and science, 7.0% education, legal, community service, arts, and media, 6.6% healthcare practitioners, 14.0% service, 16.9% sales and office, 12.8% natural resources, construction, and maintenance, 33.7% production, transportation, and material moving

Income: Per capita: $25,694; Median household: $46,438; Average household: $57,197; Households with income of $100,000 or more: 11.6%; Poverty rate: 10.1%

Educational Attainment: High school diploma or higher: 83.8%; Bachelor's degree or higher: 15.4%; Graduate/professional degree or higher: 5.7%

School District(s)

Tri-county School Corporation (PK-12)
Enrollment: 730. . . . . (219) 279-2418

Housing: Homeownership rate: 66.0%; Median home value: $90,000; Median year structure built: 1945; Homeowner vacancy rate: 1.6%; Median selected monthly owner costs: $925 with a mortgage, $310 without a mortgage; Median gross rent: $679 per month; Rental vacancy rate: 7.2%

Health Insurance: 87.5% have insurance; 72.0% have private insurance; 33.1% have public insurance; 12.5% do not have insurance; 1.1% of children under 18 do not have insurance

Transportation: Commute: 91.8% car, 0.0% public transportation, 3.8% walk, 0.6% work from home; Mean travel time to work: 16.4 minutes

---

RENSSELAER (city). County seat. Covers a land area of 3.800 square miles and a water area of 0.060 square miles. Located at 40.93° N. Lat; 87.15° W. Long. Elevation is 663 feet.

History: Rensselaer was founded in 1837 by James Van Rensselaer, a merchant from New York who operated a gristmill here. Rensselaer soon became a trading center for the surrounding farming community.

Population: 5,631; Growth (since 2000): 6.4%; Density: 1,481.8 persons per square mile; Race: 93.8% White, 2.7% Black/African American, 0.8% Asian, 0.0% American Indian/Alaska Native, 0.0% Native Hawaiian/Other Pacific Islander, 1.0% Two or more races, 5.7% Hispanic of any race; Average household size: 2.38; Median age: 41.1; Age under 18: 23.9%; Age 65 and over: 16.0%; Males per 100 females: 92.2; Marriage status: 27.1% never married, 53.8% now married, 1.3% separated, 6.9% widowed, 12.3% divorced; Foreign born: 1.8%; Speak English only: 95.6%; With disability: 18.6%; Veterans: 9.3%; Ancestry: 28.3% German, 13.8% Irish, 6.4% American, 6.2% English, 3.3% Dutch
Employment: 8.2% management, business, and financial, 1.4% computer, engineering, and science, 8.1% education, legal, community service, arts, and media, 5.4% healthcare practitioners, 21.9% service, 20.3% sales and office, 10.8% natural resources, construction, and maintenance, 23.9% production, transportation, and material moving
Income: Per capita: $22,835; Median household: $42,912; Average household: $54,230; Households with income of $100,000 or more: 15.9%; Poverty rate: 16.5%
Educational Attainment: High school diploma or higher: 82.8%; Bachelor's degree or higher: 17.2%; Graduate/professional degree or higher: 5.8%

School District(s)

Rensselaer Central School Corp (PK-12)
Enrollment: 1,624 . . . . (219) 866-7822
Housing: Homeownership rate: 57.1%; Median home value: $120,200; Median year structure built: 1959; Homeowner vacancy rate: 4.8%; Median selected monthly owner costs: $908 with a mortgage, $312 without a mortgage; Median gross rent: $712 per month; Rental vacancy rate: 7.9%
Health Insurance: 90.9% have insurance; 68.2% have private insurance; 37.1% have public insurance; 9.1% do not have insurance; 8.3% of children under 18 do not have insurance
Hospitals: Jasper County Hospital (86 beds)
Newspapers: Rensselaer Republican (daily circulation 2,100)
Transportation: Commute: 94.7% car, 0.8% public transportation, 2.7% walk, 1.3% work from home; Mean travel time to work: 17.8 minutes; Amtrak: Train service available.
Additional Information Contacts
City of Rensselaer. . . . . (219) 866-5213
http://www.cityofrensselaerin.com

WHEATFIELD (town). Covers a land area of 0.558 square miles and a water area of 0 square miles. Located at 41.19° N. Lat; 87.05° W. Long. Elevation is 663 feet.
Population: 921; Growth (since 2000): 19.3%; Density: 1,651.5 persons per square mile; Race: 89.3% White, 1.2% Black/African American, 0.0% Asian, 0.0% American Indian/Alaska Native, 0.0% Native Hawaiian/Other Pacific Islander, 6.4% Two or more races, 10.5% Hispanic of any race; Average household size: 2.84; Median age: 32.6; Age under 18: 29.3%; Age 65 and over: 10.7%; Males per 100 females: 97.5; Marriage status: 30.9% never married, 46.2% now married, 0.0% separated, 6.7% widowed, 16.2% divorced; Foreign born: 2.7%; Speak English only: 95.6%; With disability: 15.0%; Veterans: 3.7%; Ancestry: 27.7% German, 19.1% Irish, 9.9% Polish, 8.4% French, 7.2% Dutch
Employment: 4.6% management, business, and financial, 5.1% computer, engineering, and science, 8.1% education, legal, community service, arts, and media, 6.2% healthcare practitioners, 24.7% service, 18.3% sales and office, 19.6% natural resources, construction, and maintenance, 13.4% production, transportation, and material moving
Income: Per capita: $19,048; Median household: $44,667; Average household: $53,533; Households with income of $100,000 or more: 9.5%; Poverty rate: 8.3%
Educational Attainment: High school diploma or higher: 90.3%; Bachelor's degree or higher: 8.3%; Graduate/professional degree or higher: 3.7%

School District(s)

Kankakee Valley School Corp (PK-12)
Enrollment: 3,415 . . . . (219) 987-4711
Housing: Homeownership rate: 66.0%; Median home value: $113,800; Median year structure built: 1973; Homeowner vacancy rate: 0.0%; Median selected monthly owner costs: $1,049 with a mortgage, $385 without a mortgage; Median gross rent: $814 per month; Rental vacancy rate: 16.0%
Health Insurance: 86.4% have insurance; 68.4% have private insurance; 29.1% have public insurance; 13.6% do not have insurance; 10.1% of children under 18 do not have insurance
Transportation: Commute: 98.8% car, 0.6% public transportation, 0.6% walk, 0.0% work from home; Mean travel time to work: 35.4 minutes

Jay County

Located in eastern Indiana; bounded on the east by Ohio; drained by the Salamonie River. Covers a land area of 383.905 square miles, a water area of 0.177 square miles, and is located in the Eastern Time Zone at 40.43° N. Lat., 85.00° W. Long. The county was founded in 1835. County seat is Portland.

Weather Station: Portland 1 SW — Elevation: 910 feet

	Jan	Feb	Mar	Apr	May	Jun	Jul	Aug	Sep	Oct	Nov	Dec
High	33	37	48	61	71	80	84	82	76	64	50	38
Low	17	19	28	38	49	59	62	60	52	41	32	22
Precip	1.8	2.0	2.4	3.5	4.1	3.9	4.7	3.7	2.6	2.6	2.9	2.4
Snow	6.3	5.3	2.6	0.3	0.0	0.0	0.0	0.0	0.0	0.2	0.7	4.5

High and Low temperatures in degrees Fahrenheit; Precipitation and Snow in inches

Population: 21,107; Growth (since 2000): -3.2%; Density: 55.0 persons per square mile; Race: 97.5% White, 0.3% Black/African American, 0.5% Asian, 0.1% American Indian/Alaska Native, 0.0% Native Hawaiian/Other Pacific Islander, 1.0% two or more races, 3.0% Hispanic of any race; Average household size: 2.54; Median age: 39.8; Age under 18: 25.8%; Age 65 and over: 17.1%; Males per 100 females: 97.4; Marriage status: 27.1% never married, 53.2% now married, 1.7% separated, 7.2% widowed, 12.5% divorced; Foreign born: 1.7%; Speak English only: 94.7%; With disability: 16.5%; Veterans: 7.2%; Ancestry: 22.9% German, 14.7% American, 8.6% Irish, 6.1% English, 2.1% Dutch
Religion: Six largest groups: 10.8% Methodist/Pietist, 8.1% Catholicism, 6.1% Holiness, 5.6% European Free-Church, 2.0% Lutheran, 2.0% Non-denominational Protestant
Economy: Unemployment rate: 3.6%; Leading industries: 14.6 % other services (except public administration); 14.4 % retail trade; 12.4 % construction; Farms: 836 totaling 175,770 acres; Company size: 0 employ 1,000 or more persons, 1 employs 500 to 999 persons, 9 employ 100 to 499 persons, 386 employ less than 100 persons; Business ownership: 427 women-owned, n/a Black-owned, 50 Hispanic-owned, n/a Asian-owned, n/a American Indian/Alaska Native-owned
Employment: 10.9% management, business, and financial, 0.9% computer, engineering, and science, 5.4% education, legal, community service, arts, and media, 5.3% healthcare practitioners, 15.6% service, 16.3% sales and office, 14.2% natural resources, construction, and maintenance, 31.4% production, transportation, and material moving
Income: Per capita: $20,193; Median household: $42,878; Average household: $51,770; Households with income of $100,000 or more: 10.8%; Poverty rate: 17.9%
Educational Attainment: High school diploma or higher: 82.8%; Bachelor's degree or higher: 10.5%; Graduate/professional degree or higher: 3.8%
Housing: Homeownership rate: 74.1%; Median home value: $85,000; Median year structure built: 1958; Homeowner vacancy rate: 1.6%; Median selected monthly owner costs: $859 with a mortgage, $316 without a mortgage; Median gross rent: $608 per month; Rental vacancy rate: 8.7%
Vital Statistics: Birth rate: 139.4 per 10,000 population; Death rate: 103.6 per 10,000 population; Age-adjusted cancer mortality rate: 189.4 deaths per 100,000 population
Health Insurance: 88.5% have insurance; 64.1% have private insurance; 38.3% have public insurance; 11.5% do not have insurance; 9.4% of children under 18 do not have insurance
Health Care: Physicians: 5.7 per 10,000 population; Dentists: 2.9 per 10,000 population; Hospital beds: 16.6 per 10,000 population; Hospital admissions: 497.1 per 10,000 population
Transportation: Commute: 89.2% car, 0.6% public transportation, 2.2% walk, 5.9% work from home; Mean travel time to work: 19.6 minutes
2016 Presidential Election: 71.3% Trump, 23.7% Clinton, 4.7% Johnson, 0.3% Stein
National and State Parks: Limberlost State Game Reserve
Additional Information Contacts
Jay Government . . . . (260) 726-4951
http://www.jaycounty.net

Jay County Communities

BRYANT (town). Covers a land area of 0.304 square miles and a water area of 0 square miles. Located at 40.54° N. Lat; 84.96° W. Long. Elevation is 873 feet.

Population: 225; Growth (since 2000): -17.3%; Density: 740.0 persons per square mile; Race: 95.6% White, 0.0% Black/African American, 4.4% Asian, 0.0% American Indian/Alaska Native, 0.0% Native Hawaiian/Other Pacific Islander, 0.0% Two or more races, 0.0% Hispanic of any race; Average household size: 2.39; Median age: 40.6; Age under 18: 23.1%; Age 65 and over: 16.0%; Males per 100 females: 96.9; Marriage status: 28.4% never married, 51.9% now married, 0.0% separated, 3.3% widowed, 16.4% divorced; Foreign born: 2.2%; Speak English only: 97.7%; With disability: 18.7%; Veterans: 4.0%; Ancestry: 15.6% German, 13.3% American, 5.3% Irish, 4.9% English, 0.9% British

Employment: 7.1% management, business, and financial, 1.0% computer, engineering, and science, 6.1% education, legal, community service, arts, and media, 0.0% healthcare practitioners, 24.2% service, 24.2% sales and office, 0.0% natural resources, construction, and maintenance, 37.4% production, transportation, and material moving

Income: Per capita: $16,049; Median household: $36,250; Average household: $38,782; Households with income of $100,000 or more: n/a; Poverty rate: 22.2%

Educational Attainment: High school diploma or higher: 92.1%; Bachelor's degree or higher: 4.6%; Graduate/professional degree or higher: 1.3%

School District(s)

Jay School Corporation (PK-12)
Enrollment: 3,428 . . . . (260) 726-9341

Housing: Homeownership rate: 81.9%; Median home value: $41,900; Median year structure built: Before 1940; Homeowner vacancy rate: 0.0%; Median selected monthly owner costs: $806 with a mortgage, $272 without a mortgage; Median gross rent: n/a per month; Rental vacancy rate: 15.0%

Health Insurance: 84.0% have insurance; 59.1% have private insurance; 34.7% have public insurance; 16.0% do not have insurance; 13.2% of children under 18 do not have insurance

Transportation: Commute: 87.2% car, 0.0% public transportation, 5.3% walk, 7.4% work from home; Mean travel time to work: 15.9 minutes

DUNKIRK (city). Covers a land area of 1.257 square miles and a water area of 0 square miles. Located at 40.37° N. Lat; 85.21° W. Long. Elevation is 948 feet.

Population: 2,277; Growth (since 2000): -13.9%; Density: 1,811.9 persons per square mile; Race: 98.6% White, 0.2% Black/African American, 0.0% Asian, 0.0% American Indian/Alaska Native, 0.0% Native Hawaiian/Other Pacific Islander, 1.2% Two or more races, 0.1% Hispanic of any race; Average household size: 2.39; Median age: 39.6; Age under 18: 25.3%; Age 65 and over: 16.2%; Males per 100 females: 94.7; Marriage status: 25.6% never married, 49.6% now married, 2.5% separated, 6.6% widowed, 18.2% divorced; Foreign born: 0.3%; Speak English only: 99.9%; With disability: 21.4%; Veterans: 8.1%; Ancestry: 16.7% German, 13.8% American, 10.0% Irish, 4.6% English, 2.0% Scottish

Employment: 7.7% management, business, and financial, 1.2% computer, engineering, and science, 1.4% education, legal, community service, arts, and media, 3.1% healthcare practitioners, 21.0% service, 21.9% sales and office, 7.5% natural resources, construction, and maintenance, 36.2% production, transportation, and material moving

Income: Per capita: $17,343; Median household: $35,671; Average household: $41,471; Households with income of $100,000 or more: 6.2%; Poverty rate: 24.5%

Educational Attainment: High school diploma or higher: 77.1%; Bachelor's degree or higher: 6.3%; Graduate/professional degree or higher: 1.8%

School District(s)

Jay School Corporation (PK-12)
Enrollment: 3,428 . . . . (260) 726-9341

Housing: Homeownership rate: 62.8%; Median home value: $57,100; Median year structure built: 1957; Homeowner vacancy rate: 4.2%; Median selected monthly owner costs: $738 with a mortgage, $339 without a mortgage; Median gross rent: $615 per month; Rental vacancy rate: 10.7%

Health Insurance: 89.3% have insurance; 56.3% have private insurance; 45.8% have public insurance; 10.7% do not have insurance; 13.4% of children under 18 do not have insurance

Newspapers: Dunkirk News & Sun (weekly circulation 1,200)

Transportation: Commute: 95.0% car, 0.0% public transportation, 2.3% walk, 0.7% work from home; Mean travel time to work: 22.6 minutes

Additional Information Contacts

City of Dunkirk. . . . . (260) 726-4481
http://www.jaycountychamber.com

PENNVILLE (town). Covers a land area of 0.504 square miles and a water area of 0 square miles. Located at 40.49° N. Lat; 85.15° W. Long. Elevation is 876 feet.

Population: 794; Growth (since 2000): 12.5%; Density: 1,575.4 persons per square mile; Race: 98.5% White, 0.1% Black/African American, 1.4% Asian, 0.0% American Indian/Alaska Native, 0.0% Native Hawaiian/Other Pacific Islander, 0.0% Two or more races, 0.3% Hispanic of any race; Average household size: 2.58; Median age: 33.4; Age under 18: 31.1%; Age 65 and over: 11.2%; Males per 100 females: 90.0; Marriage status: 24.7% never married, 56.5% now married, 0.9% separated, 4.6% widowed, 14.2% divorced; Foreign born: 1.4%; Speak English only: 99.4%; With disability: 17.1%; Veterans: 9.0%; Ancestry: 30.0% German, 11.0% Irish, 9.3% American, 6.8% Scottish, 4.4% English

Employment: 7.3% management, business, and financial, 1.1% computer, engineering, and science, 4.1% education, legal, community service, arts, and media, 1.9% healthcare practitioners, 20.3% service, 16.5% sales and office, 6.8% natural resources, construction, and maintenance, 42.0% production, transportation, and material moving

Income: Per capita: $17,042; Median household: $39,444; Average household: $45,523; Households with income of $100,000 or more: 8.1%; Poverty rate: 20.5%

Educational Attainment: High school diploma or higher: 80.4%; Bachelor's degree or higher: 5.2%; Graduate/professional degree or higher: 2.2%

School District(s)

Jay School Corporation (PK-12)
Enrollment: 3,428 . . . . (260) 726-9341

Housing: Homeownership rate: 71.4%; Median home value: $63,700; Median year structure built: 1969; Homeowner vacancy rate: 3.1%; Median selected monthly owner costs: $790 with a mortgage, $346 without a mortgage; Median gross rent: $537 per month; Rental vacancy rate: 13.4%

Health Insurance: 95.8% have insurance; 67.3% have private insurance; 42.4% have public insurance; 4.2% do not have insurance; 0.0% of children under 18 do not have insurance

Transportation: Commute: 91.2% car, 0.0% public transportation, 0.8% walk, 4.7% work from home; Mean travel time to work: 20.1 minutes

PORTLAND (city). County seat. Covers a land area of 4.651 square miles and a water area of 0.003 square miles. Located at 40.44° N. Lat; 84.98° W. Long. Elevation is 906 feet.

History: Portland was the birthplace of Elwood Haynes (1857-1925) who invented the first successful clutch-driven automobile.

Population: 6,068; Growth (since 2000): -5.7%; Density: 1,304.6 persons per square mile; Race: 95.4% White, 0.8% Black/African American, 0.2% Asian, 0.3% American Indian/Alaska Native, 0.0% Native Hawaiian/Other Pacific Islander, 1.9% Two or more races, 8.4% Hispanic of any race; Average household size: 2.25; Median age: 35.5; Age under 18: 25.0%; Age 65 and over: 17.8%; Males per 100 females: 87.8; Marriage status: 31.0% never married, 42.6% now married, 2.9% separated, 10.8% widowed, 15.5% divorced; Foreign born: 3.5%; Speak English only: 91.4%; With disability: 18.0%; Veterans: 7.6%; Ancestry: 21.4% German, 10.8% American, 9.0% Irish, 8.0% English, 3.0% Dutch

Employment: 5.5% management, business, and financial, 1.1% computer, engineering, and science, 4.8% education, legal, community service, arts, and media, 4.0% healthcare practitioners, 19.1% service, 16.7% sales and office, 12.9% natural resources, construction, and maintenance, 35.8% production, transportation, and material moving

Income: Per capita: $18,553; Median household: $35,919; Average household: $42,330; Households with income of $100,000 or more: 6.2%; Poverty rate: 19.9%

Educational Attainment: High school diploma or higher: 79.1%; Bachelor's degree or higher: 8.0%; Graduate/professional degree or higher: 3.4%

School District(s)

Jay School Corporation (PK-12)
Enrollment: 3,428 . . . . (260) 726-9341

Housing: Homeownership rate: 60.0%; Median home value: $70,900; Median year structure built: 1953; Homeowner vacancy rate: 2.9%; Median

selected monthly owner costs: $769 with a mortgage, $271 without a mortgage; Median gross rent: $577 per month; Rental vacancy rate: 5.8%
Health Insurance: 88.4% have insurance; 61.6% have private insurance; 41.4% have public insurance; 11.6% do not have insurance; 7.0% of children under 18 do not have insurance
Hospitals: Jay County Hospital (25 beds)
Safety: Violent crime rate: 22.7 per 10,000 population; Property crime rate: 143.0 per 10,000 population
Newspapers: Commercial-Review (daily circulation 4,800)
Transportation: Commute: 89.6% car, 0.5% public transportation, 3.4% walk, 4.9% work from home; Mean travel time to work: 11.5 minutes
Airports: Portland Municipal (general aviation)
Additional Information Contacts
City of Portland . . . . (260) 726-9395
http://www.thecityofportland.net

REDKEY (town). Covers a land area of 0.936 square miles and a water area of 0.008 square miles. Located at 40.35° N. Lat; 85.15° W. Long. Elevation is 965 feet.
Population: 1,405; Growth (since 2000): -1.5%; Density: 1,501.6 persons per square mile; Race: 99.2% White, 0.0% Black/African American, 0.0% Asian, 0.8% American Indian/Alaska Native, 0.0% Native Hawaiian/Other Pacific Islander, 0.0% Two or more races, 0.0% Hispanic of any race; Average household size: 2.34; Median age: 41.6; Age under 18: 23.6%; Age 65 and over: 17.7%; Males per 100 females: 93.0; Marriage status: 31.5% never married, 47.9% now married, 1.2% separated, 7.3% widowed, 13.3% divorced; Foreign born: 0.5%; Speak English only: 99.4%; With disability: 20.5%; Veterans: 6.0%; Ancestry: 14.1% German, 10.2% American, 8.3% Irish, 4.2% English, 3.1% European
Employment: 7.3% management, business, and financial, 0.8% computer, engineering, and science, 6.0% education, legal, community service, arts, and media, 4.1% healthcare practitioners, 18.4% service, 18.4% sales and office, 11.1% natural resources, construction, and maintenance, 33.8% production, transportation, and material moving
Income: Per capita: $19,336; Median household: $37,344; Average household: $45,145; Households with income of $100,000 or more: 7.0%; Poverty rate: 19.1%
Educational Attainment: High school diploma or higher: 86.8%; Bachelor's degree or higher: 6.8%; Graduate/professional degree or higher: 2.0%

School District(s)

Jay School Corporation (PK-12)
Enrollment: 3,428 . . . . (260) 726-9341
Housing: Homeownership rate: 71.7%; Median home value: $48,200; Median year structure built: Before 1940; Homeowner vacancy rate: 4.4%; Median selected monthly owner costs: $657 with a mortgage, $285 without a mortgage; Median gross rent: $585 per month; Rental vacancy rate: 6.6%
Health Insurance: 89.2% have insurance; 58.2% have private insurance; 46.1% have public insurance; 10.8% do not have insurance; 5.7% of children under 18 do not have insurance
Transportation: Commute: 86.7% car, 0.0% public transportation, 2.7% walk, 10.6% work from home; Mean travel time to work: 22.7 minutes

SALAMONIA (town). Covers a land area of 0.366 square miles and a water area of 0 square miles. Located at 40.38° N. Lat; 84.87° W. Long. Elevation is 971 feet.
Population: 239; Growth (since 2000): 51.3%; Density: 652.5 persons per square mile; Race: 97.5% White, 0.0% Black/African American, 0.0% Asian, 0.0% American Indian/Alaska Native, 0.0% Native Hawaiian/Other Pacific Islander, 2.5% Two or more races, 20.9% Hispanic of any race; Average household size: 2.88; Median age: 25.3; Age under 18: 43.9%; Age 65 and over: 6.7%; Males per 100 females: 98.7; Marriage status: 34.7% never married, 38.7% now married, 0.7% separated, 4.7% widowed, 22.0% divorced; Foreign born: 0.0%; Speak English only: 100.0%; With disability: 10.9%; Veterans: 6.0%; Ancestry: 23.4% German, 16.3% American, 3.8% English, 2.9% Irish, 1.3% Norwegian
Employment: 1.1% management, business, and financial, 0.0% computer, engineering, and science, 1.1% education, legal, community service, arts, and media, 4.4% healthcare practitioners, 15.4% service, 25.3% sales and office, 3.3% natural resources, construction, and maintenance, 49.5% production, transportation, and material moving
Income: Per capita: $12,180; Median household: $27,417; Average household: $33,984; Households with income of $100,000 or more: 1.2%; Poverty rate: 40.6%
Educational Attainment: High school diploma or higher: 84.2%; Bachelor's degree or higher: n/a; Graduate/professional degree or higher: n/a
Housing: Homeownership rate: 54.2%; Median home value: $46,500; Median year structure built: 1975; Homeowner vacancy rate: 0.0%; Median selected monthly owner costs: $725 with a mortgage, $500 without a mortgage; Median gross rent: $558 per month; Rental vacancy rate: 0.0%
Health Insurance: 95.0% have insurance; 49.8% have private insurance; 65.3% have public insurance; 5.0% do not have insurance; 0.0% of children under 18 do not have insurance
Transportation: Commute: 93.2% car, 6.8% public transportation, 0.0% walk, 0.0% work from home; Mean travel time to work: 19.6 minutes

Jefferson County

Located in southeastern Indiana; bounded on the south partly by the Ohio River and the Kentucky border; drained by Big Creek. Covers a land area of 360.631 square miles, a water area of 2.258 square miles, and is located in the Eastern Time Zone at 38.78° N. Lat., 85.44° W. Long. The county was founded in 1810. County seat is Madison.

Jefferson County is part of the Madison, IN Micropolitan Statistical Area. The entire metro area includes: Jefferson County, IN

Weather Station: Madison Sewage Plant Elevation: 459 feet

	Jan	Feb	Mar	Apr	May	Jun	Jul	Aug	Sep	Oct	Nov	Dec
High	41	45	55	66	75	83	87	86	80	68	56	44
Low	24	26	34	43	53	62	66	65	58	46	37	28
Precip	3.4	3.0	4.2	4.3	5.3	4.2	4.6	4.1	3.2	3.8	3.7	3.8
Snow	4.3	3.9	1.3	0.1	tr	0.0	0.0	0.0	0.0	0.1	tr	3.4

High and Low temperatures in degrees Fahrenheit; Precipitation and Snow in inches

Population: 32,293; Growth (since 2000): 1.9%; Density: 89.5 persons per square mile; Race: 95.3% White, 2.0% Black/African American, 0.8% Asian, 0.3% American Indian/Alaska Native, 0.0% Native Hawaiian/Other Pacific Islander, 1.2% two or more races, 2.6% Hispanic of any race; Average household size: 2.34; Median age: 40.6; Age under 18: 20.7%; Age 65 and over: 16.2%; Males per 100 females: 93.1; Marriage status: 27.4% never married, 50.3% now married, 1.4% separated, 6.6% widowed, 15.8% divorced; Foreign born: 1.1%; Speak English only: 98.3%; With disability: 14.5%; Veterans: 9.9%; Ancestry: 20.6% German, 12.0% Irish, 11.0% English, 9.3% American, 2.5% Scottish
Religion: Six largest groups: 23.9% Baptist, 7.7% Catholicism, 4.4% Methodist/Pietist, 2.3% Non-denominational Protestant, 1.5% Holiness, 1.2% Presbyterian-Reformed
Economy: Unemployment rate: 3.6%; Leading industries: 18.8 % retail trade; 13.0 % health care and social assistance; 12.3 % accommodation and food services; Farms: 615 totaling 95,411 acres; Company size: 0 employ 1,000 or more persons, 4 employ 500 to 999 persons, 14 employ 100 to 499 persons, 643 employ less than 100 persons; Business ownership: 865 women-owned, n/a Black-owned, n/a Hispanic-owned, n/a Asian-owned, n/a American Indian/Alaska Native-owned
Employment: 10.8% management, business, and financial, 4.5% computer, engineering, and science, 8.3% education, legal, community service, arts, and media, 6.4% healthcare practitioners, 16.0% service, 17.7% sales and office, 9.5% natural resources, construction, and maintenance, 26.7% production, transportation, and material moving
Income: Per capita: $25,429; Median household: $50,722; Average household: $63,739; Households with income of $100,000 or more: 16.4%; Poverty rate: 13.7%
Educational Attainment: High school diploma or higher: 89.0%; Bachelor's degree or higher: 17.4%; Graduate/professional degree or higher: 6.9%
Housing: Homeownership rate: 71.7%; Median home value: $120,000; Median year structure built: 1973; Homeowner vacancy rate: 4.6%; Median selected monthly owner costs: $996 with a mortgage, $364 without a mortgage; Median gross rent: $723 per month; Rental vacancy rate: 6.5%
Vital Statistics: Birth rate: 112.5 per 10,000 population; Death rate: 106.3 per 10,000 population; Age-adjusted cancer mortality rate: 224.1 deaths per 100,000 population
Health Insurance: 90.9% have insurance; 71.1% have private insurance; 34.1% have public insurance; 9.1% do not have insurance; 4.1% of children under 18 do not have insurance
Health Care: Physicians: 15.8 per 10,000 population; Dentists: 6.2 per 10,000 population; Hospital beds: 70.4 per 10,000 population; Hospital admissions: 1,148.3 per 10,000 population

Transportation: Commute: 91.3% car, 0.4% public transportation, 3.0% walk, 3.9% work from home; Mean travel time to work: 24.2 minutes
2016 Presidential Election: 62.6% Trump, 31.7% Clinton, 4.4% Johnson, 0.2% Stein
National and State Parks: Clifty Falls State Park
Additional Information Contacts
Jefferson Government. . . . . (812) 265-8922
http://jeffersoncounty.in.gov

Jefferson County Communities

BROOKSBURG (town). Covers a land area of 0.102 square miles and a water area of 0.009 square miles. Located at 38.74° N. Lat; 85.25° W. Long. Elevation is 472 feet.
Population: 109; Growth (since 2000): 47.3%; Density: 1,072.8 persons per square mile; Race: 100.0% White, 0.0% Black/African American, 0.0% Asian, 0.0% American Indian/Alaska Native, 0.0% Native Hawaiian/Other Pacific Islander, 0.0% Two or more races, 0.0% Hispanic of any race; Average household size: 2.87; Median age: 35.6; Age under 18: 24.8%; Age 65 and over: 4.6%; Males per 100 females: 102.5; Marriage status: 31.1% never married, 42.2% now married, 0.0% separated, 10.0% widowed, 16.7% divorced; Foreign born: 0.0%; Speak English only: 100.0%; With disability: 14.7%; Veterans: 2.4%; Ancestry: 15.6% German, 7.3% American, 4.6% Irish, 1.8% English, 1.8% Greek
Employment: 6.7% management, business, and financial, 0.0% computer, engineering, and science, 0.0% education, legal, community service, arts, and media, 8.9% healthcare practitioners, 13.3% service, 11.1% sales and office, 4.4% natural resources, construction, and maintenance, 55.6% production, transportation, and material moving
Income: Per capita: $19,583; Median household: n/a; Average household: $54,139; Households with income of $100,000 or more: 13.2%; Poverty rate: 18.3%
Educational Attainment: High school diploma or higher: 73.7%; Bachelor's degree or higher: 5.3%; Graduate/professional degree or higher: n/a
Housing: Homeownership rate: 60.5%; Median home value: $92,500; Median year structure built: Before 1940; Homeowner vacancy rate: 0.0%; Median selected monthly owner costs: $1,344 with a mortgage, $433 without a mortgage; Median gross rent: $1,071 per month; Rental vacancy rate: 0.0%
Health Insurance: 92.7% have insurance; 65.1% have private insurance; 30.3% have public insurance; 7.3% do not have insurance; 3.6% of children under 18 do not have insurance
Transportation: Commute: 100.0% car, 0.0% public transportation, 0.0% walk, 0.0% work from home; Mean travel time to work: 20.3 minutes

CANAAN (CDP). Covers a land area of 0.309 square miles and a water area of <.001 square miles. Located at 38.87° N. Lat; 85.30° W. Long. Elevation is 948 feet.
Population: 89; Growth (since 2000): n/a; Density: 288.0 persons per square mile; Race: 100.0% White, 0.0% Black/African American, 0.0% Asian, 0.0% American Indian/Alaska Native, 0.0% Native Hawaiian/Other Pacific Islander, 0.0% Two or more races, 0.0% Hispanic of any race; Average household size: 1.59; Median age: 59.2; Age under 18: 0.0%; Age 65 and over: 16.9%; Males per 100 females: 114.3; Marriage status: 9.0% never married, 74.2% now married, 0.0% separated, 7.9% widowed, 9.0% divorced; Foreign born: 0.0%; Speak English only: 100.0%; With disability: 0.0%; Veterans: 7.9%; Ancestry: 22.5% German, 13.5% Scottish, 9.0% American, 9.0% European
Employment: 16.2% management, business, and financial, 0.0% computer, engineering, and science, 16.2% education, legal, community service, arts, and media, 0.0% healthcare practitioners, 28.4% service, 10.8% sales and office, 0.0% natural resources, construction, and maintenance, 28.4% production, transportation, and material moving
Income: Per capita: $50,949; Median household: n/a; Average household: $80,973; Households with income of $100,000 or more: 37.5%; Poverty rate: n/a
Educational Attainment: High school diploma or higher: 92.1%; Bachelor's degree or higher: 36.0%; Graduate/professional degree or higher: 13.5%

School District(s)

Canaan Community Academy (KG-06)
Enrollment: 89. . . . . (812) 839-0003
Housing: Homeownership rate: 62.5%; Median home value: n/a; Median year structure built: Before 1940; Homeowner vacancy rate: 0.0%; Median selected monthly owner costs: n/a with a mortgage, n/a without a mortgage; Median gross rent: n/a per month; Rental vacancy rate: 0.0%
Health Insurance: 91.0% have insurance; 83.1% have private insurance; 16.9% have public insurance; 9.0% do not have insurance; 0.0% of children under 18 do not have insurance
Transportation: Commute: 83.8% car, 0.0% public transportation, 0.0% walk, 16.2% work from home; Mean travel time to work: 0.0 minutes

DEPUTY (CDP). Covers a land area of 0.074 square miles and a water area of 0 square miles. Located at 38.80° N. Lat; 85.65° W. Long. Elevation is 627 feet.
Population: 10; Growth (since 2000): n/a; Density: 135.6 persons per square mile; Race: 100.0% White, 0.0% Black/African American, 0.0% Asian, 0.0% American Indian/Alaska Native, 0.0% Native Hawaiian/Other Pacific Islander, 0.0% Two or more races, 0.0% Hispanic of any race; Average household size: 0.00; Median age: n/a; Age under 18: 0.0%; Age 65 and over: 100.0%; Males per 100 females: 65.4; Marriage status: 0.0% never married, 0.0% now married, 0.0% separated, 100.0% widowed, 0.0% divorced; Foreign born: 0.0%; Speak English only: 100.0%; With disability: 100.0%; Veterans: 0.0%; Ancestry: n/a.
Employment: n/a management, business, and financial, n/a computer, engineering, and science, n/a education, legal, community service, arts, and media, n/a healthcare practitioners, n/a service, n/a sales and office, n/a natural resources, construction, and maintenance, n/a production, transportation, and material moving
Income: Per capita: n/a; Median household: n/a; Average household: n/a; Households with income of $100,000 or more: n/a; Poverty rate: n/a
Educational Attainment: High school diploma or higher: 100.0%; Bachelor's degree or higher: n/a; Graduate/professional degree or higher: n/a

School District(s)

Madison Consolidated Schools (PK-12)
Enrollment: 2,914 . . . . (812) 274-8001
Housing: Homeownership rate: 100.0%; Median home value: n/a; Median year structure built: n/a; Homeowner vacancy rate: 0.0%; Median selected monthly owner costs: n/a with a mortgage, n/a without a mortgage; Median gross rent: n/a per month; Rental vacancy rate: 0.0%
Health Insurance: 100.0% have insurance; 100.0% have private insurance; 100.0% have public insurance; 0.0% do not have insurance; 0.0% of children under 18 do not have insurance
Transportation: Commute: n/a car, n/a public transportation, n/a walk, n/a work from home; Mean travel time to work: 0.0 minutes

DUPONT (town). Covers a land area of 1.019 square miles and a water area of 0 square miles. Located at 38.89° N. Lat; 85.52° W. Long. Elevation is 791 feet.
History: Laid out 1849.
Population: 303; Growth (since 2000): -22.7%; Density: 297.5 persons per square mile; Race: 98.7% White, 0.0% Black/African American, 0.0% Asian, 0.0% American Indian/Alaska Native, 0.0% Native Hawaiian/Other Pacific Islander, 1.3% Two or more races, 2.3% Hispanic of any race; Average household size: 2.61; Median age: 39.5; Age under 18: 22.8%; Age 65 and over: 10.2%; Males per 100 females: 108.0; Marriage status: 24.4% never married, 62.4% now married, 8.0% separated, 1.6% widowed, 11.6% divorced; Foreign born: 0.7%; Speak English only: 99.6%; With disability: 15.2%; Veterans: 7.7%; Ancestry: 27.4% German, 27.1% Irish, 17.8% English, 7.9% American, 5.6% Scottish
Employment: 6.2% management, business, and financial, 2.5% computer, engineering, and science, 2.5% education, legal, community service, arts, and media, 1.9% healthcare practitioners, 21.7% service, 23.6% sales and office, 6.2% natural resources, construction, and maintenance, 35.4% production, transportation, and material moving
Income: Per capita: $23,137; Median household: $51,250; Average household: $63,297; Households with income of $100,000 or more: 21.6%; Poverty rate: 7.9%
Educational Attainment: High school diploma or higher: 90.4%; Bachelor's degree or higher: 4.6%; Graduate/professional degree or higher: 1.0%
Housing: Homeownership rate: 72.4%; Median home value: $75,600; Median year structure built: 1966; Homeowner vacancy rate: 4.1%; Median selected monthly owner costs: $933 with a mortgage, $350 without a mortgage; Median gross rent: $908 per month; Rental vacancy rate: 5.0%
Health Insurance: 88.4% have insurance; 60.4% have private insurance; 41.3% have public insurance; 11.6% do not have insurance; 4.2% of children under 18 do not have insurance

Transportation: Commute: 87.2% car, 0.0% public transportation, 7.7% walk, 5.1% work from home; Mean travel time to work: 25.3 minutes

HANOVER (town). Covers a land area of 2.308 square miles and a water area of 0.004 square miles. Located at 38.71° N. Lat; 85.47° W. Long. Elevation is 784 feet.

History: Hanover developed around Hanover College, founded in 1827 by the Presbyterian denomination as a manual labor academy.

Population: 3,483; Growth (since 2000): 22.9%; Density: 1,509.2 persons per square mile; Race: 93.5% White, 5.3% Black/African American, 0.1% Asian, 0.1% American Indian/Alaska Native, 0.0% Native Hawaiian/Other Pacific Islander, 0.8% Two or more races, 1.6% Hispanic of any race; Average household size: 2.49; Median age: 24.8; Age under 18: 18.0%; Age 65 and over: 13.3%; Males per 100 females: 90.7; Marriage status: 48.1% never married, 32.3% now married, 1.0% separated, 6.7% widowed, 12.9% divorced; Foreign born: 2.3%; Speak English only: 97.5%; With disability: 12.3%; Veterans: 6.8%; Ancestry: 27.4% German, 11.0% Irish, 9.0% English, 6.0% American, 2.8% Scottish

Employment: 10.3% management, business, and financial, 3.6% computer, engineering, and science, 12.9% education, legal, community service, arts, and media, 4.9% healthcare practitioners, 23.6% service, 19.6% sales and office, 5.9% natural resources, construction, and maintenance, 19.2% production, transportation, and material moving

Income: Per capita: $17,198; Median household: $45,043; Average household: $54,387; Households with income of $100,000 or more: 10.0%; Poverty rate: 17.8%

Educational Attainment: High school diploma or higher: 88.4%; Bachelor's degree or higher: 14.3%; Graduate/professional degree or higher: 5.2%

School District(s)

Southwestern-Jefferson Co Con (PK-12)
Enrollment: 1,387 . . . . (812) 866-6255

Four-year College(s)

Hanover College (Private, Not-for-profit, Presbyterian Church (USA))
Enrollment: 1,089 . . . . (812) 866-7000
Tuition: In-state $36,520; Out-of-state $36,520

Housing: Homeownership rate: 54.6%; Median home value: $84,900; Median year structure built: 1973; Homeowner vacancy rate: 2.1%; Median selected monthly owner costs: $906 with a mortgage, $358 without a mortgage; Median gross rent: $719 per month; Rental vacancy rate: 7.8%

Health Insurance: 90.1% have insurance; 72.5% have private insurance; 28.1% have public insurance; 9.9% do not have insurance; 4.7% of children under 18 do not have insurance

Transportation: Commute: 78.7% car, 0.8% public transportation, 13.7% walk, 3.8% work from home; Mean travel time to work: 21.4 minutes

Additional Information Contacts

Town of Hanover. . . . . (812) 265-3135
http://www.madisonchamber.org

KENT (CDP). Covers a land area of 0.104 square miles and a water area of 0 square miles. Located at 38.74° N. Lat; 85.54° W. Long. Elevation is 712 feet.

Population: 105; Growth (since 2000): n/a; Density: 1,013.9 persons per square mile; Race: 100.0% White, 0.0% Black/African American, 0.0% Asian, 0.0% American Indian/Alaska Native, 0.0% Native Hawaiian/Other Pacific Islander, 0.0% Two or more races, 0.0% Hispanic of any race; Average household size: 1.98; Median age: 40.8; Age under 18: 24.8%; Age 65 and over: 0.0%; Males per 100 females: 112.1; Marriage status: 0.0% never married, 59.5% now married, 0.0% separated, 0.0% widowed, 40.5% divorced; Foreign born: 0.0%; Speak English only: 100.0%; With disability: 0.0%; Veterans: 0.0%; Ancestry: 55.2% German, 20.0% American

Employment: 50.0% management, business, and financial, 0.0% computer, engineering, and science, 0.0% education, legal, community service, arts, and media, 0.0% healthcare practitioners, 0.0% service, 32.8% sales and office, 0.0% natural resources, construction, and maintenance, 17.2% production, transportation, and material moving

Income: Per capita: $24,948; Median household: n/a; Average household: $47,674; Households with income of $100,000 or more: n/a; Poverty rate: n/a

Educational Attainment: High school diploma or higher: 100.0%; Bachelor's degree or higher: n/a; Graduate/professional degree or higher: n/a

Housing: Homeownership rate: 39.6%; Median home value: n/a; Median year structure built: Before 1940; Homeowner vacancy rate: 0.0%; Median selected monthly owner costs: n/a with a mortgage, n/a without a mortgage; Median gross rent: n/a per month; Rental vacancy rate: 0.0%

Health Insurance: 100.0% have insurance; 44.8% have private insurance; 69.5% have public insurance; 0.0% do not have insurance; 0.0% of children under 18 do not have insurance

Transportation: Commute: 100.0% car, 0.0% public transportation, 0.0% walk, 0.0% work from home; Mean travel time to work: 0.0 minutes

LEXINGTON (unincorporated postal area)
ZCTA: 47138

Covers a land area of 73.705 square miles and a water area of 0.535 square miles. Located at 38.68° N. Lat; 85.58° W. Long..

Population: 5,097; Growth (since 2000): 19.4%; Density: 69.2 persons per square mile; Race: 97.4% White, 0.5% Black/African American, 0.5% Asian, 0.0% American Indian/Alaska Native, 0.0% Native Hawaiian/Other Pacific Islander, 1.5% Two or more races, 0.7% Hispanic of any race; Average household size: 2.69; Median age: 39.4; Age under 18: 26.4%; Age 65 and over: 15.3%; Males per 100 females: 103.1; Marriage status: 24.7% never married, 60.2% now married, 1.5% separated, 3.4% widowed, 11.8% divorced; Foreign born: 1.6%; Speak English only: 96.4%; With disability: 16.5%; Veterans: 8.9%; Ancestry: 16.9% English, 13.8% German, 13.4% American, 10.4% Irish, 3.2% Scottish

Employment: 7.7% management, business, and financial, 0.4% computer, engineering, and science, 4.3% education, legal, community service, arts, and media, 5.3% healthcare practitioners, 20.0% service, 11.4% sales and office, 16.0% natural resources, construction, and maintenance, 34.9% production, transportation, and material moving

Income: Per capita: $24,577; Median household: $57,964; Average household: $66,150; Households with income of $100,000 or more: 16.1%; Poverty rate: 2.1%

Educational Attainment: High school diploma or higher: 84.3%; Bachelor's degree or higher: 11.2%; Graduate/professional degree or higher: 4.1%

School District(s)

Scott County School District 2 (PK-12)
Enrollment: 2,583 . . . . (812) 752-8946

Housing: Homeownership rate: 87.6%; Median home value: $116,700; Median year structure built: 1985; Homeowner vacancy rate: 3.2%; Median selected monthly owner costs: $1,116 with a mortgage, $392 without a mortgage; Median gross rent: $734 per month; Rental vacancy rate: 0.0%

Health Insurance: 89.7% have insurance; 73.6% have private insurance; 30.6% have public insurance; 10.3% do not have insurance; 11.8% of children under 18 do not have insurance

Transportation: Commute: 95.7% car, 0.0% public transportation, 1.0% walk, 2.0% work from home; Mean travel time to work: 26.5 minutes

MADISON (city). County seat. Covers a land area of 8.575 square miles and a water area of 0.272 square miles. Located at 38.76° N. Lat; 85.40° W. Long. Elevation is 489 feet.

History: Madison was settled in 1805, and the town was platted in 1809 by Colonel John Paul, a Revolutionary War soldier, who named it for President James Madison. Shipyards flourished here in the 1830's, and by 1850 Madison was the largest city in Indiana. Tobacco was an important part of the economy in the early 1900's.

Population: 11,920; Growth (since 2000): -0.7%; Density: 1,390.1 persons per square mile; Race: 92.3% White, 3.0% Black/African American, 1.9% Asian, 0.4% American Indian/Alaska Native, 0.0% Native Hawaiian/Other Pacific Islander, 1.4% Two or more races, 6.0% Hispanic of any race; Average household size: 2.08; Median age: 42.6; Age under 18: 17.7%; Age 65 and over: 19.1%; Males per 100 females: 81.2; Marriage status: 29.6% never married, 42.0% now married, 1.7% separated, 8.5% widowed, 19.9% divorced; Foreign born: 1.8%; Speak English only: 97.1%; With disability: 18.0%; Veterans: 9.6%; Ancestry: 22.1% German, 12.8% Irish, 12.5% English, 6.5% American, 2.6% Italian

Employment: 11.1% management, business, and financial, 3.4% computer, engineering, and science, 10.3% education, legal, community service, arts, and media, 5.8% healthcare practitioners, 19.1% service, 16.0% sales and office, 6.5% natural resources, construction, and maintenance, 27.8% production, transportation, and material moving

Income: Per capita: $24,128; Median household: $46,444; Average household: $56,574; Households with income of $100,000 or more: 16.4%; Poverty rate: 19.2%

Educational Attainment: High school diploma or higher: 89.4%; Bachelor's degree or higher: 18.8%; Graduate/professional degree or higher: 7.9%

School District(s)

Indiana Department Of Corrections (07-12)
Enrollment: 391 . . . . (317) 233-3111
Madison Consolidated Schools (PK-12)
Enrollment: 2,914 . . . . (812) 274-8001

Housing: Homeownership rate: 58.4%; Median home value: $125,000; Median year structure built: 1964; Homeowner vacancy rate: 10.0%; Median selected monthly owner costs: $984 with a mortgage, $325 without a mortgage; Median gross rent: $715 per month; Rental vacancy rate: 6.7%
Health Insurance: 91.7% have insurance; 68.5% have private insurance; 41.6% have public insurance; 8.3% do not have insurance; 0.6% of children under 18 do not have insurance
Hospitals: King's Daughters' Health (142 beds)
Newspapers: Madison Courier (daily circulation 8,800)
Transportation: Commute: 91.4% car, 0.1% public transportation, 3.2% walk, 3.0% work from home; Mean travel time to work: 18.0 minutes
Airports: Madison Municipal (general aviation)
Additional Information Contacts
City of Madison . . . . (812) 265-8300
http://www.madison-in.gov

Jennings County

Located in southeastern Indiana; drained by Vernon, Graham, and Sand Creeks. Covers a land area of 376.583 square miles, a water area of 1.762 square miles, and is located in the Eastern Time Zone at 39.00° N. Lat., 85.63° W. Long. The county was founded in 1816. County seat is Vernon.

Jennings County is part of the North Vernon, IN Micropolitan Statistical Area. The entire metro area includes: Jennings County, IN

Weather Station: North Vernon 1 NW — Elevation: 745 feet

	Jan	Feb	Mar	Apr	May	Jun	Jul	Aug	Sep	Oct	Nov	Dec
High	40	45	55	67	75	83	86	85	79	68	55	43
Low	24	26	34	43	52	61	65	63	56	45	36	26
Precip	2.4	2.6	3.7	4.5	5.0	4.0	4.4	4.6	3.2	3.7	3.9	3.6
Snow	2.7	3.1	1.5	tr	tr	0.0	0.0	0.0	0.0	0.0	0.0	3.5

High and Low temperatures in degrees Fahrenheit; Precipitation and Snow in inches

Population: 27,840; Growth (since 2000): 1.0%; Density: 73.9 persons per square mile; Race: 97.1% White, 1.4% Black/African American, 0.4% Asian, 0.2% American Indian/Alaska Native, 0.0% Native Hawaiian/Other Pacific Islander, 0.3% two or more races, 2.3% Hispanic of any race; Average household size: 2.56; Median age: 39.6; Age under 18: 23.9%; Age 65 and over: 15.2%; Males per 100 females: 100.4; Marriage status: 25.6% never married, 52.6% now married, 1.4% separated, 7.1% widowed, 14.7% divorced; Foreign born: 1.3%; Speak English only: 98.2%; With disability: 16.0%; Veterans: 10.7%; Ancestry: 19.2% German, 17.8% American, 9.0% Irish, 7.5% English, 2.6% Scottish
Religion: Six largest groups: 18.6% Baptist, 7.8% Catholicism, 3.1% Methodist/Pietist, 2.0% Latter-day Saints, 1.9% Holiness, 1.3% Non-denominational Protestant
Economy: Unemployment rate: 3.5%; Leading industries: 21.6 % health care and social assistance; 15.0 % retail trade; 10.0 % manufacturing; Farms: 528 totaling 123,391 acres; Company size: 0 employ 1,000 or more persons, 1 employs 500 to 999 persons, 9 employ 100 to 499 persons, 402 employ less than 100 persons; Business ownership: 451 women-owned, n/a Black-owned, 30 Hispanic-owned, n/a Asian-owned, n/a American Indian/Alaska Native-owned
Employment: 9.9% management, business, and financial, 1.7% computer, engineering, and science, 6.3% education, legal, community service, arts, and media, 3.2% healthcare practitioners, 17.9% service, 21.7% sales and office, 11.1% natural resources, construction, and maintenance, 28.2% production, transportation, and material moving
Income: Per capita: $22,901; Median household: $48,362; Average household: $57,744; Households with income of $100,000 or more: 12.5%; Poverty rate: 13.9%
Educational Attainment: High school diploma or higher: 85.4%; Bachelor's degree or higher: 10.7%; Graduate/professional degree or higher: 3.3%
Housing: Homeownership rate: 74.3%; Median home value: $99,900; Median year structure built: 1979; Homeowner vacancy rate: 0.8%; Median selected monthly owner costs: $1,017 with a mortgage, $360 without a mortgage; Median gross rent: $735 per month; Rental vacancy rate: 4.4%
Vital Statistics: Birth rate: 108.6 per 10,000 population; Death rate: 108.2 per 10,000 population; Age-adjusted cancer mortality rate: 212.4 deaths per 100,000 population
Health Insurance: 89.2% have insurance; 66.0% have private insurance; 36.3% have public insurance; 10.8% do not have insurance; 6.4% of children under 18 do not have insurance
Health Care: Physicians: 5.4 per 10,000 population; Dentists: 1.4 per 10,000 population; Hospital beds: 6.2 per 10,000 population; Hospital admissions: 120.2 per 10,000 population
Transportation: Commute: 93.7% car, 0.4% public transportation, 1.5% walk, 3.1% work from home; Mean travel time to work: 26.3 minutes
2016 Presidential Election: 73.8% Trump, 21.2% Clinton, 4.7% Johnson, 0.1% Stein
National and State Parks: Brush Creek State Fish and Wildlife Area; Crosley State Fish and Wildlife Area; Selmier State Forest
Additional Information Contacts
Jennings Government . . . . (812) 352-3005
http://www.jenningscounty-in.gov

Jennings County Communities

BUTLERVILLE (CDP). Covers a land area of 0.378 square miles and a water area of 0 square miles. Located at 39.03° N. Lat; 85.51° W. Long. Elevation is 807 feet.
Population: 224; Growth (since 2000): n/a; Density: 591.8 persons per square mile; Race: 100.0% White, 0.0% Black/African American, 0.0% Asian, 0.0% American Indian/Alaska Native, 0.0% Native Hawaiian/Other Pacific Islander, 0.0% Two or more races, 0.0% Hispanic of any race; Average household size: 1.65; Median age: 34.4; Age under 18: 17.9%; Age 65 and over: 6.3%; Males per 100 females: 105.8; Marriage status: 34.8% never married, 0.0% now married, 0.0% separated, 7.6% widowed, 57.6% divorced; Foreign born: 0.0%; Speak English only: 100.0%; With disability: 36.6%; Veterans: 0.0%; Ancestry: 61.6% Irish, 30.4% German, 14.7% English, 6.3% American, 5.8% Italian
Employment: 40.9% management, business, and financial, 14.8% computer, engineering, and science, 0.0% education, legal, community service, arts, and media, 0.0% healthcare practitioners, 0.0% service, 21.6% sales and office, 0.0% natural resources, construction, and maintenance, 22.7% production, transportation, and material moving
Income: Per capita: $16,691; Median household: n/a; Average household: $27,236; Households with income of $100,000 or more: n/a; Poverty rate: 22.8%
Educational Attainment: High school diploma or higher: 62.0%; Bachelor's degree or higher: 11.1%; Graduate/professional degree or higher: n/a
Housing: Homeownership rate: 33.8%; Median home value: $64,700; Median year structure built: 1961; Homeowner vacancy rate: 0.0%; Median selected monthly owner costs: n/a with a mortgage, n/a without a mortgage; Median gross rent: $812 per month; Rental vacancy rate: 0.0%
Health Insurance: 92.4% have insurance; 55.8% have private insurance; 42.9% have public insurance; 7.6% do not have insurance; 0.0% of children under 18 do not have insurance
Transportation: Commute: 78.4% car, 0.0% public transportation, 0.0% walk, 21.6% work from home; Mean travel time to work: 0.0 minutes

COMMISKEY (unincorporated postal area)
ZCTA: 47227
Covers a land area of 49.146 square miles and a water area of 0.115 square miles. Located at 38.87° N. Lat; 85.65° W. Long. Elevation is 696 feet.
Population: 2,142; Growth (since 2000): 56.4%; Density: 43.6 persons per square mile; Race: 100.0% White, 0.0% Black/African American, 0.0% Asian, 0.0% American Indian/Alaska Native, 0.0% Native Hawaiian/Other Pacific Islander, 0.0% Two or more races, 0.0% Hispanic of any race; Average household size: 2.64; Median age: 37.8; Age under 18: 27.4%; Age 65 and over: 17.4%; Males per 100 females: 102.5; Marriage status: 20.5% never married, 60.8% now married, 0.0% separated, 8.3% widowed, 10.4% divorced; Foreign born: 0.0%; Speak English only: 100.0%; With disability: 15.4%; Veterans: 11.7%; Ancestry: 18.9% American, 15.8% English, 11.7% German, 9.3% Scottish, 6.0% Irish
Employment: 10.1% management, business, and financial, 1.5% computer, engineering, and science, 8.6% education, legal, community

service, arts, and media, 0.4% healthcare practitioners, 12.3% service, 32.9% sales and office, 10.5% natural resources, construction, and maintenance, 23.8% production, transportation, and material moving
Income: Per capita: $23,669; Median household: $54,745; Average household: $61,619; Households with income of $100,000 or more: 13.0%; Poverty rate: 7.0%
Educational Attainment: High school diploma or higher: 88.9%; Bachelor's degree or higher: 16.4%; Graduate/professional degree or higher: 5.1%

School District(s)

Jennings County School Corporation (PK-12)
Enrollment: 4,434 . . . . (812) 346-4483
Housing: Homeownership rate: 88.0%; Median home value: $119,400; Median year structure built: 1975; Homeowner vacancy rate: 0.0%; Median selected monthly owner costs: $1,106 with a mortgage, $319 without a mortgage; Median gross rent: $714 per month; Rental vacancy rate: 0.0%
Health Insurance: 90.2% have insurance; 79.6% have private insurance; 25.2% have public insurance; 9.8% do not have insurance; 3.1% of children under 18 do not have insurance
Transportation: Commute: 88.7% car, 3.5% public transportation, 0.0% walk, 6.3% work from home; Mean travel time to work: 34.7 minutes

COUNTRY SQUIRE LAKES (CDP). Covers a land area of 2.562 square miles and a water area of 0.139 square miles. Located at 39.04° N. Lat; 85.69° W. Long. Elevation is 702 feet.
Population: 3,235; Growth (since 2000): n/a; Density: 1,262.6 persons per square mile; Race: 95.1% White, 2.1% Black/African American, 0.5% Asian, 0.0% American Indian/Alaska Native, 0.0% Native Hawaiian/Other Pacific Islander, 0.0% Two or more races, 6.8% Hispanic of any race; Average household size: 2.78; Median age: 34.5; Age under 18: 25.4%; Age 65 and over: 10.2%; Males per 100 females: 102.3; Marriage status: 28.7% never married, 45.1% now married, 2.3% separated, 5.1% widowed, 21.1% divorced; Foreign born: 4.5%; Speak English only: 94.4%; With disability: 19.1%; Veterans: 13.1%; Ancestry: 16.5% German, 16.3% American, 9.9% Irish, 7.7% English, 2.2% French
Employment: 3.5% management, business, and financial, 2.4% computer, engineering, and science, 3.0% education, legal, community service, arts, and media, 0.9% healthcare practitioners, 24.3% service, 17.9% sales and office, 11.9% natural resources, construction, and maintenance, 36.0% production, transportation, and material moving
Income: Per capita: $15,278; Median household: $32,472; Average household: $40,504; Households with income of $100,000 or more: 7.9%; Poverty rate: 32.5%
Educational Attainment: High school diploma or higher: 71.0%; Bachelor's degree or higher: 4.4%; Graduate/professional degree or higher: 1.6%
Housing: Homeownership rate: 73.7%; Median home value: $33,900; Median year structure built: 1990; Homeowner vacancy rate: 0.0%; Median selected monthly owner costs: $950 with a mortgage, $384 without a mortgage; Median gross rent: $888 per month; Rental vacancy rate: 0.0%
Health Insurance: 80.8% have insurance; 43.7% have private insurance; 50.4% have public insurance; 19.2% do not have insurance; 13.5% of children under 18 do not have insurance
Transportation: Commute: 86.8% car, 0.0% public transportation, 3.2% walk, 2.4% work from home; Mean travel time to work: 22.1 minutes

HAYDEN (CDP). Covers a land area of 2.474 square miles and a water area of 0 square miles. Located at 38.97° N. Lat; 85.74° W. Long. Elevation is 620 feet.
Population: 1,112; Growth (since 2000): n/a; Density: 449.4 persons per square mile; Race: 86.1% White, 12.3% Black/African American, 0.0% Asian, 1.6% American Indian/Alaska Native, 0.0% Native Hawaiian/Other Pacific Islander, 0.0% Two or more races, 8.9% Hispanic of any race; Average household size: 4.09; Median age: 23.1; Age under 18: 36.1%; Age 65 and over: 3.9%; Males per 100 females: 110.9; Marriage status: 39.1% never married, 46.0% now married, 0.0% separated, 2.7% widowed, 12.1% divorced; Foreign born: 0.8%; Speak English only: 96.5%; With disability: 18.7%; Veterans: 14.1%; Ancestry: 33.2% American, 18.0% German, 2.0% Irish, 1.8% Polish, 1.1% Swedish
Employment: 0.0% management, business, and financial, 0.0% computer, engineering, and science, 7.5% education, legal, community service, arts, and media, 0.0% healthcare practitioners, 7.5% service, 36.8% sales and office, 6.6% natural resources, construction, and maintenance, 41.7% production, transportation, and material moving
Income: Per capita: $14,391; Median household: $55,375; Average household: $56,209; Households with income of $100,000 or more: 5.1%; Poverty rate: 14.6%
Educational Attainment: High school diploma or higher: 100.0%; Bachelor's degree or higher: 3.7%; Graduate/professional degree or higher: n/a

School District(s)

Jennings County School Corporation (PK-12)
Enrollment: 4,434 . . . . (812) 346-4483
Housing: Homeownership rate: 70.2%; Median home value: $111,500; Median year structure built: 1973; Homeowner vacancy rate: 0.0%; Median selected monthly owner costs: $1,033 with a mortgage, n/a without a mortgage; Median gross rent: n/a per month; Rental vacancy rate: 0.0%
Health Insurance: 98.5% have insurance; 70.1% have private insurance; 48.7% have public insurance; 1.5% do not have insurance; 4.2% of children under 18 do not have insurance
Transportation: Commute: 95.8% car, 0.0% public transportation, 4.2% walk, 0.0% work from home; Mean travel time to work: 25.3 minutes

NORTH VERNON (city). Covers a land area of 6.619 square miles and a water area of 0.010 square miles. Located at 39.01° N. Lat; 85.63° W. Long. Elevation is 718 feet.
History: North Vernon was platted in 1854 as a railroad town and trading center.
Population: 6,695; Growth (since 2000): 2.8%; Density: 1,011.5 persons per square mile; Race: 97.0% White, 1.5% Black/African American, 0.1% Asian, 0.7% American Indian/Alaska Native, 0.0% Native Hawaiian/Other Pacific Islander, 0.7% Two or more races, 1.8% Hispanic of any race; Average household size: 2.41; Median age: 37.3; Age under 18: 22.9%; Age 65 and over: 16.8%; Males per 100 females: 91.7; Marriage status: 29.5% never married, 42.6% now married, 2.6% separated, 8.9% widowed, 19.1% divorced; Foreign born: 0.7%; Speak English only: 98.7%; With disability: 19.7%; Veterans: 6.7%; Ancestry: 14.5% German, 14.3% American, 6.5% Irish, 6.0% English, 3.4% Dutch
Employment: 9.8% management, business, and financial, 2.8% computer, engineering, and science, 5.7% education, legal, community service, arts, and media, 2.9% healthcare practitioners, 17.1% service, 18.7% sales and office, 9.0% natural resources, construction, and maintenance, 34.0% production, transportation, and material moving
Income: Per capita: $23,558; Median household: $42,200; Average household: $57,103; Households with income of $100,000 or more: 13.8%; Poverty rate: 19.8%
Educational Attainment: High school diploma or higher: 81.6%; Bachelor's degree or higher: 12.6%; Graduate/professional degree or higher: 4.7%

School District(s)

Jennings County School Corporation (PK-12)
Enrollment: 4,434 . . . . (812) 346-4483
Housing: Homeownership rate: 51.9%; Median home value: $86,100; Median year structure built: 1972; Homeowner vacancy rate: 1.9%; Median selected monthly owner costs: $896 with a mortgage, $333 without a mortgage; Median gross rent: $656 per month; Rental vacancy rate: 7.0%
Health Insurance: 87.8% have insurance; 58.6% have private insurance; 39.2% have public insurance; 12.2% do not have insurance; 10.2% of children under 18 do not have insurance
Hospitals: Saint Vincent Jennings Hospital (25 beds)
Safety: Violent crime rate: 26.3 per 10,000 population; Property crime rate: 258.9 per 10,000 population
Newspapers: North Vernon Plain Dealer (weekly circulation 7,000); North Vernon Sun (weekly circulation 6,000)
Transportation: Commute: 95.8% car, 0.0% public transportation, 2.7% walk, 0.9% work from home; Mean travel time to work: 23.3 minutes
Additional Information Contacts
City of North Vernon . . . . (812) 346-5907
http://www.northvernon-in.gov

PARIS CROSSING (unincorporated postal area)
ZCTA: 47270
Covers a land area of 18.579 square miles and a water area of 0.058 square miles. Located at 38.84° N. Lat; 85.72° W. Long. Elevation is 623 feet.
Population: 545; Growth (since 2000): -33.5%; Density: 29.3 persons per square mile; Race: 100.0% White, 0.0% Black/African American, 0.0% Asian, 0.0% American Indian/Alaska Native, 0.0% Native Hawaiian/Other Pacific Islander, 0.0% Two or more races, 0.0%

Hispanic of any race; Average household size: 2.52; Median age: 32.3; Age under 18: 27.5%; Age 65 and over: 8.8%; Males per 100 females: 104.3; Marriage status: 20.0% never married, 59.2% now married, 1.5% separated, 17.3% widowed, 3.5% divorced; Foreign born: 0.0%; Speak English only: 97.8%; With disability: 17.4%; Veterans: 11.4%; Ancestry: 21.7% German, 9.5% American, 7.0% Irish, 6.4% Scotch-Irish, 5.3% Dutch
Employment: 9.5% management, business, and financial, 0.0% computer, engineering, and science, 12.6% education, legal, community service, arts, and media, 0.0% healthcare practitioners, 20.0% service, 31.4% sales and office, 10.5% natural resources, construction, and maintenance, 16.0% production, transportation, and material moving
Income: Per capita: $24,764; Median household: $57,417; Average household: $59,272; Households with income of $100,000 or more: 10.6%; Poverty rate: 7.7%
Educational Attainment: High school diploma or higher: 97.1%; Bachelor's degree or higher: 10.7%; Graduate/professional degree or higher: n/a
Housing: Homeownership rate: 92.1%; Median home value: $98,300; Median year structure built: 1993; Homeowner vacancy rate: 0.0%; Median selected monthly owner costs: $1,108 with a mortgage, $330 without a mortgage; Median gross rent: n/a per month; Rental vacancy rate: 0.0%
Health Insurance: 100.0% have insurance; 86.6% have private insurance; 18.9% have public insurance; 0.0% do not have insurance; 0.0% of children under 18 do not have insurance
Transportation: Commute: 96.0% car, 0.0% public transportation, 0.0% walk, 4.0% work from home; Mean travel time to work: 36.6 minutes

---

SCIPIO (CDP). Covers a land area of 1.148 square miles and a water area of 0.020 square miles. Located at 39.07° N. Lat; 85.72° W. Long. Elevation is 679 feet.
Population: 90; Growth (since 2000): n/a; Density: 78.4 persons per square mile; Race: 100.0% White, 0.0% Black/African American, 0.0% Asian, 0.0% American Indian/Alaska Native, 0.0% Native Hawaiian/Other Pacific Islander, 0.0% Two or more races, 0.0% Hispanic of any race; Average household size: 1.55; Median age: 67.2; Age under 18: 0.0%; Age 65 and over: 52.2%; Males per 100 females: 86.6; Marriage status: 0.0% never married, 71.1% now married, 0.0% separated, 20.0% widowed, 8.9% divorced; Foreign born: 0.0%; Speak English only: 100.0%; With disability: 20.0%; Veterans: 26.7%; Ancestry: 45.6% American, 11.1% English
Employment: 0.0% management, business, and financial, 0.0% computer, engineering, and science, 0.0% education, legal, community service, arts, and media, 0.0% healthcare practitioners, 0.0% service, 56.1% sales and office, 0.0% natural resources, construction, and maintenance, 43.9% production, transportation, and material moving
Income: Per capita: $25,764; Median household: $37,115; Average household: $39,022; Households with income of $100,000 or more: n/a; Poverty rate: n/a
Educational Attainment: High school diploma or higher: 91.1%; Bachelor's degree or higher: n/a; Graduate/professional degree or higher: n/a

School District(s)

Jennings County School Corporation (PK-12)
Enrollment: 4,434 . . . . (812) 346-4483
Housing: Homeownership rate: 100.0%; Median home value: $133,600; Median year structure built: 1965; Homeowner vacancy rate: 0.0%; Median selected monthly owner costs: $1,167 with a mortgage, n/a without a mortgage; Median gross rent: n/a per month; Rental vacancy rate: 0.0%
Health Insurance: 100.0% have insurance; 80.0% have private insurance; 80.0% have public insurance; 0.0% do not have insurance; 0.0% of children under 18 do not have insurance
Transportation: Commute: 46.3% car, 0.0% public transportation, 0.0% walk, 53.7% work from home; Mean travel time to work: 0.0 minutes

---

VERNON (town). County seat. Covers a land area of 0.238 square miles and a water area of 0 square miles. Located at 38.99° N. Lat; 85.61° W. Long. Elevation is 663 feet.
History: The land grant that established Vernon in 1815 stipulated that it should be the county seat forever.
Population: 403; Growth (since 2000): 22.1%; Density: 1,695.3 persons per square mile; Race: 100.0% White, 0.0% Black/African American, 0.0% Asian, 0.0% American Indian/Alaska Native, 0.0% Native Hawaiian/Other Pacific Islander, 0.0% Two or more races, 11.7% Hispanic of any race; Average household size: 2.08; Median age: 43.8; Age under 18: 26.3%; Age 65 and over: 18.9%; Males per 100 females: 92.7; Marriage status: 18.5% never married, 51.0% now married, 2.2% separated, 13.4% widowed, 17.2% divorced; Foreign born: 0.0%; Speak English only: 100.0%; With disability: 17.6%; Veterans: 17.8%; Ancestry: 34.5% German, 14.1% Irish, 6.7% English, 4.5% American, 4.5% Dutch
Employment: 28.9% management, business, and financial, 0.0% computer, engineering, and science, 20.8% education, legal, community service, arts, and media, 4.0% healthcare practitioners, 8.1% service, 13.3% sales and office, 11.0% natural resources, construction, and maintenance, 13.9% production, transportation, and material moving
Income: Per capita: $26,519; Median household: $39,167; Average household: $55,914; Households with income of $100,000 or more: 16.5%; Poverty rate: 15.4%
Educational Attainment: High school diploma or higher: 88.6%; Bachelor's degree or higher: 17.5%; Graduate/professional degree or higher: 3.2%
Housing: Homeownership rate: 69.1%; Median home value: $98,000; Median year structure built: Before 1940; Homeowner vacancy rate: 6.9%; Median selected monthly owner costs: $821 with a mortgage, $527 without a mortgage; Median gross rent: $807 per month; Rental vacancy rate: 14.3%
Health Insurance: 94.5% have insurance; 58.8% have private insurance; 50.4% have public insurance; 5.5% do not have insurance; 4.7% of children under 18 do not have insurance
Transportation: Commute: 76.9% car, 0.0% public transportation, 3.5% walk, 19.7% work from home; Mean travel time to work: 19.0 minutes

Johnson County

Located in central Indiana; drained by the West Fork of the White River. Covers a land area of 320.427 square miles, a water area of 1.363 square miles, and is located in the Eastern Time Zone at 39.50° N. Lat., 86.09° W. Long. The county was founded in 1822. County seat is Franklin.

Johnson County is part of the Indianapolis-Carmel-Anderson, IN Metropolitan Statistical Area. The entire metro area includes: Boone County, IN; Brown County, IN; Hamilton County, IN; Hancock County, IN; Hendricks County, IN; Johnson County, IN; Madison County, IN; Marion County, IN; Morgan County, IN; Putnam County, IN; Shelby County, IN

Population: 149,359; Growth (since 2000): 29.6%; Density: 466.1 persons per square mile; Race: 92.1% White, 2.4% Black/African American, 2.8% Asian, 0.2% American Indian/Alaska Native, 0.0% Native Hawaiian/Other Pacific Islander, 1.1% two or more races, 3.5% Hispanic of any race; Average household size: 2.68; Median age: 37.3; Age under 18: 25.3%; Age 65 and over: 13.9%; Males per 100 females: 96.8; Marriage status: 25.7% never married, 56.9% now married, 1.0% separated, 5.4% widowed, 12.0% divorced; Foreign born: 4.4%; Speak English only: 93.6%; With disability: 10.3%; Veterans: 8.5%; Ancestry: 23.0% German, 12.1% Irish, 10.6% English, 10.6% American, 2.8% Italian
Religion: Six largest groups: 13.0% Baptist, 12.7% Non-denominational Protestant, 8.3% Catholicism, 5.0% Pentecostal, 2.4% Methodist/Pietist, 1.5% Lutheran
Economy: Unemployment rate: 3.0%; Leading industries: 15.7 % retail trade; 11.5 % construction; 10.6 % other services (except public administration); Farms: 562 totaling 144,646 acres; Company size: 0 employ 1,000 or more persons, 3 employ 500 to 999 persons, 88 employ 100 to 499 persons, 3,004 employ less than 100 persons; Business ownership: 3,108 women-owned, 72 Black-owned, 162 Hispanic-owned, 486 Asian-owned, n/a American Indian/Alaska Native-owned
Employment: 17.0% management, business, and financial, 5.8% computer, engineering, and science, 9.3% education, legal, community service, arts, and media, 7.1% healthcare practitioners, 15.3% service, 23.6% sales and office, 8.6% natural resources, construction, and maintenance, 13.4% production, transportation, and material moving
Income: Per capita: $31,101; Median household: $65,272; Average household: $82,167; Households with income of $100,000 or more: 28.4%; Poverty rate: 9.4%
Educational Attainment: High school diploma or higher: 91.7%; Bachelor's degree or higher: 30.9%; Graduate/professional degree or higher: 10.1%
Housing: Homeownership rate: 71.0%; Median home value: $149,700; Median year structure built: 1989; Homeowner vacancy rate: 1.4%; Median

selected monthly owner costs: $1,212 with a mortgage, $436 without a mortgage; Median gross rent: $896 per month; Rental vacancy rate: 5.3%
Vital Statistics: Birth rate: 124.4 per 10,000 population; Death rate: 84.0 per 10,000 population; Age-adjusted cancer mortality rate: 165.9 deaths per 100,000 population
Health Insurance: 92.0% have insurance; 77.1% have private insurance; 26.5% have public insurance; 8.0% do not have insurance; 5.7% of children under 18 do not have insurance
Health Care: Physicians: 20.9 per 10,000 population; Dentists: 6.2 per 10,000 population; Hospital beds: 17.4 per 10,000 population; Hospital admissions: 201.9 per 10,000 population
Air Quality Index (AQI): Percent of Days: 90.3% good, 9.7% moderate, 0.0% unhealthy for sensitive individuals, 0.0% unhealthy, 0.0% very unhealthy; Annual median: 39; Annual maximum: 80
Transportation: Commute: 93.8% car, 0.3% public transportation, 1.3% walk, 3.8% work from home; Mean travel time to work: 26.1 minutes
2016 Presidential Election: 67.7% Trump, 25.8% Clinton, 5.1% Johnson, 0.3% Stein
National and State Parks: Atterbury State Fish and Wildlife Area
Additional Information Contacts
Johnson Government . . . . (317) 346-4700
http://www.co.johnson.in.us

Johnson County Communities

BARGERSVILLE (town). Covers a land area of 4.926 square miles and a water area of 0 square miles. Located at 39.54° N. Lat; 86.16° W. Long. Elevation is 820 feet.
Population: 6,919; Growth (since 2000): 226.4%; Density: 1,404.6 persons per square mile; Race: 98.3% White, 1.1% Black/African American, 0.2% Asian, 0.0% American Indian/Alaska Native, 0.0% Native Hawaiian/Other Pacific Islander, 0.4% Two or more races, 0.0% Hispanic of any race; Average household size: 2.83; Median age: 33.5; Age under 18: 30.2%; Age 65 and over: 11.4%; Males per 100 females: 104.8; Marriage status: 19.9% never married, 66.8% now married, 1.1% separated, 3.9% widowed, 9.4% divorced; Foreign born: 2.6%; Speak English only: 94.8%; With disability: 8.5%; Veterans: 8.4%; Ancestry: 21.6% German, 15.0% American, 12.9% English, 9.9% Irish, 4.8% Polish
Employment: 23.9% management, business, and financial, 8.1% computer, engineering, and science, 5.8% education, legal, community service, arts, and media, 8.7% healthcare practitioners, 10.7% service, 19.5% sales and office, 7.9% natural resources, construction, and maintenance, 15.4% production, transportation, and material moving
Income: Per capita: $39,347; Median household: $81,673; Average household: $110,158; Households with income of $100,000 or more: 38.6%; Poverty rate: 6.4%
Educational Attainment: High school diploma or higher: 89.2%; Bachelor's degree or higher: 35.0%; Graduate/professional degree or higher: 12.4%

School District(s)
Center Grove Community School Corp (PK-12)
Enrollment: 8,256 . . . . (317) 881-9326
Franklin Community School Corp (PK-12)
Enrollment: 4,944 . . . . (317) 738-5800
Housing: Homeownership rate: 74.1%; Median home value: $180,700; Median year structure built: 2003; Homeowner vacancy rate: 0.0%; Median selected monthly owner costs: $1,372 with a mortgage, $544 without a mortgage; Median gross rent: $955 per month; Rental vacancy rate: 4.4%
Health Insurance: 97.9% have insurance; 89.8% have private insurance; 19.8% have public insurance; 2.1% do not have insurance; 0.6% of children under 18 do not have insurance
Safety: Violent crime rate: 12.1 per 10,000 population; Property crime rate: 169.3 per 10,000 population
Transportation: Commute: 94.0% car, 0.4% public transportation, 1.1% walk, 4.5% work from home; Mean travel time to work: 27.6 minutes
Additional Information Contacts
Town of Bargersville . . . . (317) 422-5115
http://www.townofbargersville.org

EDINBURGH (town). Covers a land area of 3.109 square miles and a water area of 0 square miles. Located at 39.35° N. Lat; 85.96° W. Long. Elevation is 673 feet.
Population: 4,796; Growth (since 2000): 6.5%; Density: 1,542.4 persons per square mile; Race: 87.4% White, 3.4% Black/African American, 0.0% Asian, 0.2% American Indian/Alaska Native, 0.0% Native Hawaiian/Other Pacific Islander, 2.0% Two or more races, 9.8% Hispanic of any race; Average household size: 2.56; Median age: 38.2; Age under 18: 22.6%; Age 65 and over: 14.1%; Males per 100 females: 99.6; Marriage status: 32.0% never married, 46.4% now married, 0.7% separated, 6.4% widowed, 15.1% divorced; Foreign born: 7.0%; Speak English only: 90.0%; With disability: 14.5%; Veterans: 6.2%; Ancestry: 15.2% American, 11.6% Irish, 11.4% German, 6.7% English, 2.6% Italian
Employment: 5.9% management, business, and financial, 3.1% computer, engineering, and science, 2.9% education, legal, community service, arts, and media, 1.9% healthcare practitioners, 19.2% service, 21.1% sales and office, 3.8% natural resources, construction, and maintenance, 42.1% production, transportation, and material moving
Income: Per capita: $20,140; Median household: $42,885; Average household: $49,515; Households with income of $100,000 or more: 5.6%; Poverty rate: 17.9%
Educational Attainment: High school diploma or higher: 84.3%; Bachelor's degree or higher: 5.3%; Graduate/professional degree or higher: 1.8%

School District(s)
Edinburgh Community School Corp (PK-12)
Enrollment: 847. . . . . (812) 526-2681
Housing: Homeownership rate: 52.0%; Median home value: $85,000; Median year structure built: 1963; Homeowner vacancy rate: 0.0%; Median selected monthly owner costs: $968 with a mortgage, $348 without a mortgage; Median gross rent: $728 per month; Rental vacancy rate: 2.7%
Health Insurance: 83.3% have insurance; 64.1% have private insurance; 30.1% have public insurance; 16.7% do not have insurance; 10.2% of children under 18 do not have insurance
Safety: Violent crime rate: 43.6 per 10,000 population; Property crime rate: 1,073.6 per 10,000 population
Transportation: Commute: 92.8% car, 0.0% public transportation, 3.0% walk, 1.0% work from home; Mean travel time to work: 17.6 minutes
Additional Information Contacts
Town of Edinburgh . . . . (812) 526-3511
http://www.edinburgh.in.us

FRANKLIN (city). County seat. Covers a land area of 13.006 square miles and a water area of 0 square miles. Located at 39.49° N. Lat; 86.05° W. Long. Elevation is 725 feet.
History: Named for Benjamin Franklin, American statesman and inventor. Franklin developed as a shipping center for grain and tomatoes. In 1834 Franklin College was established as the Indiana Baptist Manual Labor Institute.
Population: 24,489; Growth (since 2000): 25.8%; Density: 1,882.9 persons per square mile; Race: 95.7% White, 1.5% Black/African American, 0.7% Asian, 0.0% American Indian/Alaska Native, 0.0% Native Hawaiian/Other Pacific Islander, 0.6% Two or more races, 2.7% Hispanic of any race; Average household size: 2.53; Median age: 38.0; Age under 18: 23.5%; Age 65 and over: 16.3%; Males per 100 females: 91.3; Marriage status: 25.4% never married, 51.7% now married, 0.8% separated, 8.1% widowed, 14.8% divorced; Foreign born: 2.0%; Speak English only: 96.2%; With disability: 12.2%; Veterans: 9.9%; Ancestry: 21.5% German, 11.6% Irish, 10.2% American, 7.8% English, 3.5% Italian
Employment: 12.7% management, business, and financial, 2.9% computer, engineering, and science, 10.6% education, legal, community service, arts, and media, 6.3% healthcare practitioners, 19.9% service, 21.3% sales and office, 9.2% natural resources, construction, and maintenance, 17.1% production, transportation, and material moving
Income: Per capita: $26,647; Median household: $56,367; Average household: $67,641; Households with income of $100,000 or more: 22.5%; Poverty rate: 10.4%
Educational Attainment: High school diploma or higher: 88.6%; Bachelor's degree or higher: 24.1%; Graduate/professional degree or higher: 8.7%

School District(s)
Clark-Pleasant Community Sch Corp (PK-12)
Enrollment: 6,826 . . . . (317) 535-7579
Franklin Community School Corp (PK-12)
Enrollment: 4,944 . . . . (317) 738-5800

Four-year College(s)
Franklin College (Private, Not-for-profit, American Baptist)
Enrollment: 1,034 . . . . (317) 738-8000
Tuition: In-state $30,920; Out-of-state $30,920
Housing: Homeownership rate: 63.1%; Median home value: $119,200; Median year structure built: 1991; Homeowner vacancy rate: 3.4%; Median

selected monthly owner costs: $1,104 with a mortgage, $380 without a mortgage; Median gross rent: $798 per month; Rental vacancy rate: 5.6%
Health Insurance: 90.9% have insurance; 76.7% have private insurance; 27.2% have public insurance; 9.1% do not have insurance; 7.4% of children under 18 do not have insurance
Hospitals: Johnson Memorial Hospital (161 beds)
Safety: Violent crime rate: 50.7 per 10,000 population; Property crime rate: 339.6 per 10,000 population
Newspapers: Daily Journal (daily circulation 17,100)
Transportation: Commute: 95.2% car, 0.4% public transportation, 1.7% walk, 1.8% work from home; Mean travel time to work: 23.1 minutes
Additional Information Contacts
City of Franklin . . . . (317) 736-3609
http://www.franklin.in.gov

GREENWOOD (city). Covers a land area of 21.230 square miles and a water area of <.001 square miles. Located at 39.61° N. Lat; 86.11° W. Long. Elevation is 804 feet.
History: Named for Samuel Greenwood who plotted the village in 1872. Greenwood developed as an industrial town with automobile-parts factories and a canning company.
Population: 55,459; Growth (since 2000): 53.9%; Density: 2,612.3 persons per square mile; Race: 86.2% White, 4.4% Black/African American, 5.7% Asian, 0.4% American Indian/Alaska Native, 0.0% Native Hawaiian/Other Pacific Islander, 1.1% Two or more races, 6.1% Hispanic of any race; Average household size: 2.57; Median age: 35.5; Age under 18: 25.4%; Age 65 and over: 13.8%; Males per 100 females: 93.9; Marriage status: 29.8% never married, 51.1% now married, 1.0% separated, 5.9% widowed, 13.2% divorced; Foreign born: 7.8%; Speak English only: 88.6%; With disability: 11.5%; Veterans: 8.9%; Ancestry: 22.9% German, 11.0% Irish, 10.7% English, 8.6% American, 2.3% Scottish
Employment: 15.7% management, business, and financial, 7.1% computer, engineering, and science, 7.6% education, legal, community service, arts, and media, 6.8% healthcare practitioners, 16.3% service, 26.5% sales and office, 7.8% natural resources, construction, and maintenance, 12.2% production, transportation, and material moving
Income: Per capita: $28,078; Median household: $55,274; Average household: $70,416; Households with income of $100,000 or more: 20.4%; Poverty rate: 12.2%
Educational Attainment: High school diploma or higher: 91.1%; Bachelor's degree or higher: 29.4%; Graduate/professional degree or higher: 8.1%

School District(s)
Center Grove Community School Corp (PK-12)
Enrollment: 8,256 . . . . (317) 881-9326
Central Nine Career Center (09-12)
Enrollment: n/a . . . . (317) 888-4401
Clark-Pleasant Community Sch Corp (PK-12)
Enrollment: 6,826 . . . . (317) 535-7579
Greenwood Community Sch Corp (PK-12)
Enrollment: 3,524 . . . . (317) 889-4060

Housing: Homeownership rate: 57.6%; Median home value: $143,100; Median year structure built: 1991; Homeowner vacancy rate: 1.1%; Median selected monthly owner costs: $1,115 with a mortgage, $432 without a mortgage; Median gross rent: $903 per month; Rental vacancy rate: 6.5%
Health Insurance: 90.0% have insurance; 71.3% have private insurance; 30.6% have public insurance; 10.0% do not have insurance; 6.4% of children under 18 do not have insurance
Safety: Violent crime rate: 51.8 per 10,000 population; Property crime rate: 323.9 per 10,000 population
Newspapers: Franklin Challenger (weekly circulation 3,600); Southside Challenger (weekly circulation 4,200)
Transportation: Commute: 93.9% car, 0.4% public transportation, 1.2% walk, 3.8% work from home; Mean travel time to work: 25.3 minutes
Airports: Greenwood Municipal (general aviation)
Additional Information Contacts
City of Greenwood. . . . . (317) 881-8527
http://www.greenwood.in.gov

NEEDHAM (unincorporated postal area)
ZCTA: 46162
Covers a land area of 11.233 square miles and a water area of 0.029 square miles. Located at 39.55° N. Lat; 85.95° W. Long. Elevation is 728 feet.
Population: 550; Growth (since 2000): 33.8%; Density: 49.0 persons per square mile; Race: 100.0% White, 0.0% Black/African American, 0.0% Asian, 0.0% American Indian/Alaska Native, 0.0% Native Hawaiian/Other Pacific Islander, 0.0% Two or more races, 0.0% Hispanic of any race; Average household size: 2.51; Median age: 35.0; Age under 18: 27.1%; Age 65 and over: 18.4%; Males per 100 females: 113.0; Marriage status: 22.7% never married, 53.7% now married, 3.4% separated, 9.5% widowed, 14.1% divorced; Foreign born: 0.0%; Speak English only: 100.0%; With disability: 5.1%; Veterans: 8.2%; Ancestry: 44.2% German, 35.8% Irish, 12.4% American, 6.9% English, 1.8% British
Employment: 17.0% management, business, and financial, 0.0% computer, engineering, and science, 15.0% education, legal, community service, arts, and media, 0.0% healthcare practitioners, 12.2% service, 15.6% sales and office, 15.6% natural resources, construction, and maintenance, 24.5% production, transportation, and material moving
Income: Per capita: $25,897; Median household: $51,563; Average household: $64,316; Households with income of $100,000 or more: 20.1%; Poverty rate: 19.6%
Educational Attainment: High school diploma or higher: 89.6%; Bachelor's degree or higher: 5.9%; Graduate/professional degree or higher: 2.7%
Housing: Homeownership rate: 77.2%; Median home value: $119,600; Median year structure built: 1967; Homeowner vacancy rate: 0.0%; Median selected monthly owner costs: $883 with a mortgage, $260 without a mortgage; Median gross rent: n/a per month; Rental vacancy rate: 0.0%
Health Insurance: 87.3% have insurance; 63.8% have private insurance; 37.6% have public insurance; 12.7% do not have insurance; 0.0% of children under 18 do not have insurance
Transportation: Commute: 97.3% car, 0.0% public transportation, 0.0% walk, 2.7% work from home; Mean travel time to work: 27.0 minutes

NEW WHITELAND (town). Covers a land area of 1.461 square miles and a water area of 0 square miles. Located at 39.56° N. Lat; 86.10° W. Long. Elevation is 807 feet.
Population: 5,881; Growth (since 2000): 28.4%; Density: 4,024.3 persons per square mile; Race: 91.0% White, 1.8% Black/African American, 0.9% Asian, 0.0% American Indian/Alaska Native, 0.0% Native Hawaiian/Other Pacific Islander, 4.6% Two or more races, 3.0% Hispanic of any race; Average household size: 2.72; Median age: 33.6; Age under 18: 28.3%; Age 65 and over: 12.3%; Males per 100 females: 94.6; Marriage status: 28.1% never married, 47.1% now married, 1.8% separated, 5.8% widowed, 19.0% divorced; Foreign born: 1.1%; Speak English only: 96.9%; With disability: 11.9%; Veterans: 5.1%; Ancestry: 19.5% German, 12.9% American, 7.4% Irish, 5.6% English, 3.8% Welsh
Employment: 8.5% management, business, and financial, 2.5% computer, engineering, and science, 11.6% education, legal, community service, arts, and media, 1.3% healthcare practitioners, 18.7% service, 27.4% sales and office, 13.5% natural resources, construction, and maintenance, 16.6% production, transportation, and material moving
Income: Per capita: $21,642; Median household: $60,381; Average household: $58,181; Households with income of $100,000 or more: 6.6%; Poverty rate: 5.0%
Educational Attainment: High school diploma or higher: 93.1%; Bachelor's degree or higher: 20.6%; Graduate/professional degree or higher: 5.1%

School District(s)
Clark-Pleasant Community Sch Corp (PK-12)
Enrollment: 6,826 . . . . (317) 535-7579

Housing: Homeownership rate: 86.2%; Median home value: $94,400; Median year structure built: 1970; Homeowner vacancy rate: 0.0%; Median selected monthly owner costs: $921 with a mortgage, $391 without a mortgage; Median gross rent: $1,261 per month; Rental vacancy rate: 0.0%
Health Insurance: 90.4% have insurance; 70.0% have private insurance; 32.2% have public insurance; 9.6% do not have insurance; 2.2% of children under 18 do not have insurance
Safety: Violent crime rate: 1.6 per 10,000 population; Property crime rate: 63.8 per 10,000 population
Transportation: Commute: 96.3% car, 1.3% public transportation, 0.5% walk, 1.9% work from home; Mean travel time to work: 24.1 minutes
Additional Information Contacts
Town of New Whiteland . . . . (317) 535-9487
http://www.townofnewwhiteland.com

PRINCES LAKES (town). Covers a land area of 1.348 square miles and a water area of 0.172 square miles. Located at 39.35° N. Lat; 86.11° W. Long. Elevation is 820 feet.
Population: 1,484; Growth (since 2000): -1.5%; Density: 1,101.2 persons per square mile; Race: 96.2% White, 0.5% Black/African American, 0.0% Asian, 0.0% American Indian/Alaska Native, 0.0% Native Hawaiian/Other Pacific Islander, 1.4% Two or more races, 3.0% Hispanic of any race; Average household size: 2.43; Median age: 44.5; Age under 18: 17.9%; Age 65 and over: 15.8%; Males per 100 females: 94.1; Marriage status: 24.1% never married, 55.1% now married, 0.5% separated, 3.5% widowed, 17.3% divorced; Foreign born: 0.4%; Speak English only: 96.6%; With disability: 12.5%; Veterans: 14.2%; Ancestry: 20.2% German, 16.8% American, 15.1% Irish, 9.4% English, 4.2% French
Employment: 13.3% management, business, and financial, 6.8% computer, engineering, and science, 3.7% education, legal, community service, arts, and media, 7.8% healthcare practitioners, 14.8% service, 24.0% sales and office, 16.9% natural resources, construction, and maintenance, 12.7% production, transportation, and material moving
Income: Per capita: $29,782; Median household: $65,650; Average household: $71,579; Households with income of $100,000 or more: 20.8%; Poverty rate: 11.4%
Educational Attainment: High school diploma or higher: 93.9%; Bachelor's degree or higher: 20.2%; Graduate/professional degree or higher: 8.5%
Housing: Homeownership rate: 88.7%; Median home value: $135,000; Median year structure built: 1969; Homeowner vacancy rate: 2.1%; Median selected monthly owner costs: $1,139 with a mortgage, $460 without a mortgage; Median gross rent: $1,125 per month; Rental vacancy rate: 4.2%
Health Insurance: 92.2% have insurance; 72.0% have private insurance; 34.9% have public insurance; 7.8% do not have insurance; 4.1% of children under 18 do not have insurance
Transportation: Commute: 95.9% car, 0.0% public transportation, 2.7% walk, 1.0% work from home; Mean travel time to work: 32.8 minutes

TRAFALGAR (town). Covers a land area of 2.638 square miles and a water area of 0 square miles. Located at 39.41° N. Lat; 86.15° W. Long. Elevation is 827 feet.
History: Laid out 1850.
Population: 1,307; Growth (since 2000): 63.8%; Density: 495.5 persons per square mile; Race: 97.6% White, 0.6% Black/African American, 0.0% Asian, 0.2% American Indian/Alaska Native, 0.0% Native Hawaiian/Other Pacific Islander, 0.8% Two or more races, 2.0% Hispanic of any race; Average household size: 2.80; Median age: 32.1; Age under 18: 31.4%; Age 65 and over: 7.0%; Males per 100 females: 97.3; Marriage status: 25.8% never married, 59.6% now married, 0.9% separated, 2.6% widowed, 12.0% divorced; Foreign born: 2.6%; Speak English only: 97.8%; With disability: 9.0%; Veterans: 8.9%; Ancestry: 21.0% German, 10.7% American, 9.9% English, 9.4% Irish, 3.4% Scottish
Employment: 12.1% management, business, and financial, 3.6% computer, engineering, and science, 4.0% education, legal, community service, arts, and media, 6.6% healthcare practitioners, 22.3% service, 25.1% sales and office, 12.4% natural resources, construction, and maintenance, 13.9% production, transportation, and material moving
Income: Per capita: $22,420; Median household: $55,268; Average household: $63,212; Households with income of $100,000 or more: 16.0%; Poverty rate: 6.5%
Educational Attainment: High school diploma or higher: 94.1%; Bachelor's degree or higher: 12.8%; Graduate/professional degree or higher: 3.3%

School District(s)

Nineveh-Hensley-Jackson United (PK-12)
Enrollment: 1,655 . . . . (317) 878-2100
Housing: Homeownership rate: 77.1%; Median home value: $120,100; Median year structure built: 1994; Homeowner vacancy rate: 0.0%; Median selected monthly owner costs: $1,105 with a mortgage, $388 without a mortgage; Median gross rent: $960 per month; Rental vacancy rate: 0.0%
Health Insurance: 88.2% have insurance; 75.0% have private insurance; 18.5% have public insurance; 11.8% do not have insurance; 7.0% of children under 18 do not have insurance
Transportation: Commute: 94.0% car, 0.0% public transportation, 2.0% walk, 3.0% work from home; Mean travel time to work: 27.7 minutes

WHITELAND (town). Covers a land area of 3.219 square miles and a water area of 0 square miles. Located at 39.55° N. Lat; 86.08° W. Long. Elevation is 794 feet.
Population: 4,570; Growth (since 2000): 15.5%; Density: 1,419.5 persons per square mile; Race: 99.5% White, 0.0% Black/African American, 0.5% Asian, 0.0% American Indian/Alaska Native, 0.0% Native Hawaiian/Other Pacific Islander, 0.0% Two or more races, 0.0% Hispanic of any race; Average household size: 2.89; Median age: 34.6; Age under 18: 22.1%; Age 65 and over: 6.8%; Males per 100 females: 96.4; Marriage status: 29.2% never married, 52.4% now married, 0.7% separated, 3.5% widowed, 15.0% divorced; Foreign born: 1.3%; Speak English only: 99.1%; With disability: 9.2%; Veterans: 8.2%; Ancestry: 24.3% German, 14.3% Irish, 12.4% American, 8.6% English, 2.5% Scottish
Employment: 21.1% management, business, and financial, 4.1% computer, engineering, and science, 5.4% education, legal, community service, arts, and media, 9.2% healthcare practitioners, 11.0% service, 26.5% sales and office, 8.2% natural resources, construction, and maintenance, 14.4% production, transportation, and material moving
Income: Per capita: $32,307; Median household: $70,455; Average household: $90,340; Households with income of $100,000 or more: 32.8%; Poverty rate: 3.1%
Educational Attainment: High school diploma or higher: 95.3%; Bachelor's degree or higher: 27.6%; Graduate/professional degree or higher: 6.6%

School District(s)

Clark-Pleasant Community Sch Corp (PK-12)
Enrollment: 6,826 . . . . (317) 535-7579
Housing: Homeownership rate: 84.9%; Median home value: $121,000; Median year structure built: 1984; Homeowner vacancy rate: 0.0%; Median selected monthly owner costs: $1,170 with a mortgage, $395 without a mortgage; Median gross rent: $1,025 per month; Rental vacancy rate: 0.0%
Health Insurance: 95.5% have insurance; 85.5% have private insurance; 15.0% have public insurance; 4.5% do not have insurance; 0.0% of children under 18 do not have insurance
Transportation: Commute: 94.7% car, 0.6% public transportation, 1.2% walk, 3.6% work from home; Mean travel time to work: 24.7 minutes
Additional Information Contacts
Town of Whiteland . . . . (317) 535-5531
http://townofwhiteland.com

Knox County

Located in southwestern Indiana; bounded on the west by the Wabash River and the Illinois border, on the east by the West Fork of the White River, and on the south by the White River. Covers a land area of 516.031 square miles, a water area of 8.014 square miles, and is located in the Eastern Time Zone at 38.69° N. Lat., 87.42° W. Long. The county was founded in 1790. County seat is Vincennes.

Knox County is part of the Vincennes, IN Micropolitan Statistical Area. The entire metro area includes: Knox County, IN

Weather Station: Freelandville Elevation: 549 feet

	Jan	Feb	Mar	Apr	May	Jun	Jul	Aug	Sep	Oct	Nov	Dec
High	37	42	52	64	74	83	86	85	79	66	54	40
Low	22	25	33	43	54	63	66	64	56	45	36	25
Precip	2.8	2.7	3.7	4.2	5.7	3.8	4.8	3.2	3.5	3.9	4.1	3.3
Snow	4.5	3.5	1.5	tr	0.0	0.0	0.0	0.0	0.0	0.2	0.2	4.1

High and Low temperatures in degrees Fahrenheit; Precipitation and Snow in inches

Weather Station: Vincennes 5 NE Elevation: 450 feet

	Jan	Feb	Mar	Apr	May	Jun	Jul	Aug	Sep	Oct	Nov	Dec
High	38	43	54	65	75	84	88	87	81	69	55	42
Low	22	24	33	43	54	63	66	64	56	44	35	25
Precip	2.7	2.6	3.7	4.4	5.7	4.3	4.4	3.4	3.5	4.0	4.3	3.4
Snow	2.0	1.3	0.7	tr	0.0	0.0	0.0	0.0	0.0	0.0	0.1	3.0

High and Low temperatures in degrees Fahrenheit; Precipitation and Snow in inches

Population: 37,763; Growth (since 2000): -3.8%; Density: 73.2 persons per square mile; Race: 94.2% White, 3.1% Black/African American, 0.8% Asian, 0.1% American Indian/Alaska Native, 0.1% Native Hawaiian/Other Pacific Islander, 1.2% two or more races, 1.8% Hispanic of any race; Average household size: 2.36; Median age: 38.1; Age under 18: 21.2%; Age 65 and over: 16.9%; Males per 100 females: 101.2; Marriage status: 28.0% never married, 49.5% now married, 1.1% separated, 7.6%

widowed, 14.9% divorced; Foreign born: 1.3%; Speak English only: 98.0%; With disability: 18.0%; Veterans: 8.7%; Ancestry: 23.9% German, 11.4% Irish, 10.6% American, 8.0% English, 3.9% French
Religion: Six largest groups: 12.7% Catholicism, 12.0% Baptist, 7.1% Holiness, 4.6% Methodist/Pietist, 3.1% Presbyterian-Reformed, 2.6% Non-denominational Protestant
Economy: Unemployment rate: 3.5%; Leading industries: 17.9 % retail trade; 13.5 % other services (except public administration); 10.5 % health care and social assistance; Farms: 496 totaling 329,289 acres; Company size: 1 employs 1,000 or more persons, 2 employ 500 to 999 persons, 15 employ 100 to 499 persons, 865 employ less than 100 persons; Business ownership: 894 women-owned, n/a Black-owned, n/a Hispanic-owned, 71 Asian-owned, n/a American Indian/Alaska Native-owned
Employment: 11.2% management, business, and financial, 2.0% computer, engineering, and science, 6.5% education, legal, community service, arts, and media, 7.4% healthcare practitioners, 21.1% service, 19.3% sales and office, 10.4% natural resources, construction, and maintenance, 22.1% production, transportation, and material moving
Income: Per capita: $23,441; Median household: $44,837; Average household: $57,308; Households with income of $100,000 or more: 13.4%; Poverty rate: 15.6%
Educational Attainment: High school diploma or higher: 88.2%; Bachelor's degree or higher: 16.1%; Graduate/professional degree or higher: 5.8%
Housing: Homeownership rate: 64.0%; Median home value: $87,200; Median year structure built: 1960; Homeowner vacancy rate: 1.1%; Median selected monthly owner costs: $923 with a mortgage, $332 without a mortgage; Median gross rent: $663 per month; Rental vacancy rate: 8.1%
Vital Statistics: Birth rate: 111.2 per 10,000 population; Death rate: 104.8 per 10,000 population; Age-adjusted cancer mortality rate: 163.8 deaths per 100,000 population
Health Insurance: 90.1% have insurance; 68.2% have private insurance; 36.3% have public insurance; 9.9% do not have insurance; 4.1% of children under 18 do not have insurance
Health Care: Physicians: 21.8 per 10,000 population; Dentists: 4.8 per 10,000 population; Hospital beds: 50.9 per 10,000 population; Hospital admissions: 1,823.0 per 10,000 population
Air Quality Index (AQI): Percent of Days: 91.0% good, 9.0% moderate, 0.0% unhealthy for sensitive individuals, 0.0% unhealthy, 0.0% very unhealthy; Annual median: 36; Annual maximum: 100
Transportation: Commute: 94.1% car, 0.4% public transportation, 2.2% walk, 1.5% work from home; Mean travel time to work: 18.4 minutes
2016 Presidential Election: 71.4% Trump, 24.3% Clinton, 4.1% Johnson, 0.2% Stein
National and State Parks: George Rogers Clark National Historical Park; George Rogers Clark State Memorial; White Oak State Fishing Area
Additional Information Contacts
Knox Government . . . . (812) 885-2521
http://www.knoxcounty.in.gov

Knox County Communities

BICKNELL (city). Covers a land area of 1.346 square miles and a water area of 0 square miles. Located at 38.77° N. Lat; 87.31° W. Long. Elevation is 515 feet.
History: Coal mining began in Bicknell in 1875, and was responsible for the growth of the community. The town was founded by a Bicknell, an ancestor of Ernest P. Bicknell (1862-1930) who directed American Red Cross activities abroad.
Population: 2,964; Growth (since 2000): -12.3%; Density: 2,201.8 persons per square mile; Race: 96.1% White, 1.0% Black/African American, 0.0% Asian, 0.0% American Indian/Alaska Native, 0.0% Native Hawaiian/Other Pacific Islander, 2.0% Two or more races, 1.5% Hispanic of any race; Average household size: 2.52; Median age: 36.1; Age under 18: 25.9%; Age 65 and over: 14.8%; Males per 100 females: 94.9; Marriage status: 27.6% never married, 49.0% now married, 2.5% separated, 9.1% widowed, 14.3% divorced; Foreign born: 0.3%; Speak English only: 99.4%; With disability: 22.2%; Veterans: 10.7%; Ancestry: 19.3% American, 17.9% English, 15.9% German, 13.4% Irish, 2.7% French
Employment: 8.6% management, business, and financial, 1.5% computer, engineering, and science, 7.6% education, legal, community service, arts, and media, 6.0% healthcare practitioners, 23.1% service, 18.3% sales and office, 11.7% natural resources, construction, and maintenance, 23.2% production, transportation, and material moving
Income: Per capita: $18,035; Median household: $37,045; Average household: $43,931; Households with income of $100,000 or more: 7.7%; Poverty rate: 25.8%
Educational Attainment: High school diploma or higher: 83.1%; Bachelor's degree or higher: 8.0%; Graduate/professional degree or higher: 2.7%

School District(s)

North Knox School Corp (KG-12)
Enrollment: 1,452 . . . . (812) 735-4434
Housing: Homeownership rate: 61.2%; Median home value: $50,800; Median year structure built: Before 1940; Homeowner vacancy rate: 0.0%; Median selected monthly owner costs: $716 with a mortgage, $299 without a mortgage; Median gross rent: $590 per month; Rental vacancy rate: 14.2%
Health Insurance: 81.1% have insurance; 46.2% have private insurance; 45.3% have public insurance; 18.9% do not have insurance; 2.0% of children under 18 do not have insurance
Transportation: Commute: 90.9% car, 0.0% public transportation, 1.0% walk, 2.4% work from home; Mean travel time to work: 23.5 minutes
Additional Information Contacts
City of Bicknell. . . . . (812) 882-6440
http://www.knoxcountychamber.com

BRUCEVILLE (town). Covers a land area of 0.343 square miles and a water area of 0 square miles. Located at 38.76° N. Lat; 87.42° W. Long. Elevation is 554 feet.
History: Bruceville was first settled by Major William Bruce in 1805, who built a fort on his land. The town was founded in 1811. Major Bruce operated a tavern and inn here, and raised his family of 25 children. Abraham Lincoln was a guest of Bruce in 1844.
Population: 454; Growth (since 2000): -3.2%; Density: 1,324.1 persons per square mile; Race: 99.1% White, 0.0% Black/African American, 0.0% Asian, 0.0% American Indian/Alaska Native, 0.0% Native Hawaiian/Other Pacific Islander, 0.9% Two or more races, 0.0% Hispanic of any race; Average household size: 2.80; Median age: 37.6; Age under 18: 28.2%; Age 65 and over: 13.9%; Males per 100 females: 92.0; Marriage status: 21.1% never married, 60.3% now married, 2.3% separated, 8.2% widowed, 10.4% divorced; Foreign born: 0.4%; Speak English only: 98.8%; With disability: 23.6%; Veterans: 6.7%; Ancestry: 25.1% German, 14.8% American, 9.3% Irish, 8.8% English, 2.6% French
Employment: 6.0% management, business, and financial, 0.0% computer, engineering, and science, 3.2% education, legal, community service, arts, and media, 8.3% healthcare practitioners, 21.6% service, 18.3% sales and office, 15.6% natural resources, construction, and maintenance, 27.1% production, transportation, and material moving
Income: Per capita: $27,267; Median household: $52,500; Average household: $73,217; Households with income of $100,000 or more: 19.7%; Poverty rate: 2.9%
Educational Attainment: High school diploma or higher: 90.9%; Bachelor's degree or higher: 6.1%; Graduate/professional degree or higher: 1.0%

School District(s)

North Knox School Corp (KG-12)
Enrollment: 1,452 . . . . (812) 735-4434
Housing: Homeownership rate: 84.0%; Median home value: $71,200; Median year structure built: Before 1940; Homeowner vacancy rate: 0.0%; Median selected monthly owner costs: $834 with a mortgage, $417 without a mortgage; Median gross rent: $625 per month; Rental vacancy rate: 0.0%
Health Insurance: 89.0% have insurance; 70.9% have private insurance; 29.5% have public insurance; 11.0% do not have insurance; 4.6% of children under 18 do not have insurance
Transportation: Commute: 97.1% car, 1.9% public transportation, 1.0% walk, 0.0% work from home; Mean travel time to work: 30.7 minutes

DECKER (town). Covers a land area of 0.181 square miles and a water area of 0 square miles. Located at 38.52° N. Lat; 87.52° W. Long. Elevation is 466 feet.
Population: 289; Growth (since 2000): 2.1%; Density: 1,600.4 persons per square mile; Race: 100.0% White, 0.0% Black/African American, 0.0% Asian, 0.0% American Indian/Alaska Native, 0.0% Native Hawaiian/Other Pacific Islander, 0.0% Two or more races, 1.0% Hispanic of any race; Average household size: 2.89; Median age: 35.1; Age under 18: 24.9%; Age 65 and over: 14.5%; Males per 100 females: 109.2; Marriage status: 30.1% never married, 52.7% now married, 0.0% separated, 2.7%

widowed, 14.6% divorced; Foreign born: 1.0%; Speak English only: 98.9%; With disability: 13.1%; Veterans: 12.4%; Ancestry: 36.0% German, 13.1% Irish, 10.0% American, 5.5% Italian, 4.2% English
Employment: 5.9% management, business, and financial, 1.5% computer, engineering, and science, 0.0% education, legal, community service, arts, and media, 7.4% healthcare practitioners, 16.9% service, 9.6% sales and office, 15.4% natural resources, construction, and maintenance, 43.4% production, transportation, and material moving
Income: Per capita: $20,607; Median household: $60,625; Average household: $57,865; Households with income of $100,000 or more: 19.0%; Poverty rate: 17.7%
Educational Attainment: High school diploma or higher: 83.7%; Bachelor's degree or higher: 3.9%; Graduate/professional degree or higher: 0.5%
Housing: Homeownership rate: 73.0%; Median home value: $31,100; Median year structure built: 1956; Homeowner vacancy rate: 5.2%; Median selected monthly owner costs: $736 with a mortgage, $250 without a mortgage; Median gross rent: $631 per month; Rental vacancy rate: 0.0%
Health Insurance: 83.7% have insurance; 65.4% have private insurance; 33.2% have public insurance; 16.3% do not have insurance; 6.8% of children under 18 do not have insurance
Transportation: Commute: 100.0% car, 0.0% public transportation, 0.0% walk, 0.0% work from home; Mean travel time to work: 23.4 minutes

EDWARDSPORT (town). Covers a land area of 0.279 square miles and a water area of 0 square miles. Located at 38.81° N. Lat; 87.25° W. Long. Elevation is 499 feet.
History: Edwardsport developed as a docking place for the flatboats on the White River. Later, the Indiana Public Service Company used water power and coal from the nearby strip mines to generate electricity for many parts of southwestern Indiana.
Population: 341; Growth (since 2000): -6.1%; Density: 1,224.0 persons per square mile; Race: 100.0% White, 0.0% Black/African American, 0.0% Asian, 0.0% American Indian/Alaska Native, 0.0% Native Hawaiian/Other Pacific Islander, 0.0% Two or more races, 2.9% Hispanic of any race; Average household size: 2.37; Median age: 47.1; Age under 18: 19.9%; Age 65 and over: 17.3%; Males per 100 females: 103.4; Marriage status: 26.7% never married, 53.3% now married, 0.0% separated, 9.8% widowed, 10.2% divorced; Foreign born: 0.0%; Speak English only: 98.4%; With disability: 17.9%; Veterans: 11.0%; Ancestry: 21.1% German, 18.2% American, 15.2% French, 6.2% English, 5.9% Irish
Employment: 4.5% management, business, and financial, 7.8% computer, engineering, and science, 8.4% education, legal, community service, arts, and media, 5.8% healthcare practitioners, 12.3% service, 17.5% sales and office, 20.8% natural resources, construction, and maintenance, 22.7% production, transportation, and material moving
Income: Per capita: $21,246; Median household: $46,875; Average household: $49,299; Households with income of $100,000 or more: 6.3%; Poverty rate: 10.9%
Educational Attainment: High school diploma or higher: 81.3%; Bachelor's degree or higher: 8.7%; Graduate/professional degree or higher: 2.1%
Housing: Homeownership rate: 86.1%; Median home value: $44,500; Median year structure built: Before 1940; Homeowner vacancy rate: 3.9%; Median selected monthly owner costs: $710 with a mortgage, $315 without a mortgage; Median gross rent: $655 per month; Rental vacancy rate: 13.0%
Health Insurance: 95.0% have insurance; 76.5% have private insurance; 33.1% have public insurance; 5.0% do not have insurance; 0.0% of children under 18 do not have insurance
Transportation: Commute: 95.9% car, 0.0% public transportation, 0.0% walk, 4.1% work from home; Mean travel time to work: 25.3 minutes

EMISON (CDP). Covers a land area of 1.570 square miles and a water area of 0.009 square miles. Located at 38.80° N. Lat; 87.46° W. Long. Elevation is 463 feet.
Population: 172; Growth (since 2000): n/a; Density: 109.5 persons per square mile; Race: 100.0% White, 0.0% Black/African American, 0.0% Asian, 0.0% American Indian/Alaska Native, 0.0% Native Hawaiian/Other Pacific Islander, 0.0% Two or more races, 0.0% Hispanic of any race; Average household size: 2.23; Median age: 63.4; Age under 18: 14.0%; Age 65 and over: 39.0%; Males per 100 females: 102.6; Marriage status: 0.0% never married, 69.6% now married, 0.0% separated, 18.9% widowed, 11.5% divorced; Foreign born: 0.0%; Speak English only: 100.0%; With disability: 48.3%; Veterans: 12.2%; Ancestry: 41.9% American, 10.5% English, 9.9% German
Employment: 0.0% management, business, and financial, 0.0% computer, engineering, and science, 0.0% education, legal, community service, arts, and media, 0.0% healthcare practitioners, 21.0% service, 39.5% sales and office, 21.0% natural resources, construction, and maintenance, 18.5% production, transportation, and material moving
Income: Per capita: $20,949; Median household: n/a; Average household: $45,581; Households with income of $100,000 or more: n/a; Poverty rate: n/a
Educational Attainment: High school diploma or higher: 76.4%; Bachelor's degree or higher: n/a; Graduate/professional degree or higher: n/a
Housing: Homeownership rate: 100.0%; Median home value: $64,300; Median year structure built: 1977; Homeowner vacancy rate: 0.0%; Median selected monthly owner costs: n/a with a mortgage, $325 without a mortgage; Median gross rent: n/a per month; Rental vacancy rate: 0.0%
Health Insurance: 90.1% have insurance; 82.0% have private insurance; 39.0% have public insurance; 9.9% do not have insurance; 0.0% of children under 18 do not have insurance
Transportation: Commute: 100.0% car, 0.0% public transportation, 0.0% walk, 0.0% work from home; Mean travel time to work: 0.0 minutes

FREELANDVILLE (CDP). Covers a land area of 5.570 square miles and a water area of 0 square miles. Located at 38.87° N. Lat; 87.31° W. Long. Elevation is 568 feet.
Population: 837; Growth (since 2000): n/a; Density: 150.3 persons per square mile; Race: 96.7% White, 0.0% Black/African American, 0.0% Asian, 0.0% American Indian/Alaska Native, 0.0% Native Hawaiian/Other Pacific Islander, 3.3% Two or more races, 0.0% Hispanic of any race; Average household size: 2.96; Median age: 43.6; Age under 18: 22.9%; Age 65 and over: 28.3%; Males per 100 females: 91.9; Marriage status: 26.5% never married, 54.9% now married, 0.0% separated, 11.2% widowed, 7.3% divorced; Foreign born: 0.0%; Speak English only: 100.0%; With disability: 19.0%; Veterans: 11.5%; Ancestry: 26.9% German, 13.3% English, 9.0% Irish, 4.3% French, 2.9% American
Employment: 8.1% management, business, and financial, 0.0% computer, engineering, and science, 2.0% education, legal, community service, arts, and media, 10.4% healthcare practitioners, 55.7% service, 2.2% sales and office, 14.6% natural resources, construction, and maintenance, 7.0% production, transportation, and material moving
Income: Per capita: $21,074; Median household: $45,643; Average household: $60,534; Households with income of $100,000 or more: 18.9%; Poverty rate: 6.8%
Educational Attainment: High school diploma or higher: 96.2%; Bachelor's degree or higher: 10.7%; Graduate/professional degree or higher: 9.5%
Housing: Homeownership rate: 77.4%; Median home value: $53,400; Median year structure built: 1945; Homeowner vacancy rate: 0.0%; Median selected monthly owner costs: $819 with a mortgage, $252 without a mortgage; Median gross rent: n/a per month; Rental vacancy rate: 0.0%
Health Insurance: 93.1% have insurance; 76.2% have private insurance; 36.8% have public insurance; 6.9% do not have insurance; 5.7% of children under 18 do not have insurance
Transportation: Commute: 100.0% car, 0.0% public transportation, 0.0% walk, 0.0% work from home; Mean travel time to work: 31.1 minutes

MONROE CITY (town). Covers a land area of 0.269 square miles and a water area of 0 square miles. Located at 38.61° N. Lat; 87.35° W. Long. Elevation is 522 feet.
Population: 607; Growth (since 2000): 10.8%; Density: 2,254.2 persons per square mile; Race: 99.0% White, 0.0% Black/African American, 0.0% Asian, 0.0% American Indian/Alaska Native, 0.0% Native Hawaiian/Other Pacific Islander, 1.0% Two or more races, 0.7% Hispanic of any race; Average household size: 2.86; Median age: 27.8; Age under 18: 35.7%; Age 65 and over: 11.4%; Males per 100 females: 89.9; Marriage status: 17.0% never married, 68.0% now married, 0.0% separated, 6.1% widowed, 9.0% divorced; Foreign born: 0.0%; Speak English only: 100.0%; With disability: 17.6%; Veterans: 5.9%; Ancestry: 22.2% German, 11.4% American, 8.4% Irish, 7.1% English, 6.9% European
Employment: 5.1% management, business, and financial, 2.9% computer, engineering, and science, 7.0% education, legal, community service, arts, and media, 19.8% healthcare practitioners, 12.1% service, 15.4% sales and office, 19.8% natural resources, construction, and maintenance, 17.9% production, transportation, and material moving

Income: Per capita: $21,231; Median household: $54,800; Average household: $60,342; Households with income of $100,000 or more: 9.9%; Poverty rate: 14.7%
Educational Attainment: High school diploma or higher: 95.3%; Bachelor's degree or higher: 11.8%; Graduate/professional degree or higher: 3.8%
Housing: Homeownership rate: 74.5%; Median home value: $71,000; Median year structure built: 1956; Homeowner vacancy rate: 0.0%; Median selected monthly owner costs: $672 with a mortgage, $331 without a mortgage; Median gross rent: $743 per month; Rental vacancy rate: 0.0%
Health Insurance: 94.4% have insurance; 75.5% have private insurance; 29.2% have public insurance; 5.6% do not have insurance; 0.0% of children under 18 do not have insurance
Transportation: Commute: 99.3% car, 0.0% public transportation, 0.0% walk, 0.7% work from home; Mean travel time to work: 26.9 minutes

OAKTOWN (town). Covers a land area of 0.272 square miles and a water area of 0 square miles. Located at 38.87° N. Lat; 87.44° W. Long. Elevation is 472 feet.
History: Laid out 1867.
Population: 694; Growth (since 2000): 9.6%; Density: 2,549.0 persons per square mile; Race: 97.7% White, 0.0% Black/African American, 0.3% Asian, 0.0% American Indian/Alaska Native, 0.0% Native Hawaiian/Other Pacific Islander, 1.7% Two or more races, 3.9% Hispanic of any race; Average household size: 2.76; Median age: 37.6; Age under 18: 24.9%; Age 65 and over: 16.4%; Males per 100 females: 82.0; Marriage status: 24.9% never married, 52.4% now married, 0.5% separated, 9.2% widowed, 13.5% divorced; Foreign born: 0.6%; Speak English only: 99.4%; With disability: 14.4%; Veterans: 13.6%; Ancestry: 26.4% German, 18.3% Irish, 8.6% American, 5.6% Welsh, 5.0% Dutch
Employment: 5.9% management, business, and financial, 1.1% computer, engineering, and science, 7.3% education, legal, community service, arts, and media, 9.0% healthcare practitioners, 25.2% service, 14.3% sales and office, 20.4% natural resources, construction, and maintenance, 16.8% production, transportation, and material moving
Income: Per capita: $20,588; Median household: $46,429; Average household: $55,415; Households with income of $100,000 or more: 11.1%; Poverty rate: 8.1%
Educational Attainment: High school diploma or higher: 92.4%; Bachelor's degree or higher: 5.5%; Graduate/professional degree or higher: 3.2%
Housing: Homeownership rate: 66.9%; Median home value: $48,900; Median year structure built: 1952; Homeowner vacancy rate: 7.4%; Median selected monthly owner costs: $891 with a mortgage, $339 without a mortgage; Median gross rent: $484 per month; Rental vacancy rate: 13.0%
Health Insurance: 81.6% have insurance; 54.6% have private insurance; 34.1% have public insurance; 18.4% do not have insurance; 24.3% of children under 18 do not have insurance
Transportation: Commute: 89.4% car, 0.0% public transportation, 7.8% walk, 2.8% work from home; Mean travel time to work: 24.7 minutes

RAGSDALE (CDP). Covers a land area of 2.228 square miles and a water area of 0 square miles. Located at 38.75° N. Lat; 87.32° W. Long. Elevation is 577 feet.
Population: 236; Growth (since 2000): n/a; Density: 105.9 persons per square mile; Race: 100.0% White, 0.0% Black/African American, 0.0% Asian, 0.0% American Indian/Alaska Native, 0.0% Native Hawaiian/Other Pacific Islander, 0.0% Two or more races, 0.0% Hispanic of any race; Average household size: 2.46; Median age: 60.2; Age under 18: 15.3%; Age 65 and over: 30.9%; Males per 100 females: 101.6; Marriage status: 23.0% never married, 35.0% now married, 0.0% separated, 10.5% widowed, 31.5% divorced; Foreign born: 4.2%; Speak English only: 100.0%; With disability: 54.7%; Veterans: 0.0%; Ancestry: 29.7% Norwegian, 3.0% Welsh
Employment: 0.0% management, business, and financial, 0.0% computer, engineering, and science, 30.6% education, legal, community service, arts, and media, 0.0% healthcare practitioners, 0.0% service, 36.4% sales and office, 9.1% natural resources, construction, and maintenance, 24.0% production, transportation, and material moving
Income: Per capita: $20,852; Median household: n/a; Average household: $48,642; Households with income of $100,000 or more: n/a; Poverty rate: 14.4%
Educational Attainment: High school diploma or higher: 91.1%; Bachelor's degree or higher: 12.0%; Graduate/professional degree or higher: 12.0%
Housing: Homeownership rate: 100.0%; Median home value: n/a; Median year structure built: Before 1940; Homeowner vacancy rate: 0.0%; Median selected monthly owner costs: n/a with a mortgage, $226 without a mortgage; Median gross rent: n/a per month; Rental vacancy rate: 0.0%
Health Insurance: 96.2% have insurance; 73.3% have private insurance; 51.7% have public insurance; 3.8% do not have insurance; 0.0% of children under 18 do not have insurance
Transportation: Commute: 100.0% car, 0.0% public transportation, 0.0% walk, 0.0% work from home; Mean travel time to work: 20.7 minutes

SANDBORN (town). Covers a land area of 0.391 square miles and a water area of 0 square miles. Located at 38.90° N. Lat; 87.18° W. Long. Elevation is 479 feet.
Population: 374; Growth (since 2000): -17.1%; Density: 955.7 persons per square mile; Race: 99.5% White, 0.0% Black/African American, 0.5% Asian, 0.0% American Indian/Alaska Native, 0.0% Native Hawaiian/Other Pacific Islander, 0.0% Two or more races, 0.0% Hispanic of any race; Average household size: 2.21; Median age: 44.9; Age under 18: 20.1%; Age 65 and over: 25.4%; Males per 100 females: 92.1; Marriage status: 24.1% never married, 46.9% now married, 0.6% separated, 9.6% widowed, 19.3% divorced; Foreign born: 0.5%; Speak English only: 99.4%; With disability: 11.0%; Veterans: 4.3%; Ancestry: 26.7% German, 10.7% English, 9.6% Irish, 8.8% American, 2.4% Dutch
Employment: 11.0% management, business, and financial, 1.6% computer, engineering, and science, 12.6% education, legal, community service, arts, and media, 11.5% healthcare practitioners, 14.8% service, 19.2% sales and office, 12.1% natural resources, construction, and maintenance, 17.0% production, transportation, and material moving
Income: Per capita: $26,727; Median household: $44,271; Average household: $56,617; Households with income of $100,000 or more: 10.1%; Poverty rate: 4.3%
Educational Attainment: High school diploma or higher: 85.6%; Bachelor's degree or higher: 17.7%; Graduate/professional degree or higher: 1.4%
Housing: Homeownership rate: 91.7%; Median home value: $71,500; Median year structure built: 1948; Homeowner vacancy rate: 6.6%; Median selected monthly owner costs: $791 with a mortgage, $304 without a mortgage; Median gross rent: $810 per month; Rental vacancy rate: 0.0%
Health Insurance: 89.8% have insurance; 65.5% have private insurance; 36.6% have public insurance; 10.2% do not have insurance; 14.5% of children under 18 do not have insurance
Transportation: Commute: 95.6% car, 0.0% public transportation, 2.2% walk, 0.0% work from home; Mean travel time to work: 30.1 minutes

VINCENNES (city). County seat. Covers a land area of 7.412 square miles and a water area of 0.068 square miles. Located at 38.68° N. Lat; 87.51° W. Long. Elevation is 420 feet.
History: Vicennes had its beginnings about 1732, when Francois Morgane de Vincennes built a fort here. The French flag flew over Vincennes until 1763, when it was ceded to Great Britain by the Treaty of Paris. The American flag replaced the Union Jack in 1779 when George Rogers Clark captured Fort Sackville. Vincennes was the first seat of government for the Indiana Territory created in 1800, with William Henry Harrison as governor.
Population: 17,944; Growth (since 2000): -4.0%; Density: 2,421.0 persons per square mile; Race: 91.0% White, 5.9% Black/African American, 0.9% Asian, 0.1% American Indian/Alaska Native, 0.1% Native Hawaiian/Other Pacific Islander, 1.4% Two or more races, 2.4% Hispanic of any race; Average household size: 2.21; Median age: 34.0; Age under 18: 19.1%; Age 65 and over: 15.3%; Males per 100 females: 101.1; Marriage status: 33.2% never married, 42.2% now married, 1.2% separated, 8.0% widowed, 16.6% divorced; Foreign born: 1.6%; Speak English only: 97.5%; With disability: 20.3%; Veterans: 8.2%; Ancestry: 21.5% German, 12.7% Irish, 8.0% American, 6.0% English, 4.0% French
Employment: 9.8% management, business, and financial, 1.3% computer, engineering, and science, 7.1% education, legal, community service, arts, and media, 5.7% healthcare practitioners, 25.6% service, 18.1% sales and office, 5.1% natural resources, construction, and maintenance, 27.3% production, transportation, and material moving
Income: Per capita: $19,529; Median household: $36,724; Average household: $46,187; Households with income of $100,000 or more: 7.4%; Poverty rate: 22.9%
Educational Attainment: High school diploma or higher: 83.7%; Bachelor's degree or higher: 15.1%; Graduate/professional degree or higher: 6.4%

School District(s)

South Knox School Corp (KG-12)
Enrollment: 1,030 . . . . (812) 726-4440
Twin Rivers Career & Tech Ed Area (09-12)
Enrollment: n/a . . . . (812) 882-0801
Vincennes Community School Corp (PK-12)
Enrollment: 2,810 . . . . (812) 882-4844

Four-year College(s)

Vincennes University (Public)
Enrollment: 18,914 . . . . (812) 888-8888
Tuition: In-state $5,737; Out-of-state $13,567

Vocational/Technical School(s)

Vincennes Beauty College (Private, For-profit)
Enrollment: 29. . . . . (812) 882-1086
Tuition: $11,075

Housing: Homeownership rate: 49.8%; Median home value: $73,700; Median year structure built: 1957; Homeowner vacancy rate: 1.9%; Median selected monthly owner costs: $808 with a mortgage, $320 without a mortgage; Median gross rent: $673 per month; Rental vacancy rate: 9.6%
Health Insurance: 89.4% have insurance; 62.7% have private insurance; 40.7% have public insurance; 10.6% do not have insurance; 3.5% of children under 18 do not have insurance
Hospitals: Good Samaritan Hospital
Safety: Violent crime rate: 13.4 per 10,000 population; Property crime rate: 572.6 per 10,000 population
Newspapers: Vincennes Sun-Commercial (daily circulation 9,500)
Transportation: Commute: 91.7% car, 0.4% public transportation, 4.2% walk, 0.9% work from home; Mean travel time to work: 14.5 minutes
Additional Information Contacts
City of Vincennes . . . . (812) 882-6426
http://www.vincennes.org

WESTPHALIA (CDP). Covers a land area of 2.062 square miles and a water area of 0 square miles. Located at 38.87° N. Lat; 87.23° W. Long. Elevation is 466 feet.
Population: 49; Growth (since 2000): n/a; Density: 23.8 persons per square mile; Race: 100.0% White, 0.0% Black/African American, 0.0% Asian, 0.0% American Indian/Alaska Native, 0.0% Native Hawaiian/Other Pacific Islander, 0.0% Two or more races, 0.0% Hispanic of any race; Average household size: 1.40; Median age: 60.4; Age under 18: 14.3%; Age 65 and over: 40.8%; Males per 100 females: 88.8; Marriage status: 40.8% never married, 44.9% now married, 16.3% separated, 14.3% widowed, 0.0% divorced; Foreign born: 0.0%; Speak English only: 100.0%; With disability: 30.6%; Veterans: 0.0%; Ancestry: 26.5% German, 14.3% European, 14.3% Scottish
Employment: 0.0% management, business, and financial, 0.0% computer, engineering, and science, 0.0% education, legal, community service, arts, and media, 0.0% healthcare practitioners, 0.0% service, 100.0% sales and office, 0.0% natural resources, construction, and maintenance, 0.0% production, transportation, and material moving
Income: Per capita: $17,112; Median household: n/a; Average household: n/a; Households with income of $100,000 or more: n/a; Poverty rate: 44.9%
Educational Attainment: High school diploma or higher: 81.0%; Bachelor's degree or higher: 47.6%; Graduate/professional degree or higher: n/a
Housing: Homeownership rate: 80.0%; Median home value: n/a; Median year structure built: Before 1940; Homeowner vacancy rate: 0.0%; Median selected monthly owner costs: n/a with a mortgage, n/a without a mortgage; Median gross rent: n/a per month; Rental vacancy rate: 0.0%
Health Insurance: 100.0% have insurance; 55.1% have private insurance; 71.4% have public insurance; 0.0% do not have insurance; 0.0% of children under 18 do not have insurance
Transportation: Commute: 100.0% car, 0.0% public transportation, 0.0% walk, 0.0% work from home; Mean travel time to work: 0.0 minutes

---

WHEATLAND (town). Covers a land area of 0.410 square miles and a water area of 0 square miles. Located at 38.66° N. Lat; 87.31° W. Long. Elevation is 492 feet.
History: Laid out 1858.
Population: 428; Growth (since 2000): -15.1%; Density: 1,045.0 persons per square mile; Race: 98.6% White, 0.0% Black/African American, 1.2% Asian, 0.0% American Indian/Alaska Native, 0.0% Native Hawaiian/Other Pacific Islander, 0.2% Two or more races, 2.8% Hispanic of any race; Average household size: 2.33; Median age: 38.3; Age under 18: 21.0%; Age 65 and over: 16.8%; Males per 100 females: 98.3; Marriage status: 32.8% never married, 43.8% now married, 0.0% separated, 5.6% widowed, 17.8% divorced; Foreign born: 0.7%; Speak English only: 100.0%; With disability: 17.8%; Veterans: 7.7%; Ancestry: 24.5% German, 15.7% Irish, 11.9% English, 8.4% American, 3.3% French
Employment: 11.5% management, business, and financial, 1.0% computer, engineering, and science, 2.6% education, legal, community service, arts, and media, 10.4% healthcare practitioners, 21.4% service, 16.1% sales and office, 9.9% natural resources, construction, and maintenance, 27.1% production, transportation, and material moving
Income: Per capita: $21,195; Median household: $40,938; Average household: $48,624; Households with income of $100,000 or more: 5.4%; Poverty rate: 14.4%
Educational Attainment: High school diploma or higher: 88.9%; Bachelor's degree or higher: 8.0%; Graduate/professional degree or higher: 1.4%
Housing: Homeownership rate: 69.6%; Median home value: $61,400; Median year structure built: 1943; Homeowner vacancy rate: 0.0%; Median selected monthly owner costs: $721 with a mortgage, $282 without a mortgage; Median gross rent: $575 per month; Rental vacancy rate: 0.0%
Health Insurance: 84.8% have insurance; 51.9% have private insurance; 42.3% have public insurance; 15.2% do not have insurance; 4.3% of children under 18 do not have insurance
Transportation: Commute: 99.5% car, 0.5% public transportation, 0.0% walk, 0.0% work from home; Mean travel time to work: 24.0 minutes

Kosciusko County

Located in northern Indiana; drained by the Tippecanoe and Eel Rivers; includes Wawasee and Winona Lakes. Covers a land area of 531.381 square miles, a water area of 23.012 square miles, and is located in the Eastern Time Zone at 41.24° N. Lat., 85.86° W. Long. The county was founded in 1835. County seat is Warsaw.

Kosciusko County is part of the Warsaw, IN Micropolitan Statistical Area. The entire metro area includes: Kosciusko County, IN

Weather Station: Warsaw Elevation: 810 feet

	Jan	Feb	Mar	Apr	May	Jun	Jul	Aug	Sep	Oct	Nov	Dec
High	32	36	47	60	71	80	83	81	75	62	49	36
Low	18	20	29	39	49	59	63	61	53	42	33	22
Precip	2.1	1.7	2.2	3.6	4.2	4.3	4.1	4.4	3.1	3.3	2.9	2.6
Snow	na	na	1.7	0.3	0.0	0.0	0.0	0.0	0.0	tr	0.3	4.3

High and Low temperatures in degrees Fahrenheit; Precipitation and Snow in inches

Population: 78,720; Growth (since 2000): 6.3%; Density: 148.1 persons per square mile; Race: 93.9% White, 0.8% Black/African American, 1.0% Asian, 0.3% American Indian/Alaska Native, 0.0% Native Hawaiian/Other Pacific Islander, 1.8% two or more races, 7.9% Hispanic of any race; Average household size: 2.55; Median age: 38.0; Age under 18: 24.4%; Age 65 and over: 15.3%; Males per 100 females: 98.9; Marriage status: 24.3% never married, 58.4% now married, 1.3% separated, 5.8% widowed, 11.5% divorced; Foreign born: 4.1%; Speak English only: 90.1%; With disability: 13.9%; Veterans: 7.9%; Ancestry: 24.8% German, 12.0% American, 10.4% Irish, 8.8% English, 2.6% Dutch
Religion: Six largest groups: 8.4% Non-denominational Protestant, 6.2% Methodist/Pietist, 5.6% Catholicism, 4.8% European Free-Church, 2.9% Holiness, 1.6% Baptist
Economy: Unemployment rate: 2.9%; Leading industries: 14.8 % retail trade; 12.2 % other services (except public administration); 10.6 % construction; Farms: 1,247 totaling 254,847 acres; Company size: 3 employ 1,000 or more persons, 6 employ 500 to 999 persons, 47 employ 100 to 499 persons, 1,894 employ less than 100 persons; Business ownership: 1,946 women-owned, n/a Black-owned, 94 Hispanic-owned, 71 Asian-owned, n/a American Indian/Alaska Native-owned
Employment: 11.2% management, business, and financial, 4.3% computer, engineering, and science, 8.5% education, legal, community service, arts, and media, 4.5% healthcare practitioners, 13.3% service, 21.1% sales and office, 8.9% natural resources, construction, and maintenance, 28.1% production, transportation, and material moving
Income: Per capita: $27,884; Median household: $57,190; Average household: $71,791; Households with income of $100,000 or more: 20.0%; Poverty rate: 11.2%
Educational Attainment: High school diploma or higher: 84.8%; Bachelor's degree or higher: 22.3%; Graduate/professional degree or higher: 7.8%

Housing: Homeownership rate: 74.8%; Median home value: $142,700; Median year structure built: 1978; Homeowner vacancy rate: 1.4%; Median selected monthly owner costs: $1,068 with a mortgage, $360 without a mortgage; Median gross rent: $733 per month; Rental vacancy rate: 5.1%
Vital Statistics: Birth rate: 128.7 per 10,000 population; Death rate: 87.6 per 10,000 population; Age-adjusted cancer mortality rate: 160.9 deaths per 100,000 population
Health Insurance: 88.2% have insurance; 71.0% have private insurance; 28.9% have public insurance; 11.8% do not have insurance; 10.5% of children under 18 do not have insurance
Health Care: Physicians: 9.1 per 10,000 population; Dentists: 3.2 per 10,000 population; Hospital beds: 11.1 per 10,000 population; Hospital admissions: 593.5 per 10,000 population
Transportation: Commute: 92.4% car, 0.1% public transportation, 1.7% walk, 3.6% work from home; Mean travel time to work: 19.7 minutes
2016 Presidential Election: 73.8% Trump, 19.5% Clinton, 5.2% Johnson, 0.2% Stein
National and State Parks: Tri-County State Fish and Game Area
Additional Information Contacts
Kosciusko Government . . . . (574) 372-2329
http://www.kcgov.com

Kosciusko County Communities

ATWOOD (unincorporated postal area)
ZCTA: 46502
Covers a land area of 0.056 square miles and a water area of 0 square miles. Located at 41.26° N. Lat; 85.98° W. Long. Elevation is 823 feet.
Population: 19; Growth (since 2000): -69.4%; Density: 338.2 persons per square mile; Race: 100.0% White, 0.0% Black/African American, 0.0% Asian, 0.0% American Indian/Alaska Native, 0.0% Native Hawaiian/Other Pacific Islander, 0.0% Two or more races, 0.0% Hispanic of any race; Average household size: 2.11; Median age: n/a; Age under 18: 0.0%; Age 65 and over: 0.0%; Males per 100 females: 94.9; Marriage status: 0.0% never married, 100.0% now married, 0.0% separated, 0.0% widowed, 0.0% divorced; Foreign born: 0.0%; Speak English only: 100.0%; With disability: 0.0%; Veterans: 0.0%; Ancestry: 100.0% German
Employment: 0.0% management, business, and financial, 0.0% computer, engineering, and science, 0.0% education, legal, community service, arts, and media, 0.0% healthcare practitioners, 0.0% service, 47.4% sales and office, 0.0% natural resources, construction, and maintenance, 52.6% production, transportation, and material moving
Income: Per capita: n/a; Median household: n/a; Average household: n/a; Households with income of $100,000 or more: n/a; Poverty rate: n/a
Educational Attainment: High school diploma or higher: 100.0%; Bachelor's degree or higher: n/a; Graduate/professional degree or higher: n/a
Housing: Homeownership rate: 100.0%; Median home value: n/a; Median year structure built: n/a; Homeowner vacancy rate: 0.0%; Median selected monthly owner costs: $0 with a mortgage, $0 without a mortgage; Median gross rent: n/a per month; Rental vacancy rate: 0.0%
Health Insurance: 100.0% have insurance; 100.0% have private insurance; 0.0% have public insurance; 0.0% do not have insurance; 0.0% of children under 18 do not have insurance
Transportation: Commute: 100.0% car, 0.0% public transportation, 0.0% walk, 0.0% work from home; Mean travel time to work: 0.0 minutes

BURKET (town). Covers a land area of 0.071 square miles and a water area of 0 square miles. Located at 41.15° N. Lat; 85.97° W. Long. Elevation is 863 feet.
Population: 166; Growth (since 2000): -14.9%; Density: 2,327.3 persons per square mile; Race: 100.0% White, 0.0% Black/African American, 0.0% Asian, 0.0% American Indian/Alaska Native, 0.0% Native Hawaiian/Other Pacific Islander, 0.0% Two or more races, 0.0% Hispanic of any race; Average household size: 2.59; Median age: 45.8; Age under 18: 24.7%; Age 65 and over: 16.3%; Males per 100 females: 80.6; Marriage status: 20.1% never married, 48.2% now married, 0.0% separated, 12.2% widowed, 19.4% divorced; Foreign born: 1.2%; Speak English only: 100.0%; With disability: 30.7%; Veterans: 13.6%; Ancestry: 31.9% American, 15.7% German, 9.6% English, 8.4% Irish, 3.0% Scotch-Irish
Employment: 12.5% management, business, and financial, 0.0% computer, engineering, and science, 8.9% education, legal, community service, arts, and media, 1.8% healthcare practitioners, 10.7% service, 5.4% sales and office, 0.0% natural resources, construction, and maintenance, 60.7% production, transportation, and material moving
Income: Per capita: $16,120; Median household: $36,250; Average household: $39,620; Households with income of $100,000 or more: 1.6%; Poverty rate: 31.3%
Educational Attainment: High school diploma or higher: 82.4%; Bachelor's degree or higher: n/a; Graduate/professional degree or higher: n/a
Housing: Homeownership rate: 90.6%; Median home value: $75,000; Median year structure built: Before 1940; Homeowner vacancy rate: 0.0%; Median selected monthly owner costs: $754 with a mortgage, $281 without a mortgage; Median gross rent: n/a per month; Rental vacancy rate: 40.0%
Health Insurance: 86.7% have insurance; 54.8% have private insurance; 46.4% have public insurance; 13.3% do not have insurance; 0.0% of children under 18 do not have insurance
Transportation: Commute: 83.9% car, 0.0% public transportation, 16.1% walk, 0.0% work from home; Mean travel time to work: 21.2 minutes

CLAYPOOL (town). Covers a land area of 0.244 square miles and a water area of 0.008 square miles. Located at 41.13° N. Lat; 85.88° W. Long. Elevation is 889 feet.
Population: 479; Growth (since 2000): 54.0%; Density: 1,965.3 persons per square mile; Race: 93.5% White, 0.8% Black/African American, 0.0% Asian, 1.9% American Indian/Alaska Native, 0.0% Native Hawaiian/Other Pacific Islander, 3.8% Two or more races, 6.1% Hispanic of any race; Average household size: 2.92; Median age: 34.8; Age under 18: 29.2%; Age 65 and over: 7.7%; Males per 100 females: 101.4; Marriage status: 30.7% never married, 50.1% now married, 4.2% separated, 5.2% widowed, 13.9% divorced; Foreign born: 1.0%; Speak English only: 97.8%; With disability: 21.1%; Veterans: 5.9%; Ancestry: 27.1% German, 17.7% Irish, 6.7% American, 4.6% European, 3.8% English
Employment: 4.6% management, business, and financial, 3.6% computer, engineering, and science, 2.0% education, legal, community service, arts, and media, 1.0% healthcare practitioners, 26.5% service, 13.8% sales and office, 7.1% natural resources, construction, and maintenance, 41.3% production, transportation, and material moving
Income: Per capita: $14,255; Median household: $35,000; Average household: $41,318; Households with income of $100,000 or more: 3.6%; Poverty rate: 24.1%
Educational Attainment: High school diploma or higher: 66.2%; Bachelor's degree or higher: 2.7%; Graduate/professional degree or higher: 0.3%

School District(s)

Warsaw Community Schools (PK-12)
Enrollment: 6,921 . . . . (574) 371-5098
Housing: Homeownership rate: 61.6%; Median home value: $71,300; Median year structure built: 1951; Homeowner vacancy rate: 0.0%; Median selected monthly owner costs: $829 with a mortgage, $438 without a mortgage; Median gross rent: $552 per month; Rental vacancy rate: 11.3%
Health Insurance: 80.4% have insurance; 48.9% have private insurance; 41.8% have public insurance; 19.6% do not have insurance; 21.7% of children under 18 do not have insurance
Transportation: Commute: 96.2% car, 0.0% public transportation, 2.7% walk, 1.1% work from home; Mean travel time to work: 25.5 minutes

ETNA GREEN (town). Covers a land area of 0.512 square miles and a water area of <.001 square miles. Located at 41.28° N. Lat; 86.04° W. Long. Elevation is 817 feet.
Population: 575; Growth (since 2000): -13.3%; Density: 1,124.1 persons per square mile; Race: 98.6% White, 0.3% Black/African American, 0.0% Asian, 0.0% American Indian/Alaska Native, 0.0% Native Hawaiian/Other Pacific Islander, 0.5% Two or more races, 3.1% Hispanic of any race; Average household size: 2.71; Median age: 37.9; Age under 18: 23.7%; Age 65 and over: 16.3%; Males per 100 females: 99.3; Marriage status: 25.7% never married, 53.6% now married, 0.4% separated, 5.6% widowed, 15.1% divorced; Foreign born: 1.7%; Speak English only: 98.3%; With disability: 17.0%; Veterans: 9.6%; Ancestry: 27.1% German, 13.7% Irish, 10.4% American, 5.2% English, 5.0% French
Employment: 3.6% management, business, and financial, 0.0% computer, engineering, and science, 3.3% education, legal, community service, arts, and media, 7.7% healthcare practitioners, 13.5% service, 20.4% sales and office, 14.2% natural resources, construction, and maintenance, 37.2% production, transportation, and material moving

Income: Per capita: $20,039; Median household: $50,625; Average household: $53,906; Households with income of $100,000 or more: 3.8%; Poverty rate: 9.2%
Educational Attainment: High school diploma or higher: 85.4%; Bachelor's degree or higher: 12.1%; Graduate/professional degree or higher: 0.5%
Housing: Homeownership rate: 80.3%; Median home value: $76,900; Median year structure built: 1958; Homeowner vacancy rate: 4.0%; Median selected monthly owner costs: $850 with a mortgage, $400 without a mortgage; Median gross rent: $664 per month; Rental vacancy rate: 0.0%
Health Insurance: 86.6% have insurance; 60.7% have private insurance; 38.3% have public insurance; 13.4% do not have insurance; 11.5% of children under 18 do not have insurance
Transportation: Commute: 96.3% car, 1.1% public transportation, 0.7% walk, 0.7% work from home; Mean travel time to work: 20.7 minutes

LEESBURG (town). Covers a land area of 0.260 square miles and a water area of 0 square miles. Located at 41.33° N. Lat; 85.85° W. Long. Elevation is 856 feet.
History: Laid out 1835.
Population: 760; Growth (since 2000): 21.6%; Density: 2,918.0 persons per square mile; Race: 91.7% White, 3.8% Black/African American, 0.0% Asian, 0.0% American Indian/Alaska Native, 0.0% Native Hawaiian/Other Pacific Islander, 0.7% Two or more races, 5.9% Hispanic of any race; Average household size: 3.10; Median age: 38.1; Age under 18: 24.1%; Age 65 and over: 8.0%; Males per 100 females: 96.8; Marriage status: 26.7% never married, 61.1% now married, 2.1% separated, 6.6% widowed, 5.6% divorced; Foreign born: 1.8%; Speak English only: 95.3%; With disability: 13.0%; Veterans: 3.1%; Ancestry: 26.3% German, 9.9% Italian, 8.0% American, 7.9% English, 6.6% Irish
Employment: 5.7% management, business, and financial, 0.9% computer, engineering, and science, 6.6% education, legal, community service, arts, and media, 3.6% healthcare practitioners, 20.7% service, 22.3% sales and office, 8.4% natural resources, construction, and maintenance, 31.8% production, transportation, and material moving
Income: Per capita: $24,621; Median household: $67,969; Average household: $76,064; Households with income of $100,000 or more: 25.7%; Poverty rate: 11.4%
Educational Attainment: High school diploma or higher: 87.6%; Bachelor's degree or higher: 10.9%; Graduate/professional degree or higher: 1.6%

School District(s)

Warsaw Community Schools (PK-12)
Enrollment: 6,921 . . . . (574) 371-5098

Housing: Homeownership rate: 87.3%; Median home value: $110,900; Median year structure built: 1958; Homeowner vacancy rate: 0.0%; Median selected monthly owner costs: $945 with a mortgage, $325 without a mortgage; Median gross rent: $1,065 per month; Rental vacancy rate: 0.0%
Health Insurance: 90.5% have insurance; 77.1% have private insurance; 20.1% have public insurance; 9.5% do not have insurance; 7.1% of children under 18 do not have insurance
Transportation: Commute: 91.1% car, 0.0% public transportation, 2.1% walk, 6.8% work from home; Mean travel time to work: 20.9 minutes

MENTONE (town). Covers a land area of 0.583 square miles and a water area of 0.012 square miles. Located at 41.17° N. Lat; 86.04° W. Long. Elevation is 840 feet.
Population: 1,299; Growth (since 2000): 44.7%; Density: 2,226.5 persons per square mile; Race: 95.7% White, 0.8% Black/African American, 0.2% Asian, 0.2% American Indian/Alaska Native, 0.0% Native Hawaiian/Other Pacific Islander, 1.5% Two or more races, 1.6% Hispanic of any race; Average household size: 2.85; Median age: 31.7; Age under 18: 30.3%; Age 65 and over: 9.9%; Males per 100 females: 98.6; Marriage status: 28.1% never married, 53.0% now married, 1.3% separated, 4.9% widowed, 14.0% divorced; Foreign born: 0.7%; Speak English only: 97.9%; With disability: 19.8%; Veterans: 5.5%; Ancestry: 31.4% German, 13.7% Irish, 13.4% American, 5.8% Scottish, 5.2% Italian
Employment: 4.8% management, business, and financial, 2.9% computer, engineering, and science, 7.3% education, legal, community service, arts, and media, 4.0% healthcare practitioners, 21.1% service, 16.6% sales and office, 9.0% natural resources, construction, and maintenance, 34.3% production, transportation, and material moving
Income: Per capita: $19,224; Median household: $48,750; Average household: $54,833; Households with income of $100,000 or more: 12.5%; Poverty rate: 15.8%
Educational Attainment: High school diploma or higher: 76.1%; Bachelor's degree or higher: 10.5%; Graduate/professional degree or higher: 2.5%

School District(s)

Tippecanoe Valley School Corp (KG-12)
Enrollment: 1,909 . . . . (574) 598-2759

Housing: Homeownership rate: 69.5%; Median home value: $75,600; Median year structure built: 1963; Homeowner vacancy rate: 3.9%; Median selected monthly owner costs: $833 with a mortgage, $331 without a mortgage; Median gross rent: $675 per month; Rental vacancy rate: 9.7%
Health Insurance: 93.2% have insurance; 70.4% have private insurance; 32.6% have public insurance; 6.8% do not have insurance; 2.8% of children under 18 do not have insurance
Transportation: Commute: 95.7% car, 0.4% public transportation, 1.6% walk, 2.0% work from home; Mean travel time to work: 23.9 minutes

MILFORD (town). Covers a land area of 1.102 square miles and a water area of 0.023 square miles. Located at 41.41° N. Lat; 85.85° W. Long. Elevation is 837 feet.
History: Laid out 1836.
Population: 1,538; Growth (since 2000): -0.8%; Density: 1,395.3 persons per square mile; Race: 95.1% White, 0.5% Black/African American, 0.8% Asian, 0.0% American Indian/Alaska Native, 0.0% Native Hawaiian/Other Pacific Islander, 3.0% Two or more races, 17.2% Hispanic of any race; Average household size: 2.51; Median age: 38.6; Age under 18: 23.3%; Age 65 and over: 17.1%; Males per 100 females: 96.7; Marriage status: 22.1% never married, 54.2% now married, 1.5% separated, 6.7% widowed, 17.1% divorced; Foreign born: 7.5%; Speak English only: 85.5%; With disability: 21.2%; Veterans: 6.9%; Ancestry: 25.0% German, 11.0% Irish, 8.3% English, 6.7% American, 3.8% Scottish
Employment: 2.5% management, business, and financial, 2.5% computer, engineering, and science, 2.6% education, legal, community service, arts, and media, 2.6% healthcare practitioners, 8.0% service, 24.3% sales and office, 7.7% natural resources, construction, and maintenance, 49.7% production, transportation, and material moving
Income: Per capita: $19,180; Median household: $40,071; Average household: $47,661; Households with income of $100,000 or more: 6.3%; Poverty rate: 17.4%
Educational Attainment: High school diploma or higher: 75.0%; Bachelor's degree or higher: 9.3%; Graduate/professional degree or higher: 1.4%

School District(s)

Wawasee Community School Corp (KG-12)
Enrollment: 3,090 . . . . (574) 457-3188

Housing: Homeownership rate: 68.6%; Median home value: $99,800; Median year structure built: 1964; Homeowner vacancy rate: 0.0%; Median selected monthly owner costs: $904 with a mortgage, $345 without a mortgage; Median gross rent: $580 per month; Rental vacancy rate: 0.0%
Health Insurance: 90.4% have insurance; 66.6% have private insurance; 38.2% have public insurance; 9.6% do not have insurance; 11.4% of children under 18 do not have insurance
Newspapers: The Papers Inc (weekly circulation 71,500)
Transportation: Commute: 93.6% car, 0.0% public transportation, 2.6% walk, 2.6% work from home; Mean travel time to work: 20.9 minutes

NORTH WEBSTER (town). Covers a land area of 0.803 square miles and a water area of 0.016 square miles. Located at 41.32° N. Lat; 85.70° W. Long. Elevation is 883 feet.
Population: 1,287; Growth (since 2000): 20.6%; Density: 1,602.0 persons per square mile; Race: 96.9% White, 0.0% Black/African American, 0.0% Asian, 0.4% American Indian/Alaska Native, 0.0% Native Hawaiian/Other Pacific Islander, 1.3% Two or more races, 2.0% Hispanic of any race; Average household size: 2.21; Median age: 46.0; Age under 18: 17.6%; Age 65 and over: 18.6%; Males per 100 females: 93.6; Marriage status: 26.7% never married, 52.2% now married, 2.1% separated, 4.6% widowed, 16.5% divorced; Foreign born: 0.3%; Speak English only: 98.0%; With disability: 16.8%; Veterans: 9.1%; Ancestry: 24.6% German, 15.2% Irish, 14.5% American, 8.0% English, 5.2% Italian
Employment: 9.0% management, business, and financial, 4.4% computer, engineering, and science, 5.2% education, legal, community service, arts, and media, 3.0% healthcare practitioners, 18.8% service, 19.2% sales and

office, 7.0% natural resources, construction, and maintenance, 33.4% production, transportation, and material moving
Income: Per capita: $25,151; Median household: $50,523; Average household: $55,590; Households with income of $100,000 or more: 10.5%; Poverty rate: 13.0%
Educational Attainment: High school diploma or higher: 87.4%; Bachelor's degree or higher: 17.9%; Graduate/professional degree or higher: 6.3%

School District(s)

Wawasee Community School Corp (KG-12)
Enrollment: 3,090 . . . . (574) 457-3188
Housing: Homeownership rate: 64.9%; Median home value: $113,000; Median year structure built: 1973; Homeowner vacancy rate: 2.9%; Median selected monthly owner costs: $957 with a mortgage, $329 without a mortgage; Median gross rent: $749 per month; Rental vacancy rate: 3.8%
Health Insurance: 89.1% have insurance; 68.9% have private insurance; 36.9% have public insurance; 10.9% do not have insurance; 7.1% of children under 18 do not have insurance
Transportation: Commute: 98.3% car, 0.0% public transportation, 1.1% walk, 0.6% work from home; Mean travel time to work: 22.1 minutes

PIERCETON (town). Covers a land area of 1.198 square miles and a water area of 0.002 square miles. Located at 41.20° N. Lat; 85.70° W. Long. Elevation is 928 feet.
Population: 832; Growth (since 2000): 19.7%; Density: 694.7 persons per square mile; Race: 98.7% White, 0.0% Black/African American, 1.3% Asian, 0.0% American Indian/Alaska Native, 0.0% Native Hawaiian/Other Pacific Islander, 0.0% Two or more races, 2.3% Hispanic of any race; Average household size: 2.36; Median age: 40.7; Age under 18: 25.5%; Age 65 and over: 20.7%; Males per 100 females: 91.9; Marriage status: 20.2% never married, 55.3% now married, 0.5% separated, 7.7% widowed, 16.8% divorced; Foreign born: 1.1%; Speak English only: 95.7%; With disability: 18.6%; Veterans: 7.9%; Ancestry: 15.1% German, 13.1% American, 8.4% Irish, 8.2% English, 4.8% French
Employment: 8.8% management, business, and financial, 6.8% computer, engineering, and science, 11.4% education, legal, community service, arts, and media, 3.6% healthcare practitioners, 17.1% service, 17.4% sales and office, 5.2% natural resources, construction, and maintenance, 29.6% production, transportation, and material moving
Income: Per capita: $21,039; Median household: $42,917; Average household: $49,488; Households with income of $100,000 or more: 7.6%; Poverty rate: 17.3%
Educational Attainment: High school diploma or higher: 82.3%; Bachelor's degree or higher: 12.6%; Graduate/professional degree or higher: 2.4%

School District(s)

Whitko Community School Corp (PK-12)
Enrollment: 1,590 . . . . (260) 327-3677
Housing: Homeownership rate: 69.3%; Median home value: $82,700; Median year structure built: 1952; Homeowner vacancy rate: 1.1%; Median selected monthly owner costs: $846 with a mortgage, $422 without a mortgage; Median gross rent: $709 per month; Rental vacancy rate: 8.5%
Health Insurance: 91.7% have insurance; 73.4% have private insurance; 30.5% have public insurance; 8.3% do not have insurance; 7.8% of children under 18 do not have insurance
Transportation: Commute: 95.3% car, 0.0% public transportation, 3.9% walk, 0.8% work from home; Mean travel time to work: 19.0 minutes

SIDNEY (town). Covers a land area of 0.125 square miles and a water area of 0.005 square miles. Located at 41.11° N. Lat; 85.74° W. Long. Elevation is 915 feet.
Population: 106; Growth (since 2000): -36.9%; Density: 850.6 persons per square mile; Race: 100.0% White, 0.0% Black/African American, 0.0% Asian, 0.0% American Indian/Alaska Native, 0.0% Native Hawaiian/Other Pacific Islander, 0.0% Two or more races, 1.9% Hispanic of any race; Average household size: 2.65; Median age: 36.5; Age under 18: 28.3%; Age 65 and over: 18.9%; Males per 100 females: 84.4; Marriage status: 24.4% never married, 39.5% now married, 9.3% separated, 10.5% widowed, 25.6% divorced; Foreign born: 0.0%; Speak English only: 100.0%; With disability: 37.7%; Veterans: 6.6%; Ancestry: 50.9% German, 27.4% American, 9.4% Irish, 2.8% English, 0.9% Canadian
Employment: 0.0% management, business, and financial, 4.3% computer, engineering, and science, 0.0% education, legal, community service, arts, and media, 0.0% healthcare practitioners, 6.4% service, 8.5% sales and office, 14.9% natural resources, construction, and maintenance, 66.0% production, transportation, and material moving
Income: Per capita: $18,335; Median household: $52,000; Average household: $46,895; Households with income of $100,000 or more: 5.0%; Poverty rate: 3.8%
Educational Attainment: High school diploma or higher: 71.4%; Bachelor's degree or higher: 1.4%; Graduate/professional degree or higher: n/a
Housing: Homeownership rate: 72.5%; Median home value: $58,300; Median year structure built: Before 1940; Homeowner vacancy rate: 0.0%; Median selected monthly owner costs: $740 with a mortgage, $450 without a mortgage; Median gross rent: n/a per month; Rental vacancy rate: 0.0%
Health Insurance: 92.5% have insurance; 74.5% have private insurance; 35.8% have public insurance; 7.5% do not have insurance; 0.0% of children under 18 do not have insurance
Transportation: Commute: 100.0% car, 0.0% public transportation, 0.0% walk, 0.0% work from home; Mean travel time to work: 24.1 minutes

SILVER LAKE (town). Covers a land area of 0.525 square miles and a water area of 0.001 square miles. Located at 41.07° N. Lat; 85.89° W. Long. Elevation is 906 feet.
History: Laid out 1859.
Population: 957; Growth (since 2000): 75.3%; Density: 1,822.1 persons per square mile; Race: 96.7% White, 0.0% Black/African American, 0.3% Asian, 1.0% American Indian/Alaska Native, 0.0% Native Hawaiian/Other Pacific Islander, 2.0% Two or more races, 2.1% Hispanic of any race; Average household size: 2.55; Median age: 35.5; Age under 18: 25.9%; Age 65 and over: 13.6%; Males per 100 females: 88.3; Marriage status: 32.0% never married, 46.2% now married, 4.4% separated, 6.2% widowed, 15.6% divorced; Foreign born: 0.8%; Speak English only: 97.2%; With disability: 20.0%; Veterans: 9.7%; Ancestry: 21.8% German, 16.1% Irish, 10.0% American, 5.9% English, 5.5% Dutch
Employment: 9.1% management, business, and financial, 0.5% computer, engineering, and science, 2.5% education, legal, community service, arts, and media, 7.3% healthcare practitioners, 10.7% service, 32.0% sales and office, 8.0% natural resources, construction, and maintenance, 30.0% production, transportation, and material moving
Income: Per capita: $21,400; Median household: $45,893; Average household: $55,260; Households with income of $100,000 or more: 6.2%; Poverty rate: 25.4%
Educational Attainment: High school diploma or higher: 82.6%; Bachelor's degree or higher: 9.2%; Graduate/professional degree or higher: 3.3%
Housing: Homeownership rate: 75.7%; Median home value: $73,900; Median year structure built: 1951; Homeowner vacancy rate: 0.0%; Median selected monthly owner costs: $752 with a mortgage, $325 without a mortgage; Median gross rent: $682 per month; Rental vacancy rate: 0.0%
Health Insurance: 90.6% have insurance; 68.1% have private insurance; 37.3% have public insurance; 9.4% do not have insurance; 4.4% of children under 18 do not have insurance
Transportation: Commute: 94.7% car, 0.5% public transportation, 0.5% walk, 4.3% work from home; Mean travel time to work: 27.9 minutes

SYRACUSE (town). Covers a land area of 1.787 square miles and a water area of 0.366 square miles. Located at 41.42° N. Lat; 85.75° W. Long. Elevation is 879 feet.
History: Syracuse was settled as a summer resort town on Lakes Syracuse, Wawasee, and Papakeechee.
Population: 2,873; Growth (since 2000): -5.4%; Density: 1,607.7 persons per square mile; Race: 94.8% White, 0.2% Black/African American, 0.3% Asian, 0.3% American Indian/Alaska Native, 0.0% Native Hawaiian/Other Pacific Islander, 2.9% Two or more races, 10.8% Hispanic of any race; Average household size: 2.35; Median age: 36.8; Age under 18: 26.3%; Age 65 and over: 16.0%; Males per 100 females: 101.4; Marriage status: 29.9% never married, 42.4% now married, 0.4% separated, 7.6% widowed, 20.1% divorced; Foreign born: 2.2%; Speak English only: 93.7%; With disability: 14.6%; Veterans: 10.9%; Ancestry: 22.7% German, 13.3% Irish, 10.5% American, 8.0% English, 6.2% Polish
Employment: 10.9% management, business, and financial, 2.8% computer, engineering, and science, 4.2% education, legal, community service, arts, and media, 3.0% healthcare practitioners, 19.9% service, 20.9% sales and office, 12.5% natural resources, construction, and maintenance, 25.8% production, transportation, and material moving

Income: Per capita: $23,694; Median household: $43,636; Average household: $54,057; Households with income of $100,000 or more: 8.1%; Poverty rate: 15.6%
Educational Attainment: High school diploma or higher: 81.3%; Bachelor's degree or higher: 15.1%; Graduate/professional degree or higher: 3.3%

School District(s)

Wawasee Community School Corp (KG-12)
Enrollment: 3,090 . . . . (574) 457-3188
Housing: Homeownership rate: 56.2%; Median home value: $120,600; Median year structure built: 1973; Homeowner vacancy rate: 2.4%; Median selected monthly owner costs: $932 with a mortgage, $359 without a mortgage; Median gross rent: $737 per month; Rental vacancy rate: 11.3%
Health Insurance: 85.7% have insurance; 62.3% have private insurance; 38.9% have public insurance; 14.3% do not have insurance; 8.8% of children under 18 do not have insurance
Transportation: Commute: 92.7% car, 0.0% public transportation, 1.1% walk, 3.6% work from home; Mean travel time to work: 19.2 minutes
Additional Information Contacts
Town of Syracuse . . . . (574) 457-3216
http://www.syracusein.org

WARSAW (city). County seat. Covers a land area of 11.576 square miles and a water area of 1.338 square miles. Located at 41.24° N. Lat; 85.85° W. Long. Elevation is 827 feet.
History: In its name, Warsaw remembers the Polish nationality of Thaddeus Kosciusko (1746-1817), for whom Kosciusko County was named. Kosciusko was an aide to General Washington during the Revolutionary War, in addition to being a Polish national hero.
Population: 14,797; Growth (since 2000): 19.2%; Density: 1,278.2 persons per square mile; Race: 87.4% White, 2.3% Black/African American, 3.3% Asian, 0.2% American Indian/Alaska Native, 0.0% Native Hawaiian/Other Pacific Islander, 3.5% Two or more races, 10.3% Hispanic of any race; Average household size: 2.46; Median age: 31.8; Age under 18: 25.6%; Age 65 and over: 13.5%; Males per 100 females: 96.4; Marriage status: 30.8% never married, 47.8% now married, 1.4% separated, 5.8% widowed, 15.7% divorced; Foreign born: 7.5%; Speak English only: 87.6%; With disability: 14.3%; Veterans: 6.8%; Ancestry: 23.4% German, 12.1% Irish, 9.6% English, 8.7% American, 3.2% Italian
Employment: 12.0% management, business, and financial, 7.7% computer, engineering, and science, 9.2% education, legal, community service, arts, and media, 5.4% healthcare practitioners, 10.0% service, 21.5% sales and office, 6.6% natural resources, construction, and maintenance, 27.7% production, transportation, and material moving
Income: Per capita: $27,137; Median household: $50,046; Average household: $68,466; Households with income of $100,000 or more: 17.4%; Poverty rate: 13.2%
Educational Attainment: High school diploma or higher: 84.9%; Bachelor's degree or higher: 28.4%; Graduate/professional degree or higher: 10.1%

School District(s)

Warsaw Community Schools (PK-12)
Enrollment: 6,921 . . . . (574) 371-5098
Housing: Homeownership rate: 56.2%; Median home value: $124,300; Median year structure built: 1976; Homeowner vacancy rate: 0.7%; Median selected monthly owner costs: $987 with a mortgage, $387 without a mortgage; Median gross rent: $803 per month; Rental vacancy rate: 4.6%
Health Insurance: 88.0% have insurance; 72.5% have private insurance; 25.4% have public insurance; 12.0% do not have insurance; 13.2% of children under 18 do not have insurance
Hospitals: Kosciusko Community Hospital (72 beds)
Safety: Violent crime rate: n/a per 10,000 population; Property crime rate: 412.8 per 10,000 population
Newspapers: Times-Union (daily circulation 10,900)
Transportation: Commute: 93.0% car, 0.0% public transportation, 1.9% walk, 2.9% work from home; Mean travel time to work: 13.5 minutes
Airports: Warsaw Municipal (general aviation)
Additional Information Contacts
City of Warsaw . . . . (574) 372-9545
http://warsaw.in.gov

WINONA LAKE (town). Covers a land area of 2.763 square miles and a water area of 0.490 square miles. Located at 41.22° N. Lat; 85.81° W. Long. Elevation is 817 feet.
History: Winona Lake is a vacation retreat area. Evangelist Billy Sunday built a tabernacle here that influenced the character of the town.
Population: 5,140; Growth (since 2000): 28.9%; Density: 1,860.4 persons per square mile; Race: 97.9% White, 0.5% Black/African American, 0.3% Asian, 0.1% American Indian/Alaska Native, 0.0% Native Hawaiian/Other Pacific Islander, 0.9% Two or more races, 11.4% Hispanic of any race; Average household size: 2.44; Median age: 30.1; Age under 18: 18.3%; Age 65 and over: 11.6%; Males per 100 females: 87.3; Marriage status: 35.6% never married, 49.4% now married, 2.6% separated, 6.3% widowed, 8.7% divorced; Foreign born: 7.8%; Speak English only: 86.2%; With disability: 10.1%; Veterans: 7.5%; Ancestry: 28.7% German, 13.8% Irish, 8.9% English, 8.4% American, 5.1% French
Employment: 17.5% management, business, and financial, 6.6% computer, engineering, and science, 16.0% education, legal, community service, arts, and media, 2.8% healthcare practitioners, 17.9% service, 22.5% sales and office, 4.7% natural resources, construction, and maintenance, 12.0% production, transportation, and material moving
Income: Per capita: $26,973; Median household: $60,456; Average household: $75,217; Households with income of $100,000 or more: 25.9%; Poverty rate: 12.6%
Educational Attainment: High school diploma or higher: 87.6%; Bachelor's degree or higher: 40.1%; Graduate/professional degree or higher: 14.2%

School District(s)

Warsaw Community Schools (PK-12)
Enrollment: 6,921 . . . . (574) 371-5098

Four-year College(s)

Grace College and Theological Seminary (Private, Not-for-profit, Brethren Church)
Enrollment: 2,156 . . . . (574) 372-5100
Tuition: In-state $23,170; Out-of-state $23,170
Housing: Homeownership rate: 59.3%; Median home value: $165,400; Median year structure built: 1984; Homeowner vacancy rate: 0.0%; Median selected monthly owner costs: $1,284 with a mortgage, $332 without a mortgage; Median gross rent: $696 per month; Rental vacancy rate: 0.0%
Health Insurance: 90.1% have insurance; 76.8% have private insurance; 20.7% have public insurance; 9.9% do not have insurance; 4.7% of children under 18 do not have insurance
Transportation: Commute: 85.3% car, 0.4% public transportation, 7.4% walk, 6.1% work from home; Mean travel time to work: 17.6 minutes
Additional Information Contacts
Town of Winona Lake . . . . (574) 267-7581
http://www.winonalake.net

LaGrange County

Located in northeastern Indiana; bounded on the north by Michigan; drained by the Pigeon and Short Little Elkhart Rivers. Covers a land area of 379.624 square miles, a water area of 7.078 square miles, and is located in the Eastern Time Zone at 41.64° N. Lat., 85.43° W. Long. The county was founded in 1832. County seat is Lagrange.

Weather Station: Lagrange Sewage Plant Elevation: 895 feet

	Jan	Feb	Mar	Apr	May	Jun	Jul	Aug	Sep	Oct	Nov	Dec
High	30	35	45	59	70	79	83	81	74	61	48	35
Low	15	18	26	37	48	57	61	59	52	40	32	21
Precip	1.8	1.7	2.3	3.5	4.0	4.0	3.7	4.1	3.4	3.2	2.9	2.5
Snow	6.9	5.7	2.6	0.9	tr	0.0	0.0	0.0	0.0	0.5	1.4	5.9

High and Low temperatures in degrees Fahrenheit; Precipitation and Snow in inches

Population: 38,720; Growth (since 2000): 10.9%; Density: 102.0 persons per square mile; Race: 97.8% White, 0.1% Black/African American, 0.2% Asian, 0.1% American Indian/Alaska Native, 0.0% Native Hawaiian/Other Pacific Islander, 1.7% two or more races, 3.9% Hispanic of any race; Average household size: 3.18; Median age: 31.5; Age under 18: 33.1%; Age 65 and over: 13.0%; Males per 100 females: 101.8; Marriage status: 25.1% never married, 61.8% now married, 1.0% separated, 4.8% widowed, 8.2% divorced; Foreign born: 1.8%; Speak English only: 56.5%; With disability: 10.5%; Veterans: 5.9%; Ancestry: 29.2% German, 13.9% American, 6.3% English, 5.7% Irish, 5.6% Pennsylvania German

Religion: Six largest groups: 41.7% European Free-Church, 5.2% Methodist/Pietist, 3.0% Baptist, 1.9% Holiness, 1.8% Catholicism, 1.7% Non-denominational Protestant
Economy: Unemployment rate: 2.8%; Leading industries: 19.6 % manufacturing; 17.6 % retail trade; 12.5 % construction; Farms: 2,419 totaling 204,092 acres; Company size: 0 employ 1,000 or more persons, 4 employ 500 to 999 persons, 18 employ 100 to 499 persons, 801 employs less than 100 persons; Business ownership: 1,118 women-owned, n/a Black-owned, 27 Hispanic-owned, 39 Asian-owned, n/a American Indian/Alaska Native-owned
Employment: 10.8% management, business, and financial, 2.2% computer, engineering, and science, 4.8% education, legal, community service, arts, and media, 3.0% healthcare practitioners, 11.1% service, 16.0% sales and office, 10.7% natural resources, construction, and maintenance, 41.5% production, transportation, and material moving
Income: Per capita: $22,780; Median household: $58,336; Average household: $71,844; Households with income of $100,000 or more: 18.5%; Poverty rate: 9.1%
Educational Attainment: High school diploma or higher: 63.3%; Bachelor's degree or higher: 9.9%; Graduate/professional degree or higher: 2.9%
Housing: Homeownership rate: 82.0%; Median home value: $172,500; Median year structure built: 1976; Homeowner vacancy rate: 1.5%; Median selected monthly owner costs: $1,069 with a mortgage, $330 without a mortgage; Median gross rent: $717 per month; Rental vacancy rate: 5.0%
Vital Statistics: Birth rate: 191.6 per 10,000 population; Death rate: 64.6 per 10,000 population; Age-adjusted cancer mortality rate: 183.3 deaths per 100,000 population
Health Insurance: 60.3% have insurance; 46.7% have private insurance; 22.4% have public insurance; 39.7% do not have insurance; 53.1% of children under 18 do not have insurance
Health Care: Physicians: 4.3 per 10,000 population; Dentists: 2.3 per 10,000 population; Hospital beds: 6.4 per 10,000 population; Hospital admissions: 241.0 per 10,000 population
Transportation: Commute: 80.0% car, 0.2% public transportation, 4.0% walk, 5.3% work from home; Mean travel time to work: 22.9 minutes
2016 Presidential Election: 73.4% Trump, 21.7% Clinton, 4.7% Johnson, 0.1% Stein
National and State Parks: Pigeon River State Fish and Wildlife Area
Additional Information Contacts
LaGrange Government . . . . (260) 499-6300
http://www.lagrangecounty.org

LaGrange County Communities

HOWE (CDP). Covers a land area of 1.788 square miles and a water area of 0 square miles. Located at 41.72° N. Lat; 85.43° W. Long. Elevation is 883 feet.
Population: 493; Growth (since 2000): n/a; Density: 275.8 persons per square mile; Race: 91.7% White, 1.0% Black/African American, 2.2% Asian, 0.0% American Indian/Alaska Native, 0.0% Native Hawaiian/Other Pacific Islander, 3.4% Two or more races, 1.6% Hispanic of any race; Average household size: 1.55; Median age: 53.7; Age under 18: 0.0%; Age 65 and over: 40.6%; Males per 100 females: 131.9; Marriage status: 30.6% never married, 44.4% now married, 0.0% separated, 8.5% widowed, 16.4% divorced; Foreign born: 2.2%; Speak English only: 96.1%; With disability: 26.2%; Veterans: 8.9%; Ancestry: 21.7% German, 16.0% Irish, 9.9% English, 7.3% American, 6.7% Swiss
Employment: 11.0% management, business, and financial, 0.0% computer, engineering, and science, 14.0% education, legal, community service, arts, and media, 0.0% healthcare practitioners, 3.5% service, 51.0% sales and office, 0.0% natural resources, construction, and maintenance, 20.5% production, transportation, and material moving
Income: Per capita: $19,361; Median household: n/a; Average household: $41,005; Households with income of $100,000 or more: n/a; Poverty rate: 24.9%
Educational Attainment: High school diploma or higher: 93.2%; Bachelor's degree or higher: 24.5%; Graduate/professional degree or higher: 10.5%

School District(s)

Lakeland School Corporation (PK-12)
Enrollment: 2,117 . . . . (260) 499-2400
Housing: Homeownership rate: 86.4%; Median home value: $119,900; Median year structure built: Before 1940; Homeowner vacancy rate: 0.0%; Median selected monthly owner costs: $990 with a mortgage, $170 without a mortgage; Median gross rent: n/a per month; Rental vacancy rate: 0.0%
Health Insurance: 99.2% have insurance; 87.0% have private insurance; 48.5% have public insurance; 0.8% do not have insurance; 10.0% of children under 18 do not have insurance
Transportation: Commute: 80.5% car, 0.0% public transportation, 11.0% walk, 4.5% work from home; Mean travel time to work: 12.9 minutes

LAGRANGE (town). County seat. Covers a land area of 1.704 square miles and a water area of 0 square miles. Located at 41.65° N. Lat; 85.42° W. Long. Elevation is 932 feet.
History: LaGrange became the seat of LaGrange County in 1844. The town was named in 1836 for the Marquis de LaFayette's country residence near Paris, by the French immigrants who settled here. LaGrange was incorporated in 1855.
Population: 2,802; Growth (since 2000): -4.0%; Density: 1,644.6 persons per square mile; Race: 95.8% White, 0.0% Black/African American, 0.3% Asian, 0.0% American Indian/Alaska Native, 0.0% Native Hawaiian/Other Pacific Islander, 3.9% Two or more races, 16.6% Hispanic of any race; Average household size: 2.41; Median age: 35.9; Age under 18: 24.8%; Age 65 and over: 17.0%; Males per 100 females: 87.8; Marriage status: 25.9% never married, 45.1% now married, 2.3% separated, 10.5% widowed, 18.5% divorced; Foreign born: 8.5%; Speak English only: 82.1%; With disability: 15.0%; Veterans: 9.8%; Ancestry: 21.3% German, 10.0% English, 9.4% Irish, 8.4% European, 7.2% American
Employment: 6.1% management, business, and financial, 2.0% computer, engineering, and science, 4.4% education, legal, community service, arts, and media, 1.2% healthcare practitioners, 19.3% service, 11.1% sales and office, 11.9% natural resources, construction, and maintenance, 44.1% production, transportation, and material moving
Income: Per capita: $21,340; Median household: $41,951; Average household: $50,533; Households with income of $100,000 or more: 10.7%; Poverty rate: 16.2%
Educational Attainment: High school diploma or higher: 78.8%; Bachelor's degree or higher: 8.1%; Graduate/professional degree or higher: 3.1%

School District(s)

Lakeland School Corporation (PK-12)
Enrollment: 2,117 . . . . (260) 499-2400
Prairie Heights Community Sch Corp (PK-12)
Enrollment: 1,286 . . . . (260) 351-3214
Housing: Homeownership rate: 64.4%; Median home value: $83,600; Median year structure built: 1960; Homeowner vacancy rate: 0.0%; Median selected monthly owner costs: $759 with a mortgage, $345 without a mortgage; Median gross rent: $569 per month; Rental vacancy rate: 13.1%
Health Insurance: 86.2% have insurance; 67.4% have private insurance; 31.8% have public insurance; 13.8% do not have insurance; 8.5% of children under 18 do not have insurance
Hospitals: Parkview Lagrange Hospital (62 beds)
Newspapers: Lagrange Publishing (weekly circulation 34,000)
Transportation: Commute: 89.7% car, 0.0% public transportation, 7.8% walk, 1.9% work from home; Mean travel time to work: 21.6 minutes
Additional Information Contacts
Town of LaGrange. . . . . (260) 463-3241
http://www.lagrangein.org

SHIPSHEWANA (town). Covers a land area of 1.180 square miles and a water area of 0 square miles. Located at 41.67° N. Lat; 85.58° W. Long. Elevation is 889 feet.
History: Shipshewana began as a trading center for Amish farmers in the area.
Population: 936; Growth (since 2000): 74.6%; Density: 793.3 persons per square mile; Race: 99.1% White, 0.0% Black/African American, 0.0% Asian, 0.0% American Indian/Alaska Native, 0.0% Native Hawaiian/Other Pacific Islander, 0.9% Two or more races, 4.6% Hispanic of any race; Average household size: 2.70; Median age: 30.8; Age under 18: 30.6%; Age 65 and over: 15.4%; Males per 100 females: 80.8; Marriage status: 30.2% never married, 56.5% now married, 2.4% separated, 4.4% widowed, 8.9% divorced; Foreign born: 0.4%; Speak English only: 66.5%; With disability: 7.7%; Veterans: 2.2%; Ancestry: 42.7% German, 15.0% American, 6.6% Scottish, 5.0% English, 4.8% Irish
Employment: 8.8% management, business, and financial, 1.1% computer, engineering, and science, 10.4% education, legal, community service, arts, and media, 3.3% healthcare practitioners, 14.6% service, 29.4% sales and

office, 4.0% natural resources, construction, and maintenance, 28.5% production, transportation, and material moving
Income: Per capita: $21,950; Median household: $41,938; Average household: $59,553; Households with income of $100,000 or more: 17.6%; Poverty rate: 12.4%
Educational Attainment: High school diploma or higher: 70.8%; Bachelor's degree or higher: 18.7%; Graduate/professional degree or higher: 6.6%

School District(s)

Westview School Corporation (PK-12)
Enrollment: 2,154 .... (260) 768-4404
Housing: Homeownership rate: 66.3%; Median home value: $160,900; Median year structure built: 1984; Homeowner vacancy rate: 0.0%; Median selected monthly owner costs: $1,221 with a mortgage, $371 without a mortgage; Median gross rent: $585 per month; Rental vacancy rate: 0.0%
Health Insurance: 74.3% have insurance; 55.2% have private insurance; 34.2% have public insurance; 25.7% do not have insurance; 22.4% of children under 18 do not have insurance
Transportation: Commute: 73.8% car, 0.0% public transportation, 22.0% walk, 1.8% work from home; Mean travel time to work: 13.2 minutes

SOUTH MILFORD (unincorporated postal area)

ZCTA: 46786

Covers a land area of 0.036 square miles and a water area of 0 square miles. Located at 41.53° N. Lat; 85.27° W. Long. Elevation is 978 feet.
Population: 167; Growth (since 2000): n/a; Density: 4,607.5 persons per square mile; Race: 100.0% White, 0.0% Black/African American, 0.0% Asian, 0.0% American Indian/Alaska Native, 0.0% Native Hawaiian/Other Pacific Islander, 0.0% Two or more races, 0.0% Hispanic of any race; Average household size: 5.06; Median age: 14.6; Age under 18: 80.2%; Age 65 and over: 0.0%; Males per 100 females: 82.1; Marriage status: 52.9% never married, 0.0% now married, 0.0% separated, 0.0% widowed, 47.1% divorced; Foreign born: 0.0%; Speak English only: 100.0%; With disability: 0.0%; Veterans: 0.0%; Ancestry: n/a
Employment: n/a management, business, and financial, n/a computer, engineering, and science, n/a education, legal, community service, arts, and media, n/a healthcare practitioners, n/a service, n/a sales and office, n/a natural resources, construction, and maintenance, n/a production, transportation, and material moving
Income: Per capita: n/a; Median household: n/a; Average household: n/a; Households with income of $100,000 or more: n/a; Poverty rate: 100.0%
Educational Attainment: High school diploma or higher: 100.0%; Bachelor's degree or higher: n/a; Graduate/professional degree or higher: n/a
Housing: Homeownership rate: 100.0%; Median home value: n/a; Median year structure built: n/a; Homeowner vacancy rate: 0.0%; Median selected monthly owner costs: $0 with a mortgage, $0 without a mortgage; Median gross rent: n/a per month; Rental vacancy rate: 0.0%
Health Insurance: 100.0% have insurance; 0.0% have private insurance; 100.0% have public insurance; 0.0% do not have insurance; 0.0% of children under 18 do not have insurance
Transportation: Commute: n/a car, n/a public transportation, n/a walk, n/a work from home; Mean travel time to work: 0.0 minutes

TOPEKA (town).

Covers a land area of 1.737 square miles and a water area of 0 square miles. Located at 41.54° N. Lat; 85.55° W. Long. Elevation is 925 feet.
History: Laid out 1843.
Population: 944; Growth (since 2000): -18.6%; Density: 543.4 persons per square mile; Race: 80.0% White, 0.0% Black/African American, 0.0% Asian, 0.0% American Indian/Alaska Native, 0.0% Native Hawaiian/Other Pacific Islander, 18.3% Two or more races, 3.1% Hispanic of any race; Average household size: 2.74; Median age: 29.5; Age under 18: 36.0%; Age 65 and over: 8.9%; Males per 100 females: 91.5; Marriage status: 29.9% never married, 56.9% now married, 1.8% separated, 2.7% widowed, 10.6% divorced; Foreign born: 6.7%; Speak English only: 61.7%; With disability: 13.2%; Veterans: 5.6%; Ancestry: 27.8% German, 12.4% European, 11.8% Swiss, 10.1% Other Arab, 7.0% American
Employment: 12.2% management, business, and financial, 1.9% computer, engineering, and science, 1.9% education, legal, community service, arts, and media, 9.6% healthcare practitioners, 12.5% service, 15.3% sales and office, 2.1% natural resources, construction, and maintenance, 44.5% production, transportation, and material moving
Income: Per capita: $19,933; Median household: $53,611; Average household: $54,265; Households with income of $100,000 or more: 7.0%; Poverty rate: 7.2%
Educational Attainment: High school diploma or higher: 71.8%; Bachelor's degree or higher: 7.9%; Graduate/professional degree or higher: 2.1%

School District(s)

Westview School Corporation (PK-12)
Enrollment: 2,154 .... (260) 768-4404
Housing: Homeownership rate: 57.3%; Median home value: $102,100; Median year structure built: 1945; Homeowner vacancy rate: 5.7%; Median selected monthly owner costs: $875 with a mortgage, $398 without a mortgage; Median gross rent: $581 per month; Rental vacancy rate: 11.4%
Health Insurance: 87.6% have insurance; 71.8% have private insurance; 23.4% have public insurance; 12.4% do not have insurance; 12.5% of children under 18 do not have insurance
Transportation: Commute: 83.3% car, 0.0% public transportation, 7.8% walk, 3.2% work from home; Mean travel time to work: 21.5 minutes

Lake County

Located in northwestern Indiana; bounded on the north by Lake Michigan, on the west by Illinois, and on the south by the Kankakee River; crossed by the Grand Calumet and Little Calumet Rivers. Covers a land area of 498.961 square miles, a water area of 127.599 square miles, and is located in the Central Time Zone at 41.47° N. Lat., 87.37° W. Long. The county was founded in 1836. County seat is Crown Point.

Lake County is part of the Chicago-Naperville-Elgin, IL-IN-WI Metropolitan Statistical Area. The entire metro area includes: Chicago-Naperville-Arlington Heights, IL Metropolitan Division (Cook County, IL; DuPage County, IL; Grundy County, IL; Kendall County, IL; McHenry County, IL; Will County, IL); Elgin, IL Metropolitan Division (DeKalb County, IL; Kane County, IL); Gary, IN Metropolitan Division (Jasper County, IN; Lake County, IN; Newton County, IN; Porter County, IN); Lake County-Kenosha County, IL-WI Metropolitan Division (Lake County, IL; Kenosha County, WI)

Weather Station: Lowell Elevation: 665 feet

	Jan	Feb	Mar	Apr	May	Jun	Jul	Aug	Sep	Oct	Nov	Dec
High	32	36	47	61	72	81	84	82	76	64	49	35
Low	15	18	28	38	48	58	62	60	52	40	31	19
Precip	1.9	1.7	2.7	3.7	4.3	4.5	3.9	4.2	3.2	3.4	3.4	2.5
Snow	9.4	9.1	3.6	0.3	tr	0.0	0.0	0.0	0.0	0.2	0.8	7.4

High and Low temperatures in degrees Fahrenheit; Precipitation and Snow in inches

Population: 488,694; Growth (since 2000): 0.9%; Density: 979.4 persons per square mile; Race: 62.0% White, 24.3% Black/African American, 1.4% Asian, 0.3% American Indian/Alaska Native, 0.0% Native Hawaiian/Other Pacific Islander, 2.9% two or more races, 18.4% Hispanic of any race; Average household size: 2.60; Median age: 38.6; Age under 18: 24.2%; Age 65 and over: 15.2%; Males per 100 females: 93.3; Marriage status: 34.8% never married, 46.7% now married, 1.6% separated, 7.0% widowed, 11.4% divorced; Foreign born: 6.7%; Speak English only: 85.5%; With disability: 13.9%; Veterans: 7.7%; Ancestry: 15.4% German, 11.4% Irish, 9.6% Polish, 4.8% Italian, 4.7% English
Religion: Six largest groups: 20.4% Catholicism, 12.6% Non-denominational Protestant, 6.3% Baptist, 3.2% Methodist/Pietist, 3.1% Presbyterian-Reformed, 2.8% Eastern Liturgical (Orthodox)
Economy: Unemployment rate: 5.0%; Leading industries: 15.4 % retail trade; 13.0 % health care and social assistance; 12.0 % other services (except public administration); Farms: 430 totaling 133,064 acres; Company size: 14 employ 1,000 or more persons, 11 employs 500 to 999 persons, 195 employ 100 to 499 persons, 9,725 employ less than 100 persons; Business ownership: 14,781 women-owned, 8,896 Black-owned, 3,391 Hispanic-owned, 1,246 Asian-owned, 302 American Indian/Alaska Native-owned
Employment: 12.2% management, business, and financial, 2.9% computer, engineering, and science, 8.7% education, legal, community service, arts, and media, 6.2% healthcare practitioners, 19.1% service, 23.5% sales and office, 9.5% natural resources, construction, and maintenance, 17.8% production, transportation, and material moving
Income: Per capita: $26,590; Median household: $52,559; Average household: $68,067; Households with income of $100,000 or more: 20.7%; Poverty rate: 16.8%

Educational Attainment: High school diploma or higher: 88.1%; Bachelor's degree or higher: 21.4%; Graduate/professional degree or higher: 7.0%
Housing: Homeownership rate: 69.3%; Median home value: $140,100; Median year structure built: 1964; Homeowner vacancy rate: 1.7%; Median selected monthly owner costs: $1,212 with a mortgage, $436 without a mortgage; Median gross rent: $852 per month; Rental vacancy rate: 6.7%
Vital Statistics: Birth rate: 118.6 per 10,000 population; Death rate: 100.1 per 10,000 population; Age-adjusted cancer mortality rate: 182.7 deaths per 100,000 population
Health Insurance: 89.8% have insurance; 66.9% have private insurance; 35.1% have public insurance; 10.2% do not have insurance; 5.3% of children under 18 do not have insurance
Health Care: Physicians: 18.8 per 10,000 population; Dentists: 6.1 per 10,000 population; Hospital beds: 47.5 per 10,000 population; Hospital admissions: 1,682.0 per 10,000 population
Air Quality Index (AQI): Percent of Days: 70.1% good, 28.5% moderate, 1.1% unhealthy for sensitive individuals, 0.3% unhealthy, 0.0% very unhealthy; Annual median: 42; Annual maximum: 167
Transportation: Commute: 91.7% car, 2.8% public transportation, 1.2% walk, 2.6% work from home; Mean travel time to work: 28.3 minutes
2016 Presidential Election: 37.3% Trump, 57.7% Clinton, 3.8% Johnson, 0.4% Stein
National and State Parks: Hoosier Prairie State Nature Preserve
Additional Information Contacts
Lake Government . . . . (219) 755-3200
http://www.lakecountyin.org

Lake County Communities

CEDAR LAKE (town). Covers a land area of 8.219 square miles and a water area of 1.387 square miles. Located at 41.37° N. Lat; 87.44° W. Long. Elevation is 709 feet.
Population: 12,024; Growth (since 2000): 29.6%; Density: 1,463.0 persons per square mile; Race: 94.0% White, 0.6% Black/African American, 0.3% Asian, 0.1% American Indian/Alaska Native, 0.0% Native Hawaiian/Other Pacific Islander, 2.9% Two or more races, 5.5% Hispanic of any race; Average household size: 2.85; Median age: 34.5; Age under 18: 27.1%; Age 65 and over: 10.0%; Males per 100 females: 102.8; Marriage status: 32.5% never married, 52.0% now married, 0.5% separated, 3.6% widowed, 12.0% divorced; Foreign born: 2.6%; Speak English only: 94.7%; With disability: 10.5%; Veterans: 8.7%; Ancestry: 29.0% German, 21.2% Irish, 16.5% Polish, 9.0% Italian, 8.3% English
Employment: 15.2% management, business, and financial, 4.4% computer, engineering, and science, 7.8% education, legal, community service, arts, and media, 3.8% healthcare practitioners, 19.2% service, 21.1% sales and office, 16.5% natural resources, construction, and maintenance, 12.1% production, transportation, and material moving
Income: Per capita: $30,271; Median household: $70,702; Average household: $85,043; Households with income of $100,000 or more: 25.9%; Poverty rate: 9.9%
Educational Attainment: High school diploma or higher: 90.3%; Bachelor's degree or higher: 20.6%; Graduate/professional degree or higher: 6.3%

School District(s)

Crown Point Community School Corp (PK-12)
Enrollment: 8,447 . . . . (219) 663-3371
Hanover Community School Corp (KG-12)
Enrollment: 2,208 . . . . (219) 374-3500
Housing: Homeownership rate: 80.1%; Median home value: $170,100; Median year structure built: 1975; Homeowner vacancy rate: 3.6%; Median selected monthly owner costs: $1,291 with a mortgage, $455 without a mortgage; Median gross rent: $861 per month; Rental vacancy rate: 11.6%
Health Insurance: 91.7% have insurance; 78.5% have private insurance; 22.5% have public insurance; 8.3% do not have insurance; 6.4% of children under 18 do not have insurance
Safety: Violent crime rate: n/a per 10,000 population; Property crime rate: 161.2 per 10,000 population
Transportation: Commute: 93.0% car, 1.2% public transportation, 1.1% walk, 3.8% work from home; Mean travel time to work: 34.7 minutes
Additional Information Contacts
Town of Cedar Lake . . . . (219) 374-7000
http://www.cedarlakein.org

CROWN POINT (city). County seat. Covers a land area of 17.713 square miles and a water area of 0.015 square miles. Located at 41.42° N. Lat; 87.35° W. Long. Elevation is 732 feet.
History: Named for Solon Robinson, a settler who was called King of the Squatters. Crown Point was founded by Solon Robinson, who came here from Connecticut in 1834 and built a cabin. Robinson, who served as Lake County's first justice of the peace, built the first courthouse for Lake County when Crown Point was chosen as the county seat. The town was first called Robinson's Prairie; the later name refers to Robinson's nickname of King of the Squatters.
Population: 28,952; Growth (since 2000): 46.2%; Density: 1,634.5 persons per square mile; Race: 86.8% White, 5.7% Black/African American, 2.4% Asian, 0.0% American Indian/Alaska Native, 0.0% Native Hawaiian/Other Pacific Islander, 2.4% Two or more races, 8.6% Hispanic of any race; Average household size: 2.47; Median age: 41.5; Age under 18: 21.9%; Age 65 and over: 19.0%; Males per 100 females: 100.0; Marriage status: 26.8% never married, 54.1% now married, 0.5% separated, 8.4% widowed, 10.7% divorced; Foreign born: 7.9%; Speak English only: 87.8%; With disability: 11.2%; Veterans: 8.6%; Ancestry: 22.3% German, 13.8% Irish, 11.8% Polish, 8.4% Italian, 6.2% English
Employment: 15.7% management, business, and financial, 4.1% computer, engineering, and science, 10.6% education, legal, community service, arts, and media, 9.3% healthcare practitioners, 15.7% service, 21.8% sales and office, 9.0% natural resources, construction, and maintenance, 13.9% production, transportation, and material moving
Income: Per capita: $33,636; Median household: $69,471; Average household: $84,875; Households with income of $100,000 or more: 30.3%; Poverty rate: 7.8%
Educational Attainment: High school diploma or higher: 91.9%; Bachelor's degree or higher: 33.3%; Graduate/professional degree or higher: 10.0%

School District(s)

Crown Point Community School Corp (PK-12)
Enrollment: 8,447 . . . . (219) 663-3371
NW Indiana Special Education Coop (KG-12)
Enrollment: 110 . . . . (219) 663-6500
Housing: Homeownership rate: 79.0%; Median home value: $178,400; Median year structure built: 1983; Homeowner vacancy rate: 1.3%; Median selected monthly owner costs: $1,384 with a mortgage, $478 without a mortgage; Median gross rent: $989 per month; Rental vacancy rate: 3.8%
Health Insurance: 95.5% have insurance; 81.4% have private insurance; 29.5% have public insurance; 4.5% do not have insurance; 3.4% of children under 18 do not have insurance
Hospitals: Franciscan Saint Anthony Health - Crown Point (411 beds); Pinnacle Hospital (18 beds)
Safety: Violent crime rate: 3.4 per 10,000 population; Property crime rate: 113.3 per 10,000 population
Newspapers: Crown Point Star (weekly circulation 2,700)
Transportation: Commute: 92.0% car, 1.4% public transportation, 1.5% walk, 3.1% work from home; Mean travel time to work: 28.0 minutes
Additional Information Contacts
City of Crown Point . . . . (219) 662-3235
http://www.crownpoint.in.gov

DYER (town). Covers a land area of 6.104 square miles and a water area of 0 square miles. Located at 41.50° N. Lat; 87.51° W. Long. Elevation is 640 feet.
History: On January 24, 1910, citizens of Dyer decided by a vote of 57 to 35 to incorporate as a town under the laws of the State of Indiana. The Town of Dyer was formally incorporated on February 8, 1910.
Population: 16,077; Growth (since 2000): 15.7%; Density: 2,633.9 persons per square mile; Race: 83.9% White, 4.6% Black/African American, 3.1% Asian, 0.7% American Indian/Alaska Native, 0.0% Native Hawaiian/Other Pacific Islander, 1.3% Two or more races, 10.1% Hispanic of any race; Average household size: 2.61; Median age: 45.5; Age under 18: 18.8%; Age 65 and over: 19.5%; Males per 100 females: 93.8; Marriage status: 25.3% never married, 58.3% now married, 1.0% separated, 7.9% widowed, 8.5% divorced; Foreign born: 6.9%; Speak English only: 86.9%; With disability: 9.8%; Veterans: 8.0%; Ancestry: 21.6% German, 20.2% Polish, 16.2% Irish, 10.2% Italian, 6.3% Dutch
Employment: 15.0% management, business, and financial, 3.6% computer, engineering, and science, 11.0% education, legal, community service, arts, and media, 8.3% healthcare practitioners, 12.7% service, 22.6% sales and office, 10.2% natural resources, construction, and maintenance, 16.6% production, transportation, and material moving

Income: Per capita: $40,173; Median household: $79,167; Average household: $104,417; Households with income of $100,000 or more: 37.3%; Poverty rate: 3.6%
Educational Attainment: High school diploma or higher: 94.3%; Bachelor's degree or higher: 30.4%; Graduate/professional degree or higher: 10.4%

School District(s)

Lake Central School Corporation (PK-12)
Enrollment: 9,630 . . . . (219) 558-2707

Housing: Homeownership rate: 91.0%; Median home value: $199,400; Median year structure built: 1986; Homeowner vacancy rate: 1.1%; Median selected monthly owner costs: $1,425 with a mortgage, $550 without a mortgage; Median gross rent: $999 per month; Rental vacancy rate: 0.0%
Health Insurance: 96.3% have insurance; 84.4% have private insurance; 26.3% have public insurance; 3.7% do not have insurance; 0.9% of children under 18 do not have insurance
Hospitals: Franciscan Saint Margaret Health - Dyer (794 beds)
Safety: Violent crime rate: 2.5 per 10,000 population; Property crime rate: 85.1 per 10,000 population
Transportation: Commute: 92.0% car, 3.0% public transportation, 1.1% walk, 2.8% work from home; Mean travel time to work: 29.9 minutes; Amtrak: Train service available.
Additional Information Contacts

Town of Dyer. . . . . (219) 865-2421
http://www.townofdyer.com

EAST CHICAGO (city). Covers a land area of 14.088 square miles and a water area of 2.065 square miles. Located at 41.65° N. Lat; 87.45° W. Long. Elevation is 591 feet.
History: Named for its location east of the city of Chicago. East Chicago was incorporated as a town in 1889. Growth was slow until 1901, when a steel mill was built and work was begun on the Indiana Harbor and Ship Canal. Other industries followed, and East Chicago became an important petroleum refining area.
Population: 28,728; Growth (since 2000): -11.4%; Density: 2,039.2 persons per square mile; Race: 24.5% White, 36.4% Black/African American, 0.2% Asian, 0.4% American Indian/Alaska Native, 0.0% Native Hawaiian/Other Pacific Islander, 2.7% Two or more races, 57.0% Hispanic of any race; Average household size: 2.79; Median age: 31.7; Age under 18: 30.1%; Age 65 and over: 12.3%; Males per 100 females: 88.1; Marriage status: 46.7% never married, 36.3% now married, 2.3% separated, 6.6% widowed, 10.5% divorced; Foreign born: 15.7%; Speak English only: 55.1%; With disability: 18.5%; Veterans: 4.6%; Ancestry: 2.4% Polish, 1.4% German, 0.8% American, 0.7% Irish, 0.4% French
Employment: 7.6% management, business, and financial, 0.9% computer, engineering, and science, 7.0% education, legal, community service, arts, and media, 3.5% healthcare practitioners, 27.9% service, 19.6% sales and office, 8.3% natural resources, construction, and maintenance, 25.1% production, transportation, and material moving
Income: Per capita: $15,159; Median household: $30,205; Average household: $40,367; Households with income of $100,000 or more: 6.3%; Poverty rate: 34.6%
Educational Attainment: High school diploma or higher: 72.1%; Bachelor's degree or higher: 8.6%; Graduate/professional degree or higher: 2.9%

School District(s)

East Chicago Lighthouse Charter (KG-07)
Enrollment: 440. . . . . (219) 378-7451
East Chicago Urban Enterprise Acad (KG-08)
Enrollment: 431. . . . . (219) 392-3650
School City Of East Chicago (PK-12)
Enrollment: 4,632 . . . . (219) 391-4100

Housing: Homeownership rate: 43.8%; Median home value: $73,300; Median year structure built: 1942; Homeowner vacancy rate: 2.1%; Median selected monthly owner costs: $1,023 with a mortgage, $366 without a mortgage; Median gross rent: $673 per month; Rental vacancy rate: 9.0%
Health Insurance: 82.9% have insurance; 43.8% have private insurance; 49.6% have public insurance; 17.1% do not have insurance; 7.5% of children under 18 do not have insurance
Hospitals: Saint Catherine Hospital (290 beds)
Safety: Violent crime rate: 66.6 per 10,000 population; Property crime rate: 345.6 per 10,000 population
Transportation: Commute: 90.4% car, 3.4% public transportation, 2.8% walk, 0.4% work from home; Mean travel time to work: 23.7 minutes
Additional Information Contacts

City of East Chicago . . . . (219) 391-8491
http://www.eastchicago.com

GARY (city). Covers a land area of 49.865 square miles and a water area of 7.310 square miles. Located at 41.60° N. Lat; 87.34° W. Long. Elevation is 600 feet.
History: Named for Judge Elbet H. Gary, chairman of the board of directors of U.S. Steel. The site of Gary was selected by the United States Steel Corporation in 1905 as the location of a new plant, as reported by Judge Elbert H. Gary in the Corporation's annual report. What was at first a work camp was expanded by the Gary Land Company into the city of Gary. Since the area was all sand where no grass would grow, soil had to be imported and trees and shrubs planted. Other industries soon joined the steel company, and Gary's industrial character was fixed.
Population: 77,416; Growth (since 2000): -24.7%; Density: 1,552.5 persons per square mile; Race: 14.0% White, 81.0% Black/African American, 0.4% Asian, 0.2% American Indian/Alaska Native, 0.2% Native Hawaiian/Other Pacific Islander, 2.1% Two or more races, 5.8% Hispanic of any race; Average household size: 2.43; Median age: 38.6; Age under 18: 25.4%; Age 65 and over: 17.2%; Males per 100 females: 85.1; Marriage status: 45.1% never married, 31.4% now married, 2.7% separated, 9.1% widowed, 14.3% divorced; Foreign born: 2.0%; Speak English only: 95.3%; With disability: 18.3%; Veterans: 8.6%; Ancestry: 2.6% German, 2.1% Irish, 2.0% American, 1.0% English, 0.9% Polish
Employment: 7.6% management, business, and financial, 1.4% computer, engineering, and science, 9.0% education, legal, community service, arts, and media, 4.6% healthcare practitioners, 29.9% service, 23.1% sales and office, 5.9% natural resources, construction, and maintenance, 18.6% production, transportation, and material moving
Income: Per capita: $17,392; Median household: $29,293; Average household: $40,917; Households with income of $100,000 or more: 6.8%; Poverty rate: 35.8%
Educational Attainment: High school diploma or higher: 84.9%; Bachelor's degree or higher: 12.8%; Graduate/professional degree or higher: 4.8%

School District(s)

21st Century Charter Sch Of Gary (KG-12)
Enrollment: 888. . . . . (317) 536-1027
Aspire Charter Academy (KG-08)
Enrollment: 695. . . . . (219) 944-7400
Charter School Of The Dunes (KG-08)
Enrollment: 463. . . . . (219) 939-9690
Edison Learning Roosevelt (07-12)
Enrollment: 602. . . . . (312) 554-9340
Gary Community School Corp (PK-12)
Enrollment: 6,009 . . . . (219) 881-5401
Gary Lighthouse Charter School (KG-12)
Enrollment: 1,515 . . . . (219) 880-1762
Gary Middle College (09-12)
Enrollment: 237. . . . . (317) 536-1027
Lake Ridge New Tech Schools (PK-12)
Enrollment: 1,921 . . . . (219) 838-1819
Steel City Academy (07-09)
Enrollment: 152. . . . . (219) 750-1010
Thea Bowman Leadership Academy (KG-12)
Enrollment: 1,199 . . . . (219) 883-4826

Four-year College(s)

Indiana University-Northwest (Public)
Enrollment: 4,055 . . . . (219) 980-6501
Tuition: In-state $7,207; Out-of-state $19,038

Vocational/Technical School(s)

Lil Lou's Beauty and Barber College LLC (Private, For-profit)
Enrollment: 85. . . . . (219) 884-9954
Tuition: $14,600

Housing: Homeownership rate: 52.0%; Median home value: $66,300; Median year structure built: 1955; Homeowner vacancy rate: 3.2%; Median selected monthly owner costs: $985 with a mortgage, $393 without a mortgage; Median gross rent: $751 per month; Rental vacancy rate: 8.4%
Health Insurance: 87.0% have insurance; 44.1% have private insurance; 55.6% have public insurance; 13.0% do not have insurance; 3.4% of children under 18 do not have insurance
Hospitals: Methodist Hospitals (469 beds)
Safety: Violent crime rate: 62.1 per 10,000 population; Property crime rate: 340.5 per 10,000 population

Transportation: Commute: 88.1% car, 6.0% public transportation, 2.0% walk, 1.8% work from home; Mean travel time to work: 27.0 minutes; Amtrak: Bus service available.
Airports: Gary/Chicago International (commercial service–non-primary)
Additional Information Contacts
City of Gary . . . . (219) 881-4730
http://www.gary.in.us

GRIFFITH (town). Covers a land area of 7.733 square miles and a water area of 0 square miles. Located at 41.53° N. Lat; 87.42° W. Long. Elevation is 630 feet.
History: Named for Benjamin Griffith, a civil engineer for the railroad. Settled c.1854. Incorporated 1904.
Population: 16,468; Growth (since 2000): -5.0%; Density: 2,129.6 persons per square mile; Race: 73.5% White, 15.8% Black/African American, 1.7% Asian, 0.0% American Indian/Alaska Native, 0.0% Native Hawaiian/Other Pacific Islander, 2.3% Two or more races, 15.9% Hispanic of any race; Average household size: 2.50; Median age: 36.7; Age under 18: 21.7%; Age 65 and over: 13.5%; Males per 100 females: 90.9; Marriage status: 37.3% never married, 44.0% now married, 0.4% separated, 6.2% widowed, 12.6% divorced; Foreign born: 4.4%; Speak English only: 90.8%; With disability: 13.2%; Veterans: 7.7%; Ancestry: 21.8% German, 13.0% Irish, 11.4% Polish, 5.5% English, 5.0% Dutch
Employment: 10.8% management, business, and financial, 3.1% computer, engineering, and science, 5.5% education, legal, community service, arts, and media, 5.0% healthcare practitioners, 18.4% service, 27.2% sales and office, 9.7% natural resources, construction, and maintenance, 20.2% production, transportation, and material moving
Income: Per capita: $27,430; Median household: $57,452; Average household: $67,290; Households with income of $100,000 or more: 21.7%; Poverty rate: 8.9%
Educational Attainment: High school diploma or higher: 93.0%; Bachelor's degree or higher: 18.8%; Graduate/professional degree or higher: 4.2%

School District(s)

Griffith Public Schools (PK-12)
Enrollment: 2,373 . . . . (219) 924-4250
Housing: Homeownership rate: 65.8%; Median home value: $135,600; Median year structure built: 1967; Homeowner vacancy rate: 0.2%; Median selected monthly owner costs: $1,188 with a mortgage, $417 without a mortgage; Median gross rent: $857 per month; Rental vacancy rate: 6.2%
Health Insurance: 92.1% have insurance; 70.3% have private insurance; 32.7% have public insurance; 7.9% do not have insurance; 3.9% of children under 18 do not have insurance
Safety: Violent crime rate: 15.5 per 10,000 population; Property crime rate: 219.8 per 10,000 population
Transportation: Commute: 91.8% car, 2.9% public transportation, 0.4% walk, 2.6% work from home; Mean travel time to work: 25.7 minutes
Additional Information Contacts
Town of Griffith . . . . (219) 924-7500
http://www.grffith.in.gov

HAMMOND (city). Covers a land area of 22.776 square miles and a water area of 2.106 square miles. Located at 41.62° N. Lat; 87.49° W. Long. Elevation is 600 feet.
History: Named for George H. Hammond, a Detroit butcher who adapted the refrigeration boxcar. George H. Hammond, a Detroit butcher, opened a slaughterhouse in what was to become Hammond in 1869, when the refrigerator box was invented by the Davis brothers in Detroit and shipping of dressed beef became possible. Before Hammond was incorporated as a city in 1884, it had been known as Hohman for an early settler, and as State Line for its location on the Indiana-Illinois border. Hammond 's slaughterhouse was the beginning of much industry in Hammond.
Population: 77,827; Growth (since 2000): -6.3%; Density: 3,417.1 persons per square mile; Race: 51.5% White, 21.4% Black/African American, 1.3% Asian, 0.3% American Indian/Alaska Native, 0.0% Native Hawaiian/Other Pacific Islander, 3.9% Two or more races, 36.6% Hispanic of any race; Average household size: 2.70; Median age: 33.9; Age under 18: 25.8%; Age 65 and over: 11.0%; Males per 100 females: 96.2; Marriage status: 40.9% never married, 41.1% now married, 2.5% separated, 6.1% widowed, 11.9% divorced; Foreign born: 11.3%; Speak English only: 74.2%; With disability: 15.5%; Veterans: 6.7%; Ancestry: 10.2% German, 8.6% Irish, 7.6% Polish, 3.3% English, 3.1% Italian
Employment: 8.7% management, business, and financial, 2.3% computer, engineering, and science, 7.8% education, legal, community service, arts, and media, 3.6% healthcare practitioners, 21.2% service, 23.6% sales and office, 10.2% natural resources, construction, and maintenance, 22.7% production, transportation, and material moving
Income: Per capita: $20,337; Median household: $44,427; Average household: $53,796; Households with income of $100,000 or more: 11.4%; Poverty rate: 22.2%
Educational Attainment: High school diploma or higher: 80.3%; Bachelor's degree or higher: 14.0%; Graduate/professional degree or higher: 3.7%

School District(s)

Hammond Academy Of Science & Tech (06-12)
Enrollment: 549. . . . . (219) 852-0500
School City Of Hammond (PK-12)
Enrollment: 14,193 . . . . (219) 933-2400

Four-year College(s)

Purdue University Northwest (Public)
Enrollment: 12,071 . . . . (219) 989-2400
Tuition: In-state $7,582; Out-of-state $17,129

Vocational/Technical School(s)

Brightwood College-Hammond (Private, For-profit)
Enrollment: 298. . . . . (219) 844-0100
Tuition: $15,760
Housing: Homeownership rate: 59.7%; Median home value: $87,600; Median year structure built: 1951; Homeowner vacancy rate: 2.0%; Median selected monthly owner costs: $984 with a mortgage, $393 without a mortgage; Median gross rent: $852 per month; Rental vacancy rate: 5.5%
Health Insurance: 84.9% have insurance; 57.2% have private insurance; 37.6% have public insurance; 15.1% do not have insurance; 6.5% of children under 18 do not have insurance
Hospitals: Franciscan Saint Margaret Health - Hammond (475 beds)
Safety: Violent crime rate: 63.5 per 10,000 population; Property crime rate: 391.4 per 10,000 population
Transportation: Commute: 92.7% car, 3.0% public transportation, 2.4% walk, 1.2% work from home; Mean travel time to work: 26.7 minutes; Amtrak: Train service available.
Additional Information Contacts
City of Hammond. . . . . (219) 853-6346
http://www.gohammond.com/web

HIGHLAND (town). Covers a land area of 6.936 square miles and a water area of 0.023 square miles. Located at 41.55° N. Lat; 87.46° W. Long. Elevation is 623 feet.
History: Named origianlly Clough, then for its location on an area of high ground, in 1888. Highland was settled by people of Dutch descent, who established truck-gardening farms in the area.
Population: 22,938; Growth (since 2000): -2.6%; Density: 3,307.2 persons per square mile; Race: 83.9% White, 4.4% Black/African American, 1.9% Asian, 0.4% American Indian/Alaska Native, 0.0% Native Hawaiian/Other Pacific Islander, 3.5% Two or more races, 15.5% Hispanic of any race; Average household size: 2.40; Median age: 42.5; Age under 18: 20.8%; Age 65 and over: 18.7%; Males per 100 females: 92.3; Marriage status: 28.6% never married, 50.6% now married, 1.2% separated, 7.6% widowed, 13.2% divorced; Foreign born: 5.9%; Speak English only: 88.5%; With disability: 13.3%; Veterans: 8.6%; Ancestry: 21.7% German, 18.0% Polish, 13.8% Irish, 6.7% English, 5.4% Dutch
Employment: 14.9% management, business, and financial, 3.7% computer, engineering, and science, 8.3% education, legal, community service, arts, and media, 5.4% healthcare practitioners, 17.2% service, 24.8% sales and office, 9.4% natural resources, construction, and maintenance, 16.2% production, transportation, and material moving
Income: Per capita: $31,371; Median household: $62,345; Average household: $73,803; Households with income of $100,000 or more: 24.8%; Poverty rate: 7.7%
Educational Attainment: High school diploma or higher: 93.1%; Bachelor's degree or higher: 26.7%; Graduate/professional degree or higher: 8.0%
Housing: Homeownership rate: 78.4%; Median home value: $155,400; Median year structure built: 1966; Homeowner vacancy rate: 1.6%; Median selected monthly owner costs: $1,205 with a mortgage, $435 without a mortgage; Median gross rent: $1,017 per month; Rental vacancy rate: 1.1%
Health Insurance: 93.4% have insurance; 78.9% have private insurance; 29.6% have public insurance; 6.6% do not have insurance; 4.8% of children under 18 do not have insurance

Safety: Violent crime rate: 15.9 per 10,000 population; Property crime rate: 325.6 per 10,000 population
Transportation: Commute: 92.3% car, 3.0% public transportation, 0.8% walk, 3.1% work from home; Mean travel time to work: 26.9 minutes
Additional Information Contacts
Town of Highland . . . . (219) 838-1080
http://www.highland.in.gov

HOBART (city). Covers a land area of 26.331 square miles and a water area of 0.375 square miles. Located at 41.51° N. Lat; 87.28° W. Long. Elevation is 623 feet.
History: Hobart was founded by George Earle, an Englishman who built a home here and named the town for his brother. The town was platted in 1849.
Population: 28,573; Growth (since 2000): 12.7%; Density: 1,085.1 persons per square mile; Race: 84.8% White, 7.7% Black/African American, 0.9% Asian, 0.7% American Indian/Alaska Native, 0.0% Native Hawaiian/Other Pacific Islander, 2.3% Two or more races, 11.8% Hispanic of any race; Average household size: 2.53; Median age: 39.1; Age under 18: 23.1%; Age 65 and over: 16.7%; Males per 100 females: 94.2; Marriage status: 28.1% never married, 53.0% now married, 1.7% separated, 6.9% widowed, 12.0% divorced; Foreign born: 2.8%; Speak English only: 93.5%; With disability: 13.2%; Veterans: 10.3%; Ancestry: 22.3% German, 20.3% Irish, 9.3% Polish, 9.0% English, 5.0% Italian
Employment: 12.0% management, business, and financial, 3.3% computer, engineering, and science, 10.2% education, legal, community service, arts, and media, 6.2% healthcare practitioners, 19.0% service, 22.6% sales and office, 9.1% natural resources, construction, and maintenance, 17.5% production, transportation, and material moving
Income: Per capita: $27,550; Median household: $58,366; Average household: $68,836; Households with income of $100,000 or more: 20.7%; Poverty rate: 11.1%
Educational Attainment: High school diploma or higher: 89.9%; Bachelor's degree or higher: 21.5%; Graduate/professional degree or higher: 6.6%

School District(s)
River Forest Community Sch Corp (PK-12)
Enrollment: 1,389 . . . . (219) 962-2909
School City Of Hobart (PK-12)
Enrollment: 4,038 . . . . (219) 942-8885
Housing: Homeownership rate: 75.1%; Median home value: $134,300; Median year structure built: 1966; Homeowner vacancy rate: 1.0%; Median selected monthly owner costs: $1,162 with a mortgage, $439 without a mortgage; Median gross rent: $873 per month; Rental vacancy rate: 5.2%
Health Insurance: 93.1% have insurance; 76.9% have private insurance; 31.2% have public insurance; 6.9% do not have insurance; 3.7% of children under 18 do not have insurance
Hospitals: Saint Mary Medical Center (190 beds)
Safety: Violent crime rate: 33.1 per 10,000 population; Property crime rate: 416.5 per 10,000 population
Transportation: Commute: 93.4% car, 0.9% public transportation, 0.3% walk, 4.1% work from home; Mean travel time to work: 26.8 minutes
Additional Information Contacts
City of Hobart . . . . (219) 942-1940
http://www.city.hobart.in.us

LAKE DALECARLIA (CDP). Covers a land area of 1.130 square miles and a water area of 0.257 square miles. Located at 41.34° N. Lat; 87.40° W. Long. Elevation is 712 feet.
Population: 1,595; Growth (since 2000): 24.1%; Density: 1,411.3 persons per square mile; Race: 98.3% White, 0.0% Black/African American, 0.0% Asian, 0.0% American Indian/Alaska Native, 0.0% Native Hawaiian/Other Pacific Islander, 1.7% Two or more races, 0.0% Hispanic of any race; Average household size: 3.01; Median age: 34.8; Age under 18: 22.5%; Age 65 and over: 12.0%; Males per 100 females: 111.1; Marriage status: 35.7% never married, 42.7% now married, 0.5% separated, 2.1% widowed, 19.5% divorced; Foreign born: 0.0%; Speak English only: 99.3%; With disability: 2.8%; Veterans: 14.6%; Ancestry: 43.4% Irish, 30.7% German, 29.3% English, 11.3% Polish, 7.9% Dutch
Employment: 13.7% management, business, and financial, 2.4% computer, engineering, and science, 1.9% education, legal, community service, arts, and media, 2.4% healthcare practitioners, 27.6% service, 17.2% sales and office, 15.6% natural resources, construction, and maintenance, 19.2% production, transportation, and material moving
Income: Per capita: $33,689; Median household: $94,674; Average household: $99,188; Households with income of $100,000 or more: 47.0%; Poverty rate: 2.5%
Educational Attainment: High school diploma or higher: 99.0%; Bachelor's degree or higher: 8.8%; Graduate/professional degree or higher: 2.9%
Housing: Homeownership rate: 93.2%; Median home value: $168,900; Median year structure built: 1959; Homeowner vacancy rate: 8.2%; Median selected monthly owner costs: $1,350 with a mortgage, $395 without a mortgage; Median gross rent: n/a per month; Rental vacancy rate: 0.0%
Health Insurance: 85.3% have insurance; 73.4% have private insurance; 20.5% have public insurance; 14.7% do not have insurance; 16.0% of children under 18 do not have insurance
Transportation: Commute: 95.0% car, 0.0% public transportation, 0.0% walk, 2.4% work from home; Mean travel time to work: 32.5 minutes

LAKE STATION (city). Covers a land area of 8.296 square miles and a water area of 0.131 square miles. Located at 41.58° N. Lat; 87.25° W. Long. Elevation is 620 feet.
Population: 12,157; Growth (since 2000): -12.8%; Density: 1,465.4 persons per square mile; Race: 81.1% White, 3.2% Black/African American, 0.8% Asian, 1.0% American Indian/Alaska Native, 0.0% Native Hawaiian/Other Pacific Islander, 5.3% Two or more races, 33.0% Hispanic of any race; Average household size: 2.97; Median age: 35.4; Age under 18: 28.1%; Age 65 and over: 13.0%; Males per 100 females: 99.9; Marriage status: 33.5% never married, 48.5% now married, 3.2% separated, 5.8% widowed, 12.2% divorced; Foreign born: 5.9%; Speak English only: 78.6%; With disability: 15.3%; Veterans: 8.5%; Ancestry: 14.9% Irish, 11.1% German, 10.1% Polish, 7.9% Italian, 5.4% American
Employment: 3.9% management, business, and financial, 1.3% computer, engineering, and science, 3.5% education, legal, community service, arts, and media, 6.0% healthcare practitioners, 25.4% service, 22.3% sales and office, 13.2% natural resources, construction, and maintenance, 24.3% production, transportation, and material moving
Income: Per capita: $17,217; Median household: $41,930; Average household: $50,090; Households with income of $100,000 or more: 8.7%; Poverty rate: 25.4%
Educational Attainment: High school diploma or higher: 78.8%; Bachelor's degree or higher: 6.0%; Graduate/professional degree or higher: 2.1%

School District(s)
Lake Station Community Schools (PK-12)
Enrollment: 1,365 . . . . (219) 962-1159
River Forest Community Sch Corp (PK-12)
Enrollment: 1,389 . . . . (219) 962-2909
Housing: Homeownership rate: 69.2%; Median home value: $78,700; Median year structure built: 1958; Homeowner vacancy rate: 6.1%; Median selected monthly owner costs: $939 with a mortgage, $411 without a mortgage; Median gross rent: $907 per month; Rental vacancy rate: 0.0%
Health Insurance: 84.9% have insurance; 56.1% have private insurance; 40.0% have public insurance; 15.1% do not have insurance; 7.2% of children under 18 do not have insurance
Safety: Violent crime rate: 12.7 per 10,000 population; Property crime rate: 280.1 per 10,000 population
Transportation: Commute: 97.5% car, 0.3% public transportation, 0.7% walk, 0.8% work from home; Mean travel time to work: 26.5 minutes
Additional Information Contacts
City of Lake Station . . . . (219) 962-2081
http://www.lakestation.in.gov

LAKES OF THE FOUR SEASONS (CDP). Covers a land area of 2.681 square miles and a water area of 0.416 square miles. Located at 41.40° N. Lat; 87.22° W. Long. Elevation is 764 feet.
History: Lakes of the Four Seasons (LOFS) is a private, gated community of about 10,000 residents located half-way between Crown Point and Valparaiso, Indiana. The community has its own private security force, four lakes, an 18 hole championship golf course, parks, playgrounds, athletic fields, tennis courts, beaches, a swimming pool, two restaurants, a clubhouse, and pro-shop. A set of restrictive covenants governs construction, maintenance, and general rules of the community through the POA.
Population: 7,061; Growth (since 2000): -3.2%; Density: 2,634.0 persons per square mile; Race: 94.2% White, 1.3% Black/African American, 0.4% Asian, 0.0% American Indian/Alaska Native, 0.0% Native Hawaiian/Other Pacific Islander, 1.8% Two or more races, 10.8% Hispanic of any race;

Average household size: 2.76; Median age: 44.0; Age under 18: 20.4%; Age 65 and over: 14.8%; Males per 100 females: 96.0; Marriage status: 21.6% never married, 63.6% now married, 0.2% separated, 5.5% widowed, 9.3% divorced; Foreign born: 7.5%; Speak English only: 88.3%; With disability: 9.6%; Veterans: 5.2%; Ancestry: 29.8% German, 19.7% Irish, 13.4% Polish, 6.3% Croatian, 5.3% English
Employment: 13.8% management, business, and financial, 4.9% computer, engineering, and science, 8.8% education, legal, community service, arts, and media, 8.0% healthcare practitioners, 12.0% service, 27.8% sales and office, 8.4% natural resources, construction, and maintenance, 16.2% production, transportation, and material moving
Income: Per capita: $33,764; Median household: $89,906; Average household: $91,926; Households with income of $100,000 or more: 40.2%; Poverty rate: 5.4%
Educational Attainment: High school diploma or higher: 94.8%; Bachelor's degree or higher: 27.7%; Graduate/professional degree or higher: 7.1%
Housing: Homeownership rate: 93.9%; Median home value: $184,500; Median year structure built: 1978; Homeowner vacancy rate: 0.0%; Median selected monthly owner costs: $1,408 with a mortgage, $511 without a mortgage; Median gross rent: $1,193 per month; Rental vacancy rate: 0.0%
Health Insurance: 94.3% have insurance; 80.5% have private insurance; 26.1% have public insurance; 5.7% do not have insurance; 3.1% of children under 18 do not have insurance
Transportation: Commute: 93.2% car, 0.0% public transportation, 0.4% walk, 4.6% work from home; Mean travel time to work: 35.4 minutes

LOWELL (town). Covers a land area of 5.180 square miles and a water area of 0.086 square miles. Located at 41.29° N. Lat; 87.42° W. Long. Elevation is 669 feet.
History: Settled 1849, laid out 1853.
Population: 9,502; Growth (since 2000): 26.6%; Density: 1,834.4 persons per square mile; Race: 95.0% White, 0.2% Black/African American, 0.1% Asian, 0.2% American Indian/Alaska Native, 0.2% Native Hawaiian/Other Pacific Islander, 0.6% Two or more races, 6.9% Hispanic of any race; Average household size: 2.79; Median age: 37.3; Age under 18: 26.4%; Age 65 and over: 15.2%; Males per 100 females: 96.9; Marriage status: 30.9% never married, 52.8% now married, 1.6% separated, 6.7% widowed, 9.5% divorced; Foreign born: 1.3%; Speak English only: 95.0%; With disability: 11.6%; Veterans: 9.1%; Ancestry: 34.9% German, 21.5% Irish, 14.1% Polish, 9.4% English, 7.0% American
Employment: 13.3% management, business, and financial, 1.8% computer, engineering, and science, 14.3% education, legal, community service, arts, and media, 4.6% healthcare practitioners, 13.1% service, 21.9% sales and office, 10.9% natural resources, construction, and maintenance, 20.0% production, transportation, and material moving
Income: Per capita: $25,645; Median household: $62,574; Average household: $70,662; Households with income of $100,000 or more: 22.0%; Poverty rate: 9.1%
Educational Attainment: High school diploma or higher: 91.1%; Bachelor's degree or higher: 20.4%; Graduate/professional degree or higher: 7.9%

School District(s)

Tri-creek School Corporation (KG-12)
Enrollment: 3,299 . . . . (219) 696-6661
Housing: Homeownership rate: 81.0%; Median home value: $152,200; Median year structure built: 1978; Homeowner vacancy rate: 0.0%; Median selected monthly owner costs: $1,219 with a mortgage, $420 without a mortgage; Median gross rent: $986 per month; Rental vacancy rate: 0.0%
Health Insurance: 91.2% have insurance; 77.6% have private insurance; 24.9% have public insurance; 8.8% do not have insurance; 7.2% of children under 18 do not have insurance
Safety: Violent crime rate: 2.1 per 10,000 population; Property crime rate: 6.3 per 10,000 population
Newspapers: Pilcher Publishing (weekly circulation 8,800)
Transportation: Commute: 98.3% car, 0.0% public transportation, 0.3% walk, 0.7% work from home; Mean travel time to work: 36.7 minutes
Additional Information Contacts
Town of Lowell . . . . (219) 696-7794
http://www.lowell.net

MERRILLVILLE (town). Covers a land area of 33.216 square miles and a water area of 0.035 square miles. Located at 41.47° N. Lat; 87.32° W. Long. Elevation is 656 feet.
History: Named for Dudley Merrill, a local storekeeper. Merrillville was settled at the place where many smaller trails met with the Sauk Trail.
Population: 35,183; Growth (since 2000): 15.1%; Density: 1,059.2 persons per square mile; Race: 41.2% White, 46.1% Black/African American, 1.3% Asian, 0.3% American Indian/Alaska Native, 0.0% Native Hawaiian/Other Pacific Islander, 4.5% Two or more races, 14.6% Hispanic of any race; Average household size: 2.49; Median age: 38.2; Age under 18: 24.0%; Age 65 and over: 14.7%; Males per 100 females: 88.6; Marriage status: 35.3% never married, 44.6% now married, 2.0% separated, 6.7% widowed, 13.3% divorced; Foreign born: 4.9%; Speak English only: 90.2%; With disability: 13.3%; Veterans: 8.6%; Ancestry: 11.1% German, 8.6% Irish, 4.9% Polish, 2.5% Italian, 2.5% English
Employment: 10.9% management, business, and financial, 2.8% computer, engineering, and science, 9.1% education, legal, community service, arts, and media, 6.8% healthcare practitioners, 17.4% service, 24.7% sales and office, 9.4% natural resources, construction, and maintenance, 18.9% production, transportation, and material moving
Income: Per capita: $26,749; Median household: $56,330; Average household: $65,178; Households with income of $100,000 or more: 18.6%; Poverty rate: 10.9%
Educational Attainment: High school diploma or higher: 92.0%; Bachelor's degree or higher: 23.4%; Graduate/professional degree or higher: 8.4%

School District(s)

Heritage Institute Of Arts & Tech (KG-05)
Enrollment: 153. . . . . (219) 381-5908
Merrillville Community School Corp (PK-12)
Enrollment: 6,558 . . . . (219) 650-5300

Four-year College(s)

Brown Mackie College-Merrillville (Private, For-profit)
Enrollment: n/a . . . . (219) 769-3321
DeVry University-Indiana (Private, For-profit)
Enrollment: 86. . . . . (219) 736-7440
Tuition: In-state $18,148; Out-of-state $18,148

Vocational/Technical School(s)

Denmark College (Private, For-profit)
Enrollment: 136. . . . . (219) 736-9999
Tuition: $18,800
Paul Mitchell the School-Merrillville (Private, For-profit)
Enrollment: 74. . . . . (219) 793-9246
Tuition: $15,750
Housing: Homeownership rate: 65.1%; Median home value: $128,600; Median year structure built: 1974; Homeowner vacancy rate: 1.0%; Median selected monthly owner costs: $1,195 with a mortgage, $402 without a mortgage; Median gross rent: $1,026 per month; Rental vacancy rate: 7.7%
Health Insurance: 90.4% have insurance; 71.6% have private insurance; 30.2% have public insurance; 9.6% do not have insurance; 6.6% of children under 18 do not have insurance
Safety: Violent crime rate: n/a per 10,000 population; Property crime rate: 367.4 per 10,000 population
Transportation: Commute: 93.1% car, 1.8% public transportation, 0.5% walk, 2.4% work from home; Mean travel time to work: 27.3 minutes
Additional Information Contacts
Town of Merrillville. . . . . (219) 769-3501
http://www.merrillville.in.gov

MUNSTER (town). Covers a land area of 7.570 square miles and a water area of 0.081 square miles. Located at 41.55° N. Lat; 87.50° W. Long. Elevation is 610 feet.
History: Named for Eldert Munster, who settled here in 1855. Settled 1855.
Population: 23,005; Growth (since 2000): 6.9%; Density: 3,038.9 persons per square mile; Race: 84.2% White, 3.0% Black/African American, 4.8% Asian, 0.2% American Indian/Alaska Native, 0.1% Native Hawaiian/Other Pacific Islander, 1.4% Two or more races, 14.5% Hispanic of any race; Average household size: 2.59; Median age: 45.2; Age under 18: 20.8%; Age 65 and over: 19.4%; Males per 100 females: 92.5; Marriage status: 28.8% never married, 53.7% now married, 1.0% separated, 8.5% widowed, 9.1% divorced; Foreign born: 10.7%; Speak English only: 80.5%; With disability: 11.6%; Veterans: 6.4%; Ancestry: 17.3% German, 15.5% Irish, 14.8% Polish, 9.8% Italian, 7.0% English

Employment: 22.4% management, business, and financial, 5.0% computer, engineering, and science, 10.7% education, legal, community service, arts, and media, 10.4% healthcare practitioners, 12.1% service, 24.6% sales and office, 5.8% natural resources, construction, and maintenance, 9.0% production, transportation, and material moving
Income: Per capita: $39,915; Median household: $78,251; Average household: $100,558; Households with income of $100,000 or more: 38.2%; Poverty rate: 4.8%
Educational Attainment: High school diploma or higher: 94.7%; Bachelor's degree or higher: 42.7%; Graduate/professional degree or higher: 14.9%

School District(s)

School Town Of Munster (PK-12)
Enrollment: 3,825 . . . . (219) 836-9111
Housing: Homeownership rate: 86.0%; Median home value: $217,700; Median year structure built: 1971; Homeowner vacancy rate: 1.6%; Median selected monthly owner costs: $1,580 with a mortgage, $556 without a mortgage; Median gross rent: $1,072 per month; Rental vacancy rate: 0.0%
Health Insurance: 95.1% have insurance; 85.1% have private insurance; 23.1% have public insurance; 4.9% do not have insurance; 0.8% of children under 18 do not have insurance
Hospitals: Community Hospital (354 beds); Franciscan Healthcare - Munster (63 beds)
Safety: Violent crime rate: 10.1 per 10,000 population; Property crime rate: 201.8 per 10,000 population
Newspapers: The Times (daily circulation 81,200)
Transportation: Commute: 85.6% car, 6.7% public transportation, 0.5% walk, 5.2% work from home; Mean travel time to work: 29.2 minutes
Additional Information Contacts
Town of Munster . . . . (219) 836-6900
http://www.ci.munster.in.us

NEW CHICAGO (town). Covers a land area of 0.669 square miles and a water area of 0 square miles. Located at 41.56° N. Lat; 87.27° W. Long. Elevation is 636 feet.
History: New Chicago was the home of the United States Electric Carriage Company, which built the first electric buggy in 1898.
Population: 1,803; Growth (since 2000): -12.6%; Density: 2,693.5 persons per square mile; Race: 82.5% White, 3.2% Black/African American, 0.7% Asian, 0.8% American Indian/Alaska Native, 0.0% Native Hawaiian/Other Pacific Islander, 3.6% Two or more races, 36.2% Hispanic of any race; Average household size: 2.50; Median age: 38.7; Age under 18: 22.1%; Age 65 and over: 14.9%; Males per 100 females: 99.9; Marriage status: 37.5% never married, 39.3% now married, 1.3% separated, 5.5% widowed, 17.6% divorced; Foreign born: 11.6%; Speak English only: 75.4%; With disability: 17.7%; Veterans: 7.8%; Ancestry: 14.9% German, 13.6% Irish, 6.7% Italian, 4.9% Polish, 4.6% English
Employment: 4.7% management, business, and financial, 0.6% computer, engineering, and science, 2.4% education, legal, community service, arts, and media, 5.1% healthcare practitioners, 24.5% service, 23.8% sales and office, 17.0% natural resources, construction, and maintenance, 22.0% production, transportation, and material moving
Income: Per capita: $19,545; Median household: $38,553; Average household: $47,727; Households with income of $100,000 or more: 10.0%; Poverty rate: 27.7%
Educational Attainment: High school diploma or higher: 72.6%; Bachelor's degree or higher: 5.0%; Graduate/professional degree or higher: 0.5%
Housing: Homeownership rate: 65.8%; Median home value: $78,800; Median year structure built: 1963; Homeowner vacancy rate: 7.2%; Median selected monthly owner costs: $1,024 with a mortgage, $399 without a mortgage; Median gross rent: $806 per month; Rental vacancy rate: 6.4%
Health Insurance: 83.6% have insurance; 51.1% have private insurance; 46.2% have public insurance; 16.4% do not have insurance; 6.3% of children under 18 do not have insurance
Transportation: Commute: 93.2% car, 0.4% public transportation, 0.6% walk, 4.2% work from home; Mean travel time to work: 24.4 minutes

SAINT JOHN (town). Covers a land area of 11.387 square miles and a water area of 0.091 square miles. Located at 41.44° N. Lat; 87.47° W. Long. Elevation is 725 feet.
History: St. John was founded in 1837. It is generally agreed that the Town of St. John had its beginning when John Hack, a German immigrant farmer and his family arrived in 1837, in the area then known asWestern prairie or Prairie West.
Population: 16,391; Growth (since 2000): 95.5%; Density: 1,439.4 persons per square mile; Race: 94.2% White, 0.6% Black/African American, 0.7% Asian, 0.1% American Indian/Alaska Native, 0.0% Native Hawaiian/Other Pacific Islander, 2.9% Two or more races, 9.1% Hispanic of any race; Average household size: 2.88; Median age: 43.6; Age under 18: 26.0%; Age 65 and over: 14.7%; Males per 100 females: 99.6; Marriage status: 22.8% never married, 65.2% now married, 0.1% separated, 4.8% widowed, 7.2% divorced; Foreign born: 4.4%; Speak English only: 93.1%; With disability: 9.1%; Veterans: 8.2%; Ancestry: 22.6% German, 18.8% Polish, 16.4% Irish, 11.3% Italian, 7.5% English
Employment: 20.3% management, business, and financial, 6.0% computer, engineering, and science, 9.7% education, legal, community service, arts, and media, 10.6% healthcare practitioners, 11.0% service, 23.5% sales and office, 9.1% natural resources, construction, and maintenance, 9.8% production, transportation, and material moving
Income: Per capita: $42,503; Median household: $103,701; Average household: $121,622; Households with income of $100,000 or more: 53.4%; Poverty rate: 3.2%
Educational Attainment: High school diploma or higher: 96.1%; Bachelor's degree or higher: 38.9%; Graduate/professional degree or higher: 13.6%

School District(s)

Lake Central School Corporation (PK-12)
Enrollment: 9,630 . . . . (219) 558-2707
Housing: Homeownership rate: 98.3%; Median home value: $274,300; Median year structure built: 1998; Homeowner vacancy rate: 0.1%; Median selected monthly owner costs: $1,706 with a mortgage, $571 without a mortgage; Median gross rent: $842 per month; Rental vacancy rate: 0.0%
Health Insurance: 96.5% have insurance; 89.7% have private insurance; 18.8% have public insurance; 3.5% do not have insurance; 2.2% of children under 18 do not have insurance
Safety: Violent crime rate: 1.2 per 10,000 population; Property crime rate: 83.5 per 10,000 population
Transportation: Commute: 90.6% car, 3.3% public transportation, 0.2% walk, 4.6% work from home; Mean travel time to work: 36.3 minutes
Additional Information Contacts
Town of Saint John . . . . (219) 365-6465
http://www.stjohnin.com

SCHERERVILLE (town). Covers a land area of 14.712 square miles and a water area of 0.053 square miles. Located at 41.49° N. Lat; 87.44° W. Long. Elevation is 669 feet.
History: Named for Nicholas Scherer, who plotted the town in 1866. Laid out 1866.
Population: 28,778; Growth (since 2000): 15.8%; Density: 1,956.1 persons per square mile; Race: 82.6% White, 5.1% Black/African American, 3.3% Asian, 0.4% American Indian/Alaska Native, 0.0% Native Hawaiian/Other Pacific Islander, 3.5% Two or more races, 11.8% Hispanic of any race; Average household size: 2.46; Median age: 43.2; Age under 18: 20.1%; Age 65 and over: 17.9%; Males per 100 females: 94.2; Marriage status: 29.1% never married, 54.5% now married, 0.8% separated, 6.5% widowed, 9.8% divorced; Foreign born: 10.7%; Speak English only: 83.3%; With disability: 10.3%; Veterans: 7.2%; Ancestry: 22.1% German, 17.1% Irish, 16.9% Polish, 7.2% Italian, 4.7% English
Employment: 16.0% management, business, and financial, 4.0% computer, engineering, and science, 10.5% education, legal, community service, arts, and media, 7.6% healthcare practitioners, 14.2% service, 24.0% sales and office, 10.3% natural resources, construction, and maintenance, 13.4% production, transportation, and material moving
Income: Per capita: $36,641; Median household: $68,166; Average household: $89,007; Households with income of $100,000 or more: 32.5%; Poverty rate: 4.5%
Educational Attainment: High school diploma or higher: 93.6%; Bachelor's degree or higher: 31.7%; Graduate/professional degree or higher: 12.6%

School District(s)

Lake Central School Corporation (PK-12)
Enrollment: 9,630 . . . . (219) 558-2707

Vocational/Technical School(s)

Don Roberts School of Hair Design (Private, For-profit)
Enrollment: 50. . . . . (219) 864-1600
Tuition: $16,500

Housing: Homeownership rate: 77.9%; Median home value: $206,300; Median year structure built: 1987; Homeowner vacancy rate: 1.3%; Median selected monthly owner costs: $1,408 with a mortgage, $462 without a mortgage; Median gross rent: $940 per month; Rental vacancy rate: 4.6%
Health Insurance: 91.4% have insurance; 79.7% have private insurance; 25.2% have public insurance; 8.6% do not have insurance; 8.7% of children under 18 do not have insurance
Transportation: Commute: 92.3% car, 2.5% public transportation, 0.2% walk, 3.4% work from home; Mean travel time to work: 30.2 minutes
Additional Information Contacts
Town of Schererville . . . . (219) 322-2211
http://www.ci.schererville.in.us

SCHNEIDER (town). Covers a land area of 0.861 square miles and a water area of 0 square miles. Located at 41.19° N. Lat; 87.45° W. Long. Elevation is 633 feet.
Population: 249; Growth (since 2000): -21.5%; Density: 289.1 persons per square mile; Race: 97.2% White, 0.0% Black/African American, 0.0% Asian, 0.0% American Indian/Alaska Native, 0.0% Native Hawaiian/Other Pacific Islander, 2.4% Two or more races, 0.4% Hispanic of any race; Average household size: 2.86; Median age: 33.1; Age under 18: 23.7%; Age 65 and over: 10.8%; Males per 100 females: 106.7; Marriage status: 34.3% never married, 47.5% now married, 1.0% separated, 5.1% widowed, 13.1% divorced; Foreign born: 0.4%; Speak English only: 100.0%; With disability: 16.5%; Veterans: 7.9%; Ancestry: 40.2% Irish, 35.3% German, 26.5% Polish, 8.8% American, 6.8% Dutch
Employment: 6.4% management, business, and financial, 0.0% computer, engineering, and science, 1.8% education, legal, community service, arts, and media, 5.5% healthcare practitioners, 26.6% service, 19.3% sales and office, 22.0% natural resources, construction, and maintenance, 18.3% production, transportation, and material moving
Income: Per capita: $20,327; Median household: $46,042; Average household: $55,572; Households with income of $100,000 or more: 5.7%; Poverty rate: 22.1%
Educational Attainment: High school diploma or higher: 93.7%; Bachelor's degree or higher: 9.4%; Graduate/professional degree or higher: 0.6%
Housing: Homeownership rate: 63.2%; Median home value: $94,100; Median year structure built: 1951; Homeowner vacancy rate: 0.0%; Median selected monthly owner costs: $1,054 with a mortgage, $606 without a mortgage; Median gross rent: $783 per month; Rental vacancy rate: 0.0%
Health Insurance: 90.8% have insurance; 54.2% have private insurance; 46.2% have public insurance; 9.2% do not have insurance; 7.7% of children under 18 do not have insurance
Transportation: Commute: 84.4% car, 0.0% public transportation, 11.0% walk, 2.8% work from home; Mean travel time to work: 30.3 minutes

SHELBY (CDP). Covers a land area of 1.287 square miles and a water area of 0 square miles. Located at 41.19° N. Lat; 87.34° W. Long. Elevation is 640 feet.
Population: 465; Growth (since 2000): n/a; Density: 361.2 persons per square mile; Race: 100.0% White, 0.0% Black/African American, 0.0% Asian, 0.0% American Indian/Alaska Native, 0.0% Native Hawaiian/Other Pacific Islander, 0.0% Two or more races, 8.4% Hispanic of any race; Average household size: 2.31; Median age: 39.4; Age under 18: 38.1%; Age 65 and over: 8.8%; Males per 100 females: 108.9; Marriage status: 37.9% never married, 34.9% now married, 0.0% separated, 10.2% widowed, 17.0% divorced; Foreign born: 0.0%; Speak English only: 100.0%; With disability: 11.0%; Veterans: 4.9%; Ancestry: 59.4% German, 16.3% Irish, 14.6% Polish, 8.6% French, 8.6% Scottish
Employment: 16.2% management, business, and financial, 0.0% computer, engineering, and science, 0.0% education, legal, community service, arts, and media, 21.6% healthcare practitioners, 27.0% service, 17.6% sales and office, 8.8% natural resources, construction, and maintenance, 8.8% production, transportation, and material moving
Income: Per capita: $20,995; Median household: n/a; Average household: $48,348; Households with income of $100,000 or more: 14.5%; Poverty rate: 20.0%
Educational Attainment: High school diploma or higher: 74.7%; Bachelor's degree or higher: 11.3%; Graduate/professional degree or higher: 6.2%
Housing: Homeownership rate: 68.7%; Median home value: $97,700; Median year structure built: 1955; Homeowner vacancy rate: 0.0%; Median selected monthly owner costs: $950 with a mortgage, $309 without a mortgage; Median gross rent: n/a per month; Rental vacancy rate: 0.0%
Health Insurance: 94.6% have insurance; 58.1% have private insurance; 42.6% have public insurance; 5.4% do not have insurance; 0.0% of children under 18 do not have insurance
Transportation: Commute: 91.9% car, 0.0% public transportation, 8.1% walk, 0.0% work from home; Mean travel time to work: 21.2 minutes

WHITING (city). Covers a land area of 1.798 square miles and a water area of 1.429 square miles. Located at 41.68° N. Lat; 87.48° W. Long. Elevation is 587 feet.
History: Whiting was settled by German immigrants. For many years a Standard Oil Company plant, established in 1889, was the major industry.
Population: 4,858; Growth (since 2000): -5.4%; Density: 2,702.5 persons per square mile; Race: 73.4% White, 3.3% Black/African American, 0.0% Asian, 0.0% American Indian/Alaska Native, 0.2% Native Hawaiian/Other Pacific Islander, 2.5% Two or more races, 36.7% Hispanic of any race; Average household size: 2.85; Median age: 34.4; Age under 18: 25.7%; Age 65 and over: 9.3%; Males per 100 females: 96.6; Marriage status: 41.6% never married, 41.8% now married, 3.9% separated, 7.8% widowed, 8.8% divorced; Foreign born: 7.6%; Speak English only: 81.0%; With disability: 15.6%; Veterans: 4.6%; Ancestry: 15.8% German, 14.1% Polish, 10.8% Irish, 6.3% Slovak, 6.2% English
Employment: 11.5% management, business, and financial, 1.1% computer, engineering, and science, 4.9% education, legal, community service, arts, and media, 1.5% healthcare practitioners, 22.1% service, 24.4% sales and office, 10.4% natural resources, construction, and maintenance, 24.1% production, transportation, and material moving
Income: Per capita: $24,677; Median household: $57,625; Average household: $67,944; Households with income of $100,000 or more: 24.9%; Poverty rate: 16.3%
Educational Attainment: High school diploma or higher: 87.6%; Bachelor's degree or higher: 13.3%; Graduate/professional degree or higher: 4.0%

School District(s)
School City Of Hammond (PK-12)
Enrollment: 14,193 . . . . (219) 933-2400
School City Of Whiting (PK-12)
Enrollment: 923. . . . . (219) 659-0656

Four-year College(s)
Calumet College of Saint Joseph (Private, Not-for-profit, Roman Catholic)
Enrollment: 834. . . . . (219) 473-7770
Tuition: In-state $17,920; Out-of-state $17,920

Housing: Homeownership rate: 62.9%; Median home value: $123,300; Median year structure built: Before 1940; Homeowner vacancy rate: 2.9%; Median selected monthly owner costs: $1,093 with a mortgage, $371 without a mortgage; Median gross rent: $832 per month; Rental vacancy rate: 25.1%
Health Insurance: 89.6% have insurance; 68.6% have private insurance; 32.0% have public insurance; 10.4% do not have insurance; 7.4% of children under 18 do not have insurance
Safety: Violent crime rate: n/a per 10,000 population; Property crime rate: 212.3 per 10,000 population
Transportation: Commute: 90.6% car, 1.6% public transportation, 5.0% walk, 0.5% work from home; Mean travel time to work: 28.9 minutes; Amtrak: Train service available.
Additional Information Contacts
City of Whiting . . . . (219) 659-3100
http://whitingindiana.com

WINFIELD (town). Covers a land area of 11.975 square miles and a water area of 0.066 square miles. Located at 41.41° N. Lat; 87.26° W. Long. Elevation is 709 feet.
History: The town was incorporated 1993, making it one of newest towns in Indiana. Prior to that time it had been part of Winfield Township as an unincorporated town. Winfield is named for General Winfield Scott.
Population: 5,395; Growth (since 2000): 134.8%; Density: 450.5 persons per square mile; Race: 80.7% White, 6.1% Black/African American, 3.0% Asian, 0.0% American Indian/Alaska Native, 0.0% Native Hawaiian/Other Pacific Islander, 2.2% Two or more races, 18.4% Hispanic of any race; Average household size: 3.10; Median age: 37.3; Age under 18: 28.1%; Age 65 and over: 15.3%; Males per 100 females: 95.0; Marriage status: 25.6% never married, 60.2% now married, 0.6% separated, 8.5% widowed, 5.7% divorced; Foreign born: 6.0%; Speak English only: 91.1%; With disability: 9.0%; Veterans: 6.1%; Ancestry: 23.3% German, 14.9% Irish, 8.8% English, 7.7% Polish, 4.4% Italian

Employment: 26.0% management, business, and financial, 1.6% computer, engineering, and science, 6.0% education, legal, community service, arts, and media, 10.3% healthcare practitioners, 12.6% service, 23.6% sales and office, 11.4% natural resources, construction, and maintenance, 8.4% production, transportation, and material moving
Income: Per capita: $38,314; Median household: $96,272; Average household: $117,726; Households with income of $100,000 or more: 48.4%; Poverty rate: 2.2%
Educational Attainment: High school diploma or higher: 94.0%; Bachelor's degree or higher: 30.1%; Graduate/professional degree or higher: 9.8%
Housing: Homeownership rate: 89.2%; Median home value: $275,200; Median year structure built: 2001; Homeowner vacancy rate: 2.6%; Median selected monthly owner costs: $1,732 with a mortgage, $709 without a mortgage; Median gross rent: $1,308 per month; Rental vacancy rate: 20.0%
Health Insurance: 94.7% have insurance; 84.2% have private insurance; 21.5% have public insurance; 5.3% do not have insurance; 2.6% of children under 18 do not have insurance
Newspapers: Winfield American (weekly circulation 5,000)
Transportation: Commute: 92.0% car, 0.4% public transportation, 0.0% walk, 4.8% work from home; Mean travel time to work: 26.7 minutes
Additional Information Contacts
Town of Winfield . . . . (219) 662-2665
http://www.winfieldgov.com

LaPorte County

Located in northwestern Indiana; bounded on the northwest by Lake Michigan, on the north by Michigan, and partly on the south by the Kankakee River. Covers a land area of 598.299 square miles, a water area of 14.960 square miles, and is located in the Central Time Zone at 41.55° N. Lat., 86.74° W. Long. The county was founded in 1832. County seat is La Porte.

LaPorte County is part of the Michigan City-La Porte, IN Metropolitan Statistical Area. The entire metro area includes: LaPorte County, IN

Weather Station: La Porte Elevation: 810 feet

	Jan	Feb	Mar	Apr	May	Jun	Jul	Aug	Sep	Oct	Nov	Dec
High	31	35	46	58	70	79	82	80	74	62	48	35
Low	18	21	29	40	50	60	64	63	55	44	34	23
Precip	2.6	2.3	2.9	3.6	3.8	4.2	4.3	4.4	3.7	3.8	3.9	3.2
Snow	20.6	13.9	7.2	1.4	tr	0.0	0.0	0.0	0.0	0.4	3.8	14.9

High and Low temperatures in degrees Fahrenheit; Precipitation and Snow in inches

Population: 110,839; Growth (since 2000): 0.7%; Density: 185.3 persons per square mile; Race: 83.1% White, 11.0% Black/African American, 0.6% Asian, 0.3% American Indian/Alaska Native, 0.0% Native Hawaiian/Other Pacific Islander, 2.9% two or more races, 6.3% Hispanic of any race; Average household size: 2.38; Median age: 40.2; Age under 18: 21.9%; Age 65 and over: 16.3%; Males per 100 females: 107.1; Marriage status: 30.4% never married, 48.9% now married, 1.2% separated, 6.1% widowed, 14.6% divorced; Foreign born: 3.3%; Speak English only: 94.0%; With disability: 13.5%; Veterans: 9.0%; Ancestry: 27.4% German, 13.8% Irish, 11.1% Polish, 6.5% English, 5.9% American
Religion: Six largest groups: 13.3% Catholicism, 4.8% Lutheran, 3.9% Baptist, 3.5% Methodist/Pietist, 3.4% Non-denominational Protestant, 1.8% Presbyterian-Reformed
Economy: Unemployment rate: 4.5%; Leading industries: 18.6 % retail trade; 11.3 % other services (except public administration); 10.4 % accommodation and food services; Farms: 731 totaling 227,865 acres; Company size: 2 employ 1,000 or more persons, 2 employ 500 to 999 persons, 47 employ 100 to 499 persons, 2,244 employ less than 100 persons; Business ownership: 2,540 women-owned, 515 Black-owned, 152 Hispanic-owned, 96 Asian-owned, 49 American Indian/Alaska Native-owned
Employment: 11.0% management, business, and financial, 2.4% computer, engineering, and science, 7.8% education, legal, community service, arts, and media, 5.4% healthcare practitioners, 19.5% service, 22.7% sales and office, 10.2% natural resources, construction, and maintenance, 21.0% production, transportation, and material moving
Income: Per capita: $25,004; Median household: $49,921; Average household: $64,800; Households with income of $100,000 or more: 17.0%; Poverty rate: 16.6%
Educational Attainment: High school diploma or higher: 87.9%; Bachelor's degree or higher: 17.8%; Graduate/professional degree or higher: 6.3%
Housing: Homeownership rate: 71.5%; Median home value: $126,700; Median year structure built: 1966; Homeowner vacancy rate: 1.9%; Median selected monthly owner costs: $1,036 with a mortgage, $393 without a mortgage; Median gross rent: $729 per month; Rental vacancy rate: 4.9%
Vital Statistics: Birth rate: 119.4 per 10,000 population; Death rate: 107.6 per 10,000 population; Age-adjusted cancer mortality rate: 179.9 deaths per 100,000 population
Health Insurance: 90.4% have insurance; 66.9% have private insurance; 37.0% have public insurance; 9.6% do not have insurance; 5.5% of children under 18 do not have insurance
Health Care: Physicians: 13.4 per 10,000 population; Dentists: 5.1 per 10,000 population; Hospital beds: 27.2 per 10,000 population; Hospital admissions: 1,087.9 per 10,000 population
Air Quality Index (AQI): Percent of Days: 76.6% good, 20.6% moderate, 2.8% unhealthy for sensitive individuals, 0.0% unhealthy, 0.0% very unhealthy; Annual median: 40; Annual maximum: 147
Transportation: Commute: 92.2% car, 0.8% public transportation, 2.0% walk, 3.7% work from home; Mean travel time to work: 22.1 minutes
2016 Presidential Election: 49.7% Trump, 43.4% Clinton, 5.5% Johnson, 0.4% Stein
National and State Parks: Kingsbury State Fish and Wildlife Area
Additional Information Contacts
LaPorte Government. . . . . (219) 326-6808
http://www.laportecounty.org

LaPorte County Communities

FISH LAKE (CDP). Covers a land area of 1.541 square miles and a water area of 0.344 square miles. Located at 41.56° N. Lat; 86.55° W. Long. Elevation is 702 feet.
Population: 1,500; Growth (since 2000): n/a; Density: 973.5 persons per square mile; Race: 99.3% White, 0.0% Black/African American, 0.0% Asian, 0.7% American Indian/Alaska Native, 0.0% Native Hawaiian/Other Pacific Islander, 0.0% Two or more races, 0.7% Hispanic of any race; Average household size: 2.63; Median age: 52.5; Age under 18: 21.9%; Age 65 and over: 26.3%; Males per 100 females: 97.7; Marriage status: 17.2% never married, 57.7% now married, 0.7% separated, 7.0% widowed, 18.1% divorced; Foreign born: 0.0%; Speak English only: 99.3%; With disability: 17.5%; Veterans: 16.6%; Ancestry: 23.6% Polish, 15.6% German, 12.1% Irish, 8.7% French, 7.4% English
Employment: 10.4% management, business, and financial, 0.0% computer, engineering, and science, 3.4% education, legal, community service, arts, and media, 4.9% healthcare practitioners, 38.3% service, 20.9% sales and office, 7.8% natural resources, construction, and maintenance, 14.3% production, transportation, and material moving
Income: Per capita: $23,284; Median household: $59,740; Average household: $61,880; Households with income of $100,000 or more: 6.7%; Poverty rate: 1.2%
Educational Attainment: High school diploma or higher: 84.9%; Bachelor's degree or higher: 14.1%; Graduate/professional degree or higher: 4.2%
Housing: Homeownership rate: 87.7%; Median home value: $96,500; Median year structure built: 1956; Homeowner vacancy rate: 7.9%; Median selected monthly owner costs: $800 with a mortgage, $266 without a mortgage; Median gross rent: $729 per month; Rental vacancy rate: 0.0%
Health Insurance: 93.4% have insurance; 73.7% have private insurance; 38.6% have public insurance; 6.6% do not have insurance; 0.0% of children under 18 do not have insurance
Transportation: Commute: 96.4% car, 2.1% public transportation, 1.5% walk, 0.0% work from home; Mean travel time to work: 27.4 minutes

HANNA (CDP). Covers a land area of 0.978 square miles and a water area of 0 square miles. Located at 41.41° N. Lat; 86.78° W. Long. Elevation is 705 feet.
Population: 280; Growth (since 2000): n/a; Density: 286.2 persons per square mile; Race: 100.0% White, 0.0% Black/African American, 0.0% Asian, 0.0% American Indian/Alaska Native, 0.0% Native Hawaiian/Other Pacific Islander, 0.0% Two or more races, 0.0% Hispanic of any race; Average household size: 2.04; Median age: 47.6; Age under 18: 22.9%; Age 65 and over: 10.0%; Males per 100 females: 98.7; Marriage status: 6.5% never married, 68.0% now married, 0.0% separated, 4.8% widowed, 20.8% divorced; Foreign born: 0.0%; Speak English only: 100.0%; With

disability: 6.8%; Veterans: 7.9%; Ancestry: 30.7% German, 14.3% Irish, 10.7% Czech, 8.2% English, 5.4% Polish
Employment: 14.9% management, business, and financial, 4.6% computer, engineering, and science, 3.6% education, legal, community service, arts, and media, 8.8% healthcare practitioners, 4.6% service, 30.9% sales and office, 22.7% natural resources, construction, and maintenance, 9.8% production, transportation, and material moving
Income: Per capita: $33,474; Median household: n/a; Average household: $67,491; Households with income of $100,000 or more: 37.2%; Poverty rate: 15.0%
Educational Attainment: High school diploma or higher: 95.4%; Bachelor's degree or higher: 20.4%; Graduate/professional degree or higher: 7.4%
Housing: Homeownership rate: 100.0%; Median home value: $121,200; Median year structure built: 1953; Homeowner vacancy rate: 18.9%; Median selected monthly owner costs: $1,207 with a mortgage, $256 without a mortgage; Median gross rent: n/a per month; Rental vacancy rate: 0.0%
Health Insurance: 90.7% have insurance; 77.5% have private insurance; 18.9% have public insurance; 9.3% do not have insurance; 0.0% of children under 18 do not have insurance
Transportation: Commute: 86.1% car, 0.0% public transportation, 4.6% walk, 9.3% work from home; Mean travel time to work: 27.6 minutes

HUDSON LAKE (CDP). Covers a land area of 1.925 square miles and a water area of 0.759 square miles. Located at 41.72° N. Lat; 86.55° W. Long. Elevation is 771 feet.
Population: 1,257; Growth (since 2000): n/a; Density: 653.0 persons per square mile; Race: 100.0% White, 0.0% Black/African American, 0.0% Asian, 0.0% American Indian/Alaska Native, 0.0% Native Hawaiian/Other Pacific Islander, 0.0% Two or more races, 0.0% Hispanic of any race; Average household size: 2.26; Median age: 44.0; Age under 18: 16.3%; Age 65 and over: 15.9%; Males per 100 females: 105.2; Marriage status: 19.3% never married, 58.1% now married, 0.0% separated, 2.1% widowed, 20.5% divorced; Foreign born: 0.0%; Speak English only: 98.9%; With disability: 22.0%; Veterans: 4.0%; Ancestry: 33.8% German, 13.7% Polish, 12.7% Irish, 9.9% Swedish, 8.1% Dutch
Employment: 13.5% management, business, and financial, 0.0% computer, engineering, and science, 0.0% education, legal, community service, arts, and media, 14.7% healthcare practitioners, 4.5% service, 30.0% sales and office, 24.0% natural resources, construction, and maintenance, 13.2% production, transportation, and material moving
Income: Per capita: $22,276; Median household: $47,549; Average household: $51,342; Households with income of $100,000 or more: 9.9%; Poverty rate: 14.0%
Educational Attainment: High school diploma or higher: 91.0%; Bachelor's degree or higher: 15.3%; Graduate/professional degree or higher: 7.4%
Housing: Homeownership rate: 94.8%; Median home value: $116,500; Median year structure built: 1948; Homeowner vacancy rate: 0.0%; Median selected monthly owner costs: $937 with a mortgage, $323 without a mortgage; Median gross rent: n/a per month; Rental vacancy rate: 0.0%
Health Insurance: 89.1% have insurance; 61.7% have private insurance; 36.4% have public insurance; 10.9% do not have insurance; 0.0% of children under 18 do not have insurance
Transportation: Commute: 96.4% car, 0.0% public transportation, 0.0% walk, 3.6% work from home; Mean travel time to work: 22.9 minutes

KINGSBURY (town). Covers a land area of 0.573 square miles and a water area of 0 square miles. Located at 41.53° N. Lat; 86.70° W. Long. Elevation is 748 feet.
History: Kingsbury developed around the Wabash and the Grand Trunk Railroads in the mid-1800's.
Population: 205; Growth (since 2000): -10.5%; Density: 357.8 persons per square mile; Race: 94.6% White, 0.0% Black/African American, 0.0% Asian, 0.0% American Indian/Alaska Native, 0.0% Native Hawaiian/Other Pacific Islander, 0.0% Two or more races, 7.3% Hispanic of any race; Average household size: 2.53; Median age: 46.4; Age under 18: 24.9%; Age 65 and over: 17.1%; Males per 100 females: 98.4; Marriage status: 18.5% never married, 67.9% now married, 0.0% separated, 4.8% widowed, 8.9% divorced; Foreign born: 3.4%; Speak English only: 90.2%; With disability: 17.1%; Veterans: 13.6%; Ancestry: 38.0% German, 21.5% Irish, 5.9% American, 4.9% Polish, 4.4% Italian
Employment: 7.2% management, business, and financial, 1.8% computer, engineering, and science, 0.9% education, legal, community service, arts, and media, 3.6% healthcare practitioners, 23.4% service, 8.1% sales and office, 23.4% natural resources, construction, and maintenance, 31.5% production, transportation, and material moving
Income: Per capita: $27,523; Median household: $70,625; Average household: $64,940; Households with income of $100,000 or more: 8.6%; Poverty rate: 2.0%
Educational Attainment: High school diploma or higher: 85.7%; Bachelor's degree or higher: 1.3%; Graduate/professional degree or higher: n/a
Housing: Homeownership rate: 79.0%; Median home value: $110,000; Median year structure built: 1983; Homeowner vacancy rate: 1.5%; Median selected monthly owner costs: $903 with a mortgage, $322 without a mortgage; Median gross rent: $915 per month; Rental vacancy rate: 0.0%
Health Insurance: 93.7% have insurance; 85.4% have private insurance; 35.1% have public insurance; 6.3% do not have insurance; 0.0% of children under 18 do not have insurance
Transportation: Commute: 96.4% car, 0.0% public transportation, 0.0% walk, 1.8% work from home; Mean travel time to work: 22.0 minutes

KINGSFORD HEIGHTS (town). Covers a land area of 0.942 square miles and a water area of 0 square miles. Located at 41.48° N. Lat; 86.69° W. Long. Elevation is 725 feet.
Population: 1,370; Growth (since 2000): -5.7%; Density: 1,454.9 persons per square mile; Race: 85.4% White, 7.0% Black/African American, 0.0% Asian, 1.2% American Indian/Alaska Native, 0.0% Native Hawaiian/Other Pacific Islander, 5.3% Two or more races, 3.9% Hispanic of any race; Average household size: 2.73; Median age: 32.1; Age under 18: 27.3%; Age 65 and over: 11.3%; Males per 100 females: 89.8; Marriage status: 29.0% never married, 47.7% now married, 1.6% separated, 6.5% widowed, 16.8% divorced; Foreign born: 1.2%; Speak English only: 97.9%; With disability: 19.1%; Veterans: 8.0%; Ancestry: 23.9% German, 22.3% Irish, 9.3% American, 6.1% English, 4.0% Polish
Employment: 6.2% management, business, and financial, 1.3% computer, engineering, and science, 5.1% education, legal, community service, arts, and media, 0.4% healthcare practitioners, 27.7% service, 11.5% sales and office, 6.2% natural resources, construction, and maintenance, 41.6% production, transportation, and material moving
Income: Per capita: $15,113; Median household: $33,984; Average household: $42,769; Households with income of $100,000 or more: 2.0%; Poverty rate: 25.4%
Educational Attainment: High school diploma or higher: 75.6%; Bachelor's degree or higher: 6.2%; Graduate/professional degree or higher: 1.2%

School District(s)

Laporte Community School Corp (PK-12)
Enrollment: 6,694 . . . . (219) 362-7056
Housing: Homeownership rate: 66.7%; Median home value: $66,800; Median year structure built: 1962; Homeowner vacancy rate: 2.9%; Median selected monthly owner costs: $818 with a mortgage, $300 without a mortgage; Median gross rent: $680 per month; Rental vacancy rate: 0.0%
Health Insurance: 82.5% have insurance; 45.9% have private insurance; 43.2% have public insurance; 17.5% do not have insurance; 8.5% of children under 18 do not have insurance
Transportation: Commute: 99.4% car, 0.0% public transportation, 0.0% walk, 0.0% work from home; Mean travel time to work: 24.0 minutes

LA CROSSE (town). Covers a land area of 0.531 square miles and a water area of 0 square miles. Located at 41.32° N. Lat; 86.89° W. Long. Elevation is 676 feet.
Population: 552; Growth (since 2000): -1.6%; Density: 1,039.5 persons per square mile; Race: 98.0% White, 0.9% Black/African American, 0.0% Asian, 0.0% American Indian/Alaska Native, 0.0% Native Hawaiian/Other Pacific Islander, 1.1% Two or more races, 0.4% Hispanic of any race; Average household size: 2.44; Median age: 35.6; Age under 18: 25.9%; Age 65 and over: 16.7%; Males per 100 females: 96.8; Marriage status: 25.6% never married, 55.1% now married, 3.8% separated, 3.8% widowed, 15.5% divorced; Foreign born: 1.1%; Speak English only: 99.6%; With disability: 13.0%; Veterans: 8.1%; Ancestry: 33.7% German, 11.4% Polish, 8.7% Irish, 8.0% English, 4.7% Belgian
Employment: 3.6% management, business, and financial, 1.2% computer, engineering, and science, 5.7% education, legal, community service, arts, and media, 8.9% healthcare practitioners, 13.0% service, 30.0% sales and office, 21.5% natural resources, construction, and maintenance, 16.2% production, transportation, and material moving

Income: Per capita: $25,185; Median household: $50,000; Average household: $63,578; Households with income of $100,000 or more: 14.6%; Poverty rate: 14.6%
Educational Attainment: High school diploma or higher: 92.7%; Bachelor's degree or higher: 10.1%; Graduate/professional degree or higher: 3.6%

School District(s)

Tri-township Cons School Corp (PK-12)
Enrollment: 479. . . . . (219) 754-2709
Housing: Homeownership rate: 73.9%; Median home value: $93,000; Median year structure built: 1951; Homeowner vacancy rate: 0.0%; Median selected monthly owner costs: $940 with a mortgage, $373 without a mortgage; Median gross rent: $930 per month; Rental vacancy rate: 0.0%
Health Insurance: 86.4% have insurance; 63.2% have private insurance; 35.0% have public insurance; 13.6% do not have insurance; 9.1% of children under 18 do not have insurance
Transportation: Commute: 98.0% car, 0.0% public transportation, 0.8% walk, 1.2% work from home; Mean travel time to work: 27.9 minutes

LA PORTE (city). County seat. Covers a land area of 11.660 square miles and a water area of 0.710 square miles. Located at 41.61° N. Lat; 86.71° W. Long. Elevation is 814 feet.
History: La Porte was founded in 1830 when the Michigan Road was under construction. Its name is French for "the door," and through La Porte passed much commerce.
Population: 21,825; Growth (since 2000): 0.9%; Density: 1,871.7 persons per square mile; Race: 88.4% White, 2.8% Black/African American, 0.3% Asian, 0.3% American Indian/Alaska Native, 0.1% Native Hawaiian/Other Pacific Islander, 2.4% Two or more races, 12.3% Hispanic of any race; Average household size: 2.31; Median age: 36.5; Age under 18: 25.2%; Age 65 and over: 17.7%; Males per 100 females: 93.2; Marriage status: 31.0% never married, 43.2% now married, 1.3% separated, 8.1% widowed, 17.8% divorced; Foreign born: 5.8%; Speak English only: 88.5%; With disability: 15.0%; Veterans: 8.9%; Ancestry: 29.4% German, 14.7% Irish, 11.5% Polish, 7.1% English, 5.6% American
Employment: 6.1% management, business, and financial, 2.7% computer, engineering, and science, 6.4% education, legal, community service, arts, and media, 4.8% healthcare practitioners, 22.0% service, 24.9% sales and office, 8.6% natural resources, construction, and maintenance, 24.6% production, transportation, and material moving
Income: Per capita: $19,980; Median household: $36,734; Average household: $47,451; Households with income of $100,000 or more: 7.5%; Poverty rate: 22.4%
Educational Attainment: High school diploma or higher: 84.9%; Bachelor's degree or higher: 16.1%; Graduate/professional degree or higher: 5.3%

School District(s)

Indiana Department Of Corrections (07-12)
Enrollment: 391. . . . . (317) 233-3111
Laporte Community School Corp (PK-12)
Enrollment: 6,694 . . . . (219) 362-7056
Renaissance Academy Charter School (KG-08)
Enrollment: 247. . . . . (219) 878-8711
Housing: Homeownership rate: 57.2%; Median home value: $93,400; Median year structure built: 1955; Homeowner vacancy rate: 2.3%; Median selected monthly owner costs: $929 with a mortgage, $407 without a mortgage; Median gross rent: $672 per month; Rental vacancy rate: 5.0%
Health Insurance: 85.7% have insurance; 59.3% have private insurance; 40.6% have public insurance; 14.3% do not have insurance; 8.0% of children under 18 do not have insurance
Hospitals: Indiana University Health La Porte Hospital (227 beds)
Safety: Violent crime rate: 47.5 per 10,000 population; Property crime rate: 254.6 per 10,000 population
Newspapers: Herald-Argus (daily circulation 12,500)
Transportation: Commute: 91.0% car, 0.2% public transportation, 3.4% walk, 3.2% work from home; Mean travel time to work: 19.3 minutes
Airports: La Porte Municipal (general aviation)
Additional Information Contacts
City of La Porte . . . . (219) 362-9512
http://www.cityoflaporte.com

LONG BEACH (town). Covers a land area of 1.062 square miles and a water area of 2.086 square miles. Located at 41.75° N. Lat; 86.86° W. Long. Elevation is 620 feet.
Population: 1,126; Growth (since 2000): -27.8%; Density: 1,060.1 persons per square mile; Race: 96.8% White, 1.6% Black/African American, 0.8% Asian, 0.8% American Indian/Alaska Native, 0.0% Native Hawaiian/Other Pacific Islander, 0.0% Two or more races, 0.5% Hispanic of any race; Average household size: 2.05; Median age: 60.1; Age under 18: 14.2%; Age 65 and over: 37.7%; Males per 100 females: 93.0; Marriage status: 11.0% never married, 71.9% now married, 0.6% separated, 10.2% widowed, 6.9% divorced; Foreign born: 4.4%; Speak English only: 93.3%; With disability: 10.8%; Veterans: 8.2%; Ancestry: 29.7% Irish, 27.9% German, 12.3% Polish, 10.9% English, 8.7% Italian
Employment: 24.7% management, business, and financial, 5.4% computer, engineering, and science, 16.5% education, legal, community service, arts, and media, 12.0% healthcare practitioners, 7.2% service, 25.1% sales and office, 2.8% natural resources, construction, and maintenance, 6.4% production, transportation, and material moving
Income: Per capita: $61,879; Median household: $104,444; Average household: $130,270; Households with income of $100,000 or more: 52.2%; Poverty rate: 2.5%
Educational Attainment: High school diploma or higher: 98.9%; Bachelor's degree or higher: 64.1%; Graduate/professional degree or higher: 29.2%
Housing: Homeownership rate: 96.4%; Median home value: $418,900; Median year structure built: 1955; Homeowner vacancy rate: 5.6%; Median selected monthly owner costs: $2,112 with a mortgage, $696 without a mortgage; Median gross rent: $1,094 per month; Rental vacancy rate: 0.0%
Health Insurance: 98.1% have insurance; 83.5% have private insurance; 40.4% have public insurance; 1.9% do not have insurance; 0.0% of children under 18 do not have insurance
Transportation: Commute: 79.6% car, 4.5% public transportation, 2.6% walk, 12.6% work from home; Mean travel time to work: 32.9 minutes

MICHIANA SHORES (town). Covers a land area of 0.351 square miles and a water area of 0 square miles. Located at 41.76° N. Lat; 86.82° W. Long. Elevation is 610 feet.
Population: 262; Growth (since 2000): -20.6%; Density: 746.3 persons per square mile; Race: 99.2% White, 0.0% Black/African American, 0.0% Asian, 0.0% American Indian/Alaska Native, 0.0% Native Hawaiian/Other Pacific Islander, 0.8% Two or more races, 0.8% Hispanic of any race; Average household size: 1.96; Median age: 60.7; Age under 18: 13.0%; Age 65 and over: 39.3%; Males per 100 females: 96.9; Marriage status: 15.9% never married, 66.8% now married, 0.9% separated, 5.6% widowed, 11.6% divorced; Foreign born: 4.6%; Speak English only: 94.1%; With disability: 11.8%; Veterans: 11.0%; Ancestry: 22.1% German, 18.3% Irish, 11.1% Polish, 7.3% English, 6.9% Italian
Employment: 28.3% management, business, and financial, 1.8% computer, engineering, and science, 20.4% education, legal, community service, arts, and media, 4.4% healthcare practitioners, 6.2% service, 24.8% sales and office, 5.3% natural resources, construction, and maintenance, 8.8% production, transportation, and material moving
Income: Per capita: $61,372; Median household: $80,000; Average household: $120,584; Households with income of $100,000 or more: 39.5%; Poverty rate: 8.8%
Educational Attainment: High school diploma or higher: 95.9%; Bachelor's degree or higher: 56.8%; Graduate/professional degree or higher: 25.5%
Housing: Homeownership rate: 93.3%; Median home value: $359,600; Median year structure built: 1957; Homeowner vacancy rate: 1.5%; Median selected monthly owner costs: $1,786 with a mortgage, $596 without a mortgage; Median gross rent: $850 per month; Rental vacancy rate: 0.0%
Health Insurance: 95.8% have insurance; 83.6% have private insurance; 44.7% have public insurance; 4.2% do not have insurance; 5.6% of children under 18 do not have insurance
Transportation: Commute: 80.7% car, 11.0% public transportation, 3.7% walk, 4.6% work from home; Mean travel time to work: 36.0 minutes

MICHIGAN CITY (city). Covers a land area of 19.588 square miles and a water area of 3.265 square miles. Located at 41.71° N. Lat; 86.88° W. Long. Elevation is 627 feet.
History: It was in Michigan City that Daniel Webster made a Fourth of July speech in 1837. The city was founded in 1832 at the northern end of the

Michigan Road, on Lake Michigan. From the early 1840's it served as a port for shipping interests and later for a fishing fleet.
Population: 31,352; Growth (since 2000): -4.7%; Density: 1,600.6 persons per square mile; Race: 63.2% White, 28.7% Black/African American, 0.9% Asian, 0.2% American Indian/Alaska Native, 0.0% Native Hawaiian/Other Pacific Islander, 5.5% Two or more races, 6.1% Hispanic of any race; Average household size: 2.22; Median age: 37.1; Age under 18: 22.2%; Age 65 and over: 14.0%; Males per 100 females: 105.8; Marriage status: 39.4% never married, 36.9% now married, 1.7% separated, 6.2% widowed, 17.4% divorced; Foreign born: 3.5%; Speak English only: 94.6%; With disability: 14.7%; Veterans: 7.9%; Ancestry: 20.0% German, 12.1% Irish, 9.9% Polish, 4.1% English, 4.0% American
Employment: 10.2% management, business, and financial, 1.6% computer, engineering, and science, 8.0% education, legal, community service, arts, and media, 3.9% healthcare practitioners, 23.6% service, 22.8% sales and office, 8.7% natural resources, construction, and maintenance, 21.1% production, transportation, and material moving
Income: Per capita: $20,279; Median household: $38,631; Average household: $50,213; Households with income of $100,000 or more: 9.5%; Poverty rate: 25.5%
Educational Attainment: High school diploma or higher: 85.6%; Bachelor's degree or higher: 16.6%; Graduate/professional degree or higher: 5.8%

School District(s)

Michigan City Area Schools (PK-12)
Enrollment: 6,006 .... (219) 873-2000
Housing: Homeownership rate: 54.0%; Median home value: $89,000; Median year structure built: 1961; Homeowner vacancy rate: 2.1%; Median selected monthly owner costs: $898 with a mortgage, $366 without a mortgage; Median gross rent: $741 per month; Rental vacancy rate: 5.6%
Health Insurance: 87.9% have insurance; 54.2% have private insurance; 44.4% have public insurance; 12.1% do not have insurance; 5.1% of children under 18 do not have insurance
Hospitals: Franciscan Saint Anthony Health - Michigan City (310 beds)
Newspapers: News-Dispatch (daily circulation 10,700)
Transportation: Commute: 91.6% car, 2.0% public transportation, 3.1% walk, 2.4% work from home; Mean travel time to work: 19.6 minutes; Amtrak: Train service available.
Additional Information Contacts
City of Michigan City .... (219) 873-1410
http://www.emichigancity.com

MILL CREEK (unincorporated postal area)
ZCTA: 46365

Covers a land area of 23.266 square miles and a water area of 0.328 square miles. Located at 41.61° N. Lat; 86.55° W. Long..
Population: 761; Growth (since 2000): -24.1%; Density: 32.7 persons per square mile; Race: 100.0% White, 0.0% Black/African American, 0.0% Asian, 0.0% American Indian/Alaska Native, 0.0% Native Hawaiian/Other Pacific Islander, 0.0% Two or more races, 0.0% Hispanic of any race; Average household size: 2.06; Median age: 52.8; Age under 18: 7.1%; Age 65 and over: 18.1%; Males per 100 females: 107.0; Marriage status: 19.7% never married, 68.6% now married, 0.0% separated, 8.1% widowed, 3.6% divorced; Foreign born: 1.8%; Speak English only: 98.5%; With disability: 15.1%; Veterans: 12.2%; Ancestry: 37.6% German, 9.3% English, 6.8% Irish, 5.8% American, 5.4% Dutch
Employment: 12.4% management, business, and financial, 3.0% computer, engineering, and science, 9.9% education, legal, community service, arts, and media, 3.9% healthcare practitioners, 34.2% service, 15.6% sales and office, 6.7% natural resources, construction, and maintenance, 14.4% production, transportation, and material moving
Income: Per capita: $26,873; Median household: $45,000; Average household: $56,125; Households with income of $100,000 or more: 11.9%; Poverty rate: n/a
Educational Attainment: High school diploma or higher: 94.0%; Bachelor's degree or higher: 10.2%; Graduate/professional degree or higher: 4.2%
Housing: Homeownership rate: 75.1%; Median home value: $149,200; Median year structure built: 1984; Homeowner vacancy rate: 0.0%; Median selected monthly owner costs: $1,148 with a mortgage, $475 without a mortgage; Median gross rent: n/a per month; Rental vacancy rate: 0.0%
Health Insurance: 93.0% have insurance; 81.9% have private insurance; 28.6% have public insurance; 7.0% do not have insurance; 0.0% of children under 18 do not have insurance
Transportation: Commute: 81.9% car, 0.0% public transportation, 7.1% walk, 8.5% work from home; Mean travel time to work: 26.7 minutes

POTTAWATTAMIE PARK (town). Covers a land area of 0.246 square miles and a water area of 0 square miles. Located at 41.72° N. Lat; 86.87° W. Long. Elevation is 620 feet.
Population: 262; Growth (since 2000): n/a; Density: 1,066.5 persons per square mile; Race: 99.2% White, 0.8% Black/African American, 0.0% Asian, 0.0% American Indian/Alaska Native, 0.0% Native Hawaiian/Other Pacific Islander, 0.0% Two or more races, 3.8% Hispanic of any race; Average household size: 2.36; Median age: 49.2; Age under 18: 19.8%; Age 65 and over: 24.4%; Males per 100 females: 91.1; Marriage status: 19.6% never married, 64.4% now married, 0.5% separated, 7.8% widowed, 8.2% divorced; Foreign born: 1.9%; Speak English only: 95.1%; With disability: 14.1%; Veterans: 7.6%; Ancestry: 40.5% German, 31.7% Irish, 12.6% American, 7.6% English, 6.5% Polish
Employment: 14.1% management, business, and financial, 0.0% computer, engineering, and science, 25.9% education, legal, community service, arts, and media, 9.6% healthcare practitioners, 19.3% service, 12.6% sales and office, 6.7% natural resources, construction, and maintenance, 11.9% production, transportation, and material moving
Income: Per capita: $37,935; Median household: $86,250; Average household: $92,534; Households with income of $100,000 or more: 39.2%; Poverty rate: 5.7%
Educational Attainment: High school diploma or higher: 95.4%; Bachelor's degree or higher: 52.6%; Graduate/professional degree or higher: 22.2%
Housing: Homeownership rate: 92.5%; Median home value: $160,500; Median year structure built: 1956; Homeowner vacancy rate: 0.0%; Median selected monthly owner costs: $1,271 with a mortgage, $475 without a mortgage; Median gross rent: n/a per month; Rental vacancy rate: 0.0%
Health Insurance: 94.7% have insurance; 82.8% have private insurance; 29.4% have public insurance; 5.3% do not have insurance; 7.1% of children under 18 do not have insurance
Transportation: Commute: 92.5% car, 2.2% public transportation, 0.0% walk, 4.5% work from home; Mean travel time to work: 22.5 minutes

ROLLING PRAIRIE (CDP). Covers a land area of 1.053 square miles and a water area of 0.015 square miles. Located at 41.67° N. Lat; 86.62° W. Long. Elevation is 827 feet.
Population: 681; Growth (since 2000): n/a; Density: 646.8 persons per square mile; Race: 98.5% White, 1.5% Black/African American, 0.0% Asian, 0.0% American Indian/Alaska Native, 0.0% Native Hawaiian/Other Pacific Islander, 0.0% Two or more races, 0.0% Hispanic of any race; Average household size: 3.11; Median age: 37.3; Age under 18: 27.8%; Age 65 and over: 9.3%; Males per 100 females: 94.6; Marriage status: 20.1% never married, 57.7% now married, 0.0% separated, 0.0% widowed, 22.2% divorced; Foreign born: 0.0%; Speak English only: 100.0%; With disability: 6.8%; Veterans: 11.0%; Ancestry: 38.2% German, 28.9% Irish, 20.4% American, 13.2% English, 7.2% French
Employment: 12.5% management, business, and financial, 3.9% computer, engineering, and science, 17.4% education, legal, community service, arts, and media, 0.0% healthcare practitioners, 17.8% service, 21.4% sales and office, 18.8% natural resources, construction, and maintenance, 8.2% production, transportation, and material moving
Income: Per capita: $21,403; Median household: $78,375; Average household: $67,948; Households with income of $100,000 or more: 22.8%; Poverty rate: 19.8%
Educational Attainment: High school diploma or higher: 98.2%; Bachelor's degree or higher: 35.6%; Graduate/professional degree or higher: 13.6%

School District(s)

New Prairie United School Corp (PK-12)
Enrollment: 2,537 .... (574) 654-7273
Housing: Homeownership rate: 68.9%; Median home value: $160,400; Median year structure built: 1947; Homeowner vacancy rate: 0.0%; Median selected monthly owner costs: $911 with a mortgage, n/a without a mortgage; Median gross rent: n/a per month; Rental vacancy rate: 0.0%
Health Insurance: 78.7% have insurance; 57.4% have private insurance; 28.3% have public insurance; 21.3% do not have insurance; 37.0% of children under 18 do not have insurance
Transportation: Commute: 94.1% car, 0.0% public transportation, 0.0% walk, 5.9% work from home; Mean travel time to work: 15.6 minutes

TRAIL CREEK (town). Covers a land area of 1.212 square miles and a water area of 0 square miles. Located at 41.70° N. Lat; 86.86° W. Long. Elevation is 627 feet.

Population: 2,000; Growth (since 2000): -12.9%; Density: 1,650.8 persons per square mile; Race: 82.9% White, 12.8% Black/African American, 1.2% Asian, 0.0% American Indian/Alaska Native, 0.0% Native Hawaiian/Other Pacific Islander, 2.5% Two or more races, 1.3% Hispanic of any race; Average household size: 2.44; Median age: 42.9; Age under 18: 26.4%; Age 65 and over: 18.2%; Males per 100 females: 101.6; Marriage status: 19.2% never married, 58.0% now married, 0.1% separated, 9.3% widowed, 13.5% divorced; Foreign born: 2.4%; Speak English only: 96.4%; With disability: 10.7%; Veterans: 12.9%; Ancestry: 24.7% German, 17.3% Polish, 9.6% English, 8.9% American, 8.7% Irish

Employment: 16.8% management, business, and financial, 2.7% computer, engineering, and science, 9.4% education, legal, community service, arts, and media, 9.7% healthcare practitioners, 14.7% service, 19.9% sales and office, 6.3% natural resources, construction, and maintenance, 20.6% production, transportation, and material moving

Income: Per capita: $28,830; Median household: $64,063; Average household: $71,822; Households with income of $100,000 or more: 25.0%; Poverty rate: 8.0%

Educational Attainment: High school diploma or higher: 94.5%; Bachelor's degree or higher: 19.4%; Graduate/professional degree or higher: 6.7%

Housing: Homeownership rate: 91.3%; Median home value: $131,200; Median year structure built: 1964; Homeowner vacancy rate: 4.2%; Median selected monthly owner costs: $993 with a mortgage, $315 without a mortgage; Median gross rent: $1,000 per month; Rental vacancy rate: 0.0%

Health Insurance: 95.3% have insurance; 77.5% have private insurance; 32.0% have public insurance; 4.7% do not have insurance; 1.5% of children under 18 do not have insurance

Transportation: Commute: 96.3% car, 0.4% public transportation, 0.0% walk, 3.0% work from home; Mean travel time to work: 19.2 minutes

Additional Information Contacts

Town of Trail Creek . . . . (219) 874-6221
http://www.michigancitychamber.com

UNION MILLS (unincorporated postal area)

ZCTA: 46382

Covers a land area of 48.759 square miles and a water area of 0.032 square miles. Located at 41.46° N. Lat; 86.76° W. Long. Elevation is 732 feet.

Population: 1,839; Growth (since 2000): -7.6%; Density: 37.7 persons per square mile; Race: 98.6% White, 0.0% Black/African American, 0.8% Asian, 0.0% American Indian/Alaska Native, 0.0% Native Hawaiian/Other Pacific Islander, 0.0% Two or more races, 6.0% Hispanic of any race; Average household size: 2.57; Median age: 45.3; Age under 18: 24.5%; Age 65 and over: 16.6%; Males per 100 females: 97.7; Marriage status: 18.1% never married, 68.3% now married, 1.0% separated, 6.6% widowed, 6.9% divorced; Foreign born: 1.4%; Speak English only: 97.9%; With disability: 11.9%; Veterans: 10.2%; Ancestry: 24.7% German, 13.8% Irish, 9.0% American, 6.7% English, 6.6% Polish

Employment: 20.1% management, business, and financial, 0.0% computer, engineering, and science, 6.3% education, legal, community service, arts, and media, 6.4% healthcare practitioners, 12.4% service, 13.8% sales and office, 12.8% natural resources, construction, and maintenance, 28.1% production, transportation, and material moving

Income: Per capita: $31,885; Median household: $75,625; Average household: $84,595; Households with income of $100,000 or more: 34.9%; Poverty rate: 5.3%

Educational Attainment: High school diploma or higher: 92.2%; Bachelor's degree or higher: 19.4%; Graduate/professional degree or higher: 2.9%

School District(s)

South Central Com School Corp (PK-12)
Enrollment: 752 . . . . (219) 767-2263

Housing: Homeownership rate: 98.5%; Median home value: $175,300; Median year structure built: 1981; Homeowner vacancy rate: 0.0%; Median selected monthly owner costs: $1,223 with a mortgage, $448 without a mortgage; Median gross rent: n/a per month; Rental vacancy rate: 0.0%

Health Insurance: 94.2% have insurance; 80.8% have private insurance; 30.5% have public insurance; 5.8% do not have insurance; 4.2% of children under 18 do not have insurance

Transportation: Commute: 92.3% car, 0.0% public transportation, 3.2% walk, 4.5% work from home; Mean travel time to work: 29.4 minutes

WANATAH (town). Covers a land area of 1.421 square miles and a water area of 0 square miles. Located at 41.43° N. Lat; 86.89° W. Long. Elevation is 732 feet.

History: Wanatah is named for an Indian chief whose name means "keep knee deep in mud."

Population: 1,234; Growth (since 2000): 21.8%; Density: 868.2 persons per square mile; Race: 94.9% White, 0.0% Black/African American, 0.0% Asian, 0.0% American Indian/Alaska Native, 0.0% Native Hawaiian/Other Pacific Islander, 3.6% Two or more races, 9.4% Hispanic of any race; Average household size: 2.44; Median age: 39.9; Age under 18: 20.7%; Age 65 and over: 18.5%; Males per 100 females: 100.0; Marriage status: 21.2% never married, 59.6% now married, 0.7% separated, 8.4% widowed, 10.8% divorced; Foreign born: 0.5%; Speak English only: 99.3%; With disability: 9.2%; Veterans: 9.9%; Ancestry: 26.0% German, 17.0% Irish, 10.6% English, 8.3% American, 5.0% French

Employment: 5.9% management, business, and financial, 5.1% computer, engineering, and science, 5.0% education, legal, community service, arts, and media, 3.7% healthcare practitioners, 31.7% service, 20.9% sales and office, 10.9% natural resources, construction, and maintenance, 16.7% production, transportation, and material moving

Income: Per capita: $26,789; Median household: $61,250; Average household: $68,142; Households with income of $100,000 or more: 14.7%; Poverty rate: 9.2%

Educational Attainment: High school diploma or higher: 92.1%; Bachelor's degree or higher: 15.9%; Graduate/professional degree or higher: 4.2%

School District(s)

Tri-township Cons School Corp (PK-12)
Enrollment: 479 . . . . (219) 754-2709

Housing: Homeownership rate: 86.5%; Median home value: $135,700; Median year structure built: 1966; Homeowner vacancy rate: 0.0%; Median selected monthly owner costs: $1,137 with a mortgage, $400 without a mortgage; Median gross rent: $875 per month; Rental vacancy rate: 0.0%

Health Insurance: 93.8% have insurance; 77.8% have private insurance; 32.7% have public insurance; 6.2% do not have insurance; 0.0% of children under 18 do not have insurance

Transportation: Commute: 89.4% car, 0.0% public transportation, 4.6% walk, 4.1% work from home; Mean travel time to work: 24.5 minutes

WESTVILLE (town). Covers a land area of 3.088 square miles and a water area of 0 square miles. Located at 41.54° N. Lat; 86.91° W. Long. Elevation is 794 feet.

History: Settled 1836, laid out 1851.

Population: 6,659; Growth (since 2000): 214.7%; Density: 2,156.5 persons per square mile; Race: 72.2% White, 24.2% Black/African American, 0.3% Asian, 0.2% American Indian/Alaska Native, 0.1% Native Hawaiian/Other Pacific Islander, 2.5% Two or more races, 6.8% Hispanic of any race; Average household size: 2.35; Median age: 35.1; Age under 18: 8.0%; Age 65 and over: 4.2%; Males per 100 females: 333.2; Marriage status: 51.1% never married, 24.1% now married, 2.6% separated, 2.3% widowed, 22.6% divorced; Foreign born: 1.1%; Speak English only: 96.0%; With disability: 9.4%; Veterans: 5.7%; Ancestry: 19.8% German, 15.3% Irish, 3.8% Polish, 3.5% English, 2.8% Italian

Employment: 8.8% management, business, and financial, 2.6% computer, engineering, and science, 4.1% education, legal, community service, arts, and media, 6.3% healthcare practitioners, 20.2% service, 23.4% sales and office, 13.1% natural resources, construction, and maintenance, 21.4% production, transportation, and material moving

Income: Per capita: $9,439; Median household: $40,724; Average household: $53,814; Households with income of $100,000 or more: 15.5%; Poverty rate: 25.8%

Educational Attainment: High school diploma or higher: 79.8%; Bachelor's degree or higher: 5.3%; Graduate/professional degree or higher: 0.9%

School District(s)

M S D Of New Durham Township (PK-12)
Enrollment: 820 . . . . (219) 785-2239

Housing: Homeownership rate: 77.7%; Median home value: $88,800; Median year structure built: 1983; Homeowner vacancy rate: 5.8%; Median selected monthly owner costs: $1,103 with a mortgage, $454 without a mortgage; Median gross rent: $608 per month; Rental vacancy rate: 7.3%

Health Insurance: 90.6% have insurance; 69.1% have private insurance; 30.8% have public insurance; 9.4% do not have insurance; 3.5% of children under 18 do not have insurance
Newspapers: Regional News (weekly circulation 2,000); Westville Indicator (weekly circulation 2,000)
Transportation: Commute: 95.9% car, 1.7% public transportation, 0.3% walk, 2.0% work from home; Mean travel time to work: 23.5 minutes
Additional Information Contacts
Town of Westville .... (219) 785-2123
http://westville.us

Lawrence County

Located in southern Indiana; drained by Salt Creek and the East Fork of the White River. Covers a land area of 449.168 square miles, a water area of 2.761 square miles, and is located in the Eastern Time Zone at 38.84° N. Lat., 86.49° W. Long. The county was founded in 1819. County seat is Bedford.

Lawrence County is part of the Bedford, IN Micropolitan Statistical Area. The entire metro area includes: Lawrence County, IN

Weather Station: Oolitic Purdue Exp Farm Elevation: 649 feet

	Jan	Feb	Mar	Apr	May	Jun	Jul	Aug	Sep	Oct	Nov	Dec
High	38	43	53	64	74	82	85	85	79	67	55	42
Low	20	23	30	41	51	60	64	62	54	41	33	23
Precip	2.9	2.7	3.8	4.4	5.8	4.1	4.5	3.7	3.2	3.7	3.7	3.5
Snow	4.6	4.1	2.0	0.1	tr	0.0	0.0	0.0	0.0	0.1	0.1	3.9

High and Low temperatures in degrees Fahrenheit; Precipitation and Snow in inches

Population: 45,669; Growth (since 2000): -0.6%; Density: 101.7 persons per square mile; Race: 96.6% White, 0.3% Black/African American, 0.4% Asian, 0.5% American Indian/Alaska Native, 0.0% Native Hawaiian/Other Pacific Islander, 1.6% two or more races, 1.6% Hispanic of any race; Average household size: 2.44; Median age: 42.6; Age under 18: 22.2%; Age 65 and over: 18.7%; Males per 100 females: 97.7; Marriage status: 19.4% never married, 59.0% now married, 1.4% separated, 6.8% widowed, 14.8% divorced; Foreign born: 1.5%; Speak English only: 97.8%; With disability: 17.4%; Veterans: 10.7%; Ancestry: 16.4% German, 12.4% Irish, 11.9% American, 8.8% English, 2.9% Italian
Religion: Six largest groups: 21.5% Baptist, 7.8% Non-denominational Protestant, 4.1% Catholicism, 3.8% Holiness, 2.3% Methodist/Pietist, 1.4% Pentecostal
Economy: Unemployment rate: 3.8%; Leading industries: 18.1 % retail trade; 14.6 % health care and social assistance; 13.0 % other services (except public administration); Farms: 800 totaling 134,689 acres; Company size: 0 employ 1,000 or more persons, 1 employs 500 to 999 persons, 20 employ 100 to 499 persons, 870 employ less than 100 persons; Business ownership: 1,023 women-owned, n/a Black-owned, n/a Hispanic-owned, 29 Asian-owned, n/a American Indian/Alaska Native-owned
Employment: 11.0% management, business, and financial, 4.1% computer, engineering, and science, 7.7% education, legal, community service, arts, and media, 7.2% healthcare practitioners, 18.0% service, 24.3% sales and office, 9.9% natural resources, construction, and maintenance, 17.9% production, transportation, and material moving
Income: Per capita: $25,036; Median household: $49,985; Average household: $60,768; Households with income of $100,000 or more: 13.3%; Poverty rate: 11.5%
Educational Attainment: High school diploma or higher: 89.0%; Bachelor's degree or higher: 16.1%; Graduate/professional degree or higher: 6.1%
Housing: Homeownership rate: 78.8%; Median home value: $109,200; Median year structure built: 1977; Homeowner vacancy rate: 2.3%; Median selected monthly owner costs: $988 with a mortgage, $385 without a mortgage; Median gross rent: $674 per month; Rental vacancy rate: 10.2%
Vital Statistics: Birth rate: 107.1 per 10,000 population; Death rate: 117.2 per 10,000 population; Age-adjusted cancer mortality rate: 181.0 deaths per 100,000 population
Health Insurance: 90.5% have insurance; 70.7% have private insurance; 36.2% have public insurance; 9.5% do not have insurance; 8.3% of children under 18 do not have insurance
Health Care: Physicians: 8.6 per 10,000 population; Dentists: 4.6 per 10,000 population; Hospital beds: 11.0 per 10,000 population; Hospital admissions: 443.7 per 10,000 population
Transportation: Commute: 95.2% car, 0.1% public transportation, 1.2% walk, 2.9% work from home; Mean travel time to work: 23.6 minutes
2016 Presidential Election: 73.3% Trump, 22.0% Clinton, 4.3% Johnson, 0.3% Stein
National and State Parks: Spring Mill State Park
Additional Information Contacts
Lawrence Government .... (812) 275-7543
http://bedfordonline.com/government/lawrence

Lawrence County Communities

AVOCA (CDP). Covers a land area of 2.095 square miles and a water area of 0 square miles. Located at 38.92° N. Lat; 86.56° W. Long. Elevation is 623 feet.
Population: 893; Growth (since 2000): n/a; Density: 426.2 persons per square mile; Race: 100.0% White, 0.0% Black/African American, 0.0% Asian, 0.0% American Indian/Alaska Native, 0.0% Native Hawaiian/Other Pacific Islander, 0.0% Two or more races, 0.0% Hispanic of any race; Average household size: 3.05; Median age: 28.4; Age under 18: 40.6%; Age 65 and over: 12.1%; Males per 100 females: 97.6; Marriage status: 15.5% never married, 79.1% now married, 4.3% separated, 4.1% widowed, 1.3% divorced; Foreign born: 0.0%; Speak English only: 100.0%; With disability: 10.8%; Veterans: 17.4%; Ancestry: 47.1% German, 31.1% Irish, 7.1% English, 3.8% Scotch-Irish, 3.1% Italian
Employment: 15.6% management, business, and financial, 20.4% computer, engineering, and science, 2.8% education, legal, community service, arts, and media, 3.3% healthcare practitioners, 11.8% service, 31.7% sales and office, 3.5% natural resources, construction, and maintenance, 10.8% production, transportation, and material moving
Income: Per capita: $22,673; Median household: $75,396; Average household: $69,941; Households with income of $100,000 or more: 16.4%; Poverty rate: 16.2%
Educational Attainment: High school diploma or higher: 90.9%; Bachelor's degree or higher: 26.8%; Graduate/professional degree or higher: 5.8%
Housing: Homeownership rate: 65.5%; Median home value: $137,500; Median year structure built: 1980; Homeowner vacancy rate: 0.0%; Median selected monthly owner costs: $1,354 with a mortgage, $368 without a mortgage; Median gross rent: $807 per month; Rental vacancy rate: 0.0%
Health Insurance: 100.0% have insurance; 87.6% have private insurance; 24.5% have public insurance; 0.0% do not have insurance; 0.0% of children under 18 do not have insurance
Transportation: Commute: 96.5% car, 0.0% public transportation, 0.0% walk, 3.5% work from home; Mean travel time to work: 19.3 minutes

BEDFORD (city). County seat. Covers a land area of 12.161 square miles and a water area of 0 square miles. Located at 38.86° N. Lat; 86.49° W. Long. Elevation is 686 feet.
History: Beford developed as the center of a limestone industry, providing stone for such buildings as the Empire State Building and the Chicago Museum of Fine Arts.
Population: 13,292; Growth (since 2000): -3.5%; Density: 1,093.0 persons per square mile; Race: 95.3% White, 0.6% Black/African American, 0.5% Asian, 0.5% American Indian/Alaska Native, 0.2% Native Hawaiian/Other Pacific Islander, 1.9% Two or more races, 2.1% Hispanic of any race; Average household size: 2.27; Median age: 41.8; Age under 18: 21.1%; Age 65 and over: 19.8%; Males per 100 females: 89.8; Marriage status: 22.8% never married, 47.5% now married, 0.8% separated, 9.8% widowed, 19.9% divorced; Foreign born: 1.7%; Speak English only: 98.2%; With disability: 19.2%; Veterans: 9.9%; Ancestry: 17.7% German, 13.0% Irish, 11.5% American, 9.1% English, 3.5% Italian
Employment: 8.1% management, business, and financial, 3.5% computer, engineering, and science, 6.8% education, legal, community service, arts, and media, 8.1% healthcare practitioners, 20.6% service, 22.6% sales and office, 10.9% natural resources, construction, and maintenance, 19.4% production, transportation, and material moving
Income: Per capita: $23,627; Median household: $40,076; Average household: $53,289; Households with income of $100,000 or more: 10.5%; Poverty rate: 17.9%
Educational Attainment: High school diploma or higher: 87.5%; Bachelor's degree or higher: 14.8%; Graduate/professional degree or higher: 5.7%

School District(s)
North Lawrence Com Schools (PK-12)
Enrollment: 4,910 .... (812) 279-3521

Housing: Homeownership rate: 64.9%; Median home value: $87,600; Median year structure built: 1959; Homeowner vacancy rate: 4.1%; Median selected monthly owner costs: $896 with a mortgage, $384 without a mortgage; Median gross rent: $656 per month; Rental vacancy rate: 11.7%
Health Insurance: 89.8% have insurance; 63.4% have private insurance; 41.6% have public insurance; 10.2% do not have insurance; 6.2% of children under 18 do not have insurance
Hospitals: Indiana University Health Bedford Hospital (49 beds); Saint Vincent Dunn Hospital (137 beds)
Safety: Violent crime rate: 8.3 per 10,000 population; Property crime rate: 252.8 per 10,000 population
Newspapers: Times-Mail (daily circulation 12,600)
Transportation: Commute: 94.4% car, 0.0% public transportation, 2.4% walk, 2.5% work from home; Mean travel time to work: 18.9 minutes
Airports: Virgil I Grissom Municipal (general aviation)
Additional Information Contacts
City of Bedford. . . . . (812) 279-6555
http://www.bedford.in.us

HELTONVILLE (unincorporated postal area)

ZCTA: 47436

Covers a land area of 45.799 square miles and a water area of 0.314 square miles. Located at 38.95° N. Lat; 86.39° W. Long. Elevation is 653 feet.

Population: 1,533; Growth (since 2000): 24.4%; Density: 33.5 persons per square mile; Race: 91.7% White, 0.0% Black/African American, 2.3% Asian, 4.3% American Indian/Alaska Native, 0.0% Native Hawaiian/Other Pacific Islander, 0.7% Two or more races, 1.0% Hispanic of any race; Average household size: 2.39; Median age: 48.6; Age under 18: 18.7%; Age 65 and over: 22.5%; Males per 100 females: 109.4; Marriage status: 15.7% never married, 60.6% now married, 2.7% separated, 9.7% widowed, 14.1% divorced; Foreign born: 3.3%; Speak English only: 95.5%; With disability: 23.3%; Veterans: 13.7%; Ancestry: 23.5% American, 13.2% German, 9.2% Irish, 7.1% English, 5.9% European
Employment: 16.8% management, business, and financial, 1.6% computer, engineering, and science, 9.8% education, legal, community service, arts, and media, 17.6% healthcare practitioners, 5.2% service, 20.2% sales and office, 9.3% natural resources, construction, and maintenance, 19.5% production, transportation, and material moving
Income: Per capita: $28,084; Median household: $51,375; Average household: $66,649; Households with income of $100,000 or more: 20.6%; Poverty rate: 6.2%
Educational Attainment: High school diploma or higher: 94.7%; Bachelor's degree or higher: 32.1%; Graduate/professional degree or higher: 16.7%

School District(s)

North Lawrence Com Schools (PK-12)
Enrollment: 4,910 . . . . (812) 279-3521
Housing: Homeownership rate: 82.7%; Median home value: $108,400; Median year structure built: 1984; Homeowner vacancy rate: 0.0%; Median selected monthly owner costs: $1,033 with a mortgage, $376 without a mortgage; Median gross rent: $669 per month; Rental vacancy rate: 29.3%
Health Insurance: 90.9% have insurance; 73.0% have private insurance; 45.7% have public insurance; 9.1% do not have insurance; 8.0% of children under 18 do not have insurance
Transportation: Commute: 94.0% car, 0.0% public transportation, 0.0% walk, 6.0% work from home; Mean travel time to work: 41.1 minutes

MITCHELL (city). Covers a land area of 3.276 square miles and a water area of 0.005 square miles. Located at 38.74° N. Lat; 86.47° W. Long. Elevation is 682 feet.

History: The first settlers came to Mitchell in 1813. The town was platted about 1852 when the Louisville, New Albany, & Salem Railroad came through Lawrence County. The town was named for O.M. Mitchell, a construction engineer for the Ohio & Mississippi Railroad which crossed the original line in 1856.
Population: 4,280; Growth (since 2000): -6.3%; Density: 1,306.5 persons per square mile; Race: 93.7% White, 0.2% Black/African American, 1.0% Asian, 0.0% American Indian/Alaska Native, 0.0% Native Hawaiian/Other Pacific Islander, 2.3% Two or more races, 5.3% Hispanic of any race; Average household size: 2.31; Median age: 43.7; Age under 18: 20.8%; Age 65 and over: 20.1%; Males per 100 females: 86.9; Marriage status: 18.0% never married, 50.4% now married, 2.5% separated, 10.4% widowed, 21.2% divorced; Foreign born: 2.1%; Speak English only: 95.0%; With disability: 24.5%; Veterans: 11.2%; Ancestry: 13.0% German, 9.6% American, 8.9% English, 7.1% Irish, 5.4% Italian
Employment: 13.6% management, business, and financial, 0.5% computer, engineering, and science, 8.2% education, legal, community service, arts, and media, 4.7% healthcare practitioners, 21.6% service, 27.8% sales and office, 7.8% natural resources, construction, and maintenance, 15.7% production, transportation, and material moving
Income: Per capita: $20,972; Median household: $38,598; Average household: $48,372; Households with income of $100,000 or more: 7.7%; Poverty rate: 12.0%
Educational Attainment: High school diploma or higher: 81.3%; Bachelor's degree or higher: 11.2%; Graduate/professional degree or higher: 4.7%

School District(s)

Mitchell Community Schools (PK-12)
Enrollment: 1,719 . . . . (812) 849-4481
Housing: Homeownership rate: 74.9%; Median home value: $71,500; Median year structure built: 1966; Homeowner vacancy rate: 4.8%; Median selected monthly owner costs: $848 with a mortgage, $314 without a mortgage; Median gross rent: $540 per month; Rental vacancy rate: 17.9%
Health Insurance: 85.9% have insurance; 59.1% have private insurance; 40.8% have public insurance; 14.1% do not have insurance; 10.4% of children under 18 do not have insurance
Transportation: Commute: 95.4% car, 0.0% public transportation, 2.7% walk, 1.9% work from home; Mean travel time to work: 22.1 minutes
Additional Information Contacts
City of Mitchell. . . . . (812) 849-3831
http://www.mitchell-in.gov

OOLITIC (town). Covers a land area of 0.783 square miles and a water area of 0 square miles. Located at 38.89° N. Lat; 86.53° W. Long. Elevation is 600 feet.

History: Oolitic was named for the oolitic texture of the limestone in the quarries that surround it, which provided the town with its early industry.
Population: 1,128; Growth (since 2000): -2.1%; Density: 1,441.2 persons per square mile; Race: 96.5% White, 0.0% Black/African American, 1.3% Asian, 0.0% American Indian/Alaska Native, 0.0% Native Hawaiian/Other Pacific Islander, 2.2% Two or more races, 1.4% Hispanic of any race; Average household size: 2.34; Median age: 43.1; Age under 18: 23.0%; Age 65 and over: 17.4%; Males per 100 females: 101.0; Marriage status: 18.7% never married, 53.7% now married, 2.4% separated, 7.3% widowed, 20.3% divorced; Foreign born: 2.1%; Speak English only: 98.1%; With disability: 15.9%; Veterans: 8.8%; Ancestry: 16.5% German, 14.1% American, 9.0% Irish, 8.0% English, 3.5% Italian
Employment: 8.5% management, business, and financial, 6.1% computer, engineering, and science, 6.9% education, legal, community service, arts, and media, 5.0% healthcare practitioners, 19.7% service, 19.5% sales and office, 11.7% natural resources, construction, and maintenance, 22.6% production, transportation, and material moving
Income: Per capita: $24,866; Median household: $43,194; Average household: $57,000; Households with income of $100,000 or more: 10.3%; Poverty rate: 23.7%
Educational Attainment: High school diploma or higher: 84.7%; Bachelor's degree or higher: 6.1%; Graduate/professional degree or higher: 2.6%

School District(s)

North Lawrence Com Schools (PK-12)
Enrollment: 4,910 . . . . (812) 279-3521
Housing: Homeownership rate: 71.0%; Median home value: $92,400; Median year structure built: 1968; Homeowner vacancy rate: 2.2%; Median selected monthly owner costs: $917 with a mortgage, $340 without a mortgage; Median gross rent: $489 per month; Rental vacancy rate: 16.7%
Health Insurance: 90.5% have insurance; 66.6% have private insurance; 37.4% have public insurance; 9.5% do not have insurance; 6.4% of children under 18 do not have insurance
Transportation: Commute: 91.8% car, 0.0% public transportation, 3.5% walk, 1.7% work from home; Mean travel time to work: 23.1 minutes

SPRINGVILLE (unincorporated postal area)

ZCTA: 47462

Covers a land area of 75.862 square miles and a water area of 0.040 square miles. Located at 38.96° N. Lat; 86.65° W. Long. Elevation is 640 feet.

Population: 4,479; Growth (since 2000): -7.3%; Density: 59.0 persons per square mile; Race: 98.1% White, 0.4% Black/African American, 0.5% Asian, 0.0% American Indian/Alaska Native, 0.0% Native Hawaiian/Other Pacific Islander, 0.6% Two or more races, 0.8% Hispanic of any race; Average household size: 2.85; Median age: 32.9; Age under 18: 22.2%; Age 65 and over: 9.5%; Males per 100 females: 107.3; Marriage status: 20.6% never married, 64.4% now married, 1.2% separated, 2.8% widowed, 12.1% divorced; Foreign born: 1.5%; Speak English only: 98.7%; With disability: 13.4%; Veterans: 10.5%; Ancestry: 23.9% German, 19.8% Irish, 13.2% American, 8.7% English, 2.8% French

Employment: 22.3% management, business, and financial, 4.0% computer, engineering, and science, 4.1% education, legal, community service, arts, and media, 4.3% healthcare practitioners, 22.7% service, 18.9% sales and office, 12.1% natural resources, construction, and maintenance, 11.6% production, transportation, and material moving

Income: Per capita: $26,370; Median household: $64,444; Average household: $72,694; Households with income of $100,000 or more: 17.4%; Poverty rate: 6.9%

Educational Attainment: High school diploma or higher: 88.7%; Bachelor's degree or higher: 14.5%; Graduate/professional degree or higher: 3.8%

School District(s)

North Lawrence Com Schools (PK-12)
Enrollment: 4,910 . . . . (812) 279-3521

Housing: Homeownership rate: 86.5%; Median home value: $139,000; Median year structure built: 1991; Homeowner vacancy rate: 1.5%; Median selected monthly owner costs: $1,057 with a mortgage, $450 without a mortgage; Median gross rent: $684 per month; Rental vacancy rate: 0.0%

Health Insurance: 89.4% have insurance; 77.5% have private insurance; 24.3% have public insurance; 10.6% do not have insurance; 7.3% of children under 18 do not have insurance

Transportation: Commute: 96.7% car, 0.0% public transportation, 0.0% walk, 3.3% work from home; Mean travel time to work: 24.5 minutes

TUNNELTON (unincorporated postal area)
ZCTA: 47467

Covers a land area of 0.055 square miles and a water area of 0 square miles. Located at 38.77° N. Lat; 86.34° W. Long. Elevation is 571 feet.

Population: 125; Growth (since 2000): 115.5%; Density: 2,283.1 persons per square mile; Race: 100.0% White, 0.0% Black/African American, 0.0% Asian, 0.0% American Indian/Alaska Native, 0.0% Native Hawaiian/Other Pacific Islander, 0.0% Two or more races, 0.0% Hispanic of any race; Average household size: 5.43; Median age: n/a; Age under 18: 60.8%; Age 65 and over: 0.0%; Males per 100 females: 105.7; Marriage status: 0.0% never married, 100.0% now married, 0.0% separated, 0.0% widowed, 0.0% divorced; Foreign born: 0.0%; Speak English only: 100.0%; With disability: 0.0%; Veterans: 0.0%; Ancestry: 79.2% Irish

Employment: 0.0% management, business, and financial, 0.0% computer, engineering, and science, 0.0% education, legal, community service, arts, and media, 0.0% healthcare practitioners, 53.1% service, 0.0% sales and office, 46.9% natural resources, construction, and maintenance, 0.0% production, transportation, and material moving

Income: Per capita: n/a; Median household: n/a; Average household: n/a; Households with income of $100,000 or more: n/a; Poverty rate: n/a

Educational Attainment: High school diploma or higher: n/a; Bachelor's degree or higher: n/a; Graduate/professional degree or higher: n/a

Housing: Homeownership rate: 100.0%; Median home value: n/a; Median year structure built: n/a; Homeowner vacancy rate: 0.0%; Median selected monthly owner costs: $0 with a mortgage, $0 without a mortgage; Median gross rent: n/a per month; Rental vacancy rate: 0.0%

Health Insurance: 100.0% have insurance; 100.0% have private insurance; 0.0% have public insurance; 0.0% do not have insurance; 0.0% of children under 18 do not have insurance

Transportation: Commute: 100.0% car, 0.0% public transportation, 0.0% walk, 0.0% work from home; Mean travel time to work: 0.0 minutes

WILLIAMS (CDP). Covers a land area of 3.577 square miles and a water area of 0.003 square miles. Located at 38.82° N. Lat; 86.64° W. Long. Elevation is 574 feet.

Population: 438; Growth (since 2000): n/a; Density: 122.5 persons per square mile; Race: 100.0% White, 0.0% Black/African American, 0.0% Asian, 0.0% American Indian/Alaska Native, 0.0% Native Hawaiian/Other Pacific Islander, 0.0% Two or more races, 0.0% Hispanic of any race; Average household size: 1.94; Median age: 50.8; Age under 18: 5.9%; Age 65 and over: 20.8%; Males per 100 females: 107.2; Marriage status: 17.4% never married, 45.7% now married, 0.0% separated, 15.1% widowed, 21.9% divorced; Foreign born: 0.0%; Speak English only: 94.1%; With disability: 24.7%; Veterans: 13.6%; Ancestry: 20.3% Swedish, 13.9% American, 11.9% German, 8.4% Irish, 6.4% English

Employment: 7.5% management, business, and financial, 0.0% computer, engineering, and science, 0.0% education, legal, community service, arts, and media, 0.0% healthcare practitioners, 26.3% service, 30.0% sales and office, 17.4% natural resources, construction, and maintenance, 18.8% production, transportation, and material moving

Income: Per capita: $29,082; Median household: $41,786; Average household: $55,364; Households with income of $100,000 or more: 21.7%; Poverty rate: 25.8%

Educational Attainment: High school diploma or higher: 96.7%; Bachelor's degree or higher: 26.2%; Graduate/professional degree or higher: 13.3%

Housing: Homeownership rate: 64.6%; Median home value: $103,300; Median year structure built: 2002; Homeowner vacancy rate: 0.0%; Median selected monthly owner costs: $842 with a mortgage, $425 without a mortgage; Median gross rent: n/a per month; Rental vacancy rate: 0.0%

Health Insurance: 79.0% have insurance; 59.6% have private insurance; 52.1% have public insurance; 21.0% do not have insurance; 0.0% of children under 18 do not have insurance

Transportation: Commute: 100.0% car, 0.0% public transportation, 0.0% walk, 0.0% work from home; Mean travel time to work: 33.0 minutes

Madison County

Located in east central Indiana; drained by the West Fork of the White River and by many creeks. Covers a land area of 451.915 square miles, a water area of 0.989 square miles, and is located in the Eastern Time Zone at 40.17° N. Lat., 85.72° W. Long. The county was founded in 1823. County seat is Anderson.

Madison County is part of the Indianapolis-Carmel-Anderson, IN Metropolitan Statistical Area. The entire metro area includes: Boone County, IN; Brown County, IN; Hamilton County, IN; Hancock County, IN; Hendricks County, IN; Johnson County, IN; Madison County, IN; Marion County, IN; Morgan County, IN; Putnam County, IN; Shelby County, IN

Weather Station: Anderson Sewage Plant — Elevation: 845 feet

	Jan	Feb	Mar	Apr	May	Jun	Jul	Aug	Sep	Oct	Nov	Dec
High	34	39	49	62	72	81	84	82	76	64	51	38
Low	20	23	31	41	51	61	64	63	55	44	35	24
Precip	2.4	2.3	3.3	3.8	4.4	4.2	4.4	3.5	3.0	3.1	3.7	3.1
Snow	7.2	4.2	1.6	0.2	0.0	0.0	0.0	0.0	0.0	0.1	0.5	4.1

High and Low temperatures in degrees Fahrenheit; Precipitation and Snow in inches

Weather Station: Elwood Wastewater Plant — Elevation: 839 feet

	Jan	Feb	Mar	Apr	May	Jun	Jul	Aug	Sep	Oct	Nov	Dec
High	33	38	49	62	72	81	85	83	77	64	51	38
Low	17	20	28	38	49	59	62	60	52	40	32	21
Precip	2.6	2.0	2.9	3.7	4.3	4.4	4.3	3.8	3.4	2.8	3.6	3.0
Snow	na	na	0.8	tr	0.0	0.0	0.0	0.0	0.0	tr	0.1	2.8

High and Low temperatures in degrees Fahrenheit; Precipitation and Snow in inches

Population: 129,641; Growth (since 2000): -2.8%; Density: 286.9 persons per square mile; Race: 87.9% White, 7.7% Black/African American, 0.5% Asian, 0.2% American Indian/Alaska Native, 0.0% Native Hawaiian/Other Pacific Islander, 2.7% two or more races, 3.8% Hispanic of any race; Average household size: 2.39; Median age: 40.2; Age under 18: 22.1%; Age 65 and over: 17.3%; Males per 100 females: 99.8; Marriage status: 27.6% never married, 49.9% now married, 1.7% separated, 6.7% widowed, 15.8% divorced; Foreign born: 1.9%; Speak English only: 96.4%; With disability: 17.9%; Veterans: 9.1%; Ancestry: 19.1% German, 12.2% American, 10.7% Irish, 7.9% English, 2.4% Italian

Religion: Six largest groups: 9.5% Baptist, 7.3% Holiness, 6.0% Catholicism, 5.7% Non-denominational Protestant, 3.6% Methodist/Pietist, 2.0% Pentecostal

Economy: Unemployment rate: 4.0%; Leading industries: 14.7 % retail trade; 14.3 % other services (except public administration); 12.8 % health care and social assistance; Farms: 737 totaling 205,147 acres; Company size: 3 employ 1,000 or more persons, 5 employ 500 to 999 persons, 46

employ 100 to 499 persons, 2,209 employ less than 100 persons; Business ownership: 3,093 women-owned, 377 Black-owned, 271 Hispanic-owned, 84 Asian-owned, n/a American Indian/Alaska Native-owned
Employment: 10.1% management, business, and financial, 3.3% computer, engineering, and science, 8.6% education, legal, community service, arts, and media, 7.2% healthcare practitioners, 20.8% service, 24.0% sales and office, 8.7% natural resources, construction, and maintenance, 17.3% production, transportation, and material moving
Income: Per capita: $23,680; Median household: $45,432; Average household: $58,194; Households with income of $100,000 or more: 14.6%; Poverty rate: 17.4%
Educational Attainment: High school diploma or higher: 87.7%; Bachelor's degree or higher: 17.5%; Graduate/professional degree or higher: 5.8%
Housing: Homeownership rate: 69.1%; Median home value: $91,900; Median year structure built: 1964; Homeowner vacancy rate: 2.4%; Median selected monthly owner costs: $974 with a mortgage, $364 without a mortgage; Median gross rent: $742 per month; Rental vacancy rate: 7.6%
Vital Statistics: Birth rate: 114.1 per 10,000 population; Death rate: 109.8 per 10,000 population; Age-adjusted cancer mortality rate: 186.0 deaths per 100,000 population
Health Insurance: 89.7% have insurance; 65.6% have private insurance; 39.8% have public insurance; 10.3% do not have insurance; 4.6% of children under 18 do not have insurance
Health Care: Physicians: 11.7 per 10,000 population; Dentists: 5.5 per 10,000 population; Hospital beds: 22.9 per 10,000 population; Hospital admissions: 998.2 per 10,000 population
Air Quality Index (AQI): Percent of Days: 76.4% good, 23.3% moderate, 0.3% unhealthy for sensitive individuals, 0.0% unhealthy, 0.0% very unhealthy; Annual median: 41; Annual maximum: 105
Transportation: Commute: 92.3% car, 0.2% public transportation, 2.2% walk, 3.7% work from home; Mean travel time to work: 25.9 minutes
2016 Presidential Election: 59.5% Trump, 34.2% Clinton, 4.9% Johnson, 0.4% Stein
National and State Parks: Mounds State Park
Additional Information Contacts
Madison Government . . . . (765) 641-9470
http://www.madisoncty.com

Madison County Communities

ALEXANDRIA (city). Covers a land area of 2.627 square miles and a water area of 0 square miles. Located at 40.26° N. Lat; 85.68° W. Long. Elevation is 869 feet.
History: In Alexandria the Johns-Manville Company operated the first rock-wool insulation factory in the world, utilizing the argillaceous limestone found here.
Population: 5,045; Growth (since 2000): -19.4%; Density: 1,920.2 persons per square mile; Race: 99.1% White, 0.0% Black/African American, 0.0% Asian, 0.0% American Indian/Alaska Native, 0.0% Native Hawaiian/Other Pacific Islander, 0.7% Two or more races, 4.1% Hispanic of any race; Average household size: 2.54; Median age: 33.6; Age under 18: 24.2%; Age 65 and over: 19.1%; Males per 100 females: 91.6; Marriage status: 26.0% never married, 50.5% now married, 1.5% separated, 9.5% widowed, 14.1% divorced; Foreign born: 0.8%; Speak English only: 96.3%; With disability: 13.5%; Veterans: 6.6%; Ancestry: 14.4% American, 14.0% Irish, 13.4% German, 9.4% English, 5.4% Italian
Employment: 10.3% management, business, and financial, 1.9% computer, engineering, and science, 5.5% education, legal, community service, arts, and media, 8.5% healthcare practitioners, 23.3% service, 21.1% sales and office, 14.3% natural resources, construction, and maintenance, 15.1% production, transportation, and material moving
Income: Per capita: $21,336; Median household: $50,375; Average household: $53,608; Households with income of $100,000 or more: 8.0%; Poverty rate: 23.6%
Educational Attainment: High school diploma or higher: 82.3%; Bachelor's degree or higher: 14.8%; Graduate/professional degree or higher: 4.3%

School District(s)
Alexandria Community School Corp (PK-12)
Enrollment: 1,551 . . . . (765) 724-4496

Vocational/Technical School(s)
Alexandria School of Scientific Therapeutics (Private, For-profit)
Enrollment: 33. . . . . (765) 724-9152
Tuition: $10,255
Housing: Homeownership rate: 65.5%; Median home value: $75,600; Median year structure built: 1962; Homeowner vacancy rate: 3.4%; Median selected monthly owner costs: $958 with a mortgage, $357 without a mortgage; Median gross rent: $769 per month; Rental vacancy rate: 10.7%
Health Insurance: 92.9% have insurance; 70.7% have private insurance; 40.3% have public insurance; 7.1% do not have insurance; 0.0% of children under 18 do not have insurance
Safety: Violent crime rate: 18.0 per 10,000 population; Property crime rate: 199.8 per 10,000 population
Newspapers: Alexandria Times-Tribune (weekly circulation 2,100)
Transportation: Commute: 94.1% car, 0.0% public transportation, 1.0% walk, 2.8% work from home; Mean travel time to work: 25.8 minutes
Additional Information Contacts
City of Alexandria . . . . (765) 724-2541
http://www.alexandriaindiana.net

ANDERSON (city). County seat. Covers a land area of 41.371 square miles and a water area of 0.109 square miles. Located at 40.09° N. Lat; 85.69° W. Long. Elevation is 879 feet.
History: Anderson was platted in 1823 and named for Delaware Chief Kikthawenund, who was called Captain Anderson by the settlers. It was incorporated as Andersontown in 1838, and reincorporated as a city in 1865. The discovery of natural gas in 1886 brought industrial development, followed by the automotive industry.
Population: 54,986; Growth (since 2000): -7.9%; Density: 1,329.1 persons per square mile; Race: 79.0% White, 13.8% Black/African American, 0.9% Asian, 0.3% American Indian/Alaska Native, 0.0% Native Hawaiian/Other Pacific Islander, 4.1% Two or more races, 5.3% Hispanic of any race; Average household size: 2.25; Median age: 37.4; Age under 18: 22.2%; Age 65 and over: 17.0%; Males per 100 females: 91.9; Marriage status: 32.8% never married, 40.8% now married, 2.3% separated, 7.3% widowed, 19.1% divorced; Foreign born: 3.0%; Speak English only: 94.6%; With disability: 21.2%; Veterans: 9.2%; Ancestry: 17.8% German, 11.0% Irish, 9.2% American, 6.5% English, 2.6% Italian
Employment: 8.0% management, business, and financial, 2.6% computer, engineering, and science, 8.7% education, legal, community service, arts, and media, 5.6% healthcare practitioners, 25.0% service, 23.9% sales and office, 8.1% natural resources, construction, and maintenance, 18.0% production, transportation, and material moving
Income: Per capita: $20,207; Median household: $34,693; Average household: $45,965; Households with income of $100,000 or more: 8.3%; Poverty rate: 25.8%
Educational Attainment: High school diploma or higher: 84.8%; Bachelor's degree or higher: 14.5%; Graduate/professional degree or higher: 4.8%

School District(s)
Anderson Community School Corp (PK-12)
Enrollment: 8,674 . . . . (765) 641-2028
Anderson Preparatory Academy (KG-12)
Enrollment: 812. . . . . (765) 649-8472
Excel Center - Anderson (11-12)
Enrollment: 314. . . . . (888) 959-9062

Four-year College(s)
Anderson University (Private, Not-for-profit, Church of God)
Enrollment: 1,877 . . . . (765) 649-9071
Tuition: In-state $29,710; Out-of-state $29,710

Vocational/Technical School(s)
Summit Salon Academy-Anderson (Private, For-profit)
Enrollment: 102. . . . . (765) 649-5555
Tuition: $13,800
Housing: Homeownership rate: 56.0%; Median home value: $70,500; Median year structure built: 1960; Homeowner vacancy rate: 3.9%; Median selected monthly owner costs: $866 with a mortgage, $350 without a mortgage; Median gross rent: $724 per month; Rental vacancy rate: 8.2%
Health Insurance: 86.8% have insurance; 54.1% have private insurance; 47.5% have public insurance; 13.2% do not have insurance; 6.1% of children under 18 do not have insurance
Hospitals: Community Hospital of Anderson & Madison County; Saint Vincent Anderson Regional Hospital (225 beds)
Safety: Violent crime rate: 47.3 per 10,000 population; Property crime rate: 440.0 per 10,000 population

Newspapers: Herald-Bulletin (daily circulation 22,000)
Transportation: Commute: 90.5% car, 0.3% public transportation, 3.8% walk, 3.1% work from home; Mean travel time to work: 23.7 minutes
Airports: Anderson Municipal-Darlington Field (general aviation)
Additional Information Contacts
City of Anderson . . . . (765) 648-6000
http://www.cityofanderson.com

CHESTERFIELD (town). Covers a land area of 1.323 square miles and a water area of 0 square miles. Located at 40.11° N. Lat; 85.59° W. Long. Elevation is 909 feet.
History: The Chesterfield Spiritualist Camp was built here in 1890 by Dr. J. Westerfield and his followers.
Population: 2,499; Growth (since 2000): -15.8%; Density: 1,889.5 persons per square mile; Race: 96.8% White, 0.8% Black/African American, 0.5% Asian, 0.0% American Indian/Alaska Native, 0.0% Native Hawaiian/Other Pacific Islander, 1.9% Two or more races, 4.6% Hispanic of any race; Average household size: 2.36; Median age: 40.1; Age under 18: 21.1%; Age 65 and over: 18.1%; Males per 100 females: 94.3; Marriage status: 28.7% never married, 48.2% now married, 1.1% separated, 7.7% widowed, 15.4% divorced; Foreign born: 1.5%; Speak English only: 97.9%; With disability: 18.4%; Veterans: 10.7%; Ancestry: 17.9% German, 14.2% American, 11.7% Irish, 9.0% English, 6.7% French
Employment: 5.1% management, business, and financial, 1.4% computer, engineering, and science, 7.1% education, legal, community service, arts, and media, 4.8% healthcare practitioners, 26.4% service, 31.1% sales and office, 6.9% natural resources, construction, and maintenance, 17.1% production, transportation, and material moving
Income: Per capita: $19,735; Median household: $41,536; Average household: $46,386; Households with income of $100,000 or more: 5.9%; Poverty rate: 15.0%
Educational Attainment: High school diploma or higher: 91.5%; Bachelor's degree or higher: 10.7%; Graduate/professional degree or higher: 4.8%
Housing: Homeownership rate: 64.5%; Median home value: $65,200; Median year structure built: 1960; Homeowner vacancy rate: 2.4%; Median selected monthly owner costs: $820 with a mortgage, $336 without a mortgage; Median gross rent: $719 per month; Rental vacancy rate: 8.5%
Health Insurance: 86.7% have insurance; 57.8% have private insurance; 45.4% have public insurance; 13.3% do not have insurance; 4.2% of children under 18 do not have insurance
Transportation: Commute: 97.8% car, 0.0% public transportation, 0.5% walk, 0.5% work from home; Mean travel time to work: 23.5 minutes
Additional Information Contacts
Town of Chesterfield . . . . (765) 378-3331
http://www.chesterfield.in.gov

COUNTRY CLUB HEIGHTS (town). Covers a land area of 0.283 square miles and a water area of 0 square miles. Located at 40.12° N. Lat; 85.69° W. Long. Elevation is 879 feet.
Population: 119; Growth (since 2000): 30.8%; Density: 420.1 persons per square mile; Race: 89.1% White, 10.9% Black/African American, 0.0% Asian, 0.0% American Indian/Alaska Native, 0.0% Native Hawaiian/Other Pacific Islander, 0.0% Two or more races, 0.0% Hispanic of any race; Average household size: 2.83; Median age: 61.2; Age under 18: 13.4%; Age 65 and over: 44.5%; Males per 100 females: 107.9; Marriage status: 29.6% never married, 49.1% now married, 0.0% separated, 16.7% widowed, 4.6% divorced; Foreign born: 0.0%; Speak English only: 99.2%; With disability: 20.2%; Veterans: 17.5%; Ancestry: 24.4% German, 19.3% Czech, 15.1% English, 12.6% Irish, 10.1% European
Employment: 7.3% management, business, and financial, 0.0% computer, engineering, and science, 17.1% education, legal, community service, arts, and media, 29.3% healthcare practitioners, 4.9% service, 31.7% sales and office, 4.9% natural resources, construction, and maintenance, 4.9% production, transportation, and material moving
Income: Per capita: $49,119; Median household: $118,750; Average household: $135,686; Households with income of $100,000 or more: 69.0%; Poverty rate: 1.7%
Educational Attainment: High school diploma or higher: 100.0%; Bachelor's degree or higher: 60.0%; Graduate/professional degree or higher: 37.5%
Housing: Homeownership rate: 100.0%; Median home value: $227,300; Median year structure built: 1946; Homeowner vacancy rate: 0.0%; Median selected monthly owner costs: $1,734 with a mortgage, $525 without a mortgage; Median gross rent: n/a per month; Rental vacancy rate: 0.0%
Health Insurance: 94.1% have insurance; 82.4% have private insurance; 48.7% have public insurance; 5.9% do not have insurance; 17.1% of children under 18 do not have insurance
Transportation: Commute: 75.6% car, 0.0% public transportation, 0.0% walk, 24.4% work from home; Mean travel time to work: 18.9 minutes

EDGEWOOD (town). Covers a land area of 0.809 square miles and a water area of 0 square miles. Located at 40.10° N. Lat; 85.74° W. Long. Elevation is 879 feet.
History: Edgewood grew as a residential suburb for employees of the manufacturing plants in nearby Anderson.
Population: 1,960; Growth (since 2000): -1.4%; Density: 2,424.1 persons per square mile; Race: 94.6% White, 4.2% Black/African American, 1.0% Asian, 0.0% American Indian/Alaska Native, 0.0% Native Hawaiian/Other Pacific Islander, 0.2% Two or more races, 2.7% Hispanic of any race; Average household size: 2.20; Median age: 46.1; Age under 18: 22.1%; Age 65 and over: 23.1%; Males per 100 females: 88.8; Marriage status: 19.3% never married, 57.1% now married, 0.3% separated, 8.8% widowed, 14.8% divorced; Foreign born: 1.0%; Speak English only: 96.9%; With disability: 11.9%; Veterans: 6.9%; Ancestry: 21.5% German, 18.8% English, 14.9% Irish, 10.7% American, 3.2% French
Employment: 14.0% management, business, and financial, 3.3% computer, engineering, and science, 15.0% education, legal, community service, arts, and media, 5.5% healthcare practitioners, 10.8% service, 33.4% sales and office, 7.2% natural resources, construction, and maintenance, 10.9% production, transportation, and material moving
Income: Per capita: $30,585; Median household: $63,500; Average household: $66,845; Households with income of $100,000 or more: 15.6%; Poverty rate: 3.2%
Educational Attainment: High school diploma or higher: 95.0%; Bachelor's degree or higher: 37.1%; Graduate/professional degree or higher: 12.0%
Housing: Homeownership rate: 92.8%; Median home value: $98,400; Median year structure built: 1957; Homeowner vacancy rate: 1.8%; Median selected monthly owner costs: $1,032 with a mortgage, $416 without a mortgage; Median gross rent: $1,088 per month; Rental vacancy rate: 0.0%
Health Insurance: 96.2% have insurance; 85.8% have private insurance; 28.2% have public insurance; 3.8% do not have insurance; 0.7% of children under 18 do not have insurance
Transportation: Commute: 96.7% car, 0.0% public transportation, 0.5% walk, 2.1% work from home; Mean travel time to work: 25.4 minutes

ELWOOD (city). Covers a land area of 3.774 square miles and a water area of 0 square miles. Located at 40.27° N. Lat; 85.84° W. Long. Elevation is 863 feet.
History: Elwood was the birthplace of Wendell L. Wilkie, presidential nominee in 1940, who lived here until 1919. His speech accepting the nomination was made in Elwood.
Population: 8,458; Growth (since 2000): -13.1%; Density: 2,241.2 persons per square mile; Race: 98.2% White, 0.3% Black/African American, 0.2% Asian, 0.1% American Indian/Alaska Native, 0.0% Native Hawaiian/Other Pacific Islander, 0.9% Two or more races, 3.5% Hispanic of any race; Average household size: 2.40; Median age: 38.9; Age under 18: 21.7%; Age 65 and over: 16.1%; Males per 100 females: 94.9; Marriage status: 27.7% never married, 47.6% now married, 1.9% separated, 8.6% widowed, 16.1% divorced; Foreign born: 0.9%; Speak English only: 98.2%; With disability: 19.1%; Veterans: 7.3%; Ancestry: 21.4% German, 15.6% American, 12.5% Irish, 5.2% English, 2.6% European
Employment: 5.6% management, business, and financial, 1.5% computer, engineering, and science, 3.3% education, legal, community service, arts, and media, 8.0% healthcare practitioners, 25.8% service, 19.2% sales and office, 6.9% natural resources, construction, and maintenance, 29.5% production, transportation, and material moving
Income: Per capita: $21,425; Median household: $36,342; Average household: $50,921; Households with income of $100,000 or more: 9.7%; Poverty rate: 22.5%
Educational Attainment: High school diploma or higher: 82.7%; Bachelor's degree or higher: 10.8%; Graduate/professional degree or higher: 2.8%

School District(s)

Elwood Community School Corp (PK-12)
Enrollment: 1,787 . . . . (765) 552-9861
Housing: Homeownership rate: 62.5%; Median home value: $66,600; Median year structure built: 1942; Homeowner vacancy rate: 3.9%; Median

selected monthly owner costs: $820 with a mortgage, $356 without a mortgage; Median gross rent: $683 per month; Rental vacancy rate: 5.9%
Health Insurance: 86.6% have insurance; 58.3% have private insurance; 41.4% have public insurance; 13.4% do not have insurance; 4.1% of children under 18 do not have insurance
Hospitals: Saint Vincent Mercy Hospital (25 beds)
Safety: Violent crime rate: 14.3 per 10,000 population; Property crime rate: 263.5 per 10,000 population
Newspapers: Call-Leader (daily circulation 3,100)
Transportation: Commute: 92.4% car, 0.0% public transportation, 1.7% walk, 2.6% work from home; Mean travel time to work: 23.3 minutes
Additional Information Contacts
City of Elwood .... (765) 552-5078
http://www.elwoodcity-in.org

FRANKTON (town). Covers a land area of 1.054 square miles and a water area of 0 square miles. Located at 40.22° N. Lat; 85.77° W. Long. Elevation is 833 feet.
Population: 1,879; Growth (since 2000): -1.4%; Density: 1,782.2 persons per square mile; Race: 96.5% White, 0.0% Black/African American, 1.3% Asian, 0.0% American Indian/Alaska Native, 0.3% Native Hawaiian/Other Pacific Islander, 1.5% Two or more races, 2.0% Hispanic of any race; Average household size: 2.52; Median age: 37.7; Age under 18: 26.7%; Age 65 and over: 14.6%; Males per 100 females: 94.8; Marriage status: 30.4% never married, 49.2% now married, 1.1% separated, 6.9% widowed, 13.5% divorced; Foreign born: 1.3%; Speak English only: 98.7%; With disability: 15.3%; Veterans: 7.9%; Ancestry: 20.2% German, 13.8% American, 7.7% Irish, 6.9% English, 2.1% Italian
Employment: 8.4% management, business, and financial, 3.8% computer, engineering, and science, 8.5% education, legal, community service, arts, and media, 2.8% healthcare practitioners, 20.5% service, 25.3% sales and office, 11.0% natural resources, construction, and maintenance, 19.7% production, transportation, and material moving
Income: Per capita: $22,571; Median household: $48,879; Average household: $56,857; Households with income of $100,000 or more: 12.1%; Poverty rate: 7.1%
Educational Attainment: High school diploma or higher: 89.6%; Bachelor's degree or higher: 15.5%; Graduate/professional degree or higher: 5.9%

School District(s)

Frankton-Lapel Community Schools (PK-12)
Enrollment: 2,288 .... (765) 734-1261
Housing: Homeownership rate: 74.4%; Median home value: $87,400; Median year structure built: 1961; Homeowner vacancy rate: 4.8%; Median selected monthly owner costs: $945 with a mortgage, $341 without a mortgage; Median gross rent: $727 per month; Rental vacancy rate: 0.0%
Health Insurance: 89.3% have insurance; 74.6% have private insurance; 32.2% have public insurance; 10.7% do not have insurance; 6.1% of children under 18 do not have insurance
Transportation: Commute: 90.9% car, 0.5% public transportation, 2.4% walk, 6.3% work from home; Mean travel time to work: 27.6 minutes

INGALLS (town). Covers a land area of 1.512 square miles and a water area of 0.033 square miles. Located at 39.96° N. Lat; 85.81° W. Long. Elevation is 866 feet.
Population: 2,388; Growth (since 2000): 104.5%; Density: 1,579.6 persons per square mile; Race: 91.2% White, 3.4% Black/African American, 0.0% Asian, 0.0% American Indian/Alaska Native, 0.0% Native Hawaiian/Other Pacific Islander, 4.7% Two or more races, 3.1% Hispanic of any race; Average household size: 2.80; Median age: 31.1; Age under 18: 35.2%; Age 65 and over: 9.3%; Males per 100 females: 98.2; Marriage status: 32.1% never married, 53.3% now married, 2.4% separated, 2.8% widowed, 11.7% divorced; Foreign born: 1.5%; Speak English only: 96.9%; With disability: 9.4%; Veterans: 7.2%; Ancestry: 20.2% German, 15.7% American, 7.7% Irish, 6.1% English, 3.4% African
Employment: 16.0% management, business, and financial, 7.0% computer, engineering, and science, 8.3% education, legal, community service, arts, and media, 2.5% healthcare practitioners, 18.5% service, 21.6% sales and office, 8.2% natural resources, construction, and maintenance, 17.9% production, transportation, and material moving
Income: Per capita: $19,808; Median household: $45,577; Average household: $54,805; Households with income of $100,000 or more: 11.3%; Poverty rate: 16.6%
Educational Attainment: High school diploma or higher: 87.8%; Bachelor's degree or higher: 13.9%; Graduate/professional degree or higher: 3.4%
Housing: Homeownership rate: 78.6%; Median home value: $100,800; Median year structure built: 2000; Homeowner vacancy rate: 1.9%; Median selected monthly owner costs: $987 with a mortgage, $352 without a mortgage; Median gross rent: $910 per month; Rental vacancy rate: 0.0%
Health Insurance: 92.3% have insurance; 72.0% have private insurance; 26.1% have public insurance; 7.7% do not have insurance; 3.3% of children under 18 do not have insurance
Transportation: Commute: 94.4% car, 0.0% public transportation, 0.9% walk, 3.3% work from home; Mean travel time to work: 29.0 minutes

LAPEL (town). Covers a land area of 1.379 square miles and a water area of 0 square miles. Located at 40.07° N. Lat; 85.85° W. Long. Elevation is 860 feet.
History: Laid out 1876.
Population: 2,201; Growth (since 2000): 18.7%; Density: 1,596.1 persons per square mile; Race: 99.6% White, 0.4% Black/African American, 0.0% Asian, 0.0% American Indian/Alaska Native, 0.0% Native Hawaiian/Other Pacific Islander, 0.0% Two or more races, 0.0% Hispanic of any race; Average household size: 2.17; Median age: 44.4; Age under 18: 19.5%; Age 65 and over: 18.5%; Males per 100 females: 93.5; Marriage status: 18.2% never married, 62.5% now married, 2.1% separated, 7.8% widowed, 11.5% divorced; Foreign born: 0.0%; Speak English only: 100.0%; With disability: 18.9%; Veterans: 11.7%; Ancestry: 18.8% American, 15.1% German, 10.3% English, 9.7% Irish, 3.9% Scottish
Employment: 11.1% management, business, and financial, 10.2% computer, engineering, and science, 10.2% education, legal, community service, arts, and media, 7.9% healthcare practitioners, 17.5% service, 20.7% sales and office, 11.3% natural resources, construction, and maintenance, 11.0% production, transportation, and material moving
Income: Per capita: $32,317; Median household: $54,896; Average household: $70,307; Households with income of $100,000 or more: 21.2%; Poverty rate: 11.1%
Educational Attainment: High school diploma or higher: 92.5%; Bachelor's degree or higher: 23.2%; Graduate/professional degree or higher: 5.3%

School District(s)

Frankton-Lapel Community Schools (PK-12)
Enrollment: 2,288 .... (765) 734-1261
Housing: Homeownership rate: 77.4%; Median home value: $106,300; Median year structure built: 1968; Homeowner vacancy rate: 0.0%; Median selected monthly owner costs: $1,096 with a mortgage, $358 without a mortgage; Median gross rent: $779 per month; Rental vacancy rate: 3.4%
Health Insurance: 93.7% have insurance; 81.1% have private insurance; 28.9% have public insurance; 6.3% do not have insurance; 5.2% of children under 18 do not have insurance
Transportation: Commute: 94.5% car, 0.0% public transportation, 1.0% walk, 3.7% work from home; Mean travel time to work: 29.6 minutes

MARKLEVILLE (town). Covers a land area of 0.563 square miles and a water area of 0 square miles. Located at 39.98° N. Lat; 85.62° W. Long. Elevation is 951 feet.
History: Laid out 1852.
Population: 489; Growth (since 2000): 27.7%; Density: 868.7 persons per square mile; Race: 98.4% White, 0.4% Black/African American, 0.0% Asian, 0.0% American Indian/Alaska Native, 0.0% Native Hawaiian/Other Pacific Islander, 1.2% Two or more races, 0.4% Hispanic of any race; Average household size: 2.42; Median age: 41.2; Age under 18: 25.4%; Age 65 and over: 11.9%; Males per 100 females: 95.6; Marriage status: 24.6% never married, 54.1% now married, 1.0% separated, 3.6% widowed, 17.8% divorced; Foreign born: 0.2%; Speak English only: 99.6%; With disability: 15.7%; Veterans: 7.1%; Ancestry: 17.2% German, 16.8% American, 8.0% English, 6.1% Irish, 3.5% Scottish
Employment: 10.6% management, business, and financial, 0.0% computer, engineering, and science, 11.4% education, legal, community service, arts, and media, 3.3% healthcare practitioners, 18.3% service, 25.6% sales and office, 15.4% natural resources, construction, and maintenance, 15.4% production, transportation, and material moving
Income: Per capita: $24,819; Median household: $58,889; Average household: $62,349; Households with income of $100,000 or more: 11.4%; Poverty rate: 7.0%

Educational Attainment: High school diploma or higher: 92.6%; Bachelor's degree or higher: 16.7%; Graduate/professional degree or higher: 6.3%
Housing: Homeownership rate: 80.2%; Median home value: $87,000; Median year structure built: 1962; Homeowner vacancy rate: 6.9%; Median selected monthly owner costs: $957 with a mortgage, $342 without a mortgage; Median gross rent: $788 per month; Rental vacancy rate: 0.0%
Health Insurance: 89.8% have insurance; 77.3% have private insurance; 25.6% have public insurance; 10.2% do not have insurance; 2.2% of children under 18 do not have insurance
Transportation: Commute: 86.3% car, 0.0% public transportation, 3.3% walk, 7.5% work from home; Mean travel time to work: 28.0 minutes

ORESTES (town). Covers a land area of 0.623 square miles and a water area of 0 square miles. Located at 40.27° N. Lat; 85.73° W. Long. Elevation is 873 feet.
Population: 405; Growth (since 2000): 21.3%; Density: 649.8 persons per square mile; Race: 95.3% White, 0.0% Black/African American, 0.7% Asian, 0.0% American Indian/Alaska Native, 0.0% Native Hawaiian/Other Pacific Islander, 2.5% Two or more races, 6.4% Hispanic of any race; Average household size: 2.50; Median age: 42.3; Age under 18: 27.4%; Age 65 and over: 12.1%; Males per 100 females: 106.0; Marriage status: 28.0% never married, 55.7% now married, 1.6% separated, 7.2% widowed, 9.1% divorced; Foreign born: 1.7%; Speak English only: 93.8%; With disability: 22.5%; Veterans: 7.8%; Ancestry: 20.5% German, 17.0% American, 12.3% English, 9.6% Italian, 7.9% Irish
Employment: 3.5% management, business, and financial, 0.5% computer, engineering, and science, 1.5% education, legal, community service, arts, and media, 2.0% healthcare practitioners, 24.6% service, 24.1% sales and office, 12.1% natural resources, construction, and maintenance, 31.7% production, transportation, and material moving
Income: Per capita: $21,192; Median household: $44,167; Average household: $52,251; Households with income of $100,000 or more: 9.3%; Poverty rate: 11.4%
Educational Attainment: High school diploma or higher: 90.7%; Bachelor's degree or higher: 7.8%; Graduate/professional degree or higher: 2.2%
Housing: Homeownership rate: 77.8%; Median home value: $57,700; Median year structure built: 1955; Homeowner vacancy rate: 5.8%; Median selected monthly owner costs: $730 with a mortgage, $264 without a mortgage; Median gross rent: $790 per month; Rental vacancy rate: 34.5%
Health Insurance: 86.9% have insurance; 53.0% have private insurance; 42.6% have public insurance; 13.1% do not have insurance; 13.5% of children under 18 do not have insurance
Transportation: Commute: 93.8% car, 0.0% public transportation, 1.5% walk, 3.6% work from home; Mean travel time to work: 19.2 minutes

PENDLETON (town). Covers a land area of 11.166 square miles and a water area of 0.067 square miles. Located at 40.01° N. Lat; 85.76° W. Long. Elevation is 846 feet.
History: Pendleton was the county seat in the 1820's.
Population: 4,269; Growth (since 2000): 10.2%; Density: 382.3 persons per square mile; Race: 96.9% White, 1.0% Black/African American, 0.0% Asian, 0.0% American Indian/Alaska Native, 0.0% Native Hawaiian/Other Pacific Islander, 2.2% Two or more races, 0.9% Hispanic of any race; Average household size: 2.35; Median age: 38.9; Age under 18: 23.2%; Age 65 and over: 16.8%; Males per 100 females: 89.7; Marriage status: 21.2% never married, 56.5% now married, 0.8% separated, 6.2% widowed, 16.1% divorced; Foreign born: 0.0%; Speak English only: 99.1%; With disability: 12.9%; Veterans: 10.9%; Ancestry: 26.8% German, 16.0% Irish, 12.5% American, 8.8% English, 6.8% Polish
Employment: 14.2% management, business, and financial, 5.0% computer, engineering, and science, 11.9% education, legal, community service, arts, and media, 7.9% healthcare practitioners, 12.0% service, 31.0% sales and office, 11.3% natural resources, construction, and maintenance, 6.7% production, transportation, and material moving
Income: Per capita: $30,117; Median household: $62,500; Average household: $71,869; Households with income of $100,000 or more: 25.0%; Poverty rate: 5.4%
Educational Attainment: High school diploma or higher: 95.3%; Bachelor's degree or higher: 29.0%; Graduate/professional degree or higher: 11.3%

School District(s)

Indiana Department Of Corrections (07-12)
Enrollment: 391 . . . . (317) 233-3111
South Madison Com Sch Corp (PK-12)
Enrollment: 4,218 . . . . (765) 778-2152
Housing: Homeownership rate: 65.6%; Median home value: $134,400; Median year structure built: 1973; Homeowner vacancy rate: 0.0%; Median selected monthly owner costs: $1,125 with a mortgage, $430 without a mortgage; Median gross rent: $852 per month; Rental vacancy rate: 12.1%
Health Insurance: 91.4% have insurance; 79.8% have private insurance; 25.5% have public insurance; 8.6% do not have insurance; 1.8% of children under 18 do not have insurance
Newspapers: Times-Post (weekly circulation 1,000)
Transportation: Commute: 89.5% car, 0.0% public transportation, 4.3% walk, 5.9% work from home; Mean travel time to work: 32.0 minutes
Additional Information Contacts
Town of Pendleton . . . . (765) 778-7937
http://www.town.pendleton.in.us

RIVER FOREST (town). Covers a land area of 0.017 square miles and a water area of 0 square miles. Located at 40.11° N. Lat; 85.73° W. Long. Elevation is 873 feet.
Population: 18; Growth (since 2000): -35.7%; Density: 1,032.2 persons per square mile; Race: 100.0% White, 0.0% Black/African American, 0.0% Asian, 0.0% American Indian/Alaska Native, 0.0% Native Hawaiian/Other Pacific Islander, 0.0% Two or more races, 0.0% Hispanic of any race; Average household size: 2.57; Median age: 54.0; Age under 18: 0.0%; Age 65 and over: 22.2%; Males per 100 females: 144.4; Marriage status: 16.7% never married, 83.3% now married, 0.0% separated, 0.0% widowed, 0.0% divorced; Foreign born: 0.0%; Speak English only: 94.4%; With disability: 27.8%; Veterans: 22.2%; Ancestry: 16.7% Irish, 11.1% American, 5.6% French, 5.6% German, 5.6% Italian
Employment: 11.1% management, business, and financial, 0.0% computer, engineering, and science, 33.3% education, legal, community service, arts, and media, 22.2% healthcare practitioners, 11.1% service, 11.1% sales and office, 11.1% natural resources, construction, and maintenance, 0.0% production, transportation, and material moving
Income: Per capita: $45,283; Median household: $113,750; Average household: $110,086; Households with income of $100,000 or more: 57.2%; Poverty rate: n/a
Educational Attainment: High school diploma or higher: 100.0%; Bachelor's degree or higher: 61.1%; Graduate/professional degree or higher: 11.1%
Housing: Homeownership rate: 100.0%; Median home value: $218,800; Median year structure built: 1954; Homeowner vacancy rate: 0.0%; Median selected monthly owner costs: $1,708 with a mortgage, n/a without a mortgage; Median gross rent: n/a per month; Rental vacancy rate: 0.0%
Health Insurance: 94.4% have insurance; 72.2% have private insurance; 44.4% have public insurance; 5.6% do not have insurance; 0.0% of children under 18 do not have insurance
Transportation: Commute: 66.7% car, 0.0% public transportation, 0.0% walk, 11.1% work from home; Mean travel time to work: 0.0 minutes

SUMMITVILLE (town). Covers a land area of 0.489 square miles and a water area of 0 square miles. Located at 40.34° N. Lat; 85.64° W. Long. Elevation is 883 feet.
History: Laid out 1867.
Population: 975; Growth (since 2000): -10.6%; Density: 1,993.9 persons per square mile; Race: 97.9% White, 0.4% Black/African American, 0.0% Asian, 0.0% American Indian/Alaska Native, 0.0% Native Hawaiian/Other Pacific Islander, 1.4% Two or more races, 1.5% Hispanic of any race; Average household size: 2.55; Median age: 35.0; Age under 18: 25.6%; Age 65 and over: 11.9%; Males per 100 females: 99.8; Marriage status: 22.8% never married, 55.3% now married, 1.5% separated, 5.3% widowed, 16.6% divorced; Foreign born: 0.6%; Speak English only: 98.2%; With disability: 20.8%; Veterans: 8.1%; Ancestry: 22.2% German, 12.4% American, 12.0% Irish, 11.7% English, 4.2% British
Employment: 6.3% management, business, and financial, 0.5% computer, engineering, and science, 1.3% education, legal, community service, arts, and media, 2.3% healthcare practitioners, 25.4% service, 17.0% sales and office, 18.5% natural resources, construction, and maintenance, 28.7% production, transportation, and material moving
Income: Per capita: $17,721; Median household: $41,349; Average household: $46,098; Households with income of $100,000 or more: 6.3%; Poverty rate: 21.6%
Educational Attainment: High school diploma or higher: 86.6%; Bachelor's degree or higher: 10.6%; Graduate/professional degree or higher: 1.4%

School District(s)

Madison-Grant United School Corp (PK-12)
Enrollment: 1,291 . . . . (765) 948-4143

Housing: Homeownership rate: 71.4%; Median home value: $59,000; Median year structure built: 1963; Homeowner vacancy rate: 0.0%; Median selected monthly owner costs: $776 with a mortgage, $381 without a mortgage; Median gross rent: $617 per month; Rental vacancy rate: 0.0%
Health Insurance: 85.1% have insurance; 56.0% have private insurance; 39.9% have public insurance; 14.9% do not have insurance; 9.1% of children under 18 do not have insurance
Transportation: Commute: 92.8% car, 0.8% public transportation, 3.6% walk, 1.8% work from home; Mean travel time to work: 33.3 minutes

WOODLAWN HEIGHTS (town). Covers a land area of 0.116 square miles and a water area of 0 square miles. Located at 40.12° N. Lat; 85.70° W. Long. Elevation is 866 feet.
Population: 67; Growth (since 2000): -8.2%; Density: 579.4 persons per square mile; Race: 95.5% White, 0.0% Black/African American, 0.0% Asian, 0.0% American Indian/Alaska Native, 0.0% Native Hawaiian/Other Pacific Islander, 4.5% Two or more races, 14.9% Hispanic of any race; Average household size: 2.39; Median age: 60.5; Age under 18: 16.4%; Age 65 and over: 46.3%; Males per 100 females: 83.7; Marriage status: 5.4% never married, 80.4% now married, 0.0% separated, 10.7% widowed, 3.6% divorced; Foreign born: 7.5%; Speak English only: 82.5%; With disability: 16.4%; Veterans: 8.9%; Ancestry: 17.9% German, 13.4% English, 11.9% Irish, 7.5% American, 3.0% European
Employment: 22.5% management, business, and financial, 5.0% computer, engineering, and science, 25.0% education, legal, community service, arts, and media, 15.0% healthcare practitioners, 5.0% service, 27.5% sales and office, 0.0% natural resources, construction, and maintenance, 0.0% production, transportation, and material moving
Income: Per capita: $60,310; Median household: $110,000; Average household: $143,332; Households with income of $100,000 or more: 64.3%; Poverty rate: n/a
Educational Attainment: High school diploma or higher: 96.4%; Bachelor's degree or higher: 50.0%; Graduate/professional degree or higher: 17.9%
Housing: Homeownership rate: 100.0%; Median home value: $241,700; Median year structure built: 1966; Homeowner vacancy rate: 0.0%; Median selected monthly owner costs: $1,813 with a mortgage, $763 without a mortgage; Median gross rent: n/a per month; Rental vacancy rate: 0.0%
Health Insurance: 95.5% have insurance; 68.7% have private insurance; 52.2% have public insurance; 4.5% do not have insurance; 0.0% of children under 18 do not have insurance
Transportation: Commute: 100.0% car, 0.0% public transportation, 0.0% walk, 0.0% work from home; Mean travel time to work: 19.4 minutes

Marion County

Located in central Indiana; drained by the West Fork of the White River. Covers a land area of 396.298 square miles, a water area of 6.710 square miles, and is located in the Eastern Time Zone at 39.78° N. Lat., 86.14° W. Long. The county was founded in 1821. County seat is Indianapolis. Marion County is consolidated with Indianapolis through an arrangement known as Unigov.

Marion County is part of the Indianapolis-Carmel-Anderson, IN Metropolitan Statistical Area. The entire metro area includes: Boone County, IN; Brown County, IN; Hamilton County, IN; Hancock County, IN; Hendricks County, IN; Johnson County, IN; Madison County, IN; Marion County, IN; Morgan County, IN; Putnam County, IN; Shelby County, IN

Weather Station: Indianapolis Int'l Arpt Elevation: 791 feet

	Jan	Feb	Mar	Apr	May	Jun	Jul	Aug	Sep	Oct	Nov	Dec
High	36	41	52	63	73	82	85	84	78	65	52	39
Low	21	24	32	42	52	62	66	64	56	45	35	25
Precip	2.7	2.4	3.6	3.8	5.0	4.1	4.6	3.4	3.2	3.1	3.6	3.1
Snow	8.5	6.4	2.7	0.3	tr	tr	0.0	tr	tr	0.4	0.8	6.4

High and Low temperatures in degrees Fahrenheit; Precipitation and Snow in inches

Weather Station: Indianapolis SE Side Elevation: 845 feet

	Jan	Feb	Mar	Apr	May	Jun	Jul	Aug	Sep	Oct	Nov	Dec
High	35	39	50	62	72	81	84	83	77	65	52	39
Low	19	22	30	41	52	61	65	63	55	43	34	23
Precip	2.3	2.1	3.3	4.1	5.0	4.3	4.7	3.4	3.0	3.2	3.6	3.1
Snow	5.0	3.6	1.0	0.1	tr	0.0	0.0	0.0	0.0	0.2	0.2	3.3

High and Low temperatures in degrees Fahrenheit; Precipitation and Snow in inches

Population: 939,964; Growth (since 2000): 9.2%; Density: 2,371.9 persons per square mile; Race: 62.7% White, 27.4% Black/African American, 2.9% Asian, 0.3% American Indian/Alaska Native, 0.0% Native Hawaiian/Other Pacific Islander, 3.1% two or more races, 10.1% Hispanic of any race; Average household size: 2.51; Median age: 34.3; Age under 18: 24.8%; Age 65 and over: 11.7%; Males per 100 females: 93.2; Marriage status: 40.8% never married, 40.8% now married, 2.0% separated, 5.3% widowed, 13.1% divorced; Foreign born: 9.1%; Speak English only: 86.8%; With disability: 13.7%; Veterans: 7.2%; Ancestry: 15.6% German, 9.4% Irish, 6.4% American, 6.3% English, 2.5% African
Religion: Six largest groups: 11.1% Catholicism, 10.4% Baptist, 6.4% Non-denominational Protestant, 5.0% Methodist/Pietist, 2.1% Presbyterian-Reformed, 1.6% Pentecostal
Economy: Unemployment rate: 3.6%; Leading industries: 12.6 % retail trade; 12.2 % health care and social assistance; 11.6 % professional, scientific, and technical services; Farms: 231 totaling 20,075 acres; Company size: 36 employ 1,000 or more persons, 53 employ 500 to 999 persons, 808 employ 100 to 499 persons, 22,353 employ less than 100 persons; Business ownership: 29,976 women-owned, 14,110 Black-owned, 3,617 Hispanic-owned, 2,245 Asian-owned, 457 American Indian/Alaska Native-owned
Employment: 14.1% management, business, and financial, 4.8% computer, engineering, and science, 9.8% education, legal, community service, arts, and media, 6.2% healthcare practitioners, 17.7% service, 25.0% sales and office, 7.5% natural resources, construction, and maintenance, 14.9% production, transportation, and material moving
Income: Per capita: $26,284; Median household: $44,869; Average household: $63,906; Households with income of $100,000 or more: 17.0%; Poverty rate: 19.8%
Educational Attainment: High school diploma or higher: 85.6%; Bachelor's degree or higher: 29.7%; Graduate/professional degree or higher: 10.5%
Housing: Homeownership rate: 54.0%; Median home value: $123,500; Median year structure built: 1971; Homeowner vacancy rate: 2.2%; Median selected monthly owner costs: $1,123 with a mortgage, $408 without a mortgage; Median gross rent: $836 per month; Rental vacancy rate: 8.2%
Vital Statistics: Birth rate: 150.8 per 10,000 population; Death rate: 83.3 per 10,000 population; Age-adjusted cancer mortality rate: 182.5 deaths per 100,000 population
Health Insurance: 87.4% have insurance; 60.8% have private insurance; 35.8% have public insurance; 12.6% do not have insurance; 6.1% of children under 18 do not have insurance
Health Care: Physicians: 45.9 per 10,000 population; Dentists: 8.7 per 10,000 population; Hospital beds: 47.5 per 10,000 population; Hospital admissions: 1,873.3 per 10,000 population
Air Quality Index (AQI): Percent of Days: 60.0% good, 38.9% moderate, 1.1% unhealthy for sensitive individuals, 0.0% unhealthy, 0.0% very unhealthy; Annual median: 47; Annual maximum: 122
Transportation: Commute: 91.6% car, 1.9% public transportation, 1.8% walk, 3.2% work from home; Mean travel time to work: 23.3 minutes
2016 Presidential Election: 35.5% Trump, 58.0% Clinton, 5.0% Johnson, 0.2% Stein
National and State Parks: Fort Benjamin Harrison State Park and Nature Preserve; White River State Park

Additional Information Contacts

Marion Government. . . . . (317) 327-4740
http://www.indygov.org

Marion County Communities

BEECH GROVE (city). Covers a land area of 4.395 square miles and a water area of 0 square miles. Located at 39.72° N. Lat; 86.09° W. Long. Elevation is 804 feet.
History: Named for the many local beech trees. Incorporated 1906.
Population: 14,943; Growth (since 2000): 0.4%; Density: 3,400.3 persons per square mile; Race: 89.8% White, 6.9% Black/African American, 0.5% Asian, 0.0% American Indian/Alaska Native, 0.0% Native Hawaiian/Other Pacific Islander, 1.8% Two or more races, 3.9% Hispanic of any race; Average household size: 2.52; Median age: 36.5; Age under 18: 26.6%; Age 65 and over: 16.1%; Males per 100 females: 86.8; Marriage status: 35.1% never married, 40.5% now married, 1.7% separated, 7.4% widowed, 17.0% divorced; Foreign born: 1.9%; Speak English only: 96.8%;

With disability: 16.2%; Veterans: 9.3%; Ancestry: 22.7% German, 15.2% Irish, 7.4% American, 6.8% English, 3.4% Italian
Employment: 9.5% management, business, and financial, 3.2% computer, engineering, and science, 7.2% education, legal, community service, arts, and media, 5.3% healthcare practitioners, 18.1% service, 31.2% sales and office, 7.1% natural resources, construction, and maintenance, 18.4% production, transportation, and material moving
Income: Per capita: $20,388; Median household: $37,819; Average household: $49,446; Households with income of $100,000 or more: 11.0%; Poverty rate: 21.1%
Educational Attainment: High school diploma or higher: 86.8%; Bachelor's degree or higher: 15.1%; Graduate/professional degree or higher: 4.8%

School District(s)

Beech Grove City Schools (PK-12)
Enrollment: 2,194 .... (317) 788-4481
Housing: Homeownership rate: 53.5%; Median home value: $96,200; Median year structure built: 1961; Homeowner vacancy rate: 2.0%; Median selected monthly owner costs: $952 with a mortgage, $361 without a mortgage; Median gross rent: $753 per month; Rental vacancy rate: 1.8%
Health Insurance: 89.7% have insurance; 56.4% have private insurance; 45.8% have public insurance; 10.3% do not have insurance; 3.7% of children under 18 do not have insurance
Safety: Violent crime rate: n/a per 10,000 population; Property crime rate: 227.9 per 10,000 population
Transportation: Commute: 93.3% car, 1.7% public transportation, 2.2% walk, 2.0% work from home; Mean travel time to work: 22.7 minutes
Additional Information Contacts
City of Beech Grove .... (317) 788-4977
http://www.beechgrove.com

CLERMONT (town). Covers a land area of 0.672 square miles and a water area of 0 square miles. Located at 39.82° N. Lat; 86.32° W. Long. Elevation is 833 feet.
History: When Clermont was platted in 1849 it was called Mechanicsburg, but the name was changed in 1855.
Population: 1,361; Growth (since 2000): -7.9%; Density: 2,025.5 persons per square mile; Race: 91.3% White, 4.7% Black/African American, 0.5% Asian, 0.2% American Indian/Alaska Native, 0.0% Native Hawaiian/Other Pacific Islander, 1.9% Two or more races, 1.2% Hispanic of any race; Average household size: 2.56; Median age: 45.7; Age under 18: 18.1%; Age 65 and over: 17.0%; Males per 100 females: 96.8; Marriage status: 27.7% never married, 50.6% now married, 0.7% separated, 4.9% widowed, 16.8% divorced; Foreign born: 1.1%; Speak English only: 98.3%; With disability: 11.5%; Veterans: 10.4%; Ancestry: 25.6% German, 12.7% Irish, 10.1% English, 9.0% American, 2.8% French
Employment: 17.1% management, business, and financial, 5.4% computer, engineering, and science, 10.9% education, legal, community service, arts, and media, 3.1% healthcare practitioners, 11.0% service, 24.6% sales and office, 15.9% natural resources, construction, and maintenance, 12.1% production, transportation, and material moving
Income: Per capita: $29,547; Median household: $65,385; Average household: $72,879; Households with income of $100,000 or more: 23.5%; Poverty rate: 7.6%
Educational Attainment: High school diploma or higher: 92.6%; Bachelor's degree or higher: 32.1%; Graduate/professional degree or higher: 8.9%
Housing: Homeownership rate: 85.9%; Median home value: $114,100; Median year structure built: 1964; Homeowner vacancy rate: 0.7%; Median selected monthly owner costs: $1,099 with a mortgage, $345 without a mortgage; Median gross rent: $1,042 per month; Rental vacancy rate: 25.7%
Health Insurance: 87.2% have insurance; 74.9% have private insurance; 24.6% have public insurance; 12.8% do not have insurance; 9.1% of children under 18 do not have insurance
Transportation: Commute: 92.9% car, 0.3% public transportation, 2.6% walk, 3.7% work from home; Mean travel time to work: 23.6 minutes

---

CROWS NEST (town). Covers a land area of 0.429 square miles and a water area of 0 square miles. Located at 39.86° N. Lat; 86.17° W. Long. Elevation is 774 feet.
History: Joined Indianapolis in 1970.
Population: 90; Growth (since 2000): -6.3%; Density: 209.6 persons per square mile; Race: 96.7% White, 3.3% Black/African American, 0.0% Asian, 0.0% American Indian/Alaska Native, 0.0% Native Hawaiian/Other Pacific Islander, 0.0% Two or more races, 0.0% Hispanic of any race; Average household size: 3.60; Median age: 38.7; Age under 18: 18.9%; Age 65 and over: 21.1%; Males per 100 females: 114.7; Marriage status: 42.1% never married, 50.0% now married, 0.0% separated, 3.9% widowed, 3.9% divorced; Foreign born: 0.0%; Speak English only: 100.0%; With disability: 24.4%; Veterans: 5.5%; Ancestry: 56.7% German, 40.0% Irish, 20.0% English, 14.4% Welsh, 3.3% Norwegian
Employment: 52.9% management, business, and financial, 0.0% computer, engineering, and science, 8.8% education, legal, community service, arts, and media, 5.9% healthcare practitioners, 17.6% service, 14.7% sales and office, 0.0% natural resources, construction, and maintenance, 0.0% production, transportation, and material moving
Income: Per capita: $136,608; Median household: $198,125; Average household: $481,444; Households with income of $100,000 or more: 88.0%; Poverty rate: n/a
Educational Attainment: High school diploma or higher: 100.0%; Bachelor's degree or higher: 87.0%; Graduate/professional degree or higher: 51.9%
Housing: Homeownership rate: 100.0%; Median home value: $1,604,200; Median year structure built: 1959; Homeowner vacancy rate: 0.0%; Median selected monthly owner costs: $4,000+ with a mortgage, $1,150 without a mortgage; Median gross rent: n/a per month; Rental vacancy rate: 100.0%
Health Insurance: 94.4% have insurance; 88.9% have private insurance; 23.3% have public insurance; 5.6% do not have insurance; 0.0% of children under 18 do not have insurance
Transportation: Commute: 73.5% car, 0.0% public transportation, 0.0% walk, 8.8% work from home; Mean travel time to work: 19.0 minutes

---

CUMBERLAND (town). Covers a land area of 2.058 square miles and a water area of 0.010 square miles. Located at 39.79° N. Lat; 85.95° W. Long. Elevation is 853 feet.
History: The Town was officially platted on July 7, 1831 and originally had just six streets. The first Cumberland Post Office was established in 1842.
Population: 5,566; Growth (since 2000): 1.2%; Density: 2,704.2 persons per square mile; Race: 82.6% White, 12.2% Black/African American, 0.2% Asian, 0.0% American Indian/Alaska Native, 0.0% Native Hawaiian/Other Pacific Islander, 3.4% Two or more races, 2.9% Hispanic of any race; Average household size: 2.69; Median age: 35.5; Age under 18: 29.4%; Age 65 and over: 14.2%; Males per 100 females: 92.6; Marriage status: 36.1% never married, 48.2% now married, 1.9% separated, 4.1% widowed, 11.6% divorced; Foreign born: 1.8%; Speak English only: 97.9%; With disability: 11.8%; Veterans: 10.9%; Ancestry: 19.1% American, 18.3% German, 13.3% Irish, 12.5% English, 2.8% Polish
Employment: 16.1% management, business, and financial, 5.1% computer, engineering, and science, 8.1% education, legal, community service, arts, and media, 8.3% healthcare practitioners, 13.0% service, 27.4% sales and office, 7.7% natural resources, construction, and maintenance, 14.3% production, transportation, and material moving
Income: Per capita: $28,814; Median household: $61,025; Average household: $76,424; Households with income of $100,000 or more: 27.7%; Poverty rate: 8.0%
Educational Attainment: High school diploma or higher: 88.3%; Bachelor's degree or higher: 25.6%; Graduate/professional degree or higher: 10.1%
Housing: Homeownership rate: 72.7%; Median home value: $154,600; Median year structure built: 1982; Homeowner vacancy rate: 2.8%; Median selected monthly owner costs: $1,161 with a mortgage, $493 without a mortgage; Median gross rent: $767 per month; Rental vacancy rate: 9.5%
Health Insurance: 93.1% have insurance; 72.6% have private insurance; 32.7% have public insurance; 6.9% do not have insurance; 7.8% of children under 18 do not have insurance
Safety: Violent crime rate: 28.3 per 10,000 population; Property crime rate: 276.2 per 10,000 population
Transportation: Commute: 93.8% car, 0.1% public transportation, 1.9% walk, 2.5% work from home; Mean travel time to work: 26.5 minutes
Additional Information Contacts
Town of Cumberland .... (317) 894-6201
http://www.town.cumberland.in.us

HOMECROFT (town). Covers a land area of 0.242 square miles and a water area of 0 square miles. Located at 39.67° N. Lat; 86.13° W. Long. Elevation is 755 feet.
Population: 609; Growth (since 2000): -18.9%; Density: 2,521.1 persons per square mile; Race: 95.1% White, 1.3% Black/African American, 0.5% Asian, 0.5% American Indian/Alaska Native, 0.0% Native Hawaiian/Other

Pacific Islander, 2.3% Two or more races, 0.5% Hispanic of any race; Average household size: 2.61; Median age: 39.9; Age under 18: 21.2%; Age 65 and over: 13.8%; Males per 100 females: 87.5; Marriage status: 33.9% never married, 54.6% now married, 2.2% separated, 3.5% widowed, 8.0% divorced; Foreign born: 1.0%; Speak English only: 95.2%; With disability: 11.8%; Veterans: 8.1%; Ancestry: 36.0% German, 17.9% Irish, 8.7% American, 5.3% Italian, 4.3% English
Employment: 17.1% management, business, and financial, 3.3% computer, engineering, and science, 15.6% education, legal, community service, arts, and media, 9.0% healthcare practitioners, 9.9% service, 24.0% sales and office, 5.7% natural resources, construction, and maintenance, 15.6% production, transportation, and material moving
Income: Per capita: $35,268; Median household: $83,021; Average household: $88,773; Households with income of $100,000 or more: 36.1%; Poverty rate: 3.8%
Educational Attainment: High school diploma or higher: 95.4%; Bachelor's degree or higher: 42.0%; Graduate/professional degree or higher: 13.8%
Housing: Homeownership rate: 94.4%; Median home value: $145,300; Median year structure built: 1948; Homeowner vacancy rate: 4.3%; Median selected monthly owner costs: $1,160 with a mortgage, $435 without a mortgage; Median gross rent: $1,359 per month; Rental vacancy rate: 0.0%
Health Insurance: 93.9% have insurance; 80.0% have private insurance; 24.6% have public insurance; 6.1% do not have insurance; 0.0% of children under 18 do not have insurance
Transportation: Commute: 94.0% car, 0.0% public transportation, 1.9% walk, 2.5% work from home; Mean travel time to work: 24.4 minutes

---

INDIANAPOLIS (city). State capital. County seat. Indianapolis has a consolidated city-county government, a status it has held since 1970 under Indiana Code's Unigov provision. Many functions of the city and county governments are consolidated, though some remain separate. The statistics in this book cover the "balance" population, which excludes semi-autonomous municipalities in Marion County. Covers a land area of 361.433 square miles and a water area of 6.592 square miles. Located at 39.78° N. Lat; 86.15° W. Long. Elevation is 718 feet.
History: Settlement began in Indianapolis in 1820, when several families built cabins here and called it Fall Creek. That same year, Fall Creek was selected as the site for Indiana's capital because of its location near the center of the state. The new city was named Indianapolis in 1821; the first legislature met here in 1825. Indianapolis was incorporated as a city in 1847. Henry Ward Beecher, well-known writer, preacher, and brother of Harriet Beecher Stowe, lived in Indianapolis at that time.
Population: 853,431; Growth (since 2000): 9.2%; Density: 2,361.2 persons per square mile; Race: 61.8% White, 28.1% Black/African American, 3.0% Asian, 0.3% American Indian/Alaska Native, 0.0% Native Hawaiian/Other Pacific Islander, 3.0% Two or more races, 10.1% Hispanic of any race; Average household size: 2.51; Median age: 34.1; Age under 18: 24.7%; Age 65 and over: 11.5%; Males per 100 females: 93.5; Marriage status: 41.4% never married, 40.3% now married, 2.0% separated, 5.2% widowed, 13.1% divorced; Foreign born: 9.3%; Speak English only: 86.7%; With disability: 13.7%; Veterans: 7.0%; Ancestry: 15.4% German, 9.4% Irish, 6.3% American, 6.2% English, 2.5% African
Employment: 14.0% management, business, and financial, 4.7% computer, engineering, and science, 9.8% education, legal, community service, arts, and media, 6.3% healthcare practitioners, 17.8% service, 25.0% sales and office, 7.3% natural resources, construction, and maintenance, 15.1% production, transportation, and material moving
Income: Per capita: $26,232; Median household: $44,709; Average household: $63,698; Households with income of $100,000 or more: 16.8%; Poverty rate: 20.1%
Educational Attainment: High school diploma or higher: 85.5%; Bachelor's degree or higher: 29.7%; Graduate/professional degree or higher: 10.5%

School District(s)

Ace Preparatory Academy (KG-01)
Enrollment: 36 . . . . (317) 974-4987
Andrew J Brown Academy (KG-08)
Enrollment: 660 . . . . (317) 891-0730
Avondale Meadows Academy (KG-05)
Enrollment: 452 . . . . (317) 803-3182
Carmel Clay Schools (PK-12)
Enrollment: 16,035 . . . . (317) 844-9961
Carpe Diem - Meridian Campus (06-12)
Enrollment: 137 . . . . (317) 921-7497
Carpe Diem - Northwest (06-12)
Enrollment: 154 . . . . (317) 808-8749
Carpe Diem - Shadeland (06-12)
Enrollment: 67 . . . . (317) 677-1950
Charles A Tindley Accelerated Sch (09-12)
Enrollment: 273 . . . . (317) 545-1745
Christel House Academy South (KG-12)
Enrollment: 718 . . . . (317) 783-4690
Christel House Academy West (KG-04)
Enrollment: 265 . . . . (317) 783-4690
Christel House Dors South (09-12)
Enrollment: 265 . . . . (317) 783-4690
Christel House Dors West (09-12)
Enrollment: 192 . . . . (317) 783-4690
CSUSA Donnan (07-08)
Enrollment: 392 . . . . (954) 202-3500
CSUSA Howe (07-12)
Enrollment: 543 . . . . (954) 202-3500
CSUSA Manual (09-12)
Enrollment: 696 . . . . (954) 202-3500
Damar Charter Academy (KG-12)
Enrollment: 164 . . . . (317) 455-2400
Enlace Academy (KG-06)
Enrollment: 366 . . . . (317) 383-0607
Excel Center - Lafayette Square (11-12)
Enrollment: 382 . . . . (317) 524-3925
Excel Center - University Heights (11-12)
Enrollment: 390 . . . . (317) 524-3925
Excel Center For Adult Learners (11-12)
Enrollment: 1,036 . . . . (317) 524-3925
Franklin Township Com Sch Corp (PK-12)
Enrollment: 9,445 . . . . (317) 862-2411
Global Preparatory Academy (KG-02)
Enrollment: 269 . . . . (317) 226-4244
Herron Charter (09-12)
Enrollment: 827 . . . . (317) 231-0010
Hoosier Acad Virtual Charter (KG-12)
Enrollment: 3,342 . . . . (317) 495-6494
Hoosier Academy - Indianapolis (KG-12)
Enrollment: 247 . . . . (317) 495-6494
Hope Academy (09-12)
Enrollment: 25 . . . . (317) 572-9356
Indiana College Preparatory School (KG-08)
Enrollment: 260 . . . . (317) 554-2021
Indiana Connections Academy (KG-12)
Enrollment: 4,032 . . . . (317) 550-3188
Indiana Department Of Corrections (07-12)
Enrollment: 391 . . . . (317) 233-3111
Indiana Math & Science Academy (KG-08)
Enrollment: 587 . . . . (317) 298-0025
Indiana Math & Science Academy - North (KG-12)
Enrollment: 555 . . . . (317) 259-7300
Indiana Math & Science Academy - South (KG-08)
Enrollment: 191 . . . . (317) 780-1200
Indiana Sch For The Blind & Vis Imprd (PK-12)
Enrollment: 138 . . . . (317) 253-1481
Indiana School For The Deaf (PK-12)
Enrollment: 275 . . . . (317) 924-8400
Indiana Virtual School (06-12)
Enrollment: 2,947 . . . . (317) 581-5355
Indianapolis Academy Of Excellence (KG-05)
Enrollment: 94 . . . . (317) 608-2991
Indianapolis Lighthouse East (07-10)
Enrollment: 269 . . . . (317) 897-2472
Indianapolis Metropolitan High Sch (09-12)
Enrollment: 265 . . . . (317) 524-4627
Indianapolis Public Schools (PK-12)
Enrollment: 31,011 . . . . (317) 226-4411
Indpls Lighthouse Charter School (KG-12)
Enrollment: 902 . . . . (317) 351-1534
Insight School Of Indiana (07-12)
Enrollment: 663 . . . . (317) 495-6494
Irvington Community School (KG-12)
Enrollment: 1,025 . . . . (317) 357-3770

Kindezi Academy (KG-02)
Enrollment: 167 . . . . (317) 383-0607
Kipp Indy College Prep Middle (06-08)
Enrollment: 304 . . . . (317) 547-5477
Kipp Indy Unite Elementary (KG-02)
Enrollment: 305 . . . . (317) 547-5477
M S D Decatur Township (PK-12)
Enrollment: 6,477 . . . . (317) 856-5265
M S D Lawrence Township (PK-12)
Enrollment: 15,379 . . . . (317) 423-8200
M S D Pike Township (PK-12)
Enrollment: 11,817 . . . . (317) 293-0393
M S D Warren Township (PK-12)
Enrollment: 12,865 . . . . (317) 869-4300
M S D Washington Township (PK-12)
Enrollment: 10,834 . . . . (317) 845-9400
M S D Wayne Township (PK-12)
Enrollment: 15,472 . . . . (317) 988-8600
Marion Academy (06-12)
Enrollment: 170 . . . . (317) 983-1300
Nexus Academy Of Indianapolis (09-12)
Enrollment: 130 . . . . (317) 252-5919
Paramount School Of Excellence Inc (KG-08)
Enrollment: 719 . . . . (317) 775-6660
Perry Township Schools (PK-12)
Enrollment: 16,207 . . . . (317) 789-3700
Phalen Leadership Academy (KG-05)
Enrollment: 310 . . . . (317) 333-6980
Se Neighborhood Sch Of Excellence (KG-08)
Enrollment: 540 . . . . (317) 423-0204
Southside Sp Srvs Of Marion Co (KG-12)
Enrollment: 126 . . . . (317) 789-1650
The Mind Program High School
Enrollment: n/a . . . . (414) 364-0201
Tindley Collegiate Academy (06-08)
Enrollment: 269 . . . . (317) 777-7740
Tindley Genesis Academy (KG-04)
Enrollment: 216 . . . . (317) 777-6832
Tindley Preparatory Academy (06-08)
Enrollment: 189 . . . . (317) 777-6290
Tindley Renaissance Academy (KG-05)
Enrollment: 544 . . . . (317) 777-7290
Tindley Summit Academy (KG-05)
Enrollment: 304 . . . . (317) 777-6830
Vision Academy (KG-08)
Enrollment: 439 . . . . (317) 632-2006

Four-year College(s)

American College of Education (Private, For-profit)
Enrollment: 4,816 . . . . (800) 280-0307
Brown Mackie College-Indianapolis (Private, For-profit)
Enrollment: n/a . . . . (317) 554-8300
Butler University (Private, Not-for-profit)
Enrollment: 5,145 . . . . (317) 940-8000
Tuition: In-state $39,860; Out-of-state $39,860
Chamberlain University-Indiana (Private, For-profit)
Enrollment: 208 . . . . (317) 816-7335
Tuition: In-state $19,375; Out-of-state $19,375
Christian Theological Seminary (Private, Not-for-profit, Christian Church (Disciples of Christ))
Enrollment: 165 . . . . (317) 924-1331
Crossroads Bible College (Private, Not-for-profit, Baptist)
Enrollment: 168 . . . . (317) 789-8255
Tuition: In-state $12,400; Out-of-state $12,400
Harrison College-Indianapolis (Private, For-profit)
Enrollment: 2,045 . . . . (317) 447-6200
Tuition: In-state $16,275; Out-of-state $16,275
Horizon University (Private, Not-for-profit, Other (none of the above))
Enrollment: 16 . . . . (800) 553-4674
Tuition: In-state $9,300; Out-of-state $9,300
Indiana University-Purdue University-Indianapolis (Public)
Enrollment: 29,791 . . . . (317) 274-5555
Tuition: In-state $9,334; Out-of-state $29,806
Kaplan University-Indianapolis (Private, For-profit)
Enrollment: 603 . . . . (317) 208-5311
Tuition: In-state $14,263; Out-of-state $14,263
Marian University (Private, Not-for-profit, Roman Catholic)
Enrollment: 3,429 . . . . (317) 955-6000
Tuition: In-state $33,000; Out-of-state $33,000
Martin University (Private, Not-for-profit)
Enrollment: 346 . . . . (317) 543-3235
Tuition: In-state $13,200; Out-of-state $13,200
National American University-Indianapolis (Private, For-profit)
Enrollment: 96 . . . . (317) 810-8101
Tuition: In-state $15,000; Out-of-state $15,000
The Art Institute of Indianapolis (Private, For-profit)
Enrollment: 536 . . . . (317) 613-4800
Tuition: In-state $14,818; Out-of-state $14,818
University of Indianapolis (Private, Not-for-profit, United Methodist)
Enrollment: 5,972 . . . . (317) 788-3368
Tuition: In-state $28,390; Out-of-state $28,390
University of Phoenix-Indiana (Private, For-profit)
Enrollment: 19 . . . . (866) 766-0766

Two-year College(s)

Aviation Institute of Maintenance-Indianapolis (Private, For-profit)
Enrollment: 132 . . . . (317) 243-4519
Tuition: In-state $16,757; Out-of-state $16,757
Brightwood College-Indianapolis (Private, For-profit)
Enrollment: 463 . . . . (317) 782-0315
Fortis College-Indianapolis (Private, For-profit)
Enrollment: 334 . . . . (317) 808-4800
Tuition: In-state $20,100; Out-of-state $20,100
International Business College-Indianapolis (Private, For-profit)
Enrollment: 319 . . . . (317) 813-2300
Tuition: In-state $13,960; Out-of-state $13,960
Ivy Tech Community College (Public)
Enrollment: 75,486 . . . . (317) 921-4800
Tuition: In-state $4,255; Out-of-state $8,211
Lincoln College of Technology-Indianapolis (Private, For-profit)
Enrollment: 792 . . . . (317) 632-5553

Vocational/Technical School(s)

Aveda Fredric's Institute-Indianapolis (Private, For-profit)
Enrollment: 216 . . . . (317) 578-5500
Tuition: $19,000
Empire Beauty School-Indianapolis (Private, For-profit)
Enrollment: 236 . . . . (800) 920-4593
Tuition: $19,260
Indiana Massage College (Private, For-profit)
Enrollment: 95 . . . . (317) 376-8640
Kenny's Academy of Barbering (Private, For-profit)
Enrollment: 81 . . . . (317) 635-5900
Tuition: $15,850
MyComputerCareer.edu-Indianapolis (Private, For-profit)
Enrollment: 208 . . . . (317) 550-3044
Tuition: $18,370
Paul Mitchell the School-Indianapolis (Private, For-profit)
Enrollment: 165 . . . . (317) 885-0348
Tuition: $15,495
Textures Institute of Cosmetology (Private, For-profit)
Enrollment: 20 . . . . (317) 824-1400
Tuition: $14,800
Tricoci University of Beauty Culture-Indianapolis (Private, For-profit)
Enrollment: 179 . . . . (317) 841-9400
Tuition: $18,334

Housing: Homeownership rate: 53.4%; Median home value: $123,500; Median year structure built: 1971; Homeowner vacancy rate: 2.1%; Median selected monthly owner costs: $1,124 with a mortgage, $409 without a mortgage; Median gross rent: $840 per month; Rental vacancy rate: 8.4%

Health Insurance: 87.4% have insurance; 60.5% have private insurance; 35.9% have public insurance; 12.6% do not have insurance; 6.1% of children under 18 do not have insurance

Hospitals: Community Hospital East (1,025 beds); Community Hospital North (282 beds); Community Hospital South; Community Westview Hospital (116 beds); Eskenazi Health (354 beds); Fairbanks; Franciscan Saint Francis Health - Indianapolis; Indiana Orthopaedic Hospital; Indiana University Health (1,120 beds); Indianapolis VA Medical Center (170 beds); Saint Vincent Heart Center of Indiana (80 beds); Saint Vincent Hospital & Health Services (650 beds); The Indiana Heart Hospital (72 beds)

Safety: Violent crime rate: 133.4 per 10,000 population; Property crime rate: 441.2 per 10,000 population

Newspapers: Franklin Township Informer (weekly circulation 5,000); Indianapolis Star (daily circulation 259,000); Southside Times (weekly circulation 22,500); West Indianapolis Community News (weekly circulation 15,000)
Transportation: Commute: 91.5% car, 2.0% public transportation, 1.8% walk, 3.2% work from home; Mean travel time to work: 23.1 minutes; Amtrak: Train service available.
Airports: Eagle Creek Airpark (general aviation); Indianapolis International (primary service/medium hub)
Additional Information Contacts
City of Indianapolis . . . . (317) 327-4740
http://www.indy.gov/Pages/Home.aspx

LAWRENCE (city). Covers a land area of 20.132 square miles and a water area of 0.110 square miles. Located at 39.87° N. Lat; 85.99° W. Long. Elevation is 873 feet.
History: Named for Captain James Lawrence, U.S. Naval officer in the War of 1812. Fort Benjamin Harrison is here.
Population: 48,081; Growth (since 2000): 23.6%; Density: 2,388.3 persons per square mile; Race: 64.4% White, 27.8% Black/African American, 1.5% Asian, 0.1% American Indian/Alaska Native, 0.0% Native Hawaiian/Other Pacific Islander, 3.9% Two or more races, 12.2% Hispanic of any race; Average household size: 2.59; Median age: 35.0; Age under 18: 26.5%; Age 65 and over: 11.5%; Males per 100 females: 90.5; Marriage status: 34.8% never married, 48.6% now married, 1.6% separated, 5.5% widowed, 11.2% divorced; Foreign born: 8.0%; Speak English only: 86.5%; With disability: 13.5%; Veterans: 9.3%; Ancestry: 14.7% German, 8.1% Irish, 7.6% American, 6.4% English, 2.5% Italian
Employment: 15.7% management, business, and financial, 6.0% computer, engineering, and science, 10.1% education, legal, community service, arts, and media, 5.7% healthcare practitioners, 16.3% service, 24.7% sales and office, 11.0% natural resources, construction, and maintenance, 10.6% production, transportation, and material moving
Income: Per capita: $26,397; Median household: $50,107; Average household: $66,291; Households with income of $100,000 or more: 21.0%; Poverty rate: 15.8%
Educational Attainment: High school diploma or higher: 86.0%; Bachelor's degree or higher: 32.8%; Graduate/professional degree or higher: 10.6%
Housing: Homeownership rate: 65.4%; Median home value: $133,600; Median year structure built: 1991; Homeowner vacancy rate: 3.4%; Median selected monthly owner costs: $1,167 with a mortgage, $416 without a mortgage; Median gross rent: $823 per month; Rental vacancy rate: 6.9%
Health Insurance: 86.3% have insurance; 63.5% have private insurance; 31.8% have public insurance; 13.7% do not have insurance; 6.3% of children under 18 do not have insurance
Transportation: Commute: 93.1% car, 0.4% public transportation, 1.1% walk, 4.6% work from home; Mean travel time to work: 27.4 minutes

MERIDIAN HILLS (town). Covers a land area of 1.477 square miles and a water area of 0 square miles. Located at 39.89° N. Lat; 86.16° W. Long. Elevation is 794 feet.
History: Former municipality, merged with Indianapolis 1970.
Population: 1,813; Growth (since 2000): 5.8%; Density: 1,227.8 persons per square mile; Race: 89.4% White, 2.8% Black/African American, 1.6% Asian, 0.7% American Indian/Alaska Native, 1.3% Native Hawaiian/Other Pacific Islander, 3.1% Two or more races, 3.8% Hispanic of any race; Average household size: 2.73; Median age: 44.5; Age under 18: 28.4%; Age 65 and over: 18.1%; Males per 100 females: 96.4; Marriage status: 18.1% never married, 72.6% now married, 0.4% separated, 4.4% widowed, 4.9% divorced; Foreign born: 4.4%; Speak English only: 92.1%; With disability: 6.5%; Veterans: 6.8%; Ancestry: 23.6% German, 18.6% Irish, 12.7% English, 8.2% American, 4.7% European
Employment: 38.3% management, business, and financial, 5.5% computer, engineering, and science, 17.1% education, legal, community service, arts, and media, 13.6% healthcare practitioners, 5.1% service, 11.4% sales and office, 3.8% natural resources, construction, and maintenance, 5.3% production, transportation, and material moving
Income: Per capita: $94,867; Median household: $151,563; Average household: $259,991; Households with income of $100,000 or more: 68.8%; Poverty rate: 2.7%
Educational Attainment: High school diploma or higher: 99.7%; Bachelor's degree or higher: 80.6%; Graduate/professional degree or higher: 41.7%
Housing: Homeownership rate: 95.4%; Median home value: $453,200; Median year structure built: 1956; Homeowner vacancy rate: 0.0%; Median selected monthly owner costs: $2,326 with a mortgage, $918 without a mortgage; Median gross rent: $2,577 per month; Rental vacancy rate: 0.0%
Health Insurance: 98.6% have insurance; 90.6% have private insurance; 19.1% have public insurance; 1.4% do not have insurance; 1.7% of children under 18 do not have insurance
Transportation: Commute: 87.2% car, 0.2% public transportation, 2.2% walk, 10.3% work from home; Mean travel time to work: 21.3 minutes

NORTH CROWS NEST (town). Covers a land area of 0.065 square miles and a water area of 0 square miles. Located at 39.87° N. Lat; 86.16° W. Long. Elevation is 781 feet.
Population: 46; Growth (since 2000): 9.5%; Density: 712.3 persons per square mile; Race: 73.9% White, 0.0% Black/African American, 4.3% Asian, 0.0% American Indian/Alaska Native, 0.0% Native Hawaiian/Other Pacific Islander, 21.7% Two or more races, 0.0% Hispanic of any race; Average household size: 3.29; Median age: 41.0; Age under 18: 34.8%; Age 65 and over: 17.4%; Males per 100 females: 104.5; Marriage status: 36.4% never married, 57.6% now married, 0.0% separated, 0.0% widowed, 6.1% divorced; Foreign born: 6.5%; Speak English only: 90.7%; With disability: 6.5%; Veterans: 13.3%; Ancestry: 28.3% English, 21.7% European, 13.0% German, 4.3% Austrian, 4.3% Dutch
Employment: 21.4% management, business, and financial, 14.3% computer, engineering, and science, 14.3% education, legal, community service, arts, and media, 7.1% healthcare practitioners, 0.0% service, 42.9% sales and office, 0.0% natural resources, construction, and maintenance, 0.0% production, transportation, and material moving
Income: Per capita: $85,904; Median household: n/a; Average household: $282,000; Households with income of $100,000 or more: 71.4%; Poverty rate: 15.2%
Educational Attainment: High school diploma or higher: 96.4%; Bachelor's degree or higher: 85.7%; Graduate/professional degree or higher: 28.6%
Housing: Homeownership rate: 100.0%; Median home value: $900,000; Median year structure built: Before 1940; Homeowner vacancy rate: 0.0%; Median selected monthly owner costs: $3,700 with a mortgage, $1,500+ without a mortgage; Median gross rent: n/a per month; Rental vacancy rate: 0.0%
Health Insurance: 95.7% have insurance; 95.7% have private insurance; 17.4% have public insurance; 4.3% do not have insurance; 0.0% of children under 18 do not have insurance
Transportation: Commute: 85.7% car, 0.0% public transportation, 0.0% walk, 14.3% work from home; Mean travel time to work: 0.0 minutes

ROCKY RIPPLE (town). Covers a land area of 0.303 square miles and a water area of 0 square miles. Located at 39.85° N. Lat; 86.17° W. Long. Elevation is 705 feet.
Population: 601; Growth (since 2000): -15.6%; Density: 1,984.2 persons per square mile; Race: 87.9% White, 4.3% Black/African American, 0.0% Asian, 0.0% American Indian/Alaska Native, 0.0% Native Hawaiian/Other Pacific Islander, 7.8% Two or more races, 3.7% Hispanic of any race; Average household size: 2.32; Median age: 37.6; Age under 18: 21.5%; Age 65 and over: 13.6%; Males per 100 females: 97.4; Marriage status: 38.6% never married, 42.8% now married, 1.0% separated, 4.2% widowed, 14.4% divorced; Foreign born: 2.2%; Speak English only: 94.6%; With disability: 10.6%; Veterans: 4.4%; Ancestry: 25.3% German, 11.6% Irish, 11.3% English, 9.3% American, 5.0% European
Employment: 14.6% management, business, and financial, 3.9% computer, engineering, and science, 22.4% education, legal, community service, arts, and media, 3.9% healthcare practitioners, 15.5% service, 22.4% sales and office, 5.7% natural resources, construction, and maintenance, 11.6% production, transportation, and material moving
Income: Per capita: $25,626; Median household: $45,313; Average household: $56,034; Households with income of $100,000 or more: 15.4%; Poverty rate: 23.9%
Educational Attainment: High school diploma or higher: 94.3%; Bachelor's degree or higher: 41.2%; Graduate/professional degree or higher: 18.5%
Housing: Homeownership rate: 69.9%; Median home value: $125,300; Median year structure built: 1950; Homeowner vacancy rate: 3.7%; Median selected monthly owner costs: $1,014 with a mortgage, $367 without a mortgage; Median gross rent: $1,083 per month; Rental vacancy rate: 7.1%

Health Insurance: 83.9% have insurance; 66.2% have private insurance; 27.0% have public insurance; 16.1% do not have insurance; 0.0% of children under 18 do not have insurance
Transportation: Commute: 87.7% car, 0.0% public transportation, 0.6% walk, 8.4% work from home; Mean travel time to work: 21.2 minutes

SOUTHPORT (city). Covers a land area of 0.628 square miles and a water area of 0 square miles. Located at 39.66° N. Lat; 86.12° W. Long. Elevation is 748 feet.
History: Laid out 1852.
Population: 1,894; Growth (since 2000): 2.3%; Density: 3,014.9 persons per square mile; Race: 81.0% White, 0.9% Black/African American, 16.9% Asian, 0.0% American Indian/Alaska Native, 0.0% Native Hawaiian/Other Pacific Islander, 0.7% Two or more races, 1.2% Hispanic of any race; Average household size: 3.07; Median age: 33.5; Age under 18: 28.8%; Age 65 and over: 10.8%; Males per 100 females: 92.6; Marriage status: 31.7% never married, 53.2% now married, 0.4% separated, 5.0% widowed, 10.1% divorced; Foreign born: 17.0%; Speak English only: 81.8%; With disability: 9.1%; Veterans: 9.4%; Ancestry: 28.7% German, 9.9% Irish, 8.8% English, 6.4% American, 3.4% Italian
Employment: 12.6% management, business, and financial, 1.7% computer, engineering, and science, 10.8% education, legal, community service, arts, and media, 8.2% healthcare practitioners, 13.9% service, 22.8% sales and office, 11.9% natural resources, construction, and maintenance, 18.2% production, transportation, and material moving
Income: Per capita: $23,520; Median household: $57,159; Average household: $68,107; Households with income of $100,000 or more: 18.8%; Poverty rate: 11.5%
Educational Attainment: High school diploma or higher: 86.3%; Bachelor's degree or higher: 24.9%; Graduate/professional degree or higher: 6.0%
Housing: Homeownership rate: 76.8%; Median home value: $122,100; Median year structure built: 1962; Homeowner vacancy rate: 0.0%; Median selected monthly owner costs: $1,114 with a mortgage, $377 without a mortgage; Median gross rent: $938 per month; Rental vacancy rate: 14.2%
Health Insurance: 92.6% have insurance; 71.0% have private insurance; 32.8% have public insurance; 7.4% do not have insurance; 2.4% of children under 18 do not have insurance
Transportation: Commute: 94.0% car, 0.3% public transportation, 0.8% walk, 1.7% work from home; Mean travel time to work: 24.7 minutes

SPEEDWAY (town). Covers a land area of 4.758 square miles and a water area of 0.008 square miles. Located at 39.79° N. Lat; 86.25° W. Long. Elevation is 748 feet.
History: Named for Indianapolis Motor Speedway, located in the city. Speedway, laid out in 1912 by Carl Fisher, James T. Allison, and Frank H. Wheeler, gained fame as the home of the Indianapolis Motor Speedway.
Population: 12,229; Growth (since 2000): -5.1%; Density: 2,570.1 persons per square mile; Race: 64.4% White, 21.4% Black/African American, 4.1% Asian, 0.1% American Indian/Alaska Native, 0.2% Native Hawaiian/Other Pacific Islander, 4.9% Two or more races, 9.2% Hispanic of any race; Average household size: 2.36; Median age: 33.5; Age under 18: 23.6%; Age 65 and over: 15.3%; Males per 100 females: 93.6; Marriage status: 38.1% never married, 40.4% now married, 0.9% separated, 6.8% widowed, 14.8% divorced; Foreign born: 16.3%; Speak English only: 80.5%; With disability: 14.3%; Veterans: 6.5%; Ancestry: 19.2% German, 9.6% English, 8.4% Irish, 6.6% American, 3.5% African
Employment: 12.2% management, business, and financial, 5.8% computer, engineering, and science, 8.9% education, legal, community service, arts, and media, 6.0% healthcare practitioners, 18.4% service, 23.8% sales and office, 7.4% natural resources, construction, and maintenance, 17.5% production, transportation, and material moving
Income: Per capita: $22,873; Median household: $40,109; Average household: $51,534; Households with income of $100,000 or more: 11.3%; Poverty rate: 21.0%
Educational Attainment: High school diploma or higher: 87.1%; Bachelor's degree or higher: 30.0%; Graduate/professional degree or higher: 11.3%

School District(s)

School Town Of Speedway (PK-12)
Enrollment: 1,878 . . . . (317) 244-0236

Vocational/Technical School(s)

Empire Beauty School-Speedway (Private, For-profit)
Enrollment: 218. . . . . (800) 920-4593
Tuition: $19,260

Housing: Homeownership rate: 45.7%; Median home value: $117,000; Median year structure built: 1962; Homeowner vacancy rate: 4.0%; Median selected monthly owner costs: $1,029 with a mortgage, $367 without a mortgage; Median gross rent: $741 per month; Rental vacancy rate: 6.5%
Health Insurance: 89.1% have insurance; 63.7% have private insurance; 35.6% have public insurance; 10.9% do not have insurance; 3.5% of children under 18 do not have insurance
Safety: Violent crime rate: 31.3 per 10,000 population; Property crime rate: 410.7 per 10,000 population
Newspapers: The Press Newspapers (weekly circulation 8,500)
Transportation: Commute: 92.4% car, 3.1% public transportation, 0.9% walk, 2.4% work from home; Mean travel time to work: 21.2 minutes

Additional Information Contacts

Town of Speedway . . . . (317) 246-4300
http://www.townofspeedway.org

SPRING HILL (town). Covers a land area of 0.107 square miles and a water area of 0 square miles. Located at 39.83° N. Lat; 86.19° W. Long. Elevation is 761 feet.
Population: 70; Growth (since 2000): -27.8%; Density: 653.4 persons per square mile; Race: 94.3% White, 2.9% Black/African American, 1.4% Asian, 0.0% American Indian/Alaska Native, 0.0% Native Hawaiian/Other Pacific Islander, 0.0% Two or more races, 0.0% Hispanic of any race; Average household size: 1.63; Median age: 68.5; Age under 18: 1.4%; Age 65 and over: 65.7%; Males per 100 females: 117.8; Marriage status: 17.1% never married, 57.1% now married, 0.0% separated, 7.1% widowed, 18.6% divorced; Foreign born: 8.6%; Speak English only: 95.7%; With disability: 17.1%; Veterans: 17.4%; Ancestry: 17.1% English, 15.7% Irish, 14.3% German, 8.6% Swedish, 7.1% British
Employment: 42.9% management, business, and financial, 5.7% computer, engineering, and science, 22.9% education, legal, community service, arts, and media, 2.9% healthcare practitioners, 5.7% service, 11.4% sales and office, 0.0% natural resources, construction, and maintenance, 8.6% production, transportation, and material moving
Income: Per capita: $89,673; Median household: $103,438; Average household: $148,279; Households with income of $100,000 or more: 53.5%; Poverty rate: n/a
Educational Attainment: High school diploma or higher: 97.0%; Bachelor's degree or higher: 80.6%; Graduate/professional degree or higher: 59.7%
Housing: Homeownership rate: 95.3%; Median home value: $285,000; Median year structure built: 1983; Homeowner vacancy rate: 8.9%; Median selected monthly owner costs: $2,083 with a mortgage, $930 without a mortgage; Median gross rent: n/a per month; Rental vacancy rate: 0.0%
Health Insurance: 97.1% have insurance; 82.9% have private insurance; 62.9% have public insurance; 2.9% do not have insurance; 0.0% of children under 18 do not have insurance
Transportation: Commute: 85.7% car, 0.0% public transportation, 2.9% walk, 11.4% work from home; Mean travel time to work: 21.9 minutes

WARREN PARK (town). Covers a land area of 0.450 square miles and a water area of 0 square miles. Located at 39.78° N. Lat; 86.05° W. Long. Elevation is 827 feet.
Population: 1,863; Growth (since 2000): 12.5%; Density: 4,144.5 persons per square mile; Race: 78.0% White, 14.1% Black/African American, 0.5% Asian, 0.3% American Indian/Alaska Native, 0.0% Native Hawaiian/Other Pacific Islander, 0.5% Two or more races, 22.0% Hispanic of any race; Average household size: 2.11; Median age: 51.3; Age under 18: 18.5%; Age 65 and over: 30.4%; Males per 100 females: 72.1; Marriage status: 30.6% never married, 35.4% now married, 0.8% separated, 17.3% widowed, 16.7% divorced; Foreign born: 10.1%; Speak English only: 80.7%; With disability: 22.8%; Veterans: 8.0%; Ancestry: 10.4% German, 9.6% Irish, 7.3% English, 5.3% American, 2.7% French
Employment: 7.8% management, business, and financial, 7.8% computer, engineering, and science, 10.3% education, legal, community service, arts, and media, 3.3% healthcare practitioners, 25.7% service, 28.6% sales and office, 9.6% natural resources, construction, and maintenance, 6.8% production, transportation, and material moving
Income: Per capita: $23,680; Median household: $29,261; Average household: $47,493; Households with income of $100,000 or more: 9.6%; Poverty rate: 33.0%
Educational Attainment: High school diploma or higher: 82.6%; Bachelor's degree or higher: 16.9%; Graduate/professional degree or higher: 10.9%

Housing: Homeownership rate: 31.9%; Median home value: $124,000; Median year structure built: 1962; Homeowner vacancy rate: 0.0%; Median selected monthly owner costs: $1,038 with a mortgage, $413 without a mortgage; Median gross rent: $773 per month; Rental vacancy rate: 9.7%
Health Insurance: 89.2% have insurance; 50.1% have private insurance; 55.9% have public insurance; 10.8% do not have insurance; 8.0% of children under 18 do not have insurance
Transportation: Commute: 87.4% car, 4.8% public transportation, 5.2% walk, 1.7% work from home; Mean travel time to work: 24.1 minutes

WEST NEWTON (unincorporated postal area)
ZCTA: 46183
Covers a land area of 0.031 square miles and a water area of 0 square miles. Located at 39.65° N. Lat; 86.28° W. Long. Elevation is 738 feet.
Population: 17; Growth (since 2000): n/a; Density: 550.5 persons per square mile; Race: 100.0% White, 0.0% Black/African American, 0.0% Asian, 0.0% American Indian/Alaska Native, 0.0% Native Hawaiian/Other Pacific Islander, 0.0% Two or more races, 0.0% Hispanic of any race; Average household size: 0.00; Median age: n/a; Age under 18: 0.0%; Age 65 and over: 100.0%; Males per 100 females: 115.8; Marriage status: 0.0% never married, 0.0% now married, 0.0% separated, 100.0% widowed, 0.0% divorced; Foreign born: 0.0%; Speak English only: 100.0%; With disability: 100.0%; Veterans: 0.0%; Ancestry: 100.0% American
Employment: n/a management, business, and financial, n/a computer, engineering, and science, n/a education, legal, community service, arts, and media, n/a healthcare practitioners, n/a service, n/a sales and office, n/a natural resources, construction, and maintenance, n/a production, transportation, and material moving
Income: Per capita: n/a; Median household: n/a; Average household: n/a; Households with income of $100,000 or more: n/a; Poverty rate: n/a
Educational Attainment: High school diploma or higher: 100.0%; Bachelor's degree or higher: n/a; Graduate/professional degree or higher: n/a

School District(s)
M S D Decatur Township (PK-12)
Enrollment: 6,477 . . . . (317) 856-5265
Housing: Homeownership rate: 100.0%; Median home value: n/a; Median year structure built: n/a; Homeowner vacancy rate: 0.0%; Median selected monthly owner costs: $0 with a mortgage, $0 without a mortgage; Median gross rent: n/a per month; Rental vacancy rate: 0.0%
Health Insurance: 100.0% have insurance; 100.0% have private insurance; 100.0% have public insurance; 0.0% do not have insurance; 0.0% of children under 18 do not have insurance
Transportation: Commute: n/a car, n/a public transportation, n/a walk, n/a work from home; Mean travel time to work: 0.0 minutes

WILLIAMS CREEK (town). Covers a land area of 0.334 square miles and a water area of 0 square miles. Located at 39.90° N. Lat; 86.15° W. Long. Elevation is 774 feet.
Population: 377; Growth (since 2000): -8.7%; Density: 1,127.7 persons per square mile; Race: 89.4% White, 2.7% Black/African American, 3.7% Asian, 0.0% American Indian/Alaska Native, 0.0% Native Hawaiian/Other Pacific Islander, 4.2% Two or more races, 0.3% Hispanic of any race; Average household size: 2.73; Median age: 48.7; Age under 18: 26.5%; Age 65 and over: 19.9%; Males per 100 females: 97.6; Marriage status: 17.7% never married, 76.7% now married, 1.0% separated, 1.0% widowed, 4.7% divorced; Foreign born: 8.2%; Speak English only: 91.0%; With disability: 4.5%; Veterans: 6.1%; Ancestry: 27.3% German, 21.0% Irish, 17.5% English, 9.0% American, 5.6% French
Employment: 40.0% management, business, and financial, 4.7% computer, engineering, and science, 13.3% education, legal, community service, arts, and media, 17.3% healthcare practitioners, 5.3% service, 16.0% sales and office, 0.0% natural resources, construction, and maintenance, 3.3% production, transportation, and material moving
Income: Per capita: $117,710; Median household: $162,000; Average household: $335,117; Households with income of $100,000 or more: 71.0%; Poverty rate: 5.6%
Educational Attainment: High school diploma or higher: 99.6%; Bachelor's degree or higher: 87.9%; Graduate/professional degree or higher: 47.1%
Housing: Homeownership rate: 94.9%; Median home value: $767,000; Median year structure built: 1953; Homeowner vacancy rate: 0.0%; Median selected monthly owner costs: $3,000 with a mortgage, $1,275 without a mortgage; Median gross rent: $3,500+ per month; Rental vacancy rate: 0.0%
Health Insurance: 99.2% have insurance; 96.6% have private insurance; 21.2% have public insurance; 0.8% do not have insurance; 3.0% of children under 18 do not have insurance
Transportation: Commute: 77.6% car, 0.0% public transportation, 0.7% walk, 21.8% work from home; Mean travel time to work: 19.7 minutes

WYNNEDALE (town). Covers a land area of 0.159 square miles and a water area of 0 square miles. Located at 39.83° N. Lat; 86.20° W. Long. Elevation is 758 feet.
Population: 179; Growth (since 2000): -34.9%; Density: 1,122.7 persons per square mile; Race: 69.3% White, 25.7% Black/African American, 1.1% Asian, 0.0% American Indian/Alaska Native, 0.0% Native Hawaiian/Other Pacific Islander, 3.9% Two or more races, 0.0% Hispanic of any race; Average household size: 2.18; Median age: 56.5; Age under 18: 12.3%; Age 65 and over: 26.8%; Males per 100 females: 92.5; Marriage status: 19.4% never married, 58.2% now married, 0.0% separated, 6.7% widowed, 15.8% divorced; Foreign born: 7.8%; Speak English only: 93.3%; With disability: 16.8%; Veterans: 5.7%; Ancestry: 17.3% German, 14.5% English, 13.4% Irish, 5.6% Italian, 5.0% French
Employment: 33.3% management, business, and financial, 7.1% computer, engineering, and science, 24.2% education, legal, community service, arts, and media, 7.1% healthcare practitioners, 11.1% service, 10.1% sales and office, 3.0% natural resources, construction, and maintenance, 4.0% production, transportation, and material moving
Income: Per capita: $68,791; Median household: $118,750; Average household: $150,955; Households with income of $100,000 or more: 57.3%; Poverty rate: 2.2%
Educational Attainment: High school diploma or higher: 94.2%; Bachelor's degree or higher: 66.9%; Graduate/professional degree or higher: 33.1%
Housing: Homeownership rate: 100.0%; Median home value: $234,100; Median year structure built: 1956; Homeowner vacancy rate: 0.0%; Median selected monthly owner costs: $1,750 with a mortgage, $491 without a mortgage; Median gross rent: n/a per month; Rental vacancy rate: 0.0%
Health Insurance: 94.4% have insurance; 82.1% have private insurance; 28.5% have public insurance; 5.6% do not have insurance; 0.0% of children under 18 do not have insurance
Transportation: Commute: 91.8% car, 0.0% public transportation, 0.0% walk, 6.2% work from home; Mean travel time to work: 21.2 minutes

Marshall County

Located in northern Indiana; drained by the Yellow and Tippecanoe River; includes several lakes. Covers a land area of 443.628 square miles, a water area of 6.114 square miles, and is located in the Eastern Time Zone at 41.33° N. Lat., 86.27° W. Long. The county was founded in 1835. County seat is Plymouth.

Marshall County is part of the Plymouth, IN Micropolitan Statistical Area. The entire metro area includes: Marshall County, IN

Population: 46,752; Growth (since 2000): 3.6%; Density: 105.4 persons per square mile; Race: 92.4% White, 0.7% Black/African American, 0.5% Asian, 0.3% American Indian/Alaska Native, 0.0% Native Hawaiian/Other Pacific Islander, 1.8% two or more races, 9.7% Hispanic of any race; Average household size: 2.67; Median age: 39.8; Age under 18: 25.4%; Age 65 and over: 16.5%; Males per 100 females: 98.0; Marriage status: 26.5% never married, 55.2% now married, 1.0% separated, 5.9% widowed, 12.3% divorced; Foreign born: 4.2%; Speak English only: 88.9%; With disability: 14.3%; Veterans: 8.3%; Ancestry: 27.7% German, 10.1% Irish, 9.9% American, 7.0% English, 4.0% Polish
Religion: Six largest groups: 7.6% Methodist/Pietist, 5.3% Non-denominational Protestant, 5.3% European Free-Church, 4.3% Catholicism, 3.5% Holiness, 2.9% Lutheran
Economy: Unemployment rate: 3.4%; Leading industries: 16.4 % retail trade; 13.0 % manufacturing; 12.4 % other services (except public administration); Farms: 878 totaling 206,306 acres; Company size: 0 employ 1,000 or more persons, 1 employs 500 to 999 persons, 37 employ 100 to 499 persons, 1,008 employ less than 100 persons; Business ownership: 1,017 women-owned, n/a Black-owned, 39 Hispanic-owned, n/a Asian-owned, n/a American Indian/Alaska Native-owned
Employment: 11.2% management, business, and financial, 2.3% computer, engineering, and science, 8.3% education, legal, community

service, arts, and media, 4.8% healthcare practitioners, 13.8% service, 20.3% sales and office, 9.3% natural resources, construction, and maintenance, 30.0% production, transportation, and material moving
Income: Per capita: $24,289; Median household: $51,869; Average household: $64,124; Households with income of $100,000 or more: 17.3%; Poverty rate: 11.5%
Educational Attainment: High school diploma or higher: 85.1%; Bachelor's degree or higher: 19.8%; Graduate/professional degree or higher: 7.4%
Housing: Homeownership rate: 75.5%; Median home value: $130,100; Median year structure built: 1971; Homeowner vacancy rate: 2.2%; Median selected monthly owner costs: $1,045 with a mortgage, $364 without a mortgage; Median gross rent: $681 per month; Rental vacancy rate: 7.1%
Vital Statistics: Birth rate: 127.1 per 10,000 population; Death rate: 102.4 per 10,000 population; Age-adjusted cancer mortality rate: 161.2 deaths per 100,000 population
Health Insurance: 86.8% have insurance; 65.7% have private insurance; 32.6% have public insurance; 13.2% do not have insurance; 13.8% of children under 18 do not have insurance
Health Care: Physicians: 9.0 per 10,000 population; Dentists: 4.1 per 10,000 population; Hospital beds: 31.5 per 10,000 population; Hospital admissions: 941.4 per 10,000 population
Transportation: Commute: 90.8% car, 0.4% public transportation, 2.6% walk, 3.5% work from home; Mean travel time to work: 22.4 minutes
2016 Presidential Election: 67.4% Trump, 26.3% Clinton, 5.1% Johnson, 0.2% Stein
National and State Parks: Menominee State Wetlands
Additional Information Contacts
Marshall Government . . . . (574) 936-8922
http://www.co.marshall.in.us

Marshall County Communities

ARGOS (town). Covers a land area of 1.159 square miles and a water area of 0.010 square miles. Located at 41.24° N. Lat; 86.25° W. Long. Elevation is 804 feet.
History: Argos began as a stagecoach stop on the Michigan Road. The name was chosen by Schuyler Colfax, vice-president under the Grant administration.
Population: 1,859; Growth (since 2000): 15.3%; Density: 1,604.5 persons per square mile; Race: 98.1% White, 0.3% Black/African American, 0.0% Asian, 0.0% American Indian/Alaska Native, 0.0% Native Hawaiian/Other Pacific Islander, 1.1% Two or more races, 3.0% Hispanic of any race; Average household size: 2.81; Median age: 32.7; Age under 18: 30.2%; Age 65 and over: 13.4%; Males per 100 females: 100.8; Marriage status: 27.9% never married, 51.0% now married, 1.4% separated, 4.2% widowed, 16.9% divorced; Foreign born: 2.6%; Speak English only: 96.6%; With disability: 13.4%; Veterans: 9.9%; Ancestry: 27.1% German, 20.1% Irish, 10.7% English, 7.6% American, 3.4% Dutch
Employment: 9.9% management, business, and financial, 2.5% computer, engineering, and science, 6.0% education, legal, community service, arts, and media, 2.1% healthcare practitioners, 15.0% service, 22.1% sales and office, 10.1% natural resources, construction, and maintenance, 32.3% production, transportation, and material moving
Income: Per capita: $19,146; Median household: $44,054; Average household: $52,243; Households with income of $100,000 or more: 12.6%; Poverty rate: 15.9%
Educational Attainment: High school diploma or higher: 84.9%; Bachelor's degree or higher: 13.5%; Graduate/professional degree or higher: 3.2%

School District(s)

Argos Community Schools (PK-12)
Enrollment: 664. . . . . (574) 892-5139
Housing: Homeownership rate: 67.1%; Median home value: $82,300; Median year structure built: 1945; Homeowner vacancy rate: 6.1%; Median selected monthly owner costs: $880 with a mortgage, $375 without a mortgage; Median gross rent: $731 per month; Rental vacancy rate: 3.8%
Health Insurance: 85.3% have insurance; 65.1% have private insurance; 30.8% have public insurance; 14.7% do not have insurance; 11.4% of children under 18 do not have insurance
Transportation: Commute: 94.5% car, 0.0% public transportation, 2.4% walk, 2.5% work from home; Mean travel time to work: 24.7 minutes

BOURBON (town). Covers a land area of 0.992 square miles and a water area of 0.004 square miles. Located at 41.30° N. Lat; 86.12° W. Long. Elevation is 846 feet.
Population: 1,840; Growth (since 2000): 8.8%; Density: 1,854.9 persons per square mile; Race: 95.3% White, 0.8% Black/African American, 0.2% Asian, 0.0% American Indian/Alaska Native, 0.0% Native Hawaiian/Other Pacific Islander, 3.4% Two or more races, 4.4% Hispanic of any race; Average household size: 2.66; Median age: 36.2; Age under 18: 28.7%; Age 65 and over: 12.8%; Males per 100 females: 94.4; Marriage status: 22.2% never married, 58.1% now married, 0.0% separated, 6.6% widowed, 13.2% divorced; Foreign born: 1.9%; Speak English only: 96.0%; With disability: 13.6%; Veterans: 6.3%; Ancestry: 30.7% German, 10.1% American, 8.3% Irish, 6.8% English, 2.7% Dutch
Employment: 13.3% management, business, and financial, 1.8% computer, engineering, and science, 3.8% education, legal, community service, arts, and media, 4.5% healthcare practitioners, 15.8% service, 27.3% sales and office, 5.9% natural resources, construction, and maintenance, 27.6% production, transportation, and material moving
Income: Per capita: $21,069; Median household: $50,429; Average household: $55,013; Households with income of $100,000 or more: 10.5%; Poverty rate: 13.5%
Educational Attainment: High school diploma or higher: 87.5%; Bachelor's degree or higher: 12.7%; Graduate/professional degree or higher: 3.4%

School District(s)

Triton School Corporation (PK-12)
Enrollment: 888. . . . . (574) 342-2255
Housing: Homeownership rate: 70.1%; Median home value: $96,200; Median year structure built: 1956; Homeowner vacancy rate: 2.2%; Median selected monthly owner costs: $985 with a mortgage, $366 without a mortgage; Median gross rent: $615 per month; Rental vacancy rate: 11.9%
Health Insurance: 88.2% have insurance; 67.6% have private insurance; 30.2% have public insurance; 11.8% do not have insurance; 4.0% of children under 18 do not have insurance
Transportation: Commute: 92.8% car, 0.0% public transportation, 3.2% walk, 3.4% work from home; Mean travel time to work: 22.4 minutes
Additional Information Contacts
Town of Bourbon. . . . . (574) 342-4755
http://www.bourbon-in.gov

BREMEN (town). Covers a land area of 2.715 square miles and a water area of 0.004 square miles. Located at 41.45° N. Lat; 86.15° W. Long. Elevation is 853 feet.
History: Bremen reports that its fire department was the 1882 and 1887 winner of the hose and engine maneuvers at the state championships.
Population: 4,548; Growth (since 2000): 1.4%; Density: 1,674.9 persons per square mile; Race: 91.5% White, 0.3% Black/African American, 0.0% Asian, 0.0% American Indian/Alaska Native, 0.0% Native Hawaiian/Other Pacific Islander, 3.6% Two or more races, 16.4% Hispanic of any race; Average household size: 2.48; Median age: 34.2; Age under 18: 28.2%; Age 65 and over: 13.8%; Males per 100 females: 91.5; Marriage status: 32.2% never married, 51.1% now married, 2.5% separated, 4.0% widowed, 12.7% divorced; Foreign born: 6.0%; Speak English only: 89.2%; With disability: 17.9%; Veterans: 6.6%; Ancestry: 26.8% German, 11.5% Italian, 10.5% Irish, 8.6% American, 7.8% English
Employment: 7.9% management, business, and financial, 5.2% computer, engineering, and science, 6.4% education, legal, community service, arts, and media, 10.1% healthcare practitioners, 11.7% service, 13.4% sales and office, 6.3% natural resources, construction, and maintenance, 39.0% production, transportation, and material moving
Income: Per capita: $20,896; Median household: $44,458; Average household: $52,077; Households with income of $100,000 or more: 12.6%; Poverty rate: 14.1%
Educational Attainment: High school diploma or higher: 86.0%; Bachelor's degree or higher: 20.1%; Graduate/professional degree or higher: 9.3%

School District(s)

Bremen Public Schools (KG-12)
Enrollment: 1,304 . . . . (574) 546-3929
Housing: Homeownership rate: 55.4%; Median home value: $132,200; Median year structure built: 1974; Homeowner vacancy rate: 2.1%; Median selected monthly owner costs: $1,046 with a mortgage, $298 without a mortgage; Median gross rent: $648 per month; Rental vacancy rate: 4.1%

Health Insurance: 87.2% have insurance; 60.4% have private insurance; 37.4% have public insurance; 12.8% do not have insurance; 11.4% of children under 18 do not have insurance
Hospitals: Community Hospital of Bremen (24 beds); Doctors Neuromedical Hospital & Brain Institute
Safety: Violent crime rate: n/a per 10,000 population; Property crime rate: 134.2 per 10,000 population
Newspapers: Advance-News (weekly circulation 2,200); Bremen Enquirer (weekly circulation 1,800)
Transportation: Commute: 94.6% car, 0.0% public transportation, 2.8% walk, 2.5% work from home; Mean travel time to work: 20.6 minutes
Additional Information Contacts
Town of Bremen . . . . (574) 546-2471
http://www.bremenchamberofcommerce.com

CULVER (town). Covers a land area of 0.899 square miles and a water area of 0 square miles. Located at 41.22° N. Lat; 86.42° W. Long. Elevation is 771 feet.
History: Culver developed as a resort town near Lake Maxinkuckee. It was named for Henry Harrison Culver of St. Louis who founded Culver Military Academy in 1894.
Population: 1,261; Growth (since 2000): -18.1%; Density: 1,402.4 persons per square mile; Race: 98.1% White, 0.3% Black/African American, 0.4% Asian, 0.0% American Indian/Alaska Native, 0.0% Native Hawaiian/Other Pacific Islander, 0.9% Two or more races, 2.4% Hispanic of any race; Average household size: 2.16; Median age: 47.9; Age under 18: 17.7%; Age 65 and over: 27.4%; Males per 100 females: 83.1; Marriage status: 21.9% never married, 55.4% now married, 1.3% separated, 9.6% widowed, 13.1% divorced; Foreign born: 1.7%; Speak English only: 99.5%; With disability: 16.5%; Veterans: 12.4%; Ancestry: 31.6% German, 16.6% Irish, 13.9% English, 6.4% Polish, 5.2% American
Employment: 12.1% management, business, and financial, 4.7% computer, engineering, and science, 17.7% education, legal, community service, arts, and media, 6.7% healthcare practitioners, 20.4% service, 18.2% sales and office, 7.2% natural resources, construction, and maintenance, 13.0% production, transportation, and material moving
Income: Per capita: $28,935; Median household: $40,000; Average household: $63,134; Households with income of $100,000 or more: 17.8%; Poverty rate: 12.3%
Educational Attainment: High school diploma or higher: 91.3%; Bachelor's degree or higher: 35.1%; Graduate/professional degree or higher: 17.0%

School District(s)

Culver Community Schools Corp (PK-12)
Enrollment: 919. . . . . (574) 842-3364
Housing: Homeownership rate: 60.9%; Median home value: $151,900; Median year structure built: 1956; Homeowner vacancy rate: 10.2%; Median selected monthly owner costs: $993 with a mortgage, $404 without a mortgage; Median gross rent: $713 per month; Rental vacancy rate: 13.9%
Health Insurance: 88.2% have insurance; 67.7% have private insurance; 35.3% have public insurance; 11.8% do not have insurance; 1.2% of children under 18 do not have insurance
Transportation: Commute: 81.5% car, 0.0% public transportation, 8.0% walk, 4.5% work from home; Mean travel time to work: 18.6 minutes

LA PAZ (town). Covers a land area of 0.383 square miles and a water area of 0 square miles. Located at 41.46° N. Lat; 86.31° W. Long. Elevation is 860 feet.
Population: 714; Growth (since 2000): 46.0%; Density: 1,861.9 persons per square mile; Race: 98.9% White, 0.0% Black/African American, 0.0% Asian, 0.7% American Indian/Alaska Native, 0.0% Native Hawaiian/Other Pacific Islander, 0.0% Two or more races, 4.3% Hispanic of any race; Average household size: 2.74; Median age: 34.0; Age under 18: 30.0%; Age 65 and over: 16.5%; Males per 100 females: 88.9; Marriage status: 26.2% never married, 54.0% now married, 0.0% separated, 3.5% widowed, 16.3% divorced; Foreign born: 1.4%; Speak English only: 99.6%; With disability: 16.2%; Veterans: 11.4%; Ancestry: 24.1% German, 11.9% Irish, 7.0% American, 6.2% European, 6.2% Russian
Employment: 7.8% management, business, and financial, 4.2% computer, engineering, and science, 4.5% education, legal, community service, arts, and media, 6.0% healthcare practitioners, 13.5% service, 24.0% sales and office, 7.5% natural resources, construction, and maintenance, 32.4% production, transportation, and material moving
Income: Per capita: $20,046; Median household: $51,691; Average household: $54,292; Households with income of $100,000 or more: 6.5%; Poverty rate: 10.5%
Educational Attainment: High school diploma or higher: 84.0%; Bachelor's degree or higher: 3.9%; Graduate/professional degree or higher: n/a
Housing: Homeownership rate: 75.1%; Median home value: $84,700; Median year structure built: 1965; Homeowner vacancy rate: 4.4%; Median selected monthly owner costs: $765 with a mortgage, $260 without a mortgage; Median gross rent: $778 per month; Rental vacancy rate: 11.0%
Health Insurance: 86.4% have insurance; 66.8% have private insurance; 28.3% have public insurance; 13.6% do not have insurance; 12.5% of children under 18 do not have insurance
Transportation: Commute: 95.4% car, 0.0% public transportation, 2.5% walk, 0.0% work from home; Mean travel time to work: 20.0 minutes

PLYMOUTH (city). County seat. Covers a land area of 7.534 square miles and a water area of 0.040 square miles. Located at 41.35° N. Lat; 86.32° W. Long. Elevation is 797 feet.
History: Plymouth was founded in 1834 as a shipping center and county seat.
Population: 10,011; Growth (since 2000): 1.7%; Density: 1,328.8 persons per square mile; Race: 82.9% White, 0.6% Black/African American, 0.7% Asian, 0.6% American Indian/Alaska Native, 0.0% Native Hawaiian/Other Pacific Islander, 2.6% Two or more races, 25.5% Hispanic of any race; Average household size: 2.53; Median age: 33.9; Age under 18: 27.5%; Age 65 and over: 14.5%; Males per 100 females: 91.9; Marriage status: 33.5% never married, 44.8% now married, 1.4% separated, 6.6% widowed, 15.0% divorced; Foreign born: 9.3%; Speak English only: 79.2%; With disability: 16.1%; Veterans: 8.5%; Ancestry: 20.2% German, 8.7% Irish, 7.3% American, 6.1% English, 4.1% Polish
Employment: 7.7% management, business, and financial, 0.8% computer, engineering, and science, 9.4% education, legal, community service, arts, and media, 3.6% healthcare practitioners, 16.1% service, 20.6% sales and office, 4.8% natural resources, construction, and maintenance, 36.9% production, transportation, and material moving
Income: Per capita: $17,709; Median household: $35,713; Average household: $45,069; Households with income of $100,000 or more: 7.2%; Poverty rate: 23.9%
Educational Attainment: High school diploma or higher: 80.6%; Bachelor's degree or higher: 17.4%; Graduate/professional degree or higher: 7.0%

School District(s)

Plymouth Community School Corp (PK-12)
Enrollment: 3,489 . . . . (574) 936-3115

Two-year College(s)

Ancilla College (Private, Not-for-profit, Roman Catholic)
Enrollment: 548. . . . . (574) 936-8898
Tuition: In-state $15,830; Out-of-state $15,830
Housing: Homeownership rate: 56.0%; Median home value: $89,200; Median year structure built: 1969; Homeowner vacancy rate: 4.9%; Median selected monthly owner costs: $853 with a mortgage, $370 without a mortgage; Median gross rent: $670 per month; Rental vacancy rate: 7.7%
Health Insurance: 85.4% have insurance; 53.1% have private insurance; 43.2% have public insurance; 14.6% do not have insurance; 12.3% of children under 18 do not have insurance
Hospitals: Saint Joseph Regional Medical Center - Plymouth (58 beds)
Safety: Violent crime rate: 6.0 per 10,000 population; Property crime rate: 273.8 per 10,000 population
Newspapers: Bourbon News-Mirror (weekly circulation 1,300); Culver Citizen (weekly circulation 1,800); Pilot-News (daily circulation 6,200)
Transportation: Commute: 94.2% car, 0.2% public transportation, 3.2% walk, 1.2% work from home; Mean travel time to work: 18.4 minutes
Airports: Plymouth Municipal (general aviation)
Additional Information Contacts
City of Plymouth . . . . (574) 936-2124
http://www.plymouthin.com

TIPPECANOE (unincorporated postal area)
ZCTA: 46570
Covers a land area of 20.438 square miles and a water area of 0.026 square miles. Located at 41.20° N. Lat; 86.12° W. Long. Elevation is 781 feet.
Population: 1,025; Growth (since 2000): -2.7%; Density: 50.2 persons per square mile; Race: 95.6% White, 2.2% Black/African American,

2.1% Asian, 0.0% American Indian/Alaska Native, 0.0% Native Hawaiian/Other Pacific Islander, 0.0% Two or more races, 3.1% Hispanic of any race; Average household size: 2.87; Median age: 39.6; Age under 18: 26.9%; Age 65 and over: 7.1%; Males per 100 females: 105.4; Marriage status: 26.6% never married, 50.1% now married, 0.0% separated, 5.7% widowed, 17.6% divorced; Foreign born: 3.6%; Speak English only: 81.2%; With disability: 15.8%; Veterans: 6.0%; Ancestry: 19.1% American, 15.7% Pennsylvania German, 14.5% German, 9.7% Irish, 4.1% Welsh
Employment: 13.6% management, business, and financial, 3.3% computer, engineering, and science, 9.3% education, legal, community service, arts, and media, 1.8% healthcare practitioners, 12.5% service, 20.5% sales and office, 16.1% natural resources, construction, and maintenance, 22.9% production, transportation, and material moving
Income: Per capita: $25,629; Median household: $51,625; Average household: $71,929; Households with income of $100,000 or more: 22.7%; Poverty rate: 12.5%
Educational Attainment: High school diploma or higher: 80.2%; Bachelor's degree or higher: 15.9%; Graduate/professional degree or higher: 1.2%
Housing: Homeownership rate: 81.2%; Median home value: $141,700; Median year structure built: 1950; Homeowner vacancy rate: 0.0%; Median selected monthly owner costs: $1,122 with a mortgage, $344 without a mortgage; Median gross rent: $442 per month; Rental vacancy rate: 0.0%
Health Insurance: 72.4% have insurance; 58.0% have private insurance; 16.8% have public insurance; 27.6% do not have insurance; 37.8% of children under 18 do not have insurance
Transportation: Commute: 82.1% car, 0.0% public transportation, 2.6% walk, 4.9% work from home; Mean travel time to work: 27.2 minutes

Martin County

Located in southwestern Indiana; drained by the Lost River and East Fork of the White River. Covers a land area of 335.737 square miles, a water area of 4.669 square miles, and is located in the Eastern Time Zone at 38.71° N. Lat., 86.80° W. Long. The county was founded in 1820. County seat is Shoals.

Weather Station: Shoals Hiway 50 Bridge Elevation: 549 feet

	Jan	Feb	Mar	Apr	May	Jun	Jul	Aug	Sep	Oct	Nov	Dec
High	39	44	54	66	75	83	86	86	79	68	55	42
Low	21	23	31	41	51	60	64	62	54	42	34	25
Precip	3.1	3.0	4.3	4.5	6.1	4.3	4.4	2.9	3.6	3.7	4.2	3.8
Snow	4.1	4.1	1.9	0.1	0.0	0.0	0.0	0.0	0.0	0.1	tr	3.0

High and Low temperatures in degrees Fahrenheit; Precipitation and Snow in inches

Population: 10,219; Growth (since 2000): -1.4%; Density: 30.4 persons per square mile; Race: 97.5% White, 0.5% Black/African American, 0.2% Asian, 0.7% American Indian/Alaska Native, 0.2% Native Hawaiian/Other Pacific Islander, 0.7% two or more races, 0.4% Hispanic of any race; Average household size: 2.35; Median age: 42.0; Age under 18: 22.8%; Age 65 and over: 17.8%; Males per 100 females: 102.2; Marriage status: 21.4% never married, 55.3% now married, 1.3% separated, 6.6% widowed, 16.6% divorced; Foreign born: 0.5%; Speak English only: 98.4%; With disability: 17.8%; Veterans: 11.1%; Ancestry: 23.2% German, 13.7% Irish, 12.1% American, 6.7% English, 2.4% French
Religion: Six largest groups: 25.4% Catholicism, 9.0% Methodist/Pietist, 8.8% Baptist, 7.4% European Free-Church, 4.5% Non-denominational Protestant, 2.9% Lutheran
Economy: Unemployment rate: 3.1%; Leading industries: 16.8 % retail trade; 15.8 % professional, scientific, and technical services; 13.7 % other services (except public administration); Farms: 283 totaling 62,544 acres; Company size: 0 employ 1,000 or more persons, 0 employ 500 to 999 persons, 3 employ 100 to 499 persons, 187 employ less than 100 persons; Business ownership: 277 women-owned, n/a Black-owned, n/a Hispanic-owned, n/a Asian-owned, n/a American Indian/Alaska Native-owned
Employment: 11.2% management, business, and financial, 4.1% computer, engineering, and science, 7.5% education, legal, community service, arts, and media, 6.6% healthcare practitioners, 15.1% service, 17.0% sales and office, 12.6% natural resources, construction, and maintenance, 25.8% production, transportation, and material moving
Income: Per capita: $25,138; Median household: $49,372; Average household: $60,136; Households with income of $100,000 or more: 15.1%; Poverty rate: 13.3%
Educational Attainment: High school diploma or higher: 83.5%; Bachelor's degree or higher: 11.0%; Graduate/professional degree or higher: 4.6%
Housing: Homeownership rate: 80.5%; Median home value: $97,900; Median year structure built: 1978; Homeowner vacancy rate: 2.2%; Median selected monthly owner costs: $1,053 with a mortgage, $327 without a mortgage; Median gross rent: $506 per month; Rental vacancy rate: 2.6%
Vital Statistics: Birth rate: 121.4 per 10,000 population; Death rate: 93.0 per 10,000 population; Age-adjusted cancer mortality rate: 153.9 deaths per 100,000 population
Health Insurance: 90.9% have insurance; 71.3% have private insurance; 34.2% have public insurance; 9.1% do not have insurance; 9.6% of children under 18 do not have insurance
Health Care: Physicians: 2.9 per 10,000 population; Dentists: 2.0 per 10,000 population; Hospital beds: 0.0 per 10,000 population; Hospital admissions: 0.0 per 10,000 population
Transportation: Commute: 90.3% car, 0.2% public transportation, 3.5% walk, 4.6% work from home; Mean travel time to work: 26.4 minutes
2016 Presidential Election: 76.9% Trump, 18.3% Clinton, 4.8% Johnson, 0.0% Stein
National and State Parks: Martin County State Forest; Martin State Forest
Additional Information Contacts
Martin Government . . . . (812) 295-4093

Martin County Communities

BURNS CITY (CDP). Covers a land area of 0.735 square miles and a water area of 0.005 square miles. Located at 38.82° N. Lat; 86.89° W. Long. Elevation is 712 feet.
Population: 165; Growth (since 2000): n/a; Density: 224.6 persons per square mile; Race: 100.0% White, 0.0% Black/African American, 0.0% Asian, 0.0% American Indian/Alaska Native, 0.0% Native Hawaiian/Other Pacific Islander, 0.0% Two or more races, 0.0% Hispanic of any race; Average household size: 2.50; Median age: 56.1; Age under 18: 0.0%; Age 65 and over: 23.6%; Males per 100 females: 105.3; Marriage status: 23.0% never married, 77.0% now married, 0.0% separated, 0.0% widowed, 0.0% divorced; Foreign born: 0.0%; Speak English only: 100.0%; With disability: 14.5%; Veterans: 35.8%; Ancestry: 24.2% Irish, 23.0% English, 14.5% French, 13.9% American, 13.9% German
Employment: 11.5% management, business, and financial, 0.0% computer, engineering, and science, 0.0% education, legal, community service, arts, and media, 0.0% healthcare practitioners, 0.0% service, 40.6% sales and office, 0.0% natural resources, construction, and maintenance, 47.9% production, transportation, and material moving
Income: Per capita: $36,768; Median household: $98,281; Average household: $87,303; Households with income of $100,000 or more: 33.4%; Poverty rate: n/a
Educational Attainment: High school diploma or higher: 100.0%; Bachelor's degree or higher: 8.8%; Graduate/professional degree or higher: n/a
Housing: Homeownership rate: 84.8%; Median home value: $72,500; Median year structure built: 1995; Homeowner vacancy rate: 0.0%; Median selected monthly owner costs: n/a with a mortgage, $456 without a mortgage; Median gross rent: n/a per month; Rental vacancy rate: 0.0%
Health Insurance: 100.0% have insurance; 92.7% have private insurance; 30.9% have public insurance; 0.0% do not have insurance; 0.0% of children under 18 do not have insurance
Transportation: Commute: 100.0% car, 0.0% public transportation, 0.0% walk, 0.0% work from home; Mean travel time to work: 26.8 minutes

CRANE (town). Covers a land area of 0.118 square miles and a water area of 0 square miles. Located at 38.89° N. Lat; 86.90° W. Long. Elevation is 614 feet.
Population: 235; Growth (since 2000): 15.8%; Density: 1,986.5 persons per square mile; Race: 97.9% White, 0.0% Black/African American, 0.0% Asian, 0.4% American Indian/Alaska Native, 0.0% Native Hawaiian/Other Pacific Islander, 0.4% Two or more races, 1.3% Hispanic of any race; Average household size: 2.55; Median age: 35.8; Age under 18: 29.4%; Age 65 and over: 21.7%; Males per 100 females: 93.7; Marriage status: 22.8% never married, 57.3% now married, 1.2% separated, 5.3% widowed, 14.6% divorced; Foreign born: 0.4%; Speak English only: 100.0%; With disability: 19.9%; Veterans: 33.3%; Ancestry: 26.8% Irish, 22.6% English, 13.6% American, 12.8% German, 5.1% Italian

Employment: 7.5% management, business, and financial, 8.8% computer, engineering, and science, 6.3% education, legal, community service, arts, and media, 0.0% healthcare practitioners, 31.3% service, 15.0% sales and office, 10.0% natural resources, construction, and maintenance, 21.3% production, transportation, and material moving
Income: Per capita: $20,491; Median household: $47,500; Average household: $52,113; Households with income of $100,000 or more: 5.5%; Poverty rate: 11.9%
Educational Attainment: High school diploma or higher: 87.8%; Bachelor's degree or higher: 12.2%; Graduate/professional degree or higher: 7.5%
Housing: Homeownership rate: 64.1%; Median home value: $50,500; Median year structure built: 1948; Homeowner vacancy rate: 4.8%; Median selected monthly owner costs: $700 with a mortgage, $357 without a mortgage; Median gross rent: $675 per month; Rental vacancy rate: 8.3%
Health Insurance: 85.7% have insurance; 44.2% have private insurance; 55.8% have public insurance; 14.3% do not have insurance; 21.7% of children under 18 do not have insurance
Transportation: Commute: 90.5% car, 0.0% public transportation, 9.5% walk, 0.0% work from home; Mean travel time to work: 24.3 minutes

DOVER HILL (CDP). Covers a land area of 0.776 square miles and a water area of <.001 square miles. Located at 38.72° N. Lat; 86.80° W. Long. Elevation is 663 feet.
Population: 29; Growth (since 2000): n/a; Density: 37.4 persons per square mile; Race: 100.0% White, 0.0% Black/African American, 0.0% Asian, 0.0% American Indian/Alaska Native, 0.0% Native Hawaiian/Other Pacific Islander, 0.0% Two or more races, 0.0% Hispanic of any race; Average household size: 1.16; Median age: 45.9; Age under 18: 13.8%; Age 65 and over: 34.5%; Males per 100 females: 93.2; Marriage status: 0.0% never married, 40.0% now married, 0.0% separated, 0.0% widowed, 60.0% divorced; Foreign born: 0.0%; Speak English only: 100.0%; With disability: 41.4%; Veterans: 0.0%; Ancestry: 48.3% American
Employment: 0.0% management, business, and financial, 0.0% computer, engineering, and science, 0.0% education, legal, community service, arts, and media, 0.0% healthcare practitioners, 0.0% service, 0.0% sales and office, 0.0% natural resources, construction, and maintenance, 100.0% production, transportation, and material moving
Income: Per capita: n/a; Median household: n/a; Average household: n/a; Households with income of $100,000 or more: n/a; Poverty rate: 41.4%
Educational Attainment: High school diploma or higher: 100.0%; Bachelor's degree or higher: n/a; Graduate/professional degree or higher: n/a
Housing: Homeownership rate: 52.0%; Median home value: n/a; Median year structure built: 1982; Homeowner vacancy rate: 0.0%; Median selected monthly owner costs: n/a with a mortgage, n/a without a mortgage; Median gross rent: n/a per month; Rental vacancy rate: 0.0%
Health Insurance: 100.0% have insurance; 58.6% have private insurance; 75.9% have public insurance; 0.0% do not have insurance; 0.0% of children under 18 do not have insurance
Transportation: Commute: 100.0% car, 0.0% public transportation, 0.0% walk, 0.0% work from home; Mean travel time to work: 0.0 minutes

LOOGOOTEE (city). Covers a land area of 1.567 square miles and a water area of 0.004 square miles. Located at 38.68° N. Lat; 86.91° W. Long. Elevation is 538 feet.
History: Loogootee grew when natural gas was found here in 1899, and several glass factories were established. The town was named for Lowe, an engineer on the first railroad, and Gootee, who owned the land on which the town was built.
Population: 2,712; Growth (since 2000): -1.1%; Density: 1,730.6 persons per square mile; Race: 98.3% White, 0.4% Black/African American, 0.0% Asian, 1.1% American Indian/Alaska Native, 0.0% Native Hawaiian/Other Pacific Islander, 0.0% Two or more races, 0.4% Hispanic of any race; Average household size: 2.16; Median age: 39.4; Age under 18: 24.7%; Age 65 and over: 15.7%; Males per 100 females: 91.3; Marriage status: 26.1% never married, 40.5% now married, 1.4% separated, 8.5% widowed, 24.8% divorced; Foreign born: 0.6%; Speak English only: 97.7%; With disability: 18.5%; Veterans: 11.1%; Ancestry: 21.1% German, 19.1% Irish, 11.2% American, 7.3% English, 3.2% French
Employment: 9.3% management, business, and financial, 2.3% computer, engineering, and science, 4.0% education, legal, community service, arts, and media, 8.2% healthcare practitioners, 17.7% service, 23.5% sales and office, 7.4% natural resources, construction, and maintenance, 27.4% production, transportation, and material moving
Income: Per capita: $22,623; Median household: $43,563; Average household: $49,968; Households with income of $100,000 or more: 10.9%; Poverty rate: 21.8%
Educational Attainment: High school diploma or higher: 86.6%; Bachelor's degree or higher: 10.3%; Graduate/professional degree or higher: 5.7%

School District(s)

Loogootee Community Sch Corp (PK-12)
Enrollment: 922 . . . . (812) 295-3254
Housing: Homeownership rate: 64.5%; Median home value: $84,700; Median year structure built: 1973; Homeowner vacancy rate: 2.6%; Median selected monthly owner costs: $1,009 with a mortgage, $269 without a mortgage; Median gross rent: $521 per month; Rental vacancy rate: 0.0%
Health Insurance: 90.6% have insurance; 71.4% have private insurance; 34.4% have public insurance; 9.4% do not have insurance; 12.6% of children under 18 do not have insurance
Newspapers: The Tribune (weekly circulation 3,000)
Transportation: Commute: 96.6% car, 0.0% public transportation, 1.8% walk, 0.0% work from home; Mean travel time to work: 24.2 minutes
Additional Information Contacts
City of Loogootee . . . . (812) 295-3200
http://www.loogootee.com/government/loogooteegovernment.html

SHOALS (town). County seat. Covers a land area of 1.793 square miles and a water area of 0.093 square miles. Located at 38.67° N. Lat; 86.79° W. Long. Elevation is 505 feet.
History: Shoals was founded in 1816 and named for the shallow place in the White River that afforded a crossing. The area was known as a haven for moonshiners and bootleggers during prohibition.
Population: 844; Growth (since 2000): 4.6%; Density: 470.8 persons per square mile; Race: 97.4% White, 2.0% Black/African American, 0.0% Asian, 0.6% American Indian/Alaska Native, 0.0% Native Hawaiian/Other Pacific Islander, 0.0% Two or more races, 0.0% Hispanic of any race; Average household size: 1.89; Median age: 46.1; Age under 18: 20.1%; Age 65 and over: 26.2%; Males per 100 females: 96.4; Marriage status: 25.7% never married, 44.3% now married, 1.6% separated, 16.2% widowed, 13.8% divorced; Foreign born: 0.0%; Speak English only: 100.0%; With disability: 23.2%; Veterans: 6.1%; Ancestry: 15.6% English, 11.4% German, 5.9% Irish, 3.4% American, 2.0% French
Employment: 0.7% management, business, and financial, 0.0% computer, engineering, and science, 14.4% education, legal, community service, arts, and media, 13.4% healthcare practitioners, 18.4% service, 12.7% sales and office, 9.0% natural resources, construction, and maintenance, 31.4% production, transportation, and material moving
Income: Per capita: $26,508; Median household: $32,847; Average household: $51,784; Households with income of $100,000 or more: 10.0%; Poverty rate: 20.4%
Educational Attainment: High school diploma or higher: 80.2%; Bachelor's degree or higher: 14.4%; Graduate/professional degree or higher: 5.3%

School District(s)

Shoals Community School Corp (PK-12)
Enrollment: 588 . . . . (812) 247-2060
Housing: Homeownership rate: 71.7%; Median home value: $78,700; Median year structure built: 1973; Homeowner vacancy rate: 0.0%; Median selected monthly owner costs: $896 with a mortgage, $312 without a mortgage; Median gross rent: $425 per month; Rental vacancy rate: 6.5%
Health Insurance: 85.5% have insurance; 61.1% have private insurance; 46.3% have public insurance; 14.5% do not have insurance; 6.8% of children under 18 do not have insurance
Newspapers: Shoals News (weekly circulation 2,700)
Transportation: Commute: 90.0% car, 0.0% public transportation, 1.3% walk, 6.4% work from home; Mean travel time to work: 21.8 minutes

Miami County

Located in north central Indiana; crossed by the Wabash, Mississinewa, and Eel Rivers. Covers a land area of 373.842 square miles, a water area of 3.546 square miles, and is located in the Eastern Time Zone at 40.77° N. Lat., 86.04° W. Long. The county was founded in 1832. County seat is Peru.

Miami County is part of the Peru, IN Micropolitan Statistical Area. The entire metro area includes: Miami County, IN

Population: 36,035; Growth (since 2000): -0.1%; Density: 96.4 persons per square mile; Race: 90.9% White, 5.1% Black/African American, 0.6% Asian, 0.8% American Indian/Alaska Native, 0.1% Native Hawaiian/Other Pacific Islander, 1.5% two or more races, 3.0% Hispanic of any race; Average household size: 2.51; Median age: 39.9; Age under 18: 21.8%; Age 65 and over: 16.6%; Males per 100 females: 114.4; Marriage status: 27.5% never married, 53.3% now married, 2.2% separated, 6.2% widowed, 12.9% divorced; Foreign born: 1.3%; Speak English only: 96.3%; With disability: 16.2%; Veterans: 10.9%; Ancestry: 22.2% German, 15.6% American, 10.6% Irish, 6.6% English, 1.9% Dutch
Religion: Six largest groups: 12.5% Baptist, 7.3% Methodist/Pietist, 3.2% Non-denominational Protestant, 3.1% European Free-Church, 3.0% Catholicism, 2.9% Pentecostal
Economy: Unemployment rate: 6.5%; Leading industries: 16.5 % retail trade; 15.4 % other services (except public administration); 9.5 % construction; Farms: 666 totaling 175,276 acres; Company size: 0 employ 1,000 or more persons, 1 employs 500 to 999 persons, 9 employ 100 to 499 persons, 567 employ less than 100 persons; Business ownership: 600 women-owned, n/a Black-owned, 48 Hispanic-owned, n/a Asian-owned, n/a American Indian/Alaska Native-owned
Employment: 8.6% management, business, and financial, 1.9% computer, engineering, and science, 7.7% education, legal, community service, arts, and media, 6.5% healthcare practitioners, 18.1% service, 20.0% sales and office, 10.6% natural resources, construction, and maintenance, 26.6% production, transportation, and material moving
Income: Per capita: $22,890; Median household: $46,666; Average household: $59,206; Households with income of $100,000 or more: 13.3%; Poverty rate: 16.0%
Educational Attainment: High school diploma or higher: 85.3%; Bachelor's degree or higher: 12.6%; Graduate/professional degree or higher: 4.8%
Housing: Homeownership rate: 70.2%; Median home value: $85,500; Median year structure built: 1957; Homeowner vacancy rate: 2.6%; Median selected monthly owner costs: $920 with a mortgage, $338 without a mortgage; Median gross rent: $706 per month; Rental vacancy rate: 5.1%
Vital Statistics: Birth rate: 103.2 per 10,000 population; Death rate: 98.5 per 10,000 population; Age-adjusted cancer mortality rate: 164.6 deaths per 100,000 population
Health Insurance: 90.2% have insurance; 68.8% have private insurance; 37.9% have public insurance; 9.8% do not have insurance; 5.1% of children under 18 do not have insurance
Health Care: Physicians: 5.8 per 10,000 population; Dentists: 2.2 per 10,000 population; Hospital beds: 6.9 per 10,000 population; Hospital admissions: 310.5 per 10,000 population
Transportation: Commute: 94.5% car, 0.2% public transportation, 1.5% walk, 1.9% work from home; Mean travel time to work: 24.1 minutes
2016 Presidential Election: 74.0% Trump, 20.5% Clinton, 5.2% Johnson, 0.2% Stein
National and State Parks: Frances Slocum State Forest
Additional Information Contacts
Miami Government . . . . (765) 472-3901
http://www.miamicountyin.gov

Miami County Communities

AMBOY (town). Covers a land area of 0.350 square miles and a water area of <.001 square miles. Located at 40.60° N. Lat; 85.93° W. Long. Elevation is 817 feet.
Population: 343; Growth (since 2000): -4.7%; Density: 979.1 persons per square mile; Race: 98.0% White, 0.0% Black/African American, 0.6% Asian, 0.0% American Indian/Alaska Native, 0.0% Native Hawaiian/Other Pacific Islander, 0.9% Two or more races, 0.6% Hispanic of any race; Average household size: 2.70; Median age: 47.8; Age under 18: 23.0%; Age 65 and over: 25.7%; Males per 100 females: 93.9; Marriage status: 17.6% never married, 67.0% now married, 0.4% separated, 6.6% widowed, 8.8% divorced; Foreign born: 1.2%; Speak English only: 97.9%; With disability: 24.2%; Veterans: 9.8%; Ancestry: 32.4% German, 20.1% Irish, 12.0% American, 6.1% English, 3.5% Italian
Employment: 8.0% management, business, and financial, 1.8% computer, engineering, and science, 8.0% education, legal, community service, arts, and media, 2.7% healthcare practitioners, 16.8% service, 24.8% sales and office, 7.1% natural resources, construction, and maintenance, 31.0% production, transportation, and material moving
Income: Per capita: $19,084; Median household: $43,750; Average household: $49,243; Households with income of $100,000 or more: 6.3%; Poverty rate: 15.5%
Educational Attainment: High school diploma or higher: 83.5%; Bachelor's degree or higher: 8.9%; Graduate/professional degree or higher: 4.4%
Housing: Homeownership rate: 89.8%; Median home value: $78,000; Median year structure built: Before 1940; Homeowner vacancy rate: 4.2%; Median selected monthly owner costs: $992 with a mortgage, $365 without a mortgage; Median gross rent: $775 per month; Rental vacancy rate: 0.0%
Health Insurance: 92.1% have insurance; 67.3% have private insurance; 44.9% have public insurance; 7.9% do not have insurance; 0.0% of children under 18 do not have insurance
Transportation: Commute: 92.5% car, 4.7% public transportation, 2.8% walk, 0.0% work from home; Mean travel time to work: 28.8 minutes

BUNKER HILL (town). Covers a land area of 0.419 square miles and a water area of <.001 square miles. Located at 40.66° N. Lat; 86.10° W. Long. Elevation is 820 feet.
Population: 514; Growth (since 2000): -47.9%; Density: 1,226.1 persons per square mile; Race: 93.2% White, 5.4% Black/African American, 1.2% Asian, 0.0% American Indian/Alaska Native, 0.0% Native Hawaiian/Other Pacific Islander, 0.2% Two or more races, 0.2% Hispanic of any race; Average household size: 2.35; Median age: 40.3; Age under 18: 23.9%; Age 65 and over: 18.5%; Males per 100 females: 93.5; Marriage status: 18.0% never married, 53.5% now married, 1.9% separated, 5.1% widowed, 23.4% divorced; Foreign born: 1.4%; Speak English only: 95.9%; With disability: 18.5%; Veterans: 20.2%; Ancestry: 22.4% German, 17.7% American, 8.0% Irish, 6.4% English, 3.3% Italian
Employment: 4.1% management, business, and financial, 1.0% computer, engineering, and science, 2.6% education, legal, community service, arts, and media, 3.6% healthcare practitioners, 27.8% service, 21.1% sales and office, 12.9% natural resources, construction, and maintenance, 26.8% production, transportation, and material moving
Income: Per capita: $19,891; Median household: $36,625; Average household: $46,759; Households with income of $100,000 or more: 7.8%; Poverty rate: 19.8%
Educational Attainment: High school diploma or higher: 85.2%; Bachelor's degree or higher: 10.6%; Graduate/professional degree or higher: 2.4%

School District(s)
Maconaquah School Corp (PK-12)
Enrollment: 2,388 . . . . (765) 689-9131
Housing: Homeownership rate: 69.9%; Median home value: $66,800; Median year structure built: 1954; Homeowner vacancy rate: 12.1%; Median selected monthly owner costs: $891 with a mortgage, $379 without a mortgage; Median gross rent: $588 per month; Rental vacancy rate: 22.4%
Health Insurance: 87.2% have insurance; 59.7% have private insurance; 41.8% have public insurance; 12.8% do not have insurance; 5.3% of children under 18 do not have insurance
Transportation: Commute: 97.3% car, 0.0% public transportation, 0.5% walk, 0.0% work from home; Mean travel time to work: 20.4 minutes

CONVERSE (town). Covers a land area of 0.896 square miles and a water area of 0.003 square miles. Located at 40.58° N. Lat; 85.87° W. Long. Elevation is 830 feet.
Population: 1,139; Growth (since 2000): 0.2%; Density: 1,270.7 persons per square mile; Race: 97.0% White, 0.0% Black/African American, 0.0% Asian, 0.0% American Indian/Alaska Native, 0.0% Native Hawaiian/Other Pacific Islander, 3.0% Two or more races, 1.5% Hispanic of any race; Average household size: 2.46; Median age: 39.2; Age under 18: 27.5%; Age 65 and over: 16.2%; Males per 100 females: 92.8; Marriage status: 21.3% never married, 57.1% now married, 3.4% separated, 9.3% widowed, 12.3% divorced; Foreign born: 0.0%; Speak English only: 99.1%; With disability: 15.5%; Veterans: 11.3%; Ancestry: 19.2% German, 19.1% American, 9.3% English, 6.8% Irish, 4.6% Scottish
Employment: 12.1% management, business, and financial, 4.1% computer, engineering, and science, 10.5% education, legal, community service, arts, and media, 4.6% healthcare practitioners, 20.1% service, 24.9% sales and office, 1.8% natural resources, construction, and maintenance, 21.9% production, transportation, and material moving

Income: Per capita: $21,587; Median household: $33,068; Average household: $51,325; Households with income of $100,000 or more: 9.1%; Poverty rate: 20.1%
Educational Attainment: High school diploma or higher: 84.6%; Bachelor's degree or higher: 22.4%; Graduate/professional degree or higher: 9.0%

School District(s)

Oak Hill United School Corp (PK-12)
Enrollment: 1,304 .... (765) 395-3341
Housing: Homeownership rate: 67.0%; Median home value: $81,800; Median year structure built: 1969; Homeowner vacancy rate: 0.0%; Median selected monthly owner costs: $892 with a mortgage, $374 without a mortgage; Median gross rent: $635 per month; Rental vacancy rate: 5.6%
Health Insurance: 94.7% have insurance; 67.5% have private insurance; 38.9% have public insurance; 5.3% do not have insurance; 2.9% of children under 18 do not have insurance
Transportation: Commute: 90.3% car, 0.0% public transportation, 6.2% walk, 3.5% work from home; Mean travel time to work: 23.1 minutes

---

DENVER (town). Covers a land area of 0.233 square miles and a water area of 0 square miles. Located at 40.86° N. Lat; 86.08° W. Long. Elevation is 709 feet.
Population: 508; Growth (since 2000): -6.1%; Density: 2,181.1 persons per square mile; Race: 92.3% White, 3.1% Black/African American, 0.0% Asian, 2.0% American Indian/Alaska Native, 0.0% Native Hawaiian/Other Pacific Islander, 2.6% Two or more races, 0.0% Hispanic of any race; Average household size: 2.55; Median age: 41.9; Age under 18: 20.7%; Age 65 and over: 18.9%; Males per 100 females: 94.4; Marriage status: 25.6% never married, 55.3% now married, 2.4% separated, 5.6% widowed, 13.4% divorced; Foreign born: 0.0%; Speak English only: 99.4%; With disability: 15.9%; Veterans: 10.9%; Ancestry: 23.0% American, 14.4% German, 11.2% Irish, 5.3% English, 3.1% Dutch
Employment: 6.6% management, business, and financial, 2.6% computer, engineering, and science, 10.5% education, legal, community service, arts, and media, 1.3% healthcare practitioners, 3.5% service, 28.5% sales and office, 11.0% natural resources, construction, and maintenance, 36.0% production, transportation, and material moving
Income: Per capita: $20,861; Median household: $49,911; Average household: $51,794; Households with income of $100,000 or more: 5.5%; Poverty rate: 9.9%
Educational Attainment: High school diploma or higher: 82.8%; Bachelor's degree or higher: 12.2%; Graduate/professional degree or higher: 2.9%

School District(s)

North Miami Community Schools (PK-12)
Enrollment: 966................................ (765) 985-3891
Housing: Homeownership rate: 92.0%; Median home value: $69,300; Median year structure built: Before 1940; Homeowner vacancy rate: 0.0%; Median selected monthly owner costs: $775 with a mortgage, $313 without a mortgage; Median gross rent: $775 per month; Rental vacancy rate: 0.0%
Health Insurance: 93.9% have insurance; 75.4% have private insurance; 36.0% have public insurance; 6.1% do not have insurance; 0.0% of children under 18 do not have insurance
Transportation: Commute: 94.7% car, 0.0% public transportation, 0.9% walk, 1.3% work from home; Mean travel time to work: 36.4 minutes

---

GRISSOM AFB (CDP). Covers a land area of 4.992 square miles and a water area of 0.003 square miles. Located at 40.66° N. Lat; 86.15° W. Long.
Population: 2,499; Growth (since 2000): 51.3%; Density: 500.6 persons per square mile; Race: 81.4% White, 10.8% Black/African American, 1.0% Asian, 0.0% American Indian/Alaska Native, 0.0% Native Hawaiian/Other Pacific Islander, 1.9% Two or more races, 7.8% Hispanic of any race; Average household size: 2.86; Median age: 30.2; Age under 18: 26.9%; Age 65 and over: 7.6%; Males per 100 females: 338.1; Marriage status: 37.6% never married, 41.4% now married, 4.9% separated, 3.8% widowed, 17.2% divorced; Foreign born: 3.8%; Speak English only: 93.2%; With disability: 14.3%; Veterans: 13.2%; Ancestry: 20.5% German, 13.5% Irish, 10.0% American, 3.4% English, 2.9% French
Employment: 9.7% management, business, and financial, 0.0% computer, engineering, and science, 5.2% education, legal, community service, arts, and media, 7.3% healthcare practitioners, 26.8% service, 14.0% sales and office, 14.0% natural resources, construction, and maintenance, 23.0% production, transportation, and material moving
Income: Per capita: $17,261; Median household: $43,197; Average household: $50,815; Households with income of $100,000 or more: 10.6%; Poverty rate: 25.5%
Educational Attainment: High school diploma or higher: 87.1%; Bachelor's degree or higher: 12.4%; Graduate/professional degree or higher: 4.0%
Housing: Homeownership rate: 20.4%; Median home value: $51,900; Median year structure built: 1959; Homeowner vacancy rate: 16.5%; Median selected monthly owner costs: $850 with a mortgage, $246 without a mortgage; Median gross rent: $790 per month; Rental vacancy rate: 4.1%
Health Insurance: 90.2% have insurance; 70.0% have private insurance; 33.9% have public insurance; 9.8% do not have insurance; 3.2% of children under 18 do not have insurance
Transportation: Commute: 98.2% car, 0.0% public transportation, 1.5% walk, 0.3% work from home; Mean travel time to work: 19.8 minutes

---

MACY (town). Covers a land area of 0.134 square miles and a water area of 0 square miles. Located at 40.96° N. Lat; 86.13° W. Long. Elevation is 856 feet.
History: Laid out 1860.
Population: 253; Growth (since 2000): 2.0%; Density: 1,885.6 persons per square mile; Race: 86.2% White, 0.0% Black/African American, 0.8% Asian, 0.0% American Indian/Alaska Native, 0.0% Native Hawaiian/Other Pacific Islander, 2.4% Two or more races, 10.7% Hispanic of any race; Average household size: 3.42; Median age: 28.9; Age under 18: 36.8%; Age 65 and over: 13.0%; Males per 100 females: 101.0; Marriage status: 32.4% never married, 58.0% now married, 5.1% separated, 2.8% widowed, 6.8% divorced; Foreign born: 5.5%; Speak English only: 90.2%; With disability: 15.8%; Veterans: 6.9%; Ancestry: 30.8% German, 15.0% American, 4.7% English, 4.3% European, 4.3% Irish
Employment: 8.0% management, business, and financial, 0.0% computer, engineering, and science, 8.0% education, legal, community service, arts, and media, 0.0% healthcare practitioners, 12.6% service, 11.5% sales and office, 8.0% natural resources, construction, and maintenance, 51.7% production, transportation, and material moving
Income: Per capita: $14,030; Median household: $37,917; Average household: $43,458; Households with income of $100,000 or more: 9.5%; Poverty rate: 22.5%
Educational Attainment: High school diploma or higher: 81.8%; Bachelor's degree or higher: 8.0%; Graduate/professional degree or higher: 3.6%
Housing: Homeownership rate: 82.4%; Median home value: $36,900; Median year structure built: Before 1940; Homeowner vacancy rate: 6.2%; Median selected monthly owner costs: $640 with a mortgage, $278 without a mortgage; Median gross rent: $675 per month; Rental vacancy rate: 0.0%
Health Insurance: 95.7% have insurance; 56.5% have private insurance; 52.6% have public insurance; 4.3% do not have insurance; 0.0% of children under 18 do not have insurance
Transportation: Commute: 91.7% car, 0.0% public transportation, 8.3% walk, 0.0% work from home; Mean travel time to work: 36.2 minutes

---

MEXICO (CDP). Covers a land area of 5.419 square miles and a water area of 0.066 square miles. Located at 40.81° N. Lat; 86.11° W. Long. Elevation is 702 feet.
History: Mexico was settled largely by German Baptists as a stagecoach stop between Indianapolis and Michigan City.
Population: 751; Growth (since 2000): -23.7%; Density: 138.6 persons per square mile; Race: 98.8% White, 0.0% Black/African American, 0.0% Asian, 0.0% American Indian/Alaska Native, 0.0% Native Hawaiian/Other Pacific Islander, 1.2% Two or more races, 0.0% Hispanic of any race; Average household size: 2.07; Median age: 53.4; Age under 18: 10.9%; Age 65 and over: 26.4%; Males per 100 females: 100.5; Marriage status: 17.2% never married, 59.5% now married, 0.0% separated, 5.9% widowed, 17.4% divorced; Foreign born: 0.0%; Speak English only: 100.0%; With disability: 22.8%; Veterans: 14.9%; Ancestry: 19.2% German, 11.6% American, 8.4% English, 6.7% French, 5.9% Dutch
Employment: 18.7% management, business, and financial, 0.0% computer, engineering, and science, 1.7% education, legal, community service, arts, and media, 10.6% healthcare practitioners, 6.7% service, 19.5% sales and office, 18.5% natural resources, construction, and maintenance, 24.4% production, transportation, and material moving

Income: Per capita: $27,188; Median household: $49,801; Average household: $54,680; Households with income of $100,000 or more: 6.6%; Poverty rate: 1.2%
Educational Attainment: High school diploma or higher: 82.2%; Bachelor's degree or higher: 5.0%; Graduate/professional degree or higher: 1.1%
Housing: Homeownership rate: 91.7%; Median home value: $91,300; Median year structure built: 1959; Homeowner vacancy rate: 0.0%; Median selected monthly owner costs: $909 with a mortgage, $296 without a mortgage; Median gross rent: $588 per month; Rental vacancy rate: 0.0%
Health Insurance: 91.6% have insurance; 84.3% have private insurance; 30.8% have public insurance; 8.4% do not have insurance; 0.0% of children under 18 do not have insurance
Transportation: Commute: 94.8% car, 0.0% public transportation, 0.0% walk, 5.2% work from home; Mean travel time to work: 22.8 minutes

MIAMI (unincorporated postal area)
ZCTA: 46959

Covers a land area of 1.100 square miles and a water area of 0 square miles. Located at 40.62° N. Lat; 86.11° W. Long. Elevation is 791 feet.
Population: 540; Growth (since 2000): 110.1%; Density: 491.0 persons per square mile; Race: 97.4% White, 0.0% Black/African American, 0.0% Asian, 0.0% American Indian/Alaska Native, 0.0% Native Hawaiian/Other Pacific Islander, 2.6% Two or more races, 6.7% Hispanic of any race; Average household size: 2.07; Median age: 38.0; Age under 18: 18.0%; Age 65 and over: 4.4%; Males per 100 females: 92.5; Marriage status: 29.8% never married, 56.2% now married, 0.0% separated, 0.0% widowed, 14.0% divorced; Foreign born: 0.0%; Speak English only: 100.0%; With disability: 18.7%; Veterans: 7.2%; Ancestry: 28.0% German, 5.7% Irish, 4.6% Dutch, 4.3% Russian
Employment: 0.0% management, business, and financial, 0.0% computer, engineering, and science, 9.2% education, legal, community service, arts, and media, 0.0% healthcare practitioners, 36.8% service, 20.6% sales and office, 0.0% natural resources, construction, and maintenance, 33.5% production, transportation, and material moving
Income: Per capita: $14,352; Median household: n/a; Average household: $29,544; Households with income of $100,000 or more: n/a; Poverty rate: 25.0%
Educational Attainment: High school diploma or higher: 100.0%; Bachelor's degree or higher: 6.0%; Graduate/professional degree or higher: 6.0%
Housing: Homeownership rate: 60.9%; Median home value: $67,400; Median year structure built: Before 1940; Homeowner vacancy rate: 0.0%; Median selected monthly owner costs: $642 with a mortgage, $0 without a mortgage; Median gross rent: $703 per month; Rental vacancy rate: 0.0%
Health Insurance: 100.0% have insurance; 76.3% have private insurance; 35.0% have public insurance; 0.0% do not have insurance; 0.0% of children under 18 do not have insurance
Transportation: Commute: 100.0% car, 0.0% public transportation, 0.0% walk, 0.0% work from home; Mean travel time to work: 27.7 minutes

PERU (city). County seat. Covers a land area of 5.105 square miles and a water area of 0.073 square miles. Located at 40.76° N. Lat; 86.07° W. Long. Elevation is 653 feet.
History: Peru's reputation as the Circus City of the World, serving as winter quarters for many circuses, began in the late 1800's when Ben Wallace started the Hagenbeck-Wallace Circus.
Population: 11,510; Growth (since 2000): -11.4%; Density: 2,254.7 persons per square mile; Race: 88.1% White, 7.4% Black/African American, 0.7% Asian, 1.5% American Indian/Alaska Native, 0.0% Native Hawaiian/Other Pacific Islander, 1.7% Two or more races, 4.7% Hispanic of any race; Average household size: 2.42; Median age: 38.0; Age under 18: 24.4%; Age 65 and over: 15.4%; Males per 100 females: 90.4; Marriage status: 31.1% never married, 45.7% now married, 2.0% separated, 6.9% widowed, 16.3% divorced; Foreign born: 1.1%; Speak English only: 97.8%; With disability: 17.6%; Veterans: 10.5%; Ancestry: 17.0% German, 15.3% American, 10.0% Irish, 6.4% English, 2.9% Dutch
Employment: 5.0% management, business, and financial, 2.5% computer, engineering, and science, 7.2% education, legal, community service, arts, and media, 3.9% healthcare practitioners, 22.5% service, 19.9% sales and office, 9.9% natural resources, construction, and maintenance, 29.0% production, transportation, and material moving
Income: Per capita: $19,905; Median household: $34,991; Average household: $46,776; Households with income of $100,000 or more: 7.1%; Poverty rate: 22.7%
Educational Attainment: High school diploma or higher: 83.2%; Bachelor's degree or higher: 10.8%; Graduate/professional degree or higher: 3.3%

School District(s)

Maconaquah School Corp (PK-12)
Enrollment: 2,388 . . . . (765) 689-9131
Peru Community Schools (PK-12)
Enrollment: 2,172 . . . . (765) 473-3081

Housing: Homeownership rate: 61.1%; Median home value: $60,400; Median year structure built: Before 1940; Homeowner vacancy rate: 2.2%; Median selected monthly owner costs: $783 with a mortgage, $299 without a mortgage; Median gross rent: $633 per month; Rental vacancy rate: 2.2%
Health Insurance: 88.8% have insurance; 57.0% have private insurance; 46.4% have public insurance; 11.2% do not have insurance; 2.9% of children under 18 do not have insurance
Hospitals: Dukes Memorial Hospital (158 beds)
Safety: Violent crime rate: n/a per 10,000 population; Property crime rate: 396.0 per 10,000 population
Newspapers: Peru Tribune (daily circulation 6,400)
Transportation: Commute: 93.0% car, 0.2% public transportation, 2.7% walk, 1.0% work from home; Mean travel time to work: 19.3 minutes
Airports: Grissom ARB (general aviation)
Additional Information Contacts
City of Peru . . . . (765) 472-2400
http://www.cityofperu.org

Monroe County

Located in south central Indiana; drained by the West Fork of the White River, and several creeks. Covers a land area of 394.509 square miles, a water area of 16.812 square miles, and is located in the Eastern Time Zone at 39.16° N. Lat., 86.52° W. Long. The county was founded in 1818. County seat is Bloomington.

Monroe County is part of the Bloomington, IN Metropolitan Statistical Area. The entire metro area includes: Monroe County, IN; Owen County, IN

Weather Station: Bloomington Indiana Univ — Elevation: 830 feet

	Jan	Feb	Mar	Apr	May	Jun	Jul	Aug	Sep	Oct	Nov	Dec
High	37	42	52	64	74	82	85	85	78	66	54	41
Low	21	24	32	43	53	62	66	64	56	45	36	25
Precip	3.1	2.7	3.6	4.5	5.8	4.7	4.6	3.6	3.8	3.7	3.8	3.6
Snow	5.2	2.7	0.9	tr	0.0	0.0	0.0	0.0	0.0	0.2	0.1	3.9

High and Low temperatures in degrees Fahrenheit; Precipitation and Snow in inches

Population: 144,436; Growth (since 2000): 19.8%; Density: 366.1 persons per square mile; Race: 86.5% White, 3.1% Black/African American, 6.3% Asian, 0.2% American Indian/Alaska Native, 0.0% Native Hawaiian/Other Pacific Islander, 3.2% two or more races, 3.3% Hispanic of any race; Average household size: 2.35; Median age: 28.8; Age under 18: 16.0%; Age 65 and over: 11.8%; Males per 100 females: 99.6; Marriage status: 48.2% never married, 37.5% now married, 1.0% separated, 4.0% widowed, 10.3% divorced; Foreign born: 8.2%; Speak English only: 89.2%; With disability: 11.4%; Veterans: 5.3%; Ancestry: 21.0% German, 11.8% English, 11.7% Irish, 6.5% American, 3.4% Italian
Religion: Six largest groups: 7.5% Catholicism, 7.3% Baptist, 4.0% Methodist/Pietist, 3.5% Non-denominational Protestant, 1.5% Holiness, 1.3% Pentecostal
Economy: Unemployment rate: 3.9%; Leading industries: 14.6 % retail trade; 13.9 % health care and social assistance; 11.8 % accommodation and food services; Farms: 462 totaling 52,762 acres; Company size: 4 employ 1,000 or more persons, 1 employs 500 to 999 persons, 58 employ 100 to 499 persons, 2,971 employs less than 100 persons; Business ownership: 3,532 women-owned, 269 Black-owned, 170 Hispanic-owned, 410 Asian-owned, 65 American Indian/Alaska Native-owned
Employment: 14.2% management, business, and financial, 5.9% computer, engineering, and science, 17.4% education, legal, community service, arts, and media, 5.8% healthcare practitioners, 19.9% service, 21.6% sales and office, 5.4% natural resources, construction, and maintenance, 9.7% production, transportation, and material moving

Income: Per capita: $26,738; Median household: $45,689; Average household: $66,467; Households with income of $100,000 or more: 20.0%; Poverty rate: 24.7%
Educational Attainment: High school diploma or higher: 91.9%; Bachelor's degree or higher: 45.8%; Graduate/professional degree or higher: 22.1%
Housing: Homeownership rate: 54.2%; Median home value: $163,900; Median year structure built: 1984; Homeowner vacancy rate: 1.5%; Median selected monthly owner costs: $1,172 with a mortgage, $430 without a mortgage; Median gross rent: $869 per month; Rental vacancy rate: 5.1%
Vital Statistics: Birth rate: 92.0 per 10,000 population; Death rate: 60.8 per 10,000 population; Age-adjusted cancer mortality rate: 149.2 deaths per 100,000 population
Health Insurance: 91.6% have insurance; 76.7% have private insurance; 24.2% have public insurance; 8.4% do not have insurance; 5.8% of children under 18 do not have insurance
Health Care: Physicians: 24.5 per 10,000 population; Dentists: 4.8 per 10,000 population; Hospital beds: 23.3 per 10,000 population; Hospital admissions: 899.2 per 10,000 population
Air Quality Index (AQI): Percent of Days: 92.7% good, 7.3% moderate, 0.0% unhealthy for sensitive individuals, 0.0% unhealthy, 0.0% very unhealthy; Annual median: 27; Annual maximum: 61
Transportation: Commute: 81.7% car, 3.9% public transportation, 7.4% walk, 4.1% work from home; Mean travel time to work: 18.7 minutes
2016 Presidential Election: 35.2% Trump, 58.5% Clinton, 5.0% Johnson, 1.1% Stein
National and State Parks: Allens Creek State Recreation Area; Fairfax State Recreation Area; Morgan-Monroe State Forest; North Fork State Wildlife Refuge; Paynetown State Recreation Area
Additional Information Contacts
Monroe Government . . . . (812) 349-2550
http://www.co.monroe.in.us

Monroe County Communities

BLOOMINGTON (city). County seat. Covers a land area of 23.158 square miles and a water area of 0.199 square miles. Located at 39.16° N. Lat; 86.52° W. Long. Elevation is 771 feet.
History: Bloomington was settled in 1815 and developed around the stone quarries and mills. In 1820 Indiana University was founded here. Bloomington was named by a group of early settlers who enjoyed the many flowers on the hillsides.
Population: 83,636; Growth (since 2000): 20.7%; Density: 3,611.5 persons per square mile; Race: 81.7% White, 4.3% Black/African American, 9.6% Asian, 0.3% American Indian/Alaska Native, 0.0% Native Hawaiian/Other Pacific Islander, 3.5% Two or more races, 4.2% Hispanic of any race; Average household size: 2.26; Median age: 23.8; Age under 18: 11.4%; Age 65 and over: 8.7%; Males per 100 females: 101.1; Marriage status: 63.6% never married, 25.0% now married, 0.8% separated, 3.0% widowed, 8.4% divorced; Foreign born: 12.1%; Speak English only: 84.9%; With disability: 9.8%; Veterans: 3.3%; Ancestry: 19.9% German, 10.9% Irish, 10.8% English, 4.0% Italian, 3.8% American
Employment: 12.8% management, business, and financial, 6.1% computer, engineering, and science, 22.4% education, legal, community service, arts, and media, 4.4% healthcare practitioners, 23.0% service, 20.0% sales and office, 3.6% natural resources, construction, and maintenance, 7.8% production, transportation, and material moving
Income: Per capita: $21,972; Median household: $33,172; Average household: $55,113; Households with income of $100,000 or more: 15.5%; Poverty rate: 37.5%
Educational Attainment: High school diploma or higher: 92.6%; Bachelor's degree or higher: 56.8%; Graduate/professional degree or higher: 30.6%

School District(s)

Monroe County Community Sch Corp (PK-12)
Enrollment: 11,132 . . . . (812) 330-7700
Richland-Bean Blossom C S C (PK-12)
Enrollment: 2,690 . . . . (812) 876-7100
The Bloomington Project School (KG-08)
Enrollment: 278 . . . . (812) 558-0041

Four-year College(s)

Indiana University-Bloomington (Public)
Enrollment: 43,710 . . . . (812) 855-4848
Tuition: In-state $10,533; Out-of-state $34,845

Vocational/Technical School(s)

Tricoci University of Beauty Cuture LLC-Bloomington (Private, For-profit)
Enrollment: 68 . . . . (812) 339-1117
Tuition: $16,800
Housing: Homeownership rate: 34.5%; Median home value: $176,300; Median year structure built: 1982; Homeowner vacancy rate: 0.9%; Median selected monthly owner costs: $1,208 with a mortgage, $450 without a mortgage; Median gross rent: $863 per month; Rental vacancy rate: 5.3%
Health Insurance: 90.8% have insurance; 77.3% have private insurance; 20.1% have public insurance; 9.2% do not have insurance; 5.8% of children under 18 do not have insurance
Hospitals: Indiana University Health Bloomington Hospital (355 beds); Monroe Hospital
Safety: Violent crime rate: 52.0 per 10,000 population; Property crime rate: 303.6 per 10,000 population
Newspapers: Herald-Times (daily circulation 27,300)
Transportation: Commute: 72.0% car, 6.7% public transportation, 12.8% walk, 4.1% work from home; Mean travel time to work: 16.1 minutes
Airports: Monroe County (general aviation)
Additional Information Contacts
City of Bloomington . . . . (812) 349-3400
http://bloomington.in.gov

ELLETTSVILLE (town). Covers a land area of 4.240 square miles and a water area of 0 square miles. Located at 39.23° N. Lat; 86.62° W. Long. Elevation is 696 feet.
History: Ellettsville developed around the stone quarries, some of which specialized in fine carving and ornamentation. Ellettsville was platted in 1837 and named for Edward Elletts who had operated a tavern here in the early 1800's.
Population: 6,542; Growth (since 2000): 28.8%; Density: 1,543.0 persons per square mile; Race: 93.7% White, 1.2% Black/African American, 0.0% Asian, 0.0% American Indian/Alaska Native, 0.0% Native Hawaiian/Other Pacific Islander, 3.5% Two or more races, 3.3% Hispanic of any race; Average household size: 2.33; Median age: 39.0; Age under 18: 23.9%; Age 65 and over: 17.6%; Males per 100 females: 87.5; Marriage status: 24.4% never married, 47.3% now married, 2.5% separated, 7.5% widowed, 20.7% divorced; Foreign born: 0.2%; Speak English only: 95.8%; With disability: 17.5%; Veterans: 5.9%; Ancestry: 23.8% German, 15.1% Irish, 11.1% English, 8.7% American, 3.0% French
Employment: 10.5% management, business, and financial, 5.2% computer, engineering, and science, 8.7% education, legal, community service, arts, and media, 5.9% healthcare practitioners, 17.9% service, 28.2% sales and office, 6.9% natural resources, construction, and maintenance, 16.6% production, transportation, and material moving
Income: Per capita: $26,860; Median household: $48,657; Average household: $61,650; Households with income of $100,000 or more: 13.6%; Poverty rate: 15.3%
Educational Attainment: High school diploma or higher: 86.5%; Bachelor's degree or higher: 24.8%; Graduate/professional degree or higher: 7.0%

School District(s)

Richland-Bean Blossom C S C (PK-12)
Enrollment: 2,690 . . . . (812) 876-7100
Seven Oaks Classical School (KG-08)
Enrollment: 161 . . . . (812) 272-9716
Housing: Homeownership rate: 71.7%; Median home value: $123,100; Median year structure built: 1988; Homeowner vacancy rate: 3.3%; Median selected monthly owner costs: $978 with a mortgage, $413 without a mortgage; Median gross rent: $630 per month; Rental vacancy rate: 5.7%
Health Insurance: 92.1% have insurance; 71.0% have private insurance; 34.7% have public insurance; 7.9% do not have insurance; 7.7% of children under 18 do not have insurance
Safety: Violent crime rate: 13.5 per 10,000 population; Property crime rate: 185.6 per 10,000 population
Newspapers: The Journal (weekly circulation 2,500)
Transportation: Commute: 96.2% car, 1.2% public transportation, 1.6% walk, 1.0% work from home; Mean travel time to work: 19.4 minutes
Additional Information Contacts
Town of Ellettsville . . . . (812) 876-3860
http://ellettsville.in.us

HARRODSBURG (CDP). Covers a land area of 4.314 square miles and a water area of 0.036 square miles. Located at 39.02° N. Lat; 86.55° W. Long. Elevation is 558 feet.

Population: 790; Growth (since 2000): n/a; Density: 183.1 persons per square mile; Race: 94.6% White, 0.0% Black/African American, 0.0% Asian, 0.0% American Indian/Alaska Native, 0.0% Native Hawaiian/Other Pacific Islander, 5.4% Two or more races, 0.0% Hispanic of any race; Average household size: 3.11; Median age: 28.0; Age under 18: 38.4%; Age 65 and over: 10.8%; Males per 100 females: 90.4; Marriage status: 15.6% never married, 75.8% now married, 0.0% separated, 0.0% widowed, 8.5% divorced; Foreign born: 0.0%; Speak English only: 97.3%; With disability: 17.7%; Veterans: 11.3%; Ancestry: 41.0% Irish, 27.0% French, 22.4% German, 7.8% English, 6.3% Dutch

Employment: 12.1% management, business, and financial, 2.5% computer, engineering, and science, 5.6% education, legal, community service, arts, and media, 0.0% healthcare practitioners, 26.5% service, 32.1% sales and office, 21.1% natural resources, construction, and maintenance, 0.0% production, transportation, and material moving

Income: Per capita: $21,568; Median household: $52,083; Average household: $67,562; Households with income of $100,000 or more: 20.0%; Poverty rate: 31.0%

Educational Attainment: High school diploma or higher: 88.4%; Bachelor's degree or higher: 25.8%; Graduate/professional degree or higher: 9.4%

Housing: Homeownership rate: 96.5%; Median home value: $121,100; Median year structure built: 1967; Homeowner vacancy rate: 0.0%; Median selected monthly owner costs: $910 with a mortgage, $443 without a mortgage; Median gross rent: n/a per month; Rental vacancy rate: 0.0%

Health Insurance: 95.3% have insurance; 64.2% have private insurance; 46.7% have public insurance; 4.7% do not have insurance; 0.0% of children under 18 do not have insurance

Transportation: Commute: 100.0% car, 0.0% public transportation, 0.0% walk, 0.0% work from home; Mean travel time to work: 20.5 minutes

SMITHVILLE-SANDERS (CDP). Covers a land area of 10.720 square miles and a water area of 0 square miles. Located at 39.06° N. Lat; 86.51° W. Long.

Population: 3,362; Growth (since 2000): n/a; Density: 313.6 persons per square mile; Race: 95.7% White, 0.0% Black/African American, 2.6% Asian, 0.4% American Indian/Alaska Native, 0.0% Native Hawaiian/Other Pacific Islander, 1.0% Two or more races, 0.4% Hispanic of any race; Average household size: 2.30; Median age: 47.6; Age under 18: 17.5%; Age 65 and over: 17.4%; Males per 100 females: 101.6; Marriage status: 24.4% never married, 57.7% now married, 0.5% separated, 5.9% widowed, 11.9% divorced; Foreign born: 1.4%; Speak English only: 95.0%; With disability: 15.1%; Veterans: 11.7%; Ancestry: 27.1% German, 16.7% Irish, 16.5% English, 9.8% American, 7.8% Scottish

Employment: 22.7% management, business, and financial, 5.6% computer, engineering, and science, 9.9% education, legal, community service, arts, and media, 15.3% healthcare practitioners, 15.1% service, 13.5% sales and office, 10.1% natural resources, construction, and maintenance, 7.7% production, transportation, and material moving

Income: Per capita: $45,816; Median household: $80,690; Average household: $102,764; Households with income of $100,000 or more: 33.1%; Poverty rate: 8.9%

Educational Attainment: High school diploma or higher: 91.3%; Bachelor's degree or higher: 40.5%; Graduate/professional degree or higher: 11.4%

Housing: Homeownership rate: 81.2%; Median home value: $155,100; Median year structure built: 1984; Homeowner vacancy rate: 8.8%; Median selected monthly owner costs: $1,120 with a mortgage, $399 without a mortgage; Median gross rent: $1,086 per month; Rental vacancy rate: 0.0%

Health Insurance: 97.3% have insurance; 84.6% have private insurance; 26.4% have public insurance; 2.7% do not have insurance; 0.0% of children under 18 do not have insurance

Transportation: Commute: 97.8% car, 0.0% public transportation, 0.0% walk, 2.2% work from home; Mean travel time to work: 25.3 minutes

STINESVILLE (town). Covers a land area of 0.108 square miles and a water area of 0 square miles. Located at 39.30° N. Lat; 86.65° W. Long. Elevation is 581 feet.

History: Old limestone quarries. Laid out 1855.

Population: 209; Growth (since 2000): 7.7%; Density: 1,928.1 persons per square mile; Race: 98.6% White, 0.0% Black/African American, 0.0% Asian, 0.0% American Indian/Alaska Native, 0.0% Native Hawaiian/Other Pacific Islander, 1.4% Two or more races, 1.9% Hispanic of any race; Average household size: 2.65; Median age: 48.3; Age under 18: 16.7%; Age 65 and over: 20.1%; Males per 100 females: 98.0; Marriage status: 34.1% never married, 34.1% now married, 0.5% separated, 11.5% widowed, 20.3% divorced; Foreign born: 0.0%; Speak English only: 98.5%; With disability: 19.6%; Veterans: 7.5%; Ancestry: 22.0% German, 19.1% Irish, 13.4% English, 8.1% French, 4.3% Dutch

Employment: 10.6% management, business, and financial, 3.2% computer, engineering, and science, 10.6% education, legal, community service, arts, and media, 3.2% healthcare practitioners, 34.0% service, 9.6% sales and office, 9.6% natural resources, construction, and maintenance, 19.1% production, transportation, and material moving

Income: Per capita: $18,877; Median household: $34,688; Average household: $45,603; Households with income of $100,000 or more: 5.1%; Poverty rate: 16.7%

Educational Attainment: High school diploma or higher: 82.6%; Bachelor's degree or higher: 15.6%; Graduate/professional degree or higher: 6.0%

School District(s)

Richland-Bean Blossom C S C (PK-12)
Enrollment: 2,690 . . . . (812) 876-7100

Housing: Homeownership rate: 67.1%; Median home value: $70,300; Median year structure built: Before 1940; Homeowner vacancy rate: 10.2%; Median selected monthly owner costs: $759 with a mortgage, $250 without a mortgage; Median gross rent: $389 per month; Rental vacancy rate: 16.1%

Health Insurance: 91.4% have insurance; 50.7% have private insurance; 53.1% have public insurance; 8.6% do not have insurance; 0.0% of children under 18 do not have insurance

Transportation: Commute: 91.2% car, 0.0% public transportation, 2.2% walk, 6.6% work from home; Mean travel time to work: 19.9 minutes

UNIONVILLE (unincorporated postal area)
ZCTA: 47468

Covers a land area of 26.325 square miles and a water area of 2.417 square miles. Located at 39.27° N. Lat; 86.39° W. Long. Elevation is 879 feet.

Population: 1,431; Growth (since 2000): 17.8%; Density: 54.4 persons per square mile; Race: 97.6% White, 0.0% Black/African American, 1.3% Asian, 0.0% American Indian/Alaska Native, 0.0% Native Hawaiian/Other Pacific Islander, 1.2% Two or more races, 2.2% Hispanic of any race; Average household size: 2.54; Median age: 50.8; Age under 18: 19.1%; Age 65 and over: 28.3%; Males per 100 females: 107.0; Marriage status: 22.2% never married, 62.4% now married, 0.0% separated, 9.8% widowed, 5.6% divorced; Foreign born: 1.3%; Speak English only: 98.7%; With disability: 13.5%; Veterans: 6.1%; Ancestry: 20.7% German, 17.0% Irish, 5.3% Scottish, 4.1% European, 3.3% English

Employment: 13.8% management, business, and financial, 0.0% computer, engineering, and science, 13.5% education, legal, community service, arts, and media, 9.4% healthcare practitioners, 10.7% service, 23.3% sales and office, 15.1% natural resources, construction, and maintenance, 14.1% production, transportation, and material moving

Income: Per capita: $33,977; Median household: $56,319; Average household: $82,772; Households with income of $100,000 or more: 28.7%; Poverty rate: 6.1%

Educational Attainment: High school diploma or higher: 93.3%; Bachelor's degree or higher: 40.8%; Graduate/professional degree or higher: 22.1%

School District(s)

Monroe County Community Sch Corp (PK-12)
Enrollment: 11,132 . . . . (812) 330-7700

Housing: Homeownership rate: 90.1%; Median home value: $216,600; Median year structure built: 1985; Homeowner vacancy rate: 7.0%; Median selected monthly owner costs: $0 with a mortgage, $418 without a mortgage; Median gross rent: n/a per month; Rental vacancy rate: 0.0%

Health Insurance: 94.1% have insurance; 78.6% have private insurance; 30.8% have public insurance; 5.9% do not have insurance; 4.0% of children under 18 do not have insurance

Transportation: Commute: 85.2% car, 0.0% public transportation, 7.8% walk, 7.0% work from home; Mean travel time to work: 39.5 minutes

Montgomery County

Located in west central Indiana; drained by Sugar and Raccoon Creeks. Covers a land area of 504.613 square miles, a water area of 0.832 square miles, and is located in the Eastern Time Zone at 40.04° N. Lat., 86.89° W. Long. The county was founded in 1823. County seat is Crawfordsville.

Montgomery County is part of the Crawfordsville, IN Micropolitan Statistical Area. The entire metro area includes: Montgomery County, IN

Weather Station: Crawfordsville 5 S Elevation: 762 feet

	Jan	Feb	Mar	Apr	May	Jun	Jul	Aug	Sep	Oct	Nov	Dec
High	35	39	50	62	72	82	84	83	78	65	51	38
Low	17	20	28	38	48	58	61	59	50	40	31	20
Precip	2.5	2.5	2.9	4.0	4.7	4.5	4.4	3.7	3.2	3.3	4.2	3.1
Snow	na	5.4	2.7	0.2	tr	0.0	0.0	0.0	0.0	tr	0.6	4.7

High and Low temperatures in degrees Fahrenheit; Precipitation and Snow in inches

Population: 38,288; Growth (since 2000): 1.8%; Density: 75.9 persons per square mile; Race: 96.0% White, 0.8% Black/African American, 0.8% Asian, 0.2% American Indian/Alaska Native, 0.0% Native Hawaiian/Other Pacific Islander, 2.0% two or more races, 4.7% Hispanic of any race; Average household size: 2.47; Median age: 40.5; Age under 18: 23.0%; Age 65 and over: 17.1%; Males per 100 females: 101.5; Marriage status: 24.6% never married, 56.7% now married, 1.9% separated, 5.3% widowed, 13.4% divorced; Foreign born: 3.0%; Speak English only: 95.1%; With disability: 14.6%; Veterans: 7.9%; Ancestry: 22.4% German, 14.5% Irish, 10.3% American, 9.7% English, 2.5% French

Religion: Six largest groups: 17.6% Baptist, 7.5% Non-denominational Protestant, 6.7% Catholicism, 5.5% Methodist/Pietist, 1.1% Holiness, 1.0% Lutheran

Economy: Unemployment rate: 3.4%; Leading industries: 15.3 % retail trade; 12.9 % other services (except public administration); 11.7 % health care and social assistance; Farms: 732 totaling 286,949 acres; Company size: 1 employs 1,000 or more persons, 2 employ 500 to 999 persons, 14 employ 100 to 499 persons, 826 employ less than 100 persons; Business ownership: 921 women-owned, n/a Black-owned, 110 Hispanic-owned, 46 Asian-owned, n/a American Indian/Alaska Native-owned

Employment: 9.8% management, business, and financial, 3.1% computer, engineering, and science, 8.6% education, legal, community service, arts, and media, 4.1% healthcare practitioners, 15.6% service, 21.4% sales and office, 11.3% natural resources, construction, and maintenance, 26.2% production, transportation, and material moving

Income: Per capita: $25,519; Median household: $53,075; Average household: $63,854; Households with income of $100,000 or more: 16.7%; Poverty rate: 10.2%

Educational Attainment: High school diploma or higher: 89.7%; Bachelor's degree or higher: 18.1%; Graduate/professional degree or higher: 5.4%

Housing: Homeownership rate: 71.6%; Median home value: $118,400; Median year structure built: 1966; Homeowner vacancy rate: 1.6%; Median selected monthly owner costs: $1,004 with a mortgage, $345 without a mortgage; Median gross rent: $661 per month; Rental vacancy rate: 7.5%

Vital Statistics: Birth rate: 121.2 per 10,000 population; Death rate: 98.1 per 10,000 population; Age-adjusted cancer mortality rate: 161.5 deaths per 100,000 population

Health Insurance: 89.5% have insurance; 72.0% have private insurance; 30.9% have public insurance; 10.5% do not have insurance; 6.7% of children under 18 do not have insurance

Health Care: Physicians: 6.5 per 10,000 population; Dentists: 4.7 per 10,000 population; Hospital beds: 11.0 per 10,000 population; Hospital admissions: 331.1 per 10,000 population

Transportation: Commute: 92.2% car, 0.4% public transportation, 4.0% walk, 2.6% work from home; Mean travel time to work: 21.9 minutes

2016 Presidential Election: 73.0% Trump, 22.2% Clinton, 4.5% Johnson, 0.3% Stein

Additional Information Contacts

Montgomery Government . . . . (765) 364-6430
http://www.montgomeryco.net

Montgomery County Communities

ALAMO (town). Covers a land area of 0.067 square miles and a water area of 0 square miles. Located at 39.98° N. Lat; 87.06° W. Long. Elevation is 814 feet.

Population: 47; Growth (since 2000): -65.7%; Density: 698.5 persons per square mile; Race: 97.9% White, 0.0% Black/African American, 0.0% Asian, 0.0% American Indian/Alaska Native, 0.0% Native Hawaiian/Other Pacific Islander, 2.1% Two or more races, 4.3% Hispanic of any race; Average household size: 3.62; Median age: 30.2; Age under 18: 17.0%; Age 65 and over: 6.4%; Males per 100 females: 83.3; Marriage status: 41.0% never married, 33.3% now married, 5.1% separated, 5.1% widowed, 20.5% divorced; Foreign born: 0.0%; Speak English only: 100.0%; With disability: 6.4%; Veterans: 7.7%; Ancestry: 36.2% Irish, 25.5% Italian, 23.4% German, 12.8% Dutch, 12.8% French

Employment: 0.0% management, business, and financial, 0.0% computer, engineering, and science, 15.8% education, legal, community service, arts, and media, 0.0% healthcare practitioners, 0.0% service, 15.8% sales and office, 5.3% natural resources, construction, and maintenance, 63.2% production, transportation, and material moving

Income: Per capita: $16,238; Median household: n/a; Average household: $45,654; Households with income of $100,000 or more: 7.7%; Poverty rate: 23.4%

Educational Attainment: High school diploma or higher: 76.9%; Bachelor's degree or higher: 11.5%; Graduate/professional degree or higher: 7.7%

Housing: Homeownership rate: 92.3%; Median home value: n/a; Median year structure built: Before 1940; Homeowner vacancy rate: 14.3%; Median selected monthly owner costs: n/a with a mortgage, $375 without a mortgage; Median gross rent: n/a per month; Rental vacancy rate: 0.0%

Health Insurance: 78.7% have insurance; 59.6% have private insurance; 27.7% have public insurance; 21.3% do not have insurance; 36.4% of children under 18 do not have insurance

Transportation: Commute: 100.0% car, 0.0% public transportation, 0.0% walk, 0.0% work from home; Mean travel time to work: 22.6 minutes

CRAWFORDSVILLE (city). County seat. Covers a land area of 9.146 square miles and a water area of 0 square miles. Located at 40.04° N. Lat; 86.90° W. Long. Elevation is 794 feet.

History: Crawfordsville was laid out in 1823 by Major Ambrose Whitlock, and named for Colonel William Crawford of Virginia. A prominent resident of Crawfordsville was Civil War General Lew Wallace, better known as the author of the novel "Ben Hur."

Population: 16,075; Growth (since 2000): 5.5%; Density: 1,757.5 persons per square mile; Race: 93.0% White, 1.7% Black/African American, 0.9% Asian, 0.4% American Indian/Alaska Native, 0.0% Native Hawaiian/Other Pacific Islander, 3.5% Two or more races, 8.5% Hispanic of any race; Average household size: 2.30; Median age: 37.0; Age under 18: 22.4%; Age 65 and over: 17.2%; Males per 100 females: 100.4; Marriage status: 30.8% never married, 45.7% now married, 2.4% separated, 6.4% widowed, 17.1% divorced; Foreign born: 4.8%; Speak English only: 91.9%; With disability: 16.6%; Veterans: 7.0%; Ancestry: 20.2% German, 14.2% Irish, 10.2% American, 9.1% English, 3.0% Polish

Employment: 9.0% management, business, and financial, 2.0% computer, engineering, and science, 11.9% education, legal, community service, arts, and media, 3.2% healthcare practitioners, 17.6% service, 22.0% sales and office, 9.6% natural resources, construction, and maintenance, 24.8% production, transportation, and material moving

Income: Per capita: $21,057; Median household: $40,899; Average household: $50,570; Households with income of $100,000 or more: 10.3%; Poverty rate: 15.5%

Educational Attainment: High school diploma or higher: 85.9%; Bachelor's degree or higher: 19.2%; Graduate/professional degree or higher: 6.0%

School District(s)

Crawfordsville Community Schools (PK-12)
Enrollment: 2,384 . . . . (765) 362-2342
North Montgomery Com Sch Corp (PK-12)
Enrollment: 1,942 . . . . (765) 359-2112
South Montgomery Com Sch Corp (PK-12)
Enrollment: 1,881 . . . . (765) 866-0203

Four-year College(s)

Wabash College (Private, Not-for-profit)
Enrollment: 864 .... (765) 361-6100
Tuition: In-state $42,250; Out-of-state $42,250

Housing: Homeownership rate: 55.8%; Median home value: $91,700; Median year structure built: 1960; Homeowner vacancy rate: 2.1%; Median selected monthly owner costs: $869 with a mortgage, $304 without a mortgage; Median gross rent: $637 per month; Rental vacancy rate: 8.7%

Health Insurance: 85.3% have insurance; 63.3% have private insurance; 34.1% have public insurance; 14.7% do not have insurance; 8.6% of children under 18 do not have insurance

Hospitals: Franciscan Saint Elizabeth Health - Crawfordsville (120 beds)

Safety: Violent crime rate: 47.5 per 10,000 population; Property crime rate: 256.7 per 10,000 population

Newspapers: Journal Review (daily circulation 9,500); The Weekly (weekly circulation 7,000)

Transportation: Commute: 91.0% car, 0.0% public transportation, 6.2% walk, 1.5% work from home; Mean travel time to work: 16.8 minutes; Amtrak: Train service available.

Airports: Crawfordsville Municipal (general aviation)

Additional Information Contacts

City of Crawfordsville .... (765) 364-5150
http://www.crawfordsville.net

DARLINGTON (town). Covers a land area of 0.332 square miles and a water area of 0 square miles. Located at 40.11° N. Lat; 86.78° W. Long. Elevation is 761 feet.

Population: 860; Growth (since 2000): 0.7%; Density: 2,590.3 persons per square mile; Race: 99.2% White, 0.8% Black/African American, 0.0% Asian, 0.0% American Indian/Alaska Native, 0.0% Native Hawaiian/Other Pacific Islander, 0.0% Two or more races, 0.0% Hispanic of any race; Average household size: 2.50; Median age: 44.0; Age under 18: 21.4%; Age 65 and over: 14.2%; Males per 100 females: 102.2; Marriage status: 30.4% never married, 45.1% now married, 1.4% separated, 6.4% widowed, 18.1% divorced; Foreign born: 0.0%; Speak English only: 97.8%; With disability: 16.6%; Veterans: 7.8%; Ancestry: 26.3% German, 16.3% Irish, 8.6% English, 3.0% American, 1.9% Scotch-Irish

Employment: 15.1% management, business, and financial, 1.5% computer, engineering, and science, 7.2% education, legal, community service, arts, and media, 4.6% healthcare practitioners, 14.5% service, 22.4% sales and office, 8.3% natural resources, construction, and maintenance, 26.3% production, transportation, and material moving

Income: Per capita: $23,608; Median household: $47,500; Average household: $56,484; Households with income of $100,000 or more: 14.3%; Poverty rate: 11.7%

Educational Attainment: High school diploma or higher: 90.4%; Bachelor's degree or higher: 13.2%; Graduate/professional degree or higher: 2.3%

Housing: Homeownership rate: 67.2%; Median home value: $86,800; Median year structure built: Before 1940; Homeowner vacancy rate: 5.6%; Median selected monthly owner costs: $909 with a mortgage, $407 without a mortgage; Median gross rent: $746 per month; Rental vacancy rate: 6.6%

Health Insurance: 88.3% have insurance; 73.0% have private insurance; 29.8% have public insurance; 11.7% do not have insurance; 0.0% of children under 18 do not have insurance

Transportation: Commute: 95.2% car, 0.0% public transportation, 0.7% walk, 4.1% work from home; Mean travel time to work: 21.7 minutes

LADOGA (town). Covers a land area of 0.542 square miles and a water area of 0 square miles. Located at 39.92° N. Lat; 86.80° W. Long. Elevation is 823 feet.

Population: 1,210; Growth (since 2000): 15.6%; Density: 2,234.4 persons per square mile; Race: 98.6% White, 0.3% Black/African American, 0.0% Asian, 0.0% American Indian/Alaska Native, 0.6% Native Hawaiian/Other Pacific Islander, 0.5% Two or more races, 1.9% Hispanic of any race; Average household size: 2.76; Median age: 33.5; Age under 18: 34.5%; Age 65 and over: 14.4%; Males per 100 females: 98.6; Marriage status: 23.0% never married, 52.7% now married, 1.2% separated, 9.3% widowed, 15.1% divorced; Foreign born: 0.2%; Speak English only: 98.6%; With disability: 15.2%; Veterans: 9.3%; Ancestry: 19.9% German, 14.6% American, 11.7% Irish, 10.7% French, 8.0% English

Employment: 10.1% management, business, and financial, 5.4% computer, engineering, and science, 4.8% education, legal, community service, arts, and media, 3.3% healthcare practitioners, 18.7% service, 23.9% sales and office, 7.5% natural resources, construction, and maintenance, 26.4% production, transportation, and material moving

Income: Per capita: $20,088; Median household: $46,694; Average household: $54,581; Households with income of $100,000 or more: 8.8%; Poverty rate: 23.2%

Educational Attainment: High school diploma or higher: 93.0%; Bachelor's degree or higher: 9.8%; Graduate/professional degree or higher: 1.6%

School District(s)

South Montgomery Com Sch Corp (PK-12)
Enrollment: 1,881 .... (765) 866-0203

Housing: Homeownership rate: 73.1%; Median home value: $83,200; Median year structure built: 1946; Homeowner vacancy rate: 3.2%; Median selected monthly owner costs: $854 with a mortgage, $327 without a mortgage; Median gross rent: $803 per month; Rental vacancy rate: 7.9%

Health Insurance: 88.6% have insurance; 68.4% have private insurance; 32.7% have public insurance; 11.4% do not have insurance; 6.9% of children under 18 do not have insurance

Transportation: Commute: 90.9% car, 0.0% public transportation, 1.8% walk, 6.1% work from home; Mean travel time to work: 25.2 minutes

LAKE HOLIDAY (CDP). Covers a land area of 2.577 square miles and a water area of 0.202 square miles. Located at 39.96° N. Lat; 86.96° W. Long. Elevation is 774 feet.

Population: 960; Growth (since 2000): n/a; Density: 372.6 persons per square mile; Race: 98.9% White, 1.1% Black/African American, 0.0% Asian, 0.0% American Indian/Alaska Native, 0.0% Native Hawaiian/Other Pacific Islander, 0.0% Two or more races, 0.0% Hispanic of any race; Average household size: 2.22; Median age: 50.3; Age under 18: 12.5%; Age 65 and over: 10.3%; Males per 100 females: 106.3; Marriage status: 21.9% never married, 65.0% now married, 4.6% separated, 5.4% widowed, 7.7% divorced; Foreign born: 6.1%; Speak English only: 100.0%; With disability: 17.2%; Veterans: 5.5%; Ancestry: 18.5% American, 17.4% German, 15.9% Irish, 11.0% English, 3.1% Albanian

Employment: 6.4% management, business, and financial, 7.1% computer, engineering, and science, 5.9% education, legal, community service, arts, and media, 10.1% healthcare practitioners, 13.5% service, 15.6% sales and office, 8.0% natural resources, construction, and maintenance, 33.4% production, transportation, and material moving

Income: Per capita: $34,557; Median household: $66,579; Average household: $77,093; Households with income of $100,000 or more: 27.6%; Poverty rate: 8.5%

Educational Attainment: High school diploma or higher: 96.9%; Bachelor's degree or higher: 20.7%; Graduate/professional degree or higher: 5.9%

Housing: Homeownership rate: 91.2%; Median home value: $164,200; Median year structure built: 1977; Homeowner vacancy rate: 3.7%; Median selected monthly owner costs: $1,147 with a mortgage, $406 without a mortgage; Median gross rent: n/a per month; Rental vacancy rate: 0.0%

Health Insurance: 97.5% have insurance; 82.3% have private insurance; 25.2% have public insurance; 2.5% do not have insurance; 0.0% of children under 18 do not have insurance

Transportation: Commute: 97.9% car, 0.0% public transportation, 0.0% walk, 2.1% work from home; Mean travel time to work: 28.2 minutes

LINDEN (town). Covers a land area of 0.418 square miles and a water area of 0 square miles. Located at 40.19° N. Lat; 86.90° W. Long. Elevation is 797 feet.

Population: 743; Growth (since 2000): 6.1%; Density: 1,777.3 persons per square mile; Race: 98.5% White, 0.0% Black/African American, 0.0% Asian, 0.4% American Indian/Alaska Native, 0.0% Native Hawaiian/Other Pacific Islander, 0.7% Two or more races, 2.4% Hispanic of any race; Average household size: 2.67; Median age: 38.1; Age under 18: 27.5%; Age 65 and over: 13.9%; Males per 100 females: 104.0; Marriage status: 16.0% never married, 63.4% now married, 0.9% separated, 6.0% widowed, 14.6% divorced; Foreign born: 0.3%; Speak English only: 97.9%; With disability: 20.7%; Veterans: 7.6%; Ancestry: 27.9% German, 12.4% American, 11.3% Irish, 9.4% English, 2.3% Swedish

Employment: 10.3% management, business, and financial, 3.8% computer, engineering, and science, 3.5% education, legal, community service, arts, and media, 1.5% healthcare practitioners, 21.7% service, 23.8% sales and office, 8.2% natural resources, construction, and maintenance, 27.3% production, transportation, and material moving

Income: Per capita: $21,321; Median household: $55,500; Average household: $56,171; Households with income of $100,000 or more: 9.0%; Poverty rate: 16.8%
Educational Attainment: High school diploma or higher: 85.1%; Bachelor's degree or higher: 7.9%; Graduate/professional degree or higher: 1.7%
Housing: Homeownership rate: 71.2%; Median home value: $79,700; Median year structure built: 1960; Homeowner vacancy rate: 2.9%; Median selected monthly owner costs: $937 with a mortgage, $318 without a mortgage; Median gross rent: $650 per month; Rental vacancy rate: 17.5%
Health Insurance: 87.5% have insurance; 67.4% have private insurance; 32.4% have public insurance; 12.5% do not have insurance; 9.3% of children under 18 do not have insurance
Transportation: Commute: 95.9% car, 0.0% public transportation, 0.0% walk, 2.8% work from home; Mean travel time to work: 24.9 minutes

NEW MARKET (town). Covers a land area of 0.275 square miles and a water area of 0 square miles. Located at 39.95° N. Lat; 86.92° W. Long. Elevation is 807 feet.
Population: 560; Growth (since 2000): -15.0%; Density: 2,039.0 persons per square mile; Race: 99.3% White, 0.0% Black/African American, 0.0% Asian, 0.0% American Indian/Alaska Native, 0.0% Native Hawaiian/Other Pacific Islander, 0.7% Two or more races, 2.7% Hispanic of any race; Average household size: 2.67; Median age: 35.9; Age under 18: 26.2%; Age 65 and over: 10.4%; Males per 100 females: 95.1; Marriage status: 34.3% never married, 52.1% now married, 2.1% separated, 1.7% widowed, 11.9% divorced; Foreign born: 0.2%; Speak English only: 99.5%; With disability: 15.5%; Veterans: 4.8%; Ancestry: 23.4% German, 16.1% English, 14.1% Irish, 9.6% American, 6.3% Dutch
Employment: 9.4% management, business, and financial, 8.4% computer, engineering, and science, 5.5% education, legal, community service, arts, and media, 4.2% healthcare practitioners, 18.8% service, 19.4% sales and office, 6.5% natural resources, construction, and maintenance, 27.8% production, transportation, and material moving
Income: Per capita: $26,518; Median household: $63,125; Average household: $68,823; Households with income of $100,000 or more: 20.5%; Poverty rate: 8.8%
Educational Attainment: High school diploma or higher: 95.6%; Bachelor's degree or higher: 9.0%; Graduate/professional degree or higher: 4.4%

School District(s)

South Montgomery Com Sch Corp (PK-12)
Enrollment: 1,881 . . . . (765) 866-0203
Housing: Homeownership rate: 81.9%; Median home value: $85,900; Median year structure built: 1952; Homeowner vacancy rate: 0.0%; Median selected monthly owner costs: $956 with a mortgage, $325 without a mortgage; Median gross rent: $914 per month; Rental vacancy rate: 0.0%
Health Insurance: 93.4% have insurance; 79.5% have private insurance; 24.3% have public insurance; 6.6% do not have insurance; 3.8% of children under 18 do not have insurance
Transportation: Commute: 97.9% car, 0.0% public transportation, 2.1% walk, 0.0% work from home; Mean travel time to work: 19.9 minutes

NEW RICHMOND (town). Covers a land area of 0.198 square miles and a water area of 0 square miles. Located at 40.19° N. Lat; 86.98° W. Long. Elevation is 784 feet.
Population: 311; Growth (since 2000): -10.9%; Density: 1,574.1 persons per square mile; Race: 97.1% White, 1.9% Black/African American, 1.0% Asian, 0.0% American Indian/Alaska Native, 0.0% Native Hawaiian/Other Pacific Islander, 0.0% Two or more races, 0.0% Hispanic of any race; Average household size: 2.73; Median age: 34.4; Age under 18: 28.3%; Age 65 and over: 19.0%; Males per 100 females: 99.4; Marriage status: 24.2% never married, 61.0% now married, 0.0% separated, 4.8% widowed, 10.0% divorced; Foreign born: 1.0%; Speak English only: 99.6%; With disability: 17.4%; Veterans: 17.0%; Ancestry: 26.7% German, 21.9% English, 12.2% Irish, 8.7% American, 5.1% Italian
Employment: 11.2% management, business, and financial, 0.7% computer, engineering, and science, 0.7% education, legal, community service, arts, and media, 4.5% healthcare practitioners, 11.2% service, 32.1% sales and office, 5.2% natural resources, construction, and maintenance, 34.3% production, transportation, and material moving
Income: Per capita: $24,862; Median household: $43,750; Average household: $60,372; Households with income of $100,000 or more: 11.5%; Poverty rate: 9.0%
Educational Attainment: High school diploma or higher: 86.5%; Bachelor's degree or higher: 16.1%; Graduate/professional degree or higher: 2.6%
Housing: Homeownership rate: 86.0%; Median home value: $75,300; Median year structure built: Before 1940; Homeowner vacancy rate: 10.5%; Median selected monthly owner costs: $1,088 with a mortgage, $339 without a mortgage; Median gross rent: $713 per month; Rental vacancy rate: 5.9%
Health Insurance: 97.7% have insurance; 82.3% have private insurance; 43.1% have public insurance; 2.3% do not have insurance; 0.0% of children under 18 do not have insurance
Transportation: Commute: 93.9% car, 3.0% public transportation, 0.0% walk, 2.3% work from home; Mean travel time to work: 27.1 minutes

NEW ROSS (town). Covers a land area of 0.322 square miles and a water area of 0 square miles. Located at 39.96° N. Lat; 86.71° W. Long. Elevation is 886 feet.
History: New Ross grew as a trading center for surrounding farms.
Population: 442; Growth (since 2000): 32.3%; Density: 1,374.7 persons per square mile; Race: 100.0% White, 0.0% Black/African American, 0.0% Asian, 0.0% American Indian/Alaska Native, 0.0% Native Hawaiian/Other Pacific Islander, 0.0% Two or more races, 1.1% Hispanic of any race; Average household size: 3.01; Median age: 33.0; Age under 18: 36.4%; Age 65 and over: 13.6%; Males per 100 females: 107.8; Marriage status: 22.5% never married, 56.2% now married, 0.0% separated, 7.9% widowed, 13.3% divorced; Foreign born: 0.7%; Speak English only: 92.9%; With disability: 13.3%; Veterans: 9.3%; Ancestry: 26.7% German, 5.7% English, 5.4% American, 4.8% Irish, 1.6% Danish
Employment: 10.3% management, business, and financial, 2.6% computer, engineering, and science, 2.1% education, legal, community service, arts, and media, 2.6% healthcare practitioners, 20.5% service, 13.8% sales and office, 13.8% natural resources, construction, and maintenance, 34.4% production, transportation, and material moving
Income: Per capita: $17,945; Median household: $51,705; Average household: $53,370; Households with income of $100,000 or more: 14.3%; Poverty rate: 23.5%
Educational Attainment: High school diploma or higher: 76.2%; Bachelor's degree or higher: 13.1%; Graduate/professional degree or higher: 5.2%

School District(s)

South Montgomery Com Sch Corp (PK-12)
Enrollment: 1,881 . . . . (765) 866-0203
Housing: Homeownership rate: 81.6%; Median home value: $82,000; Median year structure built: Before 1940; Homeowner vacancy rate: 8.4%; Median selected monthly owner costs: $1,063 with a mortgage, $343 without a mortgage; Median gross rent: $850 per month; Rental vacancy rate: 0.0%
Health Insurance: 90.0% have insurance; 60.4% have private insurance; 43.7% have public insurance; 10.0% do not have insurance; 8.4% of children under 18 do not have insurance
Transportation: Commute: 93.8% car, 0.0% public transportation, 2.1% walk, 4.1% work from home; Mean travel time to work: 30.4 minutes

WAVELAND (town). Covers a land area of 0.318 square miles and a water area of 0 square miles. Located at 39.88° N. Lat; 87.05° W. Long. Elevation is 781 feet.
History: Laid out 1835.
Population: 374; Growth (since 2000): -10.1%; Density: 1,174.9 persons per square mile; Race: 99.2% White, 0.0% Black/African American, 0.0% Asian, 0.3% American Indian/Alaska Native, 0.0% Native Hawaiian/Other Pacific Islander, 0.3% Two or more races, 5.6% Hispanic of any race; Average household size: 2.56; Median age: 36.2; Age under 18: 29.7%; Age 65 and over: 16.3%; Males per 100 females: 92.7; Marriage status: 18.2% never married, 63.2% now married, 2.5% separated, 5.4% widowed, 13.2% divorced; Foreign born: 1.9%; Speak English only: 98.3%; With disability: 19.8%; Veterans: 8.7%; Ancestry: 26.5% German, 15.5% Irish, 14.4% English, 10.2% American, 4.5% French Canadian
Employment: 4.5% management, business, and financial, 3.2% computer, engineering, and science, 10.8% education, legal, community service, arts, and media, 0.6% healthcare practitioners, 8.9% service, 26.1% sales and office, 13.4% natural resources, construction, and maintenance, 32.5% production, transportation, and material moving
Income: Per capita: $19,318; Median household: $40,833; Average household: $49,336; Households with income of $100,000 or more: 11.6%; Poverty rate: 21.2%

Educational Attainment: High school diploma or higher: 85.1%; Bachelor's degree or higher: 14.0%; Graduate/professional degree or higher: 3.4%
Housing: Homeownership rate: 78.1%; Median home value: $67,800; Median year structure built: Before 1940; Homeowner vacancy rate: 5.0%; Median selected monthly owner costs: $944 with a mortgage, $330 without a mortgage; Median gross rent: $829 per month; Rental vacancy rate: 0.0%
Health Insurance: 89.8% have insurance; 59.1% have private insurance; 43.3% have public insurance; 10.2% do not have insurance; 6.2% of children under 18 do not have insurance
Transportation: Commute: 92.1% car, 0.0% public transportation, 5.3% walk, 2.6% work from home; Mean travel time to work: 24.8 minutes

WAYNETOWN (town). Covers a land area of 0.478 square miles and a water area of 0 square miles. Located at 40.09° N. Lat; 87.07° W. Long. Elevation is 764 feet.
History: Waynetown developed around the tile factories and brick kilns that made use of the clay in the area.
Population: 1,171; Growth (since 2000): 28.8%; Density: 2,450.6 persons per square mile; Race: 97.3% White, 0.0% Black/African American, 0.5% Asian, 0.0% American Indian/Alaska Native, 0.0% Native Hawaiian/Other Pacific Islander, 2.2% Two or more races, 3.3% Hispanic of any race; Average household size: 2.80; Median age: 34.9; Age under 18: 32.6%; Age 65 and over: 14.1%; Males per 100 females: 93.9; Marriage status: 24.4% never married, 58.4% now married, 1.8% separated, 4.8% widowed, 12.4% divorced; Foreign born: 1.7%; Speak English only: 97.0%; With disability: 16.7%; Veterans: 13.3%; Ancestry: 22.2% Irish, 14.0% German, 9.2% American, 6.1% English, 3.0% Scottish
Employment: 5.8% management, business, and financial, 1.1% computer, engineering, and science, 3.5% education, legal, community service, arts, and media, 3.0% healthcare practitioners, 13.6% service, 30.0% sales and office, 15.2% natural resources, construction, and maintenance, 27.9% production, transportation, and material moving
Income: Per capita: $20,883; Median household: $54,688; Average household: $58,573; Households with income of $100,000 or more: 11.5%; Poverty rate: 7.8%
Educational Attainment: High school diploma or higher: 88.4%; Bachelor's degree or higher: 11.5%; Graduate/professional degree or higher: 1.6%
Housing: Homeownership rate: 80.9%; Median home value: $80,200; Median year structure built: 1958; Homeowner vacancy rate: 4.8%; Median selected monthly owner costs: $789 with a mortgage, $387 without a mortgage; Median gross rent: $888 per month; Rental vacancy rate: 0.0%
Health Insurance: 93.0% have insurance; 73.6% have private insurance; 30.8% have public insurance; 7.0% do not have insurance; 2.1% of children under 18 do not have insurance
Transportation: Commute: 95.9% car, 0.4% public transportation, 0.7% walk, 1.8% work from home; Mean travel time to work: 25.8 minutes

WINGATE (town). Covers a land area of 0.215 square miles and a water area of 0 square miles. Located at 40.17° N. Lat; 87.07° W. Long. Elevation is 781 feet.
Population: 270; Growth (since 2000): -9.7%; Density: 1,255.9 persons per square mile; Race: 99.6% White, 0.0% Black/African American, 0.4% Asian, 0.0% American Indian/Alaska Native, 0.0% Native Hawaiian/Other Pacific Islander, 0.0% Two or more races, 0.0% Hispanic of any race; Average household size: 2.08; Median age: 40.0; Age under 18: 18.1%; Age 65 and over: 15.6%; Males per 100 females: 99.2; Marriage status: 26.4% never married, 39.6% now married, 0.9% separated, 6.4% widowed, 27.7% divorced; Foreign born: 1.1%; Speak English only: 99.3%; With disability: 21.5%; Veterans: 10.4%; Ancestry: 17.0% German, 15.9% American, 15.6% English, 11.1% Irish, 6.7% Polish
Employment: 5.5% management, business, and financial, 2.8% computer, engineering, and science, 7.6% education, legal, community service, arts, and media, 8.3% healthcare practitioners, 13.8% service, 25.5% sales and office, 13.1% natural resources, construction, and maintenance, 23.4% production, transportation, and material moving
Income: Per capita: $26,636; Median household: $50,625; Average household: $54,430; Households with income of $100,000 or more: 6.9%; Poverty rate: 13.7%
Educational Attainment: High school diploma or higher: 84.4%; Bachelor's degree or higher: 12.4%; Graduate/professional degree or higher: 1.6%
Housing: Homeownership rate: 77.7%; Median home value: $66,600; Median year structure built: 1946; Homeowner vacancy rate: 7.3%; Median selected monthly owner costs: $996 with a mortgage, $348 without a mortgage; Median gross rent: $663 per month; Rental vacancy rate: 12.1%
Health Insurance: 89.6% have insurance; 69.3% have private insurance; 36.3% have public insurance; 10.4% do not have insurance; 11.5% of children under 18 do not have insurance
Transportation: Commute: 93.8% car, 0.0% public transportation, 3.4% walk, 2.8% work from home; Mean travel time to work: 31.6 minutes

Morgan County

Located in central Indiana; drained by the West Fork of the White River, Whitelick River, and Camp Creek. Covers a land area of 403.969 square miles, a water area of 5.458 square miles, and is located in the Eastern Time Zone at 39.48° N. Lat., 86.45° W. Long. The county was founded in 1821. County seat is Martinsville.

Morgan County is part of the Indianapolis-Carmel-Anderson, IN Metropolitan Statistical Area. The entire metro area includes: Boone County, IN; Brown County, IN; Hamilton County, IN; Hancock County, IN; Hendricks County, IN; Johnson County, IN; Madison County, IN; Marion County, IN; Morgan County, IN; Putnam County, IN; Shelby County, IN

Weather Station: Martinsville 2 SW Elevation: 609 feet

	Jan	Feb	Mar	Apr	May	Jun	Jul	Aug	Sep	Oct	Nov	Dec
High	37	41	52	63	73	81	85	84	78	66	53	40
Low	19	22	30	40	50	59	63	61	52	40	32	23
Precip	2.7	2.4	3.4	4.4	5.3	4.6	4.3	3.8	3.5	3.4	3.6	3.2
Snow	5.6	4.2	2.0	0.1	0.0	0.0	0.0	0.0	0.0	0.2	0.3	3.6

High and Low temperatures in degrees Fahrenheit; Precipitation and Snow in inches

Population: 69,533; Growth (since 2000): 4.3%; Density: 172.1 persons per square mile; Race: 97.4% White, 0.4% Black/African American, 0.7% Asian, 0.1% American Indian/Alaska Native, 0.0% Native Hawaiian/Other Pacific Islander, 1.3% two or more races, 1.5% Hispanic of any race; Average household size: 2.66; Median age: 41.5; Age under 18: 23.4%; Age 65 and over: 15.4%; Males per 100 females: 98.4; Marriage status: 24.0% never married, 56.3% now married, 1.6% separated, 6.1% widowed, 13.7% divorced; Foreign born: 1.2%; Speak English only: 98.6%; With disability: 15.4%; Veterans: 10.1%; Ancestry: 20.3% German, 14.2% American, 12.3% English, 11.2% Irish, 2.5% European
Religion: Six largest groups: 14.3% Baptist, 6.0% Non-denominational Protestant, 4.4% Catholicism, 3.4% Holiness, 3.2% Methodist/Pietist, 2.0% Pentecostal
Economy: Unemployment rate: 3.3%; Leading industries: 14.6 % construction; 14.2 % retail trade; 11.9 % other services (except public administration); Farms: 583 totaling 137,189 acres; Company size: 0 employ 1,000 or more persons, 1 employs 500 to 999 persons, 14 employ 100 to 499 persons, 1,173 employ less than 100 persons; Business ownership: 1,719 women-owned, 50 Black-owned, 60 Hispanic-owned, 48 Asian-owned, n/a American Indian/Alaska Native-owned
Employment: 12.2% management, business, and financial, 3.5% computer, engineering, and science, 6.9% education, legal, community service, arts, and media, 4.6% healthcare practitioners, 15.6% service, 24.3% sales and office, 14.4% natural resources, construction, and maintenance, 18.5% production, transportation, and material moving
Income: Per capita: $27,402; Median household: $60,317; Average household: $72,492; Households with income of $100,000 or more: 22.4%; Poverty rate: 11.8%
Educational Attainment: High school diploma or higher: 87.9%; Bachelor's degree or higher: 16.1%; Graduate/professional degree or higher: 5.4%
Housing: Homeownership rate: 76.6%; Median home value: $147,200; Median year structure built: 1981; Homeowner vacancy rate: 1.0%; Median selected monthly owner costs: $1,182 with a mortgage, $390 without a mortgage; Median gross rent: $784 per month; Rental vacancy rate: 7.5%
Vital Statistics: Birth rate: 108.0 per 10,000 population; Death rate: 94.2 per 10,000 population; Age-adjusted cancer mortality rate: 182.1 deaths per 100,000 population
Health Insurance: 91.2% have insurance; 71.4% have private insurance; 32.5% have public insurance; 8.8% do not have insurance; 5.8% of children under 18 do not have insurance
Health Care: Physicians: 11.5 per 10,000 population; Dentists: 4.3 per 10,000 population; Hospital beds: 16.5 per 10,000 population; Hospital admissions: 414.6 per 10,000 population

Air Quality Index (AQI): Percent of Days: 95.0% good, 4.4% moderate, 0.6% unhealthy for sensitive individuals, 0.0% unhealthy, 0.0% very unhealthy; Annual median: 32; Annual maximum: 114
Transportation: Commute: 94.6% car, 0.1% public transportation, 1.3% walk, 3.1% work from home; Mean travel time to work: 28.1 minutes
2016 Presidential Election: 75.3% Trump, 19.2% Clinton, 4.7% Johnson, 0.2% Stein
National and State Parks: Bradford Woods State Reservation; Morgan Monroe State Forest
Additional Information Contacts
Morgan Government . . . . (765) 342-8110
http://www.morgancounty.in.gov

Morgan County Communities

BETHANY (town). Covers a land area of 0.083 square miles and a water area of 0.012 square miles. Located at 39.53° N. Lat; 86.38° W. Long. Elevation is 656 feet.
Population: 99; Growth (since 2000): 5.3%; Density: 1,189.8 persons per square mile; Race: 96.0% White, 2.0% Black/African American, 2.0% Asian, 0.0% American Indian/Alaska Native, 0.0% Native Hawaiian/Other Pacific Islander, 0.0% Two or more races, 0.0% Hispanic of any race; Average household size: 2.61; Median age: 34.5; Age under 18: 24.2%; Age 65 and over: 8.1%; Males per 100 females: 113.2; Marriage status: 29.9% never married, 49.4% now married, 0.0% separated, 5.2% widowed, 15.6% divorced; Foreign born: 2.0%; Speak English only: 97.7%; With disability: 13.1%; Veterans: 16.0%; Ancestry: 32.3% German, 12.1% American, 4.0% English, 4.0% Irish, 3.0% Italian
Employment: 8.9% management, business, and financial, 8.9% computer, engineering, and science, 0.0% education, legal, community service, arts, and media, 4.4% healthcare practitioners, 24.4% service, 13.3% sales and office, 4.4% natural resources, construction, and maintenance, 35.6% production, transportation, and material moving
Income: Per capita: $18,197; Median household: $36,250; Average household: $44,829; Households with income of $100,000 or more: 13.2%; Poverty rate: 25.8%
Educational Attainment: High school diploma or higher: 84.1%; Bachelor's degree or higher: 2.9%; Graduate/professional degree or higher: n/a
Housing: Homeownership rate: 86.8%; Median home value: $82,500; Median year structure built: Before 1940; Homeowner vacancy rate: 0.0%; Median selected monthly owner costs: $675 with a mortgage, $263 without a mortgage; Median gross rent: n/a per month; Rental vacancy rate: 0.0%
Health Insurance: 79.8% have insurance; 55.6% have private insurance; 29.3% have public insurance; 20.2% do not have insurance; 7.7% of children under 18 do not have insurance
Transportation: Commute: 87.8% car, 0.0% public transportation, 12.2% walk, 0.0% work from home; Mean travel time to work: 22.9 minutes

BROOKLYN (town). Covers a land area of 0.669 square miles and a water area of 0.013 square miles. Located at 39.54° N. Lat; 86.37° W. Long. Elevation is 669 feet.
History: A supply of clay near Brooklyn provided the material for the manufacture of drain tile and brick. A brief gold rush took place in the early 1900's at Gold Creek, near Brooklyn.
Population: 1,447; Growth (since 2000): -6.3%; Density: 2,161.9 persons per square mile; Race: 97.0% White, 0.5% Black/African American, 1.7% Asian, 0.0% American Indian/Alaska Native, 0.0% Native Hawaiian/Other Pacific Islander, 0.6% Two or more races, 0.7% Hispanic of any race; Average household size: 2.47; Median age: 38.2; Age under 18: 22.7%; Age 65 and over: 12.0%; Males per 100 females: 101.8; Marriage status: 25.7% never married, 57.6% now married, 1.1% separated, 4.9% widowed, 11.9% divorced; Foreign born: 0.8%; Speak English only: 98.3%; With disability: 17.9%; Veterans: 9.8%; Ancestry: 19.6% German, 18.2% American, 10.6% Irish, 6.9% English, 2.9% French
Employment: 7.2% management, business, and financial, 8.0% computer, engineering, and science, 4.7% education, legal, community service, arts, and media, 9.4% healthcare practitioners, 10.3% service, 20.2% sales and office, 18.7% natural resources, construction, and maintenance, 21.5% production, transportation, and material moving
Income: Per capita: $26,985; Median household: $52,917; Average household: $66,109; Households with income of $100,000 or more: 16.1%; Poverty rate: 6.8%
Educational Attainment: High school diploma or higher: 89.1%; Bachelor's degree or higher: 13.1%; Graduate/professional degree or higher: 4.0%

School District(s)

M S D Martinsville Schools (PK-12)
Enrollment: 4,856 . . . . (765) 342-6641
Housing: Homeownership rate: 77.8%; Median home value: $124,500; Median year structure built: 1985; Homeowner vacancy rate: 2.1%; Median selected monthly owner costs: $1,029 with a mortgage, $336 without a mortgage; Median gross rent: $889 per month; Rental vacancy rate: 0.0%
Health Insurance: 89.3% have insurance; 77.8% have private insurance; 22.1% have public insurance; 10.7% do not have insurance; 4.4% of children under 18 do not have insurance
Transportation: Commute: 97.2% car, 0.0% public transportation, 0.3% walk, 0.9% work from home; Mean travel time to work: 27.6 minutes

CAMBY (unincorporated postal area)
ZCTA: 46113
Covers a land area of 16.398 square miles and a water area of 0.108 square miles. Located at 39.64° N. Lat; 86.30° W. Long..
Population: 15,663; Growth (since 2000): 135.0%; Density: 955.2 persons per square mile; Race: 89.4% White, 6.6% Black/African American, 0.3% Asian, 0.0% American Indian/Alaska Native, 0.0% Native Hawaiian/Other Pacific Islander, 1.7% Two or more races, 3.5% Hispanic of any race; Average household size: 2.82; Median age: 35.9; Age under 18: 25.7%; Age 65 and over: 9.7%; Males per 100 females: 99.4; Marriage status: 27.3% never married, 57.1% now married, 0.8% separated, 4.4% widowed, 11.2% divorced; Foreign born: 3.5%; Speak English only: 97.7%; With disability: 12.3%; Veterans: 10.5%; Ancestry: 18.5% German, 14.3% American, 10.5% English, 9.6% Irish, 2.8% Dutch
Employment: 10.0% management, business, and financial, 4.3% computer, engineering, and science, 5.8% education, legal, community service, arts, and media, 7.2% healthcare practitioners, 14.6% service, 30.6% sales and office, 11.1% natural resources, construction, and maintenance, 16.5% production, transportation, and material moving
Income: Per capita: $27,075; Median household: $69,964; Average household: $74,660; Households with income of $100,000 or more: 21.4%; Poverty rate: 8.3%
Educational Attainment: High school diploma or higher: 92.1%; Bachelor's degree or higher: 17.4%; Graduate/professional degree or higher: 4.2%

School District(s)

Mooresville Con School Corp (PK-12)
Enrollment: 4,133 . . . . (317) 831-0950
Housing: Homeownership rate: 80.0%; Median home value: $140,300; Median year structure built: 2001; Homeowner vacancy rate: 1.2%; Median selected monthly owner costs: $1,175 with a mortgage, $411 without a mortgage; Median gross rent: $1,020 per month; Rental vacancy rate: 9.5%
Health Insurance: 91.4% have insurance; 79.7% have private insurance; 22.7% have public insurance; 8.6% do not have insurance; 6.3% of children under 18 do not have insurance
Transportation: Commute: 95.0% car, 0.3% public transportation, 0.3% walk, 3.5% work from home; Mean travel time to work: 23.6 minutes

EMINENCE (unincorporated postal area)
ZCTA: 46125
Covers a land area of 0.034 square miles and a water area of 0 square miles. Located at 39.52° N. Lat; 86.64° W. Long. Elevation is 791 feet.
Population: 40; Growth (since 2000): -28.6%; Density: 1,176.5 persons per square mile; Race: 100.0% White, 0.0% Black/African American, 0.0% Asian, 0.0% American Indian/Alaska Native, 0.0% Native Hawaiian/Other Pacific Islander, 0.0% Two or more races, 0.0% Hispanic of any race; Average household size: 1.82; Median age: 58.7; Age under 18: 0.0%; Age 65 and over: 0.0%; Males per 100 females: 121.7; Marriage status: 15.0% never married, 85.0% now married, 0.0% separated, 0.0% widowed, 0.0% divorced; Foreign born: 0.0%; Speak English only: 100.0%; With disability: 15.0%; Veterans: 15.0%; Ancestry: 55.0% German, 45.0% Irish, 40.0% Scotch-Irish, 15.0% Austrian
Employment: 40.0% management, business, and financial, 0.0% computer, engineering, and science, 0.0% education, legal, community service, arts, and media, 0.0% healthcare practitioners, 0.0% service,

0.0% sales and office, 60.0% natural resources, construction, and maintenance, 0.0% production, transportation, and material moving
Income: Per capita: $37,073; Median household: n/a; Average household: n/a; Households with income of $100,000 or more: n/a; Poverty rate: n/a
Educational Attainment: High school diploma or higher: 100.0%; Bachelor's degree or higher: 40.0%; Graduate/professional degree or higher: n/a

School District(s)

Eminence Community School Corp (PK-12)
Enrollment: 412 . . . . (765) 528-2101
Housing: Homeownership rate: 72.7%; Median home value: n/a; Median year structure built: n/a; Homeowner vacancy rate: 0.0%; Median selected monthly owner costs: $0 with a mortgage, $0 without a mortgage; Median gross rent: n/a per month; Rental vacancy rate: 0.0%
Health Insurance: 100.0% have insurance; 85.0% have private insurance; 15.0% have public insurance; 0.0% do not have insurance; 0.0% of children under 18 do not have insurance
Transportation: Commute: 100.0% car, 0.0% public transportation, 0.0% walk, 0.0% work from home; Mean travel time to work: 0.0 minutes

MARTINSVILLE (city). County seat. Covers a land area of 4.490 square miles and a water area of 0.018 square miles. Located at 39.42° N. Lat; 86.42° W. Long. Elevation is 604 feet.
History: Named for John Martin, a member of the board of commissioners who made this city the county seat. Prospectors drilling for gas in Martinsville discovered artesian wells of therapeutic waters, giving the town the nickname of Artesian City.
Population: 11,647; Growth (since 2000): -0.4%; Density: 2,594.2 persons per square mile; Race: 95.3% White, 1.6% Black/African American, 0.2% Asian, 0.2% American Indian/Alaska Native, 0.0% Native Hawaiian/Other Pacific Islander, 2.0% Two or more races, 1.4% Hispanic of any race; Average household size: 2.50; Median age: 39.9; Age under 18: 21.3%; Age 65 and over: 16.0%; Males per 100 females: 94.4; Marriage status: 28.0% never married, 43.4% now married, 3.7% separated, 8.1% widowed, 20.5% divorced; Foreign born: 1.4%; Speak English only: 98.1%; With disability: 22.3%; Veterans: 10.7%; Ancestry: 20.6% German, 12.7% English, 11.1% American, 11.0% Irish, 3.8% French
Employment: 8.5% management, business, and financial, 1.8% computer, engineering, and science, 5.6% education, legal, community service, arts, and media, 2.9% healthcare practitioners, 20.6% service, 24.7% sales and office, 14.2% natural resources, construction, and maintenance, 21.6% production, transportation, and material moving
Income: Per capita: $20,753; Median household: $42,092; Average household: $51,695; Households with income of $100,000 or more: 11.3%; Poverty rate: 21.6%
Educational Attainment: High school diploma or higher: 82.3%; Bachelor's degree or higher: 11.2%; Graduate/professional degree or higher: 3.4%

School District(s)

M S D Martinsville Schools (PK-12)
Enrollment: 4,856 . . . . (765) 342-6641
Mooresville Con School Corp (PK-12)
Enrollment: 4,133 . . . . (317) 831-0950
Housing: Homeownership rate: 52.9%; Median home value: $96,300; Median year structure built: 1958; Homeowner vacancy rate: 0.0%; Median selected monthly owner costs: $973 with a mortgage, $374 without a mortgage; Median gross rent: $689 per month; Rental vacancy rate: 9.9%
Health Insurance: 87.4% have insurance; 55.2% have private insurance; 43.8% have public insurance; 12.6% do not have insurance; 8.0% of children under 18 do not have insurance
Hospitals: Indiana University Health Morgan Hospital (106 beds)
Newspapers: Reporter-Times (daily circulation 5,500)
Transportation: Commute: 90.6% car, 0.0% public transportation, 3.7% walk, 5.1% work from home; Mean travel time to work: 25.7 minutes
Additional Information Contacts
City of Martinsville . . . . (765) 342-2861
http://www.martinsville.in.gov

MONROVIA (town). Covers a land area of 1.772 square miles and a water area of <.001 square miles. Located at 39.58° N. Lat; 86.48° W. Long. Elevation is 804 feet.
History: Laid out 1834.
Population: 1,652; Growth (since 2000): 163.1%; Density: 932.4 persons per square mile; Race: 95.3% White, 1.2% Black/African American, 2.1% Asian, 0.0% American Indian/Alaska Native, 0.0% Native Hawaiian/Other Pacific Islander, 0.3% Two or more races, 2.1% Hispanic of any race; Average household size: 3.17; Median age: 28.1; Age under 18: 36.7%; Age 65 and over: 5.2%; Males per 100 females: 97.2; Marriage status: 26.6% never married, 58.4% now married, 1.5% separated, 2.1% widowed, 12.9% divorced; Foreign born: 1.6%; Speak English only: 96.1%; With disability: 10.4%; Veterans: 10.1%; Ancestry: 18.9% American, 17.6% German, 12.6% English, 10.7% Irish, 5.7% European
Employment: 12.5% management, business, and financial, 5.7% computer, engineering, and science, 2.5% education, legal, community service, arts, and media, 3.7% healthcare practitioners, 13.3% service, 28.0% sales and office, 14.1% natural resources, construction, and maintenance, 20.1% production, transportation, and material moving
Income: Per capita: $26,077; Median household: $67,443; Average household: $80,488; Households with income of $100,000 or more: 20.2%; Poverty rate: 9.0%
Educational Attainment: High school diploma or higher: 91.3%; Bachelor's degree or higher: 13.4%; Graduate/professional degree or higher: 3.7%

School District(s)

Monroe-Gregg School District (PK-12)
Enrollment: 1,435 . . . . (317) 996-3720
Housing: Homeownership rate: 85.6%; Median home value: $137,000; Median year structure built: 2001; Homeowner vacancy rate: 0.0%; Median selected monthly owner costs: $1,125 with a mortgage, $381 without a mortgage; Median gross rent: $940 per month; Rental vacancy rate: 0.0%
Health Insurance: 95.8% have insurance; 80.3% have private insurance; 23.7% have public insurance; 4.2% do not have insurance; 2.7% of children under 18 do not have insurance
Transportation: Commute: 90.7% car, 0.0% public transportation, 1.5% walk, 7.0% work from home; Mean travel time to work: 28.5 minutes

MOORESVILLE (town). Covers a land area of 6.285 square miles and a water area of 0.057 square miles. Located at 39.60° N. Lat; 86.37° W. Long. Elevation is 718 feet.
History: Laid out 1824.
Population: 9,571; Growth (since 2000): 3.2%; Density: 1,522.8 persons per square mile; Race: 99.5% White, 0.0% Black/African American, 0.0% Asian, 0.0% American Indian/Alaska Native, 0.0% Native Hawaiian/Other Pacific Islander, 0.5% Two or more races, 2.0% Hispanic of any race; Average household size: 2.45; Median age: 43.9; Age under 18: 20.5%; Age 65 and over: 18.6%; Males per 100 females: 89.1; Marriage status: 26.1% never married, 49.3% now married, 1.1% separated, 9.8% widowed, 14.9% divorced; Foreign born: 0.2%; Speak English only: 99.3%; With disability: 17.8%; Veterans: 10.9%; Ancestry: 19.7% German, 16.7% American, 13.5% Irish, 12.0% English, 3.1% European
Employment: 8.7% management, business, and financial, 1.6% computer, engineering, and science, 8.3% education, legal, community service, arts, and media, 2.5% healthcare practitioners, 17.2% service, 27.7% sales and office, 12.0% natural resources, construction, and maintenance, 22.0% production, transportation, and material moving
Income: Per capita: $24,105; Median household: $52,513; Average household: $58,076; Households with income of $100,000 or more: 14.1%; Poverty rate: 14.1%
Educational Attainment: High school diploma or higher: 86.1%; Bachelor's degree or higher: 11.4%; Graduate/professional degree or higher: 3.1%

School District(s)

Mooresville Con School Corp (PK-12)
Enrollment: 4,133 . . . . (317) 831-0950
Housing: Homeownership rate: 66.9%; Median home value: $123,700; Median year structure built: 1977; Homeowner vacancy rate: 0.0%; Median selected monthly owner costs: $1,005 with a mortgage, $317 without a mortgage; Median gross rent: $770 per month; Rental vacancy rate: 5.4%
Health Insurance: 92.4% have insurance; 68.7% have private insurance; 37.4% have public insurance; 7.6% do not have insurance; 5.3% of children under 18 do not have insurance
Hospitals: Franciscan Saint Francis Health - Mooresville (64 beds)
Safety: Violent crime rate: 7.2 per 10,000 population; Property crime rate: 288.4 per 10,000 population
Transportation: Commute: 93.7% car, 0.0% public transportation, 2.1% walk, 2.3% work from home; Mean travel time to work: 21.5 minutes
Additional Information Contacts
Town of Mooresville . . . . (317) 831-1608
http://www.mooresville.org

MORGANTOWN (town). Covers a land area of 0.378 square miles and a water area of 0 square miles. Located at 39.37° N. Lat; 86.26° W. Long. Elevation is 679 feet.
History: Laid out 1831.
Population: 954; Growth (since 2000): -1.0%; Density: 2,525.1 persons per square mile; Race: 95.8% White, 1.2% Black/African American, 0.0% Asian, 0.0% American Indian/Alaska Native, 0.0% Native Hawaiian/Other Pacific Islander, 2.1% Two or more races, 0.9% Hispanic of any race; Average household size: 2.69; Median age: 38.3; Age under 18: 26.6%; Age 65 and over: 18.2%; Males per 100 females: 90.7; Marriage status: 26.1% never married, 43.8% now married, 2.0% separated, 9.8% widowed, 20.3% divorced; Foreign born: 0.5%; Speak English only: 99.0%; With disability: 20.2%; Veterans: 7.6%; Ancestry: 17.4% German, 15.5% English, 12.3% Irish, 8.5% American, 5.3% Italian
Employment: 7.8% management, business, and financial, 1.6% computer, engineering, and science, 5.1% education, legal, community service, arts, and media, 3.8% healthcare practitioners, 15.1% service, 22.3% sales and office, 24.7% natural resources, construction, and maintenance, 19.6% production, transportation, and material moving
Income: Per capita: $19,389; Median household: $37,407; Average household: $50,396; Households with income of $100,000 or more: 7.1%; Poverty rate: 21.2%
Educational Attainment: High school diploma or higher: 85.2%; Bachelor's degree or higher: 6.9%; Graduate/professional degree or higher: 3.2%

School District(s)

Brown County School Corporation (PK-12)
Enrollment: 2,107 . . . . (812) 988-6601
Housing: Homeownership rate: 54.1%; Median home value: $87,300; Median year structure built: 1960; Homeowner vacancy rate: 8.5%; Median selected monthly owner costs: $970 with a mortgage, $294 without a mortgage; Median gross rent: $802 per month; Rental vacancy rate: 6.6%
Health Insurance: 86.5% have insurance; 59.7% have private insurance; 41.5% have public insurance; 13.5% do not have insurance; 3.0% of children under 18 do not have insurance
Transportation: Commute: 98.9% car, 0.0% public transportation, 0.5% walk, 0.5% work from home; Mean travel time to work: 29.8 minutes

PAINTED HILLS (CDP). Covers a land area of 1.730 square miles and a water area of 0.222 square miles. Located at 39.40° N. Lat; 86.35° W. Long. Elevation is 722 feet.
Population: 607; Growth (since 2000): n/a; Density: 351.0 persons per square mile; Race: 100.0% White, 0.0% Black/African American, 0.0% Asian, 0.0% American Indian/Alaska Native, 0.0% Native Hawaiian/Other Pacific Islander, 0.0% Two or more races, 0.0% Hispanic of any race; Average household size: 2.70; Median age: 39.9; Age under 18: 28.7%; Age 65 and over: 27.3%; Males per 100 females: 96.2; Marriage status: 16.0% never married, 39.5% now married, 0.0% separated, 5.9% widowed, 38.6% divorced; Foreign born: 0.0%; Speak English only: 100.0%; With disability: 14.8%; Veterans: 10.6%; Ancestry: 8.7% American, 6.9% Irish, 4.0% English, 2.8% Finnish, 2.5% Austrian
Employment: 17.0% management, business, and financial, 0.0% computer, engineering, and science, 11.2% education, legal, community service, arts, and media, 4.9% healthcare practitioners, 0.0% service, 52.0% sales and office, 2.4% natural resources, construction, and maintenance, 12.5% production, transportation, and material moving
Income: Per capita: $20,079; Median household: $47,917; Average household: $53,001; Households with income of $100,000 or more: 5.8%; Poverty rate: 9.0%
Educational Attainment: High school diploma or higher: 100.0%; Bachelor's degree or higher: 14.7%; Graduate/professional degree or higher: 3.9%
Housing: Homeownership rate: 94.7%; Median home value: $227,300; Median year structure built: 1979; Homeowner vacancy rate: 0.0%; Median selected monthly owner costs: $1,540 with a mortgage, $621 without a mortgage; Median gross rent: n/a per month; Rental vacancy rate: 0.0%
Health Insurance: 95.4% have insurance; 91.6% have private insurance; 27.3% have public insurance; 4.6% do not have insurance; 0.0% of children under 18 do not have insurance
Transportation: Commute: 100.0% car, 0.0% public transportation, 0.0% walk, 0.0% work from home; Mean travel time to work: 33.0 minutes

PARAGON (town). Covers a land area of 0.344 square miles and a water area of <.001 square miles. Located at 39.39° N. Lat; 86.56° W. Long. Elevation is 581 feet.
Population: 605; Growth (since 2000): -8.7%; Density: 1,760.8 persons per square mile; Race: 95.7% White, 0.0% Black/African American, 0.0% Asian, 0.0% American Indian/Alaska Native, 0.0% Native Hawaiian/Other Pacific Islander, 4.3% Two or more races, 0.0% Hispanic of any race; Average household size: 2.80; Median age: 38.5; Age under 18: 23.0%; Age 65 and over: 8.4%; Males per 100 females: 93.8; Marriage status: 22.6% never married, 55.9% now married, 3.3% separated, 5.0% widowed, 16.6% divorced; Foreign born: 0.0%; Speak English only: 100.0%; With disability: 21.2%; Veterans: 6.0%; Ancestry: 23.0% German, 15.9% Irish, 12.7% American, 11.4% English, 1.3% Dutch
Employment: 5.2% management, business, and financial, 2.4% computer, engineering, and science, 3.5% education, legal, community service, arts, and media, 2.1% healthcare practitioners, 6.9% service, 25.3% sales and office, 25.3% natural resources, construction, and maintenance, 29.2% production, transportation, and material moving
Income: Per capita: $17,715; Median household: $46,250; Average household: $48,931; Households with income of $100,000 or more: 4.2%; Poverty rate: 29.2%
Educational Attainment: High school diploma or higher: 76.4%; Bachelor's degree or higher: 3.1%; Graduate/professional degree or higher: n/a

School District(s)

M S D Martinsville Schools (PK-12)
Enrollment: 4,856 . . . . (765) 342-6641
Housing: Homeownership rate: 63.0%; Median home value: $74,100; Median year structure built: 1966; Homeowner vacancy rate: 6.8%; Median selected monthly owner costs: $857 with a mortgage, $425 without a mortgage; Median gross rent: $742 per month; Rental vacancy rate: 0.0%
Health Insurance: 79.7% have insurance; 45.6% have private insurance; 39.3% have public insurance; 20.3% do not have insurance; 13.7% of children under 18 do not have insurance
Transportation: Commute: 96.4% car, 0.0% public transportation, 3.6% walk, 0.0% work from home; Mean travel time to work: 28.2 minutes

Newton County

Located in northwestern Indiana; bounded on the west by Illinois, and on the north by the Kankakee River; also drained by the Iroquois River. Covers a land area of 401.759 square miles, a water area of 1.679 square miles, and is located in the Central Time Zone at 40.96° N. Lat., 87.40° W. Long. The county was founded in 1857. County seat is Kentland.

Newton County is part of the Chicago-Naperville-Elgin, IL-IN-WI Metropolitan Statistical Area. The entire metro area includes: Chicago-Naperville-Arlington Heights, IL Metropolitan Division (Cook County, IL; DuPage County, IL; Grundy County, IL; Kendall County, IL; McHenry County, IL; Will County, IL); Elgin, IL Metropolitan Division (DeKalb County, IL; Kane County, IL); Gary, IN Metropolitan Division (Jasper County, IN; Lake County, IN; Newton County, IN; Porter County, IN); Lake County-Kenosha County, IL-WI Metropolitan Division (Lake County, IL; Kenosha County, WI)

Population: 14,056; Growth (since 2000): -3.5%; Density: 35.0 persons per square mile; Race: 95.6% White, 0.1% Black/African American, 0.6% Asian, 0.1% American Indian/Alaska Native, 0.0% Native Hawaiian/Other Pacific Islander, 1.8% two or more races, 6.1% Hispanic of any race; Average household size: 2.50; Median age: 42.5; Age under 18: 21.9%; Age 65 and over: 17.6%; Males per 100 females: 102.0; Marriage status: 24.2% never married, 56.4% now married, 1.3% separated, 7.3% widowed, 12.1% divorced; Foreign born: 3.6%; Speak English only: 95.5%; With disability: 15.2%; Veterans: 8.7%; Ancestry: 24.2% German, 14.9% Irish, 8.7% American, 8.4% Polish, 7.4% English
Religion: Six largest groups: 14.0% Catholicism, 9.1% Baptist, 5.8% Methodist/Pietist, 4.8% Presbyterian-Reformed, 1.1% Non-denominational Protestant, 0.7% Pentecostal
Economy: Unemployment rate: 4.0%; Leading industries: 15.6 % retail trade; 13.5 % construction; 11.9 % accommodation and food services; Farms: 348 totaling 192,030 acres; Company size: 0 employ 1,000 or more persons, 0 employ 500 to 999 persons, 3 employ 100 to 499 persons, 241 employs less than 100 persons; Business ownership: 380 women-owned, n/a Black-owned, n/a Hispanic-owned, n/a Asian-owned, n/a American Indian/Alaska Native-owned

Employment: 8.1% management, business, and financial, 1.8% computer, engineering, and science, 3.6% education, legal, community service, arts, and media, 3.4% healthcare practitioners, 15.6% service, 23.5% sales and office, 20.5% natural resources, construction, and maintenance, 23.5% production, transportation, and material moving
Income: Per capita: $24,315; Median household: $52,193; Average household: $60,390; Households with income of $100,000 or more: 14.6%; Poverty rate: 14.0%
Educational Attainment: High school diploma or higher: 86.1%; Bachelor's degree or higher: 11.0%; Graduate/professional degree or higher: 3.4%
Housing: Homeownership rate: 75.0%; Median home value: $112,500; Median year structure built: 1969; Homeowner vacancy rate: 2.0%; Median selected monthly owner costs: $998 with a mortgage, $413 without a mortgage; Median gross rent: $715 per month; Rental vacancy rate: 4.1%
Vital Statistics: Birth rate: 118.2 per 10,000 population; Death rate: 95.5 per 10,000 population; Age-adjusted cancer mortality rate: 166.5 deaths per 100,000 population
Health Insurance: 87.4% have insurance; 68.0% have private insurance; 33.8% have public insurance; 12.6% do not have insurance; 10.3% of children under 18 do not have insurance
Health Care: Physicians: 3.6 per 10,000 population; Dentists: 1.4 per 10,000 population; Hospital beds: 0.0 per 10,000 population; Hospital admissions: 0.0 per 10,000 population
Transportation: Commute: 93.3% car, 0.4% public transportation, 1.3% walk, 1.1% work from home; Mean travel time to work: 31.2 minutes
2016 Presidential Election: 70.4% Trump, 24.2% Clinton, 5.4% Johnson, 0.0% Stein
National and State Parks: Kankakee River State Park; Willow Slough State Game Preserve
Additional Information Contacts
Newton Government . . . . (219) 474-6081
http://www.newtoncountyin.com

Newton County Communities

BROOK (town). Covers a land area of 0.663 square miles and a water area of 0.009 square miles. Located at 40.87° N. Lat; 87.37° W. Long. Elevation is 653 feet.
History: An early industry in Brook was the Hess Manufacturing Company, whose cosmetics line started when a local druggist concocted witch hazel lotion in a copper clothes boiler.
Population: 1,052; Growth (since 2000): -0.9%; Density: 1,587.4 persons per square mile; Race: 90.9% White, 0.5% Black/African American, 0.0% Asian, 1.0% American Indian/Alaska Native, 0.0% Native Hawaiian/Other Pacific Islander, 3.2% Two or more races, 19.0% Hispanic of any race; Average household size: 2.67; Median age: 36.0; Age under 18: 25.0%; Age 65 and over: 12.6%; Males per 100 females: 94.0; Marriage status: 30.0% never married, 49.7% now married, 1.2% separated, 6.7% widowed, 13.6% divorced; Foreign born: 10.2%; Speak English only: 83.1%; With disability: 17.4%; Veterans: 8.5%; Ancestry: 18.1% German, 13.8% Irish, 6.8% American, 5.2% English, 3.3% Italian
Employment: 8.6% management, business, and financial, 0.4% computer, engineering, and science, 4.8% education, legal, community service, arts, and media, 7.5% healthcare practitioners, 14.1% service, 17.1% sales and office, 17.8% natural resources, construction, and maintenance, 29.7% production, transportation, and material moving
Income: Per capita: $19,399; Median household: $42,500; Average household: $49,878; Households with income of $100,000 or more: 10.7%; Poverty rate: 25.1%
Educational Attainment: High school diploma or higher: 77.5%; Bachelor's degree or higher: 7.0%; Graduate/professional degree or higher: 1.4%
Housing: Homeownership rate: 69.3%; Median home value: $74,700; Median year structure built: 1945; Homeowner vacancy rate: 7.1%; Median selected monthly owner costs: $794 with a mortgage, $353 without a mortgage; Median gross rent: $658 per month; Rental vacancy rate: 9.5%
Health Insurance: 88.9% have insurance; 59.9% have private insurance; 42.4% have public insurance; 11.1% do not have insurance; 5.0% of children under 18 do not have insurance
Transportation: Commute: 98.7% car, 0.4% public transportation, 0.4% walk, 0.0% work from home; Mean travel time to work: 20.3 minutes

GOODLAND (town). Covers a land area of 0.782 square miles and a water area of 0 square miles. Located at 40.76° N. Lat; 87.30° W. Long. Elevation is 725 feet.
Population: 990; Growth (since 2000): -9.7%; Density: 1,265.3 persons per square mile; Race: 96.6% White, 0.0% Black/African American, 0.0% Asian, 0.0% American Indian/Alaska Native, 0.0% Native Hawaiian/Other Pacific Islander, 3.4% Two or more races, 0.7% Hispanic of any race; Average household size: 2.36; Median age: 45.3; Age under 18: 21.2%; Age 65 and over: 16.0%; Males per 100 females: 101.0; Marriage status: 25.6% never married, 48.4% now married, 3.4% separated, 9.0% widowed, 17.0% divorced; Foreign born: 0.6%; Speak English only: 99.4%; With disability: 20.8%; Veterans: 10.9%; Ancestry: 23.1% German, 16.0% English, 15.4% Irish, 10.9% American, 6.0% Dutch
Employment: 11.0% management, business, and financial, 1.8% computer, engineering, and science, 11.0% education, legal, community service, arts, and media, 1.1% healthcare practitioners, 9.6% service, 20.4% sales and office, 9.6% natural resources, construction, and maintenance, 35.4% production, transportation, and material moving
Income: Per capita: $19,922; Median household: $38,929; Average household: $46,290; Households with income of $100,000 or more: 8.6%; Poverty rate: 18.7%
Educational Attainment: High school diploma or higher: 85.8%; Bachelor's degree or higher: 14.3%; Graduate/professional degree or higher: 2.7%
Housing: Homeownership rate: 65.5%; Median home value: $77,900; Median year structure built: Before 1940; Homeowner vacancy rate: 0.0%; Median selected monthly owner costs: $815 with a mortgage, $349 without a mortgage; Median gross rent: $547 per month; Rental vacancy rate: 0.0%
Health Insurance: 87.0% have insurance; 57.3% have private insurance; 43.6% have public insurance; 13.0% do not have insurance; 4.2% of children under 18 do not have insurance
Transportation: Commute: 93.5% car, 0.0% public transportation, 4.9% walk, 0.9% work from home; Mean travel time to work: 21.9 minutes

KENTLAND (town). County seat. Covers a land area of 1.530 square miles and a water area of 0 square miles. Located at 40.77° N. Lat; 87.45° W. Long. Elevation is 682 feet.
History: Kentland was the birthplace in 1866 of George Ade, Hoosier author, humorist, and playwright. An early industry here was the Whole Milk Cheese Factory.
Population: 1,911; Growth (since 2000): 4.9%; Density: 1,249.0 persons per square mile; Race: 92.7% White, 0.6% Black/African American, 0.6% Asian, 0.0% American Indian/Alaska Native, 0.0% Native Hawaiian/Other Pacific Islander, 3.6% Two or more races, 9.9% Hispanic of any race; Average household size: 2.46; Median age: 35.8; Age under 18: 24.6%; Age 65 and over: 15.0%; Males per 100 females: 96.2; Marriage status: 30.7% never married, 44.5% now married, 1.4% separated, 7.3% widowed, 17.5% divorced; Foreign born: 4.0%; Speak English only: 92.1%; With disability: 16.7%; Veterans: 11.9%; Ancestry: 26.9% German, 16.0% Irish, 6.9% English, 6.8% Italian, 6.4% American
Employment: 11.2% management, business, and financial, 2.1% computer, engineering, and science, 3.4% education, legal, community service, arts, and media, 1.4% healthcare practitioners, 14.7% service, 23.6% sales and office, 14.7% natural resources, construction, and maintenance, 28.9% production, transportation, and material moving
Income: Per capita: $21,401; Median household: $44,083; Average household: $52,368; Households with income of $100,000 or more: 9.3%; Poverty rate: 23.2%
Educational Attainment: High school diploma or higher: 85.1%; Bachelor's degree or higher: 10.9%; Graduate/professional degree or higher: 3.4%

School District(s)
South Newton School Corp (PK-12)
Enrollment: 856 . . . . (219) 474-5184
Housing: Homeownership rate: 57.6%; Median home value: $83,800; Median year structure built: 1954; Homeowner vacancy rate: 1.8%; Median selected monthly owner costs: $928 with a mortgage, $340 without a mortgage; Median gross rent: $756 per month; Rental vacancy rate: 9.7%
Health Insurance: 81.5% have insurance; 55.4% have private insurance; 37.4% have public insurance; 18.5% do not have insurance; 22.2% of children under 18 do not have insurance
Newspapers: Community Media Group (weekly circulation 4,000)
Transportation: Commute: 92.4% car, 0.0% public transportation, 3.1% walk, 0.0% work from home; Mean travel time to work: 24.8 minutes

LAKE VILLAGE (CDP). Covers a land area of 3.944 square miles and a water area of 0 square miles. Located at 41.13° N. Lat; 87.44° W. Long. Elevation is 659 feet.
History: Lake Village was located on land that had been reclaimed from a swamp. It grew as the center of a farming and goat-raising area.
Population: 750; Growth (since 2000): -12.3%; Density: 190.2 persons per square mile; Race: 100.0% White, 0.0% Black/African American, 0.0% Asian, 0.0% American Indian/Alaska Native, 0.0% Native Hawaiian/Other Pacific Islander, 0.0% Two or more races, 3.9% Hispanic of any race; Average household size: 3.10; Median age: 47.4; Age under 18: 30.1%; Age 65 and over: 11.9%; Males per 100 females: 95.2; Marriage status: 35.5% never married, 37.7% now married, 0.0% separated, 6.0% widowed, 20.8% divorced; Foreign born: 1.3%; Speak English only: 100.0%; With disability: 18.0%; Veterans: 11.6%; Ancestry: 43.3% German, 10.8% American, 6.9% Irish, 5.9% Polish, 4.8% Hungarian
Employment: 8.5% management, business, and financial, 0.0% computer, engineering, and science, 2.9% education, legal, community service, arts, and media, 0.0% healthcare practitioners, 16.0% service, 20.2% sales and office, 46.3% natural resources, construction, and maintenance, 6.2% production, transportation, and material moving
Income: Per capita: $18,306; Median household: $42,619; Average household: $53,790; Households with income of $100,000 or more: 13.6%; Poverty rate: 42.8%
Educational Attainment: High school diploma or higher: 85.9%; Bachelor's degree or higher: 10.9%; Graduate/professional degree or higher: 3.8%

School District(s)

North Newton School Corp (PK-12)
Enrollment: 1,439 . . . . (219) 285-2228
Housing: Homeownership rate: 68.6%; Median home value: $124,200; Median year structure built: 1972; Homeowner vacancy rate: 0.0%; Median selected monthly owner costs: $997 with a mortgage, $441 without a mortgage; Median gross rent: n/a per month; Rental vacancy rate: 0.0%
Health Insurance: 96.5% have insurance; 42.9% have private insurance; 61.6% have public insurance; 3.5% do not have insurance; 0.0% of children under 18 do not have insurance
Transportation: Commute: 97.1% car, 0.0% public transportation, 0.0% walk, 0.0% work from home; Mean travel time to work: 32.8 minutes

MOROCCO (town). Covers a land area of 1.133 square miles and a water area of 0 square miles. Located at 40.94° N. Lat; 87.45° W. Long. Elevation is 699 feet.
History: The area in which Morocco was sited was once known as Beaver Prairie for the abundance of beaver in the streams.
Population: 1,015; Growth (since 2000): -9.9%; Density: 896.1 persons per square mile; Race: 92.4% White, 0.0% Black/African American, 0.0% Asian, 1.0% American Indian/Alaska Native, 0.0% Native Hawaiian/Other Pacific Islander, 6.6% Two or more races, 4.0% Hispanic of any race; Average household size: 2.50; Median age: 40.7; Age under 18: 24.6%; Age 65 and over: 22.6%; Males per 100 females: 102.0; Marriage status: 26.1% never married, 51.5% now married, 1.6% separated, 11.9% widowed, 10.5% divorced; Foreign born: 1.6%; Speak English only: 96.0%; With disability: 20.3%; Veterans: 12.1%; Ancestry: 19.6% German, 19.2% Irish, 11.6% English, 8.4% American, 5.3% French
Employment: 8.8% management, business, and financial, 0.5% computer, engineering, and science, 3.3% education, legal, community service, arts, and media, 4.1% healthcare practitioners, 21.4% service, 26.0% sales and office, 7.7% natural resources, construction, and maintenance, 28.2% production, transportation, and material moving
Income: Per capita: $22,282; Median household: $45,372; Average household: $54,241; Households with income of $100,000 or more: 9.6%; Poverty rate: 11.2%
Educational Attainment: High school diploma or higher: 79.6%; Bachelor's degree or higher: 10.6%; Graduate/professional degree or higher: 4.5%

School District(s)

North Newton School Corp (PK-12)
Enrollment: 1,439 . . . . (219) 285-2228
Housing: Homeownership rate: 66.0%; Median home value: $80,300; Median year structure built: Before 1940; Homeowner vacancy rate: 1.1%; Median selected monthly owner costs: $885 with a mortgage, $414 without a mortgage; Median gross rent: $740 per month; Rental vacancy rate: 7.5%
Health Insurance: 87.9% have insurance; 57.2% have private insurance; 46.9% have public insurance; 12.1% do not have insurance; 14.9% of children under 18 do not have insurance
Transportation: Commute: 97.2% car, 0.0% public transportation, 0.8% walk, 0.8% work from home; Mean travel time to work: 36.6 minutes

MOUNT AYR (town). Covers a land area of 0.149 square miles and a water area of 0 square miles. Located at 40.95° N. Lat; 87.30° W. Long. Elevation is 709 feet.
Population: 120; Growth (since 2000): -18.4%; Density: 804.2 persons per square mile; Race: 100.0% White, 0.0% Black/African American, 0.0% Asian, 0.0% American Indian/Alaska Native, 0.0% Native Hawaiian/Other Pacific Islander, 0.0% Two or more races, 0.0% Hispanic of any race; Average household size: 2.14; Median age: 52.3; Age under 18: 16.7%; Age 65 and over: 15.0%; Males per 100 females: 114.0; Marriage status: 14.0% never married, 61.0% now married, 2.0% separated, 3.0% widowed, 22.0% divorced; Foreign born: 0.0%; Speak English only: 98.3%; With disability: 31.7%; Veterans: 13.0%; Ancestry: 21.7% German, 10.8% English, 9.2% Dutch, 5.0% American, 5.0% Italian
Employment: 1.9% management, business, and financial, 0.0% computer, engineering, and science, 0.0% education, legal, community service, arts, and media, 0.0% healthcare practitioners, 22.6% service, 20.8% sales and office, 7.5% natural resources, construction, and maintenance, 47.2% production, transportation, and material moving
Income: Per capita: $20,967; Median household: $36,250; Average household: $44,938; Households with income of $100,000 or more: 5.4%; Poverty rate: 4.3%
Educational Attainment: High school diploma or higher: 65.3%; Bachelor's degree or higher: 3.2%; Graduate/professional degree or higher: n/a
Housing: Homeownership rate: 80.4%; Median home value: $72,500; Median year structure built: Before 1940; Homeowner vacancy rate: 0.0%; Median selected monthly owner costs: $817 with a mortgage, $229 without a mortgage; Median gross rent: $438 per month; Rental vacancy rate: 0.0%
Health Insurance: 74.2% have insurance; 48.3% have private insurance; 37.5% have public insurance; 25.8% do not have insurance; 30.0% of children under 18 do not have insurance
Transportation: Commute: 100.0% car, 0.0% public transportation, 0.0% walk, 0.0% work from home; Mean travel time to work: 31.7 minutes

ROSELAWN (CDP). Covers a land area of 8.070 square miles and a water area of 0.012 square miles. Located at 41.16° N. Lat; 87.29° W. Long. Elevation is 682 feet.
Population: 4,594; Growth (since 2000): 16.8%; Density: 569.3 persons per square mile; Race: 96.0% White, 0.0% Black/African American, 0.0% Asian, 0.0% American Indian/Alaska Native, 0.0% Native Hawaiian/Other Pacific Islander, 0.7% Two or more races, 8.1% Hispanic of any race; Average household size: 2.98; Median age: 37.2; Age under 18: 26.8%; Age 65 and over: 12.5%; Males per 100 females: 102.9; Marriage status: 21.4% never married, 65.2% now married, 1.3% separated, 5.3% widowed, 8.1% divorced; Foreign born: 3.5%; Speak English only: 93.4%; With disability: 12.6%; Veterans: 5.0%; Ancestry: 23.9% German, 15.9% Irish, 11.9% Polish, 9.4% American, 4.9% Norwegian
Employment: 3.3% management, business, and financial, 1.5% computer, engineering, and science, 2.6% education, legal, community service, arts, and media, 2.6% healthcare practitioners, 15.3% service, 25.3% sales and office, 24.3% natural resources, construction, and maintenance, 25.0% production, transportation, and material moving
Income: Per capita: $21,925; Median household: $60,171; Average household: $64,349; Households with income of $100,000 or more: 16.7%; Poverty rate: 7.8%
Educational Attainment: High school diploma or higher: 84.9%; Bachelor's degree or higher: 5.9%; Graduate/professional degree or higher: 2.7%
Housing: Homeownership rate: 90.4%; Median home value: $119,100; Median year structure built: 1978; Homeowner vacancy rate: 3.7%; Median selected monthly owner costs: $979 with a mortgage, $422 without a mortgage; Median gross rent: $865 per month; Rental vacancy rate: 0.0%
Health Insurance: 88.5% have insurance; 79.3% have private insurance; 19.6% have public insurance; 11.5% do not have insurance; 8.9% of children under 18 do not have insurance
Transportation: Commute: 89.4% car, 0.0% public transportation, 1.0% walk, 1.2% work from home; Mean travel time to work: 34.5 minutes

SUMAVA RESORTS (unincorporated postal area)
ZCTA: 46379

Covers a land area of 0.463 square miles and a water area of 0 square miles. Located at 41.17° N. Lat; 87.44° W. Long. Elevation is 633 feet.
Population: 95; Growth (since 2000): -55.4%; Density: 205.2 persons per square mile; Race: 100.0% White, 0.0% Black/African American, 0.0% Asian, 0.0% American Indian/Alaska Native, 0.0% Native Hawaiian/Other Pacific Islander, 0.0% Two or more races, 21.1% Hispanic of any race; Average household size: 1.10; Median age: 57.5; Age under 18: 0.0%; Age 65 and over: 14.7%; Males per 100 females: 134.9; Marriage status: 66.3% never married, 18.9% now married, 0.0% separated, 14.7% widowed, 0.0% divorced; Foreign born: 0.0%; Speak English only: 100.0%; With disability: 24.2%; Veterans: 0.0%; Ancestry: 34.7% Irish, 30.5% Italian, 24.2% English, 10.5% American, 9.5% Dutch
Employment: 0.0% management, business, and financial, 0.0% computer, engineering, and science, 0.0% education, legal, community service, arts, and media, 27.8% healthcare practitioners, 0.0% service, 0.0% sales and office, 59.7% natural resources, construction, and maintenance, 12.5% production, transportation, and material moving
Income: Per capita: $49,999; Median household: n/a; Average household: $55,231; Households with income of $100,000 or more: n/a; Poverty rate: n/a
Educational Attainment: High school diploma or higher: 75.8%; Bachelor's degree or higher: n/a; Graduate/professional degree or higher: n/a
Housing: Homeownership rate: 100.0%; Median home value: $69,500; Median year structure built: 1946; Homeowner vacancy rate: 0.0%; Median selected monthly owner costs: $648 with a mortgage, $0 without a mortgage; Median gross rent: n/a per month; Rental vacancy rate: 0.0%
Health Insurance: 89.5% have insurance; 89.5% have private insurance; 14.7% have public insurance; 10.5% do not have insurance; 0.0% of children under 18 do not have insurance
Transportation: Commute: 100.0% car, 0.0% public transportation, 0.0% walk, 0.0% work from home; Mean travel time to work: 0.0 minutes

THAYER (unincorporated postal area)
ZCTA: 46381

Covers a land area of 0.909 square miles and a water area of 0 square miles. Located at 41.17° N. Lat; 87.32° W. Long. Elevation is 643 feet.
Population: 114; Growth (since 2000): -28.8%; Density: 125.4 persons per square mile; Race: 100.0% White, 0.0% Black/African American, 0.0% Asian, 0.0% American Indian/Alaska Native, 0.0% Native Hawaiian/Other Pacific Islander, 0.0% Two or more races, 0.0% Hispanic of any race; Average household size: 1.58; Median age: 58.8; Age under 18: 0.0%; Age 65 and over: 33.3%; Males per 100 females: 95.8; Marriage status: 24.6% never married, 45.6% now married, 0.0% separated, 10.5% widowed, 19.3% divorced; Foreign born: 0.0%; Speak English only: 100.0%; With disability: 47.4%; Veterans: 0.0%; Ancestry: 23.7% English, 22.8% German, 21.9% Dutch, 9.6% Eastern European
Employment: 17.1% management, business, and financial, 0.0% computer, engineering, and science, 14.5% education, legal, community service, arts, and media, 0.0% healthcare practitioners, 35.5% service, 0.0% sales and office, 15.8% natural resources, construction, and maintenance, 17.1% production, transportation, and material moving
Income: Per capita: $24,824; Median household: $33,750; Average household: $37,357; Households with income of $100,000 or more: n/a; Poverty rate: 11.4%
Educational Attainment: High school diploma or higher: 87.1%; Bachelor's degree or higher: n/a; Graduate/professional degree or higher: n/a
Housing: Homeownership rate: 66.7%; Median home value: $162,500; Median year structure built: 1991; Homeowner vacancy rate: 0.0%; Median selected monthly owner costs: $846 with a mortgage, $0 without a mortgage; Median gross rent: n/a per month; Rental vacancy rate: 0.0%
Health Insurance: 86.8% have insurance; 65.8% have private insurance; 44.7% have public insurance; 13.2% do not have insurance; 0.0% of children under 18 do not have insurance
Transportation: Commute: 80.3% car, 0.0% public transportation, 0.0% walk, 0.0% work from home; Mean travel time to work: 17.9 minutes

Noble County

Located in northeastern Indiana; drained by the Elkhart River; includes many small lakes. Covers a land area of 410.843 square miles, a water area of 6.590 square miles, and is located in the Eastern Time Zone at 41.40° N. Lat., 85.42° W. Long. The county was founded in 1835. County seat is Albion.

Noble County is part of the Kendallville, IN Micropolitan Statistical Area. The entire metro area includes: Noble County, IN

Population: 47,421; Growth (since 2000): 2.5%; Density: 115.4 persons per square mile; Race: 97.1% White, 0.4% Black/African American, 0.7% Asian, 0.0% American Indian/Alaska Native, 0.0% Native Hawaiian/Other Pacific Islander, 1.4% two or more races, 10.2% Hispanic of any race; Average household size: 2.56; Median age: 38.5; Age under 18: 25.5%; Age 65 and over: 14.4%; Males per 100 females: 100.1; Marriage status: 24.1% never married, 57.0% now married, 1.7% separated, 5.7% widowed, 13.2% divorced; Foreign born: 4.5%; Speak English only: 88.5%; With disability: 13.9%; Veterans: 8.1%; Ancestry: 24.8% German, 9.9% American, 9.2% Irish, 8.5% European, 8.0% English
Religion: Six largest groups: 6.1% Catholicism, 5.9% Lutheran, 5.7% Methodist/Pietist, 4.0% Non-denominational Protestant, 2.2% European Free-Church, 1.6% Holiness
Economy: Unemployment rate: 3.5%; Leading industries: 16.1 % retail trade; 13.8 % manufacturing; 13.4 % other services (except public administration); Farms: 1,163 totaling 181,491 acres; Company size: 0 employ 1,000 or more persons, 5 employ 500 to 999 persons, 24 employ 100 to 499 persons, 827 employ less than 100 persons; Business ownership: 1,074 women-owned, n/a Black-owned, 117 Hispanic-owned, 26 Asian-owned, n/a American Indian/Alaska Native-owned
Employment: 11.0% management, business, and financial, 2.7% computer, engineering, and science, 5.6% education, legal, community service, arts, and media, 4.6% healthcare practitioners, 14.0% service, 17.2% sales and office, 10.4% natural resources, construction, and maintenance, 34.4% production, transportation, and material moving
Income: Per capita: $25,260; Median household: $52,393; Average household: $64,787; Households with income of $100,000 or more: 15.7%; Poverty rate: 9.3%
Educational Attainment: High school diploma or higher: 85.0%; Bachelor's degree or higher: 14.0%; Graduate/professional degree or higher: 4.2%
Housing: Homeownership rate: 74.4%; Median home value: $114,500; Median year structure built: 1973; Homeowner vacancy rate: 2.2%; Median selected monthly owner costs: $967 with a mortgage, $354 without a mortgage; Median gross rent: $673 per month; Rental vacancy rate: 4.1%
Vital Statistics: Birth rate: 136.1 per 10,000 population; Death rate: 95.5 per 10,000 population; Age-adjusted cancer mortality rate: 178.8 deaths per 100,000 population
Health Insurance: 90.8% have insurance; 72.7% have private insurance; 29.4% have public insurance; 9.2% do not have insurance; 7.1% of children under 18 do not have insurance
Health Care: Physicians: 4.0 per 10,000 population; Dentists: 2.7 per 10,000 population; Hospital beds: 6.5 per 10,000 population; Hospital admissions: 380.3 per 10,000 population
Transportation: Commute: 94.4% car, 0.0% public transportation, 1.9% walk, 2.4% work from home; Mean travel time to work: 21.9 minutes
2016 Presidential Election: 71.3% Trump, 22.8% Clinton, 4.6% Johnson, 0.0% Stein
National and State Parks: Chain O'Lakes State Park; Gene Stratton Porter State Memorial
Additional Information Contacts
Noble Government .... (260) 636-2658
http://www.nobleco.org

Noble County Communities

ALBION (town). County seat. Covers a land area of 1.908 square miles and a water area of 0 square miles. Located at 41.40° N. Lat; 85.42° W. Long. Elevation is 955 feet.
History: Albion was first called The Center. The name was changed to Albion about 1845, when the town was successful in its bid to become the new seat of Noble County. Albion was a station on the Underground Railroad, helping slaves to escape to freedom.

Population: 2,363; Growth (since 2000): 3.5%; Density: 1,238.4 persons per square mile; Race: 96.4% White, 1.4% Black/African American, 0.0% Asian, 0.0% American Indian/Alaska Native, 0.0% Native Hawaiian/Other Pacific Islander, 1.9% Two or more races, 2.8% Hispanic of any race; Average household size: 2.32; Median age: 38.4; Age under 18: 20.7%; Age 65 and over: 12.4%; Males per 100 females: 104.6; Marriage status: 29.0% never married, 44.1% now married, 2.2% separated, 8.4% widowed, 18.5% divorced; Foreign born: 0.3%; Speak English only: 97.8%; With disability: 11.9%; Veterans: 7.7%; Ancestry: 32.6% German, 11.3% European, 9.3% Irish, 8.6% American, 8.6% English
Employment: 6.9% management, business, and financial, 2.9% computer, engineering, and science, 5.4% education, legal, community service, arts, and media, 3.0% healthcare practitioners, 15.1% service, 18.3% sales and office, 7.7% natural resources, construction, and maintenance, 40.7% production, transportation, and material moving
Income: Per capita: $21,741; Median household: $44,602; Average household: $53,759; Households with income of $100,000 or more: 10.7%; Poverty rate: 18.4%
Educational Attainment: High school diploma or higher: 86.7%; Bachelor's degree or higher: 10.5%; Graduate/professional degree or higher: 1.8%

School District(s)

Central Noble Com School Corp (KG-12)
Enrollment: 1,244 .... (260) 636-2175
Housing: Homeownership rate: 57.2%; Median home value: $89,100; Median year structure built: 1973; Homeowner vacancy rate: 2.4%; Median selected monthly owner costs: $803 with a mortgage, $359 without a mortgage; Median gross rent: $647 per month; Rental vacancy rate: 0.0%
Health Insurance: 92.0% have insurance; 71.9% have private insurance; 27.0% have public insurance; 8.0% do not have insurance; 3.0% of children under 18 do not have insurance
Safety: Violent crime rate: 43.2 per 10,000 population; Property crime rate: 125.2 per 10,000 population
Newspapers: New Era (weekly circulation 2,000)
Transportation: Commute: 92.1% car, 0.0% public transportation, 6.2% walk, 1.7% work from home; Mean travel time to work: 21.8 minutes
Additional Information Contacts
Town of Albion.................................. (260) 636-2246
http://www.albion-in.org

AVILLA (town). Covers a land area of 1.481 square miles and a water area of 0 square miles. Located at 41.36° N. Lat; 85.23° W. Long. Elevation is 968 feet.
Population: 2,332; Growth (since 2000): 13.8%; Density: 1,574.7 persons per square mile; Race: 94.0% White, 0.2% Black/African American, 4.4% Asian, 0.0% American Indian/Alaska Native, 0.0% Native Hawaiian/Other Pacific Islander, 1.4% Two or more races, 3.5% Hispanic of any race; Average household size: 2.31; Median age: 40.5; Age under 18: 22.1%; Age 65 and over: 18.8%; Males per 100 females: 87.0; Marriage status: 25.7% never married, 48.7% now married, 0.9% separated, 10.0% widowed, 15.7% divorced; Foreign born: 3.5%; Speak English only: 94.7%; With disability: 14.4%; Veterans: 5.9%; Ancestry: 29.2% German, 11.5% Irish, 10.0% American, 9.4% English, 7.3% European
Employment: 9.1% management, business, and financial, 5.1% computer, engineering, and science, 5.3% education, legal, community service, arts, and media, 5.2% healthcare practitioners, 14.2% service, 21.6% sales and office, 10.1% natural resources, construction, and maintenance, 29.3% production, transportation, and material moving
Income: Per capita: $22,228; Median household: $45,045; Average household: $51,308; Households with income of $100,000 or more: 7.9%; Poverty rate: 9.0%
Educational Attainment: High school diploma or higher: 90.9%; Bachelor's degree or higher: 12.9%; Graduate/professional degree or higher: 1.9%

School District(s)

East Noble School Corporation (PK-12)
Enrollment: 3,648 .... (260) 347-2502
Housing: Homeownership rate: 73.2%; Median home value: $109,400; Median year structure built: 1990; Homeowner vacancy rate: 1.8%; Median selected monthly owner costs: $937 with a mortgage, $263 without a mortgage; Median gross rent: $622 per month; Rental vacancy rate: 4.5%
Health Insurance: 95.9% have insurance; 79.4% have private insurance; 27.5% have public insurance; 4.1% do not have insurance; 0.0% of children under 18 do not have insurance
Transportation: Commute: 97.3% car, 0.0% public transportation, 0.3% walk, 2.4% work from home; Mean travel time to work: 20.1 minutes
Additional Information Contacts
Town of Avilla .... (260) 897-3627
http://www.avillachamber.com

CROMWELL (town). Covers a land area of 0.297 square miles and a water area of 0 square miles. Located at 41.40° N. Lat; 85.61° W. Long. Elevation is 958 feet.
Population: 437; Growth (since 2000): -3.3%; Density: 1,472.4 persons per square mile; Race: 86.0% White, 0.0% Black/African American, 1.4% Asian, 0.0% American Indian/Alaska Native, 0.2% Native Hawaiian/Other Pacific Islander, 1.4% Two or more races, 21.5% Hispanic of any race; Average household size: 2.47; Median age: 34.4; Age under 18: 27.9%; Age 65 and over: 10.5%; Males per 100 females: 86.9; Marriage status: 25.1% never married, 50.2% now married, 0.3% separated, 5.9% widowed, 18.9% divorced; Foreign born: 7.8%; Speak English only: 83.1%; With disability: 19.2%; Veterans: 8.9%; Ancestry: 17.6% German, 13.0% European, 10.8% English, 9.6% American, 5.5% Irish
Employment: 3.2% management, business, and financial, 0.0% computer, engineering, and science, 4.8% education, legal, community service, arts, and media, 1.6% healthcare practitioners, 22.8% service, 21.7% sales and office, 5.8% natural resources, construction, and maintenance, 40.2% production, transportation, and material moving
Income: Per capita: $18,425; Median household: $37,321; Average household: $45,379; Households with income of $100,000 or more: 3.9%; Poverty rate: 16.0%
Educational Attainment: High school diploma or higher: 72.8%; Bachelor's degree or higher: 8.6%; Graduate/professional degree or higher: 1.8%
Housing: Homeownership rate: 51.4%; Median home value: $76,000; Median year structure built: 1968; Homeowner vacancy rate: 10.8%; Median selected monthly owner costs: $828 with a mortgage, $273 without a mortgage; Median gross rent: $658 per month; Rental vacancy rate: 2.3%
Health Insurance: 87.2% have insurance; 56.8% have private insurance; 41.6% have public insurance; 12.8% do not have insurance; 12.7% of children under 18 do not have insurance
Transportation: Commute: 91.2% car, 0.0% public transportation, 5.5% walk, 1.7% work from home; Mean travel time to work: 24.9 minutes

KENDALLVILLE (city). Covers a land area of 6.045 square miles and a water area of 0.224 square miles. Located at 41.44° N. Lat; 85.26° W. Long. Elevation is 988 feet.
History: Kendallville was settled in 1833 when David Bundle opened a tavern to serve the many travelers that passed this way. When the New York Central Railroad came through in 1857, the village grew. The Flint & Walling Manufacturing Plant was founded here in 1865 as a machine shop, and became a producer of windmills and pumps.
Population: 9,592; Growth (since 2000): -0.2%; Density: 1,586.8 persons per square mile; Race: 95.8% White, 1.0% Black/African American, 1.2% Asian, 0.1% American Indian/Alaska Native, 0.0% Native Hawaiian/Other Pacific Islander, 1.8% Two or more races, 4.0% Hispanic of any race; Average household size: 2.27; Median age: 38.1; Age under 18: 24.9%; Age 65 and over: 16.4%; Males per 100 females: 93.0; Marriage status: 26.6% never married, 46.1% now married, 2.8% separated, 8.0% widowed, 19.3% divorced; Foreign born: 3.0%; Speak English only: 94.5%; With disability: 19.4%; Veterans: 6.4%; Ancestry: 20.2% German, 11.4% American, 10.4% European, 10.1% Irish, 8.8% English
Employment: 12.1% management, business, and financial, 2.6% computer, engineering, and science, 5.9% education, legal, community service, arts, and media, 5.6% healthcare practitioners, 14.4% service, 12.5% sales and office, 5.4% natural resources, construction, and maintenance, 41.4% production, transportation, and material moving
Income: Per capita: $20,960; Median household: $37,232; Average household: $47,133; Households with income of $100,000 or more: 8.1%; Poverty rate: 19.0%
Educational Attainment: High school diploma or higher: 84.3%; Bachelor's degree or higher: 12.9%; Graduate/professional degree or higher: 4.4%

School District(s)

Dekalb Co Eastern Com Sch Dist (PK-12)
Enrollment: 1,332 .... (260) 868-2125
East Noble School Corporation (PK-12)
Enrollment: 3,648 .... (260) 347-2502

Housing: Homeownership rate: 57.1%; Median home value: $92,900; Median year structure built: 1969; Homeowner vacancy rate: 1.9%; Median selected monthly owner costs: $817 with a mortgage, $314 without a mortgage; Median gross rent: $651 per month; Rental vacancy rate: 6.8%
Health Insurance: 86.9% have insurance; 64.7% have private insurance; 36.1% have public insurance; 13.1% do not have insurance; 7.0% of children under 18 do not have insurance
Hospitals: Parkview Noble Hospital (66 beds)
Safety: Violent crime rate: n/a per 10,000 population; Property crime rate: 227.9 per 10,000 population
Newspapers: Advance Leader (weekly circulation 3,000); News-Sun (daily circulation 8,600)
Transportation: Commute: 96.0% car, 0.0% public transportation, 2.2% walk, 0.9% work from home; Mean travel time to work: 20.5 minutes
Airports: Kendallville Municipal (general aviation)
Additional Information Contacts
City of Kendallville . . . . (260) 347-2452
http://www.kendallville-in.org

KIMMELL (CDP). Covers a land area of 0.960 square miles and a water area of 0.031 square miles. Located at 41.39° N. Lat; 85.55° W. Long. Elevation is 915 feet.
Population: 547; Growth (since 2000): n/a; Density: 570.0 persons per square mile; Race: 92.0% White, 0.0% Black/African American, 0.0% Asian, 0.0% American Indian/Alaska Native, 0.0% Native Hawaiian/Other Pacific Islander, 1.6% Two or more races, 20.1% Hispanic of any race; Average household size: 2.93; Median age: 27.8; Age under 18: 25.6%; Age 65 and over: 2.9%; Males per 100 females: 100.0; Marriage status: 32.9% never married, 53.0% now married, 0.0% separated, 1.6% widowed, 12.4% divorced; Foreign born: 3.7%; Speak English only: 89.0%; With disability: 9.3%; Veterans: 16.7%; Ancestry: 18.6% German, 12.2% Irish, 9.0% Dutch, 8.0% Scottish, 7.1% Norwegian
Employment: 0.0% management, business, and financial, 0.0% computer, engineering, and science, 9.1% education, legal, community service, arts, and media, 4.2% healthcare practitioners, 18.8% service, 2.4% sales and office, 0.0% natural resources, construction, and maintenance, 65.5% production, transportation, and material moving
Income: Per capita: $21,730; Median household: $61,750; Average household: $60,416; Households with income of $100,000 or more: 12.8%; Poverty rate: 4.0%
Educational Attainment: High school diploma or higher: 81.2%; Bachelor's degree or higher: 5.3%; Graduate/professional degree or higher: n/a
Housing: Homeownership rate: 71.7%; Median home value: $70,000; Median year structure built: 1966; Homeowner vacancy rate: 0.0%; Median selected monthly owner costs: $779 with a mortgage, $325 without a mortgage; Median gross rent: n/a per month; Rental vacancy rate: 0.0%
Health Insurance: 98.7% have insurance; 93.4% have private insurance; 6.6% have public insurance; 1.3% do not have insurance; 0.0% of children under 18 do not have insurance
Transportation: Commute: 91.6% car, 0.0% public transportation, 0.0% walk, 0.0% work from home; Mean travel time to work: 22.8 minutes

LAOTTO (unincorporated postal area)
ZCTA: 46763
Covers a land area of 22.431 square miles and a water area of 0.016 square miles. Located at 41.30° N. Lat; 85.23° W. Long. Elevation is 873 feet.
Population: 1,969; Growth (since 2000): 16.9%; Density: 87.8 persons per square mile; Race: 100.0% White, 0.0% Black/African American, 0.0% Asian, 0.0% American Indian/Alaska Native, 0.0% Native Hawaiian/Other Pacific Islander, 0.0% Two or more races, 4.9% Hispanic of any race; Average household size: 2.63; Median age: 37.3; Age under 18: 31.0%; Age 65 and over: 16.0%; Males per 100 females: 100.9; Marriage status: 18.2% never married, 65.7% now married, 0.0% separated, 6.5% widowed, 9.6% divorced; Foreign born: 1.8%; Speak English only: 98.6%; With disability: 10.2%; Veterans: 5.3%; Ancestry: 42.1% German, 22.2% European, 8.6% Irish, 7.1% American, 5.7% English
Employment: 15.2% management, business, and financial, 5.5% computer, engineering, and science, 9.7% education, legal, community service, arts, and media, 19.1% healthcare practitioners, 4.5% service, 19.1% sales and office, 6.1% natural resources, construction, and maintenance, 20.7% production, transportation, and material moving
Income: Per capita: $31,417; Median household: $56,735; Average household: $84,042; Households with income of $100,000 or more: 34.5%; Poverty rate: 11.4%
Educational Attainment: High school diploma or higher: 89.0%; Bachelor's degree or higher: 29.4%; Graduate/professional degree or higher: 9.9%
Housing: Homeownership rate: 91.6%; Median home value: $182,000; Median year structure built: 1977; Homeowner vacancy rate: 4.2%; Median selected monthly owner costs: $1,283 with a mortgage, $384 without a mortgage; Median gross rent: n/a per month; Rental vacancy rate: 0.0%
Health Insurance: 94.0% have insurance; 82.0% have private insurance; 23.4% have public insurance; 6.0% do not have insurance; 2.5% of children under 18 do not have insurance
Transportation: Commute: 91.9% car, 0.0% public transportation, 0.0% walk, 6.3% work from home; Mean travel time to work: 26.8 minutes

LIGONIER (city). Covers a land area of 2.310 square miles and a water area of <.001 square miles. Located at 41.46° N. Lat; 85.59° W. Long. Elevation is 876 feet.
History: Ligonier was settled along the Elkhart River. Many of the early residents were Jewish.
Population: 4,845; Growth (since 2000): 11.2%; Density: 2,097.8 persons per square mile; Race: 96.1% White, 0.2% Black/African American, 0.0% Asian, 0.0% American Indian/Alaska Native, 0.0% Native Hawaiian/Other Pacific Islander, 3.4% Two or more races, 59.9% Hispanic of any race; Average household size: 2.91; Median age: 31.4; Age under 18: 31.4%; Age 65 and over: 9.0%; Males per 100 females: 99.1; Marriage status: 31.9% never married, 50.2% now married, 3.3% separated, 2.9% widowed, 15.0% divorced; Foreign born: 23.8%; Speak English only: 44.3%; With disability: 10.4%; Veterans: 6.0%; Ancestry: 10.5% German, 5.2% European, 5.0% American, 3.9% English, 3.5% Irish
Employment: 5.7% management, business, and financial, 1.5% computer, engineering, and science, 1.2% education, legal, community service, arts, and media, 0.6% healthcare practitioners, 14.9% service, 11.8% sales and office, 6.2% natural resources, construction, and maintenance, 58.2% production, transportation, and material moving
Income: Per capita: $21,556; Median household: $50,919; Average household: $63,023; Households with income of $100,000 or more: 9.6%; Poverty rate: 8.5%
Educational Attainment: High school diploma or higher: 60.6%; Bachelor's degree or higher: 1.8%; Graduate/professional degree or higher: 0.4%

School District(s)
West Noble School Corporation (PK-12)
Enrollment: 2,405 . . . . (260) 894-3191
Housing: Homeownership rate: 60.0%; Median home value: $80,900; Median year structure built: 1960; Homeowner vacancy rate: 3.0%; Median selected monthly owner costs: $948 with a mortgage, $307 without a mortgage; Median gross rent: $650 per month; Rental vacancy rate: 4.2%
Health Insurance: 83.9% have insurance; 59.1% have private insurance; 33.5% have public insurance; 16.1% do not have insurance; 7.2% of children under 18 do not have insurance
Safety: Violent crime rate: 2.3 per 10,000 population; Property crime rate: 83.7 per 10,000 population
Transportation: Commute: 94.3% car, 0.0% public transportation, 2.0% walk, 1.3% work from home; Mean travel time to work: 17.4 minutes
Additional Information Contacts
City of Ligonier . . . . (260) 894-4113
http://www.ligonier-in.org

ROME CITY (town). Covers a land area of 1.157 square miles and a water area of 0.991 square miles. Located at 41.49° N. Lat; 85.36° W. Long. Elevation is 935 feet.
History: Rome City developed when a dam was built across a tributary of the Elkhart River, forming Sylvan Lake. The settlement, which became a resort community, was platted in 1839 and named by the Irish construction workers.
Population: 1,131; Growth (since 2000): -30.0%; Density: 977.8 persons per square mile; Race: 96.5% White, 0.0% Black/African American, 2.1% Asian, 0.0% American Indian/Alaska Native, 0.0% Native Hawaiian/Other Pacific Islander, 1.4% Two or more races, 4.9% Hispanic of any race; Average household size: 2.13; Median age: 51.6; Age under 18: 13.6%; Age 65 and over: 23.9%; Males per 100 females: 98.4; Marriage status: 19.2% never married, 57.9% now married, 2.9% separated, 8.6%

widowed, 14.2% divorced; Foreign born: 3.2%; Speak English only: 94.5%; With disability: 17.6%; Veterans: 9.1%; Ancestry: 36.4% German, 14.2% English, 14.1% Irish, 6.5% American, 4.4% French
Employment: 10.0% management, business, and financial, 1.4% computer, engineering, and science, 7.6% education, legal, community service, arts, and media, 5.6% healthcare practitioners, 11.6% service, 25.3% sales and office, 7.9% natural resources, construction, and maintenance, 30.6% production, transportation, and material moving
Income: Per capita: $39,896; Median household: $65,795; Average household: $84,519; Households with income of $100,000 or more: 25.8%; Poverty rate: 10.9%
Educational Attainment: High school diploma or higher: 86.0%; Bachelor's degree or higher: 18.4%; Graduate/professional degree or higher: 6.0%

School District(s)

East Noble School Corporation (PK-12)
Enrollment: 3,648 . . . . (260) 347-2502
Housing: Homeownership rate: 76.5%; Median home value: $193,800; Median year structure built: 1954; Homeowner vacancy rate: 6.5%; Median selected monthly owner costs: $1,288 with a mortgage, $367 without a mortgage; Median gross rent: $780 per month; Rental vacancy rate: 0.0%
Health Insurance: 93.9% have insurance; 79.7% have private insurance; 32.9% have public insurance; 6.1% do not have insurance; 1.7% of children under 18 do not have insurance
Transportation: Commute: 90.3% car, 0.0% public transportation, 1.0% walk, 7.4% work from home; Mean travel time to work: 24.6 minutes

WAWAKA (unincorporated postal area)
ZCTA: 46794

Covers a land area of 25.732 square miles and a water area of 0.218 square miles. Located at 41.46° N. Lat; 85.46° W. Long. Elevation is 899 feet.
Population: 1,740; Growth (since 2000): 6.1%; Density: 67.6 persons per square mile; Race: 98.2% White, 0.0% Black/African American, 0.0% Asian, 0.0% American Indian/Alaska Native, 0.0% Native Hawaiian/Other Pacific Islander, 0.5% Two or more races, 3.7% Hispanic of any race; Average household size: 2.48; Median age: 40.8; Age under 18: 24.8%; Age 65 and over: 21.1%; Males per 100 females: 103.2; Marriage status: 19.7% never married, 58.0% now married, 0.0% separated, 8.2% widowed, 14.1% divorced; Foreign born: 1.9%; Speak English only: 93.8%; With disability: 21.4%; Veterans: 8.7%; Ancestry: 24.8% German, 15.1% Irish, 13.3% American, 11.8% European, 7.5% English
Employment: 8.8% management, business, and financial, 0.7% computer, engineering, and science, 7.8% education, legal, community service, arts, and media, 2.2% healthcare practitioners, 15.4% service, 13.2% sales and office, 22.4% natural resources, construction, and maintenance, 29.6% production, transportation, and material moving
Income: Per capita: $28,032; Median household: $49,074; Average household: $69,001; Households with income of $100,000 or more: 9.6%; Poverty rate: 3.8%
Educational Attainment: High school diploma or higher: 84.0%; Bachelor's degree or higher: 15.4%; Graduate/professional degree or higher: 7.1%
Housing: Homeownership rate: 79.8%; Median home value: $102,500; Median year structure built: 1967; Homeowner vacancy rate: 9.4%; Median selected monthly owner costs: $1,122 with a mortgage, $309 without a mortgage; Median gross rent: $644 per month; Rental vacancy rate: 0.0%
Health Insurance: 90.7% have insurance; 70.5% have private insurance; 34.0% have public insurance; 9.3% do not have insurance; 19.2% of children under 18 do not have insurance
Transportation: Commute: 93.2% car, 0.0% public transportation, 2.6% walk, 2.9% work from home; Mean travel time to work: 26.2 minutes

WOLCOTTVILLE (town). Covers a land area of 1.015 square miles and a water area of 0 square miles. Located at 41.53° N. Lat; 85.37° W. Long. Elevation is 942 feet.
History: Wolcottville grew around a gristmill, sawmill, and distillery established by George Wolcott from Connecticut. The number of nearby lakes made Wolcottville a vacation center as well.
Population: 959; Growth (since 2000): 2.8%; Density: 944.6 persons per square mile; Race: 97.2% White, 0.2% Black/African American, 0.0% Asian, 0.3% American Indian/Alaska Native, 0.0% Native Hawaiian/Other Pacific Islander, 2.3% Two or more races, 1.7% Hispanic of any race; Average household size: 2.77; Median age: 35.3; Age under 18: 29.1%; Age 65 and over: 8.9%; Males per 100 females: 93.4; Marriage status: 26.5% never married, 50.1% now married, 2.0% separated, 3.2% widowed, 20.1% divorced; Foreign born: 0.4%; Speak English only: 99.0%; With disability: 23.5%; Veterans: 10.3%; Ancestry: 20.8% European, 17.2% German, 9.7% English, 8.1% Irish, 5.9% American
Employment: 4.1% management, business, and financial, 2.8% computer, engineering, and science, 0.0% education, legal, community service, arts, and media, 3.0% healthcare practitioners, 18.2% service, 21.8% sales and office, 8.4% natural resources, construction, and maintenance, 41.8% production, transportation, and material moving
Income: Per capita: $21,990; Median household: $50,000; Average household: $60,973; Households with income of $100,000 or more: 11.0%; Poverty rate: 20.0%
Educational Attainment: High school diploma or higher: 73.4%; Bachelor's degree or higher: 5.8%; Graduate/professional degree or higher: 0.8%

School District(s)

Lakeland School Corporation (PK-12)
Enrollment: 2,117 . . . . (260) 499-2400
Housing: Homeownership rate: 57.8%; Median home value: $79,100; Median year structure built: 1962; Homeowner vacancy rate: 0.0%; Median selected monthly owner costs: $886 with a mortgage, $377 without a mortgage; Median gross rent: $627 per month; Rental vacancy rate: 20.7%
Health Insurance: 85.4% have insurance; 54.3% have private insurance; 39.5% have public insurance; 14.6% do not have insurance; 9.0% of children under 18 do not have insurance
Transportation: Commute: 94.9% car, 0.0% public transportation, 3.0% walk, 1.6% work from home; Mean travel time to work: 25.1 minutes

Ohio County

Located in southeastern Indiana; bounded on the east by the Ohio River and the Kentucky border. Covers a land area of 86.140 square miles, a water area of 1.294 square miles, and is located in the Eastern Time Zone at 38.94° N. Lat., 84.96° W. Long. The county was founded in 1844. County seat is Rising Sun.

Ohio County is part of the Cincinnati, OH-KY-IN Metropolitan Statistical Area. The entire metro area includes: Dearborn County, IN; Ohio County, IN; Union County, IN; Boone County, KY; Bracken County, KY; Campbell County, KY; Gallatin County, KY; Grant County, KY; Kenton County, KY; Pendleton County, KY; Brown County, OH; Butler County, OH; Clermont County, OH; Hamilton County, OH; Warren County, OH

Population: 5,911; Growth (since 2000): 5.1%; Density: 68.6 persons per square mile; Race: 97.2% White, 1.3% Black/African American, 0.3% Asian, 0.1% American Indian/Alaska Native, 0.0% Native Hawaiian/Other Pacific Islander, 0.4% two or more races, 1.0% Hispanic of any race; Average household size: 2.36; Median age: 46.8; Age under 18: 19.5%; Age 65 and over: 20.1%; Males per 100 females: 98.0; Marriage status: 21.1% never married, 63.7% now married, 1.4% separated, 6.8% widowed, 8.4% divorced; Foreign born: 0.7%; Speak English only: 98.8%; With disability: 12.9%; Veterans: 11.4%; Ancestry: 29.5% German, 16.1% American, 11.2% Irish, 8.0% English, 5.3% Italian
Religion: Six largest groups: 20.1% Baptist, 3.3% Methodist/Pietist, 2.4% Non-denominational Protestant, 1.6% Presbyterian-Reformed, 1.3% Holiness, 0.0% Other Groups
Economy: Unemployment rate: 3.7%; Leading industries: 15.7 % other services (except public administration); 13.3 % construction; 12.0 % retail trade; Farms: 171 totaling 21,461 acres; Company size: 0 employ 1,000 or more persons, 1 employs 500 to 999 persons, 0 employ 100 to 499 persons, 82 employ less than 100 persons; Business ownership: 66 women-owned, n/a Black-owned, n/a Hispanic-owned, n/a Asian-owned, n/a American Indian/Alaska Native-owned
Employment: 10.9% management, business, and financial, 3.0% computer, engineering, and science, 6.4% education, legal, community service, arts, and media, 4.7% healthcare practitioners, 23.3% service, 18.1% sales and office, 11.1% natural resources, construction, and maintenance, 22.6% production, transportation, and material moving
Income: Per capita: $27,715; Median household: $58,359; Average household: $65,245; Households with income of $100,000 or more: 20.9%; Poverty rate: 5.0%

Educational Attainment: High school diploma or higher: 88.3%; Bachelor's degree or higher: 14.2%; Graduate/professional degree or higher: 5.4%
Housing: Homeownership rate: 79.0%; Median home value: $142,400; Median year structure built: 1977; Homeowner vacancy rate: 0.5%; Median selected monthly owner costs: $1,181 with a mortgage, $404 without a mortgage; Median gross rent: $716 per month; Rental vacancy rate: 7.6%
Vital Statistics: Birth rate: 87.5 per 10,000 population; Death rate: 128.7 per 10,000 population; Age-adjusted cancer mortality rate: 195.1 deaths per 100,000 population
Health Insurance: 93.3% have insurance; 76.7% have private insurance; 31.3% have public insurance; 6.7% do not have insurance; 3.6% of children under 18 do not have insurance
Health Care: Physicians: 1.7 per 10,000 population; Dentists: 3.4 per 10,000 population; Hospital beds: 0.0 per 10,000 population; Hospital admissions: 0.0 per 10,000 population
Transportation: Commute: 93.5% car, 0.2% public transportation, 3.9% walk, 1.7% work from home; Mean travel time to work: 31.3 minutes
2016 Presidential Election: 72.5% Trump, 23.5% Clinton, 3.9% Johnson, 0.1% Stein
Additional Information Contacts
Ohio Government . . . . (812) 438-2062

Ohio County Communities

RISING SUN (city). County seat. Covers a land area of 1.449 square miles and a water area of 0.119 square miles. Located at 38.95° N. Lat; 84.85° W. Long. Elevation is 502 feet.
History: Rising Sun was platted in 1814 along the Ohio River, and grew as a shipping center.
Population: 2,219; Growth (since 2000): -10.2%; Density: 1,531.4 persons per square mile; Race: 94.6% White, 3.5% Black/African American, 0.2% Asian, 0.2% American Indian/Alaska Native, 0.0% Native Hawaiian/Other Pacific Islander, 0.2% Two or more races, 2.6% Hispanic of any race; Average household size: 2.18; Median age: 50.0; Age under 18: 16.2%; Age 65 and over: 23.6%; Males per 100 females: 91.2; Marriage status: 24.0% never married, 55.4% now married, 3.0% separated, 7.8% widowed, 12.9% divorced; Foreign born: 1.0%; Speak English only: 98.5%; With disability: 17.2%; Veterans: 11.0%; Ancestry: 24.2% German, 11.9% American, 10.3% Irish, 6.8% English, 2.4% Italian
Employment: 10.3% management, business, and financial, 3.6% computer, engineering, and science, 7.1% education, legal, community service, arts, and media, 3.9% healthcare practitioners, 29.6% service, 21.2% sales and office, 8.5% natural resources, construction, and maintenance, 15.9% production, transportation, and material moving
Income: Per capita: $24,222; Median household: $44,286; Average household: $53,220; Households with income of $100,000 or more: 12.3%; Poverty rate: 7.9%
Educational Attainment: High school diploma or higher: 85.1%; Bachelor's degree or higher: 12.0%; Graduate/professional degree or higher: 3.5%

School District(s)

Rising Sun-Ohio Co Com (PK-12)
Enrollment: 784. . . . . (812) 438-2655
Housing: Homeownership rate: 62.8%; Median home value: $100,700; Median year structure built: 1959; Homeowner vacancy rate: 1.6%; Median selected monthly owner costs: $1,083 with a mortgage, $370 without a mortgage; Median gross rent: $700 per month; Rental vacancy rate: 10.4%
Health Insurance: 89.5% have insurance; 68.1% have private insurance; 37.3% have public insurance; 10.5% do not have insurance; 2.3% of children under 18 do not have insurance
Newspapers: News Sun Recorder (weekly circulation 2,000)
Transportation: Commute: 89.6% car, 0.0% public transportation, 7.4% walk, 1.8% work from home; Mean travel time to work: 24.6 minutes
Additional Information Contacts
City of Rising Sun . . . . (812) 438-2475
http://www.cityofrisingsun.com

Orange County

Located in southern Indiana; drained by the Lick, Lost, and Potoka Rivers. Covers a land area of 398.387 square miles, a water area of 9.805 square miles, and is located in the Eastern Time Zone at 38.55° N. Lat., 86.49° W. Long. The county was founded in 1815. County seat is Paoli.

Weather Station: Paoli Elevation: 560 feet

	Jan	Feb	Mar	Apr	May	Jun	Jul	Aug	Sep	Oct	Nov	Dec
High	40	45	55	66	76	84	87	87	80	68	56	43
Low	21	24	32	41	51	60	64	62	54	42	34	24
Precip	3.3	3.1	4.4	5.0	5.4	4.1	4.2	3.4	3.8	3.4	4.0	3.7
Snow	3.3	3.2	1.1	tr	0.0	0.0	0.0	0.0	0.0	0.0	tr	3.6

High and Low temperatures in degrees Fahrenheit; Precipitation and Snow in inches

Population: 19,623; Growth (since 2000): 1.6%; Density: 49.3 persons per square mile; Race: 96.6% White, 1.3% Black/African American, 0.5% Asian, 0.1% American Indian/Alaska Native, 0.0% Native Hawaiian/Other Pacific Islander, 1.1% two or more races, 1.4% Hispanic of any race; Average household size: 2.47; Median age: 41.3; Age under 18: 23.6%; Age 65 and over: 18.2%; Males per 100 females: 98.8; Marriage status: 23.2% never married, 52.9% now married, 1.1% separated, 7.9% widowed, 16.0% divorced; Foreign born: 1.5%; Speak English only: 98.1%; With disability: 20.8%; Veterans: 8.9%; Ancestry: 18.1% German, 12.2% American, 10.8% Irish, 9.5% English, 2.4% Italian
Religion: Six largest groups: 23.6% Baptist, 6.8% Methodist/Pietist, 4.5% European Free-Church, 3.5% Holiness, 1.9% Catholicism, 1.5% Non-denominational Protestant
Economy: Unemployment rate: 3.9%; Leading industries: 15.7 % retail trade; 14.1 % health care and social assistance; 13.6 % other services (except public administration); Farms: 478 totaling 98,251 acres; Company size: 0 employ 1,000 or more persons, 1 employs 500 to 999 persons, 11 employs 100 to 499 persons, 371 employs less than 100 persons; Business ownership: 374 women-owned, n/a Black-owned, n/a Hispanic-owned, n/a Asian-owned, n/a American Indian/Alaska Native-owned
Employment: 13.6% management, business, and financial, 3.1% computer, engineering, and science, 5.5% education, legal, community service, arts, and media, 3.7% healthcare practitioners, 18.7% service, 18.1% sales and office, 12.8% natural resources, construction, and maintenance, 24.6% production, transportation, and material moving
Income: Per capita: $22,715; Median household: $42,803; Average household: $55,694; Households with income of $100,000 or more: 12.4%; Poverty rate: 15.0%
Educational Attainment: High school diploma or higher: 83.3%; Bachelor's degree or higher: 11.8%; Graduate/professional degree or higher: 4.7%
Housing: Homeownership rate: 75.4%; Median home value: $90,400; Median year structure built: 1976; Homeowner vacancy rate: 3.0%; Median selected monthly owner costs: $936 with a mortgage, $356 without a mortgage; Median gross rent: $589 per month; Rental vacancy rate: 8.6%
Vital Statistics: Birth rate: 118.4 per 10,000 population; Death rate: 109.1 per 10,000 population; Age-adjusted cancer mortality rate: 218.1 deaths per 100,000 population
Health Insurance: 90.6% have insurance; 63.9% have private insurance; 40.7% have public insurance; 9.4% do not have insurance; 5.3% of children under 18 do not have insurance
Health Care: Physicians: 8.7 per 10,000 population; Dentists: 3.6 per 10,000 population; Hospital beds: 12.8 per 10,000 population; Hospital admissions: 108.8 per 10,000 population
Transportation: Commute: 91.6% car, 0.0% public transportation, 2.3% walk, 4.7% work from home; Mean travel time to work: 25.6 minutes
2016 Presidential Election: 70.8% Trump, 25.0% Clinton, 4.2% Johnson, 0.0% Stein
National and State Parks: Hoosier National Forest; Jackson State Recreation Area; Newton-Stewart State Recreation Area; Pioneer Mothers State Wayside Park; Springs Valley State Fish and Wildlife Area; Tillery Hill State Recreation Area
Additional Information Contacts
Orange Government . . . . (812) 723-2649
http://www.co.orange.in.us

Orange County Communities

FRENCH LICK (town). Covers a land area of 1.766 square miles and a water area of 0.001 square miles. Located at 38.55° N. Lat; 86.62° W. Long. Elevation is 499 feet.
History: French Lick was founded in 1811 on the site of mineral springs where a trading post had been operated by the French in the early 1700 's. The French Lick Springs Hotel was opened in 1840 by Dr. William A. Bowles, who not only entertained visitors to the medicinal springs, but marketed the spring water by boiling and bottling it as Pluto Water.

Population: 1,924; Growth (since 2000): -0.9%; Density: 1,089.3 persons per square mile; Race: 86.0% White, 8.6% Black/African American, 1.1% Asian, 0.4% American Indian/Alaska Native, 0.0% Native Hawaiian/Other Pacific Islander, 4.0% Two or more races, 6.5% Hispanic of any race; Average household size: 2.29; Median age: 38.6; Age under 18: 25.7%; Age 65 and over: 19.0%; Males per 100 females: 88.4; Marriage status: 28.3% never married, 37.8% now married, 0.2% separated, 11.9% widowed, 22.0% divorced; Foreign born: 9.1%; Speak English only: 98.6%; With disability: 23.5%; Veterans: 7.8%; Ancestry: 19.6% German, 8.6% American, 7.8% Irish, 7.1% English, 3.0% Jamaican
Employment: 10.9% management, business, and financial, 2.0% computer, engineering, and science, 4.0% education, legal, community service, arts, and media, 2.9% healthcare practitioners, 39.8% service, 12.8% sales and office, 8.3% natural resources, construction, and maintenance, 19.2% production, transportation, and material moving
Income: Per capita: $21,201; Median household: $32,599; Average household: $48,736; Households with income of $100,000 or more: 3.6%; Poverty rate: 26.7%
Educational Attainment: High school diploma or higher: 76.6%; Bachelor's degree or higher: 7.2%; Graduate/professional degree or higher: 2.3%

School District(s)

Springs Valley Com School Corp (PK-12)
Enrollment: 879 . . . . (812) 936-4474
Housing: Homeownership rate: 54.8%; Median home value: $72,800; Median year structure built: 1967; Homeowner vacancy rate: 1.9%; Median selected monthly owner costs: $857 with a mortgage, $294 without a mortgage; Median gross rent: $644 per month; Rental vacancy rate: 14.8%
Health Insurance: 84.2% have insurance; 54.8% have private insurance; 41.9% have public insurance; 15.8% do not have insurance; 11.9% of children under 18 do not have insurance
Newspapers: Springs Valley Herald (weekly circulation 2,200)
Transportation: Commute: 86.6% car, 0.0% public transportation, 8.2% walk, 3.5% work from home; Mean travel time to work: 15.9 minutes
Airports: French Lick Municipal (general aviation)

ORLEANS (town). Covers a land area of 1.709 square miles and a water area of <.001 square miles. Located at 38.66° N. Lat; 86.45° W. Long. Elevation is 633 feet.
History: Orleans was founded in 1815 shortly after General Jackson's victory at New Orleans, and the town was named for that event. Orleans developed as an orchard and dairy center.
Population: 2,037; Growth (since 2000): -10.4%; Density: 1,191.8 persons per square mile; Race: 97.7% White, 2.3% Black/African American, 0.0% Asian, 0.0% American Indian/Alaska Native, 0.0% Native Hawaiian/Other Pacific Islander, 0.0% Two or more races, 1.2% Hispanic of any race; Average household size: 2.30; Median age: 41.6; Age under 18: 22.7%; Age 65 and over: 17.8%; Males per 100 females: 89.4; Marriage status: 22.9% never married, 49.4% now married, 3.5% separated, 10.1% widowed, 17.5% divorced; Foreign born: 0.0%; Speak English only: 99.0%; With disability: 24.5%; Veterans: 8.4%; Ancestry: 16.5% German, 15.7% American, 10.6% English, 6.0% Irish, 4.0% French
Employment: 7.4% management, business, and financial, 1.2% computer, engineering, and science, 2.1% education, legal, community service, arts, and media, 2.7% healthcare practitioners, 21.6% service, 24.1% sales and office, 8.3% natural resources, construction, and maintenance, 32.6% production, transportation, and material moving
Income: Per capita: $19,579; Median household: $35,216; Average household: $45,234; Households with income of $100,000 or more: 5.5%; Poverty rate: 23.7%
Educational Attainment: High school diploma or higher: 78.3%; Bachelor's degree or higher: 6.3%; Graduate/professional degree or higher: 1.8%

School District(s)

Orleans Community Schools (PK-12)
Enrollment: 730 . . . . (812) 865-2688
Housing: Homeownership rate: 56.9%; Median home value: $82,900; Median year structure built: 1968; Homeowner vacancy rate: 2.5%; Median selected monthly owner costs: $841 with a mortgage, $345 without a mortgage; Median gross rent: $554 per month; Rental vacancy rate: 7.5%
Health Insurance: 92.4% have insurance; 55.0% have private insurance; 50.8% have public insurance; 7.6% do not have insurance; 3.2% of children under 18 do not have insurance
Newspapers: Progress-Examiner (weekly circulation 2,100)
Transportation: Commute: 94.4% car, 0.0% public transportation, 2.0% walk, 2.7% work from home; Mean travel time to work: 19.3 minutes
Additional Information Contacts
Town of Orleans . . . . (812) 865-2539
http://www.town.orleans.in.us

PAOLI (town). County seat. Covers a land area of 3.743 square miles and a water area of 0.014 square miles. Located at 38.56° N. Lat; 86.47° W. Long. Elevation is 623 feet.
History: The Orange County Courthouse was constructed in 1850 in Paoli, the county seat.
Population: 3,665; Growth (since 2000): -4.7%; Density: 979.1 persons per square mile; Race: 97.1% White, 0.5% Black/African American, 2.0% Asian, 0.0% American Indian/Alaska Native, 0.0% Native Hawaiian/Other Pacific Islander, 0.5% Two or more races, 0.1% Hispanic of any race; Average household size: 2.38; Median age: 40.2; Age under 18: 20.1%; Age 65 and over: 18.0%; Males per 100 females: 93.3; Marriage status: 26.1% never married, 41.6% now married, 1.6% separated, 11.2% widowed, 21.1% divorced; Foreign born: 2.0%; Speak English only: 98.9%; With disability: 19.5%; Veterans: 7.4%; Ancestry: 24.0% German, 17.2% Irish, 12.1% American, 8.5% English, 3.4% Italian
Employment: 11.6% management, business, and financial, 1.1% computer, engineering, and science, 5.0% education, legal, community service, arts, and media, 5.2% healthcare practitioners, 21.4% service, 18.6% sales and office, 10.1% natural resources, construction, and maintenance, 27.0% production, transportation, and material moving
Income: Per capita: $18,612; Median household: $33,779; Average household: $43,888; Households with income of $100,000 or more: 8.8%; Poverty rate: 16.4%
Educational Attainment: High school diploma or higher: 79.7%; Bachelor's degree or higher: 8.3%; Graduate/professional degree or higher: 3.9%

School District(s)

Lost River Career Cooperative (09-12)
Enrollment: n/a . . . . (812) 723-4818
Paoli Community School Corp (PK-12)
Enrollment: 1,465 . . . . (812) 723-4717
South Central Area Special Ed (KG-12)
Enrollment: n/a . . . . (812) 723-2089
Housing: Homeownership rate: 63.0%; Median home value: $75,300; Median year structure built: 1964; Homeowner vacancy rate: 8.3%; Median selected monthly owner costs: $846 with a mortgage, $327 without a mortgage; Median gross rent: $598 per month; Rental vacancy rate: 0.0%
Health Insurance: 88.3% have insurance; 57.6% have private insurance; 41.0% have public insurance; 11.7% do not have insurance; 6.3% of children under 18 do not have insurance
Hospitals: Indiana University Health Paoli Hospital
Newspapers: Orange Co. Publishing (weekly circulation 19,000)
Transportation: Commute: 93.1% car, 0.2% public transportation, 3.3% walk, 3.3% work from home; Mean travel time to work: 19.6 minutes
Additional Information Contacts
Town of Paoli. . . . . (812) 723-4769
http://www.paolichamber.com

WEST BADEN SPRINGS (town). Covers a land area of 1.089 square miles and a water area of 0.008 square miles. Located at 38.57° N. Lat; 86.61° W. Long. Elevation is 479 feet.
Population: 526; Growth (since 2000): -14.9%; Density: 483.1 persons per square mile; Race: 92.2% White, 4.8% Black/African American, 2.1% Asian, 0.0% American Indian/Alaska Native, 0.0% Native Hawaiian/Other Pacific Islander, 0.0% Two or more races, 1.9% Hispanic of any race; Average household size: 1.96; Median age: 46.0; Age under 18: 14.3%; Age 65 and over: 22.4%; Males per 100 females: 100.7; Marriage status: 21.0% never married, 53.0% now married, 2.8% separated, 12.1% widowed, 14.0% divorced; Foreign born: 4.0%; Speak English only: 98.3%; With disability: 21.3%; Veterans: 7.3%; Ancestry: 15.8% German, 15.2% Irish, 14.4% American, 5.1% English, 3.2% Dutch
Employment: 21.7% management, business, and financial, 1.7% computer, engineering, and science, 5.4% education, legal, community service, arts, and media, 2.3% healthcare practitioners, 20.7% service, 13.0% sales and office, 12.7% natural resources, construction, and maintenance, 22.4% production, transportation, and material moving
Income: Per capita: $28,273; Median household: $38,125; Average household: $54,690; Households with income of $100,000 or more: 12.3%; Poverty rate: 12.4%

Educational Attainment: High school diploma or higher: 85.5%; Bachelor's degree or higher: 10.1%; Graduate/professional degree or higher: 2.9%
Housing: Homeownership rate: 67.3%; Median home value: $91,000; Median year structure built: 1961; Homeowner vacancy rate: 1.1%; Median selected monthly owner costs: $1,000 with a mortgage, $397 without a mortgage; Median gross rent: $570 per month; Rental vacancy rate: 12.0%
Health Insurance: 92.6% have insurance; 72.1% have private insurance; 34.6% have public insurance; 7.4% do not have insurance; 1.3% of children under 18 do not have insurance
Transportation: Commute: 92.5% car, 0.0% public transportation, 4.4% walk, 1.4% work from home; Mean travel time to work: 21.4 minutes

Owen County

Located in southwest central Indiana; drained by the West Fork of the White River and Mill Creek. Covers a land area of 385.288 square miles, a water area of 2.537 square miles, and is located in the Eastern Time Zone at 39.32° N. Lat., 86.84° W. Long. The county was founded in 1818. County seat is Spencer.

Owen County is part of the Bloomington, IN Metropolitan Statistical Area. The entire metro area includes: Monroe County, IN; Owen County, IN

Weather Station: Spencer Elevation: 549 feet

	Jan	Feb	Mar	Apr	May	Jun	Jul	Aug	Sep	Oct	Nov	Dec
High	36	41	52	63	73	81	85	84	78	66	53	40
Low	19	21	29	39	49	59	63	61	52	40	32	22
Precip	2.9	2.7	3.7	4.7	5.4	5.0	4.9	4.0	3.6	3.7	4.0	3.5
Snow	5.7	4.5	1.4	tr	0.0	0.0	0.0	0.0	0.0	0.1	0.3	3.2

High and Low temperatures in degrees Fahrenheit; Precipitation and Snow in inches

Population: 20,957; Growth (since 2000): -3.8%; Density: 54.4 persons per square mile; Race: 97.3% White, 0.8% Black/African American, 0.5% Asian, 0.3% American Indian/Alaska Native, 0.0% Native Hawaiian/Other Pacific Islander, 1.2% two or more races, 1.2% Hispanic of any race; Average household size: 2.43; Median age: 44.6; Age under 18: 21.6%; Age 65 and over: 18.0%; Males per 100 females: 100.6; Marriage status: 22.5% never married, 56.8% now married, 1.2% separated, 6.3% widowed, 14.4% divorced; Foreign born: 1.2%; Speak English only: 97.5%; With disability: 17.0%; Veterans: 9.5%; Ancestry: 23.4% German, 12.9% Irish, 11.8% American, 7.7% English, 2.8% Scottish
Religion: Six largest groups: 9.7% Baptist, 4.6% Non-denominational Protestant, 3.9% Methodist/Pietist, 1.8% Holiness, 1.3% Catholicism, 1.0% Pentecostal
Economy: Unemployment rate: 4.4%; Leading industries: 13.7 % retail trade; 13.0 % construction; 12.7 % other services (except public administration); Farms: 549 totaling 95,527 acres; Company size: 0 employ 1,000 or more persons, 1 employs 500 to 999 persons, 2 employ 100 to 499 persons, 296 employ less than 100 persons; Business ownership: 380 women-owned, n/a Black-owned, n/a Hispanic-owned, n/a Asian-owned, n/a American Indian/Alaska Native-owned
Employment: 9.9% management, business, and financial, 2.7% computer, engineering, and science, 7.0% education, legal, community service, arts, and media, 5.2% healthcare practitioners, 17.7% service, 18.9% sales and office, 17.6% natural resources, construction, and maintenance, 21.0% production, transportation, and material moving
Income: Per capita: $24,220; Median household: $48,315; Average household: $59,649; Households with income of $100,000 or more: 15.3%; Poverty rate: 15.6%
Educational Attainment: High school diploma or higher: 85.3%; Bachelor's degree or higher: 12.7%; Graduate/professional degree or higher: 5.8%
Housing: Homeownership rate: 79.1%; Median home value: $110,200; Median year structure built: 1983; Homeowner vacancy rate: 3.4%; Median selected monthly owner costs: $1,065 with a mortgage, $415 without a mortgage; Median gross rent: $673 per month; Rental vacancy rate: 2.9%
Vital Statistics: Birth rate: 113.2 per 10,000 population; Death rate: 113.7 per 10,000 population; Age-adjusted cancer mortality rate: 158.8 deaths per 100,000 population
Health Insurance: 87.3% have insurance; 63.4% have private insurance; 37.0% have public insurance; 12.7% do not have insurance; 13.6% of children under 18 do not have insurance
Health Care: Physicians: 1.9 per 10,000 population; Dentists: 1.4 per 10,000 population; Hospital beds: 0.0 per 10,000 population; Hospital admissions: 0.0 per 10,000 population
Transportation: Commute: 92.4% car, 1.1% public transportation, 2.5% walk, 2.7% work from home; Mean travel time to work: 30.8 minutes
2016 Presidential Election: 71.9% Trump, 22.7% Clinton, 4.9% Johnson, 0.3% Stein
National and State Parks: McCormicks Creek State Park
Additional Information Contacts
Owen Government . . . . (812) 829-5015
http://www.owencounty.in.gov

Owen County Communities

BOWLING GREEN (unincorporated postal area)
ZCTA: 47833

Covers a land area of 37.149 square miles and a water area of 0.007 square miles. Located at 39.36° N. Lat; 86.98° W. Long..
Population: 1,106; Growth (since 2000): 16.1%; Density: 29.8 persons per square mile; Race: 98.8% White, 0.0% Black/African American, 0.0% Asian, 0.0% American Indian/Alaska Native, 0.0% Native Hawaiian/Other Pacific Islander, 0.0% Two or more races, 1.2% Hispanic of any race; Average household size: 2.36; Median age: 40.0; Age under 18: 21.0%; Age 65 and over: 12.8%; Males per 100 females: 97.3; Marriage status: 21.3% never married, 55.4% now married, 1.0% separated, 0.8% widowed, 22.5% divorced; Foreign born: 1.2%; Speak English only: 98.0%; With disability: 25.0%; Veterans: 5.9%; Ancestry: 25.6% German, 13.1% English, 10.9% Scottish, 10.5% Irish, 9.1% Italian
Employment: 14.8% management, business, and financial, 5.2% computer, engineering, and science, 0.0% education, legal, community service, arts, and media, 1.1% healthcare practitioners, 21.7% service, 25.4% sales and office, 15.6% natural resources, construction, and maintenance, 16.3% production, transportation, and material moving
Income: Per capita: $25,563; Median household: $57,679; Average household: $63,797; Households with income of $100,000 or more: 18.4%; Poverty rate: 5.7%
Educational Attainment: High school diploma or higher: 90.7%; Bachelor's degree or higher: 12.8%; Graduate/professional degree or higher: 3.5%
Housing: Homeownership rate: 97.0%; Median home value: $99,200; Median year structure built: 1966; Homeowner vacancy rate: 0.0%; Median selected monthly owner costs: $881 with a mortgage, $547 without a mortgage; Median gross rent: n/a per month; Rental vacancy rate: 0.0%
Health Insurance: 85.0% have insurance; 54.5% have private insurance; 40.6% have public insurance; 15.0% do not have insurance; 0.0% of children under 18 do not have insurance
Transportation: Commute: 87.1% car, 6.1% public transportation, 1.9% walk, 0.0% work from home; Mean travel time to work: 28.6 minutes

COAL CITY (unincorporated postal area)
ZCTA: 47427

Covers a land area of 53.257 square miles and a water area of 0.287 square miles. Located at 39.23° N. Lat; 87.02° W. Long. Elevation is 653 feet.
Population: 721; Growth (since 2000): -33.9%; Density: 13.5 persons per square mile; Race: 100.0% White, 0.0% Black/African American, 0.0% Asian, 0.0% American Indian/Alaska Native, 0.0% Native Hawaiian/Other Pacific Islander, 0.0% Two or more races, 0.0% Hispanic of any race; Average household size: 2.41; Median age: 51.4; Age under 18: 18.2%; Age 65 and over: 11.7%; Males per 100 females: 103.2; Marriage status: 11.2% never married, 68.5% now married, 1.1% separated, 7.1% widowed, 13.3% divorced; Foreign born: 0.0%; Speak English only: 100.0%; With disability: 21.5%; Veterans: 11.2%; Ancestry: 29.5% American, 17.2% German, 7.5% Norwegian, 5.7% English, 5.5% Irish
Employment: 18.8% management, business, and financial, 0.0% computer, engineering, and science, 7.6% education, legal, community service, arts, and media, 0.0% healthcare practitioners, 14.5% service, 20.3% sales and office, 11.6% natural resources, construction, and maintenance, 27.2% production, transportation, and material moving
Income: Per capita: $23,882; Median household: $54,732; Average household: $57,400; Households with income of $100,000 or more: 3.0%; Poverty rate: 6.1%
Educational Attainment: High school diploma or higher: 87.5%; Bachelor's degree or higher: 1.7%; Graduate/professional degree or higher: n/a

Housing: Homeownership rate: 89.0%; Median home value: $106,500; Median year structure built: 1974; Homeowner vacancy rate: 0.0%; Median selected monthly owner costs: $1,161 with a mortgage, $409 without a mortgage; Median gross rent: n/a per month; Rental vacancy rate: 0.0%
Health Insurance: 90.0% have insurance; 73.0% have private insurance; 33.4% have public insurance; 10.0% do not have insurance; 8.4% of children under 18 do not have insurance
Transportation: Commute: 87.0% car, 5.4% public transportation, 0.0% walk, 7.6% work from home; Mean travel time to work: 35.0 minutes

FREEDOM (unincorporated postal area)
ZCTA: 47431
Covers a land area of 36.963 square miles and a water area of 0.029 square miles. Located at 39.24° N. Lat; 86.90° W. Long. Elevation is 538 feet.
Population: 1,267; Growth (since 2000): -0.9%; Density: 34.3 persons per square mile; Race: 97.2% White, 0.0% Black/African American, 0.0% Asian, 0.0% American Indian/Alaska Native, 0.0% Native Hawaiian/Other Pacific Islander, 2.8% Two or more races, 0.0% Hispanic of any race; Average household size: 2.51; Median age: 50.3; Age under 18: 20.7%; Age 65 and over: 24.3%; Males per 100 females: 107.6; Marriage status: 16.2% never married, 65.6% now married, 2.0% separated, 8.8% widowed, 9.5% divorced; Foreign born: 0.0%; Speak English only: 100.0%; With disability: 24.6%; Veterans: 14.9%; Ancestry: 21.9% German, 21.7% American, 7.3% Irish, 6.9% English, 6.9% French
Employment: 0.0% management, business, and financial, 0.0% computer, engineering, and science, 14.3% education, legal, community service, arts, and media, 3.0% healthcare practitioners, 26.3% service, 18.3% sales and office, 15.2% natural resources, construction, and maintenance, 22.9% production, transportation, and material moving
Income: Per capita: $20,726; Median household: $44,943; Average household: $54,016; Households with income of $100,000 or more: 8.0%; Poverty rate: 17.8%
Educational Attainment: High school diploma or higher: 80.6%; Bachelor's degree or higher: 7.8%; Graduate/professional degree or higher: 1.7%
Housing: Homeownership rate: 90.3%; Median home value: $89,900; Median year structure built: 1980; Homeowner vacancy rate: 7.1%; Median selected monthly owner costs: $960 with a mortgage, $415 without a mortgage; Median gross rent: n/a per month; Rental vacancy rate: 0.0%
Health Insurance: 93.0% have insurance; 59.5% have private insurance; 49.5% have public insurance; 7.0% do not have insurance; 16.0% of children under 18 do not have insurance
Transportation: Commute: 87.8% car, 0.0% public transportation, 3.3% walk, 8.8% work from home; Mean travel time to work: 32.8 minutes

GOSPORT (town). Covers a land area of 0.385 square miles and a water area of 0 square miles. Located at 39.35° N. Lat; 86.67° W. Long. Elevation is 696 feet.
History: Gosport was laid out in 1829 as a shipping point for trade on the White River.
Population: 829; Growth (since 2000): 15.9%; Density: 2,152.7 persons per square mile; Race: 99.4% White, 0.0% Black/African American, 0.6% Asian, 0.0% American Indian/Alaska Native, 0.0% Native Hawaiian/Other Pacific Islander, 0.0% Two or more races, 0.0% Hispanic of any race; Average household size: 2.15; Median age: 45.3; Age under 18: 16.4%; Age 65 and over: 22.3%; Males per 100 females: 85.2; Marriage status: 23.2% never married, 50.6% now married, 0.0% separated, 9.0% widowed, 17.2% divorced; Foreign born: 1.9%; Speak English only: 97.3%; With disability: 17.2%; Veterans: 7.6%; Ancestry: 24.7% German, 12.5% Irish, 11.1% English, 4.6% Scottish, 3.6% European
Employment: 8.4% management, business, and financial, 0.0% computer, engineering, and science, 9.2% education, legal, community service, arts, and media, 6.3% healthcare practitioners, 20.8% service, 17.6% sales and office, 7.6% natural resources, construction, and maintenance, 30.0% production, transportation, and material moving
Income: Per capita: $22,516; Median household: $39,550; Average household: $49,773; Households with income of $100,000 or more: 9.5%; Poverty rate: 21.1%
Educational Attainment: High school diploma or higher: 84.4%; Bachelor's degree or higher: 15.8%; Graduate/professional degree or higher: 10.1%

School District(s)
Spencer-Owen Community Schools (PK-12)
Enrollment: 2,730 . . . . (812) 829-2233
Housing: Homeownership rate: 53.5%; Median home value: $78,800; Median year structure built: 1950; Homeowner vacancy rate: 3.0%; Median selected monthly owner costs: $868 with a mortgage, $379 without a mortgage; Median gross rent: $630 per month; Rental vacancy rate: 8.7%
Health Insurance: 81.5% have insurance; 53.8% have private insurance; 45.3% have public insurance; 18.5% do not have insurance; 5.1% of children under 18 do not have insurance
Transportation: Commute: 96.4% car, 0.0% public transportation, 2.2% walk, 0.0% work from home; Mean travel time to work: 24.9 minutes

POLAND (unincorporated postal area)
ZCTA: 47868
Covers a land area of 58.105 square miles and a water area of 1.644 square miles. Located at 39.41° N. Lat; 86.90° W. Long..
Population: 3,195; Growth (since 2000): -0.5%; Density: 55.0 persons per square mile; Race: 98.4% White, 0.0% Black/African American, 0.0% Asian, 0.5% American Indian/Alaska Native, 0.0% Native Hawaiian/Other Pacific Islander, 1.1% Two or more races, 0.0% Hispanic of any race; Average household size: 2.52; Median age: 42.9; Age under 18: 25.0%; Age 65 and over: 19.3%; Males per 100 females: 103.1; Marriage status: 23.4% never married, 59.8% now married, 1.5% separated, 6.4% widowed, 10.5% divorced; Foreign born: 0.7%; Speak English only: 98.8%; With disability: 19.3%; Veterans: 8.8%; Ancestry: 25.8% German, 21.0% Irish, 8.0% American, 6.2% English, 3.2% Scottish
Employment: 7.8% management, business, and financial, 0.0% computer, engineering, and science, 4.4% education, legal, community service, arts, and media, 7.3% healthcare practitioners, 14.3% service, 14.0% sales and office, 22.7% natural resources, construction, and maintenance, 29.6% production, transportation, and material moving
Income: Per capita: $21,756; Median household: $42,868; Average household: $55,742; Households with income of $100,000 or more: 15.7%; Poverty rate: 19.6%
Educational Attainment: High school diploma or higher: 83.9%; Bachelor's degree or higher: 11.0%; Graduate/professional degree or higher: 7.2%
Housing: Homeownership rate: 72.2%; Median home value: $99,700; Median year structure built: 1991; Homeowner vacancy rate: 9.2%; Median selected monthly owner costs: $1,143 with a mortgage, $434 without a mortgage; Median gross rent: $781 per month; Rental vacancy rate: 0.0%
Health Insurance: 91.5% have insurance; 66.4% have private insurance; 40.5% have public insurance; 8.5% do not have insurance; 6.6% of children under 18 do not have insurance
Transportation: Commute: 93.0% car, 4.4% public transportation, 0.0% walk, 0.7% work from home; Mean travel time to work: 43.9 minutes

QUINCY (unincorporated postal area)
ZCTA: 47456
Covers a land area of 26.271 square miles and a water area of 0.154 square miles. Located at 39.47° N. Lat; 86.69° W. Long. Elevation is 738 feet.
Population: 1,672; Growth (since 2000): 109.3%; Density: 63.6 persons per square mile; Race: 96.1% White, 2.8% Black/African American, 0.0% Asian, 0.0% American Indian/Alaska Native, 0.0% Native Hawaiian/Other Pacific Islander, 1.2% Two or more races, 2.8% Hispanic of any race; Average household size: 2.82; Median age: 43.5; Age under 18: 20.9%; Age 65 and over: 11.5%; Males per 100 females: 112.8; Marriage status: 30.2% never married, 55.4% now married, 0.5% separated, 3.9% widowed, 10.4% divorced; Foreign born: 2.8%; Speak English only: 97.2%; With disability: 11.7%; Veterans: 7.0%; Ancestry: 17.7% American, 10.7% German, 9.8% Irish, 6.8% English, 2.0% Italian
Employment: 10.3% management, business, and financial, 0.7% computer, engineering, and science, 5.7% education, legal, community service, arts, and media, 2.8% healthcare practitioners, 14.9% service, 30.5% sales and office, 18.1% natural resources, construction, and maintenance, 17.0% production, transportation, and material moving
Income: Per capita: $23,050; Median household: $53,264; Average household: $63,917; Households with income of $100,000 or more: 12.5%; Poverty rate: 12.7%

Educational Attainment: High school diploma or higher: 90.6%; Bachelor's degree or higher: 6.2%; Graduate/professional degree or higher: 3.3%
Housing: Homeownership rate: 79.2%; Median home value: $109,800; Median year structure built: 1984; Homeowner vacancy rate: 6.2%; Median selected monthly owner costs: $1,089 with a mortgage, $416 without a mortgage; Median gross rent: $906 per month; Rental vacancy rate: 0.0%
Health Insurance: 91.6% have insurance; 66.1% have private insurance; 33.0% have public insurance; 8.4% do not have insurance; 2.3% of children under 18 do not have insurance
Transportation: Commute: 95.5% car, 0.0% public transportation, 0.0% walk, 4.5% work from home; Mean travel time to work: 33.3 minutes

SPENCER (town). County seat. Covers a land area of 1.261 square miles and a water area of 0 square miles. Located at 39.29° N. Lat; 86.77° W. Long. Elevation is 564 feet.
History: Spencer was a farming, coal mining, and quarrying center named for Captain Spencer of Kentucky, who was killed at the Battle of Tippecanoe. Spencer was the hometown of poets William Herschell (1873-1939) and William Vaughn Moody (1869-1910).
Population: 2,260; Growth (since 2000): -9.9%; Density: 1,792.6 persons per square mile; Race: 91.4% White, 2.2% Black/African American, 2.8% Asian, 0.7% American Indian/Alaska Native, 0.0% Native Hawaiian/Other Pacific Islander, 2.9% Two or more races, 5.6% Hispanic of any race; Average household size: 2.12; Median age: 42.0; Age under 18: 23.3%; Age 65 and over: 23.5%; Males per 100 females: 89.5; Marriage status: 25.6% never married, 42.2% now married, 3.2% separated, 10.3% widowed, 22.0% divorced; Foreign born: 2.8%; Speak English only: 96.3%; With disability: 19.5%; Veterans: 9.2%; Ancestry: 19.9% Irish, 18.6% German, 10.4% English, 7.5% American, 4.4% French
Employment: 9.7% management, business, and financial, 1.5% computer, engineering, and science, 4.8% education, legal, community service, arts, and media, 5.8% healthcare practitioners, 28.5% service, 19.7% sales and office, 9.3% natural resources, construction, and maintenance, 20.6% production, transportation, and material moving
Income: Per capita: $19,874; Median household: $35,208; Average household: $42,576; Households with income of $100,000 or more: 7.6%; Poverty rate: 21.2%
Educational Attainment: High school diploma or higher: 85.0%; Bachelor's degree or higher: 11.4%; Graduate/professional degree or higher: 3.0%

School District(s)

Spencer-Owen Community Schools (PK-12)
Enrollment: 2,730 . . . . (812) 829-2233
Housing: Homeownership rate: 57.3%; Median home value: $88,800; Median year structure built: 1957; Homeowner vacancy rate: 2.6%; Median selected monthly owner costs: $849 with a mortgage, $341 without a mortgage; Median gross rent: $564 per month; Rental vacancy rate: 3.5%
Health Insurance: 84.7% have insurance; 55.4% have private insurance; 46.3% have public insurance; 15.3% do not have insurance; 13.0% of children under 18 do not have insurance
Newspapers: Owen Leader (weekly circulation 400); Spencer Evening World (daily circulation 3,600)
Transportation: Commute: 88.2% car, 0.0% public transportation, 10.6% walk, 0.0% work from home; Mean travel time to work: 18.5 minutes
Additional Information Contacts
Town of Spencer . . . . (812) 829-3213
http://www.spencer.in.gov

Parke County

Located in western Indiana; bounded on the west by the Wabash River; drained by Sugar and Raccoon Creeks. Covers a land area of 444.663 square miles, a water area of 5.316 square miles, and is located in the Eastern Time Zone at 39.77° N. Lat., 87.20° W. Long. The county was founded in 1821. County seat is Rockville.

Weather Station: Rockville Elevation: 689 feet

	Jan	Feb	Mar	Apr	May	Jun	Jul	Aug	Sep	Oct	Nov	Dec
High	37	42	54	66	76	84	87	85	79	67	54	40
Low	21	24	33	43	52	61	65	64	55	44	35	25
Precip	2.8	2.5	3.4	4.1	5.4	4.5	5.1	4.0	3.3	3.8	4.2	3.6
Snow	5.1	2.9	1.7	0.1	tr	0.0	0.0	0.0	0.0	tr	0.1	3.9

High and Low temperatures in degrees Fahrenheit; Precipitation and Snow in inches

Population: 17,062; Growth (since 2000): -1.0%; Density: 38.4 persons per square mile; Race: 95.9% White, 1.0% Black/African American, 0.0% Asian, 0.2% American Indian/Alaska Native, 0.5% Native Hawaiian/Other Pacific Islander, 2.0% two or more races, 1.5% Hispanic of any race; Average household size: 2.55; Median age: 42.2; Age under 18: 21.5%; Age 65 and over: 17.8%; Males per 100 females: 88.1; Marriage status: 23.6% never married, 53.3% now married, 1.8% separated, 5.5% widowed, 17.6% divorced; Foreign born: 1.1%; Speak English only: 94.7%; With disability: 19.2%; Veterans: 10.3%; Ancestry: 21.6% German, 17.6% American, 9.8% English, 9.4% Irish, 2.8% French
Religion: Six largest groups: 12.6% Baptist, 8.7% European Free-Church, 6.3% Non-denominational Protestant, 3.6% Methodist/Pietist, 1.3% Catholicism, 1.2% Pentecostal
Economy: Unemployment rate: 4.1%; Leading industries: 16.6 % other services (except public administration); 14.6 % retail trade; 9.5 % accommodation and food services; Farms: 574 totaling 176,571 acres; Company size: 0 employ 1,000 or more persons, 0 employ 500 to 999 persons, 3 employ 100 to 499 persons, 250 employ less than 100 persons; Business ownership: 307 women-owned, n/a Black-owned, n/a Hispanic-owned, n/a Asian-owned, n/a American Indian/Alaska Native-owned
Employment: 9.1% management, business, and financial, 2.3% computer, engineering, and science, 6.4% education, legal, community service, arts, and media, 4.2% healthcare practitioners, 17.7% service, 22.1% sales and office, 14.6% natural resources, construction, and maintenance, 23.6% production, transportation, and material moving
Income: Per capita: $21,636; Median household: $44,643; Average household: $58,637; Households with income of $100,000 or more: 12.7%; Poverty rate: 13.9%
Educational Attainment: High school diploma or higher: 85.5%; Bachelor's degree or higher: 12.6%; Graduate/professional degree or higher: 3.8%
Housing: Homeownership rate: 77.2%; Median home value: $86,700; Median year structure built: 1974; Homeowner vacancy rate: 5.1%; Median selected monthly owner costs: $898 with a mortgage, $327 without a mortgage; Median gross rent: $563 per month; Rental vacancy rate: 1.6%
Vital Statistics: Birth rate: 126.1 per 10,000 population; Death rate: 100.7 per 10,000 population; Age-adjusted cancer mortality rate: 172.1 deaths per 100,000 population
Health Insurance: 86.3% have insurance; 62.5% have private insurance; 37.8% have public insurance; 13.7% do not have insurance; 16.4% of children under 18 do not have insurance
Health Care: Physicians: 6.5 per 10,000 population; Dentists: 1.8 per 10,000 population; Hospital beds: 0.0 per 10,000 population; Hospital admissions: 0.0 per 10,000 population
Transportation: Commute: 91.0% car, 0.5% public transportation, 2.3% walk, 4.0% work from home; Mean travel time to work: 27.0 minutes
2016 Presidential Election: 73.3% Trump, 21.7% Clinton, 4.1% Johnson, 0.1% Stein
National and State Parks: Raccoon Lake State Recreation Area; Turkey Run State Park
Additional Information Contacts
Parke Government . . . . (765) 569-5132
http://www.parkecounty-in.gov

Parke County Communities

BLOOMINGDALE (town). Covers a land area of 0.582 square miles and a water area of 0 square miles. Located at 39.83° N. Lat; 87.25° W. Long. Elevation is 643 feet.
Population: 309; Growth (since 2000): -3.1%; Density: 531.3 persons per square mile; Race: 99.4% White, 0.0% Black/African American, 0.0% Asian, 0.0% American Indian/Alaska Native, 0.0% Native Hawaiian/Other Pacific Islander, 0.6% Two or more races, 0.0% Hispanic of any race; Average household size: 2.66; Median age: 40.5; Age under 18: 26.2%; Age 65 and over: 16.8%; Males per 100 females: 101.8; Marriage status: 12.9% never married, 73.8% now married, 2.1% separated, 3.3% widowed, 10.0% divorced; Foreign born: 0.0%; Speak English only: 100.0%; With disability: 14.9%; Veterans: 13.2%; Ancestry: 26.5% German, 17.2% American, 12.9% English, 10.7% Irish, 4.9% Swiss
Employment: 9.2% management, business, and financial, 3.9% computer, engineering, and science, 5.9% education, legal, community service, arts, and media, 1.3% healthcare practitioners, 21.6% service, 15.0% sales and office, 15.7% natural resources, construction, and maintenance, 27.5% production, transportation, and material moving

Income: Per capita: $21,760; Median household: $46,250; Average household: $56,463; Households with income of $100,000 or more: 9.6%; Poverty rate: 18.1%
Educational Attainment: High school diploma or higher: 90.5%; Bachelor's degree or higher: 14.1%; Graduate/professional degree or higher: 3.6%
Housing: Homeownership rate: 85.3%; Median home value: $63,500; Median year structure built: Before 1940; Homeowner vacancy rate: 0.0%; Median selected monthly owner costs: $809 with a mortgage, $277 without a mortgage; Median gross rent: $678 per month; Rental vacancy rate: 0.0%
Health Insurance: 85.4% have insurance; 70.2% have private insurance; 29.1% have public insurance; 14.6% do not have insurance; 19.8% of children under 18 do not have insurance
Transportation: Commute: 94.8% car, 0.0% public transportation, 0.0% walk, 4.6% work from home; Mean travel time to work: 21.2 minutes

---

BRIDGETON (unincorporated postal area)
ZCTA: 47836
Covers a land area of 0.197 square miles and a water area of 0 square miles. Located at 39.65° N. Lat; 87.18° W. Long. Elevation is 564 feet.
Population: 46; Growth (since 2000): -63.5%; Density: 233.9 persons per square mile; Race: 100.0% White, 0.0% Black/African American, 0.0% Asian, 0.0% American Indian/Alaska Native, 0.0% Native Hawaiian/Other Pacific Islander, 0.0% Two or more races, 0.0% Hispanic of any race; Average household size: 3.07; Median age: 56.5; Age under 18: 32.6%; Age 65 and over: 0.0%; Males per 100 females: 80.8; Marriage status: 32.6% never married, 67.4% now married, 0.0% separated, 0.0% widowed, 0.0% divorced; Foreign born: 0.0%; Speak English only: 100.0%; With disability: 0.0%; Veterans: 0.0%; Ancestry: 100.0% British
Employment: 48.4% management, business, and financial, 0.0% computer, engineering, and science, 0.0% education, legal, community service, arts, and media, 51.6% healthcare practitioners, 0.0% service, 0.0% sales and office, 0.0% natural resources, construction, and maintenance, 0.0% production, transportation, and material moving
Income: Per capita: $23,926; Median household: n/a; Average household: n/a; Households with income of $100,000 or more: n/a; Poverty rate: n/a
Educational Attainment: High school diploma or higher: 100.0%; Bachelor's degree or higher: 48.4%; Graduate/professional degree or higher: n/a
Housing: Homeownership rate: 100.0%; Median home value: n/a; Median year structure built: n/a; Homeowner vacancy rate: 0.0%; Median selected monthly owner costs: $0 with a mortgage, $0 without a mortgage; Median gross rent: n/a per month; Rental vacancy rate: 0.0%
Health Insurance: 100.0% have insurance; 100.0% have private insurance; 0.0% have public insurance; 0.0% do not have insurance; 0.0% of children under 18 do not have insurance
Transportation: Commute: 51.6% car, 0.0% public transportation, 48.4% walk, 0.0% work from home; Mean travel time to work: 0.0 minutes

---

MARSHALL (town). Covers a land area of 0.256 square miles and a water area of 0 square miles. Located at 39.85° N. Lat; 87.19° W. Long. Elevation is 702 feet.
History: Covered bridges in area. Laid out 1878.
Population: 261; Growth (since 2000): -27.5%; Density: 1,019.8 persons per square mile; Race: 96.6% White, 0.0% Black/African American, 0.0% Asian, 0.0% American Indian/Alaska Native, 0.0% Native Hawaiian/Other Pacific Islander, 3.4% Two or more races, 0.0% Hispanic of any race; Average household size: 2.64; Median age: 50.1; Age under 18: 16.5%; Age 65 and over: 13.0%; Males per 100 females: 88.4; Marriage status: 9.5% never married, 67.6% now married, 2.3% separated, 7.7% widowed, 15.3% divorced; Foreign born: 0.0%; Speak English only: 100.0%; With disability: 21.5%; Veterans: 6.0%; Ancestry: 14.9% German, 14.6% American, 6.9% English, 5.0% Irish, 4.6% Welsh
Employment: 1.4% management, business, and financial, 4.2% computer, engineering, and science, 4.9% education, legal, community service, arts, and media, 4.2% healthcare practitioners, 17.6% service, 21.1% sales and office, 12.7% natural resources, construction, and maintenance, 33.8% production, transportation, and material moving
Income: Per capita: $24,725; Median household: $56,458; Average household: $61,667; Households with income of $100,000 or more: 24.2%; Poverty rate: 9.2%
Educational Attainment: High school diploma or higher: 93.0%; Bachelor's degree or higher: 10.0%; Graduate/professional degree or higher: 4.0%

School District(s)
North Central Parke Comm Schl Corp (PK-12)
Enrollment: 1,242 . . . . (765) 597-2750
Housing: Homeownership rate: 85.9%; Median home value: $72,300; Median year structure built: Before 1940; Homeowner vacancy rate: 6.6%; Median selected monthly owner costs: $906 with a mortgage, $271 without a mortgage; Median gross rent: $675 per month; Rental vacancy rate: 0.0%
Health Insurance: 90.0% have insurance; 73.2% have private insurance; 30.7% have public insurance; 10.0% do not have insurance; 0.0% of children under 18 do not have insurance
Transportation: Commute: 88.4% car, 0.0% public transportation, 3.6% walk, 8.0% work from home; Mean travel time to work: 26.1 minutes

---

MECCA (town). Covers a land area of 0.393 square miles and a water area of 0 square miles. Located at 39.73° N. Lat; 87.33° W. Long. Elevation is 512 feet.
History: Covered bridges in area. Laid out 1890.
Population: 385; Growth (since 2000): 8.5%; Density: 980.1 persons per square mile; Race: 98.7% White, 0.0% Black/African American, 0.0% Asian, 0.0% American Indian/Alaska Native, 0.0% Native Hawaiian/Other Pacific Islander, 1.3% Two or more races, 0.0% Hispanic of any race; Average household size: 2.94; Median age: 37.3; Age under 18: 37.4%; Age 65 and over: 23.6%; Males per 100 females: 113.4; Marriage status: 18.0% never married, 59.4% now married, 2.0% separated, 9.4% widowed, 13.3% divorced; Foreign born: 0.0%; Speak English only: 98.0%; With disability: 20.5%; Veterans: 15.4%; Ancestry: 24.2% American, 13.2% German, 10.4% Irish, 6.2% English, 4.4% Czechoslovakian
Employment: 2.8% management, business, and financial, 0.0% computer, engineering, and science, 3.7% education, legal, community service, arts, and media, 8.3% healthcare practitioners, 36.1% service, 12.0% sales and office, 6.5% natural resources, construction, and maintenance, 30.6% production, transportation, and material moving
Income: Per capita: $14,266; Median household: $36,250; Average household: $41,722; Households with income of $100,000 or more: 5.4%; Poverty rate: 29.7%
Educational Attainment: High school diploma or higher: 79.8%; Bachelor's degree or higher: 2.2%; Graduate/professional degree or higher: n/a
Housing: Homeownership rate: 74.8%; Median home value: $43,800; Median year structure built: 1942; Homeowner vacancy rate: 0.0%; Median selected monthly owner costs: $730 with a mortgage, $285 without a mortgage; Median gross rent: $655 per month; Rental vacancy rate: 0.0%
Health Insurance: 89.1% have insurance; 47.0% have private insurance; 59.0% have public insurance; 10.9% do not have insurance; 2.1% of children under 18 do not have insurance
Transportation: Commute: 100.0% car, 0.0% public transportation, 0.0% walk, 0.0% work from home; Mean travel time to work: 26.0 minutes

---

MONTEZUMA (town). Covers a land area of 0.600 square miles and a water area of 0 square miles. Located at 39.79° N. Lat; 87.37° W. Long. Elevation is 505 feet.
History: When the Wabash & Erie Canal was completed in 1848, Montezuma became a commercial center on the Wabash River. Montezuma was settled by Samuel Hill in 1821, and named for the Aztec emperor of Mexico.
Population: 914; Growth (since 2000): -22.5%; Density: 1,522.2 persons per square mile; Race: 96.1% White, 0.0% Black/African American, 0.0% Asian, 0.3% American Indian/Alaska Native, 0.0% Native Hawaiian/Other Pacific Islander, 2.1% Two or more races, 1.9% Hispanic of any race; Average household size: 2.62; Median age: 39.4; Age under 18: 24.6%; Age 65 and over: 21.3%; Males per 100 females: 102.0; Marriage status: 24.9% never married, 49.9% now married, 0.0% separated, 6.7% widowed, 18.5% divorced; Foreign born: 3.2%; Speak English only: 96.6%; With disability: 22.9%; Veterans: 10.0%; Ancestry: 23.5% American, 17.1% German, 11.6% Irish, 7.2% English, 1.6% Yugoslavian
Employment: 4.0% management, business, and financial, 0.9% computer, engineering, and science, 0.0% education, legal, community service, arts, and media, 0.0% healthcare practitioners, 26.1% service, 25.6% sales and office, 8.0% natural resources, construction, and maintenance, 35.3% production, transportation, and material moving

Income: Per capita: $19,007; Median household: $47,875; Average household: $49,389; Households with income of $100,000 or more: 4.6%; Poverty rate: 14.1%
Educational Attainment: High school diploma or higher: 84.2%; Bachelor's degree or higher: 6.4%; Graduate/professional degree or higher: 3.7%

School District(s)

Southwest Parke Com Sch Corp (KG-12)
Enrollment: 924 . . . . (765) 569-2073
Housing: Homeownership rate: 79.7%; Median home value: $57,700; Median year structure built: 1941; Homeowner vacancy rate: 0.0%; Median selected monthly owner costs: $750 with a mortgage, $294 without a mortgage; Median gross rent: $699 per month; Rental vacancy rate: 12.3%
Health Insurance: 86.1% have insurance; 62.4% have private insurance; 40.5% have public insurance; 13.9% do not have insurance; 9.1% of children under 18 do not have insurance
Transportation: Commute: 93.1% car, 0.0% public transportation, 2.3% walk, 4.6% work from home; Mean travel time to work: 23.5 minutes

ROCKVILLE (town). County seat. Covers a land area of 1.492 square miles and a water area of 0 square miles. Located at 39.77° N. Lat; 87.23° W. Long. Elevation is 712 feet.
History: Joseph A. Wright, a governor of Indiana, began his law practice in Rockville.
Population: 2,562; Growth (since 2000): -7.3%; Density: 1,716.6 persons per square mile; Race: 97.4% White, 0.0% Black/African American, 0.0% Asian, 0.0% American Indian/Alaska Native, 0.0% Native Hawaiian/Other Pacific Islander, 2.6% Two or more races, 0.7% Hispanic of any race; Average household size: 2.24; Median age: 40.6; Age under 18: 20.3%; Age 65 and over: 18.9%; Males per 100 females: 87.8; Marriage status: 23.5% never married, 50.5% now married, 0.0% separated, 9.1% widowed, 16.8% divorced; Foreign born: 1.5%; Speak English only: 98.2%; With disability: 21.0%; Veterans: 11.6%; Ancestry: 18.5% German, 13.8% English, 11.0% American, 9.3% Irish, 4.1% French
Employment: 8.6% management, business, and financial, 2.2% computer, engineering, and science, 11.5% education, legal, community service, arts, and media, 3.4% healthcare practitioners, 18.3% service, 22.5% sales and office, 11.4% natural resources, construction, and maintenance, 22.0% production, transportation, and material moving
Income: Per capita: $20,407; Median household: $36,375; Average household: $45,378; Households with income of $100,000 or more: 6.0%; Poverty rate: 19.6%
Educational Attainment: High school diploma or higher: 85.8%; Bachelor's degree or higher: 14.0%; Graduate/professional degree or higher: 6.9%

School District(s)

North Central Parke Comm Schl Corp (PK-12)
Enrollment: 1,242 . . . . (765) 597-2750
Housing: Homeownership rate: 65.5%; Median home value: $75,600; Median year structure built: 1962; Homeowner vacancy rate: 10.8%; Median selected monthly owner costs: $758 with a mortgage, $285 without a mortgage; Median gross rent: $498 per month; Rental vacancy rate: 0.0%
Health Insurance: 89.5% have insurance; 63.4% have private insurance; 40.9% have public insurance; 10.5% do not have insurance; 0.0% of children under 18 do not have insurance
Newspapers: Parke County Sentinel (weekly circulation 4,500)
Transportation: Commute: 87.8% car, 0.0% public transportation, 4.4% walk, 3.2% work from home; Mean travel time to work: 22.9 minutes
Additional Information Contacts
Town of Rockville . . . . (765) 569-5226
http://www.new.rockvilleindiana.org

ROSEDALE (town). Covers a land area of 0.395 square miles and a water area of 0 square miles. Located at 39.62° N. Lat; 87.28° W. Long. Elevation is 538 feet.
History: Settled c.1819.
Population: 682; Growth (since 2000): -9.1%; Density: 1,727.5 persons per square mile; Race: 90.6% White, 0.0% Black/African American, 0.0% Asian, 0.1% American Indian/Alaska Native, 0.0% Native Hawaiian/Other Pacific Islander, 7.9% Two or more races, 1.3% Hispanic of any race; Average household size: 2.24; Median age: 46.1; Age under 18: 23.5%; Age 65 and over: 19.9%; Males per 100 females: 86.4; Marriage status: 20.8% never married, 51.4% now married, 2.2% separated, 6.7% widowed, 21.2% divorced; Foreign born: 0.0%; Speak English only: 98.1%; With disability: 24.9%; Veterans: 13.6%; Ancestry: 22.0% German, 16.6% English, 13.6% Irish, 10.6% American, 5.4% Hungarian
Employment: 6.0% management, business, and financial, 4.1% computer, engineering, and science, 4.8% education, legal, community service, arts, and media, 5.7% healthcare practitioners, 24.8% service, 18.1% sales and office, 8.3% natural resources, construction, and maintenance, 28.3% production, transportation, and material moving
Income: Per capita: $22,041; Median household: $35,208; Average household: $49,260; Households with income of $100,000 or more: 9.2%; Poverty rate: 20.4%
Educational Attainment: High school diploma or higher: 88.7%; Bachelor's degree or higher: 14.1%; Graduate/professional degree or higher: 6.4%

School District(s)

Southwest Parke Com Sch Corp (KG-12)
Enrollment: 924 . . . . (765) 569-2073
Housing: Homeownership rate: 76.4%; Median home value: $64,500; Median year structure built: 1952; Homeowner vacancy rate: 2.1%; Median selected monthly owner costs: $793 with a mortgage, $331 without a mortgage; Median gross rent: $620 per month; Rental vacancy rate: 14.9%
Health Insurance: 91.2% have insurance; 58.9% have private insurance; 44.4% have public insurance; 8.8% do not have insurance; 7.9% of children under 18 do not have insurance
Transportation: Commute: 91.4% car, 0.0% public transportation, 3.5% walk, 5.1% work from home; Mean travel time to work: 30.3 minutes

Perry County

Located in southern Indiana; bounded on the south and partly on the east by the Ohio River and the Kentucky border; drained by the Anderson River. Covers a land area of 381.727 square miles, a water area of 4.563 square miles, and is located in the Central Time Zone at 38.08° N. Lat., 86.63° W. Long. The county was founded in 1814. County seat is Cannelton.

Weather Station: Tell City Elevation: 399 feet

	Jan	Feb	Mar	Apr	May	Jun	Jul	Aug	Sep	Oct	Nov	Dec
High	42	46	56	67	76	84	87	87	81	70	57	45
Low	26	28	36	45	55	64	68	67	59	47	39	29
Precip	3.3	3.2	4.3	4.3	5.8	4.4	4.5	3.4	3.6	3.4	3.8	4.1
Snow	1.8	2.2	0.4	tr	0.0	0.0	0.0	0.0	0.0	0.0	0.1	0.8

High and Low temperatures in degrees Fahrenheit; Precipitation and Snow in inches

Population: 19,229; Growth (since 2000): 1.7%; Density: 50.4 persons per square mile; Race: 94.5% White, 2.8% Black/African American, 0.3% Asian, 0.2% American Indian/Alaska Native, 0.0% Native Hawaiian/Other Pacific Islander, 1.8% two or more races, 1.3% Hispanic of any race; Average household size: 2.35; Median age: 41.9; Age under 18: 21.2%; Age 65 and over: 17.4%; Males per 100 females: 112.8; Marriage status: 24.6% never married, 54.2% now married, 1.3% separated, 6.8% widowed, 14.5% divorced; Foreign born: 0.7%; Speak English only: 98.5%; With disability: 15.5%; Veterans: 8.6%; Ancestry: 25.3% German, 12.5% American, 10.0% Irish, 7.9% English, 7.4% French
Religion: Six largest groups: 30.8% Catholicism, 6.3% Baptist, 2.9% Methodist/Pietist, 2.6% Presbyterian-Reformed, 1.6% Latter-day Saints, 1.3% Lutheran
Economy: Unemployment rate: 3.7%; Leading industries: 17.8 % retail trade; 12.2 % health care and social assistance; 10.8 % other services (except public administration); Farms: 413 totaling 66,275 acres; Company size: 1 employs 1,000 or more persons, 1 employs 500 to 999 persons, 6 employ 100 to 499 persons, 352 employ less than 100 persons; Business ownership: 289 women-owned, n/a Black-owned, n/a Hispanic-owned, n/a Asian-owned, n/a American Indian/Alaska Native-owned
Employment: 9.5% management, business, and financial, 2.9% computer, engineering, and science, 6.9% education, legal, community service, arts, and media, 4.4% healthcare practitioners, 18.3% service, 18.5% sales and office, 11.9% natural resources, construction, and maintenance, 27.6% production, transportation, and material moving
Income: Per capita: $23,003; Median household: $49,689; Average household: $59,070; Households with income of $100,000 or more: 15.3%; Poverty rate: 14.5%
Educational Attainment: High school diploma or higher: 87.9%; Bachelor's degree or higher: 14.3%; Graduate/professional degree or higher: 7.0%

Housing: Homeownership rate: 77.3%; Median home value: $103,000; Median year structure built: 1970; Homeowner vacancy rate: 1.5%; Median selected monthly owner costs: $920 with a mortgage, $325 without a mortgage; Median gross rent: $585 per month; Rental vacancy rate: 6.6%
Vital Statistics: Birth rate: 120.0 per 10,000 population; Death rate: 90.1 per 10,000 population; Age-adjusted cancer mortality rate: 142.1 deaths per 100,000 population
Health Insurance: 92.5% have insurance; 73.0% have private insurance; 34.2% have public insurance; 7.5% do not have insurance; 3.3% of children under 18 do not have insurance
Health Care: Physicians: 9.5 per 10,000 population; Dentists: 3.1 per 10,000 population; Hospital beds: 13.2 per 10,000 population; Hospital admissions: 442.9 per 10,000 population
Air Quality Index (AQI): Percent of Days: 87.2% good, 12.3% moderate, 0.4% unhealthy for sensitive individuals, 0.0% unhealthy, 0.0% very unhealthy; Annual median: 40; Annual maximum: 101
Transportation: Commute: 95.5% car, 0.2% public transportation, 0.9% walk, 2.2% work from home; Mean travel time to work: 23.5 minutes
2016 Presidential Election: 56.6% Trump, 38.0% Clinton, 5.1% Johnson, 0.3% Stein
National and State Parks: Ferdinand State Forest; Harrison-Crawford State Forest
Additional Information Contacts
Perry Government. . . . . (812) 547-6427
http://www.perrycounty.in.gov

Perry County Communities

BRANCHVILLE (unincorporated postal area)
ZCTA: 47514

Covers a land area of 4.398 square miles and a water area of 0 square miles. Located at 38.16° N. Lat; 86.59° W. Long. Elevation is 433 feet.
Population: 1,757; Growth (since 2000): 594.5%; Density: 399.5 persons per square mile; Race: 78.1% White, 21.6% Black/African American, 0.0% Asian, 0.0% American Indian/Alaska Native, 0.0% Native Hawaiian/Other Pacific Islander, 0.0% Two or more races, 1.3% Hispanic of any race; Average household size: 2.86; Median age: 35.6; Age under 18: 5.8%; Age 65 and over: 2.9%; Males per 100 females: ***.*; Marriage status: 47.6% never married, 27.3% now married, 0.6% separated, 0.8% widowed, 24.3% divorced; Foreign born: 0.6%; Speak English only: 99.7%; With disability: 0.0%; Veterans: 2.9%; Ancestry: 5.4% German, 3.5% American, 2.4% Irish, 1.3% French, 1.0% Polish
Employment: 16.1% management, business, and financial, 6.0% computer, engineering, and science, 9.5% education, legal, community service, arts, and media, 4.2% healthcare practitioners, 20.8% service, 0.0% sales and office, 25.6% natural resources, construction, and maintenance, 17.9% production, transportation, and material moving
Income: Per capita: $5,601; Median household: $49,022; Average household: $60,409; Households with income of $100,000 or more: 8.8%; Poverty rate: 5.1%
Educational Attainment: High school diploma or higher: 80.6%; Bachelor's degree or higher: 2.8%; Graduate/professional degree or higher: 1.1%
Housing: Homeownership rate: 93.1%; Median home value: n/a; Median year structure built: 1983; Homeowner vacancy rate: 0.0%; Median selected monthly owner costs: $0 with a mortgage, $230 without a mortgage; Median gross rent: n/a per month; Rental vacancy rate: 0.0%
Health Insurance: 98.1% have insurance; 76.2% have private insurance; 32.0% have public insurance; 1.9% do not have insurance; 0.0% of children under 18 do not have insurance
Transportation: Commute: 82.7% car, 3.6% public transportation, 3.6% walk, 10.1% work from home; Mean travel time to work: 20.4 minutes

BRISTOW (unincorporated postal area)
ZCTA: 47515

Covers a land area of 55.762 square miles and a water area of 0.235 square miles. Located at 38.18° N. Lat; 86.70° W. Long. Elevation is 410 feet.
Population: 980; Growth (since 2000): -11.8%; Density: 17.6 persons per square mile; Race: 100.0% White, 0.0% Black/African American, 0.0% Asian, 0.0% American Indian/Alaska Native, 0.0% Native Hawaiian/Other Pacific Islander, 0.0% Two or more races, 0.0% Hispanic of any race; Average household size: 2.39; Median age: 46.2; Age under 18: 23.1%; Age 65 and over: 22.6%; Males per 100 females: 102.7; Marriage status: 15.7% never married, 70.3% now married, 0.0% separated, 6.4% widowed, 7.6% divorced; Foreign born: 0.0%; Speak English only: 96.8%; With disability: 15.2%; Veterans: 7.2%; Ancestry: 26.7% German, 17.1% American, 15.1% French, 11.0% Belgian, 7.0% Irish
Employment: 5.2% management, business, and financial, 0.0% computer, engineering, and science, 3.8% education, legal, community service, arts, and media, 1.8% healthcare practitioners, 11.6% service, 24.5% sales and office, 14.9% natural resources, construction, and maintenance, 38.2% production, transportation, and material moving
Income: Per capita: $29,215; Median household: $67,500; Average household: $73,002; Households with income of $100,000 or more: 25.2%; Poverty rate: 8.6%
Educational Attainment: High school diploma or higher: 76.8%; Bachelor's degree or higher: 8.1%; Graduate/professional degree or higher: 1.2%
Housing: Homeownership rate: 91.7%; Median home value: $153,200; Median year structure built: 1985; Homeowner vacancy rate: 0.0%; Median selected monthly owner costs: $1,013 with a mortgage, $272 without a mortgage; Median gross rent: n/a per month; Rental vacancy rate: 0.0%
Health Insurance: 95.9% have insurance; 72.2% have private insurance; 32.9% have public insurance; 4.1% do not have insurance; 0.0% of children under 18 do not have insurance
Transportation: Commute: 100.0% car, 0.0% public transportation, 0.0% walk, 0.0% work from home; Mean travel time to work: 40.2 minutes

CANNELTON (city). County seat. Covers a land area of 1.482 square miles and a water area of 0.102 square miles. Located at 37.91° N. Lat; 86.74° W. Long. Elevation is 410 feet.
History: Cannelton was founded in 1837 as a coal-mining town and shipping port on the Ohio River.
Population: 1,622; Growth (since 2000): 34.2%; Density: 1,094.6 persons per square mile; Race: 91.7% White, 2.5% Black/African American, 0.0% Asian, 0.0% American Indian/Alaska Native, 0.0% Native Hawaiian/Other Pacific Islander, 4.4% Two or more races, 2.3% Hispanic of any race; Average household size: 2.19; Median age: 37.8; Age under 18: 25.5%; Age 65 and over: 14.1%; Males per 100 females: 95.1; Marriage status: 29.2% never married, 46.4% now married, 1.7% separated, 5.3% widowed, 19.0% divorced; Foreign born: 1.8%; Speak English only: 96.7%; With disability: 26.2%; Veterans: 11.0%; Ancestry: 19.0% German, 11.6% English, 9.6% American, 7.5% Irish, 2.6% Italian
Employment: 6.0% management, business, and financial, 3.3% computer, engineering, and science, 3.3% education, legal, community service, arts, and media, 5.0% healthcare practitioners, 29.2% service, 21.8% sales and office, 6.0% natural resources, construction, and maintenance, 25.4% production, transportation, and material moving
Income: Per capita: $15,653; Median household: $25,581; Average household: $33,349; Households with income of $100,000 or more: 3.0%; Poverty rate: 28.5%
Educational Attainment: High school diploma or higher: 87.1%; Bachelor's degree or higher: 9.5%; Graduate/professional degree or higher: 2.8%

School District(s)

Cannelton City Schools (PK-12)
Enrollment: 287. . . . . (812) 547-2637
Housing: Homeownership rate: 45.3%; Median home value: $67,100; Median year structure built: 1957; Homeowner vacancy rate: 0.0%; Median selected monthly owner costs: $774 with a mortgage, $276 without a mortgage; Median gross rent: $537 per month; Rental vacancy rate: 9.8%
Health Insurance: 91.3% have insurance; 56.7% have private insurance; 48.2% have public insurance; 8.7% do not have insurance; 7.4% of children under 18 do not have insurance
Transportation: Commute: 92.7% car, 0.0% public transportation, 0.0% walk, 3.4% work from home; Mean travel time to work: 18.9 minutes

DERBY (unincorporated postal area)
ZCTA: 47525

Covers a land area of 28.878 square miles and a water area of 0.452 square miles. Located at 38.03° N. Lat; 86.56° W. Long. Elevation is 453 feet.
Population: 381; Growth (since 2000): -8.9%; Density: 13.2 persons per square mile; Race: 100.0% White, 0.0% Black/African American, 0.0% Asian, 0.0% American Indian/Alaska Native, 0.0% Native

Hawaiian/Other Pacific Islander, 0.0% Two or more races, 0.0% Hispanic of any race; Average household size: 2.05; Median age: 53.0; Age under 18: 12.6%; Age 65 and over: 31.8%; Males per 100 females: 103.2; Marriage status: 13.2% never married, 69.4% now married, 0.0% separated, 13.8% widowed, 3.6% divorced; Foreign born: 0.0%; Speak English only: 100.0%; With disability: 15.2%; Veterans: 2.4%; Ancestry: 26.2% German, 21.5% American, 11.8% English, 11.5% French, 6.6% European

Employment: 10.5% management, business, and financial, 4.5% computer, engineering, and science, 13.5% education, legal, community service, arts, and media, 0.0% healthcare practitioners, 0.0% service, 23.3% sales and office, 12.0% natural resources, construction, and maintenance, 36.1% production, transportation, and material moving

Income: Per capita: $29,343; Median household: $38,750; Average household: $62,063; Households with income of $100,000 or more: 21.5%; Poverty rate: 2.4%

Educational Attainment: High school diploma or higher: 88.9%; Bachelor's degree or higher: 24.9%; Graduate/professional degree or higher: 10.2%

Housing: Homeownership rate: 84.9%; Median home value: $166,100; Median year structure built: 1981; Homeowner vacancy rate: 0.0%; Median selected monthly owner costs: $1,413 with a mortgage, $260 without a mortgage; Median gross rent: n/a per month; Rental vacancy rate: 0.0%

Health Insurance: 91.9% have insurance; 75.3% have private insurance; 38.8% have public insurance; 8.1% do not have insurance; 0.0% of children under 18 do not have insurance

Transportation: Commute: 85.7% car, 0.0% public transportation, 0.0% walk, 4.5% work from home; Mean travel time to work: 30.6 minutes

LEOPOLD (unincorporated postal area)

ZCTA: 47551

Covers a land area of 32.182 square miles and a water area of 0.011 square miles. Located at 38.11° N. Lat; 86.57° W. Long. Elevation is 725 feet.

Population: 862; Growth (since 2000): 51.8%; Density: 26.8 persons per square mile; Race: 100.0% White, 0.0% Black/African American, 0.0% Asian, 0.0% American Indian/Alaska Native, 0.0% Native Hawaiian/Other Pacific Islander, 0.0% Two or more races, 0.0% Hispanic of any race; Average household size: 2.60; Median age: 30.7; Age under 18: 33.5%; Age 65 and over: 14.7%; Males per 100 females: 107.3; Marriage status: 24.0% never married, 51.2% now married, 0.0% separated, 13.4% widowed, 11.4% divorced; Foreign born: 0.0%; Speak English only: 100.0%; With disability: 14.2%; Veterans: 5.2%; Ancestry: 42.9% German, 31.7% Irish, 12.6% French, 10.1% American, 6.4% Hungarian

Employment: 13.6% management, business, and financial, 5.6% computer, engineering, and science, 4.9% education, legal, community service, arts, and media, 9.5% healthcare practitioners, 4.6% service, 29.0% sales and office, 19.2% natural resources, construction, and maintenance, 13.6% production, transportation, and material moving

Income: Per capita: $26,290; Median household: $59,375; Average household: $71,375; Households with income of $100,000 or more: 22.0%; Poverty rate: 13.1%

Educational Attainment: High school diploma or higher: 91.5%; Bachelor's degree or higher: 21.6%; Graduate/professional degree or higher: 9.8%

School District(s)

Perry Central Com Schools Corp (PK-12)
Enrollment: 995 .... (812) 843-5576

Housing: Homeownership rate: 97.3%; Median home value: $124,800; Median year structure built: 1976; Homeowner vacancy rate: 0.0%; Median selected monthly owner costs: $987 with a mortgage, $342 without a mortgage; Median gross rent: n/a per month; Rental vacancy rate: 0.0%

Health Insurance: 99.0% have insurance; 91.5% have private insurance; 27.3% have public insurance; 1.0% do not have insurance; 0.0% of children under 18 do not have insurance

Transportation: Commute: 90.8% car, 2.9% public transportation, 0.0% walk, 6.3% work from home; Mean travel time to work: 32.4 minutes

ROME (unincorporated postal area)

ZCTA: 47574

Covers a land area of 14.548 square miles and a water area of 0.493 square miles. Located at 37.95° N. Lat; 86.56° W. Long. Elevation is 410 feet.

Population: 292; Growth (since 2000): 74.9%; Density: 20.1 persons per square mile; Race: 100.0% White, 0.0% Black/African American, 0.0% Asian, 0.0% American Indian/Alaska Native, 0.0% Native Hawaiian/Other Pacific Islander, 0.0% Two or more races, 0.0% Hispanic of any race; Average household size: 2.86; Median age: 49.7; Age under 18: 8.9%; Age 65 and over: 17.8%; Males per 100 females: 102.7; Marriage status: 34.2% never married, 39.8% now married, 0.0% separated, 19.5% widowed, 6.4% divorced; Foreign born: 0.0%; Speak English only: 100.0%; With disability: 28.4%; Veterans: 2.3%; Ancestry: 21.6% German, 16.8% French, 6.8% English, 4.5% American, 3.4% Belgian

Employment: 0.0% management, business, and financial, 17.0% computer, engineering, and science, 13.3% education, legal, community service, arts, and media, 0.0% healthcare practitioners, 48.9% service, 3.7% sales and office, 0.0% natural resources, construction, and maintenance, 17.0% production, transportation, and material moving

Income: Per capita: $29,845; Median household: $58,542; Average household: $88,598; Households with income of $100,000 or more: 28.4%; Poverty rate: 7.9%

Educational Attainment: High school diploma or higher: 93.8%; Bachelor's degree or higher: 25.3%; Graduate/professional degree or higher: 21.1%

Housing: Homeownership rate: 100.0%; Median home value: n/a; Median year structure built: 1971; Homeowner vacancy rate: 0.0%; Median selected monthly owner costs: $0 with a mortgage, $215 without a mortgage; Median gross rent: n/a per month; Rental vacancy rate: 0.0%

Health Insurance: 91.1% have insurance; 79.1% have private insurance; 32.5% have public insurance; 8.9% do not have insurance; 0.0% of children under 18 do not have insurance

Transportation: Commute: 88.9% car, 0.0% public transportation, 0.0% walk, 11.1% work from home; Mean travel time to work: 30.8 minutes

SAINT CROIX (unincorporated postal area)

ZCTA: 47576

Covers a land area of 21.766 square miles and a water area of 0.209 square miles. Located at 38.18° N. Lat; 86.62° W. Long. Elevation is 725 feet.

Population: 280; Growth (since 2000): -39.4%; Density: 12.9 persons per square mile; Race: 100.0% White, 0.0% Black/African American, 0.0% Asian, 0.0% American Indian/Alaska Native, 0.0% Native Hawaiian/Other Pacific Islander, 0.0% Two or more races, 0.0% Hispanic of any race; Average household size: 2.28; Median age: 40.9; Age under 18: 18.2%; Age 65 and over: 9.6%; Males per 100 females: 112.0; Marriage status: 24.8% never married, 39.5% now married, 0.0% separated, 5.5% widowed, 30.3% divorced; Foreign born: 0.0%; Speak English only: 100.0%; With disability: 13.6%; Veterans: 0.0%; Ancestry: 35.7% German, 21.1% Irish, 9.3% Belgian, 8.2% American, 5.0% English

Employment: 0.0% management, business, and financial, 4.8% computer, engineering, and science, 0.0% education, legal, community service, arts, and media, 14.8% healthcare practitioners, 0.0% service, 3.7% sales and office, 23.3% natural resources, construction, and maintenance, 53.4% production, transportation, and material moving

Income: Per capita: $25,534; Median household: $69,107; Average household: $61,940; Households with income of $100,000 or more: 9.8%; Poverty rate: 27.5%

Educational Attainment: High school diploma or higher: 100.0%; Bachelor's degree or higher: 12.8%; Graduate/professional degree or higher: n/a

Housing: Homeownership rate: 72.4%; Median home value: $88,100; Median year structure built: 1965; Homeowner vacancy rate: 0.0%; Median selected monthly owner costs: $871 with a mortgage, $285 without a mortgage; Median gross rent: n/a per month; Rental vacancy rate: 0.0%

Health Insurance: 100.0% have insurance; 96.1% have private insurance; 13.6% have public insurance; 0.0% do not have insurance; 0.0% of children under 18 do not have insurance

Transportation: Commute: 100.0% car, 0.0% public transportation, 0.0% walk, 0.0% work from home; Mean travel time to work: 30.6 minutes

TELL CITY (city). Covers a land area of 4.534 square miles and a water area of 0.105 square miles. Located at 37.95° N. Lat; 86.76° W. Long. Elevation is 420 feet.
History: Tell City was settled in 1857 by a group of Swiss immigrants, and named for the legendary Swiss hero William Tell. An early industry was furniture making.
Population: 7,295; Growth (since 2000): -7.0%; Density: 1,609.0 persons per square mile; Race: 95.1% White, 1.2% Black/African American, 0.2% Asian, 0.6% American Indian/Alaska Native, 0.0% Native Hawaiian/Other Pacific Islander, 2.7% Two or more races, 1.7% Hispanic of any race; Average household size: 2.29; Median age: 40.1; Age under 18: 23.4%; Age 65 and over: 19.4%; Males per 100 females: 90.3; Marriage status: 21.9% never married, 52.9% now married, 2.2% separated, 9.1% widowed, 16.1% divorced; Foreign born: 0.7%; Speak English only: 99.6%; With disability: 17.1%; Veterans: 9.6%; Ancestry: 29.2% German, 12.1% American, 11.7% Irish, 8.3% French, 7.8% English
Employment: 8.3% management, business, and financial, 3.2% computer, engineering, and science, 5.6% education, legal, community service, arts, and media, 2.2% healthcare practitioners, 21.3% service, 22.2% sales and office, 7.2% natural resources, construction, and maintenance, 30.0% production, transportation, and material moving
Income: Per capita: $22,152; Median household: $42,145; Average household: $52,072; Households with income of $100,000 or more: 11.5%; Poverty rate: 20.0%
Educational Attainment: High school diploma or higher: 88.7%; Bachelor's degree or higher: 15.5%; Graduate/professional degree or higher: 9.0%

School District(s)

Tell City-Troy Twp School Corp (PK-12)
Enrollment: 1,692 . . . . (812) 547-3300
Housing: Homeownership rate: 69.5%; Median home value: $91,000; Median year structure built: 1961; Homeowner vacancy rate: 1.4%; Median selected monthly owner costs: $804 with a mortgage, $326 without a mortgage; Median gross rent: $611 per month; Rental vacancy rate: 2.3%
Health Insurance: 89.5% have insurance; 65.4% have private insurance; 39.5% have public insurance; 10.5% do not have insurance; 4.9% of children under 18 do not have insurance
Hospitals: Perry County Memorial Hospital (38 beds)
Safety: Violent crime rate: 6.8 per 10,000 population; Property crime rate: 179.0 per 10,000 population
Newspapers: The Perry County News (weekly circulation 7,400)
Transportation: Commute: 96.8% car, 0.0% public transportation, 1.6% walk, 1.4% work from home; Mean travel time to work: 17.7 minutes
Additional Information Contacts
City of Tell City . . . . (812) 547-2349
http://www.tellcityindiana.com

TROY (town). Covers a land area of 0.318 square miles and a water area of 0 square miles. Located at 38.00° N. Lat; 86.80° W. Long. Elevation is 472 feet.
History: Troy was founded by families from Virginia. It served as the seat of Perry County until 1818.
Population: 344; Growth (since 2000): -12.2%; Density: 1,080.5 persons per square mile; Race: 100.0% White, 0.0% Black/African American, 0.0% Asian, 0.0% American Indian/Alaska Native, 0.0% Native Hawaiian/Other Pacific Islander, 0.0% Two or more races, 0.9% Hispanic of any race; Average household size: 1.95; Median age: 52.9; Age under 18: 12.8%; Age 65 and over: 32.8%; Males per 100 females: 86.0; Marriage status: 22.0% never married, 58.1% now married, 1.3% separated, 7.0% widowed, 12.8% divorced; Foreign born: 0.0%; Speak English only: 98.8%; With disability: 36.6%; Veterans: 20.0%; Ancestry: 35.5% German, 12.2% French, 11.3% American, 11.0% Irish, 5.8% English
Employment: 7.3% management, business, and financial, 5.1% computer, engineering, and science, 2.2% education, legal, community service, arts, and media, 3.6% healthcare practitioners, 13.1% service, 21.9% sales and office, 0.7% natural resources, construction, and maintenance, 46.0% production, transportation, and material moving
Income: Per capita: $23,631; Median household: $40,000; Average household: $45,207; Households with income of $100,000 or more: 1.7%; Poverty rate: 9.1%
Educational Attainment: High school diploma or higher: 83.8%; Bachelor's degree or higher: 9.7%; Graduate/professional degree or higher: 2.4%
Housing: Homeownership rate: 92.6%; Median home value: $69,800; Median year structure built: 1959; Homeowner vacancy rate: 2.4%; Median selected monthly owner costs: $820 with a mortgage, $358 without a mortgage; Median gross rent: $713 per month; Rental vacancy rate: 50.0%
Health Insurance: 96.8% have insurance; 79.7% have private insurance; 45.9% have public insurance; 3.2% do not have insurance; 0.0% of children under 18 do not have insurance
Transportation: Commute: 99.3% car, 0.0% public transportation, 0.0% walk, 0.7% work from home; Mean travel time to work: 29.4 minutes

Pike County

Located in southwestern Indiana; bounded on the north by the White River; drained by the Patoka River. Covers a land area of 334.238 square miles, a water area of 6.856 square miles, and is located in the Eastern Time Zone at 38.40° N. Lat., 87.23° W. Long. The county was founded in 1816. County seat is Petersburg.

Pike County is part of the Jasper, IN Micropolitan Statistical Area. The entire metro area includes: Dubois County, IN; Pike County, IN

Population: 12,471; Growth (since 2000): -2.9%; Density: 37.3 persons per square mile; Race: 97.2% White, 1.0% Black/African American, 1.0% Asian, 0.0% American Indian/Alaska Native, 0.0% Native Hawaiian/Other Pacific Islander, 0.7% two or more races, 0.5% Hispanic of any race; Average household size: 2.40; Median age: 43.9; Age under 18: 22.4%; Age 65 and over: 19.2%; Males per 100 females: 99.9; Marriage status: 19.8% never married, 59.8% now married, 1.0% separated, 8.4% widowed, 12.0% divorced; Foreign born: 1.5%; Speak English only: 98.5%; With disability: 18.3%; Veterans: 8.7%; Ancestry: 26.1% German, 16.8% English, 14.7% Irish, 13.6% American, 1.9% French
Religion: Six largest groups: 7.6% Methodist/Pietist, 7.3% Baptist, 4.2% Holiness, 2.9% Catholicism, 2.1% Lutheran, 1.0% Pentecostal
Economy: Unemployment rate: 3.7%; Leading industries: 20.8 % other services (except public administration); 16.2 % retail trade; 8.6 % health care and social assistance; Farms: 321 totaling 80,016 acres; Company size: 0 employ 1,000 or more persons, 0 employ 500 to 999 persons, 4 employ 100 to 499 persons, 193 employ less than 100 persons; Business ownership: 226 women-owned, n/a Black-owned, 27 Hispanic-owned, n/a Asian-owned, n/a American Indian/Alaska Native-owned
Employment: 10.7% management, business, and financial, 2.5% computer, engineering, and science, 6.5% education, legal, community service, arts, and media, 4.7% healthcare practitioners, 15.7% service, 17.2% sales and office, 14.2% natural resources, construction, and maintenance, 28.5% production, transportation, and material moving
Income: Per capita: $25,648; Median household: $50,196; Average household: $61,900; Households with income of $100,000 or more: 18.0%; Poverty rate: 10.6%
Educational Attainment: High school diploma or higher: 86.0%; Bachelor's degree or higher: 13.1%; Graduate/professional degree or higher: 4.7%
Housing: Homeownership rate: 82.8%; Median home value: $89,300; Median year structure built: 1972; Homeowner vacancy rate: 0.9%; Median selected monthly owner costs: $959 with a mortgage, $352 without a mortgage; Median gross rent: $634 per month; Rental vacancy rate: 3.0%
Vital Statistics: Birth rate: 107.6 per 10,000 population; Death rate: 115.6 per 10,000 population; Age-adjusted cancer mortality rate: 195.9 deaths per 100,000 population
Health Insurance: 94.1% have insurance; 76.0% have private insurance; 34.4% have public insurance; 5.9% do not have insurance; 4.0% of children under 18 do not have insurance
Health Care: Physicians: 1.6 per 10,000 population; Dentists: 0.8 per 10,000 population; Hospital beds: 0.0 per 10,000 population; Hospital admissions: 0.0 per 10,000 population
Air Quality Index (AQI): Percent of Days: 100.0% good, 0.0% moderate, 0.0% unhealthy for sensitive individuals, 0.0% unhealthy, 0.0% very unhealthy; Annual median: 1; Annual maximum: 43
Transportation: Commute: 96.6% car, 0.1% public transportation, 1.0% walk, 1.7% work from home; Mean travel time to work: 25.2 minutes
2016 Presidential Election: 73.6% Trump, 21.7% Clinton, 4.7% Johnson, 0.0% Stein
National and State Parks: Patoka State Fish and Wildlife Area; Pike State Forest
Additional Information Contacts
Pike Government. . . . . (812) 354-8448

Pike County Communities

OTWELL (CDP). Covers a land area of 1.785 square miles and a water area of 0.004 square miles. Located at 38.46° N. Lat; 87.10° W. Long. Elevation is 499 feet.
Population: 426; Growth (since 2000): n/a; Density: 238.7 persons per square mile; Race: 96.5% White, 0.0% Black/African American, 0.0% Asian, 0.0% American Indian/Alaska Native, 0.0% Native Hawaiian/Other Pacific Islander, 0.0% Two or more races, 3.5% Hispanic of any race; Average household size: 2.07; Median age: 51.0; Age under 18: 9.9%; Age 65 and over: 8.7%; Males per 100 females: 87.9; Marriage status: 21.6% never married, 59.4% now married, 2.1% separated, 2.1% widowed, 16.9% divorced; Foreign born: 3.5%; Speak English only: 94.9%; With disability: 9.2%; Veterans: 5.7%; Ancestry: 26.8% German, 18.5% Irish, 14.6% American, 12.0% English, 1.6% Dutch
Employment: 9.8% management, business, and financial, 0.0% computer, engineering, and science, 2.8% education, legal, community service, arts, and media, 0.0% healthcare practitioners, 11.8% service, 18.7% sales and office, 5.7% natural resources, construction, and maintenance, 51.2% production, transportation, and material moving
Income: Per capita: $21,229; Median household: $38,750; Average household: $46,050; Households with income of $100,000 or more: 3.4%; Poverty rate: 14.1%
Educational Attainment: High school diploma or higher: 77.8%; Bachelor's degree or higher: 17.8%; Graduate/professional degree or higher: 2.9%
Housing: Homeownership rate: 86.9%; Median home value: $100,800; Median year structure built: 1974; Homeowner vacancy rate: 0.0%; Median selected monthly owner costs: $1,018 with a mortgage, $339 without a mortgage; Median gross rent: $172 per month; Rental vacancy rate: 0.0%
Health Insurance: 86.2% have insurance; 73.7% have private insurance; 18.5% have public insurance; 13.8% do not have insurance; 0.0% of children under 18 do not have insurance
Transportation: Commute: 100.0% car, 0.0% public transportation, 0.0% walk, 0.0% work from home; Mean travel time to work: 19.7 minutes

PETERSBURG (city). County seat. Covers a land area of 1.466 square miles and a water area of 0.004 square miles. Located at 38.49° N. Lat; 87.28° W. Long. Elevation is 482 feet.
History: Laid out 1817, incorporated 1924.
Population: 2,477; Growth (since 2000): -3.6%; Density: 1,689.6 persons per square mile; Race: 97.4% White, 2.6% Black/African American, 0.0% Asian, 0.0% American Indian/Alaska Native, 0.0% Native Hawaiian/Other Pacific Islander, 0.0% Two or more races, 0.6% Hispanic of any race; Average household size: 2.47; Median age: 39.0; Age under 18: 24.6%; Age 65 and over: 19.8%; Males per 100 females: 94.5; Marriage status: 23.4% never married, 52.7% now married, 0.7% separated, 11.4% widowed, 12.5% divorced; Foreign born: 0.0%; Speak English only: 99.5%; With disability: 19.4%; Veterans: 4.9%; Ancestry: 18.7% German, 17.2% Irish, 14.3% American, 11.4% English, 3.0% Slovak
Employment: 9.7% management, business, and financial, 1.5% computer, engineering, and science, 9.7% education, legal, community service, arts, and media, 1.3% healthcare practitioners, 14.8% service, 28.5% sales and office, 8.8% natural resources, construction, and maintenance, 25.8% production, transportation, and material moving
Income: Per capita: $21,065; Median household: $43,380; Average household: $53,559; Households with income of $100,000 or more: 14.5%; Poverty rate: 13.5%
Educational Attainment: High school diploma or higher: 81.5%; Bachelor's degree or higher: 14.4%; Graduate/professional degree or higher: 5.8%

School District(s)

Pike County School Corp (PK-12)
Enrollment: 1,923 . . . . (812) 354-8731
Housing: Homeownership rate: 64.5%; Median home value: $75,400; Median year structure built: 1966; Homeowner vacancy rate: 1.0%; Median selected monthly owner costs: $786 with a mortgage, $277 without a mortgage; Median gross rent: $626 per month; Rental vacancy rate: 5.4%
Health Insurance: 90.0% have insurance; 64.3% have private insurance; 40.3% have public insurance; 10.0% do not have insurance; 7.7% of children under 18 do not have insurance
Newspapers: Press Dispatch (weekly circulation 5,700)
Transportation: Commute: 96.8% car, 0.7% public transportation, 1.8% walk, 0.3% work from home; Mean travel time to work: 25.0 minutes

Additional Information Contacts
City of Petersburg . . . . (812) 354-8511
http://www.petersburg.in.gov

SPURGEON (town). Covers a land area of 0.175 square miles and a water area of <.001 square miles. Located at 38.26° N. Lat; 87.26° W. Long. Elevation is 502 feet.
History: Laid out 1860.
Population: 138; Growth (since 2000): -39.2%; Density: 786.9 persons per square mile; Race: 100.0% White, 0.0% Black/African American, 0.0% Asian, 0.0% American Indian/Alaska Native, 0.0% Native Hawaiian/Other Pacific Islander, 0.0% Two or more races, 0.0% Hispanic of any race; Average household size: 1.84; Median age: 55.3; Age under 18: 9.4%; Age 65 and over: 24.6%; Males per 100 females: 105.0; Marriage status: 13.3% never married, 64.8% now married, 2.3% separated, 3.9% widowed, 18.0% divorced; Foreign born: 1.4%; Speak English only: 98.4%; With disability: 23.2%; Veterans: 9.6%; Ancestry: 18.8% English, 15.2% American, 13.8% German, 10.9% Irish, 5.1% Italian
Employment: 13.2% management, business, and financial, 0.0% computer, engineering, and science, 5.9% education, legal, community service, arts, and media, 7.4% healthcare practitioners, 17.6% service, 30.9% sales and office, 4.4% natural resources, construction, and maintenance, 20.6% production, transportation, and material moving
Income: Per capita: $25,288; Median household: $42,679; Average household: $46,029; Households with income of $100,000 or more: 2.7%; Poverty rate: 7.2%
Educational Attainment: High school diploma or higher: 92.4%; Bachelor's degree or higher: 9.2%; Graduate/professional degree or higher: 2.5%
Housing: Homeownership rate: 84.0%; Median home value: $63,800; Median year structure built: 1957; Homeowner vacancy rate: 0.0%; Median selected monthly owner costs: $786 with a mortgage, $357 without a mortgage; Median gross rent: $633 per month; Rental vacancy rate: 0.0%
Health Insurance: 89.9% have insurance; 71.7% have private insurance; 38.4% have public insurance; 10.1% do not have insurance; 0.0% of children under 18 do not have insurance
Transportation: Commute: 97.1% car, 0.0% public transportation, 0.0% walk, 2.9% work from home; Mean travel time to work: 28.6 minutes

STENDAL (unincorporated postal area)
ZCTA: 47585
Covers a land area of 35.405 square miles and a water area of 0.635 square miles. Located at 38.27° N. Lat; 87.16° W. Long. Elevation is 610 feet.
Population: 695; Growth (since 2000): 46.9%; Density: 19.6 persons per square mile; Race: 74.8% White, 7.2% Black/African American, 14.4% Asian, 0.0% American Indian/Alaska Native, 0.0% Native Hawaiian/Other Pacific Islander, 3.6% Two or more races, 0.0% Hispanic of any race; Average household size: 3.66; Median age: 18.4; Age under 18: 48.3%; Age 65 and over: 6.3%; Males per 100 females: 98.7; Marriage status: 37.6% never married, 55.4% now married, 0.0% separated, 0.0% widowed, 7.0% divorced; Foreign born: 18.0%; Speak English only: 96.2%; With disability: 28.9%; Veterans: 14.2%; Ancestry: 42.2% German, 20.0% English, 9.1% American, 3.6% French, 3.6% Irish
Employment: 9.7% management, business, and financial, 0.0% computer, engineering, and science, 0.0% education, legal, community service, arts, and media, 4.0% healthcare practitioners, 11.9% service, 20.6% sales and office, 29.2% natural resources, construction, and maintenance, 24.5% production, transportation, and material moving
Income: Per capita: $17,691; Median household: $51,111; Average household: $63,415; Households with income of $100,000 or more: 14.8%; Poverty rate: 33.1%
Educational Attainment: High school diploma or higher: 78.9%; Bachelor's degree or higher: 14.6%; Graduate/professional degree or higher: 12.0%
Housing: Homeownership rate: 69.5%; Median home value: $86,300; Median year structure built: 1992; Homeowner vacancy rate: 0.0%; Median selected monthly owner costs: $968 with a mortgage, $400 without a mortgage; Median gross rent: $674 per month; Rental vacancy rate: 0.0%
Health Insurance: 100.0% have insurance; 65.0% have private insurance; 40.1% have public insurance; 0.0% do not have insurance; 0.0% of children under 18 do not have insurance

Transportation: Commute: 100.0% car, 0.0% public transportation, 0.0% walk, 0.0% work from home; Mean travel time to work: 27.4 minutes

VELPEN (unincorporated postal area)

ZCTA: 47590

Covers a land area of 39.432 square miles and a water area of 0.494 square miles. Located at 38.36° N. Lat; 87.10° W. Long. Elevation is 492 feet.

Population: 410; Growth (since 2000): -45.1%; Density: 10.4 persons per square mile; Race: 100.0% White, 0.0% Black/African American, 0.0% Asian, 0.0% American Indian/Alaska Native, 0.0% Native Hawaiian/Other Pacific Islander, 0.0% Two or more races, 0.0% Hispanic of any race; Average household size: 1.65; Median age: 59.8; Age under 18: 5.9%; Age 65 and over: 19.8%; Males per 100 females: 114.8; Marriage status: 21.1% never married, 53.1% now married, 0.0% separated, 1.2% widowed, 24.6% divorced; Foreign born: 0.0%; Speak English only: 100.0%; With disability: 18.3%; Veterans: 6.0%; Ancestry: 37.8% German, 13.9% American, 12.0% Irish, 9.5% English, 6.6% Polish

Employment: 3.7% management, business, and financial, 0.0% computer, engineering, and science, 3.3% education, legal, community service, arts, and media, 4.1% healthcare practitioners, 10.6% service, 42.4% sales and office, 11.0% natural resources, construction, and maintenance, 24.9% production, transportation, and material moving

Income: Per capita: $25,092; Median household: $36,094; Average household: $41,602; Households with income of $100,000 or more: 7.6%; Poverty rate: 8.8%

Educational Attainment: High school diploma or higher: 85.7%; Bachelor's degree or higher: 9.9%; Graduate/professional degree or higher: n/a

Housing: Homeownership rate: 92.8%; Median home value: $66,500; Median year structure built: 1969; Homeowner vacancy rate: 9.8%; Median selected monthly owner costs: $572 with a mortgage, $275 without a mortgage; Median gross rent: n/a per month; Rental vacancy rate: 0.0%

Health Insurance: 93.2% have insurance; 74.6% have private insurance; 29.3% have public insurance; 6.8% do not have insurance; 0.0% of children under 18 do not have insurance

Transportation: Commute: 100.0% car, 0.0% public transportation, 0.0% walk, 0.0% work from home; Mean travel time to work: 25.9 minutes

WINSLOW (town).

Covers a land area of 0.634 square miles and a water area of 0.009 square miles. Located at 38.38° N. Lat; 87.21° W. Long. Elevation is 443 feet.

History: Winslow developed as a coal-mining town

Population: 1,022; Growth (since 2000): 16.0%; Density: 1,613.2 persons per square mile; Race: 96.5% White, 0.4% Black/African American, 0.0% Asian, 0.0% American Indian/Alaska Native, 0.0% Native Hawaiian/Other Pacific Islander, 2.7% Two or more races, 3.5% Hispanic of any race; Average household size: 2.96; Median age: 29.6; Age under 18: 35.2%; Age 65 and over: 8.9%; Males per 100 females: 88.2; Marriage status: 27.8% never married, 45.5% now married, 1.6% separated, 4.6% widowed, 22.1% divorced; Foreign born: 0.2%; Speak English only: 99.1%; With disability: 17.0%; Veterans: 6.3%; Ancestry: 24.4% German, 20.9% English, 15.1% Irish, 7.9% American, 2.6% Italian

Employment: 6.8% management, business, and financial, 0.0% computer, engineering, and science, 6.1% education, legal, community service, arts, and media, 5.2% healthcare practitioners, 25.3% service, 11.1% sales and office, 8.1% natural resources, construction, and maintenance, 37.5% production, transportation, and material moving

Income: Per capita: $16,192; Median household: $40,298; Average household: $46,338; Households with income of $100,000 or more: 5.0%; Poverty rate: 21.5%

Educational Attainment: High school diploma or higher: 87.9%; Bachelor's degree or higher: 5.8%; Graduate/professional degree or higher: 2.3%

School District(s)

Pike County School Corp (PK-12)

Enrollment: 1,923 . . . . (812) 354-8731

Housing: Homeownership rate: 79.3%; Median home value: $51,000; Median year structure built: 1953; Homeowner vacancy rate: 3.1%; Median selected monthly owner costs: $865 with a mortgage, $358 without a mortgage; Median gross rent: $783 per month; Rental vacancy rate: 10.1%

Health Insurance: 83.2% have insurance; 61.4% have private insurance; 34.4% have public insurance; 16.8% do not have insurance; 15.0% of children under 18 do not have insurance

Transportation: Commute: 94.5% car, 0.0% public transportation, 3.0% walk, 1.4% work from home; Mean travel time to work: 25.8 minutes

Porter County

Located in northwestern Indiana; bounded on the north by Lake Michigan, and on the south by the Kankakee River; drained by the Little Calumet and Grand Calumet Rivers. Covers a land area of 418.153 square miles, a water area of 103.628 square miles, and is located in the Central Time Zone at 41.51° N. Lat., 87.07° W. Long. The county was founded in 1835. County seat is Valparaiso.

Porter County is part of the Chicago-Naperville-Elgin, IL-IN-WI Metropolitan Statistical Area. The entire metro area includes: Chicago-Naperville-Arlington Heights, IL Metropolitan Division (Cook County, IL; DuPage County, IL; Grundy County, IL; Kendall County, IL; McHenry County, IL; Will County, IL); Elgin, IL Metropolitan Division (DeKalb County, IL; Kane County, IL); Gary, IN Metropolitan Division (Jasper County, IN; Lake County, IN; Newton County, IN; Porter County, IN); Lake County-Kenosha County, IL-WI Metropolitan Division (Lake County, IL; Kenosha County, WI)

Weather Station: Valparaiso Waterworks Elevation: 799 feet

	Jan	Feb	Mar	Apr	May	Jun	Jul	Aug	Sep	Oct	Nov	Dec
High	32	37	47	60	71	80	83	81	75	63	49	36
Low	17	21	29	39	49	58	63	62	54	43	34	23
Precip	2.2	1.9	2.6	3.5	4.1	4.5	4.2	3.9	3.3	3.2	3.8	2.6
Snow	12.7	8.1	6.0	1.1	tr	0.0	0.0	0.0	0.0	0.2	2.2	9.5

High and Low temperatures in degrees Fahrenheit; Precipitation and Snow in inches

Weather Station: Wanatah 2 WNW Elevation: 734 feet

	Jan	Feb	Mar	Apr	May	Jun	Jul	Aug	Sep	Oct	Nov	Dec
High	32	36	47	60	71	80	83	82	76	63	49	36
Low	15	18	27	37	47	57	61	59	50	40	31	20
Precip	1.9	1.7	2.5	3.3	3.8	4.1	4.2	4.3	3.4	3.5	3.4	2.3
Snow	11.9	9.5	4.9	0.8	tr	0.0	0.0	0.0	0.0	0.3	1.8	9.0

High and Low temperatures in degrees Fahrenheit; Precipitation and Snow in inches

Population: 167,391; Growth (since 2000): 14.0%; Density: 400.3 persons per square mile; Race: 91.6% White, 3.6% Black/African American, 1.4% Asian, 0.2% American Indian/Alaska Native, 0.1% Native Hawaiian/Other Pacific Islander, 2.1% two or more races, 9.6% Hispanic of any race; Average household size: 2.58; Median age: 39.4; Age under 18: 22.7%; Age 65 and over: 14.9%; Males per 100 females: 96.6; Marriage status: 29.1% never married, 53.9% now married, 1.2% separated, 5.9% widowed, 11.1% divorced; Foreign born: 3.8%; Speak English only: 93.7%; With disability: 10.9%; Veterans: 7.7%; Ancestry: 25.8% German, 15.5% Irish, 11.1% Polish, 8.2% English, 5.9% Italian

Religion: Six largest groups: 18.0% Catholicism, 4.7% Lutheran, 4.3% Methodist/Pietist, 3.9% Non-denominational Protestant, 2.9% Holiness, 2.4% Baptist

Economy: Unemployment rate: 3.8%; Leading industries: 13.1 % retail trade; 11.2 % health care and social assistance; 11.0 % other services (except public administration); Farms: 481 totaling 120,554 acres; Company size: 3 employ 1,000 or more persons, 3 employ 500 to 999 persons, 69 employ 100 to 499 persons, 3,455 employ less than 100 persons; Business ownership: 3,866 women-owned, 281 Black-owned, 413 Hispanic-owned, 192 Asian-owned, 31 American Indian/Alaska Native-owned

Employment: 14.2% management, business, and financial, 4.2% computer, engineering, and science, 10.6% education, legal, community service, arts, and media, 6.7% healthcare practitioners, 16.0% service, 22.0% sales and office, 11.1% natural resources, construction, and maintenance, 15.2% production, transportation, and material moving

Income: Per capita: $31,879; Median household: $65,979; Average household: $82,157; Households with income of $100,000 or more: 29.6%; Poverty rate: 11.0%

Educational Attainment: High school diploma or higher: 92.3%; Bachelor's degree or higher: 27.5%; Graduate/professional degree or higher: 10.3%

Housing: Homeownership rate: 75.4%; Median home value: $173,100; Median year structure built: 1979; Homeowner vacancy rate: 1.1%; Median

selected monthly owner costs: $1,349 with a mortgage, $464 without a mortgage; Median gross rent: $899 per month; Rental vacancy rate: 4.3%
Vital Statistics: Birth rate: 99.0 per 10,000 population; Death rate: 93.8 per 10,000 population; Age-adjusted cancer mortality rate: 178.5 deaths per 100,000 population
Health Insurance: 92.3% have insurance; 77.8% have private insurance; 27.0% have public insurance; 7.7% do not have insurance; 2.9% of children under 18 do not have insurance
Health Care: Physicians: 18.5 per 10,000 population; Dentists: 5.3 per 10,000 population; Hospital beds: 17.4 per 10,000 population; Hospital admissions: 857.2 per 10,000 population
Air Quality Index (AQI): Percent of Days: 77.5% good, 20.0% moderate, 2.5% unhealthy for sensitive individuals, 0.0% unhealthy, 0.0% very unhealthy; Annual median: 41; Annual maximum: 136
Transportation: Commute: 90.9% car, 1.5% public transportation, 2.1% walk, 4.4% work from home; Mean travel time to work: 27.2 minutes
2016 Presidential Election: 49.6% Trump, 43.0% Clinton, 5.4% Johnson, 0.5% Stein
National and State Parks: Indiana Dunes National Lakeshore; Indiana Dunes State Park
Additional Information Contacts
Porter Government . . . . (219) 926-2255
http://www.porterco.org

Porter County Communities

ABERDEEN (CDP). Covers a land area of 1.257 square miles and a water area of 0 square miles. Located at 41.44° N. Lat; 87.12° W. Long. Elevation is 725 feet.
Population: 1,602; Growth (since 2000): n/a; Density: 1,274.0 persons per square mile; Race: 89.8% White, 2.7% Black/African American, 3.2% Asian, 1.0% American Indian/Alaska Native, 0.0% Native Hawaiian/Other Pacific Islander, 3.3% Two or more races, 10.4% Hispanic of any race; Average household size: 2.35; Median age: 35.5; Age under 18: 24.9%; Age 65 and over: 15.9%; Males per 100 females: 95.5; Marriage status: 20.0% never married, 64.4% now married, 2.9% separated, 6.3% widowed, 9.2% divorced; Foreign born: 3.2%; Speak English only: 98.4%; With disability: 13.1%; Veterans: 2.8%; Ancestry: 27.3% German, 15.0% Dutch, 10.3% American, 9.1% Italian, 8.5% Irish
Employment: 24.3% management, business, and financial, 2.8% computer, engineering, and science, 14.9% education, legal, community service, arts, and media, 15.1% healthcare practitioners, 8.5% service, 17.9% sales and office, 3.0% natural resources, construction, and maintenance, 13.6% production, transportation, and material moving
Income: Per capita: $45,614; Median household: $87,227; Average household: $107,068; Households with income of $100,000 or more: 45.4%; Poverty rate: 1.4%
Educational Attainment: High school diploma or higher: 99.1%; Bachelor's degree or higher: 49.5%; Graduate/professional degree or higher: 18.3%
Housing: Homeownership rate: 62.4%; Median home value: $330,700; Median year structure built: 2000; Homeowner vacancy rate: 0.0%; Median selected monthly owner costs: $1,869 with a mortgage, $488 without a mortgage; Median gross rent: $1,209 per month; Rental vacancy rate: 4.8%
Health Insurance: 97.9% have insurance; 95.6% have private insurance; 14.5% have public insurance; 2.1% do not have insurance; 0.0% of children under 18 do not have insurance
Transportation: Commute: 86.1% car, 0.0% public transportation, 0.0% walk, 8.3% work from home; Mean travel time to work: 29.9 minutes

BEVERLY SHORES (town). Covers a land area of 3.583 square miles and a water area of 2.245 square miles. Located at 41.69° N. Lat; 86.98° W. Long. Elevation is 620 feet.
Population: 614; Growth (since 2000): -13.3%; Density: 171.4 persons per square mile; Race: 97.2% White, 1.8% Black/African American, 0.5% Asian, 0.0% American Indian/Alaska Native, 0.0% Native Hawaiian/Other Pacific Islander, 0.5% Two or more races, 2.1% Hispanic of any race; Average household size: 1.96; Median age: 63.8; Age under 18: 7.2%; Age 65 and over: 43.5%; Males per 100 females: 101.0; Marriage status: 14.9% never married, 67.9% now married, 0.7% separated, 7.5% widowed, 9.7% divorced; Foreign born: 13.7%; Speak English only: 84.6%; With disability: 12.4%; Veterans: 13.0%; Ancestry: 30.3% German, 13.2% Lithuanian, 11.2% Irish, 10.7% English, 7.2% Polish
Employment: 28.5% management, business, and financial, 7.0% computer, engineering, and science, 16.1% education, legal, community service, arts, and media, 14.5% healthcare practitioners, 1.7% service, 15.7% sales and office, 5.0% natural resources, construction, and maintenance, 11.6% production, transportation, and material moving
Income: Per capita: $71,470; Median household: $89,375; Average household: $140,063; Households with income of $100,000 or more: 47.0%; Poverty rate: 3.7%
Educational Attainment: High school diploma or higher: 97.5%; Bachelor's degree or higher: 71.6%; Graduate/professional degree or higher: 43.6%
Housing: Homeownership rate: 90.7%; Median home value: $456,900; Median year structure built: 1973; Homeowner vacancy rate: 0.7%; Median selected monthly owner costs: $2,117 with a mortgage, $778 without a mortgage; Median gross rent: n/a per month; Rental vacancy rate: 0.0%
Health Insurance: 98.0% have insurance; 89.9% have private insurance; 42.3% have public insurance; 2.0% do not have insurance; 0.0% of children under 18 do not have insurance
Transportation: Commute: 77.9% car, 3.0% public transportation, 4.3% walk, 14.9% work from home; Mean travel time to work: 50.0 minutes

BURNS HARBOR (town). Covers a land area of 6.665 square miles and a water area of 0.119 square miles. Located at 41.62° N. Lat; 87.12° W. Long. Elevation is 610 feet.
Population: 1,452; Growth (since 2000): 89.6%; Density: 217.9 persons per square mile; Race: 94.1% White, 2.5% Black/African American, 0.7% Asian, 0.0% American Indian/Alaska Native, 0.0% Native Hawaiian/Other Pacific Islander, 2.3% Two or more races, 9.7% Hispanic of any race; Average household size: 2.58; Median age: 35.2; Age under 18: 24.9%; Age 65 and over: 8.1%; Males per 100 females: 103.2; Marriage status: 33.9% never married, 44.6% now married, 0.5% separated, 3.6% widowed, 17.9% divorced; Foreign born: 2.5%; Speak English only: 95.9%; With disability: 7.3%; Veterans: 9.0%; Ancestry: 25.3% German, 18.7% Irish, 8.7% Polish, 8.0% Italian, 7.4% English
Employment: 15.6% management, business, and financial, 6.6% computer, engineering, and science, 7.7% education, legal, community service, arts, and media, 4.2% healthcare practitioners, 14.0% service, 26.3% sales and office, 7.5% natural resources, construction, and maintenance, 18.1% production, transportation, and material moving
Income: Per capita: $28,565; Median household: $72,632; Average household: $70,179; Households with income of $100,000 or more: 21.8%; Poverty rate: 8.7%
Educational Attainment: High school diploma or higher: 95.6%; Bachelor's degree or higher: 28.4%; Graduate/professional degree or higher: 4.8%
Housing: Homeownership rate: 73.8%; Median home value: $162,100; Median year structure built: 2000; Homeowner vacancy rate: 0.0%; Median selected monthly owner costs: $1,314 with a mortgage, $471 without a mortgage; Median gross rent: $1,085 per month; Rental vacancy rate: 0.0%
Health Insurance: 92.3% have insurance; 79.3% have private insurance; 19.9% have public insurance; 7.7% do not have insurance; 2.9% of children under 18 do not have insurance
Transportation: Commute: 90.8% car, 1.1% public transportation, 0.9% walk, 6.7% work from home; Mean travel time to work: 26.1 minutes

CHESTERTON (town). Covers a land area of 9.332 square miles and a water area of 0.113 square miles. Located at 41.60° N. Lat; 87.05° W. Long. Elevation is 640 feet.
History: Chesterton was first incorporated on October 5, 1869, ending the use of the former name, Calumet.
Population: 14,052; Growth (since 2000): 34.0%; Density: 1,505.7 persons per square mile; Race: 94.3% White, 1.1% Black/African American, 2.0% Asian, 0.2% American Indian/Alaska Native, 0.0% Native Hawaiian/Other Pacific Islander, 2.1% Two or more races, 7.4% Hispanic of any race; Average household size: 2.56; Median age: 39.8; Age under 18: 23.5%; Age 65 and over: 15.1%; Males per 100 females: 94.8; Marriage status: 27.4% never married, 54.4% now married, 1.6% separated, 6.3% widowed, 11.9% divorced; Foreign born: 4.0%; Speak English only: 94.0%; With disability: 8.8%; Veterans: 8.4%; Ancestry: 28.5% German, 15.6% Irish, 11.0% Polish, 7.9% English, 7.7% Italian
Employment: 16.4% management, business, and financial, 3.7% computer, engineering, and science, 12.7% education, legal, community service, arts, and media, 6.4% healthcare practitioners, 16.4% service,

20.5% sales and office, 11.7% natural resources, construction, and maintenance, 12.3% production, transportation, and material moving
Income: Per capita: $36,568; Median household: $66,861; Average household: $92,194; Households with income of $100,000 or more: 32.5%; Poverty rate: 8.1%
Educational Attainment: High school diploma or higher: 93.2%; Bachelor's degree or higher: 31.0%; Graduate/professional degree or higher: 12.5%

School District(s)

Duneland School Corporation (KG-12)
Enrollment: 5,667 . . . . (219) 983-3600
Housing: Homeownership rate: 68.1%; Median home value: $176,300; Median year structure built: 1980; Homeowner vacancy rate: 0.0%; Median selected monthly owner costs: $1,358 with a mortgage, $494 without a mortgage; Median gross rent: $885 per month; Rental vacancy rate: 1.0%
Health Insurance: 95.4% have insurance; 84.5% have private insurance; 23.0% have public insurance; 4.6% do not have insurance; 1.8% of children under 18 do not have insurance
Safety: Violent crime rate: 5.9 per 10,000 population; Property crime rate: 86.7 per 10,000 population
Newspapers: Chesterton Tribune (daily circulation 5,100)
Transportation: Commute: 90.2% car, 2.3% public transportation, 1.4% walk, 5.7% work from home; Mean travel time to work: 26.3 minutes
Additional Information Contacts
Town of Chesterton . . . . (219) 926-1641
http://www.chestertonin.org

DUNE ACRES (town). Covers a land area of 2.172 square miles and a water area of 1.266 square miles. Located at 41.65° N. Lat; 87.10° W. Long. Elevation is 627 feet.
Population: 173; Growth (since 2000): -18.8%; Density: 79.6 persons per square mile; Race: 98.3% White, 0.0% Black/African American, 1.7% Asian, 0.0% American Indian/Alaska Native, 0.0% Native Hawaiian/Other Pacific Islander, 0.0% Two or more races, 0.6% Hispanic of any race; Average household size: 2.01; Median age: 65.3; Age under 18: 8.7%; Age 65 and over: 50.9%; Males per 100 females: 109.2; Marriage status: 14.4% never married, 74.4% now married, 0.6% separated, 5.0% widowed, 6.3% divorced; Foreign born: 6.4%; Speak English only: 91.7%; With disability: 13.3%; Veterans: 9.5%; Ancestry: 23.7% German, 19.7% Irish, 16.2% English, 12.7% American, 12.1% Italian
Employment: 34.7% management, business, and financial, 1.4% computer, engineering, and science, 25.0% education, legal, community service, arts, and media, 8.3% healthcare practitioners, 1.4% service, 25.0% sales and office, 1.4% natural resources, construction, and maintenance, 2.8% production, transportation, and material moving
Income: Per capita: $115,257; Median household: $152,500; Average household: $226,865; Households with income of $100,000 or more: 61.6%; Poverty rate: 2.9%
Educational Attainment: High school diploma or higher: 98.0%; Bachelor's degree or higher: 74.3%; Graduate/professional degree or higher: 45.3%
Housing: Homeownership rate: 94.2%; Median home value: $693,200; Median year structure built: 1965; Homeowner vacancy rate: 0.0%; Median selected monthly owner costs: $3,208 with a mortgage, $1,000 without a mortgage; Median gross rent: $3,000 per month; Rental vacancy rate: 0.0%
Health Insurance: 98.8% have insurance; 83.2% have private insurance; 50.3% have public insurance; 1.2% do not have insurance; 0.0% of children under 18 do not have insurance
Transportation: Commute: 75.0% car, 11.1% public transportation, 2.8% walk, 11.1% work from home; Mean travel time to work: 44.1 minutes

HEBRON (town). Covers a land area of 1.976 square miles and a water area of 0 square miles. Located at 41.32° N. Lat; 87.20° W. Long. Elevation is 709 feet.
Population: 3,968; Growth (since 2000): 10.3%; Density: 2,008.3 persons per square mile; Race: 92.4% White, 7.6% Black/African American, 0.0% Asian, 0.0% American Indian/Alaska Native, 0.0% Native Hawaiian/Other Pacific Islander, 0.0% Two or more races, 9.2% Hispanic of any race; Average household size: 2.77; Median age: 32.7; Age under 18: 32.4%; Age 65 and over: 10.2%; Males per 100 females: 93.5; Marriage status: 31.2% never married, 52.1% now married, 1.3% separated, 4.7% widowed, 12.0% divorced; Foreign born: 0.8%; Speak English only: 98.5%; With disability: 10.6%; Veterans: 5.9%; Ancestry: 25.9% German, 14.1% Polish, 11.5% Irish, 10.9% Italian, 7.9% English
Employment: 12.9% management, business, and financial, 0.0% computer, engineering, and science, 6.0% education, legal, community service, arts, and media, 8.9% healthcare practitioners, 19.6% service, 13.5% sales and office, 18.5% natural resources, construction, and maintenance, 20.7% production, transportation, and material moving
Income: Per capita: $23,154; Median household: $54,375; Average household: $63,830; Households with income of $100,000 or more: 30.0%; Poverty rate: 17.3%
Educational Attainment: High school diploma or higher: 89.6%; Bachelor's degree or higher: 13.2%; Graduate/professional degree or higher: 3.5%

School District(s)

M S D Boone Township (KG-12)
Enrollment: 1,058 . . . . (219) 996-4771
Porter Township School Corp (KG-12)
Enrollment: 1,314 . . . . (219) 477-4933
Housing: Homeownership rate: 71.7%; Median home value: $136,300; Median year structure built: 1986; Homeowner vacancy rate: 0.0%; Median selected monthly owner costs: $1,189 with a mortgage, $505 without a mortgage; Median gross rent: $760 per month; Rental vacancy rate: 0.0%
Health Insurance: 93.6% have insurance; 78.4% have private insurance; 28.9% have public insurance; 6.4% do not have insurance; 0.0% of children under 18 do not have insurance
Transportation: Commute: 93.2% car, 0.0% public transportation, 4.7% walk, 1.1% work from home; Mean travel time to work: 29.3 minutes
Additional Information Contacts
Town of Hebron . . . . (219) 996-4641
http://www.visithebron.org

KOUTS (town). Covers a land area of 1.118 square miles and a water area of 0 square miles. Located at 41.32° N. Lat; 87.03° W. Long. Elevation is 682 feet.
History: Laid out 1864.
Population: 1,950; Growth (since 2000): 14.8%; Density: 1,744.4 persons per square mile; Race: 98.3% White, 0.2% Black/African American, 0.0% Asian, 0.4% American Indian/Alaska Native, 0.0% Native Hawaiian/Other Pacific Islander, 1.2% Two or more races, 3.2% Hispanic of any race; Average household size: 2.42; Median age: 39.9; Age under 18: 23.7%; Age 65 and over: 20.1%; Males per 100 females: 92.9; Marriage status: 23.8% never married, 54.2% now married, 0.0% separated, 7.2% widowed, 14.9% divorced; Foreign born: 1.9%; Speak English only: 96.5%; With disability: 11.6%; Veterans: 12.4%; Ancestry: 34.4% German, 19.1% Irish, 11.6% Polish, 6.4% English, 5.8% American
Employment: 11.8% management, business, and financial, 4.3% computer, engineering, and science, 11.5% education, legal, community service, arts, and media, 8.6% healthcare practitioners, 9.5% service, 28.3% sales and office, 10.1% natural resources, construction, and maintenance, 15.8% production, transportation, and material moving
Income: Per capita: $28,551; Median household: $62,014; Average household: $68,166; Households with income of $100,000 or more: 14.5%; Poverty rate: 5.5%
Educational Attainment: High school diploma or higher: 89.9%; Bachelor's degree or higher: 19.4%; Graduate/professional degree or higher: 4.8%

School District(s)

East Porter County School Corp (KG-12)
Enrollment: 2,313 . . . . (219) 766-2214
Housing: Homeownership rate: 79.3%; Median home value: $138,100; Median year structure built: 1968; Homeowner vacancy rate: 2.5%; Median selected monthly owner costs: $1,139 with a mortgage, $367 without a mortgage; Median gross rent: $775 per month; Rental vacancy rate: 11.2%
Health Insurance: 92.6% have insurance; 75.8% have private insurance; 31.8% have public insurance; 7.4% do not have insurance; 2.9% of children under 18 do not have insurance
Transportation: Commute: 90.8% car, 0.9% public transportation, 4.1% walk, 2.9% work from home; Mean travel time to work: 29.9 minutes
Additional Information Contacts
Town of Kouts . . . . (219) 766-2244
http://www.kouts.info

OGDEN DUNES (town). Covers a land area of 0.736 square miles and a water area of 0.722 square miles. Located at 41.63° N. Lat; 87.19° W. Long. Elevation is 610 feet.

History: In 1916, on the site that became Ogden Dunes, a woman was found living alone and avoiding contact with other people. The newspapers called her Diana of the Dunes, and many stories were told about her.

Population: 1,195; Growth (since 2000): -9.0%; Density: 1,623.2 persons per square mile; Race: 94.8% White, 0.0% Black/African American, 1.5% Asian, 0.2% American Indian/Alaska Native, 0.0% Native Hawaiian/Other Pacific Islander, 3.5% Two or more races, 1.7% Hispanic of any race; Average household size: 2.28; Median age: 56.7; Age under 18: 11.9%; Age 65 and over: 28.5%; Males per 100 females: 98.9; Marriage status: 16.7% never married, 66.6% now married, 1.6% separated, 7.0% widowed, 9.8% divorced; Foreign born: 4.3%; Speak English only: 96.4%; With disability: 11.5%; Veterans: 9.8%; Ancestry: 21.9% German, 20.0% Irish, 15.4% English, 7.7% Polish, 5.3% Italian

Employment: 26.8% management, business, and financial, 10.9% computer, engineering, and science, 14.2% education, legal, community service, arts, and media, 13.2% healthcare practitioners, 3.9% service, 14.5% sales and office, 7.4% natural resources, construction, and maintenance, 9.0% production, transportation, and material moving

Income: Per capita: $61,074; Median household: $108,375; Average household: $136,556; Households with income of $100,000 or more: 52.4%; Poverty rate: 3.7%

Educational Attainment: High school diploma or higher: 99.3%; Bachelor's degree or higher: 67.5%; Graduate/professional degree or higher: 31.2%

Housing: Homeownership rate: 93.3%; Median home value: $334,800; Median year structure built: 1957; Homeowner vacancy rate: 0.0%; Median selected monthly owner costs: $1,841 with a mortgage, $608 without a mortgage; Median gross rent: $1,375 per month; Rental vacancy rate: 0.0%

Health Insurance: 95.6% have insurance; 84.7% have private insurance; 29.4% have public insurance; 4.4% do not have insurance; 11.0% of children under 18 do not have insurance

Transportation: Commute: 86.9% car, 6.2% public transportation, 0.0% walk, 6.2% work from home; Mean travel time to work: 38.0 minutes

PORTAGE (city). Covers a land area of 25.628 square miles and a water area of 1.984 square miles. Located at 41.59° N. Lat; 87.18° W. Long. Elevation is 636 feet.

History: Named for Portage, Ohio. A new port, accommodating ocean vessels, began operating here in the early 1970s (Burns International Harbor). Incorporated 1959.

Population: 36,849; Growth (since 2000): 10.0%; Density: 1,437.8 persons per square mile; Race: 83.7% White, 9.6% Black/African American, 1.9% Asian, 0.2% American Indian/Alaska Native, 0.1% Native Hawaiian/Other Pacific Islander, 2.3% Two or more races, 19.3% Hispanic of any race; Average household size: 2.55; Median age: 39.1; Age under 18: 22.1%; Age 65 and over: 14.4%; Males per 100 females: 93.7; Marriage status: 33.1% never married, 46.7% now married, 1.9% separated, 7.0% widowed, 13.2% divorced; Foreign born: 5.3%; Speak English only: 89.2%; With disability: 13.1%; Veterans: 7.2%; Ancestry: 18.0% German, 13.1% Irish, 10.5% Polish, 5.9% English, 4.0% Italian

Employment: 9.6% management, business, and financial, 3.5% computer, engineering, and science, 6.9% education, legal, community service, arts, and media, 5.0% healthcare practitioners, 22.0% service, 22.9% sales and office, 9.4% natural resources, construction, and maintenance, 20.7% production, transportation, and material moving

Income: Per capita: $25,498; Median household: $54,566; Average household: $62,924; Households with income of $100,000 or more: 19.2%; Poverty rate: 17.2%

Educational Attainment: High school diploma or higher: 88.3%; Bachelor's degree or higher: 15.7%; Graduate/professional degree or higher: 5.6%

School District(s)

Neighbors' New Vistas High School (09-12)
Enrollment: 243. . . . . (219) 850-4448
Portage Township Schools (KG-12)
Enrollment: 7,799 . . . . (219) 762-6511

Vocational/Technical School(s)

Lil Lou's Beauty and Barber College-Portage (Private, For-profit)
Enrollment: 38. . . . . (219) 940-3572
Tuition: $14,600

Housing: Homeownership rate: 68.5%; Median home value: $141,000; Median year structure built: 1978; Homeowner vacancy rate: 1.6%; Median selected monthly owner costs: $1,236 with a mortgage, $462 without a mortgage; Median gross rent: $884 per month; Rental vacancy rate: 4.8%

Health Insurance: 89.6% have insurance; 70.4% have private insurance; 32.6% have public insurance; 10.4% do not have insurance; 3.3% of children under 18 do not have insurance

Transportation: Commute: 92.9% car, 1.0% public transportation, 1.6% walk, 3.0% work from home; Mean travel time to work: 26.6 minutes

Additional Information Contacts

City of Portage. . . . . (219) 762-7784
http://www.ci.portage.in.us

PORTER (town). Covers a land area of 6.200 square miles and a water area of 0.284 square miles. Located at 41.63° N. Lat; 87.08° W. Long. Elevation is 640 feet.

History: Laid out 1855.

Population: 4,855; Growth (since 2000): -2.4%; Density: 783.1 persons per square mile; Race: 96.3% White, 0.0% Black/African American, 1.7% Asian, 0.2% American Indian/Alaska Native, 0.0% Native Hawaiian/Other Pacific Islander, 0.9% Two or more races, 12.2% Hispanic of any race; Average household size: 3.13; Median age: 32.8; Age under 18: 27.2%; Age 65 and over: 8.0%; Males per 100 females: 98.1; Marriage status: 32.0% never married, 57.5% now married, 0.0% separated, 1.7% widowed, 8.8% divorced; Foreign born: 1.8%; Speak English only: 95.9%; With disability: 5.1%; Veterans: 11.1%; Ancestry: 23.8% German, 14.5% Polish, 12.3% Irish, 7.8% Scottish, 7.1% Swedish

Employment: 14.6% management, business, and financial, 2.5% computer, engineering, and science, 11.4% education, legal, community service, arts, and media, 6.2% healthcare practitioners, 11.9% service, 25.3% sales and office, 8.3% natural resources, construction, and maintenance, 19.9% production, transportation, and material moving

Income: Per capita: $33,659; Median household: $94,519; Average household: $103,690; Households with income of $100,000 or more: 45.4%; Poverty rate: 8.5%

Educational Attainment: High school diploma or higher: 91.9%; Bachelor's degree or higher: 31.9%; Graduate/professional degree or higher: 12.1%

School District(s)

Discovery Charter School (KG-08)
Enrollment: 518. . . . . (219) 983-9800
Duneland School Corporation (KG-12)
Enrollment: 5,667 . . . . (219) 983-3600

Housing: Homeownership rate: 82.0%; Median home value: $171,800; Median year structure built: 1988; Homeowner vacancy rate: 0.0%; Median selected monthly owner costs: $1,391 with a mortgage, $480 without a mortgage; Median gross rent: $1,255 per month; Rental vacancy rate: 0.0%

Health Insurance: 91.3% have insurance; 74.1% have private insurance; 22.8% have public insurance; 8.7% do not have insurance; 0.0% of children under 18 do not have insurance

Safety: Violent crime rate: 18.6 per 10,000 population; Property crime rate: 80.5 per 10,000 population

Transportation: Commute: 93.3% car, 1.3% public transportation, 1.5% walk, 2.7% work from home; Mean travel time to work: 25.9 minutes

Additional Information Contacts

Town of Porter. . . . . (219) 926-2771
http://www.townofporter.com

SALT CREEK COMMONS (CDP). Covers a land area of 0.370 square miles and a water area of 0 square miles. Located at 41.51° N. Lat; 87.14° W. Long.

Population: 2,515; Growth (since 2000): n/a; Density: 6,790.3 persons per square mile; Race: 93.8% White, 0.5% Black/African American, 1.5% Asian, 0.0% American Indian/Alaska Native, 0.0% Native Hawaiian/Other Pacific Islander, 3.4% Two or more races, 6.6% Hispanic of any race; Average household size: 3.38; Median age: 32.4; Age under 18: 33.7%; Age 65 and over: 5.2%; Males per 100 females: 101.0; Marriage status: 30.9% never married, 56.3% now married, 0.5% separated, 3.5% widowed, 9.3% divorced; Foreign born: 3.7%; Speak English only: 92.4%; With disability: 10.8%; Veterans: 4.6%; Ancestry: 23.4% Irish, 15.1% Polish, 14.7% German, 4.2% Italian, 3.8% English

Employment: 13.0% management, business, and financial, 4.5% computer, engineering, and science, 3.0% education, legal, community service, arts, and media, 3.5% healthcare practitioners, 16.9% service,

21.4% sales and office, 12.2% natural resources, construction, and maintenance, 25.5% production, transportation, and material moving
Income: Per capita: $24,368; Median household: $71,583; Average household: $79,700; Households with income of $100,000 or more: 33.6%; Poverty rate: 7.3%
Educational Attainment: High school diploma or higher: 87.3%; Bachelor's degree or higher: 14.4%; Graduate/professional degree or higher: 4.3%
Housing: Homeownership rate: 86.3%; Median home value: $125,600; Median year structure built: 1978; Homeowner vacancy rate: 0.0%; Median selected monthly owner costs: $1,144 with a mortgage, $424 without a mortgage; Median gross rent: $977 per month; Rental vacancy rate: 0.0%
Health Insurance: 93.4% have insurance; 75.0% have private insurance; 25.3% have public insurance; 6.6% do not have insurance; 0.2% of children under 18 do not have insurance
Transportation: Commute: 95.2% car, 1.2% public transportation, 0.0% walk, 3.6% work from home; Mean travel time to work: 29.1 minutes

SHOREWOOD FOREST (CDP). Covers a land area of 1.899 square miles and a water area of 0.338 square miles. Located at 41.46° N. Lat; 87.15° W. Long. Elevation is 722 feet.
Population: 2,512; Growth (since 2000): n/a; Density: 1,323.1 persons per square mile; Race: 91.2% White, 3.4% Black/African American, 4.1% Asian, 0.6% American Indian/Alaska Native, 0.0% Native Hawaiian/Other Pacific Islander, 0.2% Two or more races, 1.3% Hispanic of any race; Average household size: 2.63; Median age: 50.1; Age under 18: 22.4%; Age 65 and over: 24.0%; Males per 100 females: 94.7; Marriage status: 19.9% never married, 66.1% now married, 0.3% separated, 6.1% widowed, 7.9% divorced; Foreign born: 5.9%; Speak English only: 94.3%; With disability: 8.6%; Veterans: 11.0%; Ancestry: 31.2% German, 14.3% Polish, 13.4% Irish, 12.2% Italian, 8.1% English
Employment: 24.3% management, business, and financial, 2.5% computer, engineering, and science, 12.1% education, legal, community service, arts, and media, 12.1% healthcare practitioners, 15.5% service, 21.5% sales and office, 8.2% natural resources, construction, and maintenance, 3.8% production, transportation, and material moving
Income: Per capita: $45,210; Median household: $102,950; Average household: $117,556; Households with income of $100,000 or more: 52.8%; Poverty rate: 3.5%
Educational Attainment: High school diploma or higher: 96.6%; Bachelor's degree or higher: 50.4%; Graduate/professional degree or higher: 20.0%
Housing: Homeownership rate: 97.6%; Median home value: $350,300; Median year structure built: 1985; Homeowner vacancy rate: 0.0%; Median selected monthly owner costs: $2,349 with a mortgage, $582 without a mortgage; Median gross rent: n/a per month; Rental vacancy rate: 0.0%
Health Insurance: 96.8% have insurance; 81.3% have private insurance; 26.2% have public insurance; 3.2% do not have insurance; 1.4% of children under 18 do not have insurance
Transportation: Commute: 93.9% car, 1.4% public transportation, 2.2% walk, 1.9% work from home; Mean travel time to work: 30.9 minutes

SOUTH HAVEN (CDP). Covers a land area of 1.243 square miles and a water area of 0 square miles. Located at 41.54° N. Lat; 87.14° W. Long. Elevation is 653 feet.
Population: 5,064; Growth (since 2000): -9.9%; Density: 4,074.8 persons per square mile; Race: 93.4% White, 4.3% Black/African American, 0.1% Asian, 0.0% American Indian/Alaska Native, 0.0% Native Hawaiian/Other Pacific Islander, 1.8% Two or more races, 11.3% Hispanic of any race; Average household size: 2.63; Median age: 37.9; Age under 18: 22.7%; Age 65 and over: 12.3%; Males per 100 females: 96.3; Marriage status: 26.8% never married, 56.0% now married, 1.6% separated, 4.9% widowed, 12.2% divorced; Foreign born: 1.3%; Speak English only: 98.6%; With disability: 12.2%; Veterans: 12.3%; Ancestry: 19.1% German, 18.7% Irish, 10.9% Italian, 7.7% English, 5.7% Polish
Employment: 10.4% management, business, and financial, 2.7% computer, engineering, and science, 4.7% education, legal, community service, arts, and media, 5.3% healthcare practitioners, 18.9% service, 21.9% sales and office, 17.5% natural resources, construction, and maintenance, 18.5% production, transportation, and material moving
Income: Per capita: $24,222; Median household: $49,901; Average household: $61,682; Households with income of $100,000 or more: 17.4%; Poverty rate: 17.6%
Educational Attainment: High school diploma or higher: 88.6%; Bachelor's degree or higher: 9.0%; Graduate/professional degree or higher: 3.3%
Housing: Homeownership rate: 73.3%; Median home value: $112,300; Median year structure built: 1967; Homeowner vacancy rate: 3.4%; Median selected monthly owner costs: $1,142 with a mortgage, $379 without a mortgage; Median gross rent: $944 per month; Rental vacancy rate: 0.0%
Health Insurance: 87.7% have insurance; 67.4% have private insurance; 32.1% have public insurance; 12.3% do not have insurance; 2.9% of children under 18 do not have insurance
Transportation: Commute: 94.0% car, 2.1% public transportation, 1.8% walk, 1.5% work from home; Mean travel time to work: 27.3 minutes

TOWN OF PINES (town). Covers a land area of 2.255 square miles and a water area of 0 square miles. Located at 41.69° N. Lat; 86.95° W. Long. Elevation is 627 feet.
Population: 731; Growth (since 2000): -8.4%; Density: 324.2 persons per square mile; Race: 91.7% White, 1.6% Black/African American, 0.4% Asian, 0.0% American Indian/Alaska Native, 0.0% Native Hawaiian/Other Pacific Islander, 6.0% Two or more races, 5.2% Hispanic of any race; Average household size: 2.41; Median age: 43.1; Age under 18: 16.8%; Age 65 and over: 17.9%; Males per 100 females: 101.7; Marriage status: 29.3% never married, 51.7% now married, 2.1% separated, 7.0% widowed, 12.0% divorced; Foreign born: 3.1%; Speak English only: 94.9%; With disability: 15.3%; Veterans: 13.5%; Ancestry: 20.7% Irish, 20.0% German, 11.6% Italian, 10.8% Polish, 8.6% English
Employment: 7.0% management, business, and financial, 1.5% computer, engineering, and science, 15.2% education, legal, community service, arts, and media, 2.9% healthcare practitioners, 17.2% service, 21.3% sales and office, 13.4% natural resources, construction, and maintenance, 21.6% production, transportation, and material moving
Income: Per capita: $23,647; Median household: $47,250; Average household: $55,839; Households with income of $100,000 or more: 12.6%; Poverty rate: 19.3%
Educational Attainment: High school diploma or higher: 85.1%; Bachelor's degree or higher: 12.6%; Graduate/professional degree or higher: 6.1%
Housing: Homeownership rate: 70.6%; Median home value: $96,200; Median year structure built: 1962; Homeowner vacancy rate: 0.0%; Median selected monthly owner costs: $932 with a mortgage, $323 without a mortgage; Median gross rent: $758 per month; Rental vacancy rate: 12.7%
Health Insurance: 85.4% have insurance; 66.9% have private insurance; 38.0% have public insurance; 14.6% do not have insurance; 4.4% of children under 18 do not have insurance
Transportation: Commute: 91.2% car, 0.0% public transportation, 4.4% walk, 3.5% work from home; Mean travel time to work: 23.8 minutes

VALPARAISO (city). County seat. Covers a land area of 15.530 square miles and a water area of 0.048 square miles. Located at 41.48° N. Lat; 87.05° W. Long. Elevation is 794 feet.
History: Named for the city in Chile, near which Captain David Porter fought in the War of 1812. Valparaiso was sited on the Old Sauk Trail. In 1859 the Valparaiso Male and Female College was founded here by the Methodist Church. The College, purchased by the Lutheran Church in 1925, became Valparaiso University.
Population: 32,501; Growth (since 2000): 18.5%; Density: 2,092.8 persons per square mile; Race: 92.0% White, 3.1% Black/African American, 2.5% Asian, 0.2% American Indian/Alaska Native, 0.2% Native Hawaiian/Other Pacific Islander, 1.5% Two or more races, 6.7% Hispanic of any race; Average household size: 2.31; Median age: 34.2; Age under 18: 21.2%; Age 65 and over: 16.0%; Males per 100 females: 94.7; Marriage status: 37.4% never married, 43.8% now married, 1.4% separated, 6.4% widowed, 12.5% divorced; Foreign born: 5.2%; Speak English only: 92.8%; With disability: 10.9%; Veterans: 6.1%; Ancestry: 28.0% German, 19.3% Irish, 10.2% Polish, 9.6% English, 6.3% Italian
Employment: 14.7% management, business, and financial, 5.3% computer, engineering, and science, 16.0% education, legal, community service, arts, and media, 6.5% healthcare practitioners, 15.5% service, 25.9% sales and office, 5.7% natural resources, construction, and maintenance, 10.4% production, transportation, and material moving
Income: Per capita: $29,067; Median household: $52,507; Average household: $71,440; Households with income of $100,000 or more: 21.1%; Poverty rate: 13.6%

Educational Attainment: High school diploma or higher: 94.7%; Bachelor's degree or higher: 39.5%; Graduate/professional degree or higher: 14.4%

School District(s)

Duneland School Corporation (KG-12)
Enrollment: 5,667 . . . . (219) 983-3600
East Porter County School Corp (KG-12)
Enrollment: 2,313 . . . . (219) 766-2214
Portage Township Schools (KG-12)
Enrollment: 7,799 . . . . (219) 762-6511
Porter County Education Services (KG-12)
Enrollment: n/a . . . . (219) 464-9607
Porter Township School Corp (KG-12)
Enrollment: 1,314 . . . . (219) 477-4933
Union Township School Corp (KG-12)
Enrollment: 1,468 . . . . (219) 759-2531
Valparaiso Community Schools (KG-12)
Enrollment: 6,372 . . . . (219) 531-3000

Four-year College(s)

Valparaiso University (Private, Not-for-profit, Lutheran Church in America)
Enrollment: 4,026 . . . . (219) 464-5000
Tuition: In-state $38,760; Out-of-state $38,760

Two-year College(s)

College of Court Reporting Inc (Private, For-profit)
Enrollment: 238. . . . . (219) 531-1459
Tuition: In-state $14,450; Out-of-state $14,450

Vocational/Technical School(s)

Don Roberts Beauty School (Private, For-profit)
Enrollment: 45. . . . . (219) 462-5189
Tuition: $16,500

Housing: Homeownership rate: 56.1%; Median home value: $175,000; Median year structure built: 1976; Homeowner vacancy rate: 1.9%; Median selected monthly owner costs: $1,370 with a mortgage, $458 without a mortgage; Median gross rent: $897 per month; Rental vacancy rate: 6.4%
Health Insurance: 91.1% have insurance; 75.2% have private insurance; 26.8% have public insurance; 8.9% do not have insurance; 3.0% of children under 18 do not have insurance
Hospitals: Porter Regional Hospital (402 beds)
Safety: Violent crime rate: 14.4 per 10,000 population; Property crime rate: 151.2 per 10,000 population
Transportation: Commute: 86.2% car, 1.3% public transportation, 5.5% walk, 4.8% work from home; Mean travel time to work: 22.0 minutes
Airports: Porter County Regional (general aviation)
Additional Information Contacts
City of Valparaiso . . . . (219) 462-1161
http://www.ci.valparaiso.in.us

WHEELER (CDP). Covers a land area of 2.656 square miles and a water area of 0 square miles. Located at 41.51° N. Lat; 87.17° W. Long. Elevation is 666 feet.
Population: 405; Growth (since 2000): n/a; Density: 152.5 persons per square mile; Race: 93.3% White, 0.0% Black/African American, 0.0% Asian, 0.0% American Indian/Alaska Native, 0.0% Native Hawaiian/Other Pacific Islander, 6.7% Two or more races, 8.9% Hispanic of any race; Average household size: 2.35; Median age: 50.0; Age under 18: 14.3%; Age 65 and over: 17.8%; Males per 100 females: 92.6; Marriage status: 38.6% never married, 41.8% now married, 0.0% separated, 9.2% widowed, 10.4% divorced; Foreign born: 6.9%; Speak English only: 97.7%; With disability: 18.3%; Veterans: 12.1%; Ancestry: 21.2% American, 16.8% German, 10.6% Dutch, 8.6% Irish, 8.1% Italian
Employment: 14.4% management, business, and financial, 0.0% computer, engineering, and science, 14.4% education, legal, community service, arts, and media, 5.2% healthcare practitioners, 13.9% service, 17.5% sales and office, 29.9% natural resources, construction, and maintenance, 4.6% production, transportation, and material moving
Income: Per capita: $31,921; Median household: $63,750; Average household: $73,449; Households with income of $100,000 or more: 22.1%; Poverty rate: n/a
Educational Attainment: High school diploma or higher: 64.7%; Bachelor's degree or higher: 15.8%; Graduate/professional degree or higher: 4.6%
Housing: Homeownership rate: 76.2%; Median home value: $131,300; Median year structure built: 1973; Homeowner vacancy rate: 13.8%; Median selected monthly owner costs: $1,400 with a mortgage, $438 without a mortgage; Median gross rent: n/a per month; Rental vacancy rate: 0.0%
Health Insurance: 83.5% have insurance; 64.4% have private insurance; 42.0% have public insurance; 16.5% do not have insurance; 0.0% of children under 18 do not have insurance
Transportation: Commute: 100.0% car, 0.0% public transportation, 0.0% walk, 0.0% work from home; Mean travel time to work: 37.5 minutes

Posey County

Located in southwestern Indiana; bounded on the west by the Wabash River and the Illinois border, and on the south by the Ohio River and the Kentucky border; drained by Big Creek. Covers a land area of 409.571 square miles, a water area of 9.754 square miles, and is located in the Central Time Zone at 38.03° N. Lat., 87.87° W. Long. The county was founded in 1814. County seat is Mount Vernon.

Posey County is part of the Evansville, IN-KY Metropolitan Statistical Area. The entire metro area includes: Posey County, IN; Vanderburgh County, IN; Warrick County, IN; Henderson County, KY

Weather Station: Mount Vernon Elevation: 419 feet

	Jan	Feb	Mar	Apr	May	Jun	Jul	Aug	Sep	Oct	Nov	Dec
High	41	45	55	66	76	85	88	87	81	69	57	44
Low	24	27	35	45	56	65	68	66	58	47	38	28
Precip	3.5	3.1	4.3	4.4	5.7	3.9	3.8	2.9	3.0	3.4	4.0	3.9
Snow	2.3	3.2	1.3	0.1	0.0	0.0	0.0	0.0	0.0	0.1	0.1	1.8

High and Low temperatures in degrees Fahrenheit; Precipitation and Snow in inches

Population: 25,599; Growth (since 2000): -5.4%; Density: 62.5 persons per square mile; Race: 96.9% White, 1.5% Black/African American, 0.4% Asian, 0.0% American Indian/Alaska Native, 0.0% Native Hawaiian/Other Pacific Islander, 1.0% two or more races, 1.1% Hispanic of any race; Average household size: 2.50; Median age: 42.5; Age under 18: 22.3%; Age 65 and over: 17.1%; Males per 100 females: 99.0; Marriage status: 22.1% never married, 60.2% now married, 0.4% separated, 6.1% widowed, 11.6% divorced; Foreign born: 0.6%; Speak English only: 98.6%; With disability: 12.5%; Veterans: 9.6%; Ancestry: 37.9% German, 13.4% English, 11.9% American, 11.6% Irish, 2.2% French
Religion: Six largest groups: 22.7% Catholicism, 7.8% Methodist/Pietist, 6.9% Baptist, 5.3% Presbyterian-Reformed, 3.3% Non-denominational Protestant, 1.8% Pentecostal
Economy: Unemployment rate: 3.0%; Leading industries: 16.0 % construction; 12.0 % other services (except public administration); 11.4 % retail trade; Farms: 408 totaling 228,748 acres; Company size: 2 employ 1,000 or more persons, 0 employ 500 to 999 persons, 10 employ 100 to 499 persons, 506 employ less than 100 persons; Business ownership: 499 women-owned, 25 Black-owned, n/a Hispanic-owned, n/a Asian-owned, n/a American Indian/Alaska Native-owned
Employment: 11.6% management, business, and financial, 6.0% computer, engineering, and science, 7.8% education, legal, community service, arts, and media, 6.4% healthcare practitioners, 17.6% service, 19.4% sales and office, 10.9% natural resources, construction, and maintenance, 20.3% production, transportation, and material moving
Income: Per capita: $30,763; Median household: $60,992; Average household: $75,709; Households with income of $100,000 or more: 25.3%; Poverty rate: 9.5%
Educational Attainment: High school diploma or higher: 93.6%; Bachelor's degree or higher: 20.7%; Graduate/professional degree or higher: 7.3%
Housing: Homeownership rate: 83.1%; Median home value: $138,800; Median year structure built: 1973; Homeowner vacancy rate: 1.2%; Median selected monthly owner costs: $1,075 with a mortgage, $380 without a mortgage; Median gross rent: $698 per month; Rental vacancy rate: 7.9%
Vital Statistics: Birth rate: 111.0 per 10,000 population; Death rate: 95.3 per 10,000 population; Age-adjusted cancer mortality rate: 180.9 deaths per 100,000 population
Health Insurance: 94.9% have insurance; 79.3% have private insurance; 29.4% have public insurance; 5.1% do not have insurance; 1.0% of children under 18 do not have insurance
Health Care: Physicians: 4.7 per 10,000 population; Dentists: 2.7 per 10,000 population; Hospital beds: 0.0 per 10,000 population; Hospital admissions: 0.0 per 10,000 population
Air Quality Index (AQI): Percent of Days: 82.5% good, 16.6% moderate, 0.9% unhealthy for sensitive individuals, 0.0% unhealthy, 0.0% very unhealthy; Annual median: 42; Annual maximum: 126

Transportation: Commute: 94.5% car, 0.0% public transportation, 0.9% walk, 3.5% work from home; Mean travel time to work: 23.6 minutes
2016 Presidential Election: 67.4% Trump, 28.2% Clinton, 4.3% Johnson, 0.0% Stein
National and State Parks: Harmonie State Park; New Harmony State Memorial; The Labyrinth State Memorial
Additional Information Contacts
Posey Government . . . . (812) 838-3317
http://www.poseycountygov.org

Posey County Communities

CYNTHIANA (town). Covers a land area of 0.399 square miles and a water area of 0 square miles. Located at 38.19° N. Lat; 87.71° W. Long. Elevation is 472 feet.
Population: 572; Growth (since 2000): -17.5%; Density: 1,434.3 persons per square mile; Race: 98.8% White, 0.0% Black/African American, 0.0% Asian, 0.0% American Indian/Alaska Native, 0.0% Native Hawaiian/Other Pacific Islander, 1.2% Two or more races, 2.1% Hispanic of any race; Average household size: 2.23; Median age: 45.9; Age under 18: 16.6%; Age 65 and over: 13.5%; Males per 100 females: 98.9; Marriage status: 26.7% never married, 55.1% now married, 0.4% separated, 2.9% widowed, 15.3% divorced; Foreign born: 1.0%; Speak English only: 99.4%; With disability: 14.2%; Veterans: 10.5%; Ancestry: 44.1% German, 17.5% English, 15.9% Irish, 5.2% American, 3.5% European
Employment: 8.9% management, business, and financial, 2.6% computer, engineering, and science, 5.6% education, legal, community service, arts, and media, 1.3% healthcare practitioners, 15.7% service, 24.3% sales and office, 9.5% natural resources, construction, and maintenance, 32.1% production, transportation, and material moving
Income: Per capita: $24,612; Median household: $48,250; Average household: $54,033; Households with income of $100,000 or more: 10.5%; Poverty rate: 12.4%
Educational Attainment: High school diploma or higher: 82.6%; Bachelor's degree or higher: 12.3%; Graduate/professional degree or higher: 4.1%
Housing: Homeownership rate: 76.3%; Median home value: $77,900; Median year structure built: 1953; Homeowner vacancy rate: 0.0%; Median selected monthly owner costs: $882 with a mortgage, $357 without a mortgage; Median gross rent: $544 per month; Rental vacancy rate: 18.7%
Health Insurance: 95.6% have insurance; 81.3% have private insurance; 26.9% have public insurance; 4.4% do not have insurance; 0.0% of children under 18 do not have insurance
Transportation: Commute: 93.1% car, 0.0% public transportation, 2.3% walk, 4.6% work from home; Mean travel time to work: 22.8 minutes

GRIFFIN (town). Covers a land area of 0.068 square miles and a water area of 0 square miles. Located at 38.20° N. Lat; 87.91° W. Long. Elevation is 387 feet.
History: Laid out 1881.
Population: 151; Growth (since 2000): -5.6%; Density: 2,208.6 persons per square mile; Race: 100.0% White, 0.0% Black/African American, 0.0% Asian, 0.0% American Indian/Alaska Native, 0.0% Native Hawaiian/Other Pacific Islander, 0.0% Two or more races, 0.0% Hispanic of any race; Average household size: 2.29; Median age: 51.2; Age under 18: 17.2%; Age 65 and over: 25.8%; Males per 100 females: 75.5; Marriage status: 23.0% never married, 55.6% now married, 0.0% separated, 10.3% widowed, 11.1% divorced; Foreign born: 0.7%; Speak English only: 100.0%; With disability: 31.1%; Veterans: 9.6%; Ancestry: 29.8% German, 28.5% English, 8.6% American, 7.9% Irish, 2.6% Welsh
Employment: 4.9% management, business, and financial, 0.0% computer, engineering, and science, 6.6% education, legal, community service, arts, and media, 3.3% healthcare practitioners, 31.1% service, 6.6% sales and office, 32.8% natural resources, construction, and maintenance, 14.8% production, transportation, and material moving
Income: Per capita: $17,652; Median household: $29,615; Average household: $39,439; Households with income of $100,000 or more: 4.5%; Poverty rate: 28.5%
Educational Attainment: High school diploma or higher: 80.6%; Bachelor's degree or higher: 2.4%; Graduate/professional degree or higher: n/a
Housing: Homeownership rate: 86.4%; Median home value: $36,300; Median year structure built: 1951; Homeowner vacancy rate: 0.0%; Median selected monthly owner costs: $667 with a mortgage, $295 without a mortgage; Median gross rent: n/a per month; Rental vacancy rate: 0.0%
Health Insurance: 85.4% have insurance; 70.2% have private insurance; 36.4% have public insurance; 14.6% do not have insurance; 0.0% of children under 18 do not have insurance
Transportation: Commute: 96.7% car, 0.0% public transportation, 0.0% walk, 1.6% work from home; Mean travel time to work: 27.9 minutes

MOUNT VERNON (city). County seat. Covers a land area of 2.808 square miles and a water area of 0.050 square miles. Located at 37.94° N. Lat; 87.90° W. Long. Elevation is 400 feet.
History: Mount Vernon, founded in 1805 by Irish trader Andrew McFadden, was first called McFadden's Landing. The name was changed in 1816.
Population: 6,548; Growth (since 2000): -12.4%; Density: 2,332.2 persons per square mile; Race: 92.6% White, 4.1% Black/African American, 0.5% Asian, 0.0% American Indian/Alaska Native, 0.0% Native Hawaiian/Other Pacific Islander, 2.8% Two or more races, 1.1% Hispanic of any race; Average household size: 2.35; Median age: 42.2; Age under 18: 19.6%; Age 65 and over: 17.8%; Males per 100 females: 91.4; Marriage status: 29.1% never married, 49.7% now married, 0.7% separated, 5.7% widowed, 15.5% divorced; Foreign born: 0.7%; Speak English only: 99.1%; With disability: 16.5%; Veterans: 6.8%; Ancestry: 29.8% German, 20.8% English, 10.8% Irish, 9.4% American, 2.1% French
Employment: 11.8% management, business, and financial, 6.7% computer, engineering, and science, 4.4% education, legal, community service, arts, and media, 5.1% healthcare practitioners, 19.9% service, 22.1% sales and office, 7.9% natural resources, construction, and maintenance, 22.3% production, transportation, and material moving
Income: Per capita: $29,511; Median household: $53,750; Average household: $68,950; Households with income of $100,000 or more: 23.1%; Poverty rate: 15.0%
Educational Attainment: High school diploma or higher: 89.2%; Bachelor's degree or higher: 16.2%; Graduate/professional degree or higher: 5.4%

School District(s)

M S D Mount Vernon (PK-12)
Enrollment: 2,107 . . . . (812) 838-4471
Housing: Homeownership rate: 67.5%; Median home value: $97,500; Median year structure built: 1967; Homeowner vacancy rate: 3.7%; Median selected monthly owner costs: $958 with a mortgage, $370 without a mortgage; Median gross rent: $689 per month; Rental vacancy rate: 4.9%
Health Insurance: 94.2% have insurance; 74.7% have private insurance; 34.4% have public insurance; 5.8% do not have insurance; 0.7% of children under 18 do not have insurance
Newspapers: Mt. Vernon Democrat (weekly circulation 3,900)
Transportation: Commute: 96.0% car, 0.0% public transportation, 1.1% walk, 2.4% work from home; Mean travel time to work: 16.6 minutes
Additional Information Contacts
City of Mount Vernon. . . . . (812) 838-3317
http://www.mountvernon.in.gov

NEW HARMONY (town). Covers a land area of 0.636 square miles and a water area of 0.009 square miles. Located at 38.13° N. Lat; 87.93° W. Long. Elevation is 381 feet.
History: New Harmony was the site of two social experiments. In 1815 the Rappites, a religious group of Germans from Pennsylvania, founded the village of Harmonie, trying to create a society based on cooperative living. After ten years their hard work had created a prosperous town out of the wilderness, but also created discontent. They sold the village to Robert Owen, a Welsh philanthropist and social reformer whose dream was to found a communal society. Owen called his community New Harmony. The experiment as Owen envisioned it was a failure within two years, but New Harmony continued to be an intellectual center.
Population: 738; Growth (since 2000): -19.4%; Density: 1,161.1 persons per square mile; Race: 92.1% White, 1.2% Black/African American, 6.4% Asian, 0.3% American Indian/Alaska Native, 0.0% Native Hawaiian/Other Pacific Islander, 0.0% Two or more races, 0.0% Hispanic of any race; Average household size: 2.23; Median age: 56.2; Age under 18: 14.5%; Age 65 and over: 32.5%; Males per 100 females: 76.1; Marriage status: 16.8% never married, 51.5% now married, 0.9% separated, 14.8% widowed, 16.9% divorced; Foreign born: 4.9%; Speak English only: 95.6%; With disability: 13.8%; Veterans: 13.9%; Ancestry: 33.1% German, 29.3% English, 21.7% Irish, 7.7% French, 5.3% American
Employment: 12.3% management, business, and financial, 5.5% computer, engineering, and science, 10.1% education, legal, community service, arts, and media, 6.8% healthcare practitioners, 11.0% service,

21.8% sales and office, 10.7% natural resources, construction, and maintenance, 21.8% production, transportation, and material moving
Income: Per capita: $28,745; Median household: $58,056; Average household: $64,273; Households with income of $100,000 or more: 17.6%; Poverty rate: 4.9%
Educational Attainment: High school diploma or higher: 83.5%; Bachelor's degree or higher: 22.9%; Graduate/professional degree or higher: 13.4%
Housing: Homeownership rate: 72.8%; Median home value: $100,300; Median year structure built: Before 1940; Homeowner vacancy rate: 3.7%; Median selected monthly owner costs: $989 with a mortgage, $384 without a mortgage; Median gross rent: $792 per month; Rental vacancy rate: 25.0%
Health Insurance: 88.9% have insurance; 63.4% have private insurance; 38.6% have public insurance; 11.1% do not have insurance; 16.4% of children under 18 do not have insurance
Newspapers: Posey County News (weekly circulation 4,800)
Transportation: Commute: 87.2% car, 0.0% public transportation, 3.7% walk, 7.4% work from home; Mean travel time to work: 24.4 minutes

PARKERS SETTLEMENT (CDP). Covers a land area of 1.752 square miles and a water area of 0 square miles. Located at 38.04° N. Lat; 87.71° W. Long. Elevation is 446 feet.
Population: 663; Growth (since 2000): n/a; Density: 378.5 persons per square mile; Race: 100.0% White, 0.0% Black/African American, 0.0% Asian, 0.0% American Indian/Alaska Native, 0.0% Native Hawaiian/Other Pacific Islander, 0.0% Two or more races, 0.0% Hispanic of any race; Average household size: 2.55; Median age: 44.1; Age under 18: 17.6%; Age 65 and over: 17.6%; Males per 100 females: 100.8; Marriage status: 10.9% never married, 73.8% now married, 0.0% separated, 6.1% widowed, 9.1% divorced; Foreign born: 0.0%; Speak English only: 100.0%; With disability: 12.8%; Veterans: 11.2%; Ancestry: 47.5% German, 21.9% American, 6.0% English, 2.7% French, 2.6% Polish
Employment: 13.6% management, business, and financial, 2.4% computer, engineering, and science, 6.9% education, legal, community service, arts, and media, 5.1% healthcare practitioners, 13.9% service, 28.8% sales and office, 12.0% natural resources, construction, and maintenance, 17.3% production, transportation, and material moving
Income: Per capita: $31,961; Median household: $66,912; Average household: $77,467; Households with income of $100,000 or more: 21.2%; Poverty rate: 3.0%
Educational Attainment: High school diploma or higher: 92.4%; Bachelor's degree or higher: 15.7%; Graduate/professional degree or higher: 6.7%
Housing: Homeownership rate: 86.2%; Median home value: $136,200; Median year structure built: 1982; Homeowner vacancy rate: 0.0%; Median selected monthly owner costs: $1,113 with a mortgage, $416 without a mortgage; Median gross rent: $643 per month; Rental vacancy rate: 0.0%
Health Insurance: 91.1% have insurance; 84.9% have private insurance; 24.9% have public insurance; 8.9% do not have insurance; 0.0% of children under 18 do not have insurance
Transportation: Commute: 98.9% car, 0.0% public transportation, 0.0% walk, 0.0% work from home; Mean travel time to work: 25.5 minutes

POSEYVILLE (town). Covers a land area of 0.645 square miles and a water area of 0 square miles. Located at 38.17° N. Lat; 87.78° W. Long. Elevation is 440 feet.
Population: 1,085; Growth (since 2000): -8.6%; Density: 1,681.7 persons per square mile; Race: 99.7% White, 0.0% Black/African American, 0.0% Asian, 0.3% American Indian/Alaska Native, 0.0% Native Hawaiian/Other Pacific Islander, 0.0% Two or more races, 0.0% Hispanic of any race; Average household size: 2.39; Median age: 43.9; Age under 18: 24.3%; Age 65 and over: 26.5%; Males per 100 females: 93.9; Marriage status: 20.6% never married, 61.0% now married, 0.0% separated, 9.3% widowed, 9.1% divorced; Foreign born: 0.0%; Speak English only: 99.3%; With disability: 20.0%; Veterans: 13.5%; Ancestry: 40.2% German, 13.6% American, 12.3% Irish, 11.6% English, 4.6% French
Employment: 12.8% management, business, and financial, 7.2% computer, engineering, and science, 9.5% education, legal, community service, arts, and media, 3.7% healthcare practitioners, 18.4% service, 25.8% sales and office, 9.8% natural resources, construction, and maintenance, 12.8% production, transportation, and material moving
Income: Per capita: $25,423; Median household: $45,526; Average household: $58,667; Households with income of $100,000 or more: 13.7%; Poverty rate: 10.6%
Educational Attainment: High school diploma or higher: 92.2%; Bachelor's degree or higher: 19.6%; Graduate/professional degree or higher: 6.9%

School District(s)

M S D North Posey Co Schools (PK-12)
Enrollment: 1,464 . . . . (812) 874-2243
Housing: Homeownership rate: 85.0%; Median home value: $106,300; Median year structure built: 1957; Homeowner vacancy rate: 0.0%; Median selected monthly owner costs: $1,039 with a mortgage, $353 without a mortgage; Median gross rent: $758 per month; Rental vacancy rate: 0.0%
Health Insurance: 98.4% have insurance; 80.7% have private insurance; 40.9% have public insurance; 1.6% do not have insurance; 0.0% of children under 18 do not have insurance
Transportation: Commute: 90.9% car, 0.0% public transportation, 2.3% walk, 5.6% work from home; Mean travel time to work: 28.6 minutes

WADESVILLE (unincorporated postal area)
ZCTA: 47638
Covers a land area of 49.196 square miles and a water area of 0.021 square miles. Located at 38.07° N. Lat; 87.78° W. Long. Elevation is 479 feet.
Population: 3,747; Growth (since 2000): 8.8%; Density: 76.2 persons per square mile; Race: 99.4% White, 0.0% Black/African American, 0.0% Asian, 0.0% American Indian/Alaska Native, 0.0% Native Hawaiian/Other Pacific Islander, 0.2% Two or more races, 1.4% Hispanic of any race; Average household size: 2.59; Median age: 42.3; Age under 18: 25.1%; Age 65 and over: 14.9%; Males per 100 females: 99.6; Marriage status: 15.9% never married, 70.8% now married, 0.0% separated, 4.3% widowed, 9.0% divorced; Foreign born: 0.6%; Speak English only: 98.1%; With disability: 6.9%; Veterans: 10.9%; Ancestry: 42.8% German, 13.2% English, 11.4% American, 6.7% Irish, 3.0% Dutch
Employment: 11.3% management, business, and financial, 5.3% computer, engineering, and science, 5.8% education, legal, community service, arts, and media, 7.2% healthcare practitioners, 15.7% service, 20.9% sales and office, 13.5% natural resources, construction, and maintenance, 20.3% production, transportation, and material moving
Income: Per capita: $33,110; Median household: $67,125; Average household: $83,846; Households with income of $100,000 or more: 27.2%; Poverty rate: 5.0%
Educational Attainment: High school diploma or higher: 95.6%; Bachelor's degree or higher: 18.3%; Graduate/professional degree or higher: 4.7%

School District(s)

M S D North Posey Co Schools (PK-12)
Enrollment: 1,464 . . . . (812) 874-2243
Housing: Homeownership rate: 90.4%; Median home value: $165,000; Median year structure built: 1977; Homeowner vacancy rate: 0.0%; Median selected monthly owner costs: $1,118 with a mortgage, $420 without a mortgage; Median gross rent: $626 per month; Rental vacancy rate: 0.0%
Health Insurance: 96.1% have insurance; 83.5% have private insurance; 22.4% have public insurance; 3.9% do not have insurance; 0.0% of children under 18 do not have insurance
Transportation: Commute: 93.9% car, 0.0% public transportation, 0.5% walk, 5.0% work from home; Mean travel time to work: 30.3 minutes

Pulaski County

Located in northwestern Indiana; drained by the Tippecanoe River. Covers a land area of 433.649 square miles, a water area of 0.885 square miles, and is located in the Eastern Time Zone at 41.05° N. Lat., 86.69° W. Long. The county was founded in 1835. County seat is Winamac.

Weather Station: Winamac 2 SSE Elevation: 689 feet

	Jan	Feb	Mar	Apr	May	Jun	Jul	Aug	Sep	Oct	Nov	Dec
High	32	36	48	61	72	80	83	82	76	63	50	36
Low	16	19	28	39	50	59	63	61	53	41	32	21
Precip	2.1	1.9	2.5	3.3	4.0	3.9	4.6	4.1	3.2	3.4	3.1	2.5
Snow	8.0	5.5	3.2	0.7	0.0	0.0	0.0	0.0	0.0	0.1	0.9	5.9

High and Low temperatures in degrees Fahrenheit; Precipitation and Snow in inches

Population: 12,761; Growth (since 2000): -7.2%; Density: 29.4 persons per square mile; Race: 95.9% White, 0.5% Black/African American, 0.6% Asian, 0.1% American Indian/Alaska Native, 0.0% Native Hawaiian/Other

Pacific Islander, 1.6% two or more races, 2.9% Hispanic of any race; Average household size: 2.38; Median age: 41.8; Age under 18: 22.8%; Age 65 and over: 18.1%; Males per 100 females: 102.0; Marriage status: 21.0% never married, 57.3% now married, 1.0% separated, 6.9% widowed, 14.9% divorced; Foreign born: 1.1%; Speak English only: 97.7%; With disability: 16.6%; Veterans: 10.0%; Ancestry: 33.4% German, 14.5% Irish, 7.7% American, 6.9% English, 4.7% Polish
Religion: Six largest groups: 9.0% Baptist, 9.0% Catholicism, 6.1% Methodist/Pietist, 5.8% Non-denominational Protestant, 2.7% European Free-Church, 2.7% Lutheran
Economy: Unemployment rate: 3.1%; Leading industries: 17.4 % retail trade; 15.4 % other services (except public administration); 11.1 % construction; Farms: 536 totaling 216,503 acres; Company size: 0 employ 1,000 or more persons, 1 employs 500 to 999 persons, 3 employ 100 to 499 persons, 301 employs less than 100 persons; Business ownership: 255 women-owned, n/a Black-owned, 28 Hispanic-owned, n/a Asian-owned, n/a American Indian/Alaska Native-owned
Employment: 11.8% management, business, and financial, 2.4% computer, engineering, and science, 6.3% education, legal, community service, arts, and media, 6.4% healthcare practitioners, 14.2% service, 16.7% sales and office, 14.3% natural resources, construction, and maintenance, 28.1% production, transportation, and material moving
Income: Per capita: $24,445; Median household: $47,633; Average household: $57,966; Households with income of $100,000 or more: 13.7%; Poverty rate: 13.2%
Educational Attainment: High school diploma or higher: 88.7%; Bachelor's degree or higher: 11.8%; Graduate/professional degree or higher: 3.6%
Housing: Homeownership rate: 76.4%; Median home value: $92,600; Median year structure built: 1962; Homeowner vacancy rate: 0.0%; Median selected monthly owner costs: $957 with a mortgage, $325 without a mortgage; Median gross rent: $665 per month; Rental vacancy rate: 8.0%
Vital Statistics: Birth rate: 101.3 per 10,000 population; Death rate: 106.9 per 10,000 population; Age-adjusted cancer mortality rate: 180.5 deaths per 100,000 population
Health Insurance: 89.9% have insurance; 69.4% have private insurance; 35.0% have public insurance; 10.1% do not have insurance; 7.7% of children under 18 do not have insurance
Health Care: Physicians: 7.9 per 10,000 population; Dentists: 2.4 per 10,000 population; Hospital beds: 19.8 per 10,000 population; Hospital admissions: 547.1 per 10,000 population
Transportation: Commute: 90.6% car, 0.1% public transportation, 2.8% walk, 4.7% work from home; Mean travel time to work: 21.7 minutes
2016 Presidential Election: 70.6% Trump, 24.3% Clinton, 4.7% Johnson, 0.2% Stein
National and State Parks: Winamac State Fish and Wildlife Area
Additional Information Contacts
Pulaski Government . . . . (574) 946-3313
http://www.pulaskionline.org

Pulaski County Communities

FRANCESVILLE (town). Covers a land area of 0.304 square miles and a water area of 0 square miles. Located at 40.99° N. Lat; 86.88° W. Long. Elevation is 679 feet.
Population: 913; Growth (since 2000): 0.9%; Density: 3,007.4 persons per square mile; Race: 97.8% White, 0.0% Black/African American, 0.0% Asian, 0.0% American Indian/Alaska Native, 0.0% Native Hawaiian/Other Pacific Islander, 0.9% Two or more races, 2.7% Hispanic of any race; Average household size: 2.39; Median age: 47.9; Age under 18: 21.7%; Age 65 and over: 19.6%; Males per 100 females: 97.1; Marriage status: 24.6% never married, 55.0% now married, 0.4% separated, 9.0% widowed, 11.4% divorced; Foreign born: 0.3%; Speak English only: 99.3%; With disability: 18.1%; Veterans: 7.6%; Ancestry: 39.2% German, 9.2% Irish, 4.9% American, 4.6% English, 3.9% Italian
Employment: 8.9% management, business, and financial, 1.1% computer, engineering, and science, 4.3% education, legal, community service, arts, and media, 2.1% healthcare practitioners, 18.9% service, 26.2% sales and office, 14.6% natural resources, construction, and maintenance, 23.9% production, transportation, and material moving
Income: Per capita: $21,828; Median household: $50,417; Average household: $52,097; Households with income of $100,000 or more: 5.2%; Poverty rate: 11.2%
Educational Attainment: High school diploma or higher: 93.4%; Bachelor's degree or higher: 12.4%; Graduate/professional degree or higher: 3.1%

School District(s)

West Central School Corp (PK-12)
Enrollment: 820. . . . . (219) 567-9161
Housing: Homeownership rate: 83.0%; Median home value: $95,500; Median year structure built: 1951; Homeowner vacancy rate: 0.0%; Median selected monthly owner costs: $812 with a mortgage, $315 without a mortgage; Median gross rent: $717 per month; Rental vacancy rate: 11.0%
Health Insurance: 93.3% have insurance; 78.3% have private insurance; 27.6% have public insurance; 6.7% do not have insurance; 6.9% of children under 18 do not have insurance
Newspapers: Francesville Tribune (weekly circulation 900)
Transportation: Commute: 89.1% car, 1.9% public transportation, 4.4% walk, 3.0% work from home; Mean travel time to work: 17.6 minutes

MEDARYVILLE (town). Covers a land area of 0.459 square miles and a water area of 0 square miles. Located at 41.08° N. Lat; 86.89° W. Long. Elevation is 689 feet.
Population: 538; Growth (since 2000): -4.8%; Density: 1,172.3 persons per square mile; Race: 94.1% White, 0.0% Black/African American, 0.0% Asian, 0.0% American Indian/Alaska Native, 0.0% Native Hawaiian/Other Pacific Islander, 0.0% Two or more races, 7.8% Hispanic of any race; Average household size: 2.65; Median age: 35.5; Age under 18: 33.1%; Age 65 and over: 23.4%; Males per 100 females: 95.5; Marriage status: 19.2% never married, 56.0% now married, 3.7% separated, 10.1% widowed, 14.7% divorced; Foreign born: 0.2%; Speak English only: 99.8%; With disability: 22.5%; Veterans: 8.3%; Ancestry: 26.6% German, 22.7% Irish, 9.7% English, 4.3% American, 3.0% Czech
Employment: 4.1% management, business, and financial, 0.0% computer, engineering, and science, 2.0% education, legal, community service, arts, and media, 2.7% healthcare practitioners, 14.2% service, 14.2% sales and office, 14.2% natural resources, construction, and maintenance, 48.6% production, transportation, and material moving
Income: Per capita: $15,758; Median household: $33,068; Average household: $42,032; Households with income of $100,000 or more: 9.4%; Poverty rate: 22.5%
Educational Attainment: High school diploma or higher: 73.5%; Bachelor's degree or higher: 2.6%; Graduate/professional degree or higher: 1.5%
Housing: Homeownership rate: 74.4%; Median home value: $60,800; Median year structure built: 1953; Homeowner vacancy rate: 0.0%; Median selected monthly owner costs: $782 with a mortgage, $358 without a mortgage; Median gross rent: $675 per month; Rental vacancy rate: 0.0%
Health Insurance: 87.5% have insurance; 49.6% have private insurance; 54.5% have public insurance; 12.5% do not have insurance; 2.2% of children under 18 do not have insurance
Transportation: Commute: 81.9% car, 0.0% public transportation, 13.9% walk, 1.4% work from home; Mean travel time to work: 30.1 minutes

MONTEREY (town). Covers a land area of 0.183 square miles and a water area of 0 square miles. Located at 41.16° N. Lat; 86.48° W. Long. Elevation is 725 feet.
History: Laid out 1849.
Population: 327; Growth (since 2000): 41.6%; Density: 1,786.6 persons per square mile; Race: 88.7% White, 0.0% Black/African American, 0.0% Asian, 0.0% American Indian/Alaska Native, 0.0% Native Hawaiian/Other Pacific Islander, 0.0% Two or more races, 22.3% Hispanic of any race; Average household size: 3.34; Median age: 39.2; Age under 18: 24.2%; Age 65 and over: 8.6%; Males per 100 females: 109.6; Marriage status: 33.5% never married, 53.3% now married, 0.0% separated, 2.2% widowed, 11.0% divorced; Foreign born: 0.0%; Speak English only: 92.7%; With disability: 13.1%; Veterans: 6.5%; Ancestry: 30.0% German, 23.9% Irish, 4.3% American, 3.4% French, 2.8% English
Employment: 4.4% management, business, and financial, 0.5% computer, engineering, and science, 6.6% education, legal, community service, arts, and media, 10.9% healthcare practitioners, 6.0% service, 31.1% sales and office, 9.8% natural resources, construction, and maintenance, 30.6% production, transportation, and material moving
Income: Per capita: $20,579; Median household: $59,000; Average household: $62,733; Households with income of $100,000 or more: 2.0%; Poverty rate: 4.0%

Educational Attainment: High school diploma or higher: 87.8%; Bachelor's degree or higher: 5.9%; Graduate/professional degree or higher: n/a
Housing: Homeownership rate: 74.5%; Median home value: $65,800; Median year structure built: 1946; Homeowner vacancy rate: 0.0%; Median selected monthly owner costs: $790 with a mortgage, $286 without a mortgage; Median gross rent: $781 per month; Rental vacancy rate: 16.7%
Health Insurance: 86.5% have insurance; 74.6% have private insurance; 21.1% have public insurance; 13.5% do not have insurance; 13.0% of children under 18 do not have insurance
Transportation: Commute: 93.4% car, 0.0% public transportation, 3.8% walk, 0.5% work from home; Mean travel time to work: 27.5 minutes

STAR CITY (CDP). Covers a land area of 1.036 square miles and a water area of 0 square miles. Located at 40.97° N. Lat; 86.56° W. Long. Elevation is 715 feet.
History: Laid out 1859.
Population: 248; Growth (since 2000): -34.2%; Density: 239.3 persons per square mile; Race: 100.0% White, 0.0% Black/African American, 0.0% Asian, 0.0% American Indian/Alaska Native, 0.0% Native Hawaiian/Other Pacific Islander, 0.0% Two or more races, 0.0% Hispanic of any race; Average household size: 2.05; Median age: 28.7; Age under 18: 27.4%; Age 65 and over: 10.9%; Males per 100 females: 106.0; Marriage status: 0.0% never married, 73.9% now married, 0.0% separated, 0.0% widowed, 26.1% divorced; Foreign born: 2.8%; Speak English only: 97.0%; With disability: 9.3%; Veterans: 42.2%; Ancestry: 51.6% German, 19.0% Scottish, 16.1% Irish, 10.5% Swedish, 8.1% Italian
Employment: 0.0% management, business, and financial, 11.2% computer, engineering, and science, 0.0% education, legal, community service, arts, and media, 0.0% healthcare practitioners, 6.0% service, 17.2% sales and office, 10.4% natural resources, construction, and maintenance, 55.2% production, transportation, and material moving
Income: Per capita: $24,212; Median household: $45,121; Average household: $51,851; Households with income of $100,000 or more: 25.6%; Poverty rate: 14.5%
Educational Attainment: High school diploma or higher: 100.0%; Bachelor's degree or higher: 19.9%; Graduate/professional degree or higher: n/a
Housing: Homeownership rate: 57.0%; Median home value: $73,200; Median year structure built: Before 1940; Homeowner vacancy rate: 0.0%; Median selected monthly owner costs: $856 with a mortgage, n/a without a mortgage; Median gross rent: n/a per month; Rental vacancy rate: 0.0%
Health Insurance: 62.5% have insurance; 49.6% have private insurance; 16.1% have public insurance; 37.5% do not have insurance; 39.7% of children under 18 do not have insurance
Transportation: Commute: 83.6% car, 0.0% public transportation, 0.0% walk, 10.4% work from home; Mean travel time to work: 18.2 minutes

WINAMAC (town). County seat. Covers a land area of 1.361 square miles and a water area of 0 square miles. Located at 41.05° N. Lat; 86.60° W. Long. Elevation is 705 feet.
History: Winamac was founded in 1835 along the Tippecanoe River, and was named for Potawatomi Chief Winamac.
Population: 2,709; Growth (since 2000): 12.0%; Density: 1,989.9 persons per square mile; Race: 91.1% White, 0.8% Black/African American, 1.8% Asian, 0.0% American Indian/Alaska Native, 0.0% Native Hawaiian/Other Pacific Islander, 3.7% Two or more races, 4.7% Hispanic of any race; Average household size: 2.35; Median age: 38.9; Age under 18: 24.6%; Age 65 and over: 17.2%; Males per 100 females: 95.3; Marriage status: 28.8% never married, 46.3% now married, 1.0% separated, 7.9% widowed, 16.9% divorced; Foreign born: 2.3%; Speak English only: 95.3%; With disability: 20.6%; Veterans: 9.7%; Ancestry: 36.5% German, 18.2% Irish, 6.5% American, 5.9% English, 3.8% Dutch
Employment: 9.4% management, business, and financial, 4.0% computer, engineering, and science, 9.0% education, legal, community service, arts, and media, 7.1% healthcare practitioners, 25.6% service, 11.4% sales and office, 7.1% natural resources, construction, and maintenance, 26.5% production, transportation, and material moving
Income: Per capita: $21,120; Median household: $38,696; Average household: $49,708; Households with income of $100,000 or more: 10.7%; Poverty rate: 17.9%
Educational Attainment: High school diploma or higher: 88.6%; Bachelor's degree or higher: 13.6%; Graduate/professional degree or higher: 4.9%

School District(s)
Eastern Pulaski Community Sch Corp (PK-12)
Enrollment: 1,122 . . . . (574) 946-4010
Housing: Homeownership rate: 62.2%; Median home value: $82,100; Median year structure built: 1948; Homeowner vacancy rate: 0.0%; Median selected monthly owner costs: $851 with a mortgage, $315 without a mortgage; Median gross rent: $626 per month; Rental vacancy rate: 8.5%
Health Insurance: 87.5% have insurance; 67.1% have private insurance; 34.4% have public insurance; 12.5% do not have insurance; 10.4% of children under 18 do not have insurance
Hospitals: Pulaski Memorial Hospital
Newspapers: Pulaski County Journal (weekly circulation 3,700)
Transportation: Commute: 93.2% car, 0.0% public transportation, 2.9% walk, 2.0% work from home; Mean travel time to work: 16.8 minutes
Additional Information Contacts
Town of Winamac . . . . (574) 946-3451
http://www.townofwinamac.com

Putnam County

Located in central Indiana; drained by the Eel River. Covers a land area of 480.528 square miles, a water area of 2.164 square miles, and is located in the Eastern Time Zone at 39.67° N. Lat., 86.85° W. Long. The county was founded in 1821. County seat is Greencastle.

Putnam County is part of the Indianapolis-Carmel-Anderson, IN Metropolitan Statistical Area. The entire metro area includes: Boone County, IN; Brown County, IN; Hamilton County, IN; Hancock County, IN; Hendricks County, IN; Johnson County, IN; Madison County, IN; Marion County, IN; Morgan County, IN; Putnam County, IN; Shelby County, IN

Weather Station: Greencastle 1 SE Elevation: 859 feet

	Jan	Feb	Mar	Apr	May	Jun	Jul	Aug	Sep	Oct	Nov	Dec
High	35	40	50	63	73	82	85	84	78	65	52	39
Low	19	22	30	41	51	61	64	62	55	43	34	23
Precip	2.6	2.5	3.5	4.0	5.3	4.5	5.2	3.6	3.9	3.6	3.9	3.2
Snow	7.8	5.9	2.3	0.3	tr	0.0	0.0	0.0	0.0	0.2	0.9	5.1

High and Low temperatures in degrees Fahrenheit; Precipitation and Snow in inches

Population: 37,543; Growth (since 2000): 4.2%; Density: 78.1 persons per square mile; Race: 93.8% White, 3.1% Black/African American, 1.0% Asian, 0.2% American Indian/Alaska Native, 0.0% Native Hawaiian/Other Pacific Islander, 1.4% two or more races, 2.5% Hispanic of any race; Average household size: 2.44; Median age: 37.8; Age under 18: 19.6%; Age 65 and over: 15.5%; Males per 100 females: 111.9; Marriage status: 32.9% never married, 47.6% now married, 0.9% separated, 6.2% widowed, 13.4% divorced; Foreign born: 1.7%; Speak English only: 97.3%; With disability: 14.9%; Veterans: 8.5%; Ancestry: 18.8% German, 11.2% Irish, 9.1% American, 8.1% English, 2.3% Italian
Religion: Six largest groups: 17.3% Baptist, 4.3% Non-denominational Protestant, 2.8% Methodist/Pietist, 2.8% Catholicism, 2.0% Presbyterian-Reformed, 1.3% Pentecostal
Economy: Unemployment rate: 3.6%; Leading industries: 13.8 % retail trade; 13.3 % other services (except public administration); 13.0 % construction; Farms: 847 totaling 197,619 acres; Company size: 1 employs 1,000 or more persons, 3 employ 500 to 999 persons, 13 employ 100 to 499 persons, 681 employs less than 100 persons; Business ownership: 777 women-owned, n/a Black-owned, n/a Hispanic-owned, 46 Asian-owned, n/a American Indian/Alaska Native-owned
Employment: 11.6% management, business, and financial, 3.6% computer, engineering, and science, 9.2% education, legal, community service, arts, and media, 4.1% healthcare practitioners, 17.5% service, 22.8% sales and office, 11.5% natural resources, construction, and maintenance, 19.8% production, transportation, and material moving
Income: Per capita: $23,842; Median household: $55,295; Average household: $67,334; Households with income of $100,000 or more: 18.0%; Poverty rate: 11.6%
Educational Attainment: High school diploma or higher: 88.2%; Bachelor's degree or higher: 15.4%; Graduate/professional degree or higher: 6.5%
Housing: Homeownership rate: 73.6%; Median home value: $120,300; Median year structure built: 1977; Homeowner vacancy rate: 2.5%; Median selected monthly owner costs: $1,130 with a mortgage, $381 without a mortgage; Median gross rent: $734 per month; Rental vacancy rate: 4.3%

Vital Statistics: Birth rate: 96.5 per 10,000 population; Death rate: 90.2 per 10,000 population; Age-adjusted cancer mortality rate: 210.4 deaths per 100,000 population
Health Insurance: 90.8% have insurance; 73.5% have private insurance; 31.8% have public insurance; 9.2% do not have insurance; 6.0% of children under 18 do not have insurance
Health Care: Physicians: 7.2 per 10,000 population; Dentists: 4.2 per 10,000 population; Hospital beds: 6.7 per 10,000 population; Hospital admissions: 231.9 per 10,000 population
Transportation: Commute: 88.9% car, 0.0% public transportation, 7.4% walk, 2.9% work from home; Mean travel time to work: 25.0 minutes
2016 Presidential Election: 72.3% Trump, 22.8% Clinton, 4.7% Johnson, 0.1% Stein
National and State Parks: Owen-Putnam State Forest; Richard Lieber State Park
Additional Information Contacts
Putnam Government . . . . (765) 653-2648
http://www.co.putnam.in.us

Putnam County Communities

BAINBRIDGE (town). Covers a land area of 0.401 square miles and a water area of 0 square miles. Located at 39.76° N. Lat; 86.81° W. Long. Elevation is 932 feet.
Population: 765; Growth (since 2000): 3.0%; Density: 1,909.8 persons per square mile; Race: 99.7% White, 0.0% Black/African American, 0.0% Asian, 0.0% American Indian/Alaska Native, 0.0% Native Hawaiian/Other Pacific Islander, 0.0% Two or more races, 2.7% Hispanic of any race; Average household size: 2.47; Median age: 41.7; Age under 18: 18.3%; Age 65 and over: 16.7%; Males per 100 females: 97.9; Marriage status: 24.8% never married, 64.5% now married, 0.5% separated, 4.4% widowed, 6.2% divorced; Foreign born: 0.3%; Speak English only: 99.1%; With disability: 19.7%; Veterans: 8.2%; Ancestry: 15.9% German, 14.0% American, 12.0% Irish, 6.8% English, 3.0% Scottish
Employment: 6.0% management, business, and financial, 0.5% computer, engineering, and science, 0.5% education, legal, community service, arts, and media, 3.1% healthcare practitioners, 15.1% service, 20.9% sales and office, 17.5% natural resources, construction, and maintenance, 36.3% production, transportation, and material moving
Income: Per capita: $24,345; Median household: $49,722; Average household: $61,266; Households with income of $100,000 or more: 15.4%; Poverty rate: 10.9%
Educational Attainment: High school diploma or higher: 83.6%; Bachelor's degree or higher: 7.2%; Graduate/professional degree or higher: 1.9%

School District(s)

North Putnam Community Schools (PK-12)
Enrollment: 1,549 . . . . (765) 522-6218
Housing: Homeownership rate: 60.0%; Median home value: $87,200; Median year structure built: 1958; Homeowner vacancy rate: 3.4%; Median selected monthly owner costs: $964 with a mortgage, $316 without a mortgage; Median gross rent: $779 per month; Rental vacancy rate: 13.3%
Health Insurance: 89.8% have insurance; 68.6% have private insurance; 37.7% have public insurance; 10.2% do not have insurance; 8.7% of children under 18 do not have insurance
Transportation: Commute: 94.8% car, 0.0% public transportation, 4.2% walk, 1.0% work from home; Mean travel time to work: 33.9 minutes

CLOVERDALE (town). Covers a land area of 3.458 square miles and a water area of 0.064 square miles. Located at 39.52° N. Lat; 86.80° W. Long. Elevation is 820 feet.
Population: 1,669; Growth (since 2000): -25.6%; Density: 482.6 persons per square mile; Race: 96.2% White, 0.1% Black/African American, 0.0% Asian, 0.5% American Indian/Alaska Native, 0.0% Native Hawaiian/Other Pacific Islander, 2.6% Two or more races, 1.9% Hispanic of any race; Average household size: 2.31; Median age: 37.7; Age under 18: 20.7%; Age 65 and over: 21.6%; Males per 100 females: 93.2; Marriage status: 24.1% never married, 50.6% now married, 2.1% separated, 7.8% widowed, 17.5% divorced; Foreign born: 1.0%; Speak English only: 98.8%; With disability: 15.2%; Veterans: 12.8%; Ancestry: 20.0% German, 14.9% Irish, 11.8% American, 5.0% English, 4.7% French
Employment: 7.7% management, business, and financial, 1.9% computer, engineering, and science, 7.1% education, legal, community service, arts, and media, 1.6% healthcare practitioners, 25.3% service, 20.5% sales and office, 13.3% natural resources, construction, and maintenance, 22.5% production, transportation, and material moving
Income: Per capita: $22,427; Median household: $51,433; Average household: $54,525; Households with income of $100,000 or more: 7.0%; Poverty rate: 13.8%
Educational Attainment: High school diploma or higher: 86.9%; Bachelor's degree or higher: 11.0%; Graduate/professional degree or higher: 4.2%

School District(s)

Cloverdale Community Schools (PK-12)
Enrollment: 1,205 . . . . (765) 795-4664
Housing: Homeownership rate: 61.6%; Median home value: $84,300; Median year structure built: 1986; Homeowner vacancy rate: 11.2%; Median selected monthly owner costs: $916 with a mortgage, $404 without a mortgage; Median gross rent: $755 per month; Rental vacancy rate: 12.9%
Health Insurance: 90.4% have insurance; 67.3% have private insurance; 39.1% have public insurance; 9.6% do not have insurance; 11.4% of children under 18 do not have insurance
Newspapers: Hoosier Topics (weekly circulation 20,000)
Transportation: Commute: 97.4% car, 0.6% public transportation, 0.4% walk, 1.7% work from home; Mean travel time to work: 24.3 minutes
Additional Information Contacts
Town of Cloverdale . . . . (765) 653-2648
http://www.co.putnam.in.us

FILLMORE (town). Covers a land area of 1.948 square miles and a water area of 0 square miles. Located at 39.67° N. Lat; 86.75° W. Long. Elevation is 837 feet.
History: Laid out 1837.
Population: 574; Growth (since 2000): 5.3%; Density: 294.6 persons per square mile; Race: 99.3% White, 0.0% Black/African American, 0.3% Asian, 0.0% American Indian/Alaska Native, 0.0% Native Hawaiian/Other Pacific Islander, 0.3% Two or more races, 0.2% Hispanic of any race; Average household size: 2.35; Median age: 42.1; Age under 18: 20.2%; Age 65 and over: 15.0%; Males per 100 females: 94.5; Marriage status: 31.0% never married, 49.7% now married, 0.4% separated, 5.0% widowed, 14.3% divorced; Foreign born: 0.9%; Speak English only: 98.3%; With disability: 14.8%; Veterans: 8.3%; Ancestry: 23.7% German, 14.6% American, 9.4% English, 7.5% Irish, 5.4% Polish
Employment: 5.5% management, business, and financial, 4.9% computer, engineering, and science, 6.8% education, legal, community service, arts, and media, 5.2% healthcare practitioners, 23.5% service, 13.4% sales and office, 21.2% natural resources, construction, and maintenance, 19.5% production, transportation, and material moving
Income: Per capita: $24,352; Median household: $48,182; Average household: $57,391; Households with income of $100,000 or more: 12.7%; Poverty rate: 10.6%
Educational Attainment: High school diploma or higher: 88.1%; Bachelor's degree or higher: 7.2%; Graduate/professional degree or higher: 2.6%

School District(s)

South Putnam Community Schools (PK-12)
Enrollment: 1,113 . . . . (765) 653-3119
Housing: Homeownership rate: 75.4%; Median home value: $84,200; Median year structure built: 1955; Homeowner vacancy rate: 0.0%; Median selected monthly owner costs: $853 with a mortgage, $442 without a mortgage; Median gross rent: $772 per month; Rental vacancy rate: 0.0%
Health Insurance: 93.6% have insurance; 70.9% have private insurance; 37.3% have public insurance; 6.4% do not have insurance; 5.8% of children under 18 do not have insurance
Transportation: Commute: 96.4% car, 0.0% public transportation, 0.0% walk, 2.0% work from home; Mean travel time to work: 31.8 minutes

GREENCASTLE (city). County seat. Covers a land area of 5.242 square miles and a water area of 0.051 square miles. Located at 39.64° N. Lat; 86.85° W. Long. Elevation is 843 feet.
History: Indiana Asbury University, which later became DePauw University, was founded in 1837 in Greencastle by the Methodist Episcopal Church.
Population: 10,426; Growth (since 2000): 5.5%; Density: 1,988.9 persons per square mile; Race: 92.8% White, 2.1% Black/African American, 2.6% Asian, 0.0% American Indian/Alaska Native, 0.1% Native Hawaiian/Other Pacific Islander, 1.9% Two or more races, 3.7% Hispanic of any race; Average household size: 2.25; Median age: 26.3; Age under 18: 18.0%;

Age 65 and over: 15.4%; Males per 100 females: 87.5; Marriage status: 46.1% never married, 31.4% now married, 0.4% separated, 8.1% widowed, 14.4% divorced; Foreign born: 3.2%; Speak English only: 95.6%; With disability: 17.7%; Veterans: 6.8%; Ancestry: 17.6% German, 9.6% Irish, 8.6% English, 8.1% American, 3.7% European
Employment: 6.8% management, business, and financial, 2.6% computer, engineering, and science, 15.4% education, legal, community service, arts, and media, 3.4% healthcare practitioners, 20.1% service, 21.5% sales and office, 4.6% natural resources, construction, and maintenance, 25.6% production, transportation, and material moving
Income: Per capita: $19,689; Median household: $46,029; Average household: $58,373; Households with income of $100,000 or more: 9.7%; Poverty rate: 13.8%
Educational Attainment: High school diploma or higher: 88.0%; Bachelor's degree or higher: 17.8%; Graduate/professional degree or higher: 8.6%

School District(s)

Area 30 Career Center Edu Inter (09-12)
Enrollment: n/a . . . . (765) 653-3515
Greencastle Community School Corp (PK-12)
Enrollment: 1,918 . . . . (765) 653-4700
South Putnam Community Schools (PK-12)
Enrollment: 1,113 . . . . (765) 653-3119

Four-year College(s)

DePauw University (Private, Not-for-profit)
Enrollment: 2,158 . . . . (765) 658-4800
Tuition: In-state $47,838; Out-of-state $47,838
Housing: Homeownership rate: 51.4%; Median home value: $103,900; Median year structure built: 1963; Homeowner vacancy rate: 2.1%; Median selected monthly owner costs: $1,021 with a mortgage, $380 without a mortgage; Median gross rent: $689 per month; Rental vacancy rate: 5.5%
Health Insurance: 91.9% have insurance; 72.1% have private insurance; 33.9% have public insurance; 8.1% do not have insurance; 3.4% of children under 18 do not have insurance
Hospitals: Putnam County Hospital (85 beds)
Newspapers: Banner-Graphic (daily circulation 6,600)
Transportation: Commute: 70.8% car, 0.0% public transportation, 24.4% walk, 3.0% work from home; Mean travel time to work: 15.6 minutes
Airports: Putnam County (general aviation)
Additional Information Contacts
City of Greencastle . . . . (765) 653-3100
http://www.cityofgreencastle.com

HERITAGE LAKE (CDP). Covers a land area of 3.012 square miles and a water area of 0.469 square miles. Located at 39.73° N. Lat; 86.71° W. Long. Elevation is 860 feet.
Population: 3,000; Growth (since 2000): n/a; Density: 995.9 persons per square mile; Race: 99.3% White, 0.0% Black/African American, 0.0% Asian, 0.7% American Indian/Alaska Native, 0.0% Native Hawaiian/Other Pacific Islander, 0.0% Two or more races, 1.2% Hispanic of any race; Average household size: 2.56; Median age: 43.1; Age under 18: 18.5%; Age 65 and over: 15.4%; Males per 100 females: 102.7; Marriage status: 28.5% never married, 60.9% now married, 0.5% separated, 3.8% widowed, 6.8% divorced; Foreign born: 0.2%; Speak English only: 98.5%; With disability: 12.9%; Veterans: 9.4%; Ancestry: 30.6% German, 21.9% Irish, 15.3% English, 7.2% Italian, 6.0% American
Employment: 16.2% management, business, and financial, 1.3% computer, engineering, and science, 12.9% education, legal, community service, arts, and media, 6.8% healthcare practitioners, 11.4% service, 27.8% sales and office, 12.5% natural resources, construction, and maintenance, 11.2% production, transportation, and material moving
Income: Per capita: $31,880; Median household: $65,500; Average household: $81,234; Households with income of $100,000 or more: 24.4%; Poverty rate: 7.5%
Educational Attainment: High school diploma or higher: 95.9%; Bachelor's degree or higher: 25.4%; Graduate/professional degree or higher: 13.8%
Housing: Homeownership rate: 93.2%; Median home value: $156,800; Median year structure built: 1994; Homeowner vacancy rate: 0.9%; Median selected monthly owner costs: $1,295 with a mortgage, $430 without a mortgage; Median gross rent: n/a per month; Rental vacancy rate: 0.0%
Health Insurance: 90.0% have insurance; 80.3% have private insurance; 23.0% have public insurance; 10.0% do not have insurance; 5.6% of children under 18 do not have insurance
Transportation: Commute: 97.6% car, 0.0% public transportation, 0.0% walk, 2.4% work from home; Mean travel time to work: 36.2 minutes

REELSVILLE (unincorporated postal area)
ZCTA: 46171
Covers a land area of 36.343 square miles and a water area of 0.067 square miles. Located at 39.53° N. Lat; 86.96° W. Long. Elevation is 702 feet.
Population: 1,656; Growth (since 2000): -1.4%; Density: 45.6 persons per square mile; Race: 95.3% White, 0.0% Black/African American, 0.5% Asian, 1.1% American Indian/Alaska Native, 0.0% Native Hawaiian/Other Pacific Islander, 3.1% Two or more races, 1.6% Hispanic of any race; Average household size: 2.51; Median age: 42.8; Age under 18: 23.7%; Age 65 and over: 17.6%; Males per 100 females: 99.6; Marriage status: 15.3% never married, 63.4% now married, 0.0% separated, 8.4% widowed, 12.9% divorced; Foreign born: 0.5%; Speak English only: 97.9%; With disability: 22.5%; Veterans: 11.3%; Ancestry: 16.1% German, 10.7% American, 9.6% Irish, 6.6% English, 4.8% Scotch-Irish
Employment: 8.6% management, business, and financial, 4.7% computer, engineering, and science, 8.3% education, legal, community service, arts, and media, 0.0% healthcare practitioners, 16.0% service, 27.1% sales and office, 22.5% natural resources, construction, and maintenance, 12.8% production, transportation, and material moving
Income: Per capita: $22,415; Median household: $45,610; Average household: $55,046; Households with income of $100,000 or more: 11.9%; Poverty rate: 16.7%
Educational Attainment: High school diploma or higher: 86.7%; Bachelor's degree or higher: 9.2%; Graduate/professional degree or higher: 2.7%
Housing: Homeownership rate: 96.8%; Median home value: $107,500; Median year structure built: 1980; Homeowner vacancy rate: 5.9%; Median selected monthly owner costs: $1,013 with a mortgage, $363 without a mortgage; Median gross rent: n/a per month; Rental vacancy rate: 0.0%
Health Insurance: 85.0% have insurance; 61.6% have private insurance; 36.8% have public insurance; 15.0% do not have insurance; 2.3% of children under 18 do not have insurance
Transportation: Commute: 96.9% car, 0.0% public transportation, 0.0% walk, 1.1% work from home; Mean travel time to work: 33.5 minutes

ROACHDALE (town). Covers a land area of 0.507 square miles and a water area of 0 square miles. Located at 39.85° N. Lat; 86.80° W. Long. Elevation is 843 feet.
History: Laid out 1879.
Population: 877; Growth (since 2000): -10.1%; Density: 1,730.8 persons per square mile; Race: 98.6% White, 0.0% Black/African American, 0.0% Asian, 0.0% American Indian/Alaska Native, 0.0% Native Hawaiian/Other Pacific Islander, 0.6% Two or more races, 0.2% Hispanic of any race; Average household size: 2.48; Median age: 43.5; Age under 18: 24.2%; Age 65 and over: 11.3%; Males per 100 females: 98.7; Marriage status: 29.5% never married, 48.0% now married, 1.3% separated, 5.8% widowed, 16.6% divorced; Foreign born: 0.3%; Speak English only: 99.7%; With disability: 15.3%; Veterans: 12.9%; Ancestry: 18.1% American, 18.1% German, 14.4% Irish, 7.8% English, 7.0% Italian
Employment: 13.6% management, business, and financial, 5.1% computer, engineering, and science, 4.6% education, legal, community service, arts, and media, 1.0% healthcare practitioners, 22.1% service, 16.2% sales and office, 22.9% natural resources, construction, and maintenance, 14.4% production, transportation, and material moving
Income: Per capita: $22,028; Median household: $43,558; Average household: $56,102; Households with income of $100,000 or more: 15.0%; Poverty rate: 22.0%
Educational Attainment: High school diploma or higher: 82.5%; Bachelor's degree or higher: 12.6%; Graduate/professional degree or higher: 2.0%

School District(s)

North Putnam Community Schools (PK-12)
Enrollment: 1,549 . . . . (765) 522-6218
Housing: Homeownership rate: 67.7%; Median home value: $76,800; Median year structure built: 1950; Homeowner vacancy rate: 7.7%; Median selected monthly owner costs: $922 with a mortgage, $462 without a mortgage; Median gross rent: $808 per month; Rental vacancy rate: 0.0%

Health Insurance: 83.8% have insurance; 55.1% have private insurance; 39.8% have public insurance; 16.2% do not have insurance; 8.6% of children under 18 do not have insurance
Transportation: Commute: 96.0% car, 0.0% public transportation, 0.0% walk, 0.8% work from home; Mean travel time to work: 28.9 minutes

RUSSELLVILLE (town). Covers a land area of 0.201 square miles and a water area of 0 square miles. Located at 39.86° N. Lat; 86.98° W. Long. Elevation is 820 feet.
History: Laid out 1828.
Population: 329; Growth (since 2000): -3.2%; Density: 1,633.0 persons per square mile; Race: 100.0% White, 0.0% Black/African American, 0.0% Asian, 0.0% American Indian/Alaska Native, 0.0% Native Hawaiian/Other Pacific Islander, 0.0% Two or more races, 6.4% Hispanic of any race; Average household size: 2.44; Median age: 39.1; Age under 18: 22.2%; Age 65 and over: 10.6%; Males per 100 females: 100.0; Marriage status: 24.2% never married, 51.9% now married, 3.4% separated, 4.9% widowed, 18.9% divorced; Foreign born: 0.0%; Speak English only: 98.7%; With disability: 16.4%; Veterans: 9.0%; Ancestry: 20.1% German, 15.8% American, 10.0% Irish, 7.6% English, 3.6% Polish
Employment: 8.2% management, business, and financial, 2.0% computer, engineering, and science, 1.4% education, legal, community service, arts, and media, 3.4% healthcare practitioners, 9.5% service, 8.2% sales and office, 17.0% natural resources, construction, and maintenance, 50.3% production, transportation, and material moving
Income: Per capita: $18,777; Median household: $41,250; Average household: $43,970; Households with income of $100,000 or more: 4.4%; Poverty rate: 19.8%
Educational Attainment: High school diploma or higher: 80.9%; Bachelor's degree or higher: 4.7%; Graduate/professional degree or higher: 0.9%
Housing: Homeownership rate: 66.7%; Median home value: $65,500; Median year structure built: 1949; Homeowner vacancy rate: 0.0%; Median selected monthly owner costs: $791 with a mortgage, $375 without a mortgage; Median gross rent: $1,044 per month; Rental vacancy rate: 0.0%
Health Insurance: 92.7% have insurance; 61.4% have private insurance; 38.3% have public insurance; 7.3% do not have insurance; 0.0% of children under 18 do not have insurance
Transportation: Commute: 98.6% car, 0.0% public transportation, 1.4% walk, 0.0% work from home; Mean travel time to work: 31.1 minutes

VAN BIBBER LAKE (CDP). Covers a land area of 0.258 square miles and a water area of 0.097 square miles. Located at 39.73° N. Lat; 86.93° W. Long. Elevation is 804 feet.
Population: 643; Growth (since 2000): n/a; Density: 2,490.4 persons per square mile; Race: 100.0% White, 0.0% Black/African American, 0.0% Asian, 0.0% American Indian/Alaska Native, 0.0% Native Hawaiian/Other Pacific Islander, 0.0% Two or more races, 0.0% Hispanic of any race; Average household size: 2.19; Median age: 48.5; Age under 18: 19.0%; Age 65 and over: 32.3%; Males per 100 females: 106.4; Marriage status: 37.6% never married, 31.8% now married, 0.0% separated, 1.9% widowed, 28.6% divorced; Foreign born: 0.0%; Speak English only: 100.0%; With disability: 10.7%; Veterans: 4.8%; Ancestry: 20.4% German, 13.8% French, 11.0% American, 2.5% Swedish, 2.3% English
Employment: 12.5% management, business, and financial, 0.0% computer, engineering, and science, 0.0% education, legal, community service, arts, and media, 0.0% healthcare practitioners, 27.5% service, 15.0% sales and office, 0.0% natural resources, construction, and maintenance, 45.0% production, transportation, and material moving
Income: Per capita: $18,023; Median household: $25,313; Average household: $38,744; Households with income of $100,000 or more: 14.3%; Poverty rate: 51.9%
Educational Attainment: High school diploma or higher: 65.4%; Bachelor's degree or higher: n/a; Graduate/professional degree or higher: n/a
Housing: Homeownership rate: 85.7%; Median home value: $63,300; Median year structure built: 1988; Homeowner vacancy rate: 0.0%; Median selected monthly owner costs: $898 with a mortgage, $331 without a mortgage; Median gross rent: n/a per month; Rental vacancy rate: 0.0%
Health Insurance: 79.8% have insurance; 31.6% have private insurance; 65.0% have public insurance; 20.2% do not have insurance; 27.0% of children under 18 do not have insurance
Transportation: Commute: 100.0% car, 0.0% public transportation, 0.0% walk, 0.0% work from home; Mean travel time to work: 31.4 minutes

Randolph County

Located in eastern Indiana; bounded on the east by Ohio; drained by the Mississinewa and Whitewater Rivers and the West Fork of the White River; includes the highest point in Indiana (1,240 ft). Covers a land area of 452.379 square miles, a water area of 0.935 square miles, and is located in the Eastern Time Zone at 40.16° N. Lat., 85.01° W. Long. The county was founded in 1818. County seat is Winchester.

Weather Station: Farmland 5 NNW Elevation: 964 feet

	Jan	Feb	Mar	Apr	May	Jun	Jul	Aug	Sep	Oct	Nov	Dec
High	34	38	48	61	72	81	84	83	77	64	51	38
Low	17	19	28	38	49	59	62	60	52	40	32	22
Precip	2.1	1.9	2.8	3.7	4.3	4.2	4.8	3.6	3.0	3.0	3.3	2.6
Snow	7.1	5.9	3.1	0.4	tr	0.0	0.0	0.0	0.0	0.3	1.0	4.8

High and Low temperatures in degrees Fahrenheit; Precipitation and Snow in inches

Weather Station: Winchester Airport 3E Elevation: 1,109 feet

	Jan	Feb	Mar	Apr	May	Jun	Jul	Aug	Sep	Oct	Nov	Dec
High	33	37	47	60	71	80	83	82	76	63	50	37
Low	18	20	29	40	51	60	63	61	54	43	33	22
Precip	2.1	1.7	2.7	3.7	4.4	4.5	4.4	3.5	2.9	3.0	3.3	2.8
Snow	5.9	5.4	2.5	0.3	0.0	0.0	0.0	0.0	0.0	0.1	0.5	3.9

High and Low temperatures in degrees Fahrenheit; Precipitation and Snow in inches

Population: 25,203; Growth (since 2000): -8.0%; Density: 55.7 persons per square mile; Race: 96.4% White, 0.7% Black/African American, 0.2% Asian, 0.0% American Indian/Alaska Native, 0.0% Native Hawaiian/Other Pacific Islander, 1.6% two or more races, 3.3% Hispanic of any race; Average household size: 2.36; Median age: 42.1; Age under 18: 23.5%; Age 65 and over: 18.9%; Males per 100 females: 97.4; Marriage status: 23.5% never married, 55.9% now married, 1.2% separated, 8.0% widowed, 12.5% divorced; Foreign born: 1.7%; Speak English only: 97.4%; With disability: 16.1%; Veterans: 8.1%; Ancestry: 18.9% German, 13.6% American, 10.0% Irish, 8.1% English, 2.1% Italian
Religion: Six largest groups: 9.2% Baptist, 7.1% Methodist/Pietist, 3.9% European Free-Church, 3.2% Holiness, 2.7% Catholicism, 2.3% Presbyterian-Reformed
Economy: Unemployment rate: 3.9%; Leading industries: 15.4 % retail trade; 14.1 % other services (except public administration); 10.0 % manufacturing; Farms: 772 totaling 241,074 acres; Company size: 0 employ 1,000 or more persons, 1 employs 500 to 999 persons, 8 employ 100 to 499 persons, 460 employ less than 100 persons; Business ownership: 605 women-owned, n/a Black-owned, 55 Hispanic-owned, n/a Asian-owned, n/a American Indian/Alaska Native-owned
Employment: 10.6% management, business, and financial, 2.8% computer, engineering, and science, 7.6% education, legal, community service, arts, and media, 5.1% healthcare practitioners, 15.5% service, 19.3% sales and office, 12.4% natural resources, construction, and maintenance, 26.8% production, transportation, and material moving
Income: Per capita: $23,427; Median household: $44,985; Average household: $56,392; Households with income of $100,000 or more: 10.4%; Poverty rate: 17.0%
Educational Attainment: High school diploma or higher: 85.8%; Bachelor's degree or higher: 13.7%; Graduate/professional degree or higher: 5.8%
Housing: Homeownership rate: 75.9%; Median home value: $79,500; Median year structure built: 1954; Homeowner vacancy rate: 2.0%; Median selected monthly owner costs: $879 with a mortgage, $339 without a mortgage; Median gross rent: $623 per month; Rental vacancy rate: 4.4%
Vital Statistics: Birth rate: 116.0 per 10,000 population; Death rate: 106.7 per 10,000 population; Age-adjusted cancer mortality rate: 192.0 deaths per 100,000 population
Health Insurance: 87.7% have insurance; 63.6% have private insurance; 39.6% have public insurance; 12.3% do not have insurance; 10.3% of children under 18 do not have insurance
Health Care: Physicians: 4.0 per 10,000 population; Dentists: 2.8 per 10,000 population; Hospital beds: 6.4 per 10,000 population; Hospital admissions: 223.5 per 10,000 population
Transportation: Commute: 92.4% car, 0.4% public transportation, 1.6% walk, 4.7% work from home; Mean travel time to work: 24.5 minutes
2016 Presidential Election: 71.4% Trump, 23.2% Clinton, 4.7% Johnson, 0.0% Stein
Additional Information Contacts
Randolph Government . . . . (800) 905-0514
http://www.randolphcounty.us

Randolph County Communities

FARMLAND (town). Covers a land area of 0.531 square miles and a water area of 0 square miles. Located at 40.19° N. Lat; 85.13° W. Long. Elevation is 1,040 feet.
History: Farmland was settled as a trading town for the surrounding farming area.
Population: 1,283; Growth (since 2000): -11.9%; Density: 2,416.7 persons per square mile; Race: 94.7% White, 0.0% Black/African American, 0.0% Asian, 0.6% American Indian/Alaska Native, 0.0% Native Hawaiian/Other Pacific Islander, 4.7% Two or more races, 0.2% Hispanic of any race; Average household size: 2.39; Median age: 40.9; Age under 18: 25.1%; Age 65 and over: 16.3%; Males per 100 females: 92.4; Marriage status: 23.6% never married, 53.6% now married, 0.4% separated, 4.2% widowed, 18.6% divorced; Foreign born: 0.9%; Speak English only: 97.2%; With disability: 13.8%; Veterans: 8.7%; Ancestry: 24.7% German, 15.4% American, 13.7% Irish, 6.4% English, 5.6% Italian
Employment: 10.0% management, business, and financial, 3.8% computer, engineering, and science, 11.6% education, legal, community service, arts, and media, 5.7% healthcare practitioners, 15.2% service, 22.0% sales and office, 6.4% natural resources, construction, and maintenance, 25.3% production, transportation, and material moving
Income: Per capita: $23,035; Median household: $46,333; Average household: $55,886; Households with income of $100,000 or more: 12.1%; Poverty rate: 13.5%
Educational Attainment: High school diploma or higher: 90.8%; Bachelor's degree or higher: 16.5%; Graduate/professional degree or higher: 6.0%
Housing: Homeownership rate: 80.6%; Median home value: $68,200; Median year structure built: 1952; Homeowner vacancy rate: 5.3%; Median selected monthly owner costs: $824 with a mortgage, $365 without a mortgage; Median gross rent: $675 per month; Rental vacancy rate: 13.3%
Health Insurance: 96.7% have insurance; 78.6% have private insurance; 31.0% have public insurance; 3.3% do not have insurance; 0.3% of children under 18 do not have insurance
Transportation: Commute: 94.0% car, 0.5% public transportation, 0.5% walk, 3.6% work from home; Mean travel time to work: 29.9 minutes

LOSANTVILLE (town). Covers a land area of 0.189 square miles and a water area of 0 square miles. Located at 40.02° N. Lat; 85.18° W. Long. Elevation is 1,132 feet.
History: Also called Bronson.
Population: 252; Growth (since 2000): -10.0%; Density: 1,336.0 persons per square mile; Race: 100.0% White, 0.0% Black/African American, 0.0% Asian, 0.0% American Indian/Alaska Native, 0.0% Native Hawaiian/Other Pacific Islander, 0.0% Two or more races, 0.0% Hispanic of any race; Average household size: 2.12; Median age: 50.2; Age under 18: 13.5%; Age 65 and over: 23.0%; Males per 100 females: 99.2; Marriage status: 18.1% never married, 47.3% now married, 4.0% separated, 7.1% widowed, 27.4% divorced; Foreign born: 0.0%; Speak English only: 100.0%; With disability: 31.3%; Veterans: 9.2%; Ancestry: 25.4% German, 12.3% English, 9.5% Irish, 4.0% American, 2.0% Eastern European
Employment: 10.1% management, business, and financial, 4.2% computer, engineering, and science, 6.7% education, legal, community service, arts, and media, 0.0% healthcare practitioners, 16.0% service, 26.1% sales and office, 12.6% natural resources, construction, and maintenance, 24.4% production, transportation, and material moving
Income: Per capita: $20,720; Median household: $32,625; Average household: $45,954; Households with income of $100,000 or more: 9.2%; Poverty rate: 21.4%
Educational Attainment: High school diploma or higher: 74.9%; Bachelor's degree or higher: 10.8%; Graduate/professional degree or higher: 1.5%
Housing: Homeownership rate: 69.7%; Median home value: $61,000; Median year structure built: Before 1940; Homeowner vacancy rate: 3.5%; Median selected monthly owner costs: $773 with a mortgage, $308 without a mortgage; Median gross rent: $575 per month; Rental vacancy rate: 0.0%
Health Insurance: 87.7% have insurance; 54.8% have private insurance; 48.8% have public insurance; 12.3% do not have insurance; 0.0% of children under 18 do not have insurance
Transportation: Commute: 94.9% car, 0.0% public transportation, 0.0% walk, 4.2% work from home; Mean travel time to work: 29.5 minutes

LYNN (town). Covers a land area of 0.565 square miles and a water area of 0 square miles. Located at 40.05° N. Lat; 84.94° W. Long. Elevation is 1,181 feet.
History: Lynn was established in 1847. The arrival of the railroad in 1852 brought a period of prosperity.
Population: 1,091; Growth (since 2000): -4.5%; Density: 1,931.6 persons per square mile; Race: 96.5% White, 1.9% Black/African American, 1.1% Asian, 0.0% American Indian/Alaska Native, 0.0% Native Hawaiian/Other Pacific Islander, 0.3% Two or more races, 2.0% Hispanic of any race; Average household size: 2.50; Median age: 42.1; Age under 18: 21.1%; Age 65 and over: 17.7%; Males per 100 females: 93.5; Marriage status: 26.9% never married, 59.5% now married, 1.5% separated, 4.7% widowed, 8.9% divorced; Foreign born: 1.6%; Speak English only: 97.7%; With disability: 22.2%; Veterans: 11.1%; Ancestry: 22.8% American, 17.9% German, 12.2% Irish, 7.2% English, 2.4% Dutch
Employment: 7.2% management, business, and financial, 0.6% computer, engineering, and science, 8.7% education, legal, community service, arts, and media, 6.9% healthcare practitioners, 26.2% service, 13.0% sales and office, 8.0% natural resources, construction, and maintenance, 29.4% production, transportation, and material moving
Income: Per capita: $23,418; Median household: $45,491; Average household: $57,484; Households with income of $100,000 or more: 5.0%; Poverty rate: 18.5%
Educational Attainment: High school diploma or higher: 89.7%; Bachelor's degree or higher: 13.7%; Graduate/professional degree or higher: 6.3%

School District(s)

Randolph Southern School Corp (PK-12)
Enrollment: 508 . . . . (765) 874-1181
Housing: Homeownership rate: 63.4%; Median home value: $66,600; Median year structure built: 1941; Homeowner vacancy rate: 3.1%; Median selected monthly owner costs: $862 with a mortgage, $293 without a mortgage; Median gross rent: $702 per month; Rental vacancy rate: 15.3%
Health Insurance: 92.4% have insurance; 68.3% have private insurance; 37.9% have public insurance; 7.6% do not have insurance; 6.0% of children under 18 do not have insurance
Transportation: Commute: 96.6% car, 0.0% public transportation, 1.7% walk, 1.7% work from home; Mean travel time to work: 27.3 minutes

MODOC (town). Covers a land area of 0.103 square miles and a water area of 0 square miles. Located at 40.05° N. Lat; 85.13° W. Long. Elevation is 1,175 feet.
Population: 200; Growth (since 2000): -11.1%; Density: 1,935.6 persons per square mile; Race: 78.0% White, 8.0% Black/African American, 0.0% Asian, 0.0% American Indian/Alaska Native, 0.0% Native Hawaiian/Other Pacific Islander, 14.0% Two or more races, 1.0% Hispanic of any race; Average household size: 2.63; Median age: 33.9; Age under 18: 28.5%; Age 65 and over: 12.0%; Males per 100 females: 117.8; Marriage status: 36.7% never married, 30.7% now married, 1.3% separated, 10.0% widowed, 22.7% divorced; Foreign born: 0.0%; Speak English only: 98.9%; With disability: 17.0%; Veterans: 3.5%; Ancestry: 35.0% German, 19.5% Irish, 4.5% American, 3.0% English, 2.5% French
Employment: 12.0% management, business, and financial, 0.0% computer, engineering, and science, 0.0% education, legal, community service, arts, and media, 1.3% healthcare practitioners, 32.0% service, 14.7% sales and office, 6.7% natural resources, construction, and maintenance, 33.3% production, transportation, and material moving
Income: Per capita: $22,022; Median household: $36,667; Average household: $54,297; Households with income of $100,000 or more: 2.6%; Poverty rate: 13.5%
Educational Attainment: High school diploma or higher: 90.7%; Bachelor's degree or higher: 3.4%; Graduate/professional degree or higher: n/a

School District(s)

Union School Corporation (PK-12)
Enrollment: 420 . . . . (765) 853-5464
Housing: Homeownership rate: 65.8%; Median home value: $39,300; Median year structure built: Before 1940; Homeowner vacancy rate: 0.0%; Median selected monthly owner costs: $750 with a mortgage, $275 without a mortgage; Median gross rent: $671 per month; Rental vacancy rate: 0.0%
Health Insurance: 81.5% have insurance; 50.0% have private insurance; 34.5% have public insurance; 18.5% do not have insurance; 12.5% of children under 18 do not have insurance

Transportation: Commute: 90.7% car, 0.0% public transportation, 0.0% walk, 0.0% work from home; Mean travel time to work: 36.2 minutes

PARKER CITY (town). Covers a land area of 0.566 square miles and a water area of 0 square miles. Located at 40.19° N. Lat; 85.20° W. Long. Elevation is 1,024 feet.
History: Parker City was settled as a center for trading for the nearby farming communities.
Population: 1,352; Growth (since 2000): -4.5%; Density: 2,386.7 persons per square mile; Race: 95.8% White, 0.0% Black/African American, 1.5% Asian, 0.0% American Indian/Alaska Native, 0.0% Native Hawaiian/Other Pacific Islander, 2.7% Two or more races, 1.3% Hispanic of any race; Average household size: 2.19; Median age: 43.8; Age under 18: 19.0%; Age 65 and over: 24.0%; Males per 100 females: 86.5; Marriage status: 21.2% never married, 52.4% now married, 0.6% separated, 10.9% widowed, 15.5% divorced; Foreign born: 1.5%; Speak English only: 97.9%; With disability: 16.7%; Veterans: 7.2%; Ancestry: 19.6% American, 16.5% German, 9.2% Irish, 6.7% English, 1.2% Scotch-Irish
Employment: 8.9% management, business, and financial, 3.4% computer, engineering, and science, 7.9% education, legal, community service, arts, and media, 1.6% healthcare practitioners, 30.5% service, 15.6% sales and office, 13.4% natural resources, construction, and maintenance, 18.7% production, transportation, and material moving
Income: Per capita: $23,826; Median household: $42,250; Average household: $53,897; Households with income of $100,000 or more: 4.5%; Poverty rate: 17.2%
Educational Attainment: High school diploma or higher: 83.9%; Bachelor's degree or higher: 14.9%; Graduate/professional degree or higher: 4.2%

School District(s)

Monroe Central School Corp (PK-12)
Enrollment: 961 . . . . (765) 468-6868
Housing: Homeownership rate: 76.6%; Median home value: $65,300; Median year structure built: 1962; Homeowner vacancy rate: 2.7%; Median selected monthly owner costs: $796 with a mortgage, $320 without a mortgage; Median gross rent: $625 per month; Rental vacancy rate: 0.0%
Health Insurance: 86.5% have insurance; 60.9% have private insurance; 43.0% have public insurance; 13.5% do not have insurance; 11.9% of children under 18 do not have insurance
Transportation: Commute: 96.1% car, 0.0% public transportation, 0.7% walk, 1.8% work from home; Mean travel time to work: 26.5 minutes

RIDGEVILLE (town). Covers a land area of 0.555 square miles and a water area of 0.001 square miles. Located at 40.29° N. Lat; 85.03° W. Long. Elevation is 997 feet.
History: Settled 1817, laid out 1837, incorporated 1868.
Population: 566; Growth (since 2000): -32.9%; Density: 1,020.6 persons per square mile; Race: 96.6% White, 0.0% Black/African American, 0.0% Asian, 0.4% American Indian/Alaska Native, 0.0% Native Hawaiian/Other Pacific Islander, 2.7% Two or more races, 0.9% Hispanic of any race; Average household size: 2.33; Median age: 37.9; Age under 18: 28.3%; Age 65 and over: 17.7%; Males per 100 females: 103.3; Marriage status: 20.8% never married, 51.4% now married, 1.4% separated, 10.7% widowed, 17.1% divorced; Foreign born: 0.4%; Speak English only: 98.5%; With disability: 15.9%; Veterans: 9.6%; Ancestry: 19.6% American, 13.8% German, 8.8% English, 4.1% Irish, 1.4% Scottish
Employment: 10.2% management, business, and financial, 0.0% computer, engineering, and science, 0.4% education, legal, community service, arts, and media, 4.3% healthcare practitioners, 12.8% service, 28.1% sales and office, 15.7% natural resources, construction, and maintenance, 28.5% production, transportation, and material moving
Income: Per capita: $18,825; Median household: $36,719; Average household: $43,995; Households with income of $100,000 or more: 4.5%; Poverty rate: 21.7%
Educational Attainment: High school diploma or higher: 77.7%; Bachelor's degree or higher: 6.0%; Graduate/professional degree or higher: 0.8%

School District(s)

Randolph Central School Corp (PK-12)
Enrollment: 1,485 . . . . (765) 584-1401
Housing: Homeownership rate: 74.5%; Median home value: $46,100; Median year structure built: Before 1940; Homeowner vacancy rate: 2.6%; Median selected monthly owner costs: $704 with a mortgage, $256 without a mortgage; Median gross rent: $564 per month; Rental vacancy rate: 0.0%
Health Insurance: 89.2% have insurance; 60.8% have private insurance; 55.5% have public insurance; 10.8% do not have insurance; 3.0% of children under 18 do not have insurance
Transportation: Commute: 86.0% car, 0.0% public transportation, 6.0% walk, 8.1% work from home; Mean travel time to work: 26.9 minutes

SARATOGA (town). Covers a land area of 0.265 square miles and a water area of 0 square miles. Located at 40.24° N. Lat; 84.92° W. Long. Elevation is 1,050 feet.
History: Laid out 1875.
Population: 226; Growth (since 2000): -21.5%; Density: 853.8 persons per square mile; Race: 98.2% White, 0.0% Black/African American, 0.0% Asian, 0.0% American Indian/Alaska Native, 0.0% Native Hawaiian/Other Pacific Islander, 0.0% Two or more races, 1.8% Hispanic of any race; Average household size: 2.09; Median age: 35.8; Age under 18: 23.5%; Age 65 and over: 19.0%; Males per 100 females: 84.1; Marriage status: 30.6% never married, 39.9% now married, 1.6% separated, 5.5% widowed, 24.0% divorced; Foreign born: 0.9%; Speak English only: 95.7%; With disability: 10.6%; Veterans: 12.1%; Ancestry: 19.5% German, 19.0% English, 11.9% American, 8.8% Irish, 3.5% French
Employment: 4.3% management, business, and financial, 0.0% computer, engineering, and science, 2.2% education, legal, community service, arts, and media, 1.1% healthcare practitioners, 20.4% service, 28.0% sales and office, 8.6% natural resources, construction, and maintenance, 35.5% production, transportation, and material moving
Income: Per capita: $16,569; Median household: $33,500; Average household: $36,297; Households with income of $100,000 or more: 2.8%; Poverty rate: 22.2%
Educational Attainment: High school diploma or higher: 80.8%; Bachelor's degree or higher: 4.6%; Graduate/professional degree or higher: 2.6%
Housing: Homeownership rate: 69.4%; Median home value: $38,800; Median year structure built: Before 1940; Homeowner vacancy rate: 0.0%; Median selected monthly owner costs: $579 with a mortgage, $325 without a mortgage; Median gross rent: $525 per month; Rental vacancy rate: 13.2%
Health Insurance: 88.9% have insurance; 66.4% have private insurance; 34.1% have public insurance; 11.1% do not have insurance; 0.0% of children under 18 do not have insurance
Transportation: Commute: 82.9% car, 2.6% public transportation, 13.2% walk, 1.3% work from home; Mean travel time to work: 22.8 minutes

UNION CITY (city). Covers a land area of 2.200 square miles and a water area of 0.009 square miles. Located at 40.20° N. Lat; 84.82° W. Long. Elevation is 1,122 feet.
History: Union City was formed straddling the state line with Ohio. Isaac Pusey Gray, governor of Indiana from 1885-1889, lived here.
Population: 3,505; Growth (since 2000): -3.2%; Density: 1,593.0 persons per square mile; Race: 95.5% White, 0.0% Black/African American, 0.0% Asian, 0.0% American Indian/Alaska Native, 0.0% Native Hawaiian/Other Pacific Islander, 2.0% Two or more races, 17.7% Hispanic of any race; Average household size: 2.37; Median age: 37.0; Age under 18: 31.5%; Age 65 and over: 15.7%; Males per 100 females: 94.7; Marriage status: 34.6% never married, 32.3% now married, 1.2% separated, 10.4% widowed, 22.6% divorced; Foreign born: 6.8%; Speak English only: 91.2%; With disability: 17.7%; Veterans: 7.8%; Ancestry: 20.6% German, 8.6% Irish, 8.4% American, 4.3% English, 1.9% French
Employment: 2.7% management, business, and financial, 5.1% computer, engineering, and science, 3.7% education, legal, community service, arts, and media, 4.5% healthcare practitioners, 18.4% service, 9.3% sales and office, 13.3% natural resources, construction, and maintenance, 43.0% production, transportation, and material moving
Income: Per capita: $15,433; Median household: $31,587; Average household: $38,000; Households with income of $100,000 or more: 1.8%; Poverty rate: 28.0%
Educational Attainment: High school diploma or higher: 75.9%; Bachelor's degree or higher: 4.8%; Graduate/professional degree or higher: 2.4%

School District(s)

Randolph Eastern School Corp (PK-12)
Enrollment: 928 . . . . (765) 964-4994
Housing: Homeownership rate: 61.6%; Median home value: $48,400; Median year structure built: 1960; Homeowner vacancy rate: 5.4%; Median selected monthly owner costs: $749 with a mortgage, $340 without a mortgage; Median gross rent: $558 per month; Rental vacancy rate: 4.4%

Health Insurance: 82.6% have insurance; 43.3% have private insurance; 52.4% have public insurance; 17.4% do not have insurance; 11.6% of children under 18 do not have insurance
Transportation: Commute: 96.2% car, 0.0% public transportation, 2.5% walk, 0.6% work from home; Mean travel time to work: 22.7 minutes
Additional Information Contacts
City of Union City. . . . . (765) 964-6534
http://www.myunioncity.com

WINCHESTER (city). County seat. Covers a land area of 3.328 square miles and a water area of 0.013 square miles. Located at 40.17° N. Lat; 84.98° W. Long. Elevation is 1,093 feet.
History: Winchester developed as a grain and livestock shipping center, and as the seat of Randolph County.
Population: 5,061; Growth (since 2000): 0.5%; Density: 1,520.6 persons per square mile; Race: 94.3% White, 0.2% Black/African American, 0.6% Asian, 0.0% American Indian/Alaska Native, 0.0% Native Hawaiian/Other Pacific Islander, 2.3% Two or more races, 1.3% Hispanic of any race; Average household size: 2.30; Median age: 38.1; Age under 18: 24.2%; Age 65 and over: 18.3%; Males per 100 females: 91.0; Marriage status: 25.2% never married, 52.9% now married, 2.0% separated, 9.5% widowed, 12.4% divorced; Foreign born: 1.5%; Speak English only: 97.7%; With disability: 16.0%; Veterans: 6.4%; Ancestry: 21.8% German, 11.9% Irish, 10.2% English, 10.2% American, 2.9% Italian
Employment: 8.2% management, business, and financial, 1.5% computer, engineering, and science, 8.9% education, legal, community service, arts, and media, 4.6% healthcare practitioners, 15.1% service, 27.0% sales and office, 9.1% natural resources, construction, and maintenance, 25.7% production, transportation, and material moving
Income: Per capita: $22,972; Median household: $42,415; Average household: $55,393; Households with income of $100,000 or more: 9.4%; Poverty rate: 19.9%
Educational Attainment: High school diploma or higher: 83.8%; Bachelor's degree or higher: 14.5%; Graduate/professional degree or higher: 5.1%

School District(s)

Randolph Central School Corp (PK-12)
Enrollment: 1,485 . . . . (765) 584-1401
Housing: Homeownership rate: 64.4%; Median home value: $72,400; Median year structure built: 1954; Homeowner vacancy rate: 1.9%; Median selected monthly owner costs: $784 with a mortgage, $344 without a mortgage; Median gross rent: $633 per month; Rental vacancy rate: 5.1%
Health Insurance: 86.4% have insurance; 58.7% have private insurance; 42.6% have public insurance; 13.6% do not have insurance; 11.6% of children under 18 do not have insurance
Hospitals: Saint Vincent Randolph Hospital (25 beds)
Safety: Violent crime rate: 2.1 per 10,000 population; Property crime rate: 409.1 per 10,000 population
Newspapers: News-Gazette (daily circulation 3,700)
Transportation: Commute: 92.5% car, 0.0% public transportation, 1.9% walk, 2.9% work from home; Mean travel time to work: 16.2 minutes
Additional Information Contacts
City of Winchester. . . . . (765) 584-1351
http://www.winchester-in.gov

Ripley County

Located in southeastern Indiana; drained by Laughery and Graham Creeks. Covers a land area of 446.425 square miles, a water area of 1.636 square miles, and is located in the Eastern Time Zone at 39.10° N. Lat., 85.26° W. Long. The county was founded in 1816. County seat is Versailles.
Population: 28,372; Growth (since 2000): 7.0%; Density: 63.6 persons per square mile; Race: 97.2% White, 0.5% Black/African American, 1.0% Asian, 0.5% American Indian/Alaska Native, 0.0% Native Hawaiian/Other Pacific Islander, 0.6% two or more races, 1.8% Hispanic of any race; Average household size: 2.50; Median age: 40.6; Age under 18: 24.0%; Age 65 and over: 16.7%; Males per 100 females: 97.3; Marriage status: 22.4% never married, 59.6% now married, 1.4% separated, 6.7% widowed, 11.2% divorced; Foreign born: 1.5%; Speak English only: 97.5%; With disability: 13.6%; Veterans: 10.3%; Ancestry: 37.5% German, 11.2% Irish, 8.6% American, 7.5% English, 2.1% French
Religion: Six largest groups: 27.2% Catholicism, 14.8% Baptist, 6.3% Lutheran, 4.8% Methodist/Pietist, 2.2% Non-denominational Protestant, 1.4% Latter-day Saints
Economy: Unemployment rate: 3.8%; Leading industries: 15.4 % retail trade; 13.1 % other services (except public administration); 12.4 % construction; Farms: 876 totaling 166,711 acres; Company size: 0 employ 1,000 or more persons, 3 employ 500 to 999 persons, 12 employ 100 to 499 persons, 620 employ less than 100 persons; Business ownership: 582 women-owned, n/a Black-owned, n/a Hispanic-owned, n/a Asian-owned, n/a American Indian/Alaska Native-owned
Employment: 12.0% management, business, and financial, 2.5% computer, engineering, and science, 8.6% education, legal, community service, arts, and media, 4.6% healthcare practitioners, 16.3% service, 20.4% sales and office, 13.1% natural resources, construction, and maintenance, 22.6% production, transportation, and material moving
Income: Per capita: $25,385; Median household: $53,698; Average household: $64,227; Households with income of $100,000 or more: 15.8%; Poverty rate: 10.5%
Educational Attainment: High school diploma or higher: 88.0%; Bachelor's degree or higher: 18.2%; Graduate/professional degree or higher: 6.0%
Housing: Homeownership rate: 76.7%; Median home value: $139,500; Median year structure built: 1975; Homeowner vacancy rate: 1.8%; Median selected monthly owner costs: $1,114 with a mortgage, $384 without a mortgage; Median gross rent: $682 per month; Rental vacancy rate: 7.0%
Vital Statistics: Birth rate: 107.9 per 10,000 population; Death rate: 110.4 per 10,000 population; Age-adjusted cancer mortality rate: 183.3 deaths per 100,000 population
Health Insurance: 92.4% have insurance; 74.8% have private insurance; 30.7% have public insurance; 7.6% do not have insurance; 5.5% of children under 18 do not have insurance
Health Care: Physicians: 0.7 per 10,000 population; Dentists: 1.1 per 10,000 population; Hospital beds: 8.8 per 10,000 population; Hospital admissions: 596.7 per 10,000 population
Transportation: Commute: 92.8% car, 0.2% public transportation, 1.5% walk, 4.1% work from home; Mean travel time to work: 27.2 minutes
2016 Presidential Election: 75.8% Trump, 19.1% Clinton, 4.0% Johnson, 0.1% Stein
National and State Parks: Versailles State Park
Additional Information Contacts
Ripley Government . . . . (812) 689-6115
http://www.ripleycounty.com

Ripley County Communities

BATESVILLE (city). Covers a land area of 6.087 square miles and a water area of 0.066 square miles. Located at 39.30° N. Lat; 85.21° W. Long. Elevation is 971 feet.
History: Batesville was settled by German immigrants, and developed as a furniture manufacturing center.
Population: 6,389; Growth (since 2000): 5.9%; Density: 1,049.5 persons per square mile; Race: 95.5% White, 0.7% Black/African American, 3.3% Asian, 0.0% American Indian/Alaska Native, 0.0% Native Hawaiian/Other Pacific Islander, 0.5% Two or more races, 0.8% Hispanic of any race; Average household size: 2.36; Median age: 42.0; Age under 18: 23.4%; Age 65 and over: 20.5%; Males per 100 females: 91.3; Marriage status: 20.6% never married, 61.0% now married, 2.4% separated, 9.6% widowed, 8.8% divorced; Foreign born: 3.5%; Speak English only: 95.4%; With disability: 12.3%; Veterans: 10.3%; Ancestry: 44.0% German, 11.5% Irish, 7.8% English, 7.7% American, 3.7% Italian
Employment: 17.7% management, business, and financial, 6.1% computer, engineering, and science, 12.5% education, legal, community service, arts, and media, 7.4% healthcare practitioners, 11.0% service, 24.4% sales and office, 6.2% natural resources, construction, and maintenance, 14.7% production, transportation, and material moving
Income: Per capita: $29,211; Median household: $53,344; Average household: $69,730; Households with income of $100,000 or more: 20.2%; Poverty rate: 9.8%
Educational Attainment: High school diploma or higher: 93.4%; Bachelor's degree or higher: 32.8%; Graduate/professional degree or higher: 10.7%

School District(s)

Batesville Community School Corp (PK-12)
Enrollment: 1,970 . . . . (812) 934-2194
Housing: Homeownership rate: 68.1%; Median home value: $165,700; Median year structure built: 1976; Homeowner vacancy rate: 3.6%; Median selected monthly owner costs: $1,204 with a mortgage, $369 without a mortgage; Median gross rent: $727 per month; Rental vacancy rate: 3.8%

Health Insurance: 94.1% have insurance; 78.6% have private insurance; 30.5% have public insurance; 5.9% do not have insurance; 5.3% of children under 18 do not have insurance
Hospitals: Margaret Mary Community Hospital (79 beds)
Safety: Violent crime rate: 23.9 per 10,000 population; Property crime rate: 144.7 per 10,000 population
Newspapers: The Herald-Tribune (weekly circulation 4,000)
Transportation: Commute: 91.3% car, 0.0% public transportation, 1.6% walk, 4.7% work from home; Mean travel time to work: 21.6 minutes
Airports: Batesville (general aviation)
Additional Information Contacts
City of Batesville . . . . (812) 933-6101
http://www.batesvilleindiana.us

CROSS PLAINS (unincorporated postal area)
ZCTA: 47017
Covers a land area of 15.410 square miles and a water area of 0.080 square miles. Located at 38.94° N. Lat; 85.19° W. Long. Elevation is 961 feet.
Population: 376; Growth (since 2000): -22.3%; Density: 24.4 persons per square mile; Race: 100.0% White, 0.0% Black/African American, 0.0% Asian, 0.0% American Indian/Alaska Native, 0.0% Native Hawaiian/Other Pacific Islander, 0.0% Two or more races, 0.0% Hispanic of any race; Average household size: 2.16; Median age: 49.4; Age under 18: 18.1%; Age 65 and over: 17.6%; Males per 100 females: 103.6; Marriage status: 14.2% never married, 71.8% now married, 2.2% separated, 6.6% widowed, 7.3% divorced; Foreign born: 0.0%; Speak English only: 96.6%; With disability: 5.6%; Veterans: 8.8%; Ancestry: 36.2% German, 14.6% American, 7.4% Irish, 3.7% Scotch-Irish
Employment: 8.8% management, business, and financial, 3.4% computer, engineering, and science, 21.4% education, legal, community service, arts, and media, 5.5% healthcare practitioners, 10.9% service, 25.2% sales and office, 13.0% natural resources, construction, and maintenance, 11.8% production, transportation, and material moving
Income: Per capita: $47,892; Median household: $71,500; Average household: $103,757; Households with income of $100,000 or more: 34.5%; Poverty rate: 6.6%
Educational Attainment: High school diploma or higher: 94.8%; Bachelor's degree or higher: 11.1%; Graduate/professional degree or higher: 4.4%
Housing: Homeownership rate: 92.5%; Median home value: $176,800; Median year structure built: 1962; Homeowner vacancy rate: 0.0%; Median selected monthly owner costs: $0 with a mortgage, $313 without a mortgage; Median gross rent: n/a per month; Rental vacancy rate: 0.0%
Health Insurance: 93.6% have insurance; 83.2% have private insurance; 27.9% have public insurance; 6.4% do not have insurance; 0.0% of children under 18 do not have insurance
Transportation: Commute: 95.0% car, 0.0% public transportation, 0.0% walk, 5.0% work from home; Mean travel time to work: 33.7 minutes

HOLTON (town). Covers a land area of 1.807 square miles and a water area of 0 square miles. Located at 39.08° N. Lat; 85.38° W. Long. Elevation is 909 feet.
Population: 494; Growth (since 2000): 21.4%; Density: 273.4 persons per square mile; Race: 99.4% White, 0.0% Black/African American, 0.0% Asian, 0.0% American Indian/Alaska Native, 0.0% Native Hawaiian/Other Pacific Islander, 0.6% Two or more races, 0.8% Hispanic of any race; Average household size: 2.89; Median age: 32.1; Age under 18: 33.6%; Age 65 and over: 7.1%; Males per 100 females: 99.2; Marriage status: 21.4% never married, 58.6% now married, 1.1% separated, 2.2% widowed, 17.8% divorced; Foreign born: 0.0%; Speak English only: 97.8%; With disability: 15.0%; Veterans: 8.5%; Ancestry: 24.9% Irish, 20.9% German, 14.4% English, 12.1% American, 2.6% Polish
Employment: 7.2% management, business, and financial, 0.0% computer, engineering, and science, 7.2% education, legal, community service, arts, and media, 0.0% healthcare practitioners, 24.0% service, 17.2% sales and office, 13.6% natural resources, construction, and maintenance, 30.8% production, transportation, and material moving
Income: Per capita: $16,966; Median household: $41,583; Average household: $48,842; Households with income of $100,000 or more: 7.0%; Poverty rate: 18.0%
Educational Attainment: High school diploma or higher: 83.2%; Bachelor's degree or higher: 5.7%; Graduate/professional degree or higher: 3.0%
Housing: Homeownership rate: 80.1%; Median home value: $81,600; Median year structure built: 1967; Homeowner vacancy rate: 2.8%; Median selected monthly owner costs: $863 with a mortgage, $400 without a mortgage; Median gross rent: $894 per month; Rental vacancy rate: 11.9%
Health Insurance: 83.4% have insurance; 60.1% have private insurance; 28.9% have public insurance; 16.6% do not have insurance; 16.6% of children under 18 do not have insurance
Transportation: Commute: 95.9% car, 1.4% public transportation, 0.0% walk, 0.0% work from home; Mean travel time to work: 28.8 minutes

MILAN (town). Covers a land area of 1.950 square miles and a water area of 0.034 square miles. Located at 39.12° N. Lat; 85.13° W. Long. Elevation is 991 feet.
History: Laid out 1854.
Population: 1,934; Growth (since 2000): 6.5%; Density: 991.8 persons per square mile; Race: 98.0% White, 0.0% Black/African American, 0.3% Asian, 0.5% American Indian/Alaska Native, 0.0% Native Hawaiian/Other Pacific Islander, 0.5% Two or more races, 0.3% Hispanic of any race; Average household size: 2.49; Median age: 37.9; Age under 18: 25.1%; Age 65 and over: 17.2%; Males per 100 females: 87.3; Marriage status: 27.5% never married, 49.1% now married, 1.2% separated, 9.9% widowed, 13.5% divorced; Foreign born: 1.0%; Speak English only: 99.1%; With disability: 15.6%; Veterans: 12.2%; Ancestry: 27.3% German, 12.8% Irish, 7.3% English, 5.4% American, 1.7% Greek
Employment: 6.6% management, business, and financial, 0.5% computer, engineering, and science, 5.3% education, legal, community service, arts, and media, 2.6% healthcare practitioners, 26.6% service, 19.4% sales and office, 12.6% natural resources, construction, and maintenance, 26.4% production, transportation, and material moving
Income: Per capita: $21,051; Median household: $46,458; Average household: $54,567; Households with income of $100,000 or more: 7.1%; Poverty rate: 11.9%
Educational Attainment: High school diploma or higher: 82.9%; Bachelor's degree or higher: 9.8%; Graduate/professional degree or higher: 2.5%

School District(s)

Milan Community Schools (PK-12)
Enrollment: 1,070 . . . . (812) 654-2365
Housing: Homeownership rate: 64.1%; Median home value: $84,600; Median year structure built: 1969; Homeowner vacancy rate: 0.0%; Median selected monthly owner costs: $916 with a mortgage, $363 without a mortgage; Median gross rent: $746 per month; Rental vacancy rate: 11.8%
Health Insurance: 84.9% have insurance; 64.4% have private insurance; 33.5% have public insurance; 15.1% do not have insurance; 11.7% of children under 18 do not have insurance
Transportation: Commute: 91.0% car, 0.0% public transportation, 4.7% walk, 4.0% work from home; Mean travel time to work: 24.7 minutes

NAPOLEON (town). Covers a land area of 0.198 square miles and a water area of 0 square miles. Located at 39.20° N. Lat; 85.33° W. Long. Elevation is 965 feet.
History: Laid out 1820.
Population: 152; Growth (since 2000): -36.1%; Density: 767.1 persons per square mile; Race: 95.4% White, 0.0% Black/African American, 0.0% Asian, 0.0% American Indian/Alaska Native, 0.0% Native Hawaiian/Other Pacific Islander, 4.6% Two or more races, 2.0% Hispanic of any race; Average household size: 1.71; Median age: 49.3; Age under 18: 5.9%; Age 65 and over: 23.0%; Males per 100 females: 103.5; Marriage status: 25.9% never married, 41.3% now married, 2.8% separated, 14.7% widowed, 18.2% divorced; Foreign born: 3.3%; Speak English only: 100.0%; With disability: 11.8%; Veterans: 12.6%; Ancestry: 23.0% German, 12.5% Italian, 3.9% Irish, 2.6% American, 2.6% Czechoslovakian
Employment: 5.6% management, business, and financial, 3.3% computer, engineering, and science, 0.0% education, legal, community service, arts, and media, 8.9% healthcare practitioners, 38.9% service, 12.2% sales and office, 12.2% natural resources, construction, and maintenance, 18.9% production, transportation, and material moving
Income: Per capita: $21,466; Median household: $25,750; Average household: $36,682; Households with income of $100,000 or more: 2.2%; Poverty rate: 32.9%
Educational Attainment: High school diploma or higher: 81.9%; Bachelor's degree or higher: 4.3%; Graduate/professional degree or higher: 3.4%
Housing: Homeownership rate: 64.0%; Median home value: $95,500; Median year structure built: 1962; Homeowner vacancy rate: 6.6%; Median

selected monthly owner costs: $850 with a mortgage, $342 without a mortgage; Median gross rent: $390 per month; Rental vacancy rate: 11.1%
Health Insurance: 93.4% have insurance; 63.8% have private insurance; 45.4% have public insurance; 6.6% do not have insurance; 0.0% of children under 18 do not have insurance
Transportation: Commute: 80.0% car, 0.0% public transportation, 20.0% walk, 0.0% work from home; Mean travel time to work: 20.2 minutes

OSGOOD (town). Covers a land area of 1.451 square miles and a water area of 0.034 square miles. Located at 39.13° N. Lat; 85.29° W. Long. Elevation is 984 feet.
History: Laid out 1857.
Population: 1,827; Growth (since 2000): 9.5%; Density: 1,259.1 persons per square mile; Race: 97.6% White, 0.0% Black/African American, 1.4% Asian, 0.0% American Indian/Alaska Native, 0.0% Native Hawaiian/Other Pacific Islander, 1.0% Two or more races, 4.4% Hispanic of any race; Average household size: 2.66; Median age: 35.6; Age under 18: 27.4%; Age 65 and over: 16.3%; Males per 100 females: 90.4; Marriage status: 25.8% never married, 49.2% now married, 1.3% separated, 7.1% widowed, 17.9% divorced; Foreign born: 1.4%; Speak English only: 96.2%; With disability: 19.6%; Veterans: 10.0%; Ancestry: 27.1% German, 14.3% Irish, 13.4% American, 5.0% English, 3.7% French
Employment: 9.7% management, business, and financial, 1.0% computer, engineering, and science, 4.1% education, legal, community service, arts, and media, 7.3% healthcare practitioners, 26.5% service, 14.5% sales and office, 7.5% natural resources, construction, and maintenance, 29.3% production, transportation, and material moving
Income: Per capita: $18,764; Median household: $42,896; Average household: $50,053; Households with income of $100,000 or more: 6.7%; Poverty rate: 12.8%
Educational Attainment: High school diploma or higher: 79.7%; Bachelor's degree or higher: 6.5%; Graduate/professional degree or higher: 1.1%

School District(s)

Jac-cen-del Community Sch Corp (PK-12)
Enrollment: 890 . . . . (812) 689-4114
Housing: Homeownership rate: 60.0%; Median home value: $94,500; Median year structure built: 1960; Homeowner vacancy rate: 2.5%; Median selected monthly owner costs: $891 with a mortgage, $375 without a mortgage; Median gross rent: $675 per month; Rental vacancy rate: 9.3%
Health Insurance: 90.2% have insurance; 69.4% have private insurance; 36.2% have public insurance; 9.8% do not have insurance; 7.2% of children under 18 do not have insurance
Transportation: Commute: 92.8% car, 0.0% public transportation, 5.9% walk, 1.3% work from home; Mean travel time to work: 25.0 minutes

SUNMAN (town). Covers a land area of 1.171 square miles and a water area of 0 square miles. Located at 39.24° N. Lat; 85.09° W. Long. Elevation is 1,020 feet.
History: Laid out 1856.
Population: 1,136; Growth (since 2000): 41.1%; Density: 970.3 persons per square mile; Race: 97.9% White, 0.0% Black/African American, 0.0% Asian, 0.0% American Indian/Alaska Native, 0.0% Native Hawaiian/Other Pacific Islander, 0.3% Two or more races, 24.4% Hispanic of any race; Average household size: 2.63; Median age: 37.6; Age under 18: 26.9%; Age 65 and over: 18.9%; Males per 100 females: 104.9; Marriage status: 22.1% never married, 62.9% now married, 2.7% separated, 6.0% widowed, 9.0% divorced; Foreign born: 6.1%; Speak English only: 86.3%; With disability: 21.8%; Veterans: 10.0%; Ancestry: 32.7% German, 14.8% Irish, 7.3% English, 6.8% American, 2.7% French
Employment: 7.0% management, business, and financial, 0.4% computer, engineering, and science, 3.3% education, legal, community service, arts, and media, 1.2% healthcare practitioners, 23.2% service, 16.2% sales and office, 10.7% natural resources, construction, and maintenance, 38.1% production, transportation, and material moving
Income: Per capita: $18,571; Median household: $38,654; Average household: $49,941; Households with income of $100,000 or more: 8.6%; Poverty rate: 14.3%
Educational Attainment: High school diploma or higher: 77.8%; Bachelor's degree or higher: 9.4%; Graduate/professional degree or higher: 3.5%

School District(s)

Ripley-Ohio-Dearborn Sp Ed Coop (PK-12)
Enrollment: n/a . . . . (812) 623-2212
Sunman-Dearborn Com Sch Corp (KG-12)
Enrollment: 3,977 . . . . (812) 623-2291
Housing: Homeownership rate: 70.2%; Median home value: $105,100; Median year structure built: 1959; Homeowner vacancy rate: 2.8%; Median selected monthly owner costs: $986 with a mortgage, $364 without a mortgage; Median gross rent: $572 per month; Rental vacancy rate: 15.8%
Health Insurance: 91.1% have insurance; 60.9% have private insurance; 45.3% have public insurance; 8.9% do not have insurance; 0.0% of children under 18 do not have insurance
Transportation: Commute: 88.8% car, 1.3% public transportation, 3.6% walk, 5.7% work from home; Mean travel time to work: 27.8 minutes

VERSAILLES (town). County seat. Covers a land area of 1.514 square miles and a water area of 0 square miles. Located at 39.06° N. Lat; 85.26° W. Long. Elevation is 965 feet.
History: Versailles was founded in 1818 as a farming center. General John Morgan and his men came to Versailles in 1863 and looted the office of the county treasurer.
Population: 2,326; Growth (since 2000): 30.4%; Density: 1,536.2 persons per square mile; Race: 92.8% White, 1.6% Black/African American, 0.0% Asian, 4.0% American Indian/Alaska Native, 0.0% Native Hawaiian/Other Pacific Islander, 0.4% Two or more races, 1.9% Hispanic of any race; Average household size: 2.42; Median age: 36.8; Age under 18: 27.0%; Age 65 and over: 16.4%; Males per 100 females: 90.5; Marriage status: 27.0% never married, 43.4% now married, 1.1% separated, 7.3% widowed, 22.3% divorced; Foreign born: 0.3%; Speak English only: 99.1%; With disability: 14.8%; Veterans: 6.7%; Ancestry: 28.3% German, 10.9% American, 9.0% Irish, 5.3% English, 4.1% Italian
Employment: 5.8% management, business, and financial, 3.2% computer, engineering, and science, 6.7% education, legal, community service, arts, and media, 3.8% healthcare practitioners, 17.6% service, 18.9% sales and office, 11.6% natural resources, construction, and maintenance, 32.4% production, transportation, and material moving
Income: Per capita: $20,700; Median household: $41,318; Average household: $50,784; Households with income of $100,000 or more: 9.8%; Poverty rate: 22.8%
Educational Attainment: High school diploma or higher: 85.3%; Bachelor's degree or higher: 17.1%; Graduate/professional degree or higher: 7.4%

School District(s)

South Ripley Com Sch Corp (PK-12)
Enrollment: 1,151 . . . . (812) 689-6282
Southeastern Career Center (09-12)
Enrollment: n/a . . . . (812) 689-5253
Housing: Homeownership rate: 62.1%; Median home value: $104,500; Median year structure built: 1974; Homeowner vacancy rate: 0.0%; Median selected monthly owner costs: $1,011 with a mortgage, $334 without a mortgage; Median gross rent: $535 per month; Rental vacancy rate: 13.2%
Health Insurance: 93.8% have insurance; 69.5% have private insurance; 41.4% have public insurance; 6.2% do not have insurance; 0.0% of children under 18 do not have insurance
Newspapers: Osgood Journal (weekly circulation 5,300); Versailles Republican (weekly circulation 5,000)
Transportation: Commute: 93.0% car, 0.0% public transportation, 2.5% walk, 4.5% work from home; Mean travel time to work: 26.3 minutes

Rush County

Located in east central Indiana; drained by the Big Blue River and Flatrock Creek. Covers a land area of 408.124 square miles, a water area of 0.337 square miles, and is located in the Eastern Time Zone at 39.62° N. Lat., 85.47° W. Long. The county was founded in 1821. County seat is Rushville.

Weather Station: Rushville Sewage Plant — Elevation: 959 feet

	Jan	Feb	Mar	Apr	May	Jun	Jul	Aug	Sep	Oct	Nov	Dec
High	35	39	50	62	73	81	84	83	77	65	52	39
Low	19	21	29	40	51	60	64	61	53	42	33	23
Precip	2.9	2.5	3.3	4.6	5.5	4.3	4.6	3.4	3.0	3.1	3.5	3.3
Snow	4.6	4.1	1.7	0.1	tr	0.0	0.0	0.0	0.0	0.3	0.2	3.7

High and Low temperatures in degrees Fahrenheit; Precipitation and Snow in inches

Population: 16,765; Growth (since 2000): -8.2%; Density: 41.1 persons per square mile; Race: 97.2% White, 1.4% Black/African American, 0.1% Asian, 0.0% American Indian/Alaska Native, 0.0% Native Hawaiian/Other

Pacific Islander, 0.8% two or more races, 1.5% Hispanic of any race; Average household size: 2.48; Median age: 41.6; Age under 18: 23.0%; Age 65 and over: 17.6%; Males per 100 females: 97.3; Marriage status: 21.5% never married, 57.8% now married, 0.9% separated, 7.3% widowed, 13.4% divorced; Foreign born: 0.5%; Speak English only: 97.8%; With disability: 14.5%; Veterans: 8.4%; Ancestry: 21.7% German, 13.3% American, 9.5% English, 9.3% Irish, 2.5% Dutch
Religion: Six largest groups: 24.6% Baptist, 9.4% Catholicism, 5.9% Methodist/Pietist, 2.9% Non-denominational Protestant, 2.1% Holiness, 2.0% European Free-Church
Economy: Unemployment rate: 3.1%; Leading industries: 13.6 % other services (except public administration); 12.8 % retail trade; 9.7 % health care and social assistance; Farms: 601 totaling 207,572 acres; Company size: 0 employ 1,000 or more persons, 0 employ 500 to 999 persons, 4 employ 100 to 499 persons, 356 employ less than 100 persons; Business ownership: 392 women-owned, n/a Black-owned, n/a Hispanic-owned, n/a Asian-owned, n/a American Indian/Alaska Native-owned
Employment: 12.2% management, business, and financial, 1.8% computer, engineering, and science, 5.0% education, legal, community service, arts, and media, 5.4% healthcare practitioners, 14.2% service, 22.8% sales and office, 14.3% natural resources, construction, and maintenance, 24.3% production, transportation, and material moving
Income: Per capita: $23,749; Median household: $47,955; Average household: $59,903; Households with income of $100,000 or more: 16.4%; Poverty rate: 18.3%
Educational Attainment: High school diploma or higher: 84.8%; Bachelor's degree or higher: 14.8%; Graduate/professional degree or higher: 5.1%
Housing: Homeownership rate: 72.6%; Median home value: $100,000; Median year structure built: 1955; Homeowner vacancy rate: 2.7%; Median selected monthly owner costs: $949 with a mortgage, $376 without a mortgage; Median gross rent: $650 per month; Rental vacancy rate: 11.8%
Vital Statistics: Birth rate: 108.7 per 10,000 population; Death rate: 111.1 per 10,000 population; Age-adjusted cancer mortality rate: 134.3 deaths per 100,000 population
Health Insurance: 87.1% have insurance; 68.2% have private insurance; 32.7% have public insurance; 12.9% do not have insurance; 12.0% of children under 18 do not have insurance
Health Care: Physicians: 4.8 per 10,000 population; Dentists: 4.2 per 10,000 population; Hospital beds: 15.0 per 10,000 population; Hospital admissions: 383.6 per 10,000 population
Transportation: Commute: 93.8% car, 0.5% public transportation, 0.9% walk, 4.7% work from home; Mean travel time to work: 26.0 minutes
2016 Presidential Election: 73.4% Trump, 21.1% Clinton, 5.5% Johnson, 0.0% Stein
Additional Information Contacts
Rush Government . . . . (765) 932-5451
http://www.rushcounty.in.gov

Rush County Communities

ARLINGTON (CDP). Covers a land area of 1.465 square miles and a water area of 0.018 square miles. Located at 39.65° N. Lat; 85.58° W. Long. Elevation is 922 feet.
Population: 434; Growth (since 2000): n/a; Density: 296.2 persons per square mile; Race: 100.0% White, 0.0% Black/African American, 0.0% Asian, 0.0% American Indian/Alaska Native, 0.0% Native Hawaiian/Other Pacific Islander, 0.0% Two or more races, 0.0% Hispanic of any race; Average household size: 2.25; Median age: 53.7; Age under 18: 25.1%; Age 65 and over: 17.5%; Males per 100 females: 104.2; Marriage status: 11.4% never married, 75.1% now married, 2.2% separated, 8.6% widowed, 4.9% divorced; Foreign born: 0.0%; Speak English only: 98.2%; With disability: 23.0%; Veterans: 14.8%; Ancestry: 17.5% German, 12.7% English, 10.1% American, 4.8% European, 2.5% Italian
Employment: 11.6% management, business, and financial, 0.0% computer, engineering, and science, 0.0% education, legal, community service, arts, and media, 0.0% healthcare practitioners, 12.3% service, 25.3% sales and office, 28.1% natural resources, construction, and maintenance, 22.6% production, transportation, and material moving
Income: Per capita: $18,158; Median household: $41,181; Average household: $41,654; Households with income of $100,000 or more: 3.6%; Poverty rate: 21.2%
Educational Attainment: High school diploma or higher: 86.5%; Bachelor's degree or higher: 2.2%; Graduate/professional degree or higher: n/a

School District(s)
Rush County Schools (PK-12)
Enrollment: 2,108 . . . . (765) 932-4186
Housing: Homeownership rate: 96.4%; Median home value: $80,400; Median year structure built: 1951; Homeowner vacancy rate: 0.0%; Median selected monthly owner costs: $746 with a mortgage, $390 without a mortgage; Median gross rent: n/a per month; Rental vacancy rate: 80.6%
Health Insurance: 96.3% have insurance; 81.1% have private insurance; 31.8% have public insurance; 3.7% do not have insurance; 0.0% of children under 18 do not have insurance
Transportation: Commute: 88.9% car, 11.1% public transportation, 0.0% walk, 0.0% work from home; Mean travel time to work: 34.2 minutes

CARTHAGE (town). Covers a land area of 0.582 square miles and a water area of 0 square miles. Located at 39.74° N. Lat; 85.57° W. Long. Elevation is 876 feet.
Population: 849; Growth (since 2000): -8.5%; Density: 1,459.7 persons per square mile; Race: 99.6% White, 0.0% Black/African American, 0.0% Asian, 0.0% American Indian/Alaska Native, 0.0% Native Hawaiian/Other Pacific Islander, 0.4% Two or more races, 8.0% Hispanic of any race; Average household size: 2.39; Median age: 37.4; Age under 18: 26.4%; Age 65 and over: 14.6%; Males per 100 females: 99.8; Marriage status: 19.0% never married, 54.3% now married, 0.8% separated, 7.0% widowed, 19.8% divorced; Foreign born: 0.9%; Speak English only: 100.0%; With disability: 18.6%; Veterans: 13.9%; Ancestry: 18.7% German, 14.3% Irish, 9.5% American, 8.5% English, 4.0% Scottish
Employment: 6.5% management, business, and financial, 1.7% computer, engineering, and science, 1.7% education, legal, community service, arts, and media, 10.1% healthcare practitioners, 17.1% service, 18.8% sales and office, 23.3% natural resources, construction, and maintenance, 20.8% production, transportation, and material moving
Income: Per capita: $18,321; Median household: $35,625; Average household: $42,611; Households with income of $100,000 or more: 3.1%; Poverty rate: 23.6%
Educational Attainment: High school diploma or higher: 83.0%; Bachelor's degree or higher: 16.5%; Graduate/professional degree or higher: 6.0%
Housing: Homeownership rate: 63.7%; Median home value: $77,300; Median year structure built: 1950; Homeowner vacancy rate: 2.9%; Median selected monthly owner costs: $843 with a mortgage, $390 without a mortgage; Median gross rent: $597 per month; Rental vacancy rate: 15.5%
Health Insurance: 86.8% have insurance; 59.4% have private insurance; 39.8% have public insurance; 13.2% do not have insurance; 1.3% of children under 18 do not have insurance
Transportation: Commute: 96.2% car, 0.0% public transportation, 1.2% walk, 2.7% work from home; Mean travel time to work: 33.2 minutes

FALMOUTH (unincorporated postal area)
ZCTA: 46127
Covers a land area of 23.642 square miles and a water area of 0 square miles. Located at 39.71° N. Lat; 85.31° W. Long. Elevation is 1,047 feet.
Population: 249; Growth (since 2000): -33.4%; Density: 10.5 persons per square mile; Race: 100.0% White, 0.0% Black/African American, 0.0% Asian, 0.0% American Indian/Alaska Native, 0.0% Native Hawaiian/Other Pacific Islander, 0.0% Two or more races, 0.0% Hispanic of any race; Average household size: 2.39; Median age: 48.9; Age under 18: 15.3%; Age 65 and over: 40.6%; Males per 100 females: 89.1; Marriage status: 19.0% never married, 36.0% now married, 0.0% separated, 14.7% widowed, 30.3% divorced; Foreign born: 0.0%; Speak English only: 89.6%; With disability: 23.7%; Veterans: 6.6%; Ancestry: 22.9% German, 20.1% English, 8.8% Scotch-Irish, 3.2% Irish, 2.8% American
Employment: 7.6% management, business, and financial, 0.0% computer, engineering, and science, 0.0% education, legal, community service, arts, and media, 7.6% healthcare practitioners, 0.0% service, 11.4% sales and office, 35.2% natural resources, construction, and maintenance, 38.1% production, transportation, and material moving
Income: Per capita: $45,683; Median household: n/a; Average household: $88,381; Households with income of $100,000 or more: 41.4%; Poverty rate: 4.8%
Educational Attainment: High school diploma or higher: 87.2%; Bachelor's degree or higher: n/a; Graduate/professional degree or higher: n/a
Housing: Homeownership rate: 90.4%; Median home value: $57,400; Median year structure built: Before 1940; Homeowner vacancy rate:

0.0%; Median selected monthly owner costs: $1,077 with a mortgage, $284 without a mortgage; Median gross rent: n/a per month; Rental vacancy rate: 0.0%
Health Insurance: 92.0% have insurance; 44.2% have private insurance; 65.9% have public insurance; 8.0% do not have insurance; 0.0% of children under 18 do not have insurance
Transportation: Commute: 100.0% car, 0.0% public transportation, 0.0% walk, 0.0% work from home; Mean travel time to work: 40.8 minutes

GLENWOOD (town). Covers a land area of 0.176 square miles and a water area of 0 square miles. Located at 39.63° N. Lat; 85.30° W. Long. Elevation is 1,086 feet.
Population: 221; Growth (since 2000): -30.5%; Density: 1,254.0 persons per square mile; Race: 99.1% White, 0.0% Black/African American, 0.9% Asian, 0.0% American Indian/Alaska Native, 0.0% Native Hawaiian/Other Pacific Islander, 0.0% Two or more races, 0.0% Hispanic of any race; Average household size: 2.60; Median age: 41.9; Age under 18: 26.2%; Age 65 and over: 13.1%; Males per 100 females: 83.8; Marriage status: 20.6% never married, 62.3% now married, 1.1% separated, 5.7% widowed, 11.4% divorced; Foreign born: 0.9%; Speak English only: 97.4%; With disability: 17.2%; Veterans: 11.0%; Ancestry: 27.1% German, 16.3% Irish, 13.6% American, 8.1% English, 3.2% Dutch
Employment: 2.0% management, business, and financial, 2.0% computer, engineering, and science, 1.0% education, legal, community service, arts, and media, 4.0% healthcare practitioners, 22.0% service, 27.0% sales and office, 11.0% natural resources, construction, and maintenance, 31.0% production, transportation, and material moving
Income: Per capita: $20,349; Median household: $46,875; Average household: $54,573; Households with income of $100,000 or more: 7.1%; Poverty rate: 12.1%
Educational Attainment: High school diploma or higher: 88.7%; Bachelor's degree or higher: 0.7%; Graduate/professional degree or higher: 0.7%
Housing: Homeownership rate: 74.1%; Median home value: $70,600; Median year structure built: 1942; Homeowner vacancy rate: 14.9%; Median selected monthly owner costs: $872 with a mortgage, $367 without a mortgage; Median gross rent: $850 per month; Rental vacancy rate: 0.0%
Health Insurance: 86.9% have insurance; 56.6% have private insurance; 41.2% have public insurance; 13.1% do not have insurance; 5.0% of children under 18 do not have insurance
Transportation: Commute: 93.9% car, 0.0% public transportation, 5.1% walk, 0.0% work from home; Mean travel time to work: 27.6 minutes

HOMER (unincorporated postal area)
ZCTA: 46146
Covers a land area of 0.778 square miles and a water area of 0 square miles. Located at 39.59° N. Lat; 85.57° W. Long. Elevation is 906 feet.
Population: 73; Growth (since 2000): n/a; Density: 93.9 persons per square mile; Race: 100.0% White, 0.0% Black/African American, 0.0% Asian, 0.0% American Indian/Alaska Native, 0.0% Native Hawaiian/Other Pacific Islander, 0.0% Two or more races, 0.0% Hispanic of any race; Average household size: 2.43; Median age: 24.6; Age under 18: 28.8%; Age 65 and over: 0.0%; Males per 100 females: 116.7; Marriage status: 40.4% never married, 59.6% now married, 0.0% separated, 0.0% widowed, 0.0% divorced; Foreign born: 0.0%; Speak English only: 100.0%; With disability: 0.0%; Veterans: 0.0%; Ancestry: 12.3% German, 12.3% Irish
Employment: 0.0% management, business, and financial, 0.0% computer, engineering, and science, 0.0% education, legal, community service, arts, and media, 0.0% healthcare practitioners, 48.1% service, 23.1% sales and office, 17.3% natural resources, construction, and maintenance, 11.5% production, transportation, and material moving
Income: Per capita: $21,979; Median household: $54,375; Average household: $56,757; Households with income of $100,000 or more: n/a; Poverty rate: n/a
Educational Attainment: High school diploma or higher: 100.0%; Bachelor's degree or higher: n/a; Graduate/professional degree or higher: n/a
Housing: Homeownership rate: 80.0%; Median home value: n/a; Median year structure built: 1964; Homeowner vacancy rate: 0.0%; Median selected monthly owner costs: $0 with a mortgage, $0 without a mortgage; Median gross rent: n/a per month; Rental vacancy rate: 0.0%
Health Insurance: 100.0% have insurance; 100.0% have private insurance; 0.0% have public insurance; 0.0% do not have insurance; 0.0% of children under 18 do not have insurance
Transportation: Commute: 100.0% car, 0.0% public transportation, 0.0% walk, 0.0% work from home; Mean travel time to work: 0.0 minutes

MANILLA (CDP). Covers a land area of 0.226 square miles and a water area of 0 square miles. Located at 39.57° N. Lat; 85.62° W. Long. Elevation is 892 feet.
Population: 297; Growth (since 2000): n/a; Density: 1,317.1 persons per square mile; Race: 100.0% White, 0.0% Black/African American, 0.0% Asian, 0.0% American Indian/Alaska Native, 0.0% Native Hawaiian/Other Pacific Islander, 0.0% Two or more races, 0.0% Hispanic of any race; Average household size: 2.43; Median age: 37.2; Age under 18: 32.3%; Age 65 and over: 12.8%; Males per 100 females: 107.0; Marriage status: 34.4% never married, 29.4% now married, 0.0% separated, 17.9% widowed, 18.3% divorced; Foreign born: 0.0%; Speak English only: 100.0%; With disability: 23.9%; Veterans: 3.5%; Ancestry: 35.4% English, 13.5% American, 8.1% German, 5.7% Dutch, 2.4% Irish
Employment: 0.0% management, business, and financial, 29.6% computer, engineering, and science, 8.6% education, legal, community service, arts, and media, 0.0% healthcare practitioners, 24.7% service, 8.6% sales and office, 19.8% natural resources, construction, and maintenance, 8.6% production, transportation, and material moving
Income: Per capita: $15,708; Median household: n/a; Average household: $39,339; Households with income of $100,000 or more: 5.7%; Poverty rate: 61.6%
Educational Attainment: High school diploma or higher: 88.1%; Bachelor's degree or higher: 6.5%; Graduate/professional degree or higher: 3.5%
Housing: Homeownership rate: 73.0%; Median home value: $59,300; Median year structure built: Before 1940; Homeowner vacancy rate: 0.0%; Median selected monthly owner costs: $759 with a mortgage, $385 without a mortgage; Median gross rent: n/a per month; Rental vacancy rate: 0.0%
Health Insurance: 65.0% have insurance; 38.4% have private insurance; 41.1% have public insurance; 35.0% do not have insurance; 17.7% of children under 18 do not have insurance
Transportation: Commute: 100.0% car, 0.0% public transportation, 0.0% walk, 0.0% work from home; Mean travel time to work: 33.1 minutes

MAYS (unincorporated postal area)
ZCTA: 46155
Covers a land area of 0.023 square miles and a water area of 0 square miles. Located at 39.74° N. Lat; 85.43° W. Long. Elevation is 1,010 feet.
Population: 244; Growth (since 2000): 48.8%; Density: 10,681.6 persons per square mile; Race: 100.0% White, 0.0% Black/African American, 0.0% Asian, 0.0% American Indian/Alaska Native, 0.0% Native Hawaiian/Other Pacific Islander, 0.0% Two or more races, 0.0% Hispanic of any race; Average household size: 2.68; Median age: 31.6; Age under 18: 29.9%; Age 65 and over: 0.0%; Males per 100 females: 102.0; Marriage status: 19.6% never married, 57.5% now married, 0.0% separated, 22.9% widowed, 0.0% divorced; Foreign born: 0.0%; Speak English only: 100.0%; With disability: 0.0%; Veterans: 0.0%; Ancestry: 42.6% European, 15.2% Irish, 14.3% Northern European
Employment: 0.0% management, business, and financial, 28.5% computer, engineering, and science, 18.8% education, legal, community service, arts, and media, 0.0% healthcare practitioners, 25.7% service, 0.0% sales and office, 27.1% natural resources, construction, and maintenance, 0.0% production, transportation, and material moving
Income: Per capita: $24,852; Median household: $60,304; Average household: $65,076; Households with income of $100,000 or more: 14.3%; Poverty rate: n/a
Educational Attainment: High school diploma or higher: 100.0%; Bachelor's degree or higher: 18.8%; Graduate/professional degree or higher: 18.8%

School District(s)

Mays Community Academy (KG-06)
Enrollment: 180 . . . . (765) 645-5577
Housing: Homeownership rate: 59.3%; Median home value: n/a; Median year structure built: 1945; Homeowner vacancy rate: 0.0%; Median selected monthly owner costs: $0 with a mortgage, $0 without a mortgage; Median gross rent: n/a per month; Rental vacancy rate: 0.0%
Health Insurance: 100.0% have insurance; 100.0% have private insurance; 0.0% have public insurance; 0.0% do not have insurance; 0.0% of children under 18 do not have insurance

Transportation: Commute: 100.0% car, 0.0% public transportation, 0.0% walk, 0.0% work from home; Mean travel time to work: 0.0 minutes

MILROY (CDP). Covers a land area of 0.662 square miles and a water area of 0 square miles. Located at 39.50° N. Lat; 85.47° W. Long. Elevation is 965 feet.
Population: 715; Growth (since 2000): n/a; Density: 1,079.6 persons per square mile; Race: 98.5% White, 0.0% Black/African American, 0.0% Asian, 0.0% American Indian/Alaska Native, 0.0% Native Hawaiian/Other Pacific Islander, 1.5% Two or more races, 0.0% Hispanic of any race; Average household size: 2.77; Median age: 39.7; Age under 18: 22.7%; Age 65 and over: 15.5%; Males per 100 females: 93.0; Marriage status: 17.7% never married, 66.5% now married, 2.0% separated, 9.1% widowed, 6.6% divorced; Foreign born: 0.0%; Speak English only: 100.0%; With disability: 20.6%; Veterans: 6.1%; Ancestry: 17.1% German, 11.9% American, 8.1% English, 6.2% Irish, 3.5% Scottish
Employment: 2.4% management, business, and financial, 0.0% computer, engineering, and science, 5.5% education, legal, community service, arts, and media, 0.0% healthcare practitioners, 31.8% service, 22.9% sales and office, 11.6% natural resources, construction, and maintenance, 25.7% production, transportation, and material moving
Income: Per capita: $16,693; Median household: $45,431; Average household: $46,260; Households with income of $100,000 or more: 6.3%; Poverty rate: 29.4%
Educational Attainment: High school diploma or higher: 65.0%; Bachelor's degree or higher: 4.3%; Graduate/professional degree or higher: 0.8%

School District(s)

Rush County Schools (PK-12)
Enrollment: 2,108 . . . . (765) 932-4186
Housing: Homeownership rate: 84.1%; Median home value: $65,700; Median year structure built: 1953; Homeowner vacancy rate: 0.0%; Median selected monthly owner costs: $993 with a mortgage, $249 without a mortgage; Median gross rent: $540 per month; Rental vacancy rate: 0.0%
Health Insurance: 89.7% have insurance; 64.1% have private insurance; 38.6% have public insurance; 10.3% do not have insurance; 0.0% of children under 18 do not have insurance
Transportation: Commute: 96.5% car, 0.0% public transportation, 1.4% walk, 2.1% work from home; Mean travel time to work: 21.3 minutes

RUSHVILLE (city). County seat. Covers a land area of 3.091 square miles and a water area of 0 square miles. Located at 39.62° N. Lat; 85.45° W. Long. Elevation is 958 feet.
History: Rushville was founded in 1822 and named for Benjamin F. Rush, a Revolutionary War soldier and a signer of the Declaration of Independence.
Population: 6,160; Growth (since 2000): 2.8%; Density: 1,993.0 persons per square mile; Race: 93.9% White, 3.9% Black/African American, 0.0% Asian, 0.0% American Indian/Alaska Native, 0.0% Native Hawaiian/Other Pacific Islander, 0.9% Two or more races, 2.3% Hispanic of any race; Average household size: 2.30; Median age: 41.5; Age under 18: 21.8%; Age 65 and over: 20.5%; Males per 100 females: 90.5; Marriage status: 22.4% never married, 50.4% now married, 1.6% separated, 9.2% widowed, 18.0% divorced; Foreign born: 0.9%; Speak English only: 98.4%; With disability: 15.8%; Veterans: 9.8%; Ancestry: 23.9% German, 15.0% American, 10.2% Irish, 9.0% English, 2.5% Italian
Employment: 10.3% management, business, and financial, 1.2% computer, engineering, and science, 7.8% education, legal, community service, arts, and media, 2.7% healthcare practitioners, 16.4% service, 26.0% sales and office, 6.8% natural resources, construction, and maintenance, 28.9% production, transportation, and material moving
Income: Per capita: $21,523; Median household: $40,154; Average household: $50,802; Households with income of $100,000 or more: 13.3%; Poverty rate: 18.5%
Educational Attainment: High school diploma or higher: 81.7%; Bachelor's degree or higher: 14.5%; Graduate/professional degree or higher: 4.6%

School District(s)

Rush County Schools (PK-12)
Enrollment: 2,108 . . . . (765) 932-4186
Housing: Homeownership rate: 56.9%; Median home value: $84,700; Median year structure built: 1951; Homeowner vacancy rate: 4.4%; Median selected monthly owner costs: $881 with a mortgage, $314 without a mortgage; Median gross rent: $649 per month; Rental vacancy rate: 10.6%
Health Insurance: 88.9% have insurance; 67.9% have private insurance; 37.7% have public insurance; 11.1% do not have insurance; 5.5% of children under 18 do not have insurance
Hospitals: Rush Memorial Hospital (25 beds)
Safety: Violent crime rate: n/a per 10,000 population; Property crime rate: 385.3 per 10,000 population
Newspapers: Rushville Republican (daily circulation 2,700)
Transportation: Commute: 95.8% car, 0.0% public transportation, 0.9% walk, 3.1% work from home; Mean travel time to work: 23.5 minutes
Additional Information Contacts
City of Rushville. . . . . (765) 932-2672
http://www.cityofrushville.in.gov

Saint Joseph County

Located in northern Indiana; bounded on the north by Michigan; drained by the Saint Joseph, Yellow, and Kankakee Rivers. Covers a land area of 457.850 square miles, a water area of 3.535 square miles, and is located in the Eastern Time Zone at 41.62° N. Lat., 86.29° W. Long. The county was founded in 1830. County seat is South Bend.

Saint Joseph County is part of the South Bend-Mishawaka, IN-MI Metropolitan Statistical Area. The entire metro area includes: St. Joseph County, IN; Cass County, MI

Weather Station: South Bend Michiana Regional Elevation: 772 feet

	Jan	Feb	Mar	Apr	May	Jun	Jul	Aug	Sep	Oct	Nov	Dec
High	32	36	47	60	70	80	83	81	74	62	49	36
Low	18	21	29	39	49	59	63	62	54	43	34	23
Precip	2.3	2.0	2.5	3.3	3.7	3.8	4.0	4.0	3.7	3.4	3.2	2.7
Snow	20.3	15.1	7.4	1.5	tr	tr	tr	tr	tr	0.5	5.0	17.5

High and Low temperatures in degrees Fahrenheit; Precipitation and Snow in inches

Population: 268,613; Growth (since 2000): 1.2%; Density: 586.7 persons per square mile; Race: 79.0% White, 13.0% Black/African American, 2.2% Asian, 0.4% American Indian/Alaska Native, 0.1% Native Hawaiian/Other Pacific Islander, 3.1% two or more races, 8.3% Hispanic of any race; Average household size: 2.55; Median age: 36.5; Age under 18: 23.9%; Age 65 and over: 14.7%; Males per 100 females: 94.1; Marriage status: 35.0% never married, 47.4% now married, 1.5% separated, 6.1% widowed, 11.6% divorced; Foreign born: 6.3%; Speak English only: 90.6%; With disability: 13.7%; Veterans: 7.0%; Ancestry: 21.4% German, 12.2% Irish, 10.4% Polish, 6.6% American, 6.3% English
Religion: Six largest groups: 29.7% Methodist/Pietist, 19.7% Catholicism, 3.5% Non-denominational Protestant, 2.5% Baptist, 1.9% Lutheran, 1.7% Pentecostal
Economy: Unemployment rate: 3.7%; Leading industries: 15.3 % retail trade; 11.5 % health care and social assistance; 11.0 % other services (except public administration); Farms: 691 totaling 151,975 acres; Company size: 6 employ 1,000 or more persons, 7 employ 500 to 999 persons, 181 employs 100 to 499 persons, 5,608 employ less than 100 persons; Business ownership: 6,518 women-owned, 2,314 Black-owned, 543 Hispanic-owned, 534 Asian-owned, 165 American Indian/Alaska Native-owned
Employment: 12.5% management, business, and financial, 4.0% computer, engineering, and science, 11.9% education, legal, community service, arts, and media, 6.3% healthcare practitioners, 17.6% service, 24.0% sales and office, 6.7% natural resources, construction, and maintenance, 17.1% production, transportation, and material moving
Income: Per capita: $25,893; Median household: $48,121; Average household: $66,247; Households with income of $100,000 or more: 18.3%; Poverty rate: 17.1%
Educational Attainment: High school diploma or higher: 87.9%; Bachelor's degree or higher: 28.4%; Graduate/professional degree or higher: 11.0%
Housing: Homeownership rate: 67.9%; Median home value: $118,600; Median year structure built: 1967; Homeowner vacancy rate: 1.7%; Median selected monthly owner costs: $1,011 with a mortgage, $348 without a mortgage; Median gross rent: $743 per month; Rental vacancy rate: 12.8%
Vital Statistics: Birth rate: 128.2 per 10,000 population; Death rate: 90.2 per 10,000 population; Age-adjusted cancer mortality rate: 180.6 deaths per 100,000 population
Health Insurance: 90.0% have insurance; 68.8% have private insurance; 32.2% have public insurance; 10.0% do not have insurance; 5.1% of children under 18 do not have insurance

Health Care: Physicians: 29.7 per 10,000 population; Dentists: 5.7 per 10,000 population; Hospital beds: 30.3 per 10,000 population; Hospital admissions: 1,340.7 per 10,000 population
Transportation: Commute: 89.9% car, 1.5% public transportation, 3.7% walk, 3.8% work from home; Mean travel time to work: 21.0 minutes
2016 Presidential Election: 46.5% Trump, 46.7% Clinton, 4.6% Johnson, 0.4% Stein
National and State Parks: Potato Creek State Park
Additional Information Contacts
Saint Joseph Government.......................... (574) 235-9635
http://www.stjosephcountyindiana.com

Saint Joseph County Communities

GRANGER (CDP). Covers a land area of 25.567 square miles and a water area of 0.001 square miles. Located at 41.74° N. Lat; 86.14° W. Long. Elevation is 801 feet.
Population: 30,717; Growth (since 2000): 8.6%; Density: 1,201.4 persons per square mile; Race: 87.2% White, 3.6% Black/African American, 6.7% Asian, 0.2% American Indian/Alaska Native, 0.2% Native Hawaiian/Other Pacific Islander, 1.9% Two or more races, 2.6% Hispanic of any race; Average household size: 2.94; Median age: 42.0; Age under 18: 27.9%; Age 65 and over: 14.5%; Males per 100 females: 98.2; Marriage status: 21.8% never married, 68.5% now married, 0.7% separated, 4.2% widowed, 5.5% divorced; Foreign born: 7.9%; Speak English only: 91.0%; With disability: 8.0%; Veterans: 6.8%; Ancestry: 24.6% German, 13.0% Irish, 11.4% Polish, 9.6% English, 7.0% American
Employment: 20.3% management, business, and financial, 6.4% computer, engineering, and science, 14.9% education, legal, community service, arts, and media, 10.6% healthcare practitioners, 9.8% service, 24.1% sales and office, 4.7% natural resources, construction, and maintenance, 9.2% production, transportation, and material moving
Income: Per capita: $45,182; Median household: $100,182; Average household: $131,022; Households with income of $100,000 or more: 50.1%; Poverty rate: 4.1%
Educational Attainment: High school diploma or higher: 96.6%; Bachelor's degree or higher: 52.7%; Graduate/professional degree or higher: 23.0%

School District(s)

Penn-Harris-Madison School Corp (PK-12)
Enrollment: 10,051 .... (574) 259-7941

Two-year College(s)

Ross Medical Education Center-Granger (Private, For-profit)
Enrollment: 156.............................. (574) 273-4479
Housing: Homeownership rate: 95.5%; Median home value: $203,500; Median year structure built: 1987; Homeowner vacancy rate: 0.3%; Median selected monthly owner costs: $1,379 with a mortgage, $429 without a mortgage; Median gross rent: $1,472 per month; Rental vacancy rate: 14.7%
Health Insurance: 95.8% have insurance; 87.0% have private insurance; 19.5% have public insurance; 4.2% do not have insurance; 3.8% of children under 18 do not have insurance
Transportation: Commute: 93.1% car, 0.2% public transportation, 0.4% walk, 6.0% work from home; Mean travel time to work: 23.3 minutes

INDIAN VILLAGE (town). Covers a land area of 0.089 square miles and a water area of 0 square miles. Located at 41.71° N. Lat; 86.23° W. Long. Elevation is 728 feet.
Population: 129; Growth (since 2000): -10.4%; Density: 1,451.5 persons per square mile; Race: 72.1% White, 4.7% Black/African American, 0.8% Asian, 22.5% American Indian/Alaska Native, 0.0% Native Hawaiian/Other Pacific Islander, 0.0% Two or more races, 0.0% Hispanic of any race; Average household size: 2.48; Median age: 47.6; Age under 18: 11.6%; Age 65 and over: 17.8%; Males per 100 females: 114.5; Marriage status: 35.6% never married, 45.8% now married, 0.0% separated, 3.4% widowed, 15.3% divorced; Foreign born: 1.6%; Speak English only: 99.2%; With disability: 28.7%; Veterans: 4.4%; Ancestry: 23.3% German, 20.2% Irish, 7.8% Polish, 5.4% Italian, 3.9% American
Employment: 19.0% management, business, and financial, 7.9% computer, engineering, and science, 14.3% education, legal, community service, arts, and media, 1.6% healthcare practitioners, 22.2% service, 23.8% sales and office, 1.6% natural resources, construction, and maintenance, 9.5% production, transportation, and material moving
Income: Per capita: $34,451; Median household: $60,000; Average household: $77,273; Households with income of $100,000 or more: 26.9%; Poverty rate: 11.6%
Educational Attainment: High school diploma or higher: 89.5%; Bachelor's degree or higher: 20.0%; Graduate/professional degree or higher: 12.6%
Housing: Homeownership rate: 78.8%; Median home value: $130,200; Median year structure built: 1974; Homeowner vacancy rate: 0.0%; Median selected monthly owner costs: $880 with a mortgage, $265 without a mortgage; Median gross rent: $1,138 per month; Rental vacancy rate: 0.0%
Health Insurance: 92.2% have insurance; 65.1% have private insurance; 41.9% have public insurance; 7.8% do not have insurance; 0.0% of children under 18 do not have insurance
Transportation: Commute: 85.0% car, 0.0% public transportation, 3.3% walk, 5.0% work from home; Mean travel time to work: 15.8 minutes

LAKEVILLE (town). Covers a land area of 0.607 square miles and a water area of 0.003 square miles. Located at 41.53° N. Lat; 86.28° W. Long. Elevation is 843 feet.
Population: 857; Growth (since 2000): 51.1%; Density: 1,410.9 persons per square mile; Race: 92.9% White, 0.0% Black/African American, 5.7% Asian, 0.6% American Indian/Alaska Native, 0.0% Native Hawaiian/Other Pacific Islander, 0.8% Two or more races, 2.3% Hispanic of any race; Average household size: 2.34; Median age: 37.1; Age under 18: 22.5%; Age 65 and over: 14.7%; Males per 100 females: 96.0; Marriage status: 28.0% never married, 43.7% now married, 1.7% separated, 6.8% widowed, 21.6% divorced; Foreign born: 6.2%; Speak English only: 94.9%; With disability: 13.1%; Veterans: 7.2%; Ancestry: 23.3% German, 13.5% Irish, 7.5% Polish, 6.4% English, 4.4% Dutch
Employment: 5.0% management, business, and financial, 0.0% computer, engineering, and science, 3.1% education, legal, community service, arts, and media, 3.1% healthcare practitioners, 21.4% service, 28.1% sales and office, 15.5% natural resources, construction, and maintenance, 23.8% production, transportation, and material moving
Income: Per capita: $22,201; Median household: $52,000; Average household: $51,323; Households with income of $100,000 or more: 7.9%; Poverty rate: 15.5%
Educational Attainment: High school diploma or higher: 86.9%; Bachelor's degree or higher: 8.6%; Graduate/professional degree or higher: 4.0%

School District(s)

Union-North United School Corp (PK-12)
Enrollment: 1,134 .... (574) 784-8141
Housing: Homeownership rate: 59.0%; Median home value: $90,000; Median year structure built: 1963; Homeowner vacancy rate: 0.0%; Median selected monthly owner costs: $940 with a mortgage, $329 without a mortgage; Median gross rent: $728 per month; Rental vacancy rate: 17.7%
Health Insurance: 90.7% have insurance; 67.4% have private insurance; 34.7% have public insurance; 9.3% do not have insurance; 0.0% of children under 18 do not have insurance
Transportation: Commute: 96.6% car, 0.0% public transportation, 1.7% walk, 1.7% work from home; Mean travel time to work: 25.1 minutes

MISHAWAKA (city). Covers a land area of 16.997 square miles and a water area of 0.348 square miles. Located at 41.67° N. Lat; 86.17° W. Long. Elevation is 722 feet.
History: Mishawaka, situated along the St. Joseph River, developed around the Mishawaka Woolen and Rubber Manufacturing Company plant where felt, rubberboots, and raincoats were produced. Mishawaka was named for the daughter of Shawnee Chief Elkhart.
Population: 48,582; Growth (since 2000): 4.3%; Density: 2,858.3 persons per square mile; Race: 84.9% White, 7.2% Black/African American, 1.9% Asian, 0.8% American Indian/Alaska Native, 0.1% Native Hawaiian/Other Pacific Islander, 3.9% Two or more races, 6.3% Hispanic of any race; Average household size: 2.31; Median age: 35.4; Age under 18: 22.7%; Age 65 and over: 15.4%; Males per 100 females: 88.9; Marriage status: 35.8% never married, 40.2% now married, 1.2% separated, 7.7% widowed, 16.4% divorced; Foreign born: 5.4%; Speak English only: 93.8%; With disability: 15.0%; Veterans: 8.2%; Ancestry: 21.9% German, 12.3% Irish, 10.1% American, 9.0% Polish, 6.3% English
Employment: 10.1% management, business, and financial, 3.3% computer, engineering, and science, 9.8% education, legal, community service, arts, and media, 5.8% healthcare practitioners, 19.0% service,

25.9% sales and office, 7.0% natural resources, construction, and maintenance, 19.0% production, transportation, and material moving
Income: Per capita: $22,124; Median household: $39,821; Average household: $50,312; Households with income of $100,000 or more: 9.8%; Poverty rate: 18.8%
Educational Attainment: High school diploma or higher: 88.0%; Bachelor's degree or higher: 24.3%; Graduate/professional degree or higher: 8.4%

School District(s)

Penn-Harris-Madison School Corp (PK-12)
Enrollment: 10,051 . . . . (574) 259-7941
School City Of Mishawaka (PK-12)
Enrollment: 4,771 . . . . (574) 254-4537

Four-year College(s)

Bethel College-Indiana (Private, Not-for-profit, Missionary Church Inc)
Enrollment: 1,513 . . . . (574) 807-7000
Tuition: In-state $28,030; Out-of-state $28,030
Housing: Homeownership rate: 50.2%; Median home value: $93,300; Median year structure built: 1974; Homeowner vacancy rate: 1.7%; Median selected monthly owner costs: $931 with a mortgage, $356 without a mortgage; Median gross rent: $730 per month; Rental vacancy rate: 14.8%
Health Insurance: 86.7% have insurance; 64.5% have private insurance; 33.6% have public insurance; 13.3% do not have insurance; 6.9% of children under 18 do not have insurance
Hospitals: Saint Joseph Regional Medical Center (125 beds); Unity Medical & Surgical Hospital
Safety: Violent crime rate: 21.5 per 10,000 population; Property crime rate: n/a per 10,000 population
Newspapers: The Enterprise (weekly circulation 1,800)
Transportation: Commute: 93.6% car, 1.8% public transportation, 2.2% walk, 2.0% work from home; Mean travel time to work: 20.8 minutes
Additional Information Contacts
City of Mishawaka . . . . (574) 258-1616
http://www.mishawakacity.com

NEW CARLISLE (town). Covers a land area of 2.085 square miles and a water area of 0 square miles. Located at 41.71° N. Lat; 86.51° W. Long. Elevation is 814 feet.
History: New Carlisle was founded in 1835 and named for its founder, Richard R. Carlisle, who was an adventurer. The town became a trading center for the surrounding farm lands.
Population: 1,867; Growth (since 2000): 24.1%; Density: 895.5 persons per square mile; Race: 96.6% White, 0.5% Black/African American, 1.7% Asian, 0.2% American Indian/Alaska Native, 0.0% Native Hawaiian/Other Pacific Islander, 1.0% Two or more races, 2.4% Hispanic of any race; Average household size: 2.70; Median age: 36.7; Age under 18: 26.7%; Age 65 and over: 13.9%; Males per 100 females: 91.9; Marriage status: 26.8% never married, 56.3% now married, 2.1% separated, 6.2% widowed, 10.7% divorced; Foreign born: 2.5%; Speak English only: 97.4%; With disability: 10.1%; Veterans: 7.7%; Ancestry: 31.6% German, 15.5% Irish, 9.0% English, 8.6% Polish, 6.0% American
Employment: 8.7% management, business, and financial, 4.3% computer, engineering, and science, 14.9% education, legal, community service, arts, and media, 5.1% healthcare practitioners, 18.1% service, 28.0% sales and office, 7.3% natural resources, construction, and maintenance, 13.6% production, transportation, and material moving
Income: Per capita: $23,582; Median household: $54,722; Average household: $62,187; Households with income of $100,000 or more: 15.6%; Poverty rate: 11.7%
Educational Attainment: High school diploma or higher: 92.5%; Bachelor's degree or higher: 24.9%; Graduate/professional degree or higher: 7.9%

School District(s)

New Prairie United School Corp (PK-12)
Enrollment: 2,537 . . . . (574) 654-7273
Housing: Homeownership rate: 74.9%; Median home value: $135,700; Median year structure built: 1970; Homeowner vacancy rate: 3.9%; Median selected monthly owner costs: $1,010 with a mortgage, $374 without a mortgage; Median gross rent: $711 per month; Rental vacancy rate: 4.9%
Health Insurance: 93.2% have insurance; 75.4% have private insurance; 28.9% have public insurance; 6.8% do not have insurance; 0.6% of children under 18 do not have insurance
Transportation: Commute: 91.4% car, 0.7% public transportation, 2.2% walk, 3.2% work from home; Mean travel time to work: 23.9 minutes

NORTH LIBERTY (town). Covers a land area of 0.980 square miles and a water area of 0 square miles. Located at 41.53° N. Lat; 86.43° W. Long. Elevation is 732 feet.
History: Laid out 1836.
Population: 1,939; Growth (since 2000): 38.3%; Density: 1,977.6 persons per square mile; Race: 98.8% White, 0.0% Black/African American, 0.4% Asian, 0.0% American Indian/Alaska Native, 0.0% Native Hawaiian/Other Pacific Islander, 0.6% Two or more races, 3.9% Hispanic of any race; Average household size: 2.74; Median age: 31.1; Age under 18: 37.6%; Age 65 and over: 11.3%; Males per 100 females: 87.5; Marriage status: 23.5% never married, 53.5% now married, 0.5% separated, 6.1% widowed, 16.8% divorced; Foreign born: 0.5%; Speak English only: 99.1%; With disability: 14.2%; Veterans: 7.4%; Ancestry: 22.0% German, 13.7% Irish, 8.9% Polish, 5.8% American, 5.2% Scottish
Employment: 13.4% management, business, and financial, 2.6% computer, engineering, and science, 10.4% education, legal, community service, arts, and media, 7.2% healthcare practitioners, 19.3% service, 21.1% sales and office, 10.4% natural resources, construction, and maintenance, 15.5% production, transportation, and material moving
Income: Per capita: $19,971; Median household: $41,250; Average household: $53,849; Households with income of $100,000 or more: 15.6%; Poverty rate: 18.7%
Educational Attainment: High school diploma or higher: 90.9%; Bachelor's degree or higher: 19.6%; Graduate/professional degree or higher: 4.1%

School District(s)

John Glenn School Corporation (PK-12)
Enrollment: 1,668 . . . . (574) 586-3129
Housing: Homeownership rate: 65.6%; Median home value: $103,000; Median year structure built: 1956; Homeowner vacancy rate: 3.3%; Median selected monthly owner costs: $1,067 with a mortgage, $366 without a mortgage; Median gross rent: $475 per month; Rental vacancy rate: 3.2%
Health Insurance: 90.8% have insurance; 66.0% have private insurance; 35.4% have public insurance; 9.2% do not have insurance; 5.8% of children under 18 do not have insurance
Transportation: Commute: 95.8% car, 0.4% public transportation, 1.0% walk, 2.7% work from home; Mean travel time to work: 26.2 minutes

NOTRE DAME (CDP). Covers a land area of 1.208 square miles and a water area of 0.066 square miles. Located at 41.70° N. Lat; 86.24° W. Long.
History: Notre Dame is located north of South Bend in St. Joseph County, Indiana, and it includes the campuses of three colleges: University of Notre Dame, Saint Mary's College, and Holy Cross College.
Population: 6,720; Growth (since 2000): n/a; Density: 5,562.7 persons per square mile; Race: 82.6% White, 3.0% Black/African American, 9.6% Asian, 0.1% American Indian/Alaska Native, 0.0% Native Hawaiian/Other Pacific Islander, 4.3% Two or more races, 7.4% Hispanic of any race; Average household size: 2.29; Median age: 20.6; Age under 18: 0.3%; Age 65 and over: 1.0%; Males per 100 females: 111.5; Marriage status: 97.7% never married, 0.7% now married, 0.0% separated, 0.3% widowed, 1.4% divorced; Foreign born: 10.0%; Speak English only: 84.9%; With disability: 5.9%; Veterans: 1.0%; Ancestry: 25.5% Irish, 20.0% German, 12.2% Italian, 6.3% Polish, 5.0% English
Employment: 5.3% management, business, and financial, 6.6% computer, engineering, and science, 32.4% education, legal, community service, arts, and media, 0.4% healthcare practitioners, 20.1% service, 30.2% sales and office, 2.0% natural resources, construction, and maintenance, 3.0% production, transportation, and material moving
Income: Per capita: $5,995; Median household: $15,625; Average household: $18,193; Households with income of $100,000 or more: n/a; Poverty rate: 80.2%
Educational Attainment: High school diploma or higher: 96.1%; Bachelor's degree or higher: 76.5%; Graduate/professional degree or higher: 37.1%

Four-year College(s)

Holy Cross College (Private, Not-for-profit, Roman Catholic)
Enrollment: 557 . . . . (574) 239-8377
Tuition: In-state $29,734; Out-of-state $29,734
Saint Mary's College (Private, Not-for-profit, Roman Catholic)
Enrollment: 1,637 . . . . (574) 284-4000
Tuition: In-state $40,800; Out-of-state $40,800
University of Notre Dame (Private, Not-for-profit, Roman Catholic)
Enrollment: 12,467 . . . . (574) 631-5000
Tuition: In-state $51,505; Out-of-state $51,505

Housing: Homeownership rate: n/a; Median home value: n/a; Median year structure built: 1993; Homeowner vacancy rate: 0.0%; Median selected monthly owner costs: n/a with a mortgage, n/a without a mortgage; Median gross rent: $646 per month; Rental vacancy rate: 3.2%
Health Insurance: 97.5% have insurance; 95.4% have private insurance; 4.3% have public insurance; 2.5% do not have insurance; 0.7% of children under 18 do not have insurance
Transportation: Commute: 10.4% car, 0.2% public transportation, 70.5% walk, 12.3% work from home; Mean travel time to work: 10.6 minutes

OSCEOLA (town). Covers a land area of 1.357 square miles and a water area of 0.007 square miles. Located at 41.66° N. Lat; 86.08° W. Long. Elevation is 738 feet.
Population: 2,712; Growth (since 2000): 45.9%; Density: 1,999.0 persons per square mile; Race: 91.0% White, 0.3% Black/African American, 5.6% Asian, 0.1% American Indian/Alaska Native, 0.0% Native Hawaiian/Other Pacific Islander, 2.7% Two or more races, 4.9% Hispanic of any race; Average household size: 2.92; Median age: 38.3; Age under 18: 27.1%; Age 65 and over: 16.2%; Males per 100 females: 102.4; Marriage status: 25.2% never married, 59.9% now married, 0.1% separated, 5.5% widowed, 9.5% divorced; Foreign born: 6.2%; Speak English only: 91.3%; With disability: 12.2%; Veterans: 7.6%; Ancestry: 21.9% German, 14.6% American, 12.5% Irish, 9.5% English, 8.5% Polish
Employment: 9.9% management, business, and financial, 3.1% computer, engineering, and science, 9.9% education, legal, community service, arts, and media, 8.0% healthcare practitioners, 8.9% service, 27.0% sales and office, 6.9% natural resources, construction, and maintenance, 26.3% production, transportation, and material moving
Income: Per capita: $23,680; Median household: $58,083; Average household: $65,121; Households with income of $100,000 or more: 13.8%; Poverty rate: 6.7%
Educational Attainment: High school diploma or higher: 84.3%; Bachelor's degree or higher: 18.7%; Graduate/professional degree or higher: 6.0%

School District(s)

Penn-Harris-Madison School Corp (PK-12)
Enrollment: 10,051 . . . . (574) 259-7941

Housing: Homeownership rate: 87.5%; Median home value: $109,200; Median year structure built: 1964; Homeowner vacancy rate: 0.0%; Median selected monthly owner costs: $1,026 with a mortgage, $285 without a mortgage; Median gross rent: $972 per month; Rental vacancy rate: 0.0%
Health Insurance: 91.6% have insurance; 73.5% have private insurance; 26.8% have public insurance; 8.4% do not have insurance; 0.0% of children under 18 do not have insurance
Transportation: Commute: 95.7% car, 0.5% public transportation, 0.4% walk, 2.5% work from home; Mean travel time to work: 24.9 minutes

ROSELAND (town). Covers a land area of 0.383 square miles and a water area of 0 square miles. Located at 41.72° N. Lat; 86.25° W. Long. Elevation is 728 feet.
History: Wild roses that grew in the countryside were the inspiration for the name of Roseland. In 1855 St. Mary's College was founded here by the Roman Catholic Church as a sister institution to Notre Dame University.
Population: 484; Growth (since 2000): -73.2%; Density: 1,264.4 persons per square mile; Race: 87.8% White, 7.4% Black/African American, 1.9% Asian, 0.6% American Indian/Alaska Native, 0.0% Native Hawaiian/Other Pacific Islander, 1.4% Two or more races, 9.7% Hispanic of any race; Average household size: 2.17; Median age: 37.9; Age under 18: 10.5%; Age 65 and over: 18.6%; Males per 100 females: 95.7; Marriage status: 36.9% never married, 38.1% now married, 0.7% separated, 8.5% widowed, 16.5% divorced; Foreign born: 14.0%; Speak English only: 89.3%; With disability: 26.8%; Veterans: 5.1%; Ancestry: 22.1% German, 15.9% Irish, 13.6% Polish, 8.9% American, 8.3% Italian
Employment: 12.1% management, business, and financial, 7.7% computer, engineering, and science, 18.2% education, legal, community service, arts, and media, 5.3% healthcare practitioners, 18.6% service, 15.8% sales and office, 6.5% natural resources, construction, and maintenance, 15.8% production, transportation, and material moving
Income: Per capita: $26,143; Median household: $40,625; Average household: $53,687; Households with income of $100,000 or more: 5.8%; Poverty rate: 25.6%
Educational Attainment: High school diploma or higher: 92.8%; Bachelor's degree or higher: 34.3%; Graduate/professional degree or higher: 12.4%
Housing: Homeownership rate: 57.8%; Median home value: $84,300; Median year structure built: 1958; Homeowner vacancy rate: 2.8%; Median selected monthly owner costs: $844 with a mortgage, $276 without a mortgage; Median gross rent: $695 per month; Rental vacancy rate: 8.4%
Health Insurance: 93.2% have insurance; 68.9% have private insurance; 32.0% have public insurance; 6.8% do not have insurance; 3.7% of children under 18 do not have insurance
Transportation: Commute: 84.0% car, 1.6% public transportation, 5.8% walk, 2.1% work from home; Mean travel time to work: 17.5 minutes

SOUTH BEND (city). County seat. Covers a land area of 41.458 square miles and a water area of 0.417 square miles. Located at 41.68° N. Lat; 86.27° W. Long. Elevation is 692 feet.
History: South Bend was founded in 1823 by Alexis Coquillard, who called it Big St. Joseph Station. The location at a bend of the St. Joseph River caused settlers to refer to their community as The Bend, and in 1830 the Post Office officially named it South Bend. Early industries in South Bend were the Studebaker blacksmith and wagon shop which later became an automobile manufacturer, and the Oliver Chilled Plow Works, which used a process for chilling and hardening steel to increase its uses.
Population: 101,928; Growth (since 2000): -5.4%; Density: 2,458.6 persons per square mile; Race: 63.1% White, 26.4% Black/African American, 1.4% Asian, 0.5% American Indian/Alaska Native, 0.1% Native Hawaiian/Other Pacific Islander, 4.2% Two or more races, 14.4% Hispanic of any race; Average household size: 2.54; Median age: 33.4; Age under 18: 26.8%; Age 65 and over: 12.6%; Males per 100 females: 93.9; Marriage status: 41.5% never married, 38.9% now married, 2.4% separated, 6.5% widowed, 13.1% divorced; Foreign born: 8.5%; Speak English only: 85.1%; With disability: 15.4%; Veterans: 6.2%; Ancestry: 15.9% German, 9.3% Irish, 8.0% Polish, 4.9% English, 4.5% American
Employment: 9.7% management, business, and financial, 3.9% computer, engineering, and science, 11.9% education, legal, community service, arts, and media, 5.1% healthcare practitioners, 21.8% service, 22.8% sales and office, 5.3% natural resources, construction, and maintenance, 19.4% production, transportation, and material moving
Income: Per capita: $21,100; Median household: $37,441; Average household: $52,434; Households with income of $100,000 or more: 10.9%; Poverty rate: 25.4%
Educational Attainment: High school diploma or higher: 83.4%; Bachelor's degree or higher: 24.3%; Graduate/professional degree or higher: 9.8%

School District(s)

Career Academy High School (09-12)
Enrollment: 266. . . . . (574) 299-9800
Career Academy Middle School (05-08)
Enrollment: 399. . . . . (574) 299-9800
Excel Center - South Bend (09-12)
Enrollment: 360. . . . . (574) 472-7330
South Bend Community School Corp (PK-12)
Enrollment: 20,274 . . . . (574) 283-8000
Success Academy Primary School (KG-04)
Enrollment: 475. . . . . (574) 299-9800
Veritas Academy (KG-08)
Enrollment: 90. . . . . (574) 287-3230
Xavier School Of Excellence (KG-08)
Enrollment: 214. . . . . (574) 231-6600

Four-year College(s)

Brown Mackie College-South Bend (Private, For-profit)
Enrollment: n/a . . . . (574) 237-0774
Indiana University-South Bend (Public)
Enrollment: 5,385 . . . . (574) 520-4872
Tuition: In-state $7,207; Out-of-state $19,038
Radiological Technologies University VT (Private, For-profit)
Enrollment: 99. . . . . (574) 232-2408

Housing: Homeownership rate: 57.2%; Median home value: $81,100; Median year structure built: 1955; Homeowner vacancy rate: 2.9%; Median selected monthly owner costs: $905 with a mortgage, $337 without a mortgage; Median gross rent: $741 per month; Rental vacancy rate: 13.2%
Health Insurance: 86.2% have insurance; 56.0% have private insurance; 39.5% have public insurance; 13.8% do not have insurance; 5.6% of children under 18 do not have insurance
Hospitals: Memorial Hospital of South Bend (526 beds)
Safety: Violent crime rate: 104.5 per 10,000 population; Property crime rate: 500.7 per 10,000 population

Newspapers: South Bend Tribune (daily circulation 69,600); Tri County News (weekly circulation 1,000)
Transportation: Commute: 89.4% car, 2.8% public transportation, 3.1% walk, 2.9% work from home; Mean travel time to work: 19.9 minutes; Amtrak: Train service available.
Airports: South Bend International (primary service/non-hub)
Additional Information Contacts
City of South Bend . . . . (574) 235-9221
http://www.ci.south-bend.in.us

WALKERTON (town). Covers a land area of 1.961 square miles and a water area of 0 square miles. Located at 41.47° N. Lat; 86.48° W. Long. Elevation is 725 feet.
History: Walkerton was known as one of the largest peppermint-growing centers in the country.
Population: 2,098; Growth (since 2000): -7.7%; Density: 1,070.0 persons per square mile; Race: 98.0% White, 0.4% Black/African American, 0.0% Asian, 0.4% American Indian/Alaska Native, 0.0% Native Hawaiian/Other Pacific Islander, 0.4% Two or more races, 2.1% Hispanic of any race; Average household size: 2.42; Median age: 40.4; Age under 18: 24.8%; Age 65 and over: 14.9%; Males per 100 females: 88.4; Marriage status: 26.7% never married, 50.3% now married, 1.6% separated, 9.3% widowed, 13.6% divorced; Foreign born: 0.7%; Speak English only: 98.6%; With disability: 14.0%; Veterans: 11.3%; Ancestry: 29.1% German, 23.6% Irish, 9.9% American, 7.1% English, 7.1% Polish
Employment: 11.7% management, business, and financial, 2.4% computer, engineering, and science, 7.8% education, legal, community service, arts, and media, 1.9% healthcare practitioners, 15.0% service, 23.9% sales and office, 7.4% natural resources, construction, and maintenance, 29.9% production, transportation, and material moving
Income: Per capita: $22,604; Median household: $42,600; Average household: $53,806; Households with income of $100,000 or more: 13.3%; Poverty rate: 11.8%
Educational Attainment: High school diploma or higher: 85.7%; Bachelor's degree or higher: 14.8%; Graduate/professional degree or higher: 6.5%

School District(s)

John Glenn School Corporation (PK-12)
Enrollment: 1,668 . . . . (574) 586-3129
Housing: Homeownership rate: 71.6%; Median home value: $92,700; Median year structure built: 1952; Homeowner vacancy rate: 0.0%; Median selected monthly owner costs: $893 with a mortgage, $358 without a mortgage; Median gross rent: $661 per month; Rental vacancy rate: 4.4%
Health Insurance: 92.2% have insurance; 73.5% have private insurance; 33.8% have public insurance; 7.8% do not have insurance; 1.1% of children under 18 do not have insurance
Transportation: Commute: 88.6% car, 0.5% public transportation, 4.9% walk, 1.8% work from home; Mean travel time to work: 26.2 minutes
Additional Information Contacts
Town of Walkerton . . . . (574) 586-3100
http://www.walkerton.org

WYATT (unincorporated postal area)
ZCTA: 46595
Covers a land area of 0.228 square miles and a water area of 0 square miles. Located at 41.53° N. Lat; 86.17° W. Long. Elevation is 830 feet.
Population: 135; Growth (since 2000): 15.4%; Density: 591.8 persons per square mile; Race: 100.0% White, 0.0% Black/African American, 0.0% Asian, 0.0% American Indian/Alaska Native, 0.0% Native Hawaiian/Other Pacific Islander, 0.0% Two or more races, 0.0% Hispanic of any race; Average household size: 2.45; Median age: 26.7; Age under 18: 41.5%; Age 65 and over: 8.9%; Males per 100 females: 89.5; Marriage status: 35.9% never married, 25.0% now married, 0.0% separated, 13.0% widowed, 26.1% divorced; Foreign born: 0.0%; Speak English only: 100.0%; With disability: 9.2%; Veterans: 0.0%; Ancestry: 49.6% German, 28.9% Irish, 22.2% Polish, 11.9% Pennsylvania German, 4.4% Italian
Employment: 0.0% management, business, and financial, 0.0% computer, engineering, and science, 0.0% education, legal, community service, arts, and media, 12.5% healthcare practitioners, 18.8% service, 17.2% sales and office, 25.0% natural resources, construction, and maintenance, 26.6% production, transportation, and material moving
Income: Per capita: $20,020; Median household: $36,641; Average household: $47,293; Households with income of $100,000 or more: 12.7%; Poverty rate: 25.9%
Educational Attainment: High school diploma or higher: 100.0%; Bachelor's degree or higher: 6.8%; Graduate/professional degree or higher: n/a
Housing: Homeownership rate: 100.0%; Median home value: n/a; Median year structure built: 1956; Homeowner vacancy rate: 0.0%; Median selected monthly owner costs: $1,063 with a mortgage, $365 without a mortgage; Median gross rent: n/a per month; Rental vacancy rate: 0.0%
Health Insurance: 73.1% have insurance; 73.1% have private insurance; 9.2% have public insurance; 26.9% do not have insurance; 44.6% of children under 18 do not have insurance
Transportation: Commute: 82.6% car, 10.1% public transportation, 0.0% walk, 0.0% work from home; Mean travel time to work: 35.4 minutes

Scott County

Located in southeastern Indiana; bounded on the north by the Muscatatuck River, and drained by its tributaries. Covers a land area of 190.397 square miles, a water area of 2.351 square miles, and is located in the Eastern Time Zone at 38.68° N. Lat., 85.75° W. Long. The county was founded in 1820. County seat is Scottsburg.

Scott County is part of the Louisville/Jefferson County, KY-IN Metropolitan Statistical Area. The entire metro area includes: Clark County, IN; Floyd County, IN; Harrison County, IN; Scott County, IN; Washington County, IN; Bullitt County, KY; Henry County, KY; Jefferson County, KY; Oldham County, KY; Shelby County, KY; Spencer County, KY; Trimble County, KY

Weather Station: Scottsburg Elevation: 549 feet

	Jan	Feb	Mar	Apr	May	Jun	Jul	Aug	Sep	Oct	Nov	Dec
High	40	44	55	66	75	84	87	87	80	68	55	43
Low	22	24	32	42	53	61	65	63	54	42	34	25
Precip	3.2	2.9	4.3	4.5	5.2	4.2	4.3	4.3	3.1	3.1	3.7	3.5
Snow	3.3	4.1	2.5	0.1	0.0	0.0	0.0	0.0	0.0	0.2	0.1	2.5

High and Low temperatures in degrees Fahrenheit; Precipitation and Snow in inches

Population: 23,722; Growth (since 2000): 3.3%; Density: 124.6 persons per square mile; Race: 97.6% White, 0.3% Black/African American, 0.4% Asian, 0.2% American Indian/Alaska Native, 0.0% Native Hawaiian/Other Pacific Islander, 1.3% two or more races, 2.1% Hispanic of any race; Average household size: 2.63; Median age: 40.7; Age under 18: 23.2%; Age 65 and over: 15.9%; Males per 100 females: 97.7; Marriage status: 25.1% never married, 56.6% now married, 1.1% separated, 6.0% widowed, 12.3% divorced; Foreign born: 1.2%; Speak English only: 97.1%; With disability: 17.9%; Veterans: 7.6%; Ancestry: 14.9% German, 14.5% American, 10.6% English, 9.8% Irish, 3.0% Scottish
Religion: Six largest groups: 25.8% Baptist, 4.1% Non-denominational Protestant, 3.7% Pentecostal, 2.9% Methodist/Pietist, 1.7% Catholicism, 1.0% Latter-day Saints
Economy: Unemployment rate: 4.1%; Leading industries: 20.3 % retail trade; 13.0 % health care and social assistance; 10.2 % other services (except public administration); Farms: 321 totaling 51,472 acres; Company size: 0 employ 1,000 or more persons, 1 employs 500 to 999 persons, 14 employ 100 to 499 persons, 369 employ less than 100 persons; Business ownership: 395 women-owned, n/a Black-owned, n/a Hispanic-owned, n/a Asian-owned, n/a American Indian/Alaska Native-owned
Employment: 8.1% management, business, and financial, 2.0% computer, engineering, and science, 8.1% education, legal, community service, arts, and media, 4.7% healthcare practitioners, 15.7% service, 19.8% sales and office, 8.5% natural resources, construction, and maintenance, 33.1% production, transportation, and material moving
Income: Per capita: $24,186; Median household: $49,243; Average household: $62,721; Households with income of $100,000 or more: 17.6%; Poverty rate: 13.7%
Educational Attainment: High school diploma or higher: 84.9%; Bachelor's degree or higher: 12.9%; Graduate/professional degree or higher: 5.1%
Housing: Homeownership rate: 75.0%; Median home value: $98,800; Median year structure built: 1977; Homeowner vacancy rate: 2.9%; Median selected monthly owner costs: $996 with a mortgage, $394 without a mortgage; Median gross rent: $769 per month; Rental vacancy rate: 10.0%
Vital Statistics: Birth rate: 124.4 per 10,000 population; Death rate: 126.9 per 10,000 population; Age-adjusted cancer mortality rate: 272.1 deaths per 100,000 population

Health Insurance: 90.7% have insurance; 71.1% have private insurance; 33.6% have public insurance; 9.3% do not have insurance; 5.0% of children under 18 do not have insurance
Health Care: Physicians: 6.7 per 10,000 population; Dentists: 2.5 per 10,000 population; Hospital beds: 10.5 per 10,000 population; Hospital admissions: 348.8 per 10,000 population
Transportation: Commute: 94.8% car, 0.0% public transportation, 0.7% walk, 2.9% work from home; Mean travel time to work: 26.0 minutes
2016 Presidential Election: 66.7% Trump, 29.0% Clinton, 3.8% Johnson, 0.3% Stein
Additional Information Contacts
Scott Government .... (812) 752-8420

Scott County Communities

AUSTIN (city). Covers a land area of 2.577 square miles and a water area of 0 square miles. Located at 38.74° N. Lat; 85.81° W. Long. Elevation is 558 feet.
History: The Morgan Packing Company plant established the community of Austin as a canning center.
Population: 3,960; Growth (since 2000): -16.2%; Density: 1,536.7 persons per square mile; Race: 98.0% White, 0.0% Black/African American, 0.0% Asian, 0.9% American Indian/Alaska Native, 0.0% Native Hawaiian/Other Pacific Islander, 0.8% Two or more races, 3.6% Hispanic of any race; Average household size: 2.60; Median age: 39.7; Age under 18: 25.2%; Age 65 and over: 15.7%; Males per 100 females: 94.7; Marriage status: 26.0% never married, 54.0% now married, 1.2% separated, 7.2% widowed, 12.8% divorced; Foreign born: 1.5%; Speak English only: 96.4%; With disability: 19.5%; Veterans: 6.2%; Ancestry: 11.9% American, 10.1% German, 6.9% Irish, 6.4% English, 1.5% Polish
Employment: 5.6% management, business, and financial, 2.3% computer, engineering, and science, 6.4% education, legal, community service, arts, and media, 3.7% healthcare practitioners, 18.9% service, 15.4% sales and office, 2.7% natural resources, construction, and maintenance, 44.9% production, transportation, and material moving
Income: Per capita: $15,915; Median household: $34,920; Average household: $40,382; Households with income of $100,000 or more: 4.6%; Poverty rate: 25.5%
Educational Attainment: High school diploma or higher: 72.4%; Bachelor's degree or higher: 6.8%; Graduate/professional degree or higher: 1.4%

School District(s)
Scott County School District 1 (PK-12)
Enrollment: 1,258 .... (812) 794-8750
Housing: Homeownership rate: 67.2%; Median home value: $72,900; Median year structure built: 1968; Homeowner vacancy rate: 0.0%; Median selected monthly owner costs: $918 with a mortgage, $309 without a mortgage; Median gross rent: $758 per month; Rental vacancy rate: 14.7%
Health Insurance: 89.8% have insurance; 63.3% have private insurance; 38.9% have public insurance; 10.2% do not have insurance; 4.3% of children under 18 do not have insurance
Transportation: Commute: 96.6% car, 0.0% public transportation, 0.0% walk, 1.2% work from home; Mean travel time to work: 20.0 minutes
Additional Information Contacts
Town of Austin.................................... (812) 752-4080
http://www.greatscottindiana.com

SCOTTSBURG (city). County seat. Covers a land area of 5.053 square miles and a water area of 0.019 square miles. Located at 38.69° N. Lat; 85.78° W. Long. Elevation is 564 feet.
History: Laid out 1871.
Population: 6,687; Growth (since 2000): 10.7%; Density: 1,323.4 persons per square mile; Race: 97.4% White, 0.9% Black/African American, 0.3% Asian, 0.2% American Indian/Alaska Native, 0.0% Native Hawaiian/Other Pacific Islander, 1.0% Two or more races, 2.9% Hispanic of any race; Average household size: 2.48; Median age: 37.2; Age under 18: 20.3%; Age 65 and over: 15.9%; Males per 100 females: 90.4; Marriage status: 29.2% never married, 52.2% now married, 2.0% separated, 6.0% widowed, 12.6% divorced; Foreign born: 0.3%; Speak English only: 95.3%; With disability: 19.2%; Veterans: 8.4%; Ancestry: 15.8% German, 15.7% English, 11.8% Irish, 10.3% American, 2.7% Scottish
Employment: 10.5% management, business, and financial, 2.8% computer, engineering, and science, 9.9% education, legal, community service, arts, and media, 4.2% healthcare practitioners, 13.8% service, 22.6% sales and office, 10.2% natural resources, construction, and maintenance, 26.2% production, transportation, and material moving
Income: Per capita: $23,077; Median household: $46,090; Average household: $57,702; Households with income of $100,000 or more: 20.8%; Poverty rate: 15.4%
Educational Attainment: High school diploma or higher: 88.1%; Bachelor's degree or higher: 15.1%; Graduate/professional degree or higher: 3.6%

School District(s)
Scott County School District 2 (PK-12)
Enrollment: 2,583 .... (812) 752-8946
Housing: Homeownership rate: 59.9%; Median home value: $97,200; Median year structure built: 1971; Homeowner vacancy rate: 4.0%; Median selected monthly owner costs: $970 with a mortgage, $382 without a mortgage; Median gross rent: $754 per month; Rental vacancy rate: 8.5%
Health Insurance: 92.0% have insurance; 68.5% have private insurance; 38.1% have public insurance; 8.0% do not have insurance; 0.7% of children under 18 do not have insurance
Hospitals: Scott Memorial Hospital (90 beds)
Safety: Violent crime rate: n/a per 10,000 population; Property crime rate: 460.3 per 10,000 population
Transportation: Commute: 94.6% car, 0.0% public transportation, 1.2% walk, 1.9% work from home; Mean travel time to work: 25.3 minutes
Additional Information Contacts
City of Scottsburg .... (812) 752-4343
http://www.cityofscottsburg.com

UNDERWOOD (unincorporated postal area)
ZCTA: 47177
Covers a land area of 16.667 square miles and a water area of 0.119 square miles. Located at 38.59° N. Lat; 85.79° W. Long..
Population: 1,014; Growth (since 2000): 63.5%; Density: 60.8 persons per square mile; Race: 93.0% White, 0.0% Black/African American, 0.0% Asian, 0.0% American Indian/Alaska Native, 0.0% Native Hawaiian/Other Pacific Islander, 0.0% Two or more races, 7.0% Hispanic of any race; Average household size: 2.29; Median age: 49.6; Age under 18: 17.4%; Age 65 and over: 16.0%; Males per 100 females: 102.8; Marriage status: 23.4% never married, 57.3% now married, 0.9% separated, 7.8% widowed, 11.6% divorced; Foreign born: 1.9%; Speak English only: 94.6%; With disability: 23.1%; Veterans: 4.7%; Ancestry: 21.6% German, 19.3% American, 11.0% Irish, 4.9% Italian, 3.6% Scottish
Employment: 7.7% management, business, and financial, 2.0% computer, engineering, and science, 11.5% education, legal, community service, arts, and media, 2.0% healthcare practitioners, 14.9% service, 28.9% sales and office, 10.2% natural resources, construction, and maintenance, 22.8% production, transportation, and material moving
Income: Per capita: $30,913; Median household: $51,111; Average household: $68,752; Households with income of $100,000 or more: 13.8%; Poverty rate: 20.0%
Educational Attainment: High school diploma or higher: 84.3%; Bachelor's degree or higher: 7.9%; Graduate/professional degree or higher: 2.7%
Housing: Homeownership rate: 88.0%; Median home value: $110,000; Median year structure built: 1982; Homeowner vacancy rate: 3.0%; Median selected monthly owner costs: $1,012 with a mortgage, $322 without a mortgage; Median gross rent: n/a per month; Rental vacancy rate: 0.0%
Health Insurance: 86.4% have insurance; 66.0% have private insurance; 31.2% have public insurance; 13.6% do not have insurance; 20.5% of children under 18 do not have insurance
Transportation: Commute: 95.5% car, 0.0% public transportation, 0.0% walk, 4.5% work from home; Mean travel time to work: 25.2 minutes

Shelby County

Located in central Indiana; drained by the Big Blue River. Covers a land area of 411.147 square miles, a water area of 1.609 square miles, and is located in the Eastern Time Zone at 39.52° N. Lat., 85.79° W. Long. The county was founded in 1821. County seat is Shelbyville.

Shelby County is part of the Indianapolis-Carmel-Anderson, IN Metropolitan Statistical Area. The entire metro area includes: Boone County, IN; Brown County, IN; Hamilton County, IN; Hancock County, IN;

Hendricks County, IN; Johnson County, IN; Madison County, IN; Marion County, IN; Morgan County, IN; Putnam County, IN; Shelby County, IN

Weather Station: Shelbyville Sewage Plant Elevation: 750 feet

	Jan	Feb	Mar	Apr	May	Jun	Jul	Aug	Sep	Oct	Nov	Dec
High	36	40	51	63	73	82	85	84	78	66	53	39
Low	20	22	31	42	52	61	64	62	54	43	34	23
Precip	2.8	2.4	3.3	4.2	5.0	4.1	4.0	3.3	3.0	2.9	3.2	3.0
Snow	2.4	1.7	0.9	tr	0.0	0.0	0.0	0.0	0.0	tr	tr	0.8

High and Low temperatures in degrees Fahrenheit; Precipitation and Snow in inches

Population: 44,339; Growth (since 2000): 2.1%; Density: 107.8 persons per square mile; Race: 94.4% White, 1.0% Black/African American, 0.7% Asian, 0.1% American Indian/Alaska Native, 0.0% Native Hawaiian/Other Pacific Islander, 1.4% two or more races, 4.0% Hispanic of any race; Average household size: 2.48; Median age: 41.3; Age under 18: 23.1%; Age 65 and over: 15.8%; Males per 100 females: 98.2; Marriage status: 24.0% never married, 54.9% now married, 1.6% separated, 7.8% widowed, 13.2% divorced; Foreign born: 2.3%; Speak English only: 95.8%; With disability: 13.8%; Veterans: 9.2%; Ancestry: 24.1% German, 17.8% American, 12.7% Irish, 8.4% English, 1.6% Italian
Religion: Six largest groups: 10.8% Baptist, 8.1% Catholicism, 5.7% Methodist/Pietist, 4.9% Non-denominational Protestant, 2.1% Presbyterian-Reformed, 1.8% Holiness
Economy: Unemployment rate: 3.1%; Leading industries: 12.9 % retail trade; 12.8 % construction; 10.6 % other services (except public administration); Farms: 569 totaling 233,059 acres; Company size: 0 employ 1,000 or more persons, 6 employ 500 to 999 persons, 22 employ 100 to 499 persons, 899 employ less than 100 persons; Business ownership: 1,096 women-owned, n/a Black-owned, 56 Hispanic-owned, n/a Asian-owned, n/a American Indian/Alaska Native-owned
Employment: 12.6% management, business, and financial, 3.0% computer, engineering, and science, 7.2% education, legal, community service, arts, and media, 6.0% healthcare practitioners, 17.1% service, 19.9% sales and office, 11.4% natural resources, construction, and maintenance, 22.9% production, transportation, and material moving
Income: Per capita: $27,317; Median household: $57,216; Average household: $67,800; Households with income of $100,000 or more: 19.9%; Poverty rate: 10.6%
Educational Attainment: High school diploma or higher: 88.1%; Bachelor's degree or higher: 18.0%; Graduate/professional degree or higher: 6.0%
Housing: Homeownership rate: 73.4%; Median home value: $125,300; Median year structure built: 1967; Homeowner vacancy rate: 0.5%; Median selected monthly owner costs: $1,116 with a mortgage, $399 without a mortgage; Median gross rent: $754 per month; Rental vacancy rate: 9.8%
Vital Statistics: Birth rate: 108.1 per 10,000 population; Death rate: 97.5 per 10,000 population; Age-adjusted cancer mortality rate: 203.8 deaths per 100,000 population
Health Insurance: 90.0% have insurance; 72.5% have private insurance; 29.6% have public insurance; 10.0% do not have insurance; 7.8% of children under 18 do not have insurance
Health Care: Physicians: 7.9 per 10,000 population; Dentists: 3.8 per 10,000 population; Hospital beds: 16.3 per 10,000 population; Hospital admissions: 642.1 per 10,000 population
Air Quality Index (AQI): Percent of Days: 86.0% good, 13.6% moderate, 0.4% unhealthy for sensitive individuals, 0.0% unhealthy, 0.0% very unhealthy; Annual median: 41; Annual maximum: 108
Transportation: Commute: 94.6% car, 0.2% public transportation, 1.8% walk, 2.5% work from home; Mean travel time to work: 23.5 minutes
2016 Presidential Election: 70.7% Trump, 23.6% Clinton, 5.4% Johnson, 0.2% Stein
Additional Information Contacts
Shelby Government. . . . . (317) 392-6330
http://www.co.shelby.in.us

Shelby County Communities

BOGGSTOWN (unincorporated postal area)
ZCTA: 46110
Covers a land area of 14.544 square miles and a water area of 0.092 square miles. Located at 39.56° N. Lat; 85.92° W. Long. Elevation is 748 feet.
Population: 509; Growth (since 2000): 1.6%; Density: 35.0 persons per square mile; Race: 99.2% White, 0.0% Black/African American, 0.0% Asian, 0.0% American Indian/Alaska Native, 0.0% Native Hawaiian/Other Pacific Islander, 0.8% Two or more races, 0.0% Hispanic of any race; Average household size: 2.80; Median age: 31.1; Age under 18: 39.1%; Age 65 and over: 7.9%; Males per 100 females: 106.6; Marriage status: 18.9% never married, 45.1% now married, 5.4% separated, 11.3% widowed, 24.8% divorced; Foreign born: 0.8%; Speak English only: 100.0%; With disability: 1.6%; Veterans: 6.8%; Ancestry: 14.7% American, 14.3% Irish, 8.6% German, 7.9% Italian, 2.9% French
Employment: 0.0% management, business, and financial, 0.0% computer, engineering, and science, 2.6% education, legal, community service, arts, and media, 0.0% healthcare practitioners, 25.4% service, 27.6% sales and office, 16.4% natural resources, construction, and maintenance, 28.0% production, transportation, and material moving
Income: Per capita: $17,787; Median household: $43,214; Average household: $48,112; Households with income of $100,000 or more: 2.2%; Poverty rate: 24.8%
Educational Attainment: High school diploma or higher: 87.2%; Bachelor's degree or higher: 7.3%; Graduate/professional degree or higher: 2.1%
Housing: Homeownership rate: 72.0%; Median home value: $170,800; Median year structure built: 1965; Homeowner vacancy rate: 0.0%; Median selected monthly owner costs: $1,127 with a mortgage, $0 without a mortgage; Median gross rent: $721 per month; Rental vacancy rate: 0.0%
Health Insurance: 90.4% have insurance; 69.0% have private insurance; 36.0% have public insurance; 9.6% do not have insurance; 0.0% of children under 18 do not have insurance
Transportation: Commute: 78.4% car, 0.0% public transportation, 21.6% walk, 0.0% work from home; Mean travel time to work: 13.9 minutes

FAIRLAND (town). Covers a land area of 0.164 square miles and a water area of <.001 square miles. Located at 39.59° N. Lat; 85.86° W. Long. Elevation is 774 feet.
Population: 641; Growth (since 2000): -49.8%; Density: 3,908.7 persons per square mile; Race: 97.7% White, 0.0% Black/African American, 0.0% Asian, 0.0% American Indian/Alaska Native, 0.0% Native Hawaiian/Other Pacific Islander, 1.2% Two or more races, 3.6% Hispanic of any race; Average household size: 2.48; Median age: 41.9; Age under 18: 19.3%; Age 65 and over: 18.6%; Males per 100 females: 93.3; Marriage status: 29.5% never married, 46.7% now married, 0.2% separated, 13.1% widowed, 10.7% divorced; Foreign born: 2.0%; Speak English only: 97.1%; With disability: 13.6%; Veterans: 10.1%; Ancestry: 24.0% German, 22.2% American, 15.6% Irish, 13.6% English, 2.5% Dutch
Employment: 15.2% management, business, and financial, 9.0% computer, engineering, and science, 1.9% education, legal, community service, arts, and media, 1.3% healthcare practitioners, 3.5% service, 32.3% sales and office, 14.2% natural resources, construction, and maintenance, 22.6% production, transportation, and material moving
Income: Per capita: $26,917; Median household: $55,500; Average household: $63,122; Households with income of $100,000 or more: 21.3%; Poverty rate: 7.0%
Educational Attainment: High school diploma or higher: 93.5%; Bachelor's degree or higher: 11.9%; Graduate/professional degree or higher: 4.8%

School District(s)

Northwestern Con School Corp (PK-12)
Enrollment: 1,332 . . . . (317) 835-7461
Housing: Homeownership rate: 83.7%; Median home value: $98,000; Median year structure built: 1950; Homeowner vacancy rate: 0.0%; Median selected monthly owner costs: $1,026 with a mortgage, $291 without a mortgage; Median gross rent: $811 per month; Rental vacancy rate: 8.7%
Health Insurance: 94.5% have insurance; 79.7% have private insurance; 31.7% have public insurance; 5.5% do not have insurance; 3.7% of children under 18 do not have insurance
Transportation: Commute: 95.8% car, 0.0% public transportation, 0.0% walk, 3.5% work from home; Mean travel time to work: 35.2 minutes

FLAT ROCK (unincorporated postal area)
ZCTA: 47234
Covers a land area of 33.039 square miles and a water area of 0 square miles. Located at 39.38° N. Lat; 85.77° W. Long. Elevation is 689 feet.
Population: 1,765; Growth (since 2000): 22.5%; Density: 53.4 persons per square mile; Race: 100.0% White, 0.0% Black/African American, 0.0% Asian, 0.0% American Indian/Alaska Native, 0.0% Native Hawaiian/Other Pacific Islander, 0.0% Two or more races, 0.0%

Hispanic of any race; Average household size: 3.04; Median age: 36.9; Age under 18: 30.5%; Age 65 and over: 11.2%; Males per 100 females: 106.7; Marriage status: 18.9% never married, 67.7% now married, 0.0% separated, 6.7% widowed, 6.8% divorced; Foreign born: 0.0%; Speak English only: 98.9%; With disability: 7.9%; Veterans: 6.8%; Ancestry: 33.1% American, 20.6% German, 11.6% Irish, 5.6% English, 1.5% European

Employment: 10.8% management, business, and financial, 2.7% computer, engineering, and science, 1.2% education, legal, community service, arts, and media, 10.1% healthcare practitioners, 14.3% service, 19.8% sales and office, 15.3% natural resources, construction, and maintenance, 25.8% production, transportation, and material moving

Income: Per capita: $26,627; Median household: $65,179; Average household: $79,981; Households with income of $100,000 or more: 28.1%; Poverty rate: n/a

Educational Attainment: High school diploma or higher: 96.8%; Bachelor's degree or higher: 12.8%; Graduate/professional degree or higher: 2.8%

Housing: Homeownership rate: 86.0%; Median home value: $132,300; Median year structure built: 1951; Homeowner vacancy rate: 0.0%; Median selected monthly owner costs: $1,015 with a mortgage, $376 without a mortgage; Median gross rent: $763 per month; Rental vacancy rate: 0.0%

Health Insurance: 84.9% have insurance; 76.4% have private insurance; 17.8% have public insurance; 15.1% do not have insurance; 21.6% of children under 18 do not have insurance

Transportation: Commute: 97.4% car, 0.0% public transportation, 1.8% walk, 0.8% work from home; Mean travel time to work: 24.4 minutes

FOUNTAINTOWN (unincorporated postal area)

ZCTA: 46130

Covers a land area of 29.775 square miles and a water area of 0.036 square miles. Located at 39.67° N. Lat; 85.84° W. Long. Elevation is 850 feet.

Population: 2,430; Growth (since 2000): 9.5%; Density: 81.6 persons per square mile; Race: 97.0% White, 0.9% Black/African American, 0.0% Asian, 0.0% American Indian/Alaska Native, 0.0% Native Hawaiian/Other Pacific Islander, 2.2% Two or more races, 4.5% Hispanic of any race; Average household size: 2.60; Median age: 43.9; Age under 18: 19.8%; Age 65 and over: 15.9%; Males per 100 females: 102.1; Marriage status: 25.5% never married, 56.4% now married, 0.0% separated, 1.7% widowed, 16.4% divorced; Foreign born: 4.6%; Speak English only: 94.0%; With disability: 12.8%; Veterans: 9.9%; Ancestry: 23.8% German, 21.7% American, 8.1% Irish, 5.8% English, 5.3% French

Employment: 13.6% management, business, and financial, 3.1% computer, engineering, and science, 13.9% education, legal, community service, arts, and media, 9.4% healthcare practitioners, 16.0% service, 13.0% sales and office, 15.8% natural resources, construction, and maintenance, 15.0% production, transportation, and material moving

Income: Per capita: $31,186; Median household: $74,130; Average household: $79,227; Households with income of $100,000 or more: 21.4%; Poverty rate: 1.7%

Educational Attainment: High school diploma or higher: 91.3%; Bachelor's degree or higher: 22.7%; Graduate/professional degree or higher: 2.4%

Housing: Homeownership rate: 83.8%; Median home value: $179,300; Median year structure built: 1967; Homeowner vacancy rate: 0.0%; Median selected monthly owner costs: $1,357 with a mortgage, $399 without a mortgage; Median gross rent: $788 per month; Rental vacancy rate: 0.0%

Health Insurance: 87.5% have insurance; 76.9% have private insurance; 19.7% have public insurance; 12.5% do not have insurance; 0.2% of children under 18 do not have insurance

Transportation: Commute: 86.8% car, 0.0% public transportation, 7.5% walk, 5.0% work from home; Mean travel time to work: 26.4 minutes

GWYNNEVILLE (unincorporated postal area)

ZCTA: 46144

Covers a land area of 0.519 square miles and a water area of 0 square miles. Located at 39.66° N. Lat; 85.65° W. Long. Elevation is 909 feet.

Population: 170; Growth (since 2000): -11.5%; Density: 327.9 persons per square mile; Race: 82.9% White, 0.0% Black/African American, 0.0% Asian, 0.0% American Indian/Alaska Native, 0.0% Native Hawaiian/Other Pacific Islander, 17.1% Two or more races, 0.0% Hispanic of any race; Average household size: 2.13; Median age: 52.7; Age under 18: 10.6%; Age 65 and over: 21.8%; Males per 100 females: 102.9; Marriage status: 13.1% never married, 74.4% now married, 39.4% separated, 12.5% widowed, 0.0% divorced; Foreign born: 0.0%; Speak English only: 95.3%; With disability: 10.6%; Veterans: 6.6%; Ancestry: 35.3% Irish, 30.0% German, 15.9% English, 14.1% Scottish

Employment: 0.0% management, business, and financial, 0.0% computer, engineering, and science, 13.7% education, legal, community service, arts, and media, 0.0% healthcare practitioners, 19.6% service, 19.6% sales and office, 18.6% natural resources, construction, and maintenance, 28.4% production, transportation, and material moving

Income: Per capita: $27,889; Median household: $54,052; Average household: $59,508; Households with income of $100,000 or more: n/a; Poverty rate: n/a

Educational Attainment: High school diploma or higher: 86.3%; Bachelor's degree or higher: 29.5%; Graduate/professional degree or higher: 22.3%

Housing: Homeownership rate: 83.8%; Median home value: $68,600; Median year structure built: 1959; Homeowner vacancy rate: 0.0%; Median selected monthly owner costs: $562 with a mortgage, $0 without a mortgage; Median gross rent: n/a per month; Rental vacancy rate: 0.0%

Health Insurance: 70.0% have insurance; 54.1% have private insurance; 21.8% have public insurance; 30.0% do not have insurance; 100.0% of children under 18 do not have insurance

Transportation: Commute: 62.7% car, 0.0% public transportation, 0.0% walk, 37.3% work from home; Mean travel time to work: 0.0 minutes

MORRISTOWN (town). Covers a land area of 2.348 square miles and a water area of 0.018 square miles. Located at 39.67° N. Lat; 85.70° W. Long. Elevation is 833 feet.

History: Laid out 1828.

Population: 1,228; Growth (since 2000): 8.4%; Density: 523.1 persons per square mile; Race: 98.0% White, 0.0% Black/African American, 0.0% Asian, 0.0% American Indian/Alaska Native, 0.0% Native Hawaiian/Other Pacific Islander, 1.5% Two or more races, 1.3% Hispanic of any race; Average household size: 2.38; Median age: 42.0; Age under 18: 19.0%; Age 65 and over: 19.1%; Males per 100 females: 83.2; Marriage status: 33.3% never married, 45.8% now married, 0.6% separated, 9.0% widowed, 12.0% divorced; Foreign born: 0.0%; Speak English only: 100.0%; With disability: 14.0%; Veterans: 8.4%; Ancestry: 21.7% American, 16.1% German, 11.8% Irish, 9.5% English, 3.0% Scottish

Employment: 12.2% management, business, and financial, 2.9% computer, engineering, and science, 4.9% education, legal, community service, arts, and media, 2.0% healthcare practitioners, 20.8% service, 16.9% sales and office, 15.3% natural resources, construction, and maintenance, 24.9% production, transportation, and material moving

Income: Per capita: $21,457; Median household: $45,104; Average household: $52,995; Households with income of $100,000 or more: 8.6%; Poverty rate: 12.3%

Educational Attainment: High school diploma or higher: 91.3%; Bachelor's degree or higher: 9.6%; Graduate/professional degree or higher: 2.0%

School District(s)

Shelby Eastern Schools (PK-12)
Enrollment: 1,272 . . . . (765) 544-2246

Housing: Homeownership rate: 67.6%; Median home value: $102,200; Median year structure built: 1973; Homeowner vacancy rate: 0.0%; Median selected monthly owner costs: $954 with a mortgage, $455 without a mortgage; Median gross rent: $705 per month; Rental vacancy rate: 0.0%

Health Insurance: 90.8% have insurance; 74.1% have private insurance; 33.2% have public insurance; 9.2% do not have insurance; 2.7% of children under 18 do not have insurance

Transportation: Commute: 89.9% car, 0.0% public transportation, 8.4% walk, 1.7% work from home; Mean travel time to work: 26.5 minutes

SHELBYVILLE (city). County seat. Covers a land area of 11.564 square miles and a water area of 0.285 square miles. Located at 39.53° N. Lat; 85.77° W. Long. Elevation is 764 feet.

History: Shelbyville was laid out in 1822 and named for the first governor of Kentucky. Shelbyville was the home of Vice President Thomas A. Hendricks (1819-1885).

Population: 19,034; Growth (since 2000): 6.0%; Density: 1,646.0 persons per square mile; Race: 89.7% White, 2.1% Black/African American, 1.3% Asian, 0.3% American Indian/Alaska Native, 0.0% Native Hawaiian/Other

Pacific Islander, 1.4% Two or more races, 8.4% Hispanic of any race; Average household size: 2.40; Median age: 36.7; Age under 18: 24.6%; Age 65 and over: 14.2%; Males per 100 females: 95.2; Marriage status: 28.8% never married, 46.1% now married, 2.2% separated, 8.9% widowed, 16.1% divorced; Foreign born: 4.7%; Speak English only: 92.0%; With disability: 16.3%; Veterans: 8.3%; Ancestry: 24.4% German, 17.4% American, 11.0% Irish, 6.9% English, 1.6% European
Employment: 9.8% management, business, and financial, 2.5% computer, engineering, and science, 5.2% education, legal, community service, arts, and media, 5.4% healthcare practitioners, 17.2% service, 22.3% sales and office, 10.5% natural resources, construction, and maintenance, 27.1% production, transportation, and material moving
Income: Per capita: $24,675; Median household: $48,071; Average household: $59,757; Households with income of $100,000 or more: 15.3%; Poverty rate: 16.2%
Educational Attainment: High school diploma or higher: 83.9%; Bachelor's degree or higher: 17.0%; Graduate/professional degree or higher: 6.3%

School District(s)

Blue River Career Programs (09-12)
Enrollment: n/a . . . . (317) 392-4191
Excel Center - Shelbyville (11-11)
Enrollment: 84. . . . . (317) 524-4627
Shelbyville Central Schools (PK-12)
Enrollment: 4,065 . . . . (317) 392-2505
Southwestern Con Sch Shelby Co (PK-12)
Enrollment: 632. . . . . (317) 729-5746

Housing: Homeownership rate: 59.3%; Median home value: $96,300; Median year structure built: 1967; Homeowner vacancy rate: 1.2%; Median selected monthly owner costs: $1,041 with a mortgage, $402 without a mortgage; Median gross rent: $757 per month; Rental vacancy rate: 11.3%
Health Insurance: 88.0% have insurance; 66.9% have private insurance; 32.6% have public insurance; 12.0% do not have insurance; 10.4% of children under 18 do not have insurance
Hospitals: Major Hospital (89 beds)
Safety: Violent crime rate: n/a per 10,000 population; Property crime rate: 279.8 per 10,000 population
Newspapers: Shelbyville News (daily circulation 8,300)
Transportation: Commute: 95.9% car, 0.1% public transportation, 1.6% walk, 1.1% work from home; Mean travel time to work: 19.9 minutes
Airports: Shelbyville Municipal (general aviation)
Additional Information Contacts
City of Shelbyville . . . . (317) 392-5103
http://www.cityofshelbyvillein.com

WALDRON (CDP). Covers a land area of 1.256 square miles and a water area of 0 square miles. Located at 39.45° N. Lat; 85.66° W. Long. Elevation is 823 feet.
Population: 581; Growth (since 2000): n/a; Density: 462.5 persons per square mile; Race: 99.3% White, 0.7% Black/African American, 0.0% Asian, 0.0% American Indian/Alaska Native, 0.0% Native Hawaiian/Other Pacific Islander, 0.0% Two or more races, 0.0% Hispanic of any race; Average household size: 2.26; Median age: 47.2; Age under 18: 15.8%; Age 65 and over: 19.1%; Males per 100 females: 88.7; Marriage status: 20.6% never married, 56.6% now married, 0.0% separated, 13.3% widowed, 9.5% divorced; Foreign born: 0.0%; Speak English only: 97.8%; With disability: 17.6%; Veterans: 6.1%; Ancestry: 26.5% American, 19.4% German, 11.9% English, 4.3% Irish, 2.8% British
Employment: 17.0% management, business, and financial, 2.1% computer, engineering, and science, 5.6% education, legal, community service, arts, and media, 3.5% healthcare practitioners, 25.3% service, 15.6% sales and office, 9.4% natural resources, construction, and maintenance, 21.5% production, transportation, and material moving
Income: Per capita: $29,307; Median household: $64,583; Average household: $71,272; Households with income of $100,000 or more: 19.7%; Poverty rate: 4.7%
Educational Attainment: High school diploma or higher: 86.9%; Bachelor's degree or higher: 6.1%; Graduate/professional degree or higher: n/a

School District(s)

Shelby Eastern Schools (PK-12)
Enrollment: 1,272 . . . . (765) 544-2246

Housing: Homeownership rate: 67.4%; Median home value: $93,800; Median year structure built: 1946; Homeowner vacancy rate: 0.0%; Median selected monthly owner costs: $1,028 with a mortgage, $396 without a mortgage; Median gross rent: $728 per month; Rental vacancy rate: 0.0%
Health Insurance: 87.7% have insurance; 68.0% have private insurance; 32.6% have public insurance; 12.3% do not have insurance; 7.4% of children under 18 do not have insurance
Transportation: Commute: 100.0% car, 0.0% public transportation, 0.0% walk, 0.0% work from home; Mean travel time to work: 23.7 minutes

Spencer County

Located in southwestern Indiana; bounded on the south by the Ohio River and the Kentucky border; drained by the Anderson River and Little Pigeon Creek. Covers a land area of 396.744 square miles, a water area of 4.682 square miles, and is located in the Central Time Zone at 38.01° N. Lat., 87.01° W. Long. The county was founded in 1818. County seat is Rockport.

Weather Station: Saint Meinrad Elevation: 509 feet

	Jan	Feb	Mar	Apr	May	Jun	Jul	Aug	Sep	Oct	Nov	Dec
High	42	47	57	68	76	84	87	87	80	70	57	45
Low	25	28	36	45	54	63	66	65	58	46	38	28
Precip	3.4	3.3	4.4	4.4	5.3	4.1	4.4	3.1	3.7	3.4	4.0	3.8
Snow	2.5	2.1	1.2	tr	0.0	0.0	0.0	0.0	0.0	tr	tr	1.4

High and Low temperatures in degrees Fahrenheit; Precipitation and Snow in inches

Population: 20,610; Growth (since 2000): 1.1%; Density: 51.9 persons per square mile; Race: 96.7% White, 0.6% Black/African American, 0.2% Asian, 0.3% American Indian/Alaska Native, 0.1% Native Hawaiian/Other Pacific Islander, 1.1% two or more races, 2.9% Hispanic of any race; Average household size: 2.51; Median age: 43.2; Age under 18: 22.5%; Age 65 and over: 18.1%; Males per 100 females: 101.3; Marriage status: 21.3% never married, 60.9% now married, 0.4% separated, 7.6% widowed, 10.1% divorced; Foreign born: 1.4%; Speak English only: 96.7%; With disability: 14.9%; Veterans: 9.9%; Ancestry: 34.0% German, 12.8% Irish, 9.3% English, 8.7% American, 2.0% French
Religion: Six largest groups: 20.6% Catholicism, 12.6% Methodist/Pietist, 5.9% Baptist, 2.5% Lutheran, 2.4% Presbyterian-Reformed, 1.5% Holiness
Economy: Unemployment rate: 3.6%; Leading industries: 16.5 % retail trade; 13.2 % other services (except public administration); 11.4 % construction; Farms: 597 totaling 170,406 acres; Company size: 0 employ 1,000 or more persons, 0 employ 500 to 999 persons, 10 employ 100 to 499 persons, 385 employ less than 100 persons; Business ownership: 421 women-owned, n/a Black-owned, n/a Hispanic-owned, n/a Asian-owned, n/a American Indian/Alaska Native-owned
Employment: 13.2% management, business, and financial, 2.9% computer, engineering, and science, 7.1% education, legal, community service, arts, and media, 5.4% healthcare practitioners, 14.4% service, 20.8% sales and office, 12.0% natural resources, construction, and maintenance, 24.3% production, transportation, and material moving
Income: Per capita: $29,114; Median household: $55,280; Average household: $71,264; Households with income of $100,000 or more: 19.0%; Poverty rate: 9.7%
Educational Attainment: High school diploma or higher: 89.8%; Bachelor's degree or higher: 15.9%; Graduate/professional degree or higher: 5.6%
Housing: Homeownership rate: 82.0%; Median home value: $117,900; Median year structure built: 1977; Homeowner vacancy rate: 1.5%; Median selected monthly owner costs: $1,021 with a mortgage, $393 without a mortgage; Median gross rent: $650 per month; Rental vacancy rate: 7.7%
Vital Statistics: Birth rate: 90.7 per 10,000 population; Death rate: 116.7 per 10,000 population; Age-adjusted cancer mortality rate: 137.2 deaths per 100,000 population
Health Insurance: 93.5% have insurance; 77.9% have private insurance; 31.1% have public insurance; 6.5% do not have insurance; 2.8% of children under 18 do not have insurance
Health Care: Physicians: 4.4 per 10,000 population; Dentists: 2.9 per 10,000 population; Hospital beds: 0.0 per 10,000 population; Hospital admissions: 0.0 per 10,000 population
Air Quality Index (AQI): Percent of Days: 79.7% good, 20.3% moderate, 0.0% unhealthy for sensitive individuals, 0.0% unhealthy, 0.0% very unhealthy; Annual median: 32; Annual maximum: 67
Transportation: Commute: 92.3% car, 0.2% public transportation, 1.0% walk, 5.3% work from home; Mean travel time to work: 26.8 minutes
2016 Presidential Election: 65.9% Trump, 28.7% Clinton, 5.3% Johnson, 0.2% Stein

National and State Parks: Lincoln Boyhood National Memorial; Lincoln State Park; Nancy Hanks Lincoln State Memorial; Spencer County State Forest

Additional Information Contacts

Spencer Government . . . . (812) 649-2242
http://spencercounty.in.gov

Spencer County Communities

CHRISNEY (town). Covers a land area of 0.706 square miles and a water area of 0.029 square miles. Located at 38.01° N. Lat; 87.03° W. Long. Elevation is 469 feet.

Population: 546; Growth (since 2000): 0.4%; Density: 773.7 persons per square mile; Race: 97.8% White, 0.0% Black/African American, 0.0% Asian, 0.0% American Indian/Alaska Native, 0.0% Native Hawaiian/Other Pacific Islander, 2.2% Two or more races, 2.4% Hispanic of any race; Average household size: 2.60; Median age: 40.8; Age under 18: 21.4%; Age 65 and over: 15.4%; Males per 100 females: 89.4; Marriage status: 23.4% never married, 59.4% now married, 2.0% separated, 5.5% widowed, 11.8% divorced; Foreign born: 1.6%; Speak English only: 98.2%; With disability: 18.1%; Veterans: 14.9%; Ancestry: 36.8% German, 21.2% Irish, 11.5% English, 6.0% American, 4.8% French

Employment: 12.7% management, business, and financial, 2.1% computer, engineering, and science, 5.3% education, legal, community service, arts, and media, 4.9% healthcare practitioners, 14.1% service, 26.4% sales and office, 4.6% natural resources, construction, and maintenance, 29.9% production, transportation, and material moving

Income: Per capita: $23,220; Median household: $51,875; Average household: $56,509; Households with income of $100,000 or more: 11.9%; Poverty rate: 15.0%

Educational Attainment: High school diploma or higher: 91.6%; Bachelor's degree or higher: 17.2%; Graduate/professional degree or higher: 4.7%

School District(s)

North Spencer County Sch Corp (PK-12)
Enrollment: 2,087 . . . . (812) 937-2400

Housing: Homeownership rate: 77.6%; Median home value: $73,500; Median year structure built: 1954; Homeowner vacancy rate: 3.6%; Median selected monthly owner costs: $943 with a mortgage, $427 without a mortgage; Median gross rent: $436 per month; Rental vacancy rate: 11.3%

Health Insurance: 95.4% have insurance; 77.1% have private insurance; 33.5% have public insurance; 4.6% do not have insurance; 0.0% of children under 18 do not have insurance

Transportation: Commute: 95.7% car, 0.0% public transportation, 0.0% walk, 2.8% work from home; Mean travel time to work: 30.5 minutes

DALE (town). Covers a land area of 1.546 square miles and a water area of 0.010 square miles. Located at 38.17° N. Lat; 86.99° W. Long. Elevation is 466 feet.

History: Dale was named for Robert Dale Owen, who founded the colony at New Harmony.

Population: 1,552; Growth (since 2000): -1.0%; Density: 1,003.7 persons per square mile; Race: 89.2% White, 0.0% Black/African American, 0.0% Asian, 0.3% American Indian/Alaska Native, 1.0% Native Hawaiian/Other Pacific Islander, 1.5% Two or more races, 22.4% Hispanic of any race; Average household size: 2.35; Median age: 42.2; Age under 18: 24.9%; Age 65 and over: 22.7%; Males per 100 females: 101.6; Marriage status: 21.3% never married, 55.2% now married, 0.6% separated, 11.2% widowed, 12.4% divorced; Foreign born: 9.5%; Speak English only: 83.6%; With disability: 17.5%; Veterans: 5.2%; Ancestry: 31.9% German, 8.2% Irish, 7.0% English, 4.4% American, 4.2% French

Employment: 8.1% management, business, and financial, 1.7% computer, engineering, and science, 2.7% education, legal, community service, arts, and media, 2.6% healthcare practitioners, 16.6% service, 23.9% sales and office, 4.9% natural resources, construction, and maintenance, 39.6% production, transportation, and material moving

Income: Per capita: $20,798; Median household: $48,450; Average household: $50,386; Households with income of $100,000 or more: 7.1%; Poverty rate: 9.8%

Educational Attainment: High school diploma or higher: 75.2%; Bachelor's degree or higher: 8.6%; Graduate/professional degree or higher: 1.2%

School District(s)

North Spencer County Sch Corp (PK-12)
Enrollment: 2,087 . . . . (812) 937-2400

Housing: Homeownership rate: 69.6%; Median home value: $93,000; Median year structure built: 1974; Homeowner vacancy rate: 0.0%; Median selected monthly owner costs: $899 with a mortgage, $360 without a mortgage; Median gross rent: $538 per month; Rental vacancy rate: 0.0%

Health Insurance: 91.5% have insurance; 79.7% have private insurance; 25.4% have public insurance; 8.5% do not have insurance; 8.0% of children under 18 do not have insurance

Newspapers: Spencer County Leader (weekly circulation 2,000)

Transportation: Commute: 95.4% car, 0.0% public transportation, 1.7% walk, 2.5% work from home; Mean travel time to work: 16.4 minutes

EVANSTON (unincorporated postal area)
ZCTA: 47531

Covers a land area of 36.936 square miles and a water area of 0.506 square miles. Located at 38.04° N. Lat; 86.85° W. Long. Elevation is 413 feet.

Population: 819; Growth (since 2000): 14.5%; Density: 22.2 persons per square mile; Race: 100.0% White, 0.0% Black/African American, 0.0% Asian, 0.0% American Indian/Alaska Native, 0.0% Native Hawaiian/Other Pacific Islander, 0.0% Two or more races, 0.0% Hispanic of any race; Average household size: 2.41; Median age: 46.4; Age under 18: 27.1%; Age 65 and over: 13.7%; Males per 100 females: 114.5; Marriage status: 7.0% never married, 76.7% now married, 0.0% separated, 10.2% widowed, 6.0% divorced; Foreign born: 0.0%; Speak English only: 90.6%; With disability: 15.5%; Veterans: 7.4%; Ancestry: 53.0% German, 13.2% English, 10.0% Irish, 7.6% American, 3.5% Italian

Employment: 7.5% management, business, and financial, 2.4% computer, engineering, and science, 0.0% education, legal, community service, arts, and media, 3.9% healthcare practitioners, 24.7% service, 14.3% sales and office, 7.0% natural resources, construction, and maintenance, 40.2% production, transportation, and material moving

Income: Per capita: $22,351; Median household: $42,228; Average household: $53,534; Households with income of $100,000 or more: 10.3%; Poverty rate: 13.7%

Educational Attainment: High school diploma or higher: 100.0%; Bachelor's degree or higher: 16.5%; Graduate/professional degree or higher: 5.3%

Housing: Homeownership rate: 97.1%; Median home value: $129,500; Median year structure built: 1978; Homeowner vacancy rate: 0.0%; Median selected monthly owner costs: $1,026 with a mortgage, $340 without a mortgage; Median gross rent: n/a per month; Rental vacancy rate: 0.0%

Health Insurance: 98.9% have insurance; 81.8% have private insurance; 29.1% have public insurance; 1.1% do not have insurance; 0.0% of children under 18 do not have insurance

Transportation: Commute: 95.8% car, 0.0% public transportation, 0.0% walk, 0.0% work from home; Mean travel time to work: 26.2 minutes

GENTRYVILLE (town). Covers a land area of 0.394 square miles and a water area of 0.001 square miles. Located at 38.11° N. Lat; 87.03° W. Long. Elevation is 410 feet.

History: Abraham Lincoln was a clerk in the store of James Gentry, one of the first merchants in Gentryville and the man for whom the town was named.

Population: 342; Growth (since 2000): 30.5%; Density: 867.8 persons per square mile; Race: 95.9% White, 0.0% Black/African American, 0.0% Asian, 0.3% American Indian/Alaska Native, 0.0% Native Hawaiian/Other Pacific Islander, 0.0% Two or more races, 4.1% Hispanic of any race; Average household size: 2.80; Median age: 33.5; Age under 18: 26.6%; Age 65 and over: 11.4%; Males per 100 females: 91.4; Marriage status: 20.6% never married, 43.1% now married, 0.4% separated, 14.2% widowed, 22.1% divorced; Foreign born: 0.6%; Speak English only: 98.6%; With disability: 13.5%; Veterans: 5.2%; Ancestry: 43.9% German, 9.6% English, 8.8% Irish, 4.4% Scottish, 3.2% American

Employment: 7.1% management, business, and financial, 1.9% computer, engineering, and science, 5.1% education, legal, community service, arts, and media, 2.6% healthcare practitioners, 10.9% service, 21.8% sales and office, 5.8% natural resources, construction, and maintenance, 44.9% production, transportation, and material moving

Income: Per capita: $19,811; Median household: $49,750; Average household: $54,679; Households with income of $100,000 or more: 9.8%; Poverty rate: 28.7%

Educational Attainment: High school diploma or higher: 88.4%; Bachelor's degree or higher: 11.2%; Graduate/professional degree or higher: n/a
Housing: Homeownership rate: 73.8%; Median home value: $56,700; Median year structure built: 1978; Homeowner vacancy rate: 5.3%; Median selected monthly owner costs: $761 with a mortgage, $382 without a mortgage; Median gross rent: $812 per month; Rental vacancy rate: 0.0%
Health Insurance: 95.3% have insurance; 62.9% have private insurance; 46.5% have public insurance; 4.7% do not have insurance; 0.0% of children under 18 do not have insurance
Transportation: Commute: 96.8% car, 0.0% public transportation, 3.2% walk, 0.0% work from home; Mean travel time to work: 26.8 minutes

GRANDVIEW (town). Covers a land area of 0.959 square miles and a water area of 0.002 square miles. Located at 37.94° N. Lat; 86.98° W. Long. Elevation is 394 feet.
History: Grandview was named for its location on a bluff which afforded a view for five miles up and down the river.
Population: 803; Growth (since 2000): 15.4%; Density: 837.4 persons per square mile; Race: 93.4% White, 1.9% Black/African American, 0.0% Asian, 0.0% American Indian/Alaska Native, 0.0% Native Hawaiian/Other Pacific Islander, 3.6% Two or more races, 2.4% Hispanic of any race; Average household size: 2.54; Median age: 36.4; Age under 18: 26.2%; Age 65 and over: 12.1%; Males per 100 females: 84.5; Marriage status: 20.5% never married, 61.0% now married, 0.9% separated, 7.3% widowed, 11.2% divorced; Foreign born: 0.2%; Speak English only: 100.0%; With disability: 16.8%; Veterans: 5.2%; Ancestry: 17.8% German, 11.3% Irish, 9.8% English, 8.5% American, 1.4% British
Employment: 11.3% management, business, and financial, 1.0% computer, engineering, and science, 4.5% education, legal, community service, arts, and media, 2.1% healthcare practitioners, 13.1% service, 19.1% sales and office, 9.2% natural resources, construction, and maintenance, 39.8% production, transportation, and material moving
Income: Per capita: $19,858; Median household: $45,833; Average household: $50,189; Households with income of $100,000 or more: 10.8%; Poverty rate: 10.8%
Educational Attainment: High school diploma or higher: 87.1%; Bachelor's degree or higher: 6.3%; Graduate/professional degree or higher: 1.8%
Housing: Homeownership rate: 71.2%; Median home value: $79,400; Median year structure built: 1979; Homeowner vacancy rate: 0.0%; Median selected monthly owner costs: $862 with a mortgage, $390 without a mortgage; Median gross rent: $820 per month; Rental vacancy rate: 0.0%
Health Insurance: 92.4% have insurance; 72.9% have private insurance; 31.6% have public insurance; 7.6% do not have insurance; 1.0% of children under 18 do not have insurance
Transportation: Commute: 97.4% car, 0.0% public transportation, 1.3% walk, 1.0% work from home; Mean travel time to work: 27.9 minutes

HATFIELD (CDP). Covers a land area of 1.172 square miles and a water area of <.001 square miles. Located at 37.90° N. Lat; 87.22° W. Long. Elevation is 387 feet.
Population: 902; Growth (since 2000): n/a; Density: 769.9 persons per square mile; Race: 100.0% White, 0.0% Black/African American, 0.0% Asian, 0.0% American Indian/Alaska Native, 0.0% Native Hawaiian/Other Pacific Islander, 0.0% Two or more races, 0.0% Hispanic of any race; Average household size: 2.70; Median age: 33.4; Age under 18: 23.5%; Age 65 and over: 12.5%; Males per 100 females: 100.7; Marriage status: 15.6% never married, 67.9% now married, 0.0% separated, 5.9% widowed, 10.6% divorced; Foreign born: 0.0%; Speak English only: 97.7%; With disability: 9.9%; Veterans: 10.1%; Ancestry: 30.0% German, 21.8% Irish, 11.2% American, 6.4% English, 1.4% Slovene
Employment: 6.6% management, business, and financial, 0.0% computer, engineering, and science, 2.7% education, legal, community service, arts, and media, 10.3% healthcare practitioners, 8.7% service, 18.3% sales and office, 18.7% natural resources, construction, and maintenance, 34.7% production, transportation, and material moving
Income: Per capita: $19,030; Median household: $44,000; Average household: $49,981; Households with income of $100,000 or more: 5.7%; Poverty rate: 22.9%
Educational Attainment: High school diploma or higher: 90.2%; Bachelor's degree or higher: 2.7%; Graduate/professional degree or higher: 1.3%
Housing: Homeownership rate: 85.0%; Median home value: $74,300; Median year structure built: 1970; Homeowner vacancy rate: 0.0%; Median selected monthly owner costs: $825 with a mortgage, $319 without a mortgage; Median gross rent: $927 per month; Rental vacancy rate: 0.0%
Health Insurance: 96.1% have insurance; 72.0% have private insurance; 36.4% have public insurance; 3.9% do not have insurance; 0.0% of children under 18 do not have insurance
Transportation: Commute: 100.0% car, 0.0% public transportation, 0.0% walk, 0.0% work from home; Mean travel time to work: 36.8 minutes

LAMAR (unincorporated postal area)
ZCTA: 47550
Covers a land area of 35.126 square miles and a water area of 0.276 square miles. Located at 38.07° N. Lat; 86.92° W. Long. Elevation is 413 feet.
Population: 740; Growth (since 2000): -4.1%; Density: 21.1 persons per square mile; Race: 95.9% White, 0.0% Black/African American, 0.0% Asian, 0.0% American Indian/Alaska Native, 0.0% Native Hawaiian/Other Pacific Islander, 4.1% Two or more races, 1.5% Hispanic of any race; Average household size: 2.90; Median age: 41.0; Age under 18: 30.4%; Age 65 and over: 6.9%; Males per 100 females: 102.9; Marriage status: 18.2% never married, 65.0% now married, 0.0% separated, 7.7% widowed, 9.0% divorced; Foreign born: 0.0%; Speak English only: 100.0%; With disability: 6.9%; Veterans: 6.0%; Ancestry: 35.3% German, 16.4% American, 13.9% Irish, 3.9% English, 3.5% Polish
Employment: 13.1% management, business, and financial, 4.5% computer, engineering, and science, 7.6% education, legal, community service, arts, and media, 3.1% healthcare practitioners, 17.1% service, 21.9% sales and office, 8.1% natural resources, construction, and maintenance, 24.5% production, transportation, and material moving
Income: Per capita: $32,348; Median household: $82,583; Average household: $94,069; Households with income of $100,000 or more: 32.5%; Poverty rate: 2.3%
Educational Attainment: High school diploma or higher: 93.2%; Bachelor's degree or higher: 16.3%; Graduate/professional degree or higher: 3.7%

School District(s)

North Spencer County Sch Corp (PK-12)
Enrollment: 2,087 . . . . (812) 937-2400
Housing: Homeownership rate: 94.9%; Median home value: $131,900; Median year structure built: 1993; Homeowner vacancy rate: 0.0%; Median selected monthly owner costs: $1,211 with a mortgage, $524 without a mortgage; Median gross rent: n/a per month; Rental vacancy rate: 0.0%
Health Insurance: 100.0% have insurance; 87.8% have private insurance; 14.7% have public insurance; 0.0% do not have insurance; 0.0% of children under 18 do not have insurance
Transportation: Commute: 94.5% car, 0.0% public transportation, 0.0% walk, 2.4% work from home; Mean travel time to work: 48.9 minutes

LINCOLN CITY (unincorporated postal area)
ZCTA: 47552
Covers a land area of 5.162 square miles and a water area of 0.126 square miles. Located at 38.11° N. Lat; 87.00° W. Long. Elevation is 436 feet.
Population: 310; Growth (since 2000): 75.1%; Density: 60.1 persons per square mile; Race: 91.9% White, 0.0% Black/African American, 0.0% Asian, 0.0% American Indian/Alaska Native, 0.0% Native Hawaiian/Other Pacific Islander, 8.1% Two or more races, 0.0% Hispanic of any race; Average household size: 2.74; Median age: 53.2; Age under 18: 0.0%; Age 65 and over: 0.0%; Males per 100 females: 97.8; Marriage status: 26.8% never married, 73.2% now married, 0.0% separated, 0.0% widowed, 0.0% divorced; Foreign born: 0.0%; Speak English only: 100.0%; With disability: 18.7%; Veterans: 9.4%; Ancestry: 56.5% German, 10.0% Dutch, 8.1% English, 4.8% Norwegian, 4.2% Irish
Employment: 65.3% management, business, and financial, 5.1% computer, engineering, and science, 5.1% education, legal, community service, arts, and media, 0.0% healthcare practitioners, 5.9% service, 5.9% sales and office, 5.5% natural resources, construction, and maintenance, 7.2% production, transportation, and material moving
Income: Per capita: $195,068; Median household: n/a; Average household: $447,748; Households with income of $100,000 or more: 36.3%; Poverty rate: n/a

Educational Attainment: High school diploma or higher: 100.0%; Bachelor's degree or higher: 28.3%; Graduate/professional degree or higher: 4.0%

School District(s)

North Spencer County Sch Corp (PK-12)
Enrollment: 2,087 . . . . (812) 937-2400

Housing: Homeownership rate: 100.0%; Median home value: n/a; Median year structure built: 1965; Homeowner vacancy rate: 0.0%; Median selected monthly owner costs: $957 with a mortgage, $1,501 without a mortgage; Median gross rent: n/a per month; Rental vacancy rate: 0.0%

Health Insurance: 100.0% have insurance; 90.3% have private insurance; 9.7% have public insurance; 0.0% do not have insurance; 0.0% of children under 18 do not have insurance

Transportation: Commute: 39.8% car, 0.0% public transportation, 0.0% walk, 60.2% work from home; Mean travel time to work: 15.5 minutes

RICHLAND (town). Covers a land area of 0.515 square miles and a water area of <.001 square miles. Located at 37.95° N. Lat; 87.17° W. Long. Elevation is 390 feet.

Population: 468; Growth (since 2000): n/a; Density: 908.9 persons per square mile; Race: 98.1% White, 1.5% Black/African American, 0.0% Asian, 0.2% American Indian/Alaska Native, 0.0% Native Hawaiian/Other Pacific Islander, 0.2% Two or more races, 1.5% Hispanic of any race; Average household size: 2.74; Median age: 33.3; Age under 18: 30.6%; Age 65 and over: 11.8%; Males per 100 females: 100.5; Marriage status: 21.6% never married, 61.5% now married, 1.2% separated, 5.2% widowed, 11.7% divorced; Foreign born: 0.0%; Speak English only: 98.8%; With disability: 12.2%; Veterans: 6.5%; Ancestry: 32.9% German, 14.3% Irish, 9.2% American, 8.3% English, 5.1% Scottish

Employment: 9.5% management, business, and financial, 2.3% computer, engineering, and science, 14.1% education, legal, community service, arts, and media, 0.9% healthcare practitioners, 16.8% service, 17.3% sales and office, 19.1% natural resources, construction, and maintenance, 20.0% production, transportation, and material moving

Income: Per capita: $22,004; Median household: $55,139; Average household: $59,923; Households with income of $100,000 or more: 16.4%; Poverty rate: 5.0%

Educational Attainment: High school diploma or higher: 92.1%; Bachelor's degree or higher: 9.0%; Graduate/professional degree or higher: 2.8%

School District(s)

South Spencer County Sch Corp (PK-12)
Enrollment: 1,217 . . . . (812) 649-2591

Housing: Homeownership rate: 88.3%; Median home value: $80,900; Median year structure built: 1953; Homeowner vacancy rate: 9.5%; Median selected monthly owner costs: $876 with a mortgage, $475 without a mortgage; Median gross rent: $513 per month; Rental vacancy rate: 0.0%

Health Insurance: 85.5% have insurance; 63.2% have private insurance; 35.9% have public insurance; 14.5% do not have insurance; 7.4% of children under 18 do not have insurance

Transportation: Commute: 100.0% car, 0.0% public transportation, 0.0% walk, 0.0% work from home; Mean travel time to work: 31.8 minutes

ROCKPORT (city). County seat. Covers a land area of 1.571 square miles and a water area of 0.034 square miles. Located at 37.89° N. Lat; 87.05° W. Long. Elevation is 440 feet.

History: Rockport was first settled by Daniel Grass in 1807. The Lincoln family, and especially Abraham Lincoln, were visitors in Rockport when they lived 16 miles north. John Pitcher, a Rockport attorney, was a friend of Abe's who allowed him to use his extensive library of law, history, and fiction.

Population: 2,359; Growth (since 2000): 9.2%; Density: 1,501.5 persons per square mile; Race: 92.4% White, 3.5% Black/African American, 0.4% Asian, 0.9% American Indian/Alaska Native, 0.0% Native Hawaiian/Other Pacific Islander, 2.0% Two or more races, 3.6% Hispanic of any race; Average household size: 2.38; Median age: 40.5; Age under 18: 26.9%; Age 65 and over: 17.8%; Males per 100 females: 94.0; Marriage status: 25.4% never married, 44.4% now married, 0.4% separated, 11.1% widowed, 19.1% divorced; Foreign born: 1.4%; Speak English only: 98.3%; With disability: 19.4%; Veterans: 7.9%; Ancestry: 21.0% German, 12.3% Irish, 11.1% English, 8.8% American, 1.7% Scotch-Irish

Employment: 2.5% management, business, and financial, 2.9% computer, engineering, and science, 4.9% education, legal, community service, arts, and media, 3.6% healthcare practitioners, 22.9% service, 23.0% sales and office, 16.4% natural resources, construction, and maintenance, 23.8% production, transportation, and material moving

Income: Per capita: $17,136; Median household: $32,695; Average household: $40,747; Households with income of $100,000 or more: 3.7%; Poverty rate: 22.3%

Educational Attainment: High school diploma or higher: 79.6%; Bachelor's degree or higher: 8.5%; Graduate/professional degree or higher: 1.9%

School District(s)

South Spencer County Sch Corp (PK-12)
Enrollment: 1,217 . . . . (812) 649-2591

Housing: Homeownership rate: 52.6%; Median home value: $74,700; Median year structure built: 1961; Homeowner vacancy rate: 2.6%; Median selected monthly owner costs: $860 with a mortgage, $343 without a mortgage; Median gross rent: $688 per month; Rental vacancy rate: 15.2%

Health Insurance: 87.5% have insurance; 54.9% have private insurance; 51.8% have public insurance; 12.5% do not have insurance; 2.6% of children under 18 do not have insurance

Newspapers: Spencer County Journal Democrat (weekly circulation 6,000)

Transportation: Commute: 95.0% car, 0.0% public transportation, 2.2% walk, 1.3% work from home; Mean travel time to work: 25.2 minutes

SAINT MEINRAD (CDP). Covers a land area of 1.644 square miles and a water area of 0.023 square miles. Located at 38.17° N. Lat; 86.83° W. Long. Elevation is 443 feet.

Population: 607; Growth (since 2000): n/a; Density: 369.3 persons per square mile; Race: 97.4% White, 0.0% Black/African American, 2.6% Asian, 0.0% American Indian/Alaska Native, 0.0% Native Hawaiian/Other Pacific Islander, 0.0% Two or more races, 0.0% Hispanic of any race; Average household size: 2.06; Median age: 45.1; Age under 18: 17.8%; Age 65 and over: 15.3%; Males per 100 females: 166.4; Marriage status: 36.5% never married, 49.3% now married, 2.9% separated, 6.0% widowed, 8.3% divorced; Foreign born: 2.6%; Speak English only: 97.4%; With disability: 15.2%; Veterans: 6.6%; Ancestry: 55.5% German, 25.5% Irish, 8.4% English, 5.4% Italian, 3.0% Polish

Employment: 3.7% management, business, and financial, 0.0% computer, engineering, and science, 31.9% education, legal, community service, arts, and media, 0.0% healthcare practitioners, 9.3% service, 24.6% sales and office, 18.4% natural resources, construction, and maintenance, 12.1% production, transportation, and material moving

Income: Per capita: $28,538; Median household: $56,295; Average household: $58,192; Households with income of $100,000 or more: 17.0%; Poverty rate: 10.5%

Educational Attainment: High school diploma or higher: 95.6%; Bachelor's degree or higher: 22.5%; Graduate/professional degree or higher: 10.8%

Four-year College(s)

Saint Meinrad School of Theology (Private, Not-for-profit, Roman Catholic)
Enrollment: 171 . . . . (812) 357-6611

Housing: Homeownership rate: 87.3%; Median home value: $103,400; Median year structure built: 1959; Homeowner vacancy rate: 0.0%; Median selected monthly owner costs: $981 with a mortgage, $249 without a mortgage; Median gross rent: n/a per month; Rental vacancy rate: 0.0%

Health Insurance: 94.9% have insurance; 79.2% have private insurance; 23.1% have public insurance; 5.1% do not have insurance; 0.0% of children under 18 do not have insurance

Transportation: Commute: 85.5% car, 0.0% public transportation, 9.5% walk, 5.0% work from home; Mean travel time to work: 18.3 minutes

SANTA CLAUS (town). Covers a land area of 6.443 square miles and a water area of 0.421 square miles. Located at 38.12° N. Lat; 86.93° W. Long. Elevation is 472 feet.

History: Santa Claus was laid out in 1846. The suggested name of Santa Fe was rejected by the post office, and Santa Claus was suggested as a joke, since it was near Christmas. The name served to bring hundreds of letters through the Santa Claus post office each December, where Jim Martin, postmaster from 1897 to 1935, played Santa Claus.

Population: 2,738; Growth (since 2000): 34.1%; Density: 425.0 persons per square mile; Race: 97.5% White, 0.2% Black/African American, 0.0% Asian, 0.3% American Indian/Alaska Native, 0.0% Native Hawaiian/Other Pacific Islander, 1.0% Two or more races, 2.1% Hispanic of any race; Average household size: 2.74; Median age: 41.4; Age under 18: 25.4%; Age 65 and over: 15.9%; Males per 100 females: 91.9; Marriage status: 19.2% never married, 68.2% now married, 0.6% separated, 5.8%

widowed, 6.8% divorced; Foreign born: 0.9%; Speak English only: 96.5%; With disability: 11.2%; Veterans: 10.6%; Ancestry: 35.8% German, 14.7% Irish, 10.8% English, 10.1% American, 4.7% Polish
Employment: 16.4% management, business, and financial, 7.7% computer, engineering, and science, 12.0% education, legal, community service, arts, and media, 7.9% healthcare practitioners, 18.7% service, 19.6% sales and office, 5.8% natural resources, construction, and maintenance, 11.8% production, transportation, and material moving
Income: Per capita: $33,228; Median household: $75,474; Average household: $90,899; Households with income of $100,000 or more: 32.0%; Poverty rate: 4.8%
Educational Attainment: High school diploma or higher: 96.5%; Bachelor's degree or higher: 34.7%; Graduate/professional degree or higher: 14.7%
Housing: Homeownership rate: 89.2%; Median home value: $167,800; Median year structure built: 1995; Homeowner vacancy rate: 3.5%; Median selected monthly owner costs: $1,255 with a mortgage, $449 without a mortgage; Median gross rent: $955 per month; Rental vacancy rate: 13.6%
Health Insurance: 97.3% have insurance; 86.9% have private insurance; 24.2% have public insurance; 2.7% do not have insurance; 0.0% of children under 18 do not have insurance
Transportation: Commute: 93.5% car, 0.0% public transportation, 0.5% walk, 5.0% work from home; Mean travel time to work: 26.1 minutes
Additional Information Contacts
Town of Santa Claus . . . . (812) 937-2551
http://www.townofsantaclaus.com

Starke County

Located in northwestern Indiana; bounded on the northwest by the Kankakee River; drained by the Yellow River. Covers a land area of 309.134 square miles, a water area of 3.072 square miles, and is located in the Central Time Zone at 41.28° N. Lat., 86.65° W. Long. The county was founded in 1835. County seat is Knox.
Population: 22,966; Growth (since 2000): -2.5%; Density: 74.3 persons per square mile; Race: 96.5% White, 0.3% Black/African American, 0.5% Asian, 0.1% American Indian/Alaska Native, 0.0% Native Hawaiian/Other Pacific Islander, 1.3% two or more races, 3.5% Hispanic of any race; Average household size: 2.61; Median age: 41.7; Age under 18: 23.4%; Age 65 and over: 16.9%; Males per 100 females: 97.5; Marriage status: 25.2% never married, 53.9% now married, 1.3% separated, 6.7% widowed, 14.2% divorced; Foreign born: 2.0%; Speak English only: 96.7%; With disability: 15.9%; Veterans: 8.2%; Ancestry: 22.4% German, 15.1% Irish, 8.4% American, 6.6% English, 6.0% Polish
Religion: Six largest groups: 9.8% Catholicism, 5.1% Lutheran, 4.1% Methodist/Pietist, 2.4% Baptist, 2.3% Non-denominational Protestant, 1.6% Pentecostal
Economy: Unemployment rate: 4.2%; Leading industries: 19.8 % retail trade; 13.8 % other services (except public administration); 10.1 % accommodation and food services; Farms: 511 totaling 133,459 acres; Company size: 0 employ 1,000 or more persons, 0 employ 500 to 999 persons, 3 employ 100 to 499 persons, 295 employ less than 100 persons; Business ownership: 565 women-owned, n/a Black-owned, n/a Hispanic-owned, n/a Asian-owned, n/a American Indian/Alaska Native-owned
Employment: 11.2% management, business, and financial, 0.5% computer, engineering, and science, 7.6% education, legal, community service, arts, and media, 5.0% healthcare practitioners, 16.9% service, 20.0% sales and office, 12.1% natural resources, construction, and maintenance, 26.7% production, transportation, and material moving
Income: Per capita: $22,153; Median household: $45,526; Average household: $56,211; Households with income of $100,000 or more: 11.8%; Poverty rate: 16.7%
Educational Attainment: High school diploma or higher: 83.1%; Bachelor's degree or higher: 11.4%; Graduate/professional degree or higher: 3.8%
Housing: Homeownership rate: 80.2%; Median home value: $101,600; Median year structure built: 1972; Homeowner vacancy rate: 2.5%; Median selected monthly owner costs: $945 with a mortgage, $363 without a mortgage; Median gross rent: $665 per month; Rental vacancy rate: 3.5%
Vital Statistics: Birth rate: 111.8 per 10,000 population; Death rate: 122.7 per 10,000 population; Age-adjusted cancer mortality rate: 198.3 deaths per 100,000 population
Health Insurance: 91.9% have insurance; 66.6% have private insurance; 41.3% have public insurance; 8.1% do not have insurance; 3.0% of children under 18 do not have insurance
Health Care: Physicians: 4.8 per 10,000 population; Dentists: 1.3 per 10,000 population; Hospital beds: 6.5 per 10,000 population; Hospital admissions: 158.8 per 10,000 population
Transportation: Commute: 94.2% car, 0.2% public transportation, 1.4% walk, 3.5% work from home; Mean travel time to work: 30.3 minutes
2016 Presidential Election: 68.3% Trump, 26.7% Clinton, 4.0% Johnson, 0.0% Stein
National and State Parks: Bass Lake State Beach; Kaukakee State Fish and Wildlife Area
Additional Information Contacts
Starke Government . . . . (574) 772-9107
http://co.starke.in.us

Starke County Communities

BASS LAKE (CDP). Covers a land area of 9.088 square miles and a water area of 2.191 square miles. Located at 41.22° N. Lat; 86.59° W. Long. Elevation is 718 feet.
Population: 1,409; Growth (since 2000): 12.8%; Density: 155.0 persons per square mile; Race: 95.6% White, 0.0% Black/African American, 0.0% Asian, 0.0% American Indian/Alaska Native, 0.0% Native Hawaiian/Other Pacific Islander, 4.4% Two or more races, 0.0% Hispanic of any race; Average household size: 2.76; Median age: 47.2; Age under 18: 31.4%; Age 65 and over: 21.1%; Males per 100 females: 94.0; Marriage status: 20.3% never married, 59.8% now married, 0.6% separated, 6.4% widowed, 13.6% divorced; Foreign born: 3.5%; Speak English only: 95.4%; With disability: 18.5%; Veterans: 10.8%; Ancestry: 24.3% German, 15.1% Romanian, 12.8% English, 11.6% Irish, 11.3% Italian
Employment: 18.2% management, business, and financial, 1.7% computer, engineering, and science, 10.0% education, legal, community service, arts, and media, 4.1% healthcare practitioners, 14.5% service, 21.5% sales and office, 11.3% natural resources, construction, and maintenance, 18.7% production, transportation, and material moving
Income: Per capita: $25,834; Median household: $50,000; Average household: $69,407; Households with income of $100,000 or more: 9.4%; Poverty rate: 22.2%
Educational Attainment: High school diploma or higher: 85.6%; Bachelor's degree or higher: 13.0%; Graduate/professional degree or higher: 6.3%
Housing: Homeownership rate: 86.5%; Median home value: $148,900; Median year structure built: 1974; Homeowner vacancy rate: 12.8%; Median selected monthly owner costs: $933 with a mortgage, $510 without a mortgage; Median gross rent: $795 per month; Rental vacancy rate: 0.0%
Health Insurance: 94.3% have insurance; 75.5% have private insurance; 42.6% have public insurance; 5.7% do not have insurance; 0.0% of children under 18 do not have insurance
Transportation: Commute: 98.9% car, 0.0% public transportation, 0.0% walk, 0.0% work from home; Mean travel time to work: 29.0 minutes

GROVERTOWN (unincorporated postal area)
ZCTA: 46531
Covers a land area of 21.421 square miles and a water area of 0.010 square miles. Located at 41.36° N. Lat; 86.52° W. Long. Elevation is 728 feet.
Population: 1,519; Growth (since 2000): 13.8%; Density: 70.9 persons per square mile; Race: 94.0% White, 3.6% Black/African American, 0.0% Asian, 0.0% American Indian/Alaska Native, 0.0% Native Hawaiian/Other Pacific Islander, 0.9% Two or more races, 1.8% Hispanic of any race; Average household size: 2.59; Median age: 48.8; Age under 18: 17.4%; Age 65 and over: 17.5%; Males per 100 females: 104.8; Marriage status: 17.5% never married, 69.9% now married, 1.0% separated, 5.7% widowed, 6.8% divorced; Foreign born: 0.0%; Speak English only: 98.7%; With disability: 13.7%; Veterans: 12.0%; Ancestry: 22.4% German, 20.9% Irish, 7.7% English, 6.9% Polish, 6.5% American
Employment: 8.1% management, business, and financial, 0.0% computer, engineering, and science, 4.0% education, legal, community service, arts, and media, 5.4% healthcare practitioners, 26.2% service, 25.2% sales and office, 10.2% natural resources, construction, and maintenance, 20.9% production, transportation, and material moving

Income: Per capita: $21,227; Median household: $50,500; Average household: $55,062; Households with income of $100,000 or more: 12.2%; Poverty rate: 14.3%
Educational Attainment: High school diploma or higher: 87.7%; Bachelor's degree or higher: 9.1%; Graduate/professional degree or higher: 2.5%
Housing: Homeownership rate: 88.6%; Median home value: $111,900; Median year structure built: 1986; Homeowner vacancy rate: 0.0%; Median selected monthly owner costs: $938 with a mortgage, $367 without a mortgage; Median gross rent: $813 per month; Rental vacancy rate: 0.0%
Health Insurance: 89.5% have insurance; 71.4% have private insurance; 35.4% have public insurance; 10.5% do not have insurance; 3.3% of children under 18 do not have insurance
Transportation: Commute: 98.0% car, 1.2% public transportation, 0.8% walk, 0.0% work from home; Mean travel time to work: 26.6 minutes

HAMLET (town). Covers a land area of 0.965 square miles and a water area of 0.010 square miles. Located at 41.38° N. Lat; 86.58° W. Long. Elevation is 705 feet.
History: Hamlet was sited at the crossing of the Pennsylvania and New York Central Railroads. It was platted in 1863 by John Hamlet, for whom it was named, and soon became a shipping center.
Population: 721; Growth (since 2000): -12.1%; Density: 747.0 persons per square mile; Race: 96.0% White, 0.0% Black/African American, 0.0% Asian, 1.7% American Indian/Alaska Native, 0.0% Native Hawaiian/Other Pacific Islander, 1.7% Two or more races, 1.7% Hispanic of any race; Average household size: 2.84; Median age: 32.1; Age under 18: 30.5%; Age 65 and over: 10.4%; Males per 100 females: 98.0; Marriage status: 32.0% never married, 47.1% now married, 1.5% separated, 6.5% widowed, 14.4% divorced; Foreign born: 1.9%; Speak English only: 92.8%; With disability: 14.4%; Veterans: 9.8%; Ancestry: 17.9% German, 10.8% English, 9.4% Irish, 7.6% Scottish, 6.4% American
Employment: 9.7% management, business, and financial, 0.0% computer, engineering, and science, 6.3% education, legal, community service, arts, and media, 6.0% healthcare practitioners, 13.8% service, 17.9% sales and office, 11.0% natural resources, construction, and maintenance, 35.4% production, transportation, and material moving
Income: Per capita: $16,583; Median household: $41,875; Average household: $46,433; Households with income of $100,000 or more: 3.6%; Poverty rate: 16.0%
Educational Attainment: High school diploma or higher: 81.8%; Bachelor's degree or higher: 11.3%; Graduate/professional degree or higher: 2.5%

School District(s)

Oregon-Davis School Corp (PK-12)
Enrollment: 642. . . . . (574) 867-2111
Housing: Homeownership rate: 73.2%; Median home value: $69,600; Median year structure built: 1953; Homeowner vacancy rate: 3.1%; Median selected monthly owner costs: $954 with a mortgage, $320 without a mortgage; Median gross rent: $682 per month; Rental vacancy rate: 0.0%
Health Insurance: 89.9% have insurance; 66.0% have private insurance; 35.4% have public insurance; 10.1% do not have insurance; 6.5% of children under 18 do not have insurance
Transportation: Commute: 97.8% car, 0.0% public transportation, 0.6% walk, 0.6% work from home; Mean travel time to work: 27.9 minutes

KNOX (city). County seat. Covers a land area of 3.920 square miles and a water area of 0 square miles. Located at 41.29° N. Lat; 86.62° W. Long. Elevation is 712 feet.
History: Knox developed as a trading center for the surrounding farmlands.
Population: 3,520; Growth (since 2000): -5.4%; Density: 897.9 persons per square mile; Race: 98.7% White, 0.1% Black/African American, 0.0% Asian, 0.0% American Indian/Alaska Native, 0.0% Native Hawaiian/Other Pacific Islander, 0.1% Two or more races, 5.3% Hispanic of any race; Average household size: 2.52; Median age: 40.1; Age under 18: 18.2%; Age 65 and over: 15.5%; Males per 100 females: 86.2; Marriage status: 35.8% never married, 33.9% now married, 1.9% separated, 8.9% widowed, 21.4% divorced; Foreign born: 0.9%; Speak English only: 98.2%; With disability: 20.9%; Veterans: 6.2%; Ancestry: 27.4% Irish, 23.7% German, 7.5% American, 7.2% English, 5.5% Polish
Employment: 6.2% management, business, and financial, 1.3% computer, engineering, and science, 6.5% education, legal, community service, arts, and media, 3.7% healthcare practitioners, 27.9% service, 18.5% sales and office, 6.3% natural resources, construction, and maintenance, 29.5% production, transportation, and material moving
Income: Per capita: $20,389; Median household: $33,709; Average household: $48,825; Households with income of $100,000 or more: 6.3%; Poverty rate: 21.5%
Educational Attainment: High school diploma or higher: 76.8%; Bachelor's degree or higher: 7.3%; Graduate/professional degree or higher: 2.9%

School District(s)

Knox Community School Corp (PK-12)
Enrollment: 1,868 . . . . (574) 772-1600

Vocational/Technical School(s)

Knox Beauty College (Private, For-profit)
Enrollment: 41. . . . . (574) 772-5500
Tuition: $5,385
Housing: Homeownership rate: 55.2%; Median home value: $76,600; Median year structure built: 1958; Homeowner vacancy rate: 2.5%; Median selected monthly owner costs: $940 with a mortgage, $324 without a mortgage; Median gross rent: $636 per month; Rental vacancy rate: 8.9%
Health Insurance: 88.4% have insurance; 52.3% have private insurance; 49.0% have public insurance; 11.6% do not have insurance; 1.0% of children under 18 do not have insurance
Hospitals: Indiana University Health Starke Hospital (53 beds)
Safety: Violent crime rate: 11.2 per 10,000 population; Property crime rate: 547.5 per 10,000 population
Newspapers: The Leader (weekly circulation 2,500)
Transportation: Commute: 92.9% car, 0.0% public transportation, 7.1% walk, 0.0% work from home; Mean travel time to work: 22.7 minutes
Additional Information Contacts
City of Knox. . . . . (574) 772-3032
http://www.cityofknox.net

KOONTZ LAKE (CDP). Covers a land area of 3.370 square miles and a water area of 0.522 square miles. Located at 41.41° N. Lat; 86.48° W. Long. Elevation is 732 feet.
Population: 1,521; Growth (since 2000): -2.1%; Density: 451.4 persons per square mile; Race: 93.0% White, 0.8% Black/African American, 5.1% Asian, 0.0% American Indian/Alaska Native, 0.0% Native Hawaiian/Other Pacific Islander, 1.1% Two or more races, 5.3% Hispanic of any race; Average household size: 2.44; Median age: 48.1; Age under 18: 17.0%; Age 65 and over: 22.6%; Males per 100 females: 102.7; Marriage status: 26.2% never married, 53.4% now married, 0.9% separated, 6.2% widowed, 14.2% divorced; Foreign born: 3.1%; Speak English only: 94.6%; With disability: 19.2%; Veterans: 7.4%; Ancestry: 31.4% German, 11.0% American, 9.7% English, 9.3% Irish, 9.3% Polish
Employment: 12.5% management, business, and financial, 0.0% computer, engineering, and science, 6.0% education, legal, community service, arts, and media, 1.4% healthcare practitioners, 14.5% service, 22.7% sales and office, 10.7% natural resources, construction, and maintenance, 32.2% production, transportation, and material moving
Income: Per capita: $21,101; Median household: $42,750; Average household: $48,984; Households with income of $100,000 or more: 9.2%; Poverty rate: 14.9%
Educational Attainment: High school diploma or higher: 79.7%; Bachelor's degree or higher: 16.4%; Graduate/professional degree or higher: 7.9%
Housing: Homeownership rate: 84.8%; Median home value: $106,500; Median year structure built: 1971; Homeowner vacancy rate: 5.2%; Median selected monthly owner costs: $883 with a mortgage, $466 without a mortgage; Median gross rent: $731 per month; Rental vacancy rate: 0.0%
Health Insurance: 91.8% have insurance; 79.3% have private insurance; 36.0% have public insurance; 8.2% do not have insurance; 0.0% of children under 18 do not have insurance
Transportation: Commute: 94.7% car, 0.0% public transportation, 0.0% walk, 3.1% work from home; Mean travel time to work: 31.2 minutes

NORTH JUDSON (town). Covers a land area of 1.104 square miles and a water area of 0 square miles. Located at 41.22° N. Lat; 86.78° W. Long. Elevation is 712 feet.
History: Laid out 1861.
Population: 2,026; Growth (since 2000): 21.0%; Density: 1,834.4 persons per square mile; Race: 96.0% White, 0.2% Black/African American, 0.0% Asian, 0.0% American Indian/Alaska Native, 0.0% Native Hawaiian/Other Pacific Islander, 2.4% Two or more races, 4.0% Hispanic of any race; Average household size: 2.57; Median age: 34.5; Age under 18: 28.5%;

Age 65 and over: 16.0%; Males per 100 females: 92.4; Marriage status: 24.5% never married, 55.0% now married, 3.4% separated, 6.4% widowed, 14.1% divorced; Foreign born: 1.7%; Speak English only: 96.4%; With disability: 16.0%; Veterans: 6.0%; Ancestry: 22.5% German, 20.2% Irish, 7.0% Polish, 6.1% American, 5.5% English
Employment: 2.3% management, business, and financial, 0.4% computer, engineering, and science, 9.7% education, legal, community service, arts, and media, 6.6% healthcare practitioners, 14.0% service, 25.7% sales and office, 9.4% natural resources, construction, and maintenance, 32.0% production, transportation, and material moving
Income: Per capita: $19,512; Median household: $41,250; Average household: $50,196; Households with income of $100,000 or more: 9.2%; Poverty rate: 20.1%
Educational Attainment: High school diploma or higher: 80.4%; Bachelor's degree or higher: 10.6%; Graduate/professional degree or higher: 3.7%

School District(s)

North Judson-San Pierre Sch Corp (PK-12)
Enrollment: 1,160 . . . . (574) 896-2155
Housing: Homeownership rate: 64.7%; Median home value: $86,600; Median year structure built: 1952; Homeowner vacancy rate: 0.6%; Median selected monthly owner costs: $793 with a mortgage, $379 without a mortgage; Median gross rent: $583 per month; Rental vacancy rate: 0.0%
Health Insurance: 94.4% have insurance; 69.8% have private insurance; 35.7% have public insurance; 5.6% do not have insurance; 0.0% of children under 18 do not have insurance
Transportation: Commute: 96.7% car, 0.0% public transportation, 1.0% walk, 1.5% work from home; Mean travel time to work: 27.9 minutes

ORA (unincorporated postal area)
ZCTA: 46968

Covers a land area of 0.365 square miles and a water area of 0 square miles. Located at 41.18° N. Lat; 86.55° W. Long. Elevation is 718 feet.
Population: 57; Growth (since 2000): -34.5%; Density: 156.1 persons per square mile; Race: 100.0% White, 0.0% Black/African American, 0.0% Asian, 0.0% American Indian/Alaska Native, 0.0% Native Hawaiian/Other Pacific Islander, 0.0% Two or more races, 10.5% Hispanic of any race; Average household size: 1.43; Median age: 62.1; Age under 18: 10.5%; Age 65 and over: 29.8%; Males per 100 females: 102.8; Marriage status: 0.0% never married, 41.2% now married, 0.0% separated, 58.8% widowed, 0.0% divorced; Foreign born: 0.0%; Speak English only: 89.5%; With disability: 52.6%; Veterans: 21.6%; Ancestry: 47.4% Polish, 40.4% American, 29.8% French Canadian, 29.8% Pennsylvania German, 29.8% Swedish
Employment: 0.0% management, business, and financial, 0.0% computer, engineering, and science, 0.0% education, legal, community service, arts, and media, 0.0% healthcare practitioners, 0.0% service, 47.6% sales and office, 52.4% natural resources, construction, and maintenance, 0.0% production, transportation, and material moving
Income: Per capita: $21,739; Median household: n/a; Average household: $29,423; Households with income of $100,000 or more: n/a; Poverty rate: 29.8%
Educational Attainment: High school diploma or higher: 66.7%; Bachelor's degree or higher: n/a; Graduate/professional degree or higher: n/a
Housing: Homeownership rate: 100.0%; Median home value: n/a; Median year structure built: 1952; Homeowner vacancy rate: 0.0%; Median selected monthly owner costs: $0 with a mortgage, $0 without a mortgage; Median gross rent: n/a per month; Rental vacancy rate: 0.0%
Health Insurance: 100.0% have insurance; 47.4% have private insurance; 52.6% have public insurance; 0.0% do not have insurance; 0.0% of children under 18 do not have insurance
Transportation: Commute: 100.0% car, 0.0% public transportation, 0.0% walk, 0.0% work from home; Mean travel time to work: 0.0 minutes

SAN PIERRE (CDP). Covers a land area of 0.141 square miles and a water area of 0 square miles. Located at 41.20° N. Lat; 86.89° W. Long. Elevation is 696 feet.
Population: 104; Growth (since 2000): -33.3%; Density: 738.9 persons per square mile; Race: 100.0% White, 0.0% Black/African American, 0.0% Asian, 0.0% American Indian/Alaska Native, 0.0% Native Hawaiian/Other Pacific Islander, 0.0% Two or more races, 0.0% Hispanic of any race; Average household size: 1.93; Median age: 55.8; Age under 18: 0.0%; Age 65 and over: 38.5%; Males per 100 females: 100.0; Marriage status: 20.2% never married, 23.1% now married, 0.0% separated, 10.6% widowed, 46.2% divorced; Foreign born: 0.0%; Speak English only: 100.0%; With disability: 12.5%; Veterans: 0.0%; Ancestry: 40.4% German, 21.2% Polish, 20.2% English, 19.2% Irish, 13.5% Italian
Employment: 0.0% management, business, and financial, 0.0% computer, engineering, and science, 15.2% education, legal, community service, arts, and media, 0.0% healthcare practitioners, 16.7% service, 15.2% sales and office, 31.8% natural resources, construction, and maintenance, 21.2% production, transportation, and material moving
Income: Per capita: $32,397; Median household: $50,536; Average household: $62,431; Households with income of $100,000 or more: 18.5%; Poverty rate: n/a
Educational Attainment: High school diploma or higher: 100.0%; Bachelor's degree or higher: 14.9%; Graduate/professional degree or higher: n/a
Housing: Homeownership rate: 100.0%; Median home value: $105,400; Median year structure built: 1970; Homeowner vacancy rate: 0.0%; Median selected monthly owner costs: n/a with a mortgage, $309 without a mortgage; Median gross rent: n/a per month; Rental vacancy rate: 0.0%
Health Insurance: 100.0% have insurance; 81.7% have private insurance; 38.5% have public insurance; 0.0% do not have insurance; 0.0% of children under 18 do not have insurance
Transportation: Commute: 100.0% car, 0.0% public transportation, 0.0% walk, 0.0% work from home; Mean travel time to work: 38.3 minutes

Steuben County

Located in northeastern Indiana; bounded on the north by Michigan, and on the east by Ohio; drained by Pigeon Creek; includes several lakes. Covers a land area of 308.939 square miles, a water area of 13.527 square miles, and is located in the Eastern Time Zone at 41.64° N. Lat., 85.00° W. Long. The county was founded in 1835. County seat is Angola.

Steuben County is part of the Angola, IN Micropolitan Statistical Area. The entire metro area includes: Steuben County, IN

Weather Station: Angola Elevation: 1,009 feet

	Jan	Feb	Mar	Apr	May	Jun	Jul	Aug	Sep	Oct	Nov	Dec
High	30	34	44	58	69	78	82	80	73	60	47	34
Low	15	16	24	36	47	57	61	59	50	39	30	20
Precip	2.3	2.1	2.7	3.4	4.3	3.8	4.1	4.2	3.3	3.0	3.1	2.8
Snow	10.6	8.4	4.8	1.0	tr	0.0	0.0	0.0	0.0	0.3	2.1	9.2

High and Low temperatures in degrees Fahrenheit; Precipitation and Snow in inches

Population: 34,459; Growth (since 2000): 3.7%; Density: 111.5 persons per square mile; Race: 97.3% White, 0.2% Black/African American, 0.5% Asian, 0.1% American Indian/Alaska Native, 0.0% Native Hawaiian/Other Pacific Islander, 1.7% two or more races, 3.5% Hispanic of any race; Average household size: 2.40; Median age: 42.7; Age under 18: 20.9%; Age 65 and over: 18.2%; Males per 100 females: 101.9; Marriage status: 26.0% never married, 56.7% now married, 1.0% separated, 5.5% widowed, 11.8% divorced; Foreign born: 2.2%; Speak English only: 96.0%; With disability: 14.6%; Veterans: 8.6%; Ancestry: 34.3% German, 12.1% Irish, 9.9% American, 9.6% English, 7.1% European
Religion: Six largest groups: 9.8% Catholicism, 4.7% Methodist/Pietist, 4.5% Holiness, 4.2% Lutheran, 2.6% Baptist, 1.7% Non-denominational Protestant
Economy: Unemployment rate: 2.9%; Leading industries: 18.5 % retail trade; 12.6 % other services (except public administration); 9.3 % construction; Farms: 562 totaling 104,570 acres; Company size: 1 employs 1,000 or more persons, 0 employ 500 to 999 persons, 28 employ 100 to 499 persons, 931 employs less than 100 persons; Business ownership: 696 women-owned, 35 Black-owned, 25 Hispanic-owned, 26 Asian-owned, n/a American Indian/Alaska Native-owned
Employment: 10.7% management, business, and financial, 3.7% computer, engineering, and science, 7.5% education, legal, community service, arts, and media, 3.7% healthcare practitioners, 15.3% service, 23.8% sales and office, 8.6% natural resources, construction, and maintenance, 26.7% production, transportation, and material moving
Income: Per capita: $26,902; Median household: $52,749; Average household: $66,684; Households with income of $100,000 or more: 17.1%; Poverty rate: 10.1%
Educational Attainment: High school diploma or higher: 89.3%; Bachelor's degree or higher: 20.3%; Graduate/professional degree or higher: 7.6%
Housing: Homeownership rate: 77.8%; Median home value: $136,300; Median year structure built: 1979; Homeowner vacancy rate: 2.5%; Median

selected monthly owner costs: $1,031 with a mortgage, $391 without a mortgage; Median gross rent: $729 per month; Rental vacancy rate: 6.6%
Vital Statistics: Birth rate: 117.2 per 10,000 population; Death rate: 90.5 per 10,000 population; Age-adjusted cancer mortality rate: 164.8 deaths per 100,000 population
Health Insurance: 90.6% have insurance; 72.1% have private insurance; 31.9% have public insurance; 9.4% do not have insurance; 8.2% of children under 18 do not have insurance
Health Care: Physicians: 6.4 per 10,000 population; Dentists: 3.8 per 10,000 population; Hospital beds: 7.3 per 10,000 population; Hospital admissions: 360.9 per 10,000 population
Transportation: Commute: 92.0% car, 0.2% public transportation, 2.6% walk, 3.7% work from home; Mean travel time to work: 22.0 minutes
2016 Presidential Election: 69.6% Trump, 25.7% Clinton, 4.5% Johnson, 0.1% Stein
National and State Parks: Cedar Lake Marsh State Fish and Wildlife Area; Marsh Lake Wetlands State Fish and Wildlife Area; Pokagon State Park
Additional Information Contacts
Steuben Government . . . . (260) 668-1000
http://www.co.steuben.in.us

Steuben County Communities

ANGOLA (city). County seat. Covers a land area of 6.344 square miles and a water area of 0.047 square miles. Located at 41.64° N. Lat; 85.00° W. Long. Elevation is 1,063 feet.
Population: 8,636; Growth (since 2000): 17.6%; Density: 1,361.4 persons per square mile; Race: 95.6% White, 0.7% Black/African American, 0.4% Asian, 0.0% American Indian/Alaska Native, 0.1% Native Hawaiian/Other Pacific Islander, 2.7% Two or more races, 4.8% Hispanic of any race; Average household size: 2.33; Median age: 29.8; Age under 18: 20.8%; Age 65 and over: 16.5%; Males per 100 females: 102.4; Marriage status: 38.3% never married, 40.2% now married, 2.5% separated, 7.5% widowed, 14.0% divorced; Foreign born: 2.9%; Speak English only: 94.9%; With disability: 17.8%; Veterans: 6.5%; Ancestry: 30.9% German, 12.2% Irish, 10.6% English, 7.9% American, 7.2% European
Employment: 7.4% management, business, and financial, 6.5% computer, engineering, and science, 12.9% education, legal, community service, arts, and media, 3.4% healthcare practitioners, 16.5% service, 23.3% sales and office, 5.7% natural resources, construction, and maintenance, 24.2% production, transportation, and material moving
Income: Per capita: $20,515; Median household: $41,568; Average household: $54,217; Households with income of $100,000 or more: 11.5%; Poverty rate: 16.9%
Educational Attainment: High school diploma or higher: 87.2%; Bachelor's degree or higher: 23.1%; Graduate/professional degree or higher: 10.3%

School District(s)
M S D Steuben County (PK-12)
Enrollment: 2,668 . . . . (260) 665-2854

Four-year College(s)
Trine University (Private, Not-for-profit)
Enrollment: 4,296 . . . . (260) 665-4100
Tuition: In-state $31,540; Out-of-state $31,540
Housing: Homeownership rate: 48.3%; Median home value: $120,500; Median year structure built: 1981; Homeowner vacancy rate: 6.1%; Median selected monthly owner costs: $965 with a mortgage, $378 without a mortgage; Median gross rent: $725 per month; Rental vacancy rate: 1.5%
Health Insurance: 87.3% have insurance; 64.1% have private insurance; 34.8% have public insurance; 12.7% do not have insurance; 12.2% of children under 18 do not have insurance
Hospitals: Cameron Memorial Community Hospital (25 beds)
Newspapers: Herald-Republican (daily circulation 4,700)
Transportation: Commute: 86.5% car, 0.4% public transportation, 6.2% walk, 4.9% work from home; Mean travel time to work: 14.5 minutes
Additional Information Contacts
City of Angola . . . . (260) 665-2514
http://www.angolain.org

CLEAR LAKE (town). Covers a land area of 1.040 square miles and a water area of 1.336 square miles. Located at 41.73° N. Lat; 84.84° W. Long. Elevation is 1,040 feet.
Population: 472; Growth (since 2000): 93.4%; Density: 453.8 persons per square mile; Race: 99.8% White, 0.0% Black/African American, 0.0% Asian, 0.0% American Indian/Alaska Native, 0.0% Native Hawaiian/Other Pacific Islander, 0.2% Two or more races, 0.0% Hispanic of any race; Average household size: 1.96; Median age: 66.5; Age under 18: 8.3%; Age 65 and over: 54.7%; Males per 100 females: 105.5; Marriage status: 9.7% never married, 70.6% now married, 0.7% separated, 9.3% widowed, 10.4% divorced; Foreign born: 0.6%; Speak English only: 98.7%; With disability: 17.4%; Veterans: 8.5%; Ancestry: 44.5% German, 13.8% Irish, 11.9% English, 7.4% American, 6.8% Scottish
Employment: 26.6% management, business, and financial, 2.9% computer, engineering, and science, 4.0% education, legal, community service, arts, and media, 8.7% healthcare practitioners, 5.8% service, 28.3% sales and office, 9.2% natural resources, construction, and maintenance, 14.5% production, transportation, and material moving
Income: Per capita: $53,728; Median household: $73,958; Average household: $104,246; Households with income of $100,000 or more: 34.4%; Poverty rate: 3.4%
Educational Attainment: High school diploma or higher: 98.8%; Bachelor's degree or higher: 53.5%; Graduate/professional degree or higher: 19.6%
Housing: Homeownership rate: 89.2%; Median home value: $635,400; Median year structure built: 1976; Homeowner vacancy rate: 9.7%; Median selected monthly owner costs: $1,938 with a mortgage, $664 without a mortgage; Median gross rent: $767 per month; Rental vacancy rate: 21.1%
Health Insurance: 98.7% have insurance; 79.2% have private insurance; 56.8% have public insurance; 1.3% do not have insurance; 0.0% of children under 18 do not have insurance
Transportation: Commute: 85.1% car, 0.0% public transportation, 1.8% walk, 13.1% work from home; Mean travel time to work: 28.0 minutes

FREMONT (town). Covers a land area of 2.215 square miles and a water area of 0.006 square miles. Located at 41.73° N. Lat; 84.93° W. Long. Elevation is 1,053 feet.
Population: 2,148; Growth (since 2000): 26.7%; Density: 969.8 persons per square mile; Race: 94.7% White, 0.0% Black/African American, 1.4% Asian, 0.0% American Indian/Alaska Native, 0.0% Native Hawaiian/Other Pacific Islander, 3.8% Two or more races, 0.0% Hispanic of any race; Average household size: 2.22; Median age: 41.2; Age under 18: 18.4%; Age 65 and over: 18.5%; Males per 100 females: 93.7; Marriage status: 23.4% never married, 50.4% now married, 0.0% separated, 6.0% widowed, 20.1% divorced; Foreign born: 1.4%; Speak English only: 96.8%; With disability: 15.1%; Veterans: 8.8%; Ancestry: 38.9% German, 11.0% Irish, 9.0% European, 8.6% English, 4.7% Scotch-Irish
Employment: 16.2% management, business, and financial, 3.0% computer, engineering, and science, 2.3% education, legal, community service, arts, and media, 2.9% healthcare practitioners, 15.0% service, 22.2% sales and office, 9.2% natural resources, construction, and maintenance, 29.2% production, transportation, and material moving
Income: Per capita: $28,197; Median household: $41,617; Average household: $60,447; Households with income of $100,000 or more: 13.0%; Poverty rate: 12.1%
Educational Attainment: High school diploma or higher: 89.3%; Bachelor's degree or higher: 12.8%; Graduate/professional degree or higher: 3.2%

School District(s)
Fremont Community Schools (PK-12)
Enrollment: 966 . . . . (260) 495-5005
Housing: Homeownership rate: 82.6%; Median home value: $102,300; Median year structure built: 1990; Homeowner vacancy rate: 0.0%; Median selected monthly owner costs: $842 with a mortgage, $364 without a mortgage; Median gross rent: $609 per month; Rental vacancy rate: 0.0%
Health Insurance: 87.8% have insurance; 69.1% have private insurance; 31.4% have public insurance; 12.2% do not have insurance; 0.0% of children under 18 do not have insurance
Transportation: Commute: 95.7% car, 0.0% public transportation, 3.1% walk, 1.1% work from home; Mean travel time to work: 19.5 minutes

HAMILTON (town). Covers a land area of 2.393 square miles and a water area of 0.758 square miles. Located at 41.54° N. Lat; 84.92° W. Long. Elevation is 902 feet.
History: Hamilton was called Enterprise when it was founded in 1836 at a site that provided water power. The town was incorporated in 1914.
Population: 1,516; Growth (since 2000): n/a; Density: 633.5 persons per square mile; Race: 95.3% White, 0.2% Black/African American, 0.6% Asian, 0.7% American Indian/Alaska Native, 0.0% Native Hawaiian/Other Pacific Islander, 2.8% Two or more races, 0.4% Hispanic of any race;

Average household size: 2.20; Median age: 47.7; Age under 18: 18.5%; Age 65 and over: 21.2%; Males per 100 females: 96.2; Marriage status: 27.0% never married, 54.4% now married, 1.7% separated, 5.5% widowed, 13.2% divorced; Foreign born: 1.3%; Speak English only: 98.9%; With disability: 16.2%; Veterans: 9.0%; Ancestry: 47.4% German, 14.0% Irish, 7.6% English, 6.4% European, 5.3% American
Employment: 8.9% management, business, and financial, 3.0% computer, engineering, and science, 7.0% education, legal, community service, arts, and media, 5.8% healthcare practitioners, 16.3% service, 21.4% sales and office, 8.1% natural resources, construction, and maintenance, 29.4% production, transportation, and material moving
Income: Per capita: $29,489; Median household: $50,000; Average household: $64,694; Households with income of $100,000 or more: 14.8%; Poverty rate: 13.7%
Educational Attainment: High school diploma or higher: 92.9%; Bachelor's degree or higher: 20.8%; Graduate/professional degree or higher: 7.6%

School District(s)

Hamilton Community Schools (KG-12)
Enrollment: 385 . . . . (260) 488-2513
Housing: Homeownership rate: 73.3%; Median home value: $170,000; Median year structure built: 1960; Homeowner vacancy rate: 1.9%; Median selected monthly owner costs: $1,033 with a mortgage, $447 without a mortgage; Median gross rent: $548 per month; Rental vacancy rate: 10.7%
Health Insurance: 91.9% have insurance; 72.4% have private insurance; 34.4% have public insurance; 8.1% do not have insurance; 2.9% of children under 18 do not have insurance
Newspapers: Hamilton News (weekly circulation 1,000)
Transportation: Commute: 96.5% car, 0.0% public transportation, 2.2% walk, 0.9% work from home; Mean travel time to work: 24.3 minutes

HUDSON (town). Covers a land area of 0.692 square miles and a water area of 0 square miles. Located at 41.53° N. Lat; 85.08° W. Long. Elevation is 991 feet.
Population: 584; Growth (since 2000): -2.0%; Density: 843.6 persons per square mile; Race: 98.6% White, 0.3% Black/African American, 0.2% Asian, 0.0% American Indian/Alaska Native, 0.0% Native Hawaiian/Other Pacific Islander, 0.7% Two or more races, 3.3% Hispanic of any race; Average household size: 2.81; Median age: 36.1; Age under 18: 28.6%; Age 65 and over: 12.7%; Males per 100 females: 102.3; Marriage status: 28.8% never married, 53.0% now married, 0.2% separated, 4.0% widowed, 14.3% divorced; Foreign born: 1.7%; Speak English only: 98.2%; With disability: 11.6%; Veterans: 8.6%; Ancestry: 44.3% German, 9.8% English, 7.7% American, 5.7% Dutch, 5.0% Irish
Employment: 13.6% management, business, and financial, 2.4% computer, engineering, and science, 5.2% education, legal, community service, arts, and media, 0.3% healthcare practitioners, 15.7% service, 19.6% sales and office, 14.7% natural resources, construction, and maintenance, 28.3% production, transportation, and material moving
Income: Per capita: $18,027; Median household: $50,000; Average household: $51,428; Households with income of $100,000 or more: 1.9%; Poverty rate: 15.9%
Educational Attainment: High school diploma or higher: 91.8%; Bachelor's degree or higher: 14.4%; Graduate/professional degree or higher: 2.3%
Housing: Homeownership rate: 74.0%; Median home value: $75,000; Median year structure built: Before 1940; Homeowner vacancy rate: 5.4%; Median selected monthly owner costs: $780 with a mortgage, $357 without a mortgage; Median gross rent: $838 per month; Rental vacancy rate: 6.9%
Health Insurance: 83.0% have insurance; 70.4% have private insurance; 26.0% have public insurance; 17.0% do not have insurance; 17.7% of children under 18 do not have insurance
Transportation: Commute: 93.5% car, 0.0% public transportation, 2.5% walk, 2.9% work from home; Mean travel time to work: 18.8 minutes

ORLAND (town). Covers a land area of 0.663 square miles and a water area of 0 square miles. Located at 41.73° N. Lat; 85.17° W. Long. Elevation is 961 feet.
History: Laid out 1838.
Population: 419; Growth (since 2000): 22.9%; Density: 632.3 persons per square mile; Race: 96.2% White, 0.0% Black/African American, 0.2% Asian, 0.0% American Indian/Alaska Native, 0.0% Native Hawaiian/Other Pacific Islander, 3.6% Two or more races, 5.3% Hispanic of any race; Average household size: 2.35; Median age: 41.7; Age under 18: 17.9%; Age 65 and over: 13.8%; Males per 100 females: 100.0; Marriage status: 31.4% never married, 47.8% now married, 0.5% separated, 4.1% widowed, 16.7% divorced; Foreign born: 2.9%; Speak English only: 91.6%; With disability: 20.8%; Veterans: 5.8%; Ancestry: 31.7% German, 28.4% Irish, 11.5% English, 9.5% European, 6.7% American
Employment: 2.0% management, business, and financial, 0.8% computer, engineering, and science, 13.8% education, legal, community service, arts, and media, 2.8% healthcare practitioners, 14.6% service, 24.8% sales and office, 9.3% natural resources, construction, and maintenance, 31.7% production, transportation, and material moving
Income: Per capita: $22,521; Median household: $43,958; Average household: $53,426; Households with income of $100,000 or more: 10.1%; Poverty rate: 12.3%
Educational Attainment: High school diploma or higher: 85.3%; Bachelor's degree or higher: 6.0%; Graduate/professional degree or higher: 2.3%
Housing: Homeownership rate: 75.3%; Median home value: $84,100; Median year structure built: Before 1940; Homeowner vacancy rate: 2.8%; Median selected monthly owner costs: $835 with a mortgage, $325 without a mortgage; Median gross rent: $611 per month; Rental vacancy rate: 6.4%
Health Insurance: 94.3% have insurance; 73.3% have private insurance; 34.1% have public insurance; 5.7% do not have insurance; 2.5% of children under 18 do not have insurance
Transportation: Commute: 90.3% car, 0.0% public transportation, 6.2% walk, 0.9% work from home; Mean travel time to work: 19.8 minutes

PLEASANT LAKE (unincorporated postal area)
ZCTA: 46779
Covers a land area of 35.411 square miles and a water area of 0.653 square miles. Located at 41.58° N. Lat; 85.04° W. Long. Elevation is 978 feet.
Population: 2,124; Growth (since 2000): -3.1%; Density: 60.0 persons per square mile; Race: 98.2% White, 0.2% Black/African American, 0.7% Asian, 0.0% American Indian/Alaska Native, 0.0% Native Hawaiian/Other Pacific Islander, 0.9% Two or more races, 0.3% Hispanic of any race; Average household size: 2.63; Median age: 34.0; Age under 18: 28.4%; Age 65 and over: 14.8%; Males per 100 females: 101.5; Marriage status: 22.8% never married, 57.8% now married, 0.0% separated, 6.7% widowed, 12.8% divorced; Foreign born: 0.8%; Speak English only: 99.8%; With disability: 9.9%; Veterans: 12.0%; Ancestry: 29.2% German, 12.0% Irish, 9.1% European, 8.7% English, 7.2% American
Employment: 9.7% management, business, and financial, 0.9% computer, engineering, and science, 6.7% education, legal, community service, arts, and media, 3.3% healthcare practitioners, 19.0% service, 28.4% sales and office, 12.0% natural resources, construction, and maintenance, 20.2% production, transportation, and material moving
Income: Per capita: $23,915; Median household: $56,122; Average household: $62,016; Households with income of $100,000 or more: 13.2%; Poverty rate: 6.7%
Educational Attainment: High school diploma or higher: 95.5%; Bachelor's degree or higher: 10.9%; Graduate/professional degree or higher: 4.7%

School District(s)

M S D Steuben County (PK-12)
Enrollment: 2,668 . . . . (260) 665-2854
Housing: Homeownership rate: 78.2%; Median home value: $96,100; Median year structure built: 1950; Homeowner vacancy rate: 0.0%; Median selected monthly owner costs: $979 with a mortgage, $446 without a mortgage; Median gross rent: $597 per month; Rental vacancy rate: 12.0%
Health Insurance: 91.6% have insurance; 78.0% have private insurance; 28.5% have public insurance; 8.4% do not have insurance; 1.4% of children under 18 do not have insurance
Transportation: Commute: 96.8% car, 0.0% public transportation, 0.9% walk, 1.5% work from home; Mean travel time to work: 20.8 minutes

Sullivan County

Located in southwestern Indiana; bounded on the west by the Wabash River and the Illinois border; drained by Busseron and Maria Creeks. Covers a land area of 447.142 square miles, a water area of 6.974 square miles, and is located in the Eastern Time Zone at 39.09° N. Lat., 87.42° W. Long. The county was founded in 1816. County seat is Sullivan.

Sullivan County is part of the Terre Haute, IN Metropolitan Statistical Area. The entire metro area includes: Clay County, IN; Sullivan County, IN; Vermillion County, IN; Vigo County, IN

Population: 20,900; Growth (since 2000): -3.9%; Density: 46.7 persons per square mile; Race: 93.3% White, 3.9% Black/African American, 0.8% Asian, 0.2% American Indian/Alaska Native, 0.0% Native Hawaiian/Other Pacific Islander, 1.6% two or more races, 1.7% Hispanic of any race; Average household size: 2.47; Median age: 41.4; Age under 18: 20.2%; Age 65 and over: 16.7%; Males per 100 females: 119.0; Marriage status: 26.3% never married, 49.9% now married, 1.4% separated, 7.8% widowed, 16.0% divorced; Foreign born: 1.0%; Speak English only: 98.9%; With disability: 19.1%; Veterans: 8.2%; Ancestry: 17.1% German, 11.4% Irish, 10.7% English, 10.1% American, 4.3% Scottish
Religion: Six largest groups: 18.5% Baptist, 6.1% Methodist/Pietist, 4.2% Non-denominational Protestant, 2.3% Catholicism, 2.2% Presbyterian-Reformed, 2.1% Pentecostal
Economy: Unemployment rate: 4.6%; Leading industries: 13.5 % retail trade; 13.2 % other services (except public administration); 10.8 % accommodation and food services; Farms: 433 totaling 170,245 acres; Company size: 0 employ 1,000 or more persons, 1 employs 500 to 999 persons, 5 employ 100 to 499 persons, 327 employ less than 100 persons; Business ownership: 469 women-owned, n/a Black-owned, 30 Hispanic-owned, n/a Asian-owned, n/a American Indian/Alaska Native-owned
Employment: 9.1% management, business, and financial, 2.6% computer, engineering, and science, 7.3% education, legal, community service, arts, and media, 7.2% healthcare practitioners, 18.7% service, 18.0% sales and office, 16.5% natural resources, construction, and maintenance, 20.6% production, transportation, and material moving
Income: Per capita: $22,239; Median household: $45,031; Average household: $59,088; Households with income of $100,000 or more: 15.2%; Poverty rate: 15.6%
Educational Attainment: High school diploma or higher: 86.5%; Bachelor's degree or higher: 12.5%; Graduate/professional degree or higher: 4.0%
Housing: Homeownership rate: 72.7%; Median home value: $80,900; Median year structure built: 1970; Homeowner vacancy rate: 2.7%; Median selected monthly owner costs: $867 with a mortgage, $343 without a mortgage; Median gross rent: $668 per month; Rental vacancy rate: 8.8%
Vital Statistics: Birth rate: 95.0 per 10,000 population; Death rate: 97.4 per 10,000 population; Age-adjusted cancer mortality rate: 223.2 deaths per 100,000 population
Health Insurance: 87.8% have insurance; 64.6% have private insurance; 38.7% have public insurance; 12.2% do not have insurance; 6.7% of children under 18 do not have insurance
Health Care: Physicians: 7.2 per 10,000 population; Dentists: 2.4 per 10,000 population; Hospital beds: 12.1 per 10,000 population; Hospital admissions: 367.9 per 10,000 population
Air Quality Index (AQI): Percent of Days: 85.6% good, 14.4% moderate, 0.0% unhealthy for sensitive individuals, 0.0% unhealthy, 0.0% very unhealthy; Annual median: 32; Annual maximum: 65
Transportation: Commute: 96.9% car, 0.2% public transportation, 1.8% walk, 0.9% work from home; Mean travel time to work: 22.8 minutes
2016 Presidential Election: 71.7% Trump, 24.7% Clinton, 3.6% Johnson, 0.0% Stein
National and State Parks: Greene-Sullivan State Forest
Additional Information Contacts
Sullivan Government. . . . . (812) 398-4924

Sullivan County Communities

CARLISLE (town). Covers a land area of 0.518 square miles and a water area of 0 square miles. Located at 38.96° N. Lat; 87.40° W. Long. Elevation is 482 feet.
History: Carlisle was settled in 1803 on land granted to Samuel Ledgerwood for services to the U.S. government. Its early industry was coal mining.
Population: 678; Growth (since 2000): -74.5%; Density: 1,308.2 persons per square mile; Race: 95.6% White, 0.0% Black/African American, 0.0% Asian, 0.0% American Indian/Alaska Native, 0.0% Native Hawaiian/Other Pacific Islander, 4.4% Two or more races, 0.0% Hispanic of any race; Average household size: 2.54; Median age: 40.0; Age under 18: 24.2%; Age 65 and over: 19.0%; Males per 100 females: 98.3; Marriage status: 24.0% never married, 44.8% now married, 0.6% separated, 10.3% widowed, 20.8% divorced; Foreign born: 0.0%; Speak English only: 99.7%; With disability: 23.2%; Veterans: 9.1%; Ancestry: 21.2% Irish, 18.0% American, 12.5% English, 12.1% German, 10.2% Scotch-Irish
Employment: 2.5% management, business, and financial, 2.1% computer, engineering, and science, 16.2% education, legal, community service, arts, and media, 7.9% healthcare practitioners, 19.5% service, 23.2% sales and office, 9.5% natural resources, construction, and maintenance, 19.1% production, transportation, and material moving
Income: Per capita: $19,426; Median household: $32,589; Average household: $47,890; Households with income of $100,000 or more: 11.2%; Poverty rate: 24.5%
Educational Attainment: High school diploma or higher: 91.4%; Bachelor's degree or higher: 13.1%; Graduate/professional degree or higher: 5.4%

School District(s)
Southwest School Corporation (PK-12)
Enrollment: 1,607 . . . . (812) 268-6311
Housing: Homeownership rate: 73.8%; Median home value: $54,000; Median year structure built: Before 1940; Homeowner vacancy rate: 0.0%; Median selected monthly owner costs: $860 with a mortgage, $272 without a mortgage; Median gross rent: $600 per month; Rental vacancy rate: 11.4%
Health Insurance: 91.0% have insurance; 49.3% have private insurance; 55.3% have public insurance; 9.0% do not have insurance; 0.0% of children under 18 do not have insurance
Transportation: Commute: 88.7% car, 0.0% public transportation, 7.6% walk, 3.8% work from home; Mean travel time to work: 20.4 minutes
Additional Information Contacts
Town of Carlisle. . . . . (812) 847-4846
http://www.lintonchamber.org

DUGGER (town). Covers a land area of 0.586 square miles and a water area of 0 square miles. Located at 39.07° N. Lat; 87.26° W. Long. Elevation is 577 feet.
Population: 893; Growth (since 2000): -6.5%; Density: 1,524.4 persons per square mile; Race: 90.6% White, 5.3% Black/African American, 0.0% Asian, 0.3% American Indian/Alaska Native, 0.0% Native Hawaiian/Other Pacific Islander, 3.8% Two or more races, 3.7% Hispanic of any race; Average household size: 2.62; Median age: 41.0; Age under 18: 18.9%; Age 65 and over: 15.6%; Males per 100 females: 97.0; Marriage status: 29.1% never married, 55.1% now married, 0.8% separated, 4.0% widowed, 11.9% divorced; Foreign born: 0.0%; Speak English only: 99.8%; With disability: 12.4%; Veterans: 6.6%; Ancestry: 12.4% Irish, 9.1% American, 8.6% German, 8.2% English, 1.0% Welsh
Employment: 3.0% management, business, and financial, 2.7% computer, engineering, and science, 8.7% education, legal, community service, arts, and media, 6.6% healthcare practitioners, 32.4% service, 14.4% sales and office, 15.3% natural resources, construction, and maintenance, 16.9% production, transportation, and material moving
Income: Per capita: $21,892; Median household: $46,328; Average household: $52,274; Households with income of $100,000 or more: 8.3%; Poverty rate: 6.6%
Educational Attainment: High school diploma or higher: 92.9%; Bachelor's degree or higher: 10.2%; Graduate/professional degree or higher: 4.8%

School District(s)
Dugger Union Community School Corp (KG-12)
Enrollment: 306. . . . . (812) 648-7109
Housing: Homeownership rate: 90.3%; Median home value: $59,000; Median year structure built: 1947; Homeowner vacancy rate: 0.0%; Median selected monthly owner costs: $843 with a mortgage, $363 without a mortgage; Median gross rent: $605 per month; Rental vacancy rate: 21.4%
Health Insurance: 90.4% have insurance; 77.0% have private insurance; 29.9% have public insurance; 9.6% do not have insurance; 3.8% of children under 18 do not have insurance
Transportation: Commute: 97.2% car, 0.0% public transportation, 0.7% walk, 0.7% work from home; Mean travel time to work: 25.3 minutes

FAIRBANKS (unincorporated postal area)
ZCTA: 47849
Covers a land area of 26.057 square miles and a water area of 0.499 square miles. Located at 39.20° N. Lat; 87.56° W. Long. Elevation is 551 feet.
Population: 277; Growth (since 2000): -33.3%; Density: 10.6 persons per square mile; Race: 100.0% White, 0.0% Black/African American,

0.0% Asian, 0.0% American Indian/Alaska Native, 0.0% Native Hawaiian/Other Pacific Islander, 0.0% Two or more races, 0.0% Hispanic of any race; Average household size: 2.10; Median age: 54.8; Age under 18: 10.1%; Age 65 and over: 23.5%; Males per 100 females: 113.8; Marriage status: 20.7% never married, 49.6% now married, 3.9% separated, 9.0% widowed, 20.7% divorced; Foreign born: 0.0%; Speak English only: 100.0%; With disability: 18.8%; Veterans: 14.1%; Ancestry: 28.9% American, 8.7% German, 3.2% Scotch-Irish, 2.9% English, 2.9% Swedish
Employment: 5.5% management, business, and financial, 0.0% computer, engineering, and science, 0.0% education, legal, community service, arts, and media, 0.0% healthcare practitioners, 25.0% service, 22.7% sales and office, 21.1% natural resources, construction, and maintenance, 25.8% production, transportation, and material moving
Income: Per capita: $37,795; Median household: $52,344; Average household: $77,221; Households with income of $100,000 or more: 11.4%; Poverty rate: 16.2%
Educational Attainment: High school diploma or higher: 88.6%; Bachelor's degree or higher: 24.8%; Graduate/professional degree or higher: n/a
Housing: Homeownership rate: 86.4%; Median home value: $111,500; Median year structure built: 1991; Homeowner vacancy rate: 0.0%; Median selected monthly owner costs: $956 with a mortgage, $287 without a mortgage; Median gross rent: n/a per month; Rental vacancy rate: 0.0%
Health Insurance: 92.4% have insurance; 73.3% have private insurance; 40.1% have public insurance; 7.6% do not have insurance; 0.0% of children under 18 do not have insurance
Transportation: Commute: 100.0% car, 0.0% public transportation, 0.0% walk, 0.0% work from home; Mean travel time to work: 23.8 minutes

FARMERSBURG (town). Covers a land area of 0.743 square miles and a water area of 0 square miles. Located at 39.25° N. Lat; 87.38° W. Long. Elevation is 561 feet.
History: Farmersburg developed as a supply center for the surrounding farming community.
Population: 1,263; Growth (since 2000): 7.0%; Density: 1,699.9 persons per square mile; Race: 100.0% White, 0.0% Black/African American, 0.0% Asian, 0.0% American Indian/Alaska Native, 0.0% Native Hawaiian/Other Pacific Islander, 0.0% Two or more races, 5.0% Hispanic of any race; Average household size: 2.54; Median age: 34.0; Age under 18: 32.6%; Age 65 and over: 14.2%; Males per 100 females: 92.4; Marriage status: 24.3% never married, 46.5% now married, 0.4% separated, 6.3% widowed, 22.9% divorced; Foreign born: 0.6%; Speak English only: 100.0%; With disability: 15.9%; Veterans: 5.2%; Ancestry: 20.3% Irish, 14.7% German, 8.1% English, 6.9% American, 4.0% Czech
Employment: 6.8% management, business, and financial, 1.9% computer, engineering, and science, 1.9% education, legal, community service, arts, and media, 11.8% healthcare practitioners, 18.4% service, 22.2% sales and office, 8.2% natural resources, construction, and maintenance, 28.8% production, transportation, and material moving
Income: Per capita: $21,792; Median household: $39,196; Average household: $54,465; Households with income of $100,000 or more: 14.8%; Poverty rate: 16.1%
Educational Attainment: High school diploma or higher: 94.3%; Bachelor's degree or higher: 10.8%; Graduate/professional degree or higher: 3.1%

School District(s)

Northeast School Corp (PK-12)
Enrollment: 1,067 .... (812) 383-5761
Housing: Homeownership rate: 70.1%; Median home value: $74,500; Median year structure built: 1963; Homeowner vacancy rate: 8.4%; Median selected monthly owner costs: $823 with a mortgage, $383 without a mortgage; Median gross rent: $672 per month; Rental vacancy rate: 6.4%
Health Insurance: 93.3% have insurance; 73.2% have private insurance; 38.2% have public insurance; 6.7% do not have insurance; 3.8% of children under 18 do not have insurance
Transportation: Commute: 97.9% car, 0.0% public transportation, 0.8% walk, 0.0% work from home; Mean travel time to work: 21.4 minutes

HYMERA (town). Covers a land area of 0.712 square miles and a water area of 0 square miles. Located at 39.19° N. Lat; 87.30° W. Long. Elevation is 525 feet.
History: Hymera was platted in 1870 and named Pittsburg, after coal was discovered nearby. Postmaster John Badders changed the name to High Mary, referring to his daughter, and the name was later shortened to Hymera.
Population: 723; Growth (since 2000): -13.2%; Density: 1,015.2 persons per square mile; Race: 99.4% White, 0.0% Black/African American, 0.0% Asian, 0.6% American Indian/Alaska Native, 0.0% Native Hawaiian/Other Pacific Islander, 0.0% Two or more races, 0.0% Hispanic of any race; Average household size: 2.42; Median age: 41.6; Age under 18: 24.8%; Age 65 and over: 17.4%; Males per 100 females: 98.8; Marriage status: 28.5% never married, 43.4% now married, 3.6% separated, 9.5% widowed, 18.6% divorced; Foreign born: 0.0%; Speak English only: 99.7%; With disability: 25.0%; Veterans: 5.5%; Ancestry: 15.9% German, 12.7% Irish, 11.3% American, 7.5% Scottish, 5.4% English
Employment: 5.2% management, business, and financial, 0.0% computer, engineering, and science, 9.5% education, legal, community service, arts, and media, 8.7% healthcare practitioners, 27.3% service, 10.4% sales and office, 11.7% natural resources, construction, and maintenance, 27.3% production, transportation, and material moving
Income: Per capita: $16,192; Median household: $30,625; Average household: $38,024; Households with income of $100,000 or more: 4.0%; Poverty rate: 25.9%
Educational Attainment: High school diploma or higher: 79.9%; Bachelor's degree or higher: 6.3%; Graduate/professional degree or higher: 2.4%

School District(s)

Northeast School Corp (PK-12)
Enrollment: 1,067 .... (812) 383-5761
Housing: Homeownership rate: 74.6%; Median home value: $59,800; Median year structure built: 1959; Homeowner vacancy rate: 0.0%; Median selected monthly owner costs: $719 with a mortgage, $290 without a mortgage; Median gross rent: $670 per month; Rental vacancy rate: 0.0%
Health Insurance: 91.7% have insurance; 51.9% have private insurance; 51.0% have public insurance; 8.3% do not have insurance; 1.6% of children under 18 do not have insurance
Transportation: Commute: 97.0% car, 0.0% public transportation, 1.3% walk, 0.9% work from home; Mean travel time to work: 30.2 minutes

MEROM (town). Covers a land area of 0.355 square miles and a water area of 0 square miles. Located at 39.06° N. Lat; 87.57° W. Long. Elevation is 548 feet.
History: From 1817 to 1842 Merom was the seat of Sullivan County and a shipping center. The name, which means "high ground along the waters," reflects Merom's location on a bluff of the Wabash River.
Population: 225; Growth (since 2000): -23.5%; Density: 632.9 persons per square mile; Race: 97.8% White, 0.0% Black/African American, 0.0% Asian, 0.0% American Indian/Alaska Native, 0.0% Native Hawaiian/Other Pacific Islander, 2.2% Two or more races, 12.0% Hispanic of any race; Average household size: 2.56; Median age: 36.1; Age under 18: 27.1%; Age 65 and over: 9.8%; Males per 100 females: 101.8; Marriage status: 19.5% never married, 53.4% now married, 0.0% separated, 6.3% widowed, 20.7% divorced; Foreign born: 0.0%; Speak English only: 95.6%; With disability: 8.9%; Veterans: 1.2%; Ancestry: 27.6% German, 25.3% English, 20.4% Irish, 8.9% French, 4.0% Welsh
Employment: 2.2% management, business, and financial, 0.0% computer, engineering, and science, 6.7% education, legal, community service, arts, and media, 5.6% healthcare practitioners, 34.8% service, 18.0% sales and office, 18.0% natural resources, construction, and maintenance, 14.6% production, transportation, and material moving
Income: Per capita: $17,128; Median household: $39,375; Average household: $42,153; Households with income of $100,000 or more: 2.3%; Poverty rate: 24.9%
Educational Attainment: High school diploma or higher: 92.1%; Bachelor's degree or higher: 5.3%; Graduate/professional degree or higher: 1.3%
Housing: Homeownership rate: 65.9%; Median home value: $53,800; Median year structure built: 1953; Homeowner vacancy rate: 1.4%; Median selected monthly owner costs: $815 with a mortgage, $270 without a mortgage; Median gross rent: $631 per month; Rental vacancy rate: 0.0%
Health Insurance: 80.9% have insurance; 45.3% have private insurance; 44.0% have public insurance; 19.1% do not have insurance; 19.4% of children under 18 do not have insurance

Transportation: Commute: 98.9% car, 0.0% public transportation, 0.0% walk, 0.0% work from home; Mean travel time to work: 31.5 minutes

PAXTON (unincorporated postal area)
ZCTA: 47865

Covers a land area of 0.136 square miles and a water area of 0 square miles. Located at 39.02° N. Lat; 87.39° W. Long. Elevation is 522 feet.
Population: 345; Growth (since 2000): 385.9%; Density: 2,535.8 persons per square mile; Race: 100.0% White, 0.0% Black/African American, 0.0% Asian, 0.0% American Indian/Alaska Native, 0.0% Native Hawaiian/Other Pacific Islander, 0.0% Two or more races, 0.0% Hispanic of any race; Average household size: 3.56; Median age: 22.7; Age under 18: 44.3%; Age 65 and over: 2.0%; Males per 100 females: 61.2; Marriage status: 40.7% never married, 28.9% now married, 0.0% separated, 0.0% widowed, 30.4% divorced; Foreign born: 0.0%; Speak English only: 100.0%; With disability: 0.0%; Veterans: 2.1%; Ancestry: 9.0% British, 7.0% American, 2.0% Irish
Employment: 2.2% management, business, and financial, 0.0% computer, engineering, and science, 0.0% education, legal, community service, arts, and media, 2.2% healthcare practitioners, 33.7% service, 21.7% sales and office, 0.0% natural resources, construction, and maintenance, 40.2% production, transportation, and material moving
Income: Per capita: $15,909; Median household: n/a; Average household: $53,590; Households with income of $100,000 or more: 18.6%; Poverty rate: 8.1%
Educational Attainment: High school diploma or higher: 100.0%; Bachelor's degree or higher: n/a; Graduate/professional degree or higher: n/a
Housing: Homeownership rate: 95.9%; Median home value: n/a; Median year structure built: 1994; Homeowner vacancy rate: 0.0%; Median selected monthly owner costs: $0 with a mortgage, $361 without a mortgage; Median gross rent: n/a per month; Rental vacancy rate: 0.0%
Health Insurance: 74.5% have insurance; 70.7% have private insurance; 5.8% have public insurance; 25.5% do not have insurance; 28.1% of children under 18 do not have insurance
Transportation: Commute: 100.0% car, 0.0% public transportation, 0.0% walk, 0.0% work from home; Mean travel time to work: 19.3 minutes

SHELBURN (town). Covers a land area of 0.686 square miles and a water area of 0 square miles. Located at 39.18° N. Lat; 87.40° W. Long. Elevation is 541 feet.
History: Shelburn was founded in 1818. Growth was seen when the first coal mine was established in 1868.
Population: 1,317; Growth (since 2000): 3.9%; Density: 1,920.0 persons per square mile; Race: 99.6% White, 0.0% Black/African American, 0.0% Asian, 0.0% American Indian/Alaska Native, 0.0% Native Hawaiian/Other Pacific Islander, 0.4% Two or more races, 0.9% Hispanic of any race; Average household size: 2.91; Median age: 32.2; Age under 18: 29.1%; Age 65 and over: 12.0%; Males per 100 females: 94.1; Marriage status: 27.7% never married, 49.1% now married, 1.4% separated, 7.3% widowed, 15.9% divorced; Foreign born: 0.3%; Speak English only: 98.5%; With disability: 21.9%; Veterans: 6.9%; Ancestry: 14.1% German, 12.7% English, 9.3% Irish, 7.6% American, 4.1% British
Employment: 4.7% management, business, and financial, 1.2% computer, engineering, and science, 4.1% education, legal, community service, arts, and media, 7.5% healthcare practitioners, 20.7% service, 19.7% sales and office, 6.9% natural resources, construction, and maintenance, 35.3% production, transportation, and material moving
Income: Per capita: $15,351; Median household: $40,568; Average household: $42,497; Households with income of $100,000 or more: 1.8%; Poverty rate: 23.0%
Educational Attainment: High school diploma or higher: 81.9%; Bachelor's degree or higher: 8.0%; Graduate/professional degree or higher: 2.7%

School District(s)

Northeast School Corp (PK-12)
Enrollment: 1,067 . . . . (812) 383-5761
Housing: Homeownership rate: 71.0%; Median home value: $53,000; Median year structure built: 1973; Homeowner vacancy rate: 2.9%; Median selected monthly owner costs: $722 with a mortgage, $329 without a mortgage; Median gross rent: $683 per month; Rental vacancy rate: 19.6%
Health Insurance: 81.7% have insurance; 48.3% have private insurance; 48.4% have public insurance; 18.3% do not have insurance; 7.7% of children under 18 do not have insurance
Transportation: Commute: 99.0% car, 0.0% public transportation, 0.0% walk, 1.0% work from home; Mean travel time to work: 23.7 minutes

SULLIVAN (city). County seat. Covers a land area of 1.876 square miles and a water area of 0 square miles. Located at 39.10° N. Lat; 87.41° W. Long. Elevation is 528 feet.
History: Sullivan was laid out in 1842 as the seat of Sullivan County, which was moved from Merom to the more central location. The early economy of Sullivan was based on coal mining.
Population: 4,122; Growth (since 2000): -10.7%; Density: 2,197.5 persons per square mile; Race: 96.7% White, 0.0% Black/African American, 2.1% Asian, 0.4% American Indian/Alaska Native, 0.0% Native Hawaiian/Other Pacific Islander, 0.8% Two or more races, 0.7% Hispanic of any race; Average household size: 2.11; Median age: 45.1; Age under 18: 15.6%; Age 65 and over: 19.4%; Males per 100 females: 86.3; Marriage status: 23.8% never married, 43.3% now married, 0.5% separated, 12.3% widowed, 20.5% divorced; Foreign born: 1.4%; Speak English only: 99.9%; With disability: 27.6%; Veterans: 7.4%; Ancestry: 15.4% German, 14.3% Scottish, 12.2% English, 9.8% Irish, 7.3% American
Employment: 4.3% management, business, and financial, 3.6% computer, engineering, and science, 5.1% education, legal, community service, arts, and media, 5.9% healthcare practitioners, 20.1% service, 14.7% sales and office, 27.1% natural resources, construction, and maintenance, 19.2% production, transportation, and material moving
Income: Per capita: $18,890; Median household: $29,344; Average household: $40,423; Households with income of $100,000 or more: 11.4%; Poverty rate: 23.6%
Educational Attainment: High school diploma or higher: 81.7%; Bachelor's degree or higher: 10.9%; Graduate/professional degree or higher: 4.7%

School District(s)

Rural Community Schools Inc (KG-08)
Enrollment: 168 . . . . (812) 382-4500
Southwest School Corporation (PK-12)
Enrollment: 1,607 . . . . (812) 268-6311
Housing: Homeownership rate: 54.4%; Median home value: $72,300; Median year structure built: 1955; Homeowner vacancy rate: 0.0%; Median selected monthly owner costs: $759 with a mortgage, $334 without a mortgage; Median gross rent: $659 per month; Rental vacancy rate: 8.0%
Health Insurance: 80.0% have insurance; 52.1% have private insurance; 43.8% have public insurance; 20.0% do not have insurance; 13.0% of children under 18 do not have insurance
Hospitals: Sullivan County Community Hospital (34 beds)
Newspapers: Sullivan Daily Times (daily circulation 4,100)
Transportation: Commute: 96.2% car, 0.0% public transportation, 3.1% walk, 0.7% work from home; Mean travel time to work: 17.6 minutes
Additional Information Contacts
City of Sullivan. . . . . (812) 268-6077
http://sullivancountyindiana.us

Switzerland County

Located in southeastern Indiana; bounded on the east and south by the Ohio River and the Kentucky border. Covers a land area of 220.633 square miles, a water area of 2.806 square miles, and is located in the Eastern Time Zone at 38.83° N. Lat., 85.03° W. Long. The county was founded in 1814. County seat is Vevay.

Weather Station: Vevay — Elevation: 470 feet

	Jan	Feb	Mar	Apr	May	Jun	Jul	Aug	Sep	Oct	Nov	Dec
High	41	47	56	68	77	85	89	87	81	69	56	44
Low	25	27	34	43	53	62	66	65	57	46	37	28
Precip	3.3	2.9	3.9	4.1	5.2	4.3	3.8	3.9	2.8	3.4	3.7	3.8
Snow	5.1	5.3	2.5	0.2	tr	0.0	0.0	0.0	0.0	0.3	0.4	4.9

High and Low temperatures in degrees Fahrenheit; Precipitation and Snow in inches

Population: 10,617; Growth (since 2000): 17.1%; Density: 48.1 persons per square mile; Race: 96.6% White, 0.8% Black/African American, 0.5% Asian, 0.0% American Indian/Alaska Native, 0.0% Native Hawaiian/Other Pacific Islander, 1.6% two or more races, 1.4% Hispanic of any race; Average household size: 2.47; Median age: 40.0; Age under 18: 25.2%; Age 65 and over: 17.3%; Males per 100 females: 104.1; Marriage status:

22.4% never married, 56.1% now married, 0.9% separated, 6.6% widowed, 14.9% divorced; Foreign born: 1.4%; Speak English only: 95.7%; With disability: 16.9%; Veterans: 12.0%; Ancestry: 20.5% German, 10.3% Irish, 8.8% American, 6.9% English, 2.6% Scottish
Religion: Six largest groups: 14.5% Baptist, 4.4% European Free-Church, 2.7% Methodist/Pietist, 1.0% Non-denominational Protestant, 0.8% Catholicism, 0.1% Presbyterian-Reformed
Economy: Unemployment rate: 4.0%; Leading industries: 15.2 % retail trade; 12.0 % health care and social assistance; 12.0 % other services (except public administration); Farms: 383 totaling 50,519 acres; Company size: 0 employ 1,000 or more persons, 1 employs 500 to 999 persons, 0 employ 100 to 499 persons, 124 employ less than 100 persons; Business ownership: 223 women-owned, n/a Black-owned, n/a Hispanic-owned, n/a Asian-owned, n/a American Indian/Alaska Native-owned
Employment: 7.2% management, business, and financial, 0.8% computer, engineering, and science, 4.0% education, legal, community service, arts, and media, 4.6% healthcare practitioners, 23.2% service, 19.9% sales and office, 18.4% natural resources, construction, and maintenance, 21.9% production, transportation, and material moving
Income: Per capita: $21,511; Median household: $43,468; Average household: $53,953; Households with income of $100,000 or more: 11.3%; Poverty rate: 19.7%
Educational Attainment: High school diploma or higher: 82.6%; Bachelor's degree or higher: 8.7%; Graduate/professional degree or higher: 2.4%
Housing: Homeownership rate: 70.6%; Median home value: $114,300; Median year structure built: 1989; Homeowner vacancy rate: 4.2%; Median selected monthly owner costs: $997 with a mortgage, $383 without a mortgage; Median gross rent: $763 per month; Rental vacancy rate: 4.9%
Vital Statistics: Birth rate: 109.4 per 10,000 population; Death rate: 101.9 per 10,000 population; Age-adjusted cancer mortality rate: 207.5 deaths per 100,000 population
Health Insurance: 86.7% have insurance; 64.1% have private insurance; 38.0% have public insurance; 13.3% do not have insurance; 12.9% of children under 18 do not have insurance
Health Care: Physicians: 0.9 per 10,000 population; Dentists: 1.9 per 10,000 population; Hospital beds: 0.0 per 10,000 population; Hospital admissions: 0.0 per 10,000 population
Transportation: Commute: 92.0% car, 0.0% public transportation, 1.2% walk, 5.7% work from home; Mean travel time to work: 37.4 minutes
2016 Presidential Election: 69.2% Trump, 25.1% Clinton, 4.1% Johnson, 0.1% Stein
Additional Information Contacts
Switzerland Government . . . . (800) 435-5688
http://www.switzerland-county.com

Switzerland County Communities

BENNINGTON (unincorporated postal area)
ZCTA: 47011
Covers a land area of 35.717 square miles and a water area of 0.070 square miles. Located at 38.88° N. Lat; 85.08° W. Long. Elevation is 889 feet.
Population: 640; Growth (since 2000): -5.0%; Density: 17.9 persons per square mile; Race: 100.0% White, 0.0% Black/African American, 0.0% Asian, 0.0% American Indian/Alaska Native, 0.0% Native Hawaiian/Other Pacific Islander, 0.0% Two or more races, 7.2% Hispanic of any race; Average household size: 2.84; Median age: 31.2; Age under 18: 29.5%; Age 65 and over: 16.9%; Males per 100 females: 108.7; Marriage status: 26.8% never married, 40.8% now married, 3.3% separated, 9.5% widowed, 22.8% divorced; Foreign born: 2.0%; Speak English only: 80.5%; With disability: 14.4%; Veterans: 21.7%; Ancestry: 23.0% American, 17.3% German, 7.2% Irish, 4.7% Italian, 3.3% European
Employment: 0.0% management, business, and financial, 0.0% computer, engineering, and science, 4.6% education, legal, community service, arts, and media, 9.1% healthcare practitioners, 32.3% service, 11.0% sales and office, 20.2% natural resources, construction, and maintenance, 22.8% production, transportation, and material moving
Income: Per capita: $27,032; Median household: $56,750; Average household: $80,182; Households with income of $100,000 or more: 21.7%; Poverty rate: 27.4%
Educational Attainment: High school diploma or higher: 69.0%; Bachelor's degree or higher: 5.9%; Graduate/professional degree or higher: n/a
Housing: Homeownership rate: 83.6%; Median home value: $94,300; Median year structure built: 1991; Homeowner vacancy rate: 0.0%; Median selected monthly owner costs: $822 with a mortgage, $322 without a mortgage; Median gross rent: n/a per month; Rental vacancy rate: 0.0%
Health Insurance: 78.8% have insurance; 38.8% have private insurance; 45.8% have public insurance; 21.3% do not have insurance; 36.0% of children under 18 do not have insurance
Transportation: Commute: 96.2% car, 0.0% public transportation, 0.0% walk, 3.8% work from home; Mean travel time to work: 44.5 minutes

EAST ENTERPRISE (CDP). Covers a land area of 0.519 square miles and a water area of 0 square miles. Located at 38.87° N. Lat; 84.99° W. Long. Elevation is 879 feet.
Population: 438; Growth (since 2000): n/a; Density: 844.1 persons per square mile; Race: 100.0% White, 0.0% Black/African American, 0.0% Asian, 0.0% American Indian/Alaska Native, 0.0% Native Hawaiian/Other Pacific Islander, 0.0% Two or more races, 0.0% Hispanic of any race; Average household size: 3.04; Median age: 38.0; Age under 18: 41.3%; Age 65 and over: 8.0%; Males per 100 females: 92.2; Marriage status: 33.4% never married, 35.7% now married, 0.0% separated, 0.0% widowed, 30.8% divorced; Foreign born: 0.0%; Speak English only: 97.7%; With disability: 18.0%; Veterans: 2.3%; Ancestry: 3.4% Irish, 3.4% Italian, 2.7% Scottish, 2.3% German, 1.4% American
Employment: 0.0% management, business, and financial, 0.0% computer, engineering, and science, 0.0% education, legal, community service, arts, and media, 0.0% healthcare practitioners, 57.7% service, 12.8% sales and office, 9.7% natural resources, construction, and maintenance, 19.9% production, transportation, and material moving
Income: Per capita: $17,085; Median household: $34,069; Average household: $49,343; Households with income of $100,000 or more: 15.3%; Poverty rate: 51.1%
Educational Attainment: High school diploma or higher: 62.7%; Bachelor's degree or higher: n/a; Graduate/professional degree or higher: n/a

School District(s)
Switzerland County School Corp (PK-12)
Enrollment: 1,577 . . . . (812) 427-2611
Housing: Homeownership rate: 66.7%; Median home value: $107,400; Median year structure built: 1993; Homeowner vacancy rate: 0.0%; Median selected monthly owner costs: $1,210 with a mortgage, n/a without a mortgage; Median gross rent: n/a per month; Rental vacancy rate: 0.0%
Health Insurance: 92.2% have insurance; 85.6% have private insurance; 8.0% have public insurance; 7.8% do not have insurance; 0.0% of children under 18 do not have insurance
Transportation: Commute: 100.0% car, 0.0% public transportation, 0.0% walk, 0.0% work from home; Mean travel time to work: 46.9 minutes

FLORENCE (CDP). Covers a land area of 0.135 square miles and a water area of 0.017 square miles. Located at 38.78° N. Lat; 84.92° W. Long. Elevation is 476 feet.
Population: 18; Growth (since 2000): n/a; Density: 133.4 persons per square mile; Race: 100.0% White, 0.0% Black/African American, 0.0% Asian, 0.0% American Indian/Alaska Native, 0.0% Native Hawaiian/Other Pacific Islander, 0.0% Two or more races, 0.0% Hispanic of any race; Average household size: 1.80; Median age: n/a; Age under 18: 0.0%; Age 65 and over: 0.0%; Males per 100 females: 90.5; Marriage status: 0.0% never married, 0.0% now married, 0.0% separated, 0.0% widowed, 100.0% divorced; Foreign born: 0.0%; Speak English only: 100.0%; With disability: 0.0%; Veterans: 0.0%; Ancestry: n/a.
Employment: n/a management, business, and financial, n/a computer, engineering, and science, n/a education, legal, community service, arts, and media, n/a healthcare practitioners, n/a service, n/a sales and office, n/a natural resources, construction, and maintenance, n/a production, transportation, and material moving
Income: Per capita: n/a; Median household: n/a; Average household: n/a; Households with income of $100,000 or more: n/a; Poverty rate: 100.0%
Educational Attainment: High school diploma or higher: 44.4%; Bachelor's degree or higher: n/a; Graduate/professional degree or higher: n/a
Housing: Homeownership rate: n/a; Median home value: n/a; Median year structure built: n/a; Homeowner vacancy rate: 0.0%; Median selected monthly owner costs: n/a with a mortgage, n/a without a mortgage; Median gross rent: n/a per month; Rental vacancy rate: 0.0%

Health Insurance: 0.0% have insurance; 0.0% have private insurance; 0.0% have public insurance; 100.0% do not have insurance; 0.0% of children under 18 do not have insurance
Transportation: Commute: n/a car, n/a public transportation, n/a walk, n/a work from home; Mean travel time to work: 0.0 minutes

PATRIOT (town). Covers a land area of 0.219 square miles and a water area of 0.041 square miles. Located at 38.84° N. Lat; 84.83° W. Long. Elevation is 472 feet.
History: Suffered during flood of 1937. Laid out 1820.
Population: 449; Growth (since 2000): 122.3%; Density: 2,052.8 persons per square mile; Race: 100.0% White, 0.0% Black/African American, 0.0% Asian, 0.0% American Indian/Alaska Native, 0.0% Native Hawaiian/Other Pacific Islander, 0.0% Two or more races, 0.0% Hispanic of any race; Average household size: 3.77; Median age: 26.2; Age under 18: 43.7%; Age 65 and over: 6.9%; Males per 100 females: 117.7; Marriage status: 26.9% never married, 52.1% now married, 2.8% separated, 0.7% widowed, 20.3% divorced; Foreign born: 0.0%; Speak English only: 100.0%; With disability: 7.8%; Veterans: 10.7%; Ancestry: 39.0% Irish, 14.0% Dutch, 8.0% German, 5.3% American, 4.9% English
Employment: 0.0% management, business, and financial, 0.0% computer, engineering, and science, 0.0% education, legal, community service, arts, and media, 0.0% healthcare practitioners, 7.0% service, 39.9% sales and office, 27.3% natural resources, construction, and maintenance, 25.9% production, transportation, and material moving
Income: Per capita: $11,363; Median household: $41,875; Average household: $44,591; Households with income of $100,000 or more: 4.2%; Poverty rate: 22.9%
Educational Attainment: High school diploma or higher: 68.3%; Bachelor's degree or higher: 2.2%; Graduate/professional degree or higher: n/a
Housing: Homeownership rate: 55.5%; Median home value: $61,800; Median year structure built: 1974; Homeowner vacancy rate: 15.9%; Median selected monthly owner costs: $934 with a mortgage, $438 without a mortgage; Median gross rent: $904 per month; Rental vacancy rate: 15.9%
Health Insurance: 89.1% have insurance; 57.0% have private insurance; 46.5% have public insurance; 10.9% do not have insurance; 10.0% of children under 18 do not have insurance
Transportation: Commute: 90.8% car, 0.0% public transportation, 0.0% walk, 7.7% work from home; Mean travel time to work: 33.4 minutes

VEVAY (town). County seat. Covers a land area of 1.451 square miles and a water area of 0.097 square miles. Located at 38.74° N. Lat; 85.08° W. Long. Elevation is 482 feet.
History: Vevay was founded in 1801 by Swiss immigrants, who planted vineyards and became known for their fine wines. Vevay was the birthplace of Edward Eggleston, author of "The Hoosier Schoolmaster."
Population: 1,633; Growth (since 2000): -5.9%; Density: 1,125.1 persons per square mile; Race: 95.3% White, 0.2% Black/African American, 2.0% Asian, 0.0% American Indian/Alaska Native, 0.0% Native Hawaiian/Other Pacific Islander, 1.5% Two or more races, 0.9% Hispanic of any race; Average household size: 1.98; Median age: 42.0; Age under 18: 17.2%; Age 65 and over: 21.0%; Males per 100 females: 95.2; Marriage status: 27.6% never married, 38.9% now married, 0.8% separated, 12.6% widowed, 20.9% divorced; Foreign born: 1.9%; Speak English only: 96.5%; With disability: 21.2%; Veterans: 12.4%; Ancestry: 24.2% German, 15.0% Irish, 8.8% English, 5.9% American, 2.6% Scotch-Irish
Employment: 7.1% management, business, and financial, 1.7% computer, engineering, and science, 8.6% education, legal, community service, arts, and media, 2.4% healthcare practitioners, 30.2% service, 20.0% sales and office, 4.5% natural resources, construction, and maintenance, 25.5% production, transportation, and material moving
Income: Per capita: $23,662; Median household: $35,707; Average household: $49,247; Households with income of $100,000 or more: 9.4%; Poverty rate: 18.1%
Educational Attainment: High school diploma or higher: 84.2%; Bachelor's degree or higher: 10.8%; Graduate/professional degree or higher: 4.3%

School District(s)

Switzerland County School Corp (PK-12)
Enrollment: 1,577 . . . . (812) 427-2611
Housing: Homeownership rate: 55.4%; Median home value: $92,600; Median year structure built: 1958; Homeowner vacancy rate: 5.5%; Median selected monthly owner costs: $881 with a mortgage, $323 without a mortgage; Median gross rent: $574 per month; Rental vacancy rate: 5.8%
Health Insurance: 87.3% have insurance; 60.1% have private insurance; 42.2% have public insurance; 12.7% do not have insurance; 1.6% of children under 18 do not have insurance
Newspapers: Reveille-Enterprise (weekly circulation 2,900); Switzerland Democrat (weekly circulation 600)
Transportation: Commute: 92.1% car, 0.0% public transportation, 7.6% walk, 0.3% work from home; Mean travel time to work: 23.6 minutes
Additional Information Contacts
Town of Vevay. . . . . (812) 265-3135
http://www.madisonchamber.org

Tippecanoe County

Located in west central Indiana; crossed by the Wabash River; drained by the Tippecanoe River. Covers a land area of 499.806 square miles, a water area of 3.437 square miles, and is located in the Eastern Time Zone at 40.39° N. Lat., 86.89° W. Long. The county was founded in 1826. County seat is Lafayette.

Tippecanoe County is part of the Lafayette-West Lafayette, IN Metropolitan Statistical Area. The entire metro area includes: Benton County, IN; Carroll County, IN; Tippecanoe County, IN

Weather Station: Lafayette 8 S Elevation: 732 feet

	Jan	Feb	Mar	Apr	May	Jun	Jul	Aug	Sep	Oct	Nov	Dec
High	33	38	49	62	72	82	84	83	78	65	51	37
Low	17	20	29	40	51	60	63	62	54	42	33	21
Precip	2.1	2.0	2.7	3.4	4.6	4.4	4.1	3.8	2.8	2.8	3.2	2.6
Snow	6.9	5.3	2.4	0.6	tr	0.0	0.0	0.0	0.0	0.5	0.5	5.1

High and Low temperatures in degrees Fahrenheit; Precipitation and Snow in inches

Weather Station: West Lafayette 6 NW Elevation: 705 feet

	Jan	Feb	Mar	Apr	May	Jun	Jul	Aug	Sep	Oct	Nov	Dec
High	33	37	48	61	72	81	84	83	77	65	51	37
Low	17	20	29	40	50	60	63	61	53	42	33	21
Precip	1.9	1.9	2.6	3.6	4.6	3.9	4.2	3.6	2.8	3.1	3.2	2.5
Snow	6.4	5.4	2.3	0.5	0.0	0.0	0.0	0.0	0.0	0.2	0.6	4.7

High and Low temperatures in degrees Fahrenheit; Precipitation and Snow in inches

Population: 186,081; Growth (since 2000): 24.9%; Density: 372.3 persons per square mile; Race: 83.2% White, 4.8% Black/African American, 8.0% Asian, 0.2% American Indian/Alaska Native, 0.0% Native Hawaiian/Other Pacific Islander, 2.2% two or more races, 8.1% Hispanic of any race; Average household size: 2.47; Median age: 28.1; Age under 18: 20.7%; Age 65 and over: 10.6%; Males per 100 females: 103.9; Marriage status: 44.3% never married, 41.6% now married, 0.9% separated, 3.9% widowed, 10.2% divorced; Foreign born: 11.3%; Speak English only: 84.4%; With disability: 10.7%; Veterans: 5.4%; Ancestry: 26.5% German, 13.6% Irish, 8.3% English, 5.8% American, 3.4% Polish
Religion: Six largest groups: 11.6% Catholicism, 4.8% Methodist/Pietist, 3.4% Baptist, 2.8% Presbyterian-Reformed, 2.8% Lutheran, 2.3% Non-denominational Protestant
Economy: Unemployment rate: 3.2%; Leading industries: 15.0 % retail trade; 13.2 % health care and social assistance; 12.2 % accommodation and food services; Farms: 702 totaling 220,199 acres; Company size: 5 employ 1,000 or more persons, 3 employ 500 to 999 persons, 96 employ 100 to 499 persons, 3,466 employ less than 100 persons; Business ownership: 3,645 women-owned, 471 Black-owned, 398 Hispanic-owned, 636 Asian-owned, 44 American Indian/Alaska Native-owned
Employment: 11.8% management, business, and financial, 7.5% computer, engineering, and science, 14.7% education, legal, community service, arts, and media, 5.1% healthcare practitioners, 17.7% service, 20.6% sales and office, 6.7% natural resources, construction, and maintenance, 15.8% production, transportation, and material moving
Income: Per capita: $25,481; Median household: $50,486; Average household: $66,595; Households with income of $100,000 or more: 19.7%; Poverty rate: 20.9%
Educational Attainment: High school diploma or higher: 91.3%; Bachelor's degree or higher: 36.9%; Graduate/professional degree or higher: 16.3%
Housing: Homeownership rate: 54.2%; Median home value: $144,300; Median year structure built: 1979; Homeowner vacancy rate: 1.3%; Median selected monthly owner costs: $1,121 with a mortgage, $379 without a mortgage; Median gross rent: $823 per month; Rental vacancy rate: 4.7%

Vital Statistics: Birth rate: 125.6 per 10,000 population; Death rate: 59.7 per 10,000 population; Age-adjusted cancer mortality rate: 144.6 deaths per 100,000 population
Health Insurance: 90.0% have insurance; 75.8% have private insurance; 23.2% have public insurance; 10.0% do not have insurance; 5.5% of children under 18 do not have insurance
Health Care: Physicians: 22.3 per 10,000 population; Dentists: 4.7 per 10,000 population; Hospital beds: 25.5 per 10,000 population; Hospital admissions: 1,178.5 per 10,000 population
Air Quality Index (AQI): Percent of Days: 80.9% good, 19.1% moderate, 0.0% unhealthy for sensitive individuals, 0.0% unhealthy, 0.0% very unhealthy; Annual median: 36; Annual maximum: 81
Transportation: Commute: 84.7% car, 3.1% public transportation, 6.7% walk, 3.2% work from home; Mean travel time to work: 17.7 minutes
2016 Presidential Election: 48.6% Trump, 43.1% Clinton, 6.3% Johnson, 0.5% Stein
Additional Information Contacts
Tippecanoe Government.......................... (765) 423-9326
http://www.tippecanoe.in.gov

Tippecanoe County Communities

AMERICUS (CDP). Covers a land area of 1.263 square miles and a water area of 0.029 square miles. Located at 40.52° N. Lat; 86.75° W. Long. Elevation is 558 feet.
Population: 394; Growth (since 2000): n/a; Density: 311.9 persons per square mile; Race: 100.0% White, 0.0% Black/African American, 0.0% Asian, 0.0% American Indian/Alaska Native, 0.0% Native Hawaiian/Other Pacific Islander, 0.0% Two or more races, 0.0% Hispanic of any race; Average household size: 2.54; Median age: 39.8; Age under 18: 22.8%; Age 65 and over: 11.9%; Males per 100 females: 115.8; Marriage status: 13.9% never married, 81.0% now married, 0.0% separated, 0.0% widowed, 5.1% divorced; Foreign born: 0.0%; Speak English only: 100.0%; With disability: 10.4%; Veterans: 4.6%; Ancestry: 27.2% German, 23.6% American, 9.9% Irish, 5.8% Lithuanian, 5.3% Norwegian
Employment: 21.8% management, business, and financial, 0.0% computer, engineering, and science, 28.0% education, legal, community service, arts, and media, 0.0% healthcare practitioners, 0.0% service, 20.7% sales and office, 0.0% natural resources, construction, and maintenance, 29.5% production, transportation, and material moving
Income: Per capita: $37,197; Median household: $82,824; Average household: $95,182; Households with income of $100,000 or more: 34.9%; Poverty rate: n/a
Educational Attainment: High school diploma or higher: 94.7%; Bachelor's degree or higher: 28.6%; Graduate/professional degree or higher: 11.2%
Housing: Homeownership rate: 89.7%; Median home value: $211,100; Median year structure built: 1984; Homeowner vacancy rate: 0.0%; Median selected monthly owner costs: $1,174 with a mortgage, n/a without a mortgage; Median gross rent: n/a per month; Rental vacancy rate: 0.0%
Health Insurance: 100.0% have insurance; 100.0% have private insurance; 11.9% have public insurance; 0.0% do not have insurance; 0.0% of children under 18 do not have insurance
Transportation: Commute: 100.0% car, 0.0% public transportation, 0.0% walk, 0.0% work from home; Mean travel time to work: 25.4 minutes

BATTLE GROUND (town). Covers a land area of 0.865 square miles and a water area of 0 square miles. Located at 40.51° N. Lat; 86.85° W. Long. Elevation is 587 feet.
History: A memorial park marks scene of the Battle of Tippecanoe (1811) between Native Americans and U.S. soldiers under Gen. W. H. Harrison.
Population: 1,717; Growth (since 2000): 29.8%; Density: 1,985.9 persons per square mile; Race: 93.3% White, 0.0% Black/African American, 3.7% Asian, 0.0% American Indian/Alaska Native, 0.0% Native Hawaiian/Other Pacific Islander, 2.9% Two or more races, 1.3% Hispanic of any race; Average household size: 2.72; Median age: 41.0; Age under 18: 21.2%; Age 65 and over: 11.5%; Males per 100 females: 93.6; Marriage status: 33.9% never married, 56.5% now married, 0.7% separated, 2.4% widowed, 7.2% divorced; Foreign born: 5.5%; Speak English only: 93.8%; With disability: 10.1%; Veterans: 4.3%; Ancestry: 30.8% German, 20.6% English, 19.5% Irish, 4.7% American, 3.3% Polish
Employment: 18.0% management, business, and financial, 7.2% computer, engineering, and science, 13.0% education, legal, community service, arts, and media, 7.1% healthcare practitioners, 18.7% service, 21.3% sales and office, 4.7% natural resources, construction, and maintenance, 10.0% production, transportation, and material moving
Income: Per capita: $34,283; Median household: $85,139; Average household: $91,220; Households with income of $100,000 or more: 40.5%; Poverty rate: 8.2%
Educational Attainment: High school diploma or higher: 97.8%; Bachelor's degree or higher: 42.7%; Graduate/professional degree or higher: 17.8%

School District(s)

Tippecanoe School Corp (PK-12)
Enrollment: 13,431 .... (765) 474-2481
Housing: Homeownership rate: 87.5%; Median home value: $167,800; Median year structure built: 1987; Homeowner vacancy rate: 0.0%; Median selected monthly owner costs: $1,228 with a mortgage, $405 without a mortgage; Median gross rent: $1,277 per month; Rental vacancy rate: 0.0%
Health Insurance: 96.2% have insurance; 90.2% have private insurance; 15.0% have public insurance; 3.8% do not have insurance; 0.9% of children under 18 do not have insurance
Transportation: Commute: 95.9% car, 0.0% public transportation, 0.3% walk, 3.3% work from home; Mean travel time to work: 19.2 minutes
Additional Information Contacts
Town of Battle Ground .... (765) 567-2603
http://battleground.in.gov

BUCK CREEK (CDP). Covers a land area of 0.116 square miles and a water area of 0 square miles. Located at 40.49° N. Lat; 86.76° W. Long. Elevation is 659 feet.
Population: 166; Growth (since 2000): n/a; Density: 1,430.7 persons per square mile; Race: 100.0% White, 0.0% Black/African American, 0.0% Asian, 0.0% American Indian/Alaska Native, 0.0% Native Hawaiian/Other Pacific Islander, 0.0% Two or more races, 0.0% Hispanic of any race; Average household size: 1.82; Median age: 49.8; Age under 18: 0.0%; Age 65 and over: 28.3%; Males per 100 females: 95.3; Marriage status: 5.4% never married, 36.7% now married, 0.0% separated, 9.0% widowed, 48.8% divorced; Foreign born: 0.0%; Speak English only: 100.0%; With disability: 9.0%; Veterans: 0.0%; Ancestry: 9.6% German, 9.0% French
Employment: 0.0% management, business, and financial, 24.6% computer, engineering, and science, 0.0% education, legal, community service, arts, and media, 0.0% healthcare practitioners, 28.6% service, 0.0% sales and office, 0.0% natural resources, construction, and maintenance, 46.8% production, transportation, and material moving
Income: Per capita: $34,171; Median household: $78,361; Average household: $65,542; Households with income of $100,000 or more: n/a; Poverty rate: n/a
Educational Attainment: High school diploma or higher: 100.0%; Bachelor's degree or higher: 10.2%; Graduate/professional degree or higher: 10.2%
Housing: Homeownership rate: 100.0%; Median home value: n/a; Median year structure built: Before 1940; Homeowner vacancy rate: 0.0%; Median selected monthly owner costs: $663 with a mortgage, n/a without a mortgage; Median gross rent: n/a per month; Rental vacancy rate: 0.0%
Health Insurance: 100.0% have insurance; 91.0% have private insurance; 18.7% have public insurance; 0.0% do not have insurance; 0.0% of children under 18 do not have insurance
Transportation: Commute: 100.0% car, 0.0% public transportation, 0.0% walk, 0.0% work from home; Mean travel time to work: 0.0 minutes

CLARKS HILL (town). Covers a land area of 0.272 square miles and a water area of 0 square miles. Located at 40.25° N. Lat; 86.72° W. Long. Elevation is 827 feet.
Population: 734; Growth (since 2000): 7.9%; Density: 2,694.0 persons per square mile; Race: 97.8% White, 0.0% Black/African American, 0.0% Asian, 0.0% American Indian/Alaska Native, 0.0% Native Hawaiian/Other Pacific Islander, 2.2% Two or more races, 0.3% Hispanic of any race; Average household size: 2.66; Median age: 39.0; Age under 18: 27.8%; Age 65 and over: 13.9%; Males per 100 females: 102.3; Marriage status: 21.1% never married, 58.2% now married, 3.8% separated, 4.3% widowed, 16.4% divorced; Foreign born: 0.0%; Speak English only: 100.0%; With disability: 21.5%; Veterans: 8.9%; Ancestry: 23.8% German, 19.1% Irish, 9.1% American, 5.7% English, 1.6% European
Employment: 10.1% management, business, and financial, 2.5% computer, engineering, and science, 3.2% education, legal, community service, arts, and media, 2.2% healthcare practitioners, 22.7% service,

18.3% sales and office, 11.4% natural resources, construction, and maintenance, 29.7% production, transportation, and material moving
Income: Per capita: $18,114; Median household: $37,500; Average household: $47,249; Households with income of $100,000 or more: 10.1%; Poverty rate: 16.4%
Educational Attainment: High school diploma or higher: 83.6%; Bachelor's degree or higher: 5.2%; Graduate/professional degree or higher: 1.7%
Housing: Homeownership rate: 67.0%; Median home value: $73,900; Median year structure built: 1962; Homeowner vacancy rate: 0.0%; Median selected monthly owner costs: $897 with a mortgage, $332 without a mortgage; Median gross rent: $636 per month; Rental vacancy rate: 22.9%
Health Insurance: 82.2% have insurance; 59.9% have private insurance; 35.8% have public insurance; 17.8% do not have insurance; 14.5% of children under 18 do not have insurance
Transportation: Commute: 92.9% car, 2.3% public transportation, 2.3% walk, 2.6% work from home; Mean travel time to work: 22.9 minutes

COLBURN (CDP). Covers a land area of 0.096 square miles and a water area of 0 square miles. Located at 40.52° N. Lat; 86.71° W. Long. Elevation is 663 feet.
Population: 325; Growth (since 2000): n/a; Density: 3,399.4 persons per square mile; Race: 100.0% White, 0.0% Black/African American, 0.0% Asian, 0.0% American Indian/Alaska Native, 0.0% Native Hawaiian/Other Pacific Islander, 0.0% Two or more races, 0.0% Hispanic of any race; Average household size: 2.01; Median age: 25.0; Age under 18: 17.2%; Age 65 and over: 7.7%; Males per 100 females: 107.5; Marriage status: 50.9% never married, 9.3% now married, 0.0% separated, 0.0% widowed, 39.8% divorced; Foreign born: 0.0%; Speak English only: 100.0%; With disability: 3.4%; Veterans: 0.0%; Ancestry: 28.3% English, 24.0% Irish, 16.9% German, 4.3% Dutch
Employment: 0.0% management, business, and financial, 0.0% computer, engineering, and science, 8.2% education, legal, community service, arts, and media, 0.0% healthcare practitioners, 39.3% service, 0.0% sales and office, 16.8% natural resources, construction, and maintenance, 35.7% production, transportation, and material moving
Income: Per capita: $24,119; Median household: $42,866; Average household: $47,702; Households with income of $100,000 or more: n/a; Poverty rate: n/a
Educational Attainment: High school diploma or higher: 84.8%; Bachelor's degree or higher: 12.2%; Graduate/professional degree or higher: n/a
Housing: Homeownership rate: 46.3%; Median home value: $134,600; Median year structure built: 1955; Homeowner vacancy rate: 0.0%; Median selected monthly owner costs: n/a with a mortgage, n/a without a mortgage; Median gross rent: n/a per month; Rental vacancy rate: 0.0%
Health Insurance: 85.8% have insurance; 70.8% have private insurance; 18.5% have public insurance; 14.2% do not have insurance; 0.0% of children under 18 do not have insurance
Transportation: Commute: 100.0% car, 0.0% public transportation, 0.0% walk, 0.0% work from home; Mean travel time to work: 0.0 minutes

DAYTON (town). Covers a land area of 1.064 square miles and a water area of 0 square miles. Located at 40.38° N. Lat; 86.77° W. Long. Elevation is 676 feet.
Population: 1,619; Growth (since 2000): 44.6%; Density: 1,521.6 persons per square mile; Race: 97.8% White, 0.4% Black/African American, 0.6% Asian, 0.2% American Indian/Alaska Native, 0.0% Native Hawaiian/Other Pacific Islander, 1.1% Two or more races, 6.2% Hispanic of any race; Average household size: 2.63; Median age: 37.8; Age under 18: 26.4%; Age 65 and over: 10.7%; Males per 100 females: 98.9; Marriage status: 22.2% never married, 57.4% now married, 0.4% separated, 3.5% widowed, 16.9% divorced; Foreign born: 2.6%; Speak English only: 94.5%; With disability: 14.6%; Veterans: 11.5%; Ancestry: 28.0% German, 23.2% Irish, 9.0% American, 7.4% English, 3.2% Italian
Employment: 5.8% management, business, and financial, 1.3% computer, engineering, and science, 8.1% education, legal, community service, arts, and media, 5.9% healthcare practitioners, 12.6% service, 27.7% sales and office, 11.2% natural resources, construction, and maintenance, 27.6% production, transportation, and material moving
Income: Per capita: $24,964; Median household: $51,536; Average household: $64,806; Households with income of $100,000 or more: 18.9%; Poverty rate: 14.6%
Educational Attainment: High school diploma or higher: 92.1%; Bachelor's degree or higher: 16.6%; Graduate/professional degree or higher: 5.2%

School District(s)

Tippecanoe School Corp (PK-12)
Enrollment: 13,431 . . . . (765) 474-2481
Housing: Homeownership rate: 73.7%; Median home value: $117,100; Median year structure built: 1982; Homeowner vacancy rate: 3.0%; Median selected monthly owner costs: $1,004 with a mortgage, $393 without a mortgage; Median gross rent: $858 per month; Rental vacancy rate: 5.9%
Health Insurance: 90.7% have insurance; 74.5% have private insurance; 26.6% have public insurance; 9.3% do not have insurance; 5.2% of children under 18 do not have insurance
Transportation: Commute: 95.7% car, 0.2% public transportation, 0.7% walk, 3.3% work from home; Mean travel time to work: 16.2 minutes

LAFAYETTE (city). County seat. Covers a land area of 27.742 square miles and a water area of 0 square miles. Located at 40.40° N. Lat; 86.86° W. Long. Elevation is 702 feet.
History: Lafayette was founded in 1824 by William Digby, and named for the Marquis de Lafayette. Lafayette was an early shipping center along the Wabash River. It was from Lafayette that the balloon carrying the first airmail in the U.S. was launched. The flight failed to reach its destination and the mail continued on by train.
Population: 72,174; Growth (since 2000): 28.0%; Density: 2,601.6 persons per square mile; Race: 85.0% White, 8.5% Black/African American, 1.6% Asian, 0.2% American Indian/Alaska Native, 0.0% Native Hawaiian/Other Pacific Islander, 2.3% Two or more races, 12.2% Hispanic of any race; Average household size: 2.27; Median age: 32.4; Age under 18: 22.3%; Age 65 and over: 12.7%; Males per 100 females: 94.9; Marriage status: 37.0% never married, 42.4% now married, 1.6% separated, 5.1% widowed, 15.5% divorced; Foreign born: 7.1%; Speak English only: 88.1%; With disability: 15.2%; Veterans: 7.6%; Ancestry: 25.4% German, 13.6% Irish, 8.4% English, 6.1% American, 2.6% Dutch
Employment: 10.6% management, business, and financial, 5.7% computer, engineering, and science, 8.8% education, legal, community service, arts, and media, 5.9% healthcare practitioners, 19.1% service, 21.9% sales and office, 7.1% natural resources, construction, and maintenance, 20.9% production, transportation, and material moving
Income: Per capita: $24,117; Median household: $43,894; Average household: $54,473; Households with income of $100,000 or more: 11.5%; Poverty rate: 18.9%
Educational Attainment: High school diploma or higher: 87.6%; Bachelor's degree or higher: 24.5%; Graduate/professional degree or higher: 8.4%

School District(s)

Excel Center - Lafayette (11-12)
Enrollment: 319. . . . . (317) 524-3641
Lafayette School Corporation (PK-12)
Enrollment: 7,390 . . . . (765) 771-6000
New Community School (KG-08)
Enrollment: 149. . . . . (765) 420-9617
Tippecanoe School Corp (PK-12)
Enrollment: 13,431 . . . . (765) 474-2481

Two-year College(s)

Ross Medical Education Center-Lafayette (Private, For-profit)
Enrollment: 139. . . . . (765) 755-0048
Saint Elizabeth School of Nursing (Private, Not-for-profit, Roman Catholic)
Enrollment: 111. . . . . (765) 423-6400
Tuition: In-state $20,230; Out-of-state $20,230

Vocational/Technical School(s)

Tricoci University of Beauty Culture-Lafayette (Private, For-profit)
Enrollment: 122. . . . . (765) 742-0068
Tuition: $17,407
Housing: Homeownership rate: 46.6%; Median home value: $105,300; Median year structure built: 1971; Homeowner vacancy rate: 1.9%; Median selected monthly owner costs: $931 with a mortgage, $321 without a mortgage; Median gross rent: $789 per month; Rental vacancy rate: 5.2%
Health Insurance: 86.7% have insurance; 62.9% have private insurance; 33.8% have public insurance; 13.3% do not have insurance; 5.5% of children under 18 do not have insurance
Hospitals: Franciscan Saint Elizabeth Health - Lafayette Central (375 beds); Franciscan Saint Elizabeth Health - Lafayette East (263 beds); Indiana University Health Arnett Hospital

Safety: Violent crime rate: 50.4 per 10,000 population; Property crime rate: 364.9 per 10,000 population
Newspapers: Journal & Courier (daily circulation 35,900); Lafayette Leader (weekly circulation 2,000)
Transportation: Commute: 89.4% car, 3.6% public transportation, 2.3% walk, 2.4% work from home; Mean travel time to work: 16.7 minutes; Amtrak: Train service available.
Airports: Purdue University (general aviation)
Additional Information Contacts
City of Lafayette . . . . (765) 807-1021
http://www.lafayette.in.gov

MONTMORENCI (CDP). Covers a land area of 1.358 square miles and a water area of 0 square miles. Located at 40.47° N. Lat; 87.04° W. Long. Elevation is 699 feet.
Population: 250; Growth (since 2000): n/a; Density: 184.1 persons per square mile; Race: 100.0% White, 0.0% Black/African American, 0.0% Asian, 0.0% American Indian/Alaska Native, 0.0% Native Hawaiian/Other Pacific Islander, 0.0% Two or more races, 0.0% Hispanic of any race; Average household size: 3.05; Median age: 44.0; Age under 18: 22.4%; Age 65 and over: 26.0%; Males per 100 females: 109.5; Marriage status: 14.4% never married, 70.8% now married, 0.0% separated, 0.0% widowed, 14.9% divorced; Foreign born: 3.6%; Speak English only: 100.0%; With disability: 3.2%; Veterans: 5.2%; Ancestry: 17.6% American, 12.8% German, 3.2% Swiss
Employment: 7.2% management, business, and financial, 0.0% computer, engineering, and science, 0.0% education, legal, community service, arts, and media, 7.2% healthcare practitioners, 29.6% service, 49.6% sales and office, 0.0% natural resources, construction, and maintenance, 6.4% production, transportation, and material moving
Income: Per capita: $30,122; Median household: $96,786; Average household: $89,745; Households with income of $100,000 or more: 23.2%; Poverty rate: 5.6%
Educational Attainment: High school diploma or higher: 93.6%; Bachelor's degree or higher: 31.8%; Graduate/professional degree or higher: 16.2%
Housing: Homeownership rate: 89.0%; Median home value: $161,900; Median year structure built: 1979; Homeowner vacancy rate: 0.0%; Median selected monthly owner costs: $1,090 with a mortgage, n/a without a mortgage; Median gross rent: n/a per month; Rental vacancy rate: 0.0%
Health Insurance: 100.0% have insurance; 94.4% have private insurance; 31.6% have public insurance; 0.0% do not have insurance; 0.0% of children under 18 do not have insurance
Transportation: Commute: 94.4% car, 0.0% public transportation, 0.0% walk, 5.6% work from home; Mean travel time to work: 22.2 minutes

ROMNEY (unincorporated postal area)
ZCTA: 47981
Covers a land area of 36.371 square miles and a water area of 0 square miles. Located at 40.25° N. Lat; 86.93° W. Long. Elevation is 735 feet.
Population: 921; Growth (since 2000): 17.2%; Density: 25.3 persons per square mile; Race: 92.5% White, 0.0% Black/African American, 0.0% Asian, 0.0% American Indian/Alaska Native, 0.0% Native Hawaiian/Other Pacific Islander, 7.5% Two or more races, 0.0% Hispanic of any race; Average household size: 3.05; Median age: 33.3; Age under 18: 39.6%; Age 65 and over: 11.1%; Males per 100 females: 100.2; Marriage status: 33.1% never married, 51.3% now married, 0.0% separated, 1.2% widowed, 14.5% divorced; Foreign born: 0.9%; Speak English only: 99.1%; With disability: 11.0%; Veterans: 6.5%; Ancestry: 39.7% German, 25.8% Irish, 12.7% American, 10.1% French, 7.8% Dutch
Employment: 22.1% management, business, and financial, 2.1% computer, engineering, and science, 6.0% education, legal, community service, arts, and media, 7.5% healthcare practitioners, 10.6% service, 28.1% sales and office, 4.9% natural resources, construction, and maintenance, 18.7% production, transportation, and material moving
Income: Per capita: $40,206; Median household: $90,313; Average household: $122,557; Households with income of $100,000 or more: 45.0%; Poverty rate: 14.9%
Educational Attainment: High school diploma or higher: 96.1%; Bachelor's degree or higher: 26.0%; Graduate/professional degree or higher: 6.1%
Housing: Homeownership rate: 82.8%; Median home value: $206,800; Median year structure built: 1992; Homeowner vacancy rate: 0.0%; Median selected monthly owner costs: $1,520 with a mortgage, $667 without a mortgage; Median gross rent: $829 per month; Rental vacancy rate: 0.0%
Health Insurance: 97.0% have insurance; 87.9% have private insurance; 19.2% have public insurance; 3.0% do not have insurance; 0.0% of children under 18 do not have insurance
Transportation: Commute: 100.0% car, 0.0% public transportation, 0.0% walk, 0.0% work from home; Mean travel time to work: 22.7 minutes

SHADELAND (town). Covers a land area of 27.104 square miles and a water area of 0.232 square miles. Located at 40.34° N. Lat; 86.96° W. Long. Elevation is 620 feet.
History: Laid out 1824.
Population: 1,841; Growth (since 2000): 9.5%; Density: 67.9 persons per square mile; Race: 98.6% White, 0.0% Black/African American, 0.7% Asian, 0.2% American Indian/Alaska Native, 0.0% Native Hawaiian/Other Pacific Islander, 0.6% Two or more races, 2.3% Hispanic of any race; Average household size: 2.47; Median age: 48.9; Age under 18: 15.4%; Age 65 and over: 26.6%; Males per 100 females: 96.8; Marriage status: 24.4% never married, 58.8% now married, 0.5% separated, 5.3% widowed, 11.4% divorced; Foreign born: 1.8%; Speak English only: 97.6%; With disability: 12.0%; Veterans: 7.2%; Ancestry: 29.2% German, 12.8% Irish, 11.2% English, 8.5% American, 6.6% Dutch
Employment: 11.8% management, business, and financial, 3.2% computer, engineering, and science, 5.7% education, legal, community service, arts, and media, 6.7% healthcare practitioners, 19.3% service, 20.9% sales and office, 12.2% natural resources, construction, and maintenance, 20.1% production, transportation, and material moving
Income: Per capita: $29,675; Median household: $68,864; Average household: $72,119; Households with income of $100,000 or more: 22.7%; Poverty rate: 5.3%
Educational Attainment: High school diploma or higher: 92.0%; Bachelor's degree or higher: 23.7%; Graduate/professional degree or higher: 8.2%
Housing: Homeownership rate: 83.0%; Median home value: $166,300; Median year structure built: 1978; Homeowner vacancy rate: 0.0%; Median selected monthly owner costs: $1,225 with a mortgage, $404 without a mortgage; Median gross rent: $738 per month; Rental vacancy rate: 0.0%
Health Insurance: 93.9% have insurance; 79.0% have private insurance; 35.0% have public insurance; 6.1% do not have insurance; 1.4% of children under 18 do not have insurance
Transportation: Commute: 96.7% car, 0.0% public transportation, 2.2% walk, 0.4% work from home; Mean travel time to work: 20.4 minutes

STOCKWELL (CDP). Covers a land area of 2.613 square miles and a water area of 0 square miles. Located at 40.28° N. Lat; 86.77° W. Long. Elevation is 771 feet.
Population: 579; Growth (since 2000): n/a; Density: 221.6 persons per square mile; Race: 100.0% White, 0.0% Black/African American, 0.0% Asian, 0.0% American Indian/Alaska Native, 0.0% Native Hawaiian/Other Pacific Islander, 0.0% Two or more races, 4.3% Hispanic of any race; Average household size: 2.33; Median age: 39.5; Age under 18: 23.1%; Age 65 and over: 9.0%; Males per 100 females: 106.4; Marriage status: 22.6% never married, 44.6% now married, 5.1% separated, 2.0% widowed, 30.7% divorced; Foreign born: 0.0%; Speak English only: 100.0%; With disability: 4.0%; Veterans: 3.8%; Ancestry: 40.6% German, 10.7% Irish, 5.9% Dutch, 5.9% Portuguese, 4.3% Scotch-Irish
Employment: 8.1% management, business, and financial, 0.0% computer, engineering, and science, 5.2% education, legal, community service, arts, and media, 0.0% healthcare practitioners, 21.4% service, 29.5% sales and office, 17.0% natural resources, construction, and maintenance, 18.9% production, transportation, and material moving
Income: Per capita: $24,718; Median household: $59,375; Average household: $54,648; Households with income of $100,000 or more: n/a; Poverty rate: 5.0%
Educational Attainment: High school diploma or higher: 100.0%; Bachelor's degree or higher: 11.4%; Graduate/professional degree or higher: 5.8%
Housing: Homeownership rate: 69.9%; Median home value: $100,400; Median year structure built: 1968; Homeowner vacancy rate: 0.0%; Median selected monthly owner costs: $1,035 with a mortgage, $335 without a mortgage; Median gross rent: $717 per month; Rental vacancy rate: 0.0%
Health Insurance: 85.5% have insurance; 85.5% have private insurance; 9.0% have public insurance; 14.5% do not have insurance; 0.0% of children under 18 do not have insurance

Transportation: Commute: 97.8% car, 0.0% public transportation, 0.0% walk, 2.2% work from home; Mean travel time to work: 18.9 minutes

WEST LAFAYETTE (city). Covers a land area of 7.615 square miles and a water area of 0.010 square miles. Located at 40.46° N. Lat; 86.91° W. Long. Elevation is 610 feet.
History: Purdue University was founded in 1874 in West Lafayette.
Population: 45,110; Growth (since 2000): 56.8%; Density: 5,923.6 persons per square mile; Race: 69.2% White, 3.2% Black/African American, 23.8% Asian, 0.3% American Indian/Alaska Native, 0.1% Native Hawaiian/Other Pacific Islander, 2.9% Two or more races, 4.2% Hispanic of any race; Average household size: 2.34; Median age: 21.7; Age under 18: 10.4%; Age 65 and over: 6.8%; Males per 100 females: 118.3; Marriage status: 72.1% never married, 22.2% now married, 0.3% separated, 2.7% widowed, 2.9% divorced; Foreign born: 24.5%; Speak English only: 71.3%; With disability: 6.2%; Veterans: 2.0%; Ancestry: 24.2% German, 11.1% Irish, 7.4% English, 5.5% Polish, 4.8% Italian
Employment: 8.8% management, business, and financial, 12.7% computer, engineering, and science, 29.4% education, legal, community service, arts, and media, 3.2% healthcare practitioners, 19.6% service, 18.5% sales and office, 3.5% natural resources, construction, and maintenance, 4.3% production, transportation, and material moving
Income: Per capita: $19,421; Median household: $31,230; Average household: $59,259; Households with income of $100,000 or more: 18.8%; Poverty rate: 41.1%
Educational Attainment: High school diploma or higher: 94.7%; Bachelor's degree or higher: 71.9%; Graduate/professional degree or higher: 45.6%

School District(s)

Tippecanoe School Corp (PK-12)
Enrollment: 13,431 . . . . (765) 474-2481
West Lafayette Com School Corp (PK-12)
Enrollment: 2,248 . . . . (765) 746-1602

Four-year College(s)

Purdue University-Main Campus (Public)
Enrollment: 42,699 . . . . (765) 494-4600
Tuition: In-state $9,992; Out-of-state $28,794

Housing: Homeownership rate: 34.4%; Median home value: $192,600; Median year structure built: 1981; Homeowner vacancy rate: 0.5%; Median selected monthly owner costs: $1,374 with a mortgage, $465 without a mortgage; Median gross rent: $860 per month; Rental vacancy rate: 5.2%
Health Insurance: 94.5% have insurance; 89.6% have private insurance; 11.2% have public insurance; 5.5% do not have insurance; 5.1% of children under 18 do not have insurance
Safety: Violent crime rate: 10.5 per 10,000 population; Property crime rate: 100.1 per 10,000 population
Transportation: Commute: 57.7% car, 6.1% public transportation, 26.6% walk, 4.8% work from home; Mean travel time to work: 15.6 minutes
Additional Information Contacts
City of West Lafayette . . . . (765) 775-5150
http://www.westlafayette.in.gov

WEST POINT (CDP). Covers a land area of 4.856 square miles and a water area of 0 square miles. Located at 40.34° N. Lat; 87.04° W. Long.
Population: 708; Growth (since 2000): n/a; Density: 145.8 persons per square mile; Race: 100.0% White, 0.0% Black/African American, 0.0% Asian, 0.0% American Indian/Alaska Native, 0.0% Native Hawaiian/Other Pacific Islander, 0.0% Two or more races, 23.2% Hispanic of any race; Average household size: 3.77; Median age: 32.4; Age under 18: 46.3%; Age 65 and over: 7.5%; Males per 100 females: 105.5; Marriage status: 36.4% never married, 53.4% now married, 0.0% separated, 0.0% widowed, 10.3% divorced; Foreign born: 0.0%; Speak English only: 81.3%; With disability: 5.8%; Veterans: 9.7%; Ancestry: 51.4% German, 15.5% Italian, 8.5% Dutch, 7.1% Polish, 5.5% English
Employment: 27.5% management, business, and financial, 0.0% computer, engineering, and science, 9.0% education, legal, community service, arts, and media, 0.0% healthcare practitioners, 5.3% service, 15.2% sales and office, 23.0% natural resources, construction, and maintenance, 20.1% production, transportation, and material moving
Income: Per capita: $19,311; Median household: n/a; Average household: $77,520; Households with income of $100,000 or more: 38.8%; Poverty rate: 17.3%
Educational Attainment: High school diploma or higher: 100.0%; Bachelor's degree or higher: 15.3%; Graduate/professional degree or higher: 15.3%
Housing: Homeownership rate: 100.0%; Median home value: $140,300; Median year structure built: 1966; Homeowner vacancy rate: 0.0%; Median selected monthly owner costs: $1,146 with a mortgage, $526 without a mortgage; Median gross rent: n/a per month; Rental vacancy rate: 0.0%
Health Insurance: 77.0% have insurance; 53.4% have private insurance; 34.3% have public insurance; 23.0% do not have insurance; 17.6% of children under 18 do not have insurance
Transportation: Commute: 100.0% car, 0.0% public transportation, 0.0% walk, 0.0% work from home; Mean travel time to work: 19.6 minutes

WESTPOINT (unincorporated postal area)
ZCTA: 47992
Covers a land area of 36.444 square miles and a water area of 0.263 square miles. Located at 40.32° N. Lat; 87.05° W. Long. Elevation is 673 feet.
Population: 1,660; Growth (since 2000): 25.0%; Density: 45.5 persons per square mile; Race: 98.9% White, 0.0% Black/African American, 0.0% Asian, 0.0% American Indian/Alaska Native, 0.0% Native Hawaiian/Other Pacific Islander, 0.0% Two or more races, 12.8% Hispanic of any race; Average household size: 2.89; Median age: 39.0; Age under 18: 29.3%; Age 65 and over: 12.5%; Males per 100 females: 106.3; Marriage status: 29.3% never married, 50.8% now married, 1.5% separated, 3.4% widowed, 16.5% divorced; Foreign born: 1.1%; Speak English only: 88.6%; With disability: 13.0%; Veterans: 3.8%; Ancestry: 37.4% German, 15.2% Irish, 10.2% English, 9.5% Italian, 6.0% Dutch
Employment: 22.3% management, business, and financial, 0.0% computer, engineering, and science, 11.9% education, legal, community service, arts, and media, 0.0% healthcare practitioners, 19.4% service, 15.3% sales and office, 12.1% natural resources, construction, and maintenance, 19.0% production, transportation, and material moving
Income: Per capita: $36,298; Median household: $63,092; Average household: $100,239; Households with income of $100,000 or more: 28.6%; Poverty rate: 11.2%
Educational Attainment: High school diploma or higher: 97.1%; Bachelor's degree or higher: 16.4%; Graduate/professional degree or higher: 7.8%
Housing: Homeownership rate: 95.3%; Median home value: $147,500; Median year structure built: 1975; Homeowner vacancy rate: 0.0%; Median selected monthly owner costs: $1,141 with a mortgage, $414 without a mortgage; Median gross rent: n/a per month; Rental vacancy rate: 0.0%
Health Insurance: 83.7% have insurance; 67.6% have private insurance; 28.3% have public insurance; 16.3% do not have insurance; 12.0% of children under 18 do not have insurance
Transportation: Commute: 93.8% car, 0.0% public transportation, 0.0% walk, 6.2% work from home; Mean travel time to work: 24.3 minutes

Tipton County

Located in central Indiana; drained by Cicero and Turkey Creeks. Covers a land area of 260.541 square miles, a water area of 0.026 square miles, and is located in the Eastern Time Zone at 40.31° N. Lat., 86.06° W. Long. The county was founded in 1844. County seat is Tipton.
Population: 15,290; Growth (since 2000): -7.8%; Density: 58.7 persons per square mile; Race: 96.1% White, 0.2% Black/African American, 0.0% Asian, 0.0% American Indian/Alaska Native, 0.4% Native Hawaiian/Other Pacific Islander, 2.0% two or more races, 2.6% Hispanic of any race; Average household size: 2.37; Median age: 44.5; Age under 18: 21.2%; Age 65 and over: 19.3%; Males per 100 females: 97.0; Marriage status: 22.7% never married, 56.9% now married, 0.9% separated, 7.5% widowed, 12.8% divorced; Foreign born: 1.3%; Speak English only: 97.6%; With disability: 17.4%; Veterans: 10.6%; Ancestry: 23.2% German, 18.1% American, 9.1% Irish, 8.6% English, 2.0% Dutch
Religion: Six largest groups: 13.1% Baptist, 6.9% Catholicism, 5.7% Non-denominational Protestant, 3.6% Methodist/Pietist, 3.1% Lutheran, 2.8% Holiness
Economy: Unemployment rate: 4.7%; Leading industries: 14.0 % retail trade; 13.4 % construction; 13.4 % health care and social assistance; Farms: 377 totaling 145,181 acres; Company size: 0 employ 1,000 or more persons, 0 employ 500 to 999 persons, 6 employ 100 to 499 persons, 301 employs less than 100 persons; Business ownership: 238 women-owned, n/a Black-owned, n/a Hispanic-owned, n/a Asian-owned, n/a American Indian/Alaska Native-owned
Employment: 14.3% management, business, and financial, 4.8% computer, engineering, and science, 8.2% education, legal, community

service, arts, and media, 5.0% healthcare practitioners, 15.8% service, 16.5% sales and office, 13.8% natural resources, construction, and maintenance, 21.6% production, transportation, and material moving
Income: Per capita: $28,507; Median household: $53,931; Average household: $68,263; Households with income of $100,000 or more: 19.6%; Poverty rate: 9.4%
Educational Attainment: High school diploma or higher: 89.0%; Bachelor's degree or higher: 21.3%; Graduate/professional degree or higher: 7.3%
Housing: Homeownership rate: 79.7%; Median home value: $110,300; Median year structure built: 1961; Homeowner vacancy rate: 1.7%; Median selected monthly owner costs: $1,042 with a mortgage, $373 without a mortgage; Median gross rent: $725 per month; Rental vacancy rate: 3.4%
Vital Statistics: Birth rate: 94.5 per 10,000 population; Death rate: 105.8 per 10,000 population; Age-adjusted cancer mortality rate: 153.0 deaths per 100,000 population
Health Insurance: 91.8% have insurance; 75.7% have private insurance; 32.2% have public insurance; 8.2% do not have insurance; 6.5% of children under 18 do not have insurance
Health Care: Physicians: 5.9 per 10,000 population; Dentists: 5.3 per 10,000 population; Hospital beds: 16.5 per 10,000 population; Hospital admissions: 597.2 per 10,000 population
Transportation: Commute: 93.8% car, 0.3% public transportation, 1.3% walk, 2.7% work from home; Mean travel time to work: 23.7 minutes
2016 Presidential Election: 74.4% Trump, 21.1% Clinton, 4.4% Johnson, 0.0% Stein
Additional Information Contacts
Tipton Government . . . . (765) 675-4165
http://www.tiptoncounty.in.gov

Tipton County Communities

GOLDSMITH (unincorporated postal area)
ZCTA: 46045

Covers a land area of 0.034 square miles and a water area of 0 square miles. Located at 40.29° N. Lat; 86.15° W. Long. Elevation is 912 feet.
Population: 67; Growth (since 2000): 21.8%; Density: 1,967.7 persons per square mile; Race: 100.0% White, 0.0% Black/African American, 0.0% Asian, 0.0% American Indian/Alaska Native, 0.0% Native Hawaiian/Other Pacific Islander, 0.0% Two or more races, 0.0% Hispanic of any race; Average household size: 1.68; Median age: 60.5; Age under 18: 0.0%; Age 65 and over: 41.8%; Males per 100 females: 138.5; Marriage status: 11.9% never married, 62.7% now married, 0.0% separated, 10.4% widowed, 14.9% divorced; Foreign born: 0.0%; Speak English only: 100.0%; With disability: 25.4%; Veterans: 0.0%; Ancestry: 31.3% American, 31.3% German, 31.3% Irish
Employment: 0.0% management, business, and financial, 0.0% computer, engineering, and science, 23.8% education, legal, community service, arts, and media, 23.8% healthcare practitioners, 0.0% service, 26.2% sales and office, 0.0% natural resources, construction, and maintenance, 26.2% production, transportation, and material moving
Income: Per capita: $36,099; Median household: n/a; Average household: $62,095; Households with income of $100,000 or more: 27.5%; Poverty rate: 22.4%
Educational Attainment: High school diploma or higher: 89.6%; Bachelor's degree or higher: n/a; Graduate/professional degree or higher: n/a
Housing: Homeownership rate: 100.0%; Median home value: n/a; Median year structure built: Before 1940; Homeowner vacancy rate: 0.0%; Median selected monthly owner costs: $0 with a mortgage, $0 without a mortgage; Median gross rent: n/a per month; Rental vacancy rate: 0.0%
Health Insurance: 100.0% have insurance; 58.2% have private insurance; 41.8% have public insurance; 0.0% do not have insurance; 0.0% of children under 18 do not have insurance
Transportation: Commute: 73.8% car, 0.0% public transportation, 0.0% walk, 26.2% work from home; Mean travel time to work: 0.0 minutes

HOBBS (unincorporated postal area)
ZCTA: 46047

Covers a land area of 0.013 square miles and a water area of 0 square miles. Located at 40.28° N. Lat; 85.95° W. Long. Elevation is 869 feet.
Population: 73; Growth (since 2000): -2.7%; Density: 5,507.4 persons per square mile; Race: 100.0% White, 0.0% Black/African American, 0.0% Asian, 0.0% American Indian/Alaska Native, 0.0% Native Hawaiian/Other Pacific Islander, 0.0% Two or more races, 0.0% Hispanic of any race; Average household size: 2.43; Median age: 45.7; Age under 18: 31.5%; Age 65 and over: 0.0%; Males per 100 females: 87.0; Marriage status: 0.0% never married, 0.0% now married, 0.0% separated, 0.0% widowed, 100.0% divorced; Foreign born: 0.0%; Speak English only: 100.0%; With disability: 27.4%; Veterans: 0.0%; Ancestry: 100.0% German
Employment: 0.0% management, business, and financial, 0.0% computer, engineering, and science, 0.0% education, legal, community service, arts, and media, 0.0% healthcare practitioners, 0.0% service, 0.0% sales and office, 100.0% natural resources, construction, and maintenance, 0.0% production, transportation, and material moving
Income: Per capita: n/a; Median household: n/a; Average household: n/a; Households with income of $100,000 or more: n/a; Poverty rate: 27.4%
Educational Attainment: High school diploma or higher: 100.0%; Bachelor's degree or higher: 40.0%; Graduate/professional degree or higher: n/a
Housing: Homeownership rate: n/a; Median home value: n/a; Median year structure built: n/a; Homeowner vacancy rate: 0.0%; Median selected monthly owner costs: $0 with a mortgage, $0 without a mortgage; Median gross rent: n/a per month; Rental vacancy rate: 0.0%
Health Insurance: 100.0% have insurance; 100.0% have private insurance; 27.4% have public insurance; 0.0% do not have insurance; 0.0% of children under 18 do not have insurance
Transportation: Commute: 100.0% car, 0.0% public transportation, 0.0% walk, 0.0% work from home; Mean travel time to work: 0.0 minutes

KEMPTON (town). Covers a land area of 0.165 square miles and a water area of 0 square miles. Located at 40.29° N. Lat; 86.23° W. Long. Elevation is 928 feet.
Population: 320; Growth (since 2000): -15.8%; Density: 1,940.7 persons per square mile; Race: 99.4% White, 0.0% Black/African American, 0.0% Asian, 0.0% American Indian/Alaska Native, 0.0% Native Hawaiian/Other Pacific Islander, 0.6% Two or more races, 0.9% Hispanic of any race; Average household size: 2.54; Median age: 42.7; Age under 18: 19.7%; Age 65 and over: 15.6%; Males per 100 females: 113.4; Marriage status: 22.1% never married, 54.8% now married, 1.1% separated, 9.1% widowed, 14.1% divorced; Foreign born: 0.0%; Speak English only: 100.0%; With disability: 20.0%; Veterans: 13.6%; Ancestry: 24.4% German, 15.3% English, 11.6% American, 9.1% Irish, 3.8% Italian
Employment: 6.5% management, business, and financial, 5.1% computer, engineering, and science, 7.2% education, legal, community service, arts, and media, 2.9% healthcare practitioners, 15.9% service, 8.7% sales and office, 8.7% natural resources, construction, and maintenance, 44.9% production, transportation, and material moving
Income: Per capita: $21,458; Median household: $49,250; Average household: $55,146; Households with income of $100,000 or more: 12.7%; Poverty rate: 18.5%
Educational Attainment: High school diploma or higher: 85.3%; Bachelor's degree or higher: 8.9%; Graduate/professional degree or higher: 1.3%
Housing: Homeownership rate: 77.0%; Median home value: $69,700; Median year structure built: 1950; Homeowner vacancy rate: 0.0%; Median selected monthly owner costs: $1,008 with a mortgage, $425 without a mortgage; Median gross rent: $763 per month; Rental vacancy rate: 0.0%
Health Insurance: 92.5% have insurance; 70.6% have private insurance; 39.7% have public insurance; 7.5% do not have insurance; 0.0% of children under 18 do not have insurance
Transportation: Commute: 97.1% car, 0.0% public transportation, 0.0% walk, 0.0% work from home; Mean travel time to work: 32.1 minutes

SHARPSVILLE (town). Covers a land area of 0.239 square miles and a water area of 0 square miles. Located at 40.38° N. Lat; 86.09° W. Long. Elevation is 879 feet.
History: Laid out 1850.
Population: 781; Growth (since 2000): 26.4%; Density: 3,263.7 persons per square mile; Race: 91.4% White, 0.0% Black/African American, 0.0% Asian, 0.4% American Indian/Alaska Native, 0.0% Native Hawaiian/Other Pacific Islander, 8.2% Two or more races, 7.3% Hispanic of any race; Average household size: 2.56; Median age: 42.9; Age under 18: 23.7%; Age 65 and over: 14.0%; Males per 100 females: 97.7; Marriage status: 21.9% never married, 55.0% now married, 2.0% separated, 8.7% widowed, 14.5% divorced; Foreign born: 0.0%; Speak English only: 99.6%;

With disability: 26.4%; Veterans: 8.9%; Ancestry: 23.2% German, 15.1% American, 10.9% Irish, 9.3% English, 5.0% Dutch
Employment: 8.4% management, business, and financial, 3.1% computer, engineering, and science, 3.9% education, legal, community service, arts, and media, 3.9% healthcare practitioners, 18.2% service, 14.6% sales and office, 15.4% natural resources, construction, and maintenance, 32.5% production, transportation, and material moving
Income: Per capita: $23,146; Median household: $54,792; Average household: $60,938; Households with income of $100,000 or more: 14.2%; Poverty rate: 12.9%
Educational Attainment: High school diploma or higher: 87.5%; Bachelor's degree or higher: 13.5%; Graduate/professional degree or higher: 3.7%

School District(s)

Tri-central Community Schools (PK-12)
Enrollment: 728 . . . . (765) 963-2585
Housing: Homeownership rate: 76.1%; Median home value: $82,400; Median year structure built: 1943; Homeowner vacancy rate: 0.0%; Median selected monthly owner costs: $904 with a mortgage, $375 without a mortgage; Median gross rent: $784 per month; Rental vacancy rate: 0.0%
Health Insurance: 85.8% have insurance; 68.8% have private insurance; 31.0% have public insurance; 14.2% do not have insurance; 15.0% of children under 18 do not have insurance
Transportation: Commute: 92.4% car, 0.0% public transportation, 5.4% walk, 2.0% work from home; Mean travel time to work: 23.9 minutes

TIPTON (city). County seat. Covers a land area of 2.504 square miles and a water area of 0 square miles. Located at 40.28° N. Lat; 86.04° W. Long. Elevation is 869 feet.
History: Laid out 1839.
Population: 5,151; Growth (since 2000): -1.9%; Density: 2,057.3 persons per square mile; Race: 94.8% White, 0.4% Black/African American, 0.0% Asian, 0.0% American Indian/Alaska Native, 1.1% Native Hawaiian/Other Pacific Islander, 2.8% Two or more races, 2.8% Hispanic of any race; Average household size: 2.32; Median age: 38.8; Age under 18: 26.9%; Age 65 and over: 17.5%; Males per 100 females: 88.4; Marriage status: 25.0% never married, 53.0% now married, 0.8% separated, 9.7% widowed, 12.3% divorced; Foreign born: 2.3%; Speak English only: 97.0%; With disability: 16.2%; Veterans: 13.8%; Ancestry: 22.2% German, 16.5% American, 8.5% English, 7.2% Irish, 2.6% Scottish
Employment: 12.8% management, business, and financial, 5.1% computer, engineering, and science, 7.7% education, legal, community service, arts, and media, 2.2% healthcare practitioners, 22.1% service, 16.0% sales and office, 12.5% natural resources, construction, and maintenance, 21.5% production, transportation, and material moving
Income: Per capita: $25,652; Median household: $46,310; Average household: $59,595; Households with income of $100,000 or more: 10.9%; Poverty rate: 13.3%
Educational Attainment: High school diploma or higher: 87.3%; Bachelor's degree or higher: 17.6%; Graduate/professional degree or higher: 4.4%

School District(s)

Tipton Community School Corp (PK-12)
Enrollment: 1,674 . . . . (765) 675-2147
Housing: Homeownership rate: 65.9%; Median home value: $86,600; Median year structure built: 1951; Homeowner vacancy rate: 2.9%; Median selected monthly owner costs: $898 with a mortgage, $353 without a mortgage; Median gross rent: $719 per month; Rental vacancy rate: 4.6%
Health Insurance: 92.9% have insurance; 75.9% have private insurance; 32.7% have public insurance; 7.1% do not have insurance; 1.6% of children under 18 do not have insurance
Hospitals: Indiana University Health Tipton Hospital (102 beds)
Safety: Violent crime rate: 15.7 per 10,000 population; Property crime rate: 151.2 per 10,000 population
Newspapers: Tipton Co. Tribune (daily circulation 2,500)
Transportation: Commute: 94.7% car, 0.0% public transportation, 0.3% walk, 3.0% work from home; Mean travel time to work: 21.2 minutes
Additional Information Contacts
City of Tipton . . . . (765) 675-4165
http://www.tiptonguide.com

WINDFALL CITY (town). Covers a land area of 0.293 square miles and a water area of 0 square miles. Located at 40.36° N. Lat; 85.96° W. Long. Elevation is 863 feet.
Population: 876; Growth (since 2000): 23.0%; Density: 2,985.3 persons per square mile; Race: 99.2% White, 0.0% Black/African American, 0.0% Asian, 0.0% American Indian/Alaska Native, 0.0% Native Hawaiian/Other Pacific Islander, 0.8% Two or more races, 4.0% Hispanic of any race; Average household size: 2.71; Median age: 33.5; Age under 18: 24.9%; Age 65 and over: 12.7%; Males per 100 females: 97.8; Marriage status: 23.3% never married, 54.5% now married, 1.3% separated, 9.1% widowed, 13.2% divorced; Foreign born: 1.1%; Speak English only: 92.9%; With disability: 21.1%; Veterans: 7.0%; Ancestry: 21.1% American, 19.9% German, 12.6% Irish, 8.0% English, 2.4% French
Employment: 4.8% management, business, and financial, 2.8% computer, engineering, and science, 0.8% education, legal, community service, arts, and media, 2.5% healthcare practitioners, 22.5% service, 11.5% sales and office, 16.9% natural resources, construction, and maintenance, 38.2% production, transportation, and material moving
Income: Per capita: $18,966; Median household: $41,645; Average household: $53,245; Households with income of $100,000 or more: 15.1%; Poverty rate: 18.6%
Educational Attainment: High school diploma or higher: 75.1%; Bachelor's degree or higher: 10.1%; Graduate/professional degree or higher: 1.7%
Housing: Homeownership rate: 82.0%; Median home value: $60,200; Median year structure built: 1951; Homeowner vacancy rate: 5.6%; Median selected monthly owner costs: $858 with a mortgage, $383 without a mortgage; Median gross rent: $721 per month; Rental vacancy rate: 15.9%
Health Insurance: 83.4% have insurance; 46.3% have private insurance; 49.0% have public insurance; 16.6% do not have insurance; 6.8% of children under 18 do not have insurance
Transportation: Commute: 98.9% car, 0.0% public transportation, 0.9% walk, 0.0% work from home; Mean travel time to work: 30.0 minutes

Union County

Located in eastern Indiana; bounded on the east by Ohio; drained by the East Fork of the Whitewater River. Covers a land area of 161.224 square miles, a water area of 3.953 square miles, and is located in the Eastern Time Zone at 39.62° N. Lat., 84.93° W. Long. The county was founded in 1821. County seat is Liberty.

Union County is part of the Cincinnati, OH-KY-IN Metropolitan Statistical Area. The entire metro area includes: Dearborn County, IN; Ohio County, IN; Union County, IN; Boone County, KY; Bracken County, KY; Campbell County, KY; Gallatin County, KY; Grant County, KY; Kenton County, KY; Pendleton County, KY; Brown County, OH; Butler County, OH; Clermont County, OH; Hamilton County, OH; Warren County, OH

Population: 7,225; Growth (since 2000): -1.7%; Density: 44.8 persons per square mile; Race: 95.8% White, 0.1% Black/African American, 0.5% Asian, 0.0% American Indian/Alaska Native, 0.0% Native Hawaiian/Other Pacific Islander, 3.6% two or more races, 0.0% Hispanic of any race; Average household size: 2.50; Median age: 43.3; Age under 18: 23.2%; Age 65 and over: 18.0%; Males per 100 females: 97.7; Marriage status: 25.6% never married, 52.0% now married, 1.5% separated, 7.1% widowed, 15.3% divorced; Foreign born: 0.5%; Speak English only: 99.4%; With disability: 15.5%; Veterans: 11.5%; Ancestry: 25.6% German, 15.0% American, 10.8% English, 10.0% Irish, 4.1% Scottish
Religion: Six largest groups: 11.4% Methodist/Pietist, 7.0% Catholicism, 6.8% Baptist, 5.1% Non-denominational Protestant, 1.9% Holiness, 1.1% Presbyterian-Reformed
Economy: Unemployment rate: 3.1%; Leading industries: 19.8 % retail trade; 18.0 % other services (except public administration); 9.9 % construction; Farms: 242 totaling 74,491 acres; Company size: 0 employ 1,000 or more persons, 0 employ 500 to 999 persons, 1 employs 100 to 499 persons, 110 employ less than 100 persons; Business ownership: 204 women-owned, n/a Black-owned, n/a Hispanic-owned, n/a Asian-owned, n/a American Indian/Alaska Native-owned
Employment: 8.6% management, business, and financial, 2.8% computer, engineering, and science, 5.8% education, legal, community service, arts, and media, 4.5% healthcare practitioners, 24.1% service, 23.0% sales and office, 12.1% natural resources, construction, and maintenance, 19.0% production, transportation, and material moving

Income: Per capita: $22,527; Median household: $45,531; Average household: $54,189; Households with income of $100,000 or more: 11.7%; Poverty rate: 8.2%
Educational Attainment: High school diploma or higher: 88.4%; Bachelor's degree or higher: 17.6%; Graduate/professional degree or higher: 5.9%
Housing: Homeownership rate: 72.6%; Median home value: $109,900; Median year structure built: 1967; Homeowner vacancy rate: 1.6%; Median selected monthly owner costs: $976 with a mortgage, $417 without a mortgage; Median gross rent: $741 per month; Rental vacancy rate: 9.2%
Vital Statistics: Birth rate: 84.7 per 10,000 population; Death rate: 90.3 per 10,000 population; Age-adjusted cancer mortality rate: 204.8 deaths per 100,000 population
Health Insurance: 86.5% have insurance; 66.8% have private insurance; 32.4% have public insurance; 13.5% do not have insurance; 9.3% of children under 18 do not have insurance
Health Care: Physicians: 4.2 per 10,000 population; Dentists: 0.0 per 10,000 population; Hospital beds: 0.0 per 10,000 population; Hospital admissions: 0.0 per 10,000 population
Transportation: Commute: 94.1% car, 0.1% public transportation, 1.5% walk, 2.7% work from home; Mean travel time to work: 23.6 minutes
2016 Presidential Election: 74.3% Trump, 21.7% Clinton, 3.8% Johnson, 0.2% Stein
National and State Parks: Whitewater State Park
Additional Information Contacts
Union Government . . . . (765) 458-5464

Union County Communities

BROWNSVILLE (unincorporated postal area)
ZCTA: 47325
Covers a land area of 20.348 square miles and a water area of 0.122 square miles. Located at 39.69° N. Lat; 85.02° W. Long. Elevation is 794 feet.
Population: 525; Growth (since 2000): -32.3%; Density: 25.8 persons per square mile; Race: 100.0% White, 0.0% Black/African American, 0.0% Asian, 0.0% American Indian/Alaska Native, 0.0% Native Hawaiian/Other Pacific Islander, 0.0% Two or more races, 0.0% Hispanic of any race; Average household size: 2.26; Median age: 51.0; Age under 18: 13.5%; Age 65 and over: 19.4%; Males per 100 females: 109.7; Marriage status: 24.2% never married, 63.3% now married, 2.8% separated, 3.8% widowed, 8.7% divorced; Foreign born: 4.6%; Speak English only: 100.0%; With disability: 35.0%; Veterans: 10.6%; Ancestry: 30.5% German, 25.3% American, 10.3% Irish, 8.8% English, 1.5% Scottish
Employment: 11.2% management, business, and financial, 2.6% computer, engineering, and science, 7.9% education, legal, community service, arts, and media, 0.0% healthcare practitioners, 12.2% service, 28.6% sales and office, 15.1% natural resources, construction, and maintenance, 22.4% production, transportation, and material moving
Income: Per capita: $25,756; Median household: $63,452; Average household: $60,488; Households with income of $100,000 or more: 12.9%; Poverty rate: 5.3%
Educational Attainment: High school diploma or higher: 87.6%; Bachelor's degree or higher: 19.2%; Graduate/professional degree or higher: 3.5%
Housing: Homeownership rate: 85.3%; Median home value: $91,700; Median year structure built: 1957; Homeowner vacancy rate: 0.0%; Median selected monthly owner costs: $1,041 with a mortgage, $439 without a mortgage; Median gross rent: $486 per month; Rental vacancy rate: 0.0%
Health Insurance: 94.5% have insurance; 77.7% have private insurance; 38.3% have public insurance; 5.5% do not have insurance; 0.0% of children under 18 do not have insurance
Transportation: Commute: 86.1% car, 0.0% public transportation, 0.0% walk, 7.5% work from home; Mean travel time to work: 37.2 minutes

LIBERTY (town). County seat. Covers a land area of 0.857 square miles and a water area of 0.002 square miles. Located at 39.64° N. Lat; 84.93° W. Long. Elevation is 984 feet.
History: Liberty was the home from 1824 to 1843 of Ambrose Burnside who achieved military distinction during the Civil War, and later served as governor of Rhode Island and as a U.S. senator.
Population: 1,829; Growth (since 2000): -11.3%; Density: 2,133.3 persons per square mile; Race: 95.0% White, 0.3% Black/African American, 1.9% Asian, 0.0% American Indian/Alaska Native, 0.0% Native Hawaiian/Other Pacific Islander, 2.8% Two or more races, 0.0% Hispanic of any race; Average household size: 2.80; Median age: 37.0; Age under 18: 28.0%; Age 65 and over: 18.8%; Males per 100 females: 87.4; Marriage status: 26.4% never married, 46.5% now married, 0.5% separated, 9.1% widowed, 18.0% divorced; Foreign born: 0.7%; Speak English only: 99.7%; With disability: 15.6%; Veterans: 11.2%; Ancestry: 16.2% German, 11.5% Irish, 10.7% English, 9.0% American, 2.2% Italian
Employment: 7.5% management, business, and financial, 1.6% computer, engineering, and science, 5.3% education, legal, community service, arts, and media, 6.9% healthcare practitioners, 31.2% service, 20.8% sales and office, 9.5% natural resources, construction, and maintenance, 17.1% production, transportation, and material moving
Income: Per capita: $17,195; Median household: $40,977; Average household: $46,097; Households with income of $100,000 or more: 6.3%; Poverty rate: 14.9%
Educational Attainment: High school diploma or higher: 80.2%; Bachelor's degree or higher: 12.9%; Graduate/professional degree or higher: 3.1%

School District(s)

Union Co/Clg Corner Joint Sch Dist (KG-12)
Enrollment: 1,328 . . . . (765) 458-7471
Housing: Homeownership rate: 59.1%; Median home value: $83,300; Median year structure built: 1959; Homeowner vacancy rate: 6.5%; Median selected monthly owner costs: $895 with a mortgage, $337 without a mortgage; Median gross rent: $727 per month; Rental vacancy rate: 13.1%
Health Insurance: 86.9% have insurance; 57.5% have private insurance; 39.1% have public insurance; 13.1% do not have insurance; 7.4% of children under 18 do not have insurance
Newspapers: Liberty Herald (weekly circulation 2,600); Union County Review (weekly circulation 4,600)
Transportation: Commute: 91.8% car, 0.4% public transportation, 4.6% walk, 1.6% work from home; Mean travel time to work: 19.6 minutes

WEST COLLEGE CORNER (town). Covers a land area of 0.267 square miles and a water area of 0 square miles. Located at 39.57° N. Lat; 84.82° W. Long. Elevation is 988 feet.
Population: 697; Growth (since 2000): 9.9%; Density: 2,611.3 persons per square mile; Race: 82.1% White, 0.0% Black/African American, 0.0% Asian, 0.0% American Indian/Alaska Native, 0.0% Native Hawaiian/Other Pacific Islander, 17.9% Two or more races, 0.0% Hispanic of any race; Average household size: 2.27; Median age: 30.5; Age under 18: 31.7%; Age 65 and over: 12.1%; Males per 100 females: 91.0; Marriage status: 44.2% never married, 27.0% now married, 0.0% separated, 9.5% widowed, 19.3% divorced; Foreign born: 0.0%; Speak English only: 99.1%; With disability: 16.8%; Veterans: 7.8%; Ancestry: 21.5% German, 17.5% American, 12.3% Irish, 8.2% English, 3.7% Italian
Employment: 7.6% management, business, and financial, 1.0% computer, engineering, and science, 5.3% education, legal, community service, arts, and media, 6.4% healthcare practitioners, 43.4% service, 12.6% sales and office, 7.2% natural resources, construction, and maintenance, 16.5% production, transportation, and material moving
Income: Per capita: $17,572; Median household: $32,137; Average household: $37,178; Households with income of $100,000 or more: 2.3%; Poverty rate: 11.2%
Educational Attainment: High school diploma or higher: 87.8%; Bachelor's degree or higher: 14.9%; Graduate/professional degree or higher: 5.1%

School District(s)

Union Co/Clg Corner Joint Sch Dist (KG-12)
Enrollment: 1,328 . . . . (765) 458-7471
Housing: Homeownership rate: 64.8%; Median home value: $77,700; Median year structure built: 1953; Homeowner vacancy rate: 3.4%; Median selected monthly owner costs: $754 with a mortgage, $412 without a mortgage; Median gross rent: $691 per month; Rental vacancy rate: 27.0%
Health Insurance: 93.1% have insurance; 80.9% have private insurance; 25.1% have public insurance; 6.9% do not have insurance; 1.3% of children under 18 do not have insurance
Transportation: Commute: 92.5% car, 0.0% public transportation, 1.5% walk, 6.1% work from home; Mean travel time to work: 15.2 minutes

Vanderburgh County

Located in southwestern Indiana; bounded on the south by the Ohio River and the Kentucky border; drained by Pigeon Creek. Covers a land area of

233.475 square miles, a water area of 2.855 square miles, and is located in the Central Time Zone at 38.02° N. Lat., 87.59° W. Long. The county was founded in 1818. County seat is Evansville.

Vanderburgh County is part of the Evansville, IN-KY Metropolitan Statistical Area. The entire metro area includes: Posey County, IN; Vanderburgh County, IN; Warrick County, IN; Henderson County, KY

Weather Station: Evansville Dress Regional Arpt Elevation: 380 feet

	Jan	Feb	Mar	Apr	May	Jun	Jul	Aug	Sep	Oct	Nov	Dec
High	41	46	56	67	77	85	88	88	81	69	56	44
Low	25	28	36	45	55	64	68	66	57	46	37	28
Precip	3.1	3.2	4.3	4.4	5.4	3.9	4.0	3.0	3.1	3.3	4.1	3.7
Snow	3.4	3.8	1.3	0.2	tr	tr	0.0	0.0	tr	0.2	0.1	2.5

High and Low temperatures in degrees Fahrenheit; Precipitation and Snow in inches

Weather Station: Evansville Museum Elevation: 379 feet

	Jan	Feb	Mar	Apr	May	Jun	Jul	Aug	Sep	Oct	Nov	Dec
High	43	48	59	70	79	87	90	90	83	72	59	46
Low	27	29	38	48	57	66	70	69	61	49	41	30
Precip	3.0	3.4	4.5	4.3	5.0	3.6	4.3	3.3	3.6	3.6	4.2	3.8
Snow	3.1	2.9	1.5	0.1	tr	0.0	0.0	0.0	0.0	tr	0.1	3.3

High and Low temperatures in degrees Fahrenheit; Precipitation and Snow in inches

Population: 181,831; Growth (since 2000): 5.8%; Density: 778.8 persons per square mile; Race: 85.7% White, 9.1% Black/African American, 1.2% Asian, 0.2% American Indian/Alaska Native, 0.1% Native Hawaiian/Other Pacific Islander, 2.6% two or more races, 2.5% Hispanic of any race; Average household size: 2.34; Median age: 37.9; Age under 18: 21.8%; Age 65 and over: 15.7%; Males per 100 females: 93.2; Marriage status: 31.5% never married, 47.4% now married, 1.2% separated, 6.3% widowed, 14.8% divorced; Foreign born: 3.0%; Speak English only: 95.9%; With disability: 15.5%; Veterans: 8.2%; Ancestry: 30.1% German, 11.6% Irish, 11.4% English, 8.1% American, 2.0% French
Religion: Six largest groups: 16.2% Catholicism, 15.1% Baptist, 7.2% Non-denominational Protestant, 4.7% Methodist/Pietist, 3.6% Presbyterian-Reformed, 2.5% Lutheran
Economy: Unemployment rate: 3.4%; Leading industries: 15.3 % retail trade; 13.2 % health care and social assistance; 10.8 % other services (except public administration); Farms: 275 totaling 76,554 acres; Company size: 6 employ 1,000 or more persons, 10 employ 500 to 999 persons, 145 employ 100 to 499 persons, 4,834 employ less than 100 persons; Business ownership: 3,974 women-owned, 525 Black-owned, 130 Hispanic-owned, 305 Asian-owned, 50 American Indian/Alaska Native-owned
Employment: 12.7% management, business, and financial, 4.8% computer, engineering, and science, 9.6% education, legal, community service, arts, and media, 6.1% healthcare practitioners, 18.1% service, 23.6% sales and office, 7.7% natural resources, construction, and maintenance, 17.4% production, transportation, and material moving
Income: Per capita: $26,917; Median household: $44,815; Average household: $63,702; Households with income of $100,000 or more: 16.8%; Poverty rate: 18.0%
Educational Attainment: High school diploma or higher: 89.5%; Bachelor's degree or higher: 26.2%; Graduate/professional degree or higher: 9.4%
Housing: Homeownership rate: 64.1%; Median home value: $121,200; Median year structure built: 1966; Homeowner vacancy rate: 1.7%; Median selected monthly owner costs: $1,050 with a mortgage, $428 without a mortgage; Median gross rent: $751 per month; Rental vacancy rate: 6.2%
Vital Statistics: Birth rate: 119.1 per 10,000 population; Death rate: 102.2 per 10,000 population; Age-adjusted cancer mortality rate: 174.1 deaths per 100,000 population
Health Insurance: 90.6% have insurance; 69.1% have private insurance; 34.7% have public insurance; 9.4% do not have insurance; 4.8% of children under 18 do not have insurance
Health Care: Physicians: 29.2 per 10,000 population; Dentists: 7.2 per 10,000 population; Hospital beds: 71.9 per 10,000 population; Hospital admissions: 2,619.7 per 10,000 population
Air Quality Index (AQI): Percent of Days: 77.5% good, 21.9% moderate, 0.5% unhealthy for sensitive individuals, 0.0% unhealthy, 0.0% very unhealthy; Annual median: 42; Annual maximum: 115
Transportation: Commute: 92.8% car, 1.6% public transportation, 2.0% walk, 2.4% work from home; Mean travel time to work: 19.6 minutes
2016 Presidential Election: 55.2% Trump, 38.9% Clinton, 4.4% Johnson, 0.3% Stein

National and State Parks: Angel Mounds State Memorial
Additional Information Contacts
Vanderburgh Government. . . . . (812) 435-5160
http://www.vanderburghgov.org

Vanderburgh County Communities

DARMSTADT (town). Covers a land area of 4.516 square miles and a water area of 0.059 square miles. Located at 38.09° N. Lat; 87.58° W. Long. Elevation is 479 feet.
History: Established 1860.
Population: 1,299; Growth (since 2000): -1.1%; Density: 287.6 persons per square mile; Race: 97.8% White, 0.2% Black/African American, 0.3% Asian, 0.0% American Indian/Alaska Native, 0.0% Native Hawaiian/Other Pacific Islander, 1.8% Two or more races, 0.0% Hispanic of any race; Average household size: 2.40; Median age: 53.8; Age under 18: 16.4%; Age 65 and over: 25.5%; Males per 100 females: 106.3; Marriage status: 19.9% never married, 64.0% now married, 0.3% separated, 5.4% widowed, 10.7% divorced; Foreign born: 0.6%; Speak English only: 98.8%; With disability: 12.8%; Veterans: 8.1%; Ancestry: 44.6% German, 16.9% English, 8.8% Irish, 6.9% American, 3.2% French
Employment: 14.6% management, business, and financial, 7.0% computer, engineering, and science, 7.7% education, legal, community service, arts, and media, 8.0% healthcare practitioners, 14.4% service, 28.6% sales and office, 8.7% natural resources, construction, and maintenance, 11.0% production, transportation, and material moving
Income: Per capita: $47,113; Median household: $90,221; Average household: $109,768; Households with income of $100,000 or more: 40.4%; Poverty rate: 6.2%
Educational Attainment: High school diploma or higher: 96.9%; Bachelor's degree or higher: 38.4%; Graduate/professional degree or higher: 15.8%
Housing: Homeownership rate: 93.0%; Median home value: $211,300; Median year structure built: 1964; Homeowner vacancy rate: 1.9%; Median selected monthly owner costs: $1,263 with a mortgage, $540 without a mortgage; Median gross rent: $819 per month; Rental vacancy rate: 17.4%
Health Insurance: 96.4% have insurance; 81.2% have private insurance; 33.9% have public insurance; 3.6% do not have insurance; 4.5% of children under 18 do not have insurance
Transportation: Commute: 95.5% car, 0.0% public transportation, 1.4% walk, 3.2% work from home; Mean travel time to work: 23.3 minutes

EVANSVILLE (city). County seat. Covers a land area of 44.153 square miles and a water area of 0.472 square miles. Located at 37.99° N. Lat; 87.53° W. Long. Elevation is 387 feet.
History: Colonel Hugh McGary established a ferry at this spot on the Ohio River in 1812, and a village called McGary's Ferry grew up around it. McGary sold part of his holdings to General Robert Evans in 1818. When the community was designated as the seat of the new Vanderburgh County, it was named Evansville. The town had a good inland harbor, and soon became a transportation hub. It was chartered as a city in 1848.
Population: 119,806; Growth (since 2000): -1.5%; Density: 2,713.4 persons per square mile; Race: 81.7% White, 12.6% Black/African American, 0.7% Asian, 0.3% American Indian/Alaska Native, 0.2% Native Hawaiian/Other Pacific Islander, 3.3% Two or more races, 3.0% Hispanic of any race; Average household size: 2.24; Median age: 37.2; Age under 18: 21.5%; Age 65 and over: 15.5%; Males per 100 females: 92.7; Marriage status: 34.3% never married, 41.0% now married, 1.6% separated, 7.0% widowed, 17.7% divorced; Foreign born: 2.7%; Speak English only: 96.2%; With disability: 17.9%; Veterans: 8.4%; Ancestry: 25.7% German, 11.6% Irish, 11.3% English, 7.1% American, 1.7% French
Employment: 10.7% management, business, and financial, 3.8% computer, engineering, and science, 9.1% education, legal, community service, arts, and media, 4.9% healthcare practitioners, 19.9% service, 24.4% sales and office, 7.5% natural resources, construction, and maintenance, 19.8% production, transportation, and material moving
Income: Per capita: $22,375; Median household: $36,956; Average household: $50,350; Households with income of $100,000 or more: 9.9%; Poverty rate: 23.3%
Educational Attainment: High school diploma or higher: 86.9%; Bachelor's degree or higher: 20.7%; Graduate/professional degree or higher: 7.0%

School District(s)

Evansville Vanderburgh School Corp (PK-12)
Enrollment: 22,879 . . . . (812) 435-8453

Joshua Academy (KG-06)
Enrollment: 165. . . . . (812) 401-6300
Signature School Inc (09-12)
Enrollment: 361. . . . . (812) 421-1820

Four-year College(s)

University of Evansville (Private, Not-for-profit, United Methodist)
Enrollment: 2,516 . . . . (812) 488-2000
Tuition: In-state $35,394; Out-of-state $35,394
University of Southern Indiana (Public)
Enrollment: 11,004 . . . . (812) 464-8600
Tuition: In-state $7,970; Out-of-state $18,626

Two-year College(s)

Ross Medical Education Center-Evansville (Private, For-profit)
Enrollment: 111. . . . . (812) 475-9685

Vocational/Technical School(s)

Rogers Academy of Hair Design (Private, For-profit)
Enrollment: 81. . . . . (812) 429-0110
Tuition: $14,850
The Salon Professional Academy-Evansville (Private, For-profit)
Enrollment: 114. . . . . (812) 437-8772
Tuition: $15,390

Housing: Homeownership rate: 54.5%; Median home value: $89,700; Median year structure built: 1958; Homeowner vacancy rate: 2.2%; Median selected monthly owner costs: $926 with a mortgage, $387 without a mortgage; Median gross rent: $738 per month; Rental vacancy rate: 6.6%
Health Insurance: 88.3% have insurance; 61.1% have private insurance; 39.9% have public insurance; 11.7% do not have insurance; 4.9% of children under 18 do not have insurance
Hospitals: Deaconess Hospital (400 beds); Saint Mary's Medical Center of Evansville (508 beds)
Safety: Violent crime rate: 69.1 per 10,000 population; Property crime rate: 500.9 per 10,000 population
Newspapers: Evansville Courier & Press (daily circulation 66,200)
Transportation: Commute: 91.9% car, 2.4% public transportation, 2.5% walk, 1.7% work from home; Mean travel time to work: 18.7 minutes
Airports: Evansville Regional (primary service/non-hub)
Additional Information Contacts
City of Evansville. . . . . (812) 436-4992
http://www.evansvillegov.org

HIGHLAND (CDP). Covers a land area of 2.267 square miles and a water area of 0.013 square miles. Located at 38.05° N. Lat; 87.56° W. Long. Elevation is 482 feet.
History: The area of Highland was almost entirely under water before it was first settled in 1848. Only a high sand ridge stood above the water. People referred to this area as 'Highlands.'.
Population: 4,539; Growth (since 2000): 10.5%; Density: 2,002.0 persons per square mile; Race: 99.1% White, 0.4% Black/African American, 0.5% Asian, 0.0% American Indian/Alaska Native, 0.0% Native Hawaiian/Other Pacific Islander, 0.0% Two or more races, 0.0% Hispanic of any race; Average household size: 2.79; Median age: 43.6; Age under 18: 23.7%; Age 65 and over: 14.6%; Males per 100 females: 95.9; Marriage status: 19.7% never married, 67.1% now married, 0.0% separated, 5.7% widowed, 7.5% divorced; Foreign born: 1.0%; Speak English only: 98.7%; With disability: 12.1%; Veterans: 7.0%; Ancestry: 42.6% German, 16.6% English, 14.9% Irish, 10.8% American, 8.7% Italian
Employment: 18.4% management, business, and financial, 6.6% computer, engineering, and science, 9.7% education, legal, community service, arts, and media, 10.0% healthcare practitioners, 10.1% service, 23.5% sales and office, 4.7% natural resources, construction, and maintenance, 17.0% production, transportation, and material moving
Income: Per capita: $31,059; Median household: $71,742; Average household: $85,980; Households with income of $100,000 or more: 24.9%; Poverty rate: 9.0%
Educational Attainment: High school diploma or higher: 95.7%; Bachelor's degree or higher: 33.3%; Graduate/professional degree or higher: 12.8%

School District(s)

School Town Of Highland (PK-12)
Enrollment: 3,191 . . . . (219) 922-5615

Vocational/Technical School(s)

Tricoci University of Beauty Culture-Highland (Private, For-profit)
Enrollment: 237. . . . . (219) 838-2004
Tuition: $19,982

Housing: Homeownership rate: 94.2%; Median home value: $158,300; Median year structure built: 1981; Homeowner vacancy rate: 2.9%; Median selected monthly owner costs: $1,242 with a mortgage, $480 without a mortgage; Median gross rent: $1,091 per month; Rental vacancy rate: 0.0%
Health Insurance: 92.6% have insurance; 81.3% have private insurance; 32.9% have public insurance; 7.4% do not have insurance; 7.6% of children under 18 do not have insurance
Transportation: Commute: 93.1% car, 0.5% public transportation, 0.8% walk, 3.2% work from home; Mean travel time to work: 19.8 minutes

MELODY HILL (CDP). Covers a land area of 1.361 square miles and a water area of 0.016 square miles. Located at 38.02° N. Lat; 87.51° W. Long. Elevation is 427 feet.
Population: 3,625; Growth (since 2000): 18.2%; Density: 2,664.1 persons per square mile; Race: 94.8% White, 5.0% Black/African American, 0.0% Asian, 0.0% American Indian/Alaska Native, 0.0% Native Hawaiian/Other Pacific Islander, 0.0% Two or more races, 1.0% Hispanic of any race; Average household size: 2.65; Median age: 41.2; Age under 18: 25.2%; Age 65 and over: 16.0%; Males per 100 females: 95.8; Marriage status: 18.6% never married, 64.6% now married, 0.8% separated, 4.0% widowed, 12.7% divorced; Foreign born: 1.4%; Speak English only: 97.3%; With disability: 12.7%; Veterans: 14.6%; Ancestry: 30.8% German, 16.2% Irish, 15.0% American, 8.4% English, 3.1% Polish
Employment: 12.8% management, business, and financial, 5.5% computer, engineering, and science, 7.7% education, legal, community service, arts, and media, 11.2% healthcare practitioners, 16.2% service, 25.8% sales and office, 7.9% natural resources, construction, and maintenance, 12.9% production, transportation, and material moving
Income: Per capita: $33,726; Median household: $78,469; Average household: $88,179; Households with income of $100,000 or more: 33.9%; Poverty rate: 6.1%
Educational Attainment: High school diploma or higher: 95.2%; Bachelor's degree or higher: 31.6%; Graduate/professional degree or higher: 11.8%
Housing: Homeownership rate: 93.5%; Median home value: $149,500; Median year structure built: 1974; Homeowner vacancy rate: 3.6%; Median selected monthly owner costs: $1,160 with a mortgage, $385 without a mortgage; Median gross rent: $1,345 per month; Rental vacancy rate: 0.0%
Health Insurance: 90.0% have insurance; 77.2% have private insurance; 28.2% have public insurance; 10.0% do not have insurance; 11.0% of children under 18 do not have insurance
Transportation: Commute: 92.7% car, 0.2% public transportation, 0.0% walk, 7.0% work from home; Mean travel time to work: 19.4 minutes

Vermillion County

Located in western Indiana; bounded on the west by Illinois, and on the east by the Wabash River; drained by the Vermilion River. Covers a land area of 256.878 square miles, a water area of 3.052 square miles, and is located in the Eastern Time Zone at 39.85° N. Lat., 87.46° W. Long. The county was founded in 1824. County seat is Newport.

Vermillion County is part of the Terre Haute, IN Metropolitan Statistical Area. The entire metro area includes: Clay County, IN; Sullivan County, IN; Vermillion County, IN; Vigo County, IN

Weather Station: Perrysville 4 WNW Elevation: 620 feet

	Jan	Feb	Mar	Apr	May	Jun	Jul	Aug	Sep	Oct	Nov	Dec
High	34	39	50	63	74	83	85	84	79	66	52	38
Low	17	21	30	40	51	60	63	61	53	42	33	22
Precip	2.2	2.1	2.7	3.6	4.5	4.4	4.4	3.4	2.8	3.3	3.5	2.7
Snow	5.5	3.8	2.5	0.3	tr	0.0	0.0	0.0	0.0	0.1	0.7	4.5

High and Low temperatures in degrees Fahrenheit; Precipitation and Snow in inches

Population: 15,644; Growth (since 2000): -6.8%; Density: 60.9 persons per square mile; Race: 97.9% White, 0.4% Black/African American, 0.2% Asian, 0.3% American Indian/Alaska Native, 0.0% Native Hawaiian/Other Pacific Islander, 1.0% two or more races, 1.1% Hispanic of any race; Average household size: 2.36; Median age: 43.2; Age under 18: 22.3%; Age 65 and over: 18.8%; Males per 100 females: 97.9; Marriage status: 23.5% never married, 50.3% now married, 1.2% separated, 9.0% widowed, 17.2% divorced; Foreign born: 0.9%; Speak English only: 97.3%; With disability: 18.0%; Veterans: 10.6%; Ancestry: 18.1% German, 15.0% American, 9.9% Irish, 9.0% English, 7.8% Italian

Religion: Six largest groups: 14.2% Baptist, 6.9% Methodist/Pietist, 6.2% Catholicism, 3.5% Latter-day Saints, 2.5% Pentecostal, 2.0% Non-denominational Protestant
Economy: Unemployment rate: 5.2%; Leading industries: 19.6 % retail trade; 14.4 % other services (except public administration); 11.9 % accommodation and food services; Farms: 270 totaling 118,394 acres; Company size: 0 employ 1,000 or more persons, 0 employ 500 to 999 persons, 8 employ 100 to 499 persons, 262 employ less than 100 persons; Business ownership: 270 women-owned, n/a Black-owned, n/a Hispanic-owned, n/a Asian-owned, n/a American Indian/Alaska Native-owned
Employment: 8.5% management, business, and financial, 3.0% computer, engineering, and science, 8.3% education, legal, community service, arts, and media, 5.6% healthcare practitioners, 15.0% service, 22.1% sales and office, 12.7% natural resources, construction, and maintenance, 24.8% production, transportation, and material moving
Income: Per capita: $23,891; Median household: $45,440; Average household: $55,255; Households with income of $100,000 or more: 12.3%; Poverty rate: 13.4%
Educational Attainment: High school diploma or higher: 90.5%; Bachelor's degree or higher: 13.0%; Graduate/professional degree or higher: 4.0%
Housing: Homeownership rate: 75.0%; Median home value: $74,600; Median year structure built: 1956; Homeowner vacancy rate: 2.3%; Median selected monthly owner costs: $854 with a mortgage, $332 without a mortgage; Median gross rent: $581 per month; Rental vacancy rate: 2.7%
Vital Statistics: Birth rate: 107.1 per 10,000 population; Death rate: 129.0 per 10,000 population; Age-adjusted cancer mortality rate: 226.3 deaths per 100,000 population
Health Insurance: 90.9% have insurance; 67.8% have private insurance; 40.4% have public insurance; 9.1% do not have insurance; 2.1% of children under 18 do not have insurance
Health Care: Physicians: 5.1 per 10,000 population; Dentists: 3.2 per 10,000 population; Hospital beds: 13.5 per 10,000 population; Hospital admissions: 554.7 per 10,000 population
Transportation: Commute: 93.5% car, 0.7% public transportation, 2.6% walk, 2.7% work from home; Mean travel time to work: 24.3 minutes
2016 Presidential Election: 64.7% Trump, 29.8% Clinton, 4.6% Johnson, 0.2% Stein
Additional Information Contacts
Vermillion Government . . . . (765) 492-5300
http://www.vermilliongov.us

Vermillion County Communities

BLANFORD (CDP). Covers a land area of 0.734 square miles and a water area of 0 square miles. Located at 39.67° N. Lat; 87.52° W. Long. Elevation is 574 feet.
Population: 233; Growth (since 2000): n/a; Density: 317.4 persons per square mile; Race: 100.0% White, 0.0% Black/African American, 0.0% Asian, 0.0% American Indian/Alaska Native, 0.0% Native Hawaiian/Other Pacific Islander, 0.0% Two or more races, 0.0% Hispanic of any race; Average household size: 2.10; Median age: 53.2; Age under 18: 5.2%; Age 65 and over: 24.5%; Males per 100 females: 120.6; Marriage status: 6.3% never married, 85.1% now married, 0.0% separated, 6.3% widowed, 2.3% divorced; Foreign born: 0.0%; Speak English only: 100.0%; With disability: 27.9%; Veterans: 12.7%; Ancestry: 33.5% American, 12.0% Italian, 6.0% English, 6.0% Polish
Employment: 0.0% management, business, and financial, 0.0% computer, engineering, and science, 0.0% education, legal, community service, arts, and media, 8.5% healthcare practitioners, 4.7% service, 0.0% sales and office, 39.6% natural resources, construction, and maintenance, 47.2% production, transportation, and material moving
Income: Per capita: $60,157; Median household: n/a; Average household: $102,403; Households with income of $100,000 or more: 18.9%; Poverty rate: 28.8%
Educational Attainment: High school diploma or higher: 85.1%; Bachelor's degree or higher: n/a; Graduate/professional degree or higher: n/a
Housing: Homeownership rate: 81.1%; Median home value: n/a; Median year structure built: Before 1940; Homeowner vacancy rate: 0.0%; Median selected monthly owner costs: $580 with a mortgage, $240 without a mortgage; Median gross rent: n/a per month; Rental vacancy rate: 0.0%
Health Insurance: 88.4% have insurance; 58.4% have private insurance; 54.9% have public insurance; 11.6% do not have insurance; 0.0% of children under 18 do not have insurance
Transportation: Commute: 100.0% car, 0.0% public transportation, 0.0% walk, 0.0% work from home; Mean travel time to work: 39.2 minutes

CAYUGA (town). Covers a land area of 1.013 square miles and a water area of 0 square miles. Located at 39.95° N. Lat; 87.46° W. Long. Elevation is 509 feet.
Population: 1,179; Growth (since 2000): 6.3%; Density: 1,163.3 persons per square mile; Race: 93.9% White, 0.0% Black/African American, 0.0% Asian, 1.7% American Indian/Alaska Native, 0.0% Native Hawaiian/Other Pacific Islander, 4.4% Two or more races, 0.3% Hispanic of any race; Average household size: 2.49; Median age: 40.9; Age under 18: 22.1%; Age 65 and over: 14.1%; Males per 100 females: 93.0; Marriage status: 24.8% never married, 54.5% now married, 2.5% separated, 7.7% widowed, 13.0% divorced; Foreign born: 0.7%; Speak English only: 98.8%; With disability: 18.1%; Veterans: 12.6%; Ancestry: 21.5% American, 13.5% German, 10.1% Irish, 10.0% English, 5.9% Dutch
Employment: 8.2% management, business, and financial, 2.2% computer, engineering, and science, 12.7% education, legal, community service, arts, and media, 4.5% healthcare practitioners, 11.7% service, 24.9% sales and office, 13.3% natural resources, construction, and maintenance, 22.5% production, transportation, and material moving
Income: Per capita: $20,432; Median household: $48,333; Average household: $50,164; Households with income of $100,000 or more: 9.1%; Poverty rate: 20.9%
Educational Attainment: High school diploma or higher: 88.7%; Bachelor's degree or higher: 12.2%; Graduate/professional degree or higher: 1.8%

School District(s)

North Vermillion Com Sch Corp (PK-12)
Enrollment: 724. . . . . (765) 492-4033
Housing: Homeownership rate: 70.7%; Median home value: $67,600; Median year structure built: 1968; Homeowner vacancy rate: 0.0%; Median selected monthly owner costs: $830 with a mortgage, $344 without a mortgage; Median gross rent: $707 per month; Rental vacancy rate: 0.0%
Health Insurance: 93.8% have insurance; 69.0% have private insurance; 33.6% have public insurance; 6.2% do not have insurance; 0.0% of children under 18 do not have insurance
Newspapers: Cayuga Herald News (weekly circulation 800)
Transportation: Commute: 93.7% car, 0.0% public transportation, 0.0% walk, 5.1% work from home; Mean travel time to work: 27.2 minutes

CLINTON (city). Covers a land area of 2.238 square miles and a water area of 0.019 square miles. Located at 39.66° N. Lat; 87.40° W. Long. Elevation is 499 feet.
History: Clinton was laid out along the Wabash River in 1829, and named for DeWitt Clinton (1769-1828), governor of New York. Clinton developed as a coal-mining town.
Population: 4,752; Growth (since 2000): -7.3%; Density: 2,123.4 persons per square mile; Race: 98.5% White, 0.9% Black/African American, 0.0% Asian, 0.0% American Indian/Alaska Native, 0.0% Native Hawaiian/Other Pacific Islander, 0.0% Two or more races, 2.7% Hispanic of any race; Average household size: 2.19; Median age: 42.4; Age under 18: 22.7%; Age 65 and over: 18.8%; Males per 100 females: 90.6; Marriage status: 27.7% never married, 36.3% now married, 0.5% separated, 12.2% widowed, 23.8% divorced; Foreign born: 0.3%; Speak English only: 96.4%; With disability: 22.9%; Veterans: 7.7%; Ancestry: 17.0% German, 12.9% American, 11.3% English, 10.0% Italian, 8.1% Irish
Employment: 2.4% management, business, and financial, 3.0% computer, engineering, and science, 7.5% education, legal, community service, arts, and media, 9.0% healthcare practitioners, 15.2% service, 33.5% sales and office, 8.6% natural resources, construction, and maintenance, 20.8% production, transportation, and material moving
Income: Per capita: $17,494; Median household: $33,577; Average household: $38,568; Households with income of $100,000 or more: 4.5%; Poverty rate: 20.2%
Educational Attainment: High school diploma or higher: 86.2%; Bachelor's degree or higher: 9.7%; Graduate/professional degree or higher: 2.7%

School District(s)

South Vermillion Com Sch Corp (PK-12)
Enrollment: 1,811 . . . . (765) 832-2426

Housing: Homeownership rate: 57.8%; Median home value: $62,500; Median year structure built: 1941; Homeowner vacancy rate: 3.3%; Median selected monthly owner costs: $776 with a mortgage, $257 without a mortgage; Median gross rent: $477 per month; Rental vacancy rate: 0.0%
Health Insurance: 90.3% have insurance; 62.2% have private insurance; 49.6% have public insurance; 9.7% do not have insurance; 2.0% of children under 18 do not have insurance
Hospitals: Union Hospital Clinton
Safety: Violent crime rate: 50.2 per 10,000 population; Property crime rate: 324.1 per 10,000 population
Newspapers: Daily Clintonian (daily circulation 5,100)
Transportation: Commute: 91.0% car, 2.6% public transportation, 5.2% walk, 1.2% work from home; Mean travel time to work: 22.0 minutes
Additional Information Contacts
City of Clinton .... (765) 832-3844
http://greaterclintonchamber.org

DANA (town). Covers a land area of 0.292 square miles and a water area of 0 square miles. Located at 39.81° N. Lat; 87.49° W. Long. Elevation is 640 feet.
History: Ernie Pyle State Memorial.
Population: 556; Growth (since 2000): -16.0%; Density: 1,904.2 persons per square mile; Race: 96.9% White, 0.0% Black/African American, 0.0% Asian, 2.3% American Indian/Alaska Native, 0.0% Native Hawaiian/Other Pacific Islander, 0.7% Two or more races, 4.3% Hispanic of any race; Average household size: 2.48; Median age: 43.6; Age under 18: 19.8%; Age 65 and over: 18.9%; Males per 100 females: 85.9; Marriage status: 22.8% never married, 54.6% now married, 0.4% separated, 8.4% widowed, 14.2% divorced; Foreign born: 0.0%; Speak English only: 99.6%; With disability: 30.6%; Veterans: 14.6%; Ancestry: 32.6% American, 17.3% German, 9.5% Irish, 5.4% English, 3.2% Dutch
Employment: 11.0% management, business, and financial, 2.0% computer, engineering, and science, 0.4% education, legal, community service, arts, and media, 0.8% healthcare practitioners, 21.1% service, 16.3% sales and office, 15.9% natural resources, construction, and maintenance, 32.5% production, transportation, and material moving
Income: Per capita: $19,535; Median household: $44,000; Average household: $48,461; Households with income of $100,000 or more: 6.3%; Poverty rate: 21.8%
Educational Attainment: High school diploma or higher: 85.1%; Bachelor's degree or higher: 5.7%; Graduate/professional degree or higher: 1.7%
Housing: Homeownership rate: 70.1%; Median home value: $56,500; Median year structure built: 1947; Homeowner vacancy rate: 3.2%; Median selected monthly owner costs: $761 with a mortgage, $350 without a mortgage; Median gross rent: $606 per month; Rental vacancy rate: 0.0%
Health Insurance: 89.9% have insurance; 63.5% have private insurance; 39.4% have public insurance; 10.1% do not have insurance; 5.1% of children under 18 do not have insurance
Transportation: Commute: 94.9% car, 0.0% public transportation, 0.8% walk, 3.4% work from home; Mean travel time to work: 28.6 minutes

FAIRVIEW PARK (town). Covers a land area of 0.880 square miles and a water area of 0 square miles. Located at 39.68° N. Lat; 87.41° W. Long. Elevation is 518 feet.
History: Laid out 1902.
Population: 1,204; Growth (since 2000): -19.5%; Density: 1,367.8 persons per square mile; Race: 98.8% White, 0.0% Black/African American, 1.2% Asian, 0.0% American Indian/Alaska Native, 0.0% Native Hawaiian/Other Pacific Islander, 0.0% Two or more races, 0.8% Hispanic of any race; Average household size: 2.12; Median age: 48.4; Age under 18: 17.7%; Age 65 and over: 22.9%; Males per 100 females: 102.9; Marriage status: 21.0% never married, 55.2% now married, 0.9% separated, 5.9% widowed, 17.9% divorced; Foreign born: 1.2%; Speak English only: 96.3%; With disability: 17.7%; Veterans: 14.8%; Ancestry: 22.0% German, 14.9% English, 11.5% Italian, 9.8% American, 8.6% Irish
Employment: 9.7% management, business, and financial, 4.5% computer, engineering, and science, 8.7% education, legal, community service, arts, and media, 7.7% healthcare practitioners, 20.5% service, 16.4% sales and office, 8.3% natural resources, construction, and maintenance, 24.1% production, transportation, and material moving
Income: Per capita: $25,167; Median household: $45,592; Average household: $53,353; Households with income of $100,000 or more: 9.6%; Poverty rate: 9.2%
Educational Attainment: High school diploma or higher: 91.3%; Bachelor's degree or higher: 15.2%; Graduate/professional degree or higher: 5.3%
Housing: Homeownership rate: 74.8%; Median home value: $90,200; Median year structure built: 1970; Homeowner vacancy rate: 4.9%; Median selected monthly owner costs: $821 with a mortgage, $389 without a mortgage; Median gross rent: $585 per month; Rental vacancy rate: 13.3%
Health Insurance: 91.2% have insurance; 72.1% have private insurance; 40.3% have public insurance; 8.8% do not have insurance; 4.7% of children under 18 do not have insurance
Transportation: Commute: 96.3% car, 0.0% public transportation, 1.2% walk, 0.6% work from home; Mean travel time to work: 26.7 minutes

HILLSDALE (unincorporated postal area)
ZCTA: 47854
Covers a land area of 28.654 square miles and a water area of 0.525 square miles. Located at 39.80° N. Lat; 87.40° W. Long. Elevation is 623 feet.
Population: 845; Growth (since 2000): -12.1%; Density: 29.5 persons per square mile; Race: 100.0% White, 0.0% Black/African American, 0.0% Asian, 0.0% American Indian/Alaska Native, 0.0% Native Hawaiian/Other Pacific Islander, 0.0% Two or more races, 0.0% Hispanic of any race; Average household size: 2.84; Median age: 42.2; Age under 18: 25.2%; Age 65 and over: 17.2%; Males per 100 females: 103.1; Marriage status: 13.3% never married, 69.0% now married, 1.6% separated, 6.8% widowed, 10.9% divorced; Foreign born: 0.8%; Speak English only: 100.0%; With disability: 9.7%; Veterans: 12.3%; Ancestry: 15.9% American, 13.4% Irish, 8.0% German, 4.4% Dutch, 3.8% Polish
Employment: 17.4% management, business, and financial, 12.8% computer, engineering, and science, 2.0% education, legal, community service, arts, and media, 0.0% healthcare practitioners, 23.8% service, 9.6% sales and office, 5.5% natural resources, construction, and maintenance, 29.0% production, transportation, and material moving
Income: Per capita: $25,883; Median household: $64,063; Average household: $67,651; Households with income of $100,000 or more: 26.2%; Poverty rate: 4.9%
Educational Attainment: High school diploma or higher: 92.3%; Bachelor's degree or higher: 14.6%; Graduate/professional degree or higher: 4.4%
Housing: Homeownership rate: 100.0%; Median home value: $107,300; Median year structure built: 1960; Homeowner vacancy rate: 0.0%; Median selected monthly owner costs: $1,010 with a mortgage, $384 without a mortgage; Median gross rent: n/a per month; Rental vacancy rate: 0.0%
Health Insurance: 89.0% have insurance; 54.9% have private insurance; 43.2% have public insurance; 11.0% do not have insurance; 0.0% of children under 18 do not have insurance
Transportation: Commute: 93.3% car, 0.0% public transportation, 6.7% walk, 0.0% work from home; Mean travel time to work: 20.0 minutes

NEWPORT (town). County seat. Covers a land area of 0.868 square miles and a water area of 0 square miles. Located at 39.88° N. Lat; 87.41° W. Long. Elevation is 528 feet.
Population: 420; Growth (since 2000): -27.3%; Density: 483.9 persons per square mile; Race: 96.9% White, 0.0% Black/African American, 0.0% Asian, 0.2% American Indian/Alaska Native, 0.0% Native Hawaiian/Other Pacific Islander, 2.9% Two or more races, 1.0% Hispanic of any race; Average household size: 2.39; Median age: 46.8; Age under 18: 13.6%; Age 65 and over: 22.4%; Males per 100 females: 97.3; Marriage status: 18.2% never married, 53.2% now married, 2.5% separated, 5.0% widowed, 23.7% divorced; Foreign born: 0.0%; Speak English only: 100.0%; With disability: 23.3%; Veterans: 10.7%; Ancestry: 27.4% German, 20.2% Irish, 15.5% American, 5.5% English, 5.2% Italian
Employment: 4.0% management, business, and financial, 2.3% computer, engineering, and science, 9.6% education, legal, community service, arts, and media, 0.0% healthcare practitioners, 11.9% service, 13.0% sales and office, 7.9% natural resources, construction, and maintenance, 51.4% production, transportation, and material moving
Income: Per capita: $23,749; Median household: $54,000; Average household: $54,153; Households with income of $100,000 or more: 5.1%; Poverty rate: 10.2%
Educational Attainment: High school diploma or higher: 89.2%; Bachelor's degree or higher: 13.7%; Graduate/professional degree or higher: 6.1%

Housing: Homeownership rate: 96.6%; Median home value: $46,000; Median year structure built: 1965; Homeowner vacancy rate: 6.1%; Median selected monthly owner costs: $594 with a mortgage, $315 without a mortgage; Median gross rent: $625 per month; Rental vacancy rate: 0.0%
Health Insurance: 91.7% have insurance; 72.1% have private insurance; 42.4% have public insurance; 8.3% do not have insurance; 7.2% of children under 18 do not have insurance
Transportation: Commute: 93.8% car, 0.0% public transportation, 2.3% walk, 4.0% work from home; Mean travel time to work: 24.8 minutes

PERRYSVILLE (town). Covers a land area of 0.255 square miles and a water area of 0 square miles. Located at 40.05° N. Lat; 87.44° W. Long. Elevation is 538 feet.
Population: 504; Growth (since 2000): 0.4%; Density: 1,975.7 persons per square mile; Race: 96.2% White, 3.0% Black/African American, 0.0% Asian, 0.4% American Indian/Alaska Native, 0.0% Native Hawaiian/Other Pacific Islander, 0.4% Two or more races, 0.6% Hispanic of any race; Average household size: 2.47; Median age: 35.6; Age under 18: 26.4%; Age 65 and over: 15.3%; Males per 100 females: 83.9; Marriage status: 24.1% never married, 53.3% now married, 3.8% separated, 5.6% widowed, 17.0% divorced; Foreign born: 0.0%; Speak English only: 98.9%; With disability: 13.9%; Veterans: 12.9%; Ancestry: 27.8% American, 16.3% German, 10.1% Irish, 3.6% Italian, 3.2% English
Employment: 4.1% management, business, and financial, 2.1% computer, engineering, and science, 1.2% education, legal, community service, arts, and media, 2.9% healthcare practitioners, 20.3% service, 25.7% sales and office, 12.4% natural resources, construction, and maintenance, 31.1% production, transportation, and material moving
Income: Per capita: $23,534; Median household: $41,923; Average household: $56,635; Households with income of $100,000 or more: 15.2%; Poverty rate: 17.5%
Educational Attainment: High school diploma or higher: 93.8%; Bachelor's degree or higher: 7.4%; Graduate/professional degree or higher: 2.8%
Housing: Homeownership rate: 64.2%; Median home value: $70,600; Median year structure built: 1946; Homeowner vacancy rate: 3.4%; Median selected monthly owner costs: $875 with a mortgage, $344 without a mortgage; Median gross rent: $717 per month; Rental vacancy rate: 6.0%
Health Insurance: 92.7% have insurance; 68.1% have private insurance; 37.7% have public insurance; 7.3% do not have insurance; 0.0% of children under 18 do not have insurance
Transportation: Commute: 99.2% car, 0.0% public transportation, 0.0% walk, 0.8% work from home; Mean travel time to work: 21.5 minutes

SAINT BERNICE (CDP). Covers a land area of 1.788 square miles and a water area of 0 square miles. Located at 39.71° N. Lat; 87.52° W. Long. Elevation is 577 feet.
Population: 390; Growth (since 2000): n/a; Density: 218.1 persons per square mile; Race: 98.2% White, 0.0% Black/African American, 0.0% Asian, 1.8% American Indian/Alaska Native, 0.0% Native Hawaiian/Other Pacific Islander, 0.0% Two or more races, 0.0% Hispanic of any race; Average household size: 2.64; Median age: 34.3; Age under 18: 32.6%; Age 65 and over: 23.8%; Males per 100 females: 98.8; Marriage status: 8.5% never married, 52.6% now married, 0.0% separated, 13.2% widowed, 25.7% divorced; Foreign born: 0.0%; Speak English only: 100.0%; With disability: 27.9%; Veterans: 5.3%; Ancestry: 41.0% German, 16.4% Scotch-Irish, 9.0% Italian, 7.4% American, 4.9% French
Employment: 0.0% management, business, and financial, 0.0% computer, engineering, and science, 5.7% education, legal, community service, arts, and media, 0.0% healthcare practitioners, 8.5% service, 24.5% sales and office, 0.0% natural resources, construction, and maintenance, 61.3% production, transportation, and material moving
Income: Per capita: $15,839; Median household: $42,000; Average household: $41,843; Households with income of $100,000 or more: 4.1%; Poverty rate: 8.7%
Educational Attainment: High school diploma or higher: 88.6%; Bachelor's degree or higher: 9.1%; Graduate/professional degree or higher: 2.3%
Housing: Homeownership rate: 85.1%; Median home value: $51,700; Median year structure built: 1940; Homeowner vacancy rate: 17.6%; Median selected monthly owner costs: $870 with a mortgage, $215 without a mortgage; Median gross rent: n/a per month; Rental vacancy rate: 0.0%
Health Insurance: 100.0% have insurance; 74.1% have private insurance; 45.4% have public insurance; 0.0% do not have insurance; 0.0% of children under 18 do not have insurance
Transportation: Commute: 100.0% car, 0.0% public transportation, 0.0% walk, 0.0% work from home; Mean travel time to work: 0.0 minutes

UNIVERSAL (town). Covers a land area of 0.362 square miles and a water area of 0 square miles. Located at 39.62° N. Lat; 87.46° W. Long. Elevation is 584 feet.
History: Laid out 1911.
Population: 246; Growth (since 2000): -41.3%; Density: 679.2 persons per square mile; Race: 98.4% White, 0.0% Black/African American, 0.0% Asian, 0.0% American Indian/Alaska Native, 0.0% Native Hawaiian/Other Pacific Islander, 0.0% Two or more races, 1.6% Hispanic of any race; Average household size: 2.20; Median age: 44.1; Age under 18: 19.5%; Age 65 and over: 22.8%; Males per 100 females: 90.5; Marriage status: 24.0% never married, 50.5% now married, 0.0% separated, 11.5% widowed, 13.9% divorced; Foreign born: 2.8%; Speak English only: 98.3%; With disability: 19.1%; Veterans: 5.6%; Ancestry: 19.5% German, 17.9% Italian, 10.6% American, 10.6% Irish, 10.2% English
Employment: 10.3% management, business, and financial, 3.4% computer, engineering, and science, 2.6% education, legal, community service, arts, and media, 0.0% healthcare practitioners, 21.6% service, 17.2% sales and office, 12.1% natural resources, construction, and maintenance, 32.8% production, transportation, and material moving
Income: Per capita: $18,767; Median household: $31,786; Average household: $40,015; Households with income of $100,000 or more: 6.3%; Poverty rate: 21.1%
Educational Attainment: High school diploma or higher: 74.3%; Bachelor's degree or higher: 4.6%; Graduate/professional degree or higher: 2.3%
Housing: Homeownership rate: 87.5%; Median home value: $51,800; Median year structure built: 1946; Homeowner vacancy rate: 0.0%; Median selected monthly owner costs: $735 with a mortgage, $285 without a mortgage; Median gross rent: $763 per month; Rental vacancy rate: 0.0%
Health Insurance: 82.5% have insurance; 56.5% have private insurance; 44.7% have public insurance; 17.5% do not have insurance; 0.0% of children under 18 do not have insurance
Transportation: Commute: 93.6% car, 0.0% public transportation, 1.8% walk, 4.6% work from home; Mean travel time to work: 26.3 minutes

Vigo County

Located in western Indiana; bounded on the west by Illinois; crossed by the Wabash River; drained by Honey Creek. Covers a land area of 403.313 square miles, a water area of 7.138 square miles, and is located in the Eastern Time Zone at 39.43° N. Lat., 87.39° W. Long. The county was founded in 1818. County seat is Terre Haute.

Vigo County is part of the Terre Haute, IN Metropolitan Statistical Area. The entire metro area includes: Clay County, IN; Sullivan County, IN; Vermillion County, IN; Vigo County, IN

Weather Station: Terre Haute Indiana State — Elevation: 506 feet

	Jan	Feb	Mar	Apr	May	Jun	Jul	Aug	Sep	Oct	Nov	Dec
High	38	42	53	65	76	84	88	87	81	68	54	41
Low	19	22	32	43	52	61	66	63	55	43	33	23
Precip	2.6	2.5	3.5	4.5	5.0	4.5	4.4	3.4	3.5	3.7	3.6	3.1
Snow	3.9	3.3	1.0	0.1	0.0	0.0	0.0	0.0	0.0	0.0	0.3	2.9

High and Low temperatures in degrees Fahrenheit; Precipitation and Snow in inches

Population: 107,723; Growth (since 2000): 1.8%; Density: 267.1 persons per square mile; Race: 87.4% White, 6.2% Black/African American, 1.9% Asian, 0.2% American Indian/Alaska Native, 0.0% Native Hawaiian/Other Pacific Islander, 3.6% two or more races, 2.6% Hispanic of any race; Average household size: 2.40; Median age: 36.1; Age under 18: 20.7%; Age 65 and over: 15.1%; Males per 100 females: 102.3; Marriage status: 35.7% never married, 43.5% now married, 1.4% separated, 6.4% widowed, 14.4% divorced; Foreign born: 3.2%; Speak English only: 95.3%; With disability: 18.6%; Veterans: 8.7%; Ancestry: 20.4% German, 12.3% American, 11.5% Irish, 9.0% English, 2.8% French
Religion: Six largest groups: 7.3% Baptist, 7.0% Catholicism, 6.5% Non-denominational Protestant, 3.9% Methodist/Pietist, 2.5% Pentecostal, 1.9% Holiness
Economy: Unemployment rate: 4.6%; Leading industries: 16.9 % retail trade; 15.5 % health care and social assistance; 11.4 % other services (except public administration); Farms: 450 totaling 117,530 acres; Company size: 2 employ 1,000 or more persons, 6 employ 500 to 999 persons, 59 employ 100 to 499 persons, 2,405 employ less than 100

persons; Business ownership: 2,132 women-owned, 157 Black-owned, 60 Hispanic-owned, 366 Asian-owned, n/a American Indian/Alaska Native-owned
Employment: 10.6% management, business, and financial, 4.1% computer, engineering, and science, 11.4% education, legal, community service, arts, and media, 6.3% healthcare practitioners, 21.0% service, 22.1% sales and office, 7.3% natural resources, construction, and maintenance, 17.1% production, transportation, and material moving
Income: Per capita: $22,932; Median household: $42,030; Average household: $56,796; Households with income of $100,000 or more: 13.7%; Poverty rate: 19.9%
Educational Attainment: High school diploma or higher: 87.8%; Bachelor's degree or higher: 23.5%; Graduate/professional degree or higher: 9.0%
Housing: Homeownership rate: 60.5%; Median home value: $90,700; Median year structure built: 1966; Homeowner vacancy rate: 2.9%; Median selected monthly owner costs: $941 with a mortgage, $371 without a mortgage; Median gross rent: $717 per month; Rental vacancy rate: 7.4%
Vital Statistics: Birth rate: 118.2 per 10,000 population; Death rate: 107.7 per 10,000 population; Age-adjusted cancer mortality rate: 194.4 deaths per 100,000 population
Health Insurance: 90.0% have insurance; 66.2% have private insurance; 36.9% have public insurance; 10.0% do not have insurance; 4.9% of children under 18 do not have insurance
Health Care: Physicians: 28.9 per 10,000 population; Dentists: 5.2 per 10,000 population; Hospital beds: 45.1 per 10,000 population; Hospital admissions: 2,148.3 per 10,000 population
Air Quality Index (AQI): Percent of Days: 65.5% good, 34.0% moderate, 0.5% unhealthy for sensitive individuals, 0.0% unhealthy, 0.0% very unhealthy; Annual median: 44; Annual maximum: 105
Transportation: Commute: 91.5% car, 1.2% public transportation, 3.1% walk, 2.9% work from home; Mean travel time to work: 19.9 minutes
2016 Presidential Election: 54.7% Trump, 39.7% Clinton, 4.3% Johnson, 0.5% Stein
Additional Information Contacts
Vigo Government . . . . (812) 462-3211
http://www.vigocounty.in.gov

Vigo County Communities

DRESSER (CDP). Covers a land area of 0.151 square miles and a water area of 0 square miles. Located at 39.46° N. Lat; 87.42° W. Long. Elevation is 469 feet.
Population: 13; Growth (since 2000): n/a; Density: 86.2 persons per square mile; Race: 100.0% White, 0.0% Black/African American, 0.0% Asian, 0.0% American Indian/Alaska Native, 0.0% Native Hawaiian/Other Pacific Islander, 0.0% Two or more races, 0.0% Hispanic of any race; Average household size: 4.33; Median age: 21.9; Age under 18: 23.1%; Age 65 and over: 0.0%; Males per 100 females: 103.9; Marriage status: 100.0% never married, 0.0% now married, 0.0% separated, 0.0% widowed, 0.0% divorced; Foreign born: 0.0%; Speak English only: 100.0%; With disability: 46.2%; Veterans: 30.0%; Ancestry: 23.1% French
Employment: 0.0% management, business, and financial, 0.0% computer, engineering, and science, 0.0% education, legal, community service, arts, and media, 0.0% healthcare practitioners, 100.0% service, 0.0% sales and office, 0.0% natural resources, construction, and maintenance, 0.0% production, transportation, and material moving
Income: Per capita: n/a; Median household: n/a; Average household: n/a; Households with income of $100,000 or more: n/a; Poverty rate: 100.0%
Educational Attainment: High school diploma or higher: 50.0%; Bachelor's degree or higher: n/a; Graduate/professional degree or higher: n/a
Housing: Homeownership rate: 100.0%; Median home value: n/a; Median year structure built: n/a; Homeowner vacancy rate: 0.0%; Median selected monthly owner costs: n/a with a mortgage, n/a without a mortgage; Median gross rent: n/a per month; Rental vacancy rate: 0.0%
Health Insurance: 76.9% have insurance; 0.0% have private insurance; 76.9% have public insurance; 23.1% do not have insurance; 0.0% of children under 18 do not have insurance
Transportation: Commute: 100.0% car, 0.0% public transportation, 0.0% walk, 0.0% work from home; Mean travel time to work: 0.0 minutes

FONTANET (CDP). Covers a land area of 3.854 square miles and a water area of 0.029 square miles. Located at 39.58° N. Lat; 87.23° W. Long. Elevation is 600 feet.
Population: 360; Growth (since 2000): n/a; Density: 93.4 persons per square mile; Race: 100.0% White, 0.0% Black/African American, 0.0% Asian, 0.0% American Indian/Alaska Native, 0.0% Native Hawaiian/Other Pacific Islander, 0.0% Two or more races, 0.0% Hispanic of any race; Average household size: 2.11; Median age: 57.8; Age under 18: 3.9%; Age 65 and over: 13.1%; Males per 100 females: 96.7; Marriage status: 14.7% never married, 68.5% now married, 0.0% separated, 6.4% widowed, 10.4% divorced; Foreign born: 0.0%; Speak English only: 100.0%; With disability: 13.1%; Veterans: 10.1%; Ancestry: 32.2% German, 26.1% American, 13.9% English, 11.1% Irish, 10.3% Polish
Employment: 11.4% management, business, and financial, 4.7% computer, engineering, and science, 14.7% education, legal, community service, arts, and media, 5.7% healthcare practitioners, 4.3% service, 11.4% sales and office, 14.7% natural resources, construction, and maintenance, 33.2% production, transportation, and material moving
Income: Per capita: $43,154; Median household: $83,875; Average household: $87,958; Households with income of $100,000 or more: 40.3%; Poverty rate: n/a
Educational Attainment: High school diploma or higher: 100.0%; Bachelor's degree or higher: 20.6%; Graduate/professional degree or higher: 13.2%
Housing: Homeownership rate: 80.7%; Median home value: $154,700; Median year structure built: 1964; Homeowner vacancy rate: 16.9%; Median selected monthly owner costs: $997 with a mortgage, $359 without a mortgage; Median gross rent: n/a per month; Rental vacancy rate: 0.0%
Health Insurance: 100.0% have insurance; 81.4% have private insurance; 29.7% have public insurance; 0.0% do not have insurance; 0.0% of children under 18 do not have insurance
Transportation: Commute: 100.0% car, 0.0% public transportation, 0.0% walk, 0.0% work from home; Mean travel time to work: 24.7 minutes

LEWIS (unincorporated postal area)
ZCTA: 47858
Covers a land area of 31.868 square miles and a water area of 0.039 square miles. Located at 39.26° N. Lat; 87.22° W. Long. Elevation is 610 feet.
Population: 696; Growth (since 2000): 0.3%; Density: 21.8 persons per square mile; Race: 100.0% White, 0.0% Black/African American, 0.0% Asian, 0.0% American Indian/Alaska Native, 0.0% Native Hawaiian/Other Pacific Islander, 0.0% Two or more races, 2.0% Hispanic of any race; Average household size: 2.67; Median age: 36.5; Age under 18: 22.8%; Age 65 and over: 18.1%; Males per 100 females: 96.1; Marriage status: 12.3% never married, 62.2% now married, 3.7% separated, 7.6% widowed, 17.9% divorced; Foreign born: 0.0%; Speak English only: 92.9%; With disability: 19.3%; Veterans: 3.4%; Ancestry: 28.7% German, 15.8% American, 11.2% English, 5.7% Dutch, 2.6% Swedish
Employment: 30.5% management, business, and financial, 7.5% computer, engineering, and science, 10.8% education, legal, community service, arts, and media, 4.1% healthcare practitioners, 2.4% service, 20.7% sales and office, 7.8% natural resources, construction, and maintenance, 16.3% production, transportation, and material moving
Income: Per capita: $51,374; Median household: $60,653; Average household: $135,067; Households with income of $100,000 or more: 16.1%; Poverty rate: 10.2%
Educational Attainment: High school diploma or higher: 91.7%; Bachelor's degree or higher: 27.6%; Graduate/professional degree or higher: 7.3%
Housing: Homeownership rate: 83.5%; Median home value: $154,700; Median year structure built: 1981; Homeowner vacancy rate: 0.0%; Median selected monthly owner costs: $1,096 with a mortgage, $375 without a mortgage; Median gross rent: n/a per month; Rental vacancy rate: 0.0%
Health Insurance: 83.5% have insurance; 51.7% have private insurance; 43.8% have public insurance; 16.5% do not have insurance; 8.8% of children under 18 do not have insurance
Transportation: Commute: 97.2% car, 0.0% public transportation, 0.0% walk, 2.8% work from home; Mean travel time to work: 28.0 minutes

NEW GOSHEN (CDP). Covers a land area of 3.310 square miles and a water area of 0.026 square miles. Located at 39.59° N. Lat; 87.47° W. Long. Elevation is 646 feet.

Population: 419; Growth (since 2000): n/a; Density: 126.6 persons per square mile; Race: 100.0% White, 0.0% Black/African American, 0.0% Asian, 0.0% American Indian/Alaska Native, 0.0% Native Hawaiian/Other Pacific Islander, 0.0% Two or more races, 0.0% Hispanic of any race; Average household size: 2.22; Median age: 52.8; Age under 18: 10.3%; Age 65 and over: 18.6%; Males per 100 females: 99.0; Marriage status: 12.5% never married, 63.3% now married, 0.0% separated, 4.8% widowed, 19.4% divorced; Foreign born: 0.0%; Speak English only: 100.0%; With disability: 19.6%; Veterans: 13.6%; Ancestry: 34.6% German, 32.7% Irish, 20.8% English, 16.2% American, 8.6% Scottish

Employment: 13.2% management, business, and financial, 14.2% computer, engineering, and science, 0.0% education, legal, community service, arts, and media, 9.0% healthcare practitioners, 10.8% service, 12.7% sales and office, 9.9% natural resources, construction, and maintenance, 30.2% production, transportation, and material moving

Income: Per capita: $34,302; Median household: $67,697; Average household: $74,758; Households with income of $100,000 or more: 31.2%; Poverty rate: 4.8%

Educational Attainment: High school diploma or higher: 97.8%; Bachelor's degree or higher: 6.3%; Graduate/professional degree or higher: n/a

Housing: Homeownership rate: 85.2%; Median home value: $126,700; Median year structure built: 1947; Homeowner vacancy rate: 0.0%; Median selected monthly owner costs: $1,176 with a mortgage, $450 without a mortgage; Median gross rent: n/a per month; Rental vacancy rate: 0.0%

Health Insurance: 100.0% have insurance; 86.9% have private insurance; 40.6% have public insurance; 0.0% do not have insurance; 0.0% of children under 18 do not have insurance

Transportation: Commute: 78.8% car, 0.0% public transportation, 0.0% walk, 10.4% work from home; Mean travel time to work: 20.4 minutes

NORTH TERRE HAUTE (CDP). Covers a land area of 3.568 square miles and a water area of 0 square miles. Located at 39.54° N. Lat; 87.37° W. Long. Elevation is 495 feet.

History: The Markle Mill was built in 1816 on the banks of Otter Creek, near the site of North Terre Haute, and the town developed around it.

Population: 4,231; Growth (since 2000): -8.1%; Density: 1,185.9 persons per square mile; Race: 96.0% White, 1.3% Black/African American, 0.0% Asian, 0.6% American Indian/Alaska Native, 0.0% Native Hawaiian/Other Pacific Islander, 2.0% Two or more races, 0.4% Hispanic of any race; Average household size: 2.62; Median age: 37.0; Age under 18: 23.4%; Age 65 and over: 16.6%; Males per 100 females: 96.9; Marriage status: 28.1% never married, 46.8% now married, 0.2% separated, 7.6% widowed, 17.4% divorced; Foreign born: 0.2%; Speak English only: 98.5%; With disability: 20.3%; Veterans: 8.8%; Ancestry: 19.3% German, 17.7% Irish, 17.1% American, 10.8% English, 4.1% French

Employment: 6.5% management, business, and financial, 3.6% computer, engineering, and science, 8.3% education, legal, community service, arts, and media, 2.7% healthcare practitioners, 26.8% service, 20.7% sales and office, 9.3% natural resources, construction, and maintenance, 22.0% production, transportation, and material moving

Income: Per capita: $18,821; Median household: $41,340; Average household: $49,095; Households with income of $100,000 or more: 6.8%; Poverty rate: 18.6%

Educational Attainment: High school diploma or higher: 86.9%; Bachelor's degree or higher: 13.6%; Graduate/professional degree or higher: 5.0%

Housing: Homeownership rate: 69.5%; Median home value: $90,500; Median year structure built: 1967; Homeowner vacancy rate: 2.3%; Median selected monthly owner costs: $836 with a mortgage, $324 without a mortgage; Median gross rent: $725 per month; Rental vacancy rate: 8.5%

Health Insurance: 90.5% have insurance; 65.2% have private insurance; 38.7% have public insurance; 9.5% do not have insurance; 2.8% of children under 18 do not have insurance

Transportation: Commute: 95.9% car, 0.0% public transportation, 0.0% walk, 3.6% work from home; Mean travel time to work: 20.7 minutes

PIMENTO (unincorporated postal area)
ZCTA: 47866

Covers a land area of 17.801 square miles and a water area of 0.093 square miles. Located at 39.29° N. Lat; 87.32° W. Long. Elevation is 600 feet.

Population: 505; Growth (since 2000): 22.6%; Density: 28.4 persons per square mile; Race: 100.0% White, 0.0% Black/African American, 0.0% Asian, 0.0% American Indian/Alaska Native, 0.0% Native Hawaiian/Other Pacific Islander, 0.0% Two or more races, 36.8% Hispanic of any race; Average household size: 2.30; Median age: 39.1; Age under 18: 25.5%; Age 65 and over: 17.8%; Males per 100 females: 104.1; Marriage status: 9.3% never married, 80.9% now married, 0.0% separated, 9.8% widowed, 0.0% divorced; Foreign born: 0.0%; Speak English only: 100.0%; With disability: 4.6%; Veterans: 10.9%; Ancestry: 55.0% American, 10.9% English, 6.5% Irish, 5.5% German, 4.0% Pennsylvania German

Employment: 15.6% management, business, and financial, 0.0% computer, engineering, and science, 0.0% education, legal, community service, arts, and media, 0.0% healthcare practitioners, 10.0% service, 18.5% sales and office, 8.5% natural resources, construction, and maintenance, 47.4% production, transportation, and material moving

Income: Per capita: $14,454; Median household: n/a; Average household: $32,249; Households with income of $100,000 or more: n/a; Poverty rate: 53.7%

Educational Attainment: High school diploma or higher: 96.8%; Bachelor's degree or higher: 3.2%; Graduate/professional degree or higher: n/a

Housing: Homeownership rate: 100.0%; Median home value: $86,100; Median year structure built: 1983; Homeowner vacancy rate: 0.0%; Median selected monthly owner costs: $823 with a mortgage, $456 without a mortgage; Median gross rent: n/a per month; Rental vacancy rate: 0.0%

Health Insurance: 100.0% have insurance; 39.4% have private insurance; 78.4% have public insurance; 0.0% do not have insurance; 0.0% of children under 18 do not have insurance

Transportation: Commute: 100.0% car, 0.0% public transportation, 0.0% walk, 0.0% work from home; Mean travel time to work: 27.7 minutes

PRAIRIE CREEK (unincorporated postal area)
ZCTA: 47869

Covers a land area of 0.109 square miles and a water area of 0 square miles. Located at 39.27° N. Lat; 87.50° W. Long. Elevation is 531 feet.

Population: 56; Growth (since 2000): n/a; Density: 516.0 persons per square mile; Race: 50.0% White, 50.0% Black/African American, 0.0% Asian, 0.0% American Indian/Alaska Native, 0.0% Native Hawaiian/Other Pacific Islander, 0.0% Two or more races, 0.0% Hispanic of any race; Average household size: 1.24; Median age: 35.0; Age under 18: 0.0%; Age 65 and over: 0.0%; Males per 100 females: 117.5; Marriage status: 50.0% never married, 0.0% now married, 0.0% separated, 0.0% widowed, 50.0% divorced; Foreign born: 0.0%; Speak English only: 100.0%; With disability: 50.0%; Veterans: 50.0%; Ancestry: 50.0% German, 30.4% French

Employment: 0.0% management, business, and financial, 0.0% computer, engineering, and science, 0.0% education, legal, community service, arts, and media, 0.0% healthcare practitioners, 0.0% service, 50.0% sales and office, 19.6% natural resources, construction, and maintenance, 30.4% production, transportation, and material moving

Income: Per capita: $44,479; Median household: n/a; Average household: n/a; Households with income of $100,000 or more: n/a; Poverty rate: n/a

Educational Attainment: High school diploma or higher: 100.0%; Bachelor's degree or higher: n/a; Graduate/professional degree or higher: n/a

Housing: Homeownership rate: n/a; Median home value: n/a; Median year structure built: n/a; Homeowner vacancy rate: 0.0%; Median selected monthly owner costs: $0 with a mortgage, $0 without a mortgage; Median gross rent: n/a per month; Rental vacancy rate: 0.0%

Health Insurance: 100.0% have insurance; 100.0% have private insurance; 50.0% have public insurance; 0.0% do not have insurance; 0.0% of children under 18 do not have insurance

Transportation: Commute: 100.0% car, 0.0% public transportation, 0.0% walk, 0.0% work from home; Mean travel time to work: 0.0 minutes

RILEY (town). Covers a land area of 0.090 square miles and a water area of 0 square miles. Located at 39.39° N. Lat; 87.30° W. Long. Elevation is 564 feet.

History: Riley, first known as Lockport, developed around a coal mine.

Population: 162; Growth (since 2000): 1.3%; Density: 1,807.6 persons per square mile; Race: 98.8% White, 0.0% Black/African American, 0.0%

Asian, 0.0% American Indian/Alaska Native, 0.0% Native Hawaiian/Other Pacific Islander, 1.2% Two or more races, 0.0% Hispanic of any race; Average household size: 2.13; Median age: 45.3; Age under 18: 20.4%; Age 65 and over: 20.4%; Males per 100 females: 102.8; Marriage status: 34.3% never married, 39.3% now married, 3.6% separated, 14.3% widowed, 12.1% divorced; Foreign born: 0.0%; Speak English only: 100.0%; With disability: 9.3%; Veterans: 6.2%; Ancestry: 32.7% American, 21.6% German, 12.3% Irish, 9.9% English, 7.4% European
Employment: 17.4% management, business, and financial, 9.3% computer, engineering, and science, 5.8% education, legal, community service, arts, and media, 2.3% healthcare practitioners, 15.1% service, 24.4% sales and office, 3.5% natural resources, construction, and maintenance, 22.1% production, transportation, and material moving
Income: Per capita: $24,000; Median household: $43,750; Average household: $51,438; Households with income of $100,000 or more: 5.2%; Poverty rate: 1.9%
Educational Attainment: High school diploma or higher: 87.1%; Bachelor's degree or higher: 15.3%; Graduate/professional degree or higher: 1.6%

School District(s)

Vigo County School Corp (PK-12)
Enrollment: 14,811 . . . . (812) 462-4216
Housing: Homeownership rate: 81.6%; Median home value: $76,500; Median year structure built: 1958; Homeowner vacancy rate: 0.0%; Median selected monthly owner costs: $750 with a mortgage, $321 without a mortgage; Median gross rent: $594 per month; Rental vacancy rate: 0.0%
Health Insurance: 83.3% have insurance; 82.1% have private insurance; 22.2% have public insurance; 16.7% do not have insurance; 11.8% of children under 18 do not have insurance
Transportation: Commute: 96.4% car, 0.0% public transportation, 1.2% walk, 2.4% work from home; Mean travel time to work: 17.7 minutes

SAINT MARY OF THE WOODS (CDP). Covers a land area of 1.277 square miles and a water area of 0.019 square miles. Located at 39.51° N. Lat; 87.46° W. Long.
Population: 860; Growth (since 2000): n/a; Density: 673.6 persons per square mile; Race: 95.7% White, 2.9% Black/African American, 0.8% Asian, 0.0% American Indian/Alaska Native, 0.0% Native Hawaiian/Other Pacific Islander, 0.0% Two or more races, 3.0% Hispanic of any race; Average household size: 2.08; Median age: 50.5; Age under 18: 7.7%; Age 65 and over: 36.5%; Males per 100 females: 26.3; Marriage status: 44.1% never married, 24.3% now married, 1.1% separated, 23.0% widowed, 8.6% divorced; Foreign born: 4.1%; Speak English only: 96.0%; With disability: 28.9%; Veterans: 5.3%; Ancestry: 19.8% German, 16.9% English, 10.0% Irish, 5.2% French, 4.4% Scotch-Irish
Employment: 13.7% management, business, and financial, 0.0% computer, engineering, and science, 9.5% education, legal, community service, arts, and media, 2.8% healthcare practitioners, 30.8% service, 14.6% sales and office, 18.5% natural resources, construction, and maintenance, 10.1% production, transportation, and material moving
Income: Per capita: $16,579; Median household: $21,786; Average household: $45,172; Households with income of $100,000 or more: 18.3%; Poverty rate: 22.0%
Educational Attainment: High school diploma or higher: 81.8%; Bachelor's degree or higher: 16.1%; Graduate/professional degree or higher: 4.5%

Four-year College(s)

Saint Mary-of-the-Woods College (Private, Not-for-profit, Roman Catholic)
Enrollment: 959 . . . . (812) 535-5151
Tuition: In-state $29,510; Out-of-state $29,510
Housing: Homeownership rate: 32.5%; Median home value: $122,100; Median year structure built: 1976; Homeowner vacancy rate: 0.0%; Median selected monthly owner costs: $1,304 with a mortgage, $444 without a mortgage; Median gross rent: $373 per month; Rental vacancy rate: 0.0%
Health Insurance: 89.2% have insurance; 62.9% have private insurance; 42.5% have public insurance; 10.8% do not have insurance; 5.0% of children under 18 do not have insurance
Transportation: Commute: 78.4% car, 0.0% public transportation, 15.9% walk, 5.7% work from home; Mean travel time to work: 12.4 minutes

SEELYVILLE (town). Covers a land area of 0.888 square miles and a water area of 0.020 square miles. Located at 39.49° N. Lat; 87.27° W. Long. Elevation is 584 feet.
History: Seelyville was established as a mining center.
Population: 866; Growth (since 2000): -26.7%; Density: 975.5 persons per square mile; Race: 96.9% White, 0.0% Black/African American, 0.0% Asian, 0.0% American Indian/Alaska Native, 0.0% Native Hawaiian/Other Pacific Islander, 3.1% Two or more races, 5.1% Hispanic of any race; Average household size: 2.31; Median age: 38.9; Age under 18: 21.1%; Age 65 and over: 15.8%; Males per 100 females: 99.8; Marriage status: 25.9% never married, 46.6% now married, 2.7% separated, 4.8% widowed, 22.7% divorced; Foreign born: 1.6%; Speak English only: 98.0%; With disability: 21.4%; Veterans: 14.3%; Ancestry: 22.1% German, 15.9% Irish, 13.4% American, 8.0% English, 3.2% Dutch
Employment: 2.2% management, business, and financial, 0.0% computer, engineering, and science, 9.4% education, legal, community service, arts, and media, 4.1% healthcare practitioners, 17.5% service, 31.2% sales and office, 15.1% natural resources, construction, and maintenance, 20.6% production, transportation, and material moving
Income: Per capita: $22,749; Median household: $45,083; Average household: $52,680; Households with income of $100,000 or more: 13.0%; Poverty rate: 16.6%
Educational Attainment: High school diploma or higher: 92.4%; Bachelor's degree or higher: 10.9%; Graduate/professional degree or higher: 4.1%
Housing: Homeownership rate: 68.3%; Median home value: $75,500; Median year structure built: 1963; Homeowner vacancy rate: 0.0%; Median selected monthly owner costs: $945 with a mortgage, $367 without a mortgage; Median gross rent: $664 per month; Rental vacancy rate: 2.5%
Health Insurance: 83.4% have insurance; 64.2% have private insurance; 34.1% have public insurance; 16.6% do not have insurance; 3.7% of children under 18 do not have insurance
Transportation: Commute: 95.3% car, 0.0% public transportation, 0.7% walk, 0.0% work from home; Mean travel time to work: 23.9 minutes

SHEPARDSVILLE (CDP). Covers a land area of 0.919 square miles and a water area of 0.003 square miles. Located at 39.60° N. Lat; 87.42° W. Long. Elevation is 502 feet.
Population: 269; Growth (since 2000): n/a; Density: 292.6 persons per square mile; Race: 69.9% White, 21.2% Black/African American, 0.0% Asian, 0.0% American Indian/Alaska Native, 0.0% Native Hawaiian/Other Pacific Islander, 8.9% Two or more races, 0.0% Hispanic of any race; Average household size: 2.72; Median age: 46.1; Age under 18: 22.7%; Age 65 and over: 5.2%; Males per 100 females: 95.9; Marriage status: 18.5% never married, 43.1% now married, 0.0% separated, 22.2% widowed, 16.2% divorced; Foreign born: 0.0%; Speak English only: 100.0%; With disability: 20.8%; Veterans: 40.4%; Ancestry: 19.7% Greek, 17.1% Irish, 6.7% German, 6.7% Polish, 5.2% American
Employment: 7.0% management, business, and financial, 27.8% computer, engineering, and science, 0.0% education, legal, community service, arts, and media, 3.5% healthcare practitioners, 5.2% service, 0.0% sales and office, 0.0% natural resources, construction, and maintenance, 56.5% production, transportation, and material moving
Income: Per capita: $26,561; Median household: n/a; Average household: $64,503; Households with income of $100,000 or more: 27.3%; Poverty rate: n/a
Educational Attainment: High school diploma or higher: 100.0%; Bachelor's degree or higher: 20.7%; Graduate/professional degree or higher: n/a
Housing: Homeownership rate: 91.9%; Median home value: n/a; Median year structure built: 1957; Homeowner vacancy rate: 0.0%; Median selected monthly owner costs: n/a with a mortgage, n/a without a mortgage; Median gross rent: n/a per month; Rental vacancy rate: 0.0%
Health Insurance: 96.7% have insurance; 78.8% have private insurance; 17.8% have public insurance; 3.3% do not have insurance; 0.0% of children under 18 do not have insurance
Transportation: Commute: 74.8% car, 25.2% public transportation, 0.0% walk, 0.0% work from home; Mean travel time to work: 16.4 minutes

TECUMSEH (CDP). Covers a land area of 2.520 square miles and a water area of 0.079 square miles. Located at 39.57° N. Lat; 87.43° W. Long. Elevation is 554 feet.
Population: 772; Growth (since 2000): n/a; Density: 306.3 persons per square mile; Race: 98.6% White, 0.0% Black/African American, 1.0% Asian, 0.0% American Indian/Alaska Native, 0.0% Native Hawaiian/Other Pacific Islander, 0.4% Two or more races, 0.0% Hispanic of any race; Average household size: 2.90; Median age: 38.2; Age under 18: 32.6%; Age 65 and over: 14.2%; Males per 100 females: 94.7; Marriage status: 13.9% never married, 64.1% now married, 0.0% separated, 8.7%

widowed, 13.3% divorced; Foreign born: 1.0%; Speak English only: 100.0%; With disability: 8.9%; Veterans: 10.0%; Ancestry: 33.0% German, 17.1% English, 13.3% Irish, 6.1% American, 4.9% Russian
Employment: 11.6% management, business, and financial, 0.0% computer, engineering, and science, 11.6% education, legal, community service, arts, and media, 6.1% healthcare practitioners, 16.9% service, 27.0% sales and office, 2.9% natural resources, construction, and maintenance, 23.8% production, transportation, and material moving
Income: Per capita: $26,699; Median household: $69,737; Average household: $76,146; Households with income of $100,000 or more: 24.8%; Poverty rate: 7.3%
Educational Attainment: High school diploma or higher: 100.0%; Bachelor's degree or higher: 21.8%; Graduate/professional degree or higher: 7.8%
Housing: Homeownership rate: 92.9%; Median home value: $139,800; Median year structure built: 1976; Homeowner vacancy rate: 0.0%; Median selected monthly owner costs: $1,401 with a mortgage, $299 without a mortgage; Median gross rent: n/a per month; Rental vacancy rate: 0.0%
Health Insurance: 93.1% have insurance; 81.2% have private insurance; 21.4% have public insurance; 6.9% do not have insurance; 16.6% of children under 18 do not have insurance
Transportation: Commute: 95.1% car, 0.0% public transportation, 0.0% walk, 2.6% work from home; Mean travel time to work: 24.1 minutes

TERRE HAUTE (city). County seat. Covers a land area of 34.536 square miles and a water area of 0.732 square miles. Located at 39.47° N. Lat; 87.38° W. Long. Elevation is 502 feet.
History: Terre Haute's name, meaning "high land," was given to it by French traders in the early 1700's. The city itself was established in 1816 by the Terre Haute Town Company, a group of Indiana and Kentucky businessmen. It was soon selected as the seat of Vigo County, and was incorporated as a town in 1832. Coal mining was the major industry in Terre Haute after 1875. It's reputation as a "union town" was influenced in part by Eugene V. Debs who lived and worked here.
Population: 60,691; Growth (since 2000): 1.8%; Density: 1,757.3 persons per square mile; Race: 83.0% White, 9.5% Black/African American, 1.5% Asian, 0.3% American Indian/Alaska Native, 0.0% Native Hawaiian/Other Pacific Islander, 4.7% Two or more races, 3.0% Hispanic of any race; Average household size: 2.30; Median age: 32.6; Age under 18: 19.4%; Age 65 and over: 14.0%; Males per 100 females: 106.8; Marriage status: 43.0% never married, 35.9% now married, 1.6% separated, 6.2% widowed, 14.9% divorced; Foreign born: 3.1%; Speak English only: 94.9%; With disability: 20.4%; Veterans: 7.5%; Ancestry: 18.6% German, 11.6% American, 10.1% Irish, 8.0% English, 2.6% French
Employment: 8.9% management, business, and financial, 4.1% computer, engineering, and science, 13.0% education, legal, community service, arts, and media, 5.3% healthcare practitioners, 23.2% service, 23.0% sales and office, 6.3% natural resources, construction, and maintenance, 16.2% production, transportation, and material moving
Income: Per capita: $19,263; Median household: $34,746; Average household: $46,931; Households with income of $100,000 or more: 9.0%; Poverty rate: 26.0%
Educational Attainment: High school diploma or higher: 85.0%; Bachelor's degree or higher: 22.1%; Graduate/professional degree or higher: 9.0%

School District(s)

Covered Bridge Spec Ed Dist (KG-12)
Enrollment: n/a . . . . (812) 462-4030
Vigo County School Corp (PK-12)
Enrollment: 14,811 . . . . (812) 462-4216

Four-year College(s)

Indiana State University (Public)
Enrollment: 13,763 . . . . (812) 237-6311
Tuition: In-state $8,916; Out-of-state $19,452
Rose-Hulman Institute of Technology (Private, Not-for-profit)
Enrollment: 2,245 . . . . (812) 877-1511
Tuition: In-state $48,012; Out-of-state $48,012

Vocational/Technical School(s)

J Michael Harrold Beauty Academy (Private, For-profit)
Enrollment: 55 . . . . (812) 232-8334
Tuition: $12,950

Housing: Homeownership rate: 51.7%; Median home value: $76,600; Median year structure built: 1953; Homeowner vacancy rate: 3.8%; Median selected monthly owner costs: $849 with a mortgage, $360 without a mortgage; Median gross rent: $694 per month; Rental vacancy rate: 8.1%
Health Insurance: 88.4% have insurance; 61.0% have private insurance; 39.7% have public insurance; 11.6% do not have insurance; 5.7% of children under 18 do not have insurance
Hospitals: Terre Haute Regional Hospital (278 beds); Union Hospital
Newspapers: Tribune-Star (daily circulation 24,600)
Transportation: Commute: 87.6% car, 1.6% public transportation, 5.4% walk, 3.9% work from home; Mean travel time to work: 17.8 minutes
Airports: Terre Haute International-Hulman Field (general aviation)
Additional Information Contacts
City of Terre Haute . . . . (812) 232-3375
http://www.terrehaute.in.gov

TOAD HOP (CDP). Covers a land area of 0.221 square miles and a water area of 0 square miles. Located at 39.46° N. Lat; 87.46° W. Long. Elevation is 469 feet.
Population: 136; Growth (since 2000): n/a; Density: 615.7 persons per square mile; Race: 100.0% White, 0.0% Black/African American, 0.0% Asian, 0.0% American Indian/Alaska Native, 0.0% Native Hawaiian/Other Pacific Islander, 0.0% Two or more races, 0.0% Hispanic of any race; Average household size: 2.43; Median age: 34.2; Age under 18: 36.0%; Age 65 and over: 0.0%; Males per 100 females: 77.0; Marriage status: 39.1% never married, 18.4% now married, 0.0% separated, 0.0% widowed, 42.5% divorced; Foreign born: 0.0%; Speak English only: 100.0%; With disability: 0.0%; Veterans: 33.3%; Ancestry: 47.8% Irish, 21.3% American, 6.6% German
Employment: 0.0% management, business, and financial, 0.0% computer, engineering, and science, 0.0% education, legal, community service, arts, and media, 0.0% healthcare practitioners, 61.9% service, 0.0% sales and office, 0.0% natural resources, construction, and maintenance, 38.1% production, transportation, and material moving
Income: Per capita: $13,563; Median household: n/a; Average household: $35,598; Households with income of $100,000 or more: 16.1%; Poverty rate: 49.0%
Educational Attainment: High school diploma or higher: 60.9%; Bachelor's degree or higher: n/a; Graduate/professional degree or higher: n/a
Housing: Homeownership rate: 100.0%; Median home value: <$10,000; Median year structure built: 1994; Homeowner vacancy rate: 0.0%; Median selected monthly owner costs: n/a with a mortgage, n/a without a mortgage; Median gross rent: n/a per month; Rental vacancy rate: 0.0%
Health Insurance: 65.4% have insurance; 17.6% have private insurance; 47.8% have public insurance; 34.6% do not have insurance; 0.0% of children under 18 do not have insurance
Transportation: Commute: 100.0% car, 0.0% public transportation, 0.0% walk, 0.0% work from home; Mean travel time to work: 0.0 minutes

WEST TERRE HAUTE (town). Covers a land area of 0.753 square miles and a water area of 0 square miles. Located at 39.46° N. Lat; 87.45° W. Long. Elevation is 469 feet.
History: West Terre Haute began as a coal-mining town.
Population: 2,376; Growth (since 2000): 2.0%; Density: 3,156.4 persons per square mile; Race: 98.1% White, 0.4% Black/African American, 0.0% Asian, 0.0% American Indian/Alaska Native, 0.0% Native Hawaiian/Other Pacific Islander, 1.4% Two or more races, 1.9% Hispanic of any race; Average household size: 2.48; Median age: 35.9; Age under 18: 24.8%; Age 65 and over: 13.8%; Males per 100 females: 93.9; Marriage status: 30.8% never married, 41.2% now married, 1.7% separated, 8.4% widowed, 19.7% divorced; Foreign born: 0.0%; Speak English only: 98.2%; With disability: 23.9%; Veterans: 7.4%; Ancestry: 19.3% German, 14.9% American, 14.9% Irish, 7.9% English, 5.9% French
Employment: 2.4% management, business, and financial, 1.1% computer, engineering, and science, 6.4% education, legal, community service, arts, and media, 8.2% healthcare practitioners, 23.9% service, 15.2% sales and office, 18.1% natural resources, construction, and maintenance, 24.7% production, transportation, and material moving
Income: Per capita: $18,694; Median household: $31,375; Average household: $45,944; Households with income of $100,000 or more: 5.8%; Poverty rate: 23.6%
Educational Attainment: High school diploma or higher: 78.0%; Bachelor's degree or higher: 7.0%; Graduate/professional degree or higher: 2.2%

School District(s)

Vigo County School Corp (PK-12)
Enrollment: 14,811 . . . . (812) 462-4216

Housing: Homeownership rate: 63.0%; Median home value: $50,000; Median year structure built: Before 1940; Homeowner vacancy rate: 0.0%; Median selected monthly owner costs: $814 with a mortgage, $354 without a mortgage; Median gross rent: $694 per month; Rental vacancy rate: 6.3%
Health Insurance: 84.5% have insurance; 55.8% have private insurance; 42.3% have public insurance; 15.5% do not have insurance; 2.7% of children under 18 do not have insurance
Transportation: Commute: 96.5% car, 0.0% public transportation, 1.6% walk, 0.4% work from home; Mean travel time to work: 26.3 minutes
Additional Information Contacts
Town of West Terre Haute . . . . (812) 232-3375
http://www.terrehaute.in.gov

Wabash County

Located in northeast central Indiana; drained by the Wabash, Eel, Salamonie, and Mississinewa Rivers. Covers a land area of 412.434 square miles, a water area of 8.541 square miles, and is located in the Eastern Time Zone at 40.84° N. Lat., 85.80° W. Long. The county was founded in 1832. County seat is Wabash.

Wabash County is part of the Wabash, IN Micropolitan Statistical Area. The entire metro area includes: Wabash County, IN

Weather Station: Wabash — Elevation: 729 feet

	Jan	Feb	Mar	Apr	May	Jun	Jul	Aug	Sep	Oct	Nov	Dec
High	33	38	48	61	72	81	84	82	76	64	50	36
Low	16	19	27	38	48	58	61	60	51	40	32	21
Precip	2.5	2.3	2.7	3.4	4.5	4.2	4.3	4.1	3.1	3.1	3.2	2.5
Snow	7.0	5.3	3.0	0.7	0.0	0.0	0.0	0.0	0.0	0.2	0.9	5.9

High and Low temperatures in degrees Fahrenheit; Precipitation and Snow in inches

Population: 31,848; Growth (since 2000): -8.9%; Density: 77.2 persons per square mile; Race: 95.7% White, 0.9% Black/African American, 0.2% Asian, 0.7% American Indian/Alaska Native, 0.0% Native Hawaiian/Other Pacific Islander, 1.4% two or more races, 2.5% Hispanic of any race; Average household size: 2.32; Median age: 42.0; Age under 18: 21.3%; Age 65 and over: 19.5%; Males per 100 females: 94.4; Marriage status: 26.9% never married, 54.4% now married, 1.6% separated, 7.0% widowed, 11.7% divorced; Foreign born: 1.4%; Speak English only: 97.0%; With disability: 13.8%; Veterans: 8.5%; Ancestry: 29.0% German, 14.6% American, 12.6% Irish, 7.8% English, 1.9% Dutch
Religion: Six largest groups: 10.1% Baptist, 9.0% Methodist/Pietist, 7.3% European Free-Church, 4.4% Presbyterian-Reformed, 3.3% Catholicism, 2.5% Lutheran
Economy: Unemployment rate: 3.8%; Leading industries: 16.1 % retail trade; 13.6 % other services (except public administration); 10.6 % construction; Farms: 745 totaling 197,588 acres; Company size: 0 employ 1,000 or more persons, 2 employ 500 to 999 persons, 19 employ 100 to 499 persons, 706 employ less than 100 persons; Business ownership: 836 women-owned, n/a Black-owned, n/a Hispanic-owned, n/a Asian-owned, n/a American Indian/Alaska Native-owned
Employment: 12.4% management, business, and financial, 2.3% computer, engineering, and science, 9.9% education, legal, community service, arts, and media, 5.8% healthcare practitioners, 18.2% service, 20.0% sales and office, 10.3% natural resources, construction, and maintenance, 21.2% production, transportation, and material moving
Income: Per capita: $24,700; Median household: $49,052; Average household: $59,069; Households with income of $100,000 or more: 12.5%; Poverty rate: 13.3%
Educational Attainment: High school diploma or higher: 88.7%; Bachelor's degree or higher: 18.7%; Graduate/professional degree or higher: 7.8%
Housing: Homeownership rate: 74.0%; Median home value: $96,700; Median year structure built: 1956; Homeowner vacancy rate: 2.1%; Median selected monthly owner costs: $885 with a mortgage, $321 without a mortgage; Median gross rent: $663 per month; Rental vacancy rate: 5.3%
Vital Statistics: Birth rate: 103.7 per 10,000 population; Death rate: 130.4 per 10,000 population; Age-adjusted cancer mortality rate: 178.2 deaths per 100,000 population
Health Insurance: 90.7% have insurance; 71.8% have private insurance; 34.0% have public insurance; 9.3% do not have insurance; 6.4% of children under 18 do not have insurance
Health Care: Physicians: 6.7 per 10,000 population; Dentists: 4.1 per 10,000 population; Hospital beds: 7.9 per 10,000 population; Hospital admissions: 217.1 per 10,000 population
Air Quality Index (AQI): Percent of Days: 91.0% good, 8.7% moderate, 0.3% unhealthy for sensitive individuals, 0.0% unhealthy, 0.0% very unhealthy; Annual median: 35; Annual maximum: 105
Transportation: Commute: 91.3% car, 0.7% public transportation, 4.6% walk, 2.8% work from home; Mean travel time to work: 19.6 minutes
2016 Presidential Election: 72.5% Trump, 22.3% Clinton, 4.3% Johnson, 0.3% Stein
National and State Parks: Dora New Holland State Recreation Area; Frances Slocum State Recreation Area; Hogback Ridge State Recreation Area; Lost Bridge State Recreation Area; Miami State Recreation Area; Mount Hope State Recreation Area; Pearson Mill State Recreation Area; Red Bridge State Recreation Area; Salamonie River State Forest
Additional Information Contacts
Wabash Government . . . . (260) 563-0661
http://www.wabashcounty.in.gov

Wabash County Communities

LA FONTAINE (town). Covers a land area of 0.601 square miles and a water area of 0.011 square miles. Located at 40.67° N. Lat; 85.72° W. Long. Elevation is 804 feet.
Population: 779; Growth (since 2000): -13.4%; Density: 1,297.0 persons per square mile; Race: 97.3% White, 0.8% Black/African American, 0.0% Asian, 0.4% American Indian/Alaska Native, 0.0% Native Hawaiian/Other Pacific Islander, 0.0% Two or more races, 2.1% Hispanic of any race; Average household size: 1.98; Median age: 54.7; Age under 18: 14.4%; Age 65 and over: 33.1%; Males per 100 females: 83.8; Marriage status: 21.2% never married, 50.6% now married, 1.0% separated, 16.5% widowed, 11.8% divorced; Foreign born: 0.6%; Speak English only: 97.1%; With disability: 17.2%; Veterans: 10.3%; Ancestry: 22.2% German, 12.5% American, 12.1% Irish, 6.9% English, 2.1% Scottish
Employment: 9.7% management, business, and financial, 2.9% computer, engineering, and science, 7.4% education, legal, community service, arts, and media, 6.8% healthcare practitioners, 20.6% service, 23.2% sales and office, 6.2% natural resources, construction, and maintenance, 23.2% production, transportation, and material moving
Income: Per capita: $23,963; Median household: $45,000; Average household: $50,844; Households with income of $100,000 or more: 8.3%; Poverty rate: 7.2%
Educational Attainment: High school diploma or higher: 90.4%; Bachelor's degree or higher: 11.3%; Graduate/professional degree or higher: 3.0%
Housing: Homeownership rate: 74.0%; Median home value: $74,200; Median year structure built: Before 1940; Homeowner vacancy rate: 2.3%; Median selected monthly owner costs: $785 with a mortgage, $316 without a mortgage; Median gross rent: $556 per month; Rental vacancy rate: 0.0%
Health Insurance: 90.6% have insurance; 79.3% have private insurance; 32.1% have public insurance; 9.4% do not have insurance; 18.5% of children under 18 do not have insurance
Transportation: Commute: 96.3% car, 0.0% public transportation, 3.1% walk, 0.6% work from home; Mean travel time to work: 22.9 minutes

LAGRO (town). Covers a land area of 0.593 square miles and a water area of 0.014 square miles. Located at 40.84° N. Lat; 85.73° W. Long. Elevation is 705 feet.
History: The Wabash & Erie Canal was the impetus for the settlement of Lagro, named for an Indian chief, Les Gros.
Population: 472; Growth (since 2000): 4.0%; Density: 795.6 persons per square mile; Race: 96.2% White, 0.0% Black/African American, 0.0% Asian, 1.7% American Indian/Alaska Native, 0.0% Native Hawaiian/Other Pacific Islander, 1.9% Two or more races, 1.1% Hispanic of any race; Average household size: 2.70; Median age: 37.7; Age under 18: 28.8%; Age 65 and over: 8.5%; Males per 100 females: 118.4; Marriage status: 28.9% never married, 47.1% now married, 1.1% separated, 6.0% widowed, 18.0% divorced; Foreign born: 0.0%; Speak English only: 99.3%; With disability: 11.9%; Veterans: 6.5%; Ancestry: 16.9% American, 16.3% German, 12.7% Irish, 3.2% French, 2.5% Italian
Employment: 5.2% management, business, and financial, 0.0% computer, engineering, and science, 1.7% education, legal, community service, arts, and media, 2.6% healthcare practitioners, 16.5% service, 17.0% sales and

office, 15.7% natural resources, construction, and maintenance, 41.3% production, transportation, and material moving
Income: Per capita: $15,701; Median household: $39,432; Average household: $43,245; Households with income of $100,000 or more: 4.6%; Poverty rate: 26.9%
Educational Attainment: High school diploma or higher: 76.8%; Bachelor's degree or higher: 5.3%; Graduate/professional degree or higher: 2.1%
Housing: Homeownership rate: 80.6%; Median home value: $47,800; Median year structure built: Before 1940; Homeowner vacancy rate: 0.0%; Median selected monthly owner costs: $805 with a mortgage, $281 without a mortgage; Median gross rent: $600 per month; Rental vacancy rate: 10.5%
Health Insurance: 81.8% have insurance; 52.1% have private insurance; 36.2% have public insurance; 18.2% do not have insurance; 14.3% of children under 18 do not have insurance
Transportation: Commute: 97.8% car, 0.0% public transportation, 0.0% walk, 0.9% work from home; Mean travel time to work: 18.5 minutes

LAKETON (CDP). Covers a land area of 1.051 square miles and a water area of 0.140 square miles. Located at 40.98° N. Lat; 85.84° W. Long. Elevation is 755 feet.
Population: 506; Growth (since 2000): n/a; Density: 481.3 persons per square mile; Race: 95.5% White, 0.0% Black/African American, 0.0% Asian, 0.0% American Indian/Alaska Native, 0.0% Native Hawaiian/Other Pacific Islander, 1.4% Two or more races, 4.9% Hispanic of any race; Average household size: 2.30; Median age: 41.8; Age under 18: 24.1%; Age 65 and over: 21.7%; Males per 100 females: 94.7; Marriage status: 37.6% never married, 44.2% now married, 0.0% separated, 3.8% widowed, 14.4% divorced; Foreign born: 3.2%; Speak English only: 97.6%; With disability: 16.0%; Veterans: 8.3%; Ancestry: 24.9% German, 23.1% American, 9.3% Irish, 7.7% English, 3.0% Belgian
Employment: 4.2% management, business, and financial, 0.0% computer, engineering, and science, 14.6% education, legal, community service, arts, and media, 0.0% healthcare practitioners, 16.5% service, 27.7% sales and office, 6.5% natural resources, construction, and maintenance, 30.4% production, transportation, and material moving
Income: Per capita: $19,169; Median household: $35,313; Average household: $44,199; Households with income of $100,000 or more: 5.0%; Poverty rate: 15.0%
Educational Attainment: High school diploma or higher: 84.9%; Bachelor's degree or higher: 16.0%; Graduate/professional degree or higher: 11.0%

School District(s)

Manchester Community Schools (KG-12)
Enrollment: 1,484 . . . . (260) 982-7518
Housing: Homeownership rate: 70.0%; Median home value: $67,600; Median year structure built: 1975; Homeowner vacancy rate: 0.0%; Median selected monthly owner costs: $1,011 with a mortgage, $308 without a mortgage; Median gross rent: $563 per month; Rental vacancy rate: 25.8%
Health Insurance: 87.5% have insurance; 58.3% have private insurance; 50.6% have public insurance; 12.5% do not have insurance; 4.8% of children under 18 do not have insurance
Transportation: Commute: 83.5% car, 8.8% public transportation, 7.7% walk, 0.0% work from home; Mean travel time to work: 23.6 minutes

LIBERTY MILLS (unincorporated postal area)
ZCTA: 46946
Covers a land area of 0.325 square miles and a water area of 0.027 square miles. Located at 41.04° N. Lat; 85.73° W. Long. Elevation is 778 feet.
Population: 116; Growth (since 2000): -16.5%; Density: 356.6 persons per square mile; Race: 100.0% White, 0.0% Black/African American, 0.0% Asian, 0.0% American Indian/Alaska Native, 0.0% Native Hawaiian/Other Pacific Islander, 0.0% Two or more races, 0.0% Hispanic of any race; Average household size: 4.00; Median age: 38.5; Age under 18: 16.4%; Age 65 and over: 13.8%; Males per 100 females: 119.4; Marriage status: 41.8% never married, 50.9% now married, 11.8% separated, 0.0% widowed, 7.3% divorced; Foreign born: 0.0%; Speak English only: 100.0%; With disability: 58.6%; Veterans: 0.0%; Ancestry: 6.9% German, 6.9% Irish
Employment: 0.0% management, business, and financial, 0.0% computer, engineering, and science, 0.0% education, legal, community service, arts, and media, 0.0% healthcare practitioners, 0.0% service, 0.0% sales and office, 0.0% natural resources, construction, and maintenance, 100.0% production, transportation, and material moving
Income: Per capita: $8,477; Median household: n/a; Average household: $33,590; Households with income of $100,000 or more: n/a; Poverty rate: 74.1%
Educational Attainment: High school diploma or higher: 29.2%; Bachelor's degree or higher: n/a; Graduate/professional degree or higher: n/a
Housing: Homeownership rate: 55.2%; Median home value: n/a; Median year structure built: 1981; Homeowner vacancy rate: 0.0%; Median selected monthly owner costs: $0 with a mortgage, $0 without a mortgage; Median gross rent: n/a per month; Rental vacancy rate: 0.0%
Health Insurance: 100.0% have insurance; 25.9% have private insurance; 87.9% have public insurance; 0.0% do not have insurance; 0.0% of children under 18 do not have insurance
Transportation: Commute: 100.0% car, 0.0% public transportation, 0.0% walk, 0.0% work from home; Mean travel time to work: 0.0 minutes

NORTH MANCHESTER (town). Covers a land area of 3.534 square miles and a water area of 0.079 square miles. Located at 41.00° N. Lat; 85.78° W. Long. Elevation is 774 feet.
History: Among the early residents in North Manchester was a group of Dunkers, members of a religious sect founded in Germany in 1708. Thomas R. Marshall, Vice President of the United States under Woodrow Wilson, was born in North Manchester.
Population: 6,152; Growth (since 2000): -1.7%; Density: 1,740.6 persons per square mile; Race: 93.0% White, 1.4% Black/African American, 0.0% Asian, 0.0% American Indian/Alaska Native, 0.0% Native Hawaiian/Other Pacific Islander, 2.8% Two or more races, 7.1% Hispanic of any race; Average household size: 2.23; Median age: 34.6; Age under 18: 21.2%; Age 65 and over: 20.6%; Males per 100 females: 84.6; Marriage status: 38.7% never married, 41.8% now married, 3.3% separated, 9.6% widowed, 9.9% divorced; Foreign born: 3.3%; Speak English only: 94.4%; With disability: 15.1%; Veterans: 6.1%; Ancestry: 34.6% German, 9.9% American, 9.9% Irish, 9.5% English, 2.0% Italian
Employment: 12.2% management, business, and financial, 5.6% computer, engineering, and science, 9.2% education, legal, community service, arts, and media, 7.0% healthcare practitioners, 21.2% service, 17.9% sales and office, 8.4% natural resources, construction, and maintenance, 18.3% production, transportation, and material moving
Income: Per capita: $19,924; Median household: $45,775; Average household: $50,050; Households with income of $100,000 or more: 5.6%; Poverty rate: 14.1%
Educational Attainment: High school diploma or higher: 88.3%; Bachelor's degree or higher: 29.4%; Graduate/professional degree or higher: 14.5%

School District(s)

Manchester Community Schools (KG-12)
Enrollment: 1,484 . . . . (260) 982-7518

Four-year College(s)

Manchester University (Private, Not-for-profit, Church of Brethren)
Enrollment: 1,572 . . . . (260) 982-5000
Tuition: In-state $31,660; Out-of-state $31,660
Housing: Homeownership rate: 59.7%; Median home value: $91,000; Median year structure built: 1957; Homeowner vacancy rate: 3.5%; Median selected monthly owner costs: $837 with a mortgage, $302 without a mortgage; Median gross rent: $709 per month; Rental vacancy rate: 1.6%
Health Insurance: 93.1% have insurance; 73.0% have private insurance; 34.8% have public insurance; 6.9% do not have insurance; 5.7% of children under 18 do not have insurance
Newspapers: The Manchester Monitor (weekly circulation 1,100); The News-Journal (weekly circulation 1,800)
Transportation: Commute: 85.6% car, 0.6% public transportation, 9.8% walk, 3.5% work from home; Mean travel time to work: 20.9 minutes
Additional Information Contacts
Town of North Manchester . . . . (260) 982-9800
http://www.nmanchester.org

ROANN (town). Covers a land area of 0.228 square miles and a water area of 0 square miles. Located at 40.91° N. Lat; 85.92° W. Long. Elevation is 755 feet.
History: Laid out 1853.
Population: 483; Growth (since 2000): 20.8%; Density: 2,122.8 persons per square mile; Race: 98.6% White, 0.0% Black/African American, 0.0% Asian, 0.0% American Indian/Alaska Native, 0.0% Native Hawaiian/Other

Pacific Islander, 0.2% Two or more races, 1.4% Hispanic of any race; Average household size: 2.49; Median age: 34.9; Age under 18: 25.7%; Age 65 and over: 15.1%; Males per 100 females: 84.9; Marriage status: 35.3% never married, 46.0% now married, 1.8% separated, 5.5% widowed, 13.2% divorced; Foreign born: 0.0%; Speak English only: 99.1%; With disability: 15.7%; Veterans: 7.8%; Ancestry: 24.2% German, 21.5% American, 9.5% Irish, 3.5% Italian, 3.3% English
Employment: 8.1% management, business, and financial, 5.1% computer, engineering, and science, 11.9% education, legal, community service, arts, and media, 13.6% healthcare practitioners, 21.6% service, 14.4% sales and office, 4.2% natural resources, construction, and maintenance, 21.2% production, transportation, and material moving
Income: Per capita: $19,132; Median household: $38,929; Average household: $47,587; Households with income of $100,000 or more: 6.7%; Poverty rate: 18.2%
Educational Attainment: High school diploma or higher: 90.0%; Bachelor's degree or higher: 8.7%; Graduate/professional degree or higher: 3.9%
Housing: Homeownership rate: 67.5%; Median home value: $81,300; Median year structure built: Before 1940; Homeowner vacancy rate: 0.0%; Median selected monthly owner costs: $837 with a mortgage, $267 without a mortgage; Median gross rent: $775 per month; Rental vacancy rate: 0.0%
Health Insurance: 81.0% have insurance; 66.7% have private insurance; 26.9% have public insurance; 19.0% do not have insurance; 21.9% of children under 18 do not have insurance
Transportation: Commute: 94.6% car, 2.7% public transportation, 0.0% walk, 1.8% work from home; Mean travel time to work: 23.6 minutes

SOMERSET (CDP). Covers a land area of 0.663 square miles and a water area of 0.138 square miles. Located at 40.67° N. Lat; 85.83° W. Long. Elevation is 810 feet.
Population: 520; Growth (since 2000): n/a; Density: 784.1 persons per square mile; Race: 98.5% White, 0.0% Black/African American, 0.0% Asian, 0.0% American Indian/Alaska Native, 0.0% Native Hawaiian/Other Pacific Islander, 1.5% Two or more races, 0.0% Hispanic of any race; Average household size: 2.40; Median age: 36.4; Age under 18: 30.6%; Age 65 and over: 17.1%; Males per 100 females: 107.8; Marriage status: 7.6% never married, 74.9% now married, 3.0% separated, 11.9% widowed, 5.7% divorced; Foreign born: 0.0%; Speak English only: 100.0%; With disability: 14.0%; Veterans: 7.8%; Ancestry: 28.1% Irish, 17.1% German, 12.3% English, 10.4% American, 5.6% French Canadian
Employment: 28.4% management, business, and financial, 17.1% computer, engineering, and science, 10.4% education, legal, community service, arts, and media, 3.8% healthcare practitioners, 5.2% service, 14.7% sales and office, 14.7% natural resources, construction, and maintenance, 5.7% production, transportation, and material moving
Income: Per capita: $30,888; Median household: $77,829; Average household: $72,865; Households with income of $100,000 or more: 18.0%; Poverty rate: 3.8%
Educational Attainment: High school diploma or higher: 97.5%; Bachelor's degree or higher: 32.4%; Graduate/professional degree or higher: 11.1%
Housing: Homeownership rate: 69.6%; Median home value: $137,500; Median year structure built: 1973; Homeowner vacancy rate: 0.0%; Median selected monthly owner costs: $1,087 with a mortgage, $467 without a mortgage; Median gross rent: $782 per month; Rental vacancy rate: 0.0%
Health Insurance: 100.0% have insurance; 98.3% have private insurance; 24.8% have public insurance; 0.0% do not have insurance; 0.0% of children under 18 do not have insurance
Transportation: Commute: 100.0% car, 0.0% public transportation, 0.0% walk, 0.0% work from home; Mean travel time to work: 25.2 minutes

URBANA (unincorporated postal area)
ZCTA: 46990
Covers a land area of 30.118 square miles and a water area of 0.037 square miles. Located at 40.90° N. Lat; 85.73° W. Long. Elevation is 797 feet.
Population: 801; Growth (since 2000): -5.9%; Density: 26.6 persons per square mile; Race: 97.1% White, 0.0% Black/African American, 0.0% Asian, 2.9% American Indian/Alaska Native, 0.0% Native Hawaiian/Other Pacific Islander, 0.0% Two or more races, 3.2% Hispanic of any race; Average household size: 3.27; Median age: 42.0; Age under 18: 30.7%; Age 65 and over: 14.2%; Males per 100 females: 107.5; Marriage status: 25.6% never married, 66.8% now married, 1.3% separated, 1.5% widowed, 6.2% divorced; Foreign born: 1.0%; Speak English only: 95.4%; With disability: 12.4%; Veterans: 8.1%; Ancestry: 27.5% German, 18.2% American, 14.5% English, 10.5% Dutch, 5.1% Irish
Employment: 25.1% management, business, and financial, 2.9% computer, engineering, and science, 10.2% education, legal, community service, arts, and media, 2.3% healthcare practitioners, 16.4% service, 20.2% sales and office, 10.2% natural resources, construction, and maintenance, 12.6% production, transportation, and material moving
Income: Per capita: $20,322; Median household: $61,339; Average household: $63,680; Households with income of $100,000 or more: 11.4%; Poverty rate: 2.4%
Educational Attainment: High school diploma or higher: 95.1%; Bachelor's degree or higher: 32.6%; Graduate/professional degree or higher: 7.9%
Housing: Homeownership rate: 96.7%; Median home value: $130,400; Median year structure built: 1944; Homeowner vacancy rate: 0.0%; Median selected monthly owner costs: $1,131 with a mortgage, $396 without a mortgage; Median gross rent: n/a per month; Rental vacancy rate: 0.0%
Health Insurance: 93.0% have insurance; 84.0% have private insurance; 23.0% have public insurance; 7.0% do not have insurance; 0.0% of children under 18 do not have insurance
Transportation: Commute: 87.8% car, 7.0% public transportation, 0.0% walk, 2.8% work from home; Mean travel time to work: 24.5 minutes

WABASH (city). County seat. Covers a land area of 8.886 square miles and a water area of 0.238 square miles. Located at 40.80° N. Lat; 85.83° W. Long. Elevation is 712 feet.
History: Its location along the Wabash River gave the town of Wabash its name, which comes from the Indian "oubache," meaning "water over white stones." The Wabash & Erie Canal was completed through this area in 1835, bringing Irish immigrants as canal workers.
Population: 10,272; Growth (since 2000): -12.5%; Density: 1,156.0 persons per square mile; Race: 95.6% White, 0.4% Black/African American, 0.4% Asian, 0.4% American Indian/Alaska Native, 0.0% Native Hawaiian/Other Pacific Islander, 2.0% Two or more races, 2.2% Hispanic of any race; Average household size: 2.18; Median age: 41.1; Age under 18: 20.2%; Age 65 and over: 19.3%; Males per 100 females: 89.2; Marriage status: 26.4% never married, 49.3% now married, 1.3% separated, 7.2% widowed, 17.1% divorced; Foreign born: 1.0%; Speak English only: 96.2%; With disability: 14.5%; Veterans: 9.1%; Ancestry: 26.8% German, 13.8% Irish, 13.7% American, 7.1% English, 1.8% Dutch
Employment: 11.0% management, business, and financial, 0.9% computer, engineering, and science, 8.7% education, legal, community service, arts, and media, 5.7% healthcare practitioners, 22.3% service, 21.4% sales and office, 6.4% natural resources, construction, and maintenance, 23.7% production, transportation, and material moving
Income: Per capita: $24,876; Median household: $44,094; Average household: $55,348; Households with income of $100,000 or more: 9.2%; Poverty rate: 17.4%
Educational Attainment: High school diploma or higher: 86.5%; Bachelor's degree or higher: 12.3%; Graduate/professional degree or higher: 4.2%

School District(s)

Heartland Career Center (09-12)
Enrollment: n/a . . . . (260) 563-7481
M S D Wabash County Schools (PK-12)
Enrollment: 1,923 . . . . (260) 563-8050
Wabash City Schools (PK-12)
Enrollment: 1,486 . . . . (260) 563-2151

Housing: Homeownership rate: 66.2%; Median home value: $77,300; Median year structure built: 1949; Homeowner vacancy rate: 4.3%; Median selected monthly owner costs: $780 with a mortgage, $319 without a mortgage; Median gross rent: $640 per month; Rental vacancy rate: 5.8%
Health Insurance: 89.6% have insurance; 66.1% have private insurance; 37.8% have public insurance; 10.4% do not have insurance; 4.0% of children under 18 do not have insurance
Hospitals: Wabash County Hospital (25 beds)
Newspapers: Paper of Wabash County (weekly circulation 16,000); Wabash Plain Dealer (daily circulation 6,600)
Transportation: Commute: 94.0% car, 0.6% public transportation, 2.9% walk, 2.0% work from home; Mean travel time to work: 16.7 minutes
Airports: Wabash Municipal (general aviation)
Additional Information Contacts

City of Wabash . . . . (260) 563-4171
http://www.cityofwabash.com

Warren County

Located in western Indiana; bounded on the west by Illinois, and on the southeast by the Wabash River. Covers a land area of 364.681 square miles, a water area of 1.724 square miles, and is located in the Eastern Time Zone at 40.35° N. Lat., 87.38° W. Long. The county was founded in 1827. County seat is Williamsport.

Population: 8,269; Growth (since 2000): -1.8%; Density: 22.7 persons per square mile; Race: 98.0% White, 0.5% Black/African American, 0.0% Asian, 0.2% American Indian/Alaska Native, 0.0% Native Hawaiian/Other Pacific Islander, 1.2% two or more races, 1.5% Hispanic of any race; Average household size: 2.41; Median age: 44.6; Age under 18: 22.0%; Age 65 and over: 19.3%; Males per 100 females: 100.7; Marriage status: 18.1% never married, 62.6% now married, 1.5% separated, 6.3% widowed, 12.9% divorced; Foreign born: 0.5%; Speak English only: 98.9%; With disability: 15.6%; Veterans: 10.2%; Ancestry: 29.0% German, 13.7% Irish, 9.8% English, 8.6% American, 4.4% Dutch

Religion: Six largest groups: 12.5% Baptist, 10.8% Methodist/Pietist, 1.7% Presbyterian-Reformed, 1.4% Latter-day Saints, 1.2% Non-denominational Protestant, 1.1% Holiness

Economy: Unemployment rate: 3.3%; Leading industries: 13.6 % construction; 12.8 % other services (except public administration); 12.0 % retail trade; Farms: 413 totaling 175,961 acres; Company size: 0 employ 1,000 or more persons, 0 employ 500 to 999 persons, 3 employ 100 to 499 persons, 122 employ less than 100 persons; Business ownership: 204 women-owned, n/a Black-owned, n/a Hispanic-owned, n/a Asian-owned, n/a American Indian/Alaska Native-owned

Employment: 15.9% management, business, and financial, 2.3% computer, engineering, and science, 6.5% education, legal, community service, arts, and media, 6.1% healthcare practitioners, 11.9% service, 17.9% sales and office, 13.1% natural resources, construction, and maintenance, 26.2% production, transportation, and material moving

Income: Per capita: $29,312; Median household: $58,950; Average household: $70,935; Households with income of $100,000 or more: 20.2%; Poverty rate: 9.5%

Educational Attainment: High school diploma or higher: 91.0%; Bachelor's degree or higher: 19.4%; Graduate/professional degree or higher: 6.3%

Housing: Homeownership rate: 83.9%; Median home value: $112,500; Median year structure built: 1970; Homeowner vacancy rate: 0.3%; Median selected monthly owner costs: $968 with a mortgage, $366 without a mortgage; Median gross rent: $763 per month; Rental vacancy rate: 11.5%

Vital Statistics: Birth rate: 85.4 per 10,000 population; Death rate: 102.4 per 10,000 population; Age-adjusted cancer mortality rate: Unreliable deaths per 100,000 population

Health Insurance: 94.5% have insurance; 77.7% have private insurance; 33.0% have public insurance; 5.5% do not have insurance; 6.7% of children under 18 do not have insurance

Health Care: Physicians: 3.7 per 10,000 population; Dentists: 1.2 per 10,000 population; Hospital beds: 19.6 per 10,000 population; Hospital admissions: 797.7 per 10,000 population

Transportation: Commute: 96.0% car, 0.2% public transportation, 0.9% walk, 2.5% work from home; Mean travel time to work: 25.6 minutes

2016 Presidential Election: 73.7% Trump, 21.3% Clinton, 4.7% Johnson, 0.1% Stein

Additional Information Contacts

Warren Government . . . . (765) 762-3510

Warren County Communities

PINE VILLAGE (town). Covers a land area of 0.120 square miles and a water area of 0 square miles. Located at 40.45° N. Lat; 87.25° W. Long. Elevation is 692 feet.

Population: 215; Growth (since 2000): -15.7%; Density: 1,786.3 persons per square mile; Race: 89.8% White, 0.0% Black/African American, 0.5% Asian, 0.0% American Indian/Alaska Native, 0.0% Native Hawaiian/Other Pacific Islander, 9.8% Two or more races, 0.9% Hispanic of any race; Average household size: 2.03; Median age: 45.2; Age under 18: 22.3%; Age 65 and over: 16.3%; Males per 100 females: 95.5; Marriage status: 21.4% never married, 48.8% now married, 1.2% separated, 10.1% widowed, 19.6% divorced; Foreign born: 0.5%; Speak English only: 100.0%; With disability: 16.7%; Veterans: 15.6%; Ancestry: 20.9% Irish, 19.1% German, 10.7% American, 7.4% French, 5.6% English

Employment: 2.1% management, business, and financial, 2.1% computer, engineering, and science, 4.2% education, legal, community service, arts, and media, 9.4% healthcare practitioners, 32.3% service, 11.5% sales and office, 10.4% natural resources, construction, and maintenance, 28.1% production, transportation, and material moving

Income: Per capita: $23,811; Median household: $45,577; Average household: $49,692; Households with income of $100,000 or more: 9.5%; Poverty rate: 11.2%

Educational Attainment: High school diploma or higher: 88.2%; Bachelor's degree or higher: 14.5%; Graduate/professional degree or higher: 2.6%

School District(s)

M S D Warren County (PK-12)
Enrollment: 1,277 . . . . (765) 762-3364

Housing: Homeownership rate: 56.6%; Median home value: $72,500; Median year structure built: Before 1940; Homeowner vacancy rate: 0.0%; Median selected monthly owner costs: $745 with a mortgage, $383 without a mortgage; Median gross rent: $728 per month; Rental vacancy rate: 4.2%

Health Insurance: 87.4% have insurance; 66.5% have private insurance; 33.0% have public insurance; 12.6% do not have insurance; 16.7% of children under 18 do not have insurance

Transportation: Commute: 86.5% car, 0.0% public transportation, 11.5% walk, 2.1% work from home; Mean travel time to work: 27.3 minutes

STATE LINE CITY (town). Covers a land area of 0.139 square miles and a water area of 0 square miles. Located at 40.20° N. Lat; 87.53° W. Long. Elevation is 725 feet.

Population: 171; Growth (since 2000): 21.3%; Density: 1,228.8 persons per square mile; Race: 100.0% White, 0.0% Black/African American, 0.0% Asian, 0.0% American Indian/Alaska Native, 0.0% Native Hawaiian/Other Pacific Islander, 0.0% Two or more races, 5.8% Hispanic of any race; Average household size: 2.11; Median age: 46.5; Age under 18: 19.9%; Age 65 and over: 12.9%; Males per 100 females: 88.2; Marriage status: 13.9% never married, 59.7% now married, 1.4% separated, 6.9% widowed, 19.4% divorced; Foreign born: 0.0%; Speak English only: 100.0%; With disability: 13.5%; Veterans: 6.6%; Ancestry: 37.4% German, 15.2% Irish, 9.9% English, 9.4% American, 5.8% Dutch

Employment: 0.0% management, business, and financial, 0.0% computer, engineering, and science, 7.5% education, legal, community service, arts, and media, 5.4% healthcare practitioners, 21.5% service, 24.7% sales and office, 8.6% natural resources, construction, and maintenance, 32.3% production, transportation, and material moving

Income: Per capita: $25,444; Median household: $45,313; Average household: $55,099; Households with income of $100,000 or more: 8.7%; Poverty rate: 1.2%

Educational Attainment: High school diploma or higher: 87.4%; Bachelor's degree or higher: 7.9%; Graduate/professional degree or higher: n/a

Housing: Homeownership rate: 90.1%; Median home value: $57,900; Median year structure built: 1967; Homeowner vacancy rate: 2.5%; Median selected monthly owner costs: $691 with a mortgage, $300 without a mortgage; Median gross rent: $750 per month; Rental vacancy rate: 33.3%

Health Insurance: 93.0% have insurance; 78.4% have private insurance; 31.6% have public insurance; 7.0% do not have insurance; 2.8% of children under 18 do not have insurance

Transportation: Commute: 95.2% car, 1.2% public transportation, 0.0% walk, 0.0% work from home; Mean travel time to work: 23.0 minutes

WEST LEBANON (town). Covers a land area of 0.615 square miles and a water area of 0 square miles. Located at 40.27° N. Lat; 87.39° W. Long. Elevation is 718 feet.

History: Laid out 1830.

Population: 768; Growth (since 2000): -3.2%; Density: 1,247.8 persons per square mile; Race: 97.7% White, 1.6% Black/African American, 0.0% Asian, 0.0% American Indian/Alaska Native, 0.0% Native Hawaiian/Other Pacific Islander, 0.7% Two or more races, 0.9% Hispanic of any race; Average household size: 2.41; Median age: 40.2; Age under 18: 25.4%; Age 65 and over: 19.8%; Males per 100 females: 100.3; Marriage status: 25.0% never married, 50.9% now married, 1.0% separated, 11.5% widowed, 12.6% divorced; Foreign born: 0.0%; Speak English only: 99.6%; With disability: 19.0%; Veterans: 12.0%; Ancestry: 20.7% German, 18.9% Irish, 7.2% English, 6.1% American, 4.9% Welsh

Employment: 4.7% management, business, and financial, 2.9% computer, engineering, and science, 8.5% education, legal, community service, arts, and media, 7.0% healthcare practitioners, 14.0% service, 15.2% sales and office, 12.5% natural resources, construction, and maintenance, 35.3% production, transportation, and material moving
Income: Per capita: $21,951; Median household: $52,813; Average household: $53,918; Households with income of $100,000 or more: 10.0%; Poverty rate: 7.7%
Educational Attainment: High school diploma or higher: 86.9%; Bachelor's degree or higher: 8.8%; Graduate/professional degree or higher: 4.7%

School District(s)

M S D Warren County (PK-12)
Enrollment: 1,277 .... (765) 762-3364
Housing: Homeownership rate: 68.7%; Median home value: $70,200; Median year structure built: 1965; Homeowner vacancy rate: 2.6%; Median selected monthly owner costs: $857 with a mortgage, $350 without a mortgage; Median gross rent: $823 per month; Rental vacancy rate: 0.0%
Health Insurance: 92.7% have insurance; 77.6% have private insurance; 36.3% have public insurance; 7.3% do not have insurance; 10.6% of children under 18 do not have insurance
Transportation: Commute: 95.1% car, 2.4% public transportation, 0.0% walk, 2.4% work from home; Mean travel time to work: 19.0 minutes

WILLIAMSPORT (town). County seat. Covers a land area of 1.302 square miles and a water area of 0 square miles. Located at 40.29° N. Lat; 87.29° W. Long. Elevation is 633 feet.
History: The land on which Williamsport was founded was owned by General William Henry Harrison. A spur of the Wabash & Erie Canal was built to Williamsport, giving an early boost to commerce and bringing the nickname of Side Cut City.
Population: 1,852; Growth (since 2000): -4.3%; Density: 1,422.3 persons per square mile; Race: 96.2% White, 0.2% Black/African American, 0.0% Asian, 0.0% American Indian/Alaska Native, 0.0% Native Hawaiian/Other Pacific Islander, 3.6% Two or more races, 0.8% Hispanic of any race; Average household size: 2.33; Median age: 42.9; Age under 18: 19.6%; Age 65 and over: 23.1%; Males per 100 females: 90.4; Marriage status: 22.8% never married, 58.2% now married, 2.2% separated, 5.3% widowed, 13.7% divorced; Foreign born: 0.2%; Speak English only: 99.4%; With disability: 19.6%; Veterans: 10.3%; Ancestry: 18.6% German, 16.7% Irish, 13.4% American, 7.7% English, 5.0% Dutch
Employment: 7.0% management, business, and financial, 2.9% computer, engineering, and science, 6.4% education, legal, community service, arts, and media, 6.7% healthcare practitioners, 11.8% service, 19.2% sales and office, 10.7% natural resources, construction, and maintenance, 35.2% production, transportation, and material moving
Income: Per capita: $23,713; Median household: $44,327; Average household: $56,314; Households with income of $100,000 or more: 13.7%; Poverty rate: 15.6%
Educational Attainment: High school diploma or higher: 87.3%; Bachelor's degree or higher: 13.0%; Graduate/professional degree or higher: 5.1%

School District(s)

M S D Warren County (PK-12)
Enrollment: 1,277 .... (765) 762-3364
Housing: Homeownership rate: 71.7%; Median home value: $90,700; Median year structure built: 1968; Homeowner vacancy rate: 0.0%; Median selected monthly owner costs: $883 with a mortgage, $354 without a mortgage; Median gross rent: $705 per month; Rental vacancy rate: 15.7%
Health Insurance: 92.9% have insurance; 71.2% have private insurance; 43.7% have public insurance; 7.1% do not have insurance; 3.9% of children under 18 do not have insurance
Hospitals: Saint Vincent Williamsport Hospital (16 beds)
Newspapers: The Review-Republican (weekly circulation 3,500)
Transportation: Commute: 97.2% car, 0.0% public transportation, 0.6% walk, 2.2% work from home; Mean travel time to work: 22.8 minutes

Warrick County

Located in southwestern Indiana; bounded on the south by the Ohio River and the Kentucky border. Covers a land area of 384.815 square miles, a water area of 6.238 square miles, and is located in the Central Time Zone at 38.10° N. Lat., 87.27° W. Long. The county was founded in 1813. County seat is Boonville.

Warrick County is part of the Evansville, IN-KY Metropolitan Statistical Area. The entire metro area includes: Posey County, IN; Vanderburgh County, IN; Warrick County, IN; Henderson County, KY

Population: 61,581; Growth (since 2000): 17.6%; Density: 160.0 persons per square mile; Race: 94.1% White, 1.6% Black/African American, 2.5% Asian, 0.2% American Indian/Alaska Native, 0.0% Native Hawaiian/Other Pacific Islander, 1.3% two or more races, 1.8% Hispanic of any race; Average household size: 2.56; Median age: 40.5; Age under 18: 24.5%; Age 65 and over: 16.1%; Males per 100 females: 97.1; Marriage status: 21.6% never married, 62.4% now married, 1.1% separated, 5.7% widowed, 10.3% divorced; Foreign born: 3.0%; Speak English only: 96.5%; With disability: 11.6%; Veterans: 8.4%; Ancestry: 28.7% German, 12.3% Irish, 12.3% English, 10.7% American, 2.9% Italian
Religion: Six largest groups: 14.8% Baptist, 11.4% Catholicism, 8.7% Non-denominational Protestant, 4.3% Methodist/Pietist, 3.2% Presbyterian-Reformed, 1.2% Latter-day Saints
Economy: Unemployment rate: 3.1%; Leading industries: 14.9 % construction; 13.4 % health care and social assistance; 12.9 % other services (except public administration); Farms: 379 totaling 99,651 acres; Company size: 1 employs 1,000 or more persons, 1 employs 500 to 999 persons, 20 employ 100 to 499 persons, 1,111 employs less than 100 persons; Business ownership: 1,244 women-owned, 28 Black-owned, 34 Hispanic-owned, 100 Asian-owned, n/a American Indian/Alaska Native-owned
Employment: 15.8% management, business, and financial, 4.9% computer, engineering, and science, 9.4% education, legal, community service, arts, and media, 9.3% healthcare practitioners, 14.4% service, 21.6% sales and office, 10.1% natural resources, construction, and maintenance, 14.6% production, transportation, and material moving
Income: Per capita: $33,528; Median household: $66,080; Average household: $85,840; Households with income of $100,000 or more: 29.6%; Poverty rate: 7.7%
Educational Attainment: High school diploma or higher: 93.0%; Bachelor's degree or higher: 29.2%; Graduate/professional degree or higher: 11.0%
Housing: Homeownership rate: 80.5%; Median home value: $158,100; Median year structure built: 1982; Homeowner vacancy rate: 0.4%; Median selected monthly owner costs: $1,238 with a mortgage, $458 without a mortgage; Median gross rent: $826 per month; Rental vacancy rate: 5.7%
Vital Statistics: Birth rate: 109.5 per 10,000 population; Death rate: 98.8 per 10,000 population; Age-adjusted cancer mortality rate: 137.6 deaths per 100,000 population
Health Insurance: 93.7% have insurance; 81.5% have private insurance; 25.9% have public insurance; 6.3% do not have insurance; 3.5% of children under 18 do not have insurance
Health Care: Physicians: 52.4 per 10,000 population; Dentists: 3.8 per 10,000 population; Hospital beds: 29.2 per 10,000 population; Hospital admissions: 1,268.7 per 10,000 population
Air Quality Index (AQI): Percent of Days: 86.5% good, 12.2% moderate, 1.2% unhealthy for sensitive individuals, 0.0% unhealthy, 0.0% very unhealthy; Annual median: 42; Annual maximum: 112
Transportation: Commute: 95.2% car, 0.3% public transportation, 1.0% walk, 2.6% work from home; Mean travel time to work: 23.6 minutes
2016 Presidential Election: 63.8% Trump, 30.3% Clinton, 4.6% Johnson, 0.0% Stein
Additional Information Contacts
Warrick Government .... (812) 897-6160
http://www.warrickcounty.gov

Warrick County Communities

BOONVILLE (city). County seat. Covers a land area of 3.001 square miles and a water area of 0.013 square miles. Located at 38.05° N. Lat; 87.27° W. Long. Elevation is 423 feet.
History: Boonville was laid out in 1818 as a coal-mining and farming center at a place where several wagon trails crossed. It was named for Jesse Boon, the father of Ratliff Boon who was the first treasurer of Warrick County, the first state representative from Warrick County in 1816, and a representative in Congress from 1825-1839.
Population: 6,379; Growth (since 2000): -6.7%; Density: 2,125.5 persons per square mile; Race: 96.1% White, 0.5% Black/African American, 0.0% Asian, 0.3% American Indian/Alaska Native, 0.0% Native Hawaiian/Other Pacific Islander, 3.1% Two or more races, 4.4% Hispanic of any race; Average household size: 2.38; Median age: 40.3; Age under 18: 25.2%;

Age 65 and over: 20.4%; Males per 100 females: 86.3; Marriage status: 19.7% never married, 54.4% now married, 2.2% separated, 11.2% widowed, 14.7% divorced; Foreign born: 1.2%; Speak English only: 98.3%; With disability: 18.0%; Veterans: 8.1%; Ancestry: 18.1% German, 15.7% American, 15.5% English, 9.3% Irish, 2.9% Scottish
Employment: 8.5% management, business, and financial, 4.7% computer, engineering, and science, 10.6% education, legal, community service, arts, and media, 2.8% healthcare practitioners, 18.7% service, 22.7% sales and office, 9.7% natural resources, construction, and maintenance, 22.4% production, transportation, and material moving
Income: Per capita: $22,674; Median household: $41,019; Average household: $53,657; Households with income of $100,000 or more: 13.5%; Poverty rate: 17.6%
Educational Attainment: High school diploma or higher: 86.8%; Bachelor's degree or higher: 14.9%; Graduate/professional degree or higher: 6.8%

School District(s)

Warrick County School Corp (PK-12)
Enrollment: 10,211 . . . . (812) 897-0400
Housing: Homeownership rate: 70.5%; Median home value: $89,800; Median year structure built: 1959; Homeowner vacancy rate: 0.0%; Median selected monthly owner costs: $927 with a mortgage, $393 without a mortgage; Median gross rent: $655 per month; Rental vacancy rate: 5.7%
Health Insurance: 90.1% have insurance; 71.9% have private insurance; 38.0% have public insurance; 9.9% do not have insurance; 5.5% of children under 18 do not have insurance
Hospitals: Saint Mary's Warrick Hospital (25 beds)
Safety: Violent crime rate: 56.7 per 10,000 population; Property crime rate: 299.5 per 10,000 population
Newspapers: Boonville Standard & Newburgh Register (weekly circulation 4,500)
Transportation: Commute: 90.5% car, 1.6% public transportation, 3.2% walk, 2.6% work from home; Mean travel time to work: 19.7 minutes
Additional Information Contacts
City of Boonville. . . . . (812) 897-6543
http://www.cityofboonevilleindiana.com

CHANDLER (town). Covers a land area of 2.033 square miles and a water area of 0 square miles. Located at 38.04° N. Lat; 87.37° W. Long. Elevation is 413 feet.
Population: 3,450; Growth (since 2000): 11.5%; Density: 1,696.8 persons per square mile; Race: 98.7% White, 0.1% Black/African American, 0.0% Asian, 0.3% American Indian/Alaska Native, 0.0% Native Hawaiian/Other Pacific Islander, 0.9% Two or more races, 0.3% Hispanic of any race; Average household size: 2.69; Median age: 33.4; Age under 18: 30.1%; Age 65 and over: 10.4%; Males per 100 females: 95.2; Marriage status: 28.8% never married, 55.3% now married, 1.3% separated, 5.1% widowed, 10.8% divorced; Foreign born: 0.3%; Speak English only: 99.1%; With disability: 11.9%; Veterans: 8.5%; Ancestry: 26.3% German, 11.2% American, 9.6% Irish, 8.9% English, 8.0% Italian
Employment: 10.3% management, business, and financial, 2.7% computer, engineering, and science, 3.0% education, legal, community service, arts, and media, 8.0% healthcare practitioners, 15.6% service, 29.1% sales and office, 7.4% natural resources, construction, and maintenance, 23.8% production, transportation, and material moving
Income: Per capita: $21,043; Median household: $49,160; Average household: $56,373; Households with income of $100,000 or more: 9.6%; Poverty rate: 18.6%
Educational Attainment: High school diploma or higher: 90.1%; Bachelor's degree or higher: 10.7%; Graduate/professional degree or higher: 4.1%

School District(s)

Warrick County School Corp (PK-12)
Enrollment: 10,211 . . . . (812) 897-0400
Housing: Homeownership rate: 64.3%; Median home value: $85,100; Median year structure built: 1976; Homeowner vacancy rate: 3.4%; Median selected monthly owner costs: $878 with a mortgage, $364 without a mortgage; Median gross rent: $847 per month; Rental vacancy rate: 6.9%
Health Insurance: 90.1% have insurance; 74.1% have private insurance; 27.8% have public insurance; 9.9% do not have insurance; 11.2% of children under 18 do not have insurance
Transportation: Commute: 97.3% car, 0.0% public transportation, 0.0% walk, 1.1% work from home; Mean travel time to work: 24.4 minutes
Additional Information Contacts
Town of Chandler . . . . (812) 925-6882
http://www.townofchandler.org

ELBERFELD (town). Covers a land area of 0.306 square miles and a water area of 0 square miles. Located at 38.16° N. Lat; 87.45° W. Long. Elevation is 453 feet.
Population: 691; Growth (since 2000): 8.6%; Density: 2,258.8 persons per square mile; Race: 97.8% White, 0.0% Black/African American, 0.0% Asian, 0.0% American Indian/Alaska Native, 0.0% Native Hawaiian/Other Pacific Islander, 2.2% Two or more races, 0.0% Hispanic of any race; Average household size: 2.53; Median age: 36.6; Age under 18: 22.1%; Age 65 and over: 16.6%; Males per 100 females: 100.3; Marriage status: 28.3% never married, 57.1% now married, 0.9% separated, 6.7% widowed, 8.0% divorced; Foreign born: 0.0%; Speak English only: 99.5%; With disability: 15.6%; Veterans: 8.9%; Ancestry: 39.7% German, 12.4% Irish, 12.2% American, 11.4% English, 3.6% French
Employment: 5.6% management, business, and financial, 3.9% computer, engineering, and science, 7.6% education, legal, community service, arts, and media, 7.6% healthcare practitioners, 16.6% service, 21.1% sales and office, 5.4% natural resources, construction, and maintenance, 32.1% production, transportation, and material moving
Income: Per capita: $23,612; Median household: $49,063; Average household: $58,884; Households with income of $100,000 or more: 13.9%; Poverty rate: 10.2%
Educational Attainment: High school diploma or higher: 93.4%; Bachelor's degree or higher: 17.9%; Graduate/professional degree or higher: 6.0%

School District(s)

Warrick County School Corp (PK-12)
Enrollment: 10,211 . . . . (812) 897-0400
Housing: Homeownership rate: 85.3%; Median home value: $108,900; Median year structure built: 1955; Homeowner vacancy rate: 0.0%; Median selected monthly owner costs: $1,022 with a mortgage, $370 without a mortgage; Median gross rent: $560 per month; Rental vacancy rate: 0.0%
Health Insurance: 91.5% have insurance; 77.6% have private insurance; 34.7% have public insurance; 8.5% do not have insurance; 0.0% of children under 18 do not have insurance
Transportation: Commute: 94.9% car, 0.0% public transportation, 2.0% walk, 3.1% work from home; Mean travel time to work: 27.0 minutes

LYNNVILLE (town). Covers a land area of 1.742 square miles and a water area of 0.236 square miles. Located at 38.20° N. Lat; 87.32° W. Long. Elevation is 463 feet.
Population: 926; Growth (since 2000): 18.6%; Density: 531.5 persons per square mile; Race: 96.3% White, 0.3% Black/African American, 0.5% Asian, 0.0% American Indian/Alaska Native, 0.0% Native Hawaiian/Other Pacific Islander, 2.8% Two or more races, 0.0% Hispanic of any race; Average household size: 2.59; Median age: 43.2; Age under 18: 25.4%; Age 65 and over: 17.0%; Males per 100 females: 108.5; Marriage status: 23.1% never married, 57.4% now married, 1.6% separated, 6.0% widowed, 13.5% divorced; Foreign born: 1.1%; Speak English only: 98.9%; With disability: 14.0%; Veterans: 10.9%; Ancestry: 27.6% German, 15.3% American, 13.2% Irish, 10.0% English, 2.7% European
Employment: 11.2% management, business, and financial, 0.7% computer, engineering, and science, 10.5% education, legal, community service, arts, and media, 6.1% healthcare practitioners, 16.1% service, 13.8% sales and office, 14.2% natural resources, construction, and maintenance, 27.5% production, transportation, and material moving
Income: Per capita: $28,606; Median household: $62,361; Average household: $74,716; Households with income of $100,000 or more: 32.6%; Poverty rate: 8.8%
Educational Attainment: High school diploma or higher: 92.1%; Bachelor's degree or higher: 19.2%; Graduate/professional degree or higher: 7.7%

School District(s)

Warrick County School Corp (PK-12)
Enrollment: 10,211 . . . . (812) 897-0400
Housing: Homeownership rate: 84.7%; Median home value: $87,900; Median year structure built: 1975; Homeowner vacancy rate: 0.0%; Median selected monthly owner costs: $873 with a mortgage, $362 without a mortgage; Median gross rent: $722 per month; Rental vacancy rate: 6.9%
Health Insurance: 93.3% have insurance; 80.6% have private insurance; 31.6% have public insurance; 6.7% do not have insurance; 7.8% of children under 18 do not have insurance

Transportation: Commute: 97.6% car, 0.5% public transportation, 1.2% walk, 0.7% work from home; Mean travel time to work: 37.1 minutes

NEWBURGH (town). Covers a land area of 1.406 square miles and a water area of 0.001 square miles. Located at 37.95° N. Lat; 87.40° W. Long. Elevation is 394 feet.
History: Settled 1803, laid out 1818.
Population: 3,280; Growth (since 2000): 6.2%; Density: 2,332.5 persons per square mile; Race: 89.8% White, 3.9% Black/African American, 6.3% Asian, 0.0% American Indian/Alaska Native, 0.0% Native Hawaiian/Other Pacific Islander, 0.0% Two or more races, 0.3% Hispanic of any race; Average household size: 2.37; Median age: 45.1; Age under 18: 19.7%; Age 65 and over: 18.0%; Males per 100 females: 92.9; Marriage status: 24.2% never married, 58.7% now married, 0.9% separated, 4.2% widowed, 12.9% divorced; Foreign born: 5.3%; Speak English only: 95.0%; With disability: 14.7%; Veterans: 7.1%; Ancestry: 29.5% German, 12.7% Irish, 9.2% American, 8.7% English, 4.2% Italian
Employment: 14.0% management, business, and financial, 7.4% computer, engineering, and science, 7.1% education, legal, community service, arts, and media, 8.8% healthcare practitioners, 14.0% service, 22.2% sales and office, 12.0% natural resources, construction, and maintenance, 14.5% production, transportation, and material moving
Income: Per capita: $38,618; Median household: $67,816; Average household: $89,991; Households with income of $100,000 or more: 26.4%; Poverty rate: 7.3%
Educational Attainment: High school diploma or higher: 94.1%; Bachelor's degree or higher: 31.3%; Graduate/professional degree or higher: 8.7%

School District(s)

Warrick County School Corp (PK-12)
Enrollment: 10,211 . . . . (812) 897-0400
Housing: Homeownership rate: 75.0%; Median home value: $143,700; Median year structure built: 1972; Homeowner vacancy rate: 0.0%; Median selected monthly owner costs: $1,238 with a mortgage, $494 without a mortgage; Median gross rent: $785 per month; Rental vacancy rate: 14.0%
Health Insurance: 89.4% have insurance; 74.1% have private insurance; 28.9% have public insurance; 10.6% do not have insurance; 0.0% of children under 18 do not have insurance
Hospitals: The Heart Hospital at Deaconess Gateway (145 beds); The Women's Hospital
Transportation: Commute: 93.4% car, 0.0% public transportation, 3.9% walk, 2.7% work from home; Mean travel time to work: 17.7 minutes
Additional Information Contacts
Town of Newburgh . . . . (812) 853-7111
http://www.newburgh-in.gov

TENNYSON (town). Covers a land area of 0.234 square miles and a water area of 0 square miles. Located at 38.08° N. Lat; 87.12° W. Long. Elevation is 407 feet.
Population: 286; Growth (since 2000): -1.4%; Density: 1,223.2 persons per square mile; Race: 100.0% White, 0.0% Black/African American, 0.0% Asian, 0.0% American Indian/Alaska Native, 0.0% Native Hawaiian/Other Pacific Islander, 0.0% Two or more races, 0.7% Hispanic of any race; Average household size: 2.51; Median age: 39.0; Age under 18: 21.3%; Age 65 and over: 14.7%; Males per 100 females: 102.2; Marriage status: 29.7% never married, 42.8% now married, 3.8% separated, 7.6% widowed, 19.9% divorced; Foreign born: 0.0%; Speak English only: 100.0%; With disability: 25.9%; Veterans: 6.7%; Ancestry: 20.6% German, 14.3% American, 12.9% English, 9.1% Irish, 2.1% Scottish
Employment: 2.0% management, business, and financial, 5.0% computer, engineering, and science, 8.9% education, legal, community service, arts, and media, 2.0% healthcare practitioners, 21.8% service, 12.9% sales and office, 12.9% natural resources, construction, and maintenance, 34.7% production, transportation, and material moving
Income: Per capita: $15,809; Median household: $27,000; Average household: $37,759; Households with income of $100,000 or more: 7.0%; Poverty rate: 26.1%
Educational Attainment: High school diploma or higher: 72.7%; Bachelor's degree or higher: 4.3%; Graduate/professional degree or higher: 1.1%

School District(s)

Warrick County School Corp (PK-12)
Enrollment: 10,211 . . . . (812) 897-0400
Housing: Homeownership rate: 67.5%; Median home value: $53,800; Median year structure built: 1961; Homeowner vacancy rate: 4.9%; Median selected monthly owner costs: $888 with a mortgage, $378 without a mortgage; Median gross rent: $541 per month; Rental vacancy rate: 0.0%
Health Insurance: 88.5% have insurance; 54.5% have private insurance; 50.3% have public insurance; 11.5% do not have insurance; 0.0% of children under 18 do not have insurance
Transportation: Commute: 99.0% car, 1.0% public transportation, 0.0% walk, 0.0% work from home; Mean travel time to work: 28.8 minutes

Washington County

Located in southern Indiana; bounded on the north by the Muscatatuck River and the East Fork of the White River; drained by the Blue and Lost Rivers. Covers a land area of 513.725 square miles, a water area of 2.874 square miles, and is located in the Eastern Time Zone at 38.60° N. Lat., 86.10° W. Long. The county was founded in 1813. County seat is Salem.

Washington County is part of the Louisville/Jefferson County, KY-IN Metropolitan Statistical Area. The entire metro area includes: Clark County, IN; Floyd County, IN; Harrison County, IN; Scott County, IN; Washington County, IN; Bullitt County, KY; Henry County, KY; Jefferson County, KY; Oldham County, KY; Shelby County, KY; Spencer County, KY; Trimble County, KY

Weather Station: Salem — Elevation: 799 feet

	Jan	Feb	Mar	Apr	May	Jun	Jul	Aug	Sep	Oct	Nov	Dec
High	40	46	56	67	76	84	87	86	80	69	56	43
Low	23	26	34	43	52	61	65	63	55	44	36	27
Precip	3.2	2.9	4.3	4.4	5.3	3.9	3.9	3.4	3.3	3.2	3.7	3.7
Snow	4.7	4.1	2.4	0.2	0.0	0.0	0.0	0.0	0.0	0.2	0.2	2.8

High and Low temperatures in degrees Fahrenheit; Precipitation and Snow in inches

Population: 27,807; Growth (since 2000): 2.1%; Density: 54.1 persons per square mile; Race: 98.2% White, 0.1% Black/African American, 0.2% Asian, 0.3% American Indian/Alaska Native, 0.0% Native Hawaiian/Other Pacific Islander, 1.1% two or more races, 1.3% Hispanic of any race; Average household size: 2.60; Median age: 41.2; Age under 18: 23.5%; Age 65 and over: 16.0%; Males per 100 females: 99.7; Marriage status: 23.9% never married, 55.9% now married, 1.1% separated, 6.5% widowed, 13.7% divorced; Foreign born: 0.5%; Speak English only: 98.3%; With disability: 17.9%; Veterans: 10.3%; Ancestry: 22.9% American, 16.0% German, 10.6% Irish, 7.8% English, 2.0% Scottish
Religion: Six largest groups: 30.8% Baptist, 2.9% Methodist/Pietist, 2.1% European Free-Church, 1.1% Holiness, 0.9% Pentecostal, 0.9% Non-denominational Protestant
Economy: Unemployment rate: 3.6%; Leading industries: 15.9 % retail trade; 15.0 % construction; 11.3 % health care and social assistance; Farms: 831 totaling 199,529 acres; Company size: 0 employ 1,000 or more persons, 0 employ 500 to 999 persons, 8 employ 100 to 499 persons, 451 employs less than 100 persons; Business ownership: 327 women-owned, n/a Black-owned, n/a Hispanic-owned, n/a Asian-owned, n/a American Indian/Alaska Native-owned
Employment: 11.6% management, business, and financial, 2.1% computer, engineering, and science, 8.3% education, legal, community service, arts, and media, 6.0% healthcare practitioners, 13.1% service, 18.7% sales and office, 14.4% natural resources, construction, and maintenance, 25.8% production, transportation, and material moving
Income: Per capita: $23,223; Median household: $46,861; Average household: $59,180; Households with income of $100,000 or more: 12.7%; Poverty rate: 13.3%
Educational Attainment: High school diploma or higher: 85.1%; Bachelor's degree or higher: 12.1%; Graduate/professional degree or higher: 4.6%
Housing: Homeownership rate: 76.0%; Median home value: $106,200; Median year structure built: 1977; Homeowner vacancy rate: 2.0%; Median selected monthly owner costs: $987 with a mortgage, $346 without a mortgage; Median gross rent: $639 per month; Rental vacancy rate: 4.2%
Vital Statistics: Birth rate: 116.4 per 10,000 population; Death rate: 104.6 per 10,000 population; Age-adjusted cancer mortality rate: 163.6 deaths per 100,000 population
Health Insurance: 88.2% have insurance; 64.2% have private insurance; 37.8% have public insurance; 11.8% do not have insurance; 12.5% of children under 18 do not have insurance
Health Care: Physicians: 5.0 per 10,000 population; Dentists: 1.8 per 10,000 population; Hospital beds: 9.0 per 10,000 population; Hospital admissions: 55.9 per 10,000 population

Transportation: Commute: 93.0% car, 0.1% public transportation, 1.1% walk, 4.9% work from home; Mean travel time to work: 31.4 minutes
2016 Presidential Election: 72.1% Trump, 23.2% Clinton, 4.3% Johnson, 0.3% Stein
National and State Parks: Clark State Forest; Jackson-Washington State Forest
Additional Information Contacts
Washington Government . . . . (812) 883-5748
http://www.washingtoncountyindiana.com

Washington County Communities

CAMPBELLSBURG (town). Covers a land area of 0.992 square miles and a water area of 0.002 square miles. Located at 38.65° N. Lat; 86.26° W. Long. Elevation is 837 feet.
Population: 613; Growth (since 2000): 6.1%; Density: 618.0 persons per square mile; Race: 94.8% White, 0.0% Black/African American, 0.0% Asian, 0.0% American Indian/Alaska Native, 0.0% Native Hawaiian/Other Pacific Islander, 5.2% Two or more races, 0.7% Hispanic of any race; Average household size: 2.74; Median age: 30.1; Age under 18: 40.3%; Age 65 and over: 16.6%; Males per 100 females: 96.3; Marriage status: 22.9% never married, 49.3% now married, 3.5% separated, 12.7% widowed, 15.2% divorced; Foreign born: 0.7%; Speak English only: 99.6%; With disability: 22.2%; Veterans: 14.2%; Ancestry: 27.1% American, 9.6% German, 6.4% Irish, 4.7% English, 3.8% Greek
Employment: 6.6% management, business, and financial, 0.0% computer, engineering, and science, 10.4% education, legal, community service, arts, and media, 2.7% healthcare practitioners, 17.6% service, 18.1% sales and office, 11.0% natural resources, construction, and maintenance, 33.5% production, transportation, and material moving
Income: Per capita: $17,628; Median household: $34,000; Average household: $48,469; Households with income of $100,000 or more: 8.0%; Poverty rate: 34.2%
Educational Attainment: High school diploma or higher: 82.1%; Bachelor's degree or higher: 8.7%; Graduate/professional degree or higher: 6.3%

School District(s)

West Washington School Corp (PK-12)
Enrollment: 784. . . . . (812) 755-4872
Housing: Homeownership rate: 65.6%; Median home value: $64,100; Median year structure built: 1968; Homeowner vacancy rate: 0.0%; Median selected monthly owner costs: $740 with a mortgage, $286 without a mortgage; Median gross rent: $669 per month; Rental vacancy rate: 0.0%
Health Insurance: 89.6% have insurance; 44.7% have private insurance; 58.1% have public insurance; 10.4% do not have insurance; 7.6% of children under 18 do not have insurance
Transportation: Commute: 90.1% car, 0.0% public transportation, 3.3% walk, 2.7% work from home; Mean travel time to work: 25.0 minutes

FREDERICKSBURG (CDP). Covers a land area of 0.993 square miles and a water area of 0.020 square miles. Located at 38.43° N. Lat; 86.19° W. Long. Elevation is 614 feet.
History: Fredericksburg was settled in 1805 and became a toll station on the plank road between New Albany and Vincennes. Many of the settlers here were Quakers who built the Lick Creek Friends Church in 1815.
Population: 173; Growth (since 2000): 88.0%; Density: 174.3 persons per square mile; Race: 100.0% White, 0.0% Black/African American, 0.0% Asian, 0.0% American Indian/Alaska Native, 0.0% Native Hawaiian/Other Pacific Islander, 0.0% Two or more races, 0.0% Hispanic of any race; Average household size: 3.60; Median age: 22.3; Age under 18: 26.0%; Age 65 and over: 6.9%; Males per 100 females: 123.7; Marriage status: 53.9% never married, 25.8% now married, 0.0% separated, 9.4% widowed, 10.9% divorced; Foreign born: 0.0%; Speak English only: 100.0%; With disability: 21.4%; Veterans: 0.0%; Ancestry: 41.6% Irish, 31.2% German, 9.2% British, 5.2% American
Employment: 0.0% management, business, and financial, 0.0% computer, engineering, and science, 2.6% education, legal, community service, arts, and media, 0.0% healthcare practitioners, 32.9% service, 40.8% sales and office, 19.7% natural resources, construction, and maintenance, 3.9% production, transportation, and material moving
Income: Per capita: $6,768; Median household: $26,429; Average household: $25,788; Households with income of $100,000 or more: n/a; Poverty rate: 52.6%
Educational Attainment: High school diploma or higher: 50.0%; Bachelor's degree or higher: n/a; Graduate/professional degree or higher: n/a
Housing: Homeownership rate: 75.0%; Median home value: $77,800; Median year structure built: 1964; Homeowner vacancy rate: 0.0%; Median selected monthly owner costs: n/a with a mortgage, n/a without a mortgage; Median gross rent: n/a per month; Rental vacancy rate: 0.0%
Health Insurance: 83.8% have insurance; 6.9% have private insurance; 83.8% have public insurance; 16.2% do not have insurance; 0.0% of children under 18 do not have insurance
Transportation: Commute: 100.0% car, 0.0% public transportation, 0.0% walk, 0.0% work from home; Mean travel time to work: 31.0 minutes

HARDINSBURG (town). Covers a land area of 2.035 square miles and a water area of 0.003 square miles. Located at 38.47° N. Lat; 86.28° W. Long. Elevation is 689 feet.
History: Laid out 1838.
Population: 181; Growth (since 2000): -25.8%; Density: 88.9 persons per square mile; Race: 100.0% White, 0.0% Black/African American, 0.0% Asian, 0.0% American Indian/Alaska Native, 0.0% Native Hawaiian/Other Pacific Islander, 0.0% Two or more races, 3.9% Hispanic of any race; Average household size: 2.18; Median age: 48.5; Age under 18: 17.7%; Age 65 and over: 16.6%; Males per 100 females: 100.0; Marriage status: 18.3% never married, 56.2% now married, 1.3% separated, 8.5% widowed, 17.0% divorced; Foreign born: 0.0%; Speak English only: 97.2%; With disability: 21.5%; Veterans: 6.7%; Ancestry: 22.7% American, 18.2% German, 11.0% Irish, 8.8% English, 1.7% Scotch-Irish
Employment: 2.5% management, business, and financial, 0.0% computer, engineering, and science, 16.0% education, legal, community service, arts, and media, 2.5% healthcare practitioners, 24.7% service, 16.0% sales and office, 13.6% natural resources, construction, and maintenance, 24.7% production, transportation, and material moving
Income: Per capita: $23,002; Median household: $43,125; Average household: $51,901; Households with income of $100,000 or more: 13.2%; Poverty rate: 26.0%
Educational Attainment: High school diploma or higher: 87.4%; Bachelor's degree or higher: 9.6%; Graduate/professional degree or higher: 8.9%
Housing: Homeownership rate: 68.7%; Median home value: $65,000; Median year structure built: 1942; Homeowner vacancy rate: 6.6%; Median selected monthly owner costs: $757 with a mortgage, $241 without a mortgage; Median gross rent: $744 per month; Rental vacancy rate: 13.9%
Health Insurance: 87.3% have insurance; 55.8% have private insurance; 38.7% have public insurance; 12.7% do not have insurance; 0.0% of children under 18 do not have insurance
Transportation: Commute: 96.3% car, 0.0% public transportation, 2.5% walk, 1.2% work from home; Mean travel time to work: 29.6 minutes

LITTLE YORK (town). Covers a land area of 0.979 square miles and a water area of 0 square miles. Located at 38.70° N. Lat; 85.90° W. Long. Elevation is 548 feet.
History: Laid out 1831.
Population: 203; Growth (since 2000): 9.7%; Density: 207.3 persons per square mile; Race: 100.0% White, 0.0% Black/African American, 0.0% Asian, 0.0% American Indian/Alaska Native, 0.0% Native Hawaiian/Other Pacific Islander, 0.0% Two or more races, 0.0% Hispanic of any race; Average household size: 3.12; Median age: 43.1; Age under 18: 23.2%; Age 65 and over: 18.2%; Males per 100 females: 104.3; Marriage status: 20.6% never married, 64.2% now married, 1.8% separated, 1.8% widowed, 13.3% divorced; Foreign born: 0.0%; Speak English only: 100.0%; With disability: 21.2%; Veterans: 7.7%; Ancestry: 38.4% American, 11.3% Irish, 8.9% German, 7.9% English, 1.0% French
Employment: 18.1% management, business, and financial, 0.0% computer, engineering, and science, 3.2% education, legal, community service, arts, and media, 11.7% healthcare practitioners, 11.7% service, 18.1% sales and office, 6.4% natural resources, construction, and maintenance, 30.9% production, transportation, and material moving
Income: Per capita: $27,614; Median household: $60,417; Average household: $79,275; Households with income of $100,000 or more: 26.2%; Poverty rate: 16.3%
Educational Attainment: High school diploma or higher: 77.6%; Bachelor's degree or higher: 6.7%; Graduate/professional degree or higher: 3.0%
Housing: Homeownership rate: 90.8%; Median home value: $94,300; Median year structure built: 1970; Homeowner vacancy rate: 0.0%; Median

selected monthly owner costs: $1,025 with a mortgage, $416 without a mortgage; Median gross rent: n/a per month; Rental vacancy rate: 0.0%
Health Insurance: 87.2% have insurance; 58.1% have private insurance; 45.3% have public insurance; 12.8% do not have insurance; 2.0% of children under 18 do not have insurance
Transportation: Commute: 93.6% car, 3.2% public transportation, 3.2% walk, 0.0% work from home; Mean travel time to work: 27.9 minutes

LIVONIA (town). Covers a land area of 1.037 square miles and a water area of 0.002 square miles. Located at 38.55° N. Lat; 86.28° W. Long. Elevation is 787 feet.
History: Laid out 1819.
Population: 112; Growth (since 2000): 0.0%; Density: 108.0 persons per square mile; Race: 100.0% White, 0.0% Black/African American, 0.0% Asian, 0.0% American Indian/Alaska Native, 0.0% Native Hawaiian/Other Pacific Islander, 0.0% Two or more races, 9.8% Hispanic of any race; Average household size: 2.80; Median age: 43.8; Age under 18: 26.8%; Age 65 and over: 20.5%; Males per 100 females: 96.9; Marriage status: 21.3% never married, 65.2% now married, 0.0% separated, 2.2% widowed, 11.2% divorced; Foreign born: 0.0%; Speak English only: 96.2%; With disability: 17.0%; Veterans: 4.9%; Ancestry: 31.3% German, 20.5% American, 5.4% English, 2.7% Pennsylvania German, 1.8% Irish
Employment: 19.6% management, business, and financial, 3.6% computer, engineering, and science, 3.6% education, legal, community service, arts, and media, 3.6% healthcare practitioners, 17.9% service, 17.9% sales and office, 5.4% natural resources, construction, and maintenance, 28.6% production, transportation, and material moving
Income: Per capita: $20,229; Median household: $46,250; Average household: $50,430; Households with income of $100,000 or more: 7.5%; Poverty rate: n/a
Educational Attainment: High school diploma or higher: 77.9%; Bachelor's degree or higher: 9.1%; Graduate/professional degree or higher: 3.9%
Housing: Homeownership rate: 92.5%; Median home value: $72,500; Median year structure built: 1964; Homeowner vacancy rate: 0.0%; Median selected monthly owner costs: $1,075 with a mortgage, $250 without a mortgage; Median gross rent: n/a per month; Rental vacancy rate: 0.0%
Health Insurance: 88.4% have insurance; 58.9% have private insurance; 43.8% have public insurance; 11.6% do not have insurance; 3.0% of children under 18 do not have insurance
Transportation: Commute: 92.7% car, 0.0% public transportation, 0.0% walk, 7.3% work from home; Mean travel time to work: 30.0 minutes

NEW PEKIN (town). Covers a land area of 2.370 square miles and a water area of 0.034 square miles. Located at 38.50° N. Lat; 86.01° W. Long. Elevation is 712 feet.
Population: 1,570; Growth (since 2000): 17.7%; Density: 662.4 persons per square mile; Race: 95.5% White, 0.0% Black/African American, 0.0% Asian, 0.9% American Indian/Alaska Native, 0.0% Native Hawaiian/Other Pacific Islander, 3.4% Two or more races, 7.5% Hispanic of any race; Average household size: 2.64; Median age: 38.3; Age under 18: 30.4%; Age 65 and over: 11.3%; Males per 100 females: 95.4; Marriage status: 30.6% never married, 44.4% now married, 4.4% separated, 8.9% widowed, 16.1% divorced; Foreign born: 0.0%; Speak English only: 98.5%; With disability: 20.6%; Veterans: 8.8%; Ancestry: 17.3% American, 15.3% German, 9.9% English, 8.3% Irish, 0.6% French
Employment: 11.0% management, business, and financial, 2.9% computer, engineering, and science, 4.2% education, legal, community service, arts, and media, 8.1% healthcare practitioners, 14.7% service, 25.7% sales and office, 10.7% natural resources, construction, and maintenance, 22.6% production, transportation, and material moving
Income: Per capita: $18,187; Median household: $40,955; Average household: $46,634; Households with income of $100,000 or more: 7.4%; Poverty rate: 20.0%
Educational Attainment: High school diploma or higher: 81.5%; Bachelor's degree or higher: 10.2%; Graduate/professional degree or higher: 3.0%
Housing: Homeownership rate: 58.8%; Median home value: $79,400; Median year structure built: 1979; Homeowner vacancy rate: 3.3%; Median selected monthly owner costs: $908 with a mortgage, $329 without a mortgage; Median gross rent: $679 per month; Rental vacancy rate: 6.5%
Health Insurance: 90.4% have insurance; 62.2% have private insurance; 35.0% have public insurance; 9.6% do not have insurance; 6.1% of children under 18 do not have insurance
Transportation: Commute: 91.7% car, 0.6% public transportation, 1.3% walk, 2.2% work from home; Mean travel time to work: 33.0 minutes

PEKIN (unincorporated postal area)
ZCTA: 47165
Covers a land area of 82.396 square miles and a water area of 0.325 square miles. Located at 38.50° N. Lat; 86.01° W. Long..
Population: 6,285; Growth (since 2000): 7.9%; Density: 76.3 persons per square mile; Race: 98.9% White, 0.0% Black/African American, 0.0% Asian, 0.2% American Indian/Alaska Native, 0.0% Native Hawaiian/Other Pacific Islander, 0.8% Two or more races, 1.9% Hispanic of any race; Average household size: 2.75; Median age: 43.0; Age under 18: 23.6%; Age 65 and over: 13.0%; Males per 100 females: 102.8; Marriage status: 24.5% never married, 61.1% now married, 1.4% separated, 4.7% widowed, 9.7% divorced; Foreign born: 0.0%; Speak English only: 99.0%; With disability: 18.0%; Veterans: 10.3%; Ancestry: 25.1% American, 20.8% German, 10.5% Irish, 7.3% English, 3.8% French
Employment: 11.9% management, business, and financial, 2.5% computer, engineering, and science, 8.8% education, legal, community service, arts, and media, 9.0% healthcare practitioners, 12.8% service, 17.2% sales and office, 14.0% natural resources, construction, and maintenance, 23.7% production, transportation, and material moving
Income: Per capita: $24,706; Median household: $55,982; Average household: $65,876; Households with income of $100,000 or more: 14.5%; Poverty rate: 8.0%
Educational Attainment: High school diploma or higher: 90.8%; Bachelor's degree or higher: 15.6%; Graduate/professional degree or higher: 6.6%

School District(s)

East Washington School Corp (KG-12)
Enrollment: 1,468 . . . . (812) 967-3926
Housing: Homeownership rate: 79.7%; Median home value: $111,100; Median year structure built: 1981; Homeowner vacancy rate: 4.8%; Median selected monthly owner costs: $1,094 with a mortgage, $362 without a mortgage; Median gross rent: $638 per month; Rental vacancy rate: 3.5%
Health Insurance: 88.0% have insurance; 71.4% have private insurance; 26.9% have public insurance; 12.0% do not have insurance; 14.3% of children under 18 do not have insurance
Newspapers: Green Banner Publications (weekly circulation 66,000)
Transportation: Commute: 93.9% car, 0.1% public transportation, 1.1% walk, 4.0% work from home; Mean travel time to work: 36.3 minutes

SALEM (city). County seat. Covers a land area of 4.000 square miles and a water area of 0.018 square miles. Located at 38.60° N. Lat; 86.10° W. Long. Elevation is 751 feet.
History: Salem was founded in 1814 and named for Salem, North Carolina, the former home of the wife of the county surveyor. John Hay, statesman, diplomat, poet, and historian, was born in 1838 in Salem. In 1863 Salem was burned and looted by General Morgan and his raiders.
Population: 6,191; Growth (since 2000): 0.3%; Density: 1,547.8 persons per square mile; Race: 98.3% White, 0.4% Black/African American, 0.0% Asian, 0.0% American Indian/Alaska Native, 0.0% Native Hawaiian/Other Pacific Islander, 1.3% Two or more races, 0.6% Hispanic of any race; Average household size: 2.19; Median age: 39.7; Age under 18: 21.3%; Age 65 and over: 20.1%; Males per 100 females: 86.9; Marriage status: 23.6% never married, 44.9% now married, 1.4% separated, 10.6% widowed, 20.9% divorced; Foreign born: 0.1%; Speak English only: 99.4%; With disability: 20.6%; Veterans: 11.0%; Ancestry: 20.4% American, 12.5% Irish, 11.1% German, 7.9% English, 2.6% French
Employment: 12.6% management, business, and financial, 1.6% computer, engineering, and science, 8.1% education, legal, community service, arts, and media, 4.5% healthcare practitioners, 16.4% service, 20.6% sales and office, 11.3% natural resources, construction, and maintenance, 24.9% production, transportation, and material moving
Income: Per capita: $19,727; Median household: $34,483; Average household: $43,359; Households with income of $100,000 or more: 7.5%; Poverty rate: 20.4%
Educational Attainment: High school diploma or higher: 79.8%; Bachelor's degree or higher: 14.1%; Graduate/professional degree or higher: 5.6%

School District(s)

Salem Community Schools (PK-12)
Enrollment: 1,942 . . . . (812) 883-4437

Housing: Homeownership rate: 62.4%; Median home value: $81,700; Median year structure built: 1964; Homeowner vacancy rate: 4.1%; Median selected monthly owner costs: $868 with a mortgage, $288 without a mortgage; Median gross rent: $583 per month; Rental vacancy rate: 5.3%
Health Insurance: 91.7% have insurance; 60.9% have private insurance; 47.0% have public insurance; 8.3% do not have insurance; 4.4% of children under 18 do not have insurance
Hospitals: Saint Vincent Salem Hospital (70 beds)
Newspapers: Salem Democrat (weekly circulation 6,100); Salem Leader (weekly circulation 6,100)
Transportation: Commute: 93.4% car, 0.0% public transportation, 2.2% walk, 3.5% work from home; Mean travel time to work: 27.6 minutes
Additional Information Contacts
City of Salem . . . . (812) 883-4264
http://www.cityofsalemin.com

SALTILLO (town). Covers a land area of 1.151 square miles and a water area of 0.002 square miles. Located at 38.67° N. Lat; 86.30° W. Long. Elevation is 807 feet.
Population: 84; Growth (since 2000): -21.5%; Density: 73.0 persons per square mile; Race: 100.0% White, 0.0% Black/African American, 0.0% Asian, 0.0% American Indian/Alaska Native, 0.0% Native Hawaiian/Other Pacific Islander, 0.0% Two or more races, 0.0% Hispanic of any race; Average household size: 1.79; Median age: 49.8; Age under 18: 8.3%; Age 65 and over: 25.0%; Males per 100 females: 100.0; Marriage status: 9.1% never married, 54.5% now married, 0.0% separated, 14.3% widowed, 22.1% divorced; Foreign born: 0.0%; Speak English only: 98.7%; With disability: 27.4%; Veterans: 7.8%; Ancestry: 17.9% American, 7.1% English, 7.1% Irish, 6.0% German, 6.0% Scotch-Irish
Employment: 0.0% management, business, and financial, 4.7% computer, engineering, and science, 18.6% education, legal, community service, arts, and media, 0.0% healthcare practitioners, 25.6% service, 2.3% sales and office, 4.7% natural resources, construction, and maintenance, 44.2% production, transportation, and material moving
Income: Per capita: $27,167; Median household: $46,875; Average household: $49,879; Households with income of $100,000 or more: 8.5%; Poverty rate: 27.4%
Educational Attainment: High school diploma or higher: 85.5%; Bachelor's degree or higher: 10.1%; Graduate/professional degree or higher: 1.4%
Housing: Homeownership rate: 68.1%; Median home value: $48,000; Median year structure built: 1977; Homeowner vacancy rate: 0.0%; Median selected monthly owner costs: $950 with a mortgage, $529 without a mortgage; Median gross rent: n/a per month; Rental vacancy rate: 0.0%
Health Insurance: 89.3% have insurance; 72.6% have private insurance; 36.9% have public insurance; 10.7% do not have insurance; 0.0% of children under 18 do not have insurance
Transportation: Commute: 97.6% car, 0.0% public transportation, 0.0% walk, 2.4% work from home; Mean travel time to work: 28.5 minutes

Wayne County

Located in eastern Indiana; bounded on the east by Ohio; drained by the Whitewater River and its East Fork. Covers a land area of 401.740 square miles, a water area of 2.601 square miles, and is located in the Eastern Time Zone at 39.86° N. Lat., 85.01° W. Long. The county was founded in 1810. County seat is Richmond.

Wayne County is part of the Richmond, IN Micropolitan Statistical Area. The entire metro area includes: Wayne County, IN

Weather Station: Richmond Water Works Elevation: 1,015 feet

	Jan	Feb	Mar	Apr	May	Jun	Jul	Aug	Sep	Oct	Nov	Dec
High	36	40	50	63	73	81	85	83	77	64	52	39
Low	19	22	30	40	50	59	63	61	53	42	33	23
Precip	2.7	2.3	3.2	3.8	4.7	4.3	4.0	3.5	2.8	3.2	3.4	2.9
Snow	5.9	3.6	1.6	0.2	tr	0.0	0.0	0.0	0.0	0.2	0.4	3.8

High and Low temperatures in degrees Fahrenheit; Precipitation and Snow in inches

Population: 66,972; Growth (since 2000): -5.8%; Density: 166.7 persons per square mile; Race: 90.0% White, 5.1% Black/African American, 1.0% Asian, 0.2% American Indian/Alaska Native, 0.0% Native Hawaiian/Other Pacific Islander, 2.6% two or more races, 2.8% Hispanic of any race; Average household size: 2.44; Median age: 41.1; Age under 18: 22.2%; Age 65 and over: 18.2%; Males per 100 females: 94.4; Marriage status: 27.0% never married, 48.9% now married, 1.2% separated, 8.3% widowed, 15.7% divorced; Foreign born: 2.0%; Speak English only: 95.7%; With disability: 18.7%; Veterans: 9.8%; Ancestry: 21.8% German, 13.1% Irish, 10.6% American, 9.0% English, 2.3% Italian
Religion: Six largest groups: 12.3% Baptist, 7.0% Catholicism, 4.7% Methodist/Pietist, 4.0% Non-denominational Protestant, 3.9% Pentecostal, 3.7% Holiness
Economy: Unemployment rate: 3.7%; Leading industries: 16.6 % retail trade; 14.1 % health care and social assistance; 12.1 % other services (except public administration); Farms: 805 totaling 155,931 acres; Company size: 2 employ 1,000 or more persons, 0 employ 500 to 999 persons, 41 employs 100 to 499 persons, 1,428 employ less than 100 persons; Business ownership: 1,306 women-owned, 105 Black-owned, 37 Hispanic-owned, 112 Asian-owned, 53 American Indian/Alaska Native-owned
Employment: 10.5% management, business, and financial, 2.7% computer, engineering, and science, 9.2% education, legal, community service, arts, and media, 7.8% healthcare practitioners, 18.9% service, 21.9% sales and office, 7.9% natural resources, construction, and maintenance, 21.1% production, transportation, and material moving
Income: Per capita: $23,895; Median household: $41,813; Average household: $59,323; Households with income of $100,000 or more: 13.9%; Poverty rate: 18.2%
Educational Attainment: High school diploma or higher: 85.5%; Bachelor's degree or higher: 18.2%; Graduate/professional degree or higher: 7.5%
Housing: Homeownership rate: 67.4%; Median home value: $96,500; Median year structure built: 1959; Homeowner vacancy rate: 2.5%; Median selected monthly owner costs: $933 with a mortgage, $370 without a mortgage; Median gross rent: $665 per month; Rental vacancy rate: 16.3%
Vital Statistics: Birth rate: 116.6 per 10,000 population; Death rate: 130.1 per 10,000 population; Age-adjusted cancer mortality rate: 171.1 deaths per 100,000 population
Health Insurance: 87.0% have insurance; 61.4% have private insurance; 39.5% have public insurance; 13.0% do not have insurance; 10.8% of children under 18 do not have insurance
Health Care: Physicians: 22.5 per 10,000 population; Dentists: 5.7 per 10,000 population; Hospital beds: 60.2 per 10,000 population; Hospital admissions: 1,812.7 per 10,000 population
Transportation: Commute: 90.5% car, 0.4% public transportation, 3.0% walk, 3.6% work from home; Mean travel time to work: 19.6 minutes
2016 Presidential Election: 62.7% Trump, 32.5% Clinton, 4.8% Johnson, 0.0% Stein
Additional Information Contacts
Wayne Government . . . . (765) 973-9220
http://www.co.wayne.in.us

Wayne County Communities

BOSTON (town). Covers a land area of 0.211 square miles and a water area of 0 square miles. Located at 39.74° N. Lat; 84.85° W. Long. Elevation is 1,132 feet.
Population: 137; Growth (since 2000): -22.6%; Density: 650.1 persons per square mile; Race: 100.0% White, 0.0% Black/African American, 0.0% Asian, 0.0% American Indian/Alaska Native, 0.0% Native Hawaiian/Other Pacific Islander, 0.0% Two or more races, 0.0% Hispanic of any race; Average household size: 2.14; Median age: 55.9; Age under 18: 21.9%; Age 65 and over: 15.3%; Males per 100 females: 109.1; Marriage status: 6.5% never married, 77.8% now married, 8.3% separated, 12.0% widowed, 3.7% divorced; Foreign born: 0.0%; Speak English only: 100.0%; With disability: 15.3%; Veterans: 18.7%; Ancestry: 15.3% American, 12.4% German, 11.7% Irish, 4.4% Scotch-Irish, 0.7% English
Employment: 10.9% management, business, and financial, 0.0% computer, engineering, and science, 6.5% education, legal, community service, arts, and media, 0.0% healthcare practitioners, 34.8% service, 28.3% sales and office, 0.0% natural resources, construction, and maintenance, 19.6% production, transportation, and material moving
Income: Per capita: $18,468; Median household: $30,833; Average household: $40,239; Households with income of $100,000 or more: 9.4%; Poverty rate: 24.8%
Educational Attainment: High school diploma or higher: 84.3%; Bachelor's degree or higher: 11.8%; Graduate/professional degree or higher: 3.9%
Housing: Homeownership rate: 68.8%; Median home value: $80,000; Median year structure built: Before 1940; Homeowner vacancy rate: 13.7%; Median selected monthly owner costs: $788 with a mortgage, $407

without a mortgage; Median gross rent: $875 per month; Rental vacancy rate: 0.0%
Health Insurance: 90.5% have insurance; 62.0% have private insurance; 42.3% have public insurance; 9.5% do not have insurance; 0.0% of children under 18 do not have insurance
Transportation: Commute: 90.5% car, 0.0% public transportation, 9.5% walk, 0.0% work from home; Mean travel time to work: 14.6 minutes

CAMBRIDGE CITY (town). Covers a land area of 1.012 square miles and a water area of 0.007 square miles. Located at 39.81° N. Lat; 85.17° W. Long. Elevation is 935 feet.
History: Founded in 1836 as a depot on the Whitewater Canal, Cambridge City was a shipping center for Indianapolis merchants for a time.
Population: 1,980; Growth (since 2000): -6.6%; Density: 1,956.2 persons per square mile; Race: 96.7% White, 0.3% Black/African American, 0.0% Asian, 0.0% American Indian/Alaska Native, 0.0% Native Hawaiian/Other Pacific Islander, 2.8% Two or more races, 0.1% Hispanic of any race; Average household size: 2.51; Median age: 41.6; Age under 18: 23.0%; Age 65 and over: 15.1%; Males per 100 females: 95.4; Marriage status: 26.8% never married, 43.2% now married, 1.3% separated, 11.9% widowed, 18.1% divorced; Foreign born: 0.4%; Speak English only: 99.6%; With disability: 21.0%; Veterans: 8.1%; Ancestry: 27.2% German, 17.1% Irish, 12.0% American, 7.0% English, 2.3% Italian
Employment: 5.2% management, business, and financial, 3.8% computer, engineering, and science, 4.9% education, legal, community service, arts, and media, 6.0% healthcare practitioners, 18.5% service, 25.0% sales and office, 10.5% natural resources, construction, and maintenance, 26.0% production, transportation, and material moving
Income: Per capita: $19,724; Median household: $35,000; Average household: $49,249; Households with income of $100,000 or more: 7.6%; Poverty rate: 16.5%
Educational Attainment: High school diploma or higher: 80.5%; Bachelor's degree or higher: 9.2%; Graduate/professional degree or higher: 3.0%

School District(s)

Western Wayne Schools (PK-12)
Enrollment: 1,022 . . . . (765) 478-5375
Housing: Homeownership rate: 70.3%; Median home value: $70,300; Median year structure built: 1948; Homeowner vacancy rate: 0.7%; Median selected monthly owner costs: $772 with a mortgage, $376 without a mortgage; Median gross rent: $648 per month; Rental vacancy rate: 12.6%
Health Insurance: 85.3% have insurance; 56.7% have private insurance; 42.3% have public insurance; 14.7% do not have insurance; 11.8% of children under 18 do not have insurance
Newspapers: Nettle Creek Gazette (weekly circulation 1,000); Western Wayne News (weekly circulation 2,700)
Transportation: Commute: 92.4% car, 0.2% public transportation, 4.9% walk, 1.2% work from home; Mean travel time to work: 27.2 minutes
Additional Information Contacts
Town of Cambridge City . . . . (765) 478-4689
http://www.cambridgecityindiana.org

CENTERVILLE (town). Covers a land area of 2.404 square miles and a water area of <.001 square miles. Located at 39.83° N. Lat; 84.99° W. Long. Elevation is 1,014 feet.
History: Centerville was once the seat of Wayne County. It reluctantly gave up the county records to Richmond on August 14, 1873, when shots were fired into the jail where the Centerville citizens had barricaded themselves and the records.
Population: 2,579; Growth (since 2000): 6.3%; Density: 1,072.7 persons per square mile; Race: 94.2% White, 2.5% Black/African American, 0.0% Asian, 0.0% American Indian/Alaska Native, 0.0% Native Hawaiian/Other Pacific Islander, 3.3% Two or more races, 0.4% Hispanic of any race; Average household size: 2.48; Median age: 38.8; Age under 18: 26.2%; Age 65 and over: 17.4%; Males per 100 females: 90.4; Marriage status: 22.0% never married, 47.5% now married, 2.7% separated, 8.4% widowed, 22.1% divorced; Foreign born: 0.0%; Speak English only: 98.8%; With disability: 13.8%; Veterans: 11.2%; Ancestry: 25.3% German, 9.6% American, 8.6% Irish, 5.8% English, 2.1% Welsh
Employment: 18.0% management, business, and financial, 2.5% computer, engineering, and science, 8.7% education, legal, community service, arts, and media, 7.5% healthcare practitioners, 18.2% service, 23.0% sales and office, 3.8% natural resources, construction, and maintenance, 18.2% production, transportation, and material moving
Income: Per capita: $22,827; Median household: $42,703; Average household: $56,220; Households with income of $100,000 or more: 13.0%; Poverty rate: 20.4%
Educational Attainment: High school diploma or higher: 88.0%; Bachelor's degree or higher: 16.9%; Graduate/professional degree or higher: 5.2%

School District(s)

Centerville-Abington Com Schs (PK-12)
Enrollment: 1,491 . . . . (765) 855-3475
Housing: Homeownership rate: 73.6%; Median home value: $87,500; Median year structure built: 1960; Homeowner vacancy rate: 3.5%; Median selected monthly owner costs: $857 with a mortgage, $367 without a mortgage; Median gross rent: $879 per month; Rental vacancy rate: 15.7%
Health Insurance: 87.8% have insurance; 68.7% have private insurance; 33.4% have public insurance; 12.2% do not have insurance; 9.0% of children under 18 do not have insurance
Transportation: Commute: 94.7% car, 0.0% public transportation, 0.5% walk, 4.5% work from home; Mean travel time to work: 28.2 minutes
Additional Information Contacts
Town of Centerville . . . . (765) 855-5515
http://www.town.centerville.in.us/index.php

DUBLIN (town). Covers a land area of 0.532 square miles and a water area of 0.011 square miles. Located at 39.81° N. Lat; 85.21° W. Long. Elevation is 1,053 feet.
History: Located on the Old National Road, Dublin was the site of The Maples, a tavern built in 1825.
Population: 694; Growth (since 2000): -0.4%; Density: 1,304.1 persons per square mile; Race: 98.8% White, 0.3% Black/African American, 0.0% Asian, 0.0% American Indian/Alaska Native, 0.0% Native Hawaiian/Other Pacific Islander, 0.9% Two or more races, 1.7% Hispanic of any race; Average household size: 2.06; Median age: 50.5; Age under 18: 14.7%; Age 65 and over: 24.1%; Males per 100 females: 89.4; Marriage status: 20.3% never married, 57.0% now married, 0.3% separated, 8.9% widowed, 13.8% divorced; Foreign born: 0.0%; Speak English only: 97.9%; With disability: 18.9%; Veterans: 9.1%; Ancestry: 16.0% German, 14.6% English, 8.5% Irish, 4.3% American, 4.3% European
Employment: 7.4% management, business, and financial, 2.1% computer, engineering, and science, 7.1% education, legal, community service, arts, and media, 3.3% healthcare practitioners, 21.1% service, 16.7% sales and office, 14.9% natural resources, construction, and maintenance, 27.4% production, transportation, and material moving
Income: Per capita: $22,125; Median household: $31,146; Average household: $44,927; Households with income of $100,000 or more: 10.7%; Poverty rate: 20.7%
Educational Attainment: High school diploma or higher: 87.2%; Bachelor's degree or higher: 8.8%; Graduate/professional degree or higher: 0.7%
Housing: Homeownership rate: 78.6%; Median home value: $68,000; Median year structure built: Before 1940; Homeowner vacancy rate: 4.9%; Median selected monthly owner costs: $954 with a mortgage, $400 without a mortgage; Median gross rent: $531 per month; Rental vacancy rate: 7.7%
Health Insurance: 86.9% have insurance; 61.4% have private insurance; 39.2% have public insurance; 13.1% do not have insurance; 15.2% of children under 18 do not have insurance
Transportation: Commute: 97.8% car, 0.0% public transportation, 0.6% walk, 0.9% work from home; Mean travel time to work: 24.6 minutes

EAST GERMANTOWN (town). Covers a land area of 0.128 square miles and a water area of 0 square miles. Located at 39.81° N. Lat; 85.14° W. Long. Elevation is 951 feet.
Population: 331; Growth (since 2000): 36.2%; Density: 2,587.2 persons per square mile; Race: 98.8% White, 0.0% Black/African American, 0.0% Asian, 1.2% American Indian/Alaska Native, 0.0% Native Hawaiian/Other Pacific Islander, 0.0% Two or more races, 0.0% Hispanic of any race; Average household size: 2.21; Median age: 48.3; Age under 18: 15.1%; Age 65 and over: 27.5%; Males per 100 females: 94.3; Marriage status: 21.3% never married, 55.1% now married, 2.8% separated, 9.8% widowed, 13.9% divorced; Foreign born: 0.0%; Speak English only: 99.4%; With disability: 21.5%; Veterans: 6.0%; Ancestry: 16.3% Irish, 9.1% German, 7.3% Scottish, 5.1% American, 4.8% English
Employment: 17.9% management, business, and financial, 0.0% computer, engineering, and science, 6.7% education, legal, community service, arts, and media, 0.7% healthcare practitioners, 25.4% service,

20.1% sales and office, 7.5% natural resources, construction, and maintenance, 21.6% production, transportation, and material moving
Income: Per capita: $19,440; Median household: $31,000; Average household: $41,615; Households with income of $100,000 or more: 7.3%; Poverty rate: 14.5%
Educational Attainment: High school diploma or higher: 91.0%; Bachelor's degree or higher: 5.9%; Graduate/professional degree or higher: 3.5%
Housing: Homeownership rate: 68.7%; Median home value: $78,000; Median year structure built: 1956; Homeowner vacancy rate: 0.0%; Median selected monthly owner costs: $788 with a mortgage, $297 without a mortgage; Median gross rent: $658 per month; Rental vacancy rate: 9.6%
Health Insurance: 89.1% have insurance; 60.7% have private insurance; 46.5% have public insurance; 10.9% do not have insurance; 17.6% of children under 18 do not have insurance
Transportation: Commute: 99.2% car, 0.0% public transportation, 0.0% walk, 0.8% work from home; Mean travel time to work: 31.6 minutes

ECONOMY (town). Covers a land area of 0.098 square miles and a water area of 0 square miles. Located at 39.98° N. Lat; 85.09° W. Long. Elevation is 1,155 feet.
History: Economy was the site in 1936 of Dr. James R. King's experiment in cooperative medical care, the Economy Mutual Health Association.
Population: 133; Growth (since 2000): -33.5%; Density: 1,353.6 persons per square mile; Race: 98.5% White, 0.0% Black/African American, 0.0% Asian, 0.0% American Indian/Alaska Native, 0.0% Native Hawaiian/Other Pacific Islander, 1.5% Two or more races, 3.8% Hispanic of any race; Average household size: 2.42; Median age: 50.1; Age under 18: 10.5%; Age 65 and over: 21.1%; Males per 100 females: 92.8; Marriage status: 30.4% never married, 51.2% now married, 0.0% separated, 8.0% widowed, 10.4% divorced; Foreign born: 0.0%; Speak English only: 98.5%; With disability: 24.8%; Veterans: 11.8%; Ancestry: 33.1% English, 21.1% Irish, 16.5% German, 12.0% American, 3.8% Greek
Employment: 5.8% management, business, and financial, 2.9% computer, engineering, and science, 8.7% education, legal, community service, arts, and media, 1.4% healthcare practitioners, 24.6% service, 20.3% sales and office, 14.5% natural resources, construction, and maintenance, 21.7% production, transportation, and material moving
Income: Per capita: $21,822; Median household: $36,563; Average household: $48,733; Households with income of $100,000 or more: 12.7%; Poverty rate: 11.3%
Educational Attainment: High school diploma or higher: 82.9%; Bachelor's degree or higher: 12.4%; Graduate/professional degree or higher: 5.7%
Housing: Homeownership rate: 89.1%; Median home value: $71,500; Median year structure built: Before 1940; Homeowner vacancy rate: 9.3%; Median selected monthly owner costs: $817 with a mortgage, $325 without a mortgage; Median gross rent: n/a per month; Rental vacancy rate: 0.0%
Health Insurance: 88.0% have insurance; 72.2% have private insurance; 39.1% have public insurance; 12.0% do not have insurance; 0.0% of children under 18 do not have insurance
Transportation: Commute: 100.0% car, 0.0% public transportation, 0.0% walk, 0.0% work from home; Mean travel time to work: 25.9 minutes

FOUNTAIN CITY (town). Covers a land area of 0.263 square miles and a water area of 0 square miles. Located at 39.95° N. Lat; 84.92° W. Long. Elevation is 1,106 feet.
History: Fountain was incorporated as Newport in 1834, but the name was changed to Fountain City when water from an underground lake was found to rise to the surface when pipes were sunk to it. Fountain City was a major station on the Underground Railroad of freedom for fugitive slaves.
Population: 793; Growth (since 2000): 7.9%; Density: 3,014.9 persons per square mile; Race: 97.9% White, 0.0% Black/African American, 0.9% Asian, 0.0% American Indian/Alaska Native, 0.0% Native Hawaiian/Other Pacific Islander, 1.3% Two or more races, 0.0% Hispanic of any race; Average household size: 2.67; Median age: 38.6; Age under 18: 26.4%; Age 65 and over: 14.1%; Males per 100 females: 88.6; Marriage status: 21.3% never married, 56.7% now married, 0.8% separated, 9.7% widowed, 12.3% divorced; Foreign born: 0.5%; Speak English only: 98.7%; With disability: 19.2%; Veterans: 9.4%; Ancestry: 16.3% American, 15.6% German, 12.7% English, 9.5% Irish, 2.4% French
Employment: 9.3% management, business, and financial, 0.0% computer, engineering, and science, 6.8% education, legal, community service, arts, and media, 4.1% healthcare practitioners, 21.6% service, 28.2% sales and office, 11.0% natural resources, construction, and maintenance, 18.9% production, transportation, and material moving
Income: Per capita: $21,201; Median household: $42,708; Average household: $55,036; Households with income of $100,000 or more: 12.1%; Poverty rate: 14.9%
Educational Attainment: High school diploma or higher: 84.5%; Bachelor's degree or higher: 8.9%; Graduate/professional degree or higher: 2.4%

School District(s)

Northeastern Wayne Schools (PK-12)
Enrollment: 1,022 . . . . (765) 847-2821
Housing: Homeownership rate: 71.0%; Median home value: $75,900; Median year structure built: 1948; Homeowner vacancy rate: 0.9%; Median selected monthly owner costs: $986 with a mortgage, $339 without a mortgage; Median gross rent: $721 per month; Rental vacancy rate: 24.6%
Health Insurance: 82.8% have insurance; 61.9% have private insurance; 32.8% have public insurance; 17.2% do not have insurance; 13.1% of children under 18 do not have insurance
Transportation: Commute: 94.5% car, 0.0% public transportation, 2.2% walk, 2.7% work from home; Mean travel time to work: 19.7 minutes

GREENS FORK (town). Covers a land area of 0.160 square miles and a water area of 0.003 square miles. Located at 39.89° N. Lat; 85.04° W. Long. Elevation is 1,010 feet.
History: Laid out 1818.
Population: 403; Growth (since 2000): 8.6%; Density: 2,526.5 persons per square mile; Race: 95.0% White, 0.0% Black/African American, 0.7% Asian, 2.7% American Indian/Alaska Native, 0.0% Native Hawaiian/Other Pacific Islander, 1.5% Two or more races, 3.2% Hispanic of any race; Average household size: 2.63; Median age: 43.6; Age under 18: 20.3%; Age 65 and over: 14.6%; Males per 100 females: 88.0; Marriage status: 22.1% never married, 53.4% now married, 2.5% separated, 10.4% widowed, 14.1% divorced; Foreign born: 0.7%; Speak English only: 100.0%; With disability: 20.1%; Veterans: 16.8%; Ancestry: 14.1% German, 8.9% American, 6.2% Irish, 6.0% English, 2.2% Scottish
Employment: 8.5% management, business, and financial, 1.1% computer, engineering, and science, 5.1% education, legal, community service, arts, and media, 2.8% healthcare practitioners, 17.6% service, 24.4% sales and office, 11.9% natural resources, construction, and maintenance, 28.4% production, transportation, and material moving
Income: Per capita: $18,945; Median household: $42,083; Average household: $48,938; Households with income of $100,000 or more: 9.8%; Poverty rate: 23.8%
Educational Attainment: High school diploma or higher: 83.5%; Bachelor's degree or higher: 10.1%; Graduate/professional degree or higher: 2.2%
Housing: Homeownership rate: 73.9%; Median home value: $61,100; Median year structure built: Before 1940; Homeowner vacancy rate: 1.7%; Median selected monthly owner costs: $858 with a mortgage, $371 without a mortgage; Median gross rent: $650 per month; Rental vacancy rate: 11.1%
Health Insurance: 89.3% have insurance; 66.7% have private insurance; 36.0% have public insurance; 10.7% do not have insurance; 0.0% of children under 18 do not have insurance
Transportation: Commute: 98.3% car, 0.0% public transportation, 0.0% walk, 0.6% work from home; Mean travel time to work: 28.1 minutes

HAGERSTOWN (town). Covers a land area of 1.340 square miles and a water area of 0.003 square miles. Located at 39.91° N. Lat; 85.15° W. Long. Elevation is 1,007 feet.
Population: 1,621; Growth (since 2000): -8.3%; Density: 1,210.1 persons per square mile; Race: 97.5% White, 0.7% Black/African American, 0.0% Asian, 0.5% American Indian/Alaska Native, 0.0% Native Hawaiian/Other Pacific Islander, 1.3% Two or more races, 0.2% Hispanic of any race; Average household size: 2.46; Median age: 40.6; Age under 18: 22.8%; Age 65 and over: 21.6%; Males per 100 females: 93.8; Marriage status: 27.3% never married, 53.3% now married, 1.3% separated, 6.9% widowed, 12.5% divorced; Foreign born: 0.4%; Speak English only: 99.2%; With disability: 16.1%; Veterans: 11.5%; Ancestry: 21.7% German, 14.1% American, 12.0% Irish, 9.3% English, 3.1% Scottish
Employment: 6.8% management, business, and financial, 4.8% computer, engineering, and science, 11.0% education, legal, community service, arts, and media, 7.1% healthcare practitioners, 21.8% service, 19.5% sales and office, 7.5% natural resources, construction, and maintenance, 21.6% production, transportation, and material moving

Income: Per capita: $21,762; Median household: $43,393; Average household: $52,821; Households with income of $100,000 or more: 9.0%; Poverty rate: 13.8%
Educational Attainment: High school diploma or higher: 93.5%; Bachelor's degree or higher: 22.1%; Graduate/professional degree or higher: 7.6%

School District(s)

Nettle Creek School Corporation (PK-12)
Enrollment: 1,080 . . . . (765) 489-4543

Housing: Homeownership rate: 74.2%; Median home value: $92,100; Median year structure built: 1948; Homeowner vacancy rate: 1.8%; Median selected monthly owner costs: $941 with a mortgage, $386 without a mortgage; Median gross rent: $640 per month; Rental vacancy rate: 13.7%
Health Insurance: 89.0% have insurance; 71.6% have private insurance; 34.9% have public insurance; 11.0% do not have insurance; 10.7% of children under 18 do not have insurance
Safety: Violent crime rate: 35.3 per 10,000 population; Property crime rate: 58.8 per 10,000 population
Transportation: Commute: 91.9% car, 0.4% public transportation, 3.6% walk, 2.3% work from home; Mean travel time to work: 25.1 minutes

MILTON (town). Covers a land area of 0.267 square miles and a water area of 0.003 square miles. Located at 39.79° N. Lat; 85.16° W. Long. Elevation is 932 feet.
Population: 381; Growth (since 2000): -37.6%; Density: 1,424.6 persons per square mile; Race: 99.0% White, 0.0% Black/African American, 0.0% Asian, 0.0% American Indian/Alaska Native, 0.0% Native Hawaiian/Other Pacific Islander, 1.0% Two or more races, 0.0% Hispanic of any race; Average household size: 2.34; Median age: 48.1; Age under 18: 18.1%; Age 65 and over: 15.5%; Males per 100 females: 101.6; Marriage status: 19.0% never married, 44.5% now married, 1.2% separated, 9.3% widowed, 27.1% divorced; Foreign born: 0.8%; Speak English only: 98.9%; With disability: 31.0%; Veterans: 8.3%; Ancestry: 24.4% German, 13.6% Irish, 7.9% American, 6.8% English, 3.1% Italian
Employment: 6.3% management, business, and financial, 4.4% computer, engineering, and science, 5.0% education, legal, community service, arts, and media, 5.7% healthcare practitioners, 17.6% service, 27.7% sales and office, 10.7% natural resources, construction, and maintenance, 22.6% production, transportation, and material moving
Income: Per capita: $20,909; Median household: $37,125; Average household: $47,085; Households with income of $100,000 or more: 11.0%; Poverty rate: 23.8%
Educational Attainment: High school diploma or higher: 80.3%; Bachelor's degree or higher: 10.8%; Graduate/professional degree or higher: 2.9%
Housing: Homeownership rate: 73.6%; Median home value: $55,800; Median year structure built: Before 1940; Homeowner vacancy rate: 6.3%; Median selected monthly owner costs: $710 with a mortgage, $348 without a mortgage; Median gross rent: $682 per month; Rental vacancy rate: 17.3%
Health Insurance: 85.3% have insurance; 49.3% have private insurance; 45.7% have public insurance; 14.7% do not have insurance; 13.3% of children under 18 do not have insurance
Transportation: Commute: 98.1% car, 0.0% public transportation, 0.6% walk, 1.3% work from home; Mean travel time to work: 25.2 minutes

MOUNT AUBURN (town). Covers a land area of 0.215 square miles and a water area of 0.016 square miles. Located at 39.81° N. Lat; 85.19° W. Long. Elevation is 991 feet.
Population: 122; Growth (since 2000): 62.7%; Density: 567.7 persons per square mile; Race: 100.0% White, 0.0% Black/African American, 0.0% Asian, 0.0% American Indian/Alaska Native, 0.0% Native Hawaiian/Other Pacific Islander, 0.0% Two or more races, 0.0% Hispanic of any race; Average household size: 2.54; Median age: 40.2; Age under 18: 23.0%; Age 65 and over: 16.4%; Males per 100 females: 95.0; Marriage status: 22.3% never married, 31.9% now married, 0.0% separated, 17.0% widowed, 28.7% divorced; Foreign born: 0.0%; Speak English only: 100.0%; With disability: 9.8%; Veterans: 10.6%; Ancestry: 18.9% German, 13.1% Irish, 7.4% English, 4.9% American, 0.8% Czechoslovakian
Employment: 11.3% management, business, and financial, 0.0% computer, engineering, and science, 3.2% education, legal, community service, arts, and media, 9.7% healthcare practitioners, 11.3% service, 25.8% sales and office, 9.7% natural resources, construction, and maintenance, 29.0% production, transportation, and material moving
Income: Per capita: $24,457; Median household: $37,500; Average household: $58,640; Households with income of $100,000 or more: 20.9%; Poverty rate: 19.7%
Educational Attainment: High school diploma or higher: 92.8%; Bachelor's degree or higher: 10.8%; Graduate/professional degree or higher: 4.8%
Housing: Homeownership rate: 79.2%; Median home value: $75,000; Median year structure built: 1952; Homeowner vacancy rate: 0.0%; Median selected monthly owner costs: $633 with a mortgage, $375 without a mortgage; Median gross rent: $463 per month; Rental vacancy rate: 0.0%
Health Insurance: 84.4% have insurance; 71.3% have private insurance; 36.1% have public insurance; 15.6% do not have insurance; 0.0% of children under 18 do not have insurance
Transportation: Commute: 98.4% car, 0.0% public transportation, 0.0% walk, 1.6% work from home; Mean travel time to work: 24.1 minutes

RICHMOND (city). County seat. Covers a land area of 23.915 square miles and a water area of 0.157 square miles. Located at 39.83° N. Lat; 84.89° W. Long. Elevation is 981 feet.
History: Richmond was founded in 1805 by soldiers who had been with George Rogers Clark at the capture of Fort Sackville. They were joined by other settlers, many of them Quakers who founded Earlham College in 1847. Richmond was known for its greenhouses and rose cultivation, including the Richmond Rose hybrid developed in 1905.
Population: 35,819; Growth (since 2000): -8.4%; Density: 1,497.8 persons per square mile; Race: 84.6% White, 8.3% Black/African American, 1.6% Asian, 0.2% American Indian/Alaska Native, 0.0% Native Hawaiian/Other Pacific Islander, 3.5% Two or more races, 4.5% Hispanic of any race; Average household size: 2.33; Median age: 39.3; Age under 18: 21.2%; Age 65 and over: 18.4%; Males per 100 females: 91.8; Marriage status: 32.3% never married, 41.6% now married, 1.4% separated, 8.7% widowed, 17.4% divorced; Foreign born: 3.3%; Speak English only: 94.7%; With disability: 21.8%; Veterans: 10.2%; Ancestry: 18.3% German, 13.4% Irish, 9.0% English, 8.5% American, 2.3% Italian
Employment: 9.3% management, business, and financial, 2.5% computer, engineering, and science, 9.7% education, legal, community service, arts, and media, 6.8% healthcare practitioners, 22.2% service, 21.7% sales and office, 5.8% natural resources, construction, and maintenance, 21.9% production, transportation, and material moving
Income: Per capita: $20,907; Median household: $33,381; Average household: $50,371; Households with income of $100,000 or more: 11.1%; Poverty rate: 23.4%
Educational Attainment: High school diploma or higher: 82.6%; Bachelor's degree or higher: 18.1%; Graduate/professional degree or higher: 8.1%

School District(s)

Excel Center - Richmond (11-12)
Enrollment: 294. . . . . (317) 524-3734
Richmond Community Schools (PK-12)
Enrollment: 5,546 . . . . (765) 973-3300

Four-year College(s)

Bethany Theological Seminary (Private, Not-for-profit, Church of Brethren)
Enrollment: 47. . . . . (765) 983-1800
Earlham College (Private, Not-for-profit, Friends)
Enrollment: 1,128 . . . . (765) 983-1200
Tuition: In-state $45,750; Out-of-state $45,750
Indiana University-East (Public)
Enrollment: 3,490 . . . . (765) 973-8200
Tuition: In-state $7,207; Out-of-state $19,038

Vocational/Technical School(s)

PJ's College of Cosmetology-Richmond (Private, For-profit)
Enrollment: 34. . . . . (812) 285-8805
Tuition: $15,100

Housing: Homeownership rate: 56.8%; Median home value: $85,300; Median year structure built: 1956; Homeowner vacancy rate: 3.1%; Median selected monthly owner costs: $880 with a mortgage, $345 without a mortgage; Median gross rent: $653 per month; Rental vacancy rate: 18.0%
Health Insurance: 85.9% have insurance; 54.5% have private insurance; 45.4% have public insurance; 14.1% do not have insurance; 9.7% of children under 18 do not have insurance
Hospitals: Reid Hospital & Health Care Services (233 beds)
Newspapers: Palladium-Item (daily circulation 16,800)
Transportation: Commute: 88.2% car, 0.6% public transportation, 5.0% walk, 2.5% work from home; Mean travel time to work: 15.1 minutes
Airports: Richmond Municipal (general aviation)

Additional Information Contacts
City of Richmond . . . . (765) 983-7200
http://www.richmondindiana.gov

SPRING GROVE (town). Covers a land area of 0.317 square miles and a water area of 0.001 square miles. Located at 39.85° N. Lat; 84.89° W. Long. Elevation is 984 feet.
Population: 454; Growth (since 2000): 17.6%; Density: 1,432.8 persons per square mile; Race: 88.1% White, 4.6% Black/African American, 4.6% Asian, 0.0% American Indian/Alaska Native, 0.0% Native Hawaiian/Other Pacific Islander, 2.6% Two or more races, 2.0% Hispanic of any race; Average household size: 2.58; Median age: 46.9; Age under 18: 18.7%; Age 65 and over: 31.1%; Males per 100 females: 73.7; Marriage status: 18.8% never married, 48.5% now married, 2.5% separated, 19.5% widowed, 13.3% divorced; Foreign born: 6.2%; Speak English only: 98.6%; With disability: 12.0%; Veterans: 14.6%; Ancestry: 25.3% German, 16.1% Irish, 7.9% English, 5.9% American, 5.3% Dutch
Employment: 15.9% management, business, and financial, 2.4% computer, engineering, and science, 20.7% education, legal, community service, arts, and media, 9.8% healthcare practitioners, 6.7% service, 23.2% sales and office, 3.7% natural resources, construction, and maintenance, 17.7% production, transportation, and material moving
Income: Per capita: $21,515; Median household: $61,750; Average household: $64,145; Households with income of $100,000 or more: 17.2%; Poverty rate: 5.0%
Educational Attainment: High school diploma or higher: 87.1%; Bachelor's degree or higher: 25.8%; Graduate/professional degree or higher: 14.6%
Housing: Homeownership rate: 78.4%; Median home value: $101,900; Median year structure built: 1955; Homeowner vacancy rate: 3.5%; Median selected monthly owner costs: $971 with a mortgage, $375 without a mortgage; Median gross rent: $817 per month; Rental vacancy rate: 0.0%
Health Insurance: 92.5% have insurance; 77.9% have private insurance; 32.4% have public insurance; 7.5% do not have insurance; 7.8% of children under 18 do not have insurance
Transportation: Commute: 90.1% car, 0.0% public transportation, 9.9% walk, 0.0% work from home; Mean travel time to work: 17.5 minutes

WHITEWATER (town). Covers a land area of 0.080 square miles and a water area of 0 square miles. Located at 39.94° N. Lat; 84.83° W. Long. Elevation is 1,129 feet.
Population: 77; Growth (since 2000): -1.3%; Density: 964.7 persons per square mile; Race: 100.0% White, 0.0% Black/African American, 0.0% Asian, 0.0% American Indian/Alaska Native, 0.0% Native Hawaiian/Other Pacific Islander, 0.0% Two or more races, 0.0% Hispanic of any race; Average household size: 2.96; Median age: 32.3; Age under 18: 31.2%; Age 65 and over: 20.8%; Males per 100 females: 124.3; Marriage status: 12.7% never married, 72.7% now married, 0.0% separated, 1.8% widowed, 12.7% divorced; Foreign born: 0.0%; Speak English only: 100.0%; With disability: 20.8%; Veterans: 17.0%; Ancestry: 19.5% English, 14.3% German, 11.7% American, 9.1% Irish, 1.3% Dutch
Employment: 13.3% management, business, and financial, 0.0% computer, engineering, and science, 0.0% education, legal, community service, arts, and media, 6.7% healthcare practitioners, 26.7% service, 23.3% sales and office, 20.0% natural resources, construction, and maintenance, 10.0% production, transportation, and material moving
Income: Per capita: $17,008; Median household: $37,500; Average household: $47,050; Households with income of $100,000 or more: 7.7%; Poverty rate: 19.5%
Educational Attainment: High school diploma or higher: 73.1%; Bachelor's degree or higher: 3.8%; Graduate/professional degree or higher: n/a
Housing: Homeownership rate: 88.5%; Median home value: $61,300; Median year structure built: 1942; Homeowner vacancy rate: 0.0%; Median selected monthly owner costs: $813 with a mortgage, $370 without a mortgage; Median gross rent: $675 per month; Rental vacancy rate: 0.0%
Health Insurance: 75.3% have insurance; 42.9% have private insurance; 40.3% have public insurance; 24.7% do not have insurance; 54.2% of children under 18 do not have insurance
Transportation: Commute: 93.3% car, 0.0% public transportation, 0.0% walk, 6.7% work from home; Mean travel time to work: 16.6 minutes

WILLIAMSBURG (unincorporated postal area)
ZCTA: 47393
Covers a land area of 37.210 square miles and a water area of 0.079 square miles. Located at 39.96° N. Lat; 85.00° W. Long. Elevation is 1,066 feet.
Population: 1,795; Growth (since 2000): 14.9%; Density: 48.2 persons per square mile; Race: 93.6% White, 0.0% Black/African American, 0.8% Asian, 0.0% American Indian/Alaska Native, 0.0% Native Hawaiian/Other Pacific Islander, 4.2% Two or more races, 3.2% Hispanic of any race; Average household size: 3.38; Median age: 39.3; Age under 18: 29.8%; Age 65 and over: 9.5%; Males per 100 females: 102.9; Marriage status: 23.8% never married, 60.2% now married, 0.5% separated, 5.7% widowed, 10.4% divorced; Foreign born: 0.8%; Speak English only: 88.1%; With disability: 16.8%; Veterans: 6.5%; Ancestry: 37.9% German, 15.2% Irish, 10.7% American, 7.4% Welsh, 7.0% English
Employment: 15.4% management, business, and financial, 3.5% computer, engineering, and science, 11.5% education, legal, community service, arts, and media, 10.4% healthcare practitioners, 11.8% service, 18.6% sales and office, 14.9% natural resources, construction, and maintenance, 13.9% production, transportation, and material moving
Income: Per capita: $21,372; Median household: $67,723; Average household: $71,482; Households with income of $100,000 or more: 22.2%; Poverty rate: 15.1%
Educational Attainment: High school diploma or higher: 85.3%; Bachelor's degree or higher: 22.4%; Graduate/professional degree or higher: 8.0%
Housing: Homeownership rate: 87.2%; Median home value: $136,600; Median year structure built: 1966; Homeowner vacancy rate: 0.0%; Median selected monthly owner costs: $1,111 with a mortgage, $378 without a mortgage; Median gross rent: $921 per month; Rental vacancy rate: 0.0%
Health Insurance: 80.1% have insurance; 55.2% have private insurance; 33.0% have public insurance; 19.9% do not have insurance; 26.7% of children under 18 do not have insurance
Transportation: Commute: 89.5% car, 0.0% public transportation, 0.0% walk, 10.5% work from home; Mean travel time to work: 30.0 minutes

Wells County

Located in eastern Indiana; drained by the Wabash and Salamonie Rivers. Covers a land area of 368.087 square miles, a water area of 2.161 square miles, and is located in the Eastern Time Zone at 40.74° N. Lat., 85.21° W. Long. The county was founded in 1835. County seat is Bluffton.

Wells County is part of the Fort Wayne, IN Metropolitan Statistical Area. The entire metro area includes: Allen County, IN; Wells County, IN; Whitley County, IN

Weather Station: Bluffton 1 N — Elevation: 825 feet

	Jan	Feb	Mar	Apr	May	Jun	Jul	Aug	Sep	Oct	Nov	Dec
High	32	35	47	60	71	80	84	82	76	63	49	37
Low	17	19	28	39	50	60	63	61	53	41	32	22
Precip	2.1	2.1	2.5	3.4	4.5	4.0	4.3	3.6	3.0	2.8	3.1	2.7
Snow	7.3	6.7	3.3	0.7	0.0	0.0	tr	0.0	0.0	0.1	1.0	5.1

High and Low temperatures in degrees Fahrenheit; Precipitation and Snow in inches

Population: 27,832; Growth (since 2000): 0.8%; Density: 75.6 persons per square mile; Race: 96.6% White, 0.8% Black/African American, 0.5% Asian, 0.2% American Indian/Alaska Native, 0.0% Native Hawaiian/Other Pacific Islander, 0.9% two or more races, 2.8% Hispanic of any race; Average household size: 2.49; Median age: 39.8; Age under 18: 24.7%; Age 65 and over: 17.3%; Males per 100 females: 96.9; Marriage status: 22.2% never married, 60.2% now married, 1.1% separated, 7.2% widowed, 10.4% divorced; Foreign born: 1.5%; Speak English only: 96.7%; With disability: 13.1%; Veterans: 8.3%; Ancestry: 30.9% German, 11.7% American, 8.3% Irish, 7.1% English, 4.4% Swiss
Religion: Six largest groups: 8.0% Holiness, 7.1% European Free-Church, 7.0% Methodist/Pietist, 6.9% Baptist, 5.4% Non-denominational Protestant, 4.3% Lutheran
Economy: Unemployment rate: 2.8%; Leading industries: 16.4 % other services (except public administration); 13.2 % retail trade; 10.1 % construction; Farms: 636 totaling 200,334 acres; Company size: 1 employs 1,000 or more persons, 0 employ 500 to 999 persons, 24 employ 100 to 499 persons, 597 employ less than 100 persons; Business ownership: 516 women-owned, n/a Black-owned, 31 Hispanic-owned, n/a Asian-owned, n/a American Indian/Alaska Native-owned

Employment: 12.9% management, business, and financial, 3.2% computer, engineering, and science, 5.2% education, legal, community service, arts, and media, 6.0% healthcare practitioners, 15.9% service, 22.7% sales and office, 10.8% natural resources, construction, and maintenance, 23.3% production, transportation, and material moving
Income: Per capita: $25,850; Median household: $53,038; Average household: $64,490; Households with income of $100,000 or more: 17.8%; Poverty rate: 11.0%
Educational Attainment: High school diploma or higher: 91.3%; Bachelor's degree or higher: 18.6%; Graduate/professional degree or higher: 5.9%
Housing: Homeownership rate: 79.4%; Median home value: $121,000; Median year structure built: 1969; Homeowner vacancy rate: 1.2%; Median selected monthly owner costs: $1,014 with a mortgage, $355 without a mortgage; Median gross rent: $662 per month; Rental vacancy rate: 13.5%
Vital Statistics: Birth rate: 119.7 per 10,000 population; Death rate: 87.6 per 10,000 population; Age-adjusted cancer mortality rate: 187.1 deaths per 100,000 population
Health Insurance: 91.7% have insurance; 73.3% have private insurance; 31.5% have public insurance; 8.3% do not have insurance; 9.1% of children under 18 do not have insurance
Health Care: Physicians: 13.3 per 10,000 population; Dentists: 3.6 per 10,000 population; Hospital beds: 19.4 per 10,000 population; Hospital admissions: 683.9 per 10,000 population
Transportation: Commute: 93.7% car, 0.1% public transportation, 1.5% walk, 4.1% work from home; Mean travel time to work: 21.3 minutes
2016 Presidential Election: 75.3% Trump, 19.5% Clinton, 4.1% Johnson, 0.2% Stein
National and State Parks: Ouabache State Park
Additional Information Contacts
Wells Government. . . . . (260) 824-6479
http://www.wellscounty.org

Wells County Communities

BLUFFTON (city). County seat. Covers a land area of 8.232 square miles and a water area of 0.129 square miles. Located at 40.74° N. Lat; 85.17° W. Long. Elevation is 827 feet.
History: Established in the mid-1800's, Bluffton was built on the bluffs overlooking the Wabash River.
Population: 9,823; Growth (since 2000): 3.0%; Density: 1,193.3 persons per square mile; Race: 96.4% White, 1.1% Black/African American, 0.5% Asian, 0.0% American Indian/Alaska Native, 0.0% Native Hawaiian/Other Pacific Islander, 1.1% Two or more races, 3.5% Hispanic of any race; Average household size: 2.28; Median age: 38.6; Age under 18: 25.2%; Age 65 and over: 18.5%; Males per 100 females: 92.3; Marriage status: 26.9% never married, 51.7% now married, 1.6% separated, 8.2% widowed, 13.2% divorced; Foreign born: 0.7%; Speak English only: 97.1%; With disability: 14.9%; Veterans: 8.2%; Ancestry: 29.2% German, 12.5% American, 7.8% English, 7.4% Irish, 5.3% Swiss
Employment: 10.2% management, business, and financial, 2.6% computer, engineering, and science, 5.1% education, legal, community service, arts, and media, 7.1% healthcare practitioners, 19.9% service, 22.4% sales and office, 6.5% natural resources, construction, and maintenance, 26.2% production, transportation, and material moving
Income: Per capita: $23,041; Median household: $40,194; Average household: $52,946; Households with income of $100,000 or more: 11.6%; Poverty rate: 17.6%
Educational Attainment: High school diploma or higher: 90.8%; Bachelor's degree or higher: 16.6%; Graduate/professional degree or higher: 6.3%

School District(s)

M S D Bluffton-harrison (PK-12)
Enrollment: 1,463 . . . . (260) 824-2620
Northern Wells Community Schools (PK-12)
Enrollment: 2,349 . . . . (260) 622-4125

Housing: Homeownership rate: 66.2%; Median home value: $94,900; Median year structure built: 1968; Homeowner vacancy rate: 1.1%; Median selected monthly owner costs: $828 with a mortgage, $345 without a mortgage; Median gross rent: $560 per month; Rental vacancy rate: 10.5%
Health Insurance: 90.4% have insurance; 63.2% have private insurance; 42.3% have public insurance; 9.6% do not have insurance; 10.1% of children under 18 do not have insurance
Hospitals: Bluffton Regional Medical Center (79 beds)
Safety: Violent crime rate: 7.0 per 10,000 population; Property crime rate: n/a per 10,000 population
Newspapers: News-Banner (daily circulation 4,700)
Transportation: Commute: 93.6% car, 0.0% public transportation, 2.0% walk, 2.9% work from home; Mean travel time to work: 18.9 minutes
Additional Information Contacts
City of Bluffton . . . . (260) 824-1520
http://www.ci.bluffton.in.us

CRAIGVILLE (unincorporated postal area)
ZCTA: 46731
Covers a land area of 15.909 square miles and a water area of 0.029 square miles. Located at 40.79° N. Lat; 85.10° W. Long. Elevation is 850 feet.
Population: 518; Growth (since 2000): -20.4%; Density: 32.6 persons per square mile; Race: 94.0% White, 0.0% Black/African American, 0.0% Asian, 0.0% American Indian/Alaska Native, 0.0% Native Hawaiian/Other Pacific Islander, 0.0% Two or more races, 6.0% Hispanic of any race; Average household size: 2.34; Median age: 48.6; Age under 18: 16.2%; Age 65 and over: 19.1%; Males per 100 females: 104.0; Marriage status: 20.3% never married, 55.8% now married, 0.0% separated, 9.2% widowed, 14.7% divorced; Foreign born: 3.1%; Speak English only: 91.9%; With disability: 25.3%; Veterans: 5.8%; Ancestry: 24.5% German, 15.1% American, 13.5% Irish, 11.8% Swiss, 4.8% Italian
Employment: 11.4% management, business, and financial, 12.1% computer, engineering, and science, 2.9% education, legal, community service, arts, and media, 5.9% healthcare practitioners, 3.7% service, 19.9% sales and office, 32.7% natural resources, construction, and maintenance, 11.4% production, transportation, and material moving
Income: Per capita: $26,427; Median household: $45,947; Average household: $60,125; Households with income of $100,000 or more: 13.1%; Poverty rate: 6.0%
Educational Attainment: High school diploma or higher: 75.1%; Bachelor's degree or higher: 7.2%; Graduate/professional degree or higher: 2.1%
Housing: Homeownership rate: 79.2%; Median home value: n/a; Median year structure built: Before 1940; Homeowner vacancy rate: 0.0%; Median selected monthly owner costs: $1,250 with a mortgage, $286 without a mortgage; Median gross rent: $536 per month; Rental vacancy rate: 0.0%
Health Insurance: 93.6% have insurance; 73.9% have private insurance; 26.8% have public insurance; 6.4% do not have insurance; 0.0% of children under 18 do not have insurance
Transportation: Commute: 86.0% car, 0.0% public transportation, 3.3% walk, 10.7% work from home; Mean travel time to work: 21.4 minutes

KEYSTONE (unincorporated postal area)
ZCTA: 46759
Covers a land area of 29.605 square miles and a water area of 0.022 square miles. Located at 40.60° N. Lat; 85.18° W. Long. Elevation is 860 feet.
Population: 397; Growth (since 2000): -48.1%; Density: 13.4 persons per square mile; Race: 89.9% White, 0.0% Black/African American, 0.0% Asian, 0.0% American Indian/Alaska Native, 0.0% Native Hawaiian/Other Pacific Islander, 10.1% Two or more races, 0.0% Hispanic of any race; Average household size: 2.45; Median age: 39.9; Age under 18: 31.2%; Age 65 and over: 19.1%; Males per 100 females: 92.9; Marriage status: 8.9% never married, 68.6% now married, 5.4% separated, 16.8% widowed, 5.7% divorced; Foreign born: 0.0%; Speak English only: 99.0%; With disability: 10.8%; Veterans: 8.4%; Ancestry: 31.0% German, 14.9% American, 12.8% English, 7.3% Irish, 5.3% Welsh
Employment: 4.8% management, business, and financial, 0.0% computer, engineering, and science, 4.8% education, legal, community service, arts, and media, 8.2% healthcare practitioners, 21.2% service, 15.8% sales and office, 25.3% natural resources, construction, and maintenance, 19.9% production, transportation, and material moving
Income: Per capita: $16,632; Median household: $36,739; Average household: $39,902; Households with income of $100,000 or more: n/a; Poverty rate: 25.7%
Educational Attainment: High school diploma or higher: 87.2%; Bachelor's degree or higher: 7.0%; Graduate/professional degree or higher: 4.4%

Housing: Homeownership rate: 100.0%; Median home value: $92,400; Median year structure built: Before 1940; Homeowner vacancy rate: 0.0%; Median selected monthly owner costs: $773 with a mortgage, $341 without a mortgage; Median gross rent: n/a per month; Rental vacancy rate: 0.0%
Health Insurance: 72.3% have insurance; 44.1% have private insurance; 40.6% have public insurance; 27.7% do not have insurance; 40.3% of children under 18 do not have insurance
Transportation: Commute: 100.0% car, 0.0% public transportation, 0.0% walk, 0.0% work from home; Mean travel time to work: 30.0 minutes

LIBERTY CENTER (unincorporated postal area)
ZCTA: 46766
Covers a land area of 20.262 square miles and a water area of 0.062 square miles. Located at 40.71° N. Lat; 85.28° W. Long. Elevation is 853 feet.
Population: 830; Growth (since 2000): 31.5%; Density: 41.0 persons per square mile; Race: 100.0% White, 0.0% Black/African American, 0.0% Asian, 0.0% American Indian/Alaska Native, 0.0% Native Hawaiian/Other Pacific Islander, 0.0% Two or more races, 6.7% Hispanic of any race; Average household size: 2.31; Median age: 50.6; Age under 18: 16.4%; Age 65 and over: 15.3%; Males per 100 females: 110.8; Marriage status: 24.3% never married, 60.4% now married, 0.0% separated, 5.2% widowed, 10.1% divorced; Foreign born: 0.0%; Speak English only: 100.0%; With disability: 5.7%; Veterans: 2.3%; Ancestry: 45.3% German, 13.1% Scottish, 11.3% American, 8.8% Irish, 1.8% English
Employment: 20.0% management, business, and financial, 3.0% computer, engineering, and science, 3.0% education, legal, community service, arts, and media, 3.0% healthcare practitioners, 5.2% service, 24.3% sales and office, 19.4% natural resources, construction, and maintenance, 22.1% production, transportation, and material moving
Income: Per capita: $29,230; Median household: $56,574; Average household: $66,488; Households with income of $100,000 or more: 18.6%; Poverty rate: 4.5%
Educational Attainment: High school diploma or higher: 91.2%; Bachelor's degree or higher: 11.9%; Graduate/professional degree or higher: 7.0%
Housing: Homeownership rate: 76.7%; Median home value: $130,900; Median year structure built: Before 1940; Homeowner vacancy rate: 0.0%; Median selected monthly owner costs: $1,053 with a mortgage, $374 without a mortgage; Median gross rent: $726 per month; Rental vacancy rate: 0.0%
Health Insurance: 93.4% have insurance; 87.3% have private insurance; 24.2% have public insurance; 6.6% do not have insurance; 0.0% of children under 18 do not have insurance
Transportation: Commute: 88.2% car, 0.0% public transportation, 0.6% walk, 11.2% work from home; Mean travel time to work: 17.5 minutes

OSSIAN (town). Covers a land area of 1.429 square miles and a water area of 0.008 square miles. Located at 40.88° N. Lat; 85.17° W. Long. Elevation is 840 feet.
History: Laid out 1850.
Population: 3,899; Growth (since 2000): 32.5%; Density: 2,728.7 persons per square mile; Race: 96.2% White, 0.0% Black/African American, 0.8% Asian, 0.0% American Indian/Alaska Native, 0.0% Native Hawaiian/Other Pacific Islander, 0.4% Two or more races, 3.3% Hispanic of any race; Average household size: 2.67; Median age: 34.5; Age under 18: 27.6%; Age 65 and over: 14.9%; Males per 100 females: 90.7; Marriage status: 20.9% never married, 59.8% now married, 0.4% separated, 10.0% widowed, 9.3% divorced; Foreign born: 1.0%; Speak English only: 97.4%; With disability: 14.6%; Veterans: 8.6%; Ancestry: 27.7% German, 12.1% English, 11.7% Irish, 7.4% American, 4.9% French
Employment: 12.8% management, business, and financial, 4.8% computer, engineering, and science, 5.7% education, legal, community service, arts, and media, 2.3% healthcare practitioners, 22.0% service, 23.0% sales and office, 6.4% natural resources, construction, and maintenance, 23.0% production, transportation, and material moving
Income: Per capita: $23,846; Median household: $59,818; Average household: $63,385; Households with income of $100,000 or more: 15.0%; Poverty rate: 6.7%
Educational Attainment: High school diploma or higher: 90.1%; Bachelor's degree or higher: 17.5%; Graduate/professional degree or higher: 5.2%

School District(s)
Northern Wells Community Schools (PK-12)
Enrollment: 2,349 . . . . (260) 622-4125
Housing: Homeownership rate: 80.1%; Median home value: $118,900; Median year structure built: 1982; Homeowner vacancy rate: 3.1%; Median selected monthly owner costs: $843 with a mortgage, $238 without a mortgage; Median gross rent: $694 per month; Rental vacancy rate: 20.9%
Health Insurance: 88.7% have insurance; 81.3% have private insurance; 18.3% have public insurance; 11.3% do not have insurance; 17.3% of children under 18 do not have insurance
Newspapers: Ossian Journal (weekly circulation 700)
Transportation: Commute: 94.8% car, 0.0% public transportation, 0.0% walk, 5.2% work from home; Mean travel time to work: 22.4 minutes
Additional Information Contacts
Town of Ossian . . . . (260) 622-4251
http://www.ossianin.com

PONETO (town). Covers a land area of 0.115 square miles and a water area of 0.001 square miles. Located at 40.66° N. Lat; 85.22° W. Long. Elevation is 850 feet.
Population: 163; Growth (since 2000): -32.1%; Density: 1,420.8 persons per square mile; Race: 98.2% White, 0.0% Black/African American, 0.6% Asian, 0.0% American Indian/Alaska Native, 0.0% Native Hawaiian/Other Pacific Islander, 0.0% Two or more races, 4.3% Hispanic of any race; Average household size: 2.81; Median age: 37.8; Age under 18: 22.7%; Age 65 and over: 9.2%; Males per 100 females: 93.0; Marriage status: 28.7% never married, 53.7% now married, 0.7% separated, 2.9% widowed, 14.7% divorced; Foreign born: 0.6%; Speak English only: 96.8%; With disability: 12.3%; Veterans: 9.5%; Ancestry: 15.3% American, 14.7% German, 14.1% Irish, 12.9% English, 3.7% Polish
Employment: 9.6% management, business, and financial, 2.4% computer, engineering, and science, 2.4% education, legal, community service, arts, and media, 2.4% healthcare practitioners, 22.9% service, 21.7% sales and office, 10.8% natural resources, construction, and maintenance, 27.7% production, transportation, and material moving
Income: Per capita: $18,493; Median household: $47,500; Average household: $49,331; Households with income of $100,000 or more: 5.2%; Poverty rate: 17.8%
Educational Attainment: High school diploma or higher: 88.7%; Bachelor's degree or higher: 7.8%; Graduate/professional degree or higher: n/a

School District(s)
Southern Wells Com Schools (PK-12)
Enrollment: 664 . . . . (765) 728-5537
Housing: Homeownership rate: 79.3%; Median home value: $58,500; Median year structure built: Before 1940; Homeowner vacancy rate: 0.0%; Median selected monthly owner costs: $825 with a mortgage, $420 without a mortgage; Median gross rent: $600 per month; Rental vacancy rate: 0.0%
Health Insurance: 92.0% have insurance; 65.0% have private insurance; 40.5% have public insurance; 8.0% do not have insurance; 7.1% of children under 18 do not have insurance
Transportation: Commute: 94.0% car, 0.0% public transportation, 0.0% walk, 6.0% work from home; Mean travel time to work: 22.6 minutes

UNIONDALE (town). Covers a land area of 0.210 square miles and a water area of 0.002 square miles. Located at 40.83° N. Lat; 85.24° W. Long. Elevation is 814 feet.
History: Laid out 1883.
Population: 303; Growth (since 2000): 9.4%; Density: 1,443.8 persons per square mile; Race: 92.4% White, 0.0% Black/African American, 0.7% Asian, 5.9% American Indian/Alaska Native, 0.0% Native Hawaiian/Other Pacific Islander, 1.0% Two or more races, 3.6% Hispanic of any race; Average household size: 2.68; Median age: 31.3; Age under 18: 28.7%; Age 65 and over: 9.6%; Males per 100 females: 96.2; Marriage status: 21.5% never married, 54.8% now married, 1.8% separated, 5.3% widowed, 18.4% divorced; Foreign born: 2.3%; Speak English only: 94.0%; With disability: 16.2%; Veterans: 9.3%; Ancestry: 37.3% German, 14.2% English, 9.2% Irish, 3.6% American, 2.0% Scotch-Irish
Employment: 8.7% management, business, and financial, 2.2% computer, engineering, and science, 3.6% education, legal, community service, arts, and media, 6.5% healthcare practitioners, 7.2% service, 21.0% sales and office, 15.9% natural resources, construction, and maintenance, 34.8% production, transportation, and material moving

Income: Per capita: $20,163; Median household: $41,719; Average household: $52,273; Households with income of $100,000 or more: 11.5%; Poverty rate: 18.3%
Educational Attainment: High school diploma or higher: 87.6%; Bachelor's degree or higher: 10.6%; Graduate/professional degree or higher: 2.9%
Housing: Homeownership rate: 81.4%; Median home value: $74,100; Median year structure built: Before 1940; Homeowner vacancy rate: 0.0%; Median selected monthly owner costs: $675 with a mortgage, $311 without a mortgage; Median gross rent: $732 per month; Rental vacancy rate: 0.0%
Health Insurance: 92.7% have insurance; 66.0% have private insurance; 35.6% have public insurance; 7.3% do not have insurance; 0.0% of children under 18 do not have insurance
Transportation: Commute: 97.8% car, 0.0% public transportation, 1.4% walk, 0.7% work from home; Mean travel time to work: 22.1 minutes

VERA CRUZ (town). Covers a land area of 0.101 square miles and a water area of <.001 square miles. Located at 40.70° N. Lat; 85.08° W. Long. Elevation is 827 feet.
History: Laid out 1848.
Population: 95; Growth (since 2000): 72.7%; Density: 936.4 persons per square mile; Race: 90.5% White, 0.0% Black/African American, 0.0% Asian, 0.0% American Indian/Alaska Native, 0.0% Native Hawaiian/Other Pacific Islander, 9.5% Two or more races, 0.0% Hispanic of any race; Average household size: 2.38; Median age: 31.6; Age under 18: 28.4%; Age 65 and over: 12.6%; Males per 100 females: 100.0; Marriage status: 8.6% never married, 71.4% now married, 0.0% separated, 1.4% widowed, 18.6% divorced; Foreign born: 0.0%; Speak English only: 100.0%; With disability: 5.3%; Veterans: 4.4%; Ancestry: 22.1% German, 22.1% Irish, 16.8% American, 10.5% Swiss, 3.2% French
Employment: 4.5% management, business, and financial, 2.3% computer, engineering, and science, 9.1% education, legal, community service, arts, and media, 9.1% healthcare practitioners, 0.0% service, 20.5% sales and office, 15.9% natural resources, construction, and maintenance, 38.6% production, transportation, and material moving
Income: Per capita: $19,623; Median household: $42,000; Average household: $51,630; Households with income of $100,000 or more: 7.5%; Poverty rate: 26.6%
Educational Attainment: High school diploma or higher: 86.2%; Bachelor's degree or higher: 20.0%; Graduate/professional degree or higher: n/a
Housing: Homeownership rate: 65.0%; Median home value: $80,000; Median year structure built: Before 1940; Homeowner vacancy rate: 0.0%; Median selected monthly owner costs: $908 with a mortgage, $331 without a mortgage; Median gross rent: $567 per month; Rental vacancy rate: 0.0%
Health Insurance: 80.0% have insurance; 78.9% have private insurance; 12.6% have public insurance; 20.0% do not have insurance; 25.0% of children under 18 do not have insurance
Transportation: Commute: 93.2% car, 0.0% public transportation, 4.5% walk, 0.0% work from home; Mean travel time to work: 28.5 minutes

ZANESVILLE (town). Covers a land area of 0.821 square miles and a water area of 0.010 square miles. Located at 40.92° N. Lat; 85.28° W. Long. Elevation is 814 feet.
Population: 565; Growth (since 2000): -6.1%; Density: 688.0 persons per square mile; Race: 92.2% White, 0.0% Black/African American, 0.0% Asian, 0.0% American Indian/Alaska Native, 0.0% Native Hawaiian/Other Pacific Islander, 2.5% Two or more races, 6.5% Hispanic of any race; Average household size: 2.32; Median age: 44.2; Age under 18: 19.8%; Age 65 and over: 14.5%; Males per 100 females: 98.7; Marriage status: 15.7% never married, 63.3% now married, 0.0% separated, 4.6% widowed, 16.4% divorced; Foreign born: 6.0%; Speak English only: 92.0%; With disability: 13.3%; Veterans: 5.5%; Ancestry: 29.9% German, 11.9% Irish, 10.6% American, 5.5% English, 3.4% Welsh
Employment: 10.8% management, business, and financial, 0.7% computer, engineering, and science, 7.5% education, legal, community service, arts, and media, 7.5% healthcare practitioners, 15.4% service, 22.6% sales and office, 7.2% natural resources, construction, and maintenance, 28.2% production, transportation, and material moving
Income: Per capita: $25,379; Median household: $51,389; Average household: $58,829; Households with income of $100,000 or more: 13.6%; Poverty rate: 5.1%
Educational Attainment: High school diploma or higher: 89.5%; Bachelor's degree or higher: 13.4%; Graduate/professional degree or higher: 4.3%
Housing: Homeownership rate: 93.4%; Median home value: $93,600; Median year structure built: 1968; Homeowner vacancy rate: 2.6%; Median selected monthly owner costs: $855 with a mortgage, $429 without a mortgage; Median gross rent: $788 per month; Rental vacancy rate: 27.3%
Health Insurance: 95.2% have insurance; 75.8% have private insurance; 32.2% have public insurance; 4.8% do not have insurance; 0.0% of children under 18 do not have insurance
Transportation: Commute: 93.4% car, 0.0% public transportation, 0.3% walk, 6.3% work from home; Mean travel time to work: 21.7 minutes

White County

Located in northwestern Indiana; bounded on the east by the Tippecanoe River; drained by the Tippecanoe River. Covers a land area of 505.125 square miles, a water area of 3.555 square miles, and is located in the Eastern Time Zone at 40.75° N. Lat., 86.86° W. Long. The county was founded in 1834. County seat is Monticello.
Population: 24,279; Growth (since 2000): -3.9%; Density: 48.1 persons per square mile; Race: 92.0% White, 0.5% Black/African American, 0.2% Asian, 0.3% American Indian/Alaska Native, 0.0% Native Hawaiian/Other Pacific Islander, 1.7% two or more races, 7.9% Hispanic of any race; Average household size: 2.47; Median age: 42.0; Age under 18: 23.4%; Age 65 and over: 18.9%; Males per 100 females: 96.8; Marriage status: 22.6% never married, 57.3% now married, 0.8% separated, 7.7% widowed, 12.4% divorced; Foreign born: 4.6%; Speak English only: 92.0%; With disability: 16.3%; Veterans: 9.7%; Ancestry: 24.8% German, 11.5% Irish, 8.6% American, 8.1% English, 2.8% Polish
Religion: Six largest groups: 12.1% Baptist, 10.0% Catholicism, 7.7% Methodist/Pietist, 4.2% Non-denominational Protestant, 3.4% Presbyterian-Reformed, 3.4% Lutheran
Economy: Unemployment rate: 3.2%; Leading industries: 15.4 % retail trade; 11.2 % construction; 10.2 % accommodation and food services; Farms: 631 totaling 288,195 acres; Company size: 0 employ 1,000 or more persons, 1 employs 500 to 999 persons, 16 employ 100 to 499 persons, 573 employ less than 100 persons; Business ownership: 572 women-owned, n/a Black-owned, 51 Hispanic-owned, n/a Asian-owned, n/a American Indian/Alaska Native-owned
Employment: 12.2% management, business, and financial, 2.5% computer, engineering, and science, 7.0% education, legal, community service, arts, and media, 5.0% healthcare practitioners, 14.6% service, 20.1% sales and office, 13.4% natural resources, construction, and maintenance, 25.1% production, transportation, and material moving
Income: Per capita: $26,275; Median household: $51,404; Average household: $64,465; Households with income of $100,000 or more: 15.5%; Poverty rate: 9.8%
Educational Attainment: High school diploma or higher: 89.1%; Bachelor's degree or higher: 16.6%; Graduate/professional degree or higher: 6.0%
Housing: Homeownership rate: 78.4%; Median home value: $105,800; Median year structure built: 1971; Homeowner vacancy rate: 3.3%; Median selected monthly owner costs: $922 with a mortgage, $379 without a mortgage; Median gross rent: $703 per month; Rental vacancy rate: 0.5%
Vital Statistics: Birth rate: 121.2 per 10,000 population; Death rate: 120.8 per 10,000 population; Age-adjusted cancer mortality rate: 173.9 deaths per 100,000 population
Health Insurance: 90.8% have insurance; 71.5% have private insurance; 34.9% have public insurance; 9.2% do not have insurance; 7.6% of children under 18 do not have insurance
Health Care: Physicians: 5.8 per 10,000 population; Dentists: 2.9 per 10,000 population; Hospital beds: 10.4 per 10,000 population; Hospital admissions: 227.8 per 10,000 population
Transportation: Commute: 92.7% car, 0.1% public transportation, 1.7% walk, 3.6% work from home; Mean travel time to work: 24.9 minutes
2016 Presidential Election: 68.3% Trump, 25.7% Clinton, 5.2% Johnson, 0.2% Stein
Additional Information Contacts
White Government . . . . (574) 583-7755
http://www.whitecountyindiana.us

White County Communities

BROOKSTON (town). Covers a land area of 0.655 square miles and a water area of 0 square miles. Located at 40.60° N. Lat; 86.87° W. Long. Elevation is 682 feet.

Population: 1,393; Growth (since 2000): -18.9%; Density: 2,125.7 persons per square mile; Race: 97.6% White, 0.0% Black/African American, 0.2% Asian, 0.0% American Indian/Alaska Native, 0.0% Native Hawaiian/Other Pacific Islander, 2.2% Two or more races, 1.7% Hispanic of any race; Average household size: 2.31; Median age: 31.8; Age under 18: 25.7%; Age 65 and over: 14.7%; Males per 100 females: 86.6; Marriage status: 29.4% never married, 46.4% now married, 0.9% separated, 7.4% widowed, 16.8% divorced; Foreign born: 0.2%; Speak English only: 98.1%; With disability: 20.5%; Veterans: 9.1%; Ancestry: 24.3% German, 17.7% Irish, 10.8% English, 9.0% American, 4.6% Polish

Employment: 7.5% management, business, and financial, 5.9% computer, engineering, and science, 8.5% education, legal, community service, arts, and media, 6.2% healthcare practitioners, 17.6% service, 17.9% sales and office, 11.0% natural resources, construction, and maintenance, 25.4% production, transportation, and material moving

Income: Per capita: $22,860; Median household: $44,792; Average household: $52,213; Households with income of $100,000 or more: 8.9%; Poverty rate: 9.7%

Educational Attainment: High school diploma or higher: 93.3%; Bachelor's degree or higher: 16.8%; Graduate/professional degree or higher: 5.0%

School District(s)

Frontier School Corporation (PK-12)
Enrollment: 672 . . . . (219) 984-5009

Housing: Homeownership rate: 64.9%; Median home value: $91,500; Median year structure built: 1963; Homeowner vacancy rate: 0.8%; Median selected monthly owner costs: $815 with a mortgage, $354 without a mortgage; Median gross rent: $723 per month; Rental vacancy rate: 0.0%

Health Insurance: 87.9% have insurance; 70.9% have private insurance; 30.6% have public insurance; 12.1% do not have insurance; 2.7% of children under 18 do not have insurance

Transportation: Commute: 96.5% car, 0.0% public transportation, 2.2% walk, 1.3% work from home; Mean travel time to work: 24.3 minutes

BUFFALO (CDP). Covers a land area of 2.372 square miles and a water area of 0.165 square miles. Located at 40.89° N. Lat; 86.74° W. Long. Elevation is 666 feet.

Population: 915; Growth (since 2000): 36.2%; Density: 385.8 persons per square mile; Race: 89.8% White, 0.0% Black/African American, 0.0% Asian, 0.0% American Indian/Alaska Native, 0.0% Native Hawaiian/Other Pacific Islander, 0.5% Two or more races, 10.2% Hispanic of any race; Average household size: 2.26; Median age: 49.4; Age under 18: 13.6%; Age 65 and over: 26.7%; Males per 100 females: 103.5; Marriage status: 12.1% never married, 75.1% now married, 3.1% separated, 1.1% widowed, 11.6% divorced; Foreign born: 10.9%; Speak English only: 87.6%; With disability: 20.7%; Veterans: 9.4%; Ancestry: 26.6% German, 14.1% Irish, 8.7% Italian, 7.3% English, 6.3% American

Employment: 15.1% management, business, and financial, 1.3% computer, engineering, and science, 10.1% education, legal, community service, arts, and media, 2.9% healthcare practitioners, 6.1% service, 22.0% sales and office, 10.1% natural resources, construction, and maintenance, 32.5% production, transportation, and material moving

Income: Per capita: $25,206; Median household: $44,856; Average household: $56,285; Households with income of $100,000 or more: 16.1%; Poverty rate: 13.0%

Educational Attainment: High school diploma or higher: 86.4%; Bachelor's degree or higher: 10.6%; Graduate/professional degree or higher: 8.8%

Housing: Homeownership rate: 82.9%; Median home value: $94,100; Median year structure built: 1974; Homeowner vacancy rate: 0.0%; Median selected monthly owner costs: $934 with a mortgage, $343 without a mortgage; Median gross rent: $711 per month; Rental vacancy rate: 0.0%

Health Insurance: 88.5% have insurance; 56.0% have private insurance; 56.7% have public insurance; 11.5% do not have insurance; 25.6% of children under 18 do not have insurance

Transportation: Commute: 90.4% car, 0.0% public transportation, 0.0% walk, 9.6% work from home; Mean travel time to work: 42.0 minutes

BURNETTSVILLE (town). Covers a land area of 0.748 square miles and a water area of 0 square miles. Located at 40.76° N. Lat; 86.59° W. Long. Elevation is 712 feet.

Population: 449; Growth (since 2000): 20.4%; Density: 600.1 persons per square mile; Race: 95.5% White, 0.0% Black/African American, 2.0% Asian, 0.0% American Indian/Alaska Native, 0.0% Native Hawaiian/Other Pacific Islander, 2.4% Two or more races, 0.2% Hispanic of any race; Average household size: 2.55; Median age: 36.2; Age under 18: 24.7%; Age 65 and over: 14.7%; Males per 100 females: 87.0; Marriage status: 24.2% never married, 59.7% now married, 0.0% separated, 5.6% widowed, 10.4% divorced; Foreign born: 2.0%; Speak English only: 98.1%; With disability: 14.0%; Veterans: 6.2%; Ancestry: 25.2% German, 8.5% Irish, 8.0% American, 6.0% English, 3.6% French

Employment: 7.5% management, business, and financial, 3.5% computer, engineering, and science, 5.3% education, legal, community service, arts, and media, 3.1% healthcare practitioners, 17.1% service, 20.6% sales and office, 12.3% natural resources, construction, and maintenance, 30.7% production, transportation, and material moving

Income: Per capita: $22,399; Median household: $42,667; Average household: $56,115; Households with income of $100,000 or more: 8.6%; Poverty rate: 13.1%

Educational Attainment: High school diploma or higher: 87.4%; Bachelor's degree or higher: 11.6%; Graduate/professional degree or higher: 1.7%

School District(s)

Twin Lakes School Corp (PK-12)
Enrollment: 2,304 . . . . (574) 583-7211

Housing: Homeownership rate: 77.3%; Median home value: $83,500; Median year structure built: Before 1940; Homeowner vacancy rate: 3.5%; Median selected monthly owner costs: $767 with a mortgage, $318 without a mortgage; Median gross rent: $727 per month; Rental vacancy rate: 0.0%

Health Insurance: 92.7% have insurance; 70.2% have private insurance; 36.5% have public insurance; 7.3% do not have insurance; 5.8% of children under 18 do not have insurance

Transportation: Commute: 94.2% car, 0.9% public transportation, 2.7% walk, 0.9% work from home; Mean travel time to work: 23.6 minutes

CHALMERS (town). Covers a land area of 0.249 square miles and a water area of 0 square miles. Located at 40.66° N. Lat; 86.87° W. Long. Elevation is 712 feet.

Population: 426; Growth (since 2000): -17.0%; Density: 1,713.5 persons per square mile; Race: 99.3% White, 0.0% Black/African American, 0.0% Asian, 0.0% American Indian/Alaska Native, 0.0% Native Hawaiian/Other Pacific Islander, 0.7% Two or more races, 0.0% Hispanic of any race; Average household size: 2.27; Median age: 43.5; Age under 18: 25.8%; Age 65 and over: 15.7%; Males per 100 females: 96.1; Marriage status: 23.5% never married, 51.8% now married, 0.9% separated, 9.6% widowed, 15.1% divorced; Foreign born: 0.0%; Speak English only: 100.0%; With disability: 16.9%; Veterans: 7.9%; Ancestry: 26.5% German, 13.6% English, 10.3% Irish, 8.0% American, 4.9% Polish

Employment: 10.6% management, business, and financial, 0.9% computer, engineering, and science, 11.6% education, legal, community service, arts, and media, 2.8% healthcare practitioners, 8.3% service, 19.9% sales and office, 11.6% natural resources, construction, and maintenance, 34.3% production, transportation, and material moving

Income: Per capita: $23,491; Median household: $53,333; Average household: $54,047; Households with income of $100,000 or more: 10.1%; Poverty rate: 9.0%

Educational Attainment: High school diploma or higher: 93.8%; Bachelor's degree or higher: 18.1%; Graduate/professional degree or higher: 2.5%

School District(s)

Frontier School Corporation (PK-12)
Enrollment: 672 . . . . (219) 984-5009

Housing: Homeownership rate: 83.5%; Median home value: $89,000; Median year structure built: 1942; Homeowner vacancy rate: 0.0%; Median selected monthly owner costs: $863 with a mortgage, $325 without a mortgage; Median gross rent: $758 per month; Rental vacancy rate: 0.0%

Health Insurance: 94.1% have insurance; 85.0% have private insurance; 22.8% have public insurance; 5.9% do not have insurance; 0.0% of children under 18 do not have insurance

Transportation: Commute: 95.8% car, 0.0% public transportation, 1.4% walk, 2.8% work from home; Mean travel time to work: 26.2 minutes

IDAVILLE (CDP). Covers a land area of 5.836 square miles and a water area of 0 square miles. Located at 40.76° N. Lat; 86.65° W. Long. Elevation is 715 feet.
Population: 564; Growth (since 2000): n/a; Density: 96.6 persons per square mile; Race: 100.0% White, 0.0% Black/African American, 0.0% Asian, 0.0% American Indian/Alaska Native, 0.0% Native Hawaiian/Other Pacific Islander, 0.0% Two or more races, 0.0% Hispanic of any race; Average household size: 2.94; Median age: 26.3; Age under 18: 31.0%; Age 65 and over: 20.6%; Males per 100 females: 97.0; Marriage status: 35.3% never married, 55.4% now married, 3.1% separated, 5.0% widowed, 4.3% divorced; Foreign born: 0.0%; Speak English only: 100.0%; With disability: 5.9%; Veterans: 7.2%; Ancestry: 54.1% German, 18.6% Irish, 11.2% American, 3.9% Swiss, 2.5% Scotch-Irish
Employment: 0.0% management, business, and financial, 0.0% computer, engineering, and science, 0.0% education, legal, community service, arts, and media, 0.0% healthcare practitioners, 21.1% service, 21.9% sales and office, 32.2% natural resources, construction, and maintenance, 24.8% production, transportation, and material moving
Income: Per capita: $19,494; Median household: $60,455; Average household: $58,182; Households with income of $100,000 or more: 4.2%; Poverty rate: 5.9%
Educational Attainment: High school diploma or higher: 89.5%; Bachelor's degree or higher: 1.7%; Graduate/professional degree or higher: 1.7%
Housing: Homeownership rate: 38.5%; Median home value: $87,000; Median year structure built: 1955; Homeowner vacancy rate: 0.0%; Median selected monthly owner costs: n/a with a mortgage, $450 without a mortgage; Median gross rent: $882 per month; Rental vacancy rate: 0.0%
Health Insurance: 99.1% have insurance; 80.0% have private insurance; 31.4% have public insurance; 0.9% do not have insurance; 0.0% of children under 18 do not have insurance
Transportation: Commute: 82.6% car, 0.0% public transportation, 0.0% walk, 0.0% work from home; Mean travel time to work: 43.4 minutes

MONON (town). Covers a land area of 0.564 square miles and a water area of 0 square miles. Located at 40.86° N. Lat; 86.88° W. Long. Elevation is 679 feet.
History: Laid out 1853, incorporated 1879.
Population: 1,918; Growth (since 2000): 10.7%; Density: 3,400.9 persons per square mile; Race: 71.8% White, 1.5% Black/African American, 0.0% Asian, 0.0% American Indian/Alaska Native, 0.0% Native Hawaiian/Other Pacific Islander, 0.6% Two or more races, 39.7% Hispanic of any race; Average household size: 2.86; Median age: 34.8; Age under 18: 29.0%; Age 65 and over: 15.6%; Males per 100 females: 98.1; Marriage status: 26.8% never married, 50.6% now married, 0.8% separated, 6.5% widowed, 16.0% divorced; Foreign born: 21.5%; Speak English only: 64.0%; With disability: 14.3%; Veterans: 6.8%; Ancestry: 14.2% German, 7.9% Irish, 6.2% American, 4.7% English, 2.1% French
Employment: 5.5% management, business, and financial, 0.9% computer, engineering, and science, 4.4% education, legal, community service, arts, and media, 2.1% healthcare practitioners, 14.6% service, 17.8% sales and office, 16.5% natural resources, construction, and maintenance, 38.3% production, transportation, and material moving
Income: Per capita: $17,904; Median household: $37,500; Average household: $49,141; Households with income of $100,000 or more: 10.2%; Poverty rate: 17.4%
Educational Attainment: High school diploma or higher: 67.5%; Bachelor's degree or higher: 6.0%; Graduate/professional degree or higher: 1.8%

School District(s)

North White School Corp (PK-12)
Enrollment: 1,002 .... (219) 253-6618

Housing: Homeownership rate: 69.3%; Median home value: $71,800; Median year structure built: 1947; Homeowner vacancy rate: 1.9%; Median selected monthly owner costs: $765 with a mortgage, $353 without a mortgage; Median gross rent: $622 per month; Rental vacancy rate: 0.0%
Health Insurance: 77.4% have insurance; 50.4% have private insurance; 39.5% have public insurance; 22.6% do not have insurance; 17.2% of children under 18 do not have insurance
Newspapers: The News & Review (weekly circulation 1,300)
Transportation: Commute: 95.5% car, 1.0% public transportation, 2.8% walk, 0.4% work from home; Mean travel time to work: 24.3 minutes

MONTICELLO (city). County seat. Covers a land area of 3.470 square miles and a water area of 0.216 square miles. Located at 40.75° N. Lat; 86.77° W. Long. Elevation is 676 feet.
History: Monticello was established as a resort town on the Tippecanoe River. When the Indiana Hydroelectric Power Company built dams across the river in 1923 and 1925, several lakes were formed which provided recreation sites.
Population: 5,298; Growth (since 2000): -7.4%; Density: 1,527.0 persons per square mile; Race: 83.7% White, 0.2% Black/African American, 0.0% Asian, 0.0% American Indian/Alaska Native, 0.0% Native Hawaiian/Other Pacific Islander, 3.5% Two or more races, 15.1% Hispanic of any race; Average household size: 2.35; Median age: 38.1; Age under 18: 25.2%; Age 65 and over: 19.4%; Males per 100 females: 89.9; Marriage status: 25.3% never married, 44.3% now married, 0.9% separated, 16.3% widowed, 14.1% divorced; Foreign born: 7.0%; Speak English only: 86.2%; With disability: 18.0%; Veterans: 9.6%; Ancestry: 13.9% German, 11.2% American, 11.1% English, 8.5% Irish, 3.4% Italian
Employment: 5.8% management, business, and financial, 2.1% computer, engineering, and science, 5.1% education, legal, community service, arts, and media, 5.1% healthcare practitioners, 13.4% service, 23.9% sales and office, 17.1% natural resources, construction, and maintenance, 27.7% production, transportation, and material moving
Income: Per capita: $21,384; Median household: $41,136; Average household: $51,496; Households with income of $100,000 or more: 8.6%; Poverty rate: 9.3%
Educational Attainment: High school diploma or higher: 85.6%; Bachelor's degree or higher: 13.7%; Graduate/professional degree or higher: 6.5%

School District(s)

Twin Lakes School Corp (PK-12)
Enrollment: 2,304 .... (574) 583-7211

Housing: Homeownership rate: 66.1%; Median home value: $93,700; Median year structure built: 1964; Homeowner vacancy rate: 8.4%; Median selected monthly owner costs: $852 with a mortgage, $328 without a mortgage; Median gross rent: $663 per month; Rental vacancy rate: 0.0%
Health Insurance: 92.3% have insurance; 66.6% have private insurance; 41.9% have public insurance; 7.7% do not have insurance; 5.1% of children under 18 do not have insurance
Hospitals: Indiana University Health White Memorial Hospital (25 beds)
Newspapers: Herald Journal (daily circulation 5,100)
Transportation: Commute: 97.1% car, 0.0% public transportation, 0.6% walk, 0.8% work from home; Mean travel time to work: 16.0 minutes
Additional Information Contacts
City of Monticello................................ (574) 583-5712
http://www.monticelloin.gov

NORWAY (CDP). Covers a land area of 0.894 square miles and a water area of 0.064 square miles. Located at 40.77° N. Lat; 86.77° W. Long. Elevation is 633 feet.
Population: 471; Growth (since 2000): 7.8%; Density: 527.0 persons per square mile; Race: 100.0% White, 0.0% Black/African American, 0.0% Asian, 0.0% American Indian/Alaska Native, 0.0% Native Hawaiian/Other Pacific Islander, 0.0% Two or more races, 13.2% Hispanic of any race; Average household size: 2.06; Median age: 51.1; Age under 18: 11.9%; Age 65 and over: 30.1%; Males per 100 females: 96.9; Marriage status: 21.0% never married, 58.6% now married, 5.5% separated, 0.0% widowed, 20.5% divorced; Foreign born: 10.8%; Speak English only: 89.0%; With disability: 27.4%; Veterans: 16.9%; Ancestry: 23.8% German, 16.6% American, 15.7% Irish, 13.4% Polish, 7.4% English
Employment: 15.8% management, business, and financial, 0.0% computer, engineering, and science, 5.4% education, legal, community service, arts, and media, 0.0% healthcare practitioners, 30.0% service, 11.8% sales and office, 21.2% natural resources, construction, and maintenance, 15.8% production, transportation, and material moving
Income: Per capita: $33,472; Median household: n/a; Average household: $68,790; Households with income of $100,000 or more: 8.3%; Poverty rate: 1.9%
Educational Attainment: High school diploma or higher: 84.1%; Bachelor's degree or higher: 10.6%; Graduate/professional degree or higher: 2.3%
Housing: Homeownership rate: 79.9%; Median home value: n/a; Median year structure built: 1981; Homeowner vacancy rate: 0.0%; Median selected monthly owner costs: $856 with a mortgage, $374 without a mortgage; Median gross rent: $722 per month; Rental vacancy rate: 0.0%

Health Insurance: 86.6% have insurance; 47.3% have private insurance; 60.1% have public insurance; 13.4% do not have insurance; 0.0% of children under 18 do not have insurance
Transportation: Commute: 100.0% car, 0.0% public transportation, 0.0% walk, 0.0% work from home; Mean travel time to work: 25.9 minutes

REYNOLDS (town). Covers a land area of 0.553 square miles and a water area of 0 square miles. Located at 40.75° N. Lat; 86.87° W. Long. Elevation is 699 feet.
Population: 555; Growth (since 2000): 1.5%; Density: 1,002.8 persons per square mile; Race: 98.7% White, 0.0% Black/African American, 0.9% Asian, 0.0% American Indian/Alaska Native, 0.0% Native Hawaiian/Other Pacific Islander, 0.4% Two or more races, 10.8% Hispanic of any race; Average household size: 2.35; Median age: 40.4; Age under 18: 21.8%; Age 65 and over: 17.1%; Males per 100 females: 89.7; Marriage status: 27.6% never married, 52.0% now married, 0.0% separated, 3.6% widowed, 16.8% divorced; Foreign born: 2.3%; Speak English only: 87.7%; With disability: 14.2%; Veterans: 6.5%; Ancestry: 25.8% German, 16.2% Irish, 9.7% English, 8.5% American, 2.2% French
Employment: 14.8% management, business, and financial, 1.9% computer, engineering, and science, 4.1% education, legal, community service, arts, and media, 0.9% healthcare practitioners, 8.5% service, 29.0% sales and office, 17.7% natural resources, construction, and maintenance, 23.0% production, transportation, and material moving
Income: Per capita: $30,862; Median household: $53,542; Average household: $71,152; Households with income of $100,000 or more: 14.8%; Poverty rate: 8.3%
Educational Attainment: High school diploma or higher: 88.8%; Bachelor's degree or higher: 18.4%; Graduate/professional degree or higher: 3.4%
Housing: Homeownership rate: 78.8%; Median home value: $84,200; Median year structure built: 1963; Homeowner vacancy rate: 2.6%; Median selected monthly owner costs: $928 with a mortgage, $333 without a mortgage; Median gross rent: $673 per month; Rental vacancy rate: 16.7%
Health Insurance: 94.6% have insurance; 77.7% have private insurance; 26.8% have public insurance; 5.4% do not have insurance; 0.0% of children under 18 do not have insurance
Transportation: Commute: 89.6% car, 0.6% public transportation, 6.3% walk, 3.5% work from home; Mean travel time to work: 23.3 minutes

WOLCOTT (town). Covers a land area of 0.592 square miles and a water area of 0 square miles. Located at 40.76° N. Lat; 87.04° W. Long. Elevation is 718 feet.
History: Laid out 1861.
Population: 1,136; Growth (since 2000): 14.9%; Density: 1,918.3 persons per square mile; Race: 92.6% White, 1.1% Black/African American, 2.2% Asian, 0.3% American Indian/Alaska Native, 0.0% Native Hawaiian/Other Pacific Islander, 2.9% Two or more races, 2.3% Hispanic of any race; Average household size: 2.59; Median age: 37.1; Age under 18: 23.0%; Age 65 and over: 18.0%; Males per 100 females: 98.6; Marriage status: 24.0% never married, 58.0% now married, 1.0% separated, 6.0% widowed, 12.0% divorced; Foreign born: 1.8%; Speak English only: 98.0%; With disability: 15.9%; Veterans: 6.9%; Ancestry: 33.1% German, 13.2% Irish, 7.1% English, 5.8% American, 5.5% Dutch
Employment: 9.9% management, business, and financial, 2.0% computer, engineering, and science, 7.1% education, legal, community service, arts, and media, 2.7% healthcare practitioners, 17.1% service, 19.2% sales and office, 8.9% natural resources, construction, and maintenance, 33.2% production, transportation, and material moving
Income: Per capita: $22,856; Median household: $56,375; Average household: $59,427; Households with income of $100,000 or more: 9.8%; Poverty rate: 9.6%
Educational Attainment: High school diploma or higher: 92.8%; Bachelor's degree or higher: 15.4%; Graduate/professional degree or higher: 2.8%

School District(s)

Tri-county School Corporation (PK-12)
Enrollment: 730 . . . . (219) 279-2418
Housing: Homeownership rate: 77.4%; Median home value: $86,800; Median year structure built: 1953; Homeowner vacancy rate: 1.7%; Median selected monthly owner costs: $900 with a mortgage, $400 without a mortgage; Median gross rent: $686 per month; Rental vacancy rate: 0.0%
Health Insurance: 91.7% have insurance; 69.5% have private insurance; 33.5% have public insurance; 8.3% do not have insurance; 2.5% of children under 18 do not have insurance
Newspapers: The New Wolcott Enterprise (weekly circulation 700)
Transportation: Commute: 93.2% car, 0.0% public transportation, 3.4% walk, 2.0% work from home; Mean travel time to work: 22.0 minutes

Whitley County

Located in northeastern Indiana; drained by the Eel River. Covers a land area of 335.569 square miles, a water area of 2.345 square miles, and is located in the Eastern Time Zone at 41.14° N. Lat., 85.50° W. Long. The county was founded in 1835. County seat is Columbia City.

Whitley County is part of the Fort Wayne, IN Metropolitan Statistical Area. The entire metro area includes: Allen County, IN; Wells County, IN; Whitley County, IN

Weather Station: Columbia City Elevation: 850 feet

	Jan	Feb	Mar	Apr	May	Jun	Jul	Aug	Sep	Oct	Nov	Dec
High	32	35	46	59	70	79	83	81	75	62	49	36
Low	16	18	27	37	48	58	61	60	52	40	31	21
Precip	2.3	1.9	2.8	3.5	4.1	4.4	4.0	3.9	3.3	3.1	3.3	2.9
Snow	8.8	6.7	3.5	0.7	0.0	0.0	0.0	0.0	0.0	0.2	1.2	6.4

High and Low temperatures in degrees Fahrenheit; Precipitation and Snow in inches

Population: 33,481; Growth (since 2000): 9.0%; Density: 99.8 persons per square mile; Race: 96.6% White, 0.4% Black/African American, 0.5% Asian, 0.3% American Indian/Alaska Native, 0.0% Native Hawaiian/Other Pacific Islander, 1.9% two or more races, 1.9% Hispanic of any race; Average household size: 2.45; Median age: 41.0; Age under 18: 23.3%; Age 65 and over: 16.8%; Males per 100 females: 98.9; Marriage status: 22.3% never married, 60.2% now married, 0.9% separated, 5.9% widowed, 11.6% divorced; Foreign born: 1.0%; Speak English only: 97.8%; With disability: 15.9%; Veterans: 9.4%; Ancestry: 28.0% German, 9.5% American, 9.3% Irish, 8.8% English, 3.5% French
Religion: Six largest groups: 8.0% Methodist/Pietist, 6.4% Catholicism, 5.8% Presbyterian-Reformed, 5.0% Lutheran, 4.4% Holiness, 3.0% Non-denominational Protestant
Economy: Unemployment rate: 3.1%; Leading industries: 14.6 % retail trade; 14.3 % other services (except public administration); 9.8 % construction; Farms: 710 totaling 140,099 acres; Company size: 0 employ 1,000 or more persons, 3 employ 500 to 999 persons, 17 employ 100 to 499 persons, 652 employ less than 100 persons; Business ownership: 742 women-owned, n/a Black-owned, n/a Hispanic-owned, 40 Asian-owned, n/a American Indian/Alaska Native-owned
Employment: 10.0% management, business, and financial, 3.8% computer, engineering, and science, 7.2% education, legal, community service, arts, and media, 5.9% healthcare practitioners, 13.8% service, 22.6% sales and office, 10.3% natural resources, construction, and maintenance, 26.4% production, transportation, and material moving
Income: Per capita: $28,073; Median household: $57,041; Average household: $69,572; Households with income of $100,000 or more: 19.2%; Poverty rate: 9.5%
Educational Attainment: High school diploma or higher: 91.1%; Bachelor's degree or higher: 19.5%; Graduate/professional degree or higher: 7.0%
Housing: Homeownership rate: 79.5%; Median home value: $131,600; Median year structure built: 1975; Homeowner vacancy rate: 1.2%; Median selected monthly owner costs: $1,068 with a mortgage, $360 without a mortgage; Median gross rent: $645 per month; Rental vacancy rate: 3.2%
Vital Statistics: Birth rate: 114.6 per 10,000 population; Death rate: 87.7 per 10,000 population; Age-adjusted cancer mortality rate: 136.3 deaths per 100,000 population
Health Insurance: 92.4% have insurance; 76.0% have private insurance; 29.8% have public insurance; 7.6% do not have insurance; 4.4% of children under 18 do not have insurance
Health Care: Physicians: 8.7 per 10,000 population; Dentists: 4.1 per 10,000 population; Hospital beds: 9.0 per 10,000 population; Hospital admissions: 484.1 per 10,000 population
Air Quality Index (AQI): Percent of Days: 83.1% good, 16.9% moderate, 0.0% unhealthy for sensitive individuals, 0.0% unhealthy, 0.0% very unhealthy; Annual median: 33; Annual maximum: 85
Transportation: Commute: 94.9% car, 0.3% public transportation, 0.8% walk, 2.7% work from home; Mean travel time to work: 22.9 minutes
2016 Presidential Election: 72.1% Trump, 21.4% Clinton, 5.1% Johnson, 0.4% Stein
Additional Information Contacts

Whitley Government . . . . (260) 248-3140
http://www.whitleygov.com

Whitley County Communities

CHURUBUSCO (town). Covers a land area of 0.902 square miles and a water area of 0 square miles. Located at 41.23° N. Lat; 85.32° W. Long. Elevation is 896 feet.

History: Churubusco got its name from a Mexican town where American forces won a battle during the war with Mexico.

Population: 1,873; Growth (since 2000): 12.4%; Density: 2,076.2 persons per square mile; Race: 98.0% White, 0.0% Black/African American, 0.6% Asian, 0.0% American Indian/Alaska Native, 0.0% Native Hawaiian/Other Pacific Islander, 0.5% Two or more races, 4.4% Hispanic of any race; Average household size: 2.34; Median age: 34.1; Age under 18: 26.9%; Age 65 and over: 16.7%; Males per 100 females: 93.3; Marriage status: 26.3% never married, 54.0% now married, 1.1% separated, 8.4% widowed, 11.3% divorced; Foreign born: 2.3%; Speak English only: 96.6%; With disability: 11.5%; Veterans: 6.7%; Ancestry: 32.9% German, 13.0% American, 9.4% Irish, 6.2% English, 5.4% French

Employment: 5.9% management, business, and financial, 2.1% computer, engineering, and science, 6.3% education, legal, community service, arts, and media, 4.2% healthcare practitioners, 21.0% service, 18.1% sales and office, 4.8% natural resources, construction, and maintenance, 37.6% production, transportation, and material moving

Income: Per capita: $22,514; Median household: $46,974; Average household: $53,534; Households with income of $100,000 or more: 11.3%; Poverty rate: 12.0%

Educational Attainment: High school diploma or higher: 94.2%; Bachelor's degree or higher: 14.5%; Graduate/professional degree or higher: 3.9%

School District(s)

Smith-Green Community Schools (PK-12)
Enrollment: 1,061 . . . . (260) 693-2007

Housing: Homeownership rate: 78.3%; Median home value: $100,300; Median year structure built: 1969; Homeowner vacancy rate: 1.6%; Median selected monthly owner costs: $897 with a mortgage, $324 without a mortgage; Median gross rent: $717 per month; Rental vacancy rate: 14.7%

Health Insurance: 91.9% have insurance; 74.7% have private insurance; 30.5% have public insurance; 8.1% do not have insurance; 2.4% of children under 18 do not have insurance

Newspapers: The News (weekly circulation 2,200)

Transportation: Commute: 95.3% car, 0.0% public transportation, 1.5% walk, 3.2% work from home; Mean travel time to work: 24.1 minutes

COLUMBIA CITY (city). County seat. Covers a land area of 5.582 square miles and a water area of 0.021 square miles. Located at 41.16° N. Lat; 85.48° W. Long. Elevation is 860 feet.

History: Columbia City was the home of Thomas Riley Marshall (1854-1925), Vice-President under Woodrow Wilson, governor of Indiana from 1909-1913, and author of the statement, "What this country really needs is a good five-cent cigar." Also from Columbia City was historical novelist Lloyd C. Douglas, who was born here in 1877.

Population: 9,057; Growth (since 2000): 28.0%; Density: 1,622.6 persons per square mile; Race: 94.0% White, 0.8% Black/African American, 0.6% Asian, 0.1% American Indian/Alaska Native, 0.0% Native Hawaiian/Other Pacific Islander, 3.9% Two or more races, 3.9% Hispanic of any race; Average household size: 2.21; Median age: 37.8; Age under 18: 21.1%; Age 65 and over: 16.8%; Males per 100 females: 90.8; Marriage status: 30.5% never married, 47.0% now married, 0.9% separated, 6.4% widowed, 16.1% divorced; Foreign born: 1.0%; Speak English only: 98.3%; With disability: 20.1%; Veterans: 6.9%; Ancestry: 25.6% German, 9.8% American, 9.2% English, 7.3% Irish, 2.8% French

Employment: 14.5% management, business, and financial, 1.7% computer, engineering, and science, 7.2% education, legal, community service, arts, and media, 7.4% healthcare practitioners, 17.1% service, 22.7% sales and office, 6.2% natural resources, construction, and maintenance, 23.1% production, transportation, and material moving

Income: Per capita: $25,154; Median household: $46,611; Average household: $56,062; Households with income of $100,000 or more: 11.5%; Poverty rate: 14.7%

Educational Attainment: High school diploma or higher: 87.5%; Bachelor's degree or higher: 23.4%; Graduate/professional degree or higher: 7.8%

School District(s)

Whitley County Con Schools (PK-12)
Enrollment: 3,482 . . . . (260) 244-5771

Housing: Homeownership rate: 64.2%; Median home value: $106,200; Median year structure built: 1979; Homeowner vacancy rate: 0.6%; Median selected monthly owner costs: $974 with a mortgage, $388 without a mortgage; Median gross rent: $590 per month; Rental vacancy rate: 2.6%

Health Insurance: 91.4% have insurance; 69.8% have private insurance; 37.1% have public insurance; 8.6% do not have insurance; 5.2% of children under 18 do not have insurance

Hospitals: Parkview Whitley Hospital (45 beds)

Newspapers: Post & Mail (daily circulation 4,100)

Transportation: Commute: 95.7% car, 0.5% public transportation, 1.1% walk, 1.6% work from home; Mean travel time to work: 20.1 minutes

Additional Information Contacts

City of Columbia City. . . . . (260) 248-5100
http://www.columbiacity.net

LARWILL (town). Covers a land area of 0.223 square miles and a water area of 0 square miles. Located at 41.18° N. Lat; 85.62° W. Long. Elevation is 965 feet.

History: Laid out 1854.

Population: 332; Growth (since 2000): 17.7%; Density: 1,486.8 persons per square mile; Race: 95.5% White, 0.0% Black/African American, 0.0% Asian, 0.0% American Indian/Alaska Native, 0.0% Native Hawaiian/Other Pacific Islander, 4.5% Two or more races, 3.3% Hispanic of any race; Average household size: 2.79; Median age: 33.5; Age under 18: 28.6%; Age 65 and over: 14.8%; Males per 100 females: 96.5; Marriage status: 28.5% never married, 38.7% now married, 2.8% separated, 12.3% widowed, 20.6% divorced; Foreign born: 0.0%; Speak English only: 98.4%; With disability: 18.1%; Veterans: 5.1%; Ancestry: 22.6% German, 13.0% Irish, 7.8% English, 6.0% American, 3.0% French

Employment: 7.0% management, business, and financial, 1.4% computer, engineering, and science, 2.1% education, legal, community service, arts, and media, 3.5% healthcare practitioners, 14.7% service, 13.3% sales and office, 12.6% natural resources, construction, and maintenance, 45.5% production, transportation, and material moving

Income: Per capita: $17,203; Median household: $51,042; Average household: $48,739; Households with income of $100,000 or more: 5.0%; Poverty rate: 14.8%

Educational Attainment: High school diploma or higher: 80.7%; Bachelor's degree or higher: 4.3%; Graduate/professional degree or higher: n/a

School District(s)

Whitko Community School Corp (PK-12)
Enrollment: 1,590 . . . . (260) 327-3677

Housing: Homeownership rate: 83.2%; Median home value: $70,900; Median year structure built: Before 1940; Homeowner vacancy rate: 0.0%; Median selected monthly owner costs: $857 with a mortgage, $340 without a mortgage; Median gross rent: $990 per month; Rental vacancy rate: 20.0%

Health Insurance: 89.2% have insurance; 64.8% have private insurance; 43.7% have public insurance; 10.8% do not have insurance; 1.8% of children under 18 do not have insurance

Transportation: Commute: 96.4% car, 0.0% public transportation, 0.0% walk, 2.2% work from home; Mean travel time to work: 26.1 minutes

SOUTH WHITLEY (town). Covers a land area of 0.912 square miles and a water area of 0 square miles. Located at 41.08° N. Lat; 85.63° W. Long. Elevation is 804 feet.

History: Laid out 1837.

Population: 1,970; Growth (since 2000): 10.5%; Density: 2,161.1 persons per square mile; Race: 93.7% White, 0.4% Black/African American, 0.2% Asian, 0.0% American Indian/Alaska Native, 0.0% Native Hawaiian/Other Pacific Islander, 5.1% Two or more races, 6.7% Hispanic of any race; Average household size: 2.43; Median age: 36.7; Age under 18: 24.9%; Age 65 and over: 12.6%; Males per 100 females: 93.3; Marriage status: 23.6% never married, 52.8% now married, 2.2% separated, 5.0% widowed, 18.6% divorced; Foreign born: 2.6%; Speak English only: 95.2%; With disability: 12.4%; Veterans: 9.3%; Ancestry: 20.7% German, 8.5% Irish, 8.4% English, 8.3% American, 1.6% French

Employment: 4.9% management, business, and financial, 2.8% computer, engineering, and science, 5.0% education, legal, community service, arts, and media, 3.3% healthcare practitioners, 18.9% service, 22.7% sales and

office, 8.0% natural resources, construction, and maintenance, 34.3% production, transportation, and material moving
Income: Per capita: $22,698; Median household: $46,875; Average household: $55,516; Households with income of $100,000 or more: 10.1%; Poverty rate: 12.7%
Educational Attainment: High school diploma or higher: 88.5%; Bachelor's degree or higher: 9.8%; Graduate/professional degree or higher: 4.1%

School District(s)

Whitko Community School Corp (PK-12)
Enrollment: 1,590 . . . . (260) 327-3677
Housing: Homeownership rate: 72.0%; Median home value: $83,000; Median year structure built: 1958; Homeowner vacancy rate: 0.0%; Median selected monthly owner costs: $848 with a mortgage, $359 without a mortgage; Median gross rent: $568 per month; Rental vacancy rate: 7.4%
Health Insurance: 84.9% have insurance; 59.3% have private insurance; 32.4% have public insurance; 15.1% do not have insurance; 11.2% of children under 18 do not have insurance
Safety: Violent crime rate: n/a per 10,000 population; Property crime rate: 46.2 per 10,000 population
Newspapers: Tribune-News (weekly circulation 1,500)
Transportation: Commute: 91.5% car, 1.0% public transportation, 4.5% walk, 1.8% work from home; Mean travel time to work: 22.8 minutes

TRI-LAKES (CDP). Covers a land area of 3.417 square miles and a water area of 0.604 square miles. Located at 41.25° N. Lat; 85.45° W. Long. Elevation is 938 feet.
Population: 1,414; Growth (since 2000): -64.0%; Density: 413.8 persons per square mile; Race: 100.0% White, 0.0% Black/African American, 0.0% Asian, 0.0% American Indian/Alaska Native, 0.0% Native Hawaiian/Other Pacific Islander, 0.0% Two or more races, 0.0% Hispanic of any race; Average household size: 2.62; Median age: 44.0; Age under 18: 26.4%; Age 65 and over: 12.4%; Males per 100 females: 111.5; Marriage status: 17.8% never married, 69.4% now married, 0.0% separated, 5.0% widowed, 7.8% divorced; Foreign born: 1.3%; Speak English only: 98.8%; With disability: 17.5%; Veterans: 10.9%; Ancestry: 21.3% German, 17.9% American, 8.3% French, 7.5% English, 5.1% Irish
Employment: 13.3% management, business, and financial, 3.4% computer, engineering, and science, 4.9% education, legal, community service, arts, and media, 2.7% healthcare practitioners, 9.9% service, 30.6% sales and office, 3.3% natural resources, construction, and maintenance, 32.0% production, transportation, and material moving
Income: Per capita: $30,375; Median household: $70,938; Average household: $79,527; Households with income of $100,000 or more: 26.6%; Poverty rate: 2.9%
Educational Attainment: High school diploma or higher: 98.7%; Bachelor's degree or higher: 23.1%; Graduate/professional degree or higher: 6.0%
Housing: Homeownership rate: 97.4%; Median home value: $198,100; Median year structure built: 1973; Homeowner vacancy rate: 0.0%; Median selected monthly owner costs: $1,108 with a mortgage, $440 without a mortgage; Median gross rent: n/a per month; Rental vacancy rate: 0.0%
Health Insurance: 96.7% have insurance; 84.9% have private insurance; 21.4% have public insurance; 3.3% do not have insurance; 0.0% of children under 18 do not have insurance
Transportation: Commute: 93.1% car, 0.0% public transportation, 0.0% walk, 6.9% work from home; Mean travel time to work: 32.7 minutes;

Index

County and Place Name 717

The Hoosier State

The Crossroads of America

Aberdeen (cdp) Porter County, 638
Adams County, 461
Advance (town) Boone County, 472
Akron (town) Fulton County, 520
Alamo (town) Montgomery County, 613
Albany (town) Delaware County, 503
Albion (town) Noble County, 622
Alexandria (city) Madison County, 593
Alfordsville (town) Daviess County, 493
Allen County, 462
Alton (town) Crawford County, 490
Altona (town) DeKalb County, 500
Ambia (town) Benton County, 469
Amboy (town) Miami County, 608
Americus (cdp) Tippecanoe County, 679
Amo (town) Hendricks County, 542
Anderson (city) Madison County, 593
Andrews (town) Huntington County, 551
Angola (city) Steuben County, 672
Arcadia (town) Hamilton County, 532
Arcola (unincorporated postal area) Allen County, 463
Argos (town) Marshall County, 604
Arlington (cdp) Rush County, 655
Ashley (town) DeKalb County, 501
Atlanta (town) Hamilton County, 533
Attica (city) Fountain County, 515
Atwood (unincorporated postal area) Kosciusko County, 572
Auburn (city) DeKalb County, 501
Aurora (city) Dearborn County, 495
Austin (city) Scott County, 662
Avilla (town) Noble County, 623
Avoca (cdp) Lawrence County, 590
Avon (town) Hendricks County, 542
Bainbridge (town) Putnam County, 647
Bargersville (town) Johnson County, 565
Bartholomew County, 466
Bass Lake (cdp) Starke County, 669
Batesville (city) Ripley County, 652
Bath (unincorporated postal area) Franklin County, 517
Battle Ground (town) Tippecanoe County, 679
Bedford (city) Lawrence County, 590
Beech Grove (city) Marion County, 597
Bennington (unincorporated postal area) Switzerland County, 677
Benton County, 469
Berne (city) Adams County, 461
Bethany (town) Morgan County, 617
Beverly Shores (town) Porter County, 638
Bicknell (city) Knox County, 568
Birdseye (town) Dubois County, 506
Blackford County, 471
Blanford (cdp) Vermillion County, 688
Bloomfield (town) Greene County, 529
Bloomingdale (town) Parke County, 630
Bloomington (city) Monroe County, 611
Blountsville (town) Henry County, 545
Bluffton (city) Wells County, 709
Boggstown (unincorporated postal area) Shelby County, 663
Boone County, 472
Boonville (city) Warrick County, 699
Borden (town) Clark County, 481
Boston (town) Wayne County, 704
Boswell (town) Benton County, 469
Bourbon (town) Marshall County, 604
Bowling Green (unincorporated postal area) Owen County, 628
Branchville (unincorporated postal area) Perry County, 633
Brazil (city) Clay County, 485
Bremen (town) Marshall County, 604
Bridgeton (unincorporated postal area) Parke County, 631
Bright (cdp) Dearborn County, 495
Bringhurst (unincorporated postal area) Carroll County, 476
Bristol (town) Elkhart County, 509
Bristow (unincorporated postal area) Perry County, 633
Brook (town) Newton County, 620
Brooklyn (town) Morgan County, 617
Brooksburg (town) Jefferson County, 560
Brookston (town) White County, 712
Brookville (town) Franklin County, 518
Brown County, 474
Brownsburg (town) Hendricks County, 542
Brownstown (town) Jackson County, 553
Brownsville (unincorporated postal area) Union County, 685
Bruceville (town) Knox County, 568
Bryant (town) Jay County, 558
Buck Creek (cdp) Tippecanoe County, 679
Buffalo (cdp) White County, 712
Bunker Hill (town) Miami County, 608
Burket (town) Kosciusko County, 572
Burlington (town) Carroll County, 476
Burnettsville (town) White County, 712
Burns City (cdp) Martin County, 606
Burns Harbor (town) Porter County, 638
Butler (city) DeKalb County, 501
Butlerville (cdp) Jennings County, 562
Cadiz (town) Henry County, 545
Cambridge City (town) Wayne County, 705
Camby (unincorporated postal area) Morgan County, 617
Camden (town) Carroll County, 477
Campbellsburg (town) Washington County, 702
Canaan (cdp) Jefferson County, 560
Cannelburg (town) Daviess County, 493
Cannelton (city) Perry County, 633
Carbon (town) Clay County, 485
Carlisle (town) Sullivan County, 674
Carmel (city) Hamilton County, 533
Carroll County, 476
Carthage (town) Rush County, 655
Cass County, 478
Cayuga (town) Vermillion County, 688
Cedar Grove (town) Franklin County, 518
Cedar Lake (town) Lake County, 578
Celestine (unincorporated postal area) Dubois County, 506
Center Point (town) Clay County, 485
Centerpoint (unincorporated postal area) Clay County, 486
Centerville (town) Wayne County, 705
Central (unincorporated postal area) Harrison County, 538
Chalmers (town) White County, 712
Chandler (town) Warrick County, 700
Charlestown (city) Clark County, 481
Charlottesville (unincorporated postal area) Hancock County, 535
Chesterfield (town) Madison County, 594
Chesterton (town) Porter County, 638
Chrisney (town) Spencer County, 666
Churubusco (town) Whitley County, 715
Cicero (town) Hamilton County, 533
Clark County, 481
Clarks Hill (town) Tippecanoe County, 679
Clarksburg (cdp) Decatur County, 498
Clarksville (town) Clark County, 482
Clay City (town) Clay County, 486
Clay County, 484
Claypool (town) Kosciusko County, 572
Clayton (town) Hendricks County, 542
Clear Lake (town) Steuben County, 672
Clermont (town) Marion County, 598
Clifford (town) Bartholomew County, 467
Clinton (city) Vermillion County, 688
Clinton County, 487
Cloverdale (town) Putnam County, 647
Coal City (unincorporated postal area) Owen County, 628
Coalmont (cdp) Clay County, 486
Coatesville (town) Hendricks County, 543
Colburn (cdp) Tippecanoe County, 680
Colfax (town) Clinton County, 488
Collegeville (cdp) Jasper County, 555
Columbia City (city) Whitley County, 715
Columbus (city) Bartholomew County, 467
Commiskey (unincorporated postal area) Jennings County, 562
Connersville (city) Fayette County, 512
Converse (town) Miami County, 608
Cordry Sweetwater Lakes (cdp) Brown County, 475
Corunna (town) DeKalb County, 501
Cory (unincorporated postal area) Clay County, 486
Corydon (town) Harrison County, 538
Country Club Heights (town) Madison County, 594
Country Squire Lakes (cdp) Jennings County, 563
Covington (city) Fountain County, 515
Craigville (unincorporated postal area) Wells County, 709
Crandall (town) Harrison County, 538
Crane (town) Martin County, 606
Crawford County, 490
Crawfordsville (city) Montgomery County, 613
Cromwell (town) Noble County, 623
Cross Plains (unincorporated postal area) Ripley County, 653
Crothersville (town) Jackson County, 553
Crown Point (city) Lake County, 578
Crows Nest (town) Marion County, 598
Culver (town) Marshall County, 605
Cumberland (town) Marion County, 598
Cutler (unincorporated postal area) Carroll County, 477
Cynthiana (town) Posey County, 643
Dale (town) Spencer County, 666
Daleville (town) Delaware County, 503
Dana (town) Vermillion County, 689
Danville (town) Hendricks County, 543
Darlington (town) Montgomery County, 614

Index

Darmstadt (town) Vanderburgh County, 686
Daviess County, 492
Dayton (town) Tippecanoe County, 680
De Motte (town) Jasper County, 556
Dearborn County, 495
Decatur (city) Adams County, 461
Decatur County, 498
Decker (town) Knox County, 568
DeKalb County, 500
Delaware County, 503
Delphi (city) Carroll County, 477
Denver (town) Miami County, 609
Depauw (unincorporated postal area) Harrison County, 539
Deputy (cdp) Jefferson County, 560
Derby (unincorporated postal area) Perry County, 633
Dillsboro (town) Dearborn County, 496
Dover Hill (cdp) Martin County, 607
Dresser (cdp) Vigo County, 691
Dublin (town) Wayne County, 705
Dubois (cdp) Dubois County, 506
Dubois County, 505
Dugger (town) Sullivan County, 674
Dune Acres (town) Porter County, 639
Dunkirk (city) Jay County, 558
Dunlap (cdp) Elkhart County, 509
Dunreith (town) Henry County, 546
Dupont (town) Jefferson County, 560
Dyer (town) Lake County, 578
Earl Park (town) Benton County, 470
East Chicago (city) Lake County, 579
East Enterprise (cdp) Switzerland County, 677
East Germantown (town) Wayne County, 705
Eaton (town) Delaware County, 504
Eckerty (unincorporated postal area) Crawford County, 490
Economy (town) Wayne County, 706
Edgewood (town) Madison County, 594
Edinburgh (town) Johnson County, 565
Edwardsport (town) Knox County, 569
Elberfeld (town) Warrick County, 700
Elizabeth (town) Harrison County, 539
Elizabethtown (town) Bartholomew County, 467
Elkhart (city) Elkhart County, 509
Elkhart County, 508
Ellettsville (town) Monroe County, 611
Elnora (town) Daviess County, 493
Elwood (city) Madison County, 594
Eminence (unincorporated postal area) Morgan County, 617
Emison (cdp) Knox County, 569
English (town) Crawford County, 491
Etna Green (town) Kosciusko County, 572
Evanston (unincorporated postal area) Spencer County, 666
Evansville (city) Vanderburgh County, 686
Fair Oaks (unincorporated postal area) Jasper County, 556
Fairbanks (unincorporated postal area) Sullivan County, 674
Fairland (town) Shelby County, 663
Fairmount (town) Grant County, 525
Fairview Park (town) Vermillion County, 689
Falmouth (unincorporated postal area) Rush County, 655
Farmersburg (town) Sullivan County, 675
Farmland (town) Randolph County, 650
Fayette County, 512
Ferdinand (town) Dubois County, 507
Fillmore (town) Putnam County, 647
Fish Lake (cdp) LaPorte County, 585
Fishers (city) Hamilton County, 533
Flat Rock (unincorporated postal area) Shelby County, 663
Flora (town) Carroll County, 477
Florence (cdp) Switzerland County, 677
Floyd County, 512
Floyds Knobs (unincorporated postal area) Floyd County, 513
Fontanet (cdp) Vigo County, 691
Forest (unincorporated postal area) Clinton County, 488
Fort Branch (town) Gibson County, 521
Fort Wayne (city) Allen County, 463
Fortville (town) Hancock County, 535
Fountain City (town) Wayne County, 706
Fountain County, 514
Fountaintown (unincorporated postal area) Shelby County, 664
Fowler (town) Benton County, 470
Fowlerton (town) Grant County, 525
Francesville (town) Pulaski County, 645
Francisco (town) Gibson County, 522
Frankfort (city) Clinton County, 488
Franklin (city) Johnson County, 565
Franklin County, 517
Frankton (town) Madison County, 595
Fredericksburg (cdp) Washington County, 702
Freedom (unincorporated postal area) Owen County, 629
Freelandville (cdp) Knox County, 569
Freetown (cdp) Jackson County, 554
Fremont (town) Steuben County, 672
French Lick (town) Orange County, 626
Fulton (town) Fulton County, 520
Fulton County, 519
Galena (cdp) Floyd County, 513
Galveston (town) Cass County, 478
Garrett (city) DeKalb County, 502
Gary (city) Lake County, 579
Gas City (city) Grant County, 525
Gaston (town) Delaware County, 504
Geneva (town) Adams County, 462
Gentryville (town) Spencer County, 666
Georgetown (town) Floyd County, 513
Gibson County, 521
Glenwood (town) Rush County, 656
Goldsmith (unincorporated postal area) Tipton County, 683
Goodland (town) Newton County, 620
Goshen (city) Elkhart County, 510
Gosport (town) Owen County, 629
Grabill (town) Allen County, 464
Grandview (town) Spencer County, 667
Granger (cdp) Saint Joseph County, 658
Grant County, 524
Grantsburg (unincorporated postal area) Crawford County, 491
Greencastle (city) Putnam County, 647
Greendale (city) Dearborn County, 496
Greene County, 529
Greenfield (city) Hancock County, 536
Greens Fork (town) Wayne County, 706
Greensboro (town) Henry County, 546
Greensburg (city) Decatur County, 499
Greentown (town) Howard County, 549
Greenville (town) Floyd County, 514
Greenwood (city) Johnson County, 566
Griffin (town) Posey County, 643
Griffith (town) Lake County, 580
Grissom AFB (cdp) Miami County, 609
Grovertown (unincorporated postal area) Starke County, 669
Guilford (unincorporated postal area) Dearborn County, 496
Gwynneville (unincorporated postal area) Shelby County, 664
Hagerstown (town) Wayne County, 706
Hamilton (town) Steuben County, 672
Hamilton County, 532
Hamlet (town) Starke County, 670
Hammond (city) Lake County, 580
Hancock County, 535
Hanna (cdp) LaPorte County, 585
Hanover (town) Jefferson County, 561
Hardinsburg (town) Washington County, 702
Harlan (cdp) Allen County, 464
Harmony (town) Clay County, 487
Harrison County, 537
Harrodsburg (cdp) Monroe County, 612
Hartford City (city) Blackford County, 471
Hartsville (town) Bartholomew County, 468
Hatfield (cdp) Spencer County, 667
Haubstadt (town) Gibson County, 522
Hayden (cdp) Jennings County, 563
Hazleton (town) Gibson County, 522
Hebron (town) Porter County, 639
Heltonville (unincorporated postal area) Lawrence County, 591
Hendricks County, 541
Henry County, 545
Henryville (cdp) Clark County, 482
Herbst (cdp) Grant County, 525
Heritage Lake (cdp) Putnam County, 648
Hidden Valley (cdp) Dearborn County, 496
Highland (town) Lake County, 580
Highland (cdp) Vanderburgh County, 687
Hillsboro (town) Fountain County, 515
Hillsdale (unincorporated postal area) Vermillion County, 689
Hoagland (cdp) Allen County, 464
Hobart (city) Lake County, 581
Hobbs (unincorporated postal area) Tipton County, 683
Holland (town) Dubois County, 507
Holton (town) Ripley County, 653
Homecroft (town) Marion County, 598
Homer (unincorporated postal area) Rush County, 656
Hope (town) Bartholomew County, 468
Howard County, 549
Howe (cdp) LaGrange County, 576
Hudson (town) Steuben County, 673
Hudson Lake (cdp) LaPorte County, 586
Huntertown (town) Allen County, 464
Huntingburg (city) Dubois County, 507
Huntington (city) Huntington County, 551
Huntington County, 550

CDP = Census Designated Place

Hymera (town) Sullivan County, 675
Idaville (cdp) White County, 713
Indian Village (town) Saint Joseph County, 658
Indianapolis (city) Marion County, 599
Ingalls (town) Madison County, 595
Jackson County, 553
Jalapa (cdp) Grant County, 526
Jamestown (town) Boone County, 473
Jasonville (city) Greene County, 529
Jasper (city) Dubois County, 508
Jasper County, 555
Jay County, 557
Jefferson County, 559
Jeffersonville (city) Clark County, 482
Jennings County, 562
Johnson County, 564
Jonesboro (city) Grant County, 526
Jonesville (town) Bartholomew County, 468
Kempton (town) Tipton County, 683
Kendallville (city) Noble County, 623
Kennard (town) Henry County, 546
Kent (cdp) Jefferson County, 561
Kentland (town) Newton County, 620
Kewanna (town) Fulton County, 520
Keystone (unincorporated postal area) Wells County, 709
Kimmell (cdp) Noble County, 624
Kingman (town) Fountain County, 516
Kingsbury (town) LaPorte County, 586
Kingsford Heights (town) LaPorte County, 586
Kirklin (town) Clinton County, 489
Knightstown (town) Henry County, 546
Knightsville (town) Clay County, 487
Knox (city) Starke County, 670
Knox County, 567
Kokomo (city) Howard County, 550
Koontz Lake (cdp) Starke County, 670
Kosciusko County, 571
Kouts (town) Porter County, 639
La Crosse (town) LaPorte County, 586
La Fontaine (town) Wabash County, 695
La Paz (town) Marshall County, 605
La Porte (city) LaPorte County, 587
Laconia (town) Harrison County, 539
Ladoga (town) Montgomery County, 614
Lafayette (city) Tippecanoe County, 680
Lagrange (town) LaGrange County, 576
LaGrange County, 575
Lagro (town) Wabash County, 695
Lake County, 577
Lake Dalecarlia (cdp) Lake County, 581
Lake Holiday (cdp) Montgomery County, 614
Lake Santee (cdp) Decatur County, 499
Lake Station (city) Lake County, 581
Lake Village (cdp) Newton County, 621
Lakes of the Four Seasons (cdp) Lake County, 581
Laketon (cdp) Wabash County, 696
Lakeville (town) Saint Joseph County, 658
Lamar (unincorporated postal area) Spencer County, 667
Landess (cdp) Grant County, 526
Lanesville (town) Harrison County, 539
Laotto (unincorporated postal area) Noble County, 624
Lapel (town) Madison County, 595
LaPorte County, 585
Larwill (town) Whitley County, 715
Laurel (town) Franklin County, 518
Lawrence (city) Marion County, 601
Lawrence County, 590
Lawrenceburg (city) Dearborn County, 497
Leavenworth (town) Crawford County, 491
Lebanon (city) Boone County, 473
Leesburg (town) Kosciusko County, 573
Leo-Cedarville (town) Allen County, 465
Leopold (unincorporated postal area) Perry County, 634
Lewis (unincorporated postal area) Vigo County, 691
Lewisville (town) Henry County, 547
Lexington (unincorporated postal area) Jefferson County, 561
Liberty (town) Union County, 685
Liberty Center (unincorporated postal area) Wells County, 710
Liberty Mills (unincorporated postal area) Wabash County, 696
Ligonier (city) Noble County, 624
Lincoln City (unincorporated postal area) Spencer County, 667
Linden (town) Montgomery County, 614
Linton (city) Greene County, 530
Little York (town) Washington County, 702
Livonia (town) Washington County, 703
Lizton (town) Hendricks County, 543
Logansport (city) Cass County, 479
Long Beach (town) LaPorte County, 587
Loogootee (city) Martin County, 607
Losantville (town) Randolph County, 650
Lowell (town) Lake County, 582
Lucerne (unincorporated postal area) Cass County, 479
Lynn (town) Randolph County, 650
Lynnville (town) Warrick County, 700
Lyons (town) Greene County, 530
Mackey (town) Gibson County, 522
Macy (town) Miami County, 609
Madison (city) Jefferson County, 561
Madison County, 592
Manilla (cdp) Rush County, 656
Marengo (town) Crawford County, 491
Marion (city) Grant County, 526
Marion County, 597
Markle (town) Huntington County, 552
Markleville (town) Madison County, 595
Marshall (town) Parke County, 631
Marshall County, 603
Martin County, 606
Martinsville (city) Morgan County, 618
Marysville (unincorporated postal area) Clark County, 483
Matthews (town) Grant County, 527
Mauckport (town) Harrison County, 540
Mays (unincorporated postal area) Rush County, 656
McCordsville (town) Hancock County, 536
Mecca (town) Parke County, 631
Medaryville (town) Pulaski County, 645
Medora (town) Jackson County, 554
Mellott (town) Fountain County, 516
Melody Hill (cdp) Vanderburgh County, 687
Memphis (cdp) Clark County, 483
Mentone (town) Kosciusko County, 573
Meridian Hills (town) Marion County, 601
Merom (town) Sullivan County, 675
Merrillville (town) Lake County, 582
Metamora (cdp) Franklin County, 518
Mexico (cdp) Miami County, 609
Miami (unincorporated postal area) Miami County, 610
Miami County, 607
Michiana Shores (town) LaPorte County, 587
Michigan City (city) LaPorte County, 587
Michigantown (town) Clinton County, 489
Middlebury (town) Elkhart County, 510
Middletown (town) Henry County, 547
Mier (cdp) Grant County, 527
Milan (town) Ripley County, 653
Milford (town) Kosciusko County, 573
Mill Creek (unincorporated postal area) LaPorte County, 588
Millersburg (town) Elkhart County, 510
Millhousen (town) Decatur County, 499
Milltown (town) Crawford County, 492
Milroy (cdp) Rush County, 657
Milton (town) Wayne County, 707
Mishawaka (city) Saint Joseph County, 658
Mitchell (city) Lawrence County, 591
Modoc (town) Randolph County, 650
Monon (town) White County, 713
Monroe (town) Adams County, 462
Monroe City (town) Knox County, 569
Monroe County, 610
Monroeville (town) Allen County, 465
Monrovia (town) Morgan County, 618
Monterey (town) Pulaski County, 645
Montezuma (town) Parke County, 631
Montgomery (town) Daviess County, 493
Montgomery County, 613
Monticello (city) White County, 713
Montmorenci (cdp) Tippecanoe County, 681
Montpelier (city) Blackford County, 471
Mooreland (town) Henry County, 547
Moores Hill (town) Dearborn County, 497
Mooresville (town) Morgan County, 618
Morgan County, 616
Morgantown (town) Morgan County, 619
Morocco (town) Newton County, 621
Morristown (town) Shelby County, 664
Mount Auburn (town) Wayne County, 707
Mount Ayr (town) Newton County, 621
Mount Carmel (town) Franklin County, 519
Mount Etna (town) Huntington County, 552
Mount Summit (town) Henry County, 547
Mount Vernon (city) Posey County, 643
Mulberry (town) Clinton County, 489
Muncie (city) Delaware County, 504
Munster (town) Lake County, 582
Nabb (unincorporated postal area) Clark County, 483
Napoleon (town) Ripley County, 653
Nappanee (city) Elkhart County, 511
Nashville (town) Brown County, 475
Needham (unincorporated postal area) Johnson County, 566
New Albany (city) Floyd County, 514
New Amsterdam (town) Harrison County, 540

Index

CDP = Census Designated Place

New Carlisle (town) Saint Joseph County, 659
New Castle (city) Henry County, 548
New Chicago (town) Lake County, 583
New Goshen (cdp) Vigo County, 692
New Harmony (town) Posey County, 643
New Haven (city) Allen County, 465
New Market (town) Montgomery County, 615
New Middletown (town) Harrison County, 540
New Palestine (town) Hancock County, 536
New Paris (cdp) Elkhart County, 511
New Pekin (town) Washington County, 703
New Point (town) Decatur County, 499
New Richmond (town) Montgomery County, 615
New Ross (town) Montgomery County, 615
New Salisbury (cdp) Harrison County, 540
New Trenton (cdp) Franklin County, 519
New Washington (cdp) Clark County, 483
New Waverly (unincorporated postal area) Cass County, 479
New Whiteland (town) Johnson County, 566
Newberry (town) Greene County, 530
Newburgh (town) Warrick County, 701
Newport (town) Vermillion County, 689
Newton County, 619
Newtown (town) Fountain County, 516
Nineveh (unincorporated postal area) Brown County, 475
Noble County, 622
Noblesville (city) Hamilton County, 534
Norman (unincorporated postal area) Jackson County, 554
North Crows Nest (town) Marion County, 601
North Judson (town) Starke County, 670
North Liberty (town) Saint Joseph County, 659
North Manchester (town) Wabash County, 696
North Salem (town) Hendricks County, 544
North Terre Haute (cdp) Vigo County, 692
North Vernon (city) Jennings County, 563
North Webster (town) Kosciusko County, 573
Norway (cdp) White County, 713
Notre Dame (cdp) Saint Joseph County, 659
Oakland City (city) Gibson County, 523
Oaktown (town) Knox County, 570
Oakville (unincorporated postal area) Delaware County, 505
Odon (town) Daviess County, 494
Ogden Dunes (town) Porter County, 640
Ohio County, 625
Oldenburg (town) Franklin County, 519
Onward (town) Cass County, 479
Oolitic (town) Lawrence County, 591
Ora (unincorporated postal area) Starke County, 671
Orange County, 626
Orestes (town) Madison County, 596
Orland (town) Steuben County, 673
Orleans (town) Orange County, 627
Osceola (town) Saint Joseph County, 660
Osgood (town) Ripley County, 654
Ossian (town) Wells County, 710
Otisco (unincorporated postal area) Clark County, 484
Otterbein (town) Benton County, 470
Otwell (cdp) Pike County, 636
Owen County, 628
Owensburg (cdp) Greene County, 531
Owensville (town) Gibson County, 523
Oxford (town) Benton County, 470
Painted Hills (cdp) Morgan County, 619
Palmyra (town) Harrison County, 540
Paoli (town) Orange County, 627
Paragon (town) Morgan County, 619
Paris Crossing (unincorporated postal area) Jennings County, 563
Parke County, 630
Parker City (town) Randolph County, 651
Parkers Settlement (cdp) Posey County, 644
Patoka (town) Gibson County, 523
Patriot (town) Switzerland County, 678
Paxton (unincorporated postal area) Sullivan County, 676
Pekin (unincorporated postal area) Washington County, 703
Pendleton (town) Madison County, 596
Pennville (town) Jay County, 558
Perry County, 632
Perrysville (town) Vermillion County, 690
Peru (city) Miami County, 610
Petersburg (city) Pike County, 636
Pierceton (town) Kosciusko County, 574
Pike County, 635
Pimento (unincorporated postal area) Vigo County, 692
Pine Village (town) Warren County, 698
Pittsboro (town) Hendricks County, 544
Plainfield (town) Hendricks County, 544
Plainville (town) Daviess County, 494
Pleasant Lake (unincorporated postal area) Steuben County, 673
Plymouth (city) Marshall County, 605
Point Isabel (cdp) Grant County, 527
Poland (unincorporated postal area) Owen County, 629
Poneto (town) Wells County, 710
Portage (city) Porter County, 640
Porter (town) Porter County, 640
Porter County, 637
Portland (city) Jay County, 558
Posey County, 642
Poseyville (town) Posey County, 644
Pottawattamie Park (town) LaPorte County, 588
Prairie Creek (unincorporated postal area) Vigo County, 692
Princes Lakes (town) Johnson County, 567
Princeton (city) Gibson County, 524
Pulaski County, 644
Putnam County, 646
Quincy (unincorporated postal area) Owen County, 629
Raglesville (cdp) Daviess County, 494
Ragsdale (cdp) Knox County, 570
Ramsey (unincorporated postal area) Harrison County, 541
Randolph County, 649
Redkey (town) Jay County, 559
Reelsville (unincorporated postal area) Putnam County, 648
Remington (town) Jasper County, 556
Rensselaer (city) Jasper County, 556
Reynolds (town) White County, 714
Richland (town) Spencer County, 668
Richmond (city) Wayne County, 707
Ridgeville (town) Randolph County, 651
Riley (town) Vigo County, 692
Ripley County, 652
Rising Sun (city) Ohio County, 626
River Forest (town) Madison County, 596
Roachdale (town) Putnam County, 648
Roann (town) Wabash County, 696
Roanoke (town) Huntington County, 552
Rochester (city) Fulton County, 521
Rockport (city) Spencer County, 668
Rockville (town) Parke County, 632
Rocky Ripple (town) Marion County, 601
Rolling Prairie (cdp) LaPorte County, 588
Rome (unincorporated postal area) Perry County, 634
Rome City (town) Noble County, 624
Romney (unincorporated postal area) Tippecanoe County, 681
Rosedale (town) Parke County, 632
Roseland (town) Saint Joseph County, 660
Roselawn (cdp) Newton County, 621
Rossville (town) Clinton County, 489
Royal Center (town) Cass County, 480
Rush County, 654
Rushville (city) Rush County, 657
Russellville (town) Putnam County, 649
Russiaville (town) Howard County, 550
Saint Anthony (unincorporated postal area) Dubois County, 508
Saint Bernice (cdp) Vermillion County, 690
Saint Croix (unincorporated postal area) Perry County, 634
Saint Joe (town) DeKalb County, 502
Saint John (town) Lake County, 583
Saint Joseph County, 657
Saint Leon (town) Dearborn County, 497
Saint Mary of the Woods (cdp) Vigo County, 693
Saint Meinrad (cdp) Spencer County, 668
Saint Paul (town) Decatur County, 500
Salamonia (town) Jay County, 559
Salem (city) Washington County, 703
Salt Creek Commons (cdp) Porter County, 640
Saltillo (town) Washington County, 704
San Pierre (cdp) Starke County, 671
Sandborn (town) Knox County, 570
Santa Claus (town) Spencer County, 668
Saratoga (town) Randolph County, 651
Schererville (town) Lake County, 583
Schneider (town) Lake County, 584
Schnellville (unincorporated postal area) Dubois County, 508
Scipio (cdp) Jennings County, 564
Scotland (cdp) Greene County, 531
Scott County, 661
Scottsburg (city) Scott County, 662
Seelyville (town) Vigo County, 693
Sellersburg (town) Clark County, 484
Selma (town) Delaware County, 505
Seymour (city) Jackson County, 554
Shadeland (town) Tippecanoe County, 681
Shamrock Lakes (town) Blackford County, 472
Sharpsville (town) Tipton County, 683
Shelburn (town) Sullivan County, 676

CDP = Census Designated Place

Shelby (cdp) Lake County, 584
Shelby County, 662
Shelbyville (city) Shelby County, 664
Shepardsville (cdp) Vigo County, 693
Sheridan (town) Hamilton County, 534
Shipshewana (town) LaGrange County, 576
Shirley (town) Hancock County, 537
Shoals (town) Martin County, 607
Shorewood Forest (cdp) Porter County, 641
Sidney (town) Kosciusko County, 574
Silver Lake (town) Kosciusko County, 574
Simonton Lake (cdp) Elkhart County, 511
Sims (cdp) Grant County, 527
Smithville-Sanders (cdp) Monroe County, 612
Solsberry (unincorporated postal area) Greene County, 531
Somerset (cdp) Wabash County, 697
Somerville (town) Gibson County, 524
South Bend (city) Saint Joseph County, 660
South Haven (cdp) Porter County, 641
South Milford (unincorporated postal area) LaGrange County, 577
South Whitley (town) Whitley County, 715
Southport (city) Marion County, 602
Speedway (town) Marion County, 602
Spencer (town) Owen County, 630
Spencer County, 665
Spencerville (unincorporated postal area) Allen County, 466
Spiceland (town) Henry County, 548
Spring Grove (town) Wayne County, 708
Spring Hill (town) Marion County, 602
Spring Lake (town) Hancock County, 537
Springport (town) Henry County, 548
Springville (unincorporated postal area) Lawrence County, 591
Spurgeon (town) Pike County, 636
Star City (cdp) Pulaski County, 646
Starke County, 669
State Line City (town) Warren County, 698
Staunton (town) Clay County, 487
Stendal (unincorporated postal area) Pike County, 636
Steuben County, 671
Stilesville (town) Hendricks County, 544
Stinesville (town) Monroe County, 612
Stockwell (cdp) Tippecanoe County, 681
Straughn (town) Henry County, 548
Sullivan (city) Sullivan County, 676
Sullivan County, 673
Sulphur Springs (town) Henry County, 549
Sumava Resorts (unincorporated postal area) Newton County, 622
Summitville (town) Madison County, 596
Sunman (town) Ripley County, 654
Swayzee (town) Grant County, 528
Sweetser (town) Grant County, 528
Switz City (town) Greene County, 531
Switzerland County, 676
Syracuse (town) Kosciusko County, 574
Taswell (unincorporated postal area) Crawford County, 492
Taylorsville (cdp) Bartholomew County, 468
Tecumseh (cdp) Vigo County, 693
Tell City (city) Perry County, 635
Tennyson (town) Warrick County, 701
Terre Haute (city) Vigo County, 694
Thayer (unincorporated postal area) Newton County, 622
Thorntown (town) Boone County, 473
Tippecanoe (unincorporated postal area) Marshall County, 605
Tippecanoe County, 678
Tipton (city) Tipton County, 684
Tipton County, 682
Toad Hop (cdp) Vigo County, 694
Topeka (town) LaGrange County, 577
Town of Pines (town) Porter County, 641
Trafalgar (town) Johnson County, 567
Trail Creek (town) LaPorte County, 589
Tri-Lakes (cdp) Whitley County, 716
Troy (town) Perry County, 635
Tunnelton (unincorporated postal area) Lawrence County, 592
Twelve Mile (unincorporated postal area) Cass County, 480
Ulen (town) Boone County, 473
Underwood (unincorporated postal area) Scott County, 662
Union City (city) Randolph County, 651
Union County, 684
Union Mills (unincorporated postal area) LaPorte County, 589
Uniondale (town) Wells County, 710
Unionville (unincorporated postal area) Monroe County, 612
Universal (town) Vermillion County, 690
Upland (town) Grant County, 528
Urbana (unincorporated postal area) Wabash County, 697
Utica (town) Clark County, 484
Vallonia (cdp) Jackson County, 555
Valparaiso (city) Porter County, 641
Van Bibber Lake (cdp) Putnam County, 649
Van Buren (town) Grant County, 529
Vanderburgh County, 685
Veedersburg (town) Fountain County, 516
Velpen (unincorporated postal area) Pike County, 637
Vera Cruz (town) Wells County, 711
Vermillion County, 687
Vernon (town) Jennings County, 564
Versailles (town) Ripley County, 654
Vevay (town) Switzerland County, 678
Vigo County, 690
Vincennes (city) Knox County, 570
Wabash (city) Wabash County, 697
Wabash County, 695
Wadesville (unincorporated postal area) Posey County, 644
Wakarusa (town) Elkhart County, 511
Waldron (cdp) Shelby County, 665
Walkerton (town) Saint Joseph County, 661
Wallace (town) Fountain County, 517
Walton (town) Cass County, 480
Wanatah (town) LaPorte County, 589
Warren (town) Huntington County, 552
Warren County, 698
Warren Park (town) Marion County, 602
Warrick County, 699
Warsaw (city) Kosciusko County, 575
Washington (city) Daviess County, 494
Washington County, 701
Waterloo (town) DeKalb County, 502
Waveland (town) Montgomery County, 615
Wawaka (unincorporated postal area) Noble County, 625
Wayne County, 704
Waynetown (town) Montgomery County, 616
Wells County, 708
West Baden Springs (town) Orange County, 627
West College Corner (town) Union County, 685
West Harrison (town) Dearborn County, 498
West Lafayette (city) Tippecanoe County, 682
West Lebanon (town) Warren County, 698
West Newton (unincorporated postal area) Marion County, 603
West Point (cdp) Tippecanoe County, 682
West Terre Haute (town) Vigo County, 694
Westfield (city) Hamilton County, 534
Westphalia (cdp) Knox County, 571
Westpoint (unincorporated postal area) Tippecanoe County, 682
Westport (town) Decatur County, 500
Westville (town) LaPorte County, 589
Wheatfield (town) Jasper County, 557
Wheatland (town) Knox County, 571
Wheeler (cdp) Porter County, 642
White County, 711
Whiteland (town) Johnson County, 567
Whitestown (town) Boone County, 474
Whitewater (town) Wayne County, 708
Whiting (city) Lake County, 584
Whitley County, 714
Wilkinson (town) Hancock County, 537
Williams (cdp) Lawrence County, 592
Williams Creek (town) Marion County, 603
Williamsburg (unincorporated postal area) Wayne County, 708
Williamsport (town) Warren County, 699
Winamac (town) Pulaski County, 646
Winchester (city) Randolph County, 652
Windfall City (town) Tipton County, 684
Winfield (town) Lake County, 584
Wingate (town) Montgomery County, 616
Winona Lake (town) Kosciusko County, 575
Winslow (town) Pike County, 637
Wolcott (town) White County, 714
Wolcottville (town) Noble County, 625
Woodburn (city) Allen County, 466
Woodlawn Heights (town) Madison County, 597
Worthington (town) Greene County, 532
Wyatt (unincorporated postal area) Saint Joseph County, 661
Wynnedale (town) Marion County, 603
Yeoman (town) Carroll County, 478
Yoder (unincorporated postal area) Allen County, 466
Yorktown (town) Delaware County, 505
Young America (unincorporated postal area) Cass County, 480
Zanesville (town) Wells County, 711
Zionsville (town) Boone County, 474

Index

CDP = Census Designated Place

2019 Title List

Grey House Publishing

Visit **www.GreyHouse.com** for Product Information, Table of Contents, and Sample Pages.

General Reference
America's College Museums
American Environmental Leaders: From Colonial Times to the Present
Encyclopedia of African-American Writing
Encyclopedia of Constitutional Amendments
Encyclopedia of Human Rights and the United States
Encyclopedia of Invasions & Conquests
Encyclopedia of Prisoners of War & Internment
Encyclopedia of Religion & Law in America
Encyclopedia of Rural America
Encyclopedia of the Continental Congress
Encyclopedia of the United States Cabinet, 1789-2010
Encyclopedia of War Journalism
Encyclopedia of Warrior Peoples & Fighting Groups
The Environmental Debate: A Documentary History
The Evolution Wars: A Guide to the Debates
From Suffrage to the Senate: America's Political Women
Gun Debate: An Encyclopedia of Gun Rights & Gun Control in the U.S.
Opinions throughout History: National Security vs. Civil and Privacy Rights
Opinions throughout History: Immigration
Opinions throughout History: Drug Use & Abuse
Opinions throughout History: Gender: Roles & Rights
Opinions throughout History: The Environment
Opinions throughout History: Social Media Issues
Opinions throughout History: The Death Penalty
Opinions throughout History: Voters' Rights
Political Corruption in America
Privacy Rights in the Digital Age
The Religious Right: A Reference Handbook
Speakers of the House of Representatives, 1789-2009
This is Who We Were: 1880-1900
This is Who We Were: A Companion to the 1940 Census
This is Who We Were: In Colonial America
This is Who We Were: In the 1900s
This is Who We Were: In the 1910s
This is Who We Were: In the 1920s
This is Who We Were: In the 1940s
This is Who We Were: In the 1950s
This is Who We Were: In the 1960s
This is Who We Were: In the 1970s
This is Who We Were: In the 1980s
This is Who We Were: In the 1990s
This is Who We Were: In the 2000s
U.S. Land & Natural Resource Policy
The Value of a Dollar 1600-1865: Colonial Era to the Civil War
The Value of a Dollar: 1860-2019
Working Americans 1880-1999 Vol. I: The Working Class
Working Americans 1880-1999 Vol. II: The Middle Class
Working Americans 1880-1999 Vol. III: The Upper Class
Working Americans 1880-1999 Vol. IV: Their Children
Working Americans 1880-2015 Vol. V: Americans At War
Working Americans 1880-2005 Vol. VI: Women at Work
Working Americans 1880-2006 Vol. VII: Social Movements
Working Americans 1880-2007 Vol. VIII: Immigrants
Working Americans 1770-1869 Vol. IX: Revolutionary War to the Civil War
Working Americans 1880-2009 Vol. X: Sports & Recreation
Working Americans 1880-2010 Vol. XI: Inventors & Entrepreneurs
Working Americans 1880-2011 Vol. XII: Our History through Music
Working Americans 1880-2012 Vol. XIII: Education & Educators
Working Americans 1880-2016 Vol. XIV: Industry Through the Ages
Working Americans 1880-2017 Vol. XV: Politics & Politicians
World Cultural Leaders of the 20th & 21st Centuries

Education Information
Charter School Movement
The Comparative Guide to American Elementary & Secondary Schools
Complete Learning Disabilities Resource Guide
Educators Resource Guide
Special Education: A Reference Book for Policy and Curriculum Development

Health Information
Comparative Guide to American Hospitals
Complete Resource Guide for Pediatric Disorders
Complete Resource Guide for People with Chronic Illness
Complete Resource Guide for People with Disabilities
Complete Mental Health Resource Guide
Diabetes in America: Analysis of an Epidemic
Guide to Health Care Group Purchasing Organizations
Guide to U.S. HMO's & PPO's
Medical Device Market Place
Older Americans Information Resource

Business Information
Complete Television, Radio & Cable Industry Guide
Business Information Resources
Directory of Mail Order Catalogs
Guide to Venture Capital & Private Equity Firms
Environmental Resource Handbook
Financial Literacy Starter Kit
Food & Beverage Market Place
The Grey House Homeland Security Directory
The Grey House Performing Arts Industry Guide
The Grey House Safety & Security Directory
Hudson's Washington News Media Contacts Directory
New York State Directory
Sports Market Place

Statistics & Demographics
American Tally
America's Top-Rated Cities
America's Top-Rated Smaller Cities
Ancestry & Ethnicity in America
The Asian Databook
The Comparative Guide to American Suburbs
The Hispanic Databook
Nations of the World
Profiles of America
"Profiles of" Series - State Handbooks
Weather America

Financial Ratings Series
Financial Literacy Basics
TheStreet Ratings' Ultimate Guided Tour of Stock Investing
Weiss Ratings' Investment Research Guide to Bond & Money Market Mutual Funds
Weiss Ratings' Investment Research Guide to Stocks
Weiss Ratings' Investment Research Guide to Exchange-Traded Funds
Weiss Ratings' Investment Research Guide to Stock Mutual Funds
Weiss Ratings' Consumer Guides
Weiss Ratings' Financial Literary Basic Guides
Weiss Ratings' Guide to Banks
Weiss Ratings' Guide to Credit Unions
Weiss Ratings' Guide to Health Insurers
Weiss Ratings' Guide to Life & Annuity Insurers
Weiss Ratings' Guide to Property & Casualty Insurers

Bowker's Books In Print® Titles
American Book Publishing Record® Annual
American Book Publishing Record® Monthly
Books In Print®
Books In Print® Supplement
Books Out Loud™
Bowker's Complete Video Directory™
Children's Books In Print®
El-Hi Textbooks & Serials In Print®
Forthcoming Books®
Law Books & Serials In Print™
Medical & Health Care Books In Print™
Publishers, Distributors & Wholesalers of the US™
Subject Guide to Books In Print®
Subject Guide to Children's Books In Print®

Grey House Publishing

2019 Title List

Visit www.GreyHouse.com for Product Information, Table of Contents, and Sample Pages.

Canadian General Reference

Associations Canada
Canadian Almanac & Directory
Canadian Environmental Resource Guide
Canadian Parliamentary Guide
Canadian Venture Capital & Private Equity Firms
Canadian Who's Who
Financial Post Bonds
Financial Post Directory of Directors
Financial Post Equities
Financial Post Survey
Financial Services Canada
Government Canada
Health Guide Canada
The History of Canada
Libraries Canada
Major Canadian Cities

2019 Title List

Visit **www.SalemPress.com** for Product Information, Table of Contents, and Sample Pages.

Science, Careers & Mathematics

Ancient Creatures
Applied Science
Applied Science: Engineering & Mathematics
Applied Science: Science & Medicine
Applied Science: Technology
Biomes and Ecosystems
Careers in the Arts: Fine, Performing & Visual
Careers in Building Construction
Careers in Business
Careers in Chemistry
Careers in Communications & Media
Careers in Environment & Conservation
Careers in Financial Services
Careers in Green Energy
Careers in Healthcare
Careers in Hospitality & Tourism
Careers in Human Services
Careers in Law, Criminal Justice & Emergency Services
Careers in Manufacturing
Careers in Nursing
Careers Outdoors
Careers Overseas
Careers in Physics
Careers in Protective Services
Careers in Psychology
Careers in Sales, Insurance & Real Estate
Careers in Science & Engineering
Careers in Social Media
Careers in Sports & Fitness
Careers in Sports Medicine & Training
Careers in Technology Services & Equipment Repair
Careers in Transportation
Computer Technology Innovators
Contemporary Biographies in Business
Contemporary Biographies in Chemistry
Contemporary Biographies in Communications & Media
Contemporary Biographies in Environment & Conservation
Contemporary Biographies in Healthcare
Contemporary Biographies in Hospitality & Tourism
Contemporary Biographies in Law & Criminal Justice
Contemporary Biographies in Physics
Earth Science
Earth Science: Earth Materials & Resources
Earth Science: Earth's Surface and History
Earth Science: Physics & Chemistry of the Earth
Earth Science: Weather, Water & Atmosphere
Encyclopedia of Energy
Encyclopedia of Environmental Issues
Encyclopedia of Environmental Issues: Atmosphere and Air Pollution
Encyclopedia of Environmental Issues: Ecology and Ecosystems
Encyclopedia of Environmental Issues: Energy and Energy Use
Encyclopedia of Environmental Issues: Policy and Activism
Encyclopedia of Environmental Issues: Preservation/Wilderness Issues
Encyclopedia of Environmental Issues: Water and Water Pollution
Encyclopedia of Global Resources
Encyclopedia of Global Warming
Encyclopedia of Mathematics & Society
Encyclopedia of Mathematics & Society: Engineering, Tech, Medicine
Encyclopedia of Mathematics & Society: Great Mathematicians
Encyclopedia of Mathematics & Society: Math & Social Sciences
Encyclopedia of Mathematics & Society: Math Development/Concepts
Encyclopedia of Mathematics & Society: Math in Culture & Society
Encyclopedia of Mathematics & Society: Space, Science, Environment
Encyclopedia of the Ancient World
Forensic Science
Geography Basics
Internet Innovators
Inventions and Inventors
Magill's Encyclopedia of Science: Animal Life
Magill's Encyclopedia of Science: Plant life
Notable Natural Disasters
Principles of Artificial Intelligence & Robotics
Principles of Astronomy
Principles of Biology
Principles of Biotechnology
Principles of Business: Accounting
Principles of Business: Economics
Principles of Business: Entrepreneurship
Principles of Business: Finance
Principles of Business: Globalization
Principles of Business: Leadership
Principles of Business: Management
Principles of Business: Marketing
Principles of Chemistry
Principles of Climatology
Principles of Ecology
Principles of Modern Agriculture
Principles of Pharmacology
Principles of Physical Science
Principles of Physics
Principles of Programming & Coding
Principles of Research Methods
Principles of Sociology: Group Relationships & Behavior
Principles of Sociology: Personal Relationships & Behavior
Principles of Sociology: Societal Issues & Behavior
Principles of Sustainability
Science and Scientists
Solar System
Solar System: Great Astronomers
Solar System: Study of the Universe
Solar System: The Inner Planets
Solar System: The Moon and Other Small Bodies
Solar System: The Outer Planets
Solar System: The Sun and Other Stars
USA in Space
World Geography

Literature

American Ethnic Writers
Classics of Science Fiction & Fantasy Literature
Critical Approaches to Literature
Critical Insights: Authors
Critical Insights: Film
Critical Insights: Literary Collection Bundles
Critical Insights: Themes
Critical Insights: Works
Critical Survey of Drama
Critical Survey of Graphic Novels: Heroes & Superheroes
Critical Survey of Graphic Novels: History, Theme & Technique
Critical Survey of Graphic Novels: Independents/Underground Classics
Critical Survey of Graphic Novels: Manga
Critical Survey of Long Fiction
Critical Survey of Mystery & Detective Fiction
Critical Survey of Mythology and Folklore: Gods & Goddesses
Critical Survey of Mythology and Folklore: Heroes & Heroines
Critical Survey of Mythology and Folklore: Love, Sexuality & Desire
Critical Survey of Mythology and Folklore: World Mythology
Critical Survey of Poetry
Critical Survey of Poetry: American Poets
Critical Survey of Poetry: British, Irish & Commonwealth Poets
Critical Survey of Poetry: Cumulative Index
Critical Survey of Poetry: European Poets
Critical Survey of Poetry: Topical Essays
Critical Survey of Poetry: World Poets
Critical Survey of Science Fiction & Fantasy Literature
Critical Survey of Shakespeare's Plays
Critical Survey of Shakespeare's Sonnets
Critical Survey of Short Fiction
Critical Survey of Short Fiction: American Writers
Critical Survey of Short Fiction: British, Irish, Commonwealth Writers
Critical Survey of Short Fiction: Cumulative Index
Critical Survey of Short Fiction: European Writers
Critical Survey of Short Fiction: Topical Essays

2019 Title List

Visit **www.SalemPress.com** for Product Information, Table of Contents, and Sample Pages.

Critical Survey of Short Fiction: World Writers
Critical Survey of World Literature
Critical Survey of Young Adult Literature
Cyclopedia of Literary Characters
Cyclopedia of Literary Places
Holocaust Literature
Introduction to Literary Context: American Poetry of the 20th Century
Introduction to Literary Context: American Post-Modernist Novels
Introduction to Literary Context: American Short Fiction
Introduction to Literary Context: English Literature
Introduction to Literary Context: Plays
Introduction to Literary Context: World Literature
Magill's Literary Annual
Magill's Survey of American Literature
Magill's Survey of World Literature
Masterplots
Masterplots, 2002-2018 Supplement
Masterplots II: African American Literature
Masterplots II: American Fiction Series
Masterplots II: British & Commonwealth Fiction Series
Masterplots II: Christian Literature
Masterplots II: Drama Series
Masterplots II: Juvenile & Young Adult Literature, Supplement
Masterplots II: Nonfiction Series
Masterplots II: Poetry Series
Masterplots II: Short Story Series
Masterplots II: Women's Literature Series
Notable African American Writers
Notable American Novelists
Notable Playwrights
Notable Poets
Novels into Film: Adaptations & Interpretation
Recommended Reading: 600 Classics Reviewed
Short Story Writers

History and Social Science

The 1910s in America
The 2000s in America
50 States
African American History
Agriculture in History
American First Ladies
American Heroes
American Indian Culture
American Indian History
American Indian Tribes
American Presidents
American Villains
America's Historic Sites
Ancient Greece
The Bill of Rights
The Civil Rights Movement
The Cold War
Countries: Their Wars & Conflicts: A World Survey
Countries, Peoples & Cultures
Countries, Peoples & Cultures: Central & South America
Countries, Peoples & Cultures: Central, South & Southeast Asia
Countries, Peoples & Cultures: East & South Africa
Countries, Peoples & Cultures: East Asia & the Pacific
Countries, Peoples & Cultures: Eastern Europe
Countries, Peoples & Cultures: Middle East & North Africa
Countries, Peoples & Cultures: North America & the Caribbean
Countries, Peoples & Cultures: West & Central Africa
Countries, Peoples & Cultures: Western Europe
Defining Documents: American Revolution
The Criminal Justice System
Defining Documents: American West
Defining Documents: Ancient World
Defining Documents: Asia
Defining Documents: Business Ethics
Defining Documents: Capital Punishment
Defining Documents: Civil Rights
Defining Documents: Civil War
Defining Documents: Court Cases
Defining Documents: Dissent & Protest
Defining Documents: Emergence of Modern America
Defining Documents: Exploration & Colonial America
Defining Documents: The Free Press
Defining Documents: The Gun Debate
Defining Documents: Immigration & Immigrant Communities
Defining Documents: The Legacy of 9/11
Defining Documents: LGBTQ+
Defining Documents: Manifest Destiny
Defining Documents: Middle Ages
Defining Documents: Middle East
Defining Documents: Nationalism & Populism
Defining Documents: Native Americans
Defining Documents: Political Campaigns, Candidates & Debates
Defining Documents: Postwar 1940s
Defining Documents: Prison Reform
Defining Documents: Reconstruction
Defining Documents: Renaissance & Early Modern Era
Defining Documents: Secrets, Leaks & Scandals
Defining Documents: Slavery
Defining Documents: Supreme Court Decisions
Defining Documents: 1920s
Defining Documents: 1930s
Defining Documents: 1950s
Defining Documents: 1960s
Defining Documents: 1970s
Defining Documents: The 17th Century
Defining Documents: The 18th Century
Defining Documents: The 19th Century
Defining Documents: The 20th Century: 1900-1950
Defining Documents: Vietnam War
Defining Documents: Women's Rights
Defining Documents: World War I
Defining Documents: World War II
Education Today
The Eighties in America
Encyclopedia of American Immigration
Encyclopedia of Flight
Encyclopedia of the Ancient World
Ethics: Questions & Morality of Human Actions
Fashion Innovators
The Fifties in America
The Forties in America
Great Athletes
Great Athletes: Baseball
Great Athletes: Basketball
Great Athletes: Boxing & Soccer
Great Athletes: Cumulative Index
Great Athletes: Football
Great Athletes: Golf & Tennis
Great Athletes: Olympics
Great Athletes: Racing & Individual Sports
Great Contemporary Athletes
Great Events from History: 17th Century
Great Events from History: 18th Century
Great Events from History: 19th Century
Great Events from History: 20th Century (1901-1940)
Great Events from History: 20th Century (1941-1970)
Great Events from History: 20th Century (1971-2000)
Great Events from History: 21st Century (2000-2016)
Great Events from History: African American History
Great Events from History: Cumulative Indexes
Great Events from History: Human Rights
Great Events from History: LGBTQ Events
Great Events from History: Middle Ages
Great Events from History: Modern Scandals
Great Events from History: Secrets, Leaks & Scandals
Great Events from History: Renaissance & Early Modern Era
Great Lives from History: 17th Century
Great Lives from History: 18th Century

SALEM PRESS

SALEM PRESS

2019 Title List

Visit **www.SalemPress.com** for Product Information, Table of Contents, and Sample Pages.

Great Lives from History: 19th Century
Great Lives from History: 20th Century
Great Lives from History: 21st Century (2000-2017)
Great Lives from History: American Heroes
Great Lives from History: American Women
Great Lives from History: Ancient World
Great Lives from History: Asian & Pacific Islander Americans
Great Lives from History: Cumulative Indexes
Great Lives from History: Incredibly Wealthy
Great Lives from History: Inventors & Inventions
Great Lives from History: Jewish Americans
Great Lives from History: Latinos
Great Lives from History: Renaissance & Early Modern Era
Great Lives from History: Scientists & Science
Historical Encyclopedia of American Business
Issues in U.S. Immigration
Magill's Guide to Military History
Milestone Documents in African American History
Milestone Documents in American History
Milestone Documents in World History
Milestone Documents of American Leaders
Milestone Documents of World Religions
Music Innovators
Musicians & Composers 20th Century
The Nineties in America
The Seventies in America
The Sixties in America
Sociology Today
Survey of American Industry and Careers
The Thirties in America
The Twenties in America
United States at War
U.S. Court Cases
U.S. Government Leaders
U.S. Laws, Acts, and Treaties
U.S. Legal System
U.S. Supreme Court
Weapons and Warfare
World Conflicts: Asia and the Middle East

Health

Addictions, Substance Abuse & Alcoholism
Adolescent Health & Wellness
Aging
Cancer
Complementary & Alternative Medicine
Community & Family Health Issues
Genetics & Inherited Conditions
Infectious Diseases & Conditions
Magill's Medical Guide
Nutrition
Psychology & Behavioral Health
Psychology Basics
Women's Health

H.W. WILSON

2019 Title List

Visit **www.HWWilsonInPrint.com** for Product Information, Table of Contents and Sample Pages.

Current Biography
Current Biography Cumulative Index 1946-2013
Current Biography Monthly Magazine
Current Biography Yearbook: 2003
Current Biography Yearbook: 2004
Current Biography Yearbook: 2005
Current Biography Yearbook: 2006
Current Biography Yearbook: 2007
Current Biography Yearbook: 2008
Current Biography Yearbook: 2009
Current Biography Yearbook: 2010
Current Biography Yearbook: 2011
Current Biography Yearbook: 2012
Current Biography Yearbook: 2013
Current Biography Yearbook: 2014
Current Biography Yearbook: 2015
Current Biography Yearbook: 2016
Current Biography Yearbook: 2017
Current Biography Yearbook: 2018

Core Collections
Children's Core Collection
Fiction Core Collection
Graphic Novels Core Collection
Middle & Junior High School Core
Public Library Core Collection: Nonfiction
Senior High Core Collection
Young Adult Fiction Core Collection

The Reference Shelf
Affordable Housing
Aging in America
Alternative Facts: Post Truth & the Information War
The American Dream
American Military Presence Overseas
The Arab Spring
Artificial Intelligence
The Brain
The Business of Food
Campaign Trends & Election Law
Conspiracy Theories
Democracy Evolving
The Digital Age
Dinosaurs
Embracing New Paradigms in Education
Faith & Science
Families: Traditional and New Structures
The Future of U.S. Economic Relations: Mexico, Cuba, and Venezuela
Global Climate Change
Graphic Novels and Comic Books
Guns in America
Immigration
Immigration in the U.S.
Internet Abuses & Privacy Rights
Internet Safety
LGBTQ in the 21st Century
Marijuana Reform
New Frontiers in Space
The News and its Future
The Paranormal
Politics of the Ocean
Prescription Drug Abuse
Racial Tension in a "Postracial" Age
Reality Television
Representative American Speeches: 2008-2009
Representative American Speeches: 2009-2010
Representative American Speeches: 2010-2011
Representative American Speeches: 2011-2012
Representative American Speeches: 2012-2013
Representative American Speeches: 2013-2014
Representative American Speeches: 2014-2015
Representative American Speeches: 2015-2016
Representative American Speeches: 2016-2017
Representative American Speeches: 2017-2018
Representative American Speeches: 2018-2019
Rethinking Work
Revisiting Gender
Robotics
Russia
Social Networking
Social Services for the Poor
The South China Seas Conflict
Space Exploration & Development
Sports in America
The Supreme Court
The Transformation of American Cities
The Two Koreas
U.S. Infrastructure
U.S. National Debate Topic: Educational Reform
U.S. National Debate Topic: Surveillance
U.S. National Debate Topic: The Ocean
U.S. National Debate Topic: Transportation Infrastructure
Whistleblowers

Readers' Guide
Abridged Readers' Guide to Periodical Literature
Readers' Guide to Periodical Literature

Indexes
Index to Legal Periodicals & Books
Short Story Index
Book Review Digest

Sears List
Sears List of Subject Headings
Sears: Lista de Encabezamientos de Materia

Facts About Series
Facts About American Immigration
Facts About China
Facts About the 20th Century
Facts About the Presidents
Facts About the World's Languages

Nobel Prize Winners
Nobel Prize Winners: 1901-1986
Nobel Prize Winners: 1987-1991
Nobel Prize Winners: 1992-1996
Nobel Prize Winners: 1997-2001
Nobel Prize Winners: 2002-2018

World Authors
World Authors: 1995-2000
World Authors: 2000-2005

Famous First Facts
Famous First Facts
Famous First Facts About American Politics
Famous First Facts About Sports
Famous First Facts About the Environment
Famous First Facts: International Edition

American Book of Days
The American Book of Days
The International Book of Days

Monographs
American Game Changers
American Reformers

H.W. WILSON

2019 Title List

H.W. WILSON

Visit **www.HWWilsonInPrint.com** for Product Information, Table of Contents and Sample Pages.

The Barnhart Dictionary of Etymology
Celebrate the World
Guide to the Ancient World
Indexing from A to Z
Nobel Prize Winners
The Poetry Break
Radical Change: Books for Youth in a Digital Age
Speeches of American Presidents

Wilson Chronology
Wilson Chronology of Asia and the Pacific
Wilson Chronology of Human Rights
Wilson Chronology of Ideas
Wilson Chronology of the Arts
Wilson Chronology of the World's Religions
Wilson Chronology of Women's Achievements